MACMILLAN
Study
DICTIONARY

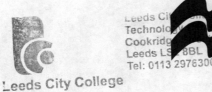

Macmillan Education
Between Towns Road, Oxford OX4 3PP
A division of Macmillan Publishers Limited
Companies and representatives throughout the world

ISBN 978 0230 40196 9

© Macmillan Publishers Limited 2010

First published 2010

The *Macmillan Study Dictionary* was conceived, compiled and edited by
A&C Black Publishers Ltd.

This Dictionary includes words on the basis of their use in the English language
today. Some words are identified as being trademarks or service marks. Neither the
presence nor absence of such identification in this Dictionary is to be regarded as
affecting in any way, or expressing a judgement on, the validity or legal status of any
trademark, service mark, or other proprietary rights anywhere in the world.

The definitions in the *Macmillan Study Dictionary* have been based on the following
corpora:

World English Corpus
The World English Corpus is made up of 200 million words of English and consists
of the Bloomsbury Corpus of World English® (owned by A&C Black Publishers Ltd)
with additional material, including a learner corpus and the Macmillan ELT corpus.

Macmillan Curriculum Corpus
The unique 20-million-word Macmillan Curriculum Corpus includes texts from
different levels, and from a wide range of school subjects, from countries where
English is used as a second language, and countries where English is the medium of
instruction in schools.

Cover design by Liz Faulkner
Typeset by Input Data Services Ltd, Bridgwater, United Kingdom
Printed and bound in Malaysia

2014 2013 2012 2011 2010
10 9 8 7 6 5 4 3 2

CONTENTS

Editor-in-Chief
Michael Rundell

Associate Editor
Gwyneth Fox

EDITORIAL TEAM

Editors
Lucy Hollingworth
Susan Jellis
Julie Plier
Elizabeth Potter
Donald Watt
Laura Wedgeworth

Editorial Consultants
Dr Siobhán O'Sullivan
(Educare Consulting and
University College Cork)
Dr Mike Taylor
Tim Webb

Phonetician
Dinah Jackson

Proofreaders
Sandra Anderson
Helen Liebeck

PROJECT TEAM

Project Manager
Katy McAdam

Database Consultant
Edmund Wright

Publishing Directors
Sue Bale
Lauren Simpson

Dictionaries' Consultant
Faye Carney

Design
Liz Faulkner

OTHER CONTRIBUTORS

Study Skills
Dr June Hassall
Elizabeth Potter
Julia Sander
Michael Vince

Illustrations
David Barnett
Stefan Chabluk
Peter Harper
Illustrated Arts
Kamae Design
Stuart Lafford
Alan Male

MPS India
Oxford Designers and
Illustrators
Redmoor Design
Peter Richardson
Touchmedia
Raymond Turvey

The publishers would like to thank the following contributors to the *Macmillan School Dictionary*, whose work laid the foundation for this dictionary:

Joel Adams
Gloria George
Michael Mayor
Stella O'Shea

Howard Sargeant
Ian M. Spackman
Nicky Thompson

INTRODUCTION

MICHAEL RUNDELL

Editor-in-chief

There is a growing trend across the world for teaching subjects in English. This movement is known as CLIL (Content and Language Integrated Learning), but also comes under a variety of other names, for example EMI (English as a Medium of Instruction), LAC (Language Across the Curriculum), CBI (Content–based Instruction) or CBLT (Content-based Language Teaching). The *Macmillan Study Dictionary* has been specially prepared for students who are studying through the medium of English. It contains a wide range of features to support successful study in any of the upper secondary and university subjects, but what makes the *Macmillan Study Dictionary* unique is the research that underlies every aspect of its design and content.

In planning the dictionary, we began by creating a database from hundreds of widely-used textbooks. This database – which forms a 'corpus' of 22 million words on every subject from agriculture to zoology – was analysed using state-of-the-art software. Using this data, we built up a detailed picture of the vocabulary that is essential for studying at upper secondary and university level. This gives us a reliable, scientific basis for selecting the words we include in the dictionary and for deciding how much information we need to provide about each word. But the corpus helps us in other ways too. It shows us how ideas and terms are explained in the textbooks which students actually use in the classroom, and this gives us a model for our own definitions.

Besides analysing this corpus of textbooks, we have consulted experienced teachers, textbook writers, and syllabus designers. Their expert advice has helped us to form a clear idea of what students at upper secondary and university really need to know. Thanks to this combination of computer technology and human expertise, we are confident that the information in the *Macmillan Study Dictionary* is not only up to date, accurate, and easy to use, but also perfectly adapted to the needs of its users.

As well as explaining general English vocabulary, the dictionary provides a wealth of useful material, making it a powerful resource for self-study. Its special features include:

- Over 10,000 words from 30 major subject areas from economics, IT and engineering, to health, social studies, and tourism

- Authentic, natural example sentences drawn from our curriculum corpus

- Helpful definitions, which are factually accurate and written in easy-to-understand language

- Over 150 specially commissioned illustrations, which help explain systems and processes such as the carbon cycle, the digestive system, and the generation of electricity

- Dozens of usage boxes with information about synonyms, word families, and other ways of building vocabulary

- A unique 38-page reference section, which includes a Study Skills section with advice on writing essays, preparing for exams, interpreting data, and so on, useful encyclopedic and scientific information, and much more besides

The *Macmillan Study Dictionary* is the product of extensive research backed by modern technology. We hope that you enjoy using it, and we are confident that it will help you to gain success in your studies and your exams.

USING YOUR DICTIONARY

Finding a word

Words with more than one entry

Sometimes the same word belongs to more than one word class: for example, the word **drum** can be a noun or a verb. Each word class is shown as a separate entry. The small number at the end of the headword tells you that a word has more than one entry.

> **drum¹** /drʌm/ noun [C] **1** MUSIC a musical instrument that consists of a tight skin stretched over a round frame. You hit it with your hands or a stick. —*picture* →
> MUSICAL INSTRUMENT, ORCHESTRA **2** a large round container for liquids: *an oil drum*

> **drum²** /drʌm/ (**drums, drumming, drummed**) verb **1** [I/T] to make a continuous sound by hitting a surface **2** [I] MUSIC to play a drum —**drumming** noun [U]
> PHRASAL VERB **,drum sth 'into sb** to make someone learn or understand something by repeating it many times

Derived words

Some words are shown at the end of the entry for the word that they are derived from. These words can be understood by reading the definition for the main entry.

chronological /ˌkrɒnəˈlɒdʒɪk(ə)l/ adj arranged or described in the order in which events happened —**chronologically** /ˌkrɒnəˈlɒdʒɪkli/ adv

Compound words

These are shown as separate entries in the alphabetical list.

> **silk** /sɪlk/ noun **1** [U] a thin smooth cloth made from the fibres produced by insects called **silkworms 2** [C] LAW a **QC**, a lawyer of high status

> **'silk ,screen** noun [U] ARTS a method of printing designs on a surface by forcing ink or paint through a thin cloth

Word classes (noun, verb etc)

There is a list of word classes on the inside front cover.

unassisted /ˌʌnəˈsɪstɪd/ adj without help

hem /hem/ noun [C] the bottom edge of something made of cloth that is folded and sewn in place

amass /əˈmæs/ verb [T] to collect a lot of money or information

Idioms and other fixed expressions

Some words are often used in idioms or other fixed expressions. These are shown at the end of the main entry, following the small box that says PHRASE . Look for fixed expressions at the entry for the first main word in the expression.

Phrasal verbs are shown after the entry for the main verb, following the small box that says PHRASAL VERB .

sake¹ /seɪk/ noun
> PHRASES **for sb's/sth's sake** or **for the sake of sb/sth** for the benefit or good of someone or something: *He agreed to resign for the sake of the party.* ♦ *We hope for her sake that the wedding goes as planned.*
> **for the sake of sth** for the purpose of doing, getting, or achieving something: *I hope you're not doing this just for the sake of the money.*

deal¹ /diːl/ (**deals, dealing, dealt** /delt/) verb [I/T] **1** to give cards to the people who are playing a game of cards: *Each player is dealt three cards.* **2** to buy and sell illegal drugs: *Many drug addicts deal as well.*
> PHRASE **deal a blow to** to harm or shock someone or something
> PHRASAL VERBS **'deal in sth** to buy and sell something: *a small company that deals in rare books*
> **'deal with sth 1** to take action to solve a problem: *The government must now deal with the problem of high unemployment.* **2** to be about a subject: *Chapter 5 deals with greenhouse gases.*

Finding the meaning of a word

Many words have more than one meaning, and each different meaning is shown by a number.

crane[1] /kreɪn/ noun [C] **1** a very tall machine that is used for moving heavy objects and for building tall buildings **2** a large water bird with long legs and a long neck —*picture* ➔ BIRD

Some words have many different meanings, and so the entries can be long. Entries with five or more meanings have a 'menu' at the top to make it easier to find the specific meaning you are looking for.

bounce /baʊns/ verb

1 hit sth & move off	**4** move in lively way
2 move up and down	**5** of email
3 of cheque	**+ PHRASAL VERB**

1 [I/T] if a ball or other object bounces, or if you bounce it, it hits a surface then immediately moves away: *The ball bounced twice before hitting the net.* ♦ *Hailstones were **bouncing off** the roof.*

Where an entry has more than five meanings and also has one or more idioms or phrasal verbs, this is shown in the 'menu' at the top of the entry by the marker **+**PHRASE or **+**PHRASAL VERB.

make[1] /meɪk/ (**makes, making, made** /meɪd/) verb

1 create/produce sth	**7** give a total
2 do sth	**8** give sth success
3 cause sth to be sth	**9** have right qualities
4 force sb to do sth	**10** reach place
5 arrange sth	**+ PHRASES**
6 earn/get money	**+ PHRASAL VERBS**

1 [T] to create or produce something: *The nail made a hole in my shirt.* ♦ *Jane **was making** coffee.* ♦ *This furniture is **made in** South America.* ♦ *a bowl **made of** wood* ♦ *They **make** paper **from** old rags.* ♦ *We **made** curtains **out of** some old material we found.*

All the definitions are written using a carefully selected 'defining vocabulary' of 3,000 words so that it is easy to understand the definitions.

epidermis /ˌepɪˈdɜːmɪs/ noun [singular] ANATOMY the outer layer of skin on top of the **dermis**. Hair and feathers grow from the epidermis. —*picture* ➔ SKIN —**epidermal** /ˌepɪˈdɜːməl/ adj

Any word in a definition that is not from this list, and that is not the entry immediately before or after the one you are looking at, is shown in **bold** letters. You can find its meaning by looking it up in the dictionary.

epiglottis /ˌepɪˈɡlɒtɪs/ noun [C] ANATOMY the small piece of flesh at the back of the tongue that closes the **windpipe** when food is swallowed

If the full definition of a word is held at a different entry, this is shown in **bold**. For example, the full definition of **pathway** can be found at **path**

hanger /ˈhæŋə/ noun [C] a **coat hanger**

pathway /ˈpɑːθˌweɪ/ noun [C] a **path**

Some words that are important in a particular specialist subject are shown in **bold**. They form part of the extra information that is given in the definition.

blood /blʌd/ noun [U] **1** BIOLOGY the red liquid that is pumped around the body from the heart. Blood carries oxygen, hormones, and nutrients to the various parts of the body, and also helps to get rid of waste products. It consists of **plasma** which contains **red blood cells** and **white blood cells**, and **platelets**: *Oxygen is carried in the blood.* ♦ *His face was covered in blood.* ➔ HAEMOGLOBIN **2** the family, nation, or group that someone belongs to through their parents and grandparents **3** violence and death: *There was a lot of **blood spilled** (=deaths and injuries caused) on both sides.* ➔ DRAW[1], FLESH

Finding out more about a word

Pronunciation

The International Phonetic Alphabet
shows you how a word is pronounced.
A list of the symbols used is given at
the end of the dictionary.

acclimatize /əˈklaɪmətaɪz/ verb [I/T] to become
familiar with a new place or situation —**acclimatization**
/əˌklaɪmətaɪˈzeɪʃ(ə)n/ noun [U]

When British and American
pronunciations are very different,
both are given.

lieutenant /lefˈtenənt, *American* luːˈtenənt/ noun [C]
an officer of low rank in most armed forces

You can find the pronunciations for
compound entries at the main entry
for each of the words in the
compound.

Stress marks tell you which part of a
compound to stress when you are
saying it.

ˈcamber ˌangle noun [C] **ENGINEERING** the angle
between the vertical axis of a vehicle's wheel and the
vertical axis of the vehicle

firefly /ˈfaɪəˌflaɪ/ (plural **fireflies**) noun [C] an insect
that produces a flashing light when it flies

Inflections

Inflections are shown at irregular
verbs, nouns, and adjectives.

lengthy /ˈleŋθi/ (**lengthier, lengthiest**) adj continuing
for a long time, especially for too long: *a lengthy period
of negotiation*

blot¹ /blɒt/ (**blots, blotting, blotted**) verb [T] to
remove liquid from the surface of something using a
piece of paper or cloth

Labels

Subject labels (in red) show whether
a word belongs to a specialized
subject.

platinum /ˈplætɪnəm/ noun [U] **CHEMISTRY** a silver-
grey metal element that is used in industry and for
making expensive jewellery. Chemical symbol: **Pt**

Other labels in *italic* tell you whether
a word is used only in American
English, or in formal or informal
contexts. Lists of these labels are
given on the inside front cover.

graduate² /ˈɡrædʒueɪt/ verb [I] **1 EDUCATION** to
complete your studies at a university or college and
get a degree: *He **graduated** from Yale University in 1936.*
♦ *one of the first women to **graduate in** engineering*
2 EDUCATION *American* to finish your studies at a high
school **3 graduate (from sth) to sth** to make progress,
or to reach a higher position: *He eventually graduated
from clerical work to his present role.*

bomb² /bɒm/ verb **1** [T] to attack a place with bombs:
NATO aircraft bombed the town again last night. **2** [I]
COMPUTING *informal* if a computer program bombs,
it stops working because of a problem

Examples

Example sentences in *italic* show you
how a word is used in context.

generous /ˈdʒenərəs/ adj **1** giving people more of your
time or money than is usual or expected: *It was very
generous of you to lend me your bike.* **2** larger than is
usual or necessary: *a generous helping of rice*
—**generously** adv

Information about collocation and
syntax – how words combine and
which structures they can be used
with – is shown in **bold type** in
examples.

impatient /ɪmˈpeɪʃ(ə)nt/ adj **1** annoyed because
something is not happening as quickly as you want or
in the way that you want ≠ PATIENT: *'Come on!' said
Maggie, becoming impatient.* ♦ *He gets **impatient with**
people who don't agree with him.* **2** wanting something
to happen as soon as possible: *They were **impatient
for** news of their father.* ♦ *After a couple of days, she
was **impatient to** get back to work.* —**impatience**
/ɪmˈpeɪʃ(ə)ns/ noun [U], **impatiently** adv

Grammar Boxes

Grammar boxes give extra information to help you to learn more about how a word is used.

> When **none** is the subject of a sentence and refers to members of a group, it can be used with a singular or plural verb: *None of his friends lives nearby/live nearby*. However, some people think that it is more correct to use a singular verb in these cases.

Notes are also given to help you to avoid common errors.

> **Information** is never used in the plural and cannot be used with an: *I've just discovered an interesting piece of information* (NOT *an interesting information*) *about the company.* ♦ *Do you have any information about local attractions?* ♦ *I found some information in the library to help with my project.*

Expanding your vocabulary

There are many ways that you can use this dictionary to expand your vocabulary.

Sometimes the opposite of a word is shown.

,low 'tide noun [C/U] GEOGRAPHY the time when the sea is at its lowest level ≠ HIGH TIDE

Some definitions give you synonyms.

highest common factor /ˌhaɪəst ˌkɒmən ˈfæktə/ noun [singular] MATHS the highest number that can be divided exactly into each number in a particular set = GREATEST COMMON DIVISOR

Sometimes you are told to look at another word or page in the dictionary where you will find additional information, a related entry, or a picture.

hardback /ˈhɑːdˌbæk/ noun [C] a book that has a hard cover → PAPERBACK

'Word family' boxes bring together groups of words that are formed from the same 'base word'.

> **Word family: deceive**
> *Words in the same family as **deceive***
> - **deceit** *n*
> - **deceptive** *adj*
> - **deceptively** *adv*
> - **deceitful** *adj*
> - **deception** *n*

'Build your vocabulary' boxes bring together words that are related to a particular subject, or suggest more specific alternatives for very common words.

> **Build your vocabulary: words you can use instead of cause**
> - **bring about** to make something happen, especially something positive that improves the situation
> - **give rise to** to make something happen, especially something unpleasant or unexpected
> - **lead to** to begin a process that makes something happen later
> - **contribute to** to be one of several causes that help to make something happen

NUMBERS THAT ARE ENTRIES

1 /wʌn/ abbrev COMPUTING used in emails and **text messages** to replace '-one': *NE1* (=anyone)

101 /ˌwʌn əʊ 'wʌn/ adj *American* consisting of only very basic information about a particular subject

112 /ˌwʌn wʌn 'tuː/ in Europe and the UK, the telephone number that you use in an emergency to call the police, the fire brigade, or an ambulance

2 /tuː/ abbrev **1** COMPUTING to or too: used in emails and **text messages**: *it's up 2 U* (=it's up to you) ♦ *me 2* (=me too) **2** used for replacing 'to-' in other words: *2day* (=today)

2-D /ˌtuː'diː/ adj MATHS flat and able to be measured only in length and breadth, not in depth

3-D /ˌθriː'diː/ adj a 3-D film, picture etc looks as if it has length, depth, and width

3G /ˌθriː 'dʒiː/ abbrev COMPUTING third generation: a technology that provides a high-speed connection to the Internet, video, and **multimedia** on your mobile phone

4 /fɔː/ abbrev COMPUTING for: used in emails and **text messages**: *4 U* (=for you)

4x4 /ˌfɔː baɪ 'fɔː/ noun [C] a **four-wheel drive** vehicle

4WD /ˌfɔː wiːl 'draɪv/ abbrev a **four-wheel drive** vehicle

8 /eɪt/ abbrev COMPUTING used in emails and **text messages** to replace '-ate' or '-eat': *C U L8R* (=see you later) ♦ *GR8* (=great)

9/11 /ˌnaɪn ɪ'lev(ə)n/ 11 September, the date in 2001 when **terrorists** attacked the US, flying planes into the World Trade Center and killing thousands of people

20/20 vision /ˌtwenti ˌtwenti 'vɪʒ(ə)n/ noun [U] the ability to see normally without wearing glasses

the 24 hour clock /ˌtwenti fɔː ˌaʊə 'klɒk/ noun [singular] a system for measuring time that uses all the twenty-four hours of the day instead of dividing it into two periods of twelve hours

24/7 /ˌtwenti fɔː 'sev(ə)n/ adv *informal* all the time: *He thinks about her 24/7.*

the $64,000 question /ˌsɪkstifɔːθaʊz(ə)nd dɒlə 'kwestʃ(ə)n/ noun [singular] a question that is the most important and most difficult to answer concerning a particular problem or situation

SYMBOLS THAT ARE ENTRIES

& a symbol meaning 'and'. It is short for 'ampersand'

* a symbol meaning 'asterisk'. It is used to mark an important word, or to show that more information is given in a footnote

@ a symbol meaning 'at'. It is used especially in email addresses

a symbol called 'hash' (or in the US, the 'pound sign'). It is used on telephones or to mean 'number'

© a symbol meaning 'copyright'

¢ the symbol for 'cent'. There are 100 cents in a dollar

$ the symbol for 'dollar', the unit of currency in the US, Australia, Canada, Singapore and some other countries

€ the symbol for 'euro', the unit of currency in most countries in the European Union

μ SCIENCE the symbol for 'micro'

Ω PHYSICS the symbol for 'ohm'

£ the symbol for 'pound'

® a symbol meaning that a word is registered as a trademark. It is used mainly in the UK

TM a symbol meaning that a word is registered as a trademark. It is used mainly in the US

¥ the symbol for 'yen', the unit of currency in Japan

Mathematical symbols

+	add	≥	is greater than or equal to
−	subtract		
×	multiply	≤	is less than or equal to
÷	divide		
=	equals	≠	does not equal
%	per cent	≈	approximately equals
√	square root		
>	is greater than	∞	infinity
<	is less than		

Examples

10+2=12	ten plus two equals/is twelve
10−2=8	ten minus two equals/is eight
10÷2=5	ten divided by two equals/is five
10×2=20	ten multiplied by two *or* ten times two is twenty *or* ten two's are twenty
√16=4	the square root of 16 is four

Roman numerals

Roman numerals were used in ancient Rome to represent numbers. They are still sometimes used today, for example on clocks and watches and in official documents.

I	one	XVII	seventeen
II	two	XVIII	eighteen
III	three	XIX	nineteen
IV	four	XX	twenty
V	five	XXI	twenty-one
VI	six	XXX	thirty
VII	seven	XL	forty
VIII	eight	L	fifty
IX	nine	LX	sixty
X	ten	LXX	seventy
XI	eleven	LXXX	eighty
XII	twelve	XC	ninety
XIII	thirteen	C	one hundred
XIV	fourteen	CC	two hundred
XV	fifteen	D	five hundred
XVI	sixteen	M	one thousand

A a

a¹ /eɪ/ (plural **a's**) or **A** (plural **A's**) noun **1** [C/U] the first letter of the English alphabet **2 A** [C/U] MUSIC the sixth note in the musical scale of C major **3 A** [U] HEALTH a common blood group in the **ABO system**

a² /*strong* eɪ, *weak* ə/ or **an** /*strong* æn, *weak* ən/ determiner
1 used when you are mentioning a person or a thing for the first time: *I have an idea.* ♦ *There's a concert on Sunday night.*
2 one: *I have a sister and two brothers.* ♦ *a million dollars*
3 used when you mean any person or thing of a particular type: *Have you got a car?* ♦ *My mother is a teacher.* ♦ *Abdul is a Muslim.* ♦ *When did France become a republic?*
4 used before a singular noun that represents every person or thing of a particular type: *A dog needs regular exercise.* ♦ *A molecule consists of two or more atoms.*
5 used in phrases showing prices, rates, or speeds to mean 'each' or 'every': *Meetings are held four times a year.* ♦ *90 miles an hour*
6 used before a noun that is formed from a verb and means a single action of that verb: *Can I have a try?* ♦ *Let's take a walk round the garden.*

A3 /ˌeɪ 'θriː/ noun [U] a large size of paper about 16.5 inches or 420 millimetres wide and 11.5 inches or 297 millimetres long

A4 /ˌeɪ 'fɔː/ noun [U] a standard size of paper about 8.5 inches or 210 millimetres wide and 11.5 inches or 297 millimetres long

A5 /ˌeɪ 'faɪv/ noun [U] a small size of paper about 6 inches or 148 millimetres wide and 8.5 inches or 210 millimetres long

A&E /ˌeɪ ənd 'iː/ noun [C/U] HEALTH accident and emergency: the part of a hospital where people go when they are injured or suddenly become ill = CASUALTY

aardvark /'ɑːdˌvɑːk/ noun [C] a southern African mammal that lays eggs, has a long nose, and uses its long sticky tongue to eat **ants**

AB /ˌeɪ 'biː/ noun [U] HEALTH a blood group in the **ABO system**

aback /ə'bæk/ adv **be taken aback** to be very shocked or surprised

abacus /'æbəkəs/ noun [C] MATHS an object used for counting or doing simple calculations. An abacus consists of a frame with small balls in rows.

abalone /ˌæbə'ləʊni/ noun [C/U] a **shellfish** that can be eaten as food. Its shell contains **mother-of-pearl**.

abandon /ə'bændən/ verb [T] **1** to leave someone or something and never come back: *His mother abandoned him when he was five days old.* ♦ *The stolen car was abandoned only five miles away.* **2** to stop doing something before it is finished, or before you have achieved your aims: *The game had to be abandoned because of rain.* ♦ *The climbers finally abandoned their attempt on the mountain.* —**abandonment** noun [U]

abandoned /ə'bændənd/ adj **1** left empty or no longer used: *an abandoned farm* **2** an abandoned child has been left alone by the person who should look after them

abashed /ə'bæʃt/ adj someone who is abashed is embarrassed or ashamed about something that they have done

abate /ə'beɪt/ verb [I] *formal* to gradually become less serious or extreme —**abatement** noun [U]

abattoir /'æbəˌtwɑː/ noun [C] AGRICULTURE a place where animals are killed for meat

abbey /'æbi/ noun [C] a large church with buildings connected to it for **monks** or **nuns** to live in

abbreviated /ə'briːviˌeɪtɪd/ adj shorter because some parts have been removed

abbreviation /əˌbriːvi'eɪʃ(ə)n/ noun [C] LANGUAGE a short form of a word or phrase: *MIA is an abbreviation for 'Missing in Action'.*

abdicate /'æbdɪkeɪt/ verb **1** [I/T] if a king or queen abdicates, he or she formally gives up being king or queen **2** [T] *formal* to stop accepting responsibility for something —**abdication** /ˌæbdɪ'keɪʃ(ə)n/ noun [C/U]

abdomen /'æbdəmən/ noun [C] **1** ANATOMY the front part of the body below the chest and above the pelvis. It contains the stomach and several other organs, including the intestines and the **liver. 2** BIOLOGY the back part of the three parts into which the body of insects or some other **arthropods** is divided. The other parts are the head and the **thorax.** —*picture* → CATERPILLAR, INSECT, SPIDER

abdominal /æb'dɒmɪn(ə)l/ adj in the abdomen

abduct /æb'dʌkt/ verb [T] to take someone away using force= KIDNAP —**abduction** /æb'dʌkʃ(ə)n/ noun [C/U]

abductor /æb'dʌktə/ noun [C] **1** someone who abducts someone **2** ANATOMY a muscle that pulls a part of the body away from its normal position, for example one that raises the arm → ADDUCTOR

aberrant /æ'berənt/ adj *formal* not normal or not what people would usually expect= ABNORMAL

aberration /ˌæbə'reɪʃ(ə)n/ noun [C] *formal* something that is not normal, or not what people would usually expect

abeyance /ə'beɪəns/ noun *formal* **in abeyance** not happening until later, or not being used at the present time

ABH /ˌeɪ biː 'eɪtʃ/ noun [U] LAW actual bodily harm: the crime of attacking and injuring someone

abhorrent /əb'hɒrənt/ adj *formal* if something, especially something someone does, is abhorrent, you hate it because it is immoral —**abhorrence** noun [U]

abide /ə'baɪd/ verb **can't abide sth** to hate something
  PHRASAL VERB **a'bide by sth** to follow a rule, decision, or instruction

abiding /ə'baɪdɪŋ/ adj *formal* an abiding feeling or belief is one that you have had for a long time

ability /ə'bɪləti/ (plural **abilities**) noun [C/U] the skill that you need in order to do something ≠ INABILITY: *She has good organizational abilities.* ♦ *Tiredness can affect your **ability to** drive.*
  PHRASE **to the best of your ability** as well as you can: *Just try to do the job to the best of your ability.*

abiotic /ˌeɪbaɪ'ɒtɪk/ adj BIOLOGY **1** relating to the non-living aspects of an organism's environment, such as air, water, and soil type **2** not containing or supporting life

abject /ˈæbdʒekt/ adj formal **1** used for emphasizing how bad something is: *abject poverty* **2** used for describing the behaviour of someone who is showing that they feel ashamed: *a look of abject embarrassment*

ablative /ˈæblətɪv/ noun [C/U] LANGUAGE the form of a noun, pronoun, or adjective that is used in languages such as Latin in order to show who something is done by, what something is done with, or where something comes from —**ablative** adj

ablaze /əˈbleɪz/ adj burning with a lot of flames

able /ˈeɪb(ə)l/ adj intelligent, or good at doing something

PHRASE be able to do sth used for saying that it is possible for someone to do something: *I don't know if I'll be able to come.* ♦ *I'd love to be able to sing like you.*

Word family: **able**

Words in the same family as able
- **ability** n
- **ably** adv
- **disabled** adj
- **enable** v
- **disability** n
- **unable** adj
- **inability** n

able-bodied /ˌeɪb(ə)l ˈbɒdid/ adj not suffering from any disability

ably /ˈeɪbli/ adv very well, or very skilfully

abnormal /æbˈnɔːm(ə)l/ adj not normal, and therefore a sign that there is a problem: *abnormal behaviour* ♦ *abnormal eating habits* —**abnormality** /ˌæbnɔːˈmæləti/ noun [C/U], **abnormally** adv: *Her blood pressure was abnormally high.*

aboard /əˈbɔːd/ adv, preposition in or on a ship, train, or plane

abode /əˈbəʊd/ noun [C] literary the place where someone lives= residence

PHRASE of no fixed abode LAW without a permanent home

abolish /əˈbɒlɪʃ/ verb [T] to officially get rid of a law or system: *Britain abolished slavery in 1807.*

abolition /ˌæbəˈlɪʃ(ə)n/ noun [U] the official end to a law or system

abolitionist /ˌæbəˈlɪʃ(ə)nɪst/ noun [C] SOCIAL STUDIES someone who supported the abolition of **slavery** in the 19th century

abominable /əˈbɒmɪnəb(ə)l/ adj formal extremely bad —**abominably** adv

Aboriginal /ˌæbəˈrɪdʒ(ə)n(ə)l/ or **Aborigine** /ˌæbəˈrɪdʒəni/ noun [C] an Australian who belongs to the race of people who were living in Australia before Europeans arrived —**Aboriginal** adj

abort /əˈbɔːt/ verb [T] **1** to stop something before it is finished: *The mission had to be aborted because of a technical problem.* **2** to remove a foetus from a woman's body, so that it is not born alive

abortion /əˈbɔːʃ(ə)n/ noun [C/U] a medical operation in which a foetus is removed from a woman's body, so that it is not born alive

abortive /əˈbɔːtɪv/ adj not finished, and therefore not successful: *abortive peace negotiations*

ABO system /ˌeɪ biː ˈəʊ ˌsɪstəm/ noun [singular] HEALTH the system that divides human blood into four main groups, A, B, AB, and O

abound /əˈbaʊnd/ verb [I] to be present in large numbers or amounts

about /əˈbaʊt/ adv, preposition **1** used for stating who or what is being considered or discussed: *a book about American history* ♦ *They were talking about their holiday.* **2** used for giving an amount, number, or time that is not exact= APPROXIMATELY: *About 250 people were killed in the explosion.* ♦ *I woke up at about 3 am.* **3** almost: *Pam's about the only person that I can trust.* **4** in or to many different parts or areas= AROUND: *The children were running about the room.*

PHRASES be about to do sth to be going to do something very soon: *The show was just about to begin.*

how about/what about ...? spoken used for making a suggestion: *'When shall we meet?' 'What about Tuesday, after school?'* ♦ *How about joining us for a game of basketball?*

a,bout-'turn noun [C] a change from one opinion or decision to the opposite opinion or decision

above /əˈbʌv/ adj, adv, preposition **1** at a higher level than something, or directly over it: *We lived in the room above the shop.* ♦ *Her leg was broken above the knee.* **2** more than a particular amount, level, or standard: *In most subjects the students scored well above average.* ♦ *A captain is above a sergeant.* **3** louder or higher than the other sounds that you can hear: *I couldn't hear his voice above all the noise.* **4** in an earlier part of a piece of writing, or higher up on the same page: *Many of the documents mentioned above are now available on the Internet.* ♦ *Convert the scores in the above table to positive and negative numbers.*

PHRASE above all used for saying what is most important: *We hope you will learn new skills, meet new people, and above all enjoy yourself.*

- Use **above** when something is not directly over something else, but at a higher level: *on the hillside above the river.*
- Use **over** when something crosses the space above something else: *flying over London* ♦ *the bridge over the river.*
- Use **over** when something covers something else: *She put a scarf over her hair.*

a,bove 'board adj completely honest and legal

abrasion /əˈbreɪʒ(ə)n/ noun **1** [C] HEALTH an injured area of skin on the body, caused by the skin rubbing hard against something **2** [U] formal the action of rubbing a surface hard enough to damage it

abrasive /əˈbreɪsɪv/ adj **1** someone who is abrasive behaves in a way that seems rude **2** an abrasive substance has a rough surface that is used for rubbing other surfaces

abreast /əˈbrest/ adv next to each other, facing or moving in the same direction

PHRASE keep abreast of sth to make sure that you know the most recent information about something

abridged /əˈbrɪdʒd/ adj an abridged book or play is shorter than the original

abroad /əˈbrɔːd/ adv in or to a foreign country: *We try to go abroad at least once a year.* ♦ *special arrangements for voters living abroad*

abrupt /əˈbrʌpt/ adj **1** sudden and unexpected, often in an unpleasant way **2** someone who is abrupt speaks in an unfriendly way using very few words —**abruptly** adv

ABS /ˌeɪ biː ˈes/ noun [U] ENGINEERING antilock braking system: a system of electronically controlled brakes that prevents a vehicle's wheels from locking, if the driver brakes suddenly

abscess /ˈæbses/ noun [C] HEALTH a painful swollen area on the skin or inside the body

abscond /əbˈskɒnd/ verb [I] *formal* **1** if someone absconds, they escape from a place where they are being kept as a punishment **2** if someone absconds with something that does not belong to them, they take it without permission when they leave a place

abseil /ˈæbseɪl/ verb [I] to come down from a high place by sliding down a rope —**abseiling** noun [U]

absence /ˈæbs(ə)ns/ noun **1** [C/U] a time when someone is not where they should be or where they usually are: *We are concerned about his frequent absences from school.* ♦ *Mark will be in charge in my absence* (=while I am away). **2** [singular/U] the fact that something does not exist or is not present: *a complete absence of humour*

absent /ˈæbs(ə)nt/ adj **1** not in the place where you should be ≠ PRESENT: *He's been absent from school for three days.* **2** *formal* missing from a place or situation: *The story has been absent from the news for weeks.*

absentee /ˌæbs(ə)nˈtiː/ adj used for describing someone who is not able to do a job well because they are not in the place where they should be: *an absentee father*

absenteeism /ˌæbs(ə)nˈtiːˌɪz(ə)m/ noun [U] the fact that a child often deliberately does not go to school when they should

absentee ˈlandlord noun [C] someone who does not live in or visit very frequently a property that they rent to someone else

absent-minded /ˌæbsənt ˈmaɪndɪd/ adj someone who is absent-minded is likely to forget or not notice things because they are not paying attention —**absent-ˈmindedly** adv

absolute /ˈæbsəluːt, ˌæbsəˈluːt/ adj **1** used for emphasizing an opinion, feeling, or statement = TOTAL: *The way they've been treated is an absolute disgrace.* ♦ *I have absolute confidence in her.* **2** used for emphasizing that something is the most or least possible in a particular situation: *£9,000 is the absolute maximum we can spend.* **3** POLITICS an absolute political system is one in which complete power is held by one person, and is not shared with a parliament or other political group

absolutely adv **1** /ˈæbsəluːtli/ completely: *Are you absolutely certain you saw him?* ♦ *The food was absolutely fantastic.* **2** /ˌæbsəˈluːtli/ *spoken* used for emphasizing that you agree or mean 'yes': *'Are you sure it's OK?' 'Absolutely!'*

absolute maˈjority noun [C] POLITICS a result in an election when one person or political party wins more than half the votes or seats

absolute ˈzero noun [U] PHYSICS -273°C, the lowest temperature that scientists believe is possible

absolution /ˌæbsəˈluːʃ(ə)n/ noun [U] RELIGION the act of forgiving someone for the things they have done wrong, especially for a religious fault

absolve /əbˈzɒlv/ verb [T] RELIGION if a priest absolves someone, especially in the Roman Catholic Church, he says formally that God has forgiven them for the things they have done wrong

absorb /əbˈzɔːb/ verb [T]

1 take in heat, liquid etc	4 reduce harmful effects
2 make sth part of sth else	5 hold attention
	6 of cell
3 learn new information	7 take in nutrients

1 to take in heat, light, liquid, or some other substance: *When wood gets wet, it absorbs water and expands.* ♦ *a device that produces energy by absorbing sunlight* **2** to make something become a part of something

larger: *After the war, the whole region was absorbed into the Roman Empire.* **3** to learn and understand new facts: *We had to absorb a lot of information.* **4** BUSINESS if the people who run a business absorb an increase in their costs, they do not increase the prices that they charge **5** to be very interesting and take all someone's attention **6** BIOLOGY to absorb liquid into a living cell through its cell membranes, for example by **osmosis** **7** BIOLOGY to take in nutrients through the walls of the intestines into the blood

absorbance /əbˈzɔːbəns/ noun [U] PHYSICS the measurement of how much light an object can absorb

absorbed /əbˈzɔːbd/ adj completely interested or involved in something: *Richard was totally absorbed in his book.*

absorbent /əbˈzɔːbənt/ adj an absorbent material can take in and hold liquids

absorbing /əbˈzɔːbɪŋ/ adj taking all your attention: *an absorbing book*

absorption /əbˈzɔːpʃ(ə)n/ noun [U] **1** BIOLOGY the process by which liquid is absorbed into a living cell through its cell membranes, for example by **osmosis** **2** BIOLOGY the process by which nutrients are taken in through the walls of the intestines into the blood **3** PHYSICS the process by which a substance absorbs heat, light, or other form of energy without reflecting it **4** the process of becoming part of something larger

abstain /əbˈsteɪn/ verb [I] **1** to deliberately avoid doing something enjoyable **2** to decide not to vote

abstention /əbˈstenʃ(ə)n/ noun [C] a decision not to vote

abstinence /ˈæbstɪnəns/ noun [U] the practice of avoiding something such as alcohol or sex

abstract /ˈæbstrækt/ adj **1** abstract ideas are not related to physical objects or real events **2** ARTS abstract art expresses ideas or feelings, rather than showing the exact appearance of people or things —**abstraction** /æbˈstrækʃ(ə)n/ noun [C/U]

abstract exˈpressionism noun [U] ARTS a style in abstract art in which the artist emphasizes emotions and reactions to things, rather than showing objects as they really appear

abstract ˈnoun noun [C] LANGUAGE a word that names a quality, idea, or feeling, such as 'happiness' or 'beauty'

abstruse /æbˈstruːs/ adj *formal* abstruse ideas or arguments are hard to understand, and are more complicated than necessary = OBSCURE

absurd /əbˈsɜːd/ adj silly, unreasonable, or impossible to believe = RIDICULOUS —**absurdity** noun [C/U], **absurdly** adv

abundance /əˈbʌndəns/ noun [singular/U] *formal* a very large quantity of something ≠ SCARCITY

abundant /əˈbʌndənt/ adj *formal* existing or available in large quantities ≠ SCARCE

abuse¹ /əˈbjuːs/ noun **1** [C/U] cruel, violent, or unfair treatment: *human rights abuses* ♦ *Many of the children were victims of sexual abuse.* **2** [C/U] the use of something in a bad, dishonest, or harmful way: *This is clearly an abuse of power.* ♦ *alcohol abuse* **3** [U] angry offensive comments: *racist abuse*

abuse² /əˈbjuːz/ verb [T] **1** to have sex with someone who is unable to refuse, especially a child: *She was abused as a child.* **2** to treat someone in a cruel or violent way **3** to use something in a bad, dishonest, or harmful way: *Those with access to private information must not abuse that trust.* **4** to speak to someone in an angry, offensive way —**abuser** noun [C]

abusive /ə'bju:sɪv/ adj **1** offensive or insulting= RUDE: *abusive language* ♦ *When we asked him to leave, he became abusive.* **2** treating someone in a cruel way, either by being violent or by forcing them to have sex: *an abusive parent* —**abusively** adv

abutment /ə'bʌtmənt/ noun [C] CONSTRUCTION **1** the point where the ends of an **arch** rest on a wall and support the weight of the structure above them **2** a place where two edges meet, for example the point where the edge of a **parapet** joins the edge of a roof

abysmal /ə'bɪzm(ə)l/ adj extremely bad= APPALLING —**abysmally** adv

abyss /ə'bɪs/ noun [C] *literary* a large deep hole

ac abbrev COMPUTING academic organization: used in the email and website addresses of universities, colleges, and schools

AC abbrev PHYSICS **alternating current**

acacia /ə'keɪʃə/ noun [C] a tree with small white or yellow flowers that grows in warm countries

academic¹ /,ækə'demɪk/ adj **1** EDUCATION relating to education, especially in colleges and universities: *We expect our students to meet high academic standards.* **2** EDUCATION based on learning from study rather than practical skills and experience: *The college offers both academic and vocational qualifications.* **3** not relating to a real situation, and therefore not relevant: *Given the lack of funding, any discussion of future plans was somewhat academic.* —**academically** /,ækə'demɪkli/ adv

academic² /,ækə'demɪk/ noun [C] EDUCATION a teacher at a college or university

academic 'year noun [C] EDUCATION the time during the year when there is teaching at schools, colleges, and universities

academy /ə'kædəmi/ (plural **academies**) noun [C] **1** EDUCATION a school or college that teaches a particular subject or skill **2** an organization that was created to encourage interest and development in a particular subject

a cappella /,æ kə'pelə/ adj, adv MUSIC sung by voices only, without musical instruments

accede /ək'si:d/ verb [I] *formal* **1** to do what someone wants or agree with what they say **2** to formally take a position of authority, especially as a king, queen, or president

accelerando /æk,selə'rændəʊ, ə,tʃelə'rændəʊ/ adj, adv MUSIC an instruction to play a section of music more and more quickly

accelerate /ək'seləreɪt/ verb **1** [I] if a vehicle or object accelerates, it moves faster **2** [I/T] to happen at a faster rate, or to make something do this: *Can we accelerate the development process?*

acceleration /ək,selə'reɪʃ(ə)n/ noun **1** [U] PHYSICS the rate at which an object increases its speed **2** [singular/U] an increase in the rate at which something happens, changes, or grows **3** [U] the ability of a vehicle to increase its speed

accelerator /ək'seləreɪtə/ noun [C] the pedal in a vehicle that the driver presses with their foot to make the vehicle go faster

accent /'æks(ə)nt/ noun **1** [C] a way of pronouncing words that shows what country, region, or social class the speaker comes from: *an upper-class British accent* **2** [C] LANGUAGE a mark above a letter that shows how you pronounce it **3** [singular] LANGUAGE the

emphasis on a particular part of a word or phrase when you say it: *The accent is on the first syllable.*

accentuate /æk'sentʃueɪt/ verb [T] to make something more noticeable

accept /ək'sept/ verb **1** [T] to take something that someone gives you: *It gives me great pleasure to accept this award.* ♦ *Two police officers were accused of accepting bribes.* **2** [I/T] to say yes to an invitation, offer, or suggestion ≠ REJECT: *They offered her a job, and she accepted without hesitation.* **3** [T] to recognize that something is true or right, or recognize that something bad exists and cannot be changed: *This argument is unlikely to be accepted by the court.* ♦ *We cannot accept responsibility for any damage.* ♦ *He could not accept that she was dead.* **4** [T] to allow someone to become part of an organization or group: *The children soon accepted her into the family.*

■ Use **accept** to mean that you take something that someone gives you, or that you recognize that something is true or right: *We accepted her gifts.* ♦ *They accepted the court's decision.*
■ Use **agree** to mean that you are willing to do something: *She agreed to work at the weekend.*
■ You **accept** something, but you **agree to do** something.

acceptable /ək'septəb(ə)l/ adj **1** if something is acceptable, most people approve of it or accept it ≠ UNACCEPTABLE: *That kind of behaviour is not acceptable.* ♦ *an agreement that is acceptable to both sides* **2** good enough= REASONABLE ≠ UNACCEPTABLE: *A success rate of 65% is acceptable.* —**acceptability** /ək,septə'bɪləti/ noun [U]

acceptance /ək'septəns/ noun [U] **1** agreement that something is true, reasonable, or cannot be changed ≠ REJECTION: *There is widespread acceptance of these principles.* **2** agreement to a plan, offer, or suggestion ≠ REJECTION: *The union has recommended acceptance of the pay offer.* **3** an attitude of accepting a bad situation because it cannot be changed: *a religion that teaches acceptance of suffering* **4** the fact of being accepted into an organization or group: *her acceptance into Cambridge University*

accepted /ək'septɪd/ adj thought by most people to be reasonable, right, or normal

access¹ /'ækses/ noun [U] **1** the right or opportunity to have or to use something: *Only a small number of our students have access to the Internet.* ♦ *Some groups still have difficulty gaining access to health care.* **2** the means by which you get to a place: *A lift provides access to the upper floors.* **3** official permission to see someone: *All prisoners have access to a lawyer.*

access² /'ækses/ verb [T] COMPUTING to get information, especially from a computer

'access ,course noun [C] EDUCATION a course of study in which you learn enough about a subject to allow you to go to a college or university to continue studying the subject

accessible /ək'sesəb(ə)l/ adj **1** easy to obtain, use, or understand ≠ INACCESSIBLE: *information that should be accessible to the public* **2** easy to find or get to ≠ INACCESSIBLE: *The city is easily accessible by road, rail, or air.* **3** suitable for disabled people: *accessible toilets* —**accessibility** /ək,sesə'bɪləti/ noun [U]

accession /ək'seʃ(ə)n/ noun *formal* **1** [C/U] the occasion on which someone formally takes a position of authority, especially as a king, queen, or president **2** [U] POLITICS the occasion when a country formally joins a group of countries or accepts an agreement

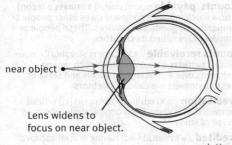

near object ●

Lens widens to
focus on near object.

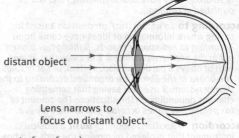

distant object

Lens narrows to
focus on distant object.

accommodation (adjustment of eye focus)

3 [C] something that is added to a collection, especially
a work of art

'access ,number noun [C] COMPUTING the telephone
number that is used to connect to an **Internet service
provider**

accessory /əkˈsesəri/ (plural **accessories**) noun [C] **1**
an additional object or piece of equipment that makes
something more attractive or useful **2** a small thing that
someone wears, for example a piece of jewellery or a
belt **3** LAW someone who helps a criminal, for example
by hiding them from the police. An **accessory before
the fact** helps before the crime. An **accessory after the
fact** helps after the crime.

'access ,profile noun [C] COMPUTING information kept
on a computer that gives details about a user, for
example their name, **password**, and the parts of the
system they are allowed to use

accident /ˈæksɪd(ə)nt/ noun [C] **1** a crash involving a
car, train, or other vehicle: *The accident was caused by
ice on the road*. **2** an unexpected event that causes
injury or damage: *He was killed in a climbing accident*.
♦ *I didn't mean to break the vase, it was an accident*.
   PHRASE **by accident** by chance, without being planned
or intended: *I discovered the answer by accident*.

accidental¹ /ˌæksɪˈdent(ə)l/ adj not intended ≠
DELIBERATE: *accidental injury* ♦ *an accidental release of
dangerous chemicals* —**accidentally** adv

accidental² /ˌæksɪˈdent(ə)l/ noun [C] MUSIC a
musical note marked with a sharp, flat, or natural sign
in order to show it is different from the **key signature**
(=symbols that show what key a piece of music is in)
—*picture* → MUSIC

,accidental 'death noun [C/U] LAW a death that was
not caused on purpose: used for reporting the decision
of a **coroner** (=an official who examines the cause of
someone's death)

'accident-,prone adj someone who is accident-prone
often hurts themselves or breaks things = CLUMSY

acclaim¹ /əˈkleɪm/ verb [T] to publicly praise someone
for a major achievement

acclaim² /əˈkleɪm/ noun [U] public praise

acclaimed /əˈkleɪmd/ adj publicly praised

acclimatize /əˈklaɪmətaɪz/ verb [I/T] to become
familiar with a new place or situation —
acclimatization /əˌklaɪmətaɪˈzeɪʃ(ə)n/ noun [U]

accolade /ˈækəleɪd/ noun [C] an honour or praise that
someone is given for their work

accommodate /əˈkɒmədeɪt/ verb [T] **1** to provide a
room or a place for someone to stay: *The teams will
be accommodated in luxury hotels*. **2** to provide enough
space for something or someone: *The new office will
easily accommodate 50 desks*. **3** *formal* to do what
someone asks you to do: *We will do our best to
accommodate your request*.

accommodating /əˈkɒməˌdeɪtɪŋ/ adj helpful and
easy to work with: *The staff were very accommodating*.

accommodation /əˌkɒməˈdeɪʃ(ə)n/ noun [U] **1** a
place for someone to stay, live, or work in: *The hotel
provides accommodation for up to 100 people*. ♦ *We
live in **rented accommodation***. **2** ANATOMY the change
in shape of the lens of the eye when it changes its **focus**
to look at something nearer or further away

accommo'dation ,centre noun [C] a place to live for
people who have entered a country without first
getting permission, until officials decide whether or not
they can live in the country permanently

accommodations /əˌkɒməˈdeɪʃ(ə)nz/ noun [plural]
American a place to live, especially a temporary place
such as a hotel room

accompanied /əˈkʌmp(ə)nid/ adj TOURISM
travelling with an adult passenger

ac,companied 'baggage noun [U] TOURISM bags or
suitcases belonging to a passenger who is travelling in
the same plane

accompaniment /əˈkʌmp(ə)nɪmənt/ noun **1** [C/U]
MUSIC music that supports someone who is singing
or playing the main tune **2** [C] something that someone
provides as an addition, especially to a meal

accompanist /əˈkʌmpənɪst/ noun [C] MUSIC
someone who plays the supporting music while
someone else sings or plays the main tune

accompany /əˈkʌmp(ə)ni/ (**accompanies,
accompanying, accompanied**) verb [T] **1** *formal* to go
with someone to a place or event: *Children must be
accompanied by an adult*. **2** *formal* to happen or exist
with something else: *A sore throat sometimes
accompanies a fever*. ♦ *The book is accompanied by a
CD-ROM*. **3** MUSIC to play music while someone sings
or plays the main tune

accomplice /əˈkʌmplɪs/ noun [C] someone who helps
another person to do something illegal

accomplish /əˈkʌmplɪʃ/ verb [T] to succeed in doing
something difficult

accomplished /əˈkʌmplɪʃt/ adj good at doing
something that needs a lot of skill

accomplishment /əˈkʌmplɪʃmənt/ noun [C/U]
something difficult that you succeed in doing

accord /əˈkɔːd/ noun [C] a formal agreement between
countries or groups
   PHRASE **do sth of your own accord** to do something
without being asked, forced, or helped to do it

accordance /əˈkɔːd(ə)ns/ noun **in accordance with** in
a way that follows a rule, system, or someone's wishes

accordingly /əˈkɔːdɪŋli/ adv **1** as a result of something
= CONSEQUENTLY: *No formal complaint was made;
accordingly, the police took no action*. **2** in a way that

is suitable: *They have broken the rules and will be punished accordingly.*

according to /əˈkɔːdɪŋ ˌtuː/ preposition **1** used for saying where information or ideas have come from: *According to newspaper reports, fighting has broken out in the northern provinces.* **2** in a way that agrees with or obeys a particular plan, system, or set of rules: *The books in the library are organized according to the Dewey system.* **3** used for saying that something changes depending on the situation: *The amount of tax people pay varies according to where they live.*

accordion /əˈkɔːdiən/ noun [C] MUSIC a musical instrument that is played by moving the ends of a box in and out while pressing buttons

account¹ /əˈkaʊnt/ noun

1 agreement with bank	4 agreement with shop
2 report/description	5 regular customer
3 financial records	+ PHRASES

1 [C] an arrangement in which a bank looks after your money: *There was only £6 in his bank account.* ♦ *How do I* ***open an account*** (=start having an account)*?*
2 [C] a written or spoken report about something that has happened: *a brief* ***account of*** *the meeting* ♦ *He was too shocked to* ***give a*** *clear* ***account*** *of events.*
3 accounts [plural] BUSINESS a detailed record that a business keeps of the money it receives and spends: *The accounts showed a loss of £498 million.*
4 [C] an arrangement that a customer has with a shop or other business that allows the customer to pay for goods or services at a later time: *I have an account with the university bookshop.*
5 [C] BUSINESS a company that regularly buys goods or services from another company
PHRASES **by/from all accounts** according to what people say
on account of because of someone or something: *She can't work much on account of the children.*
on no account used for emphasizing that something must not happen
take account of sth or **take sth into account** to consider something when you are trying to make a decision: *A good transport strategy must take account of the environmental issues.* ♦ *If you take inflation into account, the cost of computers has fallen in the last ten years.*

account² /əˈkaʊnt/ PHRASAL VERB **acˈcount for sth 1** to form a particular amount or part of something: *Electronic goods account for over 30% of our exports.* **2** to be the reason for something: *The increase in carbon dioxide emissions may account for changes in the climate.* **3** to give an explanation for something: *How do you account for this sudden improvement in his test scores?*

accountable /əˈkaʊntəb(ə)l/ adj in a position where other people have the right to criticize or ask for explanations —**accountability** /əˌkaʊntəˈbɪləti/ noun [U]

accountancy /əˈkaʊntənsi/ noun [U] the work or profession of an accountant

accountant /əˈkaʊntənt/ noun [C] someone whose job is to prepare or check financial records

accounting /əˈkaʊntɪŋ/ noun [U] the work of accountants, or the methods they use

acˈcounting ˌpackage noun [C] COMPUTING a piece of software that a business uses to organize its financial records

acˈcount ˌname noun [C] COMPUTING the name of a user on a **network** or Internet system

acˌcounts ˈpayable noun [plural] BUSINESS a record of how much money a company owes other people or companies for goods and services. These people or companies are called its **creditors**.

accounts receivable /əˌkaʊnts rɪˈsiːvəb(ə)l/ noun [plural] BUSINESS a record of how much money customers owe a company for goods and services. These customers are called its **debtors**.

accreditation /əˌkredɪˈteɪʃ(ə)n/ noun [U] official approval that is given to an organization, worker, or course of study

accredited /əˈkredɪtɪd/ adj having official approval

accretion /əˈkriːʃ(ə)n/ noun [C/U] GEOLOGY a layer of a substance that gradually forms on a rock or area of land, making it bigger

accrue /əˈkruː/ verb formal **1** [I/T] BUSINESS if money accrues or is accrued, it gradually increases in amount **2** [I] if benefits accrue to you, you receive them

accumulate /əˈkjuːmjʊleɪt/ verb **1** [T] to get more and more of something over a period of time: *Over the years, I had accumulated hundreds of books.* **2** [I] to increase in quantity over a period of time: *Rubbish accumulated in the streets.* —**accumulative** /əˈkjuːmjʊlətɪv/ adj

accumulation /əˌkjuːmjʊˈleɪʃ(ə)n/ noun [U] the process by which something increases in amount or is collected together over time

accumulator /əˈkjuːmjʊˌleɪtə/ noun [C] PHYSICS a battery that can replace its own electrical charge from stored chemical energy

accuracy /ˈækjʊrəsi/ noun [U] the ability to do something in an accurate way, or the quality of being accurate ≠ INACCURACY: *The accuracy of the report is being checked.*

accurate /ˈækjʊrət/ adj **1** correct in every detail, and without any mistakes= PRECISE ≠ INACCURATE: *accurate measurements* ♦ *an accurate description of the events* **2** an accurate throw or shot goes where it is intended to go —**accurately** adv

accusation /ˌækjʊˈzeɪʃ(ə)n/ noun [C] a claim that someone has done something wrong or illegal: *The Minister denied the accusation that she had lied.*

accusative /əˈkjuːzətɪv/ noun [singular] LANGUAGE the form of a noun or pronoun that shows that it is the **direct object** of a verb —**accusative** adj

accuse /əˈkjuːz/ verb [T] to say that someone has done something wrong or illegal: *Are you* ***accusing*** *me of lying?* —**accuser** noun [C]

the accused /əˈkjuːzd/ (plural **the accused**) noun [C] LAW someone who is accused of a crime in a court of law

accusing /əˈkjuːzɪŋ/ adj showing that you think someone has done something wrong: *an accusing stare* —**accusingly** adv

accustomed /əˈkʌstəmd/ adj **be/get accustomed to sth** to think that something is normal or natural because you have experienced it regularly over a period of time: *He had become accustomed to living without electricity.*

ace /eɪs/ noun [C] **1** in card games, a card with only one symbol and either the highest or lowest value **2** SPORTS in tennis, a very fast **serve** (=first hit of the ball) that an opponent cannot reach with their **racket**

acetate /ˈæsəˌteɪt/ noun [U] CHEMISTRY a chemical substance that is used to make products such as plastic or fibres for cloth

acetic acid /ə,siːtɪk 'æsɪd/ noun [U] CHEMISTRY a type of acid that is the main part of vinegar. It is used in making drugs, plastics, fibres, and other products.

acetone /'æsə,təʊn/ noun [U] CHEMISTRY a liquid that can be used to remove nail polish. It is also used in some types of paint and varnish to prevent them from becoming too thick.

acetylene /ə'setə,liːn/ noun [U] CHEMISTRY a gas that is burned with oxygen to produce a flame that can cut metal. Chemical formula: C_2H_2

a'cetylene ,soot noun [U] TECHNOLOGY **soot** (=black powder) that is produced in the process of **oxyacetylene welding**

ache¹ /eɪk/ verb [I] to feel a continuous but not very strong pain in part of your body

ache² /eɪk/ noun [C] a pain that is continuous but usually not very strong

achieve /ə'tʃiːv/ verb **1** [T] to succeed in doing or having something: *We have achieved what we set out to do.* ♦ *Most of the students achieved high test scores.* **2** [I] to be successful and do things that people admire: *Many managers are driven by a desire to achieve.* — **achievable** adj

achievement /ə'tʃiːvmənt/ noun **1** [C] a particular thing that someone has achieved: *Winning the gold medal was a remarkable achievement.* **2** [U] the fact of achieving something: *It was hard work, but the **sense of achievement** is huge.*

Achilles' heel /ə,kɪliːz 'hiːl/ noun [singular] a weak feature of someone or something that could cause them to fail

Achilles tendon /ə,kɪliːz 'tendən/ noun [C] ANATOMY the **tendon** that joins the muscles in the back of the lower leg to the muscles in the heel

acid /'æsɪd/ noun [C/U] CHEMISTRY a substance with a pH of less than 7. Acid turns damp litmus paper red. Some acids, for example **citric acid** in lemons, are weak and not harmful, while others, such as strong **sulphuric acid**, can seriously damage other substances. → ALKALI, BASE¹

acidic /ə'sɪdɪk/ adj **1** containing acid **2** very sour

acidification /ə,sɪdɪfɪ'keɪʃ(ə)n/ noun [U] ENVIRONMENT the process of becoming an acid, or starting to contain more acid

acidify /ə'sɪdɪ,faɪ/ verb [I/T] CHEMISTRY to become an acid, or cause a substance to become an acid —*picture* → POLLUTION

acidity /ə'sɪdəti/ noun [U] CHEMISTRY the amount of acid in a substance, often measured in pH

,acid 'rain noun [U] ENVIRONMENT, CHEMISTRY rain that contains a high concentration of acid and so can damage the environment. The acid forms when harmful gases from industry and vehicles mix with water in the atmosphere. —*picture* → POLLUTION

,acid 'test noun [singular] a fact, event, or situation that proves whether something is true or effective

acknowledge /ək'nɒlɪdʒ/ verb [T] **1** to accept that something exists, is true, or has a particular quality: *She won't acknowledge that there's a problem.* ♦ *He is **acknowledged** as one of our greatest medical experts.* **2** to thank someone for something that they have given you, or for helping you: *We gratefully acknowledge the efforts of everyone who helped us.* **3** to show that you have seen someone or that you recognize them, for example by smiling or speaking to them

acknowledgment or **acknowledgement** /ək'nɒlɪdʒmənt/ noun **1** [singular/U] something that shows that you accept that something exists or is true

2 [C/U] something that you say or write to thank someone, or to tell them that you have received something that they sent you

Acme thread /'ækmi ,θred/ noun [C/U] TECHNOLOGY a raised line curving around a screw that has straight sides at an angle of 29° to the screw

acne /'ækni/ noun [U] HEALTH a disease of the skin that causes spots to appear on the face, neck, and shoulders

acolyte /'ækəlaɪt/ noun [C] *formal* someone who helps an important person and supports their ideas, often without ever criticizing them

acorn /'eɪkɔːn/ noun [C] the nut of an **oak** tree

acoustic /ə'kuːstɪk/ adj **1** PHYSICS relating to sound **2** MUSIC an acoustic musical instrument does not use electricity to make sounds louder: *an acoustic guitar* —**acoustically** /ə'kuːstɪkli/ adv

acoustics /ə'kuːstɪks/ noun [plural] PHYSICS the way in which a sound can be heard within an enclosed room or space, as the result of its shape and size

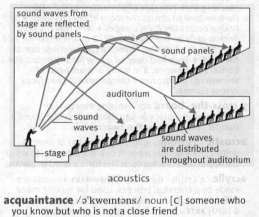

sound waves from stage are reflected by sound panels

sound panels

auditorium

sound waves

sound waves are distributed throughout auditorium

stage

acoustics

acquaintance /ə'kweɪntəns/ noun [C] someone who you know but who is not a close friend

acquainted /ə'kweɪntɪd/ adj *formal* **1** if two people are acquainted, they know each other, but usually not very well **2** if you are acquainted with something, you know about it

acquiesce /,ækwi'es/ verb [I] *formal* to agree to something, or to accept something, without really wanting to

acquire /ə'kwaɪə/ verb [T] **1** to get something: *She has acquired an impressive reputation as a negotiator.* **2** BUSINESS to buy something, especially a company or a share in a company

ac,quired im,mune de'ficiency ,syndrome noun [U] HEALTH see **AIDS**

acquisition /,ækwɪ'zɪʃ(ə)n/ noun **1** [U] the process of getting something: *the acquisition of knowledge* **2** [C] BUSINESS something that someone has bought

acquisitive /ə'kwɪzətɪv/ adj *formal* trying to get things, especially because you want them, rather than because you need them —**acquisitiveness** noun [U]

acquit /ə'kwɪt/ (**acquits, acquitting, acquitted**) verb [T] LAW to state officially that someone is not guilty of a crime: *He was eventually **acquitted of** the charges.*

acquittal /ə'kwɪt(ə)l/ noun [C/U] LAW an official judgment that someone is not guilty of a crime

acre /'eɪkə/ noun [C] a unit for measuring large areas of land, equal to 4,047 square metres

acrid /ˈækrɪd/ adj very strong, bitter, and unpleasant: *an acrid smell*

acrimonious /ˌækrɪˈməʊniəs/ adj unpleasant because people feel angry towards each other —**acrimoniously** adv

acrobat /ˈækrəˌbæt/ noun [C] a performer who balances, jumps, and turns their body in skilful ways

acrobatic /ˌækrəˈbætɪk/ adj involving balancing, jumping, or turning your body with great skill

acrolect /ˈækrəʊlekt/ noun [C] LANGUAGE a **dialect** (=way of speaking a language) that is considered better than all others

acronym /ˈækrənɪm/ noun [C] LANGUAGE a word made from the first letters of a series of words: *NATO is an acronym for the North Atlantic Treaty Organization.*

acrosome /ˈækrəʊsəʊm/ noun [C] BIOLOGY an area in the head of a sperm cell containing enzymes that break down the outer membrane of the egg during fertilization —*picture* → SEX CELL

across /əˈkrɒs/ preposition **1** moving, looking, or reaching from one side of something to the other: *Barbara looked across the room at her husband.* ♦ *a bridge across the River Ganges* ♦ *Who was the first person to fly across the Atlantic?* **2** on the opposite side of a road, river, or line: *There's a bus stop just across the road.* ♦ *They had opened a new factory across the border in Botswana.* **3** in many or most parts of something: *an insurance company with 120 offices across Europe*

a,cross-the-'board adj involving everyone or everything in a place or situation: *across-the-board budget cuts* —**a,cross the 'board** adv

acrostic /əˈkrɒstɪk/ noun [C] a number of lines of writing, for example a poem or a word **puzzle**, in which particular letters from each line form a word or phrase

acrylic /əˈkrɪlɪk/ noun **1** [U] CHEMISTRY a substance made by a chemical process, used for making many different things, for example fibres for cloth, or paint **2** [C/U] ARTS a type of paint that is made from acrylic —**acrylic** adj

act¹ /ækt/ noun

1 single thing sb does	5 part of play
2 behaviour hiding truth	6 law
3 performance	+ PHRASE
4 performer	

1 [C] a single thing that someone does: *an act of violence against innocent people* ♦ *a simple act of kindness* ♦ *groups committing criminal acts*
2 [singular] a way of behaving that is not sincere: *She isn't really upset: it's all an act.*
3 [C] a short performance: *Her act includes singing and dancing.*
4 [C] a person or group who performs on stage: *They're one of rock music's most exciting live acts.*
5 [C] ARTS, MUSIC one of the major divisions of a play, opera, or **ballet**
6 [C] LAW a law: *the Data Protection Act* ♦ *an act of Parliament*
   PHRASE   **act of God** something bad such as a flood that people cannot control because it is caused by natural forces

act² /ækt/ verb **1** [I] to do something: *Now is the time to act.* ♦ *I'm acting on the advice of my doctor.* ♦ *She claims that she acted out of necessity* (=because she had to). **2** [I] to behave in a particular way: *He's been acting strangely all day.* ♦ *Despite her problems, she acted as if nothing was wrong.* **3** [I/T] to perform in

plays or films: *I've always wanted to act.* ♦ *Philip Schofield acted the part of Joseph.* **4** [I] to have a particular effect: *Don't expect the medicine to act immediately.* ♦ *The measures are intended to act as a deterrent to criminals.*
   PHRASAL VERBS   **'act as sth** to do the job of a particular kind of person
   ,act sth 'out to copy events that happened by pretending to be the people involved

acting /ˈæktɪŋ/ noun [U] the job or skill of being an actor

actinide /ˈæktɪnaɪd/ noun [C/U] CHEMISTRY any of the metallic elements with atomic numbers 89 to 103 in the periodic table

actinium /ækˈtɪniəm/ noun [U] CHEMISTRY a silvery radioactive metallic element in the **actinide** group of the periodic table. Chemical symbol: **Ac**

action /ˈækʃ(ə)n/ noun

1 process of doing sth	5 effect of
2 fighting in war	drug/chemical
3 events in play/film	+ PHRASE
4 movement of object	

1 [C/U] something that you do: *Police say they will take tough action against drug dealers.* ♦ *What's the best course of action for dealing with a fire in the laboratory?* ♦ *It's interesting to watch a good salesman in action* (=doing his job). ♦ *How can you justify your actions?*
2 [U] fighting in a war: *a list of soldiers missing in action*
3 [singular] the events that form part of a play or film: *In Scene 1, the action takes place in an expensive restaurant.*
4 [singular] the movement of an object or machine: *This switch slows down the action of the pump.*
5 [singular] the effect that a drug or chemical has: *the action of certain chemicals on the brain*
   PHRASE   **out of action 1** unable to do your usual activities because you are injured or ill **2** equipment that is out of action is unable to be used because it is broken or being repaired

actionable /ˈækʃ(ə)nəb(ə)l/ adj LAW if someone's behaviour is actionable, it is so bad that you could start a legal case against them because of it

'action-,packed adj full of exciting events

,action 'replay noun [C] on television, an important moment in a sports game that is shown a second time, just after it happens

activate /ˈæktɪveɪt/ verb [T] to make a machine or a piece of equipment start working or a process start happening —**activation** /ˌæktɪˈveɪʃ(ə)n/ noun [U]

activated charcoal /ˌæktɪveɪtəd ˈtʃɑːkəʊl/ noun [U] ENVIRONMENT **charcoal** (=a black substance made from burnt wood) that has been treated with oxygen so that it absorbs unwanted substances, for example in water

acti'vation ,energy noun [U] CHEMISTRY the energy that is needed to make molecules of a substance take part in a chemical reaction

active /ˈæktɪv/ adj

1 doing many activities	4 producing a reaction
2 of a volcano	5 in computing
3 in grammar	

1 always doing things, especially with energy and enthusiasm: *Rose is still active at the age of 87.* ♦ *She continues to be active in politics.* ♦ *He is an active member of the American Cancer Society.*
2 GEOLOGY an active volcano is likely to erupt at any time → EXTINCT

3 LANGUAGE an active verb or sentence has the person or thing doing the action as the subject → PASSIVE
4 CHEMISTRY producing a chemical reaction: *What is the active ingredient in detergents?*
5 COMPUTING the active area of a computer screen is being used, or is ready to accept information from the user—**actively** adv

> Word family: **active**
> *Words in the same family as* **active**
> - activate v
> - inactive adj
> - actively adv
> - interactive adj
> - proactive adj
> - deactivate v
> - inactively adv
> - activity n
> - interactively adv
> - reactive adj

the active /'æktɪv/ noun [singular] LANGUAGE the active form of a verb → PASSIVE

,**active 'duty** noun [U] a soldier, pilot etc who is on active duty belongs to a military force as their main job

,**active 'flux** noun [C] TECHNOLOGY a substance that is used during **soldering** to reduce the amount of **oxide** (=rust) that is formed, and to clean the surface of the metal

,**active 'service** noun [U] a soldier, pilot etc who is on active service is ready to take part in a battle that is taking place, rather than simply preparing for one

activist /'æktɪvɪst/ noun [C] POLITICS someone who is an active member of an organization that aims to achieve political or social change: *environmental activists.* ♦ *The meeting was disrupted by environmental activists.* —**activism** noun [U]

activity /æk'tɪvəti/ (plural **activities**) noun **1** [C] something that someone does in order to achieve an aim: *Employees should not engage in political activities without a manager's permission.* ♦ *She coordinates the activities of all senior managers.* ♦ *We plan to expand our business activities in East Africa.* **2** [U] a situation in which a lot of things are happening: *On Saturdays, there's always lots of activity in the streets.* ♦ *There was a high level of electrical activity in the atmosphere.* **3** [C] something enjoyable or interesting that people do: *Guests can enjoy activities like swimming and surfing.*

ac'tivity ,holiday noun [C] TOURISM a holiday that involves a particular activity such as walking, painting, cooking, etc

actor /'æktə/ noun [C] someone who performs in plays and films

actress /'æktrəs/ noun [C] a woman who performs in plays and films. Many women performers prefer to be called actors rather than actresses.

actual /'æktʃuəl/ adj real, true, or exact: *The actual number of people killed is not yet known.* ♦ *The actual situation was quite different from the way she described it.* ♦ *The play is based on actual events.*

,**actual ,bodily 'harm** noun [U] LAW the crime of attacking and injuring someone

actually /'æktʃuəli/ adv **1** used for emphasizing what is really true or what really happened: *We've spoken on the phone but we've never actually met.* ♦ *Actually my name is Tim, not Jim.* **2** used for emphasizing that something is surprising: *I think she actually agreed to go out with him.*

actuarial /,æktʃu'eəriəl/ adj BUSINESS involving calculations about the cost of insurance based on the examination of how often deaths, accidents etc happen

acumen /'ækjʊmən/ noun [U] the ability to make good quick decisions

acupressure /'ækjʊ,preʃə/ noun [U] HEALTH a medical treatment from China that involves pressing on different parts of the body with the hands

acupuncture /'ækjʊ,pʌŋktʃə/ noun [U] HEALTH a traditional Chinese medical treatment that involves putting very thin needles into particular points on the patient's body —**acupuncturist** /'ækjʊ,pʌŋktʃərɪst/ noun [C]

acute /ə'kjuːt/ adj **1** very serious or severe: *an acute pain in his chest* ♦ *acute food shortages* **2** able to notice things very quickly and easily: *an acute sense of smell* **3** an acute accent is the mark · above a letter in some languages that shows it is pronounced in a particular way → GRAVE³

a,**cute 'angle** noun [C] MATHS an angle of less than 90° → OBTUSE ANGLE, RIGHT ANGLE —*picture* → ANGLE

acutely /ə'kjuːtli/ adv used for emphasizing that a feeling is very strong: *He was acutely aware of his public image.*

ad /æd/ noun [C] informal an **advertisement** → AD HOC

AD /,eɪ 'diː/ abbrev used after a date to show that it is later than the birth of Jesus Christ → BC, BCE

adage /'ædɪdʒ/ noun [C] a well-known phrase about life and human experience

adagio¹ /ə'dɑːdʒiəʊ/ adv MUSIC slowly: used as an instruction in music —**adagio** adj

adagio² /ə'dɑːdʒiəʊ/ noun [C] MUSIC a piece of music that should be played or sung slowly

adamant /'ædəmənt/ adj determined not to change a belief or decision: *He was adamant that he was right.* —**adamantly** adv

Adam's apple /,ædəmz 'æp(ə)l/ noun [C] ANATOMY the lump at the front of a man's throat

adapt /ə'dæpt/ verb **1** [I] to change your ideas or behaviour in order to deal with a new situation: *The children adapted quickly to the new school.* **2** [T] to make something more suitable for a new use or situation **3** [T] ARTS to change a book or play and make a film or TV programme from it

adaptable /ə'dæptəb(ə)l/ adj able to easily change, or to be easily changed, in order to deal with new situations —**adaptability** /ə,dæptə'bɪləti/ noun [U]

adaptation /,ædæp'teɪʃ(ə)n/ noun **1** [U] BIOLOGY the changes that happen in animals and plants that make them especially suitable for living in a particular environment **2** [C] ARTS a film or television programme made from a book or play **3** [U] the process of changing something so that it can be used for a different purpose

adapter or **adaptor** /ə'dæptə/ noun [C] **1** an object for connecting several pieces of electrical equipment to one electricity supply **2** an object for connecting two pieces of equipment of different types

adaptive /ə'dæptɪv/ adj changing in order to deal with new situations

add /æd/ verb **1** [T] to put something with another thing: *When the sauce has thickened, add the cheese.* ♦ *They've added more names to the petition.* **2** [I/T] MATHS to calculate the total of two or more numbers: *What do you get if you add 75 and 63?* **3** [T] to say something more: *'Don't worry,' Jenny added hastily.* **4** [T] to give something an extra quality: *The Italian chairs add a touch of elegance to the room.*

PHRASAL VERBS ,**add sth 'on** to include something extra: *If you add on legal fees, the total cost is over $1000.*
'**add to sth** to make a quality more extreme: *The arrival of five more guests only added to the confusion.*
,**add (sth) 'up** MATHS to calculate the total of several numbers or amounts

,**add 'up to sth** to combine to produce a particular result or effect: *These new measures do not add up to genuine reform.*

ADD /ˌeɪ diː 'diː/ noun [U] **HEALTH** attention deficit disorder: a medical condition that makes someone more active than normal, makes it difficult for them to concentrate, and causes problems with their behaviour

added /'ædɪd/ adj extra or additional: *Baby food should contain no added sugar or salt.*

addict /'ædɪkt/ noun [C] **1 HEALTH** someone who cannot stop taking illegal or harmful drugs: *a heroin addict* **2** someone who does a particular activity all the time: *a TV addict*

addicted /ə'dɪktɪd/ adj **1 HEALTH** unable to stop taking a harmful drug, to stop smoking cigarettes, to stop drinking alcohol etc: *He was **addicted to** cocaine.* **2** doing a particular activity as much as you can: *I admit I'm **addicted to** that TV programme.*

addiction /ə'dɪkʃ(ə)n/ noun [C/U] **1 HEALTH** a strong need to keep taking a harmful drug, to keep drinking harmful amounts of alcohol, to keep smoking cigarettes etc **2** a strong need or wish to spend as much time as possible doing a particular activity

addictive /ə'dɪktɪv/ adj **1 HEALTH** an addictive drug is difficult to stop taking **2** an addictive activity is difficult to stop doing

addition /ə'dɪʃ(ə)n/ noun **1** [U] **MATHS** the process of adding two or more numbers or amounts together to make a total **2** [C] something that is added to something else: *The latest **addition to** her business empire is a chain of clothes shops.*

PHRASE in addition as well as something else: *About 30 people were killed in the explosion. In addition, 120 people were injured.* ♦ ***In addition to*** *the twins, Jason has another child by his first wife.*

additional /ə'dɪʃ(ə)nəl/ adj extra: *The new factory will create an additional 400 jobs.* —**additionally** adv: *150 trucks were sent with supplies, and additionally, two cargo ships brought food and medicine.*

additionality /əˌdɪʃə'næləti/ noun [U] **BUSINESS** a way of paying for a project in which an organization or government gives money to another organization or government only if it also pays part of the cost itself

ad'dition sign noun [C] **MATHS** the symbol + that shows that one number is to be added to another

additive /'ædətɪv/ noun [C] **CHEMISTRY** a chemical substance that is added to food to make it last longer or look or taste better

'**additive ,colour** noun [C] **PHYSICS** any of the colours red, green, or blue, which produce white light when they are combined. Additive colours involve light that comes from a direct source.

'**add-,on** noun [C] **1** something that is added to something else **2 add-on** or **add-in COMPUTING** a computer program or a piece of computer equipment that you can add to a computer in order to increase the number of things it is able to do

address[1] /ə'dres/ noun [C] **1** the exact name of the place where someone lives or works: *I'll need your name and address.* ♦ *My address is 125 Carter Street.* **2 COMPUTING** a series of letters, numbers, and symbols that you use to find a particular website on the Internet, or to send someone an email **3** a formal speech

address[2] /ə'dres/ verb [T] **1** to write a name and address on an envelope or parcel: *This letter is **addressed to** Alice McQueen.* **2** to speak to a person or group: *He stood up to address the meeting.* **3** to call

someone a particular name or title when you are speaking to them: *The prince should be **addressed as** 'Sir' at all times.* **4** to try to deal with a problem or question: *Governments have been slow to **address the problem** of global warming.*

ad'dress ,book noun [C] a book or a piece of software in which you write people's names, addresses, telephone numbers, and email addresses in alphabetical order

adductor /ə'dʌktə/ noun [C] **ANATOMY** a muscle that pulls a part of the body back to its normal position → ABDUCTOR

adept /ə'dept/ adj skilful at doing something: *He had quickly become **adept at** handling difficult customers.*

adequate /'ædɪkwət/ adj **1** good enough or large enough= SUFFICIENT ≠ INADEQUATE: *The state has an adequate supply of trained teachers.* ♦ *It's a small office but it's **adequate for** our needs.* **2** satisfactory, but not extremely good ≠ INADEQUATE: *an adequate knowledge of the subject* —**adequately** adv

ADH /ˌeɪ diː 'eɪtʃ/ noun [U] **BIOLOGY** antidiuretic hormone: a hormone that controls the water balance in the body through the kidneys. It is produced when the body loses too much water, for example through sweating.

adhere /əd'hɪə/ verb [I] *formal* to stick to something

PHRASAL VERB ad'here to sth to do the things that are stated in a rule, law, or agreement

adherent /əd'hɪərənt/ noun [C] *formal* a supporter of a set of ideas, an organization, or a person — **adherence** noun [U]

adhesion /əd'hiːʒ(ə)n/ noun [U] **SCIENCE** the tendency of one thing to stick to another, for example for one type of molecule to stick to another type of molecule

adhesive /əd'hiːsɪv/ noun [C] a substance that you use for making things stick together —**adhesive** adj

ad hoc /ˌæd 'hɒk/ adj done only when it is needed for a specific purpose: *Members of the committee are elected on an ad hoc basis.*

adiabatic /ˌædiə'bætɪk/ adj **PHYSICS** an adiabatic process is a **thermodynamic** process that happens without loss or gain of heat

ad infinitum /ˌæd ɪnfɪ'naɪtəm/ adv if you do something ad infinitum, you repeat it again and again

adj. abbrev **LANGUAGE** adjective

adjacent /ə'dʒeɪs(ə)nt/ adj next to or near something else: *The fire spread to an adjacent office block.*

ad,jacent 'angles noun [plural] **MATHS** two angles that are formed when one angle is divided into two parts by a straight line —*picture* → ANGLE

adjective /'ædʒɪktɪv/ noun [C] **LANGUAGE** a word used for describing a noun or pronoun. The word 'big' is an adjective in 'a big house' and 'the house is big'. Many adjectives are **comparative**, which means you can have greater degrees of the quality they describe, for example 'small' and 'smaller', and 'sensible' and 'more sensible', or **superlative**, which means you can have the greatest degree of the quality they describe, for example 'small' and 'smallest', and 'sensible' and 'most sensible': *Adjectives you might use to describe someone's mood are 'happy', 'bad-tempered' or 'cheerful'.* —**adjectival** /ˌædʒɪk'taɪv(ə)l/ adj

adjoining /ə'dʒɔɪnɪŋ/ adj next to and connected to another building, room, or area

adjourn /əˈdʒɜːn/ verb [I/T] to stop something such as a meeting or a trial for a short time and then continue it later —**adjournment** noun [C/U]

adjudicate /əˈdʒuːdɪkeɪt/ verb [I/T] to make an official decision about a problem or legal disagreement —**adjudication** /ə,dʒuːdɪˈkeɪʃ(ə)n/ noun [U], **adjudicator** noun [C]

adjunct /ˈædʒʌŋkt/ noun [C] **LANGUAGE** a word or phrase that adds information to a sentence. In 'I put the box on the table', 'on the table' is an adjunct.

adjust /əˈdʒʌst/ verb **1** [T] to change or move something slightly so that it works or fits better: *She stopped to adjust the strap on her sandal.* ♦ *Use the thermostat to adjust the temperature.* **2** [I] to get used to a new situation by changing your ideas or the way you do things: *It took her two years to **adjust to** life in England.* —**adjuster** noun [C]

adjustable /əˈdʒʌstəb(ə)l/ adj something that is adjustable can be changed in order to make it work or fit better: *an adjustable strap*

ad.justable 'spanner noun [C] **ENGINEERING** a **spanner** (=metal tool for making things tighter or looser) with a head that can be moved to work on nuts and **bolts** of different sizes —*picture* → TOOL

adjustment /əˈdʒʌs(t)mənt/ noun [C/U] **1** a small change that you make to improve something: *I've made a few adjustments – I think it's working better now.* **2 SCIENCE** the way in which you **focus** a microscope. **Fine adjustment** gives you a focus that is very sharp and detailed, and **coarse adjustment** gives you a focus that is not so sharp. —*picture* → MICROSCOPE

ad-lib /ˌæd ˈlɪb/ (**ad-libs, ad-libbing, ad-libbed**) verb [I/T] to say something in a speech or play without preparing or writing it: *I lost the notes for my talk and had to ad-lib.*

administer /ədˈmɪnɪstə/ verb [T] **1** to be responsible for managing or organizing something **2** *formal* to give someone a drug or medical treatment

administration /əd,mɪnɪˈstreɪʃ(ə)n/ noun [U] the activities, processes, or people involved in managing a business, organization, or institution: *Too much money is spent on administration.* —**administrative** /ədˈmɪnɪstrətɪv/ adj

ad,ministrative as'sistant noun [C] someone whose job is to help other people by doing office work

administrator /ədˈmɪnɪ,streɪtə/ noun [C] someone whose job is to manage a business, organization, or institution

admirable /ˈædm(ə)rəb(ə)l/ adj an admirable quality, action, or person deserves to be admired and respected —**admirably** adv

admiral /ˈædm(ə)rəl/ noun [C] an officer of high rank in the navy

admiration /,ædməˈreɪʃ(ə)n/ noun [U] a feeling of respect and approval: *We're full of **admiration for** all your hard work.*

admire /ədˈmaɪə/ verb [T] **1** to respect and approve of someone or something: *I've always admired her dedication and commitment.* ♦ *Ferguson is widely **admired for** his team management skills.* **2** to look at someone or something that you think is attractive: *We stopped to admire the view.* —**admirer** noun [C]

Word family: **admire**

*Words in the same family as **admire***
- admirable *adj*
- admiring *adj*
- admirer *n*
- admirably *adv*
- admiringly *adv*
- admiration *n*

admiring /ədˈmaɪərɪŋ/ adj full of admiration for someone or something —**admiringly** adv

admission /ədˈmɪʃ(ə)n/ noun **1** [C] a statement accepting that something bad is true, or that you have done something wrong: *an **admission of** guilt* **2** [U] the act of accepting someone into a place, organization, or institution: *Several people were **refused admission*** (=not allowed in). **3** [U] the amount that you pay to enter a place or event: ***Admission to** the game is free.*

admit /ədˈmɪt/ (**admits, admitting, admitted**) verb **1** [I/T] to agree that something bad is true, or to agree that you have done something wrong: *Davis admitted causing death by careless driving.* ♦ *In court he **admitted to** lying about the accident.* ♦ *She freely admits that she made mistakes.* **2** [T] to allow someone to enter a place, join an organization, or be treated in a hospital: *Children under five will not be admitted.* ♦ *The Baltic States were **admitted to** the United Nations in 1991.*
PHRASE admit defeat to accept that you cannot succeed at something, and stop trying to do it

admittance /ədˈmɪt(ə)ns/ noun [U] *formal* permission to enter a place or to join an organization

admonish /ədˈmɒnɪʃ/ verb [T] *formal* **1** to tell someone that they have done something wrong **2** to advise someone to do or not do something

ad nauseam /,æd ˈnɔːziæm/ adv if you do or say something ad nauseam, you repeat it so many times that it annoys other people

adolescence /,ædəˈles(ə)ns/ noun [U] the period of someone's life when they are changing from being a child to being an adult, especially the period when they are a young teenager

adolescent /,ædəˈles(ə)nt/ noun [C] a young teenager who is changing from being a child into being an adult —**adolescent** adj

adopt /əˈdɒpt/ verb **1** [I/T] to legally become the parent of another person's child: *The couple are hoping to adopt a baby girl.* **2** [T] to start using a new or different way of doing something: *He decided to adopt a more radical approach to the problem.* **3** [T] to formally accept a proposal, usually by voting

adopted /əˈdɒptɪd/ adj an adopted child has been legally made the son or daughter of someone who is not their natural parent

adoption /əˈdɒpʃ(ə)n/ noun **1** [C/U] the process of making a child legally part of your family: *For many childless couples, adoption is the best solution.* **2** [U] the decision to start using a new or different way of doing something

adoptive /əˈdɒptɪv/ adj adoptive parents have **adopted** a child

adorable /əˈdɔːrəb(ə)l/ adj extremely attractive

adoration /,ædəˈreɪʃ(ə)n/ noun [U] a feeling of great love and respect for someone

adore /əˈdɔː/ verb [T] **1** to love someone very much **2** *informal* to like something very much

adorn /əˈdɔːn/ verb [T] to decorate something —**adornment** noun [C/U]

adrenal gland /əˈdriːn(ə)l ,glænd/ noun [C] **ANATOMY** one of two small glands above the kidneys that produce adrenalin

adrenalin or **adrenaline** /əˈdrenəlɪn/ noun [U] **BIOLOGY** a hormone that is produced in someone's body when they are frightened, excited, or angry

adrift /əˈdrɪft/ adj floating on the water without being tied to anything or controlled by anyone

'**A** ,**drive** noun [C] COMPUTING the disk drive for **floppy disks** on a computer system

adroit /ə'drɔɪt/ adj formal clever or skilful

ADSL /,eɪ diː es 'el/ noun [U] COMPUTING asymmetric digital subscriber line: a method of connecting a computer to the Internet that allows very fast exchange of information, and allows you to be connected at all times without having to pay any extra money

adsorb /æd'zɔːb/ verb [T] CHEMISTRY if a solid substance adsorbs a liquid or gas, a very thin layer of the liquid or gas forms on its surface

adsorption /æd'zɔːpʃ(ə)n/ noun [U] CHEMISTRY the way in which a thin layer of molecules of a substance can stick to the surface of a solid or liquid

aduki bean /ə'duːki ,biːn/ noun [C] a small dark red bean

adulation /,ædjʊ'leɪʃ(ə)n/ noun [U] great praise or admiration, especially for someone who is famous

adult[1] /'ædʌlt, ə'dʌlt/ noun [C] **1** someone who is no longer a child and is legally responsible for their own actions **2** a fully grown animal or bird

adult[2] /'ædʌlt, ə'dʌlt/ adj **1** relating to or typical of adults: About 59% of the adult population said they were suffering from stress. **2** an adult animal, bird etc is fully grown **3** adult magazines, films, and books are about sex

adulterate /ə'dʌltəreɪt/ verb [T] to make a substance less pure by adding something else to it — **adulteration** /ə,dʌltə'reɪʃ(ə)n/ noun [U]

adultery /ə'dʌlt(ə)ri/ noun [U] sex between a married person and someone who is not their husband or wife

adulthood /'ædʌlt,hʊd, ə'dʌlt,hʊd/ noun [U] the period of someone's life when they are an adult

adumbrate /'ædʌm,breɪt/ verb [T] formal to describe or suggest something in a very general way

adv. abbrev LANGUAGE adverb

advance[1] /əd'vɑːns/ noun **1** [C] an instance of progress in science, technology, human knowledge etc: major **advances in** computer technology **2** [C] a payment for work that is given before the work is complete **3** [C] a forward movement towards someone or something, especially by an army **4** advances [plural] an attempt to have a sexual relationship with someone, especially when the other person does not want this

PHRASE **in advance** done in preparation for a particular time or event in the future: You have to make reservations six months in advance.

advance[2] /əd'vɑːns/ verb **1** [I/T] to progress and become better or more developed, or to help something to do this: Technology has advanced dramatically since the 1960s. ◆ He will do anything to advance his career. **2** [I] if an army advances, it moves forward and towards something — **advancement** noun [C/U]

advance[3] /əd'vɑːns/ adj **1** done before a particular time or event: advance warning **2** sent to a place before a larger group that will arrive later: an advance party

advanced /əd'vɑːnst/ adj **1** based on the most recent methods or ideas: advanced technology **2** having achieved a high standard or level: She is very advanced for her age. **3** EDUCATION at a high academic level: a dictionary for advanced students

ad,vance 'guard noun [C] a small group of people, especially soldiers, that is sent to a place before other people to start the work that needs to be done there

advantage /əd'vɑːntɪdʒ/ noun **1** [C/U] something that makes one person or thing more likely to succeed than others = BENEFIT: the advantages of a good education ◆ Her teaching experience **gives** her **an advantage** when working with children. ◆ The home team always **has an advantage over** their opponents. **2** [C] a good feature or quality that something has ≠ DISADVANTAGE: Having children when you're older has both advantages and disadvantages.

PHRASES **take advantage of sb** if someone takes advantage of you, they unfairly use the fact that you are nice in order to get what they want from you: salesmen who take advantage of elderly customers
take advantage of sth to use a situation or opportunity in a way that will help you or be good for you: Planting is timed to **take full advantage of** the rainy season.

advantaged /əd'vɑːntɪdʒd/ adj having benefits or advantages that other people do not have ≠ DISADVANTAGED

advantageous /,ædvən'teɪdʒəs/ adj likely to make someone or something more successful

advent /'ædvent/ noun **the advent of sth** formal the introduction of a new product, idea, custom etc

Advent /'ædvent/ noun [C/U] RELIGION in the Christian religion, the four-week period before Christmas Day

adventure /əd'ventʃə/ noun [C/U] an exciting, unusual, and sometimes dangerous experience: The trip was quite an adventure. ◆ The children were looking for adventure.

ad'venture ,game noun [C] COMPUTING a game you play on a computer in which you take part in an adventure

ad'venture ,holiday noun [C] TOURISM a type of organized holiday in which people do new and exciting things, for example a **trek** or a **safari**

adventurer /əd'ventʃ(ə)rə/ noun [C] someone who uses slightly dishonest methods to become rich or achieve high social status

adventurous /əd'ventʃ(ə)rəs/ adj keen to try new or exciting things

adverb /'ædvɜːb/ noun [C] LANGUAGE a word used for describing a verb, an adjective, another adverb, or a whole sentence. Adverbs in English often consist of an adjective with '-ly' added, for example 'quietly': Think of some adverbs describing the speed at which something is moving, such as 'slowly', 'fast' or 'quickly'.

adverbial[1] /əd'vɜːbiəl/ adj LANGUAGE relating to or containing an adverb —**adverbially** adv

adverbial[2] /əd'vɜːbiəl/ noun [C] LANGUAGE a word or group of words used as an adverb

adversarial /,ædvə'seəriəl/ adj formal involving people arguing with or opposing each other

adversary /'ædvəs(ə)ri/ (plural **adversaries**) noun [C] formal an enemy or opponent

adverse /'ædvɜːs/ adj not good, or likely to cause problems: adverse weather conditions ◆ an adverse reaction from the public —**adversely** adv

adversity /əd'vɜːsəti/ noun [U] a time in someone's life during which a lot of bad things happen to them

advert /'ædvɜːt/ noun [C] an **advertisement**

advertise /'ædvətaɪz/ verb [I/T] **1** to announce a product, service, or event on television, on the Internet, in newspapers etc so that people will buy it, use it, or go to it: The perfume has been advertised in all the major women's magazines. **2** to invite people to

apply for a job by announcing it in a newspaper, on the Internet etc: *We need to **advertise for** a new chef.*
—**advertiser** noun [C]

advertisement /əd'vɜːtɪsmənt/ noun [C] an announcement in a newspaper, on television, on the Internet etc that is designed to persuade people to buy a product or service, go to an event, or apply for a job

advertising /'ædvə,taɪzɪŋ/ noun [U] the business of making advertisements, or advertisements in general: *an advertising agency*

advice /əd'vaɪs/ noun [U] an opinion that someone gives you about the best thing to do in a particular situation: *Ask your father for advice.* ♦ *We are here to **give** people **advice about** health issues.* ♦ *I **took** his **advice** (=did what he advised) and left.* ♦ *She's **acting on** her lawyer's **advice**.*

> **Advice** is never used in the plural and cannot be used with **an**: *She gave me **a** useful **piece of advice** (NOT a useful advice).* ♦ *Do you have **any advice** about the best places to eat?* ♦ *His son asked him for **some advice**.*

ad'vice ,column noun [C] an **agony column** —**ad'vice ,columnist** noun [C]

advisable /əd'vaɪzəb(ə)l/ adj if something is advisable, it is a good idea to do it, especially in order to avoid problems: *It is advisable to keep your belongings with you at all times.* —**advisability** /əd,vaɪzə'bɪləti/ noun [U]

advise /əd'vaɪz/ verb [I/T] **1** to tell someone what you think is the best thing for them to do in a particular situation: *Her doctor advised her **to** rest.* ♦ *I **strongly** advise you to reject the offer.* ♦ *Police are advising the public **against** travelling in the fog.* ♦ *Experts advise the dam-building project should be abandoned.* **2** *formal* to tell someone facts or information that they need to know: *The committee will **advise** all applicants **of** its decision by 30th June.*

> Word family: **advise**
>
> *Words in the same family as **advise***
> - advice *n*
> - advisable *adj*
> - advisability *n*
> - advisory *adj*
> - inadvisable *adj*
> - adviser *n*

adviser or **advisor** /əd'vaɪzə/ noun [C] someone whose job is to give advice on subjects that they know a lot about: *the Prime Minister's advisers* ♦ *a financial adviser*

advisory /əd'vaɪz(ə)ri/ adj existing in order to give advice about a particular subject: *an advisory committee*

advocacy /'ædvəkəsi/ noun [U] strong public support for something

advocate¹ /'ædvəkeɪt/ verb [T] to publicly support a particular policy or way of doing something

advocate² /'ædvəkət/ noun [C] **1** someone who strongly and publicly supports someone or something: *an advocate of political reform* **2** LAW a **lawyer**

adzuki bean /æd'zuːki ,biːn/ noun [C] an **aduki bean**

aegis /'iːdʒɪs/ noun **under the aegis of** *formal* under the protection or authority of a particular group, government, or person

aerate /'eəreɪt/ verb [T] CHEMISTRY, ENVIRONMENT to force air into a liquid, for example to provide oxygen

aeration /eə'reɪʃ(ə)n/ noun [U] CHEMISTRY, ENVIRONMENT the process by which oxygen is dissolved in water, in order to improve its taste or to help living things breathe

aerial¹ /'eəriəl/ adj **1** from a plane: *an aerial view* **2** taking place in the air: *an aerial display*

aerial² /'eəriəl/ noun [C] a piece of equipment made of wire or thin metal, used for receiving radio or television signals

'aerial ,root noun [C] BIOLOGY a root that grows down from a plant part that is above the ground

aerobe /'eərəʊb/ noun [C] BIOLOGY a microorganism that needs oxygen in order to carry out **metabolism**

aerobic /eə'rəʊbɪk/ adj **1** BIOLOGY using oxygen **2** aerobic exercise is a very active type of exercise that makes your heart and lungs stronger

ae,robic respi'ration noun [U] BIOLOGY the process by which the body uses oxygen in order to break down food and produce energy → ANAEROBIC RESPIRATION

aerobics /eə'rəʊbɪks/ noun [U] very active physical exercises done to music. Aerobics is usually done by a group of people in a class.

aerodynamic /,eərəʊdaɪ'næmɪk/ adj PHYSICS shaped in a way that makes it easier for something to move through the air smoothly and quickly

aerodynamics /,eərəʊdaɪ'næmɪks/ noun [U] PHYSICS the science of how objects move through the air

aerofoil /'eərə,fɔɪl/ noun [C] PHYSICS a part of the surface of a plane or other vehicle that changes the direction of the air flow to allow it to be lifted into the air or to be controlled in other ways

aerogramme /'eərəʊ,græm/ noun [C] a piece of very thin paper, used for writing letters that are sent by **airmail**

aeronautics /,eərə'nɔːtɪks/ noun [U] SCIENCE the science of making or flying planes —**aeronautical** adj

aerophone /'eərə,fəʊn/ noun [C] MUSIC a technical name for a **wind instrument**

aeroplane /'eərə,pleɪn/ noun [C] a **plane**

aerosol /'eərə,sɒl/ noun [C] a container in which a liquid such as paint or perfume is kept under high pressure so that it can be **sprayed**: *an aerosol spray*

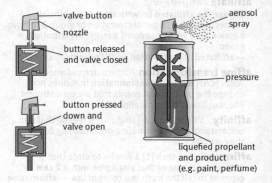

valve button
nozzle
button released and valve closed
aerosol spray
pressure
button pressed down and valve open
liquefied propellant and product (e.g. paint, perfume)

aerosol can

aerospace¹ /'eərəʊ,speɪs/ adj SCIENCE relating to the science or business of building and flying planes and space vehicles

aerospace² /'eərəʊ,speɪs/ noun [U] SCIENCE the atmosphere of the Earth surrounded by outer space

aesthetic /iːs'θetɪk/ adj relating to beauty —**aesthetically** /iːs'θetɪkli/ adv

aesthetics /iːs'θetɪks/ noun [U] ARTS the study of beauty, especially in art

AET abbrev agriculture, education, and training

aetiology /ˌiːtiˈɒlədʒi/ noun HEALTH **1** [C/U] the cause of a disease **2** [U] the study of the causes of diseases

AF abbrev PHYSICS **audio frequency**

affable /ˈæfəb(ə)l/ adj friendly, relaxed, and easy to talk to = FRIENDLY —**affably** adv

affair /əˈfeə/ noun **1 affairs** [plural] events and activities relating to the government, politics, economy etc of a country or region: *The Senator is an expert on foreign affairs.* ♦ *a government spokesperson on consumer affairs* → CURRENT AFFAIRS **2 affairs** [plural] things relating to your personal life, for example what is happening in your family or with your financial situation: *We are friends, but I don't know much about their private affairs.* **3** [C] something that happens, especially something shocking, in public or political life: *The president's popularity was unaffected by the whole affair.* **4** [C] a sexual relationship between two people, especially when one of them is married to someone else: *Her husband denied that he was* **having an affair**.

affect /əˈfekt/ verb [T] **1** to change or influence something, often in a negative way: *Did the newspapers really affect the outcome of the election?* ♦ *The disease affects many different organs of the body.* **2** to have a strong effect on someone's emotions: *She had been deeply affected by her parents' divorce.*

affected /əˈfektɪd/ adj not natural, but done in order to impress other people

affection /əˈfekʃ(ə)n/ noun [U] a feeling of liking and caring about someone or something: *He has great* **affection for** *the country.*

affectionate /əˈfekʃ(ə)nət/ adj showing that you love or care about someone or something —**affectionately** adv

affective /əˈfektɪv/ adj relating to the emotions or to someone's moods

affidavit /ˌæfɪˈdeɪvɪt/ noun [C] LAW a legal document containing a written promise that something is true

affiliate /əˈfɪlieɪt/ verb

    PHRASE **be affiliated to/with sth 1** to be officially connected with a larger organization or group **2** to have a connection with or support a larger organization or group
—**affiliated** adj, **affiliation** /əˌfɪliˈeɪʃ(ə)n/ noun [C/U]

affine transformation /ˈæfaɪn ˌtrænsfəmeɪʃ(ə)n/ noun [C/U] MATHS a **transformation** that does not change the positions of points that are on a straight line, but keeps them parallel

affinity /əˈfɪnəti/ noun [singular] a feeling that you understand and like someone or something because they are like you

affirm /əˈfɜːm/ verb [T] **1** *formal* to state that something is true or that you agree with it **2** LAW to promise to tell the truth in a court of law —**affirmation** /ˌæfəˈmeɪʃ(ə)n/ noun [C]

affirmative /əˈfɜːmətɪv/ adj an affirmative statement or answer means 'yes'

af,firmative 'action noun [U] *American* the practice of choosing someone for a job or course of education who belongs to a group that is often treated unfairly because of their race, sex, health etc

affix /ˈæfɪks/ noun [C] LANGUAGE a part added to the beginning or end of a word that changes its meaning. For example, the affix '-ly' added to the end of the word 'slow' makes the word 'slowly', and the affix 'un-'

added to the beginning of the word 'kind' makes the word 'unkind'. → PREFIX, SUFFIX

afflict /əˈflɪkt/ verb [T] *formal* if someone is afflicted by an illness or serious problem, they suffer from it

affluent /ˈæfluːənt/ adj having enough money to afford a high standard of living —**affluence** /ˈæfluːəns/ noun [U]

afford /əˈfɔːd/ verb [T] **1 can afford** or **be able to afford** to have enough money to pay for something: *I'm not sure how they are able to afford such expensive holidays.* ♦ *The company simply cannot afford to keep all its staff.* **2 can afford** or **be able to afford** to be able to do something without having to worry about the problems that it might cause you: *We can't afford any more delays.* ♦ *No politician can afford to ignore the power of television.* **3** *formal* to provide something

affordable /əˈfɔːdəb(ə)l/ adj cheap enough for ordinary people to be able to afford to buy: *a shortage of affordable housing* —**affordability** /əˌfɔːdəˈbɪləti/ noun [U]

afforestation /əˌfɒrɪˈsteɪʃ(ə)n/ noun [U] ENVIRONMENT the process of planting many trees on an area of land → DEFORESTATION

affray /əˈfreɪ/ noun [C/U] LAW a noisy argument or fight in a public place = DISPUTE

affricate /ˈæfrɪkət/ adj LANGUAGE affricate sounds are sounds like the 'ch' sound in 'church' or the 'j' sound in 'judge' —**affricate** noun [C]

afield /əˈfiːld/ adv **far afield** far away

afloat /əˈfləʊt/ adj floating on water

aforementioned /əˈfɔːˌmenʃ(ə)nd/ adj *formal* mentioned before in an earlier part of a piece of writing

aforethought /əˈfɔːˌθɔːt/ adj LAW **with malice aforethought** with a deliberate intention of causing harm

a fortiori /ˌeɪ fɔːtiˈɔːraɪ/ adj, adv LAW used for saying that something that is true for one case is even more true in another case

afraid /əˈfreɪd/ adj **1** worried that something bad might happen: *I was afraid that you'd miss the flight.* ♦ *The boy was* **afraid to** *say that he didn't know the answer.* ♦ *A lot of people are* **afraid of** *losing their jobs.* **2** frightened: *Don't be afraid – I won't hurt you.* ♦ *Everyone seems to be* **afraid of** *her.*
    PHRASE **I'm afraid** *spoken* used for politely telling someone something that might make them sad, disappointed, or angry: *I can't help you, I'm afraid.* ♦ *I'm afraid I really don't agree.*

afresh /əˈfreʃ/ adv *formal* in a new or different way

Africa /ˈæfrɪkə/ GEOGRAPHY the second largest continent. It is south of Europe, with the Atlantic Ocean to the west and the Indian Ocean to the east. —*picture* → CONTINENT

African-American /ˌæfrɪkən əˈmerɪkən/ noun [C] someone from the US who belongs to a race of people that has dark skin and whose family originally came from Africa —,**African-A'merican** adj

African-Caribbean /ˌæfrɪkən ˌkærəˈbiːən/ noun [C] someone from the Caribbean who belongs to a race of people that has dark skin and whose family originally came from Africa —,**African-Carib'bean** adj

Afro-Caribbean /ˌæfrəʊ ˌkærɪˈbiən/ noun [C] an **African-Caribbean** —,**Afro-Carib'bean** adj

after /ˈɑːftə/ adv, preposition, conjunction

1 later than	4 because of
2 next in order	5 despite
3 trying to get	+ PHRASES

1 later than a particular time or date, or when an event or action has ended: *You can call us any time after 6.00.* ♦ *After the war, I went back to work on the farm.* ♦ *Her birthday is two days after mine.* ♦ *This message arrived after everyone had gone home.* ♦ *Wash your hands after touching raw meat.*

2 next in order, position, or space: *N comes after M in the alphabet.* ♦ *You should turn right just after the market.*

3 trying to catch, find, or get someone or something: *Watch out, he's only after your money.* ♦ *The police are after him for burglary.*

4 because of something that happened in the past: *After what happened last time, I was careful not to make the same mistake again.*

5 despite everything that was done in the past: *After everything that I'd done for her, she didn't even say thank you.*

PHRASES **after all 1** despite what was said or planned before: *I'm sorry, but we've decided not to come after all.* **2** used when giving a reason to explain what you have just said: *She shouldn't be working so hard – she is 70, after all.*

day after day/year after year etc happening again and again every day/year etc for a long time: *Many families come back to our hotel year after year.*
→ ONE

the afterbirth /ˈɑːftəˌbɜːθ/ noun [singular] HEALTH the tissues, including the **placenta**, that come out of the uterus after a birth has taken place

aftercare /ˈɑːftəˌkeə/ noun [U] AGRICULTURE, ENVIRONMENT the process of continuing to manage the soil or the plants in an area that has been returned to **cultivation**, or where a new crop has been planted

ˈafter-efˌfects noun [plural] the unpleasant effects that last for a long time after a situation or event

afterlife /ˈɑːftəˌlaɪf/ noun [singular] RELIGION another life that some people believe begins after death

aftermarket /ˈɑːftəˌmɑːkɪt/ noun [singular] BUSINESS opportunities to sell other things related to a product that has already been sold, for example opportunities to sell spare parts and services for a car

the aftermath /ˈɑːftəˌmæθ/ noun [singular] the effects and results of something bad or important: *In the aftermath of the shootings, there were calls for new gun laws.*

afternoon /ˌɑːftəˈnuːn/ noun [C/U] the period of time between the middle of the day and the beginning of the evening: *What are you doing tomorrow afternoon?* ♦ *an afternoon class* ♦ *I might go shopping this afternoon.*

aftershock /ˈɑːftəˌʃɒk/ noun [C] GEOLOGY a small earthquake that happens after a bigger one

aftertaste /ˈɑːftəˌteɪst/ noun [C] a taste that remains in your mouth after you eat or drink something

afterthought /ˈɑːftəˌθɔːt/ noun [C] something that you say or do after something else because you did not think of it at first

afterwards /ˈɑːftəwədz/ adv after something else that you have already mentioned: *Let's go and see a film and afterwards we could go for a meal.* ♦ *I didn't see her until a few days afterwards.*

afterword /ˈɑːftəˌwɜːd/ noun [C] LITERATURE a part at the end of a book that has a few final remarks → FOREWORD

again /əˈɡen/ adv **1** one more time: *If you fail the exam you will have to take it again.* ♦ *Oh no, now I'll have to start all over again* (=a second time from the

beginning). ♦ *I read through her letter again and again* (=many times). → ONCE **2** returning to the same condition as before: *I turned over and went back to sleep again.*

against /əˈɡenst/ preposition

1 opposing	**4** touching/hitting
2 competing with	**5** for preventing
3 directed towards	+ PHRASES

1 disagreeing with or opposing an action, idea, or plan: *I'm against all forms of censorship.* ♦ *She argued against changing the design.*

2 competing with and trying to defeat someone in a game, race, or fight: *England's World Cup game against Argentina* ♦ *the fight against AIDS*

3 directed towards someone or something in a negative way: *Police are expected to bring criminal charges against Warren.* ♦ *She took the children away, against her husband's wishes* (=although her husband did not want her to do this). ♦ *There was growing resentment against the government.*

4 touching, hitting, or supported by the surface of something: *I fell heavily against the bookshelves.* ♦ *Ron's bike was leaning against a tree.*

5 intended to prevent something or to protect people from it: *All the children have been vaccinated against polio.* ♦ *new, tougher laws against drunken driving*

PHRASES **against the law/rules** not allowed by the law or rules: *It is against the law to park here.*

against your will if someone makes you do something against your will, you do not want to do it: *No one will be forced to leave home against their will.*

have something against sb/sth to dislike someone or something for a particular reason: *I think he's got something against journalists.*

agar /ˈeɪɡɑː/ noun [U] **1** CHEMISTRY a substance similar to **jelly** that is obtained from **seaweed**, used for making liquids thicker. It is a type of carbohydrate. **2** BIOLOGY a substance in which bacteria and other microorganisms are grown in laboratories

agate /ˈæɡət/ noun [C/U] a stone with bands of paler colour that is used for making jewellery

agave /əˈɡeɪvi, əˈɡɑːvi/ noun [C] a plant with leaves with sharp points and flowers on a long stem that grows in the southern part of the US and in Central America

age¹ /eɪdʒ/ noun

1 how old sb is	**5** period of history
2 how old sth is	**6** long time
3 time of life for sth	+ PHRASE
4 becoming old	

1 [C/U] the number of years that someone has lived: *The average age of the delegates was over 60.* ♦ *At the age of 10, I went to live with my aunt.* ♦ *The film is designed to appeal to people of all ages.* ♦ *Ali's very tall for his age.*

2 [C/U] the number of years that something has existed: *The value of the furniture depends on its age and condition.* ♦ *It's hard to guess the age of the object.*

3 [C/U] the time of life when it is possible, legal, or typical for people to do something: *young people who have reached voting age*

4 [U] the state of being old or of becoming old: *His face is starting to show signs of age.* ♦ *Good wines improve with age.*

5 [C] a period of history: *We live in a materialistic age.* ♦ *It was an age of great scientific progress.*

6 ages [plural] *informal* a long time: *She's lived here for ages.* ♦ *He took ages to answer the phone.* ♦ *We* *spent ages trying to print this out.* ♦ *After what seemed like ages, the doctor came back.*

PHRASE come of age when someone comes of age, they reach the age when they are legally an adult

---

Build your vocabulary: talking about age

asking about age
- **how old** used for asking someone their age
- **what age** used for talking about someone's age at a time in the past or future. Say 'How old are you?', not 'What age are you?', when you are asking someone their age

saying how old someone is
- **be 2/10/40 etc (years old)** the most usual way of saying how old someone is
- **be 2/9/18 months old** used for saying how old a baby or young child is
- **aged 2/10/40 etc** used in writing, for example in newspapers, for saying how old someone is
- **a 2-/10-/40-year-old** someone who is 2/10/40 years old
- **a 2-year-old child/a 10-year-old girl/a 40-year-old man** used for saying that someone is 2/10/40 years old

when you are not saying exactly how old someone is
- **in your teens/twenties/thirties etc** used for saying that someone is aged between 13–19, 20–29, 30–39 etc
- **twenty-something/thirty-something etc** used as an adjective or noun for talking about someone aged between 20–29, 30–39 etc
- **teenage** aged between 13 and 19
- **teenager** someone aged between 13 and 19
- **middle-aged** no longer young, but not yet old; usually used for someone aged between about 35 and 55

---

age² /eɪdʒ/ (**ages, ageing, aged**) verb [I/T] to become older or look older, or to make someone do this: *Her father had aged a lot since she had last seen him.*

aged¹ /eɪdʒd/ adj someone who is aged 18, 35, 70 etc is 18, 35, 70 etc years old

aged² /ˈeɪdʒɪd/ adj very old

'age ,group noun [C] all the people between two particular ages, considered as a group: *a game for children in the 7–10 age group*

ageing¹ /ˈeɪdʒɪŋ/ adj becoming old: *a town with an ageing population*

ageing² /ˈeɪdʒɪŋ/ noun [U] the process of becoming old

ageism /ˈeɪdʒɪz(ə)m/ noun [U] the practice of treating older people in an unfair way, for example by not giving them jobs

ageist /ˈeɪdʒɪst/ adj treating older people in an unfair or insulting way

'age ,limit noun [C] the oldest or the youngest age at which someone is allowed to do something

agency /ˈeɪdʒ(ə)nsi/ (plural **agencies**) noun [C] **1** a business that provides a service: *an employment agency* **2** a government department or organization that deals with a particular subject: *the official Chinese news agency* ♦ *law enforcement agencies*

agenda /əˈdʒendə/ noun [C] **1** all the things that need to be done or thought about: *Cutting the number of workers is not on the agenda.* **2** someone's plans or intentions for what they want to achieve: *Beth wanted to get married, but her boyfriend had his own agenda.* ♦ *Getting a good job is at the top of my agenda.* **3** a list of things that people will discuss at a meeting

agent /ˈeɪdʒ(ə)nt/ noun [C] **1** someone whose job is to help a person by finding work for them, or to help a person or company by dealing with their business for them: *a literary agent* **2** someone who works for a government and collects secret information = SPY **3** **CHEMISTRY** a substance that has a particular effect

'age-,old adj having existed for a long time: *the age-old problem of poverty*

agglutination /əˌgluːtɪˈneɪʃ(ə)n/ noun [U] **BIOLOGY** the process by which particles such as blood cells stick together and form a larger mass —**agglutinate** verb [I]

agglutinative /əˈgluːtɪnətɪv/ adj **LANGUAGE** an agglutinative language joins words together to make new words

aggravate /ˈægrəveɪt/ verb [T] to make something bad become worse: *His headache was aggravated by all the noise.* —**aggravation** /ˌægrəˈveɪʃ(ə)n/ noun [C/U], **aggravating** /ˈægrəˌveɪtɪŋ/ adj

aggravated /ˈægrəˌveɪtɪd/ adj **LAW** an aggravated crime has features, such as the use of violence, that make it worse

aggregate /ˈægrɪgət/ noun **1** [C] a total **2** [C/U] **CONSTRUCTION** crushed rock or **gravel** that is mixed with cement, sand, and water to make concrete

aggression /əˈgreʃ(ə)n/ noun [U] **1** an angry feeling that makes people want to behave violently or attack someone **2** a situation in which a person or country attacks another person or country: *an act of aggression against a neighbouring country*

aggressive /əˈgresɪv/ adj **1** someone who is aggressive is behaving in an angry or rude way that shows they want to fight, attack, or argue with other people: *The taxis have features that protect drivers from aggressive passengers.* ♦ *aggressive behaviour* **2** very determined to win or be successful: *an aggressive election strategy* —**aggressively** adv

aggressor /əˈgresə/ noun [C] *formal* a country that starts a war, or someone who starts a fight

aggrieved /əˈgriːvd/ adj someone who is aggrieved feels angry and unhappy because they think that they have been treated unfairly

agile /ˈædʒaɪl/ adj able to move your body quickly and easily —**agility** /əˈdʒɪləti/ noun [U]

agitate /ˈædʒɪteɪt/ verb [I] to try to cause social or political changes by arguing or protesting, or through other political activity: *students agitating for more freedom* —**agitator** noun [C]

agitated /ˈædʒɪˌteɪtɪd/ adj worried or upset ≠ CALM: *She became increasingly agitated as the interview proceeded.*

agitation /ˌædʒɪˈteɪʃ(ə)n/ noun [U] **1** a feeling of being worried or upset = CONCERN **2** *formal* the action of shaking or being shaken

aglow /əˈgləʊ/ adj bright and warm-looking

AGM /ˌeɪ dʒiː ˈem/ noun [C] **BUSINESS** Annual General Meeting: a meeting that a business or organization has every year to discuss issues and elect new officials

agnostic /ægˈnɒstɪk/ noun [C] **RELIGION** someone who believes that it is not possible to know whether God exists or not —**agnostic** adj, **agnosticism** /ægˈnɒstɪˌsɪz(ə)m/ noun [U]

ago /əˈgəʊ/ adv used for saying how much time has passed since something happened: *Your wife phoned a few minutes ago.* ♦ *How long ago did this happen?*

- Use **ago** to say how long before the present time something happened: *He died two years ago.*

- Use **before** to say how long before a time in the past something happened: *I remembered that I had met her ten years before.*
- Use **for** to say how long something in the past continued: *They were married for almost 30 years.*

agonize /ˈæɡənaɪz/ verb [I] to spend a long time worrying about something, especially when you have to make a decision: *For days I agonized over whether to accept his offer.*

agonizing /ˈæɡənaɪzɪŋ/ adj **1** making you feel very worried and upset for a long time **2** very painful

agony /ˈæɡəni/ (plural **agonies**) noun [C/U] **1** great pain **2** great worry or sadness: *She had to go through the agony of leaving her children.*

'agony ˌcolumn noun [C] part of a magazine or newspaper where someone gives advice to readers by answering letters about their problems

agoraphobia /ˌæɡ(ə)rəˈfəʊbiə/ noun [U] **HEALTH** a fear of going outside and being in public places —**agoraphobe** /ˈæɡ(ə)rəˌfəʊb/ noun [C]

agoraphobic /ˌæɡ(ə)rəˈfəʊbɪk/ adj **HEALTH** suffering from agoraphobia —**agoraphobic** noun [C]

agranulocyte /əˈɡrænjʊləʊsaɪt/ noun [C] **BIOLOGY** a white blood cell that does not have **granules** in its cytoplasm

agrarian /əˈgreəriən/ adj *formal* relating to or involving farming or farmers= AGRICULTURAL

agree /əˈgriː/ (**agrees, agreeing, agreed**) verb **1** [I/T] to have the same opinion as someone else: *Doreen thought that the house was too small, and Jim agreed.* ♦ *I agree with my mother about most things.* ♦ *The committee members all agree on the need for more information.* ♦ *We all agree that we should celebrate this event.* **2** [I] to say that you will do something that someone else wants or suggests: *I asked her to marry me, and she agreed.* ♦ *We have agreed to their request for a full investigation.* ♦ *The school agreed to send the students on the course.* **3** [I/T] to decide together what will be done and how it will be done: *Management and unions have agreed a pay deal.* ♦ *We need to agree on a date for our next meeting.* **4** [I] if two pieces of information agree, they are the same or they suggest the same thing: *The observations agree with the predictions we made earlier.* → ACCEPT

PHRASAL VERB **aˈgree with sth 1** to think that something is the right thing to do: *I don't agree with corporal punishment in schools.* **2 LANGUAGE** if a word such as a verb or adjective agrees with a noun or pronoun, it has the correct form for the noun or pronoun, according to whether it is singular or plural, **masculine** or **feminine**

Word family: **agree**

Words in the same family as agree
- **agreeable** *adj*
- **disagreeable** *adj*
- **agreement** *n*
- **disagree** *v*
- **agreeably** *adv*
- **disagreeably** *adv*
- **disagreement** *n*

agreeable /əˈgriːəb(ə)l/ adj **1** acceptable: *a compromise that is agreeable to both sides* **2** *formal* friendly or nice ≠ DISAGREEABLE **3** *formal* willing to do or accept something —**agreeably** adv

agreed /əˈgriːd/ adj **1** an agreed price, limit, date etc is one that people have talked about and accepted **2** if people are agreed, they all agree about what to do

agreement /əˈgriːmənt/ noun **1** [C] an arrangement or decision about what to do, made by two or more people, groups, or organizations: *an agreement between political parties* ♦ *Management announced that it had reached an agreement with the unions.* ♦ *an agreement on military cooperation* **2** [U] a situation when people have the same opinion or make the same decision: *After a long discussion, there was still no agreement about what to do next.* ♦ *We are all in agreement that Mr Ross should resign.* **3** [U] **LANGUAGE** a situation in which a word such as a verb or adjective has the correct form for the noun or pronoun that it refers to, according to its number, **gender**, and person: *In the sentence 'They are happy', the verb 'are' is in agreement with the pronoun 'they'.*

agribusiness /ˈæɡrɪˌbɪznəs/ noun [U] **AGRICULTURE, BUSINESS** the business of operating a very large farm

agricultural /ˌæɡrɪˈkʌltʃ(ə)rəl/ adj relating to farming and farmers —*picture* → on next page —**agriculturally** adv

agriculture /ˈæɡrɪˌkʌltʃə/ noun [U] **AGRICULTURE** the work, business, or study of farming

agriculturist /ˌæɡrɪˈkʌltʃ(ə)rɪst/ or **agriculturalist** /ˌæɡrɪˈkʌltʃ(ə)rəlɪst/ noun [C] a scientist who is an expert in a particular area of agriculture and who gives advice and information to people who work in agriculture

agri-industry /ˈæɡri ˌɪndəstri/ noun [C/U] **BUSINESS, AGRICULTURE agro-industry**

agritourism /ˈæɡrɪˌtʊərɪz(ə)m/ noun [U] **TOURISM** a type of holiday in which visitors stay on a farm and sometimes learn about or join in some of the farming activities

agro-ecology /ˈæɡrəʊ ɪˌkɒlədʒi/ noun [U] **AGRICULTURE** the science of applying environmental knowledge and principles to agriculture, so that it does not damage the environment —**agro-ecological** /ˌæɡrəʊiːkəˈlɒdʒɪk(ə)l/ adj

agro-industry /ˈæɡrəʊ ˌɪndəstri/ noun [U] **BUSINESS, AGRICULTURE 1** the business of producing goods in farming **2** an industry that makes a particular farming product

agronomics /ˌæɡrəˈnɒmɪks/ noun [U] **AGRICULTURE, ECONOMICS** the branch of economics that deals with the way land is used and the things that are produced by farming

agronomy /əˈgrɒnəmi/ noun [U] **AGRICULTURE** the study of crops and the types of soil they grow in —**agronomic** /ˌæɡrəˈnɒmɪk/ adj, **agronomically** /ˌæɡrəˈnɒmɪkli/ adv, **agronomist** noun [C]

aground /əˈgraʊnd/ adv **run/go aground** if a ship runs aground, it becomes stuck on a piece of ground or a rock under the water

ah /ɑː/ interjection **1** used for showing that you see or understand something **2** used for showing that you are interested, surprised, pleased, or annoyed

aha /ɑːˈhɑː/ interjection used for showing that you have suddenly realized or understood something

ahead /əˈhed/ adv **1** in the direction in front of you: *There's a petrol station just a few miles ahead.* ♦ *She walked ahead of him along the corridor.* ♦ *Instead of turning left, he drove straight ahead towards the river.* **2** used for saying what will happen in the future: *Looking ahead to next summer, where would you like to go?* ♦ *We have a busy day ahead of us.* → LIE AHEAD **3** leaving, arriving, or doing something before someone else: *You go on ahead and tell them we're coming.* ♦ *David finished ahead of me in last year's race.*

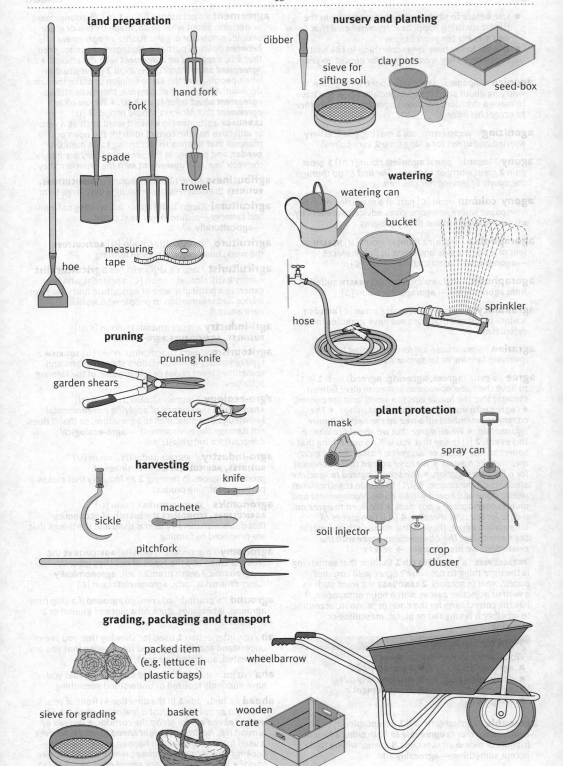

land preparation

dibber

sieve for sifting soil

hand fork

fork

spade

trowel

hoe

measuring tape

nursery and planting

clay pots

seed-box

watering

watering can

bucket

sprinkler

hose

pruning

pruning knife

garden shears

secateurs

plant protection

mask

spray can

soil injector

crop duster

harvesting

knife

machete

sickle

pitchfork

grading, packaging and transport

packed item (e.g. lettuce in plastic bags)

wheelbarrow

sieve for grading

basket

wooden crate

agricultural tools

PHRASES ahead of your/its time very advanced or modern: *As a writer, Sterne was ahead of his time.*
ahead of time/schedule at an earlier time than was planned
→ GO AHEAD

AI /ˌeɪ ˈaɪ/ noun [U] AGRICULTURE the process of **artificial insemination**

aid¹ /eɪd/ noun 1 [U] ECONOMICS money, food, or other help that a government or organization gives to people who need it: *financial aid* ♦ *The UN provided emergency economic aid to the refugees.* 2 [U] help with doing something: *Chromosomes can be seen with the aid of a microscope.* ♦ *Several people heard her screams, but no one went to her aid.* 3 [C] something that makes it easier to do something: *Hypnosis can be an aid to giving up smoking.*
PHRASE in aid of in order to make money to help an organization or group: *a concert in aid of victims of the war*

aid² /eɪd/ verb [T] *formal* 1 to help someone to do something, or to help to make something happen more easily: *Gently exercise the injured leg to aid recovery.* 2 ECONOMICS to give money, food, or other help to a country or organization that needs it
PHRASE aid and abet LAW to help someone to commit a crime

'aid ˌagency noun [C] an organization that gives money, food, or other help to people who have been affected by situations such as wars or floods

aide /eɪd/ noun [C] someone whose job is to help another person in their work

AIDS or Aids /eɪdz/ noun [U] HEALTH acquired immune deficiency syndrome: a serious disease that destroys the body's ability to defend itself against infection. It is caused by the virus, HIV.

'aid ˌworker noun [C] someone who works for an international organization giving help in a place where people need it

aileron /ˈeɪlərɒn/ noun [C] a part on the back edge of an aircraft's wing that is used in making one side of the aircraft move higher than the other

ailing /ˈeɪlɪŋ/ adj not strong, healthy, or successful: *an ailing business*

ailment /ˈeɪlmənt/ noun [C] a minor illness

aim¹ /eɪm/ noun 1 [C] the thing that you hope to achieve by doing something= GOAL: *My main aim on this course is to gain confidence.* ♦ *We visit schools with the aim of getting young people interested in the theatre.* 2 [singular] your ability to hit something when you throw, kick, or shoot something at it: *My aim isn't very good.*
PHRASE take aim (at) to point a gun at something before shooting

aim² /eɪm/ verb 1 [I] to intend or hope to achieve something: *Most of the students were aiming for jobs in manufacturing.* ♦ *The project aims to provide support for young musicians.* 2 [I/T] to point something such as a gun at a person or thing: *He was aiming at the tree but he missed.* ♦ *I looked up to see Betty aiming a gun at me.* 3 [T] **be aimed at sb** to be intended to be read, watched, or used by people of a particular type: *The book is aimed at people with no specialized knowledge.* 4 [T] **be aimed at doing sth** to have the goal of achieving a particular thing: *an energy programme that is aimed at reducing our dependence on fossil fuels*

aimless /ˈeɪmləs/ adj without any particular purpose or plan —**aimlessly** adv

air¹ /eə/ noun 1 [U] SCIENCE the mixture of gases that we breathe and that makes up the atmosphere of the Earth. Air contains about 78% nitrogen and 21% oxygen, with the rest being made up of **argon**, carbon dioxide, **helium**, and other gases: *Do we really want all these cars polluting the air?* ♦ *She breathed in the cold air.* ♦ *I'd like to open the window: I need some air.* 2 the air [singular] the space around things and above the ground: *They threw their hats up into the air.* ♦ *birds flying through the air* 3 [singular] a feeling or attitude: *She spoke with her usual air of authority.* 4 airs [plural] the false behaviour of someone who is trying to impress other people: *My friends are people I trust, and I don't have to put on airs with them.*
PHRASES by air travelling in a plane
sth is in the air used for saying that people all have a similar feeling, especially a feeling that something exciting or new is happening: *Spring is in the air.*
on air or on the air on radio or television
up in the air if a plan is up in the air, you have not yet decided what will happen
→ CLEAR², FRESH AIR, OPEN AIR

air² /eə/ verb 1 [T] to publicly make a complaint or state your opinion: *In an interview, the singer aired his views on family life.* 2 [T] to broadcast something on radio or television: *The show was first aired in 2001.* 3 [I/T] if you air a place or piece of clothing, or if they air, you let fresh air pass through them until they smell clean and fresh

'air ˌbag noun [C] a piece of equipment in a car that protects people in a crash by immediately filling with air

'air ˌbladder noun [C] BIOLOGY 1 a small bag inside the body of some types of fish that helps them to swim or to breathe 2 a small space inside some types of seaweed that helps them to float

airborne /ˈeəbɔːn/ adj moving or carried in the air

'air ˌbrake noun [C] a type of brake that works by air pressure, for example on a bus or lorry

air-breather /ˈeə ˌbriːðə/ noun [C] BIOLOGY an animal that can live in water but that needs to breathe air, for example a frog

'air ˌbrick noun [C] CONSTRUCTION a brick with holes in it that fits into the wall of a house to allow air through it, especially into the space beneath a floor

'air ˌcleaner noun [C] ENGINEERING an **air filter**

air conditioning /ˌeə kənˈdɪʃ(ə)nɪŋ/ noun [U] a system that makes the air inside a building, room, or vehicle colder —**'air-conˌditioned** adj: *air-conditioned rooms*

'air ˌcorridor noun [C] a narrow area that an aircraft must not fly outside when flying over a country

aircraft /ˈeəkrɑːft/ (plural **aircraft**) noun [C] a plane, **helicopter**, or other vehicle that flies

'aircraft ˌcarrier noun [C] a ship that carries military planes

aircrew /ˈeəkruː/ noun [C] the pilot and other people who work on a plane when it is flying

airdrop /ˈeədrɒp/ noun [C] an operation to deliver supplies to a place by dropping them from an aircraft

airfare /ˈeəfeə/ noun [C] the money that someone pays to go somewhere by plane

airfield /ˈeəfiːld/ noun [C] a small airport for military or private aircraft

'air ˌfilter noun [C] ENGINEERING a piece of equipment that removes dust and dirt from the air that is taken into an engine '**air ,float** noun [C] BIOLOGY an air-filled **sac** (=bag) on each side of the egg of the *Anopheles* mosquito, which helps the egg to float on the surface of water —*picture* → MOSQUITO

'**air ,force** noun [C] the part of a country's military forces that fights using planes

'**air ,hole** noun [C] SCIENCE a hole at the base of a Bunsen burner that allows air to mix with the flammable gas so that it burns properly

'**air ,letter** noun [C] a letter written on one piece of light paper that is folded over to form a type of envelope and is sent by **airmail**

airlift /'eə,lɪft/ noun [C] an action by which people or things are taken into or away from a dangerous place by aircraft —**airlift** verb [T]

airline /'eə,laɪn/ noun [C] a company that owns aircraft and takes people or goods by plane from one place to another

airlink /'eə,lɪŋk/ noun [C] TOURISM a way of travelling between two places, in planes or helicopters

airmail /'eə,meɪl/ noun [U] the system for sending post by plane

air marshal /'eə ,mɑːʃ(ə)l/ noun [C] a **sky marshal**

'**air ,mass** noun [C] GEOGRAPHY a very large mass of air in the atmosphere in which the temperature is almost constant, and which is divided from another mass by a weather front

airplane /'eə,pleɪn/ noun [C] *American* a **plane**

'**air ,pocket** noun [C] **1** an area where the **air pressure** is low that makes an aircraft fall suddenly to a lower level **2** a small enclosed area that becomes filled with air

airport /'eə,pɔːt/ noun [C] a place where planes arrive and leave

'**air ,pressure** noun [U] PHYSICS, GEOGRAPHY **atmospheric pressure**

'**air ,rage** noun [U] violent behaviour by an aircraft passenger towards other people on the aircraft

'**air ,raid** noun [C] an **air strike**

'**air ,resistance** noun [U] PHYSICS the effect of air in slowing down a moving object

'**air ,sac** noun [C] BIOLOGY **1** an **alveolus** —*picture* → LUNG **2** in birds, a space formed by the growth of the lungs into the bones. It reduces the bones' total weight. **3** in insects, a wider area formed in the tubes that carry air through the body. It helps respiration.

,**air-sea 'rescue** noun [U] the activity of saving someone from the sea using a helicopter

airside /'eə,saɪd/ adj, adv TOURISM next to the part of an airport where aircraft stand

airspace /'eə,speɪs/ noun [U] the sky above a particular country

airspeed /'eə,spiːd/ noun [C/U] the speed at which an aircraft flies

airstream /'eə,striːm/ noun [C] a wind, especially one blowing high in the sky

'**air ,strike** noun [C] an attack in which one or more planes drop bombs on a place

airstrip /'eə,strɪp/ noun [C] a long narrow piece of ground where planes can land and fly from

'**air ,terminal** noun [C] TOURISM a large building at an airport, where passengers **check in** (=show their tickets and leave their bags) before flying and collect their bags after flying. Air terminals are usually simply called **terminals**.

airtight /'eə,taɪt/ adj not allowing air to enter or leave: *an airtight container*

,**air traffic con'trol** noun [U] the activity of organizing the movement of planes

,**air traffic con'troller** noun [C] someone whose job is to organize the movement of planes in a particular area by giving instructions to pilots by radio

airwaves /'eə,weɪvz/ noun [plural] radio waves that are used for sending signals for radio, television, and mobile phones

airway /'eə,weɪ/ noun [C] **1** ANATOMY a tube that carries air into the lungs from the nose or mouth **2** a path through the sky that planes regularly use

airy /'eəri/ adj with a lot of fresh air and space

aisle /aɪl/ noun [C] a passage between rows of seats, for example in a theatre, church, or plane

'**aisle ,seat** noun [C] TOURISM a seat in a train, plane, etc, next to an aisle

ajar /ə'dʒɑː/ adj a door that is ajar is slightly open

à la carte /,ɑ: lɑ: 'kɑːt/ adj, adv TOURISM priced separately on a menu rather than as part of a meal

alacrity /ə'lækrəti/ noun **with alacrity** *formal* quickly and with enthusiasm

alarm¹ /ə'lɑːm/ noun **1** [U] the worried feeling that something unpleasant or dangerous might happen: *She is a little unwell but there is no **cause for alarm*** (=reason to worry). ♦ *There was a note of alarm in her voice.* **2** [C] a piece of electrical equipment that warns you of danger by making a loud noise: *a fire alarm* ♦ *My car **alarm went off** in the middle of the night.* **3** [C] an **alarm clock**: *I'll **set the alarm** for eight.*

PHRASE **raise/sound the alarm** to tell people about something dangerous that is happening: *The crash was seen by a farmer, who raised the alarm on his mobile phone.*
→ FALSE ALARM

alarm² /ə'lɑːm/ verb [T] to make someone worried that something unpleasant or dangerous might happen: *School officials were alarmed by the number of children with the disease.*

a'**larm ,bell** noun **1** [C] a bell that rings to warn you of danger **2 alarm bells** [plural] something that makes you feel something unpleasant or dangerous is going to happen

a'**larm ,clock** noun [C] a clock that wakes you up at a particular time by making a noise

alarmed /ə'lɑːmd/ adj **1** worried that something unpleasant or dangerous might happen **2** protected by an **alarm**

alarming /ə'lɑːmɪŋ/ adj frightening or worrying —**alarmingly** adv

alarmist /ə'lɑːmɪst/ adj causing unnecessary fear or worry

alas /ə'læs/ interjection an old word used for saying that you are sad about something

albatross /'ælbə,trɒs/ noun [C] a large white ocean bird with long narrow wings

albeit /ɔːl'biːɪt/ conjunction *formal* used for introducing a comment that slightly changes or reduces the effect of what was said before it

album /'ælbəm/ noun [C] **1** a CD, record, or **cassette** with several songs or pieces of music on it **2** a book in which you can collect things such as photographs or stamps

albumen /'ælbjʊmɪn/ noun [U] BIOLOGY the clear protein that surrounds the yolk of an egg and provides some of the food for the embryo

alcohol /'ælkə,hɒl/ noun **1** [U] drinks such as wine and beer that can make people drunk: *a ban on the advertising of alcohol* **2** [U] the colourless substance in drinks such as wine and beer that can make people drunk: *The alcohol content in wine is usually about 12%.* **3** [C] CHEMISTRY an organic compound that contains the **-OH** group. The names of alcohols usually end in '-ol', for example **ethanol**.

alcoholic¹ /,ælkə'hɒlɪk/ adj **1** containing alcohol: *alcoholic drinks* **2** affected by alcoholism: *alcoholic patients*

alcoholic² /,ælkə'hɒlɪk/ noun [C] someone who finds it difficult to control the amount of alcohol that they drink

alcoholism /'ælkəhɒl,ɪz(ə)m/ noun [U] the medical condition that someone has when they cannot control the amount of alcohol that they drink

alcove /'ælkəʊv/ noun [C] a small area in a room that has been created by building part of a wall further back than the rest of the wall

ale /eɪl/ noun [C/U] a type of dark-coloured beer

alert¹ /ə'lɜːt/ adj **1** able to think clearly: *She's remained physically fit and mentally alert.* **2** paying attention to what is happening and ready to react to it: *Parents must be alert to the symptoms of the disease.* —**alertness** noun [U]

alert² /ə'lɜːt/ noun [C] a warning about something dangerous

PHRASE **on the alert** or **on full alert** ready to deal with a dangerous situation

A level /'eɪ ˌlev(ə)l/ noun [C] EDUCATION an examination that students in England and Wales take before going to university → AS LEVEL

alfalfa /æl'fælfə/ noun [U] AGRICULTURE a plant with purple flowers that is fed to animals. Some people eat alfalfa **sprouts** (=young plant stems) in salads.

algae /'ældʒiː, 'ælgiː/ (singular **alga** /'ælgə/) noun [plural] BIOLOGY simple plants that have no roots, stems, or leaves and that usually grow in water. Most types of algae are small and green but some are large and brown, like some types of **seaweed**. Algae are an important part of **food chains** as many fish, insects, larvae etc feed on them.

algal bloom /,ælgəl 'bluːm/ noun [C] ENVIRONMENT a large area of algae on the surface of water, caused for example by the nutrients in pollution. Algal blooms can be harmful to fish, birds, and other organisms.

algebra /'ældʒɪbrə/ noun [U] MATHS a type of mathematics that uses letters and symbols to represent numbers —**algebraic** /,ældʒɪ'breɪɪk/ adj, **algebraically** adv

algorithm /'ælgə,rɪð(ə)m/ noun [C] COMPUTING a set of rules for solving problems or doing calculations —**algorithmic** /,ælgə'rɪðmɪk/ adj

alias¹ /'eɪliəs/ preposition used before a different name that someone uses instead of their real name: *James Bond, alias Agent 007*

alias² /'eɪliəs/ noun [C] a different name that someone uses instead of their real name

alibi /'ælɪbaɪ/ (plural **alibis**) noun [C] evidence that someone was not in a particular place when a crime was committed there

alien¹ /'eɪliən/ adj **1** not familiar= STRANGE **2** from another planet

alien² /'eɪliən/ noun [C] a creature from another planet

alienate /'eɪliəneɪt/ verb [T] **1** to make someone dislike you or not want to help you: *Their campaign has alienated the public.* **2** to make someone feel that they do not belong in a place or group **3** LAW to give someone something such as property or rights

alienated /'eɪliə,neɪtɪd/ adj feeling that you do not belong in a place or group: *angry and alienated teenagers*

alienation /,eɪliə'neɪʃ(ə)n/ noun [U] **1** the feeling that you do not belong in a particular society, place, or group = ISOLATION **2** the process of making someone dislike you, or not want to help or support you **3** LAW the process of giving someone something such as property or rights

alight¹ /ə'laɪt/ adj burning

alight² /ə'laɪt/ verb [I] *formal* **1** to get off a train, bus, or other vehicle **2** if a bird, insect, or other flying creature alights on something, it flies onto it and stops there= LAND

align /ə'laɪn/ verb [T] **1** to give your support to a group or country: *Many women do not want to **align themselves with** the movement.* **2** to organize things so that they are in the correct position in relation to other things —**alignment** noun [C/U]

alike¹ /ə'laɪk/ adj similar: *The sisters don't really look alike.*

alike² /ə'laɪk/ adv **1** in the same way, or in a similar way: *Students of both sexes dressed alike.* **2** used for referring to two people or things equally: *It's a show that appeals to young and old alike.*

alimentary canal /,ælɪ,ment(ə)ri kə'næl/ noun [singular] ANATOMY the system of organs in humans and other animals that breaks down food into a form that the cells can absorb and use. The oesophagus, the stomach, and the intestines are all part of the alimentary canal.

alive /ə'laɪv/ adj **1** living and not dead: *My father died last year but my mother is still alive.* ♦ *The family was stealing food just to **stay alive**.* **2** still existing and not gone or forgotten: *Memories of the war are still very much alive.* ♦ *They struggled to **keep** their language and traditions **alive**.* **3** full of excitement or activity: *The village really **comes alive** at Christmas.* ♦ *The street was **alive with** the sound of children playing.*

alkali /'ælkə,laɪ/ noun [C/U] CHEMISTRY a base that dissolves in water and has a pH of more than 7. Alkalis turn litmus paper blue. A common alkali used for cleaning is **ammonium hydroxide**. → ACID

alkali ˌmetal noun [C] CHEMISTRY a soft, white, metallic, very active element belonging to group 1 of the periodic table. For example, **lithium**, **sodium**, and **potassium** are alkali metals.

alkaline /'ælkə,laɪn/ adj CHEMISTRY containing an alkali or consisting of an alkali

alkaline ˌearth ˌmetal noun [C] CHEMISTRY one of a group of silvery, soft, low-density elements that belong to group 2 of the periodic table. For example, **magnesium**, **calcium**, and **radium** are alkaline earth metals.

alkalinity /,ælkə'lɪnəti/ noun [U] CHEMISTRY the amount of alkali in a substance, often measured in pH

alkaloid /'ælkə,lɔɪd/ noun [C/U] CHEMISTRY a substance found in plants that is used in medicines, drugs, and poisons. **Morphine**, **nicotine**, and **strychnine** are all alkaloids.

alkane /ˈælkeɪn/ noun [C] CHEMISTRY a chemical compound that contains only carbon and hydrogen and whose atoms share one pair of electrons between two carbon atoms

alkene /ˈælkiːn/ noun [C] CHEMISTRY a chemical compound that contains only carbon and hydrogen and whose atoms share two pairs of electrons between two carbon atoms

alkyl benzene /ˌælkɪl ˈbenziːn/ noun [U] CHEMISTRY a chemical that is used to make **detergents**

all /ɔːl/ adv, determiner, pronoun **1** the whole of an amount, thing, situation, or period of time: *Have you spent all your money?* ♦ *There's no cake left. They've eaten it all.* ♦ *I've been awake all night worrying.* ♦ *Just three pounds – that's all I've got left.* **2** every person or thing: *We all enjoyed the party.* ♦ *No one can solve all these problems.* ♦ *All seven astronauts were killed in the explosion.* ♦ *I want all of you to listen carefully.* ♦ *We play all kinds of music – rock, reggae, jazz, even classical.* **3** used for emphasizing something: *I'm all in favour of giving children more freedom.* ♦ *We're going to be late, and it's all because of you.* ♦ *The exam season is so stressful – I'll be glad when it's all over* (=completely finished). **4** used for showing the score in a game when the two teams or players have an equal number of points: *The score at half time was one all.*

PHRASES **all along** during the whole time that something is happening: *Mary knew all along what I was planning to do.*
all but almost: *The job is all but finished.*
for all sth despite something: *For all its faults, she loved the city.*
in all or **all told** when the whole of an amount or number is included: *In all, there are over 120 languages spoken in London's schools.*
→ SUDDEN²

all-age ˈschool noun [C] EDUCATION a school that provides education for students of all ages

Allah /ˈælə/ RELIGION the name of God in Islam

allay /əˈleɪ/ verb [T] *formal* if you allay feelings such as fears or worries, you make someone feel less afraid or worried

the ˌall-ˈclear noun [singular] **1** a statement from a doctor that someone is well again **2** a signal or statement that a period of danger has ended

ˌall-ˈday adj continuing or available for the whole day: *an all-day meeting* ♦ *an all-day breakfast*

allegation /ˌælɪˈɡeɪʃ(ə)n/ noun [C] a statement claiming that someone has done something wrong or illegal

allege /əˈledʒ/ verb [T] to say that someone has done something wrong or illegal, even though this has not been proved

alleged /əˈledʒd/ adj claimed to be true but not proved: *his alleged part in a terrorist plot* —**allegedly** /əˈledʒɪdli/ adv

allegiance /əˈliːdʒ(ə)ns/ noun [C/U] loyalty to a person, group, idea, or country

allegory /ˈæləɡ(ə)ri/ (plural **allegories**) noun [C/U] LITERATURE a story, poem, or picture in which events and characters are used as symbols to express a moral or political idea —**allegorical** /ˌæləˈɡɒrɪk(ə)l/ adj

allegro¹ /əˈleɡrəʊ/ adv MUSIC quickly: used as an instruction in music —**allegro** adj

allegro² /əˈleɡrəʊ/ noun [C] MUSIC a piece of music that should be played or sung quickly

allele /əˈliːl/ noun [C] BIOLOGY one of the alternative forms of a gene. Alleles exist on the same **locus** (=position) on paired chromosomes, and control the same **inherited** characteristic.

all-embracing /ˌɔːl ɪmˈbreɪsɪŋ/ adj including everyone or everything

allergen /ˈælə(r)dʒen/ noun [C] HEALTH a substance such as pollen, mould, or a type of food that is harmless to most people but that produces a severe allergic reaction in others

allergic /əˈlɜː(r)dʒɪk/ adj HEALTH **1** affected by an allergy: *I'm allergic to nuts.* **2** caused by an allergy: *an allergic reaction*

allergy /ˈælə(r)dʒi/ (plural **allergies**) noun [C/U] HEALTH a medical condition in which someone becomes ill as a reaction to something that they eat, breathe, or touch

alleviate /əˈliːvieɪt/ verb [T] *formal* to make something less painful, severe, or serious —**alleviation** /əˌliːviˈeɪʃ(ə)n/ noun [U]

alley /ˈæli/ (plural **alleys**) or **alleyway** /ˈæliˌweɪ/ noun [C] a narrow street or passage between buildings

alliance /əˈlaɪəns/ noun [C] **1** an arrangement in which people, groups, or countries agree to work together: *The two companies have formed a strategic alliance.* ♦ *an alliance between the two parties* **2** an arrangement in which two or more countries join together to defend themselves against an enemy

allied /ˈælaɪd/ adj **1** joined together in a military alliance: *the allied army* **2** /əˈlaɪd, ˈælaɪd/ if something is allied to or with something else, it is connected with it

alligator /ˈælɪˌɡeɪtə(r)/ noun [C] a large reptile with a long pointed mouth and sharp teeth. Alligators look like **crocodiles**. —*picture* → REPTILE

alliteration /əˌlɪtəˈreɪʃ(ə)n/ noun [U] LITERATURE the use of the same letter or sound at the beginning of words in a sentence, especially in poetry

ˌall-ˈnight adj continuing or available for the whole night: *an all-night restaurant*

allocate /ˈæləkeɪt/ verb [T] **1** to provide something for someone: *We allocate a personal tutor to each student.* **2** to decide to use something for a particular purpose: *Extra money has been allocated for equipment.* —**allocation** /ˌæləˈkeɪʃ(ə)n/ noun [C/U]

allomorph /ˈæləmɔːf/ noun [C] LANGUAGE one of the forms that a **morpheme** can have. For example, the plural **ending** '-s' has three allomorphs: /s/, /z/, and /ɪz/, as in the words 'trucks', 'cars', and 'buses'.

allophone /ˈæləfəʊn/ noun [C] LANGUAGE one of the slightly different ways that a **phoneme** can be pronounced. For example, the /p/ in the word 'pill' is slightly different from the /p/ in the word 'spill'.

allot /əˈlɒt/ (**allots**, **allotting**, **allotted**) verb [T] to give someone a share of something, such as time, money, or work

ˌall-ˈout adj using everything available in order to succeed in something

allow /əˈlaʊ/ verb [T] **1** to give someone permission to do something or have something: *I'm sorry, sir, but smoking is not allowed.* ♦ *She only allows the children to watch television at weekends.* ♦ *Some prisoners are allowed visitors.* **2** to give someone or something the time or opportunity to do something: *Allow the cake to cool for five minutes before taking it out of the tin.* ♦ *a program that allows you to create web pages* **3** to make certain that you have enough of something such as time, food, or money for a particular purpose: *How much rice do you allow for each person?* **4** LAW to decide that a piece of information is acceptable in a court of law

PHRASAL VERB **al·low ˌfor sth** to consider something when you are making a plan or calculation: *The cost will be about £17 million, allowing for inflation.*

allowance /əˈlaʊəns/ noun [C] **1** an amount of money that someone receives regularly to pay for things that they need: *a clothing allowance* **2** an amount of something that you are officially allowed: *Your baggage allowance is 30 kilos.*

PHRASE **make allowances (for)** to accept behaviour that you would not normally accept because you know why someone has behaved that way: *We have to make allowances for his lack of experience.*

alloy /ˈælɔɪ/ noun [C/U] **CHEMISTRY** a metal made by combining two or more other metals

ˈall-ˌpurpose adj able to be used in a lot of different ways

ˌall ˈright¹ adj, adv *spoken* **1** satisfactory or fairly nice, but not excellent: *Manchester's all right, but I'd rather live in London.* **2** well, successfully, or not ill or upset: *Did the party go all right?* ♦ *You look terrible – are you all right?* **3** used for asking for or giving permission to do something: *Is it all right if I open the window?* ♦ *It's all right to use that computer.* **4** used for making someone feel less worried or upset: *It's all right. I'm here.*

ˌall ˈright² interjection **1** used for agreeing to something: *'Can't we stay a bit longer?' 'Oh, all right, but just five minutes.'* **2** used for checking that someone understands or agrees: *I'm playing football after school today, all right?* **3** used for showing that you have heard or understood what someone has said: *'We need to leave in ten minutes.' 'All right, I'll be ready.'*

ˌall-ˈround adj good at doing a lot of different things, especially in sport —**ˌall-ˈrounder** noun [C]

all-seater /ˌɔːl ˈsiːtə/ adj **SPORTS** an all-seater sports ground has seats for everyone and no areas where people stand

ˈall-ˌtime adj used for comparing all the people or things of a particular type that have ever existed: *Interest rates are at an all-time high.*

alluring /əˈlʊərɪŋ, əˈljʊərɪŋ/ adj attractive in an exciting way

allusion /əˈluːʒ(ə)n/ noun [C/U] *formal* a statement that refers to something in an indirect way = REFERENCE

allusive /əˈluːsɪv/ adj *formal* containing allusions

alluvial /əˈluːviəl/ adj **GEOLOGY** made of earth and sand left by rivers or floods: *an alluvial plain*

alluvium /əˈluːviəm/ noun [C/U] **GEOLOGY** soil containing earth and sand that is left by rivers or floods

ally /ˈælaɪ/ (plural **allies**) noun [C] **1** a country that makes an agreement to help another country, especially in a war: *the United States and its European allies* **2** someone who helps you, especially against people who are causing problems for you: *If you're going to succeed in this job you will need allies.*

almanac /ˈɔːlməˌnæk/ noun [C] **1** a book published every year that tells you about the movements of the planets, the times of the tides, and the dates of important events **2** a book published every year that tells you about what happened in a particular subject or activity

Almighty /ɔːlˈmaɪti/ adj with power over everyone and everything: *Almighty God*

almond /ˈɑːmənd/ noun [C] a flat white nut that has a brown skin and can be eaten

almost /ˈɔːlməʊst/ adv nearly but not completely or not all: *'Are you ready?' 'Almost! I'm just putting my shoes on.'* ♦ *It's almost a year since she died.* ♦ *Almost all of the students here are from Malaysia.*

alnico /ˈælnɪkəʊ/ noun [U] **CHEMISTRY** an alloy of iron, aluminium, and **nickel** together with one or more of copper, **cobalt**, and **titanium**

aloe /ˈæləʊ/ noun [C] a plant with thick pointed leaves that contain a lot of liquid

alone /əˈləʊn/ adj, adv **1** if you are alone, no one else is with you: *Shelley is a widow and lives alone.* ♦ *She was all alone in a dark forest.* ♦ *It was the first time he had been alone with Maria* (=just the two of them and nobody else). ♦ *Was the killer acting alone* (=without help from anyone else)? **2** without including numbers or amounts from anywhere else: *Last year, she earned over a million pounds from television advertisements alone.* **3** used for emphasizing that you are referring only to one particular person or thing: *Time alone will show whether the voters made the right choice.*

PHRASE **go it alone** to live, work, or make decisions on your own, without any help from other people

along /əˈlɒŋ/ adv, preposition **1** moving forwards on a line, path, or near the edge of something: *Mrs Barnes was hurrying along the path towards us.* ♦ *We walked along in silence.* ♦ *They were sailing along the southern coast of Australia.* **2** placed in a line beside a road, river, wall etc: *a line of trees along the river bank* **3** going somewhere with someone, or taking someone or something with you: *Do you mind if I come along too?* **4** coming to the place where someone is: *Finally a taxi came along, and we jumped in.*

PHRASE **along with** in addition to: *Ramos was arrested along with 11 other men.*

alongside /əˈlɒŋˌsaɪd/ adv, preposition **1** next to someone or something, or close to their side: *The railway runs alongside the road.* **2** together with someone in the same place: *We worked alongside people from 71 other countries.* **3** existing at the same time as another system, process, or idea: *World Trade talks continue alongside the Geneva negotiations.*

aloof /əˈluːf/ adj **1** not friendly **2** not willing to be involved in something

aloud /əˈlaʊd/ adv loud enough for other people to hear

alpaca /ælˈpækə/ noun [C] a South American mammal with a long neck and long hair

alpha /ˈælfə/ noun [C] the first letter of the Greek alphabet

alphabet /ˈælfəˌbet/ noun [C] a set of letters in a particular order that are used for writing a language

alphabetical /ˌælfəˈbetɪk(ə)l/ adj arranged according to the order of letters in the alphabet: *Here is a list of words in alphabetical order.* —**alphabetically** /ˌælfəˈbetɪkli/ adv

alphabetize /ˈælfəbətaɪz/ verb [T] to put a list in alphabetical order

ˌalpha ˈmale noun [C] a man or male animal that behaves in a confident or threatening way

alphanumeric /ˌælfənjʊˈmerɪk/ adj using letters and numbers

ˈalpha ˌparticle noun [C] **PHYSICS** the nucleus of a **helium** atom that is produced by some radioactive substances

ˈalpha ˌtest noun [C] **COMPUTING** a first test by a company of its new computer equipment or software

'alpha ,version noun [C] COMPUTING the first form of a new piece of computer hardware or software, made to be tested and usually changed several times before the final product is sold

alpine /'ælpaɪn/ adj GEOGRAPHY relating to high mountains: *alpine plants*

already /ɔːl'redi/ adv **1** before now, or before another point in time: *He's only 24, but he's already achieved worldwide fame.* ♦ *By the time the doctor arrived, I was already feeling better.* **2** sooner than you expected: *Is it time to go already?* → YET

alright /ɔːl'raɪt/ adj, adv **all right**. Many people think that this spelling is incorrect.

also /'ɔːlsəʊ/ adv used for adding another fact or idea to what you have said: *Khaled is a keen photographer who also loves to paint.* ♦ *The electric drill can also be used as a screwdriver.* ♦ *Not only is it more expensive, it's also a horrible colour.* ♦ *Jeremy is now at Dartmouth College, where his father also studied.*

> **Also, as well**, and **too** all have a similar meaning.
> ■ **As well** and **too** come at the end of a clause: *My wife speaks French as well/too.* **Also** usually comes before the verb, or after an auxiliary or modal verb or the verb **to be**: *She also speaks French.* ♦ *She can also speak French.* ♦ *He was also a fine musician.*
> ■ **Also** is not normally used with negatives. **Not...either** is used instead: *I don't speak French, and I don't speak German either.*

altar /'ɔːltə/ noun [C] RELIGION a table where religious ceremonies are performed

alter /'ɔːltə/ verb [I/T] to change, or to make changes to something = MODIFY: *He had altered all the information on the forms.* ♦ *After all these years, the town has hardly altered.*

alteration /,ɔːltə'reɪʃ(ə)n/ noun [C] a change in something or someone = MODIFICATION

altercation /,ɔːltə'keɪʃ(ə)n/ noun [C] *formal* a noisy argument

,alter 'ego noun [C] **1** a part of someone's personality that is different from their usual personality and that other people do not usually see **2** a very close friend

alternate[1] /'ɔːltəneɪt/ verb [I/T] to change from one thing, idea, or feeling to another, and keep repeating that pattern: *The government **alternates between** tough talk and silence.* ♦ *The course allows students to **alternate** work **with** education.*

alternate[2] /ɔːl'tɜːnət/ adj **1** happening or coming one after another, in a regular pattern: *alternate periods of good and bad weather* **2** happening on one day, week etc, but not on the day, week etc that immediately follows: *I go and visit him on alternate weekends.* —**alternately** adv

al,ternate 'angles noun [plural] MATHS a pair of angles of equal size on opposite sides and at opposite ends of a line that cuts across two other parallel lines —*picture* → ANGLE

alternating current /,ɔːltəneɪtɪŋ 'kʌrənt/ noun [U] PHYSICS a flow of electric current that keeps changing direction at a very fast rate → DIRECT CURRENT

alternative[1] /ɔːl'tɜːnətɪv/ noun [C] something that you can choose to do instead of something else: *There was no alternative – we had to close the school.*

alternative[2] /ɔːl'tɜːnətɪv/ adj **1** able to be used or done instead of something else: *We are now looking for an alternative method.* **2** not traditional, or not done in the usual way: *an alternative lifestyle*

al,ternative 'energy noun [U] ENVIRONMENT natural sources of energy such as wind power, wave power, and solar power

alternatively /ɔːl'tɜːnətɪvli/ adv used for making another suggestion: *We could drive all the way. Alternatively, we could fly.*

al,ternative 'medicine noun [U] HEALTH medical treatments that are based on traditional ideas, not on modern scientific methods

alternator /'ɔːltə,neɪtə/ noun [C] PHYSICS, ENGINEERING a piece of equipment that produces an electric current that changes as it flows. Alternators in vehicle engines provide power for the battery and the vehicle's electrical system.

although /ɔːl'ðəʊ/ conjunction **1** used for introducing a statement that makes your main statement seem surprising = THOUGH: *She used to call me 'Tiny', although I was at least as tall as she was.* **2** used for introducing a statement that makes what you have just said seem less true: *The Lamberts liked their new home, although they missed their friends.*

altimeter /'æltɪ,miːtə, æl'tɪmɪtə/ noun [C] a piece of equipment in an aircraft that tells you the height of the aircraft above sea level

altitude /'æltɪ,tjuːd/ noun [C] **1** GEOGRAPHY the height of a place or object above sea level **2** MATHS a perpendicular line from an angle of a triangle to the opposite side

'altitude ,sickness noun [U] HEALTH an illness caused by the small amount of oxygen in the air when you are very high up, for example on a mountain

Alt key /'ɔːlt ,kiː/ noun [C] COMPUTING a key on a computer keyboard that you use with another key to perform a particular action

alto /'æltəʊ/ noun [C] MUSIC **1** a woman who has the lowest female singing voice **2** a musical instrument in the same range as an alto singing voice

'alto ,clef noun [singular] MUSIC the symbol 𝄡 used at the beginning of a line of music to show that the note on the third line of the **staff** represents **middle C** —*picture* → MUSIC

altogether /,ɔːltə'geðə/ adv **1** completely: *These rare animals may soon disappear altogether.* **2** including everyone or everything: *How many guests will there be altogether?*

> Do not confuse **altogether** with **all together**, which means 'everyone or everything together': *Write down the numbers, then add them all together.*

altostratus /,æltəʊ'streɪtəs/ noun [U] GEOGRAPHY light grey cloud in the form of thin layers or sheets, through which you can see the sun —*picture* → CLOUD

altruistic /,æltru'ɪstɪk/ adj doing something for the benefit of other people ≠ SELFISH —**altruism** /'æltru,ɪz(ə)m/ noun [U]

alum /'æləm/ noun [C] CHEMISTRY a chemical substance used in dyes and for **purifying** water (=making dirty water safe to drink)

aluminium /,ælə'mɪniəm/ noun [U] CHEMISTRY a light silver-coloured metal element that does not **corrode** easily. Chemical symbol: **Al**

alumna /ə'lʌmnə/ (plural **alumnae** /ə'lʌmniː/) noun [C] *formal* a woman who was a student at a particular school, college, or university

alumnus /ə'lʌmnəs/ (plural **alumni** /ə'lʌmnaɪ/) noun [C] *formal* someone who was a student at a particular school, college, or university

alveolar /ˌælvɪˈəʊlə, ælˈviːələ/ adj LANGUAGE alveolar sounds are made with the tongue touching the skin behind the top front teeth, for example 'l', 'd', 'n', or 't' —**alveolar** noun [C]

alveolus /ælˈvɪələs/ (plural **alveoli** /ælˈvɪəlaɪ/) noun [C] ANATOMY an extremely small **air sac** (=space like a bag) with very thin walls, of which there are a great many in the lungs. In the alveoli, oxygen is taken into the blood from air that is breathed into the lungs, and carbon dioxide is passed into the air that is breathed out. —*picture* ➔ LUNG

always /ˈɔːlweɪz/ adv **1** on every occasion: *I always get the eight o'clock train.* ♦ *Starting a new job is always a bit of a shock.* **2** all the time: *Is he always this silly?* **3** for all time in the past or future: *I'll always remember how kind she was.* ♦ *Jimmy was always a difficult boy.* **4** used for saying that something happens often, especially when this annoys you: *He's always forgetting my name.*

always-'on adj COMPUTING an always-on Internet connection allows you to remain **online** (=connected to the Internet) all the time

Alzheimer's disease /ˈæltshaɪməz dɪˌziːz/ noun [U] HEALTH a serious illness that affects someone's brain and memory

am[1] /*strong* æm, *weak* əm/ *see* **be**

am[2] /ˌeɪ ˈem/ abbrev used for showing that a time is between midnight and noon ➔ PM

amalgam /əˈmælɡəm/ noun [C/U] **1** CHEMISTRY a mixture of two or more metals, one of which is mercury **2** a substance like this that is used for filling holes in teeth

amalgamate /əˈmælɡəmeɪt/ verb [I/T] to join two or more organizations, companies etc to make a single large one, or to be joined in this way —**amalgamation** /əˌmælɡəˈmeɪʃ(ə)n/ noun [C/U]

amanuensis /əˌmænjuˈensɪs/ noun [C] *very formal* a **secretary**, especially one who helps a writer or artist

amass /əˈmæs/ verb [T] to collect a lot of money or information

amateur[1] /ˈæmətə, ˈæmətʃʊə/ adj **1** done for pleasure instead of as a job ≠ PROFESSIONAL: *amateur photography* **2** done or made badly: *a very amateur performance*

amateur[2] /ˈæmətə, ˈæmətʃʊə/ noun [C] **1** someone who does something because they enjoy it, instead of as a job ≠ PROFESSIONAL **2** someone who does not do something very well

amaze /əˈmeɪz/ verb [T] to surprise someone very much by being very impressive or unusual: *What amazes me is that they never get tired.*

amazed /əˈmeɪzd/ adj very surprised: *Frankly, I was amazed that he was interested.*

amazement /əˈmeɪzmənt/ noun [U] a feeling of being very surprised: *They were shaking their heads in amazement.*

amazing /əˈmeɪzɪŋ/ adj very good, surprising, or impressive: *Her story was quite amazing.* ♦ *Their last CD sold an amazing 2 million copies.* —**amazingly** adv

ambassador /æmˈbæsədə/ noun [C] a senior official who lives in a foreign country and represents his or her own country there

amber /ˈæmbə/ noun [U] a hard yellow-brown substance used for making jewellery

ambidextrous /ˌæmbiˈdekstrəs/ adj able to use both hands with equal skill

ambience /ˈæmbiəns/ noun [C/U] the character of a place, or the general feeling that you have in a place = ATMOSPHERE

ambient /ˈæmbiənt/ adj SCIENCE existing or present around you

ambiguity /ˌæmbɪˈɡjuːəti/ (plural **ambiguities**) noun [C/U] something that is not clear because it has more than one possible meaning

ambiguous /æmˈbɪɡjuəs/ adj something that is ambiguous is not clear because it has more than one possible meaning or intention ≠ UNAMBIGUOUS: *The wording of his statement was highly ambiguous.* —**ambiguously** adv

ambition /æmˈbɪʃ(ə)n/ noun **1** [C] something that you very much want to achieve: *His ambition was to become a successful writer.* ♦ *I had no idea about Jesse's political ambitions.* **2** [U] determination to become successful, rich, or famous

ambitious /æmˈbɪʃəs/ adj **1** determined to become successful, rich, or famous: *an ambitious young lawyer* **2** an ambitious plan or attempt will need a lot of hard work and skill in order for it to be successful

ambivalent /æmˈbɪvələnt/ adj having two different opinions about something at the same time —**ambivalence** /æmˈbɪvələns/ noun [U]

amble /ˈæmb(ə)l/ verb [I] to walk in a slow relaxed way

ambulance /ˈæmbjʊləns/ noun [C] a vehicle for taking people to hospital

ambush /ˈæmbʊʃ/ verb [T] to attack someone suddenly from a hidden position —**ambush** noun [C/U]

ameliorate /əˈmiːliəreɪt/ verb [T] *very formal* to improve something

amen /ˌɑːˈmen, ˌeɪˈmen/ interjection RELIGION said at the end of a Christian or Jewish prayer

amenable /əˈmiːnəb(ə)l/ adj willing to do something, or willing to agree with someone

amend /əˈmend/ verb [T] to make changes that improve a document, law, or agreement

amendment /əˈmen(d)mənt/ noun [C] a change to a document, law, or agreement

amends /əˈmendz/ noun **make amends** to try to make a situation better after you have done something wrong

amenities /əˈmiːnətiz/ noun [plural] things that make it comfortable or enjoyable to live or work somewhere: *Amenities include a gym and a pool.*

amenorrhoea /eɪˌmenəˈrɪə/ noun [U] HEALTH a medical condition in which a woman who is not pregnant does not **menstruate** (=produce a flow of blood once a month)

America /əˈmerɪkə/ **1** GEOGRAPHY the **land mass** that consists of North America, South America, and Central America —*picture* ➔ CONTINENT **2** the USA. This meaning is not accurate geographically, so do not use it in writing or discussions about geography or geology. —**American** adj, noun [C]

American football /əˌmerɪkən ˈfʊtbɔːl/ noun [U] a game in which two teams throw, carry, or kick an oval ball and try to cross their opponents' goal line

American Indian /əˌmerɪkən ˈɪndiən/ noun [C] a **Native American** —**American Indian** adj

americium /ˌæməˈrɪsiəm/ noun [U] CHEMISTRY a silvery radioactive metallic element in the **actinide** group of the periodic table. Chemical symbol: **Am**

amethyst /'æməθɪst/ noun [C/U] a purple stone that is used in jewellery

amiable /'eɪmiəb(ə)l/ adj friendly and easy to like

amicable /'æmɪkəb(ə)l/ adj friendly and without arguments: *an amicable divorce* —**amicably** adv

amid /ə'mɪd/ or **amidst** /ə'mɪdst/ preposition while something is happening or changing: *Banks and shops closed yesterday amid growing fears of violence.*

amino acid /ə,mi:nəʊ 'æsɪd/ noun [C] BIOLOGY one of the substances in the body that combine to make proteins

amiss /ə'mɪs/ adj if something is amiss, it is not as it should be

ammeter /'æm,mi:tə/ noun [C] PHYSICS a piece of equipment used for measuring the number of amps in an electric current —*picture* → ELECTRICITY

ammonia /ə'məʊniə/ noun [U] CHEMISTRY a poisonous gas, with a strong unpleasant smell, or the gas dissolved in water. It is used in cleaning products. Chemical formula: NH_3

ammonite /'æmənaɪt/ noun [C] an extinct sea animal with a flat spiral shell. It is often found as a fossil.

ammonium chloride /ə,məʊniəm 'klɔ:raɪd/ noun [U] CHEMISTRY a white crystalline solid. Chemical formula: NH_4Cl

ammonium hydroxide /ə,məʊniəm haɪ'drɒksaɪd/ noun [U] CHEMISTRY a strong alkali that is a solution of **ammonia** in water. Chemical formula: NH_4OH

ammonium salt /ə'məʊniəm ,sɔ:lt/ noun [U] CHEMISTRY a chemical compound formed by the reaction of ammonia with an acid substance that turns red litmus paper blue

ammunition /,æmjʊ'nɪʃ(ə)n/ noun [U] **1** bullets and bombs that can be fired from a weapon **2** facts that can be used against someone in an argument

amnesia /æm'ni:ziə/ noun [U] HEALTH a medical condition that makes someone unable to remember things

amnesty /'æmnəsti/ (plural **amnesties**) noun [C] an official order not to punish people who have committed a particular crime

amniocentesis /,æmniəʊsen'ti:sɪs/ noun [C/U] HEALTH a test that is carried out on **amniotic fluid** (=the liquid surrounding the foetus) from the uterus of a pregnant woman, in order to find out if the baby has any genetic **abnormalities**

amnion /'æmniən/ noun [C] BIOLOGY the inner of two membranes that forms around the embryo of a mammal, bird, or reptile —*picture* → EMBRYO

amniotic fluid /,æmniɒtɪk 'flu:ɪd/ noun [U] BIOLOGY fluid inside the amnion that surrounds an embryo while it is developing inside its mother —*picture* → EMBRYO

amoeba /ə'mi:bə/ (plural **amoebae** /ə'mi:bi:/ or **amoebas**) noun [C] BIOLOGY a microorganism found in wet places, that consists of a single cell. Amoebas feed and move by pushing out a part of the cell to form a **pseudopodium** (=false foot). Amoebas are a type of protozoan. —**amoebic** /ə'mi:bɪk/ adj

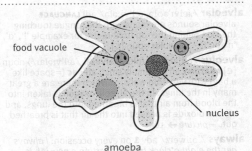

food vacuole

nucleus

amoeba

a,moebic 'dysentery noun [U] HEALTH a serious disease of the lower intestine that causes severe diarrhoea. It is the result of infection by an amoeba.

among /ə'mʌŋ/ or **amongst** /ə'mʌŋst/ preposition **1** included in a particular group of people or things: *Robert was the only one among them who had ever ridden a horse.* ♦ *They discussed, among other things, the future of the oil industry.* **2** happening within a particular group of people: *The suicide rate among young male prisoners is high.* **3** so that different people receive parts of something when it is divided up: *The money has to be shared out among several projects.* **4** with other people or things all around: *It was pleasant strolling among the olive trees.*

Between and among have a similar meaning.
- Use **between**, not **among**, when just two people are mentioned: *It was an agreement between Carl and me.*
- When three or more people are mentioned, you can use either, but **among** is more formal: *The money was divided up among/between the four children.*
- Use **between** for saying that there are people or things on two sides of someone or something: *I sat between my parents.*

amoral /,eɪ'mɒrəl/ adj someone who is amoral does not care if their behaviour is right or wrong

amorous /'æmərəs/ adj involving sexual love

amorphous /ə'mɔ:fəs/ adj *formal* with no clear shape, design, or structure

amortize /ə'mɔ:taɪz/ verb [T] BUSINESS to **pay back** a debt by making payments at regular times —**amortization** /ə,mɔ:taɪ'zeɪʃ(ə)n/ noun [C/U]

amount¹ /ə'maʊnt/ noun [C] a quantity of something: *This amount* (=quantity of money) *should be paid within two weeks.* ♦ *A computer can store vast **amounts** of information.*

Amount and number are both used for talking about quantities, but they are used in different ways.
- **Number** is used with plural nouns: *a small number of cars* ♦ *a certain number of people.*
- **Amount** is used with uncountable nouns: *a small amount of milk* ♦ *a certain amount of confidence.*
- Say a **large** or **small** number/amount and NOT a **big** or **little** number/amount.

amount² /ə'maʊnt/ PHRASAL VERB **a'mount to sth 1** to be the same as something else, or to have the same effect as something else: *Most people believe his statements amount to a declaration of war.* **2** to add up to a particular total: *His monthly earnings amount to about £2,000.*

amp /æmp/ or **ampere** /'æmpeə/ noun [C] PHYSICS a unit for measuring the amount of flow of an electric current. Symbol A

amperage /ˈæmpərɪdʒ/ noun [singular/U] PHYSICS the amount of electrical current, measured in **amperes**

ampere /ˈæmpeə/ noun [C] PHYSICS an **amp**

amphetamine /æmˈfetəmiːn/ noun [C/U] HEALTH a drug that was previously used in the treatment of **depression** but is now taken illegally for the feeling of great energy and excitement it produces

amphibian /æmˈfɪbiən/ noun [C] BIOLOGY a vertebrate that lives for some of the time on land, but breeds, lays its eggs, and develops into its adult form in water. **Frogs** and **toads** are amphibians. —*picture* → REPTILE

amphibious /æmˈfɪbiəs/ adj living, being used, or happening both in water and on land

amphitheatre /ˈæmfɪˌθɪətə/ noun [C] a large circular building without a roof and with rows of seats that slope up and away from a central area, used for sports competitions or plays

amphoteric /ˌæmfəˈterɪk/ adj CHEMISTRY able to act with both acids and alkalis. Many metals and metal oxides, for example zinc, lead, and aluminium, are amphoteric.

ample /ˈæmp(ə)l/ adj **1** enough, and often more than you need **2** used for referring to a part of someone's body that is large: *an ample bosom* —**amply** adv

amplifier /ˈæmplɪˌfaɪə/ noun [C] PHYSICS a piece of electronic equipment that makes sounds louder

amplify /ˈæmplɪˌfaɪ/ (**amplifies, amplifying, amplified**) verb [T] to make sounds louder — **amplification** /ˌæmplɪfɪˈkeɪʃ(ə)n/ noun [C/U]

amplitude /ˈæmplɪˌtjuːd/ noun [U] PHYSICS half of the total height of a wave, for example of sound or electricity, used as a measurement of how strong it is. The amplitude of a sea wave is its height above the level of water when the water is calm and still. —*picture* → WAVE

ampoule /ˈæmpuːl/ noun [C] a small glass container used for holding liquid medicine

amputate /ˈæmpjʊteɪt/ verb [I/T] HEALTH to cut off a part of someone's body in a medical operation —**amputation** /ˌæmpjʊˈteɪʃ(ə)n/ noun [C/U]

amputee /ˌæmpjʊˈtiː/ noun [C] someone who has had a part of their body amputated

amuse /əˈmjuːz/ verb [T] **1** to do or say something that other people think is funny or entertaining **2** to keep someone interested or entertained, so that they do not get bored: *We need something that will amuse a 10-year-old for an afternoon.*

amused /əˈmjuːzd/ adj showing that you think that something is funny or entertaining: *an amused expression*

amusement /əˈmjuːzmənt/ noun **1** [U] a feeling of being amused **2** [C] an enjoyable activity

aˈmusement arˌcade noun [C] a place where you can play games on machines by putting coins in them

aˈmusement ˌpark noun [C] a place where people pay money to go on **rides** (=machines that you ride on or in for pleasure) = FUNFAIR

amusing /əˈmjuːzɪŋ/ adj funny or entertaining: *an amusing birthday card*

amylase /ˈæmɪˌleɪz/ noun [C] BIOLOGY an enzyme that helps the body to make a type of sugar from starch. Amylase is found in saliva, in the pancreas, and in plants.

an /strong æn, weak ən/ determiner used instead of 'a' when the next word begins with a vowel sound: *an accident* ♦ *an hour* ♦ *an X-ray* → A²

anabolic steroid /ˌænəbɒlɪk ˈsterɔɪd/ noun [C] BIOLOGY, SPORTS a drug that makes muscles larger and stronger. It is used illegally by some sportspeople.

anachronism /əˈnækrəˌnɪz(ə)m/ noun [C] something that is no longer suitable for modern times — **anachronistic** /əˌnækrəˈnɪstɪk/ adj

anaconda /ˌænəˈkɒndə/ noun [C] a large tropical South American snake —*picture* → REPTILE

anaemia /əˈniːmiə/ noun [U] HEALTH a medical condition in which there are too few red blood cells in the blood —**anaemic** /əˈniːmɪk/ adj

anaerobe /ˈænərəʊb, ænˈeərəʊb/ noun [C] BIOLOGY a microorganism that does not need oxygen in order to carry out **metabolism**

anaerobic /ˌænəˈrəʊbɪk/ adj BIOLOGY not using, involving, or needing oxygen: *anaerobic bacteria*

anaerobic respiˈration noun [U] BIOLOGY respiration that takes place where there is little or no oxygen. This produces less energy than **aerobic respiration**, and a lot of it is lost as heat. Examples of organisms that use anaerobic respiration are some bacteria and yeast. In animal muscles, it is responsible for making **lactic acid** as a waste product. → AEROBIC RESPIRATION

anaesthetic /ˌænəsˈθetɪk/ noun [C/U] HEALTH a drug or gas that is given to someone before a medical operation to stop them feeling pain

anaesthetist /əˈniːsθətɪst/ noun [C] HEALTH a doctor who is trained to give people anaesthetics

anaesthetize /əˈniːsθətaɪz/ verb [T] HEALTH to give someone an anaesthetic so that they do not feel pain during a medical operation

anagram /ˈænəˌgræm/ noun [C] a word or phrase that you can form from another word or phrase by putting the letters in a different order

anal /ˈeɪn(ə)l/ adj ANATOMY relating to the **anus**

analgesia /ˌæn(ə)lˈdʒiːziə/ noun [U] HEALTH **1** the condition of being unable to feel pain while conscious **2** medical treatment to reduce pain

analgesic /ˌæn(ə)lˈdʒiːzɪk/ noun [C] HEALTH a drug such as **aspirin** that reduces pain

analogous /əˈnæləgəs/ adj *formal* similar to another situation, process etc

analogue /ˈænəˌlɒg/ adj **1** using signals or information that do not have fixed values but vary continuously → DIGITAL sense 1 **2** an analogue clock or instrument shows information on dials with hands or numbers that point to them

analogy /əˈnælədʒi/ (plural **analogies**) noun [C/U] a comparison between two things that shows how they are similar: *He uses the analogy of the family to explain the role of the state.*

analyse /ˈænəlaɪz/ verb [T] **1** to examine something in detail in order to understand or explain it: *Scientists analysed samples of leaves taken from the area.* **2** to examine someone's thoughts, feelings, or behaviour as a way of understanding and dealing with their emotional or mental problems

analysis /əˈnæləsɪs/ (plural **analyses** /əˈnæləsiːz/) noun **1** [C/U] the process of examining something in order to understand it or to find out what it contains: *The blood samples have been sent away for analysis.* ♦ *The study included an **analysis of** accident statistics.* **2** [U] HEALTH psychoanalysis

analyst /'ænəlɪst/ noun [C] **1** someone whose job is to carefully examine a situation, event etc in order to provide other people with information about it: *a stock market analyst* **2** HEALTH a **psychoanalyst**

analytical /,ænə'lɪtɪk(ə)l/ or **analytic** /,ænə'lɪtɪk/ adj examining a problem or issue by separating it into its different parts or aspects: *analytical skills* —**analytically** /,ænə'lɪtɪkli/ adv

anaphora /ə'næfərə/ noun [U] LANGUAGE the use of a word such as a pronoun or the verb 'do' in a sentence, instead of repeating the word used earlier. Examples of anaphora are the use of the word 'she' in the sentence 'Sue was hungry when she got home', or the word 'does' in the sentence 'I love pizza and so does my brother'.

anaphylactic shock /,ænəfɪlæktɪk 'ʃɒk/ noun [U] HEALTH a serious medical reaction caused by someone eating, touching, or being **injected** with something that they have an allergy to. Common causes are nuts, eggs, and drugs such as **penicillin**.

anaphylaxis /,ænəfɪ'læksɪs/ noun [U] HEALTH anaphylactic shock

anarchic /ə'nɑːkɪk/ adj behaving in a way that ignores the normal rules or limits of your society or group, especially when this causes trouble

anarchist /'ænəkɪst/ noun [C] POLITICS someone who believes that there should be no government or laws

anarchy /'ænəki/ noun [U] a situation in which people ignore normal rules and laws, and are unable to be controlled

anatomy /ə'nætəmi/ (plural **anatomies**) noun **1** [C] the body of a human or other animal, or the structure of a plant **2** [U] the scientific study of the internal structure of an animal or plant —**anatomical** /,ænə'tɒmɪk(ə)l/ adj

the ANC /,eɪ en 'siː/ the African National Congress: a political party in South Africa that for many years fought against the system of **apartheid**. In 1994, the ANC formed the first government in South Africa to be elected by both black and white people and it has stayed in power since then.

ancestor /'ænsestə/ noun [C] someone who lived a long time ago and is related to you —**ancestral** /æn'sestrəl/ adj ➔ DESCENDANT

'ancestor ,worship noun [U] RELIGION in Africa and Australasia, the practice of giving special respect to dead family members

ancestry /'ænsestri/ noun [singular/U] your ancestors and family history: *His family was of Danish ancestry.*

anchor¹ /'æŋkə/ noun [C] **1** a heavy object that is dropped into the water from a boat in order to prevent it from moving **2** a **newsreader**

anchor² /'æŋkə/ verb **1** [I/T] to prevent a boat from moving by dropping its anchor into the water **2** [T] to fix something firmly somewhere

anchovy /'æntʃəvi/ (plural **anchovies**) noun [C/U] a type of small fish that is often preserved in salt and oil

ancient /'eɪnʃ(ə)nt/ adj **1** very old: *an ancient tradition* **2** relating to a period of history a very long time ago: *the ancient Egyptians*

ancillary /æn'sɪləri/ adj **1** ancillary staff work with professional people such as doctors and teachers, in order to help them in their work **2** connected with something, but less important than the main thing

and /strong ænd, weak ən, ənd/ conjunction

1 used for connecting	**4** for emphasis
2 then/after that	**5** for adding
3 showing purpose	**6** in numbers

1 used for connecting words or phrases together, and sometimes for connecting sentences: *Everyone was singing and dancing.* ♦ *You cook the lunch, and I'll look after the children.* ♦ *The telephone isn't working. And that's not the only problem.*

When more than two words or phrases are joined in a list, **and** is used only between the last two: *She speaks German, French, Spanish, and English.*

2 used for showing that one thing happens after another: *He switched off the television and went to bed.* **3** used after verbs such as 'go', 'come', 'try', or 'wait', for showing what your purpose is: *I'll try and find out where we can buy tickets.* ♦ *Come and see our new kitchen.* **4** used for connecting words that are repeated for emphasis: *I've tried and tried, but I can't understand it.* **5** *spoken* added to: *Two and two is four.* **6** MATHS *spoken* used in numbers after the word 'hundred' or 'thousand', or between whole numbers and fractions: *a hundred and ten metres* ♦ *two and three quarters* (=2 3/4)

andante¹ /æn'dænti, æn'dænteɪ/ adv MUSIC fairly slowly: used as an instruction in music —**andante** adj

andante² /æn'dænti, æn'dænteɪ/ noun [C] MUSIC a piece of music that should be played or sung at a fairly slow speed

,and/'or conjunction used for saying that either or both of two situations are possible

androgynous /æn'drɒdʒ(ə)nəs/ adj **1** neither definitely male nor definitely female **2** BIOLOGY an androgynous animal or plant has both male and female parts

the Andromeda Galaxy /æn'drɒmədə ,gæləksi/ noun ASTRONOMY a group of stars and planets about two million light years away and about twice as large as our galaxy

anecdotal /,ænɪk'dəʊt(ə)l/ adj based on someone's personal experience or on what they say rather than on facts that can be checked

anecdote /'ænɪk,dəʊt/ noun [C] a story that you tell people about something interesting or funny that has happened to you

anemometer /,ænɪ'mɒmɪtə/ noun [C] GEOGRAPHY an instrument that measures the force and direction of the wind

aneuploid /'ænjʊplɔɪd/ adj BIOLOGY aneuploid cells have fewer or more chromosomes than is usual —**aneuploidy** /'ænjʊplɔɪdi/ noun [U]

aneurysm or **aneurism** /'ænjə,rɪz(ə)m/ noun [C] HEALTH a serious swelling in the wall of an artery

angel /'eɪndʒ(ə)l/ noun [C] RELIGION a spirit that in some religions is believed to live in heaven with God. In pictures, angels are usually shown as beautiful people with wings. —**angelic** /æn'dʒelɪk/ adj

anger¹ /'æŋgə/ noun [U] the strong feeling that makes someone want to hurt another person or shout at them: *Some people express their anger through violence.*

anger² /'æŋgə/ verb [T] to make someone feel angry: *The school board's decision angered many students and parents alike.*

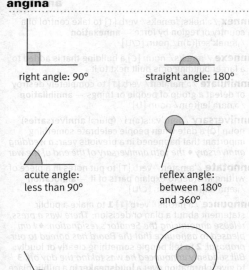

right angle: 90°

straight angle: 180°

acute angle:
less than 90°

reflex angle:
between 180°
and 360°

obtuse angle:
between 90°
and 180°

round angle: 360°

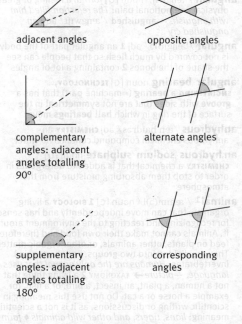

adjacent angles

opposite angles

complementary
angles: adjacent
angles totalling
90°

alternate angles

supplementary
angles: adjacent
angles totalling
180°

corresponding
angles

angles

angina /ænˈdʒaɪnə/ noun [U] HEALTH a medical condition in which not enough blood gets to the heart, which causes pains in the chest

angioplasty /ˈændʒiəˌplæsti/ noun [U] HEALTH a medical operation to repair an artery that has become blocked or too narrow

angiosperm /ˈændʒiəʊˌspɜːm/ noun [C] BIOLOGY a plant in which the sex organs are located in the flowers, and the seeds are enclosed in a fruit that develops from the flowers → GYMNOSPERM

angle¹ /ˈæŋɡ(ə)l/ noun [C] **1** MATHS the shape that is made where two lines or surfaces join each other, measured in degrees. The greatest possible number of degrees is 360: *An angle that measures 90° is called a right angle.* **2** the direction from which something comes, or the direction from which you look at something, especially when it is not directly in front of you: *Guns were firing at them from several different angles.* **3** a particular way of thinking about something: *We have considered the whole subject from many different angles.*

PHRASES **angle of incidence** PHYSICS the angle between a ray of light and a line that is perpendicular to a surface, at the point where the ray touches it —*picture* → WAVE

angle of reflection PHYSICS the angle between a reflected ray of light and a line that is perpendicular to a surface, at the point where the ray is reflected —*picture* → WAVE

angle of refraction PHYSICS the angle between a **refracted** (=bent) ray of light and a line that is perpendicular to a surface, at the point where the ray is refracted —*picture* → WAVE

at an angle not straight, but leaning to one side: *Hold the knife at a slight angle.*

angle² /ˈæŋɡ(ə)l/ verb [T] to make something move or point in a direction that is not directly in front of you

ˈangle ˌbracket noun [C] either of a pair of symbols < or >, used to surround words, numbers, or other

symbols, especially in instructions for a computer

angle grinder /ˈæŋɡ(ə)l ˌɡraɪndə/ noun [C] ENGINEERING a **power tool** that uses a disc with a rough surface to cut, **grind**, and **polish** metal or stone

Anglican /ˈæŋɡlɪkən/ noun [C] RELIGION a Christian who is a member of the Anglican Church —**Anglican** adj

the ˌAnglican ˈChurch noun RELIGION a group of Christian Protestant churches that includes the Church of England, the Church of Wales, the Church of Nigeria, and churches of many other countries around the world

anglicism /ˈæŋɡlɪˌsɪz(ə)m/ noun [C] LANGUAGE **1** a word that is used in British English but not in other types of English **2** an English word that is used in another language

angling /ˈæŋɡlɪŋ/ noun [U] the sport of catching fish —**angler** /ˈæŋɡlə/ noun [C]

Anglo- /ˈæŋɡləʊ/ prefix involving or related to England or the UK: *an Anglo-Russian trading agreement*

anglophone /ˈæŋɡləʊˌfəʊn/ adj LANGUAGE **1** an anglophone country is one where English is spoken as one of the main languages **2** an anglophone person is one who speaks English, especially as their main or first language —**anglophone** noun [C]

Anglo-Saxon /ˌæŋɡləʊ ˈsæks(ə)n/ adj **1** relating to the history, culture, or language of the Anglo-Saxons **2** relating to the US and the UK, rather than the countries of Europe

angry /ˈæŋɡri/ (**angrier, angriest**) adj very annoyed: *There's no point in getting angry.* ♦ *His attitude makes me really angry.* ♦ *He is very angry about the way he's been treated.* ♦ *Are you angry with me?* ♦ *Anne was angry that no one told her about the party.* —**angrily** adv

angst /æŋst/ noun [U] a strong feeling of worry

anguish /'æŋgwɪʃ/ noun [U] *formal* a feeling of great physical or emotional pain: *The rejection filled him with anguish.* —**anguished** /'æŋgwɪʃt/ adj: *an anguished cry*

angular /'æŋgjʊlə/ adj **1** an angular part of the body is not covered by much flesh so that people can see the shape of the bones **2** containing a lot of angles

'angular ,bearing noun [C] TECHNOLOGY, ENGINEERING a **bearing** (=machine part) that has a **groove** with sides that are not **symmetrical** in the surface of the ring in which **ball bearings** move

anhydrous /æn'haɪdrəs/ adj CHEMISTRY an anhydrous chemical compound contains no water

an,hydrous ,sodium 'sulphate noun [U] CHEMISTRY a chemical that is added to **detergents** in order to stop them absorbing moisture from the atmosphere

animal¹ /'ænɪm(ə)l/ noun [C] **1** BIOLOGY a living organism that can move independently and has senses for recognizing and reacting to the environment around it. Animals cannot make their own food and therefore feed on plants, other animals, or other organic matter. They are divided into two groups, vertebrates and invertebrates: *Humans are the only animal that uses language.* —*picture* → TAXONOMY **2** a living thing that is not a human, a plant, an insect, a bird, or a fish, for example a horse or a cat. Do not use this meaning in scientific writing or discussions, as it is not a scientific meaning: *lions, tigers, and other wild animals* ♦ *farm animals* ♦ *He is accused of cruelty to animals.*

animal² /'ænɪm(ə)l/ adj **1** relating to animals: *animal behaviour* **2** relating to people's basic physical needs such as food and sex: *animal instincts*

,animal 'husbandry noun [U] AGRICULTURE the type of farming that involves the care of cows, sheep, horses, pigs etc

animal-pollinated /'ænɪm(ə)l ,pɒlɪneɪtɪd/ adj BIOLOGY an animal-pollinated plant is fertilized by having pollen moved to it from another plant by means of an animal. The pollen grains stick to the animal's body. —**animal pollination** noun [U]

animated /'ænɪˌmeɪtɪd/ adj **1** lively or active: *an animated conversation* **2** ARTS an animated film consists of a series of drawings that look as if they are moving

animation /,ænɪ'meɪʃ(ə)n/ noun [U] **1** ARTS animated films, or the process of making them **2** energy and excitement

animatronics /,ænɪmə'trɒnɪks/ noun [U] technology that uses electronic systems to operate **puppets** (=models of people or animals)

animism /'ænɪˌmɪz(ə)m/ noun [U] RELIGION a religion in which people believe that things in nature, such as animals, trees, and mountains, have spirits

animosity /,ænɪ'mɒsəti/ noun [U] a strong feeling of disliking someone or something= HOSTILITY

anion /'æn,aɪən/ noun [C] PHYSICS, CHEMISTRY an ion with a negative electrical charge

ankle /'æŋk(ə)l/ noun [C] the part at the bottom of the leg where the foot joins the leg —*picture* → BODY

anneal /ə'niːl/ verb [T] TECHNOLOGY, ENGINEERING to soften a metal by heating it and then cooling it slowly

annelid /'ænəlɪd/ noun [C] BIOLOGY an invertebrate organism with a body that is divided into **segments** (=parts), for example an **earthworm** or a **leech**

annex /ə'neks, 'æneks/ verb [T] to take control of a country or region by force —**annexation** /,ænek'seɪʃ(ə)n/ noun [C/U]

annexe /'æneks/ noun [C] a building that is added to a larger building or is built next to it

annihilate /ə'naɪəleɪt/ verb [T] to completely destroy or defeat a group of people or things —**annihilation** /ə,naɪə'leɪʃ(ə)n/ noun [U]

anniversary /,ænɪ'vɜːs(ə)ri/ (plural **anniversaries**) noun [C] a date when people celebrate something important that happened in a previous year: *a wedding anniversary* ♦ *the 10th anniversary of the end of the war*

annotate /'ænəteɪt/ verb [T] to put notes in a piece of writing in order to explain parts of it —**annotation** /,ænə'teɪʃ(ə)n/ noun [C/U]

announce /ə'naʊns/ verb [T] **1** to make a public statement about a plan or decision: *There was a press release announcing the Senator's resignation.* ♦ *I am pleased to announce that the Board has agreed to our proposal.* **2** to tell people something clearly or loudly: *Bill suddenly announced he was taking the day off.* **3** to give information over a **loudspeaker** in a public place such as an airport: *When your flight is announced, make your way to the departure lounge.*

announcement /ə'naʊnsmənt/ noun **1** [C] a public statement that gives people information about something: *Observers expect the president to make an announcement about his plans tonight.* ♦ *Ms Baker stunned her fans with an announcement that she was quitting the music business.* **2** [U] the act of publicly stating something: *The announcement of Prince Charles' visit caused widespread media interest.*

annoy /ə'nɔɪ/ verb [T] to make someone feel slightly angry or impatient= IRRITATE: *I don't dislike her — she just annoys me sometimes.*

annoyance /ə'nɔɪəns/ noun **1** [U] a slightly angry or impatient feeling **2** [C] something that makes you feel slightly angry

annoyed /ə'nɔɪd/ adj feeling slightly angry or impatient: *We were all annoyed with him for forgetting.* ♦ *I was really annoyed that I hadn't been invited.*

annoying /ə'nɔɪɪŋ/ adj making you feel slightly angry or impatient: *an annoying habit* ♦ *What's really annoying is that we made the same mistake last time.*

annual¹ /'ænjuəl/ adj **1** happening once a year= YEARLY: *an annual holiday* **2** calculated over a period of one year= YEARLY: *an annual salary* —**annually** adv

annual² /'ænjuəl/ noun [C] **1** BIOLOGY a plant that grows, reproduces, and dies in the same year → PERENNIAL **2** a book or magazine published once every year

,annual re'port noun [C] BUSINESS a document that gives details of the financial activities of a company or other organization over the past year

annuity /ə'njuːəti/ noun [C] a fixed amount of money that someone receives regularly each year for the rest of their life

anode /'ænəʊd/ noun [C] CHEMISTRY, PHYSICS one of the electrodes in a piece of electrical equipment such as a battery to which negative ions are attracted. It has a positive charge. → CATHODE

anodize /'ænədaɪz/ verb [T] CHEMISTRY to coat a metal such as aluminium with an oxide layer, in order to prevent any more oxygen from getting into it

anodyne /'ænəˌdaɪn/ adj *formal* containing nothing that will offend anyone or cause disagreements, and therefore rather boring

anomalous /ə'nɒmələs/ adj *formal* unusual or unexpected

anomaly /ə'nɒməli/ (plural **anomalies**) noun [C] *formal* something unusual or unexpected

anon. abbrev anonymous

anonymity /,ænə'nɪməti/ noun [U] a situation in which the name of a person is not known or is kept secret

anonymizer /ə'nɒnɪ,maɪzə/ noun [C] **COMPUTING** a website that allows someone to use the Internet without leaving any sign of who they are

anonymous /ə'nɒnɪməs/ adj **1** if someone is anonymous, no one knows their name: *an anonymous caller* **2** done or written by someone whose name is not known: *an anonymous phone call* —**anonymously** adv

anorak /'ænə,ræk/ noun [C] a short coat with a **hood**

anorexia /,ænə'reksiə/ noun [U] **HEALTH** a serious mental illness that makes someone want to stop eating because they think they are too fat → BULIMIA

anorexic /,ænə'reksɪk/ adj extremely thin and suffering from anorexia —**anorexic** noun [C]

another /ə'nʌðə/ determiner, pronoun **1** one more person or thing of the same type as before: *Peter's mum is expecting another baby.* ♦ *We're changing from one system to another.* ♦ *Another 2,000 nurses are needed in our hospitals.* ♦ *We're doing a big concert tomorrow night and another one on Saturday.* **2** a different person or thing of the same type: *Isn't there another word that has the same meaning?* ♦ *Her husband was working in another part of the country.* → ONE ANOTHER

A. N. Other /,eɪ en 'ʌðə/ noun [singular] a member of a sports team who has not been chosen yet, so that you cannot give their real name in a list of players

answer¹ /'ɑːnsə/ noun [C] **1** a spoken or written reply to something such as a question, a letter, or a telephone call: *I wrote to him in May but I never got an answer.* ♦ *I'll give you a definite answer tomorrow.* ♦ *The answer to your question is yes.* **2** a spoken or written reply to a question in a test or competition: *I'm sorry, but 'Paris' is the wrong answer.* ♦ *Do you know the answer to question 10?* **3** a way of dealing with a problem= SOLUTION: *There are no easy answers to this crisis.*

answer² /'ɑːnsə/ verb **1** [I/T] to give a spoken or written reply to a question, letter etc: *Mark answered my letter right away.* ♦ *I'm still waiting for you to answer.* ♦ *What's the matter? Answer me!* ♦ *'I don't have it,' he answered truthfully.* ♦ *We asked him if he agreed with us, and he answered that he did.* **2** [I/T] to come to the door when someone calls at your house, or to pick up the phone when it rings: *I knocked and a young man answered the door.* **3** [I/T] to try to give the correct reply to a question in a test or competition: *Not everyone answered correctly.* **4** [T] to provide what is needed or wanted, especially in order to deal with a bad situation: *When they saw the plane, they knew their prayers had been answered.*

PHRASAL VERB **'answer for sth** to be responsible for explaining something that you have done: *You have to answer for any problems that happen during the show.*

answerable /'ɑːns(ə)rəb(ə)l/ adj **1** if you are answerable to someone, you have to explain to them the reasons for your actions or mistakes **2** if you are answerable for something, you are considered to be responsible for it = RESPONSIBLE

answering machine /'ɑːns(ə)rɪŋ mə,ʃiːn/ noun [C] a machine that answers your telephone and records messages that people leave for you

answerphone /'ɑːnsə,fəʊn/ noun [C] an **answering machine**

ant /ænt/ noun [C] a small insect with a sting. Many ants live under the ground in large organized groups called **colonies**. —*picture* → INSECT

antacid /ænt'æsɪd/ noun [C] **HEALTH** a medicine that reduces the amount of acid in the stomach

antagonism /æn'tægə,nɪz(ə)m/ noun [U] a strong feeling of disliking someone, or of opposing something: *the growing antagonism between the two groups* —**antagonistic** /æn,tægə'nɪstɪk/ adj

an,tagonistic 'pair noun [C] **ANATOMY** a pair of muscles that always work together, so that when one is contracting the other is relaxing

antagonize /æn'tægənaɪz/ verb [T] to make someone feel angry with you and dislike you

the Antarctic /æn'tɑːktɪk/ **GEOGRAPHY** the continent of Antarctica and the seas around it → ARCTIC

Antarctica /æn'tɑːktɪkə/ **GEOGRAPHY** the continent around the South Pole, consisting of ice-covered land and high mountains —*picture* → CONTINENT

the An'tarctic 'Circle noun **GEOGRAPHY** the line of **latitude** at about 66° S that forms a circle around Antarctica and the seas around it —*picture* → EARTH

ante- /ænti/ prefix before: used with some nouns, adjectives, and verbs

antecedent /,æntɪ'siːd(ə)nt/ noun **1 antecedents** [plural] *formal* the members of someone's family who lived a long time ago **2** [C] **LANGUAGE** the antecedent of a word is the noun or phrase nearer the beginning of the sentence that it refers to. In the sentence 'I threw the keys to him and he caught them', 'keys' is the antecedent of 'them'.

antedate /,ænti'deɪt/ verb [T] *formal* to exist or happen before something else

antelope /'ænti,ləʊp/ noun [C] a brown mammal like a **deer**, with horns and long thin legs. It can run very fast. **Impala** and **gazelles** are both types of antelope.

antenatal /,ænti'neɪt(ə)l/ adj **HEALTH** relating to the medical care of pregnant women, or to the time before a baby is born

antenna /æn'tenə/ (plural **antennae** /æn'teniː/) noun [C] **BIOLOGY** one of the two long thin parts on the head of an insect, crustacean, **centipede**, or **millipede** that it uses to feel things with —*picture* → INSECT

anterior /æn'tɪəriə/ adj near the front of a part of the body: *the anterior part of the brain*

anteroom /'ænti,ruːm/ noun [C] a small room that leads to a larger and more important room

anthem /'ænθəm/ noun [C] the official song of a particular country

anther /'ænθə/ noun [C] **BIOLOGY** the male part of a flower that produces the pollen. It is the top part of the stamen. —*picture* → FLOWER

anthill /'ænt,hɪl/ noun [C] a pile of earth that **ants** make above the underground place where they live

anthology /æn'θɒlədʒi/ (plural **anthologies**) noun [C] **LITERATURE** a book containing poems, stories, or songs that were written by different people

anthracite /'ænθrə,saɪt/ noun [U] a type of very hard coal

anthrax /'ænθræks/ noun [U] **HEALTH** a very serious disease of cows and sheep that affects the skin and lungs. It can be passed on to humans.

anthropoid /ˈænθrəˌpɔɪd/ adj an anthropoid **ape** or other animal is very similar to a human —**anthropoid** noun [C]

anthropology /ˌænθrəˈpɒlədʒi/ noun [U] **SOCIAL STUDIES** the study of human societies, customs, and beliefs —**anthropological** /ˌænθrəpəˈlɒdʒɪk(ə)l/ adj, **anthropologist** /ˌænθrəˈpɒlədʒɪst/ noun [C]

anthropomorphic /ˌænθrəpəˈmɔːfɪk/ adj considering something such as a god, animal, or object as having human features or qualities —**anthropomorphism** /ˌænθrəpəˈmɔːfɪz(ə)m/ noun [U]

anti- /ˈænti/ prefix **1** opposing: antiwar protesters **2** with the opposite qualities: an anti-hero **3** preventing or curing: antibacterial

antibacterial /ˌæntibækˈtɪəriəl/ adj **HEALTH** an antibacterial substance stops or limits the growth of bacteria

antibiotic /ˌæntibaɪˈɒtɪk/ noun [C] **HEALTH** a drug, for example **penicillin**, that cures illnesses and infections caused by bacteria

antibody /ˈæntiˌbɒdi/ (plural **antibodies**) noun [C] **HEALTH** a substance that the body produces to fight illnesses and infections. Antibodies are an important part of the **immune system** that protects the body against disease.

anticipate /ænˈtɪsɪpeɪt/ verb [T] **1** to think that something will probably happen: Organizers say they do not anticipate any difficulties. **2** to guess that something will happen, and be ready to deal with it: The businesses that survive are those that anticipate changes in technology.

anticipation /ænˌtɪsɪˈpeɪʃ(ə)n/ noun [U] a feeling of excitement about something enjoyable that is going to happen soon

    PHRASE **in anticipation of sth** if you do something in anticipation of an event, you do something to prepare for it

anticlerical /ˌæntiˈklerɪk(ə)l/ adj **SOCIAL STUDIES** disliking priests and churches, or not wanting them to have power in political or social issues

anticlimax /ˌæntiˈklaɪmæks/ noun [C] something that is not as exciting as you expected it to be

anticlinal /ˌæntiˈklaɪn(ə)l/ adj **GEOLOGY** having the form of an **anticline**

anticline /ˈæntiklaɪn/ noun [C] **GEOLOGY** a bend in a layer of underground rock that curves upwards. It has the oldest rock is at its core.

anticlockwise /ˌæntiˈklɒkwaɪz/ adj, adv moving in the direction opposite to the direction of the hands of a clock

anticoagulant /ˌæntikəʊˈægjələnt/ noun [C/U] **HEALTH** a substance that prevents blood from **coagulating** (=becoming more solid) —**anticoagulant** adj

anticyclone /ˌæntiˈsaɪkləʊn/ noun [C] **GEOGRAPHY** an area of high air pressure that brings calm weather with very little wind

anti-ˈD noun [C] **HEALTH** an injection of a **blood product** that is given to **Rhesus negative** mothers in order to prevent **Rhesus disease** in their **Rhesus positive** baby

antidepressant /ˌæntidɪˈpres(ə)nt/ noun [C] **HEALTH** a drug that is used for treating someone who is suffering from **depression**

antidiuretic hormone /ˌæntidaɪjʊˌretɪk ˈhɔːməʊn/ noun [U] **BIOLOGY** see **ADH**

antidote /ˈæntiˌdəʊt/ noun [C] **1** **HEALTH** a substance that prevents or reduces the harmful effects of a poison **2** something that helps to improve the effects of something bad: The game was a welcome antidote to the day's worries.

antifreeze /ˈæntiˌfriːz/ noun [U] a chemical that is added to the water in a car engine to prevent it from freezing

antigen /ˈæntidʒ(ə)n/ noun [C] **HEALTH** a harmful substance in the body that causes the body to produce antibodies to fight it. Bacteria, viruses, and some other chemicals are antigens.

ˈanti-ˌhero noun [C] a main character in a story who does not have the qualities that a **hero** usually has, such as being morally good

antihistamine /ˌæntiˈhɪstəmiːn/ noun [C/U] **HEALTH** a drug that is used to treat allergies

anti-inflammatory /ˌænti ɪnˈflæmət(ə)ri/ adj **HEALTH** relating to a drug or medicine that is taken to reduce **inflammation** (=swelling and pain)

antilog /ˈæntiˌlɒg/ noun [C] **MATHS** an **antilogarithm**

antilogarithm /ˌæntiˈlɒgərɪð(ə)m/ noun [C] **MATHS** the number that has a **logarithm** with a particular number

antimatter /ˈæntiˌmætə/ noun [U] **PHYSICS** particles that are the exact opposites of all the particles in the universe

antimony /ˈæntiməni/ noun [U] **CHEMISTRY** a rare toxic chemical element that exists in the form of a metal and a non-metal. Chemical symbol: **Sb**

antioxidant /ˌæntiˈɒksɪd(ə)nt/ noun [C] **1** **CHEMISTRY** a substance that prevents oxygen from combining with other substances and damaging them. Antioxidants are used in industry for making substances such as rubber and plastic stronger, and they are often added to processed foods to make them stay fresh for longer. **2** **HEALTH** a substance in the body that prevents cells and tissue from being damaged by harmful substances. Some vitamins are antioxidants.

antiparticle /ˈæntiˌpɑːtɪk(ə)l/ noun [C] **PHYSICS** a type of particle in an atom that has the opposite electrical **charge** to the charge that a normal particle has, although they both have the same mass

antipathy /ænˈtɪpəθi/ noun [U] formal a strong feeling of not liking someone or something

antiperspirant /ˌæntiˈpɜːsp(ə)rənt/ noun [C/U] a substance that you put on your skin to stop you from sweating

the Antipodes /ænˈtɪpəˌdiːz/ Australia and New Zealand —**Antipodean** /ænˌtɪpəˈdiːən/ adj, noun [C]

antiquated /ˈæntiˌkweɪtɪd/ adj too old or old-fashioned to be useful

antique /ænˈtiːk/ noun [C] an old valuable object such as a piece of furniture or jewellery

antiquity /ænˈtɪkwəti/ noun **1** [U] ancient times **2** **antiquities** [plural] objects or buildings that existed in ancient times and still exist

antiretroviral /ˌæntiretrəʊˈvaɪr(ə)l/ adj antiretroviral drugs are used to treat certain types of virus, especially HIV

ˌanti-ˈroll ˌbar noun [C] **ENGINEERING** a metal bar in the **suspension** system of a vehicle, designed to stop the vehicle from swinging dangerously or turning over

anti-Semitic /ˌænti səˈmɪtɪk/ adj showing a feeling of hate towards Jewish people —**anti-Semitism** /ˌænti ˈseməˌtɪz(ə)m/ noun [U]

antiseptic /ˌænti'septɪk/ noun [C/U] HEALTH a substance that is used for cleaning injured skin and preventing infections —**antiseptic** adj

antisocial /ˌænti'səʊʃ(ə)l/ adj 1 not interested in meeting other people, or not enjoying friendly relationships with them 2 showing a lack of care for other people: *antisocial activities*

antithesis /æn'tɪθəsɪs/ noun [singular] *formal* the exact opposite of something

antitoxin /ˌænti'tɒksɪn/ noun [C] HEALTH a substance that reduces or prevents the harmful effects of a **toxin** (=a poison)

antitrust /ˌænti'trʌst/ adj LAW American intended to prevent companies from controlling prices and reducing competition

antivirus /ˌænti'vaɪrəs/ adj COMPUTING an antivirus computer program finds and removes viruses before they can damage the computer system

antlers /'æntləz/ noun [plural] BIOLOGY the horns on the head of a male **deer**

antonym /'æntənɪm/ noun [C] LANGUAGE a word that means the opposite of another word → SYNONYM

anus /'eɪnəs/ noun [C] ANATOMY the opening at the end of the alimentary canal through which solid waste passes out of the body —*picture* → CATERPILLAR, DIGESTIVE SYSTEM, ORGAN

anvil /'ænvɪl/ noun 1 [C] a metal block on which a **blacksmith** shapes metal objects with a hammer 2 [singular] ANATOMY a small bone in the **middle ear** between the **hammer** and the **stirrup** —*picture* → EAR

anxiety /æŋ'zaɪəti/ (plural **anxieties**) noun 1 [U] a worried feeling that someone has because they think that something bad might happen: *There was a lot of anxiety about the results of the talks.* 2 [C] something that someone is worried about

anxious /'æŋkʃəs/ adj 1 someone who is anxious is worried because they think that something bad might happen: *His silence made me anxious.* ♦ *We had an anxious few moments while the results were coming through.* ♦ *People are naturally anxious about these tests.* 2 wanting something very much and feeling nervous, excited, or impatient: *We were all anxious for peace.* ♦ *We're anxious to hear from anyone who can help.* ♦ *They were anxious that everyone should enjoy themselves.* —**anxiously** adv

any /'eni/ adv, determiner, pronoun 1 used instead of 'some' in negatives, questions, and **conditional** sentences: *Did you bring any warm clothes?* ♦ *I tried to get a ticket but there weren't any left.* ♦ *If you need any help, just let me know.* ♦ *Did any of her friends come?* 2 used when something is true for every person or thing in a group: *Pick any design you want – they're all the same price.* ♦ *It was the first time that any of us had been in a plane.* 3 in any way, or by any amount: *If your headache gets any worse, you should see a doctor.* ♦ *I was too tired to walk any further.*
PHRASE **not...any more/longer** used for saying that a situation has ended: *The Campbells don't live here any more.*

anybody /'eniˌbɒdi/ pronoun anyone: *Would anybody like a cup of coffee?*

anymore /ˌeni'mɔː/ adv used when talking or asking about a situation that has ended: *Don't you love me anymore?*

anyone /'eniwʌn/ pronoun 1 used instead of 'someone' in negatives, questions, and **conditional** sentences: *I don't know anyone here.* ♦ *Was there anyone at home?* ♦ *If anyone wants coffee, here it is.*

♦ *Is anyone else coming with us?* 2 used for referring to any person, when it does not matter which one: *Anyone can make a mistake.* ♦ *You can invite anyone you like.*

anything /'eniθɪŋ/ pronoun 1 used instead of 'something' in negatives, questions, and **conditional** sentences: *Don't do anything stupid.* ♦ *He never does anything to help.* ♦ *Do you know anything about cricket?* ♦ *If anything happens, call me.* ♦ *Do you want anything else to eat?* 2 used when something is true for every thing in a group, or for every possible thing: *You can buy anything you want on the Internet.* ♦ *She would do anything for her children.*

anytime /'eniˌtaɪm/ adv at any time: *You can come and see me anytime you like.*

anyway /'eniˌweɪ/ adv *spoken* 1 used when you want to change the subject of a conversation, or end the conversation: *What are you doing here, anyway?* ♦ *Anyway, I have to go now.* 2 used for showing why something is not important, or is not a problem: *I don't understand politics, and anyway I'm not really interested.* ♦ *I'll get some bread – I was going to the shops anyway.* 3 despite something that you have previously mentioned: *It's illegal to park here, but people do it anyway.*

anywhere /'eniˌweə/ adv 1 used instead of 'somewhere' in negatives, questions, and **conditional** sentences: *He never travels anywhere without his camera.* ♦ *Have you seen Mike anywhere?* 2 used when something is true for every place, and it is not important which: *You can sit anywhere you like.* 3 used for saying that a number or amount is within a particular range: *The journey can take anywhere from 20 minutes to an hour.*
PHRASE **not be getting/going anywhere** not making any progress
→ NEAR

AOB abbrev any other business: things that are discussed at the end of a meeting

aorta /eɪ'ɔːtə/ noun [C] ANATOMY the main artery that carries blood with a high oxygen level from the heart to other parts of the body —*picture* → CIRCULATION

apart /ə'pɑːt/ adj, adv 1 at a distance away from each other, or away from someone or something else: *Stand with your feet apart.* ♦ *Their two farms are about a mile apart.* ♦ *He doesn't like being apart from his family.* 2 broken or separated into different pieces: *The book came apart in my hands.* 3 used for saying how much time there is between events: *The two brothers were born six years apart.*
PHRASE **apart from** not including someone or something: *Do you speak any languages apart from English?*
→ TELL SB/STH APART

apartheid /ə'pɑːtˌheɪt, ə'pɑːtˌhaɪt/ noun [U] POLITICS the political system that existed in the past in South Africa, in which only white people had political rights and power

apartment /ə'pɑːtmənt/ noun [C] American a **flat** for living in

a'partment ˌblock noun [C] a block of flats

a'partment ˌbuilding noun [C] American a block of flats

a'partment hoˌtel noun [C] TOURISM a set of furnished rooms or suites, each with a small kitchen, where all normal hotel services are provided

apathetic /ˌæpə'θetɪk/ adj not interested in anything, or not enthusiastic about anything —**apathetically** /ˌæpə'θetɪkli/ adv

apathy /'æpəθi/ noun [U] a feeling of not being interested in anything or not being enthusiastic about anything

ape /eɪp/ noun [C] a large monkey without a tail

aperitif /ə,perə'tiːf/ noun [C] an alcoholic drink that you have before a meal

aperture /'æpətʃə/ noun [C] **1** formal a small hole or space **2** the hole in a camera that lets light in —picture → CAMERA

apex /'eɪpeks/ noun **1** [singular] the top or highest part of something that ends in a point **2** [singular] CONSTRUCTION the top or highest part of a roof **3** [C] BIOLOGY the end of a leaf, opposite the place where it joins the stem —picture → LEAF

aphasia /ə'feɪziə/ noun [U] HEALTH a medical condition in which someone is unable to use or understand some words. It is caused by damage to the brain.

aphid /'eɪfɪd/ noun [C] a small insect that feeds on plant juices and destroys the plant

aphorism /'æfə,rɪz(ə)m/ noun [C] LANGUAGE a short statement that says something wise and true

apiary /'eɪpiəri/ noun [C] a place where bees are kept so that their **honey** can be collected

apical /'æpɪk(ə)l/ adj situated at or affecting the top or tip of something

apiece /ə'piːs/ adv for each one: Tickets were being sold for £20 apiece.

aplomb /ə'plɒm/ noun [U] a confident relaxed manner, when dealing with a difficult situation

apocalypse /ə'pɒkə,lɪps/ noun [singular] **1** a time when the whole world will be destroyed **2** a situation in which many people die and many things are destroyed

apocalyptic /ə,pɒkə'lɪptɪk/ adj describing a time when very bad things will happen

apocryphal /ə'pɒkrəf(ə)l/ adj probably not true, but believed by a lot of people to be true

apogee /'æpədʒiː/ noun [C] **1** formal the time when something is at its most successful or important **2** ASTRONOMY the point furthest from the Earth that the Moon or a satellite reaches while it moves around the Earth

apolitical /,eɪpə'lɪtɪk(ə)l/ adj **1** not interested in politics **2** not connected with a particular political party

apologetic /ə,pɒlə'dʒetɪk/ adj showing that you are sorry for doing something wrong —**apologetically** /ə,pɒlə'dʒetɪkli/ adv

apologise /ə'pɒlədʒaɪz/ another spelling of **apologize**

apologize /ə'pɒlədʒaɪz/ verb [I] to tell someone that you are sorry for doing something wrong: I **apologize for** taking so long to reply. ♦ You should **apologize to** your brother.

apology /ə'pɒlədʒi/ (plural **apologies**) noun [C] a statement that tells someone that you are sorry for doing something wrong: They were kind enough to **accept my apology**. ♦ I think I **owe you an apology**.

apoplectic /,æpə'plektɪk/ adj formal extremely angry

apostle /ə'pɒs(ə)l/ noun [C] **1** one of the 12 **disciples** (=men chosen by Jesus Christ to help him spread Christianity around the world) **2** someone who has a strong belief in an idea and tries to get other people to support it= SUPPORTER

apostolic /,æpə'stɒlɪk/ adj **1** relating to the **Pope** (=the leader of the Roman Catholic Church) **2** relating to the 12 apostles of Jesus Christ or their work

apostrophe /ə'pɒstrəfi/ noun [C] LANGUAGE the symbol ' used in English to show the **possessive** form of a noun, for example 'Bob's car', or to mark the place where a letter has been removed to make a word shorter, for example 'isn't'

apotheosis /ə,pɒθi'əʊsɪs/ noun [singular] very formal **1** the perfect example of something **2** the best point in someone's life or career

appalled /ə'pɔːld/ adj offended or shocked: I'm appalled that a doctor would behave like that. —**appal** verb [T]

appalling /ə'pɔːlɪŋ/ adj extremely bad or shocking: The conditions they live in are appalling. ♦ appalling weather

apparatchik /,æpə'rætʃɪk/ noun [C] someone who works in an organization, especially a political party or large company, but is considered to have no views or beliefs of their own

apparatus /,æpə'reɪtəs/ noun [U] equipment: They were setting up the apparatus for the experiment. ♦ divers wearing underwater breathing apparatus

apparel /ə'pærəl/ noun [U] American a word for clothes, used especially in stores or other businesses

apparent /ə'pærənt/ adj **1** easy to see or understand = OBVIOUS: It was apparent that the two women knew each other. ♦ It should be **apparent to** anyone that the letter was written by a child. **2** an apparent quality, feeling, or situation seems to exist although it may not be real: His apparent lack of interest in her work always annoyed her.

ap,parent 'depth noun [U] PHYSICS the distance that there appears to be between the surface of the water and an object that is beneath the surface. This distance is smaller than the real depth.

apparently /ə'pærəntli/ adv **1** based only on what you have heard, not on what you are certain is true: Apparently, she resigned because she had an argument with her boss. **2** used for saying what seems to be true when people do not yet know all the facts of a situation: Seven people were shot yesterday in two apparently unrelated incidents.

apparition /,æpə'rɪʃ(ə)n/ noun [C] formal a strange image or creature that someone sees

appeal¹ /ə'piːl/ noun **1** [C] an urgent request for people to do something or give something: There have been several **appeals for** an end to the fighting. ♦ The organization has **launched an appeal** to send food to the flood victims. **2** [U] a quality that something has that makes people like it or want it: How do you explain **the appeal of** horror films? **3** [C] LAW a formal request for a court of law to change its decision

appeal² /ə'piːl/ verb [I] **1** to make an urgent request for people to do something or give something: She **appealed to** her former husband **to** return their baby son. ♦ They're **appealing to** local businesses for money. **2** if something appeals to you, you like it or want it: The show's mixture of comedy and songs will **appeal to** children. **3** LAW to formally ask a court of law to change its decision: Green's family say they will **appeal against** the verdict.

appealing /ə'piːlɪŋ/ adj **1** attractive and interesting: The building has an appealing old-fashioned charm. ♦ We've tried to make the design more **appealing to** young people. **2** an appealing look, voice etc shows that someone wants help, approval, or agreement

appear /ə'pɪə/ verb [I]

1 seem	4 be written/printed
2 begin to be seen	5 be on TV etc
3 start to exist	

1 to make other people think that you are something, or that you feel something = SEEM: *Matt appears unaffected by all the media attention.* ♦ *There appears to be very little we can do about the problem.* ♦ *It appears that she's changed her mind.*
2 if someone or something appears somewhere, you see them suddenly or for the first time: *Cracks began to appear in the ceiling.*
3 to start to exist, or to start to be available for the first time: *the latest Internet guide to appear on the market*
4 to be written or printed somewhere: *Jane's name did not appear on the list.*
5 to be on television or in a play, film, or concert: *She is currently appearing in a Broadway musical.*

appearance /ə'pɪərəns/ noun **1** [U] the way that someone or something looks: *The twins are almost identical in appearance.* ♦ *His thinning hair gave him the appearance of a much older man.* ♦ *He always gives the appearance of being very busy.* **2** [U] the time when something starts to exist, or starts to be seen: *the appearance of fast food restaurants on every high street* **3** [U] the fact that someone arrives somewhere: *She was startled by Julie's sudden appearance in the doorway.* **4** [C] an occasion when someone is on television or in a play, film, or concert: *a public appearance* ♦ *She has made numerous appearances on TV game shows.*

appease /ə'piːz/ verb [T] to give someone what they want in order to avoid an argument or fight with them —**appeasement** noun [U]

appellant /ə'pelənt/ noun [C] LAW someone who appeals against a decision of a court of law

appellate court /ə,pelət 'kɔːt/ noun [C] LAW a court of law that can change the decision made in other courts

append /ə'pend/ verb [T] *formal* to add something to the end of a piece of writing

appendage /ə'pendɪdʒ/ noun [C] *formal* something that is joined to something larger, for example a hand or foot

appendectomy /,æpən'dektəmi/ (plural **appendectomies**) noun [C] HEALTH a medical operation in which the **appendix** is removed

appendicitis /ə,pendɪ'saɪtɪs/ noun [U] HEALTH a serious medical condition in which the appendix becomes infected and sometimes has to be removed

appendix /ə'pendɪks/ noun [C] **1** (plural **appendixes**) ANATOMY a small tube attached to the lower end of the **small intestine** in humans and some other mammals. There is no known use for the appendix in humans. —*picture* → DIGESTIVE SYSTEM, ORGAN **2** (plural **appendices** /ə'pendɪsiːz/) an extra section at the end of a book

appetite /'æpətaɪt/ noun [C] **1** the natural feeling of wanting to eat: *a child with a healthy appetite* ♦ *Don't have any more chocolate – it'll spoil your appetite* (=make you want to eat less at the next meal). **2** a feeling of wanting something: *Young children have a natural appetite for stories.*

appetizer /'æpə,taɪzə/ noun [C] a food that people eat before the main part of a meal

appetizing /'æpə,taɪzɪŋ/ adj appetizing food smells or looks very good

applaud /ə'plɔːd/ verb **1** [I/T] to show that you enjoyed someone's performance by hitting the palms of your hands together = CLAP **2** [T] to praise a decision or action

applause /ə'plɔːz/ noun [U] the sound made by people applauding: *Let's have a round of applause for all the organizers.*

apple /'æp(ə)l/ noun [C/U] a hard round green or red fruit that is white inside and grows on trees —*picture* → FRUIT

appliance /ə'plaɪəns/ noun [C] a piece of electrical equipment that people have in their homes: *appliances such as washing machines and refrigerators*

applicable /ə'plɪkəb(ə)l/ adj relevant to a particular situation or group of people: *This section of the law is applicable only to businesses.* —**applicability** /ə,plɪkə'bɪləti/ noun [U]

applicant /'æplɪkənt/ noun [C] someone who applies for a job

application /,æplɪ'keɪʃ(ə)n/ noun [C] **1** a formal request to do something or have something, for example a job: *His application for membership was rejected.* ♦ *her application to study at Columbia University* **2** a particular use that something has: *the practical applications of this technology* **3** COMPUTING a piece of computer software that is used for a particular purpose

appli'cation ,form noun [C] a printed list of questions that someone answers as part of a formal request for something

appli'cation ,software noun [U] COMPUTING software used for writing documents, creating **charts**, building **databases** etc that is not part of the computer's **operating system** → SYSTEM SOFTWARE

applicator /'æplɪ,keɪtə/ noun [C] an object used for putting a substance on the surface of something

applied linguistics /ə,plaɪd lɪŋ'gwɪstɪks/ noun [U] LANGUAGE the study of language for its practical uses, for example in teaching or **speech therapy**

apply /ə'plaɪ/ (**applies, applying, applied**) verb

1 request a job etc	4 put sth on surface
2 affect/be relevant to	5 use physical force
3 use method/process etc	

1 [I] to make a formal request to do something or have something: *Students can apply for money to help with their living costs.* ♦ *You have to apply to the passport office for a visa.* ♦ *Bill is applying to join the fire service.*
2 [I] to be relevant to a particular person or thing: *The rule no longer applies to him, because he's over 18.*
3 [T] to use something: *A similar technique can be applied to the treatment of cancer.*
4 [T] to put a layer of something such as paint onto a surface
5 [T] *formal* to use physical force in order to make something happen or work

appoint /ə'pɔɪnt/ verb [T] to choose someone to do a particular job: *We need to appoint a new school secretary.*

appointee /ə,pɔɪn'tiː/ noun [C] someone who has been chosen to do a particular job

appointment /ə'pɔɪntmənt/ noun **1** [C] an arrangement to see someone, for example a doctor, at a particular time: *Why don't you make an appointment with one of our doctors?* ♦ *I have an appointment to see my lawyer next Saturday.* **2** [C] a job: *academic appointments* **3** [U] the decision to give someone a job: *his appointment as head of the education department*

apportion /əˈpɔːʃ(ə)n/ verb [T] *formal* to divide something such as payments between two or more people, organizations etc

PHRASE apportion blame to say who should be blamed for something

apposite /ˈæpəzɪt/ adj *formal* relevant and appropriate to what is happening or being discussed

apposition /ˌæpəˈzɪʃ(ə)n/ noun [U] **LANGUAGE** the relationship between two **noun phrases** that are used in the same way and refer to the same person or thing. For example, in 'My best friend, Jane, likes swimming', 'my best friend' and 'Jane' are **in apposition**.

appraisal /əˈpreɪz(ə)l/ noun [C/U] **1** an opinion about how successful, effective etc someone or something is **2 BUSINESS** an interview between a manager and an employee that allows the manager to judge how well the employee is doing their job

appraise /əˈpreɪz/ verb [T] **1** *formal* to form an opinion about how successful, effective etc someone or something is **2 BUSINESS** to interview people who work for a company and tell them how well they are doing their job

appreciable /əˈpriːʃəb(ə)l/ adj enough to be noticed: *an appreciable improvement in the student's test scores* —**appreciably** adv

appreciate /əˈpriːʃiˌeɪt/ verb **1** [T] to understand a situation and know why it is important or serious= REALIZE: *Doctors are beginning to appreciate how dangerous this drug can be.* ♦ *We appreciate that you cannot make a decision immediately.* **2** [T] to be grateful for something: *I really appreciate all your help.* **3** [T] to realize that someone or something has good qualities: *She feels that her family doesn't really appreciate her.* **4** [I] to increase in value ≠ DEPRECIATE

appreciation /əˌpriːʃiˈeɪʃ(ə)n/ noun **1** [U] the feeling of being grateful: *The award is given in appreciation of her huge contribution to the film industry.* **2** [U] the ability to understand a situation and know why it is important or serious: *Most people have no appreciation of the dangers involved in the process.* **3** [singular/U] pleasure that comes from understanding something good or beautiful: *We share an appreciation of music.* **4** [singular/U] an increase in the value of something ≠ DEPRECIATION

appreciative /əˈpriːʃətɪv/ adj showing that you are grateful, or that you enjoyed something: *an appreciative audience* —**appreciatively** adv

apprehend /ˌæprɪˈhend/ verb [T] *formal* to arrest someone

apprehension /ˌæprɪˈhenʃ(ə)n/ noun [C/U] a feeling of worry that something bad might happen= ANXIETY

apprehensive /ˌæprɪˈhensɪv/ adj slightly worried or nervous —**apprehensively** adv

apprentice /əˈprentɪs/ noun [C] someone who is learning how to do a particular job

apprenticeship /əˈprentɪʃɪp/ noun [C/U] the time when someone works as an apprentice

approach¹ /əˈprəʊtʃ/ noun **1** [C] a way of dealing with something: *He has a relaxed approach to life.* **2** [singular] the fact that something is coming closer in time or in distance: *the approach of war* **3** [C] the action of asking for something, or of formally offering something: *The company has made some approaches to the government.* **4** [C] a path or road: *All approaches to the palace have been closed by the police.*

approach² /əˈprəʊtʃ/ verb **1** [I/T] to move closer in distance or time: *She heard footsteps approaching from behind.* ♦ *A strange boat was approaching the shore.*

♦ *The day of the election approached.* **2** [T] to formally ask someone for something, or formally offer something: *I have already approached my boss about a pay rise.* **3** [T] to almost reach a particular level or condition: *They played in temperatures approaching 40 degrees.* **4** [T] to deal with a situation in a particular way: *There are several ways of approaching this problem.*

approachable /əˈprəʊtʃəb(ə)l/ adj friendly and easy to talk to

approbation /ˌæprəˈbeɪʃ(ə)n/ noun [U] *formal* approval

appropriate¹ /əˈprəʊpriət/ adj suitable for a particular situation ≠ INAPPROPRIATE: *This isn't the appropriate time to discuss the problem.* —**appropriately** adv, **appropriateness** noun [U]

appropriate² /əˈprəʊpriˌeɪt/ verb [T] *formal* to take something for yourself

ap,propriate tech'nology noun [U] **ECONOMICS** technology that is suitable for the place in which it will be used, usually involving skills or materials that are easily available in the local area

appropriation /əˌprəʊpriˈeɪʃ(ə)n/ noun [C/U] *formal* **1** money that must be used in a particular way, according to an official decision **2** the action of taking something, especially when someone has no right to take it

approval /əˈpruːv(ə)l/ noun [U] **1** a positive opinion about someone or something ≠ DISAPPROVAL: *Children are constantly looking for signs of approval from their parents.* **2** official permission: *The government has not yet given the scheme its approval.*

approve /əˈpruːv/ verb **1** [I] to think that someone or something is good ≠ DISAPPROVE: *You're leaving college! Do your parents approve?* ♦ *He seemed to approve of my choice.* ♦ *I don't really approve of children wearing make-up.* **2** [T] to give official permission for something: *The new stamps were personally approved by the Queen.*

approving /əˈpruːvɪŋ/ adj showing that you like someone or something ≠ DISAPPROVING: *an approving smile* —**approvingly** adv

approx. abbrev **1** approximate **2** approximately

approximate¹ /əˈprɒksɪmət/ adj not exact, but close to an exact amount or number: *the approximate cost of the repairs*

approximate² /əˈprɒksɪmeɪt/ verb [T] to calculate something in a way that is not exact

approximately /əˈprɒksɪmətli/ adv used for showing that an amount or number is not exact= ROUGHLY: *Approximately 60,000 people filled the stadium.* ♦ *We have approximately 300 copies left.*

approximation /əˌprɒksɪˈmeɪʃ(ə)n/ noun [C/U] a nearly exact calculation, amount, number, time etc

APR /ˌeɪ piː ˈɑː/ noun [C] annual percentage rate: the percentage that a bank makes you pay in **interest** when you borrow money from it, calculated over a period of one year

apricot /ˈeɪprɪˌkɒt/ noun [C] a fruit with an orange-yellow skin and a large hard seed inside —*picture* → FRUIT

April /ˈeɪprəl/ noun [U] the fourth month of the year, between March and May: *Her birthday is in April.* ♦ *My appointment is on 8th April.*

apron /ˈeɪprən/ noun [C] something that someone wears to protect the front of their clothes when they are cooking

apt /æpt/ adj **1** very suitable: *It seemed apt that the winning goal was scored by the captain.* **2** good at learning= ABLE —**aptly** adv

aptitude /ˈæptɪˌtjuːd/ noun [C/U] natural ability that makes it easy for you to do something well: *an aptitude for maths*

aquaculture /ˈækwəˌkʌltʃə/ noun [U] AGRICULTURE the farming of plants and animals from the sea and rivers for people to eat

aqualung /ˈækwəˌlʌŋ/ noun [C] a piece of equipment that provides air for someone when they are swimming under water

aquamarine /ˌækwəməˈriːn/ noun [C/U] a green-blue stone used for making jewellery

aquaplane /ˈækwəˌpleɪn/ verb [I] ENGINEERING if a car aquaplanes, it slides across water on the road in an uncontrolled way

aquarium /əˈkweəriəm/ noun [C] **1** a glass container for fish and other water animals **2** a building with aquariums in it

Aquarius /əˈkweəriəs/ noun [U] one of the 12 signs of the zodiac. An **Aquarius** or **Aquarian** is someone who is born between 20 January and 19 February.

aquatic /əˈkwætɪk/ adj **1** BIOLOGY living in or near water: *aquatic birds* **2** relating to or involving water

aquatint /ˈækwəˌtɪnt/ noun [C] ARTS a picture like a **watercolour** that is printed by using acid to cut a design into a sheet of metal

aqueduct /ˈækwɪˌdʌkt/ noun [C] a structure like a bridge that takes water across a valley

aqueous /ˈeɪkwiəs, ˈækwiəs/ adj SCIENCE containing water

aqueous 'humour noun [C] ANATOMY the transparent liquid that fills the eye between the back of the **cornea** and the front of the **iris** and lens —*picture* → EYE, RETINA

aquifer /ˈækwɪfə/ noun [C] GEOLOGY a layer of earth or rock that contains water, or that water can pass through —*picture* → WATER SUPPLY

aquiline /ˈækwɪˌlaɪn/ adj *formal* an aquiline nose is large and curved

Arab /ˈærəb/ noun [C] someone from the Middle East or North Africa who speaks Arabic —**Arab** adj

Arabic /ˈærəbɪk/ noun [U] the language that most people speak in the Middle East and North Africa —**Arabic** adj

Arabic 'numeral noun [C] MATHS one of the written symbols 0, 1, 2, 3, 4, 5, 6, 7, 8, and 9 that are used in the writing systems of many countries to represent numbers → ROMAN NUMERAL

arable /ˈærəb(ə)l/ adj AGRICULTURE relating to, used for, or involved in the growing of crops: *arable land* ♦ *an arable farm* ♦ *arable crops*

arachnid /əˈræknɪd/ noun [C] BIOLOGY a member of a class of animals called **arthropods**. They have four pairs of legs, and include spiders, **scorpions**, **mites**, and **ticks**.

arbiter /ˈɑːbɪtə/ noun [C] **1** someone who has the official power to settle disagreements **2** someone whose opinions about art, fashion, food etc have a lot of influence

arbitrary /ˈɑːbɪtrəri/ adj not done for any particular reason and therefore often unfair: *an arbitrary decision* —**arbitrarily** /ˈɑːbɪtrərəli, ˌɑːbɪˈtreərəli/ adv

arbitration /ˌɑːbɪˈtreɪʃ(ə)n/ noun [U] LAW, BUSINESS the official process of trying to settle a

disagreement —**arbitrate** /ˈɑːbɪˌtreɪt/ verb [I], **arbitrator** /ˈɑːbɪˌtreɪtə/ noun [C]

arboreal /ɑːˈbɔːriəl/ adj BIOLOGY relating to or living in trees

arboretum /ˌɑːbəˈriːtəm/ noun [C] a place where trees are grown so that they can be studied

arboriculture /ˈɑːbəriˌkʌltʃə/ noun [U] the work, business, or study of growing trees and bushes

arc /ɑːk/ noun [C] **1** a curved shape, or a curved line **2** MATHS a part of the line that forms the outside of a circle —*picture* → CIRCLE

arcade /ɑːˈkeɪd/ noun [C] **1** an amusement arcade **2** a covered area with shops on both sides

arcane /ɑːˈkeɪn/ adj *formal* mysterious and difficult to understand

arch[1] /ɑːtʃ/ noun [C] **1** a shape or structure with straight sides and a curved top. The curved top part is also called an arch. **2** the curved bottom part of the foot **3** GEOLOGY a piece of rock in the shape of an arch that sticks out into the sea. The sea has worn a hole in the rock. —*picture* → EROSION

arch[2] /ɑːtʃ/ verb [T] to make something curve: *The cat arched its back.*

archaeology /ˌɑːkiˈɒlədʒi/ noun [U] the study of ancient societies, done by looking at old bones, buildings, and other objects —**archaeological** /ˌɑːkiəˈlɒdʒɪk(ə)l/ adj, **archaeologist** noun [C]

archaeopteryx /ˌɑːkiˈɒptərɪks/ noun [C] the first bird known to have existed, which lived during the **Jurassic** period, about 150 to 200 million years ago

archaic /ɑːˈkeɪɪk/ adj old and no longer used or useful

archaism /ˈɑːkeɪˌɪz(ə)m/ noun [C] LANGUAGE an old word or phrase that is no longer used

archangel /ˈɑːkˌeɪndʒ(ə)l/ noun [C] an important **angel** (=a spirit that lives in heaven) in the Muslim, Jewish, and Christian religions

archbishop /ɑːtʃˈbɪʃəp/ noun [C] RELIGION a priest of the highest rank in some Christian churches

archdeacon /ɑːtʃˈdiːkən/ noun [C] RELIGION a priest of a high rank in the **Anglican Church** whose job is to help a bishop

archdiocese /ɑːtʃˈdaɪəsɪs/ noun [C] RELIGION the area that an **archbishop** is responsible for

arch-'enemy noun [C] someone who is your main enemy

archeology /ˌɑːkiˈɒlədʒi/ an American spelling of **archaeology**

archery /ˈɑːtʃəri/ noun [U] SPORTS the sport of shooting arrows from a **bow** —**archer** noun [C]

archetypal /ˌɑːkɪˈtaɪp(ə)l/ adj very typical of a particular type of person or thing

archetype /ˈɑːkɪˌtaɪp/ noun [C] a very typical example of a particular type of person or thing

Archimedean spiral /ˌɑːkɪmiːdiən ˈspaɪrəl/ noun [C] MATHS, TECHNOLOGY a spiral formed by a point moving away from a fixed central point in a circular movement, at a fixed speed and at a fixed angle

archipelago /ˌɑːkɪˈpeləɡəʊ/ noun [C] GEOGRAPHY **1** a large group of small islands **2** a sea or area of ocean with many small islands in it

architect /ˈɑːkɪˌtekt/ noun [C] someone whose job is to design buildings

architecture /ˈɑːkɪˌtektʃə/ noun [U] **1** a particular style of building: *The church is a typical example of Gothic architecture.* **2** the study or practice of designing buildings **3 COMPUTING** the design and structure of a computer system or program and the way that it works in relation to other systems and programs —**architectural** /ˌɑːkɪ'tektʃ(ə)rəl/ adj

architrave /'ɑːkɪtreɪv/ noun [C] **CONSTRUCTION** a piece of wood fixed around a door frame to cover the joint between the **plaster** and the frame

archive¹ /'ɑːkaɪv/ noun [C] **1** a collection of historical documents, or the place where it is kept **2 COMPUTING** a collection of computer files that have been saved together in **compressed** form

archive² /'ɑːkaɪv/ verb [T] **1 COMPUTING** to collect and store computer files in an archive **2** to collect and store historical documents and records

archway /'ɑːtʃweɪ/ noun [C] a curved roof over an entrance or passage

'arc ,light noun [C] a light that is produced when electricity flows between two separated points

arctic /'ɑːktɪk/ adj extremely cold= FREEZING

the Arctic /'ɑːktɪk/ **GEOGRAPHY** the cold region that is the most northern part of the world —**Arctic** adj → ANTARCTIC

the ,Arctic 'Circle GEOGRAPHY the line of **latitude** at about 66° N that encloses the Arctic —*picture* → EARTH

the ,Arctic 'Ocean GEOGRAPHY the world's smallest ocean. It is north of the Arctic Circle and is mostly covered in ice. —*picture* → CONTINENT

arc welding /'ɑːk ˌweldɪŋ/ noun [U] **TECHNOLOGY** welding that uses heat produced by an **electric arc** (=continuous spark) between two electrodes, or between an electrode and the metal being welded

ardent /'ɑːd(ə)nt/ adj feeling a particular emotion very strongly: *ardent supporters of the president* —**ardently** adv

ardour /'ɑːdə/ noun [U] very strong feelings of admiration, determination, or love

arduous /'ɑːdjuəs/ adj extremely difficult and involving a lot of effort

are /strong ɑː, weak ə/ see **be**

area /'eəriə/ noun **1** [C] a part of a place or building: *Bus services in rural areas are not very good.* ♦ *My family has lived in this area of Zimbabwe for years.* **2** [C] a particular subject or type of activity: *His area of expertise is engineering.* ♦ *What is your main area of concern?* **3** [C] a place on the surface of something, for example on a part of your body: *sensitive areas of your skin* **4** [U] **MATHS** the amount of space that the surface of a place or shape covers: *The screen has a large surface area.*

'area ,code noun [C] a series of numbers that people have to **dial** when they are making a telephone call to someone in a different area

arena /ə'riːnə/ noun [C] **1** a large area surrounded by seats, used for sports or entertainment **2** the people and activities that are involved with a particular subject: *Today, businesses must be able to compete in the international arena.*

aren't /ɑːnt/ short form **1** the usual way of saying 'are not': *We aren't going to Spain this year.* **2** the usual way of saying 'am not' in questions: *I'm looking thinner, aren't I?*

arête /ə'reɪt, ə'ret/ noun [C] **GEOLOGY** a narrow line of bare rock between two **cirques** (=valleys), found in an area of mountains that has been covered by glaciers

argon /'ɑːɡɒn/ noun [U] **CHEMISTRY** a gas that is an element that does not produce a chemical reaction with other substances. It is an **inert** gas that is used in

electric lights, and also forms about 1% of air. Chemical symbol: **Ar**

arguable /'ɑːɡjuəb(ə)l/ adj **1** not clearly true or correct: *Whether good students make good teachers is arguable.* **2** *formal* if a fact or statement is arguable, there is evidence that it may be true

arguably /'ɑːɡjuəbli/ adv used for stating your opinion or belief, especially when you think that other people may disagree: *Ali was arguably the best boxer of all time.*

argue /'ɑːɡjuː/ verb **1** [I] to discuss something that you disagree about, usually in an angry way= QUARREL: *Those girls are always arguing!* ♦ *Don't argue with me – you know I'm right.* ♦ *We used to argue about who should drive.* **2** [I/T] to give reasons why you believe that something is right or true: *Woolf's report argued for* (=supported) *an improvement in prison conditions.* ♦ *Several people stood up to argue against* (=to oppose) *moving the students to the new school.* ♦ *Reuben opposed the new road, arguing that it wasn't worth $25 million.*

argument /'ɑːɡjʊmənt/ noun **1** [C] an angry disagreement between people= QUARREL: *The decision led to a heated argument* (=extremely angry disagreement). ♦ *My girlfriend and I have had an argument.* ♦ *Every time we visit my family, he gets into an argument with my sister.* ♦ *I try to avoid arguments about money.* **2** [C/U] a set of reasons that you use for persuading people to support your opinion: *There are powerful arguments against releasing them from prison.* ♦ *You could make an argument for working shorter hours.*

argumentative /ˌɑːɡjʊ'mentətɪv/ adj *showing disapproval* often arguing or disagreeing with people

aria /'ɑːriə/ noun [C] **MUSIC** a song for one of the main singers in an opera or **oratorio**

arid /'ærɪd/ adj **GEOGRAPHY** very dry with few plants

Aries /'eəriːz/ noun [C/U] one of the 12 signs of the zodiac. An **Aries** is someone who is born between 21 March and 20 April.

arise /ə'raɪz/ (**arises, arising, arose** /ə'rəʊz/, **arisen** /ə'rɪz(ə)n/) verb [I] to begin to exist or develop: *Problems arose over plans to build a new supermarket here.* ♦ *We can have another meeting if the need arises.*

aristocracy /ˌærɪ'stɒkrəsi/ (plural **aristocracies**) noun [C] **SOCIAL STUDIES** the people in the highest class of some societies, who usually have money, land, and power and who often have special titles

aristocrat /'ærɪstəˌkræt/ noun [C] **SOCIAL STUDIES** a member of the aristocracy —**aristocratic** /ˌærɪstə'krætɪk/ adj

arithmetic /ə'rɪθmətɪk/ noun [U] **MATHS** the part of mathematics that involves basic calculations such as adding or multiplying numbers —**arithmetical** /ˌærɪθ'metɪk(ə)l/ adj, **arithmetically** adv

,arithmetic 'mean noun [C] **MATHS** an average number or amount

,arithmetic pro'gression noun [singular] **MATHS** a series of numbers in which the same number is added to each number to produce the next, for example 3, 6, 9, 12 → GEOMETRIC PROGRESSION

arm¹ /ɑːm/ noun [C] **1** one of the two long parts of the body with the hands at the end: *She was holding the baby in her arms.* ♦ *Jim was carrying a parcel under his arm.* ♦ *She folded her arms across her chest.* ♦ *Lovers were strolling by arm in arm.* —*picture* → BODY **2** the part of a chair that you rest your arm on when you are sitting in it **3** the part of a piece of clothing that your arm fits into **4** a part of an organization that deals with a particular subject or activity: *the insurance arm of a major bank*

PHRASE **up in arms** angry and complaining about something: *Residents are up in arms about the closure of the local library.*
→ ARMS

arm² /ɑːm/ verb [T] to provide someone with weapons

Armageddon /ˌɑːməˈged(ə)n/ a battle in the future that will destroy the world

armaments /ˈɑːməmənts/ noun [plural] weapons and military equipment used by the armed forces

armature /ˈɑːmətʃə/ noun [C] **1** BIOLOGY a protective outer covering or structure, for example **quills** on a **porcupine** or spines on a plant **2** PHYSICS the moving part of an electric motor. It turns electric current into **rotary motion** (=movement around a central point).

armchair /ˈɑːmˌtʃeə/ noun [C] a large comfortable chair with parts for you to rest your arms on

armed /ɑːmd/ adj **1** carrying a weapon, or involving the use of weapons: *armed robbery* ♦ *a bank robber* **armed with** *a shotgun* **2** having useful or impressive equipment, information etc: *a group of reporters armed with long-lens cameras*

the ˌarmed ˈforces noun [plural] a country's army, navy, and air force

armistice /ˈɑːmɪstɪs/ noun [C] a formal agreement to stop fighting a war → CEASEFIRE

armor /ˈɑːmə/ the American spelling of **armour**

armour /ˈɑːmə/ noun [U] metal clothing that soldiers wore in the past to protect their bodies

armoured /ˈɑːməd/ adj an armoured vehicle is covered with layers of hard metal to protect it from attack

armoury /ˈɑːməri/ noun [C] **1** a building where weapons are kept **2** a set of skills, equipment, or powers that is available for someone if they need it

armpit /ˈɑːmˌpɪt/ noun [C] the part of the body under the arm, where the arm joins the body —*picture* → BODY

arms /ɑːmz/ noun [plural] weapons such as guns or bombs: *the international arms trade*

ˈarms conˌtrol noun [U] agreements between countries to reduce or limit the number of weapons in the world

ˈarm's-ˌlength adj used for describing something such as a business deal in which the different sides avoid having a close relationship with each other

ˈarms ˌrace noun [C] competition between countries to increase the number or power of their weapons

arm-twisting /ˈɑːm ˌtwɪstɪŋ/ noun [U] *informal* an attempt to persuade, threaten, or force someone to do something that they do not want to do

ˈarm-ˌwrestling noun [U] a competition between two people to find out who is stronger, in which they sit opposite each other and place an elbow on a table between them. Each holds the other's hand and tries to force their arm down onto the table to win.

army /ˈɑːmi/ (plural **armies**) noun [C] **1** a large organization of soldiers who are trained to fight wars on land: *an army officer* ♦ *Both of her sons are* **in the army.** **2** a large group of people who are doing the same thing or are in the same situation: *Armies of rescue workers are sorting through the rubble.*

aroma /əˈrəʊmə/ noun [C] a smell that is strong but nice —**aromatic** /ˌærəˈmætɪk/ adj

arose /əˈrəʊz/ the past tense of **arise**

around /əˈraʊnd/ adv, preposition

1 in many places	**5** moving in a circle
2 in opposite direction	**6** surrounding
3 to the other side of	**7** not exactly
4 in a place	**8** existing now

1 in or to many different parts or areas: *We drove around looking for a hotel.* ♦ *I glanced around the room, but I couldn't see him.* ♦ *The Games were watched by millions of people around the world.*
2 moving so that you face in the opposite direction: *I turned around to see what the noise was.*
3 moving to the other side of something: *At that moment a truck came around the corner.*
4 in or close to a place: *the quiet country roads around Chester* ♦ *Is your wife around? I'd like to talk to her.*
5 moving in a circular way: *The Earth goes around the Sun.*
6 surrounding or enclosing something: *a cottage with woods all around* ♦ *Sam had his arm around Mandy's waist.*
7 used for giving a number that is not exact = APPROXIMATELY: *There were around 500 people there.* ♦ *We got back at around 11.*
8 available or existing at this time: *There are some really good new video games around.*
→ ROUND¹

arouse /əˈraʊz/ verb [T] **1** to cause an emotion or attitude: *These rumours have aroused interest among investors.* **2** to make someone feel sexually excited

arpeggio /ɑːˈpedʒiəʊ/ noun [C] MUSIC the musical notes in a **chord** played quickly one after the other, instead of together

arraign /əˈreɪn/ verb [T] LAW to order someone to go to a court of law to be formally charged with a crime —**arraignment** noun [C/U]

arrange /əˈreɪndʒ/ verb [T] **1** to make plans for something to happen, and to manage the details of it: *I'm trying to arrange a meeting with the sales director.* ♦ *They* **arranged to** *go swimming the following day.* ♦ *Please* **arrange for** *a taxi to pick me up at six.* **2** to put things in a tidy, attractive, or useful order: *Here is the list arranged chronologically.* ♦ *We'll need to arrange the chairs around the table.* **3** MUSIC to change a piece of music so that it is suitable for a particular type of voice or instrument

arranged marriage /əˌreɪndʒd ˈmærɪdʒ/ noun [C] a marriage that is arranged by the parents of the man and woman getting married, instead of the man and woman choosing to marry each other

arrangement /əˈreɪndʒmənt/ noun **1 arrangements** [plural] practical plans for organizing and managing the details of something: *seating arrangements* ♦ *Her husband is away, so she'll have to* **make** *other childcare* **arrangements.** **2** [C] an agreement or plan that you make with someone else: *They have* **an arrangement with** *a neighbouring school to share facilities.* **3** [C/U] a set of things that have been arranged to look attractive, or the way that they have been arranged: *a floral arrangement* **4** [C] MUSIC a piece of music that has been changed so that it can be performed by a particular type of voice or instrument

array /əˈreɪ/ noun [C] **1** a large group of people or things that are related in some way: *a dazzling array of products* **2** COMPUTING an arrangement of numbers and symbols organized in rows and **columns**

arrears /əˈrɪəz/ noun **in arrears** late in making a regular payment: *We are writing to inform you that your mortgage payment is a month in arrears.*

arrest¹ /əˈrest/ verb [T] **1** if the police arrest someone, they take that person to a police station because they think that he or she has committed a crime: *Police raided the building and arrested six men.* ♦ *He was **arrested for** possession of illegal drugs.* **2** *formal* to stop a process or bad situation from continuing or developing: *A cut in interest rates failed to arrest the decline in prices.*

arrest² /əˈrest/ noun [C/U] a situation in which the police arrest someone: *The information led to the arrest of three suspects.* ♦ *Six men are **under arrest** in connection with the drug-smuggling operation.* ♦ *We hope to **make an arrest** in the near future.* → CARDIAC ARREST, HOUSE ARREST

arris /ˈærɪs/ noun [C] **CONSTRUCTION** the edge of a brick

arrival /əˈraɪv(ə)l/ noun **1** [U] the time when someone or something arrives at a place from somewhere else: *Her arrival livened up the party.* ♦ *The arrival of BA 106 from Boston has been delayed.* **2** [U] the time when something begins: *the arrival of spring* **3** [C] someone who has arrived or who has joined a group

arrivals /əˈraɪv(ə)lz/ noun [U] **TOURISM** the part of an airport that deals with passengers who are arriving

arrive /əˈraɪv/ verb [I] **1** to reach a place: *What time does your plane arrive?* ♦ *Four police officers suddenly **arrived at** their house.* **2** to happen, or to begin to exist: *Society changed forever when television arrived.* ♦ *The baby arrived (=was born) earlier than we expected.*

PHRASAL VERB **ar'rive at sth** to reach a result, decision, or solution to a problem: *The two studies arrive at very different conclusions.*

> ■ You **arrive in** a town or country, and you **arrive at** a building or place: *What time will she arrive in New York?* ♦ *He arrived at the airport early.*
> ■ You can also say that you **reach** or **get to** a town, country, or building. **Reach** is more formal than **get to**: *The ambulance took 30 minutes to reach the hospital.* ♦ *I'll call you when I get to my hotel.*

arrogant /ˈærəɡənt/ adj someone who is arrogant thinks that they are better or more important than other people —**arrogance** /ˈærəɡəns/ noun [U], **arrogantly** adv

arrow /ˈærəʊ/ noun [C] **1** a weapon in the form of a thin straight stick with a sharp point at one end and feathers at the other. It is fired using a **bow**. —*picture* → WEAPON **2** a sign that looks like an arrow →, used for showing people where to go or look

arrowhead /ˈærəʊˌhed/ noun [C] the sharp pointed part of an arrow

'arrow ˌkey noun [C] **COMPUTING** one of four computer keys marked with an up, down, left, or right arrow, used for moving the cursor

arrowroot /ˈærəʊˌruːt/ noun [U] the edible root of a tropical plant. It is made into starch and used in cooking and medicine.

arsenal /ˈɑːs(ə)n(ə)l/ noun [C] a large collection of weapons

arsenic /ˈɑːs(ə)nɪk/ noun [U] **CHEMISTRY** a poisonous grey solid element that is a **metalloid**. It is used to make alloys. Chemical symbol: **As**

arson /ˈɑːs(ə)n/ noun [U] **LAW** the crime of deliberately burning a building —**arsonist** noun [C]

art /ɑːt/ noun **1** [U] **ARTS** paintings, drawings, and similar objects, or the activity of creating or studying these objects: *the art of ancient Mexico* ♦ *Do you like modern art?* ♦ *She studied art at university.* **2** arts [plural] **EDUCATION** subjects of study that are not

scientific, such as history, literature, and languages: *the Faculty of Arts* **3** the arts [plural] activities such as art, music, film, theatre, and dance **4** [C] an activity that needs special skill: *the art of letter-writing*

art deco or **Art Deco** /ˌɑːt ˈdekəʊ/ noun [U] **ARTS** a style of art, decoration, and architecture with simple strong lines. It was especially popular in the 1920s and 1930s in Europe and the US

artefact /ˈɑːtɪˌfækt/ noun [C] an interesting object from the past

arteriosclerosis /ɑːˌtɪəriəʊskləˈrəʊsɪs/ noun [U] **HEALTH** a serious medical condition in which the sides of the arteries become thick, hard, and stiff, so that the heart has to work harder to pump blood through the body

artery /ˈɑːtəri/ (plural **arteries**) noun [C] **1** **ANATOMY** one of the blood vessels in the body that carries blood from the heart to the rest of the body. The blood in most arteries has a high level of oxygen, except for the **pulmonary artery** that takes blood from the heart to the lungs: *the coronary artery* → VEIN —*picture* → BLOOD VESSEL, CIRCULATION **2** an important road, railway, or river —**arterial** /ɑːˈtɪəriəl/ adj

artesian well /ɑːˌtiːziən ˈwel/ noun [C] a place where natural pressure under the ground forces water to the earth's surface

'art ˌform noun [C] **ARTS, MUSIC** an activity that involves creating or expressing something, such as painting, poetry, or music

'art ˌgallery noun [C] **ARTS** a building where people go to see paintings and other art

arthritis /ɑːˈθraɪtɪs/ noun [U] **HEALTH** a serious medical condition that causes swollen and painful joints —**arthritic** /ɑːˈθrɪtɪk/ adj

arthropod /ˈɑːθrəppd/ noun [C] **BIOLOGY** a type of invertebrate that has **jointed** legs, a body divided into several parts, and an external skeleton. Insects, **arachnids**, **centipedes**, and crustaceans are arthropods.

article /ˈɑːtɪk(ə)l/ noun

1 piece of writing	**4** in grammar
2 object	**5** legal training
3 part of legal document	

1 [C] a piece of writing in a newspaper or magazine: *He has written several articles for The Times.* ♦ *an article about women in politics*
2 [C] an object: *The shop sells small household articles.* ♦ *an article of clothing*
3 [C] **LAW** a part of a legal document
4 [C] **LANGUAGE** a type of word that is used before a noun. The **indefinite article** in English is 'a' or 'an' and the **definite article** is 'the'.
5 articles [plural] the final part of the education of a professional person, for example a lawyer, during which they work for a company: *She is doing her articles with a firm of architects in Guildford.* → GENUINE

articulate¹ /ɑːˈtɪkjʊlət/ adj **1** someone who is articulate speaks very well because they use words effectively ≠ INARTICULATE **2** **BIOLOGY** an articulate animal has joints —*picture* → VERTEBRA —**articulately** adv

articulate² /ɑːˈtɪkjʊleɪt/ verb **1** [T] to use words effectively to express your ideas **2** [I/T] to pronounce words clearly

articulated lorry /ɑːˌtɪkjʊleɪtɪd ˈlɒri/ noun [C] a large truck that consists of two separate parts joined together

articulation /ɑːˌtɪkjʊˈleɪʃ(ə)n/ noun [U] **1** the production of speech or music **2** the expression of thoughts, ideas, or feelings in words **3** BIOLOGY a part of the skeleton of a vertebrate where bones connect, or the way in which they connect —*picture* → VERTEBRA

artifact /ˈɑːtɪˌfækt/ another spelling of **artefact**

artificial /ˌɑːtɪˈfɪʃ(ə)l/ adj **1** not natural or real, but made by people: *The growers use both natural and artificial light.* ♦ *artificial flowers* ♦ *The product contains no artificial colours or flavours.* **2** not sincere= FALSE: *an artificial laugh* —**artificially** /ˌɑːtɪˈfɪʃəli/ adv

artificial 'fertilizer noun [C] AGRICULTURE an inorganic substance that is obtained by mining or is produced by a chemical process and is used to help plants to grow in a healthy way

artificial foun'dation noun [C] CONSTRUCTION the structure that lies between a building and its **natural foundation**

artificial insemi'nation noun [U] **1** HEALTH a medical treatment in which a man's sperm are put into a woman's **womb** (=the part of her body where a baby can grow) so that she can become pregnant **2** AGRICULTURE a process in which the sperm of a male animal is put into the uterus of a female animal so that she becomes pregnant. Artificial insemination is commonly used in the breeding of animals such as cows and pigs.

artificial in'telligence noun [U] COMPUTING the use of computer technology to make computers and machines think like people

artificial respi'ration noun [U] HEALTH the process of forcing air into the lungs of a person who has stopped breathing by blowing into their mouth or nose in order to make them start breathing again

artificial 'satellite noun [C] ASTRONOMY a man-made **satellite**

artillery /ɑːˈtɪləri/ noun [U] large powerful guns that soldiers use

artisan /ˌɑːtɪˈzæn/ noun [C] someone who uses traditional skills and tools to make things

artist /ˈɑːtɪst/ noun [C] **1** someone who creates paintings or other objects that are beautiful or interesting **2** a professional performer in music, dance, or the theatre

artiste /ɑːˈtiːst/ noun [C] a singer, dancer, or other professional entertainer

artistic /ɑːˈtɪstɪk/ adj **1** good at drawing and painting: *You don't need to be very artistic to produce great designs.* **2** relating to painting, music, or other forms of art: *high artistic standards* —**artistically** /ɑːˈtɪstɪkli/ adv

artistry /ˈɑːtɪstri/ noun [U] great skill

artless /ˈɑːtləs/ adj very sincere and willing to trust other people —**artlessly** adv, **artlessness** noun [U]

art nouveau or **Art Nouveau** /ˌɑːt nuːˈvəʊ, ˌɑː nuːˈvəʊ/ noun [U] ARTS a style of art, decoration, and architecture that uses curved patterns of leaves, flowers, and other natural objects, and was popular at the end of the 19th century in Europe and the US

'art ,therapy noun [U] a type of treatment for people with a mental illness in which they express their feelings by painting, drawing, or making **sculptures**

artwork /ˈɑːtˌwɜːk/ noun [U] ARTS **1** paintings, drawings, and other objects that artists create **2** the pictures or photographs in a book or magazine

arty /ˈɑːti/ adj very enthusiastic about art, in a way that might not be sincere

arum lily /ˈeərəm ˌlɪli/ noun [C/U] an African plant with a single large white flower shaped like a **funnel**

Aryan /ˈeəriən, ˈæriən/ noun [C] in Nazi theories of race, a white **non-Jewish** person regarded as better than other races

as /strong æz, weak əz/ adv, conjunction, preposition

1 in comparisons	4 what sb/sth is
2 referring to what is known	5 when/while
	6 because
3 in a particular way	+ PHRASES

1 used for comparing one person, thing, or situation with another: *Simon isn't **as** tall **as** his brother.* ♦ *There were twice **as many** visitors **as** last weekend.* ♦ *We need to collect **as much** information **as** possible.* ♦ *Barbara's hair looks exactly **the same as** mine.* ♦ *We all need exercise, but a healthy diet is **just as** (=equally) important.* → LESS

2 used for referring to something that has already been talked about: *As you know, Jack is leaving next month.*
3 happening or done in a particular way: *Leave everything just as you found it.* ♦ *Judith was late, as usual.*
4 used when saying what someone or something is or what people think of them: *As a parent, you naturally want the best for your children.* ♦ *An electric drill can also be used as a screwdriver.* ♦ *Van Dyck was regarded as the greatest painter of his time.*
5 happening at the same time as something else: *As we were sitting down to dinner, the phone rang.* ♦ *I'm ready to go out **as soon as** it stops raining.*
6 used for giving a reason: *As it was getting late, we decided to go home.*

PHRASES **as for** used for introducing a subject that is related to what you have just been talking about: *As for me, I went home and left them to get on with it.*
as if or **as though 1** in such a way that something seems to be true: *It looks as if it's going to rain.* **2** used when you are giving an explanation that you know is not the real one: *My car looked as if an elephant had sat on it.*
as to formal concerning: *There is some doubt as to his true identity.*

asap /ˌeɪ es eɪ ˈpiː/ adv as soon as possible: *I want those files on my desk asap.*

asbestos /æsˈbestəs/ noun [U] a substance that was used in buildings in the past. People get very ill if they breathe the dust from it.

ascend /əˈsend/ verb [I/T] formal to go upwards, or to climb something ≠ DESCEND

ascendancy /əˈsendənsi/ noun [U] the advantage, power, or influence that one person or group has over another= SUPERIORITY

ascent /əˈsent/ noun **1** [C/U] the process of climbing or of going upwards ≠ DESCENT: *the plane's ascent to 35,000 feet* **2** [C] a path that goes up a hill

ascertain /ˌæsəˈteɪn/ verb [T] formal to find out something: *Police are trying to ascertain the facts of the case.*

ascetic /əˈsetɪk/ adj living a very simple life, especially for religious reasons —**ascetic** noun [C]

ASCII /ˈæski/ noun [U] COMPUTING American Standard Code for Information Interchange: a system for changing computer information into numbers, so that different types of computers and software can exchange information

'ASCII ,file noun [C] COMPUTING a computer file that contains only ASCII characters

ascorbic acid /əˌskɔːbɪk ˈæsɪd/ noun [U] HEALTH vitamin C

aseptic /eɪˈseptɪk/ adj HEALTH not infected with bacteria, or preventing infection from bacteria

asexual /eɪˈsekʃuəl/ adj **1** BIOLOGY without sex or sex organs **2** not seeming to be interested in or to involve sex or **sexuality** —**asexually** /eɪˈsekʃuəli/ adv

asexual repro'duction noun [U] BIOLOGY reproduction in which there is no joining of male and female **gametes** (=male or female reproductive cells), for example **cloning** or **vegetative propagation**

ash /æʃ/ noun **1** [U] the grey powder that remains after something has burned **2** [C] a tree with a smooth grey bark **3 ashes** [plural] the substance that remains after a person's body has been **cremated** (=burned after death)

ashamed /əˈʃeɪmd/ adj someone who is ashamed feels guilty or embarrassed about something that they have done: *He's extremely **ashamed of** his behaviour last night.*

PHRASE **ashamed of sb** disappointed and upset by someone else's behaviour: *I'm ashamed of you – lying to your teacher!*

ashen /ˈæʃ(ə)n/ adj someone whose face is ashen looks very pale because they are shocked, upset, or ill

ashore /əˈʃɔː/ adv onto land from the sea: *He quickly rowed ashore.*

ashram /ˈæʃrəm/ noun [C] RELIGION the home of a small religious community of Hindus

ashtray /ˈæʃˌtreɪ/ noun [C] a small container for ash and cigarettes that have been smoked

Asia /ˈeɪʒə/ GEOGRAPHY the largest continent in the world. Its borders are the Ural and Caucasus mountains and the Arctic, Pacific, and Indian Oceans. —*picture* → CONTINENT

Asia-Pa'cific noun [U] GEOGRAPHY a region that includes some of the countries of East and South-East Asia and the Pacific Rim

Asiatic /ˌeɪʃiˈætɪk, ˌeɪʒiˈætɪk/ adj relating to Asia or its culture

aside¹ /əˈsaɪd/ adv

PHRASES **aside from** except for: *Aside from hanging about in the street, there's nothing for kids to do here.* **leave sth aside** to deliberately not consider something: *Let's leave aside the issue of money.* **move/step aside** to move away from someone or something: *Helen stepped aside to let him pass.* **set/put sth aside** to keep something such as time or money for a particular purpose: *Try to set aside half an hour every day for something you really enjoy doing.*

aside² /əˈsaɪd/ noun [C] **1** a remark about something that is not the main subject of your discussion **2** LITERATURE, ARTS something that a character in a play or film says that they want the audience but not the other characters to hear

ask /ɑːsk/ verb **1** [I/T] to speak to someone in order to get information from them: *I wondered who had given her the ring but was afraid to ask.* ♦ *The police wanted to **ask** us a few **questions**.* ♦ *She asked me how I knew about it.* ♦ *Did you **ask about** the money?* **2** [I/T] to speak to someone because you want them to give you something, or do something for you: *If you need any help, just ask.* ♦ *Can I **ask you a favour**?* ♦ *The children were **asking for** drinks.* ♦ *He **asked** us to move over a little.* ♦ *I **asked** to see the manager.* **3** [T] to invite someone to do something, or to go somewhere with you: *We waited for half an hour before he **asked us in** (=invited us to come inside).* ♦ *They **asked** me to stay the night.* **4** [T] to expect someone to do something, or to give you something: *It's a nice house, but they're asking over half a million pounds.*

askance /əˈskæns/ adv **look askance (at sb/sth)** to show that you do not approve of someone or something or that you do not feel certain about them

askew /əˈskjuː/ adj not as straight as it should be

asking price /ˈɑːskɪŋ ˌpraɪs/ noun [singular] BUSINESS the price that someone wants for something they are selling

asleep /əˈsliːp/ adj not awake: *The children are **fast asleep** (=sleeping deeply).* ♦ *She was so tired she **fell asleep** (=began sleeping) in her chair.*

AS level /ˌeɪ ˈes ˌlev(ə)l/ noun [C] an examination taken by students in England and Wales after their GCSEs and before their final year of school or college, usually at the age of 17. AS levels are part of the A level qualification. → A LEVEL

asparagus /əˈspærəgəs/ noun [U] a long thin green vegetable consisting of long green stems with pointed ends —*picture* → VEGETABLE

aspartame /əˈspɑːteɪm/ noun [U] an artificial substance that does not contain many **calories** that is added to food or drink to make it taste sweeter

aspect /ˈæspekt/ noun **1** [C] a particular part, feature, or quality of something: *The Internet affects every **aspect of** our business.* ♦ *This chapter considers several important aspects of the teaching process.* **2** [C/U] LANGUAGE the form of a verb that shows whether an action is continuing, is repeated, or happens only once

Asperger's syndrome /ˈæspɜːdʒəz ˌsɪndrəʊm/ noun [U] HEALTH a mental condition that makes it difficult for someone to react to and communicate with other people. It is similar to **autism** but less severe. Some people who have it are very intelligent.

aspersions /əˈspɜːʃ(ə)nz/ noun **cast aspersions (on)** to criticize someone or something

asphalt /ˈæsfælt/ noun [U] a black sticky substance that is used for making the surface of a road

asphyxiate /æsˈfɪksɪˌeɪt/ verb [I/T] to kill someone by preventing them from breathing, or to die in this way = SUFFOCATE —**asphyxiation** /æsˌfɪksiˈeɪʃ(ə)n/ noun [U]

aspirate¹ /ˈæspɪreɪt/ verb [T] **1** LANGUAGE to breathe out air while pronouncing a sound, for example the 'h' in 'hat' **2** HEALTH to remove liquid from inside someone's body

aspirate² /ˈæspɪrət/ adj LANGUAGE aspirate sounds are ones that are produced while breathing out air, for example the sound of the 'h' in 'hat' —**aspirate** noun [C]

aspiration /ˌæspɪˈreɪʃ(ə)n/ noun **1** [C] a strong wish to achieve something= AMBITION: *He has no political aspirations.* **2** [U] LANGUAGE the sound that is produced when pronouncing something by breathing air out through the mouth

aspirational /ˌæspɪˈreɪʃ(ə)nəl/ adj wanting to be successful and have a better job, home etc than you already have

aspire /əˈspaɪə/ verb [I] **+to** to want to achieve something or be successful: *She aspires to nothing less than the chairmanship of the company.*

PHRASAL VERB **a'spire to sth** to want to achieve something: *students who aspire to be professional actors*

aspirin /ˈæsprɪn/ (plural **aspirin** or **aspirins**) noun [C/U] HEALTH a drug that cures minor pain, or a pill that contains this drug

aspiring /əˈspaɪərɪŋ/ adj trying to be successful at something: *an aspiring actor*

assail /əˈseɪl/ verb [T] **1** make someone feel worried or upset **2** *formal* to physically attack or severely criticize someone

assailant /əˈseɪlənt/ noun [C] *formal* someone who violently attacks another person

assassin /əˈsæsɪn/ noun [C] someone who deliberately kills an important person

assassinate /əˈsæsɪneɪt/ verb [T] to kill an important person deliberately —**assassination** /əˌsæsɪˈneɪʃ(ə)n/ noun [C/U]

assault¹ /əˈsɔːlt/ noun [C/U] a violent attack, or the crime of physically attacking someone: *an assault on a young student*

   PHRASE assault and battery LAW the crime of threatening someone and then physically attacking them

assault² /əˈsɔːlt/ verb [T] to attack someone violently: *An elderly woman was assaulted and robbed.*

asˈsault ˌcourse noun [C] a series of objects or structures that you have to get over, under, or through in a training exercise, especially in the armed forces

assemble /əˈsemb(ə)l/ verb **1** [I/T] to bring a group together, or to come together and form a group: *The children assembled outside the building.* **2** [T] to build something by putting all its parts together: *You have to assemble the shelves yourself.* ♦ *They are assembling a peace-keeping force to send to the region.*

assembler /əˈsemblə/ noun [C] COMPUTING a computer program that changes a program written in **assembly language** into **machine language**

assembly /əˈsembli/ (plural **assemblies**) noun **1** [C] a group of people who have been chosen to make laws or deal with particular issues: *the French National Assembly* **2** [C/U] EDUCATION a regular meeting of students and teachers in a school **3** [U] the process of building something by putting all its parts together **4** [C] TECHNOLOGY a group of parts that are connected and that form one unit

asˈsembly ˌdrawing noun [C] MATHS, PHYSICS a drawing made using **orthographic projection** that shows the parts of a complete unit

asˈsembly ˌlanguage noun [C] COMPUTING a computer language that consists of symbols, used for writing computer programs

asˈsembly ˌline noun [C] BUSINESS a system for making products in a factory. Each worker or machine does a single job as the product moves past them.

assent /əˈsent/ noun [U] formal agreement or approval

assert /əˈsɜːt/ verb [T] **1** to state firmly that something is true **2** to behave in a determined or confident way: *He quickly asserted his authority as a leader.* ♦ *It's hard for shy people to assert themselves in a group.*

assertion /əˈsɜːʃ(ə)n/ noun [C] a statement in which you say that something is definitely true

assertive /əˈsɜːtɪv/ adj expressing your opinions firmly and confidently = FORCEFUL —**assertiveness** noun [U]

assess /əˈses/ verb [T] to think about something carefully and make a judgment about it: *We tried to assess his suitability for the job.* —*Our agent will assess the value of your property.* —**assessor** noun [C]

assessment /əˈsesmənt/ noun **1** [U] the process of making a judgment or forming an opinion, after considering something or someone carefully: *The investigation was reopened after careful assessment of new evidence.* **2** [C] a judgment or opinion that is the result of this process **3** [U] EDUCATION the process or methods of marking a student's work and

judging their ability: *continuous assessment* (=the method of judging ability that considers all the work that a student produces, not just the examination at the end of the year)

asset /ˈæset/ noun [C] **1** something such as money or property that a company owns **2** something that gives you benefits: *He is a definite asset to the team.* ♦ *Youth is a tremendous asset in this job.*

assiduous /əˈsɪdjʊəs/ adj formal someone who is assiduous works very hard and does things carefully —**assiduously** adv

assign /əˈsaɪn/ verb [T] **1** to give someone a particular job: *We assigned her the job of maintaining our website.* **2** to put someone in a particular group, or send them to a particular place: *Tina has been assigned to the intermediate learners' group.* **3** to give someone money or equipment so that they can use it for a particular purpose **4** LAW to give someone the **ownership** of or rights to property

assignment /əˈsaɪnmənt/ noun [C] **1** a piece of work that you must do, for example at school: *a homework assignment* ♦ *His first assignment as a reporter was to cover the local election.* **2** LAW the act of giving the **ownership** of or rights to property to someone

assimilate /əˈsɪmɪleɪt/ verb **1** [I/T] SOCIAL STUDIES to feel that you belong to the new community that you have started to live in, or to make someone feel like this **2** [T] to learn, understand, and begin to use new ideas or information: *Picasso assimilated an amazing variety of techniques in his art.*

assimilation /əˌsɪmɪˈleɪʃ(ə)n/ noun [U] **1** BIOLOGY the process of making use of food in the body, for example for growth and repair **2** SOCIAL STUDIES the process of becoming part of a community or culture **3** the process of making new ideas or pieces of information part of your knowledge so that you can use them effectively

assist /əˈsɪst/ verb **1** [I/T] to help someone or something: *Her job is to assist the head chef.* ♦ *Several designers assisted in the creation of the garden.* **2** [T] to make a job or piece of work easier to do: *information that will assist the police with their search* ♦ *The scheme assists young people to find work.*

assistance /əˈsɪst(ə)ns/ noun [U] help: *financial assistance* ♦ *He's been running the company with the assistance of his son.* ♦ *Can I be of assistance* (=can I help)*?*

assistant¹ /əˈsɪst(ə)nt/ noun [C] someone whose job is to help another person in their work, for example by doing the easier parts of it: *a personal assistant*

assistant² /əˈsɪst(ə)nt/ adj an assistant manager, teacher etc is someone whose job is to help the main manager or teacher

asˌsistant proˈfessor noun [C] EDUCATION a teacher who works at a college or university in the US who is below the level of an **associate professor**

assisted reproduction /əˌsɪstɪd ˌriːprəˈdʌkʃ(ə)n/ noun [U] HEALTH the medical processes that doctors use to help couples who cannot have a baby naturally, including processes such as **IVF**

associate¹ /əˈsəʊsiˌeɪt/ verb [T] **1** to connect people or things in your mind: *Most people associate food with pleasure.* **2** if one thing is associated with another, they are connected: *The problem is often associated with heavy drinking.*

associate² /əˈsəʊsiət/ adj an associate position or job is not at the highest level

as,sociate pro'fessor noun [C] EDUCATION a teacher who works at a college or university in the US who is above the level of an **assistant professor** and below the level of a **full professor**

association /ə,səʊsi'eɪʃ(ə)n/ noun **1** [C] an organization for people who have similar interests or aims: *the Parent-Teacher Association* **2** [C] a connection between people or things: *Smoking has a close association with lung cancer.* **3 associations** [plural] memories or feelings that are connected with a particular place or event: *The town has many happy childhood associations for me.*

PHRASE **in association with** with the help of a person or organization

the as,sociative 'law noun [singular] MATHS the feature of a group of three or more numbers or symbols according to which, if they are kept in the same order, they can be put in different groups and the result of adding them or multiplying them will be the same. For example, $(a + b) + c = a + (b + c)$ and $(a \times b) \times c = a \times (b \times c)$.

assonance /'æs(ə)nəns/ noun [U] LITERATURE, LANGUAGE the use of repeated sounds in words that are close together, especially vowel sounds, for example 'read' and 'ride' or 'wish list' → RHYME[1]

assorted /ə'sɔːtɪd/ adj including various types

assortment /ə'sɔːtmənt/ noun [C] a group of things of various types

assuage /ə'sweɪdʒ/ verb [T] *formal* to make a bad feeling less severe

assume /ə'sjuːm/ verb [T] **1** to believe that something is true, even though you cannot be certain: *I'm assuming everyone understands the importance of this meeting.* **2** *formal* to start to control something or take an important position: *His first priority was assuming control of the army.* **3** *formal* to pretend to have a particular feeling or attitude: *Fay assumed an air of innocence.* **4** to begin to have a particular quality, shape, expression etc: *The animals assumed their normal resting position.*

assumed name /ə,sjuːmd 'neɪm/ noun [C] a name that someone uses so that no one will know their real name

assuming /ə'sjuːmɪŋ/ conjunction if: sometimes used for emphasizing that something may not be true

assumption /ə'sʌmpʃ(ə)n/ noun **1** [C] something that you think is likely to be true, although you cannot be certain **2** [U] the process of starting to have power or responsibility

assurance /ə'ʃɔːrəns/ noun **1** [U] the feeling of being certain or confident about something **2** [C] a statement in which you tell someone that something is definitely true or will definitely happen **3** [U] BUSINESS insurance, especially **life insurance**

assure /ə'ʃɔː/ verb [T] **1** *formal* to tell someone that something is definitely true or will definitely happen: *There's no mistake, I can assure you.* **2** to make certain that something happens

assured /ə'ʃɔːd/ adj confident and certain —**assuredly** /ə'ʃɔːrɪdli/ adv

astatine /'æstətiːn/ noun [U] CHEMISTRY a radioactive element that is the heaviest element in the halogen series. Chemical symbol: **At**

asterisk /'æst(ə)rɪsk/ noun [C] the symbol *, used for showing that more information is given in a **footnote**

asteroid /'æstə,rɔɪd/ noun [C] ASTRONOMY a mass of rock that moves around in space. Most asteroids are found in the region of space between the planets Jupiter and Mars, a region known as the **asteroid belt**. —*picture* → SOLAR SYSTEM

asthma /'æsmə/ noun [U] HEALTH a medical condition that makes it difficult to breathe

asthmatic /æs'mætɪk/ noun [C] someone who suffers from asthma —**asthmatic** adj

astigmatism /ə'stɪgmə,tɪz(ə)m/ noun [U] HEALTH a condition in which someone's eyes cannot **focus** correctly without the help of glasses —**astigmatic** /,æstɪg'mætɪk/ adj

astonish /ə'stɒnɪʃ/ verb [T] to surprise someone very much

astonished /ə'stɒnɪʃt/ adj very surprised: *We were astonished to hear that she'd lost her job.*

astonishing /ə'stɒnɪʃɪŋ/ adj very surprising: *It's astonishing that so many people watch that programme.* —**astonishingly** adv

astonishment /ə'stɒnɪʃmənt/ noun [U] very great surprise

astound /ə'staʊnd/ verb [T] to surprise or shock someone very much

astounded /ə'staʊndɪd/ adj very surprised or shocked

astounding /ə'staʊndɪŋ/ adj very surprising or shocking

astray /ə'streɪ/ adv **lead sb astray** to make someone behave badly

astride /ə'straɪd/ preposition with one leg on each side of something: *sitting astride a bicycle*

astringent /ə'strɪndʒ(ə)nt/ adj **1** HEALTH an astringent substance or liquid makes the skin drier, or helps to stop a cut from bleeding **2** an astringent taste is one that is strong and bitter **3** an astringent remark is one that criticizes someone severely —**astringency** noun [U]

astro- /æstrəʊ/ prefix the planets and stars or space: used with some nouns, adjectives, and adverbs: *astronomer* ♦ *astronaut*

astrology /ə'strɒlədʒi/ noun [U] the study of how the stars and planets influence people's lives —**astrologer** noun [C], **astrological** /,æstrə'lɒdʒɪk(ə)l/ adj

astronaut /'æstrə,nɔːt/ noun [C] ASTRONOMY someone who travels in space —*picture* → on next page

astronomical /,æstrə'nɒmɪk(ə)l/ adj ASTRONOMY relating to the scientific study of the stars and planets

astronomical 'telescope noun [C] ASTRONOMY a telescope that is used to view distant objects such as stars and planets by using either reflected or **refracted** light

astronomical 'unit noun [C] ASTRONOMY a unit of distance in space that is equal to the average distance between the Earth and the Sun, about 150 million km

astronomy /ə'strɒnəmi/ noun [U] ASTRONOMY the scientific study of stars and planets —**astronomer** noun [C]

astrophysics /,æstrəʊ'fɪzɪks/ noun [U] ASTRONOMY the scientific study of the physical and chemical structure of the stars, planets, and other objects in the universe —**astrophysical** adj

astute /ə'stjuːt/ adj good at making decisions that benefit you: *an astute judge of the stock market* —**astutely** adv, **astuteness** noun [U]

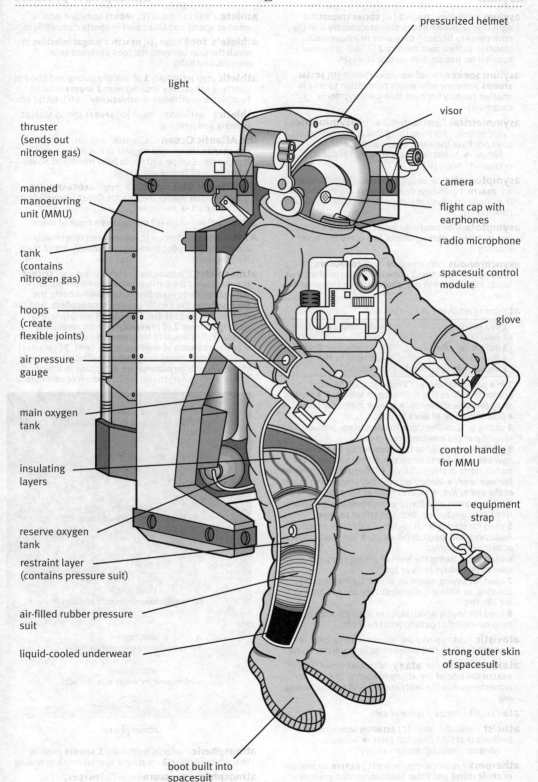

pressurized helmet

light

visor

camera

thruster
(sends out
nitrogen gas)

flight cap with
earphones

radio microphone

manned
manoeuvring
unit (MMU)

spacesuit control
module

tank
(contains
nitrogen gas)

glove

hoops
(create
flexible joints)

air pressure
gauge

control handle
for MMU

main oxygen
tank

insulating
layers

equipment
strap

reserve oxygen
tank

restraint layer
(contains pressure suit)

air-filled rubber pressure
suit

strong outer skin
of spacesuit

liquid-cooled underwear

boot built into
spacesuit

astronaut

asylum /əˈsaɪləm/ noun **1** [U] SOCIAL STUDIES the right that someone has to stay in a country that they have come to because they were in a dangerous situation in their own country **2** [C] *old-fashioned* a hospital for people with mental illnesses

asylum seeker /əˈsaɪləm ˌsiːkə/ noun [C] SOCIAL STUDIES someone who wants permission to stay in another country because their own country is dangerous

asymmetrical /ˌeɪsɪˈmetrɪk(ə)l/ or **asymmetric** /ˌeɪsɪˈmetrɪk/ adj something that is asymmetrical does not have the same shape and size on both sides —*picture* → SYMMETRY —**asymmetry** /æˈsɪmətri, eɪˈsɪmətri/ noun [U]

asymptomatic /ˌæ.sɪmptəˈmætɪk, ˌeɪsɪmptəˈmætɪk/ adj HEALTH if a disease or a person is asymptomatic, they show no physical signs of a particular medical condition

asymptote /ˈæsɪmptəʊt/ noun [C] MATHS a straight line that keeps getting nearer to a curve but never touches it

asynchronous /eɪˈsɪŋkrənəs/ adj COMPUTING relating to an electronic communication method that sends information in one direction, one character at a time

at /*strong* æt, *weak* ət/ preposition

1 in a place	**6** indicating a number/
2 near sth	level
3 indicating when	**7** in a particular direction
4 doing sth	**8** referring to sb's
5 showing how sb reacts	abilities

1 in a particular place: *I'll meet you at the main entrance.* ♦ *Does this train stop at Newport?* ♦ *We live at 23 Brookfield Avenue.* ♦ *Is your mother at home?* ♦ *Dad should be at work by now.*
2 sitting or standing close to something: *She was standing at the window, staring out.*
3 used for saying what time something happens, or how old someone is when something happens: *The match starts at three o'clock.* ♦ *What are you doing at the weekend?* ♦ *Mozart was already composing music at the age of five.* ♦ *He dies right at the start of the film.*
4 taking part in an activity, or involved in a situation: *Has Karen graduated, or is she still at college?*
5 used for stating what causes a particular reaction: *Audiences still laugh at his jokes.* ♦ *She was annoyed at being interrupted.*
6 used for showing the level of prices, temperatures, speeds etc: *Water boils at 100°C.*
7 used for saying where an action such as looking, pointing, or hitting is directed: *Why are you staring at me like that?*
8 used for saying which skills or abilities someone has: *He is an expert at getting what he wants.*

atavistic /ˌætəˈvɪstɪk/ adj *formal* relating back to feelings or ideas that people had in the distant past

ataxia /əˈtæksiə/ or **ataxy** /əˈtæksi/ noun [U] HEALTH the loss of the ability to control the movements that the body makes —**ataxic** /əˈtæksɪk/ adj

ate /et, eɪt/ the past tense of **eat**

atheist /ˈeɪθiːɪst/ noun [C] RELIGION someone who believes that God does not exist → AGNOSTIC —**atheism** /ˈeɪθiˌɪz(ə)m/ noun [U]

atheroma /ˌæθəˈrəʊmə/ noun [C] HEALTH an amount of **cholesterol** and other substances that gradually forms on the inside wall of an artery and can block the flow of blood

athlete /ˈæθliːt/ noun [C] SPORTS someone who is good at sports and takes part in sports competitions

athlete's ˈfoot noun [U] HEALTH a fungal infection in which the skin between the toes becomes sore, cracked, and **itchy**

athletic /æθˈletɪk/ adj **1** physically strong and good at sports: *a tall athletic looking man* **2** SPORTS relating to athletes or athletics —**athletically** /æθˈletɪkli/ adv

athletics /æθˈletɪks/ noun [U] SPORTS sports such as running and jumping

the Atlantic Ocean /ət,læntɪk ˈəʊʃ(ə)n/ GEOGRAPHY the second biggest ocean in the world. It separates Europe and Africa from North and South America. —*picture* → CONTINENT

the Atlantic Rim /ət,læntɪk ˈrɪm/ GEOGRAPHY the countries that border the Atlantic Ocean, especially its northern part → PACIFIC RIM

atlas /ˈætləs/ noun [C] GEOGRAPHY a book of maps

ATM /ˌeɪ tiː ˈem/ noun [C] automated teller machine: a machine that people use to take money out of their bank account

atmosphere /ˈætməsˌfɪə/ noun **1** [singular] SCIENCE the air around the Earth or around another planet. It consists of three main layers, the lowest being the **troposphere**, the middle one the **stratosphere**, and the highest the **ionosphere**: *The Earth's atmosphere is getting warmer.* **2** [C] PHYSICS a unit for measuring pressure. It is equal to the pressure needed to support a 760mm **column** of mercury at sea level. **3** [singular] the mood that exists in a place and affects the people there: *There is an atmosphere of tension in the city today.* **4** [singular] the air inside a room or other place

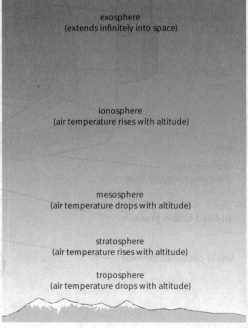

exosphere
(extends infinitely into space)

ionosphere
(air temperature rises with altitude)

mesosphere
(air temperature drops with altitude)

stratosphere
(air temperature rises with altitude)

troposphere
(air temperature drops with altitude)

atmosphere

atmospheric /ˌætməsˈferɪk/ adj **1** SCIENCE existing in the atmosphere **2** creating a special mood or feeling

atmospheric ˈpressure noun [U] PHYSICS, GEOGRAPHY the downward pressure of the atmosphere on the surface of the Earth. It has an average value of one **atmosphere** at sea level, but this value gets lower as height above sea level increases.

atoll /'ætɒl/ noun [C] GEOGRAPHY an island in the form of a ring, made of **coral**

atom /'ætəm/ noun [C] SCIENCE the smallest unit of all matter that has all the chemical properties of a particular element. An atom consists of a nucleus that is made of protons, which are positive, and neutrons, which are **neutral**. The nucleus has electrons, which are negative, travelling around it. The numbers of protons and electrons are equal so that atoms are **neutral**.

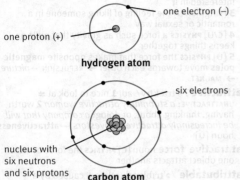

one electron (–)
one proton (+)
hydrogen atom

six electrons

nucleus with six neutrons and six protons
carbon atom

simple atomic structure

'**atom ,bomb** or a,**tomic 'bomb** noun [C] a bomb that causes a very large nuclear explosion

atomic /ə'tɒmɪk/ adj SCIENCE **1** using the energy that is produced by **splitting** atoms **2** relating to the atoms in a substance

a,**tomic 'energy** noun [U] PHYSICS nuclear energy

a,**tomic 'mass** noun [C] CHEMISTRY relative atomic mass

a,**tomic 'mass ,unit** noun [C] CHEMISTRY a unit of mass that is used to express the masses of atoms and molecules. The abbreviations are u and Da.

a,**tomic 'nucleus** noun [C] CHEMISTRY, PHYSICS the central part of an atom, consisting of protons and neutrons, and containing most of its mass

a,**tomic 'number** noun [C] CHEMISTRY the number of protons in the nucleus of an atom of an element and its isotopes. The element's position in the periodic table depends upon this number.

a,**tomic 'weight** noun [C] CHEMISTRY relative atomic mass

atomize /'ætəmaɪz/ verb [T] **1** CHEMISTRY to change a substance or liquid into very small parts or drops **2** to break or divide something into very small parts — **atomization** /,ætəmaɪ'zeɪʃ(ə)n/ noun [U]

atonal /,eɪ'təʊn(ə)l/ adj MUSIC atonal music is not written or played in any one **key** (=a set of notes) —**atonality** /,eɪtəʊ'næləti/ noun [U], **atonally** adv

atone /ə'təʊn/ verb [I] formal to do something that shows that you are very sorry for something bad that you did —**atonement** noun [U]

ATP /,eɪ ti: 'pi:/ noun [U] BIOLOGY a chemical in the **mitochondria** (=part where food molecules are broken down) of cells that stores and then releases energy for chemical reactions

atrio-ventricular /,eɪtrɪəʊ ven'trɪkjʊlə/ adj ANATOMY relating to the atrium and **ventricle**, two

enclosed spaces in the heart, or the connection between them

atrium /'eɪtriəm/ (plural **atria** /'eɪtriə/ or **atriums**) noun [C] ANATOMY one of the two upper spaces in the heart which force blood into the **ventricles** (=lower spaces) —picture → CIRCULATION

atrocious /ə'trəʊʃəs/ adj extremely bad: atrocious weather conditions —**atrociously** adv

atrocity /ə'trɒsəti/ (plural **atrocities**) noun [C/U] something very cruel and violent that someone does

atrophy /'ætrəfi/ (**atrophies, atrophying, atrophied**) verb [I/T] HEALTH if a part of the body atrophies or is atrophied, it becomes weaker or smaller because it is not being used or because blood is not reaching it

attach /ə'tætʃ/ verb [T] **1** attach sth to sth to fasten one thing to another: Attach the rope to the branch of a tree. **2** to send another document with a letter or an email: I attach a copy of his reply. **3** be attached to if one thing is attached to another, it is part of it: There is a riding school attached to the farm. **4** be attached to to be sent to work temporarily in a different place: She is now attached to the American Embassy in Beijing.

PHRASE **attach importance/significance/value/weight to sth** to think that something is important or true and that it should be considered seriously

attached /ə'tætʃt/ adj **1** joined or fixed to something **2 attached to sth/sb** if you are attached to something or someone, you like them very much: Danny is very attached to his teddy bear.

attachment /ə'tætʃmənt/ noun **1** [C] a special tool that is attached to something in order to do a particular job **2** [C/U] a feeling of liking a person or place very much **3** [C] COMPUTING a computer file that you send with an email

attack¹ /ə'tæk/ verb **1** [I/T] to use violence against a person or place: It was shortly before midnight when the terrorists attacked. ♦ Two prison officers were brutally **attacked with** a knife. **2** [T] to strongly criticize someone or something: Parliament has been **attacked for** failing to take action. **3** [I/T] to cause damage or disease in something: The virus attacks the body's red blood cells. **4** [I/T] SPORTS to try to score points in a game: They attack well, but their defence is weak. —**attacker** noun [C]

attack² /ə'tæk/ noun **1** [C/U] a violent attempt to harm someone or something: a vicious **attack on** an unarmed man ♦ The city was **under attack** throughout the night. **2** [C] strong criticism: McCann **launched an attack on** his own players. **3** [C] an occasion when someone is affected by an illness, or when they have a particular strong feeling: an asthma attack ♦ **an attack of** nerves → HEART ATTACK **4** [C] SPORTS an attempt to score points in a game

attain /ə'teɪn/ verb [T] formal to succeed in achieving something that involves a lot of effort = ACHIEVE —**attainable** adj, **attainment** noun [C/U]

attempt¹ /ə'tempt/ noun [C] **1** an effort to do something: This was the president's final attempt to reach a settlement with the rebel forces. ♦ **an attempt on** the world record ♦ It's his fourth **attempt at** flying a balloon around the world. **2** an attack on someone that is intended to kill them but fails: an assassination attempt

attempt² /ə'tempt/ verb [T] to try to do something: Few people knew that she had once attempted suicide. ♦ The book **attempts to** explain the origins of the war.

attempted /ə'temptɪd/ adj used about crimes that someone tries to commit without success: attempted murder

attend /ə'tend/ verb [I/T] **1** to be present at an event or activity: *Most of his colleagues attended the wedding.* **2** to go regularly to a place such as a school or a church: *Born in India, he attended high school in Madras.*

PHRASAL VERB **at'tend to sth** to deal with something: *We still have a number of other matters to attend to.*

attendance /ə'tendəns/ noun **1** [C/U] the number of people who are present at an event or in a place such as a school or church: *Church attendance dropped sharply in the 1970s.* ♦ *Attendance at the first meeting was high* (=there were a lot of people). **2** [U] the fact that someone is present in a place, or goes there regularly

attendant /ə'tendənt/ noun [C] someone whose job is to help customers or people who visit a public place: *a museum attendant*

attention /ə'tenʃ(ə)n/ noun [U] **1** the fact that you are listening to someone or something, or you are looking at them: *May I please have your attention – I have an important announcement.* ♦ *The man paid no attention to them.* **2** the fact that you know about something or notice something: *I have been asked to draw your attention to the following matters.* ♦ *We should bring the problem to their attention.* **3** special care, help, or treatment: *She needs urgent medical attention.*

PHRASE **stand to/at attention** if people in the armed forces stand to attention or stand at attention, they stand straight with their feet together to show respect or to receive orders

at'tention ,line noun [C] **BUSINESS** a line in a letter to an organization that states which member of staff the letter is intended for

at'tention ,span noun [singular] the length of time that you can pay attention to one thing without becoming bored or thinking about something else

attentive /ə'tentɪv/ adj **1** listening to or watching something carefully **2** behaving in a way that shows that you care about someone —**attentively** adv

attest /ə'test/ verb **1** [I] *formal* to give proof or be evidence that something is true **2** [I/T] **LAW** to state formally that you believe something is true, correct, or real

attestation /ˌæteˈsteɪʃ(ə)n/ noun [C/U] **LAW** a formal statement in which someone states that they believe something is true, correct, or real

attic /'ætɪk/ noun [C] a room in a house under the roof

attire /ə'taɪə/ noun [U] *formal* the clothes that someone is wearing

attired /ə'taɪəd/ adj *formal* dressed

attitude /'ætɪˌtjuːd/ noun [C/U] opinions or feelings that you show by your behaviour: *We can win if we keep a positive attitude.* ♦ *People here have a more relaxed attitude to their work.* ♦ *Attitudes towards the older members of the group will have to change.*

attorney /ə'tɜːni/ noun [C] **LAW** *American* a lawyer

at,torney 'general noun [C] **LAW** the most senior lawyer in some countries or US states

attract /ə'trækt/ verb [T] **1** to make someone like something, or be interested in something: *What first attracted you to geology?* **2** **PHYSICS** if a magnet or similar object attracts things, it produces a force that pulls things towards it: *the magnetic force that makes magnets attract pins* **3** to cause people to behave in a particular way towards something: *The trial attracted a lot of media interest.* **4** if one person is attracted to another person, they are interested in the other person

in a romantic or sexual way: *I was attracted to her the first time I met her.*

PHRASE **attract (sb's) attention** to make someone notice someone or something

attraction /ə'trækʃ(ə)n/ noun

1 sb/sth interesting	4 gravity etc
2 cause for liking	5 between magnets
3 romantic/sexual	

1 [C] an interesting place or object that people come to see
2 [C/U] a reason for liking something or being interested in it
3 [singular/U] the feeling of liking someone in a romantic or sexual way
4 [C/U] **PHYSICS** a force such as gravity that pulls or keeps things together
5 [U] **PHYSICS** the force that makes opposite **magnetic poles** move towards each other → REPULSION —*picture* → MAGNET

attractive /ə'træktɪv/ adj **1** nice to look at ≠ UNATTRACTIVE: *a stunningly attractive woman* **2** worth having, thinking about, or doing: *a company that will be increasingly attractive to investors* —**attractiveness** noun [U]

at,tractive 'force noun [C] **PHYSICS** the force by which one object attracts another

attributable /ə'trɪbjʊtəb(ə)l/ adj caused by a particular event, situation, or activity

attribute¹ /ə'trɪbjuːt/ **PHRASAL VERB** **at'tribute sth to sb/sth** to believe that something was caused by something else, or done by someone else: *a painting attributed to Picasso*

attribute² /'ætrɪˌbjuːt/ noun [C] *formal* a quality or feature

attributive /ə'trɪbjʊtɪv/ adj **LANGUAGE** an attributive adjective, or a word in an attributive position, comes before the noun it describes. For example in the phrase 'a nice man', 'nice' is attributive. —**attributively** /ə'trɪbjʊtɪvli/ adv → PREDICATIVE

attrition /ə'trɪʃ(ə)n/ noun [U] **1** *formal* the process of making an enemy physically and mentally weaker by continuously attacking them **2** a reduction in size, numbers, or strength **3** **BUSINESS** natural wastage

attuned /ə'tjuːnd/ adj familiar with something and able to deal with it in a sensitive way

atypical /,eɪ'tɪpɪk(ə)l/ adj not usual or typical

AU /,eɪ 'juː/ abbrev **ASTRONOMY** an astronomical unit

the AU /,eɪ 'juː/ noun [singular] **ECONOMICS, POLITICS** the African Union: an organization of African countries that tries to help its member states to work together in order to produce political and economic improvements in Africa

aubergine /'əʊbəˌʒiːn/ noun [C/U] a vegetable that has smooth dark purple skin and white flesh= EGGPLANT —*picture* → VEGETABLE

auburn /'ɔːbən/ adj auburn hair is red-brown in colour

auction¹ /'ɔːkʃ(ə)n/ noun [C] a public occasion when things are sold to the people who offer the most money for them

auction² /'ɔːkʃ(ə)n/ verb [T] to sell something at an auction

auctioneer /,ɔːkʃəˈnɪə/ noun [C] someone whose job is to sell people at an auction

audacious /ɔː'deɪʃəs/ adj done with extreme confidence, or behaving with extreme confidence

audacity /ɔːˈdæsəti/ noun [U] the confidence to say or do what you want, despite difficulties, risks, or the negative attitudes of other people

audible /ˈɔːdəb(ə)l/ adj loud enough for people to hear —**audibly** adv

audience /ˈɔːdiəns/ noun [C] **1** the people who watch or listen to a performance: *His jokes offended many people in the audience.* **2** all the people who watch a particular television programme, read a particular book etc: *The series has attracted an audience of more than 10 million.* **3** a formal meeting with a very important person: *an audience with* the Pope

> Audience can be used with a singular or plural verb. You can say *The audience was cheering* OR *The audience were cheering.*

audio /ˈɔːdiəʊ/ adj relating to sound that is recorded or broadcast

audio- /ˈɔːdiəʊ/ prefix sound or hearing: used with some adjectives and nouns

audio frequency noun [U] **PHYSICS** a frequency that is audible to the human ear, between 20 and 20,000 hertz in people with normal hearing

audiotape /ˈɔːdiəʊˌteɪp/ noun [C/U] **magnetic tape** on which sound can be recorded

audiotypist /ˈɔːdiəʊˌtaɪpɪst/ noun [C] someone whose job is to type letters, reports etc that someone else has **dictated** (=spoken) into a machine

audiovisual /ˌɔːdiəʊˈvɪʒuəl/ adj using both recorded sounds and images

audit /ˈɔːdɪt/ noun [C] **BUSINESS** an official examination of a company's financial records —**audit** verb [T]

audition /ɔːˈdɪʃ(ə)n/ noun [C] an occasion when someone sings, dances, or acts so that other people can decide if they are good enough to perform —**audition** verb [I]

auditor /ˈɔːdɪtə/ noun [C] **BUSINESS** a person whose job is to officially examine the financial records of a company, organization, or person in order to make sure that they are accurate

auditorium /ˌɔːdɪˈtɔːriəm/ noun [C] **1** **ARTS** the part of a theatre or cinema where the audience sits —*picture* → ACOUSTICS **2** a large room or building used for meetings, lectures, or public performances

auditory /ˈɔːdɪt(ə)ri/ adj formal relating to hearing

auditory ca,nal noun [singular] **ANATOMY** the passage that leads from the **outer ear** to the **inner ear**

auditory ,nerve noun [C] **ANATOMY** a nerve in the ear that sends signals relating to hearing and balance from the **inner ear** to the brain —*picture* → EAR

auger /ˈɔːgə/ noun [C] **CONSTRUCTION** a spiral-shaped tool used for removing a cylinder of wood or soil

augment /ɔːgˈment/ verb [T] formal to increase the size, amount, or value of something —**augmentation** /ˌɔːgmenˈteɪʃ(ə)n/ noun [C/U]

augur /ˈɔːgə/ verb [I/T] formal to be a sign of what may happen in the future: *The look on her face did not augur well.*

august /ɔːˈgʌst/ adj formal old, serious, and respected

August /ˈɔːgəst/ noun [U] the eighth month of the year, between July and September: *We'll be on holiday in August.* ♦ *It's my birthday on August 6th.*

aunt /ɑːnt/ noun [C] the sister of your mother or father, or the wife of your uncle: *I loved visiting my aunt and uncle.* ♦ *Hello, Aunt Betty.*

au pair /ˌəʊ ˈpeə/ noun [C] a young woman who lives with a family in a foreign country and helps to look after their children

aura /ˈɔːrə/ noun [C] a quality that seems to come from a person or place: *an aura of innocence*

aural /ˈɔːrəl/ adj relating to the ears or hearing —**aurally** adv

auricle /ˈɔːrɪk(ə)l/ noun [C] **ANATOMY** an **atrium**

auspices /ˈɔːspɪsɪz/ noun **under the auspices of** formal with the help and support of a particular person or organization

auspicious /ɔːˈspɪʃəs/ adj formal showing signs that suggest that something will be successful

austere /ɔːˈstɪə/ adj **1** plain or simple in style **2** severe or strict in manner

austerity /ɔːˈsterəti/ noun [U] **1** a bad economic situation in which people do not have much money **2** the quality of being austere

Australasia /ˌɒstrəˈleɪʒə/ **GEOGRAPHY** a region that includes Australia, New Zealand, New Guinea, and some South Pacific islands

Australia /ɒˈstreɪliə/ **GEOGRAPHY** a country that is made up of the continent of Australia and the island of Tasmania —*picture* → CONTINENT

authentic /ɔːˈθentɪk/ adj **1** real, not false or copied = GENUINE: *The letter is certainly authentic.* **2** based on facts: *an authentic account of life in rural China* —**authenticity** /ˌɔːθenˈtɪsəti/ noun [U]

author /ˈɔːθə/ noun [C] **1** **LITERATURE** someone who writes books or articles as their job **2** the person who wrote a particular document or other piece of writing: *the author of the report*

authorial /ɔːˈθɔːriəl/ adj **LITERATURE** relating to the author of a book, play etc

authoring /ˈɔːθərɪŋ/ noun [U] **COMPUTING** the process of creating documents and programs on a computer using special software

authoritarian /ɔːˌθɒrɪˈteəriən/ adj controlling everything and forcing people to obey strict rules

authoritative /ɔːˈθɒrɪtətɪv/ adj based on careful research and the most reliable information: *an authoritative report on climate change*

authority /ɔːˈθɒrəti/ (plural **authorities**) noun **1** [U] the power to make decisions and make people do things: *The president's authority is being questioned in the press.* ♦ *Parents have legal authority over their children.* ♦ *I don't have the authority to hire staff.* **2 the authorities** [plural] the police or other organizations with legal power to make people obey laws: *The French authorities have refused to issue him a visa.* **3** [C] an organization or institution that controls a public service: *She took her complaint to the local health authority.* **4** [C] an expert on a particular subject: *Charles was an authority on antique musical instruments.*

au'thority ,figure noun [C] someone who is or seems strong and powerful

authorize /ˈɔːθəraɪz/ verb [T] to give official permission for something: *The guard is authorized to carry a gun.* —**authorization** /ˌɔːθəraɪˈzeɪʃ(ə)n/ noun [U]

autism /ˈɔːtɪz(ə)m/ noun [U] **HEALTH** a serious mental condition, usually present from a very early age, that affects the person's ability to communicate with other people and to form relationships —**autistic** /ɔːˈtɪstɪk/ adj

au'tistic ,spectrum dis,order noun [C] HEALTH a medical condition that is similar to autism, but less severe

auto- /ɔːtəʊ/ prefix **1** relating to yourself **2** operating without a person being involved

autobiography /ˌɔːtəʊbaɪˈɒɡrəfi/ (plural **autobiographies**) noun [C] LITERATURE a book that someone writes about their own life —**autobiographical** /ˌɔːtəʊbaɪəˈɡræfɪk(ə)l/ adj

autocratic /ˌɔːtəˈkrætɪk/ adj ruling in a strict or cruel way —**autocrat** /ˈɔːtəˌkræt/ noun [C]

autocross /ˈɔːtəʊˌkrɒs/ noun [U] SPORTS a sport in which cars race over rough ground

,auto-de,struct sy'ringe adj HEALTH a plastic tube with a needle that is designed so that it can be used only once for putting drugs into someone's body

'auto elec,trician noun [C] someone whose job is to fit and repair electrical and electronic parts in cars

autograph /ˈɔːtəˌɡrɑːf/ noun [C] a famous person's name that they sign on something —**autograph** verb [T]

autoimmune /ˌɔːtəʊɪˈmjuːn/ adj HEALTH relating to conditions and diseases in which the body's **immune system** attacks normal cells instead of harmful ones

autolysis /ɔːˈtɒlɪsɪs/ noun [U] BIOLOGY a process in which plant or animals cells are destroyed by their own natural chemicals

automated /ˈɔːtəˌmeɪtɪd/ adj using machines instead of people

automatic¹ /ˌɔːtəˈmætɪk/ adj **1** an automatic machine can work by itself without being operated by people: *an automatic door* → MANUAL² **2** an automatic action is something that you do without thinking, or without intending to do it: *an automatic response* **3** happening as part of an established process, without a special decision being made: *Taxpayers who do not send in their forms face an automatic fine.* —**automatically** /ˌɔːtəˈmætɪkli/ adv: *He automatically assumed that the engineer would be a man.*

automatic² /ˌɔːtəˈmætɪk/ noun [C] **1** a car in which the **gears** change by themselves **2** a weapon that shoots bullets until the person firing it takes their finger off the **trigger**

,automatic 'gearbox noun [C] ENGINEERING a **gearbox** in a vehicle that can change **gears** automatically as the vehicle moves

automatic hyphenation /ˌɔːtəmætɪk ˌhaɪfəˈneɪʃ(ə)n/ noun [U] COMPUTING a feature of software that automatically divides words and puts hyphens in them in the correct places

,automatic 'pilot noun [C/U] a system that controls the direction of a plane, ship, or spacecraft

    PHRASE **on automatic pilot** doing things without thinking about what you are doing, especially because you have done the same thing many times before

,automatic trans'mission noun [C/U] ENGINEERING a system in which the **gears** of a car change by themselves without any action by the driver

automation /ˌɔːtəˈmeɪʃ(ə)n/ noun [U] a system that uses machines to do work instead of people, or the process of changing to such a system

automobile /ˈɔːtəməˌbiːl/ noun [C] a car

automotive /ˌɔːtəˈməʊtɪv/ adj **1** relating to cars **2** ENGINEERING containing a motor or engine and therefore not needing anything to pull or push it

autonomy /ɔːˈtɒnəmi/ noun [U] **1** the right of a state, region, or organization to govern itself = INDEPENDENCE **2** the power to make your own decisions = INDEPENDENCE —**autonomous** /ɔːˈtɒnəməs/ adj

autopilot /ˈɔːtəʊˌpaɪlət/ noun [C] an **automatic pilot**

autopsy /ˈɔːtɒpsi/ (plural **autopsies**) noun [C] HEALTH a medical examination of a dead person's body that is done in order to find out why they died = POSTMORTEM

autoresponder /ˈɔːtəʊrɪˌspɒndə/ noun [C] COMPUTING a piece of software that automatically sends you a message telling you another Internet user cannot reply to your email

autosave /ˈɔːtəʊˌseɪv/ noun [U] COMPUTING a feature of software that automatically saves your information every few minutes, so that you lose only a small amount of information if the computer system fails

autotrophic /ˌɔːtəˈtrɒfɪk/ adj BIOLOGY relating to organisms, especially green plants, that are capable of making food for themselves —**autotroph** /ˈɔːtətrəʊf/ noun [C], **autotrophy** /ɔːˈtɒtrəfi/ noun [U]

autumn /ˈɔːtəm/ noun [C/U] the season of the year that comes between summer and winter: *We haven't heard from him since last autumn.* ♦ *They were married in the autumn of 1953.* ♦ *a cold autumn afternoon* —**autumnal** /ɔːˈtʌmn(ə)l/ adj

auxiliary /ɔːɡˈzɪliəri/ adj **1** additional and available for use: *an auxiliary engine* **2** helping more senior or permanent workers: *auxiliary nurses*

aux'iliary de,vice noun [C] COMPUTING a piece of equipment that you can connect to your computer and use with it, for example a printer

aux'iliary ,plane noun [C] MATHS, PHYSICS a plane (=flat surface) in **orthographic projection** that shows an object at an angle to the **horizontal plane** or the **vertical plane**

aux'iliary 'verb noun [C] LANGUAGE a verb that is used with another verb to form questions, tenses, and negative or passive phrases. The main auxiliary verbs in English are 'be', 'have', and 'do'.

aux'iliary ,view noun [C/U] MATHS, PHYSICS a view in **orthographic projection** that is at an angle to the **horizontal plane** or the **vertical plane**

auxin /ˈɔːksɪn/ noun [C] BIOLOGY a natural or artificial substance that controls the growth and development of plants

avail /əˈveɪl/ noun **to no avail** *formal* without getting the effect that you wanted

available /əˈveɪləb(ə)l/ adj **1** able to be obtained, taken, or used ≠ UNAVAILABLE: *We'll notify you as soon as tickets become available.* ♦ *Not all the facts are made available to us.* ♦ *There is no money available for this project.* **2** not too busy to do something ≠ UNAVAILABLE: *I'm available next Tuesday if you want to meet then.* ♦ *My tutor is always available to talk to her students.* —**availability** /əˌveɪləˈbɪləti/ noun [U]: *The success of the crop depends on the availability of water.*

avalanche /ˈævəˌlɑːntʃ/ noun [C] **1** GEOGRAPHY a large amount of snow that suddenly falls down a mountain **2** a large quantity of things that arrive suddenly: *an avalanche of letters*

avant-garde /ˌævɒŋˈɡɑːd/ adj very modern in style

avarice /ˈævərɪs/ noun [U] *formal* a strong feeling of wanting to have a lot of money and possessions —**avaricious** /ˌævəˈrɪʃəs/ adj

avatar /'ævə,tɑ:/ noun [C] COMPUTING a picture on a computer screen that represents a particular computer user, especially one of several users who are having a conversation with each other on the Internet

Ave abbrev Avenue: used in addresses

avenge /ə'vendʒ/ verb [T] formal to react to something wrong that has been done to you or someone close to you by punishing the person who did it: He swore to avenge his father's death.

avenue /'ævə,nju:/ noun [C] **1** a wide straight road in a town or city **2** a method of achieving something: We tried every avenue, but couldn't borrow the money we needed.

average¹ /'æv(ə)rɪdʒ/ noun **1** [C/U] the typical amount or level: Unemployment here is twice the national average. ♦ Her performance in the test was **below average**. **2** [C] MATHS an amount that is calculated by adding several numbers together and dividing the total by the number of things that you added together= MEAN

PHRASE **on average** used for talking about what is usually true, although it may not be true in every situation: On average, women live longer than men.

average² /'æv(ə)rɪdʒ/ adj **1** usual or ordinary: He's about average height. **2** not very good= MEDIOCRE: a very average performance **3** MATHS calculated by adding several numbers together and dividing the total by the number of things that you added together: winds with an average speed of 15 miles per hour

average³ /'æv(ə)rɪdʒ/ verb [T] to usually do, have, or involve a particular level or amount: The cost of developing a new drug now averages around £500 million.

averse /ə'vɜ:s/ adj **not be averse to sth** to like or enjoy something, especially something that other people think is bad or harmful

aversion /ə'vɜ:ʃ(ə)n/ noun [C/U] formal a strong feeling that you dislike someone or something

avert /ə'vɜ:t/ verb [T] to prevent something bad from happening: We managed to avert disaster this time.

avian flu /'eɪviən ,flu:/ noun [U] HEALTH bird flu

aviation /,eɪvi'eɪʃ(ə)n/ noun [U] the activity of flying or making planes

avi'ation ,fuel noun [U] a type of petroleum, used as a fuel by aircraft

avid /'ævɪd/ adj very enthusiastic —**avidly** adv

avocado /,ævə'kɑ:dəʊ/ (plural **avocados**) noun [C/U] a fruit with green or black skin, a very large seed in the middle, and pale green flesh —picture → FRUIT

avoid /ə'vɔɪd/ verb [T] **1** to try to prevent something from happening: Try to avoid confrontation. ♦ I want to **avoid being** drawn into the argument. **2** to stay away from someone or something: We went early to avoid the crowds. **3** to choose not to do something: He will avoid work whenever he can. ♦ Where possible, we have avoided using technical terms. —**avoidance** /ə'vɔɪd(ə)ns/ noun [U]: the avoidance of confrontation

avoidable /ə'vɔɪdəb(ə)l/ adj capable of being prevented ≠ UNAVOIDABLE: avoidable mistakes

avowed /ə'vaʊd/ adj publicly claimed or promised —**avowedly** /ə'vaʊɪdli/ adv

avuncular /ə'vʌŋkjʊlə/ adj an avuncular man is kind and helpful to younger or less experienced people

await /ə'weɪt/ verb [T] formal **1** to wait for something: They were awaiting the birth of their first child. **2** if something awaits you, it will happen to you: Well, I wonder what surprises await us today.

awake¹ /ə'weɪk/ adj not sleeping: I've been awake for hours. ♦ Do you **lie awake** at night, worrying about things? ♦ I managed to **stay awake** long enough to watch the film. ♦ We've been **kept awake** all night by the noise. ♦ When the alarm went off, I was already **wide awake** (=completely awake).

awake² /ə'weɪk/ (**awakes**, **awaking**, **awoke** /ə'wəʊk/, **awoken** /ə'wəʊkən/) verb [I/T] to wake up, or to wake someone up: They awoke to find that several inches of snow had fallen.

awaken /ə'weɪkən/ verb formal **1** [T] to make someone have a particular feeling **2** [I/T] to wake up, or to wake someone up

awakening /ə'weɪk(ə)nɪŋ/ noun [singular] the moment when someone first realizes or experiences something

award¹ /ə'wɔ:d/ noun [C] **1** a prize that is given to someone who has achieved something: She won the Player of the Year award. ♦ an **award for** outstanding services to the industry **2** an amount of money that is given by a court of law or other authority: an **award for** compensation

award² /ə'wɔ:d/ verb [T] **1** to give someone a prize: Students who complete the course successfully will be awarded a diploma. **2** to officially give someone something such as a contract or an amount of money: He has been awarded a scholarship to do research. **3** LAW to make a legal decision to give someone the right to do something, for example to care for a child

aware /ə'weə/ adj **1** knowing about a situation or fact ≠ UNAWARE: As far as I'm aware, he didn't tell her anything. ♦ I was not aware that she had already spoken to you. ♦ They're **aware of** the dangers. **2** interested and involved in something: People are becoming much more **environmentally aware**. **3** if you become aware of someone or something, you notice them: I became aware of someone following me. ♦ He suddenly became aware that the music had stopped. —**awareness** noun [U]: The aim of our campaign is to **raise awareness about** (=make people learn about) heart disease.

awash /ə'wɒʃ/ adj **1** thoroughly covered with a liquid **2** full of something, or having a lot of something: The town is **awash with** tourists this time of year.

away¹ /ə'weɪ/ adv

1 further from	**5** gradually disappearing
2 not in your usual place	**6** doing sth continuously
3 not near	**7** in the usual place
4 removing sth	

1 in a direction that takes you further from a person, place, or thing: When Sykes saw the police, he ran away. ♦ Please move **away from** the doors.
2 not at home, or not at the place where someone works or studies: My brother looks after the farm while I'm away. ♦ Amy has spent a lot of time **away from** school.
3 at a distance: The nearest hospital is 30 miles away. ♦ The examinations are less than three weeks away.
4 used for showing that something is removed: We need to have this rubbish taken away. ♦ She wiped away her tears.
5 used for saying that something gradually disappears: The sound of their voices faded away into the distance.
6 doing something continuously or for a long time: Molly was at her desk working away as usual.
7 in the place where something is usually kept, or in a safe place: Put your toys away before you go to bed.

away² /ə'weɪ/ adj SPORTS an away game is one in which a team goes to their opponents' ground to play

awe /ɔː/ noun [U] a feeling of great respect and admiration: *He is totally in awe of his father.*

'awe-in,spiring adj making you feel great respect and admiration

awesome /'ɔːs(ə)m/ adj very impressive and sometimes a little frightening

awestruck /'ɔːstrʌk/ adj feeling extremely impressed by something

awful /'ɔːf(ə)l/ adj extremely bad = TERRIBLE: *This wine tastes awful.* ♦ *There were these awful people sitting behind us who talked all through the film.* —**awfully** adv

awkward /'ɔːkwəd/ adj **1** difficult and embarrassing: *Luckily, nobody asked any awkward questions.* **2** not comfortable, relaxed, or confident: *He stood there looking stiff and awkward in his uniform.* **3** an object that is awkward is difficult to use or carry because of its shape or position

awkwardly /'ɔːkwədli/ adv **1** in a way that shows you are not comfortable, relaxed, or confident: *They smiled awkwardly at the camera.* **2** in a way that is not graceful: *He moved to get out of the way and fell awkwardly.*

awning /'ɔːnɪŋ/ noun [C] a sheet of cloth above a window or door, used as protection against the rain or sun

awoke /ə'wəʊk/ the past tense of **awake²**

awoken /ə'wəʊkən/ the past participle of **awake²**

awry /ə'raɪ/ adj not in the correct position
PHRASE **go awry** to not happen in the way that was planned

ax /æks/ an American spelling of **axe**

axe¹ /æks/ noun [C] a tool used for cutting wood, consisting of a long wooden handle and a heavy metal blade —*picture* → TOOL

axe² /æks/ verb [T] to end or reduce something: *Almost 1,000 jobs were axed.*

axil /'æksɪl/ noun [C] BIOLOGY the space between a leaf or branch and the stem to which it is attached

axillary /æk'sɪləri/ adj BIOLOGY relating to or growing in the axil of a plant

axiom /'æksiəm/ noun [C] a statement that is generally believed to be obvious or true

axiomatic /,æksiə'mætɪk/ adj generally believed to be obvious or true —**axiomatically** /,æksiə'mætɪkli/ adv

axis /'æksɪs/ (plural **axes** /'æksiːz/) noun [C] **1** MATHS one of the two fixed lines that are used for recording measurements on a graph —*picture* → GRAPH **2** MATHS an imaginary line that divides a square, circle, or other regular shape into two equal halves: *an axis of symmetry* **3** PHYSICS an imaginary line through the middle of an object such as a planet, around which it seems to spin

axle /'æks(ə)l/ noun [C] a metal bar that connects a pair of wheels on a car or other vehicle

axon /'æksɒn/ noun [C] ANATOMY the long part of a **neuron** (=nerve cell) that carries signals away from the **cell body** of a neuron —*picture* → NEURON

ayatollah /,aɪə'tɒlə/ noun [C] RELIGION an important religious leader in Iran who often has political as well as religious influence

Ayurvedic medicine /,ɑːjʊəvedɪk 'med(ə)s(ə)n/ noun [U] HEALTH a traditional system of medicine from India that gives people advice on food and the way they live —**Ayurvedic** adj

azimuth /'æzɪməθ/ noun [C] ASTRONOMY the angle of the imaginary line between the position of a plane, ship etc and the position of another object

AZT /,eɪ zed 'tiː/ TRADEMARK HEALTH a drug used for treating AIDS

B b

b /biː/ (plural **b's**) or **B** (plural **B's**) noun **1** [C] the second letter of the English alphabet **2** B [U] HEALTH a common blood group in the **ABO system 3** B [C/U] MUSIC the seventh note of a musical scale in C major

B abbrev be: used in emails and **text messages**

b. abbrev born: used before the date of someone's birth

BA /,biː 'eɪ/ noun [C] EDUCATION Bachelor of Arts: a first degree from a university in a subject such as languages or history

baa /bɑː/ (**baas, baaing, baaed** /bɑːd/) verb [I] to make the sound that a sheep makes —**baa** noun [C]

babble /'bæb(ə)l/ verb [I/T] to speak quickly in a way that is boring or difficult to understand

baboon /bə'buːn/ noun [C] a type of large monkey that has a long tail, large teeth, and a large **snout** like a dog. Baboons are found in Africa and South Asia.

baby /'beɪbi/ (plural **babies**) noun [C] **1** a very young child who cannot yet talk or walk: *Sally's going to have a baby* (=give birth) *in May.* **2** a very young animal: *a baby elephant* **3** someone who is behaving in a way that is weak, silly, or not brave

baby boomer /'beɪbi ,buːmə/ noun [C] SOCIAL STUDIES someone who was born during the period after the Second World War when many babies were born

'baby ,food noun [U] special food for babies that has been cut into small pieces and cooked so that it is soft and smooth

babyish /'beɪbiɪʃ/ adj *showing disapproval* suitable only for a baby or young child

'baby ,milk noun [U] a type of milk that is made to be similar to a mother's milk

babysit /'beɪbi,sɪt/ (**babysits, babysitting, babysat** /'beɪbi,sæt/) verb [I/T] to look after children when their parents are not at home —**babysitter** noun [C], **babysitting** noun [U]

'baby ,talk noun [U] sounds and words that babies make when they are learning to speak, or similar sounds and words that adults use when talking to babies

baccalaureate /,bækə'lɔːriət/ noun [C] EDUCATION an examination taken at age 18 in some European countries, which allows students to study at a university

bachelor /'bætʃələ/ noun [C] a man who has never been married '**bachelor's de.gree** noun [C] **EDUCATION** a first university degree, such as a BA or BSc

bacillus /bəˈsɪləs/ (plural **bacilli** /bəˈsɪlaɪ/) noun [C] **BIOLOGY** a type of bacteria with a long straight shape. Bacilli mainly occur in **chains**. Some of them cause food to decay, and some cause diseases such as **anthrax**.

back¹ /bæk/ adv **1** returning to a place, situation, or time: *Put those CDs back where you found them.* ♦ *Can we go back to what we were talking about earlier?* **2** as a reply or reaction to what someone else has said or done: *Jane phoned, and I said you'd phone her back later.* **3** away from a person, thing, or position: *Get back – he's got a gun!* **4** in the direction that is behind you: *Don't look back, but there's a man following us.*
PHRASE **back and forth** moving first in one direction and then in the opposite direction many times
→ BACK-TO-BACK

back² /bæk/ adj **1** furthest from the front ≠ FRONT: *There's a map on the back page.* **2** owed from an earlier date and not yet paid: *back rent* **3** a back street or road is away from any main streets or roads

back³ /bæk/ noun [C]

1 part of your body	**4** part of chair
2 part furthest from front	**5** of page/picture etc
	6 in sports
3 outside behind a building	**7** brick surface
	+ PHRASES

1 the part of the body between the neck and bottom, on the opposite side to the chest and stomach ≠ FRONT: *She was lying **flat on her back** on the bed.* —*picture* → BODY
2 the part or side of something that is furthest from the front ≠ FRONT: *Get in **the back of** the car.* ♦ *I'll put my name **on the back of** the envelope.*
3 an outside area behind a building ≠ FRONT: *The kids are playing **out the back**.*
4 the part of a chair that you lean on when you are sitting on it: *What's that mark on **the back of** the sofa?*
5 the side of a page, card, picture etc that is not the main side: *I'll put my name **on the back of** the envelope.*
6 **SPORTS** a player in a football or **hockey** team whose job is to **defend** (=stop the other team from scoring goals)
7 **CONSTRUCTION** the vertical brick surface that makes the **opening** for a **fireplace**
PHRASES **back to front** with the back part at the front: *Your skirt is on back to front.*
behind sb's back if someone does something bad or unkind behind your back, they do it without you knowing
→ TURN

back⁴ /bæk/ verb **1** [T] to support a person, organization, or plan: *A group of local firms are backing the football tournament.* **2** [I/T] to move backwards, or to make a person or a vehicle move backwards: *She **backed out of** the room carrying a tray.* **3** [T] to risk an amount of money by saying that a particular person or animal will win a race or competition: *I'm backing India to win the match.*
PHRASAL VERBS ,**back 'down** to stop asking for something, or to stop saying that you will do something, because a lot of people oppose you: *Neither side is willing to back down.*
,**back 'out** to refuse to do something that you agreed to do: *We're hoping that no one will **back out of** the deal.*
,**back (sth) 'up** **COMPUTING** to make a copy of information on your computer
,**back sb 'up** to give support to someone by telling other people that you agree with them: *If I complain to the staff, will you back me up?*

,**back sth 'up** to show that an explanation or belief is probably true: *All the evidence backs up her story.*

backache /ˈbækeɪk/ noun [C/U] **HEALTH** pain in the back

backacter /ˈbæk,æktə/ noun [C] **CONSTRUCTION** an **excavator** (=machine for digging holes) with a **bucket** that moves the soil towards itself

backbone /ˈbæk,bəʊn/ noun [C] **ANATOMY** the row of small bones that goes down the middle of the back = SPINE, VERTEBRAL COLUMN —*picture* → SKELETON
PHRASE **the backbone of sth** the part of something that makes it successful or strong

backbreaking /ˈbæk,breɪkɪŋ/ adj physically very hard and tiring = EXHAUSTING

back burner /,bæk ˈbɜːnə/ noun **put sth on the back burner** *informal* to decide not to deal with something until later

'**back ,copy** noun [C] a **back issue** of a newspaper or magazine

backcross¹ /ˈbæk,krɒs/ verb [T] **BIOLOGY** to cross a plant or animal, especially a **hybrid**, with one of its parents, or with a plant or animal that has the same genes as that parent —**backcrossing** noun [U]

backcross² /ˈbæk,krɒs/ noun [C] **BIOLOGY** an act of backcrossing

backdate /,bækˈdeɪt/ verb [T] to make something such as a rule or law start to be effective from a date in the past

backdrop /ˈbæk,drɒp/ noun [C] the situation or place in which something happens: *Negotiations were carried out **against a backdrop of** continued fighting.*

backer /ˈbækə/ noun [C] someone who gives help or money to a plan or organization

backfill /ˈbæk,fɪl/ verb [T] **CONSTRUCTION** to fill a hole with the soil that has been dug out of it

backfire¹ /,bækˈfaɪə/ verb [I] **1** if a plan or idea backfires, it has the opposite effect to the one that you wanted **2** if a car backfires, its engine makes a loud noise like an explosion

backfire² /ˈbæk,faɪə/ noun [C] **TECHNOLOGY** a loud noise produced when the flame goes back into the tip of the **blowpipe** during **oxyacetylene welding**

backflow /ˈbæk,fləʊ/ noun [C] **PHYSICS** the process by which a liquid such as blood flows back through a **valve** because the valve does not close properly

'**back for,mation** noun [C] **LANGUAGE** a new word that is formed by removing a part of another word. In English, 'burgle' is a back formation from 'burglar'.

backgammon /ˈbæk,gæmən/ noun [U] a game for two people that you play on a board using **dice** and two sets of round pieces

background /ˈbæk,graʊnd/ noun **1** [C] the general experiences and influences that have formed someone's character, or the type of education and training they have had: *students from very different backgrounds* ♦ *We are looking for writers with a **background in** law.* **2** [U] information and details that help you to understand a situation: *The police need to know **the background to** the case.* **3** [C] **ARTS** the part of a picture or pattern that is behind the main people or things in it ≠ FOREGROUND: *a picture of palm trees with mountains **in the background*** **4** [singular] the sounds that you can hear in addition to the main thing that you are listening to: *birds singing **in the background*** ♦ *background noise*

PHRASE **in the background** in a place or situation in which people do not notice you: *Jo does the publicity work, while Ed stays very much in the background.*

'**background** ,**music** noun [U] **1** quiet music that plays in a public place **2** the music used in a film to create a particular mood

'**background** ,**noise** noun [C/U] noise that can be heard in addition to the main thing you are listening to

'**background** ,**processing** noun [U] **COMPUTING** processes that continue while a computer user is working with another program

,**background radi'ation** noun [C] **SCIENCE** radiation that is naturally present in the environment in small amounts. It comes from soil, rocks, the air etc.

backhand /'bæk,hænd/ noun [C] **SPORTS** in tennis and similar sports, a movement made to hit the ball in which the back of your hand moves towards the ball

backhanded /,bæk'hændɪd/ adj **1** said in a way that seems to express admiration but really expresses the opposite **2** **SPORTS** in tennis and similar sports, a backhanded shot is made by moving the back of your hand towards the ball

backing /'bækɪŋ/ noun [U] **1** support, help, or strong approval: *The new policy has the backing of several leading politicians.* **2** **MUSIC** music that is played or sung to add to the main singer's voice

,**back 'issue** noun [C] an old copy of a magazine or newspaper= BACK NUMBER

backlash /'bæk,læʃ/ noun [C] a strong, negative, and often angry reaction to something that has happened

backlit /'bæk,lɪt/ adj someone or something that is backlit has light shining at them from behind

backlog /'bæk,lɒg/ noun [singular] an amount of work that someone should already have finished

,**back 'number** noun [C] a **back issue**

backpack /'bæk,pæk/ noun [C] a **rucksack**

backpacker /'bæk,pækə/ noun [C] someone, especially a young person without much money, who visits a country or area and travels around on foot or public transport —**backpacking** noun [U]

,**back 'passage** noun [C] a person's **rectum** (=the part of your body where solid waste comes out), used for example by doctors to avoid embarrassing people

backpedal /'bæk,ped(ə)l/ (**backpedals, backpedalling, backpedalled**) verb [I] **1** to show that you are no longer certain about a previous opinion, intention, or promise **2** to pedal backwards on a bicycle

backroom boys /'bækru:m ,bɔɪz/ noun [plural] people who do important work in a private or secret way

,**back 'seat** noun [C] a seat behind the driver of a car
     PHRASE **take a back seat** to deliberately become less active, and give up trying to control things

backside /'bæk,saɪd/ noun [C] *informal* the part of your body that you sit on

backslash /'bæk,slæʃ/ noun [C] **COMPUTING** the symbol \ used for separating words or numbers, especially in the names of computer files → FORWARD SLASH

backsliding /'bæk,slaɪdɪŋ/ noun [U] *informal* the lazy behaviour of someone who goes back to doing something bad after not doing it for some time —**backslider** noun [C]

backspace /'bæk,speɪs/ noun [singular] **COMPUTING** the key that you press on a computer keyboard to move one space backwards in a document

backstabbing /'bæk,stæbɪŋ/ noun [U] unpleasant things that people say or do in order to harm someone's reputation

backstage /,bæk'steɪdʒ/ adv **ARTS** in the area behind the stage in a theatre, which includes the rooms where the actors get dressed

backstairs /'bæk,steəz/ adj *informal* secret and usually dishonest or illegal

backstory /'bækstɔːri/ noun [C] a set of events invented for a book, film, or play that have taken place before it begins

backstreet¹ /'bæk,striːt/ noun [C] a small street in a town or city

backstreet² /'bæk,striːt/ adj done secretly or illegally by people who are not very skilful

backstroke /'bæk,strəʊk/ noun [singular/U] **SPORTS** a style of swimming on your back

backswing /'bæk,swɪŋ/ noun [C] **SPORTS** the movement that a golf player makes when they raise the club backwards above their head in order to hit the ball in golf

,**back-to-'back** adj, adv **1** happening one after the other: *Bill won two golf tournaments back-to-back.* **2** with the back of someone or something against the back of someone or something else

backtrack /'bæk,træk/ verb [I] **1** to show that you have become less likely to do something that you said you would do: *The government is **backtracking on** its commitment to increase spending.* **2** to return to a subject you were discussing before **3** to go back in the direction from which you have come

backup /'bækʌp/ noun **1** [C] **COMPUTING** a copy of information on a computer that you make in case you lose the original information **2** [C/U] people or equipment that can be used when extra help is needed: *The gang was armed, so the police called for backup.*

'**backup u,tility** noun [C] **COMPUTING** a piece of software that makes the process of **backing up** computer information easier

backward /'bækwəd/ adj **1** moving or looking in the direction that is behind you: *a backward glance* **2** not developing quickly, normally, or successfully: *a remote and backward region*

backwards /'bækwədz/ adv **1** in the direction that is behind you: *The car rolled backwards down the hill.* **2** in the opposite way or order to usual: *Count backwards from ten to one.* **3** towards a time in the past: *We should plan for the future, not look backwards.*
     PHRASE **backwards and forwards** moving first in one direction and then in the opposite direction many times

,**backwards-com'patible** adj **COMPUTING** computer software that is backwards-compatible can operate with pieces of software of the same type that were made at an earlier time —,**backwards-compati'bility** noun [U]

backwash /'bæk,wɒʃ/ noun [U] the movement of waves as they leave the land —*picture* → on next page

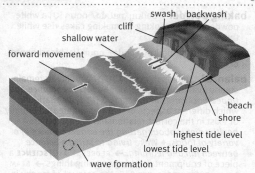

forward movement
shallow water
cliff
swash backwash
backwash
beach
shore
highest tide level
lowest tide level
wave formation

wave formation

backwater /'bæk,wɔːtə/ noun [singular] **1** a place, situation, or organization in which nothing exciting or important happens, and in which people still have old-fashioned ideas **2 GEOGRAPHY** an area of water that is connected to a river but is not affected by its current

bacon /'beɪkən/ noun [U] meat from a pig that is treated with smoke or salt, and is often cooked in **rashers** (=thin pieces)

bacteria /bæk'tɪəriə/ (singular **bacterium** /bæk'tɪəriəm/) noun [plural] **BIOLOGY, HEALTH** microorganisms consisting of a single cell, with a chromosome not inside a nucleus. Some types of bacteria cause diseases while others are responsible for decay, **fermentation**, and **nitrogen fixation**. Most reproduce **asexually** by dividing in two.

bunches, e.g.
causing food poisoning

paired spherical, e.g.
causing pneumonia

rod-shaped, e.g.
causing anthrax

spiral, e.g.
causing syphilis

bacteria

bacterial /bæk'tɪəriəl/ adj **BIOLOGY** relating to or caused by bacteria: *bacterial infections*

bacteriology /bæk,tɪəri'ɒlədʒi/ noun [U] **BIOLOGY** the scientific study of bacteria —**bacteriological** /bæk,tɪəriə'lɒdʒɪk(ə)l/ adj, **bacteriologist** /bæk,tɪəri'ɒlədʒɪst/ noun [C]

Bactrian camel /,bæktriən 'kæm(ə)l/ noun [C] a **camel** from Asia with two humps on its back → DROMEDARY

bad /bæd/ (**worse** /wɜːs/, **worst** /wɜːst/) adj

1 not nice	**5** painful
2 causing problems	**6** behaving badly
3 of low quality/skill	**7** no longer fresh
4 not suitable	**+ PHRASES**

1 not nice or enjoyable: *The weather was really bad.* ♦ *I'm afraid I have some **bad news** for you.*
2 causing major problems, harm, or damage: *a bad accident* ♦ *I tried to help, but I just made things worse.*

3 showing a lack of quality or skill: *one of this year's worst films* ♦ *I'm really **bad at** remembering people's names.*
4 not suitable or convenient: *I can come back later if this is **a bad time** for you.*
5 painful or injured: *a bad back*
6 cruel, evil, or morally wrong: *He's not a bad man, just very weak.*
7 no longer fresh or good to eat or drink: *The fish had gone **bad**.*
PHRASES **feel bad (about sth)** to feel guilty or unhappy about something
not bad *informal* fairly good, or better than you expected: *Those pictures aren't bad for someone who's a complete beginner.*
→ BADLY

Build your vocabulary: words you can use instead of bad

Bad is a very general word. Here are some words with more specific meanings that sound more natural and appropriate in particular situations.
meal/film/weather/behaviour/book
appalling, atrocious, awful, terrible
person horrible, nasty, unpleasant, wicked
illness/injury/problem major, serious, severe
performance/piece of work/teacher/singer not much good (*informal*), poor, terrible, useless (*informal*)
something that causes harm or bad effects damaging, dangerous, harmful, poisonous, toxic, unhealthy

,bad 'break noun [C] **COMPUTING** a hyphen in the wrong place in a word, sometimes caused by software that puts hyphens in words automatically

,bad 'debt noun [C] **BUSINESS** money that a person or country owes but will never pay

,bad 'faith noun [U] the fact of not being sincere or honest about your intentions

badge /bædʒ/ noun [C] **1** a special piece of metal, cloth, or plastic with words or symbols on it. Someone wears it or carries it to show their official position: *a police badge* **2** a small round object with words or symbols on it. People fasten it onto their clothes with a pin, for example to show that they support an idea or a political party.

badger¹ /'bædʒə/ noun [C] a wild animal with dark fur and a white area on its head, found in Europe, Asia, and North America. Badgers live in a system of holes in the ground called a **sett**. —*picture* → MAMMAL

badger² /'bædʒə/ verb [T] to try to make someone do something by asking them many times

,bad 'language noun [U] rude words

badly /'bædli/ (**worse** /wɜːs/, **worst** /wɜːst/) adv **1** in a way that is not skilful, effective, or successful: *She spoke English so badly I couldn't understand her.* ♦ *a badly organized meeting* **2** in a serious or severe way: *He was badly hurt in the accident.* **3** in an unkind, unfair, or unreasonable way: *She feels as though she has been badly treated.* **4** if you need or want something badly, you need or want it very much

,badly 'off (**worse off**, **worst off**) adj someone who is badly off does not have much money

badminton /'bædmɪntən/ noun [U] **SPORTS** a game in which two or four players use **rackets** to hit a **shuttlecock** (=a small light object with feathers on it) to each other across a net

bad-tempered /ˌbæd ˈtempəd/ adj becoming annoyed or angry very easily

baffle /ˈbæf(ə)l/ verb [T] to be confusing or difficult for someone to understand or solve: *Detectives remain baffled by these murders.* —**baffling** adj

bag /bæg/ noun [C] **1** a container made of paper, plastic, or cloth, used for carrying or storing things: *a plastic bag* **2** a **handbag** **3** a suitcase or similar container in which you carry clothes and other things that you need when you are travelling **4** the things in a bag, or the amount that it contains: *I've already used about half a bag of flour.*

baggage /ˈbægɪdʒ/ noun [U] **luggage**

baggage al,lowance noun [C] TOURISM the weight of bags and suitcases that a passenger is allowed to take on a plane without paying

baggage ,check noun [C] TOURISM a check of passengers' bags and suitcases at an airport to make sure they contain nothing dangerous or illegal

baggage handler /ˈbægɪdʒ ˌhændlə/ noun [C] TOURISM someone whose job is to deal with passengers' **luggage** at an airport

baggage reclaim /ˌbægɪdʒ ˈriːkleɪm/ noun [U] TOURISM the place in an airport where people get their **luggage** after a flight

baggy /ˈbægi/ (**baggier, baggiest**) adj baggy clothes are very loose and comfortable

bagpipes /ˈbægpaɪps/ noun [plural] MUSIC a musical instrument consisting of a bag with several pipes sticking out of it. You play bagpipes by blowing air through one of the pipes.

bail¹ /beɪl/ noun **1** [U] LAW money that is given to a court so that someone is allowed to stay out of prison until their trial: *She was released on bail later that day.* **2** [C] SPORTS in the game of **cricket**, one of the two small pieces of wood that are placed across the top of the **stumps** to form the **wicket**

bail² /beɪl/
PHRASAL VERBS ,bail sb ('out) LAW to give money to a court so that someone is allowed to stay out of prison while they wait for their trial
,bail sb/sth 'out to help a person or organization that is having financial problems

bailey /ˈbeɪli/ noun [C] an area of land between the outer and inner walls of a castle —*picture* → CASTLE

bailiff /ˈbeɪlɪf/ noun [C] **1** LAW an official whose job is to take away the possessions of someone who has not paid money that they owe **2** someone whose job is to look after a farm or land that belongs to someone else

bait¹ /beɪt/ noun [C/U] food that is used for attracting and catching fish, birds, insects, or other animals

bait² /beɪt/ verb [T] to put food on a hook or in a **trap** in order to catch fish, birds, insects, or other animals

bake /beɪk/ verb **1** [I/T] to cook food such as bread and cakes in an oven: *They spent the morning baking bread.* **2** [T] to use heat to make something hard: *The pottery is baked in a kiln.*

Bakelite /ˈbeɪkəlaɪt/ TRADEMARK a type of hard plastic that was used especially in the 1930s and 1940s for making things such as radios and telephones

baker /ˈbeɪkə/ noun [C] someone whose job is to make bread, cakes etc

bakery /ˈbeɪkəri/ (plural **bakeries**) noun [C] a building where bread, cakes etc are made or sold

baking powder /ˈbeɪkɪŋ ˌpaʊdə/ noun [U] a white powder used in cooking for making cakes rise while they are baking

baking soda /ˈbeɪkɪŋ ˌsəʊdə/ noun [U] **bicarbonate of soda**

balance¹ /ˈbæləns/ noun **1** [U] the ability to remain steady in an upright position: *He lost his balance and tipped backwards in the chair.* **2** [C/U] a situation in which different aspects or features are treated equally or exist in the correct relationship to each other: *A healthy diet is about getting the correct balance of a variety of foods.* ♦ *We're trying to strike a balance between fun and learning.* → REDRESS **3** [C] SCIENCE a piece of equipment used for weighing things → BEAM BALANCE, SPRING BALANCE **4** [C] the amount of money in a bank account, or the amount still to be paid for something
PHRASES **balance of payments** ECONOMICS the difference between the amount of money that a country pays to foreign countries and the amount it receives from them
balance of power the way in which military or political power is divided between countries or groups
balance of trade ECONOMICS the difference between the value of all the goods a country sells to foreign countries and all the goods it buys from them
be/hang in the balance if something is in the balance, you do not know whether it will succeed or fail
on balance after thinking about all the relevant facts: *On balance, I think we made the right decision.*

balance² /ˈbæləns/ verb **1** [I/T] to keep your body steady without falling over, or to put something in a steady position so that it does not fall: *We had to balance our plates on our knees.* **2** [T] to create or preserve a good or correct balance between two different features or aspects, so that both are equally strong or important: *There is a need to balance the demands of the workplace with those of family life.* **3** [T] to reduce the effect, strength, or amount of something= OFFSET: *In an atom, the positive charges of the protons are balanced by the negative charges of the electrons.*
PHRASAL VERB ,balance (sth) 'out *same as* **balance²** sense 3

balanced /ˈbælənst/ adj **1** thinking about all arguments, opinions, or aspects fairly and equally= UNBIASED: *We aim to provide balanced reporting of this difficult issue.* **2** with all parts combining well together or existing in the correct amounts: *a balanced diet*

,balanced e'quation noun [C] CHEMISTRY a chemical equation in which the number of atoms of each type of chemical in the **reactants** is equal to the number of products

,balanced 'forces noun [plural] PHYSICS the force pulling an object down and the force pushing it up, which are equal and opposite

'balance ,sheet noun [C] BUSINESS a written statement showing the value of a company at a particular time

balancing point /ˈbælənsɪŋ ˌpɔɪnt/ noun [singular] PHYSICS the fixed point on which a lever turns or pivots

balcony /ˈbælkəni/ (plural **balconies**) noun [C] **1** a flat surface sticking out from the outside of a building where you can sit or stand **2** ARTS the top floor in a theatre or cinema that sticks out over the main floor

bald /bɔːld/ adj **1** with little or no hair on the head **2** a bald tyre is not safe because its surface has worn smooth **3** a bald statement or fact is said in a direct way, without trying to be sensitive or polite —**baldness** noun [U]

balding /ˈbɔːldɪŋ/ adj beginning to lose hair

bale /beɪl/ noun [C] a large quantity of something such as paper, cotton, or **hay** that is tied tightly together

baleen /bəˈliːn/ noun [U] **BIOLOGY** a hard substance that grows in the shape of a **comb** from the upper jaws of some **whales**. The whale uses it to filter food, especially small crustaceans, from the water.

balk /bɔːk/ another spelling of **baulk**

ball /bɔːl/ noun [C] **1** a round object that you use in games and sports, or an object that is shaped like this: *a tennis ball* ♦ *a ball of dough* **2** the part of the foot, hand, or thumb that is slightly round and sticks out **3** a formal social event at which there is dancing and usually a meal
PHRASE get/set/start the ball rolling to make something start happening

ballad /ˈbæləd/ noun [C] **1 MUSIC** a slow popular love song **2 LITERATURE** a long poem or song that tells a story

ball-and-ˈsocket joint noun [C] **ANATOMY** a joint in the body of a person or animal where a bone with a round end fits into another bone that has a concave part, allowing the bones to move easily in many directions. The **hip** is an example of a ball-and-socket joint. —*picture* → JOINT

ballast /ˈbæləst/ noun [U] a substance such as water, sand, or metal that is carried in a ship or in a large **balloon** to help it remain steady

ˌball ˈbearing noun [C] **PHYSICS** one of several small metal balls that are used between moving parts of a machine to help the parts move smoothly

ˈball ˌboy noun [C] **SPORTS** a boy whose job is to pick up balls at a tennis match and throw them back to the players

ballcock /ˈbɔːlkɒk/ noun [C] a floating ball that opens and closes a **valve**, used for controlling a water supply, for example in a toilet

ballerina /ˌbæləˈriːnə/ noun [C] a woman who dances in ballets, especially as her job

ballet /ˈbæleɪ/ noun **1** [U] a type of complicated dancing that is used for telling a story and is performed in a theatre **2** [C] a performance of ballet

ˈballet ˌdancer noun [C] someone who dances in ballets, especially as their job

ˈball ˌgame noun [C] **1** a game played with a ball, for example tennis or football **2 SPORTS** American a baseball match
PHRASE a whole new ball game a situation that is completely different from what has happened before

ˈball ˌgirl noun [C] **SPORTS** a girl whose job is to pick up balls at a tennis match and throw them back to the players

ballgown /ˈbɔːlgaʊn/ noun [C] a special long dress worn by a woman for dancing at a **ball** (=a formal social event)

balˌlistic ˈmissile noun [C] a type of missile that travels long distances

ballistics /bəˈlɪstɪks/ noun [U] **SCIENCE** the scientific study of the movement of objects or weapons that are fired into the air

ˈball ˌjoint noun [C] **ENGINEERING** a joint in a vehicle engine that consists of a ball-shaped part and a **socket** in which the ball fits and moves

balloon /bəˈluːn/ noun [C] **1** a small coloured bag of thin rubber filled with air, used as a toy or decoration **2** a large strong bag filled with gas or hot air that can be used for travelling through the air

ballooning /bəˈluːnɪŋ/ noun [U] the activity of flying in a **hot-air balloon** —**balloonist** noun [C]

ballot¹ /ˈbælət/ noun [C/U] a secret vote to decide about an issue or to decide who wins an election

ballot² /ˈbælət/ verb [T] to ask people to vote in a ballot

ˈballot ˌbox noun **1** [C] a box in which people put a piece of paper with their vote on **2 the ballot box** [singular] **POLITICS** the democratic system of voting

ˈballot ˌpaper noun [C] a piece of paper that someone writes their vote on

ˈballot ˌrigging /ˈbælət ˌrɪgɪŋ/ noun [U] **POLITICS** the practice of cheating when counting the votes in an election to make sure that a particular person or party wins

ballpark¹ /ˈbɔːlpɑːk/ noun [C] **SPORTS** American a place where baseball games are played

ballpark² /ˈbɔːlpɑːk/ adj not calculated exactly

ˈball pein hammer /ˌbɔːl piːn ˈhæmə/ noun [C] a hammer with a steel head that has one round end and one flat end

ballpoint /ˈbɔːlpɔɪnt/ or **ˌballpoint ˈpen** noun [C] a pen with a very small ball at the end from which ink flows

ballroom /ˈbɔːlruːm/ noun [C] a very large room used for formal dances

ˌballroom ˈdancing noun [U] a type of formal dancing done by two people together, using a fixed series of movements

balm /bɑːm/ noun [C/U] an oil with a nice smell for rubbing on sore skin

baluster /ˈbæləstə/ noun [C] **CONSTRUCTION** one of the posts that supports the **handrail** on a **staircase**

balustrade /ˌbæləˈstreɪd/ noun [C] **CONSTRUCTION 1** a stone structure like a fence around the edge of a **balcony 2** the part built on the outer edge of a **staircase** to stop people falling off the edge of the stairs

bamboo /ˌbæmˈbuː/ (plural **bamboos**) noun [C/U] a type of tall grass that grows in tropical areas. Its thick light-brown stems are used for building and making things such as furniture.

bamˈboo ˌshoots noun [plural] a vegetable consisting of the stems of a young bamboo plant, used especially in Chinese cooking

ban¹ /bæn/ (**bans, banning, banned**) verb [T] **1** to say officially that something is illegal or not allowed: *a new law that bans tobacco advertising* ♦ *The book was banned from school libraries.* **2** to say officially that someone is not allowed to do something: *She was banned from competing for two years after failing a drugs test.*

ban² /bæn/ noun [C] an official statement ordering people not to do something: *There is a total ban on smoking anywhere in the college.*

banal /bəˈnɑːl/ adj boring, with no new, interesting, or unusual qualities —**banality** /bəˈnæləti/ noun [C/U]

banana /bəˈnɑːnə/ noun [C/U] a long curved fruit with a yellow skin —*picture* → FRUIT

band /bænd/ noun [C]

1 group of musicians	**4** ring-shaped thing
2 group of same type	**5** line of colour/light
3 range of levels	

1 MUSIC a group of musicians who play popular music: *He used to play in a band.*
2 a group of people who do something together or who share a particular feature: *a band of outlaws*
3 a range of values, prices etc in a system for measuring or organizing something: *students in the age band 11 to 14*
4 a flat narrow piece of something in the shape of a ring: *She wore a band around her hair.* ♦ *a rubber band*
5 a line of something such as colour or light: *The male bird has a brown band across its chest.*

> **Band** can be used with a singular or plural verb when it refers to musicians. You can say *The band was playing* OR *The band were playing.*

bandage /'bændɪdʒ/ noun [C/U] a long thin piece of cloth that is wrapped around an injured part of the body —**bandage** verb [T]

banding /'bændɪŋ/ noun [U] EDUCATION a system of putting students into groups according to their ability, so that students of different abilities are taught together

bandit /'bændɪt/ noun [C] a member of a group of thieves who attack people while they are travelling

bandwagon /'bænd,wægən/ noun [C] an idea or activity that suddenly becomes very popular
PHRASE **climb/jump on the bandwagon** *showing disapproval* to start to do something that other people are doing because it is popular or successful

bandwidth /'bænd,wɪdθ/ noun [C/U] COMPUTING the amount of data that can be sent each second through an Internet connection. A **broadband** connection has high bandwidth, and allows data to be sent at speeds of up to 1 MB per second.

bang¹ /bæŋ/ verb **1** [T] to hit or move something with a lot of force, making a loud noise: *We could hear them banging their drums.* ♦ *She banged her fist on the table.* **2** [I] to move with a lot of force, making a loud noise: *We heard a door bang.* **3** [I/T] to knock against something when you are moving: *Be careful not to bang your head.*

bang² /bæŋ/ noun [C] **1** a short loud noise, for example the sound of a door closing with a lot of force **2** a knock or hit on a part of your body: *a bang on the head*

bangle /'bæŋg(ə)l/ noun [C] a stiff circular **bracelet** (=jewellery worn around the wrist)

banish /'bænɪʃ/ verb [T] **1** to officially order someone to leave a place or a country as a punishment: *The king had banished him from the land.* **2** to make someone stop thinking about something or having particular feelings

banister /'bænɪstə/ noun [C] a structure like a fence along the edge of stairs

banisters /'bænɪstəz/ noun [plural] a **banister**

banjo /'bændʒəʊ/ (plural **banjos**) noun [C] MUSIC a musical instrument like a small round guitar

bank¹ /bæŋk/ noun [C]

1 financial institution	4 large cloud
2 raised area	5 things in row
3 large collection or store	

1 a financial institution where people can keep their money, or can borrow money: *I need to go to the bank this morning.*
2 GEOGRAPHY a raised sloping area of land, for example along the side of a river: *We climbed a steep bank.*
3 a large collection or store of something: *a blood bank*
4 a large mass of cloud or **fog**

5 a large number of things in a row, especially pieces of equipment: *a bank of TV monitors*

bank² /bæŋk/ verb **1** [I] to have a bank account with a particular bank: *Who do they bank with?* **2** [T] to put money into a bank account **3** [I] if a plane banks, it turns quickly in the air, with one wing higher than the other
PHRASAL VERB **'bank on sb/sth** to depend on someone doing something or on something happening

'bank ac,count noun [C] an arrangement with a bank that allows someone to keep their money there

'bank ,balance noun [C] the amount of money in your bank account

'bank ,card noun [C] a small plastic card that people use for making payments or for getting money from a bank

'bank ,draft noun [C] a cheque that is paid directly by a bank, rather than by money from a person's **bank account**

banker /'bæŋkə/ noun [C] someone who has an important position in a bank

,bank 'holiday noun [C] a public holiday when shops and businesses may be closed

banking /'bæŋkɪŋ/ noun [U] the work done by banks

banknote /'bæŋk,nəʊt/ noun [C] a piece of paper money

'bank ,rate noun [C] ECONOMICS the rate of interest that banks use to calculate how much to charge when they lend money to other banks → BASE RATE

bankrupt¹ /'bæŋkrʌpt/ adj a person or business that is bankrupt has officially admitted that they have no money and cannot pay what they owe

bankrupt² /'bæŋkrʌpt/ verb [T] to make a person or business bankrupt or very poor

bankruptcy /'bæŋkrʌptsi/ (plural **bankruptcies**) noun [C/U] a situation in which a person or business becomes bankrupt

banner /'bænə/ noun [C] **1** a wide piece of cloth with a message on it **2** COMPUTING an advertisement across a **website**

'banner ,ad noun [C] BUSINESS an advertisement that appears across the full width of a page or **web page**

,banner 'headline noun [C] a very large **headline** on the front of a newspaper

banquet /'bæŋkwɪt/ noun [C] a formal meal for a large number of people

banter /'bæntə/ noun [U] friendly conversation in which people make jokes about each other

banyan /'bænjən/ noun [C/U] a tree that grows in tropical regions of India. Banyans produce new roots from their branches, and these roots grow into the ground and become new **trunks**.

baobab /'beɪəbæb/ noun [C] a tree that grows in tropical regions of Africa and north-western Australia. Baobabs have a short thick **trunk** and produce large fruit that can be eaten.

baptism /'bæp,tɪz(ə)m/ noun [C/U] RELIGION a ceremony in which someone, usually a baby, is covered or touched with water in order to welcome them into the Christian religion —**baptize** /,bæp'taɪz/ verb [T]

Baptist /'bæptɪst/ noun [C] RELIGION a member of a Protestant religious group that believes that only adults should be baptized

bar¹ /bɑː/ noun

1 place serving alcohol	**7** on computer
2 surface for drinks	**8** layer of sand, mud etc
3 piece of metal	**9** unit of air pressure
4 block of sth solid	**10** in law
5 sth that prevents	**+ PHRASE**
6 in music	

1 [C] a place where people go to buy and drink alcoholic drinks
2 [C] the **counter** where alcoholic drinks are served
3 [C] a long narrow piece of metal: *an old house with iron bars on the windows*
4 [C] a solid block of a substance: *a bar of soap ♦ a chocolate bar*
5 [C] something that prevents another thing from happening: *The fact that you are a woman should not be a bar to success.*
6 [C] **MUSIC** one of the sections in a line of music
7 [C] **COMPUTING** a long narrow shape along one of the sides or along the top and bottom of a window on a computer screen: *a scroll bar*
8 [C] **GEOLOGY** a layer of sand, mud etc, usually a long thin one, that forms in a river, sea, or lake and makes the water more shallow
9 [C] **PHYSICS** a unit for measuring air pressure
10 the bar [singular] **LAW** the profession of being a **barrister**
PHRASE behind bars in prison

bar² /bɑː/ (**bars, barring, barred**) verb [T] **1** to officially say that something is not allowed: *The new rule bars the export of live animals.* **2** to put something across a door or window so that no one can get through it

barb /bɑːb/ noun [C] **BIOLOGY** one of the thin fibres that stick out from the **shaft** (=the main central part) of a feather

barbarian /bɑːˈbeəriən/ noun [C] someone who does not respect culture or who is extremely violent and cruel

barbaric /bɑːˈbærɪk/ adj extremely violent and cruel

barbecue /ˈbɑːbɪˌkjuː/ noun [C] **1** a meal at which food is cooked and eaten outside **2** a piece of equipment used for cooking food outside —**barbecue** verb [T]

barbed wire /ˌbɑːbd ˈwaɪə/ noun [U] thick wire with a lot of sharp points sticking out of it

barbell /ˈbɑːˌbel/ noun [C] **SPORTS** a long metal bar with weights at each end. People lift it in order to make their muscles stronger.

barber /ˈbɑːbə/ noun [C] someone whose job is to cut men's hair

barbiturate /bɑːˈbɪtʃərət/ noun [C] **HEALTH** a strong drug that can make people calm or help them to sleep

bar ,chart noun [C] **MATHS** a graph that represents amounts as thick lines of different lengths —*picture* → CHART

bar ,code noun [C] **COMPUTING** a set of printed lines on a product that gives a computer information about it such as its price

bare /beə/ adj **1** not covered by any clothes **2** a bare surface has nothing on it **3** basic, with nothing extra: *the bare essentials like food and clothing*
PHRASE with your bare hands without using any equipment or weapons

bare fallowing /ˌbeə ˈfæləʊɪŋ/ noun [U]
AGRICULTURE the practice of leaving land with nothing planted on it for a time. This allows air to get into the soil, and nutrients that have been used up by plant growth to be put back.

barefoot /ˈbeəˌfʊt/ adj, adv without any shoes or socks on

bare-'knuckle or **bare-knuckled** /ˌbeə ˈnʌk(ə)ld/ adj **1** used for describing situations in which people compete very hard to win and are willing to break rules or behave unfairly **2** a bare-knuckle fight is a fight between people who hit each other with their bare **fists**, without wearing gloves

barely /ˈbeəli/ adv **1** used for saying that something only just happens or exists, or is only just possible= HARDLY, SCARCELY: *He could barely stand. ♦ The roads were barely wide enough for two cars to pass.* **2** used for emphasizing that something happened a very short time before something else: *Roy had barely left the room before they started to laugh.* **3** used for emphasizing how small an amount is: *He's barely 12 years old.*

bargain¹ /ˈbɑːgɪn/ noun [C] **1** something that someone buys that costs much less than normal: *Her dress was a real bargain.* **2** an agreement in which each person or group promises something

bargain² /ˈbɑːgɪn/ verb [I] to try to persuade someone to agree to a price or deal that is better for you
PHRASAL VERB 'bargain ,on sth to expect something to happen, often because something else depends on it

bargaining counter /ˈbɑːgənɪŋ ˌkaʊntə/ noun [C] something that you can use to persuade someone to give you what you want

barge /bɑːdʒ/ noun [C] a long flat boat that is used on rivers and canals

'barge ,board noun [C] **CONSTRUCTION** a board that hides and protects the **gable end** (=triangular part on end wall) of a roof

'bar ,graph noun [C] **MATHS** a **bar chart**

baritone /ˈbærɪˌtəʊn/ noun [C] **MUSIC** a fairly deep male singing voice, between a **tenor** and a **bass**, or a man who sings with this type of voice

barium /ˈbeəriəm/ noun [U] **CHEMISTRY** a soft metal element that is a silver-white colour, used in **alloys**. Chemical symbol: **Ba**

,barium 'meal noun [C] **HEALTH** a substance that someone swallows before having an X-ray, which makes it possible for the X-ray to clearly photograph the throat, stomach, and intestines

bark¹ /bɑːk/ verb **1** [I] to make the short loud sound that a dog makes **2 bark** or **bark out** [I/T] to say or shout something in a loud angry voice

bark² /bɑːk/ noun **1** [U] the hard substance that covers a tree —*picture* → TREE **2** [C] the short loud sound that a dog makes

'bark ,cloth noun [U] a type of cloth made from the inner bark of various trees, used in Indonesia, Malaysia, and the Pacific Islands

barley /ˈbɑːli/ noun [U] **AGRICULTURE** a plant that is a type of grass that produces grain. The grain is used for making flour, beer, and whisky. —*picture* → CEREAL

'bar ,line noun [C] **MUSIC** in printed music, an upright line that separates the bars of a piece of music —*picture* → MUSIC

'bar ,magnet noun [C] **PHYSICS** a magnet in the shape of a long narrow rectangle

barman /ˈbɑːmən/ (plural **barmen** /ˈbɑːmən/) noun [C] a man who serves drinks in a bar

bar mitzvah /ˌbɑː ˈmɪtsvə/ noun [C] **RELIGION** a Jewish ceremony held when a boy is 13, after which he is considered to be an adult in his religious life

barn /bɑːn/ noun [C] a large building on a farm where animals, crops, or machines are kept

barnacle /ˈbɑːnək(ə)l/ noun [C] **BIOLOGY** a small invertebrate sea animal that sticks firmly to rocks and to the bottoms of ships

barnstorming /ˈbɑːnˌstɔːmɪŋ/ adj done with impressive energy, skill, and enthusiasm

barometer /bəˈrɒmɪtə/ noun [C] **GEOGRAPHY** a piece of equipment that measures **atmospheric pressure** (=pressure in the air) and tells you what kind of weather to expect

baron /ˈbærən/ noun [C] **1** a male member of the highest social class in some countries. A baron is of a low rank. **2** a powerful person in a particular type of business

baroque /bəˈrɒk/ adj **ARTS**, **MUSIC** relating to the very detailed style of art, building, or music that was popular in Europe in the 17th and early 18th centuries

barrack /ˈbærək/ verb [I/T] to shout at someone who is speaking, playing, or performing in public because you do not like them = HECKLE

barracks /ˈbærəks/ noun [plural] a group of buildings where members of the armed forces live and work

barracuda /ˌbærəˈkjuːdə/ noun [C] a large tropical sea fish with sharp teeth and a lower jaw that sticks out

barrage /ˈbærɑːʒ/ noun **1** [singular] a lot of criticisms, complaints, or questions that are directed at someone **2** [C] a long continuous attack of guns or bombs

barrel /ˈbærəl/ noun [C] **1** a large round container with a flat top and bottom, used for storing liquids **2** the part of a gun that a bullet is fired through **3** a unit for measuring **crude oil**: *The region's oil production has reached 2 million barrels a day.* **4** **SCIENCE** the long tube that sends the mixture of **flammable** gas and air to the mouth of a **Bunsen burner**

barren /ˈbærən/ adj barren land is dry or frozen and plants cannot grow there

barricade /ˌbærɪˈkeɪd/ noun [C] a temporary structure that is built across a road, gate, or door to prevent people from getting through

barrier /ˈbæriə/ noun [C] **1** a structure that stops people or vehicles from entering a place: *Fans broke through the barriers and rushed onto the pitch.* **2** something that prevents progress or makes it difficult for people to communicate or achieve an aim = OBSTACLE: *High levels of debt are a major barrier to economic development.* **3** something that separates one thing from another: *The coral reef provides a natural barrier between the land and the open sea.*

'barrier ˌmethod noun [C] **HEALTH** a form of contraception in which an object is used to physically reduce the possibility of the sperm getting into the vagina during sex. The use of **condoms** is a barrier method.

ˌbarrier 'reef noun [C] **GEOGRAPHY** a large long mass of **coral** in the sea, not far from land

barring /ˈbɑːrɪŋ/ preposition unless the thing mentioned happens or exists

barrister /ˈbærɪstə/ noun [C] **LAW** in English law, a lawyer who is allowed to speak in the higher law courts

barter /ˈbɑːtə/ verb [I/T] to exchange goods or services for other goods or services instead of using money —**barter** noun [U]

basal /ˈbeɪs(ə)l/ adj **BIOLOGY** at or forming the bottom of something

ˌbasal 'cell ˌlayer noun [singular] **BIOLOGY** a layer of cells at the base of the **epidermis** where **mitosis** (=cell division) takes place and new skin cells are produced

ˌbasal metaˈbolic ˌrate noun [C] **BIOLOGY** see **BMR**

basalt /ˈbæsɔːlt/ noun [U] **GEOLOGY** a dark-green or black rock formed when hot liquid rock from a volcano becomes solid. It is a type of igneous rock.

base¹ /beɪs/ noun [C]

1 lowest part	**5** number
2 place for soldiers	**6** ideas etc to start from
3 place for doing sth	**7** in baseball
4 chemical	**8** part of transistor

1 the bottom part, edge, or surface of something: *The pituitary gland is at the base of the brain.*
2 a place where members of the armed forces live and work: *a US naval base*
3 a place from which an activity can be planned, started, or carried out: *Climbers find this a convenient base for their mountain expeditions.*
4 **CHEMISTRY** a chemical substance that turns red litmus paper blue. All alkalis are bases.
5 **MATHS** a number that is used to form a system of counting. The usual system of counting uses base 10, and the **binary system** used in computers uses base 2.
6 a set of ideas, facts, achievements etc from which something can develop: *The company lacks a strong financial base.*
7 **SPORTS** one of the four places on a baseball or **rounders** field that a player must touch in order to score points
8 **PHYSICS** the part of a transistor that separates the **emitter** from the **collector**

base² /beɪs/ verb if someone is based in a place, that place is their main office or main place of work, or the place where they live: *Where are you based now?*
  PHRASAL VERB ˌbase sth 'on sth **1** to use particular ideas or facts to make a decision, do a calculation, or develop a theory: *Her theories are based largely on personal experience.* **2** to use something as a model for a film, piece of writing, or work of art: *The film is based on a true story.*

baseball /ˈbeɪsˌbɔːl/ noun [U] **SPORTS** a game played by two teams of nine players who score points by hitting a ball with a bat and then running around four bases

'base ˌboard noun [C] **CONSTRUCTION** a wooden board that supports the **base plates** of **scaffolding** on soft or uneven ground

'base ˌcurrency noun [C] **BUSINESS** a currency that a business uses in its accounts and for buying and selling

base jumping or **BASE jumping** /ˈbeɪs ˌdʒʌmpɪŋ/ noun [U] the sport of jumping with a **parachute** from high places such as buildings or mountains

baseline /ˈbeɪsˌlaɪn/ noun [C] **1** a quantity, value, or fact used as a standard for measuring other quantities, values, or facts **2** **SPORTS** the line that marks the back of the playing area in games such as tennis

basement /ˈbeɪsmənt/ noun [C] the part of a building below the level of the ground

ˌbase 'metal noun [C] a common metal that is not worth a lot of money, such as iron or lead → PRECIOUS METAL

'base ˌplate noun [C] **CONSTRUCTION** a piece of square metal that fits onto the end of a vertical piece of **scaffolding** in order to spread the weight

'base ˌrate noun [C] **ECONOMICS** the rate of interest that banks use to calculate how much interest to charge on money they lend to their customers → BANK RATE

bases 1 the plural of **basis 2** the plural of **base**[1]

bashful /ˈbæʃf(ə)l/ adj easily embarrassed when you are with other people = SHY —**bashfully** adv

basic /ˈbeɪsɪk/ adj **1** forming the main or most important part or aspect of something: *Rice is the basic ingredient of the dish.* ♦ *First you need to understand the basic principles of computers.* **2** simple, with nothing special or extra: *The state provides only basic health care.* **3** CHEMISTRY consisting of a chemical base

BASIC /ˈbeɪsɪk/ noun [U] COMPUTING a type of language for writing computer programs

basically /ˈbeɪsɪkli/ adv in the most important aspects, without thinking about the specific details: *The book is basically a love story.*

the basics /ˈbeɪsɪks/ noun [plural] the most important aspects or principles of something: **The basics of** the *game can be learned very quickly.*

basil /ˈbæz(ə)l/ noun [U] a plant with sweet leaves that are used in salads and cooking

basilect /ˈbæzɪlekt/ noun [C] LANGUAGE a **dialect** (=way of speaking a language) that is considered lower in status than other dialects

basilica /bəˈzɪlɪkə/ noun [C] **1** a large long ancient Roman building that has a round end **2** RELIGION a large important Roman Catholic church

basin /ˈbeɪs(ə)n/ noun [C] **1** a round open container that is used for holding liquids or for storing or mixing food **2** a large bowl fixed to the wall in a bathroom for washing your face and hands in **3** GEOGRAPHY a large area of land from which water flows into a particular river or lake: *the Lake Turkana basin* **4** GEOGRAPHY a large area of the Earth's surface that is lower than the surrounding area

'basin-,shaped adj having steep sides and a wide curved bottom

basis /ˈbeɪsɪs/ (plural **bases** /ˈbeɪsiːz/) noun [C] **1** a particular method or system that is used for doing or organizing something: *She looks after her younger sisters* **on a regular basis**. **2** the reason why something is done: *Don't make your decision* **on the basis of** *cost alone.* **3** the important ideas, facts, or actions from which something can develop = FOUNDATION: *The agreement provides the* **basis for** *future negotiations.*

bask /bɑːsk/ verb [I] **1** to relax and enjoy yourself by lying in the sun **2** to enjoy people's attention and approval

basket /ˈbɑːskɪt/ noun [C] **1** a container for carrying or keeping things in, made from thin pieces of plastic, wire, or wood woven together: *a laundry basket* ♦ *a* **basket of** *food* **2** SPORTS the net that you throw the ball through in basketball, or a point scored by throwing the ball through it **3** ECONOMICS a group of currencies that is used for comparing the value of another currency

basketball /ˈbɑːskɪtbɔːl/ noun [U] SPORTS a game played by two teams of five players who score points by throwing a ball through a net

basketry /ˈbɑːskɪtri/ noun [U] the art of weaving baskets

basophil /ˈbeɪsəfɪl/ noun [C] ANATOMY a white blood cell with **granules** that are easily coloured by **basic** (=alkaline) dyes

bas-relief /ˌbɑː rɪˈliːf/ noun ARTS **1** [U] a style of **sculpture** in which the artist forms shapes in stone, clay, metal etc, so that they stick out slightly from their background **2** [C] a piece of art in this style

bass /beɪs/ noun MUSIC **1** [C/U] the lowest male singing voice, or a man who sings with this type of voice **2** [U] the lower half of the full range of musical notes → TREBLE[1] sense 2 **3 bass** or **bass guitar** [C] a **bass guitar 4** [C] a **double bass** —**bass** adj

bass clef /ˌbeɪs ˈklef/ noun [C] MUSIC the symbol ᛞ used at the beginning of a line of music to show that a note on the fourth line from the bottom represents F, a **fifth** below **middle C** → TREBLE CLEF —*picture* → MUSIC

bass guitar /ˌbeɪs ɡɪˈtɑː/ noun [C] MUSIC an electric guitar that produces very low notes

bassoon /bəˈsuːn/ noun [C] MUSIC a musical instrument consisting of a long wooden tube that you hold upright and play by blowing into a thin metal pipe —*picture* → MUSICAL INSTRUMENT, ORCHESTRA

bastard /ˈbɑːstəd/ noun [C] *offensive* **1** an insulting word for an unpleasant or annoying man **2** *old-fashioned* someone whose parents are not married to each other

bastion /ˈbæstiən/ noun [C] **1** an organization, community, or system that supports and defends a particular way of life, tradition, or belief **2** a place where an army has strong defences

bat[1] /bæt/ noun [C] **1** SPORTS a wooden object used for hitting the ball in games such as baseball, **cricket**, and **table tennis 2** a small mammal that flies at night and looks like a mouse with large wings —*picture* → MAMMAL **3** CONSTRUCTION a brick that is cut across its width

bat[2] /bæt/ (**bats, batting, batted**) verb [I] SPORTS to try to hit the ball with a bat in a game such as baseball or **cricket**

batch /bætʃ/ noun [C] **1** a quantity of people or things that arrive, are made, or are dealt with at the same time: *a batch of cakes* **2** COMPUTING a series of jobs that a computer does as a set

'batch ,file noun [C] COMPUTING a file containing a series of instructions that the computer will perform in order, without the user having to do anything

'batch ,processing noun [U] COMPUTING a system of computer **processing** in which data is collected and then the program is run without the user being able to give instructions while it is in progress

bath[1] /bɑːθ/ (plural **baths** /bɑːðz/) noun [C] **1** a long deep container that you fill with water and wash yourself in **2** the process of washing your whole body, or the body of an animal, or another person, especially in a bath: *Have I got time to* **have a bath**? **3 baths** [plural] a building containing a **swimming pool**

bath[2] /bɑːθ/ verb [I/T] to wash yourself or someone else in a bath

bathe /beɪð/ verb **1** [T] to cover a part of your body with a liquid, especially in order to clean or put medicine on a cut **2** [I] *old-fashioned* to swim in a river or lake, or in the sea

bathos /ˈbeɪθɒs/ noun [U] LITERATURE a sudden change in speech or writing from a serious or important subject to one that is silly or ordinary

bathrobe /ˈbɑːθˌrəʊb/ noun [C] a loose piece of clothing like a soft coat that you wear before or after taking a bath or shower

bathroom /ˈbɑːθˌruːm/ noun [C] a room containing a bath or shower, a **washbasin**, and often a toilet

batik /bəˈtiːk, ˈbætɪk/ noun [U] a way of creating designs on cloth using **wax** and dye, or cloth made using this method

baton /'bætɒn, 'bæt(ə)n/ noun [C] **1** MUSIC a stick that the conductor of an orchestra uses **2** SPORTS a stick that a runner in a **relay** race gives to the next runner **3** a stick that a police officer can use as a weapon= TRUNCHEON

batsman /'bætsmən/ noun [C] SPORTS a player who tries to hit the ball in **cricket**

battalion /bə'tæljən/ noun [C] a large group of soldiers, usually consisting of three or more companies

batten /'bæt(ə)n/ noun [C] CONSTRUCTION a long piece of wood that is fixed to something in order to hold it in place or make it stronger

batter[1] /'bætə/ verb [I/T] to hit someone or something many times: *Huge waves battered the little ship.*

batter[2] /'bætə/ noun **1** [U] a liquid mixture of milk, flour, and eggs used in cooking. It is used to cover things before frying them or to make **pancakes**. **2** [C] SPORTS a player who is trying to hit the ball in baseball

battered /'bætəd/ adj **1** old and slightly damaged: *a battered old car* **2** having experienced a lot of problems

battering ram /'bæt(ə)rɪŋ ,ræm/ noun [C] a large heavy wooden or metal post used for breaking through gates and doors

battery /'bæt(ə)ri/ (plural **batteries**) noun [C] PHYSICS an object that fits into something such as a radio, clock, or car and supplies it with electricity. A battery consists of an **electrical cell** or a series of electrical cells. —*picture* → CIRCUIT

'battery ,pack noun [C] a type of battery used to supply electricity in electrical equipment such as **laptop** computers and video cameras

batting average /'bætɪŋ ,æv(ə)rɪdʒ/ noun [C] SPORTS the average number of points that a **cricket** player scores after playing in a number of games

battle[1] /'bæt(ə)l/ noun **1** [C/U] a fight between two armies in a war: *one of the bloodiest battles of the war* ♦ *soldiers wounded in battle* ♦ *the Battle of* Waterloo **2** [C] a situation in which people or groups compete with each other: *the battle for leadership* ♦ *a bitter legal battle* **3** [C] a situation in which someone is trying very hard to deal with something difficult: *She has lost her battle against cancer.*

battle[2] /'bæt(ə)l/ verb [I/T] to try very hard to deal with a difficult situation: *Surgeons battled to save the man's life.*

battleaxe /'bæt(ə)l,æks/ noun [C] **1** an unpleasant woman who tells people what to do in a determined and rather frightening way **2** a very large **axe** used in the past as a weapon

battlefield /'bæt(ə)l,fiːld/ or **battleground** /'bæt(ə)l,graʊnd/ noun [C] a place where a battle takes place or where one took place in the past

battlements /'bæt(ə)lmənts/ noun [plural] a wall around the top of a castle, with spaces through which weapons could be fired —*picture* → CASTLE

battleship /'bæt(ə)l,ʃɪp/ noun [C] the largest type of **warship**

baud /bɔːd/ noun [C] COMPUTING a unit for measuring the speed at which information is sent to or from a computer

baulk /bɔːk/ verb [I] to refuse to do something or let something happen: *He baulked at admitting he had done anything wrong.*

bauxite /'bɔːksaɪt/ noun [U] CHEMISTRY, GEOLOGY an ore from which aluminium is obtained. Bauxite is found in many parts of Africa, South America, and the Caribbean.

bawl /bɔːl/ verb **1** [I/T] to shout in a loud angry way **2** [I] to cry loudly

bay /beɪ/ noun [C] **1** GEOGRAPHY an area of the coast where the land curves inwards **2** an area in a building or vehicle that is used for a particular purpose: *a loading bay*

PHRASE **keep/hold sth at bay** to prevent something serious, dangerous, or unpleasant from affecting you

bayonet /'beɪənɪt/ noun [C] a long sharp blade that is fixed onto the end of a rifle

bazaar /bə'zɑː/ noun [C] a market, especially in the Middle East and South Asia

the BBC /,biː biː 'siː/ the British Broadcasting Corporation: an organization that broadcasts television and radio programmes and is owned by the British government

BC /,biː 'siː/ abbrev before Christ: used after a date to show that it refers to a time before the birth of Jesus Christ → AD, BCE

bcc abbrev used in an email for saying that a copy of the email is being sent to the person mentioned, but that the person that the email is being sent to is not being told that this person is being sent a copy

BCE /,biː siː 'iː/ abbrev before the Common Era: used especially by non-Christians after a date to show that it refers to a time before the birth of Jesus Christ

BCG /,biː siː 'dʒiː/ noun [singular/U] HEALTH a **vaccine** that is used to prevent **tuberculosis**

BDC abbrev ENGINEERING **bottom dead centre** in an engine

be /*strong* biː, *weak* bi/ verb

1 in progressive verb	**4** in descriptions
2 in passive verb	**5** defining behaviour
3 in future verb	**+** PHRASES

Be can have many different forms depending on its subject and on its tense:
present tense I **am**
he/she/it **is**
we/you/they **are**
past tense I/he/she/it **was**
we/you/they **were**
past participle **been**
present participle **being**

1 [auxiliary verb] used with a present participle for describing an action that is still happening or continuing: *I am studying English Literature.*

2 [auxiliary verb] used with a past participle for forming the passive form of a verb: *Her husband was killed in a car accident.*

3 [auxiliary verb] used with a present participle for talking about something that will happen in the future: *She's flying to Mumbai tomorrow morning.*

4 [linking verb] used for giving information about someone or something, for example their name, job, or position: *Our teacher is Miss Tiwana.* ♦ *He wants to be an actor.* ♦ *It was a very hot day.*

5 [linking verb] used for saying how someone behaves, or for telling them how to behave: *They are being very silly.* ♦ *Be quiet!*

PHRASES **have been to...** used for saying that someone has gone to a place and returned: *Have you ever been to Egypt?*

there is/are used for saying that someone or something exists, happens, or can be found: *There is a problem with the car.* ♦ *How many people were there at the party?*

types of beam

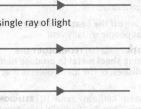

single ray of light

parallel beam of light

diverging beam
(rays spreading out from a source)

converging beam
(rays coming together)

effects of different types of material on light

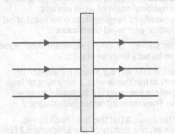

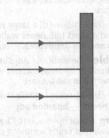

transparent materials
(e.g. clear glass, plastic wrap):
allow light to pass through completely

translucent materials
(e.g. tracing paper, grease paper,
frosted glass):
only allow some light to pass through

opaque materials
(e.g. wood, metal):
block the passage of light

beam

beach /biːtʃ/ noun [C] GEOGRAPHY an area of sand or small stones beside the sea or a lake → SHORE — picture → BACKWASH

beacon /ˈbiːkən/ noun [C] a bright light that is used as a signal to warn people or to show them the way somewhere

bead /biːd/ noun [C] **1** a small round piece of plastic, glass, metal etc that is used for making jewellery: *a string of beads* **2** a small drop of blood or sweat

beaded /ˈbiːdɪd/ adj **1** decorated with beads **2** covered in small drops of a liquid

beady /ˈbiːdi/ (**beadier, beadiest**) adj beady eyes are small, round, and bright
PHRASE **have/keep your beady eye on sb** to watch someone very closely and carefully

beak /biːk/ noun [C] the hard curved or pointed part of a bird's mouth —*picture* → BIRD

beaker /ˈbiːkə/ noun [C] **1** SCIENCE a glass or plastic container with straight sides, used in a laboratory — *picture* → LABORATORY **2** a plastic cup with straight sides

beam¹ /biːm/ noun [C] **1** a long thick piece of wood, metal, or concrete that supports a roof **2** PHYSICS a line of light or other form of energy: *a laser beam* **3** SPORTS a wooden bar used for physical exercise in a **gym**

beam² /biːm/ verb **1** [I] to have a big smile on your face because you are very happy **2** [I/T] to send out light, heat, or radio or television signals

'beam ,axle noun [C] ENGINEERING a **suspension** system in a vehicle consisting of a metal bar with a wheel on either end

'beam ,balance noun [C] PHYSICS a piece of equipment used for finding the mass of things, consisting of a bar with a small dish at each end

bean /biːn/ noun [C] **1** a seed of various plants that is cooked and eaten, or a plant that produces these seeds **2** a dried bean that is made into a powder and used to make drinks such as coffee and **cocoa**

'bean ,sprouts noun [plural] the young stems growing from the seeds of a bean plant that are eaten as food

bear¹ /beə/ (**bears, bearing, bore** /bɔː/, **borne** /bɔːn/) verb [T]

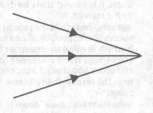

1 (not) like sb/sth	6 give birth to
2 accept bad situation	7 make fruit/flowers
3 have a quality	8 of wind/air/water
4 have words/title/	+ PHRASES
name	+ PHRASAL VERBS
5 support weight	

1 if you cannot bear someone or something, you do not like them at all or cannot accept them: *Most of her friends can't bear her brother.* ♦ *Sue **can't bear to be** parted from her mother.*
2 to accept a difficult or unpleasant situation, especially without complaining: *She bore all her suffering with incredible patience.*
3 to seem to be a particular kind of thing or to have particular qualities: *His description **bore no relation to** reality.*
4 *formal* if something bears writing or a design, it has writing or a design on it
5 to support the weight of something: *The floorboards could not **bear the weight** of the piano.*
6 *formal* to give birth to a child

7 if a plant bears flowers or fruit, it produces them
8 *formal* if something is borne along by wind, air, or water, it is moved along by it: *The logs are borne along by the current.*

PHRASES **bear fruit** if a plan or effort bears fruit, it is successful, especially after a long period of time
bear sth in mind to remember to think about something: *When you speak to Lee, bear in mind he's still upset about what happened.*
bear the responsibility/blame to be responsible for something

PHRASAL VERBS **bear 'down** to move quickly towards someone or something in a determined and threatening way: *I could see a police car bearing down on us.*
bear sb/sth 'out to show that someone is telling the truth or that something is true: *Scientific evidence bears out the claim that stress and disease are linked.*
bear 'up to behave in a brave way in a very sad or difficult situation: *Let's see how he bears up under the pressure.*

bear² /beə/ noun [C] a large wild mammal with thick fur and a short tail. Bears walk on the flat part of their **paws** and are **omnivores**. —*picture* → MAMMAL

bearable /'beərəb(ə)l/ adj something that is bearable is difficult or unpleasant, but you are able to accept or deal with it ≠ UNBEARABLE

beard /bɪəd/ noun [C] hair that grows on a man's chin and cheeks —**bearded** adj

bearing /'beərɪŋ/ noun [C] **1** PHYSICS a part of a machine that holds a moving part → BALL BEARING **2** GEOGRAPHY an exact position, usually measured from north

PHRASE **have some/no bearing on sth** to be relevant or not relevant to something

'bearing ,capacity noun [C] CONSTRUCTION the ability of soil to support the weight that is put on it

'bear ,market noun [C] BUSINESS a situation in which the prices of shares are falling → BULL MARKET

beast /biːst/ noun [C] an animal, especially a dangerous or strange one

beat¹ /biːt/ (**beats, beating, beat, beaten** /'biːt(ə)n/) verb

1 defeat sb	5 be better than sth
2 hit sb often	6 of wings
3 hit sth often	7 mix foods well
4 of heart	+ PHRASAL VERBS

1 [T] to defeat someone in a game, competition, election, or battle: *Nigeria needed to beat Cameroon to get to the final.*
2 [T] to hit someone violently several times: *The two men had been beaten to death.*
3 [I/T] to hit something many times or for a long period of time: *The rain was beating against the windows.*
4 [I] if someone's heart beats, it makes regular sounds and movements: *Exercise makes the heart beat faster.*
5 [T] *informal* to be better than something else: *I like the school holidays – it beats getting up early every day.*
6 [I/T] if a bird or insect beats its wings, or if its wings beat, it hits them together several times
7 [T] to mix foods together using a fork or a special tool or machine

PHRASAL VERBS **beat 'down** if the sun beats down, it shines very brightly
beat sb 'up *informal* to hurt someone by hitting or kicking them many times

beat² /biːt/ noun **1** [C] the regular sound or movement of the heart: *I could feel the beat of his heart.*
2 [singular] MUSIC the main pattern of regular strong sounds in a piece of music: *music with a slow beat*
3 [singular] a single regular sound, or a series of regular sounds, especially of two things hitting together: *the beat of a drum*

beaten /'biːt(ə)n/ adj **off the beaten track** far away from the places that people usually visit

,beaten 'metalwork noun [U] TECHNOLOGY the process of hammering **sheet metal** to produce items such as **trays** and dishes, or the metal objects that are produced

beatification /bi,ætɪfɪ'keɪʃ(ə)n/ noun [U] RELIGION in the Roman Catholic Church, an official statement that someone who has died was an especially good or holy person —**beatify** /bi'ætɪˌfaɪ/ verb [T]

beating /'biːtɪŋ/ noun [C] an act of hitting someone hard a number of times in a fight or as a punishment

the Beaufort scale /'bəʊfət ˌskeɪl/ noun [singular] SCIENCE an international scale of wind speeds represented by numbers ranging from o for least wind (calm) to 12 for strongest wind (**hurricane**)

beautician /bjuː'tɪʃ(ə)n/ noun [C] someone whose job is to give people beauty treatments

beautiful /'bjuːtəf(ə)l/ adj **1** a beautiful woman or child is extremely attractive ≠ UGLY **2** very nice to look at, hear, or experience = LOVELY: *a beautiful song* —**beautifully** adv: *They were all beautifully dressed.*

beauty¹ /'bjuːti/ noun **1** [U] the quality of being beautiful to look at: *the beauty of the landscape* **2** [C] a beautiful woman **3** [U] a quality of something that gives you pleasure: *the beauty of her poetry*

beauty² /'bjuːti/ adj designed to make people look more beautiful: *beauty products*

'beauty ,contest noun [C] a competition for women in which judges decide who are the most beautiful

beauty salon /'bjuːti ˌsælɒn/ noun [C] a place where you can have your hair cut, or have other beauty treatments for your skin or hair

'beauty ,spot noun [C] a beautiful place in the countryside that attracts tourists

beaver /'biːvə/ noun [C] a small mammal that has a wide flat tail, thick fur, and sharp teeth which it uses to cut down trees. It uses the wood from these trees to build **dams** across rivers. Beavers are **native** to North America, Europe, and Asia.

becalmed /bɪ'kɑːmd/ adj if a sailing boat is becalmed, it cannot move because there is no wind

became /bɪ'keɪm/ the past tense of **become**

because /bɪ'kɒz/ conjunction used for giving the reason for something: *I couldn't phone you because I hadn't got your number.* ♦ *Our profits fell because of the recession.*

beckon /'bekən/ verb [I/T] **1** to signal to someone to come towards you **2** to seem to be an attractive possibility to someone: *A bright future beckoned.*

become /bɪ'kʌm/ (**becomes, becoming, became** /bɪ'keɪm/, **become**) linking verb to change and start to be something different: *The sky became dark.*
♦ *People were becoming increasingly angry about the delay.* ♦ *Christine decided to become a writer.*
PHRASE **what has/will become of** used for asking what has happened to someone or something, or what will happen to them: *If she is sent to prison, what will become of her children?*

becquerel /'bekərəl/ noun [C] PHYSICS a unit for measuring radioactivity. Symbol Bq

bed¹ /bed/ noun

1 for sleeping on	4 for plants
2 at bottom of sea	5 bottom of brick
3 area of river/sea	+ PHRASES

1 [C/U] a piece of furniture that you sleep on: *The room had two beds in it.* ♦ *It's midnight – why aren't you in bed?*
2 [C] GEOGRAPHY the ground at the bottom of a sea or river: *fish that live close to the sea bed*
3 [C] GEOGRAPHY an area in a river, lake, or sea where there are a lot of plants or animals of a particular kind: *reed beds*
4 [C] an area of ground that has been prepared for growing plants in → FLOWERBED
5 [C] CONSTRUCTION the bottom of a brick when it is laid in a row

PHRASES **bed and board** TOURISM a hotel charge that includes all meals as well as the room charge
bed and breakfast 1 TOURISM the service of providing a room for the night and a meal the next morning **2** TOURISM a small hotel or private house that provides this service

bed² /bed/ (**beds, bedding, bedded**) verb [T] **1** to put something firmly into a base or into the ground = EMBED **2** CONSTRUCTION to lay bricks in rows

bedbug /'bed,bʌg/ noun [C] an insect with a flat round body and no wings that feeds on the blood of humans, especially when they are in bed

bedclothes /'bed,kləʊðz/ noun [plural] sheets and covers that are used on beds

bedding /'bedɪŋ/ noun [U] sheets and covers that are used on beds

'bed joint noun [C] CONSTRUCTION the horizontal joint between rows of bricks that is filled with **mortar**

bedlam /'bedləm/ noun [U] a noisy and confusing place or situation

bedlinen /'bed,lɪnɪn/ noun [U] sheets and **pillowcases** (=covers for pillows)

bednet /'bed,net/ noun [C] HEALTH a type of net that is hung over a bed to keep out mosquitos and other insects

bedraggled /bɪ'dræg(ə)ld/ adj wet, dirty, and untidy

bedridden /'bed,rɪd(ə)n/ adj someone who is bedridden is unable to get out of bed because they are too ill

bedrock /'bed,rɒk/ noun [singular] **1** GEOLOGY the solid rock under the ground that supports the soil above it —*picture* → FLOOD PLAIN **2** the principles on which a system is based

bedroom /'bedruːm/ noun [C] a room that you sleep in

bedside /'bedsaɪd/ noun [singular] the area near your bed

bedsore /'bed,sɔː/ noun [C] HEALTH a red painful area on the skin that people get from lying in one position in bed for a long time

bedspread /'bed,spred/ noun [C] a top cover for a bed

bedstead /'bed,sted/ noun [C] the wooden or metal frame of a bed

bee /biː/ noun [C] a flying insect that has a black and yellow body and lives in groups. Bees make **honey** and **wax**. —*picture* → INSECT

beech /biːtʃ/ noun **1** [C/U] a large tree with smooth grey **bark** and small nuts with three sides. Beech trees grow in **temperate** regions. **2** [U] the pale wood of a beech tree, used for making furniture

beef /biːf/ noun [U] the meat from a cow: *a slice of roast beef*

beefburger /'biːf,bɜːgə/ noun [C] a **burger**

beehive /'biː,haɪv/ noun [C] a large box that people keep bees in when they want to get the **honey** that the bees produce

beeline /'biː,laɪn/ noun **make a beeline for** *informal* to go towards someone or something in the quickest and most direct way

been /biːn/ the past participle of **be**

beep /biːp/ verb **1** [I] if a piece of electronic equipment beeps, it makes a short high sound **2** [I/T] if a driver beeps the horn in their car, it makes a short loud noise —**beep** noun [C]

beer /bɪə/ noun **1** [U] a yellow or brown alcoholic drink made from grain: *a bottle of beer* **2** [C] a glass or bottle of this drink: *Would you like another beer?*

beet /biːt/ noun [C/U] **sugar beet**

beetle /'biːt(ə)l/ noun [C] an insect with a pair of hard front wings that form its back. Dung beetles, ladybirds, and weevils are all beetles. —*picture* → INSECT

beetroot /'biːtruːt/ noun [C/U] a round purple vegetable that is cooked and eaten hot or cold —*picture* → VEGETABLE

before /bɪ'fɔː/ adv, conjunction, preposition **1** earlier than a particular time, event, or action: *I have to finish this essay before Friday.* ♦ *The others had got there before us.* ♦ *Won't you have another drink before you go?* ♦ *Haven't we met somewhere before?* ♦ *Don was here the day before yesterday.* **2** placed earlier than something else in a list or series: *'Barnes' comes before 'Brown' on the list.* **3** in a place that you reach as you go towards another place: *Our house is just before the end of the road.* **4** *formal* in front of someone or something: *He knelt before her.* → AGO

beforehand /bɪ'fɔː,hænd/ adv before a particular event: *You can collect your tickets for the game up to a week beforehand.*

befriend /bɪ'frend/ verb [T] to become someone's friend and treat them in a kind way

befuddled /bɪ'fʌd(ə)ld/ adj very confused and unable to think clearly

beg /beg/ (**begs, begging, begged**) verb [I/T] **1** if someone who is poor begs, they ask other people for money or food: *homeless children begging on the streets* **2** to ask for something in a way that shows you want it very much: *'Don't go!' he begged.*

began /bɪ'gæn/ the past tense of **begin**

beggar /'begə/ noun [C] someone who lives by asking people for money or food

begging letter /'begɪŋ ,letə/ noun [C] a letter asking for money, usually written by a poor person to someone they know is rich

begin /bɪ'gɪn/ (**begins, beginning, began** /bɪ'gæn/, **begun** /bɪ'gʌn/) verb **1** [I] to start happening ≠ END, FINISH: *The ceremony will begin at noon.* **2** [I/T] to start doing something, or to make an activity or process start or exist ≠ END, FINISH: *The police have already begun their investigation.* ♦ *He began shouting at them.* **3** [I] if a sentence, book etc begins with a particular letter, word etc, that is the first one in it ≠ END: *We usually use 'an' before a word that begins with a vowel.*

PHRASE **to begin with** before or during the first part of an activity: *How did you get involved to begin with?*

beginner /bɪˈɡɪnə/ noun [C] someone who has just started to learn or do something = NOVICE

be.ginner's 'luck noun [U] unusual success that you have when you start doing something new

beginning /bɪˈɡɪnɪŋ/ noun **1** [singular] the first part of something = START ≠ END: *I loved the beginning of the book but hated the rest.* ♦ *In the beginning I found it hard to concentrate.* **2 beginnings** [plural] the early stages of something that develops over a period of time: *It was a decade that saw the beginnings of the space programme.*

begrudge /bɪˈɡrʌdʒ/ verb [T] to feel annoyed with someone because they have got something that you think they do not deserve

beguiling /bɪˈɡaɪlɪŋ/ adj a beguiling person or thing seems attractive but may be dangerous = ALLURING

begun /bɪˈɡʌn/ the past participle of **begin**

behalf /bɪˈhɑːf/ noun

PHRASE **on sb's behalf** or **on behalf of sb 1** instead of someone, or as a representative of someone: *On behalf of everyone here, I'd like to thank Maria for all her hard work.* **2** in order to help someone: *I offered to speak to the teacher on his behalf.*

behave /bɪˈheɪv/ verb **1** [I] to act in a particular way: *The children behaved very badly.* ♦ *You behaved like a complete idiot!* **2** [I/T] to be polite and not cause trouble: *I hope the children behave themselves.* **3** [I] CHEMISTRY if a substance behaves in a particular way, it always produces the same chemical reaction because of its structure: *All three compounds behave differently when heated.*

behavior /bɪˈheɪvjə/ the American spelling of **behaviour**

behaviour /bɪˈheɪvjə/ noun **1** [C/U] the way that a person or animal behaves: *Anna was sick of her brother's behaviour.* **2** [U] CHEMISTRY the way that a substance reacts in particular conditions: *Scientists are studying the behaviour of the new gas.*

behavioural /bɪˈheɪvjərəl/ adj relating to the way someone behaves: *behavioural problems* — **behaviourally** adv

behead /bɪˈhed/ verb [T] to cut off someone's head as a punishment

behemoth /bɪˈhiːmɒθ/ noun [C] formal someone or something that is very large, especially a company

behind[1] /bɪˈhaɪnd/ adv, preposition

1 at the back	**5** responsible for
2 late	**6** encouraging
3 remaining	**7** in the past
4 less successful	

1 at the back of someone or something, or following them: *Some papers had fallen behind the cupboard.* ♦ *Someone grabbed me from behind.*
2 late, or too slow in doing things that you have to do: *The project is already a month behind schedule.* ♦ *I've been ill, and now I'm behind with my work.*
3 remaining in a place after people have left: *A few people stayed behind to clear up.*
4 with less success or progress than others: *Technology in Eastern Europe was at least 20 years behind the West.*
5 used for stating what the true cause of something is, or what the true facts are in a situation: *People want to know the truth behind these rumours.*
6 supporting a person, action, or idea: *I want you to know we're right behind you.*
7 in the past, and no longer affecting you: *All those bad times are behind me now.*

behind[2] /bɪˈhaɪnd/ noun [C] informal the part of your body that you sit on

behold /bɪˈhəʊld/ interjection literary used for telling someone to look at something

beholden /bɪˈhəʊld(ə)n/ adj formal feeling an obligation to do something for someone who has helped in the past

beige /beɪʒ/ adj very pale brown in colour —**beige** noun [U]

being /ˈbiːɪŋ/ noun [C] **1** a person: *We are social beings as well as individuals.* **2** a living creature: *All living beings require oxygen for respiration.*

belated /bɪˈleɪtɪd/ adj happening or arriving late: *a belated apology* —**belatedly** adv

belch /beltʃ/ verb [I] to let air from your stomach come out through your mouth in a noisy way = BURP —**belch** noun [C]

beleaguered /bɪˈliːɡəd/ adj having a lot of problems or criticism to deal with

belie /bɪˈlaɪ/ (**belies, belying, belied**) verb [T] formal to make something appear different from how it really is

belief /bɪˈliːf/ noun **1** [C] a strong feeling that something is true, real, or good: *a belief in the possibility of a perfect society* **2 beliefs** [plural] a set of ideas that you are certain are true: *Christian beliefs*

be'lief ˌsystem noun [C] SOCIAL STUDIES a shared set of beliefs and values, especially religious ones, that form a system

believable /bɪˈliːvəb(ə)l/ adj something that is believable seems possible or likely to be true = PLAUSIBLE

believe /bɪˈliːv/ verb **1** [T] to think that something is true or that someone is telling the truth: *The police didn't believe her.* ♦ *I don't believe she's his sister at all.* ♦ *It is widely believed* (=believed by a lot of people) *that the disease originally came from monkeys.* **2** [T] to have an opinion about what is true or what might happen, although there is no proof = THINK: *Scientists believe a cure for the disease will be discovered soon.* **3** [I] RELIGION to have a religious belief

PHRASAL VERB **be'lieve ˌin sb/sth 1** to think that someone or something exists: *I don't believe in miracles.* **2** to think that someone or something is good: *She used to say she didn't believe in marriage.*

> ### Word family: **believe**
> Words in the same family as **believe**
> - **belief** n
> - **disbelieve** v
> - **believable** adj
> - **unbelievably** adv
> - **believer** n
> - **disbelief** n
> - **unbelievable** adj

believer /bɪˈliːvə/ noun [C] someone who believes in a religion or a set of principles

belittle /bɪˈlɪt(ə)l/ verb [T] to say that someone or something is not very good or important

bell /bel/ noun [C] **1** a piece of equipment that makes a ringing sound, used for getting someone's attention: *I rang the bell.* **2** a metal object shaped like an upside-down cup that makes a noise when its sides are hit by a metal piece inside it: *the sound of church bells ringing*

PHRASE **bells and whistles** informal the additional features that make something attractive to use or look at

bellboy /ˈbelˌbɔɪ/ noun [C] TOURISM a man whose job is to carry people's bags to their room in a hotel

'**bell ,curve** noun [C] MATHS a line on a graph that is curved like a bell in the middle

belligerent /bəˈlɪdʒərənt/ adj 1 very unfriendly and angry= AGGRESSIVE 2 formal at war with someone — **belligerence** noun [U]

'**bell jar** noun [C] SCIENCE a piece of equipment that is made of glass and shaped like a bell. It is used to cover other equipment during scientific experiments in a laboratory and to prevent gases from escaping or entering. —picture → LABORATORY

bellow /ˈbeləʊ/ verb [I/T] to shout very loudly

belly /ˈbeli/ (plural **bellies**) noun [C] 1 the soft lower part of an animal's body 2 informal the stomach, or the front part of the body between the chest and legs

'**belly ,button** noun [C] informal a person's **navel**

belong /bɪˈlɒŋ/ verb [I] 1 to be in the right place: When you've finished, put the cassettes back where they belong. 2 to feel happy and comfortable in a particular place or group: I don't feel that I belong here.

PHRASAL VERBS **be'long ,to sb** to be owned by someone: Who does this coat belong to?
be'long ,to sth to be a member of a group or organization: She belongs to the school computer club.

belongings /bɪˈlɒŋɪŋz/ noun [plural] the things that you own

below /bɪˈləʊ/ adv, preposition 1 in a lower place or position: There was a party in the flat below. ♦ a gunshot wound below the left shoulder 2 less than a particular number, amount, or level: The temperature fell **below zero**. 3 lower in rank or less important than someone else: officers below the rank of captain 4 in a later part of a piece of writing: For further information, see below.

belt /belt/ noun [C] 1 a narrow piece of leather or cloth that you wear around your waist 2 PHYSICS a circular band that turns or moves something in a machine 3 GEOGRAPHY a large region or area of the Earth that has particular characteristics or a particular type of industry: the Corn Belt of the central US ♦ The Sahel is a belt of semi-arid land that stretches across Africa.

'**belt ,bomber** noun [C] American someone who hides a bomb in a special belt around their waist with the intention of killing themselves and others when it explodes

bemoan /bɪˈməʊn/ verb [T] formal to complain or say that you are disappointed about something

bemused /bɪˈmjuːzd/ adj confused

bench /bentʃ/ noun

1 long seat	4 low table in gym
2 table for working on	5 in a law court
3 in parliament	6 in sports

1 [C] a hard seat for two or more people to sit on outside: a park bench
2 [C] a long table that someone uses when they are working with tools or equipment, for example in a laboratory
3 **benches** [plural] POLITICS the seats in the British parliament where the politicians sit
4 [C] a long low table in a gym that you lie on in order to do exercises
5 **the bench** [singular] LAW the position of being a judge in a court of law, or the place where a judge sits
6 **the bench** [singular] SPORTS a place where people in a sports team sit when they are not playing

bench grinder /ˈbentʃ ˌɡraɪndə/ noun [C] ENGINEERING a **power tool** with one or two **abrasive**

(=rough) wheels that may be used, for example, for **sharpening** tools or shaping metal

benchmark /ˈbentʃˌmɑːk/ noun [C] a level or standard that you can use for judging how good other things are

bend¹ /bend/ (**bends, bending, bent** /bent/) verb 1 [I/T] to lean forwards and downwards: Helen bent **down** to pick up her pen. ♦ **Bend over** and touch your toes. 2 [I/T] to curve or fold something, or to be curved or folded: His arm was so stiff he couldn't bend it at all. 3 [I] if light bends, it changes direction

bend² /bend/ noun [C] a curve in something such as a road or river: We came to a sharp bend in the road.

the bends /bendz/ noun [plural] HEALTH **decompression sickness**

beneath /bɪˈniːθ/ adv, preposition 1 directly under something, or at a lower level: We sheltered beneath a tree. ♦ You can see through the clear water to the coral reefs beneath. 2 if something is beneath someone, they think that they are too good or important to have to do it

benediction /ˌbenɪˈdɪkʃ(ə)n/ noun [C/U] RELIGION a Christian prayer that asks God to **bless** someone

Benedict's solution /ˈbenɪdɪkts səˌluːʃ(ə)n/ noun [U] CHEMISTRY a solution that is added to a sample of food in order to test whether **reducing sugars** are present. If reducing sugars are present, a red substance is formed.

benefactor /ˈbenɪˌfæktə/ noun [C] someone who helps a person or organization by giving them money

beneficial /ˌbenɪˈfɪʃ(ə)l/ adj something that is beneficial has a good effect or influence ≠ DETRIMENTAL, HARMFUL

beneficiary /ˌbenɪˈfɪʃəri/ (plural **beneficiaries**) noun [C] someone who gets money or property from someone who has died

benefit¹ /ˈbenɪfɪt/ noun [C/U] 1 an advantage: Write about the **benefits of** taking regular exercise. ♦ Think what you could do **for the benefit of** the whole school. 2 money that some governments give to people who need financial help, for example because they are unemployed: housing benefit

PHRASE **give sb the benefit of the doubt** to accept what someone says, although you know that they might be lying

benefit² /ˈbenɪfɪt/ (**benefits, benefiting** or **benefitting, benefited** or **benefitted**) verb [I/T] to get an advantage, or to give someone an advantage: The system mainly benefited people in the cities. ♦ Some patients have **benefited** greatly **from** this treatment.

benevolent /bəˈnev(ə)lənt/ adj kind and helpful —**benevolence** noun [U]

benighted /bɪˈnaɪtɪd/ adj lacking knowledge or advantages that other people or places have

benign /bəˈnaɪn/ adj HEALTH a benign lump in the body or a benign disease is not cancer ≠ MALIGNANT

bent¹ /bent/ adj a bent object has a curved or twisted shape

bent² /bent/ the past tense and past participle of **bend¹**

benzene /ˈbenziːn/ noun [U] CHEMISTRY a colourless liquid obtained from **petroleum**. It is used for making plastics and liquids for cleaning. Benzene is a **hydrocarbon**.

benzoic acid /benˌzəʊɪk ˈæsɪd/ noun [U] CHEMISTRY a colourless solid substance found in some plant **resins**. It is used in **cosmetics** and food **preservatives**.

bequeath /bɪˈkwiːð/ verb [T] *formal* if someone bequeaths money or property to you, they say in a legal document called a **will** that you will receive the money or property after they die

bequest /bɪˈkwest/ noun [C] *formal* money or property that someone gives to another person after they die

berate /bɪˈreɪt/ verb [T] *formal* to talk to someone in an angry way because they have done something wrong

bereaved /bɪˈriːvd/ adj a bereaved person is someone whose family member or close friend has recently died

bereavement /bɪˈriːvmənt/ noun [C/U] an occasion when a family member or close friend dies

beriberi /ˌberiˈberi/ noun [U] HEALTH a serious disease that affects the nerves, caused by a lack of **thiamin** (=vitamin B_1). Its symptoms include swelling in the arms and legs and **paralysis**.

berkelium /bɜːˈkiːliəm/ noun [U] CHEMISTRY a radioactive metallic element in the **actinide** group of the periodic table. Chemical symbol: **Bk**

berry /ˈberi/ (plural **berries**) noun [C] a small fruit that does not have a **stone** inside it

berserk /bəˈzɜːk/ adj
  PHRASE **go berserk 1** *informal* to become very excited **2** to become violent because you are very angry

berth /bɜːθ/ noun [C] **1** a bed on a train or ship **2** a place at a port where a ship stays for a period of time

beryllium /bəˈrɪliəm/ noun [U] CHEMISTRY a light hard grey-white metal element that does not **oxidize** in air, used in alloys. Chemical symbol: **Be**

beseech /bɪˈsiːtʃ/ (**beseeches, beseeching, besought** /bɪˈsɔːt/ or **beseeched**) verb [T] *literary* to ask someone for something in an urgent and sincere way

beside /bɪˈsaɪd/ preposition **1** at the side of someone or something: *Who's that standing beside Jeff?* **2** used for comparing two people or things: *Their efforts were unimpressive beside Frederick's.*
  PHRASE **beside the point** not relevant to the subject that you are discussing

besides /bɪˈsaɪdz/ adv, preposition **1** in addition to someone or something else: *A lot of them are studying other things besides English.* **2** used when you are adding another reason to support what you are saying: *It's too late to invite any more people. Besides, Tim hates parties.*

besiege /bɪˈsiːdʒ/ verb [T] **1** to make more requests or complaints than someone can deal with: *The department has been besieged with letters from angry students.* **2** if soldiers besiege a place, they surround it and prevent the people there from getting food and supplies

besotted /bɪˈsɒtɪd/ adj so much in love with someone that you are always thinking about them

bespoke /bɪˈspəʊk/ adj *formal* designed and produced for particular customers

Bessemer converter /ˈbesəmə kənˌvɜːtə/ noun [C] TECHNOLOGY a type of **furnace** that is used to produce steel from **pig iron**, using a process known as the **Bessemer process**

best /best/ adj, adv, noun **1** the superlative form of 'good' and 'well', used for describing the person, thing, or way that is the most satisfactory, suitable, skilful etc ≠ WORST: *the best hotel in town* ♦ *You need to find out which program works best on your computer.* ♦ *In the world of ballet she was quite simply the best.* ♦ *The new drug is safe and effective, and, best of all, inexpensive.* **2** liked or known more than anyone or

anything else ≠ WORST: *What kind of music do you like best?*
  PHRASES **at best** used for stating what is the best or biggest possible thing, when this is not very good
  the best of both worlds a situation where you have two different advantages at the same time
  best wishes used as a polite and friendly greeting before you sign your name on a letter or card
  do/try your best to try as hard as you can
  make the best of it to try to deal with a bad or difficult situation as well as you can

best-before date noun [C] a date that is printed on a food container to show how long the food remains fresh

best man noun [singular] the friend who helps a **bridegroom** at his wedding

bestow /bɪˈstəʊ/ verb [T] *formal* to give valuable property or an important right or honour to someone

best practice noun [U] BUSINESS the best, most effective way to do something

best-seller /ˌbestˈselə/ noun [C] a book that many people buy —**best-selling** adj: *a best-selling novel*

bet¹ /bet/ (**bets, betting, bet**) verb [I/T] if someone bets, or bets money, they risk an amount of money by saying what they think will happen in a race or game: *I bet £10 on each of the horses.*
  PHRASE **I bet (that)** *spoken* used for saying that you are sure about something: *I bet the teacher will be late again.*

bet² /bet/ noun [C] an agreement in which someone bets money on what will happen, or the amount of money that they bet → BETTING

beta /ˈbiːtə/ noun [singular] the second letter of the Greek alphabet

beta-blocker /ˈbiːtə ˌblɒkə/ noun [C] HEALTH a drug that makes the heart work more slowly. It is used for treating high blood pressure.

beta site noun [C] COMPUTING a company or person that is given a **beta version** of a new piece of computer hardware or software to test

beta test noun [C] COMPUTING a test in which a new computer product is given free to customers to use, in order to find mistakes —**beta-test** verb [T]

beta version noun [C] COMPUTING a form of piece of computer hardware or software that is given to people to test before it is sold to the public

betaware /ˈbiːtəweə/ noun [U] COMPUTING software that is a **beta version**

betel /ˈbiːt(ə)l/ noun [U] a plant of South-East Asia with leaves that people chew

betel nut noun [C] the nut of a palm tree of South-East Asia that people chew together with the leaves of the betel plant

bête noire /ˌbet ˈnwɑː/ (plural **bêtes noires**) noun [C] someone or something that you dislike very much or that makes you extremely angry

betray /bɪˈtreɪ/ verb [T] **1** if someone betrays their country, their family, or their friends, they deliberately do something that harms them **2** if you betray a feeling that you want to hide, your words or face make the feeling clear to people: *The woman's face betrayed her anger.* **3** if you betray a secret, you tell it to people who do not have the right to know it —**betrayal** /bɪˈtreɪəl/ noun [C/U]

better /ˈbetə/ adj, adv **1** the comparative form of 'good' and 'well', used for describing a person, thing, or way that is more satisfactory, suitable, skilful etc than another ≠ WORSE: *The machine works better if you change the oil regularly.* ♦ *The situation started to get better.* ♦ *The results were better than we had expected.* **2** healthy again, or no longer painful ≠ WORSE: *You shouldn't go back to school until you're better.* ♦ *If you want to get better, you must take your medicine.* **3** liked or known more than someone or something else: *I've always liked Susan better than her sister.* ♦ *He is better known by the name 'Pele'.*

PHRASES **for the better** if something changes for the better, it improves

(had) better do sth *spoken* used for saying that someone should do something

the sooner the better used for saying that you want something to happen as soon as possible: *I want you to get rid of those people, and the sooner the better.*

betterment /ˈbetəmənt/ noun [U] *formal* improvement

better 'off adj someone who is better off is in a better situation than someone else, or has more money: *You'd be better off living on your own.*

betting /ˈbetɪŋ/ noun [U] the activity of trying to win money by putting a **bet** on the result of a race or game

between /bɪˈtwiːn/ adv, preposition **1** in the space separating two people or things: *Hold the needle between your finger and thumb.* ♦ *Trains running between Johannesburg and Cape Town were delayed.* ♦ *A sandwich is two slices of bread with something in between.* **2** in the period separating one time or event and another: *I have two classes this morning, with a short break in between.* **3** within a range of numbers or amounts: *children between the ages of 4 and 13* **4** used for showing which people or things are involved in something: *a conversation between the Prime Minister and the President* ♦ *Scientists believe there is a link between diet and cancer.* → AMONG

bevel /ˈbev(ə)l/ noun [C] a sloping surface along the edge of a piece of wood, glass etc

bevel gear noun [C] ENGINEERING a part of a machine in the shape of a **cone** with **teeth** (=narrow pointed parts) that fit into another set of teeth at an angle to them, in order to let power pass through them

bevelled /ˈbev(ə)ld/ adj with a sloping edge

beverage /ˈbev(ə)rɪdʒ/ noun [C] *formal* a drink of any kind

beware /bɪˈweə/ verb [I/T] if someone tells you to beware of something, they are warning you that it might be dangerous: *Beware of the dog!*

bewildered /bɪˈwɪldəd/ adj confused and not certain what to do —**bewilderment** noun [U]

bewildering /bɪˈwɪld(ə)rɪŋ/ adj making you feel confused and not certain what to do

beyond /bɪˈjɒnd/ adv, preposition **1** further away than something else, or outside a particular area: *I could see the sea beyond the fields.* **2** outside the range or limits of a subject, quality, or activity: *Their behaviour went far beyond what is acceptable.* **3** continuing after a particular time or age, or moving past a particular level: *Inflation has risen beyond 10%.* **4** used for saying that something cannot be done: *I'm afraid the watch is damaged beyond repair.* ♦ *The city centre has changed beyond recognition.*

PHRASE **be beyond sb** to be too difficult for someone to understand or deal with: *It's beyond me why anyone should want to marry him.*

bi- /baɪ/ prefix two, or twice: *bilingual* (=speaking two languages) ♦ *biped* (=an animal with two legs)

biannual /baɪˈænjʊəl/ adj happening twice every year → BIENNIAL

bias[1] /ˈbaɪəs/ noun [U] **1** an attitude that makes you treat someone in a way that is unfair or different from the way you treat other people: *a bias in favour of younger candidates* **2** emphasis on one thing more than others: *an English course with a bias towards the spoken language*

bias[2] /ˈbaɪəs/ (**biases** or **biasses**, **biasing** or **biassing**, **biased** or **biassed**) verb [T] to influence someone's opinions, decisions etc so that they behave in an unfair way —**biased** /ˈbaɪəst/ adj

bible /ˈbaɪb(ə)l/ noun RELIGION **1 the Bible** the holy book of the Christian and Jewish religions **2** [C] a copy of the Bible —**biblical** /ˈbɪblɪk(ə)l/ adj

bibliography /ˌbɪbliˈɒɡrəfi/ (plural **bibliographies**) noun [C] a list of books and articles on a particular subject

bicameral /baɪˈkæm(ə)rəl/ adj POLITICS a bicameral parliament consists of two separate groups of people involved in making laws. In a bicameral system, there is usually an **upper house** (such as the British House of Lords or the US Senate) and a **lower house** (such as the British House of Commons or the US House of Representatives).

bi,carbonate of 'soda or **bicarbonate** noun [U] a white chemical powder used in cooking to make cakes rise. It is also mixed with water and drunk as a medicine = BAKING SODA

bicentenary /ˌbaɪsenˈtiːnəri/ (plural **bicentenaries**) noun [C] the day or year exactly 200 years after an important event, or a celebration of this

biceps /ˈbaɪseps/ noun [C] ANATOMY the muscle between the shoulder and elbow on the front of the arm → TRICEPS —*picture* → BODY

bick /bɪk/ noun [C] TECHNOLOGY the front, usually pointed, part of an **anvil**

biconcave /baɪˈkɒnkeɪv/ adj a biconcave object is curved inwards on both sides

bicuspid valve /baɪˈkʌspɪd ˌvælv/ noun [C] ANATOMY the **mitral valve** on the left side of the heart that stops blood from flowing back into the **ventricle** from the **atrium** —*picture* → CIRCULATION

bicycle /ˈbaɪsɪk(ə)l/ noun [C] a vehicle with two wheels that you ride by pushing the pedals with your feet

bid[1] /bɪd/ (**bids**, **bidding**, **bid**) verb **1** [I/T] to offer a particular amount of money for something: *They bid £300 for the painting.* **2** [I] to offer to do work or provide a service for a particular amount of money: *Several firms are bidding for the job.* —**bidder** noun [C], **bidding** noun [U]

bid[2] /bɪd/ noun [C] **1** an offer to pay a particular amount of money for something **2** BUSINESS an offer to buy shares in a company and take control of it **3** BUSINESS an offer to do work or provide a service for a particular amount of money: *They've put in a bid for the catering contract.* **4** an attempt to do something: *a bid to win the championship*

biddable /ˈbɪdəb(ə)l/ adj someone who is biddable does what people tell them without arguing or complaining

bidirectional /ˌbaɪdɪˈrekʃ(ə)nəl, ˌbaɪdaɪˈrekʃ(ə)nəl/ adj operating in two directions

biennial /baɪˈeniəl/ adj **1** happening once every two years **2** BIOLOGY a biennial plant such as a **carrot** lives for only two years

bier /bɪə/ noun [C] a wooden structure for putting a **coffin** (=a container for a dead body) on

bifocals /baɪ'fəʊk(ə)lz/ noun [plural] a pair of **glasses** with special lenses that let you see things that are near if you look through the bottom part, and see things that are far away if you look through the top part

bifurcate /'baɪfəkeɪt/ verb [I] formal to divide into two separate parts, especially parts that go in different directions= FORK

big /bɪɡ/ (**bigger, biggest**) adj **1** large in size: a big house **2** powerful or successful: It was her dream to **make it big** as a singer. ♦ Her mother is **big in** the fashion business. **3** informal your big sister or big brother is older than you ≠ LITTLE: This is my big brother, Jake. **4** enthusiastic: They were big fans of the Beatles.

> **Build your vocabulary: words you can use instead of big**
>
> **Big** is a very general word. Here are some words with more specific meanings that sound more natural and appropriate in particular situations.
> **numbers/amounts** considerable, high, huge, large, massive, significant, sizeable, substantial
> **increases/decreases** considerable, great, large, major, rapid, sharp, substantial, tremendous
> **rises/falls** large, major, sharp, steep, substantial
> **changes** dramatic, drastic, major, radical, significant, sweeping
> **problems** considerable, important, major, serious
> **effects** far-reaching, major, profound, serious, significant

the ,Big 'Bang noun [singular] ASTRONOMY the explosion of a very large mass of matter that is believed to have caused the universe to begin to exist. The Big Bang is believed to have happened about 15 billion years ago, and this theory explains why the universe is still increasing in size.

,Big 'Brother noun [singular] a person or organization that watches people all the time and tries to control everything that they say or do. It is the name of the mysterious character in George Orwell's novel 1984, who is able to watch everybody wherever they are.

,big 'business noun [U] important business activity that makes a lot of money

,big 'game noun [U] large wild animals such as lions that people hunt as a sport

,big 'name noun [C] informal a famous or important person

bigot /'bɪɡət/ noun [C] someone who has very strong and unreasonable opinions about politics, race, or religion —**bigoted** adj, **bigotry** /'bɪɡətri/ noun [U]

,big 'science noun [U] scientific research that is expensive because it needs a lot of equipment and workers, and so is usually supported by large companies or by the government

the ,big 'screen noun [singular] the cinema

the 'big ,time noun [singular] the highest and most successful level in a profession

,big 'toe noun [C] the largest of the toes on the foot — picture → BODY

bike /baɪk/ noun [C] informal a **bicycle** or a **motorcycle**

bikini /bɪ'kiːni/ noun [C] a swimming suit for women, with two separate parts that cover the breasts and the lower part of the body

bilabial /baɪ'leɪbiəl/ adj LANGUAGE a bilabial sound is one that you produce using both lips, for example the sound of 'm' or 'p' —**bilabial** noun [C]

bilateral /baɪ'læt(ə)rəl/ adj involving two groups or countries: bilateral talks —**bilaterally** adv

bile /baɪl/ noun [U] HEALTH a bitter greenish-brown liquid that is produced by the liver and stored in the **gall bladder**. It helps the body to digest food. —picture → DIGESTIVE SYSTEM

'bile ,duct noun [C] ANATOMY a tube in the body that carries bile from the liver and the **gall bladder** to the **small intestine** —picture → DIGESTIVE SYSTEM

bilharzia /bɪl'hɑːtsiə/ or **bilharziasis** /ˌbɪlhɑː'tsaɪəsɪs/ noun [U] HEALTH a serious tropical disease caused by **flukes** that live in rivers, lakes etc, which enter the body through the skin and live in the bloodstream. Bilharzia causes **anaemia** and fever.

bilingual /baɪ'lɪŋɡwəl/ adj **1** able to speak two languages **2** written in two languages: a bilingual dictionary —**bilingual** noun [C]

bill¹ /bɪl/ noun [C]

1 amount that you owe	4 list of concert events
2 proposal for law	5 bird's beak
3 paper money	+ PHRASES

1 a written statement that shows how much money someone owes for goods or services that they have received: a telephone bill ♦ I always **pay** my **bills** on time. ♦ We asked the waiter for the bill.
2 POLITICS a written document that contains a proposal for a new law
3 American a **banknote**: a $100 bill
4 a list of events and performers at a show: He'll be **topping the bill** at the show next month.
5 a bird's beak, especially when the beak is large or long and thin, or when the bird has **webbed** feet — picture → BIRD

PHRASES **bill of entry** BUSINESS a list of goods that are being imported into or exported from a country, shown to **customs** officials (=people who check whether tax should be paid on imports and exports)
bill of lading BUSINESS a list of goods being sent to another country by ship or plane
bill of quantities CONSTRUCTION a document that gives the volumes, areas, and amounts of work needed to build a large structure
bill of rights POLITICS an official statement of the most important rights that the citizens of a country have
bill of sale BUSINESS a written statement describing the sale of something to someone

bill² /bɪl/ verb [T] to send or give someone a written statement that shows how much money they owe

billboard /'bɪlbɔːd/ noun [C] a large board for advertisements= HOARDING

billet /'bɪlɪt/ noun [C] TECHNOLOGY a piece of **cast** iron or steel, smaller than a **bloom**, that is ready for further processing

billiards /'bɪliədz/ noun [U] a game in which two people use long sticks called **cues** to hit balls into pockets at the edges and corners of a table → pool sense 3, SNOOKER

billion /'bɪljən/ number MATHS the number 1,000,000,000 → TRILLION

billionaire /ˌbɪljə'neə/ noun [C] someone who has more than a billion pounds or dollars

billow /'bɪləʊ/ verb [I] to rise or move in clouds: Black smoke billowed over the city.

bimetallic strip /ˌbaɪmetælɪk ˈstrɪp/ noun [C] PHYSICS a **strip** made of two metals fixed together, each of which bends a different amount when they are both heated to the same temperature. It is used in **thermostats** to turn things on and off.

bimetallic thermometer /ˌbaɪmetælɪk θəˈmɒmɪtə/ noun [C] SCIENCE a piece of equipment that uses a **bimetallic strip** to show changes in temperature on a dial. As the metal bends, it changes the figures on a **dial** so that the thermometer bends.

bin /bɪn/ noun [C] **1** a container for putting rubbish in **2** a container for storing something: *a recycling bin*

binary /ˈbaɪnəri/ adj MATHS, COMPUTING based on a system in which information is represented using combinations of the numbers o and 1

'binary ˌdigit noun [C] PHYSICS, COMPUTING either of the numbers o or 1, used as the smallest unit of information in a binary system

'binary ˌfission noun [U] BIOLOGY a form of **asexual reproduction** in which organisms reproduce by splitting into two new organisms that are identical to the parent, or are **clones** of the parent

'binary ˌnumber noun [C] PHYSICS, COMPUTING a **binary digit**

bind /baɪnd/ (**binds, binding, bound** /baʊnd/) verb [T] **1** to tie things together with rope or string: *Their hands were bound behind their backs.* **2** to limit what someone is allowed to do by making them obey a rule or agreement: *He is bound by his contract.* **3** to fasten the pages of a book together and put a cover on it **4** [I/T] if two substances bind, or if you bind two substances, they stick or mix together and become one substance

PHRASAL VERB **ˌbind sb ˈover** LAW if a court binds someone over it orders them to do something and usually makes them pay money that they lose if they do not obey

binder /ˈbaɪndə/ noun [C] a hard cover that holds loose papers together

binding[1] /ˈbaɪndɪŋ/ adj a binding agreement, contract, or decision must be obeyed

binding[2] /ˈbaɪndɪŋ/ noun [C] **1** the cover of a book **2** SPORTS the part of a **ski** that holds the boot in place

binge[1] /bɪndʒ/ noun [C] an occasion when someone does too much of something, such as eating

binge[2] /bɪndʒ/ verb [I] to do too much of something that you enjoy, such as eating

'binge ˌdrinking noun [U] the drinking of large amounts of alcohol in a short period of time, in order to get drunk

binoculars /bɪˈnɒkjʊləz/ noun [plural] a piece of equipment that you look through to see distant objects. It has a separate part for each eye.

binocular vision /bɪˌnɒkjʊlə ˈvɪʒ(ə)n/ noun [U] BIOLOGY the use of both eyes to see things with depth and in relation to each other. Humans and some other animals have binocular vision.

binomial /baɪˈnəʊmiəl/ noun [C] **1** MATHS an **expression** in algebra that contains two numbers or symbols **2** LANGUAGE a phrase containing two nouns that are joined together by a conjunction and always appear in the same order, for example 'cup and saucer' **3** BIOLOGY a scientific name for a plant, animal, or microorganism that consists of two Latin words — **binomial** adj

bio- /baɪəʊ/ prefix **1** BIOLOGY relating to living things: *biochemistry* (=the scientific study of living things) **2** relating to someone's life: *biography* (=a book about

someone's life) **3** involving chemical weapons: *bioterrorism*

bioaccumulation /ˌbaɪəʊəˌkjuːmjuːˈleɪʃ(ə)n/ noun [U] BIOLOGY, ENVIRONMENT the processes that take place when a chemical such as a **pesticide** does not break down quickly and **accumulates** in the bodies of living things

biochemical /ˌbaɪəʊˈkemɪk(ə)l/ adj BIOLOGY, CHEMISTRY involving chemical substances and processes in living things

biochemistry /ˌbaɪəʊˈkemɪstri/ noun [U] BIOLOGY, CHEMISTRY the study of chemical processes in living things —**biochemist** noun [C]

biodata /ˈbaɪəʊˌdeɪtə/ noun [C] a **CV**

biodegradable /ˌbaɪəʊdɪˈɡreɪdəb(ə)l/ adj BIOLOGY, ENVIRONMENT decaying naturally in a way that is not harmful to the environment

biodegrade /ˌbaɪəʊdɪˈɡreɪd/ verb [I] BIOLOGY, ENVIRONMENT if a substance biodegrades, bacteria cause it to separate into very small parts so that it is not harmful to the environment

biodiversity /ˌbaɪəʊdaɪˈvɜːsəti/ noun [U] BIOLOGY, ENVIRONMENT the variety of types of living thing in a particular region

bioengineering /ˌbaɪəʊendʒɪˈnɪərɪŋ/ noun [U] HEALTH, ENGINEERING the use of engineering for medical purposes, for example the use of artificial body parts, organs etc to replace damaged ones

biofuel /ˈbaɪəʊˌfjuːəl/ noun [C/U] AGRICULTURE fuel that is made from living things or from something their bodies produce, for example fuel made from cow **manure**

biogas /ˈbaɪəʊˌɡæs/ noun [U] BIOLOGY, CHEMISTRY a mixture of carbon dioxide and methane that is produced by dead animals and plants that are decaying. This gas can be burned to produce heat.

biogeography /ˌbaɪəʊdʒiːˈɒɡrəfi/ noun [C] GEOGRAPHY the study of how particular plants and animals are spread over different areas — **biogeographer** noun [C]

biography /baɪˈɒɡrəfi/ (plural **biographies**) noun [C] LITERATURE a book that someone writes about someone else's life —**biographer** noun [C], **biographical** /ˌbaɪəˈɡræfɪk(ə)l/ adj

biohazard /ˈbaɪəʊˌhæzəd/ noun [C] BIOLOGY, HEALTH something that may cause harm to people or to the environment, especially a poisonous chemical or an infectious disease

bioinformatics /ˌbaɪəʊɪnfəˈmætɪks/ noun [U] BIOLOGY, COMPUTING the use of techniques from computer science, maths, and biochemistry to analyse biological systems, especially to structure and organize data

biological /ˌbaɪəˈlɒdʒɪk(ə)l/ adj **1** BIOLOGY relating to living things **2** using dangerous bacteria or viruses to harm people: *biological weapons* —**biologically** /ˌbaɪəˈlɒdʒɪkli/ adv

ˌbiological ˈclock noun [C] a system in the body that controls when certain regular activities such as sleeping happen

ˌbiological conˈtrol noun [U] BIOLOGY, ENVIRONMENT a method of reducing the number of harmful insects and other organisms in an area by bringing in other insects or organisms that feed on them

bioˌlogical ˈfarming noun [U] AGRICULTURE farming that uses **organic** methods

biological 'shield noun [C] PHYSICS a wall of material such as concrete or steel that is placed around the central part of a **nuclear reactor** to protect people from the effects of radiation —*picture* → NUCLEAR REACTOR

biological 'warfare noun [U] the use of harmful bacteria as a weapon in war

biological 'weapon noun [C] harmful bacteria that are used as a weapon in war

biology /baɪˈɒlədʒi/ noun [U] BIOLOGY the scientific study of living things → BOTANY, ZOOLOGY —**biologist** noun [C]

biomagnification /ˌbaɪəʊˌmæɡnɪfɪˈkeɪʃ(ə)n/ noun [U] BIOLOGY, ENVIRONMENT the process by which chemicals or harmful substances become more concentrated in the bodies of living things as they move up the food chain

biomass /ˈbaɪəʊˌmæs/ noun [U] **1** BIOLOGY the mass of all the living things found in a particular area, measured in weight per unit area **2** SCIENCE plant and animal substances used for fuel. Biomass fuels produce less carbon dioxide than **fossil fuels** such as coal and oil.

biome /ˈbaɪəʊm/ noun [C] ENVIRONMENT a region that is described and **classified** on the basis of its climate and the types of animals and plants that are living in it. The **rainforest** and the **tundra** are biomes.

biomedicine /ˌbaɪəʊˈmeds(ə)n/ noun [U] HEALTH **1** the principles of biology and **biochemistry** applied to the practice of medicine **2** the study of the effect of the environment on the body under extreme conditions, especially in space travel —**biomedical** /ˌbaɪəʊˈmedɪk(ə)l/ adj

biometrics /ˌbaɪəʊˈmetrɪks/ noun [U] the recording of things such as people's **fingerprints** or the appearance of their eye, in order to identify them on an electronic system —**biometric** adj

bionic /baɪˈɒnɪk/ adj bionic body parts are artificial electronic parts that replace body parts that have been removed or do not work correctly

biophysics /ˌbaɪəʊˈfɪzɪks/ noun [U] PHYSICS the scientific study of biological processes using the laws of physics

biopiracy /ˌbaɪəʊˈpaɪrəsi/ noun [U] SCIENCE the practice of using plant or animal genes for scientific research without having the legal right to do this

biopsy /ˈbaɪɒpsi/ (plural **biopsies**) noun [C] HEALTH a medical test in which cells are taken from the body and are examined to find out if they are affected by a disease

biorhythm /ˈbaɪəʊˌrɪð(ə)m/ noun [C] BIOLOGY the pattern of physical processes that happen in someone's body over a period of time

bioscience /ˈbaɪəʊˌsaɪəns/ noun [C/U] SCIENCE an area of scientific study that relates to living things, for example biology or **biochemistry**

biosecurity /ˈbaɪəʊsɪˌkjʊərəti/ noun [U] AGRICULTURE, HEALTH the methods used to prevent an infection from spreading outside an area

the biosphere /ˈbaɪəʊˌsfɪə/ noun [singular] ENVIRONMENT the parts of the Earth's surface and atmosphere where living things can exist

biotechnology /ˌbaɪəʊtekˈnɒlədʒi/ noun [U] BIOLOGY the use of bacteria, fungi, and cells from plants and animals for industrial or scientific purposes, for example in order to make drugs, artificial hormones, or other chemicals —**biotechnological** /ˌbaɪəʊˌteknəˈlɒdʒɪk(ə)l/ adj, **biotechnologist** noun [C]

bioterrorism /ˌbaɪəʊˈterəˌrɪz(ə)m/ noun [U] terrorism that uses chemical or biological weapons

biotic /baɪˈɒtɪk/ adj BIOLOGY relating to the parts of an organism's environment that consists of living things, rather than the rock, the water etc that surrounds it: *Name some of the biotic components of the ecosystem.*

biowarfare /ˈbaɪəʊˌwɔːfeə/ noun [U] the use of biological weapons in a war

bioweapon /ˈbaɪəʊˌwep(ə)n/ noun [C] a biological or chemical weapon

bipartisan /ˌbaɪpɑːtɪˈzæn/ adj involving two political parties

bipartite /baɪˈpɑːtaɪt/ adj formal consisting of or involving two people, things, or groups

biped /ˈbaɪped/ noun [C] BIOLOGY an animal that walks on two legs

bipolar /ˌbaɪˈpəʊlə/ adj formal involving two completely opposing parts or groups

bi'polar dis,order noun [U] HEALTH a serious mental illness in which someone experiences extreme changes in mood, sometimes feeling very excited and sometimes very unhappy

birch /bɜːtʃ/ noun [C/U] **1** a tree with thin branches and bark that comes off in long thin pieces. Birch trees grow in the northern hemisphere. **2** [U] the pale wood from a birch tree

bird /bɜːd/ noun [C] BIOLOGY a vertebrate animal with feathers, two wings, and a beak. Birds are **warm-blooded** animals that build **nests**, in which female birds lay eggs. —*picture* → on next page
   PHRASES **bird of paradise** a brightly coloured bird that lives mainly in New Guinea
bird of prey a bird that hunts and eats other animals

'bird ,flu noun [U] HEALTH a type of **flu** (=an infectious disease that makes you hot and cold, tired and weak) that affects chickens and some other birds and animals and can also infect humans= AVIAN FLU

birdie /ˈbɜːdi/ noun [C] SPORTS a golf score that is one hit of the ball less than the number expected for a particular hole → BOGEY, EAGLE

'bird's-eye 'view noun [singular] a good view of something from a high position

bird-watching /ˈbɜːd ˌwɒtʃɪŋ/ noun [U] the activity of watching wild birds —**bird-watcher** noun [C]

Biro /ˈbaɪrəʊ/ (plural **Biros**) TRADEMARK a plastic pen with a metal ball at its point

birth /bɜːθ/ noun **1** [C/U] the occasion when a baby is born: *We are happy to announce the birth of our son Andrew.* ♦ *She gave birth to a baby boy.* ♦ *Her place of birth was listed as Nairobi.* → DATE OF BIRTH **2** [U] someone's position in society according to their family, or according to the place where they were born: *She's Nigerian by birth.* **3** [singular] the beginning of something: *the birth of a new era in South African politics*

'birth ,canal noun [C] ANATOMY a tube leading from the uterus to the outside of the body, along which a baby travels when it is born= VAGINA

'birth cer,tificate noun [C] an official document that shows someone's name, details of when and where they were born, and who their parents are

'birth con,trol noun [U] the practice of avoiding becoming pregnant, or the methods that people use for this= CONTRACEPTION

crane

egret

flamingo

pelican

seagull

swan

eagle

vulture

webbed foot

falcon

hawk

penguin

swallow

talon

parrot

owl

pigeon

ostrich

peacock

goose

kiwi

duck

turkey

feather

cockerel

tail

hen

bill/beak

neck

wing

leg

breast

claw

birds

birthday /'bɜːθdeɪ/ noun [C] the day each year with the same date as the day when you were born: *Her birthday is on 7th June.* ♦ *a birthday party* ♦ **Happy birthday, Tessa!**

birthmark /'bɜːθˌmɑːk/ noun [C] a red or brown mark on the skin that some people are born with

'birth ˌparent noun [C] the original mother or father of a child, not the parent who **adopts** them

birthplace /'bɜːθˌpleɪs/ noun [C] **1** the place where someone was born **2** the place where something first started

'birth ˌrate noun [C] **SOCIAL STUDIES** the official number of births in a particular year or place

birthright /'bɜːθˌraɪt/ noun [C] a basic human right, or a right to have something because you are a citizen of a particular country

'birth ˌweight noun [U] **HEALTH** [C] the weight of a baby when it is born

biscuit /'bɪskɪt/ noun [C] a small flat dry cake that is usually sweet

bisect /baɪ'sekt/ verb [T] **MATHS** to divide something into two equal parts

bisection /baɪ'sekʃ(ə)n/ noun [U] **MATHS** the process by which a straight line or **plane** (=flat surface) divides an angle or line into two equal halves

bisector /baɪ'sektə/ noun [C] **MATHS** a line that divides another line or angle into two equal parts

bisexual /baɪ'sekʃʊəl/ adj sexually attracted to both men and women → HETEROSEXUAL, HOMOSEXUAL[1] —**bisexuality** /ˌbaɪsekʃʊˈæləti/ noun [U]

bishop /'bɪʃəp/ noun [C] **1** **RELIGION** a senior Christian priest who is responsible for all the churches in a particular area **2** a piece in the game of chess, shaped like a bishop's hat

bismuth /'bɪzməθ/ noun [U] **CHEMISTRY** an element that is used to form alloys with a low **melting point**. Chemical symbol: **Bi**

bison /'baɪs(ə)n/ (plural **bison**) noun [C] a large wild mammal like a cow with long hair, a large head, and a **humped** back. Bison live in North America and Europe.

bistable /baɪ'steɪb(ə)l/ adj **PHYSICS** having two possible states, on and off

bistro /'biːstrəʊ/ noun [C] a small restaurant or bar

bit¹ /bɪt/ noun [C] **1** a small piece or part of something: *There were **bits of** broken glass everywhere.* ♦ *The **best bit** in the film is the scene in the restaurant.* **2** **COMPUTING** the basic unit of computer information → BYTE **3** a tool or part of a tool used for cutting or making holes in things **4** the part of a horse's **bridle** that fits inside the horse's mouth

PHRASES **a bit** *informal* **1** slightly, or a little: *I'm feeling a bit tired.* ♦ *The second interview was **a bit less** formal.* **2** a short time: *You'll have to wait a bit.* **3** a small amount: *'Would you like some more sauce?' '**Just a bit.**'* **bit by bit** gradually, or in small stages: *I'll move my things into the flat bit by bit.* **every bit as...** just as: *Her new book is every bit as good as the first one.* **quite a bit** *informal* a lot: *You can fly there, but it costs quite a bit.* **to bits** *informal* **1** into small pieces: *My shoes are **falling to bits.*** **2** very much: *He's thrilled to bits.*

bit² /bɪt/ the past tense of **bite¹**

bitch /bɪtʃ/ noun [C] a female dog

bitchy /'bɪtʃi/ (**bitchier, bitchiest**) adj *informal* rude or cruel towards someone

bite¹ /baɪt/ (**bites, biting, bit** /bɪt/, **bitten** /'bɪt(ə)n/) verb **1** [I/T] to use your teeth to cut or break something, usually in order to eat it: *Tom **bit into** his sandwich.* ♦ *Stop biting your nails.* **2** [I/T] if an animal such as a snake or insect bites you, it makes a small hole in your skin: *I've been bitten by a flea.* **3** [I] to have an unpleasant effect: *The economic slowdown is beginning to bite.* **4** [I] if a fish bites, it takes the **bait** that has been put on the hook in order to catch it: *The fish don't seem to be biting today.*

PHRASE **bite your tongue** to stop yourself from saying something that might upset or annoy someone

bite² /baɪt/ noun

1 act of biting food	4 very cold feeling
2 injury from being bitten	5 when fish pulls
3 small meal/piece of food	hook

1 [C] an act of cutting or breaking something with your teeth, usually in order to eat it: *Anthony ate half his burger **in one bite.*** **2** [C] a mark where an animal or insect has bitten you **3** **a bite** or **a bite to eat** [singular] a small meal, especially one that you eat in a hurry= SNACK **4** [singular] a very cold feeling **5** [C] a pull at the hook when someone is fishing, made by a fish trying to take the **bait** on the hook

bite-sized /'baɪtˌsaɪzd/ or **bite-size** /'baɪtˌsaɪz/ adj small enough to be put into your mouth whole

biting /'baɪtɪŋ/ adj **1** a biting wind is extremely cold and unpleasant **2** a biting remark is cruel

bitmap /'bɪtˌmæp/ noun [C] **COMPUTING** a computer image made up of many small points on the screen

bitstream /'bɪtˌstriːm/ noun [C] **COMPUTING** **1** a set of data sent in **binary** form **2** a flow of computer information, measured in **bits**

bitten /'bɪt(ə)n/ the past participle of **bite¹**

bitter¹ /'bɪtə/ adj **1** angry or upset because you think something is unfair, or involving people who feel angry or upset: *I'm still **bitter about** the whole affair.* ♦ *a bitter dispute* **2** making you feel very unhappy or disappointed: *It was **a bitter blow** when he lost his job.* **3** something that is bitter has a strong sharp taste that is not sweet **4** extremely cold in an unpleasant way: *a bitter north wind*

PHRASE **to the bitter end** continuing until the end of a difficult or unpleasant situation or period —**bitterness** noun [U]

bitter² /'bɪtə/ noun [C/U] a type of dark beer that tastes bitter, or a glass of this beer

bitterly /'bɪtəli/ adv **1** in an extremely angry, upset, or disappointed way: *He complained bitterly that no one had bothered to ask his opinion.* **2** in a determined and angry way: *Many people are **bitterly opposed** to the idea.*

PHRASE **bitterly cold** extremely cold

bittersweet /ˌbɪtə'swiːt/ adj involving feelings of happiness and sadness at the same time

bitumen /'bɪtʃʊmɪn/ noun [U] **CONSTRUCTION** a black sticky substance that is used for making the surfaces of roads, and for covering roofs —*picture* → REFINE

bituminous felt /bɪˌtjuːmɪnəs 'felt/ noun [U] **CONSTRUCTION** a material for covering roofs that is treated with bitumen

Biuret test /bju'ret ˌtest/ noun [C] **CHEMISTRY** a test for protein in which **sodium hydroxide** is added to a sample, followed by **copper sulphate solution**. If protein is present, the sample turns purple.

bivalve /ˈbaɪˌvælv/ noun [C] a mollusc with a shell made of two parts joined together. **Mussels** and **oysters** are bivalves.

bivariate /baɪˈveəriət, baɪˈveəriːət/ adj MATHS relating to or containing two variables

biweekly¹ /ˌbaɪˈwiːkli/ adj, adv happening or published every two weeks

biweekly² /ˌbaɪˈwiːkli/ noun [C] a magazine that is published twice a month or twice a week

bizarre /bɪˈzɑː/ adj strange and difficult to explain: *a bizarre situation* —**bizarrely** adv

black¹ /blæk/ adj

1 of darkest colour	5 angry or sad
2 with dark skin	6 sad or unpleasant
3 with no milk in it	+ PHRASE
4 causing sadness	

1 of the darkest colour, like the sky at night: *clouds of thick black smoke*
2 black or **Black** belonging to a race of people with dark skin, especially people whose families come from Africa: *a famous black actor*
3 tea or coffee that is black has no milk in it
4 making people lose hope or feel sad: *It's **a black day** for the car industry.*
5 showing angry or unhappy feelings: *a black look*
6 involving sad or unpleasant things: *black humour*
PHRASE black and blue covered in **bruises** (=dark marks on the skin where someone has been hit)
—**blackness** noun [U]

black² /blæk/ noun **1** [U] the darkest colour, like the colour of the sky at night: *You look good **in black*** (=wearing black clothes). **2 black** or **Black** [C] *offensive* a black person

black³ /blæk/
PHRASAL VERB ˌblack ˈout to suddenly become unconscious= FAINT

ˌblack-and-ˈwhite adj **1** using only black, white, and grey ≠ COLOUR: *a black-and-white photograph* **2** a black-and-white situation, description, or issue makes the difference between right and wrong seem very clear

ˌblack ˈbar noun [C/U] TECHNOLOGY a block of metal that has been rolled, pressed, or shaped after it has cooled. Its surface is black because of **oxide**.

ˈblack ˌbelt noun [C] SPORTS the highest level of skill in **judo** or **karate**, or someone who has achieved this level of skill

blackberry /ˈblækbəri/ (plural **blackberries**) noun [C] a small soft dark fruit that grows on a bush

blackboard /ˈblækˌbɔːd/ noun [C] EDUCATION a large dark board that a teacher writes on with **chalk**

ˌblack ˈbox noun [C] **1** a piece of equipment in a plane that records details about the cause of a crash **2** a computer or similar piece of equipment that performs a complicated job, although the person using it does not understand how it works

ˌblack ˈcomedy noun [C/U] LITERATURE, ARTS a play, film, or story that deals in a humorous way with unpleasant aspects of life such as illness and death

the ˌBlack ˈDeath noun [singular] a disease that killed millions of people in Europe and Asia in the 14th century. Its medical name is **bubonic plague**.

the ˌblack eˈconomy noun ECONOMICS illegal business activities that allow people to avoid paying taxes, for example selling goods or providing services without keeping any records

blacken /ˈblækən/ verb [I/T] to become black, or to make something black

ˌblack ˈeye noun [C] a dark mark on the skin around your eye that is caused by someone hitting you

ˌblack ˈhole noun [C] **1** ASTRONOMY an object in outer space that has such strong gravity that nothing near it can escape from it, not even light. Black holes are thought to be formed when a very large star stops existing. **2** *informal* a situation in which large amounts of money are spent without bringing any benefits

ˌblack ˈice noun [U] GEOGRAPHY a dangerous layer of ice that is difficult to see on a road

blacklist /ˈblækˌlɪst/ verb **be blacklisted** to be included on a list of people or things that are not approved of

ˌblack ˈmagic noun [U] magic that is used for evil purposes

blackmail /ˈblækˌmeɪl/ noun [U] **1** LAW the crime of forcing someone to do something by threatening to tell people embarrassing information about them **2** the use of threats to persuade a person or government to do what you want → EMOTIONAL BLACKMAIL —**blackmail** verb [T], **blackmailer** noun [C]

ˌblack ˈmark noun [C] something that someone has done that damages their reputation

ˌblack ˈmarket noun [singular] ECONOMICS the illegal trade in goods that are difficult or expensive to obtain legally: *Rhino horns can fetch up to £4,000 on the black market.* —**black marketeer** /ˌblæk mɑːkɪtˈɪə/ noun [C]

blackout /ˈblækaʊt/ noun [C] **1** a short period when the electricity supply is stopped= POWER CUT **2** a period during a war when the lights are turned off so that an enemy cannot see them at night **3** a period when someone suddenly becomes unconscious for a short time **4** a situation in which journalists are officially prevented from reporting news about something

ˌblack ˈpepper noun [U] pepper that is produced from dried crushed pepper seeds and their hard black cover

ˌblack ˈsheep noun [C] someone who is not approved of by the other members of their family or group

blacksmith /ˈblækˌsmɪθ/ noun [C] someone whose job is to make **horseshoes** and other objects out of metal

bladder /ˈblædə/ noun [C] ANATOMY the part inside the body like a bag where urine collects before being passed out of the body through the urethra —*picture* → ORGAN

blade /bleɪd/ noun [C]

1 sharp part of knife etc	4 flat part of machine etc
2 bar on ice skate	5 of leaf
3 of grass	

1 the thin sharp part of a knife, tool, or weapon
2 the metal bar on the bottom of an **ice skate**
3 a long thin leaf of grass
4 a flat wide part of a machine or piece of equipment
5 BIOLOGY the flat part of a leaf —*picture* → LEAF
→ SHOULDER BLADE

blame¹ /bleɪm/ verb [T] to say or think that someone or something is responsible for an accident, problem, or bad situation: *If it all goes wrong, don't blame me.*
♦ *The hospital has launched an inquiry to find out who was **to blame for** the mistake.* ♦ *You can't **blame** all your problems **on** your family.*

blame² /bleɪm/ noun [U] responsibility for an accident, problem, or bad situation: *Why do I always get **the blame for** everything?* ♦ *The management has to **take the blame** (=accept they are responsible) for recent failures.*

blameless /ˈbleɪmləs/ adj not responsible for anything bad

bland /blænd/ adj **1** not interesting or exciting: *The film is a bland adaptation of the novel*. **2** not having a strong taste and not very interesting to eat **3** bland comments or remarks are pleasant and intended not to make anyone upset or angry, but they may not be sincere

blank¹ /blæŋk/ adj **1** containing no writing, pictures, or sound: *a blank sheet of paper* ♦ *a blank tape* ♦ *The last three boxes should be **left blank***. **2** showing no emotion, or no sign of understanding something or recognizing someone: *a blank expression*

PHRASE **go blank** if your mind goes blank, you are unable to remember something

blank² /blæŋk/ noun [C] **1** an empty space on a piece of paper where you can write something: *Please put either a tick or an X in the blanks*. **2** a gun **cartridge** that explodes when the gun is fired, but contains no bullet

,**blank 'cheque** noun [C] **1** a cheque that has been signed but does not have an amount of money written on it **2** freedom and authority to do whatever is necessary to deal with a problem

blanket¹ /ˈblæŋkɪt/ noun **1** [C] a thick cover made of wool or another material that you use to keep warm in bed **2** [singular] a thick layer of something that completely covers an area

blanket² /ˈblæŋkɪt/ adj affecting everyone or everything equally, even when this is not sensible or fair: *a blanket ban on tobacco advertising*

blankly /ˈblæŋkli/ adv without showing any emotion, reaction, or understanding: *She gazed at him blankly.*

,**blank 'verse** noun [U] **LITERATURE** poetry that does not have lines that rhyme

blare /bleə/ verb [I/T] to make a loud unpleasant noise —**blare** noun [singular]

blasé /ˈblɑːzeɪ/ adj not excited, worried, or enthusiastic about something that most people think is exciting, worrying, or impressive, because you have done it many times before

blaspheme /ˌblæsˈfiːm/ verb [I] **RELIGION** to say offensive things about God or about someone's religious beliefs —**blasphemer** noun [C]

blasphemy /ˈblæsfəmi/ (plural **blasphemies**) noun [C/U] **RELIGION** something that is considered to be offensive to God or to someone's religious beliefs — **blasphemous** /ˈblæsfəməs/ adj

blast¹ /blɑːst/ noun [C] **1** an explosion: *Ten people were injured **in the blast***. **2** a strong current of air, wind, or heat: *a **blast of** cold air* **3** a sudden short loud sound: *a sudden **blast of** music*

PHRASE **(at) full blast** as loudly or with as much power as possible: *The radio was on full blast.*

blast² /blɑːst/ verb **1** [T] to damage or destroy something with a bomb or gun: *A massive car bomb blasted the police headquarters*. **2** [T] to hit something with a lot of energy or force **3** [I] to make a loud sound: *Music blasted from the open window.*

PHRASAL VERB ,**blast 'off** if a spacecraft blasts off, it leaves the ground

'**blast ,furnace** noun [C] **TECHNOLOGY** an upright furnace that is used to **smelt** iron ore

blatant /ˈbleɪt(ə)nt/ adj done in an obvious way that shows someone is not embarrassed or ashamed to be doing something bad or illegal: *a blatant lie* —**blatantly** adv

blaze¹ /bleɪz/ noun **1** [C] a large fire that causes a lot of damage: *Firefighters were called to a blaze at a warehouse yesterday*. **2** [singular] a strong bright light or area of colour

blaze² /bleɪz/ verb [I] **1** to burn strongly and brightly: *A fire blazed in the grate*. ♦ *In a few moments, the fire was blazing*. **2** to shine very brightly: *A car roared towards them, its headlights blazing*. **3** if someone's eyes blaze, they show a sudden strong emotion, especially anger **4 blaze** or **blaze away** if guns blaze or blaze away, they continue firing for a long time

blazer /ˈbleɪzə/ noun [C] a light jacket that is often worn as part of a uniform

blazing /ˈbleɪzɪŋ/ adj **1** burning very strongly: *a blazing building* **2** very hot: *the blazing sun* **3** showing a lot of anger or emotion: *a blazing row*

bleach¹ /bliːtʃ/ noun [U] a strong chemical that is used for killing bacteria or for making coloured things white

bleach² /bliːtʃ/ verb **1** [T] to remove the colour from something **2** [I] to gradually lose colour, for example because of being in the sun

bleaching agent /ˈbliːtʃɪŋ ˌeɪdʒ(ə)nt/ noun [C] **CHEMISTRY 1** a substance in a **detergent** that removes the colour from fabric and kills any bacteria in it **2** an artificial substance that is used to make some foods whiter and more attractive

bleak /bliːk/ adj **1** with no reason to feel happy or hopeful: *Textile workers face a **bleak future***. **2** cold and unpleasant: *bleak winter days* —**bleakly** adv

bleat /bliːt/ verb [I] **1** to make the sound that a sheep or goat makes **2** to complain in a weak voice, or in an annoying way

bleed /bliːd/ (**bleeds, bleeding, bled** /bled/) verb **1** [I] to have blood flowing from your body, for example from a cut: *He was **bleeding from** a wound in his shoulder*. **2** [T] to make someone pay a lot of money, especially regularly over a long period of time **3** [T] to take blood from someone's body as part of a medical treatment, especially in the past —**bleeding** noun [U]: *They had to act quickly to stop the bleeding.*

bleep /bliːp/ noun [C] a short high sound made by a piece of electronic equipment —**bleep** verb [I]

blemish /ˈblemɪʃ/ noun [C] **1** a mark or spot that spoils the appearance of something **2** a mistake or dishonest action that spoils someone's reputation

blend¹ /blend/ noun [C] **1** a combination of different tastes, styles, or qualities that produces an attractive or effective result: *a **blend of** modern and traditional songs* **2** a mixture of different types of tea, coffee, alcoholic drinks, or tobacco **3** **LANGUAGE** a word formed by combining parts of two other words, for example 'brunch' is a blend of 'breakfast' and 'lunch'

blend² /blend/ verb **1** [T] to mix things together: ***Blend** the flour **with** a little milk to make a smooth paste*. **2** [I] to combine with other things: *The pale blue of the curtains **blends** perfectly **with** the colour scheme.*

PHRASAL VERB ,**blend 'in** to be similar to the other people or things in the same place or situation: *Security men were trying to **blend in with** the crowd.*

blender /ˈblendə/ noun [C] a piece of electrical equipment that mixes foods, or turns soft food into a liquid

bless /bles/ verb [T] **RELIGION 1** to say a prayer asking God to help and protect someone or something **2** to make something holy, so that it can be used in a religious ceremony

PHRASE **be blessed with sth** to have something very good or special

blessed /'blesɪd/ adj **RELIGION** holy, or loved by God

blessing /'blesɪŋ/ noun **1** [C] something good that you feel grateful or lucky to have: *It's a blessing that your relatives live so near.* **2** [singular] permission or support for something: *They didn't want to get married without their parents' blessing.* **3** [U] **RELIGION** protection and help from God

  PHRASE **a blessing in disguise** something that seems to cause problems, but that you later realize is a good thing

blew /bluː/ the past tense of **blow¹**

blight /blaɪt/ noun **1** [U] **AGRICULTURE** a serious disease caused by various different microorganisms that quickly destroys leaves, stems, fruit and other plant parts, killing crops and any other plants it attacks **2** [singular/U] something that damages or spoils something else —**blight** verb [T]

blind¹ /blaɪnd/ adj

1 unable to see	**4** of corner
2 unable to admit sth	**5** of people as a group
3 of emotion/belief	**+ PHRASE**

1 unable to see. Some people think that this word is offensive and prefer to use the expression **visually impaired** ≠ SIGHTED: *Blind and sighted children attend the same school.* ♦ *The disease made her go blind.*
2 unable to realize or admit the truth about something: *He was blind to the importance of the occasion.*
3 a blind emotion or belief is so strong that you do not question it, even if it is unreasonable: *blind faith* ♦ *In a blind panic, I dropped the bag and ran.*
4 a blind corner is one where you cannot see what is coming towards you
5 the blind people who are blind
  PHRASE **turn a blind eye (to sth)** to pretend that you do not notice something bad or illegal
—**blindness** noun [U]

blind² /blaɪnd/ verb [T] **1** to damage someone's eyes so that they are unable to see: *Jimmy was temporarily blinded by the bright light.* **2** to prevent someone from realizing or admitting the truth about something: *Her hatred blinded her to the fact that Joe could have helped her.*

blind³ /blaɪnd/ noun [C] a window cover that you pull down from the top to the bottom

,**blind 'alley** noun [C] **1** a process that was expected to bring useful results but in fact achieves nothing **2** a narrow path between or behind buildings, that is closed at one end

,**blind 'copy** noun [C] **BUSINESS** a copy of an email that is sent to someone without telling the person the email is addressed to that that person is being sent a copy of it

blindfold¹ /'blaɪn(d)ˌfəʊld/ verb [T] to tie a cover over someone's eyes so that they cannot see

blindfold² /'blaɪn(d)ˌfəʊld/ noun [C] something that is tied over someone's eyes so that they cannot see

,**blind 'hole** noun [C] **TECHNOLOGY** a hole that does not go all the way through a piece of metal

blinding /'blaɪndɪŋ/ adj **1** extremely bright: *a blinding light* **2** very great, or severe: *a blinding headache*

blindly /'blaɪn(d)li/ adv **1** without thinking or knowing enough about what you are doing: *This group is blindly loyal to the president.* **2** without being able to see: *She felt her way blindly towards the door.* **3** without having the information you need

'**blind ,spot** noun [C] **1** a subject that you do not understand or know much about, often because you

do not want to know or admit the truth about it
2 **ANATOMY** the part of the retina in the eye that is not sensitive to light. It is the place where the **optic nerve** leaves the eye. —*picture* → EYE

,**blind 'trust** noun [C] **LAW** an arrangement in which a legal representative controls the money of someone such as a government official, who is not given specific information about how their money is being managed

bling /blɪŋ/ or ,**bling 'bling** noun [U] *informal* **1** fashionable jewellery or similar expensive shiny objects **2** behaviour deliberately aimed at showing how rich you are, for example spending money in an obvious way or wearing expensive clothes or jewellery

blink /blɪŋk/ verb **1** [I/T] to close your eyes and quickly open them again **2** [I] if a light blinks, it goes on and off continuously —**blink** noun [C]

blinkers /'blɪŋkəz/ noun [plural] things that partly cover a horse's eyes so that it can only look straight ahead

blip /blɪp/ noun [C] **1** *informal* a minor problem **2** a small flashing light on the screen of a piece of equipment

bliss /blɪs/ noun [U] complete happiness

blissful /'blɪsf(ə)l/ adj giving you great pleasure —**blissfully** adv

blister /'blɪstə/ noun [C] a swollen area on your skin that contains liquid and is caused by being burned or rubbed —**blister** verb [I/T]

'**blister ,pack** noun [C] a container in which something small is sold, consisting of a flat layer and a raised cover of plastic that protects the product.

blitz /blɪts/ noun **1** [singular] a special effort to deal with something quickly and thoroughly: *It's time we had a blitz on the paperwork.* **2** [C] a sudden military attack —**blitz** verb [T]

blizzard /'blɪzəd/ noun [C] a storm with a lot of snow and strong winds

bloated /'bləʊtɪd/ adj having an uncomfortable feeling in the stomach after eating or drinking too much

blob /blɒb/ noun [C] **1** a small amount of a thick liquid **2** something that seems to have no definite shape

bloc /blɒk/ noun [C] a group of countries or people with the same political aims

block¹ /blɒk/ noun [C]

1 large building	**6** sth stopping progress
2 solid piece of sth	**7** when you cannot think
3 amount of sth	**8** distance along street
4 area in a town	**9** at start of race
5 period of time	**+ PHRASES**

1 a large building with a lot of different levels: *an office block* ♦ *The whole block of flats was destroyed.*
2 a solid piece of wood, stone, ice etc with straight sides: *a block of marble*
3 an amount of something that you think of as a unit: *We need to find a two-hour block when we are all free for this seminar.* ♦ *You can move blocks of text using the mouse.*
4 an area of buildings in a town or city with streets on all four sides: *I was early, so I walked around the block a couple of times.*
5 a continuous period of time: *We need to find a two-hour block when we are all free for this seminar.*
6 something that stops you from doing something or making progress: *The issue of holiday pay was the major block in reaching an agreement.*
7 a short time when you are unable to think clearly or remember something: *a mental block*

8 *American* the distance along a street, from the place where one street crosses it to the place where the next street crosses it: *The school was only a few blocks from where she lived.*

9 the blocks [plural] SPORTS two pieces of metal or wood that runners use at the start of a race to push their feet against

PHRASES **block and tackle** PHYSICS a piece of equipment that consists of wheels and ropes, used for lifting heavy objects

block-and-tackle pulley PHYSICS a piece of equipment that consists of fixed and movable pulleys that are set in frames called blocks
→ STUMBLING BLOCK

block² /blɒk/ verb [T] **1** to stop something from moving along or passing through something: *A car was blocking the road.* ♦ *Something is blocking the flow of water through the pipe.* **2** to stop someone from going past you by standing in front of them: *A crowd of people blocked his way to the gate.* **3** to stop something from happening or succeeding: *The plan to build a new airport was blocked by local residents.* **4** to be in front of someone so that they cannot see something, or so that light cannot reach them: *Don't stand in the doorway, you're blocking the light.*

PHRASAL VERB ˌblock sth ˈout **1** to stop light or sound from reaching something: *That tree in the neighbour's garden blocks out a lot of light.* **2** to stop yourself from thinking about or remembering something: *He had always managed to block out the incident.*

blockade /blɒˈkeɪd/ noun [C] an official action that is intended to prevent people or goods from moving from one place to another —**blockade** verb [T]

blockage /ˈblɒkɪdʒ/ noun [C] something that blocks a tube or pipe

blockboard /ˈblɒkbɔːd/ noun [U] CONSTRUCTION a type of board made from thin layers of wood covered with **veneer** (=a top layer with an attractive appearance)

ˌblock ˈbooking noun [C] an agreement to buy a large number of tickets at one time for a concert, play etc

blockbuster /ˈblɒkbʌstə/ noun [C] a very successful film, show, or novel

ˌblock ˈcapitals noun [plural] letters of the alphabet that are written in their large form, for example 'A' rather than 'a'

ˈblock ˌgraph noun [C] MATHS a graph that shows numbers or amounts as rectangles of different sizes —*picture* → CHART

ˌblock ˈletters noun [plural] **block capitals**

ˌblock ˈrate noun [U] BUSINESS a way of charging for something in which the price varies according to the amount used. For example, if a block rate is used to charge for electricity, the cost of the electricity is higher for the first block of kilowatt hours and lower for later blocks.

ˈblock ˌwork noun [U] CONSTRUCTION part of a structure that consists of concrete blocks

blog /blɒg/ noun [C] COMPUTING a biographical weblog: a type of **diary** (=record of what someone does each day) on a website that is changed regularly, to give the latest news. The page usually contains someone's personal opinions, comments, and experiences, and provides **links** to other places on the Internet. —**blog** verb [I], **blogger** noun [C]

blogosphere /ˈblɒgəʊˌsfɪə/ noun [singular] COMPUTING the imaginary place on the Internet where people's **blogs** go so that other people can read them and react to them

bloke /bləʊk/ noun [C] *informal* a man

blonde or **blond** /blɒnd/ adj **1** blonde hair is pale yellow in colour **2** with pale yellow hair —**blonde** noun [C]

blood /blʌd/ noun [U] **1** BIOLOGY the red liquid that is pumped around the body from the heart. Blood carries oxygen, hormones, and nutrients to the various parts of the body, and also helps to get rid of waste products. It consists of **plasma** which contains **red blood cells** and **white blood cells**, and **platelets**: *Oxygen is carried in the blood.* ♦ *His face was covered in blood.* → HAEMOGLOBIN **2** the family, nation, or group that someone belongs to through their parents and grandparents **3** violence and death: *There was a lot of blood spilled* (=deaths and injuries caused) *on both sides.* → DRAW¹, FLESH

ˈblood ˌbank noun [C] HEALTH a place where blood is stored so that it can be given to people during operations

bloodbath /ˈblʌdˌbɑːθ/ noun [singular] a period of fighting in which a lot of people are killed or injured

ˈblood ˌbrother noun [C] a man who has made a very serious promise to be loyal to another man

ˈblood ˌclot noun [C] HEALTH a soft mass of almost solid blood that blocks a blood vessel

blood clotting /ˈblʌd ˌklɒtɪŋ/ noun [U] HEALTH the process by which blood becomes thick and stops flowing, forming a solid cover over any place where the skin has been cut or broken

ˈblood ˌcount noun [C] HEALTH the number of red or white cells in the blood, or a test to measure this, for example in order to find out the state of someone's **immune system**

bloodcurdling /ˈblʌdˌkɜːd(ə)lɪŋ/ adj very frightening

ˈblood ˌdonor noun [C] HEALTH someone who gives some of their blood so that hospitals can use it to treat other people

ˈblood ˌfluke noun [C] HEALTH a type of **flatworm** that is a parasite. It lives in some types of snail from where it moves into birds and mammals to complete its life cycle. It causes **bilharzia** in humans.

ˈblood ˌgroup noun [C] HEALTH one of the groups that human blood can be divided into. The groups are based on the presence or absence of chemicals that are found on the surface of a red blood cell. → ABO SYSTEM

bloodless /ˈblʌdləs/ adj not involving violence or killing, in a situation where there often is violence

ˈblood ˌpoisoning noun [U] HEALTH a serious illness caused by an infection of the blood

ˈblood ˌpressure noun [U] HEALTH the pressure at which blood flows from the heart around the body. Blood pressure that is either very high or very low can be dangerous to health.

ˈblood ˌproduct noun [C] HEALTH a substance that can be taken from the blood of one person and used in the medical treatment of someone else

ˈblood reˌlation noun [C] someone that you are related to by birth, rather than marriage

bloodshed /ˈblʌdˌʃed/ noun [U] a situation in which people are killed or injured in fighting

bloodshot /ˈblʌdˌʃɒt/ adj bloodshot eyes are red in the part where they should be white

ˈblood ˌsports noun [plural] activities such as hunting that involve killing animals or birds

bloodstained /ˈblʌdˌsteɪnd/ adj marked with blood —**bloodstain** noun [C]

bloodstock /ˈblʌdˌstɒk/ noun [U] horses that are **thoroughbred** (=belonging to a type considered of very high quality) and are produced for running in races

bloodstream /ˈblʌdˌstriːm/ noun [singular] **BIOLOGY** the blood that moves continuously around the body, going from and to the heart. It takes oxygen and nutrients to all the cells, and carries waste products such as carbon dioxide away.

blood ˈsugar noun [U] **BIOLOGY** sugars such as glucose that are present in healthy blood

ˈblood ˌtest noun [C] **HEALTH** a medical test in which a small amount of blood is taken from someone and tested to see if it shows any signs of disease, drugs etc in the body

bloodthirsty /ˈblʌdˌθɜːsti/ adj someone who is bloodthirsty enjoys being violent, or enjoys watching violence

ˈblood transˌfusion noun [C] **HEALTH** a medical treatment in which blood from one person is put into someone else's body, especially because they have lost a lot of blood through an injury or during a medical operation

ˈblood ˌtype noun [C] **HEALTH** a **blood group**

ˈblood ˌvessel noun [C] **ANATOMY** a tube that carries blood around the body. Veins, arteries, and capillaries are all blood vessels.

bloody /ˈblʌdi/ (**bloodier, bloodiest**) adj **1** covered in blood **2** a bloody fight or war is one in which a lot of people are killed or injured

bloom¹ /bluːm/ noun [C] **1** a flower: *beautiful red blooms* **2 TECHNOLOGY** a piece of **cast** iron or steel, smaller than an **ingot**, that is ready for further processing
PHRASE in (full) bloom covered with flowers

bloom² /bluːm/ verb [I] **1** if a tree or **shrub** blooms, flowers appear and open = FLOWER **2** to develop in a successful or healthy way

blossom¹ /ˈblɒs(ə)m/ noun [C/U] a flower on a tree, or all the flowers on a tree —*picture* → TREE

blossom² /ˈblɒs(ə)m/ verb [I] **1** to develop and become more successful: *Their romance blossomed on a trip to Key West.* **2** if a plant or tree blossoms, flowers appear and open

blot¹ /blɒt/ (**blots, blotting, blotted**) verb [T] to remove liquid from the surface of something using a piece of paper or cloth
PHRASAL VERB ˌblot sth ˈout to cover something so that you can no longer see it: *Dark clouds overhead had blotted out the sun.*

blot² /blɒt/ noun [C] a drop of ink or another liquid on the surface of something

blotchy /ˈblɒtʃi/ adj blotchy skin is covered with red areas

blotting paper /ˈblɒtɪŋ ˌpeɪpə/ noun [U] special thick paper that is used for drying the ink after writing with a fountain pen

blouse /blaʊz/ noun [C] a shirt for women

blow¹ /bləʊ/ (**blows, blowing, blew** /bluː/, **blown** /bləʊn/) verb

1 of air moving	**6** miss opportunity
2 move with wind	**7** of electrical failing
3 push out air	**+ PHRASE**
4 move/form sth	**+ PHRASAL VERBS**
5 play an instrument	

artery

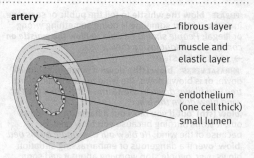

- fibrous layer
- muscle and elastic layer
- endothelium (one cell thick)
- small lumen

vein

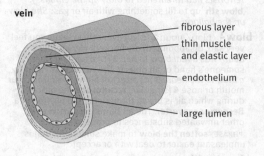

- fibrous layer
- thin muscle and elastic layer
- endothelium
- large lumen

capillary

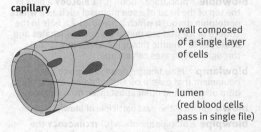

- wall composed of a single layer of cells
- lumen (red blood cells pass in single file)

blood vessels

1 [I] if wind or air blows, the air moves: *A strong wind was blowing across the island.*
2 [I/T] if something blows somewhere, or if it is blown somewhere, the wind moves it there: *The wind was blowing snow along the street.* ♦ *Newspapers and plastic bags were blowing about in the wind.*
3 [I] to push out air from your mouth: *He bent towards the candle and blew gently.*
4 [T] to move something or form something by pushing out air from your mouth: *We were sitting on the steps, blowing bubbles.* ♦ *She picked up a book and blew the dust off it.*
5 [I/T] to make a musical sound by pushing air through something: *The guard blew his whistle and the train started.* ♦ *Behind them they heard horns blowing.*
6 [T] *informal* to destroy your own chance of succeeding, or to waste a good opportunity: *We've been working very hard, and we don't intend to **blow it** now.*
7 [I/T] **PHYSICS** if something electrical blows, it stops working because a fault has caused an electrical circuit to break

PHRASE **blow the whistle** to tell the public or someone in authority that someone is doing something wrong or illegal: *People should be able to **blow the whistle on corruption** without losing their jobs.*
→ PROPORTION, STEAM[1]

PHRASAL VERBS ,**blow (sth) 'down** if something blows down, or is blown down, the wind makes it fall: *A big tree had blown down in the storm.* ♦ *A sudden gust of wind blew down the fence.*

,**blow (sth) 'out** if you blow out a flame, or if it blows out, it stops burning because you blow on it, or because of the wind: *He blew out the candle by his bed.*

,**blow 'over** if a dangerous or embarrassing situation blows over, people stop worrying about it and soon forget about it: *The scandal soon blew over.*

,**blow (sth) 'up** if something blows up, or if someone blows something up, it explodes and is destroyed: *Terrorists had threatened to blow up the embassy.*

,**blow sth 'up** to fill something with air or gas: *She blew up the balloon.*

blow² /bləʊ/ noun **1** [C] an event that makes you feel very sad, disappointed, or shocked: *Her mother's death was a real blow to her.* **2** [C] a hard hit from someone's hand or an object: *The victim was killed by a **blow to** the head.* **3** [C] an act of blowing air from your mouth or nose **4** [singular] TECHNOLOGY the process during which air is blown through melted pig iron in a **Bessemer converter.** The air burns off carbon and other unwanted substances to produce steel.
PHRASE **soften the blow** to make something that is unpleasant easier to deal with or accept

,**blow-by-'blow** adj including a lot of details: *a blow-by-blow account of her trip*

blowfly /'bləʊ,flaɪ/ noun [C] a fly that lays its eggs on meat or dead animals

blowhole /'bləʊ,həʊl/ noun [C] **1** BIOLOGY a hole in the top of the head of a sea mammal such as a **whale** or **dolphin**, through which it breathes **2** a hole in the surface of ice that sea mammals such as **whales** and **seals** use to breathe through **3** a hole in a tunnel through which gases can escape

blowlamp /'bləʊ,læmp/ noun [C] a piece of equipment that uses a controlled flame, especially to burn off paint and other substances from surfaces

blown /bləʊn/ the past participle of **blow¹**

blowpipe /'bləʊ,paɪp/ noun [C] TECHNOLOGY the equipment used to produce the flame for welding, **brazing**, or cutting metal

blowtorch /'bləʊ,tɔːtʃ/ noun [C] a tool with a flame at one end that is used for removing paint, or for joining pieces of metal together

blubber /'blʌbə/ noun [U] a layer of fat around the body of a sea mammal such as a **whale**

bludgeon /'blʌdʒ(ə)n/ verb [T] to hit someone hard with a heavy object

blue¹ /bluː/ adj **1** something that is blue is the same colour as the sky on a clear sunny day: *He looked at her with his pale blue eyes.* **2** *informal* feeling rather sad: *She usually calls her mother when she's feeling blue.*

blue² /bluː/ noun **1** [C/U] the colour of the sky on a clear sunny day: *The boy was dressed all in blue.* ♦ *bright blues and yellows* **2** blue or Blue [C] a person who has played for Oxford University or Cambridge University in a sport: *He was a cricket Blue at Oxford.*
PHRASE **out of the blue** happening in a way that is sudden and unexpected: *Out of the blue she said, 'Your name's John, isn't it?'* → BLUES

,**blue 'baby** noun [C] HEALTH a baby whose skin looks blue when it is born because its **Rhesus positive** blood cells have been attacked by **Rhesus negative** antibodies from its mother

blueberry /'bluːb(ə)ri/ (plural **blueberries**) noun [C/U] a small dark-blue fruit that grows on a bush —*picture* → FRUIT

blue-blooded /,bluː 'blʌdɪd/ adj from a royal family, or from a family of a very high social class

bluebottle /'bluː,bɒt(ə)l/ noun [C] a large fly with a shiny blue body

,**blue 'cheese** noun [C/U] a strong-tasting cheese that is white or pale yellow and has blue lines in it

'**blue ,chip** noun [C] BUSINESS a company or **investment** that is considered safe to invest in —'**blue-,chip** adj

,**blue-'collar** adj SOCIAL STUDIES blue-collar workers do physical work in places such as factories and mines → WHITE-COLLAR

blueing /'bluːɪŋ/ noun [U] TECHNOLOGY the production of a layer of blue **oxide** on **polished** steel by heating

blueprint /'bluː,prɪnt/ noun [C] **1** a detailed plan for doing something **2** a drawing that shows how to build something such as a building or a machine

'**blue ,printing** noun [U] TECHNOLOGY the process of making a copy of a drawing by shining light onto a drawing done on special paper. The copy is white on a blue background.

blues /bluːz/ noun **1** [U] MUSIC a type of slow sad music that developed from the songs of black **slaves** in the southern US **2 the blues** [plural] *informal* a feeling of sadness and loss

bluescreen /'bluː,skriːn/ noun [U] ARTS a method used in film making that involves filming the action in front of a background of a single colour and later replacing the background with a scene

Bluetooth /'bluː,tuːθ/ noun [U] TRADEMARK a type of radio technology that makes it possible for electronic communication to exist between mobile phones, the Internet, and computers

bluff¹ /blʌf/ verb [I/T] to try to trick someone by pretending that you know something or that you will do something: *They said they'd had another offer, but we knew they were just bluffing.*

bluff² /blʌf/ noun **1** [C/U] an attempt to bluff someone **2** [C] GEOGRAPHY a steep cliff by the sea or by a river —*picture* → FLOOD PLAIN
PHRASE **call sb's bluff** to tell someone to do what they are threatening to do, because you believe that they do not really intend to do it

bluish /'bluːɪʃ/ adj similar to blue

blunder /'blʌndə/ noun [C] a careless or embarrassing mistake

blunt /blʌnt/ adj **1** saying what is true or what you really think, even if this offends or upsets people **2** not pointed or sharp: *a blunt pencil* —**bluntness** noun [U]

bluntly /'blʌntli/ adv speaking in a direct and honest way, even if this offends or upsets people

blur¹ /blɜː/ (**blurs, blurring, blurred**) verb [I/T] **1** to become less clear, or to make something less clear: *The letters **blurred together** on the page.* **2** if the difference between two things blurs, or if something blurs it, they become more similar **3** if a memory or an idea blurs, it is no longer clear in your mind

blur[2] /blɜː/ noun [C] **1** a shape that is difficult to see clearly, for example because it is moving very fast: *a blur of activity* **2** a thought or memory that is not very clear in your mind: *I remember a big house, but the rest of it is a blur.*

blurred /blɜːd/ or **blurry** /ˈblɜːri/ adj difficult to see clearly, or causing difficulty in seeing something clearly: *blurred photographs ♦ blurred vision*

blurt /blɜːt/ or **,blurt sth 'out** verb [T] to say something suddenly and without thinking about the effect that it will have

blush /blʌʃ/ verb [I] if someone blushes, their cheeks become red because they feel embarrassed or ashamed

blustery /ˈblʌst(ə)ri/ adj with strong winds: *blustery weather*

BMI /ˌbiː em ˈaɪ/ noun [singular] **HEALTH** body mass index: a measurement of the amount of fat in someone's body, calculated by dividing their weight in kilograms by their height in metres

bmp abbrev **COMPUTING** bitmap: the last part of the name of a file that contains pictures

BMR /ˌbiː em ˈɑː/ noun [U] **BIOLOGY** basal metabolic rate: the rate at which an organism uses oxygen while it is awake but not active. It is measured in calories per square metre of body surface per hour.

BO /ˌbiː ˈəʊ/ noun [U] body odour: an unpleasant smell that comes from someone who has not washed or has been exercising

boa constrictor /ˈbəʊə kənˌstrɪktə/ noun [C] a large snake that kills other animals by wrapping itself around them and squeezing them

boar /bɔː/ (plural **boar** or **boars**) noun [C] **1** a male pig **2** a wild pig

board[1] /bɔːd/ noun

1 long piece of wood	**4** group of managers
2 thin flat surface	**5** meals
3 for information	**+ PHRASE**

1 [C] a long thin flat piece of wood that is used for building: *There's a loose board in the bedroom floor.*
2 [C] a thin flat piece of wood or other material that is used for a particular purpose: *a chopping board ♦ We wanted to play chess, but I couldn't find the board.*
3 [C] a flat wide surface such as a **noticeboard** or **blackboard** that is used for showing information: *The exam results were pinned up on the board.*
4 [C] a group of people who control an organization or company: *an advisory board ♦ The company's board of directors voted against the proposal.*
5 [U] meals provided for you when you stay at a hotel, live at another person's house etc → FULL BOARD, HALF BOARD

PHRASE on board on a ship or plane: *The plane had 125 passengers and crew on board.*
→ ACROSS-THE-BOARD

board[2] /bɔːd/ verb **1** [I/T] to get onto a ship, aircraft, train, or bus **2** [I] if a plane or ship is boarding, passengers are being allowed to get on it **3** [I] to live in a room in someone's house and pay them money in exchange

boarder /ˈbɔːdə/ noun [C] **1** someone who pays to live in someone else's house **2** **EDUCATION** a boy or girl who lives at a **boarding school**

'board ,game noun [C] any game in which you move objects around on a special board

boarding card /ˈbɔːdɪŋ ˌkɑːd/ noun [C] **TOURISM** a card that each passenger has to show before they are allowed to get on a plane or ship

boarding pass /ˈbɔːdɪŋ ˌpɑːs/ noun [C] **TOURISM** a boarding card

boarding school /ˈbɔːdɪŋ ˌskuːl/ noun [C] **EDUCATION** a school in which the students live during the part of the year that they go to lessons

boardroom /ˈbɔːdruːm/ noun [C] a room where the directors of a company have meetings

boast[1] /bəʊst/ verb **1** [I/T] to talk about your abilities, achievements, or possessions in a way that sounds too proud = BRAG: *The men sat in the café boasting about their win. ♦ Mrs White liked to boast that she knew every person in the town.* **2** [T] *formal* to have something good that other people admire: *The island boasts the highest number of tourists in the area.*

boast[2] /bəʊst/ noun [C] a statement in which someone talks about their abilities, achievements, or possessions in a way that sounds too proud

boastful /ˈbəʊstf(ə)l/ adj *showing disapproval* too eager to tell other people about your abilities, achievements, or possessions ≠ MODEST

boat /bəʊt/ noun [C] **1** a small vehicle for travelling on water: *The only way to get there was by boat.* → ROWING BOAT, SAILING BOAT **2** a ship that carries passengers
PHRASE in the same boat in the same difficult or unpleasant situation

boating /ˈbəʊtɪŋ/ noun [U] the activity of sailing in a boat for enjoyment

bob /bɒb/ (**bobs, bobbing, bobbed**) verb [I] to move up and down with short regular movements, especially in the water

bobsleigh /ˈbɒbˌsleɪ/ noun [C] **SPORTS** a small vehicle for two or more people designed for sliding over snow and ice and used in races down a track called a **bobsleigh run**

bode /bəʊd/ verb **bode well/ill** *formal* to be a sign that something good/bad will happen

bodily /ˈbɒdɪli/ adj relating to your body, or affecting your body: *bodily fluids*

body /ˈbɒdi/ (plural **bodies**) noun

1 of animals	**5** of car/plane
2 not arms/legs	**6** main part of sth
3 of a dead person	**7** collection of sth
4 group of people	**8** appearance of hair

1 [C] the whole physical structure of a human or other animal: *My whole body ached.* —*picture* → on next page
2 [C] the main part of a person's or animal's body, not including the head, arms, or legs
3 [C] the body of a dead person = CORPSE
4 [C] a group of people who have official responsibility for something: *the legislative body* (=group that makes laws) *of the government ♦ the school's governing body*
5 [C] the main outer part of a car or plane, not including the engine, wheels, or wings
6 [singular] the main part of something that has many parts: *You can find more details in the body of the report.*
7 [C] a large amount of knowledge, information, or work: *There is a growing body of evidence to support this theory.*
8 [U] the thick healthy appearance of someone's hair
→ FOREIGN BODY

'body ,armour noun [U] special clothes that soldiers and police officers wear to protect themselves against bullets in extremely dangerous situations

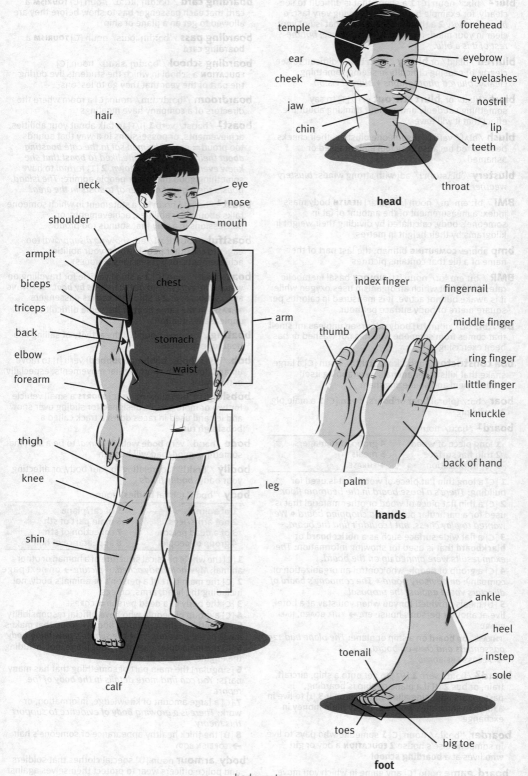

temple
forehead
ear
eyebrow
cheek
eyelashes
jaw
nostril
chin
lip
teeth
throat

head

hair
neck
eye
nose
shoulder
mouth
armpit
biceps
triceps
back
elbow
forearm
chest
arm
stomach
waist
thigh
knee
leg
shin
calf

index finger
fingernail
thumb
middle finger
ring finger
little finger
knuckle
back of hand
palm

hands

ankle
heel
instep
sole
toenail
toes
big toe

foot

body parts

'body ,bag noun [C] a large bag used for carrying a dead body

'body ,blow noun [C] a serious problem, or a great disappointment

bodyboard /'bɒdi ,bɔːd/ noun [C] a type of small **surfboard**, used for waves that are close to the land

'body ,building noun [U] regular physical exercises with weights that make the muscles bigger —**'body ,builder** noun [C]

'body ,clock noun [C] the natural system in the body that controls a person's behaviour at particular times of the day or year, for example what time they wake up or feel hungry= BIOLOGICAL CLOCK

'body ,count noun [C] the number of people killed in a battle or accident, or the process of counting them

bodyguard /'bɒdi,gɑːd/ noun [C] a person whose job is to protect an important person from being attacked

'body ,image noun [C/U] the opinion someone has about how attractive their body is

'body ,language noun [U] the movements or positions of someone's body that show other people what they are thinking or feeling

'body ,mass noun [U] HEALTH the weight of person's body in relation to their height

,body 'mass ,index noun [singular] HEALTH see BMI

the ,body 'politic noun formal all the people of a nation considered as a single group because of their combined political power

'body ,search noun [C] a search of someone's body and clothing for weapons or drugs, made by a police officer or other official

'body ,shop noun [C] a place where cars are repaired after an accident

'body ,temperature noun [U] the normal temperature of the body, measured with a **thermometer**

'body ,tube noun [C] SCIENCE the main part of a microscope, in the shape of a cylinder —picture → MICROSCOPE

bog¹ /bɒg/ noun [C/U] an area of ground that is always very wet and soft

bog² /bɒg/ verb **be/get bogged down (in sth)** to be or become so involved with one particular thing that you cannot make any progress: The trial got bogged down in legal complications.

bogey /'bəʊgi/ noun [C] SPORTS a golf score that is one hit of the ball more than the number expected for a particular hole

boggy /'bɒgi/ adj boggy ground is always very wet and soft

bogof or **BOGOF** /'bɒgɒf/ noun [U] BUSINESS buy one get one free: the practice of giving customers an extra product free each time they buy one product

,bog 'standard adj informal ordinary and not special in any way

bogus /'bəʊgəs/ adj not real, but pretending to be real: bogus insurance claims

,bogus 'caller noun [C] someone who pretends they are an official in order to enter a home to steal something

boil¹ /bɔɪl/ verb **1** [I/T] SCIENCE if a liquid boils, or if you boil it, it becomes so hot that bubbles rise to the surface as its molecules quickly turn to vapour. A pure substance always boils at the same temperature. **2** [I/T] to cook something in boiling water, or to be cooked in this way: How long does it take to boil an

egg? —picture → FOOD **3** [I] to feel something such as anger very strongly

PHRASAL VERBS **,boil 'down to sth** to be the main reason for something, or the most basic part of something: Passing exams isn't difficult; it all boils down to good preparation.

,boil 'over 1 to flow over the top of a container while boiling **2** if a situation or feeling boils over, people cannot control their anger and start to fight or argue: Racial tensions in the area were boiling over.

boil² /bɔɪl/ noun **1** [C] HEALTH a painful lump on the skin that has become infected **2** [singular] TECHNOLOGY the blow, a process in steel production PHRASES **bring sth to the boil** to heat something until it boils

come to the boil if a liquid comes to the boil, it starts to boil

boiler /'bɔɪlə/ noun [C] a machine that heats water and provides hot water for a heating system —picture → GENERATOR

boilermaker /'bɔɪlə,meɪkə/ noun [C] someone whose job is to make **boilers**

boilerplate /'bɔɪlə,pleɪt/ noun [C/U] a **template** (=a standard way of writing something that can be copied) used in legal documents, contracts etc

'boiler ,suit noun [C] a piece of clothing that you wear over your clothes to protect them. It consists of trousers and a jacket joined together.

boiling /'bɔɪlɪŋ/ or **'boiling ,hot** adj extremely hot: It was a boiling hot day.

'boiling ,point noun [C/U] SCIENCE the temperature at which a liquid boils

'boiling ,tube noun [C] SCIENCE a large **test tube** made of glass. It can be heated and is used in scientific experiments. —picture → LABORATORY

boisterous /'bɔɪst(ə)rəs/ adj lively and noisy

bold¹ /bəʊld/ adj **1** confident and not afraid of risks: a bold plan to reduce crime **2** clear, bright, and strong in colour: a shirt with bold blue and yellow stripes — **boldly** adv, **boldness** noun [U]

bold² /bəʊld/ noun [U] a way of printing letters that makes them thicker and darker than usual: Try putting the title **in bold**.

boll /bəʊl/ noun [C] the part of a cotton plant that contains the fibre and the seeds

bollard /'bɒlɑːd/ noun [C] **1** a short post that is used for stopping cars from driving into an area **2** a short post that a ship is tied to

Bolshevik /'bɒlʃəvɪk/ noun [C] POLITICS someone who supported Lenin and his political ideas at the beginning of the 20th century —**Bolshevik** adj

bolster¹ /'bəʊlstə/ or **,bolster sth 'up** verb [T] to make something stronger or more effective: The bank cut interest rates in an attempt to bolster the economy.

bolster² /'bəʊlstə/ noun [C] a very long firm **pillow** (=something you rest your head on in bed)

bolt¹ /bəʊlt/ noun [C] **1** a metal bar that you slide across a door or window in order to lock it **2** a type of screw without a point that is used for fastening things together

bolt² /bəʊlt/ verb **1** [T] to lock a door or window using a bolt **2** [T] to fasten two things together using a bolt: The chairs were all **bolted to** the floor. **3** [I] if someone bolts, they run away suddenly, especially because they are frightened: There was a gunshot and the horse bolted. **4** bolt or **bolt sth down** [T] to eat food very quickly: *She bolted down her lunch and rushed back to work*.

bolt³ /bəʊlt/ adv **bolt upright** with the back very straight

bolus /'bəʊləs/ noun [C] **1** HEALTH a very large pill **2** BIOLOGY a ball of chewed food that is swallowed and that moves down the oesophagus to the stomach by **peristalsis**

bomb¹ /bɒm/ noun **1** [C] a weapon that is made to explode at a particular time or when it hits something: *The bomb had been planted in a busy street*. ♦ *Bombs fell on the city every night for two weeks*. **2 the bomb** *old-fashioned* nuclear weapons, considered as a group

bomb² /bɒm/ verb **1** [T] to attack a place with bombs: *NATO aircraft bombed the town again last night*. **2** [I] COMPUTING *informal* if a computer program bombs, it stops working because of a problem

bombard /bɒm'bɑːd/ verb [T] to attack a place by dropping a lot of bombs on it, or by firing guns at it for a long time

PHRASE **bombard sb with questions/messages/advice etc** to ask someone so many questions or give them so much information that it is difficult for them to deal with it all
—**bombardment** noun [C/U]

bombastic /bɒm'bæstɪk/ adj using words that are intended to impress people but do not really mean anything

'bomb dis,posal noun [U] the job of dealing with bombs that have not exploded and making certain that they are safe

bombed-out /,bɒmd 'aʊt/ adj **1** destroyed by bombs **2** forced to leave a place because of being attacked by bombs

bomber /'bɒmə/ noun [C] **1** a large military plane that drops bombs **2** someone who puts a bomb in a public place

bombshell /'bɒm,ʃel/ noun [C] *informal* an event or piece of news that is unexpected and shocking

bona fide /,bəʊnə 'faɪdi/ adj a bona fide person or thing is really what they seem or claim to be

bond¹ /bɒnd/ noun [C] **1** a close special feeling of connection with other people or groups: *The experience formed a close bond between us*. **2** BUSINESS a document that a government or a company gives to someone who invests money in it. The government or company promises to pay back the money with interest. **3** LAW a legal document containing a promise that one person will pay money to another person **4** CHEMISTRY a force that holds atoms or ions together in a molecule

bond² /bɒnd/ verb **1** [I] to develop a close special feeling towards other people: *He never felt like he bonded with any of the other students*. **2** [I/T] to fix two things firmly together, or to become fixed in this way **3** [T] CONSTRUCTION to lay bricks so that they partly cover each other, with the vertical joints not in line **4** [T] PHYSICS to connect an electrical circuit to the ground so that it is safe —**bonding** noun [U]

bondage /'bɒndɪdʒ/ noun [U] *formal* a situation in which someone is a **slave** or has no freedom

bonded warehouse /,bɒndɪd 'weə,haʊs/ noun [C] BUSINESS a government building for storing goods that have been brought into a country before tax has been paid on them

'bonding ,agent noun [C] TECHNOLOGY a substance used for holding metal pieces together, for example **solder**

bone /bəʊn/ noun ANATOMY **1** [C] one of the hard parts that form the skeleton of most vertebrates: *She fell and broke a bone in her foot*. **2** [U] the **calcified** substance that bones are made of

PHRASE **a bone of contention** a subject that people disagree about: *The main bone of contention between us is money*.

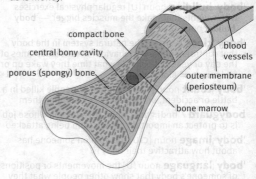

compact bone
central bony cavity
porous (spongy) bone
blood vessels
outer membrane (periosteum)
bone marrow

cross-section of a bone

'bone ,marrow noun [U] ANATOMY the soft red substance inside the spaces in the bones. Red blood cells, **platelets**, and some white blood cells are formed in the bone marrow. —*picture* → BONE

'bone ,meal noun [U] AGRICULTURE a substance made of crushed bones, used as food for animals or for helping plants to grow

bonfire /'bɒn,faɪə/ noun [C] a large fire built outside for burning rubbish or for a celebration

'Bonfire ,Night the night of 5th November, when British people have bonfires and light **fireworks**

bongos /'bɒŋgəʊz/ or **bongo drums** /'bɒŋgəʊ ,drʌmz/ noun [plural] a pair of small drums that are played with the hands

boning rod /'bəʊnɪŋ ,rɒd/ noun [C] CONSTRUCTION a T-shaped piece of wood used for checking the level of something such as a **drain**

bonnet /'bɒnɪt/ noun [C] **1** the front part of a car that covers the engine **2** a hat that ties under the chin

bonus /'bəʊnəs/ noun [C] **1** something good that someone gets in addition to what they expect: *Customers will receive a free CD as a bonus*. **2** extra money that someone is paid in addition to their usual salary: *a Christmas bonus*

bony /'bəʊni/ adj a bony part of the body is so thin that the shape of the bones can be seen: *bony fingers*

boo /buː/ (**boos, booing, booed**) verb [I/T] if people boo, they shout angrily at a performer or sports team that they think is not very good —**boo** interjection

booby prize /'buːbi ,praɪz/ noun [C] a prize that is given as a joke to someone who comes last in a competition

booby trap /'buːbi ,træp/ noun [C] a hidden bomb that explodes when someone touches something connected to it

book¹ /bʊk/ noun **1** [C] a written work that is printed on pages fastened together inside a cover: *Please open your books at page 25*. ♦ *Have you read any books by John Grisham?* ♦ *a book about American history* **2** [C] something that you write in, consisting of pages fastened together inside a cover: *an exercise book* ♦ *an address book* **3** [C] a set of small objects, such as stamps, tickets, or matches, fastened together inside a paper cover **4 the books** [plural] BUSINESS the financial records of an organization or business

PHRASES **by the book** correctly, following all the rules or systems for doing something

in sb's bad/good books *informal* used for saying that someone is annoyed with you or pleased with you

---

Build your vocabulary: types of book

- **autobiography** a book about your own life
- **biography** a book about someone's life
- **cookery book** a book of instructions for cooking
- **coursebook** a book that is used by students in class
- **guidebook** a book for tourists
- **hardback** a book with a hard cover
- **manual** a book of instructions
- **notebook** a book with empty pages for writing in
- **novel** a book that tells a story
- **paperback** a book with a thick paper cover
- **textbook** a book that you use for studying at school, college, or university
- **workbook** a book for students that contains exercises

---

book² /bʊk/ verb **1** [I/T] to arrange to have or use something at a particular time in the future: *Shall I book a room for you?* ♦ *'Can we have a table for two, please?' 'Have you booked, sir?'* ♦ *Could you book me on the 8.30 flight* (=get a ticket for me)? **2** [T] to arrange for someone to perform or speak at a public event: *Several leading businessmen were booked to speak at the conference.* **3** [T] **SPORTS** if a sports player is booked, the **referee** writes their name in an official book because they have broken the rules: *Adams was booked for dangerous play.* **4** [T] if the police book someone, they take them to the police station and make a record of their crime

PHRASAL VERB ,book (sth) 'up *see* **booked up**

bookcase /'bʊk,keɪs/ noun [C] a piece of furniture with shelves in it for books

'**book ,club** noun [C] **1** an organization that sells books at low prices to its members, usually by **mail order 2** a group of people who meet regularly to discuss books that they have read

booked up /,bʊkt 'ʌp/ adj if a hotel, restaurant, theatre etc is booked up, there are no rooms, tables, or seats available because other people have booked them

'**book ,group** noun [C] a **book club** sense 2

booking /'bʊkɪŋ/ noun [C] an arrangement to do something such as buy a travel ticket or stay in a hotel room in the future= RESERVATION: *Have you made a booking?*

'**booking ,office** noun [C] a place where people can buy tickets, for example for travelling or going to the theatre

bookkeeping /'bʊk,kiːpɪŋ/ noun [U] **BUSINESS** the job of recording a business's financial accounts — **bookkeeper** noun [C]

booklet /'bʊklət/ noun [C] a small thin book that contains information: *a 12-page booklet called 'You and Your Child's Health'*

bookmaker /'bʊk,meɪkə/ noun [C] someone whose job is to take **bets** from people on the result of a race or competition, and to pay them if they win

bookmark /'bʊk,mɑːk/ noun [C] **1** something that you put inside a book so that you can easily find a particular page again **2** COMPUTING a way of marking an Internet website so that you can easily find it again —**bookmark** verb [T]

bookseller /'bʊk,selə/ noun [C] a person or business that sells books

bookshelf /'bʊk,ʃelf/ (plural **bookshelves** /'bʊk,ʃelvz/) noun [C] a shelf that you put books on

bookshop /'bʊk,ʃɒp/ noun [C] a shop that sells books

bookstall /'bʊk,stɔːl/ noun [C] a small shop with an open front that sells books, newspapers, and magazines, for example at a railway station

bookstore /'bʊk,stɔː/ noun [C] a **bookshop**

bookworm /'bʊk,wɜːm/ noun [C] *informal* someone who spends a lot of time reading books

Boolean /'buːliən/ adj COMPUTING a Boolean search uses the words 'and', 'or', and 'not' to find a word or combination of words on the Internet using a **search engine**. For example you could search for 'bear or teddy bear', or 'England and not London'.

'**Boolean ,operator** noun [C] COMPUTING a word such as 'and', 'or', or 'not' used in a Boolean search on the Internet

boom¹ /buːm/ noun [C]

1 economic increase	**4** for blocking river
2 increase in popularity	**5** long pole
3 deep loud sound	**+** PHRASE

1 ECONOMICS a sudden increase in economic activity or success: *The island is experiencing a boom in tourism.*
2 a sudden increase in the popularity of something
3 a deep loud sound that continues for some time
4 a large floating object that is used for blocking a river or stream
5 ARTS a pole with a camera or **microphone** attached to it, used in making films

PHRASE **boom and bust** ECONOMICS a situation in which a country's economy regularly goes through periods of success followed by periods of failure

boom² /buːm/ verb [I] **1** to make a deep loud sound that continues for some time **2** ECONOMICS if a place or an industry is booming, it is experiencing a period of economic success: *The housing market is booming.* **3** if an activity is booming, it is becoming very popular

boomerang /'buːmə,ræŋ/ noun [C] a curved stick that comes back to you when you throw it

boon /buːn/ noun [singular] something that brings someone benefits or makes their life easier: *Falling book prices are a boon for consumers.*

boorish /'bʊərɪʃ/ adj rude and not caring about other people's feelings

boost¹ /buːst/ verb [T] **1** to help something to increase or improve: *The cold weather boosted demand for electricity.* **2** to make someone feel more positive or more confident: *The new coach has boosted the team's confidence.* **3** to try to make people want to buy a product, visit a place etc, by talking about it publicly in a very positive way

boost² /buːst/ noun [singular] something that helps something to increase or improve: *The festival has been a major boost for the local economy.*

booster /'buːstə/ noun [C] **1** HEALTH an extra amount of a medical drug that is given so that a drug taken at a previous time will continue to be effective **2** something that makes someone feel better: *a morale booster* **3** ASTRONOMY an extra engine on a spacecraft that gives it enough power to escape the Earth's gravity —*picture* → SPACE SHUTTLE

boot¹ /buːt/ noun [C] **1** a type of shoe that covers all of the foot and part of the leg: *riding boots* ♦ *a pair of* *black boots* **2** the covered space at the back of a car, used for carrying things in

boot² /buːt/ verb **1 boot** or **boot (sth) up** [I/T] **COMPUTING** if a computer boots, or if you boot it, it starts working and becomes ready to use **2** [T] *informal* to kick something or someone hard: *He booted the ball over the line.*

'boot ,camp noun [C] **1** a place where young criminals are treated very strictly and have to do hard physical exercise **2** a camp for training people who have just joined the US armed forces

'boot-,cut adj boot-cut trousers become slightly wider at the bottom so that they fit easily over boots

'boot ,disk noun [C] **COMPUTING** a disk that contains a program for starting a computer and the **operating system** software

booth /buːð/ noun [C] **1** a small enclosed space where people do something private, especially vote or make a phone call **2** a small enclosed space where people can buy things or use a service: *a ticket booth* **3** a private, enclosed table in a restaurant

bootleg /'buːt,leg/ adj bootleg goods are products that are made and sold illegally —**bootlegger** noun [C]

bootstrapping /'buːt,stræpɪŋ/ noun [U] **BUSINESS** the activity of building a business from nothing, with very little money put in from outside the business

bootstrap program /'buːtstræp ,prəʊɡræm/ noun [C] **COMPUTING** a program that makes a computer's **operating system** start working

booty /'buːti/ noun [U] *literary* valuable goods that are taken illegally or by force, especially in a war

booze /buːz/ noun [U] *informal* alcoholic drinks

border¹ /'bɔːdə/ noun [C] **1 GEOGRAPHY** the official line that separates two countries or regions: *the border between Hungary and Romania* ♦ *Iraq's northern border with Turkey* ♦ *Thousands of refugees were fleeing across the border.* **2** a narrow decorated area around the edge of something: *white paper with a blue border* **3** the land around the edge of something: *Rushes grew on the borders of the lake.*

border² /'bɔːdə/ verb [T] **1 GEOGRAPHY** to be next to another country or region: *Jordan holds a key position, bordering both Israel and Iraq.* **2** to form a line along the edge of something: *The canal is bordered by poplar trees.*

PHRASAL VERB 'border ,on sth to be nearly the same as a particular quality, feeling, or state: *a feeling of mistrust bordering on hatred*

'border ,crossing noun [C] a place on the border between two countries where people can cross, have their passports checked, and go through customs

borderline /'bɔːdə,laɪn/ adj **1** in a position between two standards or types, and therefore difficult to judge: *students with borderline test scores* **2** almost reaching a particular level

bore¹ /bɔː/ verb [T] **1** to make someone feel bored: *I hope I'm not boring you.* **2** to make a deep hole in something hard: *insects that bore through wood*

bore² /bɔː/ noun **1** [C] someone who talks too much about things that are not interesting **2** [singular] a boring or annoying activity or situation **3** [C] **ENGINEERING** the diameter of a cylinder in an engine

bore³ /bɔː/ the past tense of **bear¹**

bored /bɔːd/ adj feeling impatient and annoyed because nothing is interesting: *The waiter looked very bored.* ♦ *Steve was getting **bored with** the game.*

- **Bored** describes how you feel: *I hated school, and I was always bored.*
- **Boring** describes things or situations that make you feel bored: *I always found school very boring.*

boredom /'bɔːdəm/ noun [U] the feeling of being bored

borehole /'bɔː,həʊl/ noun [C] a very deep narrow hole in the ground that is made in order to get water or oil —*picture* → WATER SUPPLY

boring /'bɔːrɪŋ/ adj not at all interesting: *a boring badly-paid job* ♦ *Our maths teacher is so boring!* → BORED

born /bɔːn/ adj **1** when a baby is born, it comes out of its mother's body and starts its life: *The twins were born on 29 August, 1962.* ♦ *a German-born tennis player* (=who was born in Germany) **2** used for saying that someone has a natural ability to do something well: *a born leader* **3** if something such as a new organization or idea is born, it begins to exist

,born-again 'Christian noun [C] someone who has recently become a Christian who wants to tell other people about their strong religious beliefs

boron /'bɔːrɒn/ noun [U] **CHEMISTRY** a yellow-brown chemical element that is a **metalloid**. It is used in nuclear **reactors** and for making steel hard. It is also used for making glass and **pottery**. Chemical symbol: **B**

borough /'bʌrə/ noun [C] a town, or a district in a big city

borrow /'bɒrəʊ/ verb **1** [T] to receive and use something that belongs to someone else, and promise to give it back: *I **borrowed** a camera **from** Alex.* **2** [I/T] to borrow money from a bank and pay it back gradually: *We borrowed £20,000 to start up the business.* **3** [I/T] to use something such as an idea or word that was first used by another person or used in another place: *A lot of English words were **borrowed from** other languages.*

- If you **borrow** something from someone, they give it to you and you agree to give it back: *Can I borrow your umbrella?*
- If you **lend** something to someone, you give it to them and they agree to give it back to you: *Could you lend me your umbrella?*

borrower /'bɒrəʊə/ noun [C] someone who borrows money from a bank

borrowing /'bɒrəʊɪŋ/ noun [C] **LANGUAGE** a word or phrase that comes from another language

bosom /'bʊz(ə)m/ noun [singular] a woman's breasts

boss¹ /bɒs/ noun [C] *informal* the person who is in charge of you at work: *I'll ask my boss for a day off next week.*

boss² /bɒs/

PHRASAL VERB ,boss sb a'round or **,boss sb a'bout** *informal* to keep telling other people what to do: *He's always bossing his little brother around.*

bossy /'bɒsi/ (**bossier, bossiest**) adj someone who is bossy is annoying because they keep telling other people what to do

bot /bɒt/ noun [C] **COMPUTING** a computer program that works automatically, especially one that can find information for you on the Internet

botany /'bɒt(ə)ni/ noun [U] **BIOLOGY** the scientific study of plants —**botanical** /bə'tænɪk(ə)l/ adj, **botanist** noun [C]

botched /bɒtʃt/ adj badly done or badly planned, and therefore unsuccessful = FAILED

both /bəʊθ/ determiner, pronoun used for showing that you are referring to two people or things, and that you are saying the same thing about the two of them: *You can write on both sides of the paper.* ♦ *Both my parents are doctors.* ♦ *I like them both.* ♦ *Both of my brothers play on the football team.*

> Do not use **both** in negative sentences. Use **neither**: *Neither of my parents wanted me to leave school* (=my mother did not and my father did not).

bother¹ /'bɒðə/ verb **1** [I] if you do not bother to do something, you do not do it because it is not sensible or because you feel lazy: *It was such a stupid question, I didn't even bother to reply.* ♦ *Don't bother about driving me home, I'll walk.* **2** [T] to annoy someone by interrupting them: *I hope the children aren't bothering you.* **3** [T] to make someone feel worried, frightened, or upset: *If he keeps bothering you, you should call the police.* ♦ *Does it bother you that people think you're older than him?* **4** [T] to cause someone pain: *His knee was bothering him.*

bother² /'bɒðə/ noun [U] trouble or difficulty that is annoying but not very serious

bottle¹ /'bɒt(ə)l/ noun [C] **1** a glass or plastic container for liquids: *an empty beer bottle* ♦ *a bottle of cooking oil* **2** the amount of liquid that a bottle contains: *They drank the whole bottle.*

bottle² /'bɒt(ə)l/ verb [T] to put a liquid into bottles in order to sell it —**bottled** /'bɒt(ə)ld/ adj: *bottled beer*

'bottle ,bank noun [C] a large container in a public place where people can put empty bottles so that the glass can be **recycled** (=used again)

'bottle-,feed verb [T] to feed a baby from a bottle rather than **breastfeeding** it

bottleneck /'bɒt(ə)l,nek/ noun [C] **1** a problem that causes delays **2** a place where traffic moves slowly because the road is narrow or blocked

'bottle ,opener noun [C] a small tool that is used for removing the lid from a bottle. A bottle opener is a **second-class lever**.

bottom¹ /'bɒtəm/ noun

1 lowest part of sth	5 trousers
2 ground under sea	6 furthest part
3 lowest status	+ PHRASE
4 body part sb sits on	

1 [singular] the lowest part of something: *The page had a line missing from the bottom.* ♦ *She ran down to the bottom of the hill.* ♦ *The date and time are shown at the bottom of your screen.* ♦ *Read what is says on the bottom of the box* (=on the surface at the bottom).
2 [singular] the ground under the sea or under a lake or river
3 [singular] the lowest level or position: *She started at the bottom and ended up running the company.*
4 [C] the part of your body that you sit on
5 bottoms [plural] the trousers that are part of a set of loose clothes or sports clothes: *pyjama bottoms*
6 [singular] the part of something that is furthest away from where you are: *Go to the bottom of the street and turn left.*

PHRASE **get to the bottom of sth** to find out the true cause or explanation of a bad situation

bottom² /'bɒtəm/ adj in the lowest part or position: *the bottom half of the page* ♦ *people in the bottom 25% of the earnings table*

,bottom dead 'centre noun [U] ENGINEERING in an engine, the position of a **piston** when it is nearest to the **crankshaft**

'bottom ,feeder noun [C] BIOLOGY a fish or animal that lives and eats at the bottom of a lake, river, the sea etc

,bottom 'gear noun [U] the **gear** that you use for driving a vehicle very slowly

'bottom-,hung adj CONSTRUCTION a bottom-hung window has **hinges** at the bottom and opens inwards

,bottom 'line noun [C] BUSINESS the amount of money that a business makes or loses

PHRASES **sb's bottom line** the lowest price someone will accept, or the greatest change they are prepared to accept when they are trying to reach an agreement with someone else

the bottom line the most basic fact or issue in a situation

,bottom-'up adj starting with details rather than with a general idea ≠ TOP-DOWN: *a bottom-up approach to problem solving*

botulism /'bɒtʃʊ,lɪz(ə)m/ noun [U] HEALTH a serious illness caused by eating preserved food that contains harmful bacteria. It often causes death.

bougainvillea /,bu:gən'vɪliə/ noun [C/U] a plant with white or brightly coloured flowers. It grows up walls, especially in hot countries.

bough /baʊ/ noun [C] literary a branch of a tree

bought /bɔːt/ the past tense and past participle of **buy¹**

boulder /'bəʊldə/ noun [C] a large rock

boulevard /'bu:ləva:d/ noun [C] a wide road in a city

bounce /baʊns/ verb

1 hit sth & move off	4 move in lively way
2 move up and down	5 of email
3 of cheque	+ PHRASAL VERB

1 [I/T] if a ball or other object bounces, or if you bounce it, it hits a surface then immediately moves away: *The ball bounced twice before hitting the net.* ♦ *Hailstones were bouncing off the roof.*
2 [I/T] to move up and down, or to move something up and down: *She was bouncing the baby on her knee.*
3 [I] if a cheque bounces, the bank refuses to pay it because there is not enough money in the account of the person who wrote it
4 [I] to move quickly and with a lot of energy: *The band came bouncing onto the stage.*
5 [I] if an email message bounces, it is sent back to you without reaching the person you sent it to —**bounce** noun [C]

PHRASAL VERB **,bounce 'back 1** to become healthy, happy, or successful again after something bad has happened to you **2** BUSINESS if a market or price bounces back, it rises again after falling

bouncer /'baʊnsə/ noun [C] someone whose job is to stop violent behaviour in a bar or club

bouncy /'baʊnsi/ adj **1** a bouncy ball bounces well when it hits a surface **2** a bouncy person is happy, lively, and enthusiastic

bound¹ /baʊnd/ adj **1 bound to do sth** something that is bound to happen will almost certainly happen: *If you have problems at home, it's bound to affect your school work.* **2 bound to do sth** used for saying that you must do something or you should do something: *We felt bound to tell her that her son had been playing truant.* **3** a bound book has a leather, cloth, or paper cover: *an old book of poems, bound in dark leather*

PHRASE **bound for sth** travelling towards a place: *a taxi bound for Heathrow airport*

bound² /baʊnd/ verb [I] **1** to run or jump with large steps **2 be bounded by sth** *formal* if an area is bounded by something such as a fence, the fence goes around the edge of the area

bound³ /baʊnd/ noun [plural] **bounds** limits that affect and control what can happen or what people are able to do: *A win is not **beyond the bounds of** possibility*. PHRASE **out of bounds** if a place is out of bounds, people are not allowed to go there

bound⁴ /baʊnd/ the past tense and past participle of **bind**

boundary /'baʊnd(ə)ri/ (plural **boundaries**) noun **1** [C] the edge of an area of land, or a line that marks the edge: *The lane once formed the boundary between the two villages*. → BORDER¹ **2 boundaries** [plural] the limits of an activity or experience: *new research that pushes back **the boundaries of** genetic science* **3** [C] SPORTS the outer edge of the playing area in **cricket**

bounty /'baʊnti/ (plural **bounties**) noun [C] money that is offered as a reward for catching or killing a criminal

bouquet /buːˈkeɪ, bəʊˈkeɪ/ noun [C] flowers that are tied together in an attractive way and given to someone as a present

bourgeois /'bʊəʒwɑː/ adj SOCIAL STUDIES typical of middle-class people and their attitudes

the bourgeoisie /ˌbʊəʒwɑːˈziː/ noun [singular] SOCIAL STUDIES the middle class

bout /baʊt/ noun [C] **1** a short period when someone has a particular illness: *a bout of flu* **2** a boxing match or **wrestling** match

boutique /buːˈtiːk/ noun [C] a small fashionable shop, especially one that sells clothes

bou'tique ho,tel noun [C] TOURISM a small hotel that gives a high level of service and is considered fashionable

bovine /'bəʊvaɪn/ adj *formal* relating to cows

bow¹ /baʊ/ verb **1** [I] to bend your body forwards from the waist in order to show respect for someone **2** [I/T] to bend your head forwards so that you are looking down

bow² /baʊ/ noun [C] **1** a forward movement of the top part of your body that you make in order to show respect for someone **2** the front part of a ship

bow³ /bəʊ/ noun [C] **1** a weapon made from a curved piece of wood. It is used for shooting arrows. —*picture* → WEAPON **2** a knot that has two circular parts and two loose ends: *The ribbon was **tied in a bow***. **3** MUSIC an object that is used for playing instruments such as the **violin** and the **cello**

bowel /'baʊəl/ noun [C] ANATOMY the part of the intestine where faeces are formed. This word is often used in the plural in non-scientific language = INTESTINE

'bowel ,movement noun [C] HEALTH the action of getting rid of solid waste from the body, or the solid waste itself

bowl¹ /bəʊl/ noun [C] **1** a round container that you use for eating, serving, or preparing food **2** the food in a bowl, or the amount that a bowl contains: *I always eat **a bowl of** cereal for breakfast*. **3** a large container without a lid, used for holding liquids: *a washing-up bowl* → BOWLS

bowl² /bəʊl/ verb SPORTS **1** [I/T] to throw the ball towards the **batsman** in the sport of **cricket 2 bowl** or **bowl sb out** [T] in **cricket**, to make the **batsman** leave the field, by hitting the **wicket** with the ball **3** [I/T] to play **bowls**

bow-legged /ˌbəʊˈlegɪd/ adj with legs that curve out sideways at the knees

bowler /'bəʊlə/ noun [C] SPORTS the person who throws the ball towards the **batsman** in the sport of **cricket**

bowling /'bəʊlɪŋ/ noun [U] SPORTS an indoor game in which players roll heavy balls along a track and try to knock down a group of **pins** (=objects that look like bottles)

'bowling ,alley noun [C] a building where people go bowling

bowls /bəʊlz/ noun [U] a game in which players roll large balls across the ground towards a small ball

Bowman's capsule /ˈbəʊmənz ˌkæpsjuːl/ noun [C] ANATOMY the cup-shaped part of the **nephron** in the kidney that holds the **glomerulus**. Blood is filtered through the glomerulus into the Bowman's capsule.

bowsprit /'bəʊˌsprɪt/ noun [C] a long pole that sticks out from the front of a ship

bow tie /ˌbəʊ ˈtaɪ/ noun [C] a man's formal tie in the shape of a **bow**

box¹ /bɒks/ noun

1 container	**4** in theatre
2 things in a container	**5** area of sports ground
3 space for writing in	

1 [C] a container with straight sides and a flat base: *a cardboard box*
2 [C] the things in a box, or the amount that a box contains: *We ate the whole **box of** chocolates*.
3 [C] a space for writing information on a printed form, or a space on a computer screen with information in it: *a dialog box*
4 [C] ARTS a small private space with seats in a theatre or sports ground
5 the box SPORTS the **penalty box** in football

box² /bɒks/ verb **1** [I] SPORTS to fight in the sport of boxing **2** [T] to put something into a box

PHRASAL VERB **,box sb 'in** to surround someone so that they cannot move

boxer /'bɒksə/ noun [C] **1** SPORTS someone who takes part in the sport of boxing **2** a large dog with smooth hair and a flat face

boxercise /'bɒksəsaɪz/ noun [U] a type of exercise based on boxing

boxers /'bɒksəz/ or **'boxer ,shorts** noun [plural] loose underwear for men

boxing /'bɒksɪŋ/ noun [U] SPORTS a sport in which two people fight each other wearing large leather gloves

'Boxing ,Day noun [C/U] 26 December, the day after Christmas Day

'box ,number noun [C] an address consisting of the number of a **PO Box** (=an address you use instead of your real address)

'box ,office noun [C] ARTS **1** the place in a theatre or cinema where people buy tickets **2** the number of people who buy tickets for a film or play: *The play was a huge success at the box office* (=a lot of people went to see it).

'box ,spanner noun [C] ENGINEERING a **spanner** consisting of a tube with box-shaped ends that are designed to fit over a **nut**. It is turned with a short metal rod that goes into two holes in the tube.

boy /bɔɪ/ noun [C] **1** a male child, or a young man: *a 10-year-old boy* ♦ *Mr and Mrs Wylie have three boys.* ♦ *How old is their little boy* (=their son)? **2** a man of any age, especially used for talking about where he comes from: *The Minnesota farm boy became a national hero.*

boycott /'bɔɪ,kɒt/ verb [T] to protest about something by not taking part in an event or not buying certain products: *Turkey threatened to boycott the conference.* —**boycott** noun [C]

boyfriend /'bɔɪ,frend/ noun [C] a man or boy that someone is having a sexual or romantic relationship with: *She's got a new boyfriend.* → girlfriend sense 1

boyhood /'bɔɪ,hʊd/ noun [U] the time when someone is a boy

boyish /'bɔɪɪʃ/ adj *showing approval* like a boy, or typical of a boy: *boyish good looks*

,Boy 'Scout noun [C] a boy who is a member of the **Boy Scouts**, an organization that encourages boys to learn practical skills and help other people

bps /,bi: pi: 'es/ abbrev **COMPUTING** bits per second: a unit for measuring the rate at which information can be sent over an Internet line

bra /brɑ:/ noun [C] a piece of underwear that supports a woman's breasts

brace¹ /breɪs/ verb **1** [I/T] to get ready for something unpleasant: *Smith braced himself to give her the bad news.* ♦ *The stock market is braced for another week of falling prices.* **2** [T] to push against something solid and strong so that you do not fall down

brace² /breɪs/ noun

1 for teeth	4 for making holes
2 for holding trousers up	5 in building
3 for supporting sth	6 piece of scaffolding

1 [C] a set of wires that some people wear on their teeth to push them into the correct position
2 braces [plural] two long narrow pieces of cloth that go over a man's shoulders and are fastened to his trousers to hold them up
3 [C] an object that is designed to support something or to hold it in the correct position: *a neck brace*
4 [C] a part of a tool called a **brace and bit**, used for making holes in things
5 [C] **CONSTRUCTION** a piece of wood, metal etc that is used to strengthen a structure by spreading weight or pressure, or changing their direction
6 [C] **CONSTRUCTION** a piece of metal tube that is fixed **diagonally** in order to make a **scaffold** stronger

bracelet /'breɪslət/ noun [C] a piece of jewellery that someone wears around their wrist → BANGLE

'brace po,sition noun [singular] a position for an emergency landing of a plane, where the passenger sits bent forward with their hands behind their head

bracing /'breɪsɪŋ/ adj **1** cold in a way that makes you feel full of energy **2** shocking or unexpected in a way that is good, because it makes people notice or think about something

bracken /'brækən/ noun [U] **BIOLOGY** a plant with leaves like large wide feathers, that grows on hills and in forests. It is a type of fern.

bracket /'brækɪt/ noun **1 brackets** [plural] a pair of symbols ( ), used for showing that the words or numbers between them can be considered separately **2** [C] one of the groups that people or things are divided into, according to a feature that they all share: *people in the 20–30 age bracket* **3** [C] a piece of wood, metal, or plastic that is fixed to a wall to support something like a shelf —**bracket** verb [T]

brackish /'brækɪʃ/ adj brackish water has a slight taste of salt and so is not pure

bract /brækt/ noun [C] **BIOLOGY** a type of leaf that grows from a stem where the flower or flower **cluster** develops. Bracts may be small and green or large and brightly coloured.

brag /bræg/ (**brags, bragging, bragged**) verb [I] *showing disapproval* to talk about your achievements or possessions in a proud way that annoys other people = BOAST: *She's always bragging about her famous father.*

braided /'breɪdɪd/ adj **1** braided cloth is decorated with thick thread, especially gold thread sewn around the edges **2** braided rope consists of three or more thinner **strands** woven together

braille /breɪl/ noun [U] a reading system for blind people that uses small raised marks that they feel with their fingers

brain /breɪn/ noun [C] **1** **ANATOMY** the organ inside the skull in vertebrates that controls physical and nervous activity and intelligence: *The illness had affected his brain.* ♦ *a brain operation* —*picture* → next page **2** mental ability, or intelligence: *He's good-looking, and he's got brains.* **3** an intelligent person: *The best brains in the company can't solve the problem.* **4** **BIOLOGY** the place in the bodies of some invertebrates that is the main centre of nerve tissue

PHRASES **pick sb's brains** *informal* to talk to someone who knows more about something than you do, in order to learn more about it
rack your brain(s) to try very hard to remember something or to solve a problem

brainchild /'breɪn,tʃaɪld/ noun [singular] a clever system, organization, or plan that someone thinks of and develops

'brain ,damage noun [U] **HEALTH** damage to someone's brain as a result of an accident or illness —**'brain-,damaged** adj

'brain ,death noun [U] **HEALTH** a state in which someone's brain has stopped working, so that they are in fact dead, even though a machine may continue to make their heart continue to work —**brain-dead** adj

'brain ,drain noun [singular] *informal* a situation in which a country's most intelligent people, especially scientists, go to another country in order to make more money or to improve their living or working conditions

brainstem /'breɪn,stem/ noun [C] **ANATOMY** the part of the brain above the **spinal cord** between the left and right halves of the brain

brainstorm /'breɪn,stɔ:m/ verb [I/T] to develop new ideas through a discussion in which several people make lots of suggestions and the best ones are chosen

brain teaser /'breɪn ,ti:zə/ noun [C] a difficult question or problem that you try to solve for fun

brainwash /'breɪn,wɒʃ/ verb [T] to force someone to accept an idea by repeating it many times —**brainwashing** noun [U]

brainwave /'breɪn,weɪv/ noun [C] **1** **BIOLOGY** an electrical signal sent by the brain that can be recorded and measured **2** a sudden very good idea

brainy /'breɪni/ (**brainier, brainiest**) adj *informal* very clever

brake /breɪk/ noun [C] **1** the equipment in a vehicle or bicycle that is used for slowing down or stopping: *I saw the child run out, so I slammed on the brakes* (=stopped suddenly). **2** an action or a situation that prevents something from developing: *The high level of debt put a brake on economic recovery.*

parts of the brain

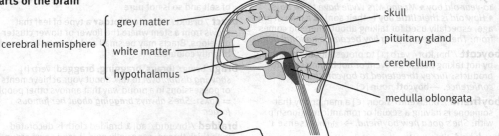

grey matter
skull
cerebral hemisphere
white matter
pituitary gland
hypothalamus
cerebellum
medulla oblongata

areas of the brain

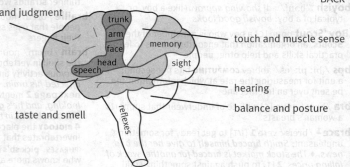

FRONT
BACK
reasoning and judgment
trunk
arm
face
memory
touch and muscle sense
head
speech
sight
hearing
taste and smell
balance and posture
reflexes

'brake ,band noun [C] **ENGINEERING** a circular piece of steel that can be tightened around a brake **shaft** to stop it turning

brake calliper /'breɪk ,kælɪpə/ noun [C] **ENGINEERING** a part of a brake system that holds the **brake pads**

'brake ,disc noun [C] **ENGINEERING** a part of a brake system that is pressed by the **brake pads** when a driver presses the brake pedal

'brake ,drum noun [C] **ENGINEERING** a cylinder attached to the wheel of a vehicle that pushes the **brake shoes** against the inner surface of the drum and slows down the vehicle when the driver presses the **brake pedal**

'brake ,fade noun [U] **ENGINEERING** a situation in which a vehicle's brakes stop working effectively, especially because they have heated up after being used a lot

'brake ,fluid noun [U] **ENGINEERING** a thick liquid used in the brakes of some vehicles that transmits force to the brake system

'brake ,light noun [C] a light on the back of a vehicle that comes on when the driver uses the brakes

'brake ,lining noun [C] **ENGINEERING** a thin piece of material attached to a **brake shoe** that can be replaced

'brake ,pad noun [C] the part of a brake that presses against a **disc** inside the wheel of a vehicle in order to stop the vehicle from moving

'brake ,pedal noun [C] **ENGINEERING** the pedal that a driver presses with their foot to make a vehicle slow down

'brake pressure ,regulator noun [C] **ENGINEERING** a part of a vehicle's brake system that stops the back wheels becoming **locked** (=fixed in one position) when the driver brakes suddenly

'brake ,shoe noun [C] **ENGINEERING** a curved metal part of a brake in some vehicles that presses on the wheel to slow it down

braking force /'breɪkɪŋ ,fɔːs/ noun [C] **ENGINEERING** the amount of resistance in a vehicle's brake system, or the amount of strength needed by a driver to stop a vehicle

bran /bræn/ noun [U] the outside parts of the grains of grass plants such as wheat or **oats**

branch¹ /brɑːntʃ/ noun [C]

1 part of tree	4 shop/office
2 part of river	5 department
3 part of subject	

1 one of the parts of a tree that grows out of its **trunk** — *picture* → TREE

2 GEOGRAPHY a part of a river that leads away from the main part

3 a part of a particular area of study or knowledge: *Mechanics is a branch of physics.*

4 a shop or office representing a large company or organization in a particular area: *The store has branches in over 50 cities.*

5 one part of a government or large organization that has particular responsibilities: *the local branch of the teachers' union*

branch² /brɑːntʃ/ verb [I] to divide into two or more parts: *The road branched into four paths.*

PHRASAL VERB **,branch 'out** to start doing something new or different

brand¹ /brænd/ noun [C] **1** a product or group of products that has its own name and is made by one particular company: *I tried using a new **brand of** soap.* **2** a particular type of something: *He has his own special **brand of** humour.* **3** a mark that is burnt onto a farm animal, in order to show who owns it

brand² /brænd/ verb [T] **1** to describe someone or something as a bad person or thing= LABEL: *The men were branded liars by the judge.* **2** to burn a mark onto a farm animal, in order to show who owns it

brandish /'brændɪʃ/ verb [T] to wave a weapon or other object around in your hand so that other people can see it

,brand 'leader noun [C] BUSINESS the product that more people buy than any other product of its type

'brand ,name noun [C] BUSINESS the name that a company chooses for its particular **brand** of product → TRADEMARK

,brand-'new adj extremely new

brandy /'brændi/ noun [U] a strong alcoholic drink made from wine

brash /bræʃ/ adj *showing disapproval* **1** a brash person talks and behaves in a loud confident way **2** big, bright, or colourful

brass /brɑːs/ noun [U] **1** a shiny yellow metal that is a mixture of copper and zinc **2** MUSIC musical instruments made of brass, for example **trumpets** —*picture* → MUSICAL INSTRUMENT, ORCHESTRA

,brass 'band noun [C] MUSIC a group of musicians who play brass instruments

bravado /brə'vɑːdəʊ/ noun [U] a brave, confident way of behaving, especially when you are in fact frightened

brave¹ /breɪv/ adj **1** able to deal with danger, pain, or trouble without being frightened or worried= COURAGEOUS ≠ COWARDLY: *the brave soldiers who fought and died for their country* ♦ *his brave fight against illness* **2** a brave decision or action is one that someone makes even though it involves risk or problems= COURAGEOUS —**bravely** adv

brave² /breɪv/ verb [T] to deal with a difficult situation in order to achieve something

bravery /'breɪvəri/ noun [U] brave behaviour= COURAGE ≠ COWARDICE

bravo /,brɑː'vəʊ/ interjection used for showing that you admire what someone has done, or that you have enjoyed their performance

brawl /brɔːl/ noun [C] a noisy fight in a public place —**brawl** verb [I]

bray /breɪ/ verb [I] to make the sound that a **donkey** makes

brazing /'breɪzɪŋ/ noun [U] TECHNOLOGY a process in which two metals being joined are heated until they are hot enough to melt the **filler metal**, so that it can flow into the joint. Brazing takes place at temperatures above 450°. —**braze** /breɪz/ verb [T]

breach¹ /briːtʃ/ noun [C] **1** an action or situation in which a law, rule, or agreement is broken: *a clear breach of copyright* ♦ *The company was in breach of environmental regulations.* **2** *formal* a serious disagreement **3** *formal* a space made in a wall, fence, or line of defence, especially during a military attack

breach² /briːtʃ/ verb [T] *formal* **1** to break a law, rule, or agreement **2** to get through something such as a wall or fence

bread /bred/ noun [U] a common food made from flour, water, and usually yeast: *a loaf of bread* ♦ *white bread* ♦ *a bread roll*

breadcrumbs /'bred,krʌmz/ noun [plural] very small pieces of bread, used in cooking

breadfruit /'bred,fruːt/ noun [C/U] a large round fruit that looks like bread after it has been cooked

breadline /'bred,laɪn/ noun **on the breadline** very poor

breadth /bredθ/ noun **1** [C/U] the distance from one side of an object to the other= WIDTH: *5 metres in breadth* **2** [U] the wide range of different things or ideas that something includes: *The book demonstrates a remarkable breadth of knowledge.* → LENGTH

breadwinner /'bred,wɪnə/ noun [C] the person who earns the money to support a family

break¹ /breɪk/ (**breaks, breaking, broke** /brəʊk/, **broken** /'brəʊkən/) verb

1 separate into pieces	**10** of wave falling
2 stop working	**11** of day starting
3 not obey rule/law	**12** of storm starting
4 not keep agreement	**13** weather: change
5 make a hole/cut	**14** when sb is upset
6 make sth end	**15** of a boy's voice
7 when news is told	**+** PHRASES
8 tell sb bad news	**+** PHRASAL VERBS
9 destroy confidence	

1 [I/T] if something breaks, or if you break it, it separates into two or more pieces when it is hit, dropped etc: *Joey broke three bones in his foot.* ♦ *The glass broke into tiny pieces.*
2 [I/T] if a piece of equipment breaks, or if you break it, it stops working correctly: *Don't play with the camera – you'll break it.*
3 [T] to fail to obey a rule or law: *Students who break these rules will be punished.*
4 [T] to not do something that you promised or agreed to do: *Elliot claims that his business partner broke her contract.*
5 [T] to make a hole or cut in the surface of something: *The dog bit his leg, but didn't break the skin.*
6 [T] to make something end: *A bird's call broke the silence.* ♦ *I found it hard to **break the habit** of eating at night.*
7 [I/T] if important news breaks, or if a newspaper or television station breaks it, it becomes publicly known: *He was back in France when the news broke.*
8 [T] to tell someone bad news in a kind way: *I didn't know how to **break** the news **to** her.*
9 [T] to destroy someone's confidence, determination, or happiness: *Twenty years in prison had not **broken** his **spirit**.*
10 [I] if waves break, they reach their highest point and start to fall
11 [I] when day breaks, it starts to get light in the morning= DAWN
12 [I] if a storm breaks, it starts
13 [I] if the weather breaks, it changes unexpectedly
14 [I] if someone's voice breaks, they cannot speak clearly, usually because they are upset
15 [I] when a boy's voice breaks, it starts to become deeper and sound like a man's

PHRASES **break even** if a person or business breaks even, they neither make a profit nor lose money
break sb's fall to stop someone who is falling from hitting the ground directly
break free 1 to escape from someone who is trying to hold you **2** to escape from an unpleasant situation that controls your life
break sb's heart to make someone feel extremely sad
break a record to do something better than anyone else has done before in a particular activity, especially a sport: *If she continues running at this pace, she'll break the world record.*

PHRASAL VERBS **,break a'way 1** to escape from a person, place, or situation: *Anna tried to break away, but he held her tight.* **2** to leave a political party or other group, especially in order to start another one

,**break** '**down 1** if a machine or vehicle breaks down, it stops working **2** if a relationship or discussion breaks down, it stops being successful: *At one point, the talks broke down completely.* **3** to start crying, especially in public: *People broke down and wept when they heard the news.*

,**break (sth)** '**down CHEMISTRY** if a substance breaks down, or if it is broken down, it separates into the parts that it is made up of: *The substance is easily broken down by bacteria.*

,**break sth** '**down** to hit something such as a door or wall very hard so that it falls down: *Firefighters had to break down the door.*

,**break** '**in** to enter a building by force, especially in order to steal things: *Someone had broken in through the bedroom window.*

,**break** '**into sth** to enter a building by force, especially in order to steal things: *A house in Brecon Place was broken into last night.*

,**break** '**off** to stop speaking: *Linda broke off, realizing that she was wrong.*

,**break (sth)** '**off** if a part of something breaks off, or if you break it off, it becomes separated from the main part: *Part of the chimney broke off and fell to the ground.*

,**break** '**sth off** to end a relationship or a discussion: *The two countries have broken off diplomatic relations.*

,**break** '**out 1** if something bad such as a war, fire, or disease breaks out, it starts **2** to start to appear on the skin: *An ugly rash broke out on my arm.*

,**break** '**through (sth)** if something that was hidden breaks through, it appears: *The sun broke through the clouds.*

,**break** '**up** if two people break up, or if a relationship breaks up, the relationship ends: *He's just broken up with his girlfriend.*

,**break (sth)** '**up** to break into smaller pieces, or to make something do this

'**break with sth 1** to leave a group because of a disagreement **2** if someone breaks with the past or with tradition, they start doing things in a new way

break² /breɪk/ noun [C]

1 time for rest	**6** pause in show
2 short holiday	**7** space in sth
3 major change	**8** in tennis
4 chance to succeed	**9** in snooker/billiards
5 where sth is broken	**+ PHRASE**

1 a period of time when you are not working and can rest or enjoy yourself: *OK, let's **take a** fifteen-minute **break**.*

2 a short holiday: *a weekend break for two in Okavanga*

3 a time at which one thing ends completely: *Lynn's decision helped her **make the break** with her past.*

4 an opportunity that helps someone to be successful: *a lucky break*

5 a place where something is broken: *a **break in** the gas pipeline*

6 a pause between television or radio programmes, especially when advertisements are broadcast: *We'll be back **after the break**.*

7 a space in something: *a **break in** the clouds*

8 SPORTS in tennis, a game that someone wins when their opponent is **serving**

9 in **snooker** or **billiards**, the number of points a player scores during a single series of shots

PHRASE give sb a break to stop being unkind or making things difficult for someone: *Give the boy a break – he's just learning.*

breakage /'breɪkɪdʒ/ noun [C] something that someone breaks

breakaway /'breɪkə,weɪ/ adj consisting of people who have decided to separate from a larger group: *a breakaway republic*

breakdown /'breɪk,daʊn/ noun [C] **1** a situation in which something has failed or is beginning to fail: *a breakdown in communication* **2** information that has been separated into different groups: *We'll need to see a breakdown of these figures.* **3 HEALTH** a **nervous breakdown 4** a situation in which a machine or vehicle stops working

'**breakdown ,truck** or '**breakdown ,lorry** noun [C] a truck used for pulling away another vehicle that has stopped working

breaker /'breɪkə/ noun [C] a large wave that comes onto a beach

breakfast /'brekfəst/ noun [C/U] the first meal that someone has in the morning: *What did you **have for breakfast** this morning?*

'**break-in** noun [C] an occasion when someone enters a building illegally using force

breaking and entering /,breɪkɪŋ ənd 'entərɪŋ/ noun [U] **LAW** the crime of entering a building illegally using force, especially in order to steal things

breaking point /'breɪkɪŋ ,pɔɪnt/ noun [singular] a situation in which there are so many problems that it is impossible to deal with them

breakneck /'breɪk,nek/ adj **at breakneck speed** very fast, in a way that is dangerous

,**break-of-**'**bulk ,point** noun [C] **BUSINESS** a place where a **cargo** of goods is divided into smaller units before it is delivered

breakout /'breɪk,aʊt/ noun [C] **1** an occasion when prisoners escape from a prison **2** one of several groups that a larger group of people has divided into to discuss something, especially at a **conference 3** a sudden appearance of a disease= OUTBREAK

'**break ,point** noun [C] **SPORTS** in tennis, a situation in which a player will win the game in which their opponent is **serving**, if they win the next point

breakthrough /'breɪkθru:/ noun [C] **1** a **discovery** or achievement that comes after a lot of hard work: *Scientists predict a **major breakthrough** within six months.* **2** a time when someone begins to be successful: *The breakthrough came when they discovered how to slow the virus down.*

breakup /'breɪkʌp/ noun [C] **1** the end of a marriage or serious relationship **2** the division of something such as an organization or country into smaller parts

'**breakup ,value** noun [C] **BUSINESS** the amount that a company would be worth if all its **assets** (=everything owned by the company) were sold

breakwater /'breɪk,wɔːtə/ noun [C] a strong wall that protects a beach from the force of the waves

breast /brest/ noun

1 part of sb's body	**4** meat
2 where feel emotions	**5** above fireplace
3 part of bird's body	

1 [C] one of the two round soft parts on the front of a woman's body that produce milk when she has a baby

2 [C] *literary* your chest and heart, thought of as the part of your body where you feel emotions

3 [C] the front part of a bird's body —*picture* → BIRD

4 [C/U] meat from the front part of a bird or some animals: *chicken breasts*

5 [C] **CONSTRUCTION** the part of a wall above a **fireplace** that sticks out into a room and contains the chimney

breastbone /'brest,bəʊn/ noun [C] ANATOMY the flat bone in the middle of the chest= STERNUM —picture → SKELETON

breastfeed /'brest,fi:d/ (**breastfeeds, breastfeeding, breastfed** /'brest,fed/) verb [I/T] if a mother breastfeeds a baby, she feeds it with milk from her breasts —**breastfeeding** noun [U]

breaststroke /'brest,strəʊk/ noun [U] SPORTS a style of swimming in which you lie on your front and pull both arms back from your chest at the same time

breath /breθ/ noun [C/U] the air that goes in and out of your body when you breathe, or the action of getting air into your lungs: *She took a deep breath* (=filled her lungs with air). ♦ *Simon held his breath* (=breathed in and held the air inside) *and dived under the water.* ♦ *I was out of breath* (=breathing fast and with difficulty) *from running.*

PHRASES **catch your breath** or **get your breath back** to have a short rest after doing something tiring, so that you can start breathing normally again

take your breath away to be extremely impressive, beautiful, or shocking
→ CATCH¹

breathe /bri:ð/ verb 1 [I/T] to take air into the lungs through the nose or mouth and let it out again: *We begin the exercise by breathing deeply* (=breathing large amounts of air). 2 [T] to bring other substances into your body as you breathe: *I don't want to breathe other people's smoke.* 3 [I] clothes that can breathe are made from cloth with very small holes that allow air in

PHRASES **breathe down sb's neck** to watch closely what someone is doing, in a way that annoys them
not breathe a word to keep something a secret
PHRASAL VERBS **,breathe (sth) 'in** to take air or other substances into the lungs through the nose or mouth = INHALE
,breathe (sth) 'out to send air or other substances out of the lungs through the nose or mouth= EXHALE

breathing /'bri:ðɪŋ/ noun [U] the process of taking air into the lungs and letting it out again → GASEOUS EXCHANGE, RESPIRATION

'breathing ,space noun [singular/U] a period of rest from a difficult situation that allows someone to get their energy back

breathless /'breθləs/ adj 1 breathing very fast and hard, for example after running 2 experiencing a very strong emotion, especially excitement —**breathlessly** adv, **breathlessness** noun [U]

breathtaking /'breθ,teɪkɪŋ/ adj extremely impressive or beautiful —**breathtakingly** adv

'breath ,test noun [C] a test in which police officers check how much alcohol a driver has drunk

breech birth /'bri:tʃ ,bɜ:θ/ or **breech delivery** /'bri:tʃ dɪ,lɪvəri/ noun [C] HEALTH a birth in which the baby's head does not come out first, as it should

breed¹ /bri:d/ (**breeds, breeding, bred** /bred/) verb 1 [I] BIOLOGY if animals breed, they become the parents of young animals 2 [T] AGRICULTURE to choose animals or plants as part of a process of improving their characteristics or keeping them pure 3 [T] AGRICULTURE to reproduce and raise animals or plants for sale, or for competitions 4 [T] to make bad feelings or situations develop: *Secrecy breeds distrust.*

breed² /bri:d/ noun [C] 1 BIOLOGY a particular type of animal that is different from others but not so different that it is another species: *different breeds of dog* 2 a particular type of person or thing: *the new breed of Internet millionaires*

breeding /'bri:dɪŋ/ noun [U] 1 BIOLOGY the process of **mating** and producing young animals 2 AGRICULTURE the activity of reproducing and raising animals or plants for sale, or for competitions 3 AGRICULTURE the development of new types of animal or plant with improved characteristics

'breeding ,ground noun [C] 1 a situation or place in which bad things easily develop 2 a place where animals breed

breeze¹ /bri:z/ noun [C] a light wind: *a gentle breeze —picture* → on next page

breeze² /bri:z/ verb [I] to go somewhere in a very confident way: *He breezed into the meeting and took charge.*
PHRASAL VERB **'breeze through sth** to do something very easily or confidently

'breeze ,block noun [C] CONSTRUCTION a large light brick made from cement and **cinders**

breezy /'bri:zi/ (**breezier, breeziest**) adj 1 with a lot of light wind= WINDY 2 lively, confident, and informal —**breezily** adv

breve /bri:v/ noun [C] MUSIC a musical note that is equal to two **semibreves** —picture → MUSIC

brevity /'brevəti/ noun [U] formal 1 the use of only a few words 2 the fact that something only lasts for a short time

brew /bru:/ verb 1 [I/T] to make beer 2 [I/T] if tea or coffee is brewing, or if someone is brewing it, they have made it and left it to develop more flavour 3 [I] to begin to happen: *A storm was brewing.*

brewery /'bru:əri/ (plural **breweries**) noun [C] 1 a company that makes beer 2 a place where beer is made

bribe¹ /braɪb/ verb [T] to give money or a present to someone in exchange for help that involves doing something wrong or illegal: *They tried to bribe the judge to find their brother not guilty.*

bribe² /braɪb/ noun [C] money or a present given in exchange for help that involves doing something wrong or illegal: *Some officials had accepted bribes from a major oil company.*

bribery /'braɪb(ə)ri/ noun [U] the act of giving money or a present to someone in exchange for help that involves doing something wrong or illegal

brick /brɪk/ noun [C/U] a small block used as a building material to make walls, houses etc: *The church was built entirely of brick.*

'brick ,gauge noun [C] CONSTRUCTION a narrow piece of wood that is used when laying bricks, with the rows marked on it

bricklayer /'brɪk,leɪə/ noun [C] someone whose job is to build walls, houses etc using bricks —**bricklaying** noun [U]

,brick-'red adj a colour that is between red and brown

brickwork /'brɪk,wɜ:k/ noun [U] the bricks in a wall or building, or the pattern that they form

brickyard /'brɪk,jɑ:d/ noun [C] a place or business where bricks are made

bridal /'braɪd(ə)l/ adj relating to a bride

bride /braɪd/ noun [C] a woman who is getting married, or one who has recently married

bridegroom /'braɪd,gru:m/ noun [C] a man who is getting married, or one who has recently married

bridesmaid /'braɪdz,meɪd/ noun [C] a girl or young woman who helps a **bride** at her wedding

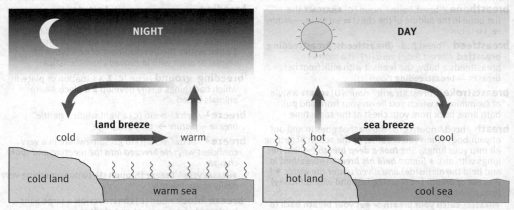

land and sea breezes

,bride-to-'be noun [C] a woman who is going to be married

bridge¹ /brɪdʒ/ noun

1 sth going over	**5** upper part of nose
2 connection	**6** on musical instrument
3 part of ship	**7** artificial tooth/teeth
4 card game	

1 [C] a structure that supports a road, railway, or path going over a river, over another road etc: *Go over the bridge and then turn right.* ♦ *a railway bridge*
2 [C] something that forms a connection between two groups or situations: *Nursery school acts as* **a bridge between** *home and school.*
3 [C] the part of a ship from which it is controlled
4 [U] a card game for four players who make two teams
5 [C] the thin part of the nose between the eyes
6 [C] MUSIC a small wooden part on an instrument such as the **violin** that holds the strings away from the main part of the instrument
7 [C] an artificial tooth or group of teeth that is fitted between natural teeth

bridge² /brɪdʒ/ verb [T] to reduce the differences that separate two things or groups: *ways to* **bridge the gap** *between income and spending*

'bridge-,building noun [U] the activity of improving relationships between people or groups

bridgehead /'brɪdʒ,hed/ noun [C] a strong position held by an army on enemy land from which they can attack

bridgeware /'brɪdʒ,weə/ noun [U] COMPUTING computer equipment or software that makes changing from one computer system to another easier, for example by changing the **file format**

bridging point /'brɪdʒɪŋ ,pɔɪnt/ noun [C] GEOGRAPHY the narrowest place where it is possible to cross a river

bridle¹ /'braɪd(ə)l/ noun [C] a set of leather bands that go over a horse's head

bridle² /'braɪd(ə)l/ verb **1** [I] to show that you are angry or offended **2** [T] to put a bridle on a horse

brief¹ /briːf/ adj **1** lasting for only a short time: *a brief visit* **2** using only a few words: *I'll make my comments brief.* **3** not covering much of the body: *She was wearing the briefest of miniskirts.*

brief² /briːf/ noun [C] **1** official instructions on how to do a job **2** LAW a document giving the facts of a legal case → BRIEFS

brief³ /briːf/ verb [T] to give someone official information about a situation: *The President's military advisors are briefing him on the situation.*

briefcase /'briːf,keɪs/ noun [C] a case for carrying documents —*picture* → WORKSTATION

briefing /'briːfɪŋ/ noun [C] a meeting or document in which people receive official information

briefly /'briːfli/ adv **1** in a way that does not take much time or give many details: *Tell me briefly what your story is about.* **2** for a short time: *I saw her briefly yesterday before she left for the airport.*

briefs /briːfs/ noun [plural] men's short tight **underpants** or women's **knickers**

brigade /brɪ'ɡeɪd/ noun [C] a large group of soldiers

brigadier /,brɪɡə'dɪə/ noun [C] an officer of high rank in the British Army

brigadier-general noun [C] an officer of high rank in the US Army, **Marines**, or Air Force

brigand /'brɪɡənd/ noun [C] *literary* someone who steals things, especially from travellers = BANDIT

bright /braɪt/ adj **1** bright colours are strong but not dark: *She was wearing a bright red scarf.* **2** full of strong shining light: *It was a bright sunny day.* ♦ *I could see a bright light in the sky.* **3** intelligent: *one of the brightest students in the class* **4** happy and lively = CHEERFUL: *She gave him a bright smile.*

PHRASES **a bright idea** a clever idea. This word is often used for showing that you think an idea is stupid.
look on the bright side to think about the good parts of a situation that is mainly bad
—**brightly** adv, **brightness** noun [U]

'bright ,bar noun [C/U] TECHNOLOGY a **black bar** (=block of shaped metal) that has been dipped in a bath of sulphuric acid to remove **oxides**

brighten /'braɪt(ə)n/ verb **1** [I/T] to start to have more colour or light, or to give something more colour or light **2** [I] to start looking or feeling happier

brilliance /'brɪljəns/ noun [U] **1** great skill or intelligence **2** great brightness

brilliant /'brɪljənt/ adj **1** very intelligent: *a brilliant scientist* **2** very skilful, impressive, or successful: *The goalkeeper made a brilliant save.* **3** shining strongly: *a brilliant light* —**brilliantly** adv: *Their plan worked brilliantly.* ♦ *brilliantly coloured birds*

brim /brɪm/ noun [C] **1** the part of a hat that sticks out from the base **2** the top edge of a cup or bowl

brine /braɪn/ noun [U] water that contains a lot of salt

bring /brɪŋ/ (**brings**, **bringing**, **brought** /brɔːt/) verb [T]

1 take sb/sth	6 start a legal case
2 move sth	7 get to a point
3 attract to a place	8 provide with sth
4 cause sth	+ PHRASES
5 make sth reach a total	+ PHRASAL VERBS

1 to take someone or something with you from one place to another: *Bring a coat in case it turns cold.* ♦ *I brought that book for you.* ♦ *Could you bring me a plate from the kitchen?*

2 to move something somewhere: *She reached up to the shelf and brought down a box.*

3 to make someone or something come to a place: *Government investment has brought thousands of new jobs to the area.*

4 to be the cause of a state, situation, or feeling: *efforts to bring peace to the region* ♦ *My work brings me into contact with all kinds of people.*

5 to make a number reach a particular total: *He scored 10 points, bringing the team's total to 85.*

6 to start a legal case against someone: *The authorities are expected to bring charges.*

7 to come to a particular point as you are talking or writing: *This brings me to the next question.*

8 to provide people with something that they can buy or use: *Our journalists work to bring you the region's most comprehensive news service.*

PHRASES **bring sth to an end/a close** to make something stop

can't bring yourself to do sth to be unable to do something because it is too unpleasant, embarrassing, or sad: *He can't even bring himself to talk to me.* → BOIL²

PHRASAL VERBS **,bring sth a'bout** to cause changes in a situation

,bring sb/sth a'long to take someone or something with you when you go somewhere

,bring sth 'back 1 to cause ideas, feelings, or memories to be in your mind again: *Do these stories bring back any memories?* **2** to start using or doing things that were used or done in the past: *They'll never bring back the death penalty.*

,bring sth 'down 1 to cause a government or politician to lose power **2** to reduce the rate, level, or amount of something: *policies designed to bring down inflation* **3** to make someone or something move or fall to the ground: *Strong winds brought down power lines across the region.*

,bring sth 'forward to change the date or time of an event so that it happens earlier: *The match has been brought forward to 1.00 pm.*

,bring sth 'in 1 to cause someone or something to get money or customers: *Renting out a spare room can bring in useful extra money.* **2** to introduce a new law or system: *She said the government would bring in the necessary legislation to deal with the problem.* **3** to use the skills of a particular group or person: *This is an opportunity to bring in new talent.*

,bring sth 'on to be the cause of something bad: *Stress can bring on headaches.*

,bring sth 'out 1 to produce a new product and start to sell it = RELEASE: *They have recently brought out a new CD.* **2** to make a particular quality appear in someone or something: *Tragedies like this sometimes bring out the best in people* (=make them show their best qualities).

,bring sb 'round to make someone who is unconscious become conscious

,bring sb 'up to look after a child until he or she becomes

an adult = RAISE: *She brought up three sons on her own.* ♦ *Our parents brought us up to believe in our own abilities.*

,bring sth 'up to start discussing a subject: *I hate to bring this up but you still owe me some money.*

> If you **bring**, **take**, or **fetch** something, you have it and go with it to another place. But which word you choose depends on the situation.
> ■ **Bring** describes movement to another place when the speaker or listener is already there: *Bring the photos when you come to visit me.* ♦ *I'll bring the photos to your house tonight.*
> ■ **Take** describes movement to another place when the speaker or listener is NOT already there: *Take the photos when you go to visit her tonight.* ♦ *I'll take the photos to her house.*
> ■ **Fetch** describes movement to another place AND back again, bringing someone or something with you: *Fetch the photos from the kitchen, will you.*

brink /brɪŋk/ noun [singular] **the brink of sth** the point in time when something very bad or very good is about to happen: *The crisis brought the two nations to the brink of war.*

brio /'briːəʊ/ noun [U] a lively manner

brisk /brɪsk/ adj **1** moving or acting quickly **2** if business is brisk, a lot of things are being sold quickly —**briskly** adv

bristle /'brɪs(ə)l/ noun [C] **1** a short stiff fibre in a brush **2** a short stiff hair

Britain /'brɪt(ə)n/ England, Scotland, and Wales → GREAT BRITAIN

British /'brɪtɪʃ/ adj **1** of the UK or from the UK **2** the **British** the people of the UK

British English /ˌbrɪtɪʃ 'ɪŋglɪʃ/ noun [U] the type of English that people speak in Great Britain

the ,British 'Isles the group of islands that consists of Great Britain, Ireland, and some smaller islands → GREAT BRITAIN

brittle /'brɪt(ə)l/ adj hard and easily broken

brittleness /'brɪt(ə)lnəs/ noun [U] TECHNOLOGY the tendency of metal to break when it is subjected to stress

broach /brəʊtʃ/ verb [T] to begin discussing a subject that may make someone upset or embarrassed: *He decided it was time to broach the subject of a pay rise.*

broad /brɔːd/ adj **1** wide ≠ NARROW: *He had very broad shoulders.* ♦ *a broad shady path* **2** including many different things or people ≠ NARROW: *I meet a broad range of people in my job.* **3** expressed in a general way, without many details: *This chapter can only give a broad outline of the subject.* **4** a broad accent is very noticeable and typical of the area that the speaker comes from

PHRASE **in broad daylight** during the day, when people can easily see what is happening: *They robbed the bank in broad daylight.* → BROADLY

broadband /'brɔːd,bænd/ noun [U] COMPUTING a type of connection between a computer and the Internet that allows you to send or receive a large amount of information in a short time

'broad-,brush adj very general and without many details

broadcast¹ /'brɔːd,kɑːst/ (**broadcasts**, **broadcasting**, **broadcast**) verb **1** [I/T] to send out messages or programmes to be received by radios or televisions: *The BBC will be broadcasting the match* *live from Cape Town.* **2** [T] to tell people something that someone wanted to be a secret —**broadcasting** noun [U]

broadcast² /ˈbrɔːdˌkɑːst/ noun [C] a programme that is broadcast: *Channel 5's main news broadcast*

broadcaster /ˈbrɔːdˌkɑːstə/ noun [C] someone whose job is to speak on radio or television programmes

broaden /ˈbrɔːd(ə)n/ verb **1** [I] to become wider, or to make something wider: *There are plans to broaden the road.* **2** [T] to start to include more things or people, or to make something include more things or people: *We have broadened the scope of the investigation.* **3** [I] if someone's smile broadens, it becomes wider because they are happy **4** [I] if someone's accent broadens, they start to speak with a more noticeable accent

broadleaved /ˈbrɔːdˌliːvd/ adj **BIOLOGY 1** relating to or belonging to **deciduous** or **evergreen** trees such as **oak** or **holly** that have wide rather than needle-shaped leaves **2** relating to all plants that have **dicotyledons** (=wide leaves) rather than **monocotyledons** (=narrow leaves), for example grasses

broadly /ˈbrɔːdli/ adv **1** in a general way, although not in every detail: *The proposal was broadly welcomed by teachers.* **2** in a way that includes a large number of people or things: *a broadly-based committee* **3** if someone smiles broadly, they smile in a very obvious way

broad-minded /ˌbrɔːdˈmaɪndɪd/ adj willing to accept different types of behaviour and not easily shocked ≠ NARROW-MINDED

broadsheet /ˈbrɔːdˌʃiːt/ noun [C] a serious type of newspaper that is printed on large sheets of paper

broadside /ˈbrɔːdˌsaɪd/ noun [C] a strong written or spoken attack

broad-'spectrum adj **1** HEALTH broad-spectrum drugs kill a wide range of microorganisms that cause illness or infection **2** AGRICULTURE, CHEMISTRY broad-spectrum **insecticides** (=chemicals for killing insects) kill a wide range of organisms that damage agricultural crops

broccoli /ˈbrɒkəli/ noun [U] a vegetable consisting of green stems with many small green or purple parts on the ends —*picture* → VEGETABLE

brochure /ˈbrəʊʃə/ noun [C] a small magazine containing details of goods or services that people can buy

'brochure ,site noun [C] BUSINESS a simple website, often consisting of just one page, that describes a company's products and gives general information about the company

broke¹ /brəʊk/ adj *informal* without any money: *Can you lend me £5? I'm completely broke.*

broke² /brəʊk/ the past tense of **break¹**

broken¹ /ˈbrəʊkən/ adj

1 in pieces	**4** extremely sad
2 not working	**5** not as promised
3 injured and cracked	

1 a broken object has been damaged with the result that it is in two or more pieces: *Nearly all the houses had broken windows.*
2 if a piece of equipment is broken, it is not working correctly: *You can't use the microwave – it's broken.*
3 a broken bone has a crack in it: *He had several broken ribs.*
4 *literary* if someone's heart is broken, they feel extremely sad
5 a broken promise is one that someone has not kept

Build your vocabulary: words you can use instead of broken

Broken is a very general word. Here are some words with more specific meanings that sound more natural and appropriate in particular situations.
cars/machines/equipment faulty, not working
houses/buildings falling down, in disrepair
systems/computers down, not working
objects chipped, cracked, dented, smashed
containers burst, leaky, split
fabric frayed, ripped, split, torn
paper in shreds, ripped, torn

broken² /ˈbrəʊkən/ the past participle of **break¹**

,broken-'down adj no longer working, or in very bad condition

broken-hearted /ˌbrəʊkən ˈhɑːtɪd/ adj extremely sad

,broken-'line ,graph noun [C] MATHS a graph where one point is joined to another by a straight line

broker /ˈbrəʊkə/ noun [C] someone who buys and sells things like property or insurance for other people

bromine /ˈbrəʊmiːn/ noun [U] CHEMISTRY a non-metal element that is usually a dark red liquid but can easily change into a gas. It belongs to the **halogen** group of elements and is used in **dyes** and in films for taking photographs. Chemical symbol: **Br**

'bromine ,vapour noun [U] CHEMISTRY the dark-red element bromine, in the form of a gas

bronchial /ˈbrɒŋkiəl/ adj ANATOMY relating to the tubes in the chest through which air goes into the lungs

bronchial tube /ˈbrɒŋkiəl ˌtjuːb/ noun [C] ANATOMY one of the tubes in the chest through which air goes into the lungs —*picture* → ORGAN

bronchiole /ˈbrɒŋkiəʊl/ noun [C] ANATOMY a very small tube inside the lungs that is connected to one of the **bronchi** (=the two main tubes inside each lung) —*picture* → LUNG

bronchitis /brɒŋˈkaɪtɪs/ noun [U] HEALTH an illness that affects someone's breathing and makes them cough. It is caused by **inflammation** of the **bronchial tubes**.

bronchus /ˈbrɒŋkəs/ (plural **bronchi**) noun [C] ANATOMY one of the two main tubes coming from the **trachea** that carry air into the lungs. It has many smaller tubes called **bronchioles** connected to it. —*picture* → LUNG

bronze /brɒnz/ noun **1** [U] a hard brown metal made from copper and **tin 2** [C] SPORTS a **bronze medal 3** [U] a red-brown colour

the 'Bronze ,Age the period of ancient history when people made tools from bronze, from around 3500 to 1500 BC

bronzed /brɒnzd/ adj with attractive brown skin because of spending time in the sun

,bronze 'medal noun [C] SPORTS a round flat piece of metal that someone gets as a prize for coming third in a competition

brooch /brəʊtʃ/ noun [C] a piece of jewellery that women fasten to their clothes

brood¹ /bruːd/ verb [I] **1** to think and worry about something a lot **2** if a bird broods, it sits on its eggs until the young birds are born

brood² /bruːd/ noun [C] a group of young birds that are born at the same time to the same mother

brook /brʊk/ noun [C] a small river

broom /bruːm/ noun [C] a brush with a long handle, used for cleaning floors

broth /brɒθ/ noun [U] a thick soup with pieces of meat or vegetables in it

brothel /ˈbrɒθ(ə)l/ noun [C] a place where men pay to have sex

brother /ˈbrʌðə/ noun [C] **1** a boy or man who has the same parents as you: *his younger brother* **2** used by men for referring to a man that they feel loyalty and friendship towards **3** RELIGION a man who is a member of a religious group, especially a **monk**

brotherhood /ˈbrʌðə,hʊd/ noun **1** [U] the friendship and support that a group of people get from one another **2** [C] a group of people who have similar interests

ˈbrother-in-ˌlaw (plural **brothers-in-law**) noun [C] **1** your sister's husband **2** the brother of your husband or wife

brotherly /ˈbrʌðəli/ adj typical of the feelings that a brother shows

brought /brɔːt/ the past tense and past participle of **bring**

brow /braʊ/ noun [C] **1** an **eyebrow 2** the highest part of a hill **3** *literary* the part of your face above your eyes

brown¹ /braʊn/ adj having the same colour as wood or coffee: *brown eyes* —**brown** noun [C/U]: *The skirt is also available in brown.*

brown² /braʊn/ verb [I/T] to cook something until it turns brown, or to become brown in this way

brownfield /ˈbraʊn,fiːld/ adj relating to land in a town that was previously used for industry and where new buildings can now be built

ˈbrown ˌgoods noun [plural] BUSINESS electrical goods such as televisions, radios, and CD and DVD equipment → WHITE GOODS

brownie points /ˈbraʊni ˌpɔɪnts/ noun [plural] *informal* approval someone gets from their teacher or boss by doing extra work or special **favours**

brownish /ˈbraʊnɪʃ/ or **browny** /ˈbraʊni/ adj similar to brown or slightly brown in colour

ˌbrown ˈsugar noun [U] sugar that is brown and has not been **refined** (=made pure) or has been only partly refined

browse /braʊz/ verb **1** [I] to look at information or pictures in a book or magazine, without looking for anything in particular: *I sat in the waiting room and browsed through the magazines.* **2** [I/T] COMPUTING to look for information on a computer, especially on the Internet **3** [I] to look at things in a shop without being sure whether to buy anything

ˈbrowse ˌmode noun [U] COMPUTING a feature of **multimedia** software that allows a user to move between pages in no fixed order

browser /ˈbraʊzə/ noun [C] COMPUTING a computer program that allows you to use the Internet

browsing /ˈbraʊzɪŋ/ noun [U] COMPUTING the activity of looking at websites on the Internet in no particular order

bruise¹ /bruːz/ verb [T] **1** to cause a dark mark on someone's skin or on a piece of fruit: *She bruised her leg quite badly when she fell.* **2** to damage a piece of fruit and cause a soft brown area to appear on its surface **3** to harm someone's reputation or confidence —**bruising** noun [U]

bruise² /bruːz/ noun [C] a dark mark on your body or on a piece of fruit where it has been hit: *He had a large bruise over his eye.*

brunette /bruːˈnet/ noun [C] a woman with dark-brown hair

brunt /brʌnt/ noun **bear/take the brunt of sth** to suffer the worst effects of something

brush¹ /brʌʃ/ verb **1** [T] to make something clean or tidy using a brush: *She hadn't bothered to brush her hair.* ♦ *How often do you brush your teeth?* **2** [T] to remove something by moving your hands or a brush quickly over a surface: *Maggie brushed away her tears as she listened.* **3** [I/T] to touch someone or something for a very short time as you go past: *She brushed past him.*
PHRASAL VERB **brush sth ˈup** or **ˌbrush ˈup on sth** to improve your skills or knowledge of something: *I took a class to brush up my German before the trip.*

brush² /brʌʃ/ noun

1 tool	4 light touch
2 for painting pictures	5 short experience
3 use of a brush	

1 [C] an object that you use for cleaning things, covering things with paint, or making your hair tidy. It consists of a handle with fibres fixed to it: *Remove any loose dirt using a soft brush.*
2 [C] ARTS an object that you use for painting pictures that consists of a short thin stick with fibres fixed to one end: *a set of artist's brushes*
3 [singular] an act of making something clean or tidy using a brush: *I'll give my teeth a brush before we leave.*
4 [singular] a very gentle movement against something
5 [C] a short experience of a dangerous or unpleasant situation: *He'd had a few brushes with the law, but nothing serious.*

brushwood /ˈbrʌʃ,wʊd/ noun [U] small branches that have fallen from or been broken off trees, often used for making fires

brushwork /ˈbrʌʃ,wɜːk/ noun [U] ARTS the way an artist creates effects using a brush

brusque /bruːsk, brʊsk/ adj speaking quickly in an unfriendly way using very few words —**brusquely** adv

Brussels /ˈbrʌs(ə)lz/ the capital city of Belgium, where the **headquarters** of the European Union is. People often use 'Brussels' for referring to the government of the European Union.

ˌBrussels ˈsprout noun [C] a small round vegetable consisting of many green leaves —*picture* → VEGETABLE

brutal /ˈbruːt(ə)l/ adj **1** extremely violent: *a brutal attack* **2** extremely honest, in a way that seems unkind: *Let's be brutal here – he's not good enough.* —**brutality** /bruːˈtæləti/ noun [C/U], **brutally** adv

brutalize /ˈbruːtəlaɪz/ verb [T] **1** to make someone unable to have normal feelings **2** to do very cruel and painful things to someone= TORMENT —**brutalization** /ˌbruːtəlaɪˈzeɪʃ(ə)n/ noun [U]

brute¹ /bruːt/ noun [C] a strong man who acts in a cruel or violent way

brute² /bruːt/ adj **brute force/strength** great physical force or strength

BSc /ˌbiː es ˈsiː/ noun [C] EDUCATION Bachelor of Science: a first degree from a university in a subject such as physics or biology

BSE /ˌbiː es ˈiː/ noun [U] AGRICULTURE, HEALTH bovine spongiform encephalopathy; a disease in cows that affects the brain and the ability to control the muscles. The disease can be spread to humans in the form of **Creutzfeldt-Jakob disease** if they eat meat from an infected cow.

b-to-'b adj BUSINESS business-to-business: used for describing a type of business activity in which companies use the Internet to trade with each other

BTW abbrev by the way: used in emails and **text messages** for introducing additional information

bubble[1] /'bʌb(ə)l/ noun [C] **1** a ball of air or gas in a liquid or other substance: *Heat the milk until bubbles form around the edge of the pan.* **2** the circle around the words said by people in a **cartoon**

bubble[2] /'bʌb(ə)l/ verb [I] **1** if liquid bubbles, bubbles form and move in it: *When the sauce starts to bubble, remove it from the heat.* **2** if something such as an emotion bubbles away, it continues to exist but is not noticeable

'bubble ,gum noun [C/U] a type of brightly coloured sweet that young people chew and blow into to form bubbles, but do not swallow

bubbly /'bʌbli/ adj **1** lively, happy, and friendly **2** full of bubbles

bubonic plague /bjuː,bɒnɪk 'pleɪg/ noun [U] a serious infectious disease that killed millions of people in Europe in the past but is now fairly rare. It is passed on by the **fleas** that live on black rats.

buccal cavity /'bʌk(ə)l ,kævəti/ noun [C] ANATOMY the inside of the mouth

buccaneer /,bʌkə'nɪə/ noun [C] **1** a sailor in the past who attacked and stole from other ships **2** someone who is determined to succeed, especially in business or politics, even if this involves taking risks or doing things that many people would not approve of

buck /bʌk/ noun [C] the male of some mammals such as **deer** or **rabbits** → DOE
PHRASE **pass the buck** to make someone else deal with something that you should take responsibility for

bucket /'bʌkɪt/ noun [C] **1** a round open container with a handle, used for carrying liquid and other substances **2** the amount that a bucket contains: *a bucket of soapy water* **3** CONSTRUCTION a part of a machine shaped like an open container, used for moving soil, stones etc

buckle[1] /'bʌk(ə)l/ verb **1** [I/T] to fasten a buckle, or to be fastened with a buckle: *The bag buckles at the side.* **2** [I/T] to bend, or to make something bend under pressure: *His legs began to buckle under the weight.* **3** [I] to stop opposing someone, because you have no energy or determination left

buckle[2] /'bʌk(ə)l/ noun [C] a metal object used for fastening a belt, shoe, or bag

buckwheat /'bʌk,wiːt/ noun [U] a type of grain that is eaten or fed to animals

bud /bʌd/ noun [C] BIOLOGY a part of a plant that opens to form a leaf or flower: *yellow rose buds* → TASTE BUD —*picture* → TREE

Buddha /'bʊdə/ RELIGION the title used for referring to Siddhartha Gautama, whose life and teachings Buddhism is based on

Buddhism /'bʊdɪz(ə)m/ noun [U] RELIGION the set of religious beliefs based on the teaching of Siddhartha Gautama, the Buddha. The basic belief of Buddhism is that people are **reincarnated** (=born again and again in different physical bodies) until they reach a state of spiritual **perfection** called **enlightenment**.
—**Buddhist** adj, **Buddhist** noun [C]

budding[1] /'bʌdɪŋ/ adj just beginning or developing and likely to succeed: *a budding musician*

budding[2] /'bʌdɪŋ/ noun [U] BIOLOGY a form of reproduction in simple organisms such as **yeasts**, in which a part of the parent becomes separate and forms a new organism

budge /bʌdʒ/ verb [I/T] **1** to move, or to make something move, especially something that is difficult to move: *I pulled again, but the wheel wouldn't budge.* **2 not budge** to refuse to change your opinion or decision

budgerigar /'bʌdʒəri,gɑː/ noun [C] a small bright blue, green, or yellow bird that is often kept as a pet

budget[1] /'bʌdʒɪt/ noun [C] **1** the amount of money a person, organization, or government has to spend, or their plan to spend it: *Two-thirds of their budget goes on labour costs.* ♦ *Try to work out a monthly budget and stick to it.* **2 the Budget** POLITICS a statement about the financial position of the UK, given in a speech to the British parliament every year

budget[2] /'bʌdʒɪt/ verb [I] if someone budgets, they carefully plan how to spend their money: *As a student, you have to learn how to budget.*

budget[3] /'bʌdʒɪt/ adj cheap: *a budget hotel*

budgetary /'bʌdʒɪt(ə)ri/ adj relating to a budget

buff[1] /bʌf/ noun [C] someone who is very interested in and knows a lot about a particular subject: *a film buff*

buff[2] /bʌf/ verb [T] TECHNOLOGY to make a metal surface shine by rubbing it with something such as a soft cloth

buffalo /'bʌfələʊ/ (plural **buffaloes** or **buffalos**) noun [C] a large mammal with curved horns similar to a cow

buffer[1] /'bʌfə/ noun [C] **1** something that protects someone or something from harm: *The air bag acts as a **buffer** between the driver and the steering wheel.* **2** COMPUTING an area in a computer's memory where information is kept temporarily when you are sending it from one system or program to another

buffer[2] /'bʌfə/ verb [T] to help protect something from harm or damage

'buffer ,state noun [C] a country that is between two other countries that are enemies but is not involved in the argument or war between them

'buffer ,zone noun [C] an area of land between two armed forces that they are not allowed to enter, making it less likely that they will attack each other

buffet[1] /'bʊfeɪ/ noun [C] a meal at which all the food is put on a table and people go and choose what they want

buffet[2] /'bʌfɪt/ verb [T] to keep hitting against something with force

'buffet ,car noun [C] the part of a train that sells drinks, sandwiches etc to passengers

bug[1] /bʌg/ noun [C]

1 infectious illness	3 sudden enthusiasm
2 computer/program fault	4 for secret listening
	5 insect

1 *informal* a minor infectious illness: *a flu bug*
2 COMPUTING a minor fault in a computer system or in a computer program
3 [singular] *informal* a sudden strong enthusiasm for doing something
4 a small piece of electronic equipment that is used for listening to people secretly
5 *informal* an insect

bug² /bʌg/ (**bugs, bugging, bugged**) verb [T] to hide a piece of electronic equipment somewhere in order to secretly listen to what people are saying

bugle /ˈbjuːg(ə)l/ noun [C] MUSIC a musical instrument, consisting of a curved metal tube that is wide at one end —*picture* → MUSICAL INSTRUMENT

build¹ /bɪld/ (**builds, building, built** /bɪlt/) verb **1** [I/T] to make a building or other large structure by putting its parts together: *Do you know when this house was built?* ♦ *The cabin was built of logs.* **2** [T] to develop something: *He set out to build a business empire and succeeded.* **3** [I/T] to increase, or to make something increase: *The company has worked hard to build sales.*

PHRASAL VERBS **,build sth 'in** to make something part of a plan, system, or calculation: *The cost of hiring equipment is built into the price.*
'build ,on sth to do something in addition to what you have already achieved: *We need to build on the ideas we have had so far.*
,build (sth) 'up *same as* **build¹** sense 3: *These exercises are good for building up leg strength.*
,build sth 'up *same as* **build¹** sense 2: *Stevens played a key role in building up the company.*
,build 'up to sth to prepare for something: *She'd been building up to telling them she was leaving.*

build² /bɪld/ noun [singular] the size and shape of someone's body: *He was of medium build and about my height.*

builder /ˈbɪldə/ noun [C] someone whose job is to build and repair houses

,builder's 'square noun [C] CONSTRUCTION a piece of wood shaped like a triangle and used for making right angles, for example when setting out the corners of a building

building /ˈbɪldɪŋ/ noun **1** [C] a structure such as a house that has a roof and walls: *The town hall was a large impressive building.* **2** [U] the process of building houses, factories, office buildings etc: *the building of a new hospital* ♦ *building materials*

'building ,block noun [C] one of the basic parts from which something is made: *Proteins are the essential building blocks of the body's cells.*

'building ,line noun [C] CONSTRUCTION a line in front of a building beyond which nothing more can be built, according to law

'building ,plan noun [C] CONSTRUCTION a drawing showing the way in which the rooms and other parts of the floors of a building are arranged

'building ,site noun [C] a place where something is being built

'building so,ciety noun [C] a financial organization in which people invest money, and from which they can borrow money to buy a house or flat

'build-,up noun [C] **1** a gradual increase in the amount or level of something: *a build-up of carbon dioxide in the atmosphere* **2** the time before an event when people are preparing for it: *the build-up to the wedding* **3** a description of someone or something in which you make people think they are very good

built /bɪlt/ the past tense and past participle of **build¹**

the ,built en'vironment noun ENVIRONMENT the buildings, roads, parks etc that are built for people to live and work in

,built-'in adj forming part of something, and not separate from it

,built-'up adj a built-up area has a lot of buildings in it

bulb /bʌlb/ noun [C] **1** a glass object with a very thin wire called a **filament** inside, that produces light when it is connected to an electricity supply= LIGHT BULB —*picture* → ELECTRICITY **2** BIOLOGY a structure growing underground that consists of a small stem, buds, and leaves that are swollen with food. The leaves provide food for the growth of a bud that makes a new plant: *An onion is a type of bulb.*

bulbous /ˈbʌlbəs/ adj big and round

'bulb ther,mometer noun [C] SCIENCE a piece of equipment for measuring temperature that has a glass bulb at one end. The bulb contains a liquid that expands into a narrow tube when it is heated.

bulge¹ /bʌldʒ/ noun [C] **1** a shape that curves outwards on the surface of something **2** an increase in something, especially a temporary one

bulge² /bʌldʒ/ verb [I] to stick out in a curved shape

bulging /ˈbʌldʒɪŋ/ adj **1** completely full: *a bulging suitcase* **2** sticking out

bulgur /ˈbʌlgə/ noun [U] a type of wheat that has been partly boiled and then dried

bulimia /bjuːˈlɪmiə/ noun [U] HEALTH a serious illness in which someone tries to control their weight by vomiting up the food they have eaten —**bulimic** adj → ANOREXIA

bulk /bʌlk/ noun [U] the fact of being large
PHRASE **the bulk of sth** the majority or largest part of something: *Women still do the bulk of domestic work in the home.*

,bulk 'buy noun [C] a large amount or number of something bought at one time, usually at a lower price

'bulk ,carrier noun [C] a ship that carries large amounts of a product

bulkhead /ˈbʌlkˌhed/ noun [C] a wall that divides the inside of a ship or plane into separate areas

bulky /ˈbʌlki/ (**bulkier, bulkiest**) adj too big to be carried or stored easily

bull /bʊl/ noun [C] a male cow —*picture* → MAMMAL

bulldog /ˈbʊlˌdɒg/ noun [C] a dog with short hair, a short neck and large head, and short thick legs

bulldoze /ˈbʊlˌdəʊz/ verb **1** [I/T] to clear an area with a bulldozer **2** [T] *informal* to force someone to do something that they do not really want to do by being very determined

bulldozer /ˈbʊlˌdəʊzə/ noun [C] a heavy vehicle with a large curved open container at the front, used for moving earth and stones and destroying buildings

bullet /ˈbʊlɪt/ noun [C] a small piece of metal that is shot from a gun

bulletin /ˈbʊlətɪn/ noun [C] **1** a short news broadcast **2** a newspaper that a club or organization produces regularly for its members

'bulletin ,board noun [C] COMPUTING a place on a computer system or on the Internet where you can leave and read messages

'bullet ,point noun [C] a printed circle, square etc before each of the notes or points on a list in order to emphasize it

bulletproof /ˈbʊlɪtˌpruːf/ adj made from a material that stops bullets from passing through

bullfrog /ˈbʊlˌfrɒg/ noun [C] a large **frog** that makes a deep loud noise

bullion /ˈbʊliən/ noun [U] gold or silver in the form of solid bars

'bull ,market noun [C] BUSINESS a situation in which prices of shares are rising → BEAR MARKET

'bull's-,eye noun [C] the circle in the centre of a **target** that you try to hit

bully¹ /'buli/ (**bullies, bullying, bullied**) verb [T] to frighten or hurt someone who is smaller or weaker than you —**bullying** noun [U]

bully² /'buli/ (plural **bullies**) noun [C] someone who uses their strength or status to threaten or frighten people

bulwark /'bulwək/ noun **1** [C] *formal* someone or something that protects or defends something such as a belief, idea, or way of life **2** [C] a wall that is built for defence **3** **bulwarks** [plural] the sides of a ship above the deck

bump¹ /bʌmp/ verb **1** [I/T] to hit against something solid, or to accidentally make something do this: *I bumped my knee on the corner of the desk.* **2** [I] to move over a surface that is not even: *The truck bumped slowly across the field.* **3** [T] TOURISM *informal* to tell someone who has bought a ticket for a plane seat that they cannot fly because the **airline** has sold too many tickets

PHRASAL VERB **,bump 'into sb** to meet someone unexpectedly: *I bumped into your mother at the local shop.*

bump² /bʌmp/ noun [C] **1** a raised part on a surface: *a bump in the road* **2** a raised part on someone's skin where they have been injured: *Her body was covered in bumps and bruises.* **3** a hit or knock against something solid: *We felt a bump as the boat hit something.*

bumper¹ /'bʌmpə/ noun [C] a long thin bar on the front or back of a vehicle that protects the vehicle if it hits anything

bumper² /'bʌmpə/ adj bigger or more successful than usual: *a bumper crowd of 80,000*

bumpy /'bʌmpi/ (**bumpier, bumpiest**) adj **1** a bumpy surface is rough **2** a bumpy journey is uncomfortable because of bad weather or a bad road **3** involving both failures and successes

bun /bʌn/ noun [C] **1** a small round cake: *a currant bun* **2** a small round piece of bread: *a burger in a bun* **3** a hairstyle in which a woman's hair is tied in a tight round ball at the back of her head

bunch¹ /bʌntʃ/ noun **1** [C] a group or set of similar things that are fastened together: *a bunch of flowers* **2** [singular] *informal* a group of people: *They're a lovely bunch who have made me feel welcome.* **3** **bunches** [plural] a girl's or woman's hairstyle in which the hair is tied together in two parts on either side of her head

bunch² /bʌntʃ/ or **,bunch (sth) 'up** verb [I/T] to form a group or a tight round shape, or to make something do this

bundle¹ /'bʌnd(ə)l/ noun [C] a group of things that have been tied together: *bundles of firewood*

bundle² /'bʌnd(ə)l/ verb [T] **1** to make someone go to a particular place by pushing them in a rough way: *He was quickly bundled into a police car.* **2** to wrap or tie things together **3** BUSINESS to put things together so that they can be sold or offered as a single product

bungalow /'bʌŋgə,ləu/ noun [C] a house that is all on one level

bungle /'bʌŋg(ə)l/ verb [I/T] to spoil something by doing it very badly

bunk /bʌŋk/ noun [C] a narrow bed fixed to a wall

bunker /'bʌŋkə/ noun [C] **1** a room with very strong walls that is built underground as a shelter against bombs **2** SPORTS in golf, a large hole dug in the ground that is filled with sand

bunny /'bʌni/ (plural **bunnies**) noun [C] a **rabbit**. This word is used by or to children.

Bunsen burner or **bunsen burner** /,bʌns(ə)n 'bɜːnə/ noun [C] SCIENCE a piece of equipment that produces a gas flame, used in a laboratory for heating substances —*picture* → LABORATORY

bunting /'bʌntɪŋ/ noun [U] a line of small flags on a string, used for decorating buildings and streets for special occasions

buoy /bɔɪ/ noun [C] an object that floats on water to show ships where there is danger

buoyancy /'bɔɪənsi/ noun [U] **1** PHYSICS the quality of being able to float, or the ability of a liquid to make things float in it **2** ECONOMICS the ability of a company, financial institution, or economy to be successful again after a difficult period **3** a feeling of happiness and confidence

buoyant /'bɔɪənt/ adj **1** happy and confident **2** capable of floating **3** ECONOMICS successful and likely to remain successful: *The housing market remains buoyant.*

burden¹ /'bɜːd(ə)n/ noun [C] **1** a serious or difficult responsibility that someone has to deal with **2** *literary* something heavy that someone has to carry **3** a negative feeling that is difficult to deal with and that you cannot get rid of

PHRASE **the burden of proof** LAW the responsibility of proving that something is true in a court of law

burden² /'bɜːd(ə)n/ verb [T] to create a problem or serious responsibility for someone

bureau /'bjuərəu/ (plural **bureaus** /'bjuərəuz/ or **bureaux** /'bjuərəuz/) noun [C] **1** an organization that collects or provides information: *an advice bureau* **2** a government department, or part of a government department: *the Federal Bureau of Investigation* **3** a piece of furniture with drawers and a top part that opens to make a writing table

bureaucracy /bjuə'rɒkrəsi/ (plural **bureaucracies**) noun **1** [U] a complicated and annoying system of rules and processes **2** [C/U] *showing disapproval* the people employed to run government organizations —**bureaucratic** /,bjuərə'krætɪk/ adj

bureaucrat /'bjuərə,kræt/ noun [C] *showing disapproval* someone who is employed to help to run an office or government department

bureau de change /,bjuərəu də 'ʃɒndʒ/ noun [C] a place where people can buy or sell foreign money

burette /bjuə'ret/ noun [C] SCIENCE a glass tube marked with a scale and with a **tap** at the bottom. It is used in laboratories for allowing a small measured amount of a liquid to flow into something. —*picture* → LABORATORY

burgeoning /'bɜːdʒ(ə)nɪŋ/ adj growing or developing quickly

burger /'bɜːgə/ noun [C] a food made by pressing small pieces of meat into a flat round shape and cooking it. It is usually eaten between two parts of a bread roll.

burglar /'bɜːglə/ noun [C] someone who enters a building illegally in order to steal things

'burglar a,larm noun [C] a piece of equipment that makes a loud noise if someone enters a building

burglary /'bɜːgləri/ (plural **burglaries**) noun [C/U] the crime of entering a building illegally in order to steal things

burgle /'bɜːg(ə)l/ verb [T] to enter a building and steal things

burial /'beriəl/ noun [C/U] the process of burying a dead body

'burial ,ground noun [C] a place where dead people are buried, especially an ancient place

burka or **burqa** /'bɜːkə/ noun [C] a loose piece of clothing that covers the head and body completely except for a space for the eyes. A burka is worn in public by Muslim women in some countries.

burly /'bɜːli/ adj a burly man is fat and strong

burn¹ /bɜːn/ (**burns, burning, burnt** /bɜːnt/ or **burned**) verb

1 damage with fire	6 of chemicals
2 be on fire	7 feel sth strongly
3 produce light/heat	8 have pink cheeks
4 spoil food	9 put on CD
5 cause injury	+ PHRASAL VERBS

1 [T] to damage or destroy something with fire: *Demonstrators burned flags outside the embassy.* ♦ *The old part of the city was **burned to the ground*** (=completely destroyed by fire).
2 [I] if something is burning, it is being damaged or destroyed by fire: *Homes were burning all over the village.*
3 [I] if a fire or flame burns, it produces light and heat
4 [I/T] if food burns, or if someone burns it, it gets spoiled by being cooked for too long or at too high a temperature: *Have you burnt the meat?*
5 [T] to injure someone or a part of your body with something hot: *The sand was so hot it burnt my feet.*
6 [I/T] if a chemical burns something, it causes damage or pain: *The acid had burnt a hole in my shirt.*
7 [I] to feel a very strong emotion or a great need for someone or something: *I was **burning with** curiosity.*
8 [I] if someone's cheeks are burning, they are red because the person feels embarrassed
9 [T] COMPUTING to put information onto a CD-ROM or DVD

PHRASAL VERBS **,burn (sth) 'down** to destroy something large with fire, or to be destroyed in this way: *The entire house burnt down in 20 minutes.*
,burn sth 'off to use up energy or get rid of fat from your body by doing physical activity: *Swimming can help you burn off calories.*
,burn (itself) 'out if a fire burns out, or if it burns itself out, it stops burning

burn² /bɜːn/ noun [C] an injury or mark caused by heat or fire

'burn-,in noun [singular] COMPUTING a final test for a piece of software in which it is used continuously to check for problems

burning /'bɜːnɪŋ/ adj **1** being destroyed by fire **2** very hot **3** painful, and feeling as if a part of your body is touching something hot: *She felt a burning sensation in her mouth.* **4** felt extremely strongly: *burning ambition*
PHRASE **burning issue/question** something that people have strong opinions about and think is very important

burnt¹ /bɜːnt/ adj injured or damaged by burning

burnt² /bɜːnt/ a past tense and past participle of **burn¹**

,burnt-'out adj **1** a burnt-out building or vehicle has had everything inside it destroyed by fire **2** someone who is burnt-out is very tired and has no energy, usually because of too much work or worry

burp /bɜːp/ verb [I] to make a noise when air from your stomach passes out through your mouth = BELCH — **burp** noun [C]

burqa /'bɜːkə/ another spelling of **burka**

burr /bɜː/ noun [C] **1** BIOLOGY the part of some plants that is covered all over with **prickles** (=small sharp parts) and contains the seed **2** TECHNOLOGY a rough edge that is left on metal when it has been cut or had a hole made in it using a **drill** or a **punch**

burrow¹ /'bʌrəʊ/ verb [I] **1** to make a hole or tunnel in the ground **2** to search for something, especially using your hands: *She **burrowed in** her bag, and found a bunch of keys.*

burrow² /'bʌrəʊ/ noun [C] a hole or tunnel in the ground made by an animal

bursary /'bɜːs(ə)ri/ (plural **bursaries**) noun [C] EDUCATION an amount of money that is given to someone to pay for their education

burst¹ /bɜːst/ (**bursts, bursting, burst**) verb **1** [I/T] if an object bursts, or if you burst it, it breaks suddenly: *Did a tyre burst?* **2** [I] to move quickly or suddenly: *A man **burst into** the room.*
PHRASAL VERBS **'burst ,into sth 1** to suddenly start doing something: *Terri keeps **bursting into tears*** (=starting to cry) *for no reason.* **2 burst into flames** to suddenly start burning
,burst 'out 1 to suddenly say or shout something: *'I hate you!' Julia suddenly burst out.* **2 burst out laughing/crying** to suddenly start laughing or crying

burst² /bɜːst/ noun [C] a sudden short noise, activity, or feeling: *After an initial **burst of** enthusiasm, she lost interest in her job.*

bursting /'bɜːstɪŋ/ adj **1** if you are bursting with something such as love or energy, you feel a lot of it **2** very keen to do something: *She was bursting to tell us what had happened.* **3** if a place is bursting, it is very full

bursty /'bɜːsti/ adj COMPUTING relating to data that is sent in at short sudden periods of activity

bury /'beri/ (**buries, burying, buried**) verb [T]

1 put body in ground	4 push sth into sth
2 put sth in ground	5 avoid feeling
3 cover sth	+ PHRASE

1 to put someone's dead body in the ground during a funeral ceremony: *All his family are buried in the same cemetery.*
2 to put something in the ground and cover it with earth: *There's supposed to be treasure buried around here.*
3 to cover something with a layer or pile of things: *My homework is buried somewhere under this pile of books.*
4 to push one thing into another very hard = SINK: *Diane screamed as the dog **buried** its teeth **in** her arm.*
5 to try to stop yourself from having a feeling or memory, by not allowing yourself to think about it: *feelings of anger that had been buried for years*
PHRASE **bury your face/head in sth** to hide your face or head with something: *She buried her face in her hands.*

bus /bʌs/ noun [C] **1** a large road vehicle that people pay to travel on: *The children go to school **by bus**.* ♦ *If you hurry, you can **catch the** next **bus**.* **2** COMPUTING a set of wires that send information from one part of a computer system to another

bush /bʊʃ/ noun **1** [C] BIOLOGY a woody plant that is smaller than a tree and has a lot of thin branches growing from the lower part of its **trunk 2 the bush** [singular] GEOGRAPHY wild areas in hot places like

Australia and Africa that are not used for growing crops

'bush ,baby noun [C] a small African mammal that lives in trees. It has a long tail and very large eyes and ears.

bushel /'buʃ(ə)l/ noun [C] a unit for measuring grain, vegetables etc equal to 36.4 litres in the UK or 35.24 litres in the US

bushmeat /'buʃ,mi:t/ noun [U] the meat of wild animals that have been killed for food

bushy /'buʃi/ (**bushier, bushiest**) adj bushy hair or fur is very thick

busily /'bɪzɪli/ adv in a busy way

business /'bɪznəs/ noun

1 buying and selling	**5** sth to deal with
2 business people	**6** sth that is private
3 the work sb does	**7** event
4 organization	**+ PHRASES**

1 [U] the work of buying or selling products or services: *They're trying to attract new business* (=get more customers) *by cutting prices.* ♦ *We have been in business since 1983.* ♦ *It was a mistake to go into business with my brother.* ♦ *I found them very easy to do business with.*
2 [U] people who work in business: *The conference brought together representatives from business, the media, and politics.* ♦ *the business community*
3 [U] the work that someone does as their job: *Jon was away on business.*
4 [C] an organization that buys or sells products or services: *a small family business* ♦ *Sheryl's parents run a clothing business.*
5 [singular/U] something that you have to deal with: *Disposing of chemicals can be a dangerous business.*
6 [U] something that affects or involves a particular person and no one else: *It's my business who I go out with.*
7 [singular] something that has happened, especially something that has caused problems: *Ever since that business with her boyfriend, Becky's been really depressed.*

PHRASES go out of business if a company goes out of business, it stops doing business permanently, usually because it has failed
have no business doing sth to do something you should not do, because it does not affect or involve you at all: *You had no business reading my private papers.*
mean business to be very serious about something you have to do: *This is not a game. We mean business.*

'business ad,ministration noun [U] **EDUCATION** a course of study for university or college students during which they learn the basic principles of business

'business ,card noun [C] **BUSINESS** a small card that has a person's name and the job that they do on it, as well as the address, telephone number, and email address of the company that they work for

'business ,class noun [U] **TOURISM** part of a plane that is more comfortable and has better service than the part where most people sit

businesslike /'bɪznəs,laɪk/ adj someone who is businesslike is serious and effective in the way that they deal with things = **EFFICIENT**

'business ,lounge noun [C] **TOURISM** a room at an airport for **business class** passengers, with comfortable chairs and a coffee bar and sometimes also computers and **fax machines**

businessman /'bɪznəsmæn/ (plural **businessmen** /'bɪznəsmən/) noun [C] a man who works at a fairly high level in business

'business ,park noun [C] a special area for offices and small factories, usually away from the centre of a town

'business ,plan noun [C] **BUSINESS** a document giving details of a company's plans for the future

'business ,school noun [C/U] **EDUCATION** a university or college where people study subjects related to business

business studies /'bɪznəs ,stʌdi:z/ noun [U] **EDUCATION** the study of how businesses work, especially the financial and management aspects

,business-to-'business adj **BUSINESS** used for describing a type of business activity in which companies use the Internet to trade with each other

'business ,traveller noun [C] **TOURISM** someone who is travelling on business

businesswoman /'bɪznəs,wʊmən/ (plural **businesswomen** /'bɪznəs,wɪmən/) noun [C] a woman who works at a fairly high level in business

'bus ,lane noun [C] a part of a wide road that only buses and taxis are allowed to travel on, especially during busy times of the day

'bus ,shelter noun [C] a structure that protects people from the weather while they are waiting for a bus

'bus ,station noun [C] a building where buses start and finish their journeys

'bus ,stop noun [C] a place marked by a sign at the side of a road where buses stop to let passengers get on and off

bust¹ /bʌst/ noun [C] **1** a model of the head and shoulders of a person **2** a woman's breasts

bust² /bʌst/ adj *informal* a company or organization that has gone bust has lost all its money and can no longer continue to operate = **BANKRUPT**

bustle¹ /'bʌs(ə)l/ noun [U] a lot of noisy activity in a crowded place

bustle² /'bʌs(ə)l/ verb [I] to do something or go somewhere quickly because you are very busy

bustling /'bʌs(ə)lɪŋ/ adj full of noise and activity: *a bustling market*

busy¹ /'bɪzi/ (**busier, busiest**) adj **1** having a lot of things to do: *He is an extremely busy man.* ♦ *We have enough work here to keep us busy for weeks.* ♦ *Irina and Marcus were busy with preparations for their wedding.* **2** full of people or vehicles: *a busy main road* ♦ *Shops are always busier at weekends.* **3** if someone's telephone is busy, it is being used when you try to call = **ENGAGED**

busy² /'bɪzi/ (**busies, busying, busied** /'bɪzid/) verb **busy yourself** to make yourself busy by doing a particular job or activity

'busy ,season noun [C] **TOURISM** the time of year when a hotel or place that people go to on holiday is busy

but /strong bʌt, weak bət/ conjunction, preposition
1 used for joining two ideas or statements when the second one is different from the first, or seems surprising after the first: *Anna's an intelligent girl, but she's lazy.* ♦ *a simple but effective way of filtering water* ♦ *I thought I had solved the problem. But I'd forgotten one thing.* **2** *spoken* used for starting to talk about a different subject: *It was really awful. But you don't want to hear about that.* **3** *spoken* used after expressions such as 'I'm sorry' and 'excuse me' to introduce a polite question, request, or statement: *I'm sorry, but I don't have time to discuss it now.* **4** used especially after words such as 'nothing', 'everyone', or 'anything' to mean 'except': *She does nothing but grumble all day long.*

PHRASE **but for** except for something, or without something: *The work was now complete, but for a final coat of paint.*

butane /'bjuːteɪn/ noun [U] **CHEMISTRY** a type of gas in liquid form that is used as a fuel. Chemical formula: C_4H_{10}

butcher¹ /'bʊtʃə/ noun [C] someone whose job is to sell meat. The shop they work in is called a **butcher's** or a **butcher's shop**.

butcher² /'bʊtʃə/ verb [T] to kill someone, often a lot of people, in a cruel way

butler /'bʌtlə/ noun [C] the most important male servant in a rich person's house

butt /bʌt/ noun [C] **1** the part of a cigarette or **cigar** that is left after someone has finished smoking it **2** the end of the handle of a gun **3** **CONSTRUCTION** a joint formed between two pieces of material with square ends that meet together
PHRASE **be the butt of sth** if you are the butt of jokes or criticism, people often make jokes about you or criticize you

butter /'bʌtə/ noun [U] a solid yellow food made from cream that people spread on bread or use in cooking —**butter** verb [T], **buttery** adj

butterfly /'bʌtəˌflaɪ/ (plural **butterflies**) noun **1** [C] an insect with two pairs of large colourful wings. Its larva is a caterpillar. —*picture* → INSECT **2 the butterfly** [singular] **SPORTS** a way of swimming in which you lie on your front and move both your arms together above your head

'**butterfly** ,**nut** noun [C] a **wing nut**

'**butterfly** ,**valve** noun [C] **ENGINEERING** a **valve** consisting of a disc that turns inside a pipe, especially one used in a carburettor

'**butt** ,**hinge** noun [C] **CONSTRUCTION** a **hinge** consisting of two separate metal parts that are held together by a pin

buttocks /'bʌtəks/ noun [plural] the two round parts of your body that you sit on

button¹ /'bʌt(ə)n/ noun [C] **1** a small object that you press to make a machine do something: *Press this button to start the computer.* **2** a small round object that is used for fastening clothes by pushing it through a hole: *He had undone the **top button** of his shirt.*

button² /'bʌt(ə)n/ or ,**button sth** '**up** verb [I/T] to fasten something with buttons, or to be fastened with buttons

buttonhole /'bʌt(ə)n,həʊl/ noun [C] **1** a small hole in a piece of clothing through which you push a button to fasten it **2** a flower that you wear on your clothes, for example at a wedding

buttress /'bʌtrəs/ noun [C] a structure made of brick or stone that sticks out from the wall of a building to support it —*picture* → CASTLE

buy¹ /baɪ/ (**buys, buying, bought** /bɔːt/) verb **1** [I/T] to get something by paying money for it: *I need to buy some clothes.* ♦ *When I go away on business, I usually buy something for my daughter.* ♦ *They offered to buy the car for £1,000.* **2** [T] *informal* to give someone something so that they will do something dishonest for you= BRIBE **3** [T] to get something you want or need, usually by losing something else that is important: *Increased profits would be bought at the expense of paying less attention to quality.*
PHRASAL VERBS ,**buy** '**into sth** to buy part of a business, especially in order to get control of it
,**buy sth** '**up** to buy large amounts of something, or all

of it that is available: *Developers bought up old theatres and converted them into cinemas.*

buy² /baɪ/ noun [C] something that someone buys

buyer /'baɪə/ noun [C] **1** someone who buys something **2** someone whose job is to choose and buy goods for a large shop to sell

'**buyer's** ,**market** noun [singular] **BUSINESS** a situation in which there is more of a product available than there are people who want to buy it, so that prices are low and people who want to buy have an advantage

buyout /'baɪaʊt/ noun [C] **BUSINESS** a situation in which a group of people buy the company that they work for

buzz¹ /bʌz/ verb [I] **1** to make a rough continuous sound like a fly or an electric tool **2** if a place is buzzing, there is a lot of noise or activity

buzz² /bʌz/ noun [singular] **1** a continuous noise like the sound of a fly **2** *informal* a strong feeling of pleasure or excitement

buzzard /'bʌzəd/ noun [C] a large bird that kills other birds and animals for food. It is a type of **hawk**.

buzzer /'bʌzə/ noun [C] a small piece of equipment that makes a sound when you press it

buzzword /'bʌz,wɜːd/ noun [C] a word relating to a particular activity or subject that has become very popular

'**B** ,**vitamin** noun [C] **HEALTH** one of the eight vitamins that make up the vitamin B group. Riboflavin (B_2) and niacin (B_3) are B vitamins.

by /baɪ/ adv, preposition

1 saying who or what does sth	**6** defining a change
2 with what method	**7** in calculations
3 before	**8** beside
4 moving past	**9** according to rules
5 of time passing	**10** how sth is held
	+ PHRASES

1 used for saying who does or makes something, or what causes something: *She was helped by her friends.* ♦ *a novel by Graham Greene* ♦ *damage caused by the storm* ♦ *Children are fascinated by TV.*
2 using a particular method, or in a particular way: *We decided to go by car.* ♦ *They keep in touch by email.* ♦ *We met completely **by chance**.*
3 not later than a particular time or date: *The meeting should have finished by 4.30.* ♦ *Application forms must be received by 31st March.*
4 moving past someone or something: *A police car drove by.* ♦ *She walked right by me without saying a word.*
5 used for saying that time passes, or how it passes: *As time went by, people's attitudes changed.* ♦ *The days seem to fly by.*
6 used for saying how large a change or difference is: *Owen broke the world record by 2.4 seconds.*
7 MATHS used for saying what numbers or units are involved in calculations and measurements: *To convert gallons to litres multiply by 4.54.*
8 beside or close to someone or something: *She was sitting by the window.*
9 according to rules, laws, or standards: *Companies are required **by law** to publish this information.*
10 used for saying which part you take in your hand when you hold someone or something: *She took me by the hand.* ♦ *Always pick up a CD by the outer edge.*
PHRASES **(all) by yourself/itself/himself etc 1** alone: *I want to be by myself for a while.* **2** without being helped by anyone else: *You can't carry that big table all by yourself.*

by night/day during the night or day: *We travelled by night to avoid the heat.*

by the way *spoken* used for adding a remark that is not relevant to the main subject of your conversation: *By the way, Jeff called this afternoon.*

bye¹ /baɪ/ or **'bye-bye** interjection goodbye: *Bye for now* – *see you later.*

bye² /baɪ/ noun [C] **SPORTS** a situation in which a player or a team does not have an opponent at a particular stage of a competition and goes straight into the next stage

'by-e,lection noun [C] an election in one particular area of the UK to choose a new representative in Parliament

bygone /'baɪɡɒn/ adj happening or existing during a period of time in the past

bypass¹ /'baɪ,pɑːs/ noun [C] **1** a road that goes round a town or city so that people can avoid going through its centre **2 HEALTH** a medical operation to make someone's blood flow past a blocked or damaged part of their heart → HEART BYPASS

bypass² /'baɪ,pɑːs/ verb [T] **1** to avoid dealing with someone or something because you think you can do something more quickly without using them **2** to avoid the centre of a town or city by using a road that goes round it

'bypass oil ,filter noun [C] **ENGINEERING** a filter in a vehicle's engine that cleans some of the oil in an engine that has already been cleaned once by the main filter

'bypass ,valve noun [C] **ENGINEERING** a **valve** that allows fluid to flow through a system without passing through a filter

'by-,product noun [C] **1** an additional product that is made as a result of an industrial or chemical process **2** something that happens unexpectedly as a result of something else

bystander /'baɪ,stændə/ noun [C] someone who sees an event happen, but who is not directly involved in it

byte /baɪt/ noun [C] **COMPUTING** a basic unit for storing computer information, used for measuring the size of a document

byzantine /bɪ'zæntaɪn/ adj *formal* complicated and difficult to understand

Cc

c¹ /siː/ (plural **c's**) or **C** (plural **C's**) noun [C/U] **1** the third letter of the English alphabet **2 C MUSIC** the first note in the musical scale of C major

c² abbrev **1** cent(s) **2** century **3** c or **ca** circa: used before a date that is not exact

C /siː/ abbrev **1** Celsius **2** see: used in emails and **text messages**

© a symbol meaning 'copyright'

C2B /,siː tə 'biː/ adj **BUSINESS** consumer-to-business: used for describing a type of business activity in which a customer deals with a company over the Internet

cab /kæb/ noun [C] **1** a taxi **2** the front part of a bus, train, or lorry where the driver sits

cabaret /'kæbəreɪ/ noun [C/U] entertainment in a restaurant or club that is performed while people eat or drink

cabbage /'kæbɪdʒ/ noun [C/U] a hard round vegetable with green or purple leaves —*picture* → VEGETABLE

cabin /'kæbɪn/ noun [C] **1** a bedroom on a ship **2** the part of a plane where the passengers sit **3** a small simple wooden house in the mountains or in a forest

'cabin ,baggage noun [U] **TOURISM** bags that passengers carry with them onto a plane, rather than those that go in the plane's **hold**

'cabin ,crew noun [C] **TOURISM** the people on a plane whose job is to look after the passengers

cabinet /'kæbɪnət/ noun [C] **1** a cupboard that is used for storing or showing things: *a medicine cabinet* → FILING CABINET **2 cabinet** or **Cabinet POLITICS** a group of advisers who are chosen by the leader of a government: *The PM called a meeting of his cabinet.*

'cabinet ,drawing noun [C/U] **MATHS, PHYSICS** a drawing that shows one side of a three-dimensional object **to scale** (=smaller or larger than it really is, but with its original shape), and the other sides at an angle of 45 degrees in order to show its depth

cable /'keɪb(ə)l/ noun **1** [C/U] thick wire used for carrying electricity or electronic signals **2** [C/U] strong thick metal rope **3** [U] **cable television**

'cable ,car noun [C] a small vehicle that hangs from a cable. It is used for taking people up and down mountains.

'cable ,modem noun [C] **COMPUTING** a high-speed **modem** that allows a computer to connect to the Internet through the same underground wires as cable television

,cable 'television or **,cable T'V** noun [U] a system for broadcasting television programmes in which signals are sent through underground wires

cacao /kə'kaʊ/ noun [U] a tropical tree, the seeds of which are used for making chocolate and **cocoa**

cache /kæʃ/ noun [C] **1** a quantity of things that have been hidden, or the place where they are hidden **2 COMPUTING cache memory**

'cache ,memory noun [C] **COMPUTING** an area of a computer's memory for storing information that is regularly needed ═ CACHE

cackle /'kæk(ə)l/ verb [I/T] to laugh in a loud unpleasant way —**cackle** noun [C]

cacophony /kə'kɒfəni/ noun [singular] an unpleasant mixture of loud sounds

cactus /'kæktəs/ (plural **cacti** or **cactuses**) noun [C] a plant with thick stems and sharp points that grows in deserts

CAD /kæd/ noun [U] **COMPUTING** computer-aided design: the use of computers to design things

cadence /'keɪd(ə)ns/ noun [C/U] **MUSIC** a short section of music that ends a longer section

cadet /kə'det/ noun [C] a young person who is training to be a police officer or military officer

cadmium /'kædmiəm/ noun [U] **CHEMISTRY** a blue-white chemical element that is a metal. It is used in electronics, in making batteries, in making **fillings** for teeth, and for **electroplating**. Chemical symbol: **Cd**

caecum /'siːkəm/ (plural **caeca** /'siːkə/) noun [C] **ANATOMY** the first section of the **large intestine**. It is

shaped like a bag and is open at one end. —*picture* →
DIGESTIVE SYSTEM

caesarean /sɪ'zeəriən/ or **cae,sarean 'section** noun
[C/U] HEALTH a medical operation in which a baby is
born by being removed through a cut in its mother's
abdomen

caesium /'siːziəm/ noun [U] CHEMISTRY a soft silver-
white **alkali metal** element. It is one of the most
reactive metals and is used to make **photoelectric
cells**. Chemical symbol: **Cs**

café /'kæfeɪ/ noun [C] a small informal restaurant
serving drinks and snacks

cafeteria /,kæfə'tɪəriə/ noun [C] a restaurant in which
people buy their food and then take it to a table
themselves

caffeine /'kæfiːn/ noun [U] a substance in coffee and
tea that makes people feel awake

cage /keɪdʒ/ noun [C] a container that is made of wire
or metal bars, used for keeping birds or other animals
in

caged /keɪdʒd/ adj kept in a cage

cajole /kə'dʒəʊl/ verb [I/T] to persuade someone to do
something by being nice to them

cake /keɪk/ noun **1** [C/U] a sweet food made by baking
a mixture of sugar, eggs, flour, and butter or oil: *a
chocolate cake* ♦ *She was **making a cake** for Peter's
birthday.* **2** [C] a small amount of food formed into a
flat round shape and cooked: *rice cakes* **3** [C] a small
hard block of something: *a cake of soap* **4 the cake** used
for talking about something, especially money, that
must be shared among several people or organizations

caked /keɪkd/ adj covered with a thick layer of
something

CAL abbrev COMPUTING computer-assisted learning:
the use of computers for learning in schools and
universities

calabash /'kæləbæʃ/ noun [C/U] a large tropical fruit
whose thick hard skin is dried and used as a container
or drum

calamitous /kə'læmɪtəs/ adj *formal* causing serious
damage, or causing a lot of people to suffer

calamity /kə'læməti/ (plural **calamities**) noun [C/U]
an event that causes serious damage or suffering=
DISASTER

calciferol /kæl'sɪfərɒl/ noun [U] HEALTH vitamin D

calcify /'kælsɪfaɪ/ (**calcifies**, **calcifying**, **calcified**) verb
[I/T] CHEMISTRY to become hard, or to make
something hard, by the addition of a substance that
contains calcium —**calcification** /,kælsɪfɪ'keɪʃ(ə)n/
noun [U]

calcite /'kælsaɪt/ noun [U] CHEMISTRY a colourless
or white mineral that is a form of **calcium carbonate**

calcium /'kælsiəm/ noun [U] CHEMISTRY a silver-
white chemical element that is very important for the
normal growth and health of most living things,
especially for bones and teeth. It is also used to make
things such as **plaster** and cement. Chemical symbol:
Ca

calcium 'carbonate noun [U] CHEMISTRY a white
solid that is one of the most common natural
substances, found as **chalk**, **limestone**, or **marble**, and
in animal shells and bone. Chemical formula: $CaCO_3$

calcium hy'droxide noun [U] CHEMISTRY a white
alkaline chemical compound used in the treatment of
acid soil and in making cement, **plaster**, and glass.
Chemical formula: $Ca(OH)_2$

calcium 'oxide noun [U] CHEMISTRY a white chemical
compound made by heating **calcium carbonate**. It is
usually called **lime**. Chemical formula: **CaO**

calcium 'sulphate noun [U] CHEMISTRY a white
powder or crystal with no smell, used as a building
material and for drying things. It is a cause of **hard
water**. Chemical formula: $CaSO_4$

calculate /'kælkjʊleɪt/ verb [T] **1** MATHS to discover
a number or amount by using mathematics: *Calculate
the size of the angle.* ♦ *He **calculates that** the proposal
would cost £4 million.* **2** to make a judgment about
what is likely to happen or be true: *It's difficult to
calculate the long-term effects of these changes.*
PHRASE **be calculated to do sth** to be deliberately
intended to have a particular result

calculated risk /,kælkjʊleɪtɪd 'rɪsk/ noun [C] a risk
that someone takes after carefully considering the
possible results

calculating /'kælkjʊ,leɪtɪŋ/ adj someone who is
calculating uses careful planning to get what they
want, even if it hurts other people

calculation /,kælkjʊ'leɪʃ(ə)n/ noun **1** [C/U] MATHS
numbers or symbols that you write when you are
calculating something, or the process of calculating
something **2** [C] a judgment about what is likely to
happen, based on available information **3** [U] careful
planning designed to achieve something, even if it
hurts other people

calculator /'kælkjʊ,leɪtə/ noun [C] MATHS a small
piece of electronic equipment that is used for doing
calculations —*picture* → WORKSTATION

calculus /'kælkjʊləs/ noun [U] MATHS a type of
mathematics used for calculating such things as the
slopes of curves

caldera /kæl'deərə/ noun [C] GEOLOGY a large hole
in a volcano, sometimes containing a lake, caused by
the walls that form the top of the volcano falling in after
an **eruption** happens

calendar /'kælɪndə/ noun [C] **1** a set of pages showing
the days, weeks, and months of a particular year **2** a
system for measuring and dividing a year **3** a list of
important events and the dates on which they take
place: *one of the major events of the sporting calendar*

calendar 'month noun [C] one of the 12 periods of
time into which a year is divided, for example January,
April, or December

calendar 'year noun [C] the period of time between
1st January and 31st December of a particular year

calf /kɑːf/ (plural **calves** /kɑːvz/) noun [C] **1** a young
cow **2** a young mammal such as a young elephant or
whale 3 the thick back part of the leg between the knee
and the ankle —*picture* → BODY

calibrate /'kælə,breɪt/ verb [T] to check or change a
piece of equipment that is used for measuring things
in order to make it accurate

calibration /,kælə'breɪʃ(ə)n/ noun SCIENCE **1** [U] the
process of regularly testing and changing a piece of
equipment that is used for measuring things, in order
to keep it accurate **2** [C/U] one of a set of regular marks
on a piece of equipment for measuring things

calibre /'kælɪbə/ noun **1** [U] the high standard or
quality of someone or something **2** [C] the width of a
bullet, or of a gun **barrel**

calico /'kælɪkəʊ/ noun [U] heavy white cloth made of
cotton

californium /,kælɪ'fɔːniəm/ noun [U] CHEMISTRY a
silvery radioactive metallic element in the **actinide**
group of the periodic table. Chemical symbol: **Cf**

caliph /ˈkeɪlɪf/ noun [C] a Muslim man who was a religious and political leader in the past

caliphate /ˈkælɪfeɪt/ noun [C] **1** the position of a caliph **2** the period of time when someone is a caliph **3** an area ruled by a caliph

call¹ /kɔːl/ verb

1 name sb/sth	**6** organize sth
2 describe sb/sth	**7** visit sb
3 telephone sb	**8** say what will happen
4 speak loudly	+ PHRASES
5 ask/tell sb to come	+ PHRASAL VERBS

1 [T] to use a particular name or title for someone or something: *They called the area the Gold Coast.* ♦ *Her name's Elizabeth, but we call her Liz.*

2 [T] to describe or refer to someone or something in a particular way: *One candidate called it a scandal.* ♦ *The other children called her names* (=said unkind things about her).

3 [I/T] to telephone someone = PHONE, RING: *He called her from the station.*

4 [I/T] to say something loudly, or to shout to someone: *Did you call me?* ♦ *When I call your name, raise your hand.*

5 [T] to ask or tell someone by phone to come to a place: *She called me up to her office.*

6 [T] to organize something such as a meeting for a particular time: *Harris wants to call a meeting.*

7 [I] to visit someone, usually for a short time: *James called to see you.*

8 [I/T] to say what you think will happen, for example in politics or business: *The situation in the East is hard to call.*

PHRASES **be called sth** to have a particular name or title
call (sb's) attention to sth to make someone notice and think about something
→ BLUFF²

PHRASAL VERBS **'call sb after sb** to give a baby the same name as someone else, especially a member of your family: *She was called after her grandmother.*
,call (sb) 'back to telephone someone again, or to telephone someone who telephoned you earlier: *Can you call me back later?*
'call for sb/sth to go and get someone or something in order to take them somewhere: *I'll call for you at eight.*
'call for sth 1 to say publicly that something must happen: *Several of the newspapers were calling for his resignation.* **2** to make something necessary or suitable = REQUIRE: *I think that calls for a celebration!* → UNCALLED FOR
,call sb 'in to ask someone to come and deal with something: *The company have called in the police to investigate.*
,call sth 'off 1 to decide that something will not happen = CANCEL: *She's called off the wedding.* **2** to decide to stop something that is already happening = ABANDON: *They've called off the search for survivors.*
'call on sb 1 to visit someone, usually for a short time **2** to officially ask someone to do something: *He called on both sides to stop fighting.*
,call (sth) 'out to shout something when you are trying to get someone's attention: *'In here!' she called out.*
,call sb 'up to force someone to join the armed forces

call² /kɔːl/ noun

1 act of telephoning	**7** announcement
2 shout	**8** decision
3 formal request	**9** guess
4 short visit	**10** strong wish to do sth
5 sth needing attention	+ PHRASE
6 animal sound	

1 [C] an act of telephoning someone = PHONE CALL: *Can*

*you wait while I **make a call**?* ♦ *Why don't you **give me a call** in the morning?*

2 [C] a loud shout to someone who is not near you: *A passer-by heard his **calls for** help.*

3 [C] a formal or public request that something should happen: *The government has rejected **calls for** tougher immigration laws.*

4 [C] a short visit to someone: *We decided to **pay** another **call** on the Browns.*

5 [C] something that needs your time, money, or attention: *Parents of young children have so many other **calls on** their time.*

6 [C/U] the sound that a bird or animal usually makes

7 [C] an announcement in an airport telling passengers to go to their plane because it is leaving soon: *This is the **last call** for flight BA6774 to Stuttgart.*

8 [C] a decision that is the responsibility of a particular person: *'Do we offer him the job?' 'It's your call.'*

9 [C] a guess about what will happen: *The election looks so close that it's **anybody's call**.*

10 [singular] a strong feeling of wanting do something or go somewhere: *Many young people are feeling the call to do charity work.* ♦ *He could not resist the **call of** the outdoor life.*

PHRASE **on call** someone such as a doctor who is on call is available in case they are needed at work: *Tim's on call this weekend.*

CALL /kɔːl/ noun [U] EDUCATION computer-assisted language learning: the use of computers to help people learn languages

callback /ˈkɔːlbæk/ noun [U] COMPUTING a system in which a **remote** computer calls back the computer that has just called its number when trying to connect to the Internet, so that only the correct person can use the Internet

'call ,box noun [C] a public telephone box = PHONE BOX

'call ,centre noun [C] a place where a large number of people are employed to deal with customers by telephone

caller /ˈkɔːlə/ noun [C] **1** someone who makes a telephone call **2** someone who comes to your house

calligraphy /kəˈlɪɡrəfi/ noun [U] ARTS beautiful writing that people do using special pens or brushes

calling /ˈkɔːlɪŋ/ noun [C] a strong feeling of wanting to do a particular type of job

callous /ˈkæləs/ adj not caring about other people's trouble or pain = HEARTLESS

callus /ˈkæləs/ noun [C] BIOLOGY a mass of **undifferentiated** cells that develops from tissue taken from a parent plant, and that can be used to form many new, identical plants

calm¹ /kɑːm/ adj **1** not affected by strong emotions: *a calm voice* ♦ *Try to **stay calm**.* **2** peaceful: *The city appears calm after last night's missile attack.* **3** if the weather is calm, there is very little wind **4** calm water does not move very much —**calmly** adv, **calmness** noun [U]

calm² /kɑːm/ verb [T] to make someone feel more relaxed and less emotional

PHRASAL VERB **,calm (sb) 'down** to begin to feel more relaxed and less emotional, or to make someone do this: *Calm down and tell us what's going on.*

calm³ /kɑːm/ noun [U] **1** a situation in which everything is peaceful: *the calm of the evening* **2** a state in which someone is not affected by strong emotions

calorie /ˈkæləri/ noun [C] **1** a unit for measuring how much energy people get from food **2 calorie** or **Calorie** SCIENCE a unit for measuring heat, equal to the amount of heat needed to raise the temperature of one kilogram of water by one degree Celsius. Most scientists now use the **joule** (J) instead. 1 calorie = 4.186 joules.

calorific /ˌkæləˈrɪfɪk/ adj containing a lot of calories and therefore likely to make people fat

calorimeter /ˌkæləˈrɪmɪtə/ noun [C] **SCIENCE** a piece of equipment used for measuring the amount of heat given out or taken in during a process such as **combustion** or change of state

calves /kɑːvz/ the plural of **calf**

calyx /ˈkeɪlɪks, ˈkælɪks/ noun [C] **BIOLOGY** the group of **sepals** that covers a flower before it opens —*picture* → FLOWER

cam /kæm/ noun [C] **ENGINEERING** a part fixed to a wheel that makes something move backwards and forwards, or up and down, when the wheel turns

CAM /kæm/ noun [U] **TECHNOLOGY** computer-aided manufacturing: the use of computers to make machines, equipment, and other products

camber /ˈkæmbə/ noun [C] a gradual curved slope from the centre of a road down to its sides

'camber ,angle noun [C] **ENGINEERING** the angle between the vertical axis of a vehicle's wheel and the vertical axis of the vehicle

cambium /ˈkæmbiəm/ noun [C/U] **BIOLOGY** a layer of cells around plant roots and stems that produces new tissue, especially tissues such as **xylem** and **phloem** that carry **sap**, and **bark**

Cambrian /ˈkæmbriən/ noun [U] **GEOLOGY** the period of geological time, 595 million to 495 million years ago, when invertebrate animals appeared and algae developed in the sea —**Cambrian** adj

camcorder /ˈkæmˌkɔːdə/ noun [C] a small camera used for recording pictures and sound onto **videotape**

came /keɪm/ the past tense of **come**

camel /ˈkæm(ə)l/ noun [C] a large desert mammal with one or two humps (=large round raised parts) on its back —*picture* → MAMMAL

camera /ˈkæm(ə)rə/ noun [C] **1** a piece of equipment for taking photographs **2** a piece of equipment for making television programmes, films, or videos
   PHRASE **in camera** LAW happening in private, without other people knowing what is said

cameraman /ˈkæm(ə)rəˌmæn/ (plural **cameramen** /ˈkæm(ə)rəˌmen/) noun [C] someone who operates a camera for making films or television programmes

cameraperson /ˈkæm(ə)rəˌpɜːsən/ noun [C] someone who operates a camera for making films or television programmes

cameraphone /ˈkæm(ə)rəˌfəʊn/ noun [C] a mobile phone that has a camera in it

camouflage[1] /ˈkæməˌflɑːʒ/ noun [singular/U] colours or clothes that hide people, objects, or animals by making them look like the natural background

camouflage[2] /ˈkæməˌflɑːʒ/ verb [T] to hide a person, object, or animal by making them look like the natural background

camp[1] /kæmp/ noun **1** [C/U] a place where people go for a holiday that often has tents or other temporary shelters: *scout camp* **2** [C] a place where soldiers or prisoners live during a war **3** [C] a group of people who support a particular person or idea, especially in politics: *People in the Brown camp* (=who support Brown) *deny this rumour.*

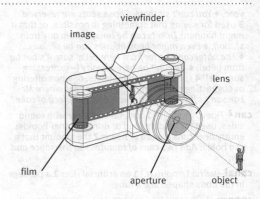

viewfinder
image
lens
film
aperture
object

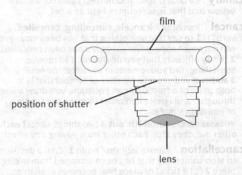

film
position of shutter
lens
camera

camp[2] /kæmp/ verb [I] **1** to stay somewhere for a short time in a tent or another temporary shelter: *They camped for two nights in the forest.* **2** if people camp somewhere, they stay there as a way of persuading people to do something or give them something: *Journalists had camped in front of the house.*

campaign[1] /kæmˈpeɪn/ noun [C] **1** a series of actions that are intended to achieve something such as a social or political change: *an election campaign* ♦ *Local people have launched a campaign against the closure of the hospital.* **2** a series of actions by an army trying to win a war: *a bombing campaign*

campaign[2] /kæmˈpeɪn/ verb [I] **1** to try to achieve a social or a political change by persuading other people or the government to do something **2** to try to win an election —**campaigner** noun [C]

'camp ,bed noun [C] a small light bed that you can fold

camper van /ˈkæmpə ˌvæn/ noun [C] a vehicle that can be used for living in when you are on holiday

camping /ˈkæmpɪŋ/ noun [U] the activity of living in a tent or another temporary shelter for fun: *We don't go camping as much as we used to.*

campsite /ˈkæmpˌsaɪt/ noun [C] a place where people on holiday can stay in tents or other temporary shelters

campus /ˈkæmpəs/ noun [C/U] **EDUCATION** an area of land containing all the main buildings of a university

camshaft /ˈkæmˌʃɑːft/ noun [C] **ENGINEERING** a bar in an engine, with one or more **cams** attached to it

can[1] /strong kæn, weak kən/ modal verb **1** to have the ability to do something: *'Can you swim?' 'No I can't.'* ♦ *The machine can translate messages into 24 different languages.* ♦ *I will help as much as I can.* ♦ *I can hear someone crying.* **2** to be allowed to do something, or to have the right or power to do it: *You can borrow my calculator if you want.* ♦ *Anyone aged 18 or over can*

vote. ♦ *You can't sit there. Those seats are reserved.*
3 used for saying that something is possible, or that it
might happen: *Tickets can be bought from any train
station.* ♦ *Even minor head injuries can be serious.*
♦ *The hotel can't be far from here* (=I'm sure it's not far
from here). ♦ *He can't be here already* (=expressing
surprise)! **4** *spoken* used in requests, or when offering
or suggesting something: *Can you tell me where Mr
Lawson's office is?* ♦ *Can I have another piece of cake?*

can² /kæn/ noun [C] **1** a metal container with round
sides, used for holding food or drink or other liquids:
empty beer cans ♦ ***a can of** beans* **2** the amount that a
can holds: *Add two **cans of** tomatoes to the sauce and
stir.*

canal /kə'næl/ noun [C] **1** an artificial river **2** a passage
in the body shaped like a tube

canary /kə'neəri/ (plural **canaries**) noun [C] a small
yellow bird that is sometimes kept as a pet

cancel /'kæns(ə)l/ (**cancels, cancelling, cancelled**)
verb [T] **1** to say that something that has been arranged
will not now happen: *The 4.05 train has been cancelled.*
2 to say officially that you do not want to receive
something: *Did you remember to cancel the taxi?*
3 MATHS if you cancel a number or symbol that is in
both parts of a fraction or an equation, you draw a line
through it and ignore it in order to make the fraction
or equation simpler

PHRASAL VERB **,cancel sth 'out** if two things cancel each
other out, they stop each other from having any effect

cancellation /,kænsə'leɪʃ(ə)n/ noun **1** [C/U] a decision
to stop something that has been arranged from taking
place **2** [C] a ticket or place that becomes available
because someone else has said they do not want it

cancer /'kænsə/ noun **1** [C/U] HEALTH a serious illness
that is caused when cells in the body increase in an
uncontrolled way: *He died of lung cancer.* **2** [C]
something harmful that affects a lot of people and is
difficult to stop: *the cancer of greed* —**cancerous** adj

Cancer /'kænsə/ noun [U] one of the 12 signs of the
zodiac. A **Cancer** or a **Cancerian** is someone who was
born between 22 June and 22 July.

candela /kæn'diːlə, kæn'delə/ noun [C] SCIENCE the
basic SI unit that measures **luminous intensity** (=the
strength of light). Symbol cd

candid /'kændɪd/ adj honest and direct, even when
the truth is not pleasant —**candidly** adv

candida /'kændɪdə/ noun [U] HEALTH a **fungal
infection** that causes a condition called **thrush**

candidate /'kændɪdeɪt, 'kændɪdət/ noun [C] **1** one of
the people who is competing in an election or
competing for a job: *an election candidate* ♦ *There were
two **candidates for** the post.* **2** a person or thing that is
likely to do or be something: *This encounter is a
candidate for the tournament's most exciting game.*
♦ *She looks like a **prime candidate** for a nervous
breakdown.* **3** *formal* someone who is taking an
examination

candidiasis /,kændɪ'daɪəsɪs/ noun [U] HEALTH an
infectious disease, **thrush**, that is caused by a fungus

candle /'kænd(ə)l/ noun [C] a stick of **wax** with a string
in it that is burned to give light

candlelight /'kænd(ə)l,laɪt/ noun [U] the light from a
burning candle

candlelit /'kænd(ə)l,lɪt/ adj lit only by **candles**

candlestick /'kænd(ə)l,stɪk/ noun [C] an object for
holding a **candle**

,can-'do adj always keen to try hard in order to succeed:
a can-do attitude

candour /'kændə/ noun [U] an expression or state of
being honest, even when the truth is not pleasant

candy /'kændi/ (plural **candies**) noun [C/U] *American*
a sweet, or sweets

cane /keɪn/ noun **1** [C/U] the hard light stem of some
plants, often used for making furniture: *cane chairs*
2 [C] a long thin stick that a person uses to help them
to walk

canine¹ /'keɪnaɪn/ adj *formal* relating to dogs

canine² /'keɪnaɪn/ or ,**canine 'tooth** noun [C]
ANATOMY one of the four pointed teeth towards the
front of the mouth. The front teeth between the canines
in humans are called **incisors**, and the large square
teeth behind them are called **premolars** and **molars**.
—*picture* → TOOTH

canister /'kænɪstə/ noun [C] a metal container for
storing a gas or dry foods such as sugar and flour

canker /'kæŋkə/ noun [U] **1** AGRICULTURE a disease
caused by a microorganism that produces swellings
on the shoots or stem of trees and other plants **2** a
disease that causes painful infected areas in the ears
of cats and dogs

cannabis /'kænəbɪs/ noun [U] HEALTH a drug that is
made from the **hemp** plant, and usually smoked. The
use of cannabis is illegal in most countries= MARIJUANA

canned /kænd/ adj canned food has been preserved
in a metal container without air= TINNED

cannibal /'kænɪb(ə)l/ noun [C] **1** someone who eats
human flesh **2** an animal that eats other animals of its
own type —**cannibalism** /'kænɪbə,lɪz(ə)m/ noun [U]

cannon /'kænən/ noun [C] **1** a large gun used in the
past to shoot heavy metal balls **2** a large gun on a ship
or tank

cannot /'kænɒt/ modal verb the negative form of **can**:
You cannot escape the law.

canoe¹ /kə'nuː/ noun [C] a light narrow boat that is
pushed through the water using a **paddle**

canoe² /kə'nuː/ (**canoes, canoeing, canoed**) verb [I]
to travel in a canoe —**canoeing** noun [U]

canon /'kænən/ noun [C] **1** *formal* a generally accepted
rule **2** all the writing, music etc that is generally
accepted as the work of one writer, musician etc: *a
lesser-known film in the Kubrick canon* **3** RELIGION a
Christian priest who works in a cathedral **4** MUSIC a
type of music in which different instruments or voices
start the same series of notes, one after another

canonical form /kə'nɒnɪk(ə)l ,fɔːm/ noun [C]
LANGUAGE the most basic or standard form of an
expression

canonize /'kænənaɪz/ verb [T] RELIGION to announce
officially that someone is a saint —**canonization**
/,kænənaɪ'zeɪʃ(ə)n/ noun [C/U]

'can ,opener noun [C] a **tin opener**

canopy /'kænəpi/ (plural **canopies**) noun **1** [C] a cloth
cover above something such as a bed or chair **2** [C] a
curved roof over part of a building **3** [singular]
ENVIRONMENT the highest branches and leaves of
the trees in a forest

can't /kɑːnt/ short form the usual informal way of
saying or writing 'cannot': *I can't remember where my
keys are.*

cantata /kæn'tɑːtə/ noun [C] MUSIC a piece of
religious music performed by singers and an orchestra

canteen /kæn'ti:n/ noun [C] a room in a factory, school, or hospital where meals are served

canter /'kæntə/ verb [I] if a horse canters, it runs fairly fast but not as fast as it can

canvas /'kænvəs/ noun **1** [U] strong heavy cotton cloth that is used for making tents, shoes, and sails **2** [C/U] ARTS cloth on which artists paint, or a painting done on this cloth

canvass /'kænvəs/ verb **1** [I/T] to encourage people to vote for someone or support something **2** [T] to ask people for their opinions about something: *We will be canvassing the views of teachers all over the country.*

canyon /'kænjən/ noun [C] GEOGRAPHY a long valley with steep sides made of rock

canyoneering /ˌkænjə'nɪərɪŋ/ noun [U] SPORTS the dangerous sport of travelling through **canyons** using skills such as climbing and swimming

cap¹ /kæp/ noun [C] **1** a soft hat with a stiff part that comes out above your eyes: *a baseball cap* **2** a lid or part that fits over the top of something: *Meg screwed the cap back on the bottle.* **3** SPORTS if a football, **rugby**, or **cricket** player wins a cap, they play for their country in an international match

cap² /kæp/ (**caps, capping, capped**) verb [T] **1** to set a limit on the amount of money that someone can spend or charge **2** to say or do something that is better than something that someone else has just said or done: *Every time I made a joke, Kim tried to cap it.* **3** SPORTS to give a player a place in a country's team for an international match in football, **rugby**, or **cricket**

capability /ˌkeɪpə'bɪləti/ (plural **capabilities**) noun [C/U] the ability to do something: *the company's manufacturing capability*

capable /'keɪpəb(ə)l/ adj **1 capable of (doing) sth** able to do something ≠ INCAPABLE: *The port is capable of handling 10 million tonnes of coal a year.* ♦ *I don't think I've achieved everything I'm capable of.* **2** very good at doing a job: *The staff all seem very capable.*

capacitance /kə'pæsɪtəns/ noun [U] PHYSICS a measure of the ability of a **capacitor** to store electricity

capacitive /kə'pæsɪtɪv/ adj PHYSICS capable of storing an electrical **charge**

capacitor /kə'pæsɪtə/ noun [C] PHYSICS a piece of electrical equipment that can store energy in the electric field between two conductors

capacity /kə'pæsəti/ (plural **capacities**) noun **1** [C/U] the most that a container, building etc can hold: *a theatre with a seating capacity of 800* ♦ *All the country's prisons are filled to capacity* (=completely full). ♦ *The computer's hard drive has a capacity of 40 gigabytes.* **2** [U] the amount of goods that a company can produce: *The factory is now operating at full capacity* (=doing as much work as possible). **3** [C/U] the ability to do something: *They are worried about their capacity to invest for the future.* ♦ *Harry had a tremendous capacity for work.* **4** [singular] the job or position that someone has when they do something: *The Princess was there in her capacity as patron of the charity.*

cape /keɪp/ noun [C] **1** a type of coat that has no sleeves and hangs from your shoulders **2** GEOGRAPHY a large area of land that continues further out into the sea than the land that it is part of

capillarity /ˌkæpɪ'lærəti/ noun [U] CHEMISTRY, PHYSICS capillary action

capillary /kə'pɪləri/ (plural **capillaries**) noun [C] ANATOMY the smallest type of blood vessel, with a wall that is only one cell thick. It carries blood to and

from individual cells in the body. → ARTERY, VEIN — *picture* → BLOOD VESSEL, SKIN

ca'pillary ˌaction noun [U] PHYSICS, CHEMISTRY the tendency of water to move up the inside of a tube because the water molecules are attracted to the walls of the tube and climb up it, bringing other molecules with them

ca'pillary ˌtube noun [C] SCIENCE a narrow tube inside a **thermometer** into which liquid expands when it is heated, measuring the temperature

capital /'kæpɪt(ə)l/ noun **1** capital or capital city [C] GEOGRAPHY the city where a country or region has its government: *Madrid is the capital of Spain.* **2** capital or **capital letter** [C] LANGUAGE the large form of a letter that is used at the beginning of a sentence or name, for example 'A' or 'B': *He wrote the title in capitals.* **3** [C] the most important place for an activity or industry: *Houston is the capital of the American oil industry.* **4** [U] BUSINESS money or property that someone invests or uses to start a business

ˌcapital 'asset noun [C] BUSINESS a **fixed asset**

ˌcapital ex'penditure noun [U] BUSINESS money that a company spends on things such as buildings and equipment that it needs to operate as a business

'capital ˌgoods noun [plural] BUSINESS goods that are used in producing other goods and are not sold to customers

ˌcapital-in'tensive adj BUSINESS a capital-intensive business or activity needs to have a lot of money invested in it → LABOUR-INTENSIVE

capitalism /'kæpɪtəˌlɪz(ə)m/ noun [U] ECONOMICS an economic system in which property and businesses are owned by individual people, not by the government

capitalist /'kæpɪt(ə)lɪst/ noun [C] ECONOMICS someone who supports the system of capitalism —**capitalist** adj

ˌcapital 'letter noun [C] LANGUAGE the large form of a letter, for example 'A' or 'B'

ˌcapital of'fence noun [C] LAW a crime for which the punishment can be death

ˌcapital 'project noun [C] BUSINESS a major project, often involving building work, which will make it possible for an organization to increase its production

ˌcapital 'punishment noun [U] LAW the punishment of legally killing someone who has committed a serious crime

Capitol Hill /ˌkæpɪt(ə)l 'hɪl/ the US Congress, or the area in Washington D.C. where members of Congress work

capitulate /kə'pɪtjuleɪt/ verb [I] *formal* to stop opposing or fighting someone, and agree to what they want —**capitulation** /kəˌpɪtjʊ'leɪʃ(ə)n/ noun [U]

caplet /'kæplət/ noun [C] a pill shaped like an oval

capricious /kə'prɪʃəs/ adj suddenly and unexpectedly changing your opinion or behaviour for no reason

Capricorn /'kæprɪˌkɔːn/ noun [C/U] one of the 12 signs of the zodiac. A **Capricorn** is someone who is born between 22 December and 19 January.

capsize /kæp'saɪz/ verb [I/T] if a boat capsizes, or if you capsize it, it turns over in the water

'caps ˌlock noun [U] COMPUTING a key on a computer keyboard or **typewriter** that causes all letters typed after it has been pressed to be capital letters

capsule /'kæpsjuːl/ noun [C] **1** a small round container filled with medicine that you swallow **2** the part of a space vehicle in which people travel **3** BIOLOGY a small container in which seeds or eggs develop in some plants and animals

captain¹ /'kæptɪn/ noun [C] **1** SPORTS the player who leads a sports team: *She was **captain of** the Olympic swimming team.* **2** the person who is in charge of a ship or aircraft **3** an officer of middle rank in the armed forces

captain² /'kæptɪn/ verb [T] to be the captain of a team, organization, ship, or aircraft

captaincy /'kæptənsi/ noun [C/U] the job of being the captain of a sports team

caption /'kæpʃ(ə)n/ noun [C] words printed near a picture that explain what the picture is about

captivate /'kæptɪveɪt/ verb [T] to attract or interest someone very much —**captivating** adj: *a captivating story*

captive¹ /'kæptɪv/ noun [C] someone who is being kept as a prisoner

captive² /'kæptɪv/ adj **1** kept as a prisoner: *She was kidnapped and **held captive** for over a week.* **2** a captive wild animal is kept in a park or zoo

,captive 'audience noun [C] a group of people who must listen to something because they cannot leave

captivity /kæp'tɪvəti/ noun [U] **1** a situation in which wild animals are kept in a place such as a park or zoo: *crocodiles that were **born in captivity*** **2** a situation in which a person is being kept as a prisoner

captor /'kæptə/ noun [C] someone who is keeping someone else as a prisoner

capture¹ /'kæptʃə/ verb [T] **1** to catch a person or animal and stop them from escaping: *Most of the men had been either killed or captured.* **2** to get control of something, for example in a war or in business: *Rebel forces have captured the village.* **3** to express what someone or something is really like in a way that people can clearly recognize: *The film succeeds in capturing the mood of the 1960s.* **4** to record an event in a film or photograph: *The whole incident was captured by a young American photographer.*

PHRASE **capture sb's interest/imagination/attention** to make someone interested in something, or excited about something: *Her story captured the interest of the world's media.*

capture² /'kæptʃə/ noun [U] **1** the act of catching a person or animal so that they become your prisoner: *He tried to avoid capture by leaving the country.* **2** the act of getting control of something, for example in a war or in business

car /kɑː/ noun [C] a road vehicle for one driver and a few passengers: *She **got into** a black car and drove away.* ♦ *It's quicker to go **by car**.* ♦ *She's learning to **drive a car**.*

carapace /'kærəpeɪs/ noun [C] BIOLOGY a hard shell on the back of an animal such as a **turtle** or a crustacean such as a **crab**

carat /'kærət/ noun [C] **1** a unit for measuring how pure gold is **2** a unit for measuring the weight of diamonds and other jewels

caravan /'kærəvæn/ noun [C] **1** a vehicle that people can live in and travel in when they are on holiday **2** a group of people and animals who are travelling together in a desert

'caravan ,park noun [C] TOURISM a **caravan site**

'caravan ,site noun [C] TOURISM a place where people can stay with their caravans, either on holiday or as a permanent place to live

carbohydrase /,kɑːbəʊ'haɪdreɪz/ noun [C] BIOLOGY any enzyme that helps the body to digest foods that are carbohydrates

carbohydrate /,kɑːbəʊ'haɪdreɪt/ noun [C/U] BIOLOGY an organic compound found in foods such as sugar, bread, and potatoes. Carbohydrates consist of oxygen, hydrogen, and carbon and they supply the body with heat and energy: *Rice and potatoes are important sources of carbohydrates.*

carbon /'kɑːbən/ noun [U] CHEMISTRY **1** an important chemical element that exists in all living things. It is unusual because although it is not a metal, some forms of it can conduct electricity. Diamonds are a very pure form of carbon, and it is a major part of coal, **petroleum**, and natural gas. Chemical symbol: **C 2** used when talking about either of the gases carbon dioxide or carbon monoxide, especially in relation to the **greenhouse effect** and **global warming**: *carbon emissions*

carbonate /'kɑːbəneɪt/ verb [T] CHEMISTRY to put carbon dioxide into a drink, producing a lot of small bubbles in it

carbonated /'kɑːbə,neɪtɪd/ adj a carbonated drink has small bubbles in it

'carbon ,chain noun [C] CHEMISTRY a number of carbon atoms joined in a row

,carbon 'copy noun [C] **1** a copy of a written document, made using **carbon paper** (=special thin blue paper with a layer of carbon on it) **2** someone or something that is almost exactly like another person or thing

the 'carbon ,cycle noun [singular] **1** BIOLOGY, CHEMISTRY the movement of carbon between living organisms and their environment. Carbon dioxide is taken from the atmosphere and is used by plants. It then moves from plants eaten as food to animals, and is returned to the atmosphere by the respiration of plants and animals and by the burning of plant material. —*picture* → on next page **2** ASTRONOMY a reaction that is believed to produce energy in a lot of stars, in which carbon is used as a **catalyst** to combine four hydrogen nuclei into one **helium** nucleus

carbon dating /,kɑːbən 'deɪtɪŋ/ noun [U] a method of finding out the age of a very old object by measuring the amount of radioactive carbon it contains

,carbon di'oxide noun [U] CHEMISTRY the gas that is produced when humans and other animals breathe out and when **fossil fuels** are burned. It is used by plants in the process of photosynthesis. Carbon dioxide is a **greenhouse gas**. Chemical formula: CO_2 —*picture* → CARBON CYCLE, POLLUTION

'carbon e,missions noun [plural] ENVIRONMENT carbon dioxide and carbon monoxide produced by vehicles and factories that spread upwards into the atmosphere

,carbon 'fibre noun [C/U] ENGINEERING a material consisting of very thin fibres that are made mostly of carbon atoms

,carbon 'footprint noun [singular] ENVIRONMENT the amount of carbon dioxide a person, organization, building etc produces, used as a measure of their effect on the environment

carbonic /kɑː'bɒnɪk/ adj CHEMISTRY containing carbon

car,bonic 'acid noun [U] CHEMISTRY a very weak acid that is formed when carbon dioxide dissolves in water

carboniferous /,kɑːbə'nɪfərəs/ adj GEOLOGY, CHEMISTRY containing or producing coal or carbon

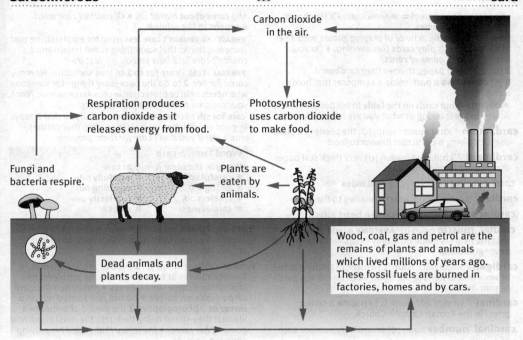

Carbon dioxide in the air.

Respiration produces carbon dioxide as it releases energy from food.

Photosynthesis uses carbon dioxide to make food.

Fungi and bacteria respire.

Plants are eaten by animals.

Dead animals and plants decay.

Wood, coal, gas and petrol are the remains of plants and animals which lived millions of years ago. These fossil fuels are burned in factories, homes and by cars.

the carbon cycle

Carboniferous /ˌkɑːbəˈnɪfərəs/ noun [U] GEOLOGY the period of geological time, 354 million to 290 million years ago, when true reptiles first appeared and much of the Earth's surface was covered by forests

carbon monˈoxide noun [U] CHEMISTRY a poisonous gas without colour or smell that is produced instead of carbon dioxide when **fossil fuels** are burnt without enough oxygen, for example in vehicle engines. Chemical formula: **CO**

carbon monˈoxide ˌpoisoning noun [U] HEALTH a serious condition leading quickly to death in which so much carbon monoxide is breathed in that the blood cannot carry oxygen around the body

carbon-ˈneutral adj ENVIRONMENT a carbon-neutral activity, company etc balances the amount of carbon dioxide and **carbon monoxide** it produces with actions that are designed to protect the environment, for example planting trees or using less electricity

ˈcarbon ˌsink noun [C] ENVIRONMENT an ocean, forest, or other area of **vegetation** (=plants and trees) that helps to protect the environment by taking in large amounts of carbon dioxide from the atmosphere

ˌcarbon ˈsteel noun [U] CHEMISTRY, ENGINEERING a type of steel whose characteristics depend on how much carbon it contains, and that only contains tiny amounts of other elements

ˈcarbon ˌtax noun [C/U] ENVIRONMENT a tax on vehicles or factories that produce a lot of **carbon emissions**

carbon trading /ˈkɑːb(ə)n ˌtreɪdɪŋ/ noun [U] ENVIRONMENT a system that allows a company or country that reduces the amount of carbon dioxide it produces to below a particular level, to sell the extra reduction as a **credit** to a company or country that has not reduced the amount it produces enough

carboxyhaemoglobin /kɑːˌbɒksiˌhiːməˈɡləʊbɪn/ noun [U] CHEMISTRY, BIOLOGY a compound that is

formed when **carbon monoxide** that has been breathed in combines with haemoglobin

carburettor /ˌkɑːbəˈretə/ noun [C] ENGINEERING the part of an engine, for example in some cars, that mixes air and petrol in order to provide power

carburizing flame /ˈkɑːbjʊraɪzɪŋ ˌfleɪm/ noun [C] TECHNOLOGY a flame used in welding that is produced by a mixture containing more **acetylene** than oxygen

carcass /ˈkɑːkəs/ noun [C] the body of a dead animal

carcinogen /kɑːˈsɪnədʒ(ə)n/ noun [C] HEALTH a substance that can cause cancer

carcinogenic /ˌkɑːsɪnəˈdʒenɪk/ adj HEALTH likely or able to cause cancer

carcinoma /ˌkɑːsɪˈnəʊmə/ noun [C] HEALTH a tumour caused by cancer

ˈcar ˌcrash noun [C] **1** an accident in which two or more vehicles crash into each other **2** something that is completely unsuccessful

card /kɑːd/ noun

1 for sending greetings	6 games
2 for money	7 thick stiff paper
3 with information	8 in a computer
4 postcard	+ PHRASE
5 for playing games	

1 [C] a folded piece of thick stiff paper with a picture and a message on it: *a birthday card*
2 [C] a small flat piece of plastic that people use for buying things, or for getting money from a bank: *I gave the waiter my card.*
3 [C] a small piece of thick stiff paper or plastic that someone carries to show who they are: *a membership card*
4 [C] a **postcard**
5 [C] one of a set of 52 small pieces of thick stiff paper,

used for various games= PLAYING CARD: *I'll teach you some new **card games**.*

6 cards [plural] the activity of playing games with a set of 52 cards: *Let's **play cards** this evening.* ♦ *Do you have time for **a game of cards**?*

7 [U] thick stiff paper, thinner than **cardboard**

8 [C] COMPUTING a part inside a computer that holds a chip

PHRASE **lay your cards on the table** to tell people exactly what you are thinking or what you are intending to do

cardamom /'kɑːdəməm/ noun [U] the seeds of a plant used for giving a particular flavour to food

cardboard /'kɑːd,bɔːd/ noun [U] very thick stiff paper that is used for making boxes

'card ,catalogue noun [C] a **card index**

cardiac /'kɑːdiæk/ adj HEALTH relating to the heart

,cardiac ar'rest noun [C] HEALTH a **heart attack**

'cardiac ,muscle noun [U] ANATOMY a type of muscle that the heart is made of. It only exists in the heart and never gets tired.

cardigan /'kɑːdɪgən/ noun [C] a piece of clothing made of wool that fastens at the front, worn on the top part of your body

cardinal /'kɑːdɪn(ə)l/ noun [C] RELIGION a senior priest in the Roman Catholic Church

,cardinal 'number noun [C] an ordinary number such as 1, 2, or 3

,cardinal 'point noun [C] one of the four main points on a **compass** (=a piece of equipment that shows direction)

'card ,index noun [C] a box of cards, each of which has different information on it, usually arranged in alphabetical order

cardio- /kɑːdiəʊ/ prefix ANATOMY connected with the heart

cardiologist /,kɑːdi'ɒlədʒɪst/ noun [C] HEALTH a doctor who studies the heart and deals with the diseases that affect it —**cardiology** noun [U]

cardiovascular /,kɑːdiəʊ'væskjʊlə/ adj HEALTH relating to the heart and the blood vessels

'card ,number noun [C] the number printed on a credit card or debit card

care¹ /keə/ noun **1** [U] the effort that you make when you avoid making mistakes or causing harm: *The label on the box said '**Handle with care**'.* ♦ *He was choosing his words **with great care**.* **2** [U] the activity of looking after someone or something: *I left him **in your care** – you should have watched him!* ♦ *advice on the **proper care of** your clothes* **3** [U] in the UK, the system in which local government looks after some children, for example because their parents are dead: *Her two children were **taken into care**.* **4** [C] something that makes someone feel worried: *She acted like she **didn't have a care in the world*** (=was not worried about anything).

PHRASES **take care** to be careful: *Take care on those steps!* ♦ ***Take care that** you don't fall.*

take care of 1 to do the necessary things for someone who needs help or protection: *Who will take care of the children?* **2** to treat something carefully so that it stays in good condition: *The booklet tells you how to take care of your camera.* **3** to deal with a person or situation: *Can you take care of this customer, please?*

care² /keə/ verb [I/T] to be interested in someone or something and think that they are important: *Her son didn't care enough to come and visit her.* ♦ *I don't think*

she **cares about** him at all. ♦ *Of course I care what happens to the school!*

PHRASE **sb couldn't care less** used for emphasizing that someone thinks that something is not important: *I couldn't care less how you do it – just do it.*

PHRASAL VERBS **'care for sb 1** to love someone: *He really cared for her.* **2** to do the necessary things for someone who needs help or protection= LOOK AFTER SB/STH: *Teach your children how to care for their pets.*

'care for sth to treat something carefully so that it stays in good condition= LOOK AFTER SB/STH: *Your clothes won't last if you don't care for them properly.*

> **Word family: care**
>
> *Words in the same family as **care***
> - **careful** *adj*
> - **caring** *adj*
> - **careless** *adj*
> - **carelessness** *n*
> - **carefully** *adv*
> - **uncaring** *adj*
> - **carelessly** *adv*
> - **carer** *n*

'care as,sistant noun [C] someone who looks after old people or people with serious illnesses, often in a special hospital

career /kə'rɪə/ noun [C] **1** a job or profession that someone works at for a long time: *the problems of combining a career and a family* ♦ *Rosen had decided on an academic career.* ♦ *He has just started out on **a career as** a photographer.* **2** the period of someone's life that they spend doing their job: *the most important game **of her career*** ♦ *the injury that ended his playing career* → CAREERS

career pathing /kə'rɪə ,pɑːθɪŋ/ noun [U] BUSINESS the process by which someone plans how they can make progress in a particular career within an organization or profession

careers /kə'rɪəz/ adj connected with the process of choosing a career: *She went to the university's **careers service** for advice.*

carefree /'keə,friː/ adj happy and without any worries, problems, or responsibilities

careful /'keəf(ə)l/ adj **1** thinking about what you do, so that you avoid problems, damage, or danger: *After careful consideration, we are giving the prize to a children's book.* ♦ *Please **be** very **careful** with those plates!* ♦ *Marta **was careful to** keep her records up to date.* **2** spending money only when it is necessary = THRIFTY: *She's always been careful with money.* —**carefully** adv: *He washed everything carefully.*

'care ,home noun [C] a home for people who need continuous medical treatment or who are unable to look after themselves, especially people who are old or mentally ill

careless /'keələs/ adj **1** not thinking about what you are doing, so that you cause problems or damage: *careless driving* ♦ *The letter was full of careless spelling mistakes.* **2** natural and relaxed: *a careless laugh* — **carelessly** adv, **carelessness** noun [U]

careline /'keə,laɪn/ noun [C] BUSINESS a telephone service provided by an organization or company to provide help and information

'care ,order noun [C] LAW a legal arrangement in the UK for the local Social Services to look after a child instead of the child's parents

carer /'keərə/ noun [C] someone who looks after a child or a person who is unable to look after themselves

caress /kə'res/ verb [T] to move your hands gently over someone's face or body in a way that shows love — **caress** noun [C]

cargo /ˈkɑːgəʊ/ (plural **cargoes**) noun [C/U] things that are being sent by ship, plane, train, or truck: *The ship and all its cargo sank.* ♦ *a cargo ship*

'cargo ,bay noun [C] the part of an aircraft or spacecraft where goods are carried —*picture* → SPACE SHUTTLE

Caribbean /ˌkærɪ'biən/ adj relating to the islands in the Caribbean Sea and the countries that surround it, the people who live there, or their culture

the Caribbean /ˌkærɪ'biən/ **1** the sea that has Central and South America to the south **2** the islands in the Caribbean Sea and the countries that surround it

caribou /ˈkærəbuː/ noun [C] a large brown mammal with long thin legs and horns on its head that lives in northern North America

caricature /ˈkærɪkətjʊə/ noun [C] **ARTS, LITERATURE** a drawing or description of someone that emphasizes particular features in order to make them seem silly —**caricature** verb [T]

caries /ˈkeəriːz/ noun [U] **HEALTH** tooth decay

caring /ˈkeərɪŋ/ adj kind, helpful, and sympathetic towards other people

carnage /ˈkɑːnɪdʒ/ noun [U] a situation in which there is a lot of death and destruction

carnation /kɑːˈneɪʃ(ə)n/ noun [C] a flower that is often worn as a decoration on formal occasions

carnival /ˈkɑːnɪv(ə)l/ noun [C/U] a festival in the streets in which people play music, dance, and wear colourful clothes

carnivore /ˈkɑːnɪvɔː/ noun [C] **BIOLOGY** an animal that eats other animals

carnivorous /kɑːˈnɪv(ə)rəs/ adj **BIOLOGY** a carnivorous animal eats other animals

carol /ˈkærəl/ noun [C] **MUSIC** a traditional song that people sing at Christmas

carotid artery /kəˌrɒtɪd ˈɑːtəri/ noun [C] **ANATOMY** one of the two main arteries on each side of the neck that carry blood from the heart to the head

carousel /ˌkærə'sel/ noun [C] **TOURISM** a moving band in an airport from which passengers collect their bags

carpal /ˈkɑːp(ə)l/ noun [C] **ANATOMY** one of the small bones in the wrist

'car ,park noun [C] an area or building where people can leave their cars for a short time

carpel /ˈkɑːpəl/ noun [C] **BIOLOGY** the female part of a flower. It consists of the **style**, the **stigma**, the ovaries and the **ovules**. —*picture* → FLOWER

carpentry /ˈkɑːpɪntri/ noun [U] the activity of making and repairing wooden things

carpet¹ /ˈkɑːpɪt/ noun **1** [C/U] a thick soft cover for a floor **2** [C] *literary* a layer of something soft covering the ground

carpet² /ˈkɑːpɪt/ verb [T] to cover a floor with a carpet

carpeted /ˈkɑːpɪtɪd/ adj a carpeted room has carpet on the floor

carriage /ˈkærɪdʒ/ noun

1 vehicle pulled by horse	4 way sb walks
2 part of train	5 support for staircase
3 for moving sth heavy	

1 [C] a vehicle pulled by horses, used in the past for carrying passengers
2 [C] one of the vehicles that are joined together to make a train
3 [C] a piece of equipment with wheels used for moving something heavy, especially a large gun

4 [singular/U] *formal* the way someone moves their body when they are walking
5 [C] **CONSTRUCTION** a support that runs down the centre of a **staircase**

'carriage re,turn noun [C] **COMPUTING** a character that tells a computer to move the cursor to the beginning of the line

carriageway /ˈkærɪdʒ,weɪ/ noun [C] one side of a major road, used by vehicles travelling in the same direction

carrier /ˈkæriə/ noun [C] **1** a company that moves goods or people from one place to another **2** a vehicle or ship used for moving goods or people → AIRCRAFT CARRIER **3** **HEALTH** someone who can pass a genetic disease to their children without suffering from it themselves, or someone who can infect another person with a disease without getting it themselves

'carrier ,bag noun [C] a cheap bag that a shop gives people for carrying their shopping home

'carrier ,wave noun [C] **PHYSICS** a high-frequency radio wave that carries sound from a radio **transmitter** to a receiver

carrot /ˈkærət/ noun **1** [C/U] a long hard orange root vegetable that has green leaves on top —*picture* → VEGETABLE **2** [C] *informal* something that someone promises you in order to encourage you to do something

carry /ˈkæri/ (**carries, carrying, carried**) verb

1 take in your hands	8 develop
2 have with you	9 accept blame
3 transport sb/sth	10 have a punishment
4 have goods for sale	11 have message
5 publish/broadcast sth	12 of sounds
6 spread disease	+ PHRASES
7 pass on gene	+ PHRASAL VERBS

1 [T] to hold someone or something using your hands, arms, or body and take them somewhere: *Do you mind carrying this box for me?* ♦ *Luke was carrying the boy on his shoulders.*
2 [T] to have something with you, usually in your pocket or bag: *I never carry much cash with me.* ♦ *British police officers don't normally carry guns.*
3 [T] to transport someone or something from one place to another: *a plane carrying 225 passengers* ♦ *They carried the message back to their villages.* ♦ *a cable carrying electricity*
4 [T] if a shop carries goods or products, it has them for sale: *We carry several models of microwaves.*
5 [T] to publish or broadcast a news story: *All the papers carried the story the next day.*
6 [T] **HEALTH** to have a disease and be capable of infecting someone else with it
7 [T] **HEALTH** to have a gene for a particular medical condition that could be passed on to your children
8 [T] to do or develop something to a particular level: *If this behaviour is carried to extremes, it can be destructive.*
9 [T] if you carry responsibility or blame for something, you accept it
10 [T] if a crime carries a particular punishment, that is the punishment that people will receive for committing it
11 [T] if something carries a message, the message is written on it: *Packets of cigarettes must carry a government health warning.*
12 [I] if a sound carries, it can be heard far away: *The child's cries carried down the quiet street.*

PHRASES **carry weight** to be respected and have influence: *Dr Watson's opinions carry a lot of weight in court.*

get carried away if someone gets carried away, they become so excited or involved in something that they lose control of their feelings or behaviour

PHRASAL VERBS **,carry sth 'off** to deal successfully with something difficult: *Both actors have the confidence needed to carry off these roles.*

,carry 'on to continue going in the same direction: *Turn left at the traffic lights and carry on up the high street.*

,carry (sth) 'on to continue doing something: *She moved to London to carry on her work.* ♦ *Just carry on with what you were doing.*

,carry sth 'out 1 to do a particular piece of work: *The building work was carried out by a local contractor.* **2** to do something that you have been told to do or that you have promised to do: *She ought to have carried out her threat to go to the police.*

carrycot /'kæri,kɒt/ noun [C] a small bed with handles that you use for carrying a baby in

carrying charge /'kæriɪŋ ,tʃɑːdʒ/ noun [C] BUSINESS a charge for storing or delivering a customer's goods

'carry-,on adj TOURISM carry-on bags or cases are ones that passengers can keep with them on a plane

cart /kɑːt/ noun [C] an open vehicle with four wheels that is pulled by a horse

carte blanche /,kɑːt 'blɑːntʃ/ noun [U] the freedom to do what you want in a particular situation

cartel /kɑː'tel/ noun [C] BUSINESS a group of companies who agree to sell something at the same price so that they do not have to compete with one another

Cartesian coordinates /kɑː,tiːziən kəʊ'ɔːdɪnəts/ noun [plural] MATHS coordinates on a graph

Cartesian plane /kɑː,tiːziən 'pleɪn/ noun [C] MATHS a **plane** (=flat surface) containing points that have been marked using coordinates

cartilage /'kɑːtəlɪdʒ/ noun [C/U] ANATOMY a type of very strong tissue that is found, for example, at the end of bones and between the **vertebrae**. It also forms parts of the ear, nose, and throat. It is a type of **connective tissue**. —*picture* → JOINT

cartilaginous /,kɑːtɪ'lædʒɪnəs/ adj ANATOMY consisting of cartilage

cartography /kɑː'tɒgrəfi/ noun [U] GEOGRAPHY the activity of making maps —**cartographer** noun [C], **cartographic** adj

carton /'kɑːt(ə)n/ noun [C] a container for liquids made of stiff thick paper

cartoon /kɑː'tuːn/ noun [C] **1** a film or television programme made by photographing a series of drawings so that things in them seem to move **2** ARTS a drawing that an artist does as preparation for doing a painting

cartoonist /kɑː'tuːnɪst/ noun [C] someone who draws cartoons, especially as their job

cartridge /'kɑːtrɪdʒ/ noun [C] **1** a small container with ink inside that is put into a printer or pen **2** a metal tube that is put into a gun, containing a bullet and a substance that will explode **3** a small container with film or **magnetic tape** inside that fits into a camera or **tape recorder**

'cartridge ,paper noun [U] thick paper with a rough surface that you use for drawing

cartwheel /'kɑːt,wiːl/ noun [C] **1** a circular movement in which someone throws themselves sideways with their hands on the floor, swing their legs over their head, then puts their feet back on the floor **2** a round shape with lines coming out from the centre, like the wheel of a cart

carve /kɑːv/ verb [I/T] **1** to make an object by cutting it from stone or wood, or to make a pattern by cutting into stone or wood **2** if someone carves a large piece of meat, they cut smaller pieces off it to serve to people

'carve-,up noun [C] *informal* the division of something such as land between different people or countries, especially in a way that seems unfair

carving /'kɑːvɪŋ/ noun [C] ARTS an object or pattern made by cutting stone or wood

'car ,wash noun [C] a place with special equipment for washing cars

cascade /kæ'skeɪd/ verb [I] to flow or hang down in large amounts —**cascade** noun [C]

case /keɪs/ noun

1 situation	**6** situation/person
2 legal matter	**7** container/cover
3 set of reasons	**8** in language
4 crime	**9** suitcase
5 instance of disease	**+** PHRASES

1 [C] a situation that involves a particular person or thing: *In the majority of cases, it's easy to keep costs down.* ♦ *If that's the case, I'm not surprised she was angry.* ♦ *It was a case of love at first sight.* ♦ 'I don't need it tonight.' 'In that case, I'll keep it until tomorrow.'
2 [C] LAW a legal matter that will be decided in a court: *He was confident that the case against him would be dropped.*
3 [C] LAW a set of facts used to support one side of an argument or legal matter: *The lawyers told me I had a strong case* (=had a good chance of winning in court).
4 [C] LAW a crime that the police are trying to solve: *a murder case*
5 [C] an instance of a disease: *a bad case of food poisoning*
6 [C] a situation or person that an official is dealing with: *Each social worker was assigned 30 cases.*
7 [C] a container or cover for something: *Have you seen my glasses' case anywhere?*
8 [C/U] LANGUAGE a form of a noun, adjective, or pronoun in some languages that shows its relationship in grammar to other words in a sentence
9 [C] a **suitcase**

PHRASES **in any case** whatever the situation is, was, or will be: *Traffic may be bad, but in any case we'll be there in time for dinner.*

in case in order to be prepared for something that may happen: *Take some sandwiches in case you get hungry later.* ♦ *It probably won't rain, but I'll take my umbrella just in case.* ♦ *In case of* (=if there is) *bad weather, the wedding will be held indoors.*

'case-,harden verb [T] ENGINEERING, TECHNOLOGY to produce a hard surface on steel by adding carbon to it, heating it, and then cooling it rapidly

casein /'keɪsiːn/ noun [U] BIOLOGY a protein that is one of a group of proteins found in milk

caseinogen /,keɪsi'ɪnədʒən/ noun [C] BIOLOGY the main protein in milk, from which casein is formed

'case ,law noun [U] LAW the system of law that has developed from judges' decisions in particular cases in the past → COMMON LAW, STATUTE LAW

caseload /'keɪsˌləʊd/ noun [C] all the cases that someone is responsible for dealing with at the same time, especially a doctor, lawyer, or **social worker**

casement /'keɪsmənt/ or ˌ**casement 'window** noun [C] **CONSTRUCTION** a window that swings open like a door → SASH WINDOW

'**case-ˌsensitive** adj **COMPUTING** a case-sensitive computer program is able to recognize the difference between the large forms of letters, A, B, C etc, and their and small forms, a, b, c etc

'**case ˌstudy** noun [C] **1** a piece of research that records details of how a situation develops over a period of time **2** a set of events that is a good example of a particular idea or situation

cash¹ /kæʃ/ noun [U] **1** money in the form of notes and coins: *Do you want to pay in cash or by credit card?* **2** money in any form, especially money that is available for someone to use when they need it: *The government has cash reserves of about £500 billion.* ♦ *Olga's short of cash so she decided to put off her trip.*

cash² /kæʃ/ verb [T] to exchange a cheque for its value in notes and coins

> PHRASAL VERB ˌ**cash 'in ˌon sth** to use an opportunity to make a profit or gain an advantage

'**cash ˌcow** noun [C] **BUSINESS** a product or business that makes a lot of money for a company, especially when this money is used to pay for other projects or businesses that the company has

'**cash ˌcrop** noun [C] **AGRICULTURE** a crop that farmers grow so that they can sell it, rather than use it themselves

'**cash disˌpenser** noun [C] a **cashpoint**

cashew /'kæʃuː, kæ'ʃuː/ or '**cashew ˌnut** noun [C] a curved nut that you can eat

'**cash ˌflow** noun [U] **BUSINESS** the process of money coming into and going out of a company

cashier /kæ'ʃɪə/ noun [C] someone whose job is to receive or give money to customers in a shop, bank etc

'**cash maˌchine** noun [C] a **cashpoint**

cashpoint /'kæʃˌpɔɪnt/ noun [C] a machine that gives someone money from their bank account when they put a **bank card** into it = ATM

casing /'keɪsɪŋ/ noun [C] a layer of a substance covering the outside of something to protect it

casino /kə'siːnəʊ/ (plural **casinos**) noun [C] a place where people gamble

casket /'kɑːskɪt/ noun [C] a small decorated box for keeping jewellery and valuable objects in

cassava /kə'sɑːvə/ noun [U] **AGRICULTURE** a tropical plant with roots that can be cooked and eaten or made into flour = MANIOC —*picture* → VEGETABLE

casserole /'kæsərəʊl/ noun [C/U] a deep dish with a lid, used for cooking in the oven, or the mixture of food that is cooked in it

cassette /kə'set/ noun [C] a flat plastic case that contains tape for playing and recording sound or pictures

Cassiopeia /ˌkæsiə'piːə/ noun [U] **ASTRONOMY** a group of stars in the northern sky that is shaped like the letter W

cast¹ /kɑːst/ (**casts**, **casting**, **cast**) verb **1** [T] to choose an actor for a particular part, or to choose all the actors for a particular play, film etc: *She was always cast as a mother.* **2** [T] to describe someone or something as belonging to a particular type = CATEGORIZE: *From his earliest days on the team he was cast as a*

troublemaker. **3** [I/T] to throw a **fishing line** or net into the water **4** [T] **TECHNOLOGY** to form an object by pouring liquid metal or liquid plastic into a mould

> PHRASES **cast doubt on sth** to make something seem less certain or less true
>
> **cast your eyes over/cast a glance at** to look at someone or something
>
> **cast a shadow over sth** to make a situation seem less hopeful or more likely to end badly
>
> **cast a vote** to vote in an election
>
> PHRASAL VERBS ˌ**cast 'off** if a boat casts off, it is untied and moves away from the land
>
> ˌ**cast sb/sth 'off** to get rid of someone or something: *It took many years for Chicago to cast off its violent reputation.*

cast² /kɑːst/ noun

1 all actors in film/play	4 particular type
2 for broken body part	5 in fishing
3 sth made in a mould	

1 [C] all the performers in a film, play etc
2 [C] **HEALTH** a hard cover for protecting a broken part of your body while it is getting better
3 [C] **TECHNOLOGY** an object made by pouring a liquid into a mould that is removed when the liquid is hard
4 [singular] a particular type of something, especially someone's mind, face, or features
5 [C] the action of swinging a fishing line or net into the water

castanets /ˌkæstə'nets/ noun [plural] a Spanish musical instrument consisting of a pair of small round pieces of wood or plastic held in one hand and brought together quickly to make a **clicking** sound. Castanets are used especially by dancers.

castaway /'kɑːstəˌweɪ/ noun [C] someone whose ship has sunk and who is left alone on an island

caste /kɑːst/ noun [C] **SOCIAL STUDIES** one of the social classes that people are born into in Hindu society

caster angle /'kɑːstə ˌæŋg(ə)l/ noun [C] **ENGINEERING** the angle between a vehicle's **suspension** and an imaginary vertical line

casting /'kɑːstɪŋ/ noun [C] **TECHNOLOGY** an object formed into a particular shape by pouring a liquid into a mould, and allowing it to become solid = CAST

ˌ**casting 'vote** noun [C] the vote that gives one group a majority when the other votes are equally divided

ˌ**cast 'iron** noun [U] very hard iron used for making objects such as cooking pans and fences

ˌ**cast-'iron** adj **1** made of cast iron **2** very definite, and certain to be effective: *a cast-iron alibi*

castle /'kɑːs(ə)l/ noun [C] **1** a large strong building with thick walls that was built in the past to protect the people inside from being attacked —*picture* → on next page **2** one of the pieces used in the game of chess

'**cast-ˌoff** noun [C] something that you give to someone else because you no longer want it

castrate /kæ'streɪt/ verb [T] to remove the **testicles** of a male animal or a man —**castration** /kæ'streɪʃ(ə)n/ noun [U]

casual /'kæʒuəl/ adj

1 relaxed/informal	4 not planned
2 comfortable	5 temporary
3 without strong feeling	

1 relaxed and informal: *The bar has a casual atmosphere.*

medieval castle

(labels: turret, battlements, buttress, keep, rampart, tower, moat, portcullis, bailey, drawbridge)

2 casual clothes are comfortable and suitable for wearing in informal situations
3 not involving strong feelings or emotions: *a casual relationship*
4 happening without being planned or thought about: *a casual remark*
5 used for describing temporary employment, and the people involved in it
—**casually** adv

casualty /ˈkæʒuəlti/ (plural **casualties**) noun **1** [C] someone who is injured or killed in an accident or war: *There were reports of **heavy casualties*** (=many people injured or killed). **2** [C] someone or something that is damaged or harmed as a result of something: *Education has again been **a casualty of** government spending cuts.* **3** [U] HEALTH the part of a hospital where people go when they are injured, or when they suddenly become ill

cat /kæt/ noun [C] **1** an animal with soft fur, a long thin tail, and **whiskers**. It is kept as a pet or for catching mice. **2** a large wild mammal that belongs to the same family, for example a lion

cataclysmic /ˌkætəˈklɪzmɪk/ adj **1** changing a situation in a sudden, violent, and unpleasant way **2** *informal* used for emphasizing that something changes things in a very bad or violent way

catalase /ˈkætəleɪz/ noun [U] BIOLOGY an enzyme found in living cells that acts as an **antioxidant**

catalepsy /ˈkætəˌlepsi/ noun [U] HEALTH a medical condition in which the body becomes stiff and stays in one position

catalogue¹ /ˈkætəlɒg/ noun [C] **1** a book that contains pictures of things that people can buy: *a mail order catalogue* **2** a list of all the things in an exhibition, sale, or library **3** a series of bad things that happen: *a catalogue of disasters*

catalogue² /ˈkætəlɒg/ verb [T] **1** to make a list of all the things in a collection **2** to list a series of related things

catalyse /ˈkætəlaɪz/ verb [T] CHEMISTRY to increase the rate of a chemical reaction by the action of a **catalyst**

catalysis /kəˈtæləsɪs/ noun [C/U] CHEMISTRY an increase in the rate of a chemical reaction as a result of the action of a catalyst

catalyst /ˈkætəlɪst/ noun [C] CHEMISTRY a substance that causes a chemical reaction to happen more quickly but is not affected itself. An enzyme is a type of catalyst.

catalytic /ˌkætəˈlɪtɪk/ adj CHEMISTRY causing a chemical reaction to happen more quickly

catalytic converter /ˌkætəlɪtɪk kənˈvɜːtə/ noun [C] ENVIRONMENT a piece of equipment fitted to a car that reduces the amount of poisonous gases that it sends into the air —*picture* → on next page

catapult /ˈkætəpʌlt/ noun [C] an object that is used for firing stones. It consists of a stick in the shape of a 'Y' with a thin band of rubber across the top.

cataract /ˈkætərækt/ noun [C] HEALTH a cloudy area that grows on someone's eye as a result of disease. It makes them gradually lose their sight.

catarrh /kəˈtɑː/ noun [U] HEALTH a medical condition in which someone's nose and throat become blocked with a thick liquid called **mucus**, usually when they have a cold

catastrophe /kəˈtæstrəfi/ noun [C] an event that causes a lot of damage or suffering **=** DISASTER: *an economic catastrophe*

catastrophic /ˌkætəˈstrɒfɪk/ adj causing a lot of damage or suffering: *catastrophic floods*
—**catastrophically** /ˌkætəˈstrɒfɪkli/ adv

catatonia /ˌkætəˈtəʊniə/ noun [U] HEALTH a medical condition in which a person cannot move or control their movements as a result of illness or shock
—**catatonic** /ˌkætəˈtɒnɪk/ adj

catch¹ /kætʃ/ (**catches, catching, caught** /kɔːt/) verb

1 stop a falling object	9 hear sth
2 stop an escape	10 find sb available
3 arrest sb	11 find a problem
4 get transport	12 make sb notice
5 find sb doing sth	13 of light
6 surprise sb	14 hit part of body
7 get stuck on sth	+ PHRASES
8 get disease/illness	+ PHRASAL VERBS

1 [I/T] to stop something that is falling or moving through the air, and hold it: *Stewart caught the ball with one hand.* ♦ *A bucket stood under the hole to catch the rain.*
2 [T] to get hold of and stop a person or animal so that they cannot escape: *She raced to catch the child before he got to the edge.* ♦ *Wolves hunt and catch their prey in packs.* ♦ *Did you **catch** any **fish*** (=using a fishing rod or net)?
3 [T] if the police catch someone, they find them and arrest them
4 [T] to get on a train, bus, plane, or boat that is travelling somewhere: *I caught the next train to London.*
5 [T] to find someone doing something that they do not expect or want you to see: *Several times she'd caught him staring at her.*
6 [T] to surprise someone in an unpleasant way, by doing something that they are not prepared for: *The question **caught** their spokesperson **by surprise**.* ♦ *Harry looked up suddenly, **catching** Emily **off her guard*** (=when she was not ready).
7 [I/T] to become stuck on something, or to make something get stuck: *I must have **caught** my shirt **on** a nail.*
8 [T] to get a disease or illness: *Brian caught chickenpox from his nephew.*
9 [T] to hear something that someone says: *I'm sorry, I didn't catch what you said.*
10 [T] to find someone available to talk by going to them or telephoning them: *Margaret caught me just as I was leaving.*
11 [T] to discover a problem or medical condition and stop it from becoming worse: *Doctors assured her that they had caught the cancer in time.*

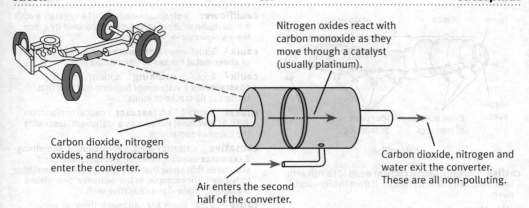

Nitrogen oxides react with carbon monoxide as they move through a catalyst (usually platinum).

Carbon dioxide, nitrogen oxides, and hydrocarbons enter the converter.

Carbon dioxide, nitrogen and water exit the converter. These are all non-polluting.

Air enters the second half of the converter.

catalytic converter

12 [T] to have a sudden effect on someone's attention or imagination: *It was Myra's red hair that first* **caught** *my* **attention**.

13 [T] if light catches something, or if something catches the light, the light makes it look bright and shiny

14 [T] to hit someone on a part of their body, or to hit a part of your body on something by accident

PHRASES **be/get caught (up) in sth** to cause someone to become unexpectedly involved in an unpleasant situation: *We were* **caught in** *a heavy storm*.

catch your breath to stop breathing suddenly for a short time because you are surprised or impressed

catch sb's eye 1 if something catches your eye, you suddenly notice it: *There was one painting that caught my eye*. **2** to get someone's attention by looking at them

catch sight of/a glimpse of to see someone or something for a very short time

PHRASAL VERBS **,catch 'on** to become popular or fashionable: *We were surprised at how quickly the idea caught on*.

,catch sb 'out to show that someone has made a mistake, or is not telling the truth: *He asked her casual questions to see if he could catch her out*.

,catch (sb/sth) 'up 1 to go faster so that you reach the person or vehicle in front of you **2** to reach the same standard or level as someone or something: *He's missed so much school that he's going to find it hard to catch up*. ♦ *Recently, salaries have* **caught up with** *inflation*.

,catch 'up on sth to do something that you have not done enough of before: *I just want to go home and catch up on some sleep*.

catch² /kætʃ/ noun

1 stopping and holding ball	3 amount of fish caught
2 sth for fastening	4 hidden problem
	5 game of throwing ball

1 [C] an act of stopping and holding a ball that is moving through the air: *Well done! Good catch!*

2 [C] an object used for fastening something such as a window, door, or container

3 [C] an amount of fish that has been caught: *Catches of Scottish salmon have declined significantly*.

4 [C] a hidden problem or difficulty in something that seems extremely good: *It sounds so cheap – is there a catch?*

5 [U] a game in which children throw a ball to each other

catch-22 situation /ˌkætʃ twentiˈtu: ˌsɪtʃueɪʃ(ə)n/ noun [C] a difficult situation that is impossible to escape from because each part of the problem must be solved first

catcher /ˈkætʃə/ noun [C] SPORTS in baseball, the person who stands behind the person who is hitting the ball and catches any balls that are not hit

catching /ˈkætʃɪŋ/ adj an illness, mood, or idea that is catching spreads quickly to other people = CONTAGIOUS

catchment area /ˈkætʃmənt ˌeəriə/ noun [C] GEOGRAPHY the area of land around a river or lake that it gets its water from

catchphrase /ˈkætʃˌfreɪz/ noun [C] a short phrase that many people know from television, movies etc

catchy /ˈkætʃi/ adj a tune or phrase that is catchy gets your attention and is easy to remember

catechism /ˈkætəˌkɪz(ə)m/ noun [singular] RELIGION a set of questions and answers used as a way of teaching people about the Christian religion

categorically /ˌkætəˈɡɒrɪkli/ adv in a very clear and definite way —**categorical** /ˌkætəˈɡɒrɪk(ə)l/ adj

,categorical 'variable noun [C] MATHS a **variable** that represents a group of things such as colours, instead of a group of numbers

categorize /ˈkætɪɡəraɪz/ verb [T] to put people or things into groups according to their qualities = CLASSIFY —**categorization** /ˌkætɪɡəraɪˈzeɪʃ(ə)n/ noun [U]

category /ˈkætəɡ(ə)ri/ (plural **categories**) noun [C] a group of people or things that have similar qualities: *There will be two winners* **in each** **category**. ♦ *The proposal would ban some* **categories of** *weapons*.

cater /ˈkeɪtə/ verb [I/T] to provide food and drinks at an event such as a party or meeting —**caterer** noun [C]

PHRASAL VERB **'cater to sb** to provide a particular group of people with something that they want or need: *There are more and more TV shows catering to young male audiences*.

catering /ˈkeɪtərɪŋ/ noun [U] the job of organizing the food and drinks for an event such as a party or meeting

caterpillar /ˈkætəˌpɪlə/ noun [C] BIOLOGY the larva of a butterfly or moth. It has a worm-like body, with three pairs of **true legs** and several pairs of **false legs**. —*picture* → on next page

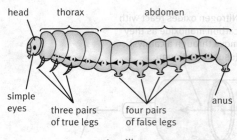

head   thorax   abdomen

simple eyes

three pairs of true legs

four pairs of false legs

anus

caterpillar

catfish /'kæt,fɪʃ/ (plural **catfish**) noun [C] a fish with long hard hairs near its mouth. It lives in lakes and rivers.

cathartic /kə'θɑːtɪk/ adj allowing someone to express strong feelings that have been affecting them, so that they do not upset them any longer

cathedral /kə'θiːdrəl/ noun [C] RELIGION the most important church in the area that a bishop controls

catheter /'kæθɪtə/ noun [C] HEALTH a thin tube put into someone's body to remove a liquid such as urine

cathode /'kæθəʊd/ noun [C] CHEMISTRY, PHYSICS the negative electrode in a battery or similar piece of electrical equipment, or the negative electrode in an **electrolytic cell** → ANODE

‚cathode 'ray ‚tube noun [C] PHYSICS a piece of equipment in televisions and some computers that creates the image on the screen. A **beam** of high-energy electrons is directed towards the screen, where it lights up different spots of colour to make a picture.

catholic /'kæθ(ə)lɪk/ adj including a wide variety of different things= VARIED

Catholic /'kæθ(ə)lɪk/ noun [C] RELIGION a member of the Roman Catholic Church —**Catholic** adj, **Catholicism** /kə'θɒlɪ,sɪz(ə)m/ noun [U]

cation /'kætaɪən/ noun [C] PHYSICS, CHEMISTRY an ion that has a positive electrical charge and is attracted towards the **cathode** during **electrolysis**

catkin /'kætkɪn/ noun [C] a long soft group of small flowers that hangs from the branches of **willows** and some other trees

CAT scan /'kæt ,skæn/ or **CT scan** /,siː 'tiː ,skæn/ noun [C] HEALTH a medical test in which computer technology is used for producing an image of the inside of a part of the body, or the image that is produced in this way

cattle /'kæt(ə)l/ noun [plural] cows and bulls that are kept by farmers for their milk or meat

'cattle ‚prod noun [C] AGRICULTURE a stick that can give an **electric shock**, used for making an animal move in a particular direction

Caucasian /kɔː'keɪziən/ adj formal used for describing a white person, for example someone from North America, Europe, or Australia —**Caucasian** noun [C]

caught¹ /kɔːt/ the past tense and past participle of **catch¹**

caught² /kɔːt/ adj if someone is caught between two opposite feelings or actions, they do not know how to react to something

cauldron /'kɔːldrən/ noun [C] a large round metal container that is used for cooking over a fire

cauliflower /'kɒli,flaʊə/ noun [C/U] a vegetable with a hard round white central part surrounded by green leaves —picture → VEGETABLE

caulk¹ /kɔːk/ verb [T] TECHNOLOGY to make the edge of **sheet metal** thicker by hammering it

caulk² /kɔːk/ or **caulking** /'kɔːkɪŋ/ noun [U] CONSTRUCTION a waterproof building material that is used to fill cracks or joints

causal /'kɔːz(ə)l/ adj LANGUAGE a causal conjunction such as 'because' introduces a statement describing the cause of something

causative /'kɔːzətɪv/ adj **1** formal causing something **2** LANGUAGE used for describing verbs, forms, and structures that show that something causes something to happen. For example, in the sentence 'She makes me laugh', 'makes' is a causative verb.

cause¹ /kɔːz/ noun **1** [C] an event, thing, or person that makes something happen: *The cause of death was found to be a heart attack.* ♦ *an essay on **the causes of** the First World War* **2** [C/U] a reason for behaving in a particular way, or for feeling a particular emotion: *He wouldn't have done it without **good cause** (=a good reason).* ♦ *The doctor's report states that there is **no cause for concern**.* **3** [C] an aim, idea, or organization that someone supports or works for: *Campaigners hope that people will be sympathetic to their cause.* ♦ *Please give as much as you can: it's **for a good cause**.* **4** [C] LAW a case in a law court

cause² /kɔːz/ verb [T] to make something happen, usually something bad: *Indigestion is **caused by** excess acid in the stomach.* ♦ *Bad weather continues to **cause problems** for travellers.* ♦ *A small sound caused him to turn his head.* ♦ *He apologizes for causing you any embarrassment.*

Build your vocabulary: words you can use instead of **cause**

- **bring about** to make something happen, especially something positive that improves the situation
- **give rise to** to make something happen, especially something unpleasant or unexpected
- **lead to** to begin a process that makes something happen later
- **contribute to** to be one of several causes that help to make something happen

‚cause-and-ef'fect adj a cause-and-effect relationship is based on the principle that one thing causes another thing

causeway /'kɔːz,weɪ/ noun [C] a raised road or path across ground that is wet or covered by water

caustic /'kɔːstɪk/ adj CHEMISTRY a caustic substance can cause burns to the skin and eyes through chemical action

caustic soda /,kɔːstɪk 'səʊdə/ noun [U] CHEMISTRY the chemical **sodium hydroxide** that is a strong alkali and is used for cleaning things that are very dirty. It is also used for making many other chemicals. It absorbs carbon dioxide gas.

cauterize /'kɔːtəraɪz/ verb [T] HEALTH to close a cut by using a hot instrument, in order to prevent infection or to stop blood flowing out

caution¹ /'kɔːʃ(ə)n/ noun **1** [U] careful thought and lack of hurry in order to try to avoid risks or danger: *He was instructed to act **with** extreme **caution**.* ♦ *Politicians should **exercise** greater **caution** with taxpayers' money.* **2** [U] advice that you should be careful: *A **word of caution**: the roads are full of potholes.* **3** [C] LAW an official warning that the police give someone who has broken the law

caution[2] /ˈkɔːʃ(ə)n/ verb [T] **1** *formal* to warn someone about a possible danger or problem: *Researchers* **cautioned that** *the drug is only partly effective.* **2** LAW if the police caution someone who has broken the law, they warn them officially

cautious /ˈkɔːʃəs/ adj careful to avoid problems or danger —**cautiously** adv

cavalier /ˌkævəˈlɪə/ adj not caring enough about other people's feelings or about a serious situation

cavalry /ˈkævəlri/ noun [singular] the part of an army that consists of soldiers who ride horses, or in modern times, of soldiers who ride in **armoured** vehicles

cave[1] /keɪv/ noun [C] a large hole in the side of a hill or under the ground

cave[2] /keɪv/ PHRASAL VERBS ,cave 'in if a roof or wall caves in, it falls down or inwards

caveat /ˈkæviˌæt/ noun [C] *formal* a warning of the limits of a particular agreement or statement

caveman /ˈkeɪvˌmæn/ (plural **cavemen** /ˈkeɪvˌmen/) noun [C] someone who lived thousands of years ago when people lived in caves

caver /ˈkeɪvə/ noun [C] someone who goes into caves to study them, or as a sport

cavern /ˈkævən/ noun [C] a large cave

caviar /ˈkæviˌɑː/ noun [U] fish eggs that are eaten as a special and expensive food

caving /ˈkeɪvɪŋ/ noun [U] the activity of going into caves to study them, or as a sport

cavity /ˈkævəti/ (plural **cavities**) noun [C] **1** a hole or space inside a solid object, especially a part of the body: *the nasal cavity* ♦ *the abdominal cavity* **2** a hole in a tooth, caused by decay

'cavity ,wall noun [C] CONSTRUCTION an outside wall of a building, built with two lines of bricks or stones with a space between them

cayenne pepper /ˌkeɪen ˈpepə/ noun [U] a red powder made from a type of pepper that has a strong flavour. It is added to food to make it taste **spicy**.

CBO /ˌsiː biː ˈəʊ/ noun [C] BUSINESS community-based organization: an organization that represents a community and provides educational, health, and other services to members of that community

CB points /ˌsiː ˈbiː ˌpɔɪnts/ noun [plural] ENGINEERING **contact breaker points** in a vehicle engine

cc /ˌsiː ˈsiː/ abbrev **1** used on a business letter or email for saying that a copy is being sent to the person mentioned: *To Jack Brown, cc: Paul Davis.* **2** cubic centimetre: used for measuring the amount of a liquid or the size of an engine: *a 75occ motorbike*

CCJ /ˌsiː siː ˈdʒeɪ/ noun [C] LAW county court judgment: a **court order** against someone who owes money that shows in public records and can make it difficult for them to borrow money

CCTV /ˌsiː siː tiː ˈviː/ noun [C/U] closed-circuit television: a system of cameras and television screens that allows someone to see what is happening in different parts of a building or town

CD /ˌsiː ˈdiː/ noun [C] compact disc: a small round piece of hard plastic with sound recorded on it or computer information stored on it

CDE /ˌsiː diː ˈiː/ noun [C] COMPUTING compact disc erasable: a CD that can have its information removed and something else recorded onto it

,C'D ,player noun [C] a piece of equipment used for playing CDs with music on them

CD-R /ˌsiː diː ˈɑː/ noun [C] COMPUTING compact disc recordable: an empty CD that you can use only once to record music or information from a computer

'C ,drive noun [C] COMPUTING the main **hard disk** drive on a computer system

CD-ROM /ˌsiː diː ˈrɒm/ noun [C/U] COMPUTING compact disc read-only memory: a CD that stores large amounts of information for use by a computer —*picture* → COMPUTER

CD-RW /ˌsiː diː ɑː ˈdʌb(ə)ljuː/ noun [C] COMPUTING compact disc rewritable: a CD that can be used for recording music or information from a computer

,CD-'video noun [C] COMPUTING a CD used for playing video pictures

,C'D ,writer noun [C] COMPUTING a piece of equipment used for recording information onto CDs

CE abbrev Common Era: the period after the birth of Jesus Christ

cease /siːs/ verb [I/T] *formal* to stop happening or continuing, or to stop something happening or continuing: *Conversation ceased when she entered the room.* ♦ *The government has ceased all contact with the rebels.*

ceasefire /ˈsiːsˌfaɪə/ noun [C] an agreement to stop fighting for a period of time

ceaseless /ˈsiːsləs/ adj *formal* continuing without stopping —**ceaselessly** adv

cedar /ˈsiːdə/ noun [C/U] a tall **evergreen** tree, or the wood from this tree

CEDAW POLITICS the Committee on the Elimination of Discrimination against Women: a group of people chosen by the United Nations to make certain that countries that have agreed to stop treating women unfairly take the action needed to achieve this

cede /siːd/ verb [T] *formal* if a ruler or country cedes power or land, they formally allow someone else to take it from them

ceiling /ˈsiːlɪŋ/ noun [C] **1** the surface that is above you in a room: *There were cracks in the walls and the ceiling.* **2** an upper limit set on the number or amount of something: *A* **ceiling of £100** *was put on all donations.*

celebrant /ˈseləbrənt/ noun [C] RELIGION someone who leads or takes part in a religious ceremony

celebrate /ˈseləˌbreɪt/ verb **1** [I/T] to do something enjoyable in order to show that an occasion or event is special: *They're celebrating the end of their exams.* **2** [T] *formal* to show admiration for someone or something in a piece of writing, music, or art, or in a ceremony: *The bravery of warriors was celebrated in song.* **3** [T] RELIGION to perform a religious ceremony, especially a Christian **mass**

celebrated /ˈseləˌbreɪtɪd/ adj famous and praised by many people: *a celebrated artist*

celebration /ˌseləˈbreɪʃ(ə)n/ noun **1** [C] a party or special event at which people celebrate something: *The whole family came for our anniversary celebration.* **2** [C/U] the activity of celebrating something: *It was a night of dancing and celebration.*

celebratory /ˌseləˈbreɪt(ə)ri/ adj a celebratory meal, drink etc is one that you have in order to celebrate a special event

celebrity /səˈlebrəti/ (plural **celebrities**) noun [C] a famous entertainer or sports personality: *a sports celebrity*

celery /ˈseləri/ noun [U] a pale green vegetable consisting of long leaf stems that are eaten raw or cooked —*picture* → VEGETABLE

celestial body /sə,lestiəl ˈbɒdi/ noun [C] ASTRONOMY a star or planet

celibate /ˈselɪbət/ adj someone who is celibate does not have sex —**celibacy** /ˈselɪbəsi/ noun [U]

cell /sel/ noun [C]

1 small part of living structure	3 on computer screen
2 small room	4 for making electricity
	5 small group of people

1 BIOLOGY the smallest unit from which all living things are made. All cells have a **cell membrane**, and plant cells also have a cellulose **cell wall**. A cell also has a nucleus that contains the **organism's** genetic information, **cytoplasm**, and very small parts called **organelles**: *brain cells*
2 a small room where a prisoner is kept
3 COMPUTING a small square in a pattern of squares on a computer **spreadsheet** for writing numbers or words in
4 PHYSICS, CHEMISTRY a piece of equipment that uses chemicals, heat, or light to produce electricity → ELECTRICAL CELL
5 a small group of people who work together as members of a larger organization, often a political one

cellar /ˈselə/ noun [C] a room under a building, below the ground

cell body noun [C] ANATOMY the main part of a neuron that contains the nucleus —*picture* → NEURON

cell division noun [C] BIOLOGY **1** mitosis **2** meiosis

cell membrane noun [C] BIOLOGY the outer layer surrounding the **cytoplasm** of all cells. The cell membrane controls which substances go in and out of the cell. —*picture* → CELL

cello /ˈtʃeləʊ/ (plural **cellos**) noun [C] MUSIC a musical instrument with strings, like a large **violin**. You hold it between your legs and play it with a **bow**. —*picture* → MUSICAL INSTRUMENT, ORCHESTRA —**cellist** /ˈtʃelɪst/ noun [C]

cellophane /ˈseləfeɪn/ noun [U] a very thin clear material that people use for wrapping things

cell phone noun [C] *American* a **mobile phone**

cellular /ˈseljələ/ adj **1** BIOLOGY relating to the cells of living things **2** relating to mobile phones **3** made up of small units or enclosed spaces

cellular phone noun [C] *formal* a **mobile phone**

cellulase /ˈseljəleɪz/ noun [U] BIOLOGY an enzyme that **breaks down** (=separates) cellulose into sugars

celluloid /ˈseljʊlɔɪd/ noun [U] a thin clear plastic material that was used in the past for making film

cellulose /ˈseljʊləʊs/ noun [U] BIOLOGY a substance that forms the walls of plant cells and plant fibres. It is **insoluble** in water, and is used to make plastics, explosives, paper, fabrics, and other products. → ROUGHAGE

cell wall noun [C] BIOLOGY a strong layer that surrounds each cell in organisms other than animals, protecting them and giving them shape. In most plants, the cell wall is made of cellulose, and in fungi it is made of **chitin**. —*picture* → CELL

Celsius /ˈselsiəs/ noun [U] SCIENCE a system for measuring temperature in the metric system. Symbol C → FAHRENHEIT

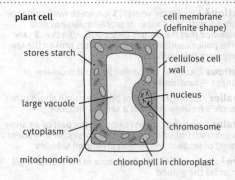

plant cell

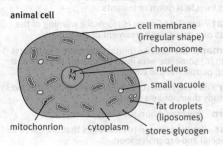

animal cell

types of animal cell

red blood cells   white blood cell

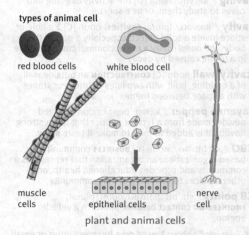

muscle cells   epithelial cells   nerve cell

plant and animal cells

Celt /kelt/ noun [C] a member of an ancient group of people who lived in parts of Western Europe —**Celtic** adj

cement[1] /səˈment/ noun [U] **1** a grey powder used in building. It becomes very hard when it is mixed with sand and water to make concrete. **2** a substance similar to bone that covers the root of a tooth —*picture* → TOOTH

cement[2] /səˈment/ verb [T] **1** to make a relationship or idea stronger or more certain **2** to cover a surface with cement

cementite /sɪˈmentaɪt/ noun [U] TECHNOLOGY a chemical compound that is a mixture of iron and carbon and is found in cast iron. It is hard and breaks easily. Chemical formula: Fe_3C

cement mixer noun [C] a machine that mixes cement, sand, and water to make concrete

cemetery /'semətri/ (plural **cemeteries**) noun [C] an area of ground where dead people are buried → GRAVEYARD

censor /'sensə/ verb [T] to remove parts of a book, film, or letter for moral, religious, or political reasons — **censor** noun [C]

censorship /'sensəʃɪp/ noun [U] the process of removing parts of books, films, or letters that are considered unsuitable for moral, religious, or political reasons

censure /'senʃə/ verb [T] formal to criticize someone severely —**censure** noun [U]

census /'sensəs/ (plural **censuses**) noun [C] SOCIAL STUDIES an occasion when government officials count all the people in a country and record information about them

cent /sent/ noun [C] ECONOMICS a small unit of money used in many countries, for example the US, South Africa and Hong Kong. There are 100 cents in a dollar or a **euro**.

centenarian /ˌsentɪ'neəriən/ noun [C] someone who is 100 years old or older

centenary /sen'tiːnəri, sen'tenəri/ (plural **centenaries**) noun [C] a day or year that people celebrate exactly 100 years after an important event

center /'sentə/ the American spelling of **centre**

centi- /senti/ prefix SCIENCE 0.01 of a unit: used with some nouns for units of measurement: centimetre

centigrade /'sentɪˌɡreɪd/ noun [U] old-fashioned **Celsius**

centilitre /'sentɪˌliːtə/ noun [C] SCIENCE a unit for measuring an amount of liquid or gas in the metric system. There are 100 centilitres in one litre. Symbol cl

centimetre /'sentɪˌmiːtə/ noun [C] SCIENCE a unit for measuring length in the metric system. There are 100 centimetres in one metre. Symbol cm

centipede /'sentɪpiːd/ noun [C] a type of **arthropod** that has a long narrow body divided into many sections, each of which has a pair of legs → MILLIPEDE

central /'sentrəl/ adj **1** in the middle of a space or area: central London ♦ The hotel is built around a central courtyard. **2** main, or major: He played a central role in the development of US economic policy. ♦ skills that are **central to** (=very important for) a child's development **3** belonging to the main organization that controls other smaller organizations: the Communist Party's central committee —**centrally** /'sentrəli/ adv

Central A'merica noun [U] GEOGRAPHY the part of the American continent between the US and South America

central 'government noun [C/U] POLITICS the government of a whole country: a new partnership between local and central government

central 'heating noun [U] a system that heats a whole building by sending hot air or water through pipes to all the rooms

centralize /'sentrəlaɪz/ verb [T] to give control of a country, organization, or industry to one group of people

central 'nervous ˌsystem noun [C] ANATOMY, BIOLOGY the part of the **nervous system** that consists of the brain and the **spinal cord**

centre¹ /'sentə/ noun

1 middle	6 player in sport
2 part of town	7 main subject
3 in maths	8 political middle
4 building for sth	+ PHRASE
5 major place for sth	

1 [C] the middle of a space or area: chocolates with soft centres ♦ **the centre of** the room
2 [C] the part of a town or city that contains most of the shops, restaurants, and places of entertainment: We caught a bus into the centre.
3 [C] MATHS the point that is in the middle of a circle or sphere —picture → CIRCLE
4 [C] a building or group of buildings that is used for a particular activity or for providing a particular service: a health centre ♦ a sports centre
5 [C] a place where a particular thing is important, or where a particular thing exists in large amounts: one of the world's most important **financial centres** ♦ people who live in the **centres** of population
6 [C] SPORTS a player in some sports whose position is in the middle of the line of attacking players
7 [singular] **the centre of sth** the main subject or cause of something: He hates being **the centre of attention**.
8 the centre [singular] POLITICS a political party, group of parties, or position that is not extreme because it is neither left-wing nor right-wing
  PHRASE   **centre of gravity** PHYSICS the point in an object around which its weight balances

centre² /'sentə/ verb [T] to put something in the centre of an area

centre 'forward noun [C] SPORTS the person in the centre of the front row of attacking players in some sports

centreline /'sentəlaɪn/ noun [C] MATHS, TECHNOLOGY a line that divides a flat shape into two symmetrical parts

centrepiece /'sentəpiːs/ noun [C] **1** the most important object or decoration in a particular place **2** the most important feature of something **3** a decoration or arrangement of flowers that you put in the middle of a table

'centre ˌpunch noun [C] TECHNOLOGY a pointed steel tool that is used to mark the position of holes that are to be drilled

centrifugal force /ˌsentrɪfjuːɡ(ə)l 'fɔːs/ noun [U] PHYSICS a force that makes things move away from the centre of something when they are moving around that centre

centring /'sentrɪŋ/ noun [C] CONSTRUCTION a curved wooden structure that supports the bricks when building an **arch**

centriole /'sentriəʊl/ noun [C] BIOLOGY in animal cells, one of two rod-shaped structures located near the nucleus of the cell. They are involved in **mitosis** (=cell division).

centripetal force /sen,trɪpɪt(ə)l 'fɔːs/ noun [U] PHYSICS a force that makes things move towards the centre of something when they are moving around that centre. Gravity is the centripetal force that keeps the planets orbiting around the Sun.

centrist /'sentrɪst/ adj POLITICS not extreme in your political beliefs = MODERATE —**centrist** noun [C]

centroid /'sentrɔɪd/ noun [C] MATHS the point considered to be the centre of the total mass of a geometric object

centromere /'sentrəmɪə/ noun [C] BIOLOGY the point at which two parts of a chromosome join

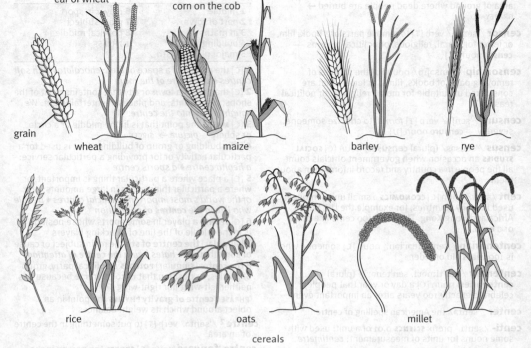

ear of wheat
corn on the cob
grain
wheat
maize
barley
rye
rice
oats
millet
cereals

centrum /'sentrəm/ (plural **centra** /'sentrə/) noun [C] ANATOMY a thick mass of bone in a **vertebra** (=bone in the spine) that is shaped like a cylinder — picture → VERTEBRA

century /'sentʃəri/ (plural **centuries**) noun [C] **1** a period of 100 years counted from a year ending in –oo: *His family has ruled Morocco since the 17th century.* **2** any period of 100 years: *the worst storm in nearly a century ♦ The tribe had died out centuries before.* **3** SPORTS a score of 100 **runs** (=points) made in **cricket** by one player

CEO /ˌsiː iː 'əʊ/ (plural **CEOs**) noun [C] BUSINESS Chief Executive Officer: the most important person in a company, who is in charge of running the whole of it

cephalopod /'sefələpɒd/ noun [C] BIOLOGY an invertebrate sea animal with a large head and **tentacles**, for example an **octopus**, **squid**, or **cuttlefish**

ceramic /sə'ræmɪk/ adj ARTS made from baked clay

ceramics /sə'ræmɪks/ noun ARTS **1** [U] the art or process of making ceramic objects **2** [plural] ceramic objects

cereal /'sɪəriəl/ noun **1** [U] AGRICULTURE grain that can be made into flour or other food **2** [C] AGRICULTURE a plant of the grass family that produces grain that can be eaten **3** [C/U] a food made from grain

cerebellum /ˌserə'beləm/ (plural **cerebella** or **cerebellums**) noun [C] ANATOMY the back part of the brain that is responsible for balance and movement —picture → BRAIN

cerebral /'serəbrəl, sə'riːbrəl/ adj ANATOMY relating to the brain, or affecting the brain

cerebral 'cortex noun [C] ANATOMY the outer layer of the **cerebrum** (=the front part of the brain) —picture → RETINA

cerebral 'haemorrhage noun [C] HEALTH an occasion when blood vessels in the brain burst, so that

blood flows into the brain and causes damage

cerebral 'hemisphere noun [C] ANATOMY one of the two halves of the front part of the brain —picture → BRAIN

cerebral palsy /ˌserəbrəl 'pɔːlzi/ noun [U] HEALTH a medical condition that affects the ability to control movement and speech. It is typically caused by damage to the brain either before or during birth.

cerebrum /sə'riːbrəm/ noun [C] ANATOMY the front part of the brain, where activities such as thinking, learning, and feeling take place. It is divided into two halves called **cerebral hemispheres**.

ceremonial /ˌserə'məʊniəl/ adj connected with a ceremony

ceremony /'serəməni/ (plural **ceremonies**) noun **1** [C] a formal public event with special traditions, actions, or words: *a ceremony to honour those who died in the war ♦ an awards ceremony* **2** [U] the formal traditions, actions, and words used for celebrating a public or religious event: *They celebrated Easter with great ceremony.*

Ceres /'sɪəriːz/ noun ASTRONOMY the first **asteroid** (=mass of rock in space) to be discovered. It is also the largest.

cerium /'sɪəriəm/ noun [U] CHEMISTRY a soft silvery-white metallic element in the **lanthanide** group of the periodic table. It is used in alloys and glass. Chemical symbol: **Ce**

certain[1] /'sɜːt(ə)n/ adj **1** having no doubts that something is true = SURE ≠ UNCERTAIN: *I'm not absolutely certain, but I think I'm right. ♦ You can be pretty certain she's not going to like it. ♦ We still can't be certain who is going to win.* **2** definitely going to happen, or definitely known: *One thing was certain: someone had been in his room. ♦ It's not certain that this method would work. ♦ Mexico is now **certain of** a place in the finals.*

PHRASE **make certain** to take action in order to be sure that something happens or be sure that something is true: *Call home to make certain everything is OK.*

certain² /ˈsɜːt(ə)n/ determiner used for referring to someone or something without being specific about who or what they are: *There are certain things we need to discuss.*

PHRASE **a certain** some, but not very much: *A certain amount of fat in your diet is good for you.*

certainly /ˈsɜːt(ə)nli/ adv used for emphasizing that something is definitely true or will definitely happen: *There certainly wasn't any point in going now.*

certainty /ˈsɜːt(ə)nti/ (plural **certainties**) noun **1** [C] something that will definitely happen, or that you feel very sure about: *Victory looked like a certainty.* **2** [U] the feeling of being completely sure about something = CONVICTION: *I can say with certainty that there will be no more information today.*

certificate /səˈtɪfɪkət/ noun [C] **1** an official document that states that particular facts are true: *a birth certificate* **2** an official document that proves that someone has passed an examination, has successfully completed a course, or has achieved the necessary qualifications to work in a particular profession

cerˈtificate auˌthority noun [C] **BUSINESS** a computer or company on the Internet that provides or checks **digital certificates** to prove that a company is who it claims it is

certification /ˌsɜːtɪfɪˈkeɪʃ(ə)n/ noun **1** [U] the process of giving someone or something an official document stating that something is of a satisfactory standard, or that someone is allowed to do a particular job **2** [C/U] an official document stating that someone is allowed to do a job, or that something is of a satisfactory standard

certify /ˈsɜːtɪfaɪ/ (**certifies**, **certifying**, **certified**) verb [T] **1** to state officially that something is true, accurate, or satisfactory **2** to give someone an official document that proves that they have passed an examination or have successfully completed a training course **3** to state officially that someone is seriously mentally ill

cervical /ˈsɜːvɪk(ə)l, səˈvaɪk(ə)l/ adj **HEALTH** relating to the cervix

ˌcervical ˈsmear noun [C] **HEALTH** a medical test in which cells taken from the opening of the uterus are examined. This can show cell changes which could develop into cancer.

ˌcervical ˈvertebra noun [C] **ANATOMY** one of the spinal bones in the neck —*picture* → VERTEBRA

cervix /ˈsɜːvɪks/ noun [C] **ANATOMY** the entrance to the uterus —*picture* → EMBRYO, REPRODUCTION

cesium /ˈsiːziəm/ noun [U] **CHEMISTRY** the American spelling of **caesium**

cessation /seˈseɪʃ(ə)n/ noun [C/U] *formal* **1** an end to something: *a cessation of hostilities* **2** **HEALTH** the act of stopping smoking

cesspit /ˈsesˌpɪt/ noun [C] **1** **CONSTRUCTION** a large covered hole or container in the ground for collecting the liquid and solid waste that flows from a building **2** a place or situation in which people behave in a way that is not moral

cesspool /ˈsesˌpuːl/ noun [C] **CONSTRUCTION** a **cesspit**

cestode /ˈsestəʊd/ noun [C] **BIOLOGY** a **tapeworm**

CFC /ˌsiː ef ˈsiː/ noun [C] **CHEMISTRY, ENVIRONMENT** chlorofluorocarbon: a gas used in refrigerators and in some **aerosols**. CFCs can damage the **ozone layer** of the Earth's atmosphere.

CGI /ˌsiː dʒiː ˈaɪ/ noun [U] **COMPUTING** computer-generated imagery: images produced by a computer

chador /ˈtʃɑːdɔː/ noun [C] a loose piece of usually black clothing that covers a woman's whole body including her head, worn by some Muslim women

chaff /tʃɑːf, tʃæf/ noun [U] the outer part of wheat and other grains that is removed before the grains are used

chain¹ /tʃeɪn/ noun **1** [C/U] a series of metal rings that are connected to each other: *The crate was attached to the deck with a chain.* ◆ *a gold chain* ◆ *Prisoners were kept in chains.* **2** [C] a series of people or things that are connected: *a chain of events that eventually led to murder* ◆ *a chain of small islands* **3** [C] a group of businesses that all belong to the same company: *Japan's leading hotel chain* ◆ *a chain of electrical goods shops* **4** [C] **PHYSICS, CHEMISTRY** a part of a molecule consisting of a series of atoms connected in a line

chain² /tʃeɪn/ verb [T] to use a chain to fasten something so that it cannot be stolen, or to fasten a prisoner with a chain so that they cannot escape

ˌchain reˈaction noun [C] **CHEMISTRY, PHYSICS** a series of chemical or physical reactions, each one of which causes the next one

chainsaw /ˈtʃeɪnˌsɔː/ noun [C] a tool with a motor, used for cutting down trees or cutting up wood —*picture* → TOOL

ˈchain ˌstore noun [C] **BUSINESS** one of a group of shops that all belong to the same company

chair¹ /tʃeə/ noun [C] **1** a piece of furniture for one person to sit on, with a back, legs, and sometimes two arms **2** the person who is in charge of a meeting, committee, company, or organization: *All questions must be addressed to the chair.* ◆ *He is the former chair of the Atomic Energy Commission.* → CHAIRMAN, CHAIRPERSON, CHAIRWOMAN **3** **EDUCATION** the position or job of being a **professor** in a university

chair² /tʃeə/ verb [T] to be the person in charge of a meeting, committee, company, or organization

chairman /ˈtʃeəmən/ (plural **chairmen** /ˈtʃeəmən/) noun [C] the person who is in charge of a meeting, committee, company, or organization

chairmanship /ˈtʃeəmənʃɪp/ noun [C/U] the position of being a chairman

chairperson /ˈtʃeəˌpɜːs(ə)n/ noun [C] the person who is in charge of a meeting, committee, company, or organization

ˈchair techˌnique noun [U] **BUSINESS** a method for solving problems in which someone sits on one chair and considers the advantages of a particular course of action, and then sits on another chair in order to consider its disadvantages

chairwoman /ˈtʃeəˌwʊmən/ (plural **chairwomen** /ˈtʃeəˌwɪmɪn/) noun [C] the woman who is in charge of a meeting, committee, company, or organization

chalk /tʃɔːk/ noun **1** [U] **GEOLOGY** a type of soft white rock that consists of almost pure **calcium carbonate**. It is a type of sedimentary rock. **2** [C/U] a stick of chalk used for writing or drawing

chalkboard /ˈtʃɔːkˌbɔːd/ noun [C] a green or black board that you write on with chalk, used especially in a classroom

chalky /ˈtʃɔːki/ adj similar to chalk, or containing chalk

challenge¹ /ˈtʃælɪndʒ/ noun **1** [C/U] something that needs a lot of skill, energy, and determination to deal with or achieve: *I felt I needed a new challenge at work.* ◆ *Are western nations ready to meet the environmental challenges that lie ahead?* ◆ *The new government faces the challenge of completing the building on time.* **2** [C] an action or idea that questions whether something is true, fair, accurate, legal etc: *Recent discoveries* **present a** serious **challenge to** *accepted views on the age of the universe.* ♦ *The strike was* **a** direct **challenge to** *the authority of the government.* **3** [C] an occasion when someone tries to win a game or competition

challenge² /'tʃælɪndʒ/ verb [T] **1** to question whether something is true, fair, accurate, legal etc: *This decision is likely to be challenged by the oil companies.* ♦ *The president has accused the governor of challenging his leadership.* **2** to invite someone to compete or fight: *The girls* **challenged** *the boys* **to** *a cricket match.* **3** to test someone's skill and abilities **4** if you are challenged by someone, they ask you who you are and why you are in a particular place

challenging /'tʃælɪndʒɪŋ/ adj difficult to deal with or achieve, but interesting and enjoyable

chalybite /'kælɪbaɪt/ noun [U] **CHEMISTRY, GEOLOGY** siderite, a type of iron ore

chamber /'tʃeɪmbə/ noun [C] **1** a room used for a particular purpose: *a torture chamber* ♦ *the debating chamber* **2** one of the sections of a parliament: *the upper chamber* **3** an enclosed space, especially one inside a machine or someone's body: *the chambers of the heart*
PHRASE **chamber of commerce BUSINESS** an organization of people who own shops and businesses in a particular town or city and work together to improve conditions for business in their area

chambermaid /'tʃeɪmbə,meɪd/ noun [C] a woman whose job is to clean the bedrooms in a hotel

'chamber ,music noun [U] **MUSIC** a type of classical music played by a small group of musicians

chameleon /kə'miːliən/ noun [C] a type of small lizard with skin that changes colour to match the colours around it —*picture* → REPTILE

chamfer /'tʃæmfə/ verb [T] **TECHNOLOGY** to cut away a right-angled edge or corner, in order to make a sloping edge

champagne /,ʃæm'peɪn/ noun [U] a type of French **sparkling** wine that some people drink on special occasions

champion /'tʃæmpiən/ noun [C] **1 SPORTS** someone who has won an important competition, especially in sport: *the world heavyweight boxing champion* **2** someone who publicly supports or defends something: *a* **champion of** *the rights of religious minorities*

championship /'tʃæmpiənʃɪp/ noun **SPORTS 1** [C] a competition to find the best player or team in a sport or game: *the World Chess Championships* **2** [singular] the position of being a champion: *Two more points and the championship will be his!*

chance¹ /tʃɑːns/ noun **1** [C] an opportunity to do something, especially something that you want to do: *Students are* **given the chance** *to learn another language.* ♦ *We work together whenever we* **get a chance.** ♦ *I warned her that this was her* **last chance.** **2** [C/U] the possibility that something will happen: *I think she has a* **good chance** *of getting the job.* ♦ *Is there* **any chance** *they will reverse their decision?* ♦ *He* **doesn't stand a chance** *of winning the tournament* (=it is not at all likely that he will win). **3** [U] the way that things happen without being planned or expected= LUCK: *The results may simply be due to chance.* ♦ *It was simply* **by chance** *that Nicholson was cast in the film.*
PHRASE **take a chance** or **take chances (on)** to do something even though it involves risk

chance² /tʃɑːns/ verb [T] to do something even though you know it involves a risk: *It looked like rain so I decided not to* **chance it** *and brought my umbrella.*

chance³ /tʃɑːns/ adj not planned or expected: *a chance meeting*

chancellor /'tʃɑːnsələ/ noun [C] **1 POLITICS** the leader of the government in some countries **2 POLITICS** the **Chancellor of the Exchequer 3 EDUCATION** someone who is the official leader of a university

Chancellor of the Exchequer /,tʃɑːnsələr əv ði ɪks'tʃekə/ noun [C] **POLITICS** the member of the British government who is responsible for taxes and public spending

chandelier /,ʃændə'lɪə/ noun [C] a light that hangs from a ceiling and has a lot of branches for holding lights or **candles**

change¹ /tʃeɪndʒ/ verb

1 become different	5 get other vehicle
2 start sth new	6 exchange money
3 replace sth	+ PHRASES
4 of clothes	+ PHRASAL VERB

1 [I/T] to become different, or to make someone or something different: *After a few days the weather changed.* ♦ *The law was changed in 1989.* ♦ *The leaves are already starting to change colour.* ♦ *The town has* **changed from** *a small fishing village* **to** *a modern tourist centre.*
2 [I/T] to stop doing one thing and start doing something different: *Dave said he might be changing jobs.* ♦ *With oil costs rising, the government is gradually* **changing to** *renewable energy.*
3 [T] to replace something with a new or different thing: *Can you help me change a tyre?*
4 [I/T] to take off the clothes that you are wearing and put on different ones: *Hang on, I'll just go and change.* ♦ *Have I got time to* **get changed** *before we go?* ♦ *You should* **change into** *some dry socks.*
5 [I/T] to leave one plane, train, bus etc to get on another: *We changed planes in Paris.*
6 [T] to exchange one type of money for another: *I need to* **change** *some dollars* **into** *pesos.*
PHRASES **change hands** to be given or sold by one person to another
change your mind to change a decision you have made or an opinion you have about something
change the subject to stop talking about one thing and start talking about another
PHRASAL VERB **'change (sth) into sth** to stop being in one condition or form and start being in another, or to make something do this: *At what point does boiling water change into steam?*

Build your vocabulary: words you can use instead of change
- **adapt** to change something in order to make it suitable for a specific situation
- **adjust** to change something slightly so that it is exactly the way you want it
- **alter** a more formal word for 'change'
- **convert** to change something so that it can be used for a different purpose
- **modify** to make small changes to a machine or system in order to make it suitable for a different situation
- **transform** to change something completely so that it looks or works much better than before

change² /tʃeɪndʒ/ noun **1** [C/U] a situation or process in which something becomes different or is replaced, or the result of this process: *A number of changes have taken place since the 1960s.* ♦ *Older people sometimes* find it hard to accept change. ♦ *We made a few changes to the team.* ♦ *a change in the law* ♦ *a change from military* **to** *civilian rule* **2** [U] the money that someone gives back to a customer when they give more money than it costs to buy something: *Here's your change.* **3** [U] coins rather than notes: *I'm sorry I haven't got any change.* ♦ *Have you got change for a five-pound note* (=notes or coins of lower value that you can exchange for it)? **4** [C] a part of a journey when you leave one plane, train, bus etc to get on another: *The journey takes five hours, with a change in Newcastle.* **PHRASES a change of heart** an occasion when you change your opinion or plan **for a change** instead of what usually happens: *It's nice to hear some good news for a change.*

changeable /'tʃeɪndʒəb(ə)l/ adj tending to change suddenly and often **= UNPREDICTABLE**

changed /tʃeɪndʒd/ adj different from before **≠ UNCHANGED**

changeover /'tʃeɪndʒ,əʊvə/ noun [C] a change from one method, system, or activity to another

changing room /'tʃeɪndʒɪŋ ,ruːm/ noun [C] **1 SPORTS** a room in which people change their clothes before and after they play a sport **2** a room in a shop in which people can try on clothes before they buy them

channel¹ /'tʃæn(ə)l/ noun [C]

1 television station	4 way to send
2 passage/cut in surface	information
3 water joining two seas	5 way of using ability

1 a television station and the programmes that it broadcasts: *What's on the other channel?* **2** a narrow passage made in the ground so that water can go along it **3 GEOGRAPHY** a narrow area of water that joins two seas **4** a way of communicating or expressing something: *It is important to keep channels of communication open.* **5** a way of showing people what you are feeling or thinking, or of using your energy or ability: *She was seeking a channel for her creative energies.*

channel² /'tʃæn(ə)l/ (**channels, channelling, channelled**) verb [T] **1** to use money or supplies for a particular purpose: *The company has channelled £1.2 million into developing new products.* **2** to use your energy, ability, feelings, or ideas for a particular purpose **3** to make something follow a particular system **4** to send something such as water along a passage

the Channel /'tʃæn(ə)l/ the narrow area of sea between England and France

chant /tʃɑːnt/ verb [I/T] **MUSIC** to shout or sing a word or phrase many times —**chant** noun [C]

Chanukah or **Chanukkah** /'hɑːnəkə/ another spelling of **Hanukkah**

chaos /'keɪɒs/ noun [U] a situation in which everything is confused and not organized

chaotic /keɪ'ɒtɪk/ adj happening in a confused way and without any order or organization —**chaotically** /keɪ'ɒtɪkli/ adv

chapel /'tʃæp(ə)l/ noun [C] **RELIGION** a small church, or a special room used as a church

chaplain /'tʃæplɪn/ noun [C] **RELIGION** a priest who works in an institution such as a school or hospital, or in the army

chaplaincy /'tʃæplɪnsi/ noun [C] **RELIGION** the job of a chaplain, or the place where a chaplain works

chapter /'tʃæptə/ noun [C] **1 LITERATURE** one of the sections of a book: *See Chapter Three for more details.* **2** a period of someone's life, or a period in history: *The war was now entering its final chapter.* **3 RELIGION** all the priests who belong to a cathedral

character /'kærɪktə/ noun

1 personality	4 attractive qualities
2 qualities of sth	5 unusual person
3 sb in book, film etc	6 letter/number

1 [C] the qualities that make up someone's personality: *This selfishness was one aspect of Steve's character that I didn't like.* ♦ *Why did Simon refuse? It seems so out of character* (=not typical of his usual behaviour). **2** [C/U] the qualities that make something clearly different from anything else: *The two villages are similar in size but very different in character.* **3** [C] **ARTS, LITERATURE** a person in a book, play, film etc: *The film's main character is played by George Clooney.* **4** [U] qualities that make someone or something good, interesting, or attractive: *a traditional hotel with a lot of character and charm* ♦ *She showed real character in standing up to her political enemies.* **5** [C] a person of a particular type: *a suspicious character* **6** [C] a letter, number, or symbol that is written or printed: *Your computer password may be up to 12 characters long.*

characterise /'kærɪktəraɪz/ another spelling of **characterize**

characteristic¹ /,kærɪktə'rɪstɪk/ noun [C] a typical quality or feature: *the main characteristics of 20th-century culture*

characteristic² /,kærɪktə'rɪstɪk/ adj typical of someone or something: *Sue answered with her characteristic truthfulness.* —**characteristically** /,kærɪktə'rɪstɪkli/ adv

characterization /,kærɪktəraɪ'zeɪʃ(ə)n/ noun [U] **LITERATURE** the way in which a writer creates characters

characterize /'kærɪktəraɪz/ verb [T] **1 be characterized by** to have something as a typical quality or feature: *The 1980s were characterized by high inflation and high unemployment.* **2 be characterized as** to be described as a particular type of person or thing: *The military is usually characterized as being conservative.*

'character recog,nition noun [U] **COMPUTING** a process by which a computer recognizes letters, numbers, or symbols and turns them into a **digital** form that a computer can use

'character ,set noun [C] **COMPUTING** a complete set of letters, numbers, or symbols that can be used by a computer

charcoal /'tʃɑː,kəʊl/ noun [U] **1** a black substance made from burnt wood, used as a fuel **2 ARTS** a black substance made from burnt wood, used for drawing

charge¹ /tʃɑːdʒ/ noun

1 amount of money	5 amount of explosive
2 when sb is accused	6 sb you take care of
3 a claim sb/sth is bad	7 materials in furnace
4 amount of electricity	+ PHRASES

1 [C/U] an amount of money that people have to pay, for example for a service or when they visit a place: *There is no charge for using the library.* ♦ *The organization provides a range of services free of charge* (=with no charge). ♦ *There's a small admission charge.* **2** [C] **LAW** an official statement that accuses someone

of committing a crime: *murder charges* ♦ *In the end we decided not to **press charges*** (=officially accuse someone of a crime). ♦ *They faced **charges of conspiracy and murder**.* ♦ *The investigation resulted in criminal **charges against** three police officers.*
3 [C] a claim that someone or something is bad, or that they have done something bad: *He was arrested on **charges** of corruption.*
4 [singular/U] **PHYSICS, CHEMISTRY** the amount or type of electrical force that something holds or carries. *The protons in an atom have a positive charge, and the electrons have a negative charge.*
5 [C] an amount of the substance that makes a bomb explode
6 [C] *formal* someone that you are responsible for and take care of
7 [C] **TECHNOLOGY** the materials that are put into a **furnace** for converting into iron or steel
PHRASES **in charge (of)** if someone is in charge, they have control over a person or situation and are responsible for them: *Who's in charge here?* ♦ *He was **put in charge of** the whole investigation.*
take charge (of) to take control and become responsible for someone or something

charge² /tʃɑːdʒ/ verb

1 ask sb for money	**4** run to attack
2 arrange payment	**5** move quickly
3 accuse sb of crime	**6** put electricity into

1 [I/T] to ask someone to pay an amount of money for something: *How much does the shop **charge for** delivery?*
2 [T] to arrange to pay for something later: *The flights were **charged to** my father's personal account.*
3 [T] **LAW** to accuse someone of committing a crime: *The police have **charged** him **with** murder.* ♦ *Two men have been **charged in connection with** the fire.*
4 [I/T] to attack someone or something by running very fast towards them
5 [I] to move somewhere quickly and carelessly: *You can't just go **charging into** the classroom.*
6 [I/T] to put electricity into a battery: *The cell phone won't work if it isn't charged.*

'charge ,carrier noun [C] **PHYSICS** a particle that carries electric current, for example an electron or ion

chariot /'tʃæriət/ noun [C] a vehicle with two wheels that was pulled by horses in races and battles in ancient times

charisma /kə'rɪzmə/ noun [U] a strong personal quality that makes people like someone and feel attracted to them= **CHARM** —**charismatic** /ˌkærɪz'mætɪk/ adj

charitable /'tʃærɪtəb(ə)l/ adj **1** intended to give money and help to people who need it **2** kind to other people and not judging them too severely

charity /'tʃærəti/ (plural **charities**) noun **1** [C/U] an organization that gives money and help to people who need it **2** [U] money or food that is given to people who need it: *The event **raised** £59,000 **for charity**.*

charlatan /'ʃɑːlətən/ noun [C] someone who cheats people by claiming to have special knowledge or abilities

charm¹ /tʃɑːm/ noun **1** [C/U] an attractive quality in a person, place etc: *The building has kept its traditional charm.* **2** [C] an object that brings luck or has magic powers
PHRASE **work like a charm** to be very effective

charm² /tʃɑːm/ verb [T] **1** to give someone pleasure or enjoyment **2** to make someone like you, or make them

want to do something for you: *He **charmed** my mother **into** giving him money.*

charming /'tʃɑːmɪŋ/ adj attractive and pleasant: *a charming smile* ♦ *a charming little house*

chart¹ /tʃɑːt/ noun **1** [C] a list, drawing, or graph that shows information —*picture* → *on next page* **2** [C] a map used for planning a journey by ship or aircraft **3 the charts** [plural] a list of the CDs that people have bought the most copies of in the previous week

chart² /tʃɑːt/ verb [T] **1** to record how something develops and changes: *A team visits every week to chart their progress.* **2** to make a map of an area **3** to plan a journey or course of action

charter¹ /'tʃɑːtə/ noun **1** [C] a document that describes the aims of an organization or the rights of a group of people **2** [C/U] the process of hiring a boat, plane, or bus, or the vehicle that is hired

charter² /'tʃɑːtə/ verb [T] to create a city, organization, university etc by giving it a charter

chartered accountant /ˌtʃɑːtəd ə'kaʊntənt/ noun [C] an **accountant** who has passed a professional examination

'charter ,flight noun [C] a plane journey that is arranged by a travel company

chase¹ /tʃeɪs/ verb **1** [I/T] to follow someone or something quickly in order to catch them= **PURSUE**: *The band have often been chased down the street by enthusiastic fans.* ♦ *I **chased after** the robbers for more than a mile.* **2** [T] to follow someone or something quickly in order to make them go away: *We chased the cat out of the house.* ♦ *Suddenly a man came out and **chased** the kids **away**.* **3** [T] to try hard to get something such as a job, prize, or money: *Tiger Woods was chasing another European title.*
PHRASAL VERB **,chase sb/sth 'up** to find out why someone is taking longer to do something than you expected: *Why don't you chase up those software people today?*

chase² /tʃeɪs/ noun **1** [C] the action of following someone or something quickly because you want to catch them: *a high-speed **car chase*** **2** [singular] the act of trying to get something that you want **3** [C] **CONSTRUCTION** a horizontal hole cut in a wall to carry things such as cables

chasm /'kæz(ə)m/ noun [C] **1** a very big difference that separates one person or group from another= **GULF** **2** **GEOGRAPHY** a very deep crack in rock or ice

chassis /'ʃæsi/ (plural **chassis** /'ʃæsiz/) noun [C] the frame and wheels of a vehicle

chasten /'tʃeɪs(ə)n/ verb [T] *formal* to make someone feel ashamed or less confident

chat¹ /tʃæt/ (**chats, chatting, chatted**) verb [I] **1** to talk in a friendly way: *They sat waiting, **chatting about** their families.* ♦ *She laughed and **chatted** happily **with** the other women.* **2** **COMPUTING** to exchange messages with someone using computers, in a way that lets you see each other's messages immediately

chat² /tʃæt/ noun [C/U] a friendly conversation: *I had an interesting chat with his sister.*

'chat ,room noun [C] **COMPUTING** a website that people can use for exchanging messages → **NEWSGROUP**

'chat ,show noun [C] a television or radio programme in which famous people talk about themselves and their work

chatter /'tʃætə/ verb [I] **1** to talk in a fast informal way about unimportant subjects **2** if your teeth chatter, they knock together from fear or cold —**chatter** noun [U]

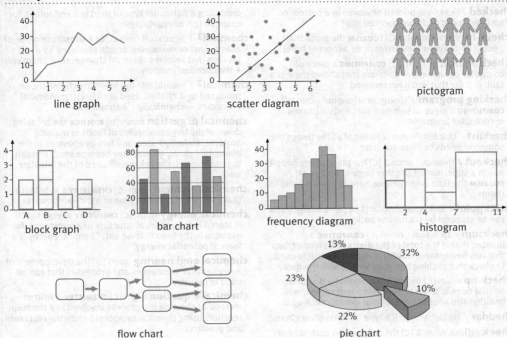

presenting statistics

chatty /ˈtʃæti/ (**chattier**, **chattiest**) adj **1** someone who is chatty enjoys talking a lot **2** a chatty writing style is friendly and informal

chauffeur /ˈʃəʊfə, ʃəʊˈfɜː/ noun [C] someone whose job is to drive a rich or important person around in a car

chauvinism /ˈʃəʊvə,nɪz(ə)m/ noun [U] the extreme belief that your own country, race, sex, or group is better than any other

cheap¹ /tʃiːp/ adj **1** not expensive: *Everyone should have access to cheap, fresh food.* **2** not expensive and not of good quality: *horrible cheap wine* **3** a cheap action or remark is unfair or unkind **4** not considered important or valuable: *It happened during the war when life was cheap.* —**cheaply** adv

cheap² /tʃiːp/ adv at a low price: *I can't believe I managed to get it so cheap.*

cheat¹ /tʃiːt/ verb **1** [I] to behave dishonestly in order to get an advantage: *Kids have always found ways of cheating in school exams.* **2** [T] to treat someone dishonestly: *He trusted these people and they cheated him.* ♦ *He was accused of **cheating** investors **out of** their life savings.* **3** [I] to do something that is not correct but makes it easier to succeed: *You can cheat by adding a little flour.*

cheat² /tʃiːt/ noun [C] someone who cheats

check¹ /tʃek/ verb **1** [I/T] to examine something in order to get information, or to find out whether it is good or correct: *Always check your spelling.* ♦ *You should have your sight checked regularly.* ♦ ***Check** our website **for** details of our special offers.* **2** [I/T] to make certain of something, for example by looking at the information again or by asking someone: *I think he's gone home – I'll just check.* ♦ *I'll check the dates.* ♦ *First, check that you have everything you need.* ♦ *For further information, **check with** your local tourist office.* ♦ *He **checked to see** if Gail was still there.* **3** [T] to give your bags and cases to an official at an airport so that they

can be put on a plane: *How many bags do you have to check?* **4** [T] to stop something bad from happening or getting worse: *They are taking measures to check the spread of the disease.* —**checker** noun [C]

PHRASAL VERBS '**check sth a,gainst sth** to find out whether information is accurate or useful by comparing it with other information

,**check 'in TOURISM** to arrive at an airport and show your ticket to an official, or to arrive at a hotel and give your details to a member of the staff

'**check on sb/sth** to look at someone or something so that you are certain they are safe, satisfactory etc: *I sent Michael to check on the kids.*

,**check 'out TOURISM** to leave a hotel after paying the bill: *Joan had already **checked out of** the hotel.*

check² /tʃek/ noun

1 examination	4 in game of chess
2 control	5 cheque
3 pattern of squares	+ PHRASE

1 [C] an examination of something that is intended to find out whether it is good or correct: *a **check for** errors* ♦ *They **do** routine **checks on** the condition of the planes.* **2** [C] something that controls another thing and stops it from becoming worse or more extreme: *Economic forces act as a **check on** political power.* **3** [C/U] a pattern of squares: *a sheet with red and white checks* **4** [U] the position of the king in the game of chess when it is threatened by another piece **5** [C] the American spelling of **cheque**

PHRASE **keep sb/sth in check** to control someone or something that might cause damage or harm: *attempts to keep global warming in check*

checkbox /ˈtʃek,bɒks/ noun [C] **COMPUTING** a small square on a computer screen that you click on with your mouse to choose a feature

checked /tʃekt/ adj printed or woven in a pattern of squares: *a red and blue checked shirt*

'check-in noun [singular/U] TOURISM the place that people go to when they arrive at an airport or hotel

'check ,indicator noun [C] COMPUTING a piece of computer equipment or software that shows there is a fault in a file that you have received

checking program /'tʃekɪŋ ,prəʊɡræm/ noun [C] COMPUTING a piece of software that finds mistakes in computer programs

checklist /'tʃek,lɪst/ noun [C] a list of all the things that someone needs to do or consider

checkout /'tʃekaʊt/ noun **1** [C] the place where people pay in a supermarket or other large shop **2** [C/U] TOURISM the time when people have to leave a hotel room

checkpoint /'tʃek,pɔɪnt/ noun [C] a place where traffic can be stopped by soldiers or police

checksum /'tʃek,sʌm/ noun [C] COMPUTING a number that is the total of the **digits** in a piece of data that has been stored or sent in **digital** form. It is used to check that nothing has gone wrong with the data.

'check-up noun [C] an examination that a doctor or dentist does in order to make sure that someone is healthy: *You should have regular dental check-ups.*

cheddar /'tʃedə/ noun [U] a type of hard yellow cheese

cheek /tʃiːk/ noun **1** [C] the soft part on each side of the face below the eyes: *Sarah kissed her on the cheek.* —*picture* → BODY **2** [singular/U] behaviour that is rude or does not show respect: *He had the cheek to suggest that I should be the one to apologize!*

cheekbone /'tʃiːk,bəʊn/ noun [C] the bone in the cheek

cheeky /'tʃiːki/ (**cheekier, cheekiest**) adj behaving in a way that does not show respect, especially towards someone who is older or more important —**cheekily** adv

cheer¹ /tʃɪə/ verb **1** [I/T] to give a loud shout of happiness or approval: *The crowd cheered and threw flowers.* **2** [T] if you are cheered by something such as a piece of news, it makes you happier or less worried

cheer² /tʃɪə/ noun [C] a loud shout of happiness or approval → CHEERS

cheerful /'tʃɪəf(ə)l/ adj **1** behaving in a happy friendly way: *Stephen was a cheerful, affectionate child.* **2** pleasant or enjoyable, and making you feel happy: *bright cheerful colours* —**cheerfully** adv, **cheerfulness** noun [U]

cheerleader /'tʃɪə,liːdə/ noun [C] **1** one of a group of young women who sing and dance together at a sports event **2** a strong supporter of a person, organization, or idea= SUPPORTER

cheers /tʃɪəz/ interjection used by people for expressing good wishes before they drink alcohol

cheese /tʃiːz/ noun [C/U] a solid food made from milk: *a slice of cheese*

cheeseburger /'tʃiːz,bɜːɡə/ noun [C] a **burger** with a piece of cheese on top of the meat

'cheese ,screw noun [C] TECHNOLOGY a screw with a flat cylindrical head

cheetah /'tʃiːtə/ noun [C] a large African wild cat that can run extremely fast —*picture* → MAMMAL

chef /ʃef/ noun [C] someone whose job is to cook food in a restaurant
PHRASE **chef de partie** a chef who is in charge of

producing a particular type of food in a restaurant, for example fish or vegetables

chemical¹ /'kemɪk(ə)l/ noun [C] a substance made of atoms, ions or molecules, or one produced by a process that involves chemical change: *toxic chemicals* ♦ *the chemical industry*

chemical² /'kemɪk(ə)l/ adj involving chemistry, or produced by a method used in chemistry: *chemical processes* —**chemically** /'kemɪkli/ adv

,chemical di'gestion noun [U] BIOLOGY the breaking down of the large molecules of foods containing proteins, carbohydrates, and fats by enzymes in the alimentary canal, so that they become small enough to pass through the cell membranes of the intestine wall

,chemical 'element noun [C] CHEMISTRY a substance that consists of only one type of atom → PERIMETER

,chemical 'energy noun [C] CHEMISTRY energy that is stored in the chemical structure of a substance, for example in the food that we eat. Chemical energy is a form of **potential energy**.

,chemical engi'neering noun [U] the development of new chemical substances and processes that can be used in industry

,chemical e'quation noun [C] CHEMISTRY a written method of showing the process involved in a chemical reaction, using chemical symbols to show the **reactants** and **products**

,chemical re'action noun [C] CHEMISTRY a process that happens when chemicals combine and form different substances. Atoms or groups of atoms move to form different molecules.

,chemical 'warfare noun [U] the use of chemical weapons in wars

,chemical 'weapon noun [C] a weapon that contains a poisonous chemical substance

,chemical 'weathering noun [U] CHEMISTRY, GEOLOGY the process by which rocks and minerals are broken into very small pieces by the action of chemicals, for example by reacting with the oxygen in the air, or by being dissolved in water or carbonic acid

chemist /'kemɪst/ noun [C] **1** chemist or chemist's a shop that sells medicines, beauty products, and toiletries= PHARMACY **2** someone whose job is preparing and selling medicines in a chemist's shop = PHARMACIST **3** CHEMISTRY a scientist who studies chemistry

chemistry /'kemɪstri/ noun [U] **1** CHEMISTRY the scientific study of the structure of substances and the way they react with other substances **2** CHEMISTRY the chemical structure of something and the reactions that take place in it **3** the emotional relationship between people

chemo /'kiːməʊ/ noun [U] *informal* **chemotherapy**

chemotherapy /,kiːməʊ'θerəpi/ noun [U] HEALTH the use of drugs in the treatment of cancer

cheque /tʃek/ noun [C] a piece of printed paper that can be used instead of money: *a cheque for £50* ♦ *Can I pay by cheque?*

chequebook /'tʃek,bʊk/ noun [C] a book of cheques

'cheque ,card noun [C] a card from someone's bank that they show in a shop when they write a cheque

cherish /'tʃerɪʃ/ verb [T] **1** to keep something pleasant in your mind for a long time **2** to think that something is very important and to want to keep it: *I cherished my independence.* **3** to look after someone or something because you love them very much

cherry /'tʃeri/ (plural **cherries**) noun [C] **1** a small round red or black fruit —picture → FRUIT **2** a tree that produces cherries, or the wood from this tree

chess /tʃes/ noun [U] a game that two people play on a board with black and white squares. The pieces used in the game have different shapes and move in different ways.

chest /tʃest/ noun [C] **1** the upper front part of the body between the neck and stomach: *a broad chest* ♦ *chest pains* —picture → BODY **2** a large strong box, used for moving or storing things

PHRASE **chest of drawers** a piece of wooden furniture with several drawers for storing clothes

chestnut /'tʃes,nʌt/ noun [C] **1** a large smooth red-brown nut that can be eaten **2** chestnut or chestnut tree a tall tree that produces chestnuts

chew /tʃu:/ verb [I/T] **1** to use your teeth to bite food in your mouth into small pieces: *She chewed her food slowly.* **2** to bite something continuously but not swallow it: *The dog was **chewing on** an old bone.*

chewing gum /'tʃu:ɪŋ ,gʌm/ noun [U] a type of sweet that people chew for a long time but do not swallow

chewy /'tʃu:i/ adj chewy food needs to be chewed a lot before you can swallow it

chic /ʃi:k/ adj fashionable and attractive in style

chick /tʃɪk/ noun [C] a baby bird

chicken /'tʃɪkɪn/ noun **1** [C] a bird that is kept for its eggs and meat. The male is called a **cockerel**, cock, or **rooster**. **2** [U] the meat of a chicken: *grilled chicken*

chickenpox /'tʃɪkɪn,pɒks/ noun [U] HEALTH an infectious disease that most children get once, in which the skin is covered with red spots

chickpea /'tʃɪk,pi:/ noun [C/U] a round yellow-brown seed that can be cooked and eaten

chief¹ /tʃi:f/ adj **1** main, or most important: *Unemployment is the chief cause of poverty.* ♦ *the company's chief competitor* **2** highest in authority, position, or rank: *the government's Chief Medical Officer*

chief² /tʃi:f/ noun [C] **1** the person who is in charge of an organization or department, or who has the main responsibility for something: *the chief of the Red Cross mission in the war zone* **2** SOCIAL STUDIES the leader of a **tribe**

,chief ex'ecutive noun [C] BUSINESS the most senior person in a company or organization who is responsible for running it

chiefly /'tʃi:fli/ adv mainly or mostly, but not completely: *He will be remembered chiefly for his years of dedicated service to the school.*

,chief superin'tendent noun [C] a senior police officer in the UK

chieftain /'tʃi:ftən/ noun [C] SOCIAL STUDIES the leader of a **tribe**

chigger /'tʃɪgə/ noun [C] a small insect larva, common in tropical regions, whose bite causes painful lumps on the skin

child /tʃaɪld/ (plural **children** /'tʃɪldrən/) noun [C] **1** a young person from the time when they are born until they are about 14 years old: *The nursery has places for 30 children.* ♦ *He can't understand – he's just a child.* **2** someone's son or daughter of any age: *All of our children are grown and married.* ♦ *They're expecting their second child in May.* ♦ *I was **an only child** (=with no brothers or sisters).* → ONLY CHILD **3** someone whose character is influenced by the main political and social attitudes of a particular period of time: *a selfish, materialistic child of the '80s*

'child a,buse noun [U] bad treatment of a child by an adult

childbearing /'tʃaɪld,beərɪŋ/ noun [U] the process of being pregnant and giving birth to children

childbirth /'tʃaɪld,bɜ:θ/ noun [U] the process of giving birth to a baby

childcare /'tʃaɪld,keə/ noun [U] the job of looking after children, especially while their parents are working: *the high cost of childcare*

childhood /'tʃaɪld,hʊd/ noun [C/U] the time of someone's life when they are a child: *We spent our childhood in a small town in the mountains.*

childish /'tʃaɪldɪʃ/ adj **1** behaving in a silly and annoying way, like a small child **2** typical of a child —**childishly** adv, **childishness** noun [U]

'child ,labour noun [U] the employment of children, especially children who have not reached the age when they are legally allowed to work

childless /'tʃaɪldləs/ adj not having any children: *childless couples*

childlike /'tʃaɪld,laɪk/ adj *showing approval* similar to the way that a child looks, behaves, or thinks: *childlike excitement*

childminder /'tʃaɪld,maɪndə/ noun [C] someone whose job is to look after children while their parents are at work, usually in his or her own home

child molester /'tʃaɪld mə,lestə/ noun [C] SOCIAL STUDIES someone who hurts a child by touching them in a sexual way or forcing them to do sexual acts

children /'tʃɪldrən/ the plural of **child**

chill¹ /tʃɪl/ verb **1** [I/T] if someone chills food or drink, or if it chills, it becomes cold enough to eat or drink **2** [T] to make someone feel extremely frightened or worried = FRIGHTEN

chill² /tʃɪl/ noun **1** [singular] a feeling of being cold: *a chill in the air* **2** [C] a minor illness like a cold **3** [C] a feeling of fear: *The cry sent a **chill down** her **spine**.*

chilled /tʃɪld/ adj chilled food or drink has been made cold in order to make it more pleasant or to keep it fresh

chilli /'tʃɪli/ (plural **chillies**) noun **1** chilli or chilli pepper [C] a red or green vegetable with a very hot taste **2** [U] a Mexican meal made from meat, beans, and chillies cooked together

chilling /'tʃɪlɪŋ/ adj **1** making someone feel suddenly very frightened or worried: *The chilling truth is that the killers are still out there.* **2** making you feel cold —**chillingly** adv

chilly /'tʃɪli/ (**chillier, chilliest**) adj **1** cold enough to be unpleasant: *The evenings are getting chilly.* **2** unfriendly

chime /tʃaɪm/ verb [I/T] to make a high ringing sound like a bell: *Somewhere a clock chimed midnight.* —**chime** noun [C]

chimera /kaɪ'mɪərə/ noun [C] *formal* a plan or course of action that is not possible to achieve —**chimerical** /kaɪ'merɪk(ə)l/ adj

chimney /'tʃɪmni/ (plural **chimneys**) noun [C] a passage that takes smoke from a fire up through a building and out through the roof

chimpanzee /,tʃɪmpæn'zi:/ noun [C] an African mammal with black or brown fur that lives and hunts in groups. It belongs to the **ape** family, which is most similar to humans. —picture → MAMMAL

chin /tʃɪn/ noun [C] the centre of the bottom part of the face, below the mouth and above the neck —*picture* → BODY

china /'tʃaɪnə/ noun [U] plates, cups etc of good quality

Chinese cabbage /,tʃaɪniːz 'kæbɪdʒ/ noun [C/U] **Chinese leaves** —*picture* → VEGETABLE

Chinese leaves /,tʃaɪniːz 'liːvz/ noun [plural] a vegetable that has large pale green leaves with thick white stalks. It can be cooked or eaten raw in salads.

Chinese medicine /,tʃaɪniːz 'med(ə)s(ə)n/ noun [U] various medical treatments developed in China over many centuries that use herbs, minerals, and animal products in addition to **acupuncture**, **massage**, and exercise

chink /tʃɪŋk/ noun [C] **1** a very small space in a wall or between two things **2** the sound that is made when two glass or metal objects hit each other= CLINK **3** a small amount of a quality

chip¹ /tʃɪp/ noun [C]

1 potato cooked in oil	**5** piece of potato
2 in computers	**6** in sport
3 small piece	**7** game money
4 missing bit of sth	

1 a long thin piece of potato cooked in hot oil: *fish and chips*
2 COMPUTING a very small piece of **silicon** that is marked with electronic connections. It is used in computers and other machines= MICROCHIP, SILICON CHIP
3 a small piece of something such as wood or glass that has broken off something: *wood chips*
4 a place on a plate, cup etc where a small piece of it has broken off: *The cup had a tiny chip in it.*
5 American a **crisp²**
6 SPORTS in sport, the action of hitting or kicking a ball so that it goes high into the air for a short distance
7 a small piece of plastic that people use instead of money when they are gambling
→ BLUE CHIP

chip² /tʃɪp/ (**chips**, **chipping**, **chipped**) verb **1** [I/T] if something hard chips, or if you chip it, a small piece of it breaks off: *These cups chip easily.* **2** [T] SPORTS to hit or kick a ball so that it goes high into the air for a short distance

Chip and 'Pin noun [U] in the UK, a system of paying for something using a credit or debit card that has information stored on it on a **microchip**. You put your **PIN number** (=a set of 4 numbers) into a machine with the card to prove who you are, instead of signing.

chipboard /'tʃɪp,bɔːd/ noun [U] CONSTRUCTION a hard material made from small pieces of waste wood pressed together to form boards

chipmunk /'tʃɪp,mʌŋk/ noun [C] a small furry Asian and North American animal with bands of darker colour on its back

chips /tʃɪps/ noun [plural] TECHNOLOGY small pieces of waste metal removed when metal is worked

chiropodist /kɪ'rɒpədɪst/ noun [C] HEALTH someone whose job is to treat problems with people's feet —**chiropody** /kɪ'rɒpədi/ noun [U]

chiropractor /'kaɪrəʊ,præktə/ noun [C] HEALTH someone whose job is to treat illnesses by pressing on bones in the body, especially the spine

chirp /tʃɜːp/ verb [I] when a bird or an insect chirps, it makes a short high sound —**chirp** noun [C]

chisel /'tʃɪz(ə)l/ noun [C] a tool with a flat metal blade used for cutting wood or stone —*picture* → TOOL

chi-square test /'kaɪ skweə ,test/ noun [C] MATHS a test used in **statistics** to find out how accurate a theory was by comparing it with the actual event

chitin /'kaɪtɪn/ noun [U] BIOLOGY a strong substance that forms part of the outer layer protecting some insects and other **arthropods**, and the cell walls of some fungi

chivalry /'ʃɪvəlri/ noun [U] polite and kind behaviour by men towards women —**chivalrous** /'ʃɪvələs/ adj

chlamydia /klə'mɪdiə/ noun [U] HEALTH a disease passed on during sex that can damage the reproductive organs

chloralkali /klɔːr'ælkəlaɪ/ adj CHEMISTRY relating to the industrial process of making chlorine from salt water by electrolysis

chloride /'klɔːraɪd/ noun [C/U] CHEMISTRY a chemical that consists partly of **chlorine**, usually with one other element

chlorinate /'klɔːrɪ,neɪt/ verb [T] CHEMISTRY to treat water with **chlorine**, especially in order to kill harmful organisms —**chlorination** /,klɔːrɪ'neɪʃ(ə)n/ noun [U]

chlorinator /'klɔːrɪneɪtə/ noun [C] CHEMISTRY a piece of equipment that is used to add **chlorine** to water to make it suitable for drinking

chlorine /'klɔːriːn/ noun [U] CHEMISTRY a non-metal element that is a strong-smelling poisonous gas. It is a **halogen**, and very **reactive**. It is added to water as a **disinfectant**. Chemical symbol: **Cl** —*picture* → WATER

chlorofluorocarbon /,klɔːrəʊ,flʊərəʊ'kɑːbən/ noun [C] CHEMISTRY a **CFC**

chloroform /'klɒrə,fɔːm/ noun [U] CHEMISTRY a clear liquid with a strong smell that makes you unconscious if you breathe it in

chlorophyll /'klɒrəfɪl, 'klɒrəfɪl/ noun [U] BIOLOGY the green substance in **chloroplasts** in plant cells. It traps the energy from sunlight which is then used to make food through the process of photosynthesis. —*picture* → PHOTOSYNTHESIS, CELL

chloroplast /'klɔːrəʊplæst/ noun [C] BIOLOGY the part of the cells of plants where photosynthesis takes place. It is shaped like a very small bag and it contains chlorophyll. —*picture* → CELL

chloroquine /'klɔːrəkwɪn/ noun [U] HEALTH a drug that people can take in order to prevent malaria

chocolate /'tʃɒklət/ noun **1** [U] a sweet brown food that is eaten as a sweet or for adding flavour to other food: *a bar of chocolate* ♦ *chocolate cake* **2** [C] a small sweet made from chocolate: *a box of chocolates*

choice¹ /tʃɔɪs/ noun **1** [singular/U] the opportunity or right to choose between different things: *We try to provide greater choice for our customers.* ♦ *Students have **a choice between** studying biology or economics.* ♦ *If you were **given the choice**, would you prefer a bicycle or a mobile phone?* ♦ *I had no choice – I had to believe what he said.* **2** [C] a decision to choose someone or something: *He was facing a difficult **choice between** staying with his family or working abroad.* ♦ *Our childhood experiences can influence our **choice of** career.* ♦ *He wants people to **make** their own **choices**.* **3** [C] a range of things that you can choose from: *The restaurant offers **a wide choice of** dishes.* **4** [C] someone or something that you choose: *Singapore is a popular choice for international conferences.* ♦ *I think Edinburgh University would be my **first choice**.*
PHRASE **by choice** if you do something by choice, you do it because you want to and not because you have to

choice² /tʃɔɪs/ adj *formal* of very high quality

choir /kwaɪə/ noun [C] **1 MUSIC** a group of singers who perform together, for example in a church or school: *the school choir* **2** the part of a church where the choir sits

choke¹ /tʃəʊk/ verb **1** [I/T] if you choke, or if something chokes you, you cannot breathe because there is not enough air, or because something is blocking your throat: *Joe took a bite of the steak and started to choke.* ◆ *Ruth almost **choked on** a mouthful of cake.* **2** [T] to squeeze someone's neck so that they cannot breathe **3** [I] if your voice chokes, you cannot speak clearly, usually because of a strong emotion or because you are laughing **4** [T] if stronger plants choke weaker ones, they surround them and stop them from growing

choke² /tʃəʊk/ noun [C] **ENGINEERING** a **valve** in a **carburettor** that controls the amount of air going into a vehicle engine, and so helps it to start

cholera /ˈkɒlərə/ noun [U] **HEALTH** a serious, highly infectious disease that causes severe vomiting and diarrhoea, and can cause death. It is typically caught from an infected water supply.

cholesterol /kəˈlestərɒl/ noun [U] **HEALTH** a substance that is found in the blood and the cells of the body. It can cause diseases of the heart and the arteries if there is too much of it.

choose /tʃuːz/ (**chooses, choosing, chose** /tʃəʊz/, **chosen** /ˈtʃəʊz(ə)n/) verb [I/T] **1** to decide which person or thing you want from a number of people or things: *Do you feel that you chose the wrong career?* ◆ *There is a huge range of clothes **to choose from.*** ◆ *She is forced to **choose between** her husband and her parents.* **2** to decide to do something: *What are the factors that make people **choose to** live in a city?*

choosy /ˈtʃuːzi/ adj someone who is choosy has definite ideas about what they like and is not willing to accept other things

chop¹ /tʃɒp/ (**chops, chopping, chopped**) verb [T] to cut something such as food or wood into pieces: *Chop the meat **into** small cubes.* —*picture* → FOOD

chop² /tʃɒp/ noun [C] a small piece of meat with a bone in it: *lamb chops*

choppy /ˈtʃɒpi/ (**choppier, choppiest**) adj choppy water has a lot of waves because the wind is blowing across it

chopsticks /ˈtʃɒpˌstɪks/ noun [plural] a pair of thin sticks used in some East Asian cultures for eating food

choral /ˈkɔːrəl/ adj **MUSIC** sung by a **choir**: *choral music*

chorale /kɒˈrɑːl/ noun [C] **MUSIC** a religious song sung by a **choir** (=a group of people singing together)

chord /kɔːd/ noun [C] **1 MUSIC** two or more musical notes played together **2 MATHS** a straight line that connects two points in a circle or curved line —*picture* → CIRCLE

PHRASE **strike/touch a chord (with sb)** to produce an emotion such as sympathy in someone

chordal /ˈkɔːd(ə)l/ adj **MUSIC** chordal music consists of a tune **accompanied** by a sequence of **chords**, rather than of two or more tunes combined with each other

chordate /ˈkɔːdeɪt/ noun [C] **BIOLOGY** an animal that has, at some stage in its development, a main nerve cord down its back, a type of backbone, and organs in the side of the head for breathing. All vertebrates and some invertebrate sea animals are chordates.

chordophone /ˈkɔːdəfəʊn/ noun [C] **MUSIC** a technical name for a **stringed instrument**

chore /tʃɔː/ noun [C] an ordinary, boring, or unpleasant job that must be done: *You can go and play after you've done your chores.*

choreography /ˌkɒriˈɒɡrəfi/ noun [U] **ARTS** the art of planning the movements of dancers, or the steps that the dancers perform —**choreographer** noun [C], **choreograph** /ˈkɒriəˌɡrɑːf/ verb [T], **choreographic** /ˌkɒriəˈɡræfɪk/ adj

choroid /ˈkɔːrɔɪd/ noun [C] **ANATOMY** the part of the eye that is between the retina and the white of the eye. The coloured **iris** at the front of the eye is part of the choroid. —*picture* → EYE

chorus /ˈkɔːrəs/ noun [C] **1 MUSIC** the part of a song that is repeated several times **2** an opinion that several people express at the same time: *a chorus of disapproval* **3 MUSIC** a piece of music that is sung by a large group of people: *the Prisoners' Chorus from Fidelio* **4 MUSIC** a large group of people who sing together= CHOIR

chose /tʃəʊz/ the past tense of **choose**

chosen /ˈtʃəʊz(ə)n/ the past participle of **choose**

chow mein /ˌtʃaʊ ˈmeɪn/ noun [U] a Chinese meal consisting of **noodles** cooked in oil with small pieces of meat and vegetables

Christ /kraɪst/ **RELIGION** Jesus Christ, whose ideas the Christian religion is based on

christen /ˈkrɪs(ə)n/ verb [T] **RELIGION** to perform a religious ceremony in which someone, especially a baby, is made a member of the Christian religion and is given a name

christening /ˈkrɪs(ə)nɪŋ/ noun [C] **RELIGION** a religious ceremony during which a baby is made a member of the Christian religion and is given a name = BAPTISM

Christian /ˈkrɪstʃən/ noun [C] **RELIGION** someone whose religion is Christianity —**Christian** adj

Christianity /ˌkrɪstiˈænəti/ noun [U] **RELIGION** the religion that is based on the ideas of Jesus Christ

'Christian ,name noun [C] someone's first name, or the name that is not someone's family name

Christmas /ˈkrɪsməs/ noun [C/U] **1** 25 December, celebrated by Christians as the day that Jesus Christ was born: *Did you get some nice Christmas presents this year?* **2** the period before and after 25 December: *We spent Christmas with my mother's family.*

'Christmas ,card noun [C] a card that people send to their friends and family at Christmas

,Christmas 'carol noun [C] a song that people sing at Christmas

,Christmas 'Day noun [C/U] 25 December, celebrated by Christians as the day that Jesus Christ was born

,Christmas 'Eve noun [C/U] the day or evening before Christmas Day

'Christmas ,tree noun [C] a tree that people cover with lights and other decorations at Christmas

chromatic /krəˈmætɪk/ adj **1 MUSIC** relating to a musical scale that uses **semitones 2 SCIENCE** relating to colour, or colours

chromatin /ˈkrəʊmətɪn/ noun [U] **BIOLOGY** the substance that forms chromosomes and contains DNA, RNA, and various proteins

chromatography /ˌkrəʊməˈtɒɡrəfi/ noun [U] **SCIENCE** a method of finding out which different gases or liquids are included in a mixture by passing it through or over substances that absorb the different parts at different rates —*picture* → on next page

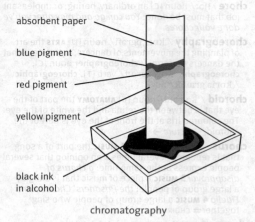

absorbent paper

blue pigment

red pigment

yellow pigment

black ink
in alcohol

chromatography

chrome /krəʊm/ noun [U] a hard metal substance used for covering other metals to make them shiny

chrominance /ˈkrəʊmɪnəns/ noun [U] PHYSICS the part of a television signal that carries colour information

chromium /ˈkrəʊmiəm/ noun [U] CHEMISTRY a white metal used for making alloys and for putting a hard shiny covering on other metals. Chemical symbol: **Cr**

chromosome /ˈkrəʊməsəʊm/ noun [C] BIOLOGY a structure that looks like a very small piece of string and that exists, usually as one of a pair, in the nucleus of all living cells. Chromosomes contain the genetic information that says whether a person, animal etc is male or female and what characteristics they get from their parents. → DNA, GENE —*picture* → CELL, SEX CELL

chronic /ˈkrɒnɪk/ adj **1** HEALTH a chronic illness or pain is serious and lasts for a long time **2** a chronic problem is always happening and is very difficult to solve: *chronic energy shortages* **3** doing something again and again, especially something harmful —**chronically** /ˈkrɒnɪkli/ adv

chronic faˈtigue ˌsyndrome noun [U] HEALTH an illness that makes you feel tired and weak all the time. Its cause is not known═ ME

chronicle /ˈkrɒnɪk(ə)l/ noun [C] a record of events that happened in the past, in the order in which they happened —**chronicle** verb [T]

chronological /ˌkrɒnəˈlɒdʒɪk(ə)l/ adj arranged or described in the order in which events happened —**chronologically** /ˌkrɒnəˈlɒdʒɪkli/ adv

chronology /krəˈnɒlədʒi/ noun [C] the order in which a series of events happened or will happen

chronometer /krəˈnɒmɪtə/ noun [C] a piece of equipment that measures time accurately

chrysalis /ˈkrɪsəlɪs/ noun [C] BIOLOGY **1** an insect such as a butterfly or moth at the stage of changing from a larva to an adult **2** the hard case in which this happens

chubby /ˈtʃʌbi/ (**chubbier, chubbiest**) adj *informal* slightly fat

chuck /tʃʌk/ verb [T] *informal* **1** to throw something **2** to get rid of something that you do not want

chuckle /ˈtʃʌk(ə)l/ verb [I] to laugh quietly —**chuckle** noun [C]

chunk /tʃʌŋk/ noun [C] **1** a large thick piece of something: *chunks of meat* **2** a large amount or part of something

chunky /ˈtʃʌŋki/ adj thick and square in shape

church /tʃɜːtʃ/ noun RELIGION **1** [C/U] a building that Christians go to in order to worship: *She doesn't go to church very often these days.* **2** [C] a group of Christian churches with its own particular beliefs and structures: *the Roman Catholic Church*

PHRASE **the Church of England** RELIGION the official Christian Church in England

churchgoer /ˈtʃɜːtʃˌɡəʊə/ noun [C] RELIGION someone who goes to church regularly

Churchillian /tʃɜːˈtʃɪliən/ adj relating to or similar to the British prime minister Winston Churchill, especially in being a good leader or being good at making speeches in public

ˈchurch ˌschool noun [C] EDUCATION a school that is connected with a church and gets some of its money from the church

churchyard /ˈtʃɜːtʃˌjɑːd/ noun [C] the area of land around a church where dead people are buried

churn /tʃɜːn/ noun [C] a container in which butter is made

ˈchurn ˌrate noun [C] BUSINESS a measurement of how often new customers try a product or service and then stop using it

chute /ʃuːt/ noun [C] a tube or narrow open structure that people or things slide down

chutney /ˈtʃʌtni/ (plural **chutneys**) noun [C/U] a cold food made from fruit, spices, and vinegar. It is eaten with meat or cheese.

chyme /kaɪm/ noun [U] BIOLOGY a thick mass of partially digested food and liquids produced by the stomach that passes from the stomach to the **small intestine** during digestion

the CIA /ˌsiː aɪ ˈeɪ/ the Central Intelligence Agency: a US government organization that collects secret information about other countries and protects secret information about the US → FBI

cicada /sɪˈkɑːdə/ noun [C] an insect that lives in trees and tall grass and makes a loud high noise by rubbing its legs together

the CID /ˌsiː aɪ ˈdiː/ the Criminal Investigation Department: the department of the police in the UK that is responsible for solving serious crimes

CI engine /ˌsiː ˈaɪ ˌendʒɪn/ noun [C] ENGINEERING a compression ignition engine

cigar /sɪˈɡɑː/ noun [C] a thick tube of dried tobacco leaves that people smoke

cigarette /ˌsɪɡəˈret/ noun [C] a narrow paper tube containing tobacco that people smoke: *a packet of cigarettes*

cilia the plural of **cilium**

ciliary muscle /ˌsɪliəri ˈmʌs(ə)l/ noun [C] ANATOMY a muscle in the eye that controls the lens —*picture* → EYE

cilium /ˈsɪliəm/ (plural **cilia** /ˈsɪliə/) noun [C] BIOLOGY one of a great many extremely small hair-like parts on a cell and on some microorganisms. The cilia beat regularly to help the movement of fluids past the cell, or, in some microorganisms, to help them to move through liquid.

cill /sɪl/ noun [C] CONSTRUCTION a horizontal piece of wood at the base of a door or window

cinchona bark /sɪŋˈkəʊnə ˌbɑːk/ noun [U] HEALTH, BIOLOGY the bark of a tree that grows in South America and that has been used for centuries to treat fevers. It is the source of the drug **quinine**.

cinder /'sɪndə/ noun [C] a small piece of something that has been burnt almost completely

'cinder ,cone adj GEOLOGY a type of volcano with a hill around the **vent** that explodes violently when it erupts

cinema /'sɪnəmə/ noun **1** [C] a building where people go to watch films: *We went to the cinema last night.* ♦ *a 10-screen cinema* **2** [U] the business of making films, or films in general

cinnamon /'sɪnəmən/ noun [U] a brown powder or small stick used for giving a special taste to food

circa /'sɜːkə/ preposition *formal* used before a date or number for showing that it is not exact

circadian /sɜː'keɪdiən/ adj BIOLOGY relating to a period of 24 hours, especially to the changes in people's or animals' bodies that happen during this period

circle¹ /'sɜːk(ə)l/ noun [C] **1** a curved line that creates a round enclosed space and is the same distance from the centre at every point —*picture* → SHAPE **2** a group of people or things arranged in a circle: *a circle of stones* **3** a group of people who know one another or are interested in the same things: *international financial circles* ♦ *They have a large circle of friends.* PHRASE **go around/round in circles** to do something for a long time without achieving any results because you always return to the same problem

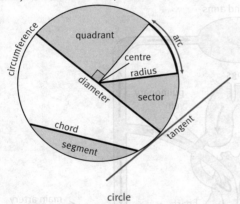

circle

circle² /'sɜːk(ə)l/ verb **1** [I/T] to move in a circle, or to move something in a circle **2** [T] to draw a circle around something **3** [I] if people are circling, they are watching a situation and waiting for an opportunity to get something they want

circuit /'sɜːkɪt/ noun [C] **1** a series of places that someone regularly goes to: *He is a performer on the New York comedy club circuit.* **2** SPORTS a track that cars, bicycles etc race around **3** PHYSICS the complete path that an electric current flows around. There are two main types of electrical circuit, a **series circuit** and a **parallel circuit**. → SHORT CIRCUIT

'circuit ,board noun [C] PHYSICS a board with electrical connections or computer chips on it, fitted inside a piece of electronic equipment

'circuit ,breaker noun [C] PHYSICS a piece of equipment that is designed to stop an electric current automatically if it becomes dangerous

'circuit ,court noun [C] LAW one of a number of courts of law in an area that a judge visits regularly in order to deal with local cases

'circuit ,judge noun [C] LAW a judge who visits a number of courts of law in an area regularly in order to deal with local cases

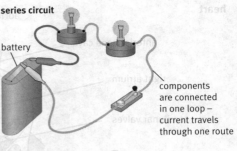

series circuit

battery

components are connected in one loop – current travels through one route

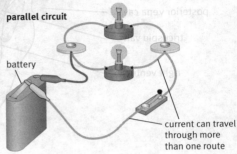

parallel circuit

battery

current can travel through more than one route

circuits

circuitous /sɜː'kjuːɪtəs/ adj **1** a circuitous journey, path etc is longer than it needs to be because it is not direct **2** taking a long time to say what you really mean when you are talking or writing about something

circular¹ /'sɜːkjʊlə/ adj **1** in the shape of a circle, or moving in a circle **2** a circular argument or theory does not mean anything because it consists of a series of causes and effects that lead you back to the original cause **3** sent to a lot of people at the same time

circular² /'sɜːkjʊlə/ noun [C] a document or advertisement that is sent to a lot of people at the same time

the ,circular 'flow noun [singular] ECONOMICS the process by which businesses get income from selling goods and services to customers, and customers get income from businesses, for example salaries, rent, or profit from investments

,circular 'orbit noun [C] ASTRONOMY a path in the shape of a circle that is taken by an object such as a planet as it moves around a larger object in space

circular overfolded seam /,sɜːkjʊlə ,əʊvəfəʊldɪd 'siːm/ noun [C] TECHNOLOGY a **knocked-up joint**

,circular 'saw noun [C] an electrical **saw** with a round metal blade

circulate /'sɜːkjʊleɪt/ verb **1** [I] if information or ideas circulate, more and more people start to know about them **2** [T] to send something to all the people in a group **3** [I/T] to move around continuously inside a system or area, or to make something do this: *a machine designed to circulate warm air* **4** [I] to move around at a party, talking to different people

circulation /,sɜːkjʊ'leɪʃ(ə)n/ noun **1** [U] BIOLOGY the movement of blood around the body —*picture* → on next page **2** [U] the continuous movement of liquid, air etc inside a system or area **3** [singular] the number of copies of a newspaper or magazine that are sold each day, week etc **4** [U] the process by which something such as information passes from one person to another

heart

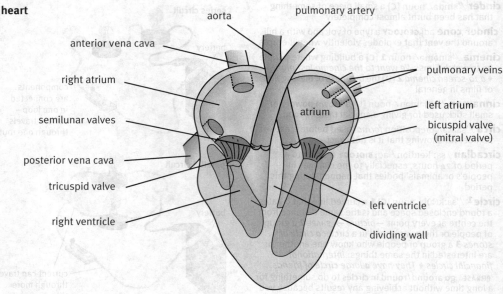

aorta

anterior vena cava

pulmonary artery

right atrium

pulmonary veins

semilunar valves

left atrium

atrium

posterior vena cava

bicuspid valve
(mitral valve)

tricuspid valve

left ventricle

right ventricle

dividing wall

circulation

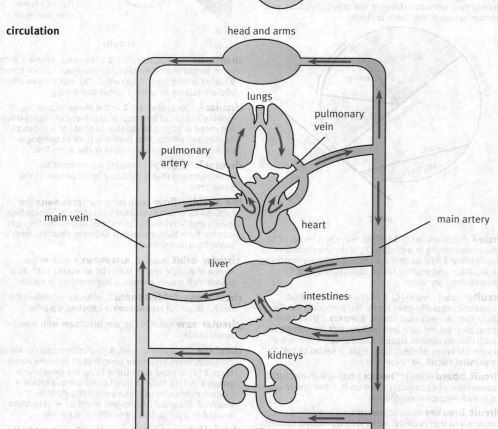

head and arms

lungs

pulmonary
vein

pulmonary
artery

main vein

heart

main artery

liver

intestines

kidneys

legs

circulatory /ˌsɜːkjʊˈleɪt(ə)ri, ˈsɜːkjələt(ə)ri/ adj **BIOLOGY** relating to the movement of blood around the body: *Smoking can lead to circulatory problems.*

circumcise /ˈsɜːkəmsaɪz/ verb [T] to remove the skin at the end of a boy's penis, or to remove part of a girl's sex organs, often for religious or cultural reasons

circumcision /ˌsɜːkəmˈsɪʒ(ə)n/ noun [C/U] the process of circumcising someone, or a religious ceremony in which someone is circumcised

circumference /səˈkʌmf(ə)rəns/ noun [C/U] **MATHS** the distance measured around the edge of a circle or a round object —*picture* → CIRCLE

circumflex /ˈsɜːkəmˌfleks/ noun [C] **LANGUAGE** the symbol – that is written above a vowel in some languages → ACUTE sense 3, GRAVE³

circumlocution /ˌsɜːkəmləˈkjuːʃ(ə)n/ noun [C/U] *formal* the use of too many words to say something, especially in order to avoid saying something clearly

circumnavigate /ˌsɜːkəmˈnævɪˌgeɪt/ verb [T] *formal* to sail or fly completely around something, especially the world or an island

circumscribing circle /ˌsɜːkəmskraɪbɪŋ ˈsɜːk(ə)l/ noun [C] **MATHS, TECHNOLOGY** a circle drawn around a geometric shape that touches all the outer angles of the shape

circumspect /ˈsɜːkəmˌspekt/ adj thinking carefully about something before you say or do it = CAUTIOUS

circumstance /ˈsɜːkəmstəns/ noun **1** [C] the facts or conditions that affect a situation: *The circumstances of this case are unusual.* ♦ *It's amazing that they did so well **under the circumstances** (=because the situation was difficult or unusual).* **2** [plural] the conditions in which someone lives, especially how much money they have: *It is very important to make a will, whatever your circumstances.* **3** [U] *formal* events and situations that cannot be controlled

PHRASE **under no circumstances** used for emphasizing that you mean 'never': *Under no circumstances will I give you any more money.*

circumstantial /ˌsɜːkəmˈstænʃ(ə)l/ adj **LAW** circumstantial evidence makes it seem likely that something is true but does not prove it

circumvent /ˌsɜːkəmˈvent/ verb [T] *formal* to find a way of avoiding a rule or law, especially using a clever trick that does not break the law

circus /ˈsɜːkəs/ noun [C] a group of people who travel from place to place and entertain people by performing tricks

cirque /sɜːk/ noun [C] **GEOLOGY** a valley with three steep sides on the slope of a mountain. It is formed by the movement of glaciers.

cirrhosis /səˈrəʊsɪs/ noun [U] **HEALTH** a serious disease of the liver, often caused by drinking too much alcohol

cirrocumulus /ˌsɪrəʊˈkjuːmjələs/ (plural **cirrocumuli** /ˌsɪrəʊˈkjumjəlaɪ/) noun [C/U] **GEOGRAPHY** small round clouds that form lines high in the sky

cirrostratus /ˌsɪrəʊˈstrɑːtəs/ (plural **cirrostrati** /ˌsɪrəʊˈstrɑːtaɪ/) noun [C/U] **GEOGRAPHY** thin white cloud that is very high in the sky. It is formed just below **cirrus** cloud. —*picture* → CLOUD

cirrus /ˈsɪrəs/ (plural **cirri** /ˈsɪraɪ/) noun [C/U] **GEOGRAPHY** a type of thin cloud that forms at the highest levels of the atmosphere —*picture* → CLOUD → CUMULUS

cistern /ˈsɪstən/ noun [C] **1** a large container for holding water **2** the part of a toilet that holds the water used for **flushing** it

citadel /ˈsɪtəd(ə)l, ˈsɪtədel/ noun [C] a castle intended originally for the defence of a city

citation /saɪˈteɪʃ(ə)n/ noun [C] a phrase or sentence taken from a piece of writing or speech = QUOTATION

cite /saɪt/ verb [T] **1** to mention something as an example, explanation, or proof **2** **LAW** to officially mention someone in a legal case **3** to officially praise someone for something that they have done

citizen /ˈsɪtɪz(ə)n/ noun [C] **1 SOCIAL STUDIES** someone who has the right to live permanently in a particular country: *She married an American and became a US citizen.* **2** someone who lives in a particular town or city: *the citizens of Edinburgh*

citizenship /ˈsɪtɪz(ə)nʃɪp/ noun [U] **SOCIAL STUDIES** the legal right to be a citizen of a particular country

citric acid /ˌsɪtrɪk ˈæsɪd/ noun [U] **CHEMISTRY** an acid contained in the juice of fruits such as oranges and lemons

citrus fruit /ˈsɪtrəs ˌfruːt/ noun [C/U] a fruit such as a lemon or orange

city /ˈsɪti/ (plural **cities**) noun [C] **1** a large important town: *an industrial city* ♦ *Lusaka is Zambia's **capital city** (=most important city).* **2** the institutions of a city: *The city has agreed to put up its taxes.* **3 the City** the British **stock exchange**, or the area in central London where the stock exchange and other major financial institutions are based

city centre noun [C] the part of a city where the main shops and businesses are

city-state noun [C] a city that in the past joined with the area around it to form an independent state

civet /ˈsɪvɪt/ noun [C] an African or Asian mammal similar to a cat

civic /ˈsɪvɪk/ adj relating to a town or city

civic centre noun [C] the building in a town or city where its government is based

civil /ˈsɪv(ə)l/ adj

1 polite	**4** of state, not religion
2 private, not criminal	**5** not military
3 involving citizens	

1 polite, but not friendly: *He could barely force himself to **be civil to** them.*
2 LAW relating to private legal disagreements between people, rather than to criminal law: *The case was tried in a civil court.*
3 involving protests or fighting by the people of a country: *civil disturbances*
4 done by the state, rather than by religious authorities: *We were married in a civil ceremony.*
5 involving ordinary people, not the armed forces: *civil employees*

civil engineering noun [U] the job of designing and building roads, bridges etc —**civil engineer** noun [C]

civilian /səˈvɪliən/ noun [C] someone who does not belong to the armed forces or the police —**civilian** adj

civilization or **civilisation** /ˌsɪvəlaɪˈzeɪʃ(ə)n/ noun [C/U] a society that has developed its own culture and institutions

civilize or **civilise** /ˈsɪvəlaɪz/ verb [T] to make someone behave in a more polite and reasonable way

civilized or **civilised** /ˈsɪvəˌlaɪzd/ adj **1** a civilized country or society has developed an advanced culture and advanced institutions **2** polite and reasonable: *Let's discuss this **in a civilized way**.*

,**civil 'law** noun [U] **LAW** the part of law that deals with disagreements between people, rather than with crime

civil liberties /ˌsɪv(ə)l 'lɪbətiz/ noun [plural] **SOCIAL STUDIES** the basic freedom that all citizens have to do or say what they want

,**civil 'partnership** noun [C] a relationship similar to marriage for two people who are of the same sex

,**civil 'rights** noun [plural] **SOCIAL STUDIES** the basic rights that all people in a society have, for example the right to be treated fairly by the law

,**civil 'servant** noun [C] **POLITICS** someone who works for a government department

the ,civil 'service noun [singular] **POLITICS** a country's government departments and the people who work in them

,**civil 'services** noun [plural] basic public services such as water, electricity, and **drainage**

,**civil tech'nology** noun [U] the study of the technological processes involved in building

,**civil 'union** noun [C] a ceremony similar to a wedding for two people who are of the same sex

,**civil 'war** noun [C/U] a war that is fought between different groups of people within the same country

CJD /ˌsiː dʒeɪ 'diː/ noun [U] **HEALTH** Creutzfeldt-Jakob disease: a serious disease that gradually destroys the brain → BSE

cl abbrev centilitre

cladding /'klædɪŋ/ noun [U] **CONSTRUCTION** a hard substance such as wood, stone, or metal that is put on the outside of a structure, especially a building, to protect it or make it look more attractive

claim¹ /kleɪm/ verb **1** [T] to say that something is true, even though there is no definite proof: *He **claims that** he is innocent.* ♦ *The organization **claims to** represent more than 20,000 firms.* **2** [I/T] to ask for something that belongs to you, or to ask for something that you have a right to: *Has anyone claimed the wallet I handed in yesterday?* ♦ *She claimed political asylum in 1986.* **3** [T] if war, disease, or an accident claims someone's life, they die as a result of it: *The flood has now claimed over 500 lives.* **4** [T] to need something such as your attention or time: *Several more urgent matters were claiming her attention.*

PHRASE claim credit/responsibility/victory etc to say that you have achieved or done something: *I can't claim all the credit for our success.*

claim² /kleɪm/ noun [C] **1** a statement that something is true but with no definite proof: ***claims of** bullying* ♦ *I don't believe his **claim that** he fought in Vietnam.* **2** an official request for something that you believe you have a right to: *an insurance claim* ♦ *a **claim for** asylum* **3** a legal or moral right to something: *She has no **claim on** her husband's estate.* **4** a right to someone's attention, love etc: *There are so many competing **claims on** our attention these days.*

claimant /'kleɪmənt/ noun [C] **1** someone who makes an official request for money **2** someone who says that they have a right to something

clairvoyant /kleə'vɔɪənt/ noun [C] someone who claims to know what will happen in the future

clam /klæm/ noun [C] a small sea mollusc with a shell in two halves and a soft body —*picture* → SEA

clamber /'klæmbə/ verb [I] to climb something with difficulty, using the hands and feet = SCRAMBLE

clammy /'klæmi/ adj cold and wet in an unpleasant way

clamour¹ /'klæmə/ noun [singular/U] *formal* **1** an urgent request for something by a lot of people **2** a very loud noise made by a lot of people or things

clamour² /'klæmə/ verb [I] if people clamour for something, they say loudly that they must have it: *children **clamouring for** attention*

clamp¹ /klæmp/ verb [T] **1** to put or hold something firmly in position **2** to hold two things together using a clamp **3** to put a piece of equipment on a wheel of a car to stop it being moved because it is illegally parked

PHRASAL VERB ,clamp 'down to make a determined attempt to stop people doing something bad or illegal

clamp² /klæmp/ noun [C] **1** a tool used for holding two things together firmly **2** a piece of equipment put on a wheel of an illegally parked car to stop it being moved

clampdown /'klæmp,daʊn/ noun [C] a determined attempt by someone in authority to stop people doing something bad or illegal

clan /klæn/ noun [C] **SOCIAL STUDIES** a large group of families that are related to each other

clandestine /klæn'destɪn, 'klænde,staɪn/ adj secret and often illegal

clang /klæŋ/ verb [I/T] if something made of metal clangs, it makes a loud sound —**clang** noun [C]

clank /klæŋk/ verb [I/T] if a heavy metal object clanks, it makes a short loud sound —**clank** noun [C]

clap¹ /klæp/ (**claps, clapping, clapped**) verb **1** [I/T] to hit your hands together many times as a way of showing that you liked something, or in order to get attention: *At the end of the speech everyone clapped.* **2** [T] to suddenly put something somewhere: *The boy **clapped** his hands **over** his ears.* —**clapping** noun [U]

clap² /klæp/ noun **1** [singular] an action of hitting your hands together, to show enjoyment or to get attention **2** [C] a sudden loud sound: *a **clap of thunder***

clapper /'klæpə/ noun [C] **MUSIC** the small metal object inside a bell that hits against the bell to make it ring

clarification /ˌklærəfɪ'keɪʃ(ə)n/ noun [U] *formal* an explanation that makes something easier to understand

clarify /'klærəfaɪ/ (**clarifies, clarifying, clarified**) verb [T] *formal* to explain something more clearly so that it is easier to understand

clarinet /ˌklærə'net/ noun [C] **MUSIC** a musical instrument consisting of a long black tube that is played by blowing into it —*picture* → MUSICAL INSTRUMENT, ORCHESTRA —**clarinettist** noun [C]

clarity /'klærəti/ noun [U] **1** the ability to be easily understood **2** the ability to think clearly or understand things clearly **3** the quality of being easy to see, hear, or understand

clash¹ /klæʃ/ noun [C] **1** a very angry argument or fight between two people or groups: *violent **clashes between** police and protesters* **2** a situation in which two people or things are so different that they cannot exist or work together: *a personality **clash between** two of the teachers* **3** a loud sound that is made when two metal objects hit each other **4** an annoying situation in which two events happen at the same time, so that it is impossible for you to go to both

clash² /klæʃ/ verb [I] **1** to argue angrily, or to fight with someone **2** if two events clash, they happen at the same time, so that it is impossible for you to go to both: *The* conference dates clash with John's wedding. **3** if colours or patterns clash, they do not look good together: *His T-shirt clashed with his shorts.*

clasp /klɑːsp/ verb [T] to hold someone or something tightly

class¹ /klɑːs/ noun

1 group of students	5 type of sth
2 teaching period	6 in biology
3 series of lessons	7 standard of service
4 group in society	8 university degree

1 [C] EDUCATION a group of students who are taught together: *What class is Sophie in now?*

> **Class** can be used with a singular or plural verb. You can say *Her class* **has** *a new teacher* or *Her class* **have** *a new teacher.*

2 [C/U] EDUCATION a period of time during which a group of students is taught together= LESSON: *I've got classes all afternoon.* ♦ *We had to write an essay* **in** *class.*
3 [C] EDUCATION a course of lessons in a particular subject: *I* **go to** *my art* **class** *on Mondays.*
4 [C/U] SOCIAL STUDIES one of the groups into which people in a society are divided according to education, income etc: *tax cuts for the* **middle class** ♦ *the relationship between* **social class** *and your level of education*
5 [C] a group of things, animals, or people with similar features or qualities: *The race has competitions for ten* **classes of** *boat.*
6 [C] BIOLOGY a group of animals or plants that are related to each other. A class includes more than an **order** and less than a **phylum**. —*picture* → TAXONOMY
7 [C] one of the standards of service that are available to someone travelling by train, plane etc
8 [C] EDUCATION one of the levels of university degree

class² /klɑːs/ verb [T] to include someone or something in a particular group: *She is now* **classed as** *a professional athlete.*

class 'action noun [C/U] LAW a legal case organized by a group of people who all have the same problem

classic¹ /ˈklæsɪk/ adj **1** completely typical: *a classic example of poor management* **2** a classic song, book, play etc is very good and has been popular for a long time **3** a classic style of clothes, furniture etc is beautiful in a very simple way

classic² /ˈklæsɪk/ noun [C] **1** a song, book, play etc that is very good and has been popular for a long time **2** something that is extremely good and likely to be remembered → CLASSICS

classical /ˈklæsɪk(ə)l/ adj **1** following the original or traditional standard for something: *classical economics* **2** relating to ancient Greece and Rome: *classical mythology* **3** ARTS based on the art or architecture of ancient Greece and Rome: *a building constructed in the classical style* **4** MUSIC relating to classical music: *classical composers* —**classically** /ˈklæsɪkli/ adv

classical 'music noun [U] MUSIC serious music that is played on instruments such as the piano and the **violin**

classic 'car noun [C] a high-quality car built between 1925 and 1948

classicism /ˈklæsɪˌsɪz(ə)m/ noun [U] ARTS, LITERATURE a style of art or literature based on ancient Greek and Roman styles that is beautiful in a simple controlled way

classics /ˈklæsɪks/ noun [U] LITERATURE the study of the language, literature, and culture of ancient Greece and Rome

classification /ˌklæsɪfɪˈkeɪʃ(ə)n/ noun [C/U] **1** the process of putting people or things into particular groups according to the features that they have, or one of these groups **2** BIOLOGY a system used for dividing living things into groups. The most popular system is the **Linnaean** system, in which the lowest level of classification is called a species and the highest level is called a **kingdom**.

classified /ˈklæsɪfaɪd/ adj classified information is officially secret and can only be known by a few government officials or military officials

classified 'ad or **classified ad'vertisement** noun [C] a short advertisement that someone puts in a newspaper, for example in order to try to sell something

classify /ˈklæsɪfaɪ/ (classifies, classifying, classified) verb [T] to put people or things into groups according to the features that they have= CATEGORIZE: *Families were* **classified according to** *their incomes.*

classless /ˈklɑːsləs/ adj SOCIAL STUDIES **1** not divided into social classes **2** not belonging to a particular social class

classmate /ˈklɑːsˌmeɪt/ noun [C] someone who is in your class at school

classroom /ˈklɑːsˌruːm/ noun **1** [C] a room in a school where classes take place **2** [singular] the activities and methods involved in teaching: *School management is often too detached from the classroom.*

classy /ˈklɑːsi/ adj *informal* **1** expensive, fashionable, and very good= EXCLUSIVE **2** someone who is classy has the natural ability to choose the best thing or behave in a suitable way in every situation

clatter /ˈklætə/ verb [I] if a hard object clatters, it makes a lot of loud short noises as it hits something hard —**clatter** noun [singular]

clause /klɔːz/ noun [C] **1** LAW a part of a legal document or law **2** LANGUAGE a group of words that contains a verb and a subject. A clause has its own meaning, but is often not a complete sentence. → MAIN CLAUSE, RELATIVE CLAUSE

claustrophobia /ˌklɔːstrəˈfəʊbiə/ noun [U] fear of being in a small space

claustrophobic /ˌklɔːstrəˈfəʊbɪk/ adj **1** someone who is claustrophobic feels afraid because they are in a small space **2** a claustrophobic place makes you uncomfortable because it is small or crowded

clavicle /ˈklævɪk(ə)l/ noun [C] ANATOMY one of the pair of bones that go across the top of the chest from the shoulder to the bottom of the neck —*picture* → SKELETON

claw¹ /klɔː/ noun [C] **1** BIOLOGY one of the sharp curved nails that some birds and other animals have on their feet **2** BIOLOGY the sharp curved end of a front leg of a sea invertebrate such as a **crab** that it uses for holding things= PINCER **3** a curved end on a tool or machine, used for pulling or picking things up

claw² /klɔː/ verb [I/T] to attack someone or damage something using claws

'claw ,hammer noun [C] a hammer with two curved metal parts on its head, used for pulling nails out of wood

clay /kleɪ/ noun [U] GEOLOGY a type of heavy wet soil that becomes hard when it is baked in a **kiln** (=oven), used for making cups, plates, and other objects

clay 'soil noun [U] AGRICULTURE a type of thick heavy soil that rain water does not easily pass through

clean¹ /kliːn/ adj **1** not dirty or polluted: *Go and put on a clean shirt.* ♦ *the clean country air* ♦ *Tom had scrubbed the floor clean.* ♦ *I like to keep the place* **clean**

and tidy. ♦ *Everything in the house was* **spotlessly clean** (=extremely clean). **2** a clean piece of paper does not have anything written on it **3** clean shapes, lines, or movements are smooth, regular, or tidy **4** not illegal or unfair, or not involved in anything illegal or unfair: *I've got a clean driving licence* (=I have not committed any driving offences).

PHRASES   **a clean slate/sheet** a situation in which everything bad that someone has done in the past has been forgiven or forgotten

come clean to tell the truth about something that you have kept secret

clean² /kliːn/ verb **1** [T] to remove the dirt from something: *Paul is cleaning his car.* ♦ *You should clean your teeth twice a day.* **2** [I/T] to remove the dirt and dust in a house: *We've cleaned the house from top to bottom.* ♦ *I was cleaning all morning.* **3** [T] to remove the inside parts of an animal, bird, or fish before cooking it

PHRASAL VERB   ,clean (sth) 'up **1** to make a place completely clean and tidy: *Let's start getting this place cleaned up.* **2** to stop bad or criminal behaviour in a place or activity: *Does the government have plans to clean up the banking system?*

> **Build your vocabulary: words you can use instead of clean**
>
> - **brush** to clean something by rubbing it with a brush
> - **cleanse** to clean your skin thoroughly using a special liquid or cream
> - **dust** to remove dust from furniture and other surfaces using a soft cloth
> - **scrub** to clean something by rubbing it hard with a brush and soap and water
> - **sweep** to clean a floor using a brush with a long handle
> - **wash** to clean something using water and soap
> - **wipe** to clean a surface such as a table using a cloth that is slightly wet

clean³ /kliːn/ noun [singular] an occasion when you clean something

,clean-'cut adj a clean-cut man looks clean and tidy

cleaner /'kliːnə/ noun **1** [C] someone whose job is to clean the rooms in a building **2** [C] a chemical substance used for cleaning things **3 the cleaner's** [singular] a place where people can get clothes **dry-cleaned** (=cleaned with chemicals)

cleaning /'kliːnɪŋ/ noun [U] the activity or job of making rooms in a building clean

'cleaning ,agent noun [C] a substance that is used to clean things, especially in the home

cleanliness /'klenlinəs/ noun [U] the process of keeping yourself and your possessions clean

cleanly /'kliːnli/ adv **1** with one smooth movement **2** without creating a lot of mess or pollution

cleanse /klenz/ verb [T] **1** to clean your skin thoroughly **2** *formal* to get rid of someone or something bad or unpleasant → ETHNIC CLEANSING

,clean-'shaven adj a clean-shaven man does not have a beard or **moustache**

clear¹ /klɪə/ adj

1 obvious	7 without clouds
2 easy to understand	8 without guilt
3 easy to see/hear	9 showing nothing
4 transparent	wrong
5 not confused	10 time: available
6 not blocked	

1 obvious and certain to be true: *It appears to be a*

---

clear case of discrimination. ♦ *It was very* **clear that** something was worrying him.

2 easy to understand: *Clear instructions are provided.* ♦ *Let me* **make** *this* **clear** *– I will not help you again!*

3 easy to see or hear: *The picture was clear and sharp.*

4 transparent: *a clear glass bottle*

5 not confused: *Are you* **clear about** *the purpose of the meeting?*

6 if a surface, road, or passage is clear, there is nothing that blocks it: *a clear view of the mountains* ♦ *All the main roads are* **clear of** *snow.*

7 if the sky is clear, there are no clouds

8 not affected by guilty feelings: *She had done her duty, and her* **conscience was clear.**

9 if a medical test is clear, it shows that there is nothing wrong: *All the tests came back clear.*

10 if a period of time is clear, you have not arranged to do anything during it = FREE: *I'll keep Thursday afternoon clear in case we need to meet.*
→ CRYSTAL CLEAR

clear² /klɪə/ verb

1 empty a place	9 accept cheque
2 remove sth	10 stop being confused
3 prove sb not guilty	etc
4 weather: improve	11 deal with problem
5 give/get permission	12 do all your work
6 pass without touching	13 in sport
7 start to disappear	+ PHRASES
8 stop looking upset etc	

1 [T] to remove people or things from a place, or to become empty when people leave or things are removed: *Millions of acres of tropical forest have been cleared.* ♦ *The room cleared quickly after the speech.* ♦ *To start with, you should* **clear** *the ground of weeds.*

2 [T] to remove something that is blocking a place: *The police cleared a path to the front of the building.*

3 [T] to prove officially that someone did not do something wrong: *The two men* **were cleared of** *murder yesterday.*

4 [I] if the sky or the weather clears, it becomes brighter with no clouds or rain

5 [T] to give or obtain permission for something to happen: *You'll have to* **clear** *this project* **with** *head office.*

6 [T] to go over, under, or past an object without touching it: *The horse cleared the fence.*

7 [I] if something such as smoke clears, it starts to disappear

8 [I] if someone's face clears, they stop looking annoyed, upset, or confused: *She frowned for a moment, then her brow cleared.*

9 [I/T] if a cheque clears, or if a bank clears it, the bank allows the money to be used

10 [I/T] if your mind or head clears, or if it is cleared, it stops being confused, tired, or affected by something such as alcohol: *Clear your mind of all negative thoughts.*

11 [T] to deal successfully with a problem: *The company has cleared the main obstacle to concluding the sale.*

12 [T] to do all the work that you have to do: *Extra staff have had to be brought in to clear the backlog.*

13 [I/T] SPORTS if someone clears a ball or if it clears in a game such as football, they succeed in kicking or hitting it away from their goal

PHRASES   **clear the air** to discuss a problem or difficult situation with someone in order to make it better

clear your throat to make a noise in your throat before you speak, so that you can speak without any difficulty

clear³ /klɪə/ noun

  PHRASE **in the clear 1** no longer believed to be guilty of something bad or illegal **2** no longer in a difficult or dangerous situation

clear⁴ /klɪə/ adv completely away from something: *Stand clear of the closing doors.*

  PHRASE **keep/stay/steer clear of** to avoid someone or something unpleasant or dangerous: *No one mentioned the divorce, so Lisa decided to steer clear of that subject.*

clearance /'klɪərəns/ noun **1** [U] official permission to do something: *Security clearance for overseas students will now be valid for four years.* **2** [U] an amount of space between two things that keeps them from touching each other **3** [C] **SPORTS** a kick or hit of a ball away from a player's goal in a game such as football

'clearance ˌfit noun [U] **TECHNOLOGY** a fit between two machine parts, for example a **shaft** and a hole, in which the limits specified for the sizes of the parts result in a slight gap being left between them

'clearance ˌsale noun [C] **BUSINESS** an occasion when a shop sells things at very low prices in order to get rid of all of them, usually because it is going to stop doing business

ˌclear-'cut adj definite and easy to understand or make a decision about

clearing /'klɪərɪŋ/ noun [C] an area in a forest where there are no trees or bushes

clearly /'klɪəli/ adv **1** used for emphasizing that what you are saying is true= OBVIOUSLY: *Both companies clearly like to do things their own way.* **2** in a way that people can easily see, hear, or understand: *His contract clearly states that he cannot leave before next year.* ♦ *The road signs were clearly visible.* **3** in a way that is sensible and not confused: *I felt too tired to think clearly.*

cleat /kliːt/ noun [C] **1** a metal object that someone ties a rope round in order to fasten something in place, especially on a ship **2** a piece of metal or hard plastic fixed to the bottom of a shoe, in order to prevent it from slipping on the ground

cleavage /'kliːvɪdʒ/ noun [C] the space between a woman's breasts

cleaver /'kliːvə/ noun [C] a knife with a large heavy blade, used for cutting large pieces of meat

clef /klef/ noun [C] **MUSIC** a symbol written at the beginning of a line of music to show the **pitch** of the notes

cleft /kleft/ noun [C] a narrow space in the surface of something, for example in a rock or in someone's chin

ˌcleft 'palate noun [C] **HEALTH** a medical condition in which there is a narrow space in the **palate** (=inside upper part) of someone's mouth, so that it is difficult for them to speak clearly

'cleft ˌsentence noun [C] **LANGUAGE** a sentence that starts with a pronoun such as 'it' or 'that' and the verb 'to be' in order to emphasize the next word, which is followed by another clause, for example 'It's you I wanted to talk to.' or 'That's my seat you're in.'

clemency /'klemənsi/ noun [U] *formal* a decision not to punish someone severely, made by someone in a position of authority

clench /klentʃ/ verb **clench your teeth/jaw/fist** to press your teeth or fingers together tightly because you are angry or upset

clergy /'klɜːdʒi/ noun [plural] **RELIGION** priests and other people who lead religious services

clerical /'klerɪk(ə)l/ adj **1** connected with the ordinary work that people do in offices **2** **RELIGION** relating to priests

clerk /klɑːk/ noun [C] someone whose job is to look after the documents in an office

clever /'klevə/ adj **1** good at learning or understanding things= INTELLIGENT: *I'd like to be a doctor but I'm not clever enough.* **2** good at achieving what you want, especially by using your intelligence or using slightly dishonest methods: *She had a clever lawyer.* **3** a clever tool or idea is effective because it was designed in an intelligent way —**cleverly** adv, **cleverness** noun [U]

cliché /'kliːʃeɪ/ noun [C] **LANGUAGE** a phrase or idea that is boring because people use it a lot and it is no longer original —**clichéd** adj

click¹ /klɪk/ verb **1** [I/T] to make a short high sound like the sound of a switch, or to make an object make this sound: *The cameras continued clicking as the President drove away.* ♦ *The young soldier clicked his heels and saluted.* **2** [I/T] **COMPUTING** to make a computer do something by pressing a button on the mouse: *To send the message, click on the 'send' button.* **3** [I] *informal* if something clicks, you suddenly understand or realize it

click² /klɪk/ noun [C] **1** a short sound like the sound of a switch **2** **COMPUTING** the action of making a computer do something by pressing a button on the mouse

clickable /'klɪkəb(ə)l/ adj **COMPUTING** if something on a computer screen is clickable, you make it work by clicking on it with the mouse

client /'klaɪənt/ noun [C] someone who uses the services of a professional person such as a lawyer, or of a business or organization that provides help or advice: *Our clients are not all wealthy people.*

clientele /ˌkliːɒn'tel/ noun [singular] the customers of a shop, hotel, or restaurant

ˌclient-'server adj **COMPUTING** used for referring to a **network** (=group of computers) in which each computer is either a **client** or a **server**. **Clients** are the individual computers that run programs, or the equipment connected to them such as printers, and **servers** are the powerful computers that supply the information that makes them work.

'client ˌstate noun [C] **POLITICS** a country that depends on another country for economic help or military protection, so that it is to some degree controlled by it

cliff /klɪf/ noun [C] **GEOGRAPHY** the steep side of an area of high land —*picture* → BACKWASH

cliffhanger /'klɪfˌhæŋə/ noun [C] *informal* **1** an exciting end to a part of a book or television programme **2** a situation in which it is not clear what will happen next

cliff jumping /'klɪf ˌdʒʌmpɪŋ/ noun [U] the sport of jumping from a high place such as a cliff into water

climactic /klaɪ'mæktɪk/ adj a climactic event or moment is the most exciting or important one in a series

climate /'klaɪmət/ noun **1** [C/U] **GEOGRAPHY** the average and usual weather conditions of a particular country or region, for example its temperature and how much rain it gets: *Japan has a temperate climate, with cool springs and autumns.* ♦ *How will the change in climate affect food production?* → CLIMATE CHANGE **2** [C] the general situation or attitudes that people have at a particular time: *We are unable to increase wages in* the current **economic climate**. ♦ *a climate of* fear and mistrust

'climate ,change noun [U] ENVIRONMENT important and possibly harmful changes that are taking place in the world's weather. Most scientists believe increased pollution in the atmosphere is the cause of the **greenhouse effect** and **global warming**.

climatic /klaɪˈmætɪk/ adj GEOGRAPHY relating to the type of weather that a place has

climatology /ˌklaɪməˈtɒlədʒi/ noun [U] GEOGRAPHY the study of climate

climax /ˈklaɪmæks/ noun [C] the most exciting or important moment in a story, event, or situation, usually near the end: *the climax to* this season's *Champions' Cup*

climb¹ /klaɪm/ verb **1** [I/T] to use your hands and feet to move up, over, down, or across something: *He climbed onto the roof.* ♦ *We escaped by climbing through a window.* ♦ *I didn't think he could climb the wall.* **2** [T] to walk up a slope or up some steps: *We left the road and climbed the hill.* **3** [I] to get into or out of something, especially by stepping to a higher or lower position: *Sara climbed wearily into bed.* **4** [I] if something such as a temperature, price, or level climbs, it becomes higher: *Their profits climbed from £20 million to £50 million last year.*

climb² /klaɪm/ noun [singular] an occasion when you go up a slope or up some steps

'climb-,down noun [C] a change of attitude in which someone admits that they were wrong

climber /ˈklaɪmə/ noun [C] someone who takes part in the activity of climbing

climbing /ˈklaɪmɪŋ/ noun [U] the activity of climbing mountains and rocks for enjoyment and exercise

'climbing ,frame noun [C] a large structure designed for children to climb on

'climbing ,wall noun [C] a wall with special holes, cracks, and lumps in it, usually in a building, that people use for practising climbing rocks

climb milling /ˈklaɪm ˌmɪlɪŋ/ noun [U] TECHNOLOGY a method of **milling** (=cutting metal with a rotating tool) in which the material moves in the same direction as the rotating cutter

climograph /ˈklaɪməˌɡrɑːf/ noun [C] GEOGRAPHY a graph that shows the average temperatures and **rainfall** in an area

clinch /klɪntʃ/ verb [T] to manage to win or achieve something by doing one final thing that makes it certain

cling /klɪŋ/ (clings, clinging, clung /klʌŋ/) verb [I] **1** to hold onto something or someone tightly, for example because you are afraid: *Some children were crying and clinging to their mothers.* **2** to stick to something, or to fit very tightly on something: *Gareth's wet clothes clung to his body.* **3** to try very hard to keep something **4** to keep believing that something is right or real, even though other people do not

clinic /ˈklɪnɪk/ noun [C] HEALTH a place where people go to receive a particular type of medical treatment or advice

clinical /ˈklɪnɪk(ə)l/ adj **1** HEALTH involving working with people who are ill, rather than in a laboratory: *a clinical study of the drug* **2** HEALTH relating to an illness: *clinical depression* **3** not showing any excitement or emotion: *a cold and clinical manner* —**clinically** /ˈklɪnɪkli/ adv

'clinical ther,mometer noun [C] HEALTH a piece of equipment for measuring the temperature of the human body

,clinical 'trial noun [C] a test of a new medicine that involves giving it to people

clinician /klɪˈnɪʃ(ə)n/ noun [C] HEALTH a doctor who works directly with people who are ill

clink /klɪŋk/ verb [I/T] to make a short high sound like glass or metal objects hitting each other —**clink** noun [singular]

clinker /ˈklɪŋkə/ noun [U] TECHNOLOGY a hard lump of waste that is left after coal has been burnt

clint /klɪnt/ noun [C] GEOLOGY one of the flat blocks of stone in a **limestone pavement**

clip¹ /klɪp/ (clips, clipping, clipped) verb **1** [I/T] to fasten something somewhere using a small object, or to be fastened somewhere in this way: *Clip the microphone to your shirt.* **2** [I/T] to be pressed or to press something into position, so that it makes a quick loud sound **3** [T] to cut off small parts of something in order to make it tidy: *I clipped my nails.* **4** [T] to hit something accidentally while passing it

clip² /klɪp/ noun [C] **1** a small object that holds something in position: *hair clips* **2** a short part of a film or television programme that is shown separately → PAPERCLIP

'clip ,art noun [U] COMPUTING pictures and designs that you can put into documents that you create on a computer

clipboard /ˈklɪpˌbɔːd/ noun [C] **1** a small board that someone carries and attaches papers to so that they can write while they are moving around **2** COMPUTING the part of a computer program where information is stored temporarily so that it can be copied to another document

clippers /ˈklɪpəz/ noun [plural] an object used for cutting things to make them tidy, consisting of two blades that you press or push together: *nail clippers*

clipping /ˈklɪpɪŋ/ noun [C] **1** an article that has been cut out of a newspaper or magazine = CUTTING **2** a small piece that you remove when you cut something to make it tidy

clique /kliːk/ noun [C] a small group of people who seem unfriendly to other people

clitoris /ˈklɪtərɪs/ noun [C] ANATOMY the small sensitive part of the female sex organs, just above the entrance to the vagina

cloak /kləʊk/ noun [C] a long coat without sleeves that fastens around the neck

cloakroom /ˈkləʊkˌruːm/ noun [C] a room in a theatre or restaurant where people can leave their coats

clock /klɒk/ noun [C] an object that shows the time. The similar object that someone wears on their wrist is called a **watch**: *The only sound was the clock ticking.* ♦ *I glanced at the kitchen clock.*

PHRASES **around/round the clock** all day and all night: *Rescuers worked around the clock to free people trapped in the wreckage.*
put/turn/set the clock back 1 to change the time on a clock to an earlier time **2** to return to a time in the past: *If we could turn the clock back, would you actually change anything?*

'clock ,speed noun [C] COMPUTING the speed at which a computer works, usually measured in **megahertz** or **gigahertz**

clockwise /ˈklɒkˌwaɪz/ adj, adv moving in a circle in the same direction as the **hands** on a clock ≠ ANTICLOCKWISE

clockwork /ˈklɒkˌwɜːk/ noun **like clockwork** happening or working correctly, with no problems

clog /klɒg/ (**clogs, clogging, clogged**) verb [I/T] to block something such as a pipe, or to become blocked

clogs /klɒgz/ noun [plural] shoes with wooden **soles**

cloister /ˈklɔɪstə/ noun [C] **RELIGION** a covered path around an open area in the centre of a large building such as a cathedral or **monastery**

clone1 /kləʊn/ noun [C] **1 BIOLOGY** an animal or plant that has been created artificially, using the DNA from one parent cell or organism to produce an animal or plant that is genetically the same as the parent, as opposed to one that **inherits** the genes of both parents through sexual reproduction **2 COMPUTING** a computer or program designed to work in the same way as another computer or program

clone2 /kləʊn/ verb [T] **BIOLOGY** to create an animal or plant in a laboratory that is an exact copy of another, using the DNA of the original animal or plant

cloning /ˈkləʊnɪŋ/ noun [U] **BIOLOGY** the artificial production of new animals or plants that are genetically exactly the same as one parent, rather than having the genetic characteristics of two parents

close1 /kləʊz/ verb

1 shut	6 reduce
2 stop doing business	distance/difference
3 stop operating	7 stop account
4 end/finish	8 of computer program
5 stop access to	+ PHRASAL VERBS

1 [I/T] if you close something, or if it closes, it moves to cover an open area: *I was just **closing** my **eyes** to go to sleep when the phone rang.* ♦ *Did you close the door?*
2 [I/T] to stop doing business for a short time: *We close the office at noon on Fridays.* ♦ *Heavy rain forced both airports to close.*
3 [I/T] to stop existing as a business, or to stop something operating as a business: *The government plans to close 10 coal mines.* ♦ *Small shops are closing because of competition from supermarkets.*
4 [I/T] if an activity or event closes, or if you close it, it ends: *Her latest show closed after only three performances.* ♦ *He closed the meeting by thanking everyone for coming.*
5 [T] to stop people from entering a place or using a road: *The bridge will have to be **closed for** repairs.*
6 close or **close up** [I/T] to reduce the distance or difference between people or things: ***Closing the gap between** rich and poor would help to improve the health of the nation.*
7 [T] to stop having an account with a bank, shop etc: *We **closed** our bank **account** and opened a new one online.*
8 [I/T] **COMPUTING** if a computer program closes, or if you close it, it stops operating and disappears from your computer screen

PHRASAL VERBS **close 'in** to move nearer to someone, especially in order to surround them: *Armed police began **closing in on** the house.*
,close sth 'off to prevent people from entering a place or using a road

close2 /kləʊs/ (**closer, closest**) adj

1 near	7 directly related
2 short time away	8 very involved
3 likely to happen soon	9 almost equal to sth
4 careful	10 not easily won
5 similar	11 warm
6 very friendly	12 guarded carefully

1 only a short distance away: *We can walk to the swimming pool – it's quite close.* ♦ *The hotel is **close to** the centre of town.*
2 only a short time away: *Sam's birthday is **close to** Christmas.*

3 likely to happen soon: *Everyone believes that a peace deal is close.* ♦ *We're **closer to** signing a contract after today's meeting.* ♦ *She was **close to tears** (=almost crying) as she said goodbye to her sister.*
4 giving careful attention to every detail: *I'll take a **closer look** at it tomorrow.* ♦ *The local police **kept a close eye on** his activities.*
5 similar to something but not exactly the same: *That's not exactly the colour I want, but it's close.* ♦ *The sensation is **close to** the feeling of floating.*
6 connected by shared feelings such as love and respect: *My brother and I are very close.* ♦ *close friends* ♦ *She's **close to** both her parents.*
7 related to you directly, for example by being your parent, child, brother, or sister: *my close relatives*
8 directly involved with someone and communicating with them a lot: *a close business associate* ♦ *We worked in close cooperation with local people.*
9 almost the same as a particular amount or number: *Unemployment on the island is **close to** 12 per cent.*
10 if a game, competition, or election is close, the scores of the players, teams etc are nearly equal
11 warm and uncomfortable because there is not enough fresh air
12 protected, watched, or guarded in a very careful and strict way: *a close secret* ♦ *The boys are being kept under close supervision for the rest of the term.*
—**closeness** noun [U]
→ CLOSELY

close3 /kləʊs/ (**closer, closest**) adv **1** only a short distance away: *She moved closer, trying to hear what Jack was saying.* ♦ *He clutched his bag **close to** his chest.* **2** only a short time away: *As the summer grew closer, we started to think about a holiday.*

PHRASES **close on/to sth** almost: *Close on 500 people attended the meeting.*
close up or **up close** from only a short distance away: *I didn't see his face close up.*
come close to (doing) sth to nearly do something: *I came close to giving up several times.*

close4 /kləʊz/ noun [singular] the end of something such as a period of time or an event: *towards the **close of** the 18th century*

close5 /kləʊs/ noun [C] **1** a street consisting of private houses at the end of which the road stops **2** the area around a cathedral including the buildings belonging to it

close corporation /ˌkləʊs ˌkɔːpəˈreɪʃ(ə)n/ noun [C] **BUSINESS** a company with a limited number of people who own its shares, often members of the same family

closed /kləʊzd/ adj

1 covering passage/hole	4 not considering ideas
2 not doing business	5 with fixed number of
3 not allowed to	sth
everyone	+ PHRASE

1 not open: *All the doors and windows were closed and locked.*
2 not operating or doing business ≠ OPEN: *All the shops were closed.* ♦ *This part of the museum is **closed to** the public.*
3 held in private, with no journalists or members of the public allowed: *Cases of this type are tried in a closed military court.*
4 not willing to consider the ideas, opinions, or beliefs of other people or groups: *You can't approach these kind of situations with a closed mind.*
5 with a fixed or limited number of parts, members, or answers = LIMITED: *The law is not a closed set of rules and principles.*

PHRASE **behind closed doors** in a place where other people cannot see or know what is happening

closed-captioned /ˌkləʊzd ˈkæpʃ(ə)nd/ adj a closed-captioned television programme has the words being spoken written at the bottom of the screen, for people who do not hear well

ˌclosed-ˌcircuit teleˈvision noun [U] **CCTV**

ˌclosed-ˌcircuit ˈvoltage noun [U] **TECHNOLOGY** the voltage between the terminals of a welding machine when there is an **electric arc** (=continuous electric spark), or when welding is in progress

ˈclosed ˌsyllable noun [C] **LANGUAGE** a syllable that has a consonant at its end

close-knit /ˌkləʊs ˈnɪt/ adj consisting of people who like and support each other: *a close-knit family*

closely /ˈkləʊsli/ adv **1** in a way that involves careful attention to every detail: *Inspectors will examine the accounts very closely.* **2** in a way that involves sharing ideas, thoughts, or feelings: *We are all working closely with each other.* **3** in a way that is very similar to something, or that has a strong connection with it: *The Northern Ireland economy is closely linked to that of the rest of the United Kingdom.* **4** with very little time or distance between one thing and another

closer /ˈkləʊzə/ noun [C] **CONSTRUCTION** a brick cut in half along its length and built into a wall, half a brick away from a corner

close-run /ˌkləʊs ˈrʌn/ adj won or settled by only a few points, votes etc

close-up /ˈkləʊs ʌp/ noun [C] a photograph of someone or something that is taken from a position very near them

close vowel /ˌkləʊs ˈvaʊəl/ noun [C] **LANGUAGE** a vowel sound made with the tongue near the top of the mouth

closing /ˈkləʊzɪŋ/ adj happening at the end of something: *the closing moments of the game*

ˈclosing ˌdate noun [C] the date by which something must be done

closure /ˈkləʊʒə/ noun [C/U] an occasion when a business or institution stops operating permanently, or the process of stopping it: *an increase in hospital closures*

clot¹ /klɒt/ noun [C] **HEALTH** a blood clot

clot² /klɒt/ (**clots, clotting, clotted**) verb [I] if blood or another liquid clots, it becomes thick and stops flowing

cloth /klɒθ/ noun **1** [C/U] material used for making things such as clothes and curtains: *cotton cloth* **2** [C] a piece of cloth that is used for a particular purpose such as cleaning or covering a table

clothe /kləʊð/ verb [T] to provide someone with clothes

clothed /kləʊðd/ adj dressed in a particular way

clothes /kləʊðz/ noun [plural] shirts, dresses, trousers, and other things that people wear: *a pile of dirty clothes* ◆ *a clothes shop* ◆ *I'm going to **put on** some clean **clothes**. ◆ Why don't you **take** those wet **clothes off**?*

> **Build your vocabulary: words you can use instead of clothes**
>
> ■ **Clothes** is a general word meaning 'things that you wear'. It is always plural: *His clothes were dirty.* ◆ *I bought some new clothes.* If you want to talk about 'one thing that you wear' use **a piece/an item of clothing**.

■ **Dress** is a less common word and refers to special clothes that are typical of a particular country or time: *men in national dress*

■ A **dress** is a single piece of clothing worn by a woman.

■ **Cloth** is material made of cotton or other fabrics, used for making clothes, curtains etc.

clothing /ˈkləʊðɪŋ/ noun [U] clothes: *a piece of clothing* ◆ *waterproof clothing* ◆ *the clothing industry*

cloud¹ /klaʊd/ noun [C] **1** **GEOGRAPHY** a white or grey mass of drops of water in the sky: *a few white clouds in the sky* ◆ *There's more cloud than yesterday.* —picture → on next page **2** a large amount of something such as smoke or dust in the air: *a huge cloud of black smoke* **3** something unpleasant that spoils a situation: *Violent protests cast a cloud over the president's visit.*

cloud² /klaʊd/ verb **1** [T] to affect your ability to think in a sensible way: *Make sure that your feelings do not cloud your judgment.* **2** [I] to become darker because grey clouds are forming in the sky **3** [T] to make something more complicated or confusing: *Unanswered questions have further clouded the issue.* **4** [I/T] if something such as glass clouds, or if something clouds it, it becomes difficult to see through

cloudless /ˈklaʊdləs/ adj a cloudless sky has no clouds in it

cloudy /ˈklaʊdi/ (**cloudier, cloudiest**) adj **1** full of clouds **2** a cloudy liquid is not clear

clove /kləʊv/ noun [C] **1** a brown dried flower bud that is a spice, used for adding flavour to food **2** a section of a bulb of **garlic**

cloven hoof /ˌkləʊv(ə)n ˈhuːf/ noun [C] **BIOLOGY** the foot of an mammal such as a cow or a sheep that has two separate parts

clover /ˈkləʊvə/ noun [U] a small flowering plant with leaves that have three round parts. Farmers grow clover for feeding cows and to improve the soil.

clown /klaʊn/ noun [C] **1** a performer in a **circus** who wears funny clothes and does silly things **2** someone who is stupid or annoying

club¹ /klʌb/ noun

1 society for activity	4 stick for golf
2 sports team & staff	5 suit of playing cards
3 place for dancing	6 stick as weapon

1 [C] an organization for people who take part in a particular activity, or the building that they use: *Why don't you **join a** chess **club**?* ◆ *Are you **a member of** the club?*
2 [C] **SPORTS** a team of sports players and the staff who work with them: *Manchester United football club*
3 [C] a place where people go in the evening to dance and drink
4 [C] **SPORTS** a long object like a stick used for hitting the ball in golf= GOLF CLUB
5 clubs [plural] the **suit** (=group) of playing cards that has a pattern of three black balls on a black stem: *the king of clubs*
6 [C] a thick heavy stick used as a weapon

club² /klʌb/ (**clubs, clubbing, clubbed**) verb [T] to hit someone with a heavy object

ˈclub ˌclass noun [U] **TOURISM** the part of a plane in which the seats cost more than **economy class** or **tourist class** but less than **first class**= BUSINESS CLASS

ˌclub ˈfoot noun [C] **HEALTH** a foot twisted to one side as a result of a medical condition —ˌclub-ˈfooted adj

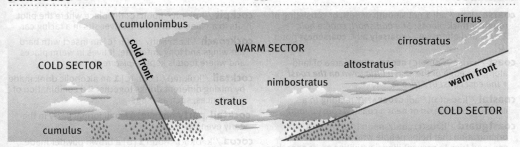

cumulonimbus

cirrus

cirrostratus

WARM SECTOR

cold front

altostratus

nimbostratus

warm front

COLD SECTOR

COLD SECTOR

stratus

cumulus

clouds

clubhouse /'klʌb,haʊs/ noun [C] the building used by members of a sports club

cluck /klʌk/ verb [I] if a chicken clucks, it makes its usual short low sound —**cluck** noun [C]

clue /klu:/ noun [C] **1** an object or fact that helps someone to solve a crime or mystery: *Detectives were brought in to help* **search for clues**. ♦ *Police still have no* **clues as to** *the identity of the killer.* **2** a piece of information that helps you to understand something: *His face gave her no* **clue as to** *what he was thinking.* **3** a word or phrase provided to help you to guess the answer in a **crossword**

PHRASE **not have a clue** *informal* to not know or understand something: *'What's wrong with him?' 'I don't have a clue.'*

clued up /,klu:d 'ʌp/ adj *informal* someone who is clued up knows about a particular subject or situation

clump[1] /klʌmp/ noun [C] a group of plants growing very close together

clump[2] /klʌmp/ verb [I] **BIOLOGY** when particles clump, they come together to form a solid mass

clumsy /'klʌmzi/ (**clumsier, clumsiest**) adj **1** a clumsy person often has accidents because they are not careful **2** a clumsy object is too large and heavy to be useful **3** showing a lack of skill in judging people or situations —**clumsily** adv, **clumsiness** noun [U]

clung /klʌŋ/ the past tense and past participle of **cling**

cluster[1] /'klʌstə/ noun [C] **1** a small group of things that are very close to each other **2** a series of events of the same type, for example cases of a disease, that all happen in the same place or around the same time **3** **ASTRONOMY** a group of stars that are close to each other

cluster[2] /'klʌstə/ verb [I] to form a small close group

clustered /'klʌstəd/ adj occurring close together

clutch[1] /klʌtʃ/ verb [T] to hold someone or something firmly

clutch[2] /klʌtʃ/ noun **1** [C] **ENGINEERING** a piece of equipment in a vehicle that a driver presses with their foot to change gear. The clutch connects or disconnects the vehicle's engine to the **transmission**. **2** [singular] a firm hold that you have on someone or something, usually because you are afraid or in pain **3 clutches** [plural] power or control over someone: *They left the country to escape the clutches of the secret police.*

clutch ,plate noun [C] **ENGINEERING** a disc in a clutch that uses **friction** to make the engine and the **transmission** turn at the same speed

clutter[1] /'klʌtə/ or ,**clutter sth 'up** verb [T] to put too many things in a place so that it looks untidy

clutter[2] /'klʌtə/ noun [U] the mess created when there are too many things in a place

cm abbrev centimetre

cm[2] abbrev **1** **MATHS** square centimetre **2** centimetre squared

cm[3] abbrev **1** **MATHS** cubic centimetre **2** centimetre cubed

CNC abbrev **COMPUTING** computer numerical control: the use of computers in **manufacturing** to control machines that cut and shape parts

cnidarian /naɪ'deəriən/ noun [C] **BIOLOGY** a type of sea animal, a **coelenterate**

CNS /,si: en 'es/ abbrev **HEALTH** **central nervous system**

Co. /kəʊ/ abbrev **1** Company **2** County

co- /kəʊ/ prefix **1** together: used with some nouns, verbs, and adjectives: *coeducation* (=the education of boys and girls together) **2** sharing a job or responsibility: used with some nouns, verbs, and adjectives: *her co-star* (=another main actor taking part with her in the film)

c/o abbrev care of: used in an address on a letter that you are sending to someone at another person's house

coach[1] /kəʊtʃ/ noun [C] **1** **SPORTS** someone who trains a sports player or team: *a baseball coach* **2** a comfortable bus for long journeys **3** one of the sections of a train = CARRIAGE **4** a vehicle pulled by horses, used in the past

coach[2] /kəʊtʃ/ verb [T] **1** **SPORTS** to train a sports player or team **2** to teach someone a particular skill **3** to tell someone what to say or do in a particular situation —**coaching** noun [U]

coach ,party noun [C] **TOURISM** a group of tourists, travelling by **coach**

coagulate /kəʊ'ægjʊleɪt/ verb [I] if a liquid coagulates, it becomes thick and almost solid

coal /kəʊl/ noun **1** [U] **GEOLOGY** a hard black substance consisting mainly of carbon that is dug from the ground and burned as fuel. It is made from **fossilized** plants and is a type of **fossil fuel**: *a lump of coal* ♦ *the coal industry* **2 coals** [plural] pieces of burning coal

PHRASE **haul sb over the coals** to speak angrily to someone because they have done something wrong

coalesce /,kəʊə'les/ verb [I/T] *formal* to come together and form a group or a single unit

coal-fired /,kəʊl 'faɪəd/ adj operated by burning coal

coalition /,kəʊə'lɪʃ(ə)n/ noun [C] a government formed by different political parties that are working together for a short time

coal ,mine noun [C] a place where coal is dug up from under the ground —**coal mining** noun [U]

coarse /kɔːs/ adj **1** not smooth or soft, or consisting of rough or thick pieces: *She had short, coarse hair.* **2** rude and offensive —**coarsely** adv, **coarseness** noun [U]

coast /kəʊst/ noun [C] **GEOGRAPHY** an area of land along the edge of the sea: *a little town on the coast* ♦ *the east coast of Africa* → SHORE

coastal /'kəʊst(ə)l/ adj **GEOGRAPHY** relating to a coast, or existing on or near a coast: *a coastal road*

coastguard /'kəʊs(t),gɑːd/ noun [C/U] a person or organization that helps people who are in trouble at sea, and tries to prevent illegal activities on or near the coast

coastline /'kəʊst,laɪn/ noun [C] **GEOGRAPHY** the land along a coast, or the shape that it makes

coat¹ /kəʊt/ noun [C] **1** a piece of clothing with long sleeves that someone wears over other clothes when they go outside in cold weather: *Put your coat on – we're going out.* **2** the fur or hair on an animal's skin **3** a layer of something such as paint on a surface
PHRASE **coat of arms** a special design that is used as the symbol of a family, institution, city etc

coat² /kəʊt/ verb [T] to cover something with a layer of a substance

'coat ,hanger noun [C] a frame used for hanging clothes on

coating /'kəʊtɪŋ/ noun [C] a thin layer that covers a surface

coax /kəʊks/ verb [T] **coax sb into/out of (doing) sth** to gently persuade someone to do something

cobalt /'kəʊ,bɔːlt/ noun [U] **1** a blue-green colour **2** a hard silver-white metal element used to make alloys and for colouring things such as clay **pottery** blue. Chemical symbol: **Co**

cobbled /'kɒb(ə)ld/ adj a cobbled street or road surface is made from many small round stones fixed closely together

cobblestones /'kɒb(ə)lstəʊnz/ noun [plural] small stones with round tops used in the past to make the surface of a road

cobra /'kəʊbrə/ noun [C] a poisonous African or Asian snake —*picture* → REPTILE

cobweb /'kɒb,web/ noun [C] a net that a spider makes out of thin sticky strings to catch insects in

cocaine /kəʊ'keɪn/ noun [U] **HEALTH** a strong illegal drug, usually sold in the form of a white powder, that causes feelings of increased energy and excitement. It is also sometimes used in medicine as a local anaesthetic.

coccyx /'kɒksɪks/ noun [C] **ANATOMY** the small bone at the bottom of the spine

cochlea /'kɒkliə/ noun [C] **ANATOMY** a part of the **inner ear** that has a spiral shape. It contains very small hairs that move when sound waves come into the ear. —*picture* → EAR

cock /kɒk/ noun [C] a male bird, especially a male chicken. A male chicken is also called a **cockerel**.

cockatoo /,kɒkə'tuː/ noun [C] a type of Australian **parrot**

cockerel /'kɒk(ə)rəl/ noun [C] a young male chicken —*picture* → BIRD

cockney /'kɒkni/ (plural **cockneys**) or **Cockney** noun **1** [U] a type of informal English spoken in London **2** [C] someone who speaks cockney —**cockney** adj

cockpit /'kɒk,pɪt/ noun [C] the place where the pilot sits in a plane or where the driver sits in a racing car

cockroach /'kɒkrəʊtʃ/ noun [C] an insect with hard flat wings and long antennae. It lives in warm places and where food is kept. —*picture* → INSECT

cocktail /'kɒk,teɪl/ noun [C] **1** an alcoholic drink made by mixing different drinks together **2** a combination of substances, such as drugs

'cocktail ,party noun [C] a small formal party in the early evening

cocoa /'kəʊkəʊ/ noun **1** [U] a brown powder made from a cocoa bean. It is used for making chocolate and chocolate-flavoured food and drinks. **2** [C/U] a hot drink made from this powder **3** [U] **AGRICULTURE** a crop plant that produces cocoa beans

'cocoa ,bean noun [C] the seed of the **cacao** tree that is crushed to make cocoa

coconut /'kəʊkə,nʌt/ noun **1** [C] a large nut that has a hard brown shell and white flesh —*picture* → FRUIT **2** [U] the white flesh of a coconut, that can be eaten

'coconut ,milk noun [U] the sweet thin liquid contained in a coconut, used in drinks and in Asian and Caribbean cooking

cocoon /kə'kuːn/ noun [C] **1** **BIOLOGY** a cover that some young insects make to protect themselves while they change into their adult form **2** something that keeps you safe, but may stop you from learning to deal with problems

cod /kɒd/ (plural **cod**) noun [C/U] a large sea fish that can be eaten

coda /'kəʊdə/ noun [C] **1** **MUSIC** the final section of a long piece of music **2** the final part of a piece of writing or a speech that acts as a summary **3** something that happens at the end of a series of events

code¹ /kəʊd/ noun

1 for secret messages	4 computer instructions
2 set of rules	5 complicated system
3 set of letters/numbers	+ PHRASE

1 [C/U] a system of words, numbers, or signs used for sending secret messages: *The message was written in code.* ♦ *They never cracked the enemy's code* (=discovered how it worked).
2 [C] a set of rules about how something should be done or how people should behave: *the company's code of conduct*
3 [C] a set of numbers, letters, or symbols used for a particular purpose, for example to give information about a product or as part of a phone number
4 [C/U] **COMPUTING** a set of instructions that a computer can understand
5 [singular] a complicated system of rules, relationships, or instructions: *the genetic code*
PHRASE **code of practice** a set of rules about how people in a particular profession should behave in their work

code² /kəʊd/ verb **1** [T] to mark something with a code that gives information about it **2** [T] to put a message in code so that it is secret **3** [I/T] **COMPUTING** to write instructions for a computer

coded /'kəʊdɪd/ adj written using a secret system of words or signs

'code ,name noun [C] a name for someone or something that is used in order to keep their real name secret

code-sharing /'kəʊd ,ʃeərɪŋ/ noun [U] **BUSINESS** an arrangement between two **airlines** in which they both sell seats on a flight using their own flight numbers

code switching /'kəʊd ˌswɪtʃɪŋ/ noun [U] LANGUAGE the practice of changing from using one language to using another when you are speaking

codicil /'kəʊdɪsɪl, 'kɒdɪsɪl/ noun [C] LAW an addition that makes changes to a **will** (=a legal document saying who gets someone's money and property when they die)

codify /'kəʊdɪfaɪ/ verb [T] to make something part of an organized system, especially an official system of laws

codomain /ˌkəʊdəʊ'meɪn/ noun [C] MATHS a set containing all the **values** (=numbers represented by letters) of a particular **function** (=a quantity that changes according to how another quantity changes)

coeducation /ˌkəʊedjʊ'keɪʃ(ə)n/ noun [U] EDUCATION the system of educating students of both sexes in the same class or college —**coeducational** adj

coefficient /ˌkəʊɪ'fɪʃ(ə)nt/ noun [C] MATHS a number written before a **variable** that shows how much the variable is to be multiplied by

coelacanth /'siːləkænθ/ noun [C] a large fish that lives in the Indian Ocean and was previously thought to be extinct

coelenterate /sɪ'lentəˌreɪt/ noun [C] BIOLOGY an invertebrate sea animal that has **tentacles** around a single opening for taking in food and getting rid of waste. **Jellyfish, sea anemones,** and **corals** are coelenterates.

coeliac disease /'siːliæk dɪˌziːz/ noun [U] HEALTH a medical condition in which the body cannot digest food that contains **gluten** (=wheat protein)

coelom /'siːləm/ noun [C] BIOLOGY the space between the body wall and the intestine of many animals. It is formed when **mesoderm** tissue divides into two layers in an embryo.

coerce /kəʊ'ɜːs/ verb [T] to make someone do something by using force or threats

coercion /kəʊ'ɜːʃ(ə)n/ noun [U] the use of force or threats to make someone do something

coexist /ˌkəʊɪg'zɪst/ verb [I] formal to live or exist at the same time or in the same place —**coexistence** /ˌkəʊɪg'zɪstəns/ noun [U]

ˌC of 'C abbrev **chamber of commerce**

C of E /ˌsiː əv 'iː/ abbrev RELIGION Church of England

coffee /'kɒfi/ noun **1** [U] a hot brown drink made by pouring hot water over crushed beans: Would you like a cup of coffee? **2** [C] a cup of this drink: Can we have three coffees please? **3** [U] a light brown colour

'coffee ˌtable noun [C] a small low table in a **living room**

coffin /'kɒfɪn/ noun [C] a box in which a dead person is buried

cog /kɒg/ noun [C] PHYSICS a wheel in a machine that fits into the edge of another wheel and makes it turn

cogent /'kəʊdʒ(ə)nt/ adj formal a cogent argument is reasonable and sensible —**cogently** adv

cogitate /'kɒdʒɪteɪt/ verb [I] formal to think about something carefully and for a long time

cognate¹ /'kɒgneɪt/ noun [C] LANGUAGE a word in a language that has the same origin as a word in a different language

cognate² /'kɒgneɪt/ adj LANGUAGE cognate words or languages have the same origin

cognition /kɒg'nɪʃ(ə)n/ noun [U] the activity of recognizing and understanding things

cognitive /'kɒgnətɪv/ adj in **psychology**, a cognitive science or process is one that is connected with recognizing and understanding things —**cognitively** adv

cognizant /'kɒgnɪz(ə)nt/ adj formal if you are cognizant of something, you know about it and understand it —**cognizance** noun [U]

cohabit /kəʊ'hæbɪt/ verb [I] formal if two people cohabit, they live together and have a sexual relationship without being married —**cohabitation** /kəʊˌhæbɪ'teɪʃ(ə)n/ noun [U]

coherent /kəʊ'hɪərənt/ adj clear and sensible, or capable of being understood ≠ INCOHERENT — **coherence** /kəʊ'hɪərəns/ noun [U], **coherently** adv

cohesion /kəʊ'hiːʒ(ə)n/ noun [U] **1** a situation in which people or things combine well to form a unit: The common threat of war produces cohesion in a community. **2** LANGUAGE a relationship between sentences or parts of a piece of writing that is shown by particular words or phrases —**cohesive** /kəʊ'hiːsɪv/ adj

coil¹ /kɔɪl/ noun [C] **1** a long piece of rope, hair, or wire, that forms several circles, each on top of the other **2** PHYSICS a piece of curved wire that produces heat or light when electricity passes through it **3** ENGINEERING a part of a vehicle's engine that supplies electricity to the **spark plugs**

coil² /kɔɪl/ verb [I/T] to make something into a coil, or to form a coil —**coiled** /kɔɪld/ adj

'coil ˌspring noun [C] ENGINEERING a type of spring used in vehicles, especially in the **suspension**

coin /kɔɪn/ noun [C] a flat round piece of metal used as money

   PHRASE **two sides of the same coin** two different aspects of the same situation

coincide /ˌkəʊɪn'saɪd/ verb [I] **1** to happen at the same time as something else: The statement was timed to coincide with the General's return to Algiers. **2** if ideas or opinions coincide, they agree with one another = CORRESPOND

coincidence /kəʊ'ɪnsɪd(ə)ns/ noun [C/U] an unusual situation in which two things happen by chance at the same time or in the same way

coincidental /kəʊˌɪnsɪ'dent(ə)l/ adj happening or existing by chance and not because of being planned or intended —**coincidentally** adv

coitus /'kəʊɪtəs/ noun [U] formal the act of having sex

coke /kəʊk/ noun [U] TECHNOLOGY fuel that is produced when coal is strongly heated in an **airtight** oven

Col abbrev Colonel

cola /'kəʊlə/ noun [U] a sweet brown **fizzy** drink

colander /'kʌləndə/ noun [C] a bowl with small holes in it. You put food into it to remove any liquid.

'cola ˌnut noun [C] a seed that is used for making the drink **cola**. It grows on a **cola tree**.

cold¹ /kəʊld/ adj **1** with a low temperature, or a temperature that is lower than normal ≠ HOT: The water was too cold for a shower. ♦ a cold winter morning ♦ I was cold and hungry. **2** not seeming friendly or sympathetic: Her father was a cold and distant man. **3** cold food has been cooked but is not eaten hot: cold chicken **4** cold colours are colours such as white, blue, and grey that make you think of things that are cold

   PHRASES **get cold feet** to suddenly feel nervous about something that you have planned or agreed to do: Two days before the wedding he got cold feet.

in cold blood in a cruel way, without showing any sympathy or emotion

cold² /kəʊld/ noun **1** [U] cold air or temperatures: *Plants need protection against extreme cold.* ◆ *Heavy curtains help to keep* ***the cold*** *out.* **2** [C] **HEALTH** a minor illness that blocks your nose and makes you cough: *I didn't go to the game because I* ***had a cold.*** ◆ *I must have* ***caught a cold*** *on my holiday.*

cold³ /kəʊld/ adv **out cold** completely unconscious

cold-blooded /ˌkəʊld ˈblʌdɪd/ adj **1** deliberately cruel and showing no emotion **2 BIOLOGY** a cold-blooded animal cannot control its body temperature from within, so it changes as the outside temperature changes → WARM-BLOODED

coldboot /ˈkəʊldˌbuːt/ verb [T] **COMPUTING** to make a computer start again by turning it off and then turning it on = HARDBOOT

'cold-,chain adj **HEALTH** the cold-chain process keeps food and medical supplies at controlled temperatures while they are being transported and stored, so that they stay fresh

'cold ,front noun [C] **GEOGRAPHY** the place where a moving mass of cold air meets a mass of warm air. Cold fronts usually cause heavy rain and they sometimes cause thunder. → WARM FRONT —*picture* → CLOUD

cold-hearted /ˌkəʊld ˈhɑːtɪd/ adj with no sympathy for other people ≠ WARM-HEARTED

coldly /ˈkəʊldli/ adv in a way that is unfriendly or not sympathetic

'cold ,sector noun [C] **GEOGRAPHY** an area of cold air behind a **cold front** → WARM SECTOR —*picture* → CLOUD

'cold ,sore noun [C] a sore area near your lips that is caused by an infection

,cold 'storage noun [U] a place that is kept very cold, where food is put in order to keep it fresh

,cold 'war noun [C/U] extremely unfriendly relations between countries that are not actually at war with each other. This often refers to the situation between the communist Soviet Union and many Western non-communist countries between 1945 and the end of the 1980s.

coleoptile /ˌkɒliˈɒptaɪl/ noun [C] **BIOLOGY** the leaf that appears first in some grasses, and that forms a protective covering around the tip of the stem

colic /ˈkɒlɪk/ noun [U] **HEALTH** severe stomach pain, especially suffered by small babies

colitis /kəˈlaɪtɪs/ noun [U] **HEALTH** a painful medical condition that affects the colon

collaborate /kəˈlæbəreɪt/ verb [I] **1** to work with someone in order to produce something **2** to work secretly to help an enemy or opponent —**collaborator** noun [C]

collaboration /kəˌlæbəˈreɪʃ(ə)n/ noun [U] **1** the process of working with someone to produce something **2** help that someone secretly gives to an enemy or opponent

collaborative /kəˈlæb(ə)rətɪv/ adj involving people or groups working together to produce something —**collaboratively** adv

collage /ˈkɒlɑːʒ/ noun [C] a picture made by sticking pieces of different materials together on a surface

collapse¹ /kəˈlæps/ verb

1 fall down suddenly	4 be folded/taken apart
2 fall because ill/tired	5 lose air inside
3 fail or stop existing	

1 [I] if a building or other structure collapses, it suddenly falls down: *There were fears that the roof would collapse.*
2 [I] to suddenly fall down and become very ill or unconscious: *A man had collapsed on the hospital steps.*
3 [I] to suddenly fail or stop existing: *The country's economy is collapsing.*
4 [I] an object that collapses can be folded or separated into parts, so that it takes up less space
5 [I/T] to lose the air that is inside and become flat, or to make this happen: *His heart was failing and one of his lungs had collapsed.*

collapse² /kəˈlæps/ noun **1** [U] a situation in which something fails or stops existing: *the collapse of the military government* **2** [U] an occasion when a building or other structure falls down **3** [C/U] an occasion when someone falls down and becomes very ill or unconscious **4** [singular] a sudden fall in the value or level of something

collapsible /kəˈlæpsəb(ə)l/ adj able to be folded into a smaller size: *a collapsible bicycle*

collar /ˈkɒlə/ noun [C] **1** the part of a coat, shirt, or dress that goes around your neck **2** a thin piece of leather or plastic put around the neck of a dog or cat that is kept as a pet **3 SCIENCE** the metal ring near the bottom of a Bunsen burner that turns to open and close the air hole

collarbone /ˈkɒləˌbəʊn/ noun [C] the bone along the front of the shoulder = CLAVICLE —*picture* → SKELETON

collate /kəˈleɪt/ verb [T] *formal* to arrange information that has been collected in a sensible order

collateral /kəˈlæt(ə)rəl/ noun [U] **BUSINESS** property that someone agrees to give to a bank if they fail to pay back money that they have borrowed

colleague /ˈkɒliːg/ noun [C] someone who works in the same organization or department as you: *Friends and colleagues will remember him with affection.*

collect /kəˈlekt/ verb

1 get and keep things	4 come together
2 go and get sb/sth	5 win/earn money/prize
3 get money	6 of crowd: form

1 [T] to get things and keep them: *I didn't know she collected stamps.*
2 [T] to go and get a person or thing = PICK SB/STH UP: *What time will you collect her from the airport?*
3 [T] to get money from someone for a particular purpose: *She is* ***collecting*** *money* ***for*** *charity.*
4 [I] to gradually come together, or to become present = GATHER: *Rain often collects in the corners of flat roofs.*
5 [T] to win or earn money or a prize = RECEIVE: *She ran well, but failed to collect a medal.*
6 [I] if a crowd of people collects, it forms

collected /kəˈlektɪd/ adj able to control your nervous or confused feelings: *She tried to stay calm and collected.*

PHRASE sb's collected works/poems/letters etc LITERATURE all of someone's work, poetry etc published together

collecting duct /kəˈlektɪŋ ˌdʌkt/ noun [C] **ANATOMY** a series of tubes in the kidney through which urine passes from the **nephrons** to the **ureter**

collecting flask /kəˈlektɪŋ ˌflɑːsk/ noun [C] **SCIENCE** a glass container used in laboratories. It is wide and flat at the bottom and has a wide neck so that liquids can flow into it easily. —*picture* → DISTILLATION

collection /kəˈlekʃ(ə)n/ noun **1** [C] a group of similar things that are kept together: *a book borrowed from Jon's huge collection* ◆ *The gallery has one of the finest*

collections of Impressionist art. **2** [C/U] the process of collecting things for a particular purpose, or an instance of this: *the **collection of** household waste* **3** [C/U] the activity of collecting money for a particular purpose, or the money that is collected: *The house-to-house collection raised £255.41.* **4** [C] a group of people: *a strange **collection of** protesters and student groups*

collective¹ /kəˈlektɪv/ adj involving all the members of a group ≠ INDIVIDUAL: *collective responsibility* —**collectively** adv

collective² /kəˈlektɪv/ noun [C] a business run by a group of workers

col,lective 'farm noun [C] AGRICULTURE a farm that is run by the people who work there but is owned by the government or another group of people

col,lective 'noun noun [C] LANGUAGE a noun that refers to a group of people and can be followed by a singular or plural verb, for example 'team' or 'family'

collector /kəˈlektə/ noun [C] **1** someone who collects things for fun: *a stamp collector* **2** someone whose job is to collect something from people: *the ticket collector* **3** PHYSICS the part of a **transistor** that **charge carriers** (=electrons that carry current) flow towards, or flow through

college /ˈkɒlɪdʒ/ noun EDUCATION **1** [C/U] a place that gives students qualifications below the level of a university degree, often in the skills that they need to do a particular job: *He teaches cookery at the local college.* ♦ *She's **at** secretarial **college**.* **2** [C] one of the parts that some universities are divided into: *King's College, Cambridge* **3** [C] American a university, often a small one **4** [U] the situation or time when someone is studying at a college or university: *It happened while my sister was away **at college**.*

collenchyma /kəˈleŋkɪmə/ noun [U] BIOLOGY a layer of tissue that helps to support a plant. It consists of living cells that are long and have walls of uneven thickness.

collide /kəˈlaɪd/ verb [I] **1** if people or things collide, they crash into each other: *The truck **collided with** a row of parked cars.* **2** PHYSICS when two or more bodies such as particles collide, they come together for a short time

collision /kəˈlɪʒ(ə)n/ noun [C/U] **1** an accident in which a person or vehicle that is moving crashes into something: *The stolen car was involved in a **head-on collision** with a truck* (=the front of the vehicles hit each other). **2** a very serious argument **3** PHYSICS an occasion when two or more bodies such as particles come together for a short time

col,lision 'damage ,waiver noun [C/U] LAW insurance that you can buy when you hire a car so that you do not pay if the car is damaged

collocate¹ /ˈkɒləkeɪt/ verb [I] LANGUAGE words that collocate are often used together

collocate² /ˈkɒləkət/ noun [C] LANGUAGE a word that is often used with another word

collocation /ˌkɒləˈkeɪʃ(ə)n/ noun [C] LANGUAGE a **collocate**²

colloid /ˈkɒlɔɪd/ noun [C] CHEMISTRY **1** a substance that contains very small particles spread through it **2** the particles that are suspended in a colloid solution

colloquial /kəˈləʊkwiəl/ adj LANGUAGE used in informal conversation rather than in writing or formal language —**colloquially** adv

colloquialism /kəˈləʊkwiəˌlɪz(ə)m/ noun [C] a colloquial word or expression

colloquium /kəˈləʊkwiəm/ noun [C] formal a large meeting to discuss something, usually an academic subject

collude /kəˈluːd/ verb [I] formal to work secretly with someone to do something dishonest

collusion /kəˈluːʒ(ə)n/ noun [U] formal the secret activities of people who work together to do something dishonest —**collusive** /kəˈluːsɪv/ adj

cologne /kəˈləʊn/ noun [C/U] a liquid with a nice smell that people put on their skin

colon /ˈkəʊlɒn/ noun [C] **1** LANGUAGE the symbol : used in writing, for example before an explanation or a list **2** ANATOMY the lower part of the **large intestine** —*picture* → DIGESTIVE SYSTEM, ORGAN

colonel /ˈkɜːn(ə)l/ noun [C] an officer of high rank in the army, the **Marines**, or the US Air Force

colonial /kəˈləʊniəl/ adj SOCIAL STUDIES relating to a system or period in which one country rules another: *years of colonial rule*

colonialism /kəˈləʊniəˌlɪz(ə)m/ noun [U] SOCIAL STUDIES a situation in which one country rules another —**colonialist** adj

colonist /ˈkɒlənɪst/ noun [C] SOCIAL STUDIES one of the people who establish a **colony** or go to live in it

colonize /ˈkɒlənaɪz/ verb [T] SOCIAL STUDIES to take control of another country by going to live there or by sending people to live there —**colonization** /ˌkɒlənaɪˈzeɪʃ(ə)n/ noun [U]

colony /ˈkɒləni/ (plural **colonies**) noun [C] **1** SOCIAL STUDIES a country that is controlled by another country **2** BIOLOGY a group of plants, birds, or other animals of the same type that live in the same area **3** SOCIAL STUDIES a group of people of the same nationality or racial group who live in the same area

color /ˈkʌlə/ the American spelling of **colour**

colossal /kəˈlɒs(ə)l/ adj extremely great or large: *It was a colossal waste of money.*

colostomy /kəˈlɒstəmi/ noun [C/U] HEALTH a medical operation in which the end of the colon is attached to an opening in the abdomen, so that faeces can leave the body

colostrum /kəˈlɒstrəm/ noun [U] BIOLOGY a yellowish fluid containing antibodies and minerals that is produced by the **mammary glands** in women and other female mammals, for a few days after they have given birth

colour¹ /ˈkʌlə/ noun **1** [C/U] red, blue, green, yellow etc: *Pink is my favourite colour.* ♦ *a light brown colour* ♦ *His hair is reddish **in colour**.* **2** [U] the quality of having colour: *Pot plants add colour to a room.* ♦ *Are the pictures **in colour** or black and white?* **3** [C/U] the colour of someone's skin as a sign of their race: *people of all creeds and colours* **4** [U] interest or excitement: *The examples chosen add colour to the writing.* → FLYING¹, OFF-COLOUR

Build your vocabulary: describing colours

general
- **hue** a particular form of a colour
- **shade** one of the light or dark types of a particular colour
- **tone** one of the different types of a particular colour

dark colours
- **dark** used for describing colours that look more like black than like white
- **deep** used for describing dark colours that look attractive

- **rich** used for describing dark colours that look attractive and expensive

bright colours
- **bright** strong and noticeable
- **colourful** brightly coloured, or having a lot of bright colours
- **garish** very bright in a way that looks ugly
- **loud** bright in a way that you think looks silly or ugly

pale colours
- **pale** like white with a small amount of a colour mixed in
- **light** used for describing colours that look more like white than like black

colour² /ˈkʌlə/ verb **1** [T] to add colour to something, or to make it a different colour: *I think I'll colour my hair.* **2** [T] to affect someone's decision or opinion about something: *Don't allow your friends' opinions to colour your judgment.* **3** [I/T] to use pens, pencils, or **crayons** to add colour to a picture

> Word family: **colour**
>
> *Words in the same family as* **colour**
> - **coloured** *adj*
> - **colourful** *adj*
> - **colourless** *adj*
> - **multicoloured** *adj*
> - **discoloured** *adj*
> - **colourfully** *adv*
> - **colouring** *n*

colour³ /ˈkʌlə/ adj **1** a colour photograph, magazine etc is in colour, not black and white **2** a colour television, **monitor** etc shows colour pictures or images

'colour-,blind adj HEALTH unable to see the difference between some colours, especially between red and green —**'colour-,blindness** noun [U]

'colour-,coded adj marked with different colours to make it easy to see different features or uses

coloured /ˈkʌləd/ adj **1** red, green, orange etc rather than black and white or transparent: *pieces of coloured paper* **2** *offensive* a coloured person has dark skin

colourful /ˈkʌləf(ə)l/ adj **1** with bright colours, or a lot of different colours: *colourful Indian rugs* **2** interesting, exciting, and sometimes funny or shocking: *a family of eccentric and colourful characters* **3** colourful language is rude or uses offensive words= OBSCENE —**colourfully** adv

colouring /ˈkʌlərɪŋ/ noun **1** [U] the colour of something, especially someone's hair, skin, and eyes **2** [C/U] a substance that is added to food to change its colour

colourless /ˈkʌləiəs/ adj **1** without any colour: *Carbon monoxide is a colourless, poisonous gas.* **2** not interesting, exciting, or original= DULL

colt /kəʊlt/ noun [C] a young male horse

column /ˈkɒləm/ noun [C]

1 tall thick post	**4** in newspaper
2 of writing/numbers	**5** sth rising into the air
3 line of people/vehicles	

1 a tall thick post that is used for supporting a roof, decorating a building, or reminding people of an important event or person: *marble columns*
2 a series of short lines of writing or numbers arranged one below the other on a page
3 a long line of people or vehicles moving together: *a column of soldiers*
4 a regular newspaper or magazine article on a particular subject or by a particular journalist
5 something that rises up into the air in a straight line: *a column of smoke and ash*

columnist /ˈkɒləmnɪst/ noun [C] a journalist who writes a regular series of articles for a particular newspaper or magazine

com /kɒm/ abbrev COMPUTING commercial organization: used in Internet addresses

coma /ˈkəʊmə/ noun [C] HEALTH a state in which someone is unconscious for a long time: *She was in a coma for a week.*

comatose /ˈkəʊmətəʊs/ adj HEALTH unconscious or in a coma

comb¹ /kəʊm/ noun [C] an object with a row of thin pointed parts that you pull through your hair in order to make it tidy

comb² /kəʊm/ verb [T] **1** to make your hair tidy with a comb **2** to search a place thoroughly: *Dozens of officers combed the area with search dogs.*

combat¹ /ˈkɒmbæt/ noun [U] fighting during a war: *servicemen killed in combat* ♦ *combat troops*

combat² /ˈkɒmbæt/ verb [T] to try to stop something bad from happening or a bad situation from becoming worse: *the need for effective action to combat global warming*

combatant /ˈkɒmbətənt/ noun [C] *formal* a person, group, or country that takes part in a war

combe or **coombe** /kuːm/ noun [C] GEOGRAPHY a valley on the downward slope of a hill

combination /ˌkɒmbɪˈneɪʃ(ə)n/ noun [C] **1** something that combines several things: *a striking colour combination* ♦ *a combination of text, illustration, and graphics* **2** a series of numbers or letters used for opening a lock: *I've forgotten the combination.*

combine /kəmˈbaɪn/ verb [I/T] if you combine things, or if they combine, they are used, done, or put together: *an attempt to combine the advantages of two systems* ♦ *High tides combined with strong winds caused severe flooding.* ♦ *One oxygen and two hydrogen atoms combine to form a molecule of water.*

combined /kəmˈbaɪnd/ adj **1** done by people or groups working together= JOINT: *a combined effort* **2** formed by adding things together: *What is your combined family income?*

combine harvester /ˌkɒmbaɪn ˈhɑːvɪstə/ noun [C] AGRICULTURE a large machine used on a farm for cutting grain crops and then removing and cleaning the seeds

combining form /kəmˈbaɪnɪŋ ˌfɔːm/ noun [C] LANGUAGE a form of a word that has its own meaning, but is used only in combination with other words to make new words, for example -footed in 'a four-footed animal'

combustible /kəmˈbʌstəb(ə)l/ adj CHEMISTRY able to burn easily —**combustibility** /kəm,bʌstəˈbɪləti/ noun [U]

combustion /kəmˈbʌstʃ(ə)n/ noun [U] **1** CHEMISTRY the chemical reaction in which oxygen combines with another substance, producing energy such as heat or light: *The release of energy from food and coal are examples of combustion.* **2** the process of burning

com'bustion ,chamber noun [C] ENGINEERING the part of a cylinder in a vehicle engine where the mixture of air and fuel **ignites** (=catches fire) and burns — *picture* → JET ENGINE

come /kʌm/ (**comes, coming, came** /keɪm/, **come**)
verb [I]

1 move (to here)	**6** happen
2 reach a state	**7** be produced/sold
3 start doing sth	**8** have position
4 reach a point	**+ PHRASES**
5 be received	**+ PHRASAL VERBS**

1 to move to the place where the person who is speaking is, or to the place that they are going, or to the place that they are talking about: *Billy, I want you to* ***come here*** *at once!* ♦ *She's got someone* ***coming*** *this morning to fix the computer.* ♦ ***Come and*** *tell me all about it.*
2 to reach a particular state: *We* ***came to the conclusion that*** *she must be telling the truth.* ♦ *All good things must* ***come to an end.*** ♦ *When the Popular Front* ***came to power*** *they continued these policies.*
3 to start being a different state or condition: *The new changes will* ***come into effect*** *next month.* ♦ *As we turned the corner, the palace* ***came into view*** (=started to be seen).
4 to reach a particular point or level: *The road* ***comes as far as*** *the post office and then ends.* ♦ *The water* ***came up to*** *my shoulders.*
5 if something such as a letter or message comes, you receive it: *The news came at the perfect time.*
6 to happen: *His resignation came after seven tough years in office.* ♦ *It* ***came as no surprise that*** *she left the company.*
7 to be produced or sold: *The dress* ***comes in*** *yellow or blue.* ♦ *All new cars* ***come with*** *one year's free insurance.*
8 to be in a particular position in a series or list or at the end of a race: *July* ***comes before*** *August.* ♦ *She* ***came first*** *in a national poetry competition.*

PHRASES **come naturally/easily (to sb)** to be easy for someone to do: *Fame and fortune have come easily to Carmen.*
come undone/untied etc to become **undone/untied** etc: *Be careful! Your shoelaces have come undone.*
to come in the future: *We were to remain enemies for years to come.*
→ CLEAN¹, MIND¹

PHRASAL VERBS **,come a'bout** to happen, especially by chance: *The company's growth has come about through the use of advanced technology.*
,come a'cross 1 to make someone have a particular opinion of you when they meet you: *She* ***comes across*** *as very self-confident.* **2 come across** or **come over** if something such as a feeling or idea comes across or comes over when you speak, you make it very clear to people: *His sense of enthusiasm comes across very clearly.*
,come a'part to separate easily into pieces= FALL APART
,come a'way 1 if one thing comes away from another that it was fixed to, it becomes separated from it by accident: *Another block of stone came away from the wall.* **2** to leave in a particular state or condition: *We* ***came away with*** *the feeling that they didn't really approve of us.*
,come be'tween sb to cause a disagreement or argument between people: *He didn't want this to come between them.*
'come by sth to get something, especially something that is hard to get: *At that time, teaching jobs were* ***hard to come by.***
'come from sth 1 to be produced by a particular place or thing, or to start from there: *The word comes from an African language.* ♦ *I can't tell where the noise is coming from, can you?* **2** to have been born or lived in a particular place: *My parents came from Italy.*
,come 'in 1 to enter a room, building, or other place: *Come in and sit down.* **2** if something such as a law or practice comes in, it starts to be used or done **3** when

the tide comes in, the sea moves higher up the beach
≠ GO OUT
,come 'into sth to get money when someone dies=
INHERIT: *He's just come into some money.*
,come 'off (sth) 1 to fall off something that you are riding: *She'd come off her new bike and hurt her knee.*
2 to stop being fixed to something: *I pulled at the drawer, and the handle came off.* ♦ *One of the legs has come off the table.*
,come 'out 1 to become known: *It eventually* ***came out*** *that she was already married.* **2** to be spoken, heard, or understood in a particular way: *She had tried to say 'sorry', but it had* ***come out all wrong.***
,come 'over 1 if a feeling comes over you, it suddenly affects you in a strong way **2** *same as* **come across** sense 2: *Stick to the facts and make sure they come over clearly.*
,come 'round to become conscious again
,come 'through if a feeling or quality that someone or something has comes through, it can be clearly understood or seen
,come 'through sth to be still alive, working, or making progress after a difficult or dangerous experience: *It's been a very upsetting time but we've come through it together.*
'come to sb if something comes to you, you think of it or remember it: *The idea came to me when we were on holiday.*
,come 'up if something such as a job comes up, it becomes available
,come 'up against sth to have to deal with something difficult or unpleasant: *In the first week, we came up against a problem.*
,come 'up with sth to think of something such as an idea or a plan: *Is that the best you can come up with?*

comeback /'kʌm,bæk/ noun [C] **1** a period when someone or something becomes successful or popular again: *Seventies styles have been* ***making a comeback.*** **2** a quick clever reply to a comment or criticism

comedian /kə'miːdiən/ noun [C] someone whose job is to entertain people by making them laugh= COMIC

comedy /'kɒmədi/ (plural **comedies**) noun **1** [C] a funny film, play, or television programme **2** [U] entertainment intended to make people laugh

comet /'kɒmɪt/ noun [C] **ASTRONOMY** an object in space that leaves a bright stream of gas and dust behind it as it moves around the sun —*picture* → SOLAR SYSTEM

comfort¹ /'kʌmfət/ noun

1 relaxed state	**4** pleasant life
2 less worried feeling	**5** sth that makes life
3 sb/sth supporting	better

1 [U] a physically relaxed state, without any pain or other unpleasant feelings: *The airline is keen to improve passenger comfort.* ♦ *There is plenty of room to lie down and sleep* ***in comfort.***
2 [U] a feeling of being less sad or worried about something than you were previously: *My mother was always there to offer comfort.*
3 [C] someone or something that makes you feel better when you are sad or worried: *Her children have been* ***a great comfort to*** *her.*
4 [U] a pleasant way of life in which someone has everything they need: *Now he can live* ***in comfort*** *for the rest of his life.*
5 comforts [plural] things that make your life easier and more pleasant: *the comforts of home*

Word family: **comfort**

Words in the same family as ***comfort***
■ **comfortable** *adj*   ■ **uncomfortable** *adj*

- **comfortably** *adv*
- **comforting** *adj*
- **comforter** *n*
- **uncomfortably** *adv*
- **discomfort** *n*

comfort2 /ˈkʌmfət/ verb [T] to make someone feel less sad, worried, or disappointed —**comforting** adj

comfortable /ˈkʌmftəb(ə)l/ adj

1 feeling pleasant
2 pleasant to use/wear
3 of furniture
4 having enough money
5 not worried about sth

1 feeling physically relaxed, without any pain or other unpleasant feelings ≠ UNCOMFORTABLE: *If you're not comfortable, try changing positions.* ♦ *Make yourself comfortable and I'll be back in a minute.*

2 making you have a pleasant satisfied feeling in your body: *loose comfortable clothes*

3 a comfortable piece of furniture feels pleasant to sit or lie on ≠ UNCOMFORTABLE: *The bed looked warm and comfortable.*

4 someone who is comfortable is rich enough to pay for everything that they need

5 not worried about something and willing to accept it: *Is everyone comfortable with the arrangement?*
—**comfortably** /ˈkʌmftəbli/ adv

comic1 /ˈkɒmɪk/ adj funny

comic2 /ˈkɒmɪk/ noun [C] 1 a magazine that contains stories told in a series of drawings 2 someone whose job is to entertain people by telling jokes and stories to make them laugh = COMEDIAN

comical /ˈkɒmɪk(ə)l/ adj funny in a strange or silly way —**comically** /ˈkɒmɪkli/ adv

'comic ,book noun [C] a magazine that contains stories told in a series of drawings

'comic ,strip noun [C] a series of drawings that tell a story, especially a funny story

coming1 /ˈkʌmɪŋ/ adj happening soon, or happening next: *the coming elections*

coming2 /ˈkʌmɪŋ/ noun
PHRASES **the coming of** the time when someone or something arrives or happens: *the coming of spring*
comings and goings activity that consists of people arriving and leaving many times

comma /ˈkɒmə/ noun [C] LANGUAGE the symbol , used in writing and printing between parts of a sentence or things in a list

command1 /kəˈmɑːnd/ noun 1 [C] an official order to do something: *Who gave the command to open fire?* 2 [U] control of a group of people, especially in the armed forces: *The President was in command of the military.* 3 [U] control of something such as a situation or your feelings: *United soon took command of the game.* 4 [C] COMPUTING an instruction that you give to a computer to make it do something
PHRASES **at your command** if you have something such as a skill at your command, you are able to use it well
command of sth knowledge of a particular subject, especially the ability to speak a foreign language

command2 /kəˈmɑːnd/ verb 1 [T] to be in charge of an activity that involves a group of people: *Lovell commanded the Apollo 13 mission to the moon.* 2 [I/T] to officially order someone to do something: *He commanded his men to retreat.* 3 [T] to have something such as people's respect or attention: *He commands the respect of everyone who works for him.*

commandant /ˈkɒməndænt/ noun [C] a military officer of high rank who controls a particular institution or group of people

com,mand e'conomy noun [C] ECONOMICS an economic system in which the government controls business and the supply of goods in a country → MARKET ECONOMY

commandeer /ˌkɒmənˈdɪə/ verb [T] to officially take someone's property for military use

commander /kəˈmɑːndə/ noun [C] 1 an officer who is in charge of a military group or operation 2 an officer of middle rank in the British Navy

com,mander in 'chief noun [C] someone in charge of the whole of the armed forces of a country

commanding /kəˈmɑːndɪŋ/ adj powerful and impressive: *a commanding voice*

com,manding 'officer noun [C] an officer of any rank who controls a particular military group or operation

com'mand ,key noun [C] COMPUTING on some computers, a key that you press together with another key to make the computer do a particular thing

com'mand ,line noun [C] COMPUTING a way of using words or letters to give a computer instructions, instead of using a mouse or computer language

commandment /kəˈmɑːn(d)mənt/ noun [C] RELIGION according to the Bible, one of the ten rules of behaviour that God gave people to obey

commando /kəˈmɑːndəʊ/ noun [C] a soldier who is trained to attack in areas controlled by an enemy

commemorate /kəˈmeməreɪt/ verb [T] if people commemorate an important person or event, they do something to show that they remember the person or event: *A huge bronze statue commemorating the poet stands in the main square.* —**commemoration** /kəˌmeməˈreɪʃ(ə)n/ noun [C/U]

commemorative /kəˈmem(ə)rətɪv/ adj produced for an important event in order to help people to remember it: *a commemorative stamp*

commence /kəˈmens/ verb [I/T] formal to begin, or to begin something: *The trial will commence in 30 days.* —**commencement** noun [singular/U]

commend /kəˈmend/ verb [T] formal to praise someone or something formally or publicly: *They were commended for the way they handled the job.* —**commendation** /ˌkɒmenˈdeɪʃ(ə)n/ noun [C/U]

commendable /kəˈmendəb(ə)l/ adj formal deserving praise or admiration

commensalism /kəˈmensəlɪz(ə)m/ noun [U] BIOLOGY a situation in which two different species live together in a way that is helpful to one species and not harmful to the other

commensurate /kəˈmenʃərət/ adj formal intended to be suitable for the quality, status, or value of someone or something

comment1 /ˈkɒment/ noun 1 [C/U] a written or spoken remark giving an opinion: *I've had enough of your sarcastic comments.* ♦ *We would welcome your comments on our work.* ♦ *Did she make any comment about Eddie?* 2 [U] written or spoken discussion of something, especially on television, radio, or in a newspaper: *a page of news and comment*

comment2 /ˈkɒment/ verb [I/T] to make a written or spoken remark about someone or something: *I'm afraid I can't comment on the matter.* ♦ *Researchers who read the report commented that it had many errors.*

commentary /ˈkɒmənt(ə)ri/ (plural **commentaries**) noun 1 [C] a spoken description of an event that is given as the event is happening, especially on radio or television 2 [C/U] a discussion of something such as an event or theory: *a **commentary on** 7th-century English life*

commentator /ˈkɒmənˌteɪtə/ noun [C] **1** someone whose job is to give a description of an event on television or radio as it happens **2** someone whose job is to write about or discuss a particular subject

commerce /ˈkɒmɜːs/ noun [U] the activity of buying and selling goods and services

commercial¹ /kəˈmɜːʃ(ə)l/ adj **1** relating to the business of buying and selling goods and services: *One of their first commercial products was an electronic typewriter.* **2** relating to making a profit: *The film's commercial success made her a star.* **3** making money by broadcasting advertisements instead of being given money by the government: *commercial radio stations* —**commercially** adv

commercial² /kəˈmɜːʃ(ə)l/ noun [C] an advertisement on television or radio

com,mercial 'break noun [C] a short interruption in a television or radio programme when advertisements are broadcast

com'mercial ,district noun [C] the part of a town where offices and shops are situated

com,mercial 'farming noun [U] AGRICULTURE the growing of crops for sale rather than as food for a family → SUBSISTENCE FARMING

commercialized /kəˈmɜːʃəlaɪzd/ adj done or changed in order to make a profit: *the increasingly commercialized world of football*

commiserate /kəˈmɪzəreɪt/ verb [I] to express sympathy to someone who is unhappy about something= SYMPATHIZE —**commiseration** /kəˌmɪzəˈreɪʃ(ə)n/ noun [U]

commission /kəˈmɪʃ(ə)n/ noun **1** [C] a group of people that is officially put in charge of something or asked to find out about something: *a special parliamentary commission* **2** [C] a request for an artist, writer, or musician to produce a piece of work for someone in exchange for payment **3** [C/U] an extra amount of money that someone earns when they sell a product or get a new customer: *All our salespeople work **on commission*** (=are paid according to how much they sell).

commissionaire /kəˌmɪʃəˈneə/ noun [C] someone whose job is to stand at the entrance to a hotel or other public building and welcome people

commissioner /kəˈmɪʃ(ə)nə/ noun [C] an official who is in charge of something: *the Metropolitan Police Commissioner*

commit /kəˈmɪt/ (**commits, committing, committed**) verb

1 do sth illegal/wrong	4 send sb to prison
2 (make sb) agree to sth	5 state sb is mentally ill
3 say sb/sth will be used	+ PHRASE

1 [T] to do something that is illegal or morally wrong: *The study aims to find out what makes people **commit** crimes.* ♦ *Reports suggest that the singer **committed** suicide* (=killed himself).
2 [I/T] to agree to do something, or to make someone agree to do something: *I do not want to **commit to** any particular date.*
3 [T] to say formally that people or things will be used for a particular purpose: *They'll have to **commit** more money to the project if it's to succeed.*
4 [T] LAW to say officially that someone must go to prison or go to court to be judged for a crime
5 [T] to officially state that someone is mentally ill and should go to a hospital to be treated

PHRASE commit yourself 1 to agree to do something: *Take a little time to think before committing yourself.* **2** to give a definite opinion, or to make a definite decision: *She won't commit herself either way.*

commitment /kəˈmɪtmənt/ noun **1** [singular/U] a strong belief that something is good and that people should support it: *The government has failed to demonstrate its **commitment** to the railways.* **2** [C/U] a promise to do something: *The Government will continue to honour its **commitment** to pensioners.* **3** [U] enthusiasm for something and a determination to work hard at it: *There is a high **level of commitment** amongst employees.* **4** [C] a duty or responsibility that someone has accepted: *I couldn't go because of **work commitments**.* ♦ *He has huge **financial commitments**.*

com'mitment ,ceremony noun [C] a ceremony similar to a wedding for two people who are of the same sex, or for two people who choose not to marry each other

committal /kəˈmɪt(ə)l/ noun [C/U] LAW the process by which a court officially sends someone to prison or for a trial in a higher court

committed /kəˈmɪtɪd/ adj loyal to a belief, organization, or group, and willing to work hard for it

committee /kəˈmɪti/ noun [C] a group of people who represent a larger group or organization and are chosen to do a particular job: *committee meetings* ♦ *He's **on the** sports **committee**.*

> **Committee** can be used with a singular or plural verb. You can say *The committee **is** meeting tomorrow* OR *The committee **are** meeting tomorrow.*

commodity /kəˈmɒdəti/ (plural **commodities**) noun [C] a product that can be bought and sold

common¹ /ˈkɒmən/ adj **1** happening frequently, or existing in large amounts or numbers: *Traffic congestion is **a common occurrence** in many major cities.* ♦ *It's **common practice** in most companies these days.* **2** used, done, or shared by two or more people: *Members also agreed to pursue a common trade policy.* ♦ *These issues are **common to** all our students.* **3** ordinary, with no special status or rank: *a common criminal*

PHRASE the common good the benefit of everyone

common² /ˈkɒmən/ noun [C] a large piece of open land in an English village or town where anyone can walk or play games

PHRASES have sth in common (with sb) to have the same interests or opinions as someone else: *We've got such a lot in common.*
have sth in common (with sth) to have the same features as something else
in common with in the same way as someone or something else
→ HOUSE OF COMMONS

commonality /ˌkɒməˈnæləti/ noun [C/U] formal the state of having the same qualities or features as other people or things

the ,common 'cold noun [singular] HEALTH a minor illness that makes you **sneeze** and cough= COLD

,common de'nominator noun [C] MATHS a number that can be divided exactly by all the **denominators** (=numbers written below the line) in a particular group of fractions. The common denominator of 1/4, 1/3, and 1/6 is 12.

,common 'factor noun [C] MATHS a number that a group of two or more other numbers can be divided by exactly, so 4 is a common factor of 8, 12, and 20

common 'fraction noun [C] MATHS a fraction written as one number above a line and another number below the line, instead of as numbers separated by a decimal point, for example, $\frac{3}{4}$ is a common fraction = VULGAR FRACTION

common 'ground noun [U] something that people can agree about when they disagree about other things

common 'knowledge noun [U] something that everyone knows

common 'law noun [U] LAW the system of law that has developed from customs and judges' decisions instead of from laws made by politicians

commonly /'kɒmənli/ adv usually, or frequently

common 'market noun [C] ECONOMICS an economic organization formed by several countries that trade with each other without charging tax on each other's goods

common 'multiple noun [C] MATHS a number that can be divided exactly by two or more other numbers, for example 12 is a common multiple of 2, 3, and 4

common 'noun noun [C] LANGUAGE a noun that is not the name of a particular person or thing. For example, 'dog' and 'paper' are common nouns, but 'Mary' and 'New York' are **proper nouns**.

commonplace /'kɒmən,pleɪs/ adj completely normal: *It is now commonplace for people to use the Internet at home.*

common ,room noun [C] EDUCATION a room in a school or college where students go to relax

the Commons /'kɒmənz/ POLITICS the **House of Commons**

common 'sense noun [U] the ability to use good judgment and make sensible decisions

the Commonwealth /'kɒmən,welθ/ POLITICS an organization of countries that used to be under the political control of the UK

commotion /kə'məʊʃ(ə)n/ noun [C/U] noise and confused activity

communal /'kɒmjʊn(ə)l, kə'mju:n(ə)l/ adj owned or used by everyone in a group: *a communal kitchen*

commune /'kɒmju:n/ noun [C] a group of people who live together and share work, food, income, and possessions

communicable /kə'mju:nɪkəb(ə)l/ adj HEALTH a communicable disease can be passed from one person or animal to another

communicate /kə'mju:nɪkeɪt/ verb **1** [I/T] to express thoughts, feelings, or information to someone else: *We communicate with each other via email.* ♦ *The information was communicated to officials in July 1981.* **2** [I/T] to make someone understand an emotion or idea without expressing it in words: *She has an amazing ability to communicate enthusiasm.* **3** [I] to let someone know what you are feeling or thinking, so that you have a good relationship: *She says that they no longer seem to communicate.* **4** [T] HEALTH to pass a disease from one person, animal, or plant to another —**communicator** noun [C]

communication /kə,mju:nɪ'keɪʃ(ə)n/ noun **1** [U] the process of giving or exchanging information or of making emotions or ideas known to someone: *There was a breakdown in communication.* ♦ *She has no communication with her family.* ♦ *a workshop to improve teachers' communication skills* **2 communications** [plural] a system for sending information: *satellite communications* **3** [C] *formal* a message such as a letter, phone call, or email

communicative /kə'mju:nɪkətɪv/ adj willing to tell things to other people

com,municative 'competence noun [U] LANGUAGE the ability to communicate well in a language

Communion /kə'mju:niən/ noun [U] RELIGION a Christian ceremony in which people eat bread and drink wine in order to remember Jesus Christ

communism /'kɒmjʊ,nɪz(ə)m/ noun [U] SOCIAL STUDIES a political and economic system in which individual people do not own property or industries and in which people of all social classes are treated equally

communist /'kɒmjʊnɪst/ noun [C] someone who believes in communism —**communist** adj

community /kə'mju:nəti/ (plural **communities**) noun **1** [C] SOCIAL STUDIES the people who live in an area: *small rural communities* ♦ *I wanted to work somewhere where I could serve the community.* **2** [C] SOCIAL STUDIES a group of people in a larger society who are the same in some way: *areas where there are large Jewish communities* **3** [U] the feeling that you belong to a group and that this is a good thing: *One of the major goals is to develop a sense of community.*

> **Community** can be used with a singular or plural verb when it refers to people. You can say: *The community is opposed to the plan* OR: *The community are opposed to the plan.*

com,munity 'service noun [U] **1** LAW work that someone does as a punishment, instead of going to prison **2** work without payment that someone does to help their local community

commutable /kə'mju:təb(ə)l/ adj **1** a place that is commutable is close enough to allow you to travel there and back to work every day **2** LAW a commutable punishment can be changed to one that is less severe

commutation /,kɒmjʊ'teɪʃ(ə)n/ noun [C/U] LAW the action of changing a punishment to one that is less severe

the com,mutative 'law noun [singular] MATHS the feature of a group of numbers or symbols according to which their order can be changed, but the result of adding them or multiplying them will be the same. For example, $a + b = b + a$ and $a \times b = b \times a$.

commute /kə'mju:t/ verb **1** [I] to travel regularly to and from your home and your work **2** [T] LAW to change a punishment to one that is less severe

commuter /kə'mju:tə/ noun [C] someone who travels regularly to and from work

compact¹ /'kɒmpækt, kəm'pækt/ adj smaller than most things of the same kind

compact² /kəm'pækt/ verb [T] to make something smaller or firmer by pressing it

com,pact 'bone noun [U] ANATOMY a type of bone tissue that forms the hard outer layer of a bone

compact 'disc noun [C] COMPUTING a CD

companion /kəm'pænjən/ noun [C] someone who is with you or who you spend a lot of time with

com'panion ,animal noun [C] an animal that someone keeps for company and enjoyment. The more usual word is 'pet'.

companionship /kəm'pænjənʃɪp/ noun [U] the relationship that you have with a good friend who spends a lot of time with you

company /'kʌmp(ə)ni/ (plural **companies**) noun **1** [C] an organization that sells services or goods: *Max* *works for a large oil company.* **2** [U] the activity of being with other people: *I thought you might want some company tonight.* ♦ *We always enjoy his company.* **3** [C] a group of actors, singers, or dancers who perform together: *the Royal Shakespeare Company*

PHRASES **be good company** to be someone who people enjoy spending time with

keep sb company to spend time with someone so that they will not feel alone

,company 'law noun [U] **LAW** the laws connected with how businesses may operate

,company re'port noun [C] **BUSINESS** a report that gives detailed information about a company's financial activities and performance during a particular period

,company 'secretary noun [C] **BUSINESS** someone who is an official of a company and whose job is to deal with financial and legal issues

comparable /ˈkɒmp(ə)rəb(ə)l/ adj fairly similar to another thing, so that it is reasonable to compare them: *The salary is **comparable with** that of a junior doctor.* —**comparability** /ˌkɒmp(ə)rəˈbɪləti/ noun [U]

comparative¹ /kəmˈpærətɪv/ adj **1** judged in comparison with something such as a previous situation or state= RELATIVE: *We expected to win with comparative ease.* **2** involving the comparison of two or more things: *a comparative analysis* **3** **LANGUAGE** the comparative form of an adjective or adverb is the form that shows that something has more of a quality than it previously had or more of a quality than something else has. For example, 'newer' is the comparative form of 'new'. → SUPERLATIVE¹

comparative² /kəmˈpærətɪv/ noun [C] **LANGUAGE** a comparative form of an adjective or adverb: *The comparative of 'good' is 'better'.*

comparatively /kəmˈpærətɪvli/ adv as compared with something else or with a previous situation or state= RELATIVELY: *The technology is still comparatively new.*

comparator /kəmˈpærətə/ noun [C] **TECHNOLOGY** a tool or piece of equipment that is used for comparing an object with a standard

compare /kəmˈpeə/ verb **1** [T] to consider the ways in which people or things are similar or different: *Compare the one that has been cleaned **with** the others.* **2** [I] to be as good or bad as someone or something else: *How does the UK's performance **compare with** performance in other European countries?* **3** [T] to say that one person or thing is similar to another: *The band has been compared to the Beatles.*

PHRASE **compare notes** to discuss something with someone who has also experienced it or thought about it

---

Word family: compare

Words in the same family as compare
- **comparative** *adj*
- **comparable** *adj*
- **comparably** *adv*
- **comparison** *n*
- **comparatively** *adv*
- **incomparable** *adj*
- **incomparably** *adv*

---

compared /kəmˈpeəd/ adj **compared with/to** used for talking about the ways in which two people or things are different, or about the ways in which someone or something has changed: *Profits were good compared with last year.*

comparison /kəmˈpærɪs(ə)n/ noun [C/U] **1** the process of considering the ways in which people or things are similar or different: *It is very difficult to **make comparisons with** other schools.* ♦ *We cannot **make a comparison between** the two languages.* **2** **LANGUAGE** changes in the form of an adjective or adverb to show

that someone or something has more of a quality, such as the change from 'good' to 'better' and 'best'

PHRASE **in/by comparison (with)** used for talking about the ways in which two people or things are different

com'parison-,shop verb [I] to compare prices and features of products for sale in different shops in order to find the best deal

compartment /kəmˈpɑːtmənt/ noun [C] **1** one of the separate parts of a container or place where things are stored **2** one of the separate spaces into which a railway **carriage** is divided

compass /ˈkʌmpəs/ noun [C] **GEOGRAPHY**, **PHYSICS** a piece of equipment used for finding your way, with a needle that always points to the north

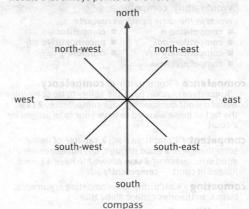

compass

compasses /ˈkʌmpəsɪz/ noun [plural] **MATHS** a piece of equipment in the shape of the letter V, used for drawing circles

compassion /kəmˈpæʃ(ə)n/ noun [U] sympathy for someone who is unhappy or in a bad situation

compassionate /kəmˈpæʃ(ə)nət/ adj caring about someone who is unhappy or in a bad situation

compatible /kəmˈpætəb(ə)l/ adj **1** able to exist together with another idea or system: *The scheme is not **compatible with** environmental principles.* **2** **COMPUTING** able to be used together with another piece of computer equipment or software **3** likely to have a good relationship because of being similar ≠ INCOMPATIBLE: *We're just not compatible.* —**compatibility** /kəmˌpætəˈbɪləti/ noun [U]

compatriot /kəmˈpætriət/ noun [C] someone who is from the same country as you

compel /kəmˈpel/ (**compels**, **compelling**, **compelled**) verb [T] to force someone to do something

compelling /kəmˈpelɪŋ/ adj **1** interesting or exciting enough to keep your attention completely: *a compelling story* **2** able to persuade someone to do or believe something: *compelling evidence*

compendium /kəmˈpendiəm/ noun [C] *formal* a detailed collection of information on a particular subject, especially in a short book

compensate /ˈkɒmpənseɪt/ verb **1** [I] to change or remove the bad effect of something: *Their enthusiasm **compensates for** their lack of skill.* **2** [I/T] to pay someone money because they have suffered an injury or loss: *They were **compensated for** the damage to the house.*

compensation /ˌkɒmpənˈseɪʃ(ə)n/ noun **1** [U] money that someone receives because something bad has happened to them: *She was awarded £2,000*

compensation for *her injuries.* **2** [C/U] something that changes or removes the bad effect of something: *He uses speed as* ***compensation for*** *his lack of strength.*

compensatory /ˌkɒmpənˈseɪtəri/ *adj formal* **1** intended to change or remove the bad result of something **2** paid as compensation to someone who has suffered injury or loss

compete /kəmˈpiːt/ *verb* [I] **1** to try to be more successful than other companies or people in business: *We're too small to* ***compete with*** *a company like that.* **2** to try to win a competition: *Her dream was to* ***compete in*** *the Olympics.* ♦ *You will be* ***competing against*** *the best athletes in the world.* ♦ *Ten teams will* ***compete for*** *the trophy.*

Word family: compete

Words in the same family as ***compete***
- **competition** *n*
- **competitor** *n*
- **competitive** *adj*
- **uncompetitive** *adj*
- **competitively** *adv*
- **competing** *adj*
- **competitiveness** *n*

---

competence /ˈkɒmpɪtəns/ or **competency** /ˈkɒmpɪtənsi/ *noun* [U] **1** the ability to do something well: *I am not questioning your competence.* **2** LAW the fact of being allowed to have your case judged by a court

competent /ˈkɒmpɪtənt/ *adj* **1** capable of doing something well **2** good enough, but not extremely good ≠ INCOMPETENT **3** LAW allowed to have a case judged in court —**competently** *adv*

competing /kəmˈpiːtɪŋ/ *adj* competing arguments, claims, or theories cannot all be true

competition /ˌkɒmpəˈtɪʃ(ə)n/ *noun* **1** [U] the activities of companies that are trying to be more successful than others: *intense* ***competition between*** *the two computer giants* **2** [U] the activities of people who are trying to get something that other people also want: *There is a lot of* ***competition for*** *jobs.* ♦ *We must emphasize that we are not* ***in competition with*** *you.* **3** [C] an organized event in which people try to win prizes by being better than other people: *He'd* ***entered a competition*** *in the local newspaper.*

> PHRASE **the competition** the person, company, or thing that someone is competing with: *Let's look at what the competition is doing and do it better.*

> **The competition** can be used with a singular or plural verb. You can say *Let's look at what the competition is doing.* OR *Let's look at what the competition* ***are*** *doing.*

competitive /kəmˈpetətɪv/ *adj* **1** a competitive activity is one in which companies or teams are competing against each other: *the struggle to survive in a* ***highly competitive*** *marketplace* **2** cheaper than others: *a wide range of goods at very competitive prices* **3** always trying to be more successful than other people: *a* ***highly competitive*** *player* —**competitively** *adv*, **competitiveness** *noun* [U]

competitor /kəmˈpetɪtə/ *noun* [C] **1** a company that sells the same goods or services as another **2** someone who takes part in a sports competition

compilation /ˌkɒmpəˈleɪʃ(ə)n/ *noun* [C] a set of things such as songs or stories that are brought together from different places

compile /kəmˈpaɪl/ *verb* [T] **1** to make a list or book using information from many different places **2** COMPUTING to use a computer program to change a set of instructions in a **programming language** into a form that can be used directly by a computer —**compiler** *noun* [C]

complacent /kəmˈpleɪs(ə)nt/ *adj* someone who is complacent is too confident and relaxed because they think they can deal with something easily, even though this may not be true —**complacently** *adv*, **complacency** /kəmˈpleɪs(ə)nsi/ *noun* [U]

complain /kəmˈpleɪn/ *verb* [I/T] to say that you are not satisfied with something: *What are you* ***complaining about?*** ♦ *He threatened to* ***complain to*** *the boss.* ♦ *She* ***complained that*** *it was too hot.*

complainant /kəmˈpleɪnənt/ *noun* [C] LAW in a court of law, the person who has asked the court to judge their case

complaint /kəmˈpleɪnt/ *noun* **1** [C/U] a statement that you are not satisfied with something: *I intend to* ***make a complaint.*** ♦ *There's been a* ***complaint about*** *your work.* **2** [C] something that someone complains about: *The main complaint was the noise.* **3** [C] an illness or other medical problem

complement[1] /ˈkɒmplɪment/ *verb* [T] to combine well with something: *a simple sweater that was complemented by elegant jewellery*

complement[2] /ˈkɒmplɪmənt/ *noun* [C] **1** something that is added to something else = ADDITION **2** something that combines well with something else: *Our sauces are the perfect* ***complement to*** *any meal.* **3** the number of people or things that something has: *We already have our* ***full complement*** *of workers.* **4** LANGUAGE a word or phrase after a verb such as 'be' that tells you about the subject. For example, in 'He was a nice man', the complement is 'a nice man'.

complementary /ˌkɒmplɪˈment(ə)ri/ *adj* combining well together, or looking attractive together

comple,mentary 'angles *noun* [plural] MATHS two angles that together form a right angle —*picture* → ANGLE

comple,mentary 'colour *noun* [C] ARTS, PHYSICS a colour that produces white light when it is mixed with a **secondary colour**

,complementary 'medicine *noun* [U] HEALTH various methods of medical treatment that are not the usual scientific methods used by most doctors but can be used in addition to them. In western societies, **acupuncture** and **hypnosis** are types of complementary medicine.

complementation /ˌkɒmplɪmənˈteɪʃ(ə)n/ *noun* [U] LANGUAGE the words or phrases used as **complements** in a sentence

complete[1] /kəmˈpliːt/ *adj* **1** used for emphasizing that someone or something has a particular quality: *He's a complete idiot!* **2** including everything ≠ INCOMPLETE: *a complete set of her novels* **3** finished: *When the chart is complete, stick it on the wall.*

> PHRASE **complete with** including something: *All our machines come complete with a three-year service warranty.*

—**completeness** *noun* [U]

complete[2] /kəmˈpliːt/ *verb* [T] **1** to finish something: *The work was completed in March.* **2** to add the missing parts of something in order to finish it: *Complete the following sentence by writing in the correct form of the present tense.*

com,plete com'bustion *noun* [U] SCIENCE burning that takes place when there is plenty of oxygen. It does not give out much light and it produces carbon dioxide but no **carbon monoxide** or **soot** (=black powder).

completely /kəmˈpliːtli/ *adv* used for emphasis: *Ellen's suggestion took us completely by surprise.*

completion /kəmˈpliːʃ(ə)n/ noun [U] the process of finishing an activity or job: *Nothing must delay the* **completion of** *the project.* ♦ *You will get a certificate* **on completion** *of the course.*

complex¹ /ˈkɒmpleks, kəmˈpleks/ adj **1** containing a lot of details or small parts and therefore difficult to understand or deal with: *These rules are* **highly complex.** **2** LANGUAGE a complex sentence contains one main clause and one or more **subordinate clauses**

complex² /ˈkɒmpleks/ noun [C] **1** a group of buildings, or a building with several parts **2** an emotional problem caused by unreasonable fears or worries: *I used to* **have a complex about** *being so tall.*

complexion /kəmˈplekʃ(ə)n/ noun [C] the appearance and colour of the skin on your face

complexity /kəmˈpleksəti/ noun **1** [U] the complicated nature of something **2** complexities [plural] the features of something that make it confusing or difficult to deal with

,**complex 'sugar** noun [C] CHEMISTRY, BIOLOGY a compound such as starch that consists of chains of glucose molecules joined together, so that they form a **polysaccharide**

compliance /kəmˈplaɪəns/ noun [U] *formal* the practice of obeying a law, rule, or request: *All building work must be carried out* **in compliance with** *safety regulations.*

compliant /kəmˈplaɪənt/ adj **1** extremely willing to do what people tell you to do ꞊ SOFT **2** designed to follow a particular law, system, or set of instructions

complicate /ˈkɒmplɪkeɪt/ verb [T] to make something more difficult to deal with or understand

complicated /ˈkɒmplɪˌkeɪtɪd/ adj difficult to do, deal with, or understand ≠ SIMPLE

complication /ˌkɒmplɪˈkeɪʃ(ə)n/ noun **1** [C/U] something that makes a process or activity more difficult to deal with **2** [C] HEALTH a new medical problem that makes an existing medical condition more serious or more difficult to treat

complicity /kəmˈplɪsəti/ noun [U] the fact that someone is involved in or knows about something bad

compliment¹ /ˈkɒmplɪmənt/ noun [C] something nice that you say to praise someone ≠ INSULT: *He kept* **paying** *me* **compliments** *on my cooking.*

compliment² /ˈkɒmplɪment/ verb [T] to say something nice to or about someone: *Everybody* **complimented** *her* **on** *the way she handled the emergency.*

complimentary /ˌkɒmplɪˈment(ə)ri/ adj **1** free: *complimentary tickets* **2** saying nice things about someone or something: *She was most* **complimentary about** *your work.*

comply /kəmˈplaɪ/ (**complies, complying, complied**) verb [I] to obey a rule or law, or to do what someone asks you to do: *You are legally obliged to* **comply with** *any investigations.*

component /kəmˈpəʊnənt/ noun [C] **1** a part of a machine or piece of equipment **2** an individual quality or feature of something

compose /kəmˈpəʊz/ verb **1** [I/T] MUSIC to write a piece of music: *The song was composed for their wedding.* **2** [T] *formal* to arrange the parts of something such as a photograph or a painting in order to get a particular effect **3** [T] *formal* to write something after thinking carefully about it: *He sat down and composed a letter of resignation.*

PHRASES **be composed of sth** to consist of something: *Muscle is composed of two different types of protein.*
compose yourself to make yourself calm after being very angry, upset, or nervous

composed /kəmˈpəʊzd/ adj calm and relaxed

composer /kəmˈpəʊzə/ noun [C] MUSIC someone who writes music

composite /ˈkɒmpəzɪt/ adj made up of separate parts —**composite** noun [C]

,**composite vol'cano** noun [C] GEOLOGY a **stratovolcano**

composition /ˌkɒmpəˈzɪʃ(ə)n/ noun **1** [U] the way in which something is formed from separate parts or people: *Households differ widely in their size and composition.* **2** [C] a piece of music, a piece of writing, or a painting **3** [U] the skill or process of producing music, writing, or paintings —**compositional** adj

compost /ˈkɒmpɒst/ noun [U] **1** AGRICULTURE, BIOLOGY a mixture of decayed plant material that is added to soil to improve it **2 potting compost**

composure /kəmˈpəʊʒə/ noun [U] the feeling of being calm and relaxed

compound¹ /ˈkɒmpaʊnd/ noun [C] **1** CHEMISTRY a chemical substance that consists of two or more elements that together form a molecule. Each different compound has a fixed ratio of elements, for example the water compound (H_2O) always consists of two hydrogen atoms and one oxygen atom. **2** an enclosed area where a particular group of people live or exercise **3** LANGUAGE a combination of two or more words that is used as a single word. The three different types of compound are **noun compounds** such as 'bus stop', **adjective compounds** such as 'self-centred', and **verb compounds** such as 'date-stamp'.

compound² /ˈkɒmpaʊnd/ adj LANGUAGE a compound noun, adjective, or verb is a combination of two or more words

,**compound ex'periment** noun [C] MATHS an experiment that consists of two or more experiments

,**compound 'eye** noun [C] BIOLOGY the type of eye that insects and crustaceans have, made from several different parts that are sensitive to light —*picture →* INSECT

,**compound 'fracture** noun [C] HEALTH a broken bone that cuts through the surface of the skin

,**compound 'interest** noun [U] interest that is based both on an amount of money that someone has borrowed or saved, and on the interest that keeps being added to it

,**compound 'leaf** noun [C] BIOLOGY a leaf that consists of two or more smaller leaves on one stalk → SIMPLE LEAF

,**compound 'outcome** noun [C] MATHS a result that consists of the results of each of the experiments that make up a particular compound experiment

comprehend /ˌkɒmprɪˈhend/ verb [I/T] *formal* to understand something

comprehensible /ˌkɒmprɪˈhensəb(ə)l/ adj able to be understood ≠ INCOMPREHENSIBLE

comprehension /ˌkɒmprɪˈhenʃ(ə)n/ noun **1** [U] the ability to understand something: *These acts of cruelty are* **beyond** *my* **comprehension** (=impossible for me to understand). **2** [C/U] EDUCATION a test of how well students understand a piece of written or spoken language

comprehensive[1] /ˌkɒmprɪˈhensɪv/ adj **1** including everything: *a comprehensive guide to university courses* **2** EDUCATION relating to a system of education in the UK in which students with different levels of ability are all taught in the same school —**comprehensively** adv

comprehensive[2] /ˌkɒmprɪˈhensɪv/ or **compreˈhensive ˌschool** noun [C] EDUCATION in the UK, a school for students of different levels of ability between the ages of 11 and 18

compress /kəmˈpres/ verb [T] **1** to press something so that it fits into a smaller space **2** COMPUTING to reduce the size of a computer file so that it can be stored using less space **3** to make something continue for less time than usual

compressed /kəmˈprest/ adj pressed or squeezed together

compression /kəmˈpreʃ(ə)n/ noun [U] PHYSICS the process of pressing or squeezing something. When sound travels through a material, the molecules in the material are alternately compressed (=pushed together) and **rarefied** (=pulled apart).

comˈpression ˌchamber noun [C] PHYSICS the part of a **jet** engine where air is put under additional pressure before it is sent into the **combustion chamber** to be mixed with fuel and burned —*picture* → JET ENGINE

comˈpression igˈnition ˌengine noun [C] ENGINEERING an engine in which air is compressed and then fuel is added to it, so that the air starts to burn

comˈpression ˌratio noun [C] ENGINEERING the ratio between the largest and smallest possible volumes in the cylinder of an **internal-combustion engine** that contains a combination of fuel and air being compressed

comˈpression ˌring noun [C] ENGINEERING a circular piece of metal that uses pressure from **combustion** to push against a cylinder wall and form a tight **seal** between the cylinder wall and a **piston**

comˈpression ˌstroke noun [C] ENGINEERING the second of four movements of the **piston** in an **internal-combustion engine** in which the air is compressed in the top of the cylinder until it starts burning

comprise /kəmˈpraɪz/ verb [T] *formal* to form something: *People aged 65 and over comprise 20% of the population.*
    PHRASE **be comprised of** to consist of two or more things: *The force is comprised of US and British troops.*

compromise[1] /ˈkɒmprəmaɪz/ noun [C/U] a way of solving a disagreement in which both people accept that they cannot have everything that they want: *Neither of them is willing to **make compromises**.*

compromise[2] /ˈkɒmprəmaɪz/ verb **1** [I] to solve a disagreement by accepting that you cannot have everything that you want: *Can we **compromise on** the schedule if not on pay?* **2** [T] to risk harming or losing something important: *We cannot compromise the safety of our workers.* **3** [T] to do things that do not agree with your beliefs or principles: *The party is obviously compromising its principles.*

compromising /ˈkɒmprəˌmaɪzɪŋ/ adj likely to damage your reputation

compulsion /kəmˈpʌlʃ(ə)n/ noun **1** [C] an extremely strong feeling of wanting to do something **2** [U] an obligation to do something

compulsive /kəmˈpʌlsɪv/ adj **1** impossible to control: *a compulsive need to succeed* **2** unable to control a habit: *a compulsive liar* —**compulsively** adv

compulsory /kəmˈpʌlsəri/ adj something that is compulsory must be done or used because of a rule or law ≠ OPTIONAL: *compulsory exams* —**compulsorily** adv

compunction /kəmˈpʌŋkʃ(ə)n/ noun [U] *formal* a feeling that you should not do something because it is wrong

computation /ˌkɒmpjʊˈteɪʃ(ə)n/ noun [C/U] *formal* the process of calculating a number or amount

computational /ˌkɒmpjʊˈteɪʃ(ə)nəl/ adj **1** COMPUTING involving the use of computers **2** relating to the ability to calculate numbers or amounts

ˌcomputational linˈguistics noun [U] LANGUAGE the study of language using computers

computer /kəmˈpjuːtə/ noun [C] COMPUTING an electronic machine that has programs on it for storing, writing, and calculating information. It also allows you to communicate on the Internet: *The job requires basic computer skills.* —*picture* → on next page

computer-aided machining /kəmˌpjuːtə ˌeɪdɪd məˈʃiːnɪŋ/ noun [U] COMPUTING, ENGINEERING the use of computers to make an object on a machine, especially a metal object

comˌputer assisted ˈlearning noun [U] EDUCATION the use of computer programs to help in developing study skills and subject knowledge

computerate /kəmˈpjuːtərət/ adj *informal* able to use a computer = COMPUTER-LITERATE

comˈputer ˌgame noun [C] COMPUTING a game that is played on a computer

computerize /kəmˈpjuːtəraɪz/ verb [T] COMPUTING to use computers to do a particular job —**computerization** /kəmˌpjuːtəraɪˈzeɪʃ(ə)n/ noun [U]

comˌputer-ˈliterate adj COMPUTING able to use a computer

comˌputer ˈscience noun [U] COMPUTING the study of how computers work and what they can be used for

computing /kəmˈpjuːtɪŋ/ noun [U] COMPUTING the activity or skill of using or programming computers

comrade /ˈkɒmreɪd/ noun [C] *formal* a friend who someone works with or who is in the same army as someone —**comradeship** noun [U]

con /kɒn/ (**cons, conning, conned**) verb [T] *informal* to make someone believe something that is not true in order to get money from them —**con** noun [C]

concatenate /kənˈkætəneɪt/ verb [T] COMPUTING to put two or more computer files or pieces of computer information together, in order to form a single unit

concave /ˈkɒnkeɪv, kɒnˈkeɪv/ adj curved inwards ≠ CONVEX —*picture* → LENS, PROJECTOR, SHAPE, SHORT-SIGHTED

conceal /kənˈsiːl/ verb [T] *formal* to hide something, or to keep something secret: *She could not conceal her annoyance.* —**concealment** noun [U]

concede /kənˈsiːd/ verb **1** [T] to admit that something is true: *Myers was forced to **concede that** competition had badly affected profits.* **2** [I/T] to stop trying to win something because you realize that you cannot: *He finally had to **concede defeat**.* **3** [T] to give something that you own or control to someone, although you do not want to: *Some territory has been conceded to the rebels.* **4** [T] SPORTS if you concede a goal, point, or game, the person or team you are playing scores a goal or point or wins a game

conceit /kənˈsiːt/ noun **1** [U] a conceited attitude or way of behaving **2** [C/U] LANGUAGE a clever and

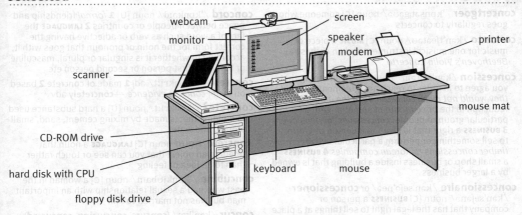

webcam

screen

monitor

speaker

modem

printer

scanner

mouse mat

CD-ROM drive

hard disk with CPU

keyboard

mouse

floppy disk drive

computer and peripherals

unusual idea or way of comparing things, especially in poetry

conceited /kən'siːtɪd/ adj *showing disapproval* someone who is conceited behaves in a way that shows they think they are very intelligent, skilful, or attractive

conceivable /kən'siːvəb(ə)l/ adj possible, or possible to imagine ≠ INCONCEIVABLE —**conceivably** adv

conceive /kən'siːv/ verb **1** [T] to think of a new idea, plan, or design: *The facilities had been conceived with families in mind.* **2** [I/T] to imagine something, or to think of doing something: *How can they even conceive of doing such an appalling thing?* **3** [I] BIOLOGY to become pregnant **4** [T] BIOLOGY to cause an embryo to start to exist by fertilizing an egg

concentrate /'kɒns(ə)n,treɪt/ verb **1** [I/T] to give all your attention to the thing that you are doing: *Shh! I'm trying to concentrate.* ♦ *Just concentrate on your work.* **2** [T] **be concentrated** to exist mainly in a particular area: *The violence was concentrated mostly in the north.*

concentrated /'kɒns(ə)n,treɪtɪd/ adj **1** CHEMISTRY concentrated liquids or substances have been made stronger by having water removed **2** directed completely at one thing, person, or place: *The presidential palace has been hit again by concentrated artillery fire.*

concentration /,kɒns(ə)n'treɪʃ(ə)n/ noun **1** [U] the process of giving all your attention to something: *It took all his concentration to stay awake.* **2** [C/U] a large number of people or things in one area: *The largest concentrations of ancient sites are around Cairo and Luxor.* **3** [C/U] CHEMISTRY the amount of a substance that is present in something: *An investigation found high concentrations of cancer-causing chemicals on the property.*

concen'tration ,camp noun [C] a prison where ordinary people are kept during a war in very unpleasant conditions

concentric /kən'sentrɪk/ adj concentric circles all have the same centre

concept /'kɒnsept/ noun [C] an idea: *It's important that children learn to understand the concept of sharing.*

conception /kən'sepʃ(ə)n/ noun **1** [C] a belief about what something is like: *His conception of the world is a very strange one.* **2** [U] BIOLOGY the moment when a woman or other female mammal becomes pregnant

conceptual /kən'septʃuəl/ adj relating to ideas and things you can imagine

con'ceptual ,art noun [U] ARTS art in which the idea the artist wants to express though a piece of work is more important than the work itself

conceptualize /kən'septʃuəlaɪz/ verb [T] *formal* to form an idea about what something is like, or how it should work

concern[1] /kən'sɜːn/ noun **1** [C/U] a feeling of worry, or something that worries you: *The trip was cancelled because of concerns about safety.* ♦ *Doctors said her condition was causing concern.* **2** [C/U] something that you think is important: *My only concern is to find my daughter.* **3** [C] a responsibility: *If children are not attending school, then that is the parents' concern.* **4** [C] a business: *a large concern employing 60 people*

concern[2] /kən'sɜːn/ verb [T] **1** to worry someone: *It concerns me that these people are not getting the support they need.* **2** to be about a particular subject: *The story concerns a friend of mine.* **3** to involve or affect someone: *My past doesn't concern you.*

PHRASE **concern yourself** to think about or worry about something: *I'm too busy to concern myself with your affairs.*

concerned /kən'sɜːnd/ adj **1** worried about something ≠ UNCONCERNED: *Police said they were very concerned about the boy's safety.* **2** involved in something, or affected by something: *I suggest you speak to the person concerned.* **3** caring about what happens to someone: *I think she's genuinely concerned about you.* **4** giving your attention to something that you think is important: *Don't be so concerned with what other people think of you.*

PHRASES **as far as I'm concerned** used for giving your opinion about something: *As far as I'm concerned, the issue is over and done with.*

as far as sb/sth is concerned used for saying which person or thing you are talking about: *I make the decisions as far as finance is concerned.*

concerning /kən'sɜːnɪŋ/ preposition *formal* about a particular subject: *the laws concerning safety in factories*

concert /'kɒnsət/ noun [C] MUSIC an event at which an orchestra, band, or musician plays or sings in front of an audience

concerted /kən'sɜːtɪd/ adj involving a lot of people working together in a determined way: *a concerted effort*

concertgoer /'kɒnsət,gəʊə/ noun [C] someone who goes regularly to concerts

concerto /kən'tʃeətəʊ/ noun [C] MUSIC a piece of music for one musical instrument and an orchestra: *Beethoven's Violin Concerto*

concession /kən'seʃ(ə)n/ noun [C] **1** something that you agree to in order to reach an agreement: *He said they would not* **make concessions to** *the union.* **2** a reduction in the price or rate of something for a particular group of people: *concessions for pensioners* **3** BUSINESS a right that is given to a person or group to sell something or perform a particular activity: *timber concessions to Korean companies* **4** BUSINESS a small shop or business inside a building that is owned by a larger business

concessionaire /kən,seʃə'neə/ or **concessioner** /kən'seʃənə/ noun [C] BUSINESS a person or company that has the legal right to sell things at a place owned by someone else

concessive clause /kən,sesɪv 'klɔːz/ noun [C] LANGUAGE a part of a sentence that usually begins with 'although', 'though', or 'while', and contains a fact or idea that seems to oppose the information in the rest of the sentence

conch /kɒŋk, kɒntʃ/ noun [C] the large curved shell of a sea animal that is also called a **conch**

concierge /'kɒnsi,eəʒ/ noun [C] TOURISM someone whose job is to help people staying in a hotel by dealing with problems and giving them information

conciliation /kən,sɪli'eɪʃ(ə)n/ noun [U] the process of trying to end an argument between two people or groups

conciliatory /kən'sɪliət(ə)ri/ adj trying to end an argument and make people feel less angry

concise /kən'saɪs/ adj expressed clearly using only a few words —**concisely** adv

conclude /kən'kluːd/ verb **1** [T] to decide that something is true after looking at all the evidence: *The report* **concluded that** *a recession was unlikely.* **2** [I/T] *formal* to end, or to end something: *The president will* **conclude** *his visit* **with** *a trip to Munich.* **3** [T] *formal* to officially arrange something: *We hope to conclude an agreement by the end of the day.*

concluding /kən'kluːdɪŋ/ adj happening or done at the end of something: *concluding remarks*

conclusion /kən'kluːʒ(ə)n/ noun **1** [C] something that you decide is true after looking at all the evidence: *I finally* **came to the conclusion** *that Lenny wasn't interested in me.* ♦ *Hubble* **reached the conclusion** *that the universe was expanding.* **2** [singular] *formal* the end of something: *a successful* **conclusion to** *the season* **3** [U] the process of officially arranging something: *The successful* **conclusion of** *the deal was announced at a press conference.*
PHRASES **in conclusion** finally: *In conclusion, I would like to thank my wife and children.*
jump to conclusions to make a decision about something before you know all the facts

conclusive /kən'kluːsɪv/ adj conclusive evidence, proof, or information proves that something is true ≠ INCONCLUSIVE —**conclusively** adv

concoct /kən'kɒkt/ verb [T] **1** to invent a false explanation or false information **2** to produce something unusual by mixing things in a new way —**concoction** /kən'kɒkʃ(ə)n/ noun [C/U]

concomitant /kən'kɒmɪtənt/ adj *formal* happening at the same time as something else

concord /'kɒnkɔːd/ noun [U] **1** *formal* friendship and peace between people or countries **2** LANGUAGE the fact of a word such as verb or adjective having the correct form for the noun or pronoun that goes with it, according to whether it is singular or plural, masculine or feminine, first person or second person etc

concrete¹ /'kɒnkriːt/ adj **1** made of concrete **2** based on facts: *concrete evidence* —**concretely** adv

concrete² /'kɒnkriːt/ noun [U] a hard substance used in building that is made by mixing cement, sand, small stones, and water

,concrete 'noun noun [C] LANGUAGE a noun that refers to an object that you can see or touch rather than to an idea or feeling

concubine /'kɒŋkjʊbaɪn/ noun [C] a woman in the past who had a sexual relationship with an important man but was not married to him

concur /kən'kɜː/ (**concurs**, **concurring**, **concurred**) verb [I] *formal* to agree

concurrent /kən'kʌrənt/ adj *formal* happening or done at the same time

concussion /kən'kʌʃ(ə)n/ noun [C/U] HEALTH a head injury that makes someone feel ill or become unconscious for a short time

condemn /kən'dem/ verb [T] **1** to say publicly that someone or something is bad or wrong: *The minister* **condemned** *the proposal* **as** *'very damaging'.* **2** to give a punishment to someone who has committed a crime: *Fifty rebels were* **condemned to death.** **3** if something condemns someone to an unpleasant situation, it forces them to experience it: *Peacock's goal* **condemned** *United* **to** *their first defeat since March.* **4** to order something such as a building or machine to be destroyed because it is not safe

condemnation /,kɒndem'neɪʃ(ə)n/ noun [C/U] a public statement in which someone severely criticizes someone or something

condemnatory /kən'demnət(ə)ri/ adj expressing severe criticism

condensation /,kɒnden'seɪʃ(ə)n/ noun SCIENCE **1** water that forms when steam or warm air changes into liquid **2** the process in which a gas changes into a liquid, usually when it becomes **cooler** —*picture →* WATER CYCLE

condense /kən'dens/ verb **1** [I/T] SCIENCE if gas or steam condenses, or if something or someone condenses it, it changes into a liquid, usually when it becomes **cooler** —*picture →* STATE **2** [T] to make something shorter or smaller

condenser /kən'densə/ noun [C] **1** SCIENCE a piece of equipment that changes gases into liquids —*picture →* DESALINATION, DISTILLATION, GENERATOR, LABORATORY, NUCLEAR REACTOR **2** ENGINEERING a piece of equipment in a vehicle's engine that stores electricity

condensing lens /kən'densɪŋ ,lenz/ noun [C] PHYSICS a lens that makes light rays move towards each other after they hit it

condescending /,kɒndɪ'sendɪŋ/ adj *showing disapproval* showing that someone thinks they are more important or intelligent than someone else —**condescension** /,kɒndɪ'senʃ(ə)n/ noun [U]

condiment /'kɒndɪmənt/ noun [C] *formal* something such as salt, pepper, or a sauce that is put on food at the table to make it taste better

condition¹ /kən'dɪʃ(ə)n/ noun **1** [singular/U] the physical state of something or someone: *Engineers will examine the condition of the damaged buildings.* ♦ *The animals that were rescued were all* **in good**

condition. 2 conditions [plural] the situation or environment in which something happens or someone lives: *Their role is to create **the conditions for** peace in the region.* ♦ *The project aims to provide better **living conditions** for elderly people.* **3** [C] something that must be true or must be done before another thing can happen: *Read the **terms and conditions** of the contract carefully.* ♦ *You will have to **meet** strict financial **conditions** to get the loan.* **4** [C] an illness or health problem that lasts a long time and affects the way someone lives: *a heart condition*

PHRASES **in no condition to do sth** too ill, upset, or drunk to do something
on condition (that) used for saying that one thing will happen only if another thing also happens: *They agreed to speak on condition that their names would not be used in the article.*

condition2 /kənˈdɪʃ(ə)n/ verb [T] **1** to influence someone over a long period so that they think or behave in a particular way **2** to make hair feel softer by putting a special liquid on it after washing it —**conditioning** /kənˈdɪʃ(ə)nɪŋ/ noun [U]

conditional /kənˈdɪʃ(ə)nəl/ adj **1** something that is conditional will only happen if something else happens: *The job offer is **conditional on** passing a medical examination.* **2** LANGUAGE a conditional clause usually begins with 'if' or 'unless' and says what must happen or exist in order for the information in the main part of the sentence to be true

the conditional /kənˈdɪʃ(ə)nəl/ noun LANGUAGE the verb form used for saying that something must happen or exist in order for something else to be true

con‚ditional 'discharge noun [C] LAW a judgment given by a court of law in which someone who has committed a crime will not be punished if they obey particular conditions and rules

conditioner /kənˈdɪʃ(ə)nə/ noun [C/U] a liquid that someone puts on their hair after washing it, in order to make it feel softer

condolences /kənˈdəʊlənsɪz/ noun [plural] the things that people say in order to show sympathy when someone has just died

condom /ˈkɒndɒm/ noun [C] HEALTH a thin rubber tube that a man covers his penis with during sex in order to reduce the chance of a woman becoming pregnant. It also helps to protect against the spread of diseases.

condone /kənˈdəʊn/ verb [T] to approve of behaviour that most people think is wrong

conducive /kənˈdjuːsɪv/ adj **conducive to sth** creating a situation that helps something to happen

conduct1 /kənˈdʌkt/ verb **1** [T] to do something in an organized way: *The interview was conducted by telephone.* **2** [T] *formal* to take someone somewhere **3** [T] PHYSICS, CHEMISTRY if something conducts heat or electricity, heat or electricity can move through it **4** [I/T] MUSIC to stand in front of an orchestra or group of singers and direct the way they play or sing

conduct2 /ˈkɒndʌkt/ noun [U] *formal* **1** the way someone behaves: *The coach criticized his team for their conduct.* **2** the way in which a process or activity is managed

conducted tour /kənˌdʌktɪd ˈtʊə/ noun [C] TOURISM a short visit to a place in which someone shows people around and tells them information about it = GUIDED TOUR

conduction /kənˈdʌkʃ(ə)n/ noun [U] PHYSICS, CHEMISTRY the process by which heat or electricity passes through a substance

conductive /kənˈdʌktɪv/ adj PHYSICS, CHEMISTRY a conductive substance allows heat or electricity to pass through it

conductivity /ˌkɒndʌkˈtɪvɪti/ noun [U] **1** PHYSICS, CHEMISTRY the ability of a substance to allow electricity or heat to move through it **2** BIOLOGY the ability of tissue to allow nerve signals to move through it

conductor /kənˈdʌktə/ noun [C] **1** MUSIC someone who directs the musicians in an orchestra or a group of singers —*picture* → ORCHESTRA **2** PHYSICS, CHEMISTRY a substance that heat or electricity can pass through: *Metals are good conductors of electricity and heat.* → INSULATOR **3** someone on a bus or a train who checks tickets and collects money

conduit /ˈkɒndjuːt, ˈkɒndɪt/ noun [C] a pipe or tube that water or electrical wires pass through

cone /kəʊn/ noun [C] **1** an object with a circular base that rises to a point —*picture* → SHAPE **2** an object shaped like a cone used for holding **ice cream** in **3** BIOLOGY the reproductive part of a conifer that contains seeds —*picture* → TREE **4** ANATOMY a cell shaped like a cone in the retina of the eye. Cones make it possible for people and animals to see colours in bright light. → ROD —*picture* → RETINA

confectionery /kənˈfekʃ(ə)n(ə)ri/ noun [U] sweets and chocolate

confederated /kənˈfedəˌreɪtɪd/ verb united with other people, states, or political parties

confederation /kənˌfedəˈreɪʃ(ə)n/ noun [C] a group of people or organizations that are united

confer /kənˈfɜː/ (**confers, conferring, conferred**) verb **1** [I] to take part in a discussion about a particular subject **2** [T] *formal* to give something such as a legal right or an honour to someone

conference /ˈkɒnf(ə)rəns/ noun [C] **1** a large meeting where people who are interested in a particular subject discuss ideas: *an international **conference on** the control of illegal drugs* **2** a meeting where a small number of people have formal discussions

'conference ‚call noun [C] a telephone call involving three or more people

'conference ‚centre noun [C] a hotel with a restaurant and meeting rooms, used for holding large meetings

confess /kənˈfes/ verb [I/T] **1** if someone confesses, or confesses something, they admit that they have done something illegal or wrong: *Simpson has **confessed to** taking the money.* ♦ *He **confessed that** he had been lying.* **2** to admit something that you are embarrassed about: *He confessed he did not understand financial matters at all.* **3** RELIGION if someone confesses, or confesses something, they tell a priest about the immoral or illegal things that they have done and they ask to be forgiven

confession /kənˈfeʃ(ə)n/ noun [C/U] **1** a statement in which someone admits that they have done something illegal or wrong **2** RELIGION a statement that someone makes to a priest about the immoral or illegal things that they have done

confessional /kənˈfeʃ(ə)nəl/ noun [C] RELIGION a small room in a Roman Catholic church where a person goes to tell a priest about the immoral or illegal things they have done

confetti /kənˈfeti/ noun [U] small pieces of coloured paper that people throw in the air to celebrate a wedding

confidante /ˈkɒnfɪdænt/ noun [C] a woman who you trust and discuss your private feelings with

confide /kənˈfaɪd/ verb [I/T] to tell someone about something that is private or secret: *She confided to friends that she was scared of her mother.*

confidence /ˈkɒnfɪd(ə)ns/ noun [U] **1** the belief that you are able to do things well: *You should have more confidence in yourself.* ♦ *The more he fails, the more he loses confidence.* **2** the belief that someone or something is good and that you can trust them: *I have complete confidence in our chairman.* ♦ *Many businesses have lost confidence in the government's economic policies.* ♦ *It took me a while to gain her confidence* (=make her feel that she could trust me). **3** the belief that something is true: *I can say with confidence that all our targets have now been met.*
PHRASE in confidence if you tell someone something in confidence, you trust them not to tell anyone else: *Any information you give us will be treated in the strictest confidence.*

ˈconfidence ˌindex noun [C] ECONOMICS a number that shows how confident people are feeling about the economy, especially about spending money on goods and services

confident /ˈkɒnfɪd(ə)nt/ adj **1** certain about your abilities and not nervous or frightened: *a confident manner* ♦ *I was starting to feel more confident about the exam.* **2** certain that something will happen or be successful: *We were confident of victory.* ♦ *They are confident that the show will open on Thursday.* —**confidently** adv

confidential /ˌkɒnfɪˈdenʃ(ə)l/ adj **1** secret: *confidential information* **2** keeping information secret: *a confidential service* —**confidentially** /ˌkɒnfɪˈdenʃ(ə)li/ adv

confidentiality /ˌkɒnfɪdenʃiˈæləti/ noun [U] a situation in which important information must be kept secret

confidentiˈality aˌgreement noun [C] a legal agreement in which a person or organization that has important information about the activities of another person or organization promises not to give it to anyone else

configuration /kənˌfɪɡjəˈreɪʃ(ə)n/ noun [C/U] COMPUTING the way in which the different parts of something such as computer software are arranged

configuˈration ˌfile noun [C] COMPUTING a file that contains information about how a particular software program or piece of equipment has been arranged

configure /kənˈfɪɡə/ verb [T] COMPUTING to arrange the parts of something, especially the software of a computer, so that it works in the way you want it to

confine /kənˈfaɪn/ verb [T] **1** to keep someone or something in a particular place: *Chris was ill, and confined to bed.* **2** formal to keep an activity within particular limits: *Try to confine the discussion to general principles.* **3** be confined to to happen only in a particular area, or to affect a particular group of people: *The risk of infection is confined to a few small groups.*

confined /kənˈfaɪnd/ adj a confined space is small and difficult to move around in

confinement /kənˈfaɪnmənt/ noun [U] a situation in which someone is forced to stay in a place → SOLITARY CONFINEMENT

confines /ˈkɒnfaɪnz/ noun [plural] the borders of a place, or the limits of an activity

confirm /kənˈfɜːm/ verb **1** [T] to show or say that something is true: *The study confirms the findings of earlier research.* ♦ *The doctor may do a test to confirm that you are pregnant.* **2** [I/T] to tell someone that something will definitely happen at the time or in the way that has been arranged: *You can make an appointment now, and then call nearer the time to confirm.* **3** [T] to formally support something and allow it to happen: *The parliament's decision still has to be confirmed in a referendum.* **4** [T] RELIGION to formally accept someone into the Christian Church in a special ceremony

confirmation /ˌkɒnfəˈmeɪʃ(ə)n/ noun **1** [U] a statement saying that something is definitely true or will definitely happen **2** [C/U] RELIGION a religious ceremony in which someone becomes a full member of a Christian Church

confirmed /kənˈfɜːmd/ adj **1** always living or behaving in a particular way, or having a particular belief: *a confirmed bachelor* **2** proved and therefore known to be true or accurate

confiscate /ˈkɒnfɪˌskeɪt/ verb [T] to officially remove someone's possessions —**confiscation** /ˌkɒnfɪˈskeɪʃ(ə)n/ noun [C/U]

conflate /kənˈfleɪt/ verb [T] formal to combine two or more things —**conflation** /kənˈfleɪʃ(ə)n/ noun [U]

conflict¹ /ˈkɒnflɪkt/ noun [C/U] **1** angry disagreement between people or groups: *a conflict between the press and the police* ♦ *The management team is keen to resolve the conflict over wages.* **2** fighting between countries or groups: *a bloody border conflict* **3** a situation in which two things cannot easily exist together, or cannot both be true: *The two recommendations seem to be in conflict with each other.*

conflict² /kənˈflɪkt/ verb [I] if different statements or suggestions conflict, they cannot all be right or they cannot all happen: *His story conflicted with reports from other journalists.*

ˈconflict resoˌlution noun [U] SOCIAL STUDIES the process of finding solutions to disagreements between people, governments etc

confluence /ˈkɒnfluəns/ noun [singular] GEOGRAPHY a place where two rivers join

conform /kənˈfɔːm/ verb [I] **1** to obey a rule, or to follow an accepted pattern: *Products are tested to make sure that they conform to safety standards.* **2** to behave in the way that people expect you to behave: *There is great pressure on women to conform.* **3** to be similar to an idea of what is usual or normal —**conformity** /kənˈfɔːməti/ noun [U]

conformist /kənˈfɔːmɪst/ adj behaving in a way that most people think is correct or suitable —**conformist** noun [C]

confound /kənˈfaʊnd/ verb [T] **1** to make someone feel surprised or confused by not behaving in the way they expect **2** formal to prove that something is wrong

confront /kənˈfrʌnt/ verb [T] **1** to go close to someone in a threatening way: *The guard was confronted by an armed man.* **2** to deal with a difficult situation: *It takes courage to confront your fears.* **3** be confronted by/with sth to be forced to deal with a difficult situation: *She was confronted with the biggest crisis of her political life.*

confrontation /ˌkɒnfrʌnˈteɪʃ(ə)n/ noun [C/U] a situation in which people are fighting or arguing angrily: *violent confrontations with the police*

confrontational /ˌkɒnfrʌnˈteɪʃ(ə)nəl/ adj behaving in a way that shows that you want to fight or have an argument = ARGUMENTATIVE

Confucian /kənˈfjuːʃən/ adj relating to or based on the moral theories and principles of Confucius —**Confucian** noun [C], **Confucianism** noun [U]

confuse /kən'fju:z/ verb [T] **1** to make someone feel that they do not understand something: *Don't confuse the reader with too much detail.* **2** to make something more complicated: *This latest piece of information just confuses the issue.* **3** to make the mistake of thinking that one thing is another thing: *It's easy to confuse the two containers because they're so similar.*

confused /kən'fju:zd/ adj **1** unable to understand something or think clearly about it: *She was completely confused.* ♦ *I'm still a little **confused about** what happened.* **2** complicated and not well organized or explained: *The situation is still fairly confused.*

confusing /kən'fju:zɪŋ/ adj not easy to understand: *She left a very confusing message.*

confusion /kən'fju:ʒ(ə)n/ noun **1** [U] a feeling that you do not understand something or cannot decide what to do: *There seems to be some **confusion about** who actually won.* ♦ *These changes have just **caused** more **confusion**.* **2** [U] a situation in which things are untidy, badly organized, or not clear: *Inside the building was a scene of total confusion.* **3** [singular/U] a situation in which you make the mistake of thinking that one person or thing is another: *I've put them in different coloured folders to **avoid confusion**.*

congeal /kən'dʒi:l/ verb [I] if a liquid congeals, it becomes thick and almost solid —**congealed** /kən'dʒi:ld/ adj

congenital /kən'dʒenɪt(ə)l/ adj **HEALTH** a congenital medical condition is one that someone was born with

conger eel /ˌkɒŋgə 'i:l/ noun [C] a sea fish with a long thin body that lives in warm parts of the Atlantic Ocean

congested /kən'dʒestɪd/ adj **1** so full of vehicles or people that it is difficult to move about: *Many of Europe's major airports are heavily congested.* **2** blocked with a liquid: *His nose was congested.*

congestion /kən'dʒestʃ(ə)n/ noun [U] a situation or condition in which something is blocked

congestion charge noun [C] a payment that people make each day for the right to drive into a city centre, introduced as a way of reducing traffic

conglomerate /kən'glɒmərət/ noun [C] **BUSINESS** a large business that was formed by joining together several businesses

congratulate /kən'grætʃʊleɪt/ verb [T] to tell someone that you are pleased about their success, good luck, or happiness on a special occasion: *I **congratulated** him **on** his recent promotion.*

congratulations /kənˌgrætʃʊ'leɪʃ(ə)nz/ noun [plural] *spoken* used for telling someone that you are pleased about their success, good luck, or happiness on a special occasion: ***Congratulations on** passing your exam!*

congratulatory /kənˌgrætʃʊ'leɪt(ə)ri/ adj *formal* offering congratulations

congregate /'kɒŋgrɪgeɪt/ verb [I] to come together in a group

congregation /ˌkɒŋgrɪ'geɪʃ(ə)n/ noun [C] **RELIGION** a group of people who go to a religious service

congress /'kɒŋgres/ noun [C] **1** a large formal meeting **2 Congress POLITICS** a group of people who are elected to make laws in some countries, such as the US

congressional /kən'greʃ(ə)n(ə)l/ adj **1** relating to a congress **2 Congressional POLITICS** relating to the US Congress

congruent /'kɒŋgruənt/ adj **MATHS** congruent shapes are exactly the same size and shape —**congruence** noun [U]

conical /'kɒnɪk(ə)l/ adj **MATHS** with a circular base that rises to a point

conical 'flask noun [C] **SCIENCE** a glass container used in laboratories. It is wide and flat at the bottom and has a long narrow neck. —*picture* → LABORATORY

conifer /'kɒnɪfə/ noun [C] **BIOLOGY** a type of **shrub** or tree that produces **cones** (=hard brown structures) and whose leaves do not fall off in winter. **Pines**, **firs**, and **yews** are conifers. —**coniferous** /kə'nɪf(ə)rəs/ adj

conjecture /kən'dʒektʃə/ noun [C/U] a theory based on information that is not complete

conjoined twin /kənˌdʒɔɪnd 'twɪn/ noun [C] **HEALTH** one of two people who are physically joined at birth

conjugal /'kɒndʒʊg(ə)l/ adj *formal* relating to marriage

conjugate /'kɒndʒʊgeɪt/ verb [T] **LANGUAGE** to state the different forms that a verb can have —**conjugation** /ˌkɒndʒʊ'geɪʃ(ə)n/ noun [C/U]

conjunction /kən'dʒʌŋkʃ(ə)n/ noun [C] **LANGUAGE** a word that is used to join other words, phrases, and sentences, for example 'and', 'because', and 'although' **PHRASE in conjunction with** combined with

conjunctiva /ˌkɒndʒʌŋk'taɪvə/ noun [C] **ANATOMY** the thin delicate skin that covers the inside of the eyelid and the **cornea** at the front of the eye —*picture* → EYE

conjunctivitis /kənˌdʒʌŋktɪ'vaɪtɪs/ noun [U] **HEALTH** an illness in which the inside of the eyelid becomes red and swollen

conjurer or **conjuror** /'kʌndʒərə/ noun [C] someone who performs magic tricks using quick hand movements

conker /'kɒŋkə/ noun [C] the large shiny brown seed of the **horse chestnut** tree

connect /kə'nekt/ verb

1 join things	4 show a relationship
2 join to energy supply	5 in changing vehicles
3 with phone/computer	6 understand sb/sth

1 [I/T] to join two things together: *She carefully connected the two wires.* ♦ *one of the bridges **connecting** Manhattan **to** the rest of New York*
2 [T] to join something to a supply of electricity, water, or gas: *Check that your printer is connected and that the power is turned on.*
3 [I/T] to make it possible for someone to communicate using a telephone or computer system: *Please wait, we are trying to connect you.* ♦ *Your modem enables you to **connect to** the Internet.*
4 [T] to show a relationship between one person or thing and another: *There was no evidence then to connect smoking and lung cancer.* ♦ *Police found nothing that **connected** him **with** the murder.*
5 [I] to arrive in time for you to continue your journey on another plane, train, bus etc: *a connecting flight*
6 [I] to feel that you have similar ideas, opinions, and beliefs to someone: *I never really connected with him.*

connected /kə'nektɪd/ adj **1** related to each other: *Were the two deaths connected?* **2** joined to each other or to something else: *connected underground tunnels* **3** able to communicate using a telephone or computer system

connecting rod /kə'nektɪŋ ˌrɒd/ noun [C] **ENGINEERING** a bar that passes movement from one part to another, especially the bar that connects the **crankshaft** to the **piston** in an **internal-combustion engine**

connection /kəˈnekʃ(ə)n/ noun

1 relationship	**5** of energy supply
2 transport	**6** people you know
3 for phone/computer	**+** PHRASE
4 where things join	

1 [C] a relationship between things or people: *I don't see **a connection between** the two cases.* ♦ *She was alleged to have **connections with** the secret police.*
2 [C] a train, bus, or plane that allows people to continue a journey: *My train was late and I **missed my connection**.*
3 [C] a means of communicating using a telephone or computer system: *high-speed Internet connections*
4 [C] a place where two things join: *The light keeps flickering – there must be a loose connection.*
5 [U] the process of joining something to a supply of electricity, water, or gas: *a connection charge*
6 connections [plural] important people who someone knows and who can help them: *He used his connections to get a government job.*

PHRASE **in connection with sth** *formal* relating to something: *Police want to talk to him **in connection with** the murder.*

connective /kəˈnektɪv/ noun [C] LANGUAGE a word that is used to join other words, phrases, clauses, and sentences, for example 'and', 'because', and 'but' = CONJUNCTION

con,nective 'tissue noun [U] HEALTH a type of very strong tissue that connects and supports organs and other parts of the body. Connective tissue can consist of fat, bone, cartilage etc.

connectivity /ˌkɒnekˈtɪvəti/ noun [U] COMPUTING the ability of computers and other types of electronic equipment to connect successfully with other computers or programs

connector /kəˈnektə/ noun [C] an object that is fixed to the end of a wire, used for connecting two pieces of equipment

conning tower /ˈkɒnɪŋ ˌtaʊə/ noun [C] the part on top of a **submarine** from which the **periscope** sticks out

connoisseur /ˌkɒnəˈsɜː/ noun [C] someone who knows a lot about a particular thing and enjoys it very much

connotation /ˌkɒnəˈteɪʃ(ə)n/ noun [C] LANGUAGE an additional idea that a word suggests to you, that is not part of its main meaning

connotative /ˈkɒnəteɪtɪv, kəˈnəʊtətɪv/ adj LANGUAGE relating to the additional ideas that are suggested by a word, rather than its literal meaning

conquer /ˈkɒŋkə/ verb **1** [I/T] to take control of land or people using force **2** [T] to gain control of a situation or emotion by making a great effort: *He managed to conquer his feelings of disgust.*

conqueror /ˈkɒŋkərə/ noun [C] someone who has taken control of land or people by force

conquest /ˈkɒŋkwest/ noun [C/U] the process of taking control of something, or the thing or place that someone takes control of

conrod /ˈkɒnˌrɒd/ noun [C] ENGINEERING the bar that connects the **crankshaft** to the **piston** in an **internal-combustion engine**

conscience /ˈkɒnʃ(ə)ns/ noun [C/U] the ideas and feelings you have that tell you whether something that you are doing is right or wrong: *Maybe he has **a guilty conscience** (=a bad feeling because he knows he has done something wrong).* ♦ *We want to leave with **a clear conscience** (=the knowledge that we have done nothing wrong).*

PHRASE **on your conscience** causing you to feel guilty

conscientious /ˌkɒnʃiˈenʃəs/ adj working hard, and careful to do things well —**conscientiously** adv

conscious /ˈkɒnʃəs/ adj **1** noticing that something exists or is happening and realizing that it is important = AWARE: *He was **conscious of** the fact that everyone was waiting for him.* ♦ *We are **conscious that** some people may not wish to work at night.* **2** awake and able to see, hear, and think ≠ UNCONSCIOUS: *The patient was fully conscious throughout the operation.* **3** done deliberately by someone who knows what the effect will be: *a conscious effort* **4** a conscious thought or experience is one that you realize you are having: *She had no conscious memory of having met him before.*

consciously /ˈkɒnʃəsli/ adv **1** in a deliberate way **2** in a way that makes you certain that something exists or has happened

consciousness /ˈkɒnʃəsnəs/ noun **1** [U] the state of being awake and able to see, hear, and think: *The pain was so bad that I **lost consciousness**.* **2** [U] the knowledge or understanding that something exists or is important: *We want to increase students' **consciousness of** health issues.* **3** [singular/U] someone's mind and thoughts

conscript¹ /kənˈskrɪpt/ verb [T] to make someone join the armed forces —**conscription** /kənˈskrɪpʃ(ə)n/ noun [U]

conscript² /ˈkɒnskrɪpt/ noun [C] someone who has been forced to join the armed forces

consecrate /ˈkɒnsɪˌkreɪt/ verb [T] RELIGION to perform a religious ceremony in order to make a place or a thing holy —**consecration** /ˌkɒnsɪˈkreɪʃ(ə)n/ noun [C/U]

consecutive /kənˈsekjʊtɪv/ adj following one after another: *her fifth consecutive defeat* —**consecutively** adv

consensual /kənˈsenʃʊəl/ adj *formal* agreed to by all the people involved

consensus /kənˈsensəs/ noun [singular/U] agreement among all the people involved: *We have finally **reached a consensus** on this issue.*

consent¹ /kənˈsent/ noun [U] permission to do something: *He entered the building without the owner's consent.*

consent² /kənˈsent/ verb [I] to give someone permission to do something, or to agree to do something: *The child's parents would not **consent to** the treatment.*

consequence /ˈkɒnsɪkwəns/ noun [C] a result or effect of something: *Climate change could have **disastrous consequences**.* ♦ *the economic **consequences of** government policies* ♦ *Demand for oil increased and, **as a consequence**, the price went up.*

PHRASE **of no consequence** *formal* not important in any way

consequently /ˈkɒnsɪkwəntli/ adv as a result: *They've employed more staff and consequently the service is better.*

conservation /ˌkɒnsəˈveɪʃ(ə)n/ noun [U]
1 ENVIRONMENT the management of land and water in ways that prevent them from being damaged or destroyed: *a wildlife conservation project* ♦ *groups calling for **the conservation of** the rainforest* **2** the careful use of supplies of things such as electricity or water, so that they are not wasted: *energy conservation*

3 the protection of buildings or objects of historical importance

conservationist /ˌkɒnsəˈveɪʃ(ə)nɪst/ noun [C] ENVIRONMENT someone who works to protect the environment from damage or destruction

conservatism /kənˈsɜːvə‚tɪz(ə)m/ noun [U] **1** a tendency to dislike change **2** POLITICS a political belief that it is better for society to change only gradually

conservative¹ /kənˈsɜːvətɪv/ adj **1** not willing to accept much change: *The small farming communities tend to be very conservative.* **2** conservative clothing or styles are traditional **3** a conservative guess about a price or a number is usually less than the actual amount —**conservatively** adv: *She dresses very conservatively.*

conservative² /kənˈsɜːvətɪv/ noun [C] someone who is not willing to accept much change

Conservative /kənˈsɜːvətɪv/ noun [C] POLITICS someone who belongs to or supports the beliefs of the Conservative Party

the Con'servative ‚Party POLITICS one of the three main political parties in the UK. It supports right-wing policies.

conservator /kənˈsɜːvətə/ noun [C] someone who protects or repairs buildings, objects, or places of historical importance

conservatory /kənˈsɜːvət(ə)ri/ (plural **conservatories**) noun [C] a room that is attached to a house and has glass walls and a glass roof

conserve /kənˈsɜːv/ verb [T] to use very little of something such as electricity or water so that it is not wasted

consider /kənˈsɪdə/ verb **1** [I/T] to think about something carefully before you make a decision: *The jury went out to consider its verdict.* ◆ *He is **considering whether to** accept another job offer.* ◆ *At one time I seriously considered leaving.* **2** [T] to have a particular opinion about someone or something: *We all considered him a hero.* **3** [I/T] to think that something may exist or be true: *Have you **considered the possibility** that he just doesn't like you?* **4** [T] to think about someone's feelings or reactions: *I'm not the only one involved – there's my daughter **to consider** as well.*

considerable /kənˈsɪd(ə)rəb(ə)l/ adj large in size, amount, or degree: *a considerable amount of money* ◆ *a matter of considerable importance*

considerably /kənˈsɪd(ə)rəbli/ adv a lot: *It was considerably colder in the mountains.*

considerate /kənˈsɪd(ə)rət/ adj thinking about the feelings and needs of other people ≠ INCONSIDERATE

consideration /kən‚sɪdəˈreɪʃ(ə)n/ noun **1** [U] careful thought before you make a decision about something: *We have **given** careful **consideration to** your request.* ◆ *Several possibilities are **under consideration** (=being thought about).* ◆ *We will **take** your good driving record **into consideration** (=think about it before deciding something).* **2** [C] something that you must think about carefully before you make a decision: *practical considerations* **3** [U] a kind way of behaving that shows that you care about other people's feelings and needs: *She treats all her patients with consideration and respect.*

considering /kənˈsɪdərɪŋ/ conjunction used for showing that your opinion about something is affected by a particular fact: *They've made remarkable progress, considering they only started last week.*

consignment /kənˈsaɪnmənt/ noun [C] goods that are being delivered somewhere

consist /kənˈsɪst/

PHRASAL VERB **con'sist of sth** to be made of particular parts or things: *My job seemed to consist of standing and smiling at people.* ◆ *Breakfast consisted of bread and a cup of tea.*

consistency /kənˈsɪstənsi/ noun **1** [U] the ability to remain the same in behaviour, attitudes, or qualities **2** [C/U] the degree to which a substance is thick, smooth, or firm

consistent /kənˈsɪstənt/ adj **1** not changing in behaviour, attitudes, or qualities ≠ INCONSISTENT: *A good teacher is flexible but consistent.* **2** continuing or developing steadily in the same way: *a consistent improvement* **3** containing statements or ideas that are similar or have the same aim: *the need for a unified and consistent policy* ◆ *These results are **consistent with** the findings of the previous study.* —**consistently** adv: *He has consistently denied the charges.*

consolation /ˌkɒnsəˈleɪʃ(ə)n/ noun [C/U] something that makes you feel less unhappy or disappointed

consolatory /kənˈsɒlət(ə)ri/ adj *formal* trying to make someone feel better when they are unhappy or disappointed

console¹ /kənˈsəʊl/ verb [T] to try to make someone feel better when they are unhappy or disappointed

console² /ˈkɒnsəʊl/ noun [C] **1** a board with switches that controls a machine or piece of equipment **2** COMPUTING a small piece of electronic equipment used for playing video games

consolidate /kənˈsɒlɪdeɪt/ verb **1** [T] to make something stronger or more effective **2** [I/T] to combine several small things into one large unit, or to become one large unit —**consolidation** /kən‚sɒlɪˈdeɪʃ(ə)n/ noun [C/U]

consonant /ˈkɒnsənənt/ noun [C] LANGUAGE **1** a letter of the alphabet used as a symbol for a consonant. All the letters of the English alphabet are consonants except for 'a', 'e', 'i', 'o', or 'u', which are **vowels**. **2** a speech sound made by stopping all or some of the air going out of your mouth, for example 'p' or 'm'

consortium /kənˈsɔːtiəm/ (plural **consortia**) noun [C] a group of companies or people with similar interests or aims who have agreed to work together

conspicuous /kənˈspɪkjʊəs/ adj very noticeable, or easy to see ≠ INCONSPICUOUS —**conspicuously** adv

conspiracy /kənˈspɪrəsi/ (plural **conspiracies**) noun **1** [C/U] a secret plan by a group of people to do something that is bad or illegal **2** [U] LAW the legal offence of planning a serious crime

conspirator /kənˈspɪrətə/ noun [C] someone who secretly makes a plan with another person or group to do something bad or illegal, especially in politics

conspiratorial /kən‚spɪrəˈtɔːriəl/ adj showing that you share knowledge of a secret with someone = SECRETIVE —**conspiratorially** adv

conspire /kənˈspaɪə/ verb [I] **1** to secretly plan with someone to do something that is bad or illegal **2** to produce a bad situation

constable /ˈkʌnstəb(ə)l/ noun [C] in the UK, a police officer of the lowest rank = POLICE CONSTABLE

constant¹ /ˈkɒnstənt/ adj **1** continuous or regular over a long period of time: *the constant noise of traffic* ◆ *His health has been a constant source of concern.* **2** continuing at the same rate, level, or amount over a particular period of time: *Maintain a constant speed.*

constant² /ˈkɒnstənt/ noun [C] **1 MATHS, SCIENCE** a number or amount in science or mathematics that is always the same **2** *formal* something that always stays the same and never changes

constantan /ˈkɒnstəntæn/ noun [U] **CHEMISTRY** an alloy of copper and nickel that is used to make **resistors**.

constantly /ˈkɒnstəntli/ adv always or regularly

constant veˈlocity ˌjoint noun [C] **ENGINEERING** in some vehicles, a joint that allows a **shaft** to turn at a constant speed, even when the vehicle is turning

constellation /ˌkɒnstəˈleɪʃ(ə)n/ noun [C] **ASTRONOMY** a group of stars that form a particular pattern in the sky. Most of the constellations we recognize have been given names, for example Orion the Hunter and the Great Bear.

consternation /ˌkɒnstəˈneɪʃ(ə)n/ noun [U] *formal* a shocked or worried feeling

constipation /ˌkɒnstɪˈpeɪʃ(ə)n/ noun [U] **HEALTH** a condition in which someone cannot easily move solid waste out of their body —**constipated** /ˈkɒnstɪˌpeɪtɪd/ adj

constituency /kənˈstɪtjuənsi/ (plural **constituencies**) noun [C] **POLITICS** an area of a country that elects a representative to a parliament, or all the people who live in that area

constituent¹ /kənˈstɪtjuənt/ noun [C] **1 POLITICS** someone who votes in a particular constituency **2** one of the parts of something

constituent² /kənˈstɪtjuənt/ adj forming part of something

constitute /ˈkɒnstɪˌtjuːt/ verb [linking verb] *formal* **1** to be one of the parts of something **2** to be a particular thing: *This letter does not constitute an offer of employment.*

constitution /ˌkɒnstɪˈtjuːʃ(ə)n/ noun **1** [C] a set of basic laws or rules that control how a country is governed or how an organization operates **2** [singular] your general physical condition

constitutional /ˌkɒnstɪˈtjuːʃ(ə)nəl/ adj **1** allowed by the constitution of a country or organization **2** relating to the constitution of a country or organization: *constitutional reform*

constrain /kənˈstreɪn/ verb [T] *formal* to limit someone's freedom to do what they want

constraint /kənˈstreɪnt/ noun [C] a limit on something = LIMITATION: *The time constraints on the project are quite strict.*

constrict /kənˈstrɪkt/ verb *formal* **1** [T] to limit what someone is able or allowed to do **2** [I/T] to become smaller or narrower, or to make something do this —**constriction** /kənˈstrɪkʃ(ə)n/ noun [C/U]

construct /kənˈstrʌkt/ verb [T] **1** to build or make something: *The tunnel was constructed in 1996.* ♦ *She is able to construct simple sentences in Spanish.* **2** to create something such as an idea or system = FORMULATE: *Police have called in an expert to construct a psychological profile of the murderer.*

construction /kənˈstrʌkʃ(ə)n/ noun **1** [U] the process of building something: *The company will finance the construction of a new sports centre.* ♦ *This website is under construction* (=being built). **2** [C] a building or other large structure: *The cathedral is a fantastic modern construction.* **3** [C/U] **LANGUAGE** the way in which words are put together to form a sentence or phrase: *difficult grammatical constructions*

constructive /kənˈstrʌktɪv/ adj intended to be useful or helpful —**constructively** adv

conˌstructive interˈference noun [U] **PHYSICS** a situation in which two sound waves or light waves are **in phase** (=have high points and low points that come at the same time), so that they produce a wave that is more intense —*picture* → WAVE

construe /kənˈstruː/ verb [T] *formal* to understand the meaning of something in a particular way

consul /ˈkɒns(ə)l/ noun [C] a government official who lives in another country and whose job is to help the citizens of their own country who go there —**consular** /ˈkɒnsjʊlə, ˈkɒnsjələ/ adj

consulate /ˈkɒnsjʊlət/ noun [C] the government building in which a consul works

consult /kənˈsʌlt/ verb **1** [T] to ask for advice from someone who has professional knowledge: *Consult your doctor before going on a diet.* ♦ *I consulted my solicitor about the matter.* **2** [I/T] to discuss something with someone before you make a decision: *Why wasn't I consulted about this?* **3** [T] to look in a book or at a document in order to find information

consultancy /kənˈsʌltənsi/ (plural **consultancies**) noun [C] a company that has expert knowledge about something and provides professional help and advice to other companies

consultant /kənˈsʌltənt/ noun [C] **1** an expert whose job is to give help and advice on a particular subject **2 HEALTH** a senior doctor in a hospital

consultation /ˌkɒns(ə)lˈteɪʃ(ə)n/ noun [C/U] **1** a process in which people give their opinions before an important decision is made **2** a meeting with a professional person in order to get advice or discuss a problem

consumable¹ /kənˈsjuːməb(ə)l/ adj **BUSINESS** intended to be bought, used, and then got rid of

consumable² /kənˈsjuːməb(ə)l/ noun [C] **BUSINESS** something that you buy and use, after which you buy a new one

consume /kənˈsjuːm/ verb [T] **1** to use a supply of something such as time, energy, or fuel **2** *formal* to eat or drink something **3** to take all of your attention so that you cannot think of anything else

consumer /kənˈsjuːmə/ noun [C] **1 ECONOMICS** someone who buys and uses goods and services: *The technology means better service for consumers.* **2 BIOLOGY** a living thing that feeds on other living things in the **food chain**. A living thing such as a plant that can make its own food is called a **producer**. —*picture* → FOOD WEB

consumer-facing /kənˈsjuːmə ˌfeɪsɪŋ/ adj **BUSINESS** dealing directly with people who buy products or services

conˌsumer ˈgoods noun [plural] **ECONOMICS** things that people buy for personal use or home use, such as clothes and furniture

consumerism /kənˈsjuːməˌrɪz(ə)m/ noun [U] **ECONOMICS 1** *showing disapproval* the belief that it is good for the economy of a country if people buy and use a lot of goods and services **2** protection for people against unfair prices, bad products, advertising claims that are not true etc —**consumerist** adj

the conˌsumer ˈprice ˌindex noun **ECONOMICS** an official list of the prices of some basic goods and services, published every month to show how much prices in general have risen or fallen

con,sumer-to-'business adj BUSINESS used for describing a type of business activity in which a customer deals with a company using the Internet

con'sumer ,unit noun [C] CONSTRUCTION a piece of electrical equipment that divides up the **mains** electricity and sends it to the various circuits in a house

consumption /kən'sʌmpʃ(ə)n/ noun [U] the use of something such as energy or fuel, or the amount of something that people use or buy: We've reduced our energy consumption by 10%.

contact¹ /'kɒntækt/ noun **1** [U] communication between people, countries, or organizations: Do you and Jo still **keep in contact**? ♦ I still haven't managed to **make contact with** Joe. ♦ There was no direct **contact between** the two sides in the dispute. ♦ I have **lost contact with** most of my university friends (=no longer talk or write to them). **2** [U] a situation in which people or things touch each other: The disease is spread through sexual contact. ♦ Are you likely to **come into contact with** any dangerous chemicals? **3** [C] someone you know who can help you, for example by giving you information **4** [C] PHYSICS a place where two electrical conductors meet and where electric current passes between them —picture → LIGHT BULB

contact² /'kɒntækt/ verb [T] to communicate with someone by phone, email, letter etc: Please contact us if you have any information.

'contact ,breaker noun [C] ENGINEERING an electrical switch in the **distributor** of a vehicle engine that controls the timing of the spark that **ignites** in the **spark plug**

'contact breaker ,points noun [plural] ENGINEERING the two metal surfaces in a **contact breaker** that create a spark when they are open

'contact ,card noun [C] BUSINESS, COMPUTING a card containing electronic information that you can read by touching the card with a special piece of equipment

'contact ,lens noun [C] one of two small pieces of plastic that people put in their eyes to help them to see more clearly

contactless card /'kɒntæktləs ,kɑːd/ noun [C] BUSINESS, COMPUTING a card containing electronic information that can be read from a distance with special equipment that uses radio waves

'contact ,sport noun [C/U] SPORTS a sport such as **rugby** or boxing in which the players have strong physical contact with each other

contagion /kən'teɪdʒ(ə)n/ noun [U] HEALTH a situation in which a disease can be spread from one person or animal to another through touch or through the air

contagious /kən'teɪdʒəs/ adj **1** HEALTH a contagious disease spreads easily from one person or animal to another **2** HEALTH a person or animal that is contagious has a disease that spreads easily to others **3** a contagious feeling spreads quickly from one person to another

contain /kən'teɪn/ verb [T] **1** to have something inside: The envelope contained a few old photographs. **2** to have or include something as a part: Milk contains many important vitamins and minerals. ♦ I disagreed with some of the points contained in the report. **3** to control something: I couldn't contain my excitement any longer. ♦ Firefighters are still battling to contain the blaze.

container /kən'teɪnə/ noun [C] **1** something used for storing or keeping things in, for example a box, bottle, or bowl **2** a very large metal or wooden box that has

been designed to be loaded easily onto ships and trucks

containment /kən'teɪnmənt/ noun [U] the process of controlling something that could become harmful or dangerous

contaminant /kən'tæmɪnənt/ noun [C] formal a substance that makes something dirty, polluted, or poisonous

contaminate /kən'tæmɪneɪt/ verb [T] **1** to make something dirty, polluted, or poisonous by adding a harmful substance: Industrial sewage continues to contaminate our beaches. **2** to affect something or someone in a negative way —**contamination** /kən,tæmɪ'neɪʃ(ə)n/ noun [U]

contaminated /kən'tæmɪ,neɪtɪd/ adj made dirty, polluted, or poisonous by the addition of a harmful substance: contaminated water

contemplate /'kɒntəm,pleɪt/ verb **1** [T] to think about something that might be possible: Have you ever contemplated working abroad? **2** [I/T] to think about or look at something very carefully for a long time —**contemplation** /,kɒntəm'pleɪʃ(ə)n/ noun [U]

contemporary¹ /kən'temp(ə)r(ə)ri/ adj **1** modern, or relating to the present time: contemporary dance **2** alive or existing at the same time as a particular event or person

contemporary² /kən'temp(ə)r(ə)ri/ (plural **contemporaries**) noun [C] someone who is or was alive at the same time as someone else: He was **a contemporary of** Charles Dickens.

contempt /kən'tempt/ noun [U] a feeling that someone or something is stupid, unimportant, or deserves no respect: I have nothing but **contempt for** their ridiculous opinions.

PHRASE **contempt of court** LAW the crime of not doing what a judge in a court of law has ordered you to do

contemptible /kən'temptəb(ə)l/ adj very bad or immoral

contemptuous /kən'temptjʊəs/ adj showing that you do not respect someone or something at all —**contemptuously** adv

contender /kən'tendə/ noun [C] someone who competes with other people for a prize or job

content¹ /'kɒntent/ noun **1** contents [plural] the things that are inside something such as a box, bottle, building, or room: The entire **contents of** the house will be sold. ♦ He emptied out the **contents of** his pockets. **2** contents [plural] the things that are contained in a book, letter, document etc, or a list of these: The **contents of** the report remain secret. **3** [U] the subject, ideas, or story that a piece of writing, television programme etc deals with: the design and content of your website **4** [singular] the amount of a substance that something contains: a breakfast cereal with a high sugar content

content² /kən'tent/ adj happy and satisfied with your life or with a particular situation: When I last saw her, she seemed content. ♦ I'm **content with** the relationship the way it is.

content³ /kən'tent/ verb **content yourself with sth** to accept what you have, although you would prefer to have something else

contented /kən'tentɪd/ adj happy and satisfied —**contentedly** adv

contention /kən'tenʃ(ə)n/ noun formal **1** [U] disagreement: The subject is a source of contention in the family. **2** [C] an opinion or statement that something is true

Arctic Ocean   Arctic Ocean

North America

Europe   Asia

Atlantic Ocean

Pacific Ocean   Pacific Ocean

Africa

South America

Indian Ocean

Australia

Southern Ocean

Antarctica

continents

contentious /kənˈtenʃəs/ adj **1** likely to cause arguments = CONTROVERSIAL **2** enjoying arguing with other people = ARGUMENTATIVE

contentment /kənˈtentmənt/ noun [U] a feeling of happiness and satisfaction

ˈcontent proˌvider noun [C] BUSINESS, COMPUTING a website that contains mostly news or information, or a business that provides the news or information for that website

contest¹ /ˈkɒntest/ noun [C] **1** a competition: *a writing contest* **2** a situation in which two or more people or groups are competing to gain power or an advantage

contest² /kənˈtest/ verb [T] **1** if someone contests something, they state formally that they disagree with it = DISPUTE **2** to compete for a job or for success in a competition

contestant /kənˈtestənt/ noun [C] someone who takes part in a contest

context /ˈkɒntekst/ noun [C/U] **1** the general situation in which something happens, that helps to explain it: *the historical context of the events* ♦ *This fall in prices has to be seen in context.* **2** LANGUAGE the words surrounding a particular word, that help to give it its meaning: *In this context, 'development' means economic growth.*

   PHRASE **take sth out of context** to use only part of something that someone said, so that the original meaning is changed
—**contextual** /kənˈtekstjʊəl/ adj

contextualize /kənˈtekstjʊəlaɪz/ verb [T] to consider an idea, event, activity etc together with everything relating to it in order to understand it better

continent /ˈkɒntɪnənt/ noun [C] GEOGRAPHY one of the very large areas of land on the Earth, for example Asia or Africa

continental /ˌkɒntɪˈnent(ə)l/ adj GEOGRAPHY relating to or belonging to a continent: *the wildlife of continental North America* —**continentally** adv

ˌcontinental ˈbreakfast noun [C] TOURISM a breakfast in a hotel consisting of bread and butter, coffee or tea, and sometimes **pastries** or **croissants** → ENGLISH BREAKFAST

ˌcontinental ˈclimate noun [C] GEOGRAPHY a climate with very hot summers, very cold winters, and not much rain that is typical of the central part of a continent

conti,nental ˈcrust noun [U] GEOLOGY the part of the outer shell of the Earth that includes the land masses and the solid rocks underneath them. It is about 35 km thick in most areas and has sedimentary rocks near the surface and metamorphic rocks lower down.

ˌcontinental ˈdrift noun [U] GEOLOGY the very gradual movement of continents across the Earth's surface

ˌcontinental ˈplate noun [C] GEOLOGY one of the large pieces into which the surface of the Earth is divided. These plates can move, and volcanoes and earthquakes are found at the places where they meet. —*picture* → on next page

ˌcontinental ˈpolar noun [C] GEOGRAPHY an air mass that forms over high cold land, and is therefore usually cold and dry

ˌcontinental ˈshelf noun [C] GEOLOGY the part of the edge of a continent that slopes gradually out into the sea and ends in a sudden steep slope that goes down into very deep water —*picture* → OCEAN

ˌcontinental ˈtropical noun [C] GEOGRAPHY an air mass that forms over tropical land, and is therefore usually hot and dry

contingency /kənˈtɪndʒ(ə)nsi/ (plural **contingencies**) noun [C] something bad that might happen in the future

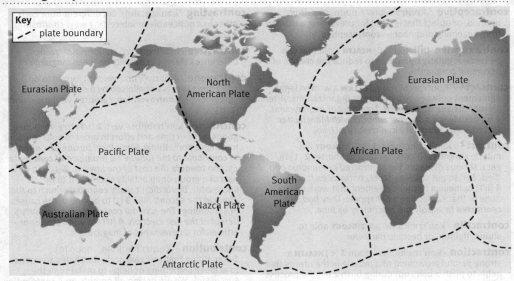

Key
-- -- plate boundary

Eurasian Plate

North American Plate

Eurasian Plate

Pacific Plate

African Plate

Australian Plate

Nazca Plate

South American Plate

Antarctic Plate

continental plates

con'tingency ,table noun [C] MATHS a way of showing the relationship between two **categorical variables** by putting the categories of the first one in rows and the categories of the second one in **columns**

contingent¹ /kən'tɪndʒ(ə)nt/ noun [C] **1** a group of people who represent a particular place or organization **2** a group of soldiers or police officers that forms part of a larger group

contingent² /kən'tɪndʒ(ə)nt/ adj *formal* able to happen only in a particular situation or if something else happens first = CONDITIONAL

continual /kən'tɪnjʊəl/ adj **1** continuing without stopping = CONSTANT **2** happening again and again, often in an annoying way —**continually** adv

continuation /kən,tɪnjʊ'eɪʃ(ə)n/ noun **1** [C/U] a situation in which something continues without stopping **2** [C] a situation in which something begins again after a pause **3** [C] something that is joined to something else so that it forms part of it

continue /kən'tɪnjuː/ verb **1** [I/T] to keep doing something, or to keep happening without stopping: *Doctors advised him to continue the treatment for another six weeks.* ♦ *She decided to **continue with** her studies for another two years.* ♦ *He continued typing while he spoke.* **2** [T] to start doing something again after stopping: *She looked up briefly, and then continued reading.* **3** [I] to go further in the same direction: *The path continued for another fifty yards.*

Word family: **continue**

*Words in the same family as **continue***
- continual *adj*
- continually *adv*
- continuation *n*
- continuity *n*
- discontinued *adj*
- continuous *adj*
- continuously *adv*
- continued *adj*
- discontinue *v*

continued /kən'tɪnjuːd/ adj provided, happening, or done regularly or for a long period: *We thank our customers for their continued support.*

continuing education /kən,tɪnjuːɪŋ ,edju'keɪʃ(ə)n/ noun [U] EDUCATION lessons for adults, often held in the evening, that give them the opportunity to study a wide variety of subjects

continuity /,kɒntɪ'njuːəti/ noun [U] **1** a situation in which something happens or exists for a long time without stopping or changing **2** the arrangement of scenes and events in a film or television programme so that it seems as if the action continues without interruption

continuous /kən'tɪnjʊəs/ adj **1** continuing without stopping: *a continuous flow of water* **2** LANGUAGE the continuous form of a verb includes 'be' and the **present participle** of a verb to show that an activity is in progress. For example in 'He is running to catch the bus', 'is running' is the continuous form of 'run' = PROGRESSIVE

continuously /kən'tɪnjʊəsli/ adv without stopping: *It rained continuously for five days.*

con,tinuous 'variable noun [C] MATHS a **variable** such as time, height, or weight that can be any possible number within a particular range of numbers, according to how detailed you make your measurements

continuum /kən'tɪnjʊəm/ noun [singular] a series of events, changes, features etc that all have a particular quality to different degrees

contort /kən'tɔːt/ verb [I/T] if your face or body contorts, or if you contort it, it twists into an unusual shape —**contortion** /kən'tɔːʃ(ə)n/ noun [C]

contorted /kən'tɔːtɪd/ adj twisted into an unusual shape or position

contour /'kɒntʊə/ noun [C] **1** the shape of the outside edge of something **2** contour or contour line GEOGRAPHY a line on a map joining points that are the same height above or below sea level

,contour 'ploughing noun [U] AGRICULTURE a method of ploughing in which sloping land such as the side of a hill or mountain is ploughed along horizontal lines across the slope. This helps to prevent **soil erosion**, as it is less likely that the soil will get washed away when it rains.

contraband /'kɒntrəbænd/ noun [U] goods that are brought into or taken out of a country illegally

contraception /,kɒntrə'sepʃ(ə)n/ noun [U] HEALTH the methods that are used for preventing a woman from becoming pregnant, or the use of these methods

contraceptive /ˌkɒntrəˈseptɪv/ noun [C] a drug, method, or object that is used for preventing a woman from becoming pregnant —**contraceptive** adj

contraˈceptive ˌpill noun [C] HEALTH a pill that can be taken regularly by women to reduce the chance of becoming pregnant

contract¹ /ˈkɒntrækt/ noun [C] LAW a written legal agreement between two people or organizations: *After six months she was offered a contract of employment.* ♦ *He has signed a six-year contract with Manchester United.* —**contractual** /kənˈtræktʃʊəl/ adj

contract² /kənˈtrækt/ verb **1** [I/T] BIOLOGY if a muscle contracts, it gets tighter and shorter **2** [T] to get a serious disease: *She contracted pneumonia and died.* **3** [I] to get smaller: *Steel contracts as it cools.* **4** [I/T] to make a formal agreement that work will be done or that something will happen: *They had contracted to supply the machinery by June.*

contractile /kənˈtræktaɪl/ adj BIOLOGY able to shrink, tighten, or become narrower

contraction /kənˈtrækʃ(ə)n/ noun **1** [C] HEALTH a strong painful movement of a muscle in the uterus that helps to push a baby out during birth **2** [U] the process of becoming smaller **3** [C] LANGUAGE a short form of a word that is made by leaving out a letter or letters. For example, 'can't' is a contraction of the word 'cannot'.

contractor /kənˈtræktə/ noun [C] a person or company that provides goods or does work for someone else

contradict /ˌkɒntrəˈdɪkt/ verb [T] **1** to say the opposite of what someone else has said **2** if one statement, piece of evidence, story etc contradicts another, they are different and cannot both be true

contradiction /ˌkɒntrəˈdɪkʃ(ə)n/ noun [C/U] a difference between two statements, ideas, stories etc that makes it impossible for both of them to be true

contradictory /ˌkɒntrəˈdɪkt(ə)ri/ adj contradictory statements, information, stories etc are different from each other and cannot both be true

contraindication /ˌkɒntrəˌɪndɪˈkeɪʃ(ə)n/ noun [C] HEALTH a medical reason why someone should not use a particular drug or medical treatment

contralto /kənˈtrɑːltəʊ/ noun [C] MUSIC the lowest female singing voice, or a woman with this singing voice

contraption /kənˈtræpʃ(ə)n/ noun [C] a machine or piece of equipment that looks strange or complicated

contrary¹ /ˈkɒntrəri/ adj completely different, or opposed to something else: *a contrary view*

contrary² /ˈkɒntrəri/ noun **on the contrary** used for emphasizing that the opposite of what has been said is true: *The situation hasn't improved – on the contrary, it's getting worse.*

contrast¹ /ˈkɒntrɑːst/ noun **1** [C/U] a noticeable difference between people or things: *There is a striking contrast between these two attitudes.* ♦ *In contrast to deserts in the south, the northern part of the state is very green.* **2** [C] something that is different from something else in a very noticeable way: *The little village was a total contrast to Athens.* **3** [U] ARTS the differences in light or colour that you can see in a painting or photograph, or on a television screen

contrast² /kənˈtrɑːst/ verb **1** [I] if one thing contrasts with another, the two things are very different from each other **2** [T] to compare two things in order to show the ways in which they are different

contrasting /kənˈtrɑːstɪŋ/ adj different from each other in a noticeable or interesting way: *contrasting colours*

contrastive /kənˈtrɑːstɪv/ adj formal showing differences clearly, especially between languages

contravene /ˌkɒntrəˈviːn/ verb [T] formal to do something that is not allowed by a rule, law, or agreement —**contravention** /ˌkɒntrəˈvenʃ(ə)n/ noun [C/U]

contribute /kənˈtrɪbjuːt/ verb **1** [I/T] to give money, goods, or your time and effort in order to help someone to achieve something: *Many local businesses offered to contribute to the fund.* ♦ *He promised to contribute £5,000 towards the cost of the lawsuit.* **2** [I/T] to be a part of a group or an activity and help it to be successful: *Davis didn't really contribute much to the game in the second half.* **3** [I] to be one of the causes of something: *The scandal contributed to the party's defeat at the last election.* **4** [I/T] to write stories or articles for a newspaper or magazine

contribution /ˌkɒntrɪˈbjuːʃ(ə)n/ noun [C] **1** something that you give or do that helps someone to achieve something or helps to make something successful: *We are asking all parents for a contribution towards the cost of the trip.* **2** a story or article that is written for a newspaper or magazine

contributor /kənˈtrɪbjʊtə/ noun [C] **1** someone who gives or does something in order to help someone to achieve something **2** someone who writes a story or article for a newspaper or magazine

contributory /kənˈtrɪbjʊt(ə)ri/ adj partly responsible for a situation or event

conˌtributory ˈnegligence noun [U] LAW the failure of a person who has been injured to take action to avoid or prevent an accident, so that they are considered partly responsible for it

contrive /kənˈtraɪv/ verb [T] formal **1** to succeed in doing something difficult by using clever or dishonest methods **2** to invent or make something in a clever or unusual way

control¹ /kənˈtrəʊl/ noun

1 power to do sth	5 computer key
2 law limiting sth	6 in experiment
3 machine part	+ PHRASES
4 checking of sth	

1 [U] the power to make decisions about what happens in a situation: *The island is now under French control.* ♦ *When they took control of the company, it was losing money.* ♦ *She lost control of the car, and it skidded off the road.*
2 [C/U] a law, agreement, or method that limits something: *new controls on the importing of live animals* ♦ *an international agreement on arms control*
3 [C] a part of a machine that you use to make it do something: *There was an experienced pilot at the controls* (=operating the controls of a plane).
4 [U] the process of checking something, or the place where it is checked: *They need higher standards of quality control in the factory.*
5 [U] COMPUTING the **control key** on a computer keyboard
6 [C] SCIENCE in an experiment, one of the people or things being studied that is not involved in the processes or treatments that the others experience. This person or thing is used as a standard that the others can be compared with. → FAIR TEST

PHRASES in control with the power to decide what happens or what someone or something does: *Dr*

*Marion is **in control of** all medical decisions at the hospital.*
out of control impossible to stop or deal with successfully: *Forest fires can easily get out of control.*
under control being managed or dealt with successfully: *He sometimes has difficulty keeping his temper under control.*

control² /kən'trəʊl/ (**controls, controlling, controlled**) verb [T] **1** to have the power to make decisions about what happens in a situation: *The rebel army now controls the northern half of the country.* ♦ *New teachers often find it difficult to control their classes.* **2** to make something operate in the way that you want: *I hit a patch of ice and couldn't control the car.* **3** to prevent something harmful from spreading or becoming more dangerous: *We must do more to control the spread of the virus.* **4** to remain calm and not show that you are angry or upset: *Carol struggled to control her anger.* —**controller** noun [C]

con'trol ,key noun [C] **COMPUTING** a key on a computer keyboard that is used in combination with other keys for doing particular operations

controlled substance /kən,trəʊld 'sʌbstəns/ noun [C] **LAW** a drug or chemical that the law does not allow you to make, own, or use

con'trol ,rod noun [C] **PHYSICS** a cylinder made of a material that can absorb neutrons. It is used to control the rate at which **nuclear reactions** take place in a **nuclear reactor.** —*picture* → NUCLEAR REACTOR

con'trol ,tower noun [C] a tall building at an airport from which planes are given permission to take off and land

controversial /,kɒntrə'vɜːʃ(ə)l/ adj causing strong feelings of disagreement: *controversial plans to build a new dam*

controversially /,kɒntrə'vɜːʃəli/ adv used for saying that people disagree about the thing you are talking about, or do not approve of it

controversy /'kɒntrəvɜːsi, kən'trɒvəsi/ (plural **controversies**) noun [C/U] a disagreement that a lot of people have strong feelings about: *the recent **controversy over** the school's new teaching methods*

contusion /kən'tjuːʒ(ə)n/ noun [C/U] **HEALTH** a blue or purple mark on the skin where it has been hit = BRUISE

conurbation /,kɒnɜː'beɪʃ(ə)n/ noun [C] **GEOGRAPHY** a large city area

convalesce /,kɒnvə'les/ verb [I] **HEALTH** to spend time resting after an illness in order to get better —**convalescent** /,kɒnvə'les(ə)nt/ adj, **convalescence** noun [U]

convection /kən'vekʃ(ə)n/ noun [U] **PHYSICS** the process by which the very small particles in a liquid or gas move and give out heat: *Land and sea breezes are caused by convection.* —**convectional** adj

con'vection ,current noun [C] **PHYSICS** a constant circular movement of warm particles upwards and cooler particles downwards

convective zone /kən'vektɪv ,zəʊn/ noun [C] **ASTRONOMY** a layer of a star across which energy is carried outwards, mainly by **convection currents** —*picture* → SUN

convenience /kən'viːniəns/ noun **1** [U] a condition that helps someone to avoid wasting time or effort: *Her hair was cut short **for convenience** rather than fashion.* **2** [C] a piece of equipment that makes things easier for you: *The kitchen was equipped with a range of modern conveniences.*

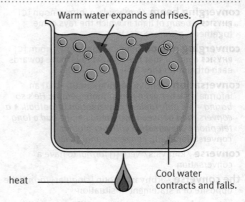

Warm water expands and rises.

heat — Cool water contracts and falls.

convection currents

con'venience ,food noun [C/U] food that is quick and easy to prepare, such as food that has already been cooked and only needs to be heated

con'venience ,store noun [C] *American* a shop that is open for long hours and sells a variety of goods

convenient /kən'viːniənt/ adj **1** easy for you to do, or suitable for your needs ≠ INCONVENIENT: *If it's convenient, call me tomorrow.* ♦ *Travelling underground is fast and convenient.* **2** near to the place where you want to go: *a house that is **convenient** for the centre of town* —**conveniently** adv

convent /'kɒnvənt/ noun [C] **RELIGION** a building where **nuns** (=women members of a religious organization) live and work

convention /kən'venʃ(ə)n/ noun **1** [C/U] a way of behaving that is generally accepted as normal and right: *social conventions* ♦ *She rebelled against convention and refused to marry.* **2** [C] a formal agreement between governments: *the Geneva Convention* **3** [C] a large meeting of people from a particular profession or organization

conventional /kən'venʃ(ə)nəl/ adj **1** someone who is conventional follows traditional ways of thinking and behaving in their society ≠ UNCONVENTIONAL **2** using ordinary or traditional methods, not new ideas or new technology: *a conventional oven* ♦ *conventional weapons* (=not nuclear or chemical weapons) **3** **HEALTH** conventional medical treatments are those that are based on drugs and operations → alternative² sense 2 —**conventionally** adv: *a conventionally dressed young man*

con,ventional 'current noun [U] **PHYSICS** a standard way of describing electrical current as a flow of positive charge from a positive region to a negative region, although in some cases the real flow is in the opposite direction

conventional milling /kən'venʃ(ə)nəl ,mɪlɪŋ/ noun [U] **TECHNOLOGY** a method of **milling** (=cutting metal with a rotating tool) in which the material moves in the opposite direction to the rotating cutter

converge /kən'vɜːdʒ/ verb **1** [I] to come to the same place from different places or directions: *Top diplomats were **converging on** Washington from all over the world.* **2** [I/T] **PHYSICS** if rays of light converge, or if they are converged, they come together at a point —*picture* → LENS, SHORT-SIGHTED

convergence /kən'vɜːdʒ(ə)ns/ noun [singular/U] a situation in which people or things gradually become the same or very similar —**convergent** adj

converging beam /kən'vɜːdʒɪŋ ˌbiːm/ noun [C] PHYSICS a beam of light in which the rays come together —*picture* → BEAM

converging mirror /kən'vɜːdʒɪŋ ˌmɪrə/ noun [C] PHYSICS a mirror that makes light rays move towards each other after they hit it

conversation /ˌkɒnvə'seɪʃ(ə)n/ noun [C/U] an informal talk between two or more people: *He's so boring – his only **topic of conversation** is football.* ♦ *a conversation between two friends* ♦ *She **had** a long telephone **conversation** with her mother.* — **conversational** adj: *conversational skills*

converse /kən'vɜːs/ verb [I] *formal* to have a conversation

the converse /'kɒnvɜːs/ noun [singular] *formal* the opposite of a statement or situation

conversely /'kɒnvɜːsli/ adv used for introducing one part of a sentence that says the opposite of an earlier part: *Some wrong answers were marked right and, conversely, some right answers had been rejected.*

conversion /kən'vɜːʃ(ə)n/ noun 1 [U] the process of changing from one system or use to another 2 [C] RELIGION a change in someone's religious beliefs 3 [C] SPORTS in rugby, a goal that is scored after a **try**

con'version ˌkick noun [C] SPORTS in rugby and American football, an occasion when a ball is kicked over a high bar in order to score more points

convert[1] /kən'vɜːt/ verb 1 [I/T] to change from one system or use to another, or to make something change in this way: *Farmers are **converting to** new production methods.* ♦ *They **converted** the old school **into** luxury flats.* 2 [I/T] RELIGION to change your religious beliefs, or to persuade someone to change their beliefs 3 [T] SPORTS to make a conversion in **rugby**

convert[2] /'kɒnvɜːt/ noun [C] someone who has changed their religious or political beliefs

convertible /kən'vɜːtəb(ə)l/ noun [C] a car with a roof that can be folded back or removed

convex /'kɒnveks/ adj a convex surface curves outwards ≠ CONCAVE —*picture* → LENS, PROJECTOR, SHAPE, SHORT-SIGHTED

convey /kən'veɪ/ (**conveys, conveying, conveyed**) verb [T] 1 to communicate ideas, feelings, or information: *A good photograph can convey far more than words.* ♦ *Please convey our thanks to the organizers.* 2 *formal* to move something from one place to another= TRANSPORT 3 LAW to make another person or organization the legal owner of a property

conveyance /kən'veɪəns/ noun 1 [U] *formal* the process of moving people, animals, or goods from one place to another 2 [C] *formal* a vehicle 3 [C] LAW a document that shows that the person who has just bought a property is now its legal owner

conveyancing /kən'veɪənsɪŋ/ noun [U] LAW the legal process by which someone becomes the new owner of a property

conveyor belt /kən'veɪə ˌbelt/ noun [C] a machine that has a flat surface that moves and carries objects from one part of a factory to another

convict[1] /kən'vɪkt/ verb [T] LAW to prove in a court of law that someone is guilty of a crime: *There wasn't enough evidence to convict her.* ♦ *Robinson was **convicted of** the murder of his brother.* —**convicted** adj: *a convicted thief*

convict[2] /'kɒnvɪkt/ noun [C] someone who is in prison because they have committed a crime

conviction /kən'vɪkʃ(ə)n/ noun 1 [C] LAW a decision by a court of law that someone is guilty of a crime: *He had two **previous convictions for** dangerous driving.* 2 [C] a strong belief or opinion: *deep religious convictions* 3 [U] the feeling or appearance of being confident: *'Everything is fine,' she said **with** as much **conviction** as she could.*

convince /kən'vɪns/ verb [T] 1 to make someone believe that something is true= PERSUADE: *He failed to **convince** the court **of** his innocence.* ♦ *Maria had convinced herself that James didn't love her.* 2 to persuade someone to do something: *They tried to **convince** him **to** buy a cheaper car.*

convinced /kən'vɪnst/ adj certain that something is true

convincing /kən'vɪnsɪŋ/ adj 1 something that is convincing makes you believe that it is true or good 2 if a player or team has a convincing win, they beat another player or team easily —**convincingly** adv

convoluted tubule /'kɒnvəluːtɪd ˌtjuːbjuːl/ noun [C] ANATOMY a tube in the **nephron** of the kidney that has many twists and turns

convoy /'kɒnvɔɪ/ noun [C] a group of vehicles or ships that are travelling together

convulsions /kən'vʌlʃ(ə)nz/ noun [plural] HEALTH sudden violent movements of someone's body that they cannot control, caused by illness

convulsive /kən'vʌlsɪv/ adj convulsive movements are sudden, violent, and difficult to control

cook[1] /kʊk/ verb 1 [I/T] to prepare and heat food so that it is ready to eat: *What's the best way to cook fish?* ♦ *Joe's cooking dinner for me tonight.* ♦ *He offered to cook me lunch.* 2 [I] when food cooks, it is heated until it is ready to eat: *The potatoes need to cook for about 20 minutes.*

PHRASE **cook the books** to change accounts and figures dishonestly, usually in order to get money —**cooked** /kʊkt/ adj

Build your vocabulary: words you can use instead of cook

- **bake** to cook food such as bread or cakes in an oven
- **boil** to cook food in very hot water
- **fry** to cook food in hot oil
- **grill** to cook food under or over a very strong heat.
- **roast** to cook meat or vegetables in an oven with fat or oil
- **simmer** to boil something very gently

cook[2] /kʊk/ noun [C] someone who cooks food, either as their job or for pleasure

cookbook /'kʊkbʊk/ noun [C] a **cookery book**

cooker /'kʊkə/ noun [C] a large piece of kitchen equipment that is used for cooking food. It usually includes an oven and a **hob**.

cookery /'kʊk(ə)ri/ noun [U] the skill or activity of preparing or cooking food

'cookery ˌbook noun [C] a book that contains **recipes** (=instructions for preparing and cooking food)

cookie /'kʊki/ noun [C] 1 *American* a **biscuit** 2 COMPUTING a file that is sent by an Internet website to a computer that visits it. If the computer visits the same website again, the file collects information about the computer user.

cooking /'kʊkɪŋ/ noun [U] the activity of preparing food, or a particular way of preparing it

cool[1] /kuːl/ adj

1 fairly cold	4 not friendly
2 calm and relaxed	5 good
3 fashionable	

1 fairly cold ≠ WARM: *The water was wonderfully cool and refreshing.* ♦ *the cool evening air*
2 calm and relaxed: *her cool way of handling the situation*
3 fashionable and attractive: *one of Britain's coolest young designers*
4 not friendly or enthusiastic: *Relations between the two countries were becoming increasingly cool.*
5 *spoken* good or enjoyable: *The restaurant was really cool.* ♦ *'We could go to see a film.' 'Cool.'*
—**coolly** adv

cool[2] /kuːl/ verb **1** [I/T] to become cooler, or to make something cooler: *Allow the cake to cool completely.* **2** [I] if an emotion such as love or anger cools, it becomes less strong

cool[3] /kuːl/ noun [U] a fashionable quality that someone or something has
PHRASES **keep your cool** to remain calm in a difficult situation
lose your cool to become angry or excited in a difficult situation

coolant /ˈkuːlənt/ noun [C/U] CHEMISTRY **1** a liquid that is used for preventing machines, car engines, and **nuclear reactors** from getting too hot —*picture* → NUCLEAR REACTOR **2** a liquid that is used for cooling and **lubricating** a cutting tool while a machine is operating

cooling-off period /ˌkuːlɪŋ ˈɒf ˌpɪəriəd/ noun [C] **1** a pause in an argument, especially one between a company's management and employees, that gives people time to think calmly about how to reach an agreement **2** a period of time in which someone is allowed to change their mind about a contract or agreement that they have signed

cooling system /ˈkuːlɪŋ ˌsɪstəm/ noun [C] ENGINEERING a system of parts and fluid for keeping a vehicle's engine cool

cooling tower /ˈkuːlɪŋ ˌtaʊə/ noun [C] a tall round structure where water used in an industrial process becomes less hot

coop /kuːp/ noun [C] a small building or large container where chickens or small animals are kept

co-op /ˈkəʊ ˌɒp/ noun [C] a **cooperative** business, for example a farm

cooped up /ˌkuːpt ˈʌp/ adj in a place that you cannot leave or cannot move around in

cooperate /kəʊˈɒpəreɪt/ verb [I] **1** to work with other people in order to achieve something: *Residents are refusing to **cooperate with** the authorities.* **2** to do what someone asks you to do: *They threatened to harm him if he didn't cooperate.*

cooperation /kəʊˌɒpəˈreɪʃ(ə)n/ noun [U] a situation in which people help each other or work together to achieve something

cooperative[1] /kəʊˈɒp(ə)rətɪv/ adj **1** someone who is cooperative is willing to do what people ask them ≠ UNCOOPERATIVE: *One of the prisoners was very cooperative.* **2** done by different groups working together: *a cooperative research project*
—**cooperatively** adv

cooperative[2] /kəʊˈɒp(ə)rətɪv/ noun [C] BUSINESS a business that is owned by all the people who work in it

coordinate[1] /kəʊˈɔːdɪneɪt/ verb [T] to organize an activity so that all the people who are involved in it work together effectively: *Jean is coordinating the project.*

coordinate[2] /kəʊˈɔːdɪnət/ noun [C] MATHS one of a set of numbers that give the exact position of something on a map or graph

co'ordinate ,clause noun [C] LANGUAGE a clause that is a main part of a sentence and is as important as another main part. Coordinate clauses are connected by words such as 'and', 'but', or 'or'.

coordinated /kəʊˈɔːdɪˌneɪtɪd/ adj able to control the movements of your body well: *She's very coordinated for a two-year-old.*

Co,ordinated Uni'versal ,Time noun [U] PHYSICS see UTC

coordinates /kəʊˈɔːdɪnəts/ noun [plural] MATHS, GEOGRAPHY a set of two numbers that give the exact position of something on a map or graph

coordinating conjunction /kəʊˌɔːdɪneɪtɪŋ kənˈdʒʌŋkʃ(ə)n/ noun [C] LANGUAGE a word such as 'and' or 'but' that joins two parts of a sentence that are of equal importance → SUBORDINATING CONJUNCTION

coordination /kəʊˌɔːdɪˈneɪʃ(ə)n/ noun [U] **1** the ability to control the parts of your body so that they move well together **2** the process of organizing people or things so that they work together effectively: *He asked for better **coordination between** NATO and the United Nations.*

cope[1] /kəʊp/ verb [I] to deal successfully with a difficult situation: *Considering how bad her injuries are, she's coping very well.* ♦ *The safety system is designed to **cope with** engine failure.*

cope[2] /kəʊp/ noun [C] TECHNOLOGY the top half of a **moulding flask**

'co-,pilot noun [C] a pilot who helps the main pilot to fly an aircraft

copious /ˈkəʊpiəs/ adj formal in large amounts

copper /ˈkɒpə/ noun [U] CHEMISTRY a red-brown metal element that is a good conductor of electricity and heat. It is used to make electric wires, water and gas pipes, and alloys. Chemical symbol: **Cu**

,copper 'sulphate so,lution noun [C] CHEMISTRY a solution of **copper sulphate** (=a chemical compound made by the action of sulphuric acid on an **oxide** of copper). It is used in the **Biuret test** for testing a sample for the presence of starch.

copra /ˈkɒprə/ noun [U] AGRICULTURE the dried white flesh of a **coconut** that is crushed to make oil

copula /ˈkɒpjʊlə/ noun [C] LANGUAGE a **linking verb**

copulate /ˈkɒpjʊleɪt/ verb [I] formal to have sex — **copulation** /ˌkɒpjʊˈleɪʃ(ə)n/ noun [U]

copy[1] /ˈkɒpi/ (plural **copies**) noun **1** [C] something that is exactly like something else: *This is not the original painting – it's a copy.* ♦ *Please send **a copy of** your birth certificate.* ♦ *I **made copies of** the report.* **2** [C] a single newspaper, book, CD etc that is one of many that are all exactly the same: *Her first album sold 100,000 copies.* ♦ *Have you got **a copy of** yesterday's newspaper?* **3** [U] writing that is published in a newspaper or magazine: *Copy for our April issue must be submitted by 20th March.* ♦ *His controversial remarks always make good copy.* → HARD COPY

copy[2] /ˈkɒpi/ (**copies, copying, copied**) verb **1** [T] to make a copy that is the same as the original thing: *They were illegally copying videotapes and selling them.* ♦ *You can use the mouse to copy text from one part of the document to another.* **2** [T] to do something in the same way as someone else= IMITATE: *Children learn by copying their parents.* **3** [T] to use someone else's ideas or methods: *Their style of music was copied by a lot of other bands.* **4** [I/T] to look at someone else's work and dishonestly write the same as they have written, especially in an examination

---

Build your vocabulary: words you can use instead of copy

- **make a copy** to copy something, especially using a machine
- **photocopy** to copy a document using a special machine
- **reproduce** to copy a picture, sound, or piece of writing, especially using modern technology
- **trace** to copy a picture by placing transparent paper on top of it and following the lines with a pencil
- **plagiarize** to copy someone else's words or ideas and pretend that they are your own
- **pirate** to make an illegal copy of something such as a book, software, or a video

---

copycat /'kɒpiˌkæt/ adj similar to something else

'copy proˌtection noun [U] COMPUTING a way of stopping people from copying computer software without getting permission from the person who wrote it

copyright /'kɒpiˌraɪt/ noun [C/U] the legal right to decide who can make and sell copies of a book, show a film, perform a piece of music etc

copywriter /'kɒpiˌraɪtə/ noun [C] someone whose job is to write the words for advertisements

coral /'kɒrəl/ noun **1** [U] a hard substance that grows in the sea. It is made from the skeletons of corals: *a coral necklace —picture* → SEA **2** [C/U] BIOLOGY a small tropical sea animal that lives in large groups that look like plants

ˌcoral 'reef noun [C] BIOLOGY, GEOGRAPHY a hard natural structure under the sea that is formed from coral. Coral reefs are an important habitat for many types of fish and other forms of sea life.

corbel /'kɔːb(ə)l/ noun [C] CONSTRUCTION a brick or a block of stone that sticks out from a wall and supports a weight

cord /kɔːd/ noun **1** [C/U] strong thick string **2** [C] an electrical wire that connects a machine to the main supply of electricity → CORDS

cordial /'kɔːdiəl/ adj *formal* friendly —**cordially** adv

cordless /'kɔːdləs/ adj a cordless piece of equipment works without being connected to the electricity supply

cords /kɔːdz/ noun [plural] trousers made of corduroy

corduroy /'kɔːdərɔɪ/ noun **1** [U] thick cotton cloth with a surface that is covered with raised lines **2** corduroys [plural] trousers made of corduroy

core¹ /kɔː/ noun [C] **1** the most important or most basic part of something: *the core of the problem* ♦ *The club has a small core of active members.* **2** the centre of something: *the seeds in an apple core* **3** GEOLOGY the central part of a planet: *the Earth's core —picture* → EARTH **4** TECHNOLOGY a metal or wooden shape that is placed in a mould, in order to create an empty space inside the part being cast in metal
PHRASE **to the core** used for emphasizing that an aspect of someone's character is very strong and will not change: *She's a feminist to the core.*

core² /kɔː/ adj most important, or most basic: *Selling insurance is the company's core business.*

ˌcore 'competence noun [C] BUSINESS a skill or type of knowledge that makes a business especially good at doing some things, and gives it an advantage over other businesses that are competing with it

coreligionist /ˌkəʊrɪ'lɪdʒənɪst/ noun [C] RELIGION *formal* someone whose religion is the same as another person's

'core ˌplug noun [C] ENGINEERING a small metal or rubber object that is used in an engine to fill spaces left after certain engine parts were made

'core ˌprint noun [C] TECHNOLOGY a small part that sticks out at the end of a **pattern** and provides a space where a **core** can be inserted in a mould for **casting**

co-respondent /ˌkəʊ rɪ'spɒndənt/ noun [C] LAW in a **divorce** case, someone accused of having sex with the husband or wife of the person who wants to get divorced

coriander /ˌkɒri'ændə/ noun [U] a plant whose leaves and seeds are used to give flavour to food

cork /kɔːk/ noun **1** [U] BIOLOGY a soft light substance from the **bark** of some cork trees **2** [C] an object made from cork, used for closing the top of a bottle such as wine

corkscrew /'kɔːkˌskruː/ noun [C] a tool used for pulling the corks out of wine bottles

corm /kɔːm/ noun [C] BIOLOGY a short swollen base of the stem in some plants that stores food underground. It is used for the growth of new shoots in the next season.

corn /kɔːn/ noun **1** [U] AGRICULTURE wheat, barley, or any other crop of grain that is grown as food **2** [U] AGRICULTURE maize plants, or their seeds when they are cooked and eaten → SWEETCORN —*picture* → CEREAL **3** [C] a small piece of painful hard skin on the foot
PHRASE **corn on the cob** the top part of a **maize** plant, cooked and eaten as a vegetable —*picture* → VEGETABLE

cornea /'kɔːniə, kɔː'niːə/ noun [C] ANATOMY the transparent layer that covers the outside of the eye —*picture* → EYE, RETINA —**corneal** adj

corner¹ /'kɔːnə/ noun [C]

1 where two sides meet	5 difficult situation
2 where roads meet	6 shot in sport
3 end of mouth/eye	7 in boxing/wrestling
4 small (quiet) area	

1 the part of an object, space, or room where two edges or sides meet: *The baby banged his head on the corner of the table.* ♦ *The 'Start' button is in the left-hand corner of the screen.*
2 a place where two roads meet, or where there is a sharp bend in the road: *I get my newspaper from the shop on the corner.* ♦ *As she turned the corner* (=went around it), *she saw us.*
3 the end of your mouth or eye: *A tear fell from the corner of her eye.*
4 a particular area, especially one that is quiet, peaceful, or private: *Plant it in a sunny corner of your garden.*
5 a difficult situation that you cannot easily escape from= PREDICAMENT: *The government is in a tight corner on the issue of taxes.*
6 SPORTS in football and other team games, an occasion when you are allowed to kick or hit the ball from a corner of the field near your opponent's goal
7 SPORTS one of the corners of the **ring** in boxing or wrestling
→ CUT¹

corner² /'kɔːnə/ verb [T] to put someone in a situation where they must talk, fight, or do what someone else wants: *Carl cornered me by the coffee machine.*

cornerstone /'kɔːnə,stəʊn/ noun [C]
CONSTRUCTION the stone at one of the bottom corners of a new building, often put there during a special ceremony

the cornerstone /'kɔːnə,stəʊn/ noun [singular] something important that everything else depends on: *Elections are **the cornerstone of** our democratic system.*

cornet /'kɔːnɪt/ noun [C] **MUSIC** a musical instrument like a small **trumpet**

cornflakes /'kɔːn,fleɪks/ noun [plural] a breakfast food made of small flat dried pieces of **maize**. People eat them with milk.

cornflour /'kɔːn,flaʊə/ noun [U] white flour made from **maize**, used in cooking to make liquids thicker

corolla /kə'rɒlə/ noun [plural] **BIOLOGY** all the petals of a flower considered as a group —*picture* → FLOWER

corollary /kə'rɒləri/ noun [C] *formal* something that will also be true if a particular idea or statement is true, or something that will also exist if a particular situation exists

corona /kə'rəʊnə/ noun [C] **ASTRONOMY 1** the circle of light around the Sun or the Moon, seen especially clearly during an **eclipse 2** the outer atmosphere of the Sun

coronary¹ /'kɒrən(ə)ri/ adj **ANATOMY** relating to the heart

coronary² /'kɒrən(ə)ri/ (plural **coronaries**) noun [C] **HEALTH** a **heart attack**

coronary 'artery noun [C] **ANATOMY** either of the two arteries that carry blood to the heart

coronary 'bypass noun [C] **HEALTH** a medical operation to make blood flow round an area of a coronary artery that has become blocked, so that the blood can flow freely to the heart muscles

coronary throm'bosis noun [C/U] **HEALTH** a **heart attack** in which the blood supply to the heart is blocked

coronation /,kɒrə'neɪʃ(ə)n/ noun [C] a ceremony at which someone officially becomes a king or queen

coroner /'kɒrənə/ noun [C] **LAW** a public official whose job is to decide how someone died

corporal /'kɔːp(ə)rəl/ noun [C] an officer of low rank in the army

corporal 'punishment noun [U] punishment that consists of hitting someone

corporate /'kɔːp(ə)rət/ adj relating to a corporation: *corporate culture*

corporate hospi'tality noun [U] **BUSINESS** entertainment provided by companies for their customers, for example at major sports events, in order to get more business

corporate 'raider noun [C] **BUSINESS** a person or organization that buys a large number of a company's shares in order to **take over** (=take control of) the company, despite its opposition to this action

corporate ,rate noun [U] **BUSINESS** a special rate for people travelling on business

corporate 'travel noun [U] **BUSINESS** travel on business by executives of a large company, paid for and organized by the company

corporation /,kɔːpə'reɪʃ(ə)n/ noun [C] **BUSINESS** a large business company: *American tobacco corporations*

corps /kɔː/ (plural **corps** /kɔːz/) noun [C] **1** a part of an army that has particular responsibilities **2** a group of people who all do the same type of job: *the press corps*

corpse /kɔːps/ noun [C] the body of a dead person

corpus /'kɔːpəs/ (plural **corpora** /'kɔːpərə/) noun [C] **LANGUAGE** a collection of written and spoken language that is stored on computer and used for language research and writing dictionaries

corpuscle /'kɔːpʌs(ə)l/ noun [C] **ANATOMY** one of the white or red cells in the blood

corpus luteum /,kɔːpəs 'luːtiəm/ noun [C] **ANATOMY** a structure that develops in a woman's ovary after an egg has been released. It produces the hormone **progesterone**, which prepares the woman's body for pregnancy.

corrasion /kə'reɪʒ(ə)n/ noun [U] **GEOLOGY** the eroding of a surface by pieces of rock carried by water, wind, or ice

correct¹ /kə'rekt/ adj **1** right according to the facts or rules ≠ INCORRECT: *The first person to give the correct answer wins the contest.* ♦ *a grammatically correct sentence* **2** behaving in a way that is considered socially acceptable or morally right: *My father was always very formal and correct.* —**correctly** adv: *She guessed my age correctly.* —**correctness** noun [U]

Word family: **correct**	
*Words in the same family as **correct***	
■ **correctly** *adv*	■ **correctness** *n*
■ **incorrect** *adj*	■ **incorrectly** *adv*
■ **correction** *n*	■ **corrective** *adj*

correct² /kə'rekt/ verb [T] **1** to show that something is wrong, and make it right: *I want to correct this false impression that people have of me.* **2** to look at a piece of writing and make marks to show where the mistakes are: *She sat correcting the students' homework.* **3** to make something work in the way that it should: *She had surgery to correct a defect in her left eye.* **4** to tell someone that something they have said is not right: *I must correct you on one point.*

correction /kə'rekʃ(ə)n/ noun **1** [C] a change that makes something correct or solves a problem: *I read the report and **made** a few small **corrections**.* ♦ *minor **corrections to** the car's steering mechanism* **2** [U] the process of changing something in order to make it correct: *some factual errors that need correction* **3** [C] **BUSINESS** an occasion when the values of company shares on the stock market become lower after a period when their values have increased a lot

corrective /kə'rektɪv/ adj *formal* designed to solve a problem or improve a bad situation

correlate /'kɒrəleɪt/ verb [I/T] *formal* if two or more things correlate, or if one thing correlates with another, they are connected

correlation /,kɒrə'leɪʃ(ə)n/ noun [C/U] *formal* a connection or relationship between things

correlative /kə'relətɪv/ adj **LANGUAGE** two words that are correlative are often used together but not usually used next to each other. For example, 'either' and 'or' are correlative conjunctions.

correspond /,kɒrɪ'spɒnd/ verb [I] **1** to be the same as something else, or very similar to something else: *Unfortunately, their statements did not correspond.* **2** *formal* if two people correspond with each other, they regularly write letters to each other

correspondence /,kɒrɪ'spɒndəns/ noun [U] the process of sending and receiving letters or emails, or the letters or emails that someone sends and receives

corre'spondence ,course noun [C] EDUCATION an educational course that people take at home. They send and receive work by post or by email.

correspondent /ˌkɒrɪ'spɒndənt/ noun [C] **1** a journalist who deals with a particular subject: *a political correspondent* **2** someone who regularly writes letters or emails to another person

corresponding /ˌkɒrɪ'spɒndɪŋ/ adj related to something, or similar to something —**correspondingly** adv

corre,sponding 'angles noun [plural] MATHS the angles that are in the same place at each point where one line crosses two other lines —*picture* ➔ ANGLE

corridor /'kɒrɪdɔː/ noun [C] **1** a long passage inside a building with doors on each side: *a hospital corridor* **2** GEOGRAPHY a long narrow area of land

corroborate /kə'rɒbəreɪt/ verb [T] *formal* to support what someone says by giving information or evidence

corrode /kə'rəʊd/ verb [I/T] CHEMISTRY if metal or another substance corrodes, or if something corrodes it, it is gradually destroyed by a chemical reaction

corrosion /kə'rəʊʒ(ə)n/ noun [U] CHEMISTRY damage that is caused to metal or stone when it is corroded

corrosive /kə'rəʊsɪv/ adj CHEMISTRY a corrosive substance contains chemicals that gradually cause damage

corrugated /'kɒrəˌɡeɪtɪd/ adj corrugated metal, paper, or cardboard has a surface of curved parallel folds —**corrugation** /ˌkɒrə'ɡeɪʃ(ə)n/ noun [C/U]

corrupt¹ /kə'rʌpt/ adj **1** doing dishonest or illegal things in order to get money or power: *corrupt officials* **2** COMPUTING corrupt computer files are damaged and do not operate correctly —**corruptly** adv

corrupt² /kə'rʌpt/ verb [T] **1** to encourage someone to do dishonest, illegal, or immoral things **2** COMPUTING to damage a computer file

corruption /kə'rʌpʃ(ə)n/ noun [U] **1** dishonest or illegal behaviour by powerful people: *The men were arrested on charges of corruption.* **2** the process of corrupting someone or something: *corruption of the database*

corsair /'kɔːseə/ noun [C] an old word for a 'pirate'

cortex /'kɔːteks/ noun [C] **1** ANATOMY the outer layer of the brain or another organ **2** BIOLOGY a layer of tissue in the stems and roots of plants. The cortex lies between the outer **epidermis** and the inner **vascular** tissue. —*picture* ➔ ROOT

cortisone /'kɔːtɪzəʊn/ noun [U] HEALTH a drug that is used to improve medical conditions such as **arthritis** and allergies

cosignatory /ˌkəʊ'sɪɡnətəri/ noun [C] *formal* someone who signs a cheque, contract, formal agreement etc together with another person

cosine /'kəʊsaɪn/ noun [C] MATHS in a right-angled triangle, the measurement of an **acute angle** that is equal to the length of the side between the angle and the right angle divided by the length of the hypotenuse

cosmetic /kɒz'metɪk/ adj **1** *showing disapproval* cosmetic changes affect only the appearance of something = SUPERFICIAL **2** relating to the improvement of someone's appearance: *cosmetic products* — **cosmetically** /kɒz'metɪkli/ adv

cosmetics /kɒz'metɪks/ noun [plural] substances that people use on their hair or skin to make themselves look more attractive

cos,metic 'surgery noun [U] medical operations that improve someone's appearance

cosmic /'kɒzmɪk/ adj ASTRONOMY relating to the planets and space

,cosmic 'dust noun [U] ASTRONOMY extremely small pieces of matter found in space, often in clouds

,cosmic radi'ation noun [U] PHYSICS a form of radiation that reaches the Earth from space

cosmology /kɒz'mɒlədʒi/ noun [U] ASTRONOMY the study of the origin and nature of the universe

cosmonaut /'kɒzmə,nɔːt/ noun [C] ASTRONOMY an astronaut in the Russian space programme

cosmopolitan /ˌkɒzmə'pɒlɪt(ə)n/ adj showing the influence of many different countries and cultures

the cosmos /'kɒzmɒs/ noun [singular] the universe

cost¹ /kɒst/ noun **1** [C/U] the amount of money that you need in order to buy something or to do something: *The cost of basic foods has risen dramatically.* ♦ *We need money to **cover the cost of** heating* (=to have enough to pay for it). ♦ *We're organizing a trip to London, **at a cost of** £15 per person.* **2** [C/U] damage or loss: *A new road is needed, but the **costs to** the environment would be too high.* ♦ *the **social costs of** unemployment* **3** costs [plural] money that someone has to spend regularly in order to live somewhere or to run a business: *Housing costs are very high in Tokyo.* ♦ *New technology has helped us to **cut costs*** (=reduce them). **4** costs [plural] LAW money that someone who is involved in a legal case must give to pay for the lawyers and the court

 PHRASES **at all costs** or **at any cost** used for saying that something must be done, even if it causes damage or harm
 the cost of living the amount of money that people need in order to pay for basic things such as food and a place to live
 to your cost if you know something to your cost, you know that it is true because of a bad experience you have had
 ➔ COUNT¹

cost² /kɒst/ (**costs, costing, cost**) verb [T] **1** if something costs an amount of money, you need that amount to pay for it or to do it: *A new computer costs around £1,000.* ♦ *Unemployment costs the taxpayer billions of pounds each year.* ♦ *How much does it cost to hire a bike?* **2** to cause someone to lose something good or valuable: *The merger of the two companies will cost jobs.* ♦ *His decision to take the car cost him his life.* **3** cost or **cost sth out** (**costs, costing, costed**) to calculate how much something will cost: *We have costed our proposals and sent them to the committee.*

costal /'kɒst(ə)l/ adj ANATOMY relating to the ribs

'co-,star noun [C] ARTS one of the main actors in a film, play, or television programme —**'co-,star** verb [I/T]

,cost-'benefit a,nalysis noun [C] BUSINESS a comparison of the likely costs of a plan or project with the benefits it will bring, done in order to help to make a decision

'cost ,curve noun [C] ECONOMICS a graph showing the relationship between the cost of producing a particular product and the amount of the product that is produced

'cost-,cutting noun [U] actions taken to reduce the costs of a business or organization

,cost-ef'fective adj a cost-effective way of doing something brings the most profit or advantage for the money that is spent —**,cost-ef'fectively** adv

costing /ˈkɒstɪŋ/ noun [C/U] calculation of the expected cost of something

costly /ˈkɒs(t)li/ adj formal **1** causing problems and wasting money **2** expensive

the ˌcost-of-ˈliving ˌindex noun BUSINESS the consumer price index

costume /ˈkɒstjuːm/ noun [C/U] **1** clothes that the actors wear in a play or film **2** clothes that are typical of a particular place or period in history

ˈcostume ˌdrama noun [C] ARTS a play or film about a particular historical period in which the actors wear clothes that are typical of that period

ˈcostume ˌjewellery noun [U] jewellery that is not valuable but looks expensive

cosy /ˈkəʊzi/ (**cosier, cosiest**) adj **1** warm and comfortable, relaxing, or friendly **2** a cosy relationship involves people who seem to be using their relationship in a dishonest way to get benefits for each other —**cosily** adv

cot /kɒt/ noun [C] a bed for a baby. It has high sides to stop the baby falling out.

cotangent /ˌkəʊˈtændʒənt/ noun [C] MATHS in a right-angled triangle, the measurement of an **acute angle** that is equal to the length of the side between the angle and the right angle divided by the length of the side opposite the angle

ˈcot ˌdeath noun [C/U] the sudden death of a young baby while he or she is sleeping

coterminous /kəʊˈtɜːmɪnəs/ adj formal **1** coterminous areas share a border **2** exactly the same as something else

cottage /ˈkɒtɪdʒ/ noun [C] a small house in a village or in the countryside

ˌcottage ˈcheese noun [U] a soft white cheese that does not contain much fat

ˌcottage ˈindustry noun [C] a small business that involves people producing things at home

cotton /ˈkɒt(ə)n/ noun [U] **1** AGRICULTURE a plant grown in warm regions that has white fibres in its fruit that are used for making cotton cloth. Cotton is an important **cash crop** in many areas of the world. **2** cloth made from the fibres of the cotton plant **3** thread used for sewing: a needle and cotton

ˌcotton ˈwool noun [U] soft fibres of cotton used for cleaning the skin or for removing **make-up**

cotyledon /ˌkɒtɪˈliːd(ə)n/ noun [C] BIOLOGY a leaf that is part of the embryo inside a seed before it **germinates** (=begins to develop into a plant). Scientists arrange plants into groups according to how many cotyledons their seeds have. → MONOCOTYLEDON, DICOTYLEDON

couch /kaʊtʃ/ noun [C] a long seat that you can sit or lie on= SETTEE, SOFA

couchette /kuːˈʃet/ noun [C] TOURISM a narrow bed attached to the wall of a train that swings down so that passengers can sleep on it

cough¹ /kɒf/ verb **1** [I] to force air up through your throat with a sudden noise, especially when you have a cold or when you want to get someone's attention: My chest felt painful, and I was coughing uncontrollably. **2** [T] to force something such as blood out of your lungs by coughing —**coughing** noun [U]

cough² /kɒf/ noun [C] **1** HEALTH an illness in which you cough a lot and your throat hurts **2** the action of coughing, or the sound that you make when you cough

could /strong kʊd, weak kəd/ modal verb **1** used for saying that someone was able to do something: Renee could read when she was four. ♦ In the distance I could see a cloud of smoke. **2** used for saying that something is possible or that it may happen: We could still win. ♦ In a situation like this, anything could happen. **3** spoken used for asking something politely: Could I have a glass of water? ♦ I wonder if we could borrow your car? **4** spoken used for suggesting to someone what they might do: You could come and stay with us.

PHRASE **could have** spoken **1** used for saying that something was possible in the past, even though it did not happen: You could have been killed. **2** used for saying that perhaps something was true, although you are not sure: The explosion could have been caused by a gas leak.

couldn't /ˈkʊd(ə)nt/ short form the usual way of saying or writing 'could not'. This is not often used in formal writing: I couldn't go to her party.

coulomb /ˈkuːlɒm/ noun [C] PHYSICS the SI unit of electric charge that is equal to the amount of charge carried by a current of one **ampere** in one second

council /ˈkaʊns(ə)l/ noun [C] **1** the elected politicians who govern a city or local area, or the organization they work for: The council has rejected their suggestion. ♦ a change in council policy **2** a group of people who are chosen to make official decisions or give advice

> Council can be used with a singular or plural verb. You can say The council **has** rejected their suggestion OR The council **have** rejected their suggestion.

ˈcouncil esˌtate noun [C] an area of a town consisting of council houses

ˈcouncil ˌhouse noun [C] a house that is owned by a local council. The people who live in it pay a low rent.

councillor /ˈkaʊns(ə)lə/ noun [C] an elected member of the council that governs a local area

counsel¹ /ˈkaʊns(ə)l/ (**counsels, counselling, counselled**) verb [T] to give someone advice about their problems, especially as your job

counsel² /ˈkaʊns(ə)l/ noun **1** [C] LAW a lawyer who represents someone in a court of law **2** [C/U] formal advice and help

counselling /ˈkaʊns(ə)lɪŋ/ noun [U] professional advice that is given to someone who has problems

counsellor /ˈkaʊns(ə)lə/ noun [C] someone whose job is to give advice to people with problems

count¹ /kaʊnt/ verb

1 say how many	5 be important
2 say numbers	+ PHRASES
3 include in calculation	+ PHRASAL VERB
4 consider as sth	

1 [I/T] to calculate how many people or things there are in a group: All the votes have been counted.

2 [I] to say numbers one after another in order: I can count up to ten in German.

3 [I/T] to include something or someone in a calculation, or to be included in a calculation: Points scored after the bell do not count. ♦ Marks for this project **count towards** your final exam result. ♦ Do national holidays **count as** part of annual leave?

4 [I/T] to consider someone or something in a particular way, or to be considered in a particular way: We can **count** ourselves **lucky** that none of us got hurt. ♦ Does geography **count as** a science subject?

5 [I] to be important: You're late, but you're here; and that's what counts.

PHRASES **count the cost** to realize what has been lost or damaged as a result of something

make sth count to make something have as useful and positive an effect as possible

PHRASAL VERB **'count on/upon sb** to trust someone to do something for you = RELY ON SB/STH: *The whole team was counting on me.* ♦ *I knew we could count on you to be on time.*

count² /kaʊnt/ noun [C] **1** the process of counting the people or things in a group, or the number of people or things that are counted: *After the count, Ellison had 25% of the votes.* **2** the process of saying numbers in order: *Hold your breath for a count of ten.* **3** the amount of a substance that is present in another substance: *the pollen count* **4** LAW each crime that someone is charged with: *Brown was jailed on three counts of corruption.*

PHRASES **keep count (of sth)** to remember or record a number as it changes over a period of time: *It seemed like a long time, but I didn't keep count of the days.*

lose count (of sth) used for emphasizing that something has happened many times

on both/several etc counts in both/several ways

countable /ˈkaʊntəb(ə)l/ adj LANGUAGE a countable noun is a noun that can have a plural and can be used after 'a' when it is singular. Countable nouns are marked [C] in this dictionary. Examples of countable nouns are 'boat', 'girl', and 'house' ≠ UNCOUNTABLE

countdown /ˈkaʊnt,daʊn/ noun [C] **1** the action of counting numbers backwards before something important happens **2** the period of time just before an important event

countenance /ˈkaʊntənəns/ verb [T] *formal* to approve of something or allow something to happen

counter¹ /ˈkaʊntə/ noun [C] **1** a long flat surface where customers are served, for example in a shop or a bank **2** a small round coloured object that you use in a **board game**

PHRASE **under the counter** bought or sold secretly and illegally

counter² /ˈkaʊntə/ verb **1** [I/T] to reply to a criticism or statement that you disagree with **2** [T] to oppose or stop something

counter- /ˈkaʊntə/ prefix opposing something: *a counter-proposal*

counteract /ˌkaʊntərˈækt/ verb [T] to reduce the negative effect of something by doing something that has an opposite effect

counterattack /ˈkaʊntərə,tæk/ verb [I] to attack someone who has just attacked you in a war, game, or argument

counterbalance /ˈkaʊntə,bæləns/ verb [T] to have an effect that is equal and opposite to something else

counterblast /ˈkaʊntə,blɑːst/ noun [C] a very strong reply to a criticism or statement that you disagree with

counterbore /ˈkaʊntə,bɔː/ verb [T] TECHNOLOGY to make a cylindrical flat-bottomed hole that can receive the head of a **slotted screw**

counterfeit /ˈkaʊntəfɪt/ adj counterfeit bank notes, documents, or products are illegal copies

counterfoil /ˈkaʊntə,fɔɪl/ noun [C] the part of something such as a cheque that someone keeps as a record of a payment they have made

counterintuitive /ˌkaʊnt(ə)rɪmˈtjuːɪtɪv/ adj opposite to what seems obvious or natural

countermand /ˌkaʊntəˈmɑːnd/ verb [T] *formal* to tell someone to ignore a previous order, usually by giving them a different order

counteroffer /ˈkaʊntə,ɒfə/ noun [C] BUSINESS an offer made as an answer to another offer that someone does not want to accept, for example an offer by the seller of a higher price than was offered by the buyer, but lower than the first price that was asked

counterpart /ˈkaʊntə,pɑːt/ noun [C] a person or thing that is similar to another in a different country or organization

counterproductive /ˌkaʊntəprəˈdʌktɪv/ adj having the opposite result to the one that you intended

countersign /ˈkaʊntə,saɪn/ verb [T] to sign a document that someone else has already signed

countersink /ˈkaʊntə,sɪŋk/ verb [T] TECHNOLOGY to shape a hole with sloping sides, so that the top of a screw in it will be level with the surface of the work

countertenor /ˌkaʊntəˈtenə/ noun [C] MUSIC a man who sings with a very high voice

counterterrorism /ˈkaʊntə,terərɪz(ə)m/ noun [U] the actions and methods of a country that are intended to stop the activities of people who use violence to achieve political aims —**counterterrorist** adj

countess /ˈkaʊntɪs/ noun [C] a woman who is the wife of an **earl**

countless /ˈkaʊntləs/ adj very many: *The temple attracts countless visitors.*

'count ,noun noun [C] LANGUAGE a countable noun

country /ˈkʌntri/ (plural **countries**) noun **1** [C] GEOGRAPHY an area of land that has its own government and official borders: *soldiers who fight for their country* ♦ *The company has offices in nine African countries.* **2 the country** [singular] areas away from towns and cities, consisting of fields, farms, villages etc = COUNTRYSIDE: *They prefer to live in the country.* **3 the country** [singular] all the people who live in a country: *a crime that has shocked the whole country* **4** [U] an area that is known for a particular product, activity, person etc: *East of here is mostly farming country.*

'country ,club noun [C] an expensive private club where the members hold social events and play sports such as golf and tennis

'country ,code noun [singular] an **international dialling code**

,country 'house noun [C] a large house in the countryside

countryman /ˈkʌntrɪmən/ (plural **countrymen** /ˈkʌntrɪmən/) noun [C] someone who is from the same country as you

'country ,music noun [U] MUSIC a type of popular music from the southern US

countryside /ˈkʌntri,saɪd/ noun [U] areas away from towns and cities, with farms, fields, and trees

county /ˈkaʊnti/ (plural **counties**) noun [C] a region that has its own local government

,county 'court noun [C/U] LAW a local court of law in parts of the UK and in some US **counties** that deals with minor legal issues but not serious crimes

coup /kuː/ noun [C] **1** coup or coup d'état an occasion when a group of people take control of a country using military force **2** an impressive and surprising success

coup de grâce /ˌkuː də ˈɡrɑːs/ noun [singular] *formal* a final action that destroys or defeats something that was already weak or failing

couple¹ /ˈkʌp(ə)l/ noun **1** [singular] two things or people of the same type: *'Has he had any serious girlfriends?' 'A couple.'* ♦ *Take a couple of aspirin – you'll* *soon feel better.* **2** [singular] a small number of things or people: *There are **a couple of** things I want to discuss.* **3** [C] two people who are married to each other, or who have a romantic relationship with each other **4** [C] two people who are doing something together: *The room was full of dancing couples.*

couple² /ˈkʌp(ə)l/ verb [T] **1** if one thing is coupled with another, they are combined **2** to join vehicles or pieces of equipment so that they work together

couplet /ˈkʌplət/ noun [C] **LITERATURE** two lines of poetry that are next to each other

coupon /ˈkuːpɒn/ noun [C] **1** a piece of paper that allows someone to buy something at a reduced price **2** a piece of paper that you write your name and address on and send to someone, for example in order to enter a competition

courage /ˈkʌrɪdʒ/ noun [U] the ability to do things that are dangerous, frightening, or very difficult: *I didn't* ***have the courage*** *to admit that I was wrong.*

courageous /kəˈreɪdʒəs/ adj very brave and determined: *It was a courageous decision to resign.*
—**courageously** adv

courgette /kɔːˈʒet/ noun [C/U] a long vegetable with dark green skin, similar to a small **marrow**= ZUCCHINI — *picture* → VEGETABLE

courier /ˈkʊriə/ noun [C] **1** someone whose job is to deliver documents or parcels **2** **TOURISM** someone whose job is to help tourists on an organized holiday

course /kɔːs/ noun [C]

1 series of lessons	**6** medical treatment
2 line of travel	**7** area for sport
3 action sb chooses	**8** row of bricks
4 way things develop	**+ PHRASES**
5 part of meal	

1 **EDUCATION** a series of lessons or lectures in an academic subject or a practical skill: *an English course* ♦ *You could **do** a language **course** abroad.* ♦ *The school* ***runs courses*** *for beginners.* ♦ *She's **on a** management* ***course*** *this week.* ♦ *an introductory **course** in economics* **2** the direction that a ship or plane is travelling in: *The captain had to **change course** quickly.* **3** the things that you choose to do in a particular situation: *What **course of action** do you recommend?* **4** the way that things develop over a period of time: *a speech that changed **the course of history*** **5** one of the parts of a meal: *We both chose fish as our* ***main course.*** **6** **HEALTH** a medical treatment that someone is given over a period of time: *It's important to take the whole course of antibiotics.* **7** **SPORTS** an area where a race or sport takes place: *a race course* **8** **CONSTRUCTION** a complete layer of bricks, including the **mortar**

PHRASES **in/during/over the course of sth** while something is happening or continuing: *In the course of the morning I learned a lot about the project.*
on course for sth or **on course to do sth** very likely to achieve something or to have a particular result
run/take its course to develop in the usual way and stop naturally: *The doctor said we just had to let the illness run its course.*
→ DUE¹, OF COURSE

coursebook /ˈkɔːsˌbʊk/ noun [C] **EDUCATION** a book that is used by students in class= TEXTBOOK

coursework /ˈkɔːsˌwɜːk/ noun [U] **EDUCATION** school work that a student must do as part of a course of study

court /kɔːt/ noun **1** [C/U] **LAW** a place where trials take place and legal cases are decided= LAW COURT: *a court case* ♦ *The man will **appear in court** on Monday.* ♦ *She threatened to **go to court** (=begin a court case) if he did not pay.* ♦ *Lynn **took** her employers **to court** (=began a court case against them).* **2** **the court** [singular] **LAW** the people in a court, especially the judge and jury: *A police officer told the court that he had seen Brown leaving the house.* **3** [C] **SPORTS** an area marked with lines where some sports are played, including tennis and basketball: *a tennis court* **4** [C/U] the place where a king or queen lives and works

PHRASES **court of appeal** **LAW** a court of law that holds **appeals** when someone is not satisfied with the original judgment
court of law **LAW** a court where legal trials take place

courteous /ˈkɜːtiəs/ adj polite in a formal way
—**courteously** adv

courtesy /ˈkɜːtəsi/ noun [U] polite behaviour: *You might have **had the courtesy to** return my calls.*
PHRASE **courtesy of** **1** used for saying who has provided something, and for thanking them for it: *The first prize is two tickets for the game, courtesy of the team's sponsors.* **2** as a result of

'courtesy ,bus noun [C] a free bus for a hotel's guests, a company's workers etc

'courtesy ,phone noun [C] a telephone that people do not have to pay to use, usually for calling taxis

courthouse /ˈkɔːtˌhaʊs/ noun [C] **LAW** a building that has one or more courts in it for legal trials

courtier /ˈkɔːtiə/ noun [C] someone who has an official position at the **court** of a king or queen, or who spends time there

,court-'martial noun [C] a military trial of a member of the armed forces who has broken military laws —,**court-'martial** verb [T]

'court ,order noun [C] **LAW** an order from a court of law that tells someone that they must do something

courtroom /ˈkɔːtˌruːm/ noun [C] **LAW** a room where legal cases are judged

courtship /ˈkɔːtʃɪp/ noun [C/U] an attempt to get someone's support, especially in business or politics

'court ,shoe noun [C] a very plain type of woman's shoe with a small heel and no fastening

courtyard /ˈkɔːtˌjɑːd/ noun [C] a square area outside that is surrounded by buildings or walls

couscous /ˈkuːskuːs/ noun [U] crushed wheat that is used in North African cooking

cousin /ˈkʌz(ə)n/ noun [C] a child of your uncle or aunt

covalent bond /kəʊˌveɪlənt ˈbɒnd/ noun [C] **CHEMISTRY** a chemical bond between two atoms produced when electrons are shared

cove /kəʊv/ noun [C] **GEOGRAPHY** a small area of sea that is partly surrounded by land

covenant¹ /ˈkʌvənənt/ noun [C] **LAW** a legal agreement, often an agreement to give money

covenant² /ˈkʌvənənt/ verb [T] **LAW** to legally agree to do something

cover¹ /ˈkʌvə/ verb [T]

1 put sth over sth	**7** travel a distance
2 be all over sth	**8** perform sb else's
3 deal with sth	song
4 report/describe	**9** point a gun at sb
5 pay for	**10** in sports
6 provide insurance	**+ PHRASE**

1 to put one thing over another in order to protect or

hide it: *Cover the food until you are ready to eat it.*
♦ *They* **covered** *the baby* **with** *a blanket.*
2 to be all over a surface or object: *Bruises covered his entire body.* ♦ *His clothes were* **covered in** *mud.*
3 to deal with a particular situation or subject: *The programme covers all aspects of health and safety at work.*
4 to give a report of an event on television or radio, or in a newspaper: *We will be covering the game on Saturday afternoon.*
5 to have enough money to pay for something: *We need £1,000 a month to cover the rent.*
6 if an insurance agreement covers a situation or person, it provides protection against loss or damage
7 to travel a particular distance: *We had to cover the last three miles on foot.*
8 MUSIC to perform or record a song that was first performed by someone else
9 to protect someone from attack by pointing a gun at someone who might shoot them: *His partner covered him while he ran across the prison yard.*
10 SPORTS to stay very close to an opposing player, in order to prevent them from scoring a goal or getting a point

PHRASE **cover your tracks** if someone covers their tracks, they try to hide evidence of something bad that they have done

cover² /ˈkʌvə/ noun

1 for putting over sth	**6** false story
2 sheets/blankets	**7** work substitute
3 outside of book/CD	**8** piece of music
4 insurance agreement	**+** PHRASES
5 place for shelter	

1 [C] something that you put over something else in order to hide it, protect it, or close it: *She put plastic covers on all the furniture.* ♦ *a cushion cover*
2 the covers [plural] sheets and blankets that someone lies under in bed
3 [C] the outside page on the front or back of a book or magazine: *Her face was once on the cover of Vogue magazine.* ♦ *On the train I* **read** *the newspaper* **from cover to cover** (=read it all).
4 [U] an agreement by an insurance company to pay money in a particular situation
5 [U] places such as buildings or trees where people or animals can hide or shelter from the weather: *Everybody* **ran for cover** *as the rain started to fall.*
6 [singular] a false story that is used for hiding who someone really is
7 [U] an arrangement in which a person does the work of someone who is away or ill
8 [C] MUSIC a song that is recorded by someone who is not the original performer

PHRASES **under cover** pretending to be someone else in order to find out secret information
under cover of night/darkness hidden by darkness

coverage /ˈkʌv(ə)rɪdʒ/ noun [U] **1** news about something on television or radio or in the newspapers: **live coverage** *of England's game against France* **2** the amount of attention that television, radio, and newspapers give to something, or the way in which something is reported

'cover ,girl noun [C] an attractive young woman whose photograph is on the front of a magazine

covering /ˈkʌv(ə)rɪŋ/ noun [singular] something that covers something else

'covering ,letter noun [C] a letter that you send with something, to explain what you are sending

'cover ,lens noun [C] TECHNOLOGY one of the outer lenses of a pair of **welding goggles**, made of clear glass

'cover ,note noun [C] BUSINESS a letter from an insurance company giving details of an insurance policy and confirming that the policy exists

'cover ,pass noun [C] TECHNOLOGY a top layer of weld that joins together the first and second layers of welding material in a joint

'cover ,slip noun [C] a piece of thin clear glass used to cover a **specimen** on a microscope slide

covert /ˈkʌvət, ˈkəʊvɜːt/ adj secret ≠ OVERT —**covertly** adv

'cover-,up noun [C] an attempt to stop people from discovering the truth about something bad

'cover ,version noun [C] MUSIC a **cover** of a popular song

covet /ˈkʌvət/ verb [T] *formal* to want something that someone else has

coveted /ˈkʌvətɪd/ adj a coveted thing is something that a lot of people want to have

cow /kaʊ/ noun [C] **1** a mammal that is kept by farmers for its milk or meat —*picture* → MAMMAL **2** the female of some types of mammal such as an elephant or a **whale**

coward /ˈkaʊəd/ noun [C] someone who is not brave enough to do something that they should do

cowardice /ˈkaʊədɪs/ noun [U] behaviour that shows that you are not brave enough to do something that you should do

cowardly /ˈkaʊədli/ adj **1** a cowardly person is not brave enough to do something that they should do **2** cruel towards someone who is weaker than you: *a cowardly attack*

cowboy /ˈkaʊˌbɔɪ/ noun [C] a man whose job is to look after cows on a ranch in the US

'cowboy ,hat noun [C] a high hat with a wide **brim**

cower /ˈkaʊə/ verb [I] to move your body down and away from someone because you are frightened ≠ CRINGE

'co-,worker noun [C] someone who works with you

cowpea /ˈkaʊˌpiː/ noun [C] AGRICULTURE a type of bean that grows well in hot, dry climates. It is used for both human and animal feed, and both the seeds and the **pods** can be eaten.

cowrie /ˈkaʊri/ noun [C] a shiny, coloured shell of a sea animal, used in the past as money in parts of Africa and Asia

cowshed /ˈkaʊˌʃed/ noun [C] a farm building where cows are kept

cox /kɒks/ noun [C] SPORTS someone who directs the people **rowing** a boat in a race —**cox** verb [I/T], **coxless** adj

coy /kɔɪ/ adj pretending to be shy in order to seem more attractive —**coyly** adv

coyote /kɔɪˈəʊti/ noun [C] a small wild North American dog

CPD /ˌsiː piː ˈdiː/ noun [U] BUSINESS continuing professional development: training and education that continues throughout a person's career, in order to improve the skills and knowledge they use in their job

CPI /ˌsiː piː ˈaɪ/ abbrev ECONOMICS the **consumer price index**

CPR /ˌsiː piː ˈɑː/ noun [U] HEALTH cardiopulmonary resuscitation: a medical treatment in which you breathe air into someone's mouth and press their chest repeatedly, so that their heart will start working again

cps /ˌsiː piː ˈes/ abbrev COMPUTING characters per second: a measure of how fast information moves from one computer or file to another

CPU /ˌsiː piː ˈjuː/ noun [C] COMPUTING a central processing unit: the part of a computer that controls what it does —picture → COMPUTER

crab /kræb/ noun **1** [C] a sea crustacean with two large claws that walks sideways —picture → SEA **2** [U] the flesh of a crab, eaten as food

crack¹ /kræk/ verb

1 break along line	**5** lose control
2 break sth open	**6** when voice shakes
3 make noise	**7** solve problem
4 hit part of body	

1 [I/T] if something cracks, or if someone cracks it, a line or long narrow hole appears on its surface, but it does not break into pieces: *The ice was starting to crack at the edges.* ♦ *I dropped a plate and cracked it.*
2 [T] to break something open in order to get what is inside: *Crack the egg open with a knife.*
3 [I] to make a short loud noise like a small explosion: *Thunder cracked overhead.*
4 [T] to accidentally hit a part of your body against something with a lot of force: *Dad fell and cracked his head against the door.*
5 [I] to say or do things that you would not normally say or do, because you are very tired or because someone is threatening you: *She won because her opponent cracked under the pressure.*
6 [I] if your voice cracks, it goes higher and lower in a way that you cannot control
7 [T] to solve a complicated problem, or to find the answer to a **mystery**: *Detectives believe they can crack the case.*

crack² /kræk/ noun [C] **1** a line on a surface where something is beginning to break apart: *cracks in the walls* **2** a narrow opening between two things: *She looked through the crack in the curtains.* **3** a sign that an organization, relationship, or plan is becoming weak: *Cracks had started to appear in their marriage.* **4** a short loud noise

ˌcrack coˈcaine noun [U] HEALTH a very pure form of the illegal drug **cocaine**

crackdown /ˈkrækˌdaʊn/ noun [C] strong action that someone in authority takes to stop a particular activity = CLAMPDOWN: *a new crackdown on drug trafficking*

cracker /ˈkrækə/ noun [C] **1** a type of thin dry **biscuit** that is often eaten with cheese **2** a decorated paper tube that makes a noise when someone pulls it apart. It usually has a small toy inside.

crackle /ˈkræk(ə)l/ verb [I] to continually make short sounds like the sound of wood burning —**crackling** /ˈkræk(ə)lɪŋ/ noun [singular/U]

cradle /ˈkreɪd(ə)l/ noun [C] **1** a small bed for a baby that can swing from side to side **2** the part of a telephone where you put the receiver **3** the place where something began = BIRTHPLACE

craft /krɑːft/ noun **1** [C] a traditional skill of making things by hand, or something such as furniture or jewellery that is made by hand: *traditional Egyptian arts and crafts* **2** (plural **craft**) [C] a boat or ship **3** [C/U] the skill needed for a particular profession

craftsman /ˈkrɑːftsmən/ (plural **craftsmen** /ˈkrɑːftsmən/) noun [C] a man who makes beautiful or practical objects using his hands

craftsmanship /ˈkrɑːftsmənʃɪp/ noun [U] the skill involved in making something beautiful or practical, or the beauty of something that has been made with skill

craftsperson /ˈkrɑːftsˌpɜːs(ə)n/ (plural **craftspeople** /ˈkrɑːftsˌpiːp(ə)l/) noun [C] someone who makes beautiful or practical objects using their hands

craftswoman /ˈkrɑːftsˌwʊmən/ (plural **craftswomen** /ˈkrɑːftsˌwɪmɪn/) noun [C] a woman who makes beautiful or practical objects using her hands

craftwork /ˈkrɑːftˌwɜːk/ noun [U] the activity of making things by hand, or things such as jewellery or furniture that are made by hand

crafty /ˈkrɑːfti/ (**craftier**, **craftiest**) adj someone who is crafty is good at getting what they want, especially dishonestly —**craftily** adv, **craftiness** /ˈkrɑːftinəs/ noun [U]

crag /kræg/ noun [C] GEOGRAPHY a very steep rough part of a cliff or mountain

craggy /ˈkrægi/ adj **1** a craggy face looks strong and has deep lines in it = RUGGED **2** steep with a lot of rough rocks

cram /kræm/ (**crams**, **cramming**, **crammed**) verb **1** [T] to put people or things into a space that is too small: *The sacks of rice were crammed under a table.* ♦ *The hall was crammed with children.* **2** [I] informal to study hard in order to learn a lot in a short time

cramp /kræmp/ noun **1** [C/U] HEALTH a sudden painful **contraction** of a muscle, often caused by tiredness or **strain 2** [C] CONSTRUCTION a metal object that holds parts in place during building

cramped /kræmpt/ adj small and crowded: *cramped offices*

crane¹ /kreɪn/ noun [C] **1** a very tall machine that is used for moving heavy objects and for building tall buildings **2** a large water bird with long legs and a long neck —picture → BIRD

crane² /kreɪn/ verb [I/T] to stretch your neck out to try to see something

cranium /ˈkreɪniəm/ noun [C] ANATOMY the bones of the head of a vertebrate = SKULL —picture → SKELETON —**cranial** adj

crank /kræŋk/ noun [C] a piece of equipment that turns to make something move or start

crankcase /ˈkræŋkˌkeɪs/ noun [C] ENGINEERING the metal cover around the **crankshaft** in some engines, especially **internal-combustion engines**

ˌcrankcase ˈventilation ˌvalve noun [C] ENGINEERING a **valve** that allows gases to leave the crankcase of an **internal-combustion engine**

crankshaft /ˈkræŋkˌʃɑːft/ noun [C] ENGINEERING a long metal bar in a vehicle's engine that is connected to the wheels and changes power into movement

crash¹ /kræʃ/ verb **1** [I/T] to make a loud noise, usually by hitting something hard: *A ball came crashing through the window.* ♦ *The waves crashed against the rocks.* **2** [I/T] if a vehicle crashes, or if someone crashes it, it hits something and is damaged or destroyed: *Three people were killed when their car crashed into a tree.* ♦ *The plane crashed a few minutes after take-off.* **3** [I] ECONOMICS if the **stock market** crashes, its value falls suddenly **4** [I] COMPUTING if a computer or a computer program crashes, it suddenly stops working

crash² /kræʃ/ noun [C] **1** an accident that happens when a vehicle hits something: *He was seriously injured in a car crash.* ♦ *It was the worst train crash in thirty years.* **2** a loud noise like the sound of things hitting each other and breaking **3** ECONOMICS a sudden fall in prices or in the value of the **stock market** **4** COMPUTING an occasion when a computer or a computer program suddenly stops working

'crash ,barrier noun [C] a low metal fence at the side of a road or along the middle of a motorway

'crash ,course noun [C] EDUCATION a course of study in which people are taught a lot about a subject in a short time

'crash ,helmet noun [C] a hard round hat that someone wears to protect their head while driving a motorcycle or **racing car**

,crash 'landing noun [C] an occasion when an aircraft has to land in a sudden and dangerous way

'crash-,test verb [T] BUSINESS to test something thoroughly in order to see whether it is safe and reliable

crate /kreɪt/ noun [C] a container for storing or moving things

crater /'kreɪtə/ noun [C] **1** GEOLOGY the round hole at the top of a volcano —*picture* → VOLCANO **2** a large round hole in the ground that is caused by an explosion

'crater ,lake noun [C] GEOLOGY a round lake that forms in the large hole in the top of a volcano after it erupts

crave /kreɪv/ verb [I/T] to feel a very strong need for something that is hard to control: *As a child he craved attention.*

craving /'kreɪvɪŋ/ noun [C] a very strong feeling of wanting something: *a **craving for** chocolate*

crawl¹ /krɔːl/ verb [I] **1** to move along the ground on your hands and knees: *We crawled through the bushes.* **2** to move or pass very slowly: *Traffic crawled along the main road.* ♦ *The hours seemed to crawl by.* **3** if an insect crawls, it moves forwards using its legs

crawl² /krɔːl/ noun **1** [singular] a very slow speed **2** [U] SPORTS a style of swimming in which you move one arm over your head and then the other while you are kicking your legs

crayon /'kreɪɒn/ noun [C] ARTS a stick of coloured **wax** that is used for drawing

craze /kreɪz/ noun [C] something that suddenly becomes very popular for a short time

crazed /kreɪzd/ adj completely crazy and uncontrolled

crazing /'kreɪzɪŋ/ noun [U] CONSTRUCTION, ARTS very small cracks that appear in the surface of **plaster** or **ceramics**

crazy /'kreɪzi/ (**crazier, craziest**) adj *informal* not at all sensible or practical: *It's crazy. Who would do a thing like that?* ♦ *She knew she would be completely crazy to refuse.*

   PHRASES   **crazy about sb** very much in love with someone
crazy about sth very enthusiastic about something
drive sb crazy to make someone very annoyed
go crazy 1 to become very angry about something **2** to become very excited
—**crazily** adv

creak /kriːk/ verb [I] if something creaks, it makes a high noise when it moves, or when you put weight on it —**creak** noun [C], **creaky** adj

cream¹ /kriːm/ noun **1** [U] a thick yellowish-white liquid that is taken from the top of milk **2** [C/U] a thick smooth substance that people put on their skin, for

example when it is too dry. Some medicines are in the form of a cream. **3** [U] a yellowish-white colour
—**creamy** adj

cream² /kriːm/ adj yellowish-white in colour

,cream 'cheese noun [U] a soft smooth white cheese that people spread on bread and similar foods

crease¹ /kriːs/ noun **1** [C] a line made on cloth or paper when it is folded or crushed **2 the crease** SPORTS in **cricket**, the line in front of the **wicket** where a **batsman** stands to hit the ball

crease² /kriːs/ verb [I/T] to make lines on cloth or paper by folding or crushing it, or to become covered in these lines

creased /kriːst/ adj creased cloth or paper is marked with a crease

create /kri'eɪt/ verb [T] to make something new exist or happen: *His comments have created a lot of confusion.* ♦ *How do I create a new file?* ♦ *In the last week, 170 new jobs have been created.* ♦ *He was only 22 when he created this masterpiece.*

creation /kri'eɪʃ(ə)n/ noun **1** [U] the act of creating something: *The government is to provide more money for job creation.* ♦ *the creation of new industries* **2** [C] something that has been created using skill or imagination: *Have you seen my latest creation?*

creationism /kri'eɪʃ(ə)n,ɪz(ə)m/ noun [U] RELIGION the belief that the universe was created exactly as the Bible describes it

creative /kri'eɪtɪv/ adj **1** involving a lot of imagination and new ideas: *Painting is a creative process.* ♦ *the creative use of technology in everyday life* **2** having a lot of imagination and new ideas: *The programme offers children the chance to be creative.* —**creatively** adv

cre,ative 'writing noun [U] LITERATURE the activity of writing stories and poems

creativity /,kriːeɪ'tɪvəti/ noun [U] the ability to create new ideas or things using your imagination: *We want to encourage creativity in our employees.*

creator /kri'eɪtə/ noun **1** [C] someone who has created something **2 the Creator** RELIGION God

creature /'kriːtʃə/ noun [C] **1** anything that lives except plants: *a small furry creature* **2** an imaginary living thing that is strange or frightening: *The Gorgon was a mythical creature.*

crèche /kreʃ/ noun [C] a place where babies and small children are looked after while their parents are busy

credentials /krɪ'denʃ(ə)lz/ noun [plural] **1** personal qualities, achievements, or experiences that make someone suitable for something: *His credentials as a football manager are impressive.* **2** documents that prove who someone is, or that show someone's qualifications

credibility /,kredə'bɪləti/ noun [U] qualities that someone or something has that make people believe them or trust them: *The government is losing credibility by its failure to act quickly.*

credible /'kredəb(ə)l/ adj **1** able to be believed or trusted: *credible evidence* **2** considered likely to happen or likely to be successful: *a credible opponent* —**credibly** adv

credit¹ /'kredɪt/ noun

1 when you pay later	5 part of course
2 praise for sth	6 list of makers
3 money added	✦ PHRASES
4 money available to you	

1 [U] an arrangement to receive money from a bank, or

receive goods from a shop, and to pay for them later: *I don't like buying things on credit.* ♦ *Some suppliers will not offer credit to their customers.*
2 [U] praise for something that you have done: *You deserve credit for all the help you gave us.* ♦ *He always takes the credit for my ideas.*
3 [C] an amount of money that is added to an account
4 [C] an amount of money that someone has a right to use: *tax credits*
5 [C] **EDUCATION** a part of a college or university course that someone has completed successfully
6 the credits [plural] a list at the beginning or end of a film or television programme that shows the people who were involved in making it

PHRASES　be a credit to sb if you are a credit to someone, they should be proud of you
give sb credit for sth to believe that someone is good at something, or that they have a particular good quality
to sb's credit used for saying that someone deserves praise

credit² /'kredɪt/ verb [T] **1** to add an amount of money to an account ≠ DEBIT: *The money will be credited to your account.* **2** to believe that something is true
PHRASAL VERB　'credit sb with sth to believe that someone has achieved something, or that they have particular good qualities

creditable /'kredɪtəb(ə)l/ adj good enough to deserve some praise or admiration

'credit ,card noun [C] a small plastic card that people use to buy things now and pay for them later

'credit ,history noun [C] **BUSINESS** a record of how someone has paid back what they owed in the past, used as a way of deciding whether to lend them money

creditor /'kredɪtə/ noun [C] **BUSINESS** a person or company that is owed money by another person or company ≠ DEBTOR

'credit ,rating noun [C] **BUSINESS** financial information about a person, company, or organization that a bank or shop uses for deciding whether to lend them money or to give them **credit**

creditworthy /'kredɪt,wɜːði/ adj likely to pay back money that you borrow

credulous /'kredjʊləs/ adj *formal* tending to believe things and therefore easily tricked or cheated = GULLIBLE

creed /kriːd/ noun [C] **RELIGION** *formal* a set of beliefs

creek /kriːk/ noun [C] **GEOGRAPHY 1** a long narrow area of sea that stretches into the land **2** a narrow stream

creep /kriːp/ (**creeps, creeping, crept** /krept/, **creeped** or **crept**) verb [I] **1** to move slowly and quietly: *Sue crept up the stairs.* ♦ *The fog was creeping across the bay.* **2** to gradually happen or start: *A smile crept over her face.*

creepy /'kriːpi/ (**creepier, creepiest**) adj *informal* unpleasant in a way that makes you feel frightened

cremate /krɪ'meɪt/ verb [T] to burn the body of a dead person —**cremation** /krɪ'meɪʃ(ə)n/ noun [C/U]

crematorium /,kremə'tɔːriəm/ noun [C] a building where the bodies of dead people are cremated

crenation /krɪ'neɪʃ(ə)n/ noun [C] **BIOLOGY** the process by which cells **shrink** (=become smaller) due to losing water through **osmosis**. Crenation particularly affects red blood cells when they are placed in a concentrated solution.

creole¹ /'kriːəʊl/ noun **1** [C/U] **LANGUAGE** a language that is a mixture of a European language and one or more other languages, spoken as the first language of a people **2** [C] a name for particular groups of people in areas outside of Europe who have European **ancestors** (=relatives who lived in the past)

creole² /'kriːəʊl/ adj **LANGUAGE** relating to languages that are creoles

creosote /'kriːəsəʊt/ noun [U] a thick brown liquid that you paint on wood to protect it from the weather —**creosote** verb [T]

crepe /kreɪp/ noun **1** [U] a light type of rubber **2** [C] a light thin **pancake 3** [U] soft thin cloth with small folds in its surface

'crepe ,paper noun [U] thin paper that stretches easily and is often used for making decorations

crept /krept/ the past tense and past participle of **creep**

crescendo /krə'ʃendəʊ/ noun [C] **MUSIC** a gradual increase in sound in a piece of music

crescent /'krez(ə)nt/ noun [C] **1** a curved shape that is wide in the middle and pointed at the ends —*picture* → SHAPE **2** a curved street: used especially in street names

cress /kres/ noun [U] a small plant with round green leaves that have a strong flavour. The leaves are eaten raw in salads or used for decorating food.

crest /krest/ noun [C] **1** the top of a hill, mountain, or wave —*picture* → WAVE **2** a set of feathers on the top of the heads of some birds

crestfallen /'krest,fɔːlən/ adj sad and disappointed

the Cretaceous /krɪ'teɪʃəs/ noun [singular] **GEOLOGY** the period from about 144 to 65 million years ago when rock containing **chalk** was formed —**Cretaceous** adj

Creutzfeldt-Jakob disease /,krɔɪtsfelt 'jækɒb dɪ,ziː z/ noun [U] **HEALTH** the disease **CJD**

crevasse /krə'væs/ noun [C] **GEOGRAPHY** a very deep crack in rock or ice

crevice /'krevɪs/ noun [C] a narrow crack in rock or in a wall

crew /kruː/ noun [C] **1** the people who work on a ship, aircraft etc: *All the passengers and crew on board the jet were killed.* **2** the people on a military ship or aircraft who are not officers **3** a group of people with a particular skill who work together: *a film crew* ♦ *an ambulance crew* **4** **SPORTS** a team of people who **row** a boat in a race

Crew can be used with a singular or plural verb. You can say *The crew **is** very experienced* OR *The crew **are** very experienced.*

crewman /'kruːmən/ (plural **crewmen** /'kruːmən/) noun [C] a man who is a member of the **crew** of a ship, aircraft etc

'crew ,neck noun [C] a **sweater** with a round neck

cricket /'krɪkɪt/ noun **1** [U] **SPORTS** a game in which teams score **runs** (=points) by hitting a ball with a **bat** and running between two sets of sticks **2** [C] a brown insect that makes a loud noise at night —*picture* → INSECT

cricketer /'krɪkɪtə/ noun [C] **SPORTS** someone who plays cricket

cried /kraɪd/ the past tense and past participle of **cry¹**

crime /kraɪm/ noun **1** [C] an illegal activity or action: *She was unaware that she had **committed a crime**.* ♦ *It took police eight years to **solve the crime** (=find out* who did it). **2** [U] illegal activities in general: *new laws to help **fight crime** ♦ **The crime rate** (=the number of crimes) in the city has risen sharply. ♦ **Rising crime** (=crime that is increasing) is a key election issue.* **3** [singular] something that is bad, wrong, or unfair: *It would be a crime to waste all that food.*

'crime ,wave noun [C] a sudden increase in the number of crimes in a particular area

criminal1 /'krɪmɪn(ə)l/ noun [C] someone who has committed a crime: *The scheme is designed to help former criminals find jobs.*

criminal2 /'krɪmɪn(ə)l/ adj **1** LAW relating to illegal acts, or to the parts of the legal system that deal with crime: *a criminal investigation* (=one that is dealing with a crime) ♦ *the criminal justice system* ♦ *a criminal offence* **2** bad, wrong, or unfair in a way that makes someone angry: *That's a criminal waste of resources.*

,criminal 'damage noun [U] LAW the crime of damaging someone's property

criminality /,krɪmɪ'næləti/ noun [U] **1** the criminal quality of someone or something **2** criminal actions

,criminal 'law noun [U] LAW the system of laws that deals with crimes and the punishment of criminals

,criminal 'negligence noun [U] LAW the crime of not doing something that would have prevented a serious accident

,criminal 'record noun [C] LAW an official list of crimes that someone has committed

criminology /,krɪmɪ'nɒlədʒi/ noun [U] the scientific study of crime and criminals —**criminologist** noun [C]

crimson /'krɪmz(ə)n/ adj dark purple-red in colour —**crimson** noun [U]

cringe /krɪndʒ/ verb [I] **1** to move back slightly from something that is unpleasant or frightening **2** to feel embarrassed or ashamed about something

crinkle /'krɪŋk(ə)l/ verb [I/T] if skin or cloth crinkles, or if you crinkle it, a lot of small folds appear in it — **crinkled** /'krɪŋk(ə)ld/ adj, **crinkly** /'krɪŋkli/ adj

cripple /'krɪp(ə)l/ verb [T] **1** to destroy something or damage it severely **2** to make someone physically disabled

crippling /'krɪplɪŋ/ adj **1** causing severe damage or problems: *crippling taxes* **2** making someone physically disabled, or causing them to have severe health problems: *a crippling disease*

crisis /'kraɪsɪs/ (plural **crises** /'kraɪsiːz/) noun [C/U] an urgent and difficult or dangerous situation: *political crisis* ♦ *The nursing profession is **in crisis**.* ♦ *the current **crisis in** the farming industry*

crisp1 /krɪsp/ adj **1** crisp food is firm in a pleasant way: *a crisp apple* **2** crisp cloth or paper is smooth, clean, and fresh: *crisp sheets* **3** crisp weather is pleasant because it is cold and dry: *crisp night air* —**crisply** adv

crisp2 /krɪsp/ noun [C] a thin flat round piece of potato that has been cooked in fat and is eaten cold

criss-cross /'krɪs,krɒs/ verb **1** [I/T] to form a pattern of straight lines that cross each other **2** [T] to go across a place and back again many times, taking a different path each time

criteria /kraɪ'tɪəriə/ (singular **criterion** /kraɪ'tɪəriən/) noun [plural] standards that are used for judging something or for making a decision about something: *Everyone whose qualifications **meet** our **criteria** will be considered.* ♦ *What **criteria** do you have **for** selecting patients for treatment?*

critic /'krɪtɪk/ noun [C] **1** someone who does not like something and states their opinion about it: *a critic of the government's tax proposals* **2** someone whose job is to give their opinions about things such as books, films, or plays

critical /'krɪtɪk(ə)l/ adj

1 saying sth is wrong	4 judging carefully
2 very important	5 according to critics
3 seriously ill/injured	

1 expressing your opinion when you think something is wrong or bad: *Her father was a very critical man.* ♦ *Warren was **critical of** the way she handled the affair.* **2** an event, time, or issue that is critical is very important, often because it affects the future: *a critical moment* ♦ *Winning the award is **critical to** our success.* **3** very seriously ill or injured: *Six of the patients were **in a critical condition.*** **4** considering something carefully and deciding what is good or bad about it: *a critical look at modern life* **5** according to the book, film, or theatre critics: *The show has won much **critical acclaim** (=admiration).*

,critical 'care noun [U] HEALTH the highest level of care in a hospital for patients who are extremely ill and could die at any time

critically /'krɪtɪkli/ adv **1** extremely and seriously: *critically ill* **2** carefully judging something: *We teach children to think critically.* **3** in a way that shows that you do not like something: *Nobody spoke critically of the government.* **4** if a book, film, or play is critically acclaimed, it is said to be good by people whose job is to give their opinion

,critical 'mass noun [C/U] PHYSICS the smallest amount of a substance needed to cause a **nuclear reaction**

,critical 'path noun [C] BUSINESS the order in which a series of operations should be done so that a project can be finished as quickly as possible and for the lowest cost possible

criticise /'krɪtɪsaɪz/ another spelling of **criticize**

criticism /'krɪtɪ,sɪz(ə)m/ noun **1** [C/U] a comment or comments that show that you think something is wrong or bad: *a fair criticism* ♦ **criticism of** *the team's performance* ♦ *The new plans drew **fierce criticism** from local people.* **2** [U] the activity of giving your professional opinion about things such as new books, films, or plays

criticize /'krɪtɪsaɪz/ verb [I/T] to say what you think is wrong or bad about something: *We were told not to criticize the policy publicly.* ♦ *The new proposals have been **criticized for** not going far enough to change the system.*

Word family: **criticize**

*Words in the same family as **criticize***
- **critic** *n*
- **critical** *adj*
- **critically** *adv*
- **criticism** *n*
- **uncritical** *adj*
- **critique** *n*

critique /krɪ'tiːk/ noun [C] a careful written examination of a subject that includes the writer's opinions

croak /krəʊk/ verb **1** [I/T] to speak or say something in a low rough voice **2** [I] when a **frog** croaks, it makes a low loud rough sound —**croak** noun [C]

crockery /'krɒkəri/ noun [U] plates, cups, bowls etc that are used for serving food

crocodile /'krɒkədaɪl/ noun [C] a large reptile with many sharp teeth that lives in water in hot countries — *picture* → REPTILE

crocus /ˈkrəʊkəs/ noun [C] a small yellow, white, or purple flower that appears early in spring

Crohn's disease /ˈkrəʊnz dɪˌziːz/ noun [U] HEALTH an **autoimmune** disease that affects the alimentary canal, especially the bowel. It causes diarrhoea and pain in the abdomen.

croissant /ˈkwæsɒ̃/ noun [C] a type of light bread with a curved shape

Cro-Magnon man /ˌkrəʊ ˌmægnɒn ˈmæn/ noun [U] a member of an ancient people who lived in Europe from 30,000 to 50,000 years ago

crony /ˈkrəʊni/ (plural **cronies**) noun [C] showing disapproval a friend or supporter of someone who is powerful

crook /krʊk/ noun [C] **1** informal someone who is dishonest or is a thief **2** the place where something bends inwards: the crook of your arm

crooked /ˈkrʊkɪd/ adj **1** not straight **2** informal dishonest= CORRUPT —**crookedly** adv

croon /kruːn/ verb [I/T] MUSIC to sing in a slow soft voice —**crooner** noun [C]

crop¹ /krɒp/ noun [C] **1** AGRICULTURE a plant that is grown for food: They're all out planting the crops today. ♦ Japan bought large amounts of rice overseas because of a **crop failure** (=the crops did not grow). **2** [C] AGRICULTURE the amount of a crop that is produced in a particular season: a good crop of potatoes **3** [singular] several things that happen or exist at the same time: this summer's **crop of** Hollywood films

crop² /krɒp/ (**crops, cropping, cropped**) verb **1** [T] to make something shorter or smaller by cutting it **2** [I] AGRICULTURE to produce a crop

'crop ˌduster noun [C] AGRICULTURE **1** a small plane used to spread liquid **insecticides** or **fungicides** onto crops from the air **2** a container held in the hands for spraying **pesticides, fertilizer** etc onto plants —picture → AGRICULTURAL

crop-dusting /ˈkrɒp ˌdʌstɪŋ/ noun [U] AGRICULTURE American **crop-spraying**

cropper /ˈkrɒpə/ noun [C] AGRICULTURE a plant variety that produces a particular type or amount of crop

'crop roˌtation noun [U] AGRICULTURE the practice of regularly changing the type of crop that is grown on a particular area of land, in order to keep the soil healthy

crop-spraying /ˈkrɒp ˌspreɪɪŋ/ noun [U] AGRICULTURE the practice of dropping liquid **fertilizers** and **pesticides** onto crops from a plane

'crop ˌyield noun [C] AGRICULTURE the amount of a particular crop that is produced

cross¹ /krɒs/ verb

1 go to other side	5 in sports
2 be across (each other)	6 oppose sb
3 appear on face	+ PHRASES
4 combine animal breeds	+ PHRASAL VERB

1 [I/T] to go from one side of something to the other: She watched the children cross the road. ♦ It was dark when we crossed the French border.
2 [I] if things such as roads or lines cross, they go across each other= INTERSECT: the point where the two paths cross
3 [T] if an expression crosses someone's face or lips, it appears there for a short time
4 [T] BIOLOGY to combine one type of animal or plant with another, in order to produce a genetic mix

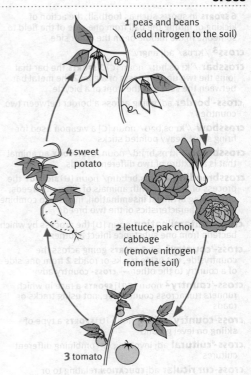

1 peas and beans (add nitrogen to the soil)

4 sweet potato

2 lettuce, pak choi, cabbage (remove nitrogen from the soil)

3 tomato

crop rotation

5 [T] SPORTS in sports such as football, to kick or hit the ball from one side of the field to someone in the middle or on the other side
6 [T] to oppose someone or disagree with them: No one ever dared cross him.

PHRASES **cross your arms** to put one arm over the other in front of your body, so that each hand is on the opposite elbow
cross your fingers or **keep your fingers crossed** to put your middle finger over your first finger as a wish for good luck
cross your legs to sit with one leg placed over the other at the knee
cross sb's mind if something crosses your mind, you think of it, but not for very long: It suddenly crossed his mind that maybe Stephanie had been right.

PHRASAL VERB **ˌcross sth ˈout** to draw a line through writing because it is wrong, or because you want to put something else

cross² /krɒs/ noun

1 symbol X	4 mixture of 2 things
2 in Christianity	5 mixed animal/plant
3 structure	6 in sport

1 [C] the symbol X, used for showing your choice on a written list, or for showing that an answer is wrong: Put a cross next to the name of the person you are voting for.
2 [C] a shape or an object with one long straight upright part and another shorter one across it, used as a symbol of Christianity —picture → SHAPE
3 the Cross [singular] RELIGION the structure on which Jesus Christ died, according to the Bible
4 [C] a mixture of two different things: Most of their music is a **cross between** jazz **and** rock.
5 [C] BIOLOGY a mixture of two different types of plant or animal

6 SPORTS in sports such as football, the action of kicking or hitting the ball from one side of the field to someone in the middle or on the other side

cross³ /krɒs/ adj angry

crossbar /'krɒs,bɑː/ noun [C] **1 SPORTS** the bar that joins the two upright posts of a goal **2** the metal bar between the seat and the front of a bicycle

,cross-'border adj going across a border between two countries

crossbow /'krɒs,bəʊ/ noun [C] a weapon used for firing short heavy pointed sticks

crossbreed /'krɒs,briːd/ noun [C] **BIOLOGY** an animal that is a mixture of two different breeds

crossbreeding /'krɒs,briːdɪŋ/ noun [U] **BIOLOGY** the process of breeding with animals of different breeds, often using **artificial insemination**, in order to combine the best characteristics of the two breeds

,cross-contami'nation noun [U] the process by which bacteria from one substance infect another

,cross-'country¹ adj **1 SPORTS** going across the countryside, not using tracks or roads **2** from one side of a country to the other —**,cross-'country** adv

,cross-'country² noun [C/U] **SPORTS** a race in which runners run across countryside, not using tracks or roads

,cross-country 'skiing noun [U] **SPORTS** a type of skiing on level ground

,cross-'cultural adj involving or combining different cultures

,cross-cur'ricular adj **EDUCATION** relating to or involving several different academic subjects at the same time

crossed line /,krɒst 'laɪn/ noun [C] a situation when two telephone conversations get mixed

,cross-exami'nation noun [C] **LAW** an occasion when someone is asked a lot of questions by a lawyer during a trial

,cross-ex'amine verb [T] **LAW** to ask a **witness** questions during a trial after another lawyer has already asked them questions

cross-eyed /,krɒs 'aɪd/ adj someone who is cross-eyed has eyes that look towards each other slightly

,cross-'fertilize verb **1** [I/T] **BIOLOGY** to fertilize one type of plant with pollen from another plant of the same species in order to produce a new genetic mix **2** [T] to add your own ideas, customs, methods etc to those of another person or group —**,cross-fertili'zation** noun [C/U]

crossfire /'krɒs,faɪə/ noun [U] **1** bullets that come from two directions **2** arguments or violence that might affect people who are not directly involved

,cross-in'fection noun [U] **HEALTH** the process by which someone infects a person who already has a different infection

crossing /'krɒsɪŋ/ noun [C] **1** a place where you are allowed to cross something such as a road or border: *a pedestrian crossing* **2** a journey across a river or sea: *a transatlantic crossing*

cross-legged /,krɒs 'leg(ɪ)d/ adj, adv in a sitting position on the floor, with your knees bent and your lower legs crossing each other

,cross-'platform adj **COMPUTING** available for more than one type of computer or **operating system**

'cross-ply ,tyre or **'cross-,ply** noun [C] **ENGINEERING** a tyre that has layers of fibres at angles to each other underneath the rubber

,cross-'pollinate verb [I/T] **BIOLOGY** to use the pollen from one plant to fertilize the flowers of another, or to be a plant that is usually fertilized in this way → SELF-POLLINATION —**,cross-polli'nation** noun [U]

'cross-,post verb [T] **COMPUTING** to send a single electronic message or article to several different **newsgroups** at the same time

,cross 'reference noun [C] a note in a book that tells you to look at another page for more information —**,cross-re'fer** verb [I/T]

crossroads /'krɒs,rəʊdz/ (plural **crossroads**) noun [C] **1** a place where one road crosses another **2** a point in time when someone has to make an important decision about what to do next

'cross ,section noun **1** [C] a group that contains an example of most types of people or things: *a cross section of the city's population* **2** [C/U] **MATHS** the inside of an object that you can see by cutting through the middle of it, or a picture of this —**cross-sectional** adj

crosstrainer /,krɒs'treɪnə/ noun [C] **SPORTS 1** someone who trains in more than one sport **2** a type of sports shoe designed for several different activities

crosswind /'krɒs,wɪnd/ noun [C] a wind that blows across the direction you are travelling in

crossword /'krɒs,wɜːd/ or **'crossword ,puzzle** noun [C] a word game in which the answers to questions are written in rows of squares that cross each other

crotch /krɒtʃ/ noun [C] the area between the legs where they join the body, or the part of a piece of clothing that covers this area

crotchet /'krɒtʃɪt/ noun [C] **MUSIC** a musical note that is a quarter of the length of a **semibreve** —*picture* → MUSIC

crouch /kraʊtʃ/ verb [I] **1** to move your body close to the ground by bending your knees and leaning forwards slightly: *She crouched down and spoke to the little boy.* **2** to lean forwards with your head and shoulders bent: *Five or six men were crouched over the desk.*

croup /kruːp/ noun [U] **HEALTH** a children's illness that makes the child cough and makes breathing difficult

crow¹ /krəʊ/ noun [C] a large black bird that makes a loud sound

crow² /krəʊ/ verb [I] **1** if a cock crows, it makes a loud high noise **2** if someone crows, they talk very proudly about something that they have done = BOAST

crowbar /'krəʊ,bɑː/ noun [C] a metal bar with a curved end, used for forcing things open

crowd¹ /kraʊd/ noun [C] **1** a large number of people in the same place: *The boys disappeared into the crowd.* ♦ *Crowds of people began making their way to the station.* **2** the audience at an event: *He came on stage and the crowd went wild.*

crowd² /kraʊd/ verb **1** [I] to move to a place at the same time as a lot of other people: *We crowded into the kitchen.* **2** [T] to fill a place: *Hundreds of people crowded the streets.*

crowded /'kraʊdɪd/ adj containing a lot of people or things: *a crowded street* ♦ *Was the pool crowded?* ♦ *a crowded schedule*

crowd pleaser /'kraʊd ,pliːzə/ noun [C] *informal* someone or something that large numbers of people, especially audiences, always like or enjoy

crown¹ /kraʊn/ noun

1 head decoration	5 top of head/hat
2 position of winner	6 top part of hill
3 government	7 top of arch
4 cover for tooth	

1 [C] a circular decoration that a king or queen wears on their head
2 [C] the position of being the winner of an important sports competition: *France lost their World Cup crown.*
3 the Crown [singular] *formal* the government of a country that has a king or queen: *a minister of the Crown*
4 [C] a cover that is used to repair a tooth, or the part of the tooth that it covers —*picture* → TOOTH
5 [C] the top part of your head or of a hat
6 [C] the round top part of a hill
7 [C] CONSTRUCTION the highest part of the upper surface of an **arch**

crown² /kraʊn/ verb [T] **1** to make someone a king or queen: *Queen Elizabeth was crowned in Westminster Abbey.* **2** to give someone a title for winning an important sports competition: *Schumacher went on to be crowned world champion.* **3** to put a cover on a tooth in order to repair it **4** to be the greatest in a series of achievements: *Iwan Roberts crowned his performance by scoring a second goal.*

,crown 'court noun [C] a court of law in England and Wales in which a judge and jury deal with serious crimes

crowning /'kraʊnɪŋ/ adj better or greater than anything else: *The garden is the hotel's crowning glory.*

the ,Crown Prose'cution ,Service noun LAW the official organization in England and Wales that decides whether the police have found enough evidence to have a court case against someone

CRT /,si: ɑː 'tiː/ abbrev **cathode ray tube**

crucial /'kruːʃ(ə)l/ adj extremely important: *Your involvement is crucial to the success of the project.* ♦ *The talks are considered crucial for ending the violence.* —**crucially** adv

crucible /'kruːsəb(ə)l/ noun [C] SCIENCE a container used for melting metals, ores, and other minerals at very high temperatures —*picture* → LABORATORY

'crucible ,furnace noun [C] TECHNOLOGY a **furnace** in which metal contained in **crucibles** is melted

crucifix /'kruːsɪfɪks/ noun [C] RELIGION a model of Jesus Christ dying on the **Cross**

crucifixion /,kruːsɪ'fɪkʃ(ə)n/ noun **1** [C/U] a method of killing someone by crucifying them **2 the Crucifixion** RELIGION the occasion when Jesus Christ was killed on the **Cross**, according to the Bible

crucify /'kruːsɪfaɪ/ (**crucifies, crucifying, crucified**) verb [T] to kill someone by fastening them to a **cross** with nails or rope

crude /kruːd/ (**cruder, crudest**) adj **1** done or made using very simple methods= BASIC: *a crude home-made bomb* **2** referring to sex in a way that offends people: *crude language* —**crudely** adv

,crude 'oil noun [U] CHEMISTRY oil in its natural state, before it has been **refined** for use —*picture* → REFINE

cruel /'kruːəl/ (**crueller, cruellest**) adj **1** causing pain to people or animals: *I can't bear to see people being cruel to animals.* **2** making someone unhappy or upset: *Closing the school would be a cruel blow to this community.* —**cruelly** adv

cruelty /'kruːəlti/ (plural **cruelties**) noun [C/U] cruel behaviour: *cruelty to children* ♦ *the cruelties he witnessed during the war*

cruise¹ /kruːz/ noun [C] a journey on a ship for pleasure, often visiting a series of places

cruise² /kruːz/ verb [I] **1** to travel at a steady speed in a car or plane **2** to sail in a ship for pleasure

,cruise 'missile noun [C] a missile that is controlled by a computer and can travel very long distances

cruiser /'kruːzə/ noun [C] **1** a fast military ship **2** a large boat with a motor that is used for sailing for pleasure

cruising altitude /'kruːzɪŋ ,æltɪtjuːd/ noun [C] the height at which a plane usually flies when it has risen into the sky

crumb /krʌm/ noun [C] **1** a very small piece that falls off a dry food such as bread or cake **2** a very small amount of something

crumbing down /,krʌmɪŋ 'daʊn/ noun [U] TOURISM the practice of removing crumbs from a table in a restaurant after the main part of the meal, before the **dessert**

crumble /'krʌmb(ə)l/ verb **1** [I/T] to break into very small pieces, or to make something do this: *The soft earth crumbled under his feet.* **2** [I] to stop existing or being effective: *My determination crumbled as soon as I saw her.*

crumple /'krʌmp(ə)l/ verb **1** [I/T] to crush something so that it forms untidy folds, or to be crushed in this way: *I quickly crumpled up the letter and put it in my pocket.* **2** [I] to fall to the ground suddenly, with your body, legs, and arms bent, because you are injured, ill, or upset

crunch¹ /krʌntʃ/ verb **1** [I/T] to bite hard food, causing it to make a loud noise **2** [I] to make a noise like something being crushed

crunch² /krʌntʃ/ noun [singular] the noise that something makes when you crunch it

crunchy /'krʌntʃi/ (**crunchier, crunchiest**) adj crunchy foods make a loud noise when you bite them

crusade /kruː'seɪd/ noun [C] an effort made by someone over a long time to achieve something that they strongly believe is right= CAMPAIGN —**crusader** /kruː'seɪdə/ noun [C]

crush¹ /krʌʃ/ verb [T] **1** to press something so hard that you damage it or break it into small pieces —*picture* → FOOD **2** to injure or kill someone by pressing on them very hard **3** to completely defeat an opponent

crush² /krʌʃ/ noun [singular] a crowd of people in an area that is too small for them

crushing /'krʌʃɪŋ/ adj **1** complete and achieved very easily: *a crushing defeat* **2** very severe: *It's a crushing blow for the president's foreign policy.*

crust /krʌst/ noun [C/U] **1** the hard brown edges of a piece of bread, or the outer part of a pie **2** GEOLOGY the outer layer of rock on the Earth or on another planet —*picture* → EARTH

crustacean /krʌ'steɪʃ(ə)n/ noun [C] BIOLOGY a small animal that is a type of **arthropod**. It has a hard shell, two pairs of antennae, and several pairs of legs. **Crabs, shrimps**, and **woodlice** are all crustaceans.

crustal /'krʌst(ə)l/ adj GEOLOGY relating to the outer layer of rock on the Earth

crusty /'krʌsti/ adj covered with a hard **crust**

crutch /krʌtʃ/ noun **1** [C] a stick that fits under your arm and that helps you to walk when your leg or foot is injured **2** [singular] *showing disapproval* something that someone depends on for support or help

crux /krʌks/ noun **the crux (of sth)** the most important aspect of something

cry¹ /kraɪ/ (**cries, crying, cried**) verb [I/T] **1** to have tears coming from your eyes because you are sad or hurt: *I'm sorry – please don't cry.* ♦ *She was crying for her mother.* ♦ *Don't waste time crying over him.* **2** to shout something: *'That's not what I meant,' Polly cried.* ♦ *Ted could hear a woman crying for help.*

cry² /kraɪ/ (plural **cries**) noun **1** [C] a loud expression of emotion: *a cry of pain* **2** [C] something that someone shouts: *There was a cry of 'Fire!'* **3** [C] the noise that an animal or bird makes **4** [singular] a period of time when you have tears coming from your eyes because you are sad or hurt: *She had a good cry.*

crypt /krɪpt/ noun [C] a room where dead people are buried, usually under a church

cryptic /ˈkrɪptɪk/ adj expressing something in a mysterious or indirect way

cryptography /krɪpˈtɒɡrəfi/ noun [U] **COMPUTING** the use of codes to put information on a website into a form that can only be read by users with permission

cryptosporidium /ˌkrɪptəʊspəˈrɪdiəm/ (plural **cryptosporidia** /ˌkrɪptəʊspəˈrɪdiə/) noun [C] **BIOLOGY, HEALTH** a parasite found in water that causes stomach infections

crystal /ˈkrɪst(ə)l/ noun **1** [C] **CHEMISTRY** a regular shape with many sides that is formed when a substance becomes solid: *ice crystals* **2** [C/U] **GEOLOGY** a clear rock that looks like glass **3** [U] very good quality glass

crystal 'ball noun [C] a glass ball that some people believe can show the future

crystal 'clear adj **1** completely transparent and very bright **2** extremely obvious or easy to understand

crystalline /ˈkrɪstəlaɪn/ adj **GEOLOGY** consisting of crystals, or looking like crystals

crystallize /ˈkrɪstəlaɪz/ verb [I/T] **1** **CHEMISTRY** to change into crystals, or to make something change into crystals **2** to become definite or easily understood, or to make something definite or easily understood

crystal meth /ˌkrɪst(ə)l ˈmeθ/ noun [U] an illegal drug that makes people feel they have a lot of energy. It is sold in the form of crystals.

CS gas /ˌsi: es ˈɡæs/ noun [U] a gas used by the police for controlling crowds of people. It hurts people's eyes and makes it difficult for them to breathe= TEAR GAS

CSR /ˌsi: es ˈɑː/ noun [U] **BUSINESS** corporate social responsibility: the belief that a company should consider the social and environmental effects of its activities on its employees and the community around it

C-to-'C adj **BUSINESS** consumer-to-consumer: used for describing a type of business activity in which a customer deals with another customer using the Internet

ctrl abbrev **COMPUTING** control: the **control key** on a computer keyboard

CT scan /ˌsi: ti: ˈskæn/ noun [C] **HEALTH** a **CAT scan**

cub /kʌb/ noun [C] **1** a young bear, lion, or other wild mammal **2** Cub a member of **the Cubs**

cube¹ /kjuːb/ noun [C] **1** an object or shape like a box with six square sides that are all the same size —*picture* → SHAPE **2 the cube of sth MATHS** the result of multiplying a number by itself twice: *The cube of 2 is 8.*

cube² /kjuːb/ verb [T] **1** **MATHS** to multiply a number by itself twice **2** to cut something into the shape of cubes= DICE

cube 'root noun [C] **MATHS** the cube root of a number is the smaller number that you multiply by itself twice to make the number, for example the cube root of 8 is 2

cubic /ˈkjuːbɪk/ adj **MATHS** cubic units are used for measuring volume

cubicle /ˈkjuːbɪk(ə)l/ noun [C] a small enclosed area in a room

cubism /ˈkjuːbɪz(ə)m/ noun [U] **ARTS** an early 20th-century style of painting in which the artist paints several different views of a person or object in a single painting, usually using straight lines —**cubist** adj, **cubist** noun [C]

cuboid¹ /ˈkjuːbɔɪd/ noun [C] **MATHS** a solid shape consisting of six flat surfaces that each have four straight sides. A cuboid is similar to a cube but its surfaces are rectangles, not squares.

cuboid² /ˈkjuːbɔɪd/ adj **MATHS** shaped like a cube or like a cuboid

the Cubs /kʌbz/ noun [plural] the division of the **Scouts** for younger boys

cuckoo /ˈkʊkuː/ (plural **cuckoos**) noun [C] a bird that leaves its eggs in other birds' nests and makes a call that sounds like its name

cucumber /ˈkjuːˌkʌmbə/ noun [C/U] a long, dark green vegetable that is usually eaten raw in salads —*picture* → VEGETABLE

cud /kʌd/ noun [U] food that animals such as cows and sheep bring back into their mouths to chew again after they have swallowed it

cuddle /ˈkʌd(ə)l/ verb [I/T] to put your arms round someone and hold them close to show that you like or love them —**cuddle** noun [C]

cue /kjuː/ noun [C] **1** an event, action, or statement that shows someone what they should do: *Greg's arrival seemed to be the cue for everyone to get up and start dancing.* **2** something that an actor does or says as a signal to another actor to do or say something **3** a long thin stick that you use for hitting the ball in games such as **snooker**

cuff /kʌf/ noun [C] the part of a sleeve that fits around your wrist

cuisine /kwɪˈziːn/ noun [C/U] **1** a particular style of cooking **2** the food you can eat in a particular place, especially a restaurant or hotel

cul-de-sac /ˈkʌl də ˌsæk/ noun [C] a short street that is closed at one end

culinary /ˈkʌlɪn(ə)ri/ adj relating to food and how to cook it

cull¹ /kʌl/ verb [T] **1** to collect something such as information from different places **2** **ENVIRONMENT, AGRICULTURE** to kill animals in order to stop the population from becoming too large

cull² /kʌl/ noun [C] **ENVIRONMENT, AGRICULTURE** an act of culling animals

culmination /ˌkʌlmɪˈneɪʃ(ə)n/ noun [singular] the final result of a process or situation —**culminate** /ˈkʌlmɪˌneɪt/ verb [I]

culpable /ˈkʌlpəb(ə)l/ adj formal responsible for doing something bad or illegal

culpable 'homicide noun [U] **LAW** in Scottish, South African, and Indian law, the crime of killing someone illegally but without intending or planning to kill them

culprit /'kʌlprɪt/ noun [C] **1** someone who is responsible for doing something bad or illegal **2** the cause of something bad that happens

cult /kʌlt/ noun [C] **1** RELIGION a religious group with beliefs that most people consider strange or dangerous **2** extreme admiration or enthusiasm for someone or something

cultivar /'kʌltɪvɑː/ noun [C] BIOLOGY a named variety of a cultivated plant that has been developed by breeding to have characteristics that are different from similar plants of the same species

cultivate /'kʌltɪveɪt/ verb [T] **1** AGRICULTURE to prepare land for growing crops or other plants **2** AGRICULTURE to grow crops or other plants: *Rice is cultivated throughout the coastal regions.* **3** to develop something: *He's trying to cultivate a more caring image.*

cultivated /'kʌltɪˌveɪtɪd/ adj **1** a cultivated person is well educated and knows how to behave politely **2** AGRICULTURE cultivated land is used for growing crops or plants **3** AGRICULTURE cultivated plants are developed from wild plants and grown on farms or in gardens

cultivation /ˌkʌltɪ'veɪʃ(ə)n/ noun [U] AGRICULTURE the process of growing crops or other plants, or the use of land for growing crops or other plants

cultivator /'kʌltɪˌveɪtə/ noun [C] AGRICULTURE a tool or machine that is used for breaking up soil

cultural /'kʌltʃ(ə)rəl/ adj **1** SOCIAL STUDIES relating to the culture of a particular group, country, or society: *cultural diversity ♦ the cultural traditions of our society* **2** relating to music, literature, and other arts: *During the summer New York offers a variety of cultural events.* —**culturally** adv

,**cultural 'fairness** noun [U] SOCIAL STUDIES the idea that all cultures are equally important

culture /'kʌltʃə/ noun **1** [U] activities involving music, literature, and other arts: *African culture ♦ Britain's literary culture* **2** [C/U] SOCIAL STUDIES a set of ideas, beliefs, and ways of behaving, especially one belonging to a particular society, race, religion etc: *societies that share the same language and culture* **3** [C] SOCIAL STUDIES a society considered as one that has its own particular beliefs, traditions, practices etc: *people from different cultures ♦ ancient cultures* **4** [C/U] BIOLOGY a group of bacteria or other cells that have been grown in a scientific experiment, or the process by which they are grown

cultured /'kʌltʃəd/ adj well educated and polite

,**culture-'fair** adj SOCIAL STUDIES giving no advantage or disadvantage to people of a particular culture

'**culture ,medium** noun [C] BIOLOGY a substance containing nutrients that is used to grow animal or plant tissues or microorganisms in a laboratory

'**culture ,shock** noun [C/U] the confused feeling that people sometimes get when they arrive in a place that has a very different culture from their own

cumbersome /'kʌmbəs(ə)m/ adj **1** complicated, slow, and difficult to use **2** large, heavy, and difficult to move or carry

cumulative /'kjuːmjʊlətɪv/ adj developing or increasing gradually as a result of more and more additions: *We studied the cumulative effect of long periods of stress on the body.*

,**cumulative 'frequency** noun [C] MATHS the total of all the frequencies that are less than, or equal to, a particular frequency

cumulonimbus /ˌkjuːmjʊləʊ'nɪmbəs/ noun [C/U] GEOGRAPHY a dark cloud stretching high into the atmosphere with a flat top containing ice. It usually brings heavy rain and sometimes thunder. —*picture* → CLOUD

cumulus /'kjuːmjʊləs/ (plural **cumuli**) noun [C/U] GEOGRAPHY a large white cloud that is round at the top and flat at the bottom. Cumulus clouds form at the lower levels of the atmosphere. → CIRRUS, STRATUS —*picture* → CLOUD

cuneiform[1] /'kjuːnɪfɔːm/ adj LANGUAGE relating to a writing system used in ancient times in the Middle East. The letters are long and thin, and wide at one end and narrow at the other.

cuneiform[2] /'kjuːnɪfɔːm/ noun [U] LANGUAGE cuneiform writing

cunning[1] /'kʌnɪŋ/ adj good at tricking or cheating people —**cunningly** adv

cunning[2] /'kʌnɪŋ/ noun [U] the use of clever methods for tricking or cheating people

cup[1] /kʌp/ noun [C] **1** a small round container for a drink, usually with a handle: *She filled my cup with hot tea.* **2** the drink contained in a cup: *Would you like a cup of coffee?* **3** a large round metal container with two handles given as a prize to the winner of a competition, or the competition for which this prize is given: *the winners of the World Cup*

cup[2] /kʌp/ (**cups**, **cupping**, **cupped**) verb [T] to hold something in your hands, with your hands in a curved shape

cupboard /'kʌbəd/ noun [C] **1** a piece of furniture that is used for storing things, with shelves inside and one or two doors at the front: *a kitchen cupboard ♦ the cupboard door* **2** a very small room with no windows used for storing things: *the cupboard under the stairs*

cupful /'kʌpfʊl/ noun [C] the amount of something that a cup contains

cupola /'kjuːpələ/ noun [C] **1** a part of a roof shaped like half a ball, often covered in shiny metal = DOME **2** TECHNOLOGY a type of cylindrical **furnace** for making **cast iron**

cupro-nickel /ˌkjuːprəʊ 'nɪk(ə)l/ noun [U] CHEMISTRY an alloy of copper and nickel that is hard and that wears well. It is used to make coins.

'**cup ,tie** noun [C] SPORTS a match in a competition that has a cup as the prize for the winners

curate /'kjʊərət/ noun [C] RELIGION an Anglican priest who helps a more senior priest

curator /kjʊ'reɪtə/ noun [C] someone whose job is to look after the objects in a museum

curb[1] /kɜːb/ verb [T] to control or limit something that is harmful or may cause problems: *efforts to curb inflation*

curb[2] /kɜːb/ noun [C] a rule or control that stops or limits something

curd /kɜːd/ noun [C/U] the solid substance that forms in milk when it becomes sour

cure[1] /kjʊə/ noun [C] **1** HEALTH a medicine or treatment that makes someone who is ill become healthy: *Doctors say there are several possible cures for the disease. ♦ There's no cure for the disease.* **2** a solution to a problem: *It's the only possible cure for high unemployment.*

cure[2] /kjʊə/ verb [T] **1** HEALTH to stop someone from being affected by an illness: *Only an operation will cure her. ♦ The disease is easy to prevent but almost impossible to cure.* **2** to solve a problem **3** to preserve meat, fish, or other foods by drying them, or by using smoke or salt

curfew /ˈkɜːfjuː/ noun [C] a period of time during which people must not go outside according to an order from the government

curiosity /ˌkjʊəriˈɒsəti/ (plural **curiosities**) noun **1** [U] a strong feeling of wanting to find out about something **2** [C] something that is unusual and interesting

curious /ˈkjʊəriəs/ adj **1** wanting to find out about something: *People were **curious to know** why the accident happened.* ♦ *Children are **curious about** animals and how they live.* **2** unusual and interesting: *He felt a curious mixture of happiness and fear.* —**curiously** /ˈkjʊəriəsli/ adv

curium /ˈkjʊəriəm/ noun [U] **CHEMISTRY** a silvery-white metallic radioactive element in the **actinide** group of the periodic table. Chemical symbol: **Cm**

curl¹ /kɜːl/ verb **1** [I/T] to form a curved or round shape, or to give something this shape: *As she talked, she curled a strand of hair on one finger.* **2** [I] to move in a curving or twisting way: *Smoke curled from tall chimneys.* **3** [I] to curve upwards or downwards at the edges: *The pages had begun to turn yellow and curl.*

curl² /kɜːl/ noun [C] **1** a section of hair that forms a curved shape **2** something long and thin that has a curved shape: *a curl of smoke*

curler /ˈkɜːlə/ noun [C] a plastic or metal tube that someone wraps their hair round in order to curl it = ROLLER

curly /ˈkɜːli/ (**curlier, curliest**) adj forming curves: *curly hair*

currant /ˈkʌrənt/ noun [C] **1** a small dark dried grape that is often used in cakes **2** a small round fruit that may be red, black, or white

currency /ˈkʌrənsi/ (plural **currencies**) noun **1** [C/U] the money that is used in a particular country: *Russian currency* **2** [U] the state of being accepted or used by many people: *The idea of withdrawing from the war has **gained** wide **currency**.*

current¹ /ˈkʌrənt/ adj **1** happening or existing now: *Production is likely to remain at current levels.* **2** believed or used by many people now: *current methods of funding research* **3** correct or legal now: *Is this your current address?* ♦ *a current driving licence*

current² /ˈkʌrənt/ noun **PHYSICS 1** [C] a strong movement of water or air in one direction **2** [C/U] a flow of electricity

current af'fairs noun [plural] political, social, and economic events that are happening now

current elec'tricity noun [U] **PHYSICS** electricity that flows from one place to another → STATIC ELECTRICITY

currently /ˈkʌrəntli/ adv at the present time: *Davis is currently appearing in a play at the National Theatre.* ♦ *the largest memory chip currently available*

curriculum /kəˈrɪkjʊləm/ noun [C] **EDUCATION** the subjects that students study at a particular school or college: *the science curriculum* —**curricular** adj

curriculum vitae /kəˌrɪkjʊləm ˈviːtaɪ/ noun [C] a **CV**

curry /ˈkʌri/ (plural **curries**) noun [C/U] an Indian food consisting of meat, fish, or vegetables cooked in a sauce with a hot flavour

curse¹ /kɜːs/ verb **1** [I] to swear: *He looked at his watch, cursed, and ran for a taxi.* **2** [T] to strongly criticize someone or something: *She cursed herself for being such a fool.* **3** [T] to use magic powers to make bad things happen to someone

curse² /kɜːs/ noun [C] **1** an offensive or very impolite word or phrase **2** the words that are used for causing bad luck **3** an unpleasant situation or influence

cursive /ˈkɜːsɪv/ adj **LANGUAGE** cursive **handwriting** is written with each letter of a word joined to the next letter

cursor /ˈkɜːsə/ noun [singular] **COMPUTING** a small flashing line on a computer screen that you move to mark the point where you are going to type or do something

cursory /ˈkɜːsəri/ adj formal quick and not thorough = SUPERFICIAL

curtail /kɜːˈteɪl/ verb [T] formal to reduce or limit something, especially something good

curtain /ˈkɜːt(ə)n/ noun **1** [C] a long piece of cloth that hangs down to cover a window: *She **closed the curtains**.* ♦ ***Open the curtains** and let some light in.* **2** [C] **ARTS** a large piece of cloth that hangs in front of the stage in a theatre: *The audience cheered wildly as the **curtain rose**.* **3** [C] a long piece of material that hangs down and separates one part of a room from another: *a shower curtain* **4** [singular/U] a large amount of a substance that is too thick to see through: *A dark **curtain of** cloud hung over the valley.*

curtsy /ˈkɜːtsi/ (plural **curtsies**) or **curtsey** noun [C] a formal greeting in which a woman bends her knees with one leg behind the other —**curtsy** verb [I]

curvature /ˈkɜːvətʃə/ noun [U] **SCIENCE** the way in which something curves

curve¹ /kɜːv/ noun [C] **1** a shape or line with a gradual smooth bend **2** **MATHS** a curved line drawn on a graph

curve² /kɜːv/ verb [I/T] to form a curve, or to make something form a curve

'curve ,ball noun [C] **SPORTS** in baseball, a throw that is difficult to hit because the ball moves in a curve

curved /kɜːvd/ adj forming a curve

CUSeeMe /ˌsiː juː siː ˈmiː/ noun [U] **COMPUTING** a computer program that allows users to take part in **videoconferencing** over the Internet

cushion¹ /ˈkʊʃ(ə)n/ noun [C] **1** a cloth bag filled with something soft, used for making a seat more comfortable **2** something that gives protection against the effects of something bad

cushion² /ˈkʊʃ(ə)n/ verb [T] to protect a person or thing from the harmful effects of something

cusp /kʌsp/ noun [C] **ANATOMY** one of the points on the surface of a **molar** or **premolar** tooth

custard /ˈkʌstəd/ noun [U] a sweet yellow sauce made from milk, eggs, and sugar

custodial /kʌˈstəʊdiəl/ adj **LAW 1** relating to the legal right to take care of someone, especially a child **2** relating to putting or keeping someone in prison

cus,todial 'parent noun [C] **LAW** the parent who has legal **custody** of a child

cus'todial ,sentence noun [C] **LAW** a punishment that involves sending someone to prison

custodian /kʌˈstəʊdiən/ noun [C] someone who is responsible for something valuable

custody /ˈkʌstədi/ noun [U] **LAW 1** the protection or care of someone or something, especially given by a court: *The father was given custody of the children.* **2** a situation in which someone is kept in prison

custom /ˈkʌstəm/ noun **1** [C/U] something that people do that is traditional or usual: *local customs and traditions* → HABIT **2** [U] the practice of buying goods or services from a particular shop or company

= BUSINESS: *Several restaurants compete for tourists' custom.* → CUSTOMS

customary /ˈkʌstəməri/ adj usual —**customarily** /ˌkʌstəˈmeərəli/ adv

custom-'built adj designed and built for one particular person

customer /ˈkʌstəmə/ noun [C] a person or company that buys goods or services: *Supermarkets use a variety of tactics to attract customers.* ♦ *customer services*

'customer ˌbase noun [C] BUSINESS the group of people who buy a particular product or who pay for a particular service

ˌcustomer 'care noun [U] BUSINESS the activity of looking after customers, and helping them with any complaints or problems

ˌcustomer 'care ˌagent noun [C] a person whose job is to look after customers and ensure that they receive satisfactory service

ˌcustomer 'services noun [U] BUSINESS the department of a company that provides customers with information about its products and services, and deals with any problems or complaints that they have

customize /ˈkʌstəmaɪz/ verb [T] to change the way that something looks or works so that it is exactly what you want or need

ˌcustom-'made adj designed and made for one particular person

customs /ˈkʌstəmz/ noun [plural] **1** the place at a port, airport, or border where officials check that people are not bringing anything into a country illegally **2** ECONOMICS a government department that collects taxes on goods that people bring into a country

cut¹ /kʌt/ (**cuts, cutting, cut**) verb [T]

1 use sth sharp	**5** stop sth working
2 injure part of body	**6** divide area into parts
3 remove parts of sth	**+ PHRASES**
4 reduce sth	**+ PHRASAL VERBS**

1 to use a knife or other sharp tool to divide something into pieces, or to remove a piece of something: *I need a sharp knife to cut the bread with.* ♦ *I'm going to* **have my hair cut** *tomorrow.* ♦ *The apples had been* **cut in half**. ♦ *Firefighters had to cut a hole in the car roof to get him out.*
2 to injure a part of your body with something sharp that cuts the skin: *Be careful not to cut your finger.* ♦ *He cut himself shaving.*
3 COMPUTING to remove parts of something such as a piece of writing or a computer document: **Cut and paste** *the file* (=cut and move a computer file) *into your 'documents' folder.* ♦ *They have cut some scenes from the film.*
4 to reduce an amount or level: *We have cut our spending by 33%.* ♦ *Manufacturing companies have already cut thousands of jobs.*
5 to stop the supply of something, or stop something working: *The injury had cut the oxygen to her brain.*
6 to divide an area into two or more parts: *The River Danube cuts Budapest in two.*

PHRASES **cut corners** if someone cuts corners, they do something quickly and carelessly because they want to save time or money
cut your losses to get out of a bad situation before it gets worse
cut sb short to interrupt someone who is talking
PHRASAL VERBS **ˌcut a'cross sth** to go across an area of land instead of going around it: *We cut across the field to save time.*

ˌcut (sth) 'down to cut through a tree and make it fall to the ground
ˌcut sth 'off 1 to stop someone from going somewhere, especially by blocking their way = BLOCK: *A second policeman cut off his escape.* **2** to make a place impossible to enter, leave, or communicate with = ISOLATE: *Our house was* **cut off from** *the rest of the village.*

cut² /kʌt/ noun [C] **1** an injury, mark, or hole that has been caused or made by something sharp: *My son's face was covered in cuts and bruises.* ♦ *Make a series of small cuts in the meat.* **2** a reduction in something: *a pay cut* ♦ **a cut in** *education spending* **3** a part that has been removed from something such as a speech or a piece of writing **4** a piece of meat: *a lean cut of beef*
PHRASE **be a cut above** to be much better than someone or something else
→ POWER CUT

cutback /ˈkʌtˌbæk/ noun [C] a reduction in something such as the amount of money that is available to spend: *Many hospitals face* **cutbacks in** *services.*

cute /kjuːt/ adj attractive: *a cute little house*

cuticle /ˈkjuːtɪk(ə)l/ noun [C] **1** ANATOMY a layer of hard skin at the base of a nail on a finger or toe **2** BIOLOGY the outer layer of a leaf that prevents it from drying out

cutlery /ˈkʌtləri/ noun [U] the knives, forks, and spoons that people use for eating food

ˌcut-'price adj cheaper than the normal price

cutter /ˈkʌtə/ noun [C] a person, machine, or tool that cuts materials

cutting¹ /ˈkʌtɪŋ/ noun **1** an article that someone has cut from a newspaper or magazine **2** AGRICULTURE a piece cut from a plant that is used for growing into a new plant

cutting² /ˈkʌtɪŋ/ adj a cutting remark is cruel and intended to upset someone

ˌcutting 'edge noun [singular] the most modern and advanced point in the development of something: *These models are* **at the cutting edge** *of computer design.*

ˌcutting-'edge adj extremely modern and advanced: *cutting-edge technology*

'cutting ˌplane noun [C] MATHS, TECHNOLOGY a line in a drawing of a solid object that shows the area that is to be cut away

cuttlefish /ˈkʌt(ə)l,fɪʃ/ noun [C/U] a flat invertebrate sea animal with ten arms and a shell inside its body

CV /ˌsiː ˈviː/ noun [C] curriculum vitae: a document that gives details of someone's qualifications and the jobs they have had

'CV ˌjoint noun [C] ENGINEERING a **constant velocity joint**

cyan /ˈsaɪən/ noun [U] a blue colour used as one of the basic colours in printing

cyanide /ˈsaɪənaɪd/ noun [U] CHEMISTRY an extremely poisonous inorganic salt

cybercafé /ˈsaɪbəˌkæfeɪ/ noun [C] a café with computers for using the Internet

cybercrime /ˈsaɪbəˌkraɪm/ noun [U] crime committed using the Internet, for example stealing someone's personal information or introducing harmful programs into someone's computer

cybershopping /ˈsaɪbəˌʃɒpɪŋ/ noun [U] shopping for goods and services on the Internet

cyberspace /'saɪbə,speɪs/ noun [U] the imaginary place that emails pass through when they are going from one computer to another

cycle¹ /'saɪk(ə)l/ noun [C] **1** a series of events that happen again and again in the same order or at the same times: *the cycle of hate and violence in the world* **2** a bicycle **3** LITERATURE, MUSIC a set of poems, songs, or pieces of music on a particular subject

cycle² /'saɪk(ə)l/ verb [I] to go somewhere on a bicycle

'cycle ,lane noun [C] a part of a road marked by painted lines and intended for use by bicycles

cyclical /'sɪklɪk(ə)l/ or **cyclic** /'saɪklɪk/ adj cyclical events happen again and again in the same order or at the same times

cyclist /'saɪklɪst/ noun [C] someone who rides a bicycle

cycloid /'saɪklɔɪd/ noun [C] MATHS a curve produced by a point on the circumference of a circle that is being rolled along a straight line

cyclone /'saɪ,kləʊn/ noun [C] GEOGRAPHY a severe storm in which the wind spins in a circle. **Hurricanes** and **tornadoes** are types of cyclone.

cyclonic storm /saɪ,klɒnɪk 'stɔːm/ noun [C] GEOGRAPHY a **cyclone**

cygnet /'sɪgnət/ noun [C] a young **swan**

cylinder /'sɪlɪndə/ noun [C] **1** an object shaped like a wide tube —*picture* → SHAPE **2** a metal container for gas or liquid **3** ENGINEERING the tube in an engine that a **piston** moves up and down in

'cylinder ,block noun [C] ENGINEERING a metal cover around the cylinders of an **internal-combustion engine**

'cylinder ,head noun [C] ENGINEERING the closed end of the cylinders in an **internal-combustion engine**

'cylinder head ,gasket noun [C] ENGINEERING a **gasket** between the cylinders and the **cylinder head** in an **internal-combustion engine**

'cylinder ,liner noun [C] ENGINEERING a circular cover that a **piston** moves inside in an engine

cylindrical /sɪ'lɪndrɪk(ə)l/ adj shaped like a cylinder

cymbal /'sɪmb(ə)l/ noun [C] MUSIC a musical instrument that is a thin circular piece of metal. You hit it with a stick, or hit two of them together. —*picture* → MUSICAL INSTRUMENT, ORCHESTRA

cynic /'sɪnɪk/ noun [C] someone who believes that people care only about themselves and are not sincere or honest

cynical /'sɪnɪk(ə)l/ adj **1** someone who is cynical believes that people care only about themselves and are not sincere or honest **2** willing to harm other people in order to get an advantage: *a cynical attempt to damage the government's reputation* —**cynically** /'sɪnɪkli/ adv

cynicism /'sɪnɪ,sɪz(ə)m/ noun [U] **1** the belief that people care only about themselves and are not sincere or honest **2** the attitude of someone who is willing to harm other people in order to get an advantage

cyst /sɪst/ noun [C] HEALTH a lump containing liquid that grows under the skin or inside the body

cystic fibrosis /,sɪstɪk faɪ'brəʊsɪs/ noun [U] HEALTH a serious medical condition that mainly affects the lungs. It is caused by a gene that is passed from parents to their children.

cystitis /sɪ'staɪtɪs/ noun [U] HEALTH a medical condition of the bladder, usually caused by an infection, that causes frequent and painful **urination**

cytology /saɪ'tɒlədʒi/ noun [U] HEALTH the study of how cells grow and change, especially cells that cause cancer

cytomegalovirus /,saɪtəʊ'megələʊ,vaɪrəs/ noun [C] HEALTH a virus that can cause serious infections in people with weak **immune systems**, for example because of AIDS. It can be passed on to babies before they are born.

cytoplasm /'saɪtəʊ,plæz(ə)m/ noun [U] BIOLOGY the substance inside the cells of living things, apart from the nucleus. It contains several different chemicals and structures. —*picture* → CELL, SEX CELL —**cytoplasmic** /,saɪtəʊ'plæzmɪk/ adj

czar /zɑː/ noun [C] **1** a senior official who is chosen by the government to make decisions about a particular subject: *the drugs czar* **2** another spelling of **tsar**

D d

d /diː/ (plural **d's**) or **D** (plural **D's**) noun [C/U] **1** the fourth letter of the English alphabet **2** D MUSIC the second note in the musical scale of C major

-'d short form a way of writing 'had' or 'would'. This is not often used in formal writing: *He realized she'd asked him something.* ♦ *I'd like a glass of milk, please.*

DA /,diː 'eɪ/ noun [C] LAW district attorney: a lawyer in the US who represents a state against a person or organization accused of committing a crime

D/A abbrev COMPUTING digital-to-analogue

dab¹ /dæb/ (**dabs, dabbing, dabbed**) verb [I/T] to touch a surface gently several times with something such as a cloth, for example in order to dry it: *Marge dabbed at her eyes with a handkerchief.*

dab² /dæb/ noun [C] a small amount of a substance that is put on a surface

DAB /,diː eɪ 'biː/ noun [U] digital audio broadcasting: a system of broadcasting radio signals using **digital** technology

dabble /'dæb(ə)l/ verb [I] to be involved in an activity in a way that is not very serious: *When he was younger he dabbled in astrology.*

dactyl /'dæktɪl/ noun [C] LITERATURE a section of a line of poetry that consists of one syllable that you emphasize when speaking, followed by two syllables that you do not emphasize. An example of this is the word 'pleasantly'.

dad /dæd/ noun [C] informal your father: *His dad works in my office.* ♦ *Can I borrow some money, Dad?*

daddy /'dædi/ (plural **daddies**) noun [C] informal your father. This word is usually used by and to young children.

daffodil /'dæfədɪl/ noun [C] a tall yellow flower that grows in **temperate** regions in the spring

dagger /'dægə/ noun [C] a weapon like a very small sword —*picture* → WEAPON

daily¹ /'deɪli/ adj **1** done or happening every day: *The information is updated on a daily basis.* **2** a daily newspaper is published every day, except Sunday **3** a daily amount is the amount for one day: *Table Six shows the daily consumption of energy per person.*

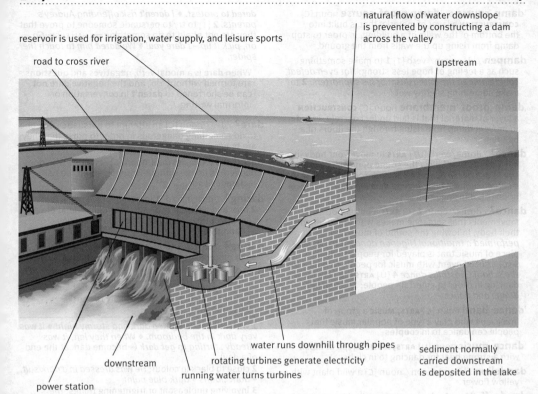

natural flow of water downslope is prevented by constructing a dam across the valley

reservoir is used for irrigation, water supply, and leisure sports

road to cross river

upstream

water runs downhill through pipes

sediment normally carried downstream is deposited in the lake

downstream

rotating turbines generate electricity

running water turns turbines

power station

dam

daily² /ˈdeɪli/ adv every day: *Fresh bread is delivered daily.*

dainty /ˈdeɪnti/ adj small and attractive in a delicate way —**daintily** adv

dairy¹ /ˈdeəri/ (plural **dairies**) noun [C] **1** a building on a farm where milk is kept and where foods such as butter and cheese are made **2** a company that sells milk and makes foods such as butter and cheese

dairy² /ˈdeəri/ adj dairy products include milk and foods such as butter and cheese

'dairy ,farming noun [U] AGRICULTURE the business of keeping cows and selling their milk

dairying /ˈdeəriɪŋ/ noun [U] AGRICULTURE **dairy farming**

daisy /ˈdeɪzi/ (plural **daisies**) noun [C] a small white flower with a yellow centre

Dalai Lama /ˌdælaɪ ˈlɑːmə/ noun [C] RELIGION the spiritual leader in Tibetan Buddhism

Dalmatian /dælˈmeɪʃ(ə)n/ noun [C] a large dog with smooth white hair and black spots

dam¹ /dæm/ noun [C] **1** a wall built across a river in a valley in order to create an artificial lake or to produce electricity. The artificial lake is called a **reservoir** and it is usually used as a water supply for towns, houses, crops etc. The electricity is called **hydroelectricity** and is produced by using the flow of water to drive a **turbine**. **2** AGRICULTURE the mother of an animal such as a horse or sheep **3** an artificial **pond** where rain and spring water is collected and stored **4** a structure made of branches built by some animals across a river or stream

dam² /dæm/ (**dams, damming, dammed**) verb [T] to stop a river or stream from flowing by building a dam across it

damage¹ /ˈdæmɪdʒ/ noun **1** [U] physical harm: *a new drug to treat nerve damage* ♦ *Luckily, no serious damage had been done.* ♦ **Damage to** *the building could take six months to repair.* **2** [U] negative effects on someone or something: *The damage to the bank's reputation is extremely serious.* **3 damages** [plural] LAW money that a court orders one person to pay to another person that they have harmed

damage² /ˈdæmɪdʒ/ verb [T] **1** to harm something physically: *Many buildings had been severely damaged in the storm.* **2** to have a negative effect on someone or something: *His political reputation has been seriously damaged by the scandal.*

damaging /ˈdæmɪdʒɪŋ/ adj causing physical harm, or having a bad or negative effect: *The chemicals have a damaging effect on the environment.*

damn¹ /dæm/ or **damned** /dæmd/ adj, adv impolite used for emphasizing something: *I can't open the damn window.* ♦ *She works damn hard.*

damn² /dæm/ verb [T] to criticize someone or something extremely severely

damning /ˈdæmɪŋ/ adj showing that something is wrong or bad: *a damning report into the way the case was handled*

damp¹ /dæmp/ adj slightly wet, often in an unpleasant way: *The wood won't burn if it's damp.* —**dampness** noun [U]

damp² /dæmp/ noun [U] slightly wet areas in the walls of a building

'**damp ,course** or '**damp proof ,course** noun [C] CONSTRUCTION a layer of material that is built into the bottom of the walls of a building, in order to stop damp from rising up the walls from the ground

dampen /'dæmpən/ verb [T] **1** to make something such as a feeling or hope less strong: *Not even defeat could dampen the enthusiasm of his supporters.* **2** to make something slightly wet

,**damp ,proof** '**membrane** noun [C] CONSTRUCTION a layer of material that is laid under concrete, in order to prevent damp from rising through the floors of a building

dance¹ /dɑːns/ verb [I/T] ARTS to move your body in movements that follow the sound of music: *I was too shy to **ask** her **to dance**.* ♦ *They **danced to** the music of a Latin band.* ♦ *Who were you **dancing with**?* —**dancer** noun [C], **dancing** noun [U]

dance² /dɑːns/ noun **1** [C] ARTS a pattern of movements that someone makes with their feet and their body, following the sound of music: *They performed a traditional Nigerian dance.* **2** [C] MUSIC a piece of music that is played for people to dance to **3** [C] a social event with music for people to dance to: *the school Christmas dance* **4** [U] ARTS the activity of dancing in order to entertain people: *She teaches drama and dance.*

'**dance ,band** noun [C] ARTS, MUSIC a group of musicians who play a type of popular music that people can dance to in **couples**

'**dance ,music** noun [U] ARTS, MUSIC a type of music with a strong beat for dancing to in clubs

dandelion /'dændɪ,laɪən/ noun [C] a wild plant with a yellow flower

dandruff /'dændrəf/ noun [U] small white pieces of dry skin in a person's hair

danger /'deɪndʒə/ noun **1** [U] a situation in which serious harm, death, or damage is possible: *The notice said 'Danger! Keep Out!'* ♦ *There is **danger from** exposure to radiation.* ♦ *His actions **put** the child's life **in danger**.* ♦ *The ship almost sank in the storm, but it's **out of danger** now.* **2** [C/U] a situation in which something unpleasant might happen: *There is a danger that the money will simply be wasted.* ♦ *The peace talks are now **in danger of** collapse.* **3** [C] a person or thing that might cause serious harm or damage: *Falling rocks **pose a** serious **danger to** tourists.* ♦ *a campaign to warn children of **the dangers of** electricity*

dangerous /'deɪndʒərəs/ adj likely to cause serious harm, or to have a bad effect: *dangerous driving* ♦ *an exciting but **highly dangerous** sport* ♦ *We don't know whether these chemicals are **dangerous to** humans.* ♦ *It's dangerous to walk around here at night.* —**dangerously** adv: *Fuel levels were dangerously low.*

dangerous driving /,deɪndʒərəs 'draɪvɪŋ/ noun [U] LAW the crime of driving a vehicle in a way that is likely to hurt or kill people

dangle /'dæŋg(ə)l/ verb [I/T] if you dangle something, or if it dangles, it hangs or swings freely: *A single light bulb dangled from the ceiling.*

dank /dæŋk/ adj unpleasantly cold and slightly wet

dapper /'dæpə/ adj a man who is dapper is wearing attractive clothes that give him a tidy appearance

dappled /'dæp(ə)ld/ adj with areas of lighter and darker colour, or light and shadow

dare¹ /deə/ verb **1** [I] to not be afraid to do something, even though it may be dangerous or may cause trouble: *I drove as fast as I dared.* ♦ *Nobody dared argue with him.* ♦ *She was one of the few people who*

dared to protest. ♦ *I **daren't** risk offending Audrey's parents.* **2** [T] to try to persuade someone to prove that they are not afraid to do something = CHALLENGE: *Go on, pick it up – I **dare you**!* ♦ *We **dared** him **to** touch the spider.*

> When **dare** is a modal verb, negatives and questions are formed without 'do', and the negative **dare not** can be shortened to **daren't** in conversation or informal writing.

dare² /deə/ noun [C] an attempt to persuade someone to do something dangerous in order to prove that they are brave = CHALLENGE

daredevil /'deə,dev(ə)l/ noun [C] someone who does dangerous things without worrying about the risk —**daredevil** adj

daring¹ /'deərɪŋ/ adj **1** involving brave behaviour **2** new and different in a way that might offend or upset some people: *a daring and highly original film* —**daringly** adv

daring² /'deərɪŋ/ noun [U] the brave attitude of someone who does new or dangerous things

dark¹ /dɑːk/ adj

1 lacking light	4 sad
2 almost black	5 likely to shock
3 frightening	

1 with little or no light: *a dark and stormy night* ♦ *It was very dark in the bedroom.* ♦ *When they left, it was already starting to **get dark** (=become dark at the end of a day).*

2 close to black in colour: *He was dressed in a dark suit.* ♦ *dark clouds* ♦ *dark blue paint*

3 involving unpleasant or frightening things: *the **darkest days** of the war*

4 dark thoughts are sad because you believe that something bad is going to happen

5 a dark secret or mystery is kept well hidden, especially because people would not approve if they knew about it

dark² /dɑːk/ noun [singular] **the dark** a situation or place in which there is little or no light: *Tim is afraid of the dark.* ♦ *Why are you sitting here **in the dark**?*

PHRASES **after dark** after it has become night: *Do not go out on your own after dark.*

before dark before it becomes night: *We were hoping to get home before dark.*

in the dark (about sth) not knowing much about something because other people have not given you information

darken /'dɑːkən/ verb [I/T] **1** to become darker, or to make something darker: *The sky darkened and heavy rain began to fall.* **2** to suddenly become serious or sad

,**dark 'horse** noun [singular] someone with a secret ability or achievement that surprises people when they discover it

darkly /'dɑːkli/ adv in an angry and threatening way

,**dark 'matter** noun [U] SCIENCE, ASTRONOMY a substance that scientists think exists out in space, but for which they have no direct proof

darkness /'dɑːknəs/ noun [U] the lack of light: *The front rooms were all **in darkness**.* ♦ *The search had to be abandoned when **darkness fell** (=it got dark).*

darling¹ /'dɑːlɪŋ/ noun [C] **1** someone who is liked or admired very much by a particular group of people: *He quickly became **the darling of** the middle classes.* **2** spoken used for talking to someone you love: *Are you coming, darling?*

darling² /ˈdɑːlɪŋ/ adj loved very much by someone: *my darling wife*

darn /dɑːn/ verb [I/T] to repair a piece of clothing by sewing stitches across the hole

dart¹ /dɑːt/ verb **1** [I] to make a sudden quick movement somewhere: *A child darted out in front of our car.* **2** [I/T] if you dart a look or a **glance**, or if your eyes dart somewhere, you look there suddenly and for a very short time

dart² /dɑːt/ noun **1** [C] a small pointed object that is thrown or fired from a gun **2** [singular] a sudden short movement= DASH **3** [C] a narrow pointed fold made in a piece of clothing by sewing, so that it has a better shape or fits better

darts /dɑːts/ noun [U] a game in which people throw darts at a round board called a **dartboard**

Darwinian /dɑːˈwɪniən/ adj relating to Darwinism

Darwinism /ˈdɑːwɪnɪz(ə)m/ noun [U] a theory of evolution developed by Charles Darwin, a 19th-century British scientist

dash¹ /dæʃ/ verb **1** [I] to go somewhere in a hurry: *I dashed out into the street, still in my pyjamas.* **2** [I/T] to hit something violently, or to throw something violently against a surface: *Huge waves dashed against the side of the boat.*

PHRASE dash sb's hopes to make it impossible for someone to do what they had hoped to do: *Saturday's defeat has dashed their hopes of success in the championship this year.*

dash² /dæʃ/ noun **1** [singular] an act of going or running somewhere quickly: *She made a dash for the door.* **2** [C] a small amount of something: *a dash of soy sauce* **3** [C] **LANGUAGE** the symbol – used in writing to separate different parts of a sentence

dashboard /ˈdæʃbɔːd/ noun [C] the part inside a car where the **speedometer** and other instruments are

data /ˈdeɪtə, ˈdɑːtə/ noun [U] **1 COMPUTING** information in a form that a computer can use **2** information that is used for making calculations or decisions, for example in maths: *The document contained data from tests of biological weapons.*

> **Data** can be used with a singular or plural verb, though the use of the plural verb is very formal.

'data ,bank noun [C] **COMPUTING** a large amount of data, especially when it is used by computers

database /ˈdeɪtəbeɪs/ noun [C] **COMPUTING** a large amount of information that is stored in a computer in an organized way

'data ,capture noun [U] **COMPUTING** the process of collecting data and putting it into a computer by electronic methods

'data com,pression noun [U] **COMPUTING** the process of changing information into a smaller form that can be stored more easily or sent more quickly

'data ,mining noun [U] **COMPUTING** the process of searching a **database** using special software in order to find out information, for example what type of people buy a product. It is often used by companies as a way of trying to increase sales.

dataport /ˈdeɪtəpɔːt/ noun [C] **COMPUTING** a part of a **laptop** computer into which you put a **cable** so that you can use the Internet

data processing /ˌdeɪtə ˈprəʊsesɪŋ/ noun [U] **COMPUTING** the operations that are performed by a computer in order to store, organize, or find information

,data pro'tection noun [U] **LAW** legal control over who can see or use information kept by computers

'data ,set noun [C] **COMPUTING** an amount of information stored as a file on a computer

datasheet /ˈdeɪtəˌʃiːt/ noun [C] **COMPUTING** an Internet document that gives a description of something in detail, especially a product

date¹ /deɪt/ noun [C] **1** a particular day, month, or year, or its name or number: *What was **the date** of the last meeting we had?* ♦ *What's **today's date**?* ♦ *Should we **set a date for** the next meeting* (=decide when it will happen)*?* ♦ *The exact details of the scheme will be worked out **at a later date*** (=at some time in the future). **2** an arrangement that two people make to meet each other in order to start or continue a romantic relationship: *I've got a date with one of the boys on my course tonight.* **3** a brown fruit that grows on a palm tree

PHRASES date of birth the day, month, and year when a person was born

to date *formal* until now: *There have been no reports of car theft to date.*
→ OUT-OF-DATE, UP-TO-DATE

date² /deɪt/ verb **1** [T] to write the date on something: *The letter was dated 23 February.* **2** [T] to discover exactly how old something is or when it was made: *The paintings have not yet been accurately dated by the museum's experts.* **3** [I] to seem to be no longer modern or fashionable: *This style has hardly dated at all.*

dated /ˈdeɪtɪd/ adj no longer modern or fashionable

'date ,rape noun [C/U] **LAW** a crime in which one person **rapes** another (=forces them to have sex) while on a date with them —**'date-,rape** verb [T]

dative /ˈdeɪtɪv/ noun [singular] **LANGUAGE** the form of a noun, pronoun, or adjective that you use in some languages when it is the **indirect object** of a verb —**dative** adj

datum level /ˈdeɪtəm ˌlev(ə)l/ noun [C] **CONSTRUCTION** a level from which all other levels are measured on maps that show the height of land

daughter /ˈdɔːtə/ noun [C] your female child

'daughter ,cell noun [C] **BIOLOGY** a cell that is formed when another cell divides

'daughter-in-,law (plural **daughters-in-law**) noun [C] the wife of your son

daunting /ˈdɔːntɪŋ/ adj something that is daunting makes you worried because you think that it will be very difficult or dangerous to do

dawdle /ˈdɔːd(ə)l/ verb [I] to go somewhere or do something so slowly that people become annoyed with you

dawn¹ /dɔːn/ noun [C/U] the beginning of the day, when it begins to get light= DAYBREAK: *We had to get up **at the crack of dawn*** (=very early in the morning). ♦ *They worked **from dawn to dusk*** (=all day).

PHRASE the dawn of sth *literary* the time when something such as a new period in history begins

dawn² /dɔːn/ verb [I] **1** if a new day dawns, it begins **2** if something such as a new period in history dawns, it begins

day /deɪ/ noun

1 24 hours	5 time for Earth to spin
2 when it is light	6 period of time
3 when sb is active	+ PHRASES
4 time in past/future	

1 [C] one of the 7 periods of time that a week is divided into. It is equal to 24 hours: *We're going away for five*

days. ♦ *The animals are kept inside for 14 hours **a day**.*
2 [C/U] the period of time when it is light outside ≠ NIGHT: *The restaurant is only open **during the day**.* ♦ ***By day** (=during the day) he is a banker, but by night he sings in a club.*
3 [C] the period of time when you are awake and doing things: *She came home exhausted after **a hard day** at the office (=a difficult or unpleasant day).* ♦ *What do you do at home **all day**?* ♦ *Next week, my father's got **a day off** (=a day when he does not have to work).*
4 [singular] a time in the past or future: *We look forward to **the day when** nuclear weapons will no longer exist.* ♦ ***The day may come** when our air becomes too polluted to breathe.*
5 [C] ASTRONOMY a unit of time equal to the time that the Earth takes to make one complete revolution. It can be measured in relation to the Sun or the stars.
6 days [plural] a period of time when something is happening or is successful: *I think **my days as** a footballer are coming to an end.* ♦ *She became famous **in the early days of** television.*

PHRASES **day after day** every day for a long time, often in a way that is boring or unpleasant
the day after tomorrow two days from now
the day before yesterday two days ago
day by day in small slow stages as each day passes: *She's getting stronger day by day.*
from day one ever since the very beginning of something
from day to day 1 in a way that changes quickly or often: *He seems to change his opinion from day to day.* **2** without thinking about what is going to happen in the future: *They lived from day to day.*
have had your/its day to have stopped being successful or fashionable: *Most people think this government has had its day.*
make sb's day to make someone feel very happy
one day 1 at some time in the future: *She hopes to own her own business one day.* **2** on a day in the past: *One day he just walked out and never came back.*
some day at some time in the future: *I'll go back there some day.*

daybreak /ˈdeɪˌbreɪk/ noun [U] the time when light first appears in the morning = DAWN

'day ˌcentre or **'day care ˌcentre** noun [C] a place where care is given during the day to people who need special help, for example because they are old or disabled

daydream /ˈdeɪˌdriːm/ verb [I] to spend time thinking about something pleasant when you should be doing something more serious —**daydream** noun [C], **daydreamer** noun [C]

daylight /ˈdeɪˌlaɪt/ noun [U] the light outside that can be seen during the day

ˌday reˈlease noun [U] EDUCATION a system by which workers go to college one day a week, in order to take a course in a subject related to their work

ˌday reˈturn noun [C] TOURISM a ticket that allows someone to travel by train or bus at a reduced price, because they go and come back on the same day

daytime /ˈdeɪˌtaɪm/ noun [U] the period of time during the day when it is light, because the part of the Earth's surface that you are on is facing the Sun

ˌday-to-ˈday adj happening every day as part of your normal life

'day ˌtrip noun [C] TOURISM a journey that someone makes for pleasure in which they go to a place and come back on the same day

daze /deɪz/ noun **in a daze** unable to think clearly or to understand what is happening

dazed /deɪzd/ adj unable to think clearly or to understand what is happening

dazzle /ˈdæz(ə)l/ verb [T] **1** if a bright light dazzles you, you cannot see for a short time **2** to impress someone a lot

dazzling /ˈdæzlɪŋ/ adj **1** a dazzling light is so bright that you cannot see for a short time **2** extremely impressive: *a dazzling display of flowers*

dB abbrev decibel

DC1 /ˌdiː ˈsiː/ noun [C] Detective Constable: a police officer of low rank in the British police force who deals with serious crimes and does not wear a uniform

DC2 /ˌdiː ˈsiː/ abbrev PHYSICS direct current

DCRP /ˌdiː siː ɑː ˈpiː/ noun [U] TECHNOLOGY direct current reversed polarity: a situation in welding in which the electrode cable is connected to the positive terminal of the welding machine, and the work cable is connected to the negative terminal

DCSP /ˌdiː siː es ˈpiː/ noun [U] TECHNOLOGY direct current straight polarity: a situation in welding in which the electrode cable is connected to the negative terminal of the welding machine, and the work cable is connected to the positive terminal

'D ˌdrive noun [C] COMPUTING the first CD drive on a computer system

DDT /ˌdiː diː ˈtiː/ noun [U] CHEMISTRY a poisonous chemical used for killing insects. It destroys crops and also kills other animals and is dangerous to humans, and so it is no longer allowed in many countries. This kind of chemical is called a **pesticide** or an **insecticide**.

dead1 /ded/ adj

1 not alive	**6** complete
2 not working	**7** people
3 not interesting	**8** no longer spoken
4 no longer important	**9** in ball games
5 having no feeling	

1 no longer alive: *The shootings left 14 people dead.* ♦ *I raked up the dead leaves.* ♦ *Rescue workers are still pulling dead bodies out of the rubble.*
2 a piece of equipment that is dead is not working: *The battery was completely dead.* ♦ *The phone suddenly **went dead**.*
3 boring because there is no activity or noise: *The street seems dead without all the children.*
4 no longer important or likely to be successful: *It seems that the peace process is now dead.*
5 if a part of someone's body is dead, they cannot feel it: *My legs had **gone** completely **dead**.*
6 complete: *dead silence* ♦ *The truck suddenly came to **a dead stop**.*
7 the dead people who have died
8 a dead language such as Latin is no longer used by people in their ordinary lives
9 SPORTS a dead ball is outside the area on which a game is being played, so that the game stops for a short time

dead2 /ded/ noun **in the dead of night/winter** *literary* in the middle of the night or in the middle of the winter, when everything is quiet

deaden /ˈded(ə)n/ verb [T] **1** to make a feeling less strong **2** to make a sound less loud

ˌdead 'end noun [C] **1** a road that has no way out at one end **2** a situation in which no more progress is possible

ˌdead-end 'job noun [C] a job that provides someone with no chance of getting a better job

dead 'heat noun [C] **SPORTS** a situation in which two people finish a race at exactly the same time, so that they both win

deadline /'dedˌlaɪn/ noun [C] a time or date by which someone has to do something: *The deadline for applications was last Friday.* ♦ *If we can't meet the deadline* (=finish something in time), *they won't give us another contract.*

'dead ˌload noun [C] **CONSTRUCTION** the weight of a fixed part of a building such as the walls, floors, or roof

deadlock /'dedˌlɒk/ noun [singular/U] a disagreement between people who are not willing to change their opinions or decisions: *Hopes of breaking the deadlock* (=ending it) *are fading.* —**deadlocked** /'dedˌlɒkt/ adj

deadly1 /'dedli/ (**deadlier, deadliest**) adj capable of killing people: *This is a potentially deadly disease.* ♦ *a deadly weapon*

deadly2 /'dedli/ adv extremely: *Politics is a deadly serious business.*

deaf /def/ adj **1** not able to hear anything, or not able to hear very well. Some people think that this word is offensive and prefer to use the expression **hearing impaired**: *I'm a little deaf in one ear.* **2** the deaf people who are deaf: *a school for the deaf* —**deafness** noun [U]

deafen /'def(ə)n/ verb [T] **1** if a noise deafens you, you cannot hear anything else because it is so loud **2** to make someone unable to hear, either for a short time or for ever

deafening /'def(ə)nɪŋ/ adj so loud that you can hear nothing else —**deafeningly** adv

deal1 /diːl/ (**deals, dealing, dealt** /delt/) verb [I/T] **1** to give cards to the people who are playing a game of cards: *Each player is dealt three cards.* **2** to buy and sell illegal drugs: *Many drug addicts deal as well.*

PHRASE **deal a blow to** to harm or shock someone or something

PHRASAL VERBS **'deal in sth** to buy and sell something: *a small company that deals in rare books*
'deal with sth 1 to take action to solve a problem: *The government must now deal with the problem of high unemployment.* **2** to be about a subject: *Chapter 5 deals with greenhouse gases.*

deal2 /diːl/ noun **1** [C] a formal agreement, especially in business or politics: *a deal with a Japanese TV company* ♦ *I got a really good deal on my new computer* (=I got it for a low price). ♦ *We think there was a deal between the CIA and the FBI.* → DEALING **2** [singular] the way in which you are treated by other people: *Disabled people have got a raw deal* (=they are treated unfairly) *under the current government.* ♦ *Unions are demanding a fair deal for nurses.* **3** [singular] the act of giving cards to the people who are playing a game of cards: *Whose deal is it next?*

PHRASE **a good/great deal of sth** a large amount of something: *A great deal of research has been done already.*

dealer /'diːlə/ noun [C] **1** a person or company that buys and sells a particular product **2** someone who sells illegal drugs

dealership /'diːləʃɪp/ noun [C] **BUSINESS** a business that sells only the products made by a particular company, especially cars

dealing /'diːlɪŋ/ noun **1** [U] the business of buying and selling: *drug dealing* **2 dealings** [plural] the business relationship that someone has with another person or organization **3** [U] the particular way in which someone does business or behaves towards other people

dealt /delt/ the past tense and past participle of **deal1**

deamination /diːˌæmɪˈneɪʃ(ə)n/ noun [U] **BIOLOGY** a process that takes place in the liver in which **amino acids** are broken down. The amino group are removed and are later used to form **urea**.

dean /diːn/ noun [C] **1 RELIGION** a senior Anglican priest **2 EDUCATION** a senior official at a college or university

dear1 /dɪə/ adj **1 Dear** used in front of someone's name or title at the beginning of a letter to them: *Dear Diana, I hope you're feeling better now.* ♦ *Dear Sir or Madam* **2** loved, or liked very much: *a dear friend* **3** expensive: *Their products are good quality, but a bit dear.*

dear2 /dɪə/ interjection **oh dear** used when you are upset, disappointed, annoyed, or worried about something: *Oh dear, I spilt the coffee.*

dearest /'dɪərəst/ adj used about something that you want or hope for more than anything else: *her dearest wish*

dearly /'dɪəli/ adv very much: *I love him dearly in spite of all his faults.*

dearth /dɜːθ/ noun [singular] *formal* a situation in which there is not enough of something = LACK

death /deθ/ noun **1** [C/U] the end of someone's life: *the rising number of deaths on the roads every year* ♦ *These people will starve to death unless they receive help soon.* ♦ *The cause of death has not yet been discovered.* **2** [singular] the end of something: *the death of apartheid in South Africa* → MATTER1

deathbed /'deθˌbed/ noun [singular] a bed in which someone has died or is about to die

deathly /'deθli/ adj **1** a deathly silence is extremely quiet and makes you feel nervous or frightened **2** someone who is deathly pale is extremely pale

the 'death ˌpenalty noun [singular] **LAW** legal punishment by death, usually for a serious crime such as murder

'death ˌrate noun [singular] **SOCIAL STUDIES** the number of deaths in a particular area in one year

'death ˌsentence noun [C] **LAW** a judge's official statement that orders someone to be punished by death

'death ˌtoll noun [singular] the number of people who are killed on a particular occasion

debacle /deɪˈbɑːk(ə)l/ noun [C] something that fails completely in an embarrassing way

debatable /dɪˈbeɪtəb(ə)l/ adj something that is debatable is not certain because it is possible for people to have different opinions about it

debate1 /dɪˈbeɪt/ noun **1** [C/U] a discussion in which people or groups state different opinions about a subject: *The proposals provoked a fierce debate.* ♦ *There has been intense debate over the treatment of illegal immigrants.* **2** [C] a formal discussion that ends with a decision made by voting

debate2 /dɪˈbeɪt/ verb [I/T] **1** to discuss a subject formally before making a decision, usually by voting: *Parliament is still debating the bill.* **2** to consider an action or situation carefully before you decide what to do: *I debated whether or not to call her parents.*

debilitating /dɪˈbɪlɪˌteɪtɪŋ/ adj *formal* making someone very weak: *a debilitating illness*

debit1 /'debɪt/ noun [C] an amount of money that is taken from a bank account ≠ CREDIT

debit2 /'debɪt/ verb [T] if a bank debits someone's account, it takes money out of it ≠ CREDIT

'debit ,card noun [C] a plastic card that moves money automatically from someone's account to the account of the person they are paying

debris /'debriː, 'deɪbriː/ noun [U] the broken pieces that are left when something large has been destroyed

debt /det/ noun **1** [C] an amount of money that someone owes: *The family had debts which they could not repay.* **2** [U] a situation in which someone owes money to other people: *I don't like being in debt to anyone.* ♦ *She was terrified of getting into debt.* **3** [U] **ECONOMICS** the total amount of money that the government of a country owes to banks and to other countries that it has borrowed from **4** [singular] an obligation to be grateful to someone because they have done something for you: *I'm forever **in your debt.***

debtor /'detə/ noun [C] **BUSINESS** a person, organization, or country that owes money ≠ CREDITOR

'debt re,lief noun [U] the practice of allowing poor countries not to pay back what they owe to rich countries

debug /diː'bʌg/ (**debugs, debugging, debugged**) verb [T] **COMPUTING** to look for and remove mistakes from a computer program so that it works correctly

debugger /diː'bʌgə/ noun [C] **COMPUTING** a computer program that looks for and removes mistakes from another program, so that it works correctly

debunk /diː'bʌŋk/ verb [T] to prove that something such as an idea or belief is false and silly

debut /'deɪbjuː/ noun [C] the first time a performer or sports player appears in public: *Easton **made his debut** in 2002.*

decade /'dekeɪd/ noun [C] a period of ten years

decadent /'dekəd(ə)nt/ adj involving a lot of immoral pleasure —**decadence** /'dekəd(ə)ns/ noun [U]

decaffeinated /diː'kæfɪ,neɪtɪd/ adj decaffeinated coffee or tea has had the **caffeine** (=a chemical substance that keeps you awake) removed

decagon /'dekəgən, 'dekəgɒn/ noun [C] **MATHS** a geometric shape with ten straight sides

decalescence /,diːkə'lesəns/ noun [U] **TECHNOLOGY** absorption of heat without a rise in temperature that takes place in iron or steel that is heated in particular conditions. It is caused by a change in the structure of the metal.

decapitate /dɪ'kæpɪteɪt/ verb [T] *formal* to cut off someone's head

decathlon /dɪ'kæθlɒn/ noun [C] **SPORTS** a sports event that consists of ten different sports

decay /dɪ'keɪ/ verb **1** [I/T] **BIOLOGY** to be gradually broken down by bacteria or fungi: *As dead plants decay, they release mineral salts into the soil.* ♦ *decaying vegetation* **2** [I] if a building or an area decays, its condition gradually gets worse because it has not been looked after —**decay** noun [U]: *tooth decay* ♦ *urban decay*

deceased /dɪ'siːst/ adj *formal* **1** dead **2 the deceased** a dead person or dead people

deceit /dɪ'siːt/ noun [C/U] dishonest behaviour that is intended to trick someone

deceitful /dɪ'siːtf(ə)l/ adj behaving dishonestly in order to trick people → DECEPTIVE sense 2

deceive /dɪ'siːv/ verb [T] **1** to trick someone by behaving in a dishonest way: *He was **deceived into** giving them all his money.* **2** to make someone believe something that is not true

Word family: deceive

Words in the same family as *deceive*
- **deceit** n
- **deceptive** adj
- **deceptively** adv
- **deceitful** adj
- **deception** n

decelerate /diː'seləreɪt/ verb [I] **PHYSICS** to move more slowly

December /dɪ'sembə/ noun [U] the twelfth month of the year, between November and January: *Coffee prices fell slightly in December.* ♦ *I received a letter from them on December 15th.*

decency /'diːs(ə)nsi/ noun [U] behaviour that is moral, good, or reasonable: *You should at least **have the decency** to say you're sorry!*

decent /'diːs(ə)nt/ adj **1** good, or good enough: *Are there any decent restaurants around here?* **2** behaving in an honest and fair way towards other people **3** considered by most people to be moral, good, or reasonable —**decently** adv

decentralize /diː'sentrəlaɪz/ verb [T] to take power from a central government or organization and give it to several smaller and more local ones — **decentralization** /,diː,sentrəlaɪ'zeɪʃ(ə)n/ noun [U]

deception /dɪ'sepʃ(ə)n/ noun [C/U] the act of tricking someone by telling them something that is not true

deceptive /dɪ'septɪv/ adj **1** if something is deceptive, it seems very different from the way it really is: *There was a deceptive calmness in his voice.* **2** if someone is being deceptive, they trick other people by telling them something that is not true: *deceptive advertising* —**deceptively** adv

deci- /desi/ prefix **MATHS, SCIENCE** used for things that are one of ten parts that make a unit

decibel /'desɪbel/ noun [C] **SCIENCE** a unit for measuring how loud a sound is. The voices of most people measure between 45 and 60 decibels. Symbol dB

decide /dɪ'saɪd/ verb **1** [I/T] to make a choice about what you are going to do: *He **decided** to stay and see what would happen.* ♦ *I decided that it would be best to tell George everything.* ♦ *I can't decide whether to go with them or stay here.* **2** [T] to produce a particular result: *Today's match will decide the championship.* **3** [T] to consider something carefully and officially state what should be done about it: *The matter will be decided by a government tribunal.*

PHRASAL VERBS **de,cide a'gainst sb/sth** to not choose someone or something: *We decided against the house because it was too small.*

de'cide on sb/sth to choose someone or something from a number of possible choices: *We finally decided on the red curtains.*

Word family: decide

Words in the same family as *decide*
- **decided** adj
- **decision** n
- **decisive** adj
- **decisively** adv
- **decisiveness** n
- **undecided** adj
- **decidedly** adv
- **indecision** n
- **indecisive** adj
- **indecisively** adv
- **indecisiveness** n

decided /dɪ'saɪdɪd/ adj *formal* impossible to doubt and easy to see: *a decided improvement on last year* —**decidedly** adv

deciduous /dɪ'sɪdjuəs/ adj **BIOLOGY** deciduous plants lose all their leaves each year at the end of the growing season and grow new ones at the start of the next growing season → EVERGREEN

decile /'desaɪl/ noun [C] **MATHS** one of the ten equal groups that a large number of people or things are divided into for comparing things such as test scores, height, salaries etc

decimal¹ /'desɪm(ə)l/ noun [C] **MATHS** a number that contains a decimal point to show that it is either smaller than 1, or that it contains parts that are smaller than a whole number. 0.5, 25.75, and 0.006 are all decimals

decimal² /'desɪm(ə)l/ adj **MATHS** relating to a counting system that has the number 10 as its base unit: *a decimal currency*

,decimal 'place noun [C] **MATHS** a position that comes after the decimal point in a decimal. 0.0164 has four decimal places

,decimal 'point noun [C] **MATHS** the symbol . in a decimal

decimate /'desɪmeɪt/ verb [T] to spoil or destroy something, for example by getting rid of a lot of people

decipher /dɪ'saɪfə/ verb [T] to discover the meaning of something that is difficult to read or understand

decision /dɪ'sɪʒ(ə)n/ noun **1** [C] a choice that you make after you have thought carefully about something: *The committee will **make a decision** by the end of the week.* ♦ *Sometimes managers need to **take decisions** quickly.* ♦ *Have you **come to a decision** yet?* **2** [U] the ability to make choices quickly, confidently, and effectively: *He acted with decision.*

de'cision-,making noun [U] the process of deciding what to do about something

decisive /dɪ'saɪsɪv/ adj **1** if something is decisive, it makes the final result of a situation certain: *The UK has played a decisive role in these negotiations.* **2** a decisive victory or defeat is one in which the winner does much better than the person who loses **3** a decisive person can decide what to do quickly and confidently ≠ INDECISIVE —**decisively** adv

deck /dek/ noun [C] **1** the outside top part of a ship that people can walk on **2** one of the levels on a ship **3** a set of cards used in card games

declaim /dɪ'kleɪm/ verb [I/T] *formal* to say something, especially in a formal or impressive way

declaration /,deklə'reɪʃ(ə)n/ noun [C] an important or official statement about something: *a **declaration of** war* ♦ *his **declaration of** love*

declarative /dɪ'klærətɪv/ adj **LANGUAGE** a declarative sentence is expressed as a statement

declare /dɪ'kleə/ verb [T] **1** to announce officially that something is true or is happening: *He was in Germany when war was **declared**.* ♦ *Mrs Armitage declared that she would fight to clear her name.* ♦ *Sarah was declared the winner.* **2** if someone declares their income, they state on an official form how much money they have earned so that they pay the correct amount of tax **3** **SPORTS** in **cricket**, to end an **innings** before all the **batsmen** have been made to leave the field

declension /dɪ'klenʃ(ə)n/ noun **LANGUAGE 1** [U] the process by which the form of nouns, adjectives, or pronouns changes in some languages, depending on their relationship to other words in a sentence **2** [C] a group of nouns, adjectives, or pronouns in some languages that all change their form in the same way, depending on their relationship to other words in a sentence

decline¹ /dɪ'klaɪn/ verb **1** [I] to become less or become worse: *Share prices **declined sharply** last week.* ♦ *The number of people dying from the disease has started to decline.* **2** [I/T] to say politely that you will not accept

something, or will not do something: *They offered to pay his fare, but he declined.* ♦ *We asked her to the reception, but she declined the invitation.* ♦ *The minister **declined to comment** on the rumours.* **3** [I] **LANGUAGE** if a noun, adjective, or pronoun declines, its form changes, depending on its relationship to other words in a sentence

decline² /dɪ'klaɪn/ noun [C/U] a reduction in the amount or quality of something: *a sharp decline* ♦ *There has been **a** steady **decline in** public services over recent years.*

decode /diː'kəʊd/ verb [T] **1** to succeed in understanding the meaning of a message that is written in code= DECIPHER **2** **COMPUTING** if a computer decodes information, it changes it into a form that you can understand **3** to change **digital** electronic signals into sound and a picture on a television screen **4** **LANGUAGE** to understand the meaning of a word, especially in a foreign language, without being able to **encode** it (=use it correctly in a sentence of your own)

decolonization /,diːkɒlənaɪ'zeɪʃ(ə)n/ noun [U] **SOCIAL STUDIES** the process by which a **colony** becomes independent from the country that used to control it —**decolonize** /diː'kɒlənaɪz/ verb [T]

decommission /,diːkə'mɪʃ(ə)n/ verb [T] to stop using something such as a weapon, ship, or **nuclear reactor**

decompose /,diːkəm'pəʊz/ verb [I] **BIOLOGY** to be broken down by a slow natural process, especially through the action of particular bacteria and fungi

decomposer /,diːkəm'pəʊzə/ noun [C] **BIOLOGY** an organism, especially a bacterium or fungus, that causes organic matter to decay —*picture* → FOOD WEB

decomposition /,diːkɒmpə'zɪʃ(ə)n/ noun [U] **BIOLOGY** the process of breaking down slowly and naturally, especially through the action of particular bacteria and fungi

decompress /,diːkəm'pres/ verb [T] **1** to reduce the pressure on something **2** **COMPUTING** to change a **compressed** computer file back to its full size

decompression /,diːkəm'preʃ(ə)n/ noun [U] **1** the process of reducing the pressure on something **2** **COMPUTING** the process of decompressing a computer file

,decom'pression ,sickness noun [U] **HEALTH** a serious medical condition that affects **divers** who come up to the surface of water too quickly

decongestant /,diːkən'dʒestənt/ noun [C] **HEALTH** a drug that helps people breathe more easily when they have a cold

deconstruct /,diːkən'strʌkt/ verb [T] **LANGUAGE** to examine a piece of writing in order to show that it can be understood in a different way by each person who reads it —**deconstruction** noun [U]

decorate /'dekəreɪt/ verb **1** [T] to make something more attractive by putting nice things on it or in it: *The room had been **decorated with** balloons.* **2** [I/T] to put new paint or paper on the walls of a room: *We decorated the kitchen last weekend.* **3** [T] to give someone a medal because they have done something brave

decoration /,dekə'reɪʃ(ə)n/ noun **1** [C/U] something nice that is used to make something else look more attractive **2** [C] a medal given to someone who has done something brave

decorative /'dek(ə)rətɪv/ adj attractive rather than useful: *decorative objects*

decorator /'dekəreɪtə/ noun [C] someone whose job is to decorate houses

decorum /dɪˈkɔːrəm/ noun [U] *formal* polite behaviour

decoy /ˈdiːkɔɪ/ noun [C] a person or thing that is used for tricking someone into going somewhere or doing something

decrease¹ /dɪˈkriːs/ verb **1** [I] to become less ≠ INCREASE: *The number of visitors has decreased significantly.* **2** [T] to reduce something

> **Build your vocabulary: words you can use instead of decrease**
>
> ■ **be/go/come down** to become less in number, value, or price
> ■ **drop/fall** to decrease in number or quality by a large amount
> ■ **dwindle** to decrease slowly and steadily until there is almost nothing left
> ■ **plummet/plunge** to decrease suddenly and very quickly
> ■ **slump** to decrease to a very low level or value, when this is seen as a bad thing

decrease² /ˈdiːkriːs/ noun [C/U] the process of becoming less, or the amount by which something is less ≠ INCREASE

decree /dɪˈkriː/ noun [C] **1** an official decision or order that is made by a leader or government **2** LAW a judgment that is made by a court of law —**decree** verb [T]

de,cree ˈabsolute noun [C] LAW an order by a court of law that ends a marriage and makes two people officially divorced

decree nisi /dɪˌkriː ˈnaɪsaɪ/ noun [C] LAW an order made by a court of law that says that a marriage will end on a particular date unless someone can show that there is a good reason not to end it

decrepit /dɪˈkrepɪt/ adj old and no longer in good condition

decrypt /diːˈkrɪpt/ verb [T] to change information that was in a code that could not be read or understood into a form that can be read and understood = DECODE

dedicate /ˈdedɪkeɪt/ verb

> PHRASAL VERBS **ˈdedicate sth to sth** to spend your time and effort doing something: *This woman has dedicated her life to helping others.*
> **ˈdedicate sth to sb** to say that a book or song that you have written was written for a person that you love or admire

dedicated /ˈdedɪkeɪtɪd/ adj **1** believing something is important and spending a lot of time and effort on it: *a dedicated teacher* **2** made or used for just one purpose: *a dedicated sports channel*

dedication /ˌdedɪˈkeɪʃ(ə)n/ noun **1** [U] a large amount of effort and time that someone spends on something, especially something that they think is good or right: *his **dedication to** the fight against AIDS* **2** [C] a statement that dedicates a song or book to someone

deduce /dɪˈdjuːs/ verb [T] *formal* to decide that something is true by considering all the available information

deduct /dɪˈdʌkt/ verb [T] to take an amount or number from a total

deduction /dɪˈdʌkʃ(ə)n/ noun [C/U] **1** an amount or number taken from a total, or the process of taking an amount or number away from a total **2** something that can be known from available information, or the process of finding something out from the information that is available

deed /diːd/ noun [C] **1** *literary* something that someone does: *a good deed* **2** LAW an official document that gives the details about who owns a building or piece of land

ˈdeed ˌpoll noun [singular/U] **change your name by deed poll** LAW to legally change your name

deem /diːm/ verb [T] *formal* to consider that someone or something has a particular quality

deep¹ /diːp/ adj

1 a long way down	6 dark/strong colour
2 of a distance	7 of big breath
3 going a long way in	8 hard to wake
4 strong feeling	9 serious
5 low sound	+ PHRASES

1 going a long way down from the top or surface of something ≠ SHALLOW: *The river is quite deep here.*
2 used for talking about the distance from the surface to the bottom of something: *The pond needs to be about four feet deep.* ♦ *How deep is the snow?*
3 going a long way in from the front, edge, or surface: *a deep cut on my arm*
4 a deep feeling is very strong: *I told him my deepest fears.*
5 a deep sound is low: *a deep voice*
6 a deep colour is dark and strong: *She wore a beautiful deep red dress.*
7 a deep breath or deep breathing brings a lot of air into and out of the lungs
8 a deep sleep is one that you do not wake up easily from
9 involving very serious thoughts, ideas, or feelings
> PHRASES **deep in thought/conversation** so involved in thinking or talking to someone that you do not notice anything else
> **thrown in at the deep end** having to deal with something difficult without being prepared for it

deep² /diːp/ adv **1** a long way down from the top or the surface, or a long way into something: *men who work deep under the ground* ♦ *They continued deep into the forest.* **2** if people or things are two deep, three deep etc, there are two, three etc rows of them
> PHRASE **deep down** used for saying that you know something is true, although you do not like to admit it: *Deep down, I knew that Caroline was right.*

deepen /ˈdiːpən/ verb **1** [I/T] to become, or to make something become, worse, stronger, deeper etc: *a deepening crisis* ♦ *a course that will deepen your understanding of economic issues* **2** [I/T] if a mystery deepens, or something deepens it, it becomes more complicated and difficult to understand **3** [I] if a colour deepens, it becomes darker

ˌdeep-ˈfocus adj GEOLOGY a deep-focus earthquake starts deeper than 300 kilometres underground

deeply /ˈdiːpli/ adv **1** very, or very much: *Your mother is deeply concerned.* **2** a long way into something: *The needle had penetrated deeply into his skin.* **3** if someone breathes or **sighs** deeply, they breathe a lot of air into or out of their lungs

ˌdeep-ˈsea adj in the deep areas of the sea

deep-seated /ˌdiːp ˈsiːtɪd/ adj a deep-seated feeling or belief is strong and difficult to change

ˌdeep-ˈset adj deep-set eyes seem to be a long way back into your face

ˈdeep-ˌstrip founˌdation noun [C] CONSTRUCTION a type of **foundation** (=part that supports a building) that is usually dug with a machine and then filled with concrete up to ground level

'deep ,structure noun [C/U] LANGUAGE the **logical** relationships on which the different parts of a phrase or sentence are based → SURFACE STRUCTURE

,deep vein throm'bosis noun [C/U] HEALTH a serious medical condition in which a blood clot forms in a vein and may stop blood flowing to other parts of the body

deer /dɪə/ (plural **deer**) noun [C] a large brown mammal with long thin legs. Male deer have horns called **antlers**.

deface /dɪˈfeɪs/ verb [T] to deliberately damage something, usually by writing on it

de facto /deɪ ˈfæktəʊ, di: ˈfæktəʊ/ adj formal actual, even though not official

defamation /ˌdefəˈmeɪʃ(ə)n/ noun [U] LAW the offence of writing or saying something bad about someone that is not true —**defamatory** /dɪˈfæmət(ə)ri/ adj

default[1] /dɪˈfɔːlt/ noun [C] COMPUTING the way that something will automatically appear or be done on a computer if the user does not change it
PHRASE **by default** if something happens by default, it happens only because you have not made any other decisions or done anything else to make it happen differently

default[2] /dɪˈfɔːlt/ verb [I] **1** to fail to pay money that is owed: They **defaulted on** the loan. **2** LAW to fail to appear in a court of law when you have been ordered to **3** SPORTS to fail to take part in a game or competition —**defaulter** noun [C]

defeat[1] /dɪˈfiːt/ noun [C/U] failure to win a competition or to succeed in doing something ≠ VICTORY: South Africa **suffered** a 2–0 **defeat**.

defeat[2] /dɪˈfiːt/ verb [T] **1** to win against someone = BEAT: Ghana defeated Senegal 3–1. **2** if something defeats someone, it is so difficult that they are unable to do it: The test completely defeated me. **3** to prevent something from happening or being successful: The proposal was defeated by 16 votes to 5.

defeatist /dɪˈfiːtɪst/ adj behaving in a way that shows that you think that you will fail = PESSIMISTIC — **defeatist** noun [C]

defecate /ˈdefəkeɪt/ verb [I] BIOLOGY to get rid of solid waste from the body through the **anus** → EXCRETION —**defecation** /ˌdefəˈkeɪʃ(ə)n/ noun [U]

defect[1] /ˈdiːfekt/ noun [C] a fault in someone or something

defect[2] /dɪˈfekt/ verb [I] to leave one country or political party and go to another one —**defection** /dɪˈfekʃ(ə)n/ noun [C/U], **defector** noun [C]

defective /dɪˈfektɪv/ adj not made correctly, or not working correctly = FAULTY

defence /dɪˈfens/ noun

1 protecting a place	4 in sport
2 protection	5 in court case
3 supporting sb	

1 [C/U] the weapons, equipment, and people that are used to protect a country or place: The government spends huge amounts of money on defence.
2 [C/U] protection for someone or something that is being attacked: Two of his friends **came to** his **defence**.
3 [C/U] something that you say to support someone or something that is being criticized: Several people **spoke in** my **defence**. ♦ a strong **defence of** government policy
4 [C/U] SPORTS the players in a team game who try to prevent the other team from scoring
5 the defence [singular] LAW the people in a court case

who try to prove that someone is not guilty
→ PROSECUTION
→ SELF-DEFENCE

defenceless /dɪˈfensləs/ adj weak and unable to protect yourself

de'fence ,mechanism noun [C] a reaction in your mind that makes you forget things that are unpleasant to think about

defend /dɪˈfend/ verb

1 protect from attack	3 support sb/sth
2 prevent sth from failing	4 in sport
	5 in law

1 [T] to protect someone or something from attack: Can the military **defend** the city **against** attack?
2 [T] to prevent something from failing, stopping, or being taken away: We will defend their right to free speech.
3 [T] to say things to support someone or something: He **vigorously defended** his party's record on human rights.
4 [I] SPORTS to try to prevent your team's opponents from scoring
5 [I/T] LAW to be the lawyer in a court case who tries to prove that someone is not guilty

> **Word family: defend**
>
> Words in the same family as **defend**
> - **defence** n
> - **defenceless** adj
> - **defensive** adj, n
> - **defensively** adv
> - **defender** n
> - **defendant** n
> - **defensible** adj
> - **indefensible** adj

defendant /dɪˈfendənt/ noun [C] LAW someone who has been accused of a crime and is on trial

defender /dɪˈfendə/ noun [C] **1** SPORTS a player who tries to stop the other team from scoring in a game **2** someone who works to prevent something from being lost or taken away

defense /dɪˈfens/ the American spelling of **defence**

defensible /dɪˈfensəb(ə)l/ adj **1** a defensible belief or idea is one that can be supported well against criticism ≠ INDEFENSIBLE **2** a defensible place can be protected against attack ≠ INDEFENSIBLE

defensive[1] /dɪˈfensɪv/ adj **1** intended or used for protecting a place during an attack **2** if someone is defensive, they are angry or offended because they think that they are being criticized: Don't get so defensive! **3** SPORTS a defensive player tries to stop the other team from scoring points —**defensively** adv

defensive[2] /dɪˈfensɪv/ noun **on the defensive** trying to defend something from attacks or criticism

defer /dɪˈfɜː/ (**defers, deferring, deferred**) verb [T] to arrange for something to happen later than you had planned = POSTPONE
PHRASAL VERB **de'fer to sb** formal to accept someone's opinion or decision, especially because you respect them

deference /ˈdef(ə)rəns/ noun [U] behaviour that shows that you respect someone —**deferential** /ˌdefəˈrenʃ(ə)l/ adj

defiance /dɪˈfaɪəns/ noun [U] refusal to obey a person or rule = DISOBEDIENCE: Goods were exported **in defiance of** the treaty.

defiant /dɪˈfaɪənt/ adj refusing to obey a person or rule = DISOBEDIENT —**defiantly** adv

defibrillator /diːˈfɪbrɪˌleɪtə/ noun [C] HEALTH a piece of equipment for giving the heart an **electric shock**, in order to make it start to beat normally again

deficiency /dɪˈfɪʃ(ə)nsi/ (plural **deficiencies**) noun [C/U] a lack of something, or a fault in someone or something: *diseases caused by mineral deficiencies in the body* ♦ *Deficiency of iron causes anaemia.*

deˈficiency diˌsease noun [C] HEALTH a disease caused by a lack of something that is necessary for good health, growth, or development. For example **scurvy** is a deficiency disease caused by a lack of vitamin C, and **beriberi** is a deficiency disease caused by a lack of vitamin B.

deficient /dɪˈfɪʃ(ə)nt/ adj lacking something, or not good enough: *a diet **deficient in** vitamin C* ♦ *a deficient education system*

deficit /ˈdefəsɪt/ noun [C] ECONOMICS the amount by which something is less than what is needed or expected, especially the amount of money an organization or country has: *the budget deficit*

define /dɪˈfaɪn/ verb [T] **1** to describe clearly and exactly what something is, or what something means: *No one has defined the aims of the project.* ♦ *Matter can be defined as anything that has mass and occupies space.* **2** to show clearly the shape or edges of something **3** to be a feature or quality that shows exactly what someone or something is like: *the high winds that **define** a storm **as** a hurricane* —**definable** adj

defined /dɪˈfaɪnd/ adj how well something such as an image is defined is how clear it is

definite /ˈdef(ə)nət/ adj **1** clearly decided and specific: *We haven't arranged a definite date for our visit yet.* **2** certain: *This book will be a definite best-seller.*

ˌdefinite ˈarticle noun [C] LANGUAGE the word 'the' in English, or a similar type of word in another language

definitely /ˈdef(ə)nətli/ adv **1** without any doubt: *That's definitely not the man I saw running away.* **2** used for emphasizing that you mean 'yes': *'So we'll see you on Sunday at 7 o'clock?' 'Definitely!'*

definition /ˌdefəˈnɪʃ(ə)n/ noun **1** [C] a statement of what a word or expression means: *The definition of 'family' has changed over the years.* **2** [U] the quality of being clear: *Some of the photographs lack definition.*

PHRASE **by definition** as a part of the basic nature of something: *Being a soldier, by definition, involves risks.*

definitive /dɪˈfɪnətɪv/ adj **1** better than all others **2** certain and unlikely to change —**definitively** adv

deflagrating spoon /ˈdefləgreɪtɪŋ ˌspuːn/ noun [C] SCIENCE a piece of equipment like a spoon that is used in laboratories for heating substances over a flame —*picture* → LABORATORY

deflate /diːˈfleɪt/ verb **1** [I/T] if a tyre or **balloon** deflates, or if you deflate it, air comes out of it ≠ INFLATE **2** [T] ECONOMICS to make changes in an economy in order to lower prices **3** [T] to make someone feel less confident or important

deflation /diːˈfleɪʃ(ə)n/ noun [U] ECONOMICS the general reduction of prices or economic activity in an economy ≠ INFLATION

deflationary /diːˈfleɪʃ(ə)n(ə)ri/ adj ECONOMICS causing prices and the level of economic activity to become lower or stop increasing ≠ INFLATIONARY

deflect /dɪˈflekt/ verb **1** [T] to direct criticism, attention, or blame away from yourself and towards someone else **2** [I/T] if something deflects, or if it is deflected, it hits something and starts to move in a different direction **3** [T] to make someone change their plans or stop what they are doing

deflection /dɪˈflekʃ(ə)n/ noun [C/U] **1** the action of making something go in a different direction **2** SCIENCE the amount by which something moves from its original position

defoliant /diːˈfəʊliənt/ noun [C/U] CHEMISTRY a chemical used for making the leaves fall off plants

defoliate /diːˈfəʊlieɪt/ verb [T] to remove the leaves from a plant or tree, for example by using a defoliant —**defoliation** /diːˌfəʊliˈeɪʃ(ə)n/ noun [U]

deforestation /diːˌfɒrɪˈsteɪʃ(ə)n/ noun [U] ENVIRONMENT the process of cutting down and removing trees, especially from large areas of land. Deforestation is bad for the environment, as there are fewer trees to take in carbon dioxide and water. This can lead to the destruction of habitats, **soil erosion**, and an increase in **global warming**: *The demand for more land for building has caused widespread deforestation.* —*picture* → on next page —**deforest** verb [T]

deform /dɪˈfɔːm/ verb [I/T] PHYSICS to change shape, or to make something change its shape

deformation /ˌdiːfɔːˈmeɪʃ(ə)n/ noun **1** [C/U] the process of changing shape in a way that is not good or attractive, or a change in shape that results from this **2** [U] PHYSICS a change in the shape of something caused by physical pressure, different temperatures etc

deformed /dɪˈfɔːmd/ adj something that is deformed is not attractive because it has a different shape from what is usual or natural

deformity /dɪˈfɔːməti/ (plural **deformities**) noun [C/U] a part of someone's body that is not the normal shape

defragment /ˌdiːfrægˈment/ (**defrags**, **defragging**, **defragged**) verb [T] COMPUTING to carry out an operation on a computer that puts all the files together and all the free space together, so that the computer operates faster

defraud /dɪˈfrɔːd/ verb [I/T] to get money from a person or organization in a dishonest way

defrost /diːˈfrɒst/ verb [I/T] **1** if frozen food defrosts, or if someone defrosts it, it becomes warmer until it is no longer frozen **2** if a **freezer** defrosts, or if someone defrosts it, it is switched off so that the ice inside it melts

deft /deft/ adj done quickly and with skill —**deftly** adv

defunct /dɪˈfʌŋkt/ adj no longer existing or working

defuse /diːˈfjuːz/ verb [T] **1** to make a situation more relaxed by making people less angry or worried **2** to stop a bomb from exploding by removing its **fuse**

defy /dɪˈfaɪ/ (**defies**, **defying**, **defied**) verb [T] **1** to refuse to obey someone or something = DISOBEY **2** if something defies description or belief, it is strange and almost impossible to describe or believe **3** to happen in a way that is different from what usually happens, or what people expect

degenerate /dɪˈdʒenəreɪt/ verb [I] to become worse —**degeneration** /dɪˌdʒenəˈreɪʃ(ə)n/ noun [U]

degenerative /dɪˈdʒen(ə)rətɪv/ adj HEALTH a degenerative disease is one that gradually gets worse

degradation /ˌdegrəˈdeɪʃ(ə)n/ noun **1** [U] ENVIRONMENT the process by which the environment or an area of land becomes damaged or polluted **2** [C/U] a situation in which someone is treated very badly and loses the respect of other people

degrade /dɪˈgreɪd/ verb **1** [T] to treat someone very badly so that they lose the respect of other people **2** [I] SCIENCE if a substance degrades, it separates into the different substances that it consists of

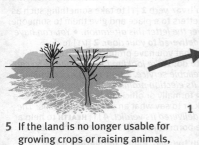

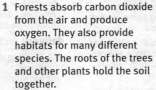

5 If the land is no longer usable for growing crops or raising animals, the human population moves to a different part of the forest.

1 Forests absorb carbon dioxide from the air and produce oxygen. They also provide habitats for many different species. The roots of the trees and other plants hold the soil together.

2 Trees are cut down and the timber is sold. The land is often cleared for agriculture or building.

4 Soil that is no longer held together by tree roots becomes exposed. The action of the rain and wind can lead to soil erosion.

3 This can lead to serious loss of habitats. Overgrazing and intensive farming can also lead to loss of nutrients from the soil.

deforestation

degrading /dɪˈɡreɪdɪŋ/ adj causing people to have less respect for themselves or for someone else

degrease /diːˈɡriːs/ verb [T] **TECHNOLOGY** to remove unwanted grease from an object, using heat or a liquid

degree /dɪˈɡriː/ noun

1 temperature unit	4 university course
2 angle unit	5 amount of sth
3 geographical unit	

1 [C] **SCIENCE** a unit for measuring temperature. Symbol °: *It will probably be a few degrees colder by the weekend.*

2 [C] **MATHS** a unit for measuring angles. Symbol °: *The two lines meet at a 90-degree angle.*

3 [C] **GEOGRAPHY** a unit for measuring **latitude** and longitude. Symbol °

4 [C] **EDUCATION** a course of study at a university, or the qualification that someone gets after finishing the course: *a biology degree* ♦ *a master's degree in English literature* ♦ *She's doing a degree at the University of Hong Kong.*

5 [C/U] an amount of something such as a feeling or a quality: *The job requires a high degree of skill.* ♦ *What you say is true to some degree* (=partly true).

dehydrate /ˌdiːhaɪˈdreɪt/ verb **1** [I] **HEALTH** if someone dehydrates, they lose so much water from their body that they feel weak or ill **2** [T] **CHEMISTRY** to remove the water from something such as food **3** [I] **CHEMISTRY** if a chemical compound dehydrates, it loses hydrogen and oxygen atoms in the ratio 2:1

dehydrated /ˌdiːhaɪˈdreɪtɪd/ adj **1 HEALTH** someone who is dehydrated feels weak or ill because they have lost a lot of water from their body **2 CHEMISTRY** dehydrated food has been preserved by having its water removed

dehydration /ˌdiːhaɪˈdreɪʃ(ə)n/ noun [U] **1 CHEMISTRY** the process of removing moisture from food as a way of preserving it **2 CHEMISTRY** the process by which a chemical compound loses

hydrogen and oxygen atoms in the ratio 2:1 **3 HEALTH** a dangerous lack of water in the body that results from not drinking enough or from extreme loss through sweating, vomiting, or diarrhoea

deictic /ˈdaɪktɪk/ adj **LANGUAGE** relating to words or phrases whose meaning depends on the situation in which they are used, for example 'you', 'there', or 'last month'

deign /deɪn/ verb [I] *showing disapproval* to do something that is useful or helpful, but in a way that shows that you do not think you should have to do it

deindustrialize /ˌdiːɪnˈdʌstriəˌlaɪz/ verb [I/T] **ECONOMICS** to take away or lose industries, especially those that involve producing things such as steel, coal, cars, and ships, from a country or region —**deindustrialization** /ˌdiːɪnˌdʌstriəlaɪˈzeɪʃ(ə)n/ noun [U]

deity /ˈdeɪəti, ˈdiːəti/ (plural **deities**) noun [C] a god

deixis /ˈdaɪksɪs/ noun [U] **LANGUAGE** the use of words or phrases such as 'you', 'there', or 'last month' whose meaning depends on the situation in which they are used

dejected /dɪˈdʒektɪd/ adj someone who is dejected has lost all of their hope or enthusiasm —**dejection** /dɪˈdʒekʃ(ə)n/ noun [U]

de jure[1] /deɪ ˈdʒʊəreɪ/ adv *very formal* legally

de jure[2] /deɪ ˈdʒʊəreɪ/ adj *very formal* legally accepted

delay[1] /dɪˈleɪ/ noun **1** [C/U] a situation in which something happens later or more slowly than was expected: *After a long delay, the plane finally took off.* ♦ *Who is responsible for the delay in reaching an agreement?* **2** [U] failure to do something quickly: *I hope that discussions will take place without delay.*

delay[2] /dɪˈleɪ/ verb **1** [I/T] to do something later than is planned or expected: *They delayed the decision for as long as possible.* **2** [T] to make someone or something late, or to slow them down: *His plane was delayed for five hours.*

delegate[1] /ˈdeləgət/ noun [C] someone who is chosen to represent a group of other people at a meeting

delegate[2] /ˈdeləgeɪt/ verb **1** [I/T] to give part of your work or responsibilities to someone else **2** [T] to choose someone to do a job for you or to represent you

delegation /ˌdeləˈgeɪʃ(ə)n/ noun **1** [C] a group of people who represent a country, government, or organization **2** [U] the process of giving some of your work or responsibilities to someone else

delete /dɪˈliːt/ verb [T] to remove something that has been written, or to remove information that has been stored in a computer —**deletion** /dɪˈliːʃ(ə)n/ noun [C/U]

deˈlete ˌkey noun [C] COMPUTING a computer key that removes characters. This key is sometimes simply referred to as **del**.

deliberate[1] /dɪˈlɪb(ə)rət/ adj **1** intended, and not done by chance or by accident = INTENTIONAL ≠ ACCIDENTAL: *This was a deliberate attack on unarmed civilians.* **2** slow and careful: *He walked with slow deliberate steps.*

deliberate[2] /dɪˈlɪbəreɪt/ verb [I/T] to think about or discuss something very carefully

deliberately /dɪˈlɪb(ə)rətli/ adv **1** with a definite intention, and not by chance or by accident: *Police believe the fire was started deliberately.* **2** in a slow careful way: *He spoke deliberately.*

delicacy /ˈdelɪkəsi/ (plural **delicacies**) noun **1** [C] a rare or expensive type of food **2** [U] a sensitive and careful way of doing something

delicate /ˈdelɪkət/ adj **1** easily damaged, broken, or hurt: *Delicate skin must be protected from the sun.* ♦ *delicate fabrics* **2** small and attractive: *delicate pink flowers* **3** needing care and skill: *The negotiations are at a very delicate stage.* **4** a delicate taste, smell, or colour is pleasant and not too strong —**delicately** adv

delicatessen /ˌdelɪkəˈtes(ə)n/ noun [C] a shop that sells food such as cooked meat and cheese

delicious /dɪˈlɪʃəs/ adj with a very pleasant taste or smell: *This sauce is delicious with fish or vegetables.* —**deliciously** adv: *a deliciously creamy dessert*

delight[1] /dɪˈlaɪt/ noun **1** [U] a feeling of great happiness: *To my great delight, she said yes.* **2** [C] something that gives you pleasure

delight[2] /dɪˈlaɪt/ verb [T] to give someone a lot of enjoyment or pleasure

PHRASAL VERB **deˈlight ˌin doing sth** to get a lot of pleasure from something

delighted /dɪˈlaɪtɪd/ adj **1** very happy about something: *They're delighted with their new grandson.* ♦ *I'm delighted that you got the job.* ♦ *I was delighted to see my old friends again.* **2** used for saying politely that you are pleased about something: *'Will you come?' 'I'd be delighted.'*

delightful /dɪˈlaɪtf(ə)l/ adj very nice —**delightfully** adv

delimit /diːˈlɪmɪt/ verb [T] formal to set the limits of something

delinquent /dɪˈlɪŋkwənt/ noun [C] a young person whose behaviour is criminal or very bad

delirious /dɪˈlɪriəs/ adj **1** HEALTH someone who is delirious is talking in a confused way because they are ill **2** extremely happy = ECSTATIC —**deliriously** adv

deliver /dɪˈlɪvə/ verb **1** [T] to take something such as goods or letters to a place and give them to someone: *I can deliver the letter this afternoon.* ♦ *You can have groceries delivered to your door.* **2** [I/T] to do something that you have promised to do or are expected to do: *We're looking for a supplier who can deliver a reliable service.* ♦ *How will the government deliver on its election promises?* **3** [T] formal to say something formally or officially, for example to give a formal talk or to say what an official decision is: *The court has delivered its verdict.* **4** [T] HEALTH to help a baby to be born: *Paramedics delivered the baby.*

delivery /dɪˈlɪv(ə)ri/ (plural **deliveries**) noun

1 bringing goods to a place	4 in computing
2 providing a service	5 way sb speaks in public
3 process of giving birth	6 style of throw or hit

1 [C/U] the process of bringing goods or letters to a place: *Please allow ten days for delivery.* ♦ *When do you make deliveries?*
2 [U] the process of providing a service: *We need to improve delivery of health care.*
3 [C/U] HEALTH the process of giving birth to a baby
4 [U] COMPUTING the process of providing information through a computer
5 [singular] the way in which someone speaks in public: *You need to work on your delivery.*
6 [singular] SPORTS the way that someone throws a ball or makes a hit in a sport

delta /ˈdeltə/ noun [C] GEOGRAPHY an area where a river divides into smaller rivers that flow into the sea. Deltas are usually very fertile areas where crops grow well: *the Nile delta* —picture → RIVER

delude /dɪˈluːd/ verb [T] to make someone believe something that is not true —**deluded** adj

deluge /ˈdeljuːdʒ/ noun [singular] **1** a lot of things all happening or arriving at the same time = FLOOD **2** a very heavy fall of rain

delusion /dɪˈluːʒ(ə)n/ noun **1** [C/U] a belief that is not true **2** [U] HEALTH a mental condition in which someone believes things that are not true

deluxe /dəˈlʌks/ adj better in quality and more expensive than other things of the same type = LUXURY

demagnifier /diːˈmægnɪfaɪə/ noun [C] PHYSICS something that makes an image appear smaller

demagogue /ˈdeməgɒg/ noun [C] POLITICS a political leader who tries to influence people by making emotional speeches

demand[1] /dɪˈmɑːnd/ noun **1** [C] a firm statement that you want something: *They made demands that our government could never accept.* **2** demands [plural] the things or qualities that are needed in a particular situation: *He's finding the demands of his new job quite tough.* ♦ *She has a lot of demands on her time.* **3** [U] ECONOMICS the amount of a product or service that people want, or the fact that they want it: *18,400 new houses will be needed to cope with the demand.* ♦ *Demand for cheap electricity is increasing.*

PHRASES **be in demand** to be wanted by a lot of people
on demand whenever people want it

demand[2] /dɪˈmɑːnd/ verb [T] **1** to say firmly that you want something: *The demonstrators demanded the release of all prisoners.* ♦ *She demanded to know what was happening.* ♦ *The panel demanded that the report be made public.* **2** to expect something, or to make something necessary: *I demand absolute loyalty from my staff.* ♦ *a situation that demands careful handling*

demanding /dɪˈmɑːndɪŋ/ adj needing a lot of attention, time, or energy: *a demanding job*

demand paging /dɪˈmɑːnd ˌpeɪdʒɪŋ/ noun [U] COMPUTING a piece of software that makes extra memory available when the computer needs to run more programs than normal

deˈmand-ˌside ecoˌnomics noun [U] ECONOMICS economic policies that are intended to increase demand for goods and services and **consumption** (=buying and using them), in order to improve the economy

demarcate /ˈdiːmɑːkeɪt/ verb [T] *formal* to decide the limits of something, especially the borders of an area

demarcation /ˌdiːmɑːˈkeɪʃ(ə)n/ noun [U] *formal* the process of establishing borders or limits between areas, groups, or things

demeaning /dɪˈmiːnɪŋ/ adj making people have less respect for someone = DEGRADING

demeanour /dɪˈmiːnə/ noun [U] *formal* the way that someone looks and behaves

dementia /dɪˈmenʃə/ noun [C/U] HEALTH a serious illness affecting the brain and memory

demersal /dɪˈmɜːs(ə)l/ adj GEOGRAPHY existing at the bottom of the sea

democracy /dɪˈmɒkrəsi/ (plural **democracies**) noun **1** [U] POLITICS a system of government in which people choose their political representatives in elections **2** [C] POLITICS a country that has democracy **3** [U] a way of running an organization in which everyone can share in making decisions

democrat /ˈdeməkræt/ noun [C] someone who supports democratic principles and democratic forms of government

democratic /ˌdeməˈkrætɪk/ adj **1** POLITICS involving elections in which people vote for their political representatives: *the democratic system* **2** based on the principle that all people should share in making decisions ≠ UNDEMOCRATIC: *a democratic organization* —**democratically** /ˌdeməˈkrætɪkli/ adv

the Demoˈcratic ˌParty POLITICS one of the two main political parties in the US

demodulate /diːˈmɒdjʊleɪt/ verb [T] PHYSICS to remove a signal that is carrying information from a **carrier wave** (=high-frequency radio wave) —**demodulation** /diːˌmɒdjʊˈleɪʃ(ə)n/ noun [U]

demographic /ˌdeməˈɡræfɪk/ adj SOCIAL STUDIES relating to populations

demographics /ˌdeməˈɡræfɪks/ noun [plural] SOCIAL STUDIES the particular features of a population

demography /dɪˈmɒɡrəfi/ noun [U] SOCIAL STUDIES the study of populations

demolish /dɪˈmɒlɪʃ/ verb [T] **1** to destroy a building **2** to completely defeat someone, or to destroy their hopes or their confidence

demolition /ˌdeməˈlɪʃ(ə)n/ noun [C/U] the deliberate destruction of a building

demon /ˈdiːmən/ noun [C] an evil spirit

demonstrate /ˈdemənstreɪt/ verb **1** [T] to show someone how to do something or how something works: *We will demonstrate various techniques.* **2** [T] to show that something is true or exists: *The study demonstrates that children are affected by advertising.* ♦ *an experiment that demonstrates Newton's second law of motion* **3** [I] to protest about something in a public place: *the right to demonstrate peacefully* ♦ *Students were demonstrating against the war.*

demonstration /ˌdemənˈstreɪʃ(ə)n/ noun **1** [C] an occasion when people protest about something in public: *Angry students held demonstrations.* **2** [C/U] an occasion when someone shows how something works or how something is done: *cookery demonstrations* **3** [C] an event or action that proves a fact: *This is a demonstration of the president's popularity.*

demonstrative /dɪˈmɒnstrətɪv/ adj **1** showing love in the way that you behave towards someone **2** LANGUAGE demonstrative adjectives and pronouns are the words 'this', 'that', 'these', and 'those' in English

demonstrator /ˈdemənstreɪtə/ noun [C] **1** someone who takes part in a public protest **2** someone whose job is to show how something works or how something is done

demoralized /dɪˈmɒrəlaɪzd/ adj feeling unhappy and without any confidence

demoralizing /dɪˈmɒrəlaɪzɪŋ/ adj causing unhappiness and loss of confidence

demote /diːˈməʊt/ verb [T] to give someone or something lower status or a less important position than they had before —**demotion** /diːˈməʊʃ(ə)n/ noun [C/U]

demotivate /diːˈməʊtɪveɪt/ verb [T] to make someone lose their enthusiasm and interest —**demotivating** adj

den /den/ noun [C] **1** a place where a wild animal such as a lion lives **2** a secret place where people meet to do illegal things

denationalize /diːˈnæʃ(ə)nəlaɪz/ verb [T] ECONOMICS to sell a business or industry that was owned and managed by the government, so that it becomes a private business —**denationalization** /diːˌnæʃ(ə)nəlaɪˈzeɪʃ(ə)n/ noun

denature /diːˈneɪtʃə/ verb [T] BIOLOGY to break down the structure of a protein so that it can no longer perform its biological function —**denaturant** /diːˈneɪtʃərənt/ noun [C], **denaturation** /diːˌneɪtʃəˈreɪʃ(ə)n/ noun [U]

dendrite /ˈdendraɪt/ noun [C] ANATOMY a very short dendron. Dendrites carry messages to the **cell body** in a neuron. —*picture* → NEURON

dendron /ˈdendrɒn/ noun [C] ANATOMY an end of a nerve cell that links it to other nerve cells, or to a sense organ, muscle, or gland —*picture* → NEURON

dengue fever /ˈdeŋɡi ˌfiːvə/ noun [U] HEALTH a very serious illness that you get if a mosquito infected with a particular virus bites you. Dengue fever causes fever, headaches, and pain in the joints.

denial /dɪˈnaɪəl/ noun **1** [C/U] a statement that something is not true **2** [U] the refusal to let someone have or do something: *the denial of health care to poor patients* **3** [U] the refusal to accept the unpleasant truth about something

denigrate /ˈdenɪɡreɪt/ verb [T] to criticize something in a way that shows that you think it has no value at all

denim /ˈdenɪm/ noun [U] thick cotton cloth that is usually blue and is used for making **jeans** and other clothes

denitrification /diːˌnaɪtrɪfɪˈkeɪʃ(ə)n/ noun [U] BIOLOGY the process in which bacteria break down **nitrates** in the soil and produce nitrogen —**denitrify** verb [T]

denitrifying bacteria /dɪˈnaɪtrɪfaɪɪŋ bækˌtɪəriə/ noun [plural] BIOLOGY bacteria in soil that break down **nitrates** in the soil and produce some of the nitrogen that exists in the air. They undo the useful work done by **nitrifying bacteria**.

denomination /dɪˌnɒmɪˈneɪʃ(ə)n/ noun [C]
1 RELIGION a religious group within one of the main religions **2** the value of a particular coin or banknote

denominator /dɪˈnɒmɪˌneɪtə/ noun [C] MATHS the number that is below the line in a fraction. The number above the line is the **numerator**. In ¾, 4 is the denominator and 3 is the numerator.

denotation /ˌdiːnəʊˈteɪʃ(ə)n/ noun [C/U] LANGUAGE the actual meaning of a word, rather than the feelings or ideas connected with the word → CONNOTATION

denotative /ˈdiːnəʊteɪtɪv/ adj relating to the actual meaning of a word, rather than to the feelings or ideas that are connected with it → CONNOTATIVE

denote /dɪˈnəʊt/ verb [T] formal **1** to be a feature that shows you what something is = INDICATE **2** to mean something = REPRESENT

denouement /deɪˈnuːmɒ̃/ noun [C] formal the end of a book, play, or series of events, when everything is explained

denounce /dɪˈnaʊns/ verb [T] to criticize someone or something severely in public

dense /dens/ adj **1** consisting of a lot of things, people, trees etc that are all very close together: *a dense forest* **2** thick and difficult to see through: *dense smoke* **3** a dense substance is very heavy in relation to its size —**densely** adv

density /ˈdensəti/ noun [U] **1** PHYSICS a measurement of how much space a particular amount of a substance takes up. It is found by dividing its mass by its volume: *The **density of** iron is greater than the density of aluminium.* **2** the number of people or things in a particular area

dent¹ /dent/ noun [C] a place where a surface has been pushed or knocked inwards

dent² /dent/ verb [T] to make a dent in a surface

dental /ˈdent(ə)l/ adj relating to teeth: *dental health*

dental hygienist /ˌdent(ə)l ˈhaɪdʒiːnɪst/ noun [C] someone whose job is to clean people's teeth and give them advice on how to care for their teeth

'dental ˌsurgeon noun [C] formal a **dentist**

dentine /ˈdentiːn/ noun [U] ANATOMY the hard substance, under the layer of **enamel**, that teeth are made of —*picture* → TOOTH

dentist /ˈdentɪst/ noun [C] someone whose job is to examine and treat people's teeth

dentistry /ˈdentɪstri/ noun [U] the job of a dentist, or the medical study of the teeth and mouth

dentition /denˈtɪʃ(ə)n/ noun [U] BIOLOGY the type, number, and arrangement of a set of teeth

dentures /ˈdentʃəz/ noun [plural] artificial teeth

denunciation /dɪˌnʌnsiˈeɪʃ(ə)n/ noun [C/U] strong public criticism of someone or something

deny /dɪˈnaɪ/ (**denies, denying, denied**) verb [T] **1** to say that something is not true: *A spokesman denied that the company had acted irresponsibly.* ♦ *He still denies murdering his wife.* **2** to not allow someone to do or have something: *Doctors were accused of denying treatment to older patients.* **3** to refuse to admit that you have a particular feeling, illness, or problem: *I had been denying this anger for years.*

deodorant /diˈəʊd(ə)rənt/ noun [C/U] a substance that is put on the skin to prevent the body from having an unpleasant smell

deodorize /diˈəʊdəˌraɪz/ verb [T] formal to make something smell better by removing odours from it

deoxidizer /diˈɒksɪdaɪzə/ verb [T] TECHNOLOGY a chemical used to remove oxygen from metal during **manufacture**

deoxygenate /diːˈɒksɪdʒəneɪt/ noun [T] CHEMISTRY, BIOLOGY to remove oxygen from a substance —**deoxygenation** /diːˌɒksɪdʒəˈneɪʃ(ə)n/ noun [U]

deoxyribonucleic acid /diːˌɒksɪraɪbəʊnjuːˌkleɪk ˈæsɪd/ noun [U] BIOLOGY see DNA

depart /dɪˈpɑːt/ verb [I] formal to leave a place and start a journey

department /dɪˈpɑːtmənt/ noun [C] **1** a section in a government, organization, or business that deals with a particular type of work: *the Department of Health* ♦ *the sales department* **2** an area in a large shop that sells a particular type of goods: *the menswear department* —**departmental** /ˌdiːpɑːtˈment(ə)l/ adj

de'partment ˌstore noun [C] BUSINESS a large shop that is divided into separate sections, with each section selling different goods

departure /dɪˈpɑːtʃə/ noun [C/U] **1** an act of leaving a place, job, or organization **2** a plane, train, ship etc that leaves to start a journey **3** a way of doing something that is different from the usual or traditional way

de'parture ˌdate noun [C] TOURISM the day on which a traveller leaves

de'parture ˌlounge noun [C] TOURISM a large room in an airport where people sit and wait before going onto a plane

departures /dɪˈpɑːtʃəz/ noun [U] TOURISM the part of an airport that deals with passengers who are leaving

depend /dɪˈpend/ verb **it/that depends** spoken used for saying that you cannot give a definite answer until certain details of the situation are described: *'How much will I have to pay for a car?' 'It depends what sort of car you want.'*
PHRASAL VERBS **de'pend on sb** if you can depend on someone to do something, you can trust them to do it: *I knew I could depend on you.*
de'pend on sb/sth to need someone or something in order to continue to exist or to be successful: *The project's success depends on the support of everyone concerned.*
de'pend on sth if one thing depends on another, it is changed or affected by the other thing: *Their future depends on how well they do in these exams.*

dependable /dɪˈpendəb(ə)l/ adj always behaving or working in the way that is expected = RELIABLE: *a dependable friend*

dependant /dɪˈpendənt/ noun [C] a child or other relative that someone is legally responsible for supporting

dependence /dɪˈpendəns/ noun [U] **1** a situation in which someone needs someone or something else in order to live or succeed = RELIANCE: *the industry's dependence on coal* **2** the fact of being **addicted** to a drug or to alcohol

dependency /dɪˈpendənsi/ noun **1** [U] a situation in which someone needs someone or something in order to live or succeed **2** [C] POLITICS a country that is controlled by another country = PROTECTORATE **3** [U] the fact that someone is **addicted** to a drug or alcohol

dependent /dɪˈpendənt/ adj **1** if you are dependent on someone or something, you need them in order to live or succeed: *a married couple with dependent* children ♦ *They hate being **dependent on** their parents.* **2** if one thing is dependent on another, it is affected by the other thing, and changes if the other thing changes: *Your pay is **dependent on** your work experience.*

de,pendent 'clause noun [C] LANGUAGE a clause in a sentence that gives more information about the **main clause** but cannot exist without it

de,pendent 'variable noun [C] MATHS a part of a mathematical expression that changes its value according to the value of the other elements that are present → INDEPENDENT VARIABLE —*picture* → GRAPH

depict /dɪˈpɪkt/ verb [T] to describe someone or something using words or pictures

depleted /dɪˈpliːtɪd/ adj with a smaller amount of something or a smaller number of things than people want or need

depletion /dɪˈpliːʃ(ə)n/ noun [U] a reduction in the amount of something or in the number of things

deplorable /dɪˈplɔːrəb(ə)l/ adj *formal* extremely bad and shocking —**deplorably** adv

deplore /dɪˈplɔː/ verb [T] *formal* to think that something is bad and immoral

deploy /dɪˈplɔɪ/ verb [T] if a government or army deploys soldiers or weapons, it uses them —**deployment** noun [U]

depopulate /diːˈpɒpjʊleɪt/ verb [T] SOCIAL STUDIES to cause an area to have far fewer people living in it than before

depopulation /ˌdiːpɒpjʊˈleɪʃ(ə)n/ noun [U] SOCIAL STUDIES a situation in which a lot of people leave a place in order to live somewhere else, leaving far fewer people in the original place: *the depopulation of the countryside*

deport /dɪˈpɔːt/ verb [T] to send someone back to the country that they came from —**deportation** /ˌdiːpɔːˈteɪʃ(ə)n/ noun [C/U]

deportee /ˌdiːpɔːˈtiː/ noun [C] *formal* someone who is sent away from a country that is not their own country, usually because they do not have a legal right to be there

depose /dɪˈpəʊz/ verb **1** [T] to force someone out of a position of power **2** [I/T] LAW to give information about something in a court of law

deposit¹ /dɪˈpɒzɪt/ noun [C] **1** a first payment that someone makes when they agree to buy something expensive such as a car or house. The rest of the money that is paid later is called the **balance**: *She paid a £500 deposit, and agreed to pay the balance within six months.* ♦ *We've **put down a deposit on** (=paid a deposit on) a new house.* **2** an amount of money that someone pays when they rent something. They get the money back if the thing is not damaged when they return it. **3** a payment that you make into a bank account **4** GEOLOGY a layer of something that is formed by natural or chemical processes: *rich mineral deposits*

deposit² /dɪˈpɒzɪt/ verb [T] **1** to pay money into a bank account **2** *formal* to put something somewhere **3** GEOLOGY if a substance is deposited in the soil or in rock, it gradually gathers there and forms a layer

deposition /ˌdepəˈzɪʃ(ə)n/ noun **1** [U] GEOLOGY a process in which layers of a substance form gradually over a period of time **2** [C] LAW a formal written statement by a **witness** that is read out in a court because the witness cannot be present at the court

depot /ˈdepəʊ/ noun [C] **1** a large building where things are stored until they are needed **2** a place where buses or trains are kept when they are not being used

depreciate /dɪˈpriːʃieɪt/ verb [I] to become less valuable —**depreciation** /dɪˌpriːʃiˈeɪʃ(ə)n/ noun [U]

depress /dɪˈpres/ verb [T] **1** to make someone feel unhappy and without any enthusiasm or hope: *It depresses me to see all that money being wasted.* **2** *formal* to make something such as a price or value go down

depressant /dɪˈpres(ə)nt/ noun [C] HEALTH a drug or substance that makes you feel relaxed and makes your body work and react more slowly

depressed /dɪˈprest/ adj **1** very unhappy and without any feelings of hope or enthusiasm **2** ECONOMICS a depressed area, industry, or economy is not successful

depressing /dɪˈpresɪŋ/ adj making someone feel very unhappy and without any feelings of hope or enthusiasm —**depressingly** adv

depression /dɪˈpreʃ(ə)n/ noun **1** [U] HEALTH a feeling of great sadness, **despair**, or anxiety that prevents the person suffering from it from enjoying life, and often includes symptoms such as loss of sleep. When depression seems to have no cause, or when it lasts for an unusually long time, it is treated as a **psychiatric** condition. **2** [C/U] ECONOMICS a period of time when there is a lot of unemployment and poverty because there is very little economic activity: *the world depression of the 1930s* **3** [C] GEOGRAPHY an area of low air pressure that usually brings colder weather and rain **4** [C] SCIENCE an area on a surface that is lower than the parts around it

deprivation /ˌdeprɪˈveɪʃ(ə)n/ noun [U] a situation in which people are very poor and do not have the basic things that they need

deprive /dɪˈpraɪv/ verb [T] to prevent someone from having something that they need or want: *people who are **deprived of** their freedom*

deprived /dɪˈpraɪvd/ adj someone who is deprived does not have enough of the basic things that they need, for example food or money

depth /depθ/ noun **1** [C/U] a distance relating to how deep something is, for example the sea, a river, or a hole: *What's **the depth of** the water here?* **2** [U] the distance from the front to the back of something: **the depth of** the shelf **3** [C/U] interesting qualities or ideas that are not obvious at first: *His first album had more depth than this one.* **4** [C/U] a high level of something such as a feeling or the amount of information that is given: *The newspaper is proud of **the depth of** its coverage.*

PHRASES **the depths of sth 1** a place that is very far inside an area: *the depths of the forest* **2** the worst part of an unpleasant time, feeling, or situation: *She was **in the depths of** despair.*
in depth in a very detailed way and giving a lot of information: *This subject will be covered in depth next term.*
out of your depth 1 not able to keep your head above water when your feet are touching the bottom of a swimming pool, the sea etc **2** in a situation that you cannot deal with because it is too difficult or dangerous

deputation /ˌdepjʊˈteɪʃ(ə)n/ noun [C] *formal* a group of people who are sent somewhere to represent a larger group at a meeting or discussion = DELEGATION

deputize /ˈdepjʊtaɪz/ verb [I] to temporarily do the work of someone more senior than you

deputy /ˈdepjʊti/ (plural **deputies**) noun [C] someone whose job is the second most important in a department or organization. A deputy does the job of the most important person in some situations.

derail /dɪˈreɪl/ verb [I/T] if a train derails, or if something derails it, it comes off its tracks —**derailment** noun [C/U]

deranged /dɪˈreɪndʒd/ adj behaving in an uncontrolled or dangerous way because of a **psychiatric** condition

deregulate /diːˈregjʊleɪt/ verb [T] to take away the rules that control something such as an industry

derelict /ˈderəlɪkt/ adj a derelict building or area is empty, not used, and in bad condition

de rigueur /də rɪˈgɜː/ adj formal necessary in order to be fashionable or to be accepted by other people in a group

derision /dɪˈrɪʒ(ə)n/ noun [U] the attitude that someone or something is stupid or useless

derisive /dɪˈraɪsɪv/ adj showing that you think that someone or something is stupid or useless

derisory /dɪˈraɪsəri/ adj if money that you are offered or given is derisory, you feel insulted because it is not very much

derivation /ˌderɪˈveɪʃ(ə)n/ noun [C/U] the original form from which something such as a word developed

derivative¹ /dɪˈrɪvətɪv/ noun [C] **LANGUAGE** a word that is formed from another word, for example an adverb that is formed from an adjective by adding '-ly'

derivative² /dɪˈrɪvətɪv/ adj something that is derivative is not very interesting or impressive because it is based on something else instead of being original

derive /dɪˈraɪv/ verb [T] **1** to get something from something else **2 CHEMISTRY** to get a chemical substance from another substance

dermatitis /ˌdɜːməˈtaɪtɪs/ noun [U] **HEALTH** a medical condition in which parts of the skin become red and painful, or covered in spots

dermatologist /ˌdɜːməˈtɒlədʒɪst/ noun [C] **HEALTH** a doctor who treats diseases of the skin — **dermatology** noun [U]

dermis /ˈdɜːmɪs/ noun [singular] **ANATOMY** the thick sensitive layer of skin that is just below the **epidermis**. It contains blood, the ends of the nerves, **blood vessels**, and **sweat glands**. —picture → SKIN

derogate /ˈderəgeɪt/ verb [T] **LAW** to state officially that a part of a law no longer has legal authority and has ended

derogatory /dɪˈrɒgət(ə)ri/ adj intended to criticize or insult someone

derrick /ˈderɪk/ noun [C] **1** a type of **crane** used for lifting things onto and off ships **2** a tall tower built over an **oil well** that is used for raising and lowering the **drill** (=the tool that makes the hole in the ground)

desalination /ˌdiːsælɪˈneɪʃ(ə)n/ noun [U] the process of removing salt from sea water so that the water can be used. A **desalination plant** is a place where this process takes place.

descant /ˈdeskænt/ noun [C/U] **MUSIC** a second tune that is higher than the main tune in a piece of music

descend /dɪˈsend/ verb **1** [I/T] formal to go down something such as a mountain, a slope, or stairs ≠ ASCEND **2** [I] to move closer to the ground from the air or from a high point **3 be descended from** to be related to a person or animal that lived long ago

descendant /dɪˈsendənt/ noun [C] a relative of a person who lived in the past

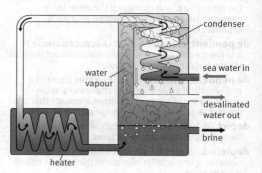

condenser
water vapour
sea water in
desalinated water out
brine
heater

desalination

descent /dɪˈsent/ noun **1** [C/U] the act of moving down to a lower place or position ≠ ASCENT: *The plane began its descent.* **2** [U] the origin of your parents or other older members of your family: *They're all of Irish descent.* **3** [singular] the process of gradually changing to a worse condition

describe /dɪˈskraɪb/ verb [T] to give details about someone or something in order to explain to another person what they are like: *It's hard to describe my feelings.* ♦ *The attacker is described as tall, with dark hair.* ♦ *Could you describe her to me?*

> **Word family: describe**
>
> *Words in the same family as describe*
> - **description** n
> - **descriptive** adj
> - **nondescript** adj
> - **indescribable** adj
> - **indescribably** adv

description /dɪˈskrɪpʃ(ə)n/ noun [C] a statement about what someone or something is like: *a brief description of the area* ♦ *Barry was unable to give the police a description of his attacker.*

descriptive /dɪˈskrɪptɪv/ adj describing something: *descriptive writing*

de,scriptive ge'ometry noun [U] **MATHS, PHYSICS** the part of geometry that deals with how three-dimensional objects are shown as **two-dimensional** (=flat) shapes

descriptor /dɪˈskrɪptə/ noun [C] **LANGUAGE** a word or expression that is used to describe something

desecrate /ˈdesɪkreɪt/ verb [T] to deliberately spoil something that is special or holy —**desecration** /ˌdesɪˈkreɪʃ(ə)n/ noun [U]

desegregation /ˌdiːsegrɪˈgeɪʃ(ə)n/ noun [U] **SOCIAL STUDIES** the process of ending a system in which people of different races are made to live or work separately —**desegregate** /diːˈsegrɪgeɪt/ verb [T]

desert¹ /ˈdezət/ noun [C/U] **GEOGRAPHY** a large area of dry land that usually gets very little rain and has no permanent rivers, lakes etc. Very few plants or animals grow or live there. Most deserts are in hot regions, but there are some in very cold regions: *The Sahara Desert is the biggest desert in the world.* ♦ *Siberia has cold, frozen deserts.* —picture → ECOSYSTEM

desert² /dɪˈzɜːt/ verb **1** [T] to leave a person or place and not come back **2** [I] if soldiers desert, they leave the army without permission **3** [T] if a feeling, quality, or skill deserts someone, they suddenly no longer have it —**desertion** /dɪˈzɜːʃ(ə)n/ noun [C/U]

deserted /dɪˈzɜːtɪd/ adj a deserted place has no people in it

deserter /dɪˈzɜːtə/ noun [C] someone who leaves the armed forces without permission

desertification /dɪˌzɜːtɪfɪˈkeɪʃ(ə)n/ noun [U] ENVIRONMENT the process of land becoming so dry that it cannot be used for farming. This is often the result of human activities such as **overgrazing** and **deforestation**.

desert island /ˌdezət ˈaɪlənd/ noun [C] a small tropical island with no people living on it

deserve /dɪˈzɜːv/ verb [T] **1** if you deserve something, it is right that you get it, because of the way that you are or the way that you have behaved: *After five hours on your feet you deserve a break.* ♦ *I think I deserve to be well paid.* **2** to be worth spending time on or thinking about: *an issue that deserves careful thought*

deservedly /dɪˈzɜːvɪdli/ adv formal used for saying that what happens is right

deserving /dɪˈzɜːvɪŋ/ adj worth supporting or helping

desiccate /ˈdesɪkeɪt/ verb [T] CHEMISTRY, BIOLOGY to remove all the water from something —**desiccation** /ˌdesɪˈkeɪʃ(ə)n/ noun [U]

desiccated /ˈdesɪˌkeɪtɪd/ adj CHEMISTRY, BIOLOGY desiccated food has had all the water taken out of it in order to preserve it

design¹ /dɪˈzaɪn/ noun **1** [C/U] the way that something is made so that it works and looks a certain way, or a drawing that shows what it will look like: *The car has a new design.* ♦ *designs for the new bridge* **2** [U] the process of deciding how something will be made, how it will work, and what it will look like, or the study of this process: *software design* ♦ *I studied design at college.* **3** [C] a pattern that decorates something: *simple geometric designs*

design² /dɪˈzaɪn/ verb [T] to decide how something will be made, how it will work, or what it will look like, and often to make drawings of it: *The bride wore a dress that she designed herself.* ♦ *She has a job designing websites.*

designate /ˈdezɪgneɪt/ verb [T] to formally choose someone or something for a particular purpose —**designation** /ˌdezɪgˈneɪʃ(ə)n/ noun [C/U]

designer /dɪˈzaɪnə/ noun [C] someone whose job is to decide how to make things, how they will work, and what they will look like: *a fashion designer*

deˈsign ˌoffice noun [C] an office where designers and **draughtsmen** work

desirable /dɪˈzaɪrəb(ə)l/ adj **1** something that is desirable has qualities that make people want it **2** sexually attractive

desire¹ /dɪˈzaɪə/ noun **1** [C/U] a strong feeling of wanting to have or do something: *a desire for peace* ♦ *his desire to travel* **2** [U] literary the strong feeling of wanting to have sex with someone

desire² /dɪˈzaɪə/ verb [T] **1** formal to want something **2** literary to want someone as a sexual partner

desired /dɪˈzaɪəd/ adj a desired aim or effect is one that you want to have or achieve

desk /desk/ noun **1** [C] a table that you sit at to write or work, often with drawers in it **2** [singular] a place that provides information or a service, for example in a hotel: *the information desk* **3** [singular] a particular department of an organization such as a television company or a newspaper: *the sports desk*

ˈdesk ˌlamp noun [C] a lamp that is used at a desk, especially in order to light documents, books etc that you are using —*picture* → WORKSTATION

ˈdesk ˌtidy noun [C] a container that you keep on top of a desk and use for holding pens and other small pieces of office equipment —*picture* → WORKSTATION

desktop /ˈdeskˌtɒp/ noun [C] COMPUTING the main screen on a computer that shows the programs that are available

desolate /ˈdesələt/ adj **1** a desolate place is completely empty with no pleasant features **2** feeling very sad and alone —**desolation** /ˌdesəˈleɪʃ(ə)n/ noun [U]

despair¹ /dɪˈspeə/ noun [U] the feeling that a situation is so bad that nothing can change it —**despairing** adj

despair² /dɪˈspeə/ verb [I] to feel that a situation is so bad that nothing can change it

despatch /dɪˈspætʃ/ another spelling of **dispatch**

desperate /ˈdesp(ə)rət/ adj **1** someone who is desperate is very upset and willing to do anything because they are in a bad situation: *The missing man's family are getting increasingly desperate.* ♦ *In a desperate attempt to escape, he killed a guard.* **2** needing or wanting something very much: *She was desperate to see him again.* **3** extremely severe or serious: *Parts of this school are in desperate need of repair.* —**desperately** adv, **desperation** /ˌdespəˈreɪʃ(ə)n/ noun [U]

despicable /dɪˈspɪkəb(ə)l/ adj extremely unpleasant or evil: *despicable crimes*

despise /dɪˈspaɪz/ verb [T] to hate someone or something and have no respect for them

despite /dɪˈspaɪt/ preposition used for saying that something happens or is true even though something else makes it seem unlikely: *He still loves her, despite the fact that she left him.*

despondent /dɪˈspɒndənt/ adj feeling very unhappy because you do not believe that an unpleasant situation will improve —**despondency** noun [U]

despot /ˈdespɒt/ noun [C] SOCIAL STUDIES someone who uses their power in a cruel and unreasonable way = TYRANT —**despotic** /dɪˈspɒtɪk/ adj, **despotism** /ˈdespəˌtɪz(ə)m/ noun [U]

dessert /dɪˈzɜːt/ noun [C/U] sweet food that is eaten after the main part of a meal = PUDDING

destabilize /diːˈsteɪbəlaɪz/ verb [T] to cause problems for a country, government, or person in authority so that they become less effective —**destabilization** /diːˌsteɪbəlaɪˈzeɪʃ(ə)n/ noun [U]

destination /ˌdestɪˈneɪʃ(ə)n/ noun [C] the place where someone or something is going

destined /ˈdestɪnd/ adj **1** certain to do something, or certain to happen: *We felt that we were destined to meet.* **2** travelling, or being sent, to a particular place

destiny /ˈdestəni/ (plural **destinies**) noun **1** [C] the things that someone will do or the type of person that they will become **2** [U] a power that some people believe controls everything that happens

destitute /ˈdestɪtjuːt/ adj with no money or possessions

destroy /dɪˈstrɔɪ/ verb [T] to damage or harm something so severely that it cannot exist as it was before: *An earthquake destroyed the town.* ♦ *This action destroyed any hope of reaching an agreement.*

Word family: **destroy**

Words in the same family as destroy
- destroyer *n*
- destruction *n*
- destructive *adj*
- indestructible *adj*
- self-destruct *v*
- self-destructive *adj*

destroyer /dɪˈstrɔɪə/ noun [C] a small fast ship that is used for fighting enemy ships

destruction /dɪˈstrʌkʃ(ə)n/ noun [U] damage that is so severe that something cannot exist as it was before: *the destruction of the environment*

destructive /dɪˈstrʌktɪv/ adj causing severe damage or harm

de,structive inter'ference noun [U] PHYSICS a situation in which two sound waves or light waves are **out of phase** (=have high points and low points that come at different times), so that they produce a wave that is less intense —*picture* → WAVE

detach /dɪˈtætʃ/ verb [I/T] to remove a part from something, or to become removed from something = SEPARATE

detachable /dɪˈtætʃəb(ə)l/ adj able to be removed and put back on again

detached /dɪˈtætʃt/ adj 1 not feeling involved in something in an emotional way 2 a detached house is not joined to another house

detail[1] /ˈdiːteɪl, *American* dɪˈteɪl/ noun 1 [C/U] one of many small facts or pieces of information relating to a situation: *No details of the offer were revealed.* ♦ *Please enter your personal details* (=information such as your name and address) *below.* ♦ *She talked in detail* (=including many smaller facts) *about her plans.* ♦ *Mr Shaw refused to go into detail* (=talk about more than general facts) *about the discussions.* 2 [U] all the small aspects or features that something has, especially when they are difficult to notice: *Attention to detail is important in this job.*

detail[2] /ˈdiːteɪl/ verb [T] to list all the facts or aspects of a situation

detailed /ˈdiːteɪld/ adj including many small facts or aspects: *a detailed description*

'detail ,paper noun [U] TECHNOLOGY thin, strong paper used by designers and **draughtsmen**

detain /dɪˈteɪn/ verb [T] 1 to not allow someone to leave a **police station** or prison 2 *formal* to delay someone who has to go somewhere

detainee /ˌdiːteɪˈniː/ noun [C] someone who is kept in prison, especially because of their political activities

detect /dɪˈtekt/ verb [T] 1 to prove that something is present by using scientific methods 2 to notice something when it is not obvious: *I thought I detected a hint of amusement in his words.* —**detection** /dɪˈtekʃ(ə)n/ noun [U]

detective /dɪˈtektɪv/ noun [C] a police officer whose job is to try to discover information about a crime

detector /dɪˈtektə/ noun [C] a piece of equipment that is used for checking whether something is present: *a smoke detector*

detention /dɪˈtenʃ(ə)n/ noun 1 [U] the state of being kept in a police station or prison and not being allowed to leave 2 [C/U] EDUCATION a punishment in which a student has to stay at school after the other students have left

de'tention ,centre noun [C] a place where people who have come into a country without permission are kept while the government decides whether they can stay

deter /dɪˈtɜː/ (**deters, deterring, deterred**) verb [T] to make someone decide not to do something

detergent /dɪˈtɜːdʒ(ə)nt/ noun [C/U] a liquid or powder that is used for washing clothes or dishes

deteriorate /dɪˈtɪəriəreɪt/ verb [I] to become worse —**deterioration** /dɪˌtɪəriəˈreɪʃ(ə)n/ noun [U]

determinant /dɪˈtɜːmɪnənt/ noun [C] *formal* something that controls or decides how something else will develop or what result it will have

determination /dɪˌtɜːmɪˈneɪʃ(ə)n/ noun [U] the refusal to let anything stop you from doing what you want to do: *The president's determination to pursue the rebels was clear.*

determine /dɪˈtɜːmɪn/ verb 1 [T] to control what something will be: *Coffee prices are determined by the world market.* 2 [I/T] to officially decide something: *The court must determine whether she is guilty.* 3 [I/T] to calculate something, or to discover it by examining evidence = FIND STH OUT: *Technicians were trying to determine why the missile didn't fire.*

determined /dɪˈtɜːmɪnd/ adj not willing to let anything stop you from doing what you want to do: *a strong, determined woman* ♦ *I was determined to become a doctor.*

determiner /dɪˈtɜːmɪnə/ noun [C] LANGUAGE a word such as 'a', 'the', 'this', or 'some' that is used before a noun for showing which thing or things are being referred to or talked about

deterrent[1] /dɪˈterənt/ noun [C] 1 something that stops people from doing something by making them afraid of what will happen if they do it 2 a weapon whose purpose is to make other countries afraid to attack the country that owns it

deterrent[2] /dɪˈterənt/ adj making people decide not to do something by making them realize that something unpleasant could happen to them

detest /dɪˈtest/ verb [T] to hate someone or something

detonate /ˈdetəneɪt/ verb [I/T] to explode, or to make something such as a bomb explode

detonation /ˌdetəˈneɪʃ(ə)n/ noun 1 [C] an explosion, or the act of making something explode 2 [U] ENGINEERING a situation in which some of the air and fuel mixture left in the **combustion chamber** of an engine explodes by setting light to itself

detonator /ˈdetəˌneɪtə/ noun [C] a piece of equipment on a bomb that makes it explode

detour /ˈdiːtʊə/ noun [C] a way of going from one place to another that is not the shortest or usual way

detract /dɪˈtrækt/ PHRASAL VERB **de'tract from sth** to make something seem less good, attractive, or important: *The ugly high-rise buildings detract from the view.*

detriment /ˈdetrɪmənt/ noun [U] *formal* harm that is caused to something as a result of something else ≠ BENEFIT

detrimental /ˌdetrɪˈment(ə)l/ adj harmful or damaging ≠ BENEFICIAL

detritus /dɪˈtraɪtəs/ noun [U] *formal* waste that remains after something has been destroyed, used, or finished

deuce /djuːs/ noun [C/U] SPORTS a situation in tennis when both players have 40 points

deus ex machina /ˌdeɪəs eks ˈmækɪnə/ noun [singular] LITERATURE ARTS someone or something that solves a situation that seemed impossible to solve in a sudden and unlikely way, especially in a book, play, film etc

deuterium /djuːˈtɪəriəm/ noun [U] CHEMISTRY an isotope of hydrogen that has double the mass of the ordinary isotope

devalue /diːˈvæljuː/ verb 1 [I/T] ECONOMICS to officially reduce the value of a country's money 2 [T] to treat someone or something as if they are not important —**devaluation** /ˌdiːvæljuˈeɪʃ(ə)n/ noun [C/U]

devastate /ˈdevəˌsteɪt/ verb [T] **1** to destroy or seriously damage something **2** to make someone feel very shocked and upset: *Mary's death devastated the family.* —**devastation** /ˌdevəˈsteɪʃ(ə)n/ noun [U]

devastated /ˈdevəˌsteɪtɪd/ adj feeling very shocked and upset

devastating /ˈdevəˌsteɪtɪŋ/ adj **1** causing a lot of harm or damage: *a devastating fire* **2** very shocking or upsetting: *a devastating loss* **3** very impressive or attractive: *devastating good looks*

develop /dɪˈveləp/ verb

1 grow/change	**5** use land for sth
2 start to exist	**6** become complete
3 be affected by	**7** make photograph
4 create sth new	

1 [I/T] to grow, change, or improve, or to make something grow, change, or improve: *All children develop at different rates.* ♦ *The area is working to develop its tourist industry.* ♦ *The cell **develops into** an embryo.*
2 [I] to start to exist, or to start to be noticeable: *A rash developed on my arm.*
3 [T] to start to have something or be affected by something: *The engine developed a problem soon after take-off.*
4 [T] to create a new product or method: *We've recently developed new communications software.*
5 [T] to use land for a particular purpose that increases its value
6 [I/T] if an idea or story develops, or if someone develops it, it becomes clear and complete as more details are added
7 [T] to treat a film with chemicals in order to make photographs

developed /dɪˈveləpt/ adj **1** ECONOMICS a developed country, region, or economy has a lot of industries and a high standard of living **2** a developed skill, idea, or quality has reached a high level: *These people had highly developed hunting techniques.*

developer /dɪˈveləpə/ noun [C] someone who buys land or buildings in order to put new or better buildings there

developing country /dɪˌveləpɪŋ ˈkʌntri/ noun [C] SOCIAL STUDIES a country that is fairly poor and does not have many industries

development /dɪˈveləpmənt/ noun **1** [U] change, growth, or improvement over a period of time: *a child's physical development* ♦ *the **development of** the region's economy* **2** [C] a new event that changes a situation: *Were there any **further developments** in the case?* **3** [U] the process of creating a new product or method, or the product or method that is created: *software development* ♦ *developments in medical research* **4** [C/U] the process of putting new buildings on land, or a group of new buildings

developmental /dɪˌveləpˈment(ə)l/ adj **1** HEALTH relating to a child's growth and ability to learn things **2** ECONOMICS relating to the development of a country or economy **3** relating to the gradual change and improvement in something over a period of time —**developmentally** adv

deviate /ˈdiːviˌeɪt/ verb [I] to start doing something different from what is expected

deviation /ˌdiːviˈeɪʃ(ə)n/ noun [C/U] a difference in the usual or expected way of doing something

device /dɪˈvaɪs/ noun [C] **1** a machine or piece of equipment that does a particular job: *a listening device* ♦ *a device for measuring humidity in the air* **2** a bomb **3** formal a way of making something happen or making someone do something: *We needed a device to get him out of the house.*

deˈvice ˌdriver noun [C] COMPUTING software that controls a piece of equipment connected to a computer

devil /ˈdev(ə)l/ noun RELIGION **1** the Devil [singular] the most powerful evil spirit in many religions **2** [C] an evil spirit

devious /ˈdiːviəs/ adj dishonest and clever = CUNNING

devise /dɪˈvaɪz/ verb [T] to invent a method of doing something

devoid /dɪˈvɔɪd/ adj **devoid of sth** lacking something, especially a good quality

the Devonian /ˈdevəʊniən/ noun [singular] GEOLOGY the geological period, 417 million to 354 million years ago, when forests and amphibians first appeared, and many fish developed —**Devonian** adj

devote /dɪˈvəʊt/ PHRASAL VERB **deˈvote sth to sth** to spend a lot of time or effort doing something: *He's devoted most of his time to his painting.*

devoted /dɪˈvəʊtɪd/ adj **1** loving someone very much: *a devoted family man* **2** **devoted to sth** containing, used for, or dealing with one particular thing = DEDICATED: *The whole area is devoted to rice farming.* **3** very enthusiastic about something

devotion /dɪˈvəʊʃ(ə)n/ noun [U] **1** great love, admiration, or loyalty **2** the process of spending a lot of time or energy on an activity **3** strong religious feeling

devour /dɪˈvaʊə/ verb [T] **1** to eat something very fast because you are hungry **2** to read, watch, or listen to something with a lot of interest **3** if someone is devoured by a feeling, they feel it very strongly and cannot get rid of it

devout /dɪˈvaʊt/ adj very religious —**devoutly** adv

dew /djuː/ noun [U] small drops of water that form on the ground at night

deworming /diːˈwɜːmɪŋ/ noun [U] HEALTH, BIOLOGY the process of giving a medicine to humans and other mammals in order to kill worms in their bodies

dexterity /dekˈsterəti/ noun [U] great skill in using the hands or the mind

dextrose /ˈdekˌstrəʊz/ noun [U] BIOLOGY a type of sugar that is found in fruit. Chemical formula: $C_6H_{12}O_6$

dhal /dɑːl/ noun [C/U] an Indian food made from cooked **lentils**

dhow /daʊ/ noun [C] an Arab ship with low sides and sails shaped like triangles

diabetes /ˌdaɪəˈbiːtiːz/ noun [U] HEALTH a serious medical condition in which the body cannot produce or use **insulin**, causing dangerously high levels of sugar in the blood

diabetic /ˌdaɪəˈbetɪk/ noun [C] HEALTH someone who has diabetes —**diabetic** adj

diachronic /ˌdaɪəˈkrɒnɪk/ adj LANGUAGE relating to or involving the changes that take place in something over a period of time, especially in a language → SYNCHRONIC —**diachronically** /ˌdaɪəˈkrɒnɪkli/ adv

diacritic /ˌdaɪəˈkrɪtɪk/ noun [C] LANGUAGE a mark written above or below a letter that shows how you should pronounce that letter

diaeresis /daɪˈerəsɪs/ noun [C] LANGUAGE the symbol ï put above a vowel to show that it is pronounced separately from another vowel, for example in the word 'naïve'

diagnose /ˈdaɪəgnəʊz/ verb [T] HEALTH to find out what physical or mental problem someone has by examining them: *Eva's been **diagnosed with** cancer.*

diagnosis /ˌdaɪəgˈnəʊsɪs/ (plural **diagnoses** /ˌdaɪəgˈnəʊsiːz/) noun [C/U] HEALTH a statement about what disease someone has, based on examining them

diagnostic /ˌdaɪəgˈnɒstɪk/ adj used for making a diagnosis

diagonal /daɪˈægən(ə)l/ adj MATHS a diagonal line is straight and sloping —**diagonally** adv

di,agonal 'scale noun [C] TECHNOLOGY a set of parallel lines **intersected** (=crossed) by another set of parallel lines at an angle. It is used for making very small measurements.

diagram /ˈdaɪəgræm/ noun [C] a drawing that explains something: *a diagram of the manufacturing process*

diagrammatic /ˌdaɪəgrəˈmætɪk/ adj in the form of a diagram —**diagrammatically** /ˌdaɪəgrəˈmætɪkli/ adv

dial[1] /ˈdaɪəl/ (**dials, dialling, dialled**) verb [I/T] to press the buttons on a telephone in order to phone someone

dial[2] /ˈdaɪəl/ noun [C] **1** the part of a clock or watch that is round and has **hands** that move to show you the time **2** a round instrument on a machine that shows you the amount of something, for example heat or pressure **3** a round control on a piece of equipment that you turn to change something such as the temperature or sound **4** a circle with holes on an old-fashioned telephone, that you turn in order to call someone

dialect /ˈdaɪəlekt/ noun [C/U] LANGUAGE a way of speaking a language that is used only in a particular area or by a particular group

dialling code /ˈdaɪəlɪŋ ˌkəʊd/ noun [C] a group of numbers at the beginning of a telephone number that represents a particular town, area, or country

dialling tone /ˈdaɪəlɪŋ ˌtəʊn/ noun [C] the sound that a telephone makes when you pick it up

dialog box /ˈdaɪəlɒg ˌbɒks/ noun [C] COMPUTING a small area that appears on a computer screen for you to type instructions

dialogue /ˈdaɪəlɒg/ noun **1** [U] LITERATURE all the words that characters speak in a book, play etc, or a particular conversation in a book, play etc **2** [C/U] a process in which two people or groups have discussions in order to solve problems

'dial-,up adj COMPUTING a dial-up service or system is one that connects with a computer using a telephone line

'dial-up ,access noun [U] COMPUTING a way of connecting to the Internet in which a **modem** calls a telephone number each time the connection is needed, and the connection is not permanent

dialysis /daɪˈæləsɪs/ noun [U] HEALTH a medical treatment that artificially removes waste substances from the blood of someone whose kidneys are not working properly

diameter /daɪˈæmɪtə/ noun [C/U] MATHS a straight line that crosses a circle through the centre, or the length of this line —*picture* → CIRCLE

diamond /ˈdaɪəmənd/ noun **1** [C/U] CHEMISTRY a very hard clear colourless stone that is used in expensive jewellery. It is a form of carbon and is the hardest known mineral: *a diamond ring* **2** [C] MATHS a shape with four straight equal sides that stands on one of its corners —*picture* → SHAPE **3** [C] a playing card with a red diamond shape on it

diaphragm /ˈdaɪəfræm/ noun [C] **1** ANATOMY the large sheet of muscle that separates the **cavity** (=area) in the chest from the cavity in the abdomen. It moves up and down, affecting the pressure in the chest and causing air to move in and out of the lungs. —*picture* → LUNG **2** HEALTH a round rubber object that some women use as a contraceptive **3** SCIENCE a piece of equipment that changes sound into electric signals and electric signals into sound, for example in a telephone receiver

diarist /ˈdaɪərɪst/ noun [C] LITERATURE someone who writes a **diary**, especially whose diary is published

diarrhoea /ˌdaɪəˈriːə/ noun [U] HEALTH an illness in which the faeces are like liquid, usually as a result of **food poisoning** or another disease. Diarrhoea can be very dangerous, especially in young children and old people, as it prevents food and important minerals from getting into the body and can cause severe **dehydration**.

diary /ˈdaɪəri/ (plural **diaries**) noun [C] **1** a book in which someone writes their experiences each day = JOURNAL: *She's **kept a diary** since she was twelve.* **2** a book that has spaces for each day of the year, where someone can write down things that they have to do

diaspora /daɪˈæsp(ə)rə/ noun [singular] SOCIAL STUDIES the movement of a large group of people from their home country to other countries in the world

diastolic pressure /ˌdaɪəstɒlɪk ˈpreʃə/ noun [U] HEALTH a person's blood pressure when the heart muscle is less tight. It is the second of the two numbers given when saying what someone's blood pressure is.

diatonic /ˌdaɪəˈtɒnɪk/ adj MUSIC based on a major or minor musical **scale**

dibber /ˈdɪbə/ noun [C] AGRICULTURE a small pointed tool that is held in one hand and is used for making holes in the soil in order to plant seeds or young plants —*picture* → AGRICULTURAL

dice[1] /daɪs/ (plural **dice**) noun [C] a small block with a number of spots on each side, used for playing games

dice[2] /daɪs/ verb [T] to cut food into small square pieces —*picture* → FOOD

di,chotomous 'key noun [C] BIOLOGY a system for identifying different species. It is based on a series of questions with 'yes' or 'no' answers that direct the user through possible choices until the final, correct choice is reached.

dichotomy /daɪˈkɒtəmi/ (plural **dichotomies**) noun [C] *formal* a difference between two opposite things or ideas —**dichotomous** adj

Dickensian /dɪˈkenziən/ adj typical of the novels of Charles Dickens, or of 19th-century England as he described it

dicotyledon /ˌdaɪˌkɒtɪˈliːd(ə)n/ noun [C] BIOLOGY a **flowering plant** that has two seed leaves (**cotyledons**) in each seed. Its other leaves have a pattern of veins. Many **herbaceous** plants, trees, and bushes are dicotyledons. → MONOCOTYLEDON —**dicotyledonous** adj

dictate /dɪkˈteɪt/ verb **1** [I/T] to say something that someone else then writes down **2** [I/T] to tell someone exactly what to do and how to behave **3** [T] to influence or control how something is done: *The situation dictates that we act cautiously.*

dictation /dɪkˈteɪʃ(ə)n/ noun **1** [U] the act of saying something that someone else then writes down **2** [C/U] **EDUCATION** a type of test in which a teacher reads sentences to students that they write down. This shows the teacher how well they understand and write a language.

dictator /dɪkˈteɪtə/ noun [C] **POLITICS** someone who uses force to take and keep power in a country —**dictatorial** /ˌdɪktəˈtɔːriəl/ adj

dictatorship /dɪkˈteɪtəʃɪp/ noun [C/U] **POLITICS** government by someone who takes power by force and does not allow elections

diction /ˈdɪkʃ(ə)n/ noun [U] the way that someone pronounces words

dictionary /ˈdɪkʃən(ə)ri/ (plural **dictionaries**) noun [C] a book that gives an alphabetical list of words with their meanings or translations

did /dɪd/ the past tense of **do**[1]

didn't /ˈdɪd(ə)nt/ short form the usual way of saying or writing 'did not'. This is not often used in formal writing: *I didn't hear the phone ringing.*

die[1] /daɪ/ (**dies**, **dying** /ˈdaɪɪŋ/, **died**) verb **1** [I/T] to stop being alive: *My grandfather died at the age of 86.* ♦ *Several people in the village have died violent deaths.* ♦ *She is dying of cancer.* **2** [I] to disappear, or to stop existing: *Our memory of her will never die.*

PHRASAL VERBS ,die 'down if something dies down, it becomes much less noisy, powerful, or active: *I waited for the laughter to die down before I spoke.*
,die 'out to gradually disappear or stop existing: *The tribe's traditional way of life is dying out.*

die[2] /daɪ/ noun [C] **TECHNOLOGY 1** a block of metal used for pressing or cutting something into a shape or pattern **2** a tool used for cutting **threads** (=raised lines curving around a screw, rod etc)

'die-,cast verb [T] **TECHNOLOGY** to **cast** an object from **molten** (=melted) metal using a metallic mould

diehard /ˈdaɪˌhɑːd/ adj loyal to particular ideas or beliefs and refusing to change= LOYAL

diesel /ˈdiːz(ə)l/ noun [U] heavy oil that is used as fuel instead of petrol in some engines —*picture* → REFINE

diet[1] /ˈdaɪət/ noun **1** [C/U] **BIOLOGY** the food that a person or animal usually eats: *Try to eat a balanced diet.* ♦ *The bird has a diet of nuts and berries.* **2** [C] **HEALTH** a limited range or amount of food that someone chooses to eat in order to be healthy or to lose weight

diet[2] /ˈdaɪət/ verb [I] to control your eating in order to lose weight —**dieting** noun [U]

dietary /ˈdaɪət(ə)ri/ adj relating to the foods that people eat

dietetics /ˌdaɪəˈtetɪks/ noun [U] the scientific study of food and nutrition

dietitian or **dietician** /ˌdaɪəˈtɪʃ(ə)n/ noun [C] someone whose job is to give people advice about the kind of food they should eat

differ /ˈdɪfə/ verb [I] **1** to be different from something else: *Our approach differs from theirs in several ways.* **2** to disagree with someone about a subject: *Experts differ on the causes of the disease.* —**differing** adj

difference /ˈdɪfrəns/ noun **1** [C/U] something that makes one person or thing not the same as another ≠ SIMILARITY: *political differences* ♦ *What's the difference between these two computers?* **2** [C] the amount by which one thing is different from another thing: *The same car costs £500 less here, which is quite a difference!* **3** differences [plural] disagreements: *Joe*

and *I have had our differences, but we work well together.*

PHRASES **make a difference** to have an important effect on something, especially a good effect: *The extra space makes a big difference.* ♦ *This scheme will certainly make a difference to the way I do my job.*
make no/little difference to not be important, or to not have any effect: *Anybody can enjoy yoga, and your age makes absolutely no difference.*
tell the difference to notice what is different between similar people or things: *How do you tell the difference between a reptile and an amphibian?*

Word family: difference
Words in the same family as difference
- **differ** v
- **different** adj
- **differently** adv
- **differential** n
- **differentiate** v
- **differentiation** n

different /ˈdɪfrənt/ adj **1** not the same as another person or thing, or not the same as before ≠ SIMILAR: *Her new glasses make her look completely different.* ♦ *The two cars are different in shape.* ♦ *Saturn's rings make it different from all the other planets.* **2** separate, but of the same type: *Six different boys asked me to dance.* **3** unusual and not like other things of the same kind: *I wanted something a bit different, so I painted the room green.* —**differently** adv: *My sister and I look at life very differently.* ♦ *six differently shaped chairs*

differential /ˌdɪfəˈrenʃ(ə)l/ noun [C] **1** the difference between two amounts, values, or rates
2 ENGINEERING a piece of equipment in a vehicle that allows the wheels to turn at different speeds, for example when a driver goes around a corner

differentiate /ˌdɪfəˈrenʃieɪt/ verb **1** [I/T] to see or show a difference between things= DISTINGUISH: *People who are colour-blind cannot usually differentiate between red and green.* **2** [T] to be the quality or fact that makes one thing different from another: *The ability to speak differentiates humans from other animals.* —**differentiation** /ˌdɪfərenʃiˈeɪʃ(ə)n/ noun [U]

differently-abled /ˌdɪfrəntli ˈeɪb(ə)ld/ adj used when someone wants to be positive and avoid using the word 'disabled'

difficult /ˈdɪfɪk(ə)lt/ adj **1** not easy to do, deal with, or understand= HARD ≠ EASY: *The exam questions were too difficult.* ♦ *Talking to teenagers can be difficult for parents.* ♦ *It's difficult to say how long the job will take.* **2** causing a lot of problems and making it hard for someone to succeed: *She had a difficult childhood.* **3** never seeming happy or satisfied: *Martin was a difficult baby.*

difficulty /ˈdɪfɪk(ə)lti/ (plural **difficulties**) noun **1** [C] a problem: *Many students have serious financial difficulties.* **2** [U] the state of not being able to do something easily ≠ EASE: *John was badly injured, and breathing with difficulty.* ♦ *She's having difficulty with her schoolwork this year.* **3** [U] the degree to which something is difficult: *The courses vary in content and difficulty.*

diffident /ˈdɪfɪdənt/ adj not confident —**diffidence** noun [U]

diffract /dɪˈfrækt/ verb [I/T] **PHYSICS** to produce diffraction in sound, water, or light waves, or to undergo diffraction

diffraction /dɪˈfrækʃ(ə)n/ noun [U] **PHYSICS** the process by which sound, water, and light waves change when they pass over an object or through a narrow space —*picture* → WAVE

diffuse¹ /dɪˈfjuːz/ verb **1** [I/T] if light diffuses, or if something diffuses it, it shines over a large area but not very brightly **2** [T] *formal* to spread something such as information, ideas, or power among a large group of people

diffuse² /dɪˈfjuːs/ adj *formal* **1** existing over a large area or in many areas **2** using too many words and not easy to understand

diffusion /dɪˈfjuːʒ(ə)n/ noun [U] **1** PHYSICS the movement of light in many directions after it hits a surface that is not smooth or when it passes though a substance that is not completely clear **2** PHYSICS, CHEMISTRY movement of molecules or ions from an area of high concentration to one of lower concentration → OSMOSIS

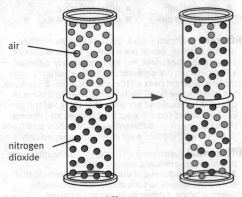

air

nitrogen dioxide

diffusion

dig /dɪg/ (**digs, digging, dug** /dʌg/) verb [I/T] to make a hole in earth using a tool, a machine, or the hands: *We dug a hole and planted the tree.* ♦ *The boys were digging for worms.*

   PHRASAL VERB **dig sth 'up 1** to find information by searching carefully: *When we investigated, we dug up some interesting facts.* **2** to remove something from under the ground by digging: *They dug up a body in his garden.*

digest /daɪˈdʒest/ verb [T] **1** BIOLOGY to break down food in the alimentary canal into **soluble** substances that the body can absorb **2** to try to understand information when it is difficult or unexpected —**digestibility** /daɪˌdʒestəˈbɪləti/ noun [U], **digestible** /daɪˈdʒestəb(ə)l/ adj

digester /daɪˈdʒestə/ noun [C] ENVIRONMENT, BIOLOGY a tank in which organic matter is left to decay without oxygen, so that a gas is produced that can be used as fuel

digestion /daɪˈdʒestʃ(ə)n/ noun [U] BIOLOGY the process by which food is broken down by the body into simple **soluble** substances that the body can absorb and then use for growth and as fuel for energy —*picture* → on next pages

digestive /daɪˈdʒestɪv/ adj BIOLOGY relating to digestion: *the digestive process*

di'gestive ˌsystem noun [C] ANATOMY the system of organs and processes in the body of humans and other animals that deals with the digestion of food —*picture* → on next pages

digestive tract noun [C] ANATOMY the **alimentary canal**

digit /ˈdɪdʒɪt/ noun [C] **1** MATHS *formal* one of the written numbers from 0 to 9 **2** ANATOMY a finger or toe

digital /ˈdɪdʒɪt(ə)l/ adj **1** COMPUTING storing information such as sound or pictures as numbers or electronic signals: *a digital recording* ♦ *a digital camera* **2** a digital clock or instrument shows information as a row of numbers —**digitally** adv

ˌdigital cer'tificate noun [C] BUSINESS, COMPUTING an electronic code that proves who someone is when they do business over the Internet or send an electronic message

ˌdigital 'signature noun [C] COMPUTING a code attached to an electronic message that proves who sent the message, and that the information in the message has not been changed. Digital signatures are used when people buy goods or make agreements on the Internet.

ˌdigital sub'scriber ˌline noun [C] COMPUTING see DSL

ˌdigital 'television or **ˌdigital T'V** noun [U] a system of television broadcasting that uses electronic signals

diglossia /daɪˈglɒsiə/ noun [U] LANGUAGE a situation in which a language exists in two forms, one formal or literary and the other informal, and people use the form that is suitable for a particular situation

dignified /ˈdɪgnɪfaɪd/ adj behaving in a calm way that people respect ≠ UNDIGNIFIED: *a dignified manner*

dignitary /ˈdɪgnɪt(ə)ri/ (plural **dignitaries**) noun [C] someone who has an important official position

dignity /ˈdɪgnəti/ noun [U] calm behaviour that makes people respect you: *She faced her death with great dignity.*

digraph /ˈdaɪgrɑːf/ noun [C] LANGUAGE a combination of two letters that represents one sound, for example 'th' or 'ay'

digress /daɪˈgres/ verb [I] to start to talk or write about something different from the subject that you were discussing —**digression** /daɪˈgreʃ(ə)n/ noun [C/U]

dilapidated /dɪˈlæpɪˌdeɪtɪd/ adj old and in bad condition: *a dilapidated farm* —**dilapidation** /dɪˌlæpɪˈdeɪʃ(ə)n/ noun [U]

dilate /daɪˈleɪt/ verb [I] if part of your body dilates, it becomes bigger and wider —**dilation** /daɪˈleɪʃ(ə)n/ noun [U]

dilemma /dɪˈlemə/ noun [C] a situation in which someone has to make a difficult decision = PREDICAMENT

dilettante /ˌdɪləˈtænti/ noun [C] *formal* someone who is interested in something such as art or music but does not know very much about it

diligent /ˈdɪlɪdʒ(ə)nt/ adj *formal* working very hard and very carefully = HARD-WORKING —**diligence** noun [U], **diligently** adv

dilute¹ /daɪˈluːt/ verb [T] to make a liquid less strong by adding water or another liquid —**dilution** /daɪˈluːʃ(ə)n/ noun [U]

dilute² /ˈdaɪluːt/ adj CHEMISTRY a dilute liquid has been mixed with another liquid to make it less concentrated

dim¹ /dɪm/ (**dimmer, dimmest**) adj **1** not bright or clear: *a dim light* **2** a dim memory is something from long ago that someone cannot remember very well ≠ CLEAR —**dimly** adv

dim² /dɪm/ (**dims, dimming, dimmed**) verb [I/T] if a light dims, or if someone dims it, it becomes less bright

DIM /ˌdiː aɪ ˈem/ abbrev COMPUTING document image management: software that allows a user to record and store printed information in a **digital** form that a computer can use

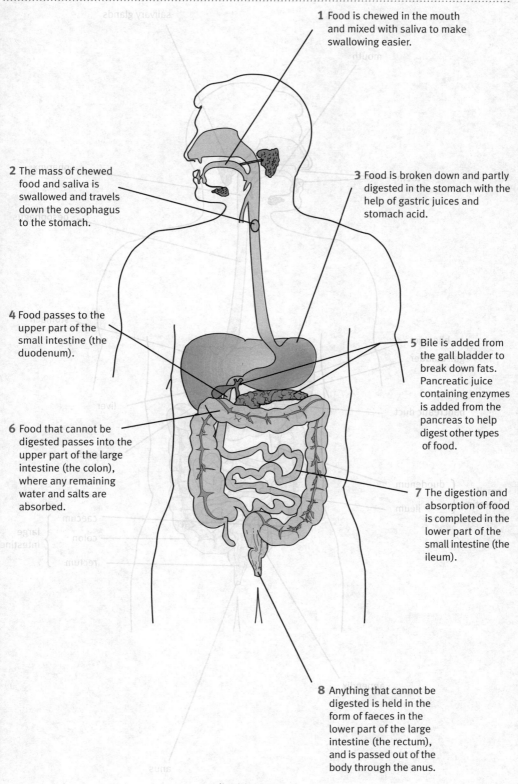

1 Food is chewed in the mouth and mixed with saliva to make swallowing easier.

2 The mass of chewed food and saliva is swallowed and travels down the oesophagus to the stomach.

3 Food is broken down and partly digested in the stomach with the help of gastric juices and stomach acid.

4 Food passes to the upper part of the small intestine (the duodenum).

5 Bile is added from the gall bladder to break down fats. Pancreatic juice containing enzymes is added from the pancreas to help digest other types of food.

6 Food that cannot be digested passes into the upper part of the large intestine (the colon), where any remaining water and salts are absorbed.

7 The digestion and absorption of food is completed in the lower part of the small intestine (the ileum).

8 Anything that cannot be digested is held in the form of faeces in the lower part of the large intestine (the rectum), and is passed out of the body through the anus.

digestive process

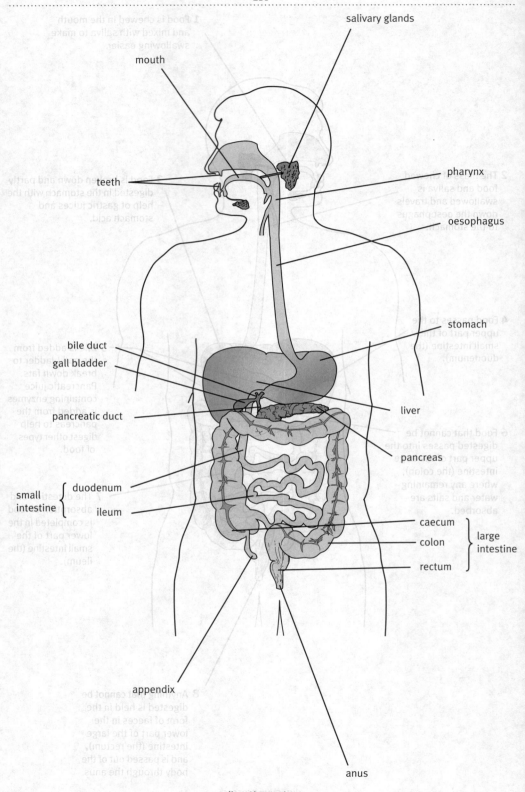

salivary glands

mouth

teeth

pharynx

oesophagus

bile duct

gall bladder

pancreatic duct

stomach

liver

pancreas

small intestine { duodenum

ileum

caecum

colon

rectum

large intestine

appendix

anus

digestive system

dimension /daɪˈmenʃ(ə)n/ noun **1** [C] an aspect of a situation that influences the way that people think about the situation: *Doing voluntary work has added a whole new dimension to my life.* **2** [C] MATHS length, height, or width **3 dimensions** [plural] the size of something: *Can you mark the dimensions of the room on the diagram?*

dimensioning /daɪˈmenʃ(ə)nɪŋ/ noun [U] TECHNOLOGY the method by which a designer provides size descriptions on a **working drawing** of a part

diminish /dɪˈmɪnɪʃ/ verb [I/T] to become less, or to make something become less: *The intensity of the sound diminished gradually.*

diminished responsibility /dɪˌmɪnɪʃt rɪˌspɒnsəˈbɪləti/ noun [U] LAW a situation in which someone cannot be considered responsible for a crime because they are mentally ill

diminishing returns /dɪˌmɪnɪʃɪŋ rɪˈtɜːnz/ noun [plural] a situation in which benefits or profits do not increase enough to make it worth making more effort or spending more money

diminuendo /dɪˌmɪnjʊˈendəʊ/ noun [C] MUSIC an instruction to play a section of music more and more quietly

diminutive¹ /dɪˈmɪnjʊtɪv/ adj *formal* very small = TINY

diminutive² /dɪˈmɪnjʊtɪv/ noun [C] LANGUAGE a word formed by adding a diminutive suffix

di,minutive 'suffix noun [C] LANGUAGE a group of letters that are added to the end of a word to show that something is smaller than things of that type usually are, for example '-let' added to 'drop' to make 'droplet'

,dim 'sum noun [U] small **steamed** or **fried** pieces of fish, meat, vegetables etc served before or with a Chinese meal

din /dɪn/ noun [singular] a very loud unpleasant noise that lasts for a long time

dinar /ˈdiːnɑː/ noun [C] ECONOMICS the unit of money used in several countries, including Iraq, Jordan, and Libya

dine /daɪn/ verb [I] *formal* to eat dinner

diner /ˈdaɪnə/ noun [C] someone who is eating a meal at a restaurant

ding-dong /ˈdɪŋ ˌdɒŋ/ noun [U] the sound that a bell makes

dinghy /ˈdɪŋi, ˈdɪŋgi/ (plural **dinghies**) noun [C] a small boat

dingy /ˈdɪndʒi/ adj dirty and dark: *a dingy room*

dining car /ˈdaɪnɪŋ ˌkɑː/ noun [C] the part of a train that is a restaurant

dining room /ˈdaɪnɪŋ ˌruːm/ noun [C] the room in a house where people eat meals

dinner /ˈdɪnə/ noun [C/U] the main meal of the day, usually eaten in the evening: *I haven't had dinner yet.* ♦ *We had chicken for dinner.*

'dinner ,jacket noun [C] a man's black or white jacket that he wears on formal occasions

'dinner ,plate noun [C] a wide flat plate for serving the main course of a meal on

dinosaur /ˈdaɪnəˌsɔː/ noun [C] a large reptile that lived a very long time ago but is now extinct

diocese /ˈdaɪəsɪs/ noun [C] RELIGION an area that a bishop is in charge of

diode /ˈdaɪəʊd/ noun [C] PHYSICS a piece of electronic equipment through which a current passes in one direction only

dioxide /daɪˈɒksaɪd/ noun [U] CHEMISTRY a compound of a metal with two atoms of oxygen

dioxin /daɪˈɒksɪn/ noun [C/U] CHEMISTRY a poisonous chemical that is produced during the process of making **pesticides** (=chemicals for killing pests). Chemical formula: $C_4H_4O_2$

dip¹ /dɪp/ (**dips, dipping, dipped**) verb **1** [T] to lower something into a liquid for a moment and then take it out again **2** [T] AGRICULTURE to put an animal into a bath filled with a liquid that kills insects on its skin **3** [I] to become less

PHRASAL VERB **,dip 'into sth** to read different parts of a book, but not the whole book

dip² /dɪp/ noun **1** [C/U] a thick cold sauce for dipping pieces of food into before eating them **2** [C] a reduction in the amount or level of something **3** [C] a place in a surface that is lower than the surrounding area: *a dip in the road* **4** [C/U] AGRICULTURE a liquid chemical that is used for killing insects on an animal's skin

diphtheria /dɪfˈθɪəriə, dɪpˈθɪəriə/ noun [U] HEALTH a serious disease affecting the throat that makes breathing difficult

diphthong /ˈdɪfθɒŋ, ˈdɪpθɒŋ/ noun [C] LANGUAGE a sound consisting of one or two vowels that is the combination of two sounds said one after the other. The vowel sounds in the words 'find' and 'fail' are diphthongs.

diploblastic /ˌdɪpləʊˈblæstɪk/ adj BIOLOGY relating to an invertebrate animal in which the adult tissues come from just two layers of tissue in the embryo, the **endoderm** and **ectoderm** → TRIPLOBLASTIC

diploid /ˈdɪplɔɪd/ adj BIOLOGY having two matched sets of chromosomes in the cell nucleus, one set from each parent. Each species has a characteristic diploid number of chromosomes. —**diploid** noun [C], **diploidy** noun [U]

diploma /dɪˈpləʊmə/ noun [C] EDUCATION **1** a course of study at a college or university in a subject that prepares someone for a particular job **2** the qualification that someone gets when they have completed a diploma course → CERTIFICATE, DEGREE

diplomacy /dɪˈpləʊməsi/ noun [U] **1** the profession of creating friendly relationships between countries **2** the ability to deal with people well, so that they are not upset or offended

diplomat /ˈdɪpləmæt/ noun [C] an official whose job is to represent their government in a foreign country

diplomatic /ˌdɪpləˈmætɪk/ adj **1** relating to the job of a diplomat: *a diplomatic mission* **2** good at dealing with people, so that they do not get upset or offended: *a diplomatic answer* —**diplomatically** /ˌdɪpləˈmætɪkli/ adv

diptych /ˈdɪptɪk/ noun [C] ARTS a painting done on two separate pieces of wood that are joined to each other

dire /ˈdaɪə/ adj very severe, serious, or bad: *dire warnings*

direct¹ /dɪˈrekt, daɪˈrekt/ adj **1** going straight to a place without stopping or changing direction: *direct flights from Scotland to North America* **2** involving only the two people or things that are mentioned and with no one or nothing else between ≠ INDIRECT: *Employees have little direct contact with management.* ♦ *Their study found a direct link between poverty and crime.*

3 saying what you really think in a very clear honest way

direct[2] /dɪˈrekt, daɪˈrekt/ verb [T] **1** to aim something at a particular person or thing: *All the criticism was directed at her rather than me.* **2** to be in charge of telling all the actors and technical staff who are involved in a film, play, or programme what to do → PRODUCE[1] sense 4 **3** to control or organize how a person or group of people does something: *The manager's job is mainly to direct the activities of others.* **4** to tell or show someone the way to go: *Could you direct me to the bus station?*

direct[3] /dɪˈrekt, daɪˈrekt/ adv **1** going straight to a place and not stopping or changing direction: *All the major airlines fly direct to Mumbai.* **2** in a way that involves only the two people or things that are mentioned, with no one or nothing else between: *You can buy direct from the manufacturer.*

'direct ,access noun [U] COMPUTING the ability to get information directly from the place on a computer where it is stored, without having to go through the information that goes before it = RANDOM ACCESS

,direct con'nection noun [C] COMPUTING a fast permanent connection between a computer and a system such as the Internet → DIAL-UP

,direct 'current noun [U] PHYSICS an electric current that flows in one direction only. It is the form in which batteries supply electricity. → ALTERNATING CURRENT

,direct 'debit noun [C/U] an order to a bank to regularly pay money from your account to a person or organization

di,rect e'lections noun [plural] POLITICS government elections in which everyone in a country can vote, not just a small group of chosen representatives

direction /dɪˈrekʃ(ə)n, daɪˈrekʃ(ə)n/ noun

1 of movement/look	4 purpose
2 instructions	5 management
3 way sb/sth changes	6 of film/play

1 [C] the place that someone or something moves, faces, or points towards: *Are you sure we're going in the right direction?* ♦ *The wind has changed direction.* ♦ *We drove off in the direction of the mountains.* ♦ *I'd give you a lift, but I'm going in the opposite direction.* ♦ *Michelle's always getting lost because of her terrible sense of direction.*
2 directions [plural] instructions for doing something or for getting to a place: *Follow the directions on the label.* ♦ *She gave the driver directions to her house.*
3 [C/U] the general development or progress of someone or something: *He was determined to change the direction of the business.*
4 [U] the feeling of having a definite purpose: *Your life seems to lack direction.*
5 [U] leadership or management: *The project was under the direction of Henry Richardson.*
6 [U] ARTS the work of directing a film, programme, or play

directional /dɪˈrekʃ(ə)n(ə)l, daɪˈrekʃ(ə)n(ə)l/ adj **1** relating to or pointing in a particular direction **2** PHYSICS designed to send or receive radio signals better in one direction than in others —**directionality** /dɪˌrekʃəˈnæləti, daɪˌrekʃəˈnæləti/ noun [U]

direction finder /dɪˈrekʃ(ə)n ˌfaɪndə/ noun [C] ASTRONOMY, PHYSICS a piece of equipment that shows where a particular radio signal is coming from. It is used by astronauts and satellite computers to find out where they are and in which direction they are facing. —*picture* → SATELLITE

directive /dɪˈrektɪv, daɪˈrektɪv/ noun [C] an official order

directly /dɪˈrek(t)li, daɪˈrek(t)li/ adv **1** in a way that involves only the two people or things that are mentioned, with no one or nothing else between: *I prefer to deal directly with the manager.* ♦ *Price is directly related to size.* **2** going straight to a place without stopping or changing direction: *They landed at the airport and went directly to the hotel.* **3** exactly: *The post office is directly opposite the town hall.* **4** in a very clear and honest way: *Jackson avoided saying directly that he disapproved.*

,direct 'object noun [C] LANGUAGE the noun or pronoun in a sentence that a verb applies to. In the sentence 'Harry was reading a book', 'a book' is the direct object of the verb 'was reading'. → INDIRECT OBJECT

director /dəˈrektə, daɪˈrektə/ noun [C] **1** ARTS someone whose job is to tell the actors and technical staff who are involved in a film, play, or TV or radio programme what to do **2** someone whose job is to manage all or part of a company, organization, or institution: *the managing director* ♦ *She's a design director.*

directory /dəˈrekt(ə)ri, daɪˈrekt(ə)ri/ (plural **directories**) noun [C] **1** a book or list of people's names, addresses, telephone numbers, or other information **2** COMPUTING a computer file that contains other files, documents, or programs

di,rect pro'portion noun [U] MATHS the relationship between quantities with a ratio that does not change

directrix /dəˈrektrɪks, daɪˈrektrɪks/ noun [C] MATHS a fixed line used for drawing a curve

,direct 'speech noun [U] LANGUAGE the actual words that someone says. In writing, these are shown inside **quotation marks**. → INDIRECT SPEECH

di,rect 'tax noun [C/U] ECONOMICS a tax that is based on the income or profits of a person or organization, instead of being paid as part of the price of a product or service —**di,rect tax'ation** noun [U]

dirge /dɜːdʒ/ noun [C] a slow sad song often sung at a funeral

dirt /dɜːt/ noun [U] **1** a substance that makes something dirty **2** soil or mud: *children playing in the dirt* ♦ *a dirt track*

'dirt ,track noun [C] a track with a loose surface for cars, horses, and motorcycles to race on

dirty[1] /ˈdɜːti/ (**dirtier, dirtiest**) adj **1** not clean: *piles of dirty washing* ♦ *dirty fingernails* **2** dealing with sex in a way that offends some people: *a dirty joke* **3** dishonest or unfair: *dirty tricks*

dirty[2] /ˈdɜːti/ (**dirties, dirtying, dirtied**) verb [T] to make something dirty

'dirty ,bomb noun [C] a bomb containing harmful nuclear waste that is sent out when the bomb explodes

disability /ˌdɪsəˈbɪləti/ (plural **disabilities**) noun [C/U] a condition in which someone is not able to use a part of their body or brain normally: *children with learning disabilities*

disabled /dɪsˈeɪb(ə)ld/ adj unable to use part of the body or brain normally

disaccharide /daɪˈsækəˌraɪd/ noun [C] CHEMISTRY a sugar made up of two simple sugars joined together

disadvantage /ˌdɪsədˈvɑːntɪdʒ/ noun [C] something that makes someone or something less effective, successful, or attractive: *One of the disadvantages of the job is the long hours I work.* ♦ *Children who don't learn to read are at a serious disadvantage.*

disadvantaged /ˌdɪsəd'vɑːntɪdʒd/ adj not having the same advantages of money or education as other people

disaffected /ˌdɪsə'fektɪd/ adj no longer feeling any loyalty towards a group or leader

disagree /ˌdɪsə'griː/ verb [I] **1** to have a different opinion from someone else ≠ AGREE: *I disagree with you – I think she's done a very good job.* ♦ *Dole and Evans disagree about many aspects of the new policy.* **2** to contain different information, or to produce different results: *Two pathologists examined the body, but their findings disagreed.*

disagreeable /ˌdɪsə'griːəb(ə)l/ adj formal **1** not nice or enjoyable **2** not friendly or polite

disagreement /ˌdɪsə'griːmənt/ noun [C/U] a situation in which people do not agree: *Bowen left the team after a disagreement with the coach.* ♦ *There has been considerable disagreement about the best way to deal with the crisis.*

disallow /ˌdɪsə'laʊ/ verb [T] to say officially that something cannot be accepted or allowed: *The referee disallowed the goal.*

disambiguate /ˌdɪsæm'bɪgjuˌeɪt/ verb [I/T] LANGUAGE to make clear the meaning of a word, phrase etc that has more than one meaning

disappear /ˌdɪsə'pɪə/ verb [I] **1** to become impossible to see or find: *The letter I had left on my desk had disappeared.* ♦ *The train disappeared from view.* **2** to no longer happen or exist: *The symptoms should disappear within a few days.* —**disappearance** noun [C/U]

disappoint /ˌdɪsə'pɔɪnt/ verb [I/T] to make someone feel unhappy or not satisfied: *I hate to disappoint you, but the cake's all gone.*

disappointed /ˌdɪsə'pɔɪntɪd/ adj unhappy because something did not happen or because someone or something was not as good as you expected: *She was disappointed that he never replied to her letter.* ♦ *I am very disappointed at not getting the job.* ♦ *I'm really disappointed in you, Ruth.*

disappointing /ˌdɪsə'pɔɪntɪŋ/ adj not as good as you had hoped or expected: *This year's exam results were very disappointing.* —**disappointingly** adv

disappointment /ˌdɪsə'pɔɪntmənt/ noun **1** [U] the feeling of being unhappy because something did not happen or because someone or something was not as good as you expected: *Diplomats expressed disappointment at the lack of progress.* **2** [C] someone or something that is not as good as you thought they would be: *The team's defeat was a big disappointment to their fans.*

disapproval /ˌdɪsə'pruːv(ə)l/ noun [U] a feeling of not thinking someone or something is good or suitable ≠ APPROVAL: *There were murmurs of disapproval in the audience.*

disapprove /ˌdɪsə'pruːv/ verb [I] to not think someone or something is good or suitable ≠ APPROVE: *Why do you always disapprove of everything I do?*

disapproving /ˌdɪsə'pruːvɪŋ/ adj a disapproving expression or reaction shows that someone does not like something or someone ≠ APPROVING —**disapprovingly** adv

disarm /dɪs'ɑːm/ verb **1** [I] if a country or organization disarms, it reduces or gets rid of its weapons or armed forces **2** [T] to take someone's weapons so that they can no longer use them ≠ ARM **3** [T] to make someone feel less angry or unfriendly: *Interviewers are disarmed by her straightforward approach.*

disarmament /dɪs'ɑːməmənt/ noun [U] the process by which a country reduces or gets rid of its weapons or armed forces

disarming /dɪs'ɑːmɪŋ/ adj making someone feel less angry or unfriendly

disarray /ˌdɪsə'reɪ/ noun [U] a situation in which people are very confused or things are not organized: *The committee was in complete disarray.*

disassembler /ˌdɪsə'semblə/ noun [C] COMPUTING a piece of software that changes **machine language** back into **assembly language**

disassociate /ˌdɪsə'səʊʃiˌeɪt/ verb [T] to **dissociate** two people or things

disaster /dɪ'zɑːstə/ noun **1** [C/U] something very bad that happens and causes a lot of damage or kills a lot of people: *A series of disasters forced the company to close down.* ♦ **natural disasters** (=floods, earthquakes etc) **2** [C] a very bad or annoying situation, or a complete failure: *Our party was a complete disaster.*

di'saster ˌarea noun [C] a place or region that has been badly affected by a disaster

disastrous /dɪ'zɑːstrəs/ adj very bad, harmful, or unsuccessful: *The spending cuts would be disastrous for schools.* ♦ *a disastrous start to the school term* —**disastrously** adv

disband /dɪs'bænd/ verb [I/T] if a group of people disbands, or if it is disbanded, its members stop working together

disbar /dɪs'bɑː/ (**disbars, disbarring, disbarred**) verb [T] LAW to officially stop a lawyer from doing any legal work

disbelief /ˌdɪsbɪ'liːf/ noun [U] the feeling of not believing someone or something

disc /dɪsk/ noun [C] **1** a flat circular object or shape **2** COMPUTING a computer disk **3** ANATOMY a round flat piece of cartilage between the **vertebrae** in the back

discard /dɪs'kɑːd/ verb [T] to get rid of something that is no longer wanted or needed

'disc ˌbrakes noun [plural] a pair of small hard surfaces inside the wheel of a car that press against a disc and stop the car from moving

discern /dɪ'sɜːn/ verb [T] formal to notice, see, or understand something: *It's hard to discern exactly what his motives are.* —**discernible** adj

discharge¹ /dɪs'tʃɑːdʒ/ verb **1** [I/T] PHYSICS if something discharges electricity, or if it discharges, electricity flows out of it **2** [I/T] to make liquid or gas leave a place **3** [T] to allow or force someone to leave a hospital, a prison, or the army ≠ RELEASE **4** [T] formal to perform a duty or responsibility

discharge² /'dɪstʃɑːdʒ/ noun

1 flow of electricity	4 when sb may leave
2 liquid/gas that leaves	5 carrying out of duty
3 liquid from sick body	

1 [C/U] PHYSICS a flow of electricity, for example from a piece of equipment or during a storm
2 [C/U] a liquid, gas, or other substance that comes out of something else
3 [C/U] HEALTH a liquid that comes out from a part of someone's body when they are ill
4 [C/U] official permission to leave a hospital, a prison, or the army
5 [U] formal the act of performing a duty or responsibility

disciple /dɪ'saɪp(ə)l/ noun [C] **1** someone who admires and is influenced by a political or religious leader **2** RELIGION one of the twelve original followers of Jesus Christ, according to the Bible

disciplinarian /ˌdɪsəplɪ'neəriən/ noun [C] someone who forces people to obey rules

disciplinary /'dɪsəˌplɪnəri/ adj connected with the punishment of people who do not obey rules

discipline¹ /'dɪsəplɪn/ noun **1** [U] the practice of making people obey rules and punishing them if they do not: *He believes in strict discipline.* **2** [C] EDUCATION a subject that people study, especially at a university: *academic disciplines* **3** [U] the ability to control your own behaviour: *Many of the students lacked the discipline to learn.*

discipline² /'dɪsəplɪn/ verb [T] to punish someone for something wrong that they have done

disciplined /'dɪsəplɪnd/ adj well organized and following rules or standards: *the team's disciplined approach*

'disc ˌjockey noun [C] MUSIC a **DJ**

disclaimer /dɪs'kleɪmə/ noun [C] a statement in which someone says that they do not take responsibility for something

disclose /dɪs'kləʊz/ verb [T] to give people information that was secret: *They failed to disclose that profits had fallen.*

disclosure /dɪs'kləʊʒə/ noun [C/U] the act of telling people information that was secret, or the information that is told: *a series of disclosures that almost wrecked his career*

disco /'dɪskəʊ/ (plural **discos**) noun MUSIC **1** [C] a place where people dance to popular music **2** [U] a type of popular **dance music** from the 1970s

discoloured /dɪs'kʌləd/ adj changed in colour and no longer looking new, clean, or healthy: *discoloured wallpaper*

discomfort /dɪs'kʌmfət/ noun **1** [U] a feeling of slight pain: *I felt discomfort in my lower back.* **2** [C] something that makes you feel slightly ill or uncomfortable: *the discomforts of life in the desert*

disconcerted /ˌdɪskən'sɜːtɪd/ adj feeling worried, confused, or surprised

disconcerting /ˌdɪskən'sɜːtɪŋ/ adj making you feel worried, confused, or surprised

disconnect /ˌdɪskə'nekt/ verb [T] **1** to separate two things that were connected to each other **2** to stop someone's telephone service or supply of gas, water, or electricity ≠ CONNECT: *His telephone has been disconnected.*

discontent /ˌdɪskən'tent/ noun [U] the unhappy feeling that you have when you are not satisfied with something: *Public discontent with the government is growing.* —**discontented** adj

discontinue /ˌdɪskən'tɪnjuː/ verb [T] to stop doing something, or to stop providing a product or service

discontinuity /ˌdɪskɒntɪ'njuːəti/ noun [C] formal a change in a process that is usually continuous

discontinuous /ˌdɪskən'tɪnjuəs/ adj formal not continuing in a steady way

discord /'dɪskɔːd/ noun **1** [U] formal disagreement between people **2** [C/U] MUSIC a strange sound in a piece of music, made by playing an unusual combination of notes at the same time

discordant /dɪs'kɔːd(ə)nt/ adj MUSIC discordant music sounds strange because it contains discords

discount¹ /'dɪsˌkaʊnt/ noun [C] a reduction in the price of something: *The store is offering a 10% discount on school textbooks.*

discount² /dɪs'kaʊnt/ verb [T] **1** to reduce the price of something **2** to decide that something is not important, possible, or likely: *Police have discounted the possibility that this was a terrorist attack.*

discourage /dɪs'kʌrɪdʒ/ verb [T] **1** to try to prevent something from happening ≠ ENCOURAGE: *We hope the bad weather won't discourage people from coming along.* **2** to make someone feel less confident or hopeful: *What she said didn't discourage me.* —**discouragement** noun [C/U]

discouraged /dɪs'kʌrɪdʒd/ adj feeling less confident or hopeful: *Don't get discouraged – just keep trying.*

discouraging /dɪs'kʌrɪdʒɪŋ/ adj making you feel less confident or hopeful ≠ ENCOURAGING

discourse /'dɪskɔːs/ noun **1** [C] formal a long serious speech or piece of writing on a particular subject **2** [U] LANGUAGE written or spoken language, especially when it is studied in order to understand how people use language

'discourse ˌmarker noun [C] LANGUAGE **1** a word that is used for showing a change in the way the conversation is developing, or for showing the other speaker how you are reacting to what they are saying. Typical discourse markers include 'well', 'oh', and 'OK'. **2** words such as 'however' or 'furthermore' that provide a connection between ideas in written language

discover /dɪ'skʌvə/ verb [T] **1** to find something that was hidden or that no one knew about before: *William Herschel discovered Uranus in 1781.* **2** to find out something that you did not know before: *He became very friendly when he discovered she was my sister.* **3** to recognize the ability of someone and help to make them famous

discovery /dɪ'skʌv(ə)ri/ (plural **discoveries**) noun **1** [C/U] the act of finding or learning about something that was hidden or not known: *Police announced the discovery of the body late last night.* ♦ *Mr Andrews told of his family's joy following the discovery that his son was alive.* **2** [C] something that is found, or something new that is learned: *This is one of the most important archaeological discoveries of the century.* **3** [U] LAW the process of making evidence and other documents available to the people involved in a legal case

discredit /dɪs'kredɪt/ verb [T] to make people stop believing or respecting someone or something: *She claims there was a conspiracy to discredit her.* —**discredit** noun [U]

discreet /dɪ'skriːt/ adj careful not to say anything that is secret or that could upset someone ≠ INDISCREET —**discreetly** adv

discrepancy /dɪs'krepənsi/ (plural **discrepancies**) noun [C/U] a difference between things that should be the same: *a discrepancy between estimated and actual spending*

discrete /dɪ'skriːt/ adj formal separate —**discretely** adv

dis,crete 'variable noun [C] MATHS a **variable** that is one of a limited group of possible numbers within a particular range of numbers, usually one used for counting

discretion /dɪ'skreʃ(ə)n/ noun [U] **1** the right or ability to make a judgment or decision rather than follow a set of rules: *The funds may be spent at the manager's* *discretion* (=according to decisions made by the manager). **2** careful and sensitive behaviour that does not upset or offend people ≠ INDISCRETION

discretionary /dɪˈskreʃ(ə)n(ə)ri/ adj based on someone's judgment of a particular situation rather than on a set of rules: *a discretionary payment*

discriminate /dɪˈskrɪmɪneɪt/ verb **1** [I] SOCIAL STUDIES to treat someone unfairly because of their religion, race, or other personal features: *laws that discriminate against women* **2** [I/T] to recognize the difference between things

discriminating /dɪˈskrɪmɪˌneɪtɪŋ/ adj able to judge whether or not something is good or suitable

discrimination /dɪˌskrɪmɪˈneɪʃ(ə)n/ noun [U] **1** SOCIAL STUDIES unfair treatment of someone because of their religion, race, or other personal features: *sex discrimination* ♦ *discrimination against disabled people* **2** the ability to judge whether something is good or suitable

discriminatory /dɪˈskrɪmɪnət(ə)ri/ adj SOCIAL STUDIES treating a particular group of people unfairly because of their religion, race, or other personal features: *discriminatory practices*

discus /ˈdɪskəs/ noun [C] SPORTS a heavy round flat object thrown as part of a sports event

discuss /dɪˈskʌs/ verb [T] **1** to talk about something with someone: *You should discuss this problem with your doctor.* **2** to write or talk about a subject in detail: *The causes of stress have already been discussed in Chapter 3.*

discussion /dɪˈskʌʃ(ə)n/ noun **1** [C] a conversation about something important: *We need to have a discussion about your school work.* ♦ *Discussions with management have broken down.* **2** [U] the process of talking about something that is important: *They're in discussion with a German company about a possible takeover.* ♦ *Proposals for changing the existing system are currently under discussion* (=being discussed).

disˈcussion ˌboard noun [C] COMPUTING a website on which a group of users exchange ideas on a particular subject

disˈcussion ˌlist noun [C] COMPUTING a website where people can discuss a particular subject

disdain /dɪsˈdeɪn/ noun [U] the feeling that someone or something is not important and does not deserve any respect —**disdainful** adj

disease /dɪˈziːz/ noun [C/U] HEALTH a medical condition in humans or other animals and plants that can cause serious health problems or death: *liver disease* ♦ *Studies have revealed that fewer vegetarians suffer from heart disease.* ♦ *Smoking can cause fatal diseases.* —**diseased** /dɪˈziːzd/ adj

disembark /ˌdɪsɪmˈbɑːk/ verb [I] *formal* to get off a ship or plane ≠ EMBARK

disembarkation card /ˌdɪsembɑːˈkeɪʃ(ə)n ˌkɑːd/ noun [C] TOURISM a card that allows a passenger to get off a plane or boat, and return after a short time

disempower /ˌdɪsɪmˈpaʊə/ verb [T] to reduce the amount of control that someone has over a situation or over their life

disenchanted /ˌdɪsɪnˈtʃɑːntɪd/ adj disappointed and no longer enthusiastic about someone or something —**disenchantment** noun [U]

disentangle /ˌdɪsɪnˈtæŋg(ə)l/ verb [T] to separate something from the thing that is holding it or that is twisted around it

disfigure /dɪsˈfɪɡə/ verb [T] to spoil the appearance of someone or something

disgrace¹ /dɪsˈɡreɪs/ noun **1** [U] the loss of other people's respect that someone suffers because they have done something bad **2** [singular] something that is so bad that it makes people angry: *The way he treats his children is a disgrace.*

disgrace² /dɪsˈɡreɪs/ verb [T] *formal* to harm the reputation of a person or group by doing something bad or immoral

disgraceful /dɪsˈɡreɪsf(ə)l/ adj extremely bad or shocking —**disgracefully** adv

disgruntled /dɪsˈɡrʌnt(ə)ld/ adj disappointed and annoyed

disguise¹ /dɪsˈɡaɪz/ verb [T] **1** to hide something such as your feelings or intentions **2** be disguised to change the way that you look or sound so that other people will not recognize you

disguise² /dɪsˈɡaɪz/ noun [C/U] **1** something that someone wears in order to change their appearance, so that other people will not recognize them: *He often went out in disguise to avoid being recognized.* **2** something that hides what something really is → BLESSING

disgust¹ /dɪsˈɡʌst/ noun [U] **1** a very strong feeling of not liking something, or of anger about something bad or immoral **2** a feeling that you are going to be physically ill that happens when you see, smell, or taste something very unpleasant

disgust² /dɪsˈɡʌst/ verb [T] **1** if something disgusts someone, it is so bad or immoral that it makes them feel angry and upset = REVOLT: *Your attitude disgusts me.* **2** to make someone feel physically ill

disgusted /dɪsˈɡʌstɪd/ adj **1** feeling very angry and upset about something that you do not approve of: *I was disgusted by the way he treated those women.* **2** feeling physically ill because something is extremely unpleasant to see, smell, or taste

disgusting /dɪsˈɡʌstɪŋ/ adj **1** extremely unpleasant = REVOLTING **2** very bad or shocking —**disgustingly** adv

dish /dɪʃ/ noun **1** [C] a container similar to a plate or bowl that is used for serving or cooking food: *Place the fruit in a large shallow dish.* **2** [C] food that has been prepared and cooked in a particular way: *Do you have any traditional Malaysian dishes?* **3 dishes** [plural] the plates, pans etc that have to be washed after a meal: *Who's going to do the dishes?* **4** [C] a round piece of equipment that sends or receives radio or television messages: *a satellite dish*

disheartened /dɪsˈhɑːt(ə)nd/ adj no longer confident or enthusiastic about something

dishevelled /dɪˈʃev(ə)ld/ adj with hair and clothes that do not look tidy

dishonest /dɪsˈɒnɪst/ adj willing to do things that are not honest ≠ HONEST —**dishonestly** adv

dishonesty /dɪsˈɒnəsti/ noun [U] behaviour that is not honest, such as telling lies ≠ HONESTY

dishonourable /dɪsˈɒn(ə)rəb(ə)l/ adj *formal* considered bad or morally wrong ≠ HONOURABLE —**dishonourably** adv

disillusioned /ˌdɪsɪˈluːʒ(ə)nd/ adj disappointed because you realize that something is not as good as you thought it was

disincentive /ˌdɪsɪnˈsentɪv/ noun [C] something that makes you not want to do something

disinfect /ˌdɪsɪnˈfekt/ verb [T] to clean something by putting a substance on it that kills bacteria —**disinfection** noun [C/U]

disinfectant /ˌdɪsɪnˈfektənt/ noun [C/U] a chemical substance that kills bacteria, used for cleaning things

disinflation /ˌdɪsɪnˈfleɪʃ(ə)n/ noun [U] ECONOMICS a reduction in the rate at which prices increase

disingenuous /ˌdɪsɪnˈdʒenjuəs/ adj formal not really honest or sincere, and only pretending to be —**disingenuously** adv

disintegrate /dɪsˈɪntɪˌɡreɪt/ verb [I] **1** to be completely destroyed by breaking into lots of very small pieces **2** to become less effective and stop working —**disintegration** /dɪsˌɪntɪˈɡreɪʃ(ə)n/ noun [U]

disinterested /dɪsˈɪntrəstɪd/ adj not involved in something and therefore able to judge it fairly → UNINTERESTED

disinvestment /ˌdɪsɪnˈvestmənt/ noun [U] BUSINESS the act of taking back all or part of the money invested in a particular country, industry, or business by selling shares in it

disjoint /dɪsˈdʒɔɪnt/ adj MATHS disjoint sets contain different numbers from each other

disjoint group noun [C] MATHS a group that contains no members that are found in another group

disk /dɪsk/ noun [C] COMPUTING a small flat circular object that is used for storing information from a computer. Different types of disks are **floppy disks**, **compact discs** (=CDs), and the **hard disk** inside a computer.

disk compression noun [U] COMPUTING a way of making more space available on a computer by **compressing** a file when you save it, and changing it back to its original form when you open it again

disk drive noun [C] COMPUTING the part of a computer that reads information from a disk or records information onto a disk

diskette /dɪˈsket/ noun [C] COMPUTING a **floppy disk** for storing computer information

dislike¹ /dɪsˈlaɪk/ verb [T] to not like someone or something: Cats dislike getting their fur wet.

> Build your vocabulary: words you can use instead of **dislike**
>
> ■ **not like** to have negative feelings about someone or something
> ■ **not be crazy about/not be keen on** (informal) used for saying that you do not like something, in situations where you do not want to sound rude
> ■ **hate** to dislike someone or something very much
> ■ **can't stand/can't bear** to dislike someone or something so strongly that it makes you feel angry or upset
> ■ **detest/loathe** used for emphasizing that you strongly dislike someone or something

dislike² /dɪsˈlaɪk/ noun **1** [singular/U] a feeling of not liking someone or something **2** [C] something that you do not like: We were asked to list our **likes and dislikes**.

dislocate /ˈdɪsləkeɪt/ verb [T] to do something that forces a bone out of its normal position —**dislocation** /ˌdɪsləˈkeɪʃ(ə)n/ noun [C]

disloyal /dɪsˈlɔɪəl/ adj someone who is disloyal is not loyal to a friend, a member of their family, or an organization that they belong to —**disloyalty** noun [U]

dismal /ˈdɪzm(ə)l/ adj **1** making you feel unhappy and without hope or enthusiasm: dismal living conditions **2** very bad —**dismally** adv

dismantle /dɪsˈmænt(ə)l/ verb [T] **1** to separate the parts of something so that they no longer form a single unit **2** to end a political or economic system, or to get rid of an institution

dismay /dɪsˈmeɪ/ noun [U] the feeling of being very worried, disappointed, or sad about something that is surprising or shocking —**dismayed** /dɪsˈmeɪd/ adj

dismiss /dɪsˈmɪs/ verb [T]

1 refuse to believe sth	4 in law
2 force sb from job	5 in cricket
3 tell sb to leave	

1 to refuse to accept that something could be true or important: Their evidence was **dismissed as** completely worthless.
2 to force someone to leave their job = FIRE, SACK: Edwards claimed that he had been unfairly dismissed from his post.
3 to give someone permission to leave a place: The class is dismissed.
4 LAW to officially decide that a court case should not continue
5 SPORTS in **cricket**, to end the **innings** of a **batsman** or a team

dismissal /dɪsˈmɪs(ə)l/ noun **1** [C/U] an act of making someone leave their job **2** [U] a refusal to accept that something could be true or important: the committee's dismissal of their complaints **3** [C/U] LAW a decision that a court case should not continue

dismissive /dɪsˈmɪsɪv/ adj showing that you do not think that something is worth paying attention to

dismount /dɪsˈmaʊnt/ verb [I] formal to get off a horse or bicycle

disobedience /ˌdɪsəˈbiːdiəns/ noun [U] behaviour in which someone refuses to obey orders or rules = DEFIANCE

disobedient /ˌdɪsəˈbiːdiənt/ adj refusing to do what someone in authority has ordered, or refusing to obey rules = DEFIANT ≠ OBEDIENT

disobey /ˌdɪsəˈbeɪ/ verb [I/T] to deliberately not pay attention to a rule or an order from someone in authority = DEFY ≠ OBEY

disorder /dɪsˈɔːdə/ noun **1** [C/U] HEALTH an illness or medical condition **2** [U] a situation in which people behave in a noisy or violent way **3** [U] a situation in which things are not tidy

disordered /dɪsˈɔːdəd/ adj not tidy, not well organized, or mentally confused

disorderly /dɪsˈɔːdəli/ adj **1** behaving in a noisy or violent way **2** not tidy

disorderly conduct noun [U] LAW the crime of being too noisy or violent in a public place

disorganized /dɪsˈɔːɡənaɪzd/ adj **1** not arranged according to a clear plan or system **2** not good at dealing with things in a clear or sensible way

disorientated /dɪsˈɔːriənˌteɪtɪd/ or **disoriented** /dɪsˈɔːriˌentɪd/ adj **1** confused about where you are or what direction you are moving in **2** unable to think clearly or make sensible decisions = CONFUSED

disown /dɪsˈəʊn/ verb [T] to say that you no longer want to be connected with someone or something: I think my parents would disown me if I ever took drugs.

disparaging /dɪˈspærɪdʒɪŋ/ adj showing that you have no respect for someone or something: disparaging comments

disparate /ˈdɪsp(ə)rət/ adj formal disparate things belong to very different groups or classes

disparity /dɪˈspærəti/ noun [singular/U] formal a difference between things

dispassionate /dɪsˈpæʃ(ə)nət/ adj formal able to make fair judgments or decisions that are not influenced by personal feelings = DETACHED
—**dispassionately** adv

dispatch /dɪˈspætʃ/ verb [T] formal to send someone or something somewhere

dispel /dɪˈspel/ (**dispels, dispelling, dispelled**) verb [T] to get rid of unpleasant feelings or false beliefs

dispensary /dɪˈspensəri/ (plural **dispensaries**) noun [C] HEALTH a place in a hospital where people can get medicines and drugs

dispense /dɪˈspens/ verb [T] to provide people with something

> PHRASAL VERB **diˈspense with sb/sth** formal to stop using someone or something because you no longer want or need them

dispenser /dɪˈspensə/ noun [C] a machine or container from which people can get something such as drinks or money

dispersal /dɪˈspɜːs(ə)l/ noun [U] **1** BIOLOGY the process by which the seeds of plants are spread over a wide area. For example in **wind dispersal**, the seeds are carried by the wind. **2** the process of spreading people or things in different directions over a wide area

disperse /dɪˈspɜːs/ verb [I/T] **1** if a crowd of people disperses, or if someone disperses it, the people separate and go in different directions: *Soldiers fired tear gas to disperse the crowds.* **2** to spread in different directions over a wide area, or to make things do this

dispersed /dɪˈspɜːst/ adj spread over a wide area

dispersion /dɪˈspɜːʃ(ə)n/ noun [U] **1** the process of dispersing something **2** PHYSICS the separation of a beam of light into several different colours

dispirited /dɪˈspɪrɪtɪd/ adj no longer feeling any hope, enthusiasm, or interest

displace /dɪsˈpleɪs/ verb [T] **1** to force someone to leave their own country and live somewhere else **2** to take the place of someone or something **3** to force something out of its position or space

displaced person /ˌdɪspleɪst ˈpɜːs(ə)n/ noun [C] someone who has been forced to leave their own country and live somewhere else, for example because there is a war in their own country

displacement /dɪsˈpleɪsmənt/ noun [U] **1** PHYSICS the amount of water that an object pushes out of the way when it is placed in water **2** the process of forcing something out of its position or space **3** a situation in which a person is forced to leave their own country and go somewhere else to live

disˈplacement acˌtivity noun [C/U] something that you do in order to avoid dealing with an unpleasant situation

display¹ /dɪˈspleɪ/ verb [T] **1** to put something in a particular place so that people can see it easily: *She displayed some of her paintings at the local arts festival.* **2** to show a feeling, quality, or attitude by the way that you behave: *From an early age he displayed a talent for singing.* **3** COMPUTING to show information on a computer screen

display² /dɪˈspleɪ/ noun [C] **1** an arrangement of things for people to look at: *a window display* **2** a performance for people to look at: *a firework display* **3** an occasion when someone shows a particular feeling, quality, or attitude: *a public **display** of Anglo-American unity* **4** COMPUTING a computer screen, or a similar piece of equipment that shows information

> PHRASE **on display** if something is on display, it is in a place where it can be seen by many people: *Her work is on display at the gallery.*

disˈplay ˌadvertising noun [U] BUSINESS advertisements in newspapers or magazines that use thick dark letters, photographs, symbols etc in order to be easy to notice

displeased /dɪsˈpliːzd/ adj formal annoyed or angry

displeasure /dɪsˈpleʒə/ noun [U] formal the feeling of being annoyed or angry

disposable /dɪˈspəʊzəb(ə)l/ adj designed to be thrown away after being used once or a few times

disˌposable ˈincome noun [U] money that someone has left to spend after they have paid their bills

disposables /dɪˈspəʊzəb(ə)lz/ noun [plural] HEALTH items such as medical equipment and supplies that are designed to be used only once

disposal /dɪˈspəʊz(ə)l/ noun [U] the process of getting rid of something: *the disposal of nuclear waste*

> PHRASE **at sb's disposal** available for someone to use at any time

disposed /dɪˈspəʊzd/ adj formal **1 be disposed to sth** likely to behave or think in a particular way **2 be disposed to do sth** to be willing to do something

disposition /ˌdɪspəˈzɪʃ(ə)n/ noun [singular] the way that someone normally thinks and behaves: *a warm and friendly disposition*

dispossessed /ˌdɪspəˈzest/ adj formal people who are dispossessed have had something valuable such as their land taken away from them

disproportionate /ˌdɪsprəˈpɔːʃ(ə)nət/ adj too big or too small in comparison with something else
—**disproportionately** adv

disprove /dɪsˈpruːv/ verb [T] to prove that something is not correct or true

dispute¹ /dɪˈspjuːt, ˈdɪspjuːt/ noun [C/U] a serious disagreement, especially one that involves groups of people and lasts for a long time: *The two companies are still in **dispute**.* ♦ *a dispute over pay* ♦ *We got involved in a **dispute with** the neighbours.*

dispute² /dɪˈspjuːt/ verb **1** [T] to say that something is not true or correct **2** [I/T] to argue about something

disqualify /dɪsˈkwɒlɪfaɪ/ (**disqualifies, disqualifying, disqualified**) verb [T] to not allow someone to take part in something, usually because they have done something wrong

disregard¹ /ˌdɪsrɪˈɡɑːd/ noun [singular/U] the attitude of someone who does not respect something or does not think that it is important

disregard² /ˌdɪsrɪˈɡɑːd/ verb [T] to not think that something is important, or to not pay any attention to it

disrepair /ˌdɪsrɪˈpeə/ noun [U] formal a broken or damaged state

disreputable /dɪsˈrepjʊtəb(ə)l/ adj not respected, and thought to be dishonest or illegal

disrepute /ˌdɪsrɪˈpjuːt/ noun [U] formal a situation in which people have no respect for someone or something

disrespect /ˌdɪsrɪˈspekt/ noun [U] a lack of respect for someone or something —**disrespectful** adj

disrupt /dɪsˈrʌpt/ verb [T] to interrupt something and prevent it from continuing: *Protesters tried to disrupt the meeting.* —**disruption** /dɪsˈrʌpʃ(ə)n/ noun [C/U]

disruptive /dɪsˈrʌptɪv/ adj causing difficulties that interrupt something and prevent it from continuing

dissatisfaction /dɪsˌsætɪsˈfækʃ(ə)n/ noun [U] the annoyed feeling that you get when something is not as good as you expected it to be ≠ SATISFACTION

dissatisfied /dɪsˈsætɪsfaɪd/ adj annoyed because something is not as good as you expected it to be ≠ SATISFIED: *a dissatisfied customer*

dissect /dɪˈsekt/ verb [T] to cut the body of a dead person or animal into pieces in order to examine it —**dissection** /dɪˈsekʃ(ə)n/ noun [C/U]

disseminate /dɪˈsemɪneɪt/ verb [T] *formal* to make something such as information or knowledge available to a lot of people —**dissemination** /dɪˌsemɪˈneɪʃ(ə)n/ noun [U]

dissent /dɪˈsent/ noun [U] strong disagreement, especially with what people in authority think or with what the majority of people think —**dissent** verb [I]

dissertation /ˌdɪsəˈteɪʃ(ə)n/ noun [C] EDUCATION a long piece of writing on a particular subject that you do as part of a university degree

dissident /ˈdɪsɪdənt/ noun [C] someone who disagrees publicly with a government —**dissident** adj

dissimilar /dɪˈsɪmɪlə/ adj different from someone or something else

dissociate /dɪˈsəʊʃieɪt/ or **disassociate** /ˌdɪsəˈsəʊʃieɪt/ verb 1 *formal* to consider two people or things to be separate, different, or not connected to each other 2 **dissociate yourself from** to show clearly that someone is not connected with someone or something —**dissociation** /dɪˌsəʊsiˈeɪʃ(ə)n/ noun [U]

dissolution /ˌdɪsəˈluːʃ(ə)n/ noun [U] the process of officially ending the existence of an organization, institution, or agreement

dissolve /dɪˈzɒlv/ verb 1 [I/T] CHEMISTRY if a solid substance dissolves in a liquid, or if someone dissolves it, it mixes into the liquid and becomes included in it 2 [T] *formal* to officially end the existence of an organization, institution, or agreement

dissonance /ˈdɪsənəns/ noun [C/U] MUSIC an unpleasant sound created when musical notes played together are not in **harmony** —**dissonant** adj

dissuade /dɪˈsweɪd/ verb [T] *formal* to persuade someone not to do something

distal /ˈdɪst(ə)l/ adj ANATOMY further away from the centre of the body, or from the point where something is attached to the body → PROXIMAL

distance /ˈdɪstəns/ noun 1 [C/U] the amount of space between two people or things: *the distance from the Earth to the Sun* ♦ *They started to walk the short distance to the camp.* ♦ *The house is within walking distance of the university.* 2 [singular/U] if there is a distance between two people, their relationship is not friendly or close

PHRASES **at/from a distance** at/from a place that is not close: *I've only ever seen him from a distance.*
in/into the distance at/to a place that is very far from where you are, although you can still see or hear things that are there: *The peaks of the Himalayas could be seen in the distance.* ♦ *He stared into the distance.*
keep your distance to avoid going near someone or something

'distance ˌlearning noun [U] EDUCATION a system in which students work at home and send work to their teachers by post or email

'distance ˌmultiplier noun [C] PHYSICS a system that places the force that is needed to move an object close to a **fulcrum**, in order to increase the distance the object can be moved → FORCE MULTIPLIER —*picture* → LEVER

distant /ˈdɪstənt/ adj 1 far away from the place where you are: *the distant sound of traffic* 2 far away in time: *our ancestors from the distant past* 3 related, but not in a close way: *a distant relative* 4 seeming unfriendly, or not showing strong feelings: *Laura was cold and distant.* —**distantly** adv: *distantly related cousins* ♦ *Ivan smiled distantly.*

distaste /dɪsˈteɪst/ noun [U] a feeling of dislike for someone or something that you do not approve of

distasteful /dɪsˈteɪstf(ə)l/ adj unpleasant in a way that upsets or offends you

distemper /dɪsˈtempə/ noun [U] 1 thick paint used for painting walls 2 a serious infectious disease that affects animals, especially dogs

distend /dɪˈstend/ verb [I/T] to swell, or to make something swell

distended /dɪˈstendɪd/ adj *formal* swollen

distil /dɪˈstɪl/ (**distils**, **distilling**, **distilled**) verb [T] 1 SCIENCE to heat a solution until it becomes a gas and then **cool** it, in order to produce a purer or more concentrated liquid by **condensation** 2 to produce a summary that contains only the most important ideas or pieces of information

distillate /ˈdɪstɪlət/ noun [C/U] SCIENCE a liquid that has been distilled

distillation /ˌdɪstɪˈleɪʃ(ə)n/ noun [U] SCIENCE the process of heating a solution until it becomes a gas and then letting it **cool** in order to produce a purer or more concentrated liquid by **condensation** —*picture* → on next page

distilled water /dɪˌstɪld ˈwɔːtə/ noun [U] SCIENCE water that has gone through the process of distillation to remove salts and other compounds

distilling flask /dɪˈstɪlɪŋ ˌflɑːsk/ noun [C] SCIENCE a piece of laboratory equipment in the form of a glass container, used for **distilling** liquids —*picture* → DISTILLATION

distinct /dɪˈstɪŋkt/ adj 1 separate and different in a way that is clear: *The animals were put into two distinct groups.* 2 able to be clearly seen, heard, smelled, or tasted ≠ INDISTINCT: *As dawn broke, the outline of a building became distinct against the sky.* ♦ *a distinct smell of burning* 3 definite and obvious: *a distinct disadvantage*

distinction /dɪˈstɪŋkʃ(ə)n/ noun 1 [C] a difference between two things: *the clear distinction between rich and poor* ♦ *The school does not make a distinction between education for girls and boys.* 2 [U] *formal* the excellent skills or features that someone or something has, or the high status that this brings: *a writer of great distinction* 3 [singular] an unusual achievement or feature that makes someone or something different: *She held the distinction of being the first woman editor of a national newspaper.* 4 [C/U] EDUCATION a very high mark in an examination

distinctive /dɪˈstɪŋktɪv/ adj easy to recognize because of being different from other people or things of the same type —**distinctively** adv

distinctly /dɪˈstɪŋk(t)li/ adv 1 clearly: *I distinctly remember seeing him.* 2 extremely: *Lucy felt distinctly uncomfortable.*

distinguish /dɪˈstɪŋgwɪʃ/ verb 1 [I/T] to recognize the differences between things = DIFFERENTIATE: *He learned to distinguish the songs of different birds.* ♦ *information on how to distinguish between the different diseases* ♦ *the ability to distinguish right from wrong* 2 [T] to be a feature that makes someone or

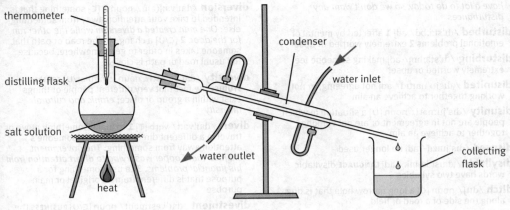

- thermometer
- condenser
- distilling flask
- water inlet
- salt solution
- water outlet
- collecting flask
- heat

distillation

something clearly different from other similar people or things **= DIFFERENTIATE:** *What distinguished Alex from the rest of us was his exceptional ability as a writer.* **3** [T] *formal* to be able to hear, see, smell, or taste something clearly

  PHRASE   distinguish yourself to do something very well so that people notice and respect you

distinguishable /dɪˈstɪŋɡwɪʃəb(ə)l/ adj **1** clearly different from other people or things of the same type **≠ INDISTINGUISHABLE 2** easy to see, hear, smell, or taste

distinguished /dɪˈstɪŋɡwɪʃt/ adj successful and respected by many people

distort /dɪˈstɔːt/ verb [T] **1** to change something so that it is no longer true or accurate: *The paper was accused of distorting the truth.* **2** to change the way that something looks, sounds, or behaves so that it becomes strange or difficult to recognize: *Her face was distorted with pain.* —**distortion** /dɪˈstɔːʃ(ə)n/ noun [C/U]

distract /dɪˈstrækt/ verb [T] to get someone's attention and prevent them from concentrating on something: *The noise was distracting me.*

distracted /dɪˈstræktɪd/ adj not able to concentrate on something —**distractedly** adv

distraction /dɪˈstrækʃ(ə)n/ noun [C/U] something that gets your attention and prevents you from concentrating on something else

distraught /dɪˈstrɔːt/ adj extremely worried, upset, or confused

distress¹ /dɪˈstres/ noun [U] **1** a feeling that someone has when they are very unhappy, worried, or upset: *It was obvious that Gina was in great distress.* **2** a situation in which a ship or aircraft is in great danger and likely to sink or crash —**distressed** /dɪˈstrest/ adj

distress² /dɪˈstres/ verb [T] to make someone feel very unhappy, worried, or upset

distressing /dɪˈstresɪŋ/ adj making someone feel extremely unhappy, worried, or upset: *distressing news*

distributary /dɪsˈtrɪbjuːtəri/ noun [C] **GEOGRAPHY** a stream that comes from, and flows away from, a main body of water

distribute /dɪˈstrɪbjuːt/ verb [T] **1** to give something such as food, clothes, or money to a group of people, especially so that each person gets an equal share: *The two men were distributing beans and maize to the refugees.* ◆ *We distributed beans and maize to the refugees.* **2 BUSINESS** to supply goods from one central place: *Hollywood movies are distributed worldwide.* **3** to

spread something over an area: *The steel beam distributes the pressure evenly across the structure.*

distribution /ˌdɪstrɪˈbjuːʃ(ə)n/ noun **1** [U] the process of giving something such as food, clothes, or money to a group of people: *the distribution of food and clothing in the disaster area* **2** [C/U] the way in which something is shared among people or spread over an area: *Brazil has a very unequal distribution of wealth.* **3** [U] **BUSINESS** the process of supplying goods from one central place: *the marketing and distribution of the software* —**distributive** adj

distri'bution ,channel noun [C] **BUSINESS** a system that a company uses to deliver a product or service to its customers

distri'bution ,pattern noun [C] **BIOLOGY** used for talking about where different plants, animals etc are found in an area

distributor /dɪˈstrɪbjʊtə/ noun [C] **1 BUSINESS** a person or company that supplies goods to shops and businesses **2 ENGINEERING** the part of a car engine that sends electricity to the **spark plugs**

district /ˈdɪstrɪkt/ noun [C] **1** an area of a town or country: *They live in one of the most exclusive districts of Mumbai.* ◆ *the city's new financial district* **2** one of the areas into which a town or country is divided for official purposes: *a district judge*

district at'torney noun [C] **LAW** a lawyer who works for a state or **county** government in the US and whose job is to bring people accused of crimes to trial

district 'court noun [C] **LAW** a court in the US that deals with cases in a particular national or state district

distrust /dɪsˈtrʌst/ noun [U] a feeling that you cannot trust someone or something **→ MISTRUST** —**distrust** verb [T]

disturb /dɪˈstɜːb/ verb [T] **1** to interrupt someone and stop them from continuing what they were doing: *Sorry to disturb you, but do you know where Miss Springer is?* **2** to upset and worry someone a lot: *He is very conservative, and any sort of change disturbs him.* **3** to make something move: *A soft breeze gently disturbed the surface of the pool.*

  PHRASE   disturb the peace LAW to commit the illegal act of behaving in a noisy way in public, especially late at night

disturbance /dɪˈstɜːbəns/ noun [C] **1** an occasion on which people behave in a noisy or violent way in a public place: *There were serious disturbances in the city last summer.* **2** something that interrupts you and stops you from continuing what you were doing: *We* have a lot to do today, so we don't want any disturbances.

disturbed /dɪ'stɜːbd/ adj **1** affected by mental or emotional problems **2** extremely worried or upset

disturbing /dɪ'stɜːbɪŋ/ adj making someone feel extremely worried or upset

disunited /,dɪsjʊ'naɪtɪd/ adj not agreeing, or not working together to achieve an aim

disunity /dɪs'juːnəti/ noun [U] a situation in which people are not in agreement or are not working together to achieve an aim

disused /dɪs'juːzd/ adj no longer used

disyllabic /,daɪsɪ'læbɪk/ adj LANGUAGE disyllabic words have two syllables

ditch /dɪtʃ/ noun [C] a long narrow hole that is dug along the side of a road or field

ditransitive /daɪ'trænsətɪv/ adj LANGUAGE a ditransitive verb has both a **direct object** and an **indirect object**. In the sentence 'Pour him some water', 'pour' is ditransitive.

diuretic /,daɪjʊ'retɪk/ noun [C] HEALTH a substance that makes the body produce more urine —**diuretic** adj

diurnal /daɪ'ɜːn(ə)l/ adj BIOLOGY a diurnal animal is awake and active during the day ≠ NOCTURNAL

dive¹ /daɪv/ verb [I] **1** to jump into water with your head first and with your arms stretched out in front of you: *I watched Paul* ***dive into*** *the pool.* **2** SPORTS to swim **underwater** using special equipment that makes it possible to breathe **3** to move quickly and suddenly towards the ground, or in a particular direction: *The plane dived suddenly.* **4** SPORTS to deliberately fall to the ground, pretending that it is the fault of an opponent

dive² /daɪv/ noun [C] **1** a jump into water with your head first and your arms stretched out in front of you **2** a quick sudden movement towards the ground, or in a particular direction: *The plane lost control and went into a dive.* **3** SPORTS a deliberate fall by a player who is pretending that an opponent made them fall

diver /'daɪvə/ noun [C] someone who swims deep under water

diverge /daɪ'vɜːdʒ/ verb **1** [I] to go in separate directions: *The two roads diverge at the entrance to the woods.* **2** [I] to develop and become different after being the same: *His ideas* ***diverge from*** *established policies.* **3** [I/T] PHYSICS if rays of light diverge, or if they are diverged, they move apart —*picture* → LENS, SHORT-SIGHTED

divergence /daɪ'vɜːdʒ(ə)ns/ noun [C/U] a difference in the way that two or more things develop from the same thing —**divergent** adj

diverging beam /daɪ'vɜːdʒɪŋ ,biːm/ noun [C] PHYSICS a beam of light in which the rays spread out from a source —*picture* → BEAM

diverging mirror /daɪ'vɜːdʒɪŋ ,mɪrə/ noun [C] PHYSICS a mirror that reflects rays of light outwards

diverse /daɪ'vɜːs/ adj very different from each other: *a diverse range of issues*

diversification /daɪ,vɜːsɪfɪ'keɪʃ(ə)n/ noun [U] BUSINESS the process of developing new products or new farming and business activities

diversify /daɪ'vɜːsɪfaɪ/ (**diversifies, diversifying, diversified**) verb [I/T] BUSINESS to develop additional products or activities

diversion /daɪ'vɜːʃ(ə)n/ noun **1** [C] something that is intended to take your attention away from something else: *One man* ***created a diversion*** *while the other ran for the door.* **2** [C/U] a change in the road or path that someone takes in order to get somewhere, because the usual road or path is closed

diversity /daɪ'vɜːsəti/ noun [singular/U] SOCIAL STUDIES the fact that very different people or things exist within a group or place: *ethnic and cultural diversity*

divert /daɪ'vɜːt/ verb [T] **1** to make something move or travel in a different direction **2** to take someone's attention away from something: *The government claimed that Cooper was trying to* ***divert attention from*** *his financial problems.* **3** to use something for a purpose that is different from its original or main purpose

divestment /daɪ'vestmənt/ noun [C/U] BUSINESS the process of selling shares or **assets** or of taking back money that you have invested

divide¹ /dɪ'vaɪd/ verb

1 separate	4 cause disagreement
2 separate and share	5 in mathematics
3 be in between	

1 [I/T] to separate into groups or parts, or to make people or things separate into groups or parts: ***Divide*** *the class* ***into*** *three groups.*
2 [T] to separate something into smaller parts and share the parts between people or things: *Decide how you would like to divide the money.* ♦ *After his death his property was* ***divided among*** *his children.* ♦ *She* ***divides*** *her time* ***between*** *teaching and research.*
3 [T] to keep two or more areas or parts separate: *A busy road* ***divides*** *the hotel* ***from*** *the beach.*
4 [T] to be the cause of disagreement between people: *This is a subject that divides the nation.*
5 [I/T] MATHS to do a calculation to find out how many times a number contains a smaller number. This is usually shown by the symbol ÷: *Divide 9 by 3.* ♦ *10 divided by 2 is 5.*

divide² /dɪ'vaɪd/ noun [C] an important difference or disagreement between people: *a political divide*

dividend /'dɪvɪdend/ noun [C] **1** BUSINESS a part of the profits of a company that is paid to the people who own shares in the company **2** MATHS a number that is going to be divided by another number

dividers /dɪ'vaɪdəz/ noun [plural] TECHNOLOGY a piece of equipment used for measuring or drawing lines and angles. It consists of two pieces of metal with pointed ends that are joined together at the top.

dividing wall /dɪ'vaɪdɪŋ ,wɔːl/ noun [C] **1** a wall inside a building that divides a large area into separate smaller rooms **2** ANATOMY a part of a cell or a body part that divides it into separate areas

divine /dɪ'vaɪn/ adj RELIGION relating to a god or God, or sent by a god or God —**divinely** adv

diving /'daɪvɪŋ/ noun [U] **1** the activity or sport of swimming deep under water **2** the activity or sport of jumping into water with your head first and your arms stretched out in front of you

'diving ,board noun [C] a long narrow board at the edge of a **swimming pool** that people can dive from

divinity /dɪ'vɪnəti/ noun [U] the state of being a god

divisible /dɪ'vɪzəb(ə)l/ adj MATHS capable of being divided by another number —**divisibility** /dɪ,vɪzə'bɪləti/ noun [U]

division /dɪ'vɪʒ(ə)n/ noun

1 split into groups	**4** a difference
2 sharing out	**5** a disagreement
3 department	**6** in mathematics

1 [C/U] the process of separating people or things into groups or parts: *The civil war led to a permanent **division** of the country.*
2 [C/U] the process of separating something into parts and sharing it between people: *the **division** of responsibilities **between** members of the class*
3 [C] one of the parts into which a large organization is divided: *the company's electronics division*
4 [C] a difference between people: *the growing **division** between rich and poor*
5 [C/U] a disagreement between people: *deep **divisions** within the Party*
6 [C/U] **MATHS** a calculation in mathematics of how many times a number is contained in a larger number

di'vision ,sign noun [C] **MATHS** the symbol ÷ that shows that one number is to be divided by another

divisive /dɪ'vaɪsɪv/ adj likely to cause arguments between people = CONTROVERSIAL

divisor /dɪ'vaɪzə/ noun [C] **MATHS** the number by which another number is divided

divorce¹ /dɪ'vɔːs/ noun [C/U] a legal way of ending a marriage: *Is it true they are **getting a divorce**?* ♦ *Both of his marriages **ended in divorce**.*

divorce² /dɪ'vɔːs/ verb **1** [I/T] to take legal action to end one's marriage to someone **2** [T] to completely separate one thing from another: *Politics should not be **divorced from** the lives of ordinary people.*

divorced /dɪ'vɔːst/ adj no longer married because the marriage has been legally ended: *After they **got divorced**, she never remarried.*

divulge /daɪ'vʌldʒ/ verb [T] *formal* to give information about something that should be kept secret

Diwali /dɪ'wɑːli/ noun [C/U] **RELIGION** an important festival in the Hindu religion that takes place in October or November

dizzy /'dɪzi/ adj **1** feeling that the things around you are spinning and that you are going to fall **2** feeling excited or confused, or making you feel like this: *We were dizzy with excitement.* —**dizziness** noun [U]

DJ /'diː,dʒeɪ/ noun [C] **MUSIC** disc jockey: someone who plays CDs and records in a club or on the radio, or who creates music by mixing pieces of recorded music

DNA /,diː en 'eɪ/ noun [U] **BIOLOGY** deoxyribonucleic acid: a chemical substance that contains genetic information and is found in all living cells and some viruses. It is in the shape of two spirals twisted together, called a **double helix**.

do¹ /duː/ (**does** /strong dʌz, weak dəz/, **doing**, **did** /dɪd/, **done** /dʌn/) verb

1 question/negative	**6** for talking about
2 referring back	health or success
3 for emphasis	**7** study
4 perform an action	**+ PHRASES**
5 have an effect	**+ PHRASAL VERBS**

1 [auxiliary verb] used before another verb for forming a question or a negative: *Do you like football?* ♦ *What did the doctor say?* ♦ *Didn't they tell you I was coming?* ♦ *Max doesn't live here any more.*

In conversation and informal written English the negative forms of the auxiliary verb 'do', **does not**, **do not**, and **did not**, are shortened to **doesn't**, **don't**, and **didn't**.

2 [I] used instead of repeating the same verb that was used earlier: *'You promised to come with me.' 'No I didn't.' ♦ 'I like drawing, but my sister doesn't.' ♦ She doesn't travel around as much as I do.* ♦ *'I enjoyed our trip to London.' 'So did I.'*
3 [auxiliary verb] used for emphasizing the meaning of a positive statement: *I've forgotten her name, but I do remember her face.*
4 [T] to perform an action or job, take part in an activity, or complete a piece of work: *Have you done that essay yet?* ♦ *I just need to **do** my hair.* ♦ *My sister often **does the cooking.*** ♦ *There's **nothing to do** around here.* ♦ *I'm not sure **what she does for a living** (=what her job is).*
5 [T] to have a particular effect on someone or something: *Frost can **do** a lot of damage.* ♦ *The fresh air will **do** you good.* ♦ *I'll never forgive him for what he **did to** me.*
6 [I] used for talking about someone's health, progress, or their general situation: *Hi Sam! How are you doing?* ♦ *He **did well** in the exams.*
7 [T] to study a subject: *I'm doing English and History.*

PHRASES do your teeth/hair/nails etc to brush your teeth/arrange your hair/paint your fingernails etc
will do used for saying that something is enough or is suitable for a particular purpose: *If you haven't got a bandage, a piece of clean cloth will do.*

PHRASAL VERBS ,do a'way with sth to get rid of something: *They discussed whether to do away with the agency completely.*
,do sth 'up 1 to fasten something ≠ UNDO: *Do up your shoelaces.* **2** to repair and decorate an old building
'do with sth 1 be/have something to do with to be connected with something: *The problem had something to do with his mother.* ♦ *Is this anything to do with school?* **2 could do with sth** *spoken* used for saying that you want or need something: *I'm sure James could do with some help.* **3 be/have nothing to do with sth** to not be connected with or involved in a particular fact or situation: *Her resignation has nothing to do with her health.*
,do with'out (sb/sth) to succeed in living or working without someone or something: *I couldn't do without my washing machine.*

do² /duː/ noun [C] **do's and don'ts** instructions and warnings about what should and should not be done in a particular situation

DO /,diː 'əʊ/ noun [C] **EDUCATION** development outcome: a goal of a particular course, project etc

docile /'dəʊsaɪl/ adj well-behaved and easy to control

dock¹ /dɒk/ noun **1** [C] an area in a port where ships stay while goods are taken on or off or while repairs are done **2 the dock** [singular] **LAW** the part of a court of law where the person who is accused of a crime stands or sits

dock² /dɒk/ verb [I] **1** if a ship docks, it arrives at a dock **2** if a spacecraft docks, it joins to another spacecraft while they are still in space

docking station /'dɒkɪŋ ,steɪʃ(ə)n/ noun [C] **COMPUTING** a piece of equipment to which you can connect a **portable** computer temporarily, for example when you are travelling between different offices, so that you can use it like a **PC**

doctor /'dɒktə/ noun [C] **1 HEALTH** someone whose job is to treat people who are ill or injured: *Have you **seen** a **doctor** yet?* ♦ *Consult your doctor before trying these exercises.* ♦ *Doctor Jones specializes in heart problems.* **2 EDUCATION** someone who has the highest degree that a university gives: *a doctor of theology* ♦ *The research team is led by Doctor Beth Levinson.*

doctorate /'dɒkt(ə)rət/ noun [C] EDUCATION the highest degree that a university gives

doctrine /'dɒktrɪn/ noun [C/U] RELIGION a set of religious or political beliefs

document[1] /'dɒkjʊmənt/ noun [C] **1** a piece of paper or a set of papers containing official information: *He refused to sign the documents.* ♦ *A secret policy document was leaked to the newspapers.* **2** COMPUTING a computer file that you can write in: *The program will automatically save any documents you have open.*

document[2] /'dɒkjʊˌment/ verb [T] **1** to record something in writing or on film: *Her report documents the effects of climate change.* **2** to support something with evidence: *Their allegations are fully documented.*

documentary[1] /ˌdɒkjʊ'ment(ə)ri/ (plural **documentaries**) noun [C] ARTS a film or television programme that deals with real people and events

documentary[2] /ˌdɒkjʊ'ment(ə)ri/ adj **1** ARTS dealing with real people and events: *a documentary film* **2** in the form of documents: *documentary evidence*

documentation /ˌdɒkjʊmen'teɪʃ(ə)n/ noun [U] **1** documents that can be used for proving that something is true **2** COMPUTING written instructions about how to use a computer or computer program

'document ˌimage ˌmanagement noun [U] COMPUTING see DIM

dodecagon /dəʊ'dekəgən, dəʊ'dekəgɒn/ noun [C] MATHS a geometric shape with twelve straight sides

dodecahedron /ˌdəʊˌdekə'hiːdr(ə)n/ noun [C] MATHS a solid shape consisting of twelve flat surfaces that each have five straight sides —*picture* → SHAPE

dodge /dɒdʒ/ verb **1** [I/T] to avoid someone or something by moving quickly **2** [T] to avoid doing something in a clever or dishonest way: *He tried to dodge the question.* —**dodge** noun [C]

doe /dəʊ/ noun [C] a female **deer** or **rabbit** —*picture* → MAMMAL

does /dəz, dʌz/ 3rd person singular of the present tense of **do**[1]

doesn't /'dʌz(ə)nt/ short form the usual way of saying or writing 'does not'. This is not often used in formal writing: *Sara doesn't live here any more.*

dog[1] /dɒg/ noun [C] **1** an animal kept as a pet, for guarding buildings, or for hunting **2** a male dog or a male animal that belongs to the same group of animals as dogs, such as a male **wolf** or **fox**: *a dog fox*

dog[2] /dɒg/ (**dogs, dogging, dogged**) verb [T] to cause trouble for someone over a long period of time: *These rumours had dogged the president for years.*

'dog ˌclutch noun [C] ENGINEERING a type of **clutch** consisting of two parts that push against each other as they turn, so that they both turn at the same speed

dog-eared /'dɒg ˌɪəd/ adj a dog-eared page or book has been used so much that the corners or edges have become damaged or torn

dogma /'dɒgmə/ noun [C/U] RELIGION a belief or set of beliefs that people are expected to accept without asking questions about them

dogmatic /dɒg'mætɪk/ adj someone who is dogmatic is so sure that their beliefs and ideas are right that they expect everyone else to accept them

do-gooder /ˌduː 'gʊdə/ noun [C] someone who always tries to help people in a way that is unnecessary or unsuitable

dogsbody /'dɒgzˌbɒdi/ noun [C] *informal* someone who is forced to do all the jobs that no one else wants to do

doh /dəʊ/ noun [C] MUSIC the first or eighth note in the **sol-fa** musical **scale**

doing /'duːɪŋ/ the present participle of **do**[1]

the doldrums /'dɒldrəmz, 'dəʊldrəmz/ noun [plural] a situation in which there is a lack of success, activity, or improvement

dole /dəʊl/ PHRASAL VERB ˌdole sth 'out *informal* to give something such as food or money to a group of people

the dole /dəʊl/ noun [singular] money that is given by the governments in some countries to people who do not have a job

doll /dɒl/ noun [C] a children's toy in the shape of a small person

dollar /'dɒlə/ noun **1** [C] ECONOMICS the unit of money used in the US and in several other countries such as Australia, Zimbabwe, and Singapore. Its symbol is $: *Payment must be in US dollars.* **2** [C] a banknote or coin that is worth a dollar **3 the dollar** [singular] ECONOMICS used for talking about the value of US money, especially in comparison with that of other countries

dolphin /'dɒlfɪn/ noun [C] a large sea animal, similar to a fish, with a long nose —*picture* → SEA

domain /dəʊ'meɪn/ noun [C] **1** a particular area of activity or life **2** COMPUTING a **domain name 3** MATHS a range of possible values of a **variable**

do'main ˌname noun [C] COMPUTING an address on the Internet

dome /dəʊm/ noun [C] a roof shaped like the top half of a ball —**domed** /dəʊmd/ adj: *a domed roof*

domestic /də'mestɪk/ adj **1** relating to a particular country: *domestic politics* ♦ *domestic and international flights* **2** relating to people's homes and family life: *domestic chores* ♦ *domestic appliances* **3** enjoying activities relating to your home, such as cooking and looking after children **4** kept as a pet or on a farm ≠ WILD: *the domestic cat*

domesticated /də'mestɪˌkeɪtɪd/ adj **1** a domesticated animal has been trained to live with or work for humans **2** enjoying activities such as cooking and cleaning, or good at them

doˌmestic 'violence noun [U] violence that takes place in the home between family members, especially adults

domicile /'dɒmɪsaɪl/ noun [C] *formal* someone's home

domiciled /'dɒmɪsaɪld/ adj *formal* living in a particular place

dominance /'dɒmɪnəns/ noun [U] a situation in which one person or thing has more influence or power than any other: *the growing dominance of the People's Party in the north of the country*

dominant /'dɒmɪnənt/ adj **1** more important, powerful, or successful than other people or things of the same type: *The company has a dominant position in the market.* **2** a dominant person or animal is stronger than the others in a group and wants to control them **3** BIOLOGY a dominant gene causes someone to be born with particular genetic features because it is stronger than other genes ≠ RECESSIVE

dominate /'dɒmɪneɪt/ verb **1** [I/T] to control someone or something by having more power or influence: *She tends to dominate the conversation.* **2** [I/T] to be the most important aspect or feature of a particular situation: *The earthquake once again dominated the news.* **3** [T] if an object dominates a place, it is so big or high that you have to notice it: *a little room dominated by a huge TV screen*

domination /ˌdɒmɪˈneɪʃ(ə)n/ noun [U] control or power over other people or things

domineering /ˌdɒmɪˈnɪərɪŋ/ adj always trying to control other people and make them obey you

dominion /dəˈmɪnjən/ noun *formal* **1** [U] control, or the right to rule over something **2** [C] an area that is ruled by one person or government

domino /ˈdɒmɪnəʊ/ (plural **dominoes**) noun **1** [C] a small flat piece of wood with spots on it, used in the game of dominoes **2 dominoes** [plural] a game in which players take turns to try to place each domino next to another one with the same number of spots on it

'domino ef,fect noun [singular] a situation in which one event causes a whole series of events to happen one after the other

donate /dəʊˈneɪt/ verb **1** [I/T] to give something such as money or goods to an organization: *Many big corporations donate to political parties.* **2** [T] HEALTH to give something such as blood, sperm, or an organ in order to help in the medical treatment of someone else

donation /dəʊˈneɪʃ(ə)n/ noun **1** [C] money or goods that someone gives to an organization: *a generous donation* **2** [C/U] HEALTH the process of giving something such as blood, sperm, or an organ to help someone else

done /dʌn/ the past participle of **do¹**

dongle /ˈdɒŋg(ə)l/ noun [C] COMPUTING a piece of equipment that must be connected to a computer before a particular program can work

donkey /ˈdɒŋki/ (plural **donkeys**) noun [C] a grey or brown mammal like a small horse with long ears —*picture* → MAMMAL

donor /ˈdəʊnə/ noun [C] **1** HEALTH someone who gives something such as blood, sperm, or an organ to help someone else **2** someone who gives something such as money or goods to an organization

don't /dəʊnt/ short form the usual way of saying or writing 'do not'. This is not often used in formal writing: *I don't believe you!*

doodle /ˈduːd(ə)l/ verb [I] to draw patterns or pictures because you are bored or thinking about other things —**doodle** noun [C]

doom /duːm/ noun [U] a bad event that cannot be avoided such as death, destruction, or complete failure

doomed /duːmd/ adj certain to end in death, destruction, or complete failure

door /dɔː/ noun [C] **1** a large flat object that you open when you want to enter or leave a building, room, or vehicle: *Shut the door.* ♦ *a car door* ♦ *the front door* ♦ *I knocked on the door* *and a voice said 'Come in'.* ♦ *Go and answer the door* (=go to see who is there)! ♦ *There's someone at the door* (=standing outside the door). ♦ *We'll deliver the goods to your door* (=directly to your house) *within 24 hours.* **2** the space created when you open a door= DOORWAY

PHRASE **out of doors** outside ≠ INDOORS
→ CLOSED

doorbell /ˈdɔːˌbel/ noun [C] a button near the front door of a house that people press to make a sound. It tells the person in the house that they are there.

doorman /ˈdɔːmən/ (plural **doormen**) noun [C] someone whose job is to be in charge of the main entrance of a building and help people when they go in or out

doormat /ˈdɔːˌmæt/ noun [C] a piece of material that people clean their shoes on before they go into a building

doorstep /ˈdɔːˌstep/ noun [C] a small step outside the main door to a building

,door-to-'door adj **1** going to all the houses in a particular area in order to sell something or ask for information or votes **2** taking someone or something directly from one place to the place they need to go to

doorway /ˈdɔːˌweɪ/ noun [C] the space that is created when you open a door

dopamine /ˈdəʊpəmiːn/ noun [U] BIOLOGY a chemical produced in the brain that carries messages from nerve cells to other nerve cells or muscles

dope /dəʊp/ noun [U] *informal* an illegal drug, especially **cannabis**

the Doppler effect /ˈdɒplər ɪˌfekt/ noun [singular] PHYSICS the change that you notice in a sound, light etc as the source of the sound or light moves closer to you, or further away from you

dormant /ˈdɔːmənt/ adj not active or developing now, but possibly becoming active in the future

dormer /ˈdɔːmə/ or ,**dormer 'window** noun [C] CONSTRUCTION an upright window in a sloping roof

dormitory /ˈdɔːmɪtri/ (plural **dormitories**) noun [C] a large room in a school or army camp where a lot of people sleep

dorsal /ˈdɔːs(ə)l/ adj BIOLOGY relating to or found on the back of a fish or other animal

'dorsal ,root noun [C] ANATOMY a structure that carries **sensory neurons** to the spinal cord

DOS /dɒs/ TRADEMARK COMPUTING Disk Operating System: the basic software in a computer that makes it work and allows you to use a program. It is usually used only in older computers.

dosage /ˈdəʊsɪdʒ/ noun [C/U] HEALTH the amount of a medicine or drug that someone takes at one time

dose /dəʊs/ noun [C] **1** HEALTH a particular amount of a drug or medicine that has been measured so that someone can take it: *a low dose of painkiller* **2** an amount of something, especially something bad: *I've just had a nasty dose of flu.*

dossier /ˈdɒsieɪ, ˈdɒsiə/ noun [C] a set of documents about a person or situation

dot¹ /dɒt/ noun [C] **1** a very small spot of ink or colour **2** COMPUTING the way you say the symbol '.' in an Internet or email address **3** something that looks very small because it is far away: *The house was a tiny dot in the valley below.*

dot² /dɒt/ (**dots, dotting, dotted**) verb [T] **1** to put people or things in many parts of a place: *The company has more than thirty branches dotted around West Africa.* **2** to put a dot over a letter of the alphabet

dotcom /ˌdɒtˈkɒm/ noun [C] a company that uses the Internet to sell its products and services

dotted line /ˌdɒtɪd ˈlaɪn/ noun [C] a line of small spots of ink that are very close together
PHRASE **sign on the dotted line** to sign a contract or other legal agreement

double¹ /ˈdʌb(ə)l/ adj **1** consisting of two things or parts: *a double murder* ♦ *She suspected his words might have a double meaning* (=two different meanings).

2 containing or consisting of twice as much as normal: *a double helping of rice* **3** large enough for two people or things: *a double bed*

double² /'dʌb(ə)l/ verb **1** [I/T] to become twice as big, twice as much, or twice as many, or to make something do this: *The number of people without work has doubled in the last five years.* ♦ *The government doubled the tax on alcohol.* ♦ *Their house has doubled in value since they bought it.* **2** [T] to fold something so that it has two layers of equal size

PHRASE **be doubled over** to be bent forwards because you are in pain or are laughing a lot

PHRASAL VERBS '**double as sth** to have another use or job as something: *an old sofa that doubled as Simon's bed*

,**double 'back** to turn and go back in the direction that you have come from = TURN BACK

double³ /'dʌb(ə)l/ determiner twice as much, or twice as many: *He now earns double the amount he used to.*

double⁴ /'dʌb(ə)l/ noun **1** [C] someone who looks very similar to another person: *He's his father's double.* **2** [C] an actor who takes the place of another actor when making difficult or dangerous parts of a film **3** [U] twice as much money: *I get double for working evenings.* **4** **doubles** [U] SPORTS a game such as tennis that is played by pairs of players

double-barrelled /,dʌb(ə)l 'bærəld/ adj **1** a double-barrelled gun has a pair of tubes that bullets come out from **2** a double-barrelled name is a family name with two parts, usually joined by a hyphen

,**double 'bass** noun [C] MUSIC a large musical instrument shaped like a **violin** that you rest on the floor and play standing up —*picture* → MUSICAL INSTRUMENT, ORCHESTRA

,**double 'bed** noun [C] a bed for two people

,**double 'bond** noun [C] CHEMISTRY a chemical bond in which two atoms share two pairs of electrons

,**double-'book** verb [I/T] to promise the same seat, table, or room to two different people

,**double-'check** verb [I/T] to check something for a second time

'**double-,click** verb [I/T] COMPUTING to give an instruction to a computer by quickly pressing the mouse twice with your finger

,**double-'cross** verb [T] if one criminal double-crosses another criminal who they are working with, one of them cheats the other, for example by taking all the stolen money

double-decker /,dʌb(ə)l 'dekə/ or ,**double-decker 'bus** noun [C] a bus that has both an upper and a lower level where people can sit

,**double-'digit** adj a double-digit number is between 10 and 99

,**double 'fault** noun [C] SPORTS a situation in which a tennis player loses a point by doing two bad **serves** one after the other

,**double 'figures** noun [plural] the numbers 10 to 99

,**double 'flat** noun [C] MUSIC a musical note that is played or sung two **semitones** lower than usual —*picture* → MUSIC

,**double 'glazing** noun [U] windows or doors that have two layers of glass, so that the building will be warmer and quieter —,**double-'glazed** adj

,**double 'helix** noun [C] BIOLOGY the DNA molecule that is made up of two chains of **nucleotides** joined by hydrogen bonds, giving it the shape of a ladder twisted into a spiral —*picture* → HELIX

,**double 'jeopardy** noun [U] LAW a situation in which someone is accused of a crime for a second time after they have already been to trial for that crime

,**double 'negative** noun [C] LANGUAGE a sentence in which two negative words such as 'not', 'don't', or 'no one' are used when only one would be correct, for example in the sentence 'I don't want no dinner.'

'**double ,room** noun [C] TOURISM a room that is large enough for two people to sleep in, especially one in a hotel or a rented property

,**double 'sharp** noun [C] MUSIC a musical note that is played or sung two **semitones** higher than usual —*picture* → MUSIC

double-sided /,dʌb(ə)l 'saɪdɪd/ adj able to be used on both sides: *double-sided disks*

,**double 'standard** noun [C] a rule or principle that is applied to some people but not to others, in a way that is unfair

,**double 'vision** noun [U] HEALTH a medical condition in which someone sees a single object as two objects

doubly /'dʌbli/ adv **1** by a much greater amount, or to a much greater degree than usual **2** for two reasons, or in two ways

doubt¹ /daʊt/ noun [C/U] a feeling of not being certain about something: *I have serious doubts about whether this system will work.* ♦ *I have no doubt that he will succeed.* ♦ ***There's no doubt about it*** – *we are in trouble.* ♦ *The accident **raises doubts about** (=makes people feel uncertain about) the safety of the aircraft.* ♦ *She is **without a doubt** one of our most talented students.*

PHRASES **be in doubt 1** if something is in doubt, it is not certain whether it will succeed or continue: *The future of the company is still in doubt.* **2** if you are in doubt about something, you do not know what to do about it

beyond (any) doubt if something is beyond doubt, it is completely certain

beyond (a) reasonable doubt LAW to a degree that the law considers to be satisfactory for making a decision → BENEFIT¹

doubt² /daʊt/ verb [T] **1** to think that something is probably not true, probably does not exist, or probably will not happen: *'Do you think they'll win?' 'I doubt it.'* ♦ *I know a few people doubted my story.* ♦ *I doubt it will work, but we can try.* **2** to feel that you cannot trust or believe someone

doubtful /'daʊtf(ə)l/ adj **1** not certain or likely to happen or to be true: *It is doubtful whether he will survive.* **2** not feeling certain about something: *Eddie looked doubtful, but agreed.* —**doubtfully** adv

doubtless /'daʊtləs/ adv used for saying that you are certain that something is true or will happen, although you have no definite proof

dough /dəʊ/ noun [C/U] a mixture of flour, water, fat etc that is baked to make bread or **pastry**

doughnut /'dəʊ,nʌt/ noun [C] a sweet food, often in the shape of a ring, that is made by cooking dough in oil

dove /dʌv/ noun [C] a white bird. Doves are often used as a sign of peace.

dowdy /'daʊdi/ adj not attractive or fashionable

dowel /'daʊəl/ noun [C] CONSTRUCTION a thick pin used for holding two pieces of wood, metal, or plastic together

the Dow Jones Average /,daʊ 'dʒəʊnz ,ævərɪdʒ/ TRADEMARK BUSINESS, ECONOMICS a number that represents an average of the share value of important companies in the US. It changes every day according to activity on the stock market, and is used as a sign of how well the US economy is performing. It is often simply called **the Dow Jones** or **the Dow**.

down¹ /daʊn/ adj, adv, preposition

1 to lower place	4 to lower level
2 in sitting position	5 sad
3 away from	+ PHRASE

1 to or in a lower place, position, or surface: *He slipped on the ice and fell down.* ♦ *Put the box down on the table.* ♦ *Tears were rolling down his cheeks.* ♦ *It was dark down in the cellar.* ♦ *Your name's further down the list.*
2 with your body in or moving into a sitting, bending, or lying position: *Why don't you lie down and rest?* ♦ *She crouched down behind the bushes.*
3 to a place that is further along: *I was walking down the street with a couple of friends.*
4 at or to a smaller amount or a lower level than before: *Turn the radio down* (=make the sound quieter). ♦ *Profits are 15% down on* (=less than) *last year.*
5 *informal* unhappy: *He's been feeling very down.*
PHRASE **be down to sb** to be someone's responsibility

down² /daʊn/ noun [U] the small soft feathers of a bird

,down-and-'out noun [C] someone who has nowhere to live and has no job or money —**,down-and-'out** adj

,down-at-'heel adj **1** looking old and no longer in good condition **2** wearing old clothes, because you do not have enough money to buy new ones = SCRUFFY

downbeat /'daʊn,biːt/ noun [C] MUSIC the first beat of music in a **bar**

downcast /'daʊn,kɑːst/ adj **1** sad or upset **2** downcast eyes are looking downwards

downfall /'daʊn,fɔːl/ noun [singular] a sudden loss of power, status, or success, or something that causes this loss: *His greed was his downfall.*

downfold /'daʊn,fəʊld/ noun [C] GEOLOGY a **syncline** (=downward bend in a layer of rock)

downgrade /'daʊn,greɪd/ verb [T] **1** to treat something in a way that makes it seem less important than before **2** to move someone to a job that is less important

downhearted /,daʊn'hɑːtɪd/ adj sad, and feeling that things will not get better

downhill¹ /,daʊn'hɪl/ adv towards the bottom of a hill or slope ≠ UPHILL
PHRASE **go downhill** to get worse

downhill² /'daʊnhɪl/ noun [C/U] SPORTS a type of skiing in which people race down a hill or slope

Downing Street /'daʊnɪŋ ,striːt/ noun [U] **1** the street in London where the British prime minister lives **2** the British prime minister, or the British government

download¹ /,daʊn'ləʊd/ verb [I/T] COMPUTING to move information to a computer from another computer system or from the Internet ≠ UPLOAD

download² /'daʊnləʊd/ noun [C/U] COMPUTING the process of downloading information to a computer, or a file that has been downloaded ≠ UPLOAD

downloadable /,daʊn'ləʊdəb(ə)l/ adj COMPUTING able or allowed to be downloaded

downmarket /'daʊn,mɑːkɪt/ adj cheap, or of low quality ≠ UPMARKET —**downmarket** adv

down-milling /'daʊn ,mɪlɪŋ/ noun [U] TECHNOLOGY **climb milling** (=a method of cutting metal)

,down 'payment noun [C] a first payment that someone makes when they buy something and will pay the rest later = DEPOSIT

downpipe /'daʊn,paɪp/ noun [C] CONSTRUCTION a **drainpipe**

downpour /'daʊn,pɔː/ noun [C] a large amount of rain that falls quickly

downright /'daʊn,raɪt/ adj, adv *informal* used to emphasize how bad something is: *She was downright rude!*

'down ,service noun [singular] CONSTRUCTION the water supply from the cold-water tank in a building

downside /'daʊn,saɪd/ noun [singular] the disadvantage or negative aspect of something ≠ UPSIDE

downsize /'daʊn,saɪz/ verb [I/T] BUSINESS to make a company or organization smaller by reducing the number of its workers

downslope /'daʊn,sləʊp/ adj, adv GEOLOGY moving down a slope

Down's syndrome /'daʊnz ,sɪndrəʊm/ noun [U] HEALTH a medical condition that someone is born with and that makes them develop in a different way from most people, mentally and physically. It is caused by an extra chromosome.

downstairs /,daʊn'steəz/ adv to or on a lower floor of a building, especially the floor at ground level ≠ UPSTAIRS: *I ran downstairs.* —**downstairs** /'daʊnsteəz/ adj: *a downstairs window*

downstream /,daʊn'striːm/ adv GEOGRAPHY in the direction that a river or stream is flowing ≠ UPSTREAM

downswing /'daʊn,swɪŋ/ noun [C] **1** ECONOMICS a reduction in economic or business activity **2** SPORTS the movement that golf players make when they bring the club down to hit the ball

'down ,time noun [U] COMPUTING time when a computer is not working

,down-to-'earth adj practical and sensible

downtown /,daʊn'taʊn/ adj, adv *American* in or near the business or shopping centre of a city

downtrodden /'daʊn,trɒd(ə)n/ adj treated in a cruel or unfair way by someone more powerful

downturn /'daʊn,tɜːn/ noun [C] ECONOMICS a reduction in economic or business activity

downward¹ /'daʊnwəd/ adj going towards a lower place or level ≠ UPWARD: *a downward slope*

downward² /'daʊnwəd/ adv *American* **downwards**

downwards /'daʊnwədz/ adv towards a lower place or level ≠ UPWARDS
PHRASE **face downwards 1** lying on the front of your body **2** lying on the side that normally faces up

downwind /,daʊn'wɪnd/ adj, adv GEOGRAPHY in the same direction that the wind is moving

dowry /'daʊri/ (plural **dowries**) noun [C] SOCIAL STUDIES money and property that, in some cultures, a woman's family gives to her husband when they get married

doze /dəʊz/ verb [I] to sleep for a short time, especially during the day

dozen /'dʌz(ə)n/ (plural **dozen**) determiner **1** a set of 12 things or people: *We need half a dozen eggs for the cake.* **2** dozens [plural] lots of things or people: *Dozens of people were injured.*

DP /,diː 'piː/ abbrev COMPUTING data processing: the use of a computer to store or make changes to information

dpc /ˌdiː piː ˈsiː/ noun [C] CONSTRUCTION a **damp (proof) course**

dpi /ˌdiː piː ˈaɪ/ abbrev COMPUTING dots per inch: a measurement of the ability of a computer screen or printer to produce a clear image

dpm /ˌdiː piː ˈem/ noun [C] CONSTRUCTION a **damp proof membrane**

Dr abbrev **1** doctor **2** Drive

drab /dræb/ adj not colourful or interesting

draconian /drəˈkəʊniən/ adj formal extremely strict and severe

draft¹ /drɑːft/ noun [C] a piece of writing or a drawing that may have changes made to it before it is finished: a **first draft** of the letter

draft² /drɑːft/ verb [T] to write a document, speech, or letter that may have changes made to it before it is finished

drag¹ /dræg/ (**drags, dragging, dragged**) verb

1 pull sth	**5** time going slowly
2 pull sb	**6** in computing
3 make sb leave	**+ PHRASE**
4 touch ground	**+ PHRASAL VERBS**

1 [T] to pull something along with difficulty, especially something heavy: She **dragged** her suitcase **down** the path.
2 [T] to pull someone strongly or violently when they do not want to go with you: I grabbed his arm and **dragged** him over **to** the window.
3 [T] to make someone leave or go to a place when they do not want to: You **dragged** me **away** from my meeting just to tell me this!
4 [I] if something drags on or along the ground, it touches the ground as you move along, because it is too long or too heavy
5 [I] if time drags, it seems to pass very slowly
6 [T] COMPUTING to move something across a computer screen using the mouse

PHRASE **drag your feet** to do something very slowly because you do not really want to do it

PHRASAL VERBS **,drag sb 'into sth** to make someone become involved in a situation when they do not want to: The US was afraid of being dragged into the war.
,drag 'on to continue for longer than you want or think is necessary: Some cases drag on for years.

drag² /dræg/ noun

1 force that slows	**3** breathing in smoke
2 sth/sb boring/ annoying	**4** clothes of opposite sex
	5 part of flask

1 [U] PHYSICS the force that slows something down when it moves through air or liquid
2 [singular] informal something that is boring or annoying
3 [C] an act of breathing in smoke from a cigarette
4 [U] women's clothes worn by a man, or men's clothes worn by a woman
5 [C] TECHNOLOGY the bottom half of a **moulding flask** for **casting** metal objects. The top half is the **cope**.

,drag-and-'drop verb [T] COMPUTING to move something across a computer screen using the mouse, and place it where you want it to be

dragon /ˈdrægən/ noun [C] in stories, an imaginary large animal that breathes out fire

dragonfly /ˈdrægənˌflaɪ/ (plural **dragonflies**) noun [C] an insect with a long narrow brightly coloured body and transparent wings. It lays its eggs in water.
—picture → INSECT

'drag ,race noun [C] a race between long and very powerful cars over a short distance —**'drag ,racing** noun [U]

drain¹ /dreɪn/ verb **1** [I/T] if liquid drains, or if someone drains it, it flows away from something: Put the meat aside to let the fat **drain off**. ♦ **Drain** the water **from** the tank. —picture → FOOD **2** [T] to get rid of the water in an area of land so that it can be used for other purposes **3** [T] to use so much of someone's energy or strength that they feel very tired **4** [T] to use so much of something that there is not enough available for other things

drain² /dreɪn/ noun **1** [C] a pipe or passage through which water or waste liquid flows away **2** [singular] something that uses a lot of something such as money or supplies

PHRASE **down the drain** informal completely lost or wasted: That's three years' work down the drain!

drainage /ˈdreɪnɪdʒ/ noun [U] a system of pipes and passages that take away water or waste liquid from an area, or the process of taking this waste away

'drainage ,basin noun [C] GEOGRAPHY an area of country from which **rainwater** flows into a particular river system

drained /dreɪnd/ adj feeling as though you have no mental or physical energy left

drainpipe /ˈdreɪnˌpaɪp/ noun [C] a pipe on the side of a building that carries **rainwater** from the roof to the ground

'drain ,plug noun [C] ENGINEERING a small metal object that you unscrew in order to remove fluid such as oil from an engine part

drama /ˈdrɑːmə/ noun **1** [C] ARTS, LITERATURE a play for the theatre, television, or radio **2** [U] ARTS, EDUCATION plays in general, or plays as a subject that people study: He teaches drama. ♦ a drama course **3** [C/U] something unusual or exciting that happens: a game full of drama

dramatic /drəˈmætɪk/ adj **1** sudden and surprising, or easy to notice: a dramatic increase in sales **2** exciting and impressive: a dramatic climax to the game **3** dramatic behaviour is done to impress other people **4** ARTS relating to the theatre or plays —**dramatically** /drəˈmætɪkli/ adv

dra,matic 'irony noun [U] ARTS, LITERATURE a situation in which an audience knows more about what is happening in a play than the characters do

dramatis personae /ˌdræmətɪs pɜːˈsəʊnaɪ/ noun [plural] ARTS, LITERATURE all the characters in a play

dramatist /ˈdræmətɪst/ noun [C] ARTS, LITERATURE someone who writes plays= PLAYWRIGHT

drank /dræŋk/ the past tense of **drink¹**

drape /dreɪp/ verb [T] to put something made of cloth over or around something

drastic /ˈdræstɪk/ adj a drastic action or change has a very big effect —**drastically** /ˈdræstɪkli/ adv

draught /drɑːft/ noun [C] cold air that blows into a room and makes people feel uncomfortable

draughts /drɑːfts/ noun [U] a game for two people, played on a board with black and white squares, using 24 round pieces

draughtsman /ˈdrɑːftsmən/ (plural **draughtsmen** /ˈdrɑːftsmən/) noun [C] someone whose job is to draw the plans for something that will be built or made

draughtsperson /ˈdrɑːftsˌpɜːsən/ noun [C] someone whose job is to draw the plans for something that will be built or made

draughty /'drɑːfti/ adj a draughty place is uncomfortable because cold air blows into it

draw¹ /drɔː/ (**draws**, **drawing**, **drew** /druː/, **drawn** /drɔːn/) verb

1 create picture	7 compare things
2 move slowly	8 make sb notice/react
3 pull sth	9 neither side wins
4 take money	+ PHRASES
5 choose sb/sth	+ PHRASAL VERBS
6 get ideas from	

1 [I/T] to create a picture by making lines with a pen or pencil: *I can't draw faces very well.* ♦ *The kids drew on the pavement with chalk.*
2 [I] to move somewhere slowly or smoothly: *As we drew nearer, I noticed that the front door was open.*
3 [T] to pull something out of, across, or down something: *He drew a handkerchief out of his pocket.* ♦ *The curtains were still drawn at noon.*
4 [T] to take money from a bank account: *Customers can draw up to £50 a day from this account.*
5 [T] to choose someone or something from a group of similar things: *Elliot's name was drawn from over 200 entries.*
6 [T] to get ideas, information, or knowledge from somewhere: *She drew inspiration for her stories from her childhood.*
7 [T] to consider the ways in which two things are different or similar: *The writer drew comparisons between the two societies.*
8 [T] to make someone notice something or react to it: *My eyes were drawn to a painting over the fireplace.* ♦ *We tried to get in without drawing attention to ourselves.*
9 [I/T] SPORTS if two teams or opponents draw, or if they draw a match, they both have the same score, so that neither wins: *They drew 1–1 with Manchester United last week.*

PHRASES **draw blood** to make someone bleed
draw a conclusion to decide what you believe about something after you have thought about all the facts
draw the line *informal* to say that you will definitely not allow or accept something: *I draw the line at breaking the law.*
draw to a close/an end to end

PHRASAL VERBS **,draw sth 'down** TECHNOLOGY to reduce the cross section of a metal bar, making it longer and thinner
'draw on sth to use something that you have gained or saved: *As an actor, you often draw on your own life experiences.*
,draw sth 'up to prepare and write something such as a document or plan: *Guidelines have been drawn up for dealing with emergencies.*

draw² /drɔː/ noun [C] **1** SPORTS a game in which both teams or players have the same number of points at the end, so that neither wins= TIE: *A last-minute goal earned Cameroon a 1–1 draw with Italy.* **2** a way of choosing something such as a name or number by chance

drawback /'drɔːˌbæk/ noun [C] a feature of something that makes it less useful than it could be: *The main drawback of the plan is its expense.*

drawbridge /'drɔːˌbrɪdʒ/ noun [C] a bridge that can be pulled up to let ships pass or to stop people getting into a castle —*picture* → CASTLE

drawer /'drɔːə/ noun [C] a part of a piece of furniture that slides in and out and is used for keeping things in

drawing /'drɔːɪŋ/ noun **1** [C] a picture that someone has drawn: *The children did drawings of themselves.*

2 [U] ARTS the activity or skill of making pictures with a pen or pencil: *I'm not very good at drawing.*

'drawing ,board noun [C] TECHNOLOGY a large board or table that designers and **draughtsmen** put their paper on when they are working
PHRASE **go back to the drawing board** to try to think of a completely new idea because the one that you tried before was not successful

'drawing ,pin noun [C] a short pin with a flat top, used for fastening paper to a wall

drawl /drɔːl/ noun [singular] a slow way of speaking, with long vowel sounds —**drawl** verb [I/T]

drawn¹ /drɔːn/ adj looking very tired, ill, or worried

drawn² /drɔːn/ the past participle of **draw¹**

dread¹ /dred/ verb [T] to feel very worried about something that will or could happen: *She started to dread seeing him.*

dread² /dred/ noun [singular/U] fear of something bad that will or could happen: *The thought of making a speech fills me with dread.*

dreadful /'dredf(ə)l/ adj **1** very unpleasant **2** used for emphasizing how bad something is

dreadfully /'dredf(ə)li/ adv **1** extremely **2** very severely

dreadlocks /'dredˌlɒks/ noun [plural] twisted pieces of long hair, worn especially by **Rastafarians**

dream¹ /driːm/ noun [C] **1** something that you experience in your mind while you are sleeping: *The idea came to him in a dream.* **2** something good that you hope that you will have or will achieve in the future: *She watched her dreams of success fade away.* ♦ *Finding my father again was a dream come true.*
PHRASE **beyond your (wildest) dreams** much better than you imagined or hoped

dream² /driːm/ (**dreams**, **dreaming**, **dreamed** or **dreamt** /dremt/) verb [I/T] **1** to experience things in your mind while you are sleeping: *He dreamt that he saw Rosa.* **2** to think about something that you hope to do: *She had always dreamed of going to America.*
PHRASE **would not dream of doing sth** used for emphasizing that you would definitely not do something: *I wouldn't dream of asking him for money.*
PHRASAL VERB **,dream sth 'up** to think of a new idea

dreamt /dremt/ a past tense and past participle of **dream¹**

dreamy /'driːmi/ adj showing that you are thinking about something pleasant rather than paying attention: *a dreamy look*

dreary /'drɪəri/ (**drearier**, **dreariest**) adj making you feel bored or unhappy: *dreary weather*

dredge /dredʒ/ verb [T] to remove dirt from the bottom of a river or lake, often in order to look for something

dregs /dregz/ noun [plural] the small solid pieces that are left in the bottom of a container of liquid: *dregs of coffee*

drench /drentʃ/ verb [T] to make someone or something very wet —**drenched** /drentʃt/ adj

dress¹ /dres/ verb **1** [I] to put clothes on yourself or on someone else ≠ UNDRESS: *It only took her ten minutes to shower and dress.* **2** [I] to wear clothes of a particular type: *The nurses dressed as clowns for Halloween.* **3** [T] to clean an injury and cover it with a piece of soft cloth **4** [T] CONSTRUCTION to cut stones into suitable shapes and sizes for building work

PHRASAL VERB ,dress 'up 1 to put on clothes that make you look like someone else, for fun: *They had dressed up as princes and princesses.* 2 to put on clothes that are more formal than the clothes that you usually wear: *Do I have to dress up for dinner?*

dress² /dres/ noun 1 [C] a piece of clothing that covers a woman's body and part of her legs: *a blue cotton dress* 2 [U] the type of clothes that are typical of a particular place, occasion, or time in history: *traditional Nigerian dress* → CLOTHES

dressed /drest/ adj 1 wearing clothes of a particular type: *She was dressed in a black suit.* ♦ *a well-dressed man* 2 someone who is dressed is wearing clothes: *Are you dressed yet?*
PHRASE get dressed to put your clothes on

dressing /'dresɪŋ/ noun 1 [C] a piece of material that is used for protecting a skin injury 2 [C/U] a mixture of liquids that people pour over salad

'dressing ,room noun [C] a room that is used by a performer or sports players for preparing for a performance or game

'dressing ,table noun [C] a piece of bedroom furniture consisting of a table or set of drawers and a mirror

'dress re,hearsal noun [C] **ARTS** the last occasion when performers practise before a concert, play etc

drew /druː/ the past tense of **draw¹**

dribble /'drɪb(ə)l/ verb 1 [I/T] if a liquid dribbles, or if someone dribbles it, it flows slowly in small drops 2 [I/T] **SPORTS** to move forwards with a ball by kicking or bouncing it 3 [I] if someone dribbles, saliva comes out onto their chin —**dribble** noun [C/U]

dried /draɪd/ adj dried food, milk, or flowers have had the water removed from them

drier /'draɪə/ another spelling of **dryer**

drift¹ /drɪft/ verb [I] 1 to be pushed along slowly by the movement of air or water: *The boat started to drift out to sea.* 2 to do something or happen in a way that is not planned: *I just drifted into nursing really.* 3 to move somewhere slowly as though you do not know where you are going: *For three months, Paul drifted from town to town.* 4 if snow or sand drifts, the wind blows it into a large pile

drift² /drɪft/ noun 1 [C] a large pile of snow or sand that has been formed by the wind 2 [singular] a slow gradual change or movement 3 [singular] *informal* the meaning that someone is trying to express

'drift ,net noun [C] a very large net for catching fish that hangs upright in the sea

drill¹ /drɪl/ noun 1 [C] a tool that is used for making a hole in something —*picture* → TOOL 2 [C] **EDUCATION** a way of teaching people something by making them repeat it several times 3 [C/U] military training that involves practising things such as marching or holding weapons

drill² /drɪl/ verb 1 [I/T] to make a hole using a drill: *Drill two holes in the wall.* 2 [T] **EDUCATION** to teach something to students by making them repeat it many times 3 [I/T] if soldiers drill, or if they are drilled, they practise things such as marching or holding weapons

drily /'draɪli/ adv in a way that expresses humour while appearing to be serious

drink¹ /drɪŋk/ (**drinks, drinking, drank** /dræŋk/, **drunk** /drʌŋk/) verb 1 [I/T] to take liquid into your body through your mouth: *Drink your juice, Thomas.* ♦ *Rosie drank thirstily from the mug.* 2 [I] to drink alcohol, especially regularly or too often: *Dan had been out drinking with his friends.*
PHRASAL VERBS 'drink to sb/sth to express a wish for

health, happiness, or success, then lift your glass and drink from it= TOAST: *We will now drink to the bride and groom.*
,drink (sth) 'up to drink all of your drink

drink² /drɪŋk/ noun [C/U] 1 an amount of liquid that someone drinks, or drinks in general: *They had had no food or drink all day.* ♦ *I need a drink of water.* 2 an alcoholic drink, or alcohol in general: *They often went for a drink after work.*

drink-driving /,drɪŋk 'draɪvɪŋ/ noun [U] driving after drinking too much alcohol

drinker /'drɪŋkə/ noun [C] 1 someone who often drinks alcohol: *a heavy drinker* (=someone who drinks a lot of alcohol) 2 someone who often drinks a particular drink: *a tea drinker*

drinking /'drɪŋkɪŋ/ noun [U] the activity of drinking alcohol

'drinking ,water noun [U] water that is safe to drink

drip¹ /drɪp/ (**drips, dripping, dripped**) verb 1 [I/T] if a liquid drips, or if someone drips it, it falls in very small drops: *Red paint had dripped on the floor.* 2 [I] to produce small drops of liquid: *The tap was dripping.*

drip² /drɪp/ noun [C] 1 a small drop of liquid that falls from something 2 **HEALTH** a piece of equipment that is used for putting a liquid such as medicine or blood directly into the body

'drip-,feed ('drip-,feeds, 'drip-,feeding, 'drip-,fed) verb [T] 1 **HEALTH** to give food or medicine to someone who is ill through a special piece of equipment with a tube that goes into their body 2 to give something to someone slowly, little by little

drive¹ /draɪv/ (**drives, driving, drove** /drəʊv/, **driven** /'drɪv(ə)n/) verb

1 control vehicle	5 provide power
2 take sb in vehicle	6 make sb try hard
3 force into bad state	7 push sth strongly
4 force sb to leave	+ PHRASAL VERBS

1 [I/T] to control a car or other vehicle so that it moves somewhere, or to go somewhere by doing this: *Usually, my sister drives and I read the map.* ♦ *You will drive carefully, won't you?*
2 [T] if someone drives you somewhere, they take you there in a vehicle that they drive: *Lee drove me to the airport.*
3 [T] to force someone or something into a bad situation or state: *Supermarkets are driving small shops out of business.* ♦ *Would you be quiet – you're driving me mad!*
4 [T] to force someone to leave the place where they live: *Thousands of people have been driven from their homes by the fighting.*
5 [T] to provide the power that makes something move: *The pump is driven by an electric motor.*
6 [T] to make someone work or try very hard: *The coach really drives his team.*
7 [T] to push, hit, or kick something using a lot of force: *He drove the nail into the wall.*
PHRASAL VERBS ,drive sb a'way to make someone stop wanting something: *Increasing your prices will only drive customers away.*
,drive sth 'up to make a price or amount rise: *The government's policies are driving up interest rates.*

- **Drive** means to move and control a vehicle such as a car or truck: *Do you walk or drive to work?* ♦ *He drives a bus.*
- **Ride** means to move and control a bicycle, motorbike, or horse. You can also **ride** in a vehicle that is driven by someone else: *She rides her bike to school.* ♦ *We rode all over town on the bus.*

drive² /draɪv/ noun

1 journey in car	5 determination
2 wide path for car	6 cause of action
3 in street names	7 effort to achieve
4 part of computer	

1 [C] a journey in a car: *The hotel is only 10 minutes' drive from the airport.* ♦ *We **went for a drive** in Jack's new car.*

2 [C] a wide path for a car that joins someone's house to a street: *There was a strange car parked in the drive.*

3 Drive [C] used in the names of streets: *25 Oakwood Drive*

4 [C] COMPUTING a part of a computer that reads and stores information: *a CD-ROM drive*

5 [U] the energy and determination that makes someone try hard to achieve something

6 [C] a feeling that makes someone act in a particular way: *the human **sex drive***

7 [C] a big effort to achieve something, especially by a company or government: *The company is launching a major recruitment drive.*

drivel /ˈdrɪv(ə)l/ noun [U] stupid and unimportant things that someone says or writes

driven /ˈdrɪv(ə)n/ the past participle of **drive¹**

driver /ˈdraɪvə/ noun [C] **1** someone who drives a vehicle, especially as their job: *a taxi driver* **2** COMPUTING software that controls a piece of equipment connected to a computer: *a printer driver*

driveshaft /ˈdraɪvˌʃɑːft/ noun [C] ENGINEERING a **shaft** that turns and carries power from the engine of a vehicle to the wheels

'drive-,through noun [C] a restaurant or other place that serves customers through a special window, so that they do not have to leave their cars

drivetime /ˈdraɪvˌtaɪm/ noun [U] the time when many people are driving to or from work and listen to the radio in their cars, especially in the afternoon

driveway /ˈdraɪvˌweɪ/ noun [C] a **drive** in front of someone's house

driving licence /ˈdraɪvɪŋ ˌlaɪs(ə)ns/ noun [C] an official document that people need in order to drive

driving test /ˈdraɪvɪŋ ˌtest/ noun [C] the official test that someone must pass before they can drive a car alone

drizzle /ˈdrɪz(ə)l/ noun [singular/U] very light rain —**drizzle** verb [I]

dromedary /ˈdrɒməd(ə)ri/ noun [C] a **camel** with one raised part on its back, called a **hump** → BACTRIAN CAMEL

drone /drəʊn/ verb [I] to make a low continuous noise —**drone** noun [singular]

drool /druːl/ verb [I] **1** *informal* to look at someone or something with great pleasure **2** to let saliva come out of your mouth

droop /druːp/ verb [I] **1** to hang downwards: *The flowers were drooping in the heat.* **2** to become tired, weak, or unhappy

drop¹ /drɒp/ (**drops, dropping, dropped**) verb

1 let sth fall	6 not continue sth
2 fall	7 not include sth/sb
3 reduce/get less	8 speak less loudly
4 take sb somewhere	+ PHRASAL VERBS
5 take sth somewhere	

1 [T] to let something fall: *The box was so heavy I almost dropped it.*

2 [I] to fall: *Teresa dropped into the chair, exhausted.*

♦ *She took off her jacket and let it drop to the floor.*

3 [I/T] to reduce the amount or rate of something, or to fall to a lower amount or rate: *Be sure to drop your speed in wet weather.* ♦ *In winter the temperature often **drops below** freezing.*

4 [T] to take someone to a place in a car: *Can you drop me at the corner of the street?*

5 [T] to take something to a place and not stay there very long: *Can you drop these magazines at Nora's house?*

6 [T] to stop doing something: *In third year, you can drop geography or history.* ♦ *He told me to **drop everything** and come over straight away.*

7 [T] to not include something or someone: *Rogers has been **dropped from** the team because of a knee injury.*

8 [I/T] if you drop your voice, or if your voice drops, you speak less loudly

PHRASAL VERBS **,drop 'by** or **,drop 'in** *informal* to make a short visit somewhere: *Why don't you drop by for coffee some time?*

,drop sb 'off *same as* **drop¹** sense 4: *Can you drop the kids off at school this morning?*

,drop 'out to leave something before you have finished what you intended to do: *Too many students **drop out** of college after only one year.*

drop² /drɒp/ noun [C] **1** a very small amount of liquid with a round shape: *a tear drop* ♦ *There were **drops of** blood on his arm.* **2** a fall in the amount or value of something: *There was **a sharp drop in** the temperature during the night.* **3** a distance down to the ground from a high place: *At the edge of the cliff is a 100-metre drop.*

PHRASE **a drop in the ocean** a very small amount that will not have much effect

'drop-down ,menu noun [C] COMPUTING a list of choices on a computer screen that goes away when one of them is chosen → PULL-DOWN MENU

'drop ,goal noun [C] SPORTS a goal scored in **rugby** by a player who drops the ball and then kicks it

droplet /ˈdrɒplət/ noun [C] a very small drop of liquid

'drop-,off adj used about the time or place that you deliver something somewhere

dropper /ˈdrɒpə/ noun [C] a small glass tube with a rubber piece at one end that you squeeze to let out single drops of liquid —*picture* → LABORATORY

'dropping ,pipette noun [C] SCIENCE a small tube that is narrow at one end and has a rubber bulb at the other. It is used to suck up liquids and then supply a few drops at a time.

droppings /ˈdrɒpɪŋz/ noun [plural] the faeces of animals or birds

'drop ,shot noun [C] SPORTS a shot in tennis, **squash** etc in which the ball falls suddenly so that an opponent cannot reach it easily

dross /drɒs/ noun [U] TECHNOLOGY a mass of solid **impurities** (=waste material) that floats on the surface of **molten** (=melted) metal

drought /draʊt/ noun [C/U] a long period of time when there is little or no rain

drove /drəʊv/ the past tense of **drive¹**

drown /draʊn/ verb **1** [I] to sink under water and die: *Thirty people drowned when the boat sank in a storm.* **2** [T] to kill someone by pushing them under water **3** [T] to cover something completely with a liquid: *shellfish drowned in a spicy sauce* **4** [T] *same as* **drown sth out**

PHRASAL VERB **,drown sth 'out** to prevent a sound from being heard by making a louder noise: *The music almost drowned out the sound of his voice.*

drowsy /ˈdraʊzi/ adj feeling that you want to sleep = SLEEPY —**drowsily** adv

drudgery /ˈdrʌdʒəri/ noun [U] boring and unpleasant work

drug¹ /drʌg/ noun [C] HEALTH **1** an illegal substance that affects someone physically or mentally when they put it into their body: *She had never taken drugs in her life.* ♦ *a drug addict* (=someone who cannot stop using illegal drugs) **2** a substance that a doctor gives someone in order to treat a disease or medical problem: *Your doctor may prescribe drugs for this condition.* ♦ *a new anti-cancer drug*

drug² /drʌg/ (**drugs, drugging, drugged**) verb [T] **1** to give a drug to someone so that they will go to sleep or become unconscious **2** to put a drug in food or drink

'drug a,buse noun [U] HEALTH the use of illegal or dangerous drugs in amounts that can damage health

'drug ,runner noun [C] someone who takes illegal drugs from one country to another —**drug running** noun [U]

drum¹ /drʌm/ noun [C] **1** MUSIC a musical instrument that consists of a tight skin stretched over a round frame. You hit it with your hands or a stick. —*picture* → MUSICAL INSTRUMENT, ORCHESTRA **2** a large round container for liquids: *an oil drum*

drum² /drʌm/ (**drums, drumming, drummed**) verb **1** [I/T] to make a continuous sound by hitting a surface **2** [I] MUSIC to play a drum —**drumming** noun [U]
PHRASAL VERB **,drum sth 'into sb** to make someone learn or understand something by repeating it many times

drumbeat /ˈdrʌm,biːt/ noun [C] MUSIC the steady beat of music played on drums

'drum ,brake noun [C] ENGINEERING a type of brake consisting of a hollow metal cylinder that **brake shoes** press against to slow down or stop a vehicle

'drum ,kit noun [C] MUSIC a set of drums and **cymbals**

drumlin /ˈdrʌmlɪn/ noun [C] GEOLOGY a long narrow hill made of rock and small pieces of stone, left by a moving glacier. One end of it is vertical and the other is sloping.

drummer /ˈdrʌmə/ noun [C] MUSIC someone who plays the drums

drumstick /ˈdrʌm,stɪk/ noun [C] MUSIC a stick used for playing a drum

drunk¹ /drʌŋk/ adj someone who is drunk is unable to control their actions or behaviour because they have drunk too much alcohol ≠ SOBER

drunk² /drʌŋk/ noun [C] someone who regularly drinks too much alcohol

drunk³ /drʌŋk/ the past participle of **drink¹**

drunkard /ˈdrʌŋkəd/ noun [C] a drunk

drunken /ˈdrʌŋkən/ adj *showing disapproval* involving or affecting someone who is drunk —**drunkenly** adv, **drunkenness** noun [U]

drupe /druːp/ noun [C] BIOLOGY a fruit with a **stone** surrounded by a soft thick part covered with skin. **Peaches, plums,** and **cherries** are all drupes.

dry¹ /draɪ/ (**drier** or **dryer, driest** or **dryest**) adj

1 with little water	5 food
2 without rain	6 joking in serious way
3 no longer liquid	7 boring/serious
4 hair/skin	

1 something that is dry has little or no water or other liquid inside or on it ≠ WET: *Are your hands dry?* ♦ *Vegetables should be stored in a cool dry place.*
2 with no rain ≠ WET: *The weather is usually dry and* sunny at this time of year. ♦ *The northern region is hot and dry.*
3 when a liquid such as paint is dry, it has become hard or solid ≠ WET
4 dry hair or skin feels rough ≠ GREASY
5 dry food contains little or no liquid: *The chicken was overcooked and dry.* ♦ *dry bread*
6 dry humour involves saying funny things in a serious way
7 very serious and boring: *The style was a little too dry for a children's book.* —**dryness** noun [U]

dry² /draɪ/ (**dries, drying, dried**) verb **1** [T] to remove the water from something by wiping it, heating it, or blowing air onto it ≠ WET: *We washed and dried all the sheets.* ♦ *Dry your hands on this towel.* **2** [I] to become dry: *I usually let my hair dry naturally.* **3** [T] to remove the water from food or plants as a way of preserving them: *dried fruit* **4** [I] when a liquid such as paint dries, it becomes hard or solid
PHRASAL VERBS **,dry (yourself/sth) 'off** if something dries off, or if you dry it off, all the water comes out of it or is wiped from its surface: *My boots dried off in the sun.*
,dry (sth) 'out if something dries out, or if it is dried out, some or all the water comes out of it: *Water the plant regularly to stop the soil from drying out.*
,dry 'up to stop being available: *What will happen when the money dries up?*
,dry (sth) 'up if something dries up, or if it is dried up, all the water comes out of it: *The land had dried up and no crops would grow.*

'dry ,battery noun [C] a battery that contains no liquid chemicals

,dry 'cell noun [C] PHYSICS a cell that produces electricity from an **electrolyte** held in a container as a thick or solid substance

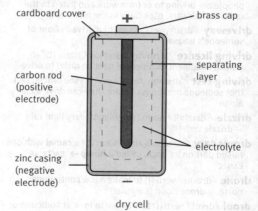
dry cell

,dry-'clean verb [T] to clean clothes using chemicals rather than water

'dry ,dock noun [C] a place where a ship or boat can be taken out of the water and repaired

dryer /ˈdraɪə/ noun [C] a machine that dries things such as clothes or hair

,dry 'land noun [U] land, rather than the sea

dryland /ˈdraɪ,lænd/ noun [U] GEOGRAPHY, AGRICULTURE areas often affected by severe lack of rain, for example deserts and **savannahs**

'dry-,line verb [T] CONSTRUCTION to finish walls with **plasterboard** instead of **plaster** —**dry-lining** noun [U]

,dry oxi'dation noun [U] CHEMISTRY the process of metal becoming destroyed by chemical action, with no water present

'dry-,point ,site noun [C] GEOGRAPHY a town, village etc that is built on higher land surrounded by water or wet ground, and that does not flood

,dry 'run noun [C] something that you do as a practice for an important event

the 'dry ,season noun GEOGRAPHY a period of the year in some countries during which rain does not usually fall ≠ RAINY SEASON, THE

,dry-sump lubri'cation noun [U] ENGINEERING a system of supplying oil to an engine in which the oil is pumped into a container and then to the **bearings** of the engine

DSL /,di: es 'el/ noun [U] COMPUTING digital subscriber line: a way of connecting to the Internet that allows a very fast exchange of information using ordinary phone connections

dual /'dju:əl/ adj with two aspects, parts, or uses: *a dual role*

,dual 'carriageway noun [C] a road with two or more lines of traffic going in each direction

,dual-'fuel adj a dual-fuel vehicle is designed to run on two different types of fuel, usually petrol and a type of fuel that does not cause pollution

,dual-'purpose adj able to be used for two different purposes

dub /dʌb/ (**dubs, dubbing, dubbed**) verb [T] to change the sound in a film by replacing the original speech with words spoken in a different language

dubious /'dju:biəs/ adj 1 not completely good, safe, or honest: *a dubious reputation* 2 not sure about something: *I'm dubious about his ability to do the job.* —**dubiously** adv

ducat /'dʌkət/ noun [C] a gold coin used in some European countries in the past

duchess /'dʌtʃɪs/ noun [C] a woman who has the same position as a **duke**, or the wife of a duke

duck¹ /dʌk/ noun 1 [C] a water bird with short legs and a large flat beak —*picture* → BIRD 2 [U] the meat of a duck 3 [C] SPORTS a score of zero points by a **batsman** in a game of **cricket**

duck² /dʌk/ verb 1 [I/T] to lower your head and body quickly, in order to move under something or to avoid being hit: *He ducked to avoid the blow.* 2 [I] to move quickly into or behind something to avoid being seen: *She ducked behind the wall.* 3 [T] to avoid something that is difficult: *Stop trying to duck the issue – who paid you for this?*

duckbilled platypus /,dʌkbɪld 'plætɪpəs/ noun [C] an unusual Australian mammal with a wide flat beak and tail. It lays eggs and feeds milk to its young. —*picture* → MAMMAL

duckling /'dʌklɪŋ/ noun [C] a young duck

duct /dʌkt/ noun [C] 1 ANATOMY a narrow tube inside the body that carries liquid: *tear ducts* 2 a tube in a building that carries air or protects wires

ductile /'dʌktaɪl/ adj SCIENCE ductile metals such as copper and aluminium can be pressed or pulled into different shapes —**ductility** /dʌk'tɪlɪti/ noun [U]

ducting /'dʌktɪŋ/ noun [U] a system of ducts in a building

ductless /'dʌktləs/ adj ANATOMY a ductless gland carries liquids directly into the blood, rather than into a **duct** (=tube)

'duct ,tape noun [U] strong and very sticky cloth that is often used for covering cracks or holes in pipes

due¹ /dju:/ adj 1 expected to happen or to be somewhere: *Her baby is due in May* (=expected to be born). ♦ *I'm due at a meeting in ten minutes.* ♦ *The case is due to go to court next month.* ♦ *The prisoners are not due for release until next year.* 2 if money is due, it is time for it to be paid: *The rent is due on the first day of each month.* 3 according to the usual standards or rules: *A driver who has due regard for the safety of other road users.* 4 if something is due to someone, they should receive it: *Some credit is due to the government for this improvement.*
PHRASE **in due course** *formal* later, when it is the right time, and not before
→ DUE TO

due² /dju:/ noun [singular] something that someone has a right to receive: *At last she has the justice that is her due.*
PHRASE **to give sb their due** used when you are going to say something good about someone, after you have been criticizing them
→ DUES

due³ /dju:/ adv **due north/south/east/west** directly towards the north, south, east, or west

duel /'dju:əl/ noun [C] a fight between two men with guns or swords —**duel** verb [I]

,due 'process noun [U] LAW the correct way of dealing with a legal trial or other legal matters, that makes sure that people's rights are protected

dues /dju:z/ noun [plural] money that someone pays regularly to be a member of a club or union

duet /dju:'et/ noun [C] MUSIC a piece of music that is sung or played by two people

'due to preposition because of something = OWING TO: *We had problems due to poor management.*

dug /dʌg/ the past tense and past participle of **dig**

dugout /'dʌgaʊt/ noun [C] 1 SPORTS a small shelter by the side of a sports field where team members sit during a game when they are not playing 2 a boat made by cutting out the inside of a **log** (=long piece of wood from a tree)

duke /dju:k/ noun [C] an **aristocrat** of high status, just below that of a prince

dull /dʌl/ adj 1 boring, or not interesting: *Life in a small village can be very dull.* 2 not bright or shiny: *hair that looks dull and lifeless* 3 a dull pain is not very strong but continues for a long time 4 a dull sound is low and not very clear

duly /'dju:li/ adv *formal* in a way that is correct or suitable

dumb /dʌm/ adj *old-fashioned* unable to speak. People now think that this word is offensive and prefer to use the expression **speech impaired**.

dumbbell /'dʌm,bel/ noun [C] SPORTS a short metal bar with a weight at both ends that people lift in order to make their muscles stronger

dumbfounded /dʌm'faʊndɪd/ adj so surprised that you do not know what to do or say

dummy /'dʌmi/ (plural **dummies**) noun [C] 1 something that is made to look like a real object 2 a model of a person's body 3 a small plastic or rubber object that a baby sucks 4 SPORTS a sudden movement of the body that a player makes, for example in football, in order to make their opponent think they are going to send the ball in a different direction

dump¹ /dʌmp/ verb [T] **1** to get rid of something that is no longer wanted or needed: *Waste chemicals were being dumped into the sea.* **2** to put something somewhere in a careless way: *She dumped her bags on the floor.* **3** COMPUTING to copy information that is stored inside a computer to another part of the same computer or onto something such as a disk **4** BUSINESS to sell goods at a very low price in a foreign country in order to keep prices higher in your own country

dump² /dʌmp/ noun [C] **1** a place where large amounts of rubbish are taken **2** COMPUTING the process of copying information that is stored inside a computer to another part of the same computer or onto something such as a disk

dumper truck /'dʌmpə ˌtrʌk/ noun [C] a truck with a large metal container that can be raised at the front end so that the material in it, such as sand or soil, falls out at the back end

dumping ground /'dʌmpɪŋ ˌɡraʊnd/ noun [C] **1** a place where large amounts of waste are taken and left **2** a place used for getting rid of things or people that are no longer wanted

dune /djuːn/ noun [C] GEOGRAPHY a hill of sand that has been formed by the wind or sea = SAND DUNE

dung /dʌŋ/ noun [U] waste from the body of a large animal

dungarees /ˌdʌŋɡəˈriːz/ noun [plural] a piece of clothing consisting of trousers and a square piece of cloth that covers the chest

'dung ˌbeetle noun [C] a beetle that lives on **dung** (=faeces), which it rolls into balls and pushes along the ground

dungeon /'dʌndʒ(ə)n/ noun [C] a dark underground room in a castle that was used as a prison in the past

dunno /dəˈnəʊ/ short form a way of writing 'don't know' that shows how it sounds in informal conversation

duo /'djuːəʊ/ (plural **duos**) noun [C] two people who perform together or do something else together

duodecimal /ˌdjuːəʊˈdesɪm(ə)l/ adj MATHS using units of 12 as a basic unit for counting or ordering, for example the division of a foot into 12 inches

duodenum /ˌdjuːəʊˈdiːnəm/ noun [C] ANATOMY the first section of the **small intestine**, just below the stomach —*picture* → DIGESTIVE SYSTEM, ORGAN — **duodenal** adj

dupe /djuːp/ verb [T] to trick someone into believing or doing something stupid or illegal

duple /'djuːp(ə)l/ adj MUSIC used to describe music that has two main beats in a bar

duplicate¹ /'djuːplɪkeɪt/ verb [T] **1** to make an exact copy of something such as a document **2** to repeat work that has been done already —**duplication** /ˌdjuːplɪˈkeɪʃ(ə)n/ noun [U]

duplicate² /'djuːplɪkət/ adj made as an exact copy of something else —**duplicate** noun [C]

durable /'djʊərəb(ə)l/ adj **1** able to stay in good condition for a long time, even after being used a lot **2** continuing to exist or be effective for a long time —**durability** /ˌdjʊərəˈbɪləti/ noun [U]

duration /djʊˈreɪʃ(ə)n/ noun [C/U] the period of time during which something continues to happen or exist

duress /djʊˈres/ noun **under duress** *formal* if you do something under duress, you do it because someone has forced or threatened you

during /'djʊərɪŋ/ preposition **1** at one point within a period of time: *During his visit to South Africa, the president met Archbishop Tutu.* **2** through the whole of a period of time: *Many creatures stay underground during daylight hours.*

dusk /dʌsk/ noun [U] the period of time at the end of the day just before it gets dark

dust¹ /dʌst/ noun [U] very small pieces of dirt or another substance that form a layer on a surface or a cloud in the air: *The books were old and covered in dust.* ♦ *He drove off, leaving us in **a cloud of dust**.*

dust² /dʌst/ verb **1** [I/T] to wipe the dust off the surface of something such as furniture **2** [T] to put a thin layer of powder on something

dustbin /'dʌs(t)bɪn/ noun [C] a container that is kept outside and used for putting rubbish in

'dust ˌbowl noun [C] GEOGRAPHY a region where there are a lot of **dust storms** because the soil has become dry from lack of rain

duster /'dʌstə/ noun [C] a cloth for removing dust from furniture

'dust ˌjacket or **'dust ˌcover** noun [C] a loose paper cover for a book

'dust ˌstorm noun [C] a storm during which a strong wind blows a lot of dry soil around

dusty /'dʌsti/ adj **1** covered with dust **2** covered with dry soil or sand

dutiable /'djuːtiəb(ə)l/ adj ECONOMICS dutiable goods must have tax paid on them, especially when they are brought into a country

dutiful /'djuːtɪf(ə)l/ adj *formal* careful to do things that other people ask for or expect —**dutifully** adv

duty /'djuːti/ (plural **duties**) noun [C/U] **1** something that you should do as a legal or moral obligation: *It is your duty as a parent to protect your children.* ♦ *The company **has a duty to** the local people.* ♦ *I was simply **doing my duty** as a good citizen.* **2** ECONOMICS a tax that people must pay on things that they buy, or on things that they bring into one country from another

PHRASES **off duty** not working at that moment **on duty** working at that moment: *The nurse on duty called for a doctor.*

ˌduty-'free adj ECONOMICS duty-free goods are cheaper than the usual price because customers do not pay any tax on them —**ˌduty-'free** adv

ˌduty 'manager noun [C] the manager who is on duty at a particular time

duvet /'duːveɪ/ noun [C] a warm cover for a bed, consisting of a large cloth bag filled with feathers or a soft material

DVD /ˌdiː viː 'diː/ noun [C] COMPUTING digital versatile disc: an object similar to a CD that has a film or television programme recorded on it

ˌDVD-'A noun [C] COMPUTING a music DVD that contains more songs than a CD and has better sound quality

ˌDVD-'R noun [C] COMPUTING a DVD that you can use only once to record information, especially images

ˌDVD-'ROM noun [C] COMPUTING a computer DVD that can hold a lot more information than a CD

ˌDVD-R'W noun [C] COMPUTING a DVD that you can use as many times as you want to record information, especially images

DVT /ˌdiː viː 'tiː/ noun [U] HEALTH deep vein thrombosis

dwarf¹ /dwɔːf/ (plural **dwarfs** or **dwarves** /dwɔːvz/) noun [C] **1** an imaginary creature in children's stories that looks like a very small old man **2** ASTRONOMY a very small star that does not shine brightly

dwarf² /dwɔːf/ adj BIOLOGY a dwarf tree, plant, or animal is much shorter or smaller than others of the same type

dwarf³ /dwɔːf/ verb [T] **1** to make someone or something seem small or unimportant **2** BIOLOGY to make a tree or other plant smaller than others of the same type by breeding, **grafting**, or other methods

dwell /dwel/ (**dwells, dwelling, dwelled** or **dwelt** /dwelt/) verb [I] *literary* to live somewhere
PHRASAL VERB **'dwell on sth** to spend a lot of time thinking or talking about something unpleasant

dweller /'dwelə/ noun [C] someone who lives in a particular type of place: *a city dweller*

dwelling /'dwelɪŋ/ noun [C] *formal* a building that someone lives in

dwindle /'dwɪnd(ə)l/ verb [I] to get gradually less or smaller over a period of time until almost nothing remains

dye¹ /daɪ/ noun [C/U] a substance used for changing the colour of cloth, hair etc

dye² /daɪ/ (**dyes, dyeing, dyed**) verb [T] to change the colour of something such as cloth or hair using dye

dying¹ /'daɪɪŋ/ adj not likely to live or exist for much longer: *a dying man*

dying² /'daɪɪŋ/ the present participle of **die¹**

dyke /daɪk/ noun [C] a wall that prevents a river, a lake, or the sea from flooding the land

dynamic¹ /daɪ'næmɪk/ adj **1** very lively and enthusiastic, with a lot of energy and determination: *dynamic leadership* **2** continuously changing, growing, or developing: *a dynamic process* **3** PHYSICS relating to the forces in nature that produce movement —**dynamically** /daɪ'næmɪkli/ adv

dynamic² /daɪ'næmɪk/ noun **1** [C] the set of forces that exist in a situation, especially a relationship, and affect how it changes or develops **2 dynamics** [U] PHYSICS the scientific study of movement

dynamite /'daɪnəmaɪt/ noun [U] a substance that is used for causing explosions

dynamo /'daɪnəməʊ/ (plural **dynamos**) noun [C] PHYSICS a piece of equipment that changes the movement of a machine into electricity

dynasty /'dɪnəsti/ (plural **dynasties**) noun [C] a family whose members rule a country or region for a long time, or are very successful in business or politics for a long time —**dynastic** /dɪ'næstɪk/ adj

dysentery /'dɪs(ə)ntri/ noun [U] HEALTH a serious disease of the lower intestine that causes severe diarrhoea

dysfunction /dɪs'fʌŋkʃ(ə)n/ noun [C/U] HEALTH any medical condition in which a part of the body does not work normally

dysfunctional /dɪs'fʌŋkʃ(ə)nəl/ adj **1** dysfunctional relationships do not work normally and are not happy or successful **2** not working normally

dyslexia /dɪs'leksiə/ noun [U] HEALTH a medical condition that makes it difficult for someone to read, write, and spell words correctly

dyslexic /dɪs'leksɪk/ adj HEALTH unable to read, write, or spell words correctly because of the medical condition of dyslexia

dyspepsia /dɪs'pepsiə/ noun [U] HEALTH indigestion

dysprosium /dɪs'prəʊziəm/ noun [U] CHEMISTRY a soft silvery metallic element in the **lanthanide** group of the periodic table. It is used in lasers and **nuclear reactors**. Chemical symbol: **Dy**

dystopia /dɪs'təʊpiə/ noun [C/U] an imaginary place in which everything is as bad as you can imagine ≠ UTOPIA

Ee

e /iː/ (plural **e's**) or **E** (plural **E's**) noun **1** [C/U] the fifth letter of the English alphabet **2 E** [C/U] MUSIC the third note in the musical scale of C major **3 E** [C/U] *informal* the illegal drug **ecstasy 4 E** [C] EDUCATION a mark that shows that a student's work is very bad

E /iː/ abbrev **1** East **2** Eastern

e- /iː/ prefix COMPUTING on or using the Internet: *e-learning ♦ e-business*

each /iːtʃ/ determiner, pronoun used for referring to all the people or things in a group, when you are thinking about every one separately: *Each child will read a poem. ♦ All five teams each won two matches. ♦ They cost about a dollar each. ♦ I locked all the doors and then checked **each one** again. ♦ **Each of** us has a job to do.*

each 'other pronoun **1** used for saying that each person or thing does something to the other or others: *The women looked at each other.* **2** used for saying that each person or thing is related in the same way to the other or others: *Suitcases were piled on top of each other.*

> You can use **one another** with the same meaning as **each other**.

eager /'iːgə/ adj very keen to do something, or excited about something that is going to happen: *The girls were **eager for** news of their families. ♦ He's so **eager to** learn that he stays late every evening.* —**eagerly** adv: *the most eagerly awaited film of the year* —**eagerness** noun [U]

eagle /'iːg(ə)l/ noun [C] **1** a large bird that eats other animals —*picture* → BIRD **2** SPORTS a golf score that is two hits of the ball less than the number expected for a particular hole

EAP /,iː eɪ 'piː/ noun [U] EDUCATION English for Academic Purposes: English taught to people whose first language is not English, but who need English for a course of study that they are doing

ear /ɪə/ noun **1** [C] ANATOMY one of the two parts on the sides of the head that you hear with and that are also important for balance. The ear is made up of three parts, the **outer ear**, the **middle ear**, and the **inner ear**. Most of the ear is protected inside the skull. —*picture* → on next page **2** [singular] the ability to hear and judge sounds: *She has **a very good ear** for music.* **3** [C] AGRICULTURE the part of a plant such as wheat or maize that contains the grain: *ears of wheat* —*picture* → CEREAL

PHRASE **play it by ear** to deal with a situation without having a plan, by reacting to things as they happen

earache /'ɪəreɪk/ noun [C/U] pain in your ear

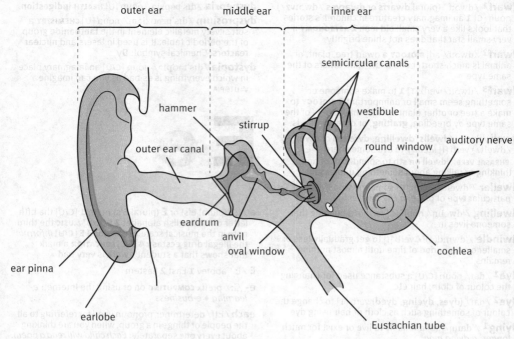

outer ear   middle ear   inner ear

semicircular canals

hammer

vestibule

stirrup

round window

auditory nerve

outer ear canal

eardrum

anvil

oval window

cochlea

ear pinna

earlobe

Eustachian tube

ear

'ear de,fenders noun [plural] **earmuffs**

eardrum /ˈɪədrʌm/ noun [C] **ANATOMY** the membrane inside the ear that vibrates when sound reaches it —*picture* → EAR

earl /ɜːl/ noun [C] a man with a very high social position in the UK

earlier /ˈɜːliə/ adj, adv used for referring to a time before the present or before the time that you are talking about: *an earlier period in history ♦ A few days earlier, he had been in Mumbai.*

the earliest /ˈɜːliəst/ noun [singular] the earliest time that something can happen or be done: *The earliest we could be there is 7.30.*

earlobe /ˈɪə,ləʊb/ noun [C] **ANATOMY** the soft part at the bottom of the ear —*picture* → EAR

early¹ /ˈɜːli/ (**earlier, earliest**) adj **1** near the beginning of a period of time ≠ LATE: *the early 19th century ♦ Julia is in her early thirties. ♦ It's too early to say what will happen.* **2** before the time that something usually happens or is expected to happen ≠ LATE: *Spring was early that year. ♦ My train was ten minutes early. ♦ I think I'll have an early night* (=go to bed before you usually do). **3** used about the first people or things of a particular type: *The early settlers built their cabins down there.*

PHRASE **the early hours** the period of time between midnight and the very early morning
→ EARLIER, EARLIEST

early² /ˈɜːli/ (**earlier, earliest**) adv **1** before the usual or expected time ≠ LATE: *I don't get up very early. ♦ The flight arrived ten minutes early.* **2** near the beginning of a period of time ≠ LATE: *Let's meet again early next week. ♦ He showed great musical talent very early in life.* **3** near the beginning of a piece of writing ≠ LATE: *This point was discussed earlier in the chapter.* **4** soon enough to avoid problems: *If we begin treatment early, we have a better chance of success.*

early adopter /ˈɜːli əˈdɒptə/ noun [C] **BUSINESS** someone who is among the first people to buy or start using a new product, technology, or idea after it becomes available or known

earmuffs /ˈɪə,mʌfs/ noun [plural] a pair of round pads, connected by a band, that are worn over the ears to protect them from cold or the noise of machinery

earn /ɜːn/ verb **1** [I/T] to receive money in exchange for working: *Most people here earn about $10 a day. ♦ She earns a good living* (=she gets a good salary) *as a financial adviser.* **2** [T] to make a profit from business or from money in the bank: *The company earned a huge profit last year.* **3** [T] to get something as a result of your efforts or your behaviour: *Have a good rest now – you've earned it. ♦ You have to earn your employees' respect.*

earned income /ˌɜːnd ˈɪnkʌm/ noun [U] the money that someone earns for doing their job, including their salary and any other payments that they receive
→ UNEARNED INCOME

earner /ˈɜːnə/ noun [C] **1** someone who earns money by working: *a wage earner* **2** something that earns money: *Tourism is a major earner of foreign currency.*

earnest /ˈɜːnɪst/ adj serious, determined, and sincere
PHRASE **in earnest 1** with more energy or determination than before: *After the rainy season, building work can begin in earnest.* **2** serious, and meaning what you say: *When I said I wanted to help you, I was in earnest.*
—**earnestly** adv

earnings /ˈɜːnɪŋz/ noun [plural] **BUSINESS 1** the amount of money that someone earns **2** the profit made by a company

earphone /ˈɪə,fəʊn/ noun [C] a piece of equipment that changes electrical signals into sound and is worn on or held close to the ear

earplug /ˈɪə,plʌg/ noun [C] a small object that you put in your ear to keep noise or water out

earring /ˈɪərɪŋ/ noun [C] a piece of jewellery that someone wears on their ear

earshot /ˈɪəˌʃɒt/ noun

PHRASES **out of earshot** too far away for you to hear
within/in earshot close enough for you to hear

earth¹ /ɜːθ/ noun

1 planet	4 animal's hole in
2 ground	ground
3 soil	5 electrical wire

1 Earth or **earth** [singular/U] **ASTRONOMY** the planet on which we live. Earth is the third planet in distance from the Sun and the fifth largest in the solar system. 75% of its surface is covered by water, its atmosphere consists of nitrogen and oxygen, and it is the only planet on which life is known to exist: *the planet Earth* ♦ *the Earth's surface* ♦ *the origins of life on Earth* —*picture* → SOLAR SYSTEM
2 the earth [singular] the land on which we live: *They felt the earth shake.*
3 [U] the substance in which plants grow, that covers most of the land: *Cover the seeds with earth, then water them.*
4 [C] a hole in the ground where an animal such as a **fox** lives
5 [singular] **PHYSICS** the wire in a piece of electrical equipment that makes it safe by connecting it to the ground —*picture* → PLUG

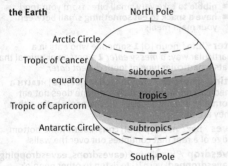

the Earth

North Pole
Arctic Circle
Tropic of Cancer
subtropics
equator
tropics
Tropic of Capricorn
Antarctic Circle
subtropics
South Pole

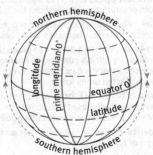

northern hemisphere
prime meridian 0°
longitude
equator 0°
latitude
southern hemisphere

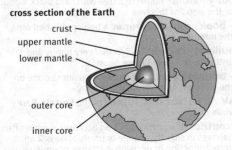

cross section of the Earth
crust
upper mantle
lower mantle
outer core
inner core

earth² /ɜːθ/ verb [T] **PHYSICS** to connect a piece of electrical equipment to the ground so that it is safe

earthenware /ˈɜːθ(ə)n,weə/ noun [U] bowls, cups etc that are made of baked clay

'earth ˌleakage ˌbreaker noun [C] **PHYSICS** a device that quickly cuts off the electric current to a piece of electrical equipment if there is a fault in the circuit, or if the person using the equipment receives an electric shock

earthly /ˈɜːθli/ adj used for giving emphasis to negative statements or to questions: *There's no earthly reason why we should pay.*

earthquake /ˈɜːθ,kweɪk/ noun [C] **GEOLOGY** a sudden movement of the ground, often causing a lot of damage to buildings etc. Earthquakes usually take place along geological faults or in volcanic areas. The strength of earthquakes is measured on the **Richter scale**. —*picture* → on next page

'earthquake-ˌproof adj not affected by earthquakes

ˌearth 'science noun [C/U] a science that involves studying the Earth, for example **geology**

earthworm /ˈɜːθ,wɜːm/ noun [C] a type of worm that lives in soil

earwig /ˈɪə,wɪg/ noun [C] a brown insect with a pair of curved parts at the end of its body —*picture* → INSECT

ease¹ /iːz/ noun [U] the ability to do something easily, or the fact that something is easy ≠ DIFFICULTY: *Our team won with ease.*

PHRASES **at ease** confident and relaxed
ill at ease not confident or relaxed

ease² /iːz/ verb **1** [I/T] to make something that is bad become less severe, or to become less severe: *Sometimes a mild painkiller is enough to ease the pain.* ♦ *The city's traffic problems are beginning to ease a little.* **2** [I/T] to move somewhere slowly and carefully, or to make something move in this way: *Joseph eased himself off the bed.* **3** [T] to make a rule or punishment less severe: *Sanctions against the country should be eased.*

easel /ˈiːz(ə)l/ noun [C] **ARTS** a frame that someone rests a painting on while they are painting it

easily /ˈiːzɪli/ adv **1** without difficulty or effort: *You could easily get there in a day.* **2** used for saying that something is likely to happen or be true: *The situation could easily get worse.* **3** definitely: *This is easily his best film in years.* **4** in a confident and relaxed way: *Sam and Luke had met before and chatted easily.*

east¹ /iːst/ noun **1** [U] **GEOGRAPHY** the direction that is in front of you when you are facing the rising sun: *driving from east to west* —*picture* → COMPASS **2 the east** [singular] the part of a place that is in the east: *They live in **the east of** the city.* ♦ *Most of the region's forests are **in the east**.* **3 the East** [singular] the eastern part of the world, especially China and Japan

east² /iːst/ adv **GEOGRAPHY** towards the east: *Drive east until you come to the river.* ♦ *She lives 40 miles east of Nairobi.*

east³ /iːst/ adj **1** **GEOGRAPHY** in the east, or facing towards the east **2** an east wind blows from the east

ˌEast 'Asia GEOGRAPHY the Far East

Easter /ˈiːstə/ noun [C/U] **RELIGION** a day when Christians celebrate the time when Jesus Christ died and then returned to life according to the Bible

'Easter ˌegg noun [C] a chocolate egg that people eat in celebration of Easter

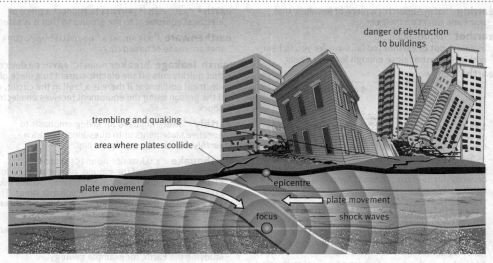

danger of destruction to buildings

trembling and quaking

area where plates collide

plate movement

epicentre

plate movement

focus   shock waves

earthquake

easterly /ˈiːstəli/ adj **1** GEOGRAPHY towards or in the east **2** an easterly wind blows from the east

eastern /ˈiːstən/ adj GEOGRAPHY in the east of a place: *eastern Nigeria* ♦ *the eastern shore of the Mediterranean*

the ˌeastern ˈhemisphere noun GEOGRAPHY countries in what is considered to be the eastern half of the world, especially the countries of Asia

eastward /ˈiːstwəd/ adj GEOGRAPHY towards or in the east

eastwards /ˈiːstwədz/ adv GEOGRAPHY towards the east

easy /ˈiːzi/ (**easier**, **easiest**) adj **1** not difficult, or not needing much work: *The test was easy.* ♦ *The easiest way to get there is on the train.* ♦ *It is easy to see why she likes him.* ♦ *This cake is very easy to make.* **2** happy, confident, and not worried about anything: *Doug had an easy charm.*

   PHRASE **the easy way out** an easy way of doing something, but not the right or best way

easygoing /ˌiːziˈɡəʊɪŋ/ adj relaxed, calm, and not easy to upset

eat /iːt/ (**eats**, **eating**, **ate** /et, eɪt/, **eaten** /ˈiːt(ə)n/) verb **1** [I/T] to put food into your mouth and swallow it: *Did you eat your sandwich?* ♦ *My sister doesn't eat meat, but she eats fish.* ♦ *Don't talk while you're eating.* ♦ *Where can we get something to eat* (=food)? **2** [I] to have a meal: *What time shall we eat?* ♦ *We ate at a small Chinese restaurant.*

   PHRASAL VERBS **ˌeat aˈway at sth** or **ˌeat ˈinto sth** to gradually destroy something = ERODE: *Inflation had eaten into all their savings.*

 ˌeat sth ˈup to use large amounts of your available time or money = CONSUME: *Having children eats up a lot of a family's income.*

> **Build your vocabulary: words you can use instead of eat**
>
> ■ **chew** to use your teeth to break up the food in your mouth
> ■ **eat up** to finish all the food that you have been given
> ■ **have breakfast/lunch/dinner** to eat a particular meal

> ■ **have something to eat** to eat something, or to have a meal
> ■ **munch** to eat something noisily
> ■ **nibble** to take very small bites from your food
> ■ **have a snack** to eat something small between your main meals

eater /ˈiːtə/ noun [C] **1** someone who eats in a particular way: *a messy eater* **2** a person or animal that eats a particular type of food: *a meat eater*

eating disorder /ˈiːtɪŋ dɪsˌɔːdə/ noun [C] HEALTH a medical condition in which someone does not eat normally, usually because they wrongly believe that they are too fat

eaves /iːvz/ noun [plural] CONSTRUCTION the bottom edge of a roof that continues out over the walls

eavesdrop /ˈiːvzˌdrɒp/ (**eavesdrops**, **eavesdropping**, **eavesdropped**) verb [I] to listen to other people's conversation secretly, without them knowing

ebb¹ /eb/ noun [singular] the process in which the sea level at the coast becomes lower twice each day

ebb² /eb/ verb [I] **1** *literary* to gradually become smaller or less: *He felt his confidence ebbing away.* **2** when the tide ebbs twice a day, the sea level at the coast gradually becomes lower

Ebola /iˈbəʊlə/ or **Eˈbola ˌvirus** noun [U] HEALTH a very serious disease that causes someone to lose blood from all parts of their body and usually results in death

ebonite /ˈebənaɪt/ noun [U] CHEMISTRY **vulcanite**, a type of hard rubber

ebony /ˈebəni/ noun [U] a tree with hard black wood, or the wood of this tree

ˈe-ˌbook noun [C] COMPUTING a book published on the Internet

ebullient /ɪˈbʌliənt/ adj *formal* very happy and enthusiastic —**ebullience** noun [U]

ˈe-ˌbusiness noun [C/U] BUSINESS business done on the Internet, or an Internet company

EBV /ˌiː biː ˈviː/ noun [U] HEALTH the **Epstein-Barr virus**

eccentric /ɪkˈsentrɪk/ adj **1** an eccentric person often behaves in slightly strange or unusual ways **2** an eccentric action or decision is strange or unusual —**eccentric** noun [C]

ecclesiastical /ɪˌkliːziˈæstɪk(ə)l/ adj **RELIGION** relating to the Christian Church

ecdysis /ˈekdɪsɪs/ noun [U] **BIOLOGY** in **arthropods** such as insects and crustaceans, and in reptiles, the regular process of **moulting** (=losing) an outer layer of the body

echelon /ˈeʃəlɒn/ noun [C] **1** one of the levels of status in an organization, or the people at that level **2** an arrangement of soldiers, ships, or aircraft in which each one is slightly to the right or left of the one in front

echinoderm /ɪˈkaɪnəʊdɜːm/ noun [C] **BIOLOGY** an invertebrate sea animal with a body that has five parts that are arranged **symmetrically** around a central point. **Starfish** and **sea urchins** are echinoderms.

echo[1] /ˈekəʊ/ (**echoes, echoing, echoed**) verb **1** [I] **PHYSICS** if a sound echoes, it is repeated because it produces **sound waves** that hit a surface and return after a short period of time: *Gunfire echoed across the streets.* **2** [I] if a place echoes, noises echo easily there **3** [T] to express the same words, ideas, or feelings that someone else has expressed: *Blake echoed the views of many players.*

echo[2] /ˈekəʊ/ (plural **echoes**) noun [C] **1** **PHYSICS** a sound that is repeated because it produces **sound waves** that hit a surface and return after a short period of time: *the echo of footsteps in the alley* **2** an idea or phrase that is like one that has been expressed before: *echoes of the past*

echolocation /ˌekəʊləˈkeɪʃ(ə)n/ noun [U] **PHYSICS, BIOLOGY** a means of knowing where an object is, based on a sound sent out being reflected back from it. Echolocation is used by animals such as **bats** to find their way.

echo sounder /ˈekəʊ ˌsaʊndə/ noun [C] **PHYSICS** a piece of equipment that uses **sound waves** to measure the depth of the sea bed, or to find objects in water

eclampsia /ɪˈklæmpsiə/ noun [U] **HEALTH** a medical condition in which a pregnant woman with high blood pressure has **convulsions** (=violent uncontrolled movements)

eclectic /ɪˈklektɪk/ adj *formal* an eclectic group of people, things, or ideas is interesting or unusual because it consists of many different types

eclipse /ɪˈklɪps/ noun **1** [C] **ASTRONOMY** a short period when all or part of the Sun or Moon becomes dark, because of the positions of the Sun, Moon, and Earth in relation to each other. A **total eclipse** is when the Sun or Moon is completely covered. An eclipse of the Sun is called a **solar eclipse**, and an eclipse of the Moon is called a **lunar eclipse**. **2** [singular/U] a time when someone or something is less successful or important, because another person or thing becomes more important

eco-ˈfriendly adj designed to cause as little harm as possible to the environment

ecolabel /ˈiːkəʊˌleɪb(ə)l/ noun [C] **BUSINESS** a label used to mark products that are produced, and can be used and got rid of, without harming the environment

E. coli /ˌiː ˈkəʊlaɪ/ noun [U] **BIOLOGY, HEALTH** a type of bacteria in the intestines that can make you very ill if it infects something that you eat or drink

ecological /ˌiːkəˈlɒdʒɪk(ə)l/ adj **BIOLOGY, ENVIRONMENT** relating to the study of the relationships between organisms and their natural or developed environment: *The oil that leaked from the damaged ship caused a massive ecological disaster.* —**ecologically** /ˌiːkəˈlɒdʒɪkli/ adv

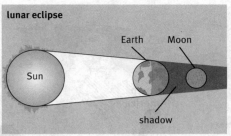
lunar eclipse

Sun | Earth | Moon | shadow

As the Moon travels into the shadow cast by the Earth, there is an eclipse of the Moon.

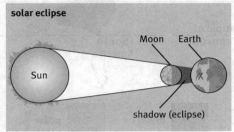
solar eclipse

Sun | Moon | Earth | shadow (eclipse)

When the Sun cannot be seen at point X on the Earth, there is an eclipse of the Sun.

ecology /ɪˈkɒlədʒi/ noun [U] **BIOLOGY, ENVIRONMENT** the study of the environment and the way organisms affect each other —**ecologist** noun [C]

e-ˈcommerce noun [U] **BUSINESS, ECONOMICS** the activity of buying and selling goods on the Internet

ˈe-comˌmunication noun [U] **COMPUTING** communication using the Internet, for example by email and **message boards**

economic /ˌiːkəˈnɒmɪk, ˌekəˈnɒmɪk/ adj **1** **ECONOMICS** relating to the economy, business, and trade: *economic development ♦ the government's economic policies ♦ The project will bring great social and economic benefits to the region.* **2** **BUSINESS** providing a satisfactory profit from business activities ≠ UNECONOMIC: *It is no longer economic to mine coal here.*

economical /ˌiːkəˈnɒmɪk(ə)l, ˌekəˈnɒmɪk(ə)l/ adj not spending or costing much money: *The material is an economical substitute for plastic or steel. ♦ It's more economical to run the machines at night.*

economically /ˌiːkəˈnɒmɪkli, ˌekəˈnɒmɪkli/ adv **1** relating to the economy or to money: *Politically and economically, the country is going through enormous changes.* **2** done so that not much is wasted or little money is spent: *We aim to do the job as economically as possible.*

ˌeconomic ˈcycle noun [C] **ECONOMICS** a series of changes in a country's economy, in which economic activity increases and decreases in a regular pattern that keeps being repeated

ˌeconomic ˈindicator noun [C] **ECONOMICS** a quantity used for measuring a particular feature of the economy

ˌeconomic ˈmigrant noun [C] **SOCIAL STUDIES** someone who goes to live in a new country because living conditions or opportunities for jobs are not good in their own country

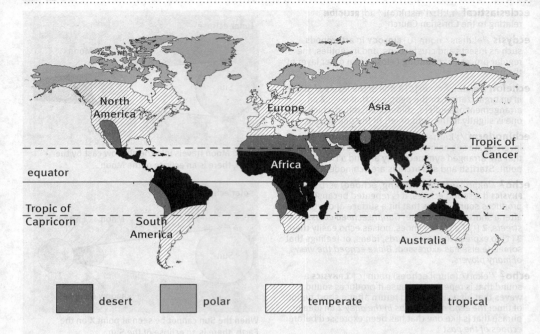

North America
Europe
Asia
Tropic of Cancer
equator
Tropic of Capricorn
South America
Africa
Australia

desert   polar   temperate   tropical

ecosystems

economics /ˌiːkəˈnɒmɪks, ˌekəˈnɒmɪks/ noun [U] ECONOMICS the study of the way that goods and services are produced and sold, and of the way that money is managed: *a degree in economics*

economist /ɪˈkɒnəmɪst/ noun [C] ECONOMICS an expert in economics

economize /ɪˈkɒnəmaɪz/ verb [I] to try to waste as little as possible of something such as money or fuel

economy¹ /ɪˈkɒnəmi/ (plural **economies**) noun **1** [C] ECONOMICS the system by which a country's trade, industry, and money are organized, and all the business, industry, and trade in that system: *a modern industrial economy* ♦ *The **economy grew** at an average of about 3 per cent per year.* ♦ *The tax cuts are designed to **boost the economy** (=make it stronger).* **2** [C/U] the careful use of something so that very little is wasted, or an example of using something carefully: *In those days, fuel economy was a central factor in car design.* ♦ *If we **make** a few **economies** (=spend money more carefully), we can afford it.* **3** [U] TOURISM the cheapest seats on a plane

PHRASE **economies of scale** BUSINESS reductions in the cost of making and selling products that are made possible because of the large quantities of them that a business produces

economy² /ɪˈkɒnəmi/ adj **1** TOURISM economy travel is the cheapest type of air travel available **2** economy goods are sold in large quantities so that they are cheaper

e'conomy ˌcar noun [C] a car that does not use much petrol

e'conomy ˌclass noun [C] TOURISM the cheapest seats on a plane —**e'conomy ˌclass** adj, adv

ecosystem /ˈiːkəʊˌsɪstəm/ noun [C] BIOLOGY, ENVIRONMENT all the plants, animals, and other organisms in a particular area, considered in relation to the environment that they live in and the way they all depend on each other: *a desert ecosystem*

ecotourism /ˈiːkəʊˌtʊərɪz(ə)m/ noun [U] TOURISM the business of organizing and selling holidays that cause as little damage to the environment as possible —**ecotourist** noun [C]

ecstasy /ˈekstəsi/ (plural **ecstasies**) noun **1** [C/U] a feeling of great happiness and pleasure **2** [U] an illegal drug that causes feelings of happiness and love

ecstatic /ɪkˈstætɪk/ adj extremely happy or pleased —**ecstatically** /ɪkˈstætɪkli/ adv

ECT /ˌiː siː ˈtiː/ noun [U] HEALTH electroconvulsive therapy: a medical treatment for serious mental illness in which electricity is passed through the brain

ectoparasite /ˌektəʊˈpærəsaɪt/ noun [C] BIOLOGY a parasite that lives on the outside of its **host**, for example on the skin or in the hair. **Fleas** are ectoparasites.

ectopic /ekˈtɒpɪk/ adj HEALTH an ectopic pregnancy is one in which a baby starts to grow outside its mother's uterus

ectotherm /ˈektəʊθɜːm/ noun [C] BIOLOGY an animal that controls its body temperature by absorbing heat from its environment. All animals other than birds and mammals are ectotherms.

ecumenical /ˌiːkjʊˈmenɪk(ə)l/ adj RELIGION encouraging different Christian churches to work and worship together

eczema /ˈeksɪmə/ noun [U] HEALTH a medical condition that makes the skin dry, sore, and **itchy**

ed. abbrev **1** edition **2** editor **3** education

EDC /ˌiː diː ˈsiː/ noun [U] COMPUTING electronic data capture: the process of collecting information using a computer

eddy /ˈedi/ (plural **eddies**) noun [C] GEOGRAPHY a current of air or water that moves against the main current in a circular pattern

edge¹ /edʒ/ noun **1** [C] the part of something that is furthest from its centre: *Victoria was sitting on the edge of the bed.* ♦ *The railway station was built on the edge of town.* **2** [C] the sharp side of a blade or tool that is used for cutting things **3** [singular] an advantage over other people or things: *Training can give you the edge over your competitors.* **4** [singular] a quality in the way that someone speaks that shows they are becoming angry or upset: *Had she imagined the slight edge to his voice?*

PHRASES on edge someone who is on edge is nervous and unable to relax because they are worried
on the edge of your seat very excited and interested, because you want to know what happens next

edge² /edʒ/ verb **1** [I/T] to move slowly and carefully, or to make something do this: *Michael was edging towards the door.* **2** [I] to gradually increase or become less: *Food prices edged up by 0.2 per cent in November.* **3** [T] to put something round the edge of another thing: *white plates edged with gold*

edgeways /'edʒweɪz/ adv sideways
PHRASE not get a word in edgeways to not manage to say something because someone else is talking a lot

EDI /ˌiː diː 'aɪ/ noun [U] **COMPUTING** electronic data interchange: the movement of information between computers in different companies using a **network**, for example the Internet

edible /'edɪb(ə)l/ adj safe to eat, or good enough to eat ≠ INEDIBLE: *edible mushrooms* ♦ *The food in the cafeteria is barely edible* (=it tastes very bad).

edict /'iːdɪkt/ noun [C] *formal* an official order that is given by a government or someone in authority

edifice /'edɪfɪs/ noun [C] *formal* **1** a large impressive building **2** a complicated system or policy

edifying /'edɪˌfaɪɪŋ/ adj *formal* teaching people something that increases their knowledge or improves their character

edit¹ /'edɪt/ verb [T] **1** to make changes to a book or document so that it is ready to be published **2** to be the **editor** in charge of a book, newspaper, or magazine **3** to make changes to a film or to a television or radio programme before it is shown or broadcast

edit² /'edɪt/ noun [U] **COMPUTING** a menu choice in some computer programs that allows you to cut, copy, or move parts of a document or file, or look for particular words in it

edition /ɪ'dɪʃ(ə)n/ noun [C] a set of copies of a book, newspaper, or magazine that are published at the same time: *the Sunday edition of the local newspaper* ♦ *the 2004 edition of the Guinness Book of Records*

editor /'edɪtə/ noun [C] **1** someone who is in charge of a newspaper or magazine, or in charge of one of its sections **2** someone whose job is to **edit** books, documents, or films **3** **COMPUTING** a computer program used for writing or **editing** documents, files, or programs

editorial /ˌedɪ'tɔːriəl/ noun [C] a newspaper article in which the editor gives their opinion on a subject in the news = LEADER

edu abbrev **COMPUTING** educational institution: used in email and Internet addresses

educate /'edjʊkeɪt/ verb **1** [T] **EDUCATION** to teach someone, especially at a school, college, or university: *Where was she educated?* ♦ *He was educated at Eton and Trinity College, Cambridge.* **2** [I/T] to give someone necessary or useful knowledge: *The mining museum was built to educate people about their local history.*
—**educator** noun [C]

educated /'edjʊˌkeɪtɪd/ adj an educated person has received a good education and has a lot of knowledge ≠ UNEDUCATED: *The people who work here are well educated and open-minded.*

education /ˌedjʊ'keɪʃ(ə)n/ noun **1** [U] **EDUCATION** the activity of educating people in schools, colleges, and universities, and all the policies and arrangements concerning this: *Education is a major concern for voters.* ♦ *the Minister of Education* **2** [singular] **EDUCATION** someone's experience of learning or being taught: *Did you have a university education?* ♦ *He wants his children to get an education.* **3** [U] the process of providing people with information about an important issue: *health education*

Word family: education

Words in the same family as education
- **educate** v
- **educator** n
- **educated** adj
- **educative** adj
- **educational** adj
- **educationally** adv
- **uneducated** adj

educational /ˌedjʊ'keɪʃ(ə)nəl/ adj **1** **EDUCATION** relating to education: *educational opportunities for women* **2** giving people useful knowledge: *The programme was educational and entertaining too.*
—**educationally** adv

edu'cational ˌleave noun [U] **BUSINESS** time away from work that your employer gives you so that you can study

educative /'edjʊkətɪv/ adj *formal* providing someone with education

edutainment /ˌedjʊ'teɪnmənt/ noun [U] television programmes, **DVDs**, software etc that entertain you while they teach you something

-ee /iː/ suffix **1** used with some verbs to make nouns meaning someone who is affected by an action **2** used with some verbs to make nouns meaning someone who performs an action

the EEA /ˌiː iː 'eɪ/ noun [singular] **ECONOMICS** European Economic Area: an economic group formed in 1994 consisting of the member states of the European Union and Iceland, Liechtenstein, and Norway

EEG /ˌiː iː 'dʒiː/ noun [C] **HEALTH** **1** electroencephalogram: a medical test of electrical activity in the brain **2** electroencephalograph: a machine that records electrical activity in the brain

eel /iːl/ noun [C] a long thin fish that looks like a snake

eerie /'ɪəri/ (**eerier, eeriest**) adj strange and mysterious, and sometimes frightening —**eerily** /'ɪərɪli/ adv

effect /ɪ'fekt/ noun **1** [C/U] a change that is produced in one person or thing by another: *Scientists are studying the chemical's effect on the environment.* ♦ *Any change in lifestyle will have an effect on your health.* ♦ *The new tax rates will have little effect on most ordinary people.* **2** [C] an appearance or reaction that is deliberately produced, for example by a writer or artist: *Students should learn how they can achieve different effects in their writing.* **3** effects [plural] special artificial images and sounds that are created for a film = SPECIAL EFFECTS **4** effects or personal effects [plural] *formal* the things that belong to you

PHRASES come into effect if a rule or law comes into effect, it starts to be used
for effect if someone does something for effect, they do it in order to impress people
in effect 1 used for giving a summary of what you think the situation really is: *In effect, this means we'll have*

to work more hours for the same pay. **2** if a law or rule is in effect, it is being applied

put sth into effect to start to use a plan or idea

take effect 1 to start to produce the results that were intended: *The tax cuts are beginning to take effect.* **2** if a rule or law takes effect, it starts to be applied
→ SIDE EFFECT

effective /ɪˈfektɪv/ adj **1** working well and producing the result that was intended ≠ INEFFECTIVE: *This is a very effective way of controlling pests and weeds.* ♦ *The new vaccine is highly effective against all strains of the disease.* **2** *formal* when a law or agreement becomes effective, it officially starts to be used: *Government ministers reached a 30-month agreement, effective from 1 July.* —**effectiveness** noun [U]

effectively /ɪˈfektɪvli/ adv **1** used for saying what the situation really is, although it might seem to be different: *With Australia 24 points ahead at half-time, the game was effectively over.* **2** in a way that works well and produces the result that you intended: *The system could deliver services to local communities more effectively.*

effector /ɪˈfektə/ noun [C] BIOLOGY something that produces an effect in the body, for example a nerve ending that produces an effect on a muscle

effervescent /ˌefəˈves(ə)nt/ adj **1** producing a lot of small bubbles as gas is released in a liquid in a **chemical reaction** = FIZZY **2** lively and enthusiastic = BUBBLY

efficiency /ɪˈfɪʃ(ə)nsi/ noun [U] the ability to work well and produce good results, using the available time, money, supplies etc in the most effective way: *new technology aimed at improving efficiency and customer service*

efficient /ɪˈfɪʃ(ə)nt/ adj working well and producing good results by using the available time, money, supplies etc in the most effective way ≠ INEFFICIENT: *The new machine is far more efficient than the old one.* ♦ *The most efficient way to plan your work is to put your tasks in order of importance.* ♦ *The hotel's staff are friendly and efficient.* —**efficiently** adv

effigy /ˈefɪdʒi/ (plural **effigies**) noun [C] a model of someone, especially one that is destroyed in a protest against them

effluent /ˈefluənt/ noun [C/U] ENVIRONMENT liquid waste that a place such as a factory or farm allows to flow into a river or the sea

effort /ˈefət/ noun **1** [C/U] an attempt to do something that is difficult or that involves hard work: *Detectives are talking to other witnesses in an effort to find out more about the girl.* ♦ *I've made an effort to be more punctual.* ♦ *The changes were part of an effort to push profits up.* **2** [singular/U] physical or mental energy needed to do something: *Writing a book takes a lot of time and effort.* ♦ *Mary put a lot of effort into this project.* **3** [C] the activities of people who are working together to achieve a particular aim: *international relief efforts* **4** [singular/U] PHYSICS the force used on a machine of any type in order to make it able to move an object —*picture* → LEVER

effortless /ˈefətləs/ adj done well or successfully and without any effort —**effortlessly** adv

effusive /ɪˈfjuːsɪv/ adj expressing happiness, praise etc in an extremely enthusiastic way

E-FIT /ˈiː ˌfɪt/ TRADEMARK a picture of the face of someone who police think committed a crime, created using software and someone's description of the person

EFL /ˌiː ef ˈel/ noun [U] EDUCATION English as a Foreign Language: English taught to people who do not live in an English-speaking country

'e-ˌfraud noun [U] the activity of obtaining money illegally using the Internet

EFTPOS /ˈeftpɒs/ noun [U] BUSINESS electronic funds transfer at point of sale: a system of paying for goods by moving money by computer from the customer's bank account to the account of the company or person they have bought from

e.g. or **eg** /ˌiː ˈdʒiː/ abbrev for example: used for giving an example of what you mean

egalitarian /ɪˌɡælɪˈteəriən/ adj supporting a social system in which everyone has the same status, money, and opportunities

egestion /ɪˈdʒestʃ(ə)n/ noun [U] BIOLOGY the process by which the body gets rid of solid waste through the **anus** → EXCRETION

egg /eɡ/ noun

1 of bird, reptile etc	**4** in plants and fungi
2 as food	**5** of insect, frog etc
3 in women or female animals	

1 [C] BIOLOGY the round object with a shell that a baby bird, reptile etc develops inside. Many eggs have a yolk that contains food for the growing embryo: *a hen's egg* ♦ *The female bird will lay about four eggs at one time.* ♦ *The eggs will hatch* (=the baby birds will come out of them) *in a couple of weeks.*
2 [C/U] a chicken's egg used as food: *We had boiled eggs for breakfast.* ♦ *an egg sandwich*
3 [C] BIOLOGY a gamete (=reproductive cell) produced inside a woman or other female animal that can develop into a baby. It is usually produced by the ovaries, and combines with a male sperm cell for fertilization to take place = OVUM
4 [C] BIOLOGY the gamete (=reproductive cell) in plants and some fungi whose nucleus joins with a male gamete to make a new organism
5 [C] BIOLOGY a small object produced by a female insect, frog etc, that a young animal comes out of: *ants' eggs* —*picture* → MOSQUITO, TADPOLE

eggplant /ˈeɡˌplɑːnt/ noun [C/U] *American* an **aubergine**

eggshell /ˈeɡˌʃel/ noun [C] the hard outer layer of an egg

'egg ˌwhite noun [C/U] the clear part of an egg that becomes white when it is cooked

EGM /ˌiː dʒiː ˈem/ noun [C] BUSINESS Extraordinary General Meeting: a special meeting of a business or organization, called by its directors, **shareholders**, or members, to discuss a particular problem or matter

ego /ˈiːɡəʊ/ (plural **egos**) noun [C] the opinion that you have of yourself and your own importance: *a guy with a huge ego* ♦ *Being asked to speak was a real boost to her ego.*

egocentric /ˌiːɡəʊˈsentrɪk/ adj someone who is egocentric behaves as if they are more important than other people, and need not care about them = ARROGANT

egotistical /ˌiːɡəʊˈtɪstɪk(ə)l/ adj *showing disapproval* someone who is egotistical thinks that they are more important than other people and need not care about them —**egotist** /ˈiːɡəʊtɪst/ noun [C]

'e-ˌgovernment noun [U] the use of the Internet by government, for example to give information to the public or to allow people to vote from their computer

egret /'iːɡrət/ noun [C] a white bird with long legs that lives near water —*picture* → BIRD

eh /eɪ/ interjection used for asking someone to agree with you: *Pretty good, eh?*

Eid /iːd/ noun [U] RELIGION a festival in the Muslim religion

eight /eɪt/ number the number 8

eighteen /ˌeɪˈtiːn/ number the number 18 —**eighteenth** /ˌeɪˈtiːnθ/ number

eighth /eɪtθ/ number **1** in the place or position counted as number 8 **2** one of 8 equal parts of something

eighties /'eɪtiz/ noun [plural]
PHRASES **the eighties 1** the years from 1980 to 1989 **2** a temperature in the eighties is between 80 and 89 degrees **Fahrenheit**
in your eighties aged between 80 and 89

eighty /'eɪti/ number the number 80 —**eightieth** /'eɪtiəθ/ number

einsteinium /eɪnˈsteɪniəm/ noun [U] CHEMISTRY a radioactive metallic element in the **actinide** group of the periodic table. Chemical symbol: **Es**

either /'aɪðə/ adv, conjunction, determiner, pronoun **1** one or the other of two people or things, especially when it does not matter which one is chosen: *Cheque or credit card – you can use either.* ◆ *We welcome candidates of either sex.* ◆ *It was a long time before either of them spoke.* **2** used instead of 'also' in negative statements: *We tried another method, but that didn't work either.* ◆ *I can't come tonight, and nobody else can either.* **3** used instead of 'both' in negative statements: *Jackie could play the piano and sing, but I couldn't do either.* ◆ *I didn't enjoy either of the books.* → ALSO
PHRASES **either...or** used for showing two or more possibilities or choices: *You must answer either yes or no.* ◆ *You can contact us either by phone, by email, or by letter.*
either side/end/hand etc each of two sides, ends, hands etc: *Her parents were sitting on either side of her.*

When **either** is the subject of a sentence, it is usually used with a singular verb: *Is either of them at home?* But in spoken English a plural verb is often used: *Are either of them at home?*

ejaculate /ɪˈdʒækjʊleɪt/ verb [I/T] BIOLOGY if a man ejaculates, semen comes out of his penis —**ejaculation** /ɪˌdʒækjʊˈleɪʃ(ə)n/ noun [C/U]

eject /ɪˈdʒekt/ verb **1** [T] to make something such as a tape or CD come out from a machine **2** [T] to make someone leave a place, especially using physical force: *A group of noisy protesters were ejected from the meeting.* **3** [I] to jump out of a plane before it crashes —**ejection** /ɪˈdʒekʃ(ə)n/ noun [U]

elaborate¹ /ɪˈlæb(ə)rət/ adj very detailed and complicated ≠ SIMPLE: *elaborate geometrical patterns* ◆ *an elaborate system of inspections*

elaborate² /ɪˈlæbəreɪt/ verb [I] to give more details or information about something: *The police refused to elaborate on the circumstances of the arrest.* —**elaboration** /ɪˌlæbəˈreɪʃ(ə)n/ noun [U]

elapse /ɪˈlæps/ verb [I] *formal* if time elapses, it passes

elastic¹ /ɪˈlæstɪk/ noun [U] a material that stretches or bends easily and can return to its original shape

elastic² /ɪˈlæstɪk/ adj **1** made of elastic **2** PHYSICS able to stretch or bend and then return to the original shape: *The elastic behaviour of some materials depends on the temperature and duration of the stress* applied. **3** ECONOMICS if the supply of something or the demand for something is elastic, it changes according to the economic conditions it operates in, for example if the price of a product changes

e,lastic col'lision noun [C] PHYSICS a **collision** in which all of the **kinetic energy** is transferred from one object to another, and kinetic energy is not wasted in the form of heat or light

elasticity /ˌiːlæˈstɪsəti/ noun [U] **1** PHYSICS the ability of a substance to stretch or bend and then return to its original shape **2** ECONOMICS the degree to which supply, **demand** etc changes according to other economic conditions that change, for example the price of goods

elated /ɪˈleɪtɪd/ adj extremely happy and excited —**elation** /ɪˈleɪʃ(ə)n/ noun [U]

elbow¹ /'elbəʊ/ noun [C] the part in the middle of the arm, where it bends: *She sat with her elbows on the table.* —*picture* → BODY, JOINT

elbow² /'elbəʊ/ verb [T] to push or hit someone with your elbow

elder¹ /'eldə/ adj older than someone, especially someone in your family: *advice from my elder brother*

elder² /'eldə/ noun [C] **1** someone in your family or community who is older than you **2** SOCIAL STUDIES an older member of an organization or community who is given respect and authority

elderly /'eldəli/ adj **1** old: *Not all elderly people can live with their relatives.* **2 the elderly** old people

eldest /'eldəst/ adj oldest of the people in a group, especially the children in a family: *He was the eldest of three sons.*

'e-,learning noun [U] EDUCATION studying by means of the Internet

elect /ɪˈlekt/ verb [T] to choose someone for an official position, or choose them to be a representative, by voting for them: *Every nation should have a right to elect its own government.* ◆ *He was elected to parliament by a large majority.* ◆ *Lee Yuan-tzu was elected the next day as Vice President.* ◆ *She was elected president of the association.*

election /ɪˈlekʃ(ə)n/ noun POLITICS **1** [C] an occasion when people vote for someone to represent them, especially in a government: *an election victory* ◆ *The new regime is promising to hold free elections as soon as possible.* ◆ *She is standing in elections for the National Assembly.* **2** [U] the process of electing a person or government: *the election of a new leader* ◆ *a candidate for election to the Council* ◆ *His election as President will mean changes in foreign policy.*

electioneering /ɪˌlekʃəˈnɪərɪŋ/ noun [U] POLITICS things that politicians say and do to persuade people to vote for them in an election, often things that do not seem sincere or fair

elective /ɪˈlektɪv/ adj **1** an elective position is one that someone holds because people have voted for them **2** done because someone chooses it, not because they have to do it: *elective surgery*

electoral /ɪˈlekt(ə)rəl/ adj relating to elections: *a new electoral system* —**electorally** adv

electorate /ɪˈlekt(ə)rət/ noun [C] POLITICS all the people who are allowed to vote in an election

electric /ɪˈlektrɪk/ adj **1** using or relating to electricity: *an electric kettle* ◆ *an electric cable* ◆ *an electric current* **2** extremely exciting: *The atmosphere was electric.*

■ **Electric** describes things that use electricity to make them work: *an electric iron/shaver/guitar*

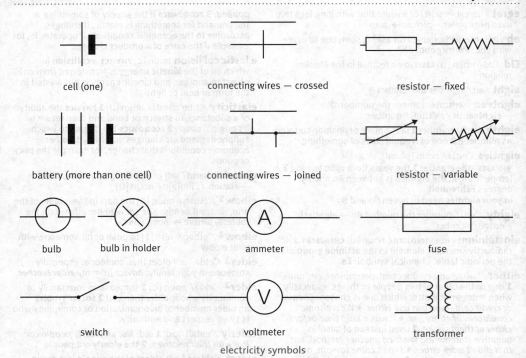

cell (one) connecting wires — crossed resistor — fixed

battery (more than one cell) connecting wires — joined resistor — variable

bulb bulb in holder ammeter fuse

switch voltmeter transformer

electricity symbols

- **Electrical** is used in more technical contexts, when you are talking about how electricity is made or used: *an electrical fault* ♦ *an electrical engineer*
- **Electronic** describes computers and other devices that use microchips: *an electronic calculator* ♦ *an electronic fuel injection system*

---

electrical /ɪˈlektrɪk(ə)l/ adj working by or relating to electricity: *electrical equipment* ♦ *an electrical fault* —**electrically** /ɪˈlektrɪkli/ adv

e,lectrical 'cell noun [C] PHYSICS a unit that produces electricity through the chemical action of electrodes

electric arc welding /ɪˌlektrɪk ˈɑːk ˌweldɪŋ/ noun [U] TECHNOLOGY the use of **arc welding** to join metals together

the e,lectric 'chair noun [singular] a chair used in parts of the US for legally killing someone as a punishment, using a strong electrical current

,electric 'current noun [C] PHYSICS a flow of electricity through a wire, **cable**, or other conductor

electrician /ɪˌlekˈtrɪʃ(ə)n/ noun [C] someone whose job is to repair or fit electrical equipment

electricity /ɪˌlekˈtrɪsəti/ noun [U] PHYSICS a form of energy that can produce light, heat, and power for computers, televisions etc. Electricity is created by the movement of **charged particles** (=particles that carry a positive or negative electric charge), especially electrons and ions: *The machines run on electricity.* ♦ *an electricity supply* —*picture* → DAM

e,lectric po'tential noun [U] PHYSICS the difference in electrical charge between two points in an electrical circuit. It is usually measured in volts.

electrics /ɪˈlektrɪks/ noun [plural] the electrical system in a building or machine

e,lectric 'shock noun [C] HEALTH a sudden strong pain that is caused by electricity passing through the body

e,lectric 'storm noun [C] a storm with thunder and lightning

electrify /ɪˈlektrɪfaɪ/ (**electrifies, electrifying, electrified**) verb [T] **1** to make someone feel extremely excited **2** PHYSICS to provide something with a supply of electricity —**electrification** /ɪˌlektrɪfɪˈkeɪʃ(ə)n/ noun [U]

electrochemical /ɪˌlektrəʊˈkemɪk(ə)l/ adj CHEMISTRY relating to electrochemistry

electrochemistry /ɪˌlektrəʊˈkemɪstri/ noun [U] CHEMISTRY the study of chemical behaviour relating to **electrolysis** and **electrical cells**

electrocute /ɪˈlektrəˌkjuːt/ verb [T] to kill or injure someone with electricity —**electrocution** /ɪˌlektrəˈkjuːʃ(ə)n/ noun [U]

electrode /ɪˈlektrəʊd/ noun [C] **1** CHEMISTRY, PHYSICS a small object inside an **electrical cell** or a battery that electricity flows through. It is made of metal or carbon. There are two electrodes, one **positive** and one **negative**. —*picture* → DRY CELL **2** TECHNOLOGY a rod or wire that carries the electric current in **arc welding**. It is made of the same metal as the pieces of metal that are to be welded.

electrodialysis /ɪˌlektrəʊdaɪˈæləsɪs/ noun [U] PHYSICS, ENVIRONMENT a method of removing unwanted substances from sea water. An electric current pulls substances through membranes and away from the water, so that it becomes clean.

electrolysis /ɪˌlekˈtrɒləsɪs/ noun [U] CHEMISTRY, PHYSICS the process of sending electricity through a solution or melted substance in order to cause chemical changes

electrolyte /ɪˈlektrəlaɪt/ noun [C] CHEMISTRY, PHYSICS a liquid containing ions that electricity can pass through —*picture* → DRY CELL

electrolytic cell /ɪˌlektrəʊlɪtɪk ˈsel/ noun [C] CHEMISTRY, PHYSICS a cell that produces electricity from the chemical reaction between two electrodes and an electrolyte held in a container

electromagnet /ɪˌlektrəʊˈmægnət/ noun [C] PHYSICS a powerful magnet that uses an electric current passed in a wire around it to produce its magnetic force. It stops being a magnet when the supply of electricity is stopped.

electromagnetic /ɪˌlektrəʊmægˈnetɪk/ adj PHYSICS relating to the use of an electric current to produce a magnetic field

e,lectromagnetic radi'ation noun [U] PHYSICS the complete range of **electromagnetic waves**, which includes light that we can see and light that we cannot see

e,lectromagnetic 'spectrum noun [singular] PHYSICS the complete range of electromagnetic waves from the shortest, which are gamma rays, to the longest, which are **radio waves**

e,lectromagnetic 'wave noun [C] PHYSICS a wave of energy within the electromagnetic spectrum

electromagnetism /ɪˌlektrəʊˈmægnəˌtɪz(ə)m/ noun [U] PHYSICS magnetism that is produced by means of an electrical current

electromechanical /ɪˌlektrəʊməˈkænɪk(ə)l/ adj PHYSICS relating to a piece of mechanical equipment that is powered or controlled by electricity

electromotive force /ɪˌlektrəʊməʊtɪv ˈfɔːs/ noun [singular] PHYSICS see **emf**

electron /ɪˈlektrɒn/ noun [C] CHEMISTRY, PHYSICS the part of an atom that has a negative electrical charge. Electrons orbit the nucleus of atoms. Electrons moving through a conductor form an electric current. → NEUTRON —*picture* → ATOM

electronegativity /ɪˌlektrəʊnegəˈtɪvɪti/ noun [C] CHEMISTRY a measure of the tendency of an atom to attract electrons in a chemical bond

electronic /ˌelekˈtrɒnɪk/ adj **1** PHYSICS, COMPUTING using electricity and extremely small electrical parts such as **microchips**: *an electronic calculator* ♦ *The information is held in electronic form* (=on computer disks). **2** COMPUTING involving the use of electronic equipment, especially computers: *an electronic voting system* —**electronically** /ˌelekˈtrɒnɪkli/ adv

electronic billing /ˌelekˌtrɒnɪk ˈbɪlɪŋ/ noun [U] BUSINESS a system for charging customers and paying bills online, by credit card or debit card

,electronic 'book noun [C] an **e-book**

,electronic 'publishing noun [U] the business of publishing books or documents in a form that you can read on a computer, for example on a CD-ROM

electronics /ˌelekˈtrɒnɪks/ noun [U] PHYSICS, COMPUTING the science and technology of electronic equipment

,electronic 'signature noun [C] BUSINESS, COMPUTING an **e-signature**

electron micrograph /ɪˌlektrɒn ˈmaɪkrəʊɡrɑːf, ɪˌlektrɒn ˈmaɪkrəʊɡræf/ noun [C] SCIENCE a photograph of an object such as a biological **specimen** taken by an electron microscope

e,lectron 'microscope noun [C] SCIENCE a very powerful microscope that uses electrons instead of light. It allows you to see things that are much too small to be seen with an ordinary microscope, because it can magnify as many as 500,000 times.

electroplate /ɪˈlektrəˌpleɪt/ verb [T] PHYSICS to cover a metal object with a thin layer of another metal, using

electricity —**electroplating** /ɪˈlektrəˌpleɪtɪŋ/ noun [U]

electrostatic /ɪˌlektrəʊˈstætɪk/ adj PHYSICS **1** produced by or relating to static electricity **2** relating to electrostatics

electrostatics /ɪˌlektrəʊˈstætɪks/ noun [U] PHYSICS the study of **static electricity**

elegant /ˈelɪɡənt/ adj **1** beautiful in a graceful simple way: *She always looks so elegant.* ♦ *an elegant room* **2** an elegant theory or solution is impressive because it is simple and effective —**elegance** noun [U], **elegantly** adv

elegiac /ˌelɪˈdʒaɪək/ adj *formal* expressing sadness, especially because someone has died or because something no longer exists

elegy /ˈelədʒi/ (plural **elegies**) noun [C] LITERATURE a poem or other piece of writing expressing sadness, usually about someone's death

element /ˈelɪmənt/ noun **1** [C] an important basic part of something, for example a system or plan: *Fieldwork is a key element of this course.* ♦ *Advertising is not the only element in the marketing process.* **2** [C] CHEMISTRY a substance that consists of only one type of atom: *hydrogen, oxygen, and other elements* → PERIMETER **3** [singular] a small but important amount of a quality or feeling: *There is an element of truth in what she said.* **4** [C] PHYSICS the part of a piece of electrical equipment that produces heat

PHRASE **be in your element** to feel very happy and comfortable in a situation

elemental /ˌelɪˈment(ə)l/ adj **1** powerful and basic **2** CHEMISTRY consisting of a single chemical element

elementary /ˌelɪˈment(ə)ri/ adj **1** relating to the most basic and important part of something= BASIC: *He made a few elementary errors.* **2** easy: *elementary tasks* **3** EDUCATION relating to the first years of school

,elementary 'particle noun [C] PHYSICS one of the extremely small pieces of matter that make up a **subatomic particle** such as a proton or neutron

ele'mentary ,school noun [C] EDUCATION in some countries, a school for children between the ages of five and about eleven

elephant /ˈelɪfənt/ noun [C] a very large wild mammal that lives in Africa and Asia. It has thick grey skin and a very long nose called a **trunk**. —*picture* → MAMMAL

elephantiasis /ˌelɪfənˈtaɪəsɪs/ noun [U] HEALTH a serious disease in which a leg or another part of the body becomes very swollen. It is caused by a parasite carried by a type of mosquito.

elevate /ˈeləveɪt/ verb [T] *formal* **1** to improve someone or something, or to make them more important: *We need to work together to elevate the position of women in society.* **2** to raise something to a higher physical position= RAISE —**elevated** /ˈeləˌveɪtɪd/ adj

elevation /ˌeləˈveɪʃ(ə)n/ noun **1** [C] GEOGRAPHY the height of an area of land, usually measured from sea level **2** [C/U] *formal* an increase in the level of something **3** [C] CONSTRUCTION a side of a building as it is shown in a drawing by an architect

elevator /ˈeləveɪtə/ noun [C] *American* a **lift** in a building

eleven /ɪˈlev(ə)n/ number the number 11

eleventh /ɪˈlev(ə)nθ/ number **1** in the place or position counted as number 11 **2** one of 11 equal parts of something

elf /elf/ (plural **elves** /elvz/) noun [C] a small imaginary person with magic powers

ELF /ˌiː el ˈef/ noun [U] English as a lingua franca: a form of English that is sometimes used as a way of communicating by people whose first languages are not English, and that has some features that are not usually considered to be correct in standard English

elicit /ɪˈlɪsɪt/ verb [T] *formal* to get something such as a reaction or information from someone: *The question elicited a positive response.*

elide /ɪˈlaɪd/ verb [T] **LANGUAGE** to leave out a sound when you say a word or group of words, for example when you say it quickly in ordinary conversation

eligible /ˈelɪdʒəb(ə)l/ adj **1** allowed by rules or laws to do something ≠ INELIGIBLE: *She will be eligible to compete in the next Olympic Games.* **2** considered to be a good marriage partner —**eligibility** /ˌelɪdʒəˈbɪləti/ noun [U]

eliminate /ɪˈlɪmɪneɪt/ verb [T] **1** to get rid of something that is not wanted or needed: *Many infectious diseases have been virtually eliminated.* ♦ *He had to **eliminate** dairy products **from** his diet.* **2** to decide that someone or something is not responsible for something: *We've eliminated the possibility that the fire was started deliberately.* **3** to remove someone from a competition: *Five candidates were eliminated after the first interview.*

elimination /ɪˌlɪmɪˈneɪʃ(ə)n/ noun **1** [U] the process of getting rid of something that is not wanted **2** [C] defeat in a competition

   PHRASE **a process of elimination** a way of solving a problem by getting rid of wrong solutions first

elision /ɪˈlɪʒ(ə)n/ noun [U] **LANGUAGE** the practice of leaving a sound out when you say a word or group of words, for example when you say it quickly in ordinary conversation

elite /ɪˈliːt/ noun [C] **1** a small group of people who have a lot of power or advantages: *the political elite* **2** the best or most skilful people in a group: *an elite group of athletes* ♦ *This book puts him **among the elite** of British novelists.*

elitism /ɪˈliːˌtɪz(ə)m/ noun [U] the belief that a small group of people should keep the most power and influence —**elitist** /ɪˈliːtɪst/ adj

ellipse /ɪˈlɪps/ noun [C] **MATHS** a shape similar to a circle that is longer than it is wide. It can be formed by crossing a **cone** with a plane. —*picture* → SHAPE

ellipsis /ɪˈlɪpsɪs/ (plural **ellipses** /ɪˈlɪpsiːz/) noun [U] **LANGUAGE** the practice of leaving a word or words out of a sentence when they are not necessary for understanding it

elliptical /ɪˈlɪptɪk(ə)l/ adj **MATHS** in the shape of a circle that is longer than it is wide

elm /elm/ noun [C] a large **deciduous** tree that grows mainly in the northern hemisphere

El Niño /el ˈniːnjəʊ/ **GEOGRAPHY, ENVIRONMENT** a change in the temperature and direction of currents of the Pacific Ocean near the South American coast. This can seriously affect the weather in different parts of the world, often causing major problems such as floods. → LA NIÑA

elongated /ˈiːlɒŋˌgeɪtɪd/ adj longer and narrower than is usual

eloquent /ˈeləkwənt/ adj expressing something clearly and effectively: *an eloquent speech* —**eloquence** noun [U], **eloquently** adv

else /els/ adv used after question words, or words such as 'anyone', 'something', 'everywhere', and 'no one', to mean 'in addition' or 'other': *No one else was willing to help.* ♦ *Would you like to go somewhere else?* ♦ *The*

police had already interviewed everyone else. ♦ *What else has gone wrong?*

   PHRASE **or else** used for saying that there will be a bad result if something does not happen: *We must leave now or else we'll miss our train.*

elsewhere /elsˈweə/ adv in or to another place or other places: *Prices in the UK are higher than elsewhere in Europe.* ♦ *Many people who come here to study are **from elsewhere**.*

ELT /ˌiː el ˈtiː/ noun [U] **EDUCATION** English Language Teaching: the teaching of English to students whose first language is not English

elude /ɪˈluːd/ verb [T] *formal* **1** if something eludes you, you cannot achieve it, understand it, or remember it: *Financial success eluded him.* **2** to manage to escape or hide from someone or something ≈ EVADE

elusive /ɪˈluːsɪv/ adj **1** difficult or impossible to find or catch **2** difficult or impossible to achieve or understand

'em /əm/ short form a way of writing 'them' that shows how it sounds in informal conversation

EM abbrev **PHYSICS 1** electron microscope **2** electromagnetic

emaciated /ɪˈmeɪsieɪtɪd/ adj someone who is emaciated is so thin that they look very ill

email /ˈiːmeɪl/ or **'e-ˌmail** noun **COMPUTING 1** [U] a system for sending messages from one computer to another: *We communicate **by email**.* ♦ *Do you know her **email address**?* **2** [C] a written message sent by email: *Send me an email with the details.* —**email** verb [T]

emanate /ˈeməneɪt/ verb [I] *formal* to come from a particular place

emancipation /ɪˌmænsɪˈpeɪʃ(ə)n/ noun [U] **SOCIAL STUDIES** the process of giving freedom and rights to someone who did not have them before —**emancipate** /ɪˈmænsɪˌpeɪt/ verb [T], **emancipated** /ɪˈmænsɪˌpeɪtɪd/ adj

embalm /ɪmˈbɑːm/ verb [T] to preserve a dead body using chemicals

embankment /ɪmˈbæŋkmənt/ noun [C] a sloping wall of earth or stone beside a road, railway, or river

embargo /ɪmˈbɑːɡəʊ/ (plural **embargoes**) noun [C] a government order preventing trade with another country: *a trade embargo*

embark /ɪmˈbɑːk/ verb [I] to get on a ship ≠ DISEMBARK —**embarkation** /ˌembɑːˈkeɪʃ(ə)n/ noun [C/U]

   PHRASAL VERB **emˈbark ˌon sth** or **emˈbark uˌpon sth** to start a new project or activity

embarrass /ɪmˈbærəs/ verb [T] to make someone feel nervous, ashamed, or stupid: *It embarrassed me to have to give my opinion in public.*

embarrassed /ɪmˈbærəst/ adj feeling slightly ashamed, and worried about what other people will think of you: *She looked embarrassed when we asked her about her boyfriend.* ♦ *I was too embarrassed to tell anyone about my illness.*

embarrassing /ɪmˈbærəsɪŋ/ adj making someone feel nervous, ashamed, or stupid: *an embarrassing situation* —**embarrassingly** /ɪmˈbærəsɪŋli/ adv

embarrassment /ɪmˈbærəsmənt/ noun **1** [U] a feeling of being embarrassed: *I felt my face burning with embarrassment.* **2** [C] a person or thing that makes someone feel embarrassed: *He is such **an embarrassment to** his family.*

embassy /ˈembəsi/ (plural **embassies**) noun [C] a group of officials who represent their government in a foreign country, or the building where they work: *the Canadian Embassy in Paris*

embattled /ɪmˈbæt(ə)ld/ adj experiencing a lot of problems and likely to be defeated or destroyed

embed /ɪmˈbed/ verb [T] **1** to fix something firmly in a surface or object **2** to make something a fixed and important part of something else **3** if a journalist, photographer etc is embedded with an army, they travel with it and report on what happens to it

embellish /ɪmˈbelɪʃ/ verb [I/T] to make a story more interesting by adding details, especially ones that are not completely true

embers /ˈembərz/ noun [plural] pieces of wood or coal that are still hot and red after a fire has stopped burning

embezzle /ɪmˈbez(ə)l/ verb [I/T] if someone embezzles money, they steal the money that they should look after as part of their job —**embezzlement** /ɪmˈbez(ə)lmənt/ noun [U]

embittered /ɪmˈbɪtəd/ adj angry and unhappy about things that have happened to you in the past

emblem /ˈembləm/ noun [C] a design or object that is a symbol of something such as a country, organization, or idea

emblematic /ˌembləˈmætɪk/ adj *formal* generally accepted as being a symbol of a quality, idea, or principle

embody /ɪmˈbɒdi/ (**embodies, embodying, embodied**) verb [T] **1** to be the best possible example of a particular idea, quality, or principle **2** *formal* to include something

embolism /ˈembəˌlɪz(ə)m/ noun [C] HEALTH something such as a blood clot that blocks a blood vessel in the body

embrace /ɪmˈbreɪs/ verb *formal* **1** [T] to accept something new with enthusiasm: *a former dictator who had embraced democracy* **2** [I/T] to put your arms around someone in order to show love or friendship —**embrace** noun [C]

embroider /ɪmˈbrɔɪdə/ verb [I/T] **1** to decorate cloth with a design of coloured stitches **2** to make a story more interesting by adding details that you have invented

embroidery /ɪmˈbrɔɪdəri/ (plural **embroideries**) noun [C/U] a design of coloured stitches on cloth, or the activity of decorating cloth in this way

embroiled /ɪmˈbrɔɪld/ adj involved in a difficult situation

embryo /ˈembriˌəʊ/ (plural **embryos**) noun [C] BIOLOGY **1** an animal in its earliest stages of development, especially in the uterus of a female mammal or in the egg of a bird, reptile etc **2** a plant in its earliest stages of development, especially contained within a seed

embryology /ˌembriˈɒlədʒi/ noun [U] BIOLOGY the scientific study of embryos

embryonic /ˌembriˈɒnɪk/ adj **1** just beginning to develop and grow: *an embryonic industry* **2** BIOLOGY relating to an embryo

emcee¹ /ˌemˈsiː/ noun [C] MUSIC someone who says the words in **rap** music

emcee² /ˌemˈsiː/ verb [I/T] MUSIC to say the words in **rap** music

emerald /ˈem(ə)rəld/ noun [C] a bright green stone used in expensive jewellery

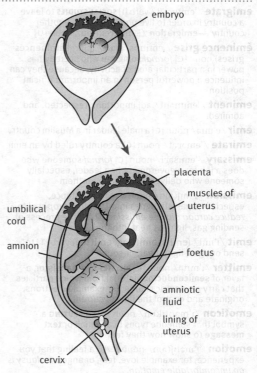

development of an embryo and foetus

(labels: embryo, placenta, muscles of uterus, umbilical cord, amnion, foetus, amniotic fluid, lining of uterus, cervix)

emerge /ɪˈmɜːdʒ/ verb [I] **1** to come out of something, or out from behind something: *After a few weeks, the caterpillar **emerges from** its cocoon.* **2** to stop being involved in a difficult situation or period of time: *The country is slowly **emerging from** a recession.* **3** to become known or recognized: *Singapore was **emerging as** an important financial centre.*

emergence /ɪˈmɜːdʒ(ə)ns/ noun [U] the process of appearing or becoming recognized: *the emergence of the modern French state*

emergency /ɪˈmɜːdʒ(ə)nsi/ (plural **emergencies**) noun [C] an unexpected situation in which immediate action is necessary, often because there is danger: *We always carry a medical kit **for emergencies**.* ♦ *In an **emergency**, call this number.* ♦ *emergency surgery*

e,mergency 'exit noun [C] a special way out of a building, used if there is a fire or other emergency

e'mergency ,room noun [C] HEALTH *American* the part of a hospital where treatment is given to people who need it immediately

e'mergency ,services noun [plural] the organizations that deal with fire, crime, accidents, and injuries

emergent /ɪˈmɜːdʒ(ə)nt/ adj starting to exist or develop: *emergent technologies*

emerging /ɪˈmɜːdʒɪŋ/ adj just beginning to exist or be noticed: *emerging markets*

emetic /ɪˈmetɪk/ noun [C] HEALTH a substance that makes you vomit —**emetic** adj

emf abbrev PHYSICS electromotive force: a force that causes the flow of electricity from one point to another = VOLTAGE

emigrant /ˈemɪgrənt/ noun [C] SOCIAL STUDIES someone who leaves their country in order to live permanently in another country

emigrate /'emɪɡreɪt/ verb [I] SOCIAL STUDIES to leave a country in order to live permanently in another country —**emigration** /ˌemɪ'ɡreɪʃ(ə)n/ noun [U]

éminence grise /ˌeminɒs 'ɡriːz/ (plural **éminences grises**) noun [C] *formal* someone who secretly has power in a particular area of activity, because they can influence a powerful person in an important official position

eminent /'emɪnənt/ adj important, respected, and admired

emir /e'mɪə/ noun [C] a male leader in a Muslim country

emirate /'emərət/ noun [C] a country ruled by an emir

emissary /'emɪsəri/ noun [C] *formal* someone who does a job for a government or a leader, especially someone who delivers a message for them

emission /ɪ'mɪʃ(ə)n/ noun **1** [C] a substance, especially a gas, that goes into the air: *a proposal to reduce carbon dioxide emissions* **2** [U] the process of sending gas, light, or heat into the air

emit /ɪ'mɪt/ (**emits**, **emitting**, **emitted**) verb [T] to send out gas, light, heat, or sound

emitter /ɪ'mɪtə/ noun [C] PHYSICS in a **transistor**, a layer of **semiconductor** material from which particles that carry an electric charge, for example electrons, originate and control the flow of current

emoticon /ɪ'məʊtɪkɒn/ noun [C] COMPUTING a symbol that someone types in an email or **text message** to show how they feel

emotion /ɪ'məʊʃ(ə)n/ noun [C/U] a feeling that you experience, for example love, fear, or anger: *Jealousy is an uncomfortable emotion.*

emotional /ɪ'məʊʃ(ə)nəl/ adj **1** relating to feelings and the way in which they affect your life: *He is in need of emotional support.* **2** affected by and expressing strong emotion: *It was an emotional reunion.* **3** causing strong emotions: *This is such an emotional issue.* —**emotionally** adv

e,motional in'telligence noun [U] the ability to understand your own personal feelings and those of other people, and to consider other people's feelings when making decisions

emotive /ɪ'məʊtɪv/ adj causing strong feelings

empathy /'empəθi/ noun [U] the ability to understand how someone else feels —**empathetic** /ˌempə'θetɪk/ adj, **empathic** /em'pæθɪk/ adj

emperor /'emp(ə)rə/ noun [C] a man who rules an **empire**

emphasis /'emfəsɪs/ (plural **emphases** /'emfəsiːz/) noun [C/U] **1** special importance or attention that is given to one thing in particular: *We place great emphasis on staff development.* **2** the extra loudness with which you say a particular phrase, word, or part of a word = STRESS: *The emphasis is on the first syllable.*

emphasize /'emfəsaɪz/ verb [T] **1** to give particular importance or attention to something: *The report emphasizes the need for better education.* ♦ *He emphasized that no one should be above the law.* **2** to say a phrase, word, or part of a word more loudly **3** to make something more noticeable: *The harsh lighting emphasized her age.*

emphatic /ɪm'fætɪk/ adj **1** said or shown in a very strong clear way: *an emphatic shake of the head* **2** with a very clear result: *an emphatic victory* —**emphatically** /ɪm'fætɪkli/ adv

emphysema /ˌemfɪ'siːmə/ noun [U] HEALTH a very serious illness that affects your lungs

empire /'empaɪə/ noun [C] **1** SOCIAL STUDIES a number of countries that are ruled by one person or government: *the Roman empire* **2** a large powerful group of companies that are controlled by one person or company: *an international media empire*

empirical /ɪm'pɪrɪk(ə)l/ adj based on scientific evidence rather than on theory —**empirically** /ɪm'pɪrɪkli/ adv

empiricism /ɪm'pɪrɪˌsɪz(ə)m/ noun [U] SCIENCE the view that ideas should be based on real experience or scientific experiments rather than on theories or beliefs

employ /ɪm'plɔɪ/ verb [T] **1** ECONOMICS, SOCIAL STUDIES to pay someone regularly to work for you: *a large car factory that employs over 800 people* ♦ *Jean was employed as a teaching assistant.* **2** *formal* to use something for a particular purpose: *They employed an imaginative marketing strategy.*

Word family: **employ**
Words in the same family as **employ**
- **employment** n   - **unemployment** n
- **employer** n   - **employee** n
- **unemployed** adj
- **employable** adj

employable /ɪm'plɔɪəb(ə)l/ adj someone who is employable has the relevant skills, qualifications, experience, or qualities to get a job —**employability** /ɪmˌplɔɪə'bɪləti/ noun [U]

employee /ɪm'plɔɪiː, ˌemplɔɪ'iː/ noun [C] ECONOMICS, SOCIAL STUDIES someone who is paid regularly to work for a person or organization: *part-time employees*

employer /ɪm'plɔɪə/ noun [C] ECONOMICS, SOCIAL STUDIES a person or organization that pays workers to work for them: *The factory is the largest single employer in the area.*

employment /ɪm'plɔɪmənt/ noun [U] **1** work that someone is paid to do: *Many qualified nurses are unable to find employment.* **2** ECONOMICS, SOCIAL STUDIES a situation in which people have regular paid work ≠ UNEMPLOYMENT: *Employment has risen among young people.*

empower /ɪm'paʊə/ verb [T] **1** to give someone more control over their life or more power to do something **2** *formal* to give a person or organization the legal authority to do something —**empowerment** noun [U]

empress /'emprəs/ noun [C] a woman who rules an **empire**, or one who is married to an **emperor**

empty¹ /'empti/ adj **1** containing no things or people ≠ FULL: *an empty jar* ♦ *The room was empty.* ♦ *empty streets* **2** lacking emotion, interest, or purpose: *Her life felt empty and meaningless.* **3** not true or serious: *an empty promise* —**emptiness** noun [U]

empty² /'empti/ (**empties**, **emptying**, **emptied**) verb **1** [T] to make something empty ≠ FILL **2** [I] if a place empties, all the people in it leave

PHRASAL VERB ,**empty sth 'out** *same as* **empty²** sense 1: *He was told to empty out his desk and leave.*

empty-handed /ˌempti 'hændɪd/ adj without getting anything for your effort: *The burglars had to leave the house empty-handed.* ♦ *They returned empty-handed from the peace negotiations.*

EMS /ˌiː em 'es/ noun [U] BUSINESS economics and management sciences: the study of economics and management

emu /'iːmjuː/ noun [C] a large Australian bird that has very long legs and cannot fly

emulate /ˈemjʊleɪt/ verb [T] *formal* to try to be like someone or something else

emulsifier /ɪˈmʌlsɪˌfaɪə/ noun [C] CHEMISTRY a substance that is added to a food or drink to stop liquid and solid parts from separating

emulsify /ɪˈmʌlsɪfaɪ/ (**emulsifies, emulsifying, emulsified**) verb [I/T] CHEMISTRY to form a liquid by mixing extremely small drops of one liquid with another liquid. By doing this, liquids that do not usually combine, such as oil and water, can be mixed together. —**emulsifiable** adj, **emulsification** /ɪˌmʌlsɪfɪˈkeɪʃ(ə)n/ noun [U]

enable /ɪnˈeɪb(ə)l/ (**enables, enabling, enabled**) verb [T] to give someone the ability or opportunity to do something: *This will enable you to work more efficiently.*

-enabled /ɪneɪb(ə)ld/ suffix COMPUTING used with some nouns to make adjectives meaning using a particular piece of software

enabling /ɪnˈeɪb(ə)lɪŋ/ adj 1 making something possible, especially by giving someone the skills to do it 2 LAW used about laws that allow a government to introduce other laws at a later date

enact /ɪnˈækt/ verb [T] to make a proposal into a law —**enactment** noun [C/U]

enamel /ɪˈnæm(ə)l/ noun [C/U] 1 ARTS a hard shiny substance that is used for protecting or decorating glass, metal, or clay 2 HEALTH the hard white outer layer of a tooth —*picture* → TOOTH

enamoured /ɪˈnæməd/ adj *formal* 1 impressed with or enthusiastic about something 2 in love with someone

enc. abbrev enclosed

encampment /ɪnˈkæmpmənt/ noun [C] a large group of tents or temporary shelters

encapsulate /ɪnˈkæpsjʊleɪt/ verb [T] to express something in a short clear form that gives the most important facts or ideas

encephalitis /enˌsefəˈlaɪtɪs, enˌkefəˈlaɪtɪs/ noun [U] HEALTH a very serious disease affecting the brain that is caused by an infection

enchanted /ɪnˈtʃɑːntɪd/ adj 1 very attracted by something, or getting great pleasure from it: *She was enchanted by the performance.* 2 affected by magic

enchanting /ɪnˈtʃɑːntɪŋ/ adj very attractive, or giving great pleasure

encircle /ɪnˈsɜːk(ə)l/ verb [T] to completely surround something

enclave /ˈenkleɪv/ noun [C] SOCIAL STUDIES an area of a country or city where a particular group of people lives

enclose /ɪnˈkləʊz/ verb [T] 1 to surround someone or something: *The swimming pool was enclosed by a high fence.* 2 to send something such as a document with a letter: *Please enclose a copy of your birth certificate with your application.* —**enclosed** /ɪnˈkləʊzd/ adj

enclosure /ɪnˈkləʊʒə/ noun [C] an area that is surrounded by a fence or wall

encode /ɪnˈkəʊd/ verb 1 [T] to put secret information into code 2 [T] COMPUTING to change a computer program into a set of instructions that a computer can use 3 [I/T] LANGUAGE to express what you want to say in a language

encomium /ɪnˈkəʊmiəm/ noun [C] *formal* a speech or piece of writing in which you express strong approval or admiration for someone or something

encompass /ɪnˈkʌmpəs/ verb [T] *formal* to include a lot of people or things: *The term 'world music' encompasses a wide range of musical styles.*

encore /ˈɒŋkɔː/ noun [C] a short performance given after the main performance, because the audience asks for more

encounter¹ /ɪnˈkaʊntə/ noun [C] 1 a meeting, especially one that was not planned 2 an experience or **discovery** of a particular kind: *my earliest encounter with the theatre*

encounter² /ɪnˈkaʊntə/ verb [T] 1 to experience or deal with something, especially a problem: *We encountered one small problem during the first test.* 2 *formal* to meet someone or see something for the first time

encourage /ɪnˈkʌrɪdʒ/ verb [T] 1 to try to persuade someone to do something that you believe would be good ≠ DISCOURAGE: *We encourage student participation in our classes.* 2 to provide conditions that make it easier for something to happen ≠ DISCOURAGE: *Bad hygiene encourages the spread of disease.* 3 to give someone confidence or hope ≠ DISCOURAGE: *His optimism encouraged me.* —**encouragement** noun [C/U]

encouraging /ɪnˈkʌrɪdʒɪŋ/ adj giving you confidence or hope ≠ DISCOURAGING: *They are testing a new malaria drug, and the first results are encouraging.* —**encouragingly** adv

encroach /ɪnˈkrəʊtʃ/ PHRASAL VERB **en'croach on sth** or **en'croach u,pon sth** 1 to gradually reduce the amount of time that someone has available to do what they want to do 2 to gradually take something such as power or authority from someone else: *The federal government is encroaching on states' rights.* 3 to gradually cover more land

encrusted /ɪnˈkrʌstɪd/ adj covered with a hard layer of something

encrypt /ɪnˈkrɪpt/ verb [T] COMPUTING to put data into a form that only someone with permission can read and understand —**encryption** noun [C/U]

encyclopedia or **encyclopaedia** /ɪnˌsaɪkləˈpiːdiə/ noun [C] a book or set of books that gives information about a lot of different subjects or about one particular subject —**encyclopedic** adj, **encyclopaedic** adj

end¹ /end/ noun [C] 1 the final part of a period of time: *We're going away at the end of this month.* ♦ *They'll make their decision at the very end of the week.* ♦ *The work should be completed by the end of the year.* 2 the time when a situation or an event stops: *Are you going to stay till the end of the game?* ♦ *After the end of the war many promises were made.* ♦ *We both knew that the partnership had come to an end.* ♦ *We want to put an end to* (=stop) *discrimination.* ♦ *the final battle that brought the war to an end* (=made it end) 3 the part of something that is furthest away from the centre: *Hold both ends of the rope.* ♦ *The only door was at the far end of the corridor.* 4 *formal* something that you want to achieve: *Governments make policies that suit their own political ends.* ♦ *She used people for her own ends.*

PHRASES **hours/days/weeks etc on end** used for emphasizing how long something continues: *He talks for hours on end about absolutely nothing.*

in the end *spoken* finally: *In the end, I decided not to buy the shoes.*

make ends meet if someone can make ends meet, they have just enough money to buy the things that they need

→ DEEP¹, ENDING, HAIR, MEANS

end² /end/ verb **1** [T] to be in a particular place or state at the end of a period: *We ended the day in a more hopeful mood.* ♦ *The team looks likely to end the season as champions.* **2** [I/T] to stop existing, or to make something stop existing: *The marriage ended after only 11 months.* ♦ *The injury ended his career.* **3** [I/T] if you end by doing or saying something, it is the last thing that you do or say: *I'd like to end by thanking everyone for their help.* ♦ *He ended his speech with a quotation from Nelson Mandela.*

PHRASAL VERBS **'end in sth** to have something as a final result: *All of our attempts ended in failure.*

,end 'up *spoken* to be in a place or state after doing something, or because of doing something: *Somehow they all ended up at my house.* ♦ *I ended up spending the night in the airport.*

endanger /ɪnˈdeɪndʒə/ verb [T] to put someone or something into a situation where they might be harmed

endangered species /ɪnˌdeɪndʒəd ˈspiːiːz/ noun [C] ENVIRONMENT, BIOLOGY a type of animal or plant that may soon become extinct, perhaps because its habitat is being destroyed or because it has been hunted or gathered too much in the past

endearing /ɪnˈdɪərɪŋ/ adj making people like you

endeavour /ɪnˈdevə/ verb [T] *formal* to try very hard to do something

'end ele,vation noun [C/U] MATHS, PHYSICS an end view

endemic /enˈdemɪk/ adj very common in a place or situation

ending /ˈendɪŋ/ noun **1** [C] the way in which a story, film, or play ends: *Children usually prefer books with a happy ending.* **2** [singular] a time when something stops permanently: *Officials have announced the ending of price controls.* **3** [C] LANGUAGE the last group of letters in a word, that can change according to the tense of a verb, the subject of a sentence, whether a word is singular or plural etc: *a plural ending* ♦ *The usual ending for verbs in the simple past tense is '-ed'.*

endless /ˈendləs/ adj lasting or continuing for a very long time: *endless questions* ♦ *There seemed to be an endless supply of food at the meeting.* —**endlessly** adv

endocarp /ˈendəʊkɑːp/ noun [C] BIOLOGY the inner layer of the **pericarp** (=skin and flesh) of a fruit

endocrine gland /ˈendəʊkraɪn ˌglænd/ noun [C] ANATOMY a gland in the body that produces hormones that go directly into the blood or into the **lymph vessels**

endoparasite /ˌendəʊˈpærəsaɪt/ noun [C] BIOLOGY a parasite that lives inside its **host**, for example a **tapeworm**

endoplasmic reticulum /ˌendəʊplæzmɪk rɪˈtɪkjʊləm/ noun [C/U] BIOLOGY a system of tube-shaped membranes in the **cytoplasm** of a cell

endorphin /enˈdɔːfɪn/ noun [C] BIOLOGY a type of hormone produced in the brain that reduces pain, especially when someone is injured or physically tired

endorse /ɪnˈdɔːs/ verb [T] if someone endorses a person or a thing, they say publicly that they support that person or thing —**endorsement** noun [C/U]

endoscopy /enˈdɒskəpi/ noun [C/U] HEALTH a medical operation in which an **endoscope** (=a very small camera on a long thin tube) is put into someone's body to examine inside it

endoskeleton /ˈendəʊˌskelɪt(ə)n/ noun [C] BIOLOGY the hard structure, usually made of bone, inside the body of a vertebrate → EXOSKELETON

endosperm /ˈendəʊspɜːm/ noun [U] BIOLOGY the substance that surrounds the embryo inside a seed and provides food for it

endospore /ˈendəʊˌspɔː/ noun [C] BIOLOGY **1** an **asexual** spore that is formed inside the cells of some bacteria and algae. It is surrounded by a thick wall and can survive difficult conditions. **2** the inner layer of the wall of a spore

endothelium /ˌendəʊˈθiːliəm/ noun [C/U] BIOLOGY the tissue that forms the inner layer of the blood vessels. It is only one cell thick. —*picture* → BLOOD VESSEL

endotherm /ˈendəʊθɜːm/ noun [C] BIOLOGY an animal that is able to keep its body temperature the same, even though the temperature of its environment changes

endothermic /ˌendəʊˈθɜːmɪk/ adj CHEMISTRY, PHYSICS an endothermic reaction is a chemical reaction in which heat is absorbed, not produced → EXOTHERMIC

endow /ɪnˈdaʊ/ verb [T] to give money to a school, hospital, or other institution

PHRASE **be endowed with sth** to have a good ability or quality

endpoint /ˈendpɔɪnt/ noun [C] MATHS the point at either end of a line

,end 'product noun [C] the thing that is produced at the end of a process

,end re'sult noun [C] the result of an activity or process

'end ,system noun [C] COMPUTING a computer that controls or performs a particular job for all the computers connected to a **network**

endurance /ɪnˈdjʊərəns/ noun [U] the ability to continue doing something that is difficult or tiring

endure /ɪnˈdjʊə/ verb **1** [T] to suffer something unpleasant without becoming upset **2** [I] to last for a long time

enduring /ɪnˈdjʊərɪŋ/ adj lasting for a long time

,end 'user noun [C] BUSINESS someone who buys a product for their own use, especially a computer or a piece of software

'end ,view noun [C/U] MATHS, PHYSICS a view of a three-dimensional object in **orthographic projection** that shows it at right angles from the side

enema /ˈenəmə/ noun [C] HEALTH a medical treatment in which liquid is forced into a person's intestines to make them go to the toilet to empty their bowels

enemy /ˈenəmi/ (plural **enemies**) noun [C] **1** someone who is opposed to someone else and tries to harm them ≠ FRIEND: *They searched for information on political enemies.* ♦ *Terrorists are described as enemies of the state.* ♦ *It's easy to make enemies in a job like this.* **2** a country that is fighting another country in a war ≠ ALLY: *They had to prevent the enemy from attacking.* ♦ *an enemy soldier*

> **Enemy** can be used with a singular or plural verb. You can say *The enemy was advancing.* OR *The enemy were advancing.*

energetic /ˌenəˈdʒetɪk/ adj an energetic person has a lot of energy and is very active —**energetically** /ˌenəˈdʒetɪkli/ adv

energy /ˈenədʒi/ noun [U] **1** the power that the body needs in order to do physical things: *She didn't even have the energy to get out of bed.* **2** a supply or source of electrical, mechanical, or other form of power:

*Switching off lights is a good way to **save energy**.* ♦ *energy supplies* **3** **PHYSICS** the ability to do work. Electricity, heat, and light are all forms of energy. Energy can change from one form to another, for example light can turn into heat.

'energy conser,vation noun [U] **ENVIRONMENT** the careful use of **resources** such as electricity, so that the fuels that produce it are not wasted

'energy ,drink noun [C] **SPORTS** a drink that contains a lot of carbohydrate, suitable for someone who is exercising very hard for a long time

,energy-ef'ficient adj **SCIENCE** using less energy to achieve the same result

'energy ,level noun [C] **PHYSICS** a possible level of energy that an electron can have in an atom

'energy-,saving adj **SCIENCE** designed to use as little energy as possible

enforce /ɪnˈfɔːs/ verb [T] to make people obey a law, rule etc: *Troops were sent in to enforce the treaty.* —**enforcement** noun [U]

Eng. abbrev England or English

engage /ɪnˈɡeɪdʒ/ verb **1** [I/T] if a part of a machine engages, or if someone engages it, it fits into another part and they start to move together **2** [T] *formal* to attract and keep someone's interest or attention **3** [T] *formal* to employ someone

 PHRASAL VERB **en'gage in sth** *formal* to take part in something

engaged /ɪnˈɡeɪdʒd/ adj **1** if two people are engaged, they have formally agreed to get married: *She's engaged to someone she met at work.* ♦ *We got engaged about this time last year.* **2** if something is engaged, you cannot use it now because someone else is using it

 PHRASE **be otherwise engaged** to be unable to do something because you have already arranged to do something else

engagement /ɪnˈɡeɪdʒmənt/ noun **1** [C] a formal agreement to get married **2** [C] an arrangement to meet someone or do something **3** [C/U] *formal* a battle between armies

engaging /ɪnˈɡeɪdʒɪŋ/ adj attractive and pleasant

engender /ɪnˈdʒendə/ verb [T] *formal* to cause a feeling or attitude to exist

engine /ˈendʒɪn/ noun [C] **1** **PHYSICS** the part of a vehicle that makes it move: *the ship's engine* ♦ *a jet engine* **2** a vehicle that pulls a train= LOCOMOTIVE

engineer /,endʒɪˈnɪə/ noun [C] **1** someone who designs things such as roads, railways, or machines **2** someone who repairs machines or electrical equipment

engineering /,endʒɪˈnɪərɪŋ/ noun [U] the activity of designing things such as roads, railways, or machines

English bond /ˈɪŋɡlɪʃ ,bɒnd/ noun [C] **CONSTRUCTION** a pattern of bricks consisting of a layer with the small side facing out, then a layer with the long side facing out

English breakfast /,ɪŋɡlɪʃ ˈbrekfəst/ noun [C] **TOURISM** in the UK, a breakfast that includes eggs and **bacon**

engrave /ɪnˈɡreɪv/ verb [T] **ARTS** to cut words or pictures into a hard surface such as stone, metal, or glass —**engraver** noun [C]

engraving /ɪnˈɡreɪvɪŋ/ noun [C] **ARTS** a picture that is printed using a piece of metal that has the picture cut into its surface

engrossed /ɪnˈɡrəʊst/ adj so interested or involved in something that you do not think about anything else

engulf /ɪnˈɡʌlf/ verb [T] **1** to cover something in a way that destroys it: *Within minutes, the car was **engulfed** in flames.* **2** to have a very strong effect on someone or something: *Feelings of panic engulfed them.*

enhance /ɪnˈhɑːns/ verb [T] to improve something, or to make something more attractive: *We've enhanced the quality of the picture.* —**enhancement** noun [U]

enigma /ɪˈnɪɡmə/ noun [C] someone or something that is mysterious and difficult to understand

enjoin /ɪnˈdʒɔɪn/ verb [T] **enjoin sb from sth** **LAW** to legally order someone not to do something

enjoy /ɪnˈdʒɔɪ/ verb [T] **1** to get pleasure from something: *Did you enjoy your meal?* ♦ *I don't enjoy going on holiday as much as I used to.* **2** *formal* to have a particular good feature: *The hotel enjoys a magnificent view of the harbour.*

 PHRASE **enjoy yourself** to get pleasure from something that you do: *I haven't enjoyed myself so much for a long time.*

enjoyable /ɪnˈdʒɔɪəb(ə)l/ adj something that is enjoyable gives you pleasure: *an enjoyable evening* ♦ *Most students find the course very enjoyable.*

enjoyment /ɪnˈdʒɔɪmənt/ noun [U] **1** pleasure that you get from an activity or experience: *their enjoyment of life* **2** **LAW** the right to own or use something

enlarge /ɪnˈlɑːdʒ/ verb [T] to make something bigger: *I sent the photos back to be enlarged.*

enlargement /ɪnˈlɑːdʒmənt/ noun **1** [C] the process of making something bigger **2** [C/U] **MATHS** a **transformation** in which a geometric shape or object is made larger without changing its shape

enlighten /ɪnˈlaɪt(ə)n/ verb [T] to give someone information about something so that they understand more about it —**enlightening** adj

enlightened /ɪnˈlaɪt(ə)nd/ adj with sensible modern attitudes: *Their parents took an enlightened approach to child-rearing.*

enlightenment /ɪnˈlaɪt(ə)nmənt/ noun [U] **1** the process of understanding something clearly **2** **RELIGION** in the Buddhist religion, the highest spiritual state that someone can achieve

enlist /ɪnˈlɪst/ verb **1** [I] to join the armed forces **2** [T] if you enlist someone or enlist their help, you ask them to help or support you

en masse /ɒn ˈmæs/ adv all together as a group

enmeshed /ɪnˈmeʃt/ adj *formal* involved in a complicated or unpleasant situation that it is difficult to escape from

enmity /ˈenməti/ noun [U] *formal* a feeling of hate

enormity /ɪˈnɔːməti/ noun [U] the fact that something is very big, important, or wrong: *the enormity of the problem*

enormous /ɪˈnɔːməs/ adj very large in size or quantity: *an enormous birthday cake* ♦ *The stress they're under is enormous.* ♦ *an enormous amount of money*

enormously /ɪˈnɔːməsli/ adv extremely, or very much: *an enormously valuable experience*

Enos salts /ˈiːnɒs ,sɔːlts/ noun [plural] **HEALTH** a medicine that reduces the amount of acid in the stomach

enough /ɪˈnʌf/ adv, determiner, pronoun **1** as much or as many as you need: *'Would you like something more to eat?' 'No thanks, I've had enough.'* ♦ *There aren't enough of us to make up a team.* ♦ *You've had more*

than enough time to finish the job. ♦ She doesn't earn **enough to** live on. ♦ Do we have **enough** books for everyone? **2** with as much of a particular quality as is necessary: You're not old **enough to** vote. ♦ They're not working hard enough. **3** used after an adjective or adverb for emphasis: It's natural **enough to** be upset, after what happened.

enquire /ɪnˈkwaɪə/ another spelling of **inquire**

enquiry /ɪnˈkwaɪri/ another spelling of **inquiry**

enrich /ɪnˈrɪtʃ/ verb [T] to make something better or more enjoyable: Doing volunteer work has enriched my life. —**enrichment** noun [U]

enrol /ɪnˈrəʊl/ (**enrols, enrolling, enrolled**) verb [I/T] EDUCATION to officially become a member of a school, course, or group, or to make someone else a member —**enrolment** noun [C/U]

en route /ɒn ˈruːt/ adv on the way: We went through London en route to Germany.

ensemble /ɒnˈsɒmb(ə)l/ noun [C] **1** ARTS, MUSIC a group of musicians, dancers, or actors who perform together **2** a group of things that look good together

enshrine /ɪnˈʃraɪn/ verb formal to officially record something such as an idea or principle in a document, so that it cannot be ignored

enslave /ɪnˈsleɪv/ verb [T] SOCIAL STUDIES to make someone a **slave**

ensue /ɪnˈsjuː/ verb [I] to happen after something else, often as a result of it —**ensuing** adj

ensure /ɪnˈʃɔː/ verb [T] to make certain that something happens or is done: Our new system ensures that everyone gets paid on time.

ENT /ˌiː en ˈtiː/ abbrev HEALTH ear, nose, and throat

entail /ɪnˈteɪl/ verb [T] formal **1** to involve something, or to make something necessary: These cuts will entail some job losses. **2** LAW an old word meaning to arrange for property to be given to someone when you die

entangled /ɪnˈtæŋɡ(ə)ld/ adj **1** so involved in a complicated situation that it is difficult to get out **2** stuck in something such as ropes or wires —**entanglement** noun [U]

enter /ˈentə/ verb

1 go or come in	**4** take part in sth
2 start to do sth	**5** start time period
3 write sth	

1 [I/T] to go into or come into a place: The man had entered through the back door. ♦ They were imprisoned for illegally entering the country.
2 [T] to start to do something: There are dozens of new companies entering the market. ♦ She had hoped to enter the legal profession.
3 [T] to write something somewhere, for example in a book, on a form, or on a computer: Enter your user name and password.
4 [I/T] to arrange to be in a race or competition, or to arrange for someone else to do this: The competition is free, and anyone over the age of 18 can enter.
5 [T] to start or reach a period of time: The war had already entered its third week.

enteritis /ˌentəˈraɪtɪs/ noun [U] HEALTH a painful medical condition that affects the intestines and causes diarrhoea

'enter ˌkey noun [C] COMPUTING a key on a computer keyboard that makes the computer perform an action or start a new line of writing

enterprise /ˈentəˌpraɪz/ noun **1** [C] a large or important project, especially a new one: an exciting scientific enterprise **2** [C] a business: Euro Disney is a much smaller enterprise than the American Disney parks. **3** [U] the ability to create new businesses or projects: The success of the band is mainly due to Jim's initiative and enterprise.

enterprising /ˈentəˌpraɪzɪŋ/ adj willing to try or think of new ideas or methods

entertain /ˌentəˈteɪn/ verb **1** [T] to give a performance that people enjoy: The children sang and danced to entertain the crowd. **2** [I/T] to receive someone as a guest and give them food and drink: I enjoy entertaining visitors. **3** [T] formal to consider an idea or feeling and allow it to develop in your mind: Jackson entertained hopes of winning the championship.

entertainer /ˌentəˈteɪnə/ noun [C] someone whose job is to entertain people

entertaining /ˌentəˈteɪnɪŋ/ adj enjoyable or interesting: an entertaining evening

entertainment /ˌentəˈteɪnmənt/ noun [C/U] performances that people enjoy: A jazz band provided entertainment for the evening. ♦ He is organizing entertainments for the children.

enthusiasm /ɪnˈθjuːziˌæzəm/ noun [U] the feeling of being very interested in something or excited by it: His enthusiasm for music has stayed strong.

enthusiast /ɪnˈθjuːziæst/ noun [C] someone who is very interested in something and spends time doing it or learning about it

enthusiastic /ɪnˌθjuːziˈæstɪk/ adj very interested in something, or excited by it: Business leaders gave an enthusiastic welcome to the proposal. ♦ For a while, we were enthusiastic about the idea. —**enthusiastically** /ɪnˌθjuːziˈæstɪkli/ adv

entice /ɪnˈtaɪs/ verb [T] to persuade someone to do something by offering them an advantage or reward —**enticing** adj: an enticing offer

entire /ɪnˈtaɪə/ adj whole or complete: She has spent her entire life in Hong Kong.

entirely /ɪnˈtaɪəli/ adv completely, or in every way: We have entirely different tastes in music. ♦ I'm not entirely sure I believe him.

entirety /ɪnˈtaɪərəti/ noun the whole of something

entitle /ɪnˈtaɪt(ə)l/ verb [T] **1** to give someone the right to do something: Membership entitles you to cheaper tickets. ♦ Some children are entitled to claim free school meals. **2** to give a title to a book, poem, or piece of music: Her first novel was entitled More Innocent Times.

entitlement /ɪnˈtaɪt(ə)lmənt/ noun [C/U] the right to receive something or to do something

entity /ˈentəti/ (plural **entities**) noun [C] formal something that exists separately from other things and has its own character

entomology /ˌentəˈmɒlədʒi/ noun [U] BIOLOGY the scientific study of insects —**entomological** /ˌentəməˈlɒdʒɪk(ə)l/ adj, **entomologist** noun [C]

entrance /ˈentrəns/ noun **1** [C] the place where you can enter a room, building, or area ≠ EXIT: I'll meet you at **the main entrance** at six o'clock. ♦ The statue stands at **the entrance to** the harbour. **2** [U] the right or ability to enter a place, or to join an organization: **Entrance to** the museum is free. ♦ There is a £5 **entrance fee**. **3** [C] the act of going into a place: Crowds cheered as she **made her entrance**.

entranced /ɪnˈtrɑːnst/ adj so impressed by someone or something that you cannot look at or think about anything else

entrant /ˈentrənt/ noun [C] someone who enters a competition or examination

entreat /ɪnˈtriːt/ verb [T] formal to keep asking someone to do something in a worried and serious way

entreaty /ɪnˈtriːti/ noun [C/U] formal a strong serious request that someone makes to another person about something that is worrying them

entrenched /ɪnˈtrentʃt/ adj entrenched attitudes or feelings have existed for a long time and are difficult to change

entrepreneur /ˌɒntrəprəˈnɜː/ noun [C] BUSINESS someone who uses money to start businesses and make business deals —**entrepreneurial** /ˌɒntrəprəˈnɜːriəl/ adj, **entrepreneurship** noun [U]

entropy /ˈentrəpi/ noun [U] SCIENCE a measurement of the amount of **disorder** within a substance that increases when the temperature goes up. For example, when water is heated and turns to vapour, entropy increases as the activity of the molecules increases.

entrust /ɪnˈtrʌst/ verb [T] to give someone responsibility for an important job or activity

entry /ˈentri/ (plural **entries**) noun

1 into a place	**4** entrance
2 information	**5** right to join
3 for a competition	

1 [U] the right or ability to go into a place: *Entry to the exhibition costs £5.50.* ♦ *They were charged with illegal entry into the US.* ♦ *We had to remove the lock on the door to gain entry* (=get in).
2 [C] a piece of information that is written in a book, on a list, or on a computer: *the dictionary entry for the word 'play'*
3 [C] a piece of work that someone does to try to win a competition: *The contest attracted entries from all over the country.*
4 [C] an entrance to a building
5 [U] the right to become a member of an organization, profession, or other group: *Older students are being denied entry into full-time education.*

'entry-,level adj **1** entry-level equipment is the most basic or simple type intended for people who are beginning an activity **2** an entry-level job is at the lowest level in a company or organization

enunciate /ɪˈnʌnsieɪt/ verb [I/T] formal to pronounce words clearly so that they can be easily understood = ARTICULATE —**enunciation** /ɪˌnʌnsiˈeɪʃ(ə)n/ noun [C/U]

envelop /ɪnˈveləp/ verb [T] to surround someone or something completely

envelope /ˈenvələʊp/ noun [C] a flat paper case that you put a letter in before you send it

enviable /ˈenviəb(ə)l/ adj an enviable quality or situation is one that someone has and that other people would like to have

envious /ˈenviəs/ adj unhappy because you want something that someone else has → JEALOUS

environment /ɪnˈvaɪrənmənt/ noun **1 the environment** [singular] ENVIRONMENT the natural world, including land, water, air, plants, and animals: *Industrial development is causing widespread damage to the environment.* ♦ *What's the impact of chemical fertilizers on the environment?* **2** [C] the place in which people live and work, including all the physical conditions that affect them: *Parents are responsible*

for providing the right environment for their children to learn in. ♦ *He grew up in a harsh urban environment.*

environmental /ɪnˌvaɪrənˈment(ə)l/ adj ENVIRONMENT **1** relating to the natural world and the effect that human activity has on it: *The Minister discussed environmental issues.* **2** intended to help or protect the environment: *Some environmental groups are opposed to tourism on the island.* —**environmentally** adv

environmentalist /ɪnˌvaɪrənˈment(ə)lɪst/ noun [C] ENVIRONMENT someone who wants to protect the environment

en,vironmental 'justice noun [U] SOCIAL STUDIES the idea that all people in all parts of the world have the right to a healthy environment

en,vironmentally 'friendly adj ENVIRONMENT not harming the natural environment

environs /ɪnˈvaɪrənz/ noun [plural] formal the area that surrounds a place

envisage /ɪnˈvɪzɪdʒ/ verb [T] to imagine that something will happen in the future

envoy /ˈenvɔɪ/ noun [C] an official who represents their government in another country

envy[1] /ˈenvi/ noun [U] the unhappy feeling that you have when you want something that someone else has
PHRASE **be the envy of** to have good qualities that people admire and would like to have themselves

envy[2] /ˈenvi/ (**envies, envying, envied**) verb [T] to have the unhappy feeling of wanting what someone else has

enzyme /ˈenzaɪm/ noun [C] BIOLOGY a protein produced by all organisms that behaves as a **catalyst** (=a substance that speeds up chemical reactions but does not itself change)

the Eocene /ˈiːəʊsiːn/ noun [singular] GEOLOGY the period of geological time, 55 million to 34 million years ago, during which mammals first appeared

EOF abbrev COMPUTING end of file

eosinophil /ˌiːəʊˈsɪnəfɪl/ noun [C] BIOLOGY a white blood cell with **granules** that are easily coloured with the acid dye **eosin**

épée /ˈepeɪ/ noun [C] SPORTS a light thin sword that bends easily, used in the sport of **fencing**

epeirogenic movement /eˌpaɪrəʊdʒenɪk ˈmuːvmənt/ noun [C/U] GEOLOGY movement of **tectonic plates** that raises or lowers the Earth's surface and causes continents to form

ephedrine /ˈefɪdriːn/ noun [U] BIOLOGY, SPORTS a drug that is used by athletes to make the heart and the **respiratory** system work better

ephemeral /ɪˈfemərəl/ adj **1** lasting for only a short time **2** BIOLOGY an ephemeral plant has only a short life

epic /ˈepɪk/ adj very long and exciting: *an epic journey*

epicarp /ˈepɪkɑːp/ noun [C] BIOLOGY the outer layer of the **pericarp** (=skin and flesh) of a fruit

epicentre /ˈepɪˌsentə/ noun [C] GEOLOGY the area of land directly over the centre of an earthquake —*picture* → EARTHQUAKE

epicyclic gear train /ˌepɪsaɪklɪk ˈgɪə ˌtreɪn/ noun [C] ENGINEERING a system of gears in which one or more wheel **axes** turn around a fixed axis

epicycloid /ˌepɪˈsaɪklɔɪd/ noun [C] MATHS a curve produced by a point on the circumference of a circle that is being rolled along the outside of another circle → HYPOCYCLOID

epidemic /ˌepɪˈdemɪk/ noun [C] **1** HEALTH a situation in which a disease spreads very quickly and infects a lot of people **2** a sudden increase in something bad or unpleasant that affects many people

epidermis /ˌepɪˈdɜːmɪs/ noun [singular] ANATOMY the outer layer of skin on top of the **dermis**. Hair and feathers grow from the epidermis. —*picture* → SKIN —**epidermal** /ˌepɪˈdɜːməl/ adj

epididymis /ˌepɪˈdɪdɪmɪs/ noun [C] ANATOMY a coiled tube above a man's **testes** that leads to the **vas deferens** (=tube that carries sperm to the urethra). Sperm made in the testes are stored in the epididymis.

epidural /ˌepɪˈdjʊərəl/ noun [C] HEALTH a medical treatment in which an anaesthetic is put into the lower back, especially of a woman who is having a baby

epigeal /eˈpɪdʒiəl/ adj BIOLOGY **1** relating to a plant part growing on, or close to, the surface of the ground → HYPOGEAL **2** relating to seed **germination** in which the embryo grows longer, so that the **cotyledons** are carried above the soil to start photosynthesis → HYPOGEAL

epiglottis /ˌepɪˈɡlɒtɪs/ noun [C] ANATOMY the small piece of flesh at the back of the tongue that closes the **windpipe** when food is swallowed

epilepsy /ˈepɪˌlepsi/ noun [U] HEALTH a brain disease that makes someone suddenly shake in an uncontrolled way or become unconscious

epileptic /ˌepɪˈleptɪk/ noun [C] someone who has epilepsy —**epileptic** adj

epilogue /ˈepɪlɒɡ/ noun [C] LITERATURE an extra comment or piece of information at the end of a book or play

EpiPen /ˈepiˌpen/ TRADEMARK HEALTH a needle fitted into a tube that looks like a pen, used for putting a drug into someone who is having a severe **allergic** reaction to something

epiphyte /ˈepɪfaɪt/ noun [C] BIOLOGY a plant that grows on top of or is supported by another plant but does not depend on it for its food. Some **mosses** and **orchids** are types of epiphyte.

episcopal /ɪˈpɪskəp(ə)l/ adj RELIGION relating to bishops

the Episcopal Church /ɪˌpɪskəp(ə)l ˈtʃɜːtʃ/ noun RELIGION a Protestant Christian church that developed from the Anglican Church

episiotomy /ɪˌpɪziˈɒtəmi/ (plural **episiotomies**) noun [C/U] HEALTH a cut made in a woman's vagina during **labour** to make it larger, so that she can give birth more easily

episode /ˈepɪsəʊd/ noun [C] **1** one part of a series in a television or radio story **2** an important event in a story, in someone's life, or during a particular period of time **3** HEALTH a time when someone is affected by an illness or a medical condition

epistasis /ɪˈpɪstəsɪs/ noun [C] BIOLOGY the situation in which a characteristic controlled by one gene does not appear, because it has been stopped by the activity of another gene

epitaph /ˈepɪtɑːf/ noun [C] LITERATURE a piece of writing that honours a dead person, especially one written on their **grave**

epithelial cell /ˌepɪˈθiːliəl ˌsel/ noun [C] BIOLOGY one of the cells in the body that makes up epithelium —*picture* → CELL

epithelium /ˌepɪˈθiːliəm/ noun [U] BIOLOGY a thin layer of cells that covers the inside of organs and spaces within the body, and forms a protective cover over openings such as cuts

epithet /ˈepɪθet/ noun [C] a word or phrase that describes the main quality of someone or something

epitome /ɪˈpɪtəmi/ noun **the epitome of** the best possible example of a particular type of person or thing

epitomize /ɪˈpɪtəmaɪz/ verb [T] to be the best possible example of a particular type of person or thing

epoch /ˈiːpɒk/ noun [C] **1** a long period of time in history **2** GEOLOGY an amount of geological time that is a division of a period

eponymous /ɪˈpɒnɪməs/ adj the eponymous character in a story has the same name as the title

epoxy resin /ɪˌpɒksi ˈrezɪn/ noun [U] a type of very strong glue

EPROM /ˈiːprɒm/ noun [U] COMPUTING erasable-programmable read-only memory: computer memory that can be changed by a user to correct a problem in the program, or to add to what the program can do

Epsom salts /ˌepsəm ˈsɔːlts/ noun [plural] CHEMISTRY **hydrated** magnesium sulphate, used to help faeces leave the body

Epstein-Barr virus /ˌepstaɪn ˈbɑː ˌvaɪrəs/ noun [U] HEALTH an infectious virus that causes **glandular fever** and makes people feel very tired and weak = GLANDULAR FEVER

equal¹ /ˈiːkwəl/ adj **1** the same in value, amount, or size: *All the workers have **an equal share** in the profits.* ◆ *One unit of alcohol **is equal to** one small glass of wine.* ◆ *The two companies are **equal in size**.* ◆ *Every game is **of equal importance** to us.* **2** having or deserving the same rights, status, and opportunities as other people: *He believed that men and women were equal.* ◆ *They are equal partners in every aspect of their lives.*

PHRASE **on an equal footing** or **on equal terms** with the same rights and conditions as someone else

equal² /ˈiːkwəl/ (**equals, equalling, equalled**) verb [T] **1** MATHS to be the same in value or amount as something else: *Five plus three equals eight.* **2** to be as good as someone or something else: *She equalled the record with a time of 27.69 seconds.*

equal³ /ˈiːkwəl/ noun [C] someone or something that has the same value, rights, or importance as another person or thing

equality /ɪˈkwɒləti/ noun [U] the state of being equal, especially in having the same rights, status, and opportunities as other people ≠ INEQUALITY

equalize /ˈiːkwəlaɪz/ verb **1** [T] to make something the same for everyone **2** [I] SPORTS to score a goal or win a point that gives a team the same score as the opposing team

equalizer /ˈiːkwəlaɪzə/ noun [C] **1** SPORTS a goal or point that gives a team the same score as the opposing team **2** something that makes all people equal

equally /ˈiːkwəli/ adv **1** in equal amounts or quantities: *The money raised will be divided equally among the charities.* **2** to the same degree: *This recipe works equally well with soft fruit.* **3** used for adding another comment that has the same importance as one that you have already made: *The views of parents are important, but equally we must listen to teachers.* **4** in a way that is fair and the same for everyone: *We will treat all the cases equally.*

equal oppor'tunity noun [C/U] SOCIAL STUDIES a situation in which people have the same opportunities in life as other people, without being treated in an unfair way because of their race, sex, religion, or age

,equal 'rights noun [plural] **SOCIAL STUDIES** a situation in which everyone in a society has the same rights, despite differences in their race, sex, religion, or age

'equals ,sign noun [C] **MATHS** the sign = used in mathematics to show that two sets of numbers are the same in quantity or amount

equanimity /,ekwə'nɪmɪti/ noun [U] *formal* a calm mental state when you deal with difficult situations

equate /ɪ'kweɪt/ verb [T] to consider something to be the same as something else: *These people seem to equate honesty with weakness.*

equation /ɪ'kweɪʒ(ə)n/ noun [C] **1 MATHS** a statement in mathematics that two sets of numbers or expressions are equal: *Solve the equation $5x - 3 = 27$.* **2 CHEMISTRY** a statement in chemistry that uses symbols to show the changes that take place in a chemical reaction → WORD EQUATION

the equator /ɪ'kweɪtə/ noun [singular] **GEOGRAPHY** an imaginary line that goes around the centre of the Earth and divides it into northern and southern parts —*picture* → EARTH

equatorial /,ekwə'tɔːriəl/ adj **GEOGRAPHY** near the equator, or typical of conditions near the equator: *an equatorial rainforest* ♦ *equatorial regions*

equestrian /ɪ'kwestriən/ adj relating to riding horses

equiangular /,iːkwi'æŋɡjʊlə/ adj **MATHS** an equiangular geometric shape contains angles that are all equal

equidistant /,iːkwɪ'dɪstənt/ adj at the same distance from two places

equilateral /,iːkwɪ'læt(ə)rəl/ adj **MATHS** an equilateral triangle has three sides that are the same length —*picture* → TRIANGLE

equilibrium /,iːkwɪ'lɪbriəm/ noun [C/U] **1** a situation in which there is a balance between different forces or aspects of something **2** a calm mental state in which you are in control of your feelings = COMPOSURE **3 PHYSICS** a state in which an object is not moving in any way or is moving at the same rate all the time because there is a balance between any forces affecting it

equinox /'iːkwɪnɒks/ noun [C] **ASTRONOMY** one of the two days in the year when the day and night are the same length. The **vernal equinox** is on 20 or 21 March and the **autumnal equinox** is on 22 or 23 September.

equip /ɪ'kwɪp/ (**equips, equipping, equipped**) verb [T] **1** to provide a person or place with the things that they need for a particular purpose: *They received a grant to build and equip a new clinic.* **2** to provide someone with the skills or qualities that they need in order to deal with a situation successfully: *The training had equipped her to deal with emergency situations.*

equipment /ɪ'kwɪpmənt/ noun [U] **SCIENCE** the tools, machines, or other things that you need for a particular job or activity: *camping equipment* ♦ *A computer is the most important piece of equipment you will buy.*

equipotential /,iːkwɪpə'tenʃ(ə)l/ adj **PHYSICS** relating to a surface that has the same **electric potential** or **gravitational potential** at all points

equitable /'ekwɪtəb(ə)l/ adj *formal* fair and reasonable because everyone is treated in the same way: *an equitable distribution of funds* —**equitably** adv

equity /'ekwəti/ noun **1** [U] *formal* a fair and reasonable way of behaving towards people, so that everyone is treated equally **2** [U] **BUSINESS** the value

of a property minus the amount of the **mortgage** (=money borrowed to buy it) that is still owed **3** equities [plural] **BUSINESS** company shares that can be bought and sold on a **stock market**

equivalent1 /ɪ'kwɪvələnt/ adj of the same size, value, importance, or meaning as something else: *The price is £500, or the equivalent amount in euros.* ♦ *a distance equivalent to a return flight from Moscow to Beijing* —**equivalence** noun [U]

equivalent2 /ɪ'kwɪvələnt/ noun [C] someone or something that has the same size, value, importance, or meaning as someone or something else

equivocal /ɪ'kwɪvək(ə)l/ adj *formal* **1** with more than one possible meaning, in order to avoid making a clear statement = NON-COMMITTAL **2** not clearly showing the real situation or providing a definite result = INCONCLUSIVE —**equivocally** /ɪ'kwɪvək(ə)li/ adv

er /ɜː/ interjection used for writing the sound that people make when they are thinking about what to say next

era /'ɪərə/ noun [C] **1** a historical period of time that has a particular quality or character: *The president promised to bring about **a new era** of peace.* **2 GEOLOGY** one of the very long periods of time that geological time is divided into

eradicate /ɪ'rædɪkeɪt/ verb [T] to completely get rid of something bad —**eradication** /ɪ,rædɪ'keɪʃ(ə)n/ noun [U]

erase /ɪ'reɪz/ verb [T] **1** to remove all the writing, sound, or pictures from something: *The virus erases all the files on your hard drive.* **2** to get rid of an unpleasant memory, feeling, or thought: *He tried to erase the memory of their painful encounter.*

eraser /ɪ'reɪzə/ noun [C] an object that you use for removing marks from a **blackboard** or **whiteboard**

erbium /'ɜːbiəm/ noun [U] **CHEMISTRY** a soft silvery metallic element in the **lanthanide** group of the periodic table. It is used in alloys and paints. Chemical symbol: **Er**

erect1 /ɪ'rekt/ verb [T] *formal* to build something, or to put something in an upright position: *Police erected barriers to control the crowds.*

erect2 /ɪ'rekt/ adj in a straight upright position: *the erect posture of a professional soldier*

erectile tissue /ɪ'rektaɪl ,tɪʃuː/ noun [U] **HEALTH** tissue in the body that is capable of becoming stiff and swollen by being filled with blood

erection /ɪ'rekʃ(ə)n/ noun **1** [C] a stiff penis **2** [U] *formal* the process of putting something such as a building or fence in an upright position

erector muscle /ɪ'rektə ,mʌs(ə)l/ noun [C] **ANATOMY** a muscle that can move a part of the body into an upright position —*picture* → SKIN

ergative /'ɜːɡətɪv/ adj **LANGUAGE** an ergative verb can have its object as its **subject** without changing its meaning. For example, 'open' is an ergative verb because you can say 'I opened the door' or 'the door opened'. —**ergative** noun [C]

ergometrine /,ɜːɡəʊ'metriːn/ noun [U] **HEALTH** a medicine that is used to stop a woman from bleeding after she has given birth to a baby

ergonomic /,ɜːɡə'nɒmɪk/ adj ergonomic furniture, equipment etc is designed to be easy and comfortable to use and to produce the most benefits to the user —**ergonomically** /,ɜːɡə'nɒmɪkli/ adv

ergonomics /,ɜːɡə'nɒmɪks/ noun [U] the study of the way that furniture, equipment etc can be designed so that it is easy and comfortable to use and produces the most benefits and the best working or living conditions for the user

erode /ɪˈrəʊd/ verb [I/T] **1** GEOLOGY to gradually damage the surface of rock or land so that it begins to disappear, or to be gradually damaged in this way **2** to gradually reduce the strength, importance, or value of something, or to be gradually reduced in this way

erosion /ɪˈrəʊʒ(ə)n/ noun [U] **1** GEOLOGY the process by which the surface of land or rock is gradually damaged by the action of water, the wind, the sea, or glaciers: *coastal erosion* —*picture* → ROCK CYCLE **2** the gradual reduction or destruction of something

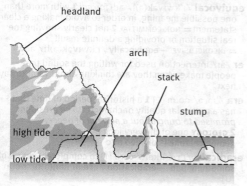

coastal erosion

erotic /ɪˈrɒtɪk/ adj containing scenes or descriptions that make people sexually excited: *erotic films*

err /ɜː/ verb [I] *formal* to make a mistake

errand /ˈerənd/ noun [C] a small job that involves going to collect or deliver something

erratic¹ /ɪˈrætɪk/ adj changing often, or not following a regular pattern = UNPREDICTABLE: *erratic behaviour* —**erratically** /ɪˈrætɪkli/ adv

erratic² /ɪˈrætɪk/ noun [C] GEOLOGY a rock that was carried to a place by a glacier and left there when the ice melted

erroneous /ɪˈrəʊniəs/ adj *formal* not correct: *reports based on erroneous information* —**erroneously** adv

error /ˈerə/ noun **1** [C/U] a mistake, for example in a calculation or a decision: *an error in our calculations* ♦ *He admitted that he'd made an error in rejecting their offer.* ♦ *I was guilty of an error of judgment in allowing myself to be placed in this situation.* ♦ *The computer had been switched off in error.* **2** [C] COMPUTING a failure in a computer process: *an error message* (=telling you that something is wrong) → TRIAL

'error ˌcode noun [C] COMPUTING a combination of letters and numbers on a computer screen that shows that there is a particular problem with a program

'error ˌmessage noun [C] COMPUTING a message that you get on your computer screen when you have made a mistake, or when something has gone wrong with the program

'error reˌcovery noun [U] COMPUTING the ability of software or equipment to continue to run after there has been a problem

erudite /ˈerʊdaɪt/ adj *formal* someone who is erudite has a lot of knowledge because they have read or studied a lot

erupt /ɪˈrʌpt/ verb [I] **1** GEOLOGY if a volcano erupts, it explodes inside and flames, rocks, and lava come out of the top **2** to start suddenly with a lot of violence or

noise: *Heavy fighting erupted in the city on Sunday.* **3** to suddenly become very angry, excited, or noisy: *The crowd erupted into wild cheers.*

eruption /ɪˈrʌpʃ(ə)n/ noun [C] GEOLOGY an occasion when a volcano explodes

erythrocyte /ɪˈrɪθrəsaɪt/ noun [C] ANATOMY a **red blood cell**

escalate /ˈeskəleɪt/ verb **1** [I/T] to become much worse or more serious, or to make something much worse or more serious **2** [I] to increase at an uncontrolled rate: *escalating costs* —**escalation** /ˌeskəˈleɪʃ(ə)n/ noun [C/U]

escalator /ˈeskəleɪtə/ noun [C] a set of moving stairs that take people from one level of a building to another

escape¹ /ɪˈskeɪp/ verb **1** [I] to get away from a dangerous or unpleasant place: *Three people died in the fire, but John escaped through the bedroom window.* ♦ *She was shot while trying to escape from prison.* **2** [I/T] to avoid a dangerous or unpleasant experience: *Two security guards escaped injury in the attack.* ♦ *Durham narrowly escaped defeat in their first match of the season.* **3** [T] if something escapes you, you cannot remember it or you do not notice it: *His name escapes me right now.* **4** [I] to come out of a container by accident: *How will we know if there's any gas escaping?* —**escaped** /ɪˈskeɪpt/ adj: *an escaped prisoner*

escape² /ɪˈskeɪp/ noun **1** [C/U] an act of avoiding or getting away from a person, place, or bad situation: *She was relieved to make her escape from the meeting.* ♦ *A couple had a narrow escape (=were almost killed) when a tree fell just in front of their car.* **2** [C/U] a way of helping yourself to stop thinking about an unpleasant situation you are in: *For him acting was a means of escape.* **3** [C] an amount of gas or liquid that escapes from a container: *There was a rapid escape of gas.* **4** [U] COMPUTING the **escape key** on a computer

esˈcape ˌclause noun [C] LAW a statement in a contract that allows someone to avoid doing something that the contract is intended to make them do

esˈcape ˌkey noun [C] COMPUTING a key on a computer keyboard that allows you to stop an action or leave a program

'escape veˌlocity noun [U] ASTRONOMY the slowest speed at which an object must travel to get away from the gravity of a planet or moon in order to orbit around it or move into space

escapism /ɪˈskeɪpɪzəm/ noun [U] a pleasant or exciting activity or entertainment that helps people to forget about real life —**escapist** adj

escarpment /ɪˈskɑːpmənt/ noun [C] GEOGRAPHY a steep slope that forms the edge of a long area of high land

escort¹ /ˈeskɔːt/ noun [C] **1** a person or a group of people or vehicles that go somewhere with someone in order to protect them or prevent them from escaping: *He arrived in court under police escort.* **2** someone, especially a man, who goes with another person to a social event as their partner

escort² /ɪˈskɔːt/ verb [T] **1** to go somewhere with a person or vehicle in order to protect them or prevent them from escaping **2** to go with another person to a social event as their partner

escrow /ˈeskrəʊ/ noun [U] LAW money, property, or a legal document that is kept by someone until a particular thing has happened

'e-,signature noun [C] **COMPUTING** electronic signature: a way of adding your name to an electronic document such as an email, used when you are buying goods or making agreements on the Internet

esker /'eskə/ noun [C] **GEOLOGY** a long narrow winding line of sand or small bits of stone, left by a stream flowing under a glacier

ESL /ˌiː es 'el/ noun [U] **EDUCATION** English as a Second Language: the activity of teaching English to people whose first language is not English, but who live in an English-speaking country

ESOL /'iːsɒl/ noun [U] **EDUCATION** English for Speakers of Other Languages: the activity of teaching English to people whose first language is not English

ESP /ˌiː es 'piː/ noun [U] **EDUCATION** English for Specific or Special Purposes: the activity of teaching English to people whose first language is not English, but who need to speak English for their job or for another purpose

esp. abbrev especially

especially /ɪ'speʃ(ə)li/ adv **1** used when mentioning conditions that make something more relevant, important, or true= **PARTICULARLY**: *It was a very cold house, especially in winter.* **2** very, or very much = **PARTICULARLY**: *I'm not especially interested in football.* **3** used for showing that what you are saying affects one person or thing more than others= **PARTICULARLY**: *Don't talk to anyone about this – especially not Jane.* **4** for a particular purpose, or for a particular person: *a service **especially for** local people*

espionage /'espiənɑːʒ/ noun [U] attempts to discover the secrets of a country that is your enemy

essay /'eseɪ/ noun [C] **EDUCATION** a short piece of writing on a particular subject, especially by a student: *We have to write **an essay about** Romantic poetry.*

essence /'es(ə)ns/ noun **1** [singular/U] the most important and typical part of something: *images that captured the essence of life in our country before the war* **2** [C/U] a liquid that contains the strong taste or smell of the plant that it is taken from
> **PHRASE** **in essence** *formal* used for emphasizing what is the most important feature of something

essential /ɪ'senʃ(ə)l/ adj **1** completely necessary: *It is absolutely **essential** that all these issues are discussed.* ♦ *A good dictionary is **essential for** learning English.* ♦ *It is **essential to** involve your staff in the decision.* **2** basic and important: *food, fuel, and other essential supplies*

essentially /ɪ'senʃ(ə)li/ adv **1** used for emphasizing the most important aspect of something: *That, essentially, is the difference between them.* **2** used for saying that something is mostly true, but not completely true: *The list is essentially complete.*

essentials /ɪ'senʃ(ə)lz/ noun [plural] things that are completely necessary or basic

establish /ɪ'stæblɪʃ/ verb [T] **1** to make something start to exist or start to happen: *A proper procedure for complaints should be established.* ♦ *Mandela was eager to **establish** good **relations** with the business community.* **2** to start an organization or company: *The company was established in 1860.* **3** to discover, prove, or decide that something is true: *The cause of death has not yet been established.* ♦ *We have established that you were present that afternoon.* **4** to achieve success, so that people recognize your skill, qualities, or power: *He quickly **established himself as** a promising film actor.*

established /ɪ'stæblɪʃt/ adj having existed or done something for a long time, and therefore recognized as good or successful: *an old established family firm*

establishment /ɪ'stæblɪʃmənt/ noun **1** *formal* an institution, organization, or business: *a research establishment* **2 the establishment** [singular] **SOCIAL STUDIES** the most important and powerful people in a country or section of society **3** [U] the process of starting or creating something: *Davis proposed the establishment of the committee.*

estate /ɪ'steɪt/ noun [C] **1** an area containing many houses or buildings of the same type= **HOUSING ESTATE**: *He grew up **on an estate**.* **2** a large area of countryside that belongs to one person with a big house on it **3** **LAW** all the property and money that belongs to someone who has just died **4** a long car with an extra door at the back and a lot of space behind the back seats

es'tate ,agent noun [C] someone whose job is to help people to buy, sell, or rent property

es'tate ,car noun [C] a car that is an **estate**

esteem /ɪ'stiːm/ noun [U] *formal* a feeling of admiration and respect for someone= **REGARD**

ester /'estə/ noun [C] **CHEMISTRY** an organic compound formed in a chemical reaction between an acid and an alcohol, with any water removed. Esters often have a pleasant smell.

estimate¹ /'estɪmeɪt/ verb [T] to guess or calculate an amount or value by using available information: *The total cost was estimated at £600,000.* ♦ *We estimate that 20 per cent of the harvest has been lost.* ♦ *It is impossible to **estimate how many** of the residents were affected.*

estimate² /'estɪmət/ noun [C] **1** an amount that you guess or calculate by using the information that is available: *The figure mentioned is just **a rough estimate**.* **2** a statement that tells a customer how much money someone will charge if the customer employs them to do a particular piece of work: *Can you give us an estimate for the repairs to the roof?*

estimation /ˌestɪ'meɪʃ(ə)n/ noun [singular] *formal* someone's opinion: *In my estimation, New York's a more interesting city than London.*

estranged /ɪ'streɪndʒd/ adj no longer living with your husband or wife

estuary /'estjuəri/ (plural **estuaries**) noun [C] **GEOGRAPHY** the part of a large river where it becomes wide and flows into the sea —*picture* → **RIVER**

'e-,tail noun [U] **BUSINESS** the activity of selling things on the Internet

etc /et 'set(ə)rə/ abbrev et cetera: used after a list of things to mean 'and others of the same type', when you do not want to mention everything

etching /'etʃɪŋ/ noun [C] **ARTS** a picture printed from a piece of metal on which marks have been made using acid

eternal /ɪ'tɜːn(ə)l/ adj continuing and never ending —**eternally** adv

eternity /ɪ'tɜːnəti/ noun **1** [U] the whole of time, with no beginning and no end **2** [singular] an extremely long time: *After what seemed like an eternity, he gave his answer.*

ethane /'iːθeɪn/ noun [U] **CHEMISTRY** a gas that has no colour and no smell and burns very easily. It is obtained from **petroleum** and **natural gas** and is used as a fuel. Chemical formula: C_2H_6

ethanol /'eθənɒl/ noun [U] CHEMISTRY the type of alcohol in alcoholic drinks. Chemical formula: C_2H_5OH

ethene /'i:θi:n/ noun [U] CHEMISTRY a gas obtained from **petroleum** and **natural gas**. It is used in making polythene and other chemicals and to ripen fruit artificially. Chemical formula: C_2H_4

ether /'i:θə/ noun [U] **1** CHEMISTRY a clear liquid that is used as a **solvent** or for making people unconscious before medical operations **2 the ether** the air or atmosphere, especially when it is thought of as the substance that radio, telephone, or Internet communications pass through

Ethernet /'i:θənet/ TRADEMARK COMPUTING a system in which several computers in an area are directly connected to each other by wires

ethic /'eθɪk/ noun **1 ethics** [plural] a set of principles that people use to decide what is right and what is wrong: *medical ethics* **2** [singular] a general principle or belief that affects the way that people behave: *a strong team ethic*

ethical /'eθɪk(ə)l/ adj **1** involving the principles that people use for deciding what is right and what is wrong: *ethical standards* **2** morally right ≠ UNETHICAL: *Is it really ethical to keep animals in zoos?* —**ethically** /'eθɪkli/ adv

ethnic /'eθnɪk/ adj **1** SOCIAL STUDIES relating to a group of people who have the same culture and traditions: *The country's population consists of three main ethnic groups.* **2** SOCIAL STUDIES belonging to a particular ethnic group that lives in a place where most people are from a different ethnic group: *ethnic Albanians living in Kosovo* **3** SOCIAL STUDIES involving people from different ethnic groups: *a rich ethnic mix* **4** ethnic clothing, food, or music comes from countries outside Western Europe and North America —**ethnically** /'eθnɪkli/ adv

ethnic cleansing /ˌeθnɪk 'klenzɪŋ/ noun [U] SOCIAL STUDIES the use of violence to force people who belong to a particular ethnic group to leave an area

ethnicity /eθ'nɪsəti/ (plural **ethnicities**) noun [C/U] SOCIAL STUDIES the fact that someone belongs to a particular **ethnic** group

ethnic mi'nority noun [C] SOCIAL STUDIES a group of people with the same culture and traditions who live in a place where most people have a different culture and different traditions

ethnology /eθ'nɒlədʒi/ noun [U] the study of the ways in which different societies and cultures have developed

ethos /'i:θɒs/ noun [singular] *formal* the set of attitudes and beliefs that are typical of an organization or a group of people

ethyl alcohol /ˌiθaɪl 'ælkəhɒl/ noun [U] CHEMISTRY ethanol

ethylene /'eθəli:n/ noun [U] CHEMISTRY the gas ethene

'e-ticket noun [C] TOURISM a ticket for a plane or train journey that has been bought on the Internet, so that there is no paper ticket

etiquette /'etɪket/ noun [U] a set of rules for behaving correctly in social situations

etymology /ˌetɪ'mɒlədʒi/ (plural **etymologies**) noun LANGUAGE **1** [U] the study of the origins and development of words **2** [C] the origin and development of a particular word —**etymological** /ˌetɪmə'lɒdʒɪk(ə)l/ adj

the EU /ˌi: 'ju:/ noun [singular] the European Union

the Eucharist /'ju:kərɪst/ noun [singular] RELIGION the Christian ceremony in which people eat bread and drink wine as a way of remembering Jesus Christ's last meal with his **disciples** as described in the Bible

Euclidean /ju'klɪdɪən/ adj MATHS relating to the system of geometry invented by the ancient Greek **mathematician** Euclid

eugenics /ju:'dʒenɪks/ noun [U] SOCIAL STUDIES the idea that society can be improved by allowing people to become parents only if they have genetic characteristics that are likely to make them produce healthy and intelligent children. Eugenics has been disapproved of since the **Nazi** period in Europe in the 1930s and 1940s.

eukaryote /ju:'kærɪɒt/ noun [C] BIOLOGY an organism whose cells contain a nucleus that is surrounded by a membrane —**eukaryotic** /juˌkæri'ɒtɪk/ adj

eulogy /'ju:lədʒi/ (plural **eulogies**) noun [C] **1** a speech at a funeral about the person who has died **2** LITERATURE a piece of writing that praises someone or something very much

euphemism /'ju:fə,mɪzəm/ noun [C] LANGUAGE a word or expression that people use when they want to talk about something unpleasant or embarrassing without mentioning the thing itself: *'Social exclusion' seems to be the latest euphemism for poverty.* —**euphemistic** /juːfə'mɪstɪk/ adj

euphoria /ju:'fɔ:riə/ noun [U] a feeling of great happiness that lasts for a short time only —**euphoric** /ju:'fɒrɪk/ adj

euro /'jʊərəʊ/ (plural **euro** or **euros**) noun [C] ECONOMICS the unit of money that is used in most countries in the European Union. Its symbol is €.

the Euromarket /'jʊərəʊˌmɑːkɪt/ noun [singular] ECONOMICS the European Union considered as a single market

Europe /'jʊərəp/ noun **1** the large area of land between Asia and the Atlantic Ocean —*picture* → CONTINENT **2** the European Union **3** the whole of Europe apart from the UK

European /ˌjʊərə'pi:ən/ adj **1** of or from Europe **2** relating to the European Union

the European 'Parliament noun [singular] POLITICS the parliament of all the countries that belong to the European Union

the European 'Union noun [singular] ECONOMICS an organization of European countries whose aim is to improve trade among its members and encourage closer political connections

europium /jʊ'rəʊpiəm/ noun [U] CHEMISTRY a soft silvery-white metallic element in the **lanthanide** group of the periodic table. It is used in **lasers**. Chemical symbol: **Eu**

the Eurozone or **the eurozone** /'jʊərəʊˌzəʊn/ noun [singular] ECONOMICS the area of Europe that consists of countries that are members of the European Union and use the **euro** as a unit of money

Eustachian tube /ju:ˌsteɪʃ(ə)n 'tju:b/ noun [C] ANATOMY one of the two tubes that connect the ears to the throat and control air pressure in the ears —*picture* → EAR

euthanasia /ˌju:θə'neɪziə/ noun [U] SOCIAL STUDIES the practice of killing a very old or very ill person in order to stop them from suffering

eutrophic /juːˈtrɒfɪk, juːˈtrɒfɪk/ adj
ENVIRONMENT relating to water that contains a large
amount of nutrients, often as a result of pollution by
fertilizers or sewage —**eutrophy** /ˈjuːtrəfi/ verb [I]

eutrophication /juːˌtrɒfɪˈkeɪʃ(ə)n,
juːˌtrɒfɪˈkeɪʃ(ə)n/ noun [U] ENVIRONMENT the
process by which rivers, lakes, or seas become polluted
by chemicals from fertilizers or sewage that cause
some types of plant to grow in large amounts. These
plants use up the oxygen in the water, which harms
other plants and organisms.

evacuate /ɪˈvækjueɪt/ verb [I/T] **1** to leave a place
because it is not safe, or to make people leave a place
because it is not safe: *The building was immediately
evacuated.* **2** HEALTH to get rid of solid waste from
the bowels —**evacuation** /ɪˌvækjuˈeɪʃ(ə)n/ noun [U]

evade /ɪˈveɪd/ verb [T] **1** to avoid dealing with someone
or something that you should deal with: *He had become
an expert at evading responsibility.* **2** to avoid being
caught: *The armed robbers managed to evade the police.*

evaluate /ɪˈvæljueɪt/ verb [T] *formal* to think carefully
about something before you make a judgment about
its value, importance, or quality —**evaluative** adj

evaluation /ɪˌvæljuˈeɪʃ(ə)n/ noun **1** [U] the process of
making a judgment about the value, importance, or
quality of something after considering it carefully **2** [C]
a judgment that you make about the value,
importance, or quality of something after considering
it carefully

evalu'ation ˌcopy noun [C] COMPUTING a piece of
software that has the most important features of a new
software product and is designed for people to try
before buying the full product

evangelical /ˌiːvænˈdʒelɪk(ə)l/ adj RELIGION relating
to a form of Christianity in which people express their
religious beliefs in an enthusiastic way

evangelism /ɪˈvændʒəˌlɪzəm/ noun [U] RELIGION the
practice of teaching people about Christianity

evangelist /ɪˈvændʒəlɪst/ noun [C] RELIGION **1** a
member of an **evangelical** church **2 evangelist** or
Evangelist one of the four writers of the parts of the
Bible called the **gospels** that tell the story of Jesus
Christ's life

evaporate /ɪˈvæpəreɪt/ verb [I] **1** SCIENCE if a liquid
evaporates, it slowly changes into a vapour at a
temperature below its **boiling point** —*picture* → STATE
2 if something such as a feeling or quality evaporates,
it suddenly disappears

evaporating dish /ɪˈvæpəreɪtɪŋ ˌdɪʃ/ noun [C]
SCIENCE a flat dish used in laboratories for allowing
substances to evaporate —*picture* → LABORATORY

evaporation /ɪˌvæpəˈreɪʃ(ə)n/ noun [U] SCIENCE a
process in which a liquid slowly changes into a vapour
without being boiled —*picture* → WATER CYCLE

evasive /ɪˈveɪsɪv/ adj not talking or answering
questions in an honest way

PHRASE **take evasive action** to do something to avoid
a dangerous situation
—**evasively** adv

eve /iːv/ noun **on the eve of sth** on the day before an
important event, or during the period of time just
before it
→ CHRISTMAS EVE, NEW YEAR'S EVE

even[1] /ˈiːv(ə)n/ adv **1** used when you are saying
something that is surprising: *This room is always cold,
even in summer.* ♦ *They
didn't even say goodbye.* ♦ *Even though the film was
bad, I enjoyed the evening.*

When emphasizing verbs, **even** comes before an
ordinary verb: *They even have a swimming pool.* But
even comes after an auxiliary verb, a modal verb, or
the verb 'to be': *She doesn't even know his name.*
♦ *Some computers can even talk to you.*

2 used for emphasizing that something is bigger, better
etc than something else that is also big, good etc: *She
was **even more** beautiful than I imagined she'd be.*
♦ *Things are bad, but they were **even worse** before.*

PHRASES **even if** used for emphasizing that although
something may happen, another situation remains the
same: *She won't apologize, even if she's proved wrong.*
even so used for introducing a statement that seems
surprising after what you said before: *Accidents are
rare. Even so, you should still drive carefully.*

even[2] /ˈiːv(ə)n/ adj **1** flat and level ≠ UNEVEN: *The table
kept wobbling because the floor wasn't quite even.*
2 not changing much in rate, level, or amount ≠ UNEVEN:
an even temperature **3** MATHS an even number can
be divided exactly by two ≠ ODD → BREAK[1]

evening /ˈiːvnɪŋ/ noun [C/U] the part of the day between
the end of the afternoon and night: *We spend most
evenings reading or listening to music.* ♦ *I'll see you on
Monday evening, OK?* ♦ *We usually go to the cinema on
Thursday evenings* (=every Thursday evening). ♦ *an
evening meal* ♦ *I'm so tired in the evenings, all I want to
do is sit and watch television.* ♦ *The incident took place
at around 9 o'clock yesterday evening.*

'evening ˌclass noun [C] EDUCATION a series of
classes in a particular subject taught in the evening

'evening ˌdress noun **1** [U] formal clothes that people
wear when they go to important social events in the
evening **2 evening dress** or **evening gown** [C] a long
dress that a woman wears when she goes to an
important social event in the evening

evening primrose /ˌiːvnɪŋ ˈprɪmrəʊz/ noun [C/U]
BIOLOGY a plant with yellow flowers that open in the
evening. An oil used in **herbal medicine** is obtained
from its seeds.

ˌevening 'star noun [C] ASTRONOMY a bright star that
appears in the western sky, usually the planet **Venus**

evenly /ˈiːvənli/ adv **1** in an equal or regular way:
Sprinkle the sugar evenly over the cake. **2** with each
person having an equal chance to win: *The two teams
are fairly evenly matched.*

event /ɪˈvent/ noun [C] **1** something that happens: *the
most important event of my life* ♦ *a series of events*
2 an organized occasion such as a party or sports
competition: *The concert is an annual event.* ♦ *Staff at
the hospital helped to organize the event.* **3** one of the
planned activities that take place during an occasion
such as a sports competition: *the winner of the first
event*

PHRASES **in any event** whatever happens or has
happened: *In any event, the project would never have
succeeded.*
in the event used for saying what happened, especially
when it was different from what was expected: *In the
event, I wasn't late.*
in the event of sth used for saying what will happen in
a particular situation: *the procedures to be followed in
the event of fire*

eventful /ɪˈventf(ə)l/ adj with a lot of exciting or
unusual things happening

e'vent ˌmanagement noun [U] BUSINESS the
planning and organization of events that **publicize** (=
make people notice) a particular company,
organization, product etc

e'vent ˌmarketing noun [U] BUSINESS activities that
are designed to advertise an event

eventual /ɪˈventʃuəl/ adj happening or existing at the end of a long process or period of time = ULTIMATE: *This mistake led to his eventual capture and imprisonment.*

eventually /ɪˈventʃuəli/ adv at the end of a long process or period of time: *Eventually, we became good friends.* ♦ *the scientific research that we hope will eventually produce a cure*

ever /ˈevə/ adv at any time in the past, present, or future: *Have you ever been to Cape Town?* ♦ *Don't ever do that again.* ♦ *It hardly ever rains here in the summer.* ♦ *Isabel's looking lovelier than ever.*

PHRASES **ever since** during the whole period of time since something happened: *They've been friends ever since they started school.*

for ever continuing always into the future: *He promised to stay with me for ever.*
→ FOREVER

evergreen /ˈevəɡriːn/ adj BIOLOGY an evergreen plant does not lose its leaves in winter or in the dry season → DECIDUOUS —**evergreen** noun [C]

everlasting /ˌevəˈlɑːstɪŋ/ adj continuing for ever

every /ˈevri/ determiner **1** used for referring to all the people or things of a particular type: *This decision affects every single one of us.* ♦ *I can remember every detail of our conversation.* **2** used for showing how often something happens or how far apart things are: *Take one tablet every four hours.* ♦ *There are army checkpoints every few miles along the road.* ♦ *I have to work every other weekend* (=on the first, third, fifth etc). **3** used for showing how common something is by giving a number as a part of a larger number: *One in every five computers was faulty.*

PHRASE **every time** whenever something happens: *She calls the doctor every time she gets a headache.*

■ A noun subject that follows **every** is used with a singular verb.
■ In formal writing, pronouns or possessive adjectives that refer back to a subject with **every** are usually singular: *Every student has his or her own copy of the text.* But in speech and informal writing, plural pronouns and possessive adjectives are more usual: *Every student has their own copy of the text.*

everybody /ˈevriˌbɒdi/ pronoun everyone: *Does everybody have a book?* ♦ *You're here, but where is everybody else?*

everyday /ˈevriˌdeɪ/ adj very common, or completely normal: *everyday life*

everyone /ˈevriˌwʌn/ pronoun **1** every person in a group: *Everyone is thrilled about Jean's baby.* ♦ *Do you know everyone's name?* ♦ *Everyone else had finished eating.* **2** used for talking about people in general: *Everyone needs a friend.* ♦ *Not everyone can afford a car.*

■ When **everyone** is a subject, it is used with a singular verb.
■ In formal writing, pronouns or possessive adjectives that refer back to **everyone** are usually singular: *Everyone should bring his or her own lunch.* But in speech and informal writing, plural pronouns and possessive adjectives are more usual: *Everyone should bring their own lunch.*

everything /ˈevriˌθɪŋ/ pronoun **1** all the things in a place, in an activity, or in general: *The earthquake destroyed everything within 25 miles.* ♦ *Everything's done by computer nowadays.* ♦ *If you do the cooking, I'll deal with everything else.* **2** someone's life, or the situation that someone is in: *You look upset – is everything all right?*

PHRASE **be/mean everything** to be more valuable or important than anyone or anything else: *Beauty isn't everything, you know!*

everywhere /ˈevriˌweə/ adv in or to every place: *Everywhere in the world people know his name.* ♦ *Rosie travels everywhere with me.* ♦ *My keys must be in the desk – I've searched everywhere else.*

evict /ɪˈvɪkt/ verb [T] LAW to legally force someone to leave the house that they are living in —**eviction** /ɪˈvɪkʃ(ə)n/ noun [C/U]

evidence /ˈevɪd(ə)ns/ noun [U] **1** facts or physical signs that help to prove something: *The study found no evidence that fish feel pain.* ♦ *the historical evidence for his theories* ♦ *We are seeing more evidence of economic growth.* **2** LAW facts, statements, or objects that help to prove whether someone has committed a crime: *The police didn't have enough evidence to convict him.* ♦ *The evidence against them is overwhelming.* ♦ *He went to court to give evidence against his attacker.*

evident /ˈevɪd(ə)nt/ adj formal easy to see, notice, or understand

evidently /ˈevɪd(ə)ntli/ adv **1** used for saying that something is obvious: *Evidently annoyed, he left the room.* **2** used for showing that a statement is based on known facts: *Evidently, these plants don't do well in a cold climate.*

evil¹ /ˈiːv(ə)l/ adj **1** very bad or cruel: *a dangerous and evil dictator* **2** very unpleasant: *an evil-smelling chemical*

evil² /ˈiːv(ə)l/ noun [U] a power that is believed to make people do very bad and cruel things ≠ GOOD

PHRASE **the evils of sth** the bad effects that something can have
→ LESSER¹

evocative /ɪˈvɒkətɪv/ adj formal an evocative smell or sound makes someone think of something, often something that they experienced in the past

evoke /ɪˈvəʊk/ verb [T] formal to bring a particular emotion, idea, or memory into your mind

evolution /ˌiːvəˈluːʃ(ə)n/ noun [U] **1** BIOLOGY the process by which plants, animals, and other organisms change over long periods of time to become more suitable for their environment, each generation being very slightly different from the previous one → NATURAL SELECTION **2** the way in which something gradually changes and develops —**evolutionary** /ˌiːvəˈluːʃ(ə)n(ə)ri/ adj

evolutionist /ˌiːvəˈluːʃənɪst/ adj connected with the scientific theory of evolution —**evolutionism** noun [U]

evolve /ɪˈvɒlv/ verb **1** [I] to gradually change and develop over a period of time: *Computer software will continue to evolve in response to users' needs.* ♦ *a debate as to whether birds evolved from dinosaurs* **2** [T] to develop something gradually: *Teachers are evolving new ways of working.*

'e-,voting noun [U] POLITICS the process of voting in an election using the Internet

'e-,wallet noun [C] COMPUTING a feature of **web browsers** that allows a user to store personal details about their credit card or **bank account** on the Internet

ewe /juː/ noun [C] a female sheep —picture → MAMMAL

ex- /eks/ prefix used with nouns that describe someone's job, rank, or relationship to someone, showing that they no longer have that job, rank, or relationship: *an ex-boyfriend*

exacerbate /ɪgˈzæsəbeɪt/ verb [T] *formal* to make a problem become worse

exact¹ /ɪgˈzækt/ adj done, made, or described in a very thorough way, with all the details correct: *the exact sequence of events leading up to the accident* ♦ *The exact number of wounded people is unknown.*
PHRASE **the exact opposite** used for emphasizing that two things or people are completely different: *She's very friendly, the exact opposite of her sister.*

exact² /ɪgˈzækt/ verb [T] *formal* to get something from someone by threatening or forcing them

exactly /ɪgˈzæk(t)li/ adv **1** no more and no less than a particular amount or time= PRECISELY: *It's exactly three o'clock.* ♦ *The wood should measure five centimetres exactly.* **2** in every way, or in every detail= JUST: *She sounds **exactly like** her mother.* ♦ *The house is **exactly the same** as it was 20 years ago.* **3** used for emphasizing that you are referring to one particular thing and no other= JUST: *She was standing exactly where you are now.*
PHRASE **what/where/when etc exactly** used for asking someone for more details about something: *What exactly did he say?*

exaggerate /ɪgˈzædʒəreɪt/ verb [I/T] to describe something in a way that makes it seem better, worse, larger, more important etc than it really is: *Don't exaggerate! It wasn't that bad!* ♦ *We should not exaggerate the importance of this agreement.*

exaggerated /ɪgˈzædʒə,reɪtɪd/ adj **1** describing something in a way that makes it seem better, worse, larger, more important etc than it really is: *exaggerated claims* **2** done in a way that does not seem sincere or natural: *a tone of exaggerated politeness*

exaggeration /ɪg,zædʒəˈreɪʃ(ə)n/ noun **1** [C] a comment or description that makes something seem better, worse, larger, more important etc than it really is **2** [U] the act of making a comment or description of this type

exam /ɪgˈzæm/ noun [C] EDUCATION an important test of knowledge, especially one that people take at school or university: *I'm **taking** the **exam** in June.* ♦ *She really needs to **pass** this **exam**.*

examination /ɪg,zæmɪˈneɪʃ(ə)n/ noun **1** [C] EDUCATION *formal* an exam: *Students will **take** an **examination** at the end of the year.* **2** [C/U] a careful look at something or someone: *The doctor will give you **a full examination**.* ♦ *Engineers made **a thorough examination of** the wreckage.* **3** [C/U] a careful study of something: *a close examination of the language of the text* **4** [C/U] an occasion when a lawyer asks someone questions in court

examine /ɪgˈzæmɪn/ verb [T] **1** to look at something or someone carefully: *She opened the suitcase and examined the contents.* ♦ *Dr Greene has come to examine the patient.* **2** to study or consider something carefully: *The committee will examine four proposals.* **3** to ask someone questions in a legal trial **4** EDUCATION *formal* to give students an examination to test their knowledge

examiner /ɪgˈzæmɪnə/ noun [C] EDUCATION someone whose job is to test people's knowledge or ability

ex'am ,paper noun [C] EDUCATION **1** the list of questions that someone must answer during an exam **2** the paper that you write your answers on in an exam

example /ɪgˈzɑːmp(ə)l/ noun [C] **1** something that you mention in order to show the type of thing that you are talking about and to help to explain what you mean: *Many sports are still dominated by men – football is an obvious example.* ♦ *He gave several **examples of** how we could change things.* ♦ *The Mini is **a classic example** (=a typical example) of a great British car.* **2** a person or way of behaving that is considered as a model for other people to copy: *You should be **setting an example** for your little brother.*
PHRASE **for example** used when mentioning something that shows the type of thing that you are talking about and helps to explain what you mean: *There are good deals available – people under 25, for example, can get discounts of up to 50%.*

exasperated /ɪgˈzɑːspə,reɪtɪd/ adj extremely annoyed —**exasperate** verb [T]

exasperating /ɪgˈzɑːspə,reɪtɪŋ/ adj making you feel extremely annoyed

excavate /ˈekskəveɪt/ verb [I/T] **1** to dig in the ground in order to find things from the past **2** CONSTRUCTION to dig a large hole in the ground —**excavation** /,ekskəˈveɪʃ(ə)n/ noun [C/U]

excavator /ˈekskə,veɪtə/ noun [C] CONSTRUCTION a large machine for digging holes in the ground

exceed /ɪkˈsiːd/ verb [T] *formal* **1** to be greater than a number or amount: *a claim exceeding £500* **2** to go above an official limit: *drivers who exceed the speed limit*

exceedingly /ɪkˈsiːdɪŋli/ adv *formal* extremely

excel /ɪkˈsel/ (**excels, excelling, excelled**) verb [I] to do something extremely well
PHRASE **excel yourself** to do something much better than you usually do

excellence /ˈeksələns/ noun [U] the quality of being extremely good: *academic excellence*

excellent /ˈeksələnt/ adj extremely good: *The food was absolutely excellent.* ♦ *It's quite an old bike, but it's **in excellent condition**.* —**excellently** adv

except /ɪkˈsept/ conjunction, preposition used for introducing the only thing, person, or fact that is not included in your main statement: *All the team were there except Eddie.* ♦ *He's done nothing all day except watch television.* ♦ *She was dressed all in black **except for** a white scarf.* ♦ *He's never relaxed, **except when** he's asleep.*

excepting /ɪkˈseptɪŋ/ preposition *formal* used for saying that you are not including a particular person or thing in what you are saying

exception /ɪkˈsepʃ(ə)n/ noun [C/U] someone or something that is different and cannot be included in a general statement: *There are some exceptions to every grammatical rule.* ♦ *The boat race always attracts a large crowd and this year **is no exception**.* ♦ ***With the exception of** the Metropole, all the hotels have their own restaurants.*
PHRASE **make an exception** to deal with something in a different way on one particular occasion only: *I don't usually lend people money, but in your case I'll make an exception.*

exceptional /ɪkˈsepʃ(ə)nəl/ adj **1** extremely good or impressive in a way that is unusual: *Her scores were quite exceptional.* **2** much more or greater than usual: *the exceptional difficulty of this task* **3** unusual and not likely to happen or exist very often= EXTREME: *exceptional circumstances* —**exceptionally** adv

excess¹ /ɪkˈses/ noun **1** [singular/U] a larger amount of something than is usual or necessary: *Tests revealed **an excess of** alcohol in the driver's blood.* **2 excesses** [plural] behaviour that is thought to be wrong because it is too extreme: *the worst excesses of the regime* **3** [singular] BUSINESS an amount of money that someone making an insurance claim has to pay, when the insurance company is going to pay the rest of the cost of the claim

PHRASE **in excess of sth** more than a particular amount

excess² /'ekses/ adj **1** more than is usual or necessary: *Drain off any excess liquid.* **2** an excess amount of money is an extra amount that someone must pay

‚excess 'baggage noun [U] **TOURISM** bags that weigh more than the official limit that each person is allowed to take on a plane without paying

‚excess 'fare noun [C] **TOURISM** an extra amount of money to pay, such as for travelling **first-class** with a **second-class** ticket

excessive /ɪk'sesɪv/ adj much more than is reasonable or necessary —**excessively** adv

exchange¹ /ɪks'tʃeɪndʒ/ noun **1** [C/U] a situation in which one person gives, does, or says something and another person gives, does, or says something in return: *a frank **exchange of** views* ♦ *an exchange of prisoners of war* ♦ *Russia supplied crude oil to Cuba in exchange for raw sugar.* **2** [U] the process of changing the money of one country for the money of another country: *What is **the rate of exchange** for US dollars?* ♦ *a foreign exchange dealer* → FOREIGN EXCHANGE **3** [C] an arrangement in which people or groups from different countries visit each other: *an educational exchange* ♦ *an **exchange student** from Spain* → STOCK EXCHANGE

exchange² /ɪks'tʃeɪndʒ/ verb [T] **1** to give someone something in return for something that they give you: *We exchanged addresses and promised to write to one another.* ♦ *The tokens can be **exchanged for** goods in any of our shops.* **2** to change the money of one country for the money of another country **3** to say or do something to someone who says or does something to you: *We exchanged greetings.*

ex'change ‚rate noun [C] **ECONOMICS** the value of the money of one country when people change it for the money of another country

excise /'eksaɪz/ noun [U] **ECONOMICS** a government tax on services used and goods sold within a country

excite /ɪk'saɪt/ verb [T] **1** to make someone feel very happy and enthusiastic about something good that is going to happen: *The idea of working in Australia really excites me.* **2** to make someone feel lively, nervous, or upset: *We were warned by the doctors not to excite him.* **3** to make someone feel that they want to have sex

excited /ɪk'saɪtɪd/ adj **1** very happy and enthusiastic because something good is going to happen: *I was so excited I couldn't sleep.* ♦ *I'm so **excited about** the trip!* ♦ *He's **excited at** the prospect of showing his work in New York.* **2** upset, worried, or angry about something: *Look, Dad, stop getting so excited – I'm sure she'll be home soon.* **3** someone who is excited feels that they want to have sex —**excitedly** adv: *He talked excitedly about his plans.*

- **Excited** describes how you feel: *I'm excited about my holiday.* ♦ *She didn't seem very excited.*
- **Exciting** describes things or situations that make you feel excited: *I find circuses very exciting.* ♦ *It was such an exciting adventure.*

excitement /ɪk'saɪtmənt/ noun [U] the feeling of being excited: *The long wait only added to our excitement.* ♦ *the **excitement of** winning a major championship*

exciting /ɪk'saɪtɪŋ/ adj **1** making you feel excited and enthusiastic ≠ UNEXCITING: *an exciting opportunity* **2** interesting and full of action ≠ BORING: *an exciting story of adventure* —**excitingly** adv

exclaim /ɪk'skleɪm/ verb [I/T] to say something suddenly and loudly because you are surprised or angry

exclamation /‚eksklə'meɪʃ(ə)n/ noun [C] something that you say because you are surprised or angry

excla'mation ‚mark noun [C] **LANGUAGE** the mark ! used in writing to show that someone says something suddenly and loudly because they are surprised or angry

exclude /ɪk'sklu:d/ verb [T] **1** to deliberately not include something ≠ INCLUDE: *These figures exclude administration costs.* **2** to deliberately prevent someone or something from being part of something or from entering a place ≠ INCLUDE: *I felt as though the other women were excluding me.* ♦ *The committee has decided to **exclude** him **from** the competition.* **3** to decide that something is not possible or not worth considering: *We cannot **exclude the possibility** that the patient has cancer.* **4** **EDUCATION** to officially tell a child to leave a school because their behaviour is very bad

excluding /ɪk'sklu:dɪŋ/ preposition not including: *The cost of hiring equipment, excluding insurance, is around £600 a year.*

exclusion /ɪk'sklu:ʒ(ə)n/ noun **1** [U] a situation in which someone or something is deliberately prevented from being part of something or from entering a place ≠ INCLUSION: *the team's **exclusion from** the competition* **2** [C/U] **EDUCATION** a situation in which a child is told to leave a school because their behaviour is very bad

PHRASE **to the exclusion of sth** when you do something to the exclusion of other things, you only do that one thing and not the other things

ex'clusion ‚order noun [C] **LAW** an official order by a court that tells someone not to go to a particular place

exclusive /ɪk'sklu:sɪv/ adj **1** very expensive and available only to people who have a lot of money: *an exclusive neighbourhood* **2** limited to a particular person or group and not shared with others: *The road is for the exclusive use of residents.* **3** published or reported by only one newspaper, magazine, or television station: *an exclusive interview*

PHRASE **exclusive of sth** not including something: *The cost is £20 exclusive of delivery charges.*

exclusively /ɪk'sklu:sɪvli/ adv only, or limited to: *a club exclusively for women*

excrement /'ekskrɪmənt/ noun [U] **BIOLOGY** the solid waste that the body gets rid of= FAECES

excreta /ɪk'skri:tə/ noun [plural] **BIOLOGY** the liquid and solid waste that the body gets rid of

excrete /ɪk'skri:t/ verb [I/T] **BIOLOGY** to get rid of waste produced in the body during **metabolism**

excretion /ɪk'skri:ʃ(ə)n/ noun [U] **BIOLOGY** the process by which the body gets rid of waste products. Excretion includes the process of getting rid of carbon dioxide from the lungs, sweat from the **sweat glands**, and **urea** from the body in urine. → EGESTION

excretory /ɪk'skri:təri/ adj **BIOLOGY** relating to excretion

ex'cretory ‚organ noun [C] **BIOLOGY** one of the organs in the body that remove waste products not needed by the body. The lungs, the skin, and the kidneys are the three main excretory organs.

excruciating /ɪk'skru:ʃieɪtɪŋ/ adj causing extreme physical pain —**excruciatingly** adv

excursion /ɪk'skɜ:ʃ(ə)n/ noun [C] a short journey that someone makes for pleasure

ex'cursion ,fare noun [C] TOURISM a special cheap fare offered on particular journeys

excursionist /ɪkˈskɜːʃ(ə)nɪst/ noun [C] TOURISM someone who goes on an excursion

excuse[1] /ɪkˈskjuːs/ noun [C] **1** a reason that you give to explain why you have done something bad, or why you have not done something that you should have done: *a reasonable excuse* ♦ *He made some excuse about having a lot of work to do.* ♦ *What excuse did they give for the delay?* **2** a reason for doing something that you want to do: *Birthdays are always a good excuse for a party.* ♦ *Emily was glad of an excuse to change the subject.*

excuse[2] /ɪkˈskjuːz/ verb [T] **1** to forgive someone for something: *Please excuse my untidy handwriting.* ♦ *I hope you'll excuse us for leaving so early.* **2** to provide a reason or explanation for something bad that someone has done, in order to make it seem less bad: *I know he's unhappy, but that doesn't excuse his rudeness.* **3** to give someone permission not to do something that they usually have to do: *You're excused from doing the washing-up tonight.* **4** to give someone permission to leave: *Now if you'll excuse us, we have to get going.*

PHRASE **excuse me** *spoken* **1** used for politely getting someone's attention, or for showing that you are sorry for interrupting or touching them: *Excuse me, do you know what time it is?* **2** used for politely asking someone to move so that you can get past them **3** used for politely telling someone that you are leaving: *Excuse me for a moment – I have to make a phone call.*

exe abbrev COMPUTING executable file: the last part of the name of a program file

executable /ˈeksɪˌkjuːtəb(ə)l/ adj COMPUTING an executable program or file can be used on a computer

execute /ˈeksɪˌkjuːt/ verb [T] **1** to kill someone as a punishment for a crime: *The prisoner is due to be executed next week.* **2** *formal* to complete something that you have agreed or planned to do: *They were able to execute their task successfully.* **3** LAW to make certain that the instructions in someone's **will** are followed after they die **4** COMPUTING to make a computer use a program or carry out an instruction

execution /ˌeksɪˈkjuːʃ(ə)n/ noun **1** [C/U] the act of killing someone as a punishment for a crime **2** [U] *formal* the act of completing something that you have agreed or planned to do

executive[1] /ɪɡˈzekjʊtɪv/ noun **1** [C] a senior manager in a business or other organization: *a meeting with some of the company's top executives* **2** [C] a group of people who are responsible for making important decisions in an organization: *This matter will be decided by the party's national executive.* **3 the executive** LAW the part of government that makes certain that laws are being applied as planned. The other two parts of government are the **legislature** and the **judiciary**.

executive[2] /ɪɡˈzekjʊtɪv/ adj **1** involved in making important decisions in an organization or government: *the executive director of the museum* ♦ *executive powers* **2** designed for rich or important people: *an executive jet*

ex,ecutive di'rector noun [C] BUSINESS a director of a company who is employed by the company in a senior management position

ex'ecutive ,lounge noun [C] TOURISM a room at an airport or hotel with comfortable chairs, free drinks etc for people who are travelling **first class** or **business class**

ex,ecutive 'officer noun [C] BUSINESS a person in a senior management position in an organization

executor /ɪɡˈzekjʊtə/ noun [C] LAW someone who arranges for the instructions of a dead person's **will** to be followed

exemplar /ɪɡˈzemplɑː/ noun [C] *formal* a perfect or typical example of something

exemplary /ɪɡˈzempləri/ adj *formal* excellent, or done in a way that other people should try to copy

exemplify /ɪɡˈzemplɪfaɪ/ (**exemplifies, exemplifying, exemplified**) verb [T] to be a typical example of something

exempt[1] /ɪɡˈzempt/ adj allowed to ignore something such as a rule, obligation, or payment

exempt[2] /ɪɡˈzempt/ verb [T] to allow someone to ignore something such as a rule, obligation, or payment —**exemption** /ɪɡˈzempʃ(ə)n/ noun [C/U]

exercise[1] /ˈeksəsaɪz/ noun

1 physical activity	4 for particular purpose
2 learning activity	5 use of power etc
3 written questions	

1 [U] physical activity or a particular physical activity that someone does in order to stay healthy and make their body stronger: *exercises such as press-ups and curl-ups* ♦ *breathing exercises* ♦ *I try to get plenty of exercise.* ♦ *You should take more exercise.* ♦ *I try to do a few exercises every day.*
2 [C] an activity or set of activities that you do in order to learn or practise a skill: *a drawing exercise* ♦ *piano exercises* ♦ *I'd like you to do the exercises on page 10.*
3 [C] a set of written questions that you answer in order to help you to learn something: *Next I'd like you to do the exercises on page 10.*
4 [singular] *formal* an action that has a particular plan, purpose, or result: *a cost-cutting exercise* ♦ *Good management is often an exercise in compromise.*
5 [U] *formal* the use of your power, rights, or skills: *General de Gaulle's military training influenced his exercise of power.*

exercise[2] /ˈeksəsaɪz/ verb **1** [I/T] to do a physical activity in order to stay healthy and to make your body stronger: *Do you eat properly and exercise regularly?* ♦ *The doctor said I should exercise my knee every morning.* **2** [T] *formal* to use power, skill, or a personal quality: *For centuries, the Catholic Church exercised authority over people's lives.*

exert /ɪɡˈzɜːt/ verb [T] *formal* to use influence, authority, or strength in order to affect or achieve something

exertion /ɪɡˈzɜːʃ(ə)n/ noun [C/U] great physical or mental effort

exhale /eksˈheɪl/ verb [I/T] BIOLOGY to breathe air out through the mouth or nose ≠ INHALE —**exhalation** /ˌekshəˈleɪʃ(ə)n/ noun [C/U]

exhaust[1] /ɪɡˈzɔːst/ verb [T] **1** to make someone feel extremely tired and without energy: *Caring for young children can exhaust you physically and mentally.* **2** to use all that you have of something: *The expedition was forced to turn back when it exhausted its food supply.*

exhaust[2] /ɪɡˈzɔːst/ noun **1** [C] an exhaust pipe **2** [U] gases or steam that are produced by an engine as it works

exhausted /ɪɡˈzɔːstɪd/ adj **1** extremely tired and without enough energy to do anything else: *After two days of travel the children were completely exhausted.* **2** completely used

exhausting /ɪɡˈzɔːstɪŋ/ adj extremely tiring

exhaustion /ɪɡˈzɔːstʃ(ə)n/ noun [U] a feeling of being extremely tired and without energy

exhaustive /ɪɡˈzɔːstɪv/ adj thorough, or complete: *The list is by no means exhaustive.*

exhaust manifold /ɪɡˈzɔːst ˌmænɪfəʊld/ noun [C] ENGINEERING a set of tubes through which gases pass into and out of a vehicle's engine

exˈhaust ˌpipe noun [C] a pipe that carries the gases or steam out of an engine

exhaust silencer /ɪɡˈzɔːst ˌsaɪlənsə/ noun [C] ENGINEERING a piece of equipment that reduces the noise made by a vehicle's **exhaust**

ˈexhaust ˌstroke noun [C] ENGINEERING the last of four movements of the **piston** in an **internal-combustion engine** in which the gases that are left in a cylinder are removed

exhibit¹ /ɪɡˈzɪbɪt/ verb **1** [I/T] ARTS to put something interesting in a public place so that people can go and look at it: *His work will be exhibited in Moscow later this year.* **2** [T] *formal* to show a particular feeling, quality, ability, or type of behaviour: *She was **exhibiting symptoms** of stress.*

exhibit² /ɪɡˈzɪbɪt/ noun [C] **1** ARTS an object that is part of an exhibition **2** LAW an object or document that is used as evidence in a court of law

exhibition /ˌeksɪˈbɪʃ(ə)n/ noun [C] **1** ARTS a public show where art or other interesting things are put so that people can go and look at them: *an **exhibition** of paintings by Henri Matisse* ♦ *an exhibition hall* **2** a particular way of behaving or performing= DISPLAY: *a fine **exhibition of** skilful and exciting football*

exhilarating /ɪɡˈzɪləˌreɪtɪŋ/ adj making you feel extremely happy, excited, and full of energy

exile¹ /ˈeksaɪl/ noun **1** [U] a situation in which someone is forced to live in a foreign country, usually for political reasons: *He died in exile in 1986.* **2** [C] someone who has been forced to live in a foreign country

exile² /ˈeksaɪl/ verb [T] to force someone to live in a foreign country, usually for political reasons

exist /ɪɡˈzɪst/ verb [I] **1** to be present in a particular place, time, or situation: *Several exciting career opportunities exist in our company.* ♦ *The company officially **ceased to exist** at midnight on March 31st.* **2** to be real, not imaginary: *Dragons don't exist.* **3** to manage to live, especially when conditions are difficult = SURVIVE: *You can't exist for long without water.*

existence /ɪɡˈzɪst(ə)ns/ noun **1** [U] the state of being a real or living thing, or of being present in a particular place, time, or situation: *The tests confirm **the existence of** a brain tumour.* ♦ *the only copy of the book that is still **in existence*** ♦ *The company **came into existence** at the end of the 1980s.* **2** [C] the way that someone lives their life: *Jones **led** a miserable **existence** in an isolated village.*

existing /ɪɡˈzɪstɪŋ/ adj used for describing something that exists now, especially when it might soon be changed or replaced: *The existing system needs to be changed.*

exit¹ /ˈeksɪt/ noun [C] **1** a door that leads out of a public place such as a room or building ≠ ENTRANCE: *Passengers should leave the plane by the nearest **emergency exit**.* **2** a minor road that people use to drive off a motorway: *Take the next exit going north.* **3** the act of leaving a place: *They **made a** hasty **exit** through the back door.*

exit² /ˈeksɪt/ verb [I/T] **1** *formal* to leave a place **2** COMPUTING to stop using a computer program

ˈexit-ˌlevel adj EDUCATION at the level of students who are leaving school

exocrine gland /ˈeksəkraɪn ˌɡlænd/ noun [C] ANATOMY a gland such as a **sweat gland** or **lymph gland** that contains tubes and produces enzymes that are not released into the bloodstream

exodus /ˈeksədəs/ noun [singular] a situation in which a lot of people leave a place at the same time: *There is a **mass exodus** from the city every Friday.*

exonerate /ɪɡˈzɒnəreɪt/ verb [T] *formal* to officially say that someone is not to blame for something

exorbitant /ɪɡˈzɔːbɪt(ə)nt/ adj an exorbitant price or amount of money is much more than is reasonable

exorcize /ˈeksɔːsaɪz/ verb [T] RELIGION to get rid of an evil spirit using prayers or a special religious ceremony —**exorcism** noun [C/U], **exorcist** noun [C]

exoskeleton /ˈeksəʊˌskelɪt(ə)n/ noun [C] BIOLOGY a hard covering on the outside of organisms such as crustaceans, insects, and **turtles**, that provides support and protection → ENDOSKELETON

the exosphere /ˈeksəʊˌsfɪə/ noun [singular] SCIENCE the outer layer of the Earth's atmosphere, which starts about 500 to 1,000 kilometres above the Earth's surface —*picture* → ATMOSPHERE

exothermic /ˌeksəʊˈθɜːmɪk/ adj CHEMISTRY, PHYSICS an exothermic reaction is a chemical reaction in which heat is produced, not absorbed → ENDOTHERMIC

exotic /ɪɡˈzɒtɪk/ adj interesting or exciting because of being unusual or not familiar

expand /ɪkˈspænd/ verb **1** [I/T] to become larger, or to make something larger: *The population is expanding rapidly.* ♦ *There are plans to expand the national park.* **2** [I/T] if a business or service expands, or if someone expands it, it grows by including more people and moving into new areas: *We are expanding the programme to provide more student places.* **3** [T] MATHS to write a mathematical expression in a longer form

PHRASAL VERB **exˈpand on sth** to talk or write more about something, adding more details or information: *The interviewer asked him to expand on his earlier statement.*

expanse /ɪkˈspæns/ noun [C] a large area of land, water, or sky

expansion /ɪkˈspænʃ(ə)n/ noun **1** [U] an increase in size ≠ CONTRACTION **2** [U] the process of developing to include more people, places, or things **3** [C/U] MATHS in mathematics, an expression written in a longer form **4** [U] CHEMISTRY, PHYSICS an increase in the size of something that is caused by an increase in temperature or a reduction in the pressure on it

exˈpansion ˌcard noun [C] COMPUTING a **circuit board** that makes a computer more powerful or able to do more things

exˈpansion ˌslot noun [C] COMPUTING a place on a computer where you can connect another piece of equipment to it and make it more powerful

expansive /ɪkˈspænsɪv/ adj friendly, generous, or willing to talk

expansivity /ˌɪkspænˈsɪvɪti/ noun [U] PHYSICS the extent to which a solid or liquid **expands** or contracts in different temperatures

expatriate /eksˈpætriət/ noun [C] someone who lives in a foreign country —**expatriate** adj

expect /ɪk'spekt/ verb [T] **1** to think that something will happen: *We're expecting good weather at the weekend.* ♦ *I didn't really **expect** you **to** understand.* ♦ *Investors expect that interest rates will rise.* ♦ *As expected, the party was a great success.* **2** to be waiting for someone or something to arrive: *Are you expecting a parcel?* ♦ *What time do you **expect** Sara **home**?* **3** to think that it is right or reasonable that something should happen: *Our customers expect good service.* ♦ *I **expect to** get paid on time.* ♦ *It's not fair to **expect** me **to** do all the housework.*

PHRASE **be expecting (a baby)** to be pregnant

Word family: expect

Words in the same family as expect
- **expected** *adj*
- **expectation** *n*
- **expectant** *adj*
- **expectantly** *adv*
- **unexpected** *adj*
- **unexpectedly** *adv*
- **expectancy** *n*

expectant /ɪk'spektənt/ adj **1** feeling excited about something that you think is going to happen **2** an expectant mother or father will soon be a parent of a new baby —**expectancy** noun [U], **expectantly** adv

expectation /ˌekspek'teɪʃ(ə)n/ noun **1** [C] a belief or hope that something will be good, or that someone will do well: *We have **high expectations** of our students* (=expect them to succeed). ♦ *We had heard so much about the restaurant, but it did not **live up to** our expectations* (=was not as good as we expected). **2** [C/U] the belief that something will happen: *The team set off without any **expectation of** success.*

expected /ɪk'spektɪd/ adj likely to happen or be true: *Events did not follow their expected course.*

expectorant /ɪk'spektərənt/ noun [C] HEALTH a medicine used for helping someone to cough liquid up from the lungs

expediency /ɪk'spiːdiənsi/ (plural **expediencies**) noun [C/U] *formal* a way of dealing with something that produces the result that you want in a particular situation, especially when this is not the best or most honest thing to do

expedition /ˌekspə'dɪʃ(ə)n/ noun [C] **1** a long journey to a dangerous or distant place **2** a short journey for pleasure

expel /ɪk'spel/ (**expels, expelling, expelled**) verb [T] **1** to officially force someone to leave a place, organization, or school, for example because of their bad behaviour **2** *formal* to force something out of a container or out of the body

expend /ɪk'spend/ verb [T] *formal* to spend time, energy, or money on something

expendable /ɪk'spendəb(ə)l/ adj no longer useful or necessary

expenditure /ɪk'spendɪtʃə/ noun [C/U] **1** the amount of money that is spent by a government, organization, or person= SPENDING **2** [U] *formal* the use of time, money, or energy to do something

expense /ɪk'spens/ noun **1** [C] an amount of money that someone spends in order to buy or do something: *medical expenses* ♦ *Rent is our biggest expense.* **2** [U] the high cost of something: *A powerful computer is worth the expense if you use it regularly.* ♦ *Previously, the chemical had to be imported **at great expense**.* **3 expenses** [plural] money that someone spends as part of their job that their employer pays back later: *Your salary will be £20,000 a year, **plus expenses**.*

PHRASES **at sb's expense 1** used for saying who pays for something: *He did a six-month training course at his own expense.* **2** if someone has a joke at your expense, you are the person that the joke is about

at the expense of sth if one thing exists or happens at the expense of another, the second thing suffers because of the first

expensive /ɪk'spensɪv/ adj **1** something that is expensive costs a lot of money= DEAR ≠ INEXPENSIVE: *He always wears expensive clothes.* ♦ *It can be very expensive to train new personnel.* **2** an expensive mistake or decision is one that causes serious problems= COSTLY —**expensively** adv

experience¹ /ɪk'spɪəriəns/ noun **1** [U] knowledge and skill that someone gets by doing a particular job or activity: *You don't need any experience to work here.* ♦ *teaching experience* ♦ *Do you have any previous **experience with** children?* ♦ *She **has** years of **experience** in manufacturing.* **2** [U] the knowledge that someone gets from life and from being in different situations: *I can say **from personal experience** that it's hard not having a job.* ♦ *Helen knew **from past experience** that there was no point in arguing with him.* **3** [C] something that happens to you, or a situation that you are involved in: *our childhood experiences* ♦ *I had **a bad experience** in my last school.*

experience² /ɪk'spɪəriəns/ verb [T] **1** if you experience a problem or situation, you have that problem or are in that situation: *Almost every country in the industrial world is experiencing economic problems.* ♦ *How can we end the discrimination experienced by older people?* **2** to feel an emotion or a physical feeling: *Are you experiencing any pain?*

experienced /ɪk'spɪəriənst/ adj someone who is experienced has skill at something because they have done it a lot ≠ INEXPERIENCED: *I'm a lot more experienced than him.* ♦ *an experienced sailor* ♦ *She's **experienced in** dealing with difficult customers.*

experiential /ɪkˌspɪəri'enʃ(ə)l/ adj *very formal* relating to or based on experience

experiment¹ /ɪk'sperɪmənt/ noun [C] **1** SCIENCE a scientific test to find out what happens to someone or something in particular conditions: *laboratory experiments* ♦ *a series of **experiments on** volunteers* ♦ *Researchers now need to **conduct** further experiments.* **2** an occasion when someone tests a new idea, method, or activity in order to find out what the result will be: *an experiment in tax reform*

experiment² /ɪk'sperɪˌment/ verb [I] **1** to try new ideas, methods, or activities in order to find out what results they will have: *a designer who is not afraid to experiment* **2** SCIENCE to perform scientific tests in order to find out what happens to someone or something in particular conditions: *This lab does not experiment on animals.*

experimental /ɪkˌsperɪ'ment(ə)l/ adj **1** using new ideas or methods that no one has tried before **2** SCIENCE relating to scientific experiments —**experimentally** adv

experimentation /ɪkˌsperɪmen'teɪʃ(ə)n/ noun [U] the process of testing ideas, methods, or activities to see what effect they have

expert¹ /'ekspɜːt/ noun [C] someone who has a particular skill or knows a lot about a particular subject: *an educational expert* ♦ *an **expert in** radio communications*

expert² /'ekspɜːt/ adj having special skills in or knowledge about something —**expertly** adv

expertise /ˌekspə'tiːz/ noun [U] special skill or knowledge that someone gets from experience, training, or study

expert 'system noun [C] COMPUTING computer software that uses a process similar to the way humans think, in order to provide people with solutions to problems relating to a particular subject

expert 'witness noun [C] LAW an expert in a particular subject who is asked to give a court of law their opinion about the technical details of a case

expire /ɪkˈspaɪə/ verb [I] if an agreement, offer, or official document expires, the period of time during which it can be used comes to an end= RUN OUT

expiry /ɪkˈspaɪəri/ noun [U] the end of a period of time during which an agreement, offer, or official document can be used

ex'piry ,date noun [C] the date after which something can no longer be used, or after which food is no longer safe to eat

explain /ɪkˈspleɪn/ verb **1** [T] to tell someone something in a way that helps them to understand it better: *The doctor explained the risks to me before the operation.* ♦ *I will try to **explain how** a car engine works.* ♦ *He explained that he would be moving to another city.* **2** [I/T] to give a reason for something that happens: *Science cannot explain everything.* ♦ *'Tom is in hospital.' 'That **explains why** he wasn't in school today.'* ♦ *Wait! Let me explain!*

> Word family: **explain**
>
> *Words in the same family as explain*
> - **explanation** *n*
> - **explanatory** *adj*
> - **unexplained** *adj*
> - **inexplicable** *adj*
> - **inexplicably** *adv*

explanation /ˌekspləˈneɪʃ(ə)n/ noun [C/U] **1** a reason that you give for something that has happened or something that you have done: *I expected an explanation and an apology.* ♦ ***The explanation for** this is simple.* ♦ *He gave **a detailed explanation of** the events leading up to the accident.* **2** a description of how something works or of how to do something: *This book provides a clear **explanation of** how to use the Internet.*

explanatory /ɪkˈsplænət(ə)ri/ adj intended to help you to understand something

explicit /ɪkˈsplɪsɪt/ adj **1** extremely clear ≠ IMPLICIT **2** showing or describing sex or violence in a lot of detail —**explicitly** adv

explode /ɪkˈspləʊd/ verb **1** [I/T] to burst with a lot of force and a loud noise, or to make something do this, usually in a way that causes a lot of damage: *Bombs were exploding all over the city.* ♦ *France first exploded a nuclear device in 1960.* **2** [I] to suddenly express a strong emotion, especially anger: *She suddenly **exploded with** rage, and stormed off.* **3** [I] to increase a lot over a very short period of time: *The city's population is exploding.*

exploded drawing /ɪkˌspləʊdɪd ˈdrɔːɪŋ/ noun [C/U] MATHS, PHYSICS a drawing that shows the parts of something separately, but in a way that makes clear how they are connected or put together

exploit¹ /ɪkˈsplɔɪt/ verb [T] **1** to treat someone unfairly in order to get some benefit for yourself: *Children are being exploited in many of these factories.* **2** to use a fact or situation in order to get an advantage, even if it is wrong or unfair to do this: *A lot of advertisements just exploit our insecurities.* **3** to make the best use of something so that you get as much as possible from it: *They're just beginning to **exploit** the country's natural resources.* —**exploitation** /ˌeksplɔɪˈteɪʃ(ə)n/ noun [U], **exploitative** adj

exploit² /ˈeksplɔɪt/ noun [C] something unusual that someone does that you think is brave, exciting, or entertaining

exploration /ˌekspləˈreɪʃ(ə)n/ noun [C/U] **1** a journey around an area in order to learn about it or in order to search for something valuable such as oil **2** a thorough examination or discussion of something

exploratory /ɪkˈsplɒrət(ə)ri/ adj done in order to learn more about something

explore /ɪkˈsplɔː/ verb **1** [I/T] to travel around an area in order to learn about it, or in order to search for something valuable such as oil: *The town is a good base from which to explore this part of Italy.* **2** [T] to examine or discuss something in order to see if it is possible or is worth doing: *We are **exploring the possibility** of taking legal action against the company.*

explorer /ɪkˈsplɔːrə/ noun [C] someone who travels around a place that other people do not know much about in order to find out what is there

explosion /ɪkˈspləʊʒ(ə)n/ noun [C] **1** an occasion when something such as a bomb explodes: *a gas explosion* ♦ *The explosion could be heard for miles around.* **2** a very large increase in something over a very short period of time: *a **population explosion*** **3** a sudden expression of a strong emotion, especially anger

explosive¹ /ɪkˈspləʊsɪv/ adj **1** SCIENCE used for causing an explosion or capable of exploding: *This gas is highly explosive.* **2** likely to become violent or very difficult: *an explosive issue* **3** increasing quickly: *the explosive growth in street crime*

explosive² /ɪkˈspləʊsɪv/ noun [C/U] SCIENCE a substance or object that can cause an explosion

exponent /ɪkˈspəʊnənt/ noun [C] **1** *formal* someone who tries to persuade other people to support an idea, theory, policy etc: *a leading **exponent** of free trade* **2** MATHS a small number or letter written above and to the right of another number. It shows how many times you should multiply that number by itself.

exponential /ˌekspəˈnenʃ(ə)l/ adj **1** increasing or growing very fast **2** MATHS showing how many times a number should be multiplied by itself —**exponentially** adv

export¹ /ˈekspɔːt/ noun **1** [C] ECONOMICS, BUSINESS a product that is sold to another country ≠ IMPORT: *Agricultural produce is the country's largest export.* ♦ *There has been a rapid increase in oil **exports to** the West.* **2** [U] ECONOMICS, SOCIAL STUDIES the business or process of selling goods to other countries ≠ IMPORT: *They are now manufacturing more goods for export.*

export² /ɪkˈspɔːt/ verb **1** [I/T] ECONOMICS, BUSINESS to send a product to another country so that it can be sold there ≠ IMPORT: *Their flowers are exported around the world.* ♦ *Weapons are being illegally **exported to** other countries.* **2** [T] COMPUTING to copy information from one part of a computer to another part, or to copy it to a place where it can be stored ≠ IMPORT **3** [T] to introduce an idea, tradition, or activity into another country ≠ IMPORT: *Blues music was exported throughout the Western world.* —**exporter** noun [C], **exportation** /ˌekspɔːˈteɪʃ(ə)n/ noun [U]

expose /ɪkˈspəʊz/ verb [T] **1** to remove something that is covering something else so that it is no longer hidden or protected: *The snow had melted and exposed the rock underneath.* **2** to put someone or something into a particular situation or give them a particular experience, especially one that involves danger or risk: *Many of the soldiers had been **exposed to** radiation.* ♦ *The children are **exposed to** the world of work at an early age.* **3** to tell the public about something shocking or illegal that was previously not known **4** to allow light to reach the film in a camera so that a photograph can be taken

exposed /ɪkˈspəʊzd/ adj **1** not covered or hidden **2** not protected from attack or from the bad effects of something

exposition /ˌekspəˈzɪʃ(ə)n/ noun **1** [C/U] formal a detailed explanation of something such as an idea or process, or the action of giving such an explanation **2** [C] a public event or show of industrial products or technology= EXHIBITION

expository /ekˈzˈpɒzɪtəri/ adj formal intended to explain or describe something

exposure /ɪkˈspəʊzə/ noun

1 being in danger	4 being out in cold
2 telling public sth	5 single photograph
3 experience of sth	

1 [C/U] the state of not being protected from something harmful: *exposure to the sun*
2 [C/U] the act of making something publicly known, for example on television or in newspapers, or the situation in which this happens: *the exposure of corruption within the government* ♦ *The affair got a good deal of exposure in the press.*
3 [C/U] the act of giving someone a particular experience: *Children who have exposure to books in their early years are likely to read earlier.*
4 [U] the harmful effect of very cold weather on your body: *Two of the climbers died of exposure.*
5 [C] the amount of film that is used for taking one photograph

expound /ɪkˈspaʊnd/ verb [I/T] formal to explain something or to express an opinion about it in detail

express¹ /ɪkˈspres/ verb [T] **1** to say in speech or writing what your opinion is or what your feelings are about something: *His teachers expressed concern about his progress at school.* ♦ *The government has expressed an interest in the scheme.* **2** to show your feelings in the way that you look or behave: *Her eyes expressed total shock.* **3** MATHS to show a mathematical quantity or problem in a particular way: *Dalton's Law can be expressed mathematically.* ♦ *A ratio can be expressed as a percentage.*

PHRASE **express yourself 1** to talk in a way that other people can understand: *She finds it difficult to express herself in English.* **2** to show your feelings in a particular way

express² /ɪkˈspres/ adj **1** much faster than the usual service: *an express train* ♦ *express delivery* **2** formal said in a clear way so that people understand what you mean or want= EXPLICIT

express³ /ɪkˈspres/ noun **1** [C] a fast train or bus **2** [U] a service that delivers letters or parcels more quickly than the ordinary service

expression /ɪkˈspreʃən/ noun **1** [C] a look on someone's face that shows what their thoughts or feelings are: *She had a puzzled expression on her face.* ♦ *I noticed his expression of disgust.* **2** [C] a word or phrase: *He uses childish expressions like 'easy-peasy'.* **3** [C/U] the act of showing what your thoughts or feelings are **4** [C] MATHS in mathematics, a group of signs and numbers that show a particular quantity or idea: *algebraic expressions*

expressionism /ɪkˈspreʃənˌɪz(ə)m/ noun [U] ARTS a style in art, literature, or music in which the artist emphasizes emotions and reactions to things rather than objects as they really appear —**expressionist** adj, noun [C]

expressive /ɪkˈspresɪv/ adj clearly showing your thoughts or feelings: *She has wonderfully expressive features.* —**expressively** adv, **expressiveness** noun [U]

expressly /ɪkˈspresli/ adv formal in a way that is clear and definite: *Smoking is expressly forbidden.*

expulsion /ɪkˈspʌlʃ(ə)n/ noun [C/U] an occasion when someone is officially forced to leave an organization, institution, or country

exquisite /ɪkˈskwɪzɪt/ adj extremely beautiful and delicate: *an exquisite hand-painted vase*

ex-ˈserviceman (plural ˌex-ˈservicemen) noun [C] a man who used to be in the armed services

ex-ˈservicewoman (plural ˌex-ˈservicewomen) noun [C] a woman who used to be in the armed services

extend /ɪkˈstend/ verb **1** [T] to increase the size, time, or range of something: *The ground floor could be extended to allow for an extra bedroom.* ♦ *The course has been extended to include the history of art.* ♦ *I asked if I could extend my holiday.* **2** [I] to continue for a particular distance or time: *an area extending from the Baltic coast to the Alps* **3** [I] to include someone or something: *This law extends to children under the age of 14 only.* **4** [T] to stretch out an arm or a leg

extended family /ɪkˌstendɪd ˈfæm(ə)li/ noun [C] SOCIAL STUDIES the family that you belong to, including people such as your grandparents, cousins etc → NUCLEAR FAMILY

extension /ɪkˈstenʃ(ə)n/ noun [C]

1 extra part	4 sth that develops
2 extra time allowed	5 computer file
3 telephone line	

1 an extra part that is added to a building: *We are building an extension on the back of our house.*
2 an extra period of time that is added to the original period: *Brady wants a two-year extension to his contract.* ♦ *Will the bank give you an extension on the loan?*
3 a telephone line that is one of two or more lines in the same building: *I'm on extension 334.*
4 something that develops from something else: *He sees local history as an extension of family history.*
5 COMPUTING a file extension

extensive /ɪkˈstensɪv/ adj **1** very large in amount or degree: *The accident caused extensive damage to both cars.* **2** involving a lot of details and information: *extensive knowledge* **3** spreading over a large area: *The hotel has extensive grounds.* —**extensively** adv: *The book was extensively revised.*

ex,tensive ˈfarming noun [U] AGRICULTURE farming activity that takes place over a large area of land ≠ INTENSIVE FARMING

extensor muscle /ɪkˈstensə ˌmʌs(ə)l/ noun [C] ANATOMY a muscle that is used when **extending** (=stretching out) part of the body

extent /ɪkˈstent/ noun **1** [singular/U] the degree to which something happens, or the degree to which something is affected: *They were shocked at the extent of the damage.* ♦ *Languages vary in the extent to which they rely on word order.* **2** [U] the size or area of something: *Open the table to its fullest extent.*

PHRASES **to a large/great extent** mainly: *The complaints were to a large extent valid.*

to some/a certain/a limited extent partly, but not completely: *To a certain extent, I was relieved.*

exterior¹ /ɪkˈstɪəriə/ noun [C] **1** the outside part of a building ≠ INTERIOR **2** the way that someone seems to be: *Beneath that gruff exterior is a very kind person.*

exterior[2] /ɪkˈstɪəriə/ adj on the outside of something ≠ INTERIOR: *exterior walls*

exterminate /ɪkˈstɜːmɪneɪt/ verb [T] to kill all the insects, animals, or people in a particular area —**extermination** /ɪkˌstɜːmɪˈneɪʃ(ə)n/ noun [C/U]

external /ɪkˈstɜːn(ə)l/ adj **1** on, or relating to, the outside of something ≠ INTERNAL: *an external door* ♦ *Her external appearance was calm and cool.* **2** from outside an organization or country ≠ INTERNAL: *We will need to find external sources of finance.* —**externally** adv

ex,ternal 'ear noun [C] ANATOMY the outside part of the ear

ex,ternal 'force noun [C] PHYSICS a force that is outside an object and that acts on it

extinct /ɪkˈstɪŋkt/ adj **1** if something such as a type of animal or plant is extinct, it no longer exists **2** GEOLOGY an extinct volcano is no longer active and no longer erupts

extinction /ɪkˈstɪŋkʃ(ə)n/ noun [U] a situation in which something such as a type of animal or plant stops existing: *Several species of monkey are in danger of extinction.*

extinguish /ɪkˈstɪŋgwɪʃ/ verb [T] *formal* to make a fire or cigarette stop burning

extinguisher /ɪkˈstɪŋgwɪʃə/ noun [C] a fire extinguisher

extortion /ɪkˈstɔːʃ(ə)n/ noun [U] LAW the crime of getting money or information from someone by using force or threats —**extortionist** noun [C]

extortionate /ɪkˈstɔːʃ(ə)nət/ adj an extortionate price is much higher than it should be

extra[1] /ˈekstrə/ adj in addition to the usual amount: *There's no extra money for emergencies.* ♦ *We need extra space for guests.*

extra[2] /ˈekstrə/ noun [C] **1** something that is added to a basic service, product etc: *A virus checker is available as **an optional extra** for your computer.* **2** ARTS someone who has a very small part in a film

extra[3] /ˈekstrə/ adv **1** more than a particular amount of money: *You have to pay extra for insurance.* **2** very: *Be extra careful when you go out alone at night.*

extract[1] /ɪkˈstrækt/ verb [T] **1** to remove something from something else: *a method of extracting sulphur from copper ore* **2** to get information from someone using force

extract[2] /ˈekstrækt/ noun **1** [C] a short piece of writing that is taken from something such as a book or letter **2** [C/U] a substance that has been taken from a plant or from another substance

extraction /ɪkˈstrækʃ(ə)n/ noun [C/U] the process of taking something from somewhere

extracurricular /ˌekstrəkəˈrɪkjʊlə/ adj EDUCATION extracurricular activities are things that students do at school or college that are not part of their usual classes

extraditable /ˈekstrəˌdaɪtəb(ə)l/ adj LAW someone who is accused of an extraditable crime can be sent back to the country where the crime was committed for a trial

extradite /ˈekstrədaɪt/ verb [T] LAW to send someone accused of a crime back to the country where the crime was committed for a trial

extradition /ˌekstrəˈdɪʃ(ə)n/ noun [C/U] LAW the process of extraditing someone

extrados /ekˈstreɪdɒs/ noun [C] CONSTRUCTION the upper surface of an **arch**

extramural /ˌekstrəˈmjʊərəl/ adj EDUCATION extramural courses are given by a university or college for people who are not its usual students

extranet /ˈekstrənet/ noun [C] COMPUTING a network of websites and email systems that can be used by people who belong to an organization, and by some others outside the organization who have signed an agreement

extraordinary /ɪkˈstrɔːd(ə)n(ə)ri/ adj **1** very unusual and surprising: *It's an extraordinary story.* ♦ *It's extraordinary that no one disagreed with him.* **2** much better or worse than is usual: *The picture does not capture her extraordinary beauty.* —**extraordinarily** /ɪkˌstrɔːd(ə)n'eərəli/ adv

extra,ordinary ,general 'meeting noun [C] BUSINESS an EGM

extrapolate /ɪkˈstræpəleɪt/ verb [I/T] *formal* to say what is likely to happen or be true by using information that you already have —**extrapolation** /ɪkˌstræpəˈleɪʃ(ə)n/ noun [C/U]

extraterrestrial /ˌekstrətəˈrestriəl/ adj existing on planets other than Earth

extraterritorial /ˌekstrəˌterɪˈtɔːriəl/ adj LAW extraterritorial rights allow you to obey your own country's laws rather than the laws of the country where you are living

,extra 'time noun [U] SPORTS a period of time that can be added to the end of a match if both teams have the same score

extravagance /ɪkˈstrævəgəns/ noun **1** [U] the act of spending a lot of money, especially on something that is not really necessary **2** [C] something that you spend a lot of money on, especially something that is not necessary

extravagant /ɪkˈstrævəgənt/ adj **1** spending or costing a lot of money: *an extravagant lifestyle* **2** extreme or unreasonable: *an extravagant claim* —**extravagantly** adv

extreme[1] /ɪkˈstriːm/ adj **1** very great in degree: *extreme poverty* **2** extreme actions or opinions are considered unreasonable by most people: *It seemed a bit extreme to call the police.* ♦ *extreme right-wing views* **3** very unusual = EXCEPTIONAL: *In extreme cases, your membership may be cancelled.* **4** furthest away from the centre of something: *My friend is on the extreme left of the picture.*

extreme[2] /ɪkˈstriːm/ noun [C] a very large or very small degree of something: *extremes of temperature* PHRASE **go to extremes** or **take/carry sth to extremes** to do something much more than is usual or reasonable: *This is political correctness taken to extremes.*

extremely /ɪkˈstriːmli/ adv very: *He knows the area extremely well.* ♦ *It is extremely important to record everything that happens.*

ex'treme ,sport noun [C] SPORTS a sport or activity that is exciting and dangerous

extremist /ɪkˈstriːmɪst/ noun [C] someone who has political or religious beliefs that most people think are unreasonable —**extremism** noun [U], **extremist** adj

extremity /ɪkˈstreməti/ (plural **extremities**) noun *formal* **1** [C] a part of something that is furthest from the main part: *the southern extremity of the island* **2 extremities** [plural] your fingers or toes

extricate /ˈekstrɪkeɪt/ verb [T] *formal* to get yourself or someone else out of a difficult situation or a dangerous place

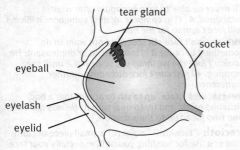

tear gland
socket
eyeball
eyelash
eyelid

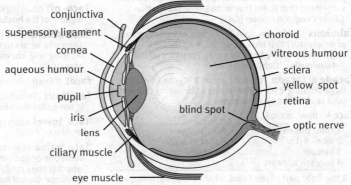

conjunctiva
suspensory ligament
cornea
aqueous humour
pupil
iris
lens
ciliary muscle
eye muscle

choroid
vitreous humour
sclera
yellow spot
retina
blind spot
optic nerve

eye

extrovert /'ekstrə,vɜ:t/ noun [C] someone who is very confident, lively, and likes social situations ≠ INTROVERT —**extroverted** adj

exuberant /ɪg'zju:bərənt/ adj happy, excited, and full of energy —**exuberance** noun [U]

exudation /,eksju'deɪʃ(ə)n/ noun [U] BIOLOGY the slow release of a substance to the surface of an organism through pores or a cut, for example the release of sweat from the body

exude /ɪg'zju:d/ verb formal **1** [T] to clearly have a lot of a particular quality **2** [I/T] if a smell or liquid exudes from something, or if something exudes a smell or liquid, it comes out of it slowly

eye¹ /aɪ/ noun [C] **1** ANATOMY one of the two organs in the face that are used for seeing. Light goes through the **cornea** into the **pupil** and onto the lens. The lens **focuses** the image on the retina. The **optic nerve** carries the image to the brain: *Close your eyes and go to sleep.* ♦ *He has blond hair and blue eyes.* —*picture* → BODY **2** the hole at the top of a needle **3** the calm area at the centre of a storm —*picture* → HURRICANE

PHRASES **have/keep your eye on sb** to watch someone carefully because you think they are going to do something wrong: *I've got my eye on you Sarah. Any more trouble and you're out.*
in sb's eyes according to what someone thinks or feels: *In his mother's eyes, the boy can do no wrong.* → BLIND¹, CATCH¹

eye² /aɪ/ (**eyes, eyeing** or **eying, eyed**) verb [T] to look at someone or something carefully

eyeball /'aɪ,bɔːl/ noun [C] ANATOMY the round ball that forms the eye —*picture* → EYE, SHORT-SIGHTED

eyebrow /'aɪ,braʊ/ noun [C] the line of hair above an eye —*picture* → BODY

PHRASE **raise your eyebrows** to make your eyebrows go higher as a way of showing surprise, or as a way of showing you are asking a question

'eye-,catching adj something that is eye-catching is attractive, impressive, or unusual, so that you notice it very easily

eyelashes /'aɪlæʃɪz/ noun [plural] the hairs along the edges of your eyelids —*picture* → BODY, EYE

eyelid /'aɪ,lɪd/ noun [C] one of the two pieces of skin that cover the eye when it is closed —*picture* → EYE

eyepiece /'aɪ,piːs/ noun [C] SCIENCE the lens or set of lenses in a microscope or telescope that is closest to the eye and that you look through —*picture* → MICROSCOPE

'eye ,shadow noun [U] a type of coloured **make-up** that someone puts on their eyelids

eyesight /'aɪ,saɪt/ noun [U] the ability to see = SIGHT: *Reading in poor light can damage your eyesight.*

'eye ,socket noun [C] ANATOMY one of the two parts of the face that the eyes fit into —*picture* → SKELETON

eyewitness /'aɪ,wɪtnəs/ noun [C] someone who has seen a crime or an accident happen: *Eyewitnesses describe the man as tall with brown hair.*

f /ef/ (plural **f's**) or **F** (plural **F's**) noun [C/U] **1** the sixth letter of the English alphabet **2** F MUSIC the fourth note in the musical scale of C major

F abbrev **1** SCIENCE Fahrenheit **2** false **3** female

f. abbrev MUSIC forte

the FA /ˌef ˈeɪ/ SPORTS the Football Association: the organization that controls professional football in England and Wales

fable /ˈfeɪb(ə)l/ noun [C] LITERATURE a traditional story about animals that teaches a moral lesson

fabric /ˈfæbrɪk/ noun **1** [C/U] cloth that is used for making things such as clothes or curtains = MATERIAL: *a wide range of fabrics* **2** [singular] the basic structure of something: *a major threat to the fabric of society* **3** [singular] CONSTRUCTION the roof and walls of a building

fabricate /ˈfæbrɪkeɪt/ verb [T] to make up a story or piece of information in order to make someone believe something that is not true = INVENT —**fabrication** /ˌfæbrɪˈkeɪʃ(ə)n/ noun [C/U]

fabulous /ˈfæbjʊləs/ adj **1** *informal* extremely good = WONDERFUL: *You look fabulous.* ♦ *a fabulous opportunity* **2** very large or great: *fabulous wealth* —**fabulously** /ˈfæbjʊləsli/ adv

facade or **façade** /fəˈsɑːd/ noun **1** [C] the front of a large building **2** [singular] a way of behaving that hides your real feelings or character

face¹ /feɪs/ noun [C]

1 front of head	**5** a flat side
2 side of sth	**6** part of brick
3 person	**+ PHRASES**
4 way sth appears	

1 the front part of the head, where the eyes, nose, and mouth are: *She wiped her face.* ♦ *He had a big smile on his face.* ♦ *The ball hit me in the face.* —*picture* → SKELETON

2 a side of something: *the mountain's north face* ♦ *one of the faces of a coin*

3 a person: *There were a lot of famous faces at the party.* ♦ *Look out for a couple of new faces in the team.*

4 the way that something appears to people: *players who changed the face of tennis* ♦ *This is the new face of banking in America.*

5 MATHS one flat side of an object such as a cube

6 CONSTRUCTION the part of a brick that you see when it forms part of a wall

PHRASES **face down** with the front or face towards the ground

face to face 1 in a situation where you are talking to another person directly: *It would be better if we talked face to face.* ♦ *I came face to face with his mother.* **2** in a situation where you are forced to deal directly with a problem: *Her work brings her face to face with human suffering.*

face up with the front or face upwards

in the face of sth despite something unpleasant or difficult: *They won in the face of stiff competition from all over the country.*

lose face to lose people's respect

make/pull a face to put a silly or rude expression on your face, or an expression that shows that you dislike someone or something

save face to avoid being embarrassed or losing people's respect

to sb's face if you say something to someone's face, you say it to them directly

face² /feɪs/ verb **1** [I/T] to have your face or front towards someone or something: *The two men faced each other across the table.* ♦ *I turned to face the sun.* ♦ *My room faces north.* **2** [T] if you face a problem, or if it faces you, you have to accept it or deal with it: *The country is now faced with the prospect of war.* ♦ *Many of the shipyard workers face losing their jobs.* ♦ *She had to face the fact that she still missed him.* **3** [T] to talk to someone when this is difficult or embarrassing:

I'll never be able to face her again after what happened. **4** [T] to compete against someone: *Williams will face Capriati for the title.*

PHRASE **can't face sth** *spoken* to not want to do something because it is too difficult or unpleasant: *He couldn't face the washing-up, so he left it until the morning.* ♦ *I just can't face attending another conference.*

PHRASAL VERB ˌface ˈup to sth to accept that a bad situation exists and try to deal with it: *He was the only one who faced up to the situation.*

facecloth /ˈfeɪsˌklɒθ/ noun [C] a small piece of cloth that you use for washing yourself, especially your face

ˈface-ˌoff noun [C] SPORTS the method used for starting a game of **ice hockey**

ˈface ˌshield noun [C] TECHNOLOGY a **mask** that someone wears to protect their face when they are working with chemicals, or with hot or sharp flying objects

facet /ˈfæsɪt/ noun [C] an aspect of something

facetious /fəˈsiːʃəs/ adj trying to be funny in a way that is not suitable —**facetiously** adv

ˈface ˌtowel noun [C] a small towel for drying the hands and face

ˌface ˈvalue noun **take sb/sth at face value** to accept someone or something without thinking about whether they really are what they claim to be: *The evidence should not be taken at face value.*

facial /ˈfeɪʃ(ə)l/ adj on your face: *a facial injury*

facilitate /fəˈsɪləteɪt/ verb [T] *formal* to make it possible or easier for something to happen —**facilitation** /fəˌsɪlɪˈteɪʃ(ə)n/ noun [U]

facilitator /fəˈsɪləteɪtə/ noun [C] *formal* someone who leads people in a discussion, course, or other activity

facility /fəˈsɪləti/ (plural **facilities**) noun **1** [C] a feature of a machine or system that allows you to do something: *the text messaging facility on your phone* ♦ *Do you have an overdraft facility at your bank?* **2 facilities** [plural] places, services, or pieces of equipment that are provided for people: *There are plans to improve toilet facilities at the station.* ♦ *Does the company offer any facilities for employees with young children?*

facing sand /ˈfeɪsɪŋ ˌsænd/ noun [U] TECHNOLOGY fresh sand that is used for preparing moulds for making metal **casts**

facsimile /fækˈsɪməli/ noun [C] **1** an exact copy of a book or document **2** *formal* a **fax**

fact /fækt/ noun **1** [C] a piece of true information: *The classes are designed to help children discover basic scientific facts.* ♦ *The fact is, he lost because he didn't try very hard.* ♦ *He has never hidden the fact that he doesn't like me.* ♦ *The fact remains that* (=it is still true that) *women are paid less than men.* ♦ *I know for a fact that he was lying.* **2** [U] things that are true or that really happened, rather than things that are imaginary or not true: *The story is based on historical fact.* ♦ *Children soon learn the difference between fact and fiction.*

PHRASES **the facts of life** the facts about sex and how babies are made

in (actual) fact 1 used for saying what is really true, when this is surprising or different from what people think: *He was paid money for a job that did not in fact exist.* ♦ *In actual fact, she was quite right.* **2** used when you are adding something to what you have just said, especially something surprising: *She's a friend of mine, a very close friend in fact.*

→ MATTER¹

faction /'fækʃ(ə)n/ noun [C] a small group within a larger group, consisting of people with different opinions from the rest

factor /'fæktə/ noun [C] **1** one of the things that influence whether an event happens or the way that it happens: *Several factors have contributed to the increase in the number of road accidents.* ♦ *Public pressure was a factor in the government's decision.* **2 MATHS** a number that a larger number can be exactly divided by: *2 and 3 are factors of 6.*

PHRASE **by a factor of sth** used for saying how many times bigger something is now than it was before: *The volume of traffic has grown by a factor of four.*

factorial /fæk'tɔːriəl/ noun [C] **MATHS** the total that you get when you multiply a number by all the whole numbers below it

factorize /'fæktəraɪz/ verb [T] **MATHS** to divide a number exactly into smaller numbers that can be multiplied together to make the original number —**factorization** /ˌfæktəraɪ'zeɪʃ(ə)n/ noun [U]

factory /'fæktri/ (plural **factories**) noun [C] a building where large quantities of goods are produced using machines: *She works in a factory.* ♦ *a car factory* ♦ *factory workers*

'factory ˌfarm noun [U] **AGRICULTURE** a farm in which farm animals and birds are kept inside buildings in small spaces and are made to grow or produce eggs very quickly —**'factory ˌfarming** noun [U]

factual /'fæktʃuəl/ adj based on facts, rather than on theories or opinions: *factual information* —**factually** adv: *factually correct*

faculty /'fæk(ə)lti/ (plural **faculties**) noun **1** [C] **EDUCATION** a department or group of departments in a university: *the Faculty of Medicine* **2** [U] **EDUCATION** American all the teachers in a university, college, or school **3** [C] a natural ability that most people have: *the faculty of speech*

fad /fæd/ noun [C] something that is popular or fashionable for a short time only

fade /feɪd/ verb [I] **1** to gradually become less clear, bright, loud, or strong: *It was late afternoon and the light was fading.* ♦ *Hopes that he will be found alive are fading.* ♦ *They heard footsteps go past the room, then fade into the distance.* **2** to become less famous or less important: *After one hit record he faded into obscurity.* —**faded** adj

PHRASAL VERB ˌfade aˈway same as **fade** sense 2: *Most of these fashions just fade away and are forgotten.*

faeces /'fiːsiːz/ noun [plural] **BIOLOGY** solid waste from the body= EXCREMENT

fah /fɑː/ noun [C] **MUSIC** the fourth note in the **sol-fa** musical **scale**

Fahrenheit /'færənhaɪt/ noun [U] **SCIENCE** a system for measuring temperature in which water freezes at 32° F and boils at 212° F

fail¹ /feɪl/ verb **1** [I] to be unsuccessful ≠ SUCCEED: *It looks as if the negotiations are going to fail.* ♦ *He failed in his attempt to get compensation.* ♦ *They have failed to think of any practical solutions.* **2** [I] to not do something that people expect you to do: *He failed to come home at the usual time.* **3** [I/T] **EDUCATION** to not achieve a satisfactory standard in a test, or to decide that someone or something has not achieved a satisfactory standard, for example in an exam ≠ PASS: *The new plane failed a safety test.* ♦ *Examiners failed nearly 30% of the candidates.* **4** [I] to stop working, developing, or existing: *The brakes failed and the van*

crashed into a tree. ♦ *He is old now and his health is starting to fail.* ♦ *If interest rates go up, more small businesses will fail.*

PHRASE **if all else fails** used for saying that if other methods do not succeed, there is one last thing that you can try

fail² /feɪl/ noun [C] **EDUCATION** a result that shows that someone or something has not achieved a satisfactory standard, for example in an exam ≠ PASS

PHRASE **without fail** used for emphasizing that something always happens in the same way or at the same time

failed /feɪld/ adj unsuccessful: *a failed attempt*

failing /'feɪlɪŋ/ noun [C] a fault that makes someone or something less effective: *the failings of the educational system*

failure /'feɪljə/ noun **1** [U] a lack of success ≠ SUCCESS: *Their first attempt to climb Everest ended in failure.* ♦ *The failure of the talks has made the situation worse.* ♦ *She is depressed by her continued failure to find a job.* **2** [U] a situation in which you do not do something that someone expects you to do: *the failure of teachers to inform parents about the problem* ♦ *Failure to follow safety procedures could put people in danger.* **3** [U] a situation in which a machine or a part of the body stops working correctly: *The crash seems to have been caused by engine failure.* ♦ *He died from liver failure.* **4** [C] someone or something that has not been successful ≠ SUCCESS: *I feel such a failure.* ♦ *The party was a total failure.*

faint¹ /feɪnt/ adj **1** not strong or clear: *the faint glow of a light through the fog* ♦ *a faint memory* **2** a faint hope or possibility is very slight **3** feeling that you are going to become unconscious —**faintly** adv

faint² /feɪnt/ verb [I] to suddenly become unconscious for a short time

fair¹ /feə/ adj

1 treating all equally	**4** not very good
2 quite large in amount	**5** with no rain
3 light in colour	**+ PHRASES**

1 reasonable and morally right, especially when this involves treating people well ≠ UNFAIR: *free and fair elections* ♦ *Life is not always fair.* ♦ *a fair wage* ♦ *It wouldn't be fair to the others if she is paid more.* ♦ *It's not fair to blame him for our mistakes.*
2 used for emphasizing that an amount, size, or number is large: *We walked 3 miles to school, which is a fair distance.*
3 fair hair is **blonde** (=light yellow) or very light brown in colour ≠ DARK
4 not bad, but not very good= AVERAGE: *His knowledge of Russian is very good though his Japanese is only fair.*
5 if the weather is fair, it is pleasant and not raining = FINE

PHRASES **have your fair share of sth** to have a lot of something, especially something bad
to be fair used for making your criticism of someone or something seem less strong: *I don't like their music but, to be fair, millions of people disagree with me.*

fair² /feə/ noun [C] **1** an event where companies bring their products for customers to look at or buy **2** a place where people ride on special machines and play games to win prizes

fair³ /feə/ adv

PHRASES **fair and square** in a way that is clear and fair, so that no one can complain or disagree
play fair to behave in a fair and honest way

fairground /ˈfeəɡraʊnd/ noun [C] an area of land where people ride on special machines and play games to win prizes

fairly /ˈfeəli/ adv **1** to some degree, but not completely or extremely = RATHER, REASONABLY: *We go to the theatre fairly often.* ♦ *He enjoys fairly good health.* **2** in a fair way: *I do my best to treat all my children fairly.*

fairness /ˈfeənəs/ noun [U] behaviour that is fair and reasonable

fair 'test noun [C] SCIENCE a scientific test or experiment in which only one **variable** is changed, so the reason for the result can be clearly seen

'fair ,trade noun [U] ECONOMICS a system by which people producing goods in **developing countries** (=poorer countries with less industry) receive fair prices for their goods from the richer countries they trade with. They are also encouraged to pay their workers fair wages and to take care of the environment.

fairway /ˈfeəweɪ/ noun [C] SPORTS the long part of a **golf course** that players hit the ball along to get to the hole

fairy /ˈfeəri/ (plural **fairies**) noun [C] an imaginary creature with magic powers that looks like a small person with wings

'fairy ,tale or **'fairy ,story** (plural **'fairy ,stories**) noun [C] LITERATURE a traditional children's story in which magic things happen

fait accompli /ˌfeɪt əˈkɒmpliː/ noun [C] formal something that has already been done and cannot be changed

faith /feɪθ/ noun **1** [U] a strong belief that someone or something is good: *I'm delighted to know you have such faith in me.* ♦ *The public have lost faith in what the government is doing.* ♦ *Maybe we put too much faith in doctors and medicine.* **2** [U] RELIGION religious belief: *Faith in God helped him through his illness.* **3** [C] RELIGION a religion: *people of many different faiths*
  PHRASE **in good faith** if you do something in good faith, you honestly believe that it is right or fair

'faith com,munity noun [C] RELIGION the people who belong to a particular church or a particular religious group

faithful /ˈfeɪθf(ə)l/ adj **1** continuing to support someone or something, even in difficult situations = LOYAL: *He had always been a faithful friend.* ♦ *He remained faithful to his beliefs.* **2** showing or describing something in a way that is exactly correct: *a faithful reproduction of the original painting* **3** not having sex with anyone other than your partner ≠ UNFAITHFUL: *Ken has always been faithful to his wife.* **4** **the faithful** the people who support a particular political party, sports team, musician etc —**faithfulness** noun [U]

faithfully /ˈfeɪθf(ə)li/ adv **1** in a loyal and honest way **2** accurately
  PHRASE **Yours faithfully** used at the end of a formal letter that begins with 'Dear Sir' or 'Dear Madam'

'faith ,school noun [C] EDUCATION a school, started or paid for by a religious group, that gives children a general education

fake¹ /feɪk/ adj **1** made to look like something real in order to trick people ≠ GENUINE: *a fake passport* **2** made to look like something expensive: *fake jewels*

fake² /feɪk/ noun [C] **1** a copy of something such as a painting that is intended to trick people **2** someone who pretends to have skills that they do not really have

fake³ /feɪk/ verb [T] **1** to pretend to do something: *He left the country after faking his own death.* **2** to make an exact copy of something in order to trick people

falafel /fəˈlɑːf(ə)l/ noun [U] a Middle Eastern food made from **chickpeas**, onion, and spices made into balls and cooked in oil

falcon /ˈfɔːlkən/ noun [C] a bird that is often trained to hunt small animals —*picture* → BIRD

fall¹ /fɔːl/ (**falls, falling, fell** /fel/, **fallen** /ˈfɔːlən/) verb [I]

1 move quickly down	**7** happen
2 go down by accident	**8** lose power
3 come from sky	**9** be controlled by sb else
4 get lower in level	**+ PHRASES**
5 belong to group	**+ PHRASAL VERBS**
6 start to be/do sth	

1 to move quickly downwards from a higher position by accident: *I keep falling off my bike.* ♦ *It's not unusual for small children to fall out of bed.*
2 to go quickly down onto the ground from an upright position by accident: *I slipped and almost fell.* ♦ *We heard the crash of falling trees.* ♦ *He collapsed and fell to the ground.*
3 to come down to the ground from the sky: *Rain began to fall.* ♦ *Bombs fell on the city throughout the night.*
4 to become lower in level or amount ≠ RISE: *The temperature has been falling all day.* ♦ *Inflation has fallen to 3%.*
5 to belong to a particular group or area of activity: *Those items fall into the category of luxury goods.*
6 to change into another state or condition: *Shortly afterwards she fell ill.* ♦ *I climbed into bed and fell into a deep sleep.*
7 to happen on a particular day or date: *Christmas falls on a Saturday this year.*
8 to lose a position of power: *The government finally fell in June 2002.*
9 if a place falls in a war, a different army takes control of it: *The city is expected to fall within days.*
  PHRASES **fall in love** to start to love someone
fall into place if something falls into place, you suddenly understand how the different pieces of it are connected
fall short to not reach a particular level
fall to bits/pieces to be in a very bad condition because of being old or badly made
  → FOOT
  PHRASAL VERBS **,fall a'part** to break because of being old or badly made
,fall 'back on sth to do something else after other things have failed: *She always has her teaching experience to fall back on.*
,fall be'hind sb to make less progress than other people
,fall 'down 1 same as **fall¹** sense 2: *I fell down and hurt my knee.* **2** if a building is falling down, it is in very bad condition
'fall for sb to fall in love with someone
'fall for sth to believe that a trick or a joke is true
,fall 'out informal to stop being friendly with someone because you have had a disagreement with them: *Have you two fallen out?* ♦ *I'd fallen out with my parents.*
,fall 'over 1 if something falls over, it falls so that its side is on the ground **2** if you fall over, you fall to the ground
,fall 'through if something such as a plan or arrangement falls through, it fails to happen

fall² /fɔːl/ noun

1 when sb/sth falls	**5** waterfall
2 amount that falls	**6** autumn
3 when level falls	**7** in wrestling/judo
4 loss of power	

1 [C] an occasion when someone or something falls to the ground: *Her brother was killed in **a fall from** a horse.*
2 [C] an amount of rain or snow that falls to the ground: *a heavy **fall of snow***
3 [C] an occasion when an amount or level falls ≠ RISE: *There has been **a sharp fall in** unemployment.* ♦ *We have seen **a fall of** 5% in sales this month.*
4 [singular] someone's defeat or loss of power: ***the fall of** the Roman Empire*
5 falls [plural] a **waterfall**
6 [singular] *American* autumn
7 [C] SPORTS an act of pushing an opponent to the ground in **wrestling** or **judo**

fallacy /ˈfæləsi/ (plural **fallacies**) noun [C] an idea or belief that is false but that many people think is true

fallen /ˈfɔːlən/ the past participle of **fall**¹

fallible /ˈfæləb(ə)l/ adj not perfect, and likely to be wrong or to make mistakes

fallopian tube or **Fallopian tube** /fəˌləʊpiən ˈtjuːb/ noun [C] ANATOMY one of the two tubes in the body of a woman or other female mammal that carry eggs produced in the ovaries to the uterus

fallout /ˈfɔːlaʊt/ noun **1** [U] PHYSICS the dangerous dust produced by a nuclear explosion **2** [singular/U] the unpleasant effects of something

fallow /ˈfæləʊ/ adj AGRICULTURE fallow land has been deliberately left for a time without any crops or animals on it, in order to improve the soil

false /fɔːls/ adj **1** something that is false is not true, either deliberately or because of being based on incorrect information ≠ TRUE: *a false statement* ♦ *I got the false impression that she was fairly rich.* ♦ *The accusations are totally false.* **2** made to look like something real = ARTIFICIAL: *false eyelashes* **3** not real and intended to trick people = FAKE: *a false passport* **4** not showing what you really feel or intend = INSINCERE: *a false smile*
PHRASE **under false pretences** by tricking people
—**falsely** adv

Build your vocabulary: words you can use instead of **false**

- **artificial** made to have the same qualities as something else that exists naturally
- **counterfeit** made to look exactly like real money and used illegally to trick people
- **fake** made to look like something valuable or important, often in order to trick people
- **forged** made to look exactly like something valuable or important and used illegally to trick people
- **pirate** used for describing copies of things such as books or videos that have been made and sold illegally

false a'larm noun [C] a situation in which you think that something bad is going to happen, but it does not

false be'ginner noun [C] EDUCATION someone who starts to study a language from the beginning again, although they already have a slight knowledge of it

false 'fruit noun [C] BIOLOGY a fruit such as a **strawberry** that consists of a fully developed ovary and other parts such as the **bract** (=leaf near the top of the stem) → TRUE FRUIT

false im'prisonment noun [U] LAW the crime of preventing someone from leaving a place when you have no legal right to do this

false 'leg noun [C] BIOLOGY a part that comes out from the abdomen of a caterpillar, that it uses to hold

on to a surface while it is moving —*picture* → CATERPILLAR

false 'positive noun [C] SCIENCE an incorrect result of a scientific test in which it wrongly shows a particular condition to be present

false 'start noun [C] **1** an unsuccessful attempt to start something or to do something **2** SPORTS a situation at the beginning of a race when one person starts too soon

falsetto /fɔːlˈsetəʊ/ noun [C] MUSIC a man's singing or speaking voice that is much higher than normal —**falsetto** adj, adv

falsify /ˈfɔːlsɪfaɪ/ (**falsifies, falsifying, falsified**) verb [T] to change something deliberately in order to trick other people

falter /ˈfɔːltə/ verb [I] **1** to stop being effective **2** if someone falters, they do something in a way that shows that they are weak or are not confident

fame /feɪm/ noun [U] the state of being famous: *Albert Finney rose to fame in the British cinema of the early Sixties.*

famed /feɪmd/ adj famous: *a restaurant **famed for** its seafood*

familial /fəˈmɪliəl/ adj SOCIAL STUDIES relating to families

familiar /fəˈmɪliə/ adj **1** well known to you, or easily recognized by you ≠ UNFAMILIAR: *People are more relaxed in familiar surroundings.* ♦ *His face looked vaguely familiar but I couldn't think why.* ♦ *I'm pleased to see so many **familiar faces** here tonight.* ♦ *The name Harry Potter will be **familiar to** many readers.*
2 something that is familiar happens a lot or exists in most places: *Horses used to be **a familiar sight** in our streets.* ♦ *an **all-too familiar** problem* **3** behaving in an informal way that shows a lack of respect for someone: *Don't be too **familiar with** the customers.*
PHRASE **familiar with sth** if you are familiar with something, you know about it: *Are you familiar with this system?*

familiarity /fəˌmɪliˈærəti/ noun **1** [U] knowledge that you have of something because you have dealt with it before: *a **familiarity with** international law* **2** [C/U] informal behaviour that shows a lack of respect for someone

familiarize /fəˈmɪliəraɪz/ verb [T] to show or teach someone something: *It's my job to **familiarize** new employees **with** office procedures.*

family¹ /ˈfæm(ə)li/ (plural **families**) noun **1** [C] a group consisting of parents and children: *Is the Watson family going to be there?* ♦ *The tent is big enough for a family of six.* **2** [C/U] all the people who are related to you, including people who are now dead: *Does your family have any history of heart disease?* ♦ *She did not want the property to go to anyone outside the family.* ♦ *The business had been **in his family** (=belonged to his family) **for four generations**.*

Family can be used with a singular or plural verb. You can say *His family **was** not at the wedding* or *His family **were** not at the wedding*.

3 [C] children: *It's difficult to **bring up a family** on one salary.* ♦ *They want to get married and **start a family** (=have children).* **4** [C] BIOLOGY a group of living things that are related to one other. A family includes more than a **genus** and less than an **order**: *The cat family includes lions and tigers as well as domestic cats.* —*picture* → TAXONOMY

family² /ˈfæm(ə)li/ adj **1** relating to families, or typical of families: *Quarrels are a normal part of family life.*

2 suitable for a family with children: *family entertainment*

'family ,name noun [C] the part of your name that all the people in your family have= LAST NAME, SURNAME

,family 'planning noun [U] HEALTH the practice of controlling the number of children born into a family and when they are born, for example, by using contraceptives

'family ,room noun [C] TOURISM a room in a hotel with enough beds for a family to sleep in

,family 'tree noun [C] SOCIAL STUDIES a drawing that shows the names of everyone in a family and shows the relationship between them

famine /ˈfæmɪn/ noun [C/U] a serious lack of food that causes many people to become ill or to die

famous /ˈfeɪməs/ adj if someone or something is famous, a lot of people know their name or have heard about them: *He dreamed of becoming a famous footballer.* ♦ *The town of Gouda is **famous for** its cheese.* ♦ *She became **famous as** a teacher and a writer.* → INFAMOUS —**famously** adv

> **Build your vocabulary: words you can use instead of famous**
> - **eminent** famous and respected for doing important work
> - **legendary** very famous and admired by many people
> - **notorious** or **infamous** famous for something bad
> - **renowned** famous for a special skill or achievement
> - **well-known** fairly famous

fan¹ /fæn/ noun [C] **1** someone who likes someone or something very much: *a crowd of football fans* ♦ *I'm a big fan of Madonna.* **2** a machine with blades that turn and move the air in a room, so that it feels less hot **3** a flat object that you move backwards and forwards in front of your face, in order to make yourself feel less hot

fan² /fæn/ (**fans, fanning, fanned**) verb [T] **1** to wave a flat object in front of your face in order to make yourself feel less hot **2** to make a fire burn more strongly by moving air onto it **3** *formal* to make a feeling or belief stronger

fanatic /fəˈnætɪk/ noun [C] **1** someone who has strong beliefs that make them behave in an unreasonable way **2** someone who likes a sport or activity very much —**fanatical** /fəˈnætɪk(ə)l/ adj

'fan ,belt noun [C] a belt in a car engine that turns a device that prevents the engine from getting too hot

fancy¹ /ˈfænsi/ (**fancies, fancying, fancied**) verb [T] **1** *informal* to want to have or to do something: *What do you fancy for your lunch?* ♦ *Do you fancy going to the cinema?* **2** used for showing that you are surprised about something: *Fancy you knowing my sister!*

fancy² /ˈfænsi/ (**fancier, fanciest**) adj **1** expensive and fashionable: *a fancy hotel* **2** with a lot of features or decorations: *fancy computer graphics*

fancy³ /ˈfænsi/ noun [singular] a feeling of wanting or liking someone or something: *One of the boys has taken a fancy to my daughter.*

fanfare /ˈfænfeə/ noun [C] MUSIC a short loud piece of music played on a musical instrument such as a **trumpet** to announce a special person or event

fang /fæŋ/ noun [C] BIOLOGY **1** one of the long pointed teeth that some animals have **2** one of the two parts of the mouth of **arachnids** that is used, for example, to catch other animals —*picture* → SPIDER

fantasize /ˈfæntəsaɪz/ verb [I/T] to imagine that something pleasant, exciting, or unusual is happening to you

fantastic /fænˈtæstɪk/ adj *informal* extremely good or pleasant: *You've done a fantastic job.* ♦ *He looked absolutely fantastic.* —**fantastically** /fænˈtæstɪkli/ adv

fantasy /ˈfæntəsi/ (plural **fantasies**) noun **1** [C] a pleasant, exciting, or unusual experience that you imagine is happening to you **2** [C/U] LITERATURE a story that shows a lot of imagination and is very different from real life

FAQ /ˌef eɪ ˈkjuː/ noun [C] COMPUTING frequently asked questions: a list of typical questions that people ask and the answers to them

far /fɑː/ (**farther** /ˈfɑːðə/ or **further** /ˈfɜːðə/, **farthest** /ˈfɑːðɪst/ or **furthest** /ˈfɜːðɪst/) adj, adv

> | | |
> |---|---|
> | **1** a long distance | **5** to what degree |
> | **2** most distant | **6** of time |
> | **3** for emphasis | **+** PHRASES |
> | **4** of progress | |

1 used for talking about a long distance, or for asking or saying how long a distance is: *You can go outside and play, but don't go far.* ♦ *We can't walk to the cinema – it's **too far**.* ♦ *The church is not **far from** the library.* ♦ ***How far** is it to the next town?*

> **Far** is used mainly in questions and negatives when talking about distance. In positive statements we usually say **a long way**: *It's a long way to the nearest hospital.*

2 most distant from someone or from the centre: *She was standing at the far end of the bar.* ♦ *I'm the one on the far left.*

3 used for emphasis, often when you are making a comparison: *You eat **far too** much.* ♦ *The situation is bad in England, but it's **far worse** in Scotland.* ♦ *The last question was the hardest **by far**.*

4 used for saying or asking how much progress someone or something has made: *How **far** have you **got** with your homework?*

5 used for talking about the degree to which something happens or how extreme an action is: *This result shows how far his popularity has fallen.* ♦ *Do you think feminism has **gone too far** (=become too extreme)?*

6 a long time before or after: *Some churches were built **as far back as** 1200.* ♦ *Do you always buy your ticket so **far in advance**?*

PHRASES **as far as possible** as much as possible: *We should keep to the original plan as far as possible.*

far from used for saying that the real situation is the opposite of the way you describe it: *The battle is far from over.*

so far 1 until now: *So far we have considered only the local area.* **2** up to a particular point or degree: *You can only get so far on good looks alone.*
→ CONCERNED, FARTHER, FARTHEST

> - **Further, farther, furthest**, and **farthest** can all be used for talking about distance: *Stand further/farther away from me.* ♦ *Who can jump furthest/farthest?*
> - **Further** is often used for talking about the degree to which something happens: *I expect prices to rise further* (=rise more). But **farther, farthest,** and **furthest** are not often used in this way.
> - **Further** is also used as an **adjective** to mean 'more': *There has been no further news.* But **farther** cannot be used in this way.

farad /'færəd, 'færæd/ noun [C] **PHYSICS** the SI unit of **capacitance**, which is equal to that of a **capacitor** carrying one **coulomb** of charge when a **potential difference** of one **volt** is applied. Symbol F

faraway /ˌfɑːrəˈweɪ/ adj **1** a long way from you or from a particular place **2** showing that you are not concentrating on what is happening: *a faraway look in her eyes*

farce /fɑːs/ noun **1** [singular/U] a situation that is silly because it is very badly organized or is unsuccessful **2** [C] **LITERATURE** a funny play that involves silly situations

fare¹ /feə/ noun **1** [C] the money that someone pays for a journey **2** [U] *formal* the type of food that is available somewhere

fare² /feə/ verb [I] *formal* used for saying how well or how badly someone does something = **DO**

the ˌFar ˈEast GEOGRAPHY the countries of the eastern part of Asia, including China and Japan

ˈfare ˌcode noun [C] **TOURISM** a code on an airline ticket that indicates which class the passenger will be travelling in

farewell¹ /ˌfeəˈwel/ noun [C/U] *old-fashioned* an occasion when you say goodbye to someone

farewell² /ˌfeəˈwel/ adj done in order to celebrate the fact that someone is leaving a place or job: *a farewell party*

far-fetched /ˌfɑː ˈfetʃt/ adj very unlikely to be true and therefore difficult to believe

farm¹ /fɑːm/ noun [C] **AGRICULTURE** an area of land that is used for growing crops or keeping animals

farm² /fɑːm/ verb [I/T] **AGRICULTURE** to use land for growing crops or keeping animals

farmer /'fɑːmə/ noun [C] **AGRICULTURE** someone who owns or manages a farm

farmhand /'fɑːmˌhænd/ noun [C] **AGRICULTURE** someone whose job is to work on a farm

farmhouse /'fɑːmˌhaʊs/ noun [C] **AGRICULTURE** the main house on a farm

farming /'fɑːmɪŋ/ noun [U] **AGRICULTURE** the business of being a farmer

farmland /'fɑːmˌlænd/ noun [U] **AGRICULTURE** land that is used for farming

farmstay /'fɑːmˌsteɪ/ noun [C] **TOURISM** a stay on a farm as a paying guest

farmyard /'fɑːmˌjɑːd/ noun [C] **AGRICULTURE** an area that is surrounded by the buildings on a farm

ˌfar-ˈoff adj far away in distance or in time

far-reaching /ˌfɑː ˈriːtʃɪŋ/ adj affecting a lot of people or things in an important way

farther /'fɑːðə/ adj, adv in or to a place that is more distant: *I live farther up the road.* ♦ *The children were too tired to walk any farther.*

farthest /'fɑːðɪst/ adj, adv in or to a place that is most distant: *Sam had chosen to sit farthest away from the door.*

fascia /'feɪʃə/ noun [C] **CONSTRUCTION** a wooden board that covers the ends of the beams supporting a roof

fascicle /'fæskɪk(ə)l/ noun [C] **ANATOMY** a tight group of structures in the body, for example nerve fibres or muscle fibres

fascinate /'fæsɪneɪt/ verb [T] to attract and interest someone very much

fascinated /'fæsɪneɪtɪd/ adj very interested in, or attracted by, someone or something

fascinating /'fæsɪneɪtɪŋ/ adj extremely interesting: *a fascinating story* ♦ *It will be fascinating to see who they appoint.* ♦ *I find him absolutely fascinating.*

fascination /ˌfæsɪˈneɪʃ(ə)n/ noun [singular/U] **1** the power to interest or attract people very strongly **2** the state of being very interested in, or attracted by, someone or something

fascism /'fæʃɪz(ə)m/ noun [U] **POLITICS** a very right-wing political system in which the government completely controls society and the economy

fascist /'fæʃɪst/ noun [C] **1 POLITICS** someone who supports or believes in fascism **2** an insulting word for someone who has very right-wing opinions —**fascist** adj

fashion /'fæʃ(ə)n/ noun **1** [U] the activity or business that involves styles of clothes and people's appearance: *the world of fashion* ♦ *an Italian fashion designer* **2** [U] the state of being popular at a particular time: *High heels are back in fashion.* ♦ *His ideas have gone right out of fashion.* **3** [C] a style of dress or an activity that is popular at a particular time: *She was always dressed in the latest fashions.* ♦ *the fashion for naming children after pop stars* **4** [singular] a particular way of doing something: *The elections took place in a peaceful and orderly fashion.*

fashionable /'fæʃ(ə)nəb(ə)l/ adj **1** popular at a particular time ≠ **UNFASHIONABLE**: *fashionable clothes* ♦ *It is now fashionable to buy organic food.* **2** popular with rich and successful people, and often expensive: *London's most fashionable shopping district* —**fashionably** adv: *a fashionably dressed young woman*

ˈfashion-ˌconscious adj very interested in fashion and wanting to wear fashionable clothes, spend time in fashionable places etc

ˈfashion ˌshow noun [C] an event at which models show new styles of clothes

ˈfashion ˌstatement noun [C] something unusual that you wear, own, or use that is intended to show people that you know a lot about fashion

fast¹ /fɑːst/ adj **1** moving, happening, or doing something quickly: *Simon loves fast cars.* ♦ *The government has promised a fast response to the crisis.* ♦ *We were expected to work at a fast pace.* **2** if a clock is fast, it shows a time that is later than the correct time ≠ **SLOW**: *My watch is a few minutes fast.* **3** a fast film is used for taking photographs of something that is moving quickly, or when there is not very much light

fast² /fɑːst/ adv **1** quickly: *I can't run very fast.* ♦ *You need to get help fast!* **2** firmly and strongly or tightly: *She held fast to the railings and refused to move.* ♦ *The van was stuck fast in the mud.*

PHRASE fast asleep sleeping in a way that makes it difficult to wake you

fast³ /fɑːst/ verb [I] to eat no food or very little food for a period of time, usually for religious reasons —**fast** noun [C]

fasten /'fɑːs(ə)n/ verb **1** [I/T] to close something such as a piece of clothing or a bag by fixing together the two parts of it, or to be closed in this way ≠ **UNFASTEN**: *Please keep your seat belts fastened.* **2** [T] to fix one thing to another using something such as string or nails so that it is held firmly in position: *We fastened our boat to a post in the river.* **3** [T] to use something such as a lock in order to close a door, gate, or window: *I checked that all the windows were properly fastened.*

fastening /'fɑːsnɪŋ/ or **fastener** /'fɑːsnə/ noun [C]
1 something such as a lock that you use to keep a door, gate, or window closed **2** something that you use to fix together the two parts of something such as a piece of clothing or a bag

fast-flowing /'fɑːst ˌfləʊɪŋ/ adj flowing very quickly

fast 'food noun [U] food that is made and served very quickly, and that people can take away with them

fast-'forward verb [I/T] if you fast-forward a tape, or if it fast-forwards, it goes forwards quickly —**fast 'forward** noun [U]

fastidious /fæ'stɪdiəs/ adj caring a lot about small details and wanting everything to be correct and tidy

fat¹ /fæt/ (**fatter, fattest**) adj **1** a person or animal that is fat has too much flesh on their body and weighs too much: *She can eat whatever she likes and she never gets fat.* **2** a fat object is thicker than other objects of the same type: *a big fat book*

> Build your vocabulary: words you can use instead of **fat**
> - **big/large** tall and fairly fat
> - **chubby** used especially for describing babies and children who look fat in a healthy attractive way
> - **obese** very fat in a way that is dangerous to your health
> - **overweight** heavier than you should be
> - **plump** slightly fat in a way that looks nice

fat² /fæt/ noun **1** [U] BIOLOGY a soft white or yellow substance that mammals and birds store under the skin. It is used as an energy store and to protect the body against heat loss. —*picture* → SKIN **2** [C/U] BIOLOGY a food substance like oil that is used by the body for energy: *Reduce the amount of fat in your diet.* **3** [C/U] oil in a solid or liquid form that is obtained from plants or animals and is used in cooking: *Fry the meat in a small amount of fat.*

fatal /'feɪt(ə)l/ adj **1** causing someone to die: *a fatal car accident* ♦ *The condition can **prove fatal** (=cause death).* **2** with very bad effects: *I made **the fatal mistake** of falling in love with him.* **3** COMPUTING a fatal **error** is one that stops a program from working correctly —**fatally** adv

fatality /fə'tæləti/ (plural **fatalities**) noun [C] formal a death that is caused by an accident, war, violence, or disease

fate /feɪt/ noun **1** [C] the things that happen to someone: *a meeting that would decide **the fate of** thousands of employees* **2** [U] a power that some people believe controls everything that happens in their lives: *Fate has dealt these people a cruel blow.*

fateful /'feɪtf(ə)l/ adj affecting what happens in the future in an important and usually bad way

father /'fɑːðə/ noun **1** [C] a male parent: *My father taught me to drive.* **2** Father RELIGION used for talking to or about a Roman Catholic priest **3** fathers [plural] people in your family who lived long before you: *Spanish was the language of their fathers.*

Father 'Christmas an imaginary old man with a long white beard and red clothes who brings children their Christmas presents= SANTA CLAUS

father-in-law noun [C] the father of someone's husband or wife

fatherly /'fɑːðəli/ adj typical of a good, kind father

fathom /'fæðəm/ verb [T] to understand something that is complicated or mysterious: *For some reason she couldn't fathom, he seemed angry.*

fatigue /fə'tiːg/ noun [U] **1** a feeling of being extremely tired: *He was suffering from fatigue.* **2** PHYSICS, CHEMISTRY a tendency for metal to break as a result of too much pressure —**fatigued** /fə'tiːgd/ adj

fat-'soluble adj BIOLOGY fat-soluble vitamins dissolve in fat

fatten /'fæt(ə)n/ verb [T] to make an animal fat so that it will be more suitable for eating

fattening /'fæt(ə)nɪŋ/ adj likely to make people fat: *Avoid fattening foods and take more exercise.*

fatty /'fæti/ adj containing a lot of fat: *fatty foods*

fatty 'acid noun [C] BIOLOGY, CHEMISTRY one of a large group of acids that, together with **glycerol**, are found in animal and vegetable fats and oils

fault /fɔːlt/ noun

1 responsibility for sth	4 in tennis
3 problem with machine etc	5 in geology
	+ PHRASE

1 [C/U] the fact of being responsible for a bad or unpleasant situation: *It's my fault – I forgot to give him the message.* ♦ *If you didn't get enough sleep, **it's your own fault**.* ♦ *The teacher **was at fault** for not telling the child's parents.*
2 [C] a feature that makes someone or something less good= FLAW: *She has her faults, but on the whole she's very nice.* ♦ *The book's main fault is that it is too long.*
3 [C] a problem with a machine or piece of equipment that stops it from working correctly: *The fire was caused by **an electrical fault**.*
4 [C] SPORTS a situation in tennis in which the ball does not land inside the correct area during a **serve**
5 [C] GEOLOGY a crack on or below the Earth's surface: *the San Andreas Fault*
PHRASE **find fault with** to criticize someone or something after deliberately looking for mistakes

fault-finding /'fɔːlt ˌfaɪndɪŋ/ noun [U] the practice of looking for mistakes in everything and criticizing people or things because of them, especially in an unfair way

faultless /'fɔːltləs/ adj containing no mistakes at all —**faultlessly** adv

faultline /'fɔːlt,laɪn/ noun [C] GEOLOGY a feature on the Earth's surface in which layers of rock that have become separated from the main layer of rock appear through the surface of the Earth

faulty /'fɔːlti/ adj not working correctly, or not made correctly: *faulty brakes*

fauna /'fɔːnə/ noun [U] BIOLOGY all the animals that live in a particular area

Faustian /'faʊstiən/ adj formal relating to Faust, a German doctor who sold his **soul** (=the spirit part of his body) to the **Devil** (=a powerful evil spirit) in exchange for knowledge and power

faux pas /ˌfəʊ 'pɑː/ (plural **faux pas**) noun [C] formal something embarrassing that someone says or does in a social situation

favour¹ /'feɪvə/ noun **1** [C] something that you do for someone in order to help them: *Could you **do me a favour**?* ♦ *He wouldn't take any money for his work: he insisted he was doing it **as a favour**.* **2** [U] support or admiration from people: *Nuclear power stations have lost favour in recent years.*
PHRASES **in favour** popular at a particular time
in sb's favour helping you, or giving you an advantage: *The delay might actually work in our favour.*
in favour of 1 supporting a person, idea, or proposal: *Those in favour of the proposal, please raise your*

hands. **2** preferring to choose someone or something that you believe is better: _Manchester was rejected in favour of Liverpool as the site for the new stadium._
out of favour not popular at a particular time

favour² /'feɪvə/ verb [T] **1** to prefer to choose someone or something that you believe is better: _The report strongly favours reform of the electoral system._ **2** to give someone an unfair advantage: _These tax cuts will favour the rich._

favourable /'feɪv(ə)rəb(ə)l/ adj

1 showing approval	**4** showing sth good
2 giving advantage or benefit	likely to happen
3 price: cheap or reasonable	**5** agreeing to sth

1 showing that you like or approve of someone or something **=** POSITIVE **≠** UNFAVOURABLE: _Reaction to the plan has been generally favourable._
2 giving someone or something an advantage or a benefit **=** BENEFICIAL
3 a favourable price is cheap or reasonable
4 showing that something good is likely to happen: _a favourable weather forecast_
5 giving agreement to something **=** POSITIVE
—**favourably** /'feɪv(ə)rəbli/ adv

favourite¹ /'feɪv(ə)rət/ adj your favourite person or thing of a particular type is the one that you like the best: _What's your favourite food?_

favourite² /'feɪv(ə)rət/ noun [C] **1** the person or thing that you like the best: _Fish and chips is still a national favourite._ **2** someone who is treated better than others because someone such as a teacher or parent prefers them: _Colin's always been mum's favourite._ **3** SPORTS the person, team, or animal that is expected to win a race or competition: _Chelsea are favourites to win the Premier League._

favouritism /'feɪv(ə)rətɪzəm/ noun [U] the unfair practice of giving help or advantages to only one person in a group

fawn¹ /fɔːn/ noun [C] a young **deer**

fawn² /fɔːn/ adj light brown in colour

fax¹ /fæks/ noun **1** fax or **fax machine** [C] a piece of equipment that is used for sending copies of documents in electronic form and printing them when they are received: _What's your fax number?_ —_picture_ → WORKSTATION **2** [C] a document that has been sent by a fax machine **3** [U] the system of sending documents using a fax machine: _Send me the details by fax._

fax² /fæks/ verb [T] to send a message to someone using a fax machine: _Could you fax me the application form?_

the FBI /ˌef biː 'aɪ/ the Federal Bureau of Investigation: a US government department that deals with serious crimes that affect more than one state

FBO /ˌef biː 'əʊ/ noun [C] RELIGION faith-based organization: a religious organization such as a charity that provides a service to the public

fear¹ /fɪə/ noun **1** [U] the feeling that you have when you are frightened: _She eventually managed to overcome her fear of the dark._ ♦ _Martin screamed in fear._ ♦ _She was shaking with fear._ ♦ _Many of these people live in fear_ (=are afraid all the time). **2** [C] something bad or unpleasant that you are afraid might happen: _There are fears that the building might collapse._ ♦ _He expressed fears for his wife's safety._ ♦ _This latest case has raised fears of an epidemic._ ♦ _There are fears about the safety of the nuclear plant._
PHRASE **for fear of (doing) sth** or **for fear (that)** in case

you make something bad happen: _I didn't tell Susan about our meeting for fear of upsetting her._

fear² /fɪə/ verb [T] **1** to feel worried and afraid that something bad will happen: _The refugees fear persecution if they return to their own country._ ♦ _Health experts fear that a flu epidemic will hit Britain this winter._ ♦ _One person is still missing, feared dead._ **2** to feel afraid of someone or something because they might harm you: _He was hated and feared by his colleagues._

fearful /'fɪəf(ə)l/ adj frightened —**fearfully** adv

fearless /'fɪələs/ adj _showing approval_ not afraid of anyone or anything —**fearlessly** adv

feasi'bility ,study noun [C] a study to see if something can be done

feasible /'fiːzəb(ə)l/ adj possible, or likely to succeed: _There seems to be only one feasible solution._ —**feasibility** /ˌfiːzə'bɪləti/ noun [U]

feasible 'region noun [C] MATHS the set of all the possible solutions to a problem in mathematics

feast /fiːst/ noun [C] a large meal, usually for a special occasion

feat /fiːt/ noun [C] something impressive that someone does

feather /'feðə/ noun [C] BIOLOGY one of the narrow tubes with connected parts like hairs on each side that cover a bird's body —_picture_ → BIRD

feature¹ /'fiːtʃə/ noun [C] **1** an important part or aspect of something: _The latest model has a lot of new safety features._ ♦ _the natural features of the landscape_ **2** a part of your face such as your eyes, nose, or mouth: _Her large blue eyes were her best feature._ **3** a newspaper or magazine article, or a part of a television or radio programme that concentrates on a particular subject: _a special feature on new children's books_

feature² /'fiːtʃə/ verb **1** [T] if something features a particular person or thing, they are an important part of it: _a concert featuring music by Haydn and Mozart_ ♦ _The film features Diane Ashmann as a young French student._ **2** [I] to be an important part or aspect of something: _She has already featured in two award-winning films this year._

Feb. abbrev February

February /'febrʊəri/ noun [U] the second month of the year, between January and March: _I'm starting my new job in February._ ♦ _They fly to Spain on February 16th._

fed /fed/ the past tense and past participle of **feed¹**

federal /'fed(ə)rəl/ adj POLITICS **1** a federal country or system is one in which individual states make their own laws, but in which there is a national government that is responsible for areas such as defence and foreign policy **2** relating to the national government of a country rather than with the government of one of its member states —**federally** adv

federation /ˌfedə'reɪʃ(ə)n/ noun [C] **1** POLITICS a country that is made up of individual states with the power to make their own decisions, but with a national government that is responsible for areas such as defence and foreign policy **2** a large organization that is made up of several smaller organizations that share similar aims

fed 'up adj _informal_ someone who is fed up is annoyed or bored with something that they feel they have accepted for too long: _I'm fed up with this job._

fee /fiː/ noun [C] **1** money that someone pays to a professional person or institution for their work: _tuition fees_ ♦ _He will have to pay legal fees of £200._

2 an amount of money that someone pays in order to be allowed to do something such as visit a museum or join an organization: *The gallery charges a small entrance fee.*

feeble /ˈfiːb(ə)l/ adj **1** physically weak **2** not good enough to achieve the intended result: *a feeble attempt* ♦ *a feeble excuse* **3** not strong enough to be seen or heard clearly: *a feeble light* —**feebly** /ˈfiːbli/ adv

feed¹ /fiːd/ (**feeds**, **feeding**, **fed** /fed/) verb **1** [T] to give food to a person or an animal: *We've been feeding the ducks on the river.* ♦ *All the children will be properly fed and cared for.* ♦ *The dogs were fed on raw meat.* ♦ *The leftover food is fed to the pigs.* **2** [I] if an animal or baby feeds, it eats: *Young babies need to feed every three to four hours.* **3** [T] to provide a supply of something for a person or a machine: *Information is fed into the computer and stored in a database.* ♦ *He's been feeding the police with information about terrorist activities.* **4** [T] to push something into a machine: *She saw him feeding documents into the shredder.*

> **PHRASAL VERB** **'feed on sth** if an animal feeds on something, it eats it as its usual food

feed² /fiːd/ noun **1** [C] an occasion on which someone gives milk to a baby: *She had her last feed at two o'clock.* **2** [C/U] food that is given to animals: *Hay is used as winter feed for the cows.*

feedback /ˈfiːdbæk/ noun [U] comments about how well or how badly someone is doing something, which are intended to help them to do it better: *Initial feedback from parents has been very positive.*

'feedback ,mechanism noun [U] **BIOLOGY** a mechanism for controlling reactions, for example in the body, in which one action produces another action, which then reduces the effect of the first action

feeder /ˈfiːdə/ noun [C] **1** the part of a machine through which you put things into the machine **2** **GEOGRAPHY** a stream that flows into a larger river **3** a minor road, railway line, or air service that leads to a major one **4** an animal or insect that eats a particular food or eats food in a particular way: *The fish is mainly a plankton feeder* (=feeds on plankton).

feeding ground /ˈfiːdɪŋ ˌɡraʊnd/ noun [C] a place where a group of animals regularly go to look for food and eat it

feel¹ /fiːl/ (**feels**, **feeling**, **felt** /felt/) verb

1 be in state mentioned	**7** have an opinion
2 have emotion/feeling	**8** be affected by sth
3 give sb a feeling	**9** search with hands
4 touch sth	**+ PHRASE**
5 seem when touched	**+ PHRASAL VERB**
6 notice sth	

1 [linking verb] to be in a particular state as a result of an emotion or a physical feeling: *I was feeling quite cheerful when we set out.* ♦ *Are you feeling ill?* ♦ *I feel such a fool for believing him.* ♦ *How do you feel now?* ♦ *I felt as though someone had just punched me in the stomach.* ♦ *When I came back to England, I felt like a stranger.*
2 [T] to experience a particular emotion or physical feeling: *He felt a sudden pain in his chest.* ♦ *Richard felt no guilt at all for what he had done.* ♦ *Cara felt the need to talk to someone.* ♦ *Children don't seem to feel the cold as much as adults do.*
3 [linking verb] if something feels nice, good, strange etc, it gives you this feeling: *It certainly felt good to be back home.*
4 [T] to touch something with your hand so that you

can discover what it is like: *She felt the child's forehead to see if he was hot.*
5 [linking verb] if something feels soft, hard etc, that is what it is like when you touch it: *Your hair feels so soft.*
6 [T] to notice something that is touching you or something that is happening to you or near you: *Can you feel the draught coming from under the door?* ♦ *I felt I was being watched.*
7 [I/T] to have a particular way of thinking about something: *I feel that more should be done to help young people.* ♦ *I know that Sally feels strongly about this issue.*
8 [T] to be affected by something: *People should feel the benefits of the tax cuts by next month.*
9 [I] to try to find something with your hands: *I felt around on the ground but couldn't find the torch.*

> **PHRASE** **feel your way 1** to move slowly and carefully, touching things with your hands because you cannot see **2** to make decisions and changes slowly, because you are not certain about what you are doing → HOME¹

> **PHRASAL VERB** **'feel for sb** to feel sympathy for someone: *I really feel for people who suffer from depression.*

feel² /fiːl/ noun [singular] **1** the way that something seems when you touch it or when it touches you: *Ben was enjoying the feel of the breeze in his hair.* **2** the way that something such as a place generally seems to you: *The village has a lovely friendly feel.* **3** an act of touching someone or something

> **PHRASE** **get a feel for sth** or **get the feel of sth** *informal* to develop a good knowledge or understanding of something

feeler /ˈfiːlə/ noun [C] **BIOLOGY** an organ of touch in various animals, for example an insect's **antenna** —*picture* → SPIDER

feeling /ˈfiːlɪŋ/ noun **1** [C] an emotional state, for example anger or happiness: *He found it difficult to express his feelings.* ♦ *I didn't want to hurt his feelings* (=upset him). ♦ *Stephen had a sudden feeling of panic.* **2** [C] an opinion that you have about something, which is based on general thoughts: *My feeling is that we should wait a week or two.* ♦ *Sarah has very strong feelings about environmental issues.* **3** [C] something that you feel physically in your body: *a feeling of nausea* **4** [U] the ability to feel something such as pain or heat in your body: *She had lost all feeling in her right arm.*

> **PHRASES** **bad/ill feeling** angry feelings that remain between people after a disagreement
> **have/get a/the feeling (that)** to be conscious of something but not certain about it: *I have a feeling we've met before.*

fee-paying /ˈfiː ˌpeɪɪŋ/ adj **1** **EDUCATION** a fee-paying school charges parents money for teaching their children **2** a fee-paying passenger, student etc pays money for a service

feet /fiːt/ the plural of **foot**

feign /feɪn/ verb [T] *formal* to pretend to have a particular feeling

feint /feɪnt/ verb [I/T] to pretend to make a movement, especially to trick an opponent

feldspar /ˈfelspɑː/ noun [U] **GEOLOGY** a type of hard pale stone

feline /ˈfiːlaɪn/ adj **BIOLOGY** connected with cats —**feline** noun [C]

fell¹ /fel/ verb [T] to cut down a tree

fell² /fel/ the past tense of **fall**¹

fellow /ˈfeləʊ/ adj used for talking about people who are similar to you or are in the same situation as you: *Ali is one of my fellow students.*

fellowship /ˈfeləʊʃɪp/ noun **1** [U] a feeling of friendship and support between people who do the same work or have the same interests **2** [C] **EDUCATION** the status of a senior member of a university or college

felon /ˈfelən/ noun [C] **LAW** American someone who has committed a serious crime such as murder or **robbery** = **CRIMINAL**

felony /ˈfeləni/ noun [C/U] **LAW** American a serious crime such as murder or **robbery** → MISDEMEANOUR

felt¹ /felt/ noun [U] a thick soft cloth made from wool, hair, or fur fibres that have been rolled and pressed flat

felt² /felt/ the past tense and past participle of **feel¹**

female¹ /ˈfiːmeɪl/ adj **BIOLOGY 1** belonging to the sex that can give birth or lay eggs ≠ MALE: *a female elephant* ♦ *a female police officer* **2** relating to a part of a plant, for example an ovary or **pistil**, that produces seeds after fertilization **3** relating to a **gamete** that is not male

female² /ˈfiːmeɪl/ noun [C] **BIOLOGY** a female person or animal ≠ MALE

feminine /ˈfemənɪn/ adj **1** having qualities that are traditionally considered to be typical of women ≠ MASCULINE: *The look this year is soft and feminine.* ♦ *conventional notions of feminine beauty* **2** **LANGUAGE** in some languages, feminine nouns, pronouns, and adjectives have different forms from **masculine** or neuter words

femininity /ˌfeməˈnɪnəti/ noun [U] qualities that are considered to be typical of women ≠ MASCULINITY

feminism /ˈfemənɪz(ə)m/ noun [U] **SOCIAL STUDIES** the belief that women should have the same rights and opportunities as men —**feminist** /ˈfemənɪst/ adj, noun [C]

femto- /femtəʊ/ prefix 10⁻¹⁵: used with some nouns

femur /ˈfiːmə/ noun [C] **ANATOMY** the bone in the top part of the leg, above the knee —*picture* → SKELETON

fence¹ /fens/ noun [C] **1** a flat upright structure made of wood or wire that surrounds an area of land **2** **SPORTS** a structure that horses jump over in a competition or race

fence² /fens/ verb **1** [I] **SPORTS** to fight with a light thin sword as a sport **2** [T] to put a fence around something

fencing /ˈfensɪŋ/ noun [U] **1** **SPORTS** the sport of fighting with a light thin sword **2** fences, or the materials that are used for making them

fend /fend/

PHRASAL VERBS ,**fend for your**'**self** to look after yourself without help from anyone else: *The kittens have been fending for themselves since they were six weeks old.* ,**fend sb/sth** '**off** to defend yourself against criticism or an attack: *He tried to fend off accusations of corruption.*

feng shui /ˌfʌŋ ˈʃweɪ/ noun [U] a Chinese system of designing buildings according to special rules about the flow of energy that is thought to influence people's lives

fennel /ˈfen(ə)l/ noun [U] a pale green vegetable with seeds and leaves that are used for adding flavour to food —*picture* → VEGETABLE

feral /ˈferəl, ˈfɪərəl/ adj *formal* a feral cat or other animal is one that lives in a wild state but was once kept as a pet or lived on a farm

ferment /fəˈment/ verb [I/T] **BIOLOGY, CHEMISTRY** if organic molecules ferment, or if they are fermented, microorganisms cause them to separate into simpler substances and to produce heat and gases when doing this. For example, sugar is changed to alcohol by the action of yeast.

fermentation /ˌfɜːmenˈteɪʃ(ə)n/ noun [U] **BIOLOGY, CHEMISTRY** the process by which microorganisms cause organic molecules to separate into simpler substances and to produce heat and gases while doing this. An example of this is the way sugar is changed to alcohol by the action of yeast.

fermium /ˈfɜːmiəm/ noun [U] **CHEMISTRY** a radioactive metallic element in the **actinide** group of the periodic table. Chemical symbol: **Fm**

fern /fɜːn/ noun [C] **BIOLOGY** a plant without flowers that usually has feather-shaped leaves. It reproduces by means of spores.

ferocious /fəˈrəʊʃəs/ adj violent and able to cause serious damage or injury: *a ferocious attack* —**ferociously** adv

ferocity /fəˈrɒsəti/ noun [U] violence, or extreme force

ferret /ˈferɪt/ noun [C] a small thin furry mammal with a long tail that people sometimes use for hunting

ferrite /ˈferaɪt/ noun [C] **CHEMISTRY** a mixed **oxide** of iron and another metal such as **cobalt** or **nickel**

ferromagnetic /ˌferəʊmægˈnetɪk/ adj **PHYSICS** ferromagnetic substances are attracted by a magnet. Iron, **cobalt**, and **nickel** are ferromagnetic metals. —**ferromagnetism** /ˌferəʊˈmægnətɪz(ə)m/ noun [U]

ferromanganese /ˌferəʊmæŋɡəˈniːz/ noun [U] **CHEMISTRY, TECHNOLOGY** an iron alloy with a high content of **manganese**. It is used to remove oxygen from steel.

ferrous metal /ˌferəs ˈmet(ə)l/ noun [C] **CHEMISTRY, TECHNOLOGY** a metal containing iron

ferry¹ /ˈferi/ (plural **ferries**) or **ferryboat** /ˈferiˌbəʊt/ noun [C] a boat that makes short regular journeys between two or more places: *They took the ferry to Dover.*

ferry² /ˈferi/ (**ferries**, **ferrying**, **ferried**) verb [T] to carry people or goods between two or more places: *Passengers were ferried to the island in a small plane.*

fertile /ˈfɜːtaɪl/ adj **1** **BIOLOGY** a fertile person, animal, or plant is able to produce babies, young animals, or new plants ≠ INFERTILE **2** **AGRICULTURE** fertile land is able to produce good crops or plants **3** a fertile mind or situation is able to produce good ideas or results: *a child's fertile imagination*

fertility /fɜːˈtɪləti/ noun [U] **1** **BIOLOGY** the ability of a woman or female animal to produce young: *fertility treatment* **2** **AGRICULTURE** the ability of the soil to produce a lot of good crops or other plants **3** **SOCIAL STUDIES** the number of children born into a family, a group, or into society generally

fertilization /ˌfɜːtəlaɪˈzeɪʃ(ə)n/ noun [U] **1** **BIOLOGY** the joining together of a female and a male gamete (=reproductive cell) in order to make a **zygote** (=fertilized egg) that will develop into a completely new plant, human being or other organism. In mammals, birds, and reptiles, fertilization takes place inside the female's body, while in animals such as fish and amphibians, the eggs are fertilized in water. In plants, fertilization takes place inside the flower. —*picture* → on next page **2** **AGRICULTURE** the process of fertilizing soil

fertilization in flowers

1 The tip of the stigma is covered with a sugary solution. Each species has a different composition of sugar solution. This prevents the germination of pollen grains from different species.

5 The male nucleus enters the ovule and fuses with the egg nucleus. This is fertilization. A zygote is formed.

stigma

ovary

style

ovule

male nucleus

2 The sugar solution stimulates the pollen grain of the same species to develop a pollen tube.

3 The pollen tube grows and digests its way slowly through the stigma and style. The pollen tube carries the male nucleus towards the ovule.

egg nucleus

4 The pollen tube grows towards the ovule. It is guided by chemicals.

fertilization in mammals

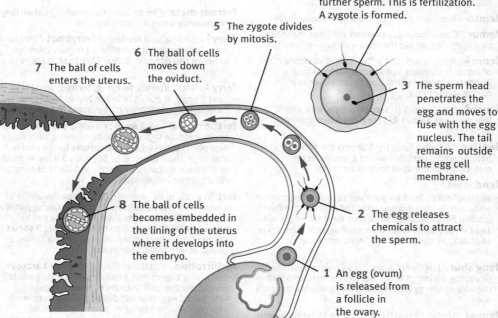

4 When the sperm penetrates the egg, a barrier forms to prevent the entry of further sperm. This is fertilization. A zygote is formed.

5 The zygote divides by mitosis.

6 The ball of cells moves down the oviduct.

7 The ball of cells enters the uterus.

3 The sperm head penetrates the egg and moves to fuse with the egg nucleus. The tail remains outside the egg cell membrane.

8 The ball of cells becomes embedded in the lining of the uterus where it develops into the embryo.

2 The egg releases chemicals to attract the sperm.

1 An egg (ovum) is released from a follicle in the ovary.

fertilize /ˈfɜːtəlaɪz/ verb [T] **1** BIOLOGY to provide the male gamete that will join with a female gamete to make a new organism **2** AGRICULTURE to add a substance to soil in order to help plants to grow

fertilizer /ˈfɜːtəlaɪzə/ noun [C/U] AGRICULTURE a substance that is added to soil in order to help plants grow

fervent /ˈfɜːv(ə)nt/ adj very enthusiastic and sincere about something that you believe in or support —**fervently** adv

fervour /ˈfɜːvə/ noun [U] excitement caused by strong feelings or beliefs

fester /ˈfestə/ verb [I] **1** if an injury festers, it becomes infected **2** if a problem or unpleasant feeling festers, it becomes worse because no one has dealt with it: *Racial tension had been festering in the community for years.*

festival /ˈfestɪv(ə)l/ noun [C] **1** a series of performances of films, plays, music, or dancing that is usually organized in the same place at the same time each year **2** a day or period when there is a public holiday, often to celebrate a religious event: *the Indian festival of Diwali*

festive /ˈfestɪv/ adj connected with a festival or celebration: *the festive season* (=Christmas)

festivities /feˈstɪvətiz/ noun [plural] lively and enjoyable activities in which people celebrate something

fetal /ˈfiːt(ə)l/ adj BIOLOGY **foetal**

fetch /fetʃ/ verb [T] **1** to go and get someone or something: *He went to fetch his coat.* ♦ *Peter was sent to fetch the doctor.* → BRING **2** to be sold for a particular amount of money: *The painting is expected to fetch up to £2,000.*

fetched test data /ˌfetʃt ˈtest ˌdeɪtə/ noun [U] COMPUTING data that will produce known results, which is prepared for the purpose of testing a new program

fetus /ˈfiːtəs/ noun [C] BIOLOGY a **foetus**

feud /fjuːd/ noun [C] an angry disagreement between two people or groups that continues for a long time: *a bitter feud between rival gangs* —**feud** verb [I]

feudal /ˈfjuːd(ə)l/ adj SOCIAL STUDIES relating to the social system that existed in Europe in the Middle Ages, in which most people worked and fought for the powerful people who owned their land —**feudalism** noun [U]

fever /ˈfiːvə/ noun **1** [C/U] HEALTH a medical condition in which the temperature of the body is very high = TEMPERATURE **2** [U] strong excitement and enthusiasm: *The country was gripped by World Cup fever.* —**fevered** /ˈfiːvəd/ adj

feverish /ˈfiːvərɪʃ/ adj **1** affected by fever **2** extremely excited: *There was a lot of feverish activity backstage.* —**feverishly** adv

few /fjuː/ (**fewer**, **fewest**) determiner, pronoun **1** some, but not many: *A few of the plates were chipped.* ♦ *We've only invited a few friends.* ♦ *We'll need a few more chairs.* ♦ *The situation will change in the next few years.* ♦ *Clean the cage every few days.* **2** very small in number: *Few managers attend the meetings.* ♦ *She approached several people, but few were interested.* ♦ *Few of his friends know the truth.* ♦ *Why were there so few women in Parliament?* ♦ *The few who saw the movie enjoyed it.*

■ **A few** usually has a positive meaning and refers to a number of people or things that is not very large: *I've got a few questions for you.* **Few** usually has a negative meaning and refers to a number that is smaller than you would like or expect: *Very few people came to her party.* **Few** is rather formal when used in this negative way and in spoken English it is more usual to say **not many**.

→ LESS

Both **fewer** and **less** can be used to refer to an amount that is smaller than another amount.
■ Use **fewer** before plural nouns: *Fewer people came than we expected.* ♦ *There are fewer restaurants in the area these days.*
■ Use **less** before uncountable nouns: *It took less time than I thought.* ♦ *You should use less paint.*

fiancé /fiˈɒnseɪ/ noun [C] the man that a woman is going to marry

fiancée /fiˈɒnseɪ/ noun [C] the woman that a man is going to marry

fiasco /fiˈæskəʊ/ (plural **fiascos**) noun [C] a complete and embarrassing failure

fibre /ˈfaɪbə/ noun **1** [U] BIOLOGY, HEALTH the parts of fruit, vegetables, and grains containing cellulose that help food to pass through the body but that the body does not use: *foods that are high in fibre* **2** [C] a type of cloth, or one of the very thin natural or artificial pieces that cloth is made from: *natural fibres such as linen and cotton* **3** [C/U] ANATOMY one of the thin pieces that form the nerves and muscles in the body

fibreglass /ˈfaɪbəɡlɑːs/ noun [U] a light hard substance made from very thin pieces of glass

fibre 'optics noun [U] the use of long thin pieces of glass or plastic to carry information from one place to another as light signals —**fibre-optic** adj

fibril /ˈfaɪbrɪl/ noun [C] ANATOMY a small thin muscle fibre

fibrin /ˈfɪbrɪn/ noun [U] BIOLOGY a type of protein that is produced by the blood near an injury to the flesh. It forms threads that catch red blood cells, and **platelets** so that a clot forms.

fibrous /ˈfaɪbrəs/ adj containing fibres, or similar to fibres

fibrous 'capsule noun [C] ANATOMY the outer layer of the knee —*picture* → JOINT

fibrous 'root noun [C] BIOLOGY a root system in some plants such as grasses that consists of very many thin roots of about the same length

fibula /ˈfɪbjʊlə/ noun [C] ANATOMY the outer narrow bone in the bottom part of the leg. The wider bone next to it is called the **tibia**. —*picture* → SKELETON

fiction /ˈfɪkʃ(ə)n/ noun **1** [U] LITERATURE books and stories about imaginary events and people: *Hardy wrote poetry as well as fiction.* **2** [C/U] a report, story, or explanation that is not true: *His account of what happened was pure fiction.* → NON-FICTION, SCIENCE FICTION

fictional /ˈfɪkʃ(ə)nəl/ adj LITERATURE invented for a book, play etc: *a fictional character*

fictitious /fɪkˈtɪʃəs/ adj invented and not real or true

fiddle /ˈfɪd(ə)l/ verb [I] to keep touching or moving something: *Mary fiddled with her keys.*

fiddly /ˈfɪd(ə)li/ adj *informal* complicated or detailed and needing attention or care

fidelity /fɪˈdeləti/ noun [U] **1** the attitude or behaviour of someone who is willing to have sex only with their partner ≠ INFIDELITY **2** *formal* loyalty to someone or something

fidget /ˈfɪdʒɪt/ verb [I] to keep making small quick movements because you are bored, nervous, or impatient —**fidgety** adj

fiduciary¹ /fɪˈdjuːʃiəri/ adj LAW involving responsibility for looking after money or property that belongs to someone else

fiduciary² /fɪˈdjuːʃiəri/ noun [C] LAW a person or company that is responsible for looking after money or property that belongs to someone else

field¹ /fiːld/ noun [C]

1 area for farming	6 area with gas, coal etc
2 subject or type of work	7 area that can be seen
3 area for sport	8 everyone in
4 space for information	competition
5 where force has effect	9 team throwing ball

1 an area of land that is used for keeping animals or growing food: *a field of wheat*
2 a subject that someone studies, or a type of work that someone does: *Professor Edwards is one of the main experts in his field.* ♦ *the field of organic chemistry*
3 SPORTS an area of land that is covered in grass and used for sport: *a football field*
4 COMPUTING a space where you can type information in a computer program: *Type your name in the User field.*
5 PHYSICS an area where a particular force has an effect: *a magnetic field*
6 GEOLOGY an area where gas, coal, oil, or other useful substances are found
7 an area that a person or piece of equipment can see at one time: *A man walked into my field of vision.* ♦ *a telescope's field of view*
8 [singular] SPORTS all the people or animals taking part in a race or competition
9 the field SPORTS the team in a sport such as **cricket** that is throwing the ball and trying to catch it when the other team hits it

field² /fiːld/ verb [T] **1** SPORTS to catch or pick up the ball in a sport such as **cricket** when a player from the other team hits it **2** to use a person or group of people as your representative or team: *The Labour Party will be fielding over 400 candidates in the election.* **3** to deal with something such as a difficult question or a telephone call

fielder /ˈfiːldə/ noun [C] SPORTS a player in a sport such as **cricket** whose job is to catch or pick up the ball when a player from the other team hits it

'field e,vent noun [C] SPORTS a sports event that is not a race, for example throwing a **javelin** or jumping

'field ,hospital noun [C] a temporary hospital for injured soldiers near an area of fighting

field marshal /ˈfiːld ˌmɑːʃ(ə)l/ noun [C] an officer of the highest rank in the British Army

'field ,trip noun [C] EDUCATION a visit to a place that gives students the chance to study something in a real environment, rather than in a classroom or laboratory

fieldwork /ˈfiːldˌwɜːk/ noun [U] EDUCATION work that involves going outside the classroom or laboratory to study something in a real environment

fierce /fɪəs/ adj **1** very angry, or ready to attack: *a fierce dog* **2** involving very strong feelings such as determination, anger, or hate: *a fierce debate* **3** very strong, or severe: *a fierce storm* ♦ *fierce competition* —**fiercely** adv

fiery /ˈfaɪri/ adj becoming angry very easily and quickly

FIFO /ˈfaɪfəʊ/ BUSINESS first in, first out: a method used for calculating the value of **stock** (=goods available for sale) according to which the goods that a

business has bought first are considered to be the ones that it sells first

fifteen /ˌfɪfˈtiːn/ number the number 15

fifteenth /ˌfɪfˈtiːnθ/ number **1** in the place or position counted as number 15 **2** one of 15 equal parts of something

fifth /fɪfθ/ number **1** in the place or position counted as number five **2** one of five equal parts of something

,fifth-gene'ration adj COMPUTING fifth-generation computer technology is very advanced and includes **artificial intelligence**

fifties /ˈfɪftiz/ noun [plural]
PHRASES **the fifties 1** the years from 1950 to 1959 **2** a temperature in the fifties is between 50 and 59 degrees Fahrenheit
in your fifties aged between 50 and 59

fiftieth /ˈfɪftiəθ/ number **1** in the place or position counted as number 50 **2** one of 50 equal parts of something

fifty /ˈfɪfti/ number the number 50

,fifty-'fifty adj, adv equal, or into two equal parts: *a fifty-fifty chance of winning* ♦ *Expenses were shared fifty-fifty.*

fig /fɪg/ noun [C] a fruit with purple or green skin and many small seeds —*picture* → FRUIT

fig. abbrev figure: a picture, graph, or table in a book

fight¹ /faɪt/ (**fights, fighting, fought** /fɔːt/) verb **1** [I/T] to violently oppose and try to defeat someone, using weapons or physical strength: *He fought in the last war.* ♦ *We were fighting for freedom.* ♦ *Protestors fought with the police outside.* ♦ *Children were fighting over scraps of food.* **2** [I] to disagree or argue about something: *I don't want to fight over this.* ♦ *What are you two fighting about now?* **3** [I/T] to try very hard to achieve something, or to stop something bad from happening: *She spent her life fighting racism.* ♦ *We fought hard for our rights.* ♦ *Local campaigners are fighting to save the building.* **4** [T] to try very hard not to show a feeling, or not to do something that you want to do: *She fought the urge to run after him.*
PHRASE **fight a fire/blaze** to try to stop a large fire from burning
PHRASAL VERBS **,fight 'back** to hit or kick someone who is attacking you, or to argue when someone criticizes you
,fight sth 'back to try very hard not to show an emotion: *Mary fought back her tears.*
,fight sb 'off to stop someone who is trying to attack you

fight² /faɪt/ noun [C]

1 hitting and kicking	4 attempt to
2 between soldiers	stop/achieve
3 disagreement/	5 in boxing
argument	+ PHRASE

1 a situation in which people hit each other: *He had a fight with a man in the pub.* ♦ *fights between rival fans*
2 a battle between soldiers or armies
3 a situation in which people disagree or argue with each other= DISAGREEMENT: *Most teenagers have fights with their parents.*
4 a determined attempt to achieve something, or to stop something bad from happening= STRUGGLE: *the fight against terrorism* ♦ *the fight to protect our children*
5 SPORTS an occasion when people fight in a boxing match
PHRASE **put up a good fight** to try hard to achieve something even though you do not succeed

fighter /'faɪtə/ noun [C] **1** a military aircraft that is designed for battles with other aircraft **2** someone who refuses to be defeated even in the most difficult situations **3 SPORTS** someone who takes part in the sport of boxing

figurative /'fɪɡərətɪv/ adj **1 LANGUAGE** a figurative meaning is not the usual **literal** meaning of a word or phrase, but makes a description more interesting: *'My love is like a red, red rose' is an example of the figurative use of language.* **2 ARTS** figurative art represents people, objects, and scenes, rather than representing feelings or ideas —**figuratively** adv

figure¹ /'fɪɡə/ noun [C]

1 number	5 drawing in a book
2 amount of money	6 mathematical shape
3 person	+ PHRASE
4 woman's shape	

1 MATHS a number that has been counted or calculated: *This year's sales figures were excellent.*
2 a price, cost, or other amount of money: *It's difficult to put an exact figure on the rebuilding work.*
3 a person: *A small figure appeared in the doorway.*
♦ *She was the dominant figure in British politics in the 1980s.*
4 the shape of a woman's body: *She has a beautiful figure.*
5 ARTS a drawing in a book that gives information
= DIAGRAM, ILLUSTRATION
6 MATHS a mathematical shape: *a five-sided figure*
PHRASE **figure of speech LANGUAGE** an expression in which the words are used in a figurative way

figure² /'fɪɡə/ verb **1** [I] to be an important part of something **2** [I/T] *informal* to think that something is true, although you do not know for certain
PHRASAL VERB **,figure sth 'out** to be able to understand something, or to solve a problem

figurehead /'fɪɡə,hed/ noun [C] a leader who has no power or influence

'figure ,skating noun [U] **SPORTS** a type of **skating** in which someone has to jump, spin, and move round the ice in a particular way —**'figure-,skater** noun [C]

figurine /'fɪɡəriːn/ noun [C] **ARTS** a small model of a person kept as a decoration

filament /'fɪləmənt/ noun [C] **1 PHYSICS** the thin wire inside a **light bulb** —*picture* → LIGHT BULB **2 BIOLOGY** the long thin stem of a stamen of a flower. It supports the **anther.** —*picture* → FLOWER

file¹ /faɪl/ noun [C] **1** a set of documents or records that someone keeps because they contain information: *medical files* ♦ *We have all your details on file* (=kept in a file). ♦ *The police file on the case has now been closed.* **2 COMPUTING** a set of information that is stored on a computer and is given a particular name **3** a metal tool that is used for making wood or metal smooth —*picture* → TOOL **4** a box or container in which papers are kept together —*picture*
→ WORKSTATION

file² /faɪl/ verb **1** [T] to put a document into a container with other documents: *File the forms in alphabetical order.* **2** [T] to make an official statement or complaint by giving it to people in authority: *The family has filed a lawsuit against the company.* ♦ *The couple filed for divorce* (=told the court that they wanted to get divorced) *last month.* **3** [I] if people file somewhere, they walk there in a line: *Students filed into the lecture hall.* **4** [T] to rub something with a metal tool in order to make it smooth, or in order to cut it

'file ex,tension noun [C] **COMPUTING** the second part of the name of a computer file, that tells you what kind of file it is. For example, 'exe' and 'doc' are file extensions.

'file ,format noun [C] **COMPUTING** the way that a particular computer program stores information in a file

file locking /'faɪl ,lɒkɪŋ/ noun [U] **COMPUTING** a feature of software that prevents information in a file from being changed by two different users at the same time

'file ,manager noun [C] **COMPUTING** a computer program that organizes computer files into groups and shows you where they are when you need to find them again

filename /'faɪl,neɪm/ noun [C] **COMPUTING** the name that someone gives to a particular computer file

'file pro,tection noun [U] **COMPUTING** a feature of computer equipment or software that prevents a file from being changed or destroyed by accident

'file ,server noun [C] **COMPUTING** a computer that stores information that can be used by people with other computers connected to the same **network**

file-sharing /'faɪl ,ʃeərɪŋ/ noun [U] **COMPUTING** the sharing of computer files by several people working on different computers, especially using a computer **network**

'file transfer u,tility noun [C] **COMPUTING** a feature of a piece of software that connects two computers and allows files to pass from to the other

'filing ,cabinet noun [C] a tall piece of furniture with drawers in for storing documents —*picture*
→ WORKSTATION

filings /'faɪlɪŋz/ noun [plural] very small pieces of metal that have been **filed** from a larger piece: *iron filings*

fill /fɪl/ verb

1 make sth full	6 feel emotion strongly
2 become full of sth	7 spend time doing sth
3 put sth in hole/gap	+ PHRASE
4 of sound/smell/light	+ PHRASAL VERBS
5 be given job/position	

1 [T] to make something full: *Let me fill your glass.*
♦ *The room was filled with thick smoke.*
2 [I] to become full of something: *The bar was slowly filling with people.*
3 [T] to put something into a hole or **gap** so that the hole or **gap** no longer exists: *We used cement to fill the cracks.*
4 [T] if sound, smell, or light fills a place, it is very strong or noticeable: *Brilliant sunlight filled the whole room.*
5 [T] if someone fills a job or position, they are given that job or position: *All the vacancies have now been filled.*
6 [T] if something fills you with a particular emotion, you feel that emotion very strongly: *The sound of his voice filled me with dread.*
7 [T] if you fill a period of time, you spend it doing something
PHRASE **fill a need/gap/void/vacuum** to provide something that is missing or needed
PHRASAL VERBS **,fill sth 'in** to add information in the empty spaces on an official document: *Please fill in the application form.*
,fill sth 'out to add information in the empty spaces on an official document: *Have you filled out the form?*
,fill 'up *same as* **fill** sense 2: *The room was beginning to fill up.*

,fill sth 'up same as **fill** sense 1: *Would you fill up that jug for me?*

filler metal /ˈfɪlə ˌmet(ə)l/ noun [C] **TECHNOLOGY** a metal rod that melts to fill and strengthen the joint between two pieces of metal during welding, **soldering**, or **brazing**

filler rod /ˈfɪlə ˌrɒd/ noun [C] **TECHNOLOGY** a **filler metal**

fillet¹ /ˈfɪlɪt/ noun **1** [C/U] a piece of meat or fish with no bones in it **2** [C] **CONSTRUCTION** a narrow piece of wood or metal, for example one that fills a gap in a roof

fillet² /ˈfɪlɪt/ verb [T] to prepare fish or meat for cooking by removing the bones

'fillet ,weld noun [C] **TECHNOLOGY** a weld formed where two surfaces meet at right angles

filling¹ /ˈfɪlɪŋ/ noun **1** [C/U] the cream, fruit etc that forms the inside part of a cake or pie **2** [C] a small amount of metal or plastic that is used for filling a hole in a tooth

filling² /ˈfɪlɪŋ/ adj food that is filling makes you feel full

film¹ /fɪlm/ noun **1** [C] **ARTS** a set of moving pictures that tell a story = MOVIE: *Have you seen the new James Bond film?* ◆ *We watched a **film about** prison life.* **2** [U] **ARTS** the job or business of making films **3** [C/U] the material that is used for taking photographs or for recording moving pictures: *I need a new film for my camera.* —*picture* → CAMERA **4** [C] a very thin layer of something that forms on a surface: *a film of oil on the water*

film² /fɪlm/ verb [I/T] **ARTS** to use a camera to record moving pictures: *The programme was filmed in South Africa.*

filming /ˈfɪlmɪŋ/ noun [U] **ARTS** the activity of making a film

'film ,script noun [C] **ARTS** a film as it is written down, including the words that the actors say, stage instructions, instructions to the people operating the cameras etc

filter¹ /ˈfɪltə/ noun [C] **1** **SCIENCE** a piece of equipment that removes substances that are present in a liquid or gas **2** a glass or plastic object that is put on a camera to change the colour or amount of light that passes through the lens **3** **COMPUTING** a computer program that prevents some types of information from appearing on a computer when someone searches the Internet

filter² /ˈfɪltə/ verb **1** [T] to pass a liquid or gas through a filter in order to remove substances that are contained in it **2** [I] if light or sound filters into a place, only a little of it enters that place: *The August sunlight filtered in through the blinds.* **3** [I] if information filters out or through to people, they receive it after a period of time: *News of the decision filtered out to reporters.*

'filter ,element noun [C] **ENGINEERING** a piece of equipment in a vehicle's engine that prevents harmful particles from getting into the engine's cylinders

'filter ,funnel noun [C] **SCIENCE** a **funnel** that holds the **filter paper** during **filtration** —*picture* → LABORATORY

'filter ,lens noun [C] **TECHNOLOGY** one of the inner lenses of a pair of **welding goggles**, usually green in colour

'filter ,paper noun [U] **SCIENCE** paper that is used inside a filter and prevents some substances passing through —*picture* → FILTER

filth /fɪlθ/ noun [U] very unpleasant dirt

filthy /ˈfɪlθi/ (**filthier, filthiest**) adj very dirty

filtrate /ˈfɪltreɪt/ noun [C] **CHEMISTRY** a material that has passed through a filter, usually a liquid or gas from which **impurities** have been removed —*picture* → FILTER

filtration /fɪlˈtreɪʃ(ə)n/ noun [U] **CHEMISTRY** the process of removing the solid parts from a mixture, for example water or air, by passing it through a filter

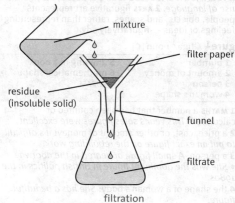

mixture

filter paper

residue (insoluble solid)

funnel

filtrate

filtration

fin /fɪn/ noun [C] **BIOLOGY** a thin flat part that sticks out of the body of a fish

final¹ /ˈfaɪn(ə)l/ adj **1** existing at the end of a process: *These issues will be discussed in the final report.* ◆ *The **final score** was 2–2.* **2** last in a series: *The final payment is due next month.* **3** if something is final, it cannot be changed: *The editor's decision is final.* **4** showing that something has finished: *the final whistle of the match*

final² /ˈfaɪn(ə)l/ noun **1** [C] **SPORTS** the last game, race etc in a competition that decides who wins the whole competition **2 finals** [plural] **EDUCATION** the last set of examinations that students take before they finish at a college or university

,final desti'nation noun [C] **TOURISM** a place that someone reaches at the end of a journey after stopping at several places on the way

finale /fɪˈnɑːli/ noun [C] **MUSIC** the last part of a performance with the most exciting music and dancing

finalist /ˈfaɪn(ə)lɪst/ noun [C] **SPORTS** a player or team that takes part in the final game in a competition

finalize /ˈfaɪnəlaɪz/ verb [T] to make the final decisions or arrangements for something

finally /ˈfaɪn(ə)li/ adv **1** after a long time, process, or series of events: *We finally arrived home at midnight.* **2** *spoken* as the last thing that you want to say: *Finally, I'd like to say thank you.* **3** *formal* in a way that cannot be changed: *The exact amount has not been finally decided.*

finance¹ /ˈfaɪnæns, faɪˈnæns/ noun **1** [U] decisions on how money is spent or invested: *the company's finance committee* **2** [U] **BUSINESS** money that is used to pay for something such as a large project: *Where will the finance for this project come from?* **3 finances** [plural] the money that someone has, and how well they spend it or save it: *My finances are in a terrible mess at the moment.*

finance² /ˈfaɪnæns, faɪˈnæns/ verb [T] to pay for something such as a large project: *The scheme is being financed by the Arts Council.*

financial /faɪˈnænʃ(ə)l/ adj involving money: *banks and other **financial institutions*** ◆ *We offer a range of* *financial services.* —**financially** adv: *The decision does not affect us financially.*

fi,nancial 'year noun [C] **BUSINESS** a period of twelve months that a company or organization uses for producing its accounts, which show how much profit it has made and how much it owes.

find¹ /faɪnd/ (**finds, finding, found** /faʊnd/) verb [T]

1 discover	5 make decision
2 get sth	6 have enough of sth
3 experience sth	+ PHRASES
4 have as opinion	+ PHRASAL VERB

1 to discover or notice something, often after searching: *Have you found your shoes?* ♦ *We hope to find the answers to these questions.* ♦ *I found her wandering in the streets.*
2 to get something: *Have you found accommodation yet?* ♦ *It is very difficult for young people in this area to find work.*
3 to experience something in a particular way: *William now finds walking very difficult.*
4 to have something as an opinion because of things that you have experienced: *I find that children need a lot of encouragement.*
5 to make a formal decision about something after listening to all the facts: *The court found that the company had broken the law.* ♦ *He was found guilty and sentenced to three years in prison.*
6 if someone finds the time or money to do something, they have enough time or money to do it
PHRASES be found if something is found in a particular place, it lives, grows, or exists there: *The flower is found only in the French Alps.*
find your way to manage to arrive in a place that you were not sure how to get to
find yourself doing sth to realize that you are doing something that you had not intended to do: *I found myself agreeing with everything she said.*
PHRASAL VERB ,find sth 'out to discover a fact or piece of information: *Her parents found out that she had a boyfriend.* ♦ *I don't want Jerry to find out about this.* ♦ *I want to find out what happened.*

find² /faɪnd/ noun [C] something good that you find by chance

findings /'faɪndɪŋz/ noun [plural] information or opinions that come from doing research

fine¹ /faɪn/ adj

1 good enough	4 difficult to notice
2 healthy	5 thin and narrow
3 of high quality	+ PHRASE

1 good enough, or acceptable: *'Is your room all right?' 'Yes, fine, thanks.'* ♦ *Your blood pressure is absolutely fine.*
2 healthy and happy: *'How are you?' 'Fine, thanks.'*
3 of very good quality: *fine bone china*
4 fine details are small and difficult to notice: *He spent hours explaining the finer points of the scheme.*
5 very thin and narrow, not thick or heavy: *fine hair* ♦ *a fine layer of dust*
PHRASE a fine line between if there is a fine line between two things, they are almost the same as each other

fine² /faɪn/ adv *informal* in a way that is acceptable and good enough: *My car's working fine now.*

fine³ /faɪn/ noun [C] an amount of money that someone must pay because they have broken the law: *I had to pay a $10 fine for parking on the street overnight.* ♦ *The court has the right to impose heavy fines* (=large fines).

fine⁴ /faɪn/ verb [T] to make someone pay an amount of money as a punishment for breaking the law: *She was fined £20 for speeding.*

,fine 'art noun [U] **ARTS** objects such as paintings that are created to be beautiful or interesting

finely /'faɪnli/ adv **1** into very small pieces: *Add one onion, finely chopped.* **2** exactly, or with great care: *a finely crafted machine*

,fine-tooth 'comb noun [C] a **comb** with very thin parts and very narrow spaces between them
PHRASE with a fine-tooth comb very carefully, so that you notice everything

,fine-'tune verb [T] to make small changes to something in order to make it as good as possible

finger /'fɪŋgə/ noun [C] **1** one of the four long thin parts on the end of the hands **2** a long thin piece of something: *Serve with fingers of toast.* → CROSS¹, LAY¹, PULSE, SLIP¹

fingering /'fɪŋgərɪŋ/ noun [C/U] **MUSIC** the positions of your fingers and the way that you move them when you are playing a musical instrument

fingernail /'fɪŋgəneɪl/ noun [C] the hard smooth part at the end of a finger —*picture* → BODY

fingerprint /'fɪŋgəprɪnt/ noun [C] a mark on something that someone has touched that shows the pattern of lines on their fingers

fingertip /'fɪŋgətɪp/ noun [C] the end of a finger

finish¹ /'fɪnɪʃ/ verb **1** [I/T] to do the last part of something so that it is complete: *I've nearly finished my work.* ♦ *I haven't finished eating yet.* **2** [I] to stop happening: *Lessons finish at midday.* ♦ *The game finished with the score at 1–1.* **3** [T] to eat, drink, or use all of something so that there is none left: *We finished the bottle of water.* **4** [I/T] to be in a particular position at the end of a race or competition: *She finished fifth.*
PHRASE the finishing touch/touches the last small details that make something complete
PHRASAL VERBS ,finish sth 'off 1 same as **finish¹** sense 1: *They hired a smaller company to finish off the job.* **2** same as **finish¹** sense 3: *Do you want to finish off these sandwiches?*
,finish 'up to be in a particular place or situation at the end of a long series of events: *She eventually finished up in Singapore.*
'finish with sth if you have finished with something, you have stopped using it and no longer need it: *Have you finished with the scissors yet?*

finish² /'fɪnɪʃ/ noun [C] **1** the end of something **2** the appearance of a surface, for example whether it is smooth or rough

finished /'fɪnɪʃt/ adj **1** something that is finished has been completed: *the finished product* **2** if you are finished, you have completed something that you were doing

finishing line /'fɪnɪʃɪŋ ˌlaɪn/ noun [C] **SPORTS** a line on the ground, used for showing where a race finishes

'finish ,line noun [C] **SPORTS** a finishing line

finite /'faɪnaɪt/ adj **1** existing only in limited numbers or amounts, or continuing only for a limited time or distance ≠ INFINITE **2** LANGUAGE a finite verb is a form of a verb that matches the form of other words in a sentence → INFINITIVE

f.i.o. abbrev **BUSINESS** for information only: written on a business letter or email to show that it is being sent to someone in order to give them information, and they are not expected to reply or take any action

fiord /'fiːɔːd, fjɔːd/ **GEOGRAPHY** another spelling of **fjord**

fir /fɜː/ noun [C] a tree that grows mainly in the northern half of the world and has thin sharp leaves that do not fall off in winter

fire[1] /'faɪə/ noun **1** [C/U] flames and heat from something that is burning in an uncontrolled way: *Lightning may have **started the fire**.* ◆ *A tree in the middle of the field was **on fire** (=burning).* ◆ *Suddenly the curtains **caught fire** (=began to burn).* ◆ *That night a **fire broke out** in the nightclub.* ◆ *The boys **set fire to** (=started a fire on) an old couch.* **2** [C] a small pile of burning wood, coal etc that is made in order to produce heat: *a coal fire* ◆ *Bill started to **build a fire**.* **3** [C] a piece of equipment that uses electricity or gas to heat a room: *a gas fire* **4** [U] shots from a gun: *machine gun fire* ◆ *One of the men **opened fire on** (=started shooting at) the police.* → OPEN[2]

fire[2] /'faɪə/ verb **1** [I/T] if a weapon fires, or if someone fires it, someone uses it to shoot something: *The rebels **fired** their guns into the air.* ◆ *Jed lifted his rifle and **fired at** the target.* **2** [T] to make someone leave their job as a punishment = SACK: *She was fired for theft.* **3** [T] to ask someone questions quickly: *Reporters **fired questions** at her as she left the court house.*

'fire a,larm noun [C] a piece of equipment that makes a loud noise to warn people that there is a fire

firearm /'faɪə,ɑːm/ noun [C] *formal* a gun

'fire ,blanket noun [C] a thick piece of fabric that is placed over a fire in order to put out the flames

'fire bri,gade noun [C] the organization whose job is dealing with fires in a particular area

'fire ,door noun [C] a very strong door that you close in order to prevent fire from spreading from one room to another

'fire ,drill noun [C] an occasion when all the people in a building pretend that there is a fire inside, and practise getting out safely

'fire ,engine noun [C] a large vehicle that takes firefighters and their equipment to a fire

'fire e,scape noun [C] a metal **staircase** on the outside of a building that people use to get out of the building when there is a fire

'fire ex,tinguisher noun [C] a metal container that is filled with water or with a chemical that stops fires

firefighter /'faɪə,faɪtə/ noun [C] someone whose job is to stop fires burning, and to help people to escape from other dangerous situations

firefighting /'faɪə,faɪtɪŋ/ noun [U] **1** the job of making fires stop burning **2** the activity of trying to solve a serious problem that suddenly happens by reacting quickly and effectively

firefly /'faɪə,flaɪ/ (plural **fireflies**) noun [C] an insect that produces a flashing light when it flies

fireguard /'faɪə,gɑːd/ noun [C] a metal screen that someone puts in front of a fire in a room to make it safer

'fire ,hose noun [C] a long thick rubber tube used for sending water onto a fire to stop it burning

firelight /'faɪə,laɪt/ noun [U] the light that a fire produces

fireman /'faɪəmən/ (plural **firemen** /'faɪəmən/) noun [C] a male firefighter

fireplace /'faɪə,pleɪs/ noun [C] a place in a room where a fire burns

firepower /'faɪə,paʊə/ noun [U] the weapons available to use against an enemy

fireproof /'faɪə,pruːf/ adj a fireproof object cannot be damaged by fire

'fire-re,sistant adj CONSTRUCTION fire-resistant material does not burn for a period of time when there is a fire —**fire resistance** noun [U]

firewall /'faɪə,wɔːl/ noun [C] COMPUTING a computer program that prevents people from entering a computer system illegally

firewood /'faɪə,wʊd/ noun [U] wood that is used as fuel for a fire

firework /'faɪə,wɜːk/ noun [C] an object that explodes and produces coloured lights and loud noises

firing order /'faɪərɪŋ ,ɔːdə/ noun [C] ENGINEERING the order in which **combustion** happens in the cylinders of an engine

firing squad /'faɪərɪŋ ,skwɒd/ noun [C] a group of soldiers who shoot and kill someone as a punishment

firm[1] /fɜːm/ noun [C] a business or company: *an engineering firm* ◆ *a firm of solicitors*

firm[2] /fɜːm/ adj

1 solid	4 determined
2 steady	5 tight
3 definite	

1 solid but not hard ≠ SOFT: *a firm mattress*

2 steady and not moving ≠ UNSTABLE: *Make sure the ladder is firm before you start to climb.*

3 definite and not changing: *Have you set a firm date for the meeting?* ◆ *The institution has the firm support of the local people.* ◆ *Mark's a **firm believer in** discipline for children.*

4 showing that you are in control of a situation: *What the party needs now is firm leadership.* ◆ *You sometimes have to **be firm with** young children.*

5 physically or mentally strong: *She took a firm hold of the stick and pulled.*

—**firmly** adv: *I firmly believe that we must act at once.* —**firmness** noun [U]

firring /'fɜːrɪŋ/ noun [C] CONSTRUCTION a sloping piece of wood fixed to the top of a flat roof to get rid of **rainwater**

first /fɜːst/ adv, number, pronoun, noun

1 before any others	5 better than others
2 before doing sth	6 university degree
3 at the beginning	+ PHRASES
4 most important	

1 coming, happening, or starting before any others: *What was your first job?* ◆ *Julia got there first.* ◆ *He's had a lot of girlfriends, but Lucy was **the first**.*

2 before you do something else: *Can't I just finish reading this article first?* ◆ *First, let's introduce ourselves.*

3 at the beginning of a period of time, a situation, an activity etc: *the first few days of term* ◆ *When I first knew him, he had a beard.*

4 used for referring to the main or most important thing: *His first love was music.* ◆ *My children will always **come first**.*

5 better than anyone or anything else in a game, competition etc: *Phil Gray **came first** in the under-12 section.* ◆ *His painting won **first prize** in a competition.*

6 EDUCATION in the UK and Australia, the highest mark for an **undergraduate** degree from a college or university

PHRASES **at first** in the beginning, before something changes: *At first he wouldn't even talk about it.*

at first sight/glance when you first see something or find out about something, before you know more details: *At first glance, the theory seems to make a lot of sense.*

first of all *spoken* **1** used for introducing the first of several things that you are going to say: *First of all, I'd like to thank my teacher.* **2** before doing anything else: *First of all, switch the machine off.*

,first 'aid noun [U] HEALTH basic medical treatment that is given as soon as someone is injured or becomes ill

,first 'aid ,kit noun [C] HEALTH a small box or bag with the equipment that someone needs in order to give first aid

,first-angle pro'jection noun [C/U] MATHS, PHYSICS a type of orthographic projection used in Europe and Asia in which an object is shown above and in front of two planes (=flat surfaces) that cross each other at right angles

,first 'base noun [singular] SPORTS in baseball, the first of four places the batter must run to after hitting the ball

,first 'class noun [U] 1 TOURISM the most expensive form of travel on a plane, train, or ship 2 the class of post that is the quickest and most expensive

,first-'class adj 1 of the best quality, or of the highest standard 2 TOURISM providing the most expensive form of travel or postal service —first-class adv

,first-class 'lever noun [C] PHYSICS a type of lever where the fulcrum is between the effort and the load. Hammers, scissors, and seesaws are first-class levers.

,first 'cousin noun [C] a child of your aunt or uncle

,first de'gree noun [C] EDUCATION a university course of study or qualification such as a BA or BSc for someone who does not already have such a qualification

,first-de'gree adj 1 HEALTH a first-degree burn is the least serious type 2 LAW American a first-degree murder is the most serious type, in which someone deliberately plans to kill someone

,first e'dition noun [C] one of the first printed copies of a book, newspaper, or magazine

'first-,ever adj happening for the first time

first filler pass /,fɜːst 'fɪlə ,pɑːs/ noun [singular] TECHNOLOGY in arc-welding, the first layer of weld that is laid on top of the stringer bead

the ,first 'floor noun in British English, the floor of a building that is just above the ground floor

,first 'gear noun [U] the lowest gear in a vehicle, used for starting or moving slowly

,first gene'ration noun [singular] 1 SOCIAL STUDIES the generation of people in a family who were the first from their country to go and live in another country 2 the first type of a particular machine or piece of equipment to be produced —,first-gene'ration adj

,first 'half noun [C] the first part of a sports match

,first-'hand adj, adv obtained by experiencing something yourself, not by learning about it from other people: *first-hand experience ♦ a first-hand account of the situation*

the ,First 'Lady the wife of the president of the US or of some other countries

,first 'language noun [C] LANGUAGE 1 the first language that someone learns to speak= MOTHER TONGUE 2 the main language that people speak in a region or country

,first law of 'motion noun [singular] PHYSICS one of the laws about movement that were first expressed by

Isaac Newton. It states that an object at rest will remain at rest, and an object in motion will move in a straight line with constant speed, unless it is acted on by an external force.

firstly /'fɜːs(t)li/ adv used for beginning a list of things that are in a particular order

'first ,name noun [C] the name that comes before your family name

,first of'fender noun [C] LAW someone who has committed their first crime

,first 'option noun [U] the right to be able to be the first to decide whether to buy or take something

,first-past-the-'post adj POLITICS a first-past-the-post system is one in which only the person or political party that gets the most votes is elected

the ,first 'person noun [singular] LANGUAGE the pronouns 'I' and 'we' and the verbs and object pronouns that are used with them

,first 'quarter noun [C] ASTRONOMY the shape of the Moon when it appears as half a moon, about a week after the new moon

,first-'rate adj of the highest quality

,first 'reading noun [C] POLITICS the first time that a parliament considers a proposal for a new law

first responder /,fɜːst rɪ'spɒndə/ noun [C] the person who arrives first at the scene of an accident or other emergency situation, for example a police officer or firefighter

'first-,time adj doing something for the first time

,first vio'lin noun [C] MUSIC a musician who plays the violin in an orchestra and belongs to the most important group of violinists —picture → ORCHESTRA

the ,First World 'War a war that was fought mainly in Europe between 1914 and 1918

fiscal¹ /'fɪsk(ə)l/ adj ECONOMICS relating to money and financial matters, especially taxes —fiscally adv

fiscal² /'fɪsk(ə)l/ noun [C] LAW in some countries, a public prosecutor (=lawyer for the government)

,fiscal 'year noun [C] BUSINESS American a financial year

fish¹ /fɪʃ/ (plural fish or fishes) noun 1 [C/U] BIOLOGY a vertebrate covered in scales that lives in water and swims. It breathes by using its gills and moves by using its tail and fins. Saltwater fish live in the sea and freshwater fish live in rivers and lakes. 2 [U] fish eaten as food. Fish and other sea animals such as shrimps are called seafood: *They serve the best fresh fish and seafood dishes.*

fish² /fɪʃ/ verb [I] 1 to try to catch fish 2 to try to find something by feeling inside a bag, a box etc: *She fished around in her bag for the keys.* 3 to try to make someone tell you something without asking directly: *'Having trouble?' he asked casually, fishing for information.*

fishcake /'fɪʃ,keɪk/ noun [C] 1 a flat round food made from pieces of fish and potato covered in breadcrumbs and then cooked 2 a type of Asian food that is made from fish and is usually served with rice and vegetables

fisherman /'fɪʃəmən/ (plural fishermen /'fɪʃəmən/) noun [C] a man who catches fish for fun, or as his job

fishery /'fɪʃəri/ noun [C] 1 an area of the sea where fish can be caught to be sold 2 a place where fish are bred, either to be sold for food, or to be put into lakes and rivers to catch as sport

'fish ,farm noun [C] AGRICULTURE an enclosed area of water where fish are bred

'fish ,farming noun [U] **AGRICULTURE** the practice of breeding fish to sell

fishing /'fɪʃɪŋ/ noun [U] the activity, sport, or business of catching fish: *We're going fishing tomorrow.*

'fishing ,line noun [C/U] strong string used with a fishing rod for catching fish

'fishing ,rod noun [C] a long thin pole that is used for catching fish

fishmonger /'fɪʃ,mʌŋgə/ noun [C] someone whose job is to sell fish

fishy /'fɪʃi/ adj **1** tasting or smelling like fish **2** not completely right, honest, or legal

fissile /'fɪsaɪl/ adj **PHYSICS** a fissile atom or element can be separated into parts by **nuclear fission**

fission /'fɪʃ(ə)n/ noun [U] **1 PHYSICS** the process of dividing an atom in order to make energy available → NUCLEAR FUSION **2 BIOLOGY** the process in which a cell divides into two or more parts

fist /fɪst/ noun [C] the hand when the fingers are closed tightly: *She was holding something tightly in her fist.*

fit¹ /fɪt/ (**fits, fitting, fitted** or **fit**) verb **1** [I/T] to be small enough or the right size and shape to go somewhere, or to manage to put someone or something in a space: *I don't think that box will fit.* ♦ *The book is small enough to **fit in** your pocket.* ♦ *The cover **fits** neatly **over** the chair.* ♦ *She can **fit** two more people **into** her car.* **2** [I/T] if clothes fit, they are the right size for you: *It is important that children's shoes fit correctly.* ♦ *I like the suit, but the jacket doesn't fit me.* **3** [I/T] to match, be suitable for, or be right for something: *We need a name that fits our image.* ♦ *He fits the description of a man seen running from the scene.* ♦ *Something in her story did not fit.* ♦ *A dark wooden table wouldn't **fit with** the decoration in here.* **4** [T] to add a piece of equipment to something else: *Some cars are **fitted** with hand controls for people with physical disabilities.* ♦ *You can **fit** a bike rack **to** the rear of your car.*

PHRASAL VERBS **,fit 'in** to be accepted by a group of people because you are similar to them: *I tried to fit in, but they were all much younger than I was.*

,fit sb/sth 'in to have enough time to deal with someone or something: *Dr Halden can fit you in this morning at 10.*

,fit sth 'out to put equipment into a room or building so that it can be used for a particular purpose: *The kitchen has been fitted out with pine cupboards.*

fit² /fɪt/ (**fitter, fittest**) adj **1 HEALTH** healthy, strong, and able to do physical exercise ≠ UNFIT: *Running around after the kids keeps me fit.* ♦ *I need to **get fit** before the football season starts.* **2** of a good enough standard for something ≠ UNFIT: *The house was not **fit** for human habitation.* ♦ *I don't think he's **fit** to be a teacher.*

PHRASE **see/think fit** to decide that something is the best thing to do: *The court will deal with the matter as it thinks fit.*

fit³ /fɪt/ noun **1** [C] a strong sudden physical reaction or emotion that someone cannot control: *a sneezing fit* ♦ *a **fit** of rage* **2** [C] *informal* an occasion when someone becomes unconscious for a short time and their body shakes **3** [singular] used for saying whether something is the right size and shape for someone or something: *When buying shoes, it is important to get a good fit.*

PHRASE **have/throw a fit** *informal* to get very angry and shout or become violent

fitment /'fɪtmənt/ noun [C] a piece of furniture or other object that is built into a room

fitness /'fɪtnəs/ noun [U] **1 HEALTH** the state of being physically healthy and strong: *a high level of physical fitness* **2** the degree to which someone or something is suitable: *There are questions as to his fitness for office.*

fitted /'fɪtɪd/ adj **1** made to fit the shape of something closely: *a fitted shirt* **2** built or made to fit a particular space: *fitted cupboards*

fitting /'fɪtɪŋ/ adj suitable for a particular situation: *The dinner was a fitting end to Carter's 25 years with the company.* —**fittingly** adv

five /faɪv/ number the number 5

'five-,star adj **TOURISM** a five-star hotel or restaurant is of the best quality

fix¹ /fɪks/ verb [T]

1 fasten so cannot move	4 make sth work again
2 set price/amount/date	5 stop colour change
3 cheat	+ PHRASE

1 to fasten something somewhere so that it cannot move: *Smoke detectors should be **fixed to** the ceiling.*
2 to decide what a price, amount, or date will be: *Interest rates have been **fixed at** 5%.* ♦ *A delivery date has not yet been fixed.*
3 to dishonestly arrange the result of something such as a game or election
4 to repair something: *Jessica fixed my watch.* ♦ *I have to get my car fixed.*
5 to use chemicals on something so that its colours do not change or disappear= SET: *The substance fixes the dye so it won't wash out.*

PHRASE **fix your eyes on sb/sth** to look straight at someone or something and at nothing else

fix² /fɪks/ noun **1** [C] something that solves a problem or corrects a mistake: *We need a long-term solution, not just **a quick fix** (=a fast solution but one that is usually only temporary).* **2** [singular] an amount of a drug that someone feels that they need to take regularly

fixation /fɪk'seɪʃ(ə)n/ noun [C] a very strong interest in something that prevents you from paying attention to anything else: *Doug has a fixation with sports cars.* —**fixated** /fɪk'seɪtɪd/ adj

fixed /fɪkst/ adj **1** not changing, or not able to be changed: *a fixed price* ♦ *a fixed smile* ♦ *My mother has fixed ideas about how to bring up children.* **2** fastened in one position and not able to be moved: *Make sure bookcases are securely fixed to the wall.* **3** if something such as a game or election is fixed, it is dishonestly arranged so that it has the result someone wants

,fixed 'asset noun [C] **BUSINESS** something such as buildings, land, or equipment that a company owns and uses in doing its business, but does not sell

,fixed 'capital noun [U] **BUSINESS** money that a company has invested in fixed assets

,fixed 'cost noun [C] **BUSINESS** a cost such as rent that a company has to pay that does not change according to how much it produces

,fixed 'point noun [C] **PHYSICS** the point on which a lever turns or **pivots**

,fixed 'pulley noun [C] **PHYSICS** a type of pulley where the pulley is attached to a fixed surface with a rope passing over it. Pulling on one end of the rope raises or lowers the load on the other. A **flagpole** is an example of a fixed pulley.

fixture /'fɪkstʃə/ noun [C] **1** a piece of furniture or equipment that is built as part of a building so that people do not take it with them when they move house: *light fixtures* **2 SPORTS** a sports event that happens at a regular time and place

fizz /fɪz/ noun [U] the small gas bubbles that are in some drinks —**fizz** verb [I]

fizzle /'fɪz(ə)l/ or ,**fizzle 'out** verb [I] to gradually fail, become less enthusiastic, or disappear: *The group's efforts at reform fizzled out after their leader left*.

fizzy /'fɪzi/ adj a fizzy drink is a sweet drink without alcohol that has bubbles

fjord /'fiːɔːd, fjɔːd/ noun [C] **GEOGRAPHY** a narrow section of sea that continues into the land between high rocks

flabby /'flæbi/ adj with a lot of loose fat: *a flabby stomach*

flag¹ /flæg/ noun [C] a piece of cloth with colours or a pattern on it, used as a signal or for representing a country or organization

flag² /flæg/ (**flags, flagging, flagged**) verb **1** [I] to become tired or weak, or to begin to lose enthusiasm: *After a long day, his energy flagged*. **2** [T] to mark something so that you will be able to find it again
PHRASAL VERB ,**flag sb/sth 'down** to wave at the driver of a car so that they stop: *tourists trying to flag down a cab*

'**flag ,airline** or '**flag ,carrier** noun [C] **TOURISM** the main national **airline** of a country

flagpole /'flæg,pəʊl/ noun [C] a tall thin pole, used for hanging a flag on

flagrant /'fleɪgrənt/ adj done in an obvious way that shows that someone does not care what people think: *a flagrant disregard for the law* —**flagrantly** adv

flair /fleə/ noun [U] an attractive, skilful, or interesting way of doing something: *She always dresses with flair*.

flake¹ /fleɪk/ noun [C] a small flat piece of something

flake² /fleɪk/ or ,**flake 'off** verb [I] to come off a surface in small flat pieces: *Her skin was itchy and beginning to flake*.

'**flake ,graphite** noun [U] **TECHNOLOGY** the form in which carbon is held in **grey cast iron**, in which the carbon is not chemically combined with the iron

flaky /'fleɪki/ (**flakier, flakiest**) adj breaking off easily into small flat pieces: *flaky chocolate*

flamboyant /flæm'bɔɪənt/ adj behaving or dressed in a way that deliberately attracts attention —**flamboyantly** adv

flame /fleɪm/ noun [C] **1** an amount of brightly burning gas that you see coming from a fire: *He sat by the fire staring at the flames*. ♦ *The whole building was soon in flames*. ♦ *A car had overturned and burst into flames*. **2** **COMPUTING** an angry email, or an email that insults someone

flaming /'fleɪmɪŋ/ adj **1** burning brightly: *flaming torches* **2** involving a lot of angry emotion = BLAZING: *a flaming row*

flamingo /flə'mɪŋgəʊ/ (plural **flamingos**) noun [C] a large pink tropical water bird with a long neck and long legs —*picture* → BIRD

flammable /'flæməb(ə)l/ adj **CHEMISTRY** likely to burn very quickly and easily = INFLAMMABLE ≠ NON-FLAMMABLE

> **Flammable** and **inflammable** both describe something that burns easily and quickly, but most people use **flammable** because **inflammable** looks as if it means **not flammable**.

flank /flæŋk/ noun [C] **1** the side of an animal's body **2** a position on the right or left side of a team or army, or the people in that position **3** **GEOGRAPHY** a side of a mountain, volcano, or other large natural structure

flannel /'flæn(ə)l/ noun **1** [U] soft cloth that is used for making clothes and sheets **2** [C] a small piece of cloth that you use for washing yourself

flannelboard /'flæn(ə)l,bɔːd/ noun [C] **EDUCATION** a cloth-covered board to which pictures can be stuck. It is used in primary education, especially for telling stories.

flannelgraph /'flæn(ə)l,grɑːf/ noun [C] **EDUCATION** a **flannelboard**

flap¹ /flæp/ noun [C] **1** a thin flat piece of something that is fixed to something else along one edge **2** a part of the wing of a plane that moves up and down to help control the plane —*picture* → SPACE SHUTTLE

flap² /flæp/ (**flaps, flapping, flapped**) verb **1** [I/T] if a bird's wings flap, or if the bird flaps them, they move quickly up and down **2** [I] to be blown noisily by the wind: *My coat was flapping in the wind*.

flare¹ /fleə/ noun **1** [C] a bright light or flame that is used as a signal in the dark **2** [C] a bright flame that burns for a short time **3** [singular] a shape that becomes wider at one end **4** **flares** [plural] a type of trousers that become wider at the bottom

flare² /fleə/ verb [I] **1** to suddenly burn or shine brightly **2** to suddenly become angry or violent **3** to suddenly become worse or more violent

flared /fleəd/ adj much wider at the bottom than at the top: *flared jeans*

'**flare-,up** noun [C] **1** an occasion when people suddenly start behaving in an angry or violent way **2** **HEALTH** an occasion when a disease or painful medical condition suddenly returns

flash¹ /flæʃ/ verb **1** [I/T] to shine on and off very quickly, or to make a light do this: *A truck behind me was flashing its headlights*. ♦ *His watch flashed in the sunlight*. **2** [I/T] to appear, or to make something appear, for a very short time before disappearing: *Tom flashed me a smile from across the room*. ♦ *The headlines flashed across the screen*. **3** [I] to pass very quickly: *The thought that I might die flashed through my mind*. —**flashing** adj: *flashing lights*

flash² /flæʃ/ noun [C] **1** a bright light that appears for a very short time: *a flash of lightning* **2** a bright light on a camera that flashes as someone takes a photograph **3** a moment when you suddenly understand or feel something: *a flash of inspiration* **4** a sudden instance of a particular emotion

flashback /'flæʃ,bæk/ noun **1** [C] a sudden clear memory of something that happened in the past **2** [C/U] **ARTS, LITERATURE** a part of a story, for example in a book or play, that tells you what happened earlier **3** [C] **TECHNOLOGY** an explosion produced in a **hose** (=pipe) or cylinder in **oxyacetylene welding**, when the flame begins to move back up the hose

flashcard /'flæʃ,kɑːd/ noun [C] **EDUCATION** a small card printed with words, pictures, or numbers that helps someone to learn something

'**flash distil,lation** noun [U] **CHEMISTRY, ENVIRONMENT** a method of making sea water pure by heating it so that it changes into steam. The steam is then condensed into fresh water by contact with pipes that are cooled by cool water.

'**flash ,drive** noun [C] **COMPUTING** a small plastic disk drive that stores information and that you can carry around with you. You connect the flash drive to a computer when you want to use the information.

flasher unit /'flæʃə ,juːnɪt/ noun [C] **ENGINEERING** a piece of electrical equipment in a vehicle's **indicator** lights that makes them flash

,flash 'flood noun [C] a sudden unexpected flood

flashing /'flæʃɪŋ/ noun [U] CONSTRUCTION a metal covering that protects joints and angles on a roof from **rainwater**

flashlight /'flæʃ,laɪt/ noun [C] *American* a **torch** sense 1

'flash ,memory noun [U] COMPUTING a type of computer memory that does not lose information when electrical power stops being available, and from which you can **erase** (=get rid of) information and then program it again

flashy /'flæʃi/ adj very bright, fashionable, or expensive in a way that is intended to impress people: *a flashy car*

flask /flɑːsk/ noun [C] **1** a **vacuum flask 2** a small flat bottle that fits in your pocket, used especially for carrying alcohol **3** SCIENCE a glass container with a wide base and a narrow top used in science laboratories —*picture* → LABORATORY **4** TECHNOLOGY a **moulding flask** for **casting** metal objects in sand

flat¹ /flæt/ (**flatter, flattest**) adj

1 level/smooth	7 tyre: no air
2 object: not thick	8 battery: no power
3 lying on surface	9 drink: no bubbles
4 rate/amount: fixed	10 musical note: lower
5 lacking emotion	11 out of tune
6 spoken directly	

1 smooth and level on the surface, with no lumps or slopes: *The farmland is very flat.* ♦ *a firm flat stomach* ♦ *You need a flat surface to work on.*

2 not curving inwards or outwards, and not very thick: *a monitor with a flat screen*

3 stretched out, or lying on a surface: *She was flat on her back asleep.*

4 a flat rate or amount is the same in all situations: *The bank charges a flat fee of £5 for money transfers.*

5 not showing any emotion, interest, or excitement: *The celebrations seemed rather flat.*

6 said directly and definitely: *a flat refusal*

7 a flat tyre does not have enough air in it

8 a flat battery does not have enough power left in it

9 a drink that is flat has lost its gas bubbles

10 MUSIC a B flat, E flat etc is a musical note that is one **semitone** lower than B, E etc ≠ SHARP —*picture* → MUSIC

11 MUSIC slightly lower than the musical note that should be played or sung ≠ SHARP

flat² /flæt/ noun **1** [C] a set of rooms for living in, usually on one floor of a large building: *The family live in a fourth-floor flat.* ♦ *a block of flats* (=a building with a lot of flats in it) **2** [C] MUSIC a musical note that is one **semitone** lower than a particular note —*picture* → MUSIC **3 flats** [plural] GEOGRAPHY a low flat area of land, usually wet land near a large area of water **4** [C] *informal* a **puncture¹** sense 2

flat³ /flæt/ (**flatter, flattest**) adv **1** stretched out, or lying on a surface: *He laid the map out flat on the table.* ♦ *Carole was lying flat on her back.* **2** MUSIC singing or playing musical notes that are slightly lower than they should be ≠ SHARP

flatfish /'flæt,fɪʃ/ (plural **flatfish**) noun [C] a type of sea fish with a thin flat body. **Sole** and **plaice** are types of flatfish.

flat-footed /,flæt 'fʊtɪd/ adj HEALTH having a medical condition in which the whole of the bottom of the foot touches the ground. Feet that do this are called **flat feet**.

flatland /'flæt,lænd/ noun GEOGRAPHY **1** [U] level land without mountains, hills, or valleys **2 flatlands** [plural] a region in which the land is level

flatly /'flætli/ adv **1** in a firm, definite way: *He flatly denied being near the scene of the crime.* **2** without showing any emotion or interest: *'How can I help you?'* the clerk asked flatly.

,flat panel 'monitor noun [C] COMPUTING a very thin computer screen with a flat surface that you look at

'flat ,race noun [C] SPORTS a horse race on flat ground with no fences or jumping

'flat ,racing noun [U] SPORTS horse racing on flat ground with no fences or jumping

,flat 'rate noun [C] BUSINESS a way of charging for something where the price always remains the same. For example, if a flat rate is used to charge for electricity, the cost of the electricity is same for each kilowatt hour, however much electricity is used overall.

'flat ,screen noun [C] COMPUTING a computer **monitor** that has a flat, square front

flatten /'flæt(ə)n/ verb **1** [I/T] to become flat, or to make something flat: *This exercise helps to flatten a flabby stomach.* **2** [T] to destroy something completely **3** [T] *informal* to completely defeat someone in a fight, argument etc

flatter /'flætə/ verb [T] **1** to praise someone in order to make them feel special, often in a way that is not sincere: *She flattered him and told him what he wanted to hear.* **2** if something flatters you, it makes you look good when you use it or wear it

PHRASE **flatter yourself** to persuade yourself that you are better, more attractive, more important etc than you are

—**flatterer** noun [C], **flattering** adj

flattery /'flætəri/ noun [U] praise that is not sincere: *She decided that a bit of flattery might bring results.*

flatworm /'flæt,wɜːm/ noun [C] BIOLOGY an invertebrate worm with a long soft flat body. Many flatworms, for example **tapeworms**, are parasites.

flaunt /flɔːnt/ verb [T] to deliberately try to make people notice something that you have so that they admire you: *Lawrence didn't flaunt his wealth.*

flautist /'flɔːtɪst/ noun [C] MUSIC someone who plays the **flute**

flavour¹ /'fleɪvə/ noun **1** [C] the particular taste that food or drink has: *The drink has a very strong flavour of citrus fruit.* ♦ *What flavour is the ice cream?* **2** [U] the quality of having a pleasant or strong taste: *This coffee has no flavour.* ♦ *Add flavour to your meal by using herbs and garlic.* **3** [singular/U] a particular quality that is typical of something: *The foreign visitors added an international flavour to the occasion.*

flavour² /'fleɪvə/ verb [T] to add something to food or drink that changes its taste or gives it a particular taste

flavouring /'fleɪvərɪŋ/ noun [C/U] a substance that is added to food or drink to give it a particular taste

flaw /flɔː/ noun [C] a mark, mistake, or fault that makes someone or something less than perfect: *There was a tiny flaw in the diamond.* ♦ *My father definitely had his flaws and failings.*

flawed /flɔːd/ adj spoiled by something such as a mark, fault, or mistake: *The current system is seriously flawed.*

flawless /'flɔːləs/ adj with no mistakes, marks, or bad features = PERFECT: *a flawless performance*
—**flawlessly** adv

flax /flæks/ noun [U] a plant with small blue flowers that is grown for the fibres in its stem and the oil in its seeds

flea /fliː/ noun [C] a small jumping insect that feeds on the blood of mammals and birds —*picture* → INSECT

fleck /flek/ noun [C] a small mark, piece, or amount of something: *flecks of grey in his hair*

fled /fled/ the past tense and past participle of **flee**

fledgling or **fledgeling** /ˈfledʒlɪŋ/ noun [C] **BIOLOGY** a young bird that has just learnt to fly

flee /fliː/ (**flees, fleeing, fled** /fled/) verb [I/T] to escape from a dangerous situation or place

fleece /fliːs/ noun **1** [C/U] the wool on a sheep **2** [U] a type of soft artificial cloth that is used for making clothes **3** [C] a short jacket or **pullover** made of soft artificial material

fleet /fliːt/ noun [C] **1** a group of vehicles that are owned by one organization or person **2** a group of ships, or all the ships in a nation's navy: *Europe's largest fishing fleet*

Flemish bond /ˈflemɪʃ ˌbɒnd/ noun [C] **CONSTRUCTION** a pattern of bricks in which the small end of one brick is followed by two long sides, then another small end etc in a single row

flesh /fleʃ/ noun [U] **1** the soft substance under the skin that consists mostly of muscle and fat: *The dog's teeth sank into my flesh.* **2** the soft part of a fruit or vegetable that is under the skin: *Cut the avocado in half and scoop out the flesh.*
PHRASES **in the flesh** present here and now, instead of on a screen or in a picture: *He was finally going to see her in the flesh.*
sb's (own) flesh and blood someone's relative

fleshy /ˈfleʃi/ adj with a lot of flesh

flew /fluː/ the past tense of **fly¹**

flex¹ /fleks/ verb [T] to bend a part of your body in order to stretch it or exercise it

flex² /fleks/ noun [C] a plastic covered wire that is used for carrying electricity

flexibility /ˌfleksəˈbɪləti/ noun [U] **1** the ability to make changes or to deal with a situation that is changing **2** the ability to bend or move easily

flexible /ˈfleksəb(ə)l/ adj **1** able to make changes or deal with a situation that is changing: *A more flexible approach is needed.* ♦ *The job offers flexible working hours.* **2** able to bend or move easily ≠ RIGID: *a flexible rubber strip* —**flexibly** adv

flexible working noun [U] **BUSINESS** ways of working that allow you to organize your work in the way you want, for example working from home, or working hours that are different from the usual 9 to 5 day

flexor muscle /ˈfleksə ˌmʌs(ə)l/ noun [C] **ANATOMY** a muscle that is used when bending part of the body

flick /flɪk/ verb **1** [I/T] to move quickly and suddenly, or to make something move quickly and suddenly: *She flicked back her long dark hair.* **2** [T] to move a switch in order to turn something on or off: *He flicked on the light.* —**flick** noun [C]

flicker¹ /ˈflɪkə/ verb [I] if a flame or light flickers, it does not burn evenly, or it goes on and off

flicker² /ˈflɪkə/ noun [C] a light that goes quickly on and off

flier /ˈflaɪə/ another spelling of **flyer**

flies /flaɪz/ noun [plural] the opening at the front of a pair of trousers

flight /flaɪt/ noun

1 journey in plane	**4** act of escaping
2 movement in air	**5** set of stairs
3 moving through air	

1 [C] a journey in a plane: *My flight has been delayed.* ♦ *The flight from Nairobi to Heathrow took about 8 hours.*
2 [C] a movement through the air by a bird or object: *Pigeons make flights of over 10,000 miles.* ♦ *Several factors control the ball's flight.*
3 [U] the process of moving through the air, or the ability to move through the air: *a flock of geese in flight*
4 [C/U] the act of running away, or of trying to escape from someone or something: *the refugees' desperate flight from their city*
5 [C] a set of stairs that go from one level to another: *The toilets are two flights up.* ♦ *A flight of stairs leads down to the courtyard.*

flight at,tendant noun [C] **TOURISM** someone whose job is to look after passengers on a plane

flight ,coupon noun [C] **TOURISM** the part of an airline ticket that shows where the passenger will leave from and arrive at during a single flight, or part of a journey

flight ,crew or **flight deck ,crew** noun [C] the people involved with flying a plane including the pilots, the **flight engineer**, and the **navigator**

flight ,deck noun [C] **1** the area at the front of a large plane or a spacecraft where the pilot works = COCKPIT —*picture* → SPACE SHUTTLE **2** the open area on an **aircraft carrier** where aircraft can take off and land

flight engi,neer noun [C] someone whose job is to be responsible for the engines, electrical systems etc of a plane while it is flying somewhere

flightless /ˈflaɪtləs/ adj a flightless bird, insect etc cannot fly even though it has wings

flimsy /ˈflɪmzi/ (**flimsier, flimsiest**) adj **1** made of a thin or light substance: *a flimsy cotton blouse* **2** badly made and likely to break easily: *a flimsy wooden fence* **3** not very reliable, or not easy to believe: *a flimsy excuse*

flinch /flɪntʃ/ verb [I] to make a sudden small movement because you are afraid, surprised, or in pain
PHRASE **not flinch from (doing) something** to deal with a situation or responsibility even though it is difficult

fling /flɪŋ/ (**flings, flinging, flung** /flʌŋ/) verb [T] **1** to throw something carelessly or with a lot of force: *She pulled off her coat and flung it on the chair.* **2** to move something quickly and with a lot of force: *He flung open the window.*

flint /flɪnt/ noun [U] **GEOLOGY** a hard grey stone that was used in the past for making tools. It is a type of sedimentary rock.

flip¹ /flɪp/ (**flips, flipping, flipped**) verb **1** flip or **flip over** [I/T] to turn over quickly, or to make something turn over: *His car flipped over and crashed.* ♦ *Flip a coin to decide who goes first.* **2** [I] *informal* to become very angry or excited

flip² /flɪp/ noun [C] an action of jumping up and completely turning over in the air

flip ,chart noun [C] large sheets of paper that are connected at the top. They are used by someone who is talking to a group for showing pictures or for writing things on.

'flip-,flop noun [C] a rubber shoe without a top or back, held to the foot by a **strap** in the shape of a 'V' that goes between the toes

flippant /'flɪpənt/ adj treating a serious subject or situation in a way that is not serious enough

flipper /'flɪpə/ noun [C] **1** BIOLOGY a wide flat part like an arm on the bodies of some sea animals and birds, for example **penguins** and **seals** —*picture* → REPTILE, SEA **2** a wide flat rubber shoe that someone wears when they swim under water

flirt /flɜːt/ verb [I] if people flirt, they behave towards each other in a way that shows that they are sexually attracted to each other

flirtation /flɜːˈteɪʃ(ə)n/ noun **1** [U] the behaviour of people who are showing that they are sexually attracted to each other **2** [C] a short period of time when someone is interested in a new idea or activity

flit /flɪt/ (**flits**, **flitting**, **flitted**) verb [I] to move quickly from one place to another without stopping long

float¹ /fləʊt/ verb

1 rest on surface	4 about money
2 be lighter than air	5 start to sell shares
3 about sound/smell	6 suggest idea

1 [I] to rest or move slowly on the surface of a liquid and not sink ≠ SINK: *Leaves and twigs floated on the water.*
2 [I] to move slowly through the air: *A cloud floated across the moon.*
3 [I] if a sound or smell floats, it can be heard or smelled in different places: *Music floated up from the garden.*
4 [I/T] ECONOMICS to allow the value of a country's money to change in relation to the money of other countries
5 [T] BUSINESS to start to sell a company's shares
6 [T] to suggest an idea for people to consider

float² /fləʊt/ noun [C] **1** a large vehicle that is decorated and driven through the streets as part of a **parade 2** an object that floats and supports someone's body when they are learning to swim **3** ENGINEERING an object linked to a **valve** in a **carburettor** that controls the level of petrol

'float ,chamber noun [C] ENGINEERING an enclosed space in a **carburettor** that has a **float** to control the level of petrol

floc /flɒk/ noun [C] CHEMISTRY a mass of large particles that forms when **alum** is added to water in order to make it pure

flock /flɒk/ noun [C] a group of birds, sheep, or goats

flog /flɒg/ (**flogs**, **flogging**, **flogged**) verb [T] to hit someone very hard with a stick or **whip** as a punishment

flood¹ /flʌd/ verb **1** [I/T] to cover a place with water, or to become covered with water: *Water burst through the dam and flooded local villages.* ♦ *The ground floor of the house was flooded.* **2** [I] when a river floods, water rises up over its banks and covers the land around it **3** [I/T] if people or things flood somewhere, they go there or arrive there in large numbers: *Two million visitors flood into our city each year.* ♦ *The TV station was flooded with complaints.* **4** [I/T] to fill a place with light, or to become filled with light: *I opened the curtains and light flooded into the room.*

flood² /flʌd/ noun **1** [C/U] a large amount of water that covers an area that was dry before: *The region has been badly hit by floods.* ♦ *After three weeks the flood waters finally receded.* **2** [C] a large number of people or things that move somewhere or arrive somewhere at the same time: *We received a flood of letters*

protesting against the change. **3** [C] a flood of memories or feelings is a lot of strong memories or feelings that suddenly affect you: *The song brought back a flood of memories.*

floodgates /'flʌd,ɡeɪts/ noun [plural] **open the floodgates** to suddenly make it possible for a lot of things to happen

flooding /'flʌdɪŋ/ noun [U] a situation in which water from a river or from heavy rain covers large areas of land

floodlight /'flʌd,laɪt/ noun [C] a very strong light that is used for lighting a public building or sports event at night

floodlit /'flʌdlɪt/ adj lit at night using floodlights

'flood ,plain noun [C] GEOGRAPHY a flat area of land near a river that often floods when the water level rises —*picture* → on next page

floodwater /'flʌd,wɔːtə/ noun [U/plural] GEOGRAPHY water that is carried over the banks of rivers and streams during a flood so that it covers previously dry land

floor¹ /flɔː/ noun

1 flat area you walk on	4 audience at debate
2 level in building	5 where shares are sold
3 of ocean/valley etc	6 lowest level allowed

1 [C] the flat area that you walk on inside a building or room: *The house has polished wooden floors.* ♦ *We were sitting on the floor watching TV.*
2 [C] one of the levels in a building: *a first-floor flat* ♦ *The toy department is on the second floor.*
3 [C] the ground at the bottom of something: *a map of the ocean floor*
4 [singular] the audience at a public discussion or debate: *The speaker will now take questions from the floor.*
5 [C] BUSINESS a large room in a **stock exchange** where shares in companies are bought and sold
6 [singular] BUSINESS the lowest level that prices, salaries, **interest rates** etc are allowed to reach → SHOP FLOOR

floor² /flɔː/ verb [T] **1** to make someone feel so surprised and confused that they cannot react **2** to hit someone so hard that they fall to the ground

floorboard /'flɔː,bɔːd/ noun [C] a long wooden board that is part of a floor

'floor ,plan noun [C] a drawing that shows the shape, size, and arrangement of rooms in a building from above

flop¹ /flɒp/ (**flops**, **flopping**, **flopped**) verb [I] **1** to sit or lie down in a heavy way by letting your body fall: *He got home and flopped into a chair.* **2** to move or hang in a loose way: *Her long hair flopped down over her eyes.* **3** *informal* if a play, film, or new product flops, it is completely unsuccessful

flop² /flɒp/ noun [C] *informal* a complete failure

floppy /'flɒpi/ (**floppier**, **floppiest**) adj soft and hanging down in a loose or heavy way

,floppy 'disk or **floppy** /'flɒpi/ noun [C] COMPUTING a small square plastic object that you use for storing information from a computer —*picture* → COMPUTER

flora /'flɔːrə/ noun [U] BIOLOGY all the plants that grow in a particular region

floral /'flɔːrəl/ adj made of flowers, or decorated with pictures of flowers

florist /'flɒrɪst/ noun [C] **1** someone whose job is to arrange and sell flowers **2** florist or florist's a shop that sells flowers

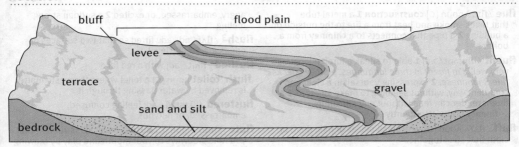

flood plain

flotation /fləʊˈteɪʃ(ə)n/ noun [C/U] **BUSINESS, ECONOMICS** the sale of shares in a company for the first time

floˈtation deˌvice noun [C] *formal* a lifebelt or lifejacket

flotilla /fləˈtɪlə/ noun [C] a group of small ships

flotsam /ˈflɒtsəm/ noun [U] things that you find floating in the sea or lying on the beach → JETSAM

flounce /flaʊns/ verb [I] to walk in an impatient angry way

flounder /ˈflaʊndə/ verb [I] **1** to experience difficulties and be likely to fail **2** to feel confused and not know what to say or do next

flour /flaʊə/ noun [U] a white or brown powder made from grain. It is used for making bread, cakes, and pasta.

flourish /ˈflʌrɪʃ/ verb [I] **1** to grow well and be healthy: *Most plants flourish in this rich soil.* **2** to be very successful= THRIVE: *His new business is flourishing.*

flout /flaʊt/ verb [T] to deliberately refuse to obey a rule or custom

flow¹ /fləʊ/ noun **1** [C/U] the continuous movement of something: *the flow of blood to the heart* **2** [C/U] a supply of something that continues without stopping: *The television provided a steady flow of information about the war.* **3** [C/U] a way of talking or thinking in an easy natural way, without any pauses or difficulties: *The phone rang, interrupting the flow of his thoughts.* **4** [singular] the movement of the sea towards the land: *the ebb and flow of the tide*

flow² /fləʊ/ verb [I]

1 move continuously	4 about hair/clothing
2 when supply continues	5 when sea moves
3 about words/ideas	

1 to move continuously: *The water flows through these pipes.* ♦ *A constant stream of people flowed past.* ♦ *Blood flowed from the wound on her face.*
2 if a supply of something flows, it continues without stopping: *Millions of pounds of new investment are flowing into the region.*
3 if words or ideas flow, they follow each other in an easy, natural, continuous way: *The conversation did not flow smoothly.*
4 if hair or clothing flows, it falls or moves in a smooth graceful way around someone's body
5 if the tide flows, the sea comes in towards the land

ˈflow ˌchart or **ˈflow ˌdiagram** noun [C] a drawing that represents a complicated process by a series of lines that show the different possibilities —*picture* → CHART

flower¹ /ˈflaʊə/ noun [C] **1 BIOLOGY** the reproductive part of a plant. Flowers are often brightly coloured or **scented** to attract insects for the purposes of

pollination. The female reproductive part of a flower is called the **pistil** and the male part is the **stamen**. These are usually enclosed by **petals** and **sepals**: *The plant has small white flowers.* **2** a plant that is grown because its flowers are attractive: *I'm going to plant more flowers in the garden this year.*

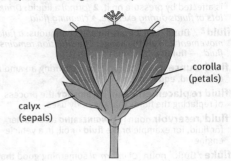

corolla (petals)

calyx (sepals)

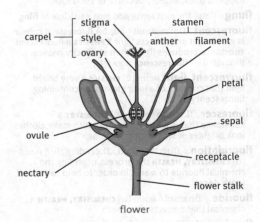

stigma
carpel
style
ovary

stamen
anther   filament

petal

sepal

ovule

receptacle

nectary

flower stalk

flower

flower² /ˈflaʊə/ verb [I] **BIOLOGY** to produce flowers

flowerbed /ˈflaʊəˌbed/ noun [C] an area of ground where flowers are grown

flowering plant /ˈflaʊərɪŋ ˌplɑːnt/ noun [C] **BIOLOGY** a plant that produces flowers and fruits

flown /fləʊn/ the past participle of **fly¹**

ˈflow-ˌon adj happening as the direct result of something

fl. oz. abbrev **fluid ounce**

flu /fluː/ noun [U] **HEALTH** influenza

fluctuate /ˈflʌktʃueɪt/ verb [I] to change frequently —**fluctuation** /ˌflʌktʃuˈeɪʃ(ə)n/ noun [C/U]

flue /fluː/ noun [C] CONSTRUCTION **1** a metal tube that takes smoke and heat from a fire to the outside of a building **2** a pipe that connects to a **chimney** from a **boiler**

fluent /ˈfluːənt/ adj **1** able to speak a foreign language very well: *I'm fluent in three languages.* ♦ *Steve speaks fluent Japanese.* **2** expressing yourself in a clear and confident way, without seeming to make an effort **3** a fluent **reader** can read without any difficulties —**fluency** noun [U], **fluently** adv

fluff /flʌf/ noun [U] very small pieces of hair, dust, or cloth that stick together

fluffy /ˈflʌfi/ (**fluffier, fluffiest**) adj **1** covered with very soft hair or feathers **2** made of something that is very soft

flugelhorn /ˈfluːɡ(ə)lˌhɔːn/ noun [C] MUSIC a small brass instrument similar to a **trumpet**

fluid¹ /ˈfluːɪd/ noun [C/U] **1** SCIENCE a liquid or gas. A fluid flows easily, takes the shape of its container, and is affected by pressure on it. **2** *formal* a liquid: *Drink lots of fluids during exercise.* ♦ *cleaning fluid*

fluid² /ˈfluːɪd/ adj **1** graceful and continuous: *a fluid movement* **2** likely to change: *The situation remains fluid.* —**fluidity** /fluˈɪdəti/ noun [U]

fluid ˈounce noun [C] a unit for measuring an amount of a liquid, equal to 0.02841 litres

ˈfluid reˌplacement noun [U] BIOLOGY the process of replacing the fluids that the body uses

ˈfluid ˌreservoir noun [C] ENGINEERING a container for fluid, for example **brake fluid** or oil, in a vehicle engine

fluke /fluːk/ noun [C] *informal* something good that happens unexpectedly because of good luck

flung /flʌŋ/ the past tense and past participle of **fling**

fluorescent /flɔːˈres(ə)nt/ adj **1** a fluorescent colour is very bright and reflects light **2** PHYSICS a fluorescent substance produces light when electricity passes through it —**fluorescence** noun [U]

fluoˈrescent ˌlight noun [C] PHYSICS a very bright light that consists of a long glass tube containing fluorescent gas

fluorescer /flɔːˈresə/ noun [C] CHEMISTRY a substance that is added to **detergent** to make clothes look brighter or whiter after washing

fluoridation /ˌflʊərɪˈdeɪʃ(ə)n, ˌflɔːrɪˈdeɪʃ(ə)n/ noun [U] CHEMISTRY, HEALTH the process of adding the chemical fluoride to water, in order to help to prevent **tooth decay**

fluoride /ˈflʊəraɪd/ noun [U] CHEMISTRY, HEALTH a chemical that protects your teeth

fluorine /ˈflʊəriːn/ noun [U] CHEMISTRY a poisonous yellow gas that is an element in the **halogen** group and is the most **reactive** element known. It is used in the treatment of water. Chemical symbol: **F**

fluorocarbon /ˌflʊərəʊˈkɑːbən, ˌflɔːrəʊˈkɑːbən/ noun [C] CHEMISTRY a compound of carbon and fluorine that is thought to damage the **ozone layer** of the Earth's atmosphere

flush¹ /flʌʃ/ verb **1** [I] if someone flushes, their face becomes red because they feel hot, angry, embarrassed, or excited: *Mark flushed with annoyance, but said nothing.* **2** [I/T] if you flush a toilet, or if it flushes, water passes through it **3** [T] to get rid of something by putting it into a toilet and flushing it

flush² /flʌʃ/ noun [singular] **1** a red colour that appears on someone's face because they feel hot,

angry, embarrassed, or excited **2** a sudden strong feeling

flush³ /flʌʃ/ adj, adv fitted so that two surfaces or edges are exactly level

flushed /flʌʃt/ adj with a red face

ˌflush ˈtoilet noun [C] a toilet where the waste matter is removed by water passing through it

flustered /ˈflʌstəd/ adj feeling confused, embarrassed, or nervous

flute /fluːt/ noun [C] MUSIC a musical instrument that you hold sideways to your mouth and play by blowing over a hole near one end —*picture* → MUSICAL INSTRUMENT, ORCHESTRA

flutter /ˈflʌtə/ verb **1** [I/T] to move with quick light movements, or to make something move in this way: *The bird fluttered from branch to branch.* **2** [I] if your heart or stomach flutters, you feel excited or nervous —**flutter** noun [singular]

fluvial /ˈfluːviəl/ adj GEOGRAPHY relating to rivers

flux /flʌks/ noun **1** [U] a condition of continuous change: *The climate appears to be in a state of flux.* **2** [C/U] PHYSICS the rate at which matter or energy flows across a surface or area **3** [C/U] TECHNOLOGY a chemical used to prevent oxidation of metal during **soldering** and **brazing**. Some fluxes also clean the surface of the metal.

fly¹ /flaɪ/ (**flies, flying, flew** /fluː/, **flown** /fləʊn/) verb

1 move with wings	**6** move quickly
2 travel on plane	**7** about time
3 take on plane	**8** of flag in air
4 control plane	**+** PHRASE
5 move through air	

1 [I] to use wings to move through the air: *Not all insects can fly.*
2 [I] to travel on a plane: *Sometimes it's cheaper to fly.* ♦ *I flew from London to Riyadh.* ♦ *We flew into Johannesburg on Monday evening.*
3 [T] to take people or goods somewhere on a plane: *They flew her to the city for urgent medical treatment.* ♦ *Helicopters are being used to fly in supplies.*
4 [I/T] to control a plane when it is in the air: *He had always wanted to learn to fly.* ♦ *The pilots refused to fly the planes until the tyres had been checked.*
5 [I] to move very fast through the air: *A bullet flew past his head.*
6 [I] to move suddenly or quickly: *The door flew open and the head teacher marched in.*
7 [I] if time flies, it seems to pass very quickly
8 [I/T] if someone flies a flag, or if it is flying, it is on the top of a pole or building

PHRASE **fly into a rage** to suddenly become extremely angry

fly² /flaɪ/ (plural **flies**) noun [C] **1** BIOLOGY one of the group of insects with one pair of true wings, for example, mosquitoes, **houseflies**, and **tsetse flies** —*picture* → INSECT **2** a small hook made to look like an insect, fixed to the end of a fishing line and used for catching fish → FLIES

ˈfly-ˌdrive adj TOURISM a fly-drive holiday includes the cost of a flight on a plane and the hire of a car

flyer or **flier** /ˈflaɪə/ noun [C] **1** an announcement or advertisement that is printed on paper and given to people = LEAFLET **2** an aircraft pilot or passenger

flying¹ /ˈflaɪɪŋ/ adj **1** able to fly: *a flying insect* **2** moving fast through the air: *About 20 people were injured by flying glass.*

PHRASE **with flying colours** very successfully

flying² /ˈflaɪɪŋ/ noun [U] **1** the activity of travelling in an aircraft: *I'm afraid of flying.* **2** the activity of operating or controlling an aircraft

ˌflying ˈfish noun [C] a fish that can move through the air by using its large fins as wings

ˌflying ˈstart noun [C] a very good beginning

ˌflying ˈtackle noun [C] a way of stopping someone by jumping at them and holding them around the legs so that they fall

ˌflying ˈvisit noun [C] a very short visit

flyover /ˈflaɪˌəʊvə/ noun [C] a road that crosses above another road like a bridge

ˈfly-ˌstay adj **TOURISM** relating to an arrangement where someone books a hotel at the same time as booking a plane ticket

flywheel /ˈflaɪˌwiːl/ noun [C] **ENGINEERING** a heavy wheel in a machine or engine that keeps it operating at a steady speed

FM /ˌef ˈem/ noun [U] **PHYSICS** frequency modulation: a system that is used for broadcasting radio signals of high quality

foal /fəʊl/ noun [C] a young horse

foam /fəʊm/ noun [U] **1** a lot of bubbles that stick together on the surface of a liquid **2** a soft thick substance that contains a lot of bubbles. It is used for cleaning, washing, or stopping fires. **3** a soft light rubber or plastic substance that contains a lot of small holes: *a foam mattress*

focal length /ˌfəʊk(ə)l ˈleŋθ/ noun [C] **PHYSICS** the distance from the centre of a lens or mirror to its focal point

focal point /ˈfəʊk(ə)l ˌpɔɪnt/ noun [C] **1** **PHYSICS** the point where light rays meet after being reflected by a mirror or passing through a lens, or the point from which they seem to start to spread **2** the most important, interesting, or attractive part of something

focus¹ /ˈfəʊkəs/ (**focuses** or **focusses**, **focusing** or **focussing**, **focused** or **focussed**) verb [I/T] **1** if your eyes focus, or if you focus your eyes, you look at something carefully until you start to see it clearly: *It took a while for my eyes to focus in the dim light of the cave.* **2** to turn a camera towards something: *The television cameras were focused on the crowd.* **3** **SCIENCE** if a lens or mirror focuses rays of light, or if they focus, they meet at a particular point

PHRASAL VERB ˈfocus on sth to concentrate on something and pay particular attention to it: *The course focuses on three main topics.*

focus² /ˈfəʊkəs/ noun

1 thing concentrated on	5 place where earthquake starts
2 attention paid to sth	+ PHRASES
3 concentrating on aim	
4 focal point	

1 [singular] the thing that people are concentrating on or paying particular attention to: *The animal's behaviour was the focus of our research.* ♦ *We have chosen six communities as the focus for our study.*
2 [singular/U] particular attention that people pay to something: *The report calls for greater focus on the needs of the poor.*
3 [singular/U] the act of concentrating on a particular aim: *All the lessons have a very clear focus.* ♦ *I think this campaign has lost its focus.*
4 (plural **foci** /ˈfəʊsaɪ/) [C] **PHYSICS** a focal point
5 [C] **GEOLOGY** the place below the Earth's surface where an earthquake begins → EPICENTRE —*picture* → EARTHQUAKE

PHRASES in focus able to be seen clearly
out of focus unable to be seen clearly: *Some of these photographs are out of focus.*

focused /ˈfəʊkəst/ adj **1** *showing approval* concentrating on a particular aim and not wasting time or energy on other things **2** a focused sound or image is very clear

fodder /ˈfɒdə/ noun [U] **AGRICULTURE** food for farm animals such as cows and horses, in the form of crops that are grown and harvested before being used

foe /fəʊ/ noun [C] *literary* an enemy

foetal /ˈfiːt(ə)l/ adj **BIOLOGY** relating to a foetus

foetus /ˈfiːtəs/ noun [C] **BIOLOGY** a mammal that is developing inside its mother's body, especially one that is not capable of existing independently —*picture* → EMBRYO

fog /fɒg/ noun [U] **GEOGRAPHY** thick clouds that form close to the ground and are difficult to see through

foggy /ˈfɒgi/ (**foggier, foggiest**) adj **GEOGRAPHY** full of fog, or covered with fog

foil¹ /fɔɪl/ noun **1** [U] very light thin sheets of metal that are used for wrapping food **2** [C] **SPORTS** a light thin sword used in the sport of **fencing**

foil² /fɔɪl/ verb [T] to prevent someone from doing something that they want to do

fold¹ /fəʊld/ verb **1** [T] to bend a piece of paper or cloth and press one part of it over another part: *Carrie folded the letter and slid it into a drawer.* ♦ *Fold the paper in half.* **2** [I/T] if something folds, or if you fold it, you bend part of it so that it becomes smaller and easier to carry or store: *Jim folded the penknife and slipped it into his pocket.* ♦ *The bed folds away conveniently for storage.* **3** [I] if a business folds, it closes because it is not able to make enough money
PHRASE fold your arms to cross one arm over the other
PHRASAL VERB ˌfold sth ˈup to make something smaller by bending it over on itself more than once: *His clothes were neatly folded up on a chair.*

fold² /fəʊld/ noun [C] **1** a line that you make on a piece of paper or cloth when you press one part of it over another **2** a curved piece of cloth that hangs in a loose way **3** **GEOLOGY** a bend in an underground layer of rock

-fold /fəʊld/ suffix used with numbers to make adjectives and adverbs describing how much something increases: *a fivefold increase in his salary*

folder /ˈfəʊldə/ noun [C] **1** a thin flat container for sheets of paper **2** **COMPUTING** a computer file that contains a group of other programs or documents

foliage /ˈfəʊliɪdʒ/ noun [U] **BIOLOGY** the leaves of a plant

folic acid /ˌfəʊlɪk ˈæsɪd/ noun [U] **HEALTH** an important **B vitamin**, found in green vegetables and liver. It is especially important for pregnant women.

folk¹ /fəʊk/ noun **1** [plural] *informal* people: *city folk* **2** [U] **MUSIC** folk music

folk² /fəʊk/ adj **SOCIAL STUDIES** **1** traditional in a particular region: *folk art* **2** based on the beliefs and methods of ordinary people: *folk medicine*

folklore /ˈfəʊkˌlɔː/ noun [U] **SOCIAL STUDIES** traditional stories, sayings, and beliefs from a particular region or community

ˈfolk ˌmusic noun [U] **MUSIC** traditional music from a particular country, region, or community, or music played in a traditional style

'folk ,song noun [C] **MUSIC 1** a traditional song from a particular region or community, especially one that was developed by people who were not professional musicians **2** a modern popular song developed from traditional songs that has a simple tune and is played on a guitar

'folk ,tale noun [C] **LITERATURE** an old traditional story

follicle /ˈfɒlɪk(ə)l/ noun [C] **ANATOMY** a small hole in the skin that contains the root of a hair —*picture* → FERTILIZATION, SKIN

follow /ˈfɒləʊ/ verb

1 move behind sb	**8** do same as sb else
2 be after sth else	**9** happen in a pattern
3 pay attention	**10** believe in religion etc
4 obey order/advice	**11** to have to be true
5 go along road/river	**12** about book/film etc
6 watch progress	**+ PHRASAL VERBS**
7 understand sth	

1 [I/T] to walk, drive etc behind someone who is going in the same direction as you: *Ralph set off down the hill, and I followed.* ♦ *Jim opened the door and followed me down the corridor.*
2 [I/T] to happen or come after something else: *The weather report follows shortly.* ♦ *In the weeks that followed the situation was very tense.*
3 [T] to pay attention to what someone or something is doing or saying: *He followed every word of the trial.*
4 [T] to obey an order, or to do what someone has advised you to do: *She refused to **follow** our **advice**.* ♦ *The soldiers claimed they were only **following orders**.* ♦ ***Follow** the **instructions** carefully.*
5 [T] to go along a road, river etc in the same direction as it does: *Follow the road down the hill into the village.*
6 [T] to be interested in the progress of someone or something: *My father's followed the same football team for 40 years.*
7 [T] to understand something that is long or complicated: *I couldn't follow what Professor Hope was saying.*
8 [I/T] to do the same thing that someone else has done: *Other students **followed** her **lead** and boycotted lectures.* ♦ *We have banned these products, and other countries should **follow** our **example**.*
9 [T] to happen according to a particular pattern or order: *All the murders have followed the same horrible pattern.*
10 [T] to believe what a religion or system of ideas teaches and do the things that it tells you to do: *I follow the teachings of the Buddha.* ♦ *those who follow Christianity*
11 [I] if something follows, it must be true because of something else that is true: *If the two groups have the same goal, then it should follow that they work together.*
12 [T] to deal with the progress or development of someone or something in a book, film, or television programme: *The film follows the adventures of an ant called Flick.* → FOOTSTEP

PHRASAL VERBS ,**follow sb a'round** or ,**follow sb a'bout** to follow someone wherever they go: *Henry's been following me around like a puppy!*
,**follow (sth) 'through** to continue doing something until it is finished
,**follow sth 'up** to try to find out more about something or do something more to deal with it: *They never followed my complaint up.*

follower /ˈfɒləʊə/ noun [C] **1** someone who believes in a religion or system of ideas, or who supports the person who established it **2** someone who is interested in the progress of something = SUPPORTER

3 **ENGINEERING** a machine part that receives movement from another part

following¹ /ˈfɒləʊɪŋ/ adj, preposition, pronoun **1** after something happens, or as a result of something that happens: *The team blossomed following the appointment of the new manager.* **2** the following day, month, page etc is the next one: *The problem will be discussed in the following chapter.* **3** used for referring to something that you are going to say or mention next: *Combine the following ingredients: brown sugar, flour, and butter.* ♦ *Make sure you have the following: a pencil, a rubber, and a ruler.* **4** a following wind blows behind a boat, plane, or other vehicle and makes it travel faster

following² /ˈfɒləʊɪŋ/ noun [C] a group of people who support or admire someone

,**follow-'through** noun **1** [C/U] **SPORTS** the final part of the movement that a player makes when they hit, kick, or throw a ball **2** [U] something that is done in order to complete a plan or activity

'follow-,up noun **1** [C/U] something that is done in order to complete something **2** [C] a book, film, or article that is based on or develops an earlier one = SEQUEL —**'follow-,up** adj

folly /ˈfɒli/ (plural **follies**) noun [C/U] *formal* stupid or careless behaviour

fond /fɒnd/ adj **1 fond of sb/sth** liking and caring about someone or something very much: *I'm very fond of my Uncle Jim.* **2 fond of (doing) sth** getting enjoyment and satisfaction from something that you do —**fondness** noun [U]

fondle /ˈfɒnd(ə)l/ verb [T] to squeeze or touch someone or something gently, often for sexual pleasure

font /fɒnt/ noun [C] a set of letters and numbers in a particular size and style

food /fuːd/ noun **1** [U] the things that people or animals eat: *Prices of food and clothing have risen recently.* ♦ *good fresh food* —*picture* → on next page **2** [U] the things that plants need in order to grow **3** [C/U] a particular type of food: *I can't eat spicy food.*

'food ,chain noun **1 BIOLOGY, ENVIRONMENT** the natural process in which one organism is eaten by another, which is then eaten by another etc **2 ECONOMICS** the series of processes in which food is grown, treated, stored, and sold

'food ,mile noun [C] a measure of the distance travelled by foods between the place where they are produced and the place where they are eaten. Long distances are considered bad because the quality of the food is worse and energy is wasted in transporting it.

'food ,poisoning noun [U] **HEALTH** an illness caused by eating food that contains harmful bacteria or **toxins**

'food ,processor noun [C] a piece of electrical equipment that is used for cutting food into very small pieces or for mixing foods together

foodstuff /ˈfuːdstʌf/ noun [C/U] *formal* a type of food

'food ,vacuole noun [C] **BIOLOGY** a space inside the cell where food is digested in some protozoa (=organisms consisting of one cell only)

'food ,web noun [C] **BIOLOGY, ENVIRONMENT** all the connected **food chains** involving all the organisms in a particular area —*picture* → on p.300

fool¹ /fuːl/ noun [C] someone who does not behave in an intelligent or sensible way
PHRASE make a fool (out) of sb to deliberately make someone seem stupid

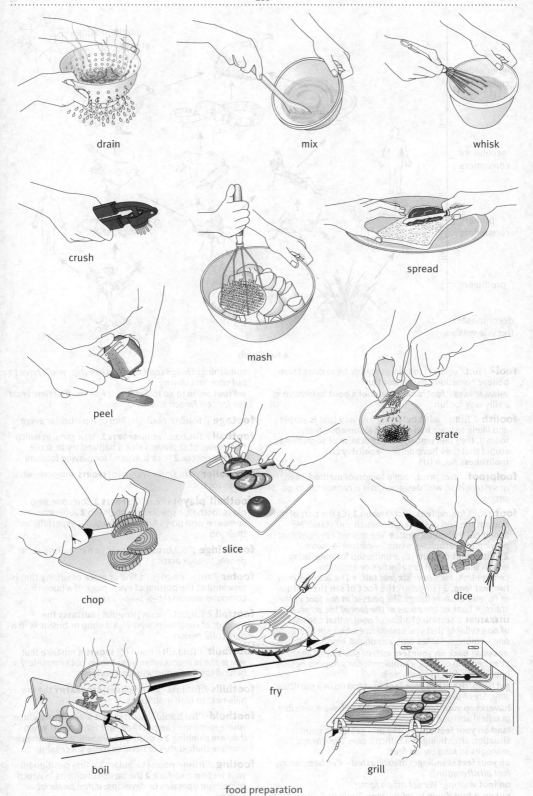

drain

mix

whisk

crush

spread

mash

peel

grate

slice

chop

dice

fry

boil

grill

food preparation

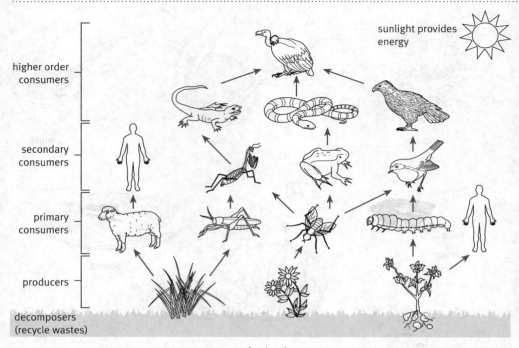

higher order consumers

sunlight provides energy

secondary consumers

primary consumers

producers

decomposers (recycle wastes)

a food web

fool² /fuːl/ verb [T] to trick someone by making them believe something that is not true

PHRASAL VERB ,fool 'around or ,fool a'bout to behave in a silly way for fun

foolish /'fuːlɪʃ/ adj **1** behaving in a way that is stupid and likely to have bad results **2** if someone feels foolish, they feel embarrassed because of something stupid that they have done —**foolishly** adv, **foolishness** noun [U]

foolproof /'fuːl,pruːf/ adj a foolproof method, plan, or system is so well designed that it cannot fail or go wrong

foot /fʊt/ (plural **feet** /fiːt/) noun **1** [C] the part of the body at the end of the leg, on which you stand: *He wiped his feet on the mat.* ♦ *She injured her right foot playing basketball.* → STAND¹ —*picture* → BODY **2** (plural **feet** or **foot**) [C] a unit used for measuring length that is equal to 12 inches or about 30 centimetres: *He's over six foot tall.* ♦ *The lizard is over two feet long.* **3** [singular] **the foot of sth** the bottom or far end of something: *She paused at the foot of the stairs.* ♦ *Look at the notes at the foot of the page.* **4** [C] LITERATURE a section of a line of poetry that consists of one syllable that you emphasize when speaking and one or more syllables that you do not emphasize

PHRASES **back on your feet** well or successful again after being ill or having problems: *Jim's hoping he'll be back on his feet by next week.*
get/leap/rise etc to your feet to stand up in a particular way: *Steve jumped to his feet.*
have/keep your feet on the ground to have a sensible practical attitude to life
land on your feet to be lucky and get into a good situation after being in a difficult one: *Tim always manages to land on his feet.*
on your feet standing: *I'm exhausted – I've been on my feet all afternoon!*
on foot walking: *We set off on foot.*
put your foot down to refuse very firmly to do or accept

something: *Things can't carry on like this; you'll have to put your foot down.*
set foot on/in to go to a place: *It was the first time I had set foot on French soil.*

footage /'fʊtɪdʒ/ noun [U] film of a particular event

football /'fʊt,bɔːl/ noun SPORTS **1** [U] a game in which two teams of 11 players kick a ball and try to score goals = SOCCER **2** [C] a ball used for playing football

footballer /'fʊt,bɔːlə/ noun [C] SPORTS someone who plays football

'football ,player noun [C] SPORTS **1** someone who plays football, especially as their job **2** *American* someone who plays American football, especially as their job

footbridge /'fʊt,brɪdʒ/ noun [C] a narrow bridge for people to walk across

footer /'fʊtə/ noun [C] a line or piece of writing that is repeated at the bottom of every page of a book or computer document → header sense 1

footfall /'fʊt,fɔːl/ noun [singular] BUSINESS the number of customers who visit a shop or business in a particular period

footfault /'fʊt,fɔːlt/ noun [C] SPORTS a mistake that you make in tennis when your foot is not completely behind the line when you are **serving**

foothills /'fʊt,hɪlz/ noun [plural] GEOGRAPHY the low hills next to high mountains

foothold /'fʊt,həʊld/ noun [C] **1** a place on a surface where someone can put their foot for support when they are climbing **2** a position from which someone can improve their status or become more successful

footing /'fʊtɪŋ/ noun [singular] **1** a firm position for your feet on a surface **2** the basic conditions in which something operates or develops: *a firm financial footing*

footnote /ˈfʊt,nəʊt/ noun [C] **1** a note at the bottom of a page that gives more detailed information about something on the page **2** an additional fact, event, or comment that is not very important = ADJUNCT

footpath /ˈfʊt,pɑːθ/ noun [C] a path that is used only for walking along, usually in the countryside

footprint /ˈfʊt,prɪnt/ noun [C] a mark made by a human or animal foot in a soft surface such as earth, sand, or snow

ˈfoot ,soldier noun [C] **1** a soldier who fights on foot, not on a horse or in a vehicle **2** someone with a junior position in a company, whose job is to do necessary but boring work

footstep /ˈfʊt,step/ noun [C] the sound of a foot touching the ground as someone walks
PHRASE **follow in sb's footsteps** to do the same work, or to achieve the same success, as someone else has done before you: *She followed in her mother's footsteps and became a doctor.*

footwear /ˈfʊt,weə/ noun [U] things that you wear on your feet, such as shoes or boots

footwork /ˈfʊt,wɜːk/ noun [U] the way that someone moves their feet when they are dancing or playing sports

for /*strong* fɔː, *weak* fə/ preposition

1 given to who/what	**8** representing sb
2 with what reason	**9** going to a place
3 of what period	**10** at what time
4 employed by sb/sth	**11** considering what
5 what sth costs	sb/sth is
6 of who is affected	**12** what sth means
7 who/what does sth	+ PHRASE

1 used for saying who or what is intended to receive something or get the benefit of it: *This present is for you. ♦ We're buying furniture for the new house. ♦ The academy provides training for young musicians. ♦ I feel very sorry for him.*
2 used for stating a purpose or reason: *We use the basement for storage. ♦ Is there enough time for a game of football? ♦ There's a lot of support for the decision.*
3 used for saying how long a period of time or a distance is: *I've been waiting for 20 minutes. ♦ The road continues for about three miles.* → SINCE
4 used for stating the person or organization that employs someone: *She works for a firm of accountants.*
5 used for stating the cost or price of something: *Dad sold our car for £900.*
6 used for saying who is affected by a situation or feeling: *Living conditions for most people have improved.*
7 used after some adjectives, nouns, and verbs for saying who or what does an action: *It's time for us to go. ♦ All I want is for you to be happy.*
8 used for saying who someone represents when they say or do something: *I'm speaking for all of us when I say how sorry we are.*
9 used for saying where you are going when you leave a place: *What time are you leaving for home? ♦ the next plane for San Francisco*
10 used for saying the time or date when something is planned to happen: *The meeting was set for 10 o'clock.*
11 used for saying that something is surprising: *She sings amazingly well for a child.*
12 used for saying what something means or represents: *What's the Italian word for 'Goodbye'?*
PHRASE **for now** or **for the moment** or **for the time being** for a short time, until a situation changes: *You'll have to stay here for now.*

forage¹ /ˈfɒrɪdʒ/ verb [I] to search in a wide area for food

forage² /ˈfɒrɪdʒ/ noun [U] AGRICULTURE food for farm animals such as cows and horses, in the form of crops that are eaten in the fields while they are still growing

forbade /fəˈbæd/ the past tense of **forbid**

forbearance /fɔːˈbeərəns/ noun [U] *formal* the ability to be polite, calm, and patient in difficult situations
—**forbearing** adj

forbid /fəˈbɪd/ (**forbids, forbidding, forbade** /fəˈbeɪd/ or **forbad** /fəˈbæd/, **forbidden** /fəˈbɪd(ə)n/) verb [T] to say that something is not allowed = PROHIBIT: *The army forbids soldiers from talking to the news media. ♦ She was forbidden to see him again.*

forbidden /fəˈbɪd(ə)n/ adj **1** not allowed according to a rule or law: *Smoking is forbidden in all parts of the building. ♦ The use of mobile phones in the library is strictly forbidden.* **2** forbidden activities or subjects are things you should not do, talk about, or know about: *forbidden books*

forbidding /fəˈbɪdɪŋ/ adj someone who is forbidding seems unfriendly or threatening

force¹ /fɔːs/ noun

1 physical strength	**5** an influence
2 power to influence	**6** strength of wind
3 scientific effect	+ PHRASES
4 group of police etc	

1 [U] physical strength, violence, or energy: *The force of the bomb blast shattered windows in 15 buildings. ♦ They accused the police of using excessive force during the arrest. ♦ The army took control of the region by force.*
2 [U] the power that something or someone has to influence people or events: *We have convinced people by the force of our argument.*
3 [C] PHYSICS a power that makes an object move or that changes the way it moves: *the force of gravity ♦ electromagnetic forces*
4 [C] a group of people doing military or police work: *Both countries have now withdrawn their forces from the area. ♦ a UN peacekeeping force*
5 [C] someone or something that has a lot of influence on what happens: *the political forces that shape people's lives ♦ The UN should be a major force for stability in the area.*
6 [U] GEOGRAPHY used with a number for describing how strong a wind is
PHRASES **force of attraction** PHYSICS a force that is attracted to another force, for example a negative charge to a positive charge —*picture* → MAGNET
in force 1 if a law or rule is in force, it is being applied and people must obey it: *The ban on arms exports remains in force.* **2** if people are somewhere in force, a lot of people are there
join/combine forces to work with someone else in order to achieve something together: *Aid workers have joined forces with police to get supplies to the town.*
through/from force of habit without thinking, because you always do a particular thing: *I locked the door from force of habit.*

force² /fɔːs/ verb [T] **1** to make someone do something that they do not want to do = COMPEL: *The judge was forced to resign. ♦ Despite the pain, she forced herself to get out of bed.* **2** to use physical force to move something or to move somewhere: *She forced the package through the slot. ♦ We had to force the windows open.* **3** to make something happen: *Opposition to the plans forced a rapid change of policy.* **4** BIOLOGY to make a plant grow faster than it would normally, for example by giving it extra heat or light

PHRASAL VERBS ,force sth 'down to eat or drink something even though you do not want to

'force sth on/upon sb to make someone accept something that they do not want: *She took over the meeting and forced her views on everyone.*

forced /fɔːst/ adj **1** not sincere or natural: *a forced smile* **2** done or happening because the situation makes it necessary or because someone makes you do it

,forced 'labour noun [U] hard physical work that someone is forced to do

'force-field a,nalysis noun [C] **SOCIAL STUDIES** a way of examining a situation in which there are **driving forces** that make a goal or a change more likely, and **restraining forces** that make it less likely

forceful /'fɔːsf(ə)l/ adj **1** confident and good at influencing people **2** likely to persuade people: *a forceful argument* —**forcefully** adv

force majeure /ˌfɔːs mæˈʒɜː/ noun [U] **1 LAW** an unexpected event that stops you doing something that you promised to do in a contract **2** greater strength or power

'force ,multiplier noun [C] **PHYSICS** a system that reduces the force needed to move something, while increasing the distance over which the force acts —*picture* → LEVER

forceps /'fɔːseps/ noun [plural] a medical tool that is used for holding or pulling things

forearm /'fɔːr,ɑːm/ noun [C] the lower part of the arm, between the elbow and the wrist —*picture* → BODY

forebears /'fɔːbeəz/ noun [plural] the people in your family who lived before you

foreboding /fɔːˈbəʊdɪŋ/ noun [U] a strong feeling that something very bad is going to happen

forecast¹ /'fɔːˌkɑːst/ noun [C] a statement about what is likely to happen, usually relating to the weather, business, or the economy

forecast² /'fɔːˌkɑːst/ (**forecasts, forecasting, forecasted, forecast** or **forecasted**) verb [T] to make a statement about what is likely to happen, usually relating to the weather, business, or the economy

foreclose /fɔːˈkləʊz/ verb [I] **LAW** to take someone's property because they failed to pay back the money that they borrowed to buy it —**foreclosure** /fɔːˈkləʊʒə/ noun [C/U]

forecourt /'fɔːˌkɔːt/ noun [C] an open area in front of a large building or a petrol station

forefathers /'fɔːˌfɑːðəz/ noun [plural] *formal* people belonging to your family or nation who lived a long time ago

forefinger /'fɔːˌfɪŋɡə/ noun [C] the finger that is next to the thumb = INDEX FINGER

the forefront /'fɔːˌfrʌnt/ noun [singular] a leading or important position

foregoing /'fɔːˌɡəʊɪŋ/ adj **LAW** used for referring to something that has just been mentioned

foregone conclusion /ˌfɔːɡɒn kənˈkluːʒ(ə)n/ noun [singular] a result that you can be certain about before it happens

the foreground /'fɔːˌɡraʊnd/ noun [singular] the front part of a scene or picture ≠ BACKGROUND

forehand /'fɔːˌhænd/ noun [C] **SPORTS** a way of hitting the ball in tennis in which the palm of the player's hand is towards their opponent

forehead /'fɒrɪd, 'fɔːˌhed/ noun [C] the upper part of the face, between the eyes and the hair —*picture* → BODY

foreign /'fɒrɪn/ adj **1** from another country, or in another country: *Working in a foreign country takes some getting used to.* ♦ *Do you speak any foreign languages?* **2** dealing with, or relating to, other countries: *foreign policy* **3 HEALTH** not forming a normal part of the body's **immune system 4** not typical of something or someone and therefore not expected or familiar = ALIEN: *emotions that were totally foreign to her nature*

,foreign 'body noun [C] *formal* something that has entered a place where it should not be: *a foreign body in her eye*

foreigner /'fɒrɪnə/ noun [C] someone who comes from another country

,foreign ex'change noun [C/U] **ECONOMICS** a system for changing the money of one country for the money of another, or the money used in this system

foreman /'fɔːmən/ (plural **foremen** /'fɔːmən/) noun [C] **1** a man who is in charge of a team of workers **2 LAW** the person who is chosen to be the leader of a jury

foremost /'fɔːˌməʊst/ adj most important, or most well known

forename /'fɔːˌneɪm/ noun [C] *formal* a **first name**

forensic /fəˈrensɪk/ adj relating to the use of scientific methods to solve crimes

forerunner /'fɔːˌrʌnə/ noun [C] an institution, custom, or thing that existed before a newer but similar thing = PRECURSOR

foresee /fɔːˈsiː/ (**foresees, foreseeing, foresaw** /fɔːˈsɔː/, **foreseen** /fɔːˈsiːn/) verb [T] to see or know something that will happen in the future = PREDICT

foreseeable /fɔːˈsiːəb(ə)l/ adj a foreseeable event or time is one that can easily be imagined or known about before it happens = PREDICTABLE ≠ UNFORESEEABLE

PHRASE the foreseeable future the time in the near future in which you can guess what might happen

foreshore /'fɔːˌʃɔː/ noun [C] **GEOGRAPHY 1** a narrow area of land beside a sea, a lake, or a wide river, between the water and where trees or houses begin **2** the **intertidal zone**

foreshortened /fɔːˈʃɔːt(ə)nd/ adj if something in a picture is foreshortened, it seems shorter or smaller than it is

foresight /'fɔːˌsaɪt/ noun [U] the ability to think about and plan for what might happen

foreskin /'fɔːˌskɪn/ noun [C] **ANATOMY** the loose skin that covers the front part of a man's penis

forest /'fɒrɪst/ noun [C/U] a large area of land that is covered by trees and other plants growing close together. Forests exist in most areas of the world apart from in deserts or where it is extremely cold. They provide important habitats for many different types of plants, animals, and insects, and also use up carbon dioxide in the air: *Acid rain is already destroying large areas of forest.* ♦ *a forest fire* → DEFORESTATION, RAINFOREST

forestall /fɔːˈstɔːl/ verb [T] to do something to prevent something from happening

forested /'fɒrɪstɪd/ adj covered with trees

forestry /'fɒrɪstri/ noun [U] **AGRICULTURE** the science or activity of caring for forests

foretell /fɔːˈtel/ (**foretells, foretelling, foretold** /fɔːˈtəʊld/) verb [T] *literary* to say what will happen in the future = PREDICT

forever /fər'evə/ or ‚for 'ever adv **1** for all time in the future, or for as long as you can imagine: *They promised to love each other forever.* **2** *informal* for a long time, usually longer than you would like: *The film seemed to go on forever.*

forewoman /'fɔːˌwʊmən/ noun [C] LAW a woman who is chosen to be the leader of a jury

foreword /'fɔːˌwɜːd/ noun [C] LITERATURE a short introduction to a book

forfeit /'fɔːfɪt/ noun [C] something that someone must give, pay, or do because they have done something wrong= PENALTY

forfeiture /'fɔːfɪtʃə/ noun [C/U] LAW the loss of a right, a benefit, or something that you own because you have failed to do something, or have done something wrong

forgave /fə'geɪv/ the past tense of **forgive**

forge¹ /fɔːdʒ/ verb [T] **1** to develop or achieve something: *During the 1970s, the US forged trade links with China.* **2** to make an illegal copy of something in order to cheat people: *Someone forged my signature.* **3** TECHNOLOGY to shape heated metal, or to join a heated piece of metal to another one, by hammering or bending it

forge² /fɔːdʒ/ noun [C] a place where metal objects are made

forgery /'fɔːdʒəri/ (plural **forgeries**) noun **1** [U] LAW the crime of making illegal copies of documents or works of art **2** [C] an illegal copy of a document or a work of art

forget /fə'get/ (**forgets**, **forgetting**, **forgot** /fə'gɒt/, **forgotten** /fə'gɒt(ə)n/) verb [I/T] **1** to be unable to remember something: *I'd forgotten that you'd already given me the money.* ◆ *I've forgotten her phone number.* ◆ *Did you forget about our agreement?* ◆ *She always forgets where her car is parked.* **2** to not remember to do something that you intended to do: *She had forgotten all about posting the letter.* ◆ *Don't forget to lock the door when you leave.* **3** to not take something with you when you should have taken it = LEAVE SB/STH BEHIND: *She forgot her glasses.* ◆ *I remembered everything else for the meal but I forgot about the rice.* **4** to stop thinking or worrying about something: *People forget that women didn't always have the right to vote.* ◆ *Try to forget about him.*

> Word family: **forget**
>
> *Words in the same family as forget*
> - forgetful *adj*
> - forgetfulness *n*
> - unforgettable *adj*
> - unforgettably *adv*

forgetful /fə'getf(ə)l/ adj often unable to remember things —**forgetfulness** noun [U]

forge welding /'fɔːdʒ ˌweldɪŋ/ noun [U] TECHNOLOGY the process of joining two pieces of metal together by heating them and hammering them together

forgework /'fɔːdʒˌwɜːk/ noun [U] TECHNOLOGY the shaping of metal that has been heated, using a tool such as a hammer

forgive /fə'gɪv/ (**forgives**, **forgiving**, **forgave** /fə'geɪv/, **forgiven** /fə'gɪv(ə)n/) verb [T] **1** to decide to stop being angry with someone who has done something that is bad: *John has never forgiven himself for the accident.* ◆ *She eventually forgave him for forgetting her birthday.* **2** ECONOMICS if a country or bank forgives a debt, they decide that the debt does not have to be paid back= CANCEL

forgiveness /fə'gɪvnəs/ noun [U] the action of forgiving someone

forgiving /fə'gɪvɪŋ/ adj willing to forget your anger towards someone

forgo /fɔː'gəʊ/ (**forgoes**, **forgoing**, **forwent** /fɔː'went/, **forgone** /fɔː'gɒn/) verb [T] *formal* to decide not to do or have something

forgot /fə'gɒt/ the past tense of **forget**

forgotten¹ /fə'gɒt(ə)n/ adj a forgotten thing is something that most people no longer remember

forgotten² /fə'gɒt(ə)n/ the past participle of **forget**

fork¹ /fɔːk/ noun [C] **1** an object that you use for eating, with a handle and three or four long points on the end **2** a garden tool that is used for breaking up soil, with a long handle and metal points on the end —picture → AGRICULTURAL **3** a place where a road divides into two parts to form a shape like a 'Y'

fork² /fɔːk/ verb [I] if a road forks, it divides into two separate parts

forked /fɔːkt/ adj divided into two separate parts in a 'Y' shape

forklift truck /ˌfɔːklɪft 'trʌk/ noun [C] a vehicle that uses two long metal bars at the front for lifting and moving heavy objects

forlorn /fə'lɔːn/ adj someone who is forlorn looks sad and alone

form¹ /fɔːm/ noun

1 type of sth	4 level of ability
2 way sth appears/exists	5 shape of sb/sth
3 official document	6 one of parts of word

1 [C] a type of something: *He developed a rare form of cancer.* ◆ *Everyone agrees that the kids must receive some form of punishment.*
2 [C/U] the particular way in which something appears or exists: *The information is also available in electronic form.* ◆ *Help arrived in the form of six police officers.* ◆ *The aid might take the form of food or medical supplies.*
3 [C] an official document with spaces where people write information: *Use the order form to get new office supplies.* ◆ *Make sure you fill in the application form.*
4 [U] SPORTS the level of someone's ability at a particular time, especially in a sport
5 [C] the body of a person, or the shape of an object: *Three forms gradually emerged out of the darkness.*
6 [C] LANGUAGE one part of a verb or other word that has several different parts

form² /fɔːm/ verb

1 start to exist/develop	4 make/shape sth
2 be sth	5 make part of word
3 influence development	

1 [I/T] to start to exist, or to make something develop: *The club was formed in 1972.* ◆ *A change in temperature causes moisture to form on the windows.* ◆ *The interview will give you a chance to form an impression of the company.*
2 [linking verb] to be something, or to be the parts that something consists of: *Research forms an important part of the course.* ◆ *Mountains form a natural barrier that keeps invaders out.*
3 [T] to influence the development of something: *His political views were formed by years of service in the army.*
4 [T] to make or shape something: *Use your hands to form the damp clay into a small ball.* ◆ *The children formed a line behind their teacher.*

5 [T] LANGUAGE to make one of the parts of a verb or other word that has several different parts

formal /ˈfɔːm(ə)l/ adj **1** following the correct official methods ≠ INFORMAL: *The government is promising a formal investigation.* ♦ *We intend to make a formal written complaint.* **2** suitable for serious situations or occasions ≠ INFORMAL: *'Ameliorate' is a more formal way of saying 'improve'.* **3** you get a formal education or formal training from studying rather than from working at a job **4** relating to the form or structure of something such as a piece of writing, art, or music: *the formal innovations in Mozart's music* —**formally** adv

formaldehyde /fɔːˈmældɪˌhaɪd/ noun [U] SCIENCE a gas with no colour and a strong smell, used mixed with water for preserving dead things in a laboratory

formalin /ˈfɔːməlɪn/ noun [U] SCIENCE a chemical made by mixing **formaldehyde** with water, used for preserving dead things in a laboratory

formality /fɔːˈmæləti/ (plural **formalities**) noun **1** [C] something that you must do as part of an official process, even though it may not seem necessary or sensible: *We went through the usual formalities at customs and passport control.* **2** [U] a formal style of writing, speaking, behaving, or dressing

formalize /ˈfɔːməlaɪz/ verb [T] to make something such as a plan, system, or agreement official

format¹ /ˈfɔːmæt/ noun [C/U] **1** the arrangement, size, or shape of something: *Changes have been proposed to the format of the competition.* **2** COMPUTING the way that information is arranged and organized on a computer disk **3** COMPUTING the structure and design of a computer document or file, for example the size and type of the letters and the width of the page

format² /ˈfɔːmæt/ (**formats, formatting, formatted**) verb [T] COMPUTING **1** to prepare a computer disk so that information can be stored on it **2** to change the size, shape, or arrangement of the words in a computer file

formation /fɔːˈmeɪʃ(ə)n/ noun **1** [U] the process of starting or developing something: *factors that affect the formation of children's personalities* **2** [C/U] a pattern that people or things are arranged into: *planes flying in formation*

formative /ˈfɔːmətɪv/ adj strongly influencing the development of someone's character and beliefs

former /ˈfɔːmə/ adj, pronoun **1** used for stating the job, title, status etc that someone or something had in the past: *former US president Bill Clinton* ♦ *the former Soviet Union* **2** *formal* used for referring to times in the past: *in former years* **3** **the former** *formal* used for referring to the first of two people or things that you have mentioned: *He attended with his wife and daughter, the former wearing a black dress.* → LATTER

formerly /ˈfɔːməli/ adv in the past

Formica /fɔːˈmaɪkə/ TRADEMARK a hard plastic used for covering tables and working areas in kitchens

formic acid /ˌfɔːmɪk ˈæsɪd/ noun [U] CHEMISTRY, HEALTH an acid that makes the skin painful or swollen. It is present in **ant** bites.

formidable /ˈfɔːmɪdəb(ə)l, fəˈmɪdəb(ə)l/ adj very impressive in size, power, or skill and therefore deserving respect

formula /ˈfɔːmjələ/ (plural **formulae** /ˈfɔːmjəliː/ or **formulas**) noun [C] **1** MATHS, SCIENCE a group of letters, numbers, or symbols that represents a rule in mathematics or science: *the formula for calculating the area of a circle* ♦ *a mathematical formula* **2** CHEMISTRY an exact description of the chemical elements that make up a particular chemical

compound, written with chemical symbols **3** a way of achieving something, or of dealing with a problem: *There is no magic formula for economic success.* **4** a list of the substances that must be mixed in order to make something

formulaic /ˌfɔːmjʊˈleɪɪk/ adj using a standard pattern that has been used many times before and is therefore not interesting or original

formulate /ˈfɔːmjʊleɪt/ verb [T] **1** to develop something by thinking carefully about its details: *He formulated a plan to improve the team's performance.* **2** to express an idea in words that you choose carefully —**formulation** /ˌfɔːmjʊˈleɪʃ(ə)n/ noun [C/U]

forsake /fəˈseɪk/ (**forsakes, forsaking, forsook** /fəˈsʊk/, **forsaken** /fəˈseɪkən/) verb [T] *literary* to leave someone when they still need you = ABANDON

fort /fɔːt/ noun [C] a strong building that is used by soldiers for defending a place

forte¹ /ˈfɔːteɪ/ noun **1** [singular] something that someone is very good at: *Cooking isn't my forte, I'm afraid.* **2** [C] MUSIC a musical note or piece of music that should be played or sung loudly —*picture* → MUSIC

forte² /ˈfɔːteɪ, ˈfɔːti/ adv MUSIC loudly: used as an instruction in music —**forte** adj

forthcoming /fɔːθˈkʌmɪŋ/ adj **1** happening or coming soon: *the forthcoming general election* **2** helpful and willing to tell you things: *James was more forthcoming than I expected.*

forthright /ˈfɔːθraɪt/ adj saying exactly what you think without being afraid of other people's reactions —**forthrightly** adv

forties /ˈfɔːtiz/ noun [plural]

PHRASES **the forties 1** the years from 1940 to 1949 **2** a temperature in the forties is between 40 and 49 degrees Fahrenheit

in your forties aged between 40 and 49

fortieth /ˈfɔːtiəθ/ number **1** in the place or position counted as number 40 **2** one of 40 equal parts of something

fortifications /ˌfɔːtɪfɪˈkeɪʃ(ə)nz/ noun [plural] strong buildings and walls that have been built to defend a place

fortify /ˈfɔːtɪfaɪ/ (**fortifies, fortifying, fortified**) verb [T] **1** to protect a place against attack by building strong walls, towers, or other structures around it **2** to give someone energy or confidence **3** to make yourself or someone else feel more determined, powerful, or full of energy **4** to add a substance to food in order to make it healthier

fortissimo /fɔːˈtɪsɪməʊ/ adv MUSIC very loudly: used as an instruction in music —*picture* → MUSIC —**fortissimo** adj

fortnight /ˈfɔːtnaɪt/ noun [C] a period of two weeks

fortnightly /ˈfɔːtnaɪtli/ adj, adv happening every two weeks

fortress /ˈfɔːtrəs/ noun [C] a strong building that is used by soldiers for defending a place

fortuitous /fɔːˈtjuːɪtəs/ adj *formal* happening by chance, especially in a way that is lucky or convenient —**fortuitously** adv

fortunate /ˈfɔːtʃənət/ adj lucky ≠ UNFORTUNATE: *It's fortunate that the doctor was here today.* ♦ *Not everyone is as fortunate as we are.* ♦ *She was extremely fortunate to escape without injury.* ♦ *I was fortunate enough to have a supportive family.*

fortunately /'fɔːtʃənətli/ adv used for emphasizing that something good has happened by chance = LUCKILY ≠ UNFORTUNATELY: *I arrived at the station late, but fortunately the train was delayed.*

fortune /'fɔːtʃən/ noun **1** [C] a large amount of money: *He had made a fortune from mining.* **2 fortunes** [plural] the good or bad things that happen to someone: *a career that illustrates the changing fortunes of the Labour Party* **3** [U] good luck: *I had the good fortune to know the manager of the company.*

fortune-teller /'fɔːtʃ(ə)n ˌtelə/ noun [C] someone who tells people what will happen to them in the future, for example by looking at the lines on their hand

forty /'fɔːti/ number the number 40

forum /'fɔːrəm/ noun [C] **1** a large meeting where people discuss something **2** a website, newspaper, television programme etc where people can express their ideas and opinions

forward¹ /'fɔːwəd/ adj, adv **1** moving or looking in the direction in front of you: *The car started to roll forward.* ♦ *a sudden forward movement* **2** in a position that is towards the front of a room or vehicle: *Let's sit further forward.* ♦ *the forward part of the train* **3** if you put a clock or watch forward, you change the time on it to a later time

forward² /'fɔːwəd/ verb [T] to send a letter, parcel, email etc that has been sent to your address to someone else at another address

forward³ /'fɔːwəd/ noun [C] SPORTS a player in a game such as football or basketball whose job is to attack and score

forwarding address /'fɔːwədɪŋ əˌdres/ noun [C] an address that people can send someone's letters to after they leave a place

forward ˈroll noun [C] SPORTS an exercise in which someone bends down and puts the top of their head on the floor in front of them, and pushes their body and legs over their head

forwards /'fɔːwədz/ adv forward

ˈforward ˌslash noun [C] COMPUTING the symbol / used in Internet addresses and computer instructions

fossil /'fɒs(ə)l/ noun [C] GEOLOGY, BIOLOGY an animal or plant that lived hundreds of thousands of years ago and has been preserved in rock or in the form of rock. Common fossils include **trilobites** and **ammonites**, sea animals that no longer exist. Someone who studies fossils is called a **palaeontologist**.

ˈfossil ˌfuel noun [C/U] ENVIRONMENT a fuel such as coal, oil, or **natural gas** made from decayed material from organisms that lived many millions of years ago

fossilization /ˌfɒsəlaɪ'zeɪʃ(ə)n/ noun [U] GEOLOGY the process by which things that were living become preserved in rock, or in the form of rock

fossilize /'fɒsəlaɪz/ verb [I/T] GEOLOGY to become a fossil by being preserved in rock for thousands or millions of years, or to preserve something in this way

fossilized /'fɒsəlaɪzd/ adj GEOLOGY preserved in rock

foster¹ /'fɒstə/ verb **1** [T] to help something to develop over a period of time = PROMOTE **2** [I/T] to look after someone else's child as part of your family for a period of time → ADOPT

foster² /'fɒstə/ adj a foster child is a child who is being temporarily looked after in someone else's family

fought /fɔːt/ the past tense and past participle of **fight¹**

foul¹ /faʊl/ adj **1** very dirty, or very unpleasant: *a foul smell* **2** SPORTS not allowed by the rules **3** if someone

has a foul **temper** or is in a foul mood, they are very angry

foul² /faʊl/ verb **1** [I/T] SPORTS to break the rules of a game **2** [T] to make something very dirty

foul³ /faʊl/ noun [C] SPORTS something that a player does in a game that is not allowed by the rules

ˌfoul ˈplay noun [U] **1** violence or criminal actions that cause someone's death **2** dishonest or illegal behaviour

found¹ /faʊnd/ verb [T] to start an organization or institution: *The newspaper was founded in 1909.*

PHRASE **be founded on sth** to be based on a particular idea or principle: *a society founded on the belief that all people are equal*

found² /faʊnd/ the past tense and past participle of **find¹**

foundation /faʊn'deɪʃ(ə)n/ noun

1 basic part of sth	**4** creating an
2 base of building	organization
3 an organization	**5** face cream

1 [C] the most basic part of something from which the rest of it develops = BASIS: *The first two years of study provide a solid foundation in computing.* ♦ *a business partnership that lays the foundation for future success* ♦ *He believes that religion is the foundation of a civilized society.*
2 [C] CONSTRUCTION the part of a building that is below the ground and that supports the rest of the building
3 [C] an organization that provides money for things such as medical research or for a charity
4 [U] the process of starting an organization or institution: *the foundation of democracy in the country*
5 [C/U] a cream that is the same colour as skin that someone puts on their face before the rest of their **make-up**

founˈdation ˌcourse noun [C] EDUCATION in the UK, a course at university or college that covers a range of subjects at a basic level and prepares students for a longer, more advanced course

founder /'faʊndə/ noun [C] someone who starts an organization or institution

foundry /'faʊndri/ (plural **foundries**) noun [C] a factory where metal is melted and made into different objects

foundrywork /'faʊndriˌwɜːk/ noun [U] TECHNOLOGY the making of metal articles by melting a metal, pouring it into moulds, and allowing it to become solid

fountain /'faʊntɪn/ noun [C] a decoration for gardens and streets in which a stream of water is sent up into the air

ˈfountain ˌpen noun [C] a type of pen that you fill with ink

four¹ /fɔː/ number the number 4

four² /fɔː/ noun [C] SPORTS the score in a game of **cricket** when a player hits the ball and it reaches the **boundary** (=edge of the playing area)
PHRASE **on all fours** with your hands, knees, and feet on the ground

ˌfour-by-ˈfour noun [C] a **four-wheel drive**

fourfold /'fɔːˌfəʊld/ adj **1** four times as much, or four times as many **2** consisting of four parts

foursome /'fɔːsəm/ noun [C] a group of four people

,four-stroke 'cycle noun [C] ENGINEERING an internal-combustion engine that completes the processes of **intake**, **compression**, **combustion**, and **exhaust** in four **strokes** (=movements of the piston)

fourteen /ˌfɔːˈtiːn/ number the number 14

fourteenth /ˌfɔːˈtiːnθ/ number **1** in the place or position counted as number 14 **2** one of 14 equal parts of something

fourth /fɔːθ/ number in the place or position counted as number four

,four-wheel 'drive noun **1** [U] ENGINEERING a system of sending power from the driving **mechanism** to all four wheels of a vehicle, so that the wheels slip less in difficult conditions **2** [C] a car with big wheels that is designed for driving on rough ground

fovea /ˈfəʊviə/ noun [C] ANATOMY a part of the retina that contains only **cones** (=cells that make it possible to see detailed images). It is the area where we see things most sharply.

fowl /faʊl/ (plural **fowl** or **fowls**) noun [C] a chicken or other bird that is kept on a farm for its eggs and meat

fox /fɒks/ noun [C] a wild animal similar to a small dog, with red-brown fur and a thick tail —picture → MAMMAL

foyer /ˈfɔɪeɪ/ noun [C] a large open space just inside the entrance to a hotel or theatre = LOBBY

FPS /ˌef piː ˈes/ noun [U] COMPUTING frames per second: a measure of the rate in which still pictures pass to create a moving image. The higher the FPS, the better the image will look.

fractal /ˈfrækt(ə)l/ noun [C] MATHS a geometric shape that can be divided many times into parts that are smaller copies of the original shape

fraction /ˈfrækʃ(ə)n/ noun [C] **1** a small part or amount of something: *His investment is now worth only a fraction of its original value.* **2** MATHS a part of a whole number, for example $\frac{1}{2}$ or $\frac{3}{4}$ —**fractional** /ˈfrækʃ(ə)nəl/ adj

,fractional 'distillation noun [U] CHEMISTRY the process of using a **volatile** mixture to separate substances that have different boiling points, by first heating the mixture and then condensing and collecting the separated parts as they turn to liquids

fractionally /ˈfrækʃ(ə)nəli/ adv by a very small amount

fractionating column /ˈfrækʃ(ə)neɪtɪŋ ˌkɒləm/ noun [C] CHEMISTRY a long tube in which substances are separated during **fractional distillation** —picture → REFINE

fracture¹ /ˈfræktʃə/ noun [C] a break or crack in a bone or piece of rock

fracture² /ˈfræktʃə/ verb [I/T] if something hard such as a bone fractures, or if it is fractured, it breaks or cracks —**fractured** adj

fragile /ˈfrædʒaɪl/ adj **1** easy to break or damage **2** not very strong or healthy: *His health has always been fragile.* —**fragility** /frəˈdʒɪləti/ noun [U]

fragment /ˈfrægmənt/ noun [C] **1** a small piece of a larger object that has broken into a lot of pieces: *Police found fragments of glass on his clothing.* **2** a small part of something: *fragments of conversation*

fragrance /ˈfreɪɡrəns/ noun [C/U] **1** a nice smell **2** perfume

fragrant /ˈfreɪɡrənt/ adj with a nice smell

frail /freɪl/ adj **1** physically weak and not very healthy **2** not strong and therefore likely to be damaged or destroyed

frailty /ˈfreɪlti/ (plural **frailties**) noun [C/U] the condition of being physically or morally weak

frame¹ /freɪm/ noun

1 border of door etc	**5** box on Internet page
2 border of picture	**6** of pair of glasses
3 basic structure	+ PHRASE
4 one photograph	

1 [C] a structure that forms the border of something such as a door or window: *The window frames need painting.*
2 [C] a structure that forms the border of a picture and holds it in place: *a silver picture frame*
3 [C] the part of an object that forms its basic structure: *the frame of a bed*
4 [C] ARTS one of the single photographs that form a film
5 [C] COMPUTING a box on an Internet page that contains information that you can **scroll** through (=go up and down by using the mouse)
6 frames [plural] the part of a pair of glasses that holds the lenses and that has pieces that go over the ears

PHRASE **frame of mind** the mood that someone is in

frame² /freɪm/ verb [T] **1** to put a picture or photograph in a frame **2** to develop or make up something such as a plan or law **3** *informal* to make someone seem guilty of a crime when they are not, for example by lying to the police or by producing false evidence **4** to express something carefully in a particular way

framework /ˈfreɪmwɜːk/ noun [C] **1** a set of principles or rules: *a framework for the study of television's effect on society* **2** a structure that supports something and makes it a particular shape: *the wooden framework of the roof*

franchise /ˈfræntʃaɪz/ noun **1** [singular/U] SOCIAL STUDIES the right to vote in elections **2** [C] BUSINESS an arrangement in which someone operates a business using the name and the products of a big company **3** [C] BUSINESS a business that operates under this arrangement

francium /ˈfrænsiəm/ noun [U] CHEMISTRY a radioactive metallic element. Chemical symbol: **Fr**

francophone¹ /ˈfræŋkəʊˌfəʊn/ adj LANGUAGE **1** a francophone country is one where French is spoken as one of the main languages **2** a francophone person speaks French, especially as their main or first language

francophone² /ˈfræŋkəʊˌfəʊn/ noun [C] LANGUAGE a francophone is someone who speaks French, especially as their main or first language

frank /fræŋk/ adj honest about a situation or your opinions, even if this offends people: *He was completely frank about the problems we face.* —**frankness** noun [U]

frankincense /ˈfræŋkɪnsens/ noun [U] a substance that is burned to produce a nice smell in some religious ceremonies. Frankincense is a type of **incense**.

frankly /ˈfræŋkli/ adv **1** used for emphasizing that you are speaking honestly: *Frankly, I don't care what you think.* **2** in an honest and direct manner: *She talks frankly about her unhappy childhood.*

frantic /ˈfræntɪk/ adj **1** done in a very urgent way: *frantic attempts to rescue people from the fire* **2** very worried —**frantically** /ˈfræntɪkli/ adv

fraternal /frəˈtɜːn(ə)l/ adj **1** of a brother, or like a brother **2** belonging to brothers or between brothers **3** between friends or people who share the same interests or opinions

fra,ternal 'twin noun [C] BIOLOGY a twin born at the same time as another baby from the same mother but from two different eggs → IDENTICAL TWIN

fraternity /frə'tɜːnəti/ (plural **fraternities**) noun **1** [C/U] people who do the same job or share the same interests, or the organization that they belong to **2** [C] American a type of private club for male students at a university or college in the US

fraud /frɔːd/ noun **1** [C/U] LAW the crime of obtaining money from someone by tricking them: *tax fraud* **2** [C] someone who pretends to be an official or professional person in order to trick people **3** [C] something that is not what people claim it is, and is designed to trick people **4** [U] the action of producing false documents or information in order to get what you want

fraudulent /'frɔːdjʊlənt/ adj done dishonestly or illegally with the intention of tricking someone —**fraudulently** adv

fraught /frɔːt/ adj very worried, or involving people who are very worried

fray /freɪ/ verb **1** [I/T] if cloth frays, or if something frays it, its fibres come apart at the edge **2** [I] if someone's nerves fray, they get nervous, and if someone's **temper** frays, they get angry

the fray /freɪ/ noun [singular] **1** an exciting situation in which people compete with each other **2** a fight, or an argument

frayed /freɪd/ adj **1** with fibres that are coming apart at the edge **2** if your nerves are frayed, you are nervous, and if your **temper** is frayed, you are angry

freak1 /friːk/ noun [C] a very strange person or thing

freak2 /friːk/ adj extremely unusual and unexpected: *He was killed in a freak accident.*

freckles /'frek(ə)lz/ noun [plural] small brown spots on someone's skin

free1 /friː/ (**freer, freest**) adj **1** something that is free does not cost anything: *There is plenty of free parking.* ♦ *The swimming pool is free for hotel guests.* **2** not held, tied, or fixed somewhere: *Hand me the free end of the rope.* ♦ *Sally struggled to get free from the branches.* **3** able to do what you like, go where you like, make your own decisions etc without being prevented or limited by other people: *He longed to be a free man again (=not in prison).* ♦ *a free society (=one in which people are politically free)* ♦ *You're free to choose whatever books you like.* **4** available to do something or to be used: *I'm busy at the moment, but I'll be free this afternoon.* ♦ *free time (=time that is available for you to use)* ♦ *Is this seat free?*
PHRASES **be free from/of sth** to be not containing or involving something that is unpleasant: *a world free from violence* ♦ *Doctors try to keep their patients free of pain.*
a free hand the right to make your own decisions without asking someone's permission

free2 /friː/ (**frees, freeing, freed**) verb [T] **1** to let someone leave a prison or a place where they have been forced to stay= RELEASE: *Amnesty International works to free political prisoners.* ♦ *The hostages were freed unharmed.* **2** to help someone to get out of a place: *Rescuers managed to free the trapped climbers.* ♦ *They helped free the injured driver from the wreckage.* **3** to remove something unpleasant that affects someone: *The new president will take action to free the media from government control.* ♦ *He has been freed of direct responsibility for his staff.* **4** to make someone or something available to be used: *We need to free more police officers for street duties.* ♦ *A classroom assistant frees teachers to concentrate on teaching.*

free3 /friː/ adv **1** without paying any money: *We got in free.* ♦ *Children can stay free of charge.* **2** out of a place where you are being kept: *The prisoner suddenly broke free and ran towards the car.* **3** without being controlled or stopped: *dogs running free in the streets*

freediving /'friːˌdaɪvɪŋ/ noun [U] SPORTS the sport of staying under deep water for as long as possible without using oxygen containers

freedom /'friːdəm/ noun **1** [U] the right or opportunity to do what you want: *a law that restricts religious freedom* ♦ *The school gives students freedom of choice about what to wear.* ♦ *Police road blocks were seen as an attempt to restrict freedom of movement.* **2 freedoms** [plural] SOCIAL STUDIES different types of freedom: *basic freedoms* **3** [C] something you have or should have a right to do or have: *basic freedoms such as the right to an education*
PHRASES **freedom from sth** a situation in which you are not affected by something that is unpleasant: *freedom from hunger*
freedom of speech the legal right to express your opinions without being prevented or punished

'freedom ,fighter noun [C] showing approval someone who fights against a cruel or unfair government

free 'enterprise noun [U] ECONOMICS an economic system in which businesses can compete with each other without being controlled by government

'free ,fall noun [U] **1** an occasion when a price or value suddenly becomes much lower **2** the part of a **parachute** jump when someone falls quickly towards the ground before the **parachute** opens —**'free-,fall** verb [I]

'free-for-,all noun [C] informal **1** a situation in which people compete with each other using unfair or cruel methods **2** a noisy fight or argument that involves a lot of people= BRAWL

freeform /'friːˌfɔːm/ adj MUSIC, ARTS freeform music or art does not obey the usual rules for creating a piece of music or art

freehand /'friːˌhænd/ adj ARTS drawn without using a ruler or other equipment —**freehand** adv

free 'kick noun [C] SPORTS in football, an occasion when a player in one team is allowed to kick the ball without any opposition because a player in the other team has broken a rule

freelancer /'friːlɑːnsə/ or **freelance** /'friːlɑːns/ noun [C] a **self-employed** person who works for different companies

freely /'friːli/ adv

1 without limits	4 not exactly
2 without pauses	5 in an honest way
3 generously	6 in many places

1 without being controlled by rules: *Players can move freely between clubs.*
2 without being stopped or interrupted: *The traffic is moving quite freely this morning.*
3 generously, or in a willing way: *They give their time freely to support our cause.*
4 not in an exact way, but giving a general idea of the meaning of something: *Poems have to be translated quite freely.*
5 without trying to hide anything= OPENLY: *I freely admit I've made mistakes.*
6 something that is freely available is easy to obtain or buy

free 'market noun [C] ECONOMICS an economic system in which the government does not control trade and prices

,free 'pardon noun [C] LAW an official statement that someone who has previously been found guilty of a crime is now known not to have committed it

,free 'period noun [C] EDUCATION a part of the school day when a student or teacher does not have a lesson

,free 'port noun [C] ECONOMICS a port or airport where no tax is paid on goods that are delivered because they are then going to be sent to other countries

,free 'radical noun [C] SCIENCE a molecule that has an extra electron and can react very easily with other molecules. Free radicals sometimes form in the human body and can cause cancer.

,free 'speech noun [U] the legal or natural right of people to say what they believe is true, without being prevented or punished

freestyle /'friː,staɪl/ adj SPORTS 1 in swimming, using the **crawl** 2 in sports, using whatever style or method you want to —**freestyle** adv

,free-to-'air adj free-to-air television programmes can be watched without having to pay anything extra

,free 'trade noun [U] ECONOMICS a system in which companies do not pay high taxes on goods that are bought from other countries or are sold in other countries

,free 'verse noun [U] LITERATURE a type of poetry that does not have a regular rhythm or rhyme

freeware /'friː,weə/ noun [U] COMPUTING computer software that is available free on CD-ROM or from the Internet

freeway /'friː,weɪ/ noun [C] American a wide fast road in a US city that drivers do not pay to use

freewheel /,friː'wiːl/ verb [I] to move on a bicycle without moving the pedals, or to move in a car without switching on the engine, usually down a slope= COAST

,free 'will noun [U] people's ability to control their own lives, based on their own decisions

> PHRASE of your own free will if you do something of your own free will, you do it because you want to do it, not because you are forced to

freeze¹ /friːz/ (freezes, freezing, froze /frəʊz/, frozen /'frəʊz(ə)n/) verb

1 become solid with cold	5 not increase a level
2 become hard with cold	6 stop moving/working
3 preserve food	7 of computer screen
4 feel extremely cold	

1 [I/T] SCIENCE if a liquid freezes, or if something freezes it, it has **cooled** to the temperature at which it becomes solid. When water freezes, at 0° C, it becomes ice: Liquid nitrogen freezes at minus 209 degrees Celsius. ♦ The lake freezes in winter. ♦ The water had **frozen** solid. —picture → STATE

2 [I/T] if a substance freezes, or if something freezes it, it becomes very cold and hard: The soil was frozen.

3 [T] to preserve food or drink by making it extremely cold in a freezer: We decided to freeze half the meat.

4 [I] to feel extremely cold: You'll freeze if you go out in that thin coat.

5 [T] ECONOMICS to decide officially that the level of something such as salaries will not increase: Wages were frozen until the end of December.

6 [I] to stop moving and keep completely still: Kate froze in horror when she saw all the blood.

7 [I/T] COMPUTING if a computer screen freezes, or if something freezes it, the images on it become completely still and you cannot move them because there is something wrong with the computer

freeze² /friːz/ noun [C] 1 ECONOMICS an official decision to prevent any increase in something such as prices or wages: a wage freeze 2 a period of extremely cold weather

freezer /'friːzə/ noun [C] a large piece of electrical equipment that is used for freezing food

freezing¹ /'friːzɪŋ/ adj informal very cold: It's absolutely freezing in here.

freezing² /'friːzɪŋ/ noun [U] SCIENCE the temperature of 0° Celsius at which water freezes and becomes ice: five degrees below freezing

'freezing ,point noun [C] SCIENCE the temperature at which a particular liquid freezes

'free ,zone noun [C] ECONOMICS an area at a port or in a city where goods can be received or stored without tax having to be paid

freight /freɪt/ noun [U] goods that are carried by vehicles

freighter /'freɪtə/ noun [C] a large ship or plane that carries goods

'freight ,train noun [C] a train that carries only goods
→ PASSENGER TRAIN

French horn /,frentʃ 'hɔːn/ noun [C] MUSIC a musical instrument consisting of a long curved metal tube that is very wide at one end —picture → MUSICAL INSTRUMENT

French windows /,frentʃ 'wɪndəʊz/ noun [plural] a pair of glass doors that lead to a garden

frenzied /'frenzid/ adj done in an extremely uncontrolled way, often by someone who is crazy

frenzy /'frenzi/ noun [singular] 1 the feeling of being unable to control your feelings or behaviour: She was in a frenzy of rage. 2 a period when there is a lot of activity

frequency /'friːkwənsi/ (plural frequencies) noun 1 [U] the number of times that something happens during a period: We hope this treatment will reduce the frequency of heart disease. 2 [C/U] PHYSICS the rate at which a sound wave, light wave, or radio wave vibrates 3 [C] PHYSICS the wavelength on which a radio programme is broadcast

'frequency ,modulation noun [U] PHYSICS see FM

'frequency ,polygon noun [C] MATHS a geometric shape formed by the line joining the points on a graph and the **x-axis** along the bottom

frequent /'friːkwənt/ adj happening often ≠ INFREQUENT: Their arguments were becoming more and more frequent. ♦ He was a frequent visitor to our house. ♦ Inspections must be carried out at frequent intervals (=regularly).

frequentative /frɪ'kwentətɪv/ adj LANGUAGE expressing an action that is often repeated

,frequent 'flyer noun [C] TOURISM 1 someone who often travels by plane, especially with the same airline 2 relating to a system in which people who often travel by air can get airline tickets free or at a reduced price

frequently /'friːkwəntli/ adv often ≠ RARELY, SELDOM: He has frequently been compared to Michael Jackson. ♦ The ten most frequently asked questions are listed below.

fresco /'freskəʊ/ (plural frescoes) noun [C] ARTS a picture that is painted onto wet **plaster** on a wall

fresh /freʃ/ adj

1 new	**7** with energy
2 food: not preserved	**8** of flowers
3 food: not too old	**9** water: with no salt
4 replacing sth	**+ PHRASE**
5 recently done	
6 smelling/tasting natural	

1 clearly new and different: *We need a completely fresh approach to the problem.* ♦ *The programme takes a fresh look at this difficult issue.* ♦ *She regarded the birth of her children as a fresh start* (=a chance to start living in a better way).
2 fresh food has not been preserved in any way: *You can use fresh or tinned tomatoes for this recipe.*
3 food that is fresh is still good to eat because it was prepared or produced recently: *Cooked meat will keep fresh for several days in the fridge.*
4 replacing or adding to a previous thing: *The police made a fresh appeal for witnesses.* ♦ *I've put fresh towels in the bathroom.*
5 recently made or experienced: *fresh footprints in the sand* ♦ *The details are still fresh in my mind.*
6 if something smells or tastes fresh, it smells or tastes pleasant and clean: *The air smelled clean and fresh after the smoky little hut.* ♦ *I like drinks with a fresh fruity flavour.*
7 if you feel fresh, you have a lot of energy
8 fresh flowers have been recently picked
9 SCIENCE fresh water is water in lakes and rivers that does not contain any salt
  PHRASE **fresh from/out of sth** if someone is fresh from a particular place or situation, they have recently come from there: *He was just a kid, fresh out of law school.*
—**freshness** noun [U]

,fresh 'air noun [U] the air outside that is nice to breathe

fresher /ˈfreʃə/ noun [C] EDUCATION a student in their first year at university

freshly /ˈfreʃli/ adv recently: *freshly washed clothes*

freshwater /ˈfreʃˌwɔːtə/ adj **1** BIOLOGY living in water that does not contain salt: *freshwater fish* **2** SCIENCE consisting of water that does not contain salt: *a freshwater lake* → SALTWATER

fret /fret/ (**frets, fretting, fretted**) verb [I] to worry about something continuously

Fri. abbrev Friday

friable /ˈfraɪəb(ə)l/ adj easily broken into smaller pieces= CRUMBLY

friar /ˈfraɪə/ noun [C] RELIGION a man who is a type of **monk** (=a member of a Christian religious community)

fricative /ˈfrɪkətɪv/ adj LANGUAGE fricative sounds such as 'f', 'z', and 'th' are made by pushing air out through a small space between the teeth and the tongue or lips, or between the tongue and **palate** (=the inside upper part of the mouth) —**fricative** noun [C]

friction /ˈfrɪkʃ(ə)n/ noun [U] **1** PHYSICS the force that **resists** the movement of one object against another. Rough surfaces and objects create more friction than smooth ones: *energy loss due to friction* ♦ *Friction can be reduced by using oil.* **2** disagreement: *There is some friction between the various departments.*

Friday /ˈfraɪdeɪ/ noun [C/U] the day after Thursday and before Saturday: *Let's go swimming on Friday.* ♦ *We usually meet on Fridays* (=every Friday).

fridge /frɪdʒ/ noun [C] a piece of equipment that is used for storing food at low temperatures
= REFRIGERATOR

fried /fraɪd/ adj cooked in hot oil

friend /frend/ noun [C] someone who you know well and like who is not a member of your family: *She's visiting friends in Scotland.* ♦ *Helga is a close friend of mine.* ♦ *I'm having lunch with an old friend* (=someone who has been a friend for a long time). ♦ *May I introduce Peter Flint, a very old friend of the family.* ♦ *She has a wide circle of friends* (=group of friends). ♦ *They used to be friends* (=with each other). ♦ *They made friends with the children next door* (=started to be their friends).

friendly¹ /ˈfren(d)li/ (**friendlier, friendliest**) adj **1** someone who is friendly is always pleasant and helpful towards other people ≠ UNFRIENDLY: *He will be remembered as a kind, friendly person.* ♦ *The local people were very friendly towards us.* → SYMPATHETIC **2** if you are friendly with someone, you are their friend: *Janet and I used to be very friendly.* ♦ *Doctors shouldn't get too friendly with their patients.* **3** SPORTS a friendly game is not part of a competition but is played for fun or to practise skills —**friendliness** noun [U]

friendly² /ˈfren(d)li/ noun [C] SPORTS a game that is not part of a competition but is played for fun or in order to practise skills

-friendly /fren(d)li/ suffix **1** used for showing that something does not harm something else: *wildlife-friendly farming methods* ♦ *environmentally-friendly cleaning materials* **2** suitable for a particular type of person: *child-friendly restaurants*

,friendly 'fire noun [U] shots fired at you accidentally by soldiers from your own army

friendship /ˈfren(d)ʃɪp/ noun [C/U] a relationship between people who are friends: *Whatever happened, I did not want to lose Sarah's friendship.* ♦ *his friendship with a local fisherman* ♦ *She formed a close friendship with Vera Brittain.*

frieze /friːz/ noun [C] a line of decoration around the walls of a room or building

fright /fraɪt/ noun [singular/U] a sudden strong feeling of being afraid: *He was shaking with fright.* ♦ *Kelly cried out in fright.*

frighten /ˈfraɪt(ə)n/ verb [T] to make someone feel afraid= SCARE: *The thought of war frightens me.*
  PHRASAL VERB **,frighten sb/sth a'way/off** to make a person or animal so afraid that they run away

frightened /ˈfraɪt(ə)nd/ adj feeling or showing fear = SCARED: *The puppy looked cold and frightened.* ♦ *Bruckner was watching him with wide, frightened eyes.* ♦ *I was frightened that he might see us.* ♦ *There's nothing to be frightened about.* ♦ *I've always been frightened of snakes.*

> ■ **Frightened** describes how you feel: *I am frightened of spiders.* ♦ *She looked very frightened.*
> ■ **Frightening** describes things or situations that make you feel frightened: *The look on his face was frightening.* ♦ *It was a very frightening experience.*

frightening /ˈfraɪt(ə)nɪŋ/ adj making you feel afraid, nervous, or worried: *That's a frightening thought!* ♦ *It was supposed to be a horror film but it wasn't very frightening.* ♦ *It's frightening that people like him get elected.* —**frighteningly** adv

frill /frɪl/ noun [C] a decoration that consists of a long narrow piece of cloth with many small folds in it

frilly /ˈfrɪli/ adj decorated with a lot of frills

fringe /frɪndʒ/ noun [C] **1** short hair that hangs down over your forehead **2** the outer edge of something: *factories on the northern fringe of the city* **3** people or activities that are considered strange: *He has been* forced to live on the fringes of society. **4** a decoration that consists of a row of fibres or thin pieces of cloth that hang down

frisk /frɪsk/ verb [T] to search someone with your hands in order to see if they are carrying anything illegal such as a gun or drugs

frivolous /ˈfrɪvələs/ adj **1** someone who is frivolous behaves in a silly way in situations in which they should be serious or sensible **2** lacking any real purpose or importance: *frivolous complaints*

frizzy /ˈfrɪzi/ adj frizzy hair has small tight stiff curls

frog /frɒg/ noun [C] a small vertebrate animal with smooth skin and long back legs that lives near water. Frogs are amphibians. → TOAD —*picture* → REPTILE

frogman /ˈfrɒgmən/ (plural **frogmen**) noun [C] someone who does police or military work under water. Frogmen wear special clothes and use special equipment.

frogspawn /ˈfrɒgˌspɔːn/ noun [U] BIOLOGY an almost transparent substance containing **frog**'s eggs that is laid in water —*picture* → REPTILE

from /strong frɒm, weak frəm/ preposition

1 provided by sb	**6** when sth starts
2 stating sb's origin	**7** giving a reason
3 saying where sb/sth started	**8** in what place
4 giving distances	**9** made of sth
5 giving a range	**10** showing differences

1 used for saying who gives, sends, or provides something: *She got a letter from Tom.* ♦ *He borrowed the money from the bank.*

2 used for saying where someone was born, where they live or work, or the type of family they were born with: *I'm originally from Kenya.* ♦ *children from the village* ♦ *a team of experts from the university*

3 used for saying where someone or something started a journey, or where they were before moving: *the 3 o'clock flight from Sydney* ♦ *He took a hammer from his tool box.* ♦ *We drove from Seoul to Taegeuk.*

4 used for saying how far away something is in relation to something else: *We live a few miles from the city.*

5 used for giving a range of things, times, prices etc: *music ranging from classical to punk*

6 starting at a point in time and continuing: *He wanted to be an actor from the age of 10.* ♦ *From now on, things are going to be different.*

7 used for saying what has caused something: *Her hair was wet from the rain.* ♦ *She's been suffering from stress.*

8 used for saying where someone is when they see, hear, or do something: *Let's watch the fireworks from the roof.*

9 used for saying what substance has been used for making something: *The toys are made from plastic.*

10 used for talking about differences between two or more people or things: *This recipe is different from the one I usually use.* ♦ *He should know right from wrong by now.*

frond /frɒnd/ noun [C] BIOLOGY a large long leaf on a fern that is usually divided into many narrow sections

front[1] /frʌnt/ noun

1 part facing forwards	**5** not sincere behaviour
2 part furthest forwards	**6** in war
3 aspect of situation	**7** in weather
4 way of hiding sth	+ PHRASES

1 the front [singular] the surface of something that faces forwards ≠ BACK: *Go round to the front* (=of the building) *and I'll let you in.* ♦ *Attach a recent*

photograph to **the front of** your application. ♦ *a book with a picture of a tiger on the front*

2 the front [singular] the part of something that is nearest the direction it faces ≠ BACK: *If you can't see the blackboard, come and sit at the front.* ♦ *Tom was sitting at the front of the bus.* ♦ *He had signed his name in the front of the book.*

3 [C] a particular aspect of a situation: *There's bad news on the job front – two factories are going to close.* ♦ *His main problems were in maths and science, but he has made progress on both fronts.*

4 [C] an organization or activity that exists in order to hide something that is secret or illegal: *They kept a shop as a front for dealing in stolen goods.*

5 [singular] behaviour that is not sincere because you want to hide your real feelings: *He always pretended he didn't care but we knew it was just a front.* ♦ *She's putting on a brave front, but she's really very worried.*

6 [C] a **front line** in a war

7 [C] GEOGRAPHY a line where a large area of cold air meets a large area of warm air

PHRASES **in front 1** a little further forwards than someone or something else: *I overtook the car in front.* **2** winning a competition, game, or election that is not yet finished: *Owen scored to put his team in front.*

in front of sb 1 in a situation where someone is there with you: *I would never say this in front of my mother.* **2** in a situation where someone is watching you do something: *The match took place in front of a crowd of 60,000 people.*

→ BACK[3], UP FRONT

front[2] /frʌnt/ adj **1** at, in, or on the front of something: *the front seat of the car* **2** LANGUAGE a front vowel is made in the front part of your mouth

frontal /ˈfrʌnt(ə)l/ adj formal at, in, or on the front part of something

'frontal ˌlobe noun [C] ANATOMY either of the two front parts of the brain

'frontal ˌsystem noun [C] GEOGRAPHY a system of air masses with particular characteristics

ˌfront 'desk noun [C] TOURISM a reception desk at the entrance to a hotel or restaurant

ˌfront 'door noun [C] the main door at the front of a house

'front eleˌvation noun [C/U] MATHS, PHYSICS a **front view**

'front ˌend noun [C] COMPUTING the parts of a computer system that the user sees and uses

'front-ˌend adj BUSINESS relating to the start of a business process or project

'front-end ˌprocessor noun [C] COMPUTING a computer that deals with information before passing it to another computer that does something else with it

frontier /frʌnˈtɪə, ˈfrʌntɪə/ noun **1** [C] a border between two countries: *the frontier between Israel and Lebanon* **2 the frontiers** [plural] the most advanced or recent ideas about something: *Their work was on the frontiers of science.*

ˌfront 'line noun [C] the area where two armies face each other and fight during a war —**ˌfront-'line** adj

ˌfront-'page adj important enough to be printed on the first page of a newspaper: *front-page news*

'front ˌview noun [C/U] MATHS, PHYSICS a view of a three-dimensional object in **orthographic projection** that shows it at right angles from the front

ˌfront-wheel 'drive noun [U] ENGINEERING a system of sending power from the driving **mechanism** to the front two wheels of a vehicle, so that the wheels slip less in difficult conditions

frost /frɒst/ noun GEOGRAPHY **1** [U] a thin white layer of ice that looks like powder and that forms on things outside when the weather is very cold: *bushes covered with frost* **2** [C/U] a period of weather that is cold enough to form frost

frostbite /'frɒs(t)ˌbaɪt/ noun [U] HEALTH a medical condition in which cold weather seriously damages the fingers, toes, ears, or nose

frostbitten /'frɒs(t)ˌbɪt(ə)n/ adj HEALTH affected by frostbite

frosty /'frɒsti/ (**frostier, frostiest**) adj **1** cold enough to produce frost, or covered with frost: *a frosty morning* **2** unfriendly: *a frosty look*

froth¹ /frɒθ/ noun [singular/U] a mass of small air bubbles that form on the surface of a liquid

froth² /frɒθ/ verb [I] to produce froth

frothy /'frɒθi/ adj covered with or consisting of froth

frown¹ /fraʊn/ verb [I] to move your eyebrows down and closer together because you are annoyed, worried, or thinking hard

PHRASAL VERB 'frown ˌon sb/sth to not approve of someone or something: *Being late for class is frowned on by the teachers.*

frown² /fraʊn/ noun [C] an expression on your face that is made by moving your eyebrows down and closer together. It shows that you are annoyed, worried, or thinking hard.

froze /frəʊz/ the past tense of **freeze¹**

frozen¹ /'frəʊz(ə)n/ adj **1** preserved by being made extremely cold and stored at a very low temperature: *frozen food* ♦ *frozen vegetables* **2** covered with a layer of ice, or made very hard because the weather is very cold: *a frozen pond* ♦ *the frozen ground*

frozen² /'frəʊz(ə)n/ the past participle of **freeze¹**

fructose /'frʌktəʊs/ noun [U] BIOLOGY a type of sugar found in some fruits and **honey**. Chemical formula: $C_6H_{12}O_6$

frugal /'fruːg(ə)l/ adj **1** spending very little money and only on things that are really necessary **2** a frugal meal is simple, cheap, and not very big —**frugally** adv

fruit /fruːt/ noun BIOLOGY **1** (plural **fruit** or **fruits**) [C/U] a type of food that grows on a **flowering plant**, for example apples or oranges. A fruit usually contains a seed or some seeds: *fruit and vegetables* ♦ *If you're hungry, have a piece of fruit* (=an apple, orange etc). —*picture* → on next page **2** [C] the part of a tree or plant that contains its seeds such as a tomato or **cucumber**. A fruit is usually made from the developed ovary of the plant.

PHRASE **the fruit/fruits of sth** something that happens or is produced as a result of something such as hard work: *The book is the fruit of a collaboration between several groups.*

fruitbat /'fruːtˌbæt/ noun [C] a bat that eats fruit and lives in tropical regions

'fruit ˌfly noun [C] a very small fly that eats decaying fruit

fruitful /'fruːtf(ə)l/ adj producing good results ≠ FRUITLESS: *a fruitful meeting*

fruition /fruː'ɪʃ(ə)n/ noun [U] *formal* the result that someone wanted to achieve from a plan or idea

fruitless /'fruːtləs/ adj producing no good results ≠ FRUITFUL: *a fruitless search*

fruity /'fruːti/ adj tasting or smelling like fruit

frustrated /frʌ'streɪtɪd/ adj **1** feeling annoyed and impatient because you are prevented from achieving something: *People are frustrated with a legal system they don't understand.* **2** wanting to be involved in a particular activity but not successful at it —**frustratedly** adv

frustrating /'frʌˌstreɪtɪŋ/ adj making you feel annoyed and impatient because you are prevented from achieving something: *It's frustrating to wait all day for a bus that doesn't turn up.*

frustration /frʌ'streɪʃ(ə)n/ noun [C/U] an annoyed or impatient feeling that you get when you are prevented from doing what you want: *a growing sense of frustration among the staff*

frustum /'frʌstəm/ noun [C] MATHS the part of a **cone** or **pyramid** between its base and a **plane** (=flat surface) that cuts through it parallel to the base

fry /fraɪ/ (**fries, frying, fried**) verb [T] to cook food in hot oil or fat, or to be cooked in this way: *the smell of chicken frying in the kitchen* ♦ *Heat the oil in a large pan and fry the onion and garlic for 5 minutes.* → STIR-FRY —*picture* → FOOD

'frying pan /'fraɪɪŋ ˌpæn/ noun [C] a flat metal pan with a long handle that is used for cooking food in hot oil or fat

ft abbrev foot or feet: *a 3 ft deep pond*

FT or **F/T** abbrev full-time

FTP /ˌef tiː 'piː/ noun [U] COMPUTING file transfer protocol: a set of rules for moving computer files from one computer to another in a **network**, especially over the Internet

fuel /'fjuːəl/ noun **1** [C/U] a substance such as oil, gas, coal, or wood that releases energy when it is burned. Coal and wood are sometimes called **solid fuel**: *a shortage of food and fuel* **2** [U] petrol or **diesel** used in vehicles: *The stolen car was abandoned when it ran out of fuel.* **3** [U] BIOLOGY a substance in the body such as glucose that provides energy through the process of respiration

'fuel ˌcell noun [C] PHYSICS, ENGINEERING the piece of equipment that produces the power in an electric vehicle

'fuel ˌelement noun [C] PHYSICS a piece of nuclear fuel in a reactor —*picture* → NUCLEAR REACTOR

'fuel ˌoil noun [C/U] CHEMISTRY a liquid produced from **petroleum** that is used for heating or in engines —*picture* → REFINE

'fuel ˌpump noun [C] ENGINEERING a pump that moves fuel from a fuel tank to an engine

fugitive /'fjuːdʒətɪv/ noun [C] someone who has done something that is illegal and is trying to avoid being caught by the police

fugue /fjuːg/ noun [C] MUSIC a piece of classical music that repeats a simple tune and develops it into a complicated pattern, using different instruments or voices

fulcrum /'fʊlkrəm/ noun [C] PHYSICS the point on which a lever balances or turns —*picture* → LEVER

fulfil /fʊl'fɪl/ (**fulfils, fulfilling, fulfilled**) verb [T] **1** to do a particular job, or to have a particular purpose: *The bus really **fulfils a need** for this community.* **2** to achieve a particular standard or achieve something that you had been aiming for: *Do you **fulfil the** entry requirements for the course?* ♦ *She never really **fulfilled** her **potential*** (=achieved as much as she could have done). **3** to do what you must do or what you have said you will do: *Landlords who refuse to **fulfil** their obligations may be liable to fines.* ♦ *The government*

orange

lemon

lime

grapefruit

mandarin

apple

pear

peach

nectarine

plum

grapes

apricot

cherries

strawberries

raspberries

blueberries

watermelon

melon

papaya

banana

coconut

kiwi fruit

mango

pineapple

avocado

fig

fruit

has failed to *fulfil* its election *promises*. **4** to make you happy and satisfied because you are using your skills and abilities: *This job doesn't really fulfil me.*

fulfilled /fʊlˈfɪld/ adj happy and satisfied because you are doing something important or are using your skills and abilities ≠ UNFULFILLED

fulfilling /fʊlˈfɪlɪŋ/ adj making you feel fulfilled: *a fulfilling career*

fulfilment /fʊlˈfɪlmənt/ noun **1** [U] a feeling of happiness and satisfaction that you get when you are doing something important or are using your skills and abilities: *Being a doctor gives him a real sense of fulfilment.* **2** [U] the act of doing or achieving something that is promised or expected: *Is there anything that might interfere with the fulfilment of your duties?* **3** [C/U] the act of something happening or being made to happen: *the fulfilment of a prediction*

full /fʊl/ adj

1 with all that fits	**5** busy
2 unable to eat more	**6** body: large
3 complete	+ PHRASES
4 as much as possible	

1 containing the largest amount that will fit in a particular place ≠ EMPTY: *The petrol tank is almost full.* ♦ *a full car park* ♦ *This bottle is only half full.* ♦ *bins full of rubbish*
2 full or **full up** not wanting to eat any more because you have eaten a lot
3 complete: *She is expected to make a full recovery.* ♦ *Please give your full name and address.*
4 used for emphasizing that something is as loud, powerful, fast etc as possible: *He turned the radio on full volume.* ♦ *He drove at full speed along the road.*
5 busy: *a full day at the office* ♦ *She leads a very full life* (=she takes part in many different activities).
6 if part of someone's body is full, it is large, wide, or has a round shape: *full lips*

PHRASES be full of sth to have or contain a lot of something: *Your trousers are full of holes!*
in full completely, including the whole of something: *Fines must be paid in full within 30 days.*
to the full as much as possible: *My aim is to enjoy life to the full.*

fullback /ˈfʊlbæk/ noun [C/U] SPORTS in football, hockey etc, a **defensive** position near your team's goal, or a player in this position

full-'blown adj in the most complete and developed form: *The wind had now become a full-blown gale.*

full 'board noun [U] TOURISM an arrangement in which a guest at a hotel eats all their meals there

full-'bodied adj **1** a full-bodied wine, beer etc has a strong pleasant taste **2** a full-bodied sound is loud and deep in a pleasant way

full em'ployment noun [U] ECONOMICS an economic situation in which everyone who is available for work has a job

fullering /ˈfʊlərɪŋ/ noun [U] TECHNOLOGY the process of making **ridges** in a piece of metal that is to be flattened, using two tools called **fullers**

full 'fare noun [C] TOURISM a ticket for a journey by an adult paying the full price

full-'grown adj American **fully-grown**

full-'length adj **1** a full-length coat, dress, or skirt goes down to someone's feet **2** a full-length mirror or picture shows someone's whole body including their feet **3** a full-length book, film etc is the normal length

full 'marks noun [plural] EDUCATION the highest score that a student can get in an examination: *She got full marks in French.*

full 'moon noun [C] the moon when it looks like a complete circle —*picture* → PHASE

full-motion 'video noun [C] COMPUTING a part of a film shown on a computer screen, for example in a computer game

full 'name noun [C] your whole name, including your **first name**, **middle name**, and **family name**

full-'on adj *informal* used for emphasizing that someone or something has a lot of a particular quality: *Things were developing into a full-on catastrophe.*

full pro'fessor noun [C] EDUCATION American the highest level of professor

full-,scale adj **1** complete, or not limited in any way: *a full-scale investigation into the murder* **2** a full-scale model or drawing of something is as big as the real thing

full 'stop noun [C] LANGUAGE the mark . used in writing at the end of sentences and abbreviations

full-,time[1] adj done or doing something for the number of hours that people normally work or study in a complete week: *a full-time student* ♦ *a full-time job* —**'full-,time** adv

full-,time[2] noun [U] the end of a sports match, after the teams have played for the usual amount of time

fully /ˈfʊli/ adv completely: *He was lying on the bed, fully dressed.* ♦ *I did not fully appreciate the seriousness of the situation.* ♦ *She still hasn't fully recovered from her shoulder injury.*

fully-'grown adj a fully-grown person or animal has reached its biggest size and will not grow any more

fumble /ˈfʌmb(ə)l/ verb [I] to try to hold, move, or find something using your hands in a way that is not skilful or graceful

fume /fjuːm/ verb [I] **1** to be very angry **2** to send out smoke or gas

fumes /fjuːmz/ noun [plural] smoke or gas that has an unpleasant smell and that may be harmful: *traffic fumes*

fun[1] /fʌn/ noun [U] enjoyment from an activity that is not important or serious: *I hate to spoil your fun but it's time to go home now.* ♦ *We haven't had such fun for years.* ♦ *The kids had a lot of fun with that old tent.* ♦ *Do come – it'll be good fun.*

PHRASE make fun of to make jokes about someone or something in an unkind way: *The other children made fun of her because she was always so serious.*

fun[2] /fʌn/ adj enjoyable: *a fun day at the beach*

■ **Fun** is used for talking about something that is enjoyable or someone that you enjoy being with: *Tokyo is a fun city.* ♦ *Our day at the beach was really fun.* ♦ *My sister is a fun person.*
■ **Funny** is used for talking about something or someone that makes you laugh: *He told a funny joke.* ♦ *She's one of the funniest people I know.* ♦ *Don't laugh; it isn't funny.*

function[1] /ˈfʌŋkʃ(ə)n/ noun **1** [C/U] a job that something is designed to do, or the duties or responsibilities that someone has in their job: *The function of the triceps muscle is to straighten the arm.* **2** [C] a social event such as a party: *an official function* **3** [C/U] something that happens in the body, or something that a part of the body does: *He has no muscle function in his upper arms.* **4** [C] COMPUTING an operation performed by a computer

function² /ˈfʌŋkʃ(ə)n/ verb [I] to work or operate in a particular way: *We need to get this department functioning efficiently.*

functional /ˈfʌŋkʃ(ə)nəl/ adj **1** designed to be effective, practical, and simple, with no unnecessary features or decorations **2** operating in the correct way: *The new hospital isn't fully functional as yet.* **3** relating to the purpose or function of something —**functionally** adv

functionality /ˌfʌŋkʃəˈnælɪti/ noun [C/U] **COMPUTING** the range of things that a computer or other electronic system can do

'function ˌkey noun [C] **COMPUTING** a special button on a computer keyboard that is used for a particular operation in a program

'function ˌword noun [C] **LANGUAGE** a word used mainly for expressing relationships between other words in a sentence, for example a conjunction like 'but' or a preposition like 'with'

fund¹ /fʌnd/ noun **1** [C] an amount of money that someone collects, saves, or invests: *a pension fund* **2 funds** [plural] money: *The business is a little low on funds just now.* **3** [C] a large supply of something, especially something useful: *She had a huge fund of knowledge, skill, and experience.* → FUNDING, TRUST FUND

fund² /fʌnd/ verb [T] to provide the money for something

fundamental /ˌfʌndəˈment(ə)l/ adj relating to the basic nature or character of something

fundamentalist /ˌfʌndəˈment(ə)lɪst/ noun [C] someone who believes that religious or political laws should be followed very strictly and in their most extreme form, and should not be changed —**fundamentalism** noun

fundamentally /ˌfʌndəˈment(ə)li/ adv **1** in a very important or basic way: *His entire approach to the problem is fundamentally flawed.* **2** used for emphasizing the basic nature or character of something: *Fundamentally, she is a political writer.*

the fundamentals /ˌfʌndəˈment(ə)lz/ noun [plural] the most basic and important aspects of something: *the fundamentals of classic French cookery*

funding /ˈfʌndɪŋ/ noun [U] money that a government or organization provides for a specific purpose

fundraiser /ˈfʌndˌreɪzə/ noun [C] **1** someone whose job is to persuade people or organizations to give money for a specific purpose, especially for a charity or a political party **2** a social event organized to make money for a specific purpose, especially for a charity or a political party

funeral /ˈfjuːn(ə)rəl/ noun [C] a ceremony that takes place after someone dies, and the formal process of taking the body to the place where it is buried or **cremated**

'funeral diˌrector noun [C] *American* someone whose job is to organize funerals = UNDERTAKER

'funeral ˌhome or **'funeral ˌparlour** noun [C] a place where the body of a dead person is prepared and kept before a funeral

funfair /ˈfʌnˌfeə/ noun [C] an event that is held outside at which people go on **rides** (=machines that people ride on for pleasure) and play games to win prizes

'fungal inˌfection noun [C] **HEALTH** an infection caused by a fungus, for example in the hair, nails, or skin

ˌfungal 'parasite noun [C] **BIOLOGY** a fungus that lives and feeds on another living organism such as a plant or an animal. Mould on decaying food and **athlete's foot** are both caused by fungal parasites.

fungi /ˈfʌngiː/ **BIOLOGY** the plural of **fungus**

'fungicidal ˌcream noun [C] **HEALTH** a cream that is used to treat a skin fungus such as **athlete's foot**

fungicide /ˈfʌngɪsaɪd, ˈfʌndʒɪsaɪd/ noun [C/U] **AGRICULTURE** a chemical used for killing fungi —**fungicidal** /ˌfʌngɪˈsaɪd(ə)l, ˌfʌndʒɪˈsaɪd(ə)l/ adj

fungus /ˈfʌngəs/ (plural **fungi** /ˈfʌngiː/ or **funguses**) noun [C/U] **BIOLOGY** a type of organism without chlorophyll that grows especially in wet conditions or on decaying matter. It reproduces by means of spores. There are many types of fungi, including mushrooms, yeasts, and moulds. Fungi are important to the environment as they naturally break down dead animal and plant material. —**fungal** adj

funicular railway /fjuːˌnɪkjʊlə ˈreɪlweɪ/ noun [C] a railway attached to a cable going up the side of a mountain, often with one car going up as another is coming down

funnel /ˈfʌn(ə)l/ noun [C] **1** a tube that is wide at the top and narrow at the bottom. It is used for pouring a liquid or powder into a container. —*picture* → FILTER **2** a tube that lets out smoke and steam from the engine of a boat or a steam train

funny /ˈfʌni/ (**funnier, funniest**) adj **1** someone or something that is funny makes you laugh: *a funny story* ♦ *one of Britain's funniest comedians* ♦ *I don't think that's at all funny.* ♦ *Wouldn't it be funny if we played a trick on him?* → FUN² **2** strange or unusual: *This tea tastes funny.* ♦ *You're in a funny mood today.* ♦ *That's funny* – she was here a minute ago.

'funny ˌbone noun [singular] *informal* the part of the elbow that hurts when you knock it against something

fur /fɜː/ noun **1** [U] the soft hair that covers the body of some animals **2** [C/U] an animal skin that is covered with soft hair, used for making clothes: *a fur coat*

furious /ˈfjʊəriəs/ adj **1** extremely angry: *Mum was absolutely furious that I'd taken the money without asking.* **2** done with a lot of speed, energy, or determination: *The game was played at a furious pace.* —**furiously** adv

furnace /ˈfɜːnɪs/ noun [C] a large enclosed container in which fuel is burned. It is used for heating a building or for industrial processes such as melting metal.

furnish /ˈfɜːnɪʃ/ verb [T] **1** to provide furniture for a room or house **2** to provide someone with something that they need, especially information: *Lyall's evidence may have furnished police with a vital clue.*

furnishings /ˈfɜːnɪʃɪŋz/ noun [plural] the things in a room such as furniture, carpets, and curtains

furniture /ˈfɜːnɪtʃə/ noun [U] the chairs, tables, beds, cupboards etc that someone puts in a room or house so that they can live in it

> **Furniture** is never used in the plural and cannot be used with a: *That's a lovely piece of furniture* (NOT *a lovely furniture*). ♦ *We don't need any more furniture for this room.* ♦ *I helped her to move some furniture.*

furrow¹ /ˈfʌrəʊ/ noun [C] **1** **AGRICULTURE** a line that a farmer digs in the soil with a plough in order to grow plants **2** a deep line in the skin of someone's face

furrow² /ˈfʌrəʊ/ verb [I/T] if your **brow** furrows, or if you furrow it, deep lines appear on your forehead

furry /'fɜːri/ adj covered with fur or with something like fur

further /'fɜːðə/ adj, adv **1** to or at a greater distance from a place: *I don't want to drive **any further** today.* ♦ *A little **further ahead**, you'll come to a crossroads.* ♦ *I would like to live **further from** the main road.* ♦ *Paul threw the ball **further than** Steve.* **2** additional: *I have nothing further to say on the subject.* ♦ *We need a further £10,000 to complete the work.* **3** more: *The situation was further complicated by Stuart's arrival.* **4** some time before or after a particular point: *Six years **further on** and still there's been no decision.* ♦ *Most of the songs date back no further than the last century.*
PHRASE **go further 1** to say or do something more extreme: *The judge went further than the law allows.* **2** to continue talking about something: *Before we go any further, shall we break for lunch?*
→ FAR, NOTICE²

further edu'cation noun [U] **EDUCATION** courses of study or training that some people do after they have left school when they do not go to university. Courses of study at a university are called **higher education**.

furthermore /'fɜːðə,mɔː/ adv *formal* used before adding another statement to what you have just said: *What you did was extremely irresponsible. Furthermore, it achieved nothing.*

furthermost /'fɜːðə,məʊst/ adj *formal* most distant

furthest /'fɜːðɪst/ adj, adv **1** at the greatest distance from something: *My desk is furthest away from the blackboard.* **2** most distant: *Merlin's fame had spread to the furthest corners of the land.* **3** the longest distance: *Trevor travelled furthest to get here.* **4** to a greater degree than anyone else or than ever before
→ FAR

furtive /'fɜːtɪv/ adj done quickly and secretly in order to avoid being noticed: *a furtive glance* —**furtively** adv

fury /'fjʊəri/ noun [singular/U] **1** a feeling of very strong anger: *She was speechless with fury.* **2** the noise and force of a strong wind, storm, or flood

fuse¹ /fjuːz/ noun [C] **1** **PHYSICS** an object in electrical equipment that contains a thin piece of wire that breaks and makes the equipment stop working when there is too much electricity flowing through it —*picture*
→ ELECTRICITY, PLUG **2** an object like string, or a piece of electrical equipment, that is used for making a bomb explode

fuse² /fjuːz/ verb [I/T] **1** **PHYSICS** if a piece of electrical equipment fuses, or if someone fuses it, it stops working when a thin piece of wire in it breaks because there is too much electricity flowing through it: *All the lights downstairs have fused.* **2** to join two substances together to form one thing, or to become joined together in this way

'fuse ,box noun [C] a box containing the fuses for the electrical system in a building

fuselage /'fjuːzəlɑːʒ/ noun [C] the main part of an aircraft that the wings are fixed to

fusion /'fjuːʒ(ə)n/ noun **1** [C/U] a process in which different things combine to form something new **2** [C/U] a process in which two substances or pieces of a substance join together to form one thing **3** [U] **PHYSICS** nuclear fusion **4** [singular/U] **MUSIC** a type of modern music that is a mixture of different styles

fusion welding /'fjuːʒ(ə)n ,weldɪŋ/ noun [U] **TECHNOLOGY** any welding process in which the metal pieces are heated until they melt, then flow together and become solid

fuss¹ /fʌs/ noun [singular/U] unnecessary worry or excitement about something: *What is all the fuss about?*
PHRASE **make a fuss of** to give a person or animal a lot of attention in order to show that you love them

fuss² /fʌs/ verb [I] to behave in a way that shows that you are nervous or worried, especially about unimportant things

fussy /'fʌsi/ (**fussier, fussiest**) adj **1** someone who is fussy is only satisfied if things are exactly as they want them to be **2** containing too many small parts or details

futile /'fjuːtaɪl/ adj certain to fail or be unsuccessful: *a futile attempt* —**futility** /fjuːˈtɪləti/ noun [U]

future¹ /'fjuːtʃə/ noun **1** **the future** [singular] the time that follows the present time: *It's important to plan for the future.* ♦ *Check if the computer can be upgraded **in the future**.* ♦ *The government plans to hold elections **in the near future**.* **2** [C] the things that will happen to someone or something after the present time: *The people of this village face an uncertain future.* **3** [U] the chance that something will continue to exist or be successful: *We see no future in continuing the negotiations.* **4** **the future** [singular] **LANGUAGE** the **future tense** of a verb
PHRASE **in future** from the present time continuing forwards in time: *In future, please ask before you borrow my clothes.*
→ FORESEEABLE

future² /'fjuːtʃə/ adj **1** expected to exist or happen during the time following the present time: *at some future date* ♦ *future developments* ♦ *We need to protect the countryside for future generations.* ♦ *his future wife* (=the woman he is going to marry) **2** **LANGUAGE** relating to the future tense of a verb

the ,future 'perfect noun [singular] **LANGUAGE** the verb tense that is used for showing that an action will be finished at a particular time in the future, as in 'He will have finished the work by Friday'.

'future-,proof adj something that is future-proof will not stop being used because it has been replaced by something newer and more effective

the ,future 'tense noun [singular] **LANGUAGE** the verb tense that is used for talking about future time

futurism /'fjuːtʃərɪz(ə)m/ noun [U] **ARTS, LITERATURE** a movement in art and literature in the early 20th century that used technology as its subject

fuzzy /'fʌzi/ adj **1** a fuzzy picture or image is not clear so that you cannot see all its details **2** covered with short soft hairs or fibres like hair

,fuzzy 'logic noun [U] **COMPUTING** a type of **logic** used in computers that are designed to behave like humans

,fuzzy 'search noun [C] **COMPUTING** a computer search that gives results that are similar to what you asked for, as well as ones that are exactly what you asked for

FYI abbrev **COMPUTING** for your information: used in emails and **text messages** as a way of introducing a useful piece of information

Gg

g¹ /dʒiː/ (plural **g's**) or **G** (plural **G's**) noun [C/U] **1** the seventh letter of the English alphabet **2 G** MUSIC the fifth note in the musical scale of C major

g² abbrev gram

G /dʒiː/ (plural **Gs**) noun [C] SCIENCE gravity: a measurement of the force of gravity

GAAP abbrev BUSINESS Generally Accepted Accounting Practice: a set of rules that **accountants** use for preparing financial records for companies

gable /ˈgeɪb(ə)l/ or **ˌgable 'end** noun [C] CONSTRUCTION the top part of the end wall of a building just below the roof. A gable is shaped like a triangle.

gadget /ˈgædʒɪt/ noun [C] a small tool or piece of equipment that does something that is useful or impressive

gadolinium /ˌgædəˈlɪniəm/ noun [U] CHEMISTRY a rare silvery-white metallic element in the **lanthanide** group of the periodic table. Chemical symbol: **Gd**

gag¹ /gæg/ (gags, gagging, gagged) verb [T] **1** to tie a piece of cloth over someone's mouth so that they cannot speak or make a noise **2** to officially prevent someone from talking about or publishing something

gag² /gæg/ noun [C] **1** a piece of cloth that is tied over someone's mouth in order to stop them from speaking or making a noise **2** POLITICS an official order that prevents someone from talking about or publishing something

gain¹ /geɪn/ verb **1** [T] to get or achieve something, usually as a result of a lot of effort: *Bolivia gained independence from Spain in 1825.* ♦ *He **gained entry** to the building by showing a fake pass.* **2** [T] to get more of something, usually as a result of a gradual process: *The property has **gained in** value since they bought it.* ♦ *She hopes to gain experience by working abroad for a year.* **3** [I/T] if shares or the markets gain, the value of shares increases **4** [I/T] to get a benefit or advantage for yourself: *Even if you fail, you are sure to **gain from** the experience.* ♦ *When the business is sold, all the brothers **stand to gain** (=are likely to benefit).*

PHRASE gain ground to become more successful, popular, or accepted

PHRASAL VERB ˈgain on sb/sth to gradually get closer to someone or something that you are trying to catch

gain² /geɪn/ noun **1** [C/U] an improvement or increase in something: *We have seen impressive gains in productivity over the last 12 months.* **2** [C] a benefit, or an advantage: *It is a policy that will bring significant gains to all sections of the community.* **3** [U] the money or other benefits that can be obtained from something: *He entered politics only for personal gain.*

gait /geɪt/ noun [singular] *formal* the way that someone walks

gala /ˈgɑːlə/ noun [C] **1** a special performance or event that celebrates something **2** SPORTS a sports competition

galactose /gəˈlæktəʊs/ noun [U] BIOLOGY a **simple sugar** that is found in **lactose**. Chemical formula: $C_6H_{12}O_6$

galaxy /ˈgæləksi/ (plural **galaxies**) noun **1** [C] ASTRONOMY an extremely large group of stars and planets **2 the Galaxy** the large group of stars and planets that the Earth and Sun are part of —**galactic** /gəˈlæktɪk/ adj

gale /geɪl/ noun [C] a very strong wind

galena /gəˈliːnə/ noun [U] CHEMISTRY the natural mineral form of **lead sulphide**. It is the main ore from which **lead** is obtained.

gallant /ˈgælənt/ adj a gallant effort, attempt, or fight is one in which someone tries very hard, but does not succeed —**gallantly** adv

gall bladder /ˈgɔːl ˌblædə/ noun [C] ANATOMY the organ in the body that stores **bile** —*picture* → DIGESTIVE SYSTEM

gallery /ˈgæləri/ (plural **galleries**) noun [C] **1** a building where people can look at paintings and other works of art **2** an upper level in a building such as a church or court

galley /ˈgæli/ (plural **galleys**) noun [C] **1** the kitchen on a boat or plane **2** a long ancient Greek or Roman ship that used sails and **slaves** with **oars** to move it

galling /ˈgɔːlɪŋ/ adj making you feel annoyed or angry, especially because something is not fair

gallium /ˈgæliəm/ noun [U] CHEMISTRY a rare metallic element that is blue-grey when solid, and silver when liquid. It is found in coal and **bauxite**, and melts at very low temperatures. Chemical symbol: **Ga**

gallon /ˈgælən/ noun [C] a unit for measuring an amount of liquid, equal to 4.55 litres

gallop /ˈgæləp/ verb [I] when a horse gallops, it runs at its fastest speed —**gallop** noun [singular]

gallows /ˈgæləʊz/ noun [singular] a wooden frame for hanging criminals in the past

galvanic cell /gælˈvænɪk ˌsel/ noun [C] CHEMISTRY, PHYSICS a **primary cell**

galvanize /ˈgælvənaɪz/ verb [T] TECHNOLOGY to protect the surface of steel or iron against **rust** by coating it in zinc

gamble¹ /ˈgæmb(ə)l/ verb [I/T] **1** to risk money in the hope of winning more: *They used to gamble at the casino in Monte Carlo.* **2** to do something that involves risks but may result in benefits if you are lucky: *Some investors are **gambling on** an economic recovery.* —**gambler** noun [C], **gambling** noun [U]

gamble² /ˈgæmb(ə)l/ noun [singular] an action or plan that involves risks but will bring benefits if it is successful

game /geɪm/ noun

1 activity done for fun	**5** sports at school
2 type of sport	**6** hunted animals etc
3 competition	**7** sth not important
4 major sports event	**+ PHRASE**

1 [C] an activity that people take part in for fun, usually one that has rules: *The children were **playing** noisy **games** in the playground.* ♦ *a computer game*
2 [C] SPORTS a type of sport: *Cricket is a popular game in India.*
3 [C] SPORTS a particular event in which people take part in a competition: *Let's **have a game of** volleyball.*
4 games [plural] SPORTS an event where people from different countries compete in sports such as running, jumping, and swimming: *the Olympic Games*

5 games [singular] EDUCATION sports as a subject at school
6 [U] wild animals, birds, and fish that people hunt, usually for food
7 [C] an activity or situation that someone seems to be treating less seriously than it should be treated: *He behaves as if studying was just a game.*
PHRASE **give the game away** to let people know a secret when you did not intend to let them know: *The expression on her face gave the game away.*
→ BALL GAME, BOARD GAME

'game con,troller noun [C] COMPUTING a small piece of electronic equipment that you connect to a **games console** or computer, with parts that you press or move to control a game

gamelan /'gæmǝlæn/ [C] MUSIC an Indonesian orchestra consisting mainly of **percussion** instruments (=instruments that you hit or shake)

gamepad /'geɪm,pæd/ noun [C] COMPUTING a small piece of electronic equipment that you connect to a **games console** or computer, with parts that you press or move to control a game

'game ,point noun [C/U] SPORTS in tennis, a situation in which a player will win the game if they win the next point

'games ,console noun [C] COMPUTING a piece of electronic equipment that plays digital games. You connect it to a screen and **game controller**s.

'game ,show noun [C] a television programme in which people play games or answer questions in order to win prizes

gamesmanship /'geɪmzmǝn,ʃɪp/ noun [U] a way of increasing the chances of beating an opponent by doing things to make them lose confidence

gamete /'gæmiːt/ noun [C] BIOLOGY a male or female cell that unites with a cell from the opposite sex to form a new organism in the process of sexual reproduction. Gametes have half the number of chromosomes of other cells. The egg and sperm cells in animals and the nuclei in grains of pollen are all gametes= REPRODUCTIVE CELL —*picture* → SEX CELL

gametophyte /gǝ'miːtǝʊfaɪt/ noun [C] BIOLOGY the stage in the life of organisms such as fungi, algae, and **mosses**, which have both sexual and **asexual** forms, in which sex organs and gametes are produced
→ SPOROPHYTE

gaming /'geɪmɪŋ/ noun [U] the business of gambling, especially when it is legal

gamma /'gæmǝ/ noun [C/U] the third letter of the Greek alphabet

gamma globulin /,gæmǝ 'glɒbjʊlɪn/ noun [U] HEALTH a natural protein that is part of the blood of humans and other mammals and helps to protect the body against some types of disease

'gamma radi,ation noun [U] SCIENCE electromagnetic waves that have a higher frequency and shorter wavelength than X-rays. Gamma radiation is given off by some radioactive isotopes and in some **nuclear reactions.**

'gamma ,rays noun [plural] SCIENCE gamma radiation

gammon /'gæmǝn/ noun [U] a type of **ham** that is eaten hot

gander /'gændǝ/ noun [C] a male **goose**

gang /gæŋ/ noun [C] **1** a group of young people who spend time together and often cause trouble **2** a group of criminals working together: *a gang of thieves* **3** a group of workers who do physical work **4** *informal* a group of friends

gangmaster /'gæŋ,mɑːstǝ/ noun [C] someone who organizes and uses a group of foreign workers to do temporary work for very low pay, for example on a farm

gangrene /'gæŋgriːn/ noun [U] HEALTH a serious medical condition in which a part of the body decays when the blood stops flowing to it because of an injury or disease —**gangrenous** adj

gangster /'gæŋstǝ/ noun [C] a member of an organized group of criminals

gangway /'gæŋweɪ/ noun [C] a space between two sets of seats

Gantt chart /'gænt ,tʃɑːt/ noun [C] BUSINESS a drawing used in planning a project, in which lines show pieces of work and the time periods within which they should be done

gaol /dʒeɪl/ noun another spelling of **jail**[1]

gap /gæp/ noun [C] **1** a space or opening in the middle of something or between things: *He has a gap between his front teeth.* ♦ *We waited for a gap in the busy traffic and crossed the road.* **2** something missing from a situation or a system that prevents it from being complete or perfect: *There are still some gaps in our knowledge.* **3** a large difference between things or groups: *the gap between rich and poor* **4** a period of time in which something does not happen: *The second book in the series came out after a gap of seven years.*

gape /geɪp/ verb [I] to look at someone or something with your mouth open because you are very surprised

gaping /'geɪpɪŋ/ adj a gaping hole or cut is very large: *a gaping wound*

'gap ,year noun [C] a year, usually between finishing school and starting university or college, when someone travels or works

garage /'gærɑːʒ, 'gærɪdʒ/ noun [C] **1** a building for keeping a car in **2** a place that repairs or sells cars **3** a place where drivers go to buy petrol= PETROL STATION

garam masala /,gɑːrǝm mǝ'sɑːlǝ/ noun [U] a mixture of spices that make food taste hot, often used in Indian cooking

garbage /'gɑːbɪdʒ/ noun [U] waste material that is thrown away, for example empty containers or food that is not wanted

garbled /'gɑːb(ǝ)ld/ adj not correctly organized or explained, and difficult to understand: *a garbled explanation*

garden[1] /'gɑːd(ǝ)n/ noun **1** [C] an area of land outside a house, usually with plants or grass growing in it: *The children were playing in the back garden.* ♦ *a vegetable garden* **2 gardens** [plural] a large area of grass, flowers, and trees that is open to the public for their enjoyment: *the Botanical Gardens in Kandy*

garden[2] /'gɑːd(ǝ)n/ verb [I] to look after a garden and its plants —**gardener** noun [C]

gardening /'gɑːd(ǝ)nɪŋ/ noun [U] the activity of looking after a garden

,garden 'shears noun [plural] a tool like very large scissors that is used in the garden —*picture* → AGRICULTURAL

garish /'geǝrɪʃ/ adj very bright and colourful in an ugly way

garland /'gɑːlǝnd/ noun [C] a ring of flowers or leaves used for decorating someone or something, especially during a celebration

garlic /'gɑːlɪk/ noun [U] a round white vegetable that is made up of sections called **cloves**. Its cloves are used in cooking in order to give food a strong flavour. —*picture* → VEGETABLE

garment /'gɑːmənt/ noun [C] *formal* a piece of clothing

garner /'gɑːnə/ verb [T] *formal* to collect or obtain a large amount of something useful or important

garnish /'gɑːnɪʃ/ noun [C] something that is added to a dish of food to make it look more attractive —**garnish** verb [T]

garrison¹ /'gærɪs(ə)n/ noun [C] a group of soldiers living in and defending a particular place

garrison² /'gærɪs(ə)n/ verb [T] to put soldiers in a place to live there and defend it

gas /gæs/ noun **1** [C/U] **SCIENCE** one of the three main forms that matter takes, that is neither a solid nor a liquid. A gas has no fixed shape or volume and its molecules move to fill the space available. Molecules in a gas move faster than the molecules in liquids and solids. —*picture* → STATE **2** [U] a gas that is burned as fuel, for example to heat a house or cook food: *Can you smell gas?* ♦ *a gas cooker* —*picture* → REFINE **3** [U] American **petrol** → GREENHOUSE GAS

gaseous exchange /ˌgæsiəs ɪksˈtʃeɪndʒ/ noun [U] **BIOLOGY** the movement of gases from areas where the gas is more dense to where it is less dense, for example between areas of oxygen and carbon dioxide during respiration in animals and plants. In humans and many other animals, gaseous exchange takes place in the lungs, where oxygen is breathed in and carbon dioxide is breathed out.

'gas ,giant noun [C] **ASTRONOMY** a large planet such as Jupiter or Saturn that consists mainly of hydrogen and **helium**

gash /gæʃ/ noun [C] a long deep cut in the skin or in the surface of something —**gash** verb [T]

'gas ,jar noun [C] **SCIENCE** a glass container used in laboratories for holding gases during experiments —*picture* → LABORATORY

gasket /'gæskɪt/ noun [C] **ENGINEERING** a flat ring of rubber, metal, or plastic that is put between two surfaces in a pipe or machine, so that liquid or gas cannot escape

gaskin /'gæskɪn/ noun [U] **CONSTRUCTION** a type of thread used for filling spaces in the joints between pipes

'gas ,mask noun [C] a special covering for the face that protects the person wearing it from a poisonous gas

gasohol /'gæsə,hɒl/ noun [U] a fuel made from a mixture of **ethanol** (=alcohol) and petrol

gasoline /'gæsəliːn/ noun [C/U] American **petrol** —*picture* → REFINE

gasp /gɑːsp/ verb [I] **1** to breathe in suddenly because you are surprised, shocked, or in pain **2** to make a violent effort to breathe because you need more air: *Laura coughed and spluttered as she gasped for air.* —**gasp** noun [C]: *a gasp of pain*

gastric /'gæstrɪk/ adj **ANATOMY** relating to the stomach: *a gastric ulcer*

'gastric ,gland noun [C] **ANATOMY** a gland in the inside of the stomach wall that produces gastric juices

,gastric 'juices noun [plural] **BIOLOGY** substances produced by the **gastric glands** in the stomach that contain the enzyme **pepsin** and **hydrochloric acid**. They help to digest food.

gastroenteritis /ˌgæstrəʊˌentəˈraɪtɪs/ noun [U] **HEALTH** a disease of the stomach and intestines that is caused by bacteria in food or a virus. Gastroenteritis causes severe diarrhoea and vomiting.

gastrointestinal /ˌgæstrəʊˈɪentestɪn(ə)l/ adj **HEALTH** relating to the stomach and intestines

gastronomic /ˌgæstrəˈnɒmɪk/ adj *formal* relating to skilful cooking and the enjoyment of good food

gastropod /'gæstrəpɒd/ noun [C] a mollusc such as a snail that moves by using one large flat foot

gate /geɪt/ noun **1** [C] a door in a fence or wall that you go through in order to enter or leave a place: *Be sure to shut the gate when you leave.* **2** [C] **TOURISM** the place at an airport where people get on a plane: *Your flight is now boarding at Gate 21.* **3** the gate [singular] **SPORTS** the number of people who go to see a sports event

gateway /'geɪtweɪ/ noun [C] **1** an entrance that is opened and closed with a gate **2 a gateway to sth** a way of going somewhere or doing something: *The Khyber Pass is the gateway to the north-west of Pakistan.* **3 COMPUTING** software or **hardware** that connects two different types of computer **networks** so that information can pass between them **4 COMPUTING** a place on the Internet from which you can get information about something, and which can be guarded

gather /'gæðə/ verb

1 come together	4 increase
2 find information	5 bring things together
3 find things you need	6 believe sth

1 [I/T] if people gather, or if someone gathers them, they come together in one place in order to do something: *She gathered her children and ran for shelter.* ♦ *A crowd gathered outside the hotel.*
2 [T] to look for and find information or documents in different places: *The police have been gathering evidence against him.*
3 [T] to search for and find similar things that you need or want: *Bees were gathering pollen.*
4 [T] if something gathers force, speed, or strength, its force, speed, or strength increases: *The train pulled away slowly, then **gathered speed**.*
5 [T] to bring things closer together, for example in order to make something tidy: *She gathered her hair into a knot at the back of her head.*
6 [I/T] to believe that something is true, although no one has directly told you about it: *I gather that the storm caused a power failure.*

gathering /'gæðərɪŋ/ noun [C] a group of people meeting together: *a large family gathering*

GATT /gæt/ noun **ECONOMICS** General Agreement on Tariffs and Trade: an international trade agreement and organization replaced by the **World Trade Organization**

gauge¹ /geɪdʒ/ noun [C] **1** a piece of equipment that measures the amount of something: *the fuel gauge* **2** a measurement of how thick or wide something is, or how far apart two things are: *a narrow-gauge railway* **3** a fact or event that can be used for judging someone or something: *New orders are **a gauge of** how well manufacturers are doing.*

gauge² /geɪdʒ/ verb [T] **1** to make a judgment or guess about something using the information that is available: *He looked at her, trying to gauge her response.* **2** to measure the amount, strength, or speed of something

gaunt /gɔːnt/ adj looking very thin, tired, and not healthy

gauze /gɔːz/ noun **1** [U] white cotton cloth that is very thin and has been woven in a loose way. It is often used for covering a cut or an injury. **2** [C] **SCIENCE** a hard flat square of wires woven together, often used for placing containers on while they are being heated by a Bunsen burner —*picture* → LABORATORY

gave /geɪv/ the past tense of **give**[1]

gay /geɪ/ adj **1** sexually attracted to people of the same sex **2** *old-fashioned* brightly-coloured and attractive, or happy and excited

gaze /geɪz/ verb [I] to look at someone or something for a long time: *They gazed into each other's eyes.* —**gaze** noun [singular]: *His gaze remained fixed on her face.*

gazelle /gəˈzel/ noun [C] a small brown African or Asian animal similar to a **deer**

gazette /gəˈzet/ noun [C] **1** an official newspaper that publishes lists of people in government, legal, military, or university jobs **2** used in the names of newspapers

Gb abbrev COMPUTING a **gigabyte**

GB abbrev Great Britain

GBH /ˌdʒiː biː ˈeɪtʃ/ noun [U] LAW grievous bodily harm: the crime of attacking and seriously injuring someone

GBP abbrev pounds sterling

GCSE /ˌdʒiː siː es ˈiː/ noun [C] EDUCATION General Certificate of Secondary Education: an examination taken by students in the UK, usually at the age of 15 or 16

GDP /ˌdʒiː diː ˈpiː/ noun [C] ECONOMICS gross domestic product: the total value of the goods and services that a country produces in a year. It does not include income that is received from money that is invested in other countries. → GNP

gear[1] /ɡɪə/ noun **1** [C/U] the part of an engine that changes engine power into movement: *Put the car into second gear.* ♦ *Helen **changed gear** as she approached the junction.* **2** [U] the special clothes and equipment that are used for a particular activity: *camping gear* ♦ *The police were dressed in riot gear.* **3** [U] a machine, or a part of a machine, that does a particular job: *heavy lifting gear* **4** [C] ENGINEERING, TECHNOLOGY a **gearwheel**

gear[2] /ɡɪə/ verb [I/T] **be geared to/towards/for** to be organized in a way that is suitable for a particular person or thing: *The museum is geared towards children.*

gearbox /ˈɡɪəˌbɒks/ noun [C] ENGINEERING a metal box that contains the gears of a vehicle, or the system of gears itself

gearing /ˈɡɪərɪŋ/ noun [U] BUSINESS the ratio of a company's debt to the value of its shares

'gear ˌratio noun [C] ENGINEERING the ratio between the number of **teeth** (=sharp points) on two **gears** that work together

'gear ˌstick or **'gear ˌlever** noun [C] the part in a car that a driver uses to change **gear**

gearwheel /ˈɡɪəˌwiːl/ noun [C] ENGINEERING, TECHNOLOGY a wheel with **teeth** (=sharp points) around its edge that are designed to fit into teeth on a similar wheel

gecko /ˈɡekəʊ/ noun [C] a type of small lizard that lives mainly in hot countries

geese /ɡiːs/ the plural of **goose**

Geiger counter /ˈɡaɪɡə ˌkaʊntə/ noun [C] PHYSICS a piece of equipment that measures radioactivity

gelatin or **gelatine** /ˈdʒelətɪn/ noun [U] a clear protein with no taste that is made from the bones and skin of animals. It is used for making glue and film, and in cooking for making liquids become thick and firm.

gelignite /ˈdʒelɪgnaɪt/ noun [U] CHEMISTRY a substance used for causing explosions

gem /dʒem/ noun [C] **1** a valuable stone used in making jewellery **2** someone or something that is special in some way: *a gem of an idea*

Gemini /ˈdʒemɪnaɪ/ noun [C/U] one of the 12 signs of the zodiac. A **Gemini** is someone who was born between May 22 and June 21.

gemstone /ˈdʒemˌstəʊn/ noun [C] a **gem**

gender /ˈdʒendə/ noun **1** [C/U] *formal* the fact of being either male or female= SEX: *The job is open to all applicants regardless of age, race, or gender.* **2** [C] all male people, or all female people= SEX **3** [C/U] LANGUAGE the division of words in some languages according to whether they are **masculine**, **feminine**, or neuter

'gender ˌbias noun [U] unfair difference in the treatment of men or women because of their sex

gendered /ˈdʒendəd/ adj based on ideas about differences between men and women

'gender ˌviolence noun [U] violence against women, especially in the home by a partner= DOMESTIC VIOLENCE

gene /dʒiːn/ noun [C] BIOLOGY a section of DNA on a chromosome that is responsible for a particular characteristic: *a gene for eye colour*

genealogy /ˌdʒiːniˈælədʒi/ noun **1** [C/U] the study of the history of families using historical documents to discover the relationships between people **2** [C] the history of one family, showing how all the people are related to each other —**genealogist** noun [C]

general[1] /ˈdʒen(ə)rəl/ adj **1** not specific, exact, or detailed: *Could you give us a general description of the work you do?* ♦ *I didn't understand all the details, but I got **the general idea**.* **2** involving or true for most people, things, or situations: *There was general agreement that the plan was too expensive.* ♦ *As a general rule, shorter sentences are easier to understand.* **3** used for describing the whole of something, without considering the details: *Your general health seems very good.* **4** dealing with all areas of a subject or activity, rather than concentrating on a particular area: *a good general introduction to the subject* ♦ *general knowledge*

PHRASE **in general 1** in most situations, or for most people: *I don't think people in general give much thought to the environment.* **2** as a whole, without giving details: *In general, the standard of your work is very high.*

general[2] /ˈdʒen(ə)rəl/ noun [C] an officer of high rank in the army or air force

ˌgeneral anaesˈthetic noun [C/U] HEALTH a substance that a doctor puts into a person's body so that they will sleep and not feel any pain during an operation → LOCAL ANAESTHETIC

ˌgeneral eˈlection noun [C] POLITICS an election in which every adult in a country can vote for the people who will represent them in a national parliament

generality /ˌdʒenəˈræləti/ noun **1** [C] a statement that is not specific but that covers a wide range of situations **2** [singular] *formal* the majority of something, for example most of the people in a group

generalization /ˌdʒen(ə)rəlaɪˈzeɪʃ(ə)n/ noun [C/U] a statement that seems to be true in most situations but that may not be true in all situations

generalize /ˈdʒenər(ə)laɪz/ verb [I] **1** to make a statement or remark about a group of people or things without giving details: *We can generalize and say that most of our students are middle-class.* **2** to give an

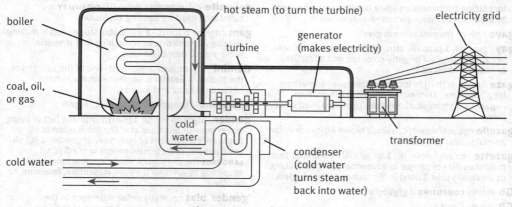

the generation of electricity

opinion about a group of people or things that is often unfair, because it makes them all seem the same when they are not

general 'knowledge noun [U] knowledge about a wide range of subjects, rather than detailed knowledge of a particular subject

generally /'dʒen(ə)rəli/ adv **1** used for saying what is usually true or typical: *The food here is generally pretty good.* **2** by most people, or in most instances: *Scientists generally agree that climate change is partly a man-made phenomenon.* **3** used for describing or considering something as a whole, without details: *His attitude to me was generally unfriendly.* → SPEAK

the ,general 'public noun [singular] ordinary people in society, rather than a particular group

> The general public can be used with a singular or plural verb. You can say *The general public has shown a lot of interest* OR *The general public have shown a lot of interest.*

,general-'purpose adj **1** a general-purpose product or vehicle is appropriate for most situations **2** not limited to one use or purpose

,general 'strike noun [C] a situation in which most or all workers stop working in order to try to get better working conditions or higher pay

generate /'dʒenəreɪt/ verb [T] **1** to produce something, or to cause something to exist: *These new policies will generate employment opportunities.* ♦ *computer-generated images* **2** to make people express feelings or opinions about something: *The advertising campaign generated a lot of interest in our work.* **3** to produce power or heat: *75% of France's electricity is generated by nuclear reactors.*

generation /,dʒenə'reɪʃ(ə)n/ noun **1** [C] SOCIAL STUDIES all the people, a group of people, or the members of a family who are born and live around the same time: *Many people from my parents' generation still remember the war.* ♦ *They want to preserve the land for future generations.* ♦ *a candidate that appeals mainly to the younger generation* ♦ *the generation gap between old and young* **2** [C] the number of years that usually pass between someone's birth and the birth of their children: *Within a generation, the family had lost all its wealth.* **3** [C] a group of products that were made at about the same time: *a new generation of mobile phones* **4** [U] the process of producing something: *cheap electricity generation*

generational /,dʒenə'reɪʃ(ə)nəl/ adj relating to a

particular generation, or to the relationship between generations

generator /'dʒenə,reɪtə/ noun [C] PHYSICS a piece of equipment, for example in a power station, that produces electricity —*picture* → NUCLEAR REACTOR

generic /dʒə'nerɪk/ adj **1** *formal* relating to, or suitable for, a particular group of similar things **2** a generic drug or other product does not have a **trademark** and is sold without a company's name on it —**generically** /dʒə'nerɪkli/ adv

generosity /,dʒenə'rɒsəti/ noun [U] kindness in giving things to people

generous /'dʒenərəs/ adj **1** giving people more of your time or money than is usual or expected: *It was very generous of you to lend me your bike.* **2** larger than is usual or necessary: *a generous helping of rice* —**generously** adv

genetic /dʒə'netɪk/ adj BIOLOGY relating to genes or to the study of genes: *a genetic disease* ♦ *We inherit genetic characteristics from our parents.* —**genetically** /dʒə'netɪkli/ adv

genetically modified /dʒə,netɪkli 'mɒdɪfaɪd/ adj BIOLOGY, AGRICULTURE *see* **GM**

ge,netic 'code noun [C] BIOLOGY the particular order of the sequence of **nucleotides** in the DNA in chromosomes that determines **heredity**

ge,netic engin'eering noun [U] BIOLOGY genetic modification

geneticist /dʒə'netɪsɪst/ noun [C] BIOLOGY a scientist who studies or works in genetics

ge,netic modifi'cation noun [U] BIOLOGY the practice or science of changing the genes of a living thing, usually so that it will develop a particular quality. For example, a crop can be changed so that it produces substances that fight disease.

genetic profiling /dʒə,netɪk 'prəʊfaɪlɪŋ/ noun [U] the scientific examination of DNA from body cells, especially in order to find out who committed a crime

genetics /dʒə'netɪks/ noun [U] BIOLOGY the study of how features of living things are passed through their genes to their children

genial /'dʒiːniəl/ adj friendly and kind

genital /'dʒenɪt(ə)l/ adj ANATOMY relating to or affecting the outer sex organs of a human or other animal: *the genital area* ♦ *genital herpes* —**genitally** adv

genital 'herpes noun [U] HEALTH a disease caused by a virus that can make painful spots appear on the sex organs. It can be passed on during sex, or during birth from a mother to her baby. There is no cure for it.

genitalia /,dʒenɪ'teɪliə/ noun [plural] ANATOMY the genitals

genitals /'dʒenɪt(ə)lz/ noun [plural] ANATOMY the outer sex organs of a human or other animal

genitive /'dʒenətɪv/ noun [singular] LANGUAGE a form of the noun or pronoun in the grammar of some languages, used to show **possession**. In English, this is shown by adding ''s' at the end of the word, for example 'Sarah's birthday'. —**genitive** adj

genius /'dʒi:niəs/ noun **1** [C] someone who is much more intelligent or skilful than other people **2** [U] a high level of intelligence or skill: *At the time, his appointment seemed like **a stroke of genius*** (=a very intelligent act or idea).

genocide /'dʒenəsaɪd/ noun [U] the murder of large numbers of people belonging to a particular race

genome /'dʒi:nəʊm/ noun [C] BIOLOGY the total amount of genetic information in the chromosomes of an organism. This includes all its genes and DNA. The human genome has about 30, 000 genes.

genotype /'dʒenətaɪp/ noun [C] BIOLOGY an organism considered as the set of genes that it has, rather than what it looks like, how big it is etc —**genotypic** /,dʒenə'tɪpɪk/ adj, **genotypical** adj, **genotypically** adv

genre /'ʒɒnrə/ noun [C] LITERATURE, ARTS a particular type of film, writing, or art, that can be recognized by specific features: *science fiction and other literary genres*

gentian violet /,dʒenʃən 'vaɪələt/ noun [U] CHEMISTRY, HEALTH a green dye that forms a purple solution in water. It is used as a biological **stain** and to kill **fungal infections**.

gentle /'dʒent(ə)l/ adj **1** kind and calm: *Joe was a gentle, loving boy.* **2** not using or needing a lot of force or effort: *gentle exercise* ♦ *Give the door a gentle push.* **3** not strong or unpleasant: *a gentle breeze* **4** a gentle slope or curve is gradual, with no sudden changes —**gently** /'dʒentli/ adv

gentleman /'dʒent(ə)lmən/ (plural **gentlemen** /'dʒent(ə)lmən/) noun [C] **1** a polite honest man who thinks about what other people want or need **2** used for referring politely to a man whose name you do not know: *Please could you call a taxi for this gentleman?*

the gentry /'dʒentri/ noun [plural] people from a high social class who own land, especially in the UK in past times

genuine /'dʒenjuɪn/ adj **1** real, and not pretended or false ≠ FAKE: *Morley looked at her with genuine concern.* ♦ *a genuine 18th-century carving* **2** honest, friendly, and sincere —**genuinely** adv

genus /'dʒi:nəs, 'dʒenəs/ (plural **genera** /'dʒenərə/) noun [C] BIOLOGY a group of living things that have similar features. The name of a genus is usually from Latin. For example, dogs and their relatives all belong to the genus *Canidae*. A genus includes more than a **species** and less than a **family**. —*picture* → TAXONOMY → SPECIES

geo- /dʒi:əʊ/ prefix earth: used to make adjectives and nouns

geocentric /,dʒi:əʊ'sentrɪk/ adj ASTRONOMY, GEOGRAPHY using the Earth as the centre from which other things are measured

geoeconomics /,dʒi:əʊ,i:kə'nɒmɪks/ noun [U] ECONOMICS the study of how the economies of the world's nations affect each other

geographical /,dʒi:ə'græfɪk(ə)l/ or **geographic** /,dʒi:ə'græfɪk/ adj GEOGRAPHY relating to an area or place, or to geography —**geographically** /,dʒi:ə'græfɪkli/ adv

geography /dʒi:'ɒgrəfi/ noun [U] GEOGRAPHY the study of the Earth's physical features and the people, plants, and animals that live in different regions of the world —**geographer** noun [C]

geohazard /'dʒi:əʊ,hæzəd/ noun [C] GEOLOGY a harmful event caused by the Earth, for example an earthquake, a **tsunami**, or a volcano

geology /dʒi:'ɒlədʒi/ noun [U] GEOLOGY the scientific study of the structure of the Earth —**geological** /,dʒi:ə'lɒdʒɪk(ə)l/ adj, **geologist** noun [C]

geometric /,dʒi:ə'metrɪk/ or **geometrical** /,dʒi:ə'metrɪk(ə)l/ adj **1** MATHS relating to geometry **2** relating to simple or regular shapes

geometric pro'gression noun [C] MATHS a series of numbers in which each number is multiplied by a particular quantity in order to get the next number, for example 1, 5, 25, 125

geometry /dʒi:'ɒmətri/ noun [U] MATHS the part of mathematics that deals with the relationships between lines, angles, and surfaces

geomorphical /,dʒi:əʊ'mɔ:fɪk(ə)l/ adj GEOLOGY relating to the **formation** and structure of the features of the Earth's surface

geomorphology /,dʒi:əʊmɔ:'fɒlədʒi/ noun [U] GEOLOGY the branch of geology that deals with the **formation** and structure of the features of the Earth's surface —**geomorphological** adj

geophysics /,dʒi:əʊ'fɪzɪks/ noun [U] PHYSICS the scientific study of the physical processes and forces that affect the Earth —**geophysical** adj

geopolitics /,dʒi:əʊ'pɒlətɪks/ noun [U] POLITICS the study of how a country's position, economy, and population influence its politics, especially in relation to other countries —**geopolitical** /,dʒi:əʊpə'lɪtɪk(ə)l/ adj

geostationary orbit /,dʒi:əʊsteɪʃ(ə)n(ə)ri 'ɔ:bɪt/ noun [C] ASTRONOMY an orbit of the Earth made by an artificial satellite that moves at the same rate as the Earth spins, with the result that it is always above the same point on the Earth's surface

geothermal energy /,dʒi:əʊθɜ:m(ə)l 'enədʒi/ noun [U] GEOLOGY, PHYSICS energy in the form of heat obtained from hot moving groundwater. It is found in areas of volcanic activity such as New Zealand.

geranium /dʒə'reɪniəm/ noun [C] a plant with soft round leaves and bright pink, red, or white flowers

geriatric /,dʒeri'ætrɪk/ adj relating to old age, or to the process of getting older

germ /dʒɜ:m/ noun **1** [C] BIOLOGY a form of bacteria that spreads disease **2** [singular] something that could develop into a greater idea or plan: *the germ of an idea*

germanium /dʒə'meɪniəm/ noun [U] CHEMISTRY a hard, easily broken grey element that is a **metalloid**. It is found in coal and zinc ore. Chemical symbol: **Ge**

German measles /,dʒɜ:mən 'mi:z(ə)lz/ noun [U] HEALTH an infectious disease that causes red spots on the skin. It is dangerous because it can cause a lot of damage to the foetus of a pregnant woman who catches it= RUBELLA

germinate /'dʒɜ:mɪneɪt/ verb [I/T] BIOLOGY to develop from a seed and begin to grow into a plant, or to make a seed begin to grow —**germination** /ˌdʒɜːmɪˈneɪʃ(ə)n/ noun [U]

'germ ˌtube noun [C] BIOLOGY a pollen tube

gerund /ˈdʒerənd/ noun [C] LANGUAGE a noun that is formed from a verb by adding '-ing', for example 'seeing' and 'believing' in the sentence 'Seeing is believing.'= VERBAL NOUN

gestation /dʒeˈsteɪʃ(ə)n/ noun [U] BIOLOGY the time and process during which a baby develops inside its mother —**gestate** /dʒeˈsteɪt/ verb

ge'station ˌperiod noun [C] BIOLOGY the period of time during which a human or animal baby develops inside its mother

gesticulate /dʒeˈstɪkjʊleɪt/ verb [I] to make movements with your hands and arms when you are talking

gesture[1] /ˈdʒestʃə/ noun [C] **1** a movement that communicates a feeling or instruction: *Joan raised her arms in a gesture of triumph.* **2** something that you do to communicate your intentions: *Offering to drive us there was a nice gesture.* ♦ *a gesture of support*

gesture[2] /ˈdʒestʃə/ verb [I] to make a movement in order to communicate something to someone

get /get/ (**gets**, **getting**, **got**, **got** or **gotten** /ˈgɒt(ə)n/) verb

1 obtain/receive	**13** send sth
2 buy sth	**14** make progress
3 bring sth	**15** fit sth in sth
4 think/feel sth	**16** understand
5 start to be ill	**17** be able to do sth
6 start to be	**18** catch/punish sb
7 be/become	**19** use a vehicle
8 cause to be	**20** reach by phone
9 make sth happen	**21** prepare meal
10 make sb do sth	+ PHRASE
11 move to/from	+ PHRASAL VERBS
12 arrive	

1 [T] to obtain, receive, or be given something: *Did you get tickets for the game?* ♦ *You get ten points for each correct answer.* ♦ *Young players will **get the chance** to meet one of their heroes.* ♦ *My uncle got me a job in the factory.*

2 [T] to buy something: *They had to stop and get some petrol.* ♦ *I got my dad a book for his birthday.*

3 [T] to go and bring something back from somewhere else: *She went and got a photograph from the desk.* ♦ *Will you get me a glass of water?*

4 [T] to start to have an idea or feeling: *I got a strange feeling as we walked towards the house.*

5 [T] to start to have an illness or a medical condition: *About 200 million people get malaria every year.*

6 [linking verb] to start to be in a particular state, or to start to have a particular quality= BECOME: *It's getting late – I have to go.* ♦ *It was raining and we all **got wet**.*

7 [linking verb] to be or become: used with past participles to form **passives**: *Somehow the paper got ripped.* ♦ *You should wash that cut – it might get infected.*

8 [T] to cause someone or something to be in a particular state: *Get the baby dressed.* ♦ *It took them three hours to get the fire under control.* ♦ *He **got** his suit **dirty**.*

9 [T] to do something, or to have it done for you: *You need to get your hair cut.* ♦ *Hal managed to **get** my email **working** again.*

10 [T] to make someone do something, or to persuade them to do it: *I'll **get** Andrew **to** give you a call.*

11 [I/T] to move to or from a position or place, or to make someone or something do this: *A car stopped and two men **got out**.* ♦ *Half the audience **got up** and*

walked out. ♦ *Get that dog out of the kitchen.*

12 [I] to arrive at a place: *What time did you **get** home last night?* ♦ *When will we **get there**?* ♦ *I usually **get to** work at about 8.30.* → ARRIVE

13 [T] to send something to a person or place: *We'll **get** the timetable **to** you as soon as we have it.*

14 [I] to make progress: *How far did you get with your homework?* ♦ *I'm **not getting anywhere** with this essay* (=not making any progress).

15 [T] to fit or put something in a place: *You can **get** a lot of things **into** this bag.*

16 [T] *informal* to understand something: *Everyone laughed, but Harold didn't **get the joke**.* ♦ *I don't **get** it – what's happening?*

17 [I/T] to have the opportunity or be able to do something: *Did you **get to** visit Table Mountain when you were in Cape Town?*

18 [T] to catch or punish someone: *The police need to get the person who did this.*

19 [T] to use a particular vehicle to travel somewhere: *It's easiest if you get a taxi from the station.*

20 [T] to succeed in talking to someone by phone: *Is there a number where I can get you this evening?*

21 [T] to prepare a meal: *It's time to start getting dinner.*

PHRASE **get it** to be punished for something → HOLD[2], KNOW

PHRASAL VERBS ˌget sth aˈcross to make people understand something: *What message are you trying to **get across to** the consumer?*

ˌget aˈhead to become more successful or progress more quickly than other people: *Sometimes you have to be ruthless to **get ahead** in business.*

ˌget aˈlong if people get along, they like each other and are friendly to each other: *I **get along** well **with** most of my colleagues.*

ˌget aˈround if news gets around, a lot of people hear it

ˌget aˈround to sth to do something after you have intended to do it for some time: *I meant to call you, but somehow I never got around to it.*

ˌget aˈway with sth to manage to do something bad without being punished or criticized for it: *How can he get away with speaking to her like that?*

ˌget sth ˈback to receive or have something again after a time when it was taken away or lost: *She left her bag on the train and she doesn't know how to get it back.*

ˌget beˈhind if you get behind with work or payments, you have not done as much work or made as many payments as you should have done: *She'd been ill so often that, she was **getting behind with** her schoolwork.*

ˌget ˈby to have just enough of something such as money or knowledge so that you can do what you need to do= MANAGE: *I couldn't possibly **get by on** £500 a month.* ♦ *You could probably **get by with** that computer, but a more powerful one would be better.*

ˌget ˈin **1** to arrive somewhere: *You got in very late last night!* ♦ *The London train gets in at 10.05.* **2** to be accepted to study at a school, or to be chosen to play for a team

ˌget ˈinto sth to become involved in a bad situation: *Those kids are always **getting into** trouble.*

ˌget ˈoff (sb/sth) to not be punished severely or at all for something you have been accused of in court: *He was charged with manslaughter, but got off.* ♦ *At best you can hope to **get off with** a £100 fine.*

ˌget ˈon **1** used for asking about or talking about how well someone has done a particular activity: *How did you **get on in** your exams?* **2** if people get on, they like each other and are friendly to each other: *My brother and I don't **get on**.* ♦ *She seems to **get on with** everybody.*

ˌget ˈonto sth to start talking about a subject: *How did we get onto this subject?*

,**get 'on with sth** to give your time to something and make progress with it: *Stop interrupting me – I want to get on with my essay.*

,**get 'out** used for telling someone to leave: *The teacher screamed at him to get out.* ♦ **Get out of** *my house!*

,**get 'out of sth** to avoid doing something that you should do, or that you said that you would do: *Ruth always tries to get out of doing the washing up.*

,**get sth 'out of sth** to get pleasure or a benefit from something: *He gets a lot of satisfaction out of being a teacher.*

,**get 'over sth** to start to feel happy or well again after something bad has happened to you: *It can take weeks to get over an illness like that.*

,**get 'round** same as **get around**: *The news soon got round that people were going to lose their jobs.*

,**get 'round to sth** same as **get around to sth**: *I finally got round to reading that book you gave me.*

,**get 'through sth** to manage to deal with a difficult situation, or to stay alive until it is over: *The refugees will need help to get through the winter.*

,**get 'through to sb** to make someone understand what you are trying to say: *I feel I'm not getting through to some of the kids in my class.*

,**get to'gether** if people get together, they meet in order to do something or in order to spend time together: *The whole family usually gets together at Christmas.*

,**get 'up** to get out of bed after sleeping: *He never gets up before eight.*

,**get sb 'up** to wake someone and tell them to get out of bed: *Will you get me up at six tomorrow?*

'get-to,gether noun [C] an informal social occasion

geyser /'gi:zə, 'gaɪzə/ noun [C] **GEOLOGY** a place where hot water and steam move very quickly and suddenly up out of the earth —*picture* → VOLCANO

ghastly /'gɑ:s(t)li/ adj very bad or unpleasant

ghetto /'getəʊ/ (plural **ghettoes** or **ghettos**) noun [C] **SOCIAL STUDIES** an area in a city or town where people live in poor conditions

ghost /gəʊst/ noun [C] the spirit of a dead person that someone believes that they can see or hear

ghostly /'gəʊs(t)li/ adj reminding you of a ghost

'ghost ,site noun [C] **COMPUTING** an old website that you can still look at

'ghost ,story noun [C] **LITERATURE** a frightening story about **ghosts**

ghostwriter /'gəʊst,raɪtə/ noun [C] someone who writes something for someone else whose name will appear on it as the writer —**ghostwrite** verb [I/T]

GHz abbrev **COMPUTING** gigahertz

GI /,dʒi: 'aɪ/ noun [C] **1** a US soldier in uniform, especially one who is not an officer **2** **HEALTH** a **glycaemic index**

giant¹ /'dʒaɪənt/ noun [C] **1** a person in stories who is much bigger than a normal human **2** a very large successful company, or a successful important person: *the Dutch electronics giant Phillips*

giant² /'dʒaɪənt/ adj extremely large: *a giant bronze statue*

Giardia /dʒi:'ɑ:diə/ noun [U] **HEALTH** an organism that lives in water and that can infect the **large intestine** of humans and other animals, causing diarrhoea

giardiasis /,dʒi:ɑ:'daɪəsɪs/ noun [U] **HEALTH** a disease of the **large intestine** that is caused by drinking water infected by the Giardia parasite

gibbon /'gɪbən/ noun [C] a mammal that looks like a monkey with long arms and no tail. It lives in the forests of India and Indonesia.

gibbous /'gɪbəs/ adj **ASTRONOMY** a gibbous moon is one that appears a few days before and after the full moon, when it is less than full but more than half visible

gibe /dʒaɪb/ noun [C] a remark that is intended to hurt someone or to make them feel stupid

giddy /'gɪdi/ adj feeling that you might become unconscious and fall = DIZZY

GIF /,dʒi: aɪ 'ef/ noun [U] **COMPUTING** Graphic Interchange Format: a type of computer file that contains an image. GIF is also used as part of a file name.

gift /gɪft/ noun [C] **1** something that you give to someone as a present: *a gift from a friend* **2** a natural ability to do something well: *She has a gift for languages.* **3** something good that you are grateful that you have: *the gift of sight*

gifted /'gɪftɪd/ adj a gifted person has an impressive natural ability

'gift ,shop noun [C] a shop selling things that people like to give and receive as presents

gig /gɪg/ noun [C] **MUSIC** informal a public performance, especially of jazz or popular music

giga- /'gɪgə/ prefix **COMPUTING** a billion (2^{30}): used with some nouns

gigabyte /'gɪgə,baɪt/ noun [C] **COMPUTING** a unit for measuring computer information, equal to 1,024 **megabytes**

gigahertz /'gɪgə,hɜːts/ (plural **gigahertz**) noun [C] **PHYSICS, COMPUTING** a unit for measuring the frequency of **sound waves**, **radio waves**, and computer speed

gigantic /dʒaɪ'gæntɪk/ adj extremely large

giggle /'gɪg(ə)l/ verb [I] to laugh in a nervous, excited, or silly way —**giggle** noun [C]

gill /gɪl/ noun [C] **BIOLOGY** one of the organs behind the head of a fish that it uses to breathe

gimmick /'gɪmɪk/ noun [C] something that is intended to impress people or get their attention but is not necessary or useful: *a sales gimmick* ♦ *a gimmick to win votes* —**gimmicky** adj

gin /dʒɪn/ noun [C/U] a strong clear alcoholic drink, or a glass of this drink

ginger¹ /'dʒɪndʒə/ noun [U] a light brown root with a strong flavour that is used in cooking —*picture* → VEGETABLE

ginger² /'dʒɪndʒə/ adj **1** ginger hair or fur is orange-brown **2** containing or tasting of ginger

gingerly /'dʒɪndʒəli/ adv in a very slow and careful way

gingivitis /,dʒɪndʒɪ'vaɪtɪs/ noun [U] **HEALTH** a medical condition that makes the **gums** painful

ginkgo /'gɪŋkəʊ/ noun [C] a tree that originally came from China and has existed since **prehistoric** times

giraffe /dʒə'rɑ:f/ noun [C] a tall African mammal that has a very long neck and very long legs —*picture* → MAMMAL

girder /'gɜːdə/ noun [C] **CONSTRUCTION** a large metal bar that is used for making the frame of a building or a bridge

girl /gɜːl/ noun [C] **1** a female child: *There are 15 girls in my class.* **2** a daughter: *Mary's two girls still live at home.* **3** a young adult woman. Some people think that this use is offensive: *Who was that beautiful girl I saw you with last night?*

girlfriend /'gɜːl,frend/ noun [C] **1** a woman that someone is having a romantic or sexual relationship with: *Has Peter got a girlfriend?* **2** a woman's female friend

girth /gɜːθ/ noun [C/U] the distance round something, for example a tree

GIS /,dʒiː aɪ 'es/ noun [U] **GEOGRAPHY, COMPUTING** Geographic Information Systems: a computer system used for collecting information about the Earth

the gist /dʒɪst/ noun [singular] the main idea, or the general meaning of something

give¹ /gɪv/ (**gives, giving, gave** /geɪv/, **given** /'gɪv(ə)n/) verb

1 provide sb with sth	**8** allow sb to do sth
2 make sb own sth	**9** pass illness to sb
3 have an effect	**10** pay money
4 communicate	**11** make sb think sth
5 perform action	**12** stretch/bend etc
6 put medicine in sb	**+ PHRASE**
7 help sb	**+ PHRASAL VERBS**

1 [T] to provide someone with something: *Could you give me that pen?* ♦ *We don't know what to give Dad for Christmas.* ♦ *I gave the keys to John.*

2 [T] to make someone the owner of something that you owned: *Ken gave me his old tennis racket.* ♦ *He gave the house to his children.*

3 [T] to cause a general result or effect: *The results gave us quite a shock.* ♦ *Some washing powders give cotton a softer feel.*

4 [T] to show or communicate information: *The answers are given on page 78.* ♦ *Someone from the university will give a talk on the future of education.* ♦ *Will you give him a message from me?*

5 [T] to perform an action: *I gave him a hug before he left.* ♦ *I'll give you a ring* (=phone you) *on Sunday.*

6 [T] to put medicine into someone's body using a particular method: *The drug is normally given by injection.*

7 [I/T] to do something good or helpful for someone: *a relationship where one partner gives more than the other*

8 [T] to allow someone to do something: *We asked to go out, and the teacher gave her permission.* ♦ *They should have given us more time to finish the test.*

9 [T] to pass an illness or disease to another person: *You could easily give the disease to your partner.*

10 [T] *spoken* to pay money for something: *Martin gave me £300 for my computer.*

11 [T] to make someone think or believe something: *We don't want to give the impression that every child is at risk.* ♦ *We were given to understand* (=we were told) *that we would be paid by Friday.*

12 [I] to stretch, bend, or break: *The bridge has to be able to give a little in the wind.*

PHRASE **give or take** used for saying that a number or quantity may be a little more or less than the number or quantity mentioned: *Each talk lasts half an hour, give or take five minutes.* → WAY¹

PHRASAL VERBS ,give sth a'way **1** to let someone know a secret, often by accident: *If captured, they might give away vital military secrets.* ♦ *Her expression gave nothing away.* **2** to provide someone with something that you no longer want or need: *I gave my plants away to the neighbours.*

,give sth 'back to give someone something that they had or owned before: *The company had to give back*

all the money. ♦ *We just want them to give us back our home.*

,give 'in to stop competing or arguing and accept that you cannot win: *The government has said that it will never give in to terrorist threats.*

,give sth 'in to give a piece of work to someone such as a teacher who is expecting it: *I have to give this essay in tomorrow.*

,give 'off sth to produce something such as heat or a smell: *When they die, plants give off gases.*

,give sth 'out **1** to give something to several people: *The office gives out financial advice to students.* **2** to produce something such as a sound or light= EMIT: *The Sun gives out energy in the form of heat and light.*

,give 'up (sth) to stop trying to do something because it is too difficult: *We've given up trying to persuade them to change.*

,give sth 'up to stop doing something that you do regularly: *I'm trying to give up smoking.*

give² /gɪv/ noun [U] the tendency to bend or stretch

,give-and-'take noun [U] a situation in which people or groups who want different things each give some things to the others, and get some things from the others

given¹ /'gɪv(ə)n/ adj **1** used for referring to a particular thing: *In a given situation, more than one method may be used.* **2** a given period has previously been decided on: *Many people pay off the money owed within a given time.*

given² /'gɪv(ə)n/ preposition because of a particular fact: *Given that conflict happens, we need to learn how to manage it.*

given³ /'gɪv(ə)n/ the past participle of **give¹**

'given ,name noun [C] the name that your parents give you when you are born= FIRST NAME → NAME¹

glacial /'gleɪʃ(ə)l/ adj **GEOLOGY** relating to, or created by, glaciers

glaciated /'gleɪsieɪtɪd/ adj **GEOLOGY** covered by glaciers or a glacier, or affected by the action of a glacier

glaciation /,gleɪsi'eɪʃ(ə)n/ noun [U] **GEOLOGY** the process in which land becomes covered by glaciers, or the fact of land being covered in glaciers

glacier /'glæsiə/ noun [C] **GEOGRAPHY, GEOLOGY** a very large mass of ice that moves very slowly down a valley. The movement of glaciers and their effects on the land they move along created the **glacial** features of many existing **landscapes**. A lot of these features were formed during the **Ice Age** when much of the Earth was covered in ice and snow. → GLACIATION

glad /glæd/ adj happy and pleased about something: *I'm glad he finally called you.* ♦ *Maggie was glad to be home.* → GLADLY

PHRASE **be glad to do sth** to be willing or ready to do something: *I'd be glad to watch the kids for you this afternoon.*

gladiator /'glædi,eɪtə/ noun [C] in ancient Rome, someone who fought people or wild animals as a form of public entertainment

gladly /'glædli/ adv in a willing or happy way

glamorous /'glæmərəs/ adj attractive or exciting in an unusual way: *a glamorous lifestyle*

glamour /'glæmə/ noun [U] a special quality that makes someone or something seem to be very attractive or exciting

glance¹ /glɑːns/ verb [I] **1** to look somewhere quickly and then look away: *'I must go,' Claudia said, **glancing at** her watch.* **2** to read something quickly and not very carefully: *I hadn't even **glanced at** the report.*

glance² /glɑːns/ noun [C] a quick look at someone or something: *She had a quick **glance at** the newspaper as she gulped down her coffee.* → FIRST

gland /glænd/ noun [C] **ANATOMY** a part of the body that produces a chemical substance that the body needs, for example a hormone —**glandular** /'glændjʊlə/ adj

glandular 'fever noun [U] **HEALTH** a disease that mainly affects young people and makes them feel very tired and weak

glans /glænz/ noun [C] **ANATOMY** the rounded head of the penis

glare¹ /gleə/ verb [I] **1** to look at someone or something in a very angry way: *Dan **glared at** me and immediately left the room.* **2** to shine with a very bright and rather unpleasant light

glare² /gleə/ noun **1** [C] an angry look **2** [singular/U] a very bright light that makes you feel uncomfortable

glaring /'gleərɪŋ/ adj **1** a glaring mistake is very obvious **2** a glaring light is very bright and rather unpleasant —**glaringly** adv: *glaringly obvious*

glass /glɑːs/ noun **1** [U] a hard clear substance used for making objects such as windows or bottles: *the sound of breaking glass ♦ a glass bowl* **2** [C] a small container made of glass that is used for drinking from, or the drink in it: *a beer glass ♦ She drank three **glasses** of milk.*

glasses /'glɑːsɪz/ noun [plural] an object that people wear in front of their eyes in order to help them see better: *a pair of glasses*

glass 'fibre noun [U] **ENGINEERING 1** a very thin fibre made of glass through which light can pass. Groups of glass fibres are used to send images. **2 fibreglass**

glassware /'glɑːs,weə/ noun [U] objects made of glass

glassy /'glɑːsi/ adj **1** glassy eyes show no interest or emotion, for example because of illness or drugs **2** smooth and shiny like glass

glaucoma /glɔː'kəʊmə/ noun [U] **HEALTH** a serious disease of the eyes that can cause blindness

glaze /gleɪz/ noun [C/U] **1 ARTS** a liquid that is put on paintings or clay objects to protect them. The liquid forms a hard shiny layer when it is dry. **2** a thin layer of milk, sugar, or egg that is put on foods to make them look shiny —**glaze** verb [T]

glazed /gleɪzd/ adj **1** made of glass, or decorated with glass: *glazed doors* **2** if someone has a glazed look or expression on their face, it shows that they are not at all interested in something

glazing /'gleɪzɪŋ/ noun [U] **CONSTRUCTION** the glass part of a window → DOUBLE GLAZING

gleam¹ /gliːm/ verb [I] **1** to shine brightly **2** if your eyes gleam, you look excited or happy= SHINE

gleam² /gliːm/ noun [C] **1** a bright light that is reflected from something **2** a look of emotion or excitement in someone's eyes

glee /gliː/ noun [U] a feeling of excitement and happiness, usually because of your own good luck or someone else's bad luck —**gleeful** adj, **gleefully** adv

glide /glaɪd/ verb [I] **1** to move in a smooth easy way with no noise **2** to fly without using power, carried by the wind

glider /'glaɪdə/ noun [C] a light plane with no engine, that flies using currents of air

'glide re,flection noun [C] **MATHS** a transformation that is a combination of a **translation** and a **reflection**

gliding /'glaɪdɪŋ/ noun [U] the activity of flying in a glider

'gliding ,joint noun [C] **ANATOMY** a **sliding joint** —*picture* → JOINT

glimmer /'glɪmə/ noun [C] a soft weak light that is not steady —**glimmer** verb [I]

glimpse /glɪmps/ noun [C] **1** an occasion when you see someone or something for a very short time: *I only caught a **glimpse** of it, but I think it was a deer.* **2** an experience that gives you an idea of what something is like: *a **glimpse of** what the future might be like* —**glimpse** verb [T]

glisten /'glɪs(ə)n/ verb [I] if something glistens, it shines because it is wet or covered with oil

glitch /glɪtʃ/ noun [C] *informal* a small problem that prevents something from operating correctly

glitter¹ /'glɪtə/ verb [I] to shine with a lot of small flashes of light= SPARKLE

glitter² /'glɪtə/ noun [U] small shiny pieces of metal or plastic that are stuck onto things to make them shine and look attractive

glittering /'glɪtərɪŋ/ adj **1** bright and shining with a lot of flashes of light **2** exciting and successful

gloat /gləʊt/ verb [I] *showing disapproval* to show that you are happy about your own success or someone else's failure

global /'gləʊb(ə)l/ adj **1** including or affecting the whole world: *The global economy has become increasingly unstable. ♦ Motor vehicles consume 60% of global oil production.* **2** complete, including all parts of something: *global changes* —**globally** adv

global 'economy noun [singular] **ECONOMICS** the economies of the world's nations, considered as a single economic system

globalization /,gləʊbəlaɪ'zeɪʃ(ə)n/ noun [U] **ECONOMICS, SOCIAL STUDIES** the idea that the world is developing a single economy and culture as a result of improved communications and the influence of large companies that operate all over the world

global warming /,gləʊb(ə)l 'wɔːmɪŋ/ noun [U] **ENVIRONMENT** the increase in the temperature of the Earth that is caused partly by increasing amounts of carbon dioxide in the atmosphere —*picture* → GREENHOUSE EFFECT

globe /gləʊb/ noun **1** [C] **GEOGRAPHY** a round object that has a map of the world on it **2** [singular] the world **3** [C] a round object

globule /'glɒbjuːl/ noun [C] a small round drop of a thick liquid —**globular** /'glɒbjʊlə/ adj

glockenspiel /'glɒkən,ʃpiːl/ noun [C] **MUSIC** a musical instrument that consists of metal bars on a wooden frame. It is played by hitting the bars with a small hammer.

glomerulus /glɒ'merʊləs/ noun [C] **ANATOMY** a dense system of tiny blood capillaries found in the kidney in the **nephron**. Blood is filtered through it into the **Bowman's capsule**.

gloom /gluːm/ noun [U] **1** a feeling of sadness and a lack of hope **2** darkness in which it is difficult to see clearly

gloomy /'gluːmi/ (**gloomier, gloomiest**) adj **1** feeling sad and without hope **2** showing that things are not going well and will probably not get better quickly: *The economic news is gloomy.* **3** dark in a way that makes you feel sad or a little afraid: *gloomy weather* —**gloomily** adv

glorified /ˈɡlɔːrɪfaɪd/ adj used for saying what something is really like when other people have described it as more impressive than it really is: *The 'yacht' we rented was just a glorified rowing boat.*

glorify /ˈɡlɔːrɪfaɪ/ (**glorifies, glorifying, glorified**) verb [T] to make someone or something seem to be more impressive than they really are —**glorification** /ˌɡlɔːrɪfɪˈkeɪʃ(ə)n/ noun [U]

glorious /ˈɡlɔːriəs/ adj **1** very beautiful in a way that makes you feel happy: *What glorious weather!* **2** extremely successful and likely to be remembered for a long time: *reminders of the country's glorious past* —**gloriously** adv

glory /ˈɡlɔːri/ (plural **glories**) noun **1** [U] admiration and praise that someone gets because they have done something impressive: *I did the hard work and someone else got all the glory.* **2** [C] an impressive example, feature, or quality that makes people admire someone or something: *one of **the glories of** Italian architecture* **3** [U] great beauty: *It will cost millions of pounds to restore the mansion to its former glory.*

gloss¹ /ɡlɒs/ noun **1** [singular/U] the shiny surface of something **2** [U] **gloss paint 3** [C] a short explanation of what something means

gloss² /ɡlɒs/ [T] **PHRASAL VERB** ,**gloss 'over sth** to ignore or avoid unpleasant facts

glossary /ˈɡlɒsəri/ (plural **glossaries**) noun [C] **LANGUAGE** a list of difficult words with explanations of their meaning

'gloss ,paint noun [U] paint that has a shiny surface when it is dry

glossy /ˈɡlɒsi/ adj **1** shiny in an attractive way **2** printed on shiny paper with a lot of bright pictures: *a glossy magazine*

glottal¹ /ˈɡlɒt(ə)l/ adj **LANGUAGE** a glottal sound is one that you make in speaking when you partly or completely stop air as it passes through the throat

glottal² /ˈɡlɒt(ə)l/ noun [C] **LANGUAGE** a **glottal stop**

,**glottal 'stop** noun [C] **LANGUAGE** a sound made by stopping air as it passes through the throat. In some varieties of spoken English a glottal stop is often used instead of a 't' sound in the middle or at the end of a word.

glottis /ˈɡlɒtɪs/ noun [C] **ANATOMY** the part of the throat where the **larynx** joins the **pharynx**, between the **vocal cords** —*picture* → LUNG

glove /ɡlʌv/ noun [C] a piece of clothing that covers the fingers and hand: *a pair of gloves*

glow¹ /ɡləʊ/ verb [I] **1** to shine with a soft warm light: *The tip of a cigarette glowed in the darkness.* **2** to show that you are happy: *She glowed with satisfaction.* **3** if your face or body is glowing, it looks pink or red, for example because you are healthy, hot, emotional, or embarrassed

glow² /ɡləʊ/ noun [singular] **1** a soft warm light **2** the pink or red colour that your skin has when you are healthy, hot, embarrassed, or emotional **3** a pleasant feeling: *Anne felt a glow of pride at Sarah's words.*

glower /ˈɡlaʊə/ verb [I] to look angrily at someone = GLARE

glowing /ˈɡləʊɪŋ/ adj **1** burning gently with an orange or red colour: *the glowing embers of the fire* **2** full of praise: *a glowing reference from her former employer*

'glow-,worm noun [C] the larva of a **firefly** that produces light from its body when it is dark

glucagon /ˈɡluːkəɡɒn/ noun [U] **BIOLOGY** a hormone produced by the pancreas that increases the levels of **blood sugar** in the body

glucose /ˈɡluːkəʊz/ noun [U] **BIOLOGY** a simple sugar that is produced in plants through photosynthesis and in animals from the breaking down of carbohydrates in the body. It is important for providing energy to all cells. Chemical formula: $C_6H_{12}O_6$

glue¹ /ɡluː/ noun [C/U] a sticky substance that is used for fixing things to each other

glue² /ɡluː/ verb [T] to stick things to each other with glue
  PHRASE be glued to sth to be looking at something and not paying attention to anything else

glum /ɡlʌm/ adj unhappy —**glumly** adv

glut /ɡlʌt/ noun [singular] a situation in which there is more of something available to buy than people want or need: *a glut of cars on the market*

gluten /ˈɡluːt(ə)n/ noun [U] **HEALTH** a sticky protein that is found in some cereals, especially wheat

gluteus /ˈɡluːtiəs/ (plural **glutei** /ˈɡluːtiːaɪ/) noun [C] **ANATOMY** a muscle in each of the **buttocks**

glutton /ˈɡlʌt(ə)n/ noun [C] someone who eats too much
  PHRASE a glutton for punishment someone who seems to enjoy doing something that is difficult or unpleasant

glycaemic index /ɡlaɪˌsiːmɪk ˈɪndeks/ noun [C] **HEALTH** a system for measuring how quickly different foods allow the sugar they contain to spread into the blood. Foods that do this slowly are thought to be better for your health.

glycerine /ˈɡlɪsərɪn, ˈɡlɪsəriːn/ noun [U] **CHEMISTRY** a thick clear sweet-tasting liquid that is used for making many things, including soap and bombs

glycerol /ˈɡlɪsərɒl/ noun [U] **CHEMISTRY** glycerine

glycogen /ˈɡlaɪkədʒən/ noun [U] **BIOLOGY** a **polysaccharide** that is found especially in the liver. Muscles use it to release the energy they need.

GM /ˌdʒiː ˈem/ adj **BIOLOGY, AGRICULTURE 1** genetically modified: relating to crops whose genes have been artificially changed **2** genetically modified: relating to foods made from these crops

GMAW abbrev **TECHNOLOGY** gas metal arc welding: a type of **arc welding** in which a continuous wire electrode and a **shielding gas** are supplied from a special tool

GMO /ˌdʒiː em ˈəʊ/ noun [C] **BIOLOGY, AGRICULTURE** genetically modified organism: a plant or animal whose genes have been changed artificially

GMT /ˌdʒiː em ˈtiː/ noun [U] Greenwich Mean Time: the time at Greenwich in England, used as an international standard

gnarled /nɑːld/ adj old and twisted and covered in lines: *gnarled hands*

gnat /næt/ noun [C] a very small flying insect that bites but is not dangerous

gnaw /nɔː/ verb [I/T] to keep biting something

gnome /nəʊm/ noun [C] an imaginary little man in children's stories who wears a pointed hat

GNP /ˌdʒiː en ˈpiː/ noun [U] **ECONOMICS** gross national product: the total value of all the goods and services that a country produces in a year → GDP

gnu /nuː/ noun [C] a **wildebeest**

go¹ /gəʊ/ (**goes, going, went** /went/, **gone** /gɒn/)
verb

1 move to place	12 be right/attractive
2 leave a place	13 when time passes
3 move to do sth	14 spend time doing sth
4 travel to activity	15 to be spent/used
5 continue to place	16 disappear
6 happen	17 move/make a sound
7 change condition	18 about story/music
8 be in state	19 begin doing sth
9 stop working	20 operate correctly
10 fit somewhere	+ PHRASES
11 be kept somewhere	+ PHRASAL VERBS

1 [I] to move or travel to a place that is away from where you are now: *She **went into** the bathroom and rinsed her face in cold water.* ♦ *He wants to **go to** England to study.* ♦ *Are you **going by train** or are you taking the bus?*

2 [I] to leave a place: *What time are you going tomorrow?* ♦ *I'm tired; let's go.*

3 [I] to move or travel to a place, or to leave a place, in order to do a particular thing: *They've **gone to** a concert in town tonight.* ♦ *He **went into hospital** for an operation last Tuesday.* ♦ *They **went for a walk**.* ♦ *On hot days the kids would **go swimming** in the river.* ♦ *Jim **went to** buy some ice cream about ten minutes ago.* ♦ *I have to **go and** pick up my friends at the airport.*

4 [I] to travel to a particular place regularly in order to take part in an activity: *None of her brothers **went to** college.* ♦ *We **go to church** every Sunday.*

5 [I] to continue from one place or time to another: *The highway going from Georgetown **to** Brazil was built with World Bank funds.*

6 [I] to happen in a particular way: *How are things going at work?* ♦ *I think the interview went very well.*

7 [linking verb] to change to another condition, usually a worse one: *Louise had **gone** completely **blind** before she died.* ♦ *The milk smells like it's **going bad**.*

8 [linking verb] to be in a particular state or situation, especially one in which you do not have something or in which something is not done: *Her comment went unnoticed.* ♦ *Thousands of people are being left to **go hungry**.*

9 [I] to start being in a worse state, or to stop working correctly, as a result of becoming old or damaged: *The brakes on the car are starting to go.*

10 [I] if something goes in a particular place, it fits there because it is the right size or shape: *There's no way all this stuff will go in the box.*

11 [I] to be usually kept or put in a particular place: *The spoons go in the other drawer.*

12 [I] to be suitable, right, or attractive in a particular place or in a particular combination: *It's the kind of furniture that would go well in any room.*

13 [I] if time goes in a particular way, it passes in that way: *This week's gone so fast – I can't believe it's Friday already.*

14 [I/T] to continue or last for a particular amount of time while doing something: *He went several days without eating a single thing.*

15 [I] to be spent or used: *We were worried because the food was going fast.* ♦ *Half of the money **went on** new shoes for the kids.*

16 [I] to disappear: *I put my book on the table, and now it's gone.*

17 [T] to make a particular sound or movement: *Cows go 'moo'.*

18 [I] to consist of a particular series of words, facts, or musical notes: *That's not the way the song goes.*

19 [I] to begin doing something: *Nobody starts until I say 'Go'.* ♦ *We've planned every detail and are **ready to**

go.* ♦ *It won't take me long once I **get going**.*

20 [I] if a machine or piece of equipment goes, it operates correctly= WORK: *My old watch is still going.*

PHRASES **be going to do sth 1** to intend to do something: *I'm going to watch TV tonight.* **2** to be about to happen or do something: *I think it's going to rain.*

go all out (to do sth/for sth) to try as hard as you can to achieve something

to go remaining: *There are just three weeks to go before the end of the term.*

PHRASAL VERBS ˌgo aˈbout sth to start dealing with a problem, situation, or job in a particular way: *I think I'd go about it quite differently.* ♦ *How did you go about finding a job?*

ˌgo aˈhead **1** to start, or continue to do something, especially after waiting for permission to do it: *The club will be **going ahead with** its plans for a new stadium.* ♦ *Go ahead and eat before everything gets cold.* **2** to go to a place before someone else that you are with: *You go ahead and we'll wait here for Sally.* ♦ *Don **went ahead of** the others to try to find help.* **3** to happen or take place: *The party went ahead as planned.*

ˌgo aˈround to behave or be dressed in a particular way: *Why do you always go around without any shoes on?*

ˌgo aˈway **1** to move away from, or to travel away from, a person or place: *If he's bothering you, tell him to go away.* **2** to stop existing or being noticeable: *The pain should go away in a couple of hours.*

ˌgo ˈback to return to a person, place, subject, or activity: *I'd left my keys in the office and had to **go back** for them.* ♦ *She should be well enough to **go back** to work on Wednesday.* ♦ *Can we go **back to** what we were discussing earlier?*

ˌgo ˈby if time goes by, it passes: *Last month went by so fast.*

ˌgo ˈdown **1** to become less: *How long will it take for the swelling to go down?* ♦ *The crime rate shows no signs of going down.* **2** COMPUTING if something such as a computer or an electrical system goes down, it stops working **3** when the sun goes down, it moves below the horizon so that it cannot be seen any longer = SET

ˌgo ˈdown with sth *informal* to become ill with a particular illness: *Three people in my office have gone down with the flu.*

ˈgo for sth **1** *informal* to try to get something that you have to compete for: *There were 200 people going for just three jobs.* **2** *informal* to choose a particular thing: *I think I'll go for the steak. What are you having?* **3** to be sold for a particular amount of money: *We expect the house to go for about £200,000.*

ˌgo ˈinto sth **1** to start working in a particular type of job or business: *Alex has decided to go into nursing.* **2** to deal with something in detail: *That's a good question, but I don't want to go into it now.* **3** to be used or spent in order to do something: *Over 50% of the budget went into the design of the equipment.* ♦ *Months of hard work have gone into making tonight's ceremony a success.*

ˌgo ˈoff **1** to leave a place for a particular purpose: *soldiers going off to war* ♦ *They went off in search of a map.* **2** to explode or be fired: *The gun went off while he was cleaning it.* **3** to start making a noise as a signal or warning: *waiting for the alarm clock to go off* **4** if something such as a light goes off, it stops working **5** if food or drink goes off, it is no longer fresh

ˌgo ˈoff sb/sth to stop liking someone or something: *I went off the idea of buying a sports car.*

ˌgo ˈon **1** to continue happening or doing something in the same way as before: *The meeting went on longer than I expected.* ♦ *Burton smiled and **went on with** his work.* ♦ *She can't go on pretending that everything is fine when it clearly isn't.* **2** if time goes on, it passes **3** if something such as a light goes on, it starts working: *I heard the TV go on in the next room.* **4** to happen: *I wonder what's going on next door – they're making a lot of noise.* **5** *spoken* used for encouraging someone to do something: *Go on, try it!*

,go 'out **1** to leave your house and go somewhere, especially to do something enjoyable: *I wanted the evenings free for going out with my friends.* **2** to stop burning or shining: *The fire must have gone out during the night.* **3** to have a romantic or sexual relationship with someone: *How long have they been going out together?* **4** when the tide goes out, the water in the sea flows away from the land

,go 'over sth to check something carefully: *Could you go over this report and correct any mistakes?*

,go 'through sth **1** to examine or search something very carefully: *Someone had broken into the office and gone through all the drawers.* **2** to experience something difficult or unpleasant: *They've gone through a really tough time.*

,go 'through with sth to do something that you have planned or agreed to do: *I can't believe he went through with the divorce.*

,go to'gether **1** if two or more things go together, they frequently exist together: *Too often greed and politics seem to go together.* **2** if two things go together, they seem good, natural, or attractive in combination with each other: *I don't think the colours go together very well.*

,go 'up **1** to increase: *The price of oil has gone up by over 50 per cent in less than a year.* **2 go up in flames** to start burning and be destroyed

'go with sth **1** to be provided or offered together with something: *Does a car go with the job?* **2** to seem good, natural, or attractive in combination with something: *Which shoes go best with this dress?*

,go with'out sth to live without something that you need or would like to have: *These villages have gone without water for several weeks.*

go² /gəʊ/ (plural **gos**) noun [C] **1** an attempt to do something: *She once had a go at writing a novel but quickly gave up.* **2** *informal* your chance to play in a game or take part in an activity: *Whose go is it?*

PHRASE make a go of sth *informal* to do something successfully

GO /gəʊ/ noun [singular] **TECHNOLOGY** one end of a **plug gauge** that is used to check the size of holes in machinery. If it fits into the hole, the hole is of an acceptable size.

goad /gəʊd/ verb [T] to deliberately make someone feel very angry or upset so that they react in a particular way

'go-a,head noun **give/get the go-ahead** to give or get permission to do something

goal /gəʊl/ noun [C] **1** **SPORTS** in games such as football, the net or structure that players try to get the ball into, in order to score points **2** **SPORTS** the action of putting a ball into a goal: *Nielsen scored two goals in the last ten minutes.* **3** something that you hope to achieve: *His goal is to win a medal at the Olympics.*

goalkeeper /'gəʊl,kiːpə/ noun [C] **SPORTS** the player whose job is to stop the ball going into the goal in games such as football

'goal ,kick noun [C] **SPORTS** an occasion when a goalkeeper kicks the ball forward during a game of football in order to start the game again

goalless /'gəʊlləs/ adj **SPORTS** with no goals scored

'goal ,line noun [C] **SPORTS** the line at each end of a sports field that a ball must cross to score a goal

goalpost /'gəʊl,pəʊst/ noun [C] **SPORTS** one of the two posts that the ball must go between in order to score a goal in games such as football

goat /gəʊt/ noun [C] a mammal similar to a sheep but with longer legs and a thinner coat —*picture* → MAMMAL

goatherd /'gəʊt,hɜːd/ noun [C] someone whose job is to look after goats

gobble /'gɒb(ə)l/ verb [T] to eat something quickly

'go-be,tween noun [C] someone who takes messages between people who cannot meet or do not want to meet

goblet /'gɒblət/ noun [C] a metal or glass cup with no handles that was used in the past

goblin /'gɒblɪn/ noun [C] a small ugly creature in children's stories that enjoys causing trouble

god /gɒd/ noun [C] **1** **RELIGION** one of the male spirits with special powers that some people believe in and worship: *The Hindu god Vishnu is often pictured as a young man herding cows.* **2** a man that many people admire very much or find very attractive

God /gɒd/ **RELIGION** the spirit or force that is believed, in many religions, to have created the universe

godchild /'gɒd,tʃaɪld/ (plural **godchildren** /'gɒd,tʃɪldrən/) noun [C] **RELIGION** a child that a **godparent** promises to look after, especially by making certain that he or she gets a religious education

goddess /'gɒdes/ noun [C] **1** **RELIGION** one of the female spirits with special powers that some people believe in and worship **2** a woman that many people admire very much or find very attractive

godfather /'gɒd,fɑːðə/ noun [C] **RELIGION** a male **godparent**

godmother /'gɒd,mʌðə/ noun [C] **RELIGION** a female **godparent**

godparent /'gɒd,peərənt/ noun [C] **RELIGION** an adult who promises to look after a child, especially by making certain that he or she gets a religious education. This promise is made during the Christian ceremony of **baptism**.

goggles /'gɒg(ə)lz/ noun [plural] special glasses that are worn to protect the eyes

going¹ /'gəʊɪŋ/ noun **1** [U] used for talking about how fast or easily you make progress: *We'd reached London by six o'clock, which was good going.* **2** [U] an occasion when someone leaves somewhere permanently: *None of us knew the reasons for his going.* → COMING² **3** [singular] **CONSTRUCTION** the horizontal distance between two **risers** (=vertical parts) on a **staircase**

going² /'gəʊɪŋ/ adj available: *It's one of the best jobs going in television.*

goitre /'gɔɪtə/ noun [C/U] **HEALTH** a disease that affects the **thyroid** gland and makes the neck swollen

gold¹ /gəʊld/ noun **1** [U] **CHEMISTRY** a valuable yellow metal element that is used for making jewellery and in alloys. Chemical symbol: **Au 2** [C/U] **SPORTS** a medal given to the winner of a race or competition: *Australia got the gold and Kenya got the silver.* **3** [C/U] the colour of gold

gold² /gəʊld/ adj **1** something that is gold is the colour of gold: *blue fabric decorated with gold stars* **2** made of gold: *a gold ring*

,gold 'disc noun [C] **1** a prize that a singer or group receives when a lot of people buy their record **2** **COMPUTING** the original **disc** from which other copies of a CD-ROM are made

golden /'gəʊld(ə)n/ adj **1** bright yellow in colour: *golden hair* ♦ *Fry the chicken joints in the oil until* **golden brown**. **2** very happy or successful: *The seventies were the* **golden years** *of Australian tennis.* **3** *literary* made of gold: *The queen wore a golden crown.*

'**golden** ,**age** noun [singular] a period of time in the past when something was the most successful that it has ever been: *the golden age of radio*

,**golden oppor'tunity** noun [C] a very good chance to do something

,**golden 'rule** noun [C] an important basic principle that should always be followed when doing a particular activity

,**golden 'wedding** noun [C] the day when two people celebrate the fact that they have been married for 50 years

goldfish /'gəʊld,fɪʃ/ (plural **goldfish**) noun [C] a small orange fish that is sometimes kept as a pet

,**gold 'medal** noun [C] **SPORTS** a medal made of gold that is given to the winner of a race or competition

goldmine /'gəʊld,maɪn/ noun [C] **1** *informal* a business or an activity that makes large amounts of money very easily **2 GEOLOGY** a place under the ground where there are rocks containing gold

golf /gɒlf/ noun [U] **SPORTS** a game in which players use **golf clubs** to hit a small white ball into a hole in the ground —**golfer** noun [C]

'**golf ,ball** noun [C] **SPORTS** a small white ball used for playing golf

'**golf ,club** noun [C] **SPORTS 1** a long stick used for hitting the ball in golf **2** a place with a golf course and **clubhouse** where people go to play golf

'**golf ,course** noun [C] **SPORTS** a large area of land that is designed for playing golf

gonad /'gəʊnæd/ noun [C] **ANATOMY** a sex organ in humans and other animals that makes cells that are used in producing babies or young. In men this sex organ is called a **testicle**, and in women it is called an **ovary**.

Gondwanaland /gɒn'dwɑːnəlænd/ **GEOLOGY** an ancient area of land that is believed to have existed in the southern hemisphere in ancient times, and to have been formed when Pangaea broke up. It consisted of South America, Africa, part of South Asia, Australia, and Antarctica and began to break up about 200 million years ago.

gone¹ /gɒn/ adj **1** someone who is gone is no longer present in a place **2** something that is gone no longer exists or has all been used

gone² /gɒn/ the past participle of **go¹**

gong /gɒŋ/ noun [C] a large circular metal object hanging from a frame. It makes a loud deep noise when it is hit with a stick.

gonorrhoea /ˌgɒnə'riːə/ noun [U] **HEALTH** a disease affecting the sex organs that is passed on during sex. If it is not treated, it can cause the infected person to become **sterile** (=unable to have children).

good¹ /gʊd/ (**better** /'betə/, **best** /best/) adj

1 of high quality	**8** giving benefits
2 able to do sth well	**9** fairly large
3 suitable	**10** able to be used
4 making sb happy	**11** thorough
5 morally correct	**12** more than sth
6 behaving well	**+ PHRASES**
7 kind/helpful	

1 of a high quality or standard: *We saw a really good film last night.* ♦ *They were all dressed in their best clothes.* ♦ *How good is his English?*
2 able to do something well: *Francine was a very good cook.* ♦ *Bob is pretty* **good at** *fixing things.* ♦ *Gina has always been* **good with** *small children.*
3 suitable and likely to produce the results or conditions that you want: *WHAT'S the best way to get to the motorway from here?* ♦ *Now would be* **a good time** *to ask for a pay rise.*
4 giving you a happy or pleasant feeling: *Here's some* **good news**: *Beth had a baby girl!* ♦ *We had a really* **good time** *at the party.*
5 honest and morally correct: *George had always tried to lead* **a good life**.
6 willing to obey and behave in a socially correct way: *I told the children to be good when they visited their grandmother.*
7 kind, generous, and willing to help: *Helen's parents were always* **good to** *us.*
8 producing benefits for someone or something: *Exercise is* **good for** *you.* ♦ *It's not good to eat so much junk food.*
9 fairly large in amount, size, range etc: *He earns a good salary as a consultant.* ♦ *They've known each other for a good many years.*
10 still able to be used: *Do you think the eggs are still good?*
11 thorough and complete: *The witness said she got a good look at his face.*
12 *informal* more than a particular distance, amount, age etc: *We've been waiting for a good half hour.*

PHRASES **as good as new** something that is as good as new is in almost the same good condition as it was before it was damaged
a good friend someone that you know very well and like a lot

> Build your vocabulary: words you can use instead of **good**
>
> **Good** is a very general word. Here are some words with more specific meanings that sound more natural and appropriate in particular situations.
> **films/books/events** brilliant, excellent, fabulous, fantastic, great, terrific
> **food/meals** delicious, tasty, wonderful
> **performance/piece of work** brilliant, excellent, outstanding
> **people** decent, kind, nice, respectable
> **ideas/suggestions** appealing, brilliant, excellent, great, interesting, clever

good² /gʊd/ noun [U] **1** advantage, or benefit: *A long rest will* **do you good**. ♦ *We should all work together* **for our own good**. **2** morally correct behaviour ≠ **EVIL**: *the battle between* **good and evil 3** the pleasant part or aspects of something: *When you're bringing up kids, you have to take the good with the bad.*

PHRASES **do no good** or **not do any good** to not have any effect or success: *I'll talk to her, but it won't do any good.*
for good permanently, without the possibility of change in the future: *It looks like Jamie has left for good this time.*
no good or **not any good** or **not much good 1** of a low quality or standard: *Most of the pictures I took weren't any good.* **2** not able to do something well: *I'm* **no good at** *chemistry.* ♦ *Ken's* **not much good with** *kids.* **3** not useful or effective: *It's no good trying to persuade her to come with us.*
→ **GOODS**

goodbye¹ /ˌgʊd'baɪ/ interjection used when you are leaving someone or when someone is leaving you, or when you are finishing a telephone call

goodbye² /ˌɡʊdˈbaɪ/ noun [C] a word or phrase that you say when you leave someone or when someone leaves you: *Emma left without even a goodbye.* ♦ *I said goodbye to everyone and left.*

Good 'Friday noun [C/U] RELIGION the Friday before Easter, when Christians believe that Jesus Christ died

good-humoured /ˌɡʊd ˈhjuːməd/ adj friendly, happy, and not easily annoyed or upset

good-looking /ˌɡʊd ˈlʊkɪŋ/ adj physically attractive

good 'looks noun [plural] the physically attractive appearance of someone

good-natured /ˌɡʊd ˈneɪtʃəd/ adj kind and friendly, and not easily annoyed —**good-'naturedly** adv

goodness /ˈɡʊdnəs/ noun [U] **1** the quality of being morally good **2** substances such as vitamins and proteins that are contained in some food and help the body to stay healthy

good 'night interjection used for saying goodbye to someone at night, or before they go to bed at night

goods /ɡʊdz/ noun [plural] **1** objects that are produced for sale: *electrical goods* ♦ *Wilkins was found in possession of £8,000 worth of stolen goods.* **2** objects that are carried in large quantities from one place to another by road or railway: *a goods train*

goods and chattels /ˌɡʊdz ən ˈtʃæt(ə)lz/ noun [plural] LAW someone's possessions, not including any houses or land that they own

goodwill /ɡʊdˈwɪl/ noun [U] **1** a feeling of wanting to be friendly and helpful to someone ≠ ILL WILL **2** BUSINESS the good reputation and good relationships that a company has with its customers, and their value if the company is sold

google /ˈɡuːɡ(ə)l/ verb [T] to search for something on the Internet using the Google™ **search engine**

googly /ˈɡuːɡli/ noun [C] SPORTS a ball in **cricket** that is difficult to hit because it has been made to go in a different direction from the one that the **batsman** is expecting

googol /ˈɡuːɡɒl/ noun [C] MATHS the number 10^{100}

goose /ɡuːs/ (plural **geese** /ɡiːs/) noun **1** [C/U] a large white or grey bird with a long beak —*picture* → BIRD **2** [U] the meat of a goose

gooseberry /ˈɡʊzb(ə)ri/ (plural **gooseberries**) noun [C] a small green fruit with a sour taste that grows on a bush, especially in **temperate** regions

gooseneck /ˈɡuːsˌnek/ noun [C] TECHNOLOGY the narrow curved part of a machine for **die-casting** metal. The liquid metal is forced along it into the **die**.

'goose ˌpimples noun [plural] very small lumps that appear on the skin when someone is cold, frightened, or excited

gore¹ /ɡɔː/ noun [U] thick blood from an injured person

gore² /ɡɔː/ verb [T] if an animal such as a bull gores someone, it injures them with its horns

gorge¹ /ɡɔːdʒ/ noun [C] GEOGRAPHY a deep valley with high straight sides —*picture* → RIVER

gorge² /ɡɔːdʒ/ verb informal **gorge yourself (on sth)** to eat or drink so much of something that you cannot eat or drink any more

gorgeous /ˈɡɔːdʒəs/ adj very beautiful or pleasant

'gorge-ˌwalking noun [U] SPORTS the sport of travelling through streams or rivers that flow through valleys, both walking and swimming and sometimes jumping down **waterfalls**

gorilla /ɡəˈrɪlə/ noun [C] a large strong African wild mammal that is similar to a monkey but much larger and without a tail. Gorillas live in forests. —*picture* → MAMMAL

gory /ˈɡɔːri/ (**gorier, goriest**) adj involving a lot of blood, killing, or injuries

gosling /ˈɡɒzlɪŋ/ noun [C] a young **goose**

gospel /ˈɡɒsp(ə)l/ noun **1** gospel or gospel music [U] MUSIC a type of Christian music that was developed by African Americans **2** [C] RELIGION one of the four books in the Bible that tell about the life of Jesus Christ **3 the gospel** [singular] RELIGION the things that Jesus Christ said and taught according to the Bible

gossip¹ /ˈɡɒsɪp/ noun **1** [U] talk about things that are not important or about people's private lives: *an interesting piece of gossip* **2** [C] someone who enjoys talking about other people

gossip² /ˈɡɒsɪp/ verb [I] to talk about other people or about things that are not important

got¹ /ɡɒt/ verb **have got** spoken used especially in speech to mean 'have': *The college has got an excellent library.* → HAVE

got² the past tense and past participle of **get**

Gothic /ˈɡɒθɪk/ adj **1** Gothic or gothic LITERATURE Gothic novels and films have frightening and mysterious subjects **2** Gothic printing or writing uses thick lines and pointed shapes

gotten /ˈɡɒt(ə)n/ the American past participle of **get**

gouache /ɡuˈɑːʃ/ noun [C] ARTS a painting made with paints mixed with water and a type of glue

gouge /ɡaʊdʒ/ verb [T] to cut long deep holes in something

gourd /ɡʊəd/ noun [C] a type of fruit with a hard thick skin. Dried gourds are sometimes used for making containers or musical instruments.

gourmet /ˈɡʊəmeɪ/ noun [C] someone who knows a lot about good food and wine

gout /ɡaʊt/ noun [U] a painful disease that makes the joints in the toes swell

gov abbrev **1** COMPUTING government: used in email and Internet addresses for government organizations **2** governor **3** government

govern /ˈɡʌvən/ verb **1** [I/T] to officially control and manage a country or area and its people = RULE: *The region is now governed by Morocco.* ♦ *The party will not be able to govern alone.* **2** [T] to control or influence the way that things happen or develop: *the laws that govern the movements of the stars* **3** [T] to control the way an organization such as a business or society operates = REGULATE: *The company is governed by strict environmental regulations.*

governance /ˈɡʌvənəns/ noun [U] formal the process of governing a country or organization

government /ˈɡʌvənmənt/ noun **1** [C/U] the people who control a country or area and make decisions about its laws and taxes: *The government has announced plans to modernize the railway system.* ♦ *a democratically elected government* ♦ *government ministers*

Government can be used with a singular or plural verb. You can say *The government is unpopular* or *The government are unpopular.*

2 [U] SOCIAL STUDIES the process, method, or effects of governing a country or area: *Will these reforms lead to more effective government?* —**governmental** /ˌɡʌv(ə)nˈment(ə)l/ adj → CENTRAL GOVERNMENT, LOCAL GOVERNMENT

governor /ˈɡʌvənə/ noun [C] **1** a political leader who is in charge of an area, especially someone who governs one of the states or regions of a country: *the governor of the Northern Region* **2** the person, or one of the people, in charge of an institution such as a bank or prison **3** a member of a group that has responsibility for an institution like a school or university —**governorship** noun [C/U]

governor 'general noun [C] a person who acts as the **head of state** instead of the British Queen or King in some countries in the British Commonwealth

gown /ɡaʊn/ noun [C] **1** a long dress that a woman wears for a special occasion **2** a long loose piece of clothing that a doctor or patient wears during a medical operation

GP /ˌdʒiː ˈpiː/ noun [C] **HEALTH** General Practitioner: a doctor who deals with general medical problems and treats the people in a local area

GPA /ˌdʒiː piː ˈeɪ/ noun [C] **EDUCATION** American a **grade point average**

GPRS /ˌdʒiː piː ɑːr ˈes/ noun [U] **COMPUTING** a system that allows you to connect to the Internet using mobile phones

GPS /ˌdʒiː piː ˈes/ noun [U] Global Positioning System: a system for finding exactly where someone or something is, anywhere in the world, using satellites

grab /ɡræb/ (**grabs**, **grabbing**, **grabbed**) verb [T] **1** to take hold of something in a rough or rude way: *He grabbed the knife before I could get to it.* ♦ *I grabbed hold of his arm.* **2** to succeed in getting something, especially by being quick or by being the best at something: *We got there early and grabbed seats at the front.* —**grab** noun [singular]

graben /ˈɡrɑːbən/ noun [C] **GEOLOGY** a wide valley, especially a **rift valley**, produced when the land between two parallel cracks in the ground sinks

grace /ɡreɪs/ noun **1** [U] a smooth and beautiful way of moving: *She moved with natural grace.* **2** [U] behaviour that is polite, fair, and shows respect for other people: *He should **have the grace to** admit he was wrong.* **3** [U] extra time that you are given to do something such as pay money that you owe **4** [singular/U] **RELIGION** a short prayer that some people say before they eat in order to thank God for the food

grace and 'favour adj a grace and favour house, flat etc has been given to someone to live in without payment by a king, queen, or government

graceful /ˈɡreɪsf(ə)l/ adj **1** a graceful shape or object is attractive **2** a graceful movement is smooth and beautiful **3** showing good manners and respect for other people: *She was extremely graceful in defeat.* —**gracefully** adv

'grace ˌnote noun [C] **MUSIC** an extra musical note added in a piece of music

gracious /ˈɡreɪʃəs/ adj showing kindness and good manners ≠ UNGRACIOUS —**graciously** adv

gradable /ˈɡreɪdəb(ə)l/ adj **LANGUAGE** a gradable adjective can be used with words such as 'very', 'more', or 'less', or have **comparative** and **superlative** forms. 'Big', 'happy', and 'expensive' are examples of gradable adjectives.

gradation /ɡrəˈdeɪʃ(ə)n/ noun [C] one of the steps in a series that shows how one thing slowly becomes something else

grade¹ /ɡreɪd/ noun [C] **1** a level of quality or importance: *He asked to be put on a higher salary grade.* **2** **EDUCATION** a letter or number that shows the quality of a student's work: *You need to improve your grades.* ♦ *I got a Grade B for art.* **3** **EDUCATION** one of the levels of school in the US that lasts for one year: *She's in the seventh grade.* **4** the rank of a person, for example in their job: *He demanded to be put on a higher grade.*

grade² /ɡreɪd/ verb [T] **1** to separate things into different groups according to quality, size, importance etc **2** **EDUCATION** to judge the quality of a student's work by giving it a letter or number

'grade point ˌaverage noun [C] **EDUCATION** American a number that is the average of the marks that students in US schools have achieved during their studies

gradient /ˈɡreɪdiənt/ noun [C] **1** a measure of how steep a slope is **2** **SCIENCE** the rate of change of something such as temperature or pressure

gradual /ˈɡrædʒuəl/ adj happening slowly and by small amounts: *a gradual change in the climate*

gradually /ˈɡrædʒuəli/ adv slowly and in small stages or amounts: *She gradually built up a reputation as a successful lawyer.* ♦ *Gradually add the flour.*

graduate¹ /ˈɡrædʒuət/ noun [C] **EDUCATION** someone who has a degree from a university: *The company recruits 30–40 graduates each year.* ♦ *a **graduate of** Hong Kong University* ♦ *Candidates should be **graduates in** science or engineering.*

graduate² /ˈɡrædʒueɪt/ verb [I] **1** **EDUCATION** to complete your studies at a university or college and get a degree: *He **graduated from** Yale University in 1936.* ♦ *one of the first women to **graduate in** engineering* **2** **EDUCATION** American to finish your studies at a high school **3** **graduate (from sth) to sth** to make progress, or to reach a higher position: *He eventually graduated from clerical work to his present role.*

graduate³ /ˈɡrædʒuət/ adj **EDUCATION** postgraduate

graduated /ˈɡrædʒuˌeɪtɪd/ adj **1** organized according to a series of levels **2** **SCIENCE** marked with divisions that show measurements

'graduate ˌschool noun [C/U] American a part of a university in the US where students who have a first degree can study for a **master's degree** or a **doctorate**

graduation /ˌɡrædʒuˈeɪʃ(ə)n/ noun **EDUCATION 1** [U] the act of receiving a degree or other qualification after finishing your studies at a college or university **2** [C/U] a ceremony at which students are given a degree or other qualification

graffiti /ɡrəˈfiːti/ noun [U] words or pictures that are drawn on walls in public places

graft¹ /ɡrɑːft/ noun [C] **1** **HEALTH** a piece of skin or bone from one part of someone's body that is used to replace or repair a part of their body that is damaged **2** **AGRICULTURE** a piece that is taken from a plant and placed in a cut that has been made in another plant, so that it can grow there

graft² /ɡrɑːft/ verb [T] **1** **HEALTH** to take a piece of skin or bone from one part of someone's body and use it to replace or repair a damaged part of their body **2** **AGRICULTURE** to take a piece from a plant and placed in a cut that has been made in another plant, so that it can grow there

grain /greɪn/ noun **1** [U] **AGRICULTURE** the seeds from cereal plants such as wheat, rice, or **maize** that are used for food, or the plants that they grow on: *harvesting grain* ♦ *grain crops* —*picture* → CEREAL **2** [C] an individual seed from one of these crops **3** [C] a very small individual piece of a substance such as sand, salt, or sugar **4** [U] the pattern or direction of the fibres in substances such as wood, cloth, or paper

PHRASE **a grain of truth** a very small amount of truth: *There was more than a grain of truth in what he'd said.*

gram /græm/ noun [C] **SCIENCE** a unit for measuring weight in the metric system

grammar /ˈgræmə/ noun **1** [U] **LANGUAGE** the set of rules that describe the structure of a language and control the way that sentences are formed: *The book covers all the essential points of English grammar.* **2** [C] a book explaining the rules of a language: *an Arabic grammar*

'grammar ˌchecker noun [C] **COMPUTING** a piece of software that checks documents to make sure they have no grammar mistakes

'grammar ˌschool noun [C] **EDUCATION** a school in some countries for children aged 11 to 18 who have passed a special examination in order to be allowed to go there

grammatical /grəˈmætɪk(ə)l/ adj **LANGUAGE** **1** relating to grammar: *grammatical errors* **2** a grammatical sentence correctly follows the rules of grammar ≠ UNGRAMMATICAL —**grammatically** /grəˈmætɪkli/ adv

granary /ˈgrænəri/ (plural **granaries**) noun [C] **AGRICULTURE** a building where grain is kept

grand /grænd/ adj **1** very impressive: *The central square is surrounded by grand buildings.* ♦ *The festival ends with a grand procession.* **2** a grand person behaves as if they are very important **3** most important: *the grand prize*

grandad /ˈgræn(d)ˌdæd/ noun [C] *informal* a **grandfather**

grandchild /ˈgræn(d)ˌtʃaɪld/ (plural **grandchildren** /ˈgræn(d)ˌtʃɪldrən/) noun [C] the son or daughter of one of your children

granddaughter /ˈgræn(d)ˌdɔːtə/ noun [C] the daughter of one of your children

grandeur /ˈgrændʒə/ noun [U] an impressive quality

grandfather /ˈgræn(d)ˌfɑːðə/ noun [C] the father of one of your parents

'grandfather ˌclock noun [C] an old-fashioned clock in a tall, narrow wooden box

ˌgrand 'jury noun [C] **LAW** a group of people in the US legal system who decide if someone accused of a crime should go to trial in a court of law

grandma /ˈgræn(d)ˌmɑː/ noun [C] *informal* a **grandmother**

ˌgrand 'mal /ˌgrɒn 'mæl/ noun [C/U] **HEALTH** a type of **seizure** (=a sudden attack of shaking) that most people associate with epilepsy

grandmother /ˈgræn(d)ˌmʌðə/ noun [C] the mother of one of your parents

grandpa /ˈgræn(d)ˌpɑː/ noun [C] *informal* a **grandfather**

grandparent /ˈgræn(d)ˌpeərənt/ noun [C] the mother or father of your mother or father

ˌgrand pi'ano noun [C] **MUSIC** a type of large piano

Grand Prix /ˌgrɒn ˈpriː/ (plural **Grand Prix** or **Grands Prix**) noun [C] **SPORTS** an international competition for **racing cars** or motorcycles that is part of a series to decide who is the best driver in the world

ˌgrand 'slam noun [C] **SPORTS** a situation in which a player wins all of a set of important competitions in a particular sport in the same year

grandson /ˈgræn(d)ˌsʌn/ noun [C] the son of one of your children

grandstand /ˈgræn(d)ˌstænd/ noun [C] **SPORTS** a large structure with rows of seats from which people watch sports events

ˌgrand 'total noun [singular] a final total of all the amounts or totals that must be added together

ˌgrand 'unified ˌtheory noun **PHYSICS** a theory that is intended to explain how **subatomic particles** behave

granite /ˈgrænɪt/ noun [U] **GEOLOGY** a type of very hard stone, used especially for building, that is grey, black, or pink in colour. It is a type of igneous rock.

granny /ˈgræni/ (plural **grannies**) noun [C] *informal* a **grandmother**

grant¹ /grɑːnt/ verb [T] *formal* to allow someone to have or to do what they want: *The Board has refused to **grant** your **request**.*

PHRASES **take sb for granted** to expect someone to always do things for you even when you do not show that you are grateful

take sth for granted to expect something always to happen or exist in a particular way and not think about any possible difficulties: *Losing my job taught me never to take anything for granted.*

grant² /grɑːnt/ noun [C] an amount of money that the government or an organization gives someone for a specific purpose: *a research grant*

granulated sugar /ˌgrænjʊˌleɪtɪd ˈʃʊgə/ noun [U] sugar in the form of small white grains, used especially for adding to cups of tea and coffee

granule /ˈgrænjuːl/ noun [C] **1** a small hard round piece of something such as sugar or coffee: *coffee granules* **2** **BIOLOGY** a small **sac** (=bag of membrane) in a cell containing enzymes that destroy microorganisms

granulocyte /ˈgrænjʊləsaɪt/ noun [C] **ANATOMY** a white blood cell that contains many **granules** in its **cytoplasm**

granum /ˈgreɪnəm/ (plural **grana** /ˈgreɪnə/) noun [C] **BIOLOGY** a set of **thylakoids** arranged one on top of the other that is found in a **chloroplast**. It contains chlorophyll and is important for photosynthesis.

grape /greɪp/ noun [C] a small green or purple fruit that grows in **bunches** on a vine. Grapes are often used for making wine. —*picture* → FRUIT

grapefruit /ˈgreɪpˌfruːt/ noun [C/U] a fruit like a large orange that is yellow on the outside, yellow or red inside, and has sour juice —*picture* → FRUIT

grapevine /ˈgreɪpˌvaɪn/ noun [singular] *informal* the way in which information spreads quickly from one person to another through conversation: *I heard **on the grapevine** that you left your job.*

graph /grɑːf, græf/ noun [C] **MATHS** a diagram that uses lines or curves to show the relationship between numbers or measurements that change. A graph usually has one set of numbers or quantities going from bottom to top (the **vertical axis**) and another set going from left to right (the **horizontal axis**): *The graph on p.28 shows how earnings have declined.* —*picture* → on next page

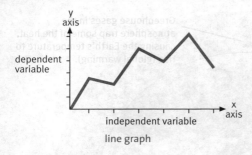

line graph

grapheme /'græfi:m/ noun [C] LANGUAGE a written letter, group of letters, number, or symbol that represents a single sound in speech

graphic /'græfik/ adj **1** containing a lot of detail that gives a very clear idea of something: *a graphic description* **2** ARTS relating to drawing —**graphically** /'græfikli/ adv

graphical 'user ,interface noun [C] COMPUTING see **GUI**

graphic de'sign noun [U] ARTS the art of designing pictures and **text** for magazines, advertisements etc —**graphic de'signer** noun [C]

graphics /'græfiks/ noun [plural] COMPUTING pictures that are produced by a computer, or that are included in a document, magazine etc

'graphics a,dapter noun [C] COMPUTING a part in a computer that changes software instructions into electrical signals that show images on a screen

'graphics ,card noun [C] COMPUTING the part inside a computer that changes information into images

'graphics ,tablet noun [C] COMPUTING a piece of equipment used for putting designs into a computer by drawing them with an electronic pen onto a special surface

graphite /'græfait/ noun [U] CHEMISTRY a soft black type of carbon that is used in pencils and for making electrodes

'graph ,paper noun [U] MATHS paper with small squares on it, used for drawing graphs

grapple /'græp(ə)l/ verb to fight with someone

grasp¹ /gra:sp/ verb [T] **1** to take and hold someone or something very tightly: *He grasped her firmly by the shoulders.* **2** to understand something: *Charlie grasped the point at once.* **3** to take advantage of an opportunity when it happens → NETTLE

grasp² /gra:sp/ noun [singular] **1** the ability to understand something: *a good grasp of English* **2** the ability to achieve something: *Victory was now within their grasp.* **3** a very tight hold of someone or something

grass /gra:s/ noun **1** [U] a very common plant with thin green leaves that covers the ground. Grass is a **monocotyledon**: *Stephen was lying on the grass.* **2** [C] a particular type of grass: *tall flowering grasses*

grasshopper /'gra:s,hɒpə/ noun [C] a large insect with long back legs that moves by jumping. It makes short high sounds. —*picture* → INSECT

grassland /'gra:s,lænd/ noun [U] GEOGRAPHY a large area of land where wild grass grows

the ,grass 'roots noun [plural] the ordinary people in a community, country, or organization rather than its leaders

'grass ,snake noun [C] a small harmless snake that lives in grass —*picture* → REPTILE

grassy /'gra:si/ adj covered in grass

grate /greit/ verb **1** [T] to rub food against a **grater** in order to cut it into small pieces —*picture* → FOOD **2** [I] to rub against something and make an unpleasant annoying sound **3** [I] to have an annoying effect on someone: *His intense stare began to grate on her nerves.*

grateful /'greitf(ə)l/ adj feeling that you want to thank someone because they have given you something or done something for you ≠ UNGRATEFUL: *Thanks for coming with me. I'm really grateful.* ♦ *I'm very grateful for all your help with the party.* ♦ *She was grateful to them for letting her stay at their house.* —**gratefully** adv

grater /'greitə/ noun [C] a tool with a rough sharp surface. Foods such as cheese and vegetables are rubbed against the surface in order to cut them into very small pieces.

grating /'greitiŋ/ noun [C] a metal frame with bars across it that is used for covering a hole or window

gratis /'grætis/ adj, adv done or provided free

gratitude /'græti,tju:d/ noun [U] the feeling of being grateful ≠ INGRATITUDE

gratuity /grə'tju:əti/ noun [C] *formal* **1** a small amount of money that someone gives another person to thank them for doing something = TIP **2** a large amount of money given to someone when they leave their job, for example in the armed forces

grave¹ /greiv/ noun [C] the place where a dead body is buried in a deep hole in the ground

grave² /greiv/ adj serious and causing worry: *You're in grave danger.* ♦ *grave concerns about the future* —**gravely** adv

grave³ /gra:v/ or **grave 'accent** noun [C] LANGUAGE the mark ` above a letter in French and some other languages that is used in order to show how it is pronounced → ACUTE sense 3, CIRCUMFLEX

gravel /'græv(ə)l/ noun [U] small pieces of stone that are used for making paths and roads

gravestone /'greiv,stəʊn/ noun [C] a stone by a **grave** that shows the name of the person who is buried there and the dates when he or she was born and died

graveyard /'greiv,ja:d/ noun [C] an area of land where dead people are buried, usually around a church

gravitas /'grævitæs/ noun [U] *formal* a serious and impressive attitude or way of behaving

gravitate /'grævi,teit/ verb [I] *formal* **1** to be attracted to someone and go to be with them **2** to be interested in something and want to do it or to have it

gravitation /,grævi'teiʃ(ə)n/ noun [U] PHYSICS the force that causes objects to move towards each other

gravitational /,grævi'teiʃ(ə)nəl/ adj PHYSICS relating to the force of gravity

gravi'tational ,field noun [singular] PHYSICS an area of space around an object in which gravity is felt

gravi,tational po'tential noun [U] PHYSICS the energy that an object or system has stored in it because of its position in a gravitational field

gravi,tational 'pull noun [U] PHYSICS the force of gravity that causes one physical object to be pulled towards another physical object such as the Earth

gravity /'grævəti/ noun [U] **1** PHYSICS the force that makes any two objects that have mass move towards each other. The most common example of this is when

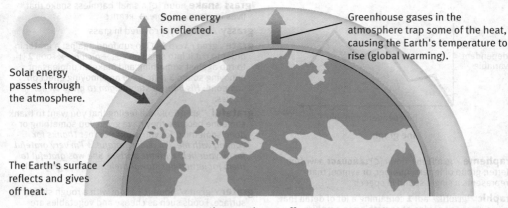

Some energy is reflected.

Greenhouse gases in the atmosphere trap some of the heat, causing the Earth's temperature to rise (global warming).

Solar energy passes through the atmosphere.

The Earth's surface reflects and gives off heat.

the greenhouse effect

an object falls to the ground: *the laws of gravity* **2** the serious or important quality of something: *I'm sure you can appreciate the gravity of the situation.*

gravy /ˈɡreɪvi/ noun [U] a sauce made from the juices of cooked meat mixed with flour

graze¹ /ɡreɪz/ verb **1** [I] to eat grass that is growing somewhere: *Goats grazed on the hillside.* **2** [T] to put an animal in a place where it can eat grass **3** [T] to break the surface of the skin: *He fell and grazed his knee.* **4** [I/T] to touch something slightly when you pass it

graze² /ɡreɪz/ noun [C] a slight injury causing a break in the surface of the skin: *a graze on my elbow*

grazing /ˈɡreɪzɪŋ/ or **grazing ˌland** noun [U] **AGRICULTURE** land on which animals eat grass

grease¹ /ɡriːs/ noun [U] a thick substance similar to oil, used on machine parts for making them work smoothly —*picture* → REFINE

grease² /ɡriːs/ verb [T] to put grease, fat, or oil on something

greasy /ˈɡriːsi/ adj **1** covered in grease or oil: *greasy hands* **2** producing a lot of natural oil ≠ DRY: *greasy hair* **3** prepared with a lot of oil or fat

great /ɡreɪt/ adj **1** bigger, or more than is usual: *in great danger* ♦ *It gives me great pleasure to welcome our next guest.* **2** important, or powerful: *a great military power* ♦ *one of the greatest writers of the modern age* **3** *informal* very good, enjoyable, or nice: *You look great in that outfit.* ♦ *We had a great view of the mountains.* **4** *spoken* used for expressing pleasure or agreement: *Great! I'll pick you up at eight, then.*

great- /ɡreɪt/ prefix **1** used with nouns describing older relatives to make other nouns meaning the grandfather, grandmother etc of your parent **2** used with nouns describing younger relatives to make other nouns meaning the child of your grandson, granddaughter etc

ˌGreat ˈBritain GEOGRAPHY the island that consists of England, Scotland, and Wales

ˌgreatest ˌcommon diˈvisor noun [singular] **MATHS** the highest common factor of a set of numbers

ˌgreat-ˈgrandchildren noun [plural] the grandchildren of someone's son or daughter

ˌgreat-ˈgrandparents noun [plural] the parents of someone's grandparents

greatly /ˈɡreɪtli/ adv very much: *Your support is greatly appreciated.*

greatness /ˈɡreɪtnəs/ noun [U] a position of power, success, or respect: *a woman destined for greatness*

greed /ɡriːd/ noun [U] **1** a strong wish to have more money, possessions, or power than you need **2** a strong wish to have more food than you need

greedy /ˈɡriːdi/ (**greedier, greediest**) adj **1** wanting to eat or drink more food than you need **2** wanting more money, possessions, or power than you need —**greedily** adv

green¹ /ɡriːn/ adj **1** something that is green is the same colour as grass: *green eyes* ♦ *bright green leaves* **2** a green area has a lot of grass, plants, or trees: *a campaign to protect the city's green spaces* **3** **ENVIRONMENT** concerned with protecting the environment: *wind farms and other green energy schemes* **4** young and without much experience of life —**greenish** adj

green² /ɡriːn/ noun **1** [C/U] the colour of grass: *She was dressed in green.* **2** [C] a large area of grass where people can walk, sit, or play games: *a house overlooking the green* **3** [C] **SPORTS** in golf, the area of short grass around a hole **4 greens** [plural] *spoken* vegetables with green leaves

ˈgreen ˌaudit noun [C] **BUSINESS** an examination of what a company is doing to prevent its business activities from harming the environment

ˌgreen ˈbean noun [C] a long thin green vegetable that grows on a tall climbing stem —*picture* → VEGETABLE

ˈgreen ˌchannel noun [singular] **TOURISM** the way through **customs** for people who are not bringing goods into the country on which they have to pay tax

greenery /ˈɡriːnəri/ noun [U] plants or leaves

greenfly /ˈɡriːnˌflaɪ/ (plural **greenfly**) noun [C] a very small green insect that damages plants

greengrocer /ˈɡriːnˌɡrəʊsə/ noun [C] **1 greengrocer's** a shop that sells fruit and vegetables **2** someone whose job is to sell fruit and vegetables in a shop

greenhouse /ˈɡriːnˌhaʊs/ noun [C] a building made of glass that is used for growing plants that need protection from the weather

the ˈgreenhouse efˌfect noun [singular] **ENVIRONMENT** the process by which the Earth's surface and lower atmosphere is getting warmer as a result of pollution by gases such as carbon dioxide. The increase in greenhouse gases means the heat from the Sun cannot escape, leading to a general increase in the Earth's temperature, called **global warming**.

greenhouse 'gas noun [C] **ENVIRONMENT** a gas that stops heat from escaping from the Earth's atmosphere and causes the greenhouse effect. Carbon dioxide is a greenhouse gas. The level of greenhouse gases in the atmosphere has increased in recent years mainly because of the burning of **fossil fuels** and also because of **deforestation**. —*picture* → GREENHOUSE EFFECT

green 'light noun [singular] official approval for something to be done

green ma'nure noun [U] **AGRICULTURE** a growing crop that is put directly back into the soil to act as a fertilizer

green 'sand noun [U] **TECHNOLOGY** wet sand used for moulding **molten** (=melted) metal

greet /griːt/ verb [T] **1** to talk to someone in a polite or friendly way when you meet them: *Natalie went to the door to greet the guests.* **2** to react to an action or news in a particular way: *The decision **was greeted by** violent demonstrations.* **3** if you are greeted by a sight, sound, or smell, it is the first thing that you notice

greeting /'griːtɪŋ/ noun **1** [C/U] something polite or friendly that you say or do when you meet someone: *They exchanged greetings and sat down.* **2** [C] a friendly message that you send to someone on a special occasion such as their birthday

grenade /grɪ'neɪd/ noun [C] a small bomb that is thrown, or fired from a gun

grew /gruː/ the past tense of **grow**

grey¹ /greɪ/ adj **1** between black and white in colour: *a **dark grey** suit* **2** if someone goes or turns grey, their hair starts to become white **3** if someone's face is grey, they look pale because they are ill or shocked **4** used for describing the weather or the light when it is not very bright because there are a lot of clouds: *grey skies* ♦ *In London it was **a grey** November **day**.* —**greyish** adj

grey² /greɪ/ noun [C/U] a colour that is between black and white

grey 'area noun [C] a situation in which the rules are not clear, or in which it is difficult to be sure what is right or wrong

grey cast 'iron noun [U] **TECHNOLOGY cast iron** in which most of the carbon exists in the form of **flake graphite**

grey ,matter noun [U] **1** **ANATOMY** the grey-brown tissue in the brain and **spinal cord** of vertebrate animals. It consists mainly of the bodies of **neurons** (=cells that carry messages to and from the brain). → WHITE MATTER —*picture* → BRAIN, SPINAL CORD **2** *informal* the brain

greyscale /'greɪ,skeɪl/ noun [C/U] **COMPUTING** the range of different colours of grey used on a black and white screen or in something printed in black and white

grid /grɪd/ noun [C] **1** a pattern of straight lines that cross each other to form squares: *streets laid out in a grid* **2** a pattern of straight lines that form squares on a map, used for finding a particular place **3** a set of wires that carry the electricity supply: *the national grid* —*picture* → GENERATOR **4** a set of metal bars that are arranged in a pattern of straight lines

gridiron /'grɪd,aɪən/ noun [C] **SPORTS** *American* a field on which American football is played

gridlock /'grɪd,lɒk/ noun [U] **1** a situation in which there are so many cars on the roads that traffic cannot move **2** a situation in which it is impossible to make progress

grid ,paper noun [C/U] **MATHS, TECHNOLOGY** paper covered with a pattern of squares or **equilateral**

triangles formed by lines or **dots**. It is used for drawing three-dimensional objects.

grid ,reference noun [C] **GEOGRAPHY** a set of numbers and letters that shows a particular position on a map. The numbers and letters relate to the lines of the map's **grid** (=an arrangement of straight lines that cross each other to form a series of squares).

grief /griːf/ noun [U] a strong feeling of sadness, usually because someone has died

grievance /'griːv(ə)ns/ noun [C] a feeling or complaint that you have been treated unfairly

grievance pro,cedure noun [C] a formal series of actions that an employee has to perform when they want to complain officially about the way that they have been treated at work

grieve /griːv/ verb [I/T] to feel extremely sad because someone has died

grievous bodily harm /,griːvəs ,bɒdɪli 'hɑːm/ noun [U] **LAW** very serious injuries caused by a violent attack

grike /graɪk/ noun [C] **GEOLOGY** one of the long deep cracks that separate the flat blocks of stone in a **limestone pavement**

grill¹ /grɪl/ noun [C] **1** the part of a cooker where food is cooked under great heat **2** a flat frame of metal bars on which food can be placed and cooked over a fire

grill² /grɪl/ verb **1** [I/T] to cook something by putting it close to great heat above or below it —*picture* → FOOD **2** [T] to ask someone a lot of difficult questions for a long period of time = INTERROGATE

grille or **grill** /grɪl/ noun [C] a metal frame with bars or wire across it that is used for protecting a door or window

grim /grɪm/ adj **1** grim news, situations, and events are unpleasant and make you feel upset and worried: *the grim reality of unemployment* **2** very serious and unfriendly: *a grim expression* —**grimly** adv

grimace /'grɪməs/ verb [I] to make an ugly expression by twisting your face, for example because you are in pain or because you do not like something —**grimace** noun [C]

grime /graɪm/ noun [U] thick dirt on a surface

grimy /'graɪmi/ adj very dirty

grin /grɪn/ (**grins, grinning, grinned**) verb [I] to smile showing your teeth —**grin** noun [C]

grind /graɪnd/ (**grinds, grinding, ground** /graʊnd/) verb [T] **1** to break something into very small pieces or powder, either by using a machine or by crushing it between two hard surfaces: *The mill is used for grinding corn.* **2** to make something such as a knife smooth or sharp by rubbing it against a hard surface **3** to press something down onto a surface using a lot of force: *He ground a half-smoked cigarette into the ashtray.*

PHRASES **grind to a halt 1** if a vehicle grinds to a halt, it moves more and more slowly until it finally stops **2** if something grinds to a halt, it stops making progress and gradually stops completely

grind your teeth to rub your top and bottom teeth together in a way that makes a noise

grip¹ /grɪp/ noun **1** [singular] a firm strong hold: *Pete tightened his grip on her arm.* **2** [singular] power and control over someone or something: *The President struggled to regain his grip on power.* **3** [singular/U] if shoes or tyres have grip, they hold a surface firmly and do not slip

PHRASES **be in the grip of sth** to be in a difficult or unpleasant situation

get/come to grips with sth to start to deal with a problem, situation, or job that must be done

grip² /grɪp/ (**grips, gripping, gripped**) verb **1** [T] to hold something tightly: *She gripped Frank's hand firmly.* **2** [T] to have a strong effect on someone: *A feeling of fear gripped the crowd.* **3** [T] to keep someone very interested in something: *The case has gripped the public because of the celebrities involved.* **4** [I/T] if shoes or tyres grip, they hold a surface firmly and therefore do not slip

gripe /graɪp/ noun [C] *informal* a complaint about something that is annoying but not very important —**gripe** verb [I]

gripping /'grɪpɪŋ/ adj very exciting and interesting

grisly /'grɪzli/ adj involving death or violence in a shocking way= GRUESOME

gristle /'grɪs(ə)l/ noun [U] a strong substance that surrounds the joints of animals and is difficult to eat when you find it in meat

grit¹ /grɪt/ noun [U] very small pieces of stone or sand

grit² /grɪt/ (**grits, gritting, gritted**) verb
PHRASE **grit your teeth 1** to press your teeth together tightly, for example because you are angry or in pain **2** to show determination in a difficult situation

gritty /'grɪti/ adj **1** showing life as it really is, even when it is not nice or attractive: *a gritty television drama* **2** firm in your intentions: *a gritty determination to succeed* **3** containing grit, or covered with grit

groan /grəʊn/ verb [I] to make a long low sound because you are unhappy or in pain: *The fans groaned at the news that the star was not fit to play.* —**groan** noun [C]

grocer /'grəʊsə/ noun [C] **1 grocer's** a small shop that sells food and other goods for the home **2** someone who owns or works in a grocer's shop

groceries /'grəʊsəriz/ noun [plural] food and other goods for the home that you buy regularly

grocery /'grəʊsəri/ adj relating to groceries or grocer's shops

groggy /'grɒgi/ adj feeling tired, weak, or confused because of illness or lack of sleep

groom¹ /gruːm/ verb [T] **1** to clean and brush an animal **2** [I/T] if an animal grooms itself or another animal, it cleans itself or another animal **3** to prepare someone for a particular job or activity

groom² /gruːm/ noun [C] **1** a **bridegroom 2** someone who looks after horses

groove /gruːv/ noun [C] a line that has been cut into a surface —**grooved** adj

grope /grəʊp/ verb **1** [I] to try to find something by feeling with your hands: *She was groping around in her bag for her keys.* **2** [I] to search for an idea or a way to say something without being certain of what you are doing **3** [T] to touch someone sexually, especially someone who does not want to be touched

gross¹ /grəʊs/ adj **1** a gross amount of money is the total amount before taxes or costs have been taken out **2** extreme and unreasonable: *a gross distortion of the truth* **3** LAW gross actions are extremely bad and are considered immoral by most people: *gross misconduct*

gross² /grəʊs/ verb [T] to earn a particular amount of money before taxes or other costs have been taken out

gross do,mestic 'product noun [U] ECONOMICS *see* **GDP**

grossly /'grəʊsli/ adv extremely: *grossly unfair*

gross ,national 'product noun [U] ECONOMICS *see* **GNP**

gross 'profit noun [C] BUSINESS the difference between the price that someone sells goods for and what it costs to produce them

grotesque /grəʊ'tesk/ adj **1** extremely ugly and strange **2** completely unreasonable, or offensive —**grotesquely** adv

ground¹ /graʊnd/ noun

1 surface of Earth	**6** reason for sth
2 layer of soil/rock	**7** subject/idea
3 area of land	**8** background colour
4 area used for sth	+ PHRASES
5 land around house	

1 [singular/U] the top part of the earth's surface: *People were sitting on the ground in small groups.* ♦ *It is gravity that makes things fall to the ground when you drop them.*
2 [singular] the layer of soil and rock that forms the Earth's surface: *getting coal out of the ground* ♦ *Plant roots grow downwards into the ground.*
3 [U] an area of land: *an acre of ground*
4 [C] an area of land that is used for a particular purpose: *soldiers on the parade ground* ♦ *a sports ground*
5 grounds [plural] the land and gardens that surround a large house or public building
6 grounds [plural] a reason that someone gives for what they say or do: *The army turned him down on medical grounds.* ♦ *The Act prohibits discrimination on the grounds of sex or marital status.*
7 [singular/U] the subject, idea, or information that people are talking about or writing about: *We'll be covering a lot of new ground in today's lecture.*
8 [C] ARTS a colour used as a background or first layer on a painting, drawing etc
PHRASES **get (sth) off the ground** to start successfully, or to get something started successfully
stand your ground 1 to not move when someone attacks you or is going to attack you **2** to refuse to change your opinions, beliefs, or decisions despite pressure to change them

ground² /graʊnd/ verb [T] **1** to stop a plane from leaving the ground: *All of their planes have been grounded.* **2** to base an idea or decision on a particular thing: *a theory that is grounded in practical experience* **3** [I/T] if a boat grounds or is grounded, it hits a rock or the ground under the water

ground³ /graʊnd/ the past tense and past participle of **grind**

groundbreaking /'graʊn(d),breɪkɪŋ/ adj using new methods, or achieving new results

ground 'floor noun [singular] the floor of a building that is at or near the level of the ground

groundless /'graʊn(d)ləs/ adj not based on evidence or good reasons

'ground ,rules noun [plural] the basic rules or principles that govern the way that something is done

'ground ,staff noun [C] **1** SPORTS the people who look after an area where sports are played **2** the people who work for an **airline** in an airport rather than on an aircraft

'ground ,stroke noun [C] SPORTS in tennis, an attempt to hit the ball after it has touched the ground

groundwater /ˈɡraʊndˌwɔːtə/ noun [U] ENVIRONMENT water that flows or collects under the ground

groundwork /ˈɡraʊnd(d)ˌwɜːk/ noun [U] work that someone does in order to prepare for something

Ground 'Zero the area that was left after the World Trade Center in New York was destroyed on 11th September, 2001

group[1] /ɡruːp/ noun [C] **1** several people or things that are together or that are related to each other in some way: *the local drama group* ♦ *The hamstring muscles are a group of muscles behind the upper leg.* **2** MUSIC a small set of musicians who play **pop music** = BAND **3** CHEMISTRY a set of chemical elements arranged one below the other in the periodic table. They have similar features and the way their electrons are arranged in rings is similar.

> **Group** can be used with a singular or plural verb. You can say *The local drama group* **meets** *every week* OR *The local drama group* **meet** *every week.*

group[2] /ɡruːp/ verb [T] to put people or things into groups: *The students are grouped according to ability.*

grouping /ˈɡruːpɪŋ/ noun [C] a set of people or things that are considered as a group

'group ˌrate noun [C] a special rate for larger groups of people travelling together

groupware /ˈɡruːpˌweə/ noun [U] COMPUTING software and other computer tools that make it possible for people in different places to work on the same project

groupwork /ˈɡruːpˌwɜːk/ noun [U] EDUCATION activities that involve students working together in a group

grove /ɡrəʊv/ noun [C] a group of trees that are arranged in lines

grovel /ˈɡrɒv(ə)l/ (**grovels, grovelling, grovelled**) verb [I] *showing disapproval* to show too much respect for someone, or to be too willing to obey someone

grow /ɡrəʊ/ (**grows, growing, grew** /ɡruː/, **grown** /ɡrəʊn/) verb

1 become taller	5 about cells etc
2 increase	6 about hair/nails
3 of plants	7 develop quality
4 look after plants	+ PHRASAL VERBS

1 [I] if children, animals, or plants grow, they develop and become taller or bigger: *She has grown at least four inches since I saw her last.* ♦ *Some of these creatures grew to a length of over 12 feet.*
2 [I] to increase in size, strength, or importance: *The world's population is still growing, but more slowly than before.* ♦ *The sound grew to a deafening roar.* ♦ *The economy has grown by 7% over the past year.* ♦ *She was growing in confidence every day.*
3 [I] BIOLOGY if plants grow somewhere, that is where they are found
4 [T] AGRICULTURE if someone grows plants, they look after them and help them to develop = CULTIVATE, PRODUCE: *They grew all their own vegetables.* ♦ *the country's largest rice-growing area*
5 [I/T] BIOLOGY if bacteria or other living cells grow or are grown, they develop
6 [I/T] if your hair or nails grow, or if you grow them, they become longer: *Her husband is growing a beard.*
7 [linking verb] *literary* used for saying that a feeling or quality gradually starts to exist: *The nights were growing darker.* ♦ *She had grown used to the old man's habits.*
—**grower** noun [C]

PHRASAL VERBS **'grow on sb** if something or someone grows on you, you start to like them more: *The new house slowly began to grow on her.*
ˌgrow 'out of sth 1 if children grow out of clothes, they grow bigger and the clothes become too small for them **2** to develop from something: *The idea grew out of a wish to improve the lives of the children in the region.*
ˌgrow 'up to change from being a child to being an adult: *She's really starting to grow up now.* ♦ *He rarely saw his father while he was growing up.*

> **Word family: grow**
> *Words in the same family as grow*
> ■ **grown** *adj*   ■ **outgrow** *v*
> ■ **growing** *adj*   ■ **overgrown** *adj*
> ■ **growth** *n*   ■ **undergrowth** *n*

growing /ˈɡrəʊɪŋ/ adj increasing or becoming more extreme: *There is growing public concern over the effects of this policy.* ♦ *the growing popularity of the Internet* ♦ *China's fastest growing city*

'growing ˌseason noun [C] AGRICULTURE the time of year during which plants grow and develop, especially farm crops

growl /ɡraʊl/ verb **1** [I] if an animal growls, it makes a frightening low noise **2** [I/T] to say something in an unfriendly and angry way —**growl** noun [C]

grown[1] /ɡrəʊn/ adj adult: *a grown woman*

grown[2] /ɡrəʊn/ the past participle of **grow**

'grown-ˌup[1] noun [C] an adult: used when talking to children

'grown-ˌup[2] adj adult, or intended for adults: *She has two grown-up sons.* ♦ *grown-up entertainment*

growth /ɡrəʊθ/ noun **1** [singular/U] BIOLOGY an increase in the size or development of a living thing, usually as the result of an increase in the number of cells: *There is no evidence that the drug increases hair growth.* ♦ *Vitamins are essential for normal growth.* **2** [singular/U] an increase in the number, size, or importance of something: *We are entering a period of rapid population growth.* ♦ *a substantial growth in the number of available jobs* **3** [C] HEALTH a lump on someone's body that is caused by a disease: *a cancerous growth* **4** [singular/U] ECONOMICS an increase in the success of a business or a country's economy, or in the amount of money invested in them = EXPANSION: *measures designed to stimulate economic growth*

'growth ˌhormone noun [C] BIOLOGY a hormone that helps the process of growth in animal and plant cells. In animals, it is produced in the **pituitary gland**.

'growth ˌindustry noun [C] an industry that is growing quickly

'growth ˌregulator noun [C] AGRICULTURE a natural or artificial substance that controls the way plants grow. Different growth regulators may encourage growth or reduce growth.

groyne /ɡrɔɪn/ noun [C] ENVIRONMENT a wall built out into the sea to protect the beach from being destroyed by the water

GRP /ˌdʒiː ɑː ˈpiː/ noun [C] ENGINEERING glass-reinforced plastic: a material made of glass fibres and plastic, **fibreglass**

grub /ɡrʌb/ noun [C] BIOLOGY the stage of an insect when it is a larva, without wings or legs

grubby /ˈɡrʌbi/ adj dirty

grudge¹ /grʌdʒ/ noun [C] a feeling of anger towards someone because they have done something unfair to you: *There's a whole list of people who might* **bear a grudge against** *him.*

grudge² /grʌdʒ/ verb [T] to give something in an unwilling way= BEGRUDGE, RESENT

gruelling /'gruːəlɪŋ/ adj involving a lot of continuous effort= PUNISHING

gruesome /'gruːs(ə)m/ adj something that is gruesome is very unpleasant because it involves violent injury or death= GRISLY

gruff /grʌf/ adj **1** rude and unfriendly **2** a gruff voice has a rough low sound —**gruffly** adv

grumble /'grʌmb(ə)l/ verb [I] to complain about something that is not important= MOAN —**grumble** noun [C]

grumpy /'grʌmpi/ adj someone who is grumpy complains a lot or is often unhappy —**grumpily** adv

grunt /grʌnt/ verb [I] **1** to make a short low sound in the throat and nose **2** if a pig grunts, it makes its usual low sound —**grunt** noun [C]

GSM /,dʒiː es 'em/ noun [U] Global System for Mobile Communication: a system used in mobile- phone communication

guano /'gwɑːnəʊ/ noun [U] AGRICULTURE the dried **droppings** (=solid waste) of birds or bats, used as an organic fertilizer

guarantee¹ /,gærən'tiː/ (guarantees, guaranteeing, guaranteed) verb [T] **1** to make it certain that something will happen or will exist= ASSURE: *The government provides help for small businesses, but it cannot guarantee their success.* ♦ *We guarantee that you will get the cheapest fare possible.* **2** if a company guarantees a product, it promises to repair the product if it stops working: *All our products are guaranteed for three years.* **3** to agree to pay back the money that someone else owes if they cannot pay it back themselves: *The loan was guaranteed by a Hong Kong property developer.*

guarantee² /,gærən'tiː/ noun [C] **1** something that makes something else certain to happen: *Massive investment is no* **guarantee of** *success.* **2** a promise that something will definitely happen: *The company has given a guarantee that there will be no job losses.* ♦ *a* **cast-iron guarantee** (=one that is completely reliable) **3** a written promise that a company will repair a product if the product stops working= WARRANTY: *My watch is still* **under guarantee** *(=protected by a guarantee).*

guaranteed /,gærən'tiːd/ adj if something is guaranteed, it will definitely happen or be provided: *a guaranteed minimum wage*

guarantor /,gærən'tɔː/ noun [C] *formal* someone who makes an official agreement to be responsible for money that someone else owes, or for someone else's behaviour

guard¹ /gɑːd/ noun **1** [C] someone whose job is to protect a place or person: *a prison guard* ♦ *There was an* **armed guard** *outside his door.* **2** [singular] a group of soldiers or police officers whose job is to protect something **3** [C] an object that covers something and protects it

PHRASES **let your guard down** or **drop your guard** to relax and trust people, even though this might be dangerous

off (your) guard not concentrating on something and therefore likely to do something that you did not intend to do

on your guard being careful not to do something that you did not intend to do

under guard protected by a guard, or prevented from escaping by a guard: *He was taken to prison under police guard.*

guard² /gɑːd/ verb [T] **1** to protect someone or something from danger or harm: *the trees that guarded the farm from the wind* **2** to prevent someone from escaping from a place: *There were two soldiers guarding the main gate.* **3** to try very hard to keep or protect something that you think is important: *The newspaper is fiercely guarding its independence.*

'guard ,cell noun [C] BIOLOGY one of the pair of cells that control the opening and closing of the **stoma** of a leaf. The guard cells close the **stomata** in order to prevent loss of water and keep them open when this is not necessary.

guarded /'gɑːdɪd/ adj careful not to give much information or show your real feelings

guardian /'gɑːdiən/ noun [C] **1** a person or organization that protects something **2** someone who is legally responsible for someone else's child

,guardian 'angel noun [C] RELIGION a helpful spirit who some people believe looks after a particular person

'guard ,rail noun [C] a bar or fence put for safety at the edge of something such as a road, a bridge, or stairs

guava /'gwɑːvə/ noun [C] a large tropical fruit with green or yellow skin. It is pink inside.

gudgeon pin /'gʌdʒən ,pɪn/ noun [C] ENGINEERING a pin in a **piston** of an **internal-combustion engine** that is attached to the small end of a **connecting rod**

guerrilla /gə'rɪlə/ noun [C] a member of a military group that fights to change a political situation

guess¹ /ges/ verb [I/T] **1** to say or decide what you think is true, without being certain about it: *Try to guess the meaning of the word before you look it up in your dictionary.* ♦ *Whoever* **guesses correctly** *will win two tickets to the show.* ♦ *Would anyone like to guess what this object is?* **2** to be correct about something that you guess: *He had already* **guessed** *the* **answer**.

guess² /ges/ noun [C] an occasion when you say what you think is true without being certain: **Have a guess** *and then check it on your calculator.*

guesswork /'ges,wɜːk/ noun [U] the guesses that you make when you try to find the answer to something

guest /gest/ noun [C] **1** someone who has been invited to your home, to a party, or to a special event: *We've got guests staying this weekend.* ♦ *He was a guest at our wedding.* ♦ *Tonight's guest speaker is Peter Bell.* → PAYING GUEST **2** someone who is paying to stay at a hotel or eat in a restaurant: *The pool is free to hotel guests.* **3** someone who appears on a television or radio programme that they do not regularly appear on: *My first guest tonight is famous for both her singing and acting talent.*

PHRASE **guest of honour** an important guest at a meeting, party, or other event

'guest ,house noun [C] a small hotel or private home where people can pay to stay the night

'guest ,ledger noun [C] a list of all the money owed by a guest to a hotel that must be paid before the guest leaves

GUI /,dʒiː juː 'aɪ/ noun [C] COMPUTING Graphical User Interface: a system that uses pictures that you click on with a computer mouse in order to perform operations or move between programs

guidance /'gaɪd(ə)ns/ noun [U] advice: *I need some* **guidance on** *which university I should choose.*

guide¹ /gaɪd/ noun **1** [C] a book that gives information: *a travel guide to South Africa* **2** [C] something or someone that helps you to make a judgment about something: *The colour of a plant's leaves is **a good guide to** its health.* ♦ *Opinion polls are **a rough guide** (=not an exact one) to how people really vote.* **3** [C] **TOURISM** someone whose job is to give information to people who are visiting a place: *a tour guide* → TOUR GUIDE **4** a piece of equipment that helps you to find the correct place or amount for something: *a cutting guide* ♦ *This chart can act as a quick reference guide.* ♦ *Draw up the plan using this pencil outline as a guide.*

guide² /gaɪd/ verb [T] **1** to show someone where to go by going with them: *He **guided** them **through** the forest.* **2** to help someone to do something or make a decision: *There was no research to guide them.* ♦ *His entire life was guided by his religious beliefs.* **3** to try to make a situation develop in a particular way: *Harry tried to **guide** the conversation **towards** the subject of money.*

guidebook /'gaɪd,bʊk/ noun [C] **TOURISM** a book for tourists that provides information about a place

'guide ,dog noun [C] a dog that is trained to lead a person who cannot see

guided tour /,gaɪdɪd 'tʊə/ noun [C] **TOURISM** a short journey around a building or place in which information is provided by a person or by a recorded description

guidelines /'gaɪd,laɪnz/ noun [plural] official instructions or advice about how to do something: *strict **guidelines on** the training of police officers*

the 'Guides Associ,ation an international organization for girls that teaches them moral values and practical skills

guild /gɪld/ noun [C] an organization of people who all have the same job or interests

guillotine /'gɪləti:n/ noun [C] a machine that was used in the past for cutting off people's heads as a punishment —**guillotine** verb [T]

guilt /gɪlt/ noun [U] **1** a feeling of being ashamed and sorry because you have done something wrong: *The accident left her with a terrible **sense of guilt**.* **2** the fact that someone has committed a crime: *The court will decide on his guilt or innocence.*

guilty /'gɪlti/ adj **1** ashamed and sorry because you have done something wrong: *I still feel **guilty about** things I said to my mother when I was a teenager.* ♦ *The look on his face showed that he had **a guilty conscience** (=a feeling that he had done something wrong).* **2** someone who is guilty has committed a crime or has done something wrong: *He was **found guilty of** murder.* —**guiltily** adv

guinea corn /'gɪni ,kɔ:n/ noun [U] **AGRICULTURE** a type of cereal plant whose grains are used to make bread

guinea grass /'gɪni ,grɑ:s/ noun [U] **BIOLOGY** a tall grass used as food for animals. It originally comes from Africa, but is also grown in Central and South America and parts of the US

guinea pig /'gɪni ,pɪg/ noun [C] **1** a small furry mammal with short ears and no tail. Guinea pigs are sometimes kept as pets. **2** someone who is used in an experiment

guinea worm /'gɪni ,wɜ:m/ noun [C] **BIOLOGY** a worm that lives as a parasite under the skin of people and animals. It can grow as long as a metre.

guinep /'gɪnɪp/ noun [C] a tropical evergreen tree that has edible fruit

guise /gaɪz/ noun [C] *formal* the way that someone or something appears to people
PHRASE **under/in the guise of** looking like someone or something else, or pretending to be them

guitar /gɪ'tɑ:/ noun [C] **MUSIC** a musical instrument with six strings that can be **acoustic** or electric: *Her son **plays the guitar** in a rock band.* —*picture* → MUSICAL INSTRUMENT —**guitarist** noun [C]

gulf /gʌlf/ noun [C] **1** **GEOGRAPHY** a large area of sea that is almost surrounded by land: *the Persian Gulf* **2** a large and important difference = CHASM: *the widening gulf between the rich and the poor*

gull /gʌl/ noun [C] a large white bird that lives near the sea = SEAGULL

gullet /'gʌlɪt/ noun [C] **ANATOMY** the oesophagus

gullible /'gʌləb(ə)l/ adj a gullible person is easy to trick because they always trust people ≠ CYNICAL

gully /'gʌli/ (plural **gullies**) noun [C] **GEOGRAPHY** **1** a long narrow valley with steep sides **2** a long narrow hole in the surface of rock or earth, usually made by the action of flowing water

'gully e,rosion noun [U] **ENVIRONMENT** a type of erosion in which flowing water cuts deep, narrow passages in the soil and wears it away

gulp /gʌlp/ verb **1** [T] to swallow food or drink quickly **2** [I] to make the movement of swallowing because you are surprised, excited, or afraid —**gulp** noun [C]

gum /gʌm/ noun **1** [C] the firm pink flesh in the mouth that the teeth are fixed to —*picture* → TOOTH **2** [U] **chewing gum 3** [U] a sticky substance that comes from some trees

gun /gʌn/ noun [C] **1** a weapon that shoots bullets or large **shells**: *Enemy guns fired a shell every two or three minutes.* ♦ *Their police officers all **carry guns**.* ♦ *He **pointed the gun** directly at me.* ♦ *Suddenly the officer **pulled a gun on** them (=took it out and pointed it at them).* —*picture* → WEAPON **2** a tool that forces something out of its container using pressure: *a paint gun*

gunboat /'gʌn,bəʊt/ noun [C] a small fast ship with large guns fixed on it

'gun ,court noun [C] **SOCIAL STUDIES** a special law court that deals with cases of children and young people who are caught carrying or using guns

gunfire /'gʌn,faɪə/ noun [U] shots from guns, or the sound they make

gunman /'gʌnmən/ (plural **gunmen** /'gʌnmən/) noun [C] someone who uses a gun when they are fighting or committing a crime

gunpoint /'gʌn,pɔɪnt/ noun **at gunpoint** in the position of threatening someone with a gun, or being threatened with a gun

gunpowder /'gʌn,paʊdə/ noun [U] **CHEMISTRY** a substance that is used for causing explosions and for making **fireworks**

gunshot /'gʌn,ʃɒt/ noun **1** [C] the sound that is made when someone fires a gun **2** [U] the bullets that are shot from a gun

guppy /'gʌpi/ (plural **guppies**) noun [C] a small brightly coloured tropical fish, often kept as a pet

gurgle /'gɜ:g(ə)l/ verb [I] to make the low sound that water makes when it is poured quickly from a bottle —**gurgle** noun [C]

guru /'gʊruː/ (plural **gurus**) noun [C] **1** RELIGION a spiritual leader in some religions **2** someone that other people respect and ask for advice about a particular subject

gush /gʌʃ/ verb [I] **1** if a liquid gushes, it flows quickly and in large quantities **2** to express a lot of admiration or pleasure in a way that does not seem to be sincere

gusset /'gʌsɪt/ noun [C] CONSTRUCTION a piece of wood or metal that joins beams together where they meet at right angles

gust /gʌst/ noun [C] a sudden strong wind —**gusty** adj

gut¹ /gʌt/ noun [C] ANATOMY the tube in the body that carries food away from the stomach

PHRASE **gut feeling/instinct** a feeling that you are certain is right, although you can give no good reason why

→ GUTS

gut² /gʌt/ (**guts**, **gutting**, **gutted**) verb [T] **1** to remove the organs from inside a fish or animal before cooking it **2** to destroy the inside of a building or vehicle: *The entire building was gutted by the fire.*

ˌgut reˈaction noun [C] something that you feel or believe strongly without stopping to think about it

guts /gʌts/ noun [plural] *informal* **1** the quality of being brave and determined: *She had the guts to go for what she wanted.* ♦ *It takes a lot of guts and hard work to get where he is.* **2** the stomach and the organs near it

gutter /'gʌtə/ noun **1** [C] the edge of a road, where water flows away **2** [C] CONSTRUCTION a piece of open pipe that is fixed along the edges of a roof to carry rain away **3 the gutter** [singular] the bad social conditions of the poorest people in society

gut-wrenching /'gʌt ˌrentʃɪŋ/ adj making you feel very sad or upset

guy /gaɪ/ noun [C] *informal* a man

gym /dʒɪm/ noun **1** [C] a room or club with equipment for doing physical exercises **2** [U] EDUCATION the activity of doing indoor physical exercises at school **3** [C] a large hall or room with special equipment for doing physical exercises **4** [C] a building or club where you go to do physical exercises, swim, and play sports

gymkhana /dʒɪmˈkɑːnə/ noun [C] SPORTS an event at which people riding horses take part in races and other competitions

gymnasium /dʒɪmˈneɪziəm/ noun [C] *formal* a **gym**

gymnast /'dʒɪmnæst/ noun [C] SPORTS someone who does gymnastics

gymnastics /dʒɪmˈnæstɪks/ noun [U] SPORTS a sport in which people perform physical exercises that involve bending and balancing —**gymnastic** adj

gymnosperm /'dʒɪmnəʊˌspɜːm/ noun [C] BIOLOGY a plant with a woody stem and seeds that are not enclosed in plant tissue but are carried naked on the scales of a **cone**. Conifers and **ginkgos** are gymnosperms. → ANGIOSPERM

gynaecology /ˌgaɪnɪˈkɒlədʒi/ noun [U] HEALTH the treatment of medical conditions that affect women, especially conditions that affect women's reproductive organs —**gynaecological** /ˌgaɪnɪkəˈlɒdʒɪk(ə)l/ adj, **gynaecologist** /ˌgaɪnɪˈkɒlədʒɪst/ noun [C]

gynoecium /dʒaɪˈniːsiəm, gaɪˈniːsiəm/ noun [C] BIOLOGY the set of **carpels** (=female reproductive part) in a flower

gypsy /'dʒɪpsi/ (plural **gypsies**) noun [C] a member of a community of people who travel from place to place and often live in **caravans**, especially in Europe

H h

h /eɪtʃ/ (plural **h's**) or **H** (plural **H's**) noun [C/U] the eighth letter of the English alphabet

ha /hɑː/ interjection **1** used for showing that you are pleased because you have discovered or achieved something **2** used for showing that you disagree with someone

habeas corpus /ˌheɪbiəs ˈkɔːpəs/ noun [U] LAW a judge's order to bring a prisoner into court, so that the court can decide whether the prisoner should stay in prison or not

habit /'hæbɪt/ noun **1** [C/U] something that you do often: *healthy eating habits* ♦ *They were in the habit of going for long walks.* ♦ *George has got into the habit of going to bed late.* **2** [C] something that is bad that you often do without realizing it, or without being able to stop: *He had the annoying habit of tapping the table when he was nervous.* **3** [C] RELIGION a simple dress that is worn by **nuns** and other members of religious communities

- A **habit** is something that someone does often or regularly, as a normal part of their life: *Eating sweets is a bad habit.* ♦ *I soon got into the habit of getting up early.*
- A **custom** is something that a particular group of people do because it is traditional and usual: *the custom of shaking hands*

habitable /'hæbɪtəb(ə)l/ adj a building that is habitable is good enough to live in

habitat /'hæbɪtæt/ noun [C] BIOLOGY, ENVIRONMENT the type of place that a particular organism usually lives in, for example a desert, forest, or lake: *Forest habitats tend to be dominated by birds and insects.* ♦ *the destruction of natural habitats* → AQUATIC, TERRESTRIAL

habitation /ˌhæbɪˈteɪʃ(ə)n/ noun [U] *formal* the fact that people are living in a place

habitual /həˈbɪtʃuəl/ adj **1** usual or typical: *He spoke to the workers with his habitual honesty.* **2** used for describing a person who has a particular bad habit: *a habitual smoker* —**habitually** adv

habituated /həˈbɪtʃueɪtɪd/ adj very familiar with something as a result of experiencing it regularly

hack /hæk/ verb [I/T] to cut something in a rough way or with a lot of energy: *The boys were hacking at the bushes with heavy sticks.*

PHRASAL VERB **ˈhack into sth** COMPUTING to use a computer in order to connect secretly and illegally to someone else's computer: *They hack into banks and transfer huge amounts of cash.*

hacker /'hækə/ noun [C] COMPUTING someone who uses a computer in order to connect secretly and illegally to someone else's computer

hacksaw /'hækˌsɔː/ noun [C] a **saw** used for cutting metal —*picture* → TOOL

had /hæd, əd, həd/ the past tense and past participle of **have**

hadn't /'hæd(ə)nt/ short form the usual way of saying or writing 'had not'. This is not often used in formal writing: *I wish I hadn't sent that letter.*

haematite /'hiːmətaɪt/ noun [U] GEOLOGY, CHEMISTRY a red mineral from which iron is obtained

haematology /ˌhiːmə'tɒlədʒi/ noun [U] HEALTH the scientific study of blood —**haematologist** noun [C]

haematoma /ˌhiːmə'təʊmə/ noun [C/U] HEALTH a soft lump in the tissues of the body consisting of blood that has become thick and stopped flowing

haemo- /hiːməʊ/ prefix involving blood: used with some nouns and adjectives

haemocoel /'hiːməsiːl/ noun [C] BIOLOGY a space in the body of spiders, crustaceans, and other **arthropods** through which blood and other fluids flows

haemoglobin /ˌhiːmə'gləʊbɪn/ noun [U] BIOLOGY a protein in red blood cells that carries oxygen from the lungs to all parts of the body → OXYHAEMOGLOBIN

haemolysis /hiː'mɒləsɪs/ noun [U] BIOLOGY the destruction of red blood cells, allowing the haemoglobin they contain to escape

haemolytic disease /ˌhiːmə'lɪtɪk dɪˌziːz/ noun [U] HEALTH a condition that can affect a Rhesus positive baby of a Rhesus negative mother. The mother's antibodies attack the baby's Rhesus positive blood cells, causing health problems and even death.

haemophilia /ˌhiːmə'fɪliə/ noun [U] HEALTH a serious genetic disease that prevents the blood from clotting, with the result that blood loss from an injury or cut cannot be stopped

haemophiliac /ˌhiːmə'fɪliæk/ noun [C] HEALTH someone who has haemophilia

haemorrhage /'hem(ə)rɪdʒ/ noun [C/U] HEALTH an occasion when someone loses a lot of blood because of an injury inside their body —**haemorrhage** verb [I/T]

haemorrhoids /'hemə,rɔɪdz/ noun [plural] HEALTH painful swollen areas around the **anus**

hafnium /'hæfniəm/ noun [U] CHEMISTRY a silvery metallic element that is used in **nuclear reactors**. Chemical symbol: **Hf**

haggard /'hægəd/ adj looking very tired, worried, or ill

haggle /'hæg(ə)l/ verb [I] to argue in order to agree on the price of something

hagiography /ˌhægi'ɒgrəfi/ noun [C] **1** RELIGION a book about the lives of saints **2** *formal* a book about a person's life that deliberately includes only good things about them

ˌha 'ha interjection used for representing the sound of laughter, or for showing that you think something is not funny

haiku /'haɪkuː/ noun [C/U] LITERATURE a short poem written in a traditional Japanese style

hail¹ /heɪl/ verb **1** [T] to say publicly how good something is= ACCLAIM **2** [T] *formal* to shout to someone as a way of attracting their attention: *I stepped out into the street and hailed a taxi.* **3** [I] GEOGRAPHY if it hails, small balls of ice fall from the sky

hail² /heɪl/ noun [U] GEOGRAPHY rain that falls as small balls of ice

    PHRASE **a hail of bullets/arrows/bottles etc** a lot of things such as bullets that come at you very quickly

hailstones /'heɪl,stəʊnz/ noun [plural] GEOGRAPHY small balls of ice that form hail

hailstorm /'heɪl,stɔːm/ noun [C] GEOGRAPHY a storm in which a lot of hail falls

hair /heə/ noun **1** [U] the mass of thin fibres that grows on the head: *long black hair* ♦ *She was brushing her hair.* —**picture →** BODY, SKIN **2** [C] a single fibre of hair: *a few grey hairs* ♦ *dog hairs on the rug* → SPLIT¹

haircare /'heə,keə/ noun [U] the activity of keeping your hair in good condition by washing it and putting substances on it

haircut /'heə,kʌt/ noun [C] **1** an act of cutting someone's hair: *He was badly dressed and needed a haircut.* **2** the style that the hair has been cut in: *a short stylish haircut*

hairdresser /'heə,dresə/ noun [C] someone whose job is to cut people's hair

hairdryer or **hairdrier** /'heə,draɪə/ noun [C] a piece of electrical equipment that you use for drying your hair after you have washed it

hairpin /'heə,pɪn/ noun [C] a metal object that is used for holding a woman's hair in position

ˌhairpin 'bend noun [C] a very sharp bend in a road, where the road forms a 'U' shape

hair-raising /'heə ˌreɪzɪŋ/ adj very frightening but exciting at the same time

ˈhair's ˌbreadth noun [singular] the smallest possible distance, amount, or degree

hairstyle /'heə,staɪl/ noun [C] the shape that your hair has been cut or arranged in

hairy /'heəri/ (**hairier, hairiest**) adj **1** covered with a lot of hair: *a hairy chest* **2** *informal* frightening, or dangerous

hajj or **haj** /hædʒ/ noun [C] RELIGION a journey to the holy city of Mecca that Muslims make as a religious duty

hajji /'hædʒi/ (plural **hajjis**) noun [C] RELIGION a Muslim who has made a hajj

halal /hə'lɑːl, 'hælæl/ adj RELIGION halal meat has been prepared according to the religious laws of Islam

half /hɑːf/ (plural **halves** /hɑːvz/) adv, determiner, noun, number, pronoun **1** one of two equal parts of a number, amount, group, or object: *Only half the population voted in the election.* ♦ *The fabric is half nylon, half cotton.* ♦ *Jasmine started school when she was four and a half.* ♦ *Half of the men were unemployed.* ♦ *Cut the potatoes in half.* **2** partly but not completely: *The door was half open.* ♦ *I only half understood the instructions.* **3** one of the two equal periods of time into which a game of football, basketball etc is divided

    PHRASE **half past one/two etc** 30 minutes after one o'clock, two o'clock etc: *The shops close at half past five.*

halfback /'hɑːf,bæk/ noun [C] SPORTS in **rugby** or **hockey**, a player who plays in front of the defending players but is not in an attacking position

ˌhalf 'board noun [U] TOURISM an arrangement in which guests stay in a hotel and have breakfast and an evening meal there → FULL BOARD

ˈhalf ˌbrother noun [C] a brother who has either the same mother or the same father as you

half-hearted /ˌhɑːf 'hɑːtɪd/ adj done with no real interest or enthusiasm —**ˌhalf-'heartedly** adv

ˌhalf-'hour¹ adj lasting for 30 minutes: *a half-hour meeting*

half-'hour² or **half an 'hour** noun [singular] a period of 30 minutes: *Shannon waited another half-hour and then left.* ♦ *We had to wait half an hour for a bus.*

'half-,life noun [C] PHYSICS the amount of time that is needed for a substance to lose one half of its radioactivity

half-'mast noun **at half-mast** a flag that is at half-mast flies at the middle of a pole, not at the top, in order to show respect for someone who has died

half 'measures noun [plural] methods that are not effective enough

half-'moon noun [C] ASTRONOMY the moon when you can see only half of it —*picture* → PHASE

'half ,pipe noun [C] SPORTS a smooth open surface that is shaped like a 'U' and made of concrete or snow that people use in **skateboarding**, **in-line skating**, or **snowboarding**

'half ,section noun [C/U] MATHS, PHYSICS a drawing of a section of a **symmetrical** object (=one with both halves exactly the same about an axis) that shows only half of the object

halfshaft /'hɑːf,ʃɑːft/ noun [C] ENGINEERING a **driveshaft** that connects a rear **differential** to a rear wheel

'half ,sister noun [C] a sister who has either the same mother or the same father as you

half 'term noun [C/U] EDUCATION a short holiday from school or university in the middle of a **term**

half 'time noun [U] SPORTS in football and some other team sports, a period of rest between the two halves of a match

halfway /hɑːf'weɪ/ adj, adv in the middle of a space or period of time: *Their house is about halfway up the street.* ♦ *at the halfway stage of the competition*

half-'yearly adj done or happening twice a year

halibut /'hælɪbət/ (plural **halibut**) noun [C/U] a large flat sea fish, or this fish eaten as food

hall /hɔːl/ noun [C] **1** a building or large room that is used for public events: *a concert at the Albert Hall* **2** an area or passage inside the front door of a building that leads to other rooms: *Leave your shoes in the hall.* ♦ *The house has a large entrance hall.*
PHRASE **hall of residence** EDUCATION a large building in or near a college or university, where students live

hallmark /'hɔːl,mɑːk/ noun [C] **1** a typical feature **2** an official mark on an object made of gold or silver that shows its quality

hallo /hə'ləʊ/ interjection **hello**

Halloween /,hæləʊ'iːn/ noun [C/U] the night of 31st October, when children in the UK and the US dress as **witches** and **ghosts**

hallucinate /hə'luːsɪneɪt/ verb [I] to see or hear something that is not really there, as a result of illness or drugs —**hallucination** /hə,luːsɪ'neɪʃ(ə)n/ noun [C/U]

hallucinogen /,hæ'luːsɪnədʒən/ noun [C] a substance, especially a drug such as **LSD**, that causes someone to hallucinate

hallway /'hɔːl,weɪ/ noun [C] an area or passage inside the front door of a building that leads to other rooms = HALL

halo /'heɪləʊ/ (plural **haloes** or **halos**) noun [C] RELIGION a circle of light that is shown around the head of a holy person in religious paintings

halogen /'hælədʒen/ noun [C] CHEMISTRY one of five non-metal elements of the periodic table that combine with metals to form salts. These include **chlorine** and **iodine**.

'halogen ,lamp noun [C] a lamp that uses a bulb containing halogen gas

halt¹ /hɔːlt/ noun [singular] the fact that someone or something stops moving or happening: *The taxi came to a halt outside his front door.* ♦ *Traffic was brought to a halt* (=stopped) *by the demonstration.* ♦ *He has appealed for a halt to the fighting.*
PHRASE **call a halt to sth** to end something formally → GRIND

halt² /hɔːlt/ verb [I/T] to stop moving or happening, or to make someone or something stop moving or happening: *Building work had been halted by the bad weather.* ♦ *She halted at the door and turned towards him.*

halting /'hɔːltɪŋ/ adj with a lot of pauses between words or movements because you are nervous or not confident —**haltingly** adv

halve /hɑːv/ verb **1** [I/T] to reduce something to half its original size or amount, or to become half the original size or amount: *Many shops have halved their prices.* ♦ *The number of hospitals in the country has halved over the last five years.* **2** [T] to cut something into two pieces of equal size

halves /hɑːvz/ the plural of **half**

ham /hæm/ noun [C/U] the meat from a pig's leg: *a slice of ham* ♦ *a ham sandwich*

hamburger /'hæm,bɜːgə/ noun [C] a **burger**

hammer¹ /'hæmə/ noun [C] **1** a tool used for hitting nails into wood. It consists of a handle and a heavy metal top. —*picture* → TOOL **2** SPORTS a heavy metal ball fixed to a chain and thrown as a sport **3** ANATOMY the **malleus** in the ear —*picture* → EAR

hammer² /'hæmə/ verb [I/T] **1** to hit something with a hammer **2** to hit something hard, or to hit it many times: *He hammered on the door.*

hammock /'hæmək/ noun [C] a bed consisting of a long piece of cloth or net that is tied at each end to a post or tree

hamper /'hæmpə/ verb [T] to prevent something from happening normally, or to prevent someone from moving normally

hamstring /'hæm,strɪŋ/ noun [C] ANATOMY a **tendon** that is behind the knee

hand¹ /hænd/ noun **1** [C] the part of the body at the end of each arm that you use for holding things: *Mrs Bennet put her hands over her ears to shut out the noise.* ♦ *The park was full of young couples holding hands* (=holding each other's hands). ♦ *The two men introduced themselves and shook hands.* ♦ *He was holding a mug of coffee in his left hand.* **2** [singular] help: *Would you like a hand with the cleaning up?* ♦ *Lydia lent a hand* (=helped) *with the costumes.* ♦ *Can you give me a hand* (=help me) *with these boxes?* **3** [C] the hands on a clock are the long parts that move round and show the time **4** [C] the cards that have been given to you in a game of cards
PHRASES **by hand 1** using your hands rather than a machine **2** if a letter is delivered by hand, someone brings it instead of sending it by post
first/second/third hand if you experience something first hand, you experience it yourself. If you experience something second hand or third hand, someone else tells you about it.
get/lay your hands on sth to manage to obtain

something: *I couldn't lay my hands on a copy of the book.*

go hand in hand to happen or exist together
have your hands full to be extremely busy
in hand if something is in hand, you are dealing with it
in sb's hands if something is in someone's hands, they are responsible for it: *The company is in the hands of the official receiver.*
off your hands if something is off your hands, you are no longer responsible for it
on hand 1 if someone is on hand, they are available to help you if you need them **2** if something is on hand, it is available to be used
on the one hand...on the other hand used for giving two different opinions about something
out of hand not well controlled: *We decided to leave before things got out of hand.*
out of your hands if something is out of your hands, someone else is now responsible for it
to hand near where you are and therefore available to use
→ OFFHAND

hand² /hænd/ verb [T] to give something to someone by holding it in your hand and offering it to them: *Talbot handed the paper to the man.* ♦ *Sarah handed me an envelope.*

PHRASAL VERBS **,hand sth 'back** to give something back to someone: *Jean handed the letter back to Doug.*
,hand sth 'down to give knowledge or skill to someone who is younger than you and will live after you have died
,hand sth 'in to give something to a person in authority: *Please hand in your keys when you leave the hotel.*
,hand sth 'out to give things to different people in a group: *Would you hand these papers out for me?*
,hand (sb) 'over to stop speaking to or dealing with someone and let someone else do it
,hand sth 'over 1 to give something to someone by holding it in your hand and offering it to them: *He handed the car keys over to Stella.* **2** to give power or control to someone else: *They formally hand power over to the new government next week.*

handbag /'hæn(d),bæg/ noun [C] a small bag that women use for carrying personal things such as money and keys

handball noun SPORTS **1** /'hænd,bɔːl/ [U] a game in which two teams of players use their hands to pass a ball and try to score goals **2** /,hænd'bɔːl/ [C/U] in football, the offence of touching the ball with the hands

handbook /'hæn(d),bʊk/ noun [C] a small book that gives information or instructions

handbrake /'hæn(d),breɪk/ noun [C] ENGINEERING the piece of equipment in a car that you pull with your hand in order to prevent the car from moving after you have stopped it

handcuff /'hæn(d),kʌf/ verb [T] to put handcuffs on someone

handcuffs /'hæn(d),kʌfs/ noun [plural] metal rings that a police officer puts round a prisoner's wrists to stop them from using their hands

'hand ,fork noun [C] AGRICULTURE a small tool that is held in one hand, used for digging small amounts of soil and for planting young plants —*picture*
→ AGRICULTURAL

handful /'hæn(d)fʊl/ noun **1** [singular] a very small number of people or things: *Only a handful of people attended the meeting.* **2** [C] the amount of something that you can hold in your hand: *a handful of coins*

'hand gre,nade noun [C] a small bomb that explodes after a soldier throws it

handgun /'hæn(d),gʌn/ noun [C] a small gun that is used with one hand

'hand-,held adj small enough to hold in the hands: *a hand-held computer*

,hand 'hot adj hand hot water is not too hot to put your hands into comfortably

handicap /'hændi,kæp/ noun [C] **1** a disadvantage that prevents someone from doing something well **2** SPORTS in golf, extra shots that a weaker player is allowed to take in order to make a competition fairer **3** SPORTS a horse race in which the best riders carry extra weights in their **saddle** to make the competition fairer

handicapped /'hændi,kæpt/ adj *old-fashioned* someone who is handicapped has a permanent injury, illness, or other problem that makes them unable to use their body or mind as well as most people can. People now think that this word is offensive and prefer to talk about **people with disabilities**.

handiwork /'hændi,wɜːk/ noun [U] something that someone has done or created

handkerchief /'hæŋkə,tʃɪf/ (plural **handkerchieves** /'hæŋkə,tʃiːvz/) noun [C] a small piece of cloth or paper that you use for wiping your nose or eyes

handle¹ /'hænd(ə)l/ verb [T] **1** to deal with someone or something: *The government was criticized for the way it handled the crisis.* ♦ *The newer computers can handle massive amounts of data.* ♦ *Flight attendants are trained to handle difficult passengers.* **2** to touch or hold something: *All chemicals must be handled with care.* **3** to control an animal or a vehicle using your hands: *She handled the horse very confidently.* **4** to buy and sell goods, especially illegally: *He denied burglary but admitted handling stolen goods.*

handle² /'hænd(ə)l/ noun [C] the part of something that you use for holding it: *knives with plastic handles* ♦ *a door handle*

handlebars /'hænd(ə)l,bɑːz/ noun [plural] the part of a bicycle that you hold with your hands and use for controlling it

handling /'hændlɪŋ/ noun [U] **1** the way that someone deals with a particular situation **2** the way in which someone touches, uses, or deals with something

'hand ,luggage noun [U] TOURISM small bags that passengers are allowed to carry with them on a plane or bus

handmade /,hæn(d)'meɪd/ adj made by a person, not by a machine

handout /'hændaʊt/ noun [C] **1** a piece of paper with information on it that a teacher gives to everyone in a class **2** *showing disapproval* money or goods that are given to people who need them

handover /'hænd,əʊvə/ noun [singular] the process of formally giving something to someone else

handphone /'hæn(d),fəʊn/ noun [C] a **mobile phone**

handrail /'hænd,reɪl/ noun [C] CONSTRUCTION a long horizontal bar that people can hold on to for support, for example at the side of stairs

handset /'hæn(d),set/ noun [C] **1** the part of a telephone that you hold next to your ear **2** a small piece of electronic equipment that you hold and use for controlling another piece of equipment from a distance

handshake /'hæn(d),ʃeɪk/ noun [C] the act of shaking someone's hand, for example as a greeting

handsome /'hæns(ə)m/ adj **1** a handsome man or boy has a very attractive face= GOOD-LOOKING **2** a handsome amount of money is large: *a handsome profit*

hands-'on adj **1** hands-on experience involves you doing something, not just reading about it **2** someone who is hands-on is involved in something and does not make other people do the work

handstand /'hænd,stænd/ noun [C] a movement in which someone puts their hands on the ground and balances their body and legs in the air

handwriting /'hænd,raitiŋ/ noun [U] the particular way that someone writes when they use a pen or pencil

handwritten /,hænd'rit(ə)n/ adj written using a pen or pencil, not printed or **typed**

handy /'hændi/ (**handier, handiest**) adj **1** useful: *a handy tool* **2** close to you and therefore easy to reach or easy to get to: *Keep your pills handy just in case you feel seasick.* **3** good at doing things with your hands: *He's very handy with a paintbrush* (=good at painting). **PHRASE come in handy** to be useful: *A spare set of keys might come in handy.*

handyman /'hændi,mæn/ (plural **handymen** /'hændi,men/) noun [C] someone who is good at making and repairing things

hang¹ /hæŋ/ (**hangs, hanging, hung** /hʌŋ/) verb **1** [I/T] to put something somewhere with its top part fixed and its bottom part free to move, or to be in this position: *Philip hung his hat on a hook behind the door.* ♦ *The children's coats were hanging on pegs behind the door.* ♦ *Her dark hair hung down over her shoulders.* **2** (**hanged**) [T] to kill someone by putting a rope around their neck and making them fall: *He was hanged for murder in 1942.* ♦ *After his wife left, he tried to hang himself.* **3** [I] if something such as smoke or a smell hangs in the air, it remains there: *A thick mist hung over the fields.* **4** [T] to fix paper to a wall as decoration: *We spent the afternoon hanging wallpaper in our bedroom.*
PHRASAL VERBS ,hang 'up to finish using the telephone at the end of a conversation: *Greg hung up and sat back in his chair.* ♦ *'Get lost!' she shouted, and hung up on me.*
,hang sth 'up to hang a piece of clothing on something: *The women hung up their coats and sat down.*

hang² /hæŋ/ noun **get the hang of sth** informal to learn to do something

hangar /'hæŋə/ noun [C] a very large building where planes are kept

hanger /'hæŋə/ noun [C] a **coat hanger**

'hang-,glider noun [C] SPORTS a simple aircraft with no engine that someone hangs under and controls by moving their body —**'hang-,gliding** noun [U]

hanging /'hæŋiŋ/ noun [C/U] a punishment in which someone is killed by putting a rope around their neck and making them fall

hangman /'hæŋmən/ (plural **hangmen** /'hæŋmən/) noun [C] someone whose job is to kill people by **hanging** them

hangover /'hæŋ,əʊvə/ noun [C] the feeling of being tired and ill as a result of having drunk too much alcohol

the Hang Seng Index /,hæŋ 'seŋ ,ındeks/ BUSINESS, ECONOMICS the value of companies in the Hong Kong **stock market** on a particular day

'hang ,time noun [U] COMPUTING the time between when a computer stops operating, preventing someone

from working, and when it starts again, allowing them to continue working

Hanukkah /'hɑːnəkə/ noun [C/U] RELIGION an important Jewish religious festival that takes place in November or December

haphazard /,hæp'hæzəd/ adj done in a way that is not carefully planned or organized —**haphazardly** adv

haploid /'hæplɔɪd/ adj BIOLOGY having a single set of unpaired chromosomes

happen /'hæpən/ verb [I] to take place, usually without being planned= OCCUR: *The accident happened at 4.30 pm yesterday.* ♦ *He seemed to be unaware of what was happening around him.* ♦ *What happens if I press this button?* ♦ *Let's just wait and see what happens.*
PHRASES happen to do sth to do something by chance: *I happened to meet an old friend in town.*
whatever happens used for saying that nothing will change a situation: *Whatever happens tomorrow, this experience has been very valuable.*
PHRASAL VERB 'happen to sb/sth if something happens to someone or something, an event or action takes place that affects them: *This is the best thing that's ever happened to me.*

happening /'hæp(ə)nıŋ/ noun [C] an unusual or important event

happily /'hæpıli/ adv **1** used when you are pleased about something: *Happily, nobody was injured.* **2** in a happy way: *He and his wife are happily settled in their new home.* **3** in a willing way: *I'll happily cook the dinner if you want me to.*

happiness /'hæpınəs/ noun [U] the feeling of being happy

happy /'hæpi/ (**happier, happiest**) adj **1** feeling pleased and relaxed, with no worries ≠ UNHAPPY: *The children seem very happy at school.* ♦ *Sarah felt happy for the first time in her life.* ♦ *Money alone will never make you happy.* ♦ *You deserve all this success. We're very happy for you.* ♦ *Anna was excited and happy about the baby.* **2** satisfied that something is good or right: *We were happy that a decision has finally been made.* ♦ *Rising profits keep the bosses happy.* ♦ *Are you happy with this arrangement?* ♦ *I'm not very happy about the children being out so late.* **3** making you feel happy, or showing that you feel happy: *a happy marriage* ♦ *a happy smile*
PHRASES be happy to do sth if you are happy to do something, you are very willing to do it
Happy Birthday/Christmas/Easter/Anniversary used as a greeting on a particular occasion

haram /hɑː'rɑːm/ adj RELIGION haram food cannot be eaten according to Islamic law

harangue /hə'ræŋ/ verb [T] to criticize someone angrily —**harangue** noun [C]

harass /'hærəs, hə'ræs/ verb [T] to annoy or upset someone, for example by regularly criticizing them or treating them in a way that is offensive

harassed /'hærəst, hə'ræst/ adj tired and upset because you do not have enough time or energy

harassment /'hærəsmənt, hə'ræsmənt/ noun [U] annoying or unpleasant behaviour towards someone that takes place regularly: *the victims of sexual harassment*

harbour /'hɑːbə/ noun [C] an area of water next to the land where boats can stop

hard¹ /hɑːd/ adj

1 not easy to break	**5** not frightened
2 difficult to do	**6** unkind/angry
3 involving effort	**+ PHRASES**
4 full of problems	

1 stiff, firm, and not easy to bend or break: *hard wooden benches* ♦ *The ice on the lake was so hard we could walk on it.*
2 difficult to do: *Some of the questions were very hard.* ♦ *It is hard for young people to get jobs in this area.* ♦ *It's hard to explain why I love this place so much.*
3 involving a lot of effort: *Lifting stones this size is pretty **hard work.*** ♦ *I need to relax at the end of **a hard day**.*
4 unpleasant and full of problems: *My grandmother had a very **hard** life.* ♦ *The family has **had a hard time** recently.* ♦ *measures that are particularly **hard on** poor people*
5 strong and not easily frightened: *He likes to pretend he's hard, but he's really soft underneath.*
6 unkind, or angry: *Don't be too **hard on** her – she was only trying to help.*

PHRASES hard and fast fixed and not able to be changed
hard of hearing unable to hear well
learn the hard way to learn how to do something by trying to do it and making a lot of mistakes
—**hardness** noun [U]

hard² /hɑːd/ adv **1** using a lot of effort or force: *I didn't mean to hit him so hard.* ♦ *The whole team has worked very hard.* ♦ *I was trying very hard to remember her name.* **2** if it is raining or snowing hard, a lot of rain or snow is falling

hardback /ˈhɑːd,bæk/ noun [C] a book that has a hard cover → PAPERBACK

hardboard /ˈhɑːd,bɔːd/ noun [U] a type of thin wooden board

hard-boiled /,hɑːd ˈbɔɪld/ adj a hard-boiled egg has been cooked in boiling water until it is solid inside

hardboot /ˈhɑːd,buːt/ verb [T] COMPUTING to make a computer start again by turning it off and on = COLDBOOT

ˈhard ,copy noun [U] COMPUTING a printed copy of information that is held on a computer → SOFT COPY

hardcore /ˈhɑːd,kɔː/ noun [U] CONSTRUCTION broken brick or stone used as a base for floors, buildings, roads etc

,hard ˈcurrency noun [U] ECONOMICS money from a country with a strong economy

,hard ˈdisk or **,hard ˈdrive** noun [C] COMPUTING the part inside a computer that stores information → FLOPPY DISK —*picture* → COMPUTER

,hard ˈdrugs noun [plural] illegal drugs that are **addictive**, for example **heroin**

harden /ˈhɑːd(ə)n/ verb [I/T] **1** to become hard or firm, or to make something hard or firm ≠ SOFTEN: *The bread will harden if you don't cover it.* **2** to become strong, or to make someone or something strong ≠ SOFTEN: *The soldiers have been hardened by months in the field.*

hardened /ˈhɑːd(ə)nd/ adj someone who is hardened has had a lot of unpleasant experiences and is no longer upset by unpleasant things: *hardened criminals*

hardfacing /ˈhɑːd,feɪsɪŋ/ noun [U] TECHNOLOGY the application of a surface layer of hard material to another metal by welding, so that it will wear better

ˈhard ,hat noun [C] a hat made of metal or hard plastic worn by workers to protect their heads

hard-hearted /,hɑːd ˈhɑːtɪd/ adj someone who is hard-hearted has no sympathy for other people

hard-hitting /,hɑːd ˈhɪtɪŋ/ adj making criticisms in a very honest and direct way

hardline /ˈhɑːd,laɪn/ adj strict or extreme in your beliefs or opinions, and not willing to change them —**hardliner** noun [C]: *He's a right-wing hardliner.*

hardly /ˈhɑːdli/ adv **1** used for saying that something is almost not true, or almost does not happen at all: *He had **hardly** changed **at all**.* ♦ ***Hardly anyone** believed the man's story.* ♦ *It **hardly ever** rains here in the summer.* ♦ *We **could hardly** afford to pay the rent.* **2** used for saying that something had only just happened when something else happened: *She had hardly arrived when she started talking about leaving again.* **3** used when you think it is obvious that something is not true, not possible, not surprising etc: *This is hardly the time to start discussing finances.*

> **Hardly** is a negative word and is often used with words like 'any' and 'ever', but it should not be used with other negative words such as 'not' or 'never'.

,hard ˈpalate noun [C] ANATOMY the top part of the mouth, just behind the front teeth. The **soft palate** is the soft part next to it further back inside the mouth. Together these parts form the **palate**.

,hard-ˈpressed adj a person or organization that is hard-pressed does not have enough money for the things that they need
PHRASE be hard-pressed to do sth used for saying that something is difficult to do, or is unlikely to happen

hardship /ˈhɑːdʃɪp/ noun [C/U] the state of having a difficult life, or something that makes life very difficult: *financial hardship*

,hard ˈshoulder noun [C] an area at the side of a motorway where drivers can stop if they have problems

ˈhard-,soldering noun [U] TECHNOLOGY brazing (=joining two metals together at high temperatures using an alloy)

,hard ˈup adj *informal* not having much money

hardware /ˈhɑːd,weə/ noun [U] **1** COMPUTING computer equipment **2** the equipment and vehicles that are used in an activity, especially in the armed forces **3** equipment such as tools, pans, and other things that you use in your home and garden

,hard ˈwater noun [U] CHEMISTRY water that comes out of pipes that contains salts of calcium and **magnesium**

hard-wired /,hɑːd ˈwaɪəd/ adj a machine that is hard-wired works in a particular way because of the way it was built, and it cannot be changed by the person using it

ˈhard-,won adj achieved only after a lot of effort: *hard-won success*

hardwood /ˈhɑːd,wʊd/ noun [C/U] hard strong wood from trees such as **oak** or **mahogany**

,hard-ˈworking adj putting a lot of effort into your work

hardy /ˈhɑːdi/ (**hardier, hardiest**) adj strong and able to deal with unpleasant or extreme conditions

hare /heə/ noun [C] a wild mammal that is similar to a **rabbit** but bigger

harem /ˈhɑːriːm/ noun [C] **1** the wives of a rich man in some Muslim societies in the past **2** a part of a Muslim home in which only women live

harm¹ /hɑːm/ noun [U] injury, damage, or problems caused by something that you do: *Eating sweets* occasionally doesn't **do** children any **harm**.

PHRASES **not mean any harm** to not intend to hurt, damage, or upset someone or something

out of harm's way in a safe place

there's no harm in (doing) sth used for saying that something may be helpful: *There's no harm in trying.*

harm² /hɑːm/ verb [T] to injure, damage, or have a bad effect on someone or something: *chemicals that harm the environment ♦ Does watching violence on TV really harm children?*

harmattan /hɑːˈmætən/ noun [singular] **GEOGRAPHY** an extremely dry dusty wind that blows from the Sahara towards the western coast of Africa, especially between November and March

harmful /ˈhɑːmf(ə)l/ adj causing harm: *the harmful effects of cigarette smoke ♦ The fungus is not harmful to humans.*

harmless /ˈhɑːmləs/ adj not causing any harm —**harmlessly** adv

harmonic¹ /hɑːˈmɒnɪk/ adj **MUSIC** relating to the way that musical notes are combined to create **chords**

harmonic² /hɑːˈmɒnɪk/ noun [C] **MUSIC** a soft high note played on a **stringed instrument** by not pressing the string all the way down

harmonica /hɑːˈmɒnɪkə/ noun [C] **MUSIC** a musical instrument that you play by blowing and sucking as you move it from side to side between your lips= MOUTH ORGAN

har,monic pro'gression noun [C] **MUSIC** a series of **chords** played in a sequence

harmonious /hɑːˈməʊniəs/ adj **1** friendly and peaceful: *a harmonious relationship* **2** looking, sounding, or combining well with each other —**harmoniously** adv

harmonize /ˈhɑːmənaɪz/ verb **1** [T] to make laws or policies that work with those of a different country, organization etc **2** [I/T] to combine with other things in a pleasant way, or to make things combine in this way **3** [I] **MUSIC** to sing or play different notes at the same time, producing a pleasant sound

harmony /ˈhɑːməni/ (plural **harmonies**) noun **1** [U] a situation in which people live and work in a friendly, peaceful way with others: *social harmony* **2** [C/U] **MUSIC** musical notes that are sung or played at the same time, making a pleasant sound

harness¹ /ˈhɑːnɪs/ noun [C] **1** strong leather bands that are used for fastening an animal to a vehicle that it pulls **2** strong bands of leather, cloth, or rope that are used for fastening someone in a particular place, or for fastening something to their body

harness² /ˈhɑːnɪs/ verb [T] **1** to get control of something in order to use it for a particular purpose: *Humans first harnessed the power of electricity over 200 years ago.* **2** to put a harness on a person or animal

harp /hɑːp/ noun [C] **MUSIC** a musical instrument that consists of a row of strings stretched over a large upright frame —*picture* → MUSICAL INSTRUMENT, ORCHESTRA

harpoon /hɑːˈpuːn/ noun [C] a pole with a blade that is fixed to a rope, used for hunting **whales** —**harpoon** verb [T]

harpsichord /ˈhɑːpsɪˌkɔːd/ noun [C] **MUSIC** a musical instrument similar to a small piano

harrow /ˈhærəʊ/ noun [C] **AGRICULTURE** a piece of farm equipment used for breaking large lumps of soil into smaller pieces before planting crops

harrowing /ˈhærəʊɪŋ/ adj extremely upsetting or frightening

harsh /hɑːʃ/ adj **1** harsh conditions, places, or weather are unpleasant and difficult to live in **2** strict, unkind, and often unfair= SEVERE: *a harsh punishment* **3** loud or bright in an unpleasant way: *the harsh glare of the sun* —**harshly** adv

harvest¹ /ˈhɑːvɪst/ noun **1** [C] **AGRICULTURE** the activity of collecting a crop, or the time when crops are collected: *the grape harvest* **2** [C] **AGRICULTURE** the amount of a crop that is collected **3** [singular] *formal* the result of something that was done in the past

harvest² /ˈhɑːvɪst/ verb **1** [I/T] **AGRICULTURE** to collect a crop from the fields **2** [T] to collect plants, animals, or other things that can be eaten or used **3** [T] **HEALTH** to take organs, cells etc from a person's body —**harvester** noun [C], **harvesting** noun [U]

has /hæz, əz, həz/ 3rd person singular of the present tense of **have**

hash /hæʃ/ noun [C] the symbol #

hasn't /ˈhæz(ə)nt/ short form the usual way of saying or writing 'has not' when 'has' is an auxiliary verb. This is not often used in formal writing: *He hasn't arrived yet.*

haste /heɪst/ noun [U] *formal* great speed in doing something because you do not have much time

hasten /ˈheɪs(ə)n/ verb [T] to make something happen sooner or more quickly

hasty /ˈheɪsti/ adj **1** done in a hurry: *a hasty inspection* **2** doing something too quickly: *Don't be too hasty about making this decision.* —**hastily** adv

hat /hæt/ noun [C] a piece of clothing that you wear on your head: *a brown fur hat*

hatch¹ /hætʃ/ verb **1** [I/T] **BIOLOGY** if a baby bird, fish, or insect hatches, or if it is hatched, it comes out of its egg **2** [T] to plan something, especially in secret

hatch² /hætʃ/ noun [C] a small door in a floor or ceiling, or above the ground in a wall

hatchet /ˈhætʃɪt/ noun [C] a tool like a small **axe**

hatching /ˈhætʃɪŋ/ noun [U] **MATHS, PHYSICS** parallel lines drawn close together at an angle over an area

hate¹ /heɪt/ verb [T] **1** to dislike someone or something very much ≠ LOVE: *I hate the smell of cigarettes. ♦ I really hate his guts* (=hate him very much). **2** if you hate a particular situation or activity, you think that it is unpleasant or upsetting: *Glen hates to lose. ♦ I hate it when my parents argue.*

hate² /heɪt/ noun [U] the feeling of disliking someone or something very much ≠ LOVE

hateful /ˈheɪtf(ə)l/ adj extremely bad, unpleasant, or cruel

hatred /ˈheɪtrɪd/ noun [U] *formal* a feeling of hate

'hat ,trick noun [C] **SPORTS** three goals scored by the same person in one game of a sport such as football

haughty /ˈhɔːti/ adj proud and unfriendly

haul¹ /hɔːl/ verb [T] **1** to pull or carry something that is heavy from one place to another with a lot of effort = DRAG: *I hauled my luggage to the nearest hotel.* **2** to move someone by pulling them= DRAG: *He grasped Judy's arm and hauled her to her feet.* → COAL

haul² /hɔːl/ noun [C] **1** a large amount of something illegal such as drugs that is found by the police **2** the amount of fish that is caught in a net → LONG-HAUL

haulier /ˈhɔːliə/ noun [C] **BUSINESS** a person or company that carries goods by road or railway

haunch /hɔːntʃ/ noun [C] **CONSTRUCTION** a sloping piece of wood fixed to the top of a flat roof to get rid of rain water

haunches /'hɔːntʃɪz/ noun [plural] the top parts of the legs and the **buttocks**

haunt /hɔːnt/ verb [T] **1** if a place is haunted by the spirit of a dead person, people believe that it appears there **2** to make someone feel worried and upset for a long time: *Images from the war still haunt him.*

haunted /'hɔːntɪd/ adj **1** believed to be lived in or visited by the spirit of a dead person **2** looking frightened or worried

haunting /'hɔːntɪŋ/ adj beautiful and sad in a way that stays in your memory: *haunting melodies*

have /strong hæv, weak əv, həv/ (**has** /strong hæz, weak əz, həz/, **having**, **had** /strong hæd, weak əd, həd/) verb

1 in perfect tense	8 arrange for sth
2 describing feature	9 suffer from sth
3 own or hold sth	10 receive sth
4 do sth	11 referring to
5 stating a relationship	arrangements
6 eat or drink sth	12 give birth
7 saying what is	+ PHRASE
available	+ PHRASAL VERBS

1 [auxiliary verb] used for forming the **perfect tenses** of verbs. The perfect tenses are used for talking about what happened or began before now, or before another point in time: *Has anybody seen Dave this afternoon?* ♦ *I've been looking for you everywhere.* ♦ *'Have you washed your hands?' 'Of course I have.'*
2 have or have got [T] used for saying what the features or qualities of someone or something are: *The house didn't have electricity.* ♦ *She's got a lot of talent.* ♦ *He has very dark eyes.*
3 have or have got [T] to own something, or to have possession of something: *If you had a computer, I could email you.* ♦ *What's that you've got in your hand?* ♦ *Do you have a pen I could borrow?* ♦ *I haven't got any money on me.* ♦ *She has a job in our London office.*
4 [T] to do or experience something: *You should have a rest.* ♦ *Have a nice weekend!* ♦ *We almost had an accident.*
5 have or have got [T] used for stating someone's relationship with another person or other people: *Stephen has a sister in Mombasa.* ♦ *I've got a friend who works at the BBC.*
6 [T] to eat or drink something: *Can I have another piece of cake?* ♦ *Why don't you stay and have lunch with us?*
7 have or have got [T] used for saying what is available: *She hadn't got space for me in her car.* ♦ *I didn't have time to cook anything.*
8 [T] to arrange for someone to do something: *I'm having my hair cut today.*
9 have or have got [T] to suffer from an illness, disease, injury, or pain: *I've got a terrible headache.* ♦ *She has a broken arm.*
10 have or have got [T] to receive a message, advice, criticism etc: *We've not had any news from home.* ♦ *Did you have any help from your friends?*
11 have or have got [T] used for saying that you have arranged or planned to do something: *I've got an appointment tomorrow afternoon.* ♦ *She has a lot of work to do today.*
12 [T] to give birth to a baby: *Linda's **having a baby** in June.*

PHRASE **have to do sth** or **have got to do sth** if you have to do something, you must do it because it is necessary: *I have to get up early tomorrow.* ♦ *You **don't***

have to come (=it is not necessary to come) *if you don't want to.*

- Questions and negatives using the auxiliary verb **have** are formed without **do**: *Has the meeting finished?* ♦ *You haven't eaten anything.*
- For many transitive senses of **have**, **have got** can also be used. Questions and negatives with these senses can be formed using **have got**, **have**, or **do**: *Has he got red hair?* ♦ *Have you any money?* ♦ *Does the car have four doors?* ♦ *I haven't got the courage to tell her.* ♦ *I'm afraid I haven't the time.* ♦ *Carol doesn't have much patience.*
- Questions and negatives with other transitive senses of **have** are formed with **do**: *Did you have a nice walk?* ♦ *I didn't have breakfast this morning.*
- In conversation or informal writing the auxiliary use of **have** is often shortened. **Have** can be shortened to **'ve**, **has** to **'s**, and **had** to **'d**: *They've already left.* ♦ *John's lost his ticket.* ♦ *I'd forgotten to tell you.* These short forms can be followed by 'not' to make negative sentences: *I've not seen anyone.* ♦ *She'd not arrived.*
- The ordinary transitive uses of **have** are not usually shortened, though **'ve** and **'d** forms are sometimes possible: *I've a sister who lives in New York.*
- Short forms are usually used before 'got': *I've got an idea.* ♦ *Jack's got the tickets.*
- Negative forms can also be shortened: **have not** can be shortened to **haven't**, **has not** can be shortened to **hasn't**, and **had not** can be shortened to **hadn't**.

PHRASAL VERBS 'have/have 'got sth a,gainst sb/sth to dislike someone or something for a particular reason: *We've got nothing against you personally.* ♦ *I've got nothing against exams for young children.*
,have sth 'on or have ,got sth 'on **1** to be wearing particular clothes, shoes etc: *Melissa had her new dress on.* **2** if you have the radio, television, heating etc on, you have switched it on and it is working

haven /'heɪv(ə)n/ noun [C] a place where people or animals can feel safe and happy

haven't /'hæv(ə)nt/ short form the usual way of saying or writing 'have not' when 'have' is an auxiliary verb. This is not often used in formal writing: *I haven't seen her all day.*

havoc /'hævək/ noun [U] a situation in which there is so much damage or trouble that something cannot continue normally: *Floods have **wreaked havoc** (=caused havoc) on the town.* → WREAK

hawk /hɔːk/ noun [C] **1** a large bird that kills other animals for food —*picture* → BIRD **2** a politician who prefers using military force to more peaceful methods ≠ DOVE

hay /heɪ/ noun [U] **AGRICULTURE** long grass that has been cut and dried so that it can be used as **fodder** for feeding farm animals

'hay ,fever noun [U] **HEALTH** a medical condition that affects the nose and eyes. It is caused by an allergy to pollen.

hayloft /'heɪ,lɒft/ noun [C] **AGRICULTURE** the area at the top of a farm building used for storing **hay**

haystack /'heɪ,stæk/ noun [C] **AGRICULTURE** a large pile of **hay** in a field, that is usually covered in order to store it

hazard /'hæzəd/ noun [C] something that could be dangerous or could cause damage: *a fire hazard* ♦ *Pollution is a major **health hazard** (=something that is dangerous to your health).*

hazardous /'hæzədəs/ adj dangerous to people's health or safety: *hazardous driving conditions*

,**hazardous 'waste** noun [U] **ENVIRONMENT** dangerous waste that is produced by something such as an industrial process

haze /heɪz/ noun [C/U] smoke, dust, or water in the air that makes it difficult to see clearly

hazy /'heɪzi/ adj **1** not clear because there is smoke, dust, or water in the air **2** not exact or sure: *hazy memories from childhood*

HCF abbrev **MATHS** highest common factor

HCI abbrev **COMPUTING** human computer interaction: the study of how people and computers communicate and react to each other

HD-DVD /,eɪtʃ di: ,di: vi: 'di:/ noun [C] a type of **DVD** that gives a much clearer picture than ordinary DVDs

HDSL /,eɪtʃ di: es 'el/ noun [C] **COMPUTING** High-Data Rate Digital Subscriber Line: a **DSL** that works at a fast speed

HDTV /,eɪtʃ di: ti: 'vi:/ noun [U] television that gives a much clearer picture than ordinary television

he /strong hi:, weak i, hi/ pronoun **1** used for referring to a man, boy, or male animal, when they have already been mentioned, or when it is obvious which one you are referring to: *I told William, but he didn't believe me.* ♦ *Like all dogs, he'll chase a rabbit if he sees one.* **2** old-fashioned used in a general way for referring to any person, whether they are male or female: *Everyone has a right to say what he thinks.*

HE abbrev **EDUCATION** higher education

head¹ /hed/ noun [C]

1 top part of body	5 where river begins
2 mind/thoughts	6 side of a coin
3 leader of group	+ PHRASES
4 top/front part	

1 the top part of the body that has the brain, eyes, mouth etc in it: *Lynn had a bruise on the side of her head.* ♦ *She **shook her head** (=moved it from side to side).* ♦ *Ron **nodded his head** (=moved it up and down) but said nothing.* —*picture* → BODY
2 your mind and thoughts: *A thought suddenly came into my head.* ♦ *He did the sums quickly **in his head**.* ♦ *I can't **get** that song **out of my head** (=cannot stop thinking about it).*
3 the leader or most important person in a group: *I'm meeting **the head of** the department tomorrow.*
4 the top or front part of something: *We walked straight to **the head of** the queue.*
5 **GEOGRAPHY** the beginning of a river, where the water comes from
6 heads [plural] the side of a coin that has a picture of a head on it. The other side is **tails**: *I'll toss a coin. You choose heads or tails.*
PHRASES a/per head for each person: *The meal cost £5 per head.*
go over sb's head if an idea, joke, or remark goes over someone's head, they cannot understand it
head of state the leader of a country, for example a king, queen, or president
head over heels completely in love with someone or something
→ BURY, NOD, SHAKE¹, TOP¹

head² /hed/ verb **1** [I] to go in a particular direction: *They headed north, across the desert.* ♦ *We decided to **head for** home.* **2** [T] to be in control of a group, organization, or activity: *Lord Justice Scott will head the inquiry.* **3** [T] to be first on a list, or first in a line of people: *Williams heads the police's list of suspects.*

4 [T] **SPORTS** to hit the ball with your head in football
PHRASE be heading/headed for sth if you are heading or headed for a situation, you are likely to be in that situation soon: *It appears that the current champions are heading for victory again.*

headache /'hedeɪk/ noun [C] a pain in your head: *I had a bad headache yesterday.*

headcam /'hed,kæm/ noun [C] a video camera that someone wears on their head

headcount /'hed,kaʊnt/ noun [C] an occasion when you count all the people in a place or organization, or the number of people that are counted

headed /'hedɪd/ adj with a particular title: *a document headed 'The Future of Farming'*

header /'hedə/ noun [C] **1** something that is printed at the top of a page or a computer document **2 SPORTS** in football, the action of hitting a ball with the head **3 CONSTRUCTION** a brick laid in a wall so that the smallest surface is showing

'**header ,bond** noun [C] **CONSTRUCTION** an arrangement of bricks in a wall that forms a pattern with the brick ends showing

,**head 'first** or **headfirst** /,hed'fɜ:st/ adv with the head in such a position that it hits something before the rest of the body

headgear /'hed,ɡɪə/ noun [U] hats and other things that you wear on your head

heading /'hedɪŋ/ noun [C] **1** the title at the top of a page or piece of writing **2** a word or phrase that gives a general description of a type of person or thing

headland /'hedlənd/ noun [C] **GEOGRAPHY** a narrow piece of land that sticks out into the sea —*picture* → EROSION

'**head ,lice** noun [plural] **HEALTH** tiny insects with six legs and no wings that live in the hair of humans. They bite the skin to suck blood, which causes **itching**. Their eggs are called **nits**.

headlight /'hed,laɪt/ noun [C] one of the two lights on the front of a vehicle

headline /'hed,laɪn/ noun **1** [C] the title of a newspaper story, printed in large letters **2 the headlines** [plural] the most important stories in the news: *The fuel crisis continues to dominate the headlines.* ♦ *Did the story **make the headlines** (=appear as one of the main reports)?*

headlong /'hed,lɒŋ/ adj, adv **1** moving with your head going first **2** very quickly and without thinking about what you are doing

headman /'hedmən/ noun [C] the leader of a village or large family group

headmaster /,hed'mɑ:stə/ noun [C] **EDUCATION** a male teacher who is in charge of a school

headmistress /,hed'mɪstrəs/ noun [C] **EDUCATION** a female teacher who is in charge of a school

,**head 'office** noun [C] the main office of an organization or company

,**head-'on** adv **1** if two vehicles crash head-on, the front of one hits the front of the other **2** if you deal with a problem head-on, you deal with it in a very direct way —'**head-,on** adj: *a head-on crash*

headphones /'hed,fəʊnz/ noun [plural] a piece of equipment that you wear over your ears in order to listen to the radio or recorded sound

headquarters /'hed'kwɔ:təz/ noun [plural] the place where a company, organization, or military unit has its main offices or its main centre of control

headrest /'hed,rest/ noun [C] the part of a chair or car seat that you lean your head against

headroom /'hed,ru:m/ noun [U] **1** the amount of space between your head and a ceiling, especially in a car **2** the amount of space between the top of a vehicle and a bridge

headset /'hed,set/ noun [C] a piece of radio or telephone equipment that you wear over your ears with a part that you can speak into

headstand /'hed,stænd/ noun [C] a position in which someone is upside down with their head and hands on the floor and their legs in the air

head 'start noun [singular] **1** an advantage over other people who are in the same situation as you: *The reading course* **gives** *young children* **a head start. 2** a situation in which you start a race before or in front of your opponent

headstone /'hed,stəʊn/ noun [C] a piece of stone that marks a **grave** (=place where a dead person is buried)

headstrong /'hed,strɒŋ/ adj determined to do what you want even if other people warn you not to do it

headteacher /,hed'ti:tʃə/ noun [C] **EDUCATION** a teacher who is in charge of a school

headwind /'hed,wɪnd/ noun [C] a wind that blows in the opposite direction to the one in which you are moving → TAILWIND

headword /'hed,wɜːd/ noun [C] one of the list of words in a dictionary. It is followed by an explanation of what it means.

heal /hiːl/ verb **1** [I/T] if an injury heals, or if someone heals it, the skin or bone grows back together and becomes healthy again: *The wound took a long time to heal.* **2** [I/T] if someone's emotional problems heal, or something heals them, they become happy again **3** [T] to make people stop fighting and become friendly again

healer /'hiːlə/ noun [C] **1** someone who is believed to be able to cure people who are ill, using special powers **2** something that heals someone

healing¹ /'hiːlɪŋ/ noun [U] the process of becoming healthy again

healing² /'hiːlɪŋ/ adj making someone feel better after they have been ill or unhappy: *a plant with healing properties*

health /helθ/ noun [U] **1 HEALTH** the condition of your body, especially whether or not you are ill: *His health improved once he stopped working.* ♦ *Lola is 85 and still* **in very good health.** ♦ *My father has been* **in poor health** *for some time.* ♦ *She's had serious* **health problems. 2** the degree to which something is successful: *Officials are worried about* **the health of** *the local technology industry.*

PHRASE **health and safety** the part of the government and legal system that deals with people's health and safety at work

'health ,care noun [U] **HEALTH** the services that look after people's health: *Homeless people need better access to health care.* —**healthcare** /'helθ,keə/ adj

'health ,centre noun [C] **HEALTH** a building where people can go to see a doctor or nurse

'health ,food noun [C/U] food that is good for you because it does not contain artificial substances

'health in,surance noun [U] a type of insurance that pays for your medical treatment when you are ill or injured

'health pro,fessional noun [C] **HEALTH** someone whose job involves providing medical care for people, for example a doctor or dentist

'health ,service noun [C] **HEALTH** a public service that is responsible for providing medical care

'health ,spa noun [C] a place similar to a hotel, or inside a hotel, with a swimming pool, **gym**, and rooms where people can have beauty treatments and **massage**

healthy /'helθi/ (**healthier, healthiest**) adj **1** physically strong and not ill ≠ UNHEALTHY: *a healthy baby* ♦ *I feel very* **healthy** *at the moment.* **2** making you strong and not ill ≠ UNHEALTHY: *a healthy diet* **3** working well and likely to continue to be successful ≠ UNHEALTHY: *The country still has a healthy economy.* **4** a healthy attitude is good and sensible ≠ UNHEALTHY —**healthily** adv

heap¹ /hiːp/ noun [C] a large untidy pile of something: *a heap of old car parts* ♦ *Dirty rags lay in a heap on the floor.*

heap² /hiːp/ verb [T] **1** to make a big untidy pile of things: *Clothing was heaped on the floor.* **2** if you heap praise or blame on someone, you praise or blame them a lot

heaped /hiːpt/ adj **1** a heaped spoon is completely full **2** filled or covered with a lot of something in a high pile: *a plate* **heaped with** *spaghetti*

hear /hɪə/ (**hears, hearing, heard** /hɜːd/) verb **1** [I/T] to realize that someone or something is making a sound: *Mary heard the sound of voices.* ♦ *Shh – I can't hear.* ♦ *He heard the door slam shut.* ♦ *She heard the dog barking outside.* ♦ *No one could* **hear what** *she said.* **2** [I/T] to receive information about something: *I heard he'd got a new job.* ♦ *Did you* **hear about** *Jim's party?* ♦ *I came home as soon as I* **heard what** *happened.* ♦ *We didn't* **hear of** *his death until many years later.* **3** [T] to listen to something such as a speech, performance, or programme: *I want to hear the news on the radio.* ♦ *He's got a great voice – you should hear him sing.* **4** [T] to listen to and judge a legal case in a court of law

PHRASAL VERBS **'hear from sb** if you hear from someone, they write to you or call you on the telephone: *It's ages since I heard from Jill.*

'hear of sb/sth if you have heard of someone or something, you know about their existence: *Have you heard of the author James Bomford?*

- When you **hear** a sound, you become conscious of it: *Did you hear the thunder last night?* ♦ *I didn't hear the door open.*
- When you **listen**, you deliberately pay attention to a sound in order to hear it: *I listened carefully but I couldn't hear what she was saying.* ♦ *I always listen to the radio in my car.*
- You **hear** something, but you **listen to** something.

hearing /'hɪərɪŋ/ noun **1** [U] the ability to hear sounds: *My hearing is getting worse as I get older.* **2** [C] **LAW** a meeting of a court of law or official organization in order to find out the facts about something **3** [singular] an opportunity to give your opinions and ideas

'hearing ,aid noun [C] a small piece of equipment that someone wears in their ear in order to help them to hear

'hearing-im,paired adj unable to hear as well as most people can

hearse /hɜːs/ noun [C] a large car that is used for carrying a dead person in a **coffin**

heart /hɑːt/ noun

1 organ in the body	**5** most important part
2 your feelings	**6** playing cards
3 central part	**+ PHRASES**
4 shape	

1 [C] **ANATOMY** in humans and most other animals, the organ in the chest that pumps blood around the body: *I could hear his **heart** beating.* ♦ *Did you know he had **a weak heart**?* —*picture* → CIRCULATION, ORGAN
2 [C] your feelings when they are considered as part of your character: *You have to do what your heart tells you is right.*
3 [singular] the central part of something: *a beautiful house deep **in the heart of** the English countryside*
4 [C] a shape that represents love —*picture* → SHAPE
5 [singular] the most important or basic part of something= CORE: *Cost-cutting **is at the heart of** their development plan.*
6 hearts [plural] the suit of playing cards that have red heart shapes on them

  PHRASES at heart used for saying what someone's basic character is: *She's really a good person at heart.*
have your heart set on (doing) sth to decide that you want something very much
sb's heart is not in sth used for saying that someone does not really care about something that they are doing
lose heart to feel disappointed and try less hard because of this
not have the heart to do sth to not want to do something because it seems cruel
(off) by heart if you know something by heart, you can remember all the words or music in it
take sth to heart to think about something seriously, often so that it upsets you
to your heart's content as much or as often as you like → BREAK¹

'heart at,tack noun [C] **HEALTH** an occasion when someone suddenly has a lot of pain in the chest because the heart stops working normally

heartbeat /'hɑːt,biːt/ noun [C] the movement or sound of the heart as it pumps blood around the body

heartbroken /'hɑːt,brəʊkən/ adj extremely sad and upset

heartburn /'hɑːt,bɜːn/ noun [U] **HEALTH** a pain that feels like burning in the chest and is a type of **indigestion**

'heart ,bypass noun [C] **HEALTH** a medical operation in which blood is directed around a blocked blood vessel in the heart

'heart ,chamber noun [C] **ANATOMY** one of the four parts that the heart is divided into

'heart dis,ease noun [U] **HEALTH** a serious medical condition that affects the heart

'heart ,failure noun [U] **HEALTH** a serious medical condition in which the heart stops working normally

heartfelt /'hɑːt,felt/ adj *formal* a heartfelt emotion, remark, or action is very sincere

hearth /hɑːθ/ noun [C] the floor around a **fireplace**

heartily /'hɑːtɪli/ adv **1** in a loud or enthusiastic way: *Jones laughed heartily at his joke.* **2** completely, or extremely: *They are heartily sorry for the trouble they've caused.* **3** if you eat heartily, you eat everything on your plate with enthusiasm

heartland /'hɑːt,lænd/ noun [C] the central part of a country

heartless /'hɑːtləs/ adj feeling or showing no sympathy or kindness= CALLOUS

,heart-'lung ma,chine noun [C] **HEALTH** a machine used for pumping blood and oxygen around someone's body when they are having a medical operation on their heart

heartwarming /'hɑːt,wɔːmɪŋ/ adj making you feel happy because people are being kind

hearty /'hɑːti/ adj **1** friendly and enthusiastic **2** a hearty meal is large

heat¹ /hiːt/ noun

1 hot quality	**5** for cooking
2 in science	**6** part of competition
3 heating for building	**+ PHRASES**
4 very hot weather	

1 [singular/U] the quality of being hot, or the degree to which something is hot: *We felt the intense heat from the fire.* ♦ *He could feel **the heat of** the sun on his back.*
2 [U] **PHYSICS** the energy that is produced when the temperature of something changes: *These chemical processes generate a lot of heat.*
3 [U] the **heating** system in a building: *The house had no heat or water.*
4 the heat [singular] very hot weather: *The local people get out of the city to escape the heat.*
5 the heat [singular] the flame or hot area on a **hob** that you cook on: *I turned the heat down a little.*
6 [C] **SPORTS** one of a set of games or races that form the first stage of a competition. The winners take part in the next stage.

  PHRASES in the heat of the moment at a time when you are too angry or excited to think carefully
on heat a female mammal that is on heat is ready to **mate** (=have sex) with a male. This is not used about humans.

heat² /hiːt/ verb [T] to make something hot, or to become hot: *Heat the oil gently in a large frying pan.*
  PHRASAL VERB ,heat (sth) 'up same as **heat²**: *I was just heating up some soup.*

heated /'hiːtɪd/ adj **1** made warm enough for people to use: *a heated swimming pool* **2** angry and excited: *a heated debate* —**heatedly** adv

heater /'hiːtə/ noun [C] a piece of equipment that is used for making a place warm, or for heating water —*picture* → DESALINATION

heath /hiːθ/ noun [C] **GEOGRAPHY** a wide area of wild land where only rough grass and bushes grow

heathen /'hiːð(ə)n/ noun [C] **RELIGION** *offensive old-fashioned* an insulting word for someone who is not a Christian or a follower of another major established religion

heather /'heðə/ noun [C/U] a plant with small purple or white flowers that grows on hills

heating /'hiːtɪŋ/ noun [U] **1** equipment that produces the heat used for heating a building **2** the process of making something warm

'heat ,pump noun [C] a piece of equipment that carries heat from one place to another, for example in a **fridge**

heatstroke /'hiːt,strəʊk/ noun [U] **HEALTH** a serious medical condition caused by being in a place that is extremely hot for too long a time

'heat ,transfer noun [U] **PHYSICS** the process by which heat moves from a hot material to a cooler material, until they both have the same temperature

heatwave /'hiːt,weɪv/ noun [C] a continuous period of very hot weather

heave /hiːv/ verb **1** [I/T] to push, pull, throw, or lift an object using a lot of effort: *Paul heaved the last box into the truck.* **2** [I] to move up and down with large regular movements: *Her chest heaved as she struggled to control her breathing.*

heaven /ˈhev(ə)n/ noun [U] RELIGION **heaven** or **Heaven** the place where God is believed to live

heavenly /ˈhev(ə)nli/ adj in or from heaven

heavily /ˈhevɪli/ adv **1** very, or to a large degree: *heavily populated areas* ♦ *Her work was heavily influenced by her father's.* ♦ *The men were heavily armed* (=carrying a lot of weapons). **2** in large amounts: *They had borrowed heavily to buy the boat.* ♦ *She had been smoking heavily since her teens.* **3** with a lot of force or effort: *She leaned heavily on the table.* ♦ *The older man was now breathing heavily.* **4** slowly, in a way that shows that you feel sad or tired: *She grabbed the chair and pulled herself up heavily.*

heavy /ˈhevi/ (**heavier, heaviest**) adj

1 with a lot of weight	**5** serious/difficult
2 many things	**6** of food
3 with physical effort	**7** big or powerful
4 with a lot of force etc	

1 a heavy object or person weighs a lot ≠ LIGHT: *She was struggling with a heavy suitcase.* ♦ *He was too heavy for the nurses to lift.*
2 used for saying that there is a lot of something, or that something is done a lot: *Traffic is very heavy on the roads tonight.* ♦ *The school places a heavy emphasis on music.* ♦ *heavy rain and strong winds* ♦ *There was heavy fighting in the capital yesterday.* ♦ *Sandra is a heavy smoker* (=she smokes a lot).
3 involving a lot of physical effort or force ≠ LIGHT: *a heavy blow to the head* ♦ *They did most of the heavy work in the morning.*
4 using a lot of bombs, guns, or other weapons: *Industrial areas came under heavy bombardment.* ♦ *reports of heavy air strikes on the capital*
5 too serious, difficult, or frightening to be good or enjoyable: *She felt their relationship was getting too heavy.* ♦ *His new book is a bit heavy.* ♦ *a heavy responsibility*
6 food that is heavy is rather solid and not enjoyable ≠ LIGHT
7 large, thick, or powerful: *The men wore heavy coats and gloves.* ♦ *a small fishing boat struggling in heavy seas* ♦ *Do not operate any heavy machinery while taking this medication.*
—**heaviness** /ˈhevinəs/ noun [U]

heavy-ˈduty adj strong and not easily damaged: *heavy-duty plastic*

heavy ˈindustry noun [U] BUSINESS industry that produces materials such as coal or steel, or large objects such as cars or ships

heavy ˈmetal noun [U] **1** CHEMISTRY a metal that has a high density **2** MUSIC a type of loud rock music that developed in the 1970s

heavy ˈwater noun [U] CHEMISTRY water with the hydrogen in it replaced by **deuterium**. It is used in **nuclear reactors**.

heavyweight /ˈheviˌweɪt/ noun [C] **1** SPORTS a **boxer** or **wrestler** in the heaviest weight group **2** someone or something that has a lot of influence, status, or knowledge: *political heavyweights*

Hebrew[1] /ˈhiːbruː/ noun **1** [U] one of the official languages of Israel **2** [C] a Jewish person in ancient times

Hebrew[2] /ˈhiːbruː/ adj **1** relating to the Hebrew language **2** of Jewish people

heckle /ˈhek(ə)l/ verb [I/T] to interrupt a speaker or performer by shouting at them —**heckler** noun [C], **heckling** noun [U]

hectare /ˈhekteə/ noun [C] a unit for measuring an area of land, equal to 10,000 square metres

hectic /ˈhektɪk/ adj full of busy activity

he'd /strong hiːd, weak iːd/ short form **1** the usual way of saying or writing 'he had' when 'had' is an auxiliary verb. This is not often used in formal writing: *He knew he'd seen her before.* **2** the usual way of saying or writing 'he would'. This is not often used in formal writing: *He'd come if you asked him.*

hedge[1] /hedʒ/ noun [C] a line of bushes or small trees that are growing close together around a garden or a field

hedge[2] /hedʒ/ verb [I] to avoid answering a question directly, or to avoid making a definite decision

ˈhedge ˌfund noun [C] BUSINESS a financial organization that invests money that has a high risk of being lost but which may make a very large profit

hedgehog /ˈhedʒˌhɒg/ noun [C] a small wild mammal with a round body that is covered with sharp **spikes**

heed /hiːd/ verb [T] formal to listen carefully to someone's advice or warning, and do what they suggest

heel /hiːl/ noun [C] **1** the back part of the foot, below the ankle —*picture* → BODY **2** the bottom part of the back of a shoe
PHRASE **(hard/hot/close) on the heels of 1** following close behind someone or something **2** happening soon after another event → HEAD[1]

hefty /ˈhefti/ adj **1** large and heavy **2** a hefty amount of money is very large

hegemony /hɪˈgeməni, ˈhedʒəməni/ noun [U] formal political control or influence, especially by one country over other countries

the Hegira /ˈhedʒɪrə, hɪˈdʒaɪrə/ noun [singular] RELIGION Muhammad's escape from Mecca to Medina in AD 622. The Muslim system of counting years is calculated from this time.

HEI abbrev EDUCATION higher education institutions

heifer /ˈhefə/ noun [C] a young cow

height /haɪt/ noun **1** [C/U] how high something is, or how tall someone is: *He was about the same height as his wife.* ♦ *What height do you want the picture at?* **2** [singular] the time or level of greatest activity: *The excitement was at its height.* ♦ *Jeans were once again the height of fashion.* **3 heights** [plural] a high place or position: *Dave was trying to overcome his fear of heights.* **4 heights** [plural] a high level of activity or success: *His popularity has reached new heights.*

heighten /ˈhaɪt(ə)n/ verb [I/T] if something heightens a feeling or emotion, or if a feeling or emotion heightens, it becomes stronger

heinous /ˈheɪnəs/ adj very formal a heinous act or crime is extremely evil

heir /eə/ noun [C] someone who will receive money, property, or a title when another person dies

heiress /ˈeəres/ noun [C] a woman or girl who will receive money or property when another person dies

heirloom /ˈeəˌluːm/ noun [C] a valuable or special possession that has belonged to one family for many years

the Hejira /'hedʒɪrə, hɪ'dʒaɪrə/ noun RELIGION the Hegira

held /held/ the past tense and past participle of **hold¹**

helicopter /'helɪˌkɒptə/ noun [C] an aircraft with large metal blades on top that spin round and lift it into the air

'helicopter ˌview noun [C] BUSINESS a general way of considering a problem

helipad /'helɪˌpæd/ noun [C] a flat area for helicopters to land on and take off from, often on top of a building

heliport /'helɪˌpɔːt/ noun [C] a small airport for helicopters

helium /'hiːliəm/ noun [U] CHEMISTRY a gas that is lighter than air and is an element. It has the lowest boiling point of any substance. Chemical symbol: **He**

helix /'hiːlɪks/ (plural **helices** /'hiːlɪsiːz/) noun [C] MATHS a shape formed by a long, continuously curving line= SPIRAL

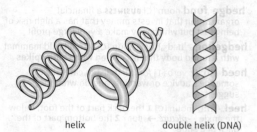

helix   double helix (DNA)

he'll /strong hiːl, weak iːl/ short form the usual way of saying or writing 'he will'. This is not often used in formal writing: He'll be here around noon.

hell /hel/ noun [U] **1** hell or Hell RELIGION in some religions, the place where bad people are believed to be sent to suffer when they die **2** a situation that is extremely unpleasant

hello /hə'ləʊ/ interjection **1** used as a greeting when you meet someone or begin to talk to someone on the telephone: Hello, my name is Anna. **2** used for calling to someone to get their attention: Hello! We're over here!

helm /helm/ noun [C] a wheel or handle used for making a boat go in the direction that you want it to go in
PHRASE **at the helm** in charge, or in the position of a leader

helmet /'helmɪt/ noun [C] a hard hat that you wear to protect your head

helminth /'helmɪnθ/ noun [C] BIOLOGY a parasitic worm such as a **tapeworm** or a **fluke**

help¹ /help/ verb **1** [I/T] to give someone support or information so that they can do something more easily: Can you help me find my glasses? ♦ Her brother offered to **help** her **with** her homework. ♦ Her work involves helping people to find jobs. **2** [I/T] to make something better or easier: Organic farming methods help the environment. ♦ We hope this **helps to** clarify the situation. **3** [T] to give someone food or drink: **Help yourselves to** more rice.
PHRASES **sb cannot/can't help sth** used for saying that someone cannot stop themselves doing something: She couldn't help laughing when she saw it.
sb cannot/can't help it if used for saying that someone cannot be blamed for a situation: I can't help it if you're upset.

PHRASAL VERB **ˌhelp (sb) 'out** to help someone by doing a particular job, or by giving them money: My family has always helped me out. ♦ He always **helped out with** the housework.

Word family: **help**
Words in the same family as **help**
■ helper n
■ helpless adj   ■ helplessly adv
■ helpful adj   ■ unhelpful adj
■ helpfully adv   ■ unhelpfully adv

help² /help/ noun **1** [U] the process of helping someone, or something that you do to help someone: Do you want some **help with** that? **2** [singular/U] a person or thing that helps: You've been a real help to me, Carrie. **3** [U] COMPUTING the part of a computer program that gives you information: Try the help menu.

help³ /help/ interjection used for asking for urgent help: Help! I'm going to fall.

helper /'helpə/ noun [C] someone who helps a person or organization

helpful /'helpf(ə)l/ adj **1** a helpful person helps you by doing something, or by giving you useful advice or information ≠ UNHELPFUL: a traditional hotel with very helpful staff **2** useful, or providing help: It's helpful to have a calculator for this exam. ♦ Exercise is helpful for controlling high blood pressure. —**helpfully** adv

helping /'helpɪŋ/ noun [C] an amount of food that is served to one person at a meal= SERVING

helpless /'helpləs/ adj not able to do anything without help —**helplessly** adv

'help ˌscreen noun [C] COMPUTING a screen in a computer program or website that contains advice on how to use the program or website

hem /hem/ noun [C] the bottom edge of something made of cloth that is folded and sewn in place

hemisphere /'hemɪˌsfɪə/ noun [C] **1** GEOGRAPHY one half of the Earth. The **northern hemisphere** is the part of the world north of the equator, and the **southern hemisphere** is the part south of it. **2** MATHS one half of a sphere → CEREBRAL HEMISPHERE —picture → SHAPE

hemorrhage /'hem(ə)rɪdʒ/ the American spelling of **haemorrhage**

hemp /hemp/ noun [U] a plant that is used for making rope. It is also used for making the drug **cannabis**.

hen /hen/ noun [C] **1** a female chicken —picture → BIRD **2** the female of any type of bird

hence /hens/ adv formal **1** therefore: Alcohol can cause liver failure and hence death. **2** used for saying how many years, months, or days from now something will happen

henceforth /ˌhens'fɔːθ/ or **henceforward** /ˌhens'fɔːwəd/ adv formal from this time into the future

hendecagon /hen'dekəgən, hen'dekəgɒn/ noun [C] MATHS a geometric shape with eleven straight sides

'hen ˌhouse noun [C] a building where **hens** are kept

'hen ˌnight or **'hen ˌparty** noun [C] a celebration for a woman who is about to be married. Only her women friends go to it.

henry /'henri/ (plural **henrys**) noun [C] PHYSICS the SI unit of electrical **inductance**, which is equal to an **electric potential** of one **volt** created in a closed circuit by a current varying by one **ampere** per second. Symbol H

hepatic /hɪˈpætɪk/ adj ANATOMY relating to the liver

hepatic portal vein /hɪˌpætɪk ˈpɔːt(ə)l veɪn/ noun [C] ANATOMY the vein that takes blood containing substances from food directly to the liver

hepatitis /ˌhepəˈtaɪtɪs/ noun [U] HEALTH an infectious disease of the liver

heptagon /ˈheptəgən/ noun [C] MATHS a geometric shape with seven straight sides —picture → SHAPE —**heptagonal** /hepˈtægən(ə)l/ adj

her /strong hɜː, weak ə, hə/ determiner, pronoun **1** the object form of 'she', used for referring to a woman, girl, or female animal when they have already been mentioned or when it is obvious which one you are referring to: Where's Susan? Has anyone seen her? ♦ Mary asked me to write to her. **2** belonging to a woman, girl, or female animal that has already been mentioned: She parked her car across the road. ♦ Emma's invited us to her party.

herald /ˈherəld/ verb [T] to announce something, or to be a sign that something is going to happen soon

herb /hɜːb/ noun [C] **1** a plant that is used as a medicine, or for adding flavour to food **2** BIOLOGY a herbaceous plant that is short and usually has a soft green stem

herbaceous /həˈbeɪʃəs/ adj BIOLOGY a herbaceous plant has a soft green stem and all its parts above ground level die after the growing season

herbal /ˈhɜːb(ə)l/ adj containing herbs, or made from herbs

herbalist /ˈhɜːbəlɪst/ noun [C] someone who grows, sells, or prepares herbs for use in medicine, or who treats ill people with herbal medicines —**herbalism** noun [U]

herbal ˈmedicine noun HEALTH **1** [C/U] medicine made from plants **2** [U] the treatment of illnesses with medicines made from plants

herbicide /ˈhɜːbɪsaɪd/ noun [C/U] AGRICULTURE a chemical used for killing weeds and other plants that are not wanted

herbivore /ˈhɜːbɪˌvɔː/ noun [C] BIOLOGY an animal that eats only plants

herbivorous /hɜːˈbɪv(ə)rəs/ adj BIOLOGY eating only or mainly grass or other plants

herd¹ /hɜːd/ noun [C] a large group of animals of the same type that live and move about together

herd² /hɜːd/ verb [T] **1** AGRICULTURE to make a group of animals move somewhere together **2** to move people as a group from one place to another

herder /ˈhɜːdə/ noun [C] AGRICULTURE a **herdsman**

herdsman /ˈhɜːdzmən/ (plural **herdsmen** /ˈhɜːdzmən/) noun [C] AGRICULTURE someone who looks after a herd of animals as their job

here /hɪə/ adv, interjection

1 in or to this place	**4** happening now
2 when offering or giving sth	**5** when sb/sth is found
3 at this point	**+ PHRASE**

1 in or to the place where you are, or where you are pointing: We've lived here for over 20 years. ♦ Come here. ♦ Sign your name here. ♦ The house looks big from here.
2 spoken used when you are offering or giving something to someone: Here, use my handkerchief. ♦ Here's £5 – go and buy yourself something nice.
3 at this point in a process, discussion, or series of events: Let's stop here and consider what we've said so far.
4 happening at the present time, or in the present situation: Summer is here at last.
5 spoken used when you have just found a particular person or thing: Oh, here are my glasses. I thought I'd lost them. ♦ Ah, here you are! I've been looking everywhere for you.

PHRASE **here and there** in or to several different places: Papers were scattered here and there.
→ NEITHER

hereby /hɪəˈbaɪ/ adv formal used for stating that something that has been said or written is now official

hereditary /həˈredət(ə)ri/ adj **1** BIOLOGY, HEALTH a hereditary disease or other characteristic is passed from a parent to their child in their genes: Cystic fibrosis is a hereditary condition. **2** LAW a hereditary title or right is officially passed from a parent to their child

heredity /həˈredəti/ noun [U] BIOLOGY, HEALTH the genetic process by which a parent's characteristics or diseases are passed to their child

heresy /ˈherəsi/ (plural **heresies**) noun [C/U] RELIGION a belief that is considered wrong because it is very different from what most people believe, or because it opposes the official principles of a religion

heretic /ˈherətɪk/ noun [C] RELIGION someone who believes things that are considered wrong because they are very different from what most people believe, or because they oppose the official principles of a religion —**heretical** /həˈretɪk(ə)l/ adj

heritage /ˈherɪtɪdʒ/ noun [C/U] SOCIAL STUDIES the art, buildings, traditions, and beliefs that a society considers to be important parts of its history and culture

ˈheritage ˌcentre noun [C] TOURISM a building where visitors get information about a place, its people, and the natural features of the area

ˈheritage ˌcoast noun [C] TOURISM a part of a coast that is considered to be of special value and that cannot therefore be built on

ˈheritage ˌlanguage noun [C] LANGUAGE in English-speaking countries, a language other than English that is the main language someone learns as a child

ˈheritage ˌsite noun [C] TOURISM a place that is legally protected because there is something of natural or cultural importance there

hermaphrodite /hɜːˈmæfrədaɪt/ noun [C] BIOLOGY a person, other animal, or plant that has both male and female sex organs

hermit /ˈhɜːmɪt/ noun [C] someone who chooses to live alone, or someone who spends most of their time alone

hermitage /ˈhɜːmɪtɪdʒ/ noun [C] RELIGION a building where a group of religious hermits live

hernia /ˈhɜːniə/ noun [C] HEALTH a medical condition in which an organ pushes itself through the muscles around it

hero /ˈhɪərəʊ/ (plural **heroes**) noun [C] **1** someone who has done something very brave **2** someone who you admire a lot **3** LITERATURE, ARTS the main male character of a book, film, or play ≠ VILLAIN

heroic /hɪˈrəʊɪk/ adj **1** very brave = COURAGEOUS **2** showing great determination to achieve something: their heroic effort to protect the future of the local hospital **3** relating to a hero —**heroically** /hɪˈrəʊɪkli/ adv

heroin /ˈherəʊɪn/ noun [U] a strong illegal drug that is very **addictive**

heroine /ˈherəʊɪn/ noun [C] **1 LITERATURE, ARTS** the main female character of a book, film, or play **2** a woman who you admire a lot = HERO

heroism /ˈherəʊ,ɪz(ə)m/ noun [U] behaviour that proves that someone is very brave

heron /ˈherən/ noun [C] a large bird with a long neck that lives near water

herpes /ˈhɜːpiːz/ noun [U] **HEALTH** an infectious disease in which sore red spots appear on someone's sex organs or near their mouth

herring /ˈherɪŋ/ (plural **herring**) noun [C] a long thin silver sea fish, or this fish eaten as food

hers /hɜːz/ pronoun a **possessive** form of 'she', used for referring to something that belongs to a woman, girl, or female animal that has already been mentioned: *His hand reached out and touched hers.* ♦ *She introduced us to some friends of hers.*

herself /*strong* həˈself, *weak* əˈself/ pronoun **1** the reflexive form of 'she', used for showing that the woman, girl, or female animal that does something is also affected by what she does: *She's going to buy herself a new jacket.* ♦ *Pam was looking at herself in the mirror.* **2** used for emphasizing that you are referring to a particular woman, girl, or female animal: *The queen herself will attend the meeting.* ♦ *She has enough money to pay for it herself.*

  PHRASES **(all) by herself 1** alone: *Annie's too young to travel by herself.* **2** without help from anyone else: *Sally had organized the whole party by herself.*
  (all) to herself not sharing something with anyone else: *Everyone had gone away, and she had the apartment all to herself.*
  be/feel/seem herself to be in a normal mental or physical state: *Beth wasn't quite herself that evening.*

hertz /hɜːts/ (plural **hertz**) noun [C] **PHYSICS** a unit for measuring the frequency of **sound waves** and **radio waves**. Symbol Hz

he's /*strong* hiːz, *weak* iːz/ short form **1** the usual way of saying or writing 'he is'. This is not often used in formal writing: *He's in Seattle this weekend.* **2** the usual way of saying or writing 'he has' when 'has' is an auxiliary verb. This is not often used in formal writing: *He's decided to move.*

hesitant /ˈhezɪtənt/ adj doing something slowly because you are nervous or not certain about it —**hesitancy** noun [U], **hesitantly** adv

hesitate /ˈhezɪteɪt/ verb [I] to pause before doing something because you are nervous or not certain about it: *He hesitated a moment, and then knocked on the door.*

hesitation /ˌhezɪˈteɪʃ(ə)n/ noun [C/U] a pause before doing something, or a feeling that you should not do it, because you are nervous or not certain about it

HET abbrev **EDUCATION** Higher Education and Training

heterogeneous /ˌhetərəʊˈdʒiːniəs/ adj *formal* consisting of many different types of people or things ≠ HOMOGENEOUS

hetero,geneous 'mixture noun [C] **CHEMISTRY** a mixture of two or more substances that can be easily separated

heterosexual /ˌhetərəʊˈsekʃuəl/ adj sexually attracted to people of the opposite sex —**heterosexual** noun [C]

heterotrophic /ˌhetərəʊˈtrɒfɪk/ adj **BIOLOGY** relating to organisms that take in food made by other organisms. Humans and other animals are

heterotrophic. —**heterotroph** /ˈhetərəʊtrəʊf/ noun [C], **heterotrophy** /ˈhetərəʊtrəʊfi/ noun [U]

heterozygous /ˌhetərəʊˈzaɪɡəs/ adj **BIOLOGY** a heterozygous cell or organism has two different forms of a particular gene for something such as eye colour

heuristic /hjʊəˈrɪstɪk/ adj relating to a method of teaching or learning in which you learn from your own discoveries and experiences

hexadecimal /ˌheksəˈdesɪm(ə)l/ adj **MATHS, COMPUTING** based on the number 16

hexagon /ˈheksəɡən/ noun [C] **MATHS** a geometric shape with six straight sides —*picture* → SHAPE —**hexagonal** /heksˈæɡən(ə)l/ adj

hexahedron /ˌheksəˈhiːdrən/ noun [C] **MATHS** a solid shape consisting of six flat surfaces. A cube is a type of hexahedron.

hexameter /hekˈsæmɪtə/ noun [C] **LITERATURE** a line of poetry that has six **metrical feet**

hey /heɪ/ interjection used for getting someone's attention, or for showing that you are surprised or annoyed

hi /haɪ/ interjection *informal* hello: *Hi, I'm Tom.*

hiatus /haɪˈeɪtəs/ noun [C] **1** *formal* a period of time when something does not happen **2 LANGUAGE** a pause between two vowel sounds that come one after the other, for example in the word **naive**

hibernate /ˈhaɪbəneɪt/ verb [I] **1 BIOLOGY** if an animal hibernates, it sleeps through the winter **2 COMPUTING** if a computer hibernates, its **operating system** closes down automatically when the computer is not being used —**hibernation** /ˌhaɪbəˈneɪʃ(ə)n/ noun [U]

hibiscus /haɪˈbɪskəs, hɪˈbɪskəs/ noun [C] a bush with large brightly coloured flowers that grows mainly in tropical regions

hiccup¹ /ˈhɪkʌp/ noun [C] a short repeated sound that you make in your throat because you have been eating or drinking too quickly

hiccup² /ˈhɪkʌp/ (**hiccups, hiccupping, hiccupped**) verb [I] to make a hiccup sound

hid /hɪd/ the past tense of **hide¹**

hidden¹ /ˈhɪd(ə)n/ adj **1** if something is hidden, most people do not know about it or understand it: *the hidden costs of being in hospital* **2** a hidden object or place is not easy to find: *a hidden camera* ♦ *hidden valleys*

hidden² /ˈhɪd(ə)n/ the past participle of **hide¹**

,hidden a'genda noun [C] a secret plan that someone has to do something, because they will get an advantage from it

,hidden 'detail ,line noun [C] **MATHS, PHYSICS** a line in a drawing showing details of the inside of a three-dimensional object that cannot be seen from the outside

,hidden 'tax noun [C] **ECONOMICS** an indirect tax

hide¹ /haɪd/ (**hides, hiding, hid** /hɪd/, **hidden** /ˈhɪd(ə)n/) verb

1 put in secret place	4 not show feelings
2 go to secret place	5 try to avoid sth
3 make hard to see	+ PHRASE

1 [T] to put something in a place so that no one can find it or see it: *She hid the key in the drawer.* ♦ *I wanted to hide his present from him until his birthday.*

2 [I] to go somewhere or be somewhere where no one can find you or see you: *Robert is **hiding from** us.* ♦ *He ran and **hid behind** a bush.*

3 [T] to make something difficult or impossible to see clearly: *Dark clouds hid the sun.*

4 [T] to prevent people from knowing your thoughts or feelings, or the truth: *He could not hide his disappointment.*

5 [I] to try not to accept something, or to try not to be affected by something: *You can't hide from your feelings forever.*

PHRASE **have nothing to hide** to not be afraid of what people may discover, because you have done nothing wrong

hide² /haɪd/ noun **1** [C/U] the skin of an animal such as a cow that is used for making leather **2** [C] a small building or structure in which someone sits in order to watch wild animals or birds

hideous /ˈhɪdiəs/ adj very ugly, frightening, or unpleasant —**hideously** adv

hiding /ˈhaɪdɪŋ/ noun **1** [U] a situation in which someone hides: *Davies, fearing arrest, went into hiding.* **2** [C] a heavy defeat in a game or competition

hierarchical /ˌhaɪəˈrɑːkɪk(ə)l/ adj a hierarchical society or organization is one in which differences in status are considered to be very important

hierarchy /ˈhaɪəˌrɑːki/ (plural **hierarchies**) noun **1** [C/U] SOCIAL STUDIES a system for organizing people according to their status **2** [C] the group of people who control an organization

hieroglyphics /ˌhaɪərəˈɡlɪfɪks/ noun [plural] **1** writing that uses pictures and symbols to represent sounds and words, especially Ancient Egyptian writing **2** written words or symbols that are difficult to read or understand

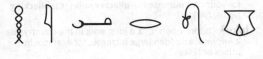

hieroglyphics

high¹ /haɪ/ adj

1 tall	7 about sounds
2 a long way up	8 winds: very strong
3 measuring things	9 affected by drugs
4 large in amount	10 most extreme
5 very good	+ PHRASE
6 important	

1 large in size from the top to the ground ≠ LOW: *Kilimanjaro is the highest mountain in Africa.* ♦ *The fence is too high to climb over.*

2 in a position that is a long way above the ground ≠ LOW: *high clouds* ♦ *the highest shelf*

3 used in measurements of how big or how far above the ground an object is: *Some of the waves are fifteen feet high.* ♦ *How high is that ceiling?*

4 large in amount ≠ LOW: *high prices* ♦ *This is an area of high unemployment.* ♦ *Ice cream is very high in calories* (=contains a lot of calories).

5 very good, or excellent ≠ LOW: *high quality products* ♦ *She has a very high opinion of herself.*

6 important in comparison with other people or things ≠ LOW: *What is the highest rank in the army?* ♦ *Both parties are giving high priority to education.*

7 MUSIC a high sound is near the upper end of a range

of sounds ≠ LOW: *Women's voices are usually higher than men's.* → HIGH-PITCHED

8 high winds are very strong

9 *informal* affected by an illegal drug: *He was high on cocaine.*

10 used in some expressions for referring to the greatest or most extreme example or part of something: *In the 1980s this was high fashion.*

PHRASE **high hopes**/**expectations** if you have high hopes or **expectations**, you hope or expect that something very good will happen

> ■ **High** is used for talking about things that are a long way from the ground. It is also used to talk about mountains: *a high shelf* ♦ *a high window* ♦ *the world's highest mountain*
> ■ **Tall** is used for talking about people or things that measure more than is usual from their bottom to their top: *a tall thin bottle* ♦ *a tall tree* ♦ *the tallest boy in the class*

high² /haɪ/ adv **1** a long distance above the ground, or above a particular position ≠ LOW: *a first-class hotel built high on a hillside* ♦ *the sound of war planes flying high above the city* **2** reaching up a long way: *She stretched her arms up high.* **3** to or at an important position ≠ LOW: *She rose high in the company.* ♦ *A colonel ranks higher than a major.* **4** MUSIC near the upper end of a range of sounds ≠ LOW: *I can't sing that high.*

high³ /haɪ/ noun **1** [C] a period or situation in which something reaches its highest level ≠ LOW: *Temperatures today are expected to reach a high of 37 degrees.* **2** [U] a high temperature in an oven or heating system ≠ LOW **3** [C] a feeling of great happiness or excitement ≠ LOW

highbrow /ˈhaɪˌbraʊ/ adj likely to interest people who enjoy learning, culture, and art

ˌHigh ˈChurch noun [U] RELIGION the part of the Anglican Church that emphasizes tradition and church authority

ˌhigh-ˈclass adj very good in quality or ability

ˌhigh-defiˈnition adj providing images that show a lot of detail very clearly

ˌhigh-ˈdensity adj having a high number or people or things in an area

ˌhigh deˈpendency ˌunit noun [C] HEALTH the department of a hospital for people who are very ill or badly injured, but who need less care than people in **intensive care**

ˈhigh-ˌend adj BUSINESS high-end goods or services are very expensive, very advanced, and of very good quality

higher¹ /ˈhaɪə/ adj **1** at a more advanced level, or involving a greater degree of knowledge: *higher mathematics* **2** higher plants and animals are the most advanced and developed

higher² /ˈhaɪə/ comparative of **high**

ˌhigher eduˈcation noun [U] EDUCATION education at a university or college

highest common factor /ˌhaɪəst ˌkɒmən ˈfæktə/ noun [singular] MATHS the highest number that can be divided exactly into each number in a particular set = GREATEST COMMON DIVISOR

ˌhigh ˈflyer noun [C] someone who has achieved a lot and is determined to continue being successful —**ˌhigh-ˈflying** adj

ˌhigh-ˈgrade adj very good in quality

the ˈhigh ˌground noun [singular] an advantage that you have in a situation or competition, especially because you have behaved more fairly or more honestly than your opponent

high-handed /ˌhaɪ ˈhændɪd/ adj speaking or acting without considering other people's opinions = ARROGANT

the ˈhigh ˌjump noun [singular] SPORTS a sports event in which people try to jump over a bar that can be raised higher after each jump

highlands /ˈhaɪləndz/ noun [plural] GEOGRAPHY an area of land that consists of hills and mountains ≠ LOWLANDS —**highland** adj

ˌhigh-ˈlevel adj **1** involving people in important or powerful positions: *a high-level meeting* **2** at a more extreme or advanced level than usual: *high-level radiation* **3** COMPUTING used for describing a computer language that is made as similar as possible to a human language ≠ LOW-LEVEL

highlife /ˈhaɪˌlaɪf/ noun [U] MUSIC a type of **dance music** that developed in West Africa from jazz

highlight¹ /ˈhaɪˌlaɪt/ verb [T] **1** to report or describe something in a way that makes people notice it and think about it: *The case highlights the need for adequate controls on such experiments.* **2** to make something easier to see or notice: *Using contrasting colours will highlight the shape and dimensions of your room.* **3** to mark a word, picture, computer file etc so that you can see it more easily

highlight² /ˈhaɪˌlaɪt/ noun [C] the most exciting, impressive, or interesting part of something: *The highlight of the trip was visiting the Great Wall of China.*

highlighter /ˈhaɪˌlaɪtə/ noun [C] a brightly coloured pen that you use for marking particular words on a document

highly /ˈhaɪli/ adv **1** used before some adjectives to mean 'very', or 'very well': *It now seems highly unlikely that the project will be finished on time.* ♦ *She's a highly educated young woman.* **2** used for saying that someone or something is very good or very important: *a highly valued member of staff* ♦ *Everyone we talked to spoke very highly of him.*

Highness /ˈhaɪnəs/ noun **Your/His/Her Highness** used for talking to or about a king, queen, prince, or princess

high-pitched /ˌhaɪ ˈpɪtʃt/ adj MUSIC a high-pitched voice or sound is very high

ˈhigh ˌpoint noun [C] the best part of something = HIGHLIGHT

ˌhigh ˈpressure noun [U] GEOGRAPHY, PHYSICS a large amount of force that the air produces in the atmosphere and that usually brings warm, calm weather —**ˌhigh-ˈpressure** adj

ˌhigh-ˈrent adj costing a lot of money to rent

ˌhigh-resoˈlution adj COMPUTING producing a very clear printed or video image by using a large number of lines or **dots**

ˈhigh-ˌrise adj very tall with many floors: *high-rise apartment blocks* —**ˈhigh-ˌrise** noun [C]

ˌhigh-ˈrisk adj involving a risk of failure, death, injury etc

ˈhigh ˌschool noun [C/U] EDUCATION a school for children aged between about 11–14 and older = SECONDARY SCHOOL

the ˌhigh ˈseas noun [plural] the parts of the sea that are far away from land and that are not owned by any country

ˌhigh ˈseason noun [singular/U] TOURISM the part of the year when many tourists visit a place ≠ LOW SEASON

ˈhigh ˌstreet noun **1** [C] the main street in a town or city, with a lot of businesses along it **2** [singular] shops and the business that they do: *Sales in the high street continue to fall.*

high-tech /ˌhaɪ ˈtek/ adj using the most advanced technology

ˌhigh ˈtide noun [C/U] GEOGRAPHY the time when the sea reaches the highest level ≠ LOW TIDE

ˌhigh ˈtreason noun [U] LAW a crime against your country, for example the crime of trying to take control of the government or helping your country's enemies

the highveld /ˈhaɪˈvelt/ noun GEOGRAPHY in South Africa, a high flat grassy area of land between 1,200 and 1,800 metres above sea level

ˌhigh ˈwater ˌmark noun [singular] GEOGRAPHY a mark that shows the highest level that the sea, a river, or a lake has risen to

highway /ˈhaɪˌweɪ/ noun [C] **1** *American* a wide road that has been built for fast travel between towns and cities **2** LAW a road or street

ˌhigh-ˈyielding ˌvariety noun [C] AGRICULTURE a type of plant that has been bred to produce a big crop every year

hijab /hɪˈdʒɑːb/ noun [C] a square of cloth that some Muslim women wear on their heads to hide their hair and neck

hijack /ˈhaɪdʒæk/ verb [T] **1** to illegally take control of a plane by using violence or threats **2** *showing disapproval* to take control of an organization or activity for your own purposes —**hijacker** noun [C], **hijacking** noun [C/U]

hike¹ /haɪk/ noun [C] **1** a long walk in the countryside **2** *informal* a sudden large increase, for example in prices or taxes

hike² /haɪk/ verb **1** [I/T] to go for a long walk in the countryside **2** [T] to suddenly increase the amount or level of something, for example a price or tax

hiking /ˈhaɪkɪŋ/ noun [U] the activity of walking for long distances in the countryside —**hiker** noun [C]

hilarious /hɪˈleəriəs/ adj extremely funny —**hilariously** adv

hill /hɪl/ noun [C] an area of land that is higher than the land surrounding it but is smaller and lower than a mountain: *They climbed slowly to the top of the hill.* ♦ *The village is built on a steep hill.*

hillside /ˈhɪlˌsaɪd/ noun [C] the land on a hill below the top

hilltop /ˈhɪlˌtɒp/ noun [C] the top of a hill

hilly /ˈhɪli/ (**hillier, hilliest**) adj with a lot of hills: *a hilly landscape*

hilt /hɪlt/ noun the handle of a sword or **dagger** —*picture* → WEAPON

hilum /ˈhaɪləm/ (plural **hila** /ˈhaɪlə/) noun [C] BIOLOGY a mark left on a seed at the place where it was attached to the plant

him /strong hɪm, weak ɪm/ pronoun **1** the object form of 'he', used for referring to a man, boy, or male animal when they have already been mentioned or when it is obvious which one you are referring to: *Luke wants me to marry him.* ♦ *I'm expecting a call from Jake. That must be him now.* **2** *old-fashioned* used in a general way for referring to any person: *Each patient should receive the treatment that suits him best.* → HE

himself /*strong* hɪmˈself, *weak* ɪmˈself/ pronoun **1** the reflexive form of 'he', used for showing that the man, boy, or male animal that does something is also affected by what he does: *William slipped once, but he didn't hurt himself.* ♦ *That man ought to be ashamed of himself.* **2** used for emphasizing that you are referring to a particular man, boy, or male animal: *You mean to tell me Jack built the whole cabin himself?* ♦ *Shakespeare himself once acted in this play.* **3** *old-fashioned* used in a general way for referring back to the subject of a sentence when they may be either male or female: *Everyone has to look after himself.* → HE

PHRASES **(all) by himself 1** alone: *I noticed Ben sitting all by himself.* **2** without help from anyone else: *There's too much work for one man to do by himself.*
(all) to himself not sharing something with anyone else: *It was the first time he'd had a room to himself.*
be/feel/seem himself to be in a normal mental or physical state: *Joe felt more himself after a good night's sleep.*

hind /haɪnd/ adj the hind legs or feet of an animal are its back legs or feet

hinder /ˈhɪndə/ verb [T] to delay or prevent someone or something from making progress ≠ HELP

hindrance /ˈhɪndrəns/ noun [C] something that delays or prevents progress

hindsight /ˈhaɪn(d),saɪt/ noun [U] the opportunity to judge or understand past events using knowledge that you have gained since then

Hindu /ˌhɪnˈduː, ˈhɪnduː/ noun [C] RELIGION someone whose religion is Hinduism —**Hindu** adj

Hinduism /ˈhɪnduˌɪz(ə)m/ noun [U] RELIGION the main religion of India. Hinduism is the oldest of the major world religions. It includes a belief in **reincarnation** and it has many gods and goddesses.

hinge /hɪndʒ/ noun [C] an object by which a door is attached to a wall, or a lid to a container, and which allows it to open and shut

ˈ**hinge joint** noun [C] ANATOMY a joint in the body that allows movement up and down in one direction only. The joints at the knees and elbows are hinge joints. —*picture* → JOINT

hint¹ /hɪnt/ noun **1** [C] something that you say in order to show what you are thinking or feeling, without saying it directly: *She hoped he would **take the hint** and leave her alone.* ♦ *Sam keeps **dropping hints** about what he wants for his birthday.* **2** [C] a small piece of information that helps someone guess something: *'You'll never guess who I saw today.' '**Give me a hint.**'* **3** [singular] a small amount of something: *There was **a hint** of impatience in his voice.* **4** [C] a useful suggestion or piece of advice= TIP: *hints on how to improve your computer skills*

hint² /hɪnt/ verb [I/T] to say what you are thinking or feeling in an indirect way: *Officials are **hinting at** the possibility of signing an agreement this week.*

hinterland /ˈhɪntəˌlænd/ noun [C] GEOGRAPHY an area that is far away from towns and cities and is not on the coast

hip /hɪp/ or ˈ**hip** ˌ**bone** noun [C] ANATOMY one of the two flat bones at either side of the body between the waist and the top of the legs: *He fell downstairs and broke his hip.* ♦ *She stood with her hands on her hips, waiting.* —*picture* → JOINT, SKELETON

ˈ**hip** ˌ**hop** noun [U] MUSIC a type of music that developed among African-American musicians using **rap** and **samples** (=short pieces of recorded music or sound)

hippie /ˈhɪpi/ (plural **hippies**) or **hippy** noun [C] someone in the 1960s who was opposed to war and traditional attitudes, and who showed this by their long hair and informal clothes

hippo /ˈhɪpəʊ/ noun [C] *informal* a hippopotamus

hippopotamus /ˌhɪpəˈpɒtəməs/ noun [C] a large African mammal with a wide head and mouth and thick grey skin —*picture* → MAMMAL

hippy /ˈhɪpi/ another spelling of **hippie**

hire¹ /ˈhaɪə/ verb **1** [T] to pay to use something such as a car or a piece of equipment for a short time: *You can hire a car at the airport.* **2** [I/T] to pay someone to work for you= EMPLOY: *I hired someone to paint the house.*

hire² /ˈhaɪə/ noun [U] the activity of paying money in order to use something for a short time: *We paid £50 for the hire of the hall.* ♦ *Bikes are available **for hire**.*

his /*strong* hɪz, *weak* ɪz/ determiner, pronoun **1** used for showing that something belongs to or is connected with a man, boy, or male animal that has already been mentioned: *She was attracted by his smile.* ♦ *The house isn't his: it's mine.* ♦ *Soon he had enough money to set up **his own** business.* **2** *old-fashioned* used in a general way for showing that something belongs to or is connected with any person, whether they are male or female: *Each child can choose his favourite story.* → HE

Hispanic /hɪˈspænɪk/ adj **1** used for describing someone whose family originally came from a country where Spanish is spoken **2** relating to countries where Spanish is spoken, or to the culture of these countries —**Hispanic** noun [C]

hiss /hɪs/ verb **1** [I/T] to say something in a quiet but angry way **2** [I] to make a long 's' sound like the sound that a snake makes —**hiss** noun [C]

histogram /ˈhɪstəˌɡræm/ noun [C] MATHS a type of **bar chart** that shows a **numerical** value on each axis —*picture* → CHART

historian /hɪˈstɔːriən/ noun [C] someone who studies history

historic /hɪˈstɒrɪk/ adj important enough to be remembered as a part of history: *historic events* ♦ *London's historic buildings*

historical /hɪˈstɒrɪk(ə)l/ adj **1** connected with history or with the past: *The painting depicts an actual historical event.* ♦ *historical research* **2** LITERATURE based on people or events that existed in the past: *a historical novel* —**historically** /hɪˈstɒrɪkli/ adv

the his,toric 'present noun LANGUAGE the present tense when it is used for writing about past events, in order to make them seem more exciting

history /ˈhɪst(ə)ri/ (plural **histories**) noun **1** [singular/U] the whole of time before now or since something began to exist, and everything that happened in that time: *Attitudes to gender roles have changed throughout history.* ♦ *The University has a distinguished history.* ♦ *the history of Nigeria* **2** [U] the study of the events of the past: *He teaches history at the local school.* ♦ *history books* **3** [C] an account of the events that happened during a particular period of the past: *He's writing **a history of** the Romans.* **4** [C/U] the length of time that something has existed: *For the first time in its 70-year history the club has admitted women members.*

PHRASE **have a history of sth** if you have a history of a medical condition or other problem, you have had it before: *He has a history of heart disease.*

'history ,list noun [C] **COMPUTING** a record of what information the previous users of a computer have put into the computer

hit¹ /hɪt/ (**hits, hitting, hit**) verb **1** [I/T] to move quickly against something, or to move an object quickly against something, touching it with force: *The glass smashed as it hit the ground.* ♦ *The child was hitting the table with a toy hammer.* **2** [I/T] to move your hand or an object hard against someone's body, so that you hurt them: *Stop hitting your brother!* ♦ *He hit me on the shoulder.* ♦ *They hit me in the stomach.* **3** [I/T] to have a sudden or bad effect on someone or something: *They were halfway down the mountain when the storm hit.* ♦ *The recession has **hit** small businesses **hard**.* **4** [T] if an idea hits you, you suddenly realize it = STRIKE: *It suddenly hit her that she would never see him again.*

PHRASAL VERBS ,hit 'back to criticize someone who has criticized you = RETALIATE
'hit on sth or 'hit u,pon sth **1** to suddenly have an idea = COME UP WITH STH: *They hit on a brilliant solution.* **2** to discover something by chance: *She was scared he might hit on the truth.*

hit² /hɪt/ noun [C]

1 successful record	**4** hitting of ball
2 sb/sth popular	**5** use of Internet
3 when sb/sth is hit	

1 a song that sells a very large number of copies: *They played a lot of old hits from the 70s and 80s.* ♦ *a CD of Madonna's **greatest hits***
2 something or someone that is very successful and popular: *The film was a massive hit at the box-office.* ♦ *His magic act was **a hit with** the children.*
3 an occasion when someone or something touches another person or thing with a lot of force
4 SPORTS an occasion when a player hits the ball in a game
5 COMPUTING an occasion when someone looks at a particular document on the Internet: *Their website gets a couple of hundred hits a day.*

hitch¹ /hɪtʃ/ verb **1** [I/T] *informal* to hitchhike **2** [T] to fasten something to something else: *We **hitched** a trailer **to** the back of our car.*

hitch² /hɪtʃ/ noun [C] a problem that is not very serious: *The plane was delayed because of a last-minute hitch.*

hitchhike /'hɪtʃ,haɪk/ verb [I] to travel by asking other people to take you in their car. You do this by standing at the side of a road and holding out your thumb or a sign. —**hitchhiker** noun [C]

hitherto /,hɪðə'tuː/ adv *very formal* until the present time = PREVIOUSLY

HIV /,eɪtʃ aɪ 'viː/ noun [U] **HEALTH** human immunodeficiency virus: a virus that attacks the **immune system** and causes AIDS. The main ways HIV is spread are by having sex without **condoms** and sharing **hypodermic** needles. Babies of infected mothers can be born with HIV. It is also called HIV/AIDS: *a campaign to warn young people of the dangers of HIV and AIDS* ♦ *Over half the children here were born with HIV.*

hive /haɪv/ noun [C] a place in which bees live and make **honey**

,HIV 'positive adj **HEALTH** infected with HIV

hm or **hmm** /m, hm/ interjection **1** used for representing a sound that you make when you pause to think before saying something else **2** used for representing a sound that you make to show you do not believe something

hoard¹ /hɔːd/ noun [C] a large amount of something that someone has hidden somewhere

hoard² /hɔːd/ verb [I/T] to get and keep a large amount of something because it might be valuable later

hoarding /'hɔːdɪŋ/ noun [C] a large board used for advertising outside

hoarse /hɔːs/ adj someone who is hoarse speaks in a low rough voice —**hoarsely** adv

hoax /həʊks/ noun [C] a trick in which someone tells people that something bad is going to happen or that something is true when it is not

hob /hɒb/ noun [C] the top part of a cooker that you put pans on

hobble /'hɒb(ə)l/ verb [I] to walk slowly and with difficulty because your feet are sore or injured

hobby /'hɒbi/ (plural **hobbies**) noun [C] something that you enjoy doing when you are not working: *Mike's hobbies include reading and chess.*

hoc see **ad hoc**

hockey /'hɒki/ noun [U] **SPORTS 1** a game that is played on grass by two teams of 11 players. They try to score goals by hitting a ball with a stick that has a curved end. **2** *American* **ice hockey**

Hodgkin's disease /'hɒdʒkɪnz dɪ,ziːz/ noun [U] **HEALTH** a type of cancer affecting the **lymph nodes**

hoe /həʊ/ noun [C] **AGRICULTURE** a tool with a long handle that is used for removing weeds (=plants that grow where they are not wanted) from the soil —*picture* → AGRICULTURAL —**hoe** verb [I/T]

hoist¹ /hɔɪst/ verb [T] to lift something or someone, often using special equipment

hoist² /hɔɪst/ noun [C] a piece of equipment that is used for lifting heavy objects

hold¹ /həʊld/ (**holds, holding, held** /held/) verb

1 carry	**10** believe
2 stop sb/sth moving	**11** keep feeling
3 put arms around sb	**12** keep control
4 be able to contain	**13** wait on telephone
5 organize event	**14** support weight
6 have a job/position	**15** have a quality
7 keep prisoner	**16** own sth
8 store information	**+** PHRASES
9 stay in same state	**+** PHRASAL VERBS

1 [T] to carry someone or something using your hands or arms: *Can you hold my bag for a moment?* ♦ *She was holding a baby in her arms.*
2 [T] to keep someone or something in a particular position so that they do not move: *Can you hold this parcel for me so I can tape it up?* ♦ *His silk tie was **held in place** with a small diamond pin.* ♦ *Four people held him down (=held him on the floor so that he could not move).*
3 [T] to put your arms around someone for a long time because you love them or because they are unhappy: *He sat beside her and held her.* ♦ *She kissed him and **held** him **tight**.*
4 [T] to be able to fit an amount of something inside: *The stadium holds 80,000 people.* ♦ *How much does this jug hold?*
5 [T] to organize something such as a meeting or event: *The government agreed to hold a referendum.*
6 [T] to have a job or position: *She is the first woman to hold this post.* ♦ *President Mitterrand **held office** for 14 years.*
7 [T] to keep someone as a prisoner: *The four men had been **held captive** for over two years.*
8 [T] to keep information, for example on a computer: *His data was held on disk.*

9 [I] to stay in the same state or at the same level: *The fine weather should hold until Tuesday.* ♦ *The coffee market has* **held steady** *for a few months.*

10 [T] to have a particular belief or opinion: *She holds some pretty unpleasant views.* ♦ *Most people* **hold** *the president* **responsible** *for the riots.*

11 [T] to continue to have a particular feeling: *I no longer hold any resentment towards him.*

12 [T] to keep control of something: *Rebel fighters have held the territory for five years.*

13 [I/T] to wait to speak to someone on the telephone: *'Do you want to call back later?' 'No, I'll hold.'*

14 [T] to support the weight of someone or something: *Do you think this branch will hold us?*

15 [T] *formal* to have a particular quality: *The project holds a great deal of promise.* ♦ *He holds no authority over us.*

16 [T] *formal* to own something, or have the right to use something: *Three per cent of our shares are now held by US investors.* ♦ *He holds a US passport.*

PHRASES **hold true** to be true, or to remain true

hold your own to be as good as other stronger or more experienced people

PHRASAL VERBS ,hold sb/sth 'back to stop someone or something from being as successful as they should be: *Her parents worried that her classmates were holding her back.*

,hold 'on **1** to hold something tightly or carefully so that you do not drop it or do not fall: *Hold on tight everyone – the driver's getting ready to go.* **2** to wait: *We'll hold on another minute, then we'll have to go.* ♦ *Hold on! You forgot your card!*

,hold 'on to sth to hold something tightly or carefully so that you do not drop it or do not fall: *Hold on to the seat in front when we go round the corner.*

,hold sth 'over to do something or deal with something at a later time or date = POSTPONE: *One session was held over until this evening.* ♦ *They intend to hold the article over for the next edition.*

'hold to sth to do what you have promised or decided: *The western democracies held to their policy of non-intervention.*

,hold sb/sth 'up to cause a delay, or to make someone late: *Sorry I'm late, but my train was held up.* ♦ *She got held up at work.*

hold² /həʊld/ noun **1** [singular] the fact that you are holding something: *His hold on her arm tightened.* ♦ *Bobby* **grabbed hold of** *the railing* (=suddenly started holding it). ♦ *She* **took hold of** *his hand* (=started holding it). **2** [singular] power or control over someone or something: *The rebels have a firm* **hold over** *the northern area.* ♦ *Does he have some sort of* **hold on** *you?* **3** [C] the area in a plane or ship that is used for goods, vehicles, or bags **4** [C] SPORTS a way of holding someone, for example in a sport: *a wrestling hold*

PHRASES **get hold of sb** to manage to talk to someone: *Can you get hold of Mike and tell him the meeting's postponed?*

get hold of sth 1 to get something that you need or want: *I've managed to get hold of some rather good wine.* **2** to start holding something with your hands: *Just get hold of the aerial and move it round to see if you can get a better picture.*

keep hold of sth 1 to not take your hands away from something that you are holding: *She kept hold of his arm.* **2** to not lose something, or not let someone else get it: *They managed to keep hold of the ball in the second half.*

on hold 1 if something is on hold, you have stopped it from happening now, but it may happen later: *After the accident her career had to be put on hold.* **2** waiting to speak to someone on the telephone, after your call has been answered: *They've put me on hold.*

take hold to become stronger and difficult to stop: *They were fortunate to escape before the fire took hold.* ♦ *A sense of dread* **took hold of** *him.*

holder /'həʊldə/ noun [C] **1** someone who owns something or who has been given something **2** something that is designed to hold or support another object

holding company /'həʊldɪŋ ,kʌmp(ə)ni/ noun [C] BUSINESS a company that owns the majority of the shares in another company and controls it

'hold-up noun [C] **1** a delay **2** a situation in which someone with a gun steals money from a bank or shop

hole /həʊl/ noun [C] **1** a space that has been dug in the surface of the ground: *Workers dug a 30-foot hole in the ground.* ♦ *rabbit holes* **2** a space in the surface of something that goes partly or completely through it: *All my socks have* **holes in** *them.* ♦ *Rain poured through a* **gaping hole** *in the roof* (=a very large hole). **3** a part of something such as an idea or explanation where important details are missing: *His argument was full of holes.* **4** SPORTS in golf, a small space in the ground that you have to hit the ball into

PHRASES **hole in one** SPORTS in golf, a situation in which a player gets the ball into a hole with just one hit

hole in the heart HEALTH a medical condition in which someone is born with a small hole in the wall that divides the heart into two sides

'hole ,punch noun [C] a piece of equipment used for putting small holes in paper —*picture* → WORKSTATION

holiday /'hɒlɪdeɪ/ noun **1** [C/U] a period of time when you do not work or study and do things for pleasure instead: *Employees are entitled to four weeks' annual holiday.* ♦ *I am away* **on holiday** *for the next two weeks.* ♦ *The kids get bored by the end of* **the summer holidays**. **2** [C] an occasion when you go and stay in another place for pleasure: *I'm* **going on holiday** *with some friends.* ♦ *a holiday resort* **3** [C] a day that is a celebration of something special, on which you do not have to work or go to school: *1st May is a holiday in many European countries.* → BANK HOLIDAY **4** [U] the number of days or weeks during a year when someone does not have to work but is paid: *Employees are entitled to four weeks' annual holiday.*

'holiday ,camp [C] TOURISM a place for families to stay on holiday, with small separate houses and organized activities

'holiday ,home noun [C] a house or flat that someone owns and uses for holidays

holidaymaker /'hɒlɪdeɪ,meɪkə/ noun [C] TOURISM a person who is visiting a place for their holiday

'holiday re,sort noun [C] TOURISM a resort

'holiday ,season noun [C] TOURISM the time of year when most people take their holidays

'holiday ,village noun [C] TOURISM a village of small houses built for people to stay in while on holiday

holistic /həʊ'lɪstɪk/ adj **1** based on the idea that people should take care of the whole body and mind, rather than just treating a part of the body that is ill **2** thinking about the whole of something, and not just dealing with particular aspects

hollow¹ /'hɒləʊ/ adj **1** empty inside: *hollow chocolate eggs* **2** not sincere or with any real meaning: *a hollow display of friendship* ♦ *a hollow victory* **3** a hollow sound is a low sound like something empty being hit **4** hollow eyes or cheeks seem to have sunk into your head

hollow² /'hɒləʊ/ noun [C] a small area in the ground that is lower than the ground around it

hollowing /'hɒləʊɪŋ/ noun [U] TECHNOLOGY the process of hammering or beating a piece of metal in order to produce shallow objects such as bowls and **trays**

holly /'hɒli/ (plural **hollies**) noun [C/U] an **evergreen** tree with dark green leaves with sharp points and small bright red berries

Hollywood /'hɒli,wʊd/ noun [U] ARTS the part of the US film industry that has a reputation for making very successful films that cost a lot of money to produce

holmium /'həʊlmiəm/ noun [U] CHEMISTRY a silvery-white metallic element in the **lanthanide** group of the periodic table. Chemical symbol: **Ho**

holocaust /'hɒlə,kɔːst/ noun [C] a war in which very many people are killed

the Holocaust /'hɒlə,kɔːst/ noun [singular] the organized killing of millions of Jews and other people by the German Nazi government during the Second World War

hologram /'hɒləgræm/ noun [C] a type of picture that is three-dimensional

holster /'həʊlstə/ noun [C] a leather container for a small gun, that is fixed to a belt

holy /'həʊli/ (**holier, holiest**) adj RELIGION
1 important in a religion, or used in worship = SACRED: _the holy book of the Sikhs_ ♦ _the holy city of Jerusalem_
2 respected for living a very religious life: _a holy man and his followers_
PHRASE **holy of holies** RELIGION the central and most holy part of a Jewish **temple**
—**holiness** noun [U]

Holy Com'munion noun [C/U] RELIGION the Christian ceremony of **Communion**

the ,Holy 'Ghost noun [singular] RELIGION the **Holy Spirit**

the ,Holy 'Spirit noun [singular] RELIGION in the Christian religion, God in the form of a spirit

Holy 'Writ noun [U] something that someone writes or says that people accept as being completely true or correct

homage /'hɒmɪdʒ/ noun [singular/U] something that someone does or says in order to show respect or admiration

home¹ /həʊm/ noun

1 where you live	**7** where sth started
2 where parents live	**8** place on sports field
3 your country/city	**9** home page
4 place to buy/rent	**10** of plants and animals
5 where people get care	+ PHRASE
6 base for sports team	

1 [C/U] the place where you live: _We go to a school close to our home._ ♦ _a child in need of a loving home_ ♦ _Peter isn't **at home** today._ ♦ _I hate being **away from home.**_ → HOUSE
2 [U] the place where your parents live and where you grew up: _He is 43 and still living **at home.**_ ♦ _I **left home** when I was 18_ (=stopped living there).
3 [U] the country or city where you live: _a great opportunity in markets both **at home** and abroad_ ♦ _**Back home**, the weather is much better._
4 [C] a building for people to buy or rent: _One thousand new homes are being built in the area._ ♦ _There is a shortage of homes for rent._
5 [C] a building where people who need special care can live and be looked after: _They didn't want to put their mother in a home._ ♦ _a **home for** orphans_
6 [U] SPORTS the place where a sports team is based

and plays most of its games: _United are playing **at home** tonight._
7 [singular] the place where something first started or was first made: _Scotland is **the home of** golf._
8 [U] SPORTS a place on a sports field that a player must try to get to in order to score a point in some sports
9 [U] COMPUTING a **home page**
10 [C] the place where a particular group of people or type of plant or animal lives: _These wetlands are **the home of** a great variety of wildlife._
PHRASE **be/feel at home** to be or feel relaxed and comfortable in a particular place or situation: _They did everything they could to make me feel at home._

home² /həʊm/ adv **1** to the place where you live: _I decided to walk home._ ♦ _What time are you **coming home?**_ ♦ _I went **home** to France._ ♦ _**On the way home** from school, I met my friend Sue._ **2** at the place where you live: _Is Kathryn home?_ ♦ _I'll be home all day Tuesday._

home³ /həʊm/ adj **1** relating to your home rather than your work: _Write your **home address** at the top of the page._ **2** done, made, or experienced at home: _home cooking_ **3** relating to things that happen within a country, rather than between different countries: _These cameras sell well in the home market._ **4** SPORTS relating to the place where a sports team is based: _a home win_ ♦ _the team's **home ground**_ (=where they usually play)

,home 'cinema noun [U] television and **DVD** equipment that is intended to copy the experience of seeing something in a cinema in someone's own home

homeland /'həʊm,lænd/ noun [C] the country where someone comes from

,Homeland Se'curity noun [U] the US government department responsible for protecting the US from attacks by **terrorists**, or the work of this department

homeless /'həʊmləs/ adj **1** without a place to live **2 the homeless** people who are homeless
—**homelessness** noun [U]

,home-'made adj made in someone's home rather than in a factory

the 'Home ,Office in the UK, the government department that is responsible for **justice** and the police, and for deciding who is allowed into the country

homeopathy /,həʊmi'ɒpəθi/ noun [U] HEALTH a way of treating illness by giving small amounts of natural substances that in large amounts would cause the illness —**homeopathic** /,həʊmiə'pæθɪk/ adj

homeostasis /,həʊmiəʊ'steɪsɪs/ noun [U] BIOLOGY the process by which a living organism or cell keeps its own state steady and continuous, despite changes in the environment around it. An example of homeostasis is the ability of **warm-blooded** animals such as humans to keep their body temperature at the correct level, despite the temperature changes around them.

homeotherm /'həʊmiəʊ'θɜːm/ noun [C] BIOLOGY an organism with a steady body temperature that is not affected by the temperature of the surrounding environment

homeothermic /,həʊmiəʊ'θɜːmɪk/ adj BIOLOGY a homeothermic animal always has the same body temperature, despite changes in the temperature of its environment. Homeothermic animals are also called **warm-blooded** animals. Animals whose body temperature changes are **cold-blooded**.

'home ,page noun [C] COMPUTING **1** a place on the Internet where a person or an organization gives information about themselves or their business **2** a place on the Internet that you choose to appear first on your computer screen each time you look at the Internet

'home ,plate noun [U] SPORTS in baseball, the place where a player stands when they hit the ball, which is also the last place they run to after hitting the ball

,home 'rule noun [U] POLITICS a form of government in which people have control in their own country, rather than being controlled by another country

,home 'run noun [C] SPORTS a point in baseball that is scored when a player hits the ball then runs around all the four **bases**

homeschool /'həʊm,skuːl/ verb [I/T] EDUCATION to educate your children completely at home, instead of in a school

homesick /'həʊm,sɪk/ adj feeling sad and alone because you are far from home

homestay /'həʊm,steɪ/ noun [U] TOURISM a visit in which people pay to stay in someone's house, rather than in a hotel

homestead /'həʊm,sted/ noun [C] American a farm, including the **farmhouse** and any other buildings on the land

the ,home 'straight noun **1** SPORTS the last part of a race **2** the last part of an activity or process

homework /'həʊm,wɜːk/ noun [U] EDUCATION work that a teacher gives a student to do at home: *Have the kids done their homework?*

homeworker /'həʊm,wɜːkə/ noun [C] a person who does paid work at home

homicidal /,hɒmɪ'saɪd(ə)l/ adj likely to kill someone, or wanting to kill someone

homicide /'hɒmɪsaɪd/ noun [C/U] LAW American the crime of killing someone

homing /'həʊmɪŋ/ adj used for describing equipment that is able to find a particular place or object: *a missile fitted with a homing device*

'homing ,instinct noun [singular] if an animal or bird has a homing instinct, it is able to find its way home across long distances

hominid /'hɒmɪnɪd/ noun [C] a member of the family from which humans developed —*picture* → TAXONOMY

Homo erectus /,həʊməʊ ɪ'rektəs/ noun [U] an extinct species of human that first appeared in Africa nearly two million years ago, and was able to walk upright

homogeneous /,həʊməʊ'dʒiːniəs/ adj consisting of things that are similar or all of the same type

homo,geneous 'mixture noun [C] CHEMISTRY a mixture of two or more substances that cannot be easily separated and that looks the same throughout

homograph /'hɒmə,grɑːf/ noun [C] LANGUAGE a word that is spelled the same as another word but has a different meaning and sometimes a different pronunciation

homologous /hɒ'mɒləgəs/ adj **1** SCIENCE sharing a similar or related structure, position, function, or value **2** BIOLOGY relating to biological structures such as the wing of a bird or the fin of a fish that share the same origin but have a different function **3** CHEMISTRY relating to a series of organic chemical compounds, such as a **methylene** group, in which each of the compounds differs from the previous one in the series by the addition of a constant component **4** BIOLOGY produced from identical tissue

homonym /'hɒmənɪm/ noun [C] LANGUAGE a word that is spelled the same, or sounds the same, as another word but has a different meaning

homophobia /,həʊməʊ'fəʊbiə/ noun [U] **hatred** of gay people —**homophobic** adj

homophone /'hɒmə,fəʊn/ noun [C] LANGUAGE a word that sounds the same as another word but has a different spelling and meaning

Homo sapiens /,həʊməʊ 'sæpienz/ noun [U] the species of human that exists at the present time. Homo sapiens first appeared about 100,000 years ago in Africa. —*picture* → TAXONOMY

homosexual[1] /,həʊməʊ'sekʃuəl/ adj attracted sexually to people of the same sex —**homosexuality** /,həʊməʊsekʃu'æləti/ noun [U]

homosexual[2] /,həʊməʊ'sekʃuəl/ noun [C] someone who is attracted sexually to people of the same sex

homozygous /,həʊməʊ'zaɪgəs/ adj BIOLOGY having two of the same form of a particular gene for something such as eye colour

honest /'ɒnɪst/ adj **1** someone who is honest does not tell lies or cheat people, and obeys the law ≠ DISHONEST: *an honest man* **2** consisting of the truth, or not intended to cheat people: *I want you to give me an honest answer.* ♦ *I gave her the wrong amount of money, but it was an honest mistake* (=not intended). **3** honest work is a job that you work fairly hard at: *When is the last time Charlie did any honest work?* ♦ *I'm just trying to earn an honest living* (=earn money by working hard).

> **Word family: honest**
>
> *Words in the same family as honest*
> - **honestly** adv
> - **honesty** n
> - **dishonestly** adv
> - **dishonest** adj
> - **dishonesty** n

honestly /'ɒnɪs(t)li/ adv **1** *spoken* used for emphasizing that what you are saying is true: *I honestly can't remember.* **2** in a way that is honest: *She was trying to do her job honestly and fairly.*

honesty /'ɒnɪsti/ noun [U] an honest way of behaving, speaking, or thinking: *She is a woman of honesty and integrity.*

honey /'hʌni/ noun [U] a sweet sticky yellow or brown food made by bees

honeymoon /'hʌni,muːn/ noun [C] a holiday that two people have after they get married

honorary /'ɒnərəri/ adj an honorary member of a group is someone who is allowed to join without applying or without having the usual qualifications

honour[1] /'ɒnə/ noun **1** [U] the respect that people have for someone who achieves something great, is very powerful, or behaves in a way that is morally right: *They were prepared to die for the honour of their country.* **2** [U] the behaviour of someone who has high moral standards≡ INTEGRITY: *a man of honour* (=someone who always behaves in a morally correct way) ♦ *It's no longer just a legal issue, it's a matter of honour.* **3** [C] something that you do that you are proud of: *Being asked to perform at La Scala is an honour for any singer.* ♦ *It's a great honour to be here with you tonight.* **4** [C] a prize that someone is given because they have done something important: *Twenty children received honours for bravery.*

PHRASE **in honour of** in order to show respect and admiration for someone or something: *St Petersburg was renamed Leningrad in honour of Lenin.*

honour[2] /'ɒnə/ verb [T] **1** to show your respect or admiration for someone by giving them a prize or a title, or by praising them publicly: *We are here today to honour the men and women who gave their lives for their country.* **2** to do what you promised to do or what it is your duty to do: *Once a contract is signed, it has to be honoured.*

honourable /ˈɒn(ə)rəb(ə)l/ adj **1** morally good and deserving respect: *Your father was an honourable man.* ♦ *the honourable thing to do* **2 Honourable** or **honourable** *formal* used for talking to judges and some politicians —**honourably** adv

honoured /ˈɒnəd/ adj **1** proud that you have been given special respect or a special opportunity: *I feel deeply honoured to have been invited here today.* **2** deserving special respect: *an honoured guest*

'honour ˌkilling noun [C] LAW the murder of a woman by a male relative because he believes that she has damaged the family's image

honours /ˈɒnəz/ noun [plural] EDUCATION a level of university degree that is higher than an ordinary degree

hood /hʊd/ noun [C] **1** the part of a coat or jacket that covers your head **2** *American* a car **bonnet**

hoof /huːf/ (plural **hoofs** or **hooves** /huːvz/) noun [C] BIOLOGY the hard part of a horse's foot

hook¹ /hʊk/ noun [C] **1** a curved piece of metal or plastic, used for hanging things on or for catching fish: *He hung his coat on a hook on the back of the door.* **2** a way of hitting someone with your arm bent: *a left hook to the jaw*

PHRASE **off the hook** if a telephone is off the hook, the part that you speak into has not been put into its place, so that you cannot receive any calls

hook² /hʊk/ verb **1** [I/T] to hang something on something else, or to be fastened to something else with a hook: *He hooked the umbrella over his arm and went outside.* **2** [T] to put your arm, finger, leg etc round something in order to hold it or bring it closer to you: *Lucy hooked her arm through Peter's.* **3** [T] to catch a fish with a hook **4** [T] SPORTS to hit, kick, or throw a ball so that it moves in a curved direction, especially in golf or football

hooked /hʊkt/ adj **1** attracted by or interested in something so much that you want to do it as much as possible **2** if someone is hooked on drugs, they cannot stop taking them **3** shaped like a hook

hooker /ˈhʊkə/ noun [C] SPORTS a player in the game of **rugby** who tries to get the ball when the players are in a **scrum**

hookworm /ˈhʊkˌwɜːm/ noun **1** [C] a small invertebrate that looks like a worm and is a parasite that lives in the intestines of humans and other animals. It can cause serious disease. **2** [U] HEALTH the disease caused by hookworms

hooligan /ˈhuːlɪɡən/ noun [C] someone who is noisy or violent in public places

hoop /huːp/ noun [C] an object in the shape of a circle, usually made of metal, plastic, or wood

hoot¹ /huːt/ noun [C] **1** a short loud sound made by people who are laughing or criticizing something **2** a short loud sound made by the horn of a car as a warning **3** the deep sound that an **owl** makes

hoot² /huːt/ verb [I/T] **1** to make a short loud sound when you laugh or criticize something **2** to use the horn of a car to make a short loud sound as a warning **3** to make the deep sound that an **owl** makes

Hoover /ˈhuːvə/ TRADEMARK a **vacuum cleaner**

hooves /huːvz/ a plural of **hoof**

hop¹ /hɒp/ (**hops**, **hopping**, **hopped**) verb [I] **1** to move forward by jumping on one foot **2** if an animal hops, it uses both or all four feet to jump forward

hop² /hɒp/ noun [C] **1** a quick jump on one foot **2** a short quick jump by a small animal

hope¹ /həʊp/ verb [I/T] to want and expect something to happen or be true: *I hope that you'll enjoy your stay with us.* ♦ *The university is hoping to raise £1,000,000.* ♦ *It wouldn't be sensible to **hope for** immediate success.*

hope² /həʊp/ noun [C/U] **1** the feeling or belief that something that you want to happen is likely to happen: *She arrived in London, young and **full of hope**.* ♦ *These young people have no **hope for** the future.* ♦ *The team's **hopes of** a championship are fading fast.* ♦ *The research **raises hopes** of a significant improvement in the treatment of cancer.* ♦ *Rescuers refused to **give up hope** of finding more survivors.* ♦ *He had **lost hope** of seeing his children again.* **2** someone or something that offers a chance of improvement: *Our **only hope** was to get her to a hospital fast.* ♦ *Many people saw the new president as their **last hope** for political change.* **3** [C] something that you wish for: *The hope is that he will eventually come to his senses.*

PHRASES **have high hopes for sb** to hope and expect that someone will be very successful

in the hope that/of wanting something to happen: *Police are carrying out a search in the hope of finding the missing girl.*

hopeful /ˈhəʊpf(ə)l/ adj **1** believing that something will happen in the way that you want it to: *In spite of our differences, we remain hopeful that a solution can be found.* ♦ *a hopeful look* **2** making you believe that something will happen in the way that you want it to: *a hopeful sign*

hopefully /ˈhəʊpf(ə)li/ adv **1** used for saying that you hope that something will happen: *Hopefully, we'll get more news next week.* **2** feeling or showing hope: *He looked at her hopefully.*

hopeless /ˈhəʊpləs/ adj **1** if a situation is hopeless, it seems very unlikely to succeed or improve **2** *informal* not skilful at all **3** feeling or showing no hope —**hopelessly** adv, **hopelessness** noun [U]

hopper /ˈhɒpə/ noun [C] **1** CONSTRUCTION a container for weighing and loading materials to go into a **cement mixer 2** CONSTRUCTION a **fitting** at the top of a rain water pipe attached to a flat roof **3** TECHNOLOGY the part at the top of a **blast furnace** through which the iron ore is poured

horizon /həˈraɪz(ə)n/ noun **1 the horizon** [singular] the line in the distance where the sky seems to meet the earth **2 horizons** [plural] the limits of your experience **3** [C] GEOLOGY a layer of soil or minerals in the ground that is different from the layer above or below it

PHRASE **on the horizon** in the near future

horizontal¹ /ˌhɒrɪˈzɒnt(ə)l/ adj **1** straight and parallel to the horizon ≠ VERTICAL **2** BUSINESS on the same level

horizontal² /ˌhɒrɪˈzɒnt(ə)l/ noun [C] MATHS a horizontal line or position —**horizontally** adv

horiˈzontal ˌaxis noun [singular] MATHS the **x-axis** in a system of coordinates

horiˌzontal 'plane noun [C] MATHS, PHYSICS a **plane** (=flat surface) in **orthographic projection** that is horizontal

horizontal welding /ˌhɒrɪˈzɒnt(ə)l ˌweldɪŋ/ noun [U] TECHNOLOGY a welding process in which a horizontal weld is used to join two pieces of metal that are placed vertically on top of each other, or two pieces of metal at right angles to each other

hormone /ˈhɔːməʊn/ noun [C] **BIOLOGY** a chemical substance produced in animals and plants that controls things such as growth and sexual development. Hormones in animals are usually produced in the **endocrine glands**: *growth hormones* ♦ *The hormone testosterone controls sexual development in boys.* —**hormonal** /hɔːˈməʊn(ə)l/ adj

horn /hɔːn/ noun [C] **1** the object in a vehicle that makes a loud warning noise when you press it **2 BIOLOGY** one of the two hard pointed parts that grow on the heads of some mammals, for example cows or goats **3 MUSIC** a metal musical instrument that is wide at one end, and that you play by blowing —*picture* → ORCHESTRA

hornbill /ˈhɔːnˌbɪl/ noun [C] a tropical bird with a large beak

hornet /ˈhɔːnɪt/ noun [C] a black and yellow flying insect like a large **wasp** that can sting you

horoscope /ˈhɒrəˌskəʊp/ noun [C] a description of someone's character and the likely events in their life that is based on **astrology** (=the position of the stars and the date they were born)

horrendous /hɒˈrendəs/ adj extremely bad or shocking —**horrendously** adv

horrible /ˈhɒrəb(ə)l/ adj very unpleasant, or very unkind: *I've had a horrible day at work.* ♦ *The medicine tasted horrible.* ♦ *Stop being so horrible to me.* —**horribly** /ˈhɒrəbli/ adv

horrid /ˈhɒrɪd/ adj very unpleasant, or very unkind

horrific /hɒˈrɪfɪk/ adj shocking and upsetting —**horrifically** /hɒˈrɪfɪkli/ adv

horrify /ˈhɒrɪfaɪ/ (**horrifies, horrifying, horrified**) verb [T] to shock someone very much —**horrifying** adj

horror /ˈhɒrə/ noun **1** [C/U] a strong feeling of shock or fear, or something that makes you feel shocked or afraid: *Millions watched in horror as the disaster unfolded on TV.* ♦ *the horrors of war* **2** [U] **ARTS, LITERATURE** a book or film that is intended to frighten people: *a horror story*

hors d'oeuvres /ˌɔː ˈdɜːv/ noun [plural] small amounts of food that are served before the main part of a meal

horse /hɔːs/ noun **1** [C] a large strong mammal that is used for riding and, especially in the past, for pulling vehicles and heavy loads —*picture* → MAMMAL **2** [C] **SPORTS** a piece of equipment shaped like a large box that is used in **gymnastics 3 the horses** [plural] **SPORTS** *informal* the sport of horse racing, or the activity of **betting** money on the results of horse races

horseback /ˈhɔːsˌbæk/ noun **on horseback** riding on a horse

horse ˈchestnut noun [C] a large tree that produces shiny hard brown seeds, or a seed from this tree. The seeds are often also called **conkers**.

horseman /ˈhɔːsmən/ (plural **horsemen** /ˈhɔːsmən/) noun [C] a man who rides horses for pleasure or sport, especially someone who is good at riding

horsepower /ˈhɔːsˌpaʊə/ (plural **horsepower**) noun [C] a unit for measuring the power of a vehicle's engine

ˈhorse-ˌriding noun [U] the activity of riding a horse

horseshoe /ˈhɔːsˌʃuː/ noun [C] a curved piece of iron that is fastened to the bottom of a horse's hoof

horst /hɔːst/ noun [C] **GEOLOGY** a raised block of land, produced when the land between two parallel cracks in the ground is forced upwards

horticulture /ˈhɔːtɪˌkʌltʃə/ noun [U] **AGRICULTURE 1** the activity of growing flowers, fruit, and vegetables in order to sell them **2** the study of growing flowers, fruit, and vegetables for selling —**horticultural** /ˌhɔːtɪˈkʌltʃərəl/ adj, **horticulturalist** noun [C]

hose /həʊz/ or **hosepipe** /ˈhəʊzˌpaɪp/ noun [C] a very long tube that water or air can flow through —*picture* → AGRICULTURAL

hospice /ˈhɒspɪs/ noun [C] **HEALTH** a hospital that looks after people who are dying

hospitable /hɒˈspɪtəb(ə)l/ adj friendly and generous towards visitors

hospital /ˈhɒspɪt(ə)l/ noun [C] **HEALTH** a place where ill or injured people receive medical treatment: *He spent a week in hospital with food poisoning.* ♦ *He went into hospital last week for a heart operation.*

hospitality /ˌhɒspɪˈtæləti/ noun [U] **1** friendly and generous behaviour towards visitors **2** food, drink, and entertainment that are given to customers by a company or organization

ˌhospiˈtality ˌindustry noun [singular] **TOURISM** all the companies involved in providing services for guests, for example hotels and restaurants, considered as a group

ˌhospiˈtality ˌtray noun [C] **TOURISM** a set of things such as an electric **kettle**, cups, milk, and tea or coffee that is provided in a hotel room for making a hot drink

host¹ /həʊst/ noun [C]

1 sb who invites	4 a lot of sth
2 on television/radio	5 plant etc lived on
3 sth arranging event	6 main computer

1 someone who invites people to a meal or a party, or to stay for a short time in their home: *They had brought a present for their hosts.*
2 someone who introduces and talks to the people taking part in a television or radio programme: *a TV game show host*
3 a place or organization that arranges a special event and provides the area, equipment, or services needed for it: *Korea and Japan played host to the 2002 World Cup.*
4 a lot of people or things: *a host of possibilities*
5 BIOLOGY a plant or animal that has another organism, called a parasite, living on it
6 COMPUTING a **host computer**

host² /həʊst/ verb [T] **1** to arrange a special event and provide the area, equipment, or services needed for it **2** to introduce and talk to the people taking part in a television or radio programme **3** to organize and be in charge of a formal or official meal or party **4 COMPUTING** to provide connections to the Internet and the equipment and software needed to run websites, usually as a business for other companies

hostage /ˈhɒstɪdʒ/ noun [C] a person who is the prisoner of someone who threatens to kill them if they do not get what they want: *Six businessmen were taken hostage by rebel groups.*

ˈhost comˌputer noun [C] **COMPUTING** the main computer in a **network** that controls particular processes or files

hostel /ˈhɒst(ə)l/ noun [C] **1** a building where people can live if they are away from home or if they have no home **2** a **youth hostel**

hostess /ˈhəʊstɪs/ noun [C] **1** a woman who invites someone to a meal or a party, or to stay for a short time in her home **2** a woman who introduces and talks to the people taking part in a television or radio programme

hostile /'hɒstaɪl/ adj **1** behaving in a very unfriendly or threatening way **2** opposing something: *The local community was hostile to plans for a new motorway.* **3** a hostile place or situation is difficult or dangerous to be in

hostility /hɒ'stɪləti/ noun **1** [U] unfriendly or threatening behaviour: *She said she had experienced hostility from her male colleagues.* **2** [U] opposition to something: *There is always some hostility to new technology.* **3** **hostilities** [plural] *formal* fighting between enemies in a war

hot /hɒt/ (**hotter, hottest**) adj **1** very high in temperature ≠ COLD: *Cook the fish under a hot grill for 5 minutes.* ♦ *Take your jacket off if you're hot.* ♦ *It's going to be hot again today.* ♦ *hot countries such as India* **2** hot food contains a lot of spices that create a burning feeling in your mouth = SPICY **3** difficult or dangerous: *When things got too hot for her at home, she'd stay with a friend.* **4** involving strong feelings

> **Build your vocabulary: words you can use instead of hot**
>
> - **baking** very hot and dry
> - **boiling (hot)** very hot in a way that is unpleasant or uncomfortable. Also used for referring to the temperature of a liquid when it starts to bubble
> - **lukewarm** used for describing water that is only slightly hot
> - **roasting** used for describing a room or building that is extremely hot
> - **scalding (hot)** used for describing a liquid that is hot enough to burn your skin
> - **sweltering** used for describing weather that is so hot that you feel uncomfortable
> - **tepid** used for describing drinks that are not hot enough
> - **warm** hot in a pleasant way

hot-'air bal,loon noun [C] an extremely large bag full of hot air, with a basket attached that people can travel through the air in

hot desking /,hɒt 'deskɪŋ/ noun [U] BUSINESS a method of working in which people do not have their own desk in an office but use any desk that is available at a particular time

hot dipping /,hɒt 'dɪpɪŋ/ noun [U] TECHNOLOGY the process of coating the surface of a metal by placing it in a bath of **molten** (=melted) metal such as zinc or aluminium

hotel /həʊ'tel/ noun [C] TOURISM a building where you pay to stay in a room: *He always stays in the best hotels.* ♦ *We booked into a luxury hotel.*

hotelier or **hotelkeeper** /həʊ'telieɪ/ noun [C] TOURISM the owner or manager of a hotel

'hot ,key noun [C] COMPUTING a key on a computer keyboard that provides a quick way of performing a set of actions

'hot ,link noun [C] COMPUTING *informal* a connection from one computer document to another by means of **hypertext**, especially on the Internet

hotly /'hɒtli/ adv **1** in a way that shows that you have very strong feelings about something: *Rumours of a split have been hotly denied by the band's manager.* **2** involving people who are competing very hard with one another: *a hotly contested election*

hotplate /'hɒt,pleɪt/ noun [C] a flat hot surface on a cooker

'hot ,spot noun [C] *informal* **1** a place that is fashionable, popular, and lively **2** COMPUTING a place in an airport, restaurant, station etc that has a device that lets you connect a portable computer to a network or the Internet without using cables

,hot 'spring noun [C] GEOLOGY a place where hot water comes up out of the ground and forms a pool

hound¹ /haʊnd/ verb [T] **1** to follow someone in a determined way in order to get something from them: *She was sick of being hounded by the press.* **2** to force someone to leave a place or job by always being unpleasant to them: *His political opponents hounded him out of office.*

hound² /haʊnd/ noun [C] a dog that is used for hunting or racing

hour /'aʊə/ noun

> | 1 60 minutes of time | 4 a time of day |
> |---|---|
> | 2 a long time | 5 point in history/life |
> | 3 time for work etc | |

1 [C] a period of time that consists of 60 minutes: *He left about an hour ago.* ♦ *Brighton is only an hour away* (=it takes an hour to get there). ♦ *I earn £2 an hour* (=for each hour spent working).
2 hours [plural] a long time: *I'm hungry and it's hours until dinner.*
3 hours [plural] the time during which you do something such as work or study: *My job is very flexible – I can fit my hours around my children.* ♦ *Jo has to work very long hours.*
4 [C] a particular time in the day or night: *You can call me at any hour of the day or night.* ♦ *You get cars coming down here at all hours* (=at any time, even at night).
5 [singular] a particular point in history or in someone's life or career: *His finest hour came in 1982 when his film Gandhi won eight Oscars.*

hourglass /'aʊə,glɑːs/ noun [C] a glass container that uses sand to measure one hour

hourly /'aʊəli/ adj **1** happening once every hour: *hourly news bulletins* **2** relating to one hour of work: *His hourly fee is £10.* —**hourly** adv: *Buses run hourly.*

house¹ /haʊs/ (plural **houses** /'haʊzɪz/) noun

> | 1 building for living in | 4 group of students |
> |---|---|
> | 2 people in a house | 5 type of music |
> | 3 area for audience | + PHRASES |

1 [C] a building for living in, usually where only one family lives: *a three-bedroom house* ♦ *We're moving house* (=going to live in a different house) *at the end of the month.*
2 [singular] the people who are in a house or who live there: *The noise woke the entire house.*
3 [C] the part of a theatre, cinema etc that contains the audience: *Her new show has been playing to packed houses.*
4 [C] EDUCATION one of the groups that students are divided into in some British schools, in order to compete against each other
5 [U] MUSIC a type of modern electronic music that developed in the 1980s, replacing **disco** as the most popular form of **dance music**. It combines deep **bass** sounds with parts that are sung or played on a **synthesizer.**

PHRASES **House of Commons** POLITICS the part of the parliament in the UK or Canada that consists of politicians who have been elected by the people
house of God RELIGION a Christian church or other building where people worship God
House of Lords POLITICS the part of the parliament in the UK that consists of politicians who are not elected by the people

- A **house** is a building for living in: *She lives in that big house.* ♦ *They're building some new houses on our street.*
- Someone's **home** is the place where they live: *This little cottage is the home of a family of eight.*
- Do not use **to** before **home**: *They all went to Dan's house, but I went home.*

house² /haʊz/ verb [T] **1** to give someone a place to live: *A large number of families are still waiting to be housed.* **2** to contain or provide a place for something: *The club is housed in a magnificent 16th-century building.*

'house ar,rest noun **be under house arrest** to be officially prevented from leaving your home because you have been accused of a political crime

houseboat /'haʊsbəʊt/ noun [C] a boat that someone lives in

housebound /'haʊsbaʊnd/ adj unable to leave your house because you are ill or disabled

housefly /'haʊsflaɪ/ (plural **houseflies**) noun [C] a very common flying insect that often lives in houses and is attracted by food. Houseflies can spread disease by landing on food, and also lay eggs in food that turn into **maggots**= FLY —*picture* → MOSQUITO

household¹ /'haʊshəʊld/ noun [C] the people who live in a house or a flat

household² /'haʊshəʊld/ adj used in homes, or relating to homes: *household goods*

householder /'haʊshəʊldə/ noun [C] a person who owns or pays the rent of a house or a flat

housekeeper /'haʊski:pə/ noun [C] someone whose job is to clean or cook in a large house or a hotel

housekeeping /'haʊski:pɪŋ/ noun [U] **1** the jobs that need to be done in a house, for example cleaning and cooking: *We try to share the housekeeping.* **2** the money that you use to pay for the things that you need at home, for example food and electricity **3** COMPUTING things that have to be done regularly on a computer system to make sure that it will run well

houseplant /'haʊsplɑ:nt/ noun [C] a plant that you keep inside your house for decoration

'house ,swap noun [C] TOURISM an arrangement where two families exchange houses for a holiday

,house-to-'house adj, adv involving visits to every house in an area

housewife /'haʊswaɪf/ (plural **housewives** /'haʊswaɪvz/) noun [C] a woman who does not work outside the home and whose main job is looking after her children, cooking, cleaning etc

housework /'haʊswɜ:k/ noun [U] the work that you do in order to keep your house clean and tidy

housing /'haʊzɪŋ/ noun **1** [U] buildings for people to live in: *Land had to be found for new housing.* ♦ *a housing shortage* **2** [C] ENGINEERING a container or cover for something such as a moving part of a machine

'housing e,state noun [C] a large group of houses that are built at the same time and in the same style

hover /'hɒvə/ verb [I] **1** if a bird, insect, or aircraft hovers, it keeps itself in the same position in the air **2** to stay somewhere because you are waiting to do something or because you cannot decide what to do: *The waiter was hovering by their table.*

hovercraft /'hɒvəkrɑ:ft/ noun [C] a vehicle that can move over both land and water, raising itself above the surface by blowing air downwards

how /haʊ/ adv, conjunction **1** used for asking or talking about the way that something happens or is done: *How did she react when you told her?* ♦ *I don't understand how the system works.* ♦ *Would you show me how to send an email?* **2** used for asking or talking about the quantity or degree of something: *How difficult was the exam?* ♦ *How old are you?* ♦ *How many grandchildren do you have now?* **3** used for asking what someone thinks about an experience: *How was school today?*

PHRASES **how are you?** *spoken* used for asking in a polite way about someone's health
how much is/are...? used for asking the price of something: *How much was that CD?*

however /haʊ'evə/ adv, conjunction **1** used for adding a statement that seems surprising or that makes a previous statement seem less true: *He worked hard. His work did not improve, however.* **2** used for saying that it makes no difference how good, bad, difficult etc something is or how much there is of something: *She would still love him however badly he behaved.* ♦ *I'm going to solve this problem, however long it takes.* **3** in whatever way someone chooses: *We let the kids decorate their rooms however they want to.*

howl /haʊl/ verb [I] **1** if a dog or other animal howls, it makes a long loud sound **2** to cry very loudly in pain, anger, or sadness **3** if the wind howls, it blows with a long loud sound **4** to laugh very loudly —**howl** noun [C]

HP /,eɪtʃ 'pi:/ noun [U] MATHS, PHYSICS a **horizontal plane**

HQ /,eɪtʃ 'kju:/ noun [plural] the **headquarters** of a company, organization, or military unit

hr abbrev hour

HR /,eɪtʃ 'ɑ:/ noun **1** [plural] SOCIAL STUDIES human rights **2** [U] BUSINESS human resources

HTML /,eɪtʃ ti: em 'el/ noun [U] COMPUTING hypertext markup language: the computer language that is used for writing pages on the Internet

http /,eɪtʃ ti: ti: 'pi:/ noun [U] COMPUTING hypertext transfer (or transport) protocol: the system that is used on the Internet to exchange documents in HTML

hub /hʌb/ noun [C] **1** the most important place where a particular activity takes place: *Mumbai is the financial hub of India.* **2** the part at the centre of a wheel **3** TOURISM a central airport that passengers can fly to from smaller local airports **4** COMPUTING a piece of computer equipment used for connecting one part of a computer system to another part, or for connecting several computers to each other to form a **network**

,hub-and-'spoke adj BUSINESS used for describing a system in which goods or people are transported from various local places to a central point, from which they travel or are sent long distances

the Hubble constant /'hʌb(ə)l ,kɒnstənt/ noun ASTRONOMY the ratio of the speed at which a galaxy (=group of stars and planets) is moving away, because the universe is expanding, to its distance from the person looking at it

the Hubble Space Telescope /,hʌb(ə)l 'speɪs ,telɪskəʊp/ noun ASTRONOMY a very powerful telescope attached to a satellite that is orbiting the Earth. It is used to look at and photograph parts of the universe that are very far away.

hubris /'hju:brɪs/ noun [U] *formal* a very proud way of talking or behaving that offends people

huddle /'hʌd(ə)l/ verb [I] to move close together in order to stay warm, feel safe, or talk

hue /hjuː/ noun [C] a particular form of a colour

hug¹ /hʌɡ/ (**hugs, hugging, hugged**) verb **1** [I/T] to put your arms round someone in order to show your love or friendship: *Mike picked up his daughter and hugged her tight.* **2** [T] to hold something close to your chest: *Emma was sitting on the floor hugging her knees.* **3** [T] to stay close to something: *They kept to the back of the crowd, hugging the wall.*

hug² /hʌɡ/ noun [C] the action of putting your arms round someone in order to show your love or friendship

huge /hjuːdʒ/ adj **1** extremely large= ENORMOUS: *She arrived carrying two huge suitcases.* ♦ *Many top players earn huge amounts of money.* ♦ *The concert turned out to be a huge success.* **2** extremely successful and well known: *The band is huge in both Britain and the US.* —**hugely** adv: *a hugely popular TV show*

hull /hʌl/ noun [C] the main part of a ship

hum¹ /hʌm/ (**hums, humming, hummed**) verb **1** [I/T] MUSIC to make musical sounds with your lips closed: *If you don't know the words, just hum the tune.* **2** [I] to make a low continuous sound: *The fridge hummed in the kitchen.* **3** [I] if a place is humming, it is full of noise and activity: *The whole stadium was humming with excitement.*

hum² /hʌm/ noun [singular] a low continuous noise made by a machine or by a lot of people talking

human¹ /ˈhjuːmən/ adj **1** relating to people: *the human brain* ♦ *the study of human behaviour* ♦ *Tests show that the meat is unfit for human consumption* (=not safe for people to eat). **2** showing normal human feelings: *It is only human to want revenge when someone hurts you.*

human² /ˈhjuːmən/ or **,human 'being** noun [C] a person: *The disease can be fatal in humans.*

humane /hjuːˈmeɪn/ adj caring about the quality of people's or animals' lives and trying to be kind to them ≠ CRUEL, INHUMANE —**humanely** adv

,human 'error noun [U] a mistake made by a person who is controlling a machine or process, rather than something wrong with the machine or process itself

,human ge'ography noun [U] GEOGRAPHY, SOCIAL STUDIES the study of how human societies developed all over the world, especially in relation to the earth's physical features

,human ,immunode'ficiency ,virus noun [singular] HEALTH HIV

humanitarian /hjuːˌmænɪˈteəriən/ adj relating to people who live in very bad conditions and to other people's efforts to help them

the humanities /hjuːˈmænətiz/ noun [plural] EDUCATION subjects that people study such as history and literature, rather than science or mathematics

humanity /hjuːˈmænəti/ noun **1** all people, thought of as a group: *Weapons of this type are a threat to the survival of humanity.* **2** a kind and sympathetic attitude towards other people ≠ INHUMANITY: *He was a man of great humanity who was deeply affected by the suffering of others.* **3** the state of being human

humankind /ˌhjuːmənˈkaɪnd/ noun [U] all people, thought of as a group

'human-,made adj something that is human-made has been made or caused by people and does not exist naturally= SYNTHETIC

,human 'nature noun [U] the attitudes, feelings, and reactions that are typical of most people

the ,human 'race noun [singular] all people, thought of as a group

,human re'sources noun [U] BUSINESS the department within a company that is responsible for employing and training people, and for looking after workers who have problems= PERSONNEL

,human 'rights noun [plural] SOCIAL STUDIES the rights that everyone should have in a society, including the right to express opinions or to have protection from harm

,human 'trafficking noun [U] the business of helping people to enter a country illegally and forcing them to work there for very little money because they have no rights

humble /ˈhʌmb(ə)l/ adj **1** not proud, and not thinking that you are better or more important than other people **2** from a low social class, or with low social status **3** simple and with only basic equipment or features —**humbly** adv

humdrum /ˈhʌmdrʌm/ adj boring because nothing new or interesting ever happens

humerus /ˈhjuːmərəs/ noun [C] ANATOMY the bone that connects the shoulder to the elbow —*picture* → SKELETON

humid /ˈhjuːmɪd/ adj hot and wet in a way that makes you feel uncomfortable: *a humid climate*

humidity /hjuːˈmɪdəti/ noun [U] GEOGRAPHY, PHYSICS the amount of water vapour that is in the air: *Banana trees are well adapted to growing in areas of high humidity.*

humiliate /hjuːˈmɪlieɪt/ verb [T] to make someone feel very embarrassed and ashamed —**humiliation** /hjuːˌmɪliˈeɪʃ(ə)n/ noun [C/U]

humiliating /hjuːˈmɪlieɪtɪŋ/ adj making you feel very embarrassed and ashamed

humility /hjuːˈmɪləti/ noun [U] a way of behaving that shows that you do not think that you are better or more important than other people

hummingbird /ˈhʌmɪŋˌbɜːd/ noun [C] a very small brightly coloured bird that makes a low continuous noise when it moves its wings

hummus /ˈhʊmʊs/ noun [U] a soft food from Greece and the Middle East that is made from **chickpeas** and eaten cold with bread

humorist /ˈhjuːmərɪst/ noun [C] LITERATURE someone who writes in a clever and funny way about real people and events, often for newspapers

humorous /ˈhjuːmərəs/ adj funny: *a humorous story* —**humorously** adv

humour¹ /ˈhjuːmə/ noun **1** [U] the quality that makes something funny: *a novel that is full of humour* **2** [U] the ability to know when something is funny and to laugh at funny situations: *Sally is a friendly person with a great sense of humour.* **3** [singular] *formal* someone's mood: *He laughed again, obviously in a good humour.*

humour² /ˈhjuːmə/ verb [T] to do what someone wants, or to pretend to agree with them, so that they do not become angry or upset

hump /hʌmp/ noun [C] **1** a large round shape that rises above a surface or above the ground **2** a large round part on the back of an animal or person

humus /ˈhjuːməs/ noun [U] AGRICULTURE, BIOLOGY plants and leaves that decay on the ground and improve the quality of the soil

hunch¹ /hʌntʃ/ noun [C] a feeling that something is true or will happen, although you do not know any definite facts about it

hunch² /hʌntʃ/ verb [I/T] to sit or stand with your back and shoulders curved forwards

hundred /'hʌndrəd/ number **1** the number 100 **2 hundreds of** a very large number or amount of people or things: *We received hundreds of applications for the job.*

hundredth /'hʌndrədθ/ number **1** in the place or position that is counted as number 100 **2** one of 100 equal parts of something

hundredweight /'hʌndrəd,weɪt/ noun [C] a unit for measuring weight that is equal to 112 pounds or 50.8 kilograms

hung /hʌŋ/ the past tense and past participle of **hang¹**

hunger /'hʌŋgə/ noun [U] **1** the feeling that you have when you need to eat: *a nutritious snack that will satisfy your hunger* **2** a lack of food that can cause illness or death: *a new chance to fight world hunger and poverty*

'hunger ,strike noun [C] a refusal to eat for a long time by someone who is protesting against something

hungry /'hʌŋgri/ (**hungrier, hungriest**) adj **1** feeling that you need to eat: *We were cold, tired, and hungry.* ♦ *She was beginning to **feel hungry** again.* **2** wanting something very much: *a hungry young actor* ♦ *People are **hungry for** news.*
  PHRASE **go hungry** to not have enough food
—**hungrily** adv

> **Build your vocabulary: words you can use instead of hungry**
> ■ **peckish** (*informal*) feeling hungry when it is not a mealtime
> ■ **ravenous** or **famished** or **starving** (*informal*) very hungry

hunt¹ /hʌnt/ verb [I/T] **1** to catch and kill animals: *Crocodiles were hunted and killed for their teeth.* ♦ *Wild dogs usually hunt in packs.* ♦ *We **hunted for** rabbits in the hills.* **2** to try to find someone or something= LOOK FOR SB/STH: *Police are still hunting the killer.* ♦ *Detectives have been **hunting for** clues to the murderer's identity.*

hunt² /hʌnt/ noun [C] **1** a search for someone or something: *the **hunt for** the missing child* **2** an attempt to catch and kill animals

hunter /'hʌntə/ noun [C] **1** a person or animal that catches and kills wild animals **2** someone who is looking for a particular type of thing

hunter-gatherer /,hʌntə 'gæðərə/ noun [C] SOCIAL STUDIES one of a group of people who live by killing wild animals and finding food, and do not keep any animals or grow any crops

hunting /'hʌntɪŋ/ noun [U] **1** the activity of catching and killing animals **2** the activity of looking for a particular thing that you want or need: *bargain hunting* ♦ *flat-hunting*

huntsman /'hʌntsmən/ (plural **huntsmen** /'hʌntsmən/) noun [C] **1** someone who hunts wild animals **2** someone who is responsible for the dogs that are used in a hunt for **foxes** in the UK

hurdle /'hɜːd(ə)l/ noun [C] **1** SPORTS an upright frame that a person or horse jumps over during a race **2** one of several problems that you must solve before you can do something successfully: *Finding investors is the biggest hurdle we face.*

hurl /hɜːl/ verb [T] **1** to throw something using a lot of force **2** to direct angry remarks or criticism at someone: *The fans began hurling abuse at each other.*

hurray /hʊ'reɪ/ or **hurrah** /hʊ'rɑː/ interjection a word that you shout to show that you are excited and happy about something

hurricane /'hʌrɪkən, 'hʌrɪkeɪn/ noun [C] GEOGRAPHY a violent storm with very strong winds that forms over warm waters in the north-east Pacific Ocean or the Atlantic Ocean. This type of storm over warm waters in the north-west Pacific Ocean is called a **typhoon**.

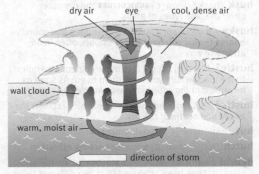

dry air   eye   cool, dense air

wall cloud

warm, moist air

direction of storm

hurricane

hurried /'hʌrid/ adj done quickly, because you do not have enough time= RUSHED —**hurriedly** adv

hurry¹ /'hʌri/ (**hurries, hurrying, hurried**) verb [I/T] to do something or to move somewhere very quickly, or to make someone do this: *We must hurry or we'll be late.* ♦ *Alex had to hurry home, but I decided to stay.* ♦ *She **hurried along** the corridor towards his office.* ♦ *Liz took Anna's arm and **hurried** her **away**.*
  PHRASAL VERB ,**hurry (sb) 'up** **1** *spoken* used for telling someone to do something more quickly: *Hurry up and finish your soup.* **2** to do something or to move somewhere more quickly, or to make someone do this: *She wished George would hurry up with her cup of tea.*

hurry² /'hʌri/ noun
  PHRASES **in a hurry** doing something or going somewhere quickly, because you do not have much time: *Donna's letter looked as though she had written it in a great hurry.*
  in no hurry or **not in any hurry** **1** able to wait to do something, because you have plenty of time: *I'm not in any hurry to get there.* **2** unwilling to do something, or not wanting to do it until a future time: *Lou's in no hurry to get married.*

hurt¹ /hɜːt/ (**hurts, hurting, hurt**) verb **1** [I] to feel pain somewhere in your body: *Fred's knees hurt after skiing all day.* **2** [I/T] to cause someone physical pain or injury: *You're hurting my arm!* ♦ *These new boots hurt.* ♦ *Don't **hurt yourself** exercising.* **3** [I/T] to cause someone emotional pain: *His comments hurt her deeply.* ♦ *I never meant to **hurt** your **feelings**.* **4** [T] to cause damage or problems, or to harm someone's chance to succeed at something: *The weakness of the dollar has hurt car sales.*

hurt² /hɜːt/ adj **1** injured, or feeling physical pain ≠ UNHURT: *I wasn't badly hurt.* **2** feeling emotional pain, usually because of someone's behaviour: *She left feeling angry and deeply hurt.*

hurt³ /hɜːt/ noun [C/U] a feeling of emotional pain that is caused by someone's behaviour

hurtful /'hɜːtf(ə)l/ adj causing emotional pain

husband /'hʌzbənd/ noun [C] the man that a woman is married to

husbandry /'hʌzbəndri/ noun [U] AGRICULTURE animal husbandry

hush /hʌʃ/ verb **1** [I] spoken used for telling someone to be quiet: *Hush! You'll wake the baby!* **2** [I/T] to stop talking, crying, or making a noise, or to make someone do this

hushed /hʌʃt/ adj very quiet: *People were talking in hushed voices.*

husk /hʌsk/ noun [C] AGRICULTURE the dry outer cover of some types of grain

husky /'hʌski/ adj a husky voice is deep and sounds **hoarse** (=as if you have a sore throat), often in an attractive way

hustle¹ /'hʌs(ə)l/ verb [T] to make someone go quickly to the place where you want them to go: *As soon as he arrived in the country, he was hustled off to prison.*

hustle² /'hʌs(ə)l/ noun [U] a lot of noisy activity: *the hustle and bustle of the city*

hut /hʌt/ noun [C] a small simple shelter

hutch /hʌtʃ/ noun [C] a box for keeping **rabbits** in

hybrid /'haɪbrɪd/ noun [C] **1** BIOLOGY an animal or plant that has been produced from two different types of animal or plant **2** a mixture of different things or styles —**hybrid** adj

hydra /'haɪdrə/ noun [C] BIOLOGY a very small invertebrate animal that lives in water and has a body shaped like a tube and a number of **tentacles** around its mouth

the Hydra /'haɪdrə/ noun [singular] a creature in Greek **mythology** (=ancient stories) that looked like a snake with many heads

hydrant /'haɪdrənt/ noun [C] an upright water pipe in the street that firefighters get water from

hydrate /'haɪˌdreɪt/ noun [C] CHEMISTRY a compound that can get rid of and absorb water

hydraulic /haɪ'drɒːlɪk/ adj SCIENCE using the pressure of water or oil to make a machine work

hydro- /'haɪdrəʊ/ prefix SCIENCE **1** relating to or using water: used with some adjectives and nouns: *hydroelectricity* **2** relating to or using hydrogen: used with some adjectives and nouns: *hydroxide*

hydrocarbon /ˌhaɪdrəʊ'kɑːbən/ noun [C] CHEMISTRY a chemical substance that contains only hydrogen and carbon, for example methane. Many fuels are hydrocarbons.

hydrochloric acid /ˌhaɪdrəˌklɒrɪk 'æsɪd/ noun [U] CHEMISTRY a strong liquid chemical that is used in industry and in laboratory work. Hydrochloric acid is present in the stomach in a weak form, and helps make conditions suitable for digestion.

hydrocortisone /ˌhaɪdrəʊ'kɔːtɪzəʊn/ noun [U] BIOLOGY a hormone that is used in medicine to treat parts of the body that have swollen and become red and painful

hydroelectric /ˌhaɪdrəʊ'ɪlektrɪk/ adj using water power to produce electricity —**hydroelectricity** /ˌhaɪdrəʊɪlek'trɪsɪti/ noun [U]

hydrofoil /'haɪdrəʊˌfɔɪl/ noun [C] a boat with wing-shaped pieces fixed to the bottom that lift the boat onto the surface of the water as it starts to travel quickly

hydrogas suspension /'haɪdrəʊgæs səˌspenʃ(ə)n/ noun [C] ENGINEERING a vehicle **suspension** system that uses balls filled with nitrogen gas instead of steel springs

hydrogen /'haɪdrədʒən/ noun [U] CHEMISTRY a chemical element that is a gas that has no colour or smell. It is the lightest element, and is the most common in the universe. Hydrogen combines with oxygen to make water, and is present in most organic compounds. In the Sun and other stars, it is turned into **helium** by **nuclear fusion** which produces heat and light. Chemical symbol: H

hydrogenated /haɪ'drɒdʒəneɪtɪd/ adj CHEMISTRY hydrogenated oils and fats have had hydrogen added to them

'hydrogen ,bomb noun [C] an extremely powerful type of nuclear bomb. It works by nuclear **fusion** and releases more energy than an **atom bomb**.

'hydrogen ,ion noun [C] CHEMISTRY an ion of hydrogen that has a positive charge and is formed by removing an electron from a hydrogen atom. It is present in solutions of acids in water. The pH of a compound is a measure of the degree to which it produces hydrogen ions.

hydrogen peroxide /ˌhaɪdrədʒən pə'rɒksaɪd/ noun [U] CHEMISTRY a chemical that is often used as a **bleach** or as a **disinfectant**. Chemical formula: H_2O_2

hydrolase /'haɪdrəleɪz/ noun [C] BIOLOGY an enzyme that speeds up the process of **hydrolysis**

hydrolastic suspension /ˌhaɪdrəʊ'læstɪk səˌspenʃ(ə)n/ noun [C] ENGINEERING a vehicle **suspension** system that uses fluid-filled objects instead of steel springs

hydrolyse /'haɪdrəlaɪz/ verb [I/T] CHEMISTRY, BIOLOGY to undergo hydrolysis, or to make a substance undergo hydrolysis

hydrolysis /haɪ'drɒləsɪs/ noun [U] BIOLOGY, CHEMISTRY a chemical reaction in which a chemical compound reacts with water and produces two or more smaller compounds. An example of this is when the body produces sugar from starch.

hydrometer /haɪ'drɒmɪtə/ noun [C] PHYSICS a piece of equipment used for measuring the density of liquids. It consists of a glass tube with a heavy glass sphere at one end that floats at a particular level in the liquid.

hydrophobic /ˌhaɪdrəʊ'fəʊbɪk/ adj CHEMISTRY, BIOLOGY hydrophobic molecules do not dissolve easily in water

hydrophyte /'haɪdrəfaɪt/ noun [C] BIOLOGY a plant that will only grow in water or in a very wet environment → MESOPHYTE, XEROPHYTE

hydroponics /ˌhaɪdrəʊ'pɒnɪks/ noun [U] AGRICULTURE a method of growing plants in water that contains all the necessary minerals for growth

hydropower /'haɪdrəʊˌpaʊə/ noun [U] ENVIRONMENT electricity produced from the energy in falling water

hydrosphere /'haɪdrəsfɪə/ noun [singular] GEOGRAPHY the part of the Earth's surface that is water, including the seas and water in the atmosphere

hydrostatic pressure /ˌhaɪdrəʊstætɪk 'preʃə/ noun [U] BIOLOGY, PHYSICS pressure created by water that is not moving

hydroxide /haɪ'drɒksaɪd/ noun [C] CHEMISTRY a chemical compound that contains oxygen and hydrogen in the form OH

hydroxyl ion /haɪˈdrɒksɪl ˌaɪən/ noun [C] CHEMISTRY a negative ion that is formed when an oxygen atom and a hydrogen atom combine

hygiene /ˈhaɪdʒiːn/ noun [U] HEALTH the practice of keeping yourself and the things around you clean in order to prevent infection and disease. Basic methods of hygiene include always washing your hands before handling food and after using the toilet, and keeping food covered up: *Hospitals need to have a high standard of hygiene.*

hygienic /haɪˈdʒiːnɪk/ adj HEALTH clean and not likely to cause illness or disease

hygrometer /haɪˈɡrɒmɪtə/ noun [C] GEOGRAPHY a piece of equipment used for measuring **humidity**

hymen /ˈhaɪmen/ noun [C] ANATOMY a thin membrane that covers the entrance to the vagina in young girls. This is usually broken before **puberty** because of normal child activity in girls, but sometimes all or part of it remains until a woman first has sex.

hymn /hɪm/ noun [C] RELIGION a religious song that Christians sing in churches

hyper- /haɪpə/ prefix more than usual or normal: used with some adjectives and nouns to make adjectives and nouns

hyperactive /ˌhaɪpərˈæktɪv/ adj very lively and finding it difficult to concentrate or relax

hyperactivity /ˌhaɪpəræk'tɪvəti/ noun [U] HEALTH a higher than normal level of activity, in an organ or in a child's behaviour

hyperbaric /ˌhaɪpəˈbærɪk/ adj PHYSICS a hyperbaric gas is at a higher pressure than it normally is

hyperbola /haɪˈpɜːbələ/ noun [C] MATHS a curve formed by the **intersection** (=crossing) of a **plane** (=flat surface) and a **right circular cone** that is produced by a set of points for which the difference in distance from two fixed points is **constant** (=always the same)

hyperbole /haɪˈpɜːbəli/ noun [C/U] LANGUAGE a way of emphasizing something by describing it as far more extreme than it really is

hypercorrection /ˌhaɪpəkəˈrekʃ(ə)n/ noun [C/U] LANGUAGE the use of incorrect grammar or pronunciation by someone who is trying to show that they know how to use correct grammar or pronunciation. An example of this is saying 'between you and I' instead of 'between you and me'.

hyperglycaemia /ˌhaɪpəɡlaɪˈsiːmiə/ noun [U] HEALTH a medical condition in which the level of sugar in someone's blood is too high

hyperinflation /ˌhaɪpərɪnˈfleɪʃ(ə)n/ noun [U] ECONOMICS very high **inflation** (=a general increase in prices) that causes serious problems for a country's economy

hyperlink /ˈhaɪpəlɪŋk/ noun [C] COMPUTING a word or image in a computer document that you can click on in order to move to a related document, word, or image —**hyperlink** verb [T]

hypermarket /ˈhaɪpəˌmɑːkɪt/ noun [C] a very large supermarket, usually built outside a town, that sells a wide range of goods

hypermedia /ˈhaɪpəˌmiːdiə/ noun [U] COMPUTING a **hypertext** system that includes images, sound, and video as well as written words

hypermetropia /ˌhaɪpəmɪˈtrəʊpiə/ noun [U] HEALTH a medical condition in which the eye cannot see objects that are close very clearly. A less technical name for this is **long-sightedness**.

hypernym /ˈhaɪpənɪm/ noun [C] LANGUAGE a superordinate

hypersensitive /ˌhaɪpəˈsensətɪv/ adj **1** very easily upset or offended **2** HEALTH extremely sensitive to certain substances

hyperspace /ˈhaɪpəˌspeɪs/ noun [U] **1** in **science fiction**, an imaginary situation in which a spacecraft can travel faster than light **2** PHYSICS space with more than three **dimensions**

hypertension /ˌhaɪpəˈtenʃ(ə)n/ noun [U] HEALTH a condition in which someone's blood pressure is extremely high

hypertext /ˈhaɪpəˌtekst/ noun [U] COMPUTING a computer system in which you can click on a word or image in order to move to a related document, word, or image

hypertonic drink /ˌhaɪpətɒnɪk ˈdrɪŋk/ noun [C] SPORTS a drink that contains sugar and a little salt, suitable for replacing body fluids quickly during exercise

hypertrophy /haɪˈpɜːtrəfi/ noun [U] BIOLOGY growth of an organ as a result of an increase in the size, rather than the number, of its cells —**hypertrophic** /ˌhaɪpəˈtrəʊfɪk/ adj, **hypertrophy** verb [I/T]

hyphen /ˈhaɪf(ə)n/ noun [C] LANGUAGE the short line – used for joining two words or parts of words, or for dividing a word at the end of a line of writing

hyphenated /ˈhaɪfəˌneɪtɪd/ adj LANGUAGE written with a hyphen

hypnosis /hɪpˈnəʊsɪs/ noun [U] a very relaxed state in which you seem to be sleeping but can still hear and react to someone else's suggestions, or the practice of putting people into this state

hypnotic /hɪpˈnɒtɪk/ adj **1** something that is hypnotic makes you feel like sleeping, because it is repeated in a regular way: *the hypnotic rhythm of the drums* **2** relating to or caused by hypnosis: *a hypnotic trance*

hypnotize /ˈhɪpnətaɪz/ verb [T] to put someone into a state that is similar to sleep, but in which they can still hear and react to someone else's suggestions

hypoallergenic /ˌhaɪpəʊælə'dʒenɪk/ adj HEALTH unlikely to cause an **allergic** reaction

hypochondriac /ˌhaɪpəʊˈkɒndriæk/ noun [C] someone who worries a lot about their health and thinks that they are ill when they are not

hypocrisy /hɪˈpɒkrəsi/ (plural **hypocrisies**) noun [C/U] behaviour in which someone pretends to be morally good or to believe something but behaves in a way that shows that they are not sincere

hypocrite /ˈhɪpəkrɪt/ noun [C] someone who pretends to be morally good or to believe something but who behaves in a way that shows that they are not sincere

hypocritical /ˌhɪpəˈkrɪtɪk(ə)l/ adj someone who is hypocritical pretends to be morally good or to believe something but behaves in a way that shows that they are not sincere —**hypocritically** /ˌhɪpəˈkrɪtɪkli/ adv

hypocycloid /ˌhaɪpəˈsaɪklɔɪd/ noun [C] MATHS a curve produced by a point on the circumference of a circle that is being rolled along the inside of another circle → EPICYCLOID

hypodermic /ˌhaɪpəˈdɜːmɪk/ or ˌhypodermic ˈneedle noun [C] HEALTH a narrow plastic tube with a needle, used for putting drugs into someone's body through the skin —**hypodermic** adj

hypogeal /ˌhaɪpəˈdʒiːəl/ adj BIOLOGY **1** relating to a plant part that remains below ground while the stem of the plant grows **2** relating to seed **germination**

hypoglycaemia /ˌhaɪpəʊɡlaɪˈsiːmiə/ noun [U] HEALTH a medical condition in which someone has a low level of sugar in their blood

hyponym /ˈhaɪpəʊnɪm/ noun [C] LANGUAGE a word with a more specific meaning than another more general word of which it is an example. For example, 'potato' is a hyponym of 'vegetable'.

hypotenuse /haɪˈpɒtənjuːz/ noun [C] MATHS the longest side of a right-angled triangle. The square of its length is equal to the squares of the lengths of the other two sides added together. —*picture* → TRIANGLE

the hypothalamus /ˌhaɪpəʊˈθæləməs/ noun [singular] ANATOMY a small area on the lower part of the brain that controls the **heartbeat** and the temperature of the body. It also affects the **pituitary gland**. —*picture* → BRAIN

hypothermia /ˌhaɪpəʊˈθɜːmiə/ noun [U] HEALTH a serious medical condition in which the body temperature gets very low

hypothesis /haɪˈpɒθəsɪs/ (plural **hypotheses** /haɪˈpɒθəsiːz/) noun [C] an idea that attempts to explain something, but has not yet been tested or been proved to be correct= THEORY

hypothesize /haɪˈpɒθəsaɪz/ verb [T] *formal* to suggest a possible explanation for something based on the information that is available, but without knowing whether the explanation is really true

hypothetical /ˌhaɪpəˈθetɪk(ə)l/ adj based on situations or events that seem possible rather than on actual ones= THEORETICAL —**hypothetically** /ˌhaɪpəˈθetɪkli/ adv

hysterectomy /ˌhɪstəˈrektəmi/ (plural **hysterectomies**) noun [C] HEALTH a medical operation to remove a woman's uterus

hysteria /hɪˈstɪəriə/ noun [U] a state of uncontrolled excitement or extreme fear

hysterical /hɪˈsterɪk(ə)l/ adj behaving in an uncontrolled way because you are extremely excited, afraid, or upset —**hysterically** /hɪˈsterɪkli/ adv

hysterics /hɪˈsterɪks/ noun [plural] an uncontrolled emotional state in which you are extremely excited, afraid, or upset

HYV abbrev AGRICULTURE a high-yielding variety of crop

Hz abbrev PHYSICS hertz

i /aɪ/ (plural **i's**) or **I** (plural **I's**) noun [C/U] the ninth letter of the English alphabet

I /aɪ/ pronoun used as the subject of a verb for referring to yourself, when you are the person speaking or writing: *I didn't hurt you, did I?* ♦ *Peter and I will do the cooking.*

iamb /ˈaɪæm/ noun [C] LITERATURE a unit of rhythm in poetry, consisting of one short or weak beat followed by one long or strong beat, as in the word 'mistake'

iambic pentameter /aɪˌæmbɪk penˈtæmɪtə/ noun [C/U] LITERATURE a common pattern used in English poetry, in which each line contains five **iambs**

ibis /ˈaɪbɪs/ noun [C] a large bird with a long neck, long legs, and a curved beak that lives near water in hot countries

ibuprofen /ˌaɪbjuːˈprəʊfen/ noun [C/U] HEALTH a medicine that people take for **headaches** and other pains that are not very serious

the ICC /ˌaɪ siː ˈsiː/ noun [singular] BUSINESS the International Chamber of Commerce: an international organization of business owners

ice /aɪs/ noun [U] water that has frozen and become solid: *a block of ice* ♦ *Ice was forming on the windscreen.* ♦ *a drink with plenty of ice*
  PHRASE **break the ice** to make people feel more relaxed and ready to talk, for example at the beginning of a party: *Joe told a few jokes, which helped to break the ice.*

the ˈIce ˌAge noun GEOLOGY a period of time thousands of years ago when large areas of the Earth were covered in ice

iceberg /ˈaɪsbɜːɡ/ noun [C] GEOGRAPHY a very large piece of ice floating in the sea with only a small amount of it above the surface of the water

ˈice ˌcap noun [C] GEOGRAPHY a large area of ice that covers the land and sea around the North or South Pole

ˌice-ˈcold adj very cold

ˌice ˈcream noun **1** [U] a frozen sweet food made from cream or milk and sugar, often with fruit or chocolate added to flavour it **2** [C] an amount of ice cream for one person

ice floe /ˈaɪs ˌfləʊ/ noun [C] GEOGRAPHY a large area of ice floating on the surface of the sea

ˈice ˌhockey noun [U] SPORTS a game that is played on ice by two teams of six players. The players use long sticks to try to hit a small round flat object called a **puck** into the other team's goal.

ˈice ˌpack noun [C] **1** a bag full of ice that you hold against an injured or painful part of your body to stop it swelling or to make it less painful **2** GEOGRAPHY an area of small pieces of ice floating in the sea

ˈice ˌrink noun [C] SPORTS a large flat area of ice inside a building, where people can go to **ice-skate**

ˈice ˌsheet noun [C] GEOGRAPHY an **ice cap**

ˈice ˌshelf noun [C] GEOGRAPHY a large area of ice that floats on the sea and is attached to the land

ˈice ˌskate noun [C] SPORTS a special boot with a metal blade on the bottom that you wear to move smoothly across ice

ˈice-ˌskate verb [I] SPORTS to move around on ice wearing ice skates —**ˈice-ˌskater** noun [C], **ˈice-ˌskating** noun [U]

icicle /ˈaɪsɪk(ə)l/ noun [C] a long thin piece of ice that hangs down from somewhere such as a roof

icing /ˈaɪsɪŋ/ noun [U] a mixture of sugar and water or butter that is used for covering cakes

icon /ˈaɪkɒn/ noun [C] **1** COMPUTING a small picture on a computer screen that you choose by pressing a button with your mouse in order to open a particular program **2** someone who is very famous and who people think represents a particular idea **3** RELIGION a picture or model of a holy person that is used in religious worship in the Russian and Greek Orthodox Church

iconic /aɪˈkɒnɪk/ adj very famous and well known, and believed to represent a particular idea

iconoclastic /aɪˌkɒnəˈklæstɪk/ adj formal attacking the beliefs, customs, and opinions that most people in a society accept

iconography /ˌaɪkəˈnɒɡrəfi/ noun [U] formal the way in which a social or religious group represent their ideas in pictures

icosahedron /ˌaɪkəsəˈhiːdrən/ noun [C] MATHS a solid geometric object with twenty flat sides

ICT /ˌaɪ siː ˈtiː/ noun [U] EDUCATION, COMPUTING information and communication technology: a school subject that deals with computers, electronics, and **telecommunications**

icy /ˈaɪsi/ (**icier, iciest**) adj **1** very cold, in an unpleasant way **2** covered with ice **3** showing that you do not like someone and do not want to be friendly with them: an icy stare

I'd /aɪd/ short form **1** the usual way of saying or writing 'I had'. This is not often used in formal writing: I'd never seen so much money in my life. **2** the usual way of saying or writing 'I would'. This is not often used in formal writing: I'd love to go to Brazil.

ID /ˌaɪˈdiː/ noun **1** [C/U] a document that gives the details of your name, address, and date of birth, sometimes with a photograph **2** [U] **intelligent design**

I'D ˌcard noun [C] an **identity card**

idea /aɪˈdɪə/ noun **1** [C] a thought that you have about how to do something or how to deal with something: What a brilliant idea! ♦ Then I **had an idea**: we could stay with Mark. ♦ Then she **got the idea of** sending the poems to a publisher. ♦ an idea for a new TV show **2** [C] an opinion, or a belief: I don't agree with his **ideas on** education. ♦ She **has** some pretty strange **ideas about** how to bring up children. **3** [singular/U] information or knowledge that you have about something: They **had no idea** what time they were supposed to arrive. ♦ I had only a basic **idea of** how the machine worked. **4** [C/U] a purpose or an intention: My parents wanted me to be a doctor, but I **had other ideas**.

PHRASES **get the idea** informal to understand something, often something that is not expressed directly: I got the idea that he didn't want to answer the question.

get the wrong idea informal to believe something that is not true: I'll explain everything to George. I wouldn't want him to get the wrong idea.

it's a good idea to do sth used for giving someone advice about what they should do: It's a good idea to get someone else's opinion about it first.

ideal¹ /aɪˈdɪəl/ adj **1** of the best or most suitable type: Upgrading your computer seems **the ideal solution**. ♦ Conditions were **ideal for** racing. **2** as good as you can imagine, and probably too good to be real = PERFECT: **In an ideal world** there would be no poverty.

ideal² /aɪˈdɪəl/ noun [C] **1** an idea that you try to follow about what is good and right= PRINCIPLE: the socialist ideal of equality for all members of society **2** the best example of something that you can think of: Sophie represented his **ideal of** beauty.

idealist /aɪˈdɪəlɪst/ noun [C] someone who is idealistic

idealistic /aɪˌdɪəˈlɪstɪk/ adj an idealistic person believes very firmly in something that is good but probably impossible to achieve

idealize /aɪˈdɪəlaɪz/ verb [T] to believe or suggest that someone or something is perfect or better than they really are —**idealization** /aɪˌdɪəlaɪˈzeɪʃ(ə)n/ noun [C/U]

ideally /aɪˈdɪəli/ adv **1** used for saying what you would like to happen or how things should be: Ideally, we should finish everything by this afternoon. **2** in the best possible way: The lake is ideally suited to sailing.

identical /aɪˈdentɪk(ə)l/ adj exactly the same: This house is almost **identical to** the one where I lived as a child. —**identically** /aɪˈdentɪkli/ adv

iˌdentical ˈtwin noun [C] BIOLOGY one of a pair of twins who are genetically exactly the same as each other because they developed from a single fertilized egg → FRATERNAL TWIN

identifiable /aɪˈdentɪˌfaɪəb(ə)l/ adj able to be recognized, or easy to recognize

identification /aɪˌdentɪfɪˈkeɪʃ(ə)n/ noun [U] **1** something that proves who you are, especially a document with your name and a photograph= ID: Can you show me some identification? **2** the action of recognizing someone or something: the identification and arrest of two suspects ♦ The identification of a problem is the first step towards solving it. **3** a feeling that you understand someone else and know how they feel

identify /aɪˈdentɪfaɪ/ (**identifies, identifying, identified**) verb [T] **1** to recognize someone and be able to say who they are: One of the thieves has been identified by witnesses. **2** to recognize something and to understand exactly what it is: Several key problems have already been identified.

identity /aɪˈdentɪti/ (plural **identities**) noun [C/U] **1** the fact of who you are or what your name is: Do you have any **proof of identity**? ♦ It was just a case of **mistaken identity** (=when you wrongly think that someone is someone else). **2** the qualities that make someone or something what they are and different from other people: The countries have kept their own political and cultural identities. ♦ Lorna went through a bit of **an identity crisis** (=was not certain about her identity) after her divorce. → MISTAKEN IDENTITY

iˈdentity ˌcard noun [C] an official document that shows who you are

iˈdentity ˌtheft noun [C/U] stealing information about someone that makes it possible to use their bank account or credit card

ideological /ˌaɪdiəˈlɒdʒɪk(ə)l/ adj based on or relating to an ideology: ideological differences —**ideologically** /ˌaɪdiəˈlɒdʒɪkli/ adv

ideology /ˌaɪdiˈɒlədʒi/ (plural **ideologies**) noun [C/U] SOCIAL STUDIES a system of ideas and principles on which a political or economic theory is based: revolutionary ideology

ideophone /ˈɪdiəʊfəʊn/ noun [C] LANGUAGE a word that gives a vivid impression of a feeling or sensory perception, for example 'clatter' or 'squelch'

idiolect /ˈɪdiəlekt/ noun [C/U] LANGUAGE one person's individual way of speaking or writing a language

idiom /ˈɪdiəm/ noun [C] LANGUAGE a fixed expression that has a **metaphorical** meaning (=when one idea, image etc represents another). For example, 'have your feet on the ground' is an idiom meaning 'to be sensible'.

idiomatic /ˌɪdiəˈmætɪk/ adj LANGUAGE **1** expressing things in a way that sounds natural: an idiomatic translation **2** containing idioms, or consisting of an idiom: idiomatic expressions —**idiomatically** /ˌɪdiəˈmætɪkli/ adv

idiophone /ˈɪdiəʊfəʊn/ noun [C] MUSIC a technical name for a musical instrument that vibrates as a whole to produce a sound when it is hit, for example a bell or a **rattle**

idiosyncrasy /ˌɪdiəʊˈsɪŋkrəsi/ (plural **idiosyncrasies**) noun [C/U] an idiosyncratic feature or way of behaving

idiosyncratic /ˌɪdiəʊsɪŋˈkrætɪk/ adj unusual or strange, and not typical of anyone or anything else: *her own idiosyncratic style of painting*

idiot /ˈɪdiət/ noun [C] informal someone who behaves in an extremely stupid way: *Diana suddenly realized what an absolute idiot she had been.*

idiotic /ˌɪdiˈɒtɪk/ adj done or behaving in an extremely stupid way —**idiotically** /ˌɪdiˈɒtɪkli/ adv

idle /ˈaɪd(ə)l/ adj **1** not working or being used: *Valuable machinery is left to lie idle for long periods.* **2** lazy **3** lacking a good reason or real purpose: *idle gossip* —**idleness** noun [U], **idly** /ˈaɪd(ə)li/ adv

idler gear /ˈaɪdlə ˌgɪə/ or **'idle ˌgear** noun [C] ENGINEERING, TECHNOLOGY a **gear** (=circular part of a machine) put between two other gears that lets movement pass through it, but does not change direction or speed

'idle ˌtime noun [U] BUSINESS a period during which a piece of equipment or someone working for an organization is not doing anything

idol /ˈaɪd(ə)l/ noun [C] **1** someone that you admire very much **2** RELIGION a picture or statue that is worshipped as a god

idolize /ˈaɪdəlaɪz/ verb [T] to think that someone is perfect

idyllic /ɪˈdɪlɪk/ adj extremely beautiful and peaceful: *an idyllic scene* —**idyllically** /ɪˈdɪlɪkli/ adv

i.e. abbrev used when you are explaining the exact meaning of something that you have mentioned: *Senior officers – i.e. anyone with the rank of colonel or above – get their own administrative staff.*

IED /ˌaɪ iː ˈdiː/ noun [C] improvised explosive device: a simple bomb that someone, especially a **terrorist** or **guerrilla**, has made themselves

IELTS /ˈaɪelts/ noun [U] International English Language Testing System: a test organized by the University of Cambridge in the UK for students who need a qualification in English in order to be able to study at a university in the UK, Canada, Australia, or New Zealand

if /ɪf/ conjunction **1** used for introducing a possible situation or a situation that you are imagining: *If we miss the last bus, we'll have to walk home.* ♦ *If you're in a hurry, take a taxi.* ♦ *I'm sorry if I've upset you.* ♦ *If you worked harder, you'd get better results.* ♦ *I'd like to be back here by 10.30 if possible.* ♦ *What if we can't solve the problem?* **2** used for introducing a situation that always has the same effect or meaning: *I get a headache if I watch too much television.* **3** used when you are asking or talking about something that is not certain: *I haven't decided if I want to play.* ♦ *She asked me if I was fond of music.* **4** spoken used when you are politely asking someone to do something, or when you are asking for permission: *I would be grateful if you would send me further details.*

PHRASES **if I were you** spoken used when you are giving someone advice: *If I were you, I'd stay away from that man.*

if only spoken used for saying that you would like a situation to be different: *If only we had a bigger house!* → AS

igloo /ˈɪgluː/ noun [C] a building made from snow or ice

igneous /ˈɪgniəs/ adj GEOLOGY igneous rocks such as **granite** and **basalt** are formed from **magma** (=liquid rock) flowing from the centre of the Earth that has cooled down and become solid. The other types of rock are metamorphic rock and sedimentary rock. —*picture* → ROCK CYCLE

ignite /ɪgˈnaɪt/ verb **1** [I/T] formal to start to burn, or to make something start to burn **2** [T] to start a fight or an argument= SPARK **3** [T] formal to start a particular feeling in someone= SPARK

ignition /ɪgˈnɪʃ(ə)n/ noun **1** [singular] TECHNOLOGY the place where you put in the key to make a car's engine start, or the system that makes it start **2** [U] formal the process of making something start to burn

ignominious /ˌɪgnəˈmɪniəs/ adj formal very embarrassing, especially because of making someone seem very unsuccessful or unimportant = HUMILIATING —**ignominiously** adv

ignorance /ˈɪgnərəns/ noun [U] lack of knowledge about something

ignorant /ˈɪgnərənt/ adj not knowing something that you should know or that you need to know —**ignorantly** adv

ignore /ɪgˈnɔː/ verb [T] **1** to not consider something, or to not let it influence you: *We had ignored the fact that it was getting darker.* ♦ *The government has ignored the advice it was given.* **2** to pretend that you have not noticed someone or something: *He completely ignored her and kept on walking.*

iguana /ɪˈgwɑːnə/ noun [C] a large lizard with sharp points on its back that lives in tropical parts of North and South America —*picture* → REPTILE

IK /ˌaɪ ˈkeɪ/ noun [U] SOCIAL STUDIES indigenous knowledge: the traditional knowledge and skills that a local community builds up over the years through living in a particular place

IKS /ˌaɪ keɪ ˈes/ noun [plural] SOCIAL STUDIES indigenous knowledge systems: the traditional knowledge and skills that a local community builds up over the years through living in a particular place

ileum /ˈɪliəm/ (plural **ilea** /ˈɪliə/) noun [C] ANATOMY the last section of the **small intestine**. It produces enzymes that help to digest food. —*picture* → DIGESTIVE SYSTEM

ill¹ /ɪl/ adj **1** HEALTH not healthy because of a medical condition or an injury: *She was too ill to travel.* ♦ *She was unlucky enough to fall ill (=become ill) on holiday.* ♦ *Her husband is seriously ill in hospital.* **2** bad or harmful: *The fish didn't taste fresh, but we suffered no ill effects.*

ill² /ɪl/ noun [C] formal a problem, or a difficulty: *a cure for all the nation's ills*

I'll /aɪl/ short form the usual way of saying or writing 'I will' or 'I shall'. This is not often used in formal writing: *I'll see you at about six o'clock.*

ill-advised /ˌɪl ədˈvaɪzd/ adj likely to have a bad effect

ill-conceived /ˌɪl kənˈsiːvd/ adj an ill-conceived idea or plan is not sensible

illegal /ɪˈliːg(ə)l/ adj not allowed by the law: *illegal drugs* ♦ *It is illegal for employers to discriminate on the grounds of race.* —**illegality** /ˌɪliːˈgæləti/ noun [U], **illegally** adv

il,legal 'immigrant noun [C] SOCIAL STUDIES someone who enters a country illegally, or who stays for a longer time than they are legally allowed

illegible /ɪˈledʒəb(ə)l/ adj difficult or impossible to read —**illegibly** /ɪˈledʒəbli/ adv

illegitimate /ˌɪləˈdʒɪtəmət/ adj **1** an illegitimate child is born to parents who are not legally married **2** formal not allowed by the rules or laws

ill-equipped /ˌɪl ɪˈkwɪpt/ adj formal lacking the necessary equipment, skills, or abilities to do something

ill-ˈfitting adj formal ill-fitting clothes are the wrong size for the person wearing them

illicit /ɪˈlɪsɪt/ adj **1** an illicit relationship, activity, or situation is one that people do not approve of **2** not allowed by the law= ILLEGAL: illicit drugs —**illicitly** adv

ill-inˈformed adj lacking knowledge of a particular subject

illiterate /ɪˈlɪtərət/ adj **1** not able to read or write **2** containing a lot of mistakes in grammar and spelling **3** lacking knowledge in a particular subject: politically illiterate —**illiteracy** /ɪˈlɪtərəsi/ noun [U]

ill-mannered /ˌɪl ˈmænəd/ adj formal not polite = RUDE ≠ WELL-MANNERED

illness /ˈɪlnəs/ noun HEALTH **1** [U] the state of feeling ill or having a disease: He missed five days of school because of illness. **2** [C] a particular disease, or a period of being ill: a serious illness

> **Build your vocabulary: words you can use instead of illness**
>
> - **bug** (informal) a minor illness that is caused by a virus or bacteria and lasts a short time only
> - **condition** a medical problem that affects someone for a long time
> - **disease** a serious illness that usually lasts a long time
> - **infection** an illness that is caused by bacteria and that usually lasts a short time only
> - **virus** an illness that is caused by a very small germ

illocutionary /ˌɪləˈkjuːʃ(ə)n(ə)ri/ adj LANGUAGE relating to an action that you perform by saying something, for example when you threaten or warn someone, or when you promise to do something for them

illogical /ɪˈlɒdʒɪk(ə)l/ adj not sensible, or not based on clear facts or reasons: an illogical argument —**illogically** /ɪˈlɒdʒɪkli/ adv

ill-ˈtreat verb [T] formal to treat someone in a cruel or unkind way: None of the prisoners was ill-treated. —**ill-ˈtreatment** noun [U]

illuminate /ɪˈluːmɪneɪt/ verb [T] formal **1** to make something bright with light or lights, or to shine a light on something= LIGHT **2** to make something clear and easier to understand

illumination /ɪˌluːmɪˈneɪʃ(ə)n/ noun **1** [U] light that is provided by something in a place **2** illuminations [plural] coloured lights that are used for decorating a town

illusion /ɪˈluːʒ(ə)n/ noun [C] **1** a false or wrong belief or idea **2** an appearance or effect that is different from the way that things really are

illusory /ɪˈluːsəri/ adj formal not real, but seeming real: the illusory benefits of the scheme

illustrate /ˈɪləstreɪt/ verb [T] **1** to show or explain something by using examples, pictures, lists of numbers etc: The process is illustrated in Figure 4. ♦ Miriam quoted three case studies to **illustrate her point**. **2** ARTS to draw the pictures in a book, or to put pictures, drawings, or photographs in a book: The

cookbook is **beautifully illustrated** with colour photographs.

illustration /ˌɪləˈstreɪʃ(ə)n/ noun **1** [C] ARTS a picture, drawing, or photograph that is used for decorating a book or for explaining something: a children's book with beautiful illustrations **2** [U] ARTS the art of illustrating books **3** [C/U] an example, event, or fact that explains something or shows that something is true: The project **provides a good illustration of** how people can work together.

illustrative /ˈɪləstrətɪv, ɪˈlʌstrətɪv/ adj formal an illustrative example, fact, document etc helps to explain something more clearly or show that something is true

illustrator /ˈɪləˌstreɪtə/ noun [C] someone whose job is to draw pictures for books or magazines

ill ˈwill noun [U] a strong feeling of disliking someone and wanting something bad to happen to them = ANIMOSITY ≠ GOODWILL

I'm /aɪm/ short form the usual way of saying or writing 'I am'. This is not often used in formal writing.

IM /ˌaɪ ˈem/ abbrev COMPUTING instant messaging

im- /ɪm/ prefix not, or no: impatient ♦ immature

image /ˈɪmɪdʒ/ noun

1 opinion	4 in writing
2 picture	5 reflection
3 in the mind	

1 [C/U] an opinion that people have about someone or something: The company needs to shake off its outdated image. ♦ We have **an image of** the US as a very rich country.
2 [C] a picture, especially one in a mirror or on a computer, television, or cinema screen: software for manipulating images after you have scanned them ♦ She stared at her image in the bathroom mirror. ♦ **Images of** the war appeared on the screen.
3 [C] a picture or idea of someone or something in your mind: I had a sudden **mental image** of Robert waiting for me with flowers.
4 [C] LITERATURE a description of something that uses language or combines ideas in an interesting way
5 [C] PHYSICS a copy of someone or something produced by light and shown by a mirror or lens = REFLECTION

imagery /ˈɪmɪdʒəri/ noun [U] **1** pictures, photographs, or objects that represent an idea **2** LITERATURE the use of words and phrases to create an image of something

imaginable /ɪˈmædʒɪnəb(ə)l/ adj possible to imagine: a situation that would have been hardly imaginable ten years ago

imaginary /ɪˈmædʒɪnəri/ adj not real, but created only in the mind: A child sometimes creates an **imaginary friend** to play with.

imagination /ɪˌmædʒɪˈneɪʃ(ə)n/ noun **1** [C/U] the ability to form pictures or original ideas in your mind: Was he scared, or was it just my imagination? ♦ a child with a **vivid imagination** ♦ Try to **use your imagination** when planning main meals. ♦ Her essay showed a remarkable **lack of imagination**. **2** [U] a feeling of interest and excitement about something: Their policies have really caught the public's imagination. → STRETCH[2]

imaginative /ɪˈmædʒɪnətɪv/ adj **1** involving new, different, or exciting ideas= CREATIVE ≠ UNIMAGINATIVE: the imaginative use of computers in the classroom **2** able to produce new, different, or exciting ideas ≠ UNIMAGINATIVE —**imaginatively** adv

imagine /ɪˈmædʒɪn/ verb [T] **1** to form a picture of someone or something in your mind: *She tried to imagine the scene.* ♦ *Imagine my surprise when they announced I had won!* ♦ *He had never imagined that digging would be such hard work.* **2** to have an idea that something exists or is happening, when in fact it does not exist or is not happening: *There's nothing there – you're just **imagining things**!* **3** to think that something is probably true= SUPPOSE: *I imagine they've left already.*

Word family: imagine

Words in the same family as imagine
- **imagination** n
- **imaginable** adj
- **imaginative** adj
- **imaginatively** adv
- **imaginary** adj
- **unimaginable** adj
- **unimaginative** adj
- **unimaginatively** adv

---

imaging /ˈɪmɪdʒɪŋ/ noun [U] **PHYSICS** the process of producing an image by using a machine that passes an electronic **beam** over something

imago /ɪˈmeɪɡəʊ, ɪˈmɑːɡəʊ/ noun [C] **BIOLOGY** an insect when it is a fully sexually developed adult

imam /ɪˈmɑːm/ noun [C] **RELIGION** a Muslim priest or leader

imbalance /ɪmˈbæləns/ noun [C/U] a situation in which the balance between two things is not equal or fair

the IMF /ˌaɪ em ˈef/ **ECONOMICS** the International Monetary Fund: an international organization that works to balance and manage the world's economies and to help countries with weak economies to develop

imitate /ˈɪmɪteɪt/ verb [T] **1** to copy something: *Italian ice cream is imitated all over the world.* **2** to copy what someone does or says, often in order to make people laugh= MIMIC —**imitator** /ˈɪmɪˌteɪtə/ noun [C]

imitation¹ /ˌɪmɪˈteɪʃ(ə)n/ noun **1** [C] the act of copying someone's actions, words, or behaviour, often in order to make people laugh **2** [C/U] the act of copying something **3** [C] something that is a copy of something else, and not as good as the original thing: *a crude imitation of Hitchcock's earlier work*

imitation² /ˌɪmɪˈteɪʃ(ə)n/ adj made to look like something that is more valuable or expensive: *imitation marble*

immaculate /ɪˈmækjʊlət/ adj **1** completely clean and tidy= SPOTLESS **2** correct or perfect in every way —**immaculately** adv

immature /ˌɪməˈtjʊə/ adj **1** behaving in a silly way, as though you are much younger than you really are ≠ MATURE **2** not fully grown or developed ≠ MATURE —**immaturity** /ˌɪməˈtjʊərəti/ noun [U]

immeasurably /ɪˈmeʒərəbli/ adv *formal* extremely

immediacy /ɪˈmiːdiəsi/ noun [U] a quality that makes someone feel as though something is happening now, and that they are involved in it

immediate /ɪˈmiːdiət/ adj

1 without delay	4 next to sb/sth
2 urgent	5 closely connected
3 directly before/after	

1 happening or done now, without delay: *Our government must take immediate action.* ♦ *My immediate response was to say yes.*
2 existing now and needing urgent action: *There doesn't seem to be any immediate danger.*
3 existing in the period of time directly before or after an event: *plans for **the immediate future***
4 next to a person or place: *There are several pleasant walks **in the immediate vicinity** (=very near).*

5 closely connected to you: *She is my immediate superior* (=the person directly in charge of me). ♦ *Only **immediate family** (=parents, children, brothers, and sisters) will be allowed to attend the ceremony.*

immediately /ɪˈmiːdiətli/ adv **1** very quickly and without delay: *She decided to leave immediately.* ♦ *I immediately realized how serious the situation was.* **2** just before or just after an event: *She was with Roosevelt immediately before his death.* **3** with no one or nothing between= DIRECTLY: *We could hear noises coming from the room immediately below us.*

immense /ɪˈmens/ adj extremely large= HUGE: *an immense amount of money*

immensely /ɪˈmensli/ adv very, or very much: *an immensely talented singer*

immensity /ɪˈmensəti/ noun [U] the very large size of something

immerse /ɪˈmɜːs/ verb [T] *formal* to put someone or something in a liquid so that they are covered completely

immersion /ɪˈmɜːʃ(ə)n/ noun **1** [U] the state of something that has been put in a liquid and is surrounded or covered by it **2** **EDUCATION** a method of teaching a foreign language in which teachers and students use only the foreign language during classes **3** [U] **RELIGION** a method of **baptizing** a new member of a Christian Church that involves putting their whole body into water

imˈmersion ˌheater noun [C] **CONSTRUCTION** a piece of electrical equipment that heats water for use in the home by direct contact with it

immigrant /ˈɪmɪɡrənt/ noun [C] **SOCIAL STUDIES** someone who comes to live in a country from another country → EMIGRANT

immigrate /ˈɪmɪɡreɪt/ verb [I] **SOCIAL STUDIES** to come into a country because you want to live there permanently → EMIGRATE

immigration /ˌɪmɪˈɡreɪʃ(ə)n/ noun [U] **1** **SOCIAL STUDIES** the process in which people come to a country in order to live there permanently **2** the place where you show your passport and are officially allowed into a country

imminent /ˈɪmɪnənt/ adj likely to happen very soon, or certain to do so —**imminence** noun [U], **imminently** adv

immiscible /ɪˈmɪsəb(ə)l/ adj **CHEMISTRY** relating to two or more liquids that will not mix together to form a single **homogeneous** substance

immobile /ɪˈməʊbaɪl/ adj **1** not moving= MOTIONLESS **2** not able to move —**immobility** /ˌɪməʊˈbɪləti/ noun [U]

immoral /ɪˈmɒrəl/ adj morally wrong: *immoral behaviour* —**immorality** /ˌɪməˈræləti/ noun [U], **immorally** adv

immortal /ɪˈmɔːt(ə)l/ adj **1** very well known and likely to be remembered for a long time **2** living or existing for all time ≠ MORTAL —**immortality** /ˌɪmɔːˈtæləti/ noun [U]

immortalize /ɪˈmɔːt(ə)laɪz/ verb [T] to make someone or something famous for a very long time

immovable /ɪˈmuːvəb(ə)l/ adj **1** with opinions or feelings that you refuse to change **2** impossible to move —**immovably** adv

immune /ɪˈmjuːn/ adj **1** **HEALTH** safe from a particular disease, because your body protects you from it **2** **HEALTH** relating to the body's immune system **3** not influenced or affected by something: *Guy seemed totally **immune to** criticism.* **4** not affected by something such as a law, because of a special arrangement: *Diplomats are **immune from** prosecution.*

im'mune ,system noun [C] HEALTH the system in the body that protects against diseases by recognizing any cells, tissues, or organisms that do not belong to it such as bacteria or viruses and taking action against them

immunity /ɪˈmjuːnəti/ (plural **immunities**) noun 1 [singular/U] HEALTH the protection that the body gives against a particular disease 2 [C/U] a situation in which someone is not affected by something such as a law because they have a special job or position

immunize /ˈɪmjʊnaɪz/ verb [T] HEALTH to prevent a person or animal from getting a particular illness by inoculating or vaccinating them —**immunization** /ˌɪmjʊnaɪˈzeɪʃ(ə)n/ noun [C/U]

immunodeficiency /ˌɪmjʊnəʊdɪˈfɪʃ(ə)nsi/ noun [U] HEALTH a medical condition in which the body does not have the normal protection against diseases —**immunodeficient** adj

immunology /ˌɪmjʊˈnɒlədʒi/ noun [U] HEALTH the study of how diseases can be prevented and how the **immune system** works —**immunologist** noun [C]

immunosuppression /ˌɪmjʊnəʊsəˈpreʃ(ə)n/ noun [U] HEALTH the process of preventing the body's **immune system** from working, or of making it work less effectively —**immunosuppressant** adj

immutable /ɪˈmjuːtəb(ə)l/ adj formal 1 impossible to change 2 always true or always the same

impact /ˈɪmpækt/ noun 1 [C] an effect or influence: *Her paper discusses the likely impact of global warming.* ♦ *Internet shopping has begun to have a serious **impact on** traditional bookshops.* 2 [C/U] the force or act of one object hitting another: *I was thrown to the ground by the impact of the blast.* ♦ *The missile exploded **on impact**.*

'impact ,crater noun [C] GEOLOGY a large round hollow area in a surface that is caused by something hitting the surface

impacted /ɪmˈpæktɪd/ adj HEALTH an impacted tooth cannot grow because it is under another tooth

impair /ɪmˈpeə/ verb [T] formal to make something less good or effective by damaging it

impaired /ɪmˈpeəd/ adj not fully able to do something

impairment /ɪmˈpeəmənt/ noun [C/U] the fact that a part of your body is unable to do something fully: *visual impairment*

impala /ɪmˈpɑːlə/ noun [C] a large brown African **deer** with long curved horns and long thin legs

impale /ɪmˈpeɪl/ verb [T] to push a pointed object through someone or something

impart /ɪmˈpɑːt/ verb [T] formal 1 to give something such as information, knowledge, or beliefs to someone 2 to give something a particular quality

impartial /ɪmˈpɑːʃ(ə)l/ adj not influenced by, or not preferring, one particular person or group —**impartiality** /ˌɪmpɑːʃiˈæləti/ noun [U], **impartially** adv

impassable /ɪmˈpɑːsəb(ə)l/ adj an impassable road or path is impossible to travel along

impasse /ˈæmpɑːs/ noun [singular] a situation in which progress is not possible because none of the people involved is willing to change their opinion or decision= DEADLOCK

impassive /ɪmˈpæsɪv/ adj not showing any emotion —**impassively** adv

impatient /ɪmˈpeɪʃ(ə)nt/ adj 1 annoyed because something is not happening as quickly as you want or in the way that you want ≠ PATIENT: *'Come on!' said Maggie, becoming impatient.* ♦ *He gets **impatient with** people who don't agree with him.* 2 wanting something to happen as soon as possible: *They were **impatient for** news of their father.* ♦ *After a couple of days, she was **impatient to** get back to work.* —**impatience** /ɪmˈpeɪʃ(ə)ns/ noun [U], **impatiently** adv

impedance /ɪmˈpiːd(ə)ns/ noun [U] PHYSICS a measure of how difficult it is for an **alternating current** of electricity to flow through a piece of electrical equipment

impede /ɪmˈpiːd/ verb [T] formal to make it more difficult for someone to do something or for something to happen

impediment /ɪmˈpedɪmənt/ noun [C] 1 formal something that makes it more difficult for someone to do something or for something to happen 2 a physical or **psychological** problem that affects how well someone can do something

impel /ɪmˈpel/ (**impels, impelling, impelled**) verb [T] formal if a feeling or idea impels someone to do something, it forces them to do it

impending /ɪmˈpendɪŋ/ adj going to happen very soon: *He was unaware of the impending disaster.*

impenetrable /ɪmˈpenɪtrəb(ə)l/ adj 1 impossible to get into, get through, or see through 2 impossible to understand: *impenetrable writing*

imperative¹ /ɪmˈperətɪv/ adj 1 formal very important and urgent 2 LANGUAGE the imperative form of a verb expresses an order to do something

imperative² /ɪmˈperətɪv/ noun 1 [C] formal something that is very important and urgent 2 **the imperative** [singular] LANGUAGE the form of a verb that expresses orders. The imperative is also called the **imperative mood**.

imperceptible /ˌɪmpəˈseptəb(ə)l/ adj something that is imperceptible is so slight or small that it is very difficult to notice —**imperceptibly** adv

imperfect /ɪmˈpɜːfɪkt/ adj 1 something that is imperfect has some faults or other bad qualities 2 LANGUAGE an imperfect form of a verb describes an action in the past that is continuous, repeated, or not finished —**imperfection** /ˌɪmpəˈfekʃ(ə)n/ noun [C/U], **imperfectly** adv

the imperfect /ɪmˈpɜːfɪkt/ noun [singular] LANGUAGE the **imperfect tense**

,imperfect 'market noun [C] ECONOMICS a market in which one or more of the producers or customers is able to affect the price of a product or service

the im,perfect 'tense noun [singular] LANGUAGE the form of a verb that describes an action in the past that is continuous, repeated, or not finished

imperial /ɪmˈpɪəriəl/ adj 1 relating to an **empire** (=a group of several countries that are ruled by one country) or the person who rules it 2 MATHS belonging to a system of measurement in which weight is measured in pounds, length is measured in feet, and volume is measured in **pints** → METRIC

imperialism /ɪmˈpɪəriəˌlɪz(ə)m/ noun [U] SOCIAL STUDIES the actions of a powerful country that tries to gain control of other countries —**imperialist** adj, noun [C]

impermeable /ɪmˈpɜːmiəb(ə)l/ adj something that is impermeable does not let liquid or gas pass through it

impersonal /ɪmˈpɜːs(ə)nəl/ adj **1** not showing your personal feelings or ideas: *His manner was cold and impersonal.* **2 LANGUAGE** an impersonal verb or sentence usually has the word 'it' as its subject, for example 'It's raining' —**impersonally** adv

im,personal 'pronoun noun [C] **LANGUAGE** a pronoun such as 'it' in English that does not refer to a particular person or thing, for example 'It's all right'

impersonate /ɪmˈpɜːsəneɪt/ verb [T] **1** to copy the way that someone speaks and behaves in order to pretend to be that person or to make people laugh= IMITATE **2** to pretend to be someone else by copying the way that they look, speak, or behave in order to trick people —**impersonation** /ɪm,pɜːs(ə)nˈeɪʃ(ə)n/ noun [C/U], **impersonator** noun [C]

impertinent /ɪmˈpɜːtɪnənt/ adj *formal* rude and not showing respect for someone —**impertinence** noun [U], **impertinently** adv

imperturbable /,ɪmpəˈtɜːbəb(ə)l/ adj *formal* always calm and not easily upset

impervious /ɪmˈpɜːviəs/ adj **1 impervious to sth** not affected by something: *He continued talking, impervious to the effect his words were having.* **2 SCIENCE** relating to a substance that does not let liquid or gas pass through it —*picture →* OIL WELL

impetigo /,ɪmpɪˈtaɪɡəʊ/ noun [U] **HEALTH** an infectious disease of the skin

impetuous /ɪmˈpetʃuəs/ adj doing things quickly, without thinking about the results= RASH —**impetuously** adv

impetus /ˈɪmpɪtəs/ noun [C] **PHYSICS** a force that makes a moving object able to continue moving at the same velocity, despite any resistance

implacable /ɪmˈplækəb(ə)l/ adj having or expressing very angry or determined feelings that will not change —**implacably** adv

implant¹ /ˈɪmplɑːnt/ noun [C] **HEALTH** something such as tissue, a hormone, or a small piece of equipment that is put into someone's body in a medical operation

implant² /ɪmˈplɑːnt/ verb [T] **1 HEALTH** to put something such as tissue, a hormone, or a small piece of equipment into someone's body in a medical operation **2** to put an idea or attitude into someone's mind

implausible /ɪmˈplɔːzəb(ə)l/ adj difficult to accept as true —**implausibly** adv

implement¹ /ˈɪmplɪ,ment/ verb [T] to make something such as an idea, plan, system, or law start to work and be used —**implementation** /,ɪmplɪmənˈteɪʃ(ə)n/ noun [U]

implement² /ˈɪmplɪmənt/ noun [C] a tool, or a simple piece of equipment

implicate /ˈɪmplɪkeɪt/ verb [T] **1** to show or claim that someone or something is involved in an activity that is illegal or morally wrong **2** to make something seem likely to be the cause of something bad

implication /,ɪmplɪˈkeɪʃ(ə)n/ noun **1** [C] a possible future effect or result: *What are **the implications of** this new technology?* ♦ *Improving your diet **has** important **implications for** your future health.* **2** [C/U] something that you suggest is true, although you do not say it directly: *I resent **the implication that** my work is not thorough.*

implicit /ɪmˈplɪsɪt/ adj **1** not stated directly, but expressed or suggested indirectly ≠ EXPLICIT: *an implicit criticism* **2** without any doubts or questions: *an implicit belief in the goodness of people* **3 implicit in sth** forming a necessary part of something —**implicitly** adv

implode /ɪmˈpləʊd/ verb [I] **1** if something such as an organization or an economic system implodes, it is completely destroyed by things that are happening within it= COLLAPSE **2** to break up violently and fall inwards

implore /ɪmˈplɔː/ verb [T] *formal* to ask someone in an emotional way to do something, because you want it very much= BEG

imply /ɪmˈplaɪ/ (**implies, implying, implied**) verb [T] to show or suggest that something exists or is true: *I didn't mean to imply that you were interfering.*

impolite /,ɪmpəˈlaɪt/ adj not polite= RUDE —**impolitely** adv

import¹ /ɪmˈpɔːt/ verb [T] **1 ECONOMICS, BUSINESS** to buy a product from another country and bring it to your country ≠ EXPORT: *We **import** most of our coal **from** other countries.* ♦ *imported luxury goods* **2 COMPUTING** to move information into a file or program ≠ EXPORT —**importation** /,ɪmpɔːˈteɪʃ(ə)n/ noun [U], **importer** noun [C]

import² /ˈɪmpɔːt/ noun [C/U] **ECONOMICS, BUSINESS** a product that is imported, or the process of importing products ≠ EXPORT: *cheap imports from Eastern Europe* ♦ *We need controls on **the import of** meat.*

importance /ɪmˈpɔːt(ə)ns/ noun [U] the fact of being important, or the degree to which something or someone is important: *The company recognizes **the importance of** training its employees.* ♦ *The issue has special **importance for** people in rural areas.*

important /ɪmˈpɔːt(ə)nt/ adj **1** something that is important has a major effect on someone or something: *Music was an important part of the life of the community.* ♦ *Winning the game yesterday was **important for** us.* ♦ *Your interest and support are **important to** your child.* ♦ *It **is important to** stress that the study only involved a small number of people.* **2** important people have a lot of influence or power: *We can't afford to lose such an important customer.*

Build your vocabulary: words you can use instead of important

Important is a very general word. Here are some words with more specific meanings that sound more natural and appropriate in particular situations.
people influential, leading, prominent, senior, top
events historic, key, landmark, main, major, momentous
issues/problems critical, major, significant
achievements/discoveries groundbreaking, historic, landmark, significant
effects far-reaching, lasting, main, major, significant
facts notable, noteworthy, significant
things that are important because you must have or do them critical, crucial, essential, necessary, urgent, vital

importantly /ɪmˈpɔːt(ə)ntli/ adv **1** used for emphasizing that something is important: *How did Jamie know? And, more importantly, what did he know?* **2** in a way that shows that you think you are important

impose /ɪmˈpəʊz/ verb **1** [T] to force people to accept something: *If she lied under oath, the court will impose a severe penalty.* ♦ *I wouldn't want to **impose** my views* *on anyone.* **2** [I] to cause extra work for someone: *Please come and stay. You wouldn't be **imposing on** us at all.*

imposing /ɪmˈpəʊzɪŋ/ adj large and impressive

imposition /ˌɪmpəˈzɪʃ(ə)n/ noun **1** [U] the introduction of something that people are forced to accept **2** [C] an unfair or unreasonable situation that you are expected to accept

impossible /ɪmˈpɒsəb(ə)l/ adj **1** if something is impossible, no one can do it or it cannot happen: *We were faced with an impossible task.* ♦ *It would be impossible to gather this information without using computers.* **2** extremely difficult to do or to deal with: *Dealing with her illness **makes** life pretty **impossible** for the rest of the family.* —**impossibility** /ɪmˌpɒsəˈbɪləti/ noun [C/U]

impostor or **imposter** /ɪmˈpɒstə/ noun [C] someone who pretends to be someone else

impotent /ˈɪmpətənt/ adj **1** unable to do anything that is effective because of a lack of power **2** a man who is impotent cannot have sex because his penis does not stay hard —**impotence** noun [U]

impoverished /ɪmˈpɒvərɪʃt/ adj very poor

impractical /ɪmˈpræktɪk(ə)l/ adj **1** not sensible, or not likely to be effective or successful **2** not good at doing practical things —**impracticality** /ɪmˌpræktɪˈkæləti/ noun [C/U]

imprecise /ˌɪmprɪˈsaɪs/ adj not exact, accurate, or clear —**imprecisely** adv

impregnate /ˈɪmpregneɪt/ verb [T] **1** to make a substance such as a liquid spread all the way through something **2** BIOLOGY to make a woman or female animal pregnant —**impregnation** /ˌɪmpregˈneɪʃ(ə)n/ noun [U]

impress /ɪmˈpres/ verb [T] if someone or something impresses you, you admire them: *I was extremely impressed by the novel.*

impression /ɪmˈpreʃ(ə)n/ noun [C] **1** an opinion, feeling, or idea about someone or something that is not based on much information, or that is only based on the way that they look, sound, or behave: *It is important to **make a** good **impression** at the interview.* ♦ *He **gave** me **the impression that** he really didn't care.* ♦ *I **have the impression that** she's very good at her job.* ♦ *I **was under the impression** (=thought) that we had met before.* **2** a performance in which someone copies the way another person speaks or behaves in order to make people laugh= IMITATION: *Jill **does impressions** of famous singers.* **3** *formal* a mark that is made when an object is pressed onto a surface

impressionable /ɪmˈpreʃ(ə)nəb(ə)l/ adj easily impressed and influenced by other people

Impressionism /ɪmˈpreʃ(ə)nˌɪz(ə)m/ noun [U] ARTS a style of painting in which artists use light and colour to give the general feeling of a scene, rather than exact detail. Impressionism began in France in the middle of the 19th century. —**Impressionist** adj, noun [C]

impressive /ɪmˈpresɪv/ adj if someone or something is impressive, you admire them: *an impressive performance* —**impressively** adv

imprint¹ /ˈɪmprɪnt/ noun [C] **1** a mark that an object leaves on a surface when it is pressed into it **2** a strong permanent influence on someone or something

imprint² /ɪmˈprɪnt/ verb [T] **1** to leave a mark on a surface by pressing an object into it **2** to make something have a strong permanent influence on someone or something

imprison /ɪmˈprɪz(ə)n/ verb [T] to put someone in a prison, or to keep them in a place that they cannot escape from —**imprisonment** noun [U]

improbable /ɪmˈprɒbəb(ə)l/ adj **1** not likely to happen or be true= UNLIKELY **2** strange and unexpected —**improbably** adv

impromptu /ɪmˈprɒmptjuː/ adj not planned or prepared —**impromptu** adv

improper /ɪmˈprɒpə/ adj **1** not suitable or right according to accepted standards of behaviour = INAPPROPRIATE **2** not legal or honest= UNLAWFUL —**improperly** adv

im,proper ˈfraction noun [C] MATHS a fraction such as 9/4 in which the number above the line is larger than the number below it → PROPER FRACTION

impropriety /ˌɪmprəˈpraɪəti/ (plural **improprieties**) noun [C/U] *formal* behaviour that is not honest, professional, or socially acceptable

improve /ɪmˈpruːv/ verb [I/T] to become better, or to make something better: *Your English will improve with practice.* ♦ *More money is needed to improve airline security.*

PHRASAL VERB **imˈprove on sth** to make something better than it was before, or to do something better than you did before: *We hope to improve on last year's performance.*

improvement /ɪmˈpruːvmənt/ noun **1** [C/U] the state of being better than before, or the process of making something better than it was before: *The school is performing well, but we recognize the need for further improvement.* ♦ *There has been **an improvement in** relations between the two countries.* **2** [C] a change that you make to something in order to make it better: *home improvements*

improvise /ˈɪmprəvaɪz/ verb **1** [I/T] to do something or to make something without any previous preparation, or using only what is available at the time: *I don't have a recipe, but we can improvise.* **2** [I] MUSIC to perform something that has not been written down or practised earlier —**improvisation** /ˌɪmprəvaɪˈzeɪʃ(ə)n/ noun [C/U]

imprudent /ɪmˈpruːd(ə)nt/ adj *formal* not sensible, especially in relation to the way that money is spent or invested ≠ PRUDENT —**imprudence** noun [C/U], **imprudently** adv

impudent /ˈɪmpjʊd(ə)nt/ adj behaving in a rude way that shows no respect —**impudence** noun [U], **impudently** adv

impulse /ˈɪmpʌls/ noun **1** [C/U] a sudden strong feeling that you must do something **2** [C] PHYSICS a short sudden electrical signal that a piece of equipment produces **3** [C] BIOLOGY an electrical signal that moves along a nerve fibre

impulsive /ɪmˈpʌlsɪv/ adj tending to do things without thinking about what will happen as a result —**impulsively** adv

impunity /ɪmˈpjuːnəti/ noun [U] *formal* freedom from any risk of being punished

impure /ɪmˈpjʊə/ adj containing another substance that should not be there ≠ PURE

impurity /ɪmˈpjʊərəti/ (plural **impurities**) noun **1** [C] a substance that is wrongly present in another substance **2** [U] the quality of not being pure ≠ PURITY

IMS abbrev COMPUTING information management system

in /ɪn/ adv, preposition

1 contained within	**9** wearing sth
2 into sth	**10** for describing a
3 inside a building	method/style
4 arriving somewhere	**11** for describing
5 during a particular	arrangement
time	**12** affected by weather
6 at the end of a period	**13** referring to an aspect
of time	of sth
7 involved with sth	**14** when the sea is high
8 for describing a	**15** in relation to a total
state/situation	

1 within a container or place: *His passport was in his coat pocket.* ♦ *Have you seen a bag with some tools in?* ♦ *a picnic in the park* ♦ *The books are printed in Hong Kong.*
2 moving, falling, or looking into a place or substance: *The door was open so I just walked in.* ♦ *The guards fired a few shots in the air.* ♦ *I invited her in for a drink.* ♦ *Look in the drawer.*
3 at home, or at work: *I asked to speak to the manager but she wasn't in.*
4 arriving somewhere, especially your home or place of work: *What time did you **get in** last night?* ♦ *Is their flight in yet?*
5 during a particular period, month, season, or year, or during a part of the day: *She was born in 1992.* ♦ *In winter the lake freezes over.* ♦ *The wedding is in April.*
6 at the end of a period of time in the future: *The exams are in six weeks' time.* ♦ *I'll be ready in a few minutes.*
7 involved with or relating to a particular type of activity: *Her husband **works in** publishing.* ♦ *a university **degree in** economics*
8 used for describing a state or situation: *Their lives were **in danger**.* ♦ *Are we all **in agreement**?*
9 used for stating what someone is wearing: *a man in a tall hat* ♦ *a woman in black* (=wearing black clothes)
10 using a particular method or style: *The houses are all built in the traditional style.* ♦ *You have to pay in cash.*
11 arranged in a particular order, shape, or pattern: *We all sat round in a circle.* ♦ *The names are listed in alphabetical order.*
12 affected by a particular type of weather: *Have you been waiting outside in the rain?*
13 used for saying what aspect of something you are referring to: *She's so selfish in her attitude to other people.* ♦ *The words are similar but there is a difference in meaning.*
14 if the tide is in, the sea has reached its highest level on the land
15 used for saying how common something is by showing it as a number in relation to the total number: *One in twelve of the adult population suffers from stress.*

in. abbrev inch

inability /ˌɪnəˈbɪləti/ noun [U] **inability to do sth** the fact of not being able to do something ≠ ABILITY

inaccessible /ˌɪnəkˈsesəb(ə)l/ adj **1** difficult or impossible to reach= REMOTE **2** difficult or impossible to understand —**inaccessibility** /ˌɪnækˌsesəˈbɪləti/ noun [U]

inaccuracy /ɪnˈækjʊrəsi/ (plural **inaccuracies**) noun [C/U] something that is not accurate, or the failure to be accurate

inaccurate /ɪnˈækjʊrət/ adj not accurate or correct —**inaccurately** adv

inaction /ɪnˈækʃ(ə)n/ noun [U] lack of action

inactive /ɪnˈæktɪv/ adj **1** not taking part in physical activity or exercise ≠ ACTIVE **2** not working or operating **3** GEOLOGY an inactive volcano is not dangerous because it is no longer capable of erupting ≠ ACTIVE **4** CHEMISTRY an inactive chemical substance does not react strongly with other substances ≠ ACTIVE —**inactivity** /ˌɪnækˈtɪvəti/ noun [U]

inadequacy /ɪnˈædɪkwəsi/ (plural **inadequacies**) noun **1** [C/U] the failure to be good enough **2** [U] a lack of confidence that makes someone feel that they are not good enough

inadequate /ɪnˈædɪkwət/ adj not enough, or not good enough: *The roads are inadequate to deal with this amount of traffic.* ♦ *Some people feel inadequate when they are faced with new responsibilities.* ♦ *The heating system is **totally inadequate**.* ♦ *The machinery is **inadequate for** the job.* —**inadequately** adv

inadmissible /ˌɪnədˈmɪsəb(ə)l/ adj LAW inadmissible evidence cannot be used in a court of law

inadvertently /ˌɪnədˈvɜːt(ə)ntli/ adv *formal* without intending to do something —**inadvertent** adj

inanimate /ɪnˈænɪmət/ adj not alive

inappropriate /ˌɪnəˈprəʊpriət/ adj not suitable in a particular situation ≠ APPROPRIATE: *inappropriate behaviour* ♦ *The material is **inappropriate for** our students.* —**inappropriately** adv

inarticulate /ˌɪnɑːˈtɪkjʊlət/ adj **1** not able to express clearly what you want to say ≠ ARTICULATE **2** not spoken or pronounced clearly —**inarticulately** adv

inasmuch as /ˌɪnəzˈmʌtʃ æz/ conjunction *formal* **1** used for adding a comment that explains or makes clearer what you have just said **2** used for adding a comment that limits what you have just said

inaudible /ɪnˈɔːdəb(ə)l/ adj difficult or impossible to hear ≠ AUDIBLE —**inaudibly** adv

inaugural /ɪˈnɔːɡjʊrəl/ adj made or happening at the beginning of something new: *the president's inaugural address*

inaugurate /ɪˈnɔːɡjʊreɪt/ verb [T] **1** *formal* to start or introduce something new and important **2** to open a new building, or to start a new organization, with an official ceremony= OPEN —**inauguration** /ɪˌnɔːɡjʊˈreɪʃ(ə)n/ noun [C/U]

inboard motor /ˌɪnbɔːd ˈməʊtə/ noun [C] a motor that is fitted inside a boat → OUTBOARD MOTOR

inborn /ˌɪnˈbɔːn/ adj something that is inborn has existed in you since you were born= INNATE

inbound /ˈɪnbaʊnd/ adj TOURISM travelling towards a station or an airport

inbox /ˈɪnbɒks/ noun [C] COMPUTING the place on a computer program where emails arrive for you

inbreeding /ˈɪnˌbriːdɪŋ/ noun [U] the process of producing children or animals from parents who are close members of the same family

Inc. abbrev BUSINESS Incorporated: used in the US after the name of a large company or a group of companies working together and using one name

incandescent /ˌɪnkænˈdes(ə)nt/ adj PHYSICS producing light as a result of being made very hot —**incandescence** noun [U]

incapable /ɪnˈkeɪpəb(ə)l/ adj **incapable of sth** unable to do something

incapacitate /ˌɪnkəˈpæsɪˌteɪt/ verb [T] *formal* to make someone or something unable to live or work normally

incapacity /ˌɪnkəˈpæsəti/ noun [U] the condition of being unable to live or work normally because you are ill or weak

incarcerate /ɪnˈkɑːsəreɪt/ verb [T] *formal* to put someone in prison= IMPRISON —**incarceration** /ɪnˌkɑːsəˈreɪʃ(ə)n/ noun [U]

incarnation /ˌɪnkɑːˈneɪʃ(ə)n/ noun [C] RELIGION according to some religions, one in a series of lives that a person may have

incense /ˈɪnsens/ noun [U] a substance that creates a strong but pleasant smell when it is burned

incensed /ɪnˈsenst/ adj extremely angry

incentive /ɪnˈsentɪv/ noun [C/U] something that makes you want to do something or to work harder, because you know that you will benefit by doing this: *The high rate of pay is a great incentive.* ♦ *Many farmers **have little incentive** to work for the environment.*

inception /ɪnˈsepʃ(ə)n/ noun [U] *formal* the beginning of something

incessant /ɪnˈses(ə)nt/ adj continuing for a long time without stopping= CONSTANT —**incessantly** adv

incest /ˈɪnsest/ noun [U] sexual activity between people who are closely related —**incestuous** /ɪnˈsestjuəs/ adj

inch /ɪntʃ/ noun [C] a unit for measuring length that is equal to 2.54 centimetres: *The insect was about **an inch long**.*
   PHRASES **every inch (of sth)** the whole of an area or place
   not give/budge an inch to completely refuse to change your opinion or decision

incidence /ˈɪnsɪd(ə)ns/ noun [singular] **1** HEALTH the number of cases of an illness or a medical condition in a particular place or group **2** the number of times that something happens

incident /ˈɪnsɪd(ə)nt/ noun [C] something that happens that is unusual, violent, or dangerous: *an embarrassing incident* ♦ *Police are appealing for witnesses to the incident.*

incidental /ˌɪnsɪˈdent(ə)l/ adj related to something, but thought to be less important than it

incidentally /ˌɪnsɪˈdent(ə)li/ adv used for adding related but less important information to what has just been said, or for suddenly introducing a new subject

incidental 'music noun [U] MUSIC music that is played in the background of a film, play, or television programme and helps to create a particular feeling or mood

'incident ,ray noun [C] PHYSICS a ray of light that hits a surface

incinerate /ɪnˈsɪnəreɪt/ verb [T] to burn something completely —**incineration** /ɪnˌsɪnəˈreɪʃ(ə)n/ noun [U]

incinerator /ɪnˈsɪnəˌreɪtə/ noun [C] a machine that destroys rubbish or other material by burning it completely

incision /ɪnˈsɪʒ(ə)n/ noun [C/U] HEALTH a cut made into someone's body during a medical operation

incisive /ɪnˈsaɪsɪv/ adj **1** expressed in a clear and direct manner **2** showing the ability to think clearly and quickly —**incisively** adv

incisor /ɪnˈsaɪzə/ noun [C] ANATOMY one of the sharp teeth at the front of the mouth —*picture* → TOOTH

incite /ɪnˈsaɪt/ verb [T] to encourage people to be violent or to commit crimes by making them angry or excited

inclination /ˌɪŋklɪˈneɪʃ(ə)n/ noun [C/U] **1** a feeling that you want to do something **2** a tendency to behave in a particular way or to have a particular interest

incline /ˈɪnˌklaɪn/ noun [C] a slope

inclined /ɪnˈklaɪnd/ adj **1** feeling that you want to do something: *Karen didn't feel **inclined to** help.* **2** tending to behave in a particular way, or to be interested in a particular thing: *Joe is **inclined to** be moody.*

inclined 'plane noun [C] PHYSICS a flat surface that forms a slope, making an angle of less than 90 degrees with a horizontal surface. It is considered to be a simple machine because it takes less force to roll or slide an object up the slope than to lift it straight upwards.

include /ɪnˈkluːd/ verb [T] **1** to contain, or to have someone or something as a part: *The book includes activities, stories, and practical advice.* **2** to make someone or something be part of a group, set, or collection of things ≠ EXCLUDE: *Please include a photograph of yourself with your application.* ♦ *His work was recently **included in** an exhibition of young painters.*

including /ɪnˈkluːdɪŋ/ preposition used for mentioning that someone or something is part of a particular group or amount ≠ EXCLUDING: *We visited several countries, including India and Pakistan.*

inclusion /ɪnˈkluːʒ(ə)n/ noun **1** [U] the action of including someone or something ≠ EXCLUSION **2** [C] someone or something that is added or included

inclusive /ɪnˈkluːsɪv/ adj **1** including all costs: *The rent is £30 a week, **inclusive of** heating and lighting.* **2** including the specific limits that have been mentioned and everything in between **3** deliberately aiming to involve all types of people

inclusivity /ˌɪnkluːˈsɪvɪti/ noun [U] SOCIAL STUDIES the practice of deliberately trying to involve all types of people in a project, workplace etc

incoherent /ˌɪnkəʊˈhɪərənt/ adj **1** badly organized or expressed and therefore difficult to understand **2** unable to express yourself clearly —**incoherence** noun [U], **incoherently** adv

income /ˈɪnkʌm/ noun [C/U] ECONOMICS money that someone gets from working, or from investing money: *What is your approximate **annual income**?* ♦ *an average household **income of** €27,000*

'income ,tax noun [C/U] ECONOMICS a tax that is based on your income

incoming /ˈɪnˌkʌmɪŋ/ adj **1** coming in, or arriving ≠ OUTGOING **2** recently elected, or recently chosen for a job or position ≠ OUTGOING

incomparable /ɪnˈkɒmp(ə)rəb(ə)l/ adj so good that nothing else can be as good —**incomparably** adv

incompatible /ˌɪnkəmˈpætəb(ə)l/ adj not able to work or exist together ≠ COMPATIBLE —**incompatibility** /ˌɪnkəmˌpætəˈbɪləti/ noun [U]

incompetent /ɪnˈkɒmpɪt(ə)nt/ adj lacking the ability or skills to do something ≠ COMPETENT —**incompetence** noun [U], **incompetently** adv

incomplete /ˌɪnkəmˈpliːt/ adj not finished, not completely developed, or lacking one or more parts ≠ COMPLETE

,incomplete com'bustion noun [U] SCIENCE burning that takes place when there is a small amount of oxygen. It produces **soot** (=black powder), **carbon monoxide**, and carbon dioxide, as well as heat and light.

incomprehensible /ɪnˌkɒmprɪˈhensəb(ə)l/ adj impossible to understand ≠ COMPREHENSIBLE —**incomprehensibly** adv

inconceivable /ˌɪnkənˈsiːvəb(ə)l/ adj impossible to believe or imagine: *It is inconceivable that he might lose his job.* —**inconceivably** adv

inconclusive /ˌɪnkənˈkluːsɪv/ adj not producing a definite result or complete proof of something: *inconclusive evidence* —**inconclusively** adv

incongruous /ɪnˈkɒŋɡruəs/ adj strange because of being very different from other things that happen or exist in the same situation —**incongruity** /ˌɪnkənˈɡruːəti/ noun [U], **incongruously** adv

inconsiderate /ˌɪnkənˈsɪdərət/ adj not thinking about other people and their feelings = THOUGHTLESS —**inconsiderately** adv

inconsistent /ˌɪnkənˈsɪstənt/ adj **1** containing parts that do not match with each other: *an inconsistent account of what happened* **2** not always behaving in the same way or producing the same results —**inconsistency** /ˌɪnkənˈsɪstənsi/ noun [C/U], **inconsistently** adv

inconspicuous /ˌɪnkənˈspɪkjuəs/ adj not easily seen or noticed ≠ NOTICEABLE —**inconspicuously** adv

incontinent /ɪnˈkɒntɪnənt/ adj HEALTH not able to control your bladder or bowels —**incontinence** noun [U]

inconvenience /ˌɪnkənˈviːniəns/ noun [C/U] a problem or situation that causes difficulties, or needs extra effort

inconvenient /ˌɪnkənˈviːniənt/ adj causing difficulties, or needing extra effort ≠ CONVENIENT —**inconveniently** adv

incorporate /ɪnˈkɔːpəreɪt/ verb **1** [T] to add or include something as a part of something else = INCLUDE: *We'll incorporate some of these ideas in the final report.* **2** [I/T] BUSINESS to form a corporation —**incorporation** /ɪnˌkɔːpəˈreɪʃ(ə)n/ noun [U]

incorrect /ˌɪnkəˈrekt/ adj wrong, or not accurate or true ≠ CORRECT —**incorrectly** adv

increase¹ /ɪnˈkriːs/ verb [I/T] to become larger in number or amount, or to make something do this: *We have managed to increase the number of patients treated.* ◆ *The population has **increased by** 15 per cent.* ◆ *The club has been **increasing in** popularity.*

> **Build your vocabulary: words you can use instead of increase**
> - **be on the increase** to be increasing steadily
> - **go up** to increase in price or level
> - **double** to increase to twice the original amount or level
> - **push sth up** to increase the price or level of something
> - **mount** to increase steadily
> - **rise** to increase
> - **rocket** (*informal*) to increase quickly and suddenly
> - **soar** to increase quickly to a very high level
> - **treble** to increase to three times the original amount or level

increase² /ˈɪnkriːs/ noun [C/U] a rise in the number, amount, or degree of something: *price increases* ◆ *There has been a significant **increase in** the number of young people who smoke.* ◆ *Workplace stress is **on the increase** (=increasing).*

increased /ɪnˈkriːst/ adj greater in size, amount, or degree: *The factory was unable to cope with the increased demand for new models.* ◆ *These conditions can lead to an **increased risk of** lung cancer.*

increasingly /ɪnˈkriːsɪŋli/ adv more and more over a period of time: *Her job has become increasingly difficult.*

incredible /ɪnˈkredəb(ə)l/ adj **1** surprising or difficult to believe: *They all have incredible stories to tell.* **2** great, extreme, or extremely good: *an incredible amount of money*

incredibly /ɪnˈkredəbli/ adv **1** extremely: *That's an incredibly important issue.* **2** used for saying that something is difficult to believe: *Incredibly, his wife did not know the truth.*

incredulous /ɪnˈkredjʊləs/ adj not believing something, or showing that you do not believe something —**incredulity** /ˌɪnkrəˈdjuːləti/ noun [U], **incredulously** adv

increment /ˈɪŋkrɪmənt/ noun [C] one in a series of increases in amount or value, for example a regular increase in pay

incriminate /ɪnˈkrɪmɪneɪt/ verb [T] to show that someone is guilty of a crime, or to make someone seem guilty of it

incubate /ˈɪŋkjʊbeɪt/ verb [I/T] **1** BIOLOGY to keep eggs warm until the young birds inside them **hatch 2** HEALTH if you incubate a disease, or if it incubates, an infection develops inside the body, although the symptoms of the disease are not yet noticeable —**incubation** /ˌɪŋkjʊˈbeɪʃ(ə)n/ noun [U]

ˌincuˈbation ˌperiod noun [C] **1** HEALTH the amount of time it takes from the start of an infection in the body until its symptoms become noticeable **2** BIOLOGY the amount of time it takes for eggs or cells to develop

inculcate /ˈɪnkʌlkeɪt/ verb [T] *formal* to fix an idea or belief firmly in someone's mind, especially by repeating it often —**inculcation** /ˌɪnkʌlˈkeɪʃ(ə)n/ noun [U]

incur /ɪnˈkɜː/ (**incurs, incurring, incurred**) verb [T] **1** to experience something that is unpleasant as a result of something that you have done **2** to lose, owe, or have to pay money as a result of doing something

incurable /ɪnˈkjʊərəb(ə)l/ adj **1** not able to be cured **2** not able to be changed: *an incurable romantic* —**incurably** adv

incursion /ɪnˈkɜːʃ(ə)n/ noun [C] **1** a sudden attack on an area controlled by other people **2** a situation in which someone or something enters an area where they do not belong

incus /ˈɪŋkəs/ noun [singular] ANATOMY a small bone in the **middle ear**. It is between the **malleus** and the **stapes** = ANVIL

indebted /ɪnˈdetɪd/ adj **1 indebted to sb** grateful to someone for their help **2** owing money

indecency /ɪnˈdiːs(ə)nsi/ noun [U] LAW a crime involving offensive sexual behaviour

indecent /ɪnˈdiːs(ə)nt/ adj offensive or shocking —**indecently** adv

inˌdecent asˈsault noun [C/U] LAW a sexual attack that does not involve **rape**

inˌdecent exˈposure noun [U] LAW the crime of deliberately showing your sexual organs in a public place

indecision /ˌɪndɪˈsɪʒ(ə)n/ noun [U] the feeling that you are unable to make a decision

indecisive /ˌɪndɪˈsaɪsɪv/ adj **1** unable to make decisions ≠ DECISIVE **2** not producing a clear result or winner: *an indecisive election* —**indecisively** adv, **indecisiveness** noun [U]

indeed /ɪnˈdiːd/ adv **1** used for emphasis with 'very': *Thank you very much indeed.* ♦ *The food was very good indeed.* **2** *formal* used for adding a statement that increases the effect of what you have just said: *The service will benefit students, and, indeed, all young people.* **3** *formal* used for emphasizing that something is true when there is some doubt about it: *Three of the pictures were indeed genuine Rembrandts.*

indefatigable /ˌɪndɪˈfætɪɡəb(ə)l/ adj *formal* never showing signs of getting tired —**indefatigably** adv

indefensible /ˌɪndɪˈfensəb(ə)l/ adj impossible to defend from criticism —**indefensibly** adv

indefinable /ˌɪndɪˈfaɪnəb(ə)l/ adj impossible to describe or explain clearly —**indefinably** adv

indefinite /ɪnˈdef(ə)nət/ adj **1** continuing into the future with no fixed end **2** not clear —**indefinitely** adv

in,definite 'article noun [C] **LANGUAGE** the word 'a' or 'an' in the English language, or a word in another language that is used in a similar way → DEFINITE ARTICLE

in,definite 'pronoun noun [C] **LANGUAGE** a pronoun that does not refer to any particular person or thing, for example 'anybody', 'everyone', or 'anything'

indemnify /ɪnˈdemnɪfaɪ/ verb [T] **LAW 1** to provide someone with insurance or protection against injury or loss **2** to make a payment to someone who has suffered injury or loss

indemnity /ɪnˈdemnəti/ (plural **indemnities**) noun **1** [U] **LAW** insurance or protection against injury or loss **2** [C] a payment that is made to someone who has suffered an injury or loss

indentation /ˌɪndenˈteɪʃ(ə)n/ noun **1** [C] a mark or hole in the surface of something **2** [C/U] the action of indenting lines of writing, or the space that is made by indenting a line

indentured /ɪnˈdentʃəd/ adj **SOCIAL STUDIES** an indentured servant worked for someone under a contract, usually for a specified period of years and in exchange for food, clothing, somewhere to live etc

independence /ˌɪndɪˈpendəns/ noun [U] **1** freedom from control by another country or organization: *Lithuania was the first of the Soviet republics to declare its independence.* **2** the ability to make decisions and live your life free from the control or influence of other people: *Employment gave young women a measure of independence.*

independent /ˌɪndɪˈpendənt/ adj **1** not controlled by another country or organization: *an independent nation* **2** not influenced by anyone else, and therefore fair: *Seek independent legal advice before entering into an agreement.* **3** not depending on other people, for example your parents ≠ DEPENDENT: *Michelle is young, independent, and confident.* **4** not connected with or joined to anything else: *The equipment has its own independent power supply.* —**independently** adv

,independent 'clause noun [C] **LANGUAGE** a part of a sentence that can exist on its own as a separate sentence = MAIN CLAUSE → DEPENDENT CLAUSE

,independent su'spension noun [C] **ENGINEERING** a vehicle **suspension** system that allows each wheel on a single **axle** to move up and down vertically without affecting the other wheel

,independent 'travel noun [U] **TOURISM** travel in which you organize flights, hotels etc yourself, rather than using a company —**,independent 'traveller** noun [C]

,independent 'variable noun [C] **MATHS** a **variable** in a mathematical statement whose value does not depend on the changing value of something else —*picture* → GRAPH

'in-,depth adj thorough and detailed: *an in-depth study*

indescribable /ˌɪndɪˈskraɪbəb(ə)l/ adj something that is indescribable is impossible to describe because it is so extreme —**indescribably** adv

indestructible /ˌɪndɪˈstrʌktəb(ə)l/ adj impossible, or very difficult, to destroy

indeterminate /ˌɪndɪˈtɜːmɪnət/ adj not known, or not clearly established = UNKNOWN

index /ˈɪndeks/ (plural **indices** /ˈɪndɪsiːz/ or **indexes**) noun [C] **1** an alphabetical list of subjects or names at the back of a book that shows on which page they are mentioned: *Look up the name you want in the index.* **2** **ECONOMICS** a number that shows the price, value, or level of something that is compared with something else: *the Dow Jones index* ♦ *a price index* **3** a measure of how something is changing: *The test provides parents with a reliable index of their child's progress.* **4** **MATHS** a second, small number above and to the right of a number. It shows how many times the main number is to be multiplied by itself.

indexation /ˌɪndekˈseɪʃ(ə)n/ noun [U] **ECONOMICS** the practice of making the value of something such as salaries or pensions rise or fall according to the general level of prices of basic things such as food and clothes

'index ,card noun [C] one of a set of small cards on which you write information

'index ,finger noun [C] the finger next to the thumb —*picture* → BODY

index-linking /ˈɪndeks ˌlɪŋkɪŋ/ noun [U] **ECONOMICS** indexation

'index ,number noun [C] **ECONOMICS** a number that shows the change in the level of something such as a price or unemployment, compared with an earlier time

'index ,page noun [C] **COMPUTING** the first page of a website that contains **links** to other parts of the website

Indian Ocean /ˌɪndiən ˈəʊʃ(ə)n/ **GEOGRAPHY** the ocean to the east of Africa —*picture* → CONTINENT

indicate /ˈɪndɪkeɪt/ verb **1** [T] to express an intention, opinion, or wish in an indirect way: *Both sides indicated a willingness to solve the problem.* ♦ *She indicated that she would like the job.* **2** [T] to show that something will happen, that it is true, or that it exists: *A survey indicated that 89 per cent of people recycle paper.* **3** [T] to point towards someone or something: *'Here it is,' she said, indicating the house.* **4** [I/T] to show that you are going to make a left or right turn in a vehicle by using an **indicator**

indication /ˌɪndɪˈkeɪʃ(ə)n/ noun [C/U] a sign that something will happen, is true, or exists

indicative¹ /ɪnˈdɪkətɪv/ adj **1** *formal* showing that something will happen, is true, or exists: *These latest figures are indicative of a slowing economy.* **2** **LANGUAGE** the indicative form of a verb is used for making statements or asking questions

indicative² /ɪnˈdɪkətɪv/ noun [singular] **LANGUAGE** a form of a verb used for making statements or asking questions. The indicative is also called the **indicative mood**.

indicator /ˈɪndɪˌkeɪtə/ noun [C] **1** something that shows you what condition something is in: *economic indicators* **2** one of the lights on a car that shows in which direction it is turning **3** **CHEMISTRY** a chemical compound that changes colour in specific conditions.

It can be used to test chemical substances, for example in order to discover how acid or alkaline something is.

'indicator ,board or **'indicator ,panel** noun [C] TOURISM a large board used at stations and airports to show when trains and flights are arriving or leaving

indices /'ɪndɪsiːz/ a plural of **index**

indict /ɪn'daɪt/ verb [T] LAW to accuse someone officially of a serious crime= CHARGE

indictable /ɪn'daɪtəb(ə)l/ adj LAW an indictable offence is one for which you can be officially accused and brought to a court for trial

indictment /ɪn'daɪtmənt/ noun **1** [C] **an indictment of sth** something that shows how bad or wrong something is **2** [C/U] LAW an official statement accusing someone of committing a serious crime = CHARGE

indie¹ /'ɪndi/ adj ARTS, MUSIC indie films and music are produced and sold by small independent companies

indie² /'ɪndi/ noun [U] MUSIC music that is produced by small independent record companies

indifferent /ɪn'dɪfrənt/ adj lacking interest or sympathy —**indifference** noun [U], **indifferently** adv

indigenous /ɪn'dɪdʒənəs/ adj **1** formal indigenous people lived in a place for a very long time before other people came to live there **2** BIOLOGY indigenous plants and animals belong to a region because they developed there

indigestible /,ɪndɪ'dʒestəb(ə)l/ adj **1** indigestible food is difficult for the body to digest **2** too difficult or complicated to understand

indigestion /,ɪndɪ'dʒestʃ(ə)n/ noun [U] HEALTH pain that you get in your stomach when your body has difficulty in digesting the food that you have eaten

indignant /ɪn'dɪgnənt/ adj angry, because a situation is unfair —**indignantly** adv

indignation /,ɪndɪg'neɪʃ(ə)n/ noun [U] anger about an unfair situation

indignity /ɪn'dɪgnəti/ (plural **indignities**) noun [C/U] a situation that makes you feel embarrassed or ashamed

indigo /'ɪndɪgəʊ/ adj between dark blue and purple in colour —**indigo** noun [U]

indirect /,ɪndə'rekt, ,ɪndaɪ'rekt/ adj **1** not using the shortest or simplest way ≠ DIRECT: We took an indirect route through the mountains. **2** an indirect effect is not the immediate result of something but happens because of some other result ≠ DIRECT: Her promotion may have an indirect effect on the morale of other employees. **3** not communicated in a direct way: He made only indirect references to his opponent. —**indirectly** adv

,indirect 'cost noun [C] BUSINESS a business cost that is not directly connected with a particular product or operation

,indirect 'object noun [C] LANGUAGE in a sentence with two objects, the person or thing that receives something through the action of the verb. For example 'me' is the indirect object in 'He gave me the book.'.

,indirect 'question noun [C] LANGUAGE the words that you use to report a question that someone else has asked, for example 'She asked me where I was going'

,indirect 'speech noun [U] LANGUAGE the words that you use for reporting what someone else has said, for example 'She said that we must leave'= REPORTED SPEECH

,indirect 'tax noun [C] ECONOMICS a tax on goods and services instead of on income

indiscreet /,ɪndɪ'skriːt/ adj telling or showing something that should be private —**indiscreetly** adv

indiscretion /,ɪndɪ'skreʃ(ə)n/ noun [U] the behaviour of someone who fails to keep something private

indiscriminate /,ɪndɪ'skrɪmɪnət/ adj done in a careless way that causes extra harm or damage —**indiscriminately** adv

indispensable /,ɪndɪ'spensəb(ə)l/ adj something that is indispensable is so useful or important that you must have it= ESSENTIAL

indisposed /,ɪndɪ'spəʊzd/ adj formal **1** unable to do something because of illness= UNWELL **2** not willing to do something= UNWILLING

indistinct /,ɪndɪ'stɪŋkt/ adj difficult to see or hear clearly= UNCLEAR ≠ CLEAR —**indistinctly** adv

indistinguishable /,ɪndɪ'stɪŋgwɪʃəb(ə)l/ adj people or things that are indistinguishable are so similar that you cannot see any difference between them

indium /'ɪndiəm/ noun [U] CHEMISTRY a soft silvery rare metallic element that is found in zinc and tin ores. Chemical symbol: **In**

individual¹ /,ɪndɪ'vɪdʒuəl/ adj **1** considered separately from other people or things: individual pieces of furniture **2** intended for one person only or for a particular person ≠ COLLECTIVE: individual liberties ♦ Choose a holiday to match your individual needs. **3** unusual or different in an interesting way: a very individual style

individual² /,ɪndɪ'vɪdʒuəl/ noun [C] a person: We believe in the freedom of the individual.

individuality /,ɪndɪ,vɪdʒu'æləti/ noun [U] the qualities that make someone or something different from all others

individually /,ɪndɪ'vɪdʒuəli/ adv as a separate person or thing, not as part of a group

indivisible /,ɪndɪ'vɪzəb(ə)l/ adj MATHS impossible to divide exactly by a particular number ≠ DIVISIBLE

indoctrinate /ɪn'dɒktrɪneɪt/ verb [T] to teach someone a set of beliefs so thoroughly that they do not accept any other ideas= BRAINWASH —**indoctrination** /ɪn,dɒktrɪ'neɪʃ(ə)n/ noun [U]

indomitable /ɪn'dɒmɪtəb(ə)l/ adj formal very determined and impossible to defeat

indoor /'ɪndɔː/ adj done or used inside a building ≠ OUTDOOR: an indoor swimming pool ♦ indoor plants

indoors /ɪn'dɔːz/ adv in or into a building ≠ OUTDOORS: I stayed indoors all day.

induce /ɪn'djuːs/ verb [T] **1** to cause a mental or physical condition **2** HEALTH to make a woman start to give birth to her baby

inducement /ɪn'djuːsmənt/ noun [C/U] something that someone offers you in order to persuade you to do something

inductance /ɪn'dʌktəns/ noun [U] PHYSICS the ability of an **inductor** to store electricity

induction /ɪn'dʌkʃ(ə)n/ noun **1** [C/U] the process of formally making someone part of a group or organization **2** [U] PHYSICS the production of electrical or magnetic forces in an object by other electrical or magnetic forces near it

in'duction ,coil noun [C] **PHYSICS** a piece of equipment used for changing low voltage to high voltage

in'duction ,loop noun [C] a system in which a wire around a room such as a theatre sends a signal to the **hearing aids** of people in the room

inductive /ɪnˈdʌktɪv/ adj **1** *formal* reasoning from particular facts or ideas to a general rule or law **2** **PHYSICS** relating to electrical or magnetic force that is produced by **induction** —**inductively** adv

inductor /ɪnˈdʌktə/ noun [C] **PHYSICS** a piece of electrical equipment that can store electrical energy in a magnetic field

indulge /ɪnˈdʌldʒ/ verb **1** [I/T] to allow yourself to have something enjoyable: *The new job gave him the chance to indulge his passion for music.* **2** [I] **indulge in sth** to do something that people do not approve of: *He had indulged in affairs with several women.* **3** [T] to allow someone to do or have what they want when you should be more strict

indulgence /ɪnˈdʌldʒ(ə)ns/ noun **1** [U] the act of doing something that is not good for you: *indulgence in alcohol* **2** [C] something enjoyable that you do for pleasure **3** [U] kind behaviour in a situation where strict behaviour is needed

indulgent /ɪnˈdʌldʒ(ə)nt/ adj allowing someone to do or have what they want when you should be more strict: *indulgent parents* —**indulgently** adv

industrial /ɪnˈdʌstriəl/ adj **1** relating to industries, or to the people who work in them: *industrial development* **2** an industrial region or country has a lot of industries in it —**industrially** adv

in,dustrial 'action noun [U] **SOCIAL STUDIES** protests in which workers deliberately work slowly or **strike** (=refuse to work)

in,dustrial e'state noun [C] an area where there are a lot of factories

industrialist /ɪnˈdʌstriəlɪst/ noun [C] someone who owns a large industrial company

industrialize /ɪnˈdʌstriəlaɪz/ verb [I/T] **ECONOMICS** if a country industrializes, or if it is industrialized, it develops industries or makes them more modern —**industrialization** /ɪn,dʌstriəlaɪˈzeɪʃ(ə)n/ noun [U]

industrialized /ɪnˈdʌstriəlaɪzd/ adj **ECONOMICS** an industrialized country or society has a lot of industries

the In,dustrial Revo'lution **SOCIAL STUDIES** the period in the 18th and 19th centuries in Europe and the US when machines began to be used for producing goods and many new industries developed

in,dustrial tri'bunal noun [C] **LAW** a court in the UK where workers can bring complaints against their employers

in'dustrial ,waste noun [U] **ENVIRONMENT** waste products such as chemicals that are produced by industrial processes

industrious /ɪnˈdʌstriəs/ adj *formal* someone who is industrious works very hard

industry /ˈɪndəstri/ (plural **industries**) noun **1** [U] **ECONOMICS** the production of goods in factories: *The town was severely hit by the decline in industry.* **2** [C] **ECONOMICS** all the businesses involved in producing a particular type of goods or service: *the oil industry* **3** [C] an activity that indirectly earns money for businesses: *the wedding industry* → COTTAGE INDUSTRY, GROWTH INDUSTRY

inebriated /ɪˈniːbrieɪtɪd/ adj *formal* drunk

inedible /ɪnˈedəb(ə)l/ adj too unpleasant or poisonous to eat

ineffective /,ɪnɪˈfektɪv/ adj something that is ineffective does not work correctly or does not do what you want it to do

inefficient /,ɪnɪˈfɪʃ(ə)nt/ adj people or methods that are inefficient do not work well because they waste time, energy, materials, or money ≠ EFFICIENT —**inefficiency** noun [C/U], **inefficiently** adv

inelastic collision /,ɪnɪlæstɪk kəˈlɪʒ(ə)n/ noun [C] **PHYSICS** a **collision** in which the objects change shape and the **kinetic energy** is changed into heat and sometimes light

ineligible /ɪnˈelɪdʒəb(ə)l/ adj not officially allowed to do something ≠ ELIGIBLE

inept /ɪˈnept/ adj someone who is inept does something badly ≠ CAPABLE —**ineptitude** /ɪˈneptɪ,tjuːd/ noun [U], **ineptly** adv

inequality /,ɪnɪˈkwɒləti/ (plural **inequalities**) noun [C/U] **1** an unfair situation in which some people have more opportunities, power, or money than other people ≠ EQUALITY **2** **MATHS** a mathematical statement that shows that two quantities are not equal

inequitable /ɪnˈekwɪtəb(ə)l/ adj *formal* unfair because people are not being treated equally

inequity /ɪnˈekwəti/ noun [C/U] *very formal* the fact of being unfair, or an unfair situation

inert /ɪˈnɜːt/ adj **1** not moving, or seeming to have no life **2** **CHEMISTRY** an inert substance such as a gas does not produce a chemical reaction with other substances

inertia /ɪˈnɜːʃə/ noun [U] **1** a feeling of not wanting to do anything **2** **PHYSICS** the force that makes an object stay in the same position until another force makes it move, or that makes an object continue moving at the same speed until another force slows it down

inescapable /,ɪnɪˈskeɪpəb(ə)l/ adj impossible to avoid or ignore = INEVITABLE

inevitable /ɪnˈevɪtəb(ə)l/ adj **1** impossible to avoid or prevent: *War now seems almost inevitable.* **2** the inevitable something that is certain to happen: *You must face the inevitable and try to deal with it.* —**inevitability** /ɪn,evɪtəˈbɪləti/ noun [U], **inevitably** adv

inexact /,ɪnɪɡˈzækt/ adj not exact or accurate ≠ EXACT

inexcusable /,ɪnɪkˈskjuːzəb(ə)l/ adj inexcusable behaviour is so bad that you cannot forgive the person who behaved like that = UNFORGIVABLE

inexhaustible /,ɪnɪɡˈzɔːstəb(ə)l/ adj never completely used up, and therefore always available

inexorable /ɪnˈeksərəb(ə)l/ adj *formal* impossible to stop —**inexorably** adv

inexpensive /,ɪnɪkˈspensɪv/ adj something that is inexpensive does not cost much money ≠ EXPENSIVE —**inexpensively** adv

inexperienced /,ɪnɪkˈspɪəriənst/ adj lacking experience ≠ EXPERIENCED —**inexperience** noun [U]

inexplicable /,ɪnɪkˈsplɪkəb(ə)l/ adj impossible to explain —**inexplicably** adv

inextricably /,ɪnɪkˈstrɪkəbli/ adv *formal* used for emphasizing that two things always exist together and cannot be considered separately

infallible /ɪnˈfæləb(ə)l/ adj **1** someone who is infallible never makes mistakes = PERFECT ≠ FALLIBLE **2** certain to work or have the effect you intended —**infallibility** /ɪn,fæləˈbɪləti/ noun [U]

infamous /ˈɪnfəməs/ adj well known for something bad = NOTORIOUS: *an infamous criminal*

infancy /ˈɪnfənsi/ noun [U] the time when you are a very young child

infant /ˈɪnfənt/ noun **1** [C] a very young child **2 infants** [plural] EDUCATION the youngest children in the UK school system, between the ages of four and seven

infanticide /ɪnˈfæntɪsaɪd/ noun [U] LAW the crime of killing a baby or a very young child

infantile /ˈɪnfəntaɪl/ adj HEALTH affecting young children

,infant morˈtality ,rate noun [C] SOCIAL STUDIES, HEALTH the number of deaths of children under a year old in a particular society. It is expressed as the number of deaths out of every 1,000 live births.

infantry /ˈɪnfəntri/ noun [U] soldiers who fight on foot, not on horses or in tanks or other vehicles

infarction /ɪnˈfɑːkʃ(ə)n/ noun [C/U] HEALTH a situation in which blood cannot get to an area of tissue, so that the tissue dies

infatuation /ɪnˌfætjuˈeɪʃ(ə)n/ noun [C/U] a strong feeling of love that seems silly or extreme to other people

infect /ɪnˈfekt/ verb [T] **1** HEALTH to make someone get a disease that is caused by bacteria or by a virus or a parasite: *Thousands of people have been infected with the disease.* **2** COMPUTING if a computer virus infects a computer, it enters the computer and causes problems

infected /ɪnˈfektɪd/ adj HEALTH **1** someone who is infected has a disease that is caused by bacteria or by a virus or a parasite **2** containing bacteria, a virus, or a parasite that cause disease

infection /ɪnˈfekʃ(ə)n/ noun HEALTH **1** [U] the process of becoming infected with a disease that is caused by bacteria or by a virus or a parasite: *There are ways to reduce your risk of infection.* **2** [C] a disease that is caused by bacteria or by a virus or a parasite: *a throat infection*

infectious /ɪnˈfekʃəs/ adj **1** HEALTH an infectious disease is caused by bacteria or by a virus or a parasite and can spread from one person to another: *The condition is highly infectious.* **2** HEALTH a person or animal that is infectious has a disease that is caused by bacteria or by a virus or a parasite and that can spread from one person or animal to another **3** behaviour that is infectious makes other people behave in the same way: *His enthusiasm was infectious.*

infectivity /ˌɪnfekˈtɪvɪti/ noun [U] HEALTH a measure of the ability of a microorganism to cause infection

infer /ɪnˈfɜː/ (**infers, inferring, inferred**) verb [T] *formal* to form an opinion about something that is based on information that you already have → IMPLY

inference /ˈɪnf(ə)rəns/ noun [C] an opinion about something that is based on information that you already have: *It's impossible to **make inferences from** such a small sample.*

inferior¹ /ɪnˈfɪəriə/ adj not good, or not as good as someone or something else ≠ SUPERIOR: *This design is **inferior to** the one the German company proposed.* —**inferiority** /ɪnˌfɪəriˈɒrəti/ noun [U]

inferior² /ɪnˈfɪəriə/ noun [C] someone who has a lower status than someone else

inferno /ɪnˈfɜːnəʊ/ (plural **infernos**) noun [C] a large and dangerous fire

infertile /ɪnˈfɜːtaɪl/ adj **1** BIOLOGY not physically able to have children or offspring **2** AGRICULTURE infertile land is not very good for growing crops —**infertility** /ˌɪnfəˈtɪləti/ noun [U]

infest /ɪnˈfest/ verb [T] if a place is infested with animals or insects, there are so many of them that they might cause damage or disease

infestation /ˌɪnfeˈsteɪʃ(ə)n/ noun [C/U] a situation in which a lot of insects or animals are in a place and are causing damage or disease

infidel /ˈɪnfɪd(ə)l, ˈɪnfɪdel/ noun [C] RELIGION, SOCIAL STUDIES an old word used as an insult for someone who has no religious beliefs or who has religious beliefs that are different from yours

infidelity /ˌɪnfɪˈdeləti/ (plural **infidelities**) noun [C/U] a situation in which someone has sex with someone other than their husband, wife, or partner

infield /ˈɪnfiːld/ noun [C] SPORTS in baseball and cricket, the central part of the field, or the players whose positions are in this part of the field

infill /ˈɪnfɪl/ noun [U] CONSTRUCTION something that fills a space, for example the **baluster** between the **handrail** and **string** of a **staircase** —**infill** verb [I/T]

infilling /ˈɪnfɪlɪŋ/ noun [U] **1** CONSTRUCTION the process of filling a gap in a row of houses by building on the empty land between them **2** GEOLOGY a process in which a layer of sand, stone, or dirt fills a gap or space in a geographical feature

infiltrate /ˈɪnfɪltreɪt/ verb [I/T] **1** to join an organization in order to secretly get information for its enemies **2** to become a feature of something gradually, without anyone noticing —**infiltrator** noun [C]

infiltration /ˌɪnfɪlˈtreɪʃ(ə)n/ noun [U] GEOGRAPHY the passing of water into the soil or into a **drainage** system

infinite /ˈɪnfɪnət/ adj **1** very great, and seeming to have no limit: *a teacher with infinite patience* ♦ *The possibilities are infinite.* **2** with no physical end or limit: *Space is infinite.*

infinitely /ˈɪnfɪnətli/ adv very, or very much: *It tastes infinitely better than the last coffee we had.* ♦ *I'm infinitely grateful for your help.*

infinitesimal /ˌɪnfɪnɪˈtesɪm(ə)l/ adj *formal* extremely small

infinitive /ɪnˈfɪnətɪv/ noun [C] LANGUAGE the basic form of a verb, for example 'take', 'sit', and 'be'. In English, it often has the word 'to' in front of it.

infinitum *see* **ad infinitum**

infinity /ɪnˈfɪnəti/ noun [U] **1** a space, time, or distance that has no limit **2** MATHS a number that is larger than any that exists

infirmary /ɪnˈfɜːməri/ (plural **infirmaries**) noun [C] HEALTH a hospital

in flagrante delicto /ɪn fləˌgrænti dɪˈlɪktəʊ/ adv LAW while having sex with someone, especially someone who is not your regular partner. In flagrante delicto is often simply called **in flagrante**.

inflamed /ɪnˈfleɪmd/ adj HEALTH swollen and painful because of an infection or injury

inflammable /ɪnˈflæməb(ə)l/ adj something that is inflammable burns easily ≠ NON-FLAMMABLE → FLAMMABLE

inflammation /ˌɪnfləˈmeɪʃ(ə)n/ noun [C/U] HEALTH an area on your body that is swollen and painful because of an infection or injury

inflatable /ɪnˈfleɪtəb(ə)l/ adj an inflatable object must be filled with air or gas before you can use it

inflate /ɪnˈfleɪt/ verb **1** [I/T] to fill something with air or gas, or to become full of air or gas ≠ DEFLATE **2** [T] to make a number or price higher than it should be —**inflated** adj

inflation /ɪnˈfleɪʃ(ə)n/ noun [U] **1** ECONOMICS an economic process in which prices increase so that money becomes less valuable ≠ DEFLATION: *Inflation has risen again this month.* ♦ *The rate of inflation is 3.2%.* **2** the process of filling something with air or gas

inflationary /ɪnˈfleɪʃ(ə)n(ə)ri/ adj ECONOMICS likely to cause an increase in prices ≠ DEFLATIONARY: *inflationary pressures*

in,flationary 'spiral noun [C] ECONOMICS an economic situation in which higher prices cause higher salaries, which in turn cause even higher prices

inflect /ɪnˈflekt/ verb [I] LANGUAGE if a word inflects, you change its form to go with the grammar of the other words you are using it with

inflected /ɪnˈflektɪd/ adj LANGUAGE an inflected form of a word is a form that is different from the basic form, for example a plural form of a noun

inflection /ɪnˈflekʃ(ə)n/ noun **1** [U] the way in which the sound of your voice becomes higher and lower when you speak **2** [C/U] LANGUAGE a change in the basic form of a word that gives information about the tense, number etc. For example 'went' and 'gone' are inflections of the verb 'go'.

inflexible /ɪnˈfleksəb(ə)l/ adj **1** not willing to change your ideas or decisions: *an inflexible attitude* **2** stiff and not able to bend ≠ FLEXIBLE

inflict /ɪnˈflɪkt/ verb [T] to cause something unpleasant to happen: *the environmental damage we are inflicting on the Earth*

'in-,flight adj TOURISM provided for passengers flying in an aircraft

inflorescence /ˌɪnfləˈresəns/ noun BIOLOGY **1** [C] a part of a plant that consists of two or more individual flowers **2** [U] the production of buds and flowers by a plant

influence¹ /ˈɪnfluəns/ noun **1** [C/U] the effect that a person or thing has on someone or something: *He couldn't hope to exert any real influence in the new department.* ♦ *Teachers have considerable influence over what is taught in the classroom.* **2** [C] a person or thing that has an effect on someone or something

influence² /ˈɪnfluəns/ verb [T] to affect someone or something: *What factors influenced your decision to take the job?* ♦ *Research has shown that the weather can influence people's behaviour.*

influential /ˌɪnfluˈenʃ(ə)l/ adj able to influence the way that other people think or behave: *He is one of the most influential figures in the government.*

influenza /ˌɪnfluˈenzə/ noun [U] HEALTH a very contagious disease caused by a virus. Influenza often appears in epidemics, and can be extremely dangerous to some groups, for example older people. The more common name for influenza is **flu**.

influx /ˈɪnflʌks/ noun [C] a large number of people or things coming to a place

inform /ɪnˈfɔːm/ verb [T] to officially tell someone about something: *The President has been fully informed of developments.* ♦ *I've been reliably informed that the delivery will arrive tomorrow.* ♦ *Please inform us of any changes in your circumstances.*

PHRASAL VERB **in'form on sb** to secretly give information about someone to the police

informal /ɪnˈfɔːm(ə)l/ adj **1** relaxed, friendly, and not official: *They cooperate with other groups on an informal basis.* **2** suitable for relaxed friendly situations. In this dictionary, words that are mainly used in relaxed situations are marked 'informal': *informal clothes* —**informality** /ˌɪnfɔːˈmæləti/ noun [U], **informally** adv

informant /ɪnˈfɔːmənt/ noun [C] someone who secretly gives information about someone to the police

information /ˌɪnfəˈmeɪʃ(ə)n/ noun [U] knowledge or facts about someone or something: *We're not allowed to give you any information about our client's medical records.* ♦ *We were able to get the information we needed from the Internet.* ♦ *He gave us a very interesting piece of information.* —**informational** adj

> **Information** is never used in the plural and cannot be used with **an**: *I've just discovered an interesting piece of information* (NOT *an interesting information*) *about the company.* ♦ *Do you have any information about local attractions?* ♦ *I found some information in the library to help with my project.*

Infor,mation and Communi'cation Tech,nology noun [U] EDUCATION, COMPUTING see ICT

infor'mation ,processing noun [U] COMPUTING the process of organizing and working with information by computer

infor,mation re'trieval noun [U] COMPUTING the process of getting particular information from all the information stored on a computer

infor,mation 'science noun [U] COMPUTING the study of the processes involved in collecting, organizing, and using computer information

infor,mation tech'nology noun [U] COMPUTING the use of computers and electronic systems for storing information

informative /ɪnˈfɔːmətɪv/ adj giving a lot of useful information

informed /ɪnˈfɔːmd/ adj **1** based on good knowledge: *an informed choice* **2** someone who is informed has a lot of knowledge about something

informer /ɪnˈfɔːmə/ noun [C] an **informant**

infrared /ˌɪnfrəˈred/ adj PHYSICS using a type of light felt as heat that cannot be seen and has wavelengths that are longer than those of light that can be seen, but shorter than those of **radio waves**: *infrared sensors*

,infrared radi'ation noun [U] PHYSICS electromagnetic radiation that cannot be seen and has wavelengths that are longer than those of light that can be seen, but shorter than those of **radio waves**

,infrared ther'mometer noun [C] SCIENCE a piece of equipment that measures the temperature of an object without touching it, using a **beam** of infrared light that is directed at the object

infrasound /ˈɪnfrəˌsaʊnd/ noun [U] SCIENCE very low frequency **sound waves** that are below the normal range that can be heard by humans

infrastructure /ˈɪnfrəˌstrʌktʃə/ noun [C] ECONOMICS the set of systems in a country or organization that affect how well it operates, for example telephone and transport systems —**infrastructural** /ˌɪnfrəˈstrʌktʃ(ə)rəl/ adj

infrequent /ɪnˈfriːkwənt/ adj something that is infrequent does not happen very often = RARE —**infrequently** adv

infuriate /ɪnˈfjʊərieɪt/ verb [T] to make someone extremely angry

infuriating /ɪnˈfjʊəri,eɪtɪŋ/ adj extremely annoying

infuse /ɪnˈfjuːz/ verb [T] to give someone or something a particular quality

infusion /ɪnˈfjuːʒ(ə)n/ noun [C/U] **1** a drink, medicine, or beauty treatment made by putting something such as leaves in hot water **2** the addition of something such as money or ideas

ingenious /ɪnˈdʒiːniəs/ adj **1** using new and clever ideas **2** good at inventing things or solving problems —**ingeniously** adv

ingenuity /ˌɪndʒəˈnjuːəti/ noun [U] the ability to solve problems in new and clever ways

ingest /ɪnˈdʒest/ verb [T] **BIOLOGY** to take food or drink into the body

ingestion /ɪnˈdʒestʃən/ noun [U] **BIOLOGY** the process of taking food or drink into the body

ingot /ˈɪŋɡət/ noun [C] **TECHNOLOGY** a block of metal formed in a mould during the process of **casting**

ingrained /ɪnˈɡreɪnd/ adj **1** an ingrained attitude or habit has existed for a long time and cannot easily be changed **2** ingrained dirt is under the surface and is difficult to remove

ingratiate /ɪnˈɡreɪʃieɪt/ verb **ingratiate yourself with sb** showing disapproval to try to get someone's approval by doing things that will please them

ingratitude /ɪnˈɡrætɪ,tjuːd/ noun [U] the fact that someone is not grateful for something when you think they should be grateful

ingredient /ɪnˈɡriːdiənt/ noun [C] **1** one of the foods or liquids that you use in making a particular meal: *Mix all the ingredients together carefully.* **2** one of the things that give something its character or make it effective: *Good communication is **an essential ingredient of** good management.*

inhabit /ɪnˈhæbɪt/ verb [T] to live in a particular place

inhabitant /ɪnˈhæbɪtənt/ noun [C] a person or animal that lives in a particular place

inhabited /ɪnˈhæbɪtɪd/ adj a place that is inhabited has people living in it ≠ UNINHABITED

inhalant /ɪnˈheɪlənt/ noun [C] **HEALTH** a medicine or drug in the form a vapour that someone breathes into their lungs

inhale /ɪnˈheɪl/ verb [I/T] **BIOLOGY** to breathe air, smoke, or other substances into the lungs= BREATHE (STH) IN ≠ EXHALE —**inhalation** /ˌmhəˈleɪʃ(ə)n/ noun [C/U]

inherent /ɪnˈherənt, ɪnˈhɪərənt/ adj an inherent quality is a basic or essential feature that gives something its character —**inherently** adv

inherit /ɪnˈherɪt/ verb [T] **1** to receive property or money from someone when they die: *He **inherited** the business **from** his father.* **2** to be born with the same appearance or character as one of your parents: *The boys inherited Derek's good looks.* **3** **HEALTH, BIOLOGY** to be born with a characteristic that has been passed from parent animals, plants, or other organisms through their genes **4** to have something because it was left by someone who was in your situation before you: *These are problems we **inherited from** the previous government.* —**inheritor** noun [C]

inheritance /ɪnˈherɪt(ə)ns/ noun **1** [C] property or money that someone receives from another person who has died **2** [U] **BIOLOGY** the process by which characteristics are passed from parent animals, plants, or other organisms to their young through their genes

inherited /ɪnˈherɪtɪd/ adj **1** inherited money or property has been given to someone when the previous owner died **2** **HEALTH, BIOLOGY** inherited characteristics are passed on from parent animals, plants, or other organisms through their genes

inhibit /ɪnˈhɪbɪt/ verb [T] **1** to prevent something from developing in a normal way **2** to make someone feel too embarrassed to behave in a normal way

inhibited /ɪnˈhɪbɪtɪd/ adj too embarrassed to do something

inhibition /ˌɪnhɪˈbɪʃ(ə)n/ noun [C/U] a feeling of being too embarrassed to do what you want to do

inhibitor /ɪnˈhɪbɪtə/ noun [C] **1** **BIOLOGY** a substance that stops or slows down a chemical reaction **2** **CHEMISTRY** a substance that prevents the action of an enzyme

inhospitable /ˌɪnhɒˈspɪtəb(ə)l/ adj **1** an inhospitable place is unpleasant to live in **2** unfriendly to guests

inhuman /ɪnˈhjuːmən/ adj someone who is inhuman does not care when other people are suffering

inhumane /ˌɪnhjuːˈmeɪn/ adj inhumane treatment is very cruel ≠ HUMANE —**inhumanely** adv

inhumanity /ˌɪnhjuːˈmænəti/ noun [U] extremely cruel behaviour

initial[1] /ɪˈnɪʃ(ə)l/ adj happening at the beginning of a process, or when you first see or hear about something: *the **initial stages** of the project* ♦ *My **initial reaction** was to panic.*

initial[2] /ɪˈnɪʃ(ə)l/ noun [C] the first letter of a name

initialize /ɪˈnɪʃəlaɪz/ verb [T] **COMPUTING** to prepare a piece of computer equipment or software for use

initially /ɪˈnɪʃ(ə)li/ adv at the beginning= ORIGINALLY: *Initially she worked for us as a secretary.*

initiate /ɪˈnɪʃieɪt/ verb [T] **1** formal to make something start **2** to teach someone about an activity that they have never done before **3** to make someone a member of a group, often with a special ceremony —**initiation** /ɪ,nɪʃiˈeɪʃ(ə)n/ noun [singular/U]

initiative /ɪˈnɪʃətɪv/ noun **1** [U] the ability to take action in an independent way: *Employees are encouraged to **use their initiative** if faced with a problem.* ♦ *He developed the plan **on his own initiative**.* **2** [C] an important action that is intended to solve a problem: *a number of initiatives designed to address the problem of child poverty* **3 the initiative** [singular] the opportunity to take action before other people do: *She would have to **take the initiative** in order to improve their relationship.*

inject /ɪnˈdʒekt/ verb [T] **1** to put a drug into someone's body through the skin using a syringe **2** to add something new to a situation: *Young designers are **injecting** new life **into** the fashion industry.*

injection /ɪnˈdʒekʃ(ə)n/ noun [C/U] **1** **HEALTH** a drug that is injected into the body, or the process of injecting it into the body: *Did the doctor give you a measles injection?* **2** the act of providing more money for something: *an injection of cash*

injunction /ɪnˈdʒʌŋkʃ(ə)n/ noun [C] **LAW** an order from a court that prevents someone from doing something

injure /ˈɪndʒə/ verb [T] to hurt someone: *Nine people died and 54 were injured in the accident.* ♦ *No one was seriously injured.*

injured /ˈɪndʒəd/ adj hurt in an accident or attack: *The injured man was taken to hospital.*

PHRASE the injured party LAW someone who has not been treated fairly

injury /ˈɪndʒəri/ (plural **injuries**) noun [C/U] **1** physical harm: *an eye injury* ♦ *All the passengers in the vehicle escaped injury.* ♦ *Both drivers sustained* (=received) *multiple injuries.* **2** LAW harm done to a person's reputation, career, or feelings by someone or something

ˈinjury ˌtime noun [U] SPORTS time added at the end of a match because time has been lost dealing with injured players

injustice /ɪnˈdʒʌstɪs/ noun [C/U] an unfair way of treating someone

ink /ɪŋk/ noun [U] a black or coloured liquid that is used for writing, drawing, or printing

ˈink-jet ˌprinter noun [C] COMPUTING a type of printer for computers that prints using very small drops of ink

inland /ɪnˈlænd/ adv in a direction away from the coast —**inland** /ˈɪnlənd/ adj

ˈin-laws noun [plural] the parents or other relatives of someone's husband or wife

inlet /ˈɪnlət/ noun [C] **1** GEOGRAPHY a long narrow area of water that continues into the land from a lake or sea **2** a tube through which a liquid or gas goes into a machine ≠ OUTLET

inlet manifold /ˈɪnlət ˌmænɪfəʊld/ noun [C] ENGINEERING a part of a vehicle engine that carries the mixture of air and fuel from the **carburettor** to the cylinders

ˌin-line ˈskating noun [U] SPORTS the activity of moving on boots called **in-line skates** that each have a single row of narrow wheels on them

in loco parentis /ɪn ˌləʊkəʊ pəˈrentɪs/ adv LAW if an adult acts in loco parentis to a child who is not their own child, they take responsibility for looking after that child

inmate /ˈɪnˌmeɪt/ noun [C] someone who is kept in a prison or similar institution

inn /ɪn/ noun [C] a small hotel or **pub**

innate /ɪˈneɪt/ adj an innate quality or ability is one that you have always had

inner /ˈɪnə/ adj **1** inside, or further towards the centre of something ≠ OUTER: *the inner ear* **2** close to the centre of a city: *inner London* **3** private, or personal: *inner feelings*

ˌinner ˈcity noun [C] GEOGRAPHY an area near the centre of a large city where a lot of social problems exist —ˌinner-ˌcity adj

ˌinner ˈcore noun [singular] GEOLOGY the central solid part of the Earth that contains **nickel** and iron —*picture* → EARTH

ˌinner ˈear noun [singular] ANATOMY the inside part of the ear that controls balance and the ability to hear. The inner ear includes the **cochlea** and the **semicircular canals**.

innermost /ˈɪnəˌməʊst/ adj **1** your innermost thoughts and feelings are very personal and private **2** closest to the centre of something ≠ OUTERMOST

inning /ˈɪnɪŋ/ noun [C] SPORTS one of the nine periods played in a baseball game

innings /ˈɪnɪŋz/ (plural **innings**) noun [C] SPORTS a period in a **cricket** match during which one player or one team tries to score runs

innocence /ˈɪnəs(ə)ns/ noun [U] **1** the state of not being guilty of a crime or anything bad ≠ GUILT: *This new evidence would hopefully prove his innocence.* **2** lack of experience of life that makes you trust people too much

innocent /ˈɪnəs(ə)nt/ adj **1** not guilty of a crime or anything bad ≠ GUILTY: *the innocent victims of terrorism* ♦ *She was completely innocent of any crime.* **2** not intended to harm or upset anyone: *an innocent remark* **3** someone who is innocent does not have much experience of life and often trusts people too much

PHRASE **the innocent party** LAW someone who has been harmed by the wrong action of another person —**innocently** adv

innocuous /ɪˈnɒkjuəs/ adj not likely to offend or upset anyone

innovation /ˌɪnəʊˈveɪʃ(ə)n/ noun [C/U] a new idea or piece of equipment, or the use of new ideas or equipment

innovative /ˈɪnəvɪtɪv, ˈɪnəvətɪv/ adj new and advanced —**innovatively** adv

innuendo /ˌɪnjuˈendəʊ/ noun [C/U] **1** the use of statements with a second possible meaning, usually referring to sex and intended as a joke, or one of these statements **2** the use of insulting or negative comments about someone that are suggested rather than stated directly, or one of these comments

innumerable /ɪˈnjuːmərəb(ə)l/ adj formal too many to be counted: *There are innumerable examples of his generous nature.*

innumeracy /ɪˈnjuːmərəsi/ noun [U] EDUCATION the inability to do simple mathematics

inoculate /ɪˈnɒkjʊleɪt/ verb [T] HEALTH to protect someone against a particular disease by **injecting** a medicine containing a small amount of the disease into them, so that their body becomes **immune** to it = IMMUNIZE, VACCINATE —**inoculation** /ɪˌnɒkjʊˈleɪʃ(ə)n/ noun [C/U]

inoperable /ɪnˈɒpərəb(ə)l/ adj **1** HEALTH an inoperable medical condition cannot be cured by an operation **2** formal not working, or not capable of being used successfully

inorganic /ˌɪnɔːˈɡænɪk/ adj CHEMISTRY **1** not consisting of or produced from any living organism ≠ ORGANIC **2** relating to simple chemical compounds with little stored energy that are not organic, especially those that do not contain carbon ≠ ORGANIC

ˌinorganic ˈchemistry noun [U] CHEMISTRY the part of chemistry that deals with chemical compounds that are not organic, especially those that do not contain carbon → ORGANIC CHEMISTRY

inpatient /ˈɪnˌpeɪʃ(ə)nt/ noun [C] HEALTH someone who stays overnight or for a period of time in hospital when they are receiving medical treatment → OUTPATIENT

input /ˈɪnpʊt/ noun

1 comments/suggestions	4 in farming
2 information	5 in industry
3 energy	

1 [U] comments and suggestions that someone makes as part of a discussion

2 [U] COMPUTING information that someone puts into a computer ≠ OUTPUT

3 [U] PHYSICS an electrical or other form of energy that is put into a machine or piece of equipment

4 [C] AGRICULTURE something that is introduced into farming that has an effect on production, for example **fertilizers**, **pesticides**, or **labour**

5 [C] something that is needed for industrial production or some other process to operate effectively

'input de,vice noun [C] **COMPUTING** a **peripheral** such as a keyboard or mouse that allows a user to put information into a computer

,input/'output noun [U] **COMPUTING** equipment or software that controls the passage of information into and out of a computer or computer part

'input ,shaft noun [C] **ENGINEERING** a **shaft** in a vehicle that sends power to another part of the engine, for example from the **clutch** to the **gears**

inquest /'ɪŋkwest/ noun [C] an official attempt by a court to find the cause of someone's death

inquire /ɪn'kwaɪə/ verb [I/T] to ask someone for information about something: *I am writing to inquire whether you have any positions available.* —**inquirer** noun [C]

inquiring /ɪn'kwaɪərɪŋ/ adj **1** keen to learn about new things: *an inquiring mind* **2** showing that you want more information about something: *an inquiring look*

inquiry /ɪn'kwaɪəri/ (plural **inquiries**) noun **1** [C] a question that is intended to get information about someone or something: *There have already been over 300 inquiries from people interested.* **2** [C/U] a process of trying to find out more information about something: *The public is demanding an official inquiry into the incident.*

inquisitive /ɪn'kwɪzətɪv/ adj keen to learn about a lot of different things, and asking a lot of questions = CURIOUS: *an inquisitive journalist* —**inquisitively** adv

insane /ɪn'seɪn/ adj **1** informal very stupid or crazy: *You'd be totally insane to see him again.* **2** **HEALTH** old-fashioned suffering from very severe mental illness —**insanely** adv

insanitary /ɪn'sænətəri/ adj insanitary conditions are dirty and dangerous to people's health, usually because there is a lack of water pipes, toilets, **drains** etc, so that it is difficult to keep things clean = UNSANITARY ≠ SANITARY

insanity /ɪn'sænəti/ noun [U] **HEALTH** old-fashioned very severe mental illness

insatiable /ɪn'seɪʃəb(ə)l/ adj always wanting more and never feeling satisfied —**insatiably** adv

inscribe /ɪn'skraɪb/ verb [T] to write or cut words on or in something: *a gold watch inscribed with her initials*

inscribing circle /ɪn,skraɪbɪŋ 'sɜːk(ə)l/ noun [C] **MATHS, TECHNOLOGY** a circle drawn inside a geometric shape that touches all the sides of the shape

inscription /ɪn'skrɪpʃ(ə)n/ noun [C] a piece of writing that is written on or cut into something

inscrutable /ɪn'skruːtəb(ə)l/ adj making it impossible for other people to understand what you are thinking or feeling

insect /'ɪnsekt/ noun [C] **1** **BIOLOGY** an **arthropod** (=type of invertebrate) that has six legs and usually two pairs of wings, such as a bee, a fly, or a beetle. An insect's body is divided into three parts: the head, the **thorax**, and the **abdomen**: *Some insects, especially sucking insects, are responsible for the spread of diseases.* —*picture* ➜ on next page **2** a small animal that is similar to an insect, for example a spider or worm. Do not use this meaning in scientific writing or discussions, as it is not a scientific meaning.

insecticide /ɪn'sektɪsaɪd/ noun [C] **AGRICULTURE, BIOLOGY** a chemical used for killing insects

insectivore /ɪn'sektɪ,vɔː/ noun [C] **BIOLOGY** an animal or plant that eats insects —**insectivorous** /,ɪnsek'tɪvərəs/ adj ➜ CARNIVORE

insect-pollinated /'ɪnsekt ,pɒləneɪtɪd/ adj **BIOLOGY** an insect-pollinated plant is fertilized by having pollen moved to it from another plant by means of an insect —**insect pollination** noun [U]

'insect re,pellent noun [U] a substance that keeps harmful insects such as mosquitoes away

insecure /,ɪnsɪ'kjʊə/ adj **1** not confident about yourself: *She's always been very insecure about the way she looks.* **2** not safe or protected: *In this economy, all our jobs are insecure.* —**insecurity** /,ɪnsɪ'kjʊərəti/ noun [C/U]

inseminate /ɪn'semɪneɪt/ verb [T] **BIOLOGY** to put sperm into a woman or a female animal to make her pregnant ➜ ARTIFICIAL INSEMINATION

insemination /ɪn,semɪ'neɪʃ(ə)n/ noun [U] **BIOLOGY** the process of putting sperm into a woman or female mammal to make her pregnant

insensitive /ɪn'sensətɪv/ adj not noticing or caring about other people's feelings and not worrying that the things you say or do may upset them —**insensitively** adv, **insensitivity** /ɪn,sensə'tɪvəti/ noun [U]

inseparable /ɪn'sep(ə)rəb(ə)l/ adj **1** people who are inseparable spend all their time together **2** things that are inseparable cannot exist or be considered separately: *His personal morality was inseparable from his religious beliefs.* —**inseparably** adv

insert /ɪn'sɜːt/ verb [T] **1** to put something into something else: *Insert the plug into the earphone socket.* **2** to add something at a particular place in a document or series **3** **COMPUTING** to add a word or letter between other words or letters in a computer document —**insertion** /ɪn'sɜːʃ(ə)n/ noun [C/U]

inset /'ɪnset/ noun [C] **1** a small picture or map inside a larger one **2** something that is put in something else: *a gold ring with diamond insets*

inside¹ /'ɪn,saɪd, ɪn'saɪd/ adj, adv, preposition **1** within a container or place, or in the inner part of something ≠ OUTSIDE: *She was standing just inside the door.* ♦ *Draw a triangle inside the circle.* ♦ *The melon was still green inside.* **2** into a place or container ≠ OUTSIDE: *As I walked past the door, I glanced inside.* ♦ *You're not allowed to go inside the museum without paying.* ♦ *She reached inside her handbag and pulled out an envelope.* **3** within an organization or group ≠ OUTSIDE: *There is a battle being fought inside the Conservative Party.* ♦ *The rumours are coming from inside the company.* **4** only known by people who belong to a particular organization or group: *The thieves clearly had inside information.*

inside² /'ɪn,saɪd/ noun [C] the inner part of something: *I had never seen the inside of a prison before.*

,inside 'out adv with the inside part facing out: *Your jumper is on inside out.*

PHRASE know sb/sth inside out to know someone or something very well

insider /,ɪn'saɪdə/ noun [C] someone within an organization or group who knows about all the things happening in it

insects

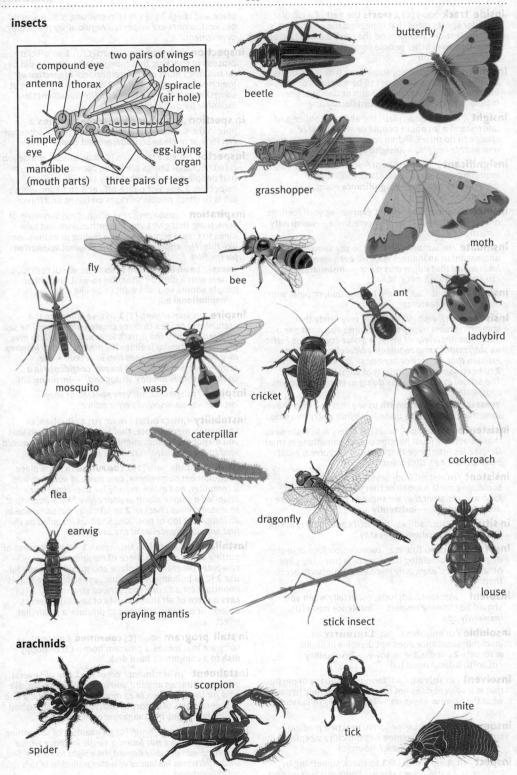

two pairs of wings

compound eye

abdomen

antenna thorax

spiracle (air hole)

simple eye

egg-laying organ

mandible (mouth parts)

three pairs of legs

butterfly

beetle

grasshopper

moth

fly

bee

ant

ladybird

mosquito

wasp

cricket

cockroach

caterpillar

flea

dragonfly

earwig

louse

praying mantis

stick insect

arachnids

scorpion

mite

tick

spider

insects and arachnids

,inside 'track noun [C] **1** SPORTS the part of a circular track for sports races that is nearest the centre and is the shortest distance around the track **2** a position of advantage over other people competing with you, especially for a job

insidious /ɪnˈsɪdiəs/ adj something that is insidious is dangerous because it seems to be harmless or not important but in fact causes harm or damage: *the insidious effects of gossip* —**insidiously** adv

insight /ˈɪnsaɪt/ noun [C/U] the ability to notice and understand a lot about people or situations, or a chance to do this: *Children can sometimes show quite remarkable insight.* —**insightful** /ˈɪnsaɪtf(ə)l/ adj

insignificant /ˌɪnsɪgˈnɪfɪkənt/ adj not large or important enough to be worth considering: *insignificant details* —**insignificance** noun [U], **insignificantly** adv

insincere /ˌɪnsɪnˈsɪə/ adj not expressing your feelings or opinions honestly: *an insincere smile* —**insincerity** /ˌɪnsɪnˈserəti/ noun [U]

insinuate /ɪnˈsɪnjueɪt/ verb [T] to say something unpleasant in an indirect way: *He even went as far as insinuating that Roger was a liar.* —**insinuation** /ɪnˌsɪnjuˈeɪʃ(ə)n/ noun [C/U]

insipid /ɪnˈsɪpɪd/ adj formal boring, dull, or pale, with no interesting features

insist /ɪnˈsɪst/ verb [I/T] **1** to say very firmly that something must happen or be done: *You must see a doctor immediately – I insist.* ♦ *Some companies insist on staff undergoing regular medical checks.* ♦ *She insisted that we stay at her house instead of a hotel.* **2** to keep saying very firmly that something is true: *The school insists that it is doing everything it can to cooperate.*

   PHRASAL VERB **in'sist ,on sth** to say that you must have something: *She insists upon fresh fruit every morning.*

insistence /ɪnˈsɪstəns/ noun [U] a very firm statement that something must happen or that something is true: *Despite his insistence that he wasn't involved, most people think he's dishonest.*

insistent /ɪnˈsɪstənt/ adj saying very firmly that something must happen or that something is true: *John was insistent that we shouldn't tell anyone else about our plans.* —**insistently** adv

in situ /ɪn ˈsɪtjuː/ adj, adv formal if something is in situ, it is in the place where it will stay

insofar as /ˌɪnsəʊˈfɑːr æz/ conjunction formal to the degree that something happens or is true: *She cites other scholars' work only insofar as it supports her own theories.*

insolent /ˈɪnsələnt/ adj rude, especially when you should be showing respect —**insolence** noun [U], **insolently** adv

insoluble /ɪnˈsɒljʊb(ə)l/ adj **1** CHEMISTRY an insoluble substance does not dissolve in liquid ≠ SOLUBLE **2** impossible to solve —**insolubility** /ɪnˌsɒljʊˈbɪləti/ noun [U]

insolvent /ɪnˈsɒlvənt/ adj formal a company or person that is insolvent does not have enough money to pay what they owe= BANKRUPT —**insolvency** /ɪnˈsɒlvənsi/ noun [U]

insomnia /ɪnˈsɒmniə/ noun [U] HEALTH a medical condition in which someone has difficulty sleeping —**insomniac** /ɪnˈsɒmniˌæk/ noun [C]

inspect /ɪnˈspekt/ verb [T] **1** to check something by looking at it carefully= EXAMINE: *Engineers will inspect the site later today.* ♦ *The young plants are regularly inspected for disease and insects.* **2** to officially visit a

place and check to see that everything is as it should be: *Restaurants are inspected regularly by the health department.*

inspection /ɪnˈspekʃ(ə)n/ noun [C/U] **1** an official process of checking that things are as they should be: *All countries must allow international inspection of their nuclear weapons sites.* **2** an action of looking at something carefully to check it: *The documents are available for public inspection.*

in'spection ,chamber noun [C] CONSTRUCTION a hole in the surface of the ground from where someone can look at or clean an underground **drain**

inspector /ɪnˈspektə/ noun [C] **1** an official whose job is to check that things are in the correct condition, or that people are doing what they should: *health inspectors* **2** a senior police officer **3** someone whose job is to check people's tickets on buses and trains

inspiration /ˌɪnspəˈreɪʃ(ə)n/ noun [C/U] someone or something that gives you the enthusiasm and new ideas to create something, or a feeling of enthusiasm like this: *Her short story was the original inspiration for the film.*

   PHRASE **be an inspiration to sb** to be so successful, or to deal with a difficult situation so well, that other people admire you and want to be like you —**inspirational** adj

inspire /ɪnˈspaɪə/ verb [T] **1** to give someone the enthusiasm or idea to do or create something: *The sea inspired many of the artist's later paintings.* **2** to give people a particular feeling: *His athletic ability inspires awe in everyone who sees him in action.* ♦ *Her resignation will do little to inspire confidence in a company that is already struggling.* —**inspiring** adj

inspired /ɪnˈspaɪəd/ adj very special, or very impressive: *an inspired performance*

instability /ˌɪnstəˈbɪləti/ noun [U] a situation, or someone's mental state, that keeps changing, so that you do not know what might happen: *This policy would lead to greater instability in the region.*

install /ɪnˈstɔːl/ verb [T] **1** COMPUTING to put a piece of equipment somewhere, or a piece of software into a computer, and make it ready for use: *Have you installed a smoke alarm in your office?* ♦ *It's important to install a virus checker.* **2** to officially put someone in an important job or position: *She was installed as the first woman chancellor of the university.*

installation /ˌɪnstəˈleɪʃ(ə)n/ noun **1** [U] the process of putting a new system, piece of equipment, or computer program in its place and making it ready for use **2** [C] a building or structure, especially one that is important for an army, industry, or government **3** [C] ARTS a piece of art that consists of several different objects or pictures arranged to produce a particular effect

in'stall ,program noun [C] COMPUTING a piece of software that moves a program from a CD or **floppy disk** to a computer's **hard disk**

instalment /ɪnˈstɔːlmənt/ noun [C] **1** one of several payments that an amount you owe is divided into: *We paid for the television in 12 monthly instalments.* **2** one of several parts of a story or article that are published at different times in a magazine or newspaper

instance /ˈɪnstəns/ noun [C] an example of something happening: *I have not found a single instance where someone was actually denied their right to vote.* ♦ *The study discusses instances of water pollution in this neighbourhood.*

   PHRASE **for instance** for example: *They intend to provide information, via the Internet for instance.*

instant¹ /ˈɪnstənt/ adj **1** immediate: *We can't promise instant solutions, but we can promise to listen.* ♦ *They took an instant liking to each other.* **2** instant food or drink can be prepared very quickly, usually by adding hot water: *instant coffee* —**instantly** adv

instant² /ˈɪnstənt/ noun [C] a moment: *It took only an instant for him to react.*

instantaneous /ˌɪnstənˈteɪniəs/ adj immediate —**instantaneously** adv

instant 'messaging noun [U] **COMPUTING** the activity of communicating with someone directly over the Internet and replying to their messages as soon as they arrive

instead /ɪnˈsted/ adv used for saying that one person or thing replaces another: *If you don't have olive oil, you can use sunflower oil instead.* ♦ *Can't we deal with this now instead of waiting until tomorrow?* ♦ *Tickets will cost only $5, instead of the usual $6.50.*

instep /ˈɪnstep/ noun [C] the raised part in the middle of the foot —*picture* → BODY

instigate /ˈɪnstɪɡeɪt/ verb [T] *formal* to make something start happening —**instigation** /ˌɪnstɪˈɡeɪʃ(ə)n/ noun [U], **instigator** noun [C]

instil /ɪnˈstɪl/ (**instils, instilling, instilled**) verb [T] to make someone have a particular feeling or belief: *His parents had instilled a lasting love of music in him.*

instinct /ˈɪnstɪŋkt/ noun [C/U] **1** a natural tendency to behave in a particular way: *the instinct of ducklings to follow their mother* ♦ *the instinct for survival* **2** a natural ability to know what to do in a particular situation: *Instinct told me that it would be unwise to return home.* ♦ *It's always best to trust your instincts.*

instinctive /ɪnˈstɪŋktɪv/ adj done without thinking, because of a natural tendency or ability: *His reaction was purely instinctive.* —**instinctively** adv

institute¹ /ˈɪnstɪˌtjuːt/ noun [C] an organization that does a particular type of research or educational work

institute² /ˈɪnstɪˌtjuːt/ verb [T] *formal* to start something such as a system or an official process: *The company has instituted new security measures for its staff.*

institution /ˌɪnstɪˈtjuːʃ(ə)n/ noun [C] **1** a large organization such as a bank, hospital, university, or prison: *an educational institution* ♦ *an institution of higher education* **2** a hospital or other building where people are looked after for a long time, for example if they are disabled or mentally ill **3** an important tradition on which society is based: *the institution of marriage* —**institutional** adj

instruct /ɪnˈstrʌkt/ verb [T] **1** *formal* to tell someone to do something, especially officially: *He instructed his men to collect information about troop movements.* **2** *formal* to teach someone a particular subject or skill: *All children are instructed in the use of the library.* **3** **LAW** to arrange for a lawyer to speak for you in court

instruction /ɪnˈstrʌkʃ(ə)n/ noun **1** [C] a statement of something that must be done, or an explanation of how to do or use something: *I tried to follow her instructions, but I got confused.* ♦ *The players were given strict instructions not to leave the hotel.* **2** [U] the teaching of a particular subject or skill

instructive /ɪnˈstrʌktɪv/ adj giving useful information

instructor /ɪnˈstrʌktə/ noun [C] **EDUCATION** someone whose job is to teach a skill or a sport

instrument /ˈɪnstrʊmənt/ noun [C] **1** **SCIENCE** a tool that is used in science, medicine, or technology: *scientific instruments such as microscopes* **2** **MUSIC** a musical instrument, for example a piano or a guitar: *Do*

you play an instrument? **3** a piece of equipment that measures something such as position, speed, or temperature: *Your compass and clock are the most important instruments in sailing.*

instrumental /ˌɪnstrʊˈment(ə)l/ adj **1** involved in an important way in making something happen: *The general was instrumental in helping both sides to reach a compromise.* **2** **MUSIC** instrumental music is played by instruments only, rather than being sung

instrumentalist /ˌɪnstrʊˈment(ə)lɪst/ noun [C] **MUSIC** someone who plays a musical instrument

instrumentation /ˌɪnstrʊmenˈteɪʃ(ə)n/ noun [U] **MUSIC** the way that a piece of music is arranged for a group of instruments

'instrument ˌdrawing noun [U] **ENGINEERING** the process of producing drawings using special tools or special computer software

'instrument ˌpanel noun [C] the board that faces the driver or pilot inside a vehicle, ship, or plane, where they can see and operate the controls

insubordinate /ˌɪnsəˈbɔːdɪnət/ adj *formal* not obeying, or not showing respect to, someone in authority —**insubordination** /ˌɪnsəbɔːdɪˈneɪʃ(ə)n/ noun [U]

insufferable /ɪnˈsʌfərəb(ə)l/ adj *formal* extremely unpleasant or annoying —**insufferably** adv

insufficient /ˌɪnsəˈfɪʃ(ə)nt/ adj not enough: *There are insufficient funds in your account.* —**insufficiently** adv

insulate /ˈɪnsjʊleɪt/ verb [T] **1** **PHYSICS, CHEMISTRY** to cover something in order to prevent heat, cold, sound, or electricity from passing through it **2** to protect someone from unpleasant knowledge or harmful experiences

insulating tape /ˈɪnsjʊleɪtɪŋ ˌteɪp/ noun [U] sticky material that you wrap around electrical wires to insulate them

insulation /ˌɪnsjʊˈleɪʃ(ə)n/ noun [U] **CHEMISTRY, PHYSICS 1** material that is used for preventing heat, cold, sound, or electricity from passing through something **2** protection from heat, cold, sound, or electricity

insulator /ˈɪnsjʊˌleɪtə/ noun [C] **PHYSICS, CHEMISTRY** a substance that reduces the amount of heat, cold, sound, or electricity that can pass through something: *insulators such as wood or plastic*

insulin /ˈɪnsjʊlɪn/ noun [U] **BIOLOGY, HEALTH** a hormone produced in the body that controls the level of sugar in the blood. People who have the disease **diabetes** do not produce enough insulin and have to **inject** artificially produced insulin.

insult¹ /ˈɪnsʌlt/ noun [C] **1** an offensive remark **2** something that seems to show a lack of respect for someone or something: *This exam is an insult to my students' intelligence.*

insult² /ɪnˈsʌlt/ verb [T] to say or do something that is offensive: *She has no right to insult us like that.* —**insulting** adj

insurance /ɪnˈʃʊərəns/ noun **1** [U] an arrangement in which you regularly pay a company an amount of money so that they will give you money if something that you own is damaged, lost, or stolen, or if you die or are ill or injured: *health insurance* ♦ *car insurance* ♦ *Do you have insurance for the house yet?* **2** [singular/U] a situation or action that is intended to prevent something bad from happening or affecting you: *The hostages were being held as insurance against further bombing raids.*

in'surance ,policy noun [C] an official document containing the details of the agreement between you and an insurance company

insure /ɪnˈʃʊə/ verb [T] to buy or provide insurance for someone or something: *They've **insured** the painting **for** over half a million pounds.*

insurgency /ɪnˈsɜːdʒ(ə)nsi/ noun [C/U] *formal* an attempt by a group of people to take control of their country by force

insurgent /ɪnˈsɜːdʒ(ə)nt/ noun [C] *formal* someone who belongs to a group of people fighting to take control of their country by force

insurmountable /ˌɪnsəˈmaʊntəb(ə)l/ adj *formal* impossible to deal with successfully = INSOLUBLE

intact /ɪnˈtækt/ adj not harmed, damaged, or lacking any parts

intake /ˈɪnteɪk/ noun **1** [singular] the amount of something that you eat or drink: *You should reduce your intake of salt.* **2** [C] the part of a machine or engine where air or fuel is taken in —*picture* → JET ENGINE **3** [singular/U] EDUCATION, BUSINESS the number of people accepted by an institution such as a school, university, or company at one time

'intake ,stroke noun [C] ENGINEERING the first of four movements of the **piston** in an **internal-combustion engine** in which a mixture of fuel and air is drawn into the cylinder

intangible /ɪnˈtændʒəb(ə)l/ adj not able to be touched or measured, and difficult to describe or explain

in,tangible 'asset noun [C] BUSINESS something that a company has, for example the good opinion of its customers, that has value to the company although it is difficult to calculate exactly how much it is worth

integer /ˈɪntɪdʒə/ noun [C] MATHS a **whole number** that can be positive, negative, or zero

integral /ˈɪntɪɡrəl, ɪnˈteɡrəl/ adj **1** forming an essential part of something and needed to make it complete: *Home visits by our trained technicians are **an integral part** of the service.* **2** built to form part of something larger and not separate from it: *a house with an integral garage* —**integrally** adv

,integral 'body con,struction noun [U] ENGINEERING a method for building vehicles in which a separate frame is used to connect the **suspension** to the main outer structure of the vehicle

integrate /ˈɪntɪˌɡreɪt/ verb **1** [I/T] SOCIAL STUDIES to become a full member of a society or group and be involved completely in its activities, or to help someone to do this **2** [T] to connect or combine two or more things so that together they form an effective unit, group, or system: *We provide resources that can be **integrated into** the national teaching programme.* —**integration** /ˌɪntɪˈɡreɪʃ(ə)n/ noun [U]

integrated /ˈɪntɪˌɡreɪtɪd/ adj **1** combining things, people, or ideas of different types in one effective unit, group, or system: *a modern, integrated approach to learning* **2** able to be used or shared by people of all races

,integrated 'circuit noun [C] COMPUTING a set of electronic parts on a single chip, used for performing the same jobs as a number of separate parts that would need much more space

,integrated 'software noun [U] COMPUTING software such as an **operating system** or **word processor** that is stored in a computer system and has been designed for that particular system

integrity /ɪnˈteɡrəti/ noun [U] **1** the quality of always behaving honestly and according to moral principles **2** *formal* the quality of being complete or whole, without any missing parts

integument /ɪnˈteɡjʊmənt/ noun [C] BIOLOGY a strong outer layer on a plant or animal that covers and protects it

intellect /ˈɪntəlekt/ noun [U] the ability to think in an intelligent way and to understand difficult or complicated ideas and subjects: *a lawyer of great intellect*

intellectual1 /ˌɪntəˈlektʃuəl/ adj **1** relating to the ability to think in an intelligent way and to understand things **2** well educated and interested in serious subjects at an advanced level —**intellectually** adv

intellectual2 /ˌɪntəˈlektʃuəl/ noun [C] someone who is well educated and interested in serious subjects at an advanced level

,intellectual 'property noun [U] LAW something that someone has created or invented and that no one else is legally allowed to make, copy, or sell

intelligence /ɪnˈtelɪdʒ(ə)ns/ noun [U] **1** the ability to understand and think about things, and to gain and use knowledge: *Maria had intelligence as well as beauty.* ♦ *a person of **average intelligence*** **2** information that is collected about the secret plans and activities of a foreign government, enemy etc: *military intelligence*

in'telligence ,test noun [C] EDUCATION a test that aims to measure how good someone is at understanding problems and thinking about them in an intelligent way

intelligent /ɪnˈtelɪdʒ(ə)nt/ adj **1** good at thinking, understanding, and learning = CLEVER: *He was **highly intelligent**, but disliked studying.* **2** COMPUTING intelligent software is able to react and deal with changes or different situations in a way that is similar to human intelligence —**intelligently** adv

> Build your vocabulary: words you can use instead of **intelligent**
> - **bright** intelligent and quick to understand things
> - **brilliant** extremely intelligent
> - **clever** able to understand and learn things quickly
> - **quick** able to understand things quickly and react to them quickly
> - **sharp** quick to notice and understand things
> - **smart** able to understand and learn things quickly
> - **wise** able to use your knowledge and experience to judge what is right or true

in,telligent de'sign noun [U] the theory that the universe was created by an intelligent force or **being**. It is opposed to the theory of **evolution**.

intelligible /ɪnˈtelɪdʒəb(ə)l/ adj clear or simple enough to understand ≠ UNINTELLIGIBLE —**intelligibly** adv

intend /ɪnˈtend/ verb [T] **1** to have a plan in your mind to do something: *What do you **intend to** do about this?* ♦ *I **intend using** the report as evidence to support my case.* **2** to want something to have a particular meaning: *Perhaps it was **intended as** a joke.* ♦ *She wondered what he **intended by** that statement.*

PHRASE **be intended for** to be made, done, or said for a particular purpose or person: *The book is intended for use in the classroom.*
—**intended** adj

intense /ɪn'tens/ *adj* **1** very great, or extreme: *The pain was intense.* ♦ *the **intense heat** of the midday sun* ♦ *He's been under **intense pressure**.* **2** involving or done with a lot of effort, energy, attention etc: *This type of work requires intense concentration.* **3** feeling and showing emotions in a very strong way: *an intense personality* —**intensely** *adv*, **intensity** *noun* [U]

intensifier /ɪn'tensɪˌfaɪə/ *noun* [C] **LANGUAGE** a word that makes the meaning of another word stronger, for example adverbs such as 'very' and 'extremely'

intensify /ɪn'tensɪfaɪ/ (**intensifies, intensifying, intensified**) *verb* [I/T] if something intensifies, or if you intensify it, it becomes greater, stronger, or more extreme —**intensification** /ɪnˌtensɪfɪ'keɪʃ(ə)n/ *noun* [U]

intensive /ɪn'tensɪv/ *adj* involving a lot of effort, energy, learning, or attention in a short period of time: *three weeks of intensive negotiations* —**intensively** *adv*

in,tensive 'care *noun* [U] **HEALTH** the department of a hospital for people who are very ill or badly injured and must be watched closely by doctors and nurses

in,tensive 'farming *noun* [U] **AGRICULTURE** a method of farming that is designed to produce as much food as possible from a small area of land → EXTENSIVE FARMING

intent¹ /ɪn'tent/ *noun* **1** [singular/U] *formal* the intention to do something **2** [U] **LAW** the intention to commit a crime or an offence

intent² /ɪn'tent/ *adj* **1** concentrating hard on something **2** determined to do something: *The people of the area are **intent on** keeping their club open.* —**intently** *adv*

intention /ɪn'tenʃ(ə)n/ *noun* [C/U] a plan in your mind to do something: *We **have no intention of** giving up.* ♦ *No one goes to college **with the intention of** failing.* ♦ *It wasn't my **intention to** upset you.*

intentional /ɪn'tenʃ(ə)nəl/ *adj* deliberate ≠ UNINTENTIONAL: *I'm sorry I hurt you, but it wasn't intentional.* —**intentionally** *adv*

inter /ɪn'tɜ:/ *verb* [T] *formal* to bury a dead person

inter- /ɪntə/ *prefix* between: used with some nouns, verbs, or adjectives

interact /ɪntər'ækt/ *verb* [I] **1** if people interact, they communicate with and react to each other: *In large classes, children feel that they cannot **interact with** the teacher properly.* **2** if things interact, they affect or change each other in some way —**interaction** /ɪntər'ækʃ(ə)n/ *noun* [C/U]

interactive /ɪntər'æktɪv/ *adj* **1** COMPUTING an interactive computer program, video etc reacts to the information and instructions that you give it **2** involving people communicating with each other and reacting to each other —**interactively** *adv*

intercede /ɪntə'si:d/ *verb* [I] *formal* to try to persuade someone in authority to help someone else or change their opinion or decision about them, especially someone who is going to be punished

intercept /ɪntə'sept/ *verb* [T] to stop, catch, or take control of someone or something before they can get

to the place they are going to —**interception** /ɪntə'sepʃ(ə)n/ *noun* [U]

interchange¹ /'ɪntəˌtʃeɪndʒ/ *noun* **1** [C] a place where you can change from a motorway to a main road using a system of smaller roads, bridges etc **2** [C] a place where you change from one **railway line** to another **3** [C/U] an exchange of things such as ideas or information

interchange² /ˌɪntə'tʃeɪndʒ/ *verb* **1** [I/T] to put one thing in the place where a second thing was and put the second thing in the place where the first one was, or to be put in different places in this way **2** [T] to exchange things such as ideas or information

interchangeable /ˌɪntə'tʃeɪndʒəb(ə)l/ *adj* things that are interchangeable can be put or used in place of each other with the same effect —**interchangeably** *adv*

intercity /ˌɪntə'sɪti/ *adj* intercity trains are fast trains that travel between major cities without stopping at small towns in between

intercom /'ɪntəˌkɒm/ *noun* [C] a system or a piece of electrical equipment that allows people in different parts of a building, aircraft, or ship to speak to each other

interconnect /ˌɪntəkə'nekt/ *verb* [I/T] to connect two things to or with each other, or to be connected to or with each other —**interconnected** *adj*, **interconnecting** *adj*

interconnection /ˌɪntəkə'nekʃ(ə)n/ *noun* [C/U] a link or relationship between two things

interconnectivity /ˌɪntəkənek'tɪvɪti/ *noun* [U] COMPUTING the ability of two or more computers to connect to each other and communicate over a **network**

interconnector /'ɪntəkəˌnektə/ *noun* [C] a **pipeline** that carries gas from one country to another

intercontinental /ˌɪntəˌkɒntɪ'nent(ə)l/ *adj* between continents

interconversion /ˌɪntəkən'vɜːʒ(ə)n/ *noun* [U] SCIENCE the process by which two things can be changed into each other

interconvert /ˌɪntəkən'vɜːt/ *verb* [I] SCIENCE to cause two things to be changed into each other

intercostal muscle /ˌɪntəkɒst(ə)l 'mʌs(ə)l/ *noun* [C] ANATOMY one of the muscles that are between the ribs —*picture* → LUNG

intercourse /'ɪntəˌkɔːs/ *noun* [U] BIOLOGY sexual intercourse

intercultural /ˌɪntə'kʌltʃərəl/ *adj* involving more than one culture

interdependent /ˌɪntədɪ'pendənt/ *adj* things that are interdependent are related to each other in such a close way that each one needs the others in order to exist —**interdependence** *noun* [U], **interdependency** *noun* [U]

interdict /'ɪntəˌdɪkt, ˌɪntə'dɪkt/ *noun* [C] LAW an order from a court of law that officially tells someone not to do something —**interdiction** /ˌɪntə'dɪkʃ(ə)n/ *noun* [C]

interdisciplinary /ˌɪntə'dɪsɪplɪnəri, ˌɪntədɪsɪ'plɪnəri/ *adj* involving different subjects of study

interest¹ /'ɪntrəst/ *noun*

1 a need to know	**4** money paid/received
2 quality attracting you	**5** advantage/benefit
3 activity you enjoy	**+ PHRASE**

1 [singular/U] a feeling of wanting to know about or take part in something: *an interest in politics* ♦ *Apparently several buyers have **expressed an interest** in the deal.* ♦ *People are **losing interest in** the election.*

2 [U] the quality that something has that makes you notice it and want to know about it or take part in it: *The city has lots of museums and places of interest.* ♦ *publications that may be of interest to the self-employed*
3 [C] an activity that you enjoy doing when you are not working: *Tell us about your interests and hobbies.*
4 [U] the money that a bank charges or pays you when you borrow or save money: *an increase in the interest charged on personal loans* ♦ *low interest rates* ♦ *We were required to repay the loan with interest.*
5 [C/U] an advantage or benefit to someone or something: *Publication of the documents is not in the public interest.* ♦ *It's in their own interest to cooperate.*
PHRASE in the interest(s) of sth in order to preserve, develop, or achieve something: *It is vital that we reform the system in the interests of fairness to everyone.*

interest² /'ɪntrəst/ verb [T] to make someone want to know about or take part in something: *Oceanography has always interested me.*

Word family: interest

Words in the same family as interest
- interest *n*
- interesting *adj*
- interested *adj*
- uninterested *adj*
- disinterested *adj*
- interestingly *adv*

---

interested /'ɪntrəstɪd/ adj **1** wanting to know about or take part in something ≠ UNINTERESTED: *Joe's always been interested in politics.* **2** willing or keen to do something: *We're going to the cinema. Are you interested?* —**interestedly** adv

- **Interested** describes how you feel: *I am interested in art.* ♦ *She didn't look very interested.*
- **Interesting** describes things or situations that make you feel interested: *I find history very interesting.* ♦ *It was a really interesting lecture.*

interesting /'ɪntrəstɪŋ/ adj making you want to pay attention or know more: *an interesting topic* ♦ *It would be interesting to hear their views on this problem.* ♦ *It's interesting that she suddenly changed her attitude.* —**interestingly** adv

'interest ,rate noun [C] ECONOMICS the percentage that a bank charges or pays someone in interest when they borrow money from it or keep money in an account

interface /'ɪntəfeɪs/ noun [C] COMPUTING a point in a computer system where information passes from one part of the system to another, or from the computer to the person using it

interfaith /ˌɪntə'feɪθ/ adj involving people who belong to different religions

interfere /ˌɪntə'fɪə/ verb [I] to deliberately become involved in a situation, although you have no right to do this: *I don't want to interfere, but maybe you'd better listen to me.* ♦ *I don't want your friends interfering in our affairs.*

PHRASAL VERB inter'fere with sth to prevent something from happening or developing in the correct way: *Mum says I can get a job if it doesn't interfere with my homework.*

interference /ˌɪntə'fɪərəns/ noun [U] **1** the process of deliberately becoming involved in a situation, although you have no right to do this: *They expressed resentment at outside interference in their domestic affairs.* **2** radio signals that make the sound or picture of a radio or television programme difficult to hear or see clearly, or the noise caused by this —*picture* → WAVE

inter'ference ,fit noun [U] TECHNOLOGY a fit between two machine parts, for example a **shaft** and a hole, in which the specified limits of the sizes result in the shaft

being slightly larger than the hole, so that force is needed to insert it

intergenerational /ˌɪntəˌdʒenə'reɪʃ(ə)n(ə)l/ adj relating to more than one generation

interior /ɪn'tɪəriə/ noun **1** [C] the inside part of something ≠ EXTERIOR: *The car has a surprisingly spacious interior.* **2 the interior** [singular] GEOGRAPHY the inner part of a country or region

in,terior 'monologue noun [C/U] LITERATURE a piece of writing in which a writer expresses what a character in a novel or story is thinking

interject /ˌɪntə'dʒekt/ verb [I/T] *formal* to say something suddenly that interrupts the person who is speaking

interjection /ˌɪntə'dʒekʃ(ə)n/ noun [C] LANGUAGE a word or phrase that you use in speech for expressing a strong emotion such as surprise or anger. 'Oh' and 'ouch' are interjections.

interlanguage /'ɪntəˌlæŋgwɪdʒ/ noun [C/U] LANGUAGE a mixture of two languages, especially one used by someone learning a new language, that contains features of the person's first language mixed with those of the language they are learning

interlingual /ˌɪntə'lɪŋgwəl/ adj LANGUAGE **1** involving two languages **2** relating to an interlanguage

interlink /ˌɪntə'lɪŋk/ verb [I/T] to connect different things with each other, or to be connected with each other

interlock¹ /ˌɪntə'lɒk/ verb [I/T] to join things together by means of parts that fit into other parts, or to be joined together in this way

interlock² /'ɪntəˌlɒk/ noun [C] ENGINEERING a piece of equipment that stops a vehicle's engine from starting in certain situations

interlocutor /ˌɪntə'lɒkjʊtə/ noun [C] *formal* **1** someone who a person is having a conversation with **2** someone who takes part in talks as a representative of another person or organization

interloper /'ɪntəˌləʊpə/ noun [C] *formal* someone who is in a place or group but is not wanted by the other people there

interlude /'ɪntəˌluːd/ noun [C] **1** a short period of time between two longer periods **2** MUSIC a short piece of music played between the separate parts of a play

intermarry /ˌɪntə'mæri/ verb [I] **1** to get married to someone from a different religion, race, or social group from you **2** to get married to someone who is related to you

intermediary /ˌɪntə'miːdiəri/ (plural **intermediaries**) noun [C] someone who talks to each of the people or groups that are involved in something, in order to help them to agree about it

intermediate /ˌɪntə'miːdiət/ adj **1** in between two stages, places, levels, times etc: *The cells have a series of intermediate stages before they develop fully.* **2** EDUCATION at an academic level below advanced: *an intermediate English course* —**intermediately** adv

inter,mediate 'neuron noun [C] ANATOMY a type of **neuron** (=nerve cell) that passes signals between two other neurons, for example between a **sensory neuron** and a **motor neuron** —*picture* → NEURON

inter'mediate ,system noun [C] COMPUTING a piece of equipment that connects a **network** or user to the Internet

inter·mediate tech·nology noun [C/U] technology used in developing countries that is based on cheap materials that are available there

intermezzo /ˌɪntəˈmetsəʊ/ noun [C] MUSIC a short piece of music played between the main parts of an opera or a longer piece of music

intermittent /ˌɪntəˈmɪt(ə)nt/ adj happening sometimes but not regularly or often: *a dull day with intermittent rain* —**intermittently** adv

internal /ɪnˈtɜːn(ə)l/ adj **1** existing or happening within a country, organization, or system ≠ EXTERNAL: *an internal memo* ♦ *They were opposed to foreign involvement in their **internal affairs**.* **2** existing or happening inside the body or the mind: *internal bleeding* ♦ *an internal struggle* **3** existing or happening inside an object or building ≠ EXTERNAL: *internal walls* —**internally** adv

in·ternal-com·bustion ·engine noun [C] ENGINEERING a type of engine used in most cars, in which fuel is burned inside the engine itself

international¹ /ˌɪntəˈnæʃ(ə)nəl/ adj involving several countries, or existing between countries: *international trade* ♦ *an international flight* —**internationally** adv

international² /ˌɪntəˈnæʃ(ə)nəl/ noun [C] **1** SPORTS a sports match between players or teams from different countries **2** a company or organization that exists, works, or has members in more than one country

inter·national ·call noun [C] a telephone call to another country

the inter·national com·munity noun [singular] political leaders and important organizations from all parts of the world

the ·international 'date ·line noun [singular] GEOGRAPHY an internationally agreed imaginary line that runs along the 180° **meridian** of longitude. The date is one day earlier to the east of it than to the west of it. —*picture* → TIME ZONE

·international 'dialling ·code noun [C] a series of numbers used to make a call to another country

the ·International 'Monetary ·Fund ECONOMICS the **IMF**

internecine /ˌɪntəˈniːsaɪn/ adj *formal* happening or existing between people who belong to the same group, organization, country etc

the Internet /ˈɪntəˌnet/ noun [singular] COMPUTING a computer system that allows people in different parts of the world to exchange information: *The group posted the names of the men **on the Internet**.* → WORLD WIDE WEB

'Internet ad·dress noun [C] COMPUTING a code for a particular computer that is used for sending messages to it on a **network** or on the Internet = IP ADDRESS

'Internet ·banking noun [U] COMPUTING a system that allows someone to use the Internet to communicate with their bank, check their account, pay bills etc

'Internet ho·tel noun [C] COMPUTING a business that consists of computers and Internet services for other businesses to use

·Internet 'Relay ·Chat noun [U] COMPUTING a method of communicating with other people immediately over the Internet, especially through **newsgroups**

·Internet 'service pro·vider noun [C] COMPUTING an **ISP**

interpenetration /ˌɪntəpenəˈtreɪʃ(ə)n/ noun [U] a process in which two substances spread into each other and become mixed

interpersonal /ˌɪntəˈpɜːs(ə)nəl/ adj involving relationships between people

interplay /ˈɪntəˌpleɪ/ noun [U] the ways that people or things affect each other or react when they are put together

interpolate /ɪnˈtɜːpəleɪt/ verb [T] **1** *formal* to add something in the middle of a piece of writing **2** *formal* to say something that interrupts someone who is speaking **3** MATHS to calculate a number or quantity between two other numbers or quantities

interpret /ɪnˈtɜːprɪt/ verb **1** [I/T] to translate what someone is saying into another language: *I speak Spanish. Would you like me to interpret for you?* **2** [T] to understand an action, situation etc in a particular way: *Low voter turnout can be **interpreted as** a sign of satisfaction with the current government.* **3** [T] to explain the meaning of something: *We'll need some help to interpret all this data.*

interpretation /ɪnˌtɜːprɪˈteɪʃ(ə)n/ noun [C/U] **1** an explanation of the meaning or importance of something: *The Catholic **interpretation of** the Bible is slightly different.* **2** ARTS a way of performing a piece of music, a part in a play etc that shows how you understand it and feel about it: *He was best known for his **interpretation of** folk music.*

interpre'tation ·centre noun [C] TOURISM a **visitor centre**

interpretative /ɪnˈtɜːrprɪˌtətɪv/ adj relating to how someone explains or understands something, or how someone performs a piece of music, a part in a play etc —**interpretatively** adv

interpreter /ɪnˈtɜːprɪtə/ noun [C] someone whose job is to translate what someone is saying into another language → TRANSLATOR

interquartile /ˌɪntəˈkwɔːtaɪl/ adj MATHS relating to the middle half of a range, above the lowest quarter and below the highest quarter

interrelated /ˌɪntərɪˈleɪtɪd/ adj things that are interrelated affect each other because they are connected in some way —**interrelatedness** noun [U]

interrelationship /ˌɪntərɪˈleɪʃ(ə)nʃɪp/ noun [C/U] the way in which two or more things affect each other because they are related in some way

interrogate /ɪnˈterəgeɪt/ verb [T] to ask someone a lot of questions in order to get information: *The suspects were interrogated by local police.* —**interrogation** /ɪnˌterəˈgeɪʃ(ə)n/ noun [C/U], **interrogator** noun [C]

interrogative¹ /ˌɪntəˈrɒgətɪv/ adj LANGUAGE an interrogative word or phrase is one that you use for asking a question

interrogative² /ˌɪntəˈrɒgətɪv/ noun [C] LANGUAGE a word or phrase that you use for asking a question, for example 'what?' or 'how?'

interrupt /ˌɪntəˈrʌpt/ verb **1** [I/T] to say or do something that stops someone when they are speaking or concentrating on something: *Please don't interrupt her while she's working.* **2** [T] to make something stop for a period of time: *Rain interrupted the tournament for an hour this afternoon.* —**interruption** /ˌɪntəˈrʌpʃ(ə)n/ noun [C/U]

intersect /ˌɪntəˈsekt/ verb [I/T] if roads or lines intersect, they cross each other, or they join

intersection /'ɪntə,sekʃ(ə)n/ noun [C] a place where roads, lines etc join or cross each other: *The school is at the intersection of two main roads.*

intersperse /,ɪntə'spɜːs/ verb [T] to put something in various places in or among something else

interstate /,ɪntə'steɪt/ adj existing or taking place between states, especially between the states in the US or Australia

interstitial /,ɪntə'stɪʃ(ə)l/ noun [C] **BUSINESS, COMPUTING** a page of advertising that appears in the middle of a website

intertidal zone /,ɪntə'taɪd(ə)l ,zəʊn/ noun [C] **GEOGRAPHY** an area of shallow water and drier land between the highest and lowest level that the sea reaches as **tides** rise and fall

intertwine /,ɪntə'twaɪn/ verb [I/T] **1** to twist things together, or to be twisted together **2** to be closely connected with something else

interval /'ɪntəv(ə)l/ noun [C] **1** a period of time between two events: *The normal interval between our meetings is six weeks.* ♦ *Payments are to be resumed after an interval of several months.* ♦ *Planes pass overhead at regular intervals.* ♦ *It may be necessary to stop at intervals* (=sometimes) *and go back over key points in the lesson.* **2** a short break between the parts of something such as a play or concert: *How long is the interval?* **3** a space or distance between two things: *There are pillars at three-foot intervals for reinforcement.* **4** **MUSIC** a difference in **pitch** between two musical notes

intervene /,ɪntə'viːn/ verb [I] **1** to become involved in a situation in order to try to stop or change it: *The police had to intervene when protesters blocked traffic.* **2** to happen between two events, often in a way that delays the second event: *Several months intervened before we met again.*

intervening /,ɪntə'viːnɪŋ/ adj happening between two events or times: *Not much has changed during the intervening six years.*

intervention /,ɪntə'venʃ(ə)n/ noun [C/U] a situation in which someone becomes involved in a particular issue, situation etc in order to influence what happens

intervertebral disc /,ɪntəvɜːtəbrəl 'dɪsk/ noun [C] **ANATOMY** a round flat piece of cartilage between the **vertebrae** in the back

interview¹ /'ɪntə,vjuː/ noun **1** [C] a meeting in which someone asks another person, especially a famous person, questions about themselves, their work, or their ideas: *He doesn't give interviews to the press.* ♦ *The magazine has an exclusive interview with the couple.* **2** [C/U] a formal meeting in which someone asks you questions in order to find out if you are suitable for a job, course of study etc: *I have an interview tomorrow for a job as an interpreter.* **3** [C/U] an official meeting in which the police ask someone questions about a crime

interview² /'ɪntə,vjuː/ verb **1** [T] to ask someone, especially someone famous, questions about themselves, their work, or their ideas: *He was interviewed on the radio this morning.* **2** [I/T] to meet someone and ask them questions in order to find out if they are suitable for a job, course of study etc: *Applicants will be interviewed early next month.* **3** [I/T] if the police interview someone about a crime, they ask them questions about it= QUESTION —**interviewer** noun [C]

interviewee /,ɪntəvjuː'iː/ noun [C] someone who is being interviewed

intervisibility /,ɪntəvɪzə'bɪləti/ noun [U] **GEOGRAPHY** the fact of being able to see place A from place B, and place B from place A

interweave /,ɪntə'wiːv/ (**interweaves, interweaving, interwove** /,ɪntə'wəʊv/, **interwoven** /,ɪntə'wəʊv(ə)n/) verb [I/T] to closely connect or mix different things together, or to be closely connected or mixed together

intestate /ɪn'testeɪt/ adj **LAW** if someone dies intestate, they die without making a **will** explaining what they want to happen to their money and possessions

intestinal /ɪn'testɪn(ə)l/ adj **ANATOMY** relating to the intestines

intestine /ɪn'testɪn/ noun [C] **ANATOMY** the long tube in the body between the stomach and the **anus** that is a major part of the digestive system. There are two parts of the intestine, the **small intestine** and the **large intestine**, where different stages of digestion take place. —*picture* → CIRCULATION, ORGAN

intimacy /'ɪntɪməsi/ noun [singular/U] a close personal relationship

intimate /'ɪntɪmət/ adj **1** an intimate friend is someone who you know very well and like very much= CLOSE **2** relating to very private or personal things: *The magazine published intimate details of their affair.* **3** private and friendly and making you feel relaxed and comfortable: *It's a small hotel with an intimate atmosphere.* **4** an intimate relationship is a very close personal relationship, especially a sexual one —**intimately** adv

intimidate /ɪn'tɪmɪdeɪt/ verb [T] to make someone feel frightened so that they will do what you want —**intimidated** adj, **intimidation** /ɪn,tɪmɪ'deɪʃ(ə)n/ noun [U]

into /strong 'ɪntuː, weak 'ɪntə, 'ɪntʊ/ preposition

1 moving to the inside	5 starting to be involved
2 hitting sth	in sth
3 facing sth	6 interested in sth
4 changing to sth	

1 moving from the outside to the inside of a place or container: *She got into her car and drove away.* ♦ *He put his hands into his pockets.* ♦ *She marched into my office without knocking.*
2 moving towards something and hitting it: *Their car had crashed into a tree.* ♦ *He was so angry he slammed his fist into the wall.*
3 used for stating the direction in which someone or something looks, faces, or points: *She was gazing into the mirror.* ♦ *Please speak into the microphone.*
4 used for stating the result of a change from one thing to another: *Jemma had grown into a beautiful woman.* ♦ *Her stories have been translated into more than 30 languages.*
5 used for saying that someone becomes involved in an activity or situation: *She always manages to get into trouble.* ♦ *He went into the army when he left school.*
6 informal used for saying what activity or subject someone is interested in and enjoys: *She's really into yoga.*

intolerable /ɪn'tɒlərəb(ə)l/ adj impossible to bear or deal with —**intolerably** adv

intolerance /ɪn'tɒlərəns/ noun **1** [U] someone's refusal to accept behaviour, beliefs, or opinions that are different from their own: *religious intolerance* **2** [C/U] **HEALTH** if someone has an intolerance to a particular food or drink, they cannot eat it or drink it because it makes them ill

intolerant /ɪnˈtɒlərənt/ adj **1** not willing to accept behaviour, beliefs, or opinions that are different from your own **2 HEALTH** unable to eat a particular type of food because it makes you ill

intonation /ˌɪntəˈneɪʃ(ə)n/ noun [C/U] **LANGUAGE** the way in which your voice rises and falls when you speak

intoxicated /ɪnˈtɒksɪˌkeɪtɪd/ adj formal drunk —**intoxication** /ɪnˌtɒksɪˈkeɪʃ(ə)n/ noun [U]

intracellular /ˌɪntrəˈseljʊlə/ adj **BIOLOGY** within a cell or cells

intrados /ɪnˈtreɪdɒs/ noun [C] **CONSTRUCTION** the lower surface of an **arch**

intramolecular /ˌɪntrəməˈlekjʊlə/ adj **CHEMISTRY** existing or taking place within a single molecule

intramuscular /ˌɪntrəˈmʌskjʊlə/ adj **HEALTH** within a muscle

intranet /ˈɪntrəˌnet/ noun [C] **COMPUTING** a **network** (=system connecting computers) that only members of a particular organization can use → INTERNET

intransigent /ɪnˈtrænsɪdʒ(ə)nt/ adj formal refusing to change ideas or behaviour with no good reason = STUBBORN —**intransigence** noun [U]

intransitive /ɪnˈtrænsətɪv/ adj **LANGUAGE** an intransitive verb has no direct object. In the sentence 'The children played', the verb 'play' is intransitive. Intransitive verbs are marked [T] in this dictionary.

intravenous /ˌɪntrəˈviːnəs/ adj **HEALTH** put directly into a vein —**intravenously** adv

'in ˌtray noun [C] a container on your desk where you keep documents that you have not dealt with yet —picture → WORKSTATION

intrepid /ɪnˈtrepɪd/ adj not afraid to do dangerous things = DARING

intricate /ˈɪntrɪkət/ adj very detailed in design or structure: an intricate tunnel system —**intricately** adv

intrigue¹ /ɪnˈtriːg/ verb [T] to make someone very interested in knowing more about something: That old house has always intrigued me.

intrigue² /ˈɪntriːg/ noun [C/U] a secret plan to harm or cheat someone, or the process of making such a plan

intriguing /ɪnˈtriːgɪŋ/ adj very interesting and making you want to know more —**intriguingly** /ɪnˈtriːgɪŋli/ adv

intrinsic /ɪnˈtrɪnsɪk/ adj formal relating to the essential qualities or features of something or someone: Providing good service is **intrinsic to** a successful business. —**intrinsically** /ɪnˈtrɪnsɪkli/ adv

intro /ˈɪntrəʊ/ noun [C] informal the introduction to something

introduce /ˌɪntrəˈdjuːs/ verb [T] **1** to tell someone another person's name when they meet for the first time: I would like to **introduce** you **to** my friend Martin. ♦ He **introduced** himself **as** (=said his name was) Major Desmond Morton. **2** to bring something into existence or use for the first time: City schools have introduced stricter rules for dealing with truancy. **3** to provide someone with a new experience: My father first **introduced** me **to** jazz when I was about five. **4** to tell an audience about a programme, performer, performance etc that they are going to see or hear: It is my pleasure to introduce tonight's speaker.

introduction /ˌɪntrəˈdʌkʃ(ə)n/ noun **1** [U] the process of bringing something into existence or use for the first time: Opposition to the tax has decreased since its introduction last year. ♦ **the introduction of** new cancer-

fighting drugs **2** [C] the part at the beginning of a book, report etc that gives a general idea of what it is about **3** [C] something that provides an opportunity to learn or experience something for the first time: My **introduction to** sailing happened on a trip to Switzerland.

introductory /ˌɪntrəˈdʌkt(ə)ri/ adj **1** providing basic information about a subject, especially for people who know nothing about it: introductory lessons **2** an introductory offer or price is a low price that is intended to encourage people to buy a new product

introspective /ˌɪntrəˈspektɪv/ adj tending to examine your own thoughts, feelings, or ideas rather than communicating with other people

introvert /ˈɪntrəˌvɜːt/ noun [C] someone who tends to concentrate on their own thoughts and feelings rather than communicating with other people ≠ EXTROVERT —**introverted** adj

intrude /ɪnˈtruːd/ verb [I] to become involved in a situation in which you are not wanted, or to enter a place where you are not allowed to go: I was very concerned about her, but I didn't want to intrude.

intruder /ɪnˈtruːdə/ noun [C] someone who enters a place where they are not allowed to go

intrusion /ɪnˈtruːʒ(ə)n/ noun [C/U] something that interrupts a peaceful situation or a private event

intrusive /ɪnˈtruːsɪv/ adj becoming involved in something in a way that is not welcome

intuition /ˌɪntjuˈɪʃ(ə)n/ noun [C/U] an ability to know or understand something through your feelings, rather than by considering facts or evidence

intuitive /ɪnˈtjuːətɪv/ adj **1** based on feelings rather than on facts or evidence **2** an intuitive system, method, piece of software etc is easy to use because the process of operating it is very obvious —**intuitively** adv

inundate /ˈɪnʌndeɪt/ verb [T] to send or provide much more of something than someone can easily deal with: We've been inundated with phone calls.

inured /ɪˈnjʊəd/ adj formal someone who is inured to an unpleasant experience is so familiar with it that they no longer become upset by it

in utero /ˌɪn ˈjuːtərəʊ/ adv inside the uterus —**in utero** adj

invade /ɪnˈveɪd/ verb **1** [I/T] to take or send an army into another country in order to get control of it: The island was invaded during the war. **2** [T] to enter a place, especially in large numbers or in a way that causes problems: The town is invaded by tourists every summer. **3** [T] to get involved in someone's life without their permission —**invader** noun [C]

invalid¹ /ɪnˈvælɪd/ adj **1** not legally effective ≠ VALID: Your ticket is invalid. **2** not based on facts, evidence, or good judgment **3 COMPUTING** not acceptable as a computer instruction or operation

invalid² /ˈɪnvəlɪd/ noun [C] **HEALTH** someone who is ill or injured and cannot look after themselves

invaluable /ɪnˈvæljuəb(ə)l/ adj extremely useful

invariably /ɪnˈveəriəbli/ adv always, or almost always

invasion /ɪnˈveɪʒ(ə)n/ noun [C/U] **1** an occasion when one country's army goes into another country in order to take control of it **2** a situation in which a very large number of people come to a place **3 HEALTH** the movement of a disease, or of the cells that cause it, from one area to another

invasive /ɪnˈveɪsɪv/ adj HEALTH **1** invasive medical treatment involves putting something into the body or cutting into the body ≠ NON-INVASIVE **2** an invasive disease spreads within the body and is difficult to treat

invective /ɪnˈvektɪv/ noun [U] *formal* insulting language or swearing

invent /ɪnˈvent/ verb [T] **1** to design or create something that did not exist before: *Alfred Nobel invented dynamite.* **2** to make up a story, excuse etc that is not true

invention /ɪnˈvenʃ(ə)n/ noun **1** [C/U] something that someone has made, designed, or thought of for the first time, or the act of inventing something: *Inventions like the electric light bulb changed the way people lived.* ♦ *the invention of the Internet* **2** [C/U] a story, excuse etc that is not true **3** [U] the ability to think of new and original ways of doing things: *By comparison, British artists seemed to lack imagination and invention.*

inventive /ɪnˈventɪv/ adj **1** good at thinking of new ideas or methods **2** used about new and original ideas, methods etc: *an inventive strategy* —**inventiveness** noun [U]

inventor /ɪnˈventə/ noun [C] someone who has invented something, or whose job is to invent things

inventory /ˈɪnvəntəri/ (plural **inventories**) noun **1** [C] a list that gives the details of all the things in a place **2** [U] BUSINESS American the **stock** available to buy in a shop

inverse¹ /ˌɪnˈvɜːs/ adj changing in the opposite way to something else, especially in position, size, or amount —**inversely** adv

inverse² /ˈɪnvɜːs, ɪnˈvɜːs/ noun [C] the complete opposite of something, for example a calculation or result in mathematics

invert¹ /ˌɪnˈvɜːt/ verb [T] *formal* to turn something upside down, or to put it in the opposite position —**inversion** /ɪnˈvɜːʃ(ə)n/ noun [C/U]

invert² /ˈɪnˌvɜːt/ noun [C] CONSTRUCTION the depth of a drain

invertebrate /ɪnˈvɜːtɪbrət/ noun [C] BIOLOGY a small animal without a backbone, for example an insect or a worm. Invertebrates are one of the two main animal groups. —**invertebrate** adj → VERTEBRATE

inverted commas /ˌɪnvɜːtɪd ˈkɒməz/ noun [plural] LANGUAGE a pair of marks " " or ' ', used in written English for showing the words that someone said, or the title of a book, film etc = QUOTATION MARKS

invest /ɪnˈvest/ verb [I/T] BUSINESS to use your money with the aim of making a profit from it, for example by buying shares in a company: *Banks invested £20 million in the scheme.* —**investor** noun [C]

    PHRASAL VERB **invest in sth** to spend money on something in order to improve it or to make it more successful: *This government believes in investing in education.*

investigate /ɪnˈvestɪɡeɪt/ verb [I/T] to try to find out all the facts about something in order to learn the truth about it: *We sent a reporter to investigate the rumour.* ♦ *The research aims to investigate why schools are not doing better.* —**investigator** noun [C]

investigation /ɪnˌvestɪˈɡeɪʃ(ə)n/ noun [C/U] the process of trying to find out all the facts about something, often in order to discover who or what caused it or how it happened: *methods of scientific investigation* ♦ *the investigation into the crash of Flight 803*

investigative /ɪnˈvestɪɡətɪv/ adj intended or intending to discover new details and facts about something

investment /ɪnˈves(t)mənt/ noun **1** [C/U] BUSINESS money that is used in a way that may earn someone more money, for example money used for buying shares in a company: *Her investments were mainly in technology stocks.* ♦ *The new laws will attract foreign investment.* **2** [U] the process of spending money in order to improve something or make it more successful: *Investment in new technology is critical to our success.* **3** [C] something that you are willing to spend money on because it will give you benefits in the future: *Computer courses are a good investment for your career.* **4** [C/U] the amount of time, energy, or emotion needed in order to make something successful: *Teachers' investment of time in class preparation is always underestimated.*

invigorate /ɪnˈvɪɡəreɪt/ verb [T] to give someone more energy = REFRESH

invincible /ɪnˈvɪnsəb(ə)l/ adj too strong to be defeated

invisible /ɪnˈvɪzəb(ə)l/ adj **1** something that is invisible cannot be seen —*picture* → PHASE **2** ECONOMICS a country's invisible income is money it earns from activities such as financial services rather than from selling goods —**invisibility** /ɪnˌvɪzəˈbɪləti/ noun [U], **invisibly** adv

invitation /ˌɪnvɪˈteɪʃ(ə)n/ noun [C] a request for someone to come to an event or to do something: *a wedding invitation* ♦ *an invitation to the party*

    PHRASE **invitation to tender** BUSINESS a formal request to a number of **suppliers** to make a detailed proposal for providing particular goods or services

invite /ɪnˈvaɪt/ verb [T] **1** to ask someone to come to see you or to spend time with you socially: *We've invited all the neighbours to the party.* ♦ *Why don't you invite them for a drink?* ♦ *They've invited me to eat at their house tonight.* **2** to formally ask someone to do something or go somewhere: *Leaders of the two countries were invited to attend peace talks in Geneva.* **3** to make something bad or unpleasant more likely to happen: *His policies invited widespread criticism.*

inviting /ɪnˈvaɪtɪŋ/ adj attractive in a way that makes you want to do something: *an inviting outdoor pool* —**invitingly** adv

in vitro /ˌɪn ˈviːtrəʊ/ adj SCIENCE done or produced outside a living organism, for example in a test tube —**in vitro** adv

ˌin ˈvitro fertiliˌzation noun [U] HEALTH *see* IVF

invoice /ˈɪnvɔɪs/ noun [C] a document giving details of goods or services that someone has bought and must pay for

invoke /ɪnˈvəʊk/ verb [T] *formal* to use a law or rule in order to achieve something

involuntary /ɪnˈvɒləntəri/ adj **1** sudden and not able to be controlled: *He gave an involuntary gasp.* **2** BIOLOGY relating to biological processes in the body, for example digestion, that are not controlled consciously by the mind but are controlled automatically by the brain —**involuntarily** adv

inˌvoluntary ˈmuscle noun [C/U] ANATOMY muscle that is involved in processes in the body that a person cannot consciously control. Heart muscle is a type of involuntary muscle.

involute /ˈɪnvəlut/ noun [C] MATHS, TECHNOLOGY a curved line that gradually becomes more distant from a central point. The teeth on most **gears** have the shape of involutes.

involve /ɪnˈvɒlv/ verb [T] **1** to include something as a necessary part of an activity, event, or situation: *The course involves a lot of hard work.* ♦ *The job involved working with a software development team.* **2** to include or affect someone or something in an important way: *Four vehicles were involved in the accident.* **3** to encourage or allow someone to take part in something: *The goal is to **involve** workers **in** the decision-making process.*

involved /ɪnˈvɒlvd/ adj **1** affected by or included in an activity, event, or situation: *They became **involved in** a lengthy dispute.* **2** someone who is involved in something takes part in it: *We want all departments to be involved.* ♦ *He denied that he was **involved with** organized crime.* ♦ *We were **involved in** the talks until today.* **3** complicated and difficult to understand: *a long, involved explanation* **4** if you are involved with someone, you have a sexual or emotional relationship with them

involvement /ɪnˈvɒlvmənt/ noun [C/U] the act of taking part in an activity, event, or situation: *Our **involvement with** this project started in 1989.* ♦ *There is no evidence of his direct **involvement in** the bombing.*

inward /ˈɪnwəd/ adj **1** felt in your own mind but not obvious to other people **2** going towards the inside or centre of something ≠ OUTWARD

inwardly /ˈɪnwədli/ adv in a hidden way that is not obvious to other people ≠ OUTWARDLY: *I tried not to smile at the news, but I was inwardly delighted.*

inwards /ˈɪnwədz/ adv towards the inside of something ≠ OUTWARDS

iodine /ˈaɪədiːn/ noun [U] CHEMISTRY, HEALTH a poisonous dark non-metal element. A solution in alcohol is put on cuts in the skin in order to prevent infection. Chemical symbol: **I**

iodine so,lution noun [C/U] CHEMISTRY a solution of iodine in **potassium iodide**, used as a test for starch. It turns blue-black when starch is present.

ion /ˈaɪən/ noun [C] CHEMISTRY an atom or group of atoms that has become **charged**. A **positive ion** has an electrical charge caused by losing electrons, and a **negative ion** has an electrical charge caused by gaining them.

ionic /aɪˈɒnɪk/ adj CHEMISTRY relating to ions

i,onic 'bond noun [C] CHEMISTRY a chemical bond that is formed between two ions with opposite charges, when one or more electrons are passed from one atom to another → COVALENT BOND

ionize /ˈaɪənaɪz/ verb [I/T] CHEMISTRY to form ions, or to make something form ions —**ionization** /ˌaɪənaɪˈzeɪʃ(ə)n/ noun [U]

the ionosphere /aɪˈɒnəˌsfɪə/ noun SCIENCE the part of the Earth's atmosphere through which radio waves can be sent —*picture* → ATMOSPHERE

IPA /ˌaɪ piː ˈeɪ/ noun [U] LANGUAGE International Phonetic Alphabet: a system of symbols that are used to represent speech sounds. The IPA spelling of words is shown in this dictionary, to show you how to pronounce the word.

IPM /ˌaɪ piː ˈem/ noun [U] AGRICULTURE integrated pest management: a system for controlling **pests** and diseases that uses different methods including natural **predators**, biological controls, and physical **barriers**, as well as the use of **pesticides**

IQ /ˌaɪ ˈkjuː/ noun [C] EDUCATION intelligence quotient: a number that represents someone's intelligence

irascible /ɪˈræsəb(ə)l/ adj formal easily becoming angry

irate /aɪˈreɪt/ adj very angry

IRC /ˌaɪ ɑː ˈsiː/ abbrev COMPUTING Internet relay chat: a system that allows many users to exchange messages in **real time** on the Internet

iridescent /ˌɪrɪˈdes(ə)nt/ adj showing changing colours in different types of light

iridium /ɪˈrɪdiəm/ noun [U] CHEMISTRY a hard silver-white metallic element that is similar to **platinum**. It is used in alloys. Chemical symbol: **Ir**

iris /ˈaɪrɪs/ noun [C] **1** a tall, usually purple, flower **2** ANATOMY the coloured part of the eye in vertebrate animals. The iris controls the amount of light that reaches the retina by changing in size. —*picture* → EYE

irk /ɜːk/ verb [T] formal to annoy someone = IRRITATE

iron¹ /ˈaɪən/ noun **1** [U] CHEMISTRY a chemical element that is a hard heavy metal. It is used especially for making steel. Chemical symbol: **Fe 2** [U] HEALTH iron that exists in small quantities in some foods and in the body. Iron is found in foods such as **red meat**, eggs, nuts, and cereals and is important in order to make **haemoglobin** (=the substance that makes red blood cells able to carry oxygen around the body). Lack of iron in the body causes **anaemia**. **3** [C] a heated object that you push across clothes in order to make them smooth **4** [C] SPORTS a **golf club** with a metal end for hitting the ball

iron² /ˈaɪən/ verb [I/T] to push an iron across clothes in order to make them smooth: *She ironed her skirt.*

iron³ /ˈaɪən/ adj **1** made of iron **2** very strong, strict, or severe: *an iron will*

the 'Iron ,Age noun the period of time when people made tools and weapons from iron, starting around 1500 BC, after the Bronze Age

iron carbide /ˌaɪən ˈkɑːbaɪd/ noun [U] CHEMISTRY, TECHNOLOGY cementite

ironic /aɪˈrɒnɪk/ adj **1** LANGUAGE expressing the opposite of what you really think, especially in order to be humorous: *an ironic comment* **2** an ironic event or situation is interesting, because it is the opposite of what you expect

ironically /aɪˈrɒnɪkli/ adv used for saying that a situation has developed in an unexpected or humorous way

ironing /ˈaɪənɪŋ/ noun [U] the job of making clothes smooth with an iron, or the clothes that must be made smooth with an iron: *I'll **do the ironing**.*

ironmongery /ˈaɪənˌmʌŋgəri/ noun [U] CONSTRUCTION the metal parts such as locks and handles that are fitted to doors and windows

,iron 'ore noun [U] GEOLOGY rock that contains iron

,iron 'oxide noun [U] CHEMISTRY a compound that consists of iron combined with oxygen. It is commonly known as **rust**.

irony /ˈaɪrəni/ (plural **ironies**) noun **1** [U] a form of humour in which you use words to express the opposite of what the words really mean **2** [C/U] a strange, funny, or sad situation in which things happen in the opposite way to what you expect

irradiate /ɪˈreɪdieɪt/ verb [T] **1** SCIENCE to treat something with radiation, especially food, in order to kill bacteria **2** HEALTH to use radiation on something as a medical treatment, for example on cancer cells in order to destroy them

irradiation /ɪˌreɪdiˈeɪʃ(ə)n/ noun [U] **1** SCIENCE the process of treating something or somebody with radiation **2** PHYSICS the **visual** effect by which a brightly lit thing appears larger against a dark background **3** HEALTH the medical use of radiation, for example X-rays, gamma rays, or neutrons

irrational /ɪˈræʃ(ə)nəl/ adj without clear or sensible reasons, or not thinking in a sensible way: *irrational panic* —**irrationally** adv

irreconcilable /ɪˌrekənˈsaɪləb(ə)l/ adj irreconcilable opinions, aims, or disagreements are so opposed to each other that it is impossible to reach an agreement

irrefutable /ˌɪrɪˈfjuːtəb(ə)l/ adj *formal* impossible to prove wrong

irregular /ɪˈregjʊlə/ adj **1** not happening regularly: *His breathing had become irregular.* **2** not even, smooth, or straight in shape or appearance: *an irregular surface* **3** not following the rules, laws, or usual ways of doing things **4** LANGUAGE not following the usual rules of grammar. For example, 'eat' is an irregular verb because its past tense is 'ate' and its past participle is 'eaten'. —**irregularly** adv

irregularity /ɪˌregjʊˈlærəti/ (plural **irregularities**) noun **1** [C] a situation in which the rules, laws, or usual ways of doing things have not been followed: *irregularities in the election process* **2** [C/U] a situation in which events do not happen at regular times **3** [C] a shape or appearance that is not even, smooth, or straight: *irregularities in the surface*

ir,regular 'polygon noun [C] MATHS a geometric shape with three or more straight sides and angles that are not equal

irrelevant /ɪˈreləvənt/ adj not important, or not relevant to what you are doing ≠ RELEVANT: *an irrelevant remark* —**irrelevance** noun [C/U]

irreparable /ɪˈrep(ə)rəb(ə)l/ adj *formal* irreparable harm or damage is extremely bad and cannot be repaired

irreplaceable /ˌɪrɪˈpleɪsəb(ə)l/ adj something irreplaceable is valuable and impossible to replace if it is used, lost, or destroyed

irresistible /ˌɪrɪˈzɪstəb(ə)l/ adj **1** strong or powerful, and impossible to control: *an irresistible urge to laugh* **2** impossible to refuse, not want, or not like: *an irresistible smile* —**irresistibly** adv

irrespective /ˌɪrɪˈspektɪv/ adv **irrespective of sth** despite a particular fact, situation, or quality

irresponsible /ˌɪrɪˈspɒnsəb(ə)l/ adj **1** done or said without thinking about the possible results ≠ RESPONSIBLE: *It was irresponsible of you to leave her alone.* **2** not sensible, or not able to be trusted to be reasonable ≠ RESPONSIBLE: *an irresponsible driver* —**irresponsibly** adv

irreverent /ɪˈrevərənt/ adj showing no respect for traditions, rules, or religious beliefs

irreversible /ˌɪrɪˈvɜːsəb(ə)l/ adj impossible to change or bring back to a previous condition or situation ≠ REVERSIBLE: *irreversible damage to the environment*

irrevocable /ɪˈrevəkəb(ə)l/ adj *formal* impossible to change or stop —**irrevocably** adv

irrigate /ˈɪrɪgeɪt/ verb [T] AGRICULTURE to bring water to land through a system of pipes, **ditches** etc in order to make plants grow

irrigation /ˌɪrɪˈgeɪʃ(ə)n/ noun [U] the process of bringing water to land though a system of pipes, **ditches** etc in order to make crops grow

irri'gation ,channel noun [C] AGRICULTURE a passage dug in the ground and used for bringing water to land in order to make plants grow

irritability /ˌɪrɪtəˈbɪləti/ noun [U] **1** a tendency to become easily annoyed or impatient **2** BIOLOGY the ability of living things to react to physical **stimuli** such as heat, light, or touch

irritable /ˈɪrɪtəb(ə)l/ adj **1** likely to become easily annoyed or made angry **2** BIOLOGY able to react to physical **stimuli** such as heat, light, or touch —**irritably** adv

irritant /ˈɪrɪt(ə)nt/ noun [C] **1** something that annoys you **2** HEALTH something that makes part of the body become painful or swollen

irritate /ˈɪrɪteɪt/ verb [T] **1** to make you feel annoyed or angry: *That little noise he makes really irritates me.* **2** HEALTH to make part of the body painful or swollen —**irritation** /ˌɪrɪˈteɪʃ(ə)n/ noun [U]

irritated /ˈɪrɪteɪtɪd/ adj **1** annoyed or angry about something: *I was beginning to get irritated.* **2** HEALTH painful or swollen

irritating /ˈɪrɪteɪtɪŋ/ adj making you feel annoyed or angry: *He had an irritating habit of cracking his knuckles.* —**irritatingly** adv

is /ɪz/ 3rd person singular of the present tense of **be**

ISBN /ˌaɪ es biː ˈen/ noun [C] International Standard Book Number: an individual number given to every book that is published

Islam /ˈɪzlɑːm/ noun [U] **1** RELIGION the religion based on the ideas of Muhammad. Its followers are called **Muslims** and they worship in a **mosque**. The holy book of Islam is the **Koran**. Muslims believe that there is only one God and that Muhammad is his **prophet**. **2** Muslim people and Muslim countries generally —**Islamic** /ɪzˈlæmɪk/ adj

Islamist /ˈɪzləmɪst/ noun [C] RELIGION someone who follows Islam very strictly —**Islamism** noun [U]

island /ˈaɪlənd/ noun [C] GEOGRAPHY a piece of land that is completely surrounded by water: *the best hotel on the island* ♦ *islands off the west coast of Canada*

islander /ˈaɪləndə/ noun [C] someone who lives on a small island

'island-,hop verb [I] TOURISM *informal* to travel from island to island within the same group of islands —**'island-,hopping** noun [U]

isle /aɪl/ noun [C] GEOGRAPHY an island

islet of Langerhans /ˌaɪlət əv ˈlæŋəhæns/ noun [C] ANATOMY one of the many groups of cells in the pancreas that produce **insulin** and other hormones

isn't /ˈɪz(ə)nt/ short form the usual way of saying or writing 'is not'. This is not often used in formal writing: *Isn't she here yet?*

isobar /ˈaɪsəʊˌbɑː/ noun [C] GEOGRAPHY a line drawn on a weather map that connects places that have the same air pressure

isolate /ˈaɪsəleɪt/ verb [T] **1** to keep someone in a place that is away from other people **2** to prevent a country or group from communicating with, doing business with, or getting support from other countries or groups **3** to separate something from other similar things so that you can consider it by itself

isolated /ˈaɪsəˌleɪtɪd/ adj **1** an isolated place is a long way from other places and is often difficult to get to = REMOTE: *isolated mountain villages* **2** happening only once, or existing only in one place: *an isolated incident* **3** feeling alone and unhappy, with no friends: *Many victims feel isolated and unable to talk about their* *experiences.* **4** an isolated country or organization is one that others refuse to deal with

isolation /ˌaɪsəˈleɪʃ(ə)n/ noun [U] **1** the state of being separated from other people, or a situation in which you do not have support from other people: *Isolation from family and friends can lead to feelings of anxiety.* **2** a situation in which a country or group is alone and without support because other countries or groups stop dealing with it **3** HEALTH a situation in which someone with an infectious disease is kept away from other people, to reduce the possibility of the disease spreading to them

PHRASE **in isolation 1** if something is considered in isolation, it is considered separately from other similar things **2** in a place that is away from other people, animals, or things: *The prisoners were kept in isolation.*

isolationism /ˌaɪsəˈleɪʃ(ə)nˌɪz(ə)m/ noun [U] **SOCIAL STUDIES** a country's policy of not having political or economic relationships with other countries —**isolationist** adj

isomer /ˈaɪsəmə/ noun [C] **CHEMISTRY** one of two or more compounds that have the same formula, but have the atoms in their molecules arranged in a different way and have different properties from each other

isometric drawing /ˌaɪsəʊmetrɪk ˈdrɔːɪŋ/ noun [C/U] **MATHS, PHYSICS** a drawing of a three-dimensional object made using vertical lines, and lines at 30° from the horizontal axis

isometric paper /ˌaɪsəʊmetrɪk ˈpeɪpə/ noun [U] **MATHS** paper covered with a pattern of **equilateral** triangles formed by lines or **dots** (=spots) that is used for drawing three-dimensional objects

ISO metric screw thread /ˌaɪ es əʊ ˌmetrɪk ˈskruː ˌθred/ noun [C] **TECHNOLOGY** a **metric screw thread**

isometric transformation /ˌaɪsəʊmetrɪk ˌtrænsfəˈmeɪʃ(ə)n/ noun [C/U] **MATHS** a **transformation** that does not change the shape or size of a geometric shape

isosceles triangle /aɪˌsɒsəliːz ˈtraɪæŋg(ə)l/ noun [C] **MATHS** a triangle in which two sides are the same length —*picture* → TRIANGLE

isotherm /ˈaɪsəʊˌθɜːm/ noun [C] **GEOGRAPHY** a line on a weather map that connects places where the temperature is the same

isotonic drink /ˌaɪsəʊtɒnɪk ˈdrɪŋk/ noun [C] **SPORTS** a drink that contains sugar and a little salt, suitable for replacing body fluid quickly during exercise

isotope /ˈaɪsətəʊp/ noun [C] **CHEMISTRY** one of the forms of a chemical element that have the same atomic number but a different number of neutrons, and therefore have a different mass

isotropic /ˌaɪsəʊˈtrɒpɪk/ adj **PHYSICS** having physical properties that are the same in all directions

ISP /ˌaɪ es ˈpiː/ noun [C] **COMPUTING** Internet service provider: a company that provides a connection to the Internet

issue[1] /ˈɪʃuː, ˈɪsjuː/ noun **1** [C] a subject or problem that people discuss or argue about: *environmental issues* ♦ *Education was one of the biggest issues in the campaign.* **2** [C] a magazine that is published at a particular time: *The article appeared in the November issue.* **3** [U] **LAW** someone's children

PHRASE **make an issue of sth** to treat something as an important problem when it is not

issue[2] /ˈɪʃuː, ˈɪsjuː/ verb [T] **1** to announce something officially: *The banks issued a warning that interest*

rates would rise. **2** if you issue someone with something, you officially give it to them: *All visitors to the factory must be **issued with** protective goggles.* **3** to officially make things available for people to buy or use: *The post office is issuing a new range of stamps.*

-ist suffix **1** used with the names of some skills and professions to describe a person practising that skill or profession **2** used with the names of some musical instruments to describe someone who plays that instrument **3** used for describing someone who has an unreasonable negative opinion a particular group of people within society

isthmus /ˈɪsməs/ noun [C] **GEOGRAPHY** a narrow piece of land that joins two larger areas and has water on both sides

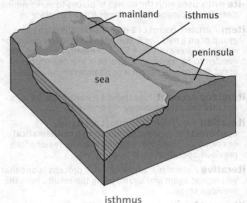

isthmus

it /ɪt/ pronoun

1 referring to sth already mentioned	**5** about times and dates
2 as subject/object	**6** about distance
3 referring to sb's life or situation	**7** emphasizing who or what you mean
4 about weather conditions	**+** PHRASE

1 used for referring to something that has already been mentioned, or when it is obvious which thing you mean: *I can't find my ticket. I think I must have lost it.* ♦ *You should come to Rome – it's a wonderful city.*

2 used instead of the subject or object of a sentence, when the real subject or object is a phrase or clause at the end of the sentence: *It's nice to be home again.* ♦ *The new law made it easier to get a divorce.*

3 used for referring to someone's life, work, or general situation: *What's it like in the army these days?*

4 used for talking about weather and other natural conditions: *It rained in the night.* ♦ *It's cooler indoors.* ♦ *It gets dark at around five.*

5 used for saying or asking what the time, day, or date is: *'What time is it?' 'It's four o'clock.'* ♦ *Thank goodness it's Saturday tomorrow.*

6 used for saying how long a distance is: *It's about ten miles from here to my home.*

7 used with the verb 'to be' for emphasizing that you are referring to a particular person or thing: *It's your brother I want to speak to.*

PHRASE **it seems/looks/appears** used for saying what seems to be true: *It seems that no one is willing to accept responsibility.* ♦ *It looks as if we're going to lose our jobs.*

IT /ˌaɪ ˈtiː/ noun [U] **COMPUTING** information technology

italics /ɪˈtælɪks/ noun [plural] italics are letters that slope to the right, like the letters in examples in this dictionary —**italic** adj

itch¹ /ɪtʃ/ verb [I] if your skin itches, you want to **scratch** it

itch² /ɪtʃ/ noun [singular] a feeling on your skin that makes you want to **scratch** it (=rub it with your nails)

itchy /ˈɪtʃi/ adj if you feel itchy, you want to **scratch** your skin (=rub it with your nails)

it'd /ɪtəd/ short form **1** a way of saying or writing 'it would'. This is not often used in formal writing: *It'd be better to wait until later.* **2** a way of saying or writing 'it had', when 'had' is an auxiliary verb. This is not often used in formal writing: *It'd been a difficult night.*

-ite suffix used with the names of places to make nouns describing someone who comes from that place

item /ˈaɪtəm/ noun [C] **1** one of several things in a group or on a list: *The first item to be discussed was the new computer system.* ♦ *Several items of equipment needed to be repaired.* **2** an article in a newspaper or magazine, or one part of a news programme on the television or radio

itemized account /ˌaɪtəmaɪzd əˈkaʊnt/ noun [C] a detailed record of money paid or owed

iteration /ˌɪtəˈreɪʃ(ə)n/ noun [C/U] **MATHS, COMPUTING** the process of repeating a **mathematical** or computer operation, starting with the result of the previous operation each time

iterative /ˈɪtərətɪv/ adj an iterative process is one that you repeat again and again, using the results from the previous stage

itinerant¹ /aɪˈtɪnərənt/ adj travelling around frequently, especially in order to get work

itinerant² /aɪˈtɪnərənt/ noun [C] someone who travels around frequently, especially in order to get work

itinerary /aɪˈtɪnərəri/ (plural **itineraries**) noun [C] a written plan that shows the details of a journey

it'll /ˈɪt(ə)l/ short form the usual way of saying or writing 'it will'. This is not often used in formal writing: *It'll be fun!*

it's /ɪts/ short form **1** the usual way of saying or writing 'it is'. This is not often used in formal writing: *It's cold outside.* **2** the usual way of saying or writing 'it has', when 'has' is an auxiliary verb. This is not often used in formal writing: *It's been raining for hours.*

its /ɪts/ determiner belonging or relating to something, when it has already been mentioned or when it is obvious which thing you are referring to: *The chair lay on its side.* ♦ *Asia and its many great cities*

Its should not be confused with it's, which is the short form of 'it is' or 'it has'.

itself /ɪtˈself/ pronoun **1** the reflexive form of 'it', used for showing that an action affects the thing that does the action: *The young bird cannot feed itself.* ♦ *The government needs to defend itself against these attacks.* **2** used for emphasizing that you are referring to a particular thing: *The problem is not with the software, but with the computer itself.*

PHRASE (all) by itself 1 not near or with any other thing: *His house stood by itself on the edge of the village.* **2** without help: *The door opened by itself.* ♦ *Can the baby stand up all by itself?*

IUD /ˌaɪ ju: ˈdi:/ noun [C] **HEALTH** intra-uterine device: a type of contraceptive that consists of a small piece of plastic or metal fitted inside a woman's uterus

I've /aɪv/ short form the usual way of saying or writing 'I have'. This is not often used in formal writing: *I've just been to the cinema.*

ivermectin /ˌaɪvəˈmektɪn/ noun [U] **HEALTH** a medicine that is used to treat a wide range of infections caused by parasites

IVF /ˌaɪ vi: ˈef/ noun [U] **HEALTH** in vitro fertilization: the medical process in which a woman's egg is fertilized outside her body and then put back into the uterus so she becomes pregnant

ivory¹ /ˈaɪvəri/ noun [U] the bone that an elephant's **tusks** are made of

ivory² /ˈaɪvəri/ adj pale yellow-white in colour

ivy /ˈaɪvi/ noun [U] a dark-green plant that spreads and grows up walls

J j

j /dʒeɪ/ (plural **j's**) or **J** (plural **J's**) noun [C/U] the tenth letter of the English alphabet

jab¹ /dʒæb/ (**jabs**, **jabbing**, **jabbed**) verb [I/T] to push something narrow or pointed into or toward something else with a sudden movement

jab² /dʒæb/ noun [C] **1** a hard straight push with something narrow or pointed **2** **HEALTH** an **injection** (=amount of medicine given through a needle) that is intended to stop someone getting a disease **3** **SPORTS** in boxing, a short quick hit with a closed hand

jack /dʒæk/ noun [C] **1** a piece of equipment for lifting and supporting a heavy object, for example a car **2** a playing card that has a picture of a young man on it **3** an electrical **socket** with one hole, or the type of **plug** that fits into it

jackal /ˈdʒækɔ:l/ noun [C] a wild African or Asian mammal like a dog

jacket /ˈdʒækɪt/ noun [C] **1** a short coat: *a denim jacket* **2** a cover for a book

jackfruit /ˈdʒækˌfru:t/ noun **1** [C] a tropical tree that produces a large fruit **2** [C/U] a piece of fruit from the jackfruit tree

jacking point /ˈdʒækɪŋ ˌpɔɪnt/ noun [C] **ENGINEERING** a place under a vehicle where a **jack** can be placed in order to lift the vehicle

jackknife /ˈdʒækˌnaɪf/ verb [I] if a truck or train jackknifes in an accident, it bends in the middle and its parts fold towards each other

jade /dʒeɪd/ noun [U] a hard green stone that is used for making jewellery

jagged /ˈdʒægɪd/ adj a jagged surface or edge has a lot of rough pointed parts

jaguar /ˈdʒægjuə/ noun [C] a large wild cat with black spots from Central and South America

jail¹ /dʒeɪl/ noun [C/U] a place where people are put as punishment for a crime = PRISON: *Adam spent 3 years in jail for drug possession.*

jail² /dʒeɪl/ verb [T] to put someone in jail: *He was jailed for drink-driving.*

Jain /dʒaɪn/ noun [C] **RELIGION** a member of a religious group in India that believes that people should not be violent towards any living creature —**Jain** adj, **Jainism** noun [U]

jam¹ /dʒæm/ noun **1** [C/U] a sweet sticky food made from boiled fruit and sugar, that is usually spread onto bread: *strawberry jam* **2** [C] a long line of vehicles that are not moving or are moving very slowly = TRAFFIC JAM **3** [C] an occasion when a machine does not work because something prevents its parts from moving: *a paper jam in the printer* → TRAFFIC JAM

jam² /dʒæm/ (**jams, jamming, jammed**) verb **1** [T] to use force to put something into a small space: *I tried to jam some paper into the cracks.* **2** [T] if people or things jam a place, there are so many of them that it is difficult to move: *The streets were jammed with cars.* **3** [I/T] if a machine, lock, window etc jams, or if something jams it, it does not work because something stops it from moving: *He fired one shot before his gun jammed.* **4** [T] to block a radio, television, or other electronic signal

jamb /dʒæm/ noun [C] **CONSTRUCTION 1** the upright side of an opening such as a door or window **2** the bricks that form the side part of a **fireplace**

'jam ,session noun [C] **MUSIC** an occasion when musicians play music together in an informal way

Jan. abbrev January

jangle /ˈdʒæŋg(ə)l/ verb [I/T] if small metal objects jangle, they make a noise when they hit against each other

January /ˈdʒænjuəri/ noun [U] the first month of the year: *My class begins in January.* ♦ *The new year begins on January 1st.*

jar¹ /dʒɑ/ noun [C] a glass container for food, with a lid and a wide opening: *a jar of marmalade*

jar² /dʒɑ/ (**jars, jarring, jarred**) verb [I/T] **1** to accidentally push something hard against something else, in a way that causes pain or damage: *The shock of the fall jarred every bone in his body.* **2** [I] to be unpleasant or not suitable in a particular situation

jargon /ˈdʒɑgən/ noun [U] **LANGUAGE** *showing disapproval* special words and phrases that are only understood by people who do the same kind of work: *computer jargon*

jaundice /ˈdʒɔːndɪs/ noun [U] **HEALTH** an illness that makes the skin and the white part of the eyes become yellow

Java /ˈdʒɑːvə/ **TRADEMARK COMPUTING** a computer language that allows computer software to be used on any kind of computer, and allows all computers to communicate with each other, for example through the Internet

javelin /ˈdʒæv(ə)lɪn/ noun [C/U] **SPORTS** a long pointed stick that is thrown in a sports competition, or the sport of throwing this stick

jaw /dʒɔː/ noun **1** [C] [C] **ANATOMY** one of the two hard parts around the mouth in vertebrates that are used for biting and for eating food. The upper jaw is joined to the skull while the lower part, the **mandible**, moves up and down. **2** [C] the lower part of the face that includes the chin and stretches back almost to the ear —*picture* → BODY **3** jaws [plural] **TECHNOLOGY** the parts of a machine or piece of equipment that open and close, either to hold something firmly, or to pick it up and move it from one place to another

jawbone /ˈdʒɔːˌbəʊn/ noun [C] **ANATOMY** the **mandible**

jazz /dʒæz/ noun [U] **MUSIC** a type of music with a strong lively beat in which players often **improvise** (=make up the music as they play)

jealous /ˈdʒeləs/ adj **1** upset because someone has something that you would like to have, or can do something that you would like to do: *I expect some of your friends will be jealous.* **2** angry and upset because someone who you love is giving a lot of attention to another person: *He would dance with other women to make her jealous.* —**jealously** adv

jealousy /ˈdʒeləsi/ noun [U] **1** a feeling of anger and sadness because someone has or does something that you would like to have or do: *Professional jealousy can cause problems at work.* **2** a strong feeling of anger and sadness because someone who you love is giving a lot of attention to someone else: *sexual jealousy*

jeans /dʒiːnz/ noun [plural] informal trousers made of **denim** (=heavy cotton cloth): *a pair of faded blue jeans*

Jeep /dʒiːp/ **TRADEMARK** a car with no roof that can drive over all types of land

'jeep sa,fari noun [C] **TOURISM** an organized journey in a **four-wheel drive** vehicle, for example to look at wild animals

jeer /dʒɪə/ verb [I/T] to shout or laugh at someone in an unkind way —**jeer** noun [C]

Jehovah /dʒɪˈhəʊvə/ **RELIGION** the name of God in the Old Testament of the Bible

Je,hovah's 'Witness noun [C] **RELIGION** a member of a Christian religious group started in the US in 1872. Jehovah's Witnesses believe it is their duty to go to people's homes and prepare them for the time when the world will end and Jesus Christ will come to Earth for the second time.

jelly /ˈdʒeli/ (plural **jellies**) noun [C/U] **1** a soft sweet food, made from fruit juice, sugar, and **gelatin**, that shakes when you touch it **2** a sweet sticky food made from boiled fruit juice and sugar, often spread on bread

jellyfish /ˈdʒeliˌfɪʃ/ (plural **jellyfish**) noun [C] **BIOLOGY** a soft transparent invertebrate sea animal that can sting you. A sting from a jellyfish can be very dangerous, and can even kill. —*picture* → SEA

'jelly-,like adj a jelly-like substance is between a liquid and a solid

jeopardize /ˈdʒepədaɪz/ verb [T] to risk damaging or destroying something important: *Cuts in funding could jeopardize our research.*

jeopardy /ˈdʒepədi/ noun **in jeopardy** likely to be damaged or destroyed

jerk¹ /dʒɜːk/ verb [I/T] to move suddenly, or to make something move suddenly: *The train jerked forwards.*

jerk² /dʒɜːk/ noun [C] a quick sudden movement

jersey /ˈdʒɜːzi/ noun [U] a soft cloth made from wool or cotton

Jesuit /ˈdʒezjuɪt/ noun [C] **RELIGION** a priest who belongs to a Christian religious organization called the **Society of Jesus**, that was started in 1534. Its members are known for teaching and studying Christianity.

Jesus Christ or **Jesus** /ˌdʒiːzəs ˈkraɪst/ **RELIGION** the man on whose ideas Christianity is based

jet /dʒet/ noun [C] **1** a plane that can fly very fast **2** a stream of liquid that comes out of something very quickly and with a lot of force: *The firefighter sprayed a jet of water on the flames.*

jet-'black adj very dark black

'jet ,engine noun [C] a type of engine that combines air and burning fuel in order to create power for a plane —*picture* → on next page

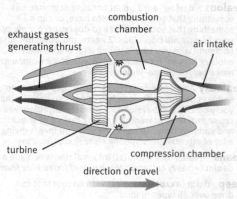

combustion chamber

exhaust gases generating thrust

air intake

turbine

compression chamber

direction of travel

a jet engine

jetsam /'dʒets(ə)m/ noun [U] things that you find floating in the sea or lying on the beach, especially parts of a ship that has sunk → FLOTSAM

'**Jet ,Ski** TRADEMARK a very small fast boat for one or two people that you drive standing up

jettison /'dʒetɪs(ə)n/ verb [T] **1** to get rid of something that is not useful or successful: *We may have to jettison some parts of the business.* **2** to throw goods, equipment, or fuel from a ship or plane in order to make it less likely to sink or crash

jetty /'dʒeti/ (plural **jetties**) noun [C] a long narrow structure that goes from the land out into a lake, sea, or river to provide a place for boats to stop

Jew /dʒuː/ noun [C] RELIGION someone who believes in Judaism, or who comes from a family that believed in Judaism in the past

jewel /'dʒuːəl/ noun [C] a hard valuable stone that has been cut and made shiny

jeweller /'dʒuːələ/ noun [C] someone who makes, repairs, or sells jewellery

jewellery /'dʒuːəlri/ noun [U] objects such as rings that you wear as decoration: *She's got some lovely pieces of jewellery.* ♦ *I don't wear very much jewellery.* → COSTUME JEWELLERY

Jewish /'dʒuːɪʃ/ adj **1** relating to Jews, their culture, or their religion **2** someone who is Jewish was born in the Jewish culture, and may practise Judaism

jib /dʒɪb/ noun [C] a small triangular sail near the front of a boat

jig /dʒɪg/ noun [C] MUSIC a fast traditional dance, or the music for this dance

jigsaw /'dʒɪgsɔː/ or **jigsaw ,puzzle** noun [C] a picture made of a lot of small pieces that you have to fit together

jihad /dʒɪ'hæd/ noun [C] a holy war or fight that Muslims take part in to defend Islam

jilbab /'dʒɪlbæb/ noun [C] a piece of clothing worn by Muslim women that covers their whole body but not their hands, feet, or head

jingle /'dʒɪŋg(ə)l/ verb [I/T] if small metal objects jingle, they make a noise when they hit against each other

jingoism /'dʒɪŋgəʊ,ɪz(ə)m/ noun [U] the belief which someone has that other countries are not as good as their own —**jingoistic** /,dʒɪŋgəʊ'ɪstɪk/ adj

jinx /dʒɪŋks/ noun [C] *informal* someone or something that causes bad luck: *There seems to be a jinx on that family.* —**jinx** verb [T], **jinxed** /dʒɪŋkst/ adj

job /dʒɒb/ noun **1** [C] work that you do regularly to earn money: *a part-time job* ♦ *Andy got a holiday job at a factory in Bristol.* ♦ *My son has been offered a job in Tokyo.* ♦ *Dan left his job.* ♦ *Many steelworkers are worried that they'll lose their jobs.* **2** [C] something that you have to do or deal with: *Our architects have done the job in record time.* ♦ *No one wanted the job of telling Mum the bad news.* → ODD JOBS **3** [singular] your duty in a particular situation or organization: *It's my job to welcome new members to the club.* **4** [C] COMPUTING something that a computer, printer etc does: *Your scan is the third job in the queue.*

PHRASE make a good/bad job of (doing) sth to do something well or badly

Build your vocabulary: talking about jobs

general
- **job** what someone does regularly to earn money
- **work** something that someone does to earn money, or the place where they go to do it
- **career** the jobs that someone does over a period of time that involve a particular type of work
- **profession** a type of job that you need a lot of education or special training to do
- **post** a particular job within a company or organization, especially a job with some responsibility
- **position** a particular job: used especially in advertisements for jobs

getting a job
- **apply** to officially say, usually in a letter or on a special form, that you would like to be considered for a particular job
- **CV** a list of your qualifications and work experience
- **applicant** someone who applies for a particular job
- **candidate** someone who is competing with other people for a particular job
- **interview** a meeting with the people you are hoping to work for where they ask you questions and find out more about you
- **interviewee** an applicant who is asked to come for an interview

not having a job
- **unemployed** or **jobless** or **out of work** used for describing someone who does not have a job
- **retired** used for describing someone who is not working because they are old

'**job de,scription** noun [C] BUSINESS a list of all the things that someone must do in their job

jobless /'dʒɒbləs/ adj without a job, or relating to people without a job = UNEMPLOYED: *a jobless steelworker*

'**job ,title** noun [C] BUSINESS the official name of someone's job

jockey /'dʒɒki/ (plural **jockeys**) noun [C] SPORTS someone whose job is to ride horses in races → DISC JOCKEY

jog¹ /dʒɒg/ (**jogs, jogging, jogged**) verb **1** [I] to run at a slow steady speed, usually for exercise: *Let's jog around the lake.* **2** [T] to knock something so that it moves a little

PHRASE jog sb's memory to make someone remember something

jog² /dʒɒg/ noun [singular] a run for exercise at a slow steady speed: *We went for a jog around the park.* —**jogger** noun [C]

jogging /'dʒɒgɪŋ/ noun [U] the activity of running for exercise at a slow steady speed: *I go jogging every morning.*

join¹ /dʒɔɪn/ verb **1** [T] to become a member of an organization, club, or group, or to start working for an organization ≠ LEAVE: *Martin joined the firm in 1999.* ♦ *He wants to join the army.* **2** [I/T] to come together with other people or things: *Wendy went off to join her friends in the bar.* ♦ *The police car was soon joined by two ambulances.* **3** [I/T] to connect two things, or to become connected at a particular point ≠ DISCONNECT, SEPARATE: *The two roads join about five miles south of the city.* ♦ *First, join the two pipes together.*

PHRASE **join forces (with sb)** to work together with someone else in order to achieve something

PHRASAL VERBS **join 'in (sth)** to do an activity with people who are already doing it: *She laughed and Tom joined in.* ♦ *Pat didn't feel like joining in the celebrations.*

join 'up to become a member of the armed forces

join (sth) 'up *same as* **join¹** *sense 3:* *You need to join up these two lines.*

join² /dʒɔɪn/ noun [C] the place where two objects have been connected together

joiner /'dʒɔɪnə/ noun [C] someone who makes the wooden parts of buildings —**joinery** noun [U]

joining /'dʒɔɪnɪŋ/ adj ENGINEERING relating to the way joints are formed in a structure

joint¹ /dʒɔɪnt/ adj involving two or more people, or done by two or more people together: *a joint decision* ♦ *The two presidents issued a joint statement.* —**jointly** adv: *a jointly owned property*

joint² /dʒɔɪnt/ noun [C] **1** ANATOMY a part of the body that can bend where two bones meet. It usually consists of **connective tissue** and cartilage: *a knee joint* **2** a place where two parts of something are connected: *Make sure you seal the joints of the pipes with tape.* **3** a large piece of meat that is cooked in an oven: *a joint of beef* **4** *informal* a cigarette that contains **cannabis**

joint 'custody noun [U] LAW an arrangement in which parents who are divorced both have responsibility for looking after a child, and both give the child a home for some of the time

jointed /'dʒɔɪntɪd/ adj a jointed arm, leg, or other part can bend because it has joints

joint 'venture noun [C] BUSINESS an agreement between two companies to work together on a particular job

joist /dʒɔɪst/ noun [C] CONSTRUCTION a steel or wooden **beam** that supports a floor or roof

joke¹ /dʒəʊk/ noun [C] something that you say or do that is intended to make people laugh: *Greg sprayed her with water as a joke.* ♦ *The kids were telling jokes* (=short stories with funny endings). ♦ *Stephen decided to play a joke on* (=trick) *his teacher.*

joke² /dʒəʊk/ verb [I] to say things that are intended to make people laugh: *You shouldn't joke about such serious things.* —**jokingly** adv

jolly /'dʒɒli/ (**jollier, jolliest**) adj friendly and happy

jolt¹ /dʒəʊlt/ noun [C] **1** a sudden violent movement: *The bus stopped with a jolt and we were all flung forward.* **2** a sudden strong feeling of surprise or shock: *I realized with a jolt that she was staring at me.* **3** a sudden strong increase in energy

jolt² /dʒəʊlt/ verb **1** [I/T] to move with a sudden violent movement, or to make something move like this **2** [T] to give someone a sudden shock

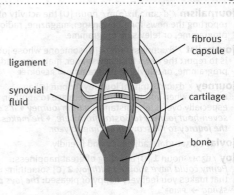

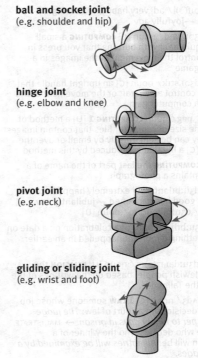

ball and socket joint
(e.g. shoulder and hip)

hinge joint
(e.g. elbow and knee)

pivot joint
(e.g. neck)

gliding or sliding joint
(e.g. wrist and foot)

joints in the body

jostle /'dʒɒs(ə)l/ verb **1** [I] to compete for something: *The two parties are jostling for control of the parliament.* **2** [I/T] to push against someone in order to move past them in a crowd: *We managed to jostle our way to the front.*

joule /dʒuːl/ noun [C] SCIENCE a unit for measuring work or energy, equal to the work done when a force of one **newton** moves an object a distance of one metre. Symbol J

journal /'dʒɜːn(ə)l/ noun [C] **1** a newspaper or magazine that contains articles relating to a particular profession or subject: *a scientific journal* ♦ *the British Medical Journal* **2** a book in which someone writes about what happens to them every day ≠ DIARY

'journal ,bearing noun [C] TECHNOLOGY a **bearing** (=machine part) in which a **shaft** (=thin metal rod) is enclosed in a cylinder. A layer of oil separates the two parts.

journalism /ˈdʒɜːnəˌlɪz(ə)m/ noun [U] the activity of reporting the news for a newspaper, magazine, radio programme, or television programme

journalist /ˈdʒɜːnəlɪst/ noun [C] someone whose job is to report the news for a newspaper, magazine, radio programme, or television programme = REPORTER

journey /ˈdʒɜːni/ (plural **journeys**) noun [C] an occasion when you travel from one place to another, especially over a long distance: *a train journey ♦ It's a seven-hour journey to Boston from here. ♦ He makes the journey to Moscow three times a year.*

jovial /ˈdʒəʊviəl/ adj happy and friendly

joy /dʒɔɪ/ noun **1** [U] a feeling of great happiness: *Penny could have shouted with joy.* **2** [C] something that makes you feel very happy or pleased: *the joys of skiing* → PRIDE¹

joyful /ˈdʒɔɪf(ə)l/ adj very happy, or causing happiness —**joyfully** adv

joypad /ˈdʒɔɪˌpæd/ noun [C] COMPUTING a small piece of equipment with buttons that you press in order to control the movement of the images in a computer game

joystick /ˈdʒɔɪˌstɪk/ noun [C] an upright handle that you use to control an aircraft or the movement of the images in a computer game

JPEG /ˈdʒeɪ ˌpeg/ noun COMPUTING **1** [U] a method of reducing the size of computer files that contain images so that they can be sent quickly by email or over the Internet **2** [C] a file that is produced by this method

jpg abbrev COMPUTING the last part of the name of a file that contains a photograph

jubilant /ˈdʒuːbɪlənt/ adj extremely happy because something good has happened —**jubilantly** adv, **jubilation** /ˌdʒuːbɪˈleɪʃ(ə)n/ noun [U]

jubilee /ˈdʒuːbɪliː/ noun [C] a celebration on a date on which something important happened in an earlier year

Judaism /ˈdʒuːdeɪˌɪz(ə)m/ noun [U] RELIGION the religion of Jewish people, based on the writings of the Torah and the Talmud

judge¹ /dʒʌdʒ/ noun [C] **1** LAW someone whose job is to make decisions in a court of law: *The judge sentenced her to ninety days in prison.* → MAGISTRATE **2** someone who decides who the winner of a competition will be: *All entries will be examined by a panel of judges.*

PHRASE **be a good/bad etc judge of sth** to be someone whose opinions about something are usually right or wrong

judge² /dʒʌdʒ/ verb **1** [I/T] to form an opinion about something after considering all the details or facts: *Schools are judged on their exam results.* ♦ *The water was judged to be of good quality.* **2** [I/T] to decide who or what is the winner of a competition: *In the end, Debbie's cake was judged the winner.* ♦ *The paintings will be judged on imagination and technique.* **3** [I/T] to criticize someone because you think their moral behaviour is not very good: *It's difficult not to judge people sometimes.* **4** [T] LAW to decide in a court of law whether or not someone is guilty

judgment or **judgement** /ˈdʒʌdʒmənt/ noun **1** [C/U] an opinion that you have after thinking carefully about something: *It is still too soon to form a judgment about this.* ♦ *She is not someone who passes judgment without knowing all the facts.* ♦ *In my judgment, he was not very good at his job.* **2** [U] your ability to understand a situation and make good decisions: *Her decision shows good judgment.* ♦ *I trust your*

judgment. **3** [C/U] LAW a decision that is made by a judge in a court of law = VERDICT

judgmental or **judgemental** /ˌdʒʌdʒˈment(ə)l/ adj too willing to criticize other people = CRITICAL

judicial /dʒuːˈdɪʃ(ə)l/ adj LAW relating to judges or to courts of law

the judiciary /dʒuːˈdɪʃəri/ noun [singular] LAW the part of government that consists of all the judges and courts of law in a country

judicious /dʒuːˈdɪʃəs/ adj formal showing intelligence and good judgment

judo /ˈdʒuːdəʊ/ noun [U] SPORTS a sport in which you fight using balance and the weight of your body to throw your opponent to the ground

jug /dʒʌg/ noun [C] a container from which you pour liquids

juggle /ˈdʒʌg(ə)l/ verb **1** [I/T] to keep objects moving through the air by catching them and throwing them back into the air **2** [T] to try to do several important things at the same time: *the pressures of juggling a career and study*

jugular /ˈdʒʌgjʊlə/ noun [C] ANATOMY a major vein in the neck that carries blood from the head to the heart. The jugular is also called the **jugular vein**.

juice /dʒuːs/ noun [C/U] **1** the liquid that comes out of fruit or vegetables, often used as a drink: *orange juice* **2** the liquid that comes out of meat when you cook it

juicy /ˈdʒuːsi/ (**juicier**, **juiciest**) adj containing a lot of juice: *a sweet juicy apple*

jujitsu /dʒuːˈdʒɪtsuː/ noun [U] SPORTS a sport in which you fight with someone by hitting them and throwing them to the ground

jukebox /ˈdʒuːkˌbɒks/ noun [C] a machine that plays music when you put money in it

Jul. abbrev July

July /dʒʊˈlaɪ/ noun [U] the seventh month of the year, between June and August: *We're moving into our new house in July.* ♦ *The wedding is on July 19th.*

jumble /ˈdʒʌmb(ə)l/ or **jumble sth 'up** verb [T] to mix things in a confusing or untidy way

jumbo /ˈdʒʌmbəʊ/ adj larger than other things of the same type: *jumbo sausages*

'jumbo ˌjet noun [C] a large plane for a lot of passengers

jump¹ /dʒʌmp/ verb

1 move off ground	4 move suddenly
2 move in shock	5 switch ideas
3 increase quickly	

1 [I/T] to push your body off the ground using your legs: *He jumped the fence and walked across the field.* ♦ *The cat jumped up onto my lap.* ♦ *The horse jumped over the stream.*
2 [I] to get a shock and suddenly move your body slightly because of this: *The noise made her jump.*
3 [I] to increase or improve very quickly: *Profits jumped by 15% last year.*
4 [I] to move somewhere quickly and suddenly: *He jumped in the car and drove off.* ♦ *Maggie jumped out of bed.*
5 [I] to move quickly from one idea to another: *The conversation suddenly jumped back to what had happened yesterday.*

jump² /dʒʌmp/ noun [C] **1** a movement in which you jump off the ground **2** a movement in which you jump from a high place: *a parachute jump* **3** a sudden increase = LEAP: *There has been another sharp jump in* property prices. **4** SPORTS a structure that a horse or runner jumps over

'jump ,ball noun [C] SPORTS in basketball, an occasion when the ball is thrown straight up so that one player from each team can jump for it

jumper /'dʒʌmpə/ noun [C] a piece of clothing that you pull over your head and that covers your upper body and arms = SWEATER

'jump ,shot noun [C] SPORTS the movement that a basketball player makes by jumping into the air and throwing the ball towards the basket

jumpy /'dʒʌmpi/ adj informal nervous

Jun. abbrev June

junction /'dʒʌŋkʃ(ə)n/ noun [C] a place where one road or railway line crosses or joins another

'junction ,box noun [C] a box in which electrical wires are connected

juncture /'dʒʌŋktʃə/ noun [C] formal a point in a process or period of time
PHRASE **at this juncture** spoken formal now

June /dʒuːn/ noun [U] the sixth month of the year, between May and July: The museum opens to the public in June. ♦ Our last class is on June 5th.

jungle /'dʒʌŋg(ə)l/ noun **1** [C/U] a thick tropical forest **2** [U] MUSIC a type of **dance music**

junior¹ /'dʒuːniə/ adj **1** a junior person does not have a lot of responsibility or power in their job ≠ SENIOR **2** intended for young people, or involving them: the world junior swimming championship

junior² /'dʒuːniə/ noun [C] EDUCATION a child in the UK who goes to a **junior school**
PHRASE **be two years/ten years etc sb's junior** to be younger than someone else by two years, ten years etc

Junior /'dʒuːniə/ adj used after the name of a man who has the same name as his father

,junior 'high school noun [C/U] EDUCATION a school in the US for children between the ages of 12 and 15

'junior ,school noun [C/U] EDUCATION a school in the UK for children between the ages of 7 and 11

junk /dʒʌŋk/ noun [U] old things that are not valuable or not wanted = RUBBISH

junkie /'dʒʌŋki/ noun [C] informal someone who is unable to stop taking illegal drugs

Jupiter /'dʒuːpɪtə/ ASTRONOMY the fifth planet from the Sun and the largest in the solar system —picture → SOLAR SYSTEM

the Jurassic /dʒʊə'ræsɪk/ noun [singular] GEOLOGY the period of geological time from 205 million years to 142 million years ago, when dinosaurs lived and the first birds and mammals developed

jurisdiction /,dʒʊərɪs'dɪkʃ(ə)n/ noun [U] LAW the right or power to make legal decisions

jurisprudence /,dʒʊərɪs'pruːd(ə)ns/ noun LAW formal **1** [singular/U] the system of laws that exists in a particular place, or that affects a particular area of activity **2** [U] the study of law

juror /'dʒʊərə/ noun [C] LAW a member of a jury

jury /'dʒʊəri/ (plural **juries**) noun [C] **1** LAW a group of members of the public who decide whether someone is guilty in a court case: The jury found him guilty. **2** a group of people who judge a competition

just¹ /dʒʌst/ adv

1 a moment ago	**5** slightly
2 at this time	**6** when sth almost does
3 only	not happen
4 exactly	+ PHRASES

1 a short time ago, or a short time before something that happened in the past: Mum's just gone down to the shops. ♦ I'd spoken to him just the day before. ♦ What were you saying to Lisa **just now** (=a moment ago)? ♦ The film has **only just** started.
2 at the same time as something else: I can't come now. I'm just putting the children to bed. ♦ **Just then** a knock at the door interrupted our conversation. ♦ Mahmud was **just about to** leave when someone called his name. ♦ I was **just going to** ask you the same question.
3 not more, bigger, more important etc than what you are mentioning: The medicine costs just a few pence to produce. ♦ It was just a silly mistake. ♦ It's **not just** me. Other people are complaining too.
4 exactly: He's just like his father. ♦ The result is just what we wanted.
5 slightly before, after etc: I spoke with him just after he won the award. ♦ Her parents were seated just behind her.
6 used for saying that although something happens, it almost does not happen: We just got there in time.
PHRASES **just about** very nearly: I think we've just about finished.
just as... (as) used for emphasizing that something is equally large, good, bad etc: Animals feel pain just as much as we do.
→ LIKE

just² /dʒʌst/ adj formal fair and morally right = FAIR ≠ UNJUST: a just society —**justly** adv

justice /'dʒʌstɪs/ noun [U] **1** treatment of people that is fair and morally right ≠ INJUSTICE: Victims are calling for justice. **2** LAW the legal process of judging and punishing people: Whoever committed these crimes must be **brought to justice** (=judged in a court of law).
PHRASE **do sb/sth justice** to show or emphasize all the good qualities of someone or something

justifiable /'dʒʌstɪ,faɪəb(ə)l/ adj if something is justifiable, there is a good reason for it = REASONABLE —**justifiably** adv

justification /,dʒʌstɪfɪ'keɪʃ(ə)n/ noun [C/U] a reason why something is correct and morally right: There can be no justification for such rude behaviour.

justified /'dʒʌstɪfaɪd/ adj if something is justified, there is a good reason for it

justify /'dʒʌstɪfaɪ/ (**justifies, justifying, justified**) verb [T] to show that there is a good reason for something: The results justify all our hard work. ♦ How can you justify spending all that money?

'just-in-,time adj BUSINESS a just-in-time system is one in which goods are produced or delivered immediately before they are needed, in order to avoid waste and reduce the cost of storing them

jute /dʒuːt/ noun [U] a substance from plants that is used for making cloth or rope

juvenile¹ /'dʒuːvənaɪl/ adj **1** relating to young people **2** silly and not suitable for an adult

juvenile² /'dʒuːvənaɪl/ noun [C] a young person

juxtapose /,dʒʌkstə'pəʊz/ verb [T] formal to place things together, or describe things together, so that people can see how they are different —**juxtaposition** /,dʒʌkstəpə'zɪʃ(ə)n/ noun [C/U]

k /keɪ/ (plural **k's**) or **K** (plural **K's**) noun [C/U] the eleventh letter of the English alphabet

K¹ /keɪ/ abbrev **1** kilometre **2** COMPUTING kilobyte

K² /keɪ/ (plural **Ks** or **K's**) noun [C] informal one thousand pounds, or one thousand dollars

Kabbalah /kəˈbɑːlə/ noun [U] RELIGION a religious system based on the ideas of Judaism that explains holy writings through **mysticism**

kafir /ˈkæfə/ noun [C] offensive a word meaning 'non-believer', used by some Muslims to describe someone who is not a Muslim

kaleidoscope /kəˈlaɪdəˌskəʊp/ noun [C] **1** a scene, situation, or experience that keeps changing and has many different aspects **2** a toy that shows changing patterns. It consists of a tube with coloured pieces inside.

kameez /kəˈmiːz/ noun [C] a piece of clothing like a long shirt, worn by women in India

kangaroo /ˌkæŋɡəˈruː/ noun [C] a large Australian mammal that moves by jumping and carries its baby in a **pouch** (=pocket on the front of its body). It is a **marsupial**. —picture → MAMMAL

kaolin or **kaoline** /ˈkeɪəlɪn/ noun [U] **1** GEOLOGY a white clay used for making **porcelain** (=a hard white substance used for making plates, cups etc) **2** HEALTH, CHEMISTRY this substance used in making some medicines

karate /kəˈrɑːti/ noun [U] SPORTS a way of fighting from Japan, in which people hit each other using their hands, feet, arms, and legs

karma /ˈkɑːmə/ noun [U] RELIGION in Hinduism and Buddhism, a belief that the way you behaved in past lives affects your present life, and the way you behave in this life will affect your future lives

karst /kɑːst/ noun [C] GEOLOGY a large area of **limestone** that has caves, deep cracks, and underground streams

kayak /ˈkaɪæk/ noun [C] a small covered **canoe**

kb abbrev COMPUTING kilobyte

kbps abbrev COMPUTING kilobits per second: a unit for measuring the speed of a **modem**

kcal abbrev SCIENCE kilocalorie

kebab /kɪˈbæb/ noun [C] a food that consists of small pieces of meat and vegetables cooked on a stick

keel /kiːl/ noun [C] a long thin piece of wood or metal along the bottom of a boat that helps it to balance in the water

keen /kiːn/ adj

1 wanting sth	4 very strong
2 wanting to do well	5 about sense
3 very interested in	

1 wanting to do something or wanting other people to do something: The government is **keen to** continue negotiations. ♦ The captain wasn't **keen on** having him in the team. ♦ I was quite **keen on** the idea of going to live in a bigger city.

2 wanting to do something well= ENTHUSIASTIC: Many of our players are very young and keen.

3 very interested in an activity that you enjoy, often in a way that makes you determined to be successful at it: a keen sportsman ♦ Luke's **keen on** swimming.

4 very strong: a keen sense of duty ♦ Mr Lindsay always took **a keen interest** in his pupils' achievements

5 keen sight, hearing etc makes you very good at seeing, hearing etc

—**keenly** /ˈkiːnli/ adv, **keenness** noun [U]

keep¹ /kiːp/ (**keeps, keeping, kept** /kept/) verb

1 stay in state	8 do what you said
2 continue/repeat	9 provide money for
3 make sb/sth continue	10 look after animals
4 continue to have	11 of food etc
5 stay within limit	+ PHRASES
6 store sth	+ PHRASAL VERBS
7 store information	

1 [linking verb] to stay in a state, position, or place without changing or moving, or to make someone or something do this: **Keep still** while I brush your hair. ♦ People **kept quiet** because they were afraid. ♦ **Keep** her **warm** and give her plenty to drink.

2 [T] to do something many times, or to continue doing something: Keep taking the tablets. ♦ I keep forgetting to put the answering machine on.

3 [T] to make someone or something continue doing something: Sorry to **keep you waiting**.

4 [T] to continue to have or own something: I've got two copies, you can keep that one.

5 [T] to control something so that it stays within a limit: Costs must be kept within reasonable limits.

6 [T] to store something in a particular place so that you know where it is: Where do you keep the washing powder? ♦ Read this letter carefully, and keep it **in a safe place**.

7 [T] to store information by writing it or putting it into a computer: Some companies do not keep detailed records. ♦ Every member of the group has to keep a diary.

8 [T] to do what you said you would do: If you cannot keep your **appointment**, please let us know. ♦ I have tried to keep my **promise**.

9 [T] to provide money for yourself or someone else, in order to pay for the food, clothes, and other things that you or they need: She keeps the family on two hundred pounds a week.

10 [T] to own animals and look after them: A few cows are kept to provide milk, cheese, and cream.

11 [I] if food or other substances keep for a particular period of time, they stay in good condition for that period of time: The sauce will **keep for** two weeks in the fridge.

PHRASES **keep going 1** to continue to do something although it is difficult: They forced themselves to keep going even though they felt exhausted. **2** to continue to move without stopping: The truck kept going and disappeared from view.

keep sth to yourself to not tell anyone else about something

PHRASAL VERBS **ˌkeep aˈway** to avoid someone or something, or to not go near someone or something: I've told him to keep away, but he won't listen. ♦ You should **keep away from** fried foods.

ˌkeep (sb) ˈback to not move towards someone or something, or to stop someone from doing this: Police were warning people to keep back. ♦ A barrier had been erected to keep back the crowds.

ˌkeep sb ˈback to prevent someone from making progress: It's only her lack of confidence that's keeping her back.

,keep sth 'back to not tell someone something, or to not show how you feel: *He said he was fine, but I knew he was keeping something back.*

,keep sth 'off (sth) to not touch something, or to prevent something from touching something: *Keep the flies off the food.* ♦ *Keep your hands off! It's mine.*

,keep 'on doing sth to continue to do something: *My sister kept on asking me question after question.*

,keep 'out used on signs to tell people not to go into a place

,keep sb/sth 'out to prevent someone or something from entering a place: *Cars should be kept out of the city centre.*

,keep 'up to move or develop at the same speed as someone or something: *By studying hard, she managed to keep up.* ♦ *He had to hurry to keep up with her.*

,keep sth 'up to continue to do something: *Keep up the good work.* ♦ *The staff continued to keep up pressure for better wages.*

keep² /kiːp/ noun [C] a large strong tower in the centre of a castle —*picture* → CASTLE

keeper /'kiːpə/ noun [C] **1** someone who is responsible for looking after a place, a group of animals, or a collection of objects **2 SPORTS** *informal* a **goalkeeper** → SHOPKEEPER

kelvin /'kelvɪn/ noun [C] **SCIENCE** the **SI unit** for measuring temperature. Symbol K

kennel /'ken(ə)l/ noun [C] **1** a small building where a dog sleeps and is protected from bad weather **2** a place where dogs or cats stay while their owners are away

kept /kept/ the past tense and past participle of **keep¹**

keratin /'kerətɪn/ noun [U] **BIOLOGY** a protein that is the main substance that hair, nails, feathers, horns, and hooves are made of

kerb /kɜːb/ noun [C] the edge of a **pavement** that is closest to the road

kernel /'kɜːn(ə)l/ noun [C] **1 AGRICULTURE** the soft seed inside a nut or other fruit **2** the central or most important part of something

kerosene /'kerəsiːn/ noun [U] **CHEMISTRY paraffin** —*picture* → REFINE

ketamine /'ketəmɪn/ noun [U] **HEALTH** a drug that is used as an anaesthetic. It is also taken illegally for enjoyment.

ketchup /'ketʃəp/ noun [U] a thick red sauce made from tomatoes

kettle /'ket(ə)l/ noun [C] a container that is used for boiling water

kettledrum /'ket(ə)l,drʌm/ noun [C] **MUSIC** a large drum with a round metal base

key¹ /kiː/ noun [C]

1 object for lock	5 in music
2 for achieving sth	6 list of symbols
3 on keyboard	7 list of answers
4 on instrument	

1 a small piece of metal that is used for opening or locking a door or a container, or for starting the engine of a vehicle: *a bunch of keys* ♦ *I could hear someone turning the key in the lock.* ♦ *Where's the key to the back door?*

2 the thing that will do most to help you to achieve something: *Proper planning is the key to success.*

♦ *Tourism holds the key to the region's economic recovery.*

3 COMPUTING one of the parts that you press on a keyboard to make it produce letters, numbers, and

symbols: *Highlight the file you want and press the RETURN key.*

4 MUSIC one of the parts that you press on a musical instrument to make it produce sounds: *piano keys*

5 MUSIC a set of musical notes that are based on one particular note: *a minor key* ♦ *in the key of D sharp*

6 GEOGRAPHY a list of the symbols that are used on a map or a drawing

7 a list of answers to the questions in a test or in a book

key² /kiː/ adj very important: *Foreign policy had been a key issue in the campaign.* ♦ *Women farmers are key to China's economic development.*

key³ /kiː/ verb [T] **COMPUTING** to put information into a computer or other electronic machine using a keyboard

keyboard /'kiːbɔːd/ noun [C] **1 COMPUTING** a piece of computer equipment with keys on it, used for putting information into a computer —*picture* → COMPUTER, WORKSTATION **2 MUSIC** the part of a musical instrument such as a piano that has the keys that you touch to make sounds **3 MUSIC** a musical instrument that has a keyboard, especially an electric piano

'key ,card noun [C] a small plastic card that has electronic information stored on it and is used for opening doors

keyhole /'kiːˌhəʊl/ noun [C] the hole in a lock where you put the key

,keyhole 'surgery noun [U] **HEALTH** a type of medical operation which is performed through a very small hole in a person's body, using very small electronic cameras

keypad /'kiːˌpæd/ noun [C] **COMPUTING** a part of a piece of equipment, for example on a computer, that has keys that you press

'key ,ring noun [C] a metal ring that you use for keeping your keys together

'key ,signature noun [C] **MUSIC** the symbols that are printed at the beginning of a piece of music to show the key in which the music is played —*picture* → MUSIC

keystone /'kiːˌstəʊn/ noun [C] **1** something that is very important to a plan, arrangement, or set of beliefs **2 CONSTRUCTION** a stone or brick at the top of an **arch** that keeps the structure together

keystroke /'kiːˌstrəʊk/ noun [C] **COMPUTING** a single action of pressing a key on a **typewriter** or computer

keyway /'kiːˌweɪ/ noun [C] **TECHNOLOGY** a prepared slot for a **key** (=a part used for locking other parts together), on a **shaft** or in a hole

keyword /'kiːˌwɜːd/ noun [C] **1** a word that represents the main feature or idea of something: *The office was extremely tidy; efficiency was the keyword.*
2 COMPUTING a word that you type into a computer in order to find information about a particular subject

kg abbrev **SCIENCE** kilogram

khaki /'kɑːki/ adj green-brown or brown-yellow in colour —**khaki** noun [U]

kHz abbrev **SCIENCE** kilohertz

kibbutz /kɪ'bʊts/ (plural **kibbutzim** /ˌkɪbʊt'siːm/) noun [C] **SOCIAL STUDIES** a farm or working community in Israel where the workers live together and share everything

kick¹ /kɪk/ verb **1** [I/T] to hit someone or something with your foot: *Mum! Jimmy kicked me!* ♦ *A couple of children were kicking a ball around.* ♦ *Southgate kicked the door open.* **2** [I/T] to move your legs as if you were kicking something: *The baby lay on its back kicking its* *legs in the air.* **3** [T] *informal* to stop doing something that is bad for you: *Do you smoke and want to **kick the habit**?*

PHRASE **kick yourself** to be annoyed with yourself because you have made a mistake, or have missed an opportunity to do something

kick² /kɪk/ noun **1** [C] a hit with your foot: *Bobby **gave** the door **a** good **kick**.* **2** [singular] *informal* a feeling of excitement or pleasure: *I **get** a real **kick out of** seeing my children do well in school.*

kickboxing /ˈkɪkˌbɒksɪŋ/ noun [U] **SPORTS** a sport in which two people kick as well as hit each other when they fight

kickoff /ˈkɪkˌɒf/ noun [C] **SPORTS** the beginning of a game of football, when one player kicks the ball down the field

,kick-'start verb [T] **1** to start a motorcycle by pressing your foot down on a pedal **2** to make something start again after it has stopped or slowed down

kid /kɪd/ noun **1** [C] *informal* a child or young adult: *There was a group of kids playing football in the street.* ♦ *a bunch of middle-class college kids* **2** [C] a young goat **3** [U] leather made from the skin of a young goat

kidnap¹ /ˈkɪdnæp/ (**kidnaps, kidnapping, kidnapped**) verb [T] to illegally take someone away and make them a prisoner, especially in order to make their family pay money or a government to take the political action you want —**kidnapper** noun [C]

kidnap² /ˈkɪdnæp/ or **kidnapping** /ˈkɪdnæpɪŋ/ noun [C/U] an act of illegally taking someone away and keeping them as a prisoner, especially in order to get money or something you want politically for releasing them

kidney /ˈkɪdni/ (plural **kidneys**) noun **1** [C] **ANATOMY** one of the two organs in the body that clean the blood by removing waste products such as **urea** and also control the level of water that the blood contains. The waste passes into the bladder in the liquid form of urine, which is then passed out of the body. —*picture* → CIRCULATION, ORGAN **2** [C/U] the kidney of some animals eaten as food

'kidney ,bean noun [C] a red bean eaten as a vegetable —*picture* → VEGETABLE

kill¹ /kɪl/ verb **1** [I/T] to make a person or other living thing die: *Each year thousands of people are killed and injured on the roads.* ♦ *Speed kills.* **2** [T] *informal* if part of your body is killing you, it is causing you a lot of pain: *My back's killing me.* **3** [T] to spend time doing a particular activity while you are waiting for something: *We killed a few hours watching videos.* **4** [T] to stop something from continuing: *The nurse will give you something to kill the pain.*

> Build your vocabulary: words you can use instead of **kill**
>
> - **assassinate** to kill an important or famous person for political reasons or for money
> - **commit suicide** to deliberately kill yourself
> - **execute** to kill someone legally as a punishment for a very serious crime
> - **massacre** to kill a very large number of people in a violent or cruel way
> - **murder** to deliberately kill someone
> - **put sth down** or **put sth to sleep** to kill an animal because it is ill or in pain

kill² /kɪl/ noun [singular] **1** an act in which a hunted animal is killed **2** an animal that has been killed, especially for food

the kill /kɪl/ noun [singular] **TECHNOLOGY** the addition of **ferromanganese** to the **molten** (=melted) metal during the **manufacture** of steel in a **Bessemer converter**

killer /ˈkɪlə/ noun [C] **1** someone who kills another person= MURDERER: *The young woman's killer has not yet been found.* **2** something that kills people: *Cancer is the second largest killer in the US.* **3** something that kills or destroys something else: *weed killer*

killing /ˈkɪlɪŋ/ noun [C] an act in which someone is deliberately killed

kiln /kɪln/ noun [C] a type of oven that is used for baking clay and bricks to make them hard

kilo /ˈkiːləʊ/ noun [C] **SCIENCE** a **kilogram**

kilo- /ˈkɪləʊ/ prefix **SCIENCE** 1,000 units: used with some nouns in the metric system

kilobit /ˈkɪləʊˌbɪt/ noun [C] **COMPUTING** a unit for measuring computer information, containing 1,024 **bits**

kilobyte /ˈkɪləʊˌbaɪt/ noun [C] **COMPUTING** a unit for measuring computer information, containing 1,024 bytes. Symbol Kb

kilocalorie /ˈkiːləʊˌkæləri/ noun [C] **SCIENCE** a unit of measurement of heat equal to 1,000 calories

kilogram /ˈkɪləˌgræm/ noun [C] **SCIENCE** a unit for measuring weight in the metric system, containing 1,000 grams. Symbol K

kilohertz /ˈkɪləʊˌhɜːts/ noun [C] **SCIENCE** a unit for measuring radio waves, containing 1,000 **hertz**

kilojoule /ˈkɪləˌdʒuːl/ noun [C] **SCIENCE** a unit for measuring an amount of energy, especially in food

kilometre /ˈkɪləˌmiːtə, kɪˈlɒmɪtə/ noun [C] **SCIENCE** a unit for measuring distance in the metric system, containing 1,000 metres

kilowatt /ˈkɪləˌwɒt/ noun [C] **PHYSICS** a unit for measuring electrical power, containing 1,000 **watts**. Symbol kW

,kilowatt-'hour noun [C] **PHYSICS** a unit for measuring electrical energy, equal to the work done by one kilowatt in one hour. Symbol kWh

kilt /kɪlt/ noun [C] a type of traditional Scottish clothing, similar to a skirt, worn by men

kimono /kɪˈməʊnəʊ/ noun [C] a type of traditional Japanese clothing, like a long coat with wide sleeves

kin /kɪn/ noun [U] *formal* all the people in your family → NEXT

kind¹ /kaɪnd/ noun [C] a type of person or thing= SORT: *The bridge is the largest **of its kind** in the world.* ♦ *We've all had disappointments **of some kind**.* ♦ *There was no financial link between us **of any kind**.* ♦ *What **kind of** person is she?* ♦ *Many people like to try lots of **different kinds of** food.*

PHRASE **in kind** payments or benefits in kind are in the form of goods or services rather than money

kind² /kaɪnd/ adj behaving in a way that shows you care about other people and want to help them ≠ UNKIND: *Thank you, Mark, you've been very **kind**.* ♦ *We are grateful for your **kind offer**.* ♦ *She was very **kind to** me when the children were ill.* ♦ *It was **kind of you to** help them.*

kindergarten /ˈkɪndəˌgɑːt(ə)n/ noun [C/U] **EDUCATION** a **nursery school**

kindly /ˈkaɪndli/ adv **1** in a kind way: *'Don't worry about it,' she said kindly.* **2** *formal* used for making a polite request when you are annoyed with someone: *Would you kindly stop making that noise?*

kindness /'kaɪn(d)nəs/ noun [U] kind behaviour, or kind feelings

kindred /'kɪndrəd/ noun [U] *formal* the whole of someone's family, considered as a group

kinetic art /kaɪ,netɪk 'ɑ:t/ noun [U] **ARTS** a type of art in which artists produce works that move, or have parts that move

kinetic energy /kaɪ,netɪk 'enədʒi/ noun [U] **PHYSICS** the energy that an object has as a result of moving. This energy depends on the mass and velocity of the object. → POTENTIAL ENERGY

king /kɪŋ/ noun [C] **1** a man who rules a country and is the senior male member of the royal family: *King George VI* **2** a man who is the best at doing a particular thing: *Elvis, the king of rock and roll* **3** a playing card with the picture of a king on it: *the king of spades* **4** one of the two most important pieces in the game of chess

kingdom /'kɪŋdəm/ noun [C] **1** a country or area that is ruled by a king or queen **2** **BIOLOGY** one of the large divisions into which living things are divided by biologists. There are five basic kingdoms: animals, plants, fungi, prokaryotes, and protists. —*picture* → TAXONOMY

kingfisher /'kɪŋ,fɪʃə/ noun [C] a blue and orange bird with a pointed beak that lives near water and eats fish

kingpin /'kɪŋ,pɪn/ noun [C] **1** the most important person in a group or organization **2** **ENGINEERING** a metal pin that enables a wheel to **pivot** and **steer** a vehicle

kingpin incli,nation noun [C] **ENGINEERING** the angle that a kingpin makes with an imaginary vertical line, measured in degrees. The kingpin inclination affects the way that a vehicle's wheels straighten after turning.

kingship /'kɪŋʃɪp/ noun [singular/U] *very formal* the position of king, or the fact that someone is king

king-,size or **king-sized** /'kɪŋ ,saɪzd/ adj bigger than usual

kinship /'kɪnʃɪp/ noun [singular/U] **SOCIAL STUDIES** the fact of being related to someone

kiosk /'ki:ɒsk/ noun [C] a very small shop selling newspapers, drinks etc

kiss[1] /kɪs/ verb [I/T] to touch someone with your lips to show love, or as a greeting: *They kissed again, and then he was gone.* ♦ *He went upstairs to kiss his son goodnight.*

kiss[2] /kɪs/ noun [C] an act of kissing someone: *Julius gave her another kiss.*
  PHRASE **the kiss of life 1** **HEALTH** mouth-to-mouth resuscitation **2** if something such as a business or project is given the kiss of life, it starts to become more successful again

kit /kɪt/ noun **1** [C] a set of tools or equipment for a particular activity: *Cyclists should carry a repair kit.* **2** [U] **SPORTS** special clothes that you wear for a sport: *a football kit* **3** [C] all the pieces that you need to build something such as a vehicle or a computer

kitchen /'kɪtʃən/ noun [C] a room where you prepare and cook food, and wash dishes: *kitchen utensils*

kite /kaɪt/ noun [C] a toy that flies in the air while you hold it by a long string

kite-,flying noun [U] **1** the activity of making a kite fly in the air **2** the use of an action or a statement to try to find out what people think about it

kitten /'kɪt(ə)n/ noun [C] a young cat

kiwi /'ki:wi:/ noun [C] **1** the bird that is the symbol of New Zealand. It has a long thin beak and cannot fly. —*picture* → BIRD **2** a **kiwi fruit**

kiwi ,fruit noun [C/U] a fruit with green flesh, small black seeds, and a brown skin —*picture* → FRUIT

kJ abbrev **SCIENCE** kilojoule

kleptomaniac /,kleptəʊ'meɪniæk/ noun [C] someone who has a mental illness that makes them want to steal things

km abbrev kilometre

knack /næk/ noun [singular] *informal* a particular skill or way of doing something: *She had a knack of making people feel really special.*

knead /ni:d/ verb [T] to prepare **dough** (=a mixture for making bread) or clay by pressing it continuously with your hands

knee /ni:/ noun [C] **1** the part in the middle of the leg, where it bends: *a serious knee injury* ♦ *Bend your knees when you pick up heavy objects.* ♦ *He got down on his knees for a closer look.* —*picture* → BODY, JOINT **2** the upper part of the legs when you are sitting down, where you can hold a child or object = LAP: *He was sitting in the armchair with the cat curled up on his knees.*

kneecap /'ni:,kæp/ noun [C] the bone at the front of the knee, the **patella** —*picture* → SKELETON

knee-jerk ,reflex noun [C] **BIOLOGY** a sudden small uncontrolled kick made by the lower leg as a reaction to being hit gently just below the knee

kneel /ni:l/ (**kneels, kneeling, knelt** /nelt/) or **kneel 'down** verb [I] to put or have your knee or both knees on the ground: *She knelt in front of the fire to warm herself.* ♦ *He was kneeling at her feet.*

knew /nju:/ the past tense of **know**

knickers /'nɪkəz/ noun [plural] a piece of underwear for a woman's lower body = PANTS

knife[1] /naɪf/ (plural **knives** /naɪvz/) noun [C] an object with a blade, used for cutting things or as a weapon: *knives and forks* ♦ *The girls were threatened with a knife.* —*picture* → AGRICULTURAL

knife[2] /naɪf/ verb [T] to injure or kill someone with a knife

knife-edged ,ridge noun [C] **GEOLOGY** an **arête**

knight /naɪt/ noun [C] **1** in the past, a European soldier from a high social class who wore a suit of **armour** (=a metal suit) and rode a horse **2** a piece in the game of chess that is shaped like a horse's head

knit /nɪt/ (**knits, knitting, knit** or **knitted**) verb [I/T] **1** to make something such as a piece of clothing using wool and **knitting needles** **2** to join together or work together as one group **3** [I] if a broken bone knits, its parts join together again → CLOSE-KNIT

knitting /'nɪtɪŋ/ noun [U] **1** the activity or process of knitting things **2** something that is being knitted

knitting ,needle noun [C] one of the metal or plastic sticks used for knitting

knives /naɪvz/ the plural of **knife**[1]

knob /nɒb/ noun [C] **1** a round handle on a door or drawer **2** a round switch on a piece of equipment

knock[1] /nɒk/ verb **1** [I] to hit a door with your hand or with a knocker: *They walked up to the door and knocked loudly.* ♦ *I knocked on his door but got no reply.* **2** [T] to hit something, or hit against something: *He knocked a couple of nails into the door.* ♦ *She had knocked her leg against a table.* **3** [T] to hit someone very hard, so that they fall or become unconscious: *They knocked him to the ground.* ♦ *The driver had been* *knocked unconscious* by the impact. **4** [T] *informal* to criticize someone or something

PHRASAL VERBS ,knock sb 'down to hit someone with a vehicle

,knock sth 'down to destroy a building or wall

,knock sb 'out 1 to make someone unconscious 2 to make someone leave a competition by defeating them

knock² /nɒk/ noun [C] **1** the sound of someone knocking on a door: *There was a loud knock at the door.* **2** damage or an injury that is caused by being knocked: *a nasty knock on the head* **3** something bad that happens to someone: *Life is full of hard knocks.*

knockabout /'nɒkəbaʊt/ noun **1** [C/U] a very lively argument, for example between politicians **2** [C] an informal game with a ball **3** [U] actions or stories that are intended to make you laugh

knockback /'nɒk,bæk/ noun [C] *informal* a refusal to accept someone or something

'knocked-up ,joint noun [C] TECHNOLOGY a joint that is used for producing a watertight joint in sheet metal

knocker /'nɒkə/ noun [C] a piece of metal on a door that you use for knocking

knockout /'nɒkaʊt/ noun [C] SPORTS **1** a hit that knocks a boxer down, so that they cannot get up **2** a competition in which a player or team that loses a game leaves the competition

'knock-up noun [C] SPORTS a period of practice before a match in tennis

knoll /nəʊl/ noun [C] GEOGRAPHY a low round hill: *a grassy knoll*

knot /nɒt/ noun [C] **1** a point where string, rope, or cloth is tied or twisted together and pulled tight: *Can you tie a knot in the end of this thread?* **2** a unit for measuring the speed of ships, aircraft, and wind, equal to one nautical mile per hour

knotted /'nɒtɪd/ adj with knots: *a scarf with knotted corners*

know /nəʊ/ (knows, knowing, knew /njuː/, known /nəʊn/) verb

1 have information	**6** experience
2 be familiar with	**7** have learned sth
3 feel certain about	**+ PHRASES**
4 call sb/sth name	**+ PHRASAL VERB**
5 remember sb for sth	

1 [I/T] to have information about something, or to understand something: *How do you know my name?* ♦ *If you don't know the answer, just guess.* ♦ *I knew she wasn't really happy.* ♦ *None of us really knew what had gone wrong.* ♦ *I don't know if she's made a decision yet.* ♦ *'Have they arrived yet?' 'I don't know.'* ♦ *Do you know anything about computers?* ♦ *Some drugs are known to cause damage to unborn children.*

2 [T] to be familiar with someone or something, for example because you have met someone before or been to a place before: *Do you know Terry Davis?* ♦ *How well do you know the city?* ♦ *Jane and I have known each other for years.*

3 [I/T] to feel certain about something: *She knew it was Steven before she'd picked up the phone.*

4 [T] to use a particular name for someone or something: *They know all their tutors by their first names.* ♦ *The village was known as Garden Mill.*

5 [T] to remember someone because of a particular skill or quality: *We know her mostly for her love poetry.* ♦ *He was best known as a painter.*

6 [T] to experience something: *It was the only comfort and warmth she had ever known.*

7 [T] to have learned a poem, story, or song, so that you can say it or sing it

PHRASES **get to know** to start to be familiar with someone or something: *It took a while to get to know the city properly.*

know best to be in the best position to decide something

know better 1 to understand that you should not do something, because you are sensible or experienced: *She should know better than to try to fool him.* **2** to know that what someone else says or thinks is wrong: *Everyone thought it was an innocent mistake, but I knew better.*

→ LET¹

PHRASAL VERB **'know of sb/sth** to know about someone or something: *I only know of one case in which this has happened.*

> **Word family: know**
>
> *Words in the same family as know*
> - knowing *adj*
> - knowingly *adv*
> - knowledge *n*
> - knowledgeable *adj*
> - known *adj*
> - unknowingly *adv*
> - unknown *adj*
> - know-how *n*

'know-how noun [U] *informal* the knowledge that is needed to do something

knowing /'nəʊɪŋ/ adj showing that you know about something: *Tom gave me a knowing look.*

knowingly /'nəʊɪŋli/ adv **1** deliberately, knowing that something is wrong or illegal: *Had her brother knowingly taken the money?* **2** in a way that shows that you know something: *She smiled knowingly.*

knowledge /'nɒlɪdʒ/ noun **1** [singular/U] what you know, or what is known about a particular subject: *She had a lot of knowledge and experience.* ♦ *Candidates should have a good knowledge of Russian.* **2** [U] the fact that you know that something is happening: *This was done without my knowledge.* ♦ *Daniels has denied all knowledge of the events.* ♦ *The staff had no knowledge that the company was in trouble.*

PHRASE **to (the best of) my knowledge** used for saying that you think that something is true, but you are not completely certain

→ COMMON KNOWLEDGE

> **Knowledge** is never used in the plural and cannot be used with **a**: *a very important piece of knowledge* (NOT *a very important knowledge*) ♦ *They claim not to have any knowledge about what happened.* ♦ *Most of the students have some knowledge of computers.*

knowledgeable /'nɒlɪdʒəb(ə)l/ adj knowing a lot about one subject or many subjects

'knowledge ,industry noun [singular] BUSINESS organizations that mainly deal with information or developing information technology

'knowledge 'management noun [U] BUSINESS the process of organizing all the information that a business has, especially the knowledge of its employees, in order to use it most effectively

'knowledge ,transfer noun [U] BUSINESS the process of communicating knowledge that has been developed in one part of an organization to other parts of the organization or to customers

'knowledge ,worker noun [C] BUSINESS someone who works for an organization who is valuable to it because of the knowledge and ideas that they have

known¹ /nəʊn/ adj **1** discovered or known about by people: *a disease with no known cure* **2** famous: *internationally known TV personalities*

known² /nəʊn/ the past participle of **know**

knuckle /'nʌk(ə)l/ noun [C] one of the parts where the fingers can bend, or where they join the hand —*picture* → BODY

koala /kəʊ'ɑːlə/ or **ko'ala ˌbear** noun [C] an Australian mammal with grey fur, large ears, and no tail. It lives in trees. —*picture* → MAMMAL

kookaburra /'kʊkə,bʌrə/ noun [C] an Australian bird that makes a sound like laughter

kora /'kɔːrə/ noun [C] MUSIC a West African musical instrument like a guitar

the Koran /kɔː'rɑːn/ RELIGION the holy book of Islam

kosher /'kəʊʃə/ adj RELIGION approved or allowed by Jewish laws concerning food

the Kremlin /'kremlɪn/ the government of Russia or, in the past, of the Soviet Union

krypton /'krɪptɒn/ noun [U] CHEMISTRY a chemical element that is a gas with no colour or smell. It is used in **fluorescent** lights and in **lasers**. Chemical symbol: **Kr**

kudos /'kjuːdɒs/ noun [U] praise and respect because of something that you have achieved

kumquat /'kʌm,kwɒt/ noun [C] a fruit like a very small orange

kung fu /ˌkʌŋ 'fuː/ noun [U] SPORTS a Chinese sport in which people fight using their hands and feet

kurta /'kɜːtə/ noun [C] a piece of clothing like a long shirt, worn by men in India

kW abbrev PHYSICS kilowatt

kwaito /'kwaɪtəʊ/ noun [U] MUSIC a type of **dance music** that started in the Soweto area of Johannesburg. It is based on **house music**.

kwashiorkor /ˌkwɒʃi'ɔːkɔː/ noun [U] HEALTH a serious disease that mainly affects children in Africa and is caused by a lack of protein in the food that they eat

kwela /'kweɪlə/ noun [U] MUSIC a type of **popular music** developed by black people in South Africa

kWh abbrev PHYSICS kilowatt-hour

L l

l¹ /el/ (plural **l's**) or **L** (plural **L's**) noun [C/U] the 12th letter of the English alphabet

l² abbrev litre

L /el/ abbrev large: used on clothes labels

lab /læb/ noun [C] *informal* a **laboratory**

label¹ /'leɪb(ə)l/ noun [C] **1** a piece of paper or material fastened to an object that gives information about the object: *Always read the label on medical products.* **2** a company that produces records: *Their album was released on the Digital Experience label.* **3** a company that designs and makes expensive clothes: *After working with Armani, he launched his own label.* **4** a word or phrase that is used for describing someone or something: *a group of writers who were given the label 'Angry Young Men'*

label² /'leɪb(ə)l/ (**labels, labelling, labelled**) verb [T] **1** to use a word or phrase in order to describe someone or something, especially in a way that is not fair or true = BRAND: *We shouldn't label these boys as criminals so early in their lives.* **2** to put a label on an object —**labelling** noun [U]

labia /'leɪbiə/ noun [plural] ANATOMY the outer folds of skin around the opening of a woman's vagina

labial /'leɪbiəl/ adj **1** LANGUAGE labial sounds such as 'p', 'b', 'f', 'v', and 'm' are ones that are pronounced with the lips closed or close together, or with the top teeth touching the bottom lip **2** HEALTH relating to the lips —**labial** noun [C]

labiodental /ˌleɪbiəʊ'dent(ə)l/ adj LANGUAGE labiodental sounds such as 'f' and 'v' are made with the top teeth touching the bottom lip —**labiodental** noun [C]

labiovelar /ˌleɪbiəʊ'viːlə/ adj LANGUAGE labiovelar sounds such as 'w' are made with the lips and upper back part of the mouth —**labiovelar** noun [C]

laboratory /lə'bɒrət(ə)ri, *American* 'læbrə,tɔːri/ (plural **laboratories**) noun [C] EDUCATION, SCIENCE a building or large room where people do scientific experiments or research: *our new research laboratory* ♦ *a laboratory test* —*picture* → on next page

laborious /lə'bɔːriəs/ adj long, difficult, and boring: *a laborious task* —**laboriously** adv

labour¹ /'leɪbə/ noun **1** [U] ECONOMICS the workers in a country, industry, or company when they are thought of as a group: *a plentiful supply of cheap labour* ♦ *the demand for skilled labour* ♦ *labour costs* **2** [U] workers' organizations and their leaders when they are thought of as a group: *a meeting between management and labour* ♦ *a labour dispute* **3** [C/U] work, especially physical work: *The price includes the cost of labour.* **4** [singular/U] the process by which a baby is pushed from its mother's body when it is being born: *labour pains* ♦ *She went into labour early this morning.* ♦ *His wife was in labour for six hours.*

labour² /'leɪbə/ verb [I] **1** to work hard, or to put a lot of effort into something **2** to move very slowly and with difficulty

laboured /'leɪbəd/ adj **1** if someone's breathing is laboured, they are breathing with difficulty **2** not natural because of being done with too much effort: *laboured jokes*

labourer /'leɪbərə/ noun [C] someone whose job involves hard physical work

'labour ˌforce noun [C] ECONOMICS all the people who work in an industry or country

ˌlabour-in'tensive adj BUSINESS needing a lot of workers rather than machines

'labour ˌmarket noun [C] ECONOMICS the number of people who are available to work

the 'Labour ˌParty one of the three main political parties in the UK. Its original aim was to try to improve conditions for workers.

Labrador /'læbrədɔː/ noun [C] a large dog with short fur

labyrinth /'læbərɪnθ/ noun [C] a place with a lot of paths or streets where you can easily become lost = MAZE

lace¹ /leɪs/ noun **1** [U] light delicate cloth with patterns of small holes in it **2** [C] a thick piece of string that is used for tying shoes or clothing

lace² /leɪs/ verb [I/T] to fasten something with a lace, or to be fastened with a lace

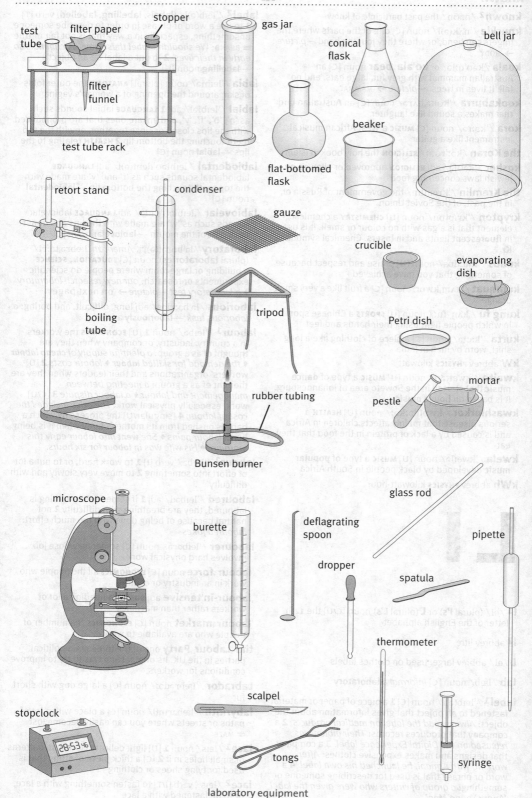

test tube

filter paper

stopper

gas jar

conical flask

bell jar

filter funnel

test tube rack

beaker

flat-bottomed flask

retort stand

condenser

gauze

crucible

evaporating dish

boiling tube

tripod

Petri dish

mortar

pestle

rubber tubing

Bunsen burner

glass rod

microscope

burette

deflagrating spoon

pipette

dropper

spatula

thermometer

scalpel

stopclock

28:53:46

tongs

syringe

laboratory equipment

lacerate /ˈlæsəreɪt/ verb [T] *formal* to make a deep cut in someone's flesh —**laceration** noun [C]

lack¹ /læk/ noun [singular/U] a situation in which you do not have something, or do not have enough of something: *The match was cancelled because of lack of support.* ♦ *a lack of confidence*

lack² /læk/ verb [T] to not have something, or to not have enough of something: *He lacked the skills required for the job.* ♦ *Many people lack confidence in their own abilities.*

lackadaisical /ˌlækəˈdeɪzɪk(ə)l/ adj doing something in a lazy or careless way that shows that you are not really interested in it —**lackadaisically** /ˌlækəˈdeɪzɪkli/ adv

lacking /ˈlækɪŋ/ adj if something is lacking, there is none of it, or not enough of it: *Concern for passenger safety has been sadly lacking.* ♦ *She seems to be lacking in common sense.*

lacklustre /ˈlækˌlʌstə/ adj not lively, exciting, or impressive

laconic /ləˈkɒnɪk/ adj using very few words —**laconically** /ləˈkɒnɪkli/ adv

lacquer /ˈlækə/ noun [C/U] a liquid that is put on wood or metal in order to make it shiny —**lacquer** verb [T]

lacrosse /ləˈkrɒs/ noun [U] **SPORTS** a game in which two teams throw and catch a ball using long sticks with nets at the end, and try to score goals

lactate /lækˈteɪt/ verb [I] **BIOLOGY** if a woman or other female mammal lactates, she produces milk in order to feed her baby or babies —**lactation** /lækˈteɪʃ(ə)n/ noun [U]

lacteal /ˈlæktiəl/ noun [C] **ANATOMY** one of the clear tubes in the small intestine that absorb **fatty acids**. Lacteals are part of the **lymphatic system**.

lactic acid /ˌlæktɪk ˈæsɪd/ noun [U] **1 BIOLOGY, HEALTH** a substance that forms in muscles after physical exercise as a result of **anaerobic respiration**. It can cause **cramp**. **2 BIOLOGY** an acid formed in sour milk

lactose /ˈlæktəʊs/ noun [U] **CHEMISTRY** a type of simple sugar that is in milk. Chemical formula: $C_{12}H_{22}O_{11}$

lacy /ˈleɪsi/ adj made of **lace**, or looking like **lace**

lad /læd/ noun [C] *informal* a boy, or a young man

ladder /ˈlædə/ noun [C] **1** a piece of equipment for reaching high places that consists of two long pieces of wood or metal joined by smaller pieces called **rungs**: *A fireman climbed the ladder.* **2** a system that has different levels through which you can progress: *She rose to a high position on the corporate ladder.* **3** a long thin hole in **stockings** or **tights**

laden /ˈleɪd(ə)n/ adj carrying or supporting something heavy: *Passengers got off the train laden with boxes and suitcases.*

ladle /ˈleɪd(ə)l/ noun [C] a large deep spoon with a long handle that is used for serving liquid food such as soup —**ladle** verb [T]

lady /ˈleɪdi/ (plural **ladies**) noun [C] **1** a woman. Some people think that this use is polite, but other people think that it is old-fashioned and prefer to use 'woman': *Go and ask that lady over there.* **2** a woman who behaves politely and in a way that was traditionally considered suitable for a woman: *She doesn't talk like a lady.*

PHRASE **ladies and gentlemen** *formal* used for addressing an audience of men and women
→ FIRST LADY

Lady /ˈleɪdi/ used as a title for some women who have important social or official positions

ladybird /ˈleɪdiˌbɜːd/ noun [C] a small insect that has a round red or yellow body with small black spots —*picture* → INSECT

ladylike /ˈleɪdiˌlaɪk/ adj behaving in a quiet polite way that was traditionally thought to be suitable for a woman

lady's finger noun [U] the vegetable **okra** —*picture* → VEGETABLE

lag¹ /læg/ (**lags, lagging, lagged**) verb [I] **1** to not be as successful or advanced as other people or organizations: *Their software tends to lag behind other producers.* **2** to walk more slowly than the people you are with

lag² /læg/ noun [singular] a period of time or delay between one event and another

lager /ˈlɑːgə/ noun [C/U] a type of light-coloured beer, or a glass of this beer

lagging /ˈlægɪŋ/ noun [U] **CONSTRUCTION** thick material used for covering water pipes or a **boiler** (=container for hot water) to prevent heat from being lost

lagoon /ləˈguːn/ noun [C] **GEOGRAPHY** an area of sea water that is separated from the sea by sand or rocks

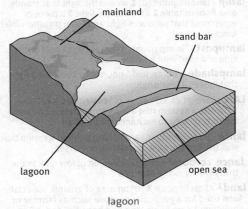

mainland
sand bar
lagoon
open sea

lagoon

lah /lɑː/ noun [C] **MUSIC** the sixth note in the **sol-fa** musical **scale**

laid /leɪd/ the past tense and past participle of **lay¹**

lain /leɪn/ the past participle of **lie¹**

lair /leə/ noun [C] a place where a wild animal lives

laissez-faire /ˌleɪseɪ ˈfeə/ adj **1 ECONOMICS** a laissez-faire policy allows companies and the economy to operate in a **free market** without government control **2** allowing someone to do what they want to do, and to do it in any way that they want to

laity /ˈleɪəti/ noun [singular/U] **RELIGION** people who are members of a church but who are not priests → CLERGY

lake /leɪk/ noun [C] **GEOGRAPHY** a large area of water surrounded by land

lamb /læm/ noun [C/U] a young sheep, or its meat

lambing /ˈlæmɪŋ/ noun [U] **AGRICULTURE** **1** the process by which a sheep gives birth to lambs: *The farm is busy this month with lambing.* **2** the time when lambs are born: *the lambing season*

lame /leɪm/ adj **1** not at all impressive or likely to persuade someone: *a lame excuse* **2** a lame animal cannot walk very well because its leg or foot is damaged —**lamely** adv

lamellaphone /ləˈmeləˌfəʊn/ noun [C] **MUSIC** a technical name for a musical instrument with a series of thin plates or **tongues** that vibrate when the free end is pushed down with the finger

lament¹ /ləˈment/ verb [I/T] to show publicly that you feel sad or disappointed about something: *Some older people lament the loss of close local communities.* —**lamentation** /ˌlæmənˈteɪʃ(ə)n/ noun [C]

lament² /ləˈment/ noun [C] **LITERATURE, MUSIC** a song, poem, piece of music etc in which sadness is expressed about a death or loss

lamentable /ˈlæməntəb(ə)l/ adj extremely bad, and deserving criticism

lamina /ˈlæmɪnə/ (plural **laminae** /ˈlæmɪnaɪ/) noun [C] **BIOLOGY** the flat part of a leaf= BLADE —*picture* → LEAF

laminar flow /ˈlæmɪnə ˌfləʊ/ noun [U] **PHYSICS** a pattern of flow in a liquid or gas in which neighbouring layers do not mix, but flow at different velocities

laminate /ˈlæmɪnət/ noun [C/U] a substance that consists of several thin layers of wood, plastic, glass etc —**laminated** /ˈlæmɪˌneɪtɪd/ adj

lamp /læmp/ noun [C] **1** an electric light that stands on a floor or table **2** an oil or gas light **3** a piece of equipment that produces light and heat: *an ultra-violet lamp*

lamppost /ˈlæmpˌpəʊst/ noun [C] a tall post at the side of a road with a light on top

lampshade /ˈlæmpˌʃeɪd/ noun [C] a cover for a light that makes it less bright

LAN /læn, ˌel eɪ ˈen/ noun [C] **COMPUTING** local area network: a system that allows computers in the same building or area to exchange information

lance /lɑːns/ noun [C] a very long pointed weapon that was used in the past by soldiers on horses

lance ˈcorporal noun [C] a person of low rank in the British Army or the **Marines**

land¹ /lænd/ noun **1** [U] an area of ground, especially one used for a particular purpose such as farming or building: *Some of his land had been flooded.* ♦ *The land around here is very fertile.* ♦ *acres of agricultural land* **2** [U] the part of the Earth's surface that is not water: *The vehicle can travel on land or in water.* **3** [C] *literary* a real or imaginary country: *a land of abundant wildlife and great beauty* → COUNTRY, NO-MAN'S-LAND

land² /lænd/ verb

1 of plane	**4** get sth you wanted
2 arrive by boat	**5** be in bad situation
3 fall or fly to the ground	

1 [I/T] if an aircraft lands, or if you land it, it comes down to the ground ≠ TAKE OFF: *The plane landed a couple of hours before dawn.* ♦ *The pilot was able to land the aircraft safely.*

2 [I] to arrive at a place by boat: *The refugees landed on the east side of the island.*

3 [I] to come down to a surface after falling or flying: *She fell from the window and landed in the bushes.*

4 [T] to get something that you wanted: *At the age of 19 she landed a part in a West End play.*

5 [I/T] to put someone in an unexpected or unpleasant situation, or to be in this kind of situation: *His attitude could land him in trouble.*

→ FOOT

land-based /ˈlænd ˌbeɪst/ adj **BUSINESS** existing in a physical place rather than as a website

ˈland ˌbreeze noun [C/U] **GEOGRAPHY** a light wind blowing towards the sea from the land, especially at night

landed /ˈlændɪd/ adj **SOCIAL STUDIES** used for describing people who own a lot of land, especially when their family has owned it for a long time

landfill /ˈlæn(d)ˌfɪl/ or **ˈlandfill ˌsite** noun [C] **ENVIRONMENT** a large hole in the ground where rubbish from people's homes or from industry is buried

landform /ˈlæn(d)ˌfɔːm/ noun [C] **GEOGRAPHY** a feature on the Earth's surface such as a mountain or a valley

landing /ˈlændɪŋ/ noun **1** [C/U] the process of moving a plane down from the air onto the ground: *The pilot was forced to make an emergency landing.* **2** [C] the area at the top of a set of stairs

ˈlanding ˌcard noun [C] **TOURISM** a card given to passengers arriving on a plane to fill in before passing through **immigration** and **passport control**

ˈlanding ˌstage noun [C] a wooden structure where people or goods leave a boat

landlady /ˈlæn(d)ˌleɪdi/ (plural **landladies**) noun [C] **1** a woman who owns a house, flat, or room that people can rent **2** a woman who owns or manages a **pub** or a small hotel → LANDLORD

landless /ˈlæn(d)ləs/ adj **SOCIAL STUDIES** too poor to own any land

landline /ˈlæn(d)ˌlaɪn/ noun [C] a telephone that is not a mobile phone

landlocked /ˈlæn(d)ˌlɒkt/ adj **GEOGRAPHY** a landlocked country is surrounded by land

landlord /ˈlæn(d)ˌlɔːd/ noun [C] **1** a man who owns a house, flat, or room that people can rent **2** a man who owns or manages a **pub** or a small hotel → LANDLADY

landmark /ˈlæn(d)ˌmɑːk/ noun [C] **1** a famous building or object that you can easily recognize **2** something that marks an important stage in a process, and influences how it will develop: *This book has become a landmark in art criticism.*

ˈland ˌmass noun [C] **GEOGRAPHY** a continent or a large area of land that is surrounded by sea

landmine /ˈlæn(d)ˌmaɪn/ noun [C] a bomb hidden under the ground that explodes when someone moves over it

landowner /ˈlændˌəʊnə/ noun [C] **SOCIAL STUDIES** someone who owns a large amount of land

landscape /ˈlæn(d)ˌskeɪp/ noun **1** [C] an area of land that has particular features: *a green, rural landscape* **2** [C] **ARTS** a painting of an area of land **3** [singular] the main features of a situation **4** [U] **COMPUTING, ENGINEERING** a way of arranging a page so that its long sides are at the top and bottom → PORTRAIT

ˌlandscape ˈgardening noun [U] the profession or activity of making a garden or area of land more attractive by planting trees and adding special features —**landscape gardener** noun [C]

landside /ˈlæn(d)ˌsaɪd/ adj **TOURISM** next to the part of an airport before passengers go through the **security** checks to get on an plane

landslide /ˈlæn(d)ˌslaɪd/ noun [C] **1** **GEOGRAPHY** a heavy fall of earth and rocks down the side of a mountain **2** **POLITICS** a victory by a very big majority in an election

landslip /'læn(d)ˌslɪp/ noun [C] GEOGRAPHY a small fall of earth or rock down the side of a hill

lane /leɪn/ noun [C] **1** a narrow road, especially in the countryside: *They live down a little country lane.* **2** one of the parts that a wide road or motorway is divided into. A lane is intended for one line of traffic: *the fast lane* ♦ *Are taxis allowed to drive in the bus lane?* **3** the part of a **racetrack** or **swimming pool** that is used by one person in a competition **4** a course that a ship or aircraft follows

language /'læŋgwɪdʒ/ noun **1** [U] LANGUAGE the method of human communication using spoken or written words: *language skills* ♦ *a new study of how a child learns language* ♦ *a comparison between spoken and written language* **2** [C] LANGUAGE the particular form of words and speech that is used by the people of a country, area, or social group: *African languages* ♦ *English and French are the official languages of Canada.* ♦ *Do you speak any other languages?* **3** [C/U] a system of signs, symbols, sounds etc, used for communicating information or ideas: *computer languages* ♦ *the language of dance* → BODY LANGUAGE, FIRST LANGUAGE, SECOND LANGUAGE

'language engiˌneering noun [U] COMPUTING the development of computer systems that process language for use in industry

langue /lɒŋg/ noun [C/U] LANGUAGE a language considered as a system of communication that belongs to the people who speak it → PAROLE

languid /'læŋgwɪd/ adj **1** very slow and relaxed **2** a languid occasion or period of time is relaxed and pleasant

La Niña /ˌlæ 'niːnjə/ noun [singular] GEOGRAPHY, ENVIRONMENT a long period of unusually cold temperatures in the Pacific Ocean near the South American coast. This can seriously affect the weather in different parts of the world. → EL NIÑO

lanky /'læŋki/ adj tall, thin, and not very graceful: *a lanky teenager*

lanolin /'lænəlɪn/ noun [U] an oil that comes from sheep's wool fibres. It is used in skin creams and soaps.

lantern /'læntən/ noun [C] a light inside a transparent container that has a handle for carrying it

lanthanide /'lænθənaɪd/ noun [U] CHEMISTRY any of the metallic elements in the group with atomic numbers 57–71

lanthanum /'lænθənəm/ noun [U] CHEMISTRY a soft silvery-white metallic element in the **lanthanide** group of the periodic table. Chemical symbol: **La**

lap¹ /læp/ noun [C] **1** the top half of your legs above your knees when you sit down: *The cat settled on Christine's lap.* **2** SPORTS one complete journey around a course in a race **3** CONSTRUCTION the horizontal distance that the end of one brick sticks out beyond the end of the one below it

lap² /læp/ (**laps, lapping, lapped**) verb **1** [T] if an animal laps water, it drinks it with its tongue **2** [I/T] if water laps against something, it moves against it gently with a soft sound **3** [T] SPORTS to pass someone else in a race when you are ahead of them by a whole lap

laparoscopy /ˌlæpə'rɒskəpi/ noun [C/U] HEALTH a medical operation in which a narrow tube called a **laparoscope** is put into a part of the body in order to operate on it or examine it

laparotomy /ˌlæpə'rɒtəmi/ noun [C/U] HEALTH a cut that is made in the stomach in order to examine the inside of it

lapel /lə'pel/ noun [C] one of the two parts on each side of the front of a coat or jacket that are folded back

lapse¹ /læps/ noun [C] **1** a short period when you fail to do something, or fail to show a particular quality: *He suffers from memory lapses.* ♦ *lapses in concentration* **2** a period of time between two events: *There was a lapse of ten years between his visits.*

lapse² /læps/ verb [I] **1** to stop gradually or for a short time: *At this point conversation lapsed.* **2** if an official document, decision, or right lapses, it stops operating or being used

laptop /'læpˌtɒp/ noun [C] COMPUTING a small computer that you can carry with you

lard /lɑːd/ noun [U] white fat that is used in cooking

larder /'lɑːdə/ noun [C] a cupboard or small room where food is stored

large /lɑːdʒ/ adj bigger than usual in size, number, or amount: *a house with a very large garden* ♦ *a large software company* ♦ *large sums of money* ♦ *A large crowd had gathered outside the American Embassy.* ♦ *She's a rather large woman with red hair.*

PHRASE **at large** not yet caught and put into prison or into a cage: *The murderer is still at large.*

ˌlarge inˈtestine noun [C] ANATOMY the wide lower part of the intestine where water is removed from food that has not been digested and is changed into solid waste —*picture* → DIGESTIVE SYSTEM

largely /'lɑːdʒli/ adv mainly: *Our success is largely due to your efforts.*

ˈlarge-ˌscale adj **1** involving a large number of people or things, or happening over a large area **2** a large-scale map is one that shows a lot of details

largo¹ /'lɑːgəʊ/ adj, adv MUSIC very slowly and in a serious way: used as an instruction in music

largo² /'lɑːgəʊ/ noun [C] MUSIC a piece of music that is played very slowly and in a serious way

lark /lɑːk/ noun [C] a small brown bird that is known for its singing

larva /'lɑːvə/ (plural **larvae** /'lɑːviː/) noun [C] BIOLOGY a form that some insects and amphibians take after they have **hatched** from the egg and before they develop into their adult form. After a period of time, an insect larva changes into a **pupa**, inside which the adult insect develops. —*picture* → MOSQUITO —**larval** adj

larvicide /'lɑːvɪsaɪd/ noun [C] CHEMISTRY a chemical used to kill larvae —**larvicidal** /ˌlɑːvɪ'saɪd(ə)l/ adj

laryngitis /ˌlærɪn'dʒaɪtɪs/ noun [U] HEALTH an illness affecting the throat and larynx, which become red and swollen, making it difficult to talk

larynx /'lærɪŋks/ noun [C] ANATOMY the organ in the throat that contains the **vocal cords**, which produce sounds —*picture* → LUNG, ORGAN

laser /'leɪzə/ noun [C] PHYSICS a piece of equipment that produces a powerful line of light that can be used as a tool, or the line of light that is produced: *laser surgery*

'laser ˌprinter noun [C] COMPUTING a type of computer printer that uses a laser to produce clear letters and images

lash¹ /læʃ/ verb **1** [T] to tie something firmly to something else **2** [I/T] to hit against something with a very strong force: *Violent storms lashed the shore.* **3** [T] to hit someone or something with a **whip** or a thin stick

lash² /læʃ/ noun [C] **1** one of your **eyelashes** **2** a hit with a **whip** or a thin stick

lasso /ləˈsuː/ (plural **lassos**) noun [C] a long rope with one end tied in a circle that is used for catching and controlling horses, cows etc, especially in North America —**lasso** verb [T]

last¹ /lɑːst/ adv, determiner, pronoun **1** happening, coming, or ending most recently: *I don't agree with that last comment.* ♦ *I last saw her three years ago.* ♦ *How did you boys sleep **last night**?* ♦ **Last year** *the company made a profit of £35 million.* ♦ *We went to the play the **night before last** (=two nights ago).* ♦ *We discussed it **the last time** we met.* **2** happening or coming at the end, after all the others: *The last of the guests had arrived.* ♦ *She finished last in the race.* ♦ *Janice was **the last to** leave.* ♦ *That's **the last time** I help you! (=I will never help you again.)* **3** remaining after all the rest have gone: *the last book left on the shelf* ♦ *Who wants **the last of** the ice cream?* **4** used for emphasizing that someone or something is not at all likely, suitable, or wanted: *Upsetting you is **the last thing** I'd want to do.*
> **PHRASE at (long) last** used for saying that something that you have been waiting for finally happens: *I'm so glad to meet you at last.*
→ LAST-MINUTE, RESORT

last² /lɑːst/ verb **1** [I] to continue happening for a particular period or until a particular time: *The game lasts 80 minutes.* ♦ *The conference will **last for** two weeks.* ♦ *The party **lasted until** the early morning.* **2** [I/T] to continue to be available or to be enough for what people need: *The water won't last long.* ♦ *Thirty pounds usually lasted him about a week.* **3** [I] to continue in a good state without changing or failing: *I hope the good weather will last.* ♦ *These cars are built **to last**.*

lasting /ˈlɑːstɪŋ/ adj continuing to exist or to have an effect for a long time: *a lasting peace*

lastly /ˈlɑːs(t)li/ adv used when you want to say one more thing before you finish speaking= FINALLY: *And lastly, remember that your essays are due tomorrow.*

last-ˈminute adj happening or done at the latest possible time: *You can do any last-minute shopping at the airport.*

ˈlast ˌname noun [C] the name that you share with the other members of your family. In English, it comes at the end of your full name= FAMILY NAME, SURNAME

the ˌLast ˈSupper noun RELIGION in the Bible, the last meal Jesus Christ ate with his 12 **disciples** on the evening before he was **crucified**. He offered them bread and wine, and the religious ceremony known as **Communion** or the **Eucharist** is based on this.

latch /lætʃ/ noun [C] **1** an object for keeping a door, gate etc shut **2** a lock for a door that needs a key to open it from the outside, although it can be opened from the inside without one

late /leɪt/ adj, adv **1** arriving somewhere or doing something after the expected or usual time≠ EARLY: *She phoned to say she'd **be late**.* ♦ *Sheila was **late for** work again this morning.* ♦ *The trains are all **running** about 15 minutes **late**.* **2** near the end of an evening or night: *Late one night I heard a knock on the door.* ♦ *It was **getting late** and all the kids were sleepy.* ♦ *We had **a late night** last night (=went to bed when it was late).* **3** near the end of a period of time≠ EARLY: *the late 18th century* ♦ *a girl in her late teens* **4** used for talking about someone who has died, especially recently: *my late aunt*
> **PHRASES better late than never** used for saying that it is good that something has happened, but that it would have been better if it had been earlier
too late if you are too late, you have missed the best or only time for doing something: *The ambulance arrived, but it was too late.*

late adopter /ˌleɪt əˈdɒptə/ noun [C] BUSINESS someone who is among the last people to buy or start using a new product, technology, or idea after it becomes available or known

ˌlate availaˈbility noun [U] TOURISM cheaper airline tickets that become available close to the time of departure

ˌlate ˈcheckout noun [C] TOURISM a guest who leaves a hotel at a later time than guests usually have to leave

lately /ˈleɪtli/ adv recently: *Have you seen either of them lately?*

ˈlate-ˌnight adj happening late at night: *a late-night film*

ˌlate-night ˈshopping noun [U] shopping in the late evening, with shops opening much later than usual

latent /ˈleɪt(ə)nt/ adj something that is latent exists, but it is not obvious or has not developed yet: *latent aggression*

ˌlatent ˈheat noun [U] PHYSICS the heat that is taken in or given out when a substance changes its physical state, without affecting the temperature of the substance

later¹ /ˈleɪtə/ adv at some time in the future, or after the time that you have been talking about: *She'll be home later.* ♦ *We can make an appointment for **later in** the week.*
> **PHRASE later on** at a time in the future, or after the time that you have been talking about: *I'll come and see you later on.*

later² /ˈleɪtə/ adj **1** happening at some time in the future, or after the time that you have been talking about: *We can settle on the price **at a later date**.* **2** near the end of a period of time, or near the end of someone's life or career: *Her views changed in her later years.*

lateral /ˈlæt(ə)rəl/ adj on the side of something, or moving sideways —**laterally** adv

ˌlateral inˈversion noun [U] PHYSICS the change that happens to an image in a flat mirror, when it appears the correct way up but with the right side on the left and the left side on the right

ˈlateral ˌline noun [C] BIOLOGY a line of sense organs along the head and sides of fish and some amphibians living in water, by which they can experience pressure changes and vibrations

ˌlateral ˈmoraine noun [C] GEOLOGY a mass of earth and pieces of rock left at the sides of a glacier as it passes

ˌlateral ˈthinking noun [U] a way of solving a problem in which someone uses their imagination to try to think about it in a different or unusual way

laterite /ˈlætəraɪt/ noun [U] GEOLOGY a red clay containing iron and aluminium that forms a layer on the top of soil in some tropical regions

latest /ˈleɪtɪst/ adj most recent or newest: *The latest figures show steady growth.*

the latest /ˈleɪtɪst/ noun [singular] the most recent event, thing, piece of news etc: *Have you heard the latest? He's getting married.*
> **PHRASE at the latest** no later than a particular time

latex /ˈleɪteks/ noun [U] CHEMISTRY a substance that is used for making rubber, paint, and glue

lathe /leɪð/ noun [C] TECHNOLOGY a machine that holds a piece of wood or metal and spins it round, so that it can be cut or shaped evenly

lather /ˈlɑːðə, ˈlæðə/ noun [singular] the white mass of bubbles that is produced when you mix soap and water

latin /'lætɪn/ noun [U] MUSIC a type of music from Latin America or influenced by music from Latin America, especially **dance music** such as **salsa**

Latin¹ /'lætɪn/ noun [U] LANGUAGE the language that people spoke in ancient Rome. Modern European languages such as Italian, Spanish, and French developed from it.

Latin² /'lætɪn/ adj LANGUAGE **1** written in Latin **2** relating to people who speak languages that developed from Latin, or to their culture

Latin A'merica noun [U] GEOGRAPHY the part of the American continent consisting of Mexico, Central America, and South America, where Spanish and Portuguese are the main languages

Latin A'merican adj GEOGRAPHY from or relating to Mexico, Central America, or South America —**Latin A'merican** noun [C]

latitude /'lætɪˌtjuːd/ noun **1** [C/U] GEOGRAPHY the distance of a point on the Earth from the equator, measured in degrees north or south → LONGITUDE —picture → EARTH **2** [U] formal freedom that someone has to use their own methods and judgment

latrine /lə'triːn/ noun [C] a toilet built or made outside in a military camp

latter /'lætə/ adj, pronoun **1** formal used for referring to the second of two people, things, or groups that have just been mentioned: He enjoys both reading and swimming, but prefers **the latter**. ♦ Treaties were signed in 1990 and 1998, but only **the latter** agreement was valid. → FORMER **2** used for describing the later part of a period of time: **the latter half** of 1998

latterly /'lætəli/ adv formal recently

laudable /'lɔːdəb(ə)l/ adj formal deserving to be praised or admired

laugh¹ /lɑːf/ verb [I] **1** to make the sound with your voice that shows that you think that something is funny: We talked and laughed late into the night. ♦ The audience didn't **laugh at** his jokes. ♦ They were still **laughing about** the experience years later. ♦ She **burst out laughing** when she saw what he was wearing. **2** to show that you think that someone or something is stupid or deserves no respect: When I told them my idea, they just laughed. ♦ Are you **laughing at** me?

laugh² /lɑːf/ noun [C] the sound that you make when you laugh: a hearty laugh

laughable /'lɑːfəb(ə)l/ adj stupid, or unreasonable —**laughably** adv

laughter /'lɑːftə/ noun [U] the sound or action of someone laughing: The children's laughter drifted down the street. ♦ The men were **roaring with laughter** (=laughing a lot) at the boy's embarrassment.

launch¹ /lɔːntʃ/ verb [T]

1 send sth into space/ the air	3 of new product
2 start activity etc	4 of boat/ship
	5 of computer program

1 ASTRONOMY to send a space vehicle, missile, or other object into space or into the air: The agency will launch a new weather satellite next month.
2 to start a major activity such as a military attack, a public project, or a new career: The armies launched their attack at dawn.
3 BUSINESS to make a new product available for the public to buy for the first time: The company will launch a new version of the software in July.
4 to put a boat or ship into water, especially for the first time
5 COMPUTING to start a computer program

launch² /lɔːntʃ/ noun [C] **1** the act of sending a missile, space vehicle, satellite, or other object into the air or into space: the launch of the space shuttle **2** the start of a major activity such as a military attack, a public **investigation**, or a new career or project **3** a large open boat with an engine **4** BUSINESS an occasion on which a company makes a new product available for the public to buy for the first time

laundry /'lɔːndri/ (plural **laundries**) noun **1** [singular/U] dirty clothes, sheets etc that you are washing, or clean clothes, sheets etc that have just been washed: a laundry basket ♦ My husband **does** (=washes) **the laundry**. **2** [C] a business that you pay to wash your clothes

'laundry ,list noun [C] TOURISM a printed list of items of clothing that a guest in a hotel may want to have washed

lava /'lɑːvə/ noun [U] GEOLOGY **1** rock in the form of extremely hot liquid that flows from a volcano —picture → VOLCANO **2** the solid rock that forms when liquid lava becomes cold

lavatory /'lævətri/ (plural **lavatories**) noun [C] a toilet

lavender¹ /'lævəndə/ noun [C] a plant with small light purple flowers that have a pleasant smell

lavender² /'lævəndə/ adj light purple in colour

lavish /'lævɪʃ/ adj given very generously, or very expensive —**lavishly** adv

law /lɔː/ noun **1** the law [singular] SOCIAL STUDIES the system of rules that must be obeyed in society: Failing to declare any extra income is **against the law**. ♦ How can I bring my boyfriend into the country without **breaking the law** (=doing something that is not allowed by the law)? **2** [C/U] an official rule that people must obey, or a set of these rules: The new **law will be passed** by Parliament in the spring. ♦ Several traffic **laws** had been **broken**. ♦ a **law against** shoplifting **3** [U] the academic study of laws, or the profession of working as a judge, lawyer etc: a degree in law ♦ Anne's been **practising law** (=working as a lawyer) for 20 years. **4** [C] SCIENCE a generally accepted explanation of a natural or scientific process: the laws of physics/gravity

PHRASES **law and order** safe and peaceful conditions in society that result when people obey the law
law of moments PHYSICS a law of physics that states that when an object is **in equilibrium** (=balanced), the sum of the clockwise movements is equal to the sum of the anticlockwise movements about the same **pivot**
law of motion PHYSICS one of the laws about movement that were first expressed by Isaac Newton
take the law into your own hands to punish someone in your own way without involving the police or the courts, often by doing something illegal

'law-a,biding adj obeying the law

'law ,court noun [C] LAW a place where trials take place and are officially judged

lawful /'lɔːf(ə)l/ adj allowed by law ≠ UNLAWFUL —**lawfully** adv

'law-,making adj responsible for making laws = LEGISLATIVE —**'law-,making** noun [U]

lawn /lɔːn/ noun [C/U] an area of grass that is cut short, especially in a garden

lawnmower /'lɔːnˌməʊə/ noun [C] a machine for cutting grass = MOWER

,lawn 'tennis noun [U] SPORTS formal the game of tennis

lawrencium /ləˈrentsiəm/ noun [U] CHEMISTRY a radioactive metallic element in the **actinide** group of the periodic table. Chemical symbol: **Lr**

lawsuit /ˈlɔːˌsuːt/ noun [C] LAW a situation in which a disagreement between people or groups is formally judged in a law court

lawyer /ˈlɔːjə/ noun [C] LAW someone whose profession is to provide people with legal advice and services: *Mayer's lawyer spoke to the press today.*

lax /læks/ adj not paying enough attention to rules, or not caring enough about quality or safety

laxative /ˈlæksətɪv/ noun [C] HEALTH a medicine, food, or drink that helps faeces to leave the body —**laxative** adj

lay¹ /leɪ/ (**lays, laying, laid** /leɪd/) verb [T] **1** to put someone or something down in a careful way, especially so that they are lying flat: *Lay the baby on her back.* ♦ *He laid his coat across the arm of the chair.* **2** if a female animal such as a bird or fish lays an egg, it produces the egg by pushing it from its body **3** if you lay the table, you prepare it for a meal by putting forks, knives, spoons, dishes etc on it = SET **4** to carefully plan and prepare something: *an agreement that laid the foundations for a lasting peace* ♦ *The police had laid a trap for the killer.*

PHRASES **lay the blame/responsibility (for sth) on** to say that someone or something is responsible for something that has happened: *Don't try to lay the blame on me.*

not lay a finger on sb to not hit or harm someone in any way

PHRASAL VERB **,lay sth 'out** to spread something out or arrange things so that you can see them easily

- Lay means to put something in a particular place or position: *I always lay my clothes carefully on the chair when I undress.* ♦ *He laid the book on the desk.*
- Lie means to be in a particular place or position: *I found the cat lying in front of the fire.* ♦ *He loves to lie on the beach all day.* ♦ *Papers were lying all over the desk.*
- Lay is also the past tense of the verb lie: *The book lay on the floor where I'd left it.*

lay² /leɪ/ the past tense of **lie¹**

lay³ /leɪ/ adj RELIGION belonging to a Christian church but not officially employed by it as a priest, minister etc

'lay-,by (plural **'lay-,bys**) noun [C] an area provided by the side of a road where vehicles can stop for a short period of time

layer /ˈleɪə/ noun [C] **1** an amount or sheet of a substance that covers a surface or lies between two things: *Glue the layers together and let them dry.* ♦ *Put a layer of grated cheese on top.* **2** a level or rank within an organization or system: *another layer of bureaucracy*

layman /ˈleɪmən/ (plural **laymen** /ˈleɪmən/) noun [C] someone who does not have professional or advanced knowledge of a particular subject

layout /ˈleɪaʊt/ noun [C] the way in which the different parts of something are arranged: *the layout of the keyboard*

laze /leɪz/ or **,laze a'round** verb [I] to relax and enjoy yourself, doing no work: *We found some time to swim and laze in the sun.*

lazy /ˈleɪzi/ (**lazier, laziest**) adj **1** not willing to work or do anything that involves effort: *Get out of bed, you lazy slob!* **2** a lazy period of time is spent resting and

relaxing: *a lazy afternoon in the sun* —**lazily** adv, **laziness** noun [U]

lb abbrev pound: a unit for measuring weight that is equal to 0.454 kilograms

LBO /ˌel biː ˈəʊ/ noun [C] BUSINESS a **leveraged buyout**

LCM abbrev MATHS lowest common multiple

LDC /ˌel diː ˈsiː/ noun [C] ECONOMICS a **less developed country**

leach /liːtʃ/ verb [I/T] GEOLOGY to remove a chemical or mineral from something such as soil as a result of water passing through it, or to be removed by this process —**leaching** noun [U]

lead¹ /liːd/ (**leads, leading, led** /led/) verb

1 take sb somewhere	**6** make sb do sth
2 go somewhere	**7** live particular way
3 be winning	+ PHRASE
4 be best	+ PHRASAL VERBS
5 be in charge	

1 [T] to take someone to a place by going there with them, usually in front of them: *The estate agent led us into the kitchen.* ♦ *She took the boy by the hand and led him from the room.*

2 [I/T] if something such as a road, river, or door leads somewhere, or if it leads you there, it goes there: *The road leads west for three miles then turns south.* ♦ *This door leads you to a large entrance hall.*

3 [I/T] to be winning at a particular time during a race or competition: *The polls show Labour leading with only 10 days left until the election.* ♦ *France was leading England at half time by 3 goals to 2.*

4 [I/T] to be the most successful, popular, or advanced of all the people or groups that are involved in a particular activity: *They lead the world in oil production.*

5 [T] to be in charge of an organization, a group of people, or an activity: *She led the team for over twelve years.*

6 [T] to influence someone to do something: *I had been led to believe that the job was mine if I wanted it.*

7 [T] to live your life in a particular way: *He had always led a quiet life until he met Emma.*

PHRASE **lead the way 1** to show other people the way to a place: *Sheila turned and led the way downstairs.* **2** to be the first person to do something and to show other people how to do it: *It is a country that has always led the way in its conservation policies.*

PHRASAL VERBS **'lead to sth** to begin a process that causes something to happen: *Stress can lead to physical illness.* → THING

,lead 'up to sth to happen in the period of time before something else happens: *the events that led up to the war*

lead² /liːd/ noun

1 first position	**6** first piece of news
2 winning amount	**7** for controlling dog
3 main part or actor	**8** electrical wire
4 useful information	+ PHRASE
5 example to others	

1 [singular] the first position at a particular time during a race or competition: *He regained his lead in the final lap.* ♦ *The latest polls show the Labour candidate in the lead* (=winning).

2 [singular] the distance, amount of time, number of points etc by which someone is winning a race or competition: *They've now increased their lead to three points.*

3 [C] the main person or part in a play, film, or television programme: *She's playing the lead in her school play.*

4 [C] a piece of information that may help to solve a

crime or help to find out the truth about something

5 [C] an action that is an example for someone to copy: *North Korea is to **follow** China's **lead** in attracting foreign investment.*

6 [C] the most important story on the front page of a newspaper, or the first piece of news in a news broadcast

7 [C] a chain or long narrow piece of leather that you fasten to a collar around a dog's neck in order to control the dog: *All dogs must be kept **on a lead** in the park.*

8 [C] an electrical wire that connects a piece of equipment to a power supply= CABLE

PHRASE **take the lead 1** to start winning a race or competition: *She took the lead ten miles into the marathon.* **2** to do something first, especially as an example for other people to follow: *British farmers took the lead by sending tons of grain to the disaster area.*

lead³ /led/ noun **1** [U] CHEMISTRY a soft heavy grey metal element whose compounds can be poisonous. It is used to make containers that protect against harmful radiation. It is also a bad conductor of electricity that does not **corrode** easily. Chemical symbol: **Pb 2** [C/U] the part of a pencil that you make marks with

leaded /'ledɪd/ adj ENVIRONMENT leaded petrol contains lead and is therefore harmful to the environment ≠ UNLEADED

leader /'liːdə/ noun [C] **1** someone who is in charge of a group, organization, or country: *a religious leader* ♦ *the leader of the Kenyan delegation* **2** someone or something that is winning at a particular time during a race or competition: *She remains the leader after the 17th hole.* **3** someone or something that is the most successful, most popular, most advanced etc: *He is a world **leader in** his field.* **4** an article in a newspaper in which the **editor** expresses their personal opinion on a subject= EDITORIAL

leadership /'liːdəʃɪp/ noun **1** [U] the position of being a leader: *The war was fought **under** the emperor's **leadership.*** **2** [U] the qualities and skills of a good leader **3** [singular] the people who are in charge of an organization or country

leading /'liːdɪŋ/ adj **1** main, most important, or most successful: *He became **a leading figure** in the London art world.* ♦ *a leading brand of toothpaste* ♦ *She played a leading role in the country's independence movement.* **2** ahead of all others in a race or competition: *Michael broke away from the leading group to win by 70 metres.*

leading economic indicator noun [C] ECONOMICS an **economic indicator** (=quantity used for measuring a particular feature of the economy) that shows how general economic activity is developing

leading-edge adj of the most modern or advanced type: *leading-edge technology*

leading light noun [C] a very important or respected person in a group, organization, or area of activity

leading question noun [C] a question that you ask in a way that tricks someone, or that forces them to give the answer that you want

lead replacement petrol /ˌled rɪˈpleɪsmənt ˌpetrəl/ noun [U] a type of petrol used by vehicles that cannot use **unleaded** petrol

lead sulphide /ˌled ˈsʌlfaɪd/ noun [U] CHEMISTRY a chemical compound obtained from the mineral **galena**. Chemical formula: **PbS**

lead time /'liːd ˌtaɪm/ noun [C/U] BUSINESS the time between planning something and starting to do it

leaf /liːf/ (plural **leaves** /liːvz/) noun [C] **1** BIOLOGY a flat, thin, usually green part of a plant that grows on a branch or stem. A leaf consists of an outer layer called the **epidermis**, inner layers of cells that contain **chloroplasts**, and veins that transport water, minerals, and food: *The autumn leaves were beginning to fall.* —*picture* → TREE **2** a page of a book **3** CONSTRUCTION one of the two separate parts of a **hinge**

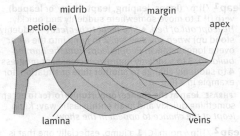

parts of a leaf

leaflet /'liːflət/ noun [C] a printed sheet of paper that is provided free and gives information about something= FLYER

leaf spring noun [C] ENGINEERING a steel **spring** shaped in a curve, used in the **suspension** of vehicles

leafy /'liːfi/ adj **1** covered with a lot of leaves: *leafy green vegetables* **2** a leafy town or area has a lot of trees: *a leafy neighbourhood*

league /liːg/ noun [C] **1** SPORTS an organized group of teams or players who regularly compete against each other: *Manchester United **are top of the league** again.* ♦ *They were the **league champions** twice during the 1990s.* **2** a group of people, organizations, or countries that have joined together because they have the same interests or aims: *the League of Nations* **3** a group of people or things that are similar in their quality, skills, or achievements: *He's not bad, but he's **not in the same league as** the others.*

leak¹ /liːk/ verb **1** [I/T] if a pipe, container, roof etc leaks, or if it leaks something, liquid or gas comes out of it through a hole: *The roof is still leaking.* **2** [I] if a liquid or gas leaks, it comes out of a pipe, container, roof etc through a hole: *Oil was leaking from the pipeline.* **3** [T] to give secret information about the organization you work for to a journalist or to the public: *The story was leaked to the press.*

leak² /liːk/ noun [C] **1** a hole or crack in something that a liquid or gas comes out of, or the liquid or gas that comes out **2** an occasion when secret information about an organization is told to a journalist or to the public

leakage /'liːkɪdʒ/ noun [C/U] an amount of liquid or gas that comes out of a hole or crack in something

leaky /'liːki/ adj a leaky object or container has a hole or crack in it so that liquid or gas comes out of it

lean¹ /liːn/ (**leans, leaning, leaned** or **leant** /lent/) verb **1** [I] to move your body by bending at the waist, bringing yourself closer to or further from someone or something: *The other girl **leaned forward** to hear what was going on.* ♦ *I **leaned over** her shoulder to study the maps.* **2** [I] to stand or be placed at an angle against something for support, instead of being upright: *There was a small ladder **leaning against** the wall.* ♦ *He walked in, **leaning heavily on** a cane.* **3** [T] to put something at an angle against an object for support: *John leaned his rake against the side of the barn.*

lean² /liːn/ adj **1** someone who is lean does not have any fat on their body and looks physically fit and healthy **2** lean meat contains very little fat **3** a lean period is very difficult to live in because many people lack money or other necessary things

leaning /'liːnɪŋ/ noun [C] a tendency to prefer, support, or be interested in a particular idea or activity

leant /lent/ a past tense and past participle of **lean¹**

leap¹ /liːp/ (**leaps, leaping, leapt** /lept/ or **leaped**) verb [I] **1** to move somewhere suddenly and quickly: *He leapt out of bed.* ♦ *She leapt to her feet* (=suddenly stood up) *when she saw me.* **2** to jump into the air or over a long distance: *People leapt from the burning building.* **3** to suddenly improve, increase, or progress **4** to suddenly change to another time or situation, for example in a film

PHRASE **leap at the chance/opportunity/offer** to accept something quickly and in an enthusiastic way: *Klein leapt at the chance to appear in the show.*

leap² /liːp/ noun [C] **1** a jump, especially one that is long or high **2** a sudden increase or improvement = JUMP: *a huge leap in the price of fuel* **3** a big change in the way someone thinks, or in what they do

leapt /lept/ a past tense and past participle of **leap¹**

'leap ,year noun [C] a year that has 366 days instead of 365. This happens once every four years.

learn /lɜːn/ (**learns, learning, learnt** /lɜːnt/ or **learned** /lɜːnd/) verb **1** [I/T] to gain knowledge or experience of something, for example by being taught: *What did you learn at school today?* ♦ *The children are learning to swim this summer.* ♦ *I want to learn how to ride a motorbike.* **2** [T] EDUCATION to study something so that you remember it exactly = MEMORIZE: *I've got a list of German verbs to learn tonight.* **3** [I/T] to gain new information about a situation, event, or person = FIND STH OUT: *We were distressed to learn that American troops were the targets of the attack.* ♦ *We didn't learn about the situation until it was too late.* **4** [I] to improve your behaviour as a result of gaining greater experience or knowledge of something: *His girlfriend's left him again. Some people never learn, do they?*

PHRASE **learn your lesson** to be unlikely to do something stupid or wrong again, because the last time you did it something unpleasant happened

■ When you **learn**, you gain knowledge or skills through experience or as a result of practising, reading, or being taught: *I am learning to play the guitar.* ♦ *He wanted to learn about life in ancient Rome.*
■ When you **study**, you make an effort to learn a particular subject, usually by going to classes or reading and doing research: *He studied geography at university.* ♦ *If you want to learn English you must study hard.*

learned /'lɜːnɪd/ adj having or showing a lot of knowledge about academic subjects: *a learned man*

learner /'lɜːnə/ noun [C] someone who is learning something: *a learner driver*

learning /'lɜːnɪŋ/ noun [U] EDUCATION **1** the process of gaining knowledge and experience, for example by studying **2** knowledge that someone has gained, especially by studying

'learning ,curve noun [C] the rate at which you learn something: *I've never done this kind of work before, so I'm on a steep learning curve* (=I have to learn a lot in a short time).

'learning disa,bility or **'learning ,difficulty** noun a condition that prevents someone from learning basic skills as quickly or easily as other people

'learning-dis,abled adj unable to learn basic skills or information at the same rate as other people

learnt /lɜːnt/ a past tense and past participle of **learn**

lease /liːs/ noun [C] LAW a legal agreement in which you agree to pay to use someone else's building, land, or equipment for a particular period of time —**lease** verb [T]

least /liːst/ adv, determiner, pronoun **1** the smallest amount ≠ MOST: *I earn the least out of all of us.* ♦ *Cooking is the thing I spend least time on.* ♦ *Let me pay for the dinner – it's the least I can do* (=I should do more).* **2** to the smallest degree: *The new taxes hurt those who are least able to pay.* ♦ *Troubles come when you least expect them.*

PHRASE **at least 1** not less than a particular amount or number: *The disease killed at least 120 people in England last year.* **2** even if nothing else happens or is true: *You might at least have waited for me.* **3** used for talking about an advantage that exists despite something else: *The work is difficult, but at least the pay is good.* **4** used when you are saying something that changes or limits what you have just said: *No one saw anything, or at least they say they didn't.*
→ SAY¹

leather /'leðə/ noun [C] a strong material made from animal skin that is used for making shoes, clothes, bags etc: *a black leather jacket*

leave¹ /liːv/ (**leaves, leaving, left** /left/) verb

1 go away from place	**8** cause a feeling
2 go away forever	**9** not do sth
3 stop doing sth	**10** let sb decide
4 cause sth that remains	**11** not use sth
5 forget to take sth	**12** give sth in death
6 end relationship	**+ PHRASAL VERBS**
7 put sth somewhere	

1 [I/T] to go away from a place: *We left London at three in the afternoon.* ♦ *Your plane leaves in ten minutes.* ♦ *She leaves for work at 7.30 every morning.*
2 [I/T] to go away from a place permanently: *He didn't leave home until he was 24.*
3 [I/T] to stop working for an organization, or to stop going to school or college: *He decided to leave the company after 15 years.*
4 [T] to produce something that remains after you have gone: *The government left the economy in ruins.* ♦ *The ants leave a trail of chemicals for others to follow.*
5 [T] to put something somewhere and forget to take it away with you: *I left my homework on the bus.*
6 [I/T] to end a relationship with someone and stop living with them: *His wife has threatened to leave him.*
7 [T] to put something somewhere, especially in a place where it will stay: *Leave your things by the door.* ♦ *I'll leave a note for Leigh.*
8 [T] to produce a feeling or opinion: *I was left with the feeling that she wasn't being quite honest.* ♦ *Kate's sudden departure left us all wondering what was going to happen.*
9 [T] to not do something that can be done later, or that can be done by someone else: *Leave the dishes and do them in the morning.* ♦ *Don't worry – just leave everything to me.*
10 [T] to not make a decision and let someone else make it: *Leave questions of guilt or innocence for the jury to decide.*
11 [T] to not use something: *I hope you've left enough hot water for me to have a shower.* ♦ *You've left half your dinner.* ♦ *We don't have much money left.* ♦ *There*

was some material **left over** when I'd finished making the dress.

12 [T] to say that you want someone to have your money, property etc after you die: *She left her jewels to her favourite niece.* ♦ *He left her all his money.*

PHRASAL VERBS ,**leave sb/sth be'hind 1** to improve or progress much faster than someone or something else **2** to forget to take someone or something with you: *When she was halfway home, she realized that she'd left her purse behind.*

,**leave sb/sth 'out** to not include someone or something: *We decided to leave the chapter out of the book altogether.* ♦ *She feels left out because the other children don't play with her.*

Build your vocabulary: words you can use instead of leave

- **depart** (*formal*) to leave a place: used mainly about planes, trains, and other types of transport
- **go** a general word used for talking about leaving a place or situation
- **go away** to leave a place: often used for ordering someone to leave
- **set off** to leave a place at the beginning of a journey
- **storm out** to leave a place in an angry way
- **walk out** to leave a job or relationship suddenly

- Both **forget** and **leave** can be used to talk about not taking something that you need with you.
- Use **leave**, not **forget**, when you mention the place where the thing is: *Oh no, I've forgotten my keys.* ♦ *Don't forget your wallet.* ♦ *I can't find my keys – I must have left them somewhere.* ♦ *Don't leave your bag in your hotel room.*

---

leave² /liːv/ noun [U] **1** a period of time when someone is officially away from their job or the armed forces: *You are entitled to six weeks' annual leave.* **2** *formal* permission

leaves /liːvz/ the plural of **leaf**

LECD /ˌel iː siː 'diː/ noun [C] ECONOMICS less economically developed country: a country that is fairly poor and does not have much industrial development → MECD

lecture¹ /'lektʃə/ noun [C] **1** EDUCATION a talk to a group of people about a particular subject, especially at a college or university: *a lecture on Dickens* ♦ *Tomorrow she will be giving a lecture at London University.* **2** *showing disapproval* a long serious talk that criticizes or warns someone: *I don't need any lectures from you about being late!*

lecture² /'lektʃə/ verb **1** [I] EDUCATION to give a lecture or a series of lectures **2** [T] *showing disapproval* to talk to someone seriously in order to criticize or warn them about something

'**lecture ,hall** noun [C] a **lecture theatre**

lecturer /'lektʃərə/ noun [C] **1** someone who gives a lecture = SPEAKER **2** EDUCATION a teacher at a university or college

'**lecture ,theatre** noun [C] a large room with rows of seats where students sit to listen to lectures

'**lecture ,tour** noun [C] TOURISM a journey that includes lectures on the places or objects that people see

led /led/ the past tense and past participle of **lead¹**

LED /ˌel iː 'diː/ noun [C] PHYSICS light-emitting diode: a piece of electronic equipment that produces light. LEDs are used in patterns to form numbers and letters, especially on computer screens, **digital** watches, and calculators.

-led /led/ suffix directed, controlled, or influenced by: used with some nouns

ledge /ledʒ/ noun [C] **1** a narrow surface that sticks out from the side of a cliff or wall **2** a narrow shelf at the bottom of a window= SILL

ledger /'ledʒə/ noun [C] **1** a book that contains the financial records of a business **2** CONSTRUCTION a horizontal part attached to a vertical surface to create a place where other horizontal parts can rest

leech /liːtʃ/ noun [C] a small soft invertebrate like a worm that attaches itself to the skin of other animals in order to feed on their blood

leek /liːk/ noun [C] a long thin vegetable that tastes similar to an onion and consists of the leaves of the plant. It is white at one end and green at the other.

leeward /'liːwəd, 'luːəd/ adj on the side of something that has shelter from the wind —**leeward** adv

left¹ /left/ adj **1** on the side of the body that is to the west if you are facing north ≠ RIGHT: *He wore a wedding ring on his left hand.* **2** on the left side of something: *the bottom left corner of the screen* ♦ *We took a left turn when we should have gone right.*

left² /left/ noun **1** [singular] the left side or direction: *On the left of the picture you can see his grandmother.* ♦ *My office is the third door on your left.* ♦ *The car swerved to the left.* **2** **the left** or **the Left** [singular] POLITICS people or groups with left-wing political opinions: *He received strong criticism from the left of the party.* **3** [C] SPORTS a hit made with the left hand, especially in boxing ≠ RIGHT

left³ /left/ adv **1** towards the left side ≠ RIGHT: *Turn left at the end of the street.* **2** POLITICS towards the left in politics ≠ RIGHT

left⁴ /left/ the past tense and past participle of **leave¹**

'**left-,click** verb [I] COMPUTING to press the button on the left side of a computer mouse with your finger

'**left-,hand** adj on the left side ≠ RIGHT-HAND: *The plates are on the left-hand side of the cupboard.*

left-handed /ˌleft 'hændɪd/ adj **1** born with a natural tendency to use the left hand to do things ≠ RIGHT-HANDED **2** designed for, or done with, the left hand ≠ RIGHT-HANDED —**left-handedness** noun [U]

,**left 'luggage ,office** noun [C] a place at an airport, railway station, or bus station where you can pay to leave your bags for a short time

leftover /'left,əʊvə/ adj remaining after you have finished using the amount that you want or need

leftovers /'left,əʊvəz/ noun [plural] the food that remains at the end of a meal after you have finished eating

,**left-'wing** adj POLITICS someone who is left-wing believes that property, money, and power should be shared more equally ≠ RIGHT-WING —,**left-'winger** noun [C]

leg /leg/ noun [C]

1 part of body	**4** part of furniture
2 clothing on leg	**5** part of journey
3 animal leg meat	

1 one of the parts of a person's or animal's body to which the feet are attached: *She sat down and crossed her legs.* —*picture* → BIRD, BODY
2 the part of a piece of clothing that covers one of your legs: *There was dirt on his trouser leg.*
3 a piece of meat that comes from an animal's leg: *roast leg of lamb*
4 the part of a piece of furniture that supports it and raises it off the floor: *a stool with three legs*

5 a part of a journey, race, or competition
→ LEGS

legacy /ˈlegəsi/ (plural **legacies**) noun [C] **1** money or property that you arrange for someone to have after you die **2** something such as a tradition or problem that exists as a result of something that happened in the past

ˈlegacy ˌsystem noun [U] COMPUTING a computer system that is still used although it is no longer the most modern or advanced, because it would be very expensive or difficult to replace it

legal /ˈliːg(ə)l/ adj LAW **1** relating to the law or lawyers: *You may wish to seek legal advice before signing the contract.* ♦ *China's legal system* ♦ *Parents are taking legal action to challenge the school's closure.* **2** allowed by the law, or done according to the law ≠ ILLEGAL: *It is perfectly legal to import these goods under European law.* ♦ *the child's legal guardians* —**legally** /ˈliːgəli/ adv

ˌlegal ˈaid noun [U] LAW a system in which the government pays for people to get legal help when they do not have much money

legality /lɪˈgæləti/ noun [U] the fact that something is legal

legalize /ˈliːgəlaɪz/ verb [T] to make something legal by creating a new law —**legalization** /ˌliːgəlaɪˈzeɪʃ(ə)n/ noun [U]

legend /ˈledʒ(ə)nd/ noun **1** [C] LITERATURE an old story about imaginary people and events in the past: *Greek myths and legends* **2** [U] LITERATURE these old stories considered as a group: *Here, according to legend, Robin Hood lies buried.* **3** [C] someone who is very famous and admired by many people: *the Hollywood legend, Elizabeth Taylor*

legendary /ˈledʒ(ə)nd(ə)ri/ adj **1** very famous or well known for a long time **2** mentioned or described in a legend

legible /ˈledʒəb(ə)l/ adj legible writing is clear and tidy enough to be read ≠ ILLEGIBLE —**legibility** /ˌledʒəˈbɪləti/ noun [U], **legibly** adv

legionnaire's disease /ˌliːdʒəˈneəz dɪˌziːz/ noun [U] HEALTH a serious disease of the lungs that leads to severe **pneumonia** and is usually spread through **air conditioning** systems

legislate /ˈledʒɪˌsleɪt/ verb [I] LAW to create a new law and have it officially accepted —**legislator** /ˈledʒɪˌsleɪtə/ noun [C]

legislation /ˌledʒɪˈsleɪʃ(ə)n/ noun [U] LAW a law, or a set of laws: *a complex piece of legislation* ♦ *The government should pass legislation to limit the powers of the police.*

legislative /ˈledʒɪslətɪv/ adj LAW **1** relating to laws or to the process of creating new laws: *the legislative power of Parliament* **2** used for talking about groups of people who have the power to create new laws: *a legislative body* —**legislatively** adv

legislature /ˈledʒɪslətʃə/ noun [singular] LAW the part of government that makes and changes laws. The other parts of government are the **executive** and the **judiciary**.

legitimate /lɪˈdʒɪtəmət/ adj **1** fair and reasonable: *Did he have a legitimate excuse for being late?* **2** allowed by the law, or correct according to the law: *Are the premises being used for legitimate business purposes?* **3** a legitimate child is born to parents who are legally married —**legitimacy** /lɪˈdʒɪtəməsi/ noun [U], **legitimately** adv

legless /ˈlegləs/ adj without legs

legroom /ˈlegˌruːm/ noun [U] the amount of space in front of your seat in which you can stretch your legs

legume /ˈlegjuːm/ noun [C] BIOLOGY **1** a seed such as a **pea** or bean that grows in a **pod 2** the plant on which seeds with **pods** such as beans and **peas** grow. Legumes are important for the environment as the bacteria in their roots carry out **nitrogen fixation**. —**leguminous** /lɪˈgjuːmɪnəs/ adj

leisure /ˈleʒə/ noun [U] **1** activities that you do in order to relax or enjoy yourself: *My busy schedule leaves little time for leisure.* ♦ **leisure activities 2** the time when you are not working or are not busy: *I'm looking forward to more leisure time in my retirement.*

leisurely /ˈleʒəli/ adj slow and relaxed

ˈleisure ˌtraveller or **ˈleisure ˌvisitor** noun [C] TOURISM someone who is on holiday, not travelling on business

leitmotif or **leitmotiv** /ˈlaɪtməʊˌtiːf/ noun [C] **1** MUSIC a tune that is repeated several times in a piece of music and represents a particular character or situation **2** a word, phrase, or idea that is repeated several times in something such as a speech or book and is important for understanding the speech or book correctly ═ THEME

lemma /ˈlemə/ (plural **lemmas** or **lemmata** /ˈlemətə/) noun [C] LANGUAGE a **headword** in a dictionary

lemon /ˈlemən/ noun [C/U] a fruit with a hard yellow skin and sour juice —*picture* → FRUIT

lemonade /ˌleməˈneɪd/ noun [C/U] a drink that has a lemon flavour, or a glass of this drink

lend /lend/ (**lends, lending, lent** /lent/) verb **1** [T] to give someone something for a short time, expecting that they will give it back to you later: *The local library will lend books for a month without charge.* ♦ *She lent me her coat.* ♦ *Joe lent this car to us for the weekend.* → BORROW **2** [I/T] to give someone money that you expect them to pay back later: *Banks will lend large amounts of money to new businesses.* **3** [T] to give something a particular quality: *The smile lent his face a certain boyish charm.* **4** [T] to give someone support or help: *Patricia is always ready to lend a hand* (=help people).

PHRASE **lend itself to sth** to be suitable for a particular purpose: *The story lends itself to being adapted for film.*

lender /ˈlendə/ noun [C] a person or financial institution that lends money

length /leŋθ/ noun

1 how long in size	5 measure of distance in races
2 how long in time	
3 how long book is	+ PHRASES
4 long thin piece	

1 [C/U] MATHS, SCIENCE a measurement of the distance from one end of something to the other. In a **two-dimensional** shape or a **three-dimensional** object, length is the greatest **dimension**: *The boat was 16 feet in length.* ♦ *He ran half the length of the pitch with the ball.* ♦ *Measure the length of the line.*
2 [C/U] a measurement of how long something takes to do or of how long it lasts: *The length of your talk must be at least 10 minutes.*
3 [C/U] a measurement of how long a book or piece of writing is: *His latest novel is twice the length of his previous one.*
4 [C] a piece of something that is long and thin: *a length of rope*

A concave lens diverges (spreads) light rays.

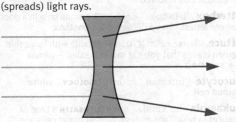

A convex lens converges (brings together) light rays.

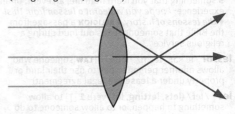

lens: concave and convex lenses

5 [C] SPORTS a measure of how far one car, horse etc is in front of another in a race, usually equal to the length of one car, horse etc

PHRASES **at (great/some) length** for a long time and with a lot of detail: *Austin was questioned at length by detectives.*

go to great/extreme/any etc lengths to try in a very determined way to achieve something: *They have gone to great lengths to make us feel welcome.*

the length and breadth of sth every part of a large area

lengthen /'leŋθ(ə)n/ verb [I/T] to become longer, or to make something longer

lengthways /'leŋθ,weɪz/ or **lengthwise** /'leŋθ,waɪz/ adv in the direction of the longest side of something

lengthy /'leŋθi/ (**lengthier, lengthiest**) adj continuing for a long time, especially for too long: *a lengthy period of negotiation*

lenient /'liːniənt/ adj punishing someone less severely than they deserve —**leniency** noun [U], **leniently** adv

lens /lenz/ noun [C] **1** SCIENCE a thin piece of curved glass or plastic that makes things seem smaller, bigger, or clearer when you look through it. Lenses are used in glasses, microscopes, and cameras: *glasses with thick lenses* —*picture* → CAMERA **2** ANATOMY the part of the eye that is the most important in bending light to produce an image on the retina —*picture* → EYE, RETINA, SHORT-SIGHTED **3** a **contact lens**

lent /lent/ the past tense and past participle of **lend**

Lent /lent/ RELIGION the period of 40 days before Easter, when, for religious reasons, some Christians stop doing or eating something that they enjoy

lenticel /'lentɪsel/ noun [C] BIOLOGY a **pore** (=tiny hole) in the outer layer of a woody plant stem, through which gases pass from inside the stem to the atmosphere, or vice versa

lentil /'lentɪl/ noun [C] a small round flat dried seed that you boil before you eat it

Leo /'liːəʊ/ (plural **Leos**) noun [C/U] one of the 12 signs of the zodiac. A **Leo** is someone who was born between 23 July and 22 August.

leopard /'lepəd/ noun [C] a large wild mammal from Africa and Southern Asia that has yellow fur with black spots —*picture* → MAMMAL

leper /'lepə/ noun [C] HEALTH someone who has leprosy

leprosy /'leprəsi/ noun [U] HEALTH a serious disease that affects the skin, nerves, and bones. In its later stages it can cause loss of fingers and toes and blindness. It can now be successfully treated.

leptospirosis /,leptəʊspaɪˈrəʊsɪs/ noun [U] HEALTH a disease caused by bacteria that affects the kidneys and liver of humans and other mammals

lesbian /'lezbiən/ noun [C] a woman who is sexually attracted to women —**lesbian** adj

lesion /'liːʒ(ə)n/ noun [C] HEALTH **1** an area of damaged skin= WOUND **2** a damaged part of an organ such as the brain or the lungs

less /les/ adv, determiner, pronoun **1** a smaller amount ≠ MORE: *You should eat less and exercise more.* ♦ *The industry operates with less government control these days.* ♦ *I aim to spend **less of** my time travelling.* ♦ *It uses **less** fuel **than** other cars.* **2** to a smaller degree, or not as often ≠ MORE: *We've been trying to use the telephone less this month.* ♦ *This week's homework was less difficult.* ♦ *My husband worries about things less than I do.* **3** used in front of a number or amount to state that it should be taken away from another number or amount that has just been mentioned: *We made £2,000 profit on the deal, less tax.*

PHRASES **less and less** gradually getting smaller in amount or degree: *Fishing was growing less and less profitable.*

the less...the less/more used for saying that when a particular activity, feeling etc is reduced, it causes something else to change at the same time: *Sometimes it seems like the less I do, the more tired I feel.*

> Both **less** and **fewer** can be used to refer to an amount that is smaller than another amount.
> ■ Use **less** before uncountable nouns: *You'll get a smoother finish if you use less paint.*
> ■ Use **fewer** before plural nouns: *Fewer people turned up than expected.*
> ■ In informal English, some people now use **less** rather than **fewer** before plural nouns, although many people think that this is not correct.

less de,veloped 'country noun [C] ECONOMICS a fairly poor country without much industrial development

lessee /le'siː/ noun [C] LAW someone who pays rent to use land or property and has signed a **lease** (=a legal agreement) with the owner

lessen /'les(ə)n/ verb [I/T] to become smaller in amount, level, or importance, or to make something do this

lesser¹ /'lesə/ adj *formal* smaller, less important, or less serious than something else: *She was encouraged by her mother and, **to a lesser extent**, her father.*

PHRASE **the lesser of two evils** the less unpleasant or harmful of two possible choices

lesser² /'lesə/ adv less: *one of the lesser known English poets*

lesson /'les(ə)n/ noun [C] **1** EDUCATION a period of time in which students are taught about a subject in school**=** CLASS: *a maths lesson* **2** a period of time in which someone is taught a skill: *a swimming lesson* **3** something that you learn from life, an event, or an experience: *I hope you've **learnt a lesson** from this!* ♦ *the lessons of history* **4** RELIGION a passage from the Bible that someone reads out loud during a religious service

lessor /le'sɔː, 'lesɔː/ noun [C] LAW someone who allows another person to pay to use their land or property under a **lease** (=a legal agreement)

let¹ /let/ (**lets, letting, let**) verb **1** [T] to allow something to happen, or to allow someone to do something: *Alice's mum won't let her come with us.* ♦ *The large windows let in a lot of light.* **2** [T] used for offering to do something: *Here, let me help you.* **3** [I/T] to rent a room, flat, house etc to someone: *There are three flats **to let** (=available to be rented) in the building.* ♦ *He's let his cottage to some people from London.* **4** [T] MATHS used in mathematics for saying that you are imagining that something is true, usually in order to prove a principle of mathematics

PHRASES **let alone** used for saying that something is even less likely to happen than another unlikely thing: *I hardly have time to think these days, let alone relax.*
let sb go to allow a person or animal to go free = RELEASE: *The police had to let her go because of insufficient evidence.*
let (sb/sth) go to stop holding someone or something: *Let me go!* ♦ *Reluctantly, he **let go** of her arm.*
let sth go/pass to not react to something annoying that someone says: *The remark made me furious, but I let it pass.*
let sb know to tell someone something: *Let us know what time your plane arrives.*
let's used for suggesting that you and one or more other people do something: *Let's eat now.*
→ STEAM¹

PHRASAL VERBS ,let sb 'down to make someone feel disappointed by not doing something that they are expecting you to do: *The families of the victims feel that the justice system has let them down.*
,let sb 'off to give someone little or no punishment for something that they did wrong: *I was pulled over for speeding, but I was let off with a warning.*
,let sb/sth 'out to allow a person or animal to leave a place

let² /let/ noun [C] **1** SPORTS in tennis, a **service** that hits the net and must be played again **2** a period of time in which a house or flat is rented to someone
PHRASE **without let or hindrance** LAW without being prevented from doing something

letdown /'let,daʊn/ noun [singular] something that makes you feel disappointed because it is not as good as you expected

lethal /'liːθ(ə)l/ adj very dangerous and capable of killing someone

lethargic /lə'θɑːdʒɪk/ adj lacking energy and not wanting to do anything

lethargy /'leθədʒi/ noun [U] the feeling of being lethargic

letter /'letə/ noun [C] **1** a piece of paper that you write a message on and send to someone: *Most of the soldiers **wrote** long **letters** home.* ♦ *I **get letters from** them every week.* ♦ *I **sent them a letter** complaining about it.* ♦ *a **letter to** a friend* **2** a symbol used for writing words: *the letter J*
PHRASES **follow/obey sth to the letter** to do something exactly as you are told to do it
letter of agreement BUSINESS a contract in the form

of a letter that has been signed by the people or organizations involved

letterbox /'letə,bɒks/ noun [C] **1** a small hole in a door where letters can be delivered **2** a **postbox**

lettuce /'letɪs/ noun [C/U] a vegetable with large thin green leaves that you eat raw in a salad —*picture* → VEGETABLE

leucocyte /'luːkəsaɪt/ noun [C] BIOLOGY a **white blood cell**

leukaemia /luːˈkiːmiə/ noun [U] HEALTH a type of cancer in which not enough normal blood cells are produced because too many white blood cells that are not normal are produced instead

leukemia /luːˈkiːmiə/ HEALTH the American spelling of **leukaemia**

leukocyte /'luːkəsaɪt/ BIOLOGY another spelling of **leucocyte**

levee /'levi/ noun [C] GEOGRAPHY a wall of soil built along the side of a river to help to prevent it from causing a flood —*picture* → FLOOD PLAIN

level¹ /'lev(ə)l/ noun

1 amount	4 part of system
2 height of sth	5 floor in building
3 standard	6 way of understanding

1 [C] the amount of something that exists at a particular time: *Unemployment is now **at** its **lowest level** for 15 years.* ♦ *Many people have to cope with high **levels of** stress at work.*
2 [C] the height of something in a container or on a surface: *The river is **at** its **highest level** for several years.* ♦ *Check **the level of** fluid in the tank.*
3 [C/U] a standard of academic ability: *This is an excellent book for **advanced level** students.*
4 [C] a part or stage in a system that has several parts or stages: *Decisions should be taken **at** local, not national, **level**.* ♦ *These social changes will affect everyone, **at all levels of** society.*
5 [C/U] one of the floors in a building: *a garage at basement level*
6 [C] a particular way of relating to someone or something: *I get on with Frank very well **on a personal level**, but we just can't work together!*

level² /'lev(ə)l/ adj **1** flat, smooth, and not sloping up or down: *We found a nice level spot for a picnic.* ♦ *Add two **level teaspoons** of salt.* **2** at the same height: *They stood so that their shoulders were level.* ♦ *My head was **level with** George's chin.* **3** next to someone or something, not behind them or further forward than them: *Make sure the edges are level before you glue them together.* ♦ *For most of the race he was **level with** the leader.* **4** equal in a competition: *At half time the two sides were level on 15 points each.* —**levelly** adv

level³ /'lev(ə)l/ (**levels, levelling, levelled**) verb [T] **1** to make something flat: *Level the ground carefully before you lay the paving stones.* **2** to destroy a building or group of buildings **3** to make something equal: *James' goal levelled the score at three all.*

level 'crossing noun [C] a place where a road crosses a railway and gates are used to stop cars when a train is coming

lever¹ /'liːvə/ noun [C] **1** a long handle that you pull or push to operate a machine **2** SCIENCE a solid bar, often made of metal, that you put under a heavy object to move it. A lever is a simple machine that turns on a **fulcrum** (=balance point) to apply the **effort** (=force) in order to move a load. —*picture* → on next page

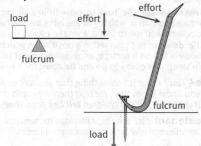

force multiplier

effort

load

effort

fulcrum

fulcrum

load

force multiplier

effort

load

effort

fulcrum

fulcrum

load

distance multiplier

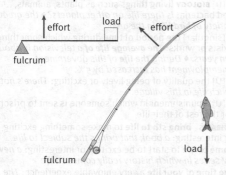

effort

load

effort

fulcrum

load

fulcrum

lever: types of lever

lever² /'liːvə/ verb [T] to move something using a lever

leverage¹ /'liːvərɪdʒ/ noun [U] **1** the power to make someone do what you want **2** PHYSICS the power that a lever provides for moving things

leverage² /'liːvərɪdʒ/ verb [T] BUSINESS to borrow money in order to buy a business, hoping to make enough profit to pay the interest on the loan

leveraged buyout /ˌliːvərɪdʒd 'baɪaʊt/ noun [C] BUSINESS a way of taking control of a company by buying its shares using borrowed money, with the intention of using money from the company to **pay back** the loan

levy¹ /'levi/ (plural **levies**) noun [C] an amount of money that you have to pay, for example as a tax

levy² /'levi/ (**levies, levying, levied**) verb [T] to officially request payment of something such as a tax

lexeme /'leksiːm/ noun [C] LANGUAGE a word or group of words that has a meaning that cannot be understood from the meaning of the parts of which it consists

lexical /'leksɪk(ə)l/ adj LANGUAGE relating to words

lexicology /ˌleksɪ'kɒlədʒi/ noun [U] LANGUAGE the study of the form and meaning of words

lexicon /'leksɪkən/ noun LANGUAGE **the lexicon** all the words and phrases in a language

lexis /'leksɪs/ noun [U] LANGUAGE all the words in a language

liability /ˌlaɪə'bɪləti/ (plural **liabilities**) noun **1** [U] legal responsibility for causing damage or injury, or for paying something **2** [C] someone or something that causes problems for someone

liable /'laɪəb(ə)l/ adj legally responsible for causing damage or injury, so that you have to pay something or be punished: *The hospital was **held liable** for negligence.*

    PHRASES **liable to sth** likely to suffer from something unpleasant: *Many parts of the country are liable to flooding.*
    liable to do sth likely to do something bad or unpleasant: *The handle is liable to break.*

liaison /li'eɪz(ə)n/ noun **1** [singular/U] an exchange of information between people or organizations, so that they understand each other and work well together **2** [C] a secret sexual or romantic relationship between two people

liar /'laɪə/ noun [C] someone who tells lies

libel¹ /'laɪb(ə)l/ noun [C/U] LAW the illegal act of writing bad things that are not true about someone → SLANDER¹

libel² /'laɪb(ə)l/ (**libels, libelling, libelled**) verb [T] LAW to write bad things that are not true about someone → SLANDER²

libellous /'laɪbələs/ adj LAW containing written statements about someone that are not true → SLANDEROUS

liberal¹ /'lɪb(ə)rəl/ adj **1** willing to accept ideas and ways of behaving that are different from your own: *Their views on marriage and divorce are very liberal.* **2** SOCIAL STUDIES believing that people should have social and political freedom, and that they should be allowed to make their own decisions about moral issues: *liberal politicians* **3** giving or consisting of a larger amount than is usual: *There was a liberal supply of food and wine.* —**liberalism** /'lɪb(ə)rəˌlɪz(ə)m/ noun [U], **liberally** adv

liberal² /'lɪb(ə)rəl/ noun [C] someone who has liberal social or political beliefs

liberate /'lɪbəreɪt/ verb [T] **1** to make a place or the people in it free from soldiers who have been controlling it **2** to give someone the freedom to do what they want —**liberation** /ˌlɪbə'reɪʃ(ə)n/ noun [U], **liberator** noun [C]

liberated /'lɪbəreɪtɪd/ adj not accepting traditional ideas or rules about the way you should behave

liberating /'lɪbəreɪtɪŋ/ adj making you feel that you have more freedom to do what you want to do

liberty /'lɪbəti/ noun [U] **1** the freedom to think or behave in the way that you want and not be controlled by anyone else **2** freedom from being kept in prison

    PHRASE **be at liberty to do sth** *formal* to be allowed to do something

libido /lɪ'biːdəʊ/ noun [C/U] *formal* someone's feelings of wanting to have sex

Libra /ˈliːbrə/ noun [C/U] one of the 12 signs of the zodiac. A **Libra** or **Libran** is someone who was born between 23 September and 22 October.

librarian /laɪˈbreəriən/ noun [C] someone who works in a library, or who is in charge of a library

library /ˈlaɪbrəri/ (plural **libraries**) noun [C] **1** a place where books, documents, CDs etc are available for people to look at or borrow: *the school library* **2** a private collection of books, or the room that it is kept in

librettist /lɪˈbretɪst/ noun [C] MUSIC someone who writes the librettos of operas

libretto /lɪˈbretəʊ/ noun [C] MUSIC the words of an opera

lice /laɪs/ noun [plural] small insects that live on people's skin and in their hair. Lice is the plural of **louse**.

licence /ˈlaɪs(ə)ns/ noun **1** [C] an official document that gives you permission to do or use something: *He was charged with possessing a shotgun **without a licence**.* **2** [U] freedom to say or do what you want: *The designers were allowed a lot of creative licence.*

'licence a,greement noun [C] COMPUTING a legal document that comes with a software product and states how you can use the software and how many people are allowed to use it

licensed /ˈlaɪs(ə)nst/ adj **1** a place that is licensed has official permission to sell alcoholic drinks **2** someone who is licensed has official permission to do something, for example to work in a particular job **3** licensed products are products that someone has official permission to use or to own

lichen /ˈlaɪkən, ˈlɪtʃ(ə)n/ (plural **lichens** or **lichen**) noun [C/U] BIOLOGY a grey, green, or yellow organism that grows on surfaces such as trees and walls. It is made of a fungus and an alga living closely together.

lick /lɪk/ verb [I/T] to move the tongue across something: *The boy licked his ice cream.* —**lick** noun [C]

lid /lɪd/ noun [C] **1** a cover for a container: *a saucepan lid* **2** the piece of skin that covers the eye when it is closed = EYELID

lie¹ /laɪ/ (**lies**, **lying**, **lay** /leɪ/, **lain** /leɪn/) verb [I]

1 be/put yourself flat	5 be in a state
2 be on surface	6 say sth untrue
3 be in position	+ PHRASES
4 consist of	+ PHRASAL VERBS

1 to be or put yourself in a position in which your body is flat on a surface such as the floor or a bed: *She was **lying on** the beach reading a book.* ♦ *Emma was **lying on her stomach** on the couch.* → LAY¹
2 to be on a particular surface: *The gun was lying on the ground next to him.*
3 to be in a particular position or place: *The farm lay a few miles to the north.*
4 used for talking about things such as plans, ideas, and qualities and what they consist of: *The difficulty **lies in** knowing what to do next.*
5 if something lies in a particular state, it is in that state: *The castle **lay in** ruins.*
6 (**lies**, **lying**, **lied** /laɪd/) to deliberately say something that is not true: *It was obvious that she was lying.* ♦ *He had to **lie about** his age to get into the army.* ♦ *She admitted **lying to** the police.*
PHRASES **lie ahead** to be going to happen in the future: *A grand future lies ahead of him.*
lie in wait (for sb) to hide so that you can attack someone when they pass you

lie low to hide, or to try to avoid attracting attention to yourself

PHRASAL VERBS **,lie 'back** to move from a sitting position into a position in which you are lying on a surface: *The doctor asked me to lie back on the couch.*
,lie 'down to put yourself in a position in which your body is flat on a surface, especially in order to rest or to sleep: *I'm going to **go and lie down** for a while.*

lie² /laɪ/ noun [C] something that you say or write that you know is not true: *He told them he could drive, but it was a lie.* ♦ *Most children **tell lies** sometimes.*

lieutenant /lefˈtenənt, American luːˈtenənt/ noun [C] an officer of low rank in most armed forces

life /laɪf/ (plural **lives** /laɪvz/) noun

1 time sb is alive	5 time sth lasts
2 way of living	6 activity/excitement
3 state of being alive	7 punishment
4 living things	+ PHRASES

1 [C/U] the period of time from someone's birth until their death: *He had a long and happy life.* ♦ *Don't **spend your** whole **life** worrying about money.* ♦ *She's lived in California **all her life**.* → WORKING LIFE
2 [C/U] your particular way of living and the experiences that you have: *His life revolves around his children.* ♦ *I never liked **city life** (=the experiences people have in a city).* ♦ *The **life of** a film star is not always a glamorous one.* ♦ *I just want to be able to **lead a normal life**.*
3 [C/U] the state of being alive: *He believed his life was in danger.* ♦ *They **risk their lives** to protect the people they love.* ♦ *Thousands of people **lost their lives** (=died) in the earthquake.* ♦ *It was a police officer who **saved her life**.*
4 [U] BIOLOGY living things such as plants, animals, and bacteria: *Is there life on other planets?* ♦ *the great variety of **bird life** in the area*
5 [singular] the period of time during which something exists or works: *The **average life of** a television is about ten years.* ♦ *During **the life of** this government, unemployment has increased by 5%.*
6 [U] the quality of being lively or exciting: *There's not much life in this village.*
7 [U] a punishment in which someone is sent to prison for the rest of their life
PHRASES **bring sth to life** to make something exciting or interesting: *a book that brings the subject to life*
come to life to start to be exciting or interesting: *a new TV series in which history really comes to life*
the time of your life a very enjoyable experience: *The children were having the time of their lives.*
→ LOSE, MATTER¹, REAL LIFE, TRUE

lifebelt /ˈlaɪfbelt/ noun [C] a large rubber ring that you throw to someone to save them when they have fallen into water

lifeboat /ˈlaɪfbəʊt/ noun [C] a small boat that is kept on a ship for emergencies

'life ,coach noun [C] someone who provides advice and support to people who want to improve their lives, helping them to make decisions, solve problems, and achieve their goals

'life ,cycle noun [C] BIOLOGY the series of changes that happen to an organism during its life

'life ,drawing noun ARTS **1** [U] the activity or skill of drawing someone, especially a model in an art class **2** [C] a drawing of someone, especially of a model in an art class

,life ex'pectancy noun [C/U] the length of time that someone is likely to live

lifeguard /ˈlaɪfˌɡɑːd/ noun [C] TOURISM someone whose job is to save swimmers who are in danger

'life in,surance noun [U] a type of insurance that pays money to your family when you die

lifejacket /ˈlaɪfˌdʒækɪt/ noun [C] something you wear on a boat to make you float if you fall into the water

lifeless /ˈlaɪfləs/ adj **1** not interesting or exciting **2** dead, or seeming to be dead **3** without any living or growing things

lifelike /ˈlaɪfˌlaɪk/ adj a lifelike picture, model etc looks real

lifeline /ˈlaɪfˌlaɪn/ noun [C] **1** someone or something that you depend on to help you when you are in a difficult situation **2** a rope that you throw to someone who has fallen into water by accident

lifelong /ˈlaɪfˌlɒŋ/ adj continuing all through your life: *a lifelong friendship*

,lifelong 'learning noun [U] EDUCATION a process of gaining knowledge and skills that continues throughout a person's life

'life ,raft noun [C] a small rubber boat used for saving people whose boat is sinking

'life ,sciences noun [plural] SCIENCE subjects that involve the study of living organisms, for example **botany** and **biology**

,life 'sentence noun [C] a punishment in which someone is sent to prison for the rest of their life, or for a very long time

'life-,size adj a life-size picture, model etc of something is the same size as the real thing

'life ,skills noun [plural] skills that help someone to deal effectively with events and problems in their life

lifespan /ˈlaɪfˌspæn/ noun [C] the length of time that someone lives for, or the length of time that something exists

lifestyle /ˈlaɪfˌstaɪl/ noun [C/U] SOCIAL STUDIES the type of life that someone has, for example the type of things that they own and the type of activities that they do: *a healthy, outdoor lifestyle*

,life sup'port ,system noun [C] **1** HEALTH a set of machines that keep someone alive when they are very ill. It is often simply called **life support. 2** a set of equipment that keeps people alive in space or under water

'life-,threatening adj HEALTH a life-threatening disease or situation is one that could kill someone

lifetime /ˈlaɪfˌtaɪm/ noun [C] **1** the period of time when someone is alive **2** the length of time that something exists or works

lift¹ /lɪft/ verb

1 move sth up	4 of weather
2 improve situation	5 dig up plants
3 officially end rule	+ PHRASAL VERB

1 [T] to move something to a higher position: *Lie on the floor and lift your legs slowly.* ♦ *The phone rang and he lifted the receiver immediately.* ♦ *Always bend your knees when lifting heavy loads.*

2 [T] to improve the situation that someone or something is in, or to make someone feel happier: *economic measures designed to lift the country out of recession* ♦ *Being outdoors can really lift your spirits.*

3 [T] to officially end a rule or law that stopped someone from doing something: *They're hoping to get the ban lifted soon.*

4 [I] if something such as cloud or **fog** lifts, it disappears

5 [T] AGRICULTURE to dig vegetables or other plants out of the ground

PHRASAL VERB ,lift 'off if a space vehicle lifts off, it goes up from the ground into the air

lift² /lɪft/ noun **1** [C] an occasion when someone takes you somewhere in their car: *I can give you a lift into town.* **2** [C] a machine that carries people up and down between different levels of a tall building **3** [C] a movement in which something is lifted **4** [U] PHYSICS the force that makes an aircraft leave the ground and stay in the air

ligament /ˈlɪɡəmənt/ noun [C] ANATOMY a strong band or sheet of tissue inside the body that holds bones together or keeps organs in place —*picture* → JOINT

ligature /ˈlɪɡətʃə/ noun [C] **1** *formal* a piece of rope or string that someone ties around something **2** HEALTH a thread or wire that doctors tie around a blood vessel to stop someone losing blood

light¹ /laɪt/ noun

1 from sun	5 energy able to be seen
2 electrical	6 energy not able to be
3 for traffic	seen
4 for cigarette	+ PHRASES

1 [U] brightness from the sun or from a light, which allows you to see things: *a beam of light* ♦ *The house could be clearly seen by the light of the moon.*

2 [C] a piece of electrical equipment that produces brightness: *Could somebody put the light on?* ♦ *I turned the lights off and shut the door.*

3 [C] one of a set of **traffic lights**: *Turn left at the lights.*

4 [singular] something that is used for lighting a cigarette: *Have you got a light?*

5 [U] SCIENCE a type of electromagnetic radiation that the eye can see and that travels in waves at a speed of nearly 300,000 kilometres a second

6 [U] SCIENCE a type of electromagnetic radiation such as **infrared** light or **ultraviolet** light that travels in waves with lengths longer or shorter than those that the eye can see

PHRASES bring sth to light or **come to light** if facts are brought to light or come to light, people discover them

in a bad/new/different etc light used for talking about someone's opinion of a particular person or thing: *This incident made me see him in a completely different light.*

in (the) light of sth because of a particular fact: *In light of your good record, we've decided to overlook this offence.*

set light to sth to make something start burning

light² /laɪt/ adj

1 bright/well lit	7 not severe
2 not dark	8 gentle
3 pale in colour	9 not serious
4 not weighing much	10 about sleep
5 about clothes	+ PHRASE
6 small/not much	

1 very bright because of light from the sun ≠ DARK: *The room is light and airy.*

2 if it is light, you can see because it is day and not night ≠ DARK: *It gets light around 5 am.*

3 pale in colour, not dark ≠ DARK: *a light blue shirt*

4 not weighing much, or weighing less than you expect ≠ HEAVY: *The table is a lot lighter than it looks.*

5 light clothes are made of thin cloth and are not very warm ≠ HEAVY: *a light summer jacket*

6 not much in quantity: *Traffic was fairly light as we left the city.* ♦ *a light frost* ♦ *light refreshments*

7 a light punishment is not very severe ≠ HARSH: *a light prison sentence*

8 not strong, hard, or loud: *a light breeze* ♦ *a light kiss on the cheek* ♦ *She heard a light knock at the window.* **9** enjoyable and not very serious or difficult: *a little light reading* **10** a light sleep is one from which you wake up easily ≠ HEAVY

PHRASE **make light of sth** to treat something as not being very serious
—**lightness** noun [U]

light³ /laɪt/ (**lights**, **lighting**, **lit** /lɪt/ or **lighted**) verb **1** [I/T] to start to burn, or to make something start to burn: *The fire won't light if the wood is wet.* ♦ *Amy lit a cigarette.* **2** [T] to make a place brighter by giving it light: *The room was lit by candlelight.* ♦ *dimly lit corridors* **3** [T] if you light someone's way, you use a light to lead them through a dark place

,light 'aircraft noun [C] a very small plane

'light ,bulb noun [C] a glass object that you put in an electric light to produce light

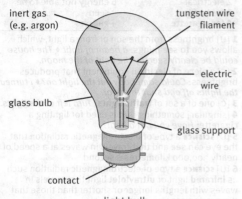

inert gas (e.g. argon)

tungsten wire filament

electric wire

glass bulb

glass support

contact

light bulb

,light-e,mitting 'diode noun [C] PHYSICS an **LED**

lighten /'laɪt(ə)n/ verb **1** [I/T] if a situation or someone's mood lightens, or if something lightens the mood, it becomes more relaxed **2** [I/T] to become brighter or lighter in colour, or to make something brighter or lighter in colour **3** [T] to reduce an amount of work **4** [I/T] to become less heavy, or to make something less heavy

'light ,energy noun [U] PHYSICS energy in the form of light that comes mainly from the Sun

lighter /'laɪtə/ noun [C] a small object that produces a flame, used for lighting cigarettes

light-hearted /,laɪt 'hɑːtɪd/ adj **1** funny and not intended to be serious **2** happy and not worried about anything

lighthouse /'laɪt,haʊs/ (plural **lighthouses** /'laɪt,haʊzɪz/) noun [C] a tower that is built next to the sea with a powerful light that warns ships of danger

,light 'industry noun [U] ECONOMICS industry in which small goods are produced, for example electronic equipment → HEAVY INDUSTRY

lighting /'laɪtɪŋ/ noun [U] light of a particular type or quality, or the equipment that produces it

,lighting 'up ,time noun [U] the time in the evening when lights in the street are put on and drivers must put their car lights on

lightly /'laɪtli/ adv

1 without much force	**4** cooked for a short time
2 without thought	**5** waking up very easily
3 in small amounts	**+** PHRASE

1 without using much force or pressure: *Her hands rested lightly on his shoulders.*
2 without considering something carefully and seriously: *The decision was not taken lightly.*
3 in small amounts, or using only a small amount of something
4 cooked for a short time: *a lightly boiled egg*
5 if you sleep lightly, you wake up very easily
PHRASE **get off/be let off lightly** to not be harmed or punished as severely as you might have been

lightning /'laɪtnɪŋ/ noun [U] GEOGRAPHY the bright flashes of light that appear in the sky during a storm: *The ship was struck by lightning soon after it left the port.* ♦ *She lay awake, listening to the thunder and lightning.*

'light ,pen noun [C] COMPUTING an object shaped like a pen and used for touching a computer screen to give instructions to the computer

'light-,sensitive adj PHYSICS affected by the presence of light

lightweight¹ /'laɪt,weɪt/ adj **1** weighing less than other similar things **2** not serious or important

lightweight² /'laɪt,weɪt/ noun [C] **1** someone who is not important or does not have much influence **2** SPORTS a **boxer** or **wrestler** who belongs to one of the lower weight divisions

'light ,year noun **1** [C] ASTRONOMY, PHYSICS the distance that light travels in a year, used as a unit for measuring distances in space. A light year is almost 9,500,000,000,000 kilometres. **2** [plural] *informal* a very long way in time, distance, or quality: *Her life in Hollywood was light years away from her childhood in the East End of London.*

lignin /'lɪgnɪn/ noun [U] BIOLOGY a chemical compound that makes the walls of plant cells hard and stiff. It is the main substance that wood is made of.

like¹ /laɪk/ conjunction, preposition **1** similar to someone or something else: *No one could play the trumpet like he did.* ♦ *Doesn't he look like Mark?* ♦ *The cloth felt like silk against her skin.* ♦ *Our car is just like yours.* **2** used for introducing an example of someone or something that you have just mentioned: *It eats small animals like birds and mice.* **3** typical of a particular person: *It's not like him to lie.*
PHRASES **like this** *spoken* used when showing someone exactly how to do something: *Click on the 'Mail' icon, like this.*
what is sb/sth like? used for asking or talking about the qualities or features that someone or something has: *I haven't met Alan – what's he like?* ♦ *She took Andrew with her to show him what the club was like.*

like² /laɪk/ verb [T] **1** to think that someone or something is pleasant or attractive: *Do you like my new hairstyle?* ♦ *We like walking along the beach.* ♦ *Which of her novels did you like best?* ♦ *He always liked to sleep late on Sundays.* **2** to prefer to do something in a particular way, or to prefer to have something done in a particular way: *How do you like your eggs?* ♦ *She likes us to hand our work in on time.*
PHRASES **would like** used for stating politely what you want: *I would like a large whisky, please.* ♦ *I'd like to thank everyone who made this evening a success.*
would you like...? used for offering something to someone or for inviting them to do something: *Would*

you like some cake?♦ Would you like me to help you with your homework?

> **Build your vocabulary: words you can use instead of like**
>
> - **adore** (*informal*) to like someone or something very much
> - **be crazy** or **mad about** (*informal*) to like someone or something very much
> - **be fond of** to like someone or something very much
> - **be keen on** to be enthusiastic about a particular person, thing, or activity
> - **enjoy** to like doing a particular activity
> - **love** to like something very much. **Love** is also used for saying that you care about someone very much
> - **prefer** to like one thing more than another

like³ /laɪk/ noun **sb's likes and dislikes** the things that someone likes or does not like

-like /laɪk/ suffix similar to something: *a childlike face* ♦ *The illness causes flu-like symptoms.*

likeable /ˈlaɪkəb(ə)l/ adj pleasant, friendly, and easy to like

likelihood /ˈlaɪklihʊd/ noun [singular/U] the chance that something might happen: *The likelihood of developing cancer is increased in people who smoke.*

likely¹ /ˈlaɪkli/ (**likelier, likeliest**) adj **1** probably going to happen, or probably true ≠ UNLIKELY: *Is anyone likely to see Fran?* ♦ *It seems likely that interest rates will rise.* **2** suitable, or almost certain to be successful ≠ UNLIKELY: *a likely candidate for the job*

likely² /ˈlaɪkli/ adv probably: *They'll quite likely ask you to pay.*

like-minded /ˌlaɪk ˈmaɪndɪd/ adj like-minded people have similar interests and opinions

liken /ˈlaɪkən/   PHRASAL VERB   **'liken sb/sth to sb/sth** *formal* to say that someone or something is similar to someone or something else

likeness /ˈlaɪknəs/ noun **1** [C/U] the quality of being similar to someone or something **2** [C] a picture, model etc of someone that looks just like them

like 'poles noun [plural] PHYSICS a situation in which the positive end of one magnet faces the positive end of another. Like poles **repel** each other (=push each other away).

likewise /ˈlaɪkwaɪz/ adv *formal* in a similar way: *Most fathers want more time with their families. Likewise, kids want to be with their dads more.*

liking /ˈlaɪkɪŋ/ noun [singular] a feeling of enjoying something: *a liking for science subjects*
  PHRASES   **for sb's liking** if something is too expensive, too dark etc for someone's liking, they do not like it because it is too expensive, too dark etc
take a liking to to begin to like someone or something
to sb's liking if something is to someone's liking, they like it

lilac /ˈlaɪlək/ noun [C/U] a small tree with pale purple or white flowers

lilt /lɪlt/ noun [singular] a pleasant rising and falling pattern of sounds in the way that someone talks or in a piece of music —**lilting** adj

lily /ˈlɪli/ (plural **lilies**) noun [C] a large flower in the shape of a bell

lima bean /ˈlaɪmə ˌbiːn, ˈliːmə ˌbiːn/ noun [C] a flat pale green bean

limb /lɪm/ noun [C] an arm or a leg

lime /laɪm/ noun **1** [C/U] a fruit with a hard green skin and sour juice —*picture* → FRUIT **2** [U] AGRICULTURE, CHEMISTRY a white chemical compound that is used for making cement or for reducing the amount of acid in soil. Lime is also called **calcium oxide**.

,lime-'green adj bright yellow-green in colour —**,lime 'green** noun [U]

'lime ,juice noun [C/U] the juice of the **lime**, which contains **citric acid**, or a glass of this juice

limerick /ˈlɪmərɪk/ noun [C] LITERATURE a humorous poem with five lines

limescale /ˈlaɪmˌskeɪl/ noun [U] CHEMISTRY a layer of hard white or grey **calcium carbonate** that forms in pipes and **kettles**

limestone /ˈlaɪmˌstəʊn/ noun [U] GEOLOGY a type of white or grey stone that consists mainly of **calcium carbonate** and is formed from the skeletons and shells of sea animals. Limestone is a sedimentary rock. —*picture* → on next page

,limestone 'pavement noun [C] GEOLOGY a flat block of limestone with deep cracks in it

limewater /ˈlaɪmˌwɔːtə/ noun [U] CHEMISTRY **1** a clear liquid consisting of **calcium hydroxide** and water. It is used to test for carbon dioxide as it stops being clear when carbon dioxide is put through it. **2** water that contains a lot of **calcium carbonate** or **calcium sulphate**

limit¹ /ˈlɪmɪt/ noun [C] **1** the greatest amount or level of something that is possible or allowed: *The speed limit here is forty miles an hour.* ♦ *There is a limit to what we can do in two weeks.* **2** the outer edge of an area: *No bombs landed within the city limits.* **3** limits [plural] TECHNOLOGY the largest and smallest sizes that a hole or **shaft** can have during **manufacturing**
  PHRASE   **off limits 1** if a place is off limits, you are not allowed to go there **2** not allowed or approved of: *Discussion of these subjects is off limits.*

limit² /ˈlɪmɪt/ verb [T] **1** to prevent a number, amount, or effect from increasing past a particular point: *The new laws should limit environmental damage.* ♦ *We want to limit classes to a maximum of 30 pupils.* **2** to reduce or control someone's freedom or ability to be effective ▬ RESTRICT: *They were limited by the amount of money they could spend on the production.* ♦ *Try to limit yourself to one teaspoonful of sugar in tea or coffee.* **3 be limited to** if something is limited to a particular place or group, it happens only in that place or within that group: *The right to vote was limited to men.*

limitation /ˌlɪmɪˈteɪʃ(ə)n/ noun **1** [C/U] a rule or situation that puts a limit on something, or the process of limiting something: *a limitation on the use of cars in the city* **2** limitations [plural] weak points that make someone or something less effective: *There are several limitations to this method.*

limited /ˈlɪmɪtɪd/ adj **1** not allowed to go above a particular number, amount, or level ≠ UNLIMITED: *The promotional pack will be on sale for a limited period only.* **2** not very good, or not very great in amount: *a limited grasp of economics* **3** BUSINESS used after the name of a company for showing that its owners are legally responsible for its debts only up to a specific amount

,limited 'company noun [C] BUSINESS a company whose owners are legally responsible for paying only a limited amount of its debts

,limited lia'bility noun [U] BUSINESS the legal position in which someone is legally responsible for

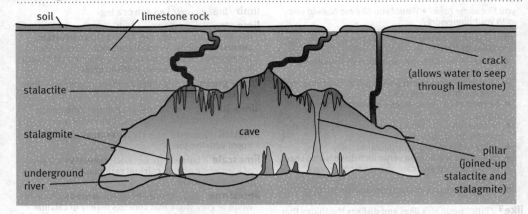

soil
limestone rock
stalactite
stalagmite
cave
underground river
crack (allows water to seep through limestone)
pillar (joined-up stalactite and stalagmite)

limestone cave

paying only a limited amount of the debts of a company they have invested in

limiting /ˈlɪmɪtɪŋ/ adj preventing someone or something from developing or improving

limonite /ˈlaɪmənaɪt/ noun [U] **CHEMISTRY, GEOLOGY** a type of yellowish-brown iron ore that contains about 30 per cent iron

limousine /ˌlɪməˈziːn/ noun [C] a large expensive comfortable car in which a rich or important person travels

limp¹ /lɪmp/ verb [I] to walk with difficulty because of an injured leg or foot —**limp** noun [singular]

limp² /lɪmp/ adj not firm, stiff, or strong —**limply** adv

line¹ /laɪn/ noun

1 long thin mark	9 transport company
2 row of things	10 set of products
3 on sb's skin	11 string/rope/wire
4 imaginary limit	12 direction/path
5 phone connection	13 series of events etc
6 part of railway	14 people waiting
7 way of thinking	+ PHRASES
8 series of words	

1 [C] a long thin mark on the surface of something: *Draw a straight line.* ♦ *It was hard to tell whether the ball had crossed the line.*
2 [C] a row of people or things: *a line of palm trees*
3 [C] a thin mark on someone's skin that appears especially as they get older= WRINKLE
4 [C] an imaginary limit or border between two situations or conditions: *There is a fine line between helping and interfering.*
5 [C] a telephone connection or service: *an advice line* ♦ *It's a very bad line – I'll call you back.*
6 [C] a part of a railway system: *the London to Brighton line*
7 [C] a way of thinking, talking, or finding out about something: *a persuasive line of argument* ♦ *The government is taking a hard line on street crime* (=dealing with it firmly).
8 [C] a series of words in a book, song, play etc: *The actors kept forgetting their lines.* ♦ *a line of poetry*
9 [C] a company that provides a transport service: *a shipping line*
10 [C] **BUSINESS** several products forming a set
11 [C] a piece of string, rope, or wire used for a particular purpose: *a washing line*
12 [C] the direction or path along which someone or something moves or looks: *He was so drunk he couldn't walk in a straight line.*

13 [C] a series of people or events that are connected: *the latest in a long line of scandals*
14 [C/U] a queue of people waiting for something: *We stood in line for an hour.*

PHRASES **along the lines of sth** similar to or based on something: *an ad campaign along the lines of the one we did last year*
along similar/different lines in a way that is similar or different
be in line for sth to be likely to receive something
down the line at a later stage in a process: *The situation will be very different two months down the line.*
line of intersection MATHS, PHYSICS a line used in **orthographic projection** for showing where two three-dimensional objects meet
on line connected to a computer system or to the Internet → ONLINE
on the line 1 at risk: *His job could be on the line if results do not improve.* **2** on the telephone: *We have a caller on the line from Bangkok.*

line² /laɪn/ verb [T] **1** to cover the inside of something with a layer of something else: *Line the dish with aluminium foil.* ♦ *He wore a black coat lined with dark grey silk.* **2** to form rows along the sides of something: *Crowds lined the streets to watch the parade.*

PHRASAL VERB **,line (sb/sth) 'up** to form a row, or to put people or things in a row: *The books are lined up on a shelf above the desk.* ♦ *All children must line up when the whistle goes.*

lineage /ˈlɪniɪdʒ/ noun [C/U] *formal* the people in your family who lived in the past, especially when you come from a rich or important family

linear /ˈlɪniə/ adj *formal* consisting of lines, or of a straight line

lined /laɪnd/ adj **1** clothing that is lined has another layer of cloth on the inside **2** lined skin has a lot of lines on it **3** lined paper has lines printed on it

'line ,graph noun [C] **MATHS** a graph that uses lines to show the relationship between numbers or measurements that change —*picture* → CHART

'line ,management noun [U] **BUSINESS 1** a management system in which each manager or employee is in charge of the person at the next level below them in the company **2** the managers who are responsible for running the main business activity of a company

'line ,manager noun [C] **BUSINESS 1** a manager who is in charge of the work of an employee at the next level below them **2** one of the managers responsible for running the main business activity of a company

linen /'lɪnɪn/ noun [C/U] **1** a cloth like thick cotton that **creases** easily **2** things made of cloth that are used in the house, such as sheets and **tablecloths**

'line-,out noun [C] **SPORTS** in **rugby**, a throw of the ball into the air between lines of players from each team, in order to continue the game after the ball has gone off the field

liner /'laɪnə/ noun [C] **1** a large passenger ship that people travel on for pleasure **2** something that you put inside another thing to keep it clean or protect it: *a bin liner*

linesman /'laɪnzmən/ (plural **linesmen**) noun [C] **SPORTS** someone whose job is to decide whether a ball has gone out of the playing area

linger /'lɪŋgə/ verb [I] **1** to stay somewhere for a long time, or to do something for a long time: *I like to linger over breakfast and read the newspapers.* **2** to continue for a long time: *Doubts still linger about his honesty.*

linguist /'lɪŋgwɪst/ noun [C] **LANGUAGE 1** someone who studies and speaks a lot of languages **2** someone who teaches or studies **linguistics**

linguistic /lɪŋ'gwɪstɪk/ adj **LANGUAGE** relating to languages, words, or linguistics —**linguistically** /lɪŋ'gwɪstɪkli/ adv

linguistics /lɪŋ'gwɪstɪks/ noun [U] **LANGUAGE** the study of language and how it works

lining /'laɪnɪŋ/ noun [C/U] **1** a piece of cloth that is fastened to the inside of something such as clothes or curtains to make them thicker **2** something that you put on the inside of another thing to keep it clean or protect it **3 CONSTRUCTION** a wooden **framework** put inside an internal wall

link¹ /lɪŋk/ verb [T] **1** if people, things, or events are linked, they are related to each other in some way: *Police suspect that the two murder cases are linked.* ♦ *Rock music has often been linked with the drug culture.* **2** to say or show that two things are related, or that one of the things causes the other: *Scientists have linked certain types of cancer to people's diets.* **3** to connect two or more places or things: *Several new roads will link the southern and northern regions of the country.* ♦ *Link the supply cable to the fitting at the rear of the machine.*

PHRASAL VERB ,link (sb/sth) 'up to make a connection between two or more things: *The space shuttle will link up with the space station this afternoon.*

link² /lɪŋk/ noun [C] **1** a connection or relationship between two or more people or things: *They are studying the links between carbon emissions and climate change.* ♦ *They were thought to have links with a terrorist group.* **2** a means of travel or communication that connects two or more places: *a rail link between Edinburgh and London* **3 COMPUTING** a connection between one Internet file or section and another, for example on a website: *Click on this link to find out more.* → HYPERLINK **4** one of the rings that are connected to each other to form a chain

linkage /'lɪŋkɪdʒ/ noun **1** [C/U] a policy of connecting two or more issues by making agreement on one issue depend on agreement on another issue **2** [C/U] a connection made between two or more things **3** [C] a physical connection, or a system of connections

linking verb /'lɪŋkɪŋ ,vɜ:b/ noun [C] **LANGUAGE** a verb such as 'be' or 'seem' that connects the subject of a sentence with its **complement** (=the part of the sentence that describes the subject)

'link ,rot noun [U] **COMPUTING** a situation in which **links** on websites do not work

'link-up noun [C] **1** a connection between machines or electronic equipment **2** an agreement between two companies to work together or to become business partners

Linnaean /lɪ'ni:ən/ adj **SCIENCE** relating to the scientific system invented by Carolus Linnaeus for giving names to plants and animals, and for putting them into particular groups according to the features that they have

linoleum /lɪ'nəʊliəm/ or **lino** /'laɪnəʊ/ noun [U] a hard flat substance with a shiny surface, used for covering floors

linseed oil /,lɪnsi:d 'ɔɪl/ noun [U] an oil from the seed of a **flax** plant that is used in making things such as paint and ink

lintel /'lɪnt(ə)l/ noun [C] **CONSTRUCTION** a **beam** that goes across the top of a door or window to support the weight of the wall above

Linux /'lɪnʌks/ noun **TRADEMARK COMPUTING** a type of computer **operating system** (=the main program in a computer that manages all the other programs) that is available free on the Internet

lion /'laɪən/ noun [C] a large African wild cat with yellow fur —*picture* → MAMMAL

lioness /'laɪənes/ noun [C] a female lion —*picture* → MAMMAL

lip /lɪp/ noun [C] **1** one of the two edges that form the top and bottom parts of the mouth —*picture* → BODY **2** the place on the edge of a glass or container where you pour out liquid

lipase /'laɪpeɪs/ noun [U] **BIOLOGY** an enzyme in the pancreas. It helps the body to turn lipids into **fatty acids** and **glycerol**.

'lip-,blown adj **MUSIC** a lip-blown musical instrument is one in which air is made to vibrate when the player vibrates their lips and blows into a mouthpiece. The **trumpet** is a lip-blown instrument.

lipid /'lɪpɪd/ noun [C] **BIOLOGY** a chemical compound in organisms, mainly in the form of fats and oils

liposome /'laɪpəʊ,səʊm/ noun [C] **BIOLOGY** a very small artificial **sac** made of **fatty acids**. It is used in medicine to carry a drug or enzyme to particular cells in the body. —*picture* → CELL

lip-read /'lɪp ,ri:d/ (**lip-reads, lip-reading, lip-read**) verb [I] to look at someone's lips in order to understand what they are saying because you cannot hear them

liquefaction /,lɪkwɪ'fækʃ(ə)n/ noun [U] **CHEMISTRY** the process of becoming a liquid, or making something become a liquid

liquefied petroleum gas /,lɪkwɪfaɪd pə'trəʊliəm ,gæs/ noun [U] **CHEMISTRY** LPG

liquid¹ /'lɪkwɪd/ noun **1** [C/U] **SCIENCE** one of the three forms of matter that has a fixed volume but a changing shape and can also flow. Water is a liquid: *a glass of colourless liquid* → GAS, SOLID¹ sense 1 —*picture* → STATE **2** [C] **LANGUAGE** the sound 'l' or 'r'

liquid² /'lɪkwɪd/ adj **1 SCIENCE** in the form of a liquid: *liquid detergent* **2 BUSINESS** easy to sell in order to get cash

,liquid 'assets noun [plural] **BUSINESS** the money that a company has, and anything else that can easily be exchanged for money

liquidate /'lɪkwɪdeɪt/ verb [I/T] **BUSINESS** to close a business and sell all its **assets** (=things that it owns), usually in order to pay its debts —**liquidation** /,lɪkwɪ'deɪʃ(ə)n/ noun [U]

'liquid crystal ther,mometer noun [C] SCIENCE a piece of equipment for measuring temperature that consists of a piece of plastic containing liquid crystals. Different coloured crystals become visible at different temperatures.

liquidity /lɪˈkwɪdəti/ noun [U] BUSINESS a situation in which a business has money or property that it can sell in order to pay its debts

,liquid 'nitrogen noun [U] CHEMISTRY the element nitrogen in liquid form. It can be used to freeze things.

liquor /ˈlɪkə/ noun [U] *American* strong alcoholic drinks

liquorice /ˈlɪkərɪs, ˈlɪkərɪʃ/ noun [U] a black substance with a strong flavour, used for making sweets and medicines

lisp /lɪsp/ noun [singular] if someone has a lisp, they pronounce 's' sounds as 'th' —**lisp** verb [I/T]

list¹ /lɪst/ noun [C] **1** a set of names, numbers etc that are written or printed one below another: *I'd better make a list, or I'll forget who I've invited.* ♦ *I couldn't see my name on the list.* ♦ *a list of the world's richest people* **2** a set of things that you put in a particular order in your mind, according to how important they are: *Decorating the house is high on our list of things to do.*

list² /lɪst/ verb **1** [T] to mention or write things one after another: *The ingredients in food must be listed on the packet.* ♦ *Chris lists his hobbies as cycling, gardening, and chess.* **2** [T] if a telephone number is listed, it is published in a book **3** [I] if a ship lists, it leans to one side

listen /ˈlɪs(ə)n/ verb [I] **1** to pay attention to a sound, or to try to hear a sound: *Do you like listening to music?* ♦ *Listen carefully to the instructions.* ♦ *She was listening for the sound of his key in the lock.* → HEAR **2** to pay attention to what someone tells you and do what they suggest: *I've tried to give Jerry advice, but he just won't listen.* ♦ *Don't listen to him – he doesn't know anything about it.*

   PHRASAL VERB **,listen 'in** to secretly listen to what someone says = EAVESDROP: *Rachel was listening in on our conversation.*

listener /ˈlɪs(ə)nə/ noun [C] **1** someone who listens to the radio, or to a particular radio programme or radio station **2** someone who listens to a person speaking

listing /ˈlɪstɪŋ/ noun **1** [C] a list, or a position on a list **2** **listings** [plural] a list of things such as films, plays, and exhibitions printed in a newspaper

listless /ˈlɪstləs/ adj feeling as if you have no energy and no interest in anything

listserv /ˈlɪst,sɜːv/ TRADEMARK COMPUTING a piece of software that automatically sends a copy of every email received to all members of a group

lit /lɪt/ a past tense and past participle of **light³**

litany /ˈlɪtəni/ noun [C] **1** a long, usually boring, list of things that someone talks or writes about **2** RELIGION a series of prayers in a religious service, usually with a priest saying some parts and the people saying other parts

lite /laɪt/ adj a spelling of 'light' that is often used in the names of foods and drinks that contain less sugar, fat, or alcohol than usual

literacy /ˈlɪt(ə)rəsi/ noun [U] EDUCATION the ability to read and write

literal /ˈlɪt(ə)rəl/ adj **1** the literal meaning of a word is its most basic meaning → FIGURATIVE **2** a literal translation is one in which each word is translated separately in a way that does not sound natural

literally /ˈlɪt(ə)rəli/ adv **1** used for showing that what you are saying is really true: *Now there are literally thousands of companies using our software.* **2** used when you are describing something in an extreme way that cannot be true: *When I told him the news he literally exploded.* **3** in the most basic, obvious meanings of the words that are used: *There's an Italian dessert called tiramisu, which literally means 'pull me up'.* **4** if you translate something literally, you translate each word separately in a way that does not sound natural

literary /ˈlɪt(ə)rəri/ adj LITERATURE **1** relating to literature **2** typical of words that are used only in stories or poems, and not in normal writing or speech

'literary ,agent noun [C] someone whose job is to help a writer to sell his or her work

literate /ˈlɪt(ə)rət/ adj **1** EDUCATION able to read and write ≠ ILLITERATE **2** having a good understanding of a particular subject

literature /ˈlɪtrətʃə/ noun [U] **1** LITERATURE stories, poems, and plays, especially those that are considered to have value as art: *She is studying German literature.* **2** books or other printed information about a subject: *Police discovered racist literature in his home.*

lithe /laɪð/ adj moving and bending in a graceful way

lithified /ˈlɪθɪfaɪd/ adj GEOLOGY changed from loose stones, sand, dirt etc into solid rock

lithium /ˈlɪθiəm/ noun [U] **1** CHEMISTRY a very soft, silver-white metal element that is lighter than all other metals. Chemical symbol: Li **2** HEALTH a drug based on the metal lithium that is used to treat some mental illnesses

lithography /lɪˈθɒɡrəfi/ noun [U] ARTS a method of printing pictures that uses flat metal or stone surfaces, parts of which are covered with ink —**lithographic** /ˌlɪθəˈɡræfɪk/ adj

the lithosphere /ˈlɪθəˌsfɪə/ noun [singular] GEOLOGY the solid outer layer of the Earth, consisting of the **crust** and the upper part of the **mantle** —**lithospheric** /ˌlɪθəˈsferɪk/ adj

litigant /ˈlɪtɪɡənt/ noun [C] LAW someone who is involved in a disagreement that is being examined in a court of law

litigate /ˈlɪtɪɡeɪt/ verb [I] LAW to ask a court of law to make a decision about a disagreement

litigation /ˌlɪtɪˈɡeɪʃ(ə)n/ noun [U] LAW use of the legal system to settle a disagreement

litmus /ˈlɪtməs/ noun [U] CHEMISTRY a substance like a powder obtained from **lichens**. Litmus is an **indicator** used to show whether something is an acid or an alkali, turning red in an acid solution and blue in an alkaline solution.

'litmus ,paper noun [U] CHEMISTRY paper that contains litmus, used for testing whether something is an acid or an alkali

'litmus ,test noun [C] CHEMISTRY a test of a chemical substance using litmus paper

litre /ˈliːtə/ noun [C] **1** SCIENCE a unit for measuring an amount of liquid or gas in the metric system, containing 1,000 millilitres. Symbol l **2** ENGINEERING a unit for measuring the size of a vehicle's engine

litter¹ /ˈlɪtə/ noun **1** [U] things that people have dropped on the ground in a public place, making it untidy **2** [C] a group of baby cats, dogs, or other mammals that are born at the same time

litter² /ˈlɪtə/ verb [T] **1** be littered with if a place is littered with things, they are spread around there: *The room was littered with books and papers.* **2** be littered

with if something is littered with things, there are many of them in it: *The book is **littered with** quotations from the Bible.*

little[1] /'lɪt(ə)l/ (**less** /les/, **least** /liːst/) adv, determiner, pronoun **1** an extremely small amount of something: *They made little effort to explain.* ♦ *Little has been revealed about his background.* ♦ *There was too much rain and **too little** sun.* ♦ *The company **did little** to prevent the disaster.* **2** not very often, or only to a small degree: *In her last years I saw her **very little**.* ♦ *They spoke of him **as little as possible**.* ♦ *a **little known** fact* (=not known by many people)

PHRASES **a little 1** a small amount: *We managed to save a little money.* ♦ *Mix in **a little of** the flour.* ♦ *I have **a little more** patience than you.* **2** to a small degree: *I held her **a little** closer.* ♦ *This may be **a little bit** painful.* **3** for a short time: *You should rest **a little**.*

little by little very gradually: *Little by little his eyes adjusted to the light.*

> **Little** and **a little** are both used for talking about a small amount of something. But they have slightly different meanings.
> - **Little** means 'not much' or 'not enough', and is used when you would like there to be more of something: *There is little hope of finding survivors.* ♦ *There has been little change since this morning.*
> - **A little** means 'some', and is used for emphasizing that an amount is small, but larger than you might expect: *There is still a little time to finish the game.* ♦ *I had a little money left so I took a taxi.*

little[2] /'lɪt(ə)l/ adj **1** small in size or number: *Use the little pan for making the sauce.* ♦ *a **tiny little** garden* → SMALL **2** young, and often small ≠ BIG: *a little girl* ♦ *Things were different when I was little.* ♦ *Is this your **little brother**?* (=younger brother) **3** short in time or distance: *Molly carried me a little way towards the house.* ♦ *I'll be with you in **a little while**.* **4** not important = MINOR: *little details*

,little 'finger noun [C] the smallest finger on the hand —*picture* → BODY

liturgy /'lɪtədʒi/ noun [C/U] **RELIGION** the way religious ceremonies are performed in church, including the words that the priest uses

live[1] /lɪv/ verb **1** [I] to have your home in a particular place: *Paris is a nice place to live.* ♦ *They **lived in** a flat in South London.* ♦ *Do you still **live at home** (=in your parents' home)?* **2** [I/T] to have a particular kind of life: *Food is inexpensive here, so you can live quite cheaply.* ♦ *people **living in** poverty* ♦ *Millions of families are living on benefits.* ♦ *Now they have retired and want to **live a quiet life**.* **3** [I] to be alive, or to stay alive: *Aunt Joan **lived to be** 86.* ♦ *Socrates **lived in** the fifth century BC.* **4** [I] to have an interesting and exciting life: *Come on, you have to **live a little!***

PHRASAL VERBS **,live sth 'down** to make people forget about something embarrassing or silly that you have done: *I'm never going to live this down!*

'live for sb/sth to think that someone or something is so important that they are your main reason for living: *She lives for her work.*

'live off sb/sth to depend on someone or something for the money or food that you need: *He's 25 and still living off his parents.*

'live on sth 1 to have a particular amount of money to buy the things that you need to live: *They have to live on a pension of £250 a month.* **2** to eat a particular kind of food: *These fish live on small sea creatures such as shrimp.*

'live through sth to experience a dangerous or unpleasant situation and still be alive after it

,live 'up to sth to be as good as what was expected or promised: *The beautiful scenery certainly lived up to expectations.*

'live with sth to accept something unpleasant that you cannot change: *How does she live with the guilt?*

live[2] /laɪv/ adj

1 living	4 with electricity
2 broadcast	5 bullets
3 performance	6 important subject

1 living and not dead: *The law deals with the transport of live animals.*
2 a live television or radio programme shows something that is happening at the same time as you are watching it or listening to it
3 a live performance is given in front of an audience: *We found a bar that has **live music** on Friday nights.*
4 a live wire or piece of equipment is connected to the electricity supply and has electricity going through it —*picture* → PLUG
5 live bullets or **ammunition** are real, rather than **blanks** or rubber or plastic bullets
6 a live issue continues to be important and relevant

live[3] /laɪv/ adv **1** if something is broadcast live, it is happening at the same time as you are watching it or listening to it **2** if something is performed live, it is performed in front of an audience

livelihood /'laɪvlihʊd/ noun [C/U] something such as your work that provides the money that you need to live

live load /,laɪv 'ləʊd/ noun [C] **CONSTRUCTION** the weight of the people, furniture, and machines in a building

lively /'laɪvli/ (**livelier, liveliest**) adj **1** full of energy and enthusiasm: *a lively debate* **2** full of people: *lively bars and restaurants*

liver /'lɪvə/ noun **1** [C] **ANATOMY** an organ in the body that changes **toxins** such as alcohol into less harmful substances, and produces **bile, urea**, and **cholesterol**. The liver controls the level of glucose and **amino acids** in the blood, and stores some important vitamins and minerals: *Excessive drinking can lead to liver failure.* —*picture* → CIRCULATION, DIGESTIVE SYSTEM, ORGAN **2** [C/U] the liver of some animals eaten as food

liverwort /'lɪvə,wɜːt/ noun [C/U] **BIOLOGY** a small green plant without stems or leaves that carries out photosynthesis. It grows on damp surfaces.

livery /'lɪvəri/ noun [C/U] a special old-fashioned type of uniform that some people wear for their job

lives /laɪvz/ the plural of **life**

livestock /'laɪv,stɒk/ noun [plural] **AGRICULTURE** animals such as cows, sheep, and pigs that are kept on farms

live wire /,laɪv 'waɪə/ noun [C] **PHYSICS** a wire through which electricity passes

living[1] /'lɪvɪŋ/ adj **1** alive at the present time: *He has no **living relatives**.* **2** living things are animals or plants that are alive, rather than objects such as rocks

PHRASE **in living memory** during the time that anyone still alive can remember: *the worst storm in living memory*

living[2] /'lɪvɪŋ/ noun **1** [singular] money that you earn to live on: *Do you know what she does **for a living** (=does as a job)?* ♦ *She makes a living as a music teacher.* **2** [U] a particular type of life: *the stresses of modern living*

'living ,room noun [C] the main room in a house where you usually relax in comfortable chairs = SITTING ROOM, LOUNGE

lizard /ˈlɪzəd/ noun [C] a small reptile with a long tail that lives mainly in hot places —*picture* → REPTILE

llama /ˈlɑːmə/ noun [C] a large South American mammal with a long neck and a thick coat

load¹ /ləʊd/ noun

1 sth carried	**4** weight sth bears
2 amount of work	**5** weight sth moves
3 amount of clothes	**+ PHRASE**

1 [C] something that a person, animal, or vehicle carries: *a lorry carrying **a load of** wood*
2 [C] an amount of work that a person, piece of equipment, or system has to do at one time
= WORKLOAD: *Teaching loads have increased this year.*
3 [C] a quantity of clothes that you put in a washing machine
4 [singular] PHYSICS the amount of weight or pressure that something has to bear
5 [singular] PHYSICS the weight moved by a machine of any type —*picture* → LEVER
PHRASE **a load of/loads of sth** *informal* a lot of something: *I've got loads of things to do today.*

load² /ləʊd/ verb **1** [I/T] to put a load onto or into something such as a vehicle or container ≠ UNLOAD: *Down at the docks, ships were loading and unloading.* **2** [T] to put something into a piece of equipment so that it is ready to use: *Did you **load the dishwasher**?* ♦ *My camera is **loaded with** a colour film.* **3** [T] to put bullets into a gun **4** [I/T] COMPUTING to put information or a program into a computer
PHRASAL VERB ˌload (sth) ˈup *same as* **load²** sense 1: *The trucks were being loaded up and driven away.*

ˈload-ˌbearing adj ENGINEERING, CONSTRUCTION strong enough to support part of a structure

loaded /ˈləʊdɪd/ adj **1** carrying a load: *a truck **loaded** with fruit* **2** having a large amount of a particular thing or quality: *mass-produced cakes that are **loaded with** fat and sugar* **3** a loaded gun has bullets in it **4** a loaded question, word, statement etc has a hidden or second meaning

ˈload-sensing ˌvalve noun [C] ENGINEERING a part of a vehicle's braking system that changes the braking pressure, depending on the weight the vehicle is carrying

loaf /ləʊf/ (plural **loaves** /ləʊvz/) noun [C] an amount of bread in a long, round, or square shape that you cut into **slices** for eating

loam /ləʊm/ noun [U] AGRICULTURE a type of soil that is extremely good for plants to grow in. It is a mixture of sand, **silt**, **clay**, and **humus**.

loan¹ /ləʊn/ noun **1** [C] an amount of money that a person, business, or country borrows, especially from a bank: *How soon do you have to **pay off the loan**?* ♦ *Jim took out a loan to pay for his car.* **2** [singular] a situation in which someone lends something to someone: *He had accepted Tom's offer of **the loan of** his cottage.*
PHRASE **on loan** if something is on loan, someone has borrowed it: *That book is already **out on loan**.* ♦ *These paintings are **on loan from** the Guggenheim Museum in Bilbao.*

loan² /ləʊn/ verb [T] to lend something to someone

ˈloan transˌlation noun [C] LANGUAGE a word or expression used in a language that has been translated from another language

loanword /ˈləʊnˌwɜːd/ noun [C] LANGUAGE a word from one language that is used in another language without being changed

loath /ləʊθ/ adj *formal* very unwilling to do something = RELUCTANT

loathe /ləʊð/ verb [T] to dislike someone or something very much= DETEST —**loathing** noun [U]

loaves /ləʊvz/ the plural of **loaf**

lob /lɒb/ (**lobs, lobbing, lobbed**) verb [T] **1** to throw, hit, or kick something so that it goes high into the air **2** SPORTS to hit or kick a ball high into the air and usually over the head of another player —**lob** noun [C]

lobby /ˈlɒbi/ (plural **lobbies**) noun [C] **1** an organized group of people who try to influence politicians **2** the area just inside the entrance to a hotel, theatre, or other large building= FOYER

lobe /ləʊb/ noun [C] **1** a round part of something, especially a part of a leaf or a large section of the brain **2** the **earlobe**

lobola /ləˈbəʊlə/ noun [U] among some South African peoples, a payment given to a woman's father in return for permission to marry her

lobster /ˈlɒbstə/ noun [C/U] a large sea crustacean with a long body and eight legs, or the meat from this fish —*picture* → SEA

local¹ /ˈləʊk(ə)l/ adj **1** in or related to a particular area, especially the place where you live: *Ask for the book in your local library.* ♦ *Local calls cost 2p a minute.* **2** HEALTH affecting only a small area of the body: *a local infection*

local² /ˈləʊk(ə)l/ noun [C] someone who lives in a particular place

ˌlocal anaesˈthetic noun [C/U] HEALTH a drug that is given to someone to stop them feeling pain in one part of their body → GENERAL ANAESTHETIC

ˌlocal ˌarea ˈnetwork noun [C] COMPUTING *see* LAN

locale /ləʊˈkɑːl/ noun [C] *formal* **1** the place where something happens **2** the place where the story of a book, film etc is set

ˌlocal ˈgovernment noun [U] the organizations that provide public services in a particular town or area and that are controlled by officials chosen in local elections

locality /ləʊˈkæləti/ (plural **localities**) noun [C] *formal* a particular area or district

localization /ˌləʊkəlaɪˈzeɪʃ(ə)n/ noun [U] BUSINESS the process of carrying out an activity only in a particular area of the world, or the process of changing it to make it suitable for a particular area of the world

localized /ˈləʊkəlaɪzd/ adj *formal* existing only in a particular area

locally /ˈləʊk(ə)li/ adv in the area where you live or that you are talking about

ˈlocal ˌtime noun [U] the time in a particular part of the world

locate /ləʊˈkeɪt/ verb [T] **1** to find out the exact place where someone or something is: *Engineers are still trying to locate the fault.* **2** to build or establish something in a particular place: *The company wants to locate the factory near the railway.*
PHRASE **be located** to exist in a particular place: *The centre is **conveniently located** close to many historical sites.* ♦ *The hotel is **located in** Wolverhampton town centre.*

location /ləʊˈkeɪʃ(ə)n/ noun **1** [C] the place or position where someone or something is, or where something happens: *The talks are taking place at a secret location.* **2** [C/U] a place where a film or television programme is made, away from a **studio**: *a thriller filmed entirely **on location***

locative /'lɒkətɪv/ noun [C/U] LANGUAGE the form of a noun, pronoun, or adjective that you use in some languages when you are talking about where someone or something is —**locative** adj

lock¹ /lɒk/ verb **1** [I/T] to fasten something such as a door with a key, or to be fastened with a key ≠ UNLOCK: *Have you locked the car?* ♦ *This drawer won't lock.* ♦ *She locked the documents in the safe.* **2** [I/T] to become fixed in one position, or to fix something in one position: *The brakes locked and the car spun off the road.* ♦ *He locked his arms around her waist.* **3** [T] COMPUTING to prevent information on a computer from being changed or looked at by someone who does not have permission

PHRASE **locked in debate/a dispute etc** involved in a discussion or argument that lasts a long time: *The two sides were locked in fierce debate.*

PHRASAL VERBS **,lock sb 'out** to prevent someone from coming into a room or building by locking the door: *I've locked myself out again – could I use your phone?* **,lock (sth) 'up** to lock all the doors and windows of a building: *I locked up and went to bed.*

lock² /lɒk/ noun [C]

1 for preventing opening	5 group of hairs
2 for preventing use	6 in rugby
3 gates on river/canal	+ PHRASE
4 in computing	

1 the thing that is used for fastening a door, drawer etc so that no one can open it: *All the windows were **fitted with locks**.*
2 a piece of equipment used for preventing someone from using a vehicle, machine etc: *a bicycle lock*
3 a place on a river or canal that allows boats to move to a higher or lower water level
4 COMPUTING something that prevents information on a computer from being changed or looked at by someone who does not have permission
5 a small piece of hair on your head: *She cut off a lock of his hair.*
6 SPORTS in **rugby**, a player in the second row of the **scrum**

PHRASE **under lock and key** in a room or container that is fastened with a lock

locker /'lɒkə/ noun [C] a cupboard that you store clothes, books, and other personal things in, for example at school

locket /'lɒkɪt/ noun [C] a piece of jewellery that consists of a very small case that you wear round your neck on a chain

lockjaw /'lɒk,dʒɔː/ noun [U] HEALTH the disease **tetanus**

locknut /'lɒk,nʌt/ noun [C] TECHNOLOGY a **nut** that is screwed on top of another nut, in order to prevent it from becoming loose

locomotion /,ləʊkə'məʊʃ(ə)n/ noun [U] **1** the way that something such as an animal or a vehicle moves **2** BIOLOGY the ability of an organism to move from place to place —**locomote** verb [I]

locomotive¹ /,ləʊkə'məʊtɪv/ noun [C] the vehicle that pulls a train= ENGINE

locomotive² /,ləʊkə'məʊtɪv/ adj BIOLOGY involving movement, or making something move

locomotor /,ləʊkə'məʊtə/ adj BIOLOGY relating to **locomotion** (=ability to move from place to place)

locus /'ləʊkəs/ (plural **loci** /'ləʊsaɪ/) noun [C] MATHS the set of points described by a particular mathematical rule or equation

locust /'ləʊkəst/ noun [C] AGRICULTURE a type of **grasshopper** that flies in very large groups and can cause a lot of damage to crops

lodge¹ /lɒdʒ/ verb **1** [T] to formally make something such as a complaint or claim: *She **lodged a complaint** with the city council.* **2** [I/T] to become firmly fixed somewhere, usually accidentally: *A piece of meat lodged in his throat.* **3** [I] to pay to live in someone else's house

lodge² /lɒdʒ/ noun [C] a small house in the countryside that people stay in, for example when they go hunting or fishing

lodger /'lɒdʒə/ noun [C] someone who pays to live in a house with the person who owns it

lodging /'lɒdʒɪŋ/ noun [C/U] a place that you pay to live in for a short time

lodgings /'lɒdʒɪŋz/ noun [plural] a room or set of rooms in someone's house that you pay to live in

loess /'ləʊɪs, lɜːs/ noun [U] GEOLOGY very small pieces of yellow, brown, or grey soil blown to a place and left there by the wind, especially in China

loft¹ /lɒft/ noun [C] a room or space under the roof of a building

loft² /lɒft/ verb [T] SPORTS to hit a ball high into the air, especially in golf

log¹ /lɒg/ noun [C] **1** a thick piece of wood that has been cut from a tree **2** an official written record of things that happen, especially on a ship or a plane

log² /lɒg/ (**logs, logging, logged**) verb **1** [T] to make an official written record of things that happen **2** [T] to travel for a particular number of hours or miles **3** [I/T] to cut down trees in an area to get wood

PHRASAL VERBS **,log 'off** or **,log 'out** COMPUTING to finish using a computer system ≠ LOG ON
,log 'on or **,log 'in** COMPUTING to start using a computer system, for example by typing a **password** ≠ LOG OFF

logarithm /'lɒgərɪð(ə)m/ noun [C] MATHS the number of times a base number must be multiplied by itself in order to produce a particular number

'log ,book noun [C] **1** an official document giving details of a vehicle and its owner **2** a book containing the official record of a journey on a ship or in a plane

logging /'lɒgɪŋ/ noun [U] AGRICULTURE, ENVIRONMENT the act of cutting down trees for wood, usually in order to sell it at a profit: *Illegal logging has led to widespread deforestation.*

logic /'lɒdʒɪk/ noun [U] **1** the way that someone connects ideas when they are explaining something or giving a reason **2** the study of the way that ideas can be connected and used to explain things

logical /'lɒdʒɪk(ə)l/ adj sensible and reasonable ≠ ILLOGICAL: *a logical argument* ♦ *It seems like the most logical solution to the problem.* —**logically** /'lɒdʒɪkli/ adv: *She presented her ideas clearly and logically.*

'logic ,gate noun [C] PHYSICS an electronic circuit that applies a **Boolean operator** to one or more **inputs** and produces an **output**

login /'lɒgɪn/ noun [C/U] COMPUTING the process of performing the necessary actions to start using a computer program or system ≠ LOGOFF

logistics /lə'dʒɪstɪks/ noun [plural] the practical arrangements that are necessary in order to organize something successfully —**logistical** adj, **logistic** adj

lo'gistics ,management noun [U] BUSINESS management of the activity of transporting goods to customers, or to places where they are bought or sold

logjam /ˈlɒɡˌdʒæm/ noun [C] a situation in which one problem is stopping anything else from being done

logo /ˈləʊɡəʊ/ (plural **logos**) noun [C] a symbol that represents an organization or company

LOGO or **Logo** /ˈləʊɡəʊ/ noun [U] COMPUTING a computer language used for creating images and designs

logoff /ˈlɒɡɒf/ noun [U] COMPUTING the process of finishing using a computer program or system ≠ LOGIN, LOGON

logon /ˈlɒɡɒn/ noun [U] COMPUTING [C/U] the process of performing the necessary actions to open a computer program or start using a computer system

logotype /ˈlɒɡəʊˌtaɪp/ noun [C] a **logo**

loll /lɒl/ verb [I] **1** to sit, stand, or lie in a relaxed position **2** if your tongue or your head lolls, it hangs down in an uncontrolled way

lone /ləʊn/ adj **1** single, or alone **2** without a husband, wife, or partner: *lone parents*

lonely /ˈləʊnli/ (**lonelier, loneliest**) adj **1** unhappy because you are alone or have no friends: *a lonely childhood* ♦ *She must **feel** desperately **lonely** with all her family in Scotland.* **2** a lonely place is far from where people live or go= REMOTE: *a lonely stretch of country road* —**loneliness** noun [U]

loner /ˈləʊnə/ noun [C] someone who likes to be alone

long¹ /lɒŋ/ adj

1 lasting a long time	**5** of document
2 not short	**6** of clothes
3 for measuring	**7** about vowel
4 seeming long	**+ PHRASES**

1 lasting for a large amount of time ≠ SHORT: *He has a long history of mental illness.* ♦ *It's **a long time** since I saw Rachel.*
2 measuring a large amount from one end to the other ≠ SHORT: *It's the longest tunnel in Europe.* ♦ *There was **a long queue** outside the bank.* ♦ *a woman with **long** blonde **hair***
3 used for saying how long something lasts, or how long something is from one end to the other: *The room was 3 metres long.* ♦ *How long was the film?*
4 seeming to last for a very long time because you are bored or tired: *It had been a long week.*
5 a long book, letter, report etc has a lot of pages ≠ SHORT
6 long dresses, trousers, sleeves etc cover your arms or legs ≠ SHORT: *a shirt with **long sleeves***
7 LANGUAGE a long vowel is pronounced for a longer time than most other vowels

PHRASES **go a long way towards doing sth** to help someone to achieve something: *The money will go a long way towards paying for her medical treatment.*
have come a long way to have achieved a lot of things and made progress: *Technology has come a long way since the days of telegrams.*
have a long way to go to need to do a lot more before you are successful: *We've raised £100 so far, but we still have a long way to go.*
in the long run/term not immediately, but at some time in the future: *In the long run, this will be a better solution for the company.*

long² /lɒŋ/ adv **1** for a long period of time: *I hope you haven't been **waiting long**.* ♦ *People are **living longer** nowadays.* **2** much earlier or later than a particular event or period: ***long before** the war* ♦ *I should have ended the relationship **long ago**.*

PHRASES **all day/week/year etc long** for the whole day, week, year etc: *I don't think I could look after children all day long.*

as/so long as used before explaining the conditions that will make something else happen or be true: *My parents don't care what job I do as long as I'm happy.*
before long soon: *She joined the company in 1999, and before long she was promoted to sales manager.*
be/take long used for saying or asking whether you will have to wait a long time for someone or something: *Dinner won't be long now.* ♦ *It didn't take long to get there.*
for long for a long period of time: *I haven't known them for long.*
no longer or **not any longer** used when something happened or was true in the past but is not true now: *He no longer plays in an orchestra.*

long³ /lɒŋ/ verb [I] to want something very much: *She longed to see him again.*

long-awaited /ˌlɒŋ əˈweɪtɪd/ adj a long-awaited event has been expected for a long time

,long-ˈdistance adj **1** travelling between two places that are far apart: *a long-distance runner* **2** a long-distance phone call is one that you make to someone far away —**,long-ˈdistance** adv

,long diˈvision noun [U] MATHS in mathematics, a calculation in which you divide one large number by another

,long-drawn-ˈout adj continuing for too long = PROTRACTED

longevity /lɒnˈdʒevəti/ noun [U] *formal* the fact of having a long life or existence

'long-,haul adj travelling a long distance, especially by air ≠ SHORT-HAUL

longing /ˈlɒŋɪŋ/ noun [C/U] a strong feeling of wanting someone or something —**longingly** adv

longitude /ˈlɒndʒɪˌtjuːd, ˈlɒŋɡɪˌtjuːd/ noun [C/U] GEOGRAPHY the position of a place in the world when it is measured in relation to east or west, not to north or south → LATITUDE —*picture* → EARTH

longitudinal /ˌlɒndʒɪˈtjuːdɪn(ə)l, ˌlɒŋɡɪˈtjuːdɪn(ə)l/ adj **1** going from the top to the bottom of something —*picture* → SECTION **2** GEOGRAPHY relating to or measured in longitude —**longitudinally** adv

,longitudinal ˈwave noun [C] PHYSICS a wave such as a **sound wave** that moves in the same direction as the vibrations of the particles of the substance it moves through —*picture* → WAVE

the ˈlong jump noun [singular] SPORTS a sports event in which each person tries to jump further than the other people

,long-ˈlasting adj continuing for a long time: *long-lasting damage*

,long-ˈlife adj long-life products remain fresh or useful for longer than other products

'long-,range adj **1** continuing or looking far into the future: *a long-range weather forecast* **2** able to travel long distances: *long-range missiles*

,long-ˈrunning adj having continued for a long time: *a long-running dispute*

longshore drift /ˈlɒŋʃɔː ˌdrɪft/ noun [U] GEOLOGY a process in which loose stones, sand, dirt etc are moved along the coast by the action of the waves

,long-ˈsighted adj not able to see things clearly when they are near to you ≠ SHORT-SIGHTED —*picture* → SHORT-SIGHTED —**long-sightedness** noun [U]

long-'standing adj having existed for a long time: *a long-standing tradition*

'long-,stay adj **1** needing to stay somewhere for a long time, or for someone who needs to do this **2** designed so that you can park your car there for a long time

,long-'suffering adj patient despite having problems, or despite being badly treated, over a long period of time

,long-'term adj **1** continuing to exist, be relevant, or have an effect for a long time in the future ≠ SHORT-TERM: *a good long-term investment* **2** having existed for a long time and unlikely to change: *long-term debt*

'long ,wave noun [U] PHYSICS a radio wave of more than 1,000 metres used for broadcasting → MEDIUM WAVE, SHORT WAVE

look¹ /lʊk/ verb

1 direct eyes at	5 how likely sth is
2 search for	6 face a direction
3 have an appearance	+ PHRASES
4 seem	+ PHRASAL VERBS

1 [I] to direct your eyes towards someone or something so that you can see them: *Dan **looked at** his watch.* ♦ *If you **look through** this window, you can see the cathedral.* → SEE
2 [I] to search for someone or something: *I don't know where the keys are. I've **looked everywhere**.* ♦ *I spent most of the morning **looking for** my passport.*
3 [linking verb] to have a particular appearance: *He looked about twenty.* ♦ *He looked very funny in his hat.* ♦ *It was a first date so Emily wanted to **look her best** (=as attractive as possible).*
4 [linking verb] to seem to be something: *That new film **looks good**.*
5 [linking verb] used for giving your opinion about how likely it is that something will happen or be true: *Martin looks certain to win.*
6 [I] if a building or room looks in a particular direction, it faces that direction: *My room looked out over the lake.*

PHRASES be looking to do sth planning to do something: *We're looking to expand the business.*
look good/bad 1 to seem to be going to have a good or bad result: *Things aren't looking too good for him at the moment.* **2** to be considered a good or bad thing to do: *Do you think it will look bad if I don't go and see him?*
look like 1 to have a particular appearance: *Kathleen looks like her dad.* ♦ *I asked him what the house looks like.* **2** to seem likely: *It looks like Bill will be able to come too.* ♦ *She looks like winning the tournament.*

PHRASAL VERBS ,look 'after sb/sth to take care of someone or something: *It's hard work looking after three children all day.*
,look a'round (sth) to walk around a room, building, or place and see what is there: *Do you want to look around the school?*
'look at sth to think about a situation or subject in a particular way = CONSIDER: *We're looking carefully at all the options before we make our decision.*
,look 'back to think about a time or event in the past: *Most people **look back on** their school days with fondness.*
,look 'down on sb to think that you are better or more important than someone else: *She looks down on anyone who hasn't had a university education.*
'look for sb/sth 1 to hope to get something that you want or need: *He was looking for work as a builder.* **2** to search for someone or something: *I'm looking for Jim. Have you seen him?*

,look 'forward to sth to feel happy and excited about something that is going to happen
,look 'into sth to try to discover the facts about something such as a problem or crime = INVESTIGATE: *The airline have promised to look into the matter.*
,look 'out for sb/sth to look carefully at people or things around you in order to try to find a particular person or thing: *We were told to look out for a blue van.*
,look 'through sth to search for something among a lot of other things: *I'll look through these files and see if I can find a copy of my CV.*
,look sth 'up to try to find a piece of information by looking in a book or on a list, or by using a computer: *I had to look the word up in a dictionary.*

look² /lʊk/ noun

1 act of looking	4 appearance/style
2 act of searching	5 appearance of face
3 expression on face	6 act of thinking

1 [C] an act of looking at someone or something: *Can I **have a look at** your new skateboard?* ♦ *Come and **take a look at** this.*
2 [C] an act of searching for someone or something: *I don't know where the book is, but I'll **have a look for** it.*
3 [C] an expression that you have on your face or in your eyes: *I could tell by **the look on his face** that he was not happy.* ♦ *She saw **the look of** surprise on Nicky's face.* ♦ *She gave me **a worried look**.*
4 [C] the appearance that someone or something has: *Let us create a stylish modern look for your home.* ♦ *I don't **like the look of** him.*
5 looks [plural] the attractive appearance of someone, especially their face: *She's got everything – looks, intelligence, and money.*
6 [C] an occasion when you think carefully about a problem or situation: *We need to **have a look at** the way we deal with orders.*

lookout /'lʊkaʊt/ noun [C] someone who watches for danger and is ready to warn other people, or the place where they watch from
PHRASE be on the lookout for or **keep a lookout for** to be watching carefully for someone or something

loom¹ /luːm/ verb [I] **1** to appear as a large shape that is not clear, usually in a threatening way: *Suddenly the mountains loomed up out of the mist.* **2** if something unpleasant or difficult looms, it seems likely to happen soon: *The government is denying that a crisis is looming.* —**looming** adj

loom² /luːm/ noun [C] a machine used for making cloth

loop¹ /luːp/ noun [C] **1** a shape made by a line that curls back towards itself, or something in this shape **2** COMPUTING a set of instructions in a computer program that are repeated until an action is completed **3** a piece of film or tape on which images or sounds are repeated again and again **4** GEOGRAPHY a part of a river where it has eroded a wide curved path in the shape of the letter S = MEANDER —*picture* → RIVER

loop² /luːp/ verb [I/T] to form a loop, or to make something into a loop

loophole /'luːp,həʊl/ noun [C] a bad feature of a law or legal document that allows people to avoid obeying it

loose¹ /luːs/ adj

1 not firmly fixed	4 free to move
2 not together	5 not exact/detailed
3 not tight	6 not official

1 not firmly fixed in position: *a loose tooth* ♦ *One of the screws had* **come loose**.

2 not kept together as part of a group or in a container: *Loose oranges are 6op each.*

3 loose clothes are large and do not fit your body tightly ≠ TIGHT

4 free to move around: *A large dog was loose in the garden.* ♦ *The woman managed to* **break loose** (=escape) *from her attacker.*

5 not exactly accurate in every detail: *This is a loose translation of the letter.*

6 not strictly organized or official: *a system in which political parties form a loose alliance*

loose² /luːs/ noun **on the loose** if a dangerous person or animal is on the loose, they have escaped from where they were being kept

loosely /'luːsli/ adv **1** not firmly or tightly **2** not in an exact or detailed way: *loosely translated* **3** not according to a strict system or official set of rules: *a loosely organized group of criminal gangs*

loosen /'luːs(ə)n/ verb **1** [I/T] to become less firmly fixed or fastened, or to make something less firmly fixed or fastened ≠ TIGHTEN: *The screws began to loosen.* ♦ *He loosened his tie.* **2** [T] to make something less strict or controlled

loot¹ /luːt/ noun [U] things that have been stolen, especially during a war

loot² /luːt/ verb [I/T] to steal things from houses or shops during a war, or after a **disaster** such as a fire —**looter** noun [C], **looting** noun [U]

lopsided /ˌlɒp'saɪdɪd/ adj not level because one side is higher than the other

loquacious /ləʊ'kweɪʃəs/ adj *formal* tending to talk a lot or too much ═ TALKATIVE

lord /lɔːd/ noun **1** [C] a man who has a high rank in the British **aristocracy 2 the Lord** RELIGION a name that Christians use for talking about God or Jesus Christ

the ˌLord's 'Prayer noun RELIGION a Christian prayer that Jesus Christ taught to his followers according to the Bible

lore /lɔː/ noun [U] traditional knowledge about nature and culture that people get from older people, not from books

lorry /'lɒri/ (plural **lorries**) noun [C] a **truck**

lose /luːz/ (**loses, losing, lost** /lɒst/) verb

1 stop having sth	**6** waste time/chance
2 be unable to find	**7** escape from sb
3 not win	**8** confuse sb
4 have less of sth	**9** about clock/watch
5 when sb dies	**+ PHRASES**

1 [T] to no longer have something: *Mike lost his job last year.* ♦ *The family lost everything when their home burned down.* ♦ *Peter lost a leg in a climbing accident.* ♦ *Jane started to lose interest in her schoolwork.* ♦ *We've lost all hope of finding him alive.*

2 [T] to be unable to find someone or something: *I've lost my bag.* ♦ *You can easily lose a child in a busy street.*

3 [I/T] to not win a race or competition ≠ WIN: *Those comments may well have lost them the election.* ♦ *England lost 2–1 to Germany.* ♦ *They lost by only one point.*

4 [T] to have less of something than before because some of it has gone: *The plane suddenly lost cabin pressure.* ♦ *He's lost a lot of weight recently.*

5 [T] if you lose a member of your close family or a close friend, they die: *She lost her son in a car accident.*

6 [T] if you lose time or an opportunity, you waste it

7 [T] to manage to escape from someone who is following you

8 [T] to make someone confused when you are explaining something: *I'm sorry, you've lost me there. Who's Andrew?*

9 [T] if a clock or watch loses time, it is operating too slowly and shows a time that is earlier than the correct time

PHRASES **have a lot/too much to lose** to be in a position where something bad might happen if you are not successful

have nothing to lose used for saying that someone should try something because their situation will not be any worse if they fail

lose count 1 to forget a total when you are counting something: *Don't talk to me or I'll lose count.* **2** used for emphasizing that something has happened many times: *I've lost count of the times he's asked to borrow money.*

lose your life to die as a result of something such as an accident, war, or illness: *He lost his life in a sailing accident.*

lose touch (with sth) to not know the most recent information about something, so that you no longer understand it completely

lose touch/contact (with sb) to not know what someone is doing because you have not talked to or communicated with them for a long time
→ COUNT²

loser /'luːzə/ noun [C] **1** someone who did not win a race or competition ≠ WINNER **2** *informal* someone who has never been successful and is never likely to be **3** someone or something that is affected in a negative way by something ≠ WINNER: *When parents split up the real losers are the children.*

loss /lɒs/ noun

1 not having sth	**5** sadness
2 having less of sth	**6** in sport
3 money lost	**+ PHRASE**
4 death of sb	

1 [C/U] the state of no longer having something: *job losses* ♦ *a loss of confidence* ♦ *The loss of his sight was a severe blow.*

2 [C/U] the state of having less of something than before: *a new treatment for hair loss* ♦ *Exercise and weight loss can help lower your blood pressure.*

3 [C/U] BUSINESS an amount of money that a person or company loses when they spend more than they earn ≠ PROFIT: *The company reported heavy losses for last year.* ♦ *We made a loss on the house sale.*

4 [C/U] the death of someone: *Jean never recovered from the loss of her husband.* ♦ *There was only minor damage and no loss of life* (=no one died).

5 [U] a feeling of sadness that you have when someone leaves or dies, or when you no longer have something: *We all felt a tremendous sense of loss when Robin left.*

6 [C] a failure to win a race or competition ═ DEFEAT ≠ WIN: *Manchester United's loss to Liverpool at Anfield last week*

PHRASE **at a loss (to do sth)** not understanding something, or not knowing what to do: *I was at a loss to understand what had happened.*
→ CUT¹

'loss ˌleader noun [C] BUSINESS a product sold at a very low price to encourage customers to buy other products in the same shop, or other products made by the same company

lossmaker /'lɒsˌmeɪkə/ noun [C] BUSINESS a business, organization, or industry that does not make a profit

'loss-,making adj BUSINESS a loss-making business, organization, or industry does not make a profit

lost¹ /lɒst/ adj

1 not knowing way	**6** unable to understand
2 when sth is missing	**7** killed
3 no longer existing	**8** not noticing
4 not relaxed	environment
5 time/chances	**+ PHRASE**

1 if you are lost, you do not know where you are: *They decided to drive to York and ended up **getting lost**.*
2 if something is lost, you cannot find it: *The keys are lost somewhere in the house.*
3 if something is lost, you no longer have it: *The strike has cost the airline £3 million in lost profits.* ♦ *lost innocence*
4 someone who feels lost does not feel confident or relaxed because they are in a new situation
5 lost time or chances have been wasted: *The team's season has been littered with missed opportunities and lost chances.*
6 unable to understand something: *I was completely lost after the first paragraph.*
7 killed, especially while fighting in the armed forces: *a memorial to all soldiers lost in battle*
8 concentrating very hard on something, and not noticing other things that are happening: *Martin was lost in thought and did not hear the door open.*
PHRASE **lost on sb** if something is lost on someone, they do not understand it or are not influenced by it: *The joke was lost on Alex.*

lost² /lɒst/ the past tense and past participle of **lose**

,lost 'property noun [U] **1** possessions that people have accidentally left in a public place that are kept until they come and claim them **2** a room where lost property is kept until the owners come to get it

lot¹ /lɒt/ adv, pronoun
PHRASE **a lot 1** to a great or greater degree: *I liked her a lot.* ♦ *I can run a lot faster than you.* → MUCH **2 a lot** or **lots** a large number, amount, or quantity: *There's a lot to see in Paris.* ♦ *Have another piece of cake – there's **lots more** in the kitchen.* ♦ *Bob used to have a **lot of** friends in New York.* ♦ *The idea has attracted **lots of** publicity.* → MANY **3** often: *I think about him a lot.* ♦ *Her youngest child cries a lot.*

lot² /lɒt/ noun **1** [C] a group of people or things: *I've just finished typing one lot of letters.* ♦ *Two lots of parents are involved.* **2 the lot** [singular] *spoken* the whole of a number or amount that has just been mentioned: *I offered him half, but he wanted the lot.*

lotion /'ləʊʃ(ə)n/ noun [C/U] a thick liquid that you put on your skin to make it feel softer

lottery /'lɒtəri/ (plural **lotteries**) noun **1** [C] a game in which people win money if they guess the correct numbers **2** [singular] *showing disapproval* a situation where everything depends on luck

lotto /'lɒtəʊ/ noun [U] a game in which each player tries to match the numbers on their card with numbers chosen by chance from a container

lotus /'ləʊtəs/ noun [C] an Asian water plant with large white or pink flowers

loud¹ /laʊd/ adj **1** a loud sound is strong and very easy to hear ≠ SOFT: *There was a loud knocking on the door.* ♦ *The music is deafeningly loud.* **2** someone who is loud talks in a loud and confident way that annoys other people ≠ QUIET **3** very bright in a way that does not show good taste: *a loud shirt* —**loudly** adv, **loudness** noun [U]

loud² /laʊd/ adv in a loud way
PHRASE **out loud** in a way that other people can hear

loudspeaker /,laʊd'spiːkə/ noun [C] a piece of electrical equipment that allows someone's voice to be heard far away

lounge /laʊndʒ/ noun [C] **1** a comfortable room in a house where people sit and relax= LIVING ROOM, SITTING ROOM **2** an area in an airport, hotel, or other public building for sitting and relaxing in

louse /laʊs/ (plural **lice** /laɪs/) noun [C] a small insect that lives on the bodies of humans and other mammals and feeds on their blood —*picture* → INSECT

lousy /'laʊzi/ adj *informal* bad or unpleasant

lout /laʊt/ noun [C] an unpleasant young man who behaves badly in public —**loutish** adj

louvred /'luːvəd/ adj CONSTRUCTION a louvred window or door is made of narrow pieces of glass or wood that slope and have spaces between them

lovable /'lʌvəb(ə)l/ adj attractive and easy to like

love¹ /lʌv/ verb [T] **1** to be very strongly attracted to someone in an emotional and sexual way: *I love you.* ♦ *We love each other, and we're getting married.* **2** to care very much about someone or something: *She loved her children with all her heart.* ♦ *She went back to the country she loved.* **3** to like or enjoy something very much: *She loves all types of music.* ♦ *I would love a cup of coffee* (=would like one very much). ♦ *I would love to see them again.* ♦ *Ben loves playing the piano.*

love² /lʌv/ noun

1 romantic feeling	**5** at end of letter
2 feeling of caring	**6** no points in tennis
3 sb in relationship	**+ PHRASE**
4 sth you enjoy	

1 [U] a very strong emotional and sexual feeling for someone: *I think I'm in love.* ♦ *They met and **fell in love*** (=started to love each other) *at college.* ♦ *the speech in which Romeo expresses his **love for** Juliet*
2 [U] the feeling of caring about someone or something very much ≠ HATE: *Children need a lot of **love and affection**.* ♦ *his **love for** his brother* ♦ *a great **love of** life*
3 [C] someone that you have a sexual or romantic relationship with: *the boy who was her **first love***
4 [C] something that you enjoy very much: *Music was his **greatest love**.*
5 [U] used at the end of a letter to someone you know well: *Hope to see you soon. Love, Ray.* ♦ *Take care. **Lots of love**, Helen.* ♦ *I can't wait to see you. **All my love**, Douglas.*
6 [U] SPORTS a score of no points in tennis
PHRASE **make love** to have sex with someone

lovebird /'lʌv,bɜːd/ noun [C] a small colourful African parrot

loveless /'lʌvləs/ adj without love ≠ LOVING

lovely /'lʌvli/ (**lovelier**, **loveliest**) adj **1** very attractive = BEAUTIFUL: *a city surrounded by lovely countryside* **2** enjoyable, or nice= WONDERFUL: *We've had a lovely evening.* ♦ *It's lovely to see you again.* **3** kind, pleasant, and easy to like= DELIGHTFUL —**loveliness** noun [U]

lover /'lʌvə/ noun [C] **1** a person that someone has a sexual relationship with, often when they are married to someone else **2** someone who likes something very much: *a music lover*

loving /'lʌvɪŋ/ adj feeling or showing love

lovingly /'lʌvɪŋli/ adv **1** in a way that expresses love **2** with great care and interest: *The old church has been lovingly restored.*

low¹ /ləʊ/ adj **1** small in height, or not far above the ground: *a low wall* ♦ *low cloud* ♦ *The water level was very low.* **2** small in amount or level ≠ HIGH: *The bigger shops are able to keep their prices low.* ♦ *low standards* ♦ *people on low incomes* ♦ *Vegetables are low in fat and high in nutrition.* **3** someone who is low feels unhappy and does not have much hope or confidence: *It was unlike her to be in such low spirits.* ♦ *She'd been feeling low for a few days.* **4** a low voice or sound is quiet and difficult to hear ≠ HIGH

low² /ləʊ/ adv **1** in or to a low position ≠ HIGH **2** quietly, or in a deep voice: *I asked them to turn the volume down low.* ♦ *She can sing high or low.* → LIE¹

low³ /ləʊ/ noun [C] **1** BUSINESS the lowest level, value, or price ≠ HIGH: *Share prices hit an all-time low.* **2** a bad time in your life ≠ HIGH: *He's experienced all the highs and lows of an actor's life.*

,low-'density adj having a low number of people or things in an area

'low-,end adj BUSINESS less expensive and less advanced than other similar goods and services ≠ HIGH-END

,low-'energy adj PHYSICS designed to use as little energy as possible

lower¹ /'ləʊə/ adj **1** below another thing of the same kind ≠ UPPER: *the upper and lower lips* **2** fairly near the bottom of something: *the lower floors of the building* **3** fairly low in status or importance ≠ HIGHER: *the lower ranks of the army*

lower² /'ləʊə/ verb [T] **1** to move something or someone slowly down from a higher position ≠ RAISE: *He lowered himself into the chair.* **2** to reduce something in number, amount, value, or strength: *The voting age was lowered from 21 to 18 years.* ♦ *Less fat in your diet lowers the risk of heart disease.*

,lower 'case noun [U] the ordinary small form in which letters of the alphabet are written: *Type the file name in lower case.* ♦ *lower-case letters* → UPPER CASE

the ,lower 'class or **the ,lower 'classes** noun SOCIAL STUDIES people who have the lowest social status —,lower-'class adj → MIDDLE CLASS, UPPER CLASS, WORKING CLASS

,lower epi'dermis noun [C] BIOLOGY the lower part of the surface of a leaf that contains most of the **stomata** (=holes that allow vapour in and out)

,lower 'jaw noun [singular] ANATOMY the **mandible** —*picture* → SKELETON

lowest common multiple /,ləʊɪst ,kɒmən 'mʌltɪp(ə)l/ noun [C] MATHS the lowest number that can be divided by all the numbers in a set = LCM

,low-'fat adj HEALTH low-fat food contains only a small amount of fat

lowlands /'ləʊləndz/ noun [plural] GEOGRAPHY the part of a country that is fairly low and flat ≠ HIGHLANDS —**lowland** adj

,low-'level adj **1** without much importance, power, or difficulty: *a low-level sales position* **2** in a low position **3** COMPUTING a low-level language is a **machine code** used for writing computer programs → HIGH-LEVEL

lowly /'ləʊli/ adj with a low status or position: *a lowly office clerk*

low-lying /,ləʊ 'laɪɪŋ/ adj in a position that is close to the level of the sea or the ground

,low-'paid adj not receiving or offering much pay

,low-pitched /,ləʊ 'pɪtʃt/ adj a low-pitched voice or sound is deep and sometimes difficult to hear

'low ,point noun [C] the worst moment in a situation

,low 'pressure noun [U] GEOGRAPHY, PHYSICS an area of less dense air in the atmosphere that usually brings wet weather → HIGH PRESSURE —,low-'pressure adj

,low-reso'lution adj COMPUTING producing a printed or video image that is not very clear because blocks of colour are used, not thin lines or small **dots**

'low-,rise adj a low-rise building has only a few levels ≠ HIGH-RISE

'low ,season noun [singular] TOURISM the time of year when a place or business is least busy, for example because there are not many tourists ≠ HIGH SEASON

low-tech /,ləʊ 'tek/ adj low-tech equipment is simple and usually old-fashioned ≠ HIGH-TECH

,low 'tide noun [C/U] GEOGRAPHY the time when the sea is at its lowest level ≠ HIGH TIDE

,low 'water ,mark noun [singular] GEOGRAPHY a mark showing the lowest level that the water in a river or the sea has ever reached

loyal /'lɔɪəl/ adj someone who is loyal continues to support a person, organization, or principle in difficult times = FAITHFUL ≠ DISLOYAL: *a loyal friend* ♦ *people who have remained loyal to the company for years* —**loyally** adv

loyalist /'lɔɪəlɪst/ noun [C] someone who supports their government

loyalty /'lɔɪəlti/ noun support that you always give to someone or something: *I was impressed by his loyalty to his brother.*

'loyalty ,card noun [C] BUSINESS a card given to customers of a supermarket or other business that gives them benefits such as price reductions

lozenge /'lɒzɪndʒ/ noun [C] **1** HEALTH a sweet that contains medicine for a sore throat **2** MATHS a shape with four sloping sides

LP /,el 'pi:/ noun [C] long-playing record: a record that turns 33 times a minute

LPG /,el pi: 'dʒi:/ noun [U] CHEMISTRY liquefied petroleum gas: a fuel that is a mixture of **hydrocarbon** gases in liquid form

LSD /,el es 'di:/ noun [U] a powerful illegal drug that makes people see things that are not real = ACID

Ltd abbrev Limited: used after the name of some companies

lubricant /'lu:brɪkənt/ noun [C/U] ENGINEERING an oil that you use to lubricate a machine

lubricate /'lu:brɪkeɪt/ verb [T] ENGINEERING to put oil on the parts of a machine in order to make them move more smoothly —**lubrication** /,lu:brɪ'keɪʃ(ə)n/ noun [U]

lucid /'lu:sɪd/ adj **1** describing things in a clear, simple way **2** capable of thinking clearly

luck /lʌk/ noun [U] **1** success that you have by chance: *We'd all like to wish you luck in your new job.* ♦ *John never had much luck with girls.* **2** an influence that seems to make good things happen to people for no particular reason: *He's had nothing but bad luck since moving to New York.* ♦ *It's a custom that is believed to bring good luck.* ♦ *Their luck is bound to run out* (=end) *sometime.*

PHRASES **good luck** or **best of luck** used for telling someone that you hope that they will be successful: *Good luck in your driving test!*

in luck able to do something that did not seem likely: *You're in luck. We've got one pair of shoes left in your size.*

out of luck unable to do something that you wanted

luckily /'lʌkɪli/ adv used for saying that something good happens in a lucky way= FORTUNATELY: *Luckily he wasn't injured.*

lucky /'lʌki/ (**luckier, luckiest**) adj if you are lucky, something good happens to you as a result of luck = FORTUNATE ≠ UNLUCKY: *You're lucky that he was there.* ♦ *It's lucky that I arrived when I did.* ♦ *Five lucky winners will each receive £1,000.* ♦ *None of his sisters had been lucky with men.* ♦ *You're really lucky to be alive.*

lucrative /'lu:krətɪv/ adj bringing a lot of money = PROFITABLE

ludicrous /'lu:dɪkrəs/ adj extremely silly= ABSURD: *a ludicrous new rule* —**ludicrously** adv: *ludicrously expensive*

luggage /'lʌgɪdʒ/ noun [U] bags and suitcases that you take on a journey= BAGGAGE

> **Luggage** is never used in the plural and cannot be used with **a**: *Someone had left a piece of luggage* (NOT *a luggage*) *in the taxi.* ♦ *Do you have any luggage?* ♦ *There was some luggage lying around in the hall.*

'luggage al,lowance noun [C] TOURISM the weight of bags and suitcases that a passenger is allowed to take on a plane without paying

'luggage ,lockers noun [plural] TOURISM a set of small cupboards in an airport, railway station etc where passengers can leave luggage safely

lukewarm /,lu:k'wɔːm/ adj **1** not hot or cold enough to be enjoyable **2** not very enthusiastic or interested

lull /lʌl/ noun [C] a short period during which noise or activity stops

lullaby /'lʌləbaɪ/ (plural **lullabies**) noun [C] MUSIC a relaxing song that helps a young child to sleep

lumbar /'lʌmbə/ adj ANATOMY relating to the lower part of the back —*picture* → VERTEBRA

,lumbar 'puncture noun [C] HEALTH a medical treatment or test in which a needle is used to **inject** medicine, or to take liquid from the lumbar part of the spine

lumbering /'lʌmbərɪŋ/ adj walking slowly because of being large and heavy

lumberjack /'lʌmbə,dʒæk/ noun [C] someone whose job is to cut down trees for wood

lumen /'lu:mɪn/ noun [C] ANATOMY the central space in an artery or vein through which blood flows —*picture* → BLOOD VESSEL

luminary /'lu:mɪnəri/ (plural **luminaries**) noun [C] *formal* one of the people most admired in a particular profession

luminescence /,lu:mɪ'nes(ə)ns/ noun [U] PHYSICS light that is produced without heat

luminous /'lu:mɪnəs/ adj PHYSICS, ASTRONOMY producing light

,luminous 'flame noun [C] PHYSICS a flame that burns when there is a small amount of oxygen available. It gives out heat and light and produces **soot** (=black powder).

lump /lʌmp/ noun [C] **1** a solid piece of something that does not have a regular shape: *a lump of metal* **2** a solid piece in a substance that should be smooth or liquid: *Stir the sauce to get rid of any lumps.* **3** a small hard part on or under the skin that is caused by illness or injury

lumpectomy /,lʌm'pektəmi/ (plural **lumpectomies**) noun [C] HEALTH a medical operation to remove a lump, usually from a woman's breast

,lump 'sum noun [C] money in a single large payment rather than in separate small payments

lumpy /'lʌmpi/ adj full of lumps: *a lumpy pillow*

lunacy /'lu:nəsi/ noun [U] stupid ideas or behaviour = MADNESS

lunar /'lu:nə/ adj relating to the Moon

,lunar e'clipse noun [C] ASTRONOMY a short period when the Moon becomes dark, because the Earth moves between the Sun and the Moon so that its shadow covers the Moon → SOLAR ECLIPSE —*picture* → ECLIPSE

,lunar 'month noun [C] ASTRONOMY the period of about 28 days during which the Moon goes through all of its **phases** while moving around the Earth

lunatic /'lu:nətɪk/ noun [C] someone who behaves in an extreme or dangerous way —**lunatic** adj

lunch /lʌntʃ/ noun [C/U] a meal that you eat in the middle of the day: *I'll get a sandwich for lunch.* ♦ *Let's have lunch at that new restaurant.* ♦ *She's usually at lunch from twelve till one.* ♦ *Mr Miller's already gone to lunch.*

lunchtime /'lʌntʃ,taɪm/ noun [U] the time in the middle of the day when people usually eat lunch: *I'm going swimming at lunchtime.*

lung /lʌŋ/ noun [C] ANATOMY one of the two organs in the chest that fill with air during breathing. Blood flowing to the lungs takes oxygen from the air breathed into the **alveoli** and puts in carbon dioxide which is then breathed out as a waste product. Air enters and leaves the lungs through the **bronchial tubes**. —*picture* → CIRCULATION, ORGAN and on next page

'lung ca,pacity noun [U] SPORTS, HEALTH the maximum amount of air that the lungs can hold

lunge /lʌndʒ/ verb [I] to move suddenly and with a lot of force —**lunge** noun [C]

lungi /'lʊŋgiː/ noun [C] a piece of cloth that you wrap around your waist like a long skirt, worn by men in India

lupus /'lu:pəs/ noun [U] HEALTH an **autoimmune** disease that affects the **immune system**, and the skin or other parts of the body

lurch /lɜːtʃ/ verb [I] **1** to move suddenly in a way that is not smooth or controlled **2** if your heart or stomach lurches, it seems to jump suddenly because you are excited or upset

lure¹ /ljʊə/ verb [T] to persuade someone to do something by making it look very attractive

lure² /ljʊə/ noun [C] **1** something that persuades someone to do something by seeming very attractive **2** an object used for attracting fish or animals

lurk /lɜːk/ verb [I] **1** to hide somewhere and wait to frighten or attack someone **2** if something is lurking, it is likely to threaten, harm, or upset you

luscious /'lʌʃəs/ adj **1** very attractive in a sexual way **2** luscious food looks, smells, and tastes extremely good= DELICIOUS

lush /lʌʃ/ adj a lush plant or area looks very green and healthy

lust /lʌst/ noun [U] **1** a strong feeling of wanting to have sex= DESIRE **2** great enthusiasm for something = PASSION

lung

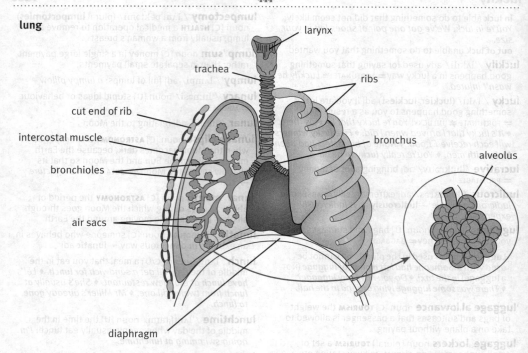

larynx

trachea

ribs

cut end of rib

intercostal muscle

bronchus

alveolus

bronchioles

air sacs

diaphragm

breathing in humans

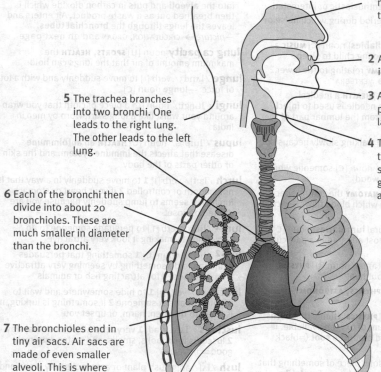

1 Air is breathed into the nasal cavity through the two nostrils in the nose.

2 Air can also be breathed in through the mouth.

3 Air passes through the pharynx (throat) to the larynx (voice box).

4 The larynx leads to the trachea, which has a narrow slit-like opening called the glottis. The vocal cords are also found in the trachea.

5 The trachea branches into two bronchi. One leads to the right lung. The other leads to the left lung.

6 Each of the bronchi then divide into about 20 bronchioles. These are much smaller in diameter than the bronchi.

7 The bronchioles end in tiny air sacs. Air sacs are made of even smaller alveoli. This is where oxygen is absorbed into the blood.

lustrous /'lʌstrəs/ adj bright and shiny

lute /lu:t/ noun [C] **MUSIC** a musical instrument similar to a guitar with a body that is round on one side and flat on the other. Lutes were popular in the past but are still sometimes played today.

lutetium /lu'ti:ʃəm/ noun [U] **CHEMISTRY** a silvery-white metallic element in the **lanthanide** group of the periodic table. Chemical symbol: **Lu**

luxurious /lʌg'zjʊəriəs/ adj very expensive and comfortable

luxury¹ /'lʌkʃəri/ (plural **luxuries**) noun **1** [U] a situation in which you are very comfortable because you have the best and most expensive things: *They live a life of absolute luxury.* **2** [C] something expensive that you enjoy but do not really need **3** [singular] something that you enjoy very much but do not have very often: *A day off was a real luxury.*

luxury² /'lʌkʃəri/ adj very expensive and of the highest quality: *a luxury hotel*

LW abbrev **PHYSICS** long wave

lychee /'laɪtʃi:, 'lɪtʃi/ noun [C] a small round white fruit from China

Lycra /'laɪkrə/ **TRADEMARK** cloth made from artificial fibres that stretches and keeps its shape. It is used for making sports clothes.

Lyme disease /'laɪm dɪ,zi:z/ noun [U] **HEALTH** a serious disease caused by insects called **ticks** that can affect the **nervous system** and heart

lymph /lɪmf/ noun [U] **BIOLOGY** a clear liquid in the body that cleans the tissues and helps to remove harmful bacteria from the blood

lymphatic /lɪm'fætɪk/ adj **BIOLOGY** relating to lymph, or involved in moving lymph around the body

the lym'phatic ,system noun [singular] **ANATOMY** a system of lymph nodes and tubes that carries lymph from the body's tissues to the bloodstream. It is part of the **immune system**.

'lymph ,node or **'lymph ,gland** noun [C] **ANATOMY** one of several small organs in the body that help to remove harmful bacteria from the blood

lymphocyte /'lɪmfəsaɪt/ noun [C] **BIOLOGY** a white blood cell that attacks antigens

lymphoma /lɪm'fəʊmə/ (plural **lymphomas** or **lymphomata** /lɪm'fəʊmətə/) noun [C/U] **HEALTH** a cancer that affects the **lymph nodes**

'lymph ,vessel noun [C] **ANATOMY** one of the many clear tubes that carry **lymph** to most parts of the body

lynch /lɪntʃ/ verb [T] if a group of angry people lynch someone, they kill that person by hanging them by the neck —**lynching** noun [C/U]

lyre /laɪə/ noun [C] **MUSIC** an ancient Greek musical instrument with strings that was shaped like the letter U

lyric /'lɪrɪk/ noun [C] **1 MUSIC** the words of a song **2 LITERATURE** a short poem that expresses feelings in a direct way, like a song

lyrical /'lɪrɪk(ə)l/ adj **1** expressing emotions in a beautiful way: *The new concerto is intensely lyrical.* **2** having the qualities of music

lyricism /'lɪrɪ,sɪz(ə)m/ noun [U] **ARTS** the expression of feeling in art

lysis /'laɪsɪs/ noun [U] **BIOLOGY** the destruction of a cell by breaking the membrane that contains it, allowing the contents of the cell to escape

lysosome /'laɪsəsəʊm/ noun [C] **BIOLOGY** a **sac** (=small bag) inside a living cell, containing enzymes that can digest the contents of the cell. Lysosomes break down proteins and old or foreign material in the cell.

M m

m¹ /em/ (plural **m's**) or **M** (plural **M's**) noun [C/U] the 13th letter of the English alphabet

m² abbrev **1** metre **2** mile

M¹ abbrev medium: used on clothes labels

M² /em/ noun motorway: used in the names of motorways in the UK

MA /,em 'eɪ/ noun [C] **EDUCATION** Master of Arts: an advanced degree in a subject such as languages or history from a university

mac /mæk/ noun [C] a coat that stops you from getting wet in the rain = RAINCOAT

macabre /mə'kɑ:brə/ adj something that is macabre is frightening because it involves death or violence

macadamia /,mækə'deɪmiə/ or **maca'damia ,nut** noun [C] a white nut that grows on a tropical tree

macaroni /,mækə'rəʊni/ noun [U] a type of pasta in the form of short curved tubes

mace /meɪs/ noun **1** [C] a decorated stick carried by an official on special occasions **2** [U] the crushed shell of **nutmeg**, used for adding flavour to food

machete /mə'ʃeti/ noun [C] a large knife that can be used as a weapon or a tool —*picture* → AGRICULTURAL, WEAPON

machine /mə'ʃi:n/ noun [C] **1** a piece of equipment with moving parts that does a particular job by using electricity, steam, gas etc: *Sue showed him how to operate the washing machine.* **2** a person or animal that does something very effectively: *The lion is an efficient killing machine.* **3 PHYSICS** a simple tool or piece of equipment that changes the size or direction of a force, for example a lever or a screw

ma'chine ,code noun [C/U] **COMPUTING** a series of instructions written in a form that a computer can read and understand

ma'chine ,gun noun [C] a gun that fires a lot of bullets very quickly —*picture* → WEAPON

mac'hine ,language noun [U] **COMPUTING** machine code

ma,chine-'readable adj **COMPUTING** able to be used by a computer

machinery /mə'ʃi:nəri/ noun [U] **1** machines: *agricultural machinery* **2** an established system for doing something: *the company's decision-making machinery*

ma'chine ,tool noun [C] **ENGINEERING** a powered machine for cutting or shaping metal, wood, and other materials

machinist /mə'ʃi:nɪst/ noun [C] someone whose job is to use a machine, especially a **sewing machine**

mackerel /'mækrəl/ (plural **mackerel**) noun [C/U] a sea fish that is eaten as food in Europe and North America. It is found in the northern Atlantic Ocean.

Macpherson strut /mək'fɪəs(ə)n ,strʌt/ noun [C] ENGINEERING a type of vehicle **suspension** system. It contains a **coil spring** and a **shock absorber**.

macro /'mækrəʊ/ (plural **macros**) noun [C] COMPUTING a short computer program that performs a longer series of operations

macrobiotic /ˌmækrəʊbaɪ'ɒtɪk/ adj HEALTH macrobiotic foods are considered healthy because they consist of grains, seeds, fruits, and vegetables produced without adding chemicals

macroeconomics /ˌmækrəʊˌiːkə'nɒmɪks, ˌmækrəʊˌekə'nɒmɪks/ noun [U] ECONOMICS the study of the general aspects of the economic systems of whole countries or large regions —**macroeconomic** adj

macroeconomy /'mækrəʊɪˌkɒnəmi/ noun [C] ECONOMICS the economic system of a whole country or large region

macroenvironment /'mækrəʊɪnˌvaɪrənmənt/ noun [C] BUSINESS all the factors that influence a business or organization but which it cannot directly control, for example changes in the law

macromolecule /'mækrəʊˌmɒlɪkjuːl/ noun [C] CHEMISTRY a large molecule, such as that of a protein or **polymer**, that is made up of smaller parts connected to one another

macronutrient /'mækrəʊˌnjuːtriənt/ noun [C] BIOLOGY, AGRICULTURE a chemical element that plants need in large amounts in order to grow and develop normally. Nitrogen, carbon, and **potassium** are macronutrients.

macrophage /'mækrəʊfeɪdʒ/ noun [C] BIOLOGY a type of white blood cell that is present in blood, **lymph**, and **connective tissue**. Macrophages surround harmful microorganisms in the body and digest them.

macroscopic /ˌmækrəʊ'skɒpɪk/ adj **1** SCIENCE large enough to be seen and examined without the help of a microscope **2** BIOLOGY, PHYSICS relating to large units or large-scale processes

mad /mæd/ (**madder, maddest**) adj **1** very silly or stupid= CRAZY: *You'll think I'm mad – I've just left my job.* ♦ *You're mad to spend so much money on clothes.* **2** *informal* angry: *My boss is mad with me for missing the meeting.* **3** done quickly or without thinking, in a way that is badly organized: *It was a mad rush to get the job finished.*

PHRASES **drive sb mad** *informal* to make someone feel angry, upset, or very impatient
go mad *informal* **1** to become extremely excited and happy: *The waiting crowd went mad when she stepped out of the car.* **2** to become crazy, for example because you are extremely bored: *I would go mad if I had to stay in bed for three weeks.* **3** to become extremely angry: *Dad went mad when he saw what I'd done to the car.*
→ MADLY, MADNESS

madam /'mædəm/ used for talking or writing politely to a woman whose name you do not know

,mad 'cow dis,ease noun [U] HEALTH *informal* BSE

made /meɪd/ the past tense and past participle of **make¹**

,made-'up adj **1** imaginary, or false **2** someone who is made-up is wearing **make-up** on their face

madly /'mædli/ adv **1** in a very excited or uncontrolled way **2** very, or very much: *He fell madly in love with her at first sight.* ♦ *madly jealous*

madness /'mædnəs/ noun [U] ideas and actions that show a lack of good judgment and careful thought: *It would be madness to give up your job just now.*

madrasa /mə'dræsə/ noun [C] a college where students are taught about Islam

the Mafia /'mæfiə/ a secret criminal organization that is involved in illegal activities, especially in Italy and the US

magazine /ˌmægə'ziːn/ noun [C] **1** a large thin book with a paper cover that is usually published once a month or once a week: *a fashion magazine* ♦ *a magazine article* **2** the part of a gun in which the bullets are placed

magenta /mə'dʒentə/ adj purple-red in colour

maggot /'mægət/ noun [C] the larva of various types of fly, shaped like a small white worm. It feeds on dead and decaying matter.

magic¹ /'mædʒɪk/ noun [U] **1** a mysterious power that makes impossible things happen if you do special actions or say special words → BLACK MAGIC **2** mysterious tricks that an entertainer performs, for example making things disappear **3** a special attractive quality that something has

magic² /'mædʒɪk/ adj **1** able to make impossible things happen: *a magic spell* **2** involving mysterious tricks performed by an entertainer: *a magic trick*

magical /'mædʒɪk(ə)l/ adj **1** involving magic: *magical powers* **2** especially enjoyable or attractive: *It was a truly magical evening.* —**magically** /'mædʒɪkli/ adv

magician /mə'dʒɪʃ(ə)n/ noun [C] **1** someone whose job is to entertain people by performing magic tricks **2** someone who is believed to use magic to make impossible things happen= SORCERER, WIZARD

,magic 'realism noun [U] ARTS, LITERATURE a type of literature or cinema in which very strange things happen in ordinary situations, as they do in dreams

magistrate /'mædʒɪ,streɪt/ noun [C] LAW a judge in a court for minor crimes

magma /'mægmə/ noun [U] GEOLOGY hot liquid rock inside the Earth. When magma becomes cool it forms igneous rock. —*picture* → ROCK CYCLE, VOLCANO

magnanimous /mæg'nænɪməs/ adj *formal* willing to forgive people, or willing to be kind and fair

magnesium /mæg'niːziəm/ noun [U] CHEMISTRY a light grey metal element that burns very brightly. It is used in **fireworks** and in the flashes used for taking photographs. It is an important element in chlorophyll. Chemical symbol: **Mg**

magnet /'mægnɪt/ noun [C] **1** PHYSICS a piece of metal that attracts iron or steel objects so that they seem to stick to it. Magnets have two **poles**, north and south. → ELECTROMAGNET —*picture* → on next page **2** someone or something that attracts people

magnetic /mæg'netɪk/ adj **1** PHYSICS able to attract iron or steel objects **2** able to attract and interest people: *his magnetic personality* —**magnetically** /mæg'netɪkli/ adv

mag,netic 'field noun [C] PHYSICS the area that the force of a magnet affects —*picture* → MAGNET

mag,netic 'north noun [U] GEOGRAPHY the direction shown as north by a **compass**, which is slightly different from **true north**

mag,netic 'pole noun [C] **1** GEOGRAPHY an area near either the North Pole or the South Pole where the Earth's magnetic field is strongest and towards which a **compass** points **2** PHYSICS either end of a magnet, where its force is strongest

mag,netic 'tape noun [U] a long narrow piece of plastic covered with a magnetic substance and used for recording sounds, images, or computer information

forces of attraction

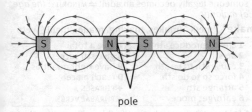

pole

magnet

forces of repulsion

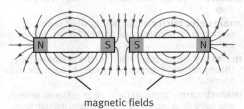

magnetic fields

magnetism /ˈmæɡnə,tɪz(ə)m/ noun [U] **1 PHYSICS** the ability that a magnet has to attract iron or steel **2** a special ability to attract and interest people

magnetite /ˈmæɡnətaɪt/ noun [U] **CHEMISTRY, GEOLOGY** a common black magnetic mineral that contains iron

magnetize /ˈmæɡnətaɪz/ verb [T] **PHYSICS** to make a piece of iron able to attract other iron or steel objects

magnification /ˌmæɡnɪfɪˈkeɪʃ(ə)n/ noun [U] the power of a piece of equipment to make something appear bigger than it really is

magnificent /mæɡˈnɪfɪs(ə)nt/ adj very impressive and beautiful, good, or skilful: *It was so exciting to see these magnificent animals in the wild.* ♦ *She gave a magnificent performance.* —**magnificence** noun [U], **magnificently** adv

magnify /ˈmæɡnɪfaɪ/ **(magnifies, magnifying, magnified)** verb [T] **1** to make something appear bigger than it really is **2** to make something appear more important or serious than it really is

magnifying glass /ˈmæɡnɪfaɪɪŋ ˌɡlɑːs/ noun [C] a small circle of glass with a handle that makes things appear bigger when you look through it

magnitude /ˈmæɡnɪtjuːd/ noun **1** [C] **ASTRONOMY** the brightness of a star, shown as a number **2** [U] great size or importance **3** [C] **MATHS** the size of a mathematical object, especially in relation to objects of the same kind

magnolia /mæɡˈnəʊliə/ noun **1** [C] a small tree with large white or pink flowers, found especially in Europe, North America, and Asia, or a flower from this tree **2** [U] a white colour that looks slightly yellow

magpie /ˈmæɡpaɪ/ noun [C] a noisy black and white bird with a long tail

mahjong /ˌmɑːˈdʒɒŋ/ noun [U] a Chinese game played on a table with small square pieces

mahogany /məˈhɒɡəni/ noun **1** [U] a hard brown-red wood that is used for making furniture **2** [C] the tropical tree that produces this wood

maid /meɪd/ noun [C] a woman whose job is to clean rooms in a hotel or large house

maiden¹ /ˈmeɪd(ə)n/ noun [C] an old word meaning a girl or young woman who is not married

maiden² /ˈmeɪd(ə)n/ adj a maiden flight or voyage is the first one made by a plane or ship

ˈmaiden ˌname noun [C] the original family name of a woman who uses her husband's family name now

mail¹ /meɪl/ noun **1** [U] letters and parcels that are delivered by the post office= POST: *The mail arrived early today.* ♦ *I haven't had a chance to open my mail yet.* ♦ *There was nothing interesting in the mail this morning.* **2** [U] the system for sending and delivering letters and parcels= POST: *All our goods can be ordered by mail.* ♦ *The letter must have got lost in the*

mail. 3 [C/U] email, or an email message: *You've got mail.* ♦ *Did you read that mail from Cindy?* **4** [U] clothing made of small metal rings or pieces joined together, worn by soldiers in the past to protect their bodies = CHAIN MAIL

mail² /meɪl/ verb [T] **1** to post a letter or parcel to someone **2** COMPUTING to send a message to someone by email

mailbox /ˈmeɪl,bɒks/ noun [C] **1** COMPUTING the part of a computer's memory where email is stored **2** American a **postbox 3** American a **letterbox** for putting letters in when they are delivered to a house

ˈmail ˌform noun [C] BUSINESS a page of a website designed to be used as a form for ordering a product or service over the Internet

mailing list /ˈmeɪlɪŋ ˌlɪst/ noun [C] BUSINESS a list of all the people that letters or email messages are sent to

ˈMail ˌMerge TRADEMARK COMPUTING a computer program that can automatically add names and addresses to copies of a letter

ˌmail ˈorder noun [U] a way of buying goods in which you order them by post or telephone and they are posted to you

mailroom /ˈmeɪl,ruːm/ noun [C] BUSINESS a room in an organization where post is received, and where it is prepared for being sent to people

ˈmail ˌserver noun [C] COMPUTING a central computer that controls the sending and receiving of email

maim /meɪm/ verb [T] to injure someone severely and permanently

main¹ /meɪn/ adj most important, or largest: *We eat our main meal in the evening.* ♦ *The main entrance to the building is on George Street.*

main² /meɪn/ noun **1** [C] a large pipe or wire that is used for carrying water, gas, or electricity **2 the mains** [plural] **mains electricity**

ˌmain ˈclause noun [C] LANGUAGE a clause that can be a sentence on its own

mainframe /ˈmeɪn,freɪm/ noun [C] COMPUTING a large powerful computer that has several smaller computers connected to it

the mainland /ˈmeɪn,lænd/ noun [singular] GEOGRAPHY a large mass of land that forms the main part of a country but does not include any islands belonging to the country —*picture* → ISTHMUS, LAGOON —**mainland** adj

mainly /ˈmeɪnli/ adv **1** used for talking about the largest or most important part of something: *This sauce is made mainly of milk and flour.* ♦ *We spent four days there – mainly visiting family.* ♦ *I didn't come mainly because I didn't feel very well.* **2** in most cases: *Our customers are mainly young mothers.*

main road noun [C] a wide road that has a lot of traffic

mainsail /'meɪn,seɪl/ noun [C] the largest sail on a ship

mains elec'tricity noun [U] the public supply of electricity for people to use in their homes, businesses etc

mainstay /'meɪn,steɪ/ noun [C] the person or thing that something depends on in order to continue or be successful

mainstream /'meɪn,striːm/ adj considered normal, and used or accepted by most people: *mainstream politics*

maintain /meɪn'teɪn/ verb [T]

1 keep sth the same	**4** provide money etc
2 keep in good condition	**5** keep up to date
3 keep saying sth	

1 to make something stay the same = KEEP: *Regular inspections ensure that high safety standards are maintained.*
2 to make regular repairs to something, so that it stays in good condition: *The car had been very well maintained.*
3 to continue to say that something is true, even though other people do not believe you = ASSERT: *She maintained her innocence throughout the trial.* ♦ *The company still maintains that the drug is safe.*
4 to provide someone with the money and other things that they need in order to live
5 COMPUTING to make sure a website, a piece of software, or something similar contains the latest information

maintenance /'meɪntənəns/ noun [U] **1** work that is done to keep something in good condition: *aircraft maintenance* **2** the process of continuing something: *the maintenance of international peace and security* **3** money that someone pays to the person they used to be married to

'maintenance rou,tine noun [C] COMPUTING a piece of software that you use to make sure that there are no problems with a computer system that could cause damage to it

maize /meɪz/ noun [U] AGRICULTURE a tall plant that produces yellow seeds on a **cob** (=thick flower stem). The seeds are called **sweetcorn** or **corn** when cooked and eaten. —*picture* → CEREAL

majestic /mə'dʒestɪk/ adj very beautiful or impressive —**majestically** /mə'dʒestɪkli/ adv

majesty /'mædʒəsti/ noun [U] the quality of being very beautiful or impressive
PHRASE Your/His/Her Majesty used for talking formally to or about a king or queen

major¹ /'meɪdʒə/ adj **1** important, large, or great ≠ MINOR: *one of the major problems facing our planet* ♦ *The major attraction is a huge clock in the entrance hall.* ♦ *Age is a major factor affecting chances of employment.* **2** MUSIC in the musical scale that is used for most tunes in western music → MINOR¹ sense 2

major² /'meɪdʒə/ noun [C] an officer of middle rank in the armed forces

major 'axis noun [C] MATHS the longer axis of an **ellipse** (=circle that is longer than it is wide)

majority /mə'dʒɒrəti/ (plural **majorities**) noun
1 [singular] most of the people or things in a group ≠ MINORITY: *The majority of our employees are women.* ♦ *Young women are in the majority in the fashion industry.* ♦ *The vast majority* (=nearly everyone) *had never travelled outside their own town.* ♦ *The majority view is that the election was unfair.* ♦ *We have to accept the majority decision.* **2** [C] the number of votes by which someone wins an election **3** [U] LAW the age at which someone legally becomes an adult ≠ MINORITY: *the age of majority*

make¹ /meɪk/ (**makes, making, made** /meɪd/) verb

1 create/produce sth	**7** give a total
2 do sth	**8** give sth success
3 cause sth to be sth	**9** have right qualities
4 force sb to do sth	**10** reach place
5 arrange sth	**+ PHRASES**
6 earn/get money	**+ PHRASAL VERBS**

1 [T] to create or produce something: *The nail made a hole in my shirt.* ♦ *Jane was making coffee.* ♦ *This furniture is made in South America.* ♦ *a bowl made of wood* ♦ *They make paper from old rags.* ♦ *We made curtains out of some old material we found.*
2 [T] used with some nouns for showing that someone performs an action: *Have you made a decision?* ♦ *Nobody's perfect – we all make mistakes.* ♦ *Helen made an attempt to stop him.* ♦ *We've made some progress, but there's still a long way to go.* ♦ *Stop making so much noise!* ♦ *Matthew made a note of the car's number* (=kept a written record of it) *and informed the police.*
3 [T] to cause someone or something to be in a particular state: *The noise in the room makes reading difficult.* ♦ *Listening to the news just makes me angry these days.* ♦ *The smell of fish makes me feel ill.* ♦ *That haircut makes you look ten years younger.* ♦ *I'd like to make it clear that I had nothing to do with this.*
4 [T] to force someone to do something: *They made us work for 12 hours a day.*
5 [T] to arrange or organize something: *I've made an appointment with the doctor.*
6 [T] to earn or get money: *She makes about a hundred dollars a month.* ♦ *You can make a lot of money playing the stock market.* ♦ *Can you make a living from painting?* ♦ *The company made a small profit in its first year.*
7 [linking verb] to give a particular total when added together: *Four multiplied by two makes eight.*
8 [T] to cause something to be successful: *It was the children's singing that really made the performance.*
9 [linking verb] to have the right qualities for a particular job or purpose: *Don't you think the novel would make a great film?*
10 [T] *informal* to reach a place, or to be present in a place: *At this rate we won't make Jedda before midnight.* ♦ *I won't be able to make tomorrow's meeting.*
PHRASES make believe to pretend that something is real
make do (with/without sth) to succeed in dealing with a situation by using what is available, or despite not having something: *There wasn't much food, but we made do.*
make it 1 to succeed in a particular activity: *She made it in films when she was still a teenager.* **2** to manage to arrive on time: *We just made it in time for the wedding.* **3** to be able to be present at a particular event: *I can't make it on Friday.* ♦ *We made it to the meeting.*
make way (for) 1 to move away so that someone or something can get past you: *We were asked to make way for the bride and groom.* **2** to be replaced by someone or something: *Most of the old buildings have made way for hotels and offices.*
—**maker** noun [C]
PHRASAL VERBS 'make for sth 1 to move towards a place: *He picked up his umbrella and made for the door.* **2** to help to make something possible: *The new computers make for much greater efficiency.*

'make sb/sth ,into sth to change someone or something so that they become something else: *The story was made into a film two years ago.*

'make sth ,of sb/sth to understand someone or the meaning of something in a particular way: *I don't know what to make of our new teacher.* ♦ *What do you make of this news?*

,make 'off to leave quickly, especially after doing something wrong= RUN AWAY: *The kids made off when they heard us coming.*

,make sth 'out to see, hear, or understand something with difficulty: *I can just make a few words out on this page.* ♦ *I couldn't make out what he was saying.*

,make 'up to become friendly with someone again after an argument: *Why don't you two forget your differences and make up?* ♦ *Tom still hasn't made up with Alice.*

,make sth 'up 1 to invent something such as a story or an explanation: *He made up some excuse about the dog eating his homework.* ♦ *She's good at making up stories for the children.* **2** to put **make-up** on someone's face: *They made my face up to look like a clown.*

,make 'up for sth 1 to take the place of something that has been lost or damaged: *Nothing can make up for the loss of a child.* **2** to provide something good, so that something bad seems less important: *He bought her some flowers to make up for being late.* → LOST¹

> **Build your vocabulary: words you can use instead of make**
>
> **Make** is a very general word. Here are some words with more specific meanings that sound more natural and appropriate in particular situations.
> **things made in factories** assemble, build, manufacture, mass-produce, produce, turn out
> **buildings/structures** build, erect, put up
> **power/heat/light** emit, generate, give off, produce
> **problems/changes/effects** cause, create, generate, produce
> **new things** come up with, create, design, develop, invent
> **things that are made quickly and not very well** churn out, cobble together, throw together

make² /meɪk/ noun [C] a product that is made by a particular company= BRAND: *a very popular make of car*

'make-be,lieve noun [U] the activity of pretending that something is real or that a situation is better than it really is —**'make-be,lieve** adj

,make-or-'break adj bringing either total success or total failure, and therefore very important

makeshift /'meɪkˌʃɪft/ adj made using whatever is available and therefore not very good

'make-,up noun [U] substances that people put on their faces to make them look attractive= COSMETICS: *Gina wears no make-up at all.* ♦ *Rachel was still putting on her make-up when the taxi arrived.*

making /'meɪkɪŋ/ noun [U] the activity or process of creating something

PHRASES **have the makings of** to have the qualities that are necessary to become a particular type of thing or person: *I believe you have the makings of a great artist.*
in the making in the process of being created or produced: *We are witnessing a piece of history in the making.*

maladministration /ˌmæləd.mɪnɪ'streɪʃ(ə)n/ noun [U] *formal* bad or dishonest management

malaria /mə'leəriə/ noun [U] HEALTH a very serious illness that you can get if a mosquito infected with a particular parasite bites you. Malaria causes fever, **shivering**, and sweating, and it can be **fatal**.

male¹ /meɪl/ adj **1** BIOLOGY belonging to the sex that does not give birth and is capable of fertilizing a female egg ≠ FEMALE: *male workers* ♦ *a male elephant* **2** BIOLOGY relating to a gamete that is not female **3** BIOLOGY relating to the part of a plant, especially a stamen or **anther**, that produces a gamete that is capable of fertilizing a female gamete **4** relating to men ≠ FEMALE: *ideas about female and male sexuality*

male² /meɪl/ noun [C] **1** BIOLOGY a male animal ≠ FEMALE **2** a man ≠ FEMALE

malevolent /mə'levələnt/ adj showing that you want to do something bad to someone

malfeasance /ˌmæl'fiːz(ə)ns/ noun [U] LAW illegal actions

malfunction /mæl'fʌŋkʃ(ə)n/ noun [C/U] an occasion when something does not operate correctly —**malfunction** verb [I]

malice /'mælɪs/ noun [U] a strong feeling of wanting to hurt someone or be unkind to them

malicious /mə'lɪʃəs/ adj intended to hurt or upset someone —**maliciously** adv

malignant /mə'lɪgnənt/ adj HEALTH a tumour that is malignant consists of cancer cells that can spread in the body ≠ BENIGN —**malignancy** noun [C/U], **malignantly** adv

mall /mɔːl, mæl/ noun [C] a large building with a lot of shops in it

malleable /'mæliəb(ə)l/ adj **1** a malleable metal is easy to press into different shapes **2** a malleable person is easy to persuade or influence —**malleability** /ˌmæliə'bɪləti/ noun [U]

mallet /'mælɪt/ noun [C] a wooden hammer —*picture* → TOOL

the malleus /'mæliəs/ noun [singular] ANATOMY the first of three small bones in the **middle ear** that carry sound from the **eardrum** to the **inner ear**

malnourished /ˌmæl'nʌrɪʃt/ adj HEALTH someone who is malnourished is weak or ill because they do not eat enough food, or they do not eat enough of the right foods

malnutrition /ˌmælnjuː'trɪʃ(ə)n/ noun [U] HEALTH a medical condition in which you are very weak or ill because you do not have enough to eat, or you do not eat enough of the right foods

Malpighian layer /mæl'pɪgiən ˌleɪə/ noun [singular] BIOLOGY the **basal cell layer**, where new skin cells are produced

Malpighian tubule /mæl'pɪgiən ˌtjuːbjuːl/ noun [C] BIOLOGY a narrow tube in the body of an insect that is involved in removing waste matter

malpractice /mæl'præktɪs/ noun [C/U] careless or illegal behaviour by someone with a professional or official job

malt /mɔːlt/ noun [U] AGRICULTURE a substance produced by keeping grain such as **barley** in water until it begins to grow and then drying it. Malt is used in making beer, **whisky**, and vinegar.

maltose /'mɔːltəʊs/ noun [U] BIOLOGY a sugar that is produced by the breaking down of starch. Chemical formula: $C_{12}H_{22}O_{11}$

malware /'mælweə/ noun [U] COMPUTING software such as a virus that is designed to damage or destroy information on a computer

mamba /'mæmbə/ noun [C] a large poisonous black or green African snake —*picture* → REPTILE

mammal /'mæm(ə)l/ noun [C] **BIOLOGY** a **warm-blooded** vertebrate animal with hair that is born from its mother's body, not from an egg, and that drinks its mother's milk as a baby. Humans, cows, and bats are all mammals. —*picture* → pp 452 and 453

mammary gland /'mæməri ˌglænd/ noun [C] **ANATOMY** a gland that produces milk in women and other female mammals

mammogram /'mæməgræm/ noun [C] **HEALTH** an X-ray photograph of a woman's breasts that is taken in order to check for diseases such as cancer

mammoth /'mæməθ/ noun [C] a very large mammal similar to an elephant with long hair that lived a very long time ago

man¹ /mæn/ (plural **men** /men/) noun **1** [C] an adult male human: *a jury of nine men and three women* ♦ *a man's overcoat* ♦ *a man of 64* (=who is 64 years old) ♦ *a nice young man* **2** [U] people in general. Some people avoid using this word because it suggests that women are not included, or that men are more important than women. They use the word **humans** instead. **3** [C] a husband, boyfriend, or sexual partner: *Have you met Jessica's new man?* **4** [C] someone who is strong and brave, as a man is traditionally expected to be

man² /mæn/ (**mans, manning, manned**) verb [T] to provide a place, machine, or system with the people who are needed to operate it. Some people avoid using this word because it suggests that women are not included. They use the word **staff** instead.

manage /'mænɪdʒ/ verb **1** [I/T] to succeed in doing or dealing with something, especially something difficult or something that needs a lot of effort: *I don't think I can manage a long walk today.* ♦ *techniques for managing stress in the workplace* ♦ *We couldn't have managed without your help.* ♦ *She managed to escape by diving into the river.* **2** [T] to be in charge of a company, an area, or people that you work with: *He manages the family business.* ♦ *Smith says he wants to manage the football team next year.* ♦ *a well-managed restaurant* **3** [T] to be able to provide something or make it available, for example money or time: *Could you manage 5 o'clock on Monday* (=will you be able to do something at that time?)*?* ♦ *We can only manage 20 dollars a week for rent.* **4** [I] to be able to live with only a limited amount of money: *I don't know how he manages on what he earns.*

manageable /'mænɪdʒəb(ə)l/ adj able to be dealt with or controlled —**manageability** /ˌmænɪdʒə'bɪləti/ noun [U]

management /'mænɪdʒmənt/ noun **1** [U] the control and operation of a business or organization: *In this company we have a new approach to management.* ♦ *a diploma in management* **2** [U] the process of controlling or managing something: *stress management* ♦ *an attack on the government's management of the economy* **3** [singular/U] the people who are in charge of a business or organization, or of the people who work there: *the company's senior management* ♦ *Talks between the workers' union and management broke down today.*

> **Management** can be used with a singular or plural verb. You can say: *The management **was** responsible.* OR: *The management **were** responsible.*

management ac'counting noun [U] **BUSINESS** the activity of preparing and using financial information to support management decisions

management 'buyout noun [C] **BUSINESS** a business deal in which the managers of a company

take control of it by buying all, or the majority of, its shares

'management con,sultant noun [C] **BUSINESS** someone whose job is to advise managers on how to control and operate their companies more effectively

manager /'mænɪdʒə/ noun [C] **1** someone whose job is to organize and control the work of a business, a department, or the people who work there: *I'd like to speak to the manager.* ♦ *an office manager* ♦ *For three years she was **the manager of** a radio station.* **2** someone whose job is to look after the business activities of an entertainer or sports player **3** **SPORTS** someone whose job is to organize and train a sports team

managerial /ˌmænə'dʒɪəriəl/ adj relating to the job of a manager, especially in a company

managing director /ˌmænɪdʒɪŋ daɪ'rektə/ noun [C] someone in charge of a company

mandarin /'mændərɪn/ noun [C] a fruit like a small orange —*picture* → FRUIT

Mandarin /'mændərɪn/ noun [U] the official language of China

mandate¹ /'mændeɪt/ noun **1** [singular] **POLITICS** the authority of an elected government or official to do the things that they promised to do before an election **2** [C] *formal* an official order to do something **3** [C/U] **POLITICS** the authority given to a country to rule another country or region

mandate² /mæn'deɪt/ verb [T] **POLITICS** to give someone the authority to do something

mandated /mæn'deɪtɪd/ adj **POLITICS** a mandated country or region is ruled by another country that has been given the authority to do this

mandatory /'mændət(ə)ri/ adj something that is mandatory has to be done because of a law or rule: *a mandatory meeting for all employees*

mandible /'mændɪb(ə)l/ noun [C] **1** **ANATOMY** the lower jaw of humans and vertebrates —*picture* → SKELETON **2** **BIOLOGY** one of the two parts of an insect's mouth that it uses for biting —*picture* → INSECT

mandolin /ˌmændə'lɪn/ noun [C] **MUSIC** a musical instrument that looks like a guitar with a curved back

mane /meɪn/ noun [C] **BIOLOGY** the long hair on the neck of a horse or lion

manganese /'mæŋgəniːz/ noun [U] **CHEMISTRY** a hard grey metal element used for making steel and glass. Chemical symbol: **Mn**

manganin /'mæŋgənɪn/ noun **TRADEMARK CHEMISTRY** an alloy of copper, manganese, and **nickel**. It is used to make **resistors**.

manger /'meɪndʒə/ noun [C] a long low open container that horses or cows eat from

mangetout /ˌmɒnʒ'tuː/ (plural **mangetout**) noun [C] a small flat green vegetable that is the fruit of the plant. It is a type of **pea** and you can eat its skin.

mango /'mæŋgəʊ/ (plural **mangos** or **mangoes**) noun [C/U] a soft sweet tropical fruit with a red or green skin and yellow flesh —*picture* → FRUIT

mangrove /'mæŋˌgrəʊv/ noun [C] a tropical tree that grows beside water and has roots that begin above the ground

'mangrove ,swamp noun [C/U] **GEOGRAPHY, BIOLOGY** an area of land covered by water where mangroves grow

manhandle /'mæn,hænd(ə)l/ verb [T] to touch, push, or pull someone in a rough way

manhole /ˈmænˌhəʊl/ noun [C] a hole in the surface of a road or street, covered with a metal lid and used for entering an underground passage

manhood /ˈmænhʊd/ noun [U] *formal* the time when a boy becomes a man

mania /ˈmeɪniə/ noun [C/U] **1** an extremely strong enthusiasm for something, especially among a lot of people: *World Cup mania* **2 HEALTH** a mental illness that makes someone behave in an unusually excited and strange way

maniac /ˈmeɪniæk/ noun [C] *informal* someone who behaves in a stupid and dangerous way = LUNATIC

manic /ˈmænɪk/ adj **1** behaving in an unusually excited way **2 HEALTH** someone who is manic is affected by a mental illness that makes them behave in an unusually excited and strange way —**manically** /ˈmænɪkli/ adv

manic deˈpression noun [U] **HEALTH** a serious mental condition that involves extreme changes in mood. Most people now use the term **bipolar disorder**. —**manic depressive** adj

manicure /ˈmænɪkjʊə/ noun [C] a beauty treatment for your hands and nails —**manicure** verb [T]

manifest /ˈmænɪfest/ verb [T] *formal* to show something such as a feeling, attitude, or ability

manifestation /ˌmænɪfeˈsteɪʃ(ə)n/ noun [C/U] *formal* evidence that something exists or is present

manifesto /ˌmænɪˈfestəʊ/ (plural **manifestos**) noun [C] a formal statement describing the aims and plans of an organization, especially a political party

manioc /ˈmæniɒk/ noun [U] **AGRICULTURE** a tropical plant whose roots can be eaten when cooked. It is an important food in many countries. —*picture* → VEGETABLE

manipulate /məˈnɪpjʊleɪt/ verb [T] **1** to influence someone, or to control something, in a clever or dishonest way **2** to skilfully handle, control, or use something **3 COMPUTING** to change, correct, or move information stored on a computer —**manipulation** /məˌnɪpjʊˈleɪʃ(ə)n/ noun [U]

manipulative /məˈnɪpjʊlətɪv/ adj *showing disapproval* someone who is manipulative makes people do what they want by influencing them in a clever or dishonest way

mankind /mænˈkaɪnd/ noun [U] all humans considered as a single group. Some people avoid using this word because it seems not to include women, and they use **humankind** instead.

manly /ˈmænli/ adj tending to behave in a way that men are traditionally expected to behave, especially by being strong and brave —**manliness** noun [U]

man-ˈmade adj something that is man-made has been made by people and does not exist naturally ≠ NATURAL: *Rayon is a man-made fibre.*

manned /mænd/ adj a manned vehicle or place has people working in or on it ≠ UNMANNED: *a manned space flight*

manned manoeuvring unit /ˌmænd məˈnuːv(ə)rɪŋ ˌjuːnɪt/ noun [C] **ASTRONOMY** an **MMU** —*picture* → ASTRONAUT

manner /ˈmænə/ noun **1** [singular] the way that you do something, or the way that something happens: *Things had been done in the same manner for centuries.* ♦ *The manner of his death aroused a lot of interest in the media.* **2** [singular] the way that you behave towards someone: *The salesman's aggressive manner put us off.* **3 manners** [plural] traditionally accepted ways of behaving that show a polite respect for other people: *Children learn manners by observing*

their parents. ♦ *It's bad manners to interrupt someone.*

mannerism /ˈmænəˌrɪz(ə)m/ noun [C] a particular way of speaking or moving that someone has

manoeuvre /məˈnuːvə/ noun **1** [C] an action or movement that you need care or skill to do **2** [C] something clever or dishonest that someone does in order to get something that they want **3 manoeuvres** [plural] a military training operation

manometer /məˈnɒmɪtə/ noun [C] **PHYSICS** a piece of equipment that is used to measure gas pressure

manor /ˈmænə/ or **ˈmanor ˌhouse** noun [C] a large house with a lot of land and small buildings around it

manpower /ˈmænˌpaʊə/ noun [U] all the people who are available to do a particular job or to work in a particular place. Some people avoid this word because they consider it offensive to women, and they use the words **staff** or **personnel** instead.

mansion /ˈmænʃən/ noun [C] a very large house

manslaughter /ˈmænˌslɔːtə/ noun [U] **LAW** the crime of causing someone's death illegally but without intending to → MURDER¹

mantelpiece /ˈmænt(ə)l,piːs/ noun [C] a shelf above a **fireplace**

mantis /ˈmæntɪs/ noun [C] a **praying mantis**

mantissa /mænˈtɪsə/ noun [C] **MATHS** the part of a **logarithm** shown after the decimal point

mantle /ˈmænt(ə)l/ noun [singular] **1** the authority or responsibility connected with someone's position, duties, or beliefs **2 GEOLOGY** the part of the Earth that is deep below the surface and surrounds the core —*picture* → EARTH

mantra /ˈmæntrə/ noun [C] **RELIGION** a sound, word, or phrase that is continuously repeated as a prayer

manual¹ /ˈmænjʊəl/ noun [C] a book that contains instructions for doing something, especially for operating a machine

manual² /ˈmænjʊəl/ adj **1** involving the use of your hands, or doing work with your hands: *The job requires manual skill.* ♦ *manual labour* **2** operated by people rather than automatically or using computers **3** a manual worker is someone whose job involves physical work, using their hands —**manually** adv

ˌmanual ˈgearbox noun [C] **ENGINEERING** a **gearbox** in a vehicle where the driver changes the gears, rather than them changing automatically

manufacture¹ /ˌmænjʊˈfæktʃə/ verb [T] to make goods in large quantities in a factory: *The firm manufactures women's clothing.* —**manufacturing** noun [U]

manufacture² /ˌmænjʊˈfæktʃə/ noun [U] the process of making goods in large quantities in a factory

manufacturer /ˌmænjʊˈfæktʃərə/ noun [C] a person or company that makes a particular type of product, especially in a factory

manure /məˈnjʊə/ noun [U] **AGRICULTURE** solid waste from farm animals, often mixed with other substances and used on crops to help them to grow

manuscript /ˈmænjʊˌskrɪpt/ noun [C] **1** a writer's original pages of a book, article, or document before it is published **2** a very old book or document that was written by hand before books began to be printed

many /ˈmeni/ (**more** /mɔː/, **most** /məʊst/) determiner, pronoun **1** a large number of people, things, places etc: *I've been to their house many times.* ♦ *We didn't sell many tickets.* ♦ *Many of the world's leading doctors have been trained here.* ♦ *There are too many*

cheetah

leopard

lion

chimpanzee

tiger

lioness

gorilla

monkey

elephant

hippopotamus

orang-utan

giraffe

zebra

rhinoceros

panda

camel

bear

koala

doe

stag

mammals

kangaroo

duckbilled platypus

bat

wolf

mongoose

fox

badger

mole

rat

mouse

squirrel

rabbit

horse

donkey

pig

ram

ewe

goat

bull

cow

mammals

map 454 **maritime polar**

rules and regulations. ♦ *He has **so many** books, he couldn't possibly read them all.* ♦ ***Not many** students can afford to buy their own computers.* ♦ *We've lived here for **a good many** years.* **2** used for asking or talking about the number of people, things etc that there are: ***How many** students are taking the test?* ♦ *They try to interview **as many** candidates **as** possible.*

PHRASE **as many as** used before a number for showing how large and surprising it is: *The rainforest contains as many as 5 million species of plant and animal.*

> ■ **Many** is used mainly in negative sentences and questions, or in positive sentences after 'too', 'so', or 'as': *You're trying to do too many things at once.* Positive statements, such as: *Many children dislike sport*, are quite formal, and in these cases **a lot of** is often used instead: *A lot of people came.*
> ■ In informal English, **lots of** is often used instead of **a lot of**: *She's got lots of friends.*

map¹ /mæp/ noun [C] **1** GEOGRAPHY a drawing of an area that shows the positions of things such as countries, rivers, cities, and streets: ***a map of** Central Asia* ♦ *They never taught us how to **read a map** at school.* **2** a drawing that shows the position of things in relation to each other: ***a map of** the human genome*

map² /mæp/ (**maps, mapping, mapped**) verb [T] **1** GEOGRAPHY to make a map of an area **2** to find the position of something, or to find the positions of the parts of something: *Scientists have succeeded in mapping the human genome.*

PHRASAL VERB **,map sth 'out** to plan or describe in detail how something will happen

maple /ˈmeɪp(ə)l/ noun [C] a tree that grows mainly in northern countries and has wide leaves that turn red and yellow in the autumn

'map ,projection noun [C/U] GEOGRAPHY a method of making a flat map of the Earth, or a map made by this method

mapwork /ˈmæp,wɜːk/ noun [U] GEOGRAPHY the activity of studying and using maps correctly

mar /mɑː/ (**mars, marring, marred**) verb [T] to spoil something

Mar. abbrev March

marabou or **marabout** /ˈmærəbuː/ noun [C] a large African **stork** (=a type of bird) with long legs and a long beak

marasmus /məˈræzməs/ noun [U] HEALTH a medical condition in which a young child gradually becomes extremely thin and weak as a result of not having enough food

marathon /ˈmærəθ(ə)n/ noun [C] **1** SPORTS a race that is run for 42 kilometres or about 26 miles **2** an activity or event that takes a long time to complete: *The meeting turned out to be a bit of a marathon.*

marble /ˈmɑːb(ə)l/ noun **1** [U] GEOLOGY a hard smooth metamorphic rock that is used for building and making statues. It is a type of **limestone** and is usually white or grey with marks of another colour in it. **2** [C] a small coloured glass ball, used in children's games

march¹ /mɑːtʃ/ verb [I] **1** when soldiers march, they walk in a group with each person matching the speed and movements of the others **2** to walk somewhere quickly and in a determined, confident, or angry way **3** to walk to a place as part of an organized group protesting about something —**marcher** noun [C]

march² /mɑːtʃ/ noun [C] **1** a long walk by an organized group, especially soldiers **2** a walk by a group of people to a place in order to protest about something **3** MUSIC a piece of music with a strong beat that matches the steps taken by marching soldiers

March /mɑːtʃ/ noun [U] the third month of the year, between February and April: *His birthday is in March.* ♦ *The concert is on 29 March.*

mare /meə/ noun [C] an adult female horse

margarine /ˌmɑːdʒəˈriːn/ noun [C/U] a yellow substance made from vegetable oil or animal fat that can be used instead of butter

margin /ˈmɑːdʒɪn/ noun [C]

1 space at side of page	**4** edge of area
2 amount sth is won by	**5** payment in case of loss
3 extra amount	**6** of leaf

1 the space at the left or right side of a page that is usually left empty: *I made a couple of notes **in the margin**.*
2 the amount by which a competition or election is won: *Members voted by **a narrow margin** (=a small amount) to accept the proposals.*
3 an additional amount of time, space, money etc that someone includes to be certain that they will be safe or successful: *There's no **margin for error** – we have to win.* ♦ *It's a business that operates with very small **profit margins** (=the difference between the cost of providing a product, and the amount that the business charges for providing it).*
4 the edge of an area
5 BUSINESS an amount of money that an **investor** gives a **stockbroker** to pay for possible losses on money that the stockbroker invests for them
6 BIOLOGY the outer edge of a leaf —*picture* → LEAF

marginal /ˈmɑːdʒɪn(ə)l/ adj **1** very small **2** not important or relevant

marginalize /ˈmɑːdʒɪnəlaɪz/ verb [T] **1** to make someone or something seem not important or relevant **2** to prevent someone from having power or influence

marginally /ˈmɑːdʒɪn(ə)li/ adv by only a very small amount

marijuana /ˌmærɪˈwɑːnə/ noun [U] **cannabis**

marimba /məˈrɪmbə/ noun [C] MUSIC a musical instrument consisting of wooden bars of different sizes fixed to a frame. You play it by hitting the bars with sticks. → XYLOPHONE

marina /məˈriːnə/ noun [C] an area of water beside the sea or a lake for keeping small boats in

marinade /ˌmærɪˈneɪd/ noun [C/U] a liquid that you put food into to give it a special flavour before cooking it —**marinade** verb [I/T]

marine¹ /məˈriːn/ adj **1** BIOLOGY living in, relating to, or happening in the sea: *marine animals* **2** involving ships or the business of moving people and goods in ships

marine² /məˈriːn/ noun [C] a soldier whose job is to fight on both land and sea

Mariner Valley /ˌmærɪnə ˈvæli/ noun ASTRONOMY a large area of deep valleys on the planet Mars

marital /ˈmærɪt(ə)l/ adj relating to marriage

,marital 'status noun [U] *formal* used for asking officially whether someone is married or not

maritime /ˈmærɪ,taɪm/ adj **1** involving ships or the business of moving people and goods in ships **2** close to the sea

,maritime 'polar noun [C] GEOGRAPHY an air mass that forms over cold ocean water, and is therefore cold and wet

,maritime 'tropical noun [C] GEOGRAPHY an air mass that forms over tropical seas, and is therefore usually warm and wet

mark¹ /mɑːk/ noun [C]

1 area of dirt/damage	4 sth printed/written
2 school score	5 of a quality
3 level/stage/total etc	+ PHRASE

1 a small area of something such as dirt, oil, or damage on the surface of something: *There was a greasy mark on his shirt.* ♦ *There were burn marks all over her hands.*

2 EDUCATION a score or grade that you are given for school work or for how well you perform in a competition: *What mark did you get for your essay?*

3 a particular level, stage, total etc that something reaches: *Esfahan was **the halfway mark** on our trip across Iran.* ♦ *The temperature had already **reached** the 45 degree **mark**.* → POINT¹ sense 5

4 a printed or written symbol that is not a letter or a number: *Put a mark by the names of the most interesting candidates.*

5 something that shows that a person or thing has a particular quality: *The mark of a good film is that it leaves you talking about it.*

PHRASE **wide of the mark** or **(way) off the mark** incorrect: *Her theory turned out to be pretty wide of the mark.*

mark² /mɑːk/ verb

1 make mark on sth	5 show sth is happening
2 write/draw on sth	6 celebrate sth
3 judge sb's work	7 in sports
4 show place of sth	+ PHRASAL VERBS

1 [T] to make a mark on the surface of something so that its appearance is spoiled or damaged: *Her cheek was **marked with** scratches.*

2 [T] to write or draw words, letters, symbols etc on something for a particular purpose: *We entered through a door marked 'Private'.* ♦ *The teacher **marked** six of the answers **wrong** (=put a symbol by them to show they were wrong).* ♦ *Names **marked with** a red star are included in the team.*

3 [I/T] EDUCATION to judge the quality of a student's work and write a mark on it: *The teacher spent the evening **marking essays**.*

4 [T] to show the position of something: *A memorial plaque will **mark the spot** where he died.*

5 [T] to show that something is happening: *This tournament **marks the** official **start of** the season.*

6 [T] to celebrate something: *A ceremony was held to **mark the occasion**.*

7 [T] SPORTS to stay close to a member of the other team in a game such as football in order to prevent them from getting the ball

PHRASAL VERBS **,mark sth 'off** to show the limits of an area using a line, fence, rope etc: *The crime scene was marked off with official police tape.*

,mark sth 'out to show the shape of something by drawing it on a surface: *The shape of the pond is marked out first with a spade.*

marked /mɑːkt/ adj clear and noticeable = DISTINCT
—**markedly** /'mɑːkɪdli/ adv

marker /'mɑːkə/ noun [C] **1** an object that is used for showing where something is or where you should go **2** a pen with a thick soft point **3** SPORTS a player whose job is to stay close to a member of the other team in a game such as football, in order to prevent them from getting the ball or playing

market¹ /'mɑːkɪt/ noun

1 public place for selling	4 stock market
2 trade in goods	5 people who buy sth
3 group product is sold to	+ PHRASE

1 [C] a place, especially outside, where people sell goods: *a vegetable market* ♦ *a street market* ♦ *a market trader*

2 [singular] ECONOMICS trade in goods of a particular type: *Changes in the weather affect **the market in** fruit and vegetables.* ♦ *We're hoping to increase our **share of the market**.*

3 [C] ECONOMICS, BUSINESS a particular place or group of people that a product is sold to: *overseas markets* ♦ *Hong Kong is the main market for our shellfish.*

4 [C] ECONOMICS a stock market: *Trading has been slow on the New York and Tokyo markets this morning.*

5 [singular] BUSINESS the number of people willing to buy a particular product

PHRASE **on the market** available to buy: *Computers as powerful as this are not yet on the market.*

market² /'mɑːkɪt/ verb [T] to use advertising and other methods to persuade people to buy something

marketable /'mɑːkɪtəb(ə)l/ adj **1** a marketable product can be sold because people want to buy it **2** marketable skills are those that employers are likely to want people to have

'market-,driven adj BUSINESS controlled by what and how much people buy, not by the government

,market e'conomy noun [C] ECONOMICS an economic system in which prices, salaries, and the supply of goods are controlled by what and how much people buy, not by the government

,market 'forces noun [plural] ECONOMICS the economic influences that affect prices, salaries, and the number of jobs available, and that are not controlled by governments

,market 'garden noun [C] AGRICULTURE a small farm where fruit and vegetables are grown to be sold
—**,market 'gardener** noun [C], **,market 'gardening** noun [U]

marketing /'mɑːkɪtɪŋ/ noun [U] the ways in which a company encourages people to buy its products

,market 'leader noun [C] BUSINESS **1** a company that sells more of a particular product than any other company **2** a product that is bought by more people than any other of its type

marketplace /'mɑːkɪt,pleɪs/ noun **1** [C] a place where people buy and sell goods in an outdoor market **2 the marketplace** [singular] ECONOMICS the part of the economy that involves buying and selling

,market 'share noun [C/U] BUSINESS the percentage of the total amount of sales of a particular product that a company has

'market ,town noun [C] a town where goods can be bought and sold in a market

marking /'mɑːkɪŋ/ noun **1** [C] a pattern of marks on the surface of something, for example the skin, fur, or feathers of an animal or bird **2** [U] EDUCATION the process of checking students' written work and giving it a mark

'mark-,up noun [U] COMPUTING instructions added to documents that tell a computer how to print or organize the information

'mark-up ,language noun [C/U] COMPUTING a system of instructions that are added to documents to tell a computer how to print or organize the information

marlin /'mɑːlɪn/ noun [C] a large fish with a long pointed top jaw that people catch for sport in the Atlantic and Pacific Oceans

marmalade /'mɑːməleɪd/ noun [C/U] a sweet food that is made from cooked fruit, especially oranges. It is usually spread on **toast**.

maroon /mə'ruːn/ adj dark red-brown in colour

marooned /mə'ruːnd/ adj left in a place and unable to leave

marriage /'mærɪdʒ/ noun **1** [C/U] the relationship between two people who are husband and wife: *a long and happy marriage* ♦ *Anne's marriage to Daniel lasted ten years.* **2** [C] a **wedding**: *Their marriage is planned for September.*

married /'mærid/ adj **1** a married person has a husband or wife ≠ SINGLE: *a married man* ♦ *He's married to my older sister.* ♦ *They're getting married next year.* **2** involving marriage or people who are married: *married life*

marrow /'mærəʊ/ noun **1** [C/U] a large long vegetable that has a dark green skin and is white inside **2** [U] ANATOMY the soft substance inside bones, where blood cells develop = BONE MARROW

marry /'mæri/ (**marries, marrying, married**) verb **1** [I/T] to become someone's husband or wife: *Marge married a lawyer.* ♦ *They married in 1996.* **2** [T] to perform the ceremony in which two people become husband and wife **3** [T] *formal* to combine one thing with another

Mars /mɑːz/ ASTRONOMY the red planet that is fourth furthest from the Sun, between Venus and Earth —*picture* → SOLAR SYSTEM

marsh /mɑːʃ/ noun [C] GEOGRAPHY an area of soft wet land —**marshy** adj

'marsh ,gas noun [U] CHEMISTRY a gas that results from the decay of plants in an area of wet land and consists mainly of methane

marshland /'mɑːʃlænd/ noun [U] GEOGRAPHY an area that consists of **marshes**

marshmallow /,mɑːʃ'mæləʊ/ noun [C/U] a soft white sweet with a thick round shape

marsupial /mɑː'suːpiəl/ noun [C] BIOLOGY a mammal whose babies feed on milk in a pocket in their mother's body until they are completely developed

martial /'mɑːʃ(ə)l/ adj *formal* relating to war or fighting → COURT-MARTIAL

,martial 'art noun [C] SPORTS a sport that is a traditional Asian form of fighting such as **karate** or **judo**

,martial 'law noun [U] direct control of a country or area by the armed forces

Martian /'mɑːʃ(ə)n/ adj ASTRONOMY relating to the planet Mars

martyr /'mɑːtə/ noun [C] RELIGION someone who suffers or is killed because of their religious or political beliefs

martyrdom /'mɑːtədəm/ noun [U] a martyr's pain or death

marvel[1] /'mɑːv(ə)l/ (**marvels, marvelling, marvelled**) verb [I/T] to show or feel surprise or admiration

marvel[2] /'mɑːv(ə)l/ noun [C] someone or something that is very surprising or impressive

marvellous /'mɑːvələs/ adj extremely enjoyable, good, or impressive: *a marvellous performance* —**marvellously** adv

Marxism /'mɑːksɪz(ə)m/ noun [U] SOCIAL STUDIES the political and economic theories of Karl Marx, from which Communist and **socialist** political systems developed

Marxist /'mɑːksɪst/ adj SOCIAL STUDIES relating to or based on Marxism —**Marxist** noun [C]

marzipan /,mɑːzɪ'pæn/ noun [U] a sweet food made from sugar and **almonds** that is used for decorating cakes

masculine[1] /'mæskjʊlɪn/ adj **1** with qualities that are considered typical of men ≠ FEMININE **2** LANGUAGE in some languages, masculine nouns, pronouns, and adjectives have different forms from **feminine** or neuter words

masculine[2] /'mæskjʊlɪn/ noun [C] LANGUAGE a word or form of a word that belongs to the masculine group of nouns, pronouns, or adjectives → FEMININE, NEUTER

masculinity /,mæskjʊ'lɪnəti/ noun [U] the qualities that are considered typical of men ≠ FEMININITY

mash /mæʃ/ or ,**mash 'up** verb [T] to crush food so that it is a soft mass: *Mash the potatoes with a little milk.* —*picture* → FOOD

masjid /'mʌsdʒɪd/ noun [C] a Muslim name for a **mosque**

mask[1] /mɑːsk/ noun [C] **1** something that you wear in order to cover part or all of your face **2** an expression on someone's face that hides their true feelings, thoughts, or character

mask[2] /mɑːsk/ verb [T] **1** to cover something in order to hide it **2** to hide the smell, taste, or sound of something with a stronger smell or taste or a louder sound **3** to hide your true feelings, thoughts, or character

masking tape /'mɑːskɪŋ ,teɪp/ noun [U] TECHNOLOGY narrow sticky paper that is used for protecting something such as a window when painting next to it, or for fixing a drawing to a **drawing board** when they are drawing

masonry /'meɪsənri/ noun [U] the bricks or stones that make a building, wall, or other structure

masquerade /,mæskə'reɪd/ verb [I] to pretend to be someone or something that you are not

mass[1] /mæs/ noun

1 large quantity	4 ordinary people
2 sth without shape	5 religious ceremony
3 scientific use	6 piece of music

1 [C] a large quantity, number, or amount: *The police had a mass of evidence.* ♦ *a mass of fallen leaves*
2 [C] a lump or amount of a substance that does not have a clear or definite shape: *The vegetables had turned into a sticky mass at the bottom of the pan.*
3 [U] CHEMISTRY, PHYSICS the amount of matter that something contains. Mass is different from weight as the effects of gravity are not taken into account when it is measured. Symbol m. → CRITICAL MASS
4 the masses [plural] SOCIAL STUDIES working-class people generally
5 mass or **Mass** [C/U] RELIGION the main religious ceremony of the Roman Catholic Church
6 [C] MUSIC a piece of music that was written to be played at a Mass

mass[2] /mæs/ adj involving or affecting a large number of people: *the problem of mass unemployment* ♦ *weapons of mass destruction*

massacre /'mæsəkə/ noun [C/U] the action of killing a lot of people —**massacre** verb [T]

massage /ˈmæsɑːʒ/ noun [C/U] the action of pressing, squeezing, and rubbing someone's body in order to reduce pain in their muscles or to make them relax —**massage** verb [T]

masse see en masse

ˌmass ˈenergy noun [U] **CHEMISTRY, PHYSICS** mass and energy considered as capable of being changed into one another, according to the laws of **relativity**

massive /ˈmæsɪv/ adj **1** very large: *a massive amount of money* **2** very severe: *a massive heart attack* —**massively** adv

ˌmass-ˈmarket adj produced in large quantities in order to be sold to many customers

the ˌmass ˈmedia noun [plural] the newspapers, television, and radio that communicate news and information to large numbers of people

ˌmass ˈmovement noun [U] **GEOLOGY** the downward movement of a large area of soil or rock, caused by gravity

ˈmass ˌnoun noun [C] **LANGUAGE** a noun such as 'coffee' that is usually uncountable but can be used in the plural or with the **indefinite** article, for example when you are talking about different types of coffee

ˈmass ˌnumber noun [C] **CHEMISTRY, PHYSICS** the number of protons and neutrons in the nucleus of an atom

mass-produced /ˌmæs prəˈdjuːst/ adj made in large quantities using machines —**mass-produce** verb [T], **mass production** noun [U]

mast /mɑːst/ noun [C] **1** a tall pole that the sails hang from on a ship **2** a tall metal structure that is used for broadcasting radio and television signals

mastectomy /mæˈstektəmi/ (plural **mastectomies**) noun [C] **HEALTH** a medical operation in which a woman's breast is removed, usually to prevent a cancer from spreading

master¹ /ˈmɑːstə/ noun [C] **1** a man who has control over servants, other people, or an animal **2** a man who is very good at something: *He's a master of the clever remark.* **3** a document, photograph, or recording from which copies are made = ORIGINAL

master² /ˈmɑːstə/ verb [T] **1** to learn something so that you know it or can do it very well **2** to manage to control a difficult situation or a strong emotion

ˌmaster ˈbedroom noun [C] the largest bedroom in a house or flat

ˈmaster ˌcylinder noun [C] **ENGINEERING** a cylinder in the braking system of a vehicle that contains **brake fluid**

ˈmaster ˌkey noun [C] a key that will open all the doors in a building

mastermind /ˈmɑːstəmaɪnd/ verb [T] to plan and organize a difficult or complicated operation

masterpiece /ˈmɑːstəpiːs/ noun [C] an excellent work of art, or the best work of art by a particular artist, writer, or musician

master's /ˈmɑːstəz/ noun [C] **EDUCATION** informal a **master's degree**

ˈmaster's deˌgree noun [C] **EDUCATION** a university degree that students get if they study for one or two years after their first degree

mastery /ˈmɑːstəri/ noun [U] **1** great knowledge or skill: *his mastery of the English language* **2** power or control over someone or something

mastic /ˈmæstɪk/ noun [U] **CONSTRUCTION** a sticky substance used as a glue for filling holes and keeping out water

mastitis /mæˈstaɪtɪs/ noun [U] **HEALTH, AGRICULTURE** an illness affecting a woman's breast, or a mammal's **udder**, that makes it sore and swollen

masturbate /ˈmæstəbeɪt/ verb [I] to rub the sexual organs in order to get sexual pleasure —**masturbation** /ˌmæstəˈbeɪʃ(ə)n/ noun [U]

mat /mæt/ noun [C] **1** a piece of thick cloth that is put on a floor to protect it or for decoration **2** a small piece of plastic, cloth, or other material that you put on a table or other surface to protect it **3** a piece of a thick soft material like rubber that you use when doing exercises

match¹ /mætʃ/ noun **1** [C] a small stick that produces a flame when it is rubbed against a rough surface: *a box of matches* ♦ *He lit a match.* **2** [C] **SPORTS** a game in which players or teams compete against each other: *a football match* ♦ *They lost the match on Saturday.* **3** [singular] a thing that forms an attractive combination with something else: *The curtains are a good match for the sofa.* **4** [C] something that looks the same as something else: *It was difficult to get an exact match for the paint.*

PHRASE **be no match for sb** to be not as good, strong, clever etc as someone

match² /mætʃ/ verb **1** [I/T] if one thing matches another, or if they match, they are the same or have similar qualities: *The two signatures match.* ♦ *He matches the description of a man seen in the area.* **2** [I/T] to be equal to something else in amount or level, or to provide something that is equal: *The rise in student numbers has not been matched by an increase in teaching staff.* **3** [I/T] if one thing matches another, or if they match, they form an attractive combination: *She wore a green dress and a hat to match.* **4** [T] to choose or provide something that is suitable for a particular situation, person, or purpose: *It is important to match the software to the task.* ♦ *The children were asked to match words with pictures.*

matchbox /ˈmætʃˌbɒks/ noun [C] a small box that contains matches

matching /ˈmætʃɪŋ/ adj with the same colour, pattern, or design

ˌmatch ˈpoint noun [C/U] **SPORTS** in tennis, the last point that a player needs to win in order to win a match

matchstick man /ˈmætʃstɪk ˌmæn/ noun [C] a very simple drawing of a person, with lines to represent the arms, legs, and body

mate¹ /meɪt/ noun [C] **1** informal a friend **2** **BIOLOGY** an animal's sexual partner

mate² /meɪt/ verb [I] **BIOLOGY** if one animal mates with another, or if two animals mate, they have sex

material¹ /məˈtɪəriəl/ noun **1** [C/U] cloth = FABRIC: *What sort of material is your dress made from?* **2** [C/U] a substance that is used for a particular purpose: *Brick was used as the main building material.* **3** [U] information or ideas that are used as the subject of a book, film, or song: *Newspaper articles are a good source of material for stories.* **4** [C/U] documents, or other things giving or showing information, that are used for a particular activity: *publicity material* ♦ *teaching materials*

material² /məˈtɪəriəl/ adj **1** relating to things such as money and possessions that affect people's physical life rather than their thoughts or emotions **2** relating to the physical world that people experience directly, rather than the world of the imagination or thoughts

3 LAW important enough to have an effect: *information that is* **material to** *the decision*

materialistic /mə,tɪəriə'lɪstɪk/ adj believing that money and possessions are the most important aspect of life

materialize /mə'tɪəriəlaɪz/ verb [I] **1** to happen, or to become real **2** to appear suddenly and unexpectedly

maternal /mə'tɜːn(ə)l/ adj **1** *showing approval* typical of a kind and caring mother **2** a maternal relative is related to you through your mother

maternity /mə'tɜːnəti/ adj designed or provided for women who are pregnant or who have just had a baby: *a maternity hospital* ♦ *maternity clothes*

math /mæθ/ noun [U] *American* mathematics

mathematical /,mæθə'mætɪk(ə)l/ adj relating to or involving mathematics —**mathematically** /,mæθə'mætɪkli/ adv

mathematician /,mæθ(ə)mə'tɪʃ(ə)n/ noun [C] someone who studies or teaches mathematics

mathematics /,mæθə'mætɪks/ noun [U] *formal* the study or use of numbers and shapes to calculate, represent, or describe things

maths /mæθs/ noun [U] mathematics

matriarch /'meɪtri,ɑːk/ noun [C] SOCIAL STUDIES a female leader of a family or community

matriarchal /,meɪtri'ɑːk(ə)l/ adj SOCIAL STUDIES a matriarchal society is one in which women have all or most of the influence and power —**matriarchy** /'meɪtri,ɑːki/ noun [C/U]

matriculate /mə'trɪkjʊleɪt/ verb [I] EDUCATION to officially become a student at a university —**matriculation** /mə,trɪkjʊ'leɪʃ(ə)n/ noun [U]

matrilineal /,mætri'lɪniəl/ adj SOCIAL STUDIES used for describing the mother's side of a family and the relations on that side

matrimonial /,mætri'məʊniəl/ adj *formal* relating to marriage

matrimony /'mætriməni/ noun [U] *formal* marriage

matrix /'meɪtrɪks/ (plural **matrices** /'meɪtrɪsiːz/ or **matrixes**) noun [C] **1** ANATOMY the substance between cells in the body from which new tissue such as bones, teeth, and fingernails grow **2** COMPUTING an arrangement of electronic parts in a computer circuit **3** GEOLOGY the rock in which hard stones or jewels form

matt or **matte** /mæt/ adj with a dull surface that is not shiny ≠ GLOSSY, SHINY

matted /'mætɪd/ adj matted hair or fur is twisted or stuck together

matter¹ /'mætə/ noun

1 sth being dealt with	5 substance/thing
2 problem	6 all substances
3 situation sb is in	+ PHRASES
4 when time is short	

1 [C] something that you are discussing, considering, or dealing with: *an extremely **important matter*** ♦ *Teachers feel this is **a matter for** discussion with parents.*

2 the matter [singular] used for talking about problems or bad situations: *You look sad. **What's the matter**?* ♦ ***What's the matter** with the car?* ♦ *I think **there's something the matter** with the printer.* ♦ ***There's nothing the matter** (=there is no problem) with you – you're just tired.*

3 matters [plural] a situation that someone is involved

in: *Her angry attitude didn't improve matters.* ♦ *To* **make matters worse**, *his wife is ill.*

4 [singular] used for emphasizing how short a period of time is: *The school could close in **a matter of** a few weeks.*

5 [U] a particular type of substance or thing: *organic matter* ♦ *Is this suitable **reading matter** for a young child?*

6 [U] SCIENCE the physical substances that everything in the universe is made of. Matter exists in the form of a solid, a liquid, or a gas.

PHRASES **as a matter of fact 1** used when you are going to give more details about something: *I haven't been here long. As a matter of fact, I just got off the plane yesterday.* **2** used when you are going to disagree with or correct what has just been said: *'Was he in a bad mood?' 'No, as a matter of fact, he seemed quite cheerful.'*

a matter of life and death a serious or dangerous situation

a matter of opinion something that different people have different opinions about

a matter of time used for saying that something will certainly happen at some time in the future: *It **was only a matter of time before** she left the company.*
→ SUBJECT MATTER

matter² /'mætə/ verb [I] to be important: *Education matters.* ♦ *Does it matter if I don't take a present?* ♦ *It **doesn't** really **matter** if we're a bit late.* ♦ *Winning this award **matters a lot** to me.*

,matter-of-'fact adj calm and showing no emotion when dealing with something —**,matter-of-'factly** adv

matting /'mætɪŋ/ noun [U] strong rough material that is used as a floor cover

mattress /'mætrəs/ noun [C] the thick soft part of a bed that you lie on

mature¹ /mə'tʃʊə/ adj **1** behaving in the sensible way that you would expect an adult to behave **2** fully developed, or fully grown —**maturely** adv

mature² /mə'tʃʊə/ verb [I] **1** to start behaving like an adult and become more sensible **2** to grow to full adult size **3** BUSINESS if something such as an **investment** or **insurance policy** matures, it reaches the end of a fixed period of time and must be paid or **paid back** —**maturation** /,mætʃʊ'reɪʃ(ə)n/ noun [U]

ma,ture 'student noun [C] EDUCATION someone who begins studying at a college or university after they are 25 years old

maturity /mə'tʃʊərəti/ noun **1** [U] the qualities and behaviour that you would expect of a sensible adult **2** [U] full growth, or completed development **3** [C/U] BUSINESS the time when the interest and profits on money that has been invested must be paid

maul /mɔːl/ verb [T] **1** if an animal mauls someone, it attacks them, usually causing serious injury **2** to touch someone in a rough unpleasant way

mauve /məʊv/ adj pale purple in colour —**mauve** noun [U]

maverick /'mævərɪk/ noun [C] an independent person who has ideas and behaviour that are very different from other people's

max /mæks/ abbrev maximum

maxim /'mæksɪm/ noun [C] LANGUAGE a phrase or saying that includes a rule or moral about how you should behave

maximize /ˈmæksɪmaɪz/ verb [T] **1** to make something as large as possible ≠ MINIMIZE **2** COMPUTING to make the image on a computer screen fill all the space on the screen ≠ MINIMIZE

maximum¹ /ˈmæksɪməm/ adj the largest in amount, size, or number that is allowed or possible ≠ MINIMUM: *This is the **maximum amount** of money we are prepared to pay.*

maximum² /ˈmæksɪməm/ noun [C] the largest number, amount, size, or degree that is allowed or is possible ≠ MINIMUM: *20 kg of luggage is the maximum we allow on the flight.* ♦ *Give yourself **a maximum of** 15 minutes to read the questions.*

,maximum-ˈminimum ther,mometer noun [C] SCIENCE a piece of equipment for measuring temperature that shows the highest and lowest temperatures over a period of time

may /meɪ/ modal verb **1** used for saying that something is possibly true or will possibly happen: *The injury may have caused brain damage.* ♦ *I may not be able to play on Saturday.* **2** *formal* used for asking or stating whether something is allowed: *May I use your phone?* ♦ *Visitors may use the swimming pool between 5.30 and 7.30 pm.*

May /meɪ/ noun [U] the fifth month of the year, between April and June: *We're taking an early holiday in May.* ♦ *They were married on 17th May.*

maybe /ˈmeɪbi/ adv **1** used for showing that you are not sure whether something is true or will happen: *Maybe it will rain tonight.* ♦ *'Do you think he really loves you?' 'Maybe, **maybe not** – I'm just not sure.'* **2** *spoken* used for asking someone to do something, without saying directly that you want them to do it: *Maybe you could do a little job for me?* ♦ *Maybe someone could explain to me what's going on around here?*

mayhem /ˈmeɪhem/ noun [U] a very confused situation = CHAOS

mayonnaise /ˌmeɪəˈneɪz/ noun [U] a thick white sauce made from eggs and oil

mayor /meə/ noun [C] the most important elected official in a town or city —**mayoral** adj

maze /meɪz/ noun **1** [C] an arrangement of closely connected paths that are separated by tall bushes, walls, or trees, designed for a game of finding your way through **2** [singular] a set of many small streets or paths that is easy to get lost in **3** [singular] a set of closely connected but complicated rules, issues, or ideas: *a maze of new legislation*

Mb or **MB** abbrev COMPUTING megabyte: a unit for measuring the size of a computer's memory, equal to just over one million bytes

MBA /ˌem biː ˈeɪ/ noun [C] EDUCATION Master of Business Administration: a **master's** degree in business management

mbira /ɒmˈbiːrə/ noun [C] MUSIC an African **percussion** instrument that consists of metal or wooden keys attached to a box. It is played by **plucking** the keys with the thumb and fingers.

mbps /ˌem biː piː ˈes/ abbrev COMPUTING megabits per second: a unit for measuring the speed of a **modem**

MD /ˌem ˈdiː/ noun [C] EDUCATION Doctor of Medicine: an advanced degree in medicine

MDF /ˌem diː ˈef/ noun [U] CONSTRUCTION medium-density fibreboard: a building material made of small pieces of wood pressed together to form boards. It is used for making furniture, doors etc.

me /strong miː, weak mi/ pronoun the object form of 'I', used for referring to yourself when you are the person who is speaking or writing: *I think Darren really likes me.* ♦ *She wrote me a letter.* ♦ *You can come with me.*

ME /ˌem ˈiː/ noun [U] HEALTH myalgic encephalitis: the illness **chronic fatigue syndrome**

meadow /ˈmedəʊ/ noun [C] a field where grass and wild flowers grow

meagre /ˈmiːɡə/ adj smaller or less than you want or need: *a meagre food supply*

meal /miːl/ noun **1** [C] an occasion when you eat, for example breakfast or lunch, or the food that you eat at that time: *He **cooked** us a delicious **meal**.* ♦ *We could see a film or **go out for a meal** (=go to a restaurant).* **2** [U] crushed grain, used as food

mealtime /ˈmiːl,taɪm/ noun [C] a time when you eat a meal

mean¹ /miːn/ (**means, meaning, meant** /ment/) verb [T]

1 have a meaning	4 make sth happen
2 intend a meaning	5 be evidence of sth
3 intend sth	+ PHRASES

1 to have a particular meaning: *What does 'meander' mean?* ♦ *The word 'serviette' means something different in French.*
2 to intend to communicate a particular meaning: *By 'partner', I mean your wife, your husband, or someone you live with.* ♦ *She didn't reply to our invitation, which probably means she isn't coming.* ♦ *Don't be offended, she **meant it as** a joke.*
3 to intend something, or to intend to do something: *She had never meant him any real harm.* ♦ *I didn't **mean to** step on your toe.*
4 to make something happen, or to have a particular result: *The company's failure could mean that hundreds of workers lose their jobs.* ♦ *The new contract will mean starting the whole project again.*
5 to be evidence that something exists: *That dark patch means that water is coming in.*

PHRASES **be meant for** to be intended, designed, or suitable for something or someone: *These books are not meant for primary school students.*
be meant to do sth to have a particular responsibility, duty, or purpose: *You were meant to keep the children out of trouble.*
mean nothing or **not mean anything** to have no importance: *He spoke in a relaxed, slow way, as if time meant nothing to him.*

mean² /miːn/ adj **1** cruel, or unkind: *Don't do that – it's mean.* ♦ *The older kids were **mean to** him.* **2** not willing to spend money: *She was **too mean to** put the heating on.* **3** MATHS average: *the mean annual temperature*

mean³ /miːn/ noun [C] MATHS an average number or amount

meander¹ /miˈændə/ verb [I] **1** GEOGRAPHY if a river or road meanders, it has a lot of turns and curves **2** to move slowly without a particular direction or purpose

meander² /miˈændə/ noun [C] GEOGRAPHY a part of a river where it has eroded a wide curved path in the shape of a letter S = LOOP —*picture* → RIVER

meˈander ,cliff noun [C] GEOGRAPHY a cliff on the side of a valley that is on the outside of the curve formed by a river running through the valley

meaning /ˈmiːnɪŋ/ noun **1** [C/U] the thing, action, feeling, or idea that a word represents: *The dictionary gives two meanings for 'meander'.* ♦ *The poem's real* *meaning has always been a puzzle.* **2** [singular/U] the special importance or purpose of something: *Times change and old customs lose their meaning.* ♦ *The book tackles important questions, such as **the meaning of** life.*

meaningful /ˈmiːnɪŋf(ə)l/ adj **1** serious, useful, or important: *a meaningful debate* **2** expressing a clear feeling or thought, but without using words: *a meaningful look* —**meaningfully** adv

meaningless /ˈmiːnɪŋləs/ adj **1** without any clear purpose or importance: *My life seems meaningless since Jim died.* **2** without a clear meaning: *a series of meaningless phrases*

means /miːnz/ noun **1** [C] a method for doing or achieving something= METHOD: *Information is not easily obtained by any other means.* ♦ *The telephone was our only **means of** communication.* ♦ *We had **no means of** warning them.* **2** [plural] *formal* the money that someone has or gets: *She doesn't **have the means to** support herself.*

PHRASES **by no means** or **not by any means** not at all: *He was by no means certain that his plan would be successful.*

a means to an end a way of getting or achieving something that you want

meant /ment/ the past tense and past participle of **mean¹**

meantime /ˈmiːnˌtaɪm/ noun **in the meantime** during the time between two events, or between the present time and a future event

meanwhile /ˈmiːnˌwaɪl/ adv between the time that two things happen, or while something is happening: *Put the eggs on to boil and meanwhile slice the onions.*

measles /ˈmiːz(ə)lz/ noun [U] HEALTH a very infectious disease caused by a virus that causes red spots to appear on the body and a high temperature. Measles can cause death in young children. → GERMAN MEASLES

measurable /ˈmeʒ(ə)rəb(ə)l/ adj large enough to be measured, noticed, or important —**measurably** adv

measure¹ /ˈmeʒə/ noun [C] **1** an action that is intended to achieve something or deal with something: *This is **a temporary measure** to stop the problem from getting any worse.* ♦ *Stronger **measures** will have to be **taken** to bring down unemployment.* **2** an amount of a particular quality that is neither large nor small: *The system gives people **a measure of** protection against dishonest salesmen.* **3** a way of judging something: *The tests are not an accurate **measure of** performance.* **4** a unit used for measuring things

measure² /ˈmeʒə/ verb **1** [I/T] to find the exact size, amount, speed, or rate of something: *We measured from the back of the house to the fence.* ♦ *a device for measuring the flow of water through a pipe* **2** [T] to form an opinion about how good or bad something is: *Success isn't measured by how much money you have.* ♦ *Their rate of economic growth is not very impressive, when you **measure** it **against** (=compare it with) that of the neighbouring countries.* **3** [linking verb] to be a particular size: *The room measures approximately 12 feet by 13 feet.*

PHRASAL VERB ˌmeasure sth ˈout to take a particular amount of something from a larger amount: *Measure out 10 grams of sugar.*

measurement /ˈmeʒəmənt/ noun **1** [C] the exact size, amount, speed, or rate of something, expressed in standard units: *They **took measurements of** noise levels inside the building.* **2** [U] the process of measuring something

measuring cylinder /ˈmeʒ(ə)rɪŋ ˌsɪlɪndə/ noun [C] SCIENCE a container in the shape of a cylinder that has marks on it to allow the measurement of volume

measuring tape /ˈmeʒ(ə)rɪŋ ˌteɪp/ noun [C] a long piece of plastic or metal tape with measurements marked on it, used for measuring things —*picture* → AGRICULTURAL

meat /miːt/ noun [U] the flesh of an animal or bird that is eaten as food

> **Build your vocabulary: words you can use instead of meat**
> - **beef** the meat of a cow
> - **chicken** the meat of a chicken
> - **lamb** the meat of a young sheep
> - **pork** the meat of a pig
> - **poultry** the meat of a chicken, duck, or other farm bird
> - **red meat** meat that is red in colour, such as beef or lamb
> - **veal** the meat of a young cow
> - **white meat** meat that is a light colour, such as chicken or pork

mebendazole /məˈbendəzəʊl/ noun [U] HEALTH a medicine that is used to treat a wide range of infections caused by worms

mecca /ˈmekə/ noun [C/U] a place that a lot of people visit

Mecca /ˈmekə/ RELIGION a city in Saudi Arabia that is holy for Muslims

MECD /ˌem iː siː ˈdiː/ noun [C] ECONOMICS more economically developed country: a country that is fairly rich and has a lot of industrial development → LECD

mechanic /mɪˈkænɪk/ noun **1** [C] someone whose job is to repair vehicles and machines **2 mechanics** [plural] the way in which something works or is done: *the mechanics of newspaper reporting* **3 mechanics** [U] PHYSICS the area of physics that deals with the forces such as gravity that affect all objects

mechanical /mɪˈkænɪk(ə)l/ adj **1** PHYSICS operated by a machine, or relating to machines: *a mechanical device* **2** PHYSICS relating to or produced by physical forces **3** done without thinking, or without any attempt to be original: *her mechanical responses to my questions* —**mechanically** /məˈkænɪkli/ adv

meˌchanical adˈvantage noun [C] PHYSICS the ratio of the load a machine can move to the effort that is needed to move the load. A machine that uses a small effort to move a heavy load will have a greater mechanical advantage.

meˌchanical diˈgestion noun [U] BIOLOGY the stages in the process of digestion in which food is physically broken up, for example by biting and chewing

meˌchanical ˈshovel noun [C] CONSTRUCTION a machine that takes off layers of soil in its **bucket**, which can be raised, lowered, or **tilted** to move soil from one place to another

meˌchanical ˈweathering noun [U] CHEMISTRY, GEOLOGY the process of **physical weathering**

mechanised /ˈmekənaɪzd/ another spelling of **mechanized**

mechanism /ˈmekəˌnɪz(ə)m/ noun [C] **1** a machine, or a part of a machine: *a locking mechanism* **2** a method or process for getting something done: *a mechanism for settling disputes* **3** behaviour that makes it possible for someone to deal with a difficult situation or problem

mechanize /ˈmekənaɪz/ verb [I/T] to start using machines to do something that was previously done by people —**mechanization** /ˌmekənaɪˈzeɪʃ(ə)n/ noun [U]

mechanized /ˈmekənaɪzd/ adj a process that is mechanized is done using machines but was previously done by people or animals

medal /ˈmed(ə)l/ noun [C] a small flat piece of metal that you are given for winning a competition or for doing something that is very brave

medallist /ˈmed(ə)lɪst/ noun [C] **SPORTS** someone who has won a medal in a competition

meddle /ˈmed(ə)l/ verb [I] to become involved in a situation that does not affect you, in a way that is annoying= INTERFERE

media /ˈmiːdiə/ a plural of **medium²**

the media /ˈmiːdiə/ noun radio, television, newspapers, the Internet, and magazines, considered as a group: *The story has been widely reported in the media.* → MASS MEDIA, MULTIMEDIA

Media can be used with a singular or plural verb. You can say: *The media **has** exaggerated the issue.* OR: *The media **have** exaggerated the issue.*

mediaeval /ˌmedɪˈiːv(ə)l/ another spelling of **medieval**

medial moraine /ˌmiːdiəl məˈreɪn/ noun [C] **GEOLOGY** a line of earth and pieces of rock formed in the centre of a glacier when the **lateral moraines** of two glaciers meet

median /ˈmiːdiən/ noun [C] **MATHS 1** a number that is in the middle of a set when the numbers are arranged in order → AVERAGE¹ sense 2 **2** a line drawn from one of the points of a triangle to the opposite side —**median** adj

media studies /ˈmiːdiə ˌstʌdiːz/ noun [U] **EDUCATION** the academic study of newspapers, television, advertising etc and their influence on society

mediate /ˈmiːdieɪt/ verb [I/T] to try to end a disagreement between two people or groups —**mediation** /ˌmiːdiˈeɪʃ(ə)n/ noun [U], **mediator** noun [C]

medic /ˈmedɪk/ noun [C] **HEALTH** informal a doctor or a medical student

medical¹ /ˈmedɪk(ə)l/ adj **HEALTH** relating to medicine and the treatment of injuries and diseases: *a career in the **medical profession** ♦ a man in need of urgent **medical care** —**medically** /ˈmedɪkli/ adv

medical² /ˈmedɪk(ə)l/ noun [C] **HEALTH** a complete examination of a person's body by a doctor= PHYSICAL

medical prac'titioner noun [C] *formal* a doctor

medication /ˌmedɪˈkeɪʃ(ə)n/ noun [C/U] **HEALTH** drugs that you take to treat or cure an illness

medicinal /məˈdɪs(ə)nəl/ adj **HEALTH** capable of treating an illness: *medicinal herbs*

me'dicinal ,drug noun [C] **HEALTH** a drug used to treat an illness or its symptoms

medicine /ˈmed(ə)s(ə)n/ noun **1** [C/U] **HEALTH** a substance that you take to treat an illness: *cough medicine ♦ You have to **take** the **medicine** three times a day.* **2** [U] the study and practice of treating or preventing illnesses and injuries: *He **studied medicine** at Harare University.*

'medicine ,man noun [C] **SOCIAL STUDIES** a man who is believed to be able to control the powers of the spiritual world and cure and prevent illness

medieval /ˌmediˈiːv(ə)l/ adj relating to the period of European history between about the year 1000 AD and the year 1500 AD: *a medieval church*

mediocre /ˌmiːdiˈəʊkə/ adj not very good: *a mediocre performance* —**mediocrity** /ˌmiːdiˈɒkrəti/ noun [U]

meditate /ˈmedɪteɪt/ verb [I] **RELIGION** to make your mind empty in order to relax, or as a religious exercise —**meditation** /ˌmedɪˈteɪʃ(ə)n/ noun [U]

Mediterranean /ˌmedɪtəˈreɪniən/ adj **GEOGRAPHY** relating to the countries that surround the Mediterranean, or to the culture of the people in those countries

the Mediterranean /ˌmedɪtəˈreɪniən/ **GEOGRAPHY 1** the sea that has Europe to the north and North Africa to the south **2** the countries that surround the Mediterranean Sea

medium¹ /ˈmiːdiəm/ adj **1** between small and large in size or amount: *Use six medium tomatoes.* ♦ *medium-length hair ♦ She's slim and **of medium height**.* **2** neither light nor dark in colour: *medium-brown hair*

medium² /ˈmiːdiəm/ noun [C] **1** something such as a piece of clothing that is between small and large in size: *Have you got a medium in this style?* **2** (plural **media** /ˈmiːdiə/) a way of communicating information and ideas: *Patients can express their emotions through **the medium of** drama.* **3** **SCIENCE** a substance that something grows in, exists in, or moves through **4** someone who communicates with the spirits of dead people → MEDIA

medium-sized /ˌmiːdiəm ˈsaɪzd/ adj neither large nor small: *Use a medium-sized saucepan.* ♦ *a medium-sized business*

'medium ,term noun [singular] the period of time that lasts a few months or years from the present time

'medium-,term adj within the period of time that begins at the present time and lasts a few months or years

'medium ,wave noun [U] **PHYSICS** a range of radio waves between 100 and 1000 metres in length, used for broadcasting → LONG WAVE, SHORT WAVE

medley /ˈmedli/ noun [C] **1** **MUSIC** a piece of music consisting of a collection of tunes or songs that someone plays or sings one after another **2** a mixture of things: *an interesting **medley of** flavours*

medulla /meˈdʌlə/ noun [C] **ANATOMY** the inner part of an organ such as the kidney

medulla oblongata /meˌdʌlə ˌɒblɒŋˈɡɑːtə/ noun [singular] **ANATOMY** the lowest part of the brain that is connected to the **spinal cord**. It controls the way the heart and lungs work. —*picture* → BRAIN

meek /miːk/ adj quiet, gentle, and easy to persuade —**meekly** adv

meerkat /ˈmɪəkæt/ noun [C] a small South African mammal that has grey fur with black marks

meet /miːt/ (**meets, meeting, met** /met/) verb

1 come together	6 do sth necessary
2 for discussions	7 do sth planned
3 meet by accident	8 of roads/lines
4 be introduced to sb	9 look into sb's eyes
5 experience result	+ PHRASAL VERBS

1 [I/T] to come together in order to spend time with someone who you have arranged to see: *I'll meet you in the bar later.* ♦ *Sally and I met after work to go and see a film.* ♦ *We're meeting for lunch tomorrow.*
2 [I/T] to come together with other people in order to discuss something formally: *The president is meeting*

world leaders in Brussels. ♦ *The council meets today to decide what action to take.*
3 [T] to see someone and speak to them without planning to: *You'll never guess who I met on the plane.*
4 [I/T] to be introduced to someone that you do not know: *Have you met my sister?* ♦ *I think they met at college.*
5 [T] to get a particular result or reaction: *The plans met strong opposition from local people.*
6 [T] to do what is necessary: *This technology can meet the challenges of the 21st century.* ♦ *The water won't meet the needs of the local population.*
7 [T] to do what you planned or promised to do = ACHIEVE: *Will the government be able to meet their spending targets?*
8 [I] if things such as roads or lines meet, they join each other: *The two rivers meet just north of the town.*
9 [I] if two people's eyes meet, they look directly into each other's eyes
PHRASAL VERBS ,meet 'up to come together with someone as you have planned to do: *We usually meet up for coffee after lunch.*
'meet with sb to have a formal meeting with someone: *Today the President met with Russian leaders in Washington.*
'meet with sth to unexpectedly experience trouble, danger, difficulty etc: *She met with an accident yesterday.*

meeting /'mi:tɪŋ/ noun [C] **1** an occasion when people come together in order to discuss things and make decisions: *We're holding a meeting for people who want to join the club.* ♦ *our meeting with the ambassador* ♦ *World leaders attended a meeting on air pollution.* **2** an occasion when two people meet **3** SPORTS an occasion when two teams or players compete

'meeting ,point noun [C] TOURISM a place at an airport or railway station where people can arrange to meet

meg /meg/ noun [C] COMPUTING *informal* a megabyte

mega- /megə/ prefix **1** SCIENCE one million: used with some units of measurement: *a 2,000-megawatt power plant* **2** very large or important: used with some nouns

megabit /'megə,bɪt/ noun [C] COMPUTING a million **bits** (=the smallest unit of information that can be used by a computer)

megabyte /'megə,baɪt/ noun [C] COMPUTING a unit for measuring the size of a computer's memory, equal to just over one million bytes

megacity /'megə,sɪti/ noun [C] GEOGRAPHY a city with a population of more than 10 million people

megahertz /'megə,hɜ:ts/ (plural **megahertz**) noun [C] COMPUTING a unit for measuring the speed of a computer, equal to one million **hertz**

megalomania /,megələʊ'meɪniə/ noun [U] **1** a strong wish to have a lot of power **2** HEALTH a mental illness in which someone believes they are very important and powerful when they are not —**megalomaniac** noun [C]

megaphone /'megə,fəʊn/ noun [C] a piece of equipment that is used for making your voice louder when you are talking to a crowd

megapixel /'megə,pɪks(ə)l/ noun [C] COMPUTING a unit for measuring the speed at which images can be sent from one computer to another, or the amount of detail you can see on a computer screen. It is equal to just over one million **pixels**.

megawatt /'megə,wɒt/ noun [C] PHYSICS a unit for measuring electrical power, equal to one million **watts**

meiosis /maɪ'əʊsɪs/ noun [U] BIOLOGY a type of cell division in which a cell divides into four cells, each of which contains half the number of chromosomes of the original cell. It takes place when **gametes** (=reproductive cells) are formed. → MITOSIS

melamine /'meləmi:n/ noun [U] hard smooth plastic used for making the surfaces of things such as tables

melancholy /'melənkəli/ noun [U] *literary* a feeling of being very sad and having no hope —**melancholy** adj: *a melancholy tone of voice*

melanin /'melənɪn/ noun [U] BIOLOGY a substance in the skin, eyes, and hair that gives them their colour

melanoma /,melə'nəʊmə/ noun [C] HEALTH a serious type of skin cancer

melatonin /,melə'təʊnɪn/ noun [U] BIOLOGY a hormone produced by vertebrates that causes changes in the skin colour of some animals

melodic /mə'lɒdɪk/ adj MUSIC pleasant to listen to

melodrama /'melə,drɑ:mə/ noun [C/U] LITERATURE, ARTS a story, play, or film in which the characters express extreme emotions

melodramatic /,melədrə'mætɪk/ adj *showing disapproval* behaving in a way that is too emotional or too serious

melody /'melədi/ (plural **melodies**) noun MUSIC **1** [C] a tune or song **2** [C/U] the main tune in a piece of music

melon /'melən/ noun [C/U] a large round fruit with orange, green, or white flesh —*picture* → FRUIT

melt /melt/ verb **1** [I/T] SCIENCE to change a solid substance into a liquid using heat, or to be changed from a solid substance into a liquid by the use of heat: *Melt the butter in a small saucepan.* ♦ *The ice will melt quickly in direct sunlight.* —*picture* → STATE **2** [I] to disappear: *My fears melted when I saw his kind expression.* **3** [I/T] to make someone more sympathetic, or to become more sympathetic **4** [I] to gradually change and combine, so that there seems to be no difference between things: *The reds and golds melted into each other as the sun sank.*

meltdown /'melt,daʊn/ noun [C/U] **1** a sudden complete failure of a company, organization, or system: *a global financial meltdown* **2** PHYSICS a very dangerous accident in which nuclear fuel becomes too hot and escapes from its container

melting point /'meltɪŋ ,pɔɪnt/ noun [C/U] SCIENCE the temperature at which a solid substance changes into a liquid

meltwater /'melt,wɔ:tə/ noun [U] GEOLOGY water formed by the melting of ice or snow, especially from a glacier

member /'membə/ noun [C] **1** someone who belongs to a group or an organization: *a trade union member* ♦ *She was the only member of the family who visited him.* **2** a plant or animal that belongs to a particular group of plants or animals: *members of the cat family* **3** CONSTRUCTION a piece that forms part of a structure
PHRASE Member of Parliament POLITICS a politician who represents people in a parliament

membership /'membəʃɪp/ noun **1** [U] the fact of being a member of a club, organization, or group: *Several countries have applied for membership of the EU.* ♦ *China's membership of the United Nations* **2** [singular] the members of a club, organization, or group: *Our membership will vote on the proposal in May.*

membrane /'mem,brem/ noun [C] **BIOLOGY** a thin layer of tissue that covers, separates, protects, or connects cells or parts of an organism: *The eye is protected by a thin membrane.* → CELL MEMBRANE

membranophone /mem'brema,fəʊn/ noun [C] **MUSIC** a technical name for a musical instrument such as a drum, in which the sound is produced by a stretched membrane

meme /mi:m/ noun [C] **SOCIAL STUDIES** a feature of a culture, for example its language, that is passed from one generation to the next

memento /mə'mentəʊ/ (plural **mementos**) noun [C] an object that you keep to remind you of someone or something: *a memento of our trip*

memo /'meməʊ/ (plural **memos**) noun [C] a short note about work that one person sends to another person that they work with

memoirs /'mem,wɑːz/ noun [plural] a book that someone famous writes about their own experiences

memorabilia /,mem(ə)rə'bɪliə/ noun [plural] objects that people collect because they are connected with someone famous or something interesting: *Beatles memorabilia*

memorable /'mem(ə)rəb(ə)l/ adj worth remembering, or easy to remember: *a memorable experience*

memorandum /,memə'rændəm/ noun [C] **1** a short official note from someone in a government or organization **2** *formal* a **memo 3** *LAW* a written summary of the details of a legal document

memorial /mə'mɔːriəl/ noun [C] a structure that is built to remind people of a famous person or event: *the Vietnam War Memorial* —**memorial** adj: *a memorial ceremony*

memorialize /mə'mɔːriəlaɪz/ verb [T] to be a memorial to someone or something, or to provide someone or something with a memorial

memorize /'meməraɪz/ verb [T] to learn something so that can you remember it perfectly: *The children had memorized a poem.*

memory /'mem(ə)ri/ (plural **memories**) noun **1** [C] something that you remember: *What are your most vivid memories* (=very clear memories) *of that period?* ♦ *I have very fond memories of my childhood.* **2** [singular] the ability to remember things: *Your memory tends to get worse as you get older.* ♦ *I've never had a very good memory for names* (=I can't remember names very well). **3** [C] **COMPUTING** the part of a computer in which information, instructions, and programs are stored

PHRASES **do sth from memory** to do something that you remember learning in the past but have not done recently: *The three of us sang the whole song from memory.*
in memory of sb something that is done in memory of someone is done so that people will remember them → LIVING[1]

'Memory ,Stick TRADEMARK COMPUTING a small disk drive that can store information for use in electronic equipment and that you can carry around with you

men /men/ the plural of **man**[1]

menace /'menəs/ noun **1** [C] someone or something that is dangerous or very annoying: *the growing menace of global pollution* **2** [U] a threatening quality or feeling

menacing /'menəsɪŋ/ adj intended to threaten someone: *a menacing look* —**menacingly** adv

mend /mend/ verb **1** [T] to repair something that is broken or damaged: *Have you mended the gate?* **2** [T] to do something to end a disagreement **3** [I] if a bone mends, it grows back together after it has broken

mendelevium /,mendə'liːviəm/ noun [U] **CHEMISTRY** a radioactive metallic element in the **actinide** group of the periodic table. Chemical symbol: **Md**

menial /'miːniəl/ adj menial work does not need much skill

meningitis /,menɪn'dʒaɪtɪs/ noun [U] **HEALTH** a serious illness affecting the brain and **spinal cord**. It is caused by a bacterium or a virus and can cause death.

meniscus /mɪ'nɪskəs/ noun [singular] **SCIENCE** the curved surface of a liquid in a tube as a result of **surface tension**. It is usually concave as the liquid sticks to the sides of the container and is slightly higher there.

menopause /'menə,pɔːz/ noun [singular] **BIOLOGY** the time in a woman's life when she no longer produces eggs, her periods stop, and she is no longer capable of getting pregnant

menorah /mə'nɔːrə/ noun [C] **RELIGION** an object that holds seven or more **candles**. It is used in the Jewish religion.

menstrual /'menstruəl/ adj **BIOLOGY** relating to **menstruation**

'menstrual ,cycle noun [C] **BIOLOGY** the repeated process in which a woman's uterus prepares for pregnancy, and which ends in a period if she does not get pregnant. The menstrual cycle usually lasts about a month, and **ovulation** usually takes place about halfway through it.

menstruate /'menstrueɪt/ verb [I] **BIOLOGY** when a woman menstruates, she has a flow of blood from her uterus called a period. This usually happens about once a month, unless she is pregnant or has reached the **menopause**.

menstruation /,menstru'eɪʃ(ə)n/ noun [U] **BIOLOGY** the process of menstruating

mensuration /,menʃə'reɪʃ(ə)n/ noun [U] **SCIENCE** **1** the calculation of quantities such as length, area, and volume from measurements and angles that are already known **2** the act or process of measuring something

mental /'ment(ə)l/ adj existing in the mind, or relating to the mind: *a child's mental development* ♦ *mental health* —**mentally** adv: *mentally ill*

,mental de'pendence noun [U] **HEALTH** the belief that a person has that they cannot do without a drug

,mental 'illness noun [C/U] **HEALTH** an illness that affects the mind

mentality /men'tæləti/ noun [singular] a particular way of thinking: *a destructive mentality*

mention[1] /'menʃ(ə)n/ verb [T] to refer to something, but not discuss it much: *He didn't mention her all evening.* ♦ *I'll mention the problem to her.* ♦ *Did I mention that I've got a new job?*

PHRASE **not to mention** used for referring to something else that emphasizes what you have just said: *The fire caused terrible loss of life, not to mention all the damage to the buildings.*

mention[2] /'menʃ(ə)n/ noun [singular/U] the act of referring to someone or something = REFERENCE: *There's no mention of these costs in the contract.*

mentor /'mentɔː/ noun [C] an experienced person who gives advice to someone with less experience —**mentoring** noun [U]

menu /ˈmenjuː/ noun [C] **1** a list of the food that is available in a restaurant: *Do you see anything you like on the menu?* **2** COMPUTING a list of choices on a computer screen: *the Edit menu*

ˈmenu ˌbar noun [C] COMPUTING a row of all the menus in a computer program that usually appears at the top of a computer screen

Mercator projection /məˈkeɪtə(r) prəˌdʒekʃ(ə)n/ noun [U] GEOGRAPHY the traditional way of showing countries on a map, in which the shapes of the countries are accurate, but not their sizes in relation to each other

mercenary /ˈmɜːs(ə)n(ə)ri/ (plural **mercenaries**) noun [C] a soldier who fights for any army that will pay him or her

merchandise /ˈmɜːtʃ(ə)ndaɪz/ noun [U] *formal* goods that people buy and sell

merchant /ˈmɜːtʃ(ə)nt/ noun [C] *formal* a person or business that buys and sells goods

ˌmerchant ˈbank noun [C] a bank that provides financial services to companies, not to individual people —**ˌmerchant ˈbanker** noun [C], **ˌmerchant ˈbanking** noun [U]

ˌmerchant ˈnavy noun [U] a country's ships that carry goods, not soldiers and weapons

merchant seaman /ˌmɜːtʃ(ə)nt ˈsiːmən/ noun [C] a sailor in the merchant navy

merciful /ˈmɜːsɪf(ə)l/ adj showing kindness, even when other people are unkind —**mercifully** adv

merciless /ˈmɜːsɪləs/ adj very cruel or severe: *a merciless beating* —**mercilessly** adv

mercury /ˈmɜːkjʊri/ noun [U] CHEMISTRY a very heavy silver metal element that is liquid at room temperature. It is used in **thermometers** and for making **pesticides**. Chemical symbol: **Hg**

Mercury /ˈmɜːkjʊri/ ASTRONOMY the planet that is smallest and nearest to the Sun —*picture* → SOLAR SYSTEM

mercy /ˈmɜːsi/ noun [U] the act of treating someone in a kind way when you could have punished them: *the mercy of God*
PHRASE **at the mercy of** in a situation that is controlled by someone or something that can harm you

mere /mɪə/ adj **1** used for emphasizing that something is small or unimportant: *Her comments are mere opinion, not fact.* **2** used for emphasizing the major effect of something that seems unimportant: *The mere fact that he came to see her made her happy.*

merely /ˈmɪəli/ adv **1** used for emphasizing that something is small or unimportant= ONLY: *This job is merely a way to pay my bills.* **2** used for emphasizing that something is not as bad, severe, or important as someone thinks it is= ONLY: *I'm not angry, I'm merely trying to explain it to you.*

merge /mɜːdʒ/ verb [I] **1** if two organizations merge, they combine to form one bigger organization: *Small publishers were forced to merge with larger companies.* **2** if two things merge, they combine so that you can no longer tell the difference between them: *The hills merged into the dark sky behind them.*

merger /ˈmɜːdʒə/ noun [C] BUSINESS an occasion when two companies combine to form a bigger company

meridian /məˈrɪdiən/ noun [C] GEOGRAPHY one of the lines on a map that goes around the Earth from the North Pole to the South Pole

meringue /məˈræŋ/ noun [C/U] a sweet food made from a mixture of sugar and the white part of eggs

meristem /ˈmeristem/ noun [C] BIOLOGY plant tissue where the cells are in the process of dividing, as found at the tip of stems and roots —**meristematic** /ˌmeristəˈmætɪk/ adj

merit¹ /ˈmerɪt/ noun **1** [C/U] a good quality that makes you admire something: *Attention to detail is one of the great merits of the book.* **2** [C] EDUCATION a mark that a school student gets as a reward for good work or behaviour

merit² /ˈmerɪt/ verb [T] *formal* to deserve something: *The case merits further investigation.*

mermaid /ˈmɜːˌmeɪd/ noun [C] an imaginary sea creature that has the body of a woman and the tail of a fish

merrily /ˈmerəli/ adv **1** in a happy or lively way **2** without knowing or thinking about any problems

merry /ˈmeri/ (**merrier, merriest**) adj *old-fashioned* happy and lively
PHRASE **Merry Christmas** used for wishing someone a happy time at Christmas

mesh /meʃ/ noun [C/U] a piece of material that is like a net made of wires or strings

mesocarp /ˈmesəʊkɑːp/ noun [C/U] BIOLOGY the middle layer of the **pericarp** (=skin and flesh) of a fruit

mesoderm /ˈmesəʊdɜːm/ noun [C/U] BIOLOGY the middle of the three cell layers in an embryo, from which muscle, blood, bone, **connective tissue**, and **dermis** develop

Mesolithic /ˌmesəʊˈlɪθɪk/ adj GEOLOGY dating from the time of the middle of the **Stone Age**

mesophyll /ˈmesəʊfɪl/ noun [C] BIOLOGY the middle section of a plant leaf between the upper and lower layers of the **epidermis**. It contains cells that have many **chloroplasts**.

mesophyte /ˈmesəʊfaɪt/ noun [C] BIOLOGY a plant that needs an average amount of water to grow successfully → HYDROPHYTE, XEROPHYTE

the mesosphere /ˈmesəʊˌsfɪə/ noun [singular] SCIENCE the layer of the Earth's atmosphere that starts about 50 to 80 kilometres above the Earth's surface, where temperatures are cooler —*picture* → ATMOSPHERE

mess¹ /mes/ noun **1** [C/U] a situation in which a place is dirty, untidy, or in bad condition: *Try not to make a mess because I've been cleaning.* ♦ *His papers were in a terrible mess.* **2** [singular] a difficult situation with a lot of problems: *an economic mess* ♦ *The company was in a complete mess.* ♦ *I don't know how we got into this mess.* ♦ *Tom felt he had made a mess of his life.* **3** [C] a room where people have their meals in the armed forces

mess² /mes/ PHRASAL VERB **ˌmess sth ˈup** to damage or spoil something: *I'm not going to let him mess up my life.*

message /ˈmesɪdʒ/ noun **1** [C] a piece of written or spoken information that you give or send to someone: *I got your email message, thank you.* ♦ *If I'm not there, just leave a message with Chris.* ♦ *She's not here at the moment – can I take a message?* **2** [singular] the main idea that is contained in something such as a speech or an advertisement: *The film sends a clear message about the dangers of drug-taking.*
PHRASE **get the message** *informal* to understand what someone is trying to tell you

'**message ,board** noun [C] **COMPUTING** a system in which a group of Internet users regularly write email messages about a particular subject for other members of the group to read

'**message code au,thentication** noun [U] **COMPUTING** a computer process that checks who emails come from and whether they are safe

messaging /'mesɪdʒɪŋ/ noun [U] **COMPUTING** the process of sending and receiving electronic messages by computer or mobile phone

messenger /'mes(ə)ndʒə/ noun [C] someone who delivers messages to people

messiah /mə'saɪə/ noun [C] **1** someone who will save people from a difficult situation **2 RELIGION** a religious leader who is sent by God to save the world **3 the Messiah RELIGION** a name that Christians use for Jesus Christ

messy /'mesi/ (**messier, messiest**) adj **1** dirty, or very untidy **2** complicated, difficult, and unpleasant to deal with: *a messy divorce*

met /met/ the past tense and past participle of **meet**

meta'bolic ,rate noun [C] **BIOLOGY** the speed at which chemical processes take place in the body, especially the processes of breaking down food

metabolism /mə'tæbə,lɪz(ə)m/ noun [C/U] **BIOLOGY** all the chemical processes by which cells produce the energy and substances necessary for life. Organic compounds taken in as food are broken down to produce heat and energy, while other compounds are used for repairing tissues and for growth. —**metabolic** /,metə'bɒlɪk/ adj

metabolize /mə'tæbəlaɪz/ verb [T] **BIOLOGY** if your body metabolizes food, oxygen etc, it changes it into a form that can be used as energy

metacarpal /,metə'kɑːp(ə)l/ noun [C] **ANATOMY** one of the five bones in the hand —*picture* → SKELETON

metadata /'metə,deɪtə/ noun [U] **COMPUTING** details of the information contained in a large computer **database**, for example who wrote the information and what **format** it is in

metal /'met(ə)l/ noun [C/U] **1 CHEMISTRY** a hard, usually shiny element that is a good conductor of heat and electricity. Metals are used to make things such as tools, machines, pans, jewellery etc. Lead, iron, and gold are all types of metal. Mercury is the only metal that is liquid at room temperature. **2** an alloy such as steel that is made of two or more metals or a metal combined with a non-metal. This is very often used to refer to anything that seems to be a metal, but it is not a scientific use of the word: *They collect old scraps of metal that they find on the beach.*

metalanguage /'metə,læŋgwɪdʒ/ noun [C/U] **LANGUAGE** a set of words used for describing and discussing language

metallic /mɪ'tælɪk/ adj consisting of metal, or similar to metal

metalloid¹ /'met(ə)lɔɪd/ noun [C] **CHEMISTRY** a chemical element such as **silicon** that is not a metal but has some of the qualities that a metal has

metalloid² /'met(ə)lɔɪd/ adj **CHEMISTRY 1** relating to or similar to a metalloid **2** similar to both a metal and a non-metal

metallophone /me'tæləfəʊn/ noun [C] **MUSIC** a musical instrument similar to a **xylophone**, with metal bars of different **pitches** that are struck with wooden hammers

metallurgy /mə'tælədʒi/ noun [U] **SCIENCE** the scientific study of metals and the ways in which they are used —**metallurgical** /,metə'lɜːdʒɪk(ə)l/ adj, **metallurgist** noun [C]

'**metal ,spatter** noun [U] **TECHNOLOGY** drops of **molten** (=melted) metal that can be thrown up during welding

metalwork /'met(ə)l,wɜːk/ noun [U] **1** the skill of making things out of metal **2** metal objects, or the metal parts of something

metamorphic /,metə'mɔːfɪk/ adj **GEOLOGY** metamorphic rock, for example **slate** and **marble**, is formed by heat or pressure. The other types of rock are igneous rock and sedimentary rock. —*picture* → ROCK CYCLE

metamorphose /,metə'mɔːfəʊz/ verb [I] **BIOLOGY** to change into a different physical form

metamorphosis /,metə'mɔːfəsɪs/ (plural **metamorphoses** /,metə'mɔːfəsiːz/) noun [C/U] **1 BIOLOGY** a major change in the physical form of an insect or amphibian as it develops. For example, when a butterfly larva **hatches** it is in the form of a caterpillar and then develops into a **pupa**. The adult butterfly then develops from this. **2** *formal* a major change that makes someone or something very different

metaphor /'metəfə, 'metəfɔː/ noun [C/U] **LITERATURE** a way of describing something in which you refer to it as something else with similar qualities: *Writers often use war as a metaphor for business activity and competition.* —**metaphorical** /,metə'fɒrɪk(ə)l/ adj, **metaphorically** /,metə'fɒrɪkli/ adv → SIMILE

metaphysical /,metə'fɪzɪk(ə)l/ adj relating to ideas about life, existence, and other things that are not part of the physical world

metastasis /me'tæstəsɪs/ (plural **metastases** /me'tæstəsiːz/) noun **HEALTH 1** [U] the process by which cancer cells spread to a new place in the body **2** [C] a new area of cancer that grows from an older one in the body —**metastatic** /,metə'stætɪk/ adj, **metastasize** verb

metatarsal /,metə'tɑːs(ə)l/ noun [C] **ANATOMY** one of the bones in the foot between the toes and the ankle —*picture* → SKELETON

meteor /'miːtiə, 'miːti,ɔː/ noun [C] **ASTRONOMY** a large piece of rock from space that passes into the Earth's atmosphere and appears as a bright light in the sky

meteoric /,miːti'ɒrɪk/ adj **1** becoming very successful very quickly **2 ASTRONOMY** from or relating to a meteor

meteorite /'miːtiəraɪt/ noun [C] **ASTRONOMY** a piece of rock that has fallen from space and landed on the Earth

meteorology /,miːtiə'rɒlədʒi/ noun [U] **GEOGRAPHY** the scientific study of weather —**meteorological** /,miːtiərə'lɒdʒɪk(ə)l/ adj, **meteorologist** noun [C]

meter /'miːtə/ noun [C] **1** a piece of equipment for measuring how much electricity or gas you have used **2** a **parking meter**

methadone /'meθədəʊn/ noun [U] **HEALTH** a strong drug that reduces pain and is often taken by people who want to stop using the drug **heroin**

methane /'mi:θeɪn/ noun [U] **CHEMISTRY** a natural gas with no colour or smell that is used as a fuel. Chemical formula: **CH₄**

methanol /'meθənɒl/ noun [U] **CHEMISTRY** a poisonous type of alcohol that can be used as a fuel

method /'meθəd/ noun [C] a way of doing something, especially a planned or established way: *a rug produced by **traditional methods** ♦ We developed new methods of pollution control.*

'method ,acting noun [U] **ARTS** preparation for an acting **role** in which the actor gets real experience of the life of the type of character that he or she will play —**'method ,actor** noun [C]

methodical /mə'θɒdɪk(ə)l/ adj always careful to do things in an organized way, or done in an organized way: *a methodical worker* —**methodically** /mə'θɒdɪkli/ adv

Methodist /'meθədɪst/ noun [C] **RELIGION** a member of a Protestant Christian church that was formed by John Wesley in the 18th century —**Methodist** adj

methodology /,meθə'dɒlədʒi/ (plural **methodologies**) noun [C/U] *formal* the methods and principles used for doing a particular kind of work, especially scientific or academic research —**methodological** /,meθədə'lɒdʒɪk(ə)l/ adj

methyl alcohol /,mi:θaɪl 'ælkəhɒl/ noun [U] **CHEMISTRY** methanol

methylated spirits /,meθəleɪtɪd 'spɪrɪts/ noun [U] a type of alcohol that is used as a fuel and is not suitable for drinking

methylene /'meθəli:n/ noun [U] **CHEMISTRY** a group of atoms obtained from methane that contains one carbon atom and two hydrogen atoms. Chemical formula: **CH₂**

meticulous /mɪ'tɪkjʊləs/ adj done with careful attention to detail: *a meticulous piece of research* —**meticulously** adv

metonymy /me'tɒnəmi/ noun [U] **LITERATURE** expressions in which you refer to something using the name of something else that is closely related to it, as, for example, when journalists use the expression **Downing Street** to refer to the British prime minister

metre /'mi:tə/ noun **1** [C] **SCIENCE** a unit for measuring length in the metric system, equal to 100 centimetres **2** [C/U] **LITERATURE** the patterns of sounds and rhythms in poetry

metric /'metrɪk/ adj **1 SCIENCE** using or relating to the metric system of measurements **2 LITERATURE metrical →** IMPERIAL sense 2

metrical /'metrɪk(ə)l/ adj **LITERATURE** relating to the patterns of sounds and rhythms in poetry —**metrically** /'metrɪkli/ adv

metrication /,metrɪ'keɪʃ(ə)n/ noun [U] *formal* the process in which a country, organization etc starts using the metric system of measurements

,metric 'screw ,thread noun [C/U] **TECHNOLOGY** a **thread** (=raised line) shaped like the letter V curving around a screw, with sides at an angle of 60° to the screw. It is the standard type of screw thread used throughout the world.

the 'metric ,system noun [singular] **SCIENCE** the system of measurement in which the basic units are metres and kilograms

metro /'metrəʊ/ (plural **metros**) noun [C] an underground railway system in a city

metronome /'metrənəʊm/ noun [C] **MUSIC** a piece of equipment that repeats a regular beat, used by musicians to help them play music at the right speed

metropolis /mə'trɒpəlɪs/ noun [C] a big city

metropolitan /,metrə'pɒlɪt(ə)n/ adj belonging to a big city, or typical of big cities: *the metropolitan area*

mezzanine /'metsəni:n/ noun [C] an area between two levels of a building

mezzo-soprano /,metsəʊ sə'prɑːnəʊ/ noun [C] **MUSIC** a woman with a fairly high singing voice, higher than an **alto** but lower than a **soprano**

mg abbrev **MATHS** milligram

MHz abbrev **COMPUTING** megahertz

mi /mi:/ noun [C] **MUSIC** the third note in the **sol-fa** musical **scale**

MIA /,em aɪ 'eɪ/ noun [C] *American* missing in action: a soldier who has disappeared during a military operation and who may be alive or dead

miaow /mjaʊ/ verb [I] when a cat miaows, it makes a short high sound —**miaow** noun [C]

mice /maɪs/ the plural of **mouse**

micelle /mɪ'sel/ noun [C] **CHEMISTRY** a tiny drop that consists of molecules of dirt and **detergent**

micro- /maɪkrəʊ/ prefix **1** extremely small: used with some nouns and adjectives: *microchip* **2 SCIENCE** one of a million equal parts of something: used to make nouns: *a microsecond*

microampere /'maɪkrəʊ,æmpeə/ noun [C] **PHYSICS** one millionth part of an ampere

microbe /'maɪkrəʊb/ noun [C] **BIOLOGY** a microorganism, especially a bacterium or virus that causes disease

microbiology /,maɪkrəʊbaɪ'ɒlədʒi/ noun [U] **BIOLOGY** the science that deals with microorganisms —**microbiological** /,maɪkrəʊ,baɪə'lɒdʒɪk(ə)l/ adj, **microbiologist** noun [C]

microbrewery /'maɪkrəʊ,bru:əri/ noun [C] a small independent company that produces small quantities of special beers

microchip /'maɪkrəʊ,tʃɪp/ noun [C] **COMPUTING** a very small piece of **silicon** that contains the electronic connections for making a computer work

microclimate /'maɪkrəʊ,klaɪmət/ noun [C] **GEOGRAPHY** the weather or temperature in a specific small area, especially when this is different from the weather or temperature in the areas surrounding it

microcomputer /'maɪkrəʊkəm,pju:tə/ noun [C] **COMPUTING** a small computer in which the **processor** is a single chip

microcosm /'maɪkrəʊ,kɒz(ə)m/ noun [C] *formal* something small that contains all the features of something larger: *The village is **a microcosm of** rural Turkish life.*

'micro-,earthquake noun [C] **GEOLOGY** a small earthquake measuring between 0 and 2 on the Richter scale

microeconomics /,maɪkrəʊ,i:kə'nɒmɪks, ,maɪkrəʊ,ekə'nɒmɪks/ noun [U] **ECONOMICS** the study of particular parts or aspects of an economy —**microeconomic** adj

microelectronics /,maɪkrəʊɪlek'trɒnɪks/ noun [U] **PHYSICS, COMPUTING** the science or industry that deals with designing very small electronic parts for computers and other equipment —**microelectronic** adj

microenvironment /ˈmaɪkrəʊˌvaɪrənmənt/ noun
[U] BUSINESS all the factors that have a direct effect
on a business or organization, for example its
employees or customers

microfarad /ˈmaɪkrəʊˌfærəd, ˈmaɪkrəʊˌfæræd/ noun
[C] PHYSICS one millionth part of a farad

microfinance /ˈmaɪkrəʊˌfaɪnæns/ noun [U]
ECONOMICS the practice of providing financial
services that involve very small amounts of money to
poor people

microgeneration /ˈmaɪkrəʊˌdʒenəreɪʃ(ə)n/ noun [U]
ENVIRONMENT the process by which a person,
group, or organization produces heat or energy for their
own use

microgram /ˈmaɪkrəˌgræm/ noun [C] SCIENCE one
millionth part of a gram

microlender /ˈmaɪkrəʊˌlendə/ noun [C] ECONOMICS
a person or financial institution that gives very small
loans given to poor people to start or run a business

micrometer /maɪˈkrɒmɪtə/ noun [C] SCIENCE,
TECHNOLOGY a piece of equipment that is used for
measuring small diameters, thicknesses, distances, or
angles very accurately

micrometre /ˈmaɪkrəʊˌmiːtə/ noun [C] SCIENCE one
millionth part of a metre

micron /ˈmaɪkrɒn/ noun [C] SCIENCE a unit for
measuring very small lengths in the **metric system**.
There are one million microns in a metre.

micronutrient /ˈmaɪkrəʊˌnjuːtriənt/ noun [C]
BIOLOGY a substance that an organism needs in very
small amounts in order to grow and develop normally.
Vitamins and minerals are micronutrients.
→ MACRONUTRIENT

microorganism /ˌmaɪkrəʊˈɔːgənɪz(ə)m/ noun [C]
BIOLOGY a very small living thing that you can see
only with a microscope

microphone /ˈmaɪkrəˌfəʊn/ noun [C] a piece of
equipment for making someone's voice louder when
they are performing or recording something

micropower /ˈmaɪkrəʊˌpaʊə/ noun [U]
ENVIRONMENT electrical power produced or used in
small quantities, usually close to the place where it is
needed so that large **power stations** are not needed

microprocessor /ˈmaɪkrəʊˌprəʊsesə/ noun [C]
COMPUTING a piece of electronic equipment inside a
computer that makes it work

micropyle /ˈmaɪkrəʊpaɪl/ noun [C] BIOLOGY 1 a
small opening in the covering of the **ovule** of a plant
through which the **pollen tube** passes before
fertilization. After fertilization, the ovule becomes a
seed, and water is absorbed through the opening. 2 a
small **pore** (=hole) in the membrane of an insect egg
that allows sperm to enter and fertilize the egg

microscope /ˈmaɪkrəˌskəʊp/ noun [C] SCIENCE a
piece of scientific equipment for looking at things that
are too small for people to see normally. **Light
microscopes** use a lens or a combination of lenses.
Electron microscopes use electrons that are sent back
from the surface of the object that is being examined:
*The virus can be seen clearly when examined **under a
microscope**.* —picture → LABORATORY

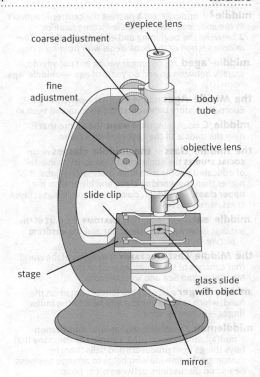

eyepiece lens
coarse adjustment
fine adjustment
body tube
objective lens
slide clip
glass slide with object
stage
mirror
microscope

microscopic /ˌmaɪkrəˈskɒpɪk/ adj **1** very small:
microscopic life **2** a microscopic examination is done
by looking at the details of something extremely
carefully —**microscopically** /ˌmaɪkrəˈskɒpɪkli/ adv

microsecond /ˈmaɪkrəʊˌsekənd/ noun [C] PHYSICS
one millionth part of a second

microsurgery /ˌmaɪkrəʊˈsɜːdʒəri/ noun [U] HEALTH
medical operations that are done using very small
pieces of equipment and a very powerful microscope
—**microsurgical** adj

microtubule /ˌmaɪkrəʊˈtjuːbjuːl/ noun [C] BIOLOGY
a tube-shaped structure in a living cell that helps to
keep the shape of the cell and transports material
within it

microwave /ˈmaɪkrəˌweɪv/ noun [C] **1** microwave or
microwave oven an oven that cooks food very quickly
by using electromagnetic waves rather than heat
2 SCIENCE a type of electromagnetic wave used in
radio communication, **radar**, and cooking

midday /ˌmɪdˈdeɪ/ noun [U] 12 o'clock, when the
morning ends and the afternoon begins= NOON

middle¹ /ˈmɪd(ə)l/ noun **1 the middle** [singular] the
part of something that is furthest from the sides,
edges, or ends= CENTRE: *a sheet with a blue stripe
down the middle* ♦ *There was a large cat sitting **in the
middle of** the road.* **2 the middle** [singular] the part that
is between the beginning and the end of a period of
time or an event: *the middle of the 15th century* ♦ *He
fell asleep **in the middle of** the film.* **3** [C] your waist
and the part of your body around your waist: *Ben was
holding a towel around his middle.*

PHRASE **in the middle of (doing) sth** busy doing
something: *He was in the middle of cooking dinner
when I arrived.*

middle² /'mɪd(ə)l/ adj **1** nearest the centre: *The map's in the middle drawer.* ♦ *middle-income families* **2** between the beginning and end of something: *The middle section of the book deals with training a dog.*

,middle-'aged adj no longer young but not yet old, usually between 40 and 60 years of age —,middle 'age noun [U]

the ,Middle 'Ages noun [plural] the period in European history between about 1000 AD and 1500 AD

,middle 'C noun [singular] MUSIC the C note that is near the middle of the keyboard on a piano

the ,middle 'class or the ,middle 'classes noun SOCIAL STUDIES the social class that consists mostly of educated people who have professional jobs. It is higher than the **working class** and lower than the **upper class**. —,middle-'class adj → LOWER CLASS, UPPER CLASS, WORKING CLASS

,middle 'ear noun [singular] ANATOMY the part of the ear that is between the **inner ear** and the **eardrum** —*picture* → EAR

the ,Middle 'East GEOGRAPHY the region of the world that consists of the countries east of the Mediterranean Sea and west of India

,middle 'finger noun [C] the longest finger on the hand, which is in the middle and next to the **index finger** —*picture* → BODY

middleman /'mɪd(ə)l,mæn/ (plural **middlemen** /'mɪd(ə)l,men/) noun [C] **1** a person or company that buys things from producers and sells them to customers **2** someone who helps to arrange business deals and discussions between other people

,middle 'management noun [U] BUSINESS managers who are in charge of parts of an organization and have less authority than senior managers —,middle 'manager noun [C]

,middle 'name noun [C] a second name that some people have between their first name and their family name

'middle ,school noun [C/U] EDUCATION a school in the UK for children between the ages of 8 and 12

midfield /'mɪd,fiːld/ noun [U] SPORTS the middle part of the field in football, **hockey,** and other ball games

midfielder /'mɪd,fiːldə/ noun [C] SPORTS a player who plays in the midfield

midget /'mɪdʒɪt/ noun [C] *offensive* an adult who has not grown to a normal size. A more polite expression is **person of restricted growth.**

midnight /'mɪd,naɪt/ noun [U] 12 o'clock at night

midpoint /'mɪd,pɔɪnt/ noun [singular] MATHS a place that is exactly in the middle of a line, shape, or object

midrib /'mɪd,rɪb/ noun [C] BIOLOGY the thick central vein that divides a leaf or a flower petal into two halves —*picture* → LEAF

midriff /'mɪdrɪf/ noun [C] the front part of the body between the waist and the chest

midsummer /,mɪd'sʌmə/ noun [U] the middle part of summer, when the weather is usually hottest

midterm /,mɪd'tɜːm/ adj happening in the middle part of a government's time in power, or in the middle part of a university or school **term**

midway /,mɪd'weɪ/ adj, adv **1** in a position that is **halfway** between two places: *He stopped midway across the room.* **2** at a time in the middle of an event or period: *Our problems started midway through the first year.*

midweek /,mɪd'wiːk/ adj, adv in the middle of the week, usually from Tuesday to Thursday: *a midweek game*

midwife /'mɪd,waɪf/ (plural **midwives** /'mɪd,waɪvz/) noun [C] HEALTH a nurse whose job is to look after women when they are having a baby

might¹ /maɪt/ modal verb **1** used for saying that something is possibly true or will possibly happen: *If you're not careful, you might start a fire.* ♦ *The disease might have come from monkeys originally.* **2** used as the past tense of 'may' when you are reporting what someone said: *Roger said they might not be able to come.* **3** used for making a suggestion: *To find out more, you might like to visit the following website.*

might² /maɪt/ noun [U] great power or strength

mightn't /'maɪt(ə)nt/ short form the usual way of saying 'might not' in questions: *It might be nice to get out of the city for a while, mightn't it?*

mighty /'maɪti/ (**mightier, mightiest**) adj very large, powerful, or impressive: *a mighty empire*

migraine /'miːgreɪn, 'maɪgreɪn/ noun [C] HEALTH a very severe **headache** that often makes you unable to bear strong light

migrant /'maɪgrənt/ noun [C] SOCIAL STUDIES someone who travels to another place in order to find work: *migrant workers*

migrate /maɪ'greɪt/ verb

1 of a bird/animal	4 change software etc
2 travel to find work	5 of cells
3 use computer system	

1 [I] BIOLOGY if a bird or other animal migrates, it travels to another part of the world or another region and then returns, especially as the seasons change. Birds and other animals usually migrate in order to find better conditions for feeding, living, and breeding.
2 [I] SOCIAL STUDIES to go to another place in order to find work
3 [I/T] COMPUTING to start to use a different computer system, or to make someone do this
4 [T] COMPUTING to move software or hardware to a different computer system
5 [I] BIOLOGY if cells migrate, they move to a specific place in the body
—**migration** /maɪ'greɪʃ(ə)n/ noun [U]

migratory /'maɪgrət(ə)ri, ,maɪ'greɪtəri/ adj BIOLOGY a migratory bird or other animal is one that **migrates**

mild /maɪld/ adj **1** not strong, serious, or severe: *They were both suffering from a mild bout of flu.* ♦ *There was a note of mild alarm in her voice.* ♦ *a mild recession* **2** mild weather is not as cold as people expect it to be: *a mild winter* **3** without a strong taste: *a mild curry* **4** very gentle and not likely to have any bad effects: *a mild soap*

mildly /'maɪldli/ adv slightly but not very: *Some of the stories were mildly amusing.*

mild-mannered /,maɪld 'mænəd/ adj gentle and kind

,mild 'steel noun [U] TECHNOLOGY steel that contains only a small amount of carbon. It is easy to shape or cut.

mile /maɪl/ noun **1** [C] a unit for measuring distance, equal to 1.609 kilometres or 1,760 yards: *We drove about 900 miles in two days.* ♦ *The island is 13 miles long.* ♦ *The car was travelling at 50 miles per hour.* **2** miles [plural] a long distance: *They live miles from the nearest town.* ♦ *The beach stretched for miles in each direction.*

mileage /'maɪlɪdʒ/ noun [singular/U] **1** the number of miles that a vehicle has travelled: *a car with high mileage* **2** the number of miles that a vehicle can travel using one gallon or one litre of petrol

milestone /'maɪl,stəʊn/ noun [C] an event or achievement that marks an important stage in a process

milieu /'miːljɜː/ (plural **milieus** or **milieux**) noun [C] *formal* the particular people and society that surround someone, and influence the way in which they behave

militant¹ /'mɪlɪtənt/ adj using violence or extreme methods in order to achieve political change: *The militant group claimed to have killed two soldiers.* —**militancy** noun [U]

militant² /'mɪlɪtənt/ noun [C] someone who uses militant methods to achieve something

military /'mɪlɪt(ə)ri/ adj relating to armed forces, or using armed forces: *military service* ♦ *The government is prepared to take **military action**.* ♦ *a huge **military operation*** —**militarily** adv

the military /'mɪlɪt(ə)ri/ noun [singular] a country's armed forces: *The military does not have the weapons it needs to defeat the rebels.*

,military po'lice noun [plural] the part of an army that deals with soldiers who break the army's rules

,military 'service noun [U] **1** the period of time that someone spends in an army, navy, or air force **2** in some countries, a system in which people must spend time in the country's army, navy, or air force= CONSCRIPTION

militia /mə'lɪʃə/ noun [C] a group of ordinary people who are trained as soldiers to fight in an emergency

milk¹ /mɪlk/ noun [U] **1** BIOLOGY, HEALTH a white liquid that women and other female mammals produce to feed their babies. Humans drink the milk of cows, goats, and sheep and use it to make cheese, butter etc. Milk provides the body with calcium: *a bowl of milk* **2** BIOLOGY a white liquid that some plants produce

milk² /mɪlk/ verb [T] **1** AGRICULTURE to take milk from a cow, goat, or sheep **2** to get a lot of personal advantage from something: *Both parties have milked the political situation for all it's worth.*

'milk ,tooth (plural **'milk ,teeth**) noun [C] ANATOMY one of the first teeth that a child has, which fall out when the adult teeth start to develop

milky /'mɪlki/ adj **1** containing milk or a liquid that looks like milk: *milky drinks* **2** white like milk

the ,Milky 'Way noun ASTRONOMY the group of planets and stars that the Earth belongs to. It can be seen at night as a band of pale light across the sky.

mill¹ /mɪl/ noun [C] **1** a building with a machine that is used for crushing grain into flour **2** a factory where a product such as cotton, wool, or steel is made: *a textile mill* **3** a small machine or tool that you use in the kitchen for crushing substances into powder: *a pepper mill*

mill² /mɪl/ verb [T] **1** to crush grain into flour **2** TECHNOLOGY to shape or **polish** metal using a machine

millennium /mɪ'leniəm/ (plural **millennia** /mɪ'leniə/ or **millenniums**) noun [C] a period of 1,000 years —**millennial** /mɪ'leniəl/ adj

millet /'mɪlɪt/ noun [U] AGRICULTURE a type of grain grown for food and for use as **fodder** (=animal food) —*picture* → CEREAL

milli- /mɪli/ prefix SCIENCE one of a thousand equal parts of something: used to make nouns: *a millilitre*

millibar /'mɪli,bɑː/ noun [C] SCIENCE a unit for measuring air pressure

milligram /'mɪli,ɡræm/ noun [C] SCIENCE a unit for measuring weight in the metric system. There are 1,000 milligrams in a **gram**. Symbol mg

millihenry /'mɪli,henri/ (plural **millihenrys**) noun [C] PHYSICS one-thousandth part of a henry

millilitre /'mɪli,liːtə/ noun [C] SCIENCE a unit for measuring volume in the metric system. There are 1,000 millilitres in a litre. Symbol ml

millimetre /'mɪli,miːtə/ noun [C] SCIENCE a unit for measuring length in the metric system. There are 1,000 millimetres in a metre. Symbol mm

million /'mɪljən/ number **1** the number 1,000,000 **2** **millions** or **a million** a large number of people or things: *I've got a million things to do before I leave.* ♦ *They received **millions of** letters asking for information.* —**millionth** /'mɪljənθ/ number

millionaire /,mɪljə'neə/ noun [C] someone who has more than a million pounds, rand, dollars etc

millipede /'mɪlɪpiːd/ noun [C] an **arthropod** with a long thin body divided into many **segments**, most of which have two pairs of small legs

mime /maɪm/ verb [I/T] **1** to tell a story using only the movements of your body and face, not using words **2** to pretend to sing or play an instrument while a piece of recorded music is being played —**mime** noun [U]

mimic /'mɪmɪk/ (**mimics, mimicking, mimicked**) verb [T] **1** to copy someone's voice, behaviour, or appearance= IMITATE: *She mimicked his accent.* **2** to behave or work in the same way as something else = IMITATE **3** BIOLOGY if a plant or animal mimics another plant or animal or something in its environment, it looks like it in order to make itself less noticeable to its enemies

mimicry /'mɪmɪkri/ noun [U] **1** BIOLOGY the way in which one organism is able to look like another organism or an object, especially as a protection from attack **2** the action of mimicking someone, or the ability to do this

mimosa /mɪ'məʊzə, mɪ'məʊsə/ noun [C/U] a small tree with yellow flowers that grows in hot countries

min abbrev **1** minute **2** minimum

minaret /,mɪnə'ret/ noun [C] RELIGION a tall tower that is traditionally part of a mosque, where someone stands to call people to prayer

mince /mɪns/ verb [T] to cut meat into very small pieces using a machine

mind¹ /maɪnd/ noun **1** [C/U] your thoughts and attention, or the part of you that thinks, knows, and remembers things: *You never know what's going on in her mind.* ♦ *I can't **keep my mind on** work when it's so sunny outside.* ♦ *She's never been able to **get him out of her mind** (=stop thinking about him).* ♦ *She shouldn't drive in her present **state of mind** (=the way she is thinking and feeling).* ♦ *Just try to **put the problem out of your mind**.* ♦ *A good night out will help you **take your mind off** your exams (=help you to stop thinking about them).* **2** [singular] someone's intelligence and ability to understand things: *a brilliant/keen mind* ♦ *Her youngest child has a very enquiring mind (=is very interested in things and always asking questions).* ♦ *My grandmother's mind is failing.*

PHRASES **at the back of your mind** if something is at the back of your mind, you are not thinking about it now, but you still remember it or know about it: *At the back of her mind, she knew he was lying.*

be in two minds (about sth) to not be certain about something, or to have difficulty in making a decision: *I'm in two minds about accepting the job.*

come/spring to mind if something comes to mind, you suddenly remember it or start to think about it

have sb/sth in mind to know the person or thing that you want: *Who do you have in mind for the job?*

have/keep an open mind to be willing to listen to other people's opinions: *I told the committee that I had an open mind on the matter.*

keep/bear sth in mind to remember or consider something: *Keep that in mind when you come to make your decision.*

keep sb in mind to remember someone because they might be suitable for something in the future: *Keep me in mind if you need some help.*

make up your mind to make a decision: *I can't make up my mind whether to go or not.* ♦ *My mind's made up. Nothing will make me change it.*

on your mind if something is on your mind, you are thinking or worrying about it: *She isn't usually so rude; she's got a lot on her mind.*

put your mind to sth to decide to do something and try very hard to achieve it
→ BEAR¹, CROSS¹

mind² /maɪnd/ verb **1** [I/T] to feel annoyed, upset, or unhappy about something: *We had to cancel, but Rosa didn't seem to mind.* ♦ *I don't mind the heat* (=the heat is not a problem to me). ♦ *I don't mind going to the shops* (=I'm willing to go) *if no one else wants to.* ♦ *He won't mind if we're a bit late.* **2** [T] to be careful about something: *Mind the step* (=do not fall over it). ♦ *Mind you don't spill that drink.* **3** [T] to look after someone or something for a short time: *Could you mind the children for me for five minutes?*

PHRASES **do you mind if I do sth?** used for politely asking someone's permission to do something
would you mind used for asking politely for something: *Would you mind closing that window?* ♦ *Would you mind if I brought a friend to the party?*

mindful /ˈmaɪn(d)f(ə)l/ adj careful about something, or conscious of something: *Travellers ought to be mindful of their surroundings.*

mindless /ˈmaɪn(d)ləs/ adj **1** done without a reason, or without thinking about the results: *mindless vandalism* **2** not needing any thought or intelligence: *a mindless task*

ˈ**mind ˌmap** noun [C] a diagram that shows how ideas, words, or actions are all connected to one important idea. It is used for organizing ideas, solving problems, or making decisions.

mine¹ /maɪn/ pronoun used for referring to people or things that belong to you or are connected with you, when you are the person who is speaking or writing: *Can I borrow your keys? I can't find mine.* ♦ *This must be your T-shirt. Mine has stains on it.* ♦ *I got the idea from a friend of mine.*

mine² /maɪn/ noun [C] **1** a large hole or tunnel in the ground from which people take coal, gold etc **2** a bomb that is hidden under the ground or under water and explodes when it is touched

mine³ /maɪn/ verb **1** [I/T] to dig a large hole or tunnel in the ground in order to get coal, gold etc: *People still mine for coal in this area.* **2** [T] to hide bombs under the ground or under water

minefield /ˈmaɪnˌfiːld/ noun **1** [singular] a situation with many possible problems or dangers: *The issue of tax cuts is a potential minefield for the government.* **2** [C] an area where bombs have been hidden under the ground or under water

miner /ˈmaɪnə/ noun [C] someone whose job is to dig coal from a mine

mineral /ˈmɪn(ə)rəl/ noun [C] **1** CHEMISTRY, GEOLOGY a natural substance found in the earth, for example coal, clay, or salt. Minerals usually have their own individual colour, chemical structure etc. **2** HEALTH an inorganic chemical in some foods that is important for good health, for example calcium: *vitamins and minerals*

mineralogy /ˌmɪnəˈrælədʒi/ noun [U] GEOLOGY the study of minerals —**mineralogist** noun [C]

ˈ**mineral ˌsalt** noun [C] CHEMISTRY one of the inorganic salts that living things need for good health and growth, for example iron and zinc

ˈ**mineral ˌwater** noun [U] water that comes from under the ground and contains minerals

mineshaft /ˈmaɪnˌʃɑːft/ noun [C] a vertical tunnel in a mine with lifts inside that carry the workers up and down

mingle /ˈmɪŋɡ(ə)l/ verb [I] **1** if things such as smells or feelings mingle, they become mixed together: *Polly felt hope mingled with fear.* **2** to move around and talk to a lot of people during a social event: *Try to get the guests to mingle.*

mini- /ˈmɪni/ prefix smaller or shorter than other things of the same kind: *a miniskirt*

miniature /ˈmɪnətʃə/ adj much smaller than other things of the same kind: *a miniature railway*

minibar /ˈmɪniˌbɑː/ noun [C] TOURISM a small cupboard of alcoholic and non-alcoholic drinks for guests in a hotel room

minibreak /ˈmɪniˌbreɪk/ noun [C] TOURISM a short holiday for only two or three days

minibus /ˈmɪniˌbʌs/ noun [C] a small bus for about 10 to 15 people

minicab /ˈmɪniˌkæb/ noun [C] a car that is used as a taxi. People must call for it by telephone and they cannot stop it in the street.

minim /ˈmɪnɪm/ noun [C] MUSIC a musical note that is half as long as a **semibreve** —*picture* → MUSIC

minimal /ˈmɪnɪm(ə)l/ adj extremely small in amount or degree: *a minimal increase* ♦ *minimal damage* —**minimally** adv

minimalism /ˈmɪnɪm(ə)lˌɪz(ə)m/ noun [U] ARTS a style of art that developed in the 1960s and uses a small number of simple shapes and colours —**minimalist** adj, **minimalist** noun [C]

ˌ**minimal ˈpair** noun [C] LANGUAGE a pair of words that are different from each other in one sound only, for example **pan** and **can**

minimarket /ˈmɪniˌmɑːkɪt/ noun [C] a very small self-service store

minimize /ˈmɪnɪmaɪz/ verb [T] **1** to make the amount of something bad as small as possible ≠ MAXIMIZE: *We must minimize the damage to innocent civilians.* **2** to make something seem much less important than it really is ≠ EXAGGERATE: *I don't want to minimize their role in the campaign.* **3** COMPUTING to make a computer program appear as only a small picture on your computer screen when you are not using it

minimum¹ /ˈmɪnɪməm/ adj as small in amount or degree as possible ≠ MAXIMUM: *the minimum voting age* ♦ *the minimum requirements for entry to college*

minimum² /ˈmɪnɪməm/ noun [singular] the smallest amount or degree of something that is necessary or possible ≠ MAXIMUM: *They can produce high-quality* results with **a minimum of** supervision. ♦ *We need to keep costs **to a minimum**.*

,minimum 'wage noun [singular/U] ECONOMICS the smallest amount of money that an employer is legally allowed to pay a worker in some countries

mining /'maɪnɪŋ/ noun [U] the process of getting coal, gold etc from under the ground: *Mining is one of the country's main industries.* ♦ *coal mining*

minister /'mɪnɪstə/ noun [C] **1** SOCIAL STUDIES an official who is in charge of a government department in the UK and in other countries: *a meeting of trade ministers* ♦ *the **Minister for** Education* **2** RELIGION a priest in some Protestant churches

ministerial /,mɪnɪ'stɪəriəl/ adj relating to the job of being a government minister: *a ministerial meeting*

ministry /'mɪnɪstri/ (plural **ministries**) noun **1** [C] a government department in the UK and in other countries: *the Dutch foreign ministry* ♦ *the **Ministry of** Defence* **2 the ministry** [singular] RELIGION the profession or work of a church minister

mink /mɪŋk/ noun [C/U] a small mammal found in Europe, Asia, and North America that is kept for its thick dark fur, or the fur of this mammal

minnow /'mɪnəʊ/ noun [C] a small fish that lives in rivers and lakes

minor¹ /'maɪnə/ adj **1** not very important in comparison with people or things of the same type ≠ MAJOR: *The damage here was only minor.* ♦ *a minor offence* ♦ *Some minor changes may be necessary.* **2** MUSIC relating to one of the two types of musical keys → MAJOR¹ sense 2

minor² /'maɪnə/ noun [C] LAW a young person who is not yet an adult, according to the law

,minor 'axis noun [C] MATHS the shorter axis of an **ellipse** (=circle that is longer than it is wide)

minority¹ /maɪ'nɒrəti/ (plural **minorities**) noun **1** [singular] a group of people or things that forms less than half of a larger group ≠ MAJORITY: *In a small minority of cases, the treatment does not help.* ♦ *Women are in the minority in the top ranks of government.* **2** [U] LAW the period of time before someone is legally an adult **3** [C] SOCIAL STUDIES a part of a population that is different in race, religion, or culture from most of the population: *The regulations are intended to prevent discrimination against minorities.* ♦ *Members of **ethnic minorities** are represented on the committee.*

minority² /maɪ'nɒrəti/ adj **1** relating to a minority, or forming a minority: *They hold a minority interest in the company.* **2** SOCIAL STUDIES belonging to a racial minority: *students from minority backgrounds*

,minor 'planet noun [C] ASTRONOMY an asteroid

mint¹ /mɪnt/ noun **1** [U] a small plant with green leaves that have a strong smell and a cool pleasant taste. It is found in northern **temperate** countries. **2** [C] a sweet with a strong fresh taste **3** [C] the place where a country makes its coins

mint² /mɪnt/ verb [T] to make a coin from metal

minus¹ /'maɪnəs/ preposition **1** MATHS used for showing that you are taking one number from another. Minus is usually represented by the symbol – ≠ PLUS: *72 minus 5 equals 67.* **2** MATHS used before a number to show that it is less than zero: *The temperature fell to minus 15 degrees.* **3** *informal* without: *Anthony returned to work minus his beard.*

PHRASE **A minus/B minus etc** EDUCATION marks given for students' work that are slightly lower than the marks A, B etc

minus² /'maɪnəs/ noun [C] *informal* a disadvantage: *Before I decide, I need to weigh up all the pluses and minuses.*

minuscule /'mɪnɪ,skjuːl/ adj extremely small in size or amount: *The risk to public health is minuscule.*

'minus ,sign noun [C] MATHS the symbol – that shows that one number is to be subtracted from another

minute¹ /'mɪnɪt/ noun [C] **1** a period of 60 seconds. There are 60 minutes in one hour: *I'll meet you downstairs in ten minutes.* ♦ *The train leaves at six minutes past ten.* **2** MATHS one of the 60 parts of a degree **3** *informal* a very short period of time: *It will only take a minute.* ♦ *For a minute I thought she had left.* ♦ *I'll be ready in a minute* (=very soon). ♦ *Within minutes I realized I was on the wrong train.*

PHRASE **the last minute** the latest possible time for doing something: *Jane always waits until the last minute to write her paper.*

minute² /maɪ'njuːt/ adj **1** very small: *The soil contained minute quantities of uranium.* **2** very careful and detailed: *a minute examination of the evidence*

minutes /'mɪnɪts/ noun [plural] an official written record of the decisions that people make at a formal meeting: *Carl usually takes the minutes but he's not here tonight.*

mips /mɪps/ noun [plural] COMPUTING million instructions per second: a unit for measuring computer speed

miracle /'mɪrək(ə)l/ noun [C] **1** something that is extremely lucky and that would not normally be possible: *It's a miracle that no one was killed.* **2** RELIGION an event that cannot be explained according to the laws of nature and is considered to be an act of God

miraculous /mə'rækjʊləs/ adj extremely lucky and unexpected —**miraculously** adv

mirage /'mɪrɑːʒ/ noun [C] PHYSICS an **optical illusion** in which you see something such as an area of water that is not really there. It happens when hot air causes light to **refract** at an angle to the surface of the ground.

mired /maɪəd/ adj caught in an unpleasant situation that you cannot easily escape from

mirror¹ /'mɪrə/ noun [C] a surface made of something such as glass that is able to reflect light, forming an image of something that is in front of it: *a bathroom mirror* ♦ *Rachel looked at herself in the mirror.* —picture → MICROSCOPE, WAVE

mirror² /'mɪrə/ verb [T] to match or express the qualities, features, or feelings of someone or something

,mirror 'image noun [C] an image or object that is exactly the same as another, but with the left and right sides the other way round, as in a mirror

misadventure /,mɪsəd'ventʃə/ noun [C/U] LAW death caused by an accident

misanthropic /,mɪs(ə)n'θrɒpɪk/ adj *formal* someone who is misanthropic dislikes people and avoids social situations

misbehave /,mɪsbɪ'heɪv/ verb [I] to behave badly

miscalculate /mɪs'kælkjʊleɪt/ verb [I/T] **1** to make a wrong judgment about what will happen or what to do in a situation **2** to make a mistake in calculating numbers —**miscalculation** /,mɪskælkjʊ'leɪʃ(ə)n/ noun [C/U]

miscarriage /'mɪskærɪdʒ/ noun [C/U] BIOLOGY a process in which a foetus comes out of the uterus before it has developed enough to live independently.

Very often there is no known reason for this, but it can be the result of illness in the mother, something wrong with the foetus itself, or an accident.

PHRASE **miscarriage of justice** LAW a situation in which a court of law punishes someone for a crime that they did not commit

miscarry /ˌmɪsˈkæri/ (**miscarries, miscarrying, miscarried**) verb [I/T] BIOLOGY to give birth to a baby before it has developed enough to live

miscellaneous /ˌmɪsəˈleɪniəs/ adj consisting of various kinds of people or things

mischief /ˈmɪstʃɪf/ noun [U] behaviour or play, especially of children, that causes trouble but not serious harm

mischievous /ˈmɪstʃɪvəs/ adj a mischievous person, especially a child, enjoys having fun by causing trouble —**mischievously** adv

miscible /ˈmɪsəb(ə)l/ adj CHEMISTRY miscible liquids mix together to form a solution

misconception /ˌmɪskənˈsepʃ(ə)n/ noun [C/U] a wrong belief or opinion that is the result of not understanding something

misconduct /mɪsˈkɒndʌkt/ noun [U] formal bad or dishonest behaviour by someone who has a position of responsibility

misdemeanour /ˌmɪsdɪˈmiːnə/ noun [C] formal an action that is bad or wrong, but not in a serious way

misdirect /ˌmɪsdaɪˈrekt/ verb [T] LAW if a judge misdirects a jury, he or she gives them the wrong information or instructions

mise-en-place /ˌmiːz ɒn ˈplæs/ noun [U] the practice of planning how to cook a particular meal, and organizing and preparing all the foods and equipment needed for it before starting to make it

miserable /ˈmɪz(ə)rəb(ə)l/ adj **1** extremely unhappy: He looked cold and miserable. **2** making you feel very unhappy: The weather was miserable. **3** a miserable amount of something is very small and not enough —**miserably** adv

misery /ˈmɪzəri/ noun [U] the state of being extremely unhappy or uncomfortable

misfire /mɪsˈfaɪə/ verb [I] **1** if a gun misfires, the bullet does not come out **2** if an engine misfires, the fuel does not burn in the right way and it does not work smoothly **3** if a plan or activity misfires, it does not have the result that you wanted

misfit /ˈmɪsfɪt/ noun [C] someone who does not seem to belong to a group, or who is not accepted by a group

misfortune /mɪsˈfɔːtʃ(ə)n/ noun [U] bad luck, or a situation in which you have bad luck

misgiving /mɪsˈɡɪvɪŋ/ noun [C/U] a feeling of doubt about whether something is right or will have a good result: Richard expressed grave misgivings about the deal.

misguided /mɪsˈɡaɪdɪd/ adj based on judgments or opinions that are wrong

mishap /ˈmɪshæp/ noun [C/U] a minor mistake or accident

mishit /mɪsˈhɪt/ verb [T] SPORTS to hit or kick a ball badly in a game —**mishit** /ˈmɪshɪt/ noun [C]

misinform /ˌmɪsɪnˈfɔːm/ verb [T] to give someone false or incorrect information —**misinformation** /ˌmɪsɪnfəˈmeɪʃ(ə)n/ noun [U]

misinterpret /ˌmɪsɪnˈtɜːprɪt/ verb [T] to understand or explain something wrongly —**misinterpretation** /ˌmɪsɪntɜːprɪˈteɪʃ(ə)n/ noun [C/U]

misjudge /mɪsˈdʒʌdʒ/ verb [T] **1** to make a wrong judgment about a person or situation **2** to make a mistake in calculating something —**misjudgment** noun [C/U]

mislay /mɪsˈleɪ/ (**mislays, mislaying, mislaid** /mɪsˈleɪd/) verb [T] to lose something for a short time, because you cannot remember where you put it

mislead /mɪsˈliːd/ (**misleads, misleading, misled** /mɪsˈled/) verb [T] to make someone believe something that is incorrect or not true

misleading /mɪsˈliːdɪŋ/ adj intended or likely to make someone believe something that is incorrect or not true: He had made misleading statements to the committee.

mismanagement /mɪsˈmænɪdʒmənt/ noun [U] the process of managing something badly: the mismanagement of public funds —**mismanage** verb [T]

misogynist /mɪˈsɒdʒənɪst/ noun [U] a man who hates women

misplaced /mɪsˈpleɪst/ adj a misplaced feeling or opinion is not suitable for a particular situation, or is directed towards the wrong person: misplaced trust

misprint /ˈmɪsˌprɪnt/ noun [C] a mistake such as a wrong spelling in a book, newspaper etc

misrepresent /ˌmɪsreprɪˈzent/ verb [T] to deliberately give a false or incorrect description of someone or something —**misrepresentation** /ˌmɪsreprɪzenˈteɪʃ(ə)n/ noun [C/U]

miss¹ /mɪs/ verb

1 not reach	**5** not take chance
2 not be present at	**6** avoid sth bad
3 be too late for	**7** feel sad about
4 not notice	**+ PHRASAL VERBS**

1 [I/T] to fail to catch, hit, or reach something: I tried to catch the ball but missed. ♦ An official said that the missiles had missed their targets.
2 [T] to fail to be present for someone or something: I had to **miss** a week of **school**. ♦ We must have missed each other by about an hour. ♦ I **wouldn't miss** your party **for the world** (=I really want to go to it).
3 [T] to be too late for something such as a train or bus: I **missed the** last **train** home again. ♦ If you don't go now you'll **miss the post**.
4 [T] to fail to notice or understand something: I missed most of what she said. ♦ Sue had **missed the point** (=not understood what someone meant). ♦ The house is next to the station – **you can't miss it** (=it is very easy to see).
5 [T] to fail to take advantage of an opportunity: She realized she had **missed a chance** to speak to Brian.
6 [T] to escape something that is unpleasant or uncomfortable: If I leave at eight o'clock, I miss the traffic.
7 [T] to feel sad because someone is not with you any longer, or because you do not have or cannot do something any longer: We miss him enormously. ♦ I'm missing our lunchtime drinks on Friday. ♦ I miss watching her ride her horse.

PHRASAL VERBS ,**miss 'out** to lose an opportunity to do or have something: Come with us or you'll **miss out on** all the fun.
,**miss sth 'out** to fail to include someone or something: An important fact had been missed out.

miss² /mɪs/ noun **1** Miss a title used in front of the last name or whole name of a girl or woman who is not married → MRS, MS **2** Miss a title used by children when talking to a woman teacher **3** [C] a failure to hit or catch something, or to score in a game

missile /'mɪsaɪl, 'mɪs(ə)l/ noun [C] **1** a weapon that travels long distances and explodes when it hits something: *a nuclear missile* → BALLISTIC MISSILE, CRUISE MISSILE **2** an object that is thrown or fired at someone or something

missing /'mɪsɪŋ/ adj **1** if someone or something is missing, they are not where they should be and you do not know where they are: *We need to look to see if anything is missing.* ♦ *a missing dog* ♦ *The young woman's boyfriend had already reported her missing.* ♦ *Important documents have mysteriously gone missing.* ♦ *The key was missing from its usual place.* **2** if someone or something is missing, they are not included in something when you would expect them to be there: *Candidates' names were missing from ballot papers.* **3** not found after a battle or accident, but not known to be dead or taken prisoner: *Five other passengers are missing, presumed dead.* ♦ *Over 8,000 soldiers are listed as missing in action.*

,**missing 'person** noun [C] someone that the police are trying to find because their family does not know where they are and is worried about them

mission /'mɪʃ(ə)n/ noun

1 important work	4 flight into space
2 group sent for sth	5 important aim
3 military operation	6 religious work

1 [C] an important piece of work that a person or group of people has to do for a government or large organization, especially one that involves travel: *a rescue mission* **2** [C] a group of people who have been sent to do an important piece of work: *members of the trade mission to Russia* **3** [C] a military operation, especially one by aircraft: *He was shot down during a mission over the Balkans.* **4** [C] a flight into space: *the possibility of a manned mission to Mars* **5** [singular] an aim that is very important to a person or organization: *Helping homeless people was Gina's mission in life.* **6** [C/U] RELIGION the work of religious people who go to other countries in order to make people believe in their religion, or the building where they do this

missionary /'mɪʃ(ə)n(ə)ri/ (plural **missionaries**) noun [C] RELIGION someone who has been sent to a foreign country by a religious organization to teach people about a particular religion

'**mission ,creep** noun [U] a tendency for military operations in foreign countries to increase gradually, and for more and more soldiers to be needed

'**mission ,statement** noun [C] a short official statement that an organization makes about its aims and principles

misspell /mɪs'spel/ (**misspells, misspelling, misspelled** or **misspelt** /mɪs'spelt/) verb [T] to spell a word wrongly —**misspelling** noun [C/U]

mist¹ /mɪst/ noun [C/U] a mass of small drops of water in the air close to the ground → FOG

mist² /mɪst/ or ,**mist 'up** verb [I] to become covered with small drops of water

mistake¹ /mɪ'steɪk/ noun [C] **1** something that you have not done correctly, or something you say or think that is not correct: *a spelling mistake* **2** something that you do that you later wish you had not done, because it causes a lot of problems: *You're making a big mistake.* ♦ *It would be a mistake to think that the trouble is over.* ♦ *I made the mistake of inviting Jennifer to the party.*
PHRASE **by mistake** if you do something by mistake,

you did not intend to do it: *I'm sorry – I opened one of your letters by mistake.*

mistake² /mɪ'steɪk/ (**mistakes, mistaking, mistook** /mɪ'stʊk/, **mistaken** /mɪ'steɪkən/) verb [T] to not understand something correctly: *I'm afraid I mistook what she was trying to tell me.*
PHRASAL VERB **mi'stake sb/sth for sb/sth** to think that a person or thing is someone or something else: *I had mistaken friendship for love.*

mistaken /mɪ'steɪkən/ adj **1** if someone is mistaken, they are wrong about something: *If you think I'm going to help, you're sadly mistaken.* **2** a mistaken belief, idea, opinion etc is not correct —**mistakenly** adv: *He mistakenly believed that she was married.*

mis,taken i'dentity noun [U] a situation in which you think a person is someone else

mistletoe /'mɪs(ə)l,təʊ/ noun [U] a plant with small white fruits, found in Europe, North America, and Asia. It is used in some countries for decorating rooms at Christmas.

mistook /mɪ'stʊk/ the past tense of **mistake²**

mistral /'mɪstrəl, mɪ'strɑːl/ noun [singular] GEOGRAPHY a cold dry wind from the north that is common in the south of France

mistreat /mɪs'triːt/ verb [T] to treat someone in an unfair or cruel way: *She felt she had been mistreated by the police.* —**mistreatment** noun [U]

mistrial /mɪs'traɪəl/ noun [C] LAW a trial that was not done correctly and has to be started again

mistrust /mɪs'trʌst/ noun [singular/U] a feeling that you should not trust someone or something: *Many voters have a deep mistrust of the government.* —**mistrust** verb [T]

misty /'mɪsti/ adj it is misty when a mass of small drops of water is in the air close to the ground

misunderstand /,mɪsʌndə'stænd/ (**misunderstands, misunderstanding, misunderstood** /,mɪsʌndə'stʊd/) verb [I/T] to not understand someone or something correctly: *I think he has misunderstood the nature of the problem.*

misunderstanding /,mɪsʌndə'stændɪŋ/ noun **1** [C/U] a failure to understand someone or something correctly: *There's been a misunderstanding: Mr Jones isn't expecting you until tomorrow.* **2** [C] an argument that is not very serious

misunderstood¹ /,mɪsʌndə'stʊd/ adj if someone or something is misunderstood, people do not realize what they are really like

misunderstood² /,mɪsʌndə'stʊd/ the past tense and past participle of **misunderstand**

misuse /mɪs'juːs/ noun [C/U] the use of something in the wrong way or for the wrong purpose: *a misuse of government money* —**misuse** /mɪs'juːz/ verb [T]

mite /maɪt/ noun [C] a very small arachnid that lives in foods, on plants, or on animals —*picture* → INSECT

mitigate /'mɪtɪɡeɪt/ verb [T] *formal* to reduce the harmful effects of something

mitigating /'mɪtɪˌɡeɪtɪŋ/ adj **mitigating circumstances** facts that help to explain a crime or mistake and make it seem less bad

mitigation /,mɪtɪ'ɡeɪʃ(ə)n/ noun [U] LAW things that are said in a court of law to explain why someone committed a crime, so that it seems less bad

mitochondrion /,maɪtəʊ'kɒndriən/ (plural **mitochondria** /,maɪtəʊ'kɒndriə/) noun [C] BIOLOGY a very small round or rod-shaped part in the **cytoplasm** of a cell. It contains enzymes for the respiration of food to release energy. —*picture* → CELL, SEX CELL

mitosis /ˌmaɪˈtəʊsɪs/ noun [U] **BIOLOGY** the process by which a cell divides into two smaller cells that each contain the same number of chromosomes as the original cell. It is the basis of **asexual reproduction** and ordinary cell division in living things. → MEIOSIS —*picture* → FERTILIZATION

mitral valve /ˈmaɪtrəl vælv/ noun [C] **ANATOMY** a **valve** on the left side of the heart. It prevents blood from flowing back from the left **ventricle** into the **atrium** = BICUSPID VALVE —*picture* → CIRCULATION

mix¹ /mɪks/ verb

1 combine substances	4 meet people socially
2 make sth by combining	5 play CDs continuously
3 combine activities, ideas, styles etc	+ PHRASAL VERB

1 [I/T] to combine two or more substances so that they become a single substance: *Add the eggs and mix thoroughly.* ♦ *Oil and water don't mix.* ♦ *Mix the flour with the eggs and butter.* ♦ *Mix the paint and water together.* —*picture* → FOOD
2 [T] to make something by combining two or more substances: *Phil was mixing a cocktail.*
3 [I/T] to combine things such as activities, ideas, or styles: *In this room, antique and modern furniture have been successfully mixed.* ♦ *Their mood was one of relief mixed with sadness.*
4 [I] to meet other people in social situations and talk to them: *The party gave me a chance to mix with the other students.*
5 [T] **MUSIC** to play records and CDs continuously, so that one piece of music begins before another finishes

PHRASAL VERB ,mix sb/sth 'up to think that someone or something is another person or thing: *They look so alike that it's easy to mix them up.* ♦ *I think I'm mixing him up with someone else.*

mix² /mɪks/ noun **1** [singular] a combination of different types of people or things: *There was a good mix of people at the party.* **2** [C/U] a powder that you buy and mix with liquid to make a particular type of food: *a cake mix*

mixed /mɪkst/ adj **1** consisting of different things: *a mixed salad* **2** involving people of different ages, abilities, races etc: *a mixed population* ♦ *students of mixed abilities* ♦ *a mixed marriage* **3** for men and women, or for boys and girls: *Lucy goes to a mixed school.* **4** partly good and partly bad: *Reactions to the new policy have been mixed.* ♦ *mixed reviews of the new film*

PHRASE mixed feelings/emotions mixed feelings or emotions make you not certain how you feel about someone or something

mixed a'bility adj **EDUCATION** including or designed for students with different levels of educational ability: *mixed ability classes*

mixed 'doubles noun [C/U] **SPORTS** a game, especially in tennis, in which a man and a woman play together against another man and woman

mixed e'conomy noun [C] **ECONOMICS** an economic system in which some businesses are controlled by the government and some are controlled by private companies

mixed 'farming noun [U] **AGRICULTURE** a system of farming that combines growing crops and keeping animals

mixed 'metaphor noun [C] **LANGUAGE** a combination of **metaphors** that sounds silly because it creates a strange image in your mind

mixed 'number noun [C] **MATHS** a number made up of a whole number and a fraction, for example 5½

mixed-'race adj **SOCIAL STUDIES** involving people of different races: *mixed-race marriage* ♦ *a mixed-race child* (=with parents who are of different races)

mixed 'up adj confused: *I got mixed up with the dates and went on the wrong day.*

PHRASE be/get mixed up in sth *informal* to be or become involved in something bad or embarrassing

mixer /ˈmɪksə/ noun [C] **1** a machine that mixes something: *a cement mixer* **2** a **non-alcoholic** drink that you mix with an alcoholic drink

mixture /ˈmɪkstʃə/ noun **1** [singular] a combination of two or more different people or things: *Her face showed a mixture of fear and excitement.* ♦ *a mixture of volunteers and paid staff* **2** [C/U] a substance such as food that is the result of mixing different things: *Spoon the mixture into the cake tins.* **3** [C] **CHEMISTRY** a substance consisting of different substances that mix together without a chemical reaction taking place. The parts of a mixture can be physically separated. —*picture* → FILTRATION

mix-,up noun [C] *informal* a mistake or problem that happens because someone is confused about details

mizzen /ˈmɪz(ə)n/ noun [C] the sail behind the main sail on a ship

mkt abbrev **BUSINESS** market

ml abbrev **SCIENCE** millilitre

mm abbrev **SCIENCE** millimetre

MMR vaccine /ˌem em ˈɑː ˌvæksiːn/ noun [singular] **HEALTH** a drug given to young children by **injection** to protect them against **measles, mumps,** and **rubella**

MMU /ˌem ˌem ˈjuː/ noun [C] **ASTRONOMY** a manned manoeuvring unit: a small vehicle that fits onto the suit of an astronaut and allows them to move around in space without being connected to a space vehicle —*picture* → ASTRONAUT

mnemonic /nɪˈmɒnɪk/ noun [C] a sentence or short poem that you use for helping you remember something

moan¹ /məʊn/ verb [I/T] **1** to complain about something in an annoying way **2** to make a long low sound because of pain, sadness, or pleasure —**moaner** noun [C]

moan² /məʊn/ noun [C] a long low sound that you make because of pain, sadness, or pleasure

moat /məʊt/ noun [C] a deep wide hole filled with water that surrounds a castle —*picture* → CASTLE

mob /mɒb/ noun [C] a large crowd of people that is dangerous or difficult to control

mobile¹ /ˈməʊbaɪl, ˈməʊb(ə)l/ adj **1** easy to move around, capable of moving, or continuously moving: *a mobile X-ray unit* ♦ *a mobile library* (=one contained in a vehicle that can move from place to place) **2** able to move and walk: *He's got a broken leg and isn't very mobile.* **3** able to travel from one place to another because you have a vehicle **4 SOCIAL STUDIES** able to move easily from one job, social class, or place to another

mobile² /ˈməʊbaɪl/ noun [C] **1** a **mobile phone 2** a decoration with parts that hang down and move in the air

mobile 'home noun [C] a large **caravan** that people live in as their home

mobile 'phone noun [C] a small phone that you can carry around with you = MOBILE —*picture* → WORKSTATION

mobility /məʊˈbɪləti/ noun [U] **1** the ability to move a part of your body **2** the ability to travel from one place to another **3 SOCIAL STUDIES** the tendency to move between places, jobs, or social classes

mobilize /ˈməʊbəlaɪz/ verb [I/T] **1** to bring together a large group of people, or to be brought together, in order to achieve something **2** to prepare an army to fight a war, or to be prepared to do this —**mobilization** /ˌməʊbəlaɪˈzeɪʃ(ə)n/ noun [U]

mock¹ /mɒk/ adj **1** not real but intended to look or seem real = FAKE **2** a mock feeling is one that you pretend to have, usually as a joke **3** a mock test, interview etc is one that you do in order to practise for a real one

mock² /mɒk/ verb [I/T] to make someone or something seem stupid by laughing at them or copying them in an unkind way

mock³ /mɒk/ noun [C] **EDUCATION** an examination that you do for practice before an important examination

mockery /ˈmɒkəri/ noun [U] remarks or behaviour intended to make someone seem stupid

  PHRASE **make a mockery of** to make someone or something seem stupid or useless

'mock-ˌup noun [C] **TECHNOLOGY** a model of an object that is the same size as the real thing and is made from wood, cardboard etc. It shows what the object will look like.

modal¹ /ˈməʊd(ə)l/ adj **LANGUAGE** relating to the **mood** of a verb (=one of the sets of verb forms that shows whether the action is a fact, an order, a wish etc)

modal² /ˈməʊd(ə)l/ noun [C] **LANGUAGE** a **modal verb**

'modal ˌverb or **ˌmodal auxˈiliary** noun [C] **LANGUAGE** a verb such as 'can', 'may', and 'should' that is used with another verb to express ideas such as possibility, permission, or intention

mode /məʊd/ noun [C] **1** a particular way of doing something **2** one of a series of ways that a machine can be made to work

model¹ /ˈmɒd(ə)l/ noun [C]

1 small copy of sth	**4** for artist
2 good example	**5** type of vehicle etc
3 sb who shows clothes	

1 a small copy of something such as a building, vehicle, or machine: *a model of the Petronas Towers*
2 someone or something that is such a good example of a particular quality or method that people should copy them: *Daisy was a model of good manners.* ♦ *The school was a model of excellence.* ♦ *The system has been used as a model for other organizations.*
3 someone whose job is to show clothes, **make-up** etc by wearing them at **fashion shows** or for magazine photographs: *a fashion model*
4 ARTS someone whose job is to be drawn or painted by an artist or photographed by a photographer
5 a particular type of vehicle or machine that a company makes: *Fiat launched a new model last week.*

model² /ˈmɒd(ə)l/ (**models, modelling, modelled**) verb **1** [I/T] to show clothes by wearing them at **fashion shows**, in magazine photographs etc, especially as a job **2** [I] to be drawn, painted, or photographed by an artist, especially as a job **3** [T] to make small objects from clay, wood etc

  PHRASAL VERB **'model on** or **'model upon** to copy a method or system

model³ /ˈmɒd(ə)l/ adj **1** a model railway, aircraft, boat etc is a small copy of a real one **2** a model student, husband etc behaves in the way a perfect student, husband etc would behave

modem /ˈməʊdem/ noun [C] **COMPUTING** a piece of equipment that allows you to connect a computer to a telephone line —*picture* → COMPUTER

moderate¹ /ˈmɒd(ə)rət/ adj **1** neither very big nor very small in amount, size, strength, or degree: *Cook the spinach over a moderate heat.* ♦ *a moderate increase in prices* **2** reasonable and avoiding extreme opinions or actions: *a moderate political party* ♦ *The tone of his speech was quite moderate.* —**moderately** adv

moderate² /ˈmɒdəreɪt/ verb **1** [I/T] to make something less extreme, or to become less extreme **2** [T] to be in charge of a discussion between people with different opinions, especially in order to make it fair to everyone **3** [I/T] **EDUCATION** to check that the marks given in an examination are fair and correct

moderate³ /ˈmɒd(ə)rət/ noun [C] someone whose opinions and actions are reasonable and not extreme, especially in politics

moderation /ˌmɒdəˈreɪʃ(ə)n/ noun [U] **1** sensible behaviour, especially behaviour that involves not eating or drinking too much of something: *In moderation, red wine is still thought to be good for health.* **2** opinions and actions, especially in politics, that are reasonable and not extreme **3 EDUCATION** the process of checking that the marks given in an examination are fair and correct

modern /ˈmɒdən/ adj **1** relating to or belonging to the present time: *the role of women in modern society* **2** using the most recent methods, ideas, designs, or equipment: *We should replace the equipment with something more modern.* **3** using new styles that are very different from the styles of the past = CONTEMPORARY: *The architecture of the hotel is strikingly modern.*

'modern-ˌday adj existing or happening in the present

modernism /ˈmɒdəˌnɪz(ə)m/ noun [U] **ARTS, LITERATURE** a style of art, literature etc that developed in the early part of the 20th century

modernity /mɒˈdɜːnəti/ noun [U] ideas and practices that use modern methods, styles etc

modernize /ˈmɒdənaɪz/ verb [I/T] to become less old-fashioned, or to make something become less old-fashioned, as a result of new methods, equipment, or ideas —**modernization** /ˌmɒdənaɪˈzeɪʃ(ə)n/ noun [U]

ˌmodern 'languages noun [plural] **EDUCATION** languages that are still used at the present time, rather than languages such as Latin and ancient Greek

modest /ˈmɒdɪst/ adj **1** fairly small in size, degree, or value: *He earned a modest income.* ♦ *She has had some modest success with her short stories.* **2** a modest person does not like to talk about themselves, their achievements, or their abilities, even if they are successful ≠ BOASTFUL: *Peter is genuinely modest about his achievements.* **3** feeling shy or embarrassed about other people seeing your body —**modestly** adv

modesty /ˈmɒdɪsti/ noun [U] **1** the tendency not to talk about yourself, your achievements, or your abilities even if you are successful **2** a feeling of being shy or embarrassed about other people seeing your body

modification /ˌmɒdɪfɪˈkeɪʃ(ə)n/ noun *formal* **1** [C/U] a small change to something = ALTERATION **2** [U] the process of changing something slightly

modifier /'mɒdɪˌfaɪə/ noun [C] LANGUAGE a word or phrase that slightly changes the meaning of another word or phrase by giving more information about it. For example, in the sentence 'He's driving extremely fast', 'extremely' is a modifier that tells you more about how fast he is driving.

modify /'mɒdɪfaɪ/ (**modifies, modifying, modified**) verb **1** [T] to change something slightly in order to improve it or in order to make it less extreme = ALTER **2** [I/T] LANGUAGE to slightly change the meaning of another word or a phrase by giving more information about it

modular /'mɒdjʊlə/ adj **1** EDUCATION a modular course of study is divided into separate sections called **modules 2** modular buildings, furniture, or other structures are made in separate sections that fit together

modulate /'mɒdjʊleɪt/ verb **1** [I/T] formal to change something, especially in order to achieve a particular effect **2** [T] PHYSICS to change the energy level or frequency of a radio wave **3** [I] MUSIC if a piece of music modulates, it changes to a different **key** —**modulation** /ˌmɒdjʊˈleɪʃ(ə)n/ noun [U]

modulated /'mɒdjʊˌleɪtɪd/ adj a modulated voice is controlled and pleasant to listen to

module /'mɒdjuːl/ noun [C] **1** EDUCATION one of the separate units of a course of study **2** one of several parts that are made separately and then joined together in order to make a building or other structure **3** COMPUTING a section of a computer program **4** ASTRONOMY a part of a space vehicle that is used separately for doing a particular job

modulus /'mɒdjʊləs/ noun [C] MATHS a number that, when it is used to divide two other numbers, produces the same **remainder** for each

modus operandi /ˌməʊdəs ˌɒpəˈrændiː/ noun [singular] formal a way of behaving or doing something that is typical of a person or group

modus vivendi /ˌməʊdəs vɪˈvendiː/ noun [singular] formal an arrangement that helps people who have very different opinions to live or work together

mogul /'məʊɡ(ə)l/ noun [C] **1** an important and powerful person in a particular activity or industry **2 Mogul** a Muslim ruler in India in the 16th to 19th centuries

mohair /'məʊˌheə/ noun [U] soft wool made from the hair of a particular type of goat

moist /mɔɪst/ adj slightly wet

moisten /'mɔɪs(ə)n/ verb [T] to make something slightly wet

moisture /'mɔɪstʃə/ noun [U] very small drops of water or other liquid in the air, on the surface of something, or in a substance

molar¹ /'məʊlə/ noun [C] ANATOMY one of the large teeth at the back of the mouth that you use for chewing food —picture→ TOOTH

molar² /'məʊlə/ adj CHEMISTRY relating to a **mole** (=a unit for measuring the number of molecules in a substance)

mole /məʊl/ noun [C] **1** a small mammal with dark fur that digs underground and cannot see well —picture→ MAMMAL **2** a dark brown lump or spot on the skin that is permanent **3** CHEMISTRY a unit for measuring the amount of a substance in the metric system. It is numerically equal to the **relative molecular mass** of the substance. Symbol mol

molecular /məˈlekjʊlə/ adj SCIENCE relating to or made up of molecules

moˌlecular ˈweight noun [C/U] CHEMISTRY the **relative molecular mass** of a molecule

molecule /'mɒlɪˌkjuːl/ noun [C] SCIENCE the smallest part of an element or compound that could exist independently, consisting of two or more atoms: water molecules ♦ a molecule of carbon dioxide

molehill /'məʊlˌhɪl/ noun [C] a small pile of earth made by a **mole** digging underground → MOUNTAIN

mollify /'mɒlɪfaɪ/ (**mollifies, mollifying, mollified**) verb [T] formal to make someone feel less angry or upset

mollusc /'mɒləsk/ noun [C] BIOLOGY an invertebrate animal that has a soft body with no bones and is usually covered by a hard shell. Snails, **octopuses**, and **mussels** are all molluscs.

mollusk /'mɒləsk/ the American spelling of **mollusc**

molten /'məʊltən/ adj molten rock, metal, or glass has become liquid because it is very hot

molybdenum /məˈlɪbdənəm/ noun [U] CHEMISTRY a metallic element that is used in steel alloys and electric **wiring**. It is essential to biological life. Chemical symbol: **Mo**

moment /'məʊmənt/ noun **1** [C] a particular point in time when something happens: *At that moment there was a knock on the door.* ♦ *Ellie had never really given it much thought up until that moment.* ♦ *This is the proudest moment of my career.* **2** [C] a very short period of time: *A moment later Jane had completely disappeared.* ♦ *He paused for a moment before giving his answer.* **3** [C] a short period of time when you have the opportunity to do something: *As he stood up, James knew his big moment had arrived.* ♦ *I saw he was alone and seized the moment.* ♦ *She waited until the last possible moment to cancel her flight.* **4** [singular/U] PHYSICS the tendency of a force to produce movement of a load. It is measured by multiplying the force by the distance from the **fulcrum**. Symbol Nm

PHRASES **at the moment** now: *They're very upset and don't want to talk at the moment.*
for the moment at the present time, but possibly not in the future
→ FOR, HEAT¹

momentarily /'məʊmənt(ə)rəli, ˌməʊmənˈteərəli/ adv for a moment

momentary /'məʊmənt(ə)ri/ adj lasting for only a very short time

momentous /məʊˈmentəs/ adj something that is momentous is very important because it will have an effect on future events

momentum /məʊˈmentəm/ noun [U] **1** PHYSICS the tendency of a moving object to keep moving unless another force stops it or slows it down. It is equal to the mass of the object multiplied by its velocity. **2** progress or development that is becoming faster or stronger

Mon. abbrev Monday

monarch /'mɒnək/ noun [C] a king or queen

monarchy /'mɒnəki/ (plural **monarchies**) noun SOCIAL STUDIES **1** [C/U] a system of government in which a country is ruled by a king or queen **2** [C] a country that is ruled by a king or queen

monastery /'mɒnəst(ə)ri/ (plural **monasteries**) noun [C] RELIGION a building where **monks** live and work

monastic /məˈnæstɪk/ adj RELIGION relating to **monks** or monasteries

Monday /'mʌndeɪ/ noun [C/U] the day after Sunday and before Tuesday: *This year's Oscar ceremony will be on a Monday.* ♦ *You can start work* **next Monday**. ♦ *The group meets* **on Mondays** (=every Monday) *at 8 pm.*

monetarism /'mʌnɪtə,rɪz(ə)m/ noun [U] ECONOMICS the belief that a government must carefully control the supply of money in its economy in order to avoid economic problems —**monetarist** adj

monetary /'mʌnɪt(ə)ri/ adj ECONOMICS relating to money

money /'mʌni/ noun [U] the coins and pieces of paper that you earn, save, invest, and use for paying for things: *I haven't got any money.* ♦ *We've* **spent** *a lot of* **money** *on this house.* ♦ *It would have* **cost us** *a lot of* **money** *to cancel the event.* ♦ *I have had to* **borrow money** *from my family.* ♦ *The business has* **made** *more* **money** *this year.* ♦ *They're trying to* **save money** (=keep it so that they can spend it later) *so that they can buy more hens.* ♦ **Have** *you got any* **money on you**?

'money ,market noun [C] ECONOMICS business activities in which banks and other financial institutions lend money to other organizations in order to make more money

money-spinner /'mʌni ,spɪnə/ noun [C] BUSINESS *informal* a project or product that makes a lot of money

'money sup,ply noun [singular] ECONOMICS all the money in the economy of a country

mongoose /'mɒŋ,guːs/ noun [C] (plural **mongooses**) a small furry mammal with a long tail that lives in Asia and Africa and eats snakes and other small animals —*picture* → MAMMAL

mongrel /'mʌŋgrəl/ noun [C] a dog that is a mixture of different breeds

monitor¹ /'mɒnɪtə/ verb [T] to regularly check something or watch someone in order to find out what is happening: *a special machine to monitor the baby's breathing* ♦ *Staff will* **monitor his progress**.

monitor² /'mɒnɪtə/ noun [C] **1** COMPUTING a screen that shows pictures or information, especially on a computer, or the piece of equipment that contains the screen —*picture* → COMPUTER, WORKSTATION **2** HEALTH a piece of equipment that shows and records what is happening in a particular part of someone's body **3** someone who checks to see that something is done fairly or correctly

monk /mʌŋk/ noun [C] RELIGION a man who lives in a religious community away from other people → NUN

monkey /'mʌŋki/ noun [C] (plural **monkeys**) a mammal with a long tail that climbs trees and uses its hands in the same way that people do —*picture* → MAMMAL

'monkey ,wrench noun [C] a **spanner** that you use for turning nuts of different sizes

monochrome /'mɒnə,krəʊm/ adj **1** able to show or produce only black, white, and grey= BLACK-AND-WHITE **2** ARTS using different **shades** of a single colour

monocline /'mɒnəʊklaɪn/ noun [C] GEOLOGY a rock structure in which all the layers slope in one direction

monocoque /'mɒnəkɒk/ noun [C] ENGINEERING a vehicle whose body and **chassis** are built as a single unit

monocotyledon /,mɒnəʊ,kɒtɪ'liːd(ə)n/ noun [C] BIOLOGY a plant that has only one **cotyledon** in the seed, for example a grass —**monocotyledonous** adj

monoculture /'mɒnəʊ,kʌltʃə/ noun [U] AGRICULTURE the practice of growing only one crop in an area

monogamous /mə'nɒgəməs/ adj SOCIAL STUDIES having only one husband, wife, or sexual relationship at a time

monogamy /mə'nɒgəmi/ noun [U] SOCIAL STUDIES the practice of having only one husband, wife, or sexual relationship at a time

monolingual /,mɒnəʊ'lɪŋgwəl/ adj LANGUAGE speaking, writing, or using only one language → BILINGUAL

monologue /'mɒnəlɒg/ noun [C] **1** a speech made by someone who talks for a long time and does not let anyone else say anything **2** ARTS a long speech made by someone in a play

monomer /'mɒnəmə/ noun [C] CHEMISTRY a simple molecule that can combine with other molecules to form a **polymer**

monomial /mɒ'nəʊmiəl/ noun [C] BIOLOGY a scientific name that consists of one element only. The names of most families of plants and animals are monomials.

monopoly /mə'nɒpəli/ (plural **monopolies**) noun **1** [C] ECONOMICS, BUSINESS a company that has complete control of the product or service it provides because it is the only company that provides it **2** [C/U] ECONOMICS complete control over something by one organization or person **3** [singular] something that only one person or group of people has

monosaccharide /,mɒnəʊ'sækə,raɪd/ noun [C] CHEMISTRY a simple sugar such as glucose or **fructose** that cannot be separated into simpler sugars by **hydrolysis**

monosodium glutamate /,mɒnəʊ,səʊdiəm 'gluːtə,meɪt/ noun [U] CHEMISTRY MSG

monosyllabic /,mɒnəʊsɪ'læbɪk/ adj **1** using very few short words **2** LANGUAGE a monosyllabic word has only one syllable

monosyllable /'mɒnəʊ,sɪləb(ə)l/ noun [C] LANGUAGE a word with only one syllable. The words 'yes' and 'no' are monosyllables.

monotonous /mə'nɒtənəs/ adj **1** a monotonous sound or voice is boring because it does not change **2** a monotonous job is boring because you have to keep repeating the same activity —**monotonously** adv

monotony /mə'nɒtəni/ noun [U] the fact that something never changes, so that it is boring

monounsaturated fat /,mɒnəʊʌn,sætʃəreɪtɪd 'fæt/ noun [C] BIOLOGY, CHEMISTRY fat that is made mainly from vegetable oils that have **fatty acids** with only one **double bond**. They are considered to be healthier than those made from **saturated** animal fats. → POLYUNSATURATED FAT

monoxide /mə'nɒksaɪd/ noun [C/U] CHEMISTRY a chemical containing one atom of oxygen in each molecule

monsoon /mɒn'suːn/ noun [C] GEOGRAPHY a period of heavy rain in India and South-East Asia: *Every monsoon, the plain gets completely flooded.*

monster /'mɒnstə/ noun [C] **1** an imaginary creature that is large, ugly, and frightening **2** something that is very large **3** someone who is very cruel

monstrosity /mɒn'strɒsəti/ (plural **monstrosities**) noun [C] something that is very large and ugly

monstrous /'mɒnstrəs/ adj **1** cruel, unfair, or morally wrong **2** very large and ugly or frightening —**monstrously** adv

month /mʌnθ/ noun **1** [C] one of the 12 periods that a year is divided into, for example January or February:

*Could we meet earlier in the month?♦ They aim to finish by **the end of the month**. ♦ A man was arrested **last month** in connection with the robbery. ♦ We try to save fifty dollars **a month** (=each month).* **2** [C] a period of about four weeks: *They're getting married **in a month's time**. ♦ I'll be leaving **a month from** today. ♦ a three-month-old baby* **3** ASTRONOMY a lunar month **4 months** [plural] a long time: *It'll take months to finish the work. ♦ We haven't been to the cinema **for months**.*

monthly /'mʌnθli/ adj **1** happening or published once a month: *a monthly newsletter* **2** relating to a single month —**monthly** adv

monument /'mɒnjʊmənt/ noun [C] **1** a structure that is built in a public place in order to celebrate an important person or event **2** a place of historical importance

moo /muː/ (**moos, mooing, mooed**) verb [I] to make the long deep sound that a cow makes —**moo** noun [C]

mood /muːd/ noun **1** [C/U] the way that someone is feeling, or the way that a group of people is feeling at a particular time: *Politicians have to be in touch with the public mood. ♦ I had never seen Ann **in such a good mood** before. ♦ Jeff's been in a **bad mood** all day. ♦ a **mood** of optimism* **2** [C] a period when you feel unhappy or angry: *She refused to put up with her husband's moods. ♦ Just leave her on her own when she's **in a mood**.* **3** [C] a quality that something such as a place, film, or piece of music has that makes you have a particular feeling: *a collection of stories that vary in mood and style ♦ Lighting was particularly important in **setting the mood of** the play.* **4** [C] LANGUAGE a group of verb forms that are used to show whether, for example, a sentence is a statement (**indicative** mood), a question (**interrogative** mood), or an order (**imperative** mood)
  PHRASE **be/feel in the mood (for sth)** to want to do something: *I'm in the mood for dancing.*

'mood ,swing noun [C] a sudden, unexpected change in the way someone feels and behaves, especially when they become very angry or unhappy

moody /'muːdi/ (**moodier, moodiest**) adj likely to become unhappy or angry for no particular reason

moon /muːn/ noun ASTRONOMY **1 the Moon** or **the moon** the natural satellite that goes around the Earth and that you can see shining in the sky at night: *The moon was shining brightly.* —*picture* → ECLIPSE, PHASE, SOLAR SYSTEM **2** [C] a natural satellite that goes around another planet: *How many moons has Jupiter got?*

moonlet /'muːnlət/ noun [C] ASTRONOMY a small moon, or an artificial satellite

moonlight /'muːnlaɪt/ noun [U] light from the moon

moonlit /'muːnˌlɪt/ adj provided with light from the moon

moor¹ /mʊə, mɔː/ verb [I/T] to stop a ship or boat from moving by fastening it to a place with ropes or chains, or by using an **anchor**

moor² /mʊə, mɔː/ noun [C] a large area of high land that is covered with grass, bushes, and **heather**, and has soil that is not good for growing crops

mooring /'mɔːrɪŋ, 'mʊərɪŋ/ noun **1 moorings** [plural] ropes, chains, or **anchors** that you use to moor a ship or boat **2** [C] a place where a ship or boat is moored with ropes, chains, or **anchors**

moose /muːs/ (plural **moose**) noun [C] a large **deer** that lives in North America, northern Europe, and Asia

mop¹ /mɒp/ noun [C] an object that has a long handle and is used for washing floors

mop² /mɒp/ (**mops, mopping, mopped**) verb **1** [I/T] to wash a floor using a mop **2** [T] to wipe sweat from your face with a cloth when you are very hot or ill

moraine /mə'reɪn/ noun [C] GEOLOGY a mass of earth and pieces of rock carried by a glacier and left behind as it passes

moral¹ /'mɒrəl/ adj **1** relating to right and wrong and the way that people should behave: *moral standards ♦ our children's religious and moral education* **2** a moral person always tries to behave in the right way —**morally** adv

moral² /'mɒrəl/ noun **1 morals** [plural] principles of right or wrong behaviour that are generally accepted by a society: *He's shown that he has no morals at all.* **2** [singular] something that you can learn from a story or an experience

morale /mə'rɑːl/ noun [U] the amount of enthusiasm that someone feels about the situation that they are in

morality /mə'ræləti/ noun [U] **1** principles of right or wrong behaviour: *standards of morality* **2** the degree to which something is thought to be right or wrong: *the continuing debate about **the morality of** genetic research*

,moral sup'port noun [U] if you give someone moral support, you try to make them more confident

morbid /'mɔːbɪd/ adj **1** interested in subjects such as death that most people think are unpleasant **2** HEALTH relating to or caused by disease

more /mɔː/ adv, determiner, pronoun **1** to a greater degree ≠ LESS: *The storm was more violent than we expected. ♦ Could you speak more slowly please?♦ You won't get better unless you practise more. ♦ Lizzie is **a lot more** intelligent than the other girls.* **2** a larger amount or number ≠ LESS: *No matter how much money he has, he always wants more. ♦ If you need more paper, there's some in the drawer. ♦ We'll have to wait for two more days. ♦ Ken already earns **more than** his father. ♦ That's all I know. I can't tell you **any more**.*
  PHRASES **more and more** an increasing number or degree: *More and more children are going to university now. ♦ I was becoming more and more hungry.*
  the more...the more/less used for saying that when one thing increases, it causes something else to change at the same time: *The more I thought about Carrie's suggestion, the more doubtful I became.*
  more or less almost: *The team is more or less the same as it was last season.*
  → ANY, OFTEN, ONCE

moreover /mɔː'rəʊvə/ adv formal used for introducing an additional important fact: *More and more people are opposed to the idea of increasing university fees. Moreover, there is now evidence that it discourages many students from coming to the UK.*

mores /'mɔːreɪz/ noun [plural] formal the traditional practices and moral values of a particular society or group of people

morgue /mɔːg/ noun [C] a building or room where dead bodies are kept for a short time

moribund /'mɒrɪbʌnd/ adj formal no longer effective and not likely to continue for much longer

morning /'mɔːnɪŋ/ noun [C/U] **1** the part of the day from when the sun rises until midday: *Call me at my office on Monday morning. ♦ We spent the morning walking in the park. ♦ What time did you get up **this morning**?♦ Let's talk about this **in the morning** (=during the morning of the next day).* **2** the part of the day between midnight and midday: *The phone woke me at 2 **o'clock in the morning**. ♦ I was working until **the early hours of the morning**.*

the life cycle of a mosquito

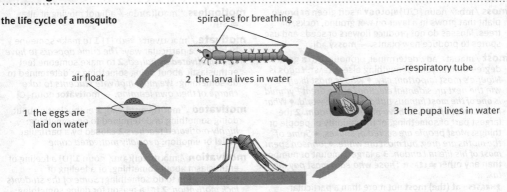

spiracles for breathing

respiratory tube

air float

2 the larva lives in water

1 the eggs are laid on water

3 the pupa lives in water

4 the adult female feeds on blood

the life cycle of a housefly

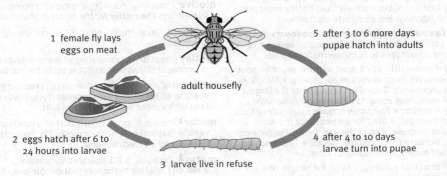

1 female fly lays eggs on meat

5 after 3 to 6 more days pupae hatch into adults

adult housefly

2 eggs hatch after 6 to 24 hours into larvae

4 after 4 to 10 days larvae turn into pupae

3 larvae live in refuse

life cycles of a mosquito and housefly

,morning 'call noun [C] a phone call or knock on the door to wake someone up in the morning

morose /məˈrəʊs/ adj unhappy and unfriendly —**morosely** adv

morpheme /ˈmɔːfiːm/ noun [C] **LANGUAGE** the smallest unit of meaning in a language. A morpheme can be a whole word, for example 'the', or part of a word, for example 'un' in 'unable'.

morphine /ˈmɔːfiːn/ noun [U] **HEALTH** a powerful drug obtained from **opium** that is used for reducing pain

morphology /mɔːˈfɒlədʒi/ noun [U] **1 LANGUAGE** the study of how words are formed in a language **2 BIOLOGY** the study of the form and structure of living things —**morphological** /ˌmɔːfəˈlɒdʒɪk(ə)l/ adj

Morse code /ˌmɔːs ˈkəʊd/ noun [U] a system of sending messages using long and short signals of sound or light that represent the letters of the alphabet

morsel /ˈmɔːs(ə)l/ noun [C] **1** formal a small piece of food **2** a small amount of something, especially something good, contained in something else

mortal /ˈmɔːt(ə)l/ adj **1** human and not able to live for ever ≠ IMMORTAL **2** serious enough to cause death **3** used for emphasizing that a particular feeling is extremely strong: *people living in mortal fear*

mortality /mɔːˈtæləti/ noun [U] **1** the number of deaths in a particular area or group of people **2** the fact that your life will end

mortally /ˈmɔːt(ə)li/ adv in a way that is likely to cause death: *He was mortally wounded.*

mortar /ˈmɔːtə/ noun **1** [U] a substance that is used in building for joining bricks **2** [C] a large gun that soldiers use for firing bombs over short distances **3** [C] a bowl in which you crush substances into a powder using a tool called a **pestle** —*picture* → LABORATORY

mortgage /ˈmɔːgɪdʒ/ noun [C] money that someone borrows from a bank and uses to buy a house

'mortgage ,bond noun [C] **BUSINESS** a legal document by which someone promises to **pay back** a mortgage on a business property or a home

mortice /ˈmɔːtɪs/ another spelling of **mortise**

mortified /ˈmɔːtɪfaɪd/ adj feeling extremely embarrassed or ashamed —**mortify** verb [T]

mortise /ˈmɔːtɪs/ noun [C] **CONSTRUCTION** a hole cut into a piece of wood or stone into which you fit the end of another piece of wood or stone

mortuary /ˈmɔːtjuəri/ (plural **mortuaries**) noun [C] a place where dead bodies are kept for a short time

mosaic /məʊˈzeɪɪk/ noun [C] **ARTS** a pattern made of small pieces of coloured stone or glass

Mosaic /məʊˈzeɪɪk/ adj relating to Moses, a leader of the Jewish people in ancient times

mosque /mɒsk/ noun [C] **RELIGION** a building in which Muslims worship

mosquito /mɒˈskiːtəʊ/ (plural **mosquitos** or **mosquitoes**) noun [C] a small flying insect of the fly family. Female mosquitos bite the skin of mammals in order to feed on their blood. Some types of mosquito can spread diseases such as **malaria**, **dengue fever**, and **yellow fever**. —*picture* → INSECT

moss /mɒs/ noun [C/U] BIOLOGY a soft green or brown plant that grows in a layer on wet ground, rocks, or trees. Mosses do not produce flowers or seeds and use spores to produce new plants. —**mossy** adj

most /məʊst/ adv, determiner, pronoun **1** to a greater degree than anyone or anything else ≠ LEAST: *Lagos is Nigeria's most important city.* ♦ *Who is most likely to win the next presidential election?* ♦ *The Great Pyramid is one of the most famous buildings in the world.* ♦ *What I want most of all is to have my own bedroom.* **2** the largest part of something, or the majority of people or things: *Most people are scared of snakes.* ♦ *Some of the moths are grey, but most are white.* ♦ *Johnson spent most of his life in London.* **3** a larger amount or number than any other ≠ LEAST: *Those who earn most pay most tax.*

PHRASES **at (the) most** not more than a particular amount, and probably less: *The whole process will take half an hour at the most.*

for the most part used for saying that something is mainly true but not completely true: *For the most part we were happy to live alongside each other.*

,most ,favoured 'nation noun [C] ECONOMICS one of the countries that a particular country agrees to give the most advantages to in its international trade

mostly /'məʊs(t)li/ adv **1** most of the time, or in most situations: *We listen to rock music mostly.* ♦ *Mostly, he avoids arguments.* **2** used for saying what the largest part of something consists of: *a group of journalists, mostly American* ♦ *The group is made up mostly of local business people.* **3** used for emphasizing the main reason or purpose of something = MAINLY: *People work mostly because they need the money.* ♦ *This machine was used mostly for agricultural work.*

motel /məʊ'tel/ noun [C] a hotel for people who are travelling by car

moth /mɒθ/ noun [C] a flying insect that flies mainly at night —*picture* → INSECT

mother /'mʌðə/ noun [C] your female parent: *My mother and father live in Rome.*

motherboard /'mʌðə,bɔːd/ noun [C] COMPUTING the main **circuit board** in a computer

motherhood /'mʌðə,hʊd/ noun [U] the state of being a mother

'mother-in-,law noun [C] the mother of someone's husband or wife

,Mother 'Nature nature, or natural forces

,mother-of-'pearl noun [U] the shiny layer inside some shells that is used for making jewellery

,Mother Su'perior noun [C] RELIGION a woman who is in charge of a **convent**

'mother ,tongue noun [C] the first language that you learn to speak

motif /məʊ'tiːf/ noun [C] **1** a shape that is repeated in a design **2** LITERATURE, MUSIC an idea or subject that is frequently repeated in a piece of music, literature, or art

motion[1] /'məʊʃ(ə)n/ noun **1** [U] the process or action of moving: *photographs of animals in motion* ♦ *He studied the motion of the planets.* **2** [C] a movement that someone or something makes: *Rub the horse's coat with a circular motion.* **3** [C] a suggestion that you make at a formal meeting

PHRASE **in motion** if something is in motion, it has already started to happen

motion[2] /'məʊʃ(ə)n/ verb [I] to move your hand in a particular direction, for example in order to point to something: *He motioned for the waiter to bring the bill.*

motionless /'məʊʃ(ə)nləs/ adj not moving at all = STILL

motivate /'məʊtɪveɪt/ verb [T] **1** to make someone behave in a particular way: *The crime appears to have been motivated by hatred.* **2** to make someone feel enthusiastic about doing something or determined to do something: *We must motivate students to take charge of their own learning.* —**motivator** noun [C]

motivated /'məʊtɪ,veɪtɪd/ adj **1** enthusiastic about doing something or determined to do something: *highly motivated teachers* **2** caused by a particular belief or emotion: *a racially motivated crime*

motivation /,məʊtɪ'veɪʃ(ə)n/ noun **1** [U] a feeling of enthusiasm about something, or a feeling of determination to do something: *Some of the students lack motivation.* **2** [C] a reason for doing something: *Our real motivation is to make a profit.* —**motivational** adj

motive /'məʊtɪv/ noun [C] a reason for doing something: *The motive for the attack is still unknown.*

mot juste /,məʊ 'ʒuːst/ noun [C] exactly the right word or phrase

motley /'mɒtli/ adj consisting of many different types of people or things that do not seem to belong together

motocross /'məʊtəʊ,krɒs/ noun [U] SPORTS a sports event in which people race on motorcycles over rough land with a lot of bends and steep hills

motor[1] /'məʊtə/ noun [C] the part of a machine or vehicle that makes it work or move: *The pump is powered by an electric motor.*

motor[2] /'məʊtə/ adj **1** operated by a motor **2** BIOLOGY relating to the way that people use muscles and control their movements **3** relating to cars: *motor insurance*

motorbike /'məʊtə,baɪk/ noun [C] a road vehicle that has two wheels and an engine

motorboat /'məʊtə,bəʊt/ noun [C] a small boat that has an engine

motorcycle /'məʊtə,saɪk(ə)l/ noun [C] *formal* a **motorbike**

motorist /'məʊtərɪst/ noun [C] someone who drives a car

,motor 'neuron noun [C] ANATOMY a type of nerve cell that passes signals from the brain or **spinal cord** to a muscle or gland —*picture* → NEURON

,motor 'neurone dis,ease noun [U] HEALTH a serious illness in which the part of a person's **nervous system** that controls movement is gradually destroyed

'motor ,racing noun [U] SPORTS a sport in which fast cars race on a track

'motor ,vehicle noun [C] *formal* a road vehicle that has an engine, for example a car or a truck

motorway /'məʊtə,weɪ/ noun [C] a wide fast road with several **lanes** of traffic going in each direction

mottled /'mɒt(ə)ld/ adj covered with areas of light and dark colours

motto /'mɒtəʊ/ (plural **mottoes** or **mottos**) noun [C] a short statement that expresses a principle or aim

mould[1] /məʊld/ noun **1** [U] a green, blue, or white substance that grows on food that is not kept fresh or on other things that are not kept clean and dry **2** [C] a container into which you pour a liquid that then becomes solid in the shape of the container

mould² /məʊld/ verb [T] **1** to give something a particular shape: *Mould the dough into loaves.* **2** to influence someone strongly so that they will have particular qualities or will behave in a particular way: *The coach must mould the group into a team.*

moulding /ˈməʊldɪŋ/ noun [C/U] a decorated edge around something such as a door or picture frame

ˈ**moulding ˌboard** noun [C] **TECHNOLOGY** in **sand-casting**, a flat wooden board placed under the lower part of a moulding flask before the shape to be moulded is inserted

ˈ**moulding ˌflask** noun [C] **TECHNOLOGY** a mould used in **sand-casting** in the shape of a wooden box that is filled with sand

ˈ**moulding ˌsand** noun [U] **TECHNOLOGY** sand used for preparing moulds in **sand-casting**. It is usually used several times.

mouldy /ˈməʊldi/ adj covered with mould: *mouldy bread*

moult /məʊlt/ verb [I] **BIOLOGY** if a bird or other animal moults, it loses its outer layer of skin or feathers so that a new layer can replace it

mound /maʊnd/ noun [C] **1** a pile of something such as earth or stones **2** a large amount of something in a pile: *a mound of papers*

mount¹ /maʊnt/ verb **1** [I] if a particular feeling mounts, it gets stronger: *Tension continues to mount between the two parties.* **2** [T] to prepare and begin an activity: *We are mounting a campaign to recruit more volunteers.* ♦ *Government forces have mounted an attack on a rebel base.* **3** [T] to fix something in position: *A machine gun was mounted on the roof.* ♦ *Each photograph is mounted on cardboard.* **4** [I/T] to get on a horse

mount² /maʊnt/ noun [C] a base that something is fixed to

Mount /maʊnt/ a word used in the names of mountains: *Mount Everest*

mountain /ˈmaʊntɪn/ noun [C] **1** **GEOGRAPHY** a very high hill: *They went walking and climbing in the mountains.* **2** a large pile or amount of something: *a mountain of paperwork*
PHRASE **make a mountain out of a molehill** to treat a minor problem as if it were a very serious problem

ˈ**mountain ˌbike** noun [C] a strong bicycle with wide tyres, used on rough ground

mountainboarding /ˈmaʊntɪnˌbɔːdɪŋ/ noun [U] the dangerous sport of travelling down hills on a board on wheels

mountaineer /ˌmaʊntɪˈnɪə/ noun [C] someone who climbs mountains

mountaineering /ˌmaʊntɪˈnɪərɪŋ/ noun [U] the activity of climbing mountains

mountainous /ˈmaʊntɪnəs/ adj **GEOGRAPHY** covered with mountains

ˈ**mountain ˌrange** noun [C] **GEOGRAPHY** a long row of mountains

mountainside /ˈmaʊntɪnˌsaɪd/ noun [C] **GEOGRAPHY** the side of a mountain

mountaintop /ˈmaʊntɪnˌtɒp/ noun [C] **GEOGRAPHY** the area at the top of a mountain

mounting /ˈmaʊntɪŋ/ adj becoming stronger, greater, or worse: *mounting debts*

mourn /mɔːn/ verb [I/T] **1** to feel extremely sad because someone has died **2** to be sad because something no longer exists

mourner /ˈmɔːnə/ noun [C] someone who is at a funeral

mournful /ˈmɔːnf(ə)l/ adj feeling sad, or expressing sadness

mourning /ˈmɔːnɪŋ/ noun [U] **1** expressions of sadness because someone has died **2** *old-fashioned* black clothes that people wear when someone has died

mouse /maʊs/ noun [C] **1** (plural **mice** /maɪs/) a small furry mammal with a long tail —*picture* → MAMMAL **2** (plural **mouses** or **mice**) **COMPUTING** a small piece of computer equipment that you move with your hand in order to do things on the screen. When you press on a part of the mouse, you **click on** it. You also **click on** things on the computer screen itself, using a mouse: *Click on the left mouse button.* —*picture* → COMPUTER

ˈ**mouse ˌbutton** noun [C] **COMPUTING** one of the two or three parts of a computer mouse that you press to give an instruction to a computer

ˈ**mouse ˌmat** noun [C] **COMPUTING** a piece of soft material that you move a computer mouse around on —*picture* → COMPUTER

mousse /muːs/ noun [U] **1** a cold sweet food made with cream, eggs, and fruit or chocolate **2** a white substance that people put in their hair in order to hold it in a particular style

moustache /məˈstɑːʃ/ noun [C] hair that grows above a man's mouth

mouth /maʊθ/ (plural **mouths** /maʊðz/) noun [C] **1** the part of the face below the nose that is used for eating and speaking. Food is chewed in the mouth by the teeth and broken down by the action of the tongue against the **hard palate** before being swallowed. Air is breathed out through the mouth from the **vocal cords** and shaped by the tongue and lips in order to produce speech: *She opened her mouth to speak.* ♦ *I've got a funny taste in my mouth.* —*picture* → BODY, DIGESTIVE SYSTEM **2** **GEOGRAPHY** the place where a river is widest and joins the sea **3** the entrance to a tunnel or cave **4** **SCIENCE** the part at the top of a Bunsen burner where the flame is applied to light it

ˈ**mouth ˌdrumming** noun [U] **MUSIC** a way of using the mouth to make sounds similar to those made by **percussion** instruments

mouthful /ˈmaʊθfʊl/ noun [C] an amount of food or drink that you put in your mouth at one time

ˈ**mouth ˌorgan** noun [C] **MUSIC** a **harmonica**

mouthparts /ˈmaʊθpɑːts/ noun [plural] **BIOLOGY** a set of body parts near the mouth of an insect or other **arthropod** that it uses to collect food

mouthpiece /ˈmaʊθpiːs/ noun [C] **1** *informal* a person or newspaper that expresses the opinions of an organization **2** the part of something that you put in or near your mouth

ˌ**mouth-to-ˌmouth reˌsusciˈtation** noun [U] **HEALTH** a way of making someone breathe again by blowing air into their lungs

mouthwash /ˈmaʊθwɒʃ/ noun [C/U] a liquid that you use for cleaning your mouth

mov abbrev **COMPUTING** the last part of the name of a film file

movable¹ /ˈmuːvəb(ə)l/ adj able to be moved easily

movable² /ˈmuːvəb(ə)l/ noun [C] **LAW** a possession that can be moved from one place to another, especially a piece of furniture

ˌ**movable ˈpulley** noun [C] **PHYSICS** a pulley that is not attached to a fixed surface, but is attached to the load and moves with it

move¹ /muːv/ verb

1 change position	6 change opinion
2 progress/change	7 cause emotion
3 change house	8 belong to group
4 do sth	+ PHRASAL VERBS
5 change subject/time etc	

1 [I/T] to change position, or to make someone or something change position: *Could you help me move the bookcase away from the wall?* ♦ *The traffic was barely moving.* ♦ *She moved quickly towards the door.*
2 [I] to progress or change in a particular way: *Events were moving rapidly.* ♦ *The country has only recently begun **moving towards** democracy.*
3 [I/T] to begin to live in a different house or area: *We're moving next week.* ♦ ***Moving house** can be quite a stressful experience.*
4 [I] to do something in order to achieve an aim or solve a problem: *The police moved swiftly to prevent a riot.*
5 [I] to change from one subject to another in a discussion, speech, piece of writing etc: *We need to **move to** the next item on the agenda.*
6 [I/T] to persuade someone to change their opinion or decision, or to be persuaded to change yours: *He refuses to move on the salary issue.*
7 [T] to make someone feel sad or sympathetic: *You can't fail to be **moved by** the plight of these people.* ♦ *Her songs can **move** me **to tears.***
8 [I] to spend time with people who belong to a particular group: *We **move in** such different **circles** that I'm surprised we ever met.*

PHRASAL VERBS ,move 'in to start living in a different house ≠ MOVE OUT: *We're moving in next week.*
,move 'into sth to start living or working in a place: *We're moving into new offices by the river.*
,move 'off if a vehicle moves off, it starts to move: *Make sure you look over your shoulder before you move off.*
,move 'out to leave your house and start to live somewhere else ≠ MOVE IN
,move 'up to change your position in order to make space for someone or something: *Could everyone move up a bit, please?*

move² /muːv/ noun [C]
1 something that you do in order to achieve an aim or solve a problem: *Getting rid of the tax would be a welcome move.* ♦ *She's going to have to plan her **next move** carefully.* **2** a change in an activity or situation: *an upward move in the value of the company* ♦ *The new law is a **move towards** equality.* ♦ *He's considering a **move into** politics.* **3** a change in the place where you live or work: *We're considering a **move to** the city.* **4** a change in the place where you live or work: *We're considering a move to the city.*

PHRASE **on the move** travelling from one place to other places

moveable /ˈmuːvəb(ə)l/ another spelling of **movable**

movement /ˈmuːvmənt/ noun

1 group with same aim	5 sb's activities
2 way of moving	6 part of classical music
3 change in situation	7 in biology
4 change of place	

1 [C] a group of people who work together in order to achieve a particular aim: *the peace movement*
2 [C/U] a way of moving the body, or the ability to move the body: *rhythmic movements* ♦ *The injury has restricted movement in his arm.*
3 [C/U] change or progress in a situation: *There has been little movement in the peace talks.*
4 [C/U] the process of moving something from one place to another: *The agreement governs the free movement of goods between countries.*

5 movements [plural] someone's activities over a period of time: *Their job is to monitor the movements of suspected terrorists.*
6 [C] MUSIC one of the main parts of a **symphony**
7 [U] BIOLOGY the ability of an organism to move itself or part of itself

'movement ,energy noun [U] PHYSICS **kinetic energy**

movie /ˈmuːvi/ noun [C] a film shown in a cinema or on television

the movies /ˈmuːviz/ noun [plural] the cinema, or the film industry

moving /ˈmuːvɪŋ/ adj **1** making you feel sad or sympathetic **2** a moving object is something that moves: *He was pushed from a moving train.* —**movingly** adv

mow /məʊ/ (**mows, mowing, mowed, mown** /məʊn/ or **mowed**) verb [T] to cut grass using a machine with blades

mower /ˈməʊə/ noun [C] a machine that is used for cutting grass = LAWNMOWER

MP /ˌem ˈpiː/ noun [C] SOCIAL STUDIES Member of Parliament: a politician who represents people in a parliament

MP3 /ˌem piː ˈθriː/ noun [U] COMPUTING a computer program that is used for sending music by email, or the part of a computer that can play these files

MP'3 ,player noun [C] a piece of equipment used for playing MP3 files

MPEG /ˈempeg/ noun COMPUTING **1** [U] a method for reducing the size of computer files that contain video images and sound so that they can be sent quickly by email or over the Internet **2** [C] a file that is produced by this method

mpg /ˌem piː ˈdʒiː/ abbrev miles per gallon: the distance in miles that a vehicle can travel using one gallon of petrol

mph /ˌem piː ˈeɪtʃ/ abbrev miles per hour: a unit for measuring the speed at which a vehicle is travelling

Mr /ˈmɪstə/ a polite or formal title used in front of a man's name: *Mr Jones* ♦ *Mr Samuel Smith*

MRI scan /ˌem ɑː ˈaɪ ˌskæn/ noun [C] HEALTH a medical test in which images are made of the organs inside the body, or the image that is produced in this way. MRI is a short form of **magnetic resonance imaging**.

Mrs /ˈmɪsɪz/ a polite or formal title used in front of the name of a married woman: *Mrs Grace Talbot* ♦ *Good morning, Mrs Adams.*

MRSA /ˌem ɑː es ˈeɪ/ noun [U] HEALTH methicillin-resistant Staphylococcus aureus: a type of bacteria that most **antibiotics** cannot kill

Ms /məz, mɪz/ a polite or formal title used in front of the name of a woman, whether she is married or not: *Ms Gloria Johnson* ♦ *Can I help you, Ms Jones?*

MS /ˌem ˈes/ noun [U] HEALTH **multiple sclerosis**

MSc /ˌem es ˈsiː/ noun [C] EDUCATION Master of Science: an advanced degree in a subject such as physics or biology from a university

MSG /ˌem es ˈdʒiː/ noun [U] CHEMISTRY monosodium glutamate: a chemical added to food to improve its flavour

Mt abbrev GEOGRAPHY Mount, or Mountain: used in the names of mountains

much /mʌtʃ/ (**more** /mɔː/, **most** /məʊst/) adv, determiner, pronoun **1** a large amount of something: *It's a small car that doesn't use much fuel.* ♦ *It wouldn't* *cost **very much** to have your old bike repaired.* ♦ *We can't talk here. There's **too much** noise.* ♦ ***Much of the** evidence was gathered in 1991.* **2** used for asking or saying what the amount of something is: ***How much** luggage is she taking with her?* ♦ ***How much** were the tickets?* ♦ *We didn't spend **as much** time at the museum **as** I had hoped.* **3** a lot, or to a great degree: *People here don't use public transport much.* ♦ *Richard's much happier now that he's got a permanent job.* ♦ *He drinks **too much**.* ♦ *We don't go out **as much as** we used to.* ♦ *It's obvious that they love each other **very much**.*

PHRASES as much as used before an amount for showing how large and surprising it is: *You can pay as much as £500,000 for a small flat in London.*
be too much for sb to be too difficult or tiring for someone to deal with

> Both **much** and **a lot** can be used for referring to a large amount or a great degree.
> ■ **Much** is mainly used in questions and negative sentences, or in positive statements after 'so', 'too', and 'as'
> ■ **A lot** is usually used instead of **much** in positive statements: *They waste a lot of time.*
> ■ **Lots** is used in more informal English: *You save lots of money if you shop there.*

muck /mʌk/ noun [U] **1** *informal* dirt **2** animal faeces

mucous membrane /ˌmjuːkəs ˈmembreɪn/ noun [C] **ANATOMY** a thin layer of skin that covers some parts of the body, for example the inside of the nose, and produces mucus to prevent itself from becoming dry

mucus /ˈmjuːkəs/ noun [U] a liquid that is produced inside the nose and other parts of your body

mud /mʌd/ noun [U] very soft wet earth

muddle /ˈmʌd(ə)l/ noun [singular] a confused situation in which mistakes happen: *She died leaving her financial affairs **in a muddle**.*

muddled /ˈmʌd(ə)ld/ adj not clear or effective

muddle-ˈheaded adj resulting from a lack of clear thought

muddy /ˈmʌdi/ (**muddier, muddiest**) adj covered with mud, or full of mud

mudflow /ˈmʌdˌfləʊ/ noun [C] **GEOGRAPHY** a fast-moving flow of mud and soil that has been made loose by rain or melting snow

mudslide /ˈmʌdˌslaɪd/ noun [C] **GEOGRAPHY** a large amount of wet earth that falls down a hill

muezzin /muˈezɪn/ noun [C] **RELIGION** the official of a mosque who calls from a tower to let Muslims know it is time to pray

muffin /ˈmʌfɪn/ noun [C] **1** a small sweet cake that often contains fruit **2** a flat round type of bread that is eaten hot with butter

muffle /ˈmʌf(ə)l/ verb [T] to make a sound quieter and less easy to hear —**muffled** /ˈmʌf(ə)ld/ adj

mug¹ /mʌg/ noun [C] **1** a cup with straight sides and no **saucer 2** *informal* someone who does not realize that they are being tricked

mug² /mʌg/ (**mugs, mugging, mugged**) verb [T] to attack someone in a public place and steal their money or possessions —**mugger** noun [C], **mugging** noun [C/U]

Muhammad /məˈhæmɪd/ **RELIGION** the main **prophet** of Islam, who lived from about 570 AD to 632 AD, on whose ideas and teaching the religion of Islam is based. In 628 AD he made Mecca the holy city of Islam. His beliefs and **teachings** are contained in the **Koran**.

mujahedin /ˌmuːdʒəheˈdiːn/ noun [plural] soldiers belonging to an Islamic armed group

mulch /mʌltʃ/ noun [C/U] **AGRICULTURE** decaying leaves or other plant material used for protecting the area underneath plants and for improving the soil —**mulch** verb [T]

mule /mjuːl/ noun [C] a mammal that has a horse as its mother and a **donkey** as its father

mullah /ˈmʌlə, ˈmʊlə/ noun [C] **RELIGION** a Muslim leader or religious teacher

mullion /ˈmʌljən/ noun [C] **CONSTRUCTION** a piece of metal, wood, or stone used for separating the pieces of glass in a window

multi- /ˈmʌlti/ prefix many or several: used with some adjectives and nouns: *multilingual* (=able to speak several languages) ♦ *multimillionaire* (=someone with many millions of pounds)

multiaccess /ˈmʌltiˌækses/ adj **COMPUTING** a multiaccess computer system allows several users to use it at the same time

multicellular /ˌmʌltiˈseljʊlə/ adj **BIOLOGY** a multicellular organism consists of many cells

multicultural /ˌmʌltiˈkʌltʃərəl/ adj **SOCIAL STUDIES** consisting of people of different cultures —**multiculturalism** noun [U]

multidisciplinary /ˌmʌltidɪsɪˈplɪnəri/ adj involving several different subjects of study or areas of professional activity

multiethnic /ˈmʌltiˌeθnɪk/ adj **SOCIAL STUDIES** involving people from different **ethnic** groups

multifaceted /ˌmʌltiˈfæsɪtɪd/ adj *formal* containing many different aspects, features, or qualities

multifunctional /ˌmʌltiˈfʌŋkʃ(ə)nəl/ adj something that is multifunctional does several different things or has several different uses

multigrade oil /ˈmʌltigreɪd ˌɔɪl/ noun [U] **ENGINEERING** engine oil that has a range of **viscosities** (=thicknesses) and is therefore effective at different temperatures

multilateral /ˌmʌltiˈlæt(ə)rəl/ adj involving several groups or countries: *a multilateral agreement*
→ BILATERAL, UNILATERAL

multilingual /ˌmʌltiˈlɪŋgwəl/ adj **LANGUAGE** someone who is multilingual is able to speak several different languages well —**multilingualism** noun [U]
→ BILINGUAL

multimedia /ˌmʌltiˈmiːdiə/ adj **COMPUTING** multimedia computers and software produce both pictures and sounds —**multimedia** noun [U]

multimodal /ˌmʌltiˈməʊd(ə)l/ adj involving more than one way of doing something

multination /ˈmʌltiˌneɪʃ(ə)n/ adj **BUSINESS** involving two or more countries

multinational /ˌmʌltiˈnæʃ(ə)nəl/ adj **1 BUSINESS** a multinational company has offices, shops, or factories in several countries **2 SOCIAL STUDIES** involving people from many different countries

multiparty /ˈmʌltiˌpɑːti/ adj **1 POLITICS** involving more than one political party **2** involving several people, groups, or organizations that take part in something

multiplatform /ˈmʌltiˌplætfɔːm/ adj **COMPUTING** multiplatform software can run on several different types of computer system

multiple¹ /ˈmʌltɪp(ə)l/ adj involving many people, things, or parts

multiple² /'mʌltɪp(ə)l/ noun [C] **MATHS** a number that you can divide by a smaller number an exact number of times: *12 is a multiple of 4.*

multiple-'choice adj giving you several answers from which you choose the correct answer

multiple sclerosis /ˌmʌltɪp(ə)l sklə'rəʊsɪs/ noun [U] **HEALTH** a serious illness that gradually makes you unable to move, speak, or see

multiplicand /ˌmʌltɪplɪ'kænd/ noun [C] **MATHS** a number that is multiplied by another number

multiplication /ˌmʌltɪplɪ'keɪʃ(ə)n/ noun [U] **MATHS** the process of adding a number to itself a particular number of times

multipli'cation ˌsign noun [C] **MATHS** the symbol x that shows that one number is to be multiplied by another

multipli'cation ˌtable noun [C] **MATHS** a list that shows the results of multiplying all the combinations of two numbers between 1 and 12 together

multiplicative /ˌmʌltɪ'plɪkətɪv/ adj **MATHS** relating to or involving **multiplication**

multiˌplicative 'inverse noun [C] **MATHS** the number used to multiply another number to produce the answer 1. For example 3 and 1/3 are multiplicative inverses of each other, since 3 x 1/3 = 1.

multiplicity /ˌmʌltɪ'plɪsəti/ noun [singular] *formal* a large quantity or variety of things

multiplier /'mʌltɪplaɪə/ noun [C] **MATHS** the number by which another number (the **multiplicand**) is multiplied, for example the number 4 is the multiplier in the statement 2 x 4 = 8

multiply /'mʌltɪplaɪ/ (**multiplies, multiplying, multiplied**) verb [I/T] **1 MATHS** to add a number to itself a particular number of times: *If you multiply 3 by 3, you get 9.* **2** to increase, or to increase something

multi-'purpose adj able to be used for several different purposes

multiracial /ˌmʌltɪ'reɪʃ(ə)l/ adj **SOCIAL STUDIES** involving people of many different races

multiresistant /ˌmʌltɪrɪ'zɪst(ə)nt/ adj **HEALTH** a multiresistant bacterium is one that can no longer be killed by the **antibiotics** that are usually used to kill it

multi-'storey adj a multi-storey building has several levels

multitasking /ˌmʌlti'tɑːskɪŋ/ noun [U] **1 COMPUTING** the ability of a computer to do several things at the same time **2** the activity of doing more than one thing at the same time —**multi-task** verb [I]

multitude /'mʌltɪˌtjuːd/ noun **a multitude of** *formal* a very large number of people or things

multiuser /'mʌltiˌjuːzə/ adj **COMPUTING** involving or capable of dealing with a lot of different users at the same time

multivariate /ˌmʌltɪ'veəriət/ adj **MATHS** relating to or containing two or more **variables**

multiview drawing /'mʌltɪvjuː ˌdrɔːɪŋ/ noun [C] **TECHNOLOGY** a drawing that shows two or more views of an object exactly

multivitamin /'mʌltiˌvɪtəmɪn/ noun [C] a pill that some people take to make them healthier, containing various vitamins and minerals

multiword /'mʌltiˌwɜːd/ adj **LANGUAGE** consisting of two or more words

mum /mʌm/ noun [C] *informal* your mother: *It's my mum's birthday tomorrow.* ♦ *What's for dinner, Mum?*

mumble /'mʌmb(ə)l/ verb [I/T] to speak in a way that is not loud enough or clear enough for people to hear

mummy /'mʌmi/ (plural **mummies**) noun [C] **1** a dead body that was preserved in special oils and wrapped in cloth in countries such as ancient Egypt **2** mum

mumps /mʌmps/ noun [U] **HEALTH** an infectious disease caused by a virus that makes the glands in the face swollen and painful

munch /mʌntʃ/ verb [I/T] to eat something in a noisy way

Munchausen's syndrome /'mʌntʃaʊzənz ˌsɪndrəʊm/ noun [U] **HEALTH** a condition in which someone pretends to have a serious illness, in order to get treatment and sympathy from medical workers

mundane /ˌmʌn'deɪn/ adj ordinary and not interesting or exciting

mung bean /'mʌŋ ˌbiːn/ noun [C] a small round green bean, usually used for producing a **bean sprout**

municipal /mjuː'nɪsɪp(ə)l/ adj relating to a town: *municipal elections* ♦ *a municipal swimming pool*

munitions /mjuː'nɪʃ(ə)nz/ noun [plural] military weapons and equipment

mural /'mjʊərəl/ noun [C] **ARTS** a large painting done on a wall

murder¹ /'mɜːdə/ noun [C/U] **LAW** the crime of deliberately killing someone: *The murder was committed over five years ago.* → MANSLAUGHTER

murder² /'mɜːdə/ verb [T] to commit the crime of deliberately killing someone

murderer /'mɜːdərə/ noun [C] someone who commits murder

murderous /'mɜːdərəs/ adj likely to kill someone, or intending to kill someone

murky /'mɜːki/ (**murkier, murkiest**) adj **1** dark and difficult to see through: *murky water* **2** involving activities that are dishonest or morally wrong: *We suspected he had a murky past.*

murmur¹ /'mɜːmə/ verb **1** [I/T] to say something in a very quiet voice: *Frances murmured an apology as she left.* ♦ *'How strange', she murmured.* **2** [I] to make a quiet continuous sound

murmur² /'mɜːmə/ noun **1** [C] something that you say in a very quiet voice **2** [C] a complaint that you make in a very quiet way **3** [singular] a quiet continuous sound **4** [C] **HEALTH** an unusual sound made by the heart that may be a sign of disease or damage

muscle /'mʌs(ə)l/ noun **1** [C/U] **ANATOMY** a piece of flesh that connects bones and produces movement of the parts of the body by contracting and relaxing: *These exercises are good for your stomach muscles.* **2** [U] power or strength: *financial muscle*

'muscle ˌcell or **'muscle ˌfibre** noun [C] **ANATOMY** one of the rod-shaped cells that form the muscles in the body. It contains **myofibrils** (=smaller fibres) that makes the muscle contract. —*picture* → CELL

muscular /'mʌskjʊlə/ adj **1** having big muscles: *muscular legs* **2** affecting your muscles

muscular dystrophy /ˌmʌskjʊlə 'dɪstrəfi/ noun [U] **HEALTH** a serious illness in which the muscles gradually become weaker

muse /mjuːz/ verb [I] to think about something in a slow careful way

museum /mjuː'ziːəm/ noun [C] a building where valuable and important objects are kept for people to see and study

mush /mʌʃ/ noun [singular/U] a solid substance that is much softer than it should be —**mushy** adj

mushroom /'mʌʃruːm/ noun [C] a small white or brown fungus with a short stem and a round top that is often eaten as a vegetable → TOADSTOOL —*picture* → VEGETABLE

'mushroom ,head noun [C] TECHNOLOGY a rounded cap that forms on the heads of tools such as **chisels** and **punches** when they have been used many times

music /'mjuːzɪk/ noun [U] MUSIC 1 pleasant sounds made by voices or instruments: *She prefers listening to classical music.* ♦ *She writes music for films.* ♦ *We need to play a new piece of music for the concert.* 2 the activity of writing, performing, or studying music: *She's planning to do a degree in music.* ♦ *a music teacher* 3 the printed symbols that represent music: *I'm learning to read music.*

musical¹ /'mjuːzɪk(ə)l/ adj MUSIC 1 involving music, or relating to music: *musical instruments* ♦ *an evening of musical entertainment* 2 a musical sound is pleasant to listen to 3 good at playing or singing music: *They're a very musical family.* —**musicality** /,mjuːzɪ'kæləti/ noun [U], **musically** /'mjuːzɪkli/ adv

musical² /'mjuːzɪk(ə)l/ noun [C] MUSIC a play or film in which there are a lot of songs

,musical 'instrument noun [C] MUSIC an object such as a piano, guitar, or drum that you use for playing music —*picture* → on next page

musician /mjuː'zɪʃ(ə)n/ noun [C] MUSIC someone who performs or writes music, especially as their job

musicology /,mjuːzɪ'kɒlədʒi/ noun [U] MUSIC the academic study of music and its history —**musicologist** noun [C]

musket /'mʌskɪt/ noun [C] a type of long gun used by soldiers before the invention of the rifle

Muslim /'mʊzləm/ noun [C] RELIGION someone whose religion is Islam —**Muslim** adj

muslin /'mʌzlɪn/ noun [U] a type of thin cotton cloth

mussel /'mʌs(ə)l/ noun [C] a small **shellfish** with a black shell and a soft body that can be eaten —*picture* → SEA

must /*strong* mʌst, *weak* məst/ modal verb 1 used for saying that something is necessary or important to do: *You must answer all the questions.* ♦ *We mustn't be late.* 2 used for saying that you think something is probably true: *You must be tired after your long journey.* ♦ *I must have fallen asleep.* 3 used for suggesting to someone that they should do something: *You must come and visit us again some time.*

mustard /'mʌstəd/ noun [U] a thick yellow sauce with a strong taste. It is eaten cold, often with meat.

muster /'mʌstə/ verb [T] to try to make yourself feel something as strongly as possible: *The job would need all the energy I could muster.*

mustn't /'mʌs(ə)nt/ short form the usual way of saying or writing 'must not'. This is not often used in formal writing: *I mustn't forget to phone Jenny.*

musty /'mʌsti/ adj smelling unpleasant and not fresh

mutant /'mjuːt(ə)nt/ noun [C] BIOLOGY a plant or animal that is different from others of its type because of a change in its genes —**mutant** adj

mutate /mjuː'teɪt/ verb [I] BIOLOGY to become physically different from other plants or animals of the same type because of a genetic change

mutation /mjuː'teɪʃ(ə)n/ noun [C/U] BIOLOGY a change in the genes of an organism that causes it to become different from others of its type

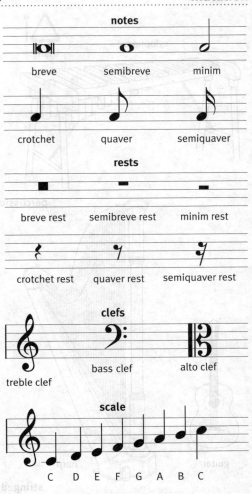

notes

breve   semibreve   minim

crotchet   quaver   semiquaver

rests

breve rest   semibreve rest   minim rest

crotchet rest   quaver rest   semiquaver rest

clefs

treble clef   bass clef   alto clef

scale

C D E F G A B C

accidentals

natural   flat   double flat

sharp   double sharp

time signature   key signature

bar line

p   *pp*   *f*   *ff*

piano   pianissimo   forte   fortissimo

musical notation

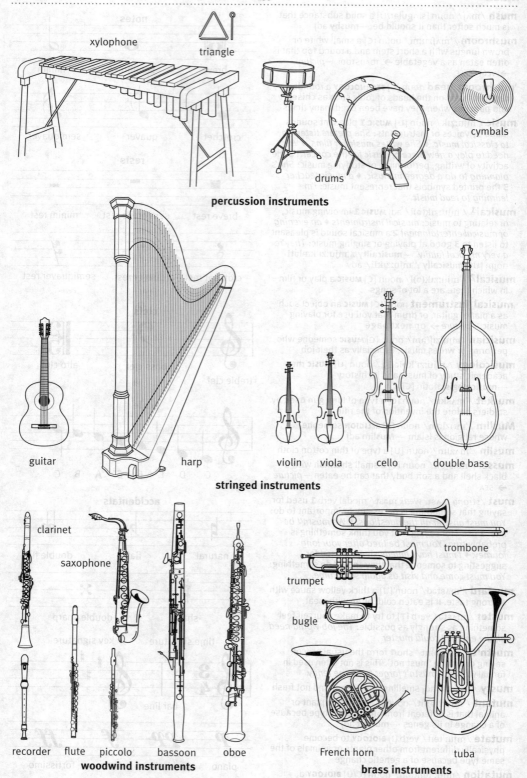

xylophone

triangle

cymbals

drums

percussion instruments

guitar

harp

violin   viola   cello   double bass

stringed instruments

clarinet

saxophone

trombone

trumpet

bugle

French horn

tuba

recorder   flute   piccolo   bassoon   oboe

woodwind instruments

brass instruments

musical instruments

mute¹ /mjuːt/ adj **1** saying nothing, or not willing to speak **2** LANGUAGE a letter that is mute is not pronounced **3** *old-fashioned* unable to speak. People now think that this word is offensive and prefer to use the expression **speech-impaired**.

mute² /mjuːt/ verb [T] **1** MUSIC to make the sound of a musical instrument softer and less loud, especially by using a mute **2** to make something less strong or extreme

mute³ /mjuːt/ noun [C] MUSIC an object used for making a musical instrument produce a sound that is softer and less loud

muti /'muːti/ noun [U] traditional South African medicine, especially medicine made from plants

mutilate /'mjuːtɪleɪt/ verb [T] to damage someone's body permanently by cutting it or cutting off part of it —**mutilation** /ˌmjuːtɪ'leɪʃ(ə)n/ noun [C/U]

mutineer /ˌmjuːtɪ'nɪə/ noun [C] someone who takes part in a **mutiny=** REBEL

mutinous /'mjuːtɪnəs/ adj refusing to obey someone who is in a position of authority

mutiny /'mjuːtəni/ (plural **mutinies**) noun [C/U] an occasion when people refuse to obey someone in a position of authority —**mutiny** verb [I]

mutter /'mʌtə/ verb [I/T] to say something in a quiet voice, especially because you are annoyed

mutton /'mʌt(ə)n/ noun [U] the meat from an adult sheep → LAMB

mutual /'mjuːtʃuəl/ adj **1** felt or done in the same way by each person: *mutual respect ♦ His contract was cancelled by mutual agreement.* **2** BUSINESS a mutual insurance company, building society etc is owned by all of its customers, who share its profits **3** belonging to two or more people: *They were introduced by a mutual friend. ♦ We have a mutual interest in hiking.*

mutually /'mjuːtʃuəli/ adv to or for each person equally

muzzle¹ /'mʌz(ə)l/ noun [C] **1** BIOLOGY the nose and mouth of an animal such as a dog or horse **2** something that you put around the nose and mouth of a dog to prevent it from biting people **3** the end of a gun **barrel** where the bullets come out

muzzle² /'mʌz(ə)l/ verb [T] **1** to prevent someone from expressing their opinions publicly **2** to put a muzzle on a dog

MW abbrev PHYSICS medium wave

my /maɪ/ determiner belonging to or connected with you, when you are the person who is speaking or writing: *I shut my eyes. ♦ When my sister went to college I got my own room.*

myelin sheath /'maɪəlɪn ˌʃiːθ/ noun [C] ANATOMY a layer of protein and fat around the **axon** (=long part) of a nerve cell. It protects the nerve cell and helps signals to travel faster along the nerve. —*picture* → NEURON

mynah bird or **myna bird** /'maɪnə ˌbɜːd/ noun [C] a black bird that can copy human speech. It is found in Asia and Australia.

myopia /maɪ'əʊpiə/ noun [U] HEALTH a medical condition in which the eye cannot see objects that are far away very clearly. A less technical name for this is **short-sightedness**.

myopic /maɪ'ɒpɪk/ adj HEALTH not able to see objects that are far away very clearly. A less technical name for this is **short-sighted**.

myrrh /mɜː/ noun [U] a sticky brown substance with a sweet smell used for making perfume, **incense**, and medicine

myself /maɪ'self/ pronoun **1** the reflexive form of 'I', used for showing that an action that you do affects you: *I fell and hurt myself. ♦ I'm going to pour myself another coffee.* **2** used for emphasizing that you are referring to yourself and not to anyone else: *I myself was once a prisoner.*

PHRASES **(all) by myself 1** alone: *I like to spend a little time by myself at weekends.* **2** without help from anyone else: *I made the whole meal all by myself.* **(all) to myself** not sharing something with anyone else: *I had the whole beach to myself.*

mysterious /mɪ'stɪəriəs/ adj **1** not explained, understood, or known: *They are investigating the mysterious disappearance of a young man. ♦ He died in mysterious circumstances.* **2** keeping things secret in a way that makes other people want to discover what they are —**mysteriously** adv

mystery /'mɪst(ə)ri/ (plural **mysteries**) noun **1** [C] something that you cannot understand, explain, or get information about: *The exact origin of the universe remains a mystery. ♦ Why she left is still a mystery to him.* **2** [U] a quality that makes someone or something difficult to explain, understand, or get information about, in a way that makes them seem interesting or exciting: *a woman with an air of mystery about her ♦ His past is shrouded in mystery.* **3** [C] a story, film, or play in which events take place that are not explained until the end: *a murder mystery*

mystic /'mɪstɪk/ noun [C] RELIGION someone who practises **mysticism**

mystical /'mɪstɪk(ə)l/ adj RELIGION **1** relating to mysticism **2** involving mysterious religious or spiritual powers

mysticism /'mɪstɪˌsɪz(ə)m/ noun [U] RELIGION the belief that you can understand God directly by praying and **meditating**

mystify /'mɪstɪfaɪ/ (**mystifies, mystifying, mystified**) verb [T] if something mystifies you, you cannot understand or explain it —**mystifying** adj

myth /mɪθ/ noun [C] **1** LITERATURE an ancient traditional story about gods, magic, and **heroes** **2** something that people wrongly believe to be true

mythical /'mɪθɪk(ə)l/ adj **1** existing only in **myths**: *mythical creatures* **2** imaginary, or not real: *Has anyone ever met this mythical boyfriend of hers?*

mythology /mɪ'θɒlədʒi/ (plural **mythologies**) noun [C/U] ancient **myths**: *Roman mythology* —**mythological** /ˌmɪθə'lɒdʒɪk(ə)l/ adj

Nn

n¹ /en/ (plural **n's**) or **N** (plural **N's**) noun [C/U] the 14th letter of the English alphabet

n² abbrev LANGUAGE noun

N abbrev **1** PHYSICS Newton **2** GEOGRAPHY North **3** GEOGRAPHY Northern

nag /næg/ (**nags, nagging, nagged**) verb [T] **1** to annoy someone by frequently criticizing them or telling them to do something: *My mum keeps nagging me to tidy my room.* **2** if a doubt, worry, or fear nags you, you cannot stop thinking about it

nagging /'nægɪŋ/ adj **1** continuously hurting you or making you feel worried: *a nagging doubt* **2** annoying you by frequently criticizing you or telling you to do something

nail¹ /neɪl/ noun [C] **1** a thin pointed piece of metal that you use for fixing one thing to another by hitting it with a hammer **2** the smooth hard part that grows over the ends of the fingers and toes

nail² /neɪl/ verb [T] to fix something with nails

'nail ,varnish or **'nail ,polish** noun [U] a shiny coloured liquid that some women put on their nails

naive /naɪˈiːv/ adj lacking experience of life, and extremely willing to trust and believe people —**naively** adv, **naivety** /naɪˈiːvəti/ noun [U]

naked /'neɪkɪd/ adj **1** not wearing any clothes **=** BARE: *a drawing of a naked woman* **2** not covered: *a naked flame* **3** a naked emotion is very strong and can be clearly seen in someone's expression
PHRASE the naked eye if you can see something with the naked eye, you can see it without using an instrument such as a telescope or a microscope

NAM /ˌen eɪ ˈem/ noun [singular] **POLITICS, ECONOMICS** non-aligned movement: an organization of countries not **allied** with with any world power that was set up in the 1950s to encourage trade between poorer countries and richer countries with more industries

name¹ /neɪm/ noun **1** [C] a word or set of words used for referring to a person or thing: *My name is Judith Kramer.* ♦ *What's **the name of** this flower?* ♦ *I think it's a great **name for** a band.* **2** [singular] a reputation: *These people have ruined the school's **good name.*** ♦ *He first **made a name for himself as** a singer.* **3** [C] a famous person or organization: *She's one of the most famous names in pop music.* ♦ *This role has turned him into a **household name** (=known by everyone).* → BIG NAME
PHRASES call sb names to insult someone by using unpleasant words to refer to them
in the name of representing someone or something

Build your vocabulary: types of name

- **alias** a false name that a criminal uses
- **first name/Christian name** a personal name that you are given when you are born
- **last name/surname** your family name
- **maiden name** a woman's last name before she was married
- **nickname** an invented name that other people call you
- **second name/middle name** the name that comes after your first name

name² /neɪm/ verb [T] **1** to give someone or something a name: *Have you named the baby yet?* ♦ *We named our puppy Patch.* **2** to know and say what the name of someone or something is: *How many world capitals can you name?* **3** to make a decision about a date, time, place, or price, and say what it is: *Name a time, and I'll be there.* **4** to choose someone for a particular job, position, or prize: *He was named player of the year.*
PHRASAL VERB 'name sb/sth after sb/sth to give someone or something the same name as someone or something else: *Albert was named after his grandfather.*

'name-,calling noun [U] the act of saying insulting things to or about someone

namely /'neɪmli/ adv used for introducing more detailed information about a subject that you are discussing: *Some groups, namely students and older people, will benefit from the new tax.*

namesake /'neɪmseɪk/ noun [C] a person or thing with the same name as someone or something else

naming ceremony /'neɪmɪŋ ˌserəməni/ noun [C] a non-religious ceremony for naming a child

nanny /'næni/ (plural **nannies**) noun [C] a woman whose job is to look after someone else's children

nano- /'nænəʊ/ prefix **SCIENCE 1** one of a thousand million equal parts: used with some nouns **2** involving the use of nanotechnology: used with some nouns

nanogram /'nænəʊgræm/ noun [C] **SCIENCE** a **billionth** (=one thousand-millionth) part of a gram

nanometre /'nænəʊˌmiːtə/ noun [C] **SCIENCE** a unit for measuring length in the metric system. There are one **billion** (=one thousand million) nanometres in a millimetre.

nanosecond /'nænəʊˌsekənd/ noun [C] **SCIENCE** a unit for measuring time. There are one **billion** (=one thousand million) nanoseconds in a second.

nanotechnology /'nænəʊtekˌnɒlədʒi/ noun [U] **SCIENCE** the skill of building very small machines from individual atoms and molecules

nap /næp/ noun [C] a short sleep, usually during the day —**nap** verb [I]

napalm /'neɪpɑːm/ noun [U] a thick sticky liquid chemical contained in some bombs that burns the person or thing it hits

nape /neɪp/ noun [singular] the back of your neck

naphtha /'næfθə, 'næpθə/ noun [U] **CHEMISTRY** one of the substances that is produced from **crude oil**. It is used in making **solvents** and in petrol. —*picture* → REFINE

napkin /'næpkɪn/ noun [C] a piece of cloth or paper that you use for protecting your clothes and wiping your mouth and hands when you are eating

nappy /'næpi/ (plural **nappies**) noun [C] a thick piece of soft cloth or paper that a baby wears to catch solid and liquid waste

narcolepsy /'nɑːkəˌlepsi/ noun [U] **HEALTH** a medical condition that makes you go to sleep very suddenly and unexpectedly at any time of the day or night

narcotic¹ /nɑːˈkɒtɪk/ noun [C] **HEALTH** a powerful, usually **addictive** drug that is used by doctors to help reduce pain and to encourage sleep, but is also taken as an illegal drug. Narcotics are usually based on **opium**.

narcotic² /nɑːˈkɒtɪk/ adj **1 HEALTH** able to make you feel less pain and help you sleep **2** relating to a narcotic, especially when used illegally

narrate /nəˈreɪt/ verb [T] **1** to tell a story in speech or writing **2** **ARTS** to give information about what is happening in a television programme or a film without appearing on the screen

narration /nəˈreɪʃ(ə)n/ noun [U] **1** the process of telling a story **2** **ARTS** spoken information about what is happening in a television programme or a film, given by someone who you do not see

narrative /'nærətɪv/ noun [C] **LITERATURE** a story or an account of something that has happened

narrator /nəˈreɪtə/ noun [C] **1 LITERATURE** someone who tells the story in a novel **2 ARTS** someone whose voice explains what is happening in a television programme or a film, but who you do not see

narrow[1] /'nærəʊ/ adj **1** if something is narrow, there is only a short distance from one side of it to the other ≠ WIDE: *narrow streets* **2** limited ≠ BROAD: *a narrow range of options* **3** used about something that you succeed in doing but nearly failed to do: *a narrow escape*

narrow[2] /'nærəʊ/ verb [I/T] to become narrower, or to make something narrower ≠ WIDEN

narrowcast /'nærəʊ,kɑːst/ verb [I/T] to make a television or radio programme available to a particular group of people only, for example people who have **cable television**

narrowly /'nærəʊli/ adv **1** by a very small amount: *Three teenagers narrowly escaped death in the crash.* **2** in a limited way that does not include many aspects of something ≠ BROADLY

narrow-minded /,nærəʊ 'maɪndɪd/ adj not interested in ideas or cultures that are different from your own ≠ BROAD-MINDED

NASA /'næsə/ ASTRONOMY the National Aeronautics and Space Administration: a government organization in the US that is responsible for space research and sending spacecraft into space

nasal[1] /'neɪz(ə)l/ adj **1** ANATOMY relating to the nose **2** someone with a nasal voice sounds as if they are speaking through their nose

nasal[2] /'neɪz(ə)l/ noun [C] LANGUAGE a speech sound such as 'm' or 'n' that is produced mainly through the nose

nasalize /'neɪzəlaɪz/ verb [T] LANGUAGE to pronounce or produce a sound mainly through the nose

nasty /'nɑːsti/ (**nastier, nastiest**) adj **1** very unpleasant = HORRIBLE: *a nasty smell* **2** unkind, offensive, or violent: *She said some very nasty things about him.* **3** serious or dangerous: *a nasty accident* —**nastily** adv

nation /'neɪʃ(ə)n/ noun [C] **1** a country: *the leaders of the main industrial nations* **2** the people of a particular country: *We want government to serve the whole nation.*

national[1] /'næʃ(ə)nəl/ adj **1** relating to one particular nation: *the national and international news* **2** relating to the whole of a nation: *House prices in the capital are 5% higher than the national average.* **3** owned or controlled by the government of a country: *the National Museum of Australia* ♦ *a national monument* —**nationally** adv

> **Word family: national**
>
> *Words in the same family as national*
> - **nation** *n*
> - **international** *adj*
> - **nationalize** *v*
> - **nationalism** *n*
> - **nationality** *n*
> - **nationally** *adv*
> - **internationally** *adv*
> - **nationalized** *adj*
> - **nationalistic** *adj*
> - **multinational** *adj, n*

national[2] /'næʃ(ə)nəl/ noun [C] SOCIAL STUDIES a citizen of a particular country

national ac'counts noun [plural] ECONOMICS a detailed record of the income and **expenditure** of all the parts of a country's economy

national 'anthem noun [C] SOCIAL STUDIES the official national song of a country

national cur'riculum noun [singular] EDUCATION a country's official programme of what children must learn at school

national 'income noun [singular] ECONOMICS the total money earned or gained by all the people who live in a country over a period of time

nationalism /'næʃ(ə)nə,lɪz(ə)m/ noun [U] **1** the attitude of people who want their country to be independent from another country that rules them **2** the belief that your country is better than all other countries

nationalist /'næʃ(ə)nəlɪst/ noun [C] **1** a member of a group of people who are trying to change the fact that their country is controlled by another country **2** someone who believes that their own country is better than all other countries —**nationalist** adj

nationalistic /,næʃ(ə)nə'lɪstɪk/ adj extremely proud of your own country and believing that it is better than all other countries

nationality /,næʃə'næləti/ (plural **nationalities**) noun **1** [U] LAW the legal status of being a citizen of a particular country: *He has British nationality.* **2** [C] a group of people who have the same race, language, or culture: *There may be as many as 20 different nationalities in a school.*

nationalize /'næʃ(ə)nəlaɪz/ verb [T] ECONOMICS if a government nationalizes a large company or industry, it takes control of it and owns it ≠ PRIVATIZE —**nationalization** /,næʃ(ə)nəlaɪ'zeɪʃ(ə)n/ noun [U]

national 'park noun [C] GEOGRAPHY, ENVIRONMENT a large area of countryside that is protected by the government in order to preserve its natural beauty

national 'product noun [singular] ECONOMICS the total value of all the goods and services produced by a country during a particular period, usually a year

national 'service noun [U] a period of time that young people in some countries must spend in the armed forces

'nation-,building noun [U] SOCIAL STUDIES the process of changing the structure of a country and giving it a new sense of identity as a nation

nationhood /'neɪʃ(ə)n,hʊd/ noun [U] the fact that a place is a nation

nation 'state noun [C] POLITICS an independent country, especially one in which all the people share the same language and culture

nationwide /,neɪʃ(ə)n'waɪd/ adj, adv in all parts of a country: *a nationwide strike*

native[1] /'neɪtɪv/ adj **1** living in a particular country or area since birth: *My wife's a native Zimbabwean, but I'm from South Africa.* ♦ *After a long stay in Singapore he's back in his native land* (=the country that he was born in). **2** native plants, animals, or people have always existed in a place: *the native population* ♦ *Elephants are native to Africa and Asia.* **3** native abilities or qualities are ones that someone has had since birth: *Pupils are encouraged to develop their native skills.* **4** your native language or tongue is the first language that you learn

native[2] /'neɪtɪv/ noun [C] **1** someone who was born in a particular place: *He's a native of Seoul but now lives in Taegeuk.* **2** *offensive* an offensive word for a member of a group of people who lived in a place before Europeans arrived there

Native A'merican noun [C] a member of one of the groups of people who lived in America before Europeans arrived

native 'speaker noun [C] someone who speaks a particular language as their first language

NATO /'neɪtəʊ/ North Atlantic Treaty Organization: an organization of North American and European countries that provides military support for its members

natural¹ /'nætʃ(ə)rəl/ adj

1 not caused by people	**4** relaxed/honest
2 reasonable/expected	**5** who you were born to
3 in sb from early age	

1 existing in nature, and not produced by people: *This cloth is made from natural fibres.* ♦ *areas of great natural beauty* ♦ *The earthquake is the worst natural disaster that Japan has experienced.* ♦ *Mr Johnson died from natural causes* (=not as a result of an accident or crime).
2 reasonable in a particular situation: *His fear was an entirely natural reaction.* ♦ *It's only natural to lose your temper occasionally.*
3 existing in someone from an early age: *The best players have natural talent.*
4 behaving in a relaxed and sincere way
5 someone's natural parents are the ones they were born to

natural² /'nætʃ(ə)rəl/ noun [C] **1** someone with a lot of skill that has developed very quickly and easily **2** **MUSIC** a musical note that is not a **sharp** or a flat, or the written sign showing this —*picture* → MUSIC

natural di'saster noun [C] **ENVIRONMENT** something that happens in the natural environment and causes a lot of damage or kills a lot of people, for example a flood or an earthquake

natural foun'dation noun [C] **CONSTRUCTION** the ground underneath the base of a building after all the soil has been removed

natural 'gas noun [U] **CHEMISTRY** a gas consisting mainly of methane and other **hydrocarbon** gases that is found underground and is used for heating and cooking

natural 'history noun [U] the study of plants and animals

naturalism /'nætʃ(ə)rə,lɪz(ə)m/ noun [U] **ARTS, LITERATURE** a style of art or literature that shows people as they are in real life

naturalist /'nætʃ(ə)rəlɪst/ noun [C] **1** someone who studies plants and animals **2** **ARTS, LITERATURE** someone who writes or paints in a naturalistic manner

naturalistic /,nætʃ(ə)rə'lɪstɪk/ adj **ARTS, LITERATURE** a naturalistic painting, novel etc shows people and things as they are in real life

naturalize /'nætʃ(ə)rə,laɪz/ verb [T] **LAW** to make someone an official citizen of a country that they were not born in —**naturalization** /,nætʃ(ə)rəlaɪ'zeɪʃ(ə)n/ noun [U], **naturalized** /'nætʃ(ə)rə,laɪzd/ adj

naturally /'nætʃ(ə)rəli/ adv **1** as most people would expect or understand= OBVIOUSLY: *Naturally, I was very keen to make a good first impression.* ♦ *His death has naturally come as a shock to us all.* **2** as a basic feature: *Her hair is naturally curly.* ♦ *Many herbs grow naturally in poor dry soils.* **3** in a normal way: *Try to act naturally in front of the camera.* → COME

natural re'sources noun [plural] **SCIENCE** useful substances such as wood, coal, minerals, and oil that occur naturally in the environment

natural 'satellite noun [C] **ASTRONOMY** a natural object such as a moon that travels around a planet

natural se'lection noun [U] **BIOLOGY** the process by which the organisms that are best able to grow and reproduce in their natural environment are the ones that usually pass their genes to the new organisms they produce. This results in very small changes in the genetic features of that particular group with each generation, and is what the theory of **evolution** is based on.

natural 'wastage noun [U] **BUSINESS** the process by which the number of workers in a company is reduced by not replacing people who leave, **retire**, or die

nature /'neɪtʃə/ noun **1** [U] the physical world and all the living things in it: *the beauty of nature* **2** [C/U] the character, qualities, or features of someone or something: *The pony has a very gentle nature.* ♦ *It isn't in my nature to be aggressive.* ♦ *Apes are curious by nature.* ♦ *It's the nature of plastic to melt at high temperatures.* **3** [singular] a particular type of thing: *His behaviour was inappropriate for a meeting of this nature.*

'nature re,serve noun [C] **ENVIRONMENT** an area of land in which the animals and plants are protected

'nature ,trail noun [C] **TOURISM** a path through the countryside with signs that tell people about the animals and plants that live there

naturopath /'neɪtʃərə,pæθ/ noun [C] **HEALTH** someone who treats people's illnesses using natural methods such as exercise and controlling what food they eat —**naturopathy** /,neɪtʃə'rɒpəθi/ noun [U]

naughty /'nɔːti/ (**naughtier, naughtiest**) adj a naughty child behaves badly —**naughtily** adv

nausea /'nɔːsiə, 'nɔːziə/ noun [U] the feeling that you are going to vomit

nauseam see ad nauseam

nautical /'nɔːtɪk(ə)l/ adj relating to ships, or to sailing them

nautical 'mile noun [C] a unit for measuring distances at sea, equal to 1,852 metres

naval /'neɪv(ə)l/ adj relating to a country's navy

navel /'neɪv(ə)l/ noun [C] **ANATOMY** the small round place in the middle of the skin on the abdomen

navigable /'nævɪgəb(ə)l/ adj deep and wide enough for ships to travel through

navigate /'nævɪgeɪt/ verb **1** [I] to use maps or other equipment in order to decide which way to go in a ship, plane, or car **2** [T] to follow a path through a difficult place **3** [T] *formal* to deal effectively with a complicated situation **4** [I/T] **COMPUTING** to move between the different areas of a website by using the **links** contained in it

navigation /,nævɪ'geɪʃ(ə)n/ noun [U] **1** the movement of a ship or an aircraft along a planned path **2** the skill of choosing a path so that a ship, plane, or car can go in a particular direction, especially by using maps or instruments **3** a way to find and follow a path through a difficult place, or deal effectively with a complicated situation **4** **COMPUTING** the process of moving between the different pages of a website by clicking on the **links** contained in it

navigator /'nævɪ,geɪtə/ noun [C] someone whose job is to plan the direction in which a ship, plane, or car should travel

navy /'neɪvi/ (plural **navies**) noun **1** [C] the part of a country's armed forces that uses ships **2** [U] navy blue

navy 'blue adj very dark blue in colour —**,navy 'blue** noun [U]

Nazi /'nɑːtsi/ (plural **Nazis**) noun [C] **POLITICS** someone who belonged to the political party that governed Germany during the Second World War —**Nazi** adj, **Nazism** noun [U]

NB /,en 'biː/ abbrev nota bene: used for saying that someone should pay particular attention to the information that follows

n/c abbrev **BUSINESS** no charge: used for showing that a customer does not have to pay anything for a particular service

NDP /ˌen diː ˈpiː/ noun [singular] **ECONOMICS** net domestic product

NDPB /ˌen diː piː ˈbiː/ noun [C] non-departmental public body: an organization that advises the government on particular policy areas or that provides a public service, but is not a government department

neap tide /ˈniːp ˌtaɪd/ noun [C] **GEOGRAPHY** a tide that has the least amount of change between the highest and lowest levels of the sea

near /nɪə/ adv, preposition **1** close to someone or something: *A group of students were standing near the entrance.* ♦ *They live on a farm 15 miles from the nearest village.* ♦ *Rosa moved a little **nearer to** the fire.* **2** close to a particular time or event: *The incident occurred near the end of the war.* ♦ *They plan to start a family **in the near future** (=soon).* **3** almost in a particular state or situation: *Julian was **near to** panic as he realized that he was trapped.* **4** close to a particular amount or number: *The temperature fell to near zero.*
 PHRASES from near and far from a very wide area
 the nearest thing to something very similar to something else
 nowhere near/not anywhere near very far from a particular place or condition: *We were nowhere near the crash when it happened.* ♦ *She doesn't look anywhere near as old as Rebecca.*

nearby¹ /ˌnɪəˈbaɪ/ adj a nearby place is not far away

nearby² /ˌnɪəˈbaɪ/ adv not far from where you are: *My cousin lives nearby.*

nearly /ˈnɪəli/ adv almost: *It took nearly six hours to do the work.* ♦ *I tripped and nearly fell down the stairs.*
 PHRASE not nearly (as/so) much less than: *It's not nearly so cold today.* ♦ *There isn't nearly enough food for everyone.*

neat /niːt/ adj **1** things that are neat look nice because they have been arranged carefully = **TIDY**: *She arranged the papers into three neat piles on her desk.* ♦ *The house was always **neat and tidy**.* **2** someone who is neat tends to keep things carefully arranged **3** producing a result in a simple but intelligent way: *a neat way of solving the problem* **4** a neat alcoholic drink is served without any ice and is not mixed with any other liquid —**neatly** adv, **neatness** noun [U]

nebula /ˈnebjʊlə/ (plural **nebulae** /ˈnebjʊliː/) noun [C] **ASTRONOMY** a very large cloud of dust and gas that exists in **outer space**

necessarily /ˈnesəsərəli, ˌnesəˈserəli/ adv always, or in every situation

necessary /ˈnesəs(ə)ri/ adj if something is necessary, you must have it or must do it: *I don't want to be disturbed unless it's **absolutely necessary**.* ♦ *I can take your place at the meeting tomorrow **if necessary**.* ♦ *It was **necessary for** all students to attend classes regularly.*

> **Word family: necessary**
>
> *Words in the same family as **necessary***
> - **necessity** n
> - **necessarily** adv
> - **necessitate** v
> - **unnecessary** adj
> - **unnecessarily** adv

necessitate /nəˈsesɪteɪt/ verb [T] *formal* to make something necessary

necessity /nəˈsesəti/ (plural **necessities**) noun **1** [U] the fact that something is necessary: *the **necessity for** a quick solution to the problem* ♦ *doubts about the*

necessity of the war **2** [C] something that you must have or must do ≠ **LUXURY**: *They lacked even **the bare necessities** (=the basic things that everyone needs).*

neck /nek/ noun [C] **1** the part of the body that joins the head to the rest of the body —*picture* → BIRD, BODY, JOINT **2** the part of a piece of clothing that fits around your neck **3** a long narrow part of something such as a bottle or a musical instrument
 PHRASE neck and neck with each person or group competing as well as the other and equally likely to win
 → BREATHE

necklace /ˈnekləs/ noun [C] a piece of jewellery that hangs round the neck

nectar /ˈnektə/ noun [U] **BIOLOGY** a sweet liquid in flowers that insects and birds drink. Bees collect it and use it for making **honey**.

nectarine /ˈnektəriːn/ noun [C] a fruit with a smooth red and yellow skin. It is yellow inside and has a large seed. —*picture* → FRUIT

nectary /ˈnektəri/ (plural **nectaries**) noun [C] **BIOLOGY** the part of a flower that produces **nectar** —*picture* → FLOWER

need¹ /niːd/ verb [T] **1** if you need something, you must have it because it is necessary: *You'll need some warm clothes for the winter.* ♦ *She **needs to** rest for a couple of weeks.* ♦ *I **need someone to** help me carry these books downstairs.* **2** used for saying that it is necessary for something to be done or to exist: *The bathroom needs cleaning.* ♦ *Food is **needed to** supply the raw materials for cell growth.*
 PHRASE needn't do sth/don't need to do sth used for saying that someone does not have to do something: *You needn't wear your uniform for the school trip.*

need² /niːd/ noun **1** [singular/U] a situation in which it is necessary for something to be done: *He recognizes **the need for** immediate action.* ♦ *We feel there is **a need to** do more research.* ♦ *There's **no need for** you to attend the meeting (=it isn't necessary).* **2** [C] something that you need in order to be healthy, comfortable etc: *People with mental health problems **have** special **needs**.*
 PHRASES in need not having enough food, money, clothing, or other things that are necessary: *families in need*
 in need of sth needing something: *He was tired and hungry, and badly in need of a bath.*

needle /ˈniːd(ə)l/ noun [C] **1** **HEALTH** a thin sharp metal tube that is used for putting medicine or drugs into the body through the skin **2** a thin metal tool that is used for sewing or **knitting 3** the part of a piece of equipment that points to a number in order to show a measurement: *a compass needle* **4** **BIOLOGY** a very thin sharp leaf that grows on some conifer trees: *pine needles* —*picture* → TREE

'needle ˌbearing noun [C] **TECHNOLOGY** a **bearing** (=machine part) that uses small metal cylinders, rather than metal balls, to reduce **friction** between moving parts

needless /ˈniːdləs/ adj unnecessary: *needless waste*
 PHRASE needless to say used for emphasizing something that people already know
 —**needlessly** adv

needlestick injury /ˈniːd(ə)lstɪk ˌɪndʒəri/ noun [C] **HEALTH** an injury that is caused when the needle of a syringe accidentally makes a hole in someone's skin, possibly infecting them with a harmful microorganism

'needle ˌvalve noun [C] **ENGINEERING** a **valve** that controls the flow of a fluid or gas very **precisely**

needn't /'niːd(ə)nt/ short form the usual way of saying or writing 'need not': *You needn't worry about me, I'll be fine.*

'need-to-,know adj used for describing the principle that secret information will only be given to people who need it to do a particular job

needy /'niːdi/ (**needier, neediest**) adj **1** without enough money, food, or clothes **2 the needy** people who are poor

negation /nɪ'ɡeɪʃ(ə)n/ noun [U] MATHS a statement that says that another statement is false

negative¹ /'neɡətɪv/ adj

1 disagreeing	**5** expressing 'no'
2 harmful/bad	**6** less than zero
3 emphasizing bad part	**7** about electrical charge
4 of medical test	

1 expressing disagreement or criticism ≠ POSITIVE: *a negative response*
2 harmful, or bad: *I hope the experience won't have a negative effect on the children.*
3 giving more attention or emphasis to bad aspects than good ones ≠ POSITIVE: *The article presents a rather negative view of professional sports.*
4 showing that someone does not have a particular disease or condition: *Her pregnancy test was negative.*
♦ *He tested negative for drugs.*
5 LANGUAGE a negative word expresses 'no' or 'not', for example 'don't' or 'never'
6 MATHS a negative number or amount is less than zero ≠ POSITIVE
7 PHYSICS with the same electrical charge as an electron ≠ POSITIVE
—**negatively** adv

negative² /'neɡətɪv/ noun [C] **1** an image on film in which dark things appear light, and light things appear dark **2** LANGUAGE a word or expression that means 'no' or 'not'

,negative 'camber noun [U] ENGINEERING a way of arranging the position of the wheels on a vehicle in which the top of the wheel leans in towards the centre of the vehicle

,negative 'earth adj ENGINEERING a negative earth electrical system in a vehicle has the negative terminal of its battery connected to the frame of the vehicle, so that the frame acts as an **earth** (=conducts electricity safely to the ground)

negativity /,neɡə'tɪvəti/ noun [U] the attitude of someone who always sees the bad aspects of a situation

neglect¹ /nɪ'ɡlekt/ verb [T] **1** to not look after someone or something: *The building had been neglected for years.* ♦ *parents who neglect their children* **2** to not do something that you should do: *He couldn't neglect his duties as an officer.* ♦ *She had neglected to inform me that the company was having problems.* **3** to not pay attention to something such as the work of a writer or an artist —**neglected** adj

neglect² /nɪ'ɡlekt/ noun [U] the failure to give someone or something the care that they need: *Our roads have suffered from years of neglect.*

negligence /'neɡlɪdʒ(ə)ns/ noun [U] the failure to be careful enough, so that something bad happens

negligent /'neɡlɪdʒ(ə)nt/ adj failing to be careful enough, so that something bad happens
—**negligently** adv

negligible /'neɡlɪdʒəb(ə)l/ adj very unimportant, or very small = INSIGNIFICANT

negotiable /nɪ'ɡəʊʃiəb(ə)l/ adj able to be changed through discussion by the people involved

negotiate /nɪ'ɡəʊʃieɪt/ verb **1** [I/T] to try to reach an agreement by discussing something formally: *The two sides have shown their willingness to negotiate.*
♦ ***Negotiating a** peace **deal** will not be an easy task.*
♦ *The airline is **negotiating a** new **contract** with the union.* **2** [T] to successfully travel on a road or path that is difficult to travel on or travel through: *Only 4-wheel-drive vehicles can negotiate the rough roads around here.* —**negotiator** noun [C]

negotiation /nɪ,ɡəʊʃi'eɪʃ(ə)n/ noun [C/U] formal discussions in which people try to reach an agreement

negroid or **Negroid** /'niːɡrɔɪd/ adj SOCIAL STUDIES someone with negroid features has the physical appearance of a black person

neighbour /'neɪbə/ noun [C] **1** someone who lives near you: *friends and neighbours* **2** a person or place that is next to another person or place: *She whispered to her neighbour that she thought the play was too long.* ♦ *Turkey and its European neighbours*

neighbourhood /'neɪbəhʊd/ noun [C] a particular area of a town

neighbouring /'neɪbərɪŋ/ adj next to each other: *a neighbouring town*

neither /'naɪðə, 'niːðə/ adv, determiner, pronoun **1** used for showing that a negative statement also applies to someone or something else: *Adams was not invited, and neither was his wife.* ♦ *'I don't like him.' 'Neither do I.'* **2** used for referring to each of two people or things, when saying something that applies to both of them: *Neither side trusts the other.* ♦ *It was an experience that **neither of** us will ever forget.*

PHRASES **neither here nor there** not important or relevant: *What he does in his private life is neither here nor there.*

neither...nor used for showing that something is not true of two people or things: *Neither his son nor his daughter were at the funeral.*

> When **neither** is the subject of a sentence, it is usually used with a singular verb: *Neither of the books was published in this country.* But in spoken English a plural verb is sometimes used: *Neither of us are planning to go.*

nematode /'nemətəʊd/ noun [C] BIOLOGY a roundworm

neocolonialism /,niːəʊkə'ləʊniə,lɪz(ə)m/ noun [U] SOCIAL STUDIES a policy in which a powerful country uses political and economic power over a poorer country for its own benefit

neocon /'niːəʊ,kɒn/ noun [C] POLITICS a neoconservative

neoconservative /,niːəʊkən'sɜːvətɪv/ adj POLITICS relating to, or expressing, conservative views of the type that existed before the liberal times of the 1960s and 1970s —**neoconservative** noun [C]

neodymium /,niːəʊ'dɪmiəm/ noun [U] CHEMISTRY a silvery-white or yellowish metallic element in the **lanthanide** group of the periodic table. Chemical symbol: **Nd**

Neolithic /,niːə'lɪθɪk/ adj the Neolithic period of history began around 10,000 BC, when humans began to make stone tools, grow their food, and live in permanent communities

neologism /ni'ɒlə,dʒɪz(ə)m, 'niːələ,dʒɪz(ə)m/ noun [C] LANGUAGE a new word or expression, or an existing word used with a new meaning

neon /'ni:ɒn/ noun [U] CHEMISTRY a colourless gas that is an element that turns orange when electricity is passed through it, used in lights and electric signs. Chemical symbol: **Ne**

neonatal /,ni:əʊ'neɪt(ə)l/ adj HEALTH relating to the first weeks of a baby's life

neonate /'ni:əʊneɪt/ noun [C] HEALTH a very young baby, no more than a few weeks old

nephew /'nefju:, 'nevju:/ noun [C] a son of your brother or sister, or a son of your husband's or wife's brother or sister

nephron /'nefrɒn/ noun [C] ANATOMY one of many small structures in the kidney that consists of the **glomerulus**, the **Bowman's capsule**, its **convoluted tubules**, and the **collecting duct**

nepotism /'nepə,tɪz(ə)m/ noun [U] the practice of giving jobs to your family and friends

Neptune /'neptju:n/ ASTRONOMY the planet that is eighth furthest from the Sun, between Uranus and Pluto. It has a very **stormy** atmosphere and is the second-coldest planet in the solar system. —*picture* → SOLAR SYSTEM

neptunium /nep'tju:niəm/ noun [U] CHEMISTRY a silvery radioactive metallic element in the **actinide** group of the periodic table. Chemical symbol: **Np**

nerve /nɜ:v/ noun **1** [C] ANATOMY one of the groups of fibres in the body that carry messages between the sense organs, the brain, and the rest of the body, communicating pain, pressure, feelings of heat and cold etc: *the optic nerve* ♦ *a nerve cell* **2 nerves** [plural] the worried feeling that you will do something badly: *He asked for a drink to **calm his nerves** before heading out to the plane.* **3** [U] the ability to control your fear and stay determined when you are doing something that is difficult= COURAGE: *Suddenly I **lost my nerve** and I couldn't move.* ♦ *After months of agonizing, she finally **found the nerve** to tell him he was wrong.* **4** [U] a rude attitude that makes other people angry: *She had **the nerve** to call me a liar.*

    PHRASE **get on sb's nerves** to annoy someone

'**nerve ,cell** noun [C] ANATOMY a **neuron** —*picture* → CELL

'**nerve ,centre** noun [C] the centre of a business, or political or other big organization, where decisions are made and activities are planned and directed

'**nerve ,cord** noun [C] ANATOMY a long set of nerve fibres running along an animal's body, especially in an invertebrate

nervous /'nɜ:vəs/ adj **1** feeling excited and worried, or slightly afraid= ANXIOUS: *Driving on mountain roads always makes him nervous.* ♦ *a nervous laugh* ♦ *I got very nervous waiting for my turn to be called.* ♦ *She was **nervous about** walking home so late.* **2** a nervous person easily becomes excited or upset because they are not relaxed **3** ANATOMY relating to the nerves in the body: *a nervous condition* —**nervously** adv, **nervousness** noun [U]

,**nervous 'breakdown** noun [C] HEALTH a mental condition in which you are so upset or unhappy that you cannot look after yourself

the '**nervous ,system** noun ANATOMY, BIOLOGY the system of nerves that control the body and the mind

nest¹ /nest/ noun [C] BIOLOGY **1** a structure that birds make to keep their eggs and young birds in **2** a home that insects or small animals make for themselves

nest² /nest/ verb **1** [I] BIOLOGY to build or use a nest **2** [T] to organize information so that one part is contained inside another

net¹ /net/ noun

1 material with large spaces	3 in sport
2 bag for catching fish/animals	4 system for computers
	5 Internet

1 [C/U] a material made of string or rope that is woven into a loose pattern with spaces in it
2 [C] a bag made of net that you use for catching fish or other animals
3 [C] SPORTS in some sports, an object made of net that you hit, kick, or throw the ball over or into
4 [C] COMPUTING a system in which a set of computers are able to communicate with each other= NETWORK
5 the Net COMPUTING the **Internet**

net² /net/ adj **1** a net amount of money is the total amount after taxes or costs have been removed → GROSS¹ sense 1 **2** a net effect or result is the final one, after everything has been considered **3** the net weight of something is its weight without its container

net³ /net/ (**nets, netting, netted**) verb [T] **1** to manage to get or do something **2** to earn a particular amount of money as profit → GROSS² **3** SPORTS in sport, to hit or throw a ball into a net

net⁴ /net/ adv after everything such as taxes or costs have been removed → GROSS

netball /'net,bɔ:l/ noun [U] SPORTS a women's game that is similar to basketball

,**net do,mestic 'product** noun [singular] ECONOMICS the total value of all the goods and services produced by a country in a year, except for income received from money invested in other countries, after taking away the value that buildings and equipment lose

netiquette /'netɪ,ket/ noun [U] *informal* the polite way of communicating with other people when using the Internet

,**net 'movement** noun [U] CHEMISTRY, PHYSICS the overall direction of the movement of a substance, for example the movement of molecules during **osmosis**

,**net ,national 'product** noun [singular] ECONOMICS the total value of all the goods and services produced by a country during a year, after taking away the value that buildings and equipment lose

netphone /'net,fəʊn/ noun [C] COMPUTING a phone that uses the Internet to make connections and carry voice messages

netting /'netɪŋ/ noun [U] a material made of string or rope that is woven into a loose pattern with spaces in it= NET

nettle /'net(ə)l/ noun [C] a wild plant with pointed leaves and small hairs that sting you if you touch them

network¹ /'net,wɜ:k/ noun [C] **1** a system of things such as roads, rivers, or wires that are connected to each other: *a mobile phone network* ♦ *a network of canals* **2** a group of people or organizations that work together: *We have a nationwide **network of** financial advisors.* **3** COMPUTING a number of computers that are connected to each other **4** a group of companies that broadcast the same television or radio programmes in all parts of a large area

network² /'netwɜ:k/ verb **1** [I] to meet people in order to make friends who will be useful, especially for business purposes **2** [I/T] COMPUTING to connect computers together **3** [T] if a television or radio programme is networked, it is broadcast by all the companies in a network at the same time

networking /'net,wɜ:kɪŋ/ noun [U] COMPUTING the activity of connecting computers together in order to form a network

network topology /ˌnetwɜːk təˈpɒlədʒi/ noun [C] **COMPUTING** the arrangement of computer equipment in a **network**

neural /ˈnjʊərəl/ adj **HEALTH** relating to the nerves or the **nervous system**

'neural ca,nal noun [C] **ANATOMY** a space inside a **vertebra** through which the **spinal cord** passes —*picture* → VERTEBRA

neuralgia /njʊˈrældʒə/ noun [U] **HEALTH** severe pain in a part of the body where there is a nerve —**neuralgic** adj

,neural 'net noun [C] **COMPUTING** a computer system or other electrical system that is designed to work in the same way as the human brain

,neural 'network noun [C] **1** **ANATOMY** a system of nerve cells that receives messages from the brain, allowing the body to do something **2** **COMPUTING** a **neural net**

neuro- /njʊərəʊ/ prefix brain, nerve, or **nervous system**: used with some nouns and adjectives

neurocognitive /ˌnjʊərəʊˈkɒgnətɪv/ adj **HEALTH** relating to or involving the brain and the ability to think

neurodegenerative /ˌnjʊərəʊdɪˈdʒenərətɪv/ adj **HEALTH** relating to medical conditions such as **Alzheimer's disease** or **Parkinson's disease** in which nerve cells in the brain or **spinal cord** die or are damaged

neurology /njʊˈrɒlədʒi/ noun [U] **HEALTH** the study of the **nervous system** and the diseases that affect it —**neurological** /ˌnjʊərəˈlɒdʒɪk(ə)l/ adj

neuron or **neurone** /ˈnjʊərɒn/ noun [C] **HEALTH** a cell that sends messages to the brain and receives messages from the brain

intermediate or relay neuron

motor neuron   **sensory neuron**

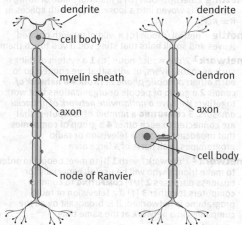

dendrite

dendrite

cell body

dendron

myelin sheath

axon

axon

cell body

node of Ranvier

neuron structures

neuroscience /ˈnjʊərəʊˌsaɪəns/ noun [U] **HEALTH** the scientific study of the **nervous system** —**neuroscientist** noun [C]

neurosis /njʊˈrəʊsɪs/ (plural **neuroses** /njʊˈrəʊsiːz/) noun [C/U] **HEALTH** a minor mental illness that may involve feelings of anxiety and **depression**, and **obsessive** behaviour

neurotic /njʊˈrɒtɪk/ adj **1** extremely worried about something in an unreasonable way **2** **HEALTH** suffering from neurosis

neurotransmitter /ˌnjʊərəʊtrænsˈmɪtə/ noun [C] **ANATOMY** a chemical substance that crosses the **synapse** (=space) between nerve cells, sending the signal from one nerve cell to another

neuter[1] /ˈnjuːtə/ verb [T] to perform an operation on an animal's sexual organs so that it cannot have babies

neuter[2] /ˈnjuːtə/ adj **LANGUAGE** a neuter word has a different form and behaviour from **masculine** or **feminine** words in some languages

neutral[1] /ˈnjuːtrəl/ adj

1 not involved	4 neither acid nor base
2 without strong feeling	5 without electric charge
3 colours: not strong	

1 not supporting a particular person, group, or country in an argument, competition, or war: *a neutral country* ♦ *The television coverage was by no means neutral.*
2 not showing strong feelings or opinions in the way you speak or behave: *Her voice remained neutral as she spoke.*
3 neutral colours are not very strong or bright
4 **CHEMISTRY** a neutral chemical is neither an acid nor a base
5 **PHYSICS** a neutral wire is not **live**. It is the wire that is blue in a **plug**. —*picture* → PLUG
—**neutrally** adv

neutral[2] /ˈnjuːtrəl/ noun [U] the position of the **gears** in a car when the car cannot move

,neutral equi'librium noun [U] **PHYSICS** a situation in which the centre of gravity of an object is always at the same height

,neutral 'flame noun [C] **TECHNOLOGY** a flame used in welding that is produced by equal amounts of oxygen and **acetylene**

neutrality /njuːˈtræləti/ noun [U] the attitude of someone who does not support either side in a war or disagreement

,neutrali'zation re,action noun [C] **CHEMISTRY** a reaction that takes place between an acid and a **base**. It produces water and a salt.

neutralize /ˈnjuːtrəlaɪz/ verb [T] **1** to stop something from having any effect **2** **CHEMISTRY** if a chemical neutralizes a substance, it makes it neither an acid nor a base —**neutralization** /ˌnjuːtrəlaɪˈzeɪʃ(ə)n/ noun [U]

,neutral ,p'H noun [singular/U] **CHEMISTRY** a pH with a value of 7 that is neither an acid nor a base

,neutral 'wire noun [C] **PHYSICS** a wire in an electrical system that does not have an electrical charge

neutrino /njuːˈtriːnəʊ/ noun [C] **PHYSICS** a particle that is smaller than an atom and has no electrical charge

neutron /ˈnjuːtrɒn/ noun [C] **PHYSICS** a part of the nucleus of an atom that does not have an electrical charge —*picture* → ATOM

,neutron 'star noun [C] **ASTRONOMY** a very small, very dense object in space that is mostly made up of neutrons

neutrophil /ˈnjuːtrəfɪl/ noun [C] BIOLOGY the most common type of white blood cell in vertebrates. Neutrophils protect the body against infection and are easily coloured with chemically neutral dyes. —**neutrophil** adj

never /ˈnevə/ adv at no time, or not at all: *I've never been in love before.* ♦ *You'll never guess who I saw today!* ♦ *He never even said goodbye.* ♦ *I never knew you two were cousins.* ♦ *I went sailing once, but never again* (=I will never want to do it again because I didn't like it).

nevertheless /ˌnevəðəˈles/ adv despite something that you have just mentioned: *It's a difficult race. Nevertheless, about 1,000 runners participate every year.*

nevirapine /neˈvɪrəpiːn/ noun [U] HEALTH a medicine that is used in the treatment of HIV and AIDS

new /njuː/ adj

1 recently made	**4** replacing sb/sth
2 recently bought	**5** recently arrived
3 not used	**6** not known before

1 recently made, invented, or developed ≠ OLD: *They are going to build a new office block here.* ♦ *the new Tom Cruise film* ♦ *I was full of new ideas.*
2 recently bought or obtained ≠ OLD: *Have you seen my new car?* ♦ *When do you start your new job?*
3 never used or owned by anyone before: *I don't need a new printer – a used one is good enough.* → SECOND-HAND
4 replacing someone or something else ≠ OLD: *I need to get a new passport – my old one's expired.*
5 recently arrived in a new place or situation: *Many firms help new employees with finding accommodation.* ♦ *We are new to this area.*
6 not previously known or discovered: *Police have now been given some new information.*
→ GOOD[1]

> Build your vocabulary: words you can use instead of **new**
>
> **New** is a very general word. Here are some words with more specific meanings that sound more natural and appropriate in particular situations.
> **equipment, computers etc made using the latest ideas and technology** advanced, cutting-edge, modern, newfangled (*showing disapproval*), state-of-the-art, up-to-date
> **ideas, methods etc that are new and not like anything that has existed before** innovative, fresh, novel, original, revolutionary
> **films, books etc that have just become available** latest, recent, just out
> **something you have just bought that has never been used** brand new

New 'Age adj not connected with the main religions or with traditional ideas and methods

newbie /ˈnjuːbi/ noun [C] COMPUTING someone who has just started to use the Internet

newborn /ˈnjuːbɔːn/ adj recently born

newbuild /ˈnjuːbɪld/ noun [C] a house that has recently been built

newcomer /ˈnjuːkʌmə/ noun [C] someone who has recently arrived somewhere

newel /ˈnjuːəl/ noun [C] CONSTRUCTION a thick vertical post that supports the **handrail** at the top or bottom of a staircase

newly /ˈnjuːli/ adv recently: *the newly appointed chairperson of the company*

new 'moon noun [singular] a moon that appears after a night when there was no moon, and looks like a thin curve in the sky —*picture* → PHASE

news /njuːz/ noun **1** [U] information about something that has happened recently: *I'm afraid I've got some bad news.* ♦ *She was delighted by this piece of news.* ♦ *Have you heard the good news? Michael's got the job!* ♦ *Friends expressed shock at the news of his death.* ♦ *The leaflet is full of up-to-date news on the environment.* **2** [U] information about recent events that is reported in newspapers or on television or radio: *sports news* ♦ *a news item* ♦ *Farming methods are back in the news this week.* **3** the news [singular] a television or radio broadcast that gives you information about recent events: *I always listen to the nine o'clock news.* ♦ *Did you see the Prime Minister on the news last night?*

> **News** looks like a plural, but it is never used with a plural verb and cannot be used with **a**: *I've got a wonderful piece of news* (NOT a wonderful news) *for you.* ♦ *Do you have any news about Laura's baby?* ♦ *Here's some news about the World Cup.*

newsagent /ˈnjuːzˌeɪdʒ(ə)nt/ noun [C] **1** someone whose job is to sell newspapers and magazines **2** newsagent or newsagent's a shop that sells newspapers and magazines

newsgroup /ˈnjuːzˌɡruːp/ noun [C] COMPUTING a place on the Internet where people can leave messages about a subject or activity that interests them

newsletter /ˈnjuːzˌletə/ noun [C] written information sent regularly to members of an organization, containing news about events, activities etc

newspaper /ˈnjuːzˌpeɪpə/ noun **1** [C] a set of large printed sheets of folded paper containing news, articles, and other information that is published every day or every week: *a local newspaper* ♦ *a newspaper article* ♦ *I saw an interesting article in the newspaper this morning.* **2** [U] sheets of paper from a newspaper: *vegetables wrapped in newspaper*

newsprint /ˈnjuːzˌprɪnt/ noun [U] the ink and paper that are used for printing newspapers

newsreader /ˈnjuːzˌriːdə/ noun [C] someone whose job is to read the news on television or radio

newt /njuːt/ noun [C] a small amphibian with a long tail that lives mainly in water

the New 'Testament RELIGION the second part of the Bible, that describes Jesus Christ's life and the things he taught → OLD TESTAMENT

newton /ˈnjuːt(ə)n/ noun [C] PHYSICS a unit for measuring force, equal to the force that causes a mass of one kilogram to accelerate at one metre a second every second. Symbol N

new variant CJ'D noun [U] HEALTH a form of the illness **CJD** that makes people ill very quickly

new 'wave noun [singular/U] ARTS a form of art that uses new styles and ideas —**new 'wave** adj

the New 'World North, Central, and South America

new 'year or **New 'Year** noun [C] the time around the beginning of a new year, when people celebrate

New Year's 'Day noun [C] 1st January, the first day of the year

New Year's 'Eve noun [C] 31st December, the last day of the year

next /nekst/ adj, adv, pronoun **1** used for referring to the time, event, or person that comes after this one, or that comes after another one: *He said he was leaving* for Rome **the next day**. ♦ I knew exactly what was going to **happen next**. ♦ I'll see you **next Friday**. ♦ A meeting has been arranged for the **weekend after next**. ♦ Who's **next** in the queue? **2** used for referring to the place that is closest to where you are: I could hear the sound of laughter in **the next room**.

PHRASES **the next best/largest/smallest etc** one that is almost as good, large, small etc as another one that you are mentioning: Britain is Europe's next largest oil producer after Norway.

next of kin your closest relative or relatives

next to 1 very close to someone or something, with nothing or no one in between: She sat down next to me. ♦ Steve lives next to the hospital. **2** used before negative words to mean 'almost, but not completely': It will be **next to impossible** to win. ♦ She earns **next to nothing**.

,**next-'door** adj **1** the next-door flat, office etc is the one next to yours **2** your next-door **neighbour** lives in the house next to yours

nexus /'neksəs/ noun [C] formal a closely connected group of people or things, often forming the central part of something

NGO /,en dʒi: 'əʊ/ noun [C] non-governmental organization: an organization such as a charity that is not owned by the government, but may work with government departments

NI abbrev **1** National Insurance **2** Northern Ireland

niacin /'naɪəsɪn/ noun [U] HEALTH a type of vitamin that exists in milk and other foods. Niacin is one of the **B vitamins**.

nib /nɪb/ noun [C] the part of a pen that the ink comes out of

nibble /'nɪb(ə)l/ verb [I/T] to eat something by taking a lot of small bites —**nibble** noun [C]

NIC /,en aɪ 'si:/ noun [C] ECONOMICS newly industrialized country: a country that has recently achieved a lot of industrial development, for example Malaysia

nice /naɪs/ adj **1** attractive, enjoyable, or pleasant: The city is a much nicer place to live nowadays. ♦ Your hair **looks nice**. **2** friendly, kind, and pleasant: She's a nice girl. ♦ He's always been **nice to** me. ♦ It was **nice of you** to come. **3** used with another adjective to emphasize that you like a particular quality about someone or something: nice warm socks ♦ It's **nice and** quiet in here.

> **Build your vocabulary: words you can use instead of nice**
>
> Nice is a very general word. Here are some words with more specific meanings that sound more natural and appropriate in particular situations.
> **people** easy-going, easy to get on with, friendly, good fun, kind, lovely, sweet
> **behaviour** helpful, kind, thoughtful
> **something that happens or something that you do** good, great, lovely, marvellous, wonderful
> **weather** fantastic, fine, glorious, good, lovely, pleasant
> **clothes** beautiful, flattering, smart, stylish
> **food/flowers/gifts/places** beautiful, delightful, fantastic, great, lovely

nicely /'naɪsli/ adv **1** in a satisfactory or suitable way: That illustrates the point nicely. **2** in an attractive way: a nicely furnished flat **3** in a polite or friendly way: If you ask Bob nicely, I'm sure he'll help.

niche /ni:ʃ/ noun [C] **1** a job or activity that is very suitable for you: She's never really found her niche in life. **2** BUSINESS an opportunity to sell a particular

product or service that no one else is selling **3** a small space in a wall where you can put small objects

'**niche** ,**market** noun [C] BUSINESS a market in which a particular product or service can be sold to the small number of customers who want it

nichrome /'naɪ,krəʊm/ noun [U] CHEMISTRY an alloy of **nickel** and **chromium**. It is used to make **resistors**.

nick /nɪk/ verb [T] to cut the surface of something slightly: He nicked his finger opening a tin. —**nick** noun [C]

nickel /'nɪk(ə)l/ noun **1** [U] CHEMISTRY a hard silver-white metal element, used in batteries and to make alloys. Chemical symbol: **Ni 2** [C] a coin in the US and Canada that is worth five **cents**

nickname /'nɪk,neɪm/ noun [C] an informal name that your friends or family call you that is not your real name

nicotine /'nɪkəti:n/ noun [U] the drug in tobacco that makes people **addicted** to it

niece /ni:s/ noun [C] a daughter of your brother or sister, or a daughter of your husband's or wife's brother or sister

night /naɪt/ noun [C/U] **1** the part of each 24-hour period when it is dark because the part of the Earth affected is facing away from the Sun ≠ DAY: It was a very warm night. ♦ I woke up **in the middle of the night**. ♦ It rained **all night (long)**. ♦ The attacks usually take place **at night**. ♦ Owls hunt **by night**. **2** the time between the end of the afternoon and the time when people go to bed= EVENING: Most nights Jan helps the kids with their homework. ♦ What are you doing Friday night? ♦ Did you watch the football on TV last night?

PHRASE **night and day** or **day and night** all the time —**nightly** adj, adv → DEAD²

nightdress /'naɪt,dres/ noun [C] a loose dress that women wear for sleeping in

nightfall /'naɪt,fɔ:l/ noun [U] literary the time in the evening when it starts to become dark

nightmare /'naɪt,meə/ noun [C] **1** a very difficult or frightening experience or situation: That maths test was a nightmare. **2** a very frightening and unpleasant dream: I still **have** terrible **nightmares about** the crash. —**nightmarish** /'naɪt,meərɪʃ/ adj

'**night** ,**school** noun [U] EDUCATION classes in the evening for people who work during the day

nighttime /'naɪt,taɪm/ noun [U] the period of time when it is night

,**night 'watchman** noun [C] someone whose job is to guard a building during the night

nil /nɪl/ noun [U] **1** spoken the number 0 in the result of a game: Brazil won three nil. **2** used for saying that something does not exist: Their chances of survival are virtually nil.

nimble /'nɪmb(ə)l/ adj able to move quickly and easily —**nimbly** /'nɪmbli/ adv

nimbostratus /,nɪmbəʊ'streɪtəs/ noun [U] GEOGRAPHY thick low cloud that carries rain and covers all of the sky —picture → CLOUD

nimbus /'nɪmbəs/ noun [C] GEOGRAPHY a dark grey rain cloud

nine /naɪn/ number the number 9

nineteen /,naɪn'ti:n/ number the number 19

nineteenth /,naɪn'ti:nθ/ number **1** in the place or position counted as number 19 **2** one of 19 equal parts of something

nineties /ˈnaɪntiz/ noun [plural]
  PHRASES **the nineties 1** if the temperature is in the nineties, it is in the range of 90 to 99 degrees Fahrenheit **2** the years from 1990 to 1999: *people who were born in the nineties*
  in your nineties to be an age in the range of 90 to 99

ninety /ˈnaɪnti/ number the number 90 —**ninetieth** number

ninth /naɪnθ/ number **1** in the place or position counted as number nine: *the ninth of January* **2** one of nine equal parts of something

niobium /naɪˈəʊbiəm/ noun [U] CHEMISTRY a shiny pale grey metallic element used in steel alloys. Chemical symbol: **Nb**

nip /nɪp/ (**nips, nipping, nipped**) verb [I/T] to bite someone gently —**nip** noun [C]

nipple /ˈnɪp(ə)l/ noun [C] ANATOMY a small round raised area of flesh on each side of the chest. In females, it is where a baby can suck to get milk.

nirvana /nɪəˈvɑːnə/ noun [U] RELIGION a state of complete spiritual happiness that Buddhists and Hindus try to achieve

nisi *see* **decree nisi**

nitpicking /ˈnɪtˌpɪkɪŋ/ noun [U] annoying criticisms about small unimportant details

nitrate /ˈnaɪtreɪt/ noun [C/U] CHEMISTRY a salt formed from nitric acid that is used for improving the quality of soil. Nitrates are an important part of the **nitrogen cycle**. Chemical formula: NO_3 —*picture* → NITROGEN CYCLE

nitric acid /ˌnaɪtrɪk ˈæsɪd/ noun [U] CHEMISTRY a very **corrosive** chemical that is used in industry, and for making bombs and in rocket fuels

nitrification /ˌnaɪtrɪfɪˈkeɪʃ(ə)n/ noun [U] BIOLOGY a process in which compounds of nitrogen in decaying plants are changed by bacteria in soil into **nitrites** and then to **nitrates** that green plants can use as food → DENITRIFICATION

nitrify /ˈnaɪtrɪfaɪ/ (**nitrifies, nitrifying, nitrified**) verb [T] **1** CHEMISTRY to add nitrogen to something **2** AGRICULTURE to improve the quality of soil by adding compounds of nitrogen to it

nitrifying bacteria /ˌnaɪtrɪfaɪɪŋ bækˈtɪəriə/ noun [plural] BIOLOGY bacteria in soil that change compounds of nitrogen in decaying plants into **nitrites** or **nitrates** → DENITRIFYING BACTERIA —*picture* → NITROGEN CYCLE

nitrite /ˈnaɪtraɪt/ noun [C] CHEMISTRY a chemical compound that is formed during the nitrogen cycle and is absorbed by plants. Chemical formula: NO_2

nitrogen /ˈnaɪtrədʒ(ə)n/ noun [U] CHEMISTRY an element that is a gas with no colour or smell. It makes up about 78% of the Earth's atmosphere. Chemical symbol: **N**

the ˈnitrogen ˌcycle noun [singular] BIOLOGY, CHEMISTRY the series of processes by which nitrogen in the atmosphere is changed into nitrogen compounds in soil, is taken up by plants, then eaten and released in waste by animals and decaying organic matter. It is then changed back into nitrogen in the atmosphere. These processes include **nitrogen fixation**, **nitrification**, and **denitrification**. —*picture* → on next page

ˌnitrogen diˈoxide noun [U] CHEMISTRY a very poisonous brown gas often present in **smog** and **exhaust** from vehicles. Chemical formula: NO_2

ˈnitrogen fiˌxation noun [U] BIOLOGY **1** the process by which nitrogen in the atmosphere is changed by bacteria into compounds in the soil that plants and other organisms can use **2** an industrial process in which chemicals are used to change nitrogen in the atmosphere into compounds used in making fertilizers

nitrogen narcosis /ˈnaɪtrədʒ(ə)n nɑːˌkəʊsɪs/ noun [U] HEALTH a condition in which nitrogen from air is absorbed into the blood of divers who use breathing equipment when they stay under water at great depths, usually more than 100 feet

nitrogenous /naɪˈtrɒdʒənəs/ adj BIOLOGY, CHEMISTRY relating to a compound, a protein, or a fertilizer that contains nitrogen

niˌtrogenous ˈwaste noun [U] BIOLOGY waste products from the body that contain nitrogen

ˌnitrogen ˈoxide noun [C/U] CHEMISTRY a chemical substance that is an **oxide** of nitrogen. **Nitrogen dioxide** and **nitrous oxide** are nitrogen oxides.

nitroglycerine or **nitroglycerin** /ˌnaɪtrəʊˈɡlɪsərɪn/ noun [U] CHEMISTRY a chemical that is used for making bombs

nitrous oxide /ˌnaɪtrəs ˈɒksaɪd/ noun [U] CHEMISTRY a sweet-smelling, sweet-tasting gas used in the past as an anaesthetic. Chemical formula: N_2O

nits /nɪts/ noun [plural] the eggs of insects called **lice** that people sometimes have in their hair

NLP /ˌen el ˈpiː/ noun [U] **1** COMPUTING natural language processing: the activity of using computers to produce or understand natural language **2** LANGUAGE neurolinguistic programming: a way of changing the relationship between someone's mind and language in order to affect their behaviour

NNP /ˌen en ˈpiː/ noun [C] ECONOMICS net national product

no¹ /nəʊ/ adv, determiner, interjection **1** used for giving a negative answer or for saying that something is not true: *'Is she still working at the clinic?' 'No, she works at the hospital now.'* ♦ *'You blame me whenever something goes wrong.' 'No, I don't.'* ♦ *'Do you want another glass of water?' 'No, thanks.'* ♦ *I asked Maria to help, but she said no.* **2** used for agreeing with a negative statement or request: *'Don't forget to make the reservation.' 'No, I won't.'* **3** not one, or not any: *There was no hospital in the town.* ♦ *I have no living cousins that I know about.* ♦ *There's no time to stop and talk.* ♦ *It's no surprise* (=it is not at all surprising) *that the company failed.* **4** used on signs or in instructions in order to say that something is not allowed: *No smoking.*
  PHRASES **in no time** in a very short time: *I'll have it fixed for you in no time.*
  no more/less/better etc not more, less, better etc than someone or something else: *The painting was no more than a few inches square.*

no² /nəʊ/ (plural **noes**) noun [C] a negative answer or vote: *His answer was a firm no.*

no. abbrev number

Noah's ark /ˌnəʊəz ˈɑːk/ in the Bible, the large boat that Noah built to save animals from a flood that covered the whole world

nobelium /nəʊˈbiːliəm/ noun [U] CHEMISTRY a radioactive metallic element in the **actinide** group of the periodic table. Chemical symbol: **No**

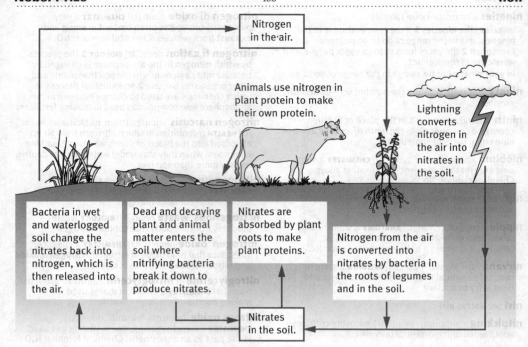

Nitrogen in the air.

Animals use nitrogen in plant protein to make their own protein.

Lightning converts nitrogen in the air into nitrates in the soil.

Bacteria in wet and waterlogged soil change the nitrates back into nitrogen, which is then released into the air.

Dead and decaying plant and animal matter enters the soil where nitrifying bacteria break it down to produce nitrates.

Nitrates are absorbed by plant roots to make plant proteins.

Nitrogen from the air is converted into nitrates by bacteria in the roots of legumes and in the soil.

Nitrates in the soil.

the nitrogen cycle

Nobel Prize /ˌnəʊˌbel ˈpraɪz/ noun [C] an international prize given each year for chemistry, physics, medicine, literature, economics, or work towards world peace

nobility /nəʊˈbɪləti/ noun **1** [U] an honest and brave way of behaving that people admire **2 the nobility** [singular] SOCIAL STUDIES people in the highest social class in a country, especially in a **monarchy** (=country with a king or queen) or a former monarchy. Members of the nobility usually have titles that are either **inherited** or given to them by the government.

noble¹ /ˈnəʊb(ə)l/ noun [C] a member of an **aristocratic** family in Europe in the past

noble² /ˈnəʊb(ə)l/ adj **1** behaving in an honest and brave way that other people admire **2** belonging to an **aristocratic** family in Europe in the past —**nobly** /ˈnəʊbli/ adv

'noble ,gas noun [C] CHEMISTRY one of the group of gases that includes **helium** and **neon**. Noble gases do not usually combine with anything else to form compounds.

nobleman /ˈnəʊb(ə)lmən/ (plural **noblemen**) noun [C] SOCIAL STUDIES a man who is a member of the **nobility**

nobody¹ /ˈnəʊbɒdi/ pronoun no one: *Nobody understands me.*

nobody² /ˈnəʊbɒdi/ noun [C] a person who is not at all important: *I'm tired of everyone treating me like a nobody.*

,no-'claims ,bonus noun [C] a reduction in the cost of insurance that people get when they have not claimed money in previous years for any accident or damage

nocturnal /nɒkˈtɜːn(ə)l/ adj **1** nocturnal animals are active at night **2** *formal* happening at night

,nocturnal e'mission noun [C] BIOLOGY a release of semen from the penis that takes place during sleep, as a result of a dream

nod /nɒd/ (**nods**, **nodding**, **nodded**) verb **1** [I/T] to move your head up and down in order to answer 'yes' or to show that you agree, approve, or understand: *I expected an argument, but she merely nodded and went out.* ♦ *Alison smiled and nodded in agreement.* ♦ *Luke was nodding his head thoughtfully.* **2** [I] to move your head once in order to make someone look at something, in order to greet someone, or in order to give someone a signal to do something: *'They're having fun', she said, **nodding towards** the kids on the beach.* ♦ *I **nodded to** my friend and she rang the bell.* —**nod** noun [C]

nodding donkey /ˌnɒdɪŋ ˈdɒŋki/ noun [C] a type of pump used for getting oil from under the ground —*picture* → OIL WELL

node /nəʊd/ noun [C] **1** HEALTH a small lump in the body **2** MATHS the place where lines cross or meet on a graph **3** the place where two parts of a structure meet **4** COMPUTING a point on a computer **network** where a message can be created or received

PHRASE **node of Ranvier** ANATOMY a gap in the protective layer around a nerve cell —*picture* → NEURON —**nodal** adj

nodule /ˈnɒdjuːl/ noun [C] **1** HEALTH a small mass of cells or tissue in the body that may be normal or may be a tumour **2** BIOLOGY a small round lump that grows on the roots of some **legumes** (=plants such as beans) that contain bacteria that carry out **nitrogen fixation** —**nodular** adj, **nodulation** noun [U]

noes noun [plural] *see* **no²**

'no-,frills adj including only the most basic features, and of acceptable quality but not very high quality

noggin /ˈnɒgɪn/ noun [C] CONSTRUCTION a piece of wood put into a wall to receive nails

noir /nwɑː/ adj ARTS, LITERATURE relating to a type of film or literature in which strong, sometimes violent, characters are involved in mysterious events —**noir** noun

noise /nɔɪz/ noun [C/U] a loud or unpleasant sound: *The dog made a deep growling noise in his throat.* ♦ *The neighbours said that we were **making** too much* ***noise.*** ♦ *We heard **the noise of** breaking glass.*

'noise pol,lution noun [U] ENVIRONMENT dangerous or annoying levels of noise

noisy /'nɔɪzi/ (**noisier, noisiest**) adj making a lot of noise, or full of noise: *noisy neighbours* ♦ *a noisy crowded bar* —**noisily** adv

nomad /'nəʊmæd/ noun [C] someone who belongs to a group of people who do not live in one place but move from place to place —**nomadic** /nəʊ'mædɪk/ adj

'no-man's-,land noun [singular/U] an area of land between two countries or armies that is not controlled by either of them

nominal /'nɒmɪn(ə)l/ adj **1** a nominal amount of money is very small and is much less than the real cost of something: *Transport can be provided **for a nominal fee**.* **2** officially described in a particular way, although this is not really true or correct: *He is still the nominal leader of the organization.* **3** the nominal amount or value of something is its official amount or value and not the real one **4** LANGUAGE concerning a noun, or used as a noun

nominalize /'nɒmɪnəlaɪz/ verb [T] LANGUAGE to change a verb or adjective in order to make a noun

nominate /'nɒmɪneɪt/ verb [T] to officially suggest that someone should be given a job, or that someone or something should receive a prize —**nomination** /,nɒmɪ'neɪʃ(ə)n/ noun [C/U]

nominative /'nɒmɪnətɪv/ noun [singular] LANGUAGE the form of a noun or pronoun when it is the **subject** of a verb —**nominative** adj

nominee /,nɒmɪ'niː/ noun [C] someone who has been officially suggested for a position or prize

non- /nɒn/ prefix not: *a non-alcoholic drink* ♦ *a non-smoker*

,non-ac'ceptance noun [U] BUSINESS the act of refusing to accept something such as a contract

nonagon /'nɒnəgɒn, 'nəʊnəgɒn/ noun [C] MATHS a geometric shape with nine straight sides

,non-alco'holic adj a non-alcoholic drink does not contain alcohol

non-aligned /,nɒn ə'laɪnd/ adj POLITICS a country that is non-aligned does not receive support from a more powerful country —**,non-a'lignment** noun [U]

,non-'aqueous adj SCIENCE not containing water

,non-biode'gradable adj ENVIRONMENT not able to decay naturally, and therefore harmful to the environment

nonchalant /'nɒnʃ(ə)lənt/ adj relaxed and not worried about anything —**nonchalance** noun [U], **nonchalantly** adv

,non-'combatant noun [C] someone who is not involved in fighting during a war

non-committal /,nɒn kə'mɪt(ə)l/ adj avoiding stating clearly what you think or what you plan to do: *He was non-committal about any future plans.*

,non-compati'bility noun [U] COMPUTING a situation in which two or more pieces of computer equipment or software cannot be used together

,non-com'petitive adj **1** not involving competition between businesses, organizations, or teams **2** BUSINESS unable to compete against other

businesses or organizations because of being too small or not efficient enough

,non-com'pliance noun [U] *formal* failure to follow an official rule or obey a law

,non-con'ductor noun [C] CHEMISTRY, PHYSICS a material that does not allow an electric current to pass through it

nonconformist /,nɒnkən'fɔːmɪst/ noun [C] someone who does not think or behave in the way that most people do —**nonconformist** adj

Nonconformist /,nɒnkən'fɔːmɪst/ noun [C] RELIGION a member of a **Protestant** church that is not part of the Church of England —**Nonconformist** adj

,non-contact 'force noun [C] PHYSICS a force that affects an object without actually touching it. Gravity is a non-contact force.

,non-'count adj LANGUAGE a non-count noun is **uncountable**

,non-'dairy adj non-dairy foods are not made from milk or cream

nondescript /'nɒndɪ,skrɪpt/ adj very ordinary, and not interesting or attractive

,non-'digital adj COMPUTING not relating to or using computers, the Internet, or other **digital** technology

,non-dis'closure a,greement noun [C] BUSINESS an agreement not to pass on information to anyone else. This often happens when companies are planning to work together and have to tell each other important information that they do not want anyone else to know.

,non-dis'criminatory adj SOCIAL STUDIES treating people from different ethnic, religious etc groups fairly, equally, and without **prejudice** —**non-discrimination** noun [U]

none /nʌn/ pronoun not any of something, or no amount of something: *I thought there was some coffee in the cupboard, but there's none there.* ♦ *The driver was killed, but **none of** the passengers was hurt.* ♦ *Some people might have only mild symptoms or **none at all**.*

PHRASES **none the better/worse etc** no better, worse etc than before

none the less see **nonetheless**

none other than used for saying who someone is when this is surprising or impressive: *The surprise guest was none other than David Beckham.*

none too not at all: *Hugo was none too pleased when I told him I was leaving.*

→ SECOND[1]

When **none** is the subject of a sentence and refers to members of a group, it can be used with a singular or plural verb: *None of his friends lives nearby/live nearby.* However, some people think that it is more correct to use a singular verb in these cases.

nonentity /nɒ'nentəti/ (plural **nonentities**) noun [C] someone who is not at all important or interesting

nonetheless /,nʌnðə'les/ adv *formal* despite what has just been said: *Everyone worked very hard. There were still problems, nonetheless.*

,non-e'vent noun [C] an event that is not as exciting as you expected it to be

non-existent /,nɒn ɪg'zɪst(ə)nt/ adj not real or present: *Wildlife is **virtually non-existent** in this area.*

,non-'fiction noun [U] LITERATURE writing that is about real people and events, not imaginary ones —**non-fiction** adj

,non-'finite adj LANGUAGE a non-finite verb is either a participle or an infinitive, and so does not show a particular tense

,non-'flammable adj not able to be burned easily

non-flowering /ˌnɒn ˈflaʊərɪŋ/ adj BIOLOGY a non-flowering plant does not produce flowers. Examples of non-flowering plants are **mosses**, ferns, and conifers.

,non-ˌgovern'mental organization noun [C] an NGO

,non-'human adj not human

,non-iˌdentical 'twin noun [C] BIOLOGY a **fraternal twin** → IDENTICAL TWIN

,non-in'vasive adj HEALTH non-invasive medical tests or treatments do not involve cutting the body or putting things inside it

,non-'linear adj **1** not moving in one direction, or not changing in one way at a regular speed **2** not telling a story in the order in which events happened

,non-'luminous adj not producing or reflecting light

,non-luminous 'flame noun [C] PHYSICS a flame that burns when there is plenty of oxygen. It gives out heat but not much light.

,non-'mammal noun [C] BIOLOGY an animal that is not a mammal

,non-'member noun [C] someone who does not belong to a particular organization

,non-'metal noun [C] CHEMISTRY a chemical element that is not a metal, for example carbon or oxygen. Non-metals are solids and gases and are not good conductors of heat and electricity. —**non-metallic** adj

,non-ne'gotiable adj fixed and not possible to change through discussions

,no-'nonsense adj doing things quickly and effectively without worrying too much about people's feelings: *a no-nonsense approach*

,non-'payment noun [U] a failure or a refusal to pay for something

,non-'perfect adj MATHS not able to be divided exactly into equal **roots**

,non-'porous adj SCIENCE a substance or object that is non-porous is one that liquids and gases cannot pass through —*picture* → OIL

,non-'profit or **,non-'profit-,making** adj a non-profit organization works to help people in some way rather than to make a profit

,non-proˌlife'ration noun [U] a policy of not increasing the number of nuclear or chemical weapons in the world

non-recoverable /ˌnɒn rɪˈkʌv(ə)rəb(ə)l/ adj COMPUTING used for describing computer information that is impossible to get back once it has been lost or deleted

,non-reducing 'sugar noun [C] CHEMISTRY, BIOLOGY a type of sugar that does not produce a reddish-brown substance when **Benedict's solution** is added to it

,non-re'newable adj ENVIRONMENT non-renewable energy, fuel, or other raw materials exist in limited amounts only and cannot be replaced once they have been used. Oil is an example of a **non-renewable resource**.

,non-'resident adj **1** not based in a particular country **2** not living in a house that you own

,non-re'strictive adj LANGUAGE a non-restrictive clause gives extra information about a noun or

pronoun, but the rest of the sentence can be understood without it. In writing, it is separated from the rest of the sentence by commas. In the sentence 'His father, who is an engineer, lives in Delhi', 'who is an engineer' is a non-restrictive clause.

nonsense /ˈnɒns(ə)ns/ noun [U] **1** ideas, behaviour, or statements that are not true or sensible: *So you believe the nonsense about ghosts?* ♦ *That's **a load of nonsense**.* ♦ *These accusations are **absolute nonsense**.* **2** unreasonable or annoying behaviour: *I won't **stand any nonsense** from anybody.* **3** words or sounds that seem like ordinary words but have no meaning: *a nonsense poem* —**nonsensical** /nɒnˈsensɪk(ə)l/ adj

non sequitur /ˌnɒn ˈsekwɪtə/ noun [C] a statement that has no connection with what was said before

,non-'smoking adj a non-smoking area is one where you are not allowed to smoke

,non-'standard adj **1** not the usual type **2** LANGUAGE non-standard forms of language are different from those that are usually considered to be correct

,non-'stop adj, adv without stopping: *a non-stop flight from Los Angeles to London* ♦ *The president spoke non-stop for two hours.*

non-unitary fraction /ˌnɒn ˌjuːnɪt(ə)ri ˈfrækʃ(ə)n/ noun [C] MATHS a fraction with a **numerator** (=number above the line) that is not 1, for example $\frac{3}{4}$

,non-'verbal adj not involving words or speech —**,non-'verbally** adv

,non-'violent adj **1** using peaceful methods to achieve political change: *a campaign of non-violent resistance* **2** non-violent crime does not involve physically hurting people —**,non-'violence** noun [U]

,non-'white adj *offensive* used for describing people who are not considered to be members of the race of people who have pale skins. This word is usually considered offensive because it suggests that the white section of the population of the world is more important than any other. —**non-white** noun [C]

noodles /ˈnuːd(ə)lz/ noun [plural] a type of long thin pasta

noon /nuːn/ noun [U] 12 o'clock in the middle of the day= MIDDAY: *We should be there by noon.*

'no ,one or **'no-,one** pronoun not any person= NOBODY: *There was no one around.* ♦ ***No one else** wanted the job.*

noose /nuːs/ noun [C] a piece of rope that is put around someone's neck and used for killing them by hanging them

nor /nɔː/ conjunction used after a negative statement when adding another negative statement: *I have not been asked to resign, nor do I intend to do so.* ♦ *She did not return that night, nor the night after.*

norm /nɔːm/ noun **1 the norm** [singular] something that is average, usual, or expected: *Students who fall below the norm should be encouraged to improve.* **2 norms** [plural] standards of behaviour that are accepted in a particular society: *Each culture develops its own **social norms**.*

normal /ˈnɔːm(ə)l/ adj **1** as expected, and not unusual or surprising in any way: *Temperatures are higher than normal.* ♦ *He didn't like anything to interrupt his normal daily routine.* ♦ *Life is beginning to **get back to normal** after the fire.* ♦ *Under normal circumstances, candidates are interviewed by the head of the department.* ♦ *It's normal to be nervous before an interview.* **2** thinking, behaving, or looking like most people: *He's no hero – just a normal human being.* ♦ *She's a perfectly normal messy child!*

normality /nɔːˈmæləti/ noun [U] a situation in which everything is normal

normalize /ˈnɔːməlaɪz/ verb **1** [I/T] to make something normal, or to become normal **2** [T] **TECHNOLOGY** to make a metal softer by heating and cooling it more quickly than when **annealing** it —**normalization** /ˌnɔːməlaɪˈzeɪʃ(ə)n/ noun [U]

normally /ˈnɔːm(ə)li/ adv **1** in most situations or cases = USUALLY: *Normally it takes about six days to arrange a visit.* ♦ *She's not normally late.* **2** in the usual way: *Bus services are operating normally.*

Norman /ˈnɔːmən/ adj relating to the 11th and 12th centuries in English history, when England was ruled by people from Normandy in northern France

normative /ˈnɔːmətɪv/ adj **SOCIAL STUDIES** *formal* relating to the parts of a culture that regulate how social activity operates and make people behave in similar ways

north¹ /nɔːθ/ noun **1** [U] **GEOGRAPHY** the direction that is on your left when you are facing the rising sun: *We were driving from north to south.* —*picture* → COMPASS **2 the north** [singular] the part of a place that is in the north: *How do you like living in the north?* ♦ *She grew up in the north of France.*

north² /nɔːθ/ adv **GEOGRAPHY** towards the north: *The geese will soon be flying north.* ♦ *a village 10 miles north of here*

north³ /nɔːθ/ adj **GEOGRAPHY 1** in the north, or facing towards the north **2** a north wind blows from the north

North Aˈmerica **GEOGRAPHY** a continent that stretches from north-west South America in the south to the Arctic Ocean in the north. The countries in it are Central America, Mexico, the USA, Canada, and Greenland. —*picture* → CONTINENT —**North Aˈmerican** adj, noun

the ˌNorth Atˌlantic ˈDrift **GEOGRAPHY** a current of warm water in the Atlantic Ocean that is part of the Gulf Stream. It makes the climate of north-west Europe warmer than it would otherwise be.

ˌnorth-ˈeast¹ noun **GEOGRAPHY 1** [U] the direction that is between north and east —*picture* → COMPASS **2 the north-east** [singular] the part of a place that is in the north-east —**ˌnorth-ˈeastern** adj

ˌnorth-ˈeast² adj **GEOGRAPHY** in the north-east, or facing towards the north-east —**ˌnorth-ˈeast** adv

northerly /ˈnɔːðəli/ adj **1** a northerly wind blows from the north **2** **GEOGRAPHY** towards or in the north

northern /ˈnɔːð(ə)n/ adj **GEOGRAPHY** in or from the north of a country or place: *northern Africa*

the ˌnorthern ˈhemisphere noun [singular] **GEOGRAPHY** the northern half of the Earth, north of the equator —*picture* → EARTH

northernmost /ˈnɔːð(ə)n,məʊst/ adj furthest towards the north

the ˌNorth ˈPole **GEOGRAPHY** the northern end of the Earth's axis —*picture* → EARTH

northward /ˈnɔːθwəd/ adj towards or in the north

northwards /ˈnɔːθwədz/ or **northward** /ˈnɔːθwəd/ adv towards the north

ˌnorth-ˈwest¹ noun **GEOGRAPHY 1** [U] the direction that is between north and west —*picture* → COMPASS **2 the north-west** [singular] the part of a place that is in the north-west —**ˌnorth-ˈwestern** adj

ˌnorth-ˈwest² adj **GEOGRAPHY** in the north-west, or facing towards the north-west —**ˌnorth-ˈwest** adv

nose /nəʊz/ noun [C] the part of the face above the mouth that is used for smelling and breathing: *I'd like to punch him on the nose.* ♦ *Can you pass me a tissue – my nose is running* (=liquid is coming out of it).
♦ *Excuse me, I just need to blow my nose* (=force liquid from it). —*picture* → BODY

PHRASES **look down your nose at sb/sth** to behave in a way that shows that you think someone or something is not good enough for you: *She looks down her nose at most boys.*

poke/stick your nose into sth to become interested or involved in something when you have no right to do this: *You have no right to poke your nose into my affairs!*

turn your nose up at sth *informal* to refuse to accept something because you do not think that it is good enough

under sb's nose if something happens under someone's nose, it happens in a place or situation where they should notice it, but they do not: *They were dealing drugs right under the noses of the police.*

nosebleed /ˈnəʊz,bliːd/ noun [C] **HEALTH** an occasion when blood comes out of someone's nose

nosedive /ˈnəʊz,daɪv/ noun [C] an occasion when a plane suddenly falls out of the sky with its front end pointing down —**nosedive** verb [I]

nosey /ˈnəʊzi/ another spelling of **nosy**

nosing /ˈnəʊzɪŋ/ noun [C] **CONSTRUCTION** on stairs, the horizontal part of the step that sticks out beyond the vertical part

nostalgia /nɒˈstældʒə/ noun [U] thoughts about happy times in the past that make someone want to be back in the past

nostalgic /nɒˈstældʒɪk/ adj remembering happy times in the past —**nostalgically** /nɒˈstældʒɪkli/ adv

nostril /ˈnɒstrəl/ noun [C] **ANATOMY** one of the two holes at the end of the nose —*picture* → BODY

nosy /ˈnəʊzi/ (**nosier, nosiest**) adj *showing disapproval* wanting to know about things that involve other people but not you —**nosiness** noun [U]

not /nɒt/ adv **1** used for giving a negative or opposite meaning to a sentence, expression, or word: *Barbara's not coming to the party.* ♦ *They told me not to worry.*
♦ *Not all children enjoy sport.* ♦ *The teacher could not even remember my name.* **2** used instead of repeating something in the negative: *Are you coming with me or not?* ♦ *I'll probably see you on Sunday; if not, it'll be Monday.* ♦ *'Is it going to be very expensive?' 'I hope not.'* **3** *spoken* used for forming a question when you expect the answer to be 'yes': *Isn't it a beautiful day?* ♦ *That was easy, wasn't it?*

PHRASES **not at all 1** in no way: *My parents were not at all pleased with my exam results.* **2** used as a polite reply when someone says 'thank you'

not one or **not a single** used for emphasizing that there are none of the people or things you are talking about: *Not one member voted in favour.*

not that used for adding a negative statement that reduces the effect of what you have just said: *You're using my pen – not that I mind* (=I don't mind).

notable /ˈnəʊtəb(ə)l/ adj unusual or interesting enough to be mentioned or noticed

notably /ˈnəʊtəbli/ adv *formal* especially

notarized /ˈnəʊtəraɪzd/ adj **LAW** signed by a notary and therefore official

notary /ˈnəʊtəri/ or **notary ˈpublic** noun [C] **LAW** someone who has the legal authority to make a document official

notation /nəʊˈteɪʃ(ə)n/ noun [U] a set of written signs or shapes that are used in something such as music or mathematics —**notational** adj

notch /nɒtʃ/ noun [C] a small cut on the edge or surface of something

note¹ /nəʊt/ noun [C]

1 short message	5 sound in music
2 sth that reminds	6 feeling/mood
3 detailed information	+ PHRASE
4 paper money	

1 a short written message to someone: *I've written him a note asking him to meet me tonight.* ♦ *We left them a note saying we'd be back later.*
2 something that you write on a piece of paper in order to remind yourself of something: *I've made a note of what needs to be repaired.*
3 notes [plural] details from something such as a lecture or a book that you write on a piece of paper so that you can remember them: *It'll help you later if you take notes.*
4 a piece of paper money: *a five-dollar note*
5 MUSIC an individual sound in music, or a written sign that represents it: *See if you can sing this note.* ♦ *He played a few notes on the piano.* —picture → MUSIC
6 a feeling or mood that is shown in the way that someone speaks or writes: *I'd like to end the discussion on a more cheerful note.* ♦ *There was a note of impatience in her voice.*
PHRASE **take note** to notice something and try to remember it because you think that it is important: *When the people speak with such passion, politicians should take note.* ♦ *I took note of what she said.*
→ COMPARE

note² /nəʊt/ verb [T] **1** formal to notice or realize something: *Liz noted the changes with satisfaction.* ♦ *Please note that all travellers must have a valid passport.* **2** to write something on a piece of paper so that you will have a record of it: *Isabel noted the details in her diary.*
PHRASAL VERB ,note sth 'down *same as* note² sense 2

notebook /ˈnəʊtbʊk/ noun [C] **1** a book with empty pages that you use for writing notes **2** COMPUTING a small flat computer that is easy to carry

noted /ˈnəʊtɪd/ adj well known and admired: *a noted British scientist* ♦ *He is particularly noted for his short stories.*

notepad /ˈnəʊtpæd/ noun [C] **1** several sheets of paper that are joined together along one edge and used for writing notes —picture → WORKSTATION **2** COMPUTING a simple wordprocessing program, used for writing notes

noteworthy /ˈnəʊtwɜːði/ adj worth giving special attention or praise to: *a noteworthy performance*

,NOT 'GO noun [singular] TECHNOLOGY the end of a plug gauge that is used to check the size of holes in machinery. If it is too big for the hole, then the hole is of an acceptable size.

nothing /ˈnʌθɪŋ/ pronoun **1** not anything: *There was nothing in the room except for a chair.* ♦ *She waited, but nothing happened.* ♦ *I saw nothing unusual in the situation.* ♦ *I knew nothing at all about looking after babies.* ♦ *If there's nothing else you want, can we go?* **2** not anything that is important or worth thinking about: *You're just making a fuss about nothing.* ♦ *A minor headache is nothing to worry about.*
PHRASES **be nothing like** to not be similar to someone or something in any way
for nothing 1 without any payment: *Some of the men volunteered to work for nothing.* **2** without a reason or

purpose: *Why did you call me down here for nothing?*
have/be nothing to do with to not be connected with or relevant to something or someone: *What I do in my own time has nothing to do with you.*
nothing but only: *The teacher has nothing but praise for the pupils in her class.*
→ STOP¹

notice¹ /ˈnəʊtɪs/ verb [T] to become conscious of someone or something by seeing, hearing, or feeling them: *After a few days here you hardly notice the noise!* ♦ *I noticed that the door was open.* ♦ *Did you notice how pale he looks?*

notice² /ˈnəʊtɪs/ noun **1** [C] a written sign or announcement that gives information or that warns people about something: *They put up a notice on the door saying they'd gone out of business.* ♦ *Have you read the notice on the board about next week's class?* **2** [U] information or a warning about something that is going to happen: *If you want to arrive early you must give advance notice.* ♦ *Finding a replacement could prove difficult at short notice.* ♦ *Lucy was ready to leave at a moment's notice.* **3** [U] the fact that someone pays attention to something, or finds out about something: *Their terrible working conditions were only brought to public notice last year.* ♦ *It has come to our notice that some cash is missing.* ♦ *It may have escaped your notice, but some of us are trying to work.*
PHRASES **give in/hand in your notice** to tell your employer that you are leaving your job
take notice to pay attention to something: *Wear what you like – no one seems to take any notice.* ♦ *Take no notice of him – he always behaves like that.*
until further notice until someone announces that a situation has changed or no longer exists: *The road is closed to traffic until further notice.*

noticeable /ˈnəʊtɪsəb(ə)l/ adj easy to see, hear, or feel: *There was a noticeable chill in the air.* —**noticeably** adv

noticeboard /ˈnəʊtɪsbɔːd/ noun [C] a board that has announcements and other information on it

notification /ˌnəʊtɪfɪˈkeɪʃ(ə)n/ noun [U] an official announcement about something

notify /ˈnəʊtɪfaɪ/ (**notifies, notifying, notified**) verb [T] to tell someone officially about something: *Winners will be notified as soon as possible.*

notion /ˈnəʊʃ(ə)n/ noun [C] an idea or belief that is wrong or silly: *Somehow he got the notion that I was interested in going out with him.*

notional /ˈnəʊʃ(ə)n(ə)l/ adj existing only as an idea, not as something real

notoriety /ˌnəʊtəˈraɪəti/ noun [U] a situation in which someone or something is famous for something that is bad

notorious /nəʊˈtɔːriəs/ adj famous for something that is bad: *This part of the city is notorious for its high crime rate.* —**notoriously** adv

notwithstanding /ˌnɒtwɪðˈstændɪŋ/ adv, preposition formal despite something

nought /nɔːt/ noun [C] **1** MATHS zero **2** nothing
PHRASE **noughts and crosses** a game for two players in which they take turns writing an X or an O in one of nine boxes until one player gets three Xs or three Os in a row

noun /naʊn/ noun [C] LANGUAGE a word or group of words used for referring to a person, thing, place, or quality. Nouns can be **countable** (=you can use the word in the plural), for example 'tree', 'car', and 'book', or **uncountable** (=you cannot use the word in the plural), for example 'peace', 'enjoyment', and 'eyesight': *'Kindness', 'mother'* and *'shopping'* are all nouns.

'noun ,phrase noun [C] LANGUAGE a phrase that is used in a sentence in the same way that a noun is used

nourish /'nʌrɪʃ/ verb [T] to give a person, animal, or plant the food or the substances in food that they need to live, grow, and be healthy

nourishing /'nʌrɪʃɪŋ/ adj nourishing food provides the substances that you need to live, grow, and be healthy

nourishment /'nʌrɪʃmənt/ noun [U] food or the substances in food that you need to live, grow, and be healthy

novel /'nɒv(ə)l/ noun [C] LITERATURE a long written story about imaginary characters and events

novelist /'nɒvəlɪst/ noun [C] LITERATURE someone who writes novels

novelty /'nɒv(ə)lti/ (plural **novelties**) noun **1** [C] something that is new and unusual **2** [U] the excitement or interest that something that is new or unusual creates

November /nəʊ'vembə/ noun [U] the eleventh month of the year, between October and December: *She's arriving in November.* ♦ *The play opens on November 15th.*

novice /'nɒvɪs/ noun [C] **1** someone who is just beginning to learn a skill or subject = BEGINNER **2** RELIGION someone who has entered a religious community but is not yet a full member

now /naʊ/ adv, conjunction, pronoun **1** at the present time: *She's been very ill, but she's much better now.* ♦ *The meeting should have finished by now.* ♦ *Nancy will be working full-time from now on.* ♦ *Prices will remain unchanged for now* (=until some future time). ♦ *'Can I ask you a question?' 'Not now – I'm busy.'* **2** immediately: *If you want to catch the bus, you'll have to leave now.* **3** used when you are saying that something happens as a result of something else: *Now I understand why she was so upset.* ♦ *Now that the war is over, there is a lot more food in the shops.* **4** *spoken* used when you want to get people's attention, or when you are going to talk about something new: *Now, are there any more questions?*

PHRASES **(every) now and then/again** sometimes, but not regularly: *Now and then I receive letters from my former students.*
just now 1 a very short time ago: *'When did you see him?' 'Just now.'* **2** at the present time: *Mrs Collins is busy just now.*

nowadays /'naʊə,deɪz/ adv at the present time: *Nowadays, doctors understand these diseases.*

nowhere /'nəʊweə/ adv **1** not in any place, or not to any place: *Nowhere does it say that we cannot have guests in our rooms.* ♦ *There is nowhere else for me to stay.* **2** in or to no particular place: *The old railway tracks lead nowhere.*

PHRASE **nowhere near 1** not nearly: *His latest album is nowhere near as good as his last.* **2** a long way away from somewhere

noxious /'nɒkʃəs/ adj harmful, or poisonous

nozzle /'nɒz(ə)l/ noun [C] a narrow part at the end of a tube through which a liquid or a gas flows —*picture* → AEROSOL

NQF /,en kju: 'ef/ noun [singular] EDUCATION National Qualifications Framework: an explanation of the levels against which a qualification can be recognized in England, Wales, and Northern Ireland

nuance /'nju:ɒns/ noun [C] a slight difference: *A translator has to be alert to every nuance of meaning.*

nuclear /'nju:kliə/ adj **1** PHYSICS, CHEMISTRY relating to energy that is released by changing the structure of the central part of an atom = ATOMIC: *a nuclear war* ♦ *nuclear weapons* ♦ *Are you in favour of nuclear disarmament* (=getting rid of nuclear weapons)? **2** PHYSICS relating to the central part of an atom: *nuclear physics*

,nuclear 'energy noun [U] PHYSICS **1** energy that is released during a **nuclear reaction 2** electricity produced by a **nuclear reactor**

,nuclear 'family noun [C] SOCIAL STUDIES a family unit that consists of a mother, a father, and their children

,nuclear 'fission noun [U] PHYSICS the process of **splitting** the nucleus of an atom, for example the nucleus of a radioactive **uranium** atom, in order to release nuclear energy → ATOM BOMB

,nuclear 'fusion noun [U] PHYSICS the process of combining the nuclei of particular atoms, for example hydrogen atoms, in order to release energy. This process takes place continuously in stars such as the Sun.

,nuclear 'physics noun [U] PHYSICS the scientific study of the nucleus of atoms

,nuclear 'power noun **1** [U] PHYSICS power, usually in the form of electricity, that is produced by making use of nuclear energy **2** [C] a country that owns nuclear weapons and is capable of using them

,nuclear re'action noun [C] PHYSICS a reaction that changes the structure of the nucleus of an atom, and produces a large amount of energy in the form of radiation

,nuclear re'actor noun [C] PHYSICS a system used for producing nuclear energy, usually in the form of electricity —*picture* → on next page

,nuclear 'weapon noun [C] a powerful bomb or other weapon that uses nuclear energy

nucleated village /,nju:klieɪtɪd 'vɪlɪdʒ/ noun [C] GEOGRAPHY a village in which houses are found around a central place such as a church

nuclei /'nju:kliaɪ/ SCIENCE the plural of **nucleus**

nucleic acid /nju:,kli:ɪk 'æsɪd/ noun [C/U] BIOLOGY an acid such as **DNA** or **RNA** that is found in the cells of all organisms

nucleolus /,njukli'əʊləs/ (plural **nucleoli** /,njukli'əʊlaɪ/) noun [C] BIOLOGY a small round body inside a cell nucleus, consisting of protein and RNA. It is involved in the formation of **ribosomes**.

nucleon number /'nju:kliɒn ,nʌmbə/ noun [C] CHEMISTRY, PHYSICS the number of protons and neutrons in the nucleus of an atom

nucleoplasm /,nju:kliəʊ'plæzəm/ noun [U] BIOLOGY the substance contained in a cell nucleus

nucleosynthesis /,nju:kliəʊ'sɪnθəsɪs/ noun [U] CHEMISTRY, PHYSICS the process by which the elements are created from protons and neutrons as a result of **nuclear reactions** within stars

nucleotide /'nju:kliə,taɪd/ noun [C] BIOLOGY an organic compound that is found in all living things and in **nucleic acids** such as DNA

nucleus /'nju:kliəs/ (plural **nuclei** /'nju:kliaɪ/) noun [C] **1** CHEMISTRY, PHYSICS the central part of an atom, consisting of protons and neutrons, and containing most of its mass —*picture* → ATOM **2** BIOLOGY the central part of a living cell that contains

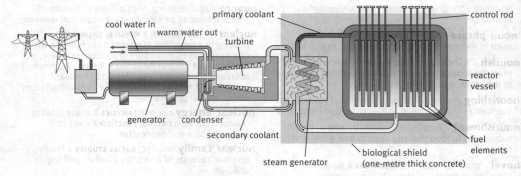

cool water in
warm water out
turbine
primary coolant
control rod
reactor vessel
generator
condenser
secondary coolant
steam generator
biological shield
(one-metre thick concrete)
fuel elements

nuclear reactor

its DNA and controls its growth and reproduction —*picture* → AMOEBA, CELL, FERTILIZATION, SEX CELL **3** the central or basic part of something: *These groups formed **the nucleus of** a new political party.*

nuclide /'nju:klaɪd/ noun [C] **CHEMISTRY** one or more nuclei in an atom that have the same number of protons and neutrons and the same energy, and so are a form of the same chemical element

nude¹ /nju:d/ adj not wearing clothes = NAKED

nude² /nju:d/ noun [C] **ARTS** a painting or other work of art showing someone who is not wearing clothes
PHRASE **in the nude** not wearing clothes

nudge /nʌdʒ/ verb **1** [T] to use a part of your body, especially your elbow, to give a little push to someone or something **2** [I/T] to move or to move something gradually or a little way —**nudge** noun [C]

nudity /'nju:dəti/ noun [U] the state of not wearing clothes, or of not covering a part of the body that is traditionally covered

nugget /'nʌgɪt/ noun [C] **GEOLOGY** a rough lump of gold or other metal as it is found in the earth

nuisance /'nju:s(ə)ns/ noun **1** [C] someone or something that annoys you or causes problems for you **2** [C/U] **LAW** illegal behaviour that is annoying or offensive to other people

null /nʌl/ adj **null and void LAW** with no legal effect

nullify /'nʌlɪfaɪ/ (**nullifies, nullifying, nullified**) verb [T] **1 LAW** to make something lose its legal effect **2** to make something lose its value or effect

numb¹ /nʌm/ adj **1** a part of your body that is numb has no feeling **2** not able to react or to show your emotions, often because of shock —**numbness** noun [U]

numb² /nʌm/ verb [T] to make a part of your body lose its ability to feel

number¹ /'nʌmbə/ noun

1 amount	4 a quantity
2 position	5 in language
3 telephone number	

1 [C] **MATHS** a sign or word that represents an amount or quantity: *Can you read the numbers on the chart?* ◆ *a number between one and ten*
2 [C] used for showing the position of something in a series: *The local trains will be arriving at platform number 4.*
3 [C] a telephone number: *Call this number to get a taxi.* ◆ *I must have dialled the **wrong number**.*
4 [C/U] a quantity of people or things: *a small **number of** shops* → AMOUNT¹
5 [U] **LANGUAGE** the form of a word that shows

whether you are referring to one thing or more than one thing: *If the subject is plural, the verb has to be in the plural number.*

number² /'nʌmbə/ verb [T] **1** to give a number to something **2** *formal* to consist of a particular quantity of people or things

number crunching /'nʌmbə ˌkrʌntʃɪŋ/ noun [U] *informal* work that involves doing a lot of calculations, especially when you think this is boring

'number ˌline noun [C] **MATHS** a line with numbers marked on it with equal spaces between them

ˌnumber 'one noun **1** [singular] the person or thing that is the first, best, or most important **2** [C] in popular music, the CD or record that has sold the most copies in a particular week

'number ˌplate noun [C] an official sign on the front and back of a car or other vehicle, with numbers and letters on it

numeracy /'nju:mərəsi/ noun [U] **EDUCATION** the ability to use numbers in mathematics

numeral /'nju:mərəl/ noun [C] **MATHS** a symbol that represents a number

numerate /'nju:mərət/ adj **EDUCATION** able to use and calculate numbers

numeration /ˌnju:mə'reɪʃ(ə)n/ noun **MATHS 1** [U] the process of giving a number to something **2** [C] a system for giving numbers to things or for counting them

numerator /'nju:məˌreɪtə/ noun [C] **MATHS** the number that appears above the line in a **common fraction** → DENOMINATOR

numerical /nju:'merɪk(ə)l/ adj expressed as numbers, or consisting of numbers —**numerically** /nju:'merɪkli/ adv

numeric keypad /nju:ˌmerɪk 'ki:ˌpæd/ noun [C] **COMPUTING** the part of a computer keyboard to the right of the main keys that has keys with numbers on them

numerous /'nju:mərəs/ adj existing in large numbers = MANY: *The machine broke down **on numerous occasions**.*

Num Lock /'nʌm ˌlɒk/ noun [U] **COMPUTING** a computer key that you press to make the number keys below it enter numbers, rather than move up and down a document

nun /nʌn/ noun [C] **RELIGION** a woman who belongs to a religious community of women → MONK

nurse¹ /nɜːs/ noun [C] **HEALTH** someone who is trained to look after ill or injured people, usually in a hospital

nurse² /nɜːs/ verb **1** [I/T] HEALTH to look after someone who is ill or injured **2** [T] to feel a strong emotion for a long time: *He had **nursed a grudge** (=had angry feelings) against them for ages.* **3** [T] to help yourself to get better after an illness or injury, for example by resting or getting medical treatment: *I took over as captain while she nursed a strained muscle.* ♦ *I'm nursing a cold.* **4** [T] if a woman nurses a baby, she feeds it by letting the baby suck milk from her breasts = BREASTFEED

nursery /'nɜːs(ə)ri/ (plural **nurseries**) noun [C] **1** a place where babies and young children are looked after, especially while their parents are at work **2** EDUCATION a school for very young children **3** AGRICULTURE a place where young trees and other plants are grown

'nursery ,rhyme noun [C] MUSIC, LITERATURE a short poem or song for young children

'nursery ,school noun [C/U] EDUCATION a school for very young children

nursing /'nɜːsɪŋ/ noun [U] HEALTH the job or skills of a nurse

'nursing ,home noun [C] HEALTH a place where old people live when they are too old or ill to look after themselves without help

nurture /'nɜːtʃə/ verb [T] **1** to provide the care and attention that are needed for a young child, animal, or plant to grow and develop **2** to help someone or something to develop

nut /nʌt/ noun [C] **1** a dry fruit that grows inside a hard shell on some types of tree. Many types of nut can be eaten: *Do you want some nuts and raisins?* **2** a small metal object with a hole in the middle that you screw a **bolt** through in order to fasten things together

nutmeg /'nʌtmeg/ noun [C/U] a brown powder used as a spice to give flavour to food. It comes from the hard seed of a tropical tree.

nutrient /'njuːtriənt/ noun [C] BIOLOGY a substance that all organisms need in order to live, grow, and be healthy. In animals, the nutrients are foods that contain energy, vitamins, and minerals. In plants, they are carbon dioxide, water, and **mineral salts**.

nutrient cycling /'njuːtriənt ,saɪklɪŋ/ noun [U] BIOLOGY, ENVIRONMENT the process by which nutrients move from the soil to plants, from plants to animals, and then back to the soil again

nutrition /njuː'trɪʃ(ə)n/ noun [U] **1** HEALTH the food that you eat and its effects on your health and growth **2** HEALTH the science of food and its effect on health and growth **3** BIOLOGY in animals, humans, and other organisms, the process of obtaining the food that is needed in order to live, grow, and be healthy **4** BIOLOGY in plants, the process of making the food that is needed in order to live, grow, and be healthy —**nutritional** /njuː'trɪʃən(ə)l/ adj, **nutritionally** /njuː'trɪʃən(ə)li/ adv

nu'tritional dis,order noun [C] HEALTH a condition or illness caused by a problem with the food someone eats

nutritious /njuː'trɪʃəs/ adj nutritious food provides the substances that you need in order to live, grow, and be healthy

nutshell /'nʌt,ʃel/ noun [C] the hard shell around a nut

nylon /'naɪlɒn/ noun [U] a strong artificial substance that is used in making plastic and clothes

nymph /nɪmf/ noun [C] **1** BIOLOGY a young insect that will become an adult by small changes without going through the stage of being a **pupa 2** LITERATURE in ancient Greek and Roman stories, one of the female spirits who live in rivers, mountains, or forests

o /əʊ/ (plural **o's**) or **O** (plural **O's**) noun **1** [C/U] the 15th letter of the English alphabet **2 O** [U] HEALTH a common blood group in the **ABO system**

oak /əʊk/ noun **1** [C] a large tree that can live for a very long time and that produces small hard fruit called **acorns 2** [U] the hard wood from an oak tree

oar /ɔː/ noun [C] a long stick with a wide flat blade at one end, used for rowing a boat

oasis /əʊ'eɪsɪs/ (plural **oases** /əʊ'eɪsiːz/) noun [C] GEOGRAPHY a place in a desert where there is water and where plants and trees grow

oath /əʊθ/ (plural **oaths** /əʊðz/) noun [C] a formal promise: *an oath of loyalty*
    PHRASE **under oath** if someone is under oath, they have officially promised to tell the truth in a court of law

oatmeal /'əʊt,miːl/ noun [U] crushed **oats** that are used in cooking

oats /əʊts/ noun [plural] AGRICULTURE a type of grain that people and animals eat *—picture* → CEREAL

OAU /,əʊ eɪ 'juː/ noun [singular] POLITICS Organization of African Unity: an organization of African countries between 1963 and 2002

obeah /əʊ'biːə/ noun SOCIAL STUDIES **1** [U] a religion from Africa based on a belief in magic, practised in the Caribbean **2** [C] an object believed to have magic power, used in obeah

obedient /ə'biːdiənt/ adj doing what a person, law, or rule says that you must do ≠ DISOBEDIENT —**obedience** noun [U], **obediently** adv

obese /əʊ'biːs/ adj extremely fat

obesity /əʊ'biːsəti/ noun [U] HEALTH a condition in which someone is extremely fat in a way that is dangerous for their health

obey /ə'beɪ/ (**obeys, obeying, obeyed**) verb [I/T] **1** to do what a person, law, or rule says that you must do: *Officers expect their troops to obey them without question.* ♦ *Drivers are not **obeying the** new traffic **laws**.* ♦ *The soldiers were used to **obeying orders**.* **2** to behave in an expected way in relation to something: *Molecules obey the laws of physics.*

Word family: obey	
*Words in the same family as **obey***	
■ obedience *n*	■ disobedience *n*
■ obedient *adj*	■ obediently *adv*
■ disobedient *adj*	■ disobey *v*

obituary /ə'bɪtʃuəri/ (plural **obituaries**) noun [C] a report in a newspaper that announces someone's death and that gives a short description of their life and achievements

object¹ /ˈɒbdʒekt/ noun [C]

1 thing you can see	**5** noun etc affected
2 sth you plan to achieve	indirectly
3 person or thing sth	**6** noun etc after
happens to	preposition
4 noun etc affected	
directly	

1 a thing that you can see and touch that is not living: *candles, vases, and other household objects* ♦ *There are 6,000 objects in the museum's collection.*
2 something that you plan to achieve: *His object was to gain time until help could arrive.* ♦ *The decision was made **with the object of** cutting costs.*
3 the person or thing that something happens to, or that people have a particular feeling about: *The band is currently **the object of** much media attention.*
4 LANGUAGE a noun, pronoun, or phrase that is affected in a direct way by the action of a verb, for example 'the report' in 'I've read the report'.
5 LANGUAGE a noun, pronoun, or phrase that is affected in an indirect way by the action of a verb, for example 'me' in 'Give me the pen'= INDIRECT OBJECT
6 LANGUAGE a noun, pronoun, or phrase that comes after a preposition, for example 'the bed' in 'He was lying on the bed'.

object² /əbˈdʒekt/ verb [I] to be opposed to something, or to say that you oppose it: *I'll take care of it, unless anyone objects.* ♦ *Local residents **objected to** the proposed development.* ♦ *I **object to** paying that much for milk.*

object code /ˈɒbdʒekt ˌkəʊd/ noun [C] COMPUTING a computer program in **binary** form that is used by the computer to run the program → SOURCE CODE

objection /əbˈdʒekʃ(ə)n/ noun [C/U] a statement that shows that you disagree with a plan, or a reason for your disagreement: *I think I'll go home now, if you **have no objection**.* ♦ *I would like to put forward several **objections to** this proposal.* ♦ *They **raised an objection** (=objected) to the plan.*

objective¹ /əbˈdʒektɪv/ noun [C] something that you plan to achieve: *I'm not sure I understand **the objective of** this exercise.* ♦ ***The main objective of** our department is to identify market opportunities.*

objective² /əbˈdʒektɪv/ adj **1** based only on facts and evidence, and not influenced by personal feelings or beliefs **2** LANGUAGE relating to the object of a verb or preposition —**objectively** adv, **objectivity** noun [U]

ob,jective 'lens noun [C] SCIENCE the lens in a microscope or similar piece of equipment that is nearest to the object that you are looking at through the equipment —*picture* → MICROSCOPE

object-oriented /ˈɒbdʒekt ˌɔːrientɪd/ adj COMPUTING an object-oriented computer language uses a system in which small parts of the program are considered as separate objects that can be put together to make the whole program

oblate /ˈɒbleɪt/ adj MATHS an oblate sphere has a smaller vertical diameter than its horizontal diameter

obligation /ˌɒblɪˈgeɪʃ(ə)n/ noun [C/U] **1** something that you must do for legal or moral reasons: *You are **under no obligation** to give anyone personal information.* ♦ *The firm **has an obligation to** its customers.* ♦ *He felt a certain **moral obligation** to help.* **2** a grateful feeling that you have towards someone who has done something for you: *She felt a certain **obligation towards** him.*

obligatory /əˈblɪgət(ə)ri/ adj *formal* something that is obligatory must be done in order to obey a law or rule

oblige /əˈblaɪdʒ/ verb **1** [T] *formal* to force someone to do something because it is the law, a rule, or a duty: *They **felt obliged to** offer him hospitality.* ♦ *You are **legally obliged to** pay this fine.* **2** [I/T] to help someone by doing something that they have asked you to do: *If there's anything else I can do, I'm always **happy to oblige**.*

oblique /əˈbliːk/ adj **1** MATHS an oblique angle is any angle that is not 90°, 180°, or 270° **2** MATHS an oblique line is a line that slopes **3** not expressing something directly: *an oblique reference to the war* —**obliquely** adv

ob'lique ˌdrawing noun [C/U] MATHS, ENGINEERING a simple three-dimensional drawing in which the side of the object you are looking at is drawn flat, and the other sides are drawn at 45° and with half the depth

obliterate /əˈblɪtəreɪt/ verb [T] to destroy something completely —**obliteration** /əˌblɪtəˈreɪʃ(ə)n/ noun [U]

oblivion /əˈblɪviən/ noun [U] **1** a situation in which someone or something has been completely forgotten **2** a state in which you do not notice what is happening around you

oblivious /əˈblɪviəs/ adj not noticing something, or not knowing about it

oblong /ˈɒblɒŋ/ noun [C] MATHS a shape with four straight sides and four right angles. Two of the parallel sides are longer than the other two sides = RECTANGLE —**oblong** adj

obnoxious /əbˈnɒkʃəs/ adj very rude, offensive, or unpleasant

oboe /ˈəʊbəʊ/ noun [C] MUSIC a musical instrument that you play by blowing air through a **reed** —*picture* → MUSICAL INSTRUMENT, ORCHESTRA

obscene /əbˈsiːn/ adj **1** offensive in a sexual way **2** extremely unfair or immoral

obscenity /əbˈsenəti/ (plural **obscenities**) noun **1** [U] behaviour or language that is sexually offensive **2** [C] a word or action that is sexually offensive

obscure¹ /əbˈskjʊə/ adj **1** not known about, or not well known **2** not clearly expressed, or not easy to understand —**obscurely** adv

obscure² /əbˈskjʊə/ verb [T] **1** to cover something so that it cannot be seen **2** to make something difficult to understand

obscurity /əbˈskjʊərəti/ noun [U] a state in which a person or thing is not well known, or is not remembered

observance /əbˈzɜːv(ə)ns/ noun **1** [U] the practice of obeying a law or rule, or of doing something according to a tradition **2** [C] a part of a religious or official ceremony

observant /əbˈzɜːv(ə)nt/ adj **1** noticing the things that happen around you **2** obeying religious laws

observation /ˌɒbzəˈveɪʃ(ə)n/ noun **1** [U] the process of watching someone or something carefully in order to find something out: *She's been admitted to hospital **for observation**.* **2** [C] a written or spoken comment about something that you have seen, heard, or felt **3** [U] the ability to notice things: *Most children have great **powers of observation**.* **4** [U] the practice of obeying a law, rule, or custom —**observational** adj

obser'vation ˌcar noun [C] TOURISM a railway carriage designed so that passengers can look at the view through large windows

observatory /əbˈzɜːvətri/ (plural **observatories**) noun [C] ASTRONOMY a building containing a large telescope that scientists use to study the stars and planets

observe /əb'zɜːv/ verb [T] **1** to notice or watch someone who is doing something, or something that is happening: *Similar trends may be observed in most modern societies.* ♦ *All evening Jane observed his behaviour closely.* **2** to accept and obey something such as a rule or agreement: *The proper procedures must be strictly observed.* **3** to accept and perform the customs connected with a particular day, festival, or event: *Russians observed a day of mourning for the victims.* **4** *formal* to make a written or spoken comment about someone or something —**observable** adj

observer /əb'zɜːvə/ noun [C] someone who watches, sees, or notices something

obsessed /əb'sest/ adj unable to stop thinking about someone or something all the time

obsession /əb'seʃ(ə)n/ noun **1** [U] an emotional condition in which someone or something is so important to you that you are always thinking about them **2** [C] someone or something that you cannot stop thinking about

obsessive /əb'sesɪv/ adj unable to stop thinking about someone or something in a way that is extreme —**obsessively** adv

ob,sessive com'pulsive dis,order noun [U] HEALTH a mental illness that makes someone keep repeating an action such as washing the hands, in order to avoid painful thoughts

obsolescent /ˌɒbsə'les(ə)nt/ adj becoming replaced by something newer and more effective

obsolete /'ɒbsəliːt, ˌɒbsə'liːt/ adj something that is obsolete is no longer used because it has been replaced by something newer

obstacle /'ɒbstək(ə)l/ noun [C] **1** a difficulty or problem that prevents you from achieving something = BARRIER **2** an object that you must remove or go around in order to move forwards = BARRIER

'obstacle ,course noun [C] **1** a series of objects or structures that someone has to get over, under, or through in an obstacle race **2** a series of problems that someone has to deal with in order to succeed in something

'obstacle ,race noun [C] a type of race in which people have to get over, under, or through a series of objects or structures

obstetrician /ˌɒbstə'trɪʃ(ə)n/ noun [C] HEALTH a doctor whose job is to check the health of a woman who is pregnant, and to help with the birth and early care of her child

obstinate /'ɒbstɪnət/ adj not willing to be reasonable and change your ideas or behaviour = STUBBORN —**obstinacy** noun [U], **obstinately** adv

obstruct /əb'strʌkt/ verb [T] **1** to block a path, passage, door etc so that it is difficult or impossible to get past **2** to take action in order to prevent something from happening

obstruction /əb'strʌkʃ(ə)n/ noun **1** [C] something that blocks a path, passage, door etc so that it is difficult or impossible to get past **2** [U] the process of taking action in order to prevent something from happening **3** [U] SPORTS an offence in a game such as football in which someone stops an opponent from moving to get the ball

obstructive /əb'strʌktɪv/ adj trying to prevent something by deliberately causing problems

obtain /əb'teɪn/ verb **1** [T] to get something that you want or need: *She has to obtain her father's permission before she does anything.* ♦ *Details can be obtained from the Department for Education.* **2** [I] *formal* if

something such as a rule or condition obtains, it exists, is used, or is accepted

obtainable /əb'teɪnəb(ə)l/ adj able to be obtained

obtrusive /əb'truːsɪv/ adj attracting attention in a way that is not pleasant or welcome ≠ UNOBTRUSIVE

obtuse /əb'tjuːs/ adj *formal* someone who is obtuse does not understand explanations or situations quickly

ob,tuse 'angle noun [C] MATHS any angle that is between 90° and 180° —*picture* → ANGLE

obvious /'ɒbviəs/ adj clear to almost anyone: *an obvious mistake* ♦ **For obvious reasons**, *I won't go into details.* ♦ *It's pretty obvious he's crazy about you.*

obviously /'ɒbviəsli/ adv **1** in a way that is clear for almost anyone to see or understand = CLEARLY: *Richards was obviously disappointed at being left out of the team.* ♦ *'Isn't he afraid?' 'Obviously not.'* **2** as most people would expect or understand = NATURALLY: *Obviously, I'll have to think about your offer carefully.*

occasion /ə'keɪʒ(ə)n/ noun [C] **1** a time at which something happens: *On one occasion* (=once) *the boat turned over in the water.* ♦ *He continues to work with us on occasion* (=sometimes). **2** a special or important time or event: *a great occasion in the nation's history* ♦ *This dress is perfect for a special occasion.* **3** [singular] *formal* a reason for something: *I've had no occasion to complain about their service.* → RISE

occasional /ə'keɪʒ(ə)nəl/ adj happening sometimes, but not frequently or regularly: *Chocolate is best kept as an occasional treat.* ♦ *He made occasional visits to the city.*

occasionally /ə'keɪʒ(ə)nəli/ adv sometimes, but not frequently or regularly: *Simmer the sauce for ten minutes, stirring occasionally.*

occluded front /əˌkluːdɪd 'frʌnt/ noun [C] GEOGRAPHY an area that forms when warm air is pushed upwards as a cold front moves past a warm front and pushes underneath it, so that cloud forms

the occult /ə'kʌlt, 'ɒkʌlt/ noun [singular] magic or **supernatural** forces and events —**occult** adj

occupant /'ɒkjʊpənt/ noun [C] **1** someone who is living in or using a place: *the current occupants of the building* **2** a person who has a particular job or position —**occupancy** noun [U]

occupation /ˌɒkjʊ'peɪʃ(ə)n/ noun **1** [C/U] a job: *Please give your name, address, and occupation.* **2** [C] something that you do in your free time: *Walking is now Dad's favourite occupation.* **3** [U] the act of living or staying in a building, room, or other place: *The new homes will be ready for occupation in August.* **4** [U] the action of using military force to go into a place and take control away from the people or government there: *the Roman occupation of Britain*

occupational /ˌɒkjʊ'peɪʃ(ə)nəl/ adj relating to, or caused by, someone's job

,occu,pational 'therapist noun [C] HEALTH someone who provides people who have been injured or very ill with special activities or equipment, in order to help them to get well again —**,occupational 'therapy** noun [U]

occupied /'ɒkjʊpaɪd/ adj **1** a seat, room etc that is occupied has someone using it **2** an area or country that is occupied has foreign military forces in it that are controlling it **3** busy doing something: *The game kept them occupied for the rest of the afternoon.*

occupier /'ɒkjʊˌpaɪə/ noun [C] **1** someone who lives in, works in, or uses a room, building, or area of land **2** someone who is in control of a place that they have entered in a group using military force

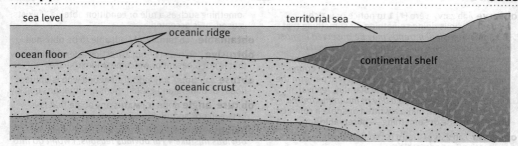

sea level

oceanic ridge

territorial sea

ocean floor

continental shelf

oceanic crust

cross section of an ocean

occupy /'ɒkjʊpaɪ/ (**occupies, occupying, occupied**) verb [T]

1 use a place	**4** keep sb busy
2 be in control of place	**5** regularly think about
3 have job/position	sth

1 to be using or in a room, building, or other place: *The family have occupied this farm for over a hundred years.* **2** to be in control of a place that you have entered in a group using military force: *The region was quickly occupied by foreign troops.* **3** to have a particular job or position in an organization or system, especially an important one: *Members of the group occupy positions of power in the country.* **4** to keep someone busy at an activity: *I need some way to occupy the kids for an hour.* **5** *formal* if something occupies someone, they think about it a lot: *My mind's been too occupied with moving house to think about a holiday.*

occur /ə'kɜː/ (**occurs, occurring, occurred**) verb [I] **1** to happen: *The police said that the accident occurred at about 4.30 pm.* **2** *formal* to exist or be found somewhere: *Radon gas occurs naturally in rocks such as granite.*

PHRASAL VERB oc'cur to sb if a thought or idea occurs to you, you suddenly start to think about it: *The thought of giving up never occurred to me.* ♦ *It suddenly occurred to her that Joe was afraid of being alone.*

occurrence /ə'kʌrəns/ noun [C/U] something that happens

OCD /,əʊ siː 'diː/ noun [U] HEALTH **obsessive compulsive disorder**

ocean /'əʊʃ(ə)n/ noun GEOGRAPHY **1** [C] one of the large areas of salt water that cover most of the Earth: *the Atlantic Ocean* —*picture* → WATER CYCLE **2 the ocean** [singular] the **sea** → DROP²

oceanarium /,əʊʃə'neəriəm/ noun [C] TOURISM a very large glass container where fish and other sea animals are kept

'ocean ,current noun [C] GEOGRAPHY a movement of the water on the surface of an ocean, caused by wind, the temperature, or the salt in the water

Oceania /,əʊsi'ɑːniə/ noun GEOGRAPHY the region of the world that includes the Pacific islands and the seas around them, sometimes also including Australia and New Zealand

oceanic /,əʊʃi'ænɪk/ adj GEOGRAPHY concerning the sea, or found in the sea

the ,oceanic 'crust noun [singular] GEOLOGY the part of the Earth's outer surface under the ocean —*picture* → OCEAN

,oceanic 'ridge noun [C] GEOGRAPHY a section of a range of mountains under the sea —*picture* → OCEAN

oceanography /,əʊʃə'nɒgrəfi/ noun [U] the scientific study of the sea —**oceanographer** noun [C]

ochre /'əʊkə/ noun [U] **1** ARTS a yellow, red, or brown type of earth used for making paint for artists **2** a brown-yellow colour —**ochre** adj

o'clock /ə'klɒk/ adv **one o'clock/four o'clock etc** used for saying what time it is when a clock shows the exact hour

OCR /,əʊ siː 'ɑː/ noun [U] COMPUTING optical character recognition: the ability of a computer to read printed or written numbers and words

octagon /'ɒktəgən/ noun [C] MATHS a shape with eight straight sides —*picture* → SHAPE —**octagonal** /ɒk'tægən(ə)l/ adj

octahedron /,ɒktə'hiːdrən/ noun [C] MATHS a solid shape consisting of eight flat surfaces with straight sides

octave /'ɒktɪv/ noun [C] MUSIC a series of eight musical notes in a musical scale

octet /ɒk'tet/ noun [C] MUSIC a group of eight musicians or singers

October /ɒk'təʊbə/ noun [U] the tenth month of the year, between September and November: *We'll begin harvesting the crops in October.* ♦ *The next meeting will be on October 9th.*

octogenarian /,ɒktəʊdʒə'neəriən/ noun [C] *formal* someone who is between 80 and 89 years old

octopus /'ɒktəpəs/ noun [C] a mollusc that lives in the sea and has a soft round body and eight long arms called **tentacles** —*picture* → SEA

odd /ɒd/ adj **1** unusual, or strange: *Harry's behaviour did seem a little odd.* ♦ *It's very odd that he hasn't sent you a birthday present.* **2** not happening frequently or regularly= OCCASIONAL: *The sky was clear blue with only the odd small cloud.* **3** MATHS an odd number is a whole number that cannot be divided exactly by two, for example 1, 3, 5, 7 etc ≠ EVEN **4** without the other thing from a pair of things: *odd socks*

PHRASE the odd one/man out someone or something that is different from the others in a group or list → ODDS

oddity /'ɒdəti/ (plural **oddities**) noun [C] someone or something that seems strange or unusual

,odd-'job ,man noun [C] a man who does general work such as repairs, in a building or for other people

odds /ɒdz/ noun [plural] **1** the chances of something happening: *The odds are* (=it is likely that) *they won't succeed.* **2** the chances that are used for calculating how much money you will get if the person or thing you **bet** on wins a race or competition

PHRASES against all (the) odds if you succeed in doing

something against all odds, you succeed in it despite problems and difficulties

at odds (with) if things are at odds with each other, they are different or opposite when they should be the same: *This statement is completely at odds with what was said last week.*

ode /əʊd/ noun [C] LITERATURE a poem that has been written for or about a particular person, thing, or event

odious /'əʊdiəs/ adj *formal* very unpleasant

odour /'əʊdə/ noun [C] a smell, especially one that is unpleasant

odourless /'əʊdələs/ adj with no smell

oedema /ɪ'diːmə/ noun [U] HEALTH an illness in which parts of the body become swollen because fluid has collected between the cells of the tissue

oesophagus /ɪ'sɒfəgəs/ noun [C] ANATOMY a tube that carries food from the **pharynx** to the stomach —*picture* → DIGESTIVE SYSTEM, ORGAN

oestrogen /'iːstrədʒ(ə)n/ noun [U] BIOLOGY, HEALTH a hormone that makes women and other female mammals develop typical female sexual features

oestrus /'iːstrəs/ noun [U] BIOLOGY the period when a female animal can produce babies if she **mates** with a male

of /əv, *strong* ɒv/ preposition

1 part of sb/sth	**6** in numbers/dates
2 concerning sb/sth	**7** created by sb
3 consisting of sth	**8** giving the cause
4 saying which	**9** stating who
5 saying who or what	

1 belonging to, connected with, or forming part of someone or something: *the colour of the sky* ♦ *The roof of the church was damaged.* ♦ *the President of Syria* ♦ *Lori is the daughter of my father's sister.* ♦ *She's one of my best friends.*

2 concerning or showing someone or something: *She had a photograph of him beside her bed.* ♦ *a history of Russia*

3 containing or formed from a particular type of person or thing: *He handed her a glass of water.* ♦ *a kilo of rice* ♦ *a collection of poems* ♦ *a group of teenage girls*

4 used after a general word for giving a specific example: *a feeling of sadness* ♦ *the month of April* ♦ *the city of Medina*

5 used after nouns that refer to actions, for saying who or what does the action or is affected by it: *the shouts of excited children* ♦ *the removal of a tumour*

6 used for giving a specific number or date: *She died at the age of 87.* ♦ *a price increase of 4 per cent* ♦ *the 27th of June*

7 written or produced by someone: *the paintings of Picasso* ♦ *the plays of Shakespeare*

8 used for saying what causes something: *He died of lung cancer.*

9 used for saying who shows a particular quality in a situation: *It was nice of you to help me.*

of 'course adv **1** used for saying 'yes' very definitely, in answer to a question **2** used for agreeing or disagreeing with someone: *'I'm sure everything's going to be OK.' 'Of course it is.'* **3** used for saying something that someone probably already knows or will not be surprised about: *He finally found out that Doug had lied, of course.* **4** used when you have just realized something: *Of course! Now I understand.*

off /ɒf/ adj, adv, preposition

1 not on	**8** not at school/ work
2 no longer attached	**9** not happening
3 away from a place	**10** reduced in price
4 leaving a vehicle	**11** a distance away
5 close to	**12** not fresh
6 not operating	+ PHRASE
7 removing clothes	

1 not on the top or surface of something: *The wind blew some tiles off the roof.* ♦ *Hold on tight so you don't slip off.*

2 no longer attached to something: *They cut a branch off the tree.* ♦ *One of the doll's legs fell off.*

3 leaving a place: *She said goodbye and went off to school.*

4 leaving a plane, train, bus etc: *They didn't see each other till they got off the plane.*

5 near a place, area, room etc: *an island five miles off the coast* ♦ *There is a bathroom off the bedroom.*

6 not switched on or operating: *All the lights were off in the house.*

7 used for saying that clothes or shoes are removed: *She kicked off her shoes and sat down.*

8 not at school or work, for example because you are ill or because it is not a working day: *Mum took two weeks off in August.* ♦ *Today is my father's* **day off**. ♦ *She's* **off sick** *today.*

9 used for saying that an event is no longer going to take place as planned: *Sorry, but the meeting's off.*

10 reduced in price by a particular amount: *There's now 30% off all carpets.*

11 used for saying how far away something is in time or space: *Christmas is only three weeks off.* ♦ *We could see a house a few miles off.*

12 food that is off is no longer fresh and is not good to eat

PHRASE **off and on** or **on and off** sometimes but not regularly: *The matter has been discussed off and on for several months now.*

offal /'ɒf(ə)l/ noun [U] the organs of animals that are eaten

,off-'balance adj in a position in which you feel that you are going to fall down

,off-'centre adj not exactly in the middle of an area or a thing

,off-'colour adj feeling slightly ill

,off-'duty adj not working: *an off-duty police officer*

offence /ə'fens/ noun **1** [C] LAW a crime or illegal activity for which there is a punishment: *motoring offences* ♦ *Killing these animals is* **a criminal offence**. ♦ **minor offences** *such as vandalism* ♦ *She had* **committed** *no* **offence** *under military law.* ♦ *Those arrested have* **been charged with** *public order* **offences**. **2** [U] the feeling of being angry, upset, or insulted by something that someone says or does: *advertisements that* **cause offence 3** [C] something that makes you feel angry and upset because it is insulting, unfair, or morally wrong: *This law is* **an offence to** *working people.*

PHRASE **take offence (at sth)** to feel angry and upset because of something that someone has said or done

offend /ə'fend/ verb **1** [T] to make someone angry and upset by doing or saying something: *They avoided saying anything that might offend their audience.* **2** [I] LAW to commit a crime —**offended** adj: *We feel saddened and offended.*

offender /ə'fendə/ noun [C] LAW someone who has committed a crime: *young offenders*

offense /əˈfens/ the American spelling of **offence**

offensive¹ /əˈfensɪv/ adj **1** unpleasant or insulting, and likely to make people upset or embarrassed: *offensive language* ♦ *offensive odours* ♦ *The advertisement **was offensive to** many women.* **2** used for attacking ≠ DEFENSIVE: *offensive weapons* —**offensively** adv

offensive² /əˈfensɪv/ noun [C] a major military attack

offer¹ /ˈɒfə/ verb [T] **1** to let someone know that you will give them something or do something for them if they want it: *They haven't offered me the job yet.* ♦ *He had **offered** cocaine **to** an undercover police officer.* ♦ *Thank you for **offering to** help.* **2** to say that you will pay a particular price for something: *I offered Jim 500 dollars for his car.* ♦ *Police are offering a reward to anyone with information.* **3** to provide something such as a product or service: *Smaller hotels can offer comfort at lower prices.* ♦ *The city **has a lot to offer** (=has many attractive features).* **4** to express your feelings towards someone: *I'd like to offer you my sympathy.* ♦ *He called the team manager to offer his congratulations.*

PHRASAL VERB ˌoffer sth ˈup to give thanks, praise, or prayers to God: *Lord, we offer up our prayers to you.*

offer² /ˈɒfə/ noun [C] **1** a statement in which you offer to give, pay, or do something if someone wants it: *a job offer* ♦ *I've decided to **accept your offer**.* ♦ *Did she **make you an offer for** (=tell you how much she would pay for) the bike?* ♦ *the government's **offer of** financial aid* **2** a special price that is lower than the usual price for something: *a half-price offer*

PHRASE **on offer 1** available, for example for people to buy or use **2** being sold for a lower price for a short time

offering /ˈɒf(ə)rɪŋ/ noun [C] **RELIGION** something that someone gives to a church or to a god

ˌoff-ˈguard adj surprised by something unexpected: *The questions **caught** her completely **off-guard**.*

offhand /ɒfˈhænd/ adj **1** unfriendly in the way that you treat someone **2** an offhand remark is one that you do not think carefully about

office /ˈɒfɪs/ noun **1** [C] a room or building where the people in an organization or department work, or the people who work there: *the company's Lusaka office* ♦ *Our offices are on the third floor.* ♦ *I left **the office** before 6.00 pm.* **2** [C] a room or building where you go for a particular service: *a tourist information office* **3** [C] a government department: *the tax office* ♦ *the Foreign Office* **4** [C/U] a position in a large powerful organization, especially a government: ***the office of** President* ♦ *Bob plans to **run for office** (=try to be elected) next year.* → PUBLIC OFFICE

ˈoffice ˌblock noun [C] a large building that contains many offices

ˈoffice ˌchair noun [C] a chair designed to be used while working at a desk or working on a **desktop** computer. It has a firm back, its height can be changed, and its seat can spin around. —*picture* → WORKSTATION

officer /ˈɒfɪsə/ noun [C] **1** someone with a position of power and authority in the armed forces: *an army officer* **2** a **police officer 3** someone with a position of authority in an organization

official¹ /əˈfɪʃ(ə)l/ adj **1** decided or done by people in authority, especially a government ≠ UNOFFICIAL: *the country's **official language*** ♦ *There will be **an official investigation** into last week's accident.* **2** relating to a job in which someone has authority or represents other people: *a list of her official duties*

official² /əˈfɪʃ(ə)l/ noun [C] someone with an important position in an organization: *a senior government official*

officially /əˈfɪʃ(ə)li/ adv **1** publicly and formally: *The new school won't be officially opened until next month.* **2** according to what governments or people in authority say, although it may not be true: *Officially, the government claims no knowledge of the subject.*

officious /əˈfɪʃəs/ adj *showing disapproval* someone who is officious is too serious about their job and duties, in a way that is annoying

ˌoff-ˈkey adj, adv **MUSIC** music or singing that is off-key does not sound good because the notes are slightly wrong

ˌoff-ˈlimits adj if a place is off-limits, you are not allowed to go there

offline /ˌɒfˈlaɪn/ adj, adv **COMPUTING 1** not directly connected to a computer **2** working on a computer but not connected to the Internet → ONLINE

offload /ˌɒfˈləʊd/ verb **1** [T] to give or sell something that you do not want to someone else **2** [T] to remove goods from a vehicle **3** [I/T] to tell someone all your problems so that you feel better

ˌoff-ˈpeak adj, adv at times when prices are lower because a service is not usually used by many people

ˌoff-ˈpiste adj **SPORTS** off-piste **skiing** is not done on the marked **pistes** (=tracks) but on snow that has not been skied on

ˌoff-ˈplan adj **BUSINESS** based on the plans of a building that has not yet been built

off-putting /ˌɒf ˈpʊtɪŋ/ adj used for describing something that you want to avoid because it is unpleasant

ˌoff-road ˈvehicle noun [C] a vehicle designed to be used in rough country such as hills and deserts

ˌoff-ˈseason noun [singular] **TOURISM** the period of the year when there is least business or activity

offset /ˈɒfˌset/ (**offsets, offsetting, offset**) verb [T] to balance the effect of something, with the result that there is no real change or difference: *Falling sales were offset by strong performances in other markets.*

offshoot /ˈɒfˌʃuːt/ noun [C] **1** a company, group, or organization that has developed from a larger one **2** a new branch or stem that grows on a plant

offshore /ˌɒfˈʃɔː/ adj, adv **1** in the sea, not on the land ≠ ONSHORE: *an offshore oil rig* ♦ *They're going to be working offshore.* **2** **ECONOMICS** involving money that is invested in another country, or referring to a business that is in another country: *offshore banking* ♦ *offshore investments*

ˌoffshore ˈbar noun [C] **GEOGRAPHY** a long raised area of sand below the surface of the sea near the land and parallel to it

offshoring /ˈɒfˌʃɔːrɪŋ/ noun [U] **BUSINESS** the practice of sending work to be done in another country where taxes, costs, or salaries are lower, or where rules are less strict, in order to save money

offside /ˌɒfˈsaɪd/ adj, adv **SPORTS** in the wrong position according to the rules in a game such as football or **hockey**

offspring /ˈɒfˌsprɪŋ/ (plural **offspring**) noun [C] **BIOLOGY** the young of any living thing, including humans

ˌoff-ˈwhite adj close to white in colour, but with slightly more yellow or grey

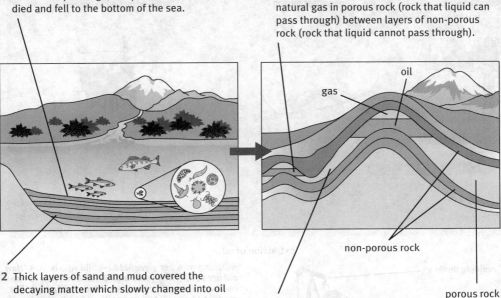

1 Millions of years ago, sea plants and animals died and fell to the bottom of the sea.

2 Thick layers of sand and mud covered the decaying matter which slowly changed into oil and natural gas.

3 Movement of the earth trapped the oil and natural gas in porous rock (rock that liquid can pass through) between layers of non-porous rock (rock that liquid cannot pass through).

oil

gas

non-porous rock

rock and water

porous rock

formation of oil

often /ˈɒf(ə)n/ adv **1** on many occasions, or in many situations: *Boredom often leads to poor behaviour.* ♦ *Very often the student can't understand the question.* ♦ *It's quite often impossible to park your car in the city.* **2** used for talking about how many times something happens in a particular period of time: *How often do you listen to the radio?*
PHRASES every so often sometimes, but not frequently: *She still visits me every so often.*
more often than not on most occasions, or in most situations: *More often than not, arguments can be avoided.*

ogive /ˈəʊdʒaɪv/ noun [C] **1** a pointed curved shape **2 MATHS** a graph showing a **cumulative frequency**

oh /əʊ/ interjection **1** used at the beginning of an answer or reply for showing that you understand or accept new information: *'Joe is her brother, not her boyfriend.' 'Oh, I see!'* ♦ *'He's just gone out.' 'Oh, has he?'* **2** used for expressing an emotion such as surprise, anger, or happiness: *Oh, what a beautiful view!* ♦ *Oh no! I've lost my keys.* **3** used when you start telling someone something, for example something that you have just remembered: *Oh Mum, did you see that note I left you?*

OHC /ˌəʊ eɪtʃ ˈsiː/ noun [C] **ENGINEERING** an **overhead camshaft**

ohm /əʊm/ noun [C] **PHYSICS** a unit used for measuring resistance in an electrical circuit. Symbol Ω

OHV /ˌəʊ eɪtʃ ˈviː/ noun [C] **ENGINEERING** an **overhead valve**

oil¹ /ɔɪl/ noun **1** [U] **GEOLOGY, CHEMISTRY** a thick dark smooth liquid used for making petrol, other fuels, and other chemicals: *The house is heated with oil.* ♦ *an oil company* **2** [C/U] **BIOLOGY** a thick smooth liquid form of animal or vegetable fat, used in cooking and medicines: *Cook the chicken in oil.* ♦ *olive oil* **3** [C/U] a thick smooth liquid used in an engine so that it will work smoothly **4** [C/U] a thick clear liquid used for protecting the skin or making it soft: *baby oil*

oil² /ɔɪl/ verb [T] to put oil on something

oil bath 'air ,cleaner noun [C] **ENGINEERING** a type of air filter in a car engine that collects particles of dirt in a container of oil

oil control 'piston ,ring noun [C] **ENGINEERING** a **piston ring** that controls the supply of oil to the piston

oilfield /ˈɔɪlˌfiːld/ noun [C] **GEOLOGY** an area where there is oil underground

'oil ,filter noun [C] **ENGINEERING** a filter that removes particles of dirt from engine oil

'oil ,gallery noun [C] **ENGINEERING** a passage in a vehicle's engine through which oil flows

'oil ,paint noun [C/U] **ARTS** a thick paint used by artists that contains oil

'oil ,painting noun [C/U] **ARTS** a picture painted with oil paint, or the art of painting this type of picture

oilpalm /ˈɔɪlˌpɑːm/ noun [C] **AGRICULTURE** a palm tree grown in tropical regions for its fruit and seeds, from which **palm oil** is obtained

'oil ,pump noun [C] **ENGINEERING** a pump that forces oil through an engine to make its moving parts move smoothly

'oil ,rig noun [C] a large structure with equipment on it for getting oil out from underground —*picture* → on next page

'oil ,slick noun [C] **ENVIRONMENT** a layer of oil on the surface of a large area of water, for example after a ship has sunk

'oil ,tanker noun [C] a large ship that carries oil

'oil ,well noun [C] a deep narrow hole that is dug in order to obtain oil —*picture* → on next page

oily /ˈɔɪli/ (**oilier, oiliest**) adj **1** covered with oil, containing oil, or like oil: *an oily rag* ♦ *oily fish* ♦ *an oily texture* **2** *showing disapproval* very polite in a way that does not seem sincere —**oiliness** noun [U]

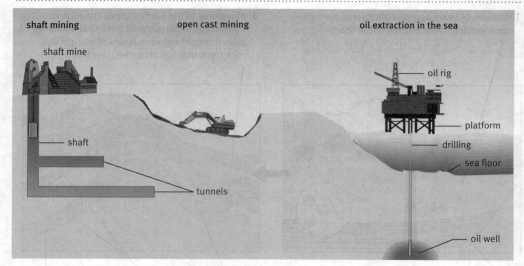

shaft mining   open cast mining   oil extraction in the sea

shaft mine

oil rig

platform

shaft

drilling

sea floor

tunnels

oil well

extraction of oil

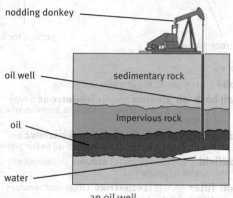

nodding donkey

oil well

sedimentary rock

oil

impervious rock

water

an oil well

ointment /'ɔɪntmənt/ noun [C/U] a thick smooth substance that you put on sore or injured skin

OK¹ /,əʊ'keɪ/ interjection **1** used for showing that you agree, approve, or understand. This is also used to ask if someone agrees, approves, or understands: *'I'd like to buy some new clothes.' 'OK.'* ◆ *So 'C' is the best answer. OK?* **2** used when you want to start or continue talking about something: *OK. Is everyone ready?* **3** used for showing that you want to end a conversation or argument: *OK! I'll try to do better next time.*

OK² /,əʊ'keɪ/ adj *spoken* **1** satisfactory, but not usually the best possible: *The food was OK.* **2** allowed, suitable, or not likely to make you upset: *The teacher said it was OK for me to leave class early.* **3** not injured, damaged, ill, or upset: *Are you OK? You look tired.* —**OK** adv: *I think I did OK in the exam.*

okapi /əʊ'kɑːpi/ noun [C] an African mammal like a **giraffe** without a long neck. It has a brown body with white stripes on its legs.

okay /,əʊ'keɪ/ another spelling of **OK**

okra /'əʊkrə/ noun [U] a vegetable with long green **pods** (=seed containers) that is used especially in African and Asian cooking —*picture* → VEGETABLE

old /əʊld/ adj **1** used for talking about the age of someone or something: *I'm older than my brother.* ◆ *She's the oldest girl in the class.* ◆ *A woman stood*

watching with her *3-year-old* (=child who is 3). ◆ *'How old are you?' 'I'm 5 years old.'* **2** someone who is old has lived a long time ≠ YOUNG: *A lot of old people live alone.* ◆ *I hope I'll still be healthy when I get old.* **3** something that is old has existed or been used for a long time: *an old belief* ◆ *I finally replaced my old sewing machine.* ◆ *He's an old friend of my father's.* **4** used for describing something that existed, happened, or was used in the past: *'Thy' is an old way of saying 'your'.* ◆ *The old road was very bumpy.* ◆ *She still gets letters from some of her old students* (=people that she taught in the past).

,old 'age noun [U] the period of time when you are old

Old English /,əʊld 'ɪŋglɪʃ/ noun [U] **LANGUAGE** the oldest form of the English language, spoken from around the year 450 to the year 1150

old-fashioned /,əʊld 'fæʃ(ə)nd/ adj **1** no longer modern or fashionable: *an old-fashioned dress* **2** no longer useful or suitable in the modern world = OUTDATED: *old-fashioned ideas about women who have jobs*

,old 'master noun [C] **ARTS** a painting by one of the famous European painters of the 16th, 17th, or 18th centuries

,old 'people's ,home noun [C] in some countries, a place where old people live and are looked after

the ,Old 'Testament **RELIGION** the first part of the Christian Bible → NEW TESTAMENT

oleum /'əʊliəm/ noun [U] **CHEMISTRY** a form of **sulphuric acid** that is used to make **detergents** that do not contain any soap

O level /'əʊ ,lev(ə)l/ noun [C] **EDUCATION** an examination taken by students at schools, usually those aged 15 to 16. O levels are taken in many countries, especially in Africa and Asia, but they are no longer taken in the UK: *She has O levels in Arabic, Maths, and English Literature.*

olfactory /ɒl'fækt(ə)ri/ adj *formal* relating to the sense of smell

oligarch /'ɒlɪgɑːk/ noun [C] **SOCIAL STUDIES** a member of a small group that runs a country or large organization

oligarchy /ˈɒlɪˌɡɑːki/ noun [C] **SOCIAL STUDIES** a small group of people who together govern a country or control an organization, often for their own purposes

olive[1] /ˈɒlɪv/ noun **1** [C] a small black or green fruit that is eaten or used for its oil **2 olive** or **olive green** [U] a dark yellow-green colour

olive[2] /ˈɒlɪv/ adj **1** olive skin is yellowish brown in colour **2** dark yellowish green in colour

,**olive 'oil** noun [C/U] a type of cooking oil that is made from **olives**

Olympiad /əˈlɪmpiˌæd/ noun [C] **SPORTS** formal a meeting of the Olympic Games

Olympian /əˈlɪmpiən/ noun [C] **1 SPORTS** someone who competes in the Olympic Games **2** one of the ancient Greek gods

Olympic /əˈlɪmpɪk/ adj **SPORTS** relating to the Olympic Games

the O,lympic 'Games or **the O'lympics** noun [plural] **SPORTS** an international sports event that takes place every four years

Olympus Mons /əˈlɪmpəs ˌmɒnz/ noun **ASTRONOMY** a volcano on Mars that is the largest volcano in the solar system

omelette /ˈɒmlət/ noun [C] a flat round food made by mixing eggs together and cooking them

omen /ˈəʊmən/ noun [C] something that shows whether good or bad things will happen in the future: *He was convinced that losing his bag was **a bad omen**.*

ominous /ˈɒmɪnəs/ adj making you think that something bad will happen: *an ominous silence* —**ominously** adv

omission /əʊˈmɪʃ(ə)n/ noun [C/U] someone or something that has not been included, or the fact of not including something: *I did notice one or two surprising **omissions from** the list.*

omit /əʊˈmɪt/ (**omits, omitting, omitted**) verb [T] to fail to include someone or something: *Important details had been **omitted from** the article.*

omnipotent /ɒmˈnɪpətənt/ adj formal powerful enough to do everything —**omnipotence** noun [U]

omnipresent /ˌɒmnɪˈprez(ə)nt/ adj formal able to be everywhere at the same time —**omnipresence** noun [U]

omniscient /ɒmˈnɪsiənt/ adj formal knowing everything —**omniscience** noun [U]

omnivore /ˈɒmnɪˌvɔː/ noun [C] **BIOLOGY** an animal that eats both plants and other animals. An animal that eats only plants is called a **herbivore** and an animal that eats only other animals is called a **carnivore**.

omnivorous /ɒmˈnɪv(ə)rəs/ adj **BIOLOGY** an omnivorous animal eats both plants and other animals

OMR /ˌəʊ em ˈɑː/ noun [U] **COMPUTING** optical mark reading

on /ɒn/ adv, preposition

1 supported by	12 operating
2 touching sth	13 taking part in sth
3 at a particular time	14 using a drug
4 in area	15 being a member
5 wearing sth	16 happening
6 being broadcast	17 immediately after
7 affecting who/what	18 giving phone
8 about sth	numbers
9 continuing	+ PHRASES
10 in or into a vehicle	
11 using particular equipment	

1 supported by something, or touching the top of it: *Chad was asleep on the floor.* ♦ *He left a note for you on the kitchen table.*

2 touching or attached to something: *There were several posters on the wall.* ♦ *The key is hanging on a hook in the hall.* ♦ *Evelyn kissed him on the cheek.*

3 used for stating the day or date when something happens: *He's coming home on Wednesday.* ♦ *My birthday is on the 27th of November.*

4 in a particular area, place, or position: *Wilson grew up on a farm.* ♦ *Look at the picture **on page** 94.*

5 wearing or carrying a particular thing on a part of your body: *Put your shoes on.* ♦ *He had a gun on him.*

6 being broadcast by radio or television: *I usually listen to the news on the radio.* ♦ *What time is the football match on?*

7 used for saying who or what is affected by something: *The attacks on Walters are very unfair.*

8 concerning a particular subject: *a report on the Civil War*

9 continuing to do something or to happen: *His lecture seemed to go **on and on** for hours.*

10 in or into a bus, train, plane etc: *We **got on** the train in Cape Town.*

11 used for saying what type of machine or equipment is used for doing something: *I recorded our conversation on my tape recorder.*

12 if a machine or piece of electrical equipment is on, it is working: *Who left the TV on?*

13 used for saying that someone takes part in an activity in which they travel or see something: *I met him when I was on a school trip to Hong Kong.*

14 using a particular drug: *She's on antibiotics for an eye infection.*

15 belonging to a team or committee: *There are only three directors on the board.*

16 happening, or planned to happen: *There's a wedding on at the church.*

17 formal immediately after another event: *Report to the reception desk on arrival.*

18 used for giving the phone number where someone can be contacted: *Call us on 0800 0900017.*

PHRASES **from now/then etc on** starting at a particular time and continuing to happen: *The new rules will apply to all members from now on.*

on the left/right at or to the left or right side: *His office is the last door on the left.*

→ FULL-ON, HEAD-ON, UPON

,**on-'board** adj fitted as part of a car, plane etc

once /wʌns/ adv, conjunction **1** on one occasion only: *Cathy's only been to visit us once.* ♦ *The class meets **once a week**.* ♦ *Take two pills once every six hours.* **2** in the past, but not now: *Did you know that Dan was once a policeman?* **3** as soon as: *Once you have completed the tests, write a report.*

PHRASES **all at once 1** at the same time: *Everybody started speaking all at once.* **2** literary suddenly: *All at once thunder shook the whole house.*

at once 1 immediately: *Bake for 35 minutes and then serve at once.* **2** at the same time: *You're trying to do too many things at once.*

(every) once in a while sometimes, but not very often

once again/once more 1 used for emphasizing that something happens again: *The concert was once again a tremendous success.* **2** used for saying that a situation becomes as it was before it changed: *We look forward to the day when there will be peace once more.*

once and for all completely and finally: *The Supreme Court's ruling should decide this matter once and for all.*

once or twice a few times, but not very often: *I've travelled on an underground train once or twice, but I don't really like it.*

once upon a time used for starting children's stories

oncology /ɒnˈkɒlədʒi/ noun [U] HEALTH the study and treatment of cancer —**oncologist** noun [C]

oncoming /ˈɒnˌkʌmɪŋ/ adj moving towards you: *oncoming traffic*

one /wʌn/ determiner, pronoun

1 number	5 the only
2 single thing	6 for emphasis
3 referring to things	7 in comparisons
4 people in general	+ PHRASES

1 the number 1: *They have one daughter and five sons.*
2 used for referring to a single person or thing when there are others of the same type: *I bought three T-shirts – do you want one?* ♦ *One passenger said she had been waiting for 13 hours.* ♦ *It's one of the best restaurants in town.* ♦ *Look at this old photo – my father is the one with the beard.*
3 (plural **ones**) used for referring to something when that type of thing has already been mentioned: *It was a problem, but not a major one.* ♦ *Paper bags aren't as strong as plastic ones.*
4 *formal* used instead of 'you' when you are making a statement about people in general: *One can never be sure what lies ahead.*
5 the only person or thing of a particular type: *My one concern is that not everyone will be able to attend.*
6 used for emphasizing a particular fact, person, or thing: *There's one thing you can be sure of – you won't get any help from him.*
7 used for mentioning the first of two or more similar people or things: *She had a glass in one hand and an empty bottle in the other.*

PHRASES **(all) in one** used for saying that someone or something can do many different things at the same time: *The device will give you telephone, television, and Internet all in one.*

one after another or **one after the other** used for saying that actions are done or things happen with very little time between them: *They visited four cities one after another.*

one by one first one, then the next, then the next, separately: *Add the eggs one by one.*

one day/night/year etc on a particular day, night, year etc in the past: *One evening Sam didn't come home.*

one or two a small number of people or things: *Carla said she had one or two ideas of her own.*

one aˈnother pronoun used for saying that each of two or more people does the same thing to the other, or has the same relationship with the other= EACH OTHER: *They all shook hands with one another.* ♦ *We respect one another's privacy.*

one-dimensional /ˌwʌn daɪˈmenʃ(ə)nəl/ adj MATHS something that is one-dimensional can only be measured in length, for example a line

ˈone-ˌman adj **1** made for just one person. Many people prefer to use the word **one-person**: *a one-man tent* **2** involving just one person. Many people prefer to use the word **one-person**: *a one-man show*

ˌone-ˈoff adj happening, done, or made only once —**ˌone-ˈoff** noun [C]

ˈone-ˌperson adj involving one person, or made for one person: *a one-person household*

onerous /ˈəʊnərəs/ adj *formal* something that is onerous causes worry or problems because it is very difficult to deal with

oneself /wʌnˈself/ pronoun *formal* the reflexive form of 'one', used for showing that people in general, including yourself, are affected by something that they do: *One has to think of oneself in these matters.*

ˈone-ˌsided /ˌwʌn ˈsaɪdɪd/ adj **1** unfair because of only showing one aspect of something: *a one-sided account of the conflict* **2** in a one-sided activity, one of the people or groups involved has a lot more skill, power etc than the other: *a one-sided contest*

ˈone-ˌtime adj used for saying what someone or something was in the past= FORMER: *the one-time Communist party leader*

ˌone-to-ˈone adj, adv involving only two people

ˈone-ˌway adj **1** with cars travelling in one direction only: *a one-way street* **2** a one-way ticket allows you to travel from one place to another but not back again ≠ RETURN

ˌone-way ˈvalve noun [C] PHYSICS, ANATOMY a **valve** (=part of an organ or tube that opens and closes to control flow) that only allows liquid or gas to flow in one direction

ˈone-ˌwoman adj involving only one woman: *a one-woman comedy act*

ongoing /ˈɒnˌɡəʊɪŋ/ adj still happening or being done: *an ongoing discussion*

onion /ˈʌnjən/ noun [C] a round vegetable with a thin dry skin and many layers of swollen leaves inside. It tastes and smells very strong and is a type of bulb. —*picture* → VEGETABLE

online /ˈɒnlaɪn/ adj COMPUTING connected to, or available through, a computer or a computer **network** such as the Internet: *an online bookshop* ♦ *online banking* —**online** /ˌɒnˈlaɪn/ adv

onlooker /ˈɒnˌlʊkə/ noun [C] someone who watches something happen but does not take part in it

only /ˈəʊnli/ adj, adv, conjunction **1** no one or nothing else except the person or thing that you are mentioning: *The flowers grow only on the island of Maui.* ♦ *Everyone promised to come, but only Ted turned up.* ♦ *This is the only letter my father ever wrote to me.* ♦ *My only reason for coming here was to see you.* ♦ *'What was that noise?' 'Don't worry – it's only the wind.'* **2** used for emphasizing that an amount, distance, or time is small: *She was only 18 when she got married.* ♦ *The police station was only 150 metres away.* ♦ *It only takes 5 minutes.* **3** not before a particular time: *They only got married last week.* **4** used for adding a comment to something that you have just said that makes it less true or correct: *Her coat is like mine, only it has four buttons.* ♦ *I'd love to come. The only thing is, I'll have to leave early.*

PHRASE **only just 1** a very short time ago: *The film's only just started, so you haven't missed much.* **2** by a small degree, or by a small amount: *I've got only just enough money for the bus fare.*

ˌonly ˈchild noun [C] a child who has no brothers or sisters

ˈon-ˌoff adj happening, stopping, and then happening again, several times: *an on-off relationship*

onomatopoeia /ˌɒnəmætəˈpiːə/ noun [U] LANGUAGE the use of words such as 'buzz' and 'thud' that sound like the sound which they refer to —**onomatopoeic** /ˌɒnəmætəˈpiːɪk/ adj

ˈon-ˌscreen adj, adv **1** COMPUTING on a computer screen: *The work is edited on-screen.* **2** happening or being in a television programme or film: *She plays his on-screen wife, Nancy.*

onset /'ɒn,set/ noun **1 the onset of sth** the beginning of something, especially something bad: *the onset of the disease* **2 LANGUAGE** the initial consonant or group of consonants in a syllable, for example 'str-' in strap

onshore /'ɒn,ʃɔː/ adj on land rather than on the sea ≠ OFFSHORE

onsite /'ɒn,saɪt/ adj, adv at the place someone is talking about

onslaught /'ɒn,slɔːt/ noun [C] **1** large numbers of people or things that come at the same time and are difficult to deal with **2** an attack

,on-the-'job adj done or happening while someone is at work

onto /'ɒntə/ preposition **1** into a position or area on an object or surface: *A tree fell onto the car, trapping the passengers inside.* ♦ *A spectator ran onto the field and attacked the referee.* **2** into a bus, train, ship, aircraft etc: *Slater tried to carry a gun onto the plane.* **3** used for saying that something is added to a list, statement, word etc: *To form the plural, just add 's' or 'es' onto the end.*

PHRASES be onto sb to have found out that someone has done something wrong: *He knew the police were onto him.*
be onto sth to have information that will help you to discover something important: *I think we may be onto something here.*

ontology /ɒn'tɒlədʒi/ noun [U] the type of **philosophy** that deals with the study of existence —**ontological** /,ɒntə'lɒdʒɪkl/ adj

onus /'əʊnəs/ noun [singular] *formal* if the onus is on someone to do something, it is their responsibility or duty to do it

onward /'ɒnwəd/ adj moving forwards, or continuing

,onward 'flight noun [C] **TOURISM** a flight to the next destination

onwards /'ɒnwədz/ adv if something happens or exists from a particular time onwards, it starts at that time and continues to happen or exist: *Most nights are busy from about 7 pm onwards.*

onyx /'ɒnɪks/ noun [U] a type of smooth stone with layers of white, brown, and pink in it, used in jewellery

ooze /uːz/ verb [I/T] **1** if a thick liquid oozes from something, or if something oozes a liquid, a small amount of it flows out slowly: *Juice oozed from the grapes.* **2** if someone or something oozes a particular quality, or if it oozes from them, they show that quality in a very obvious way: *Her brother oozes charm.*

opal /'əʊp(ə)l/ noun [U] a smooth white stone used in jewellery

opaque /əʊ'peɪk/ adj **1** opaque glass, liquid etc is difficult to see through ≠ TRANSPARENT **2 PHYSICS** an opaque substance does not allow light to pass through it —*picture* → BEAM **3** difficult to understand: *Most people found the theory rather opaque.*

op art /'ɒp ,ɑːt/ noun [U] **ARTS** a style of painting that uses lines and shapes that seem to move when you look at them

OPEC /'əʊpek/ Organization of Petroleum Exporting Countries: an organization that controls the supply and price of oil in the world market

open¹ /'əʊpən/ adj

1 when public can visit	7 for anyone
2 when you can see in	8 considering ideas
3 of a door/window	9 not decided
4 not blocked	10 when sth can be done
5 not covered	+ PHRASE
6 honest	

1 if a shop, restaurant etc is open, the public can use it or visit it ≠ CLOSED, SHUT: *The bar stays open all night.* ♦ *the campaign to keep the hospital open* ♦ *The house is only open to the general public for three weeks each year.*
2 something that is open has no cover, or has its edges separated, so that you can see what is inside: *an open drawer* ♦ *The kids were tearing open presents.* ♦ *A book lay open on the table.* ♦ *The baby's eyes were open.*
3 in a position that allows someone or something to pass through: *The bedroom door was open.* ♦ *Someone has left the gate wide open.*
4 if a road or method of communication is open, it is available for people to use
5 an open space or area is not covered or enclosed, or does not have many buildings, trees etc: *The top deck of the bus is open.* ♦ *the wide open spaces of the American West*
6 not keeping anything secret: *an open and honest discussion* ♦ *He has always been open about his drinking problem.*
7 available for anyone to take part in or see: *The meeting is open to the public.*
8 willing to consider many different possibilities: *Police are keeping an open mind about the cause of her disappearance.* ♦ *I have some ideas about where to go, but I'm open to suggestions.*
9 a situation that is open has at least two possible results: *Shall we leave it open for now, and decide at the meeting?*
10 if something is open to criticism, doubt etc, it is possible or reasonable to criticize it, doubt it etc: *The system is open to abuse.*

PHRASE the open sea/seas the wide areas of sea that are away from land

open² /'əʊpən/ verb

1 move sth to see in	6 begin
2 of a door/window	7 of a film/play
3 move part of body	8 of a flower
4 allow people in	+ PHRASE
5 first become available	+ PHRASAL VERB

1 [T] to separate the edges of something, or take off its cover, so that you can see what is inside: *She opened her shopping bag and took out an umbrella.* ♦ *Can you open this jar?* ♦ *Open your books at page 25.*
2 [I/T] if you open a door or window, or if it opens, you move it into a position that allows people or things to pass through: *Do you mind if I open a window?*
3 [I/T] if parts of your body open, or if you open them, they move to their widest position: *Open your mouth wide.* ♦ *Her eyes opened slowly.*
4 [I/T] if a shop, public building etc opens at a particular time, or if someone opens it, it becomes available for people to use or visit at that time: *The library doesn't open till 9.30.*
5 [I/T] if a new business, building etc opens, or if someone opens it, it becomes available for people to use for the first time: *They're opening a new library in the town.*
6 [T] to begin something: *I opened an account at the local bank.* ♦ *He opened his talk with a quotation from Shakespeare.* ♦ *The police have opened an investigation into his business affairs.*

7 [I] if a film or play opens, it starts being shown to the public

8 [I] if a flower opens, it moves into its widest position

PHRASE **open fire** to start shooting a gun

PHRASAL VERB **,open (sth) 'up 1** to open a locked door, container, or building: *He opens up the shop every morning.* **2** same as **open²** sense 5: *Donald wants to open up a bookshop.* **3** to make a situation possible or make something available to people, or to become possible or available in this way: *New markets are opening up every day.* ♦ *The job opened up a lot of opportunities for me.*

the open /'əʊpən/ noun [singular] any place that is outside, not in a building: *It's too hot out here in the open.*

PHRASE **(out) in the open** known about and not secret

the ,open 'air noun [singular] any place that is outside

,open-'air adj happening or existing outside

,open-'circuit ,voltage noun [U] TECHNOLOGY the voltage between the terminals of a welding machine when the machine is running but no welding is taking place

'open ,day noun [C] EDUCATION an occasion when an organization such as a school allows people to visit and see what is done there

open-ended /,əʊpən 'endɪd/ adj something that is open-ended has no limits: *an open-ended ticket*

opener /'əʊp(ə)nə/ noun [C] a tool or machine that is used for opening something

,open-'hearth ,furnace noun [C] TECHNOLOGY a type of **furnace** used to produce steel. It can produce much larger quantities than the **Bessemer converter**, but takes much longer.

,open 'house noun [U] a period of time when people are encouraged to visit a place

opening¹ /'əʊp(ə)nɪŋ/ noun [C]

1 when sth opens to public	3 opportunity
2 (hole) where sth opens	4 a job
	5 beginning

1 an occasion when a new shop, public building etc starts being available for people to use: *Lots of stars were invited to the Gallery's grand opening.* ♦ *the opening of a new section of ring-road*

2 a hole or place where something opens: *a narrow opening in the hedge*

3 an opportunity to do something: *His comments created an opening for efforts to resolve the crisis.*

4 a job that has become available: *There's an opening in the sales department.*

5 the beginning of a performance or film: *the opening of the play*

opening² /'əʊp(ə)nɪŋ/ adj **1** showing that something is open or has begun: *the opening ceremony of the Olympic Games* **2** the first of several similar things: *the opening paragraph*

'opening ,light noun [C] CONSTRUCTION the part of a window that opens

,open-'jaw adj TOURISM an open-jaw ticket allows a passenger to leave from one airport and return to a different one, or fly to one airport and return from a different one

openly /'əʊpənli/ adv in a direct or honest way that makes something obvious: *The report openly criticizes the military leadership.*

,open 'market noun [C] ECONOMICS a situation in which people can buy and sell things without any official rules about prices: *The land will be sold on the open market.*

openness /'əʊpənnəs/ noun [U] **1** an honest way of talking or behaving **2** a tendency to accept new ideas, methods, or changes

,open-'plan adj an open-plan office, house etc has few walls and a lot of open space

open sesame /,əʊpən 'sesəmi/ noun [singular] an easy way for you to get something that seems difficult or impossible

,open 'source noun [U] COMPUTING the practice of writing computer programs that are based on a code that is available for anyone to use

,open 'system noun [C] COMPUTING a computer system that is designed to work with parts or systems made by other companies

,open 'ticket noun [C] TOURISM a ticket that can be used at any time

,open 'verdict noun [C] LAW a court's decision stating that the cause of someone's death is officially not known

,open 'vowel noun [C] LANGUAGE a vowel that you pronounce with your tongue on the bottom of your mouth

opera /'ɒp(ə)rə/ noun [C/U] MUSIC a type of play that is performed by singers and an orchestra, or the art of performing these plays —**operatic** /,ɒpə'rætɪk/ adj → SOAP OPERA

'opera ,house noun [C] a theatre where operas are performed

operate /'ɒpəreɪt/ verb **1** [I/T] if equipment operates, or if you operate it, you use or control it and it works in the way it should: *The equipment was not operating properly.* ♦ *The motor operates at very high speeds.* ♦ *Do not operate machinery after taking this medication.* **2** [I/T] if an organization, company, service, or system operates, or if it is operated, it does its work: *The company has been operating in Europe for two years.* ♦ *Flights operate every day from Islamabad.* **3** [I] HEALTH to cut into part of someone's body for medical reasons: *Surgeons had to operate to remove the bullet.* ♦ *We may have to operate on your leg.* **4** [I] if something such as a rule, idea, or fact operates, it exists and has an effect in a particular situation

operating costs /'ɒpəreɪtɪŋ ,kɒsts/ noun [plural] BUSINESS the usual costs involved in running a business, not including the costs of producing the goods to be sold

operating profit /'ɒpəreɪtɪŋ ,prɒfɪt/ noun [C] BUSINESS the **gross profit** that a company makes from its normal activities of selling goods or services, before **expenses**, taxes, and payment of interest on loans are taken from it

operating system /'ɒpəreɪtɪŋ ,sɪstəm/ noun [C] COMPUTING the software that tells the parts of a computer how to work together and what to do

operating theatre /'ɒpəreɪtɪŋ ,θɪətə/ noun [C] HEALTH a room in a hospital where doctors perform medical operations

operation /,ɒpə'reɪʃ(ə)n/ noun **1** [C] a planned activity involving a lot of people, for example soldiers or police officers: *the biggest military operation for 20 years* **2** [C] an action or set of actions that is necessary to achieve something: *Connecting the water supply is a very simple operation.* **3** [C] HEALTH the process of cutting into someone's body for medical reasons: *She may need an operation on her knee.* ♦ *The baby had to have*

an operation. ♦ *A very experienced surgeon will* **perform the operation.** **4** [U] the way that something operates: *We are here to explain* **the operation of** *the new exam system.*

PHRASES **go/come into operation** to start to work or become effective: *The new production plant went into operation last month.*

in operation 1 working in the normal way: *Only one of our telephone lines is currently in operation.* **2** existing and having an effect in a situation: *Guidelines governing the use of email are now in operation.*

operational /ˌɒpəˈreɪʃ(ə)nəl/ adj **1** working correctly and able to be used: *The new computer system is* **fully operational. 2** relating to the way something works, especially a system or business: *operational efficiency*

operative /ˈɒp(ə)rətɪv/ adj working correctly and having the right effect

operator /ˈɒpəˌreɪtə/ noun [C] **1** someone who works for a telephone company and helps people with calls **2** someone whose job is to operate a machine or piece of equipment: *a crane operator* **3** a person or company that runs a business: *a bus operator*

operetta /ˌɒpəˈretə/ noun [C] MUSIC a musical entertainment that is like an opera but shorter and with a less serious story

ophthalmic /ɒfˈθælmɪk/ adj HEALTH relating to the eyes, and illnesses of the eyes

oph,thalmic opˈtician noun [C] an **optician**

ophthalmologist /ˌɒfθælˈmɒlədʒɪst/ noun [C] HEALTH a doctor who is an expert in illnesses of the eyes —**ophthalmology** /ˌɒfθælˈmɒlədʒi/ noun [U]

opiate /ˈəʊpiət/ noun [C] HEALTH a drug that contains **opium** and is used for reducing pain and making someone go to sleep

opinion /əˈpɪnjən/ noun [C] the attitude that someone has towards something, especially about how good it is: *What is your* **opinion of** *her latest novel?* ♦ *The professor* **has a high opinion of** *your work* (=thinks your work is good). ♦ *The students all* **gave their opinions.** ♦ *Despite our* **differences of opinion,** *we remained good friends.* ♦ *The book was a waste of time,* **in my opinion.** ♦ **Public opinion** *has turned against the government in recent months.*

oˈpinion ,poll noun [C] an attempt to find out what people in general think about a subject by asking a number of people questions about it

opium /ˈəʊpiəm/ noun [U] a powerful illegal drug made from the seeds of a type of **poppy**

opossum /əˈpɒsəm/ noun [C] a mammal found in North America and Australia with thick fur and a long tail

opponent /əˈpəʊnənt/ noun [C] **1** someone who is competing against you: *His opponent received only 36 per cent of the vote.* **2** someone who disagrees with something and tries to change or stop it: *opponents of the legislation*

opportunist /ˌɒpəˈtjuːnɪst/ noun [C] *showing disapproval* someone who is always trying to gain an advantage and is willing to behave in an unfair way —**opportunism** noun [U], **opportunist** adj

opportunistic /ˌɒpətjuːˈnɪstɪk/ adj **1** *showing disapproval* looking for and taking an opportunity, often in a way that is unfair or harms someone else: *opportunistic crimes* **2** HEALTH an opportunistic disease or infection is one that attacks someone who is already ill and who has a weak **immune system**

opportunity /ˌɒpəˈtjuːnəti/ (plural **opportunities**) noun **1** [C/U] a chance to do something, or a situation

in which it is easy for you to do something: *The trip sounds like a wonderful opportunity.* ♦ *We have given them* **ample opportunity** (=a lot of chances) *to voice their complaints.* ♦ *I'd like to* **take this opportunity to** *thank all of you for coming.* ♦ *We will inform you of any changes* **at the earliest opportunity** (=as soon as possible). ♦ **an opportunity for** *career advancement* ♦ *The programme gives students* **the opportunity to** *learn more about global warming.* **2** [C] a job that is available: *There are good opportunities in the marketing division.*

oppose /əˈpəʊz/ verb [T] to disagree with a plan or policy, and to try to stop it: *a group that opposes the death penalty* ♦ *There was a campaign to oppose the building of a nuclear reactor.*

opposed /əˈpəʊzd/ adj **1** someone who is opposed to something thinks that it should not happen: *He was* **bitterly opposed to** *the war.* **2** completely different: *The two ideas are directly opposed.*

PHRASE **as opposed to** used for referring to something that is very different from the thing that you have just mentioned: *The cost of these planes is 3 million dollars,* **as opposed to** *the 2 million dollars charged by their competitors.*

opposing /əˈpəʊzɪŋ/ adj **1** competing against someone else or against each other **2** opposing facts, opinions, or ideas are completely different from each other

opposite¹ /ˈɒpəzɪt/ adj **1** across from, or on the other side of, someone or something: *They sat at* **opposite ends** *of the room.* ♦ *On the* **opposite side** *of the road from the school was the church.* **2** completely different: *The car smashed into a lorry coming* **in the opposite direction.**

opposite² /ˈɒpəzɪt/ preposition across from, or facing someone or something: *the bus stop opposite the cinema* ♦ *Adam took the seat opposite her.*

opposite³ /ˈɒpəzɪt/ adv on the other side of an area from someone or something and facing towards them: *Jim and Rachel live opposite* (=on the other side of the road).

opposite⁴ /ˈɒpəzɪt/ noun [C] someone or something that is completely different from someone or something else: *Whatever I suggested, they would go and* **do the opposite.**

,opposite ˈangles noun [plural] MATHS the angles opposite each other that are formed when two lines **intersect** (=cross each other) —*picture* → ANGLE

,opposite ˈnumber noun sb's opposite number someone who has the same job as someone else in another organization or country

,opposite ˈpoles noun [plural] PHYSICS a situation in which the positive end of one magnet faces the negative end of another. Opposite poles attract each other.

the ,opposite ˈsex noun [singular] for men, women are the opposite sex, and for women, men are the opposite sex

opposition /ˌɒpəˈzɪʃ(ə)n/ noun **1** [U] strong disagreement with a plan or policy: *Public opposition* **to** *the government is growing.* **2 the opposition** [singular] a person, organization etc that someone is competing against **3 the Opposition** [singular] POLITICS the political parties in a country that are not part of the government

oppress /əˈpres/ verb [T] to treat people who are less powerful in an unfair and cruel way —**oppression** /əˈpreʃ(ə)n/ noun [U]

oppressed /əˈprest/ adj suffering from unfair and cruel treatment

oppressive /əˈpresɪv/ adj **1** unfair and cruel **2** oppressive weather is hot in an unpleasant way

opt /ɒpt/ verb [I] to choose from a range of possibilities: *We opted for the less expensive car.*

optic /ˈɒptɪk/ adj BIOLOGY, HEALTH relating to the eyes

optical /ˈɒptɪk(ə)l/ adj **1** BIOLOGY relating to sight **2** PHYSICS relating to or producing light **3** PHYSICS relating to the science of **optics**

optical brightener /ˌɒptɪk(ə)l ˈbraɪt(ə)nə/ noun [C] CHEMISTRY a substance that is added to **detergent** to make clothes look brighter or whiter after washing

ˈ**optical efˌfect** noun [C] PHYSICS the special way that something looks because of the way light is reflected

ˌ**optical ˈfibre** noun [C/U] PHYSICS a very long thin piece of transparent glass, used in telephone and computer systems for sending information in the form of light

ˌ**optical ilˈlusion** noun [C] something that looks very different from what it really is, usually because of the way it is drawn or lit

ˌ**optical ˈmark ˌreading** noun [U] COMPUTING the ability of a computer to read marks and save them in electronic form in its memory

ˈ**optical ˌpen** noun [C] COMPUTING a small piece of electronic equipment that you move across a printed page in order to store the words, either in its own memory or in your computer

optician /ɒpˈtɪʃ(ə)n/ noun [C] someone whose job is to test people's sight and make and sell glasses

ˌ**optic ˈnerve** noun [C] ANATOMY the large nerve that sends signals relating to sight from the retina in the eye to the brain —*picture* → EYE, RETINA

optics /ˈɒptɪks/ noun [U] PHYSICS the scientific study of light and seeing

optimal /ˈɒptɪm(ə)l/ adj **optimum** —**optimally** adv

optimism /ˈɒptɪˌmɪzəm/ noun [U] a tendency to be hopeful and to expect that good things will happen ≠ PESSIMISM

optimist /ˈɒptɪmɪst/ noun [C] someone who tends to be hopeful and to expect that good things will happen ≠ PESSIMIST

optimistic /ˌɒptɪˈmɪstɪk/ adj someone who is optimistic is hopeful about the future and tends to expect that good things will happen ≠ PESSIMISTIC: *She said that she was **optimistic about** the outcome of the trial.* —**optimistically** /ˌɒptɪˈmɪstɪkli/ adv

optimize /ˈɒptɪmaɪz/ verb [T] to make something such as a method or process as good or as effective as possible —**optimization** /ˌɒptɪmaɪˈzeɪʃ(ə)n/ noun [U]

optimum /ˈɒptɪməm/ adj best, or most suitable

option /ˈɒpʃ(ə)n/ noun [C] **1** something that you can choose to do: *We discussed all the options and chose what seemed the best method.* ♦ *She **had no option but to** admit the truth* (=she had to admit the truth). **2** BUSINESS the right to buy or sell something in the future **3** COMPUTING one of a range of things you can choose to do when you are using a computer program: *Choose the 'save' option from the File menu.*

PHRASE **keep/leave your options open** to avoid making a decision now so that you will still have choices later

optional /ˈɒpʃ(ə)nəl/ adj something that is optional is available if you want it, but you do not have to have it

≠ COMPULSORY: *The history course is optional.* —**optionally** adv

ˈ**opt-ˌout** noun [C] a decision not to be involved in something, or the freedom to make that decision

opulent /ˈɒpjʊlənt/ adj *formal* very impressive and expensive —**opulence** noun [U]

opus /ˈəʊpəs/ (plural **opuses** /ˈəʊpəsɪz/ or **opera** /ˈɒpərə/) noun [C] **1** MUSIC a piece of music, or a collection of pieces of music, written by a particular **composer 2** ARTS, LITERATURE an important piece of work by a writer, artist etc → MAGNUM OPUS

or /ɔː/ conjunction **1** used for connecting possibilities or choices. In a list, 'or' is usually used only before the last possibility or choice: *Which colour do you want – red, green, or blue?* ♦ *He's probably at lunch or in a meeting.* ♦ *'When will you get the results?' 'Either tomorrow or the day after.'* ♦ *The jury must decide whether the prisoner is guilty **or not**.* **2** used for including someone or something else in a negative statement: *She's had nothing to eat or drink all day.* **3** used for saying what will happen if someone does not do something: *You had better leave now, or I'll call the police.* **4** used for introducing a comment that corrects or adds more information to what you have just said: *There are six cashpoints, or ATMs, in the main airport terminal.*

PHRASE **two or three/once or twice etc** used between numbers to show that you do not mean them exactly: *There were three or four students in the corridor.* ♦ *It will only take a minute or two.*

oracy /ˈɔːrəsi/ noun [U] LANGUAGE the ability to express yourself fluently and grammatically when speaking

oral¹ /ˈɔːrəl/ adj **1** spoken, not written: *an oral agreement* **2** relating to the mouth: *oral hygiene* **3** HEALTH oral medicine is taken by mouth —**orally** adv: *The medicine is taken orally.*

oral² /ˈɔːrəl/ noun [C] EDUCATION a spoken examination, especially in a foreign language

ˌ**oral contraˈceptive** noun [C] HEALTH a pill that some women take every day to prevent themselves from becoming pregnant. It is usually called **the pill** and is a form of **birth control**.

ˌ**oral ˈhistory** noun [C/U] SOCIAL STUDIES spoken information about the past that is passed on to people in the present

orange¹ /ˈɒrɪndʒ/ noun **1** [C] a round fruit that has a thick orange-coloured skin —*picture* → FRUIT **2** [U] a colour that is between red and yellow

orange² /ˈɒrɪndʒ/ adj between red and yellow in colour

orang-utan or **orang-utang** /ɔːˈræŋ əˌtæn, əˈræŋ uːˌtæn/ noun [C] an **ape** with long orange hair —*picture* → MAMMAL

oration /əˈreɪʃ(ə)n/ noun [C] *formal* a formal public speech, especially one that is made as part of a ceremony

orator /ˈɒrətə/ noun [C] someone who is skilled at making speeches in public

oratorio /ˌɒrəˈtɔːriəʊ/ noun [C] MUSIC a long piece of classical music for singers and an orchestra, usually based on a religious story

oratory /ˈɒrət(ə)ri/ noun [U] the skill of making effective and impressive speeches in public

orbit¹ /ˈɔːbɪt/ noun **1** [C] ASTRONOMY the path that is taken by an object such as a planet that is moving around a larger object in space: *Space stations are designed to remain **in orbit** for years.* ♦ *the planet's*

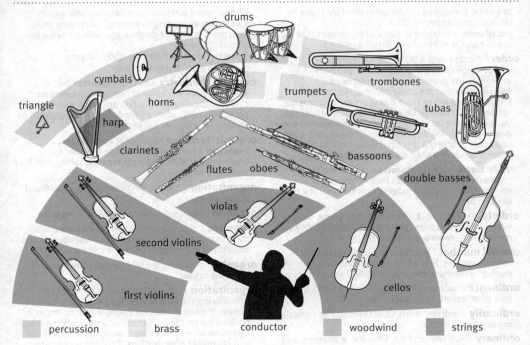

drums

cymbals

trombones

triangle

trumpets

horns

tubas

harp

clarinets

bassoons

flutes　oboes

double basses

violas

second violins

cellos

first violins

percussion　　brass　　conductor　　woodwind　　strings

orchestra

orbit around the sun **2** [singular] an area in which someone or something has power or influence **3** [C] **CHEMISTRY, PHYSICS** the path that is taken by an electron around the nucleus of an atom

orbit² /'ɔːbɪt/ verb [I/T] **1 ASTRONOMY** to make a circular movement around a large object in space such as a planet **2 CHEMISTRY, PHYSICS** to make a circular movement around the nucleus of an atom

orbital /'ɔːbɪt(ə)l/ adj **1** an orbital road goes around the outside of a large city **2 ASTRONOMY** connected with the orbit of one object around another larger object in space

orbiter /'ɔːbɪtə/ noun [C] **ASTRONOMY** a spacecraft or satellite that is designed to travel continuously around a planet or other object in space but not to land on it —picture → SPACE SHUTTLE

orchard /'ɔːtʃəd/ noun [C] **AGRICULTURE** a place where fruit trees are grown

orchestra /'ɔːkɪstrə/ noun [C] **MUSIC** a large group of musicians who use many different instruments in order to play mostly classical music —**orchestral** /ɔː'kestrəl/ adj

orchestrate /'ɔːkɪˌstreɪt/ verb [T] **1 MUSIC** to arrange a piece of music **2** to organize a complicated event or course of action so that you achieve the result that you want

orchid /'ɔːkɪd/ noun [C] a tropical flower with an unusual shape and a beautiful **scent**

ordain /ɔː'deɪn/ verb [T] **1 RELIGION** to make someone a priest, minister, or rabbi in an official religious ceremony → ORDINATION **2** formal to officially order that something should be done

ordeal /ɔː'diːl/ noun [C] an extremely unpleasant experience: They have suffered **a terrible ordeal**.

order¹ /'ɔːdə/ noun

1 arrangement	**6** general situation
2 request by customer	**7** group of people
3 official instruction	**8** group of
4 when law is obeyed	plants/animals
5 organized situation	**+ PHRASES**

1 [C/U] the way in which a set of things is arranged or done so that it is clear which thing is first, second, third etc: Please try to keep the pictures **in order** (=in the correct order). ♦ Some of the names on the list are **out of order** (=in the wrong order).

2 [C] a request for something to be made for you or brought to you: May I **take your order** (=write down what you want to eat or drink)? ♦ A major **order for** six new ships will guarantee the company's future.

3 [C] an instruction that is given by someone in a position of authority: Try to persuade your employees – don't just **give orders**. ♦ Soldiers must **obey orders**. ♦ I don't have to **take orders from** you (=obey you).

4 [U] a situation in which people obey the law: The new president's most urgent task will be to **maintain order**.

5 [U] a situation in which everything is well organized or arranged: I'm trying to bring a bit of order to the cupboard.

6 [singular] **SOCIAL STUDIES** the general situation at a particular time, especially the existing political, economic, or social system: The old **social order** was slowly breaking down.

7 [C] **RELIGION** a group of people, especially a religious group, who live according to special rules: a Buddhist order

8 [C] **BIOLOGY** a large group of plants or animals that are related to one another. An order includes more than a **family** and less than a **class**. —picture → TAXONOMY

PHRASES **in order** legally or officially correct: All your papers seem to be in order.

in order to do sth so that someone can do something,

or so that something can happen: *What do I have to do in order to convince them?*

out of order a machine or piece of equipment that is out of order is not working correctly

order² /ˈɔːdə/ verb **1** [T] to tell someone to do something, in a way that shows that you have authority: *The government has ordered an investigation into the cause of the accident.* ♦ *The judge ordered Hill to serve five years in prison for the robbery.* **2** [I/T] to ask for something to be brought to you or be made for you: *We sat down and ordered some beers.* ♦ *The airline has ordered 35 new planes.* ♦ *Are you ready to order?* **3** [T] to put things in a particular order: *The list of books is ordered alphabetically.*

'order ,book noun [C] **BUSINESS** a record of all the orders for goods or services from a company, considered as a way of judging how successful it is likely to be

orderly /ˈɔːdəli/ adj **1** arranged in a tidy way, or with everything in its correct place **2** well-behaved, or well-controlled —**orderliness** noun [U]

ordinal number /ˈɔːdɪn(ə)l ˌnʌmbə/ noun [C] a number such as 'first' or 'second' that shows what position something has in a series → CARDINAL NUMBER

ordinance /ˈɔːdɪnəns/ noun [C] *formal* an official order by a government, king, queen etc

ordinarily /ˈɔːd(ə)n(ə)rəli, ˌɔːd(ə)n'erəli/ adv usually = NORMALLY

ordinary /ˈɔːd(ə)n(ə)ri/ adj **1** normal or average, and not unusual or special: *It was just an ordinary Saturday morning.* ♦ *I didn't notice anything out of the ordinary* (=unusual). **2** not especially good, interesting, or impressive: *The inside of the house is rather ordinary.*

ordination /ˌɔːdɪ'neɪʃ(ə)n/ noun [C/U] **RELIGION** the process or religious ceremony by which someone is officially made a priest, minister, or rabbi

ordnance /ˈɔːd(ə)nəns/ noun [U] **1** military supplies, especially weapons, missiles, and bombs **2** large guns fixed to wheels

ore /ɔː/ noun [C/U] **CHEMISTRY, GEOLOGY** rock or earth from which metal can be obtained

oregano /ˌɒrɪ'gɑːnəʊ/ noun [U] a plant whose leaves are used in cooking for giving a special flavour to food. Oregano is a **herb**.

org /ɔːg/ abbrev **COMPUTING** private organization: used in email and Internet addresses

organ /ˈɔːgən/ noun [C] **1** **ANATOMY** a part of the body made up of several tissues that does a particular job, such as the heart or brain —*picture* → on next page **2** **MUSIC** a large musical instrument with pipes of different lengths, played by pressing keys on it **3** *formal* a part of an organization that is responsible for doing a particular job **4** *formal* a magazine, newspaper, or regular letter that contains official information from an organization such as a political party= MOUTHPIECE

organelle /ˌɔːgə'nel/ noun [C] **BIOLOGY** a structure in a cell that is designed to do a particular job, for example a nucleus

organic /ɔː'gænɪk/ adj

1 from living things	**4** in farming
2 containing carbon	**5** about the body's
3 not using chemicals	organs

1 **BIOLOGY** relating to or produced by organisms: *organic matter*

2 **CHEMISTRY** organic compounds contain carbon, and energy can be released from them → ORGANIC CHEMISTRY

3 **ENVIRONMENT** organic food or drink is produced

without using artificial chemicals: *organic apples*
4 **AGRICULTURE** relating to methods of farming and food production that do not use artificial chemicals: *organic farmers*
5 **HEALTH** connected with the body's organs
—**organically** /ɔː'gænɪkli/ adv

or,ganic 'chemistry noun [U] **CHEMISTRY** the scientific study of chemical compounds based on carbon, including compounds produced naturally by organisms or substances produced artificially such as plastics → INORGANIC CHEMISTRY

or,ganic 'fertilizer noun [C/U] **AGRICULTURE, CHEMISTRY** a fertilizer that is made from natural organic material, for example **manure**, rather than from artificial chemicals

organisation /ˌɔːgənaɪ'zeɪʃ(ə)n/ another spelling of **organization**

organise /ˈɔːgənaɪz/ another spelling of **organize**

organism /ˈɔːgə,nɪz(ə)m/ noun [C] **BIOLOGY** a living thing that is capable of growing and reproducing and consists of one or more cells → MICROORGANISM

organist /ˈɔːgənɪst/ noun [C] **MUSIC** someone who plays the organ

organization /ˌɔːgənaɪ'zeɪʃ(ə)n/ noun **1** [C] an officially organized group of people who work together or have the same aims, for example a company or a political party: *the human rights organization Amnesty International* ♦ *She belongs to a number of political and charitable organizations.* **2** [U] the way in which the different parts of something are arranged = STRUCTURE: *scientists investigating the organization of the human brain* ♦ *Officials have asked for help with the organization of the elections.* —**organizational** adj: *her excellent organizational skills*

organize /ˈɔːgənaɪz/ verb [T] **1** to prepare or arrange an activity or event: *Who's organizing the conference?* **2** to put things into a sensible order, or to create a system in which all the parts work well together: *Let's organize this agenda a little better.*

organized /ˈɔːgənaɪzd/ adj **1** planned carefully and effectively ≠ DISORGANIZED **2** an organized person arranges and plans activities carefully and effectively ≠ DISORGANIZED

,organized 'crime noun [U] criminal activities that are controlled by a large powerful secret organization

organizer /ˈɔːgə,naɪzə/ noun [C] someone who makes all the arrangements for an event or activity

organogram /ɔː'gænəgræm/ noun [C] **BUSINESS** a drawing or plan that gives the names and jobs of all the staff in an organization or department, showing how they are connected to each other

organophosphate /ˌɔːˌgænəʊ'fɒs,feɪt/ noun [C] **AGRICULTURE, CHEMISTRY** an organic compound containing **phosphorus** that is used as a **pesticide**. High concentrations of organophosphates are harmful to humans.

'organ ,system noun [C] **BIOLOGY** a group of organs in the body that work together to do a particular thing, for example the digestive system

orgasm /ˈɔːˌgæz(ə)m/ noun [C/U] the stage of sexual activity when sexual pleasure is strongest

orgy /ˈɔːdʒi/ (plural **orgies**) noun **1** [C] a party at which there is a lot of drinking and sexual activity **2** [singular] an occasion on which someone does something a lot, especially something bad: *an orgy of killing*

oriental /ˌɔːri'ent(ə)l/ adj of eastern Asia, or from eastern Asia

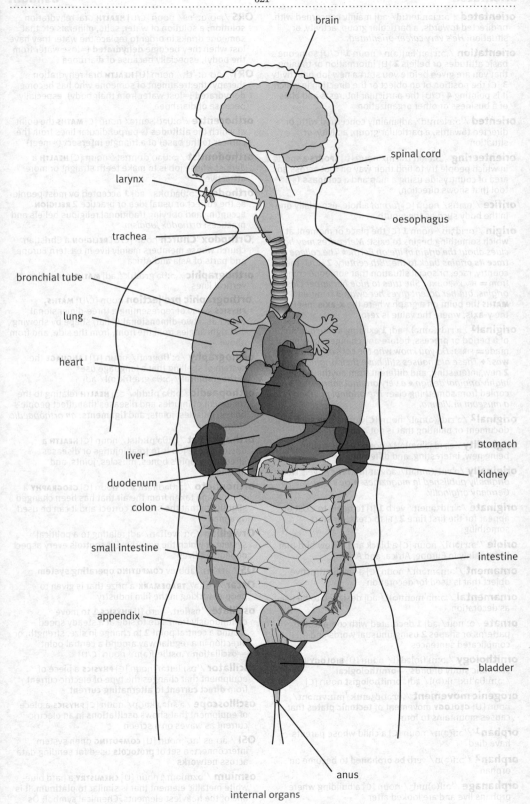

brain

spinal cord

larynx

oesophagus

trachea

bronchial tube

lung

heart

stomach

liver

kidney

duodenum

colon

small intestine

intestine

appendix

bladder

anus

internal organs

orientated /'ɔːriən,teɪtɪd/ adj mainly concerned with, or directed towards, a particular group, activity, or situation: *He's very career-orientated.*

orientation /,ɔːriən'teɪʃ(ə)n/ noun **1** [C/U] someone's basic attitudes or beliefs **2** [U] information or training that you are given before you start a new job or activity **3** [C] the position of an object or the direction in which it is pointing **4** [C/U] the particular interests and aims of a business or other organization

oriented /'ɔːrientɪd/ adj mainly concerned with, or directed towards, a particular group, activity, or situation

orienteering /,ɔːriən'tɪərɪŋ/ noun [U] **SPORTS** a sport in which people try to find their way on foot across an area of countryside using a map and a **compass** (=a tool that shows direction)

orifice /'ɒrɪfɪs/ noun [C] *formal* a hole, especially one in the body such as the mouth

origin /'ɒrɪdʒɪn/ noun **1** [C] the place or moment at which something begins to exist: *Meteorites may hold clues about **the origin of** life on Earth.* ♦ *The college can **trace its origins** back to the 18th century.* **2** [C/U] the country, race, or social situation that someone comes from= BACKGROUND: *She tries to hide her upper-class origins, but her accent gives her away.* **3** [singular] **MATHS** the point on a graph where the **x-axis** meets the **y-axis**, where the value is zero

original¹ /ə'rɪdʒ(ə)nəl/ adj **1** existing at the beginning of a period or process, before any changes have been made= FIRST: *Do you know who the car's original owner was?* ♦ *These old houses still have their original doors.* **2** new, interesting, and different from anything else: *a highly original design* ♦ *a very original songwriter* **3** not copied from something else: *The original painting is in a museum in Vienna.*

original² /ə'rɪdʒ(ə)nəl/ noun [C] something such as a document or painting that is not a copy

originality /ə,rɪdʒə'næləti/ noun [U] the quality of being new, interesting, and different

originally /ə'rɪdʒ(ə)nəli/ adv at first: *His novels were originally published in magazines.* ♦ *He's from Germany originally.*

originate /ə'rɪdʒəneɪt/ verb **1** [I] to begin to exist or appear for the first time **2** [T] to create or start something

oriole /'ɔːriəʊl/ noun [C] a black and yellow bird that lives mainly in Europe, Africa, and Asia

ornament /'ɔːnəmənt/ noun [C] a small attractive object that is used for decoration

ornamental /,ɔːnə'ment(ə)l/ adj designed to be used as decoration

ornate /ɔː'neɪt/ adj **1** decorated with complicated patterns or shapes **2** using unusual words and complicated sentences

ornithology /,ɔːnɪ'θɒlədʒi/ noun [U] **BIOLOGY** the scientific study of birds —**ornithological** /,ɔːnɪθə'lɒdʒɪk(ə)l/ adj, **ornithologist** noun [C]

orogenic movement /,ɒrəʊdʒenɪk 'muːvmənt/ noun [U] **GEOLOGY** movement of **tectonic plates** that causes mountains to form

orphan¹ /'ɔːf(ə)n/ noun [C] a child whose parents have died

orphan² /'ɔːf(ə)n/ verb **be orphaned** to become an orphan

orphanage /'ɔːf(ə)nɪdʒ/ noun [C] a building where orphans live and are looked after

ORS /,əʊ ɑː 'es/ noun [C/U] **HEALTH** oral rehydration solution: a solution of water, salts, minerals etc that someone drinks in order to replace the water they have lost when they become **dehydrated** (=lose water from the body), especially because of diarrhoea

ORT /,əʊ ɑː 'tiː/ noun [U] **HEALTH** oral rehydration therapy: the treatment of someone who has become **dehydrated** (=lost water from their body), especially because of diarrhoea

orthocentre /'ɔːθəʊ,sentə/ noun [C] **MATHS** the point at which the **altitudes** (=perpendicular lines from the corners to the base) of a triangle **intersect** (=meet)

orthodontist /,ɔːθə'dɒntɪst/ noun [C] **HEALTH** a dentist whose job is to make teeth straight or more attractive

orthodox /'ɔːθədɒks/ adj **1** accepted by most people as the correct or usual idea or practice **2** **RELIGION** accepting and obeying traditional religious beliefs and practices: *orthodox Judaism*

Orthodox 'Church noun [C/U] **RELIGION** a Christian church whose members mainly live in eastern Europe and parts of Africa

orthographic /,ɔːθə'græfɪk/ adj **MATHS** consisting of vertical lines

orthographic pro'jection noun [C/U] **MATHS**, **PHYSICS** a way of representing a three-dimensional object as a **two-dimensional** (=flat) shape by showing it at right angles from the front, from the side, and from above

orthography /ɔː'θɒgrəfi/ noun [U] **LANGUAGE** the system of spelling that a language uses — **orthographical** /,ɔːθə'græfɪk(ə)l/ adj

orthopaedic /,ɔːθə'piːdɪk/ adj **HEALTH** relating to the treatment of injuries and diseases that affect people's bones, muscles, joints, and **ligaments**: *an orthopaedic surgeon*

orthopaedist /,ɔːθə'piːdɪst/ noun [C] **HEALTH** a doctor whose job is to treat injuries or diseases affecting people's bones, muscles, joints, and **ligaments**

orthophoto /'ɔːθəʊ,fəʊtəʊ/ noun [C] **GEOGRAPHY** a photograph taken from the air that has been changed slightly, so that the scale is correct and it can be used as a map

Orwellian /ɔː'weliən/ adj relating to a political system in which the government controls every aspect of people's lives

OS /,əʊ 'es/ abbrev **COMPUTING** operating system

Oscar /'ɒskə/ **TRADEMARK** a prize that is given to people working in the film industry

oscillate /'ɒsɪleɪt/ verb [I] **PHYSICS** **1** to move continuously from side to side at a steady speed around a central point **2** to change in size, strength, or direction in a regular way around a central point —**oscillation** /,ɒsɪ'leɪʃ(ə)n/ noun [C/U]

oscillator /'ɒsɪ,leɪtə/ noun [C] **PHYSICS** a piece of equipment that changes the type of electric current from **direct current** to **alternating current**

oscilloscope /ə'sɪlə,skəʊp/ noun [C] **PHYSICS** a piece of equipment that shows **oscillations** in an electric current as waves on a screen

OSI /,əʊ es 'aɪ/ noun [U] **COMPUTING** open system interconnect: a set of **protocols** used for sending data across **networks**

osmium /'ɒzmiəm/ noun [U] **CHEMISTRY** a hard blue-white metallic element that is similar to **platinum**. It is one of the heaviest elements. Chemical symbol: **Os**

osmometer /ɒz'mɒmɪtə/ noun [C] CHEMISTRY, BIOLOGY an instrument that measures **osmotic pressure**

osmoregulation /ˌɒzməʊregjuˈleɪʃ(ə)n/ noun [U] BIOLOGY the process that controls the levels of water and salts in the cells and body fluids of an animal

osmosis /ɒz'məʊsɪs/ noun [U] PHYSICS, CHEMISTRY the process by which a **solvent**, usually water, slowly passes through a **semipermeable** membrane from a weaker solution to a stronger one, until they both have the same concentration

osmotic pressure /ɒzˌmɒtɪk 'preʃə/ noun [U] BIOLOGY the pressure that must be applied to a solution to stop osmosis

ossicle /'ɒsɪk(ə)l/ noun [C] ANATOMY a very small bone, especially in the **inner ear**

ostentatious /ˌɒstenˈteɪʃəs/ adj *showing disapproval* intended to impress people: *an ostentatious display of wealth* —**ostentation** noun [U], **ostentatiously** adv

osteoarthritis /ˌɒstiəʊɑːˈθraɪtɪs/ noun [U] HEALTH a serious medical condition that affects the body's joints, for example the knees, making it difficult to move

osteomalacia /ˌɒstiəʊməˈleɪʃiə/ noun [U] HEALTH a disease in which the bones become soft and bend. It is caused by a lack of vitamin D in food, or by a lack of sunlight on the skin.

osteopathy /ˌɒstiˈɒpəθi/ noun [U] HEALTH a treatment for conditions such as back pain or muscle injury —**osteopath** /'ɒstiəʊˌpæθ/ noun [C]

osteoporosis /ˌɒstiəʊpəˈrəʊsɪs/ noun [U] HEALTH a condition, mainly affecting women, in which the bones become weaker and more likely to break

ostinato /ˌɒstɪˈnɑːtəʊ/ noun [C] MUSIC a short musical phrase or melody that is repeated over and over, usually at the same **pitch**

ostrich /'ɒstrɪtʃ/ noun [C] a large African bird that runs very fast but cannot fly —*picture* → BIRD

OTE abbrev BUSINESS on-target earnings: used, in advertisements for jobs, after an amount of money for showing how much an employee will earn if they work as well as their employer expects them to

OTEC /'əʊtek/ noun [U] ENVIRONMENT ocean thermal energy conversion: a way of collecting and using solar energy that has been absorbed by the sea

other /'ʌðə/ determiner, pronoun **1** used for referring to additional people or things of the type that has already been mentioned: *a book aimed at teachers and others working in education* ♦ *We recycle paper, glass, and other waste materials.* **2** used for referring to a different person or thing from the one that has already been mentioned: *I wanted to go camping, but Kerry had other ideas* (=intended to do something else). ♦ *Not now. We'll talk about it some other time.* **3** used for referring to the second of two people or things: *I held onto the rope with my other hand.* ♦ *One of the twins was Reggie. What was the other one called?* **4** used for referring to the rest of the people or things in a group: *Beethoven's Ninth is much longer than his other symphonies.* ♦ *One boy fell off his chair and the others laughed.*

PHRASES **the other day/night** two or three days or nights ago: *I had a phone call from Mandy the other day.*

the other end/side/direction the opposite end, side etc, or the one that is furthest away: *Ashley sat at the other end of the sofa.* ♦ *A car was coming in the other direction.*

other than except for someone or something: *I don't*

have time to read anything other than the newspaper.
→ ANOTHER, HAND[1], NONE, WORD[1]

otherwise /'ʌðəˌwaɪz/ adv **1** used for saying that if one thing does not happen, something else will happen, usually something bad: *I hope the weather improves. Otherwise, we'll have to cancel the game.* ♦ *The programme has saved thousands of children who would otherwise have died.* **2** in a different or opposite way from what has been mentioned: *I plan to wait here unless someone tells me otherwise.* **3** except for the fact that you have just mentioned: *The show was a little long, but otherwise it was very good.*

OTP /ˌəʊ tiː 'piː/ noun [U] BUSINESS open trading protocol: a set of rules that has been developed to make buying and selling over the Internet easier and safer

otter /'ɒtə/ noun [C] a mammal that has a long body covered in brown fur and that can swim very well

ouch /aʊtʃ/ interjection *spoken* used for expressing a feeling of sudden pain

ought /ɔːt/ modal verb **1 ought to (do sth)** used for saying what is the right or sensible thing to do, or the right way to behave: *You ought to get up earlier.* ♦ *They ought to have listened to the warnings.* **2 ought to (do sth)** used when you have strong reasons for believing or expecting something: *We ought to win easily.*

oughtn't /'ɔːt(ə)nt/ short form a way of saying or writing 'ought not'. This is not often used in formal writing: *You oughtn't to make promises you can't keep.*

ounce /aʊns/ noun [C] a unit for measuring weight, equal to 28.35 grams. The written abbreviation for ounce is **oz**.

our /aʊə/ determiner belonging to or connected with us: *Most of our friends live in the village.* ♦ *When is our next meeting?*

ours /aʊəz/ pronoun the thing or things that belong to or are connected with us: *Ours is the third house on the left.* ♦ *If you don't have enough chairs, you can borrow ours.* ♦ *Some friends of ours are coming to visit.*

ourselves /aʊəˈselvz/ pronoun **1** the reflexive form of 'we', used for showing that both you and the group that you are a part of are affected by what you do together: *We kept ourselves awake by playing card games.* **2** used for emphasizing that you are referring to yourself and your group, and not to anyone else: *If nobody will help us, we will do it ourselves.*

PHRASES **(all) by ourselves 1** alone: *We had dinner by ourselves in our hotel room.* **2** without help from anyone: *We knew that we couldn't organize such a big event all by ourselves.*

(all) to ourselves not sharing something with anyone else: *Freddy's parents were away, so we had the house all to ourselves.*

oust /aʊst/ verb [T] to remove someone from a position of power

out /aʊt/ adv, preposition

1 not inside	**8** sun not hidden
2 not at home/work	**9** not burning
3 none left	**10** not possible
4 publicly available	**11** not correct
5 far away	**12** low sea level
6 unconscious	**+** PHRASES
7 not in game	

1 away from the inside of a building, vehicle, container etc: *The children are out in the fields.* ♦ *He opened the drawer and took out a large brown envelope.* ♦ *She went out, slamming the door behind her.*
2 away from your home or place of work: *Dr Hammond's*

out just now, visiting a patient. ♦ *We have young children, so we don't* **go out** *very often.*
3 with none of something left: *We're* **out of** *bread.* ♦ *What will we do when all the oil* **runs out**?
4 available for the public to buy or see: *Their new CD comes out next week.*
5 in another place that is far away: *They live out on a farm.*
6 unconscious: *I must have been out for five minutes.* ♦ *Arthur hit his head on a beam and* **knocked** *himself* **out**.
7 no longer taking part in a game or competition: *If we don't win today, we'll be* **out of** *the championships.*
8 if the sun or moon is out, it is not behind clouds
9 no longer burning or shining: *It got so cold when the fire* **went out**. ♦ *Don't forget to* **turn** *the lights* **out**.
10 *informal* if a particular idea, suggestion, or activity is out, it is not possible, or it cannot be accepted
11 used for saying that a number is not correct: *Their calculations were* **out by** *about two million pounds.*
12 if the tide is out, the sea is at a lower level on the land

PHRASES   **be out to do sth** or **be out for sth** to be aiming to do something or get something: *These are dangerous men, and they are out for revenge.*
one out of ten/99 out of 100 etc used for saying how large a part of a group or number is: *Only one out of ten graduates goes into the teaching profession.*
out of interest/respect/pity etc because of a particular feeling or attitude: *I went there out of curiosity, really.*

the outback /'aʊt,bæk/ noun [singular] **GEOGRAPHY** the large areas of land in Australia that are far away from any city or town

outboard motor /,aʊtbɔːd 'məʊtə/ noun [C] a motor that is fitted to the outside of a small boat, at the back end

outbound /'aʊt,baʊnd/ adj **TOURISM** travelling away from a particular place ≠ INBOUND

outbox /'aʊt,bɒks/ noun [C] **COMPUTING** the place on an email program where emails are stored before you send them

outbreak /'aʊt,breɪk/ noun [C] the sudden start of war, disease, violence etc

outbreeding /'aʊt,briːdɪŋ/ noun [U] **BIOLOGY**
1 breeding between two animals that are not related
2 fertilization between two or more separate plants, rather than within a single flower, or between flowers of the same plant → INBREEDING

outbuilding /'aʊt,bɪldɪŋ/ noun [C] a separate building that belongs to a house and is used, for example, for keeping animals or equipment in

outburst /'aʊt,bɜːst/ noun [C] a sudden spoken expression of a strong feeling, especially anger

outcast /'aʊt,kɑːst/ noun [C] someone who other people will not accept as a member of society or of a particular group

outcome /'aʊt,kʌm/ noun [C] the final result of a process or activity: *A second game will be played to determine the outcome.*

outcrop /'aʊt,krɒp/ noun [C] **GEOLOGY** a rock, or a group of rocks, that sticks up out of the ground

outcry /'aʊt,kraɪ/ noun [singular] an angry expression of protest or shock by a lot of people

outdated /,aʊt'deɪtɪd/ adj not modern enough to be useful

outdo /,aʊt'duː/ (**outdoes** /,aʊt'dʌz/, **outdoing**, **outdid** /,aʊt'dɪd/, **outdone** /,aʊt'dʌn/) verb [T] to be better than someone else at doing something

outdoor /,aʊt'dɔː/ adj done, used, or existing outside ≠ INDOOR

outdoors /,aʊt'dɔːz/ adv not in a building = OUTSIDE ≠ INDOORS

outer /'aʊtə/ adj **1** on or around the outside of something ≠ INNER: *The outer walls of the castle were over six feet thick.* **2** furthest away from the centre of something ≠ INNER: *the outer limits of the solar system*

outer 'core noun [singular] **GEOLOGY** the central part of the Earth that consists of **molten** (=liquid) rocks, iron, and **nickel**. It surrounds the inner core. —*picture* → EARTH

outer 'ear noun [singular] **ANATOMY** the part of the ear in humans and many other mammals that can be seen. It consists mainly of cartilage, and its job is to send **sound waves** to the **inner ear**.

outermost /'aʊtə,məʊst/ adj furthest away from a particular place or from the centre of something ≠ INNERMOST

outer 'planet noun [C] **ASTRONOMY** one of the planets in the solar system that is furthest away from the Sun

outer 'space noun [U] **ASTRONOMY** the area outside the Earth's atmosphere that contains the stars and planets

outfall /'aʊt,fɔːl/ noun [C] the place where water or liquid waste flows out of a pipe

outfield /'aʊt,fiːld/ noun [singular] **SPORTS** in baseball and **cricket**, the parts of the field that are furthest from the player who is batting

outfit /'aʊt,fɪt/ noun [C] **1** a set of clothes that are worn together **2** *informal* an organization, especially a small firm

outflow /'aʊt,fləʊ/ noun [C] a flow of water, gas etc out of a pipe

outgoing /,aʊt'gəʊɪŋ/ adj **1** someone who is outgoing is friendly and enjoys meeting and talking to people = SOCIABLE **2** soon to leave a position of authority or power ≠ INCOMING: *the outgoing prime minister* **3** going out of or away from a place ≠ INCOMING: *outgoing flights*

outgoings /'aʊt,gəʊɪŋz/ noun [plural] the amounts of money that someone has to spend regularly, for example on food

outing /'aʊtɪŋ/ noun **1** [C] a short journey that you take for enjoyment **2** [C/U] a public announcement saying that someone, especially a famous person, is gay

outlast /,aʊt'lɑːst/ verb [T] to last longer than someone or something else: *This system has outlasted many of its rivals.*

outlaw¹ /'aʊt,lɔː/ verb [T] to make something illegal: *They signed an agreement outlawing chemical weapons.*

outlaw² /'aʊt,lɔː/ noun [C] *old-fashioned* a criminal

outlet /'aʊt,let/ noun [C] **1** a way of expressing strong feelings, or of using extra physical energy **2** a pipe or hole through which gas or liquid flows out

outlier /'aʊt,laɪə/ noun [C] **MATHS 1** a point on a graph that is very far from the other points **2** a result that is very different from the other results in a set

outline¹ /'aʊtlaɪn/ verb [T] **1** to give the main ideas of a plan or a piece of writing: *The document outlines our company's recycling policy.* **2** to draw a line around the edge of something

outline² /'aʊtlaɪn/ noun [C] **1** an explanation that includes the general points about something, but not the details: *The chairman gave them a brief **outline of** the museum's history.* **2** a line that shows the outer edge or shape of something: *Through the mist we could see **the outline of** the island.*

outlive /ˌaʊtˈlɪv/ verb [T] **1** to live longer than someone else **2** to continue to exist after something else has stopped

outlook /ˈaʊtˌlʊk/ noun [singular] **1** an idea about what a situation will be like in the future: *The outlook for the economy is still uncertain.* **2** your general attitude to things: *a positive **outlook on** life*

outlying /ˈaʊtˌlaɪɪŋ/ adj existing away from a particular place: *outlying islands*

outnumber /ˌaʊtˈnʌmbə/ verb [T] if one group outnumbers another, there are more in the first group than in the second

out-of-date adj old and no longer useful

out-of-position welding /ˌaʊt əv pəˈzɪʃ(ə)n ˌweldɪŋ/ noun [U] **TECHNOLOGY** welding that takes place in anything other than a flat position. It includes **horizontal welding**, **vertical welding**, and **overhead welding**.

outpatient /ˈaʊtˌpeɪʃ(ə)nt/ noun [C] **HEALTH** someone who receives medical treatment at a hospital, but does not stay there for the night

outpost /ˈaʊtˌpəʊst/ noun [C] **1** a military camp that is far away from the army **2** a small town far away from other towns, usually where trading takes place

output¹ /ˈaʊtˌpʊt/ noun [C/U] **1** [U] the amount of something that a person, organization, or system produces ≠ INPUT: *Industrial output increased by four per cent last year.* **2** [U] **COMPUTING** the information that is shown on a screen or printed on paper by a computer: *graphics output* **3** [C] **AGRICULTURE** something that a farm produces, for example crops, meat, or silk ≠ INPUT **4** **PHYSICS** the electricity or power produced by a piece of equipment or an engine

output² /ˈaʊtˌpʊt/ (**outputs**, **outputting**, **outputted**) verb [T] **COMPUTING** to produce information from a computer, for example by showing it on a screen or printing it ≠ INPUT

ˈoutput deˌvice noun [C] **COMPUTING** a **peripheral** such as printer or **monitor** that allows a user to get information out of a computer

outrage /ˈaʊtˌreɪdʒ/ noun [singular/U] a strong feeling of anger and shock, or something that causes this feeling

outrageous /aʊtˈreɪdʒəs/ adj **1** very shocking or unreasonable **2** extremely unusual and likely to shock people or make them laugh —**outrageously** adv

outreach /ˈaʊtˌriːtʃ/ noun [U] the practice of providing help and advice to people in a community before they have to ask for it

outright¹ /ˌaʊtˈraɪt/ adv **1** completely in a single process: *Few people could afford to buy a house outright.* **2** without hiding your feelings: *I told them outright that they had to leave.*

outright² /ˈaʊtˌraɪt/ adj **1** clear and direct: *outright hostility* **2** complete and total: *an outright lie*

outset /ˈaʊtˌset/ noun [singular] the start of something: *I loved this book **from the outset**.*

outside /ˌaʊtˈsaɪd/ adj, adv, noun, preposition **1** not inside or within a room, building, or area ≠ INSIDE: *Outside the sun was shining.* ♦ *I went to the window and looked outside.* ♦ *Three police cars were parked outside their house.* **2** used for referring to the outer part or surface of something ≠ INSIDE: *The outside of the house is in urgent need of repair.* **3** not within the

limits of a particular time, range, or situation ≠ INSIDE: *classes held outside normal school hours* **4** not part of a particular group or organization ≠ INSIDE: *The company brought in advisers from outside.* ♦ *an outside consultant*

PHRASE **an outside chance** a situation in which something is possible but unlikely: *There's an outside chance that we'll both arrive on the same day.*

ˌoutside ˈcabin noun [C] **TOURISM** a cabin with a window on a ship

ˌoutside ˈline noun [C] a phone connection from a phone system in an office or building to the main **telephone exchange**

outsider /aʊtˈsaɪdə/ noun [C] someone who does not belong to a particular group

the outskirts /ˈaʊtˌskɜːts/ noun [plural] the areas of a town or city that are furthest away from the centre: *a park **on the outskirts of** Harare*

outsourcing /ˈaʊtˌsɔːsɪŋ/ noun [U] **BUSINESS** an arrangement in which work is done by people from outside a company, usually by another company that is expert in that type of work —**outsource** verb [I/T]

outspoken /ˌaʊtˈspəʊkən/ adj an outspoken person states their opinion honestly, even if other people do not like it = FORTHRIGHT

outstanding /aʊtˈstændɪŋ/ adj **1** extremely good or impressive: *an outstanding example of Indian art* ♦ *an area of outstanding natural beauty* **2** not yet completed, dealt with, or paid: *Some tasks are still outstanding.* —**outstandingly** adv

outstretched /ˌaʊtˈstretʃt/ adj stretched out

outstrip /ˌaʊtˈstrɪp/ (**outstrips**, **outstripping**, **outstripped**) verb [T] to go faster, do something better, or become larger than someone or something else: *Demand for the new computers has outstripped supply.*

ˈout ˌtray noun [C] a container on your desk where you keep letters or documents that are ready to be sent or put somewhere else —*picture* → WORKSTATION

outward¹ /ˈaʊtwəd/ adj **1** relating to something that you can see or notice = EXTERNAL ≠ INWARD: *He had no outward signs of the illness.* **2** an outward journey is one in which you are going away from home

outward² /ˈaʊtwəd/ adv **outwards**

outwardly /ˈaʊtwədli/ adv according to the way that something seems, that is not always the same way that it really is ≠ INWARDLY

outwards /ˈaʊtwədz/ adv away from the centre of something, or towards the outside of it ≠ INWARDS

outwash /ˈaʊtˌwɒʃ/ noun [C] **GEOLOGY** a flat area formed by sand and small stones that have been left by streams flowing away from a glacier

outweigh /ˌaʊtˈweɪ/ verb [T] to be more important, useful, or valuable than something else: *The possible benefits outweigh the risks involved.*

ova /ˈəʊvə/ **BIOLOGY** the plural of **ovum**

oval¹ /ˈəʊv(ə)l/ adj **MATHS** with a shape like a long narrow circle

oval² /ˈəʊv(ə)l/ noun [C] something with an oval shape —*picture* → SHAPE

ˌoval ˈwindow noun [C] **ANATOMY** an opening covered by a membrane between the middle ear and the inner ear that sound vibrations pass through —*picture* → EAR

ovary /ˈəʊv(ə)ri/ (plural **ovaries**) noun [C]
1 ANATOMY one of the two organs in the body of a woman or other female animal that produce eggs and the sex hormones **progesterone** and **oestrogen**. In mammals, the eggs travel from the ovaries down the **fallopian tubes** to the uterus. If the eggs are fertilized, an embryo will develop. —*picture* → FERTILIZATION, REPRODUCTION **2** BIOLOGY the part of a flower which, after fertilization, swells and develops into a fruit —*picture* → FERTILIZATION, FLOWER —**ovarian** /əʊˈveəriən/ adj

ovation /əʊˈveɪʃ(ə)n/ noun [C] *formal* if an audience gives someone an ovation, they **clap** their hands to express their admiration or enjoyment

oven /ˈʌv(ə)n/ noun [C] a large piece of equipment in a kitchen that you cook food in: *Preheat the oven to 220°C, Gas mark 7.*

over¹ /ˈəʊvə/ adj, adv, preposition

1 above sb/sth	**8** moving down
2 covering sb/sth	**9** concerning sth
3 across	**10** more than
4 on opposite side	**11** ended
5 in or to many parts	**12** no longer affected
6 to the side	**13** during
7 to a place	+ PHRASES

1 in a higher position above someone or something, without touching them ≠ UNDER: *Perry glanced at the clock over the door.* ♦ *Birds circled over their heads.*
2 covering someone or something: *Put a cloth over the food.* ♦ *She spilled coffee all over my new dress.*
3 from one side of something to the other: *a bridge over the river* ♦ *Three prisoners had climbed over the wall.*
4 on or to the opposite side of something: *She lives over the road from our house.* ♦ *He turned the card over.* ♦ *Roll over onto your back.*
5 in, to, or from many different parts of an area: *The drought has spread over the south of the country.* ♦ *The festival attracts music lovers from all over the world.*
6 towards the side: *She leaned over and whispered in my ear.*
7 to a particular place: *Why don't you come over and visit us sometime?* ♦ *Lawrence walked over to the window and looked out.*
8 moving down from an upright or higher position: *Carey fell over and broke his leg.* ♦ *Lava flowed over the rim of the volcano.*
9 about or concerning: *We spent a whole hour arguing over the meaning of two words.*
10 more than a particular amount or age ≠ UNDER: *Your body contains over 3 billion cells.* ♦ *The pension will be paid to people aged 65 and over.*
11 used for saying that a particular event or period has ended: *Moore's fourth marriage was over after only 18 months.* ♦ *We're all so relieved that the trial is over and done with.*
12 no longer upset or affected by an illness or a bad experience: *She still isn't over the shock of her brother's death.* ♦ *He'll soon get over his disappointment.*
13 during a period of time: *Most hotels are fully booked over the holiday weekend.*

   PHRASES **all over again** again, starting from the beginning: *I had to do my essay all over again.*
over and over (again) many times: *They keep asking the same questions over and over again.*
→ ABOVE

over² /ˈəʊvə/ noun [C] SPORTS in **cricket**, a series of six actions of **bowling** by one person

overall¹ /ˌəʊvərˈɔːl/ adj **1** considering something as a whole, rather than its details: *My overall impression of the town was not very good.* **2** including everything: *What were the overall costs of the project?*

overall² /ˌəʊvərˈɔːl/ adv when everything is considered: *Overall, our position is stronger than it was last year.*

overall³ /ˈəʊvərˌɔːl/ noun **1** [C] a light coat that someone wears over their clothes to protect them when they are working **2 overalls** [plural] a single piece of clothing with trousers and long sleeves that someone wears over their clothes to protect them when they are working

overambitious /ˌəʊvəræmˈbɪʃəs/ adj someone who is overambitious expects to achieve more than is reasonable or likely

overboard /ˈəʊvəˌbɔːd/ adv off a boat or ship and into the water

overbook /ˌəʊvəˈbʊk/ verb [I/T] TOURISM to arrange for more people to buy tickets, stay in hotel rooms etc than there are places available

overcame /ˌəʊvəˈkeɪm/ the past tense of **overcome**

overcapacity /ˌəʊvəkəˈpæsəti/ noun [singular/U] TOURISM the state of having more seats or space than there are travellers or guests

overcast /ˈəʊvəˌkɑːst/ adj an overcast sky is covered in clouds

overcharge /ˌəʊvəˈtʃɑːdʒ/ verb [I/T] to charge someone too much money for something

overcoat /ˈəʊvəˌkəʊt/ noun [C] a long warm coat

overcome /ˌəʊvəˈkʌm/ (**overcomes**, **overcoming**, **overcame** /ˌəʊvəˈkeɪm/, **overcome**) verb [T] **1** to succeed in dealing with a problem: *Jimmy overcame his difficulties to graduate with a first-class degree.* **2** to make someone very emotional, ill, or unconscious: *The entire family was overcome with grief.* ♦ *Two men died when they were overcome by smoke.* **3** to defeat someone or something: *Government troops have finally overcome rebel forces in the north.*

overconfident /ˌəʊvəˈkɒnfɪd(ə)nt/ adj more confident than it is sensible to be, often in a way that is annoying

overconsumption /ˌəʊvəkənˈsʌmpʃ(ə)n/ noun [U] a situation in which people eat, drink, or use too much of something

overcrowded /ˌəʊvəˈkraʊdɪd/ adj containing too many people or things: *overcrowded schools*

overcrowding /ˌəʊvəˈkraʊdɪŋ/ noun [U] unpleasant conditions that are caused by too many people or things being in the same place

overdose /ˈəʊvəˌdəʊs/ noun [C] too much of a drug that is taken at one time —**overdose** verb [I]

overdraft /ˈəʊvəˌdrɑːft/ noun [C] an agreement with a bank that allows someone to spend money when they have no money left in their account

overdue /ˌəʊvəˈdjuː/ adj if something is overdue, it should have been done before now

overestimate /ˌəʊvərˈestɪˌmeɪt/ verb [T] to think that something is better or bigger than it really is ≠ UNDERESTIMATE —**overestimate** /ˌəʊvərˈestɪmət/ noun [C]

overfishing /ˌəʊvəˈfɪʃɪŋ/ noun [U] ENVIRONMENT fishing that damages a river or an area of sea because too many fish are caught

overflow¹ /ˌəʊvəˈfləʊ/ verb **1** [I/T] to flow over the top of a container because it is too full **2** [I/T] if a river or lake overflows, it floods the land next to it **3** [I] if a place is overflowing with people or things, there are too many of them to fit into it

overflow² /ˈəʊvəˌfləʊ/ noun [C] a hole or pipe that allows a substance to flow out of a container when it gets too full

overfly /ˌəʊvəˈflaɪ/ (**overflies, overflying, overflew** /ˌəʊvəˈfluː/, **overflown** /ˌəʊvəˈfləʊn/) verb [T] to fly over an area in a plane

overgrazing /ˌəʊvəˈɡreɪzɪŋ/ noun [U] **ENVIRONMENT, AGRICULTURE** a situation in which land is damaged because cows or other animals have been allowed to feed on the grass for too long —**overgraze** verb [I]

overgrown /ˌəʊvəˈɡrəʊn/ adj covered with plants that have been allowed to grow in an uncontrolled way

overhang /ˌəʊvəˈhæŋ/ (**overhangs, overhanging, overhung** /ˌəʊvəˈhʌŋ/) verb [I/T] to stick out from an edge above something —**overhang** /ˈəʊvəˌhæŋ/ noun [C]

overhaul /ˌəʊvəˈhɔːl/ verb [T] to repair or change a machine or system in order to make it work better —**overhaul** /ˈəʊvəˌhɔːl/ noun [C]

overhead /ˌəʊvəˈhed/ adj, adv above your head

ˌoverhead ˈcable noun [C] a thick wire that is used for carrying electricity high above the ground

ˌoverhead ˈcamshaft noun [C] **ENGINEERING** a camshaft that is on top of the **cylinder heads** in a vehicle engine, above the **combustion chambers**

ˌoverhead ˈlocker noun [C] **TOURISM** one of a row of small cupboards above the seats in a plane where passengers can store things during a flight

overheads /ˈəʊvəˌhedz/ noun [plural] **BUSINESS** money that is paid regularly as the cost of running a business or organization, for example rent or payments for electric light and heating

ˌoverhead ˈvalve noun [C] **ENGINEERING** one of two valves in a vehicle's engine, an **inlet valve** by which fuel goes into the cylinder head, or an **exhaust valve** by which burnt gases leaves it

overhead welding /ˈəʊvəˌhed ˌweldɪŋ/ noun [U] **TECHNOLOGY** a welding position in which the joint is on the under part of the work and above the head of the operator

overhear /ˌəʊvəˈhɪə/ (**overhears, overhearing, overheard** /ˌəʊvəˈhɜːd/) verb [I/T] to hear what people are saying during a conversation that you are not involved in

overheat /ˌəʊvəˈhiːt/ verb [I/T] to become too hot, or to make something too hot

overheated /ˌəʊvəˈhiːtɪd/ adj **1** too emotional **2 ECONOMICS** if an economy is overheated, demand for goods and services is growing too fast, so that prices are rising in an uncontrolled way **3** too hot

overhung /ˌəʊvəˈhʌŋ/ the past tense and past participle of **overhang**

overjoyed /ˌəʊvəˈdʒɔɪd/ adj extremely pleased

overland /ˈəʊvəˌlænd/ adj, adv on land rather than by boat or plane: *an overland journey*

overlap /ˌəʊvəˈlæp/ (**overlaps, overlapping, overlapped**) verb [I/T] **1** if two objects overlap, or if one overlaps the other, part of one object covers part of the other **2** if subjects, activities, or ideas overlap, they are partly the same as each other —**overlapping** adj, **overlap** /ˈəʊvəˌlæp/ noun [C/U]

overleaf /ˌəʊvəˈliːf/ adv *formal* on the other side of the page

overload /ˌəʊvəˈləʊd/ verb [T] **1** to put too many people or things in or on something **2** to give someone too much work to do **3 PHYSICS** to damage an electrical system or a piece of electrical equipment by putting too much electricity through it **4 COMPUTING** to give a computer more information than it can process —**overload** /ˈəʊvəˌləʊd/ noun [C/U], **overloaded** /ˌəʊvəˈləʊdɪd/ adj

overlook /ˌəʊvəˈlʊk/ verb [T] **1** to fail to notice or do something: *Accidents happen when safety checks are overlooked.* **2** to forgive or ignore a mistake or bad behaviour: *I'm prepared to overlook what you said.* **3** to have a view of something from above: *Our hotel overlooked the river.* **4** to not consider someone or something: *He was once again overlooked when the prizes were awarded.*

overly /ˈəʊvəli/ adv *formal* very much, or too much: *It is a problem, but we're not overly worried about it.*

overnight¹ /ˌəʊvəˈnaɪt/ adv **1** during the night, or for one night: *They stayed overnight at the hotel.* **2** in a very short time: *Don't expect to become famous overnight.*

overnight² /ˈəʊvəˌnaɪt/ adj **1** working or happening during the night: *an overnight train* **2** happening after a very short time: *an overnight success*

overpopulation /ˌəʊvəˌpɒpjʊˈleɪʃ(ə)n/ noun [U] **GEOGRAPHY** a situation in which the population of area needs more **resources** (=food, water, energy etc) than the area can provide —**overpopulated** adj

overpower /ˌəʊvəˈpaʊə/ verb [T] **1** to control or defeat someone using physical strength: *Two police officers overpowered him and took the gun.* **2** to affect someone so strongly that they cannot think or behave normally

overpowering /ˌəʊvəˈpaʊərɪŋ/ adj **1** very strong, so that you do not notice or feel anything else: *an overpowering smell of fish* **2** able to control people because of having a very strong personality

overpriced /ˌəʊvəˈpraɪst/ adj worth less than the price that is being charged

overproduce /ˌəʊvəprəˈdjuːs/ verb [I/T] **BUSINESS** to produce more of something, for example a product or a crop, than is wanted or needed —**overproduction** /ˌəʊvəprəˈdʌkʃ(ə)n/ noun [U]

overran /ˌəʊvəˈræn/ the past tense of **overrun**

overrated /ˌəʊvəˈreɪtɪd/ adj not as good or important as some people believe ≠ **UNDERRATED**

overreact /ˌəʊvəriˈækt/ verb [I] to be more worried, annoyed, or offended than you should be —**overreaction** noun [C]

overregulate /ˌəʊvəˈreɡjʊˌleɪt/ verb [T] **BUSINESS** to make too many laws and rules for controlling an activity, especially a type of business or industry, so that it cannot operate or develop properly

overriding /ˌəʊvəˈraɪdɪŋ/ adj more important than anything else

overrule /ˌəʊvəˈruːl/ verb [T] to officially change someone else's decision

overrun /ˌəʊvəˈrʌn/ (**overruns, overrunning, overran** /ˌəʊvəˈræn/, **overrun**) verb **1** [I/T] to take more time or money than was intended **2** [T] to defeat an enemy in war and take the land they control **3** [T] to be present in a place in very large numbers, in a way that is unpleasant: *The mall was **overrun with** holiday shoppers.*

oversaw /ˌəʊvəˈsɔː/ the past tense of **oversee**

overseas¹ /ˈəʊvəsiːz/ adj existing in, or coming from, a country that is across the sea from your country: *overseas visitors*

overseas² /ˌəʊvəˈsiːz/ adv to or in a country that is across the sea from your country: *There are plans to move production overseas.*

oversee /ˌəʊvəˈsiː/ (**oversees, overseeing, oversaw** /ˌəʊvəˈsɔː/, **overseen** /ˌəʊvəˈsiːn/) verb [T] to watch something in order to check that it happens in the way that it should

overshadow /ˌəʊvəˈʃædəʊ/ verb [T] **1** to be a negative feature that spoils something: *Violent protests overshadowed the president's visit.* **2** to make someone or something seem less important

oversight /ˈəʊvəˌsaɪt/ noun [C] something that you do not think of that causes problems later

oversite /ˈəʊvəˌsaɪt/ adj **CONSTRUCTION** oversite concrete forms the ground floor of a building

overspend /ˌəʊvəˈspend/ (**overspends, overspending, overspent** /ˌəʊvəˈspent/) verb [I/T] to spend too much money, or more money than planned —**overspend** /ˈəʊvəˌspend/ noun [C], **overspending** noun [U]

overt /əʊˈvɜːt/ adj not hidden or secret ≠ COVERT: *overt hostility* —**overtly** adv

overtake /ˌəʊvəˈteɪk/ (**overtakes, overtaking, overtook** /ˌəʊvəˈtʊk/, **overtaken** /ˌəʊvəˈteɪkən/) verb **1** [T] to become better, bigger, or faster than someone or something else: *The women students seem to be overtaking the men.* **2** [I/T] to go past another vehicle that is travelling in the same direction: *That's a dangerous place to overtake.*

overthrow /ˌəʊvəˈθrəʊ/ (**overthrows, overthrowing, overthrew** /ˌəʊvəˈθruː/, **overthrown** /ˌəʊvəˈθrəʊn/) verb [T] to force a leader or government out of their position of power —**overthrow** /ˈəʊvəˌθrəʊ/ noun [singular]

overthrust /ˈəʊvəˌθrʌst/ noun [C] **GEOLOGY** a rock structure caused by pressure pushing the layers of rock up, until one side folds over onto the second side. This causes younger rock layers to be under older layers.

overtime /ˈəʊvəˌtaɪm/ noun [U] extra hours that someone works at their job, or money that is paid for working extra hours

overtone /ˈəʊvəˌtəʊn/ noun [C] a quality that is noticeable but not obvious

overtook /ˌəʊvəˈtʊk/ the past tense of **overtake**

overture /ˈəʊvəˌtjʊə/ noun [C] **1** MUSIC the first part of a long piece of classical music **2** *formal* a suggestion or offer

overturn /ˌəʊvəˈtɜːn/ verb **1** [I/T] if something overturns, or if you overturn it, it moves so that its bottom or side is upwards **2** [T] to officially change a decision or law

overturned fold /ˌəʊvətɜːnd ˈfəʊld/ noun [C] GEOLOGY a bend in an underground layer of rock in which both sides of the bend are nearly parallel

overview /ˈəʊvəˌvjuː/ noun [C] a description of the main features of something: *The book gives a good overview of the subject.*

overweight /ˌəʊvəˈweɪt/ adj someone who is overweight is heavier than they should be ≠ UNDERWEIGHT

overwhelm /ˌəʊvəˈwelm/ verb [T] **1** to affect someone's emotions in a very powerful way: *Her beauty completely overwhelmed him.* **2** to be too much for someone or something to deal with: *In June the town is **overwhelmed by** tourists.*

overwhelming /ˌəʊvəˈwelmɪŋ/ adj **1** making you feel a very strong emotion that you cannot control: *I had the overwhelming desire to get up and leave.* **2** much larger or more important than anything else in a situation: *An overwhelming majority voted against his proposal.* —**overwhelmingly** adv

overworked /ˌəʊvəˈwɜːkt/ adj forced to work too hard

overwrite /ˌəʊvəˈraɪt/ (**overwrites, overwriting, overwrote** /ˌəʊvəˈrəʊt/, **overwritten** /ˌəʊvəˈrɪt(ə)n/) verb [T] **COMPUTING** to get rid of information in a computer file by replacing it with other information

overzealous /ˌəʊvəˈzeləs/ adj *showing disapproval* doing something to an unnecessary degree

oviduct /ˈəʊvɪdʌkt/ noun [C] **ANATOMY** a tube in the body of a female mammal that takes eggs from an ovary to the uterus = FALLOPIAN TUBE —*picture* → FERTILIZATION, REPRODUCTION

ovulate /ˈɒvjʊleɪt/ verb [I] **BIOLOGY** when a woman or other female mammal ovulates, she produces an egg in her body and can become pregnant —**ovulatory** adj

ovulation /ˌɒvjʊˈleɪʃ(ə)n/ noun [U] **BIOLOGY** the process of ovulating

ovule /ˈɒvjuːl/ noun [C] **BIOLOGY** a small structure containing the female gamete in a plant that becomes a seed after it has been fertilized —*picture* → FERTILIZATION, FLOWER

ovum /ˈəʊvəm/ (plural **ova** /ˈəʊvə/) noun [C] **BIOLOGY** the female gamete or egg cell that can grow into a new animal after it has been fertilized. In mammals, this happens inside the female. —*picture* → FERTILIZATION, SEX CELL

ow /aʊ/ interjection used for expressing a feeling of sudden pain

owe /əʊ/ verb [T] **1** to have to give someone a particular amount of money because you have bought something from them or have borrowed money from them: *Pam still owes me five dollars.* ♦ *How much do we owe you for the tickets?* **2** to have an obligation to do something for someone or to give them something: *I think you **owe** her **an apology**.* ♦ *They **owe it to** their children to make the house safe.* **3** to have something because someone or something has helped you: *The company owes its success to its excellent training programme.* **4** to feel grateful to someone because of the way that they have helped you: *We really owe you a great deal for all your hard work this year.*

owing to /ˈəʊɪŋ ˌtuː/ preposition because of: *Owing to the high cost of drugs, the disease is difficult to control.*

Both **owing to** and **due to** mean 'because of'. They are used in exactly the same way, except that **due to** can be used after the verb 'to be': *Their failure was due to a lack of care and attention* (NOT: *was owing to*).

owl /aʊl/ noun [C] a large bird with a big head and eyes and a small sharp beak. Owls hunt at night. —*picture* → BIRD

own¹ /əʊn/ determiner, pronoun belonging to or done by a particular person or thing and not any other: *You are free to do what you like in your own home.* ♦ *It's my*

own fault I didn't get the job. ♦ She has two small children **of her own**.

PHRASE (all) on your own 1 alone: You shouldn't be out on your own at this time of night. → YOURSELF **2** without any help: Your grandfather did it all on his own. → HOLD¹

own² /əʊn/ verb [T] to legally have something, especially because you have bought it: Who owns that house by the lake?

PHRASAL VERB ,own 'up to admit that you have done something that is bad or embarrassing: Two local students later **owned up to** the prank.

owner /'əʊnə/ noun [C] someone who owns something: a restaurant owner ♦ Who is **the owner of** this car?

ownership /'əʊnəʃɪp/ noun [U] legal possession of something

,own 'goal noun [C] **1** SPORTS a goal that you accidentally score against your own team **2** something you do that accidentally harms you

ox /ɒks/ (plural **oxen** /'ɒks(ə)n/) noun [C] a large type of male cow that is used for pulling or carrying things

oxalic acid /ɒk,sælɪk 'æsɪd/ noun [U] CHEMISTRY an acid that is found in plants such as **rhubarb**

oxbow lake /,ɒksbəʊ 'leɪk/ noun [C] GEOGRAPHY a curved lake that is formed when a bend in a river becomes separated from the rest of the river —picture → RIVER

oxen /'ɒks(ə)n/ the plural of **ox**

oxidase /'ɒksɪdeɪz, 'ɒksɪdeɪs/ noun [C] BIOLOGY an enzyme that helps in the chemical reactions that produce oxidation

oxidation /,ɒksɪ'deɪʃ(ə)n/ noun [U] CHEMISTRY the process of a substance gaining oxygen or losing hydrogen

oxi'dation-re,duction noun [U] CHEMISTRY a **chemical reaction** in which one substance **oxidizes** (=loses electrons to) another substance that **reduces** (=gains them)

oxide /'ɒksaɪd/ noun [U] CHEMISTRY a chemical that consists of oxygen combined with another substance

oxidize /'ɒksɪdaɪz/ verb [I/T] CHEMISTRY if a substance oxidizes, or if something oxidizes it, it combines with oxygen or loses hydrogen

oxidizing flame /'ɒksɪdaɪzɪŋ ,fleɪm/ noun [C] TECHNOLOGY a flame used in welding that is produced by a mixture containing more oxygen than **acetylene**

oxyacetylene /,ɒksiə'setəli:n/ noun [U] CHEMISTRY a mixture of oxygen and **acetylene**, used as a fuel for making a very hot flame that cuts metal

oxyacetylene welding /,ɒksiə'setəli:n ,weldɪŋ/ noun [U] TECHNOLOGY a type of **fusion welding** that uses a combination of oxygen and **acetylene** to melt the pieces being joined

oxy-fuel welding /,ɒksi 'fju:əl ,weldɪŋ/ noun [U] TECHNOLOGY a type of **fusion welding** that uses a combination of oxygen and another gas such as **propane** to melt the pieces of metal

oxygen /'ɒksɪdʒ(ə)n/ noun [U] CHEMISTRY an important element in the air that is a gas with no smell or taste. It makes **aerobic respiration** possible in organisms. It combines with most other elements. Chemical symbol: **O**: Brain damage occurs when the supply of oxygen to the brain is interrupted. ♦ Blood absorbs oxygen from the air in the lungs.

oxygenate /'ɒksɪdʒəneɪt/ verb [T] SCIENCE to add oxygen to something: Blood is oxygenated in the lungs. —**oxygenation** /,ɒksɪdʒə'neɪʃ(ə)n/ noun [U]

the 'oxygen ,cycle noun CHEMISTRY, BIOLOGY the series of processes by which oxygen moves between the air, the seas, plants, and animals. It is released into the air by photosynthesis from plants, and is then used in respiration and **combustion** (=burning).

oxyhaemoglobin /,ɒksɪ,hi:məʊ'gləʊbɪn/ noun [U] BIOLOGY the bright red compound produced when haemoglobin in the blood combines with oxygen in the lungs → HAEMOGLOBIN

oxymoron /,ɒksi'mɔːrɒn/ noun [C] LITERATURE an expression that contains words with opposite meanings, for example 'a bitter-sweet experience' (=an experience that is both unpleasant and pleasant)

oxytocin /,ɒksi'təʊsɪn/ noun [U] BIOLOGY a hormone that makes the uterus of a woman or female mammal contract when she gives birth. It also makes her produce milk for the baby.

oyster /'ɔɪstə/ noun [C] a type of **shellfish** with a rough shell that is eaten as food, often raw —picture → SEA

oz abbrev ounce

ozone /'əʊzəʊn/ noun [U] CHEMISTRY a type of oxygen that exists high in the Earth's atmosphere. Each molecule consists of three atoms of oxygen. Chemical formula: O_3 —picture → POLLUTION

'ozone de,pletion noun [U] ENVIRONMENT, SCIENCE a reduction in the amount of ozone gas in the Earth's atmosphere

'ozone ,hole noun [C] ENVIRONMENT, SCIENCE a hole in the ozone layer thought to be caused by light reacting with some chemicals such as **CFCs**

'ozone ,layer noun [singular] ENVIRONMENT, SCIENCE a layer of **ozone** in the Earth's atmosphere that protects the Earth from some of the harmful effects of the Sun

p¹ /pi:/ (plural **p's**) or **P** (plural **P's**) noun [C/U] the 16th letter of the English alphabet

p² /pi:/ abbrev **1** page **2** pence **3** penny **4** MUSIC piano

P2P /,pi: tə 'pi:/ abbrev COMPUTING peer to peer: P2P software allows computers to communicate directly with each other without going through a **server**

PA /,pi: 'eɪ/ noun [C] **1** personal assistant: someone whose job is to help a manager by writing business letters, organizing meetings etc **2** public address system: a piece of electrical equipment for making announcements or for playing music in a public place

pace¹ /peɪs/ noun **1** [singular/U] the speed at which something happens or is done: The course allows students to progress **at their own pace**. ♦ **the pace of** technological change **2** [singular/U] the speed at which you move: a player with skill and pace (=the ability to move fast) ♦ We wandered along **at a leisurely pace**. **3** [C] a step that you take when you walk or run: I took a few **paces** towards her. **4** [U] an exciting quality that a story has, because of the quick and interesting way it develops: Her plays lack pace.

PHRASES **gather pace 1** to start to happen more quickly and have more success: *After 1946, support for European unity began to gather pace.* **2** to start to move more quickly
keep pace with sth to develop or progress at the same rate as something: *The government is not allowing salaries to keep pace with inflation.*

pace² /peɪs/ verb **1** [I/T] to walk with regular steps around a small area, because you are worried, nervous, or impatient **2** [T] to make the story in a book, film etc develop in a particular way: *His films were always well paced and exciting.*

pacemaker /ˈpeɪsˌmeɪkə/ noun [C] **1 HEALTH** a small piece of electronic equipment that is put in someone's heart in order to help the muscles to move regularly **2 SPORTS** someone who begins a race quickly so that the other people will follow them and run a fast race

pachyderm /ˈpækɪˌdɜːm/ noun [C] **BIOLOGY** a large mammal with thick skin, such as an elephant or a **rhinoceros**

Pacific Ocean /pəˌsɪfɪk ˈəʊʃ(ə)n/ **GEOGRAPHY** the biggest ocean in the world. It stretches from the Arctic Ocean in the north to Antarctica in the south, and from North and South America in the east to East Asia, the Malay Archipelago, and Australia in the west. —*picture* → CONTINENT

the Pacific Rim /pəˌsɪfɪk ˈrɪm/ **GEOGRAPHY** the countries around the Pacific Ocean, considered as a political or economic group

pacifism /ˈpæsɪˌfɪz(ə)m/ noun [U] **SOCIAL STUDIES** the belief that violence is wrong and that people should refuse to fight in wars

pacifist /ˈpæsɪfɪst/ noun [C] **SOCIAL STUDIES** someone who believes that violence is wrong and refuses to fight in wars —**pacifist** adj

pacify /ˈpæsɪfaɪ/ (**pacifies**, **pacifying**, **pacified**) verb [T] to make someone who is angry, worried, or upset feel calm

pack¹ /pæk/ verb **1** [I/T] to put your possessions into a bag, case, or box so that you can take or send them somewhere: *Haven't you packed yet?* ♦ *It didn't take her long to pack a few clothes.* ♦ *He was still packing his suitcase when the taxi came.* **2** [T] to put goods into containers so that they can be sent somewhere and sold: *This is where the fruit is packed.* **3** [T] to fill a place completely: *Eager spectators packed the courtroom.* **4** [T] to press something such as soil or snow into a solid hard mass

PHRASAL VERB ˌpack (sth) ˈup to put things into a bag, case, or box so that you can take or send them somewhere: *He simply packed up his belongings and moved out.*

pack² /pæk/ noun [C]

1 set of things	**4** group of animals
2 box of sth	**5** group of people
3 bag	**6** in rugby

1 a set of things such as products or documents that are wrapped together: *On registration we will send you a membership pack.* ♦ *Envelopes are cheaper if you buy them in packs of 100.*
2 a paper or card box for something such as playing cards or cigarettes
3 a bag that you carry on your back
4 BIOLOGY a group of animals that live and hunt together: *a pack of wolves*
5 *showing disapproval* a group of people or things: *There was a pack of reporters waiting outside.* ♦ *The whole story is a pack of lies* (=completely untrue).

6 SPORTS the group of attacking players in a **rugby** team, especially in a **scrum**

package¹ /ˈpækɪdʒ/ noun [C] **1** an object or set of objects that is wrapped in a box or in paper and sent to someone= PARCEL: *a package full of Christmas presents* **2 BUSINESS** a plan or offer that is intended to deal with a problem: *a package designed to stabilize the economy* **3** money and other benefits, for example a car, that someone gets from their employer **4 COMPUTING** a set of computer software that is sold as one unit: *the best new graphics package on the market*

package² /ˈpækɪdʒ/ verb [T] **1** to put things into boxes, or to wrap them, so that they can be sold **2** to sell several things together as one unit **3** to try to make a product, idea, or person attractive to the public: *Politicians these days are packaged to appeal to a mass market.*

ˈpackage ˌdeal noun [C] **1** a set of different things that are offered together and must be accepted together = BUNDLE **2 TOURISM** a package holiday, especially at a special low price

ˈpackage ˌholiday noun [C] **TOURISM** a holiday arranged by a travel company for a fixed price that includes the cost of a hotel, transport, and sometimes meals and entertainment

packaging /ˈpækɪdʒɪŋ/ noun [U] the boxes, plastic etc that are used for wrapping products

ˈpack ˌanimal noun [C] an animal used for carrying heavy loads, such as a horse or **donkey**

packed /pækt/ adj **1** extremely crowded: *The cinema was packed.* **2** *informal* containing a lot of something: *This new series is packed with drama.* **3** if someone is packed, they have put their possessions into bags, suitcases, or boxes

packet /ˈpækɪt/ noun [C] **1** a box, bag, or piece of plastic wrapping, containing food that is ready to be sold: *The ingredients should be listed on the packet.* ♦ *an empty crisp packet* ♦ *a 500g packet of spaghetti* **2** a small parcel or envelope containing a set of similar things: *A packet of brochures arrived in the post.* **3 COMPUTING** a small amount of computer information that has been divided up so that it can be sent across a computer **network**

ˈpack ˌice noun [U] **GEOGRAPHY** a large mass of ice that floats in the sea

pact /pækt/ noun [C] an agreement between two or more people or organizations in which they promise to do something

pad¹ /pæd/ noun [C] **1** a set of sheets of paper that are fastened together along the top or along one side: *a note pad* **2** a thick piece of a soft substance that you use for protecting something, making it more comfortable, or changing its shape: *knee pads* **3** an area of soft flesh on the end of the finger or thumb **4 BIOLOGY** an area of hard flesh on the bottom of the foot of an animal such as a dog or cat

pad² /pæd/ (**pads, padding, padded**) verb **1** [I] to walk with quiet light steps **2** [T] to cover or fill something with a soft substance in order to protect it, make it more comfortable, or change its shape —**padded** adj: *a warm padded jacket*

padding /ˈpædɪŋ/ noun [U] **1** a thick soft substance that is used for protecting something, making it more comfortable, or changing its shape **2** unnecessary information added to a speech or piece of writing to make it longer

paddle[1] /ˈpæd(ə)l/ noun [C] **1** a short pole with a flat end or with two flat ends, that is used for moving a small boat such as a **canoe 2** an act of playing or walking in water that is not very deep

paddle[2] /ˈpæd(ə)l/ verb **1** [I] to play or walk in water that is not very deep **2** [I/T] to move a small boat through the water using a paddle

paddock /ˈpædək/ noun [C] **AGRICULTURE** a small field, especially for keeping horses in

paddy /ˈpædi/ or **ˈpaddy ˌfield** noun [C] **AGRICULTURE** a field of rice growing in water

ˈpad founˌdation noun [C] **CONSTRUCTION** a hole filled with concrete that supports a **column** in the **foundation** of a building

padlock /ˈpædˌlɒk/ noun [C] a lock that you can fix to something such as a gate or suitcase. It has a curved bar on top that moves when you open the lock. —**padlock** verb [T]

paediatrician /ˌpiːdiəˈtrɪʃ(ə)n/ noun [C] **HEALTH** a doctor who deals with children and their illnesses

paediatrics /ˌpiːdiˈætrɪks/ noun [U] **HEALTH** the part of medical science that deals with children and their illnesses

pagan /ˈpeɪgən/ adj **RELIGION** relating to a religion that is not one of the main religions of the world. Many people think this word is offensive, as it is sometimes used in a disapproving way by people belonging to one of the main religions. —**pagan** noun [C]

page[1] /peɪdʒ/ noun [C] **1** a sheet of paper in a book, newspaper, or magazine: *the poem on page 125* ♦ *For information on hotels in Amsterdam, see page 20.* ♦ *She turned a page of the book in her lap.* ♦ *The football scores are on the back page.* ♦ *Lawrence ate while glancing at the sports page.* **2** a piece of paper: *Chris wrote her name at the top of the page.* **3** **COMPUTING** the writing or pictures on a computer screen that you can see at one time, for example as part of a website: *Click 'Back' to return to the previous page.*

page[2] /peɪdʒ/ verb [T] **1** to communicate with someone by sending a message to their **pager 2** to call someone's name in a public place using a public address system

pageant /ˈpædʒ(ə)nt/ noun [C] a play, concert, or other performance that is based on a historical or religious story

ˈpage ˌbreak noun [C] **COMPUTING** the place in a computer document where one page ends and another one begins

ˈpage proˌtection noun [U] **COMPUTING** a set of software controls that prevents pages being changed by accident

pager /ˈpeɪdʒə/ noun [C] a small piece of equipment that makes a noise to tell you to phone someone or go somewhere

page setup /ˈpeɪdʒ ˌsetʌp/ noun [C] **COMPUTING** the set of software choices, for example the size of pages or the size of the **margins**, that allow a user to decide how the page will look when it is printed

ˈpage ˌview noun [singular] **BUSINESS** the number of times that customers look at a website, used as a way of measuring how effective an advertisement is

pagoda /pəˈgəʊdə/ noun [C] **RELIGION** a Buddhist religious building with several roofs built on top of each other

paid[1] /peɪd/ adj **1** a paid period of time is one when you receive pay although you are not at work ≠ UNPAID: *paid holidays* **2** earning a particular amount of money: *highly paid managers* **3** working or done in exchange

for pay: *paid campaign workers* ♦ *paid work*

paid[2] /peɪd/ the past tense and past participle of **pay**[1]

pain[1] /peɪn/ noun **1** [C/U] a bad feeling in part of your body when you are hurt or become ill: *An old injury was causing him intense pain.* ♦ *He heard Leo scream in pain.* ♦ *I'm having terrible pains in my chest.* **2** [singular/U] a feeling of being very upset or unhappy: *He found it hard to cope with the pain of being separated from his children.* ♦ *The incident must have caused my parents great pain.*

pain[2] /peɪn/ verb [T] *formal* **1** to make someone feel very upset, ashamed, or unhappy **2** to make someone feel physical pain

painful /ˈpeɪnf(ə)l/ adj **1** making you feel upset, ashamed, or unhappy: *painful memories of her unhappy childhood* **2** causing physical pain: *The sting can be excruciatingly painful.* ♦ *I have a sore throat, and it's really painful when I swallow.*

painfully /ˈpeɪnf(ə)li/ adv in a way that makes you feel upset, ashamed, or unhappy: *She was painfully aware of his embarrassment.* ♦ *She looked painfully thin.*

painkiller /ˈpeɪnˌkɪlə/ noun [C] **HEALTH** a medicine that reduces pain

painless /ˈpeɪnləs/ adj **1** not causing any physical pain **2** less difficult or unpleasant than you expected: *I was dreading the interview, but in fact it was pretty painless.*

painstaking /ˈpeɪnzˌteɪkɪŋ/ adj done or doing something very carefully and slowly = METICULOUS —**painstakingly** adv

paint[1] /peɪnt/ noun **1** [U] a coloured substance that you use for changing the colour of a surface or for making a picture: *You need to apply two coats of paint.* ♦ *The paint was peeling off the doors.* **2** **paints** [plural] **ARTS** a set of small blocks or tubes containing paint that you use for making pictures

paint[2] /peɪnt/ verb **1** [I/T] to put paint onto something in order to change its colour: *Wash the walls before you start to paint.* ♦ *Will you help me paint the kitchen?* **2** [I/T] **ARTS** to create a picture of something using paints: *I painted a view of the lake.* **3** [T] to describe someone or something in a particular way: *The film paints a picture of what life was like during the war.*

paintbrush /ˈpeɪntˌbrʌʃ/ noun [C] **ARTS** a brush used for painting

painter /ˈpeɪntə/ noun [C] **1** **ARTS** an artist who paints pictures **2** someone whose job is to paint the inside or outside of buildings

painting /ˈpeɪntɪŋ/ noun **1** [C] **ARTS** a picture made using paint: *a painting by Picasso* **2** [U] the activity of using paint to make a picture or cover a surface: *After retirement he took up painting.*

ˈpaint ˌprogram noun [C] **COMPUTING** a piece of software that allows a user to draw pictures on screen in different colours, with different styles of brush and special effects

paintwork /ˈpeɪntˌwɜːk/ noun [U] the painted surface of something such as a car or the inside of a building

pair /peə/ noun [C] **1** a set of two things of the same type: *The vases were sold as a pair.* ♦ *a pair of shoes* **2** a single unit made up of two similar parts joined together: *My glasses are getting old and I probably need a new pair.* ♦ *a pair of trousers* **3** two people who are connected or who do something together: *The pair became good friends.* ♦ *a pair of identical twins* ♦ *The students worked in pairs.*

pak choi /ˌpæk ˈtʃɔɪ/ noun [U] a Chinese vegetable with long dark green leaves and white stems —*picture* → VEGETABLE

pakora /pəˈkɔːrə/ noun [C/U] an Indian food made from pieces of meat or vegetables that have been covered in a mixture of flour and egg and cooked in hot oil

palace /ˈpæləs/ noun [C] a very large building that is the official home of a royal family, president, or religious leader

Palaeolithic /ˌpæliəˈlɪθɪk, ˌpeɪliəˈlɪθɪk/ adj SOCIAL STUDIES relating to the time when humans first started to make tools out of stone

palaeontology /ˌpeɪliɒnˈtɒlədʒi/ noun [U] GEOLOGY the study of fossils —**palaeontologist** noun [C]

Palaeozoic /ˌpeɪliəˈzəʊɪk/ noun [U] GEOLOGY the **era** of geological time, about 570 million to 248 million years ago, during which fish, insects, amphibians, reptiles, and land plants first appeared

palatable /ˈpælətəb(ə)l/ adj **1** tasting good enough to eat or drink **2** acceptable

palatal /ˈpælət(ə)l/ adj LANGUAGE a palatal sound, especially a consonant, is pronounced by moving your tongue near or against the hard **palate** —**palatal** noun [C]

palatalize /ˈpælətəlaɪz/ verb [T] to make a speech sound by putting the tongue against or near the **hard palate**

palate /ˈpælət/ noun [C] **1** ANATOMY the inside upper part of the mouth **2** the ability to taste and judge flavours

palatial /pəˈleɪʃ(ə)l/ adj a palatial building is very large and impressive

pale¹ /peɪl/ adj **1** light and not bright in colour: *pale yellow* ♦ *a pale sky* **2** a pale person has skin that is lighter than usual because they are ill, shocked, or worried: *He **looked pale** and weary.* —**palely** adv

pale² /peɪl/ verb [I] to seem less important or serious: *The devastating floods of two years ago **pale in comparison with** last week's storms.*

Palestinian /ˌpæləˈstɪniən/ adj **1** someone who is Palestinian is from Palestine **2** relating to Palestine or its culture

palette /ˈpælət/ noun [C] ARTS a board that an artist uses for mixing paints on

'palette ˌknife noun [C] **1** ARTS a knife that an artist uses for mixing paints or putting paint on a picture **2** a knife with a wide blade used in cooking for spreading soft foods

palisade mesophyll /ˌpælɪˈseɪd ˌmesəʊfɪl/ noun [C] BIOLOGY the part of a leaf, close to its top surface, that is made up of cells where photosynthesis takes place

palladium /pəˈleɪdiəm/ noun [U] CHEMISTRY a silvery-white metallic element that is similar to **platinum**. It is used in electronic equipment, **catalytic converters**, and jewellery. Chemical symbol: **Pd**

palliative /ˈpæliətɪv/ adj HEALTH reducing the pain or other bad effects of an illness, but not curing it completely

pallor /ˈpælə/ noun [singular] the very pale colour that your skin has when you are ill or worried

palm /pɑːm/ noun [C] **1** the inside part of the hand, between the fingers and the wrist —*picture* → BODY **2** a **palm tree**

'palm comˌputer noun [C] COMPUTING a very small computer with a screen that you touch rather than a keyboard. It is used mainly as an address book and for email.

'palm ˌoil noun [U] a thick type of oil produced from the fruit of palm trees that is used especially for cooking and making soap

palmtop /ˈpɑːmˌtɒp/ noun [C] COMPUTING a very small computer that you can hold in your hand

'palm ˌtree noun [C] a tropical tree without branches that has large wide leaves growing from the top of its **trunk**

palpate /pælˈpeɪt, ˈpælpeɪt/ verb [T] HEALTH to examine a part of the body by pressing the fingers on it

paltry /ˈpɔːltri/ adj not at all big or important

pamper /ˈpæmpə/ verb [T] to look after someone very well, especially by making them feel very comfortable

pamphlet /ˈpæmflət/ noun [C] a very thin book with a paper cover

pan /pæn/ noun [C] **1** a round metal container with a handle that is used for cooking **2** the liquid or food contained in a pan, or the amount that a pan holds: *a **pan of** hot water*

panacea /ˌpænəˈsiːə/ noun [C] something that people think will solve all their problems

pan-African /ˌpæn ˈæfrɪkən/ adj SOCIAL STUDIES **1** relating to the nations of Africa, together or in cooperation with one another **2** supporting freedom and independence for African people

pancake /ˈpænˌkeɪk/ noun [C] a thin round flat food made by cooking a mixture of flour, eggs, and milk = CREPE

pancreas /ˈpæŋkriəs/ noun [C] ANATOMY the small organ behind the stomach that produces **insulin** and enzymes to help with the process of digestion —*picture* → DIGESTIVE SYSTEM

pancreatic /ˌpæŋkriˈætɪk/ adj ANATOMY relating to the pancreas

ˌpancreatic 'duct noun [C] ANATOMY a tube in humans and other vertebrates that carries pancreatic juice from the pancreas through the **bile duct**, and into the **small intestine** —*picture* → DIGESTIVE SYSTEM

ˌpancreatic 'juice noun [C] BIOLOGY a weak alkaline liquid produced by the pancreas. It contains enzymes that help to digest food in the **small intestine**.

panda /ˈpændə/ noun [C] a large Chinese wild mammal with black and white fur —*picture* → MAMMAL

pandemic /pænˈdemɪk/ noun [C] HEALTH a disease that affects almost everyone in a very large area —**pandemic** adj → EPIDEMIC

pandemonium /ˌpændəˈməʊniəm/ noun [C/U] a very noisy and confused situation that is caused by a lot of angry or excited people= CHAOS

pane /peɪn/ noun [C] a flat piece of glass in a window or door

panel /ˈpæn(ə)l/ noun [C] **1** a group of people who make decisions or judgments: *an interview panel* ♦ *a **panel of** judges* **2** a group of well-known people who discuss subjects on television or radio programmes **3** a flat piece of wood, glass, or other material that forms part of something such as a door or wall: *a door with stained glass panels* **4** the part of a vehicle or machine that contains the switches and other instruments: *a control panel*

pang /pæŋ/ noun [C] a sudden unpleasant physical feeling or emotion: *a pang of guilt*

Pangaea /pæn'dʒi:ə/ GEOLOGY a continent that existed between 200 and 300 million years ago. It broke up into two parts and then later into the continents that exist now.

panic¹ /'pænɪk/ noun **1** [singular/U] a sudden strong feeling of fear or worry that makes you unable to think clearly or calmly: *Panic spread quickly through the city.* ♦ *People are fleeing the area in panic.* ♦ *She gets in a panic whenever she has to speak in public.* **2** [C/U] a situation in which a lot of people are hurrying to do something because they are frightened or worried: *News of the incident caused a panic.* —**panicky** /'pænɪki/ adj

panic² /'pænɪk/ (**panics, panicking, panicked**) verb [I/T] to have a sudden strong feeling of fear or worry and be unable to think clearly or calmly, or to make someone do this

panic buying /'pænɪk ˌbaɪɪŋ/ noun [U] a situation in which large numbers of people buy a product in large quantities, because they are worried there is not enough of it available

panorama /ˌpænə'rɑːmə/ noun [C] a view of a large area of land or sea —**panoramic** /ˌpænə'ræmɪk/ adj

pant /pænt/ verb [I] to breathe very loudly with your mouth open, for example when you have been running —**pant** noun [C]

panther /'pænθə/ noun [C] a **leopard** with black fur

pantomime /'pæntəˌmaɪm/ noun [C/U] ARTS in the UK, a funny play for children that is based on a traditional story and is performed at Christmas

pantry /'pæntri/ (plural **pantries**) noun [C] a small room for storing food= LARDER

pants /pænts/ noun [plural] **1** a piece of underwear that covers the part of the body from the waist to the top of the legs **2** *American* **trousers**

the papacy /'peɪpəsi/ noun [singular] RELIGION the position of being the **Pope**

papain /pə'peɪn, pə'paɪn/ noun [U] BIOLOGY an enzyme found in the juice of **papaya** fruit. It is used in medicine to help digestion and the healing of wounds.

papal /'peɪp(ə)l/ adj RELIGION relating to the **Pope**

papaya /pə'paɪə/ noun [C/U] a fruit with green and yellow skin, orange flesh, and small black seeds inside —*picture* → FRUIT

paper¹ /'peɪpə/ noun

1 for writing/wrapping	4 examination
2 newspaper	5 writing by student
3 documents	+ PHRASE

1 [U] the thin flat substance that you use for writing on or wrapping things in: *a parcel wrapped in brown paper* ♦ *Stuart handed me a piece of paper with an address written on it.*
2 [C] a newspaper: *Is that today's paper?* ♦ *He sat down and read the paper.* ♦ *The story was in all the papers.*
3 papers [plural] official documents such as your passport, or documents relating to work, study, or personal matters: *We had to show our papers at the security desk.* ♦ *Some important papers are missing from the files.*
4 [C] EDUCATION a document containing a set of examination questions, or the answers that a student has written to them: *I had a maths paper in the afternoon.* ♦ *Please hand your papers in now.*
5 [C] EDUCATION a piece of writing done by a student

as part of a course: *I have to write a paper on the Cuban Revolution.*
PHRASE on paper in writing: *We need to have something on paper that people can take away with them.*

paper² /'peɪpə/ adj made of paper

paper³ /'peɪpə/ verb [T] to cover the walls of a room with **wallpaper**

paperback /'peɪpəˌbæk/ noun [C] a book with a cover made of thick paper → HARDBACK

paperclip /'peɪpəˌklɪp/ noun [C] a small piece of bent wire that is used for holding pieces of paper together —*picture* → WORKSTATION

paperwork /'peɪpəˌwɜːk/ noun [U] **1** the part of a job that involves producing reports, keeping records, and writing letters **2** the documents that you need for a particular activity or occasion

papier-mâché /ˌpæpieɪ 'mæʃeɪ/ noun [U] a substance consisting of pieces of paper covered in glue, used for making objects

paprika /'pæprɪkə, pə'priːkə/ noun [U] a red powder that is used in cooking for adding a slightly hot flavour to food

papyrus /pə'paɪrəs/ noun [U] a type of paper made from plants that was used in ancient Egypt

par /pɑː/ noun [U] **1** the usual or expected standard: *His performance was well below par* (=not as good as usual). **2** SPORTS in golf, the number of times that a player is expected to hit the ball to get it into the hole, or into all of the holes
PHRASE on a par with of the same quality as, or at the same level as, someone or something

par. or **para.** abbrev LANGUAGE paragraph

parable /'pærəb(ə)l/ noun [C] RELIGION a simple story with a moral or religious purpose, especially one told by Jesus Christ in the Bible

parabola /pə'ræbələ/ noun [C] MATHS, PHYSICS a curve formed when a **cone** and a **plane** (=flat surface) parallel to its side meet

paracetamol /ˌpærə'siːtəmɒl, ˌpærə'setəmɒl/ noun [C/U] HEALTH a common type of **painkiller** (=drug for curing minor pains). It can be very dangerous if too much of it is taken, causing damage to the liver or even death.

parachute /'pærəˌʃuːt/ noun [C] a large piece of cloth joined to heavy strings that is used by someone jumping out of a plane

parade¹ /pə'reɪd/ noun [C] **1** a public celebration in which a large group of people moves through an area, often with decorated vehicles and bands playing music **2** a public ceremony in which a large group of soldiers marches together **3** a row of shops in a street. This word is often used in the names of streets.

parade² /pə'reɪd/ verb **1** [I] to walk as part of an organized group in order to celebrate or publicly protest about something **2** [T] to publicly show something that you are proud of **3** [I] *showing disapproval* to walk around so that people will look at you and admire you **4** [I] if soldiers parade, they march as a group during a ceremony or public celebration

paradigm /'pærədaɪm/ noun [C] **1** *formal* a typical example or model of something **2** *formal* a set of ideas that are used for understanding or explaining something, especially in a particular subject **3** LANGUAGE the complete set of the different forms of a word, for example *student*, *student's*, *students*, and *students'*

'**paradigm ,shift** noun [C] *formal* a basic change in ideas or methods

paradise /'pærədaɪs/ noun **1** [C/U] a perfect place or situation **2 Paradise** [U] **RELIGION** Heaven, the place where some people believe that you go when you die if you have lived a good life

paradox /'pærədɒks/ noun [C] a situation or idea that is strange because it has features or qualities that you would not expect to exist together: *the paradox of people with the best qualifications not being able to get jobs*

paradoxical /,pærə'dɒksɪk(ə)l/ adj strange because of being the opposite of what you expect — **paradoxically** /,pærə'dɒksɪkli/ adv

paraffin /'pærəfɪn/ noun [U] **CHEMISTRY** a clear oil with a strong smell that is obtained from **petroleum** and is used as fuel

paragraph /'pærə,grɑːf, 'pærə,græf/ noun [C] **LANGUAGE** a section of a piece of writing that begins on a new line and contains one or more sentences

paralinguistic /,pærəlɪŋ'gwɪstɪk/ adj **LANGUAGE** expressed in ways that do not use words, for example by the look on your face or the sound of your voice

parallax /'pærəlæks/ noun [C/U] **PHYSICS** the change in the position of an object that seems to take place when the person looking at the object changes their position

parallel[1] /'pærəlel/ adj **1 MATHS** lines that are parallel are the same distance apart at every point along their length: *He leaned forward so that his body was almost **parallel to** the ground.* ✦ *The river flows **parallel with** the high street.* **2** happening at the same time or in the same way but separately: *Taxes are going up in the US, and in a parallel development, Germany is also raising taxes.* **3 COMPUTING** performing several operations at the same time

parallel[2] /'pærəlel/ noun [C] **1** a way in which separate things or people are similar to each other: *There are some interesting **parallels between** the two wars.* ✦ *Some writers have **drawn parallels between** computers and the human brain* (=shown how they are similar). **2** someone or something that is similar to another person or thing: *The proposed reforms have parallels in several other countries.* ✦ *Woods is a golfer **without parallel*** (=no one is better). **3 GEOGRAPHY** an imaginary line around the Earth at a fixed distance from the equator: *The 49th parallel marks part of the boundary between the United States and Canada.*
    PHRASE in parallel connected and happening at the same time: *Advertising has developed **in parallel with** modern industry and the mass media.*

parallel[3] /'pærəlel/ verb [T] to be similar or equal to something

,**parallel 'bars** noun [plural] **SPORTS** two bars on posts that are parallel to each other, used in the sport of **gymnastics**

,**parallel 'beam** noun [C] **PHYSICS** a beam (=line) of light in which the rays are always at an equal distance from each other

,**parallel 'circuit** noun [C] **PHYSICS** an electric circuit in which all the parts are connected directly to the voltage supply, so that each receives a part of the current —*picture* → CIRCUIT

parallelogram /,pærə'lelə,græm/ noun [C] **MATHS** a shape with four straight sides in which opposite sides are of equal length and are parallel to each other — *picture* → SHAPE

,**parallel 'port** noun [C] **COMPUTING** a connection between a computer and another piece of equipment, for example a printer, that uses more than one wire to carry information → SERIAL PORT

paralyse /'pærəlaɪz/ verb [T] **1 HEALTH** to make someone lose the ability to move their body or a part of it **2** to make something completely unable to operate normally

paralysed /'pærəlaɪzd/ adj **1 HEALTH** unable to move your body or a part of it because of an injury or illness **2** temporarily unable to move or think clearly **3** completely unable to operate normally

paralysis /pə'ræləsɪs/ noun [U] **1 HEALTH** the loss of the ability to move your body or a part of it **2** the state of being completely unable to operate normally

paramedic /,pærə'medɪk/ noun [C] **HEALTH** someone who is not a doctor but is trained to give medical treatment to people at the place where an accident has happened —**paramedical** adj

parameter /pə'ræmɪtə/ noun [C] a limit that affects how something can be done

paramilitary /,pærə'mɪlɪt(ə)ri/ adj organized and operating like an army, but not part of an official army —**paramilitary** noun [C]

paramount /'pærəmaʊnt/ adj more important than all other things

paranoia /,pærə'nɔɪə/ noun [U] **1 HEALTH** a mental illness that makes someone believe that other people do not like them and want to harm them, even though there is no proof of this **2** the worried feeling that other people do not like you and are trying to harm you, although you have no proof of this. This is not a medical meaning.

paranoid[1] /'pærə,nɔɪd/ adj **1** someone who is paranoid worries that people do not like them and are trying to harm them, although they have no proof of this **2 HEALTH** suffering from the mental illness paranoia

paranoid[2] /'pærə,nɔɪd/ noun [C] someone who suffers from paranoia

the paranormal /,pærə'nɔːm(ə)l/ noun [singular] mysterious events or facts that cannot be explained by science

parapet /'pærəpɪt, 'pærəpet/ noun [C] **CONSTRUCTION** a low wall at the edge of something high such as a bridge or roof

paraphrase /'pærə,freɪz/ verb [T] to express what someone has said or written using different words in order to make it shorter or clearer —**paraphrase** noun [C]

paraplegic /,pærə'pliːdʒɪk/ noun [C] **HEALTH** someone who cannot move the parts of their body below their waist —**paraplegic** adj

parasite /'pærəsaɪt/ noun [C] **1 BIOLOGY** an organism that lives in or on another living thing and feeds on it. Lice, fleas, and tapeworms are all types of parasite. The organism that a parasite lives on is called the **host**. **2** *showing disapproval* a lazy person who lives by getting things such as money or food from other people

parasitic /,pærə'sɪtɪk/ adj **1 BIOLOGY** a parasitic organism lives in or on another living thing and feeds on it **2 HEALTH** a parasitic disease is caused by parasites living inside the body

parasitism /'pærəsaɪt,ɪz(ə)m/ noun [U] **BIOLOGY** a situation in which one organism lives as a parasite in or on another organism

parasitology /ˌpærəsaɪˈtɒlədʒi/ noun [U] BIOLOGY the scientific study of plants and animals that live as parasites

parasol /ˈpærəsɒl/ noun [C] a type of **umbrella** that provides protection from the sun

parastatal /ˌpærəˈsteɪt(ə)l/ adj partly or completely controlled or owned by the government —**parastatal** noun [C]

parathyroid /ˌpærəˈθaɪrɔɪd/ noun [C] ANATOMY a gland next to the thyroid that produces a hormone called **parathormone** that controls levels of calcium in the body

paratrooper /ˈpærəˌtruːpə/ noun [C] a soldier who is trained to jump out of planes wearing a **parachute**

paratroops /ˈpærəˌtruːps/ noun [plural] soldiers who are paratroopers

parcel /ˈpɑːs(ə)l/ noun [C] something wrapped in paper or in a large envelope so that it can be sent by post = PACKAGE

parched /pɑːtʃt/ adj extremely dry because of hot weather

parchment /ˈpɑːtʃmənt/ noun [U] 1 a substance made from animal skin that was used in the past for writing on 2 thick pale yellow paper

pardon¹ /ˈpɑːd(ə)n/ interjection 1 used for politely asking someone to repeat something that you did not hear or did not understand 2 used for saying 'sorry' when you make a rude noise with your body

pardon² /ˈpɑːd(ə)n/ verb [T] LAW to officially forgive someone for committing a crime and to free them from prison

pardon³ /ˈpɑːd(ə)n/ noun [C] LAW an official decision to forgive someone for committing a crime and to free them from prison

parenchyma /pəˈreŋkɪmə/ noun [U] BIOLOGY 1 the soft tissue in plants that forms the greater part of leaves, roots, the **pith** in stems, and the flesh of fruit 2 the tissue of an organ that is important for what it does, as opposed to the tissue that is part of its structure

parent /ˈpeərənt/ noun [C] your mother or father: Has Joe met your parents yet?

parental /pəˈrent(ə)l/ adj involving or provided by parents

pa,rental 'leave noun [U] a period of time away from work that is allowed to a parent to care for a baby or child

'parent ,cell noun [C] BIOLOGY the cell from which other cells are produced during cell division

'parent ,company noun [C] BUSINESS a company that owns or controls a smaller company of the same type → SUBSIDIARY

parentheses /pəˈrenθəˌsiːz/ noun [plural] LANGUAGE the symbols (and), used in writing for separating a word, phrase, or number from the rest of a sentence: The students' nationalities are shown in parentheses.

parenthood /ˈpeərəntˌhʊd/ noun [U] the fact of being a parent

parenting /ˈpeərəntɪŋ/ noun [U] the activities that are involved in being a parent and bringing up children

'parent ,metal noun [C] 1 TECHNOLOGY, CHEMISTRY the main metal in an alloy 2 TECHNOLOGY a metal piece that is to be welded to another piece

parish /ˈpærɪʃ/ noun 1 [C] RELIGION in some Christian churches, a district that has its own church building

and priest 2 [singular] the people who live in a parish

parishioner /pəˈrɪʃ(ə)nə/ noun [C] RELIGION someone who lives in a particular parish and regularly goes to church

parity /ˈpærəti/ noun [U] a situation in which different people or things are equal

park¹ /pɑːk/ noun [C] 1 an open public area with grass and trees in a town. Parks often have sports fields or places for children to play. 2 ENVIRONMENT an area in the countryside that is protected by the government for people to enjoy. Parks often have important natural features such as lakes or mountains: Yellowstone National Park

park² /pɑːk/ verb [I/T] to move a vehicle into a place where you are going to leave it for a period of time: Mary parked the car at the side of the road.

parking /ˈpɑːkɪŋ/ noun [U] 1 the process of putting a vehicle into a place and leaving it there 2 space where vehicles can be left

'parking ,meter noun [C] a machine in the street that you put coins into in order to pay for leaving your car there

'parking ,ticket noun [C] an official document that is put on someone's car, telling them that they have broken a rule about parking and must pay a **fine**

Parkinson's disease /ˈpɑːkɪnsənz dɪˌziːz/ noun [U] HEALTH a serious illness that affects the nerves and makes someone shake and move slowly

parliament /ˈpɑːləmənt/ noun 1 [C] POLITICS an official elected group of people in some countries who meet to make the laws of the country and discuss national issues: the Russian parliament 2 Parliament [U] SOCIAL STUDIES the main law-making institution in some countries such as the UK: The party has a large majority in Parliament. ♦ He entered Parliament in 1997. → MEMBER OF PARLIAMENT 3 [C/U] SOCIAL STUDIES the period of time during which a particular parliament meets: The bill would be discussed in the next parliament.

parliamentary /ˌpɑːləˈment(ə)ri/ adj POLITICS relating to a parliament, or suitable for a parliament

parochial /pəˈrəʊkiəl/ adj showing disapproval not interested in things that do not affect your own local area

parody /ˈpærədi/ (plural **parodies**) noun [C/U] LITERATURE, ARTS a piece of writing, a poem, or a performance that copies a serious work of literature or music in a humorous way —**parody** verb [T]

parole /pəˈrəʊl/ noun [U] 1 LAW permission for a prisoner to leave prison before the official time, if they promise to obey particular rules: He could be out on parole in two years. 2 LANGUAGE language considered as the way that individual people use it → LANGUE

parrot /ˈpærət/ noun [C] a brightly coloured tropical bird that is often kept as a pet and can be taught to copy what people say. There are many different types of parrot. —picture → BIRD

parse /pɑːz/ verb [T] LANGUAGE to examine and describe the grammar of a sentence or a particular word in a sentence

Parsee /ˈpɑːsiː/ noun [C] RELIGION someone in India whose religion is **Zoroastrianism**

parsimonious /ˌpɑːsɪˈməʊniəs/ adj formal not willing to give or spend money —**parsimoniously** adv, **parsimony** /ˈpɑːsɪməni/ noun [U]

parsley /'pɑːsli/ noun [U] a small plant that you use for decorating food or giving it a fresh flavour

parsnip /'pɑːsnɪp/ noun [C/U] a long white hard vegetable that is the swollen root of the plant

part¹ /pɑːt/ noun

1 section	**5** piece for machine
2 sb played by actor	**6** relative quantity
3 involvement	+ PHRASES
4 section of book	

1 [C] one of the pieces, sections, or aspects that something consists of: *The top part of the shoe is made of leather.* ♦ *We walked part of the way, then took a bus.* ♦ *The hardest part of my job is controlling the budgets.* ♦ *This is one of the nicest parts of San Francisco.*
2 [C] the person played by an actor in a film, play, or television programme, or the words that the actor speaks: *She'd be really good for that part.* ♦ *He had just two weeks to learn his part.*
3 [singular] the way in which someone is involved in an activity or event, and the effect that they have on what happens: *He was jailed for 10 years for his part in the crime.*
4 [C] a section of a book, magazine, play, television series etc: *a new 12-part drama starting tonight on ITV*
5 [C] an individual piece of a machine or vehicle: *We're waiting for a part to come from Germany.*
6 [C] a particular quantity that is used for measuring equal amounts of different substances to form a mixture: *Use a mixture of one part milk to four parts water.*
  PHRASES **have/play a part (in sth)** to be involved in a particular situation or activity and influence its development: *They have worked very hard, but luck has played a part too.*
  in part to some degree: *The accidents were due in part to the bad weather.*
  on sb's part or **on the part of sb** done or experienced by someone: *a mistake on the part of the authorities*
  part of speech LANGUAGE one of the main grammatical groups that a particular word belongs to, for example noun, verb, adjective, or adverb
  take part (in sth) to be involved in an activity with other people: *They will be taking part in the discussions.*
  → MOST

part² /pɑːt/ verb **1** [I/T] to move apart, or to move two things or two sections of a single unit away from each other: *The crowd parted to let them through.* ♦ *Tony parted the curtains and looked out.* **2** [I] if two people part, they go away from each other: *They parted at the train station.* ♦ *The marriage failed, but they parted on good terms.* **3** [T] to make a line on your head by brushing or **combing** your hair in two different directions: *Her dark hair was parted down the middle.*
  PHRASE **be parted (from sb)** to be prevented from being with someone who you want to be with: *Being parted from his family made him depressed.*
  PHRASAL VERB **'part with sth** to give something to someone although you would prefer to keep it

part³ /pɑːt/ adv **part..., part...** a mixture of two things: *I am part Russian, part English.*

'part ,drawing noun [C] MATHS, PHYSICS a drawing made using **orthographic projection** that shows one part of an **assembly** (=set of parts forming a unit)

,part ex'change noun [U] a method of buying something new such as a car by giving your old one as part of the payment for the new one

partial /'pɑːʃ(ə)l/ adj **1** not complete: *a partial withdrawal from enemy territory* **2** supporting one person, group, or opinion more than others, instead of being fair to everyone ≠ IMPARTIAL

partially /'pɑːʃəli/ adv not completely = PARTLY: *A partially clothed body was discovered in the woods.*

,partially 'sighted adj someone who is partially sighted cannot see properly but is not completely blind

participant /pɑː'tɪsɪpənt/ noun [C] someone who takes part in something

participate /pɑː'tɪsɪpeɪt/ verb [I] to take part in something: *The rebels have agreed to participate in the peace talks.* —**participation** /pɑːˌtɪsɪ'peɪʃ(ə)n/ noun [U], **participative** /pɑː'tɪsɪpətɪv/ adj

participial /ˌpɑːtɪ'sɪpiəl/ adj LANGUAGE consisting of, containing, or used as a participle

participle /pɑː'tɪsɪp(ə)l, 'pɑːtɪsɪp(ə)l/ noun [C] LANGUAGE the form of a verb used in compound tenses and as an adjective. English uses the **present participle**, which ends in '-ing', and the **past participle**, which usually ends in '-ed'.

particle /'pɑːtɪk(ə)l/ noun [C] **1** an extremely small piece or amount of something **2** SCIENCE an extremely small piece of matter, for example an atom or a molecule **3** SCIENCE a **subatomic particle** that is part of an atom, for example an electron, proton, or neutron **4** LANGUAGE an adverb or preposition used with a verb to form a phrasal verb. For example in the sentence 'He put on his clothes', 'on' is a particle.

particular¹ /pə'tɪkjʊlə/ adj **1** used for emphasizing that you are talking about one specific person or thing and not anyone or anything else = SPECIFIC: *Are there any particular topics that you would like me to explain further?* **2** especially great = SPECIAL: *Two matters need to be given particular attention.* **3** someone who is particular has very clear ideas about what they like and dislike, and is difficult to please: *She's very particular about what she eats.* **4** clearly different and belonging to just one person or thing = DISTINCTIVE

particular² /pə'tɪkjʊlə/ noun
  PHRASE **in particular 1** especially: *I liked the last candidate in particular.* **2** special, or important: *'What are you doing tonight?' 'Nothing in particular.'*
  → PARTICULARS

particularly /pə'tɪkjʊləli/ adv **1** very, or very much: *His remarks were particularly helpful.* ♦ *'Did you have a good time?' 'Not particularly.'* **2** especially: *The environment has become a major political issue, particularly in the past decade.* **3** in a clear and specific way: *He particularly asked for you to be at the meeting.*

particulars /pə'tɪkjʊləz/ noun [plural] information and details about someone or something

particulate¹ /pɑː'tɪkjʊlət/ noun [C] SCIENCE a very small piece of matter, either solid or liquid, that is present in a gas

particulate² /pɑː'tɪkjʊleɪt/ adj SCIENCE made up of separate particles

parting¹ /'pɑːtɪŋ/ adj done or said by someone when they are leaving: *a parting gift*

parting² /'pɑːtɪŋ/ noun **1** [C/U] the act of leaving someone **2** [C] a line on your head that you make by brushing or **combing** your hair in two different directions

partition /pɑː'tɪʃ(ə)n/ noun **1** [C] a wall, screen, or piece of glass that is used for separating one area from another in a room **2** [U] the process of dividing a country into two or more separate countries —**partition** verb [T]

partitive /'pɑːtətɪv/ noun [C] LANGUAGE a word or expression used for showing that only part of something is being referred to, rather than all of it. In the sentence 'Have a piece of cake', 'a piece of' is a partitive.

partly /ˈpɑːtli/ adv to some degree, but not completely: *I'll admit I was partly to blame.* ♦ *We get on well together, partly because we share the same sense of humour.*

partner¹ /ˈpɑːtnə/ noun [C] **1** someone who you live with and have a sexual relationship with: *Are partners invited to the office party?* **2** someone who you do a particular activity with: *John is my tennis partner.* ♦ *Take your partners for the last dance.* **3** BUSINESS one of two or more people who own a company and share its profits and losses: *He became **a partner in** his father's law firm.* **4** BUSINESS a business, organization, or country that has an agreement with another business, organization, or country: *China is one of our major **trading partners**.*

partner² /ˈpɑːtnə/ verb [T] to be someone's partner in an activity

partnership /ˈpɑːtnəʃɪp/ noun **1** [U] BUSINESS the position of being one of two or more people who own a company as partners **2** [C] BUSINESS a company that is owned by two or more partners **3** [C/U] a relationship between two or more people, groups, or countries that are involved in an activity together

ˈpart ˌsection noun [C/U] MATHS, PHYSICS a drawing of a section of a three-dimensional object that shows only part of the object

ˌpart-ˈtime adj **1** done for only part of the time that an activity is usually performed: *a part-time job* **2** doing part-time work or study: *a part-time student* —ˌpart-ˈtime adv → FULL-TIME¹

parturition /ˌpɑːtjʊˈrɪʃ(ə)n/ noun [C/U] BIOLOGY the act of giving birth

party /ˈpɑːti/ (plural **parties**) noun [C] **1** a social event at which people meet in order to celebrate something or have fun: *Did you invite her to your **birthday party**?* ♦ *We're **having a party** on Saturday night.* **2** an organized group of people who share the same ideas about how a country should be governed, and who try to get elected: *the two main **political parties*** **3** a group of people who are going somewhere together, or who are involved in the same activity: *a rescue party* ♦ *a **party of** tourists* **4** formal a person or group involved in a contract or legal case with another person or group: *the guilty party* ♦ *the parties to the 1930 agreement*

pascal /ˈpæskəl/ noun [C] PHYSICS a unit for measuring pressure, equal to one **newton** per square metre (N/m²). Symbol Pa

PASCAL or **Pascal** /ˈpæsˈkæl/ noun [U] COMPUTING a simple computer language used for writing programs

pass¹ /pɑːs/ verb

1 go past sth	**10** kick/hit ball to sb
2 move somewhere	**11** go above amount
3 do well in test	**12** happen
4 accept in test	**13** give opinion
5 let sb have sth	**14** of body waste
6 make sth official	**15** change owner
7 be spent	**+ PHRASE**
8 spend time	**+ PHRASAL VERBS**
9 stop happening	

1 [I/T] to go past something: *The procession slowly passed us.* ♦ *They stopped at the crossing, waiting for the train to pass.*

2 [I/T] to move, or to move something, in a particular direction or to a particular place or position: *The railway line **passes through** Darlington.* ♦ *Two large birds **passed over** our heads.* ♦ *He **passed** his hand **across** his forehead.*

3 [I/T] EDUCATION to be successful in an examination or test, by achieving a satisfactory standard ≠ FAIL: *Do you think you'll pass?* ♦ *She **passed** her driving **test**.*

4 [T] EDUCATION to officially decide that someone has been successful in an examination or test ≠ FAIL: *The examiners passed only 40% of the candidates.*

5 [T] to put something into someone's hand or into a position where they can take it: *Could you pass me that newspaper?* ♦ *He **passed** the camera **to** her.*

6 [T] to make a law or proposal become official by voting to accept it: *one of the worst **laws** ever **passed***

7 [I] if time passes, it happens and comes to an end: *The summer holidays passed quickly, as usual.*

8 [T] to spend time doing something: *We passed the day swimming and lying in the sun.* ♦ *They watched videos to **pass the time** (=make it seem shorter).*

9 [I] to come to an end: *I felt a sharp pain, but it soon passed.*

10 [I/T] SPORTS to kick, hit, or throw the ball to another player in a sports team: *He **passed the ball** to Scholes who shot wide of the goal.*

11 [I] to become more than a particular amount: *The death toll has already passed 200.*

12 [I] to happen, or to be allowed to happen: *Her mistake seemed to have **passed unnoticed**.* ♦ *The rest of the meeting **passed without incident** (=without anything unpleasant happening).* ♦ *Andrew was furious and wasn't going to **let** this one **pass** (=not react to something annoying).*

13 [T] to make a comment, or to give an opinion: *He was asked for his opinion but refused to **pass comment**.*

14 [T] formal to make something leave the body as a waste product: *He had difficulty in passing water (=making liquid waste leave his body).*

15 [I] to stop being owned or controlled by one person and start being owned or controlled by another: *The estate has passed from father to son for generations.*

PHRASE **pass (a) sentence (on sb)** LAW to officially say in a court of law what a criminal's punishment will be → BUCK

PHRASAL VERBS **ˌpass sth aˈround** same as **pass sth round**
ˌpass aˈway to die. This word is used to avoid saying 'die' when you think it might upset someone.
ˌpass ˈby (sth) to go past: *Three buses passed by, but mine never came.* ♦ *I pass by her house every day on my way to school.*
ˌpass sth ˈdown to give knowledge, or to teach skills, to your children or to younger people
ˌpass sb/sth ˈoff as sth to make people believe that a person or thing is something else: *He put on a suit, intending to pass himself off as a businessman.*
ˌpass sth ˈon 1 to give someone something that someone else has given you: *When you've read this message, please pass it on.* **2** to give someone an infectious illness
ˌpass ˈout to suddenly become unconscious = FAINT
ˌpass sth ˈround to give something to one person in a group, who gives it to someone else, who then gives it to someone else and so on

pass² /pɑːs/ noun [C]

1 document allowing sth	**4** path through
2 successful test result	mountains
3 kick/hit etc of ball to sb	**5** check of information

1 an official document that gives you permission to enter a place or to use a particular form of transport without having to pay each time: *You always have to **show** your **pass** before they'll let you in.*

2 EDUCATION a successful result in an examination or test: *She got **a pass in** maths.*

3 SPORTS a kick, hit, or throw of the ball to another

player in your sports team: *a perfect pass from Ince to Owen*
4 GEOGRAPHY a path or road that goes through an area of mountains
5 one of several stages in a process that involves checking and dealing with information: *I finished my first pass on my transcript yesterday.*

passage /ˈpæsɪdʒ/ noun

1 long narrow walled area	**4** way through a place
2 short section of sth	**5** tube in body
3 movement over place	**6** process of making law

1 [C] a long narrow area with walls on each side that leads from one room or place to another: *He left his bike in the passage between the kitchen and the back door.*
2 [C] a short section of a book, article, poem, or piece of music, considered on its own: *He read me a passage from his favourite book.*
3 [U] movement past, over, or through a place: *The passage of heavy guns had left deep ruts in the field.*
4 [singular] a way through a place, especially when this is difficult: *Branches and vines blocked our passage through the jungle.*
5 [C] ANATOMY a tube in the body for air or liquid to pass through: *Her air passages were blocked.*
6 [singular] POLITICS the process by which a bill is discussed in a parliament and becomes law

passageway /ˈpæsɪdʒˌweɪ/ noun [C] a passage from one room or place to another = PASSAGE

passenger /ˈpæsɪndʒə/ noun [C] someone who travels in a vehicle, aircraft, train, or ship but is not the driver or one of the people who works on it

passenger ,manifest noun [C] TOURISM a list of passengers on a ship or plane

passenger ,train noun [C] a train that carries only passengers → FREIGHT TRAIN

passer-by /ˌpɑːsəˈbaɪ/ (plural **passers-by**) noun [C] someone who is walking past a place

passim /ˈpæsɪm/ adv *formal* used in notes for a book or article for showing that something is mentioned in many places in it

passing¹ /ˈpɑːsɪŋ/ adj **1** moving past: *He was found by a passing motorist.* **2** lasting only a short time, and usually not very important or serious: *a passing fashion*

passing² /ˈpɑːsɪŋ/ noun [U] **1** the process by which something ends or stops existing **2** the process by which time passes: *Even with the passing of time, nothing had happened to change his view.*
PHRASE in passing if you say something in passing, you mention it while you are talking about something else

passion /ˈpæʃ(ə)n/ noun **1** [C/U] a powerful emotion such as love or anger: *She spoke with great passion about the plight of the refugees.* **2** [C/U] a very strong feeling of sexual love: *I was suddenly seized by an overwhelming passion for him.* **3** [C] a strong enthusiasm or interest: *a passion for classical music*

passionate /ˈpæʃ(ə)nət/ adj **1** showing or expressing powerful emotions or very strong beliefs **2** involving or affected by very strong feelings of sexual excitement —**passionately** adv

passionflower /ˈpæʃ(ə)nˌflaʊə/ noun [C] a tropical climbing plant with large brightly coloured flowers

passive /ˈpæsɪv/ adj **1** accepting what happens without trying to change events or react to things: *a helpless and passive victim* **2** LANGUAGE in a passive sentence, the subject is the person or thing that is affected by the action of the verb. 'He was examined

by another doctor' is a passive sentence. → active sense 3 —**passively** adv

the passive /ˈpæsɪv/ or **the ,passive 'voice** noun [singular] LANGUAGE the passive form of a verb → ACTIVE

,passive 'flux noun [C] TECHNOLOGY a flux that prevents the joint from further **oxidation** during **soldering**

,passive 'smoking noun [U] HEALTH the act of breathing other people's tobacco smoke into the lungs

Passover /ˈpɑːsˌəʊvə/ noun [C/U] RELIGION a Jewish religious festival that lasts for seven or eight days in March or April

passport /ˈpɑːspɔːt/ noun [C] **1** an official document that contains someone's photograph and shows which country they are a citizen of. It is used when travelling to foreign countries: *Bill has a Canadian passport.*
♦ *You must **hold a valid passport**.* **2** something that makes it possible for you to achieve something good: *In those days a university degree was **a passport to** a secure job.*

'passport con,trol noun [U] TOURISM an area in an airport where people's passports are checked

'passport ,photo noun [C] TOURISM a small photograph of a person's face, of the type used on passports

password /ˈpɑːsˌwɜːd/ noun [C] **1** a secret word or phrase that you need in order to get into a room, building, or area **2** COMPUTING a set of numbers or letters that you have to type in order to use a computer system

'password pro,tection noun [U] COMPUTING software for which a user has to enter a password before they can use it

past¹ /pɑːst/ adv, preposition **1** later than a particular time: *It's ten past three (=3.10).* ♦ *It was **past midnight** by the time we arrived.* **2** moving near someone or something and then beyond them: *I walked past several hotels on my way to the petrol station.* ♦ *She heard music coming from inside the van as it drove past.* **3** having passed a particular stage, point, or limit: *I tried to read the book, but couldn't get past the first chapter.* ♦ *He was past his best as a player by then.* **4** used for saying that a period of time passes: *The months went past, and still no word from her.* → PUT

past² /pɑːst/ noun [singular] **1 the past** the time before the present, and everything that happened then: *Archaeology helps us to understand the past.* ♦ *He has made similar promises in the past.* **2** all the things that someone has done before now: *She was trying to remember an event from her past.* **3 the past** LANGUAGE the **past tense**

past³ /pɑːst/ adj **1** happening or existing in the period immediately before now: *He has spent the past two weeks travelling around the country.* **2** happening or existing at an earlier time: *She is a past president of the Union.* ♦ *I know from past experience that this work is very time-consuming.* **3** LANGUAGE expressing actions or events that happened or states that existed before the present time: *the past tense*

pasta /ˈpæstə/ noun [C/U] an Italian food made in many different shapes from flour and water, and sometimes eggs. **Spaghetti** and **ravioli** are types of pasta.

paste¹ /peɪst/ noun [U] **1** a glue that is used for making something stick to a surface **2** a food that is made by crushing meat, fish, or vegetables. It is spread on bread or added to other food in cooking.

paste² /peɪst/ verb [I/T] **1** to glue paper onto a surface using paste **2 COMPUTING** to copy or move words, pictures etc on a computer screen from one place to another

pastel¹ /ˈpæst(ə)l/ adj pale and not strong in colour

pastel² /ˈpæst(ə)l/ noun **1** [C] a colour that is very pale **2** [C/U] **ARTS** a stick of colour used for making drawings. It is made of **wax** mixed with powder. **3** [C] **ARTS** a drawing made using pastels

pasteurized /ˈpɑːstʃəraɪzd/ adj a pasteurized liquid such as milk has been heated to a temperature that kills all the harmful bacteria —**pasteurization** /ˌpɑːstʃəraɪˈzeɪʃ(ə)n/ noun [U]

pastime /ˈpɑːstaɪm/ noun [C] something that you do regularly for fun in your free time

pastor /ˈpɑːstə/ noun [C] **RELIGION** a priest in some Christian churches

pastoral /ˈpɑːst(ə)rəl/ adj **1** pastoral work or activities involve giving help and advice to people about personal problems **2** *literary* relating to life in the countryside

ˌpastoral ˈfarming noun [U] **AGRICULTURE** sheep or cattle farming

ˌpast ˈparticiple noun [C] **LANGUAGE** the form of a verb that is used for making perfect tenses and passive forms of verbs. Past participles are also sometimes used as adjectives, for example 'cooked' in the phrase 'cooked vegetables'.

the ˌpast ˈperfect noun [singular] **LANGUAGE** a verb tense that is formed in English with 'had' and a past participle. It is used to express an action that was completed before a particular time in the past, for example 'had finished' in the sentence 'She offered to help but I had already finished'.

pastry /ˈpeɪstri/ (plural **pastries**) noun **1** [U] a food made by mixing flour, fat, and water. The mixture is rolled flat and used for making pies and other food. **2** [C] a type of cake made from sweet pastry

the ˌpast ˈtense noun [singular] **LANGUAGE** the form of a verb that is used for expressing what existed or happened in the past, for example 'lived' in the sentence 'We lived in France until I was seven.'

pasture /ˈpɑːstʃə/ noun [C/U] **AGRICULTURE** land covered with grass where sheep or cows are kept

pat¹ /pæt/ (**pats, patting, patted**) verb [T] to touch a person or animal gently several times with a flat hand in a friendly way
PHRASE pat sb on the back to praise someone for doing something good

pat² /pæt/ noun [C] the action of gently touching a person or animal several times with a flat hand in a friendly way
PHRASE a pat on the back praise for having done something good

patch¹ /pætʃ/ noun [C]

1 different part of sth	4 cover for eye
2 piece of ground	5 piece of software
3 piece of cloth	+ PHRASE

1 an area that is different from what surrounds it: *There were damp patches on the ceiling.*
2 a piece of ground, especially one where you grow fruit or vegetables, or where a particular plant grows: *a patch of grass*
3 a piece of cloth that you sew over a hole in clothes, or over a part where holes might form
4 a cover that you wear over an injured eye
5 COMPUTING a piece of software that is added to a computer program in order to improve it or remove a fault
PHRASE a bad/rough patch a time when your life is difficult or unpleasant

patch² /pætʃ/ verb [T] to cover a hole in clothes by sewing a patch over it

patchwork /ˈpætʃˌwɜːk/ noun **1** [singular] something that consists of many different parts **2** [U] the art of sewing pieces of cloth of different colours together to make a pattern or picture

patchy /ˈpætʃi/ (**patchier, patchiest**) adj **1** happening or existing in some places but not in other places: *patchy rain* **2** not detailed enough or complete enough to be useful: *a patchy knowledge of Spanish history* **3** if someone's performance or work is patchy, it is good sometimes but not always

pâté /ˈpæteɪ/ noun [C/U] a soft food made from meat, fish, or vegetables that you spread on bread

patella /pəˈtelə/ noun [C] **ANATOMY** the bone at the front of the knee = KNEECAP —*picture* → SKELETON

patent /ˈpeɪt(ə)nt, ˈpæt(ə)nt/ noun [C] an official document that gives someone who has invented something the legal right to make or sell it for a particular period of time, and prevents anyone else from doing so

patent leather /ˌpeɪt(ə)nt ˈleðə/ noun [U] very shiny leather, used for making bags and shoes

paternal /pəˈtɜːn(ə)l/ adj **1** relating to being a father **2** a paternal relative is related to you through your father **3** *showing approval* typical of a kind and caring father —**paternally** adv

paternalism /pəˈtɜːnəˌlɪz(ə)m/ noun [U] **SOCIAL STUDIES** a system in which someone in authority advises and helps people, but also controls them by not letting them make their own decisions and choices —**paternalistic** /pəˌtɜːnəˈlɪstɪk/ adj

paternity /pəˈtɜːnəti/ noun [U] **LAW** the fact of being the father of a child

paˈternity ˌleave noun [U] a period of time when a father is allowed to be away from work after the birth of his child

path /pɑːθ/ noun [C]

1 to a place	4 sb's life
2 empty space	5 of computer file
3 direction	

1 a way from one place to another that people can walk along: *Amy walked up the path to the house.* → ROAD
2 a way from one place to another passing through a lot of people or objects: *Police tried to clear a path through the rush hour traffic.*
3 the direction that someone or something is moving in: *She ran into the path of an oncoming car.*
4 the way that someone takes to achieve something, or the way that their life develops: *Our lives began to follow separate paths.*
5 COMPUTING the set of letters or other symbols that is the full name of a computer file and shows which **directory** it is stored in

pathetic /pəˈθetɪk/ adj **1** useless or not effective in an annoying way **2** if someone or something looks or sounds pathetic, you feel sympathy for them = PITIFUL —**pathetically** /pəˈθetɪkli/ adv

pathogen /ˈpæθədʒən/ noun [C] **BIOLOGY** a microorganism such as a bacterium or virus that causes disease —**pathogenic** /ˌpæθəˈdʒenɪk/ adj

pathological /ˌpæθəˈlɒdʒɪk(ə)l/ adj **HEALTH** **1** pathological behaviour or feelings are not based on ordinary practical reasons, and cannot be controlled by the person experiencing them **2** relating to **pathology** —**pathologically** /ˌpæθəˈlɒdʒɪkli/ adv

pathologist /pəˈθɒlədʒɪst/ noun [C] **HEALTH** a scientist who studies the causes of diseases and how they affect people, especially one who studies the causes of a person's death

pathology /pəˈθɒlədʒi/ noun [U] **HEALTH** the study of the causes of diseases and how they affect people

pathos /ˈpeɪθɒs/ noun [U] a quality in a person or situation that makes you feel sad or sorry for them

pathway /ˈpɑːθˌweɪ/ noun [C] a path

patience /ˈpeɪʃ(ə)ns/ noun [U] **1** the ability to continue doing something for a long time without losing interest: *Photography* **requires** *a lot of* **patience.** **2** the ability to remain calm and not get angry, especially when something is annoying or takes too long: *I'm afraid I've* **no patience with** *people like them.* ♦ *After waiting for an hour, I was beginning to* **run out of patience** (=stop having any). ♦ *She was quickly* **losing patience with** *the whole wretched situation.*

patient¹ /ˈpeɪʃ(ə)nt/ noun [C] **HEALTH** someone who is receiving medical treatment

patient² /ˈpeɪʃ(ə)nt/ adj able to wait for a long time or deal with a difficult situation without becoming angry or upset ≠ IMPATIENT: *Susan's very patient with the children.* —**patiently** adv

patriarch /ˈpeɪtriˌɑːk/ noun [C] **1** **SOCIAL STUDIES** the oldest man in a family or organization, who is respected because of this **2** **RELIGION** a religious leader in one of the **Orthodox** Christian churches

patriarchal /ˌpeɪtriˈɑːk(ə)l/ adj **SOCIAL STUDIES** a patriarchal society, system, or organization is one in which men have all the power and influence —**patriarchy** /ˈpeɪtriˌɑːki/ noun [C/U]

patrilineal /ˌpætriˈlɪniəl/ adj **SOCIAL STUDIES** *formal* used for describing the father's side of a family and the relations on that side

patriotic /ˌpætriˈɒtɪk, ˌpeɪtriˈɒtɪk/ adj feeling a lot of love, respect, and duty towards your country —**patriot** /ˈpeɪtriət, ˈpætriət/ noun [C], **patriotism** /ˈpætriəˌtɪz(ə)m, ˈpeɪtriəˌtɪz(ə)m/ noun [U]

patrol¹ /pəˈtrəʊl/ noun **1** [C] a group of people or vehicles that move regularly around a place in order to prevent trouble or crime **2** [C/U] the movement of a patrol around a place: *Police officers will be* **on patrol** *during the carnival.*

patrol² /pəˈtrəʊl/ (**patrols, patrolling, patrolled**) verb [I/T] to move regularly around a place in order to prevent trouble or crime

patron /ˈpeɪtrən/ noun [C] **1** someone who supports the work of writers, artists, or musicians by giving them money **2** a famous person who supports an organization and allows it to use their name in its advertising **3** *formal* someone who uses a particular restaurant, hotel, or other business

patronage /ˈpætrənɪdʒ/ noun [U] help or money that is given by a patron

patronize /ˈpætrənaɪz/ verb **1** [I/T] *showing disapproval* to behave or speak in a way that shows that you think that you are more intelligent or important than someone else **2** [T] *formal* to use a particular restaurant, hotel, or other business

patronizing /ˈpætrəˌnaɪzɪŋ/ adj *showing disapproval* behaving or speaking in a way that shows that you think that you are more intelligent or important than someone else

patron 'saint noun [C] **RELIGION** a saint who is believed to protect a particular place, activity, or group of people according to the Christian religion

pattern /ˈpæt(ə)n/ noun [C] **1** a series of actions or events that together show how things normally happen or are done: *The study examined* **patterns of** *behaviour in young children.* ♦ *The four murders all seemed to* **follow** *the same* **pattern.** **2** a set of lines, shapes, or colours that are repeated regularly: *a carpet with a pretty pattern* **3** a drawing or shape that you use when you are making something, so that you get the shape and size correct **4** **TECHNOLOGY** an exact model of an object that is to be **cast** in metal

patterned /ˈpæt(ə)nd/ adj decorated with a pattern

paunch /pɔːntʃ/ noun [C] a fat stomach that a man sometimes has

pause¹ /pɔːz/ verb **1** [I] to stop moving or doing something for a short time before starting again: *She paused at the door and then left.* **2** [I/T] to make a CD, video, or computer game stop for a short time by pressing a button

pause² /pɔːz/ noun **1** [C] a short time when someone stops moving or doing something before starting again **2** [U] a button that stops a CD, video, or computer game for a short time **3** [C] **MUSIC** a mark ⌒ over a musical note that shows the note should last for longer than usual

pavement /ˈpeɪvmənt/ noun [C] a path with a hard surface next to a road

pavilion /pəˈvɪliən/ noun [C] **1** **SPORTS** a building in a sports field for players or club members to use **2** a building in a park or large garden for people to sit in **3** a building or tent at an exhibition or show

Pavlovian /pævˈləʊviən/ adj used for describing reactions that people have automatically

paw /pɔː/ noun [C] **BIOLOGY** the foot of some mammals such as cats, dogs, and bears

pawl /pɔːl/ noun [C] **ENGINEERING** a metal object that fits into a **ratchet** to move it forward, or to stop it moving backwards

pawn /pɔːn/ noun [C] **1** a person who is used by someone who is more powerful so that they can achieve an aim **2** one of the eight least important pieces that each player has in a game of chess

pawpaw /ˈpɔːpɔː/ noun [C/U] a **papaya**

pay¹ /peɪ/ (**pays, paying, paid** /peɪd/) verb

1 buy goods	**5** have good result
2 be worth in wages etc	**6** suffer for sth
3 give money for job	**+ PHRASES**
4 be successful	**+ PHRASAL VERBS**

1 [I/T] to give money in order to buy something, or to give money that you owe someone: *Let me* **pay for** *dinner.* ♦ *Will you be* **paying by** *cash, cheque, or credit card?* ♦ *Can I* **pay in** *dollars?* ♦ *There's a reduction if you* **pay cash.**
2 [I/T] if a job pays a particular amount of money, someone gets that amount for doing it: *She was in a job paying over £60,000 a year.* ♦ *My new job pays well.*
3 [I/T] to give money to someone for a job that they do for you or as their salary: *We still haven't paid them for the repairs to the roof.* ♦ *We had to pay them over £100 to sort it out.* ♦ *Some of the workers haven't been paid for weeks.*
4 [I] if a business pays, it earns money: *We have a lot of hard work ahead if we're going to make the business pay.*
5 [I/T] to have a good result: *The message is simple:*

crime doesn't pay. ♦ *It pays to cover the pool to keep out falling leaves.*

6 [I] to suffer because of something that you have done: *They had made him look like a fool and now they were going to* **pay for** *it.*

PHRASES   **pay attention (to)** to listen to, watch, or think about someone or something very carefully

pay sb a compliment to say something nice about someone

pay the penalty/price for sth to have to deal with the bad effects of something that you have done

pay tribute to sb to say or do something that shows that you respect and admire someone a lot

pay sb/sth a visit to visit someone or something

PHRASAL VERBS   **,pay sb 'back** to give someone the same amount of money that you borrowed from them

,pay sth 'in to put money into a bank account = DEPOSIT ≠ WITHDRAW

pay² /peɪ/ noun [U] money that you receive for doing your job: *They were demanding higher pay.* ♦ *holiday pay* ♦ *a pay rise*

payable /ˈpeɪəb(ə)l/ adj an amount of money that is payable must be paid

PHRASE   **payable to sb** a cheque that is payable to someone has that person's name written on it

'pay ,day noun [C/U] the day when you get your pay

payload /ˈpeɪˌləʊd/ noun **1** [C] the equipment or people in a space vehicle **2** [C/U] the amount of people or things that an aircraft or other vehicle is able to carry

payment /ˈpeɪmənt/ noun **1** [C] an amount of money that you pay or receive: *The first payment is due on 31 January.* **2** [U] the process of paying money: *We require prompt* **payment** *of all bills.*

PHRASE   **payment by results** BUSINESS a system of payment in which employees' salaries depend on how well they do their jobs

payphone /ˈpeɪfəʊn/ noun [C] a telephone in a public place that you pay to use

'pay ,scale noun [C] a range of different amounts paid for a particular type of work, or for all types of work within an organization

payware /ˈpeɪˌweə/ noun [U] COMPUTING software that you have to pay for → FREEWARE, SHAREWARE

PC /ˌpiː ˈsiː/ noun [C] **1** COMPUTING personal computer: a computer that is designed to be used by one person at home or in an office **2** police constable: a police officer of the lowest rank

PD abbrev PHYSICS potential difference

PDA /ˌpiː diː ˈeɪ/ noun [C] COMPUTING personal digital assistant: a **palmtop** (=a very small computer) on which you can store addresses and telephone numbers, and write letters and reports

PDF /ˌpiː diː ˈef/ noun [U] COMPUTING Portable Document Format: a type of computer file that can contain words, images etc and can be sent on the Internet and read on any computer

PE /ˌpiː ˈiː/ noun [U] EDUCATION physical education: a school subject in which you exercise and play sports

pea /piː/ noun [C] a small round green seed that grows in a long narrow **pod**. It is eaten as a vegetable. —*picture* → VEGETABLE

peace /piːs/ noun [U] **1** a situation in which there is no war between countries or groups: *For many years the agreement maintained peace in Europe.* ♦ *The UN Secretary General urged the two sides to* **make peace.** ♦ *peace talks* ♦ *The agreement brought* **peace between** *the two countries.* **2** a calm quiet situation in which you are not annoyed by noise or other people: *He just*

wanted to read his newspaper **in peace.** ♦ *It's not the holiday to choose if you're looking for* **peace and quiet.** **3** a state when you are calm and have no worries: *With this type of insurance, you're buying* **peace of mind.**

PHRASE   **make (your) peace (with sb)** to end an argument with someone and stop feeling angry towards them

→ DISTURB

peaceable /ˈpiːsəb(ə)l/ adj behaving or happening in a way that avoids arguments and violence —**peaceably** adv

peaceful /ˈpiːsf(ə)l/ adj **1** not involving war or violence: *talks aimed at finding a* **peaceful solution** *to the crisis* **2** calm and quiet: *The hotel is set in peaceful surroundings.* —**peacefully** adv: *The baby was sleeping peacefully.*

peacekeeper /ˈpiːsˌkiːpə/ noun [C] a soldier in a military force that has been sent to a place in order to prevent war between groups who have been fighting there

peacekeeping /ˈpiːsˌkiːpɪŋ/ noun [U] military efforts to prevent war, especially between groups who have been fighting

peacetime /ˈpiːsˌtaɪm/ noun [U] the time when a country is not involved in a war ≠ WARTIME

peach /piːtʃ/ noun **1** [C/U] a fruit with a furry yellow-pink skin that is yellow inside and has a large hard seed —*picture* → FRUIT **2** [U] a yellow-pink colour

peacock /ˈpiːˌkɒk/ noun [C] a large brightly coloured male bird with long blue-green tail feathers that it sometimes spreads out and up. The female is called a **peahen.** —*picture* → BIRD

peak¹ /piːk/ noun [C] **1** the time when something is at its highest or greatest level: *The traffic* **reaches its peak** *at about 8.30 in the morning.* **2** GEOGRAPHY the top of a mountain: *snow-covered peaks* **3** GEOGRAPHY a mountain: *one of the hardest peaks in Europe for climbers* **4** the flat curved part of a **cap** that continues beyond the main part at the front above your eyes

peak² /piːk/ adj **1** a peak period of time is when the largest number of people are doing or using something **2** a peak level of something is when it is highest

peak³ /piːk/ verb [I] to reach the highest amount, level, or standard before becoming lower

,peak 'oil noun [U] ECONOMICS the time when the production of oil in the world is at its highest level

'peak ,season noun [singular/U] TOURISM American **high season**

peanut /ˈpiːˌnʌt/ noun [C] a type of nut that you can eat that grows under the ground inside a thin shell

pear /peə/ noun [C/U] a fruit that is smaller towards the stem end, is white inside, and has yellow, green, or brown skin —*picture* → FRUIT

pearl /pɜːl/ noun [C] a small round jewel that is white and shiny. Pearls grow inside the shells of **oysters.**

pearlite /ˈpɜːlaɪt/ noun [U] TECHNOLOGY a combination of **cementite** and **ferrite** that is found in some types of steel and **cast iron**

peasant /ˈpez(ə)nt/ noun [C] SOCIAL STUDIES a poor person who works on another person's farm or on their own small farm, especially in the past

peasantry /ˈpez(ə)ntri/ noun [U] SOCIAL STUDIES peasants, considered as a social class

peat /piːt/ noun [U] AGRICULTURE, ENVIRONMENT a type of soil that consists of decaying plants. It can be used for growing young plants, for improving other soils, and for burning as fuel. As a **non-renewable**

resource peat has been used too much and alternatives are being looked for.

pebble /'peb(ə)l/ noun [C] a small stone made smooth by water

pecan /pɪ'kæn, 'piːkən/ noun [C] a sweet nut with a hard thin smooth shell

peck /pek/ verb **1** [I/T] when a bird pecks, or when it pecks something, it moves its beak quickly forward to hit or bite something **2** [T] to kiss someone in a quick light way: *She pecked him on the cheek.* —**peck** noun [C]

pectoral /'pekt(ə)rəl/ adj **1** ANATOMY in or relating to the chest: *the pectoral muscles* **2** BIOLOGY on the side of a fish's body just behind its head

pectoral 'fin noun [C] BIOLOGY the fin on each side of a fish's body just behind its head that is used for controlling the direction it moves in

pectoral girdle /'pekt(ə)rəl ,ɡɜːd(ə)l/ noun [singular] ANATOMY a space inside a **vertebra** through which the **spinal cord** passes —*picture* → SKELETON

peculiar /pɪ'kjuːliə/ adj **1** strange, often in an unpleasant way: *a peculiar smell* **2** especially true or typical of a particular person, thing, or situation = PARTICULAR: *features of the environment that are peculiar to the tropics*

peculiarity /pɪ,kjuːli'ærəti/ (plural **peculiarities**) noun [C] **1** a quality or feature that belongs to a particular person, thing, or situation **2** something strange in the way that a person or animal behaves, or in their appearance

pedagogical /,pedə'ɡɒdʒɪk(ə)l/ adj EDUCATION relating to educational methods and principles

pedal /'ped(ə)l/ noun [C] **1** a part of a bicycle, vehicle, or machine that you push with your foot in order to operate it **2** a part on some musical instruments that you press with your foot to change or make a sound —**pedal** verb [I/T]

pedantic /pɪ'dæntɪk/ adj *showing disapproval* giving too much importance to details and formal rules, especially of grammar —**pedantically** /pɪ'dæntɪkli/ adv

pedestal /'pedɪst(ə)l/ noun [C] a base on which something such as a statue stands

pedestrian /pə'destriən/ noun [C] someone who is walking, especially in a town or city, instead of driving or riding

pe,destrian 'crossing noun [C] an area where vehicles must stop for people who are walking across the street

pedestrian precinct /pə,destriən 'priːsɪŋkt/ noun [C] a street with shops, where vehicles are not allowed

pedigree1 /'pedɪɡriː/ noun **1** [C] all the past experiences, achievements, and successes of someone or something: *an investment analyst with a remarkable pedigree* **2** [C/U] the parents, grandparents etc of an animal

pedigree2 /'pedɪɡriː/ adj a pedigree animal comes from a family whose members are all of the same type

peek1 /piːk/ noun [C] a quick look at something: *Emma took a quick peek inside the box.*

peek2 /piːk/ verb [I] **1** to look at something quickly **2** to appear slightly from behind or under something

peel1 /piːl/ verb **1** [T] to remove the skin from a fruit or vegetable —*picture* → FOOD **2** [T] to remove something from the surface of something else **3** [I] if something peels, small pieces of it start to fall off: *Paint was peeling off the walls.*

peel2 /piːl/ noun [U] the skin of a fruit or vegetable

peep1 /piːp/ verb [I] **1** to look at something quickly and secretly **2** to appear from behind or under something: *His head peeped out from under the blanket.*

peep2 /piːp/ noun [C] a quick secret look at something

peer1 /pɪə/ noun [C] SOCIAL STUDIES **1** someone who is the same age or who belongs to the same social or professional group as another person **2** someone who is from a high social class in the UK and has a title such as **Lord**

peer2 /pɪə/ verb [I] to look very carefully at something because it is difficult to see

'peer ,group noun [C] SOCIAL STUDIES a group of people of the same age, social class, or education

,peer-to-'peer adj COMPUTING used for describing a computer **network** in which each computer can pass information directly to another without the need for a central **server**

peg1 /peɡ/ noun [C]

1 for fastening clothes onto line	3 for fastening together
2 for hanging things on	4 for tent
	5 for tightening strings

1 a wooden or plastic object that you use for fastening wet clothes onto a line so that they will dry
2 an object that is fixed to a wall or door and used for hanging things on
3 an object that is used for fastening things together: *The furniture is built using wooden pegs instead of nails.*
4 peg or **tent peg** an object that is pushed or hit into the ground in order to keep a tent in position
5 MUSIC a screw used for making the strings on a musical instrument tighter or looser

peg2 /peɡ/ (**pegs, pegging, pegged**) verb [T] **1** to fasten something, or to keep something in position, with pegs **2** ECONOMICS to keep prices, salaries, or amounts at a particular level

pejorative /pɪ'dʒɒrətɪv/ adj *formal* a pejorative word, phrase etc expresses criticism or a bad opinion of someone or something —**pejoratively** adv

pelagic /pə'lædʒɪk/ adj GEOGRAPHY **1** relating to the parts of the sea that are far from land **2** close to the surface of the sea

pelican /'pelɪkən/ noun [C] a large bird with a bag of skin that hangs from its beak —*picture* → BIRD

pellagra /pə'læɡrə, pə'leɪɡrə/ noun [U] HEALTH a disease in which the skin becomes very rough. It is caused by a lack of the vitamin **niacin** in food.

pellet /'pelɪt/ noun [C] a small round piece of a substance

pelt /pelt/ noun [C] the skin or fur of an animal

pelvic /'pelvɪk/ adj ANATOMY relating to the pelvis: *a pelvic fracture*

,pelvic 'fin noun [C] BIOLOGY the fin on each side of a fish towards the back of its body that controls the direction it moves in = VENTRAL FIN

,pelvic 'floor noun [C] ANATOMY the set of muscles inside the body that control the movements of sexual organs, between the abdomen and the pelvis

the ,pelvic 'girdle noun ANATOMY the bones that form the hips and pelvis

pelvis /'pelvɪs/ noun [C] ANATOMY the large circular bones that support the lower part of the back. They are connected to the bones of the legs. —*picture* → SKELETON

pen^1 /pen/ noun [C] **1** an object that you use for writing or drawing with ink: *a felt-tip pen* —*picture* → WORKSTATION **2** AGRICULTURE a small area with a fence around it, used for keeping animals in

pen^2 /pen/ (**pens, penning, penned**) verb [T] AGRICULTURE to shut an animal in a small area with a fence around it

penal /'piːn(ə)l/ adj LAW relating to the punishment of criminals

'penal ,code noun [C] LAW a system of laws dealing with the punishment of crimes

penalize /'piːnəlaɪz/ verb [T] **1** to treat someone in an unfair way and make them have a disadvantage: *The tax system seems to penalize people who save for their old age.* **2** to punish someone for breaking a rule or law

penalty /'pen(ə)lti/ (plural **penalties**) noun [C] **1** a punishment for breaking a rule or law: *the death penalty* ♦ *The maximum penalty for the offence is two years' imprisonment.* **2** something bad that happens to someone because of their behaviour or position in society: *Some growers are paying the penalty for not watering crops sufficiently in hot weather.* **3** SPORTS a chance to score a goal in a sports match when the other team has broken a rule: *Southgate missed a penalty that would have won them the match.*

'penalty ,area noun [C] SPORTS in football, the area in front of the goal where the **goalkeeper** is allowed to hold the ball, and where a penalty is given if a player breaks a rule

'penalty ,box noun [C] SPORTS a **penalty area** in football

'penalty ,kick noun [C] SPORTS in football and **rugby**, a chance for a player to kick the ball directly into the goal or between the goalposts, without other players trying to take the ball off them

,penalty 'shoot-,out noun [C] SPORTS in football, a series of chances to kick the ball into the goal, given to both teams as a way of deciding who wins the game when both teams have the same score

'penalty ,spot noun [C] SPORTS in football, the place where a player puts the ball when they are taking a **penalty kick**

penance /'penəns/ noun [C/U] RELIGION punishment or suffering that you accept in order to show that you are sorry

pence /pens/ a plural of **penny**

pencil^1 /'pens(ə)l/ noun [C] ARTS a long thin wooden object that you use for writing or drawing: *a coloured pencil* —*picture* → WORKSTATION

pencil^2 /'pens(ə)l/ (**pencils, pencilling, pencilled**) verb [T] ARTS to write or draw something with a pencil

pencil sharpener /'pens(ə)l ˌʃɑːp(ə)nə/ noun [C] an object with a blade inside, used for making a pencil sharper

'pen com,puter noun [C] COMPUTING a computer that accepts information written by hand

pending /'pendɪŋ/ adj **1** waiting to be dealt with **2** likely to happen soon

pendulum /'pendjʊləm/ noun [C] PHYSICS a long thin bar with a weight at the lower end that swings from side to side, usually in order to keep a clock working

penetrate /'penəˌtreɪt/ verb [I/T] **1** to get inside, past, or through something: *A piece of glass had penetrated the skin.* **2** to reach or affect something such as a part of society —**penetrative** adj

penetrating /'penəˌtreɪtɪŋ/ adj **1** a person who gives you a penetrating look seems to know what you are thinking= PIERCING **2** intelligent and quick to solve problems or to understand things **3** a penetrating voice or sound is so high or loud that it makes you slightly uncomfortable **4** affecting a person or thing by passing through layers that would normally protect them —**penetratingly** adv

penetration /ˌpenə'treɪʃ(ə)n/ noun [U] **1** the act of getting into a place or group **2** the act of getting inside something, especially past objects or substances that are intended to stop things getting inside

penguin /'peŋgwɪn/ noun [C] a black and white bird that cannot fly. Penguins live by the sea, especially around Antarctica. —*picture* → BIRD

penicillin /ˌpenə'sɪlɪn/ noun [U] HEALTH a drug used for treating illnesses that are caused by bacteria

peninsula /pə'nɪnsjʊlə/ noun [C] GEOGRAPHY a long piece of land that is mostly surrounded by water but is joined at one end to a larger area of land —*picture* → ISTHMUS —**peninsular** adj

penis /'piːnɪs/ noun [C] BIOLOGY in men and other male mammals, the organ that is used for sex and that carries semen and urine out of the body

penitent /'penɪtənt/ adj sorry for something bad that you have done and willing to change your behaviour —**penitence** noun [U]

penknife /'penˌnaɪf/ (plural **penknives** /'penˌnaɪvz/) noun [C] a small knife with one or more blades that fold into the handle

'pen ,name noun [C] a name that a writer uses instead of their real name

penniless /'penɪləs/ adj someone who is penniless has no money

penny /'peni/ (plural **pennies** or **pence** /pens/) noun [C] a small unit of money in the UK. There are 100 pence in one pound.

pension /'penʃ(ə)n/ noun [C] an amount of money that someone receives regularly when they no longer work because of their age or because they are ill

pensioner /'penʃ(ə)nə/ noun [C] someone who receives a pension

pensive /'pensɪv/ adj someone who is pensive seems to be thinking carefully about something —**pensively** adv

pentadactyl /ˌpentə'dækt(ə)l/ adj ANATOMY having five digits on each hand or foot

pentagon /'pentəgən/ noun [C] MATHS a shape that has five straight sides —*picture* → SHAPE

the Pentagon /'pentəgən/ the department of defence in the US government, or the building that belongs to this department

pentameter /pen'tæmɪtə/ noun [C] LITERATURE a line of poetry with five strong beats

pentathlon /pen'tæθlən/ noun [C] SPORTS a sports event that consists of five different sports → DECATHLON

pentatonic scale /ˌpentətɒnɪk 'skeɪl/ noun [C] MUSIC a scale that consists of five notes, especially five **whole tones**

pentavalent /ˌpentə'veɪlənt/ adj CHEMISTRY relating to chemical elements that have a **valency** of five

Pentecost /'pentɪkɒst/ noun [C/U] RELIGION the seventh Sunday after Easter, when Christians celebrate the time when the Holy Spirit came from Heaven to Earth

penultimate /pəˈnʌltɪmət/ adj *formal* the penultimate person or thing in a series is the one before the last

penumbra /pəˈnʌmbrə/ noun [C] **PHYSICS** an area covered by the outer part of a shadow, so that it is not completely dark

penury /ˈpenjəri/ noun [U] *formal* the state of being extremely poor

people /ˈpiːp(ə)l/ noun **1** [plural] the plural of **person**: *The accident left three people dead and many injured.* ♦ *People were running everywhere.* ♦ *a magazine full of gossip about famous people* **2 the people** [plural] **SOCIAL STUDIES** ordinary people who are not members of the government or the upper classes: *On this issue, government has failed to listen to the people.* **3** [C] **SOCIAL STUDIES** everyone who belongs to a particular nation, religion, or race: *The Mongols were regarded as a very warlike people.* **4 the people** [C] **LAW** the lawyers representing the US government or a US state in a criminal case

'people ˌskills noun [plural] the ability to communicate effectively with people in a friendly way, especially in business

pepper /ˈpepə/ noun **1** [U] a black or white powder that adds a strong flavour to food **2** [C] a green, red, yellow, or orange vegetable that is the fruit of the plant and has small white seeds inside. It can be eaten raw in salads or cooked. It is also called a **sweet pepper**. —*picture* → VEGETABLE

peppermint /ˈpepəˌmɪnt/ noun **1** [U] a strong fresh flavour that is obtained from a **mint** plant and is used in medicines or drinks **2** [C] a sweet with a peppermint flavour

pepsin /ˈpepsɪn/ noun [U] **BIOLOGY** an enzyme produced in the stomach that breaks down protein into simpler compounds

peptic ulcer /ˌpeptɪk ˈʌlsə/ noun [C] **HEALTH** a small painful area on the inside of the stomach, where it has been damaged by **hydrochloric acid**

peptide /ˈpeptaɪd/ noun [C] **CHEMISTRY, BIOLOGY** a compound that consists of two or more **amino acids** joined in a chain

per /*strong* pɜː, *weak* pə/ preposition used for stating the rate or cost for each unit of time, quantity, distance etc: *He is paid £10 per hour for the job.* ♦ *Ellen can type 100 words per minute.*

per annum /pər ˈænəm/ adv *formal* for each year

per capita /pə ˈkæpɪtə/ adj, adv *formal* based on calculations that show the average amount for each person affected

perceive /pəˈsiːv/ verb [T] **1** to understand or think about something in a particular way: *New technology is often perceived as a threat.* ♦ *The organization is generally perceived to be inefficient.* **2** *formal* to notice or realize something: *He quickly perceived that there was a problem with the figures.*

per cent¹ /pə ˈsent/ noun [singular] **MATHS** one part of every 100. Per cent is often shown using the symbol %: *Women now represent 50 per cent of the workforce.* ♦ *He owns 20% of the business.*

per cent² /pə ˈsent/ adj, adv **MATHS** equal to part of a total that has been divided by 100: *Sales increased thirty per cent compared with last year.*

percentage /pəˈsentɪdʒ/ noun [C/U] **MATHS** an amount that is equal to a particular part of a total that has been divided by 100: *Calculate what percentage of your income you spend on food.*

percentile /pəˈsentaɪl/ noun [C] **MATHS** one of the 100 equal groups that a large number of people or things are divided into for comparing something such as test scores, height, salaries etc

perception /pəˈsepʃ(ə)n/ noun **1** [C/U] a particular way of understanding or thinking about something: *There is a perception among workers that management only wants to cut costs.* **2** [U] the ability to notice something by seeing, hearing, smelling etc

perceptive /pəˈseptɪv/ adj **1** good at noticing or understanding things quickly and easily: *Children are often very perceptive about adults' moods.* **2** a perceptive remark or piece of writing is intelligent and shows good judgment= INCISIVE

perceptual /pəˈseptʃuəl/ adj *formal* relating to the ability to notice or understand things by seeing or hearing

perch¹ /pɜːtʃ/ verb **1** [I/T] to sit on something that is narrow or small, or to sit on the edge of something **2** [T] to put something high up or on the edge of something, or to be in this position **3** [I] if a bird perches somewhere, it is resting there for a time

perch² /pɜːtʃ/ noun [C] an area or object that a bird uses for resting on

percolate /ˈpɜːkəleɪt/ verb [I] **1** if a liquid or gas percolates through a substance, it gradually passes through it **2** if information or ideas percolate, they spread gradually and become known to more people —**percolation** /ˌpɜːkəˈleɪʃ(ə)n/ noun [U]

ˌpercoˈlation ˌtest noun [C] **CONSTRUCTION** a test to see how long it takes for water to filter into the soil

percussion /pəˈkʌʃ(ə)n/ noun [U] **MUSIC** musical instruments such as drums that you play by hitting them —*picture* → MUSICAL INSTRUMENT, ORCHESTRA —**percussionist** noun [C]

percussive /pəˈkʌsɪv/ adj **MUSIC** a percussive sound is short and loud like someone hitting a drum

perennating organ /ˌperəneɪtɪŋ ˈɔːgən/ noun [C] **BIOLOGY** part of a plant that stores food and can live for several years, usually with a period when it is not growing or active

perennial /pəˈreniəl/ noun [C] **BIOLOGY** a flowering plant that lasts for several years → ANNUAL¹, BIENNIAL —**perennial** adj

perfect¹ /ˈpɜːfɪkt/ adj **1** as good, accurate, or complete as possible, with no faults= FLAWLESS: *Her English was perfect.* ♦ *These recipes give perfect results every time.* **2** completely suitable or right= IDEAL: *It seemed like the perfect gift.* ♦ *Their house is absolutely perfect for parties.* **3** used for emphasizing what you are saying: *I don't want to share a room with a perfect stranger.* **4 LANGUAGE** the perfect form of a verb is used for talking about an action that has been completed before the present time → PERFECT TENSE

perfect² /pəˈfekt/ verb [T] to make something completely free from faults, or to make it as good as it can be

the perfect /ˈpɜːfɪkt/ noun [singular] **LANGUAGE** the perfect tense

perfection /pəˈfekʃ(ə)n/ noun [U] a state in which someone or something is perfect

perfectionist /pəˈfekʃənɪst/ noun [C] someone who always wants things to be done in a perfect way

perfectly /ˈpɜːfɪk(t)li/ adv **1** in a way that could not be better **2** used for emphasizing a particular quality = COMPLETELY

,perfect 'market noun [C] ECONOMICS a market with very many producers and customers in which none of them is able to affect the price of a product or service

,perfect 'pitch noun [U] MUSIC the ability to recognize or sing a musical note at the correct **pitch**

,perfect 'storm noun [C] a very unpleasant situation in which several bad things happen at once

the 'perfect ,tense noun [singular] LANGUAGE the form of a verb that is used for talking about an action that has been completed before the present time. It is formed in English with 'have' and a past participle.
→ FUTURE PERFECT, PAST PERFECT, PRESENT PERFECT

perforated /'pɜːfəˌreɪtɪd/ adj **1** with a lot of small holes in the surface **2** HEALTH if an organ or tube inside your body is perforated, it has a small hole or cut in its surface —**perforation** /ˌpɜːfə'reɪʃ(ə)n/ noun [C]

perform /pə'fɔːm/ verb **1** [T] to complete an action or activity: *He's a surgeon who has performed many heart transplant operations.* ♦ *a robot that can perform routine tasks in the home* **2** [I/T] to do something in front of an audience in order to entertain them: *The opera was first performed in 1992.* ♦ *Akram went on to perform on stage in England and India.* **3** [I] to do something with a particular amount of success: *The tyres perform well in wet conditions.*

performance /pə'fɔːməns/ noun **1** [C] ARTS the act of performing a play, dance, or other form of entertainment: *The first performance of the play was in 1936.* **2** [C/U] the standard of success that someone or something achieves: *A healthy diet can improve a child's performance in school.* ♦ *We need to test the performance of the equipment.* **3** [C/U] *formal* the process of doing a job or action

per'formance ap,praisal noun [C] BUSINESS a formal meeting between a worker and their manager in order to discuss how well the worker is doing in their job and how they can improve their performance

per'formance ,art noun [U] ARTS a type of art in which an artist gives a performance using different art forms such as acting, dance, and painting

performance-enhancing /pə'fɔːməns ɪnˌhɑːnsɪŋ/ adj HEALTH a performance-enhancing drug or substance is taken illegally by someone involved in sport, in order to make them stronger, faster etc

per,formance-re,lated 'pay noun [U] BUSINESS pay that increases when someone is successful at their job, and that is reduced when they are not successful

performer /pə'fɔːmə/ noun [C] **1** ARTS someone who performs in front of an audience, for example an actor or a musician **2** someone who does something with a particular amount of success: *He was one of the team's star performers.*

the performing arts /pəˌfɔːmɪŋ 'ɑːts/ noun [plural] ARTS types of art that are performed in front of an audience, such as plays, music, and dance

perfume /'pɜːfjuːm/ noun [C/U] a liquid with a pleasant smell that you put on your skin —**perfumed** /'pɜːfjuːmd/ adj

perfunctory /pə'fʌŋkt(ə)ri/ adj done without much effort or interest —**perfunctorily** adv

perhaps /pə'hæps/ adv used for saying that you are not certain whether something is true: *I haven't seen them for months – perhaps they've moved away.* ♦ *There were perhaps a dozen women in the audience.*

perianth /'peri,ænθ/ noun [C] BIOLOGY the outer part of a flower, consisting of the **sepals** and the petals

pericarp /'peri,kɑːp/ noun [C] BIOLOGY the part of a fruit that develops from the wall of the ovary and that surrounds the seed or seeds. It forms the fruit's skin and flesh.

peril /'perəl/ noun [U] *literary* serious danger

perilous /'perələs/ adj *literary* very dangerous —**perilously** adv

perimeter /pə'rɪmɪtə/ noun [C] **1** the outer edge of an enclosed area of ground such as a field **2** MATHS the total length of the sides of a shape such as a square

perinatal /ˌperi'neɪt(ə)l/ adj HEALTH relating to the period in the development of a baby from several weeks before its birth to several weeks after its birth

period /'pɪəriəd/ noun [C] **1** an amount of time: *The long dry period ended with heavy rain.* ♦ *a period of three months* **2** BIOLOGY the time about once a month when a woman who is not pregnant loses blood from the uterus → MENSTRUATION **3** EDUCATION a part of a school day when a particular subject is taught = LESSON

periodic /ˌpɪəri'ɒdɪk/ adj happening regularly though not frequently —**periodically** /ˌpɪəri'ɒdɪkli/ adv

periodical /ˌpɪəri'ɒdɪk(ə)l/ noun [C] a magazine on a particular subject that is published regularly

peri'odic ,function noun [C] MATHS a function that has the same value at regular intervals

periodicity /ˌpɪəriə'dɪsɪti/ noun [U] a situation in which something happens regularly

,periodic 'table noun [singular] CHEMISTRY a list of chemical elements arranged according to the structure of their atoms

periosteum /ˌperi'ɒstiəm/ noun [U] ANATOMY a strong membrane that covers the outside of bones, except at the joints —*picture* → BONE

peripheral[1] /pə'rɪf(ə)rəl/ adj connected with something but not a necessary or important part of it = MARGINAL

peripheral[2] /pə'rɪf(ə)rəl/ noun [C] COMPUTING a piece of equipment that you can connect to a computer, for example a printer

,peripheral 'nervous ,system noun [C] ANATOMY, BIOLOGY the part of the nervous system that consists of the nerve fibres, as opposed to the brain and **spinal cord**

periphery /pə'rɪf(ə)ri/ (plural **peripheries**) noun [C] the outer part of an area

periphrasis /pə'rɪfrəsɪs/ noun [C/U] LANGUAGE the practice of expressing something in a more complicated indirect way than is necessary, or something that is expressed in this way —**periphrastic** /ˌperi'fræstɪk/ adj

periscope /'peri,skəʊp/ noun [C] PHYSICS a long tube with mirrors set at a 45° angle at each end, used for looking over the top of something, for example from a **submarine**

perish /'perɪʃ/ verb [I] **1** *literary* to die **2** if a substance such as wood, rubber, or food perishes, it decays

perishable /'perɪʃəb(ə)l/ adj perishable food decays after a short time

peristalsis /ˌperi'stælsɪs/ noun [C] BIOLOGY the regular involuntary movement of the muscles in the alimentary canal as they contract and relax, pushing food along —**peristaltic** adj

peritonitis /ˌperitə'naɪtɪs/ noun [U] HEALTH a serious illness in which the membrane surrounding the stomach becomes infected and swollen

perjure /'pɜːdʒə/ verb LAW **perjure yourself** to lie when you give evidence in a court of law —**perjurer** noun [C]

perjury /'pɜːdʒəri/ noun [U] LAW the crime of lying when you give evidence in a court of law

permanent /'pɜːmənənt/ adj happening or existing for a long time, or for all time in the future ≠ TEMPORARY: *The illness can cause permanent blindness.* ♦ *They've offered me a room until I can find something more permanent.* ♦ *I don't have a permanent job.* —**permanently** adv: *She complained of feeling permanently exhausted.* ♦ *the decision to close down the factory permanently*

,**permanent 'magnet** noun [C] PHYSICS a magnet that stays as a magnet even after it is removed from a magnetic field. It is made from iron, or from iron mixed with aluminium, **nickel**, or **cobalt**.

permeable /'pɜːmiəb(ə)l/ adj GEOLOGY a permeable substance or material is one that a liquid or gas can pass through —**permeability** /,pɜːmiə'bɪləti/ noun [U]

permeate /'pɜːmieɪt/ verb [I/T] to spread gradually through every part of something

permethrin /pɜː'meθrɪn/ noun [U] CHEMISTRY an artificially made chemical that is used to kill harmful insects. It is a **pyrethroid**.

permissible /pə'mɪsəb(ə)l/ adj *formal* if something is permissible, you are allowed to do it

permission /pə'mɪʃ(ə)n/ noun [U] the right to do something that is given to you by someone in authority: *You are not allowed to camp here **without permission**.* ♦ *Children should **ask** their parents' **permission** before making phone calls.* ♦ *Who **gave** you **permission** to come in here?*

permit[1] /pə'mɪt/ (**permits, permitting, permitted**) verb **1** [T] *formal* to allow someone to do something, or to allow something to happen: *The use of mobile phones is not permitted inside the aircraft.* ♦ *The course permits students to gain practical experience as well as theoretical knowledge.* **2** [I/T] to make something possible: *The game starts at 11 o'clock, **weather permitting** (=if the weather is good enough).*

permit[2] /'pɜːmɪt/ noun [C] an official document that gives you permission to do something

permittivity /,pɜːmɪ'tɪvəti/ noun [C/U] PHYSICS the measure of the ability of a material that does not allow electricity to pass through it to store electric energy when it is placed in an electric field. Symbol ε

permutation /,pɜːmjʊ'teɪʃ(ə)n/ noun [C] one of the various ways in which you can combine or arrange a group of things

pernicious /pə'nɪʃəs/ adj *formal* dangerous or harmful

perpend /'pɜːpend/ noun [C] CONSTRUCTION **1** the vertical joint between two bricks **2** a stone linking the inner and outer walls of a building

perpendicular /,pɜːpən'dɪkjʊlə/ adj **1** completely upright **2** MATHS forming a 90° angle with another surface or line: *Line A is **perpendicular to** line B.* —**perpendicularly** adv

perpetrate /'pɜːpətreɪt/ verb [T] *formal* to do something that is harmful, illegal, or dishonest —**perpetrator** noun [C]

perpetual /pə'petʃuəl/ adj happening or continuing all the time —**perpetually** adv

perpetuate /pə'petʃueɪt/ verb [T] to make a situation or process continue for a long time, especially a bad or dangerous situation —**perpetuation** /pə,petʃu'eɪʃ(ə)n/ noun [U]

perpetuity /,pɜːpə'tjuːəti/ noun LAW **in perpetuity** for all time in the future

perplexed /pə'plekst/ adj confused because you cannot understand something = BEWILDERED

persecute /'pɜːsɪ,kjuːt/ verb [T] to treat someone very badly because of their race, religion, political beliefs etc —**persecution** /,pɜːsɪ'kjuːʃ(ə)n/ noun [U], **persecutor** noun [C]

perseverance /,pɜːsɪ'vɪərəns/ noun [U] a determined attitude that makes you continue trying to achieve something that is difficult

persevere /,pɜːsɪ'vɪə/ verb [I] to continue trying to achieve something that is difficult

persist /pə'sɪst/ verb [I] **1** to continue to do something in a determined way, especially something bad or annoying **2** to continue to exist: *Despite yesterday's stock market falls, optimism persists among investors.*

persistent /pə'sɪstənt/ adj **1** continuing to do something in a determined way, especially something bad or annoying **2** continuing to exist —**persistence** noun [U], **persistently** adv

person /'pɜːs(ə)n/ (plural **persons** or **people** /'piːp(ə)l/) noun [C] an individual human. The plural is 'people', but in formal or official language the form 'persons' is used: *Every single person in the room stopped talking.* ♦ *Some people hate camping.* ♦ *Voting is obligatory for all persons between the ages of 18 and 70.*
PHRASE **do sth in person** to do something by going to a place yourself, rather than by writing, telephoning, or sending someone else: *You have to collect your tickets in person.*
→ FIRST PERSON, SECOND PERSON, THIRD PERSON

persona /pə'səunə/ (plural **personas** or **personae** /pə'səuni/) noun [C] the part of your personality that you deliberately show to most people

personal /'pɜːs(ə)nəl/ adj **1** involving you or belonging to you, not to anyone else: *Most writers use **personal experience** as the basis for their novels.* ♦ *Many of Tim's **personal belongings** had been stolen.* **2** private and not known or available to most people: *She resigned from her job **for personal reasons**.* ♦ *My **personal life** is not your concern.* **3** aimed at one particular person, in an unfriendly or offensive way: *He saw her comments as a personal attack.* **4** done by a person directly, rather than by a representative: *The members of REM will be making a personal appearance at the awards ceremony.* ♦ *the president's **personal involvement** in the project*

,**personal com'puter** noun [C] COMPUTING the usual type of computer, designed to be used by one person on a desk

,**personal ,digital as'sistant** noun [C] COMPUTING a PDA

personality /,pɜːsə'næləti/ (plural **personalities**) noun **1** [C/U] the part of a person that makes them behave in a particular way in social situations: *He has a very outgoing personality and makes friends very easily.* ♦ *a personality disorder* **2** [U] confidence and lively behaviour that make people like you and think that you are interesting: *Mary has lots of personality.* **3** [C] a famous or well-known person = CELEBRITY: *a TV personality*

personally /'pɜːs(ə)nəli/ adv **1** *spoken* used for emphasizing that you are giving your own opinion: *Personally, I think we should stick with our original plan.* ♦ *I personally prefer pizza to burgers.* **2** used for emphasizing that you are referring to a particular person, not to anyone else: *Were you **personally**

involved in this decision? **3** in a way that is intended for you only, rather than for a group of people that you belong to: *The invitation was made to me personally, not to the committee.*

PHRASE **take sth personally** to feel that a failure or unpleasant situation is your fault and to be upset about it

personal 'organizer noun [C] a small book or simple computer that you use for keeping addresses, telephone numbers, and dates

personal 'pronoun noun [C] **LANGUAGE** a pronoun such as 'I', 'you', 'them', or 'it' that refers to a specific person, thing, or group of people or things

personal 'video re,corder noun [C] a video machine that records television programmes in **digital** form onto a computer, rather than onto a **cassette**

persona non grata /pə,səʊnə nɒn 'grɑːtə/ noun [C] *formal* someone that people in a particular place do not like or welcome

personification /pə,sɒnɪfɪ'keɪʃ(ə)n/ noun [C/U] **ARTS, LITERATURE** the practice of showing a particular quality in the form of a person, or an instance of this

PHRASE **the personification of sth** someone who is a very clear example of a particular quality

personify /pə'sɒnɪfaɪ/ (**personifies, personifying, personified**) verb [T] **1** to be a very clear example of a particular quality: *He personifies Russia's dynamic new business class.* **2 ARTS, LITERATURE** to show a particular quality in the form of a person

personnel /ˌpɜːsə'nel/ noun **BUSINESS 1** [plural] the people who work for a company or organization **2** [U] the department in an organization that is responsible for looking after all of the people who work there, and for choosing new workers= HUMAN RESOURCES

person'nel ,carrier noun [C] a military vehicle for carrying soldiers

perspective /pə'spektɪv/ noun **1** [C] a way of thinking about something: *You can call it brave or foolish, depending on your perspective.* **2** [U] a sensible way of judging something without making it seem too important: *It's important to **keep** things **in perspective** and not worry too much.* ♦ *This kind of tragedy **puts** a mere football match **into perspective**.* **3** [U] **ARTS** a method of showing distance in a picture by making far-away objects smaller

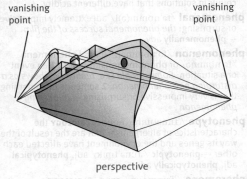

vanishing point

vanishing point

perspective

Perspex /'pɜːspeks/ **TRADEMARK** a strong transparent plastic that can be used instead of glass

perspiration /ˌpɜːspə'reɪʃ(ə)n/ noun [U] the liquid that your skin produces when you are hot, ill, or nervous= SWEAT

perspire /pə'spaɪə/ verb [I] to produce liquid on your skin as a result of being hot, ill, or nervous= SWEAT

persuade /pə'sweɪd/ verb [T] **1** to make someone agree to do something by giving them reasons why they should: *He did finally come with us, although it took a long time to persuade him.* ♦ *Nobody could persuade her to change her mind.* **2** to make someone believe that something is true= CONVINCE: *I managed to persuade him that it was not his fault.* ♦ *There was no way she could persuade him of her innocence.*

persuasion /pə'sweɪʒ(ə)n/ noun [U] the process of persuading someone to do or believe something

persuasive /pə'sweɪsɪv/ adj good at making people agree to do or believe what you want them to —**persuasively** adv

pertinent /'pɜːtɪnənt/ adj *formal* relevant

perturbed /pə'tɜːbd/ adj worried, or upset —**perturb** verb [T]

peruse /pə'ruːz/ verb [T] *formal* to read something —**perusal** noun [C/U]

pervade /pə'veɪd/ verb [T] *formal* to spread through the whole of something and become a very obvious feature of it

pervasive /pə'veɪsɪv/ adj spreading through the whole of something: *a pervasive culture of official corruption*

perverse /pə'vɜːs/ adj behaving in an unreasonable way, by deliberately doing what people do not expect you to do —**perversely** adv

pervert¹ /'pɜːvɜːt/ noun [C] *offensive* an insulting word for someone whose sexual behaviour is thought to be wrong or not normal

pervert² /pə'vɜːt/ verb [T] **pervert the course of justice** **LAW** to try to influence the result of a court case, especially by preventing the true facts about a crime from being known

pessimism /'pesə,mɪz(ə)m/ noun [U] the attitude of someone who expects the worst thing to happen in every situation ≠ OPTIMISM

pessimist /'pesəmɪst/ noun [C] someone who expects the worst thing to happen in every situation ≠ OPTIMIST

pessimistic /ˌpesə'mɪstɪk/ adj expecting the worst thing to happen in every situation ≠ OPTIMISTIC: *Doctors are pessimistic about his chances of making a full recovery.*

pest /pest/ noun [C] **1 AGRICULTURE** an insect or other small animal that damages plants or supplies of food **2** *informal* an annoying person= NUISANCE

pester /'pestə/ verb [T] to keep annoying someone by asking them for something, or by asking them to do something= NAG

pesticide /'pestɪsaɪd/ noun [C/U] **AGRICULTURE, ENVIRONMENT** a chemical used for killing insects that damage crops

pestle /'pes(ə)l/ noun [C] a short hard object like a stick with a round end. It is used for crushing food or chemical substances in a bowl called a **mortar**. —*picture* → LABORATORY

pet /pet/ noun [C] an animal, bird etc that you keep in your home and look after

petal /'pet(ə)l/ noun [C] **BIOLOGY** one of the coloured parts around the centre of a flower —*picture* → FLOWER

petiole /'petiəʊl/ noun [C] **BIOLOGY** the small stalk that attaches a leaf to a stem —*picture* → LEAF

petite /pə'tiːt/ adj a petite woman is small and thin in an attractive way

petition[1] /pəˈtɪʃ(ə)n/ noun [C] **1** a document signed by many people that asks someone in authority to do something **2 LAW** an official document in which you ask a court to take legal action

petition[2] /pəˈtɪʃ(ə)n/ verb [I/T] **1** to ask someone in authority to do something by using a petition **2 LAW** to give a court an official document in which you ask it to take legal action —**petitioner** noun [C]

petit mal /ˌpeti ˈmæl/ noun [U] **HEALTH** a type of **epilepsy** that is less serious than **grand mal**

Petri dish /ˈpiːtri ˌdɪʃ/ noun [C] **SCIENCE** a flat dish with a lid that is used in laboratories, especially for growing **cultures** of microorganisms —*picture* → LABORATORY

petrified /ˈpetrɪfaɪd/ adj extremely frightened

petrochemical /ˌpetrəʊˈkemɪk(ə)l/ noun [C] **CHEMISTRY** a chemical made from **petroleum** or natural gas

petrodollar /ˈpetrəʊˌdɒlə/ noun [C] **ECONOMICS** a unit of money earned by a country from exporting oil to other countries

petrol /ˈpetrəl/ noun [U] a liquid that is used as a fuel for cars and other vehicles

petroleum /pəˈtrəʊliəm/ noun [U] **CHEMISTRY** a mixture of oils that is found under the ground or under the bottom of the sea. It is a mixture of **hydrocarbons** and is used for making petrol and other chemical products.

petrology /pəˈtrɒlədʒi/ noun [U] **GEOLOGY** the scientific study of rocks

'petrol ,pump noun [C] a machine at a **service station**, used for putting fuel into vehicles

'petrol ,station noun [C] a **garage** that sells petrol for cars

petty /ˈpeti/ adj **1** not important and not worth worrying about: *petty arguments* **2** behaving badly towards other people, because you care too much about something that is not really important **3** minor: *a petty criminal* —**pettiness** noun [U]

,petty 'cash noun [U] **BUSINESS** a small amount of money in coins or notes that a business or organization keeps available to pay for small things

,petty 'crime noun [C] a crime that is not very serious

pew /pjuː/ noun [C] a long wooden seat in a church

PFI /ˌpiː ef ˈaɪ/ noun [singular] **BUSINESS** Private Finance Initiative: a system in which private companies work with the government to provide public services such as health services

pH /ˌpiː ˈeɪtʃ/ noun [singular] **CHEMISTRY** a number that describes how acid or alkaline a substance is. Pure water has a pH of 7, with a lower number showing a level of acidity and a higher number showing a level of **alkalinity**.

phagocyte /ˈfæɡəʊsaɪt/ noun [C] **BIOLOGY** a cell in an organism that gets rid of bacteria and other harmful cells by taking them into itself and digesting them

phagocytosis /ˌfæɡəʊsaɪˈtəʊsɪs/ noun [U] **BIOLOGY** the process by which phagocytes surround foreign particles in order to remove them

phalanx /ˈfælæŋks/ (plural **phalanxes** or **phalanges** /fəˈlændʒiːz/) noun [C] **ANATOMY** one of the bones of a finger or toe —*picture* → SKELETON

phantom /ˈfæntəm/ noun [C] the spirit of a dead person that someone believes they can see = GHOST

pharaoh /ˈfeərəʊ/ noun [C] a king in ancient Egypt

pharmaceutical /ˌfɑːməˈsjuːtɪk(ə)l/ adj **CHEMISTRY, HEALTH** relating to medicines and drugs: *the pharmaceutical industry*

pharmacist /ˈfɑːməsɪst/ noun [C] **HEALTH** someone whose job is to prepare and sell medicines = CHEMIST

pharmacology /ˌfɑːməˈkɒlədʒi/ noun [U] **CHEMISTRY, HEALTH** the scientific study of medicines and drugs —**pharmacologist** noun [C]

pharmacy /ˈfɑːməsi/ (plural **pharmacies**) noun [C] **HEALTH** a place where medicines are prepared and sold = CHEMIST

pharyngitis /ˌfærɪnˈdʒaɪtɪs/ noun [U] **HEALTH** a common condition caused by a virus or bacterium in which the throat becomes sore and swollen. A less technical word is **sore throat**.

pharynx /ˈfærɪŋks/ noun [singular] **ANATOMY** the part of the throat that leads from the mouth to the oesophagus —*picture* → DIGESTIVE SYSTEM, LUNG

phase /feɪz/ noun [C] **1** a particular period of time during the development of something: *The first phase of the project will be completed by 2010.* ♦ *Tim went through a phase of being aggressive at school.* ♦ *a depressing phase in our history* **2 ASTRONOMY** a shape of the Moon or a planet that changes according to a regular pattern and can be seen from the Earth —*picture* → on next page

PHRASES **in phase PHYSICS** if sound waves or light waves are in phase, their **crests** (=high points) and **troughs** (=low points) come at the same time

out of phase PHYSICS if sound waves or light waves are out of phase, their **crests** (=high points) and **troughs** (=low points) come at different times

phatic /ˈfætɪk/ adj **LANGUAGE** used for describing words or phrases that you use for social reasons, for example in order to be friendly, rather than in order to give information

PhD /ˌpiː eɪtʃ ˈdiː/ noun [C] **EDUCATION** Doctor of Philosophy: the highest university degree, or someone who has this degree

pheasant /ˈfez(ə)nt/ noun [C/U] a large bird with a long tail that is hunted for sport and food, or the meat from this bird

phenol /ˈfiːnɒl/ noun [U] **CHEMISTRY** a chemical made from coal, used for killing bacteria

phenolphthalein /ˌfiːnɒlˈθæliːn/ noun [U] **CHEMISTRY** a chemical that is used in scientific experiments, for example as an **indicator** that changes colour in solutions that have different acidity

phenomenal /fəˈnɒmɪn(ə)l/ adj extremely impressive or surprising: *the phenomenal success of the film* —**phenomenally** adv

phenomenon /fəˈnɒmɪnən/ (plural **phenomena** /fəˈnɒmɪnə/ or **phenomenons**) noun [C] **1** an event or a situation: *Some people see 'reality TV' shows as a disturbing new phenomenon.* **2** someone or something that is very impressive or surprising: *a publishing phenomenon*

phenotype /ˈfiːnəʊtaɪp/ noun [C] **BIOLOGY** the characteristics of an organism that are the result of the way its genes and the environment have affected each other —**phenotypic** /ˌfiːnəˈtɪpɪk/ adj, **phenotypical** adj, **phenotypically** adv

pheromone /ˈferəməʊn/ noun [C] **BIOLOGY** a chemical produced by an animal that spreads in the air and influences the behaviour of other animals of the same type

philanthropist /fɪˈlænθrəpɪst/ noun [C] someone who spends a lot of their money on things that benefit

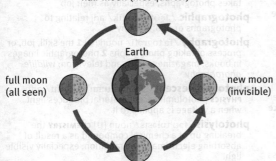

half-moon (first quarter)

Earth

full moon (all seen)

new moon (invisible)

Sun's rays

half-moon (last quarter)

phases of the Moon

society or poor people —**philanthropic** /ˌfɪlən'θrɒpɪk/ adj

philology /fɪ'lɒlədʒi/ noun [U] **LANGUAGE** the scientific study of the history and development of languages or of a particular language —**philological** /ˌfɪlə'lɒdʒɪk(ə)l/ adj, **philologist** noun [C]

philosopher /fɪ'lɒsəfə/ noun [C] someone who studies and writes about the meaning of things such as life, knowledge, or beliefs

philosophical /ˌfɪlə'sɒfɪk(ə)l/ adj **1** relating to philosophy: *a philosophical argument* **2** able to accept an unpleasant situation calmly because you know that you cannot change it —**philosophically** /ˌfɪlə'sɒfɪkli/ adv

philosophy /fɪ'lɒsəfi/ (plural **philosophies**) noun **1** [C/U] the study of theories about the meaning of things such as life, knowledge, and beliefs, or a particular theory that results from this study: *He studied politics and philosophy.* ♦ *a professor of philosophy* ♦ *Eastern philosophies* **2** [C] a belief that influences someone's decisions and behaviour: *the latest philosophies of management* ♦ *My philosophy is 'live and let live'.*

phishing /'fɪʃɪŋ/ noun [U] the practice of trying to trick someone into giving their secret bank information by sending them an email that looks as if it comes from their bank, and that asks them to give their account number or password

phlegm /flem/ noun [U] **HEALTH** a thick substance that develops in the nose and throat, especially when someone has a cold

phloem /'fləʊem/ noun [U] **BIOLOGY** one of the two main types of **vascular** tissue in plants, which takes food from the leaves to all parts of the plant —*picture* → ROOT

phobia /'fəʊbiə/ noun [C] a very strong feeling of fear or dislike for something: *a phobia about spiders* —**phobic** /'fəʊbɪk/ adj

phonation /fəʊ'neɪʃ(ə)n/ noun [U] **LANGUAGE** the production of speech sounds by vibrating the **vocal cords**

phone¹ /fəʊn/ noun [C] a telephone: *The phone rang five times in the next hour.* ♦ *I called his house but his mother answered the phone* (=picked it up when it rang). ♦ *Our teenagers spend hours on the phone* (=using the phone) *every day.* ♦ *We take orders by phone or by email.*

phone² /fəʊn/ verb [I/T] to use a telephone to call someone= CALL: *Phone me if you have any questions.*

'phone ,box noun [C] a small structure with a telephone inside it that you pay to use

'phone ,call noun [C] an act of telephoning someone: *Excuse me, I have to make a phone call.*

'phone-,in noun [C] a radio or television programme that people phone with their questions or comments

phoneme /'fəʊniːm/ noun [C] **LANGUAGE** an individual speech sound that makes one word different from another, for example the 'b' and 'f' in 'bill' and 'fill'

phonemic /fəʊ'niːmɪk/ adj **LANGUAGE** relating to a phoneme

phonemics /fəʊ'niːmɪks/ noun [U] **LANGUAGE** the study of the phonemes of a language

'phone ,number noun [C] a series of numbers that you press on a telephone in order to call someone = TELEPHONE NUMBER

phonetic /fə'netɪk/ adj **LANGUAGE** relating to the sounds used in speech, or using special symbols to show speech sounds: *the phonetic alphabet* —**phonetically** /fə'netɪkli/ adv

phonetics /fə'netɪks/ noun [U] **LANGUAGE** the study of the sounds that are used in speech

phoney /'fəʊni/ adj *informal* **1** not real and intended to trick people= FAKE: *a phoney ID card* **2** pretending to be friendly, clever, kind etc in order to impress or trick people= INSINCERE

phonic /'fɒnɪk/ adj **1** EDUCATION using phonics to teach people to read **2** LANGUAGE relating to the sounds used in speech, or to the study of these sounds

phonically /'fɒnɪkli/ adv **1** LANGUAGE in a way that relates to speech sounds **2** EDUCATION in a way that relates to phonics

phonics /'fɒnɪks/ noun [U] EDUCATION a way of teaching people to read by teaching them to recognize individual sounds, instead of whole words

phonology /fə'nɒlədʒi/ noun [U] LANGUAGE the study of the pattern of speech sounds used in a particular language —**phonological** /ˌfəʊnə'lɒdʒɪk(ə)l, ˌfɒnə'lɒdʒɪk(ə)l/ adj

phosphate /'fɒsfeɪt/ noun [C/U] CHEMISTRY, AGRICULTURE a chemical compound containing **phosphorus** that is used for making plants grow

phospholipid /ˌfɒsfəʊˈlɪpɪd/ noun [C] BIOLOGY a chemical compound that contains **phosphorus**, **fatty acids**, and nitrogen. Cell membranes contain a double layer of phospholipids.

phosphor bronze /ˈfɒsfə ˌbrɒnz/ noun [U] ENGINEERING a strong alloy of copper with tin and **phosphorus**, used in making **bearings** and **gears**

phosphorescent /ˌfɒsfəˈres(ə)nt/ adj PHYSICS a phosphorescent substance absorbs energy from radiation and releases it in the form of light, even after the source of radiation is removed —**phosphorescence** noun [U]

phosphor powder /ˈfɒsfə ˌpaʊdə/ noun [C] CHEMISTRY, PHYSICS a substance that is used in **fluorescent lights** to coat the inside surface of the glass tube. It produces a bluish light when it is hit by **ultraviolet light**.

phosphorus /ˈfɒsfərəs/ noun [U] CHEMISTRY a chemical element, especially a form called **white phosphorus** that starts to burn by itself when air touches it. Chemical symbol: **P** —**phosphorous** /ˈfɒsfərəs/ adj

photo /ˈfəʊtəʊ/ (plural **photos**) noun [C] a **photograph**: *photos of her grandchildren* ♦ *Shall I take a photo of the cathedral?*

photocell /ˈfəʊtəʊˌsel/ noun [C] PHYSICS a **photoelectric cell**

photochemical reaction /ˌfəʊtəʊˌkemɪk(ə)l riˈækʃ(ə)n/ noun [C] CHEMISTRY a chemical change that is caused by the action of light

photochemical smog /ˌfəʊtəʊˌkemɪk(ə)l ˈsmɒg/ noun [U] ENVIRONMENT polluted air that forms a cloud close to the ground. It is caused by the chemical action of light.

photochromic lens /ˌfəʊtəʊˌkrəʊmɪk ˈlenz/ noun [C] PHYSICS a type of lens that becomes darker in sunlight

photoconductivity /ˌfəʊtəʊkɒndʌkˈtɪvɪti/ noun [U] PHYSICS an increase in the ability of a substance to conduct electricity when it absorbs electromagnetic radiation, especially visible light —**photoconductive** /ˌfəʊtəʊkɒnˈdʌktɪv/ adj, **photoconductor** noun [C]

photocopier /ˈfəʊtəʊˌkɒpiə/ noun [C] a machine that copies documents or pictures from one piece of paper to another

photocopy /ˈfəʊtəˌkɒpi/ (plural **photocopies**) noun [C] a copy made by a photocopier —**photocopy** verb [T]

photoelectric /ˌfəʊtəʊɪˈlektrɪk/ adj PHYSICS relating to electrical effects caused by the action of electromagnetic radiation, especially visible light —**photoelectricity** /ˌfəʊtəʊɪlekˈtrɪsɪti/ noun [U]

photoelectric 'cell noun [C] **1** a piece of equipment that reacts to light and is used in machines such as **burglar alarms** (=machines that make a loud noise if a thief tries to get into a building) **2** PHYSICS a piece of equipment that changes light from the Sun into electricity

photoemission /ˌfəʊtəʊɪˈmɪʃ(ə)n/ noun [U] PHYSICS the release of electrons from a substance as a result of electromagnetic radiation —**photoemissive** adj

photograph¹ /ˈfəʊtəˌgrɑːf/ noun [C] a picture of something that you take with a camera: *black and white photographs* ♦ *We took lots of photographs on holiday.*

photograph² /ˈfəʊtəˌgrɑːf/ verb [T] to take a photograph of someone or something: *They were photographed shaking hands.*

photographer /fəˈtɒgrəfə/ noun [C] someone who takes photographs, especially as their job

photographic /ˌfəʊtəˈgræfɪk/ adj relating to photographs or photography

photography /fəˈtɒgrəfi/ noun [U] **1** the skill, job, or process of taking photographs **2** photographic images in books, magazines, films, and television: *wildlife photography*

photoluminescent /ˌfəʊtəʊluːmɪˈnes(ə)nt/ adj PHYSICS photoluminescent material produces light when a voltage is applied to it

photolysis /fəʊˈtɒləsɪs/ noun [U] CHEMISTRY the breaking up of a chemical compound as a result of absorbing electromagnetic radiation, especially visible light

photometer /fəʊˈtɒmɪtə/ noun [C] PHYSICS a piece of equipment that is used to measure the strength of visible light

photometry /fəʊˈtɒmɪtri/ noun [U] PHYSICS the measurement of the strength of sources of visible light

photomontage /ˈfəʊtəʊˌmɒntɑːʒ/ noun [C] a picture that consists of parts of photographs put together

photon /ˈfəʊtɒn/ noun [C] PHYSICS a unit of energy in the form of light —*picture* → SOLAR CELL

'photo oppor,tunity noun [C] an occasion when a politician or famous person appears in public and people take photographs of them

photoreceptive /ˌfəʊtəʊrɪˈseptɪv/ adj BIOLOGY photoreceptive cells are able to receive and use light, for example in processes such as photosynthesis —**photoreception** noun [U]

photosensitive /ˌfəʊtəʊˈsensətɪv/ adj reacting to light, especially by changing colour

the photosphere /ˈfəʊtəʊˌsfɪə/ noun [singular] ASTRONOMY the bright outer layer of a star, especially the Sun —*picture* → SUN

photosynthesis /ˌfəʊtəʊˈsɪnθəsɪs/ noun [U] BIOLOGY the process in which green plants combine carbon dioxide and water, by using energy from light, to produce their own food —*picture* → CARBON CYCLE —**photosynthesize** verb [I], **photosynthetic** /ˌfəʊtəʊsɪnˈθetɪk/ adj, **photosynthetically** adv

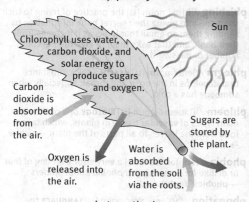

Sun

Chlorophyll uses water, carbon dioxide, and solar energy to produce sugars and oxygen.

Carbon dioxide is absorbed from the air.

Sugars are stored by the plant.

Oxygen is released into the air.

Water is absorbed from the soil via the roots.

photosynthesis

photovoltaic cell /ˌfəʊtəʊvɒlˌteɪk ˈsel/ noun [C] PHYSICS a piece of equipment that changes light into electricity

phrasal verb /ˌfreɪz(ə)l ˈvɜːb/ noun [C] LANGUAGE a combination of words that is used like a verb. It consists of a verb and an adverb or preposition, for example 'give in' or 'come up with'.

phrase[1] /freɪz/ noun [C] **1 LANGUAGE** a group of words that are used together in a fixed expression: *Several of those interviewed used the phrase 'being my own boss'.* **2 LANGUAGE** a group of words that form a unit within a clause **3 MUSIC** a series of musical notes that are part of a piece of music —**phrasal** adj

phrase[2] /freɪz/ verb [T] **1** to express something in a particular way in speech or writing **2 MUSIC** to perform music in a way that clearly shows which musical notes belong together

phraseology /ˌfreɪzɪˈɒlədʒi/ noun [U] *formal* **1** the words and phrases used in a particular profession or activity = TERMINOLOGY **2 LANGUAGE** a particular way of putting words together to express something

phrasing /ˈfreɪzɪŋ/ noun [U] **MUSIC** the way that music is performed to show clearly which musical notes belong together

phylum /ˈfaɪləm/ (plural **phyla**) noun [C] **BIOLOGY** a large group of living things that are related to one other. A phylum includes more than a **class** and less than a **kingdom**. —*picture* → TAXONOMY

physical /ˈfɪzɪk(ə)l/ adj

1 relating to body	4 sexual
2 able to be seen/ touched	5 in real world
3 when people touch a lot	6 relating to physics

1 relating to your body rather than to your mind: *children who have physical disabilities* ♦ *hard physical work* → MENTAL
2 real and able to be seen, touched, or felt: *There was no physical evidence to connect Whitman with the crime.*
3 used about activities or relationships that involve people touching or hitting each other a lot: *Rugby is a very physical game.* ♦ *There was little physical contact between mother and children.*
4 involving sex: *Did they have a physical relationship?*
5 existing in the real world, rather than in someone's imagination: *the physical universe*
6 SCIENCE relating to physics

physical 'chemistry noun [U] **PHYSICS, CHEMISTRY** the branch of chemistry that studies the way physical characteristics depend on chemical **composition**, and the physical changes that take place in chemicals

physical de'pendence noun [U] **HEALTH** a situation in which the body begins to depend on a drug

physical edu'cation noun [U] **EDUCATION** PE

physical ge'ography noun [U] **GEOGRAPHY** the type of geography that deals with the physical features of the world such as mountains and rivers → POLITICAL GEOGRAPHY

physically /ˈfɪzɪkli/ adv **1** in a way that is related to your body or appearance: *physically attractive* ♦ *physically fit* **2** used about things in the real world, rather than in your imagination or in stories: *It is physically impossible to be in two places at the same time.*

physical 'science noun [C] **SCIENCE** a science that deals with things that are not alive, for example geology or physics

physical 'weathering noun [U] **CHEMISTRY, GEOLOGY** the process by which rocks and minerals are broken into very small pieces by physical forces, for example by the action of water, ice, wind, and changes in temperature

physician /fɪˈzɪʃ(ə)n/ noun [C] *formal* a **doctor** sense 1

physics /ˈfɪzɪks/ noun [U] **PHYSICS** the science that deals with heat, light, and other forms of energy and how they affect objects —**physicist** /ˈfɪzɪsɪst/ noun [C]

physiological /ˌfɪzɪəˈlɒdʒɪk(ə)l/ adj **BIOLOGY** relating to the way that the body of an organism operates —**physiologically** /ˌfɪzɪəˈlɒdʒɪkli/ adv

physiology /ˌfɪziˈɒlədʒi/ noun [U] **BIOLOGY 1** the science that deals with the way that the bodies of organisms operate **2** the way that the body of a particular organism operates

physiotherapy /ˌfɪziəʊˈθerəpi/ noun [U] **HEALTH** the treatment of injuries using special physical exercises —**physiotherapist** noun [C]

physique /fɪˈziːk/ noun [C] the shape of someone's body: *a boxer with an impressive, muscular physique*

phytoplankton /ˌfaɪtəʊˈplæŋktən/ noun [U] **BIOLOGY** microscopic organisms that exist in large numbers in water and are eaten by fish

pi /paɪ/ noun [U] **MATHS** a number equal to 22/7 or 3.142, written as the symbol π. It describes the ratio of the circumference of a circle to its diameter.

pianissimo /ˌpiːəˈnɪsɪməʊ/ adj, adv **MUSIC** used as an instruction in music for telling you to play or sing very quietly —*picture* → MUSIC

pianist /ˈpiːənɪst/ noun [C] **MUSIC** someone who plays the piano

piano[1] /piˈænəʊ/ (plural **pianos**) noun [C] **MUSIC** a large musical instrument with a row of black and white keys that you press: *Do you play the piano?* ♦ *She was accompanied by Helen on piano.*

piano[2] /ˈpjɑːnəʊ/ adj, adv **MUSIC** used as an instruction in music for telling you to play or sing quietly —*picture* → MUSIC

pi'ano ac,cordion noun [C] **MUSIC** an **accordion** that has a row of **keys**, not buttons, that you press to produce the sound

piccolo /ˈpɪkələʊ/ (plural **piccolos**) noun [C] **MUSIC** a musical instrument like a small **flute** —*picture* → MUSICAL INSTRUMENT

pick[1] /pɪk/ verb [T] **1** to choose someone or something from a group: *Each month we pick a novel, and we all read it and discuss it.* ♦ *The following season he was picked for the national team.* **2** to get flowers or fruit by breaking them off their stems: *They spent the summer picking strawberries.* **3** to keep pulling something with your fingernails: *She sits and picks the loose skin on her feet.*

PHRASES **pick and choose (sth)** to choose the things that you prefer, rather than simply accepting what you are given: *We cannot pick and choose which laws to obey.*
pick a fight/quarrel with sb to start a fight or argument with someone
pick a lock to open a lock without a key, for example with a piece of wire

PHRASAL VERBS **'pick on sb** to keep treating someone badly or unfairly, especially by criticizing them: *Why do you always pick on Jill?*
,pick sth 'up 1 to learn a new skill, or to start to have a habit, without intending to: *She picked up a few German phrases while staying in Berlin.* **2 HEALTH** *informal* to get an illness = CATCH: *I must have picked up a bug on holiday.* **3** *informal* to receive an electronic signal on a radio or similar piece of equipment
,pick sb/sth 'up 1 to lift someone or something up from a surface: *She rushed to pick up the baby.* ♦ *Please pick those toys up and put them away.* **2** to go to a place in order to get someone or something and take them somewhere, usually in a car: *Will you pick me up at 11.00?* ♦ *Can I pick up my luggage tomorrow?*

pick² /pɪk/ noun [C] a tool with a heavy curved blade, used for breaking hard surfaces

PHRASE take your pick to choose the person or thing that you like best

pickaxe /'pɪk,æks/ noun [C] a tool with a heavy curved blade, used for breaking hard surfaces = PICK —*picture* → TOOL

picket /'pɪkɪt/ or **'picket ,line** noun [C] a group of people who are protesting outside a building, especially a group of workers who are on **strike**

pickle¹ /'pɪk(ə)l/ noun [U] a thick sauce that consists of vegetables or fruit preserved in vinegar. You eat it cold.

pickle² /'pɪk(ə)l/ verb [T] **1** to preserve food in vinegar or salt water **2 TECHNOLOGY** to remove the **oxides** that form on the surface of a metal after it is heated, by dipping it into acid —**pickled** /'pɪk(ə)ld/ adj

pickpocket /'pɪk,pɒkɪt/ noun [C] someone who steals things from people's pockets and bags in crowded places

pickup point /'pɪkʌp ,pɔɪnt/ noun [C] **TOURISM** a place where people arrange to be collected by a **coach**, taxi etc

pickup truck /'pɪkʌp ,trʌk/ noun [C] a small van with an open back and low sides

picnic /'pɪknɪk/ noun [C] a meal that you take with you to eat outside, often while sitting on the grass —**picnic** verb [I]

picofarad /'piːkəʊ,færəd/ noun [C] **PHYSICS** one million millionth part of a farad

picogram /'piːkəʊgræm/ noun [C] **SCIENCE** one million millionth part of a gram

pictogram /'pɪktəgræm/ noun [C] **MATHS** a graph that shows numbers or amounts as simple pictures —*picture* → CHART

pictograph /'pɪktəʊgrɑːf/ noun [C] a picture that represents a word or idea in some writing systems

pictorial /pɪk'tɔːriəl/ adj consisting of pictures: *a pictorial history of the Solomon Islands* —**pictorially** adv

pic'torial ,drawing noun [C/U] **MATHS, PHYSICS** a drawing representing a three-dimensional object as a picture, using **perspective** to show distance

picture¹ /'pɪktʃə/ noun

1 drawing etc	4 situation
2 description	5 image on screen
3 mental image	

1 [C] a drawing, painting, or photograph: *I'll stand over here, and you can **take the picture** (=use a camera). ♦ a picture of the house where I was born ♦ She asked children to **draw pictures** of their family.*
2 [C] a description or idea of what someone or something is like: *The book **paints a picture of** (=gives a description of) a man with a very lonely life.*
3 [C] an image in your mind: *I have this **picture** in my head **of** Sam's face when he realized it was just a joke.*
4 [singular] a situation: *The picture has changed a lot recently.*
5 [singular] the image on a television or film screen, or the quality of the image: *The picture isn't very good on this channel.*

> Build your vocabulary: types of **picture**
>
> ■ **drawing** a picture that is made using a pen or pencil
> ■ **graphics** the pictures in a magazine or a computer document

■ **illustration** a picture that appears in a book or magazine
■ **painting** a picture that is made using paints
■ **photograph/photo** a picture that is taken with a camera
■ **portrait** a picture of a person
■ **sketch** a picture that you create quickly, often in preparation for a more detailed drawing or painting

picture² /'pɪktʃə/ verb [T] **1** to imagine something: *Try to picture what life was like in those days. ♦ I pictured myself lying in the sun on a beach.* **2** to show someone in a photograph, painting etc: *Pictured above are some of the clothes from the new collection.*

'picture ,messaging noun [U] the sending of images and photographs from one mobile phone to another

picturesque /,pɪktʃə'resk/ adj a picturesque place or scene is attractive, usually because it is old and interesting

pidgin /'pɪdʒɪn/ noun [C/U] **LANGUAGE** a language made up of two or more languages, used as a way of communicating by people whose **first languages** are different from each other —**pidgin** adj

pie /paɪ/ noun [C/U] a food that consists of meat, vegetables, or fruit cooked inside a case of **pastry** → PIE CHART

piece¹ /piːs/ noun [C]

1 individual object	5 writing/art etc
2 one of a type	6 object in game
3 part of sth	+ PHRASES
4 used to make sth	

1 an individual object of a particular type: *I've used four **pieces of** paper already. ♦ a piece of furniture ♦ Police found several **pieces of** clothing.*
2 a single instance or amount of something of a particular type: ***a piece of** information ♦ an impressive **piece of** work ♦ I have another **piece of** news for you.*
3 a part that has been cut, broken, or separated from something larger: *Can I offer you another **piece of** cake? ♦ Jerry **tore** the letter **to pieces** (=tore it until it was destroyed) and threw it out.*
4 a part that you fit together with other parts to make something: *a jigsaw with 500 pieces ♦ I didn't expect the furniture to arrive **in pieces**.*
5 something that a writer, musician, or artist has produced
6 an object that you move in a **board game**: *chess pieces*

PHRASES go to pieces informal to be so nervous or worried that you cannot behave in a sensible way
in one piece not badly damaged or injured
pull/rip/tear etc sb/sth to pieces to criticize someone or something severely
→ SET PIECE

piece² /piːs/ **PHRASAL VERB ,piece sth to'gether** to make something by combining separate bits

'pie ,chart noun [C] **MATHS** a circle divided into sections, used in order to show how something is divided into different amounts —*picture* → CHART

pier /pɪə/ noun [C] **1** a structure that is built out from the land over water. It is used for getting on and off boats, fishing, walking etc. **2 CONSTRUCTION** a support made of bricks or stone that is wider than a **column**

pierce /pɪəs/ verb [T] **1** to make a hole in something using a sharp object = PENETRATE: *The knife pierced his skin.* **2** literary if sound or light pierces something, it is suddenly very loud or bright **3** if you have a part of your body pierced, you have a small hole made in it so that you can wear jewellery in it: *I had my **ears pierced** years ago.*

piercing /ˈpɪəsɪŋ/ adj **1** very loud, high, and unpleasant = PENETRATING: *a piercing scream* **2** piercing wind or cold air is so cold that it hurts you **3** piercing eyes or looks seem to show that someone understands everything

piezoelectric effect /ˌpiːzəʊɪlektrɪk ɪˈfekt/ noun [U] PHYSICS the ability of some crystals and **ceramic** materials to produce electric current when physical pressure is applied to them

pig /pɪg/ noun [C] **1** a mammal with a curly tail and usually pink skin that is kept by farmers for its meat —*picture* → MAMMAL **2** an insulting word for someone who behaves in an unpleasant way or eats too much

pigeon /ˈpɪdʒ(ə)n/ noun [C] a brown, white, and grey bird that often lives in cities —*picture* → BIRD

pigeonhole /ˈpɪdʒ(ə)n,həʊl/ noun [C] one of the open boxes in a desk or on a wall where you can put papers, letters, messages etc

pigeon-toed /ˌpɪdʒ(ə)n ˈtəʊd/ adj having feet that point inwards

'pig ,iron noun [U] TECHNOLOGY impure iron that is produced from iron ore in a **blast furnace**

piglet /ˈpɪglət/ noun [C] a young pig

pigment /ˈpɪgmənt/ noun [C/U] **1** BIOLOGY a natural chemical compound that gives colour to animal or plant tissues **2** ARTS a substance that gives colour to something such as paint or ink

pigmentation /ˌpɪgmenˈteɪʃ(ə)n/ noun [U] BIOLOGY the natural colour of something, for example someone's skin

pigsty /ˈpɪg,staɪ/ (plural **pigsties**) noun [C] AGRICULTURE a small building on a farm where pigs are kept

pike /paɪk/ (plural **pike**) noun [C] a large fish that lives in rivers and lakes

pilaf or **pilaff** /ˈpiːlæf, ˈpɪlæf/ noun [C/U] a Middle Eastern or Indian food consisting mainly of rice mixed with meat or vegetables

pilau rice /ˌpiːlaʊ ˈraɪs/ noun [U] flavoured and often coloured rice eaten with Indian food

pile¹ /paɪl/ noun

1 things put on things	**4** haemorrhoids
2 large amount of sth	**5** support post
3 surface of cloth/carpet	

1 [C] a number of things that are put on top of one another in an untidy way: *Rubbish lay **in piles** in the street.* ♦ *a pile of books and papers*
2 [C] *informal* a large amount of something: *By the time he was 40, he'd made **piles of** money.*
3 [singular/U] the surface of a carpet or cloth, formed by the ends of fibres that have been cut
4 piles [plural] *informal* **haemorrhoids**
5 [C] CONSTRUCTION a cylinder of concrete or steel that is put into the ground to support the **foundation** of a building

pile² /paɪl/ verb [T] to put a large number of things on top of one another: *A group of boys were piling branches in a heap for their bonfire.* ♦ *a plate **piled high** with food*

'pile ,driver noun [C] CONSTRUCTION a large machine that pushes posts into the ground to support new buildings

pilfer /ˈpɪlfə/ verb [I/T] to steal things that are not very valuable, especially from the place where you work

pilgrim /ˈpɪlgrɪm/ noun [C] RELIGION **1** someone who travels to a holy place that is important in their religion **2 Pilgrim** one of the people who left England and went to live in what is now the US in the early 17th century

pilgrimage /ˈpɪlgrɪmɪdʒ/ noun [C/U] RELIGION a journey that a religious person makes to a holy place

pill /pɪl/ noun HEALTH **1** [C] a small piece of solid medicine that you swallow with water = TABLET: *vitamin pills* ♦ *Did you remember to **take your pills** this morning?* **2 the pill** [singular] a pill that a woman swallows every day to prevent her from becoming pregnant: *Are you **on the pill** (=taking it)?*

pillage /ˈpɪlɪdʒ/ verb [I/T] to steal things from a place using force, especially during a war

pillar /ˈpɪlə/ noun [C] **1** a thick strong upright post that supports part of a building **2** GEOLOGY a tall thin piece of rock that stretches from the ground to the ceiling of a cave or to a higher rock structure. It is formed by **erosion**, for example by the sea. —*picture* → LIMESTONE

pillow /ˈpɪləʊ/ noun [C] a soft object on which you rest your head in bed

pillowcase /ˈpɪləʊ,keɪs/ noun [C] a cloth cover for a pillow

pilot /ˈpaɪlət/ noun [C] **1** someone who flies an aircraft: *an airline pilot* **2** ARTS a television programme that is broadcast to find out if people would like to watch a whole series —**pilot** verb [T]

pimple /ˈpɪmp(ə)l/ noun [C] a small red lump on the skin, especially on the face = SPOT

pin¹ /pɪn/ noun [C] **1** a small thin piece of metal with a sharp point, used for holding cloth in place while you are sewing **2** a thin piece of metal or wood used for holding things together **3** PHYSICS one of the long pieces of metal that stick out from an electric **plug** and make the electrical connections when it is put into a **socket**. Plugs usually have either two or three pins. —*picture* → PLUG

PHRASE **pins and needles** HEALTH the slightly painful feeling that you get in a part of your body when you move it after it has been in an uncomfortable position for a long time

pin² /pɪn/ (**pins, pinning, pinned**) verb [T] **1** to fasten something, or hold it in place, using pins: *Lucy pinned back her hair.* ♦ *Maps were **pinned** to the walls.* ♦ *She **pinned** the badge on her jacket.* **2** to hold someone very firmly so that they cannot move: *Two men **pinned** him **against** the wall.*

PHRASAL VERBS **,pin sth 'down** to understand or describe something exactly = IDENTIFY

,pin sth 'up to fix a picture or notice to a wall: *She had David Beckham's photograph pinned up above her bed.*

PIN /pɪn/ noun [C] personal identification number: a set of four numbers that you put into a cash machine in order to take money out of your bank account

pincer /ˈpɪnsə/ noun [C] BIOLOGY a large part like a hand on some insects and crustaceans. It is used for attacking and for holding things.

pinch¹ /pɪntʃ/ verb **1** [T] to squeeze someone's skin between your thumb and finger so that it hurts them: *Roger pinched my arm.* **2** [I/T] if shoes or clothes pinch, they hurt you because they fit too tightly **3** [T] *informal* to steal something = NICK

pinch² /pɪntʃ/ noun [C] **1** a small amount of something that you can hold between your finger and thumb: *a pinch of salt* **2** the action of squeezing someone's skin between your thumb and finger so that it hurts them

pine /paɪn/ noun **1** [C] a tall tree with long thin sharp leaves that do not fall off in winter **2** [U] the wood of this tree

pineapple /ˈpaɪnˌæp(ə)l/ noun [C/U] a large fruit that is yellow inside and has a thick brown skin with sharp points on it —*picture* → FRUIT

'pine ˌcone noun [C] the brown hard fruit of a pine

'pine ˌneedle noun [C] the thin sharp leaf of a pine

'pine ˌtree noun [C] a **pine**

pinion /ˈpɪnjən/ noun [C] **ENGINEERING** a small metal wheel inside a machine that moves other wheels

pink /pɪŋk/ adj between red and white in colour: *His cheeks turned pink with embarrassment.* —**pink** noun [U]

'pin ˌmould noun [C] **BIOLOGY** a type of fungus that reproduces by spores that are released from a case at the end of a long thread

pinna /ˈpɪnə/ noun [C] **ANATOMY** the part of the ear that sticks out from the side of the head. It captures sound waves which are then directed into the main part of the ear. —*picture* → EAR

pinnacle /ˈpɪnək(ə)l/ noun [C] *literary* **1** the most successful or exciting part of someone's life: *the pinnacle of her acting career* **2** **GEOLOGY** a tall thin pointed piece of stone or rock

pinnate /ˈpɪneɪt/ adj **BIOLOGY** a pinnate leaf is divided into small leaf parts

pinned /pɪnd/ adj **TECHNOLOGY** a pinned **file** has teeth that are full of metal **filings** —**pinning** noun [U]

pinpoint /ˈpɪnˌpɔɪnt/ verb [T] to discover or explain exactly what or where something is: *We couldn't pinpoint the source of the problem.*

pint /paɪnt/ noun [C] a unit for measuring liquid, equal to 0.57 litres in the UK and 0.48 litres in the US

pinworm /ˈpɪnˌwɜːm/ noun [C] **BIOLOGY** a small thin worm that is a parasite of humans. Pinworms live in the intestines.

Pinyin /pɪnˈjɪn/ noun [U] **LANGUAGE** Chinese words written using the **Roman alphabet**

pioneer¹ /ˌpaɪəˈnɪə/ noun [C] **1** one of the first people to do something important that is later developed by other people: *the pioneers of early colour photography* **2** one of the first people to travel to a new place and start living there, especially one of the first Europeans to start living in parts of North America

pioneer² /ˌpaɪəˈnɪə/ verb [T] to do something that no one else has ever done: *The approach was pioneered by Dr Bruce Fisher.* —**pioneering** adj: *pioneering research*

pious /ˈpaɪəs/ adj **1** **RELIGION** strict in your religious beliefs and practices **2** *showing disapproval* done or said with the intention of seeming religious and moral —**piously** adv

pip /pɪp/ noun [C] a small seed in a piece of fruit

pipe¹ /paɪp/ noun [C] **1** a tube that carries liquid or gas from one place to another: *A pipe runs to the hot water tap in the kitchen.* ♦ *Workers were **laying** water **pipes** outside the house.* **2** an object used for smoking tobacco, consisting of a tube with a small bowl at the end **3** **MUSIC** a musical instrument with one or more tubes that you blow through

pipe² /paɪp/ verb [T] to send liquid or gas through a pipe from one place to another

pipeline /ˈpaɪpˌlaɪn/ noun [C] a long underground pipe that carries water, gas etc from one place to another: *a 500-kilometre oil pipeline*
   PHRASE **in the pipeline** something that is in the pipeline is being planned and will happen or be available soon

pipette /pɪˈpet/ noun [C] **SCIENCE** a thin glass tube that scientists use for measuring and moving small amounts of liquid from one container to another —*picture* → LABORATORY

piping /ˈpaɪpɪŋ/ noun [U] **TECHNOLOGY** the formation of a hollow end in a piece of metal that is being **drawn down** (=hammered to a narrow point)

piracy /ˈpaɪrəsi/ noun [U] **LAW 1** the crime of making and selling illegal copies of computer programs, books, CDs, DVDs etc **2** the crime of stealing things from ships while they are sailing

piranha /pəˈrɑːnə/ noun [C] a small South American river fish that has sharp teeth and eats meat

pirate¹ /ˈpaɪrət/ noun [C] **1** someone who steals things from ships while they are sailing **2** someone who illegally makes and sells copies of computer programs, books, CDs, DVDs etc

pirate² /ˈpaɪrət/ verb [T] to illegally make copies of computer programs, books, CDs, DVDs etc —**pirated** adj

Pisces /ˈpaɪsiːz/ (plural **Pisces**) noun [C/U] one of the 12 signs of the zodiac. A **Pisces** is someone who was born between 20 February and 20 March.

pistachio /pɪˈstɑːʃiəʊ, pɪˈstæʃiəʊ/ (plural **pistachios**) noun [C/U] a small green nut

piste /piːst/ noun [C] **SPORTS** an area of ground covered in snow that has been prepared for **skiing**

pistil /ˈpɪstɪl/ noun [C] **BIOLOGY** the female part of a flower used in reproduction. It consists of one or several **carpels**.

pistol /ˈpɪst(ə)l/ noun [C] a small gun

piston /ˈpɪstən/ noun [C] **ENGINEERING** a solid cylinder that fits into a larger cylinder and moves up and down to create power in an engine

'piston ˌring noun [C] **ENGINEERING** a steel ring on the outside of a piston in an engine. It closes the space between the piston and the wall of the cylinder.

pit /pɪt/ noun **1** [C] a large hole in the ground: *a gravel pit* **2** the place in front of a stage where an orchestra sits **3** **the pits** [plural] **SPORTS** the area beside a **racetrack** where cars get fuel, have their tyres changed, or are repaired during a race

pitch¹ /pɪtʃ/ noun

1 sports ground	4 attempt to persuade
2 strength of emotions	5 of sound
3 of musical note	6 slope of roof etc

1 [C] **SPORTS** a flat area of ground that is used for playing sports on: *a football pitch* ♦ *Hundreds of fans invaded the pitch at the end of the game.*
2 [singular/U] the level of someone's emotions: *Excitement and enthusiasm **rose to fever pitch** (=reached a high level).*
3 [singular/U] **MUSIC** the high or low quality of a musical note
4 [C] the things that you say to persuade someone to buy something or support you: *Most people do not like a very obvious **sales pitch**.*
5 [U] **PHYSICS** the high or low quality of a sound that is controlled by the rate of the vibrations that produce it

6 [singular/U] **CONSTRUCTION** the slope of something such as a roof

pitch² /pɪtʃ/ verb

1 aim talk etc at group	**5** fall suddenly
2 make sound high/low	**6** try to sell/persuade
3 throw with force	**+ PHRASE**
4 in baseball	

1 [T] to make something such as a speech or explanation suitable for people who are a particular age or level of ability: *Her book is **pitched at** a teenage audience.*
2 [T] to make a sound at a particular level
3 [T] to throw something using a lot of force **= FLING**: *Jan pitched her books over the fence.*
4 [I/T] **SPORTS** to throw the ball to a **batter** in the game of baseball
5 [I] to fall suddenly in a particular direction **= PLUNGE**: *He tripped and **pitched** head first **into** the water.*
6 [T] to try to sell something, or to try to persuade someone to do something: *He tried to **pitch** the film **to** all the major Hollywood studios.*
PHRASE **pitch a tent** to put up a tent and make it ready to use

,**pitch-'black** adj completely black or dark

,**pitch-'dark** adj completely dark

pitched roof /ˌpɪtʃt 'ruːf/ noun [C] **CONSTRUCTION** a roof that slopes downwards from a central **ridge** (=high point)

pitcher /'pɪtʃə/ noun [C] **SPORTS** in baseball, the player who throws the ball to the **batter**

pitchfork /'pɪtʃfɔːk/ noun [C] **AGRICULTURE** a tool like a large fork with a long handle, used on farms for lifting and carrying **hay** —*picture* → AGRICULTURAL

pitfall /'pɪtfɔːl/ noun [C] a problem that is likely to happen in a particular situation: *the pitfalls involved in starting a business*

pith /pɪθ/ noun [U] **BIOLOGY 1** the white substance under the skin of oranges and similar fruits **2** the white substance inside the stems of some plants —*picture* → ROOT

pitiful /'pɪtɪf(ə)l/ adj **1** someone who is pitiful looks or sounds so unhappy that you feel sympathy for them **2** extremely bad: *a pitiful performance* ♦ *a pitiful excuse* **3** a pitiful amount of something is very small and not enough: *pitiful wages* —**pitifully** adv

'**pit la,trine** noun [C] a type of outside toilet that consists of a hole in the floor built over a large hole in the ground

'**pit ,stop** noun [C] **SPORTS** an occasion when a driver in a race stops for a short time to get fuel, or to let people change the tyres or repair the car

pitta bread /'pɪtə ˌbred, 'piːtə ˌbred/ or **pitta** /'pɪtə, 'piːtə/ noun [C/U] a type of flat bread that is eaten especially with Middle Eastern food

pittance /'pɪt(ə)ns/ noun [singular] an amount of money that is so small that it seems unfair

pituitary gland /pɪ'tjuːɪt(ə)ri ˌglænd/ noun [C] **ANATOMY** the small gland at the base of the brain that produces the hormones that the body needs to control its growth and development. It is the main **endocrine gland** in the body, and controls many other endocrine glands. —*picture* → BRAIN

pity¹ /'pɪti/ noun [U] a strong feeling of sympathy that you have for someone because they are very unhappy or in a bad situation: *She looked at him with a mixture of pity and disgust.*
PHRASES **(it's a) pity** used for saying that you are disappointed about something: *It's a pity we couldn't stay longer in Boston.* ♦ *It seems a pity to waste this food.*
take pity on sb to feel sorry for someone and try to help them

pity² /'pɪti/ (**pities, pitying, pitied**) verb [T] to feel sorry for someone because they are in a bad situation: *I pity the poor person who has to clean this mess up.*

pivot¹ /'pɪvət/ noun [C] **1** **SCIENCE** a fixed point or pin that something turns on or balances on **= FULCRUM** **2** the most important thing that something is based on or depends on

pivot² /'pɪvət/ verb [I/T] to turn or balance on a central point, or to make something do this

pivotal /'pɪvət(ə)l/ adj **1** extremely important and affecting how something develops **= CRUCIAL 2** like a pivot

'**pivot ,joint** noun [C] **ANATOMY** a joint in the body in which one bone turns around on another bone. This type of joint allows, for example, the head to turn from side to side. —*picture* → JOINT

pixel /'pɪks(ə)l/ noun [C] **COMPUTING** the smallest unit of an image on a computer screen

pixelated or **pixellated** /'pɪks(ə)leɪtɪd/ adj **COMPUTING** a pixelated image is divided into large pixels so that it is difficult to see clearly

pizza /'piːtsə/ noun [C/U] a food that consists of flat round bread with tomato, cheese, vegetables, meat etc on it

pizzicato /ˌpɪtsɪ'kɑːtəʊ/ adv **MUSIC** if you play a **violin** or other **stringed instrument** pizzicato, you play it by pulling the strings with your fingers instead of using the **bow**

pl. abbrev plural

placate /plə'keɪt/ verb [T] formal to stop someone feeling angry or offended by being nice to them or by giving them what they want **= PACIFY**

place¹ /pleɪs/ noun [C]

1 area/position	**5** position in a race
2 town/building etc	**6** importance
3 chance to be in sth	**7** point in book etc
4 seat/position	**+ PHRASES**

1 an area or position: *Keep your credit cards in a **safe place**.* ♦ *She pushed the couch back **into place** (=into the correct position).* ♦ *The road is very narrow and quite dangerous **in places** (=in some areas but not all).*
2 a particular town, country, building, shop etc: *They live in a small place called Clovelly.* ♦ *We went back to Jon's place (=where Jon lives) after the film.* ♦ *Is this a safe place to swim?* ♦ *Cyprus is a great **place for** a holiday.*
3 an opportunity to join an organization, team, university etc: *nursery places for children* ♦ *The organizers are expecting all the places on the course to be filled.* ♦ *Lewis has **earned a place** in the Olympic team.*
4 a seat on a train, on a bus, in a theatre etc, or a position in a queue: *There's no place to sit.* ♦ *Would you mind **saving my place** for a minute?*
5 **SPORTS** the position that you achieve in a race or competition: *Brian finished the race **in third place**.*
6 the importance that someone or something has in people's lives: *a discussion about **the place of** religion in society*
7 the point that you have reached in a book, speech etc
PHRASES **in place** existing and capable of being used: *We didn't have the systems in place to deal with so many orders.*

in place of instead of

out of place 1 if someone feels out of place, they are uncomfortable because they feel that they are not like other people around them **2** if something looks out of place, it is in a position where it does not belong or look good

place of work/business/worship *formal* the area where you work, have your business, or practise your religion

take sb's/sth's place or **take the place of sb/sth** to do something instead of someone else, or to be used instead of something else: *Joe resigned as chairperson in 1999 and I took his place.*

> Use **room** or **space**, not **place**, to mean an empty area or part of something where people or things can fit: *Is there any room* OR *any space for me in your car?*
> ♦ *I wanted a big table in here, but there wasn't enough room* OR *enough space.*

place² /pleɪs/ verb [T]

1 put sth somewhere	**4** decide importance
2 put sb in situation	**5** remember
3 make sb experience sth	**6** of advertisement

1 to put something somewhere, usually in a careful way: *Ella placed the dish on the table.*
2 to put someone or something in a particular situation or state: *Her decision places me in an awkward situation.* ♦ *At the end of the war, the island was placed under French control.*
3 if someone places limits, responsibilities, pressures etc on someone, they make them experience them: *The large influx of refugees was placing a great burden on Pakistan's resources.*
4 to decide how good or important something is in comparison with other things: *The company was accused of placing profits above safety.* ♦ *The school places great **importance on** the welfare of its students.*
5 if you can't place someone, you do not remember them or you cannot remember their name: *He looks familiar, but I can't place him.*
6 if you place an advertisement, an order, or a **bet**, you give it to someone

placebo /pləˈsiːbəʊ/ (plural **placebos**) noun [C] HEALTH a substance that a doctor gives to a patient instead of medicine, either as part of an experiment or in order to help the patient without using drugs

pla'cebo ef,fect noun [C] HEALTH an improvement in an ill person's condition when they have been given a placebo instead of real medicine

'place ,kick noun [C] SPORTS a kick of the ball in **rugby** or American football while the ball is on the ground or being held by a player

placement /ˈpleɪsmənt/ noun **1** [U] the process of finding someone a place where they can live, work, or study: *job placement* **2** [C/U] a temporary job that is part of a course of study and gives you experience of the work that you hope to do at the end of the course: *a three-month placement with the BBC* **3** [C/U] the act of putting something into a position, or the position that it is in

placenta /pləˈsentə/ noun [C] ANATOMY the organ through which a foetus is connected to its mother's blood supply in the uterus before birth —*picture* → EMBRYO

placid /ˈplæsɪd/ adj not often angry or excited

plagiarism /ˈpleɪdʒəˌrɪz(ə)m/ noun [U] the process of taking another person's work, ideas, or words, and using them as if they were your own

plagiarize /ˈpleɪdʒəraɪz/ verb [I/T] to take someone else's work, ideas, or words, and use them as if they were your own

plague¹ /pleɪg/ noun [C] **1** HEALTH a serious disease that spreads quickly and usually ends in death **2** an uncontrolled increase in the numbers of an insect or other animal in a place

plague² /pleɪg/ verb [T] **1** to cause a lot of problems for someone or something for a long period of time: *The east coast has been **plagued by** blizzards this month.* **2** to annoy someone all the time by doing something or asking for something

plaice /pleɪs/ (plural **plaice**) noun [C/U] a thin flat brown sea fish with orange spots, or the meat from this fish

plain¹ /pleɪn/ adj **1** simple, with no decoration or with nothing extra added: *a plain wooden table* ♦ *a plain white T-shirt* ♦ *plain yoghurt* **2** easily seen or understood= OBVIOUS: *Her disappointment was **plain to see**.* ♦ *Sykes **made it plain** that he had no intention of resigning.* ♦ *It was **plain to** everyone that Maude was not happy.* **3** expressing what you think honestly, using simple, direct language: *She was admired for her **plain speaking**.* **4** not very attractive

plain² /pleɪn/ noun [C] GEOGRAPHY a large flat area of land

plain³ /pleɪn/ adv used for emphasizing that someone or something has a particular negative quality: *It was just plain stupid of him to get involved.*

plainly /ˈpleɪnli/ adv **1** in a way that is easy to see, hear, or notice= CLEARLY: *The climbers were plainly visible on the hillside.* ♦ *Something was plainly wrong with the engine.* **2** in a direct and honest way: *Albright told us plainly what the situation was like.* **3** without much decoration

plaintiff /ˈpleɪntɪf/ noun [C] LAW someone who brings a legal case against someone else in a court of law

plait¹ /plæt, *American* pleɪt/ noun [C] a length of hair that is formed by twisting three separate lengths over and under each other

plait² /plæt, *American* pleɪt/ verb [T] to twist three lengths of hair or rope over and under each other in order to make one single piece

plan¹ /plæn/ noun [C] **1** an idea about what you will do in the future, usually including details about how you will do it: *We need to **make a plan** before we start.* ♦ *We don't have any **plans for** our holiday yet.* ♦ *Everything **went according to plan** (=there were no problems).* **2** a drawing that shows what something is like or how it will be made= DESIGN: *plans for the new public gardens*

plan² /plæn/ (**plans, planning, planned**) verb **1** [I/T] to think carefully about a series of actions that you need to take in order to achieve something: *They had been planning their trip to Africa for months.* ♦ *We'll need to **plan ahead** if we want to take a year off for travelling.* ♦ *The meeting has been **planned for** next week.* **2** [T] to intend to do something: *My boss is **planning to** retire at 50.* **3** [T] to think about something that you intend to build or make, and decide how it will look

PHRASAL VERB **'plan on sth** to intend to do something, or to expect something to happen: *We hadn't planned on so many people coming.*

plane /pleɪn/ noun [C] **1** an aircraft with wings and an engine or engines: *Most of the passengers got off the plane in Dublin.* ♦ *We travelled **by plane** from Mexico City.* **2** a level in society, or a level of intelligence or ability= LEVEL: *The top players are on **a higher plane***

than the rest. **3** a tool that is used for making wooden surfaces smooth —*picture* → TOOL **4** MATHS a flat surface

'plane ge,ometry noun [U] MATHS the part of geometry that deals with **two-dimensional** (=flat) shapes → SOLID GEOMETRY

planet /'plænɪt/ noun **1** [C] ASTRONOMY a very large **spherical** object such as the Earth that moves around a sun or around another star: *Mars is sometimes known as the red planet.* **2 the planet** [singular] ENVIRONMENT the planet Earth and everything on it: *policies to protect the future of the planet* —**planetary** /'plænət(ə)ri/ adj

planetarium /ˌplænə'teəriəm/ noun [C] ASTRONOMY a building with a curved roof where lights in the ceiling represent the movement of the planets and stars

planish /'plænɪʃ/ verb [T] TECHNOLOGY to flatten and smooth **sheet metal** with a special hammer, after it has been beaten

plank /plæŋk/ noun [C] **1** a long narrow piece of wood that is used for making structures such as floors **2** an important aspect of something, on which it is based: *the main plank of the party's defence policy*

plankton /'plæŋktən/ noun [U] BIOLOGY very small organisms that exist in large numbers in water and are eaten by fish

planning /'plænɪŋ/ noun [U] **1** the process of deciding how you will do something before you do it: *There was very little planning done for this project.* **2** the job of deciding where buildings and roads should be built: *urban planning* —**planner** noun [C]

plant¹ /plɑːnt/ noun **1** [C] BIOLOGY an organism that grows in soil or water and usually has green leaves. Plants have cell walls made of cellulose and cannot move from place to place. They use light energy from the sun to produce oxygen and carbohydrates by means of photosynthesis. Trees, algae, ferns, and grass are all types of plant. **2** [C] BIOLOGY a **herbaceous** plant that grows in soil, is smaller than a tree or bush, and usually has green leaves, roots, and flowers. Do not use this meaning in scientific writing or discussions, as it is not a scientific meaning: *What kind of plants did you get for the garden?* ♦ *a pot plant* **3** [C] a large factory: *a nuclear plant* **4** [U] large machines and equipment that are used in industry or on a building site: *plant hire*

plant² /plɑːnt/ verb [T]

1 of seeds etc	4 hide sth on sb
2 of land/field	5 hide bomb
3 place firmly	6 give sb an idea

1 BIOLOGY to put plants or seeds in soil so that they will grow there: *I've planted a small apple tree in the garden.*
2 AGRICULTURE to use an area of land for growing plants: *fields planted with wheat*
3 to put someone or something firmly in a particular place or position: *Henry planted himself in the seat next to me.*
4 to secretly put something that is illegal or stolen in someone's clothes so that they appear to be guilty when it is found: *Someone must have planted the gun on him.*
5 if someone plants a bomb, they hide it where they want it to explode
6 if you plant an idea in someone's mind, you mention it so that they begin to think about it

plantain /'plæntɪn/ noun [C/U] a type of banana used as a vegetable in Caribbean and African foods

plantation /plɑːn'teɪʃ(ə)n/ noun [C] AGRICULTURE **1** a large farm where crops such as tea, cotton, and **sugar cane** are grown **2** an area where trees have been planted

planter /'plɑːntə/ noun [C] AGRICULTURE **1** someone who owns or is in charge of a plantation **2** a machine used for planting seeds, potatoes etc

'plan ,view noun [C/U] MATHS, PHYSICS a view of a three-dimensional object in **orthographic projection** that shows it at right angles from above

plaque /plæk, plɑːk/ noun **1** [C] a flat piece of metal or stone that is hung on a wall for decoration, or to give information **2** [U] HEALTH a substance that forms on the teeth and in which bacteria can grow **3** [U] HEALTH a layer of fat that forms in the arteries and can be harmful

plasma /'plæzmə/ noun [U] BIOLOGY the yellow liquid that is part of blood

'plasma ,screen noun [C] COMPUTING a type of television or computer screen made by putting a mixture of gases between two sheets of glass

plasmolysis /plæz'mɒlɪsɪs/ noun [U] BIOLOGY a process in which plant cells in a concentrated solution **shrink** (=become smaller) due to **osmosis**. The cell membrane is pulled away from the cell wall, leaving a space that is filled with the concentrated solution.

plaster¹ /'plɑːstə/ noun **1** [U] a substance that is spread onto walls and ceilings to form a hard smooth surface **2** [C] a thin sticky piece of cloth or plastic that you put on your skin to cover a cut
PHRASE **in plaster** enclosed in a hard cover that protects a broken bone: *One man had his leg in plaster.*

plaster² /'plɑːstə/ verb [T] **1** to cover a surface with labels, advertisements, pictures etc: *He has posters of rock stars plastered all over the walls of his room.* **2** to cover a wall or ceiling with wet plaster or a similar substance **3** to make something lie flat against something else: *The rain had plastered her hair to her forehead.*

plasterboard /'plɑːstəˌbɔːd/ noun [U] CONSTRUCTION plaster that is put between layers of strong paper, and is used for covering walls

'plaster ,cast noun [C] **1** HEALTH a hard cover used for holding a broken bone in position while it gets better. It is made from a net over which you spread a white powder that dries quickly when mixed with water. **2** ARTS a copy of a statue, made of a white powder that dries quickly when mixed with water

plasterer /'plɑːstərə/ noun [C] someone whose job is to put **plaster** on walls or ceilings

plastic¹ /'plæstɪk/ noun [C/U] CHEMISTRY a very common light, strong, non-metal **polymer** that is produced artificially. Plastics are used for making many different things.

plastic² /'plæstɪk/ adj **1** made of plastic: *plastic bags* **2** SCIENCE a plastic substance can be bent into any shape if pressure or heat is applied to it and will keep that shape = FLEXIBLE —**plasticity** noun [U]

,plastic 'arts noun [plural] ARTS arts such as **sculpture** that produce solid objects out of materials such as clay, stone, or wood

,plastic 'surgery noun [U] HEALTH medical operations to improve the appearance of a part of someone's body → COSMETIC SURGERY —**,plastic 'surgeon** noun [C]

plate /pleɪt/ noun

1 flat round dish	4 thin metal layer
2 metal/plastic sign	5 part of Earth
3 sth flat and hard	6 wooden support

1 [C] a flat round dish that you put food on, or the amount that it will hold: *Put away the plates.* ♦ *a plate of sandwiches*

2 [C] a small piece of metal or plastic that is fixed to something and used for showing information such as someone's name or a number: *He read the name on the brass plate on the door.* → NUMBER PLATE

3 [C] a flat piece of metal or other hard substance: *steel plates*

4 [U] a thin layer of silver or gold that covers a less valuable metal to improve its appearance: *gold plate*

5 [C] GEOLOGY one of the layers of rock that form the surface of the Earth —*picture* → CONTINENTAL PLATE

6 [C] CONSTRUCTION a horizontal piece of wood placed along the top of a wall to support the roof

plateau /ˈplætəʊ/ (plural **plateaus** or **plateaux** /ˈplætəʊz/) noun [C] **1** GEOGRAPHY a large flat area of land that is higher than the land around it **2** a period of time when something stops increasing or improving: *The recent boom in mobile phone sales seems to have reached a plateau.*

,**plate 'boundary** noun [C] GEOLOGY an area where two or more **tectonic plates** meet —*picture* → CONTINENTAL PLATE

plated /ˈpleɪtɪd/ adj a metal object that is plated is covered with a thin layer of silver or gold

platelet /ˈpleɪtlət/ noun [C] BIOLOGY a small piece of a cell in the blood of humans and other mammals that helps the blood to clot

,**plate 'movement** noun [C] GEOLOGY one of the ways in which **tectonic plates** move in relation to each other, for example moving apart or moving past each other —*picture* → EARTHQUAKE

plate tectonics /ˌpleɪt tekˈtɒnɪks/ noun [U] GEOLOGY the study of the large layers of rock under the surface of the Earth, and how they were formed and move

platform /ˈplætfɔːm/ noun [C]

1 raised structure	4 policies/aims of party
2 where you get on train	5 in computing
3 chance to express sth	

1 a raised structure for someone to stand on so that they can be seen by an audience: *The two candidates shared the platform for the question and answer session.*

2 an area next to a railway track where passengers get onto and off trains: *The train to Brussels will depart from platform 3.*

3 an opportunity to express your ideas or opinions: *Radio phone-ins provide a platform for people with strong opinions.*

4 POLITICS the policies and aims of a political party, especially the ones they state in order to get people to vote for them

5 COMPUTING the type of computer system that you have and the programs that you can use with it

platinum /ˈplætɪnəm/ noun [U] CHEMISTRY a silver-grey metal element that is used in industry and for making expensive jewellery. Chemical symbol: **Pt**

platonic /pləˈtɒnɪk/ adj a platonic relationship is friendly but does not involve sex

platoon /pləˈtuːn/ noun [C] a small group of soldiers

platter /ˈplætə/ noun [C] a large plate that is used for serving food

platypus /ˈplætɪpəs/ noun [C] a **duckbilled platypus**

plausible /ˈplɔːzəb(ə)l/ adj likely to be true = REASONABLE ≠ IMPLAUSIBLE —**plausibility** /ˌplɔːzəˈbɪləti/ noun [U], **plausibly** adv

play¹ /pleɪ/ verb

1 take part in game	5 have part in play
2 compete against sb	6 of children
3 make music	+ PHRASES
4 produce sounds	+ PHRASAL VERBS

1 [I/T] SPORTS to take part in a sport or game: *The children were playing football in the park.* ♦ *He played for AC Milan before he transferred to Arsenal.*

2 [I/T] SPORTS to compete against someone in a sport or game: *She plays the winner of tomorrow's match.* ♦ *England will be playing against Brazil in the next round.*

3 [I/T] MUSIC to perform music, or to use an instrument to make music: *He played several organ pieces by Bach.* ♦ *Gloria plays the violin in the London Philharmonic.*

4 [I/T] to produce sounds, or to make something such as a radio or CD produce sounds: *They played the CD at full volume.* ♦ *I could hear a radio playing in the flat above.*

5 [T] ARTS to have a particular part in a play or film: *She played Blanche in A Streetcar Named Desire.*

6 [I] if children play, they do things that they enjoy, for example using toys: *The children were out playing in the garden.* ♦ *Which toys do you want to play with today?*

PHRASES **play games** to behave in a silly way by not saying what you really think or by not being serious enough

play (it) safe to avoid taking any risks

PHRASAL VERBS '**play at sth** to do something without being very serious about it

,**play sth 'back** to play a message or video that has been recorded in order to listen to or watch it

,**play sth 'down** to try to make a problem or difficult situation seem less important than it is

'**play with sth** to keep touching something, especially because you are bored

play² /pleɪ/ noun **1** [C] ARTS, LITERATURE a piece of writing that is intended to be performed by actors in a theatre or on television or the radio: *a Shakespeare play* ♦ *The school's going to put on a play this Christmas.* **2** [U] activities that are done because they are enjoyable and fun, especially by children: *She watched the children at play in the park.* **3** [U] SPORTS the action in a sport or game: *Rain stopped play again this afternoon.*

PHRASE **a play on words** a clever or funny use of a word that has two different meanings → FOUL PLAY

player /ˈpleɪə/ noun [C] **1** SPORTS someone who plays a particular game or sport: *a cricket player* **2** MUSIC someone who plays a musical instrument: *a piano player* **3** a person or organization that influences a situation: *Germany is seen as a key player within the European Union.*

playful /ˈpleɪf(ə)l/ adj **1** lively and full of fun: *playful kittens* **2** intended to be funny or friendly rather than serious: *a playful pat on the back* —**playfully** adv, **playfulness** noun [U]

playground /ˈpleɪˌɡraʊnd/ noun [C] EDUCATION an area of land where children can play, especially at a school

playing card /ˈpleɪɪŋ ˌkɑːd/ noun [C] a card that is used for playing card games

playing field /ˈpleɪɪŋ ˌfiːld/ noun [C] SPORTS a piece of land with lines marked on it where a particular sport is played

'play-,off noun [C] **SPORTS** an extra game that is played to decide the winner, after a game ends with an equal score

playtime /'pleɪ,taɪm/ noun [C/U] **EDUCATION** a period of time at school when children can play outside

playwright /'pleɪ,raɪt/ noun [C] **ARTS, LITERATURE** someone who writes plays

plc /,piː el 'siː/ noun [C] **BUSINESS** public limited company: a company in the UK that has shares that ordinary people can buy

PLC abbrev **COMPUTING** programmable logic controller: a type of computer that controls the machines that make products in **assembly lines**

plea /pliː/ noun [C] **1** an urgent or emotional request for something: *The police ignored her **pleas** for help.* **2** **LAW** a statement that someone makes in a court of law to say whether they are guilty of a crime or not

plea bargaining /'pliː ,bɑːgənɪŋ/ noun [U] **LAW** a process by which someone may be allowed to avoid punishment for a serious crime, if they admit they have committed a less serious crime

plead /pliːd/ verb **1** [I] to make an urgent or emotional request: *She **pleaded with** him to stay, but he would not.* **2** [I/T] **LAW** to say in a court of law whether you are guilty of a crime or not: *Both defendants **pleaded not guilty**.* **3** [T] to mention something as an excuse for doing or not doing something: *Ellie pleaded tiredness and went to bed early.* **4** [T] to try to show that something is important or worth trying to achieve: *He pleaded the case for continued cooperation with the Russians.*

pleading /'pliːdɪŋ/ noun [C/U] **LAW** an official statement of someone's case in a court of law

pleasant /'plez(ə)nt/ adj **1** enjoyable or attractive ≠ UNPLEASANT: *They spent a pleasant evening together.* **2** a pleasant person is friendly and behaves correctly in social situations ≠ UNPLEASANT —**pleasantly** adv: *I was **pleasantly surprised** by the results of the survey.*

please¹ /pliːz/ interjection **1** used as a polite way of asking for something, or of asking someone to do something: *Would you help me with these bags, please?* ♦ *Could I have change for a pound, please?* **2** used for emphasizing a request, an order, or a statement: *Please stop making all that noise!* **3** used as a polite way of accepting something that someone has offered you: *'Would you like some more coffee?' **'Yes, please.'***

please² /pliːz/ verb [I/T] to make someone feel happy and satisfied: *He'll do anything to please her.* ♦ *Some of our customers can be very **difficult to please**.*

pleased /pliːzd/ adj happy and satisfied: *We're very pleased that you've accepted our offer.* ♦ *Are you **pleased with** the way things went yesterday?* ♦ *I'm really **pleased about** your new job.* ♦ *You'll be **pleased to hear** that Dave can come tonight!*

PHRASE **pleased to meet you** *spoken* used as a polite way of greeting someone when you meet them for the first time: *'Tony, this is Mr Wilkins.' 'Pleased to meet you.'*

pleasing /'pliːzɪŋ/ adj *formal* **1** pleasant and enjoyable: *a pleasing aroma* **2** making you feel happy and satisfied: *pleasing news*

pleasurable /'pleʒ(ə)rəb(ə)l/ adj *formal* giving you a feeling of happiness, enjoyment, or satisfaction = ENJOYABLE

pleasure /'pleʒə/ noun **1** [U] a feeling of happiness, enjoyment, or satisfaction: *He smiled **with pleasure** when she walked in.* ♦ *His books have **given** enormous pleasure to many people.* ♦ *He **took great pleasure in** pointing out my mistakes.* **2** [C] something that makes you feel happy and satisfied: *Music is one of the greatest pleasures in life.* ♦ *It's a **pleasure to meet** you.* **3** [U] the activity of relaxing and enjoying yourself rather than working: *Are you travelling for **business or pleasure**?*

plectrum /'plektrəm/ noun [C] **MUSIC** a small thin piece of plastic or metal used for playing the strings of a guitar or a similar musical instrument

pledge /pledʒ/ verb [T] to promise seriously and publicly to do something = PROMISE —**pledge** noun [C]

the Pleistocene /'plaɪstəʊ,siːn/ noun [singular] **GEOLOGY** the **era** of geological time, about 1.8 million to 10,000 years ago, in which glaciers formed in the northern half of the world and humans first appeared

plenary /'pliːnəri/ adj a plenary speaker talks about a subject to all the people at a particular meeting or a **conference**

plentiful /'plentɪf(ə)l/ adj present or available in large quantities ≠ SCARCE —**plentifully** adv

plenty /'plenti/ pronoun a lot, or enough: *'How much money will I need?' 'Five pounds should be plenty.'* ♦ *There's **plenty of** room for luggage behind the seats.* ♦ *There's **plenty more** ice cream in the freezer.* ♦ *The animals give birth in the wet season, when there is **plenty to** eat.*

pleonasm /'pliːə,næz(ə)m/ noun [C/U] **LANGUAGE** the use of more words than are necessary to say something —**pleonastic** /,pliːə'næstɪk/ adj

plethora /'pleθərə/ noun [singular] *formal* a greater amount than someone needs or wants = PROFUSION ≠ DEARTH

pleural membranes /,plʊərəl 'membreɪnz/ noun [plural] **ANATOMY** the membranes in mammals that cover the lungs and the inside of the chest

pleurisy /'plɜːrɪsi/ noun [U] **HEALTH** a serious illness, usually caused by an infection, that affects the lungs, making breathing difficult

pliable /'plaɪəb(ə)l/ adj able to bend or change shape easily without breaking

pliers /'plaɪəz/ noun [plural] a metal tool that looks like a strong pair of scissors, used for holding small objects or for bending or cutting wire —*picture* → TOOL

plight /plaɪt/ noun [singular] a sad, serious, or difficult situation

plimsoll line /'plɪmsəl ,laɪn/ noun [C] a mark on the side of a ship that shows how deep it can legally be in the water when it is loaded

the Pliocene /'plaɪəʊ,siːn/ noun [singular] **GEOLOGY** [U] the **era** of geological time, 5.3 million to 1.8 million years ago. Modern humans and other mammals first appeared during this time.

plod /plɒd/ (**plods, plodding, plodded**) verb [I] to walk with slow heavy steps = TRUDGE

plop /plɒp/ (**plops, plopping, plopped**) verb [I] to fall with a short sound like the sound made by a small object falling into a liquid —**plop** /plɒp/ noun [C]

plosive /'pləʊsɪv/ adj **LANGUAGE** plosive sounds such as 'k', 'p', and 't' are made by quickly stopping the breath leaving the mouth, and then suddenly letting it go again —**plosive** noun [C]

plot¹ /plɒt/ noun **1** [C/U] **LITERATURE, ARTS** a series of related events that make up the main story in a book, film etc **2** [C] a secret plan to do something bad, made by two or more people: *a kidnap plot* ♦ *a **plot against** the government* ♦ *a plot to kill the president*

3 [C] a piece of land that is used for a particular purpose: *a burial plot*

plot² /plɒt/ (**plots, plotting, plotted**) verb **1** [I/T] to make a secret plan with other people to do something bad = SCHEME **2** [T] to make marks on a map or graph in order to show the movement or development of something **3** [T] LITERATURE, ARTS to invent the series of related events that make up the main story in a book, film etc

plough¹ /plaʊ/ noun [C] AGRICULTURE a piece of equipment that farmers use for turning over the soil before putting seeds into it

plough² /plaʊ/ verb [I/T] AGRICULTURE to turn over the soil with a plough before putting seeds into it
—**ploughing** noun [U]

the Plough /plaʊ/ noun ASTRONOMY a group of seven bright stars that you can only see in the northern part of the world

ploy /plɔɪ/ noun [C] a way of tricking someone in order to get an advantage, or to make them do what you want them to do

pluck /plʌk/ verb **1** [T] to take someone or something quickly from a particular place: *Rescue crews plucked survivors from the sea.* **2** [T] to pull the feathers off the body of a dead bird so that it can be cooked **3** [I/T] MUSIC to pull the strings of a musical instrument with your fingers in order to produce a sound

PHRASE **pluck up (the) courage (to do sth)** to persuade yourself to do something that frightens you

plucky /ˈplʌki/ (**pluckier, pluckiest**) adj brave and determined, especially when success is unlikely

plug¹ /plʌg/ noun [C] **1** an object with three straight pins that is used for connecting a piece of equipment to an electricity supply, usually by fitting it into a **socket** in a wall **2** an attempt to make people interested in a book, film etc by talking about it in an enthusiastic way on a radio or television programme **3** a small round plastic or rubber object that prevents water from flowing out of the hole in a sink or bath

plug² /plʌg/ (**plugs, plugging, plugged**) verb [T] **1** to fill a hole so that nothing can get through it: *Plug the hole with newspaper before applying the cement.* **2** to try to make people interested in a book, film, idea etc by talking about it in an enthusiastic way on a radio or television programme

PHRASAL VERBS **,plug sth 'in** to connect a piece of equipment to an electricity supply or to another piece of equipment ≠ UNPLUG: *I realized I hadn't plugged the TV in.*

,plug (sth) 'into sth to connect a piece of equipment to an electricity supply or to another piece of equipment, or to be connected in this way: *First plug the keyboard into your computer.*

,plug-and-'play adj COMPUTING plug-and-play software or computer equipment is immediately ready for use when it is connected to a computer

'plug ,gauge noun [C] TECHNOLOGY a type of **gauge** that is used for checking whether a hole or **shaft** is close enough to an acceptable standard in size

plughole /ˈplʌɡˌhəʊl/ noun [C] a hole at the bottom of a sink or bath where water flows out and where you put a plug

'plug-,in noun [C] COMPUTING a piece of software or hardware that you add to a computer to increase the range of things it can do

'plug ,spanner noun [C] ENGINEERING a tool for tightening or loosening **spark plugs** in a vehicle's engine

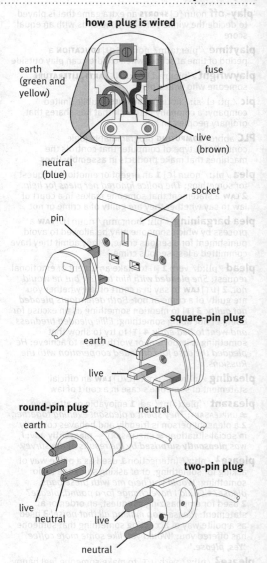

how a plug is wired

earth (green and yellow)

fuse

live (brown)

neutral (blue)

socket

pin

square-pin plug

earth

live

round-pin plug

earth

live

neutral

two-pin plug

live

neutral

live

neutral

plum /plʌm/ noun [C] a small round fruit with purple, red, or yellow skin and a large hard seed inside
—*picture* → FRUIT

plumage /ˈpluːmɪdʒ/ noun [U] BIOLOGY a bird's feathers

plumb bob /ˈplʌm ˌbɒb/ noun [C] CONSTRUCTION a weight at the end of a string, used by builders to show a vertical line

plumbing /ˈplʌmɪŋ/ noun [U] **1** the job of fitting and repairing the pipes and equipment that are used for supplying and storing water in a building **2** the system of pipes and equipment that are used for supplying and storing water in a building

plumbline /ˈplʌmˌlaɪn/ noun [C] **1** a piece of string with a metal object fixed to the bottom. It is used to check that things are straight, or to draw straight lines. **2** CONSTRUCTION a vertical line that forms a guide for building

plummet /'plʌmɪt/ verb [I] **1** if something such as an amount, rate, or value plummets, it suddenly becomes much lower: *Share prices plummeted on the New York stock exchange today.* → CRASH[1] sense 3, NOSEDIVE **2** to fall straight down very quickly from a high position = PLUNGE

plump /plʌmp/ adj **1** slightly fat, in a pleasant way ≠ SKINNY **2** large and round in an attractive way: *plump strawberries*

plumule /'pluːmjuːl/ noun [C] BIOLOGY **1** the first shoot of a plant embryo as it starts to grow **2** a soft feather that is part of the **down** of a young bird

plunder /'plʌndə/ verb [I/T] to take valuable things from a place using force —**plunder** noun [U]

plunge[1] /plʌndʒ/ verb [I] **1** to fall quickly from a high position = PLUMMET: *The helicopter plunged 500 feet into the sea.* **2** if an amount or level plunges, it suddenly becomes much lower = PLUMMET: *The temperature is expected to plunge below zero tonight.*

plunge[2] /plʌndʒ/ noun [C] **1** a quick fall from a high position: *the plane's plunge into the sea* **2** a sudden reduction in the amount or level of something: *the plunge in oil prices*

PHRASE **take the plunge** to finally do something that is important, difficult, or dangerous, after thinking about it carefully

'plunge ,pool noun [C] GEOLOGY a deep pool at the bottom of a **waterfall**. It is caused by the force of the water eroding the river bed. —*picture* → WATERFALL

the pluperfect /pluː'pɜːfɪkt/ noun [singular] LANGUAGE the **past perfect** tense of a verb

plural /'plʊərəl/ noun [C] LANGUAGE a word or form that is used for referring to more than one person or thing. For example, 'students' is the plural of 'student', and 'mice' is the plural of 'mouse'. —**plural** adj

pluralism /'plʊərə,lɪz(ə)m/ noun [U] SOCIAL STUDIES **1** the idea that people can and should live together without fighting, despite differences in race, religion, culture, politics etc **2** a social system which has different political, ethnic or religious groups living together within it —**pluralist** adj

plurality /plʊə'ræləti/ noun [U] LANGUAGE the state of being plural

plus[1] /plʌs/ preposition, conjunction **1** MATHS used for showing that one number or amount is added to another. This word is usually represented by the symbol + ≠ MINUS: *36 plus 5 is 41.* **2** *informal* and also: *He came along with his five children, plus their partners.* **3** used after a number to show that the actual number may be larger: *an audience of 500-plus*

PHRASE **A plus/B plus/C plus etc** EDUCATION marks given for students' work that are slightly higher than the marks A, B, C etc

plus[2] /plʌs/ (plural **plusses**) noun [C] an advantage: *For this job, experience in telecommunications is a plus.*

'plus ,sign noun [C] MATHS the symbol +

Pluto /'pluːtəʊ/ ASTRONOMY the planet that is furthest away from the Sun —*picture* → SOLAR SYSTEM

plutonium /pluː'təʊniəm/ noun [U] CHEMISTRY a highly toxic radioactive element in the **actinide** group of the periodic table. It is used in the production of nuclear power. Chemical symbol: **Pu**

plywood /'plaɪ,wʊd/ noun [U] a type of board that is used in building houses, furniture etc, made by sticking thin layers of wood together with glue

pm /,piː 'em/ abbrev used after a time for showing that it is between **noon** and midnight: *3.30 pm*

PM /,piː 'em/ noun [C] POLITICS *informal* a **prime minister**

pneumatic /njuː'mætɪk/ adj **1** filled with air or gas **2** a pneumatic tool or piece of equipment works by using air

pneu,matic 'drill noun [C] CONSTRUCTION a piece of equipment for breaking the surface of a road into small pieces. It is held in both hands.

pneumatics /njuː'mætɪks/ noun [U] PHYSICS the study of the mechanical properties of air and other gases

pneumatophore /njuː'mætəʊfɔː/ noun [C] BIOLOGY in plants such as **mangrove** that grow in very wet areas, a branch that grows upwards from the roots and carries out respiration

pneumonia /njuː'məʊniə/ noun [U] HEALTH a serious infection of the lungs

poach /pəʊtʃ/ verb **1** [T] to cook something in liquid that is boiling gently **2** [I/T] to illegally catch or kill an animal or fish on someone else's property **3** [T] to persuade someone to leave a group or organization and become a member of your group, organization etc

poacher /'pəʊtʃə/ noun [C] someone who illegally catches or kills animals or fish on someone else's property

'P'O ,Box noun [C] post office box: used in an address showing the number of a small box at a **post office** where your letters can be sent

pocket[1] /'pɒkɪt/ noun [C] **1** a small bag that forms part of a piece of clothing and is used for holding small objects: *She searched her pockets for the car keys.* **2** a small bag or other container that forms part of an object: *The safety instructions are in the pocket of the seat in front of you.* **3** a supply of money that is available for spending: *Our boss expects us to pay for the trip out of our own pockets* (=using our own money). **4** a small area with a particular quality that makes it different from the areas around it: *pockets of resistance to government forces*

pocket[2] /'pɒkɪt/ adj small enough to fit into your pocket: *a pocket dictionary*

pod /pɒd/ noun [C] BIOLOGY the long narrow part that holds the seeds of a bean or a similar plant

podcast /'pɒd,kɑːst/ noun [C] COMPUTING a **multimedia** file, such as a radio programme or music video, that can be downloaded from the Internet and played on an **MP3 player** or similar piece of equipment —**podcasting** noun [U]

podium /'pəʊdiəm/ noun [C] a small raised area where someone stands to give a speech or receive a prize

poem /'pəʊɪm/ noun [C] LITERATURE a piece of writing that uses beautiful or unusual language. It is arranged in lines that have a particular beat and often rhyme.

poet /'pəʊɪt/ noun [C] LITERATURE someone who writes poetry

poetic /pəʊ'etɪk/ adj **1** expressing ideas in a sensitive way and with great beauty or imagination **2** LITERATURE connected with poetry, or having the qualities of poetry

poetry /'pəʊɪtri/ noun [U] LITERATURE poems: *the poetry of Walt Whitman* ♦ *a poetry book*

poignant /'pɔɪnjənt/ adj giving you feelings of sadness —**poignancy** /'pɔɪnjənsi/ noun [U], **poignantly** adv

point¹ /pɔɪnt/ noun

1 idea/opinion	**7** particular place
2 what sb means	**8** unit for game score
3 reason	**9** measurement
4 particular time	**10** sharp end of sth
5 stage in process	**11** decimal point
6 aspect/feature	**+ PHRASES**

1 [C] one idea or opinion among a number of others: *I disagree with you on **a couple of points**.*

2 [singular] the thing that you are trying to say: ***My point is** that we're spending too much time on details.* ♦ *I **take your point** (=understand it), but I still think we should go ahead with the changes.* ♦ *She **missed the point** (=did not understand it) and thought I was blaming her.*

3 [singular] the reason for something: *I see **no point in** discussing this any further.* ♦ *What is **the point of** your visit?* ♦ *I'm sorry – I just don't **see the point of** doing this (=understand the reason).*

4 [singular] a particular moment in time: ***At that point** I left the room.* ♦ ***At this point in time** we can't afford to hire any more people.*

5 [C] a particular stage in a process: *We're just trying to **reach a point** where both sides will sit down together and talk.*

6 [C] an aspect or a feature: *Patience is **not one of his strong points**.*

7 [C] a particular place: *We'll meet at a point halfway between here and your hotel.*

8 [C] SPORTS a unit for counting the score in a game or sport: *Our team is two points behind.*

9 [C] a unit of measurement: *Interest rates fell by 2 **percentage points**.*

10 [C] the sharp end of something: *The potatoes should be soft when pierced with the point of a knife.*

11 [C] MATHS the word for a **decimal point**, used when saying a number. For example, 6.3 is said as 'six point three'.

PHRASES **come/get to the point** to stop talking about unimportant details and say what is important

have (got) a point to have made an important statement

make a point of doing sth to be certain that you do something, usually in an obvious way: *He made a point of avoiding her.*

on the point of doing sth about to do something: *We were on the point of leaving when the phone rang.*

point of reference information or experience that you already have that helps you to understand or deal with a new situation

point of view a way of judging a situation, based on a particular aspect: *From a technical point of view, the idea will work.*

up to a point to some degree but not completely
→ BESIDE, SORE¹

point² /pɔɪnt/ verb

1 show with finger etc	**4** show sb what to do
2 show with sign/	**5** stretch toes
symbol	**+ PHRASAL VERBS**
3 aim (sth) at	

1 [I/T] to show something by holding out your finger or a long thin object: *Don't point. They'll know we're looking at them.* ♦ *He pointed his stick in the direction of the path.* ♦ *'What's through there?' he asked, **pointing at** the door.*

2 [I] to show a particular direction or place, usually using a sign or symbol: *The arrow pointed left towards the exit door.*

3 [I/T] to aim an object at someone or something, or to be aimed at someone or something: *He pointed his rifle at the deer.*

4 [I/T] to show someone the direction in which they should go: *Could you **point** me **in the direction of** the exit?*

5 [I/T] to stretch the toes as if trying to make them form a straight line with the leg

PHRASAL VERBS ,point sb/sth 'out to show someone who a person is or where something is: *Which one is Jane's brother? Can you point him out to me?* ♦ *He pointed out the best beaches on the map.*

,point sth 'out to tell someone something: *Thank you for pointing that out.* ♦ *He pointed out that we had two hours of free time before dinner.*

'point to sth to show the truth or importance of something= INDICATE: *The evidence clearly points to her guilt.*

,point-and-'click adj COMPUTING used for describing a way of doing things on a computer by using a mouse to move a cursor on the screen and pressing the mouse button

,point-'blank adj, adv in a very firm and direct way: *Polly refused point-blank to let me use the car.*

PHRASE **at point-blank range** if you shoot someone at point-blank range, you hold the gun very close to their body

pointed /'pɔɪntɪd/ adj **1** with a point at the end **2** done in a way that shows that you are annoyed or do not agree: *a pointed comment* —**pointedly** adv

pointer /'pɔɪntə/ noun [C] a pole or stick for pointing at something such as a map or picture

pointing /'pɔɪntɪŋ/ noun [U] CONSTRUCTION **1** the cement or **mortar** between the stones or bricks in a wall **2** the process of filling the spaces in a wall with cement or **mortar**

'pointing de,vice noun [C] COMPUTING a piece of equipment used for moving a cursor on a computer screen, for example a computer mouse

pointless /'pɔɪntləs/ adj lacking any purpose or use —**pointlessly** adv, **pointlessness** noun [U]

points /pɔɪnts/ noun [plural] **1** a section of railway track that moves between two sets of track so that a train can cross from one to the other **2** ENGINEERING **contact breaker points** in a vehicle

,point to 'point ,protocol noun COMPUTING see PPP

poised /pɔɪzd/ adj **1** about to do or achieve something after preparing for it: *Japan was poised to become the biggest foreign investor in Vietnam.* **2** waiting in a position where you can make a movement as soon as you need to: *Two guards stood poised with their hands on their guns.* **3** behaving in a controlled and relaxed way

poison¹ /'pɔɪz(ə)n/ noun [C/U] a substance that can kill someone or make them very ill if they eat, drink, or breathe it

poison² /'pɔɪz(ə)n/ verb [T] **1** to kill someone, or make them very ill, by giving them poison: *He was suspected of poisoning his wife.* **2** to put poison in something: *Waste from the factories is poisoning the water supply.* **3** to have a bad effect on something: *The decision had poisoned relations between Britain and France.*

,poison 'gas noun [U] gas used for killing or harming people

poisoning /'pɔɪz(ə)nɪŋ/ noun [C/U] an occasion when someone is affected by poison

poisonous /'pɔɪz(ə)nəs/ adj **1** containing poison: *poisonous gases* **2** capable of producing poison: *a poisonous snake*

'poison ,pill noun [C] BUSINESS an action taken by a company in order to make someone less likely to want to get control of it

poke¹ /pəʊk/ verb **1** [I/T] to push something quickly with your finger or a pointed object: *Jane poked me in the arm to get my attention.* **2** [T] to put something into a space: *The kid was poking a stick down a drain.* ♦ *Dad poked his head into my room and said dinner was ready.* **3** [I] to stick out beyond an object or surface **4** [T] to let someone on a **social networking** site know that you are there, in order to get them to send you a message

PHRASE **poke fun (at)** to make unkind jokes about someone or something

poke² /pəʊk/ noun [C] a quick push with your finger or a pointed object

poker /'pəʊkə/ noun **1** [U] a card game in which players try to win money **2** [C] a metal stick for moving the coal or wood of a fire around

polar /'pəʊlə/ adj **1** GEOGRAPHY coming from, or relating to, an area near the North Pole or the South Pole —*picture* → ECOSYSTEM **2** *formal* as different as it is possible to be **3** SCIENCE relating to the **pole** of a battery or magnet

'polar ,bear noun [C] a large white bear that lives in areas near the North Pole

Polaris /pəʊ'lɑːrɪs/ noun ASTRONOMY the **Pole Star**

polarity /pəʊ'lærəti/ noun [U] **1** *formal* a situation in which there is a very great difference between opinions, people, or situations **2** SCIENCE the condition of having opposite electrical **charges**

polarize /'pəʊləraɪz/ verb [I/T] to form two very different groups, opinions, or situations that are completely opposite to each other, or to cause this to happen —**polarization** /ˌpəʊləraɪ'zeɪʃ(ə)n/ noun [U]

Polaroid /'pəʊlərɔɪd/ TRADEMARK a type of camera that produces photographs immediately, or a photograph from this type of camera

pole /pəʊl/ noun [C] **1** a long thin stick, often used for holding or supporting something: *There were rows of poles supporting young bean plants.* **2** GEOGRAPHY one of the points on the extreme top or bottom of the Earth, called the **North Pole** and the **South Pole 3** PHYSICS one of the two ends of a magnet —*picture* → MAGNET

polecat /'pəʊlˌkæt/ noun [C] a small European or Asian wild mammal that produces an unpleasant smell

polemical /pə'lemɪk(ə)l/ or **polemic** /pə'lemɪk/ adj *formal* using or supported by strong arguments

'pole po,sition noun [C/U] SPORTS the front position at the start of a car race

the 'Pole ,Star noun [singular] ASTRONOMY a bright star that appears in the sky very near the North Pole

the 'pole ,vault noun [singular] SPORTS a sport in which you use a long pole to push yourself over a high bar

police¹ /pə'liːs/ noun [plural] the official organization that tries to catch criminals and checks that people obey the law, or the people that work for this organization: *traffic police* ♦ *If you don't leave, I'll call the police.* ♦ *a police car*

police² /pə'liːs/ verb [T] to use police officers to control an area or event

po,lice 'constable noun [C] a police officer of the lowest rank

po'lice ,force noun [C] an organized group of police officers in charge of a country or a particular area

policeman /pə'liːsmən/ (plural **policemen** /pə'liːsmən/) noun [C] a male police officer

po'lice ,officer noun [C] a member of the police

po'lice ,station noun [C] the building where the police of a particular area work

policewoman /pə'liːsˌwʊmən/ (plural **policewomen** /pə'liːsˌwɪmɪn/) noun [C] a female police officer

policy /'pɒləsi/ (plural **policies**) noun **1** [C/U] a set of plans or actions that are agreed on by a government, political party, business, or other organization: *It is not the hospital's policy to disclose the names of patients.* ♦ *the government's economic policy* ♦ *What is the party's policy on immigration?* **2** [C] a contract between an insurance company and a person or organization: *Read the wording of your policy very carefully.*

policyholder /'pɒləsiˌhəʊldə/ noun [C] BUSINESS someone who has an **insurance policy**

poling board /'pəʊlɪŋ/ noun [C] CONSTRUCTION one of a series of vertical wooden boards that support the sides of a narrow hole dug in the ground

polio /'pəʊliəʊ/ noun [U] HEALTH a serious infectious disease caused by a virus that can destroy muscles and affect the ability to control movement. It mainly affects children and young adults. Polio is short for **poliomyelitis**.

polish¹ /'pɒlɪʃ/ verb [T] **1** to rub the surface of something in order to make it shine: *Have you polished your shoes?* **2** to improve a skill by practising: *He'd spent the summer polishing his flying skills.*

polish² /'pɒlɪʃ/ noun **1** [C/U] a substance that you rub onto an object to make it shine: *shoe polish* **2** [singular] an act of rubbing an object to make it shine: *This table needs a good polish.* **3** [U] the high quality of a performance or a piece of work

polished /'pɒlɪʃt/ adj **1** clean and shiny because of being rubbed: *a highly polished wooden floor* **2** of very high quality: *a polished performance*

polite /pə'laɪt/ adj behaving towards other people in a pleasant way that follows all the usual rules of society = COURTEOUS ≠ RUDE: *a polite refusal* ♦ *You must be more polite to the customers.* ♦ *It's not polite to talk with your mouth full of food.* —**politely** adv, **politeness** noun [U]

political /pə'lɪtɪk(ə)l/ adj **1** SOCIAL STUDIES relating to politics: *the importance of political stability* ♦ *a political party* ♦ *the political system in the US* **2** interested or involved in politics: *I'm really not very political at all.* **3** relating to relationships of power that exist between people in an organization: *It was a purely political decision to give him the job.* —**politically** /pə'lɪtɪkli/ adv

po,litical cor'rectness noun [U] language or behaviour that is **politically correct** (=not offensive, especially to people who have been affected by unfair treatment)

po,litical ge'ography noun [U] GEOGRAPHY the study of the way the world is divided up into countries rather than the way it is marked by natural things such as rivers, mountains etc → PHYSICAL GEOGRAPHY

po,litical 'prisoner noun [C] POLITICS someone who is sent to prison for opposing their government

politician /ˌpɒlə'tɪʃ(ə)n/ noun [C] POLITICS someone who has a job in politics

politicize /pəˈlɪtɪsaɪz/ verb [T] **POLITICS 1** to cause something to become involved with politics: *The tobacco issue is becoming too politicized.* **2** to make someone more interested and involved in politics

politics /ˈpɒlətɪks/ noun **1** [U] **POLITICS** the ideas and activities that are involved in getting power in an area or governing it: *She's heavily involved in local politics.* **2** [plural] **POLITICS** your beliefs and attitudes about how government should work: *Her politics became more conservative as she grew older.* **3** [U] **POLITICS** the profession of being a politician: *He entered politics at the age of 21.* **4** [U] the ideas and activities that people within a particular group use to try to get power: *Now that I'm self-employed, I don't have to worry about office politics.*

> **Word family: politics**
>
> *Words in the same family as **politics**:*
> - **political** *adj*
> - **politically** *adv*
> - **politician** *n*
> - **apolitical** *adj*
> - **politicize** *v*

poll¹ /pəʊl/ noun **1** [C] an occasion when a lot of people are asked their opinions about something, usually as research for a political party, television programme etc: *A recent poll indicated that most people supported a ban on tobacco advertising.* ♦ *According to a poll conducted last week, 75% of the public support the Prime Minister.* **2 the polls** [plural] **POLITICS** the place where people vote: *The polls close at ten o'clock.* ♦ *Citizens across the country will be **going to the polls** (=voting in an election) tomorrow.*

poll² /pəʊl/ verb [T] **1** to ask a lot of people their opinions about something, especially a political issue: *Over half of those polled said that they were satisfied with the government's performance.* **2 POLITICS** to get a particular number or percentage of votes in an election —**polling** /ˈpəʊlɪŋ/ noun [U]

pollen /ˈpɒlən/ noun [U] **BIOLOGY** a powder that flowers or **cones** produce. It is carried by the wind or by insects to other flowers and **cones** so that they can produce seeds.

ˈ**pollen ˌcount** noun [C] a measurement of how much pollen there is in the air

ˈ**pollen ˌgrain** noun [C] **BIOLOGY** a small individual particle of pollen that contains the male gametes of a plant

ˈ**pollen ˌsac** noun [C] **BIOLOGY** the part of the **anther** (=male part) of a plant that contains the pollen

ˈ**pollen ˌtube** noun [C] **BIOLOGY** a tube that develops from a grain of pollen. In a flowering plant, the tube grows down the **style** to the **ovule** which is fertilized and produces a seed. —*picture* → FERTILIZATION

pollinate /ˈpɒləneɪt/ verb [T] **BIOLOGY** to place pollen from one flower or **cone** onto another of the same type, and make fertilization possible

pollination /ˌpɒləˈneɪʃ(ə)n/ noun [U] **BIOLOGY** the process by which plant pollen gets from the male stamen or **cone** to the female **stigma** or **cone**. In plants with flowers, this is often done by insects or the wind. → FERTILIZATION

pollinator /ˈpɒləneɪtə/ noun [C] **BIOLOGY** something such as an insect or animal that moves pollen from one flower to another of the same type, and makes fertilization possible

ˈ**polling ˌstation** noun [C] **POLITICS** a building where people go to vote in an election

pollutant /pəˈluːt(ə)nt/ noun [C] **ENVIRONMENT** a substance that is harmful to the environment, especially a chemical. Large amounts of noise, heat etc can also be pollutants.

pollute /pəˈluːt/ verb [T] **ENVIRONMENT** to damage the air, water, land, or organisms with chemicals or other substances: *The oil spillage has polluted the harbour.* —**polluted** *adj*: *a heavily polluted river* —**polluter** noun [C]

pollution /pəˈluːʃ(ə)n/ noun [U] **ENVIRONMENT 1** the process of damaging the air, water, land, or organisms with chemicals or other substances. Pollution is almost always caused by human activity, for example during the process of getting rid of chemical waste from factories or the production of **carbon emissions** from cars: *the pollution of local rivers* —*picture* → on next page **2** chemicals and other substances that have a harmful effect on air, water, land, or organisms: *The agency is responsible for controlling air pollution.* ♦ *new measures to prevent pollution levels from rising*

polo /ˈpəʊləʊ/ noun [U] **SPORTS** a game played by two teams riding small horses. They get points for hitting a ball with a wooden hammer with a long handle.

polonium /pəˈləʊniəm/ noun [U] **CHEMISTRY** a very rare radioactive metallic element that is found in **uranium** ore. Chemical symbol: **Po**

polyacrylamide /ˌpɒliəˈkrɪləmaɪd/ noun [U] **CHEMISTRY** a type of plastic that absorbs water and then releases it when it comes into contact with salt. It is used in soil mixtures and in purifying water.

polycyanoacrylate /ˌpɒlisaɪənəʊˈækrɪlaɪt/ noun [U] **CHEMISTRY** a type of plastic that sticks to almost anything and sets very quickly. It is used in medical operations instead of stitches.

polyester /ˌpɒliˈestə/ noun [U] a light cloth made from artificial fibres

polygamy /pəˈlɪɡəmi/ noun [U] **SOCIAL STUDIES** the custom of having more than one husband or wife at the same time —**polygamous** /pəˈlɪɡəməs/ adj

polyglot /ˈpɒliˌɡlɒt/ adj *formal* speaking or using several languages —**polyglot** noun [C]

polygon /ˈpɒlɪɡən, ˈpɒlɪɡɒn/ noun [C] **MATHS** a flat geometric shape with three or more sides and angles

> **PHRASE** **polygon of forces PHYSICS** a polygon with sides that represent the **magnitudes** and directions of three or more forces that are **in equilibrium** (=balanced)

—**polygonal** /pəˈlɪɡən(ə)l/ adj

polyhedron /ˌpɒliˈhiːdrən/ noun [C] **MATHS** a solid geometrical shape with many flat sides

polymath /ˈpɒliˌmæθ/ noun [C] *formal* someone who has a lot of knowledge about many different subjects

polymer /ˈpɒlɪmə/ noun [C] **CHEMISTRY** a chemical compound consisting of large molecules made of groups of identical smaller ones joined together. Polymers can be natural or artificial. Starch, **nylon**, **cellulose**, and **polythene** are all polymers. —**polymerization** /ˌpɒlɪməraɪˈzeɪʃ(ə)n/ noun [U]

polymethyl methacrylate /ˌpɒlimiːθaɪl meˈθækrɪleɪt/ noun [U] **CHEMISTRY** a type of plastic that is used to make Perspex

polymorph /ˈpɒliˌmɔːf/ noun [C] **BIOLOGY** an animal or plant that has various forms at different stages of its development

polynomial /ˌpɒliˈnəʊmiəl/ noun [C] **MATHS** an expression in algebra that contains more than one **term** (=number or symbol) —**polynomial** adj

polyp /ˈpɒlɪp/ noun [C] **1 HEALTH** a small lump that grows inside the body, usually on a stalk **2 BIOLOGY** the basic form of a **coelenterate** animal such as a **coral**,

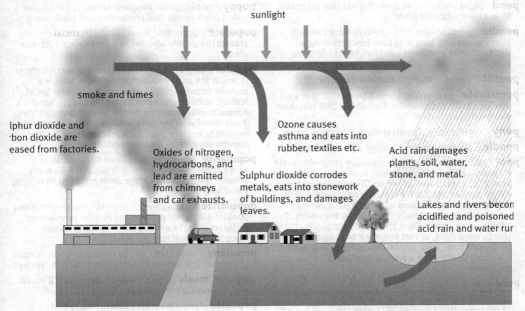

sunlight

smoke and fumes

lphur dioxide and
·bon dioxide are
eased from factories.

Oxides of nitrogen,
hydrocarbons, and
lead are emitted
from chimneys
and car exhausts.

Sulphur dioxide corrodes
metals, eats into stonework
of buildings, and damages
leaves.

Ozone causes
asthma and eats into
rubber, textiles etc.

Acid rain damages
plants, soil, water,
stone, and metal.

Lakes and rivers becon
acidified and poisoned
acid rain and water rur

Earth, lead damages brain tissue,
ecially in children, and can be
·ied long distances by wind.

Acidified soils damage roots of plants a
trees, and essential minerals are washe
while poisonous minerals are released.

effects of air pollution

that has a body like a tube and **tentacles** around its mouth

polypeptide /ˌpɒliˈpeptaɪd/ noun [C] **CHEMISTRY, BIOLOGY** a smaller unit that is formed when protein is broken down by an enzyme such as **pepsin**

polyphonic /ˌpɒliˈfɒnɪk/ adj a polyphonic **ringtone** is a sound that a mobile phone makes to tell you that someone is calling. It consists of several notes played together, so that it sounds like music.

polyphony /pəˈlɪfəni/ noun [U] **MUSIC** a type of music that combines several different tunes at the same time

polyploid /ˈpɒliplɔɪd/ adj **BIOLOGY** having more than twice the number of matched sets of chromosomes in the cell nucleus than is usual for the species —**polyploidy** noun [U]

polypropene /ˌpɒliˈprəʊpiːn/ noun [U] **CHEMISTRY** a type of plastic that is used to make clothing and carpets

polypropylene /ˌpɒliˈprəʊpəliːn/ noun [U] a type of plastic used for making fibres for ropes, carpets etc

polyrhythm /ˈpɒliˌrɪðəm/ noun [C] **MUSIC** a rhythm that consists of two or more rhythms at the same time

polysaccharide /ˌpɒliˈsækəˌraɪd/ noun [C] **CHEMISTRY** a carbohydrate such as starch or cellulose made up of simple sugar molecules joined together

polysemous /pəˈlɪsɪməs, ˌpɒliˈsiːməs/ adj **LANGUAGE** a polysemous word has more than one meaning —**polysemy** /pəˈlɪsɪmi, ˈpɒliˌsiːmi/ noun [U]

polystyrene /ˌpɒliˈstaɪriːn/ noun [U] a very light artificial substance, used especially for making containers or for protecting the things in a box

polysyllable /ˈpɒliˌsɪləb(ə)l/ noun [C] **LANGUAGE** a word that has more than two syllables —**polysyllabic** /ˌpɒlisɪˈlæbɪk/ adj

polytechnic /ˌpɒliˈteknɪk/ noun [C] **EDUCATION** a college for people who want to study scientific or technical subjects, especially in order to train for a practical job

polythene /ˈpɒliθiːn/ noun [U] **CHEMISTRY** a strong light plastic made from **ethylene**, used especially for making plastic bags and wrapping food in order to keep it fresh

polytunnel /ˈpɒliˌtʌn(ə)l/ noun [C] **AGRICULTURE** a large plastic structure shaped like the top half of a tube that is used for growing plants that need protection from the weather

polyunsaturated fat /ˌpɒliʌnˌsætʃəreɪtɪd ˈfæt/ noun [C] **CHEMISTRY, HEALTH** fat that is made mainly from vegetable oils that have **fatty acids** with several **double bonds**. They are considered to be healthier than those made from **saturated** animal fats.
→ MONOUNSATURATED FAT

polyurethane /ˌpɒliˈjʊərəˌθeɪn/ noun [U] **CHEMISTRY** a type of plastic that is used for making paint and **varnishes**

polyvinyl chloride /ˌpɒliˌvaɪn(ə)l ˈklɔːraɪd/ noun [U] **CHEMISTRY** a type of plastic that is used for making **waterproof** materials. It is more commonly called **PVC**.

pome /pəʊm/ noun [C] **BIOLOGY** a type of fruit such as an apple or pear that has a fleshy part consisting of a swollen flower base, and a hard core containing the seeds

pomegranate /ˈpɒmɪˌɡrænət/ noun [C] a round fruit that has a hard skin and a lot of thick seeds inside

pompous /ˈpɒmpəs/ adj *showing disapproval* speaking or behaving in a very serious and formal way that shows that you think you are very important —**pomposity** /pɒmˈpɒsəti/ noun [U]

pond /pɒnd/ noun [C] an area of water that is smaller than a lake: *a garden pond*

ponder /ˈpɒndə/ verb [I/T] *formal* to think carefully about something for a long time before making a decision: *Mike pondered what he should say to his wife.*

pontiff /ˈpɒntɪf/ noun [C] RELIGION the **Pope**

pontificate /pɒnˈtɪfɪkeɪt/ verb [I] *formal* to give your opinions in an annoying way that shows that you think you are definitely right

pony /ˈpəʊni/ (plural **ponies**) noun [C] a small horse

poodle /ˈpuːd(ə)l/ noun [C] a dog with thick curly fur

pool /puːl/ noun **1** [C] a large structure filled with water for people to swim in= SWIMMING POOL: *a heated indoor pool* **2** [C] a small area of liquid: *The water collected in a little pool on the floor.* ♦ *a muddy road dotted with pools of rainwater* ♦ *a pool of blood* **3** [U] a game in which two players hit balls into holes at the edges of a table using a **cue** (=long stick) **4** [C] a group that shares something, or that someone or something can be chosen from: *a car pool* ♦ *The training programme is helping to establish a pool of local qualified craftsmen.*

poor /pɔː, pʊə/ adj

1 lacking money	**4** not skilful
2 people without money	**5** lacking sth
3 of low quality	**6** feeling sorry for sb

1 having little money and few possessions ≠ RICH: *We were very poor and could barely afford the necessities of life.* ♦ *a poor area*
2 the poor people who have little money and few possessions
3 not as good as expected or needed= BAD ≠ GOOD: *poor health* ♦ *The buildings were all in poor condition.*
4 *formal* not skilful or clever ≠ GOOD: *I was always put with the poorest students in the class.*
5 not having enough of something important: *a country poor in natural resources*
6 *spoken* used for showing that you feel sorry for someone: *The poor child had lost both his parents.*

poorly /ˈpɔːli, ˈpʊəli/ adv badly: *a poorly written essay*

pop¹ /pɒp/ noun **1** [U] MUSIC pop music: *Her music combines jazz and pop.* **2** [C] a sudden short sound like a small explosion: *The balloon burst with a loud pop.*

pop² /pɒp/ adj **1** created for, or popular with, a very large number of people: *pop psychology* **2** MUSIC relating to **pop music**: *a pop singer*

pop³ /pɒp/ (**pops, popping, popped**) verb **1** [I/T] to make a sudden short sound like a small explosion, or to make something do this: *Champagne corks were popping.* **2** [I/T] if something such as a **balloon** pops, or if you pop it, it bursts **3** [T] to move something quickly to a particular position: *She picked a berry and popped it into her mouth.*

PHRASAL VERB ,pop 'up to appear very quickly or suddenly: *The daffodils and tulips are popping up everywhere.*

'pop ,art noun [U] ARTS a style of modern art that began in the 1960s and used familiar images such as advertisements as its subjects

Pope /pəʊp/ noun [C] RELIGION the leader of the Roman Catholic Church

poplar /ˈpɒplə/ noun [C] a tall thin tree

'pop ,music noun [U] MUSIC a type of music that is popular with many people, especially young people

poppy /ˈpɒpi/ (plural **poppies**) noun [C] a red flower with a black centre that produces small black seeds

populace /ˈpɒpjʊləs/ noun [singular] SOCIAL STUDIES the people who live in a particular country or area

popular /ˈpɒpjʊlə/ adj **1** liked by many people: *Jenny is one of the most popular girls in the school.* ♦ *a popular brand of breakfast cereal* **2** a popular belief, feeling, attitude etc is one that many people have: *It's a popular misconception that all women love shopping.* **3** intended for, or involving, ordinary people rather than experts or leaders: *popular science* ♦ *There is little popular support for their economic reforms.*

popularity /ˌpɒpjʊˈlærəti/ noun [U] a situation in which someone or something is popular with many people: *The popularity of the sport has been increasing steadily.*

popularize /ˈpɒpjʊləraɪz/ verb [T] to make something popular with many people: *The Beatles popularized British rock in the early 1960s.* —**popularization** /ˌpɒpjʊləraɪˈzeɪʃ(ə)n/ noun [U]

popularly /ˈpɒpjʊləli/ adv by most people, or in most situations: *The duchess is popularly known as 'Fergie'.*

,popular 'music noun [U] MUSIC **1** pop music **2** music that is accessible to a wide audience

populate /ˈpɒpjʊleɪt/ verb COMPUTING to add information to a computer file, for example to a **database**
PHRASE **be populated** GEOGRAPHY if an area is populated by people or animals, they live there: *Burundi is one of the most densely populated countries in the world.*

population /ˌpɒpjʊˈleɪʃ(ə)n/ noun **1** [C] GEOGRAPHY the number of people who live in a particular area: *Los Angeles has a population of over 3 million.* ♦ *Better health care and agriculture have led to rapid population growth.* **2** [singular] SOCIAL STUDIES all the people who live in a particular area: *Less than 40% of the population voted in the last election.* ♦ *the ageing population of the US* **3** [C] a group of people or animals of a particular type that live somewhere: *Tanzania's elephant population stands at about 55,000.*

popu'lation ex,plosion noun [C] GEOGRAPHY, SOCIAL STUDIES a very large increase in the number of people in a place over a very short period of time

populist /ˈpɒpjʊlɪst/ adj representing the interests and opinions of ordinary people —**populist** noun [C]

populous /ˈpɒpjʊləs/ adj a populous area has many people living in it

'pop-,up¹ adj **1** a pop-up book or card has pictures inside that have been cut out so that they stand up when you open the pages **2** COMPUTING used for describing something that appears suddenly on a computer screen when you are looking at the Internet, or when you click the mouse or press a key

'pop-,up² noun [C] COMPUTING something such as an advertisement that appears suddenly on a computer screen when you are looking at the Internet, or when you click the mouse or press a key

porcelain /ˈpɔːs(ə)lɪn/ noun [U] a hard shiny white substance that is used for making things such as dishes, cups, and decorations, or the things that are made from this substance

porch /pɔːtʃ/ noun [C] a small area covered by a roof at the entrance to a house or other building

porcupine /ˈpɔːkjʊpaɪn/ noun [C] a small mammal whose back is covered with stiff sharp hairs

pore /pɔː/ noun [C] ANATOMY one of the very small holes in the surface of the skin —picture → SKIN

pork /pɔːk/ noun [U] the meat from a pig → BACON, HAM

porosity /pɔːˈrɒsɪti/ noun [U] **1** SCIENCE the degree to which a substance is porous **2** TECHNOLOGY the fact of there being tiny holes in a metal **casting**, often caused by bubbles of gas from the hot metal

porous /ˈpɔːrəs/ adj SCIENCE with a lot of very small holes that air and water can pass through —picture → OIL

'porous ,bone noun [U] ANATOMY spongy bone —picture → BONE

porpoise /ˈpɔːpəs/ (plural **porpoises**) noun [C] a large sea mammal, similar to a **dolphin** —picture → SEA

porridge /ˈpɒrɪdʒ/ noun [U] a hot food made from **oats** (=a type of grain) and milk or water, often eaten at breakfast

port /pɔːt/ noun **1** [C/U] an area of water on the coast where ships stop, or a city with a port: *New York is the busiest port on the East Coast.* ♦ *At dusk they docked at **the port of** Monaco.* ♦ *We'll have to spend 10 days **in port** for repairs.* **2** [C] COMPUTING a part of a computer where you can connect another piece of equipment **3** [U] a strong sweet wine made in Portugal **4** [U] the left side of a ship or plane

portability /ˌpɔːtəˈbɪləti/ noun [U] **1** COMPUTING the ability of software or equipment to be used on several systems **2** the portability of a subject or qualification is its ability to be used in different situations, places etc

portable /ˈpɔːtəb(ə)l/ adj **1** easy to carry or move: *a portable television* **2** COMPUTING able to be used on different types of computer

portal /ˈpɔːt(ə)l/ noun [C] COMPUTING a website that has **links** to other websites

portcullis /pɔːtˈkʌlɪs/ noun [C] a heavy iron gate that can be lowered in front of the entrance to a castle as a defence —picture → CASTLE

porter /ˈpɔːtə/ noun [C] TOURISM someone in a station, airport, or hotel whose job is to help people with their bags and show them where to go

portfolio /pɔːtˈfəʊliəʊ/ (plural **portfolios**) noun [C] **1** ARTS a collection of pictures, photographs, or documents that you use as examples of work that you have done **2** all the **investments** that a person or company has made

port'folio ,working noun [U] BUSINESS a way of organizing your working life in which you work for several different employers and do several different jobs at one time instead of working all the time for one employer —**portfolio worker** noun [C]

porthole /ˈpɔːtˌhəʊl/ noun [C] a small round window in the side of a ship or plane

portion /ˈpɔːʃ(ə)n/ noun [C] **1** a part of something: *Only **a** small **portion of** the population could read.* **2** the amount of food that one person eats at a meal: *If you eat smaller portions, you will begin to lose weight.*

portmanteau word /pɔːtˈmæntəʊ ˌwɜːd/ noun [C] LANGUAGE a word that combines the sound and meaning of two words. For example 'smog' is a combination of 'smoke' and 'fog'.

portrait /ˈpɔːtrɪt/ noun **1** [C] ARTS a painting, drawing, or photograph of someone: *A **portrait of** her three children hangs behind her desk.* **2** [C] a description of someone or something, for example in a book: *an interesting **portrait of** life under communism* **3** [U] COMPUTING, ENGINEERING a way of arranging a

page so that its short sides are at the top and bottom → LANDSCAPE

portraiture /ˈpɔːtrɪtʃə/ noun [U] ARTS formal the art of making portraits of people

portray /pɔːˈtreɪ/ verb [T] **1** to show or describe someone or something in a particular way: *Opponents **portray** the president **as** weak and ineffectual.* **2** ARTS to play the part of a particular person in a film, play etc —**portrayal** noun [C]

pose¹ /pəʊz/ verb **1** [T] to create a difficult or dangerous situation: *The oil spill poses a threat to marine life in the area.* **2** [I] ARTS to sit or stand somewhere so that someone can take a photograph of you or paint a picture of you **3** [I] to dress or behave in a way that is not natural or sincere in order to make people notice you, admire you, or be impressed by you

PHRASAL VERB **'pose as sb/sth** to pretend to be a particular person or type of person in order to trick people

pose² /pəʊz/ noun [C] **1** ARTS the position that you keep your body in when someone is taking your photograph or painting your picture **2** behaviour that is not natural or sincere and is intended to make people notice you, admire you, or be impressed by you: *You get the feeling that his apparently strong religious faith is just a pose.*

posh /pɒʃ/ adj informal **1** expensive and attractive: *a posh hotel* **2** talking or behaving in a way that is typical of people from a high social class

posit /ˈpɒzɪt/ verb [T] formal to say that something is true, or that something should be accepted as true

position¹ /pəˈzɪʃ(ə)n/ noun [C]

1 way sth is placed	5 opinion about sth
2 general situation	6 job in company
3 where sth is	7 rank/status
4 in sports game	8 place in list etc

1 the way that someone's body or an object is placed: *First, get yourself into a comfortable position.* ♦ *He managed to push the vehicle back to an upright position.*
2 the situation that someone is in: *What would you do if you were in my position?* ♦ *I'm not **in a position to** say who my sources are.*
3 the place where something is in relation to other things: *Place the plant in a bright sunny position.*
♦ *Here is a chart showing **the positions of** the planets.*
♦ *Put the photographs **into position** on the page.*
4 SPORTS in team sports, the part of the field where a particular player plays: *'What position do you play?' 'Centre forward.'*
5 an opinion about an important issue: *No one was sure of his **position on** any issue.* ♦ *The President will consider the facts carefully before **taking a position** on this case.*
6 a job in a company: *There are 12 women in **management positions** within the company.* ♦ *I'm sorry, **the position has** already **been filled** (=someone has already been chosen to do the job).*
7 someone's rank or status in an organization or in society: *Such behaviour was clearly not acceptable for someone in **a position of authority**.*
8 the place that someone or something has in a list or competition: *Following behind in fourth position is car number 47.*

position² /pəˈzɪʃ(ə)n/ verb [T] **1** to put someone or something in a particular place: *Position the microphone as close as possible to the source of sound.* **2** BUSINESS to make people think of a product in a particular way

positive /'pɒzətɪv/ adj

1 completely certain	6 number: above zero
2 expecting sth good	7 trying to help/improve
3 showing agreement	8 blood type
4 situation etc: good	9 about electrical charge
5 showing condition	

1 completely certain: *Are you positive that there's been no mistake?* ♦ *We'd met before – I was **positive about** that.*
2 believing that good things will happen, or that a situation will get better = OPTIMISTIC ≠ NEGATIVE: *a positive attitude* ♦ *Try to think positive thoughts.*
3 showing agreement or approval ≠ NEGATIVE: *We couldn't be sure if her reaction would be positive.*
4 a positive experience, situation, result etc is a good one ≠ NEGATIVE: *School was **a totally positive experience** for me.* ♦ *The **positive aspects** of parenthood are rarely written about.*
5 HEALTH a positive result in a medical test means that the person has the disease or condition that was tested for ≠ NEGATIVE: *HIV positive*
6 MATHS a positive number is higher than zero ≠ NEGATIVE
7 if someone does something positive, they do something to try to improve a situation rather than doing nothing: *You must be prepared to make a positive contribution to the business.*
8 HEALTH used for saying that someone's blood contains a **Rhesus factor**. You can say that someone is **Rhesus positive** or that their blood group is, for example, **O positive** or **A positive**.
9 PHYSICS with the same electrical **charge** as a proton ≠ NEGATIVE

'positive ,camber noun [U] ENGINEERING a way of arranging the position of the wheels in a vehicle in which the top of the wheel leans away from the centre of the vehicle

,positive discrimi'nation noun [U] SOCIAL STUDIES the practice of giving special benefits to people from a group that was treated in an unfair way in the past

,positive 'feedback noun [U] PHYSICS the way in which the result of a process increases or improves the process that caused it originally

positively /'pɒzətɪvli/ adv **1** in a way that shows that you approve or agree with something: *Most people reacted quite **positively** to the proposal.* **2** in a way that shows that you believe that good things will happen, or that a situation will get better: *We need to approach this problem positively.*

positron /'pɒzɪtrɒn/ noun [C] PHYSICS a particle that is the same size as an electron but has a positive electrical charge

possess /pə'zes/ verb [T] *formal* to own or have something: *They were all found guilty of illegally possessing firearms.* —**possessor** noun [C]

possessed /pə'zest/ adj controlled by an evil spirit

possession /pə'zeʃ(ə)n/ noun **1** [C] something that you own: *Their family home and possessions were destroyed in the fire.* ♦ *Her most **prized possession** is a locket that she wears constantly.* **2** [U] *formal* a situation in which you have or own something: *The seller is entitled to retain **possession** of the goods until they are paid for.* ♦ *The town of Winterset **took possession of** (=started owning) the castle in 1947.* ♦ *Unfortunately, we no longer have those records **in our possession**.* ♦ *The brothers were caught **in possession of** stolen property.* **3** [U] SPORTS if you have possession in a team game such as football or basketball, you have the ball

possessive¹ /pə'zesɪv/ adj **1** *showing disapproval* wanting to have all of someone's love and attention: *a jealous and possessive boyfriend* **2** not willing to share things **3** LANGUAGE a possessive word or form of a word is a word such as 'her', 'its', 'Jan's', or 'dog's' that shows who or what someone or something belongs to or is connected with: *a possessive pronoun* —**possessively** adv, **possessiveness** noun [U]

possessive² /pə'zesɪv/ noun [C] LANGUAGE a possessive word, or form of a word

possibility /,pɒsə'bɪləti/ (plural **possibilities**) noun **1** [C/U] something that might happen or be true: *Is everyone **aware of the possibility** of injury when skateboarding?* ♦ *There is a **strong possibility** that they will win the next election.* **2** [C] a likely or suitable choice among several possible people or things: *We need to examine other possibilities before we make a final decision.* **3** possibilities [plural] opportunities to develop in a successful, interesting, or exciting way: *This old building has some intriguing possibilities.*

possible /'pɒsəb(ə)l/ adj **1** able to be done, or capable of happening or being true ≠ IMPOSSIBLE: *The task will not be possible without access to the Internet.* ♦ *I suppose it's possible she didn't know, but I'm fairly sure I told her.* ♦ *We need to avoid delay **if** at all **possible**.* ♦ *I walk to work **whenever possible**.* ♦ *Get **as much** information **as possible**.* ♦ *It is possible to see as far as Corsica on a clear day.* **2** likely or suitable in a particular situation or for a particular purpose: *a possible explanation* ♦ *a possible site for the new school building* **3** used with a **superlative** for emphasizing that something has the most or least of a particular quality: *Deb scored the highest score possible on the test.* ♦ *He arrived at **the worst possible** time.*

possibly /'pɒsəbli/ adv used for saying that something is likely to happen or be true, but not certain: *There is a chance of showers today and possibly a thunderstorm.* ♦ *'Do we have enough money to get a car?' 'Possibly.'* ♦ *He is **quite possibly** the most experienced climber in the world.*
PHRASE **can/could possibly 1** used for emphasizing what is or is not possible: *There was nothing more we could possibly do under the circumstances.* ♦ *You **can't possibly** ask them to risk their lives.* **2** used for emphasizing your surprise or shock at something: *How can anyone possibly spend an hour in the shower?*

post¹ /pəʊst/ noun

1 letters etc delivered	4 place for military force
2 job	5 posting in computing
3 upright pole	

1 [U] the letters and parcels that are delivered to someone, or the system used for collecting, carrying, and delivering them = MAIL: *There was **no post** for you today.* ♦ *I never **send** anything valuable **through the post**.* ♦ *Did you send the parcel **by post** or by courier?*
2 [C] a job, especially one with a lot of responsibility: *The Prime Minister appointed her to **the post of** ambassador.*
3 [C] a strong thick pole made of wood or metal that is put upright in the ground
4 [C] a place where a soldier or guard must remain in order to do their job
5 [C] COMPUTING a **posting** sense 2

post² /pəʊst/ verb [T] **1** to send a letter or parcel to someone in the post **2** to put information or a message where the public can see it, for example on a wall: *The menu and prices are posted outside the door.*
3 COMPUTING to put information on the Internet: *New job openings are posted every day on their website.*
4 to send someone somewhere to do a job, especially

in another country= STATION: *a United Nations plan to post troops along Croatia's borders*

PHRASE **keep sb posted** to regularly give someone information about how something is developing or changing

post- /pəʊst/ prefix after, or later than: *a post-match interview*

postage /ˈpəʊstɪdʒ/ noun [U] money that you pay in order to send letters and parcels in the post

ˈpostage ˌstamp noun [C] *formal* a stamp that is put on an envelope etc

postal /ˈpəʊst(ə)l/ adj **1** relating to the system that takes the post to the people it is addressed to: *postal deliveries* **2** done in a way that involves sending things by post: *a postal vote*

ˌpost-aˈpartheid adj **SOCIAL STUDIES** during or relating to the period of time after the political system of **apartheid** in South Africa that ended in 1991

postbox /ˈpəʊs(t)bɒks/ noun [C] a container in a public place where you can put post that you want to send

postcard /ˈpəʊs(t)kɑːd/ noun [C] a small card that you write on one side of and send to someone in the post

postcode /ˈpəʊs(t)kəʊd/ noun [C] a group of letters and numbers that you write at the end of a person's address

ˌpost-coˈlonial adj **SOCIAL STUDIES** during or relating to the period of time when a country is no longer a **colony** of another country and has gained its independence —**post-colonialism** noun [U]

poster /ˈpəʊstə/ noun [C] a large printed notice or picture that you put on a wall for decoration or to advertise something

poste restante /ˌpəʊst ˈrestɒnt/ noun [U] **TOURISM** an arrangement in which someone's post is sent to a **post office** in a different area so that they can collect it while they are travelling

posterior /pɒˈstɪəriə/ adj relating to the back part of something, especially the back part of the body

posterity /pɒˈsterəti/ noun [U] the people who will live in the future after you are dead: *We have a duty to preserve great works of art **for posterity**.*

ˈposter ˌpaint noun [C/U] **ARTS** a type of paint that is used especially by children for painting pictures

postgraduate¹ /ˌpəʊs(t)ˈɡrædʒʊət/ adj **EDUCATION** relating to study done after you receive your first university degree

postgraduate² /ˌpəʊs(t)ˈɡrædʒʊət/ noun [C] **EDUCATION 1** someone who is studying after receiving a first university degree **2** *American* someone who is studying after receiving an advanced degree, such as an **MA** or a **PhD**

posthumous /ˈpɒstjʊməs/ adj given or happening after someone's death: *posthumous awards for bravery* —**posthumously** adv

ˌpost-inˈdustrial adj **SOCIAL STUDIES** relating to societies or economies that had a lot of industry in the past but now depend on other types of work

posting /ˈpəʊstɪŋ/ noun [C] **1** a public notice, especially one advertising a job **2 COMPUTING** a message put on the Internet **3** a job that someone is sent somewhere to do, usually in another country

ˈPost-ˌit TRADEMARK a small piece of paper with a sticky substance on the back that is used for sticking notes on other papers and surfaces —*picture* → WORKSTATION

postman /ˈpəʊs(t)mən/ (plural **postmen** /ˈpəʊs(t)mən/) noun [C] someone whose job is to collect and deliver post

postmodernism /ˌpəʊst ˈmɒdəˌnɪz(ə)m/ noun [U] **ARTS, LITERATURE** ideas, attitudes, or styles of art, literature, or thinking that have developed after **modernism**, often as a reaction against it — **postmodernist** adj, **postmodernist** noun [C]

postmodifier /ˌpəʊstˈmɒdɪfaɪə/ noun [C] **LANGUAGE** a word, usually an adjective or adverb, that comes after the word it describes

postmortem /ˌpəʊs(t)ˈmɔːtəm/ noun [C] **HEALTH** a medical examination of a dead body to find out why the person died= AUTOPSY

postnatal /ˌpəʊs(t)ˈneɪt(ə)l/ adj **HEALTH** relating to the period of time after the birth of a baby: *postnatal care* → ANTENATAL

ˌpostnatal deˈpression noun [U] **HEALTH** a state of severe **depression** that some women suffer from after the birth of a baby

ˈpost ˌoffice noun [C] a place where you can buy stamps, send letters and parcels, collect money given to you by the government etc

postpone /pəʊs(t)ˈpəʊn/ verb [T] to decide that something will not be done at the time when it was planned for, but at a later time: *Bad weather forced us to postpone Friday's game.* —**postponement** noun [C/U]

ˌpost-proˈduction adj **ARTS** used for describing the work done on a film or television programme after the action has been filmed —**ˌpost-proˈduction** noun [U]

postscript /ˈpəʊs(t)skrɪpt/ noun [C] **1** a message that is added at the end of a letter or email, usually below your name **2 LITERATURE** a piece of information added to the end of a story, article, or report

ˌpost-traumatic ˈstress disˌorder noun [singular/U] **HEALTH** a mental condition caused by having seen or experienced something very shocking, upsetting, or frightening in the past

postulate /ˈpɒstjʊleɪt/ verb [T] *formal* to claim or imagine that something is true or that it exists —**postulation** /ˌpɒstjʊˈleɪʃ(ə)n/ noun [C/U]

posture /ˈpɒstʃə/ noun **1** [C/U] the position that your body is in when you sit, stand, or walk: *Exercise can improve your posture.* **2** [C] *formal* an attitude, or the way someone behaves toward other people —**postural** adj

ˌpost-ˈwar or **postwar** /ˌpəʊs(t)ˈwɔː/ adj happening or existing in the period of time immediately after a war, especially the Second World War

pot¹ /pɒt/ noun [C] **1** a deep round metal container that you cook food in: *a set of pots and pans* **2** a container used for making or serving hot drinks, or the amount of a drink that a pot contains: *a pot of tea* **3** a container that you grow plants in: *a plant pot* **4** a container made of glass or clay that is used for storing food= JAR: *a pot of honey*

pot² /pɒt/ (**pots, potting, potted**) verb [T] to put a plant in a container with soil

potassium /pəˈtæsiəm/ noun [U] **CHEMISTRY** a soft white metal element that is used for making soaps and fertilizers. Chemical symbol: **K**

poˌtassium hyˈdroxide noun [U] **CHEMISTRY** a white alkaline compound that is used in making soap. Chemical formula: **KOH**

potassium iodide /pəˌtæsiəm ˈaɪədaɪd/ noun [U] **CHEMISTRY** a white **crystalline** compound that tastes like salt, used in medicine and photography. The solution of this with **iodine** is used to test for starch. Chemical formula: **KI**

potassium permanganate /pəˌtæsiəm pəˈmæŋɡəneɪt/ noun [U] CHEMISTRY a dark purple compound that is used in dyes, and to kill bacteria. Chemical formula: $KMnO_4$

potato /pəˈteɪtəʊ/ (plural **potatoes**) noun [C/U] a common hard round vegetable that has a brown, red, or yellow skin and is white or yellow inside. Potatoes are **tubers** (=stems that grow under the ground) and they can be eaten in many different ways: *baked potatoes* ♦ *potato salad* —*picture* → VEGETABLE

potent /ˈpəʊt(ə)nt/ adj **1** powerful, or effective **2** if a drug, medicine, or chemical is potent, it has a strong effect —**potency** noun [U]

potential¹ /pəˈtenʃ(ə)l/ adj possible, or likely in the future: *a potential disaster* ♦ *The disease is a potential killer.* —**potentially** adv: *a potentially harmful drug*

potential² /pəˈtenʃ(ə)l/ noun **1** [U] the possibility to develop or achieve something in the future: *As a composer, she still hasn't realized her potential.* **2** [singular] a possibility that something will happen: *With so many people involved, there is always a potential for conflict.*

poˌtential ˈdifference noun [U] PHYSICS the work done in moving a unit of electrical charge between two points in an electrical circuit

poˌtential ˈenergy noun [U] PHYSICS the energy that an object or system has stored because of its position or condition. For example, a raised weight has potential energy.

pothole /ˈpɒtˌhəʊl/ noun [C] a hole in a road

potion /ˈpəʊʃ(ə)n/ noun [C] a drink that is believed to be magic, poisonous, or useful as a medicine

potted /ˈpɒtɪd/ adj **1** giving a short summary of the facts: *a potted history* **2** potted food is preserved in a pot **3** growing in a pot: *a potted geranium*

ˌpotted ˈplant noun [C] a plant in a container

potter¹ /ˈpɒtə/ noun [C] someone who makes pottery

potter² /ˈpɒtə/ verb [I] to do things in a slow and enjoyable way: *Jo spent the day pottering around the garden.*

pottery /ˈpɒtəri/ noun [U] **1** objects such as plates and cups that are made out of baked clay **2** the activity of making pottery

potting compost /ˈpɒtɪŋ ˌkɒmpɒst/ noun [U] the special soil that you use when you put a plant in a container

pouch /paʊtʃ/ noun [C] **1** a small bag made of cloth or thin leather **2** a fold of skin on the body of an animal, for example the place where a **kangaroo** carries its baby

poultry /ˈpəʊltri/ noun [U] birds such as chickens that are used for meat or eggs, or the meat of these birds

pounce /paʊns/ verb [I] **1** to quickly jump on or hold someone or something: *They pounced on their suspect.* **2** to react in a very sudden way, especially by criticizing someone: *White House aides pounced on the remark.*

pound¹ /paʊnd/ noun [C] **1** ECONOMICS a unit of money that is used in the UK and several other countries. The symbol for a pound is £: *a pound coin* ♦ *a ten pound note* **2** a unit for measuring weight, used in several countries including the US, containing 16 **ounces** and equal to 0.454 kilograms: *half a pound of cheese* ♦ *The baby weighed over 10 pounds.*

pound² /paʊnd/ verb **1** [I/T] to hit something many times with a lot of force: *I could hear them pounding on the door.* **2** [I] if your heart pounds, it beats strongly and quickly because you are nervous, excited, or afraid **3** [T] to continuously attack a place with bombs for a long period of time

pour /pɔː/ verb **1** [T] to make a liquid or substance flow out of a container that you are holding: *Sit down and I'll pour you a drink.* ♦ *Pour the mixture into a dish and bake for 45 minutes.* **2** [I] to flow continuously and in large amounts: *The village was evacuated as lava poured from the volcano.* ♦ *Tears were pouring down her face.* **3** [I] to rain very hard: *The thunder and lightning stopped, but it continued to pour.* **4** [I] to arrive or go somewhere quickly in a large group or in large amounts: *People poured out of the train.* ♦ *Election results are beginning to pour in.*

pout /paʊt/ verb [I] to push your lips out in order to show that you are annoyed, or in order to look more sexually attractive —**pout** noun [C]

poverty /ˈpɒvəti/ noun **1** [U] a situation in which someone does not have enough money to pay for their basic needs ≠ WEALTH: *Half the world's population is living in poverty.* **2** [singular] formal a lack of something ≠ WEALTH

POW /ˌpiː əʊ ˈdʌb(ə)ljuː/ noun [C] a **prisoner of war**

powder /ˈpaʊdə/ noun [C/U] a soft dry substance that looks like dust or sand: *chilli powder* —**powdery** adj

ˈpowder ˌcoating noun [U] ENGINEERING a process in which metal is covered with a dry coloured powder and heated, so that the powder sticks to the metal's surface

powdered /ˈpaʊdəd/ adj in the form of powder: *powdered milk*

power¹ /ˈpaʊə/ noun

1 ability to influence	6 strong country
2 ability to achieve	7 energy/electricity
3 natural ability	8 strength/effectiveness
4 political control	9 in mathematics
5 legal authority	+ PHRASE

1 [U] the ability to influence or control people: *Her parents still have a lot of power over her.* ♦ *Don't underestimate the power of advertising.* ♦ *a power struggle within the party* (=an attempt by each of two people or groups to get control)

2 [U] the ability to achieve something or make something happen: *purchasing power* ♦ *Willis did everything within his power for his client.*

3 [C/U] a natural or unusual ability for doing something: *He has amazing powers of concentration.*

4 [U] political control of a country or government: *The ruling Social Democratic party has been in power for ten years.* ♦ *Later that year, the generals seized power in a bloody coup.*

5 [C/U] official or legal authority to do something: *A high court has power to overturn the lower court's decision.*

6 [C] a strong country that is able to influence other countries: *China has emerged as a major economic power.*

7 [U] PHYSICS energy obtained from oil, coal, the sun etc, used for operating equipment and machines: *solar power*

8 [U] physical force or strength: *The boy was thrown backwards by the power of the blast.*

9 [C] MATHS used in mathematics for saying how many times you multiply a number by itself. For example '10 to the power of 3' means 10 x 10 x 10.

PHRASE **power of attorney** LAW the legal right to make decisions for someone else, especially because they are old or ill and cannot make decisions themselves

power² /'paʊə/ verb [T] to give power to a machine or vehicle

power³ /'paʊə/ adj operated by electricity or by a motor: *a power drill*

'power ‚cut noun [C] a period when the electricity supply stops

powerful /'paʊəf(ə)l/ adj **1** able to influence or control what people do or think ≠ WEAK: *We live in a society where the media are extremely powerful.* ♦ *a powerful argument in favour of gun control* **2** with a lot of physical strength or force: *a powerful explosion* ♦ *a powerful athlete* ♦ *The new model has a more powerful engine.* **3** with a strong effect: *powerful drugs* —**powerfully** adv

'power ‚hose noun [C] a type of **hose** that uses water at a high pressure

powerless /'paʊələs/ adj not able to control or prevent something: *She was powerless to stop him.* —**powerlessness** noun [U]

'power ‚point noun [C] a place on a wall where you can connect equipment to the electricity supply

'power ‚rating noun [C] the amount of electricity that an electrical appliance uses

'power ‚shower noun [C] a shower that produces a very strong flow of water

'power ‚station noun [C] a large building that contains machines that produce power, especially electricity —*picture* → DAM

‚power 'steering noun [U] ENGINEERING a system in which extra power from a vehicle's engine makes it possible to turn a car with only small movements of the **steering wheel**

'power ‚stroke noun [singular] ENGINEERING the third of four movements of the **piston** in an **internal-combustion engine**, which creates force

'power ‚tool noun [C] a tool that is operated by electricity or a motor

pp abbrev **1** pages **2** BUSINESS written before someone's name when you are signing a letter for them **3** MUSIC pianissimo

PPP /ˌpiː piː 'piː/ abbrev BUSINESS public-private partnership: a system in which private companies work with the government to provide public services such as health services

PPTP /ˌpiː piː tiː 'piː/ abbrev COMPUTING point-to-point tunnelling protocol: a method of sending information between computers on a public **network** so that only the people intended to see the information can see it

PR /ˌpiː 'ɑː/ noun [U] **1** public relations **2** POLITICS proportional representation

practicable /'præktɪkəb(ə)l/ adj formal able to be done or used successfully

practical¹ /'præktɪk(ə)l/ adj **1** involving or relating to real situations rather than theories or ideas alone: *Unfortunately this research has no practical use.* ♦ *Practical experience can be as valuable as academic qualifications.* **2** making sensible decisions and choices based on what can be successfully achieved ≠ IMPRACTICAL: *a practical attitude to marriage* ♦ *Despite their wealth, they were always practical about money.* **3** intended to be useful or suitable, not just fashionable or attractive: *a practical car for the family* **4** able to make repairs or do things with your hands in a skilful way

practical² /'præktɪk(ə)l/ noun [C] an examination or lesson in which you make things or do experiments

practicality /ˌpræktɪ'kæləti/ noun **1** [U] the quality of being useful or suitable for a particular purpose or situation **2 practicalities** [plural] the things that need to be dealt with, planned for, or done in order to achieve something

practically /'præktɪkli/ adv **1** almost: *I was practically begging him to think again.* **2** in a way that is useful, sensible, or practical

practice /'præktɪs/ noun [C/U] **1** occasions when you do something in order to become better at it, or the time that you spend doing this: *basketball practice* ♦ *Your typing will improve* **with practice**. **2** a way of doing something, or something that is regularly done: *It is* **good practice** *to check your work before handing it in.* ♦ *Bribery is* **common practice** *in many countries.* **3** the business or profession of a doctor, lawyer, or other professional person
PHRASES **in practice** used for talking about what really happens rather than what you think will or should happen: *It's a good idea, but I don't think it would work in practice.*
out of practice bad at doing something because you have not been doing it regularly

practise /'præktɪs/ verb **1** [I/T] to repeat an activity regularly so that you become better at it: *How many hours a day do you practise?* ♦ *Practise putting your tent up in the garden several times.* **2** [T] to do something regularly or in a particular way: *The earliest colonists seem to have practised farming.* **3** [I/T] to work in a particular profession, especially in the medical or legal profession: *She completed her medical training, though she never practised.* ♦ *He is no longer allowed to* **practise law**.

practised /'præktɪst/ adj skilful in something as a result of experience

practising /'præktɪsɪŋ/ adj active in a particular profession, religion, or way of life

practitioner /præk'tɪʃ(ə)nə/ noun [C] formal someone who works in a particular profession, especially medicine or law

pragmatic /præg'mætɪk/ adj involving or emphasizing practical results rather than theories and ideas: *a pragmatic approach to problem-solving* —**pragmatism** /'prægmə‚tɪz(ə)m/ noun [U], **pragmatist** /'prægmətɪst/ noun [C]

pragmatics /præg'mætɪks/ noun [U] LANGUAGE the study of how language is used in particular situations to express a meaning or attitude that may not be obvious from the actual words

prairie /'preəri/ noun [C] GEOGRAPHY a large flat area in central North America that is covered with grass and farms but has no trees

praise¹ /preɪz/ verb [T] to express strong approval or admiration for someone or something: *If you never praise your kids, how can they know when they're doing something right?* ♦ *The painting was* **highly praised**.

praise² /preɪz/ noun [U] an expression of strong approval or admiration

praiseworthy /'preɪz‚wɜːði/ adj formal deserving praise or admiration

pram /præm/ noun [C] a small vehicle with four wheels that you push a baby in while you are walking

prance /prɑːns/ verb [I] showing disapproval to move around in a lively way that seems silly to other people

praseodymium /ˌpreɪziəʊ'dɪmiəm/ noun [U] CHEMISTRY a soft silvery metallic element in the

lanthanide group of the periodic table. It is used in lasers and **nuclear reactors**. Chemical symbol: **Pr**

prawn /prɔːn/ noun [C] a crustacean with a hard shell around it and two pairs of claws, that can be eaten —picture → SEA

pray /preɪ/ verb **1** [I/T] RELIGION to speak to God or a saint, for example in order to give thanks or to ask for help: *We all prayed that she would soon recover.* ♦ *They **prayed for** peace.* ♦ *He **prayed to God** to save him.* **2** [I] to hope or wish very strongly for something: *Everyone prayed that the war wouldn't last long.*

prayer /preə/ noun RELIGION **1** [C] something that you say when you speak to God: *a prayer for peace* ♦ *He **said a prayer** for their safety.* **2** [U] the practice of speaking to God: *the power of prayer*

'**prayer ,book** noun [C] RELIGION a book that contains prayers

'**prayer ,mat** noun [C] RELIGION a small carpet that Muslims put on the floor under their knees when they pray

praying mantis /ˌpreɪɪŋ ˈmæntɪs/ noun [C] a large insect with long front legs —picture → INSECT

pre- /priː/ prefix before: *pre-war fashions* ♦ *pre-school programmes* (=for children who are too young for school)

preach /priːtʃ/ verb **1** [I/T] RELIGION to talk about a religious subject to a group of people, especially in a church **2** [I] *showing disapproval* to tell people how to behave= LECTURE

preacher /ˈpriːtʃə/ noun [C] RELIGION someone whose job is to give religious speeches or lead religious ceremonies in some Christian churches

preamble /priˈæmb(ə)l/ noun [C] *formal* an introduction to a document, speech, or report explaining its purpose

prearranged /ˌpriːəˈreɪndʒd/ adj planned or agreed to at an earlier time

the Precambrian /priːˈkæmbriən/ noun [singular] GEOLOGY the **era** of geological time, from 4,650 to 700 million years ago, during which the Earth's **crust** formed and simple forms of life first appeared

precancerous /priːˈkæns(ə)rəs/ adj HEALTH precancerous cells are certain to develop into cancer if the patient does not get medical treatment

precarious /prɪˈkeəriəs/ adj **1** likely to change or become dangerous without warning: *For the refugees life was always precarious.* **2** not safe, or likely to fall —**precariously** adv

precast /ˌpriːˈkɑːst/ verb [T] CONSTRUCTION already made into the correct shape to use for building a structure

precaution /prɪˈkɔːʃ(ə)n/ noun [C] something that you do in order to protect people or things against possible harm or trouble: *Doctors recommend **taking precautions** to protect your skin from the sun.*

precautionary /prɪˈkɔːʃ(ə)n(ə)ri/ adj done or used for protection against possible harm or trouble: *a precautionary measure*

precede /prɪˈsiːd/ verb [T] *formal* to happen or exist before another person or thing: *These exercises must always be preceded by a warm-up.*

precedence /ˈpresɪdəns/ noun **take precedence (over)** if something takes precedence over something else, it is more important and should be dealt with first

precedent /ˈpresɪdənt/ noun **1** [C/U] an action or event in the past that is used as an example when someone wants to do the same thing again: *This*

decision could **set a** dangerous **precedent**. **2** [C] LAW a decision by a court on which future decisions are based

preceding /prɪˈsiːdɪŋ/ adj existing or coming immediately before someone or something else

precious /ˈpreʃəs/ adj very valuable: *a precious jewel* ♦ *Our freedom is the most precious thing we have.*

,**precious ˈmetal** noun [C] a valuable metal such as gold or silver

,**precious ˈstone** noun [C] a valuable stone such as a diamond or **ruby**

precipice /ˈpresəpɪs/ noun [C] GEOGRAPHY a very steep high cliff

precipitate¹ /prɪˈsɪpɪteɪt/ verb **1** [T] *formal* to make something happen or begin to exist: *Such headaches can be precipitated by certain foods as well as stress.* **2** [I] GEOGRAPHY to rain, snow, hail etc, as a result of the condensation of water vapour in the atmosphere **3** [I/T] CHEMISTRY if a solid substance precipitates, or if something precipitates it, it becomes separate from the liquid that it is in and drops to the bottom of the container

precipitate² /prɪˈsɪpɪteɪt/ noun [C] CHEMISTRY a solid substance that has been separated from the liquid that it was in

precipitation /prɪˌsɪpɪˈteɪʃ(ə)n/ noun [U] **1** GEOGRAPHY water that falls to the ground in the form of rain, snow, hail etc. These are all formed by the condensation of water vapour in the atmosphere. **2** CHEMISTRY the process by which a solid substance separates from the liquid that it is in —picture → WATER CYCLE

précis /ˈpreɪsiː/ (plural **précis**) noun [C] a short summary of a speech or piece of writing

precise /prɪˈsaɪs/ adj **1** exact and accurate: *The precise date and place of his birth are unknown.* ♦ *Lara was able to tell me everything that had happened **in precise detail**.* **2** used for emphasizing that something is definite or clearly true: *At that precise moment, someone came round the corner.*

precisely /prɪˈsaɪsli/ adv **1** exactly: *He knows precisely what we want.* **2** clearly: *Dartman spoke very precisely.* **3** used for adding emphasis to a reason or explanation: *They have the best medical care precisely because of high taxes.*

precision /prɪˈsɪʒ(ə)n/ noun [U] the quality of being exact and accurate

preˈcision ,farming noun [U] AGRICULTURE the use of computer technology and other technologies such as **GPS** and satellite images to improve crop growing and reduce the use of fertilizers, **herbicides**, and **pesticides**

preclude /prɪˈkluːd/ verb [T] *formal* if one thing precludes another, the first thing prevents the second one from happening

precocious /prɪˈkəʊʃəs/ adj a precocious child is more intelligent than other children of his or her age or behaves in a way that is more typical of someone older

preconceived /ˌpriːkənˈsiːvd/ adj a preconceived idea or opinion is formed before you have all the facts

precursor /prɪˈkɜːsə/ noun [C] something that exists before something else

predate /ˌpriːˈdeɪt/ verb [T] to exist or happen earlier than something else

predation /prɪˈdeɪʃ(ə)n/ noun [U] BIOLOGY the relationship between two groups of animals in which one species hunts, kills, and eats the other

predator /'predətə/ noun [C] **1 BIOLOGY** an animal that hunts, kills, and eats other animals **2 BUSINESS** a company that tries to take control of other companies —**predatory** /'predət(ə)ri/ adj: *a predatory takeover bid*

predecease /ˌpriːdɪ'siːs/ verb [T] **LAW** to die before someone else

predecessor /'priːdɪˌsesə/ noun [C] the person who had a job before someone else

predetermined /ˌpriːdɪ'tɜːmɪnd/ adj happening or developing in a particular way because of things that have existed, happened, or been decided before

predeterminer /ˌpriːdɪ'tɜːmɪnə/ noun [C] **LANGUAGE** a word that can come before a **determiner** (=a word such as 'a', 'the', 'his', or 'this'), and gives more information about a noun. In the phrases 'all my fingers' and 'half a loaf', the words 'all' and 'half' are predeterminers.

predicament /prɪ'dɪkəmənt/ noun [C] a difficult or unpleasant situation that is not easy to get out of

predicate /'predɪkət/ noun [C] **LANGUAGE** the part of the sentence that contains the verb and its object or **complements**, and gives more information about the subject. For example, in the sentence 'Lisa was combing her hair', 'was combing her hair' is the predicate.

predicative /prɪ'dɪkətɪv/ adj **LANGUAGE** predicative adjectives and phrases follow a verb, for example 'afraid' in the sentence 'We were afraid.'

predict /prɪ'dɪkt/ verb [T] to say what you think will happen in the future: *They're predicting heavy rain for tomorrow.* ♦ *Industry leaders predict that another 8,000 jobs could be lost by the end of the year.*

predictable /prɪ'dɪktəb(ə)l/ adj **1** something that is predictable happens in the way that you expect it to = FORESEEABLE **2** someone who is predictable always behaves or reacts in the same way ≠ UNPREDICTABLE —**predictably** adv

prediction /prɪ'dɪkʃ(ə)n/ noun [C] a statement about what you think will happen in the future

predictive /prɪ'dɪktɪv/ adj relating to a technology that guesses and finishes the word that a computer or mobile phone user is typing before they have finished typing it

predisposition /ˌpriːdɪspə'zɪʃ(ə)n/ noun the fact that someone is likely to think or behave in a particular way, or likely to develop a particular medical condition

predominant /prɪ'dɒmɪnənt/ adj **1** most common, or greatest in number or amount **2** most important or powerful —**predominance** noun [U]

predominantly /prɪ'dɒmɪnəntli/ adv mainly: *a predominantly Catholic country*

predominate /prɪ'dɒmɪneɪt/ verb [I] *formal* to be more important, or greater in number or amount, than other things or people

pre-eminent /ˌpriː 'emɪnənt/ adj best at a particular activity: *Spain's pre-eminent guitarist*

pre-empt /ˌpriː 'empt/ verb [T] to do something in order to try to prevent something from happening

pre-emptive /ˌpriː 'emptɪv/ adj said or done before someone else has a chance to act or attack so that their plans or actions are prevented from happening

preen /priːn/ verb [I/T] **1** if an animal, especially a bird, preens, or if it preens itself, it cleans and arranges its feathers or fur **2** to spend a lot of time trying to make yourself look more attractive

pre-existing adj used for describing something that already existed before something else started

preface /'prefəs/ noun [C] an introduction to a book or a speech

prefect /'priːfekt/ noun [C] **EDUCATION** in some schools in the UK, an older student who controls the activities of younger students and makes certain that they obey the rules

prefer /prɪ'fɜː/ (**prefers, preferring, preferred**) verb [T] to like or want someone or something more than someone or something else: *Which do you prefer, the red or the blue one?* ♦ *Even today, most Americans prefer coffee to tea.* ♦ *I prefer to work alone.*
PHRASE prefer charges (against sb) LAW to officially accuse someone of a crime

preferable /'pref(ə)rəb(ə)l/ adj more suitable or useful than something else

preferably /'pref(ə)rəbli/ adv used for saying what would be best in a particular situation even if it is not possible: *The successful candidate should have a degree, preferably in a foreign language.*

preference /'pref(ə)rəns/ noun [C/U] someone or something that you prefer to something else: *Either tomorrow or Wednesday is fine for me. Do you have a preference?* ♦ *It's really just a matter of personal preference which you choose.*
PHRASE in preference to instead of someone or something else that you like or want less: *They drink coffee in preference to tea.*

preferential /ˌprefə'renʃ(ə)l/ adj giving one person or group an advantage over all others: *Neither sex should get preferential treatment.*

prefix /'priːfɪks/ noun [C] **LANGUAGE** a group of letters that is added to the beginning of a word in order to change its meaning. For example, the prefix 'un-' is added to the word 'tidy' in order to form the word 'untidy'.

pregnancy /'pregnənsi/ (plural **pregnancies**) noun [C/U] **BIOLOGY** the condition of being pregnant, or the period of time when a woman is pregnant

pregnant /'pregnənt/ adj **BIOLOGY** if a woman or other female mammal is pregnant, she has a foetus developing inside her body: *I was only 19 when I got pregnant.* ♦ *She was pregnant with twins.*

preheating flame /priː'hiːtɪŋ ˌfleɪm/ noun [C] **TECHNOLOGY** a **neutral flame** used for heating a piece of metal that is to be cut, before applying a stream of oxygen to it

prehistoric /ˌpriːhɪ'stɒrɪk/ adj relating to the period of time before anything was written down by humans: *prehistoric animals*

prehistory /ˌpriː'hɪst(ə)ri/ noun [U] the period of time before written history, or the study of this period

pre-ignition noun [U] **ENGINEERING** a situation in which the fuel in an **internal-combustion engine** starts to burn before the **spark** has been made, so that the engine does not work correctly

prejudge /ˌpriː'dʒʌdʒ/ verb [T] to form an opinion about someone or something before you know everything about them

prejudice /'predʒʊdɪs/ noun [C/U] an unreasonable opinion or feeling about someone or something, especially about a particular group of people: *We've been working hard to overcome prejudice against women in politics.*

prejudiced /'predʒʊdɪst/ adj someone who is prejudiced has an unreasonable opinion or feeling about someone or something, especially about a particular group of people

preliminary /prɪˈlɪmɪn(ə)ri/ adj coming before the main or most important part of something: *a preliminary discussion*

prelude /ˈprelju:d/ noun [C] **1** an event that happens before a more important event **2** MUSIC a short piece of music that introduces a longer piece of music

premature /ˈpremətʃə/ adj **1** happening too soon or before the usual time **2** HEALTH a premature baby is born before it should be —**prematurely** adv

premeditated /priːˈmedɪˌteɪtɪd/ adj a premeditated crime is deliberately planned —**premeditation** /priːˌmedɪˈteɪʃ(ə)n/ noun [U]

premier /ˈpremɪə, *American* prɪˈmɪr/ noun [C] POLITICS a **prime minister**

premise /ˈpremɪs/ noun [C] *formal* a principle or statement that you consider to be true, on which you base other theories and actions

premises /ˈpremɪsɪz/ noun [plural] the buildings and land that a business or organization uses

premium¹ /ˈpriːmiəm/ noun [C] BUSINESS **1** the amount by which the price of a share is higher than its original value **2** something given free or at a special low price to someone, in order to influence them to buy a particular product or service

premium² /ˈpriːmiəm/ adj premium goods or services are more expensive or of higher quality than other similar ones

premodifier /priːˈmɒdɪfaɪə/ noun [C] LANGUAGE a word, usually an adjective or adverb, that comes before the word that it describes

premolar /priːˈməʊlə/ noun [C] ANATOMY one of the two teeth on each side of both jaws that are immediately in front of the **molars** and behind the **canines**. They are used for chewing and **grinding**. —*picture* → TOOTH

premonition /ˌpreməˈnɪʃ(ə)n/ noun [C] a strong feeling that something bad is going to happen

prenatal /ˌpriːˈneɪt(ə)l/ adj HEALTH relating to the period of time when a woman is pregnant

preoccupation /priːˌɒkjʊˈpeɪʃ(ə)n/ noun **1** [singular/U] a state in which you think about something so much that you do not notice or think about other things: *a preoccupation with death* **2** [C] something that you think about and want to do because it is important= CONCERN

preoccupied /priːˈɒkjʊpaɪd/ adj thinking about something so much that you do not notice or think about other things —**preoccupy** verb [T]

prepaid /ˌpriːˈpeɪd/ adj something that is prepaid has already been paid for before you use it

preparation /ˌprepəˈreɪʃ(ə)n/ noun **1** [U] the process of making someone or something ready for something: *The experience was good **preparation** for a career in journalism.* ♦ *The flowers were ordered **in preparation** for the wedding.* **2 preparations** [plural] things that you do so that you are ready for something: *The US continued its military preparations.* ♦ *Organizers are **making** final **preparations for** next week's festival.* **3** [C] a mixture that has been made especially for use as a medicine or food

preparatory /prɪˈpærət(ə)ri/ adj done as preparation for something else

prepare /prɪˈpeə/ verb **1** [I/T] to get ready for something, or to make someone or something ready: *Medical teams are **preparing to** fly to the area tomorrow.*

2 [I/T] to make plans for a future event so that you will be ready for it: *Traders began to **prepare for** the annual surge of Christmas shoppers.* ♦ *We're preparing a special reception for him when he returns.* **3** [T] to make food ready to be cooked or eaten: *You can prepare this dish in advance and freeze it.*

> PHRASE **prepare the way/ground for sth** to do things that make it possible or easier for something to happen: *Her research prepared the way for later advances.*

prepared /prɪˈpeəd/ adj **1** ready and able to do something ≠ UNPREPARED: *We have to be **prepared for** anything.* **2** ready for use: *Make sure the room is prepared before they get there.* **3** done or made earlier: *Bonner read from a prepared statement.*

> PHRASE **prepared to do sth** willing and able to do something: *I'm not prepared to listen to excuses.*

prepayment /priːˈpeɪmənt/ noun [C/U] money that you pay before you can use a service

preponderance /prɪˈpɒnd(ə)rəns/ noun [singular] *formal* most of the people or things in a group

preposition /ˌprepəˈzɪʃ(ə)n/ noun [C] LANGUAGE a word that usually comes before a noun or a pronoun and shows its relation to another part of the sentence. In the sentences 'I left it on the table' and 'She came out of the house', the words 'on' and 'out of' are prepositions. —**prepositional** adj

prepositional 'phrase noun [C] LANGUAGE a phrase consisting of a preposition and the noun or pronoun that comes after it, for example 'in the car' or 'near her'

preposterous /prɪˈpɒst(ə)rəs/ adj *formal* extremely unreasonable or silly= ABSURD

preprocessor /priːˈprəʊsesə/ noun [C] COMPUTING a piece of software that partly prepares information before it is used

prep school /ˈprep ˌsku:l/ noun [C/U] EDUCATION **1** in the UK, a private school for children between the ages of 7 or 8 and 11 or 13 **2** in the US, a private school for children over the age of 11 that prepares them for college

prequel /ˈpriːkwəl/ noun [C] ARTS, LITERATURE a book or film about events that happened before the events in another book or film that was written or made earlier

prerecorded /ˌpriːrɪˈkɔːdɪd/ adj prerecorded messages, music, or television or radio programmes have been recorded so that they can be used later —**prerecord** verb [T], **prerecording** noun [C]

pre-regi'stration noun [U] the process of taking a person's details before they actually arrive at a hotel or a **conference**, so as to save time

prerequisite /priːˈrekwəzɪt/ noun [C] *formal* something that must exist or happen before something else is possible

prerogative /prɪˈrɒɡətɪv/ noun [C] *formal* a right that a particular person or group has

'pre-school adj EDUCATION relating to or involving children who are too young to go to school

prescribe /prɪˈskraɪb/ verb [T] **1** HEALTH if a doctor prescribes a drug or treatment, they say that you should have it **2** *formal* to state officially what should be done in a particular situation

prescription /prɪˈskrɪpʃ(ə)n/ noun [C] HEALTH a piece of paper that a doctor gives you that says what type of medicine you need: *The drug is only available **on prescription** (=if you have a prescription).* → REPEAT PRESCRIPTION

prescriptive /prɪˈskrɪptɪv/ adj **1** stating what should happen, or what someone should do **2 LANGUAGE** stating how people should use a language rather than describing how they really use it —**prescriptively** adv

presence /ˈprez(ə)ns/ noun **1** [U] the fact of being in a particular place at a particular time: *a device for detecting **the presence of** submarines* ♦ *Mr Reese didn't even **acknowledge** my **presence**.* **2** [singular] a group of people who are in a place for a particular purpose: *There is still a large **military presence** in the region.* **3** [singular/U] an impressive appearance or way of behaving or speaking

PHRASE **presence of mind** the ability to think quickly and clearly in a difficult situation

present¹ /ˈprez(ə)nt/ adj **1** existing or happening now: *The present situation cannot be allowed to continue.* ♦ *The present owners purchased the farm in 1996.* **2 LANGUAGE** the present form of a verb is used for talking about actions that are happening now or things that exist now **3** at an event, or in a place: *Among those **present at** the ceremony were the ambassador and his wife.*

PHRASE **the present day** now: *It's a tradition that has survived right up till the present day.*

present² /prɪˈzent/ verb [T]

1 give officially	**7** introduce sb formally
2 cause situation etc	**8** show sth to sb
3 offer to be considered	**9** give cheque/bill
4 describe sb/sth	**10** show signs of an
5 introduce programme	illness
6 organize sth	

1 to give something to someone formally or officially: *Who will be **presenting the prizes**?* ♦ *We are very pleased to have been **presented with** this award.* ♦ *Finally the mayor **presented** the medals **to** the winners.*
2 to cause something such as a problem, threat, or opportunity: *The group's activities **presented a threat** to national security.*
3 to offer something for people to consider: *The commission **presented** its **report** in October.*
4 to show someone or something in a particular way: *The film **presents** a disturbing **image** of youth culture.*
5 ARTS to introduce a television or radio programme: *The show will be presented by Trevor McDonald.*
6 ARTS to produce or organize something such as a play, film, or exhibition
7 to introduce someone formally to someone else, especially to an important person: *They hovered around, hoping to be **presented to** the Queen.*
8 to show something such as a passport to someone in an official position
9 to give a cheque to a bank so that it can be put into an account
10 HEALTH if a patient presents with particular signs of an illness, they have those signs

present³ /ˈprez(ə)nt/ noun **1** [C] something that you give to someone, for example on their birthday= GIFT: *a wedding present* ♦ *Yuki was wrapping **a present for** her mother.* **2 the present** [singular] the period of time that is happening now: *We must learn to **live in the present**, not in the past.* **3 the present LANGUAGE** the present tense

PHRASE **at present** now: *At present there seems to be no solution to the crisis.*

presentable /prɪˈzentəb(ə)l/ adj looking good enough for people to see

presentation /ˌprez(ə)nˈteɪʃ(ə)n/ noun **1** [U] the way in which something is shown, arranged, or explained: *Using a computer helped with the spelling and*

presentation of his school work. **2** [C] a ceremony at which something such as a prize is given to someone: *He will receive the prize at a presentation on Saturday.* **3** [C] a formal talk in which you describe or explain something to a group of people: *I'm going to ask each of you to **give a presentation**.*

presentational /ˌprez(ə)nˈteɪʃ(ə)nəl/ adj relating to the way in which someone explains or describe something to a group of people

presenˈtation ˌsoftware noun [U] **COMPUTING** software that allows a user to create a business **presentation** with words, pictures, and **charts**

present-ˈday adj relating to a situation or place as it exists now: *The novel is set in present-day Russia.*

presenter /prɪˈzentə/ noun [C] **ARTS** someone who introduces a television or radio programme

presently /ˈprez(ə)ntli/ adv formal at the present time

present ˈparticiple noun [C] **LANGUAGE** in English, the form of a verb that ends in '-ing' and that expresses continuing action, for example the word 'doing'. It can sometimes be used as an adjective, for example in 'the crying baby'.

the ˌpresent ˈperfect noun [singular] **LANGUAGE** in English, a verb tense that expresses an action that was completed recently in the past, or that started in the past and continues. The tense is formed by combining the present tense of 'have' and the past participle of a verb, as in the sentence 'She has paid the bill'.

the ˌpresent ˈtense noun [singular] **LANGUAGE** the form of a verb that expresses what exists now, what is happening now, or what happens regularly

preservation /ˌprezəˈveɪʃ(ə)n/ noun [U] **1 ENVIRONMENT** the process of working to protect something so that it is not damaged or destroyed **2** the addition of a chemical substance to food or wood in order to prevent it from decaying **3** the degree to which something has not been changed by the effects of time or weather

preservative /prɪˈzɜːvətɪv/ noun [C/U] a chemical substance used for preventing food or wood from decaying

preserve¹ /prɪˈzɜːv/ verb [T] **1 ENVIRONMENT** to take care of something in order to prevent it from being harmed or destroyed: *The society works to preserve historic buildings.* **2** to keep food fresh for a long time, for example by adding salt or chemicals to it **3** to keep an idea, quality, or situation from changing or being lost: *It's important that these traditions are preserved.*

preserve² /prɪˈzɜːv/ noun **1** [C] formal a place or activity that is considered to belong to a particular person or group: *Sailing is no longer **the preserve of** the rich.* **2** [C/U] a sweet food made by boiling fruit and sugar together= JAM

preside /prɪˈzaɪd/ verb [I] to be in charge of an official meeting, ceremony, or other event

presidency /ˈprezɪdənsi/ (plural **presidencies**) noun [C] **POLITICS** the job of being president, or the period of time that someone has this job

president /ˈprezɪdənt/ noun [C] **1 POLITICS** the political leader of a country that does not have a king or queen: *President Lincoln* ♦ *the French president* ♦ *Clinton was **elected president** in 1992.* **2** the person who has the highest position in an organization or institution: *Lily Chang, our club president* **3** American the person in charge of a business or university: *the president of Citibank Corporation*

presidential /ˌprezɪˈdenʃ(ə)l/ adj **1** POLITICS relating to a president: *a presidential election* **2** behaving like a president or an important leader

press¹ /pres/ noun

1 newspapers etc	**4** for making sth flat
2 machine for printing	**5** for crushing fruit etc
3 publishing business	

1 the press [singular] newspapers and news magazines, or the journalists who work on them: *the national press* ♦ *the popular press* ♦ *She has been criticized in the press for not speaking out on this issue.* **2** [C] a machine that is used for printing newspapers, books, or magazines → PRINTING PRESS **3** [C] a business that publishes books: *Edinburgh University Press* **4** [C] a piece of equipment that is used for making something flat or smooth: *a trouser press* **5** [C] a piece of equipment that is used for squeezing the juice or oil out of fruit or vegetables: *a garlic press*

The press can be used with a singular or plural verb when it means all of the journalists who work on a newspaper or magazine. You can say *The press was out in force* OR *The press were out in force.*

press² /pres/ verb

1 push	**5** make clothes smooth
2 button/key	**+** PHRASE
3 move forward	**+** PHRASAL VERB
4 try to make sb do sth	

1 [I/T] to push one thing against another: *Children were pressing their faces against the window.* ♦ *Even with the phone pressed to his ear, he couldn't hear what she was saying.* ♦ *He felt the enormous weight of the man pressing down on his back.* **2** [T] to push something such as a button or switch in order to make a piece of equipment do something: *To read your email, press the return key.* **3** [I] to move as a group by pushing together in a particular direction: *A wave of protesters pressed forward towards the building.* **4** [T] to try in a determined way to make someone do something or tell you something= FORCE: *She continued to press him on the reasons for his decision.* ♦ *They had all been pressed into helping with the preparations for the party.* **5** [T] to make clothes smooth using a hot iron= IRON

PHRASE **press charges (against sb)** LAW to officially accuse someone of committing a crime so that they have to go to court for a trial

PHRASAL VERB **,press a'head** to continue doing something in a determined way: *They pressed ahead regardless of objections from local people.*

pressed /prest/ adj in a difficult situation because you do not have enough time, money, or other things that you need

pressing /ˈpresɪŋ/ adj very important and urgent

pressure¹ /ˈpreʃə/ noun **1** [C/U] attempts to persuade or force someone to do something: *Pressure for political change increased in the 1990s.* ♦ *The council is still under pressure to reduce spending.* ♦ *There is now greater pressure on the White House to take action.* ♦ *He did not put any pressure on her to take the job.* **2** [C/U] a worried feeling that someone gets when they have to deal with a difficult or complicated situation= STRESS: *With greatly increased workloads, everyone is under pressure now.* ♦ *The pressure on teachers has increased dramatically.* **3** [U] a physical force that is pressing on someone or something: *She became aware of the pressure of his hand on her shoulder.* **4** [U] PHYSICS the force that a liquid, air, or

gas produces on a particular area. This is found by dividing the force acting on a surface, which is measured in **newtons**, by the area it affects, which is measured in square metres. Pressure is measured in **pascals**. Symbol *p*: *You should check your tyre pressure at least once a month.*

pressure² /ˈpreʃə/ verb [T] to try to make someone do something that they do not want to do: *Don't be pressured into making any rash decisions.*

ˈpressure ,cap noun [C] ENGINEERING a lid on a vehicle's **radiator** that controls the pressure of the water in the **cooling system**

pressured /ˈpreʃəd/ adj worried because you have a lot of problems or responsibilities

ˈpressure ,group noun [C] SOCIAL STUDIES an organized group of people who try to persuade people and influence political decisions about a particular issue

ˈpressure ,wave noun [C] GEOLOGY a type of **seismic wave** (=movement caused by an earthquake) that pushes particles of rock together and then apart as it moves through the Earth

pressurized /ˈpreʃəraɪzd/ adj **1** with air pressure that is controlled so that it is different from the air pressure outside, for example in a plane **2** a pressurized container forces a substance out when the container is opened

prestige /preˈstiːʒ/ noun [U] the good reputation and respect that someone or something has, as a result of their achievements, high social status etc

prestigious /preˈstɪdʒəs/ adj admired and respected by a lot of people

presumably /prɪˈzjuːməbli/ adv used for saying that you think something is true, because it seems reasonable or likely, although you are not completely sure: *They are students, so presumably they don't have a lot of money.*

presume /prɪˈzjuːm/ verb **1** [T] to think that something is true because it seems reasonable or likely, although you are not completely sure: *I presume you've already ordered lunch.* **2** [I] to behave as though you have the right to behave in a particular way when you do not: *He would never presume to tell me what to do.* **3** [T] LAW to accept that something is true unless someone proves that it is not true: *Everyone should be presumed innocent until proven guilty.*

presumption /prɪˈzʌmpʃ(ə)n/ noun [C] a belief that something is true because it seems reasonable or likely

presumptuous /prɪˈzʌmptʃuəs/ adj *showing disapproval* showing too much confidence and not enough respect

presuppose /ˌpriːsəˈpəʊz/ verb [T] *formal* if one thing presupposes another, it cannot exist or happen unless the other thing is also true —**presupposition** /ˌpriːsʌpəˈzɪʃ(ə)n/ noun [C/U]

pretence /prɪˈtens/ noun [C/U] a way of behaving that does not honestly express your real feelings, thoughts, or intentions

pretend¹ /prɪˈtend/ verb [I/T] **1** to behave in a particular way because you want someone to believe that something is true when it is not: *We were never going to succeed, so why pretend?* ♦ *I'm sorry, but I can't just pretend it hasn't happened.* ♦ *She closed her eyes and pretended to be asleep.* **2** to imagine that something is true when you are playing a game: *They're pretending they're astronauts again.* ♦ *The little girl was pretending to be a lion.* **3** [T] to claim that something is true when it is not: *I'm not going to pretend I wasn't angry.*

pretend² /prɪ'tend/ adj *informal* imaginary: *a pretend pet*

pretentious /prɪ'tenʃəs/ adj *showing disapproval* trying to seem more important, intelligent etc than you really are

the preterite /'pretərɪt/ noun **LANGUAGE** the **past tense**

pretext /'priː,tekst/ noun [C] a reason that you pretend to have for doing something, that is given in order to hide your real reason or intention

pretty¹ /'prɪti/ adv *spoken* **1** fairly: *My TV's getting pretty old now.* ♦ *Tom looks pretty tired.* **2** very: *The weather's been pretty awful, hasn't it?* ♦ *They've made a pretty good job of it.*
PHRASE **pretty much/well/nearly** almost: *They look pretty much the same, don't they?*

pretty² /'prɪti/ (**prettier, prettiest**) adj **1** a pretty child, girl, or woman is attractive: *His girlfriend's very pretty.* **2** attractive, or nice to look at or listen to: *It's one of the prettiest villages on the south coast.* ♦ *a pretty tune* ♦ *a pretty little cottage* —**prettiness** noun [U]

prevail /prɪ'veɪl/ verb [I] *formal* **1** to exist at a particular time or in a particular situation: *A friendly atmosphere prevailed among the crowd.* **2** to be the strongest influence or element in a situation: *We hope that common sense will prevail in the dispute.* **3** to defeat someone in a game, competition, argument etc

prevailing /prɪ'veɪlɪŋ/ adj existing or having influence at a particular time or in a particular place: *Our markets were affected by the prevailing economic environment.*

pre,vailing 'wind noun [C] **GEOGRAPHY** a wind that blows in a particular area at a particular time of year

prevalent /'prevələnt/ adj very common in a particular place or among a particular group —**prevalence** noun [singular/U]

prevent /prɪ'vent/ verb [T] **1** to stop something from happening: *Rubber seals are fitted to prevent gas from escaping.* **2** to stop someone from doing something: *The owner is prevented by law from making any major changes.*

preventative /prɪ'ventətɪv/ adj **preventive**

prevention /prɪ'venʃ(ə)n/ noun [U] the act of preventing something, or things that people do in order to prevent something: *the prevention of cancer* ♦ *crime prevention*

preventive /prɪ'ventɪv/ adj done so that something does not become worse or become a problem

pre,ventive de'tention noun [U] **LAW** a situation in which someone is kept in prison in order to prevent them from committing more crimes, rather than as a punishment

pre,ventive 'medicine noun [U] **HEALTH** medical treatments, advice etc intended to prevent disease or to discover and stop it before it becomes serious

preview /'priː,vjuː/ noun [C] **1** **ARTS** an opportunity to see something such as a play, film, or work of art before it is shown to the public **2** a short description of something that will happen or will be available later —**preview** verb [T]

previous /'priːviəs/ adj a previous event, period, or thing happened or existed before the one that you are talking about: *Mark has two children from a previous marriage.* ♦ *All the other guests had arrived the previous day.* ♦ *No previous experience is required.*

previously /'priːviəsli/ adv before the present time, or before the time that you are discussing: *She was previously employed as a nurse.*

,pre-'war or **prewar** /,priː'wɔː/ adj from a time before a particular war

prey /preɪ/ noun [U] **1** **BIOLOGY** an animal that is hunted, killed, and eaten by another animal → **BIRD OF PREY** **2** someone who is attacked, cheated, or harmed by a criminal or dishonest person= **VICTIM**

price¹ /praɪs/ noun **1** [C] the amount of money that you have to pay in order to buy something: *Oil was at its lowest price in 30 years.* ♦ *For a limited period only, all our carpets are being sold at half price.* ♦ *They'll do the work for you, at a price* (=for a lot of money). **2** [singular] the bad things that you have to accept in order to achieve something that you want: *For some of these young athletes, success comes at a heavy price.* ♦ *She has fulfilled her dream, but at what price?*
PHRASE **at any price** *showing disapproval* if you want something at any price, you are determined to get it, even if this causes serious problems **2** if you refuse to do something at any price, you refuse to do it, even for a lot of money or other benefits

price² /praɪs/ verb [T] **1** to set the price of a product or service: *The farmhouse is priced at £195,000.* **2** to compare prices at different shops or companies before buying something

'price con,trol noun [C/U] **ECONOMICS** control of the prices of goods and services by the government, usually during a period of economic difficulty

'price-,cutting noun [U] **BUSINESS** the practice of reducing prices in order to sell more than other companies

,price-'earnings ,ratio or **,price-'earnings ,multiple** noun [C] **BUSINESS** a way of measuring the value of a company's shares by dividing the price of each share by what the company earns from it

priceless /'praɪsləs/ adj **1** very valuable and impossible to replace **2** extremely useful in helping you to achieve something

'price ,point noun [C] **BUSINESS** the price, chosen from a number of possible prices, at which a product is sold in shops

prick¹ /prɪk/ verb **1** [T] to make a very small hole in the surface of something with a sharp object **2** [I/T] to cause or experience a guilty or embarrassed feeling

prick² /prɪk/ noun [C] a quick feeling of pain, caused by a sharp object making a hole in your skin

prickle¹ /'prɪk(ə)l/ verb [I/T] if your skin prickles, or something prickles it, you feel as if something sharp is touching it

prickle² /'prɪk(ə)l/ noun [C] **1** an uncomfortable feeling on your skin as if something sharp is touching it **2** a sharp pointed part on a plant or animal

prickly /'prɪkli/ adj covered with prickles

pride¹ /praɪd/ noun **1** [U] a feeling of pleasure at your own achievements or those of someone you love: *They take a lot of pride in their daughter's career.* **2** [U] a feeling of respect for yourself= **DIGNITY**: *Their win has restored national pride.* → **SWALLOW¹** **3** [U] a feeling that you are better than other people **4** [C] **BIOLOGY** a group of lions
PHRASE **sb's pride and joy** a person or possession that gives someone a lot of happiness and satisfaction

pride² /praɪd/ verb **pride yourself on sth** to feel proud about an achievement, skill, or special quality that you have

priest /priːst/ noun [C] RELIGION **1** someone whose job is to perform religious duties and ceremonies in some Christian churches: *a Roman Catholic priest* **2** a man who performs religious duties in some religions that are not Christian —**priestly** adj

priestess /ˌpriːˈstes/ noun [C] RELIGION a woman who performs religious duties in some religions that are not Christian

priesthood /ˈpriːsthʊd/ noun RELIGION **1 the priesthood** [singular] the work and responsibility of being a priest **2** [C/U] all the priests of a particular religion

prim /prɪm/ adj very careful about your behaviour and easily shocked —**primly** adv

prima facie /ˌpraɪmə ˈfeɪʃi/ adj, adv *formal* based on what seems to be true, before a situation has been examined in detail

primarily /ˈpraɪm(ə)rəli, praɪˈmerəli/ adv mainly

primary /ˈpraɪməri/ adj **1** most important= MAIN: *Dealing with crime is our primary concern*. **2** EDUCATION relating to the education of children between the ages of about five and eleven: *primary education* **3** coming or happening before other things: *primary sources of information*

primary ˌcell noun [C] PHYSICS an **electrical cell** that cannot be **recharged** after use

primary ˈcolour noun [C] ARTS, PHYSICS one of the colours red, blue, or yellow that are combined to make the other colours. They can also be combined to make white light. → SECONDARY COLOUR

primary conˌsumer noun [C] BIOLOGY, ENVIRONMENT a living thing that feeds on plants at the bottom of the **food chain**, and is itself eaten by a **secondary consumer**

primary ˈproduct noun [C] ECONOMICS, AGRICULTURE a product such as wood, milk, or fish that is a basic raw material

primary ˈschool noun [C/U] EDUCATION a school for children between the ages of four or five and eleven

primary ˈstress noun [C/U] LANGUAGE the strongest emphasis that you give to a particular syllable when you say a word. Primary stress is marked ' in this dictionary.

primate /ˈpraɪˌmeɪt/ noun [C] BIOLOGY a mammal belonging to the same group as humans, including monkeys and **apes** —*picture* → TAXONOMY

prime /praɪm/ adj **1** most important= PRIMARY: *Our prime concern is the safety of our customers*. **2** of the highest quality: *prime beef* **3** most likely to be chosen or to be suitable for something: *the prime suspect in a murder case*

prime ˈcost noun [C/U] BUSINESS the cost of the **material** and **labour** (=workers) needed for making a product, but not including **fixed costs** such as rent → OVERHEAD

prime meˈridian noun [singular] GEOGRAPHY the imaginary line on the Earth's surface that all lines of longitude are measured from. It passes through Greenwich in England. —*picture* → EARTH

prime ˈminister noun [C] POLITICS the political leader in countries such as the UK that are governed by a parliament

prime ˈnumber noun [C] MATHS a number that can only be divided exactly by itself and the number 1, for example 7

primer /ˈpraɪmə/ noun **1** [U] a substance that is used for preparing a surface for paint **2** [C] a book that gives

very simple instructions or basic information about something

prime ˌrate noun [C] ECONOMICS the lowest rate available for borrowing money

prime ˌtime noun [U] the most popular time for watching television, which is in the middle of the evening

primeval /praɪˈmiːv(ə)l/ adj relating to the period when the universe or the Earth first began to exist

primitive /ˈprɪmətɪv/ adj **1** relating to a very early stage in the development of people, animals, or plants: *primitive fish* **2** very simple or old-fashioned: *a primitive computer* **3** natural, and done or experienced without thinking: *a primitive instinct*

primogeniture /ˌpraɪməʊˈdʒenɪtʃə/ noun [U] LAW the legal right of an eldest son to get his father's property after his father dies

prince /prɪns/ noun [C] **1** a male member of a royal family who is not the king **2** the male royal leader of some small countries

princess /ˌprɪnˈses/ noun [C] **1** a female member of a royal family who is not the queen **2** the wife of a prince

principal¹ /ˈprɪnsəp(ə)l/ adj main, or most important: *The principal aim of the project is to provide an answer to this question*.

principal² /ˈprɪnsəp(ə)l/ noun

1 main actor etc in performance	3 head of school
2 head of college/university	4 money borrowed
	5 in law

1 [C] ARTS the main actor, dancer, singer etc in a performance: *The show had eight principals and more than twenty dancers*.
2 [C] EDUCATION the head of a college or university: *the Principal of Glasgow University*
3 [C] EDUCATION the head of a school in the US and some other countries
4 [singular] BUSINESS the original amount of money that someone borrows. It is paid back with additional money called **interest**.
5 [C] LAW a person or organization that has someone to represent them in legal and business matters

principality /ˌprɪnsəˈpæləti/ (plural **principalities**) noun [C] a country that is ruled by a prince

principally /ˈprɪnsəp(ə)li/ adv mainly

principal ˈparts noun [plural] LANGUAGE the basic forms of an English verb, from which other verb forms are made, such as the infinitive, **past tense**, and **past participle**

principle /ˈprɪnsəp(ə)l/ noun **1** [C] a basic belief, theory, or rule that has a major influence on the way in which something is done: *the principle that education should be free to everyone* ♦ *It is a basic principle of English law that a person is innocent until proven guilty*. **2** [C/U] a basic rule or belief about what is right that influences the way you behave: *We are opposed on principle to any further building in the valley*. ♦ *It was against their principles to join the armed forces*. **3** [C] a scientific theory or basic natural law that explains the way something works: *Windmills differ in design, but all operate on exactly the same principle*.
PHRASE **in principle** used for saying that something is possible in theory, although it has not been tried

principled /ˈprɪnsəp(ə)ld/ adj honest and able to be trusted to do the right thing ≠ UNPRINCIPLED

print¹ /prɪnt/ verb

1 produce on paper	**4** press surface
2 publish	**5** produce photo
3 write by hand	+ PHRASAL VERB

1 [I/T] to produce words, numbers, pictures etc on paper, using a printer or **printing press**: *The book is beautifully printed on quality paper.*

2 [T] to publish something in a newspaper or magazine: *They refused to print my letter.*

3 [I/T] to write by hand using individual letters that are not joined together: *Please be sure to **print your name** next to your signature.*

4 [T] to create a mark on a surface by pressing something into it: *He had printed his initials in the sand.*

5 [I/T] to produce a photograph on paper

PHRASAL VERB ,print sth 'out or ,print sth 'off **COMPUTING** to produce a copy of a computer document from a printer

print² /prɪnt/ noun

1 mark	**5** photograph
2 of fingers	**6** cloth with pattern
3 letters	+ PHRASE
4 picture	

1 [C] a mark made by pressing something onto a surface: *There were huge paw prints right outside our tent.*

2 [C] a **fingerprint**

3 [U] letters or other symbols made by pressing ink, paint etc on paper or a similar surface: *The print is too small to read.*

4 [C] **ARTS** an image that is created by pressing a raised design onto paper, or by copying an existing image: *a limited-edition print*

5 [C] a photograph: *old black and white prints*

6 [C/U] a piece of clothing or cloth with a pattern printed on it: *She was wearing a bold flowered print.*

PHRASE in print printed in a book, magazine, or newspaper

printed circuit /,prɪntɪd 'sɜːkɪt/ noun [C] **COMPUTING** a narrow line of metal in a very thin layer that is put on a board to carry an electronic signal instead of a wire. The board it is on is called a **printed circuit board**.

printer /'prɪntə/ noun [C] **1 COMPUTING** a piece of equipment that you use for printing documents that you have created on a computer *—picture* → COMPUTER **2** a person or business that prints books, newspapers etc

printing /'prɪntɪŋ/ noun **1** [U] the process of making books, newspapers etc, using a printing press **2** [C] the number of copies of something such as a book or newspaper that are printed at one time

'printing ,press noun [C] a machine that is used for printing newspapers, books etc

printmaking /'prɪnt,meɪkɪŋ/ noun [U] **ARTS** the art or process of making prints by pressing paper against a surface that has a raised design covered with ink *—***printmaker** noun [C]

printout /'prɪnt,aʊt/ noun [C/U] **COMPUTING** paper that is printed with information from a computer file

'print ,preview noun [U] **COMPUTING** a feature of a software product that lets you see how a page will look when you print it

prion /'praɪɒn, 'priːɒn/ noun [C] **BIOLOGY, HEALTH** a type of protein that is believed to be responsible for the brain diseases **BSE** and **CJD**

prior /'praɪə/ adj *formal* happening, existing, or done before a particular time= PREVIOUS: *I'm afraid I won't be able to come. I've got **a prior engagement**.* ♦ *students with no **prior knowledge** of English*

PHRASE prior to sth before something happened or existed: *The plane appeared to catch fire a few seconds prior to taking off.*

priority /praɪ'ɒrəti/ (plural **priorities**) noun **1** [C] something important that must be done first, or that needs more attention than anything else: *Health insurance will be our **top priority**.* **2** [U] the importance that you give to something that must be done: *Their marriage **took priority over** everything else.* ♦ *Safety must **be given** the highest **priority**.* **3** [U] the right to go before someone or something else, or to receive something before they do: *Buses **take priority over** other vehicles on the road.* *—***prioritize** verb [I/T]

prise /praɪz/ verb [T] to force two things apart

prism /'prɪz(ə)m/ noun [C] **1 MATHS** a solid object that has a regular shape and can be cut into **slices** that all have the same shape. A prism usually has two or more sides shaped like a triangle. *—picture* → SHAPE **2 SCIENCE** a glass or plastic object in the shape of a prism, used for dividing light into its different colours

prison /'prɪz(ə)n/ noun [C/U] an institution where people are kept as a punishment for committing a crime: *He's currently **in prison** for tax fraud.* ♦ *You can **go to prison** for that, you know.* ♦ *He was **sent to prison** for armed robbery.* ♦ *She could face a ten-year **prison term** (=period in prison).*

'prison ,camp noun [C] a place where prisoners are kept during a war

prisoner /'prɪz(ə)nə/ noun [C] someone who is in prison, or who is being kept somewhere against their will: *He was **taken prisoner** during the battle.*

PHRASE prisoner of war someone who is held as a prisoner by the enemy during a war= POW

'prison ,officer noun [C] someone whose job is to guard and take care of prisoners in a prison= WARDER

pristine /'prɪstiːn/ adj something that is pristine looks very clean, tidy, or new

privacy /'prɪvəsi, 'praɪvəsi/ noun [U] the freedom to do things without other people watching you or knowing what you are doing

private¹ /'praɪvət/ adj

1 not for everyone	**5** not government
2 secret	**6** not public
3 person	+ PHRASE
4 not work	

1 used only by a particular person or group, or available only to them: *a private bathroom*

2 used about places or situations where other people cannot see or hear you: *They found a private spot where they could talk.*

3 a private person does not talk to other people about their personal life or feelings

4 not connected with someone's work or their public position: *What you do in your **private life** has nothing to do with your boss.*

5 BUSINESS controlled or owned by individual people or companies, rather than by the government ≠ PUBLIC: *a private hospital*

6 with no position in government or public life: *a private citizen*

PHRASE in private in a place or situation where other people cannot watch or listen: *I'd like to talk with you in private, if you don't mind.*

private² /'praɪvət/ noun [C] the lowest rank of soldier in the army

private 'company noun [C] BUSINESS a company that is owned by a person or group of people who do not sell shares in it to the public

private 'enterprise noun [C/U] BUSINESS, ECONOMICS a business or industry that is owned and managed by independent people or businesses, rather than by the government

private key cryp'tography noun [U] COMPUTING a way of keeping Internet messages secret in which a single **key** (=letter or number) changes the message into code, and back again

privately /'praɪvətli/ adv **1** in a place where no other people can see or hear you: *We wanted to speak privately.* **2** used about thoughts or feelings that you do not express: *Privately, he hoped they would refuse.* **3** by people who provide money themselves, rather than by governments: *privately owned businesses*

private 'school noun [C] EDUCATION a school that the children's parents pay for directly to the school

the 'private ,sector noun [singular] ECONOMICS all the businesses, industries, and services that are not owned or managed by the government

private 'treaty noun [U] BUSINESS an agreement to sell property that is made directly between the person selling the property and the person buying it

private 'view or **private 'viewing** noun [C] ARTS an event at which certain people are invited to see something such as a film or an exhibition before it is opened to the public

privatize /'praɪvətaɪz/ verb [T] ECONOMICS to sell a business or industry that was owned and managed by the government so that it becomes a private business ≠ NATIONALIZE —**privatization** /,praɪvətaɪ'zeɪʃ(ə)n/ noun [C/U]

privilege /'prɪvəlɪdʒ/ noun **1** [C] a special benefit that is available only to a particular person or group: *Cheap air travel is one of the privileges of working for the airline.* **2** [C] something nice that you feel lucky to have: *It's been a privilege to be involved in such an interesting project.* **3** [U] a way of life that involves having many advantages and opportunities, without working hard for them: *a life of privilege* **4** [U] LAW a situation in which lawyers, doctors, and other professional people are legally allowed to keep their discussions with people secret

privileged /'prɪvəlɪdʒd/ adj **1** having advantages and opportunities that other people do not have: *a privileged background* **2** LAW privileged information is secret and does not have to be discussed in court

prize¹ /praɪz/ noun [C] **1** a reward that you get for being successful in a competition, or for being good at something: *the Nobel Prize for chemistry* ♦ *Peter Turnbull won **first prize** (=the prize that is given to the person who is first in a competition).* **2** something very important that someone tries very hard to get: *the prize of freedom/peace*

prize² /praɪz/ adj good enough to deserve or win a prize: *a prize calf*

prize³ /praɪz/ verb [T] to think that something is very important and special: *He prized his car above everything else.*

'prize ,day noun [C] EDUCATION a day at school when prizes are given to students for doing well in particular subjects or in sports

prize-giving /'praɪz ,gɪvɪŋ/ noun [C] EDUCATION a ceremony where prizes are given in a school

pro /prəʊ/ (plural **pros**) noun [C] *informal* someone who works in sport, music, or art as a professional = PROFESSIONAL
PHRASE **pros and cons** advantages and disadvantages

pro- /prəʊ/ prefix supporting or approving of something: *pro-democracy groups*

proactive /prəʊ'æktɪv/ adj taking action and making changes before they need to be made, instead of waiting until problems develop

pro-am /,prəʊ'æm/ noun [C] SPORTS a sports event in which professional and **amateur** players compete together —**pro-'am** adj

probability /,prɒbə'bɪləti/ (plural **probabilities**) noun **1** [singular/U] a measure of how likely something is to happen or be true: *What is **the probability of** success?* **2** [C/U] MATHS a calculation of how likely something is: *There is a 20% probability that he could develop the cancer.* ♦ *the laws of probability* **3** [singular] something that is likely to happen or be true: *War is now a probability rather than a possibility.*
PHRASE **in all probability** used for saying that you think that something is very likely

probable /'prɒbəb(ə)l/ adj likely to happen or be true ≠ IMPROBABLE: *It seems probable that the chairman will resign.*

probably /'prɒbəbli/ adv used for saying that you think that something is likely: *You'll probably be gone by the time I get back.* ♦ *'Are you going to accept their offer?' **'Probably not.'***

probate /'prəʊbeɪt/ noun [U] LAW the process of proving that a **will** (=a document with the details of who gets property when someone dies) can be accepted as legally correct

probation /prə'beɪʃ(ə)n/ noun [U] **1** LAW a system by which someone who has committed a crime is not sent to prison if they promise to behave well for a specific period of time **2** BUSINESS a period of time during which someone who has a new job is watched to see whether they can do the job well

probe¹ /prəʊb/ verb **1** [I/T] to try to find out the truth about something, especially by asking a lot of questions **2** [T] to examine something by using your fingers or a tool —**probing** adj

probe² /prəʊb/ noun [C] **1** HEALTH a long thin medical instrument that is used for examining things inside the body **2** ASTRONOMY a **space probe**

problem /'prɒbləm/ noun [C] **1** something that causes trouble or difficulty: *the problem of unemployment* ♦ *We've been **having problems with** our neighbours.* ♦ *They're the best cameras on the market. **The only problem is** they're incredibly expensive.* **2** a question that someone is given to answer as a test of their ability: *mathematical problems*

problematic /,prɒblə'mætɪk/ or **problematical** /,prɒblə'mætɪk(ə)l/ adj involving or causing problems

problem-solving /'prɒbləm ,sɒlvɪŋ/ noun [U] the process of finding solutions to problems

pro bono /prəʊ 'bəʊnəʊ/ adj, adv LAW done without the usual payment that a lawyer charges

proboscis /prə'bɒsɪs/ noun [C] BIOLOGY **1** the long nose of some mammals, for example an elephant's **trunk 2** a long tube on the outside of the mouth of some insects that is used for sucking

procedure /prə'siːdʒə/ noun [C] **1** a way of doing something, especially the correct or usual way: *The **procedure for** doing this is explained fully in the next chapter.* ♦ *Those ticket holders who **followed the***

proper **procedure** will receive a full refund. **2** HEALTH a medical operation that is done in a particular way —**procedural** /prəˈsiːdʒ(ə)rəl/ adj

proceed /prəˈsiːd/ verb [I] **1** formal to continue doing something: The council is **proceeding with** its plan to move the stadium. **2** formal to go in a particular direction: Passengers for flight 406 to New York should **proceed to** Gate 32. **3** used for telling other people about a surprising or annoying thing that someone has done: He placed the remainder of the apple in his mouth and proceeded to eat the core, stalk, and pips. **4** to make progress by moving to the next stage in a series of actions or events: The Australian team will **proceed to** the quarterfinals.

PHRASAL VERB proˈceed aˌgainst sb LAW to begin a case against someone in a court of law

proceedings /prəˈsiːdɪŋz/ noun [plural] **1** LAW the actions that are taken to settle a legal matter, usually in court **2** an event or series of related events **3** formal an official record giving the details of what happened in a meeting

proceeds /ˈprəʊsiːdz/ noun [plural] money that a person or organization makes from selling or winning something, or from organizing an event

process¹ /ˈprəʊses/ noun [C] **1** a series of things that happen naturally and have a particular result: Changes occur in the body because of **the process of** ageing. **2** a series of actions that you take that have a particular result: Learning a language is a slow process. ♦ an industrial process

PHRASE **in the process of doing sth** involved in doing something at the present time

process² /ˈprəʊses/ verb [T] **1** COMPUTING to put information into a computer in order to organize it: **Data** is processed as it is received. **2** to deal with a document officially: 28,000 **applications** have still to be processed. **3** to make photographs from film by treating it with chemicals **4** to treat food or another substance with chemicals or machines: processed cheese —**processing** noun [U]: the food processing industry

procession /prəˈseʃ(ə)n/ noun [C] **1** a line of people or vehicles that are moving in a slow formal way as part of an event **2** a series of people or things

processor /ˈprəʊsesə/ noun [C] **1** COMPUTING the part of a computer that controls and performs all its operations **2** a **food processor**

proclaim /prəˈkleɪm/ verb [T] to announce or state something officially or publicly

proclamation /ˌprɒkləˈmeɪʃ(ə)n/ noun [C/U] an official or public announcement, or the act of making an official or public announcement

procrastinate /prəʊˈkræstɪneɪt/ verb [I] to delay doing something until later because you do not want to do it —**procrastination** /prəʊˌkræstɪˈneɪʃ(ə)n/ noun [U]

procreate /ˈprəʊkrieɪt/ verb [I/T] formal to produce babies or young animals —**procreation** /ˌprəʊkriˈeɪʃ(ə)n/ noun [U]

procure /prəˈkjʊə/ verb [T] formal to obtain something, especially with effort or difficulty

procurement /prəˈkjʊəmənt/ noun [U] the process of buying supplies or equipment for a government department or a company

prod /prɒd/ (**prods**, **prodding**, **prodded**) verb [I/T] **1** to push someone or something quickly with your finger, or with an object that has a long thin end **2** to persuade or encourage someone to do something

prodigious /prəˈdɪdʒəs/ adj very great, or impressive: a prodigious appetite

prodigy /ˈprɒdədʒi/ (plural **prodigies**) noun [C] a young person who has a natural ability to do something extremely well

produce¹ /prəˈdjuːs/ verb **1** [T] to make or grow something: We are now producing the same quantity of goods with fewer workers. ♦ The body produces chemicals to control the pain. ♦ The region produces some of the best wine in France. **2** [T] to cause something to happen: I managed to produce the opposite effect from the one I had intended. **3** [T] to show or offer something so that it can be examined or used by someone else: They **produced** very little **evidence** in support of their argument. **4** [I/T] ARTS to organize the work and money that are involved in making a film, play, television or radio programme, CD etc: Steve McQueen produced and starred in the film.

> **Word family: produce**
>
> Words in the same family as **produce**:
> - **producer** n
> - **product** n
> - **production** n
> - **productive** adj
> - **productively** adv
> - **productivity** n
> - **reproduce** v
> - **reproduction** n
> - **reproductive** adj
> - **unproductive** adj

produce² /ˈprɒdjuːs/ noun [U] fruit, vegetables, and other things that farmers grow

producer /prəˈdjuːsə/ noun [C] **1** ARTS someone whose job is to organize the work and money that are involved in making a film, play, television or radio programme, CD etc **2** BUSINESS a person, company, or country that grows food or makes goods to be sold: a grain producer **3** BIOLOGY an organism such as a green plant that makes its own food from simple inorganic compounds and is itself used as food by other organisms —picture → FOOD WEB

proˈducer ˌgoods noun [plural] BUSINESS materials, equipment, and other goods that are used to make a product that is sold to customers

product /ˈprɒdʌkt/ noun **1** [C/U] something that is made, grown, or obtained in large quantities so that it can be sold: software products **2** [C] something or someone that is the result of particular actions, events, or influences: The system we have now is **the product of** years of research. **3** [C] MATHS a number that is the result of multiplying two other numbers **4** [C] CHEMISTRY, BIOLOGY a substance that is produced as a result of a chemical reaction in living and non-living things

production /prəˈdʌkʃ(ə)n/ noun **1** [U] BUSINESS the process of making or growing things in large quantities so that they can be sold: **the production of** goods for sale in the Far East **2** [U] the natural process of making a substance: the body's **production of** hormones **3** [C/U] ARTS a film, play, television or radio programme, CD etc, or the process of making it: the Royal Shakespeare Company's **production of** Macbeth

productive /prəˈdʌktɪv/ adj **1** making or growing things in large quantities: This is **highly productive** farming country. **2** producing or achieving a lot ≠ UNPRODUCTIVE: a very productive meeting —**productively** adv

productivity /ˌprɒdʌkˈtɪvəti/ noun [U] ECONOMICS the rate at which goods are produced, especially in relation to the time, money, and workers that are needed to produce them

ˌproduct liaˈbility noun [U] BUSINESS, LAW the legal responsibility of a company that makes or sells a product to pay someone money if their product causes damage or injury

'product ,recall noun [U] BUSINESS a request from a company to shops or customers to return a product that may not work properly or may be dangerous

Prof. /prɒf/ abbrev EDUCATION Professor: used in writing before the name of a professor

profess /prə'fes/ verb [T] formal **1** to claim something, especially when it is not true **2** to admit publicly that you have a particular feeling or belief

professed /prə'fest/ adj formal **1** admitting publicly that you have a particular feeling or belief **2** used for describing something that you claim to be true but that is possibly false

profession /prə'feʃ(ə)n/ noun [C] **1** a job that you need special skills and qualifications to do: Her father discouraged her from going into the legal profession. ♦ He was a teacher **by profession** (=as his job). **2** all the people who work in a particular profession: The medical profession is always telling us we should exercise more.

professional¹ /prə'feʃ(ə)nəl/ adj **1** relating to work that needs special skills and qualifications: Teachers must be free to exercise their **professional judgment**. **2** relating to a profession or working in a profession: professional qualifications **3** playing a sport or taking part in an activity as a job rather than for enjoyment ≠ AMATEUR: a professional actor ♦ professional football **4** showing a high level of skill or training: They did **a thoroughly professional job**. —**professionalism** noun [U]

professional² /prə'feʃ(ə)nəl/ noun [C] **1** someone who does a job that you need special skills and qualifications to do: doctors and other professionals **2** SPORTS someone who plays a sport or takes part in an activity as a job rather than for enjoyment ≠ AMATEUR **3** someone who has a lot of skill or training ≠ AMATEUR: You've got the makings of a real professional.

professionally /prə'feʃ(ə)nəli/ adv **1** with the formal qualifications that are necessary for a particular profession: professionally qualified staff **2** in a way that shows the type of behaviour and skills that someone with a professional job is expected to have: She hasn't behaved very professionally, has she? **3** in a way that is connected with your work: Without Nina's help I wouldn't be where I am today professionally. **4** as a job rather than for enjoyment: She has been acting professionally since she was 17.

professor /prə'fesə/ noun [C] EDUCATION **1** a senior teacher in a college or university. Someone begins as a **lecturer**, then becomes a **senior lecturer**, then sometimes a **reader**, and finally a **professor**. **2** American a teacher in a college or university. Someone begins as an **assistant professor**, then becomes an **associate professor**, and finally a **full professor**.

proffer /'prɒfə/ verb [T] formal **1** to offer someone something by moving it towards them **2** to offer someone something such as an explanation or **apology**

proficiency /prə'fɪʃ(ə)nsi/ noun [U] great skill

proficient /prə'fɪʃ(ə)nt/ adj very good at something —**proficiently** adv

profile /'prəʊfaɪl/ noun [C] **1** the public image of a person or organization, and the attention that they get from the public or journalists: We have done a lot to change the profile of the company. ♦ She's trying to **keep a low profile** (=avoid being noticed). **2** a short article or television or radio programme about someone: a profile of the British royal family **3** the

shape of someone's face when you look at them from the side: She turned his head so she could see his profile. **4** CONSTRUCTION a wooden board that marks the edges of **excavations** and walls

'profile ,cutting noun [U] ENGINEERING a process in which a piece of metal such as a **gear** is cut into a particular shape

profit /'prɒfɪt/ noun **1** [C/U] BUSINESS money that you get when you sell something for a price that is higher than the cost of making it or buying it ≠ LOSS: Investors have **made a** 14% **profit** in just 3 months. ♦ the practice of killing whales **for profit** (=in order to make money) ♦ They were buying computers and reselling them **at a profit** (=so that they made a profit). ♦ The **profit on** that deal was £21 million. ♦ All the **profits from** the sales of the CD will go to charity. ♦ The company's **profits rose** to £144 million last year. **2** [U] formal the advantage that you get from a situation

profitable /'prɒfɪtəb(ə)l/ adj **1** BUSINESS making a profit: a profitable business **2** giving you a benefit or advantage: The trip should be an enjoyable and profitable experience. —**profitability** /,prɒfɪtə'bɪləti/ noun [U], **profitably** adv

,profit and 'loss ac,count noun [C] BUSINESS a document that shows a company's income and **expenditure** during a particular period of time, and how much profit or loss it has made

'profit ,centre noun [C] BUSINESS a part of a company that has its own income and costs, so that it is possible to calculate how much profit it makes

'profit-,making adj BUSINESS a profit-making organization exists in order to make a profit

'profit ,margin noun [C] BUSINESS the amount by which the income from sales is greater than the costs of making a product or providing a service

profit-sharing /'prɒfɪt ,ʃeərɪŋ/ noun [U] BUSINESS a system by which all the employees of a company get a share in the profits

'profits ,warning noun [C] BUSINESS an announcement by a company that profits for a particular period will be lower than expected

profligate /'prɒflɪgət/ adj formal wasting money or other things —**profligacy** noun [U]

,pro-'form noun [C] LANGUAGE a word, usually a pronoun, that is used in place of another word to avoid repeating it

pro ,forma 'invoice noun [C] BUSINESS a document that gives details of goods or services that someone has bought and must pay for. It is sent to them before or when the goods or services are provided.

profound /prə'faʊnd/ adj **1** very great: My grandfather's death had a profound effect on my father. **2** showing intelligence and serious thought: a very profound statement **3** very severe —**profoundly** adv

profuse /prə'fjuːs/ adj existing in large amounts —**profusely** adv

profusion /prə'fjuːʒ(ə)n/ noun [singular] formal a large amount of something

progesterone /prəʊ'dʒestərəʊn/ noun [U] BIOLOGY, HEALTH a hormone produced in the bodies of women and other female mammals that makes the uterus ready for pregnancy

progestin /prɒ'dʒestɪn/ noun [U] BIOLOGY a hormone such as progesterone that prepares a woman's body for pregnancy

proglottid /prəʊˈglɒtɪd/ noun [C] BIOLOGY one of the separate parts of a **tapeworm**'s body. Each part contains a complete reproductive system.

prognosis /prɒgˈnəʊsɪs/ (plural **prognoses** /prɒgˈnəʊsiːz/) noun [C] 1 HEALTH a doctor's opinion about how a disease is likely to develop 2 formal a statement about what is likely to happen in a particular situation → DIAGNOSIS

program¹ /ˈprəʊgræm/ noun [C] 1 COMPUTING a series of instructions that makes a computer or other piece of equipment do something automatically: a word processing program 2 the American spelling of **programme**

program² /ˈprəʊgræm/ (**programs, programming, programmed**) verb [T] COMPUTING to make a computer or other piece of equipment do something automatically —**programmable** /prəʊˈgræməb(ə)l, ˈprəʊgræməb(ə)l/ adj

programme¹ /ˈprəʊgræm/ noun [C] 1 a plan of activities for achieving something: a research programme ♦ an ambitious **programme** of educational expansion ♦ the government's **programme** for economic recovery 2 a series of planned events: a festival with an exciting musical programme 3 ARTS a television or radio broadcast: More people watch the news than any other programme. 4 ARTS a document that tells you what will happen in a performance or event

programme² /ˈprəʊgræm/ verb [T] 1 to make a person or animal behave in a particular way 2 to plan something → PROGRAM²

ˈprogramme ˌmusic noun [U] MUSIC music that describes a picture, a story, or an idea

programmer /ˈprəʊˌgræmə/ noun [C] COMPUTING someone whose job is to create computer programs

programming /ˈprəʊˌgræmɪŋ/ noun [U] COMPUTING the activity of creating computer programs

ˈprogramming ˌlanguage noun [C] COMPUTING a set of words and rules for writing computer programs

progress¹ /ˈprəʊgres/ noun [U] 1 the process of developing or improving: Keep me informed about **the progress of** the project. ♦ I'm worried about my son's lack of **progress in** English. ♦ Negotiators have **made** considerable **progress** in the peace talks. 2 forward movement: the ship's slow progress across the harbour
  PHRASE **in progress** happening, or being done: The road will be closed while the maintenance work is in progress.

progress² /prəʊˈgres/ verb 1 [I] to continue to develop: Work on the project is progressing well. 2 [T] BUSINESS to cause something such as an idea or a plan to move forward

progression /prəʊˈgreʃ(ə)n/ noun 1 [U] gradual change or development = PROGRESS: The drug can slow **the progression of** the disease. 2 [C] a series of things

progressive /prəʊˈgresɪv/ adj 1 involving political change that aims to make society fairer: progressive forces 2 developing gradually: The disease causes progressive deterioration of the nervous system. 3 LANGUAGE the progressive form of a verb is used for showing that an action is continuing = CONTINUOUS 4 using the most modern ideas or methods: progressive music —**progressively** adv

proˌgressive ˈtax noun [singular] ECONOMICS a tax in which the percentage rate of tax increases as someone's income increases

prohibit /prəʊˈhɪbɪt/ verb [T] 1 to officially stop people from doing something = BAN: Smoking is prohibited inside the building. ♦ a rule prohibiting doctors **from** advertising their services 2 to prevent something from happening or being done —**prohibition** /ˌprəʊɪˈbɪʃ(ə)n/ noun [C/U]

prohibitive /prəʊˈhɪbɪtɪv/ adj a prohibitive price is so high that it prevents people from buying something —**prohibitively** adv

project¹ /ˈprɒdʒekt, ˈprəʊdʒekt/ noun [C] 1 an organized attempt to achieve something = SCHEME: The first phase of the project is now complete. ♦ an ambitious project to modernize the road network 2 a piece of work that involves collecting information: The university has set up **a** new **research project** to study language development in babies. ♦ Students must complete **a project on** a topic of their choice.

project² /prəˈdʒekt/ verb 1 [T] to calculate how something will develop in the future, using information that is available now = FORECAST, PREDICT: It is projected that the population will rise by one million by 2008. 2 [I] to stick out past the edge or surface of something: The edges of the roof project outwards and keep the rain away from the walls. 3 [T] to make people believe that someone or something has a particular quality: Ending the talks now would project an image of failure. 4 [T] to send an image to a screen or other surface

projectile /prəˈdʒektaɪl/ noun [C] formal an object that is shot or thrown as a weapon = MISSILE

projection /prəˈdʒekʃ(ə)n/ noun

1 calculation about future	3 sth that sticks out
2 sending image to screen	4 (method of making) map
	5 amount sth sticks out

1 [C] a calculation of the way that something will develop
2 [U] the action of sending an image to a screen
3 [C] something that sticks out from a surface
4 [C/U] GEOGRAPHY a method of making a flat map of the Earth, or a map made by this method
5 [U] CONSTRUCTION the distance that something sticks out

ˌproject ˈmanagement noun [U] BUSINESS the planning and organization of the work that a project involves, including deciding the **budget** (=money for spending on it) and organizing and controlling the people working on it

projector /prəˈdʒektə/ noun [C] a piece of equipment that is used for showing films or **slides** on a screen

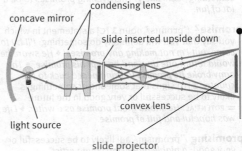

concave mirror
condensing lens
slide inserted upside down
light source
convex lens
slide projector

prokaryote /prəʊˈkærɪɒt/ noun [C] BIOLOGY an organism such as a bacterium in which the DNA is not contained within a nucleus —**prokaryotic** /prəʊˌkæriˈɒtɪk/ adj

prolapse /ˈprəʊlæps/ noun [C] HEALTH a medical condition in which an organ in the body moves out of its usual position —**prolapsed** adj

proletarian /ˌprəʊləˈteəriən/ adj SOCIAL STUDIES working-class

the proletariat /ˌprəʊləˈteəriət/ noun [singular] SOCIAL STUDIES working-class people considered as a social group

proliferate /prəˈlɪfəreɪt/ verb [I] formal to suddenly increase in number or amount

proliferation /prəˌlɪfəˈreɪʃ(ə)n/ noun [singular/U] formal a sudden increase in number or amount

prolific /prəˈlɪfɪk/ adj producing a lot of something: a prolific writer

prologue /ˈprəʊlɒg/ noun [C] LITERATURE, ARTS a short part at the start of a book, play etc that introduces the story

prolong /prəˈlɒŋ/ verb [T] to make something last longer

prolonged /prəˈlɒŋd/ adj continuing for a long time: a prolonged period of silence

promethium /prəˈmiːθiəm/ noun [U] CHEMISTRY a radioactive metallic element in the **lanthanide** group of the periodic table. Chemical symbol: **Pm**

prominence /ˈprɒmɪnəns/ noun [U] the state of being important and well known: a young actor who came **to prominence** last year

prominent /ˈprɒmɪnənt/ adj **1** important and well known: a prominent member of the government **2** easy to see or notice: prominent cheekbones ♦ a prominent feature of the landscape —**prominently** adv

promiscuous /prəˈmɪskjuəs/ adj showing disapproval someone who is promiscuous has a lot of sexual partners —**promiscuity** /ˌprɒmɪˈskjuːəti/ noun [U]

promise¹ /ˈprɒmɪs/ verb [I/T] **1** to tell someone that you will definitely do something: The police chief promised tougher action against young criminals. ♦ Promise me you'll be home before dark. ♦ She phoned at 9 am, **as promised**. ♦ Peter wished he'd never **promised to** help them. ♦ Relief organizations are promising aid to the country. **2** formal to make something seem likely: This evening promises to be a lot of fun.

promise² /ˈprɒmɪs/ noun **1** [C] a statement in which you say that you will definitely do something: I'll try to come, but I'm not **making** any **promises**! ♦ He swore he would return one day, and he **kept his promise**. ♦ The army **broke its promise** to bring peace back to the country. **2** [U] signs that someone or something is likely to be successful or very good in the future = POTENTIAL: He **shows** great **promise** as a writer. ♦ Life was hopeful and **full of promise**.

promising /ˈprɒmɪsɪŋ/ adj likely to be successful or very good: a highly promising young artist —**promisingly** adv

promontory /ˈprɒmənt(ə)ri/ (plural **promontories**) noun [C] GEOGRAPHY a narrow piece of land that sticks out into the sea

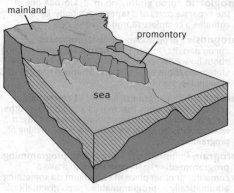
promontory

promote /prəˈməʊt/ verb [T] **1** to support something, or to help something to develop: a campaign to promote recycling ♦ Young plants are exposed to bright light to **promote growth**. **2** to attract people's attention to a product or event, for example by advertising: They are going on tour to promote their new album. **3** to move someone to a job at a higher level: Steve Burrows was recently **promoted to** senior manager.

promoter /prəˈməʊtə/ noun [C] someone who helps to start a new company or project

promotion /prəˈməʊʃ(ə)n/ noun **1** [C/U] a move to a job at a higher level: His main objective is to **get promotion**. ♦ his **promotion to** a position of leadership **2** [U] the activity of encouraging or supporting something: The campaign is concerned with **the promotion of** health. **3** [U] the process of advertising something: a ban on **the promotion of** tobacco products

promotional /prəˈməʊʃ(ə)nəl/ adj used for advertising something

prompt¹ /prɒmpt/ verb [T] **1** to cause something to happen: The birth of my first child prompted me to write this article. **2** to encourage someone to say something: Without being prompted, she began to apologize. **3** to remind an actor which words to say next —**prompting** /ˈprɒmptɪŋ/ noun [U]

prompt² /prɒmpt/ adj **1** immediate, or quick: Prompt action is required. **2** happening or arriving at exactly a particular time: The meeting got off to a prompt start at ten o'clock. —**promptly** adv, **promptness** noun [U]

prompt³ /prɒmpt/ adv at a particular time exactly: We begin at 9.00 prompt.

prompt⁴ /prɒmpt/ noun [C] **1** COMPUTING a sign on a computer screen that shows that the computer is ready for you to key something **2** a word or words that someone says to remind an actor what to say next

prone /prəʊn/ adj **1** likely to do something bad, or likely to be affected by something bad: an accident-prone child ♦ The region is **prone to** earthquakes. **2** formal lying flat with the front of your body facing downwards

prong /prɒŋ/ noun [C] one of the sharp points on a fork

pronominal¹ /prəʊˈnɒmɪn(ə)l/ adj LANGUAGE relating to a pronoun, or used as a pronoun —**pronominally** adv

pronominal² /prəʊˈnɒmɪn(ə)l/ noun [C] LANGUAGE a word that acts as a pronoun

pronoun /'prəʊnaʊn/ noun [C] LANGUAGE a word used instead of a noun that has been mentioned earlier, for example 'she', 'this', and 'yourself'

pronounce /prə'naʊns/ verb **1** [T] LANGUAGE to say the sounds of words: *I find some Japanese words very difficult to pronounce.* ♦ *Did I pronounce your name correctly?* **2** [I/T] *formal* to state an official opinion or decision: *The court pronounced her innocent of all charges.*

pronounced /prə'naʊnst/ adj very obvious or noticeable: *a pronounced German accent*

pronunciation /prə,nʌnsi'eɪʃ(ə)n/ noun [C/U] LANGUAGE the way in which a word or language is pronounced: *a guide to French pronunciation* ♦ *What is the correct pronunciation of 'cough'?*

proof /pru:f/ noun **1** [U] information or evidence that shows that something is definitely true: *Do you have any proof that this is true?* ♦ *We were unable to establish **proof of** her innocence.* ♦ *Do you have any **proof of identity** (=a document that proves who you are)?* **2** [U] the strength of an alcoholic drink **3** [C] a copy of a book or article that someone reads and corrects before the final copy is made

proofread /'pru:f,ri:d/ (**proofreads, proofreading, proofread** /'pru:f,red/) verb [I/T] to read and correct the mistakes in a piece of writing before the final copy is printed —**proofreader** /'pru:f,ri:də/ noun [C]

prop[1] /prɒp/ (**props, propping, propped**) verb [T] to hold something in position by putting an object under or against it, or by leaning it against an object: *I noticed a red bicycle **propped against** the wall.* ♦ *Prop the door open behind you so we don't get locked out.*

prop[2] /prɒp/ noun [C] **1** something that you put under or against an object in order to hold it up **2** ARTS an object that is used in a play or film **3** SPORTS one of the forward players in **rugby**

propaganda /,prɒpə'gændə/ noun [U] SOCIAL STUDIES information that a government or an organization spreads in order to influence people's opinions

propagate /'prɒpəgeɪt/ verb [T] **1** to spread ideas or beliefs to a lot of people **2** AGRICULTURE to produce plants from seed or from parts of another plant —**propagation** /,prɒpə'geɪʃ(ə)n/ noun [U]

propagator /'prɒpə,geɪtə/ noun [C] AGRICULTURE a covered box containing soil that is used for growing new plants

propane /'prəʊpeɪn/ noun [U] CHEMISTRY a hydrocarbon gas obtained from natural gas or petroleum and used as a fuel for cooking and heating. Chemical formula: C_3H_8

propel /prə'pel/ (**propels, propelling, propelled**) verb [T] **1** to move something forward: *a car propelled by solar energy* **2** to quickly put someone into a particular situation: *The film's success **propelled** him **to** stardom.*

propeller /prə'pelə/ noun [C] the part of a plane or ship that has blades that spin round to make it move

pro'peller ,shaft noun [C] ENGINEERING a **driveshaft** that connects a vehicle's **gearbox** to a rear **differential**

propensity /prə'pensəti/ (plural **propensities**) noun [C] a natural tendency to behave in a particular way

proper /'prɒpə/ adj **1** suitable for a particular purpose or situation: *You have to have the proper tools for the job.* ♦ *That's not **the proper way** to do it.* **2** considered to be real or serious: *When are you going to get a **proper job**?* **3** behaving in a way that is morally right or polite: *It's only **right and proper** that his family should be present.* **4** understood in its most exact meaning:

Does he live in Mumbai proper or in the suburbs?

,proper 'fraction noun [C] MATHS a fraction in which the number above the line is smaller than the number below the line, for example $\frac{1}{4}$ → IMPROPER FRACTION

properly /'prɒpəli/ adv in a correct or suitable way: *You're not **properly dressed** for this weather.* ♦ *If she doesn't **behave properly**, send her home.*

,proper 'noun noun [C] LANGUAGE a noun that is the name of a person, place, or thing, for example 'Mary', 'London', or 'Africa'

propertied /'prɒpətid/ adj SOCIAL STUDIES owning a lot of property, especially land

property /'prɒpəti/ (plural **properties**) noun **1** [U] the things that you own: *The books are my **personal property**.* ♦ *The police found a lot of **stolen property** in his house.* → INTELLECTUAL PROPERTY **2** [C/U] land and the buildings on it: *He owns several properties in London.* ♦ *The sign said '**Private Property**, Keep Out'.* ♦ *Property prices are rising.* **3** [C] a quality or feature of something: *The plants are believed to **have** healing **properties**.*

prophecy /'prɒfəsi/ (plural **prophecies**) noun [C] a statement about what will happen in the future

prophesy /'prɒfə,saɪ/ (**prophesies, prophesying, prophesied**) verb [T] to say what will happen in the future

prophet /'prɒfɪt/ noun [C] RELIGION **1** someone who is believed to have been sent by God to lead people and teach religious beliefs **2** the **Prophet** Muhammad, the **founder** of Islam

prophetic /prə'fetɪk/ adj saying what will happen in the future

prophylactic /,prɒfə'læktɪk/ adj HEALTH intended to prevent disease or infection

proportion /prə'pɔːʃ(ə)n/ noun

1 part of whole	4 relative importance
2 relative quantity	5 size or shape
3 of appearance	+ PHRASES

1 [C] MATHS a quantity of something that is a part of the whole: *Only a small **proportion of** graduates fail to get a job.*

2 [U] the relationship between two or more quantities or parts of a whole: ***The proportion of** trucks **to** cars on the roads has changed dramatically.*

3 [U] the correct or most attractive relationship between things: *Everything about the room **is** beautifully **in proportion**.* ♦ *His head is large **in proportion to** his body.* ♦ *The figures in the painting are completely **out of proportion with** their surroundings.*

4 [U] the importance of something in comparison with other things: *We need to keep **a sense of proportion** about what really matters.*

5 proportions [plural] the size or shape of something: *a chair of graceful proportions* ♦ *The tree can grow to massive proportions.*

PHRASES **blow sth up out of (all) proportion** to make a situation seem much worse than it really is

out of (all) proportion (to sth) too strong or serious for a particular situation

proportional /prə'pɔːʃ(ə)nəl/ adj **1** two things that are proportional to each other keep the same relationship to each other when they change in size or amount: *Proportional increases in income maintain the gap between rich and poor.* **2** not too big or too severe in relation to something else —**proportionally** /prə'pɔːʃ(ə)nəli/ adv

proportionality /prə,pɔːʃ(ə)n'æləti/ noun [U] MATHS, PHYSICS the quality that two quantities have of being related by a fixed ratio

proportionate /prə'pɔːʃ(ə)nət/ adj **1** not too big or too severe in relation to something else: *a punishment that is **proportionate to** the crime* **2** keeping the same relationship of size or amount to something else = PROPORTIONAL —**proportionately** adv

proposal /prə'pəʊz(ə)l/ noun [C] **1** an official plan or suggestion: ***Proposals for** a new health service are under discussion.* ♦ *a government **proposal to** impose a tax on fuel* **2** an occasion when you ask someone to marry you

propose /prə'pəʊz/ verb **1** [T] *formal* to suggest something: *She is proposing that we sell the house.* **2** [T] to make a formal suggestion, especially in a meeting: *I propose Sue Wilson for chairman.* ♦ *It was proposed that we postpone the next meeting.* ♦ *France has proposed creating an international force to deal with the crisis.* **3** [I] to ask someone to marry you: *He **proposed to** her in August.* **4** [T] *formal* if you propose to do something, you intend to do it

proposition /,prɒpə'zɪʃ(ə)n/ noun [C] **1** an offer or suggestion **2** a statement that people can examine in order to decide whether it is true **3** MATHS a problem or statement in mathematics or **logic** that must be solved, or must be proved true or false

proprietary /prə'praɪət(ə)ri/ adj **1** BUSINESS, LAW owned by a person or company and sold under a **trademark** or **patent 2** *formal* typical of an owner

pro'prietary ,name noun [C] BUSINESS, LAW the name of a product that is on an official list as a trademark

proprietor /prə'praɪətə/ noun [C] *formal* someone who owns a business

propulsion /prə'pʌlʃ(ə)n/ noun [U] PHYSICS the force that makes something move forwards

pro rata /,prəʊ 'rɑːtə/ adj, adv BUSINESS calculated according to how long someone works or how much of an amount is used

prorate /prəʊ'reɪt/ verb [T] BUSINESS to calculate, divide, or share something **pro rata**

prose /prəʊz/ noun [U] LITERATURE ordinary written language, not poetry

prosecute /'prɒsɪ,kjuːt/ verb LAW **1** [T] to officially accuse someone of a crime and ask a court of law to judge them **2** [I/T] to try to prove as a lawyer in court that someone is guilty of a crime

prosecution /,prɒsɪ'kjuːʃ(ə)n/ noun LAW **1** [U] the act of officially accusing someone of a crime and asking a court of law to judge them **2 the prosecution** [singular] the lawyers in a court who try to prove that someone is guilty of a crime → DEFENCE

prosody /'prɒsədi/ noun [U] LITERATURE the patterns of sounds and **beats** in poetry —**prosodic** /prə'sɒdɪk/ adj

prospect /'prɒspekt/ noun **1** [U] the possibility that something good will happen: *Doctors say there is little **prospect of** any improvement in his condition.* ♦ *We have an exciting match **in prospect**.* **2** [singular] something that you expect to happen in the future, or the thought of this: *Spending a week at his cousin's farm was an exciting prospect.* ♦ *We were very excited at **the prospect of** going home.* **3 prospects** [plural] chances of success in a career: *Your employment prospects would be much better if you finished your degree.*

prospective /prə'spektɪv/ adj likely to become a particular thing: *a prospective client*

prospectus /prə'spektəs/ noun [C] **1** EDUCATION a small book that describes a school or university and its courses **2** BUSINESS a document that provides details about a business to people who are interested in investing in it

prosper /'prɒspə/ verb [I] to be successful, or to become rich

prosperity /prɒ'sperəti/ noun [U] the situation of being successful and having a lot of money

prosperous /'prɒsp(ə)rəs/ adj rich and successful

prostate /'prɒ,steɪt/ or '**prostate ,gland** noun [C] ANATOMY the organ in men and other male mammals that produces a liquid that combines with and carries sperm

prosthesis /prɒs'θiːsɪs/ (plural **prostheses** /prɒs'θiːsiːz/) noun [C] HEALTH an artificial body part —**prosthetic** /prɒs'θetɪk/ adj

prostitute /'prɒstɪ,tjuːt/ noun [C] someone who has sex with people as their job

prostrate /'prɒstreɪt/ adj *formal* lying completely flat on the ground with the face downwards

protactinium /,prəʊtæk'tɪniəm/ noun [U] CHEMISTRY a toxic silvery metallic element in the **actinide** group of the periodic table. Chemical symbol: **Pa**

protagonist /prəʊ'tægənɪst/ noun [C] ARTS the main character in a play, film, or book

protease /'prəʊtieɪz/ noun [U] BIOLOGY an enzyme that helps the body to digest protein

protect /prə'tekt/ verb [T] **1** to keep someone or something safe: *The hat will **protect** his face **from** the sun.* ♦ *The jacket **protected** him **against** the cold.* **2** if an insurance policy protects someone against something, they will receive money if that particular thing happens: *Many of the homes weren't **protected against** flood damage.* —**protector** noun [C]

protected /prə'tektɪd/ adj ENVIRONMENT used about animals, plants, and other things that the law prevents people from damaging or destroying

protection /prə'tekʃ(ə)n/ noun [U] **1** the process of keeping someone or something safe: *the **protection** of the countryside* ♦ *A healthy diet should provide **protection against** disease.* ♦ *White clothes give your skin good **protection from** the sun.* **2** the agreement made by an insurance company to pay someone money if something bad happens to them: *protection in case of an accident*

protectionism /prə'tekʃ(ə)n,ɪz(ə)m/ noun [U] ECONOMICS a system in which a country helps its own industries by putting taxes on imports —**protectionist** adj, noun [C]

protective /prə'tektɪv/ adj **1** wanting to protect someone from being harmed or hurt: *He's very **protective towards** his sister.* **2** providing protection against something harmful or dangerous: *protective clothing*

protectorate /prə'tekt(ə)rət/ noun [C] POLITICS a country that is defended and controlled by a more powerful country

protein /'prəʊtiːn/ noun **1** [C] BIOLOGY an organic compound that is made of **amino acids**. Proteins contain carbon, hydrogen, oxygen, and nitrogen. **2** [U] HEALTH food such as meat, eggs, and milk that contain proteins and that people need in order to grow and be healthy. Protein is very important for building tissues such as muscles and for keeping them healthy:

The villagers' main source of protein is fish from the river. ♦ *a diet that is **high in protein***

'**protein ,energy malnu,trition** noun [U] HEALTH a condition in which a person's body begins to get energy from its tissues, rather than its fat, because there is no more body fat

'**protein ,synthesis** noun [U] BIOLOGY the process by which proteins are made in a cell, on the **ribosomes**. Amino acids are joined in a specific order to produce specific proteins, according to the genetic information carried in the cell.

protest¹ /'prəʊtest/ noun **1** [C/U] a strong complaint or disagreement: *a formal **protest against** nuclear testing* ♦ *She resigned **in protest** during the scandal.* **2** [C] an occasion when people show strong public opposition to something: *a protest march* ♦ *Students will **stage a protest** this weekend outside Parliament.*
PHRASE **under protest** if you do something under protest, you do it but you tell people that you think that it is unfair

protest² /prə'test/ verb **1** [I] to show publicly that you oppose something: *Workers are **protesting against** high unemployment.* ♦ *Prisoners began **protesting at** their conditions.* **2** [T] to try to make other people believe that something is true= SWEAR: *She still **protests** her **innocence**.* —**protester** noun [C]

Protestant /'prɒtɪstənt/ noun [C] RELIGION a member of a group of Christian churches that separated from the Roman Catholic Church in the 16th century —**Protestant** adj

protist /'prəʊtɪst/ noun [C] BIOLOGY a microorganism that consists of only one cell and belongs to the **kingdom** that includes protozoa such as amoebas

protocol /'prəʊtəkɒl/ noun **1** [U] rules for correct behaviour **2** [C] COMPUTING a method of sending information between computers

protoctist /prəʊ'tɒktɪst/ noun [C] BIOLOGY a single-celled organism, or a simple organism consisting of many cells

proton /'prəʊtɒn/ noun [C] CHEMISTRY, PHYSICS the part of the nucleus of an atom that has a positive electrical charge. In an atom, the number of protons equals the number of electrons and is the same as the atomic number of the element. → ELECTRON, NEUTRON —*picture* → ATOM

'**proton ,number** noun [C] CHEMISTRY the number of protons in the nucleus of an atom

protoplasm /'prəʊtəplæz(ə)m/ noun [U] BIOLOGY the substance that the cells of living things are made of. It consists of the **cytoplasm** and the nucleus.

prototype /'prəʊtətaɪp/ noun [C] the first form of something new that is made before it is produced in large quantities

protozoan /ˌprəʊtə'zəʊən/ (plural **protozoans** or **protozoa** /ˌprəʊtə'zəʊə/) noun [C] BIOLOGY a very small organism such as an amoeba that is made up of only one cell. Protozoans are able to move and live in water or as parasites in other organisms. —**protozoal** adj

protozoon /ˌprəʊtə'zəʊɒn/ noun [C] BIOLOGY a **protozoan**

protracted /prə'træktɪd/ adj formal continuing for a longer time than normal or necessary= LENGTHY, LONG

protractor /prə'træktə/ noun [C] MATHS an object that is shaped like half a circle and is used for measuring and drawing angles

protrude /prə'truːd/ verb [I] to stick out from a surface

protrusion /prə'truːʒ(ə)n/ noun [C] a part of something that sticks out from a surface

proud /praʊd/ adj **1** feeling happy about your achievements, your possessions, or people you are connected with: *We're proud that they chose our hotel for their conference.* ♦ *We're so **proud of** her for telling the truth.* ♦ *I'm **proud to say** we made the right decision.* **2** a proud person does not like other people to help them or to think that they are weak ≠ HUMBLE: *a proud and independent nation* ♦ *I was too proud to admit I didn't understand.* **3** showing disapproval someone who is proud thinks that they are better than other people= ARROGANT —**proudly** adv

prove /pruːv/ (**proves, proving, proved, proved** or **proven** /'pruːv(ə)n, 'prəʊv(ə)n/) verb **1** [T] to provide evidence that shows that something is true: *You have to prove you are sorry for what you've done.* ♦ *Recent excellent results have proved their critics wrong.* ♦ *He is still fighting to **prove his innocence**.* ♦ *She was determined to **prove to** her parents that she could live on her own.* **2** [linking verb] if something proves to have a particular quality, things happen that show that it has that quality: *The film is proving very profitable.* ♦ *My decision proved to be a good one.*
PHRASE **prove yourself** to show how good you are at doing something

> Build your vocabulary: words you can use instead of **prove**
>
> ■ **show** used for saying that an event, action, or fact proves that something exists or that something is true
> ■ **demonstrate** to prove something very clearly, by providing definite information
> ■ **confirm** to provide evidence that definitely proves something that people already believed
> ■ **indicate** to show that something is very likely to be true

proven¹ /'pruːv(ə)n, 'prəʊv(ə)n/ adj shown to be true, real, or effective

proven² /'pruːv(ə)n, 'prəʊv(ə)n/ a past participle of **prove**

proverb /'prɒvɜːb/ noun [C] a short well-known statement that gives practical advice about life = SAYING

provide /prə'vaɪd/ verb [T] **1** to give someone something that they want or need: *The hotel provides a playroom for children.* ♦ *We provide legal advice to our clients.* ♦ *Our office can **provide information** on the local area.* ♦ *The lecture **provided** him **with** an opportunity to meet one of his heroes.* **2** to cause something to exist or be available: *The film provides new insights into the problems that women in the industry face.* **3** [I/T] LAW to contain statements or plans that set conditions for dealing with a particular issue

provided /prə'vaɪdɪd/ or **providing** /prə'vaɪdɪŋ/ conjunction only if a particular thing happens or is done: *You can go out to play provided you finish your homework first.* ♦ *We'll all be there providing that Al can get time off work.*

providence /'prɒvɪdəns/ noun [U] literary a powerful force that some people believe causes everything that happens to us= DESTINY, FATE

provider /prə'vaɪdə/ noun [C] BUSINESS a company that provides a service

province /'prɒvɪns/ noun **1** [C] one of the large areas that some countries are divided into **2 the provinces**

[plural] the parts of a country that are outside the capital city or the large cities

provincial /prə'vɪnʃ(ə)l/ adj **1** in the parts of a country that are not the capital city or the large cities **2** old-fashioned or conservative: *provincial attitudes to modern art*

provision /prə'vɪʒ(ə)n/ noun **1** [U] the act of providing something that someone needs **2** [C/U] plans to provide things that you will need in the future: *We've made provision for our grandchild's education.* **3** [C] a part of a law that deals with a particular problem **4 provisions** [plural] food and other necessary supplies, especially for a journey

provisional /prə'vɪʒ(ə)nəl/ adj intended to be temporary and therefore likely to be changed —**provisionally** adv

provocation /ˌprɒvə'keɪʃ(ə)n/ noun [C/U] something that makes you react in an angry or violent way

provocative /prə'vɒkətɪv/ adj **1** intended to make you angry or upset **2** intended to make you sexually excited —**provocatively** adv

provoke /prə'vəʊk/ verb [T] **1** to deliberately try to make someone angry: *He's just trying to provoke you.* **2** to cause a particular reaction, especially an angry one: *The Minister's speech has provoked a furious reaction.*

prowess /'praʊes/ noun [U] great skill, or great ability

prowl /praʊl/ verb [I/T] to move around an area quietly, especially because you are planning to do something bad

Proxima Centauri /ˌprɒksɪmə sen'tɔːraɪ/ noun ASTRONOMY a red star that is the closest known star to the solar system

proximal /'prɒksɪm(ə)l/ adj BIOLOGY nearer to the centre of the body, or to the point where something is attached to the body → DISTAL

proximity /prɒk'sɪməti/ noun [U] *formal* the state of being near someone or something

proxy server /'prɒksi ˌsɜːvə/ noun [C] COMPUTING a computer system that allows users to go to popular websites more quickly, by storing pages that are often asked for or have been recently used

prudent /'pruːd(ə)nt/ adj careful, and using good judgment —**prudence** noun [U], **prudently** adv

prune¹ /pruːn/ verb [T] AGRICULTURE to cut off parts of a tree or plant

prune² /pruːn/ noun [C] a dried **plum**

pruning knife /'pruːnɪŋ ˌnaɪf/ noun [C] AGRICULTURE a knife used for **pruning** plants such as bushes and fruit trees —*picture* → AGRICULTURAL

prurient /'prʊəriənt/ adj *formal* involving sex in an unpleasant way

pry /praɪ/ (**pries, prying, pried**) verb [I] to be interested in someone's personal life in a way that is annoying or offensive: *I just glanced at the letter; I didn't mean to pry.* ♦ *The press continues to pry into their affairs.*

PS /ˌpiː 'es/ abbrev postscript: used for introducing additional information at the end of a letter after you have signed your name

psalm /sɑːm/ noun [C] RELIGION a song or poem from the Bible that praises God

pseudonym /'sjuːdənɪm/ noun [C] a false name that someone uses, especially when they write a book = PEN NAME

pseudopodium /ˌsjuːdəʊ'pəʊdiəm/ noun [C] BIOLOGY a part of an amoeba or other protozoan that sticks out temporarily and is used for moving around and for getting food

psoriasis /sə'raɪəsɪs/ noun [U] HEALTH a medical condition that affects the skin

psyche /'saɪki/ noun [C] the part of your mind that controls your attitudes and behaviour

psychiatric /ˌsaɪki'ætrɪk/ adj HEALTH connected with the treatment of mental illness, or involving mental illness

psychi'atric ˌhospital noun [C] HEALTH a hospital that treats people who have a mental illness

psychiatrist /saɪ'kaɪətrɪst/ noun [C] HEALTH a doctor who treats people with mental illnesses

psychiatry /saɪ'kaɪətri/ noun [U] HEALTH the study and treatment of mental illness —**psychiatric** /ˌsaɪki'ætrɪk/ adj

psychic /'saɪkɪk/ adj **1** someone who is psychic claims to be able to know what other people are thinking or what is going to happen to them **2** connected with the mind rather than the body **3** connected with mysterious mental powers that cannot be explained by science: *psychic energy* —**psychic** noun [C]

psychoanalysis /ˌsaɪkəʊə'næləsɪs/ noun [U] HEALTH medical treatment in which someone talks to a psychoanalyst about their feelings in order to help them solve their mental problems —**psychoanalyse** /ˌsaɪkəʊ'ænəˌlaɪz/ verb [T]

psychoanalyst /ˌsaɪkəʊ'ænəlɪst/ noun [C] HEALTH a doctor whose job is to talk to people about their feelings in order to help them solve their mental problems

psycholinguistics /ˌsaɪkəʊlɪŋ'gwɪstɪks/ noun [U] LANGUAGE the scientific study of the way that the brain produces and deals with language —**psycholinguistic** adj

psychological /ˌsaɪkə'lɒdʒɪk(ə)l/ adj **1** involving or affecting the mind: *Harry's problems are more psychological than physical.* **2** connected with the study of how the mind works and how this affects behaviour: *psychological theories* **3** caused by someone's feelings or thoughts: *Defeat is psychological. You lose one or two games and you stop believing you can win.* —**psychologically** /ˌsaɪkə'lɒdʒɪkli/ adv

psychologist /saɪ'kɒlədʒɪst/ noun [C] someone who studies how the mind works and how this affects behaviour

psychology /saɪ'kɒlədʒi/ noun [U] **1** the study of the mind and how it affects behaviour **2** the way that the mind affects behaviour in a particular person or group of people: *a book on the psychology of murderers*

psychopath /'saɪkəʊpæθ/ noun [C] HEALTH someone who has a serious mental illness that makes them behave very violently —**psychopathic** /ˌsaɪkəʊ'pæθɪk/ adj

psychosis /saɪ'kəʊsɪs/ (plural **psychoses** /saɪ'kəʊsiːz/) noun [C/U] HEALTH a severe form of mental illness, for example **schizophrenia** or **mania**

psychosomatic /ˌsaɪkəʊsəʊ'mætɪk/ adj HEALTH a psychosomatic illness is caused by the mind rather than having a physical cause

psychotic /saɪ'kɒtɪk/ adj HEALTH suffering from a serious mental illness —**psychotic** noun [C]

psychotropic /ˌsaɪkə'trəʊpɪk, ˌsaɪkə'trɒpɪk/ adj CHEMISTRY, HEALTH relating to drugs that are capable of affecting the mind, for example those used to treat psychiatric conditions

pt abbrev **1** pint **2** point

PTA /ˌpiː tiː ˈeɪ/ noun [C] EDUCATION Parent-Teacher Association: an organization of parents and teachers who work together in order to improve their school

PTO /ˌpiː tiː ˈəʊ/ abbrev please turn over: used at the bottom of a page when there is more writing on the other side

pub /pʌb/ noun [C] a place where people go to drink alcohol

puberty /ˈpjuːbəti/ noun [U] BIOLOGY the stage of development in the lives of humans and other **primates** when they change from being a child to being an adult. This involves the development of physical characteristics such as the growth of breasts in females and the voice getting deeper in males. Females start to produce eggs and start to **menstruate**, and males begin to produce sperm. —**pubertal** adj

pubic /ˈpjuːbɪk/ adj ANATOMY relating to the area around the sexual organs

the public /ˈpʌblɪk/ noun [singular] people in general: *The palace was* **opened to the public** *in the 1950s.* ♦ *The police should be trained to deal politely with* **members of the public.** → GENERAL PUBLIC

> **The public** can be used with a singular or plural verb. You can say *The public* **wants** *tougher sentences for terrorists* OR *The public* **want** *tougher sentences for terrorists.*

public¹ /ˈpʌblɪk/ adj **1** owned by the government, not by a private company ≠ PRIVATE: *The damage was repaired using* **public money.** **2** available for people in general to use ≠ PRIVATE: *a public library* ♦ *the city's public parks* **3** involving a lot of people, or involving people in general: *a public nuisance* ♦ *The scheme has a lot of* **public support.** **4** used about places and situations where other people can see you: *Can we go somewhere a little less public?* ♦ *She keeps her public and private lives very separate.*

PHRASES **in the public eye** well known to people in general: *Her job keeps her in the public eye.*

make sth public to tell everyone about something: *The government has decided to make the results of the inquiry public.*

public² /ˈpʌblɪk/ noun **in public** if you do something in public, people in general hear about it or see it: *It's unprofessional to criticize your colleagues in public.*

publication /ˌpʌblɪˈkeɪʃ(ə)n/ noun **1** [U] the process of producing a book for people to buy: *She became famous after* **the publication of** *her first novel.* **2** [C] a magazine, newspaper, or book: *a weekly financial publication* **3** [U] the process of making information available to the public: **Publication of** *the report is expected next week.*

public body noun [C] an organization whose work is part of the process of government, but is not a government department

public company noun [C] BUSINESS a company whose shares people can buy on the **stock exchange**

public figure noun [C] a well-known person

publicist /ˈpʌblɪsɪst/ noun [C] someone whose job is to use newspapers, television etc in order to make people notice a person, organization, or product

publicity /pʌbˈlɪsəti/ noun [U] attention in newspapers and on television: *a publicity campaign* (=an attempt to get publicity) ♦ *Her behaviour during the filming* **attracted** *a lot of* **publicity.**

publicize /ˈpʌblɪsaɪz/ verb [T] to publish or broadcast information about someone or something

public limited company noun [C] BUSINESS in the UK, a company that sells its shares to the public and provides its **shareholders** with **limited liability** for its debts. It has **plc** at the end of its name.

publicly /ˈpʌblɪkli/ adv **1** in a way that many people notice ≠ PRIVATELY: *Kent publicly disagreed with his fellow doctors on many occasions.* **2** by the government or state, or by or for people in general: *a publicly owned health service* ♦ *publicly available information* **3** for people in general to have or buy

public nuisance noun [C/U] LAW an activity that offends most of the people in a place, for example being noisy or showing offensive sexual behaviour

public opinion noun [U] the opinions that most people in a society have about something

public private partnership noun [U] BUSINESS see PPP

public prosecutor /ˌpʌblɪk ˈprɒsɪkjuːtə/ noun [C] LAW in the UK, a lawyer who works for the government and tries to prove that someone has done something illegal

public school noun [C/U] EDUCATION **1** in the UK, an expensive private school **2** a school that is controlled and paid for by the government

public sector noun [singular] ECONOMICS the industries and services that are controlled by the government

public service noun **1** [C] a service that the government pays for, for example education or health care **2** [U] the work that is done by people who are employed by the government **3** [C] a service that helps people without charging them any money

public transport noun [U] buses, trains etc that everyone can use

publish /ˈpʌblɪʃ/ verb [T] **1** to produce many copies of a book, magazine, or newspaper for people to buy: *Their company* **publishes** *a wide selection of* **books.** **2** to make information available for everyone to read: *The department's* **report** *was* **published** *in June.* **3** to have something that you have written printed and sold: *In 1934 he published another successful novel.* **4** to include something such as a letter in a newspaper or magazine: *Our* **research** *is being* **published** *in a well-known medical journal.*

publisher /ˈpʌblɪʃə/ noun [C] a person or company that produces books for people to buy

publishing /ˈpʌblɪʃɪŋ/ noun [U] the business of producing books for people to buy

puck /pʌk/ noun [C] SPORTS the round flat piece of rubber that players hit in the game of **ice hockey**

pudding /ˈpʊdɪŋ/ noun **1** [C] a soft sweet food that you eat at the end of a meal: *a sponge pudding* **2** [U] the last part of a meal when you eat sweet foods = DESSERT

puddle /ˈpʌd(ə)l/ noun [C] a small pool of water that is left on the ground after it has rained

puddling furnace /ˈpʌd(ə)lɪŋ ˌfɜːnɪs/ noun [C] TECHNOLOGY a type of **furnace** for producing **wrought iron** or steel from **pig iron**

puerile /ˈpjʊəraɪl/ adj *formal* like a silly young person, or like something they would say or do = IMMATURE, JUVENILE

puff¹ /pʌf/ verb **1** [I/T] to smoke a cigarette **2** [I] to breathe noisily after running or doing something else that is physically hard → HUFF¹

puff² /pʌf/ noun [C] **1** the action of breathing in smoke from a cigarette **2** a small amount of smoke, wind, or air

puffy /'pʌfi/ adj slightly swollen

pugnacious /pʌg'neɪʃəs/ adj formal quick to argue or fight with people

pull¹ /pʊl/ verb

1 move sth to you	6 injure muscle
2 remove sth fixed	7 take gun/knife out
3 move with force	+ PHRASES
4 move with vehicle	+ PHRASAL VERBS
5 attract people	

1 [I/T] to move someone or something towards you using your hands ≠ PUSH: *I climbed into bed and pulled the blankets over my head.* ♦ *A lifeguard had to pull her out of the water.* ♦ *Jane pulled the door open.* ♦ *Don't pull the string too tight.* ♦ *The little girl **pulled** gently **at** my sleeve.*
2 [T] to use force in order to remove something that is fixed somewhere: *She was **pulling up** the weeds in the garden.* ♦ *Someone **pulled** the handle **off** the door.*
3 [T] to move your body or part of your body using effort or force: *He needed all his energy to pull himself up off the ground.*
4 [T] to move something along behind your vehicle by fixing it to the vehicle: *Two horses were pulling the plough.*
5 [T] to attract customers, voters, or an audience: *The show is pulling huge audiences all over America.*
6 [T] to injure a muscle by stretching it too much
7 [T] to take a gun or a knife out of your pocket and be ready to use it: *His attacker suddenly pulled a knife on him.*

PHRASES **pull out all the stops** to make a big effort so that something happens or is successful
pull strings to use your influence in order to get something
pull the strings if someone is pulling the strings, they are secretly controlling a situation
pull sb/sth to pieces/to bits 1 to separate the connected pieces of something **2** to criticize someone or something severely
pull your weight to work as hard as the other people who are involved in something
pull yourself together to start to control your emotions after being very upset or angry

PHRASAL VERBS ,pull a'way if a vehicle pulls away, it starts to move away from a place: *The bus pulled away from the station around noon.*
,pull sth 'down to destroy a building that is old or dangerous= DEMOLISH
,pull 'in if a vehicle pulls in, it arrives or stops somewhere
,pull 'into sth if a vehicle pulls into a place, it stops there: *The train pulled into Central Station.*
,pull sth 'off to succeed in doing something that is difficult: *They nearly managed to get the loan but just failed to **pull it off**.*
,pull 'out 1 to decide not to take part in something: *The Columbian team pulled out at the last minute.* **2** if a train pulls out, it leaves a station
,pull (sth) 'over to stop at the side of the road, or to make a vehicle stop at the side of the road
,pull 'up if a vehicle pulls up, it stops: *Their taxi pulled up outside the church.*

pull² /pʊl/ noun **1** [C] the act of moving someone or something towards you **2** [singular] a strong physical force that causes things to move in a particular direction: *the pull of gravity* **3** [singular] the power that something has to attract people

'pull-down ,menu noun [C] COMPUTING a list of choices on a computer screen that you get by clicking on something → DROP-DOWN MENU

pullet /'pʊlɪt/ noun [C] AGRICULTURE a chicken that is less than a year old

pulley /'pʊli/ (plural **pulleys**) noun [C] a simple machine used for lifting heavy things, consisting of a wheel with a rope around it. The rope is pulled in order to raise a load.

pullover /'pʊləʊvə/ noun [C] a warm piece of **knitted** clothing without buttons that you wear on the top part of your body= JUMPER, SWEATER

pulmonary /'pʌlmən(ə)ri/ adj ANATOMY, HEALTH affecting or relating to the lungs

,pulmonary 'artery noun [C] ANATOMY one of two arteries that carry blood from the right **ventricle** of the heart to the lungs —*picture* → CIRCULATION

,pulmonary circu'lation noun [U] BIOLOGY the movement of blood from the right side of the heart to the lungs

,pulmonary 'vein noun [C] ANATOMY one of four veins that carry blood from the lungs to the left **atrium** of the heart —*picture* → CIRCULATION

pulp¹ /pʌlp/ noun **1** [U] the inside of a fruit or vegetable= FLESH **2** [U] AGRICULTURE wood or plant fibre that is crushed for making paper **3** [U] ANATOMY the soft, sensitive part in the inside of a tooth that contains nerves and blood vessels **4** [singular/U] a thick soft substance made by crushing something

pulp² /pʌlp/ adj pulp books or films are of low quality and about sex or violence

'pulp ,cavity noun [C] ANATOMY the area inside a tooth where the pulp is —*picture* → TOOTH

pulpit /'pʊlpɪt/ noun [C] RELIGION the place where a priest stands to talk to people in a church

pulsar /'pʌlsɑː/ noun [C] ASTRONOMY a type of star in space that produces a regular radio signal

pulse /pʌls/ noun [C] **1** HEALTH the regular movement of blood as the heart pumps it round the body: *The first thing the doctor does is **take** your **pulse** (=check how fast your heart is beating).* **2** PHYSICS an amount of electricity, light, or sound that something produces for a short time

pulses /'pʌlsɪz/ noun [plural] beans, peas, and other seeds that you can cook and eat

pumice /'pʌmɪs/ or **'pumice ,stone** noun **1** [U] GEOLOGY a very light grey stone from a volcano **2** [C] a piece of this stone that is used for rubbing the skin clean and smooth

pump¹ /pʌmp/ noun [C] a piece of equipment for sending a liquid or gas into or out of something: *a fuel pump* ♦ *a foot pump* —*picture* → WATER

pump² /pʌmp/ verb **1** [T] PHYSICS to send liquid or gas somewhere, especially by using a pump: *Poisonous gases are pumped into the atmosphere every day.* **2** [I/T] to move up and down with a lot of force, or to move something up and down with a lot of force: *Liz pumped the accelerator to start the car.*

PHRASAL VERBS ,pump sth 'out to make liquid or gas escape from a place: *Huge generators were pumping out black smoke.*
,pump sth 'up to fill something with air, using a pump

pumping station /'pʌmpɪŋ ,steɪʃ(ə)n/ noun [C] a place where water or gas is pumped along a pipe or out of the ground up to a tank, where it is stored —*picture* → WATER SUPPLY

pumpkin /ˈpʌmpkɪn/ noun [C/U] a large round vegetable with thick orange skin —*picture* ➔ VEGETABLE

pump-priming /ˈpʌmp ˌpraɪmɪŋ/ noun [U] BUSINESS money that is invested in something to encourage it to develop, or to encourage other people to invest in it

pun /pʌn/ noun [C] LANGUAGE a joke using words that have two meanings

punch¹ /pʌntʃ/ verb [T] **1** to hit someone or something with your **fist** (=closed hand) **2** to make a hole in something with a tool or machine

punch² /pʌntʃ/ noun **1** [C] the action of hitting someone or something with your **fist** (=closed hand) **2** [U] a sweet drink made with fruit juice and alcohol **3** [C] a tool for making a hole in something

punchbag /ˈpʌntʃˌbæg/ noun [C] **1** SPORTS a large heavy bag hanging from a rope, that people hit for exercise **2** someone who is always blamed when things go wrong, even for things that are not their fault = SCAPEGOAT

punctilious /pʌŋkˈtɪliəs/ adj formal very careful to behave well, and to follow the details of rules or instructions —**punctiliously** adv

punctual /ˈpʌŋktʃuəl/ adj someone who is punctual arrives at the time that they should arrive at —**punctuality** /ˌpʌŋktʃuˈæləti/ noun [U], **punctually** adv

punctuate /ˈpʌŋktʃueɪt/ verb [I/T] LANGUAGE to use full stops, commas, and other **punctuation marks** in a piece of writing

punctuation /ˌpʌŋktʃuˈeɪʃ(ə)n/ noun [U] LANGUAGE **1** the use of marks such as full stops and commas in writing **2** punctuation marks

punctuˈation ˌmark noun [C] LANGUAGE a mark such as a full stop, comma, or question mark that you use in order to write in a clear style

puncture¹ /ˈpʌŋktʃə/ noun [C] **1** a small hole made with a sharp point **2** a small hole that is made by accident in a tyre

puncture² /ˈpʌŋktʃə/ verb [T] to make a small hole in something

pundit /ˈpʌndɪt/ noun [C] someone who is an expert in a subject, and is often asked to talk to the public about that subject = COMMENTATOR

pungent /ˈpʌndʒənt/ adj a pungent taste or smell is very strong and sharp

punish /ˈpʌnɪʃ/ verb [T] to do something unpleasant to someone because they have done something bad or illegal: *He was punished for stealing.*

punishable /ˈpʌnɪʃəb(ə)l/ adj if someone does something that is punishable, they can be punished for doing it

punishing /ˈpʌnɪʃɪŋ/ adj extremely difficult or tiring

punishment /ˈpʌnɪʃmənt/ noun **1** [C] a way in which someone is punished: *He had to clean up the mess as a punishment.* **2** [U] the process of punishing someone: *He has cheated people and escaped punishment.*

punitive /ˈpjuːnətɪv/ adj relating to punishment, or intended as a punishment

Punnett square /ˈpʌnɪt ˌskweə/ noun [C] BIOLOGY a diagram that is used for showing the possible combination of genes in a child with particular parents

puny /ˈpjuːni/ adj a puny person or animal is small, thin, and weak

pup /pʌp/ noun [C] BIOLOGY a young dog or **seal**

pupa /ˈpjuːpə/ (plural **pupae** /ˈpjuːpiː/) noun [C] BIOLOGY an insect such as a moth while it is changing inside a **cocoon** or hard shell. A pupa is the stage between a larva and an adult insect. —*picture* ➔ MOSQUITO

pupil /ˈpjuːp(ə)l/ noun [C] **1** EDUCATION someone who goes to school or who has lessons in a particular subject ➔ STUDENT **2** ANATOMY the black round part in the centre of the **iris** of the eye, where light enters —*picture* ➔ EYE

ˈpupil ˌreflex noun [singular] BIOLOGY a **reflex** (=automatic movement of a muscle) in which the pupil of the eye gets smaller or bigger according to the amount of light reaching the retina

puppet /ˈpʌpɪt/ noun [C] **1** a toy that looks like a person or animal that you move by pulling wires or strings, or by putting your hand inside it **2** showing disapproval someone who is controlled by someone else

puppy /ˈpʌpi/ (plural **puppies**) noun [C] a very young dog

purchase¹ /ˈpɜːtʃəs/ verb [T] formal to buy something: *She purchased shares in the company.*

purchase² /ˈpɜːtʃəs/ noun formal **1** [U] the process of buying something: *the purchase of new computers* **2** [C] something that you buy: *Her latest purchase was a long black coat.*

pure /pjʊə/ adj **1** a pure substance has nothing mixed with it that might spoil its quality ≠ IMPURE: *pure gold* ♦ *clean, pure drinking water* **2** used for emphasis: *a smile of pure happiness* ♦ *Perhaps it was pure chance that the other woman happened to be there.* **3** morally good ≠ IMPURE: *He seems to have led a pure life.* **4** EDUCATION a pure subject of study, especially a science, deals only with theory and not with the way the theory can be used

> **Word family: pure**
>
> *Words in the same family as pure*
> - **purely** adv
> - **purify** v
> - **purity** n
> - **purist** n
> - **impure** adj
> - **impurity** n

purebred /ˈpjʊəbred/ adj a purebred animal comes from parents of the same breed

purée /ˈpjʊəreɪ/ noun [C/U] food that has been mixed or crushed to form a thick smooth sauce —**purée** verb [T]

purely /ˈpjʊəli/ adv completely, or only: *What I'm saying is purely my own point of view.* ♦ *We meet purely for business reasons.*

purgatory /ˈpɜːɡət(ə)ri/ noun [U] **1** RELIGION the place where Roman Catholics believe that people go to suffer after they die before they are allowed to go to heaven **2** an unpleasant place or experience

purge /pɜːdʒ/ verb [T] **1** to force people to leave an organization **2** to get rid of bad feelings —**purge** noun [C]

purify /ˈpjʊərɪfaɪ/ (**purifies, purifying, purified**) verb [T] to make something clean by removing dirty or harmful substances from it —**purification** /ˌpjʊərɪfɪˈkeɪʃ(ə)n/ noun [U]

purist /ˈpjʊərɪst/ noun [C] someone who wants people to follow rules carefully

puritanical /ˌpjʊərɪˈtænɪk(ə)l/ adj showing disapproval a puritanical person does not approve of pleasures such as sex and drinking alcohol = PIOUS

purity /'pjʊərəti/ noun [U] **1** the condition of being pure ≠ IMPURITY **2** a clear or beautiful quality in sound, writing, music etc

purlin /'pɜːlɪn/ noun [C] CONSTRUCTION a **beam** (=long piece of wood) that supports the **rafters** of a roof

purple /'pɜːp(ə)l/ adj between red and blue in colour —**purple** noun [U]

,purple 'cabbage noun [C] CHEMISTRY, BIOLOGY a type of cabbage with purple leaves that is used to make an **indicator** for chemicals

purpose /'pɜːpəs/ noun **1** [C] an aim or use: *Another meeting would serve absolutely no purpose.* ♦ *He went there for the purpose of making business contacts.* **2** [U] an aim or meaning that someone's life has, because there is something they want to achieve: *Now his life lacks purpose.* ♦ *The course gave her a new sense of purpose.*
   PHRASE **on purpose** deliberately: *They think the fire was started on purpose.*
   → ALL-PURPOSE

,purpose-'built adj made for a particular purpose

purposeful /'pɜːpəsf(ə)l/ adj showing that you are determined to do something —**purposefully** adv

purposely /'pɜːpəsli/ adv deliberately

,purpose-'made adj designed and made for a particular purpose

purr /pɜː/ verb [I] **1** if a cat purrs, it makes a continuous low sound because it is happy **2** if a machine purrs, it makes a continuous quiet sound because it is operating correctly —**purr** noun [C]

purse /pɜːs/ noun [C] **1** a small bag for carrying money **2** *American* a woman's **handbag**

pursue /pə'sjuː/ verb [T] **1** to do something, or to try to achieve something: *We're persuading both countries to pursue a peaceful solution.* ♦ *He wants to pursue a career in medicine.* ♦ *I intend to pursue the matter* (=continue to try to achieve my aim). **2** to chase someone

pursuit /pə'sjuːt/ noun **1** [U] the process of trying to achieve something: *the pursuit of happiness* **2** [U] the process of chasing someone: *Several police officers are in pursuit of the stolen car.* **3** [C] *formal* an activity that you enjoy: *his artistic pursuits*

pus /pʌs/ noun [U] HEALTH a thick yellow liquid that the body produces when it has an infection

push¹ /pʊʃ/ verb

1 move sb/sth away	**6** make sb work hard
2 press button	**7** try to sell sth
3 move through	**8** make impatient
4 bring sth to level	+ PHRASAL VERBS
5 force sb	

1 [I/T] to move someone or something away from you using your hands ≠ PULL: *Push as hard as you can.* ♦ *She gently pushed him away.* ♦ *I pushed open the door.*
2 [I/T] to press a button on a machine: *To turn on the television, you push this switch.*
3 [I/T] to move through a group of people using the force of your body: *Stop pushing and just wait your turn.* ♦ *He just pushed past Fred and left.* ♦ *I was pushing my way through the crowd.*
4 [T] to make something reach a particular level or standard: *The strong sun pushed temperatures into the nineties.* ♦ *The Bank of England had pushed up interest rates sharply to protect the pound.*
5 [T] to force someone to do something: *The police pushed her into giving evidence.*

6 [T] to make someone work very hard: *Some parents really push their children.* ♦ *You shouldn't push yourself so hard.*
7 [T] *informal* to try to make people buy a product or accept an idea= PROMOTE
8 [T] to make someone impatient or annoyed by behaving in an unreasonable way: *If you push him too far, he'll resign.*
   PHRASAL VERBS **,push a'head** to continue trying to achieve something= GO ON
'push for sth to try hard to get or achieve something: *They continue to push for more pay.*
,push sth 'through to succeed in making people accept something such as an agreement or a new law

push² /pʊʃ/ noun **1** [C] a movement in which you push someone or something: *Jan helped me give the car a push.* **2** [C] a determined attempt to do something: *The two sides began a final push to reach an agreement before the deadline.* **3** [singular] an occasion when you encourage or force someone to do something: *I knew I could do it – I just needed someone to give me an extra push.* **4** [C] a movement by an army further into or through a country or area, using force: *The army begin their push on the town at dawn.*

'push ,mail noun [U] BUSINESS, COMPUTING email sent to a particular group of people in order to advertise a product or service

'push tech,nology noun [U] COMPUTING a type of computer technology that automatically sends information to your computer over the Internet, so that you do not have to request it

pushy /'pʊʃi/ (**pushier, pushiest**) adj *informal* extremely determined to get what you want, even if it annoys other people

pustule /'pʌstjuːl/ noun [C] HEALTH a spot on the skin that is filled with liquid

put /pʊt/ (**puts, putting, put**) verb [T]

1 move sth to a place	**6** place somewhere
2 cause to be in situation	**7** give position on list
3 write/print sth	**8** state sth
4 make sb go to place	+ PHRASES
5 say in particular way	+ PHRASAL VERBS

1 to move something to a particular position using your hands: *Where did you put the newspaper?* ♦ *Did I put my wallet in your bag?* ♦ *She put her hand on Cliff's arm.*
2 to cause someone or something to be in a particular situation: *She was put in charge of the marketing department.* ♦ *The information you've given me puts me in a really difficult position.* ♦ *I hate being put under so much pressure.* ♦ *That argument put me in a bad mood for the rest of the day.* ♦ *Supermarkets have put many smaller shops out of business.*
3 to write or print something somewhere: *Put a tick by the correct answer.* ♦ *I'll put a note at the bottom of the card.* ♦ *You've put the comma in the wrong place.*
4 to make someone go to a place: *The government has promised to put more police officers on the street.* ♦ *What time do you put the kids to bed?*
5 to say or write something in a particular way: *She put it very well when she described him as 'brilliant but lazy'.*
6 to build or place something somewhere: *There are plans to put ten new houses on the site.* ♦ *We decided to put the office upstairs.*
7 to give something a particular position on a list according to importance, quality, or value: *I'd put Monet among the best artists of the century.* ♦ *They're so different, you can't even put them in the same category.*

8 to state or explain something: *You will get plenty of opportunity to **put your point of view**.*

PHRASES **put sth behind you** to stop thinking about something unpleasant that has happened to you: *I was upset at the time, but I've managed to put it behind me.*

put a stop/end to sth to make something stop happening: *You ought to put a stop to that sort of behaviour.*

PHRASAL VERBS **,put sth a'cross** to explain something in a way that people can understand: *Television can be a useful way of putting across information.*

,put sth a'side to save money for the future

,put sth a'way to put something in the place where you usually keep it: *He put the notebook away and stood up.*

,put sth 'back to put something in the place where it was before it was moved: *Can you put the book back when you've finished with it?*

,put sth 'down to put something onto a surface such as the floor or a table: *Emma put her bag down and went upstairs.*

,put sth 'in to spend time or effort doing something: *Wendy has been putting in more hours at the office recently.* → APPEARANCE

,put sb 'off to prevent someone from concentrating on something: *Stop laughing – you'll put her off.*

,put sb 'off (sb/sth) to make someone not like someone or something or not want to do something: *Robert's attitude towards women really puts me off. ♦ I put him off the idea of going shopping with me.*

,put sth 'off 1 to delay doing something that you do not want to do: *You can't put the decision off any longer.* **2** to arrange to do something at a later time than you originally planned: *They had to put the wedding off because the bride's mother had an accident.* **3** to switch off a piece of equipment

,put sth 'on 1 to cover a part of your body with a piece of clothing or jewellery so that you are wearing it ≠ TAKE STH OFF: *Dorothy put on her coat and went out.* **2** to make equipment start working: *Can you put the light on, please?*

,put sth 'out 1 to make something stop burning **2** to switch off a light

,put sb 'through sth to make someone do something difficult or unpleasant: *The team are put through a daily fitness programme.*

,put sth to'gether to make something by joining all its parts: *Will you help me put this desk together?*

,put sb 'up to let someone stay in your house: *Could you put me up for the night when I come to London?*

,put sth 'up 1 to build something such as a wall, fence, or house **2** to fix something to a wall: *The teachers will put a notice up about the new courses.*

,put 'up with sb/sth to accept someone or something unpleasant in a patient way: *How has Jan put up with him for so long?*

putlog /'pʊt,lɒg/ noun [C] CONSTRUCTION a horizontal piece of **scaffolding** that has one end built into a building

Putonghua /,puːtɒŋ'hwaː/ noun [U] LANGUAGE the standard form of the modern Chinese language

putrid /'pjuːtrɪd/ adj *formal* decaying and smelling very bad

putt /pʌt/ noun [C] SPORTS in golf, a gentle hit of the ball so that it rolls along the ground towards the hole —**putt** verb [I/T]

putter /'pʌtə/ noun [C] SPORTS a special type of stick that is used in golf for hitting the ball along the ground towards the hole

putting green /'pʌtɪŋ ,griːn/ noun [C] SPORTS a flat area covered with short, smooth grass around a hole on a **golf course**

putty /'pʌti/ noun [U] a soft grey substance that is used for fixing glass into windows

puzzle¹ /'pʌz(ə)l/ verb [T] if something puzzles you, you cannot understand it

puzzle² /'pʌz(ə)l/ noun [C] **1** someone or something that you cannot understand **2** a game or toy that is designed to test your intelligence

puzzled /'pʌz(ə)ld/ adj confused because you cannot understand something

puzzling /'pʌz(ə)lɪŋ/ adj confusing or difficult to understand

PVC /,piː viː 'siː/ noun [U] a type of plastic that is used for making clothes and cloth

pyjamas /pə'dʒɑːməz/ noun [plural] comfortable trousers and a shirt that you wear in bed

pylon /'paɪlən/ noun [C] a tall metal tower that holds electricity wires high above the ground

pyloric sphincter /paɪ,lɔːrɪk 'sfɪŋktə/ noun [C] ANATOMY the muscle between the stomach and small intestine that controls the amount of food that passes from the stomach and goes into the small intestine

pyramid /'pɪrəmɪd/ noun [C] **1** a large pointed stone structure with a square base and triangular sides **2** MATHS an object with the shape of a pyramid —*picture* → SHAPE **3** an organization or system that has fewer people at each level towards the top

pyramidal /'pɪrəmɪd(ə)l/ adj in the shape of a pyramid

pyre /paɪə/ noun [C] a high pile of wood for burning a dead body in a funeral ceremony

pyrethrin /paɪ'riːθrɪn/ noun [C/U] CHEMISTRY either of two compounds, obtained from plants, that are used as **insecticides**

pyrethroid /paɪ'riːθrɔɪd/ noun [U] CHEMISTRY an artificially made chemical that is used to kill harmful insects. It is similar to **pyrethrin**.

pyrites /paɪ'raɪtiːz/ noun [U] GEOLOGY a hard substance found in rock that is a mixture of **sulphur** and a metal, especially iron. It is also known as **fool's gold** because it looks like gold.

pyroclastic flow /,paɪrəʊklæstɪk 'fləʊ/ noun [U] GEOLOGY the large amount of hot ash, pieces of rock, and gas that flows very quickly down the side of a volcano when it erupts

Pythagoras theorem /paɪ'θægərəs ,θɪərəm/ noun [U] MATHS a rule in geometry that states that the square of the hypotenuse of a right-angled triangle is equal to the **sum** of the squares of the other two sides

Pythagorean /paɪ,θægə'riːən/ adj MATHS relating to **Pythagoras** or to Pythagoras theorem

python /'paɪθ(ə)n/ noun [C] a large snake that kills animals by wrapping itself around them

Q q

q /kju:/ (plural **q's**) or **Q** (plural **Q's**) noun [C/U] the 17th letter of the English alphabet

QC /ˌkjuː ˈsiː/ noun [C] LAW Queen's Counsel: in the UK, a lawyer of high status

quack /kwæk/ noun [C] the sound that a **duck** makes

quadrangle /ˈkwɒdˌræŋɡ(ə)l/ noun [C] MATHS a **quadrilateral**

quadrant /ˈkwɒdrənt/ noun [C] MATHS a shape that is a quarter of a circle —*picture* → CIRCLE

quadratic equation /kwɒˌdrætɪk ɪˈkweɪʒ(ə)n/ noun [C] MATHS an equation in which a **variable** (=quantity which can represent different amounts) is multiplied by itself once only, and is never multiplied by another power. $2x^2 + 2x - 15 = 0$ is a quadratic equation

quadrilateral /ˌkwɒdrɪˈlæt(ə)rəl/ noun [C] MATHS any flat shape with four sides, for example a square —*picture* → SHAPE —**quadrilateral** adj

quadruped /ˈkwɒdrʊped/ noun [C] BIOLOGY any animal that walks on four legs —**quadrupedal** adj

quadruple /ˈkwɒdrʊp(ə)l, kwɒˈdruːp(ə)l/ verb [I/T] MATHS if a number or an amount quadruples, or if you quadruple it, it becomes four times bigger than it was

quagmire /ˈkwæɡˌmaɪə, ˈkwɒɡˌmaɪə/ noun [C] a situation that is so difficult or complicated that you cannot make much progress

quaint /kweɪnt/ adj interesting or attractive with a slightly strange and old-fashioned quality

quake /kweɪk/ verb [I] **1** to feel so afraid that your body shakes slightly **2** if something such as a building quakes, it shakes violently

Quaker /ˈkweɪkə/ noun [C] RELIGION a member of a Christian religious group whose members avoid violence and hold simple religious services with no priests

qualification /ˌkwɒlɪfɪˈkeɪʃ(ə)n/ noun **1** [C] EDUCATION something such as a degree or a **diploma** that you get when you successfully finish a course of study: *Simon left school with no qualifications.* ♦ *She has a qualification in teaching.* **2** [C] an ability or quality that you need in order to do a particular job or activity: *Good communication skills are an essential qualification for the job.* **3** [U] the action or process of qualifying for something: *Their chances of World Cup qualification are high.* **4** [C/U] something that you add to a statement or rule in order to show that it is not true in some situations

qualified /ˈkwɒlɪfaɪd/ adj **1** successfully trained for a particular job: *a qualified doctor* **2** able to do something, because you have the knowledge, skill, or experience that is needed: *She is particularly well qualified to give an opinion.* **3** qualified support or agreement is not completely positive because someone has some doubts or criticisms

qualifier /ˈkwɒlɪˌfaɪə/ noun [C] **1** SPORTS a game that is played to decide which team or player may enter a competition **2** LANGUAGE a **modifier 3** SPORTS a team or person who competes successfully in an early stage of a competition and is able to go on to the next stage

qualify /ˈkwɒlɪfaɪ/ (**qualifies, qualifying, qualified**) verb

1 join profession	4 in linguistics
2 have qualities for sth	5 change a
3 reach competition stage	statement

1 [I] to become a member of a particular profession after a period of training or study, or to decide that someone can be a member of a particular profession: *Andrew qualified as a teacher in 1995.* ♦ *After qualifying in medicine, he worked for a time at City Hospital.* ♦ *At the end of the course, you will be qualified to practise law.*
2 [I/T] to have the right qualities to be or to do something: *Twenty per cent of Americans qualify as rich.* ♦ *To qualify for Olympic status, a sport must be played in 50 countries and on three continents.* ♦ *Only people over the age of 18 are qualified to vote.* ♦ *The fact that his grandparents were Irish qualified him to play in the Irish national team.*
3 [I] to reach a particular stage of a competition by competing successfully in an earlier stage: *It would be incredible if Brazil failed to qualify.* ♦ *What are your team's chances of qualifying for the finals?*
4 [T] LANGUAGE a word that qualifies another word gives more information about it. For example, in 'the dog barked furiously', the adverb 'furiously' qualifies the verb 'barked'.
5 [T] to add something to a statement in order to change it slightly, or state the situations in which it is not true: *Let me qualify that last statement by saying that your condition might improve.*

> **Word family: qualify**
> *Words in the same family as qualify*
> - qualification *n*
> - qualified *adj*
> - qualifier *n*
> - disqualified *adj*
> - disqualify *v*
> - unqualified *adj*

qualitative /ˈkwɒlɪtətɪv/ adj MATHS relating to data that cannot be counted or measured —**qualitatively** adv

quality¹ /ˈkwɒləti/ (plural **qualities**) noun **1** [C/U] the quality of something is how good or how bad it is: *poor-quality workmanship* ♦ *This cut in funding will affect the quality of education in our schools.* ♦ *The food is of the highest quality.* **2** [U] a high standard: *a company with a reputation for quality and reliability* **3** [C] a positive feature of a person's character: *What is the quality you most admire in others?* ♦ *Do you possess the right personal qualities to be a teacher?* ♦ *a woman with strong leadership qualities* (=the ability to be a good leader) **4** [C] a feature of something: *the addictive qualities of tobacco*

quality² /ˈkwɒləti/ adj of a high standard

quality con'trol noun [U] BUSINESS a method that a company uses for making sure that its products are of a satisfactory quality by doing regular checks on **samples** of the products —**quality con'troller** noun [C]

qualms /kwɑːmz/ noun [plural] thoughts that what you are doing might be bad or wrong

quandary /ˈkwɒndəri/ (plural **quandaries**) noun **be in a quandary** to not be certain what decision to take about something

quantifier /ˈkwɒntɪˌfaɪə/ noun [C] LANGUAGE a word or phrase such as 'much' or 'a few' that is used with another word in order to show quantity

quantify /ˈkwɒntɪfaɪ/ (**quantifies, quantifying, quantified**) verb [T] *formal* to measure or describe something as a quantity —**quantifiable** /ˈkwɒntɪˌfaɪəb(ə)l/ adj, **quantification** /ˌkwɒntɪfɪˈkeɪʃ(ə)n/ noun [U]

quantitative /'kwɒntɪtətɪv/ adj MATHS relating to data that can be counted or measured
—**quantitatively** adv

quantity /'kwɒntəti/ (plural **quantities**) noun **1** [U] the amount of something: *They check both the quantity and quality of materials used.* **2** [C/U] a particular amount of something: *a small **quantity of** drugs* ♦ *large **quantities of** water*

quantum /'kwɒntəm/ noun [C] PHYSICS a unit used for measuring very small amounts of energy

ˌquantum meˈchanics noun [U] PHYSICS the science that deals with the structure and behaviour of the particles of an atom and the energy they produce

ˈquantum ˌtheory noun [U] PHYSICS the belief that energy is produced in units, and that the size of these units can be calculated

quarantine /'kwɒrəntiːn/ noun [U] HEALTH a situation in which a person or animal that might have an infectious disease is kept separate from other people or animals so that they do not catch it
—**quarantine** verb [T]

quark /kwɑːk/ noun [C] PHYSICS a basic unit of matter, smaller than a **subatomic particle**. Protons and neutrons are made up of quarks.

quarrel¹ /'kwɒrəl/ noun [C] an argument

quarrel² /'kwɒrəl/ (**quarrels, quarrelling, quarrelled**) verb [I] to have an argument

quarry¹ /'kwɒri/ (plural **quarries**) noun **1** [C] a place where stone is dug up out of the ground **2** [singular] *formal* a person or animal that someone is trying to catch

quarry² /'kwɒri/ (**quarries, quarrying, quarried**) verb [T] to dig stone out of the ground

quart /kwɔːt/ noun [C] a unit for measuring an amount of liquid, equal to two **pints**

quarter /'kwɔːtə/ noun [C]

1 one of four parts	**4** part of town
2 15 minutes	**5** person/group
3 period of 3 months	**+** PHRASES

1 MATHS one of four equal parts of something: *Over a **quarter of** our income goes on food.*
2 one of four periods of 15 minutes that an hour is divided into when you are telling the time
3 one of four periods of three months that the year is divided into, especially when you are talking about financial accounts: *The company's profits fell in the third quarter.*
4 a part of a town where you find particular buildings, activities, or people: *the Chinese quarter of the city*
5 *formal* a particular person or group of people: *I knew there would be a lot of trouble **from that quarter**.*
♦ *Concern has been expressed **in some quarters** (=among some people or groups) about this policy.*
♦ *He has won support **from all quarters** (=from all people or groups).*

PHRASES **quarter past five/six etc** 15 minutes past five o'clock/six o'clock etc
quarter to five/six etc 15 minutes before five o'clock/six o'clock etc
→ QUARTERS

quarterback /'kwɔːtəˌbæk/ noun [C] SPORTS an important player in an American football team who gives instructions to other players

ˌquarter-ˈfinal noun [C] SPORTS one of the four games that are played between the eight players or teams that are still left in a competition

quarterly /'kwɔːtəli/ adj, adv done or produced four times a year

quarters /'kwɔːtəz/ noun [plural] *formal* rooms or buildings for people to live in

quartet /kwɔː'tet/ noun [C] MUSIC a group of four musicians or singers, or a piece of music for a quartet to perform

quartile /'kwɔːtaɪl/ noun [C] MATHS **1** in **statistics**, each of the four equal groups into which a **sample** can be divided **2** in **statistics**, each of the three values that divide a **sample** into four equal groups

quartz /kwɔːts/ noun [U] GEOLOGY a hard transparent mineral that forms inside rocks such as **sandstone**. It is often used inside electronic equipment and watches.

quartzite /'kwɔːtsaɪt/ noun [U] GEOLOGY a rock, made mainly of quartz, that is formed by the action of heat and pressure on **sandstone**

quasar /'kweɪzɑː/ noun [C] ASTRONOMY a very bright object in space that looks like a star and produces a lot of energy

quash /kwɒʃ/ verb [T] *formal* **1** to use force or violence to stop the political action taken by a group of people **2** to stop something from continuing **3** LAW to say officially that a decision taken by another court was wrong and no longer has legal force

quaternary consumer /kwə,tɜːnəri kən'sjuːmə/ noun [C] BIOLOGY, ENVIRONMENT a **carnivore** (=meat-eating animal) that feeds on another carnivore, that itself feeds on another carnivore. Very few animals feed as quaternary consumers.

quatrain /'kwɒˌtreɪn/ noun [C] LITERATURE a group of four lines in a poem

quaver /'kweɪvə/ noun [C] MUSIC a very short musical note that is played for one eighth of the time of a **semibreve** —*picture* → MUSIC

quay /kiː/ noun [C] a hard surface next to the sea or a river, where boats can stop

queasy /'kwiːzi/ adj feeling that you are going to vomit

queen /kwiːn/ noun [C]

1 woman who rules	**4** in cards
2 king's wife	**5** in chess
3 female insect	

1 a woman who belongs to a royal family and who rules a country: *Queen Elizabeth* ♦ *She was **crowned queen** in 1953.*
2 a woman who is married to a king
3 BIOLOGY a large female insect that can lay eggs: *a queen bee*
4 in a game of cards, a card with a picture of a queen on it
5 a piece that can move in any direction in a game of chess

ˌQueen's ˈevidence noun **turn Queen's evidence** LAW if a criminal turns Queen's evidence, they agree to give information to the police or to a court of law, in order to help them to catch other criminals

queer /kwɪə/ adj **1** *old-fashioned* strange **2** *offensive* an offensive word used for describing gay people

quell /kwel/ verb [T] *formal* **1** to get rid of unpleasant thoughts or feelings **2** to cause a violent situation to end

quench /kwentʃ/ verb [T] TECHNOLOGY to heat steel to an even temperature then cool it rapidly in a liquid, in order to make it harder
PHRASE **quench your thirst** to drink something so that you no longer feel thirsty

query[1] /'kwɪəri/ (plural **queries**) noun [C] a question

query[2] /'kwɪəri/ (**queries, querying, queried**) verb [T] to ask a question

'query ,language noun [C] COMPUTING a language used in a computer **database** that allows the database to be searched without difficulty

question[1] /'kwestʃ(ə)n/ noun **1** [C] something that someone asks you when they want information: *Why won't you **answer** my **question**?* ♦ *I wish I hadn't **asked** that **question**.* ♦ *Does anyone have any **questions about** the trip?* **2** [C] something that you are asked in a test or competition: *Only one person **answered** all three **questions** correctly.* **3** [C] an issue that needs to be discussed and dealt with: *Recent incidents are bound to **raise questions** about the level of violence in football.* ♦ *His report did not **address the question** of air warfare.* **4** [C/U] a feeling of doubt about something: *This information began to **raise questions** in her mind about Jack's innocence.* ♦ *New evidence has **called into question** (=made people have doubts about) the testimony of this witness.* ♦ *There had been some **question about** whether to interview the boy.*

PHRASES **be out of the question** used for saying that something is definitely not a possibility: *Any agreement between the groups was out of the question.*

be a/the question of used for saying what the most important issue is in a situation: *There would definitely be some job losses; it was just a question of how many.* ♦ *We all want to go ahead with the project, but there's the question of finance.*

in question the person, thing, time etc in question is the one that you are talking about: *The photograph in question was taken long before I met you.*

there is no question of sth if there is no question of something, it definitely will not happen

without question used for saying that something is definitely true: *He is without question the best player in our team.*

question[2] /'kwestʃ(ə)n/ verb [T] **1** to ask someone questions: *A hundred employers were questioned in the survey.* ♦ *Curious friends **questioned** me **about** the case.* **2** to have or express doubts about something: *I have never questioned her honesty.*

questionable /'kwestʃ(ə)nəb(ə)l/ adj **1** probably not true, accurate, or complete: *The results of the test seem highly questionable.* **2** probably not good, honest, or worth admiring: *questionable behaviour* —**questionably** adv

questioning /'kwestʃ(ə)nɪŋ/ noun [U] a situation in which people ask someone questions

'question ,mark noun [C] LANGUAGE the symbol ? that is used at the end of a sentence in order to show that it represents a question

questionnaire /ˌkwestʃə'neə/ noun [C] a set of questions that a lot of people are asked as a way of getting information about what people generally think or do

'question ,tag noun [C] LANGUAGE a word or phrase such as 'isn't it?' or 'haven't you?' that you can add to a sentence in order to make a question

queue[1] /kju:/ noun [C] **1** a line of people that are waiting for something: *There was a long **queue for** tickets.* ♦ *We stood **in a queue** for over an hour.* **2** COMPUTING a set of jobs that a computer is preparing to do

queue[2] /kju:/ (**queues, queuing** or **queueing, queued**) or **,queue 'up** verb [I] to wait for something in a queue

queue-jumping /'kju: ˌdʒʌmpɪŋ/ noun [U] the unfair behaviour of someone who moves nearer to the front of a queue than other people who have been waiting longer —**queue-jump** verb [I]

quibble /'kwɪb(ə)l/ verb [I] to argue or complain about things that are not important —**quibble** noun [C]

quick /kwɪk/ adj **1** able to move fast or to do something fast: *He's surprisingly quick for such a big man.* ♦ *a quick worker* **2** done or happening in a short time: *He took a quick glance over his shoulder.* ♦ *a quick decision* **3** able to understand things very easily: *a quick learner*

quicken /'kwɪkən/ verb [I/T] formal if something quickens, or if you quicken it, it happens or moves more quickly

quickly /'kwɪkli/ adv **1** at a fast speed: *We have to work quickly.* ♦ *She walked quickly out of the room.* **2** after only a short time, or lasting only a short time: *Something has to be done about this quickly.* ♦ *Let me explain very quickly what I mean.*

quicksand /'kwɪkˌsænd/ noun [U] soft wet sand that is dangerous to walk on because it pulls your body down into it

quid pro quo /ˌkwɪd prəʊ 'kwəʊ/ noun [C] formal something that someone offers or gives to someone in return for something that they have offered or given

quiet[1] /'kwaɪət/ adj **1** making very little or no noise: *some quiet soothing music* ♦ *Be quiet, please. I'm trying to read.* **2** not talking, or not usually talking: *He's a quiet sensitive boy.* **3** not very busy, or with not much activity: *a quiet little village* ♦ *a quiet and relaxing day at home* **4** used about feelings that someone has but does not show or talk about: *her quiet confidence*

PHRASE **keep quiet about sth** or **keep sth quiet** to not tell anyone about something: *Can we trust him to keep quiet about what he's seen?*

quiet[2] /'kwaɪət/ noun [U] a place or situation in which there is not much noise or activity: *We went into the field for some **peace and quiet**.*

quieten /'kwaɪət(ə)n/ verb [I/T] to become calmer or less noisy, or to make someone do this

quietly /'kwaɪətli/ adv **1** in a way that does not make much noise: *He closed the door quietly behind him.* **2** in a quiet voice: *'Listen,' she said quietly, 'I want to tell you something.'* **3** in a way that is not obvious to other people: *Sandra stood by, quietly amused.*

quill /kwɪl/ noun [C] a large feather from a bird, or an old-fashioned pen made from a bird's feather

quilt /kwɪlt/ noun [C] a thick cover for a bed

quinine /kwɪ'ni:n/ noun [U] HEALTH a drug used for treating someone who has malaria or another disease that causes fever

quintessential /ˌkwɪntɪ'senʃ(ə)l/ adj formal perfect as an example of a type of person or thing —**quintessentially** adv

quintet /kwɪn'tet/ noun [C] MUSIC a group of five musicians or singers, or a piece of music for a quintet to perform

quintuple /kwɪn'tju:p(ə)l/ determiner five times as much or as many

quirk /kwɜ:k/ noun [C] **1** a strange or annoying habit **2** something strange that happens

quit /kwɪt/ (**quits, quitting, quit**) verb [I/T] informal **1** to stop doing something: *She drinks so much, she could never quit now.* **2** to leave a job or school permanently

quite /kwaɪt/ adv **1** fairly but not very: *I was feeling quite tired after our walk.* ♦ *I quite like his films.* **2** completely or very: *We haven't quite finished.* ♦ *Are you quite sure you know what to do?* ♦ *'Are you ready?' 'Not quite.'* **3** used after a negative word to mean that something is not exactly correct or clear: *We couldn't quite remember where you lived.*

quiver /'kwɪvə/ verb [I] to shake with short quick movements —**quiver** noun [C]

quiz /kwɪz/ (plural **quizzes**) noun [C] a test or competition in which you answer questions

quizzical /'kwɪzɪk(ə)l/ adj showing that you are confused or surprised by something that is rather strange —**quizzically** /'kwɪzɪkli/ adv

quo see **status quo**

quoin /kɔɪn, kwɔɪn/ noun [C] **CONSTRUCTION** the external corner where two wall surfaces meet

quorum /'kwɔːrəm/ noun [singular] *formal* the smallest number of people who must be present at a meeting in order to allow official decisions to be made

quota /'kwəʊtə/ noun [C] **ECONOMICS** an official amount of a product that someone is allowed to make, sell, or buy: *The government is planning to introduce quotas on sugar production.*

quotation /kwəʊ'teɪʃ(ə)n/ noun [C] **1 LITERATURE** words from a book, play etc that are used by someone else **2** the price that someone says that they will charge you for doing a job

quo'tation ˌmarks noun [plural] **LANGUAGE** the symbols ' ' and " " that are used in writing before and after a quotation or the words that someone speaks = **INVERTED COMMAS**

quote¹ /kwəʊt/ verb **1** [I/T] to say or write words that someone else has said or written: *He was quoted as saying that he was shocked by the judge's decision.* ♦ *Robert quoted from one of Churchill's speeches.* **2** [T] to give something as an example to support what you are saying: *He quoted the example of a 40-year-old man who has been waiting nearly two years for an operation.* **3** [T] to tell someone what price you would charge them to do a particular piece of work: *They quoted us fifty dollars to replace the broken window.*

quote² /kwəʊt/ noun [C] **LITERATURE** a **quotation**

quotient /'kwəʊʃ(ə)nt/ noun [C] **MATHS** the number that is the result of dividing one number by another

the Qur'an /kɔː'rɑːn/ **RELIGION** the **Koran**

qwerty /'kwɜːti/ noun [C] **COMPUTING** a qwerty keyboard for a computer is the standard keyboard for typing in the English language. Its top row of keys starts with the letters Q, W, E, R, T, and Y.

r /ɑː/ (plural **r's**) or **R** (plural **R's**) noun [C/U] the 18th letter of the English alphabet

R abbrev **COMPUTING** are: used in emails and **text messages**

R & B /ˌɑː ən 'biː/ noun [U] **MUSIC** rhythm and blues: a type of music that combines **blues** and **soul** styles with modern beats and production methods

R & D /ˌɑː ən 'diː/ noun [U] **BUSINESS research and development**

rabbi /'ræbaɪ/ noun [C] **RELIGION** a Jewish religious leader

rabbit /'ræbɪt/ noun [C] a small furry mammal with long ears, large teeth, and a short tail —*picture* → MAMMAL

rabies /'reɪbiːz/ noun [U] **HEALTH** a very serious viral disease that affects the **central nervous system**. It is passed on in the saliva of an infected animal, and so it can be caught by being bitten.

race¹ /reɪs/ noun

1 competition for speed	**4** similar animals/plants
2 competition to be best/first	**5** competition for horses
3 similar people	**+ PHRASE**

1 [C] **SPORTS** a competition that decides who is the fastest at doing something: *He is training for a big race.* ♦ *Marlene needs to win the race to keep her title.*
2 [singular] a competition in which a person, organization, business, or country tries to win something or to be the first to do something: *There are three candidates in the race for the presidency.* ♦ *We are losing the race to find a cure for AIDS.*
3 [C/U] a group of people who are similar because they have the same skin colour or other physical features, or because they speak the same language or have the same history or customs: *We do not discriminate on the basis of race or gender.* ♦ *a disaster that could mark the end of the human race* (=all of the people of the world, considered as a single group)
4 [C] **BIOLOGY** a group of animals or plants that are similar to each other. A race of animals or plants is smaller than a **species**.
5 the races [plural] **SPORTS** a series of horse races: *a day at the races*
PHRASE a race against time a situation in which someone must do or finish something very quickly because they only have a limited amount of time to do it

race² /reɪs/ verb **1** [I/T] **SPORTS** to compete in a race: *The gun sounded and they started to race.* ♦ *I raced my brother down the street.* **2** [I] to move very quickly: *He raced to the bathroom when he heard Cheryl scream.* ♦ *Thoughts were racing through her mind.* **3** [T] to take someone somewhere quickly: *We raced the children to hospital.* **4** [I] to work or move at a faster speed than usual: *Her heart began to race madly.*

racecourse /'reɪskɔːs/ noun [C] **SPORTS** a track that is used for horse races

racegoer /'reɪsˌɡəʊə/ noun [C] someone who goes regularly to horse races

racehorse /'reɪshɔːs/ noun [C] **SPORTS** a horse that is trained to run in races

ˌrace re'lations noun [plural] **SOCIAL STUDIES** the relationships between people of different races who live in the same community

racetrack /'reɪsˌtræk/ noun [C] **SPORTS 1** a track that is used for racing cars **2** a **racecourse**

racial /'reɪʃ(ə)l/ adj **SOCIAL STUDIES 1** happening between people of different races **2** relating to someone's race —**racially** adv

racing /'reɪsɪŋ/ noun [U] **SPORTS** a sport in which cars, boats, or horses or other animals race against each other —**racing** adj

'racing ˌcar noun [C] **SPORTS** a car that is designed and used for racing

racism /'reɪ,sɪz(ə)m/ noun [U] SOCIAL STUDIES a way of behaving or thinking that treats people belonging to some races unfairly

racist /'reɪsɪst/ noun [C] SOCIAL STUDIES someone who thinks that their race is better than others —**racist** adj

rack /ræk/ noun [C] an object with shelves, spaces, or hooks, used for storing things

,**rack-and-'pinion ,steering** noun [U] ENGINEERING a vehicle **steering** system consisting of a **shaft** from the **steering wheel** with a **pinion** (=wheel with teeth) on the end that connects with a horizontal **rack** (=bar with teeth). When the driver turns the steering wheel the rack, which is connected to the wheels, moves backwards and forwards and the vehicle's wheels turn.

racket /'rækɪt/ noun 1 [singular] *informal* a loud annoying noise 2 [C] SPORTS an object used for hitting the ball in games such as tennis 3 [C] *informal* an illegal activity that makes money

'**rack ,rate** noun [C] TOURISM the price for a room in a hotel that is advertised in the hotel and does not include any **discounts**

racquetball /'rækɪt,bɔːl/ noun [U] SPORTS an indoor game in which two players use small **rackets** to hit a ball

radar /'reɪdɑː/ noun [C/U] a system that uses radio signals in order to find the position of something such as an aircraft or ship

radial1 /'reɪdɪəl/ adj a radial pattern or design consists of straight lines that all go out from the centre of a circle

radial2 /'reɪdɪəl/ or ,**radial 'tyre** noun [C] ENGINEERING a **radial-ply tyre**

'**radial ,cam** noun [C] ENGINEERING, TECHNOLOGY a machine that changes radial motion into **straight-line motion**

'**radial ,motion** noun [U] PHYSICS movement in the direction in which someone is looking

'**radial-ply ,tyre** noun [C] ENGINEERING a type of vehicle tyre with wires inside that make it firmer and safer

'**radial ,symmetry** noun [U] ANATOMY, BIOLOGY the fact of having all parts arranged equally around a central point

radian /'reɪdɪən/ noun [C] MATHS a unit for measuring angles that is equal to about 57.3°

radiance /'reɪdɪəns/ noun [singular/U] 1 happiness that you can see in someone's appearance or smile 2 light that shines from something

radiant /'reɪdɪənt/ adj 1 someone who is radiant looks extremely happy 2 very bright 3 SCIENCE radiant heat is the energy produced by hot objects. It is in the form of **infrared** light that cannot be seen. —**radiantly** adv

radiate /'reɪdɪeɪt/ verb 1 [I/T] to show a particular feeling or attitude: *John radiated charm.* 2 [I/T] PHYSICS to produce energy in the form of electromagnetic waves such as heat, light, or radio waves 3 [I] if lines, paths, or roads radiate from a central point, they spread out from it

radiation /,reɪdɪ'eɪʃ(ə)n/ noun [U] 1 CHEMISTRY, PHYSICS a form of energy that is released by radioactive substances such as **uranium** and **plutonium**. It can be very harmful to humans and other animals, and to the environment, if too much of it gets into the air or to the ground: *Some workers at the power station were **exposed to** high levels of **radiation**.* 2 PHYSICS a type of energy that is sent out in the form of radioactive waves, for example, heat, light, or radio

waves 3 PHYSICS a method by which heat can travel through empty space → CONDUCTION, CONVECTION

radiative zone /'reɪdɪətɪv ,zəʊn/ noun [C] ASTRONOMY a layer of a star between its core and the **convective zone**, across which energy is carried by means of radiation —*picture* → SUN

radiator /'reɪdɪ,eɪtə/ noun [C] 1 ENGINEERING a piece of equipment that stops a vehicle's engine from getting too hot. It consists of tubes through which heated water from the engine passes to be cooled. 2 a large metal object on a wall, used for heating a room

radical1 /'rædɪk(ə)l/ adj 1 a radical change or way of doing something is new and very different from the usual way: *a radical solution to the problem* 2 SOCIAL STUDIES believing that major political and social changes are necessary: *a radical left-wing group*

radical2 /'rædɪk(ə)l/ noun [C] 1 CHEMISTRY a group of atoms that behaves as a single unit in a chemical reaction → FREE RADICAL 2 SOCIAL STUDIES someone who believes that major political and social changes are necessary

radically /'rædɪkli/ adv if something changes radically, it changes completely or in a way that is very noticeable

radicle /'rædɪk(ə)l/ noun [C] BIOLOGY the part of a plant embryo that forms the root of the young plant

radii /'reɪdɪaɪ/ a plural of **radius**

radio1 /'reɪdɪəʊ/ (plural **radios**) noun 1 [singular/U] a system of broadcasting information and programmes that people can listen to, or the programmes that are broadcast: *an independent **radio station** ♦ **Radio and television** have had an enormous effect on people's lives. ♦ She began her career **in** local **radio**. ♦ What's **on the radio**?* 2 [C] a piece of equipment that you use for listening to radio programmes: *a car radio ♦ Let's **turn on the radio**.* 3 [U] a system of sending and receiving spoken messages by using electronic signals: *We remained **in** constant **radio contact**.* 4 [C] the piece of equipment that is used for sending or receiving spoken messages using electronic signals: *a two-way radio*

radio2 /'reɪdɪəʊ/ (**radios, radioing, radioed**) verb [I/T] to communicate with someone using a radio

radioactive /,reɪdɪəʊ'æktɪv/ adj CHEMISTRY, PHYSICS 1 a radioactive substance such as **uranium** gives off energy in the form of streams of particles, caused by the way its **unstable** atoms decay —*picture* → NUCLEAR REACTOR 2 relating to or making use of radioactivity or the radiation that some substances give off

radioactivity /,reɪdɪəʊæk'tɪvəti/ noun [U] CHEMISTRY, PHYSICS the ability that some substances have to produce energy in the form of radiation

'**radio ,button** noun [C] COMPUTING a place on a website or computer screen that looks like a button that the user can press to choose something

radiocarbon dating /,reɪdɪəʊkɑːbən 'deɪtɪŋ/ noun [U] SCIENCE **carbon dating**

radiography /,reɪdɪ'ɒgrəfi/ noun [U] HEALTH the process of taking X-ray photographs of someone's body as part of a medical treatment —**radiographer** noun [C]

radioisotope /,reɪdɪəʊ'aɪsətəʊp/ noun [C] CHEMISTRY, PHYSICS an isotope that is radioactive

,**radio 'microphone** noun [C] a **microphone** that works using radio technology and does not need to be connected by wire to other equipment

,radio 'telescope noun [C] ASTRONOMY a very large piece of equipment that receives and records the **radio waves** that come from stars and other objects in space

radiotherapy /ˌreɪdɪəʊˈθerəpi/ noun [U] HEALTH a medical treatment, especially for cancer, that uses X-rays or other forms of radiation —**radiotherapist** noun [C]

'radio ,wave noun [C] PHYSICS an electromagnetic wave that radio signals can be sent on

radish /ˈrædɪʃ/ noun [C] a small white or red vegetable that is eaten raw in salads —*picture* → VEGETABLE

radium /ˈreɪdiəm/ noun [U] CHEMISTRY a radioactive element that is used in the treatment of cancer. Chemical symbol: **Ra**

radius /ˈreɪdiəs/ (plural **radiuses** or **radii** /ˈreɪdiaɪ/) noun [C] **1** MATHS the distance from the centre of a circle to its edge, or a straight line from the centre to the edge —*picture* → CIRCLE **2** MATHS a particular distance in all directions from a central point: *Delivery is free within a five-mile radius of the city centre.* **3** ANATOMY the larger outer bone in the lower arm, next to the **ulna** —*picture* → SKELETON

'radius ,arm noun [C] ENGINEERING a metal bar in the **suspension** system of a vehicle, designed to stop the vehicle's wheel from moving forwards and backwards too much

radon /ˈreɪdɒn/ noun [U] CHEMISTRY a type of radioactive gas that is produced when **radium** breaks down. Chemical symbol: **Rn**

raffia /ˈræfiə/ noun [U] a rough substance used for making baskets and other objects that comes from the leaves of a palm tree

raffle /ˈræf(ə)l/ noun [C] a competition in which you win a prize if the number on your ticket is the same as the number on the prize

raft /rɑːft/ noun [C] **1** a simple flat boat made by tying long pieces of wood together **2** a small light boat made of rubber or plastic

rafter /ˈrɑːftə/ noun [C] a large piece of wood that supports a sloping roof

'raft foun,dation noun [C] CONSTRUCTION a type of **foundation** used on soft or loose soil, consisting of a layer of **reinforced concrete**

rafting /ˈrɑːftɪŋ/ noun [U] the activity of travelling on a river in a small boat

rag /ræg/ noun **1** [C] a piece of old cloth that is used for cleaning or wiping something **2 rags** [plural] clothes that are old, torn, and dirty: *The little girl was dressed in rags.*

raga /ˈrɑːgə/ noun [C] MUSIC a piece of Indian music based on a traditional pattern of notes

rage¹ /reɪdʒ/ noun [C/U] a very strong feeling of anger: *Her eyes filled with tears of rage and frustration.*

rage² /reɪdʒ/ verb [I] to continue with a lot of force, violence, or angry arguments: *Fierce fighting raged for several days.*

ragged /ˈrægɪd/ adj **1** torn and dirty: *a pair of ragged shorts* **2** wearing old dirty clothes: *ragged children playing in the street* **3** not smooth or regular: *a ragged edge*

raging /ˈreɪdʒɪŋ/ adj **1** happening with a lot of force or violence: *a raging battle* **2** very serious, painful, or strong: *a raging fever*

ragworm /ˈrægwɜːm/ noun [C] BIOLOGY a sea worm that is often used as fishing **bait**

rai /raɪ/ noun [U] MUSIC a type of popular North African **folk music** that has been mixed with various styles such as **rock** and **reggae**

raid¹ /reɪd/ noun [C] **1** a sudden short military attack: *Soldiers carried out raids on enemy targets.* **2** an action by police officers in which they suddenly enter a place in order to arrest people or search for something **3** a crime in which someone suddenly enters a place and uses force or threats to steal something **4** BUSINESS an attempt by one business to **take over** another (=take control of it) by buying a large number of its shares, despite its opposition to this action

raid² /reɪd/ verb [T] **1** to use force to enter a place in order to search for something **2** to suddenly attack a place and cause a lot of damage

raider /ˈreɪdə/ noun [C] someone who attacks a place using force

rail /reɪl/ noun **1** [C] a metal bar that is used for hanging clothes and other things on: *a clothes rail* **2** [C] a metal or wooden bar that you can hold onto to stop yourself from falling: *a safety rail* **3** [U] the system of travelling by train: *We ought to transport more heavy goods by rail.* ♦ *an increase in rail fares* **4** [C] one of the pair of metal bars that a train travels on

railcar /ˈreɪlˌkɑː/ noun [C] a single **coach** with its own motor, carrying passengers by rail

railcard /ˈreɪlˌkɑːd/ noun [C] TOURISM a card that allows passengers to travel by train at a lower price than usual

railhead /ˈreɪlˌhed/ noun [C] the place where a railway line ends

railing /ˈreɪlɪŋ/ noun [C] a fence made of narrow posts supporting an upper bar

railpass /ˈreɪlˌpɑːs/ noun [C] TOURISM a train ticket that allows passengers to travel anywhere in a particular area during a particular period of time

railway /ˈreɪlˌweɪ/ noun [C] **1** the system of travelling by train, and all the people and things that are connected with it: *a railway station* **2 railway** or **railway line** the metal track that trains travel on: *The path continues along a disused railway.*

rain¹ /reɪn/ noun GEOGRAPHY **1** [U] water that falls in drops from clouds in the sky: *Visibility was good, with only occasional light rain.* ♦ *People were standing in the rain.* **2 the rains** [plural] the large amounts of rain that fall in tropical regions during a particular season

rain² /reɪn/ verb [I] **1** GEOGRAPHY when it rains, water falls in drops from clouds in the sky: *It had been raining heavily all day.* **2** to fall from the air in large amounts
PHRASE **rained off** if a sports game or other outside event is rained off, it does not happen because of rain

rainbow /ˈreɪnˌbəʊ/ noun [C] a curved line of colours that appears in the sky when the sun shines while it is raining

raincoat /ˈreɪnˌkəʊt/ noun [C] a long coat made of light material that is designed to keep you dry when it is raining

raindrop /ˈreɪnˌdrɒp/ noun [C] a drop of rain

rainfall /ˈreɪnˌfɔːl/ noun [C/U] GEOGRAPHY the amount of rain that falls in a particular area during a particular period of time

rainforest /ˈreɪnˌfɒrɪst/ noun [C/U] BIOLOGY, ENVIRONMENT a forest in a tropical region of the world where it rains a lot. Rainforests are considered to be important environmental areas with large numbers of different animals and plants. The rainforests are disappearing fast because of land being cleared for development, and because of the activities of **logging** companies. → DEFORESTATION

'rain ,gauge noun [C] GEOGRAPHY a piece of equipment used for measuring the amount of rain that falls

'rain ,shadow noun [C] GEOGRAPHY a region that has little rain because it is protected by a mountain range in the direction of winds that carry rain. As the winds rise over the mountains they drop most of their water before reaching the other side.

rainstorm /'reɪn,stɔːm/ noun [C] GEOGRAPHY a storm with a lot of rain

rainwater /'reɪn,wɔːtə/ noun [U] water that falls to the ground in the form of rain

rainy /'reɪni/ (**rainier, rainiest**) adj a rainy day is one on which it rains a lot

the 'rainy ,season noun [singular] GEOGRAPHY in some regions of the world, the season in which a lot of rain falls

raise /reɪz/ verb [T]

1 lift sth higher	**6** cause feelings
2 lift yourself	**7** take care of children
3 increase	**8** of animals/crops
4 collect money	**9** in mathematics
5 mention sth	**+ PHRASE**

1 to lift something to a higher place or position: *He slowly raised the cup to his lips.* ♦ *A number of children raised their hands.*
2 to lift yourself from a sitting or lying position: *She could barely raise herself out of the chair.*
3 to increase a number, amount, or level: *They had raised their prices to unreasonable levels.*
4 to collect money for a particular purpose: *We need your help to raise money for medical research.*
5 to mention something so that it can be discussed: *Are there any other questions you would like to raise at the meeting?* ♦ *We will raise the issue of working hours with the manager.*
6 to make someone have a particular feeling or reaction: *Doubts have been raised about the company's right to use this land.*
7 to take care of children while they are growing up: *For most parents, raising a family is a positive challenge.* ♦ *This seems strange to someone born and raised in the city.*
8 AGRICULTURE to keep a particular type of animal, or to grow a particular crop: *She's been raising sheep for over 40 years.*
9 MATHS if you raise a number to the power of a particular number, you multiply the first number by itself a particular number of times
  PHRASE raise your voice to speak in a loud angry way
→ ALARM[1], EYEBROW

raisin /'reɪz(ə)n/ noun [C] a dried grape

raising agent /'reɪzɪŋ ,eɪdʒ(ə)nt/ noun [C] CHEMISTRY a chemical that is used in cooking for making cakes rise

rake[1] /reɪk/ verb **1** [T] to pull your fingers through or along something **2** [I/T] AGRICULTURE to use a rake in order to make an area of soil level or to remove leaves etc from the ground

rake[2] /reɪk/ noun [C] AGRICULTURE a tool for making soil level and for removing leaves etc from the ground. It has a long handle with a row of sharp points attached at one end.

rally[1] /'ræli/ (plural **rallies**) noun **1** [C] a public meeting that a lot of people go to in order to support something or protest against something **2** [C] SPORTS

a car race **3** [C] SPORTS an occasion when two players in a game such as tennis hit the ball to each other several times before either of them wins the point **4** [singular] an increase or improvement in something

rally[2] /'ræli/ (**rallies, rallying, rallied**) verb **1** [I/T] to join other people in order to support someone or something **2** [I] to increase or improve after being low, weak, or ill

ram[1] /ræm/ (**rams, ramming, rammed**) verb **1** [I/T] if a vehicle or boat rams something, it hits it very hard **2** [T] to push something into a place with great force: *He rammed his fist through a window.*

ram[2] /ræm/ noun [C] a male sheep —*picture* → MAMMAL

RAM /ræm/ noun **1** [U] COMPUTING random access memory: the part of a computer that programs are loaded into while you are using them. In this part of the computer you can get any piece of information directly, without needing to use several stages to get it. **2** [C] CHEMISTRY relative atomic mass

Ramadan /,ræmə'dɑːn/ noun [U] RELIGION the ninth month of the Muslim year, when Muslims do not eat or drink anything before the sun sets, for religious reasons

ramification /,ræmɪfɪ'keɪʃ(ə)n/ noun [C] formal a complicated or unexpected way in which a decision, process, or event affects other things

ramp /ræmp/ noun [C] a slope connecting two levels of a building or road

rampage /'ræmpeɪdʒ/ noun [C] uncontrolled behaviour involving damage to property

rampant /'ræmpənt/ adj existing or spreading in an uncontrolled way: *Official corruption there is rampant.*

rampart /'ræm,pɑːt/ noun [C] a high hill of earth or a stone wall built around a city or castle in the past in order to protect it against an enemy —*picture* → CASTLE

ramshackle /'ræm,ʃæk(ə)l/ adj in bad condition and likely to fall down

ran /ræn/ the past tense of **run[1]**

ranch /rɑːntʃ/ noun [C] AGRICULTURE a very large farm where cows, horses, or sheep are kept

rancher /'rɑːntʃə/ noun [C] AGRICULTURE someone who owns or manages a ranch or whose job is to work on a ranch —**ranching** noun [U]

rancour /'ræŋkə/ noun [U] formal a feeling of hate or anger that lasts a long time

rand /rænd/ (plural **rand**) noun [C] ECONOMICS the unit of money used in South Africa

random /'rændəm/ adj chosen or happening without any particular method or pattern: *a random sample of voters* ♦ *Winning tickets will be chosen at random.* —**randomly** adv, **randomness** noun [U]

,random 'access noun [U] COMPUTING the ability to get information directly from the place on a computer where it is stored, without having to search through the information that goes before it = DIRECT ACCESS

,random 'access ,memory noun [U] see **RAM**

rang /ræŋ/ the past tense of **ring[1]**

range[1] /reɪndʒ/ noun

1 things of same type	**6** open area of land
2 numbers, ages etc	**7** area of farm for
3 of responsibility etc	animals
4 distance for sth	**8** mountains
5 in music	

1 [C] a number of different things that are of the same

general type: *We discussed **a range of** issues affecting professional women.* ♦ *We stock **a wide range** of office furniture.*

2 [C] all the numbers, ages, measurements etc that are included within particular fixed limits: *books for children in the 11-to-14 **age range*** ♦ *Temperatures are expected to be **in the range of** 40 to 45 degrees.*

3 [singular] the limits within which a person or organization is able to deal with something= SCOPE: *Such a decision is not **within the range of** my responsibility.*

4 [singular/U] the distance within which you can see, hear, or reach something: *The children turned their cameras on anyone **in range**.* ♦ *It's best to stay **out of range of** recording equipment.*

5 [C] MUSIC all the musical notes that a person can sing or an instrument can play, from the highest to the lowest

6 [C] an open area of land where people can practise firing guns: *a rifle range*

7 [C] AGRICULTURE a large area of land on a farm where cows or other animals are kept

8 [C] GEOGRAPHY a number of mountains considered as a group

range² /reɪndʒ/ verb **1** [I] to be included in a group of numbers, ages, measurements etc with particular fixed limits: *Costs **range from** 50 **to** several hundred pounds.* ♦ *The team contained ten players whose ages **ranged between** 10 and 16.* **2** [I] to include a variety of things: *products **ranging from** televisions **to** computer software* **3** [I/T] to move with complete freedom around a large area: *There were buffalo ranging the plains of North America.* **4** [T] to arrange things in a particular place or position: *Boxes of books were **ranged against** the wall.*

rank¹ /ræŋk/ noun **1** [C/U] someone's position in an organization or in society: *Her rank when she retired was captain.* ♦ *She had reached **the rank of** junior minister by the time she was 30.* **2 ranks** [plural] all the people within a group or organization: *a dispute within the party ranks* ♦ *By 1939, Soviet Russia had **joined the ranks of** the leading modern industrial powers.*

PHRASE **close ranks** if members of a group close ranks, they support each other against people who are trying to defeat or criticize them

rank² /ræŋk/ verb **1** [I] to have a particular quality compared with other similar things: *This must **rank as** one of the most violent films ever made.* **2** [T] to put someone or something into a position according to their success, importance, size etc: *The survey ranked schools according to their exam results.*

ransack /ˈrænsæk/ verb [T] to go through a place stealing or damaging things

ransom /ˈræns(ə)m/ noun [C/U] an amount of money that someone asks for, in exchange for a person who they are keeping as a prisoner

rant /rænt/ verb [I] to complain or talk loudly and angrily for a long time: *He was ranting about taxes.*

rap¹ /ræp/ noun **1** [C] a quick hard hit, or the sound of this **2** [U] MUSIC a type of music in which words are spoken over a strong musical beat

rap² /ræp/ (**raps, rapping, rapped**) verb **1** [I/T] to hit something hard and quickly **2** [I] MUSIC to perform by speaking over a strong musical beat

rape /reɪp/ noun **1** [C/U] LAW the crime of forcing someone to have sex by using violence **2** [U] a plant with bright yellow flowers that is used for feeding animals or making oil —**rape** verb [T]

rapid /ˈræpɪd/ adj happening, moving, or acting quickly: *We are seeing a **rapid growth** in the use of the Internet.* ♦ *the **rapid movement** of troops into the area* —**rapidity** /rəˈpɪdəti/ noun [U], **rapidly** adv: *a rapidly expanding population*

rapids /ˈræpɪdz/ noun [plural] GEOGRAPHY a part of a river where the water moves extremely quickly over rocks —*picture* → RIVER, WATERFALL

rapier /ˈreɪpiə/ noun [C] a long thin sword with a very sharp point

rapist /ˈreɪpɪst/ noun [C] someone who forces someone else to have sex with them

rapper /ˈræpə/ noun [C] MUSIC someone who performs **rap** music

rapporteur /ˌræpɔːˈtɜː/ noun [C] *formal* someone who is chosen to study a particular situation or subject, and report what they learn to an organization or meeting

raptor /ˈræptə/ noun [C] BIOLOGY a bird that kills other birds and animals for food

rapture /ˈræptʃə/ noun [U] **be in rapture/raptures** to be in an extremely happy or excited state, and show this in talking

rare /reə/ adj **1** not happening very often: *I am late only **on rare occasions**.* ♦ *It's extremely **rare for** her to lose her temper.* **2** not often seen or found, and therefore valuable: *rare birds* ♦ *He has a rare talent for managing people.* **3** rare meat has been cooked for only a short time and is red inside → RARITY

rare-'earth adj CHEMISTRY belonging to the group of chemically similar metallic elements with atomic numbers between 57 to 71 in the periodic table

rarefaction /ˌreərɪˈfækʃ(ə)n/ noun [U] PHYSICS the process by which the molecules in a material are pulled apart as **sound waves** travel through them

rarely /ˈreəli/ adv not often ≠ FREQUENTLY: *My mother very rarely has time to rest.*

rarity /ˈreərəti/ (plural **rarities**) noun [C] something that is unusual or does not happen often

rash¹ /ræʃ/ noun **1** [C] HEALTH an area of small red spots on the skin that is caused by a disease or by a reaction to something **2** [singular] a lot of events of the same type taking place in a short period of time

rash² /ræʃ/ adj acting or done too quickly, without thinking —**rashly** adv

rasp /rɑːsp/ verb [I/T] to make an unpleasant sound as if two rough surfaces were rubbing together

raspberry /ˈrɑːzbəri/ (plural **raspberries**) noun [C] a small soft red fruit that grows on a bush —*picture* → FRUIT

Rastafarian /ˌræstəˈfeəriən/ noun [C] RELIGION a member of a religious group based in Jamaica whose main religious leader was Emperor Haile Selassie of Ethiopia

rat /ræt/ noun [C] a small furry mammal like a large mouse with a long tail. Rats are **rodents**. —*picture* → MAMMAL

ratchet /ˈrætʃɪt/ or **'ratchet ,wheel** noun [C] ENGINEERING a part of a machine consisting of a wheel or bar with **teeth** (=sharp points) on it. Another metal piece fits into it, allowing it to move in one direction only.

rate¹ /reɪt/ noun [C] **1** the number of times that something happens, or the number of examples of something within a particular period of time: *a rising **birth rate*** ♦ *areas where **the rate of** unemployment is high* **2** the speed at which something happens within a particular period of time: *The population was growing at an alarming rate.* ♦ *Doctors monitor the patient's* **heart rate**. **3** an amount of money that is paid or charged: *tax rates* ♦ *an hourly* **rate** *of pay*

PHRASE **rate of return** BUSINESS the income that a company makes in a year from money it has invested, calculated as a percentage of the amount originally invested

→ FIRST-RATE, SECOND-RATE, THIRD-RATE

rate² /reɪt/ verb **1** [T] to consider that someone or something has a particular quality or has achieved a particular standard or level: *Many voters* **rate** *the environment* **as** *the number one issue.* ♦ *She is* **rated** *very* **highly** *by her colleagues* (=they approve of her). **2** [I] to have a particular quality compared with other similar things: *The exhibition* **rates as** *one of the most successful for this museum.* **3** [T] to deserve something: *That should rate a mention in the local newspaper!*

rather /ˈrɑːðə/ adv **1** to a fairly large degree = QUITE: *Matt left rather suddenly without any explanation.* ♦ *He was a rather handsome boy.* **2** used for correcting or explaining what you have just said: *He couldn't help us,* **or rather** *he didn't want to.*

PHRASES **rather than** instead of: *Doug chose to quit rather than admit that he'd made a mistake.*

would rather used for saying what you would prefer: *They said they would rather take a pay cut than lose their jobs.* ♦ *You don't need to come if you'**d rather not**.*

ratify /ˈrætɪfaɪ/ (**ratifies, ratifying, ratified**) verb [T] to make an agreement official by signing it, or formally approving it —**ratification** /ˌrætɪfɪˈkeɪʃ(ə)n/ noun [U]

rating /ˈreɪtɪŋ/ noun **1** [C] a measurement of how good or popular someone or something is: *Labour's popularity rating fell for the first time.* **2** [C] a letter or number that shows how old someone needs to be before they are allowed to see a particular film **3** **ratings** [plural] the number of people who watch or listen to a particular television or radio programme: *Her new series had* **high ratings** *right from the start.*

ratio /ˈreɪʃiəʊ/ (plural **ratios**) noun [C] MATHS a relationship between the sizes of two or more numbers or amounts. This is expressed as x to y, or x:y, so if you have eight red pens and five black pens, the ratio of red pens to black pens is 8 to 5 or 8:5: *a teacher-student ratio of 1:20* (=1 teacher for every 20 students) ♦ *The* **ratio of** *men* **to** *women was 4:1.*

ration¹ /ˈræʃ(ə)n/ noun **1** [C] a limited amount of something that you are allowed to have when there is not much available **2** **rations** [plural] amounts of food that are provided for people

ration² /ˈræʃ(ə)n/ verb [T] **1** to control the supply of something so that people are allowed to have only a fixed amount **2** to allow someone to have only a small amount of something —**rationing** noun [U]

rational /ˈræʃ(ə)nəl/ adj a rational person makes decisions based on sensible practical reasons, rather than emotions ≠ IRRATIONAL: *There was no rational explanation for his actions.* ♦ *She was perfectly calm and rational.* —**rationally** adv

rationale /ˌræʃəˈnɑːl/ noun [C] the set of reasons that a plan, decision, or belief is based on

rattan /ræˈtæn/ noun [U] a climbing plant with long thin stems, used for making **wicker** furniture

rattle¹ /ˈræt(ə)l/ verb [I/T] to make short sharp knocking sounds, or to move or shake things so that they make these sounds: *The house shook and the windows rattled.* ♦ *She rattled her keys impatiently.*

rattle² /ˈræt(ə)l/ noun [C] **1** the sound that something makes when it rattles **2** a baby's toy that rattles when it is shaken

rave /reɪv/ verb [I] **1** to speak or write in a very enthusiastic way about something or someone: *The critics are* **raving about** *her performance.* **2** to talk in an angry and uncontrolled way

ravenous /ˈræv(ə)nəs/ adj very hungry

ravine /rəˈviːn/ noun [C] GEOGRAPHY a very deep narrow valley with steep sides

ravioli /ˌrævɪˈəʊli/ noun [U] a type of pasta made in small squares with meat, cheese, or vegetables inside

raw /rɔː/ adj

1 not cooked	**5** not examined
2 strong/natural	**6** not trained
3 not processed	**+** PHRASE
4 sore	

1 raw food has not been cooked: *raw meat* ♦ *The chicken is still raw.*

2 a raw quality is strong and natural, without being controlled or made more pleasant: *Her performance was filled with* **raw emotion**.

3 raw substances have not been processed or treated in any way: *raw silk* ♦ *There was* **raw sewage** *on the beach.* → RAW MATERIALS

4 if your skin is raw, it is very sore: *I scrubbed my hands until they were raw.*

5 raw data consists of information that has not been examined or organized

6 not trained or experienced: *raw recruits*

PHRASE **a raw deal** unfair treatment

ˌraw maˈterials noun [plural] substances that are in their natural state before being processed or made into something. Oil, wood, and iron are all raw materials.

ray /reɪ/ noun [C] **1** a line of light, heat, or energy **2** a large flat sea fish with a skeleton made of cartilage and a long pointed tail —*picture* → SEA

PHRASE **a ray of hope** something that makes you feel slightly more hopeful in a difficult situation

rayon /ˈreɪɒn/ noun [U] a light smooth cloth made from cellulose

razor /ˈreɪzə/ noun [C] a small tool or piece of electrical equipment used for **shaving**

ˈrazor ˌblade noun [C] a thin flat blade with a very sharp edge that you put in a razor

RC /ˌɑːˈsiː/ abbrev RELIGION Roman Catholic

Rd abbrev Road: used in addresses

RDA /ˌɑːdiːˈeɪ/ noun [singular] HEALTH recommended daily allowance: the amount of a nutrient such as a vitamin that people should take every day, in order to stay healthy

re¹ /riː/ preposition used in business letters for introducing the subject that you are going to write about

re² /reɪ/ noun [singular] MUSIC the second note in the **sol-fa** musical **scale**

re- /riː/ prefix again: *the re-election of the Mayor* ♦ *reheated soup* ♦ *She reappeared a few minutes later.*

reach¹ /riːtʃ/ verb

1 arrive somewhere	**6** achieve sth
2 get to point/stage	**7** programme: be seen/
3 get to level	heard
4 move hand to sth	**8** talk by phone
5 touch sth	

1 [T] to arrive somewhere: *We hoped to reach the camp before dark.* ♦ *The money should reach your bank account within three days.* → ARRIVE

2 [T] to get to a particular point in time, or to a particular stage in a process: *You **reach a point** where medicine can't help.* ♦ *The children have **reached the age** when they want more privacy.*

3 [T] to get as high as a particular level or amount: *Temperatures here can **reach** 120 degrees Fahrenheit.*

4 [I] to move your hand towards something you are trying to touch or pick up: *He turned round and **reached for** the phone.* ♦ *Travis **reached into** his pocket to get his car keys.* ♦ *I **reached across** the table and took Alice's hand.*

5 [I/T] to manage to touch something or pick it up by stretching out your arm: *We keep the bottles up here so the children can't **reach** them.*

6 [T] to achieve something after discussing it or thinking about it for a long time: *Ministers must **reach a decision** before next month.*

7 [T] if something such as a programme or message reaches people, they see or hear it: *The advertisement reached an audience of over 19 million.*

8 [T] to succeed in talking to someone by phone: *I'll leave you a number where I can be reached in an emergency.*

reach² /riːtʃ/ noun [U] **1** the distance within which you can touch something by stretching out your arm: *Put the books **within reach of** your desk.* ♦ *I kicked the knife **out of reach**.* **2** the distance that you travel to get somewhere: *The hotel is **within easy reach** of the town centre.*

PHRASE **within/beyond sb's reach** used for saying that someone can or cannot have or do something: *Achievements like these are beyond the reach of ordinary players.* ♦ *Reduced ticket prices put the best seats within everyone's reach.*

react /riˈækt/ verb [I] **1** to behave in a particular way because of things that are happening around you or things that other people are doing to you: *I wasn't sure how you would react.* ♦ *Workers **reacted** angrily **to** the news of more job cuts.* **2** CHEMISTRY if a chemical substance reacts with another substance, it changes as they are combined: *Car emissions **react with** sunlight to form ozone.* **3** HEALTH to become ill when you eat a particular food or medicine: *Some people **react** badly **to** nuts.*

reactant /riˈæktənt/ noun [C] CHEMISTRY a substance that reacts with another in a chemical reaction

reaction /riˈækʃ(ə)n/ noun

1 how you react to sth	**4** chemical change
2 bad effect on body	**5** interest in change
3 ability to act quickly	**6** opposition to change

1 [C] the way that you feel or behave as a result of something that happens: *My mother's reaction was quite unexpected.* ♦ *Shock is **a** natural **reaction to** such bad news.* ♦ *a **reaction against** her parents' values*

2 [C] HEALTH a bad effect on your body caused by food, medicine, or another substance: *an allergic **reaction to** dust*

3 reactions [plural] your ability to think and act quickly in a difficult or dangerous situation: *A tragedy was prevented by the driver's quick reactions.*

4 [C] CHEMISTRY a process in which a chemical change happens: *Temperature can affect the rate of **a** chemical **reaction**.* → CHAIN REACTION

5 [singular] an attitude of wanting to do things in a different way from the way that they were done in the past: *The **reaction against** traditional styles continued for another 50 years.*

6 [U] *formal* strong opposition to any social or political change = CONSERVATISM

reactionary /riˈækʃ(ə)n(ə)ri/ adj strongly opposed to any social or political change —**reactionary** noun [C]

reactive /riˈæktɪv/ adj **1** reacting to things that happen, rather than making things happen yourself: *We take a proactive rather than a reactive approach.* **2** CHEMISTRY a reactive substance combines easily with other substances —**reactivity** /ˌriːækˈtɪvəti/ noun [U]

reac'tivity ˌseries noun [C] CHEMISTRY a list of chemical elements in order of how reactive they are with other elements

reactor /riˈæktə/ noun [C] PHYSICS a **nuclear reactor** —*picture* → NUCLEAR REACTOR

re'actor ˌvessel noun [C] PHYSICS a very large steel cylinder in some **nuclear reactors** that contains the elements involved in **nuclear fission,** for example the fuel, **coolant,** and **control rods** —*picture* → NUCLEAR REACTOR

read¹ /riːd/ (**reads, reading, read** /red/) verb

1 understand words	**7** know sb's mind
2 speak sth written	**8** contain words
3 get information	**9** show number etc
4 understand sth	**+** PHRASE
5 examine/copy data	**+** PHRASAL VERBS
6 interpret meaning	

1 [I/T] to look at and understand words in a letter, book, newspaper etc: *I read a few chapters every night.* ♦ *He was sitting reading in the waiting room.* ♦ *By the age of five, he was able to **read and write**.*

2 [I/T] to speak the words that you are looking at: *Read me that last sentence again.* ♦ *I'm going to **read** this poem **aloud**.* ♦ ***Reading to** young children helps develop their language skills.*

3 [I/T] to get information from books, newspapers etc: *We read it in the local paper.* ♦ *He likes **reading about** wildlife.*

4 [T] to look at and understand the information, symbols, or numbers on a map or a piece of measuring equipment: *We're learning how to read a compass.*

5 [T] COMPUTING if a computer or other piece of electronic equipment reads something, it examines the information on it or copies it to a particular place

6 [T] to understand something in a particular way = INTERPRET: *They had **read the situation** accurately.* ♦ *We had **read** their decision **as** an admission of failure.*

7 [T] to be able to understand what someone is like or what they are thinking: *It was difficult to read his expression.* ♦ *Her next comment surprised me. It was as if she had **read my mind**.* → BOOK¹, MIND¹

8 [T] if a short piece of writing reads something, it contains those particular words: *The label read, 'Suitable only for children over three'.*

9 [T] if a piece of measuring equipment reads something, it shows a particular number or amount: *The thermometer has been reading over 45 degrees all day.*

PHRASE **read between the lines** to guess something that is not expressed directly

PHRASAL VERBS **ˌread sth 'into sth** to find an extra meaning in someone's words or actions that is not obvious or does not exist: *I think you're reading too much into his remark.*

ˌread sth 'off to read the measurement on a piece of equipment or graph: *He looked at the thermometer and read the temperature off.*

ˌread sth 'out to say the words that you are reading so that people can hear them: *He read the list of names out.*

,read sth 'through to read all of a piece of writing in order to check or correct it: *Read the contract through carefully before you sign.*

,read 'up on sth to get information on a particular subject by reading a lot about it: *I need to read up on Roman history.*

read² /riːd/ noun [singular] an act of reading something, or a period of time spent reading something

readable /'riːdəb(ə)l/ adj **1** easy and pleasant to read **2** clear and able to be read

reader /'riːdə/ noun [C]

1 sb who reads	**4** to say how sb reads
2 of a newspaper etc	**5** book for learning
3 electronic equipment	**6** at university

1 someone who reads: *I am an avid reader of detective novels.*
2 someone who reads a particular newspaper, book, or magazine: *The books provide the reader with an introduction to natural history.* ♦ *Readers of our magazine will be familiar with her column.*
3 a piece of electronic equipment used for reading information from plastic cards, tapes etc
4 someone who reads in a particular way or with a particular level of skill: *a special programme for slow readers*
5 a book containing simple pieces of writing for people who are learning to read or who are learning a language
6 EDUCATION someone who teaches in a university in the UK with a position just below that of a **professor**

readily /'redɪli/ adv **1** easily: *The equipment was cheap and readily available.* **2** in a way that shows that you are willing: *She had readily agreed to the interview.*

readiness /'redɪnəs/ noun **1** [U] a state of being ready and able to deal with what might or will happen **2** [singular/U] the state of being willing to do something

reading /'riːdɪŋ/ noun

1 ability to read	**4** when sb reads to group
2 act of reading sth	**5** amount measured
3 sth you read	**6** way of looking at sth

1 [U] the process of recognizing written or printed words and understanding their meaning: *My brother is having difficulty with his reading.*
2 [singular/U] the act of reading or studying a book, newspaper, document etc: *I haven't done much reading lately.* ♦ *a list of suggestions for further reading*
3 [U] something that someone reads: *This report is dull reading.* ♦ *The prisoners have limited reading material.*
4 [C] an event at which someone reads something to a group of people: *a poetry reading*
5 [C] a number or amount shown on a piece of measuring equipment: *compass readings*
6 [C] a particular way of thinking about a situation, statement, or event= INTERPRETATION: *a modern reading of Freud's work*

'reading ,group noun [C] a **book club** sense 2

,read-only 'memory noun [U] **COMPUTING** see **ROM**

read-out /'riːd ,aʊt/ noun [C] **COMPUTING** a record of information that has been produced by a piece of electronic equipment

ready /'redi/ adj **1** prepared for what is going to happen: *We'll never be ready in time.* ♦ *She was ready for a new challenge.* ♦ *Are you ready to go yet?* **2** in a suitable condition for use: *Is dinner ready?* ♦ *I'd just got tea ready when they called.* ♦ *We can have your order ready by 5.00.* **3** *formal* easily and quickly produced or available: *a ready smile* **4** willing or likely

to do something: *You are too ready to find fault with other people.*

,ready-'made adj already made or prepared and ready to be used

reaffirm /,riːə'fɜːm/ verb [T] to formally and officially state something again= CONFIRM

reafforestation /,riːəfɒrə'steɪʃ(ə)n/ noun [U] **ENVIRONMENT** the process of putting new trees in the ground in an area where trees used to grow

reagent /ri'eɪdʒ(ə)nt/ noun [C] **CHEMISTRY** a substance such as an acid that is involved in several chemical reactions

real /rɪəl/ adj

1 in physical world	**6** most important
2 not false/artificial	**7** about amount/
3 with true qualities	number
4 not just claimed	**+ PHRASE**
5 important/serious	

1 existing in the physical world, not just in someone's imagination or in stories: *Children believe that these characters are real.* ♦ *I had never met a real live pop star before.*
2 not false or artificial= GENUINE: *Is that a real diamond?* ♦ *You'd pay a lot more for the real thing.*
3 used for emphasizing that someone or something has the true qualities of a particular type of person or thing: *Few tourists see the real Thailand.* ♦ *He had no real friends.*
4 true, and not just according to what someone claims: *We all know the minister's real reason for refusing to speak.*
5 important or serious enough to be worth thinking or worrying about: *The committee had little real power.* ♦ *The journey was difficult, but we were never in any real danger.*
6 most important: *Let's deal with the real issue.*
7 ECONOMICS a real amount or number is one that someone gets after considering everything that could affect its value
PHRASE in real terms after considering all the things that affect the true value of something

realise /'rɪəlaɪz/ another spelling of **realize**

realism /'rɪə,lɪz(ə)m/ noun [U] **1** the ability to accept events and situations as they really exist and to deal with them in a practical way **2 ARTS** a style in art and literature that shows life as it really is

realist /'rɪəlɪst/ noun [C] **1** someone who accepts events and situations as they really are and deals with them in a practical way **2 ARTS, LITERATURE** an artist or writer whose work shows life as it really is

realistic /,rɪə'lɪstɪk/ adj **1** based on facts and situations as they really are ≠ UNREALISTIC: *He has a realistic chance of winning the election.* ♦ *I don't think it's very realistic to expect her to help us.* **2** able to understand and accept things as they really are: *He's never going to agree to that. Be realistic!* ♦ *The recession has made people more realistic about what they can afford to buy.* **3** made to seem natural or real ≠ UNREALISTIC: *The troops staged a realistic attack using blank ammunition.* —**realistically** /,rɪə'lɪstɪkli/ adv

reality /ri'æləti/ (plural **realities**) noun **1** [U] the real character or nature of things, not what you imagine or think is possible: *What she had to do, finally, was face reality.* ♦ *Her version of events bore no relation to reality.* ♦ *This is a man who has lost touch with reality.* **2** [C] a fact, event, or situation as it really exists: *After years of hard work, his dream has become a reality.* ♦ *the grim realities of war*
PHRASE in reality used for saying that the true situation

is different from what has been said or thought: *Reports put the death toll at 50, when in reality it was closer to 200.*

realization /ˌrɪəlaɪˈzeɪʃ(ə)n/ noun [singular/U] **1** the process of understanding something, or the moment when this happens **2** the process of achieving something that you have planned or hoped for, or the moment when this happens

realize /ˈrɪəlaɪz/ verb **1** [I/T] to know and understand something: *We realize that this is upsetting for you, but it's for the best.* ♦ *At the time I never even realized how unhappy I was.* **2** [T] to gradually begin to understand something that you did not know or notice before: *I soon realized my mistake.* ♦ *It was some time before he realized he'd offended them.* ♦ *I've just realized how much I miss him.* **3** [T] *formal* to achieve something that you have planned or hoped for: *He finally realized his dream to become a dancer.* **4** [T] BUSINESS to obtain an amount of money by selling something

real 'life noun [U] the world as it really is, rather than as it is in someone's imagination or in stories = REALITY —**real-'life** adj

really /ˈrɪəli/ adv **1** *spoken* very, or very much: *I'm really hungry.* ♦ *She really enjoys her job.* ♦ *We've all been working really hard.* **2** used for talking about what is in fact true, when something else seems to be true: *He's not really ill – he's just pretending.* ♦ *We'll never know what really happened.* **3** completely: *Rigby had never really recovered from his knee injury.* **4** used for emphasizing what you are saying: *You really must write to her.*

realm /relm/ noun [C] *formal* a particular area of knowledge, experience, interest etc

'real ˌtime noun [U] COMPUTING if a computer deals with information in real time, it deals with it immediately —**'real-ˌtime** adj

ˌreal-time authoriˈzation noun [U] COMPUTING a system that can check whether a customer's credit card is acceptable in a few seconds, so that an Internet shop can process an order immediately

the 'real ˌworld noun ordinary life with all its practical problems, rather than theories or policies that do not seem relevant to it —**ˌreal-'world** adj

ream /riːm/ verb [T] TECHNOLOGY to make a hole in metal wider and smoother, using a tool called a **reamer**

reap /riːp/ verb [T] **1** to get something as a result of something else that you do **2** AGRICULTURE to cut and gather a crop

reaper /ˈriːpə/ noun [C] AGRICULTURE a person or machine that cuts and gathers a crop such as wheat

reappear /ˌriːəˈpɪə/ verb [I] to appear again —**reappearance** noun [C/U]

reapply /ˌriːəˈplaɪ/ verb **1** [I] to make an official request for something again, especially for a job or a place in a college or university **2** [T] to put another layer of something on a surface

rear¹ /rɪə/ noun **1 the rear** [singular] the back part of a place or thing: *The main entrance is at the rear.* **2** [C] *informal* the part of your body that you sit on

rear² /rɪə/ verb **1** [T] to look after a child or young animal until it is fully grown: *Most farmers in the area rear sheep.* **2** [I] if a horse rears, it lifts its front legs up into the air

rear³ /rɪə/ adj at the back of something

rearrange /ˌriːəˈreɪndʒ/ verb [T] **1** to arrange people or things in a different way **2** to arrange for an event or meeting to take place at a different time

ˌrear-view 'mirror noun [C] a mirror fixed to the front window of a car that lets the driver see what is happening behind the car

ˌrear-wheel 'drive noun [U] ENGINEERING a system of sending the power from the driving mechanism to the back two wheels of a vehicle

reason¹ /ˈriːz(ə)n/ noun **1** [C] a fact, situation, or intention that explains why something happened, why someone did something, or why something is true: *The reason these cars are so expensive is that they are largely built by hand.* ♦ *The police asked her **the reason for** her visit.* ♦ *The council **gave** no **reason** for its decision.* ♦ *The **reason why** so many people caught the disease is still not clear.* **2** [U] a good or clear cause for doing something or thinking something: *Sometimes the dog would bark **for no reason**.* ♦ *With plenty of orders coming in, **there is reason for** optimism about the company's future.* **3** [U] a way of behaving that most people accept as sensible: *He finally **saw reason** and gave me the gun.* ♦ *Let your children have their freedom, **within reason**.* **4** [U] the human ability to think in an intelligent way, make sensible decisions, and form clear arguments: *His assessment of the situation is based on sheer emotion, not reason.*

PHRASES **all the more reason** used for emphasizing that what someone has said or done is another reason why they should do a particular thing

for some reason used for saying that you do not know why something happened: *For some reason, they wouldn't let me help them.*
→ STAND¹

Build your vocabulary: words you can use instead of **reason**

- **cause** the reason that something happens, or the reason that you feel a particular emotion
- **excuse** a reason that you give in order to explain why you did something bad
- **explanation** a set of facts that tell you why something happened
- **grounds** a good or fair reason for doing something. This word is used in official or legal situations
- **motivation** someone's personal reason for doing something
- **motive** someone's personal reason for doing something
- **pretext** a false reason that you give in order to hide your real reason for doing something
- **purpose** something that you want to achieve

reason² /ˈriːz(ə)n/ verb [T] *formal* to make a particular judgment after you have thought about the facts of a situation in an intelligent and sensible way

reasonable /ˈriːz(ə)nəb(ə)l/ adj **1** sensible and fair: *We have taken all reasonable precautions to avoid an accident.* ♦ *Come on, **be reasonable** – I didn't mean to do it!* **2** if something is reasonable, there are good reasons for thinking it is true or correct: *I'm sure there's **a reasonable explanation** for his absence.* ♦ *It's **reasonable to assume** that these measures will prove successful.* **3** fairly good, although not extremely good = ACCEPTABLE: *a reasonable standard of accommodation* **4** not too high or great: *The hotel is situated within a reasonable distance of the beach.* ♦ *reasonable prices*

reasonably /ˈriːz(ə)nəbli/ adv **1** to a fairly high degree, level, or standard: *He did reasonably well in maths.* **2** in a sensible and fair way: *She behaved very reasonably.*

reasoned /ˈriːz(ə)nd/ adj thought about and expressed in an intelligent and sensible way

reasoning /ˈriːz(ə)nɪŋ/ noun [U] the process of thinking about something in an intelligent and sensible way

reassure /ˌriːəˈʃʊə/ verb [T] to make someone feel less worried about something —**reassurance** noun [C/U]

reassuring /ˌriːəˈʃʊərɪŋ/ adj making you feel less worried —**reassuringly** adv

reawaken /ˌriːəˈweɪkən/ verb [T] *formal* to make someone have a particular feeling again or remember something they have not thought about for a long time

rebate /ˈriːbeɪt/ noun [C] **1** part of a payment that someone has made that is officially **given back** to them, usually because they have paid too much = REFUND **2 CONSTRUCTION** a line cut in a board to hold the end of another board

rebel1 /ˈreb(ə)l/ noun [C] **1** someone who tries to remove a government or leader by using organized force **2** someone who opposes people in authority or opposes accepted ways of doing things

rebel2 /rɪˈbel/ (**rebels, rebelling, rebelled**) verb [I] **1** to try to remove a government or leader by using organized force **2** to oppose someone in authority, or to oppose accepted ways of doing things

rebellion /rɪˈbeljən/ noun **1** [C/U] an attempt to remove a government or leader by using organized force = REVOLT, UPRISING **2** [U] opposition to someone in authority or to accepted ways of doing things

rebellious /rɪˈbeljəs/ adj **1** fighting to remove a government or leader by using organized force **2** opposing authority or the accepted rules of society

rebirth /riːˈbɜːθ/ noun [singular/U] a situation in which something becomes popular, important, or effective again

reboard /riːˈbɔːd/ verb [I/T] **TOURISM** to go back onto a ship, plane, train, or bus after leaving it for a time

reboot /riːˈbuːt/ verb [I/T] **COMPUTING** if a computer or system reboots, or if someone reboots it, it starts again after it has been turned off

rebound /rɪˈbaʊnd/ verb [I] **1** to hit a surface and then move quickly backwards again **2** if something bad that you try to do to someone rebounds on you, it harms you, not them

rebuff /rɪˈbʌf/ verb [T] *formal* to refuse to talk to someone or do what they suggest —**rebuff** noun [C]

rebuild /riːˈbɪld/ (**rebuilds, rebuilding, rebuilt** /riːˈbɪlt/, **rebuilt**) verb [T] **1** to build something again after it has been damaged or destroyed **2** to improve a situation so that it is as good as it was in the past

rebuke /rɪˈbjuːk/ verb [T] *formal* to tell someone angrily that they have behaved badly —**rebuke** noun [C]

rebuttal /rɪˈbʌt(ə)l/ noun [C/U] *formal* a statement showing or saying that something is not true

recalcitrant /rɪˈkælsɪtrənt/ adj *formal* refusing to obey orders —**recalcitrance** noun [U]

recalescence /ˌriːkəˈlesəns/ noun [U] **TECHNOLOGY** a sudden increase of temperature that takes place in iron or steel that is being cooled under particular conditions. It is caused by a change in the structure of the metal.

recall /rɪˈkɔːl/ verb **1** [I/T] to remember something: *He couldn't recall what had happened. ♦ I don't recall seeing the document.* **2** [T] to order someone to return to their country or the place where they work: *Spain immediately recalled its ambassador for consultations.* **3** [T] to ask for a product that people have bought to

be returned because there is something wrong with it —**recall** /rɪˈkɔːl, ˈriːˌkɔːl/ noun [singular/U]

recap /ˌriːˈkæp, ˈriːˌkæp/ (**recaps, recapping, recapped**) verb [I/T] to describe what has already been done or decided, without repeating the details —**recap** /ˈriːˌkæp/ noun [C]

recapture /riːˈkæptʃə/ verb [T] **1** to use force to get an area into your control again: *The rebels have recaptured the south.* **2** to have a memory or feeling again **3** to catch an animal or person that has escaped

recede /rɪˈsiːd/ verb [I] **1** to move further away **2** to become less strong or likely **3** if a man's hair is receding, less and less of it is growing at the front

receipt /rɪˈsiːt/ noun **1** [C] a document that you get from someone showing that you have given them money or goods: *Keep all your credit card receipts.* ♦ *Make sure you get a receipt for the taxi fare.* **2** [U] *formal* the act of receiving something: *Please acknowledge receipt of this letter.* **3 receipts** [plural] **BUSINESS** the total amount of money that a business or organization receives in a particular period of time

receivables /rɪˈsiːvəb(ə)lz/ noun [plural] **BUSINESS** amounts of money that a company is owed, which count as its **assets**

receive /rɪˈsiːv/ verb [T]

1 get sth given to you	4 welcome sb
2 have treatment etc	5 get electronic signal
3 react in particular way	+ PHRASE

1 to get something that someone gives or sends you: *We have not received your letter.* ♦ *The head teacher has received several calls from angry parents.*
2 to have a particular type of treatment or experience: *Several of the victims are receiving hospital treatment.*
3 to react to something in a particular way: *Heather's proposals were received without much enthusiasm.*
4 to formally welcome a visitor: *Her Royal Highness was received by the Deputy Mayor.*
5 to get pictures or sound on a television, radio, or mobile phone: *With a satellite dish you can receive hundreds of channels.*
PHRASE at/on the receiving end (of sth) affected by something unpleasant

Word family: receive
Words in the same family as receive
- **receipt** *n*
- **receiver** *n*
- **recipient** *n*
- **reception** *n*
- **receptive** *adj*
- **receptor** *n*

receiver /rɪˈsiːvə/ noun [C] **1** the part of a phone that you pick up in order to hear and speak **2** the part of a television or radio that receives electronic signals and changes them into pictures and sounds **3 BUSINESS** an official who is put in charge of a business with financial problems

recent /ˈriːs(ə)nt/ adj happening or starting a short time ago: *a recent discovery* ♦ *Business has boomed in recent years.*

recently /ˈriːs(ə)ntli/ adv not long ago: *She only recently discovered the truth.* ♦ *He's been back to America fairly recently.*

receptacle /rɪˈseptək(ə)l/ noun [C] **1 BIOLOGY** the wider, top part of the stem of a plant, where the flower joins the stem —*picture* → FLOWER **2** *formal* a container

reception /rɪˈsepʃ(ə)n/ noun **1** [U] the part of a building where there is someone whose job is to welcome visitors, deal with questions etc: *Visitors must report to reception first.* **2** [C] a formal party to welcome someone or to celebrate something: *a wedding reception* **3** [singular] the reaction of people to

someone or something: *a friendly reception*
♦ *Crawford's performance had **a mixed reception** from the critics.* **4** [U] the quality or strength of the picture or sound you receive on a television, radio, or mobile phone: *Mobile phone users were complaining of **poor reception**.*

re'ception ,class noun [C] **EDUCATION** a class for children aged four and five who are just starting school

receptionist /rɪ'sepʃ(ə)nɪst/ noun [C] **TOURISM** someone who works in reception at a hotel or office and whose job is to welcome visitors, deal with questions etc

receptive /rɪ'septɪv/ adj willing to listen or consider suggestions

receptor /rɪ'septə/ noun [C] **1 ANATOMY** a nerve in a sense organ such as the skin or the nose that sends messages to the **central nervous system**: *a touch receptor* (=one that tells the brain that you are touching something) —*picture* → SKIN **2** a piece of equipment that is designed to receive electronic signals

recess /rɪ'ses, 'riːses/ noun **1** [C/U] a short time between periods of work in a court of law or parliament **2** [C] a space in a room where part of a wall is further back than the rest of it

recession /rɪ'seʃ(ə)n/ noun [C/U] **ECONOMICS** a period when trade and industry are not successful and there is a lot of unemployment

recessive /rɪ'sesɪv/ adj **BIOLOGY** a recessive gene has to have been passed on by both parents in order to produce a particular feature in a child → DOMINANT

recharge /riː'tʃɑːdʒ/ verb [T] to put more power into a battery

recharger /riː'tʃɑːdʒə/ noun [C] a piece of electrical equipment that puts electricity into a battery

recipe /'resəpi/ noun [C] a set of instructions for cooking or preparing a particular food: *a recipe for apple pie*
  PHRASE **be a recipe for sth** to make it extremely likely that something will happen: *Giving your kids too much freedom can be **a recipe for disaster**.*

recipient /rɪ'sɪpiənt/ noun [C] *formal* someone who receives something

reciprocal¹ /rɪ'sɪprək(ə)l/ adj done according to an arrangement by which you do something for someone who does the same thing for you

reciprocal² /rɪ'sɪprək(ə)l/ noun [C] **MATHS** either one of a pair of numbers that make 1 when you multiply them by each other, as, for example, the numbers 2 and ½ do

re'ciprocal ,verb noun [C] **LANGUAGE** a verb that describes something that two people do to or with each other, for example the verb 'meet' in the sentences 'We always meet in the park.' and 'I meet her in the park every Friday.'

reciprocate /rɪ'sɪprəkeɪt/ verb [I/T] *formal* **1** to have the same feelings towards someone else that they have for you **2** to do the same thing for someone that they have done for you

recitative /,resɪtə'tiːv/ noun [C/U] **MUSIC** in opera, the ordinary words that are sung or spoken between the important songs

recite /rɪ'saɪt/ verb [I/T] to say a poem or story that you have learnt to an audience —**recitation** /,resɪ'teɪʃ(ə)n/ noun [C/U]

reckless /'rekləs/ adj not thinking about the possible bad effects of your actions: *reckless driving* —**recklessly** adv, **recklessness** noun [U]

reckon /'rekən/ verb *spoken* **1** [I/T] to believe that something is true: *I reckon there's something wrong with him.* ♦ *It is generally **reckoned** to be the best restaurant in town.* **2** [T] to have a particular opinion about someone or something: *I think it'll work. **What do you reckon**?*

reclaim /rɪ'kleɪm/ verb [T] **1 ENVIRONMENT** to improve an area of land so that it can be used for farming or building **2** to get something back that someone has taken from you: *He wants to reclaim the world championship title.*

reclamation /,reklə'meɪʃ(ə)n/ noun [U] **ENVIRONMENT** the improvement of an area of land or water so that it can be used

reclassify /riː'klæsɪfaɪ/ verb [T] to decide that something belongs to a different group from the group it was in before

recline /rɪ'klaɪn/ verb [I] **1** to lie or lean in a comfortable position with your back supported by something **2** if a chair reclines, you can make the back of it lean backwards to be more comfortable

reclining seat /rɪ,klaɪnɪŋ 'siːt/ noun [C] **TOURISM** a seat that lies back, so that a traveller can sleep

recluse /rɪ'kluːs/ noun [C] someone who lives alone and avoids seeing other people —**reclusive** /rɪ'kluːsɪv/ adj

recognise /'rekəgnaɪz/ another spelling of **recognize**

recognition /,rekəg'nɪʃ(ə)n/ noun **1** [singular/U] agreement that something is true or important: *official **recognition of** the need for affordable childcare* **2** [singular/U] praise, respect, or admiration for something that you have done: *His work has **gained** international **recognition**.* ♦ *She received the award **in recognition of** her work in the community.* **3** [U] the ability to recognize a person or thing: *She looked at me without recognition.*

recognize /'rekəgnaɪz/ verb [T] **1** to know someone or something because you have seen, heard, or met them before: *I recognized the house from your description.* ♦ *I thought I recognized the voice!* **2** to accept that something is true or important: *I recognize that there are some problems with the current system.* ♦ *We **recognize the need for** improvement in our performance.* **3** to give praise or approval to someone for something they have done: *Her achievement was recognized with a medal.* **4** to accept the authority or status of someone or something: *Many countries refused to recognize the new regime.* —**recognizable** /'rekəg,naɪzəb(ə)l/ adj, **recognizably** adv

recoil¹ /rɪ'kɔɪl/ verb [I] to move quickly back from someone or something that is frightening or unpleasant

recoil² /'riː,kɔɪl/ noun [U] the sudden backwards movement of a gun or rifle when it is fired

recollect /,rekə'lekt/ verb [I/T] to remember something that has happened

recollection /,rekə'lekʃ(ə)n/ noun **1** [U] the ability to remember something that has happened **2** [C] something that you remember

recombination /,riːkɒmbɪ'neɪʃ(ə)n/ noun [C/U] **BIOLOGY** any process that gives rise to **offspring** that have combinations of genes different from those of either parent —**recombine** /,riːkəm'baɪn/ verb [I]

recommend /,rekə'mend/ verb [T] **1** to advise that something should happen: *I recommend that you buy a more powerful computer.* ♦ *We **strongly recommend** booking early.* ♦ *He was **recommended for** the job.* ♦ *Students are **recommended to** read the following books.* **2** to say that someone or something is good and worth using, having, or experiencing: *Can you recommend a good restaurant?* ♦ *Please recommend our shop to your friends.*

recommendation /ˌrekəmənˈdeɪʃ(ə)n/ noun [C/U] **1** a suggestion or piece of advice about how to solve a problem, deal with a situation etc **2** a suggestion that someone or something is especially suitable or useful for a particular situation

recompense[1] /ˈrekəmpens/ noun [U] *formal* payment that someone gives to another person who has suffered injury or loss because of them, or who has done something for them

recompense[2] /ˈrekəmpens/ verb [T] *formal* to give someone recompense for something

reconcile /ˈrekənsaɪl/ verb **1** [T] to make things that are opposed to each other capable of existing together: *We can't reconcile the two versions of what happened.* **2** [I/T] if you reconcile two people or groups, or if they reconcile, they become friendly again after a disagreement **3** [T] to force someone to accept a situation that they do not like: *She couldn't reconcile herself to the idea of just giving up.*

reconciliation /ˌrekənsɪliˈeɪʃ(ə)n/ noun [singular/U] **1** a new and friendly relationship with someone who you have argued with or fought with **2** a way of making it possible for things that are opposed to each other to exist together

reconnaissance /rɪˈkɒnɪs(ə)ns/ noun [C/U] the use of soldiers or aircraft to go into an area and get information about an enemy

reconsider /ˌriːkənˈsɪdə/ verb [I/T] to think again about a decision in order to decide whether you should change it

reconstruct /ˌriːkənˈstrʌkt/ verb [T] **1** to build something again **2** to form an idea of something that happened by connecting pieces of information

reconstruction /ˌriːkənˈstrʌkʃ(ə)n/ noun **1** [U] the process of building something again **2** [C/U] a situation in which you try to form an idea of something that happened by making something similar happen again **3** [C] a copy of something that existed in the past **4** [C] a performance showing events exactly as they happened

record[1] /ˈrekɔːd/ noun **1** [C] information that is kept about something that has happened: *medical records* ♦ *Try to keep a record of everything you read this week.* ♦ *This monsoon has been the wettest on record* (=wetter than ever before). **2** [singular] the things that someone has done that give an idea of what they are like: *The company has a reasonably good safety record.* **3** [C] the best achievement so far in a particular activity, especially a sport: *She holds the world record in the 800 metres.* → BREAK[1] **4** [C] a large circular black piece of plastic containing music or other sounds: *an original Beatles' record*

PHRASES off the record used for saying that a remark is not official or is not intended to be made public

on (the) record used for stating that you are saying something officially or publicly

set/put the record straight to tell the truth about something after someone else has not told the truth about it

record[2] /rɪˈkɔːd/ verb **1** [T] to make a record of something that has happened, usually by writing it down: *They were asked to record the time at which the attack happened.* **2** [I/T] to put sounds or images onto a **cassette**, CD, or video: *Can you record the football for me at 10 o'clock?* **3** [T] if a piece of equipment records an amount, it measures it and shows it: *Temperatures as low as −70 degrees Celsius have been*

recorded. **4** [T] to officially decide something and write it down: *The coroner recorded a verdict of suicide.*

record[3] /ˈrekɔːd/ adj more, better, worse, faster etc than ever before: *I made it back to the classroom in record time.*

recorder /rɪˈkɔːdə/ noun [C] **MUSIC** a musical instrument that you play by blowing into a hole at the top while putting your fingers over other holes —*picture* → MUSICAL INSTRUMENT

recording /rɪˈkɔːdɪŋ/ noun **1** [C] a piece of music or speech that has been recorded **2** [U] the process of making recordings

record-keeping /ˈrekɔːd ˌkiːpɪŋ/ noun [U] the activity of keeping written records of something

recount[1] /rɪˈkaʊnt/ verb [T] *formal* to say what happened

recount[2] /ˈriːˌkaʊnt/ noun [C] an occasion when something is counted again, especially the votes in an election

recount[3] /ˌriːˈkaʊnt/ verb [T] to count something again, especially the votes in an election

recourse /rɪˈkɔːs/ noun [U] *formal* the use of something so that someone can get what they want or need in a difficult situation

recover /rɪˈkʌvə/ verb **1** [I] to become fit and healthy again after an illness or injury: *I haven't fully recovered from the flu.* **2** [T] to get back something that has been lost or stolen or is owed: *The thieves were caught, but many of the stolen items were never recovered.* **3** [I] to return to a previous state after a difficult period or unpleasant experience: *The economy appears to be recovering from the recession.* **4** [T] to get back the ability to do or feel something: *Sangmin never recovered the use of his arm after the crash.* ♦ *Dilip was rushed to hospital, but he never recovered consciousness.*

recovery /rɪˈkʌv(ə)ri/ noun **1** [singular/U] the process of becoming fit and healthy again after an illness or injury: *The doctors expect Josie to make a full recovery.* **2** [singular/U] the process of returning to normal activity after a period of slow activity: *signs of economic recovery* **3** [U] the act of getting something back that has been lost or stolen or is owed: *the recovery of stolen property*

the reˈcovery poˌsition noun **HEALTH** the position in which an unconscious person should be placed, in which they are lying on their side with the upper leg bent and the lower arm stretched out

recreate /ˌriːkriˈeɪt/ verb [T] to make something exist again

recreation /ˌrekriˈeɪʃ(ə)n/ noun [C/U] *formal* things that you do to enjoy yourself —**recreational** adj

recreational facilities /ˌrekriˈeɪʃən(ə)l fəˌsɪlətiz/ noun [plural] places provided for people to do sports or other **leisure** activities

recrimination /rɪˌkrɪmɪˈneɪʃ(ə)n/ noun **1** [U] a situation in which people are accusing or criticizing each other **2** [C] a statement accusing or criticizing someone who has accused or criticized you

recruit[1] /rɪˈkruːt/ verb **1** [I/T] to get someone to join a company, an organization, or the armed forces **2** [T] to get someone to help you do something —**recruitment** noun [U]

recruit[2] /rɪˈkruːt/ noun [C] a new member of a company, an organization, or the armed forces

rectangle /ˈrekˌtæŋɡ(ə)l/ noun [C] **MATHS** a shape with four straight sides and four angles of 90° —*picture* → SHAPE —**rectangular** /rekˈtæŋɡjʊlə/ adj

rectification /ˌrektɪfɪˈkeɪʃ(ə)n/ noun [U] MATHS the process of calculating the length of a curve

rectify /ˈrektɪfaɪ/ (**rectifies, rectifying, rectified**) verb [T] *formal* to correct a problem or mistake, or to make a bad situation better

rectilinear /ˌrektiˈlɪniə/ adj *formal* in the form of a straight line

rector /ˈrektə/ noun [C] **1** RELIGION a priest in an Anglican church **2** EDUCATION the person in charge in some schools, colleges, and universities

rectum /ˈrektəm/ noun [C] ANATOMY the lowest part of the tube through which solid waste leaves the body —*picture* → DIGESTIVE SYSTEM —**rectal** /ˈrekt(ə)l/ adj

recuperate /rɪˈkuːpəreɪt/ verb [I] HEALTH to get better after being ill or injured —**recuperation** /rɪˌkuːpəˈreɪʃ(ə)n/ noun [U]

recur /rɪˈkɜː/ (**recurs, recurring, recurred**) verb [I] to happen again, once or several times —**recurrence** /rɪˈkʌrəns/ noun [C/U], **recurrent** /rɪˈkʌrənt/ adj

recursive /rɪˈkɜːsɪv/ adj MATHS, COMPUTING involving a process that continues to be repeated again and again

recycle /riːˈsaɪk(ə)l/ verb [T] **1** ENVIRONMENT to treat waste materials so that they can be used again **2** to use something again, often for a different purpose —*picture* → FOOD WEB —**recyclable** adj, **recycling** noun [U]

re'cycle ˌbin noun [C] COMPUTING a place on a computer where documents, files, and programs that you have deleted are kept

red¹ /red/ (**redder, reddest**) adj **1** something that is red is the same colour as blood: *bright red lipstick* **2** red wine is dark red or purple in colour **3** red hair is a red-brown or orange colour
PHRASE **go red** to become red in the face because you are embarrassed

red² /red/ noun [C/U] the colour of blood: *She was dressed all in red.*
PHRASES **in the red** with more money being spent than there is available: *Their bank account was in the red again.*
see red to become very angry

ˌred 'blood ˌcell noun [C] ANATOMY a blood cell that contains haemoglobin and gives the blood its red colour. Red blood cells have no nucleus and are formed in the bone marrow. → WHITE BLOOD CELL —*picture* → CELL

ˌred 'card noun [C] SPORTS in football, a card that is used for telling a player that they have committed a serious **foul** and that they must leave the field → YELLOW CARD

redeem /rɪˈdiːm/ verb [T] **1** to improve something that is not very good by including something that is good: *A difficult year for the company was redeemed by a successful deal.* **2** RELIGION to make someone free from the power of evil, especially in the Christian religion

the Redeemer /rɪˈdiːmə/ noun RELIGION a word used by Christians for referring to Jesus Christ

redemption /rɪˈdempʃ(ə)n/ noun [U] RELIGION the state of being made free from the power of evil, especially in the Christian religion= SALVATION
PHRASE **beyond/past redemption** too bad to be used or made good

redeploy /ˌriːdɪˈplɔɪ/ verb [T] *formal* to move someone or something to a different place or a different job —**redeployment** noun [U]

redevelopment /ˌriːdɪˈveləpmənt/ noun [U] ECONOMICS the improvement of an area that is in bad condition by destroying or improving old buildings and building new ones

ˌred 'giant noun [C] ASTRONOMY a very large star that shines brightly, but that has a low temperature at its surface

redid /ˌriːˈdɪd/ the past tense of **redo**

rediscover /ˌriːdɪˈskʌvə/ verb [T] **1** to realize again that you like something by, doing it again after not doing it for a long time **2** to find something that has been lost for a long time

redistribute /ˌriːdɪˈstrɪbjuːt/ verb [T] to change the way that something is shared between people —**redistribution** /ˌriːdɪstrɪˈbjuːʃ(ə)n/ noun [U]

ˌred 'meat noun [U] meat such as beef or lamb that is red before it is cooked

redo /ˌriːˈduː/ (**redoes** /ˌriːˈdʌz/, **redoing, redid** /ˌriːˈdɪd/, **redone** /ˌriːˈdʌn/) verb [T] to do something again in a different way in order to correct or improve it

redox /ˈriːdɒks/ noun [U] CHEMISTRY oxidation-reduction

redress¹ /rɪˈdres/ noun [U] *formal* something that someone does for another person, or money that someone gives to another person, as a way of improving a bad situation that they are responsible for

redress² /rɪˈdres/ verb [T] *formal* if someone redresses a bad situation that they are responsible for, they improve it by doing something for someone else, or by giving them money
PHRASE **redress the balance** to change a situation in order to make things fair and equal

ˌred 'tide noun [C] ENVIRONMENT a type of **algal bloom** that causes water to have a reddish colour. It can kill fish, birds, and other animals.

reduce /rɪˈdjuːs/ verb [T] to make something smaller or less in size, amount, importance, price etc: *Try to reduce the amount of time you waste.* ♦ *The price of children's shoes has been reduced by 20%.*

reducing agent /rɪˈdjuːsɪŋ ˌeɪdʒ(ə)nt/ noun [C] CHEMISTRY the chemical or substance in an **oxidation-reduction** reaction that **oxidizes** (=combines with oxygen), so losing electrons

reducing flame /rɪˈdjuːsɪŋ ˌfleɪm/ noun [C] TECHNOLOGY a **carburizing flame** used in welding

reducing sugar /rɪˈdjuːsɪŋ ˌʃʊgə/ noun [C] CHEMISTRY, BIOLOGY a type of sugar that produces a reddish-brown substance when **Benedict's solution** is added to it and boiled

reduction /rɪˈdʌkʃ(ə)n/ noun [C/U] **1** the process or result of making something smaller or less in amount, size, price, importance etc: *price reductions* ♦ *a dramatic reduction in the birth rate* **2** CHEMISTRY a chemical reaction that produces an increase in hydrogen or a loss of oxygen

redundancy /rɪˈdʌndənsi/ (plural **redundancies**) noun **1** [C/U] a situation in which someone is told to leave their job because they are no longer needed **2** [U] a situation in which something is not needed, because the same thing or a similar thing already exists

redundant /rɪˈdʌndənt/ adj **1** if someone is made redundant, they have been told that they must leave their job because they are no longer needed **2** not needed because the same thing or a similar thing already exists

redwood /'red,wʊd/ noun [C] a very large tree with red wood that grows in the US

reed /riːd/ noun **1** [C/U] a tall thin plant that grows near water **2** [C] MUSIC a thin piece of wood in the top of some musical instruments such as **clarinets** and **oboes** that makes a sound when you blow over it

'reed-,blown adj MUSIC a reed-blown musical instrument has a **reed** (=a thin piece of wood, metal or plastic) that is made to vibrate in a current of air

reef /riːf/ noun [C] GEOGRAPHY a long line of rock or **coral** in the sea, with its top just below or just above the surface

reel¹ /riːl/ noun [C] an object shaped like a wheel that you wind string, thread, wire, or film around in order to store it

reel² /riːl/ verb [I] **1** to move in a way that is not steady = LURCH **2** to feel very shocked, upset, or confused

,re-e'lect verb [T] to elect someone again — **,re-e'lection** noun [U]

refer /rɪ'fɜː/ (**refers, referring, referred**)
PHRASAL VERBS **re'fer to sth** formal to look at a book, map, website etc for information: Please refer to our catalogue for details.
re'fer to sb/sth to mention someone or something when you are speaking or writing: She referred to the subject several times during her speech.

referee¹ /,refə'riː/ noun [C] SPORTS someone whose job is to make sure that players in a game obey the rules

referee² /,refə'riː/ (**referees, refereeing, refereed**) verb [I/T] SPORTS to be a referee in a game

reference /'ref(ə)rəns/ noun

1 mention of sb/sth	4 number for finding sth
2 statement about you	5 phrase from book/
3 search for information	poem

1 [C/U] a comment that mentions someone or something= MENTION: He **made no reference to** my untidy appearance.
2 [C] a statement giving information about you that you ask someone who knows you or has worked with you to provide when you apply for a new job: Her former employer **provided a reference** for her.
3 [U] the process of looking at something in order to get information: The sentences are numbered **for ease of reference**.
4 [C] a number that shows someone where they can find information that they need: Start your walk at map reference 2D.
5 [C] a word or phrase that comes from a book or a poem: obscure literary references

'reference ,book noun [C] a book that contains facts and information

referendum /,refə'rendəm/ (plural **referenda** /,refə'rendə/ or **referendums**) noun [C/U] SOCIAL STUDIES an occasion on which everyone in a country can vote to make a decision about one particular subject

refill /riː'fɪl/ verb [T] to put another amount of something into a container that was full but is now empty —**refill** /'riː,fɪl/ noun [C]

refine /rɪ'faɪn/ verb [T] **1** to make small changes to something in order to improve it: We've refined the system since it was first launched. **2** to remove things from a natural substance in order to make it pure

gases
(e.g. butane and propane)

fractionating
column

gasoline
(fuel for cars)

naphtha
(used for making
chemicals
such as solvents)

kerosene
(fuel for aircraft
and stoves)

diesel
(fuel for large
vehicles and
trains)

lubricating oil
(used for engines
and machines)

fuel oil

greases and
waxes

crude oil in

bitumen

refining crude oil

refined /rɪ'faɪnd/ adj **1** pure, because other things have been removed: refined sugar **2** someone who is refined is very polite and enjoys art, music etc = CULTURED

refinement /rɪ'faɪnmənt/ noun **1** [C/U] a small change that is made to something in order to improve it **2** [U] the quality of being very polite and enjoying art, music etc **3** [U] the process of removing things from a natural substance so that it is pure

refinery /rɪ'faɪnəri/ (plural **refineries**) noun [C] a factory where things are removed from a natural substance to make it pure

reflate /riː'fleɪt/ verb [I/T] ECONOMICS if a government reflates the economy of a country, it improves it by increasing the amount of money in **circulation** (=being used) → DEFLATE

reflation /riː'fleɪʃ(ə)n/ noun [U] ECONOMICS the process of improving the economy of a country by increasing the amount of money that people are earning and spending in the country

reflect /rɪ'flekt/ verb **1** [T] PHYSICS if a surface reflects something, you can see the image of that thing on the surface: I caught a glimpse of them **reflected in** the mirror. **2** [I/T] PHYSICS if something reflects light, heat etc, the light, heat etc comes back off it: Pale colours **reflect light**. **3** [T] to show that something is true of a particular situation or person: He said that the statement did not reflect his own views. **4** [I] to think about something carefully and seriously
PHRASE **reflect well/badly on sb** to give people a good or bad opinion of someone

reflected ray /rɪ,flektɪd 'reɪ/ noun [C] PHYSICS a ray of light that is reflected from a surface → INCIDENT RAY —picture → WAVE

reflection /rɪ'flekʃ(ə)n/ noun **1** [C] an image that you see when you look in a mirror or at a shiny surface: Anna stared at her **reflection in** the hall mirror. **2** [U] careful thought about something= CONSIDERATION: At the time I thought I was right, but **on reflection** I think perhaps I wasn't. **3** [C] something that shows that something is true of a particular person or situation: *The expression on your face is **a reflection of** how you are feeling.* **4** [U] **PHYSICS** the process of reflecting light, sound, or images —*picture* → WAVE

PHRASE **be a reflection on sb/sth** to show the faults of someone or something: *These crimes are a sad reflection on modern society.*

reflective /rɪˈflektɪv/ adj **PHYSICS** able to reflect light —**reflectively** adv

reflector /rɪˈflektə/ noun [C] **PHYSICS** an object that reflects light and shines when light shines onto it

reflex /ˈriːfleks/ noun [C] **1 BIOLOGY** a movement that one of your muscles makes without you thinking about it or being able to control it **2** a quick way of reacting to something, without thinking about it

ˈreflex ˌaction noun [C] **BIOLOGY** a **reflex**

ˈreflex ˌangle noun [C] **MATHS** an angle that is between 180° and 360° —*picture* → ANGLE

ˈreflex ˌarc noun [C] **BIOLOGY** the path along which nerve signals travel in a reflex. It consists of an **effector**, a **receptor**, and the spinal cord.

reflexive /rɪˈfleksɪv/ adj **LANGUAGE** a reflexive verb or pronoun refers back to the subject of the verb. In English, 'to enjoy yourself' is a **reflexive verb** and 'yourself' is a **reflexive pronoun**.

reforestation /ˌriːfɒrɪˈsteɪʃ(ə)n/ noun [U] **ENVIRONMENT** the process of planting new trees in an area where the original trees have been cut down —**reforest** /riːˈfɒrɪst/ verb [I/T]

reform¹ /rɪˈfɔːm/ noun [C/U] a change that is made in order to improve a situation or system: *economic reforms* ♦ *the most important **reform of** the police service in over 30 years*

reform² /rɪˈfɔːm/ verb **1** [T] to change a situation or system in order to improve it **2** [I/T] to improve your own or someone else's behaviour —**reformer** noun [C]

the Reformation /ˌrefəˈmeɪʃ(ə)n/ **RELIGION** a period of religious change in Europe in the 16th century, in which the Protestant Church was started

refract /rɪˈfrækt/ verb [T] **PHYSICS** if a surface such as water or glass refracts light, light travels in a slightly different direction after it hits the surface, so that the surface appears to bend it

refraction /rɪˈfrækʃ(ə)n/ noun [U] **1 PHYSICS** the way in which light bends when it passes from one substance to a different substance, for example from air to water —*picture* → WAVE **2 BIOLOGY** the ability of the eye, especially the lens, to bend light in order to **focus** it on the retina

refractor /rɪˈfræktə/ noun [C] **PHYSICS** a piece of equipment that changes the direction of a **beam** of light by passing it between two transparent materials of different density

refractory /rɪˈfrækt(ə)ri/ adj **TECHNOLOGY** able to withstand very high temperatures. Refractory materials are used on the inside of **crucibles** (=containers for melting metals).

refrain /rɪˈfreɪn/ verb [I] *formal* to stop yourself from doing something

refresh /rɪˈfreʃ/ verb [T] **1** to make you feel that you have more energy again, when you are tired or hot **2 COMPUTING** to make a web page or other computer document show the most recent changes to it

PHRASE **refresh sb's memory** to make someone remember something

refreshing /rɪˈfreʃɪŋ/ adj **1** making you feel more lively when you have been feeling tired or hot **2** *showing*

approval newer, more interesting, or more exciting than other things that have come before: *a refreshing change* —**refreshingly** adv

refreshments /rɪˈfreʃmənts/ noun [plural] food and drinks that are provided at an event

refrigerant /rɪˈfrɪdʒərənt/ noun [C] **CHEMISTRY** a substance that is used to cool or freeze something, for example the liquid that circulates in a refrigerator

refrigerate /rɪˈfrɪdʒəreɪt/ verb [T] to keep food or drinks cold by putting them in a refrigerator —**refrigeration** /rɪˌfrɪdʒəˈreɪʃ(ə)n/ noun [U]

refrigerator /rɪˈfrɪdʒəˌreɪtə/ noun [C] a machine that keeps food and drinks cold, usually with a part for freezing food too= FRIDGE

refuge /ˈrefjuːdʒ/ noun [C/U] a place you go to in order to protect yourself from something dangerous or threatening= SHELTER

refugee /ˌrefjʊˈdʒiː/ noun [C] **SOCIAL STUDIES** someone who leaves their country because of a war or other threatening event

refund¹ /ˈriːfʌnd/ noun [C] money that you get back because you have paid too much for something, or because you have decided that you do not want it

refund² /rɪˈfʌnd/ verb [T] to give money back to someone because they have paid too much for something or have decided that they do not want it

refurbish /riːˈfɜːbɪʃ/ verb [T] to improve a room or a building by cleaning and painting it, by adding new furniture or equipment etc —**refurbishment** noun [C/U]

refusal /rɪˈfjuːz(ə)l/ noun [C/U] the act of refusing to do or accept something, or of not allowing someone to do something: *The rebels' refusal to surrender led to further bloodshed.*

refuse¹ /rɪˈfjuːz/ verb [I/T] to say that you will not do or accept something, or will not let someone do something: *I asked him to apologize, but he refused.* ♦ *Judge Mackey refused the defendant the right to appeal.* ♦ *He couldn't **refuse to** help his own son.*

refuse² /ˈrefjuːs/ noun [U] *formal* things that you throw away= RUBBISH

refute /rɪˈfjuːt/ verb [T] *formal* to prove or say that a statement is false= DISPROVE

regain /rɪˈɡeɪn/ verb [T] to get back something that you had lost

regal /ˈriːɡ(ə)l/ adj typical of or suitable for a king or queen —**regally** adv

regard¹ /rɪˈɡɑːd/ verb [T] to think of someone or something in a particular way: *I **regard** him **as** a friend.*

PHRASE **as regards** *formal* concerning someone or something
→ REGARDING

regard² /rɪˈɡɑːd/ noun **1** [U] attention or care that you give to someone or something: *The road was built **without regard for** the safety of residents.* **2** [U] respect and admiration for someone or something= ESTEEM: *I have very **high regard for** her.* **3 regards** [plural] greetings: ***Give my regards to** your parents.*

PHRASE **in/with regard to** concerning a particular subject

regarding /rɪˈɡɑːdɪŋ/ preposition concerning a particular subject: *Davis had very little to say regarding the accident.*

regardless /rɪˈɡɑːdləs/ adv without being affected or influenced by something: *It seemed an impossible task, but we **carried on, regardless.*** ♦ *There must be equality for all citizens, **regardless of** nationality.*

regatta /rɪˈɡætə/ noun [C] **SPORTS** a series of boat races

regenerate /rɪˈdʒenəreɪt/ verb **1** [T] to develop something again, or to bring it back to its original state **2** [I/T] **SCIENCE** if a new body part or organ regenerates, or if someone regenerates it, it starts to grow —**regeneration** /rɪˌdʒenəˈreɪʃ(ə)n/ noun [U]

regent /ˈriːdʒ(ə)nt/ noun [C] someone who governs a country in the place of a king or queen who is ill, young, or not available to govern

reggae /ˈreɡeɪ/ noun [U] **MUSIC** a type of popular music that developed in Jamaica in the 1960s

regime /reɪˈʒiːm/ noun [C] **SOCIAL STUDIES** a system of government, especially a strict or unfair one: *a military regime*

reˈgime ˌchange noun [U] **POLITICS** a situation in which one country tries to get rid of another country's government, especially by force, and to replace it with a government that supports its own ideas and interests more

regiment /ˈredʒɪmənt/ noun [C] a large group of soldiers made up of several **battalions** —**regimental** /ˌredʒɪˈment(ə)l/ adj

regimented /ˈredʒɪˌmentɪd/ adj organized and controlled by strict rules

region /ˈriːdʒ(ə)n/ noun [C] **1** **GEOGRAPHY** a large area of land: *Peru's eastern jungle region* **2** a particular area of your body: *pain in the abdominal region* **PHRASES in the region of** used before a number for saying that it is not exact
the regions the part of a country outside the capital city

regional /ˈriːdʒ(ə)nəl/ adj **GEOGRAPHY** relating to or typical of a particular region: *a regional council* —**regionally** adv

register1 /ˈredʒɪstə/ verb **1** [I/T] to put a name or other information on an official list: *Births must be registered within 42 days.* ♦ *Have you registered for the English exam yet?* ♦ *Everyone in the village should register with the local doctor.* **2** [T] to show something as a measurement on a piece of equipment: *an earthquake registering 5.1 on the Richter scale* **3** [I/T] to realize or notice something, or to be realized or noticed: *She did tell me she'd be out, but it didn't register.* **4** [T] *formal* to show your feelings about something in your face or voice: *George's look registered his confusion.*

register2 /ˈredʒɪstə/ noun **1** [C] an official list or record of a particular type of thing: *the register of births, deaths, and marriages* ♦ *All guests must sign the hotel register.* **2** [C] **MUSIC** the range of musical sounds that a voice or a musical instrument can produce **3** [C/U] **LANGUAGE** the type of language that you use in a particular situation or when you are communicating with a particular group of people

ˈregister ˌoffice noun [C] a **registry office**

registrar /ˌredʒɪˈstrɑː/ noun [C] **1** someone whose job is to keep official records **2** **HEALTH** a doctor in a hospital who is training to be a **consultant**

registration /ˌredʒɪˈstreɪʃ(ə)n/ noun [U] the process of recording names or information on an official list

regisˈtration ˌcard noun [C] a card or form that has to be filled in when registering at a hotel, conference etc

regisˈtration ˌnumber noun [C] the official set of numbers and letters on a car's **number plate**

registry /ˈredʒɪstri/ (plural **registries**) noun [C] a collection of official records, or the place where it is kept

ˈregistry ˌoffice noun [C] in the UK, a place where births, deaths, and marriages are officially recorded, and where people can get married without a religious ceremony

regolith /ˈreɡəlɪθ/ noun [C] **GEOLOGY** the layer of loose rock particles that covers the solid rock under the ground of most land on the Earth and the Moon

regression line /rɪˈɡreʃ(ə)n ˌlaɪn/ noun [C] **MATHS** a straight line used in showing the relationship between the value of one **variable** and the values of other variables

regret1 /rɪˈɡret/ (**regrets, regretting, regretted**) verb [T] to feel sorry or sad about something that has happened, or about something that you have done: *We regret any inconvenience caused by the delay.* ♦ *I regret that I cannot attend your wedding.* ♦ *I don't regret moving to New York.*

regret2 /rɪˈɡret/ noun [C/U] a feeling of sadness about something that has happened or something that you have done —**regretful** adj, **regretfully** adv

regrettable /rɪˈɡretəb(ə)l/ adj used for talking about something that you wish had not happened —**regrettably** adv

regular /ˈreɡjʊlə/ adj

1 arranged evenly	4 with even shape
2 doing sth often	5 about grammar
3 ordinary	6 of army

1 arranged so that there is the same amount of time or space between things: *regular monthly meetings* ♦ *They come here on a regular basis.*
2 doing something, or done frequently: *a regular customer* ♦ *regular exercise*
3 ordinary, or of average size: *regular unleaded petrol*
4 arranged to form an even shape: *He was a handsome man, with strong regular features.*
5 **LANGUAGE** following the normal patterns of grammar ≠ **IRREGULAR**: *regular verbs*
6 relating to or belonging to a professional army —**regularity** /ˌreɡjʊˈlærəti/ noun [U]

regularly /ˈreɡjʊləli/ adv **1** after equal amounts of time have passed: *The committee meets regularly.* **2** frequently: *The equipment needs to be checked regularly.* **3** with an even shape, or arranged with an equal amount of space between objects = **EVENLY**: *The council planted trees along the streets at regularly spaced intervals.*

ˌregular ˈpolygon noun [C] **MATHS** a geometric shape with three or more straight sides of equal length, and angles of equal size

regulate /ˈreɡjʊleɪt/ verb [T] **1** to control something so that it operates effectively **2** to officially control an activity, process, or industry —**regulator** noun [C], **regulatory** /ˈreɡjʊlət(ə)ri, ˈreɡjʊˌleɪt(ə)ri/ adj

regulation /ˌreɡjʊˈleɪʃ(ə)n/ noun **1** [C] an official rule that controls the way things are done: *building regulations* **2** [U] official control of an activity, process, or industry: *the government's regulation of the steel industry*

regurgitate /rɪˈɡɜːdʒɪteɪt/ verb [T] **1** **BIOLOGY** to bring food up from the stomach back into the mouth **2** *formal* to repeat facts or ideas that you have heard or learnt without understanding them or thinking about them for yourself —**regurgitation** /rɪˌɡɜːdʒɪˈteɪʃ(ə)n/ noun [U]

rehabilitate /ˌriːəˈbɪlɪteɪt/ verb [T] **SOCIAL STUDIES** to help someone to return to a normal life after they have been in prison, or after they have been **addicted**

to drugs or alcohol —**rehabilitation** /ˌriːəbɪlɪˈteɪʃ(ə)n/ noun [U]

rehearsal /rɪˈhɜːs(ə)l/ noun [C/U] an occasion when you practise for the performance of a play, concert etc

rehearse /rɪˈhɜːs/ verb [I/T] to practise a play, concert etc before giving a performance

rehydration solution /ˌriːhaɪˈdreɪʃ(ə)n səˌluːʃ(ə)n/ noun [C/U] HEALTH a solution of water containing important salts, sugars, and minerals, given to someone whose body has become severely **dehydrated** (=lost a lot of water), especially through diarrhoea. The solution replaces the water, salts etc that have been lost.

reign[1] /reɪn/ noun [C] **1** the period of time when a king or queen rules a country **2** a period of time during which a particular person, group, or thing is very powerful or popular

reign[2] /reɪn/ verb [I] **1** if a king or queen reigns, they officially rule a country **2** to be very powerful or popular at a particular time **3** to be the most important feature in a situation: *For weeks, confusion reigned at the office.*

reimburse /ˌriːɪmˈbɜːs/ verb [T] to give someone back money that they have spent= PAY SB BACK —**reimbursement** noun [C/U]

reimport /ˌriːɪmˈpɔːt/ verb [T] BUSINESS to bring back into your country goods made in other places, from materials that originally came from your country

rein /reɪn/ noun [C] **1** a piece of leather fastened to a horse's head that a rider uses to control the horse **2** reins [plural] control of a company, government, or organization

reincarnation /ˌriːɪnkɑːˈneɪʃ(ə)n/ noun RELIGION **1** [U] the belief that after you die you can be born again as a different person, animal, or thing **2** [C] someone who has been born again as a different person, animal, or thing after their death

reindeer /ˈreɪnˌdɪə/ (plural **reindeer**) noun [C] a large mammal like a **deer** with large **antlers**, found in cold regions of northern Europe, northern Asia, and North America

reinforce /ˌriːɪnˈfɔːs/ verb [T] **1** to make an idea, belief, or feeling stronger: *The figures reinforce the view that economic growth is slowing.* **2** to make a building, structure, or object stronger: *Crews started work to reinforce the damaged bridge.* **3** to make a group of soldiers, police etc stronger by adding more people or equipment to it= BOLSTER —**reinforced** /ˌriːɪnˈfɔːst/ adj

reinforced concrete noun [U] CONSTRUCTION concrete that has metal bars or wires inside it to make it stronger

reinforcement /ˌriːɪnˈfɔːsmənt/ noun **1** reinforcements [plural] extra soldiers or police officers who go to help an existing group of soldiers or police officers **2** [U] the process of **reinforcing** something

reinstate /ˌriːɪnˈsteɪt/ verb [T] **1** to give someone back their previous job or position **2** to bring back something such as a law or benefit that had been stopped= RESTORE —**reinstatement** noun [U]

reissue /ˌriːˈɪʃuː/ verb [T] TOURISM to change an airline ticket so that a passenger can fly on a different date or route, or at a different time

reiterate /riːˈɪtəreɪt/ verb [T] *formal* to repeat something in order to emphasize it —**reiteration** /riːˌɪtəˈreɪʃ(ə)n/ noun [C/U]

reject[1] /rɪˈdʒekt/ verb [T] **1** to not accept or agree with something such as an offer or an argument: *Our proposal was rejected.* **2** to refuse to accept someone for a job or a course of study **3** to behave in an unkind way to someone who wants kindness or love from you **4** HEALTH if someone's body rejects an organ after a **transplant** operation, they become ill because their body has a bad reaction to the organ

reject[2] /ˈriːdʒekt/ noun [C] something or someone that is not accepted because they have not reached the necessary standard

rejection /rɪˈdʒekʃ(ə)n/ noun **1** [C/U] a refusal to accept or agree with something such as an offer or an argument ≠ ACCEPTANCE: *the rejection of the peace plan* **2** [C] a letter that tells you that you have not got a job or a place on a course of study **3** [C/U] a refusal to show someone the love or kindness that they need or expect: *fear of rejection*

rejoice /rɪˈdʒɔɪs/ verb [I] *literary* to celebrate and express feelings of great happiness —**rejoicing** noun [U]

rejoin /ˌriːˈdʒɔɪn/ verb [T] to return to a person or organization that you were with before

rejoinder /rɪˈdʒɔɪndə/ noun [C] *formal* a quick reply, especially one that is clever or rude

rejuvenate /rɪˈdʒuːvəneɪt/ verb [T] to make someone feel or look younger —**rejuvenation** /rɪˌdʒuːvəˈneɪʃ(ə)n/ noun [U]

relapse /ˈriːlæps/ noun [C/U] **1** HEALTH a period of illness after you had been getting better **2** a return to a worse state after a period of improvement —**relapse** /rɪˈlæps/ verb [I]

relate /rɪˈleɪt/ verb **1** [I/T] to show how one thing has a connection with another, or to be connected with another thing: *I can't really see how the two issues relate.* ♦ *We offer courses that relate English literature to other subjects.* **2** [T] *formal* to tell someone about something that has happened: *Philip began to relate the horrors of his childhood.*

PHRASAL VERB **reˈlate to sth** to be about something, or to be connected with something: *We're only interested in events that relate directly to the murder.*

related /rɪˈleɪtɪd/ adj **1** connected ≠ UNRELATED: *We think the two crimes are related in some way.* **2** belonging to the same family: *Annie's related to the director.*

relation /rɪˈleɪʃ(ə)n/ noun **1** relations [plural] the relationship between countries, people, or organizations: *international relations* ♦ *better relations between Japan and China* ♦ *We have very good relations with the local police.* **2** [C/U] a connection between two or more people or things: *The study found a direct relation between smoking and lung cancer.* ♦ *The tax bears no relation to people's ability to pay.* **3** [C] a member of your family such as a cousin or aunt= RELATIVE: *All our friends and relations came to our wedding.*

PHRASE **in relation to 1** in comparison to something: *Unemployment here is high in relation to national levels.* **2** concerning something: *I have nothing further to say in relation to this matter.*
—**relational** adj

Word family: **relation**

Words in the same family as relation

- **relate** *v*
- **related** *adj*
- **unrelated** *adj*
- **relative** *n*
- **relationship** *n*

re,lational 'database noun [C] COMPUTING a computer **database** that allows information to be stored and found in various ways

relationship /rɪ'leɪʃ(ə)nʃɪp/ noun [C] **1** the way in which two or more people or things are connected: *There is a close relationship between poverty and crime.* **2** the way in which two or more people or groups behave towards each other: *The relationships between players from the two teams were pretty friendly.* ♦ *What was your relationship with your mother like?* **3** a situation in which two people are sexual or romantic partners: *I was already in a relationship when I met Ben.*

relative¹ /'relətɪv/ adj used for comparing one situation with a more extreme one: *There was relative calm after the violence of the previous night.*
PHRASE **relative to** compared with

relative² /'relətɪv/ noun [C] a member of your family, especially one who does not live with you = RELATION

relative a,tomic 'mass noun [C] CHEMISTRY the mass of an atom of a particular chemical element, measured in relation to the mass of an atom of **carbon-12** (=the most common form of carbon, with six protons and six neutrons)

relative 'clause noun [C] LANGUAGE a clause that is joined to a previous one by words such as 'who', 'that', or 'which'

relative 'density noun [C] CHEMISTRY the ratio of the density of a material compared with the density of a particular substance, for example water or air

relative hu'midity noun [U] GEOGRAPHY the amount of water vapour in the air, expressed as a percentage of the highest amount that it could contain at the same temperature

relatively /'relətɪvli/ adv in comparison with someone or something similar = COMPARATIVELY: *a relatively small flat*

relative mo,lecular 'mass noun [C] PHYSICS the total of the **relative atomic masses** of the atoms in a particular molecule

relative 'pronoun noun [C] LANGUAGE a pronoun such as 'who', 'that', or 'which' that introduces a **relative clause**

relativity /,relə'tɪvəti/ noun [U] SCIENCE the relationship between time, space, and movement as described in Einstein's 'Theory of Relativity'

relax /rɪ'læks/ verb **1** [I] to rest and become calm: *Just sit down and try to relax for half an hour.* **2** [I/T] BIOLOGY if muscles relax, or if you relax them, they become less tight ≠ CONTRACT: *Relax your stomach muscles; then repeat the exercise.* **3** [T] to make rules, controls, conditions etc less strict —**relaxation** /,riːlæk'seɪʃ(ə)n/ noun [C/U]

relaxed /rɪ'lækst/ adj **1** calm and not worried: *You'll feel more relaxed after a good night's sleep.* **2** friendly, informal, and comfortable: *The atmosphere in their office is very relaxed.*

relaxing /rɪ'læksɪŋ/ adj pleasant and making you feel relaxed

relay¹ /rɪ'leɪ, 'riːleɪ/ (**relays, relaying, relayed**) verb [T] **1** to communicate information to someone **2** to send out television or radio signals to be broadcast

relay² /'riːleɪ/ or **relay ,race** noun [C] **1** SPORTS a race between two or more teams where each member of the team does part of the race and then another member continues **2** ENGINEERING, PHYSICS a switch that automatically opens or closes an electrical circuit

'relay ,neuron noun [C] ANATOMY a type of nerve cell in the **spinal cord** that passes signals between **motor neurons** and **sensory neurons** —*picture* → NEURON

release¹ /rɪ'liːs/ verb [T]

1 let sb leave	4 give information
2 let sth into area around	5 offer product
3 stop holding sth	

1 to let someone leave a place where they have been kept = FREE: *The authorities had recently released two suspects.* ♦ *He was released from prison in July.*
2 SCIENCE to let a substance or energy spread into the area or atmosphere around it, especially as part of a chemical reaction: *Oxygen from the water is released into the atmosphere.*
3 to stop holding someone or something: *She slowly released her grip on Louisa's hand.*
4 to make information or documents available: *Managers have released few details from yesterday's meeting.*
5 to make a new film, DVD, or CD available for people to see or buy: *They have just released their second album.*

release² /rɪ'liːs/ noun **1** [U] the act of letting someone leave a place such as a prison or hospital: *The release of Nelson Mandela was watched by millions of people on TV.* **2** [U] SCIENCE a situation in which something such as a chemical spreads into the area or atmosphere around it: *We're doing all we can to prevent the release of toxic waste into the oceans.* **3** [U] the act of making information or documents available: *the release of secret government information* **4** [C] a new film, DVD, or CD that is available for people to see or buy

relegate /'reləgeɪt/ verb [T] to move someone or something to a less important position —**relegation** /,relə'geɪʃ(ə)n/ noun [U]

relent /rɪ'lent/ verb [I] **1** to change your mind about not letting someone do something **2** if rain or snow relents, it stops falling so heavily

relentless /rɪ'lentləs/ adj **1** never seeming to stop or improve **2** determined and never stopping your attempts to achieve something —**relentlessly** adv

relevance /'reləv(ə)ns/ noun [U] the quality of being connected with and important to something else

relevant /'reləv(ə)nt/ adj important and directly connected with what is being discussed or considered ≠ IRRELEVANT: *How is that relevant to this discussion?*

reliable /rɪ'laɪəb(ə)l/ adj able to be trusted = DEPENDABLE ≠ UNRELIABLE: *a reliable workman* ♦ *reliable evidence* —**reliability** /rɪ,laɪə'bɪləti/ noun [U], **reliably** adv

reliance /rɪ'laɪəns/ noun [U] the state of depending on someone or something = DEPENDENCE

reliant /rɪ'laɪənt/ adj depending on someone or something = DEPENDENT

relic /'relɪk/ noun [C] an object, system, or rule that belongs to the past

relief /rɪ'liːf/ noun

1 relaxed happy feeling	4 sth with raised surface
2 reduction of pain etc	5 right not to pay in full
3 sth given to sb in need	

1 [singular/U] a relaxed happy feeling that you get because something bad has ended or has not happened: *It's a huge relief to know that everyone is safe.* ♦ *To her relief, someone had found her keys.*
2 [U] the reduction of pain or the effects of an illness: *The patients experienced no relief from their symptoms.*

3 [U] food, clothes, and money that is given to people who are in need of help: *earthquake relief*
4 [C] ARTS a design or **sculpture** consisting of a raised surface on a flat background
5 [U] the right to not have to pay the full amount of tax or interest on an amount of money

re'lief ,map noun [C] GEOGRAPHY a map that shows hills and mountains in a way that makes them easy to see by using **contour** lines and different colours

relieve /rɪˈliːv/ verb [T] **1** to make an unpleasant feeling or situation less severe or unpleasant: *Can't the doctor give you medicine to **relieve the pain**?* ♦ *Reading helped to **relieve the boredom**.* **2** to replace someone when they finish work

relieved /rɪˈliːvd/ adj happy and relaxed because something bad has ended or did not happen: *I'm so relieved to know the truth.*

religion /rɪˈlɪdʒ(ə)n/ noun [C/U] RELIGION belief in a god or in gods, or a particular system of beliefs in a god or in gods: *the Hindu religion*

religious /rɪˈlɪdʒəs/ adj **1** relating to religion: *religious beliefs* **2** believing strongly in your religion= DEVOUT: *a deeply religious man*

religiously /rɪˈlɪdʒəsli/ adv if you do something religiously, you do it regularly and are very serious about it

relinquish /rɪˈlɪŋkwɪʃ/ verb [T] *formal* to give up your power, position, or an advantage

reload /riːˈləʊd/ verb [I/T] to put something into an object such as a gun or camera so that it is ready to use again

relocate /ˌriːləʊˈkeɪt/ verb [I/T] to move to a different place, or to make someone do this —**relocation** /ˌriːləʊˈkeɪʃ(ə)n/ noun [U]

reluctant /rɪˈlʌktənt/ adj not willing to do something: *She was reluctant to leave.* —**reluctance** noun [U], **reluctantly** adv

rely /rɪˈlaɪ/ (**relies, relying, relied**)
PHRASAL VERBS **re'ly on sb/sth** to trust someone or something to do something for you: *Sometimes you just have to rely on your own judgment.* ♦ *Can we **rely on** him **to** support us?*
re'ly on sth to need something in order to continue living, existing, or operating: *The museum **relies on** voluntary donations **to** stay open.*

remain /rɪˈmeɪn/ verb **1** [linking verb] to continue to be in a particular situation or condition: *The dictator has remained in power for over 20 years.* ♦ *The economy remains fragile.* **2** [I] to stay in a particular place or position and not leave it: *You must **remain in bed** for three days after surgery.* **3** [I] to continue to exist after other things have gone or have been dealt with: *Only a handful of these rare fish remain in Scotland.*
PHRASE **it remains to be seen (whether/what/how)** used for saying that you do not know yet whether something will happen or will be possible

the remainder /rɪˈmeɪndə/ noun [singular] **1** the part of something that is left after the rest has gone or been finished **2** MATHS the amount that is left when one number cannot be divided exactly by another

remaining /rɪˈmeɪnɪŋ/ adj still left after other people or things have gone or been dealt with

remains /rɪˈmeɪnz/ noun [plural] **1** the part of something that is left after the rest has been finished, used, or destroyed **2** the body of a person or animal that has died

remand[1] /rɪˈmɑːnd/ verb **be remanded in custody** LAW someone who is remanded in custody is put in prison until their trial

remand[2] /rɪˈmɑːnd/ noun **on remand** LAW someone who is on remand is in prison waiting for their trial

re'mand ,centre noun [C] LAW a place where people are kept while they wait for the date of their trial

remark[1] /rɪˈmɑːk/ noun [C] a few words that give the facts or give your opinion about something= COMMENT: *Nicholas **made a** rude **remark about** her hair.*

remark[2] /rɪˈmɑːk/ verb [T] [I/T] to make a comment about something

remarkable /rɪˈmɑːkəb(ə)l/ adj unusual in a way that surprises or impresses you: *The play has been a remarkable success.*

remarkably /rɪˈmɑːkəbli/ adv in an unusual or surprising way: *All the students did remarkably well.*

remedial /rɪˈmiːdiəl/ adj **1** intended to improve or correct something **2** EDUCATION intended to help people who have difficulty learning basic skills such as reading and writing

remediation /rɪˌmiːdiˈeɪʃ(ə)n/ noun [U] *formal* the process of improving a situation or correcting a problem

remedy[1] /ˈremədi/ (plural **remedies**) noun [C] **1** a solution to a particular problem: *There are no easy **remedies for** learning difficulties.* **2** HEALTH a cure for pain or for a minor illness: *herbal remedies* **3** LAW a solution to a disagreement

remedy[2] /ˈremədi/ (**remedies, remedying, remedied**) verb [T] to correct or improve a situation

remember /rɪˈmembə/ verb **1** [I/T] to have an image in your mind of a person, a place, or something that happened in the past: *I can still remember every word of our conversation.* ♦ *She remembers seeing him there.* ♦ *I remember that I was really nervous on my first day at school.* ♦ *Try to remember where you put the keys.* **2** [T] to not forget to do something: *I hope she remembers my book (=brings it with her).* ♦ *He never remembers to lock the door when he goes out.*

remembrance /rɪˈmembrəns/ noun [U] a way of showing respect for someone who has died, or for an important event

remind /rɪˈmaɪnd/ verb [T] to help someone to remember something: *She reminded me that we had met before.* ♦ *I need the notes to remind me what to say.* ♦ *Can you **remind** us **of** your plans for the building?* ♦ *Remind Jenny to bring my CD when she comes.*
PHRASAL VERB **re'mind sb of sb/sth** to be very similar to someone or something else

reminder /rɪˈmaɪndə/ noun [C] something that reminds you of something

reminisce /ˌremɪˈnɪs/ verb [I] to talk, think, or write about enjoyable experiences in your past —**reminiscence** /ˌremɪˈnɪs(ə)ns/ noun [C]

reminiscent /ˌremɪˈnɪs(ə)nt/ adj reminding you of someone or something similar

remission /rɪˈmɪʃ(ə)n/ noun [C/U] **1** HEALTH a period of time when an illness or disease becomes less severe: *Her sister's cancer is **in remission**.* **2** LAW the reduction of a prison sentence because the prisoner has behaved well

remit /ˈriːmɪt/ noun [singular] *formal* a particular area of work that someone is responsible for

remittance /rɪˈmɪt(ə)ns/ noun **1** [C/U] *formal* a payment for goods or services that you send by post **2** [U] the process of sending a payment by post

remix /ˈriːˌmɪks/ noun [C] MUSIC a piece of music that is produced by combining parts of an existing piece of music with new sounds —**remix** /ˌriːˈmɪks/ verb [T]

remnant /ˈremnənt/ noun [C] a small remaining part of something

remonstrate /ˈremənˌstreɪt/ verb [I] formal to argue with, complain to, or criticize someone about something

remorse /rɪˈmɔːs/ noun [U] a strong sad and guilty feeling about something bad that you have done —**remorseful** adj, **remorsefully** adv

remorseless /rɪˈmɔːsləs/ adj 1 not feeling sad or guilty for having done something bad 2 continuing without stopping, or continuing to get worse= RELENTLESS —**remorselessly** adv

remote /rɪˈməʊt/ (**remoter, remotest**) adj 1 distant in space or time: *a remote village in China* ♦ *the remote past* 2 slight: *You have only a remote chance of winning.* 3 not showing any friendly interest in other people = ALOOF 4 not connected or relevant to something: *All these theories seem very remote from our everyday experience in the classroom.* —**remoteness** noun [U]

re,mote 'access noun [U] COMPUTING the ability to use a computer using a separate **terminal**

re,mote con'trol noun 1 [C] a piece of equipment that you use for controlling something such as a television from a short distance away 2 [U] a system of controlling a machine or a vehicle from a distance —**re,mote-con'trolled** adj

remotely /rɪˈməʊtli/ adv in a very small way: *He wasn't even remotely interested in anything we had to say.*

remote manipulator system /rɪˌməʊt məˈnɪpjʊleɪtə ˌsɪstəm/ noun [C] ASTRONOMY a mechanical arm on a spacecraft that the **crew** can use to handle objects on the outside of the spacecraft from the inside —*picture* → SPACE SHUTTLE

removable /rɪˈmuːvəb(ə)l/ adj easily removed = DETACHABLE

removal /rɪˈmuːv(ə)l/ noun [C/U] 1 the process of removing someone or something 2 the process of taking furniture from one property to another when you move to another house or office

remove /rɪˈmuːv/ verb [T] 1 to take someone or something away from a place: *Medical crews removed two people from the collapsed building.* 2 to take off a piece of clothing: *She removed her coat and sat down.* 3 to get rid of a problem, difficulty, or something that annoys you: *We need to remove any obstacles to a peaceful solution.* 4 to take away someone's power or position, especially in politics: *Officials who were involved in the scandal were removed from office.*

removed section /rɪˈmuːvd ˌsekʃ(ə)n/ noun [C/U] MATHS, PHYSICS a drawing of a section of a three-dimensional object that shows a part of the object separately

remunerate /rɪˈmjuːnəreɪt/ verb [T] formal to pay or reward someone for their work —**remuneration** /rɪˌmjuːnəˈreɪʃ(ə)n/ noun [U]

renaissance /rɪˈneɪs(ə)ns, American ˈrenəˌsɑns/ noun 1 [singular] a situation in which something becomes popular again 2 **the Renaissance** the period in Europe between the 14th and 16th centuries when there was increased interest in art, literature, and science

renal /ˈriːn(ə)l/ adj ANATOMY relating to the kidneys

'renal ˌartery noun [C] ANATOMY the blood vessel that takes blood containing waste products to the kidney

rename /riːˈneɪm/ verb [T] to change the name of someone or something

render¹ /ˈrendə/ verb [T] formal 1 to provide a service, or to give help to someone or something 2 to make someone or something be or become something

render² /ˈrendə/ noun [U] CONSTRUCTION **plaster** made from cement and sand, put on the external walls of buildings

rendering /ˈrend(ə)rɪŋ/ noun [C] the way a piece of music, poem, film, play etc is performed

renew /rɪˈnjuː/ verb [T] 1 to arrange for something to continue= EXTEND 2 to do something again after a pause 3 to replace something that is old or damaged —**renewal** noun [C/U]

renewable /rɪˈnjuːəb(ə)l/ adj 1 ENVIRONMENT renewable energy and **resources** replace themselves by natural processes, so that they are never completely used up≠ NON-RENEWABLE: *renewable sources of energy* ♦ *Sunlight is a renewable resource.* 2 a renewable contract or arrangement can be continued for a longer period of time ≠ NON-RENEWABLE

renewed /rɪˈnjuːd/ adj happening again after a pause, and with more energy or enthusiasm than before

renounce /rɪˈnaʊns/ verb [T] formal 1 to say formally that you no longer support or believe in something 2 to say formally that you want to give up a right, title, or position —**renunciation** /rɪˌnʌnsiˈeɪʃ(ə)n/ noun [C/U]

renovate /ˈrenəveɪt/ verb [T] to make something old look new again by repairing and improving it —**renovation** /ˌrenəˈveɪʃ(ə)n/ noun [C/U]

renowned /rɪˈnaʊnd/ adj famous for a special skill or achievement —**renown** noun [U]

rent¹ /rent/ noun [C/U] an amount of money that someone pays regularly for using a house, room, office etc that belongs to someone else: *After she'd paid her rent, Jan had no money left for food.*

rent² /rent/ verb 1 [I/T] to pay money regularly to use a house, room, office etc that belongs to someone else: *How long have you been renting this place?* 2 [I/T] to pay money to use a vehicle, piece of equipment etc for a short time 3 [T] to allow a house, room, office etc that you own to be used by someone who pays you regularly for using it: *All the rooms are rented out to students.*

rental /ˈrent(ə)l/ noun [C/U] the process of renting something, or an amount of money that you pay for renting something —**rental** adj

reorder /riˈɔːdə/ verb [T] to order more of something that you have bought before

reorganize /riˈɔːɡənaɪz/ verb [I/T] to organize something in a different way —**reorganization** /riˌɔːɡənaɪˈzeɪʃ(ə)n/ noun [C/U]

repackage /riːˈpækɪdʒ/ verb [T] to change the way that something is presented or sold, in order to make it seem more attractive or interesting

repair¹ /rɪˈpeə/ verb [T] 1 to fix something that is broken or damaged: *The cost of repairing the damage will be high.* 2 to improve a bad situation: *an attempt to repair the relationship between the two countries*

repair² /rɪˈpeə/ noun 1 [C/U] work that is done to fix something that is broken or damaged: *How much will the repairs cost?* ♦ *Unfortunately the engine is beyond repair* (=so badly damaged that it cannot be repaired). ♦ *Both church and tower were in need of repair.* 2 [C] a part of something that has been repaired
PHRASE **in good/bad repair** in a good or a bad condition: *Most of the paintings are in good repair.*

reparations /ˌrepəˈreɪʃ(ə)nz/ noun [plural] money paid by the country that loses a war for the damage that it has caused to other countries

repay /rɪˈpeɪ/ (**repays, repaying, repaid** /rɪˈpeɪd/) verb [T] **1** to give someone back the money that you borrowed from them **2** to reward someone who has helped you

repayment /rɪˈpeɪmənt/ noun [C] an amount of money that you pay back to the person that you borrowed it from

repeal /rɪˈpiːl/ verb [T] **LAW** to officially end a law —**repeal** noun [U]

repeat¹ /rɪˈpiːt/ verb

1 say/do again	**4** say/write again to learn
2 do same class again	**5** broadcast again
3 tell sb else	**+ PHRASE**

1 [T] to say or do something again: *Can you repeat what you just said, please?* ♦ *Repeat the exercise eight times with each leg.*

2 [I/T] **EDUCATION** to do the same class at school the next year because you did not achieve a satisfactory standard the first time: *If you don't pass this exam you'll have to repeat a year.*

3 [T] to tell someone something that someone else has told you: *I'll tell you a secret, but please don't repeat it to anyone.*

4 [T] to say or write something that you have heard or read because you are trying to learn or understand it: *The students carefully repeated the words after the teacher.*

5 [T] to broadcast a television or radio programme again

PHRASE **repeat yourself** to say the same words or idea that you said before, often without realizing you are doing it: *Sally sometimes gets confused and repeats herself.*

Word family: repeat

Words in the same family as repeat
- **repeated** *adj*
- **repeatedly** *adv*
- **repetitive** *adj*
- **repetition** *n*
- **repetitious** *adj*

repeat² /rɪˈpiːt/ noun [C] **1** a television or radio programme that is broadcast again **2** an event or situation that happens again **3** **MUSIC** a particular passage of music played again, or the symbol that tells a musician to do this

repeated /rɪˈpiːtɪd/ adj done many times —**repeatedly** adv

repel /rɪˈpel/ (**repels, repelling, repelled**) verb [T] **1** if something repels you, you think that it is extremely unpleasant **2** to keep someone or something away, or to prevent them from attacking you **3** **PHYSICS** if one thing repels another, an electrical or magnetic force pushes them away from each other

repellent /rɪˈpelənt/ noun [C/U] a substance that keeps insects or animals away

repent /rɪˈpent/ verb [I/T] **RELIGION** to be very sorry for something bad that you have done, especially something against the rules of your religion —**repentance** noun [U], **repentant** adj

repercussions /ˌriːpəˈkʌʃ(ə)nz/ noun [plural] the bad effects that something causes

repertoire /ˈrepəˌtwɑː/ noun [C] all the songs, pieces of music etc that a performer knows and is able to perform

repertory /ˈrepət(ə)ri/ noun [U] **ARTS** a system used by theatres in which a group of actors regularly

perform different plays during a particular period of time

repetition /ˌrepəˈtɪʃ(ə)n/ noun **1** [U] a situation in which someone repeats something **2** [C] something that happens in the same way as an earlier event

repetitious /ˌrepəˈtɪʃəs/ adj happening or done many times in a way that becomes boring —**repetitiously** adv

repetitive /rɪˈpetətɪv/ adj repeating the same thing, especially in a way that is boring or annoying

rephrase /ˌriːˈfreɪz/ verb [T] to say or write the same thing, using different words

replace /rɪˈpleɪs/ verb [T] **1** to get rid of someone or something and put a new person or thing in their place: *We'll have to replace all the furniture that was damaged in the flood.* ♦ *The plan is to replace state funding with private money.* **2** to do the same job that someone or something did before: *Have they found anyone to replace him yet?* ♦ *Email may completely replace traditional letters in the future.* **3** to put something back in its correct place or position: *She carefully replaced the plate on the shelf.*

replacement /rɪˈpleɪsmənt/ noun [C/U] someone or something that takes the place of another person or thing, or the process of replacing someone or something: *Have you found a **replacement for** your assistant?*

replay /ˈriːˌpleɪ/ noun [C] **SPORTS 1** part of a sports match that is broadcast again **2** a game that is played again because neither team won the first time —**replay** /ˌriːˈpleɪ/ verb [T]

replenish /rɪˈplenɪʃ/ verb [T] *formal* to make something full again, or to bring it back to its previous level by replacing what has been used

replica /ˈreplɪkə/ noun [C] an accurate copy of something

replicate /ˈreplɪkeɪt/ verb **1** [T] *formal* to do or make something again in the same way as before: *Other scientists have been unable to replicate his results.* **2** [I] **BIOLOGY** if an organism, a cell, or genetic material replicates, it reproduces itself exactly —**replication** /ˌreplɪˈkeɪʃ(ə)n/ noun [U]

reply¹ /rɪˈplaɪ/ (**replies, replying, replied**) verb **1** [I/T] to say, write, or do something as an answer: *'I know,' Corbett replied quietly.* ♦ *When I asked where he was going, he replied that it was none of my business.* ♦ *It took them a week to **reply to** my letter.* **2** [I] to do something as a reaction to what someone else has done = RESPOND

reply² /rɪˈplaɪ/ (plural **replies**) noun [C] **1** something that you say or write as an answer: *I wrote to him, but I got no reply.* ♦ *We received **a reply from** the minister herself.* ♦ *I still haven't had **a reply to** my email.* ♦ *I am writing **in reply to** your letter of 7 August.* **2** something that you do as a reaction to what someone else has done = RESPONSE

report¹ /rɪˈpɔːt/ noun [C] **1** a spoken or written description of a particular subject, situation, or event: *A new report shows violent crime is on the increase.* ♦ *We're **getting reports of** more fighting in the area.* ♦ *the company's **annual report*** ♦ *We have to write a short **report on** the conference.* **2** an article or broadcast that gives information about something in the news: *Did you see that **report about** corruption in government?* **3** **EDUCATION** a document that is written by a teacher, giving details of a student's school work

report² /rɪˈpɔːt/ verb **1** [T] to provide information about something, especially to people in authority: *Witnesses reported hearing a loud noise before the* plane crashed. ♦ *If you see anything suspicious, report it to the police.* **2** [I/T] to give information about something in a news article or broadcast: *Correspondents reported that the president had lost control of the country.* ♦ *Three journalists were sent to report on the conflict.* **3** [T] to produce an official statement or a written document about a particular subject: *The committee will report the results of its investigation tomorrow.*

PHRASAL VERBS re,port 'back to tell or send someone information that you have discovered: *He promised to report back to the committee.*

re'port to sb if you report to someone at work, they are responsible for telling you what to do

reportedly /rɪˈpɔːtɪdli/ adv used for showing that you are not certain that something you are reporting is true

reported speech /rɪˌpɔːtɪd ˈspiːtʃ/ noun [U] **LANGUAGE** a way of saying what someone has said that does not repeat their actual words= INDIRECT SPEECH

reporter /rɪˈpɔːtə/ noun [C] someone whose job is to write articles or make broadcasts about events in the news= JOURNALIST

reprehensible /ˌreprɪˈhensəb(ə)l/ adj *formal* very bad

represent /ˌreprɪˈzent/ verb

1 speak/act for sb	4 be example of
2 be sth	5 in sport
3 be sign/symbol of	6 be picture of

1 [T] to officially speak or do something for another person or group: *The vice-president will represent the United States at the ceremony.*
2 [linking verb] if something represents another thing, it consists of that thing= CONSTITUTE: *Albanians represent about 90 per cent of the population in Kosovo.*
3 [T] to be a sign or symbol of something: *The colour red commonly represents danger.*
4 [T] to be an example of a particular quality or type: *His attitude represents everything I dislike about this country.*
5 [T] to take part in a sport as a member of a particular team, country etc: *Ben's ambition is to represent Zimbabwe at the Olympics.*
6 [T] to be a picture or image of something= DEPICT: *The statue represents Jefferson as a young man.*

representation /ˌreprɪzenˈteɪʃ(ə)n/ noun **1** [C] a sign, symbol, or picture of something **2** [U] a person or group that officially speaks or does something for someone else

representational /ˌreprɪzenˈteɪʃ(ə)nəl/ adj **ARTS** representational paintings and other works of art show things as they really are

representative¹ /ˌreprɪˈzentətɪv/ noun [C]
1 someone who has been chosen by a person or group to vote, speak, or make decisions for them: *an elected representative* ♦ *The new government sent a representative to the talks.* **2** someone who is thought of as a typical member of a particular group → SALES REPRESENTATIVE

representative² /ˌreprɪˈzentətɪv/ adj **1** typical of people or things in a particular group: *His views are not representative of the majority of the population.*
2 **POLITICS** a representative form of government is one in which people vote for their politicians

Representative /ˌreprɪˈzentətɪv/ noun [C] **POLITICS** a politician who is a member of the US House of Representatives

repression /rɪˈpreʃ(ə)n/ noun [U] the use of force or violence to control people

repressive /rɪˈpresɪv/ adj ruling or controlling people with force or violence

reprieve /rɪˈpriːv/ noun [C] **1** a stop or delay in something bad or unpleasant **2** an official decision not to kill someone who was going to be killed as a punishment for a crime —**reprieve** verb [T]

reprimand /ˈreprɪˌmɑːnd/ verb [T] to tell someone officially that something that they have done is wrong —**reprimand** noun [C]

reprint /ˈriːˌprɪnt/ noun [C] a book that has been reprinted

reprise /rɪˈpriːz/ noun [C] **MUSIC** a part of a song or other piece of music that is repeated

reprivatize /riːˈpraɪvətaɪz/ verb [T] **ECONOMICS** to sell a **nationalized** business or industry so that it becomes a private business again= DENATIONALIZE

reproach¹ /rɪˈprəʊtʃ/ verb [T] to criticize someone for something that they have done

reproach² /rɪˈprəʊtʃ/ noun [C/U] a criticism that you make of someone because of something bad that they have done

PHRASE beyond reproach impossible to criticize because of being so good
—**reproachful** adj, **reproachfully** adv

reproduce /ˌriːprəˈdjuːs/ verb **1** [I/T] **BIOLOGY** to have babies, or to produce young animals, plants, or other organisms **2** [T] to make a copy of something **3** [T] to repeat something so that it happens in the same way as before —**reproducibility** /ˌriːprədjuːsəˈbɪləti/ noun [U]

reproducible /ˌriːprəˈdjuːsəb(ə)l/ adj able to be copied or repeated

reproduction /ˌriːprəˈdʌkʃ(ə)n/ noun **1** [U] **BIOLOGY** the process of having babies or producing young animals, plants, and other organisms. The form of reproduction that involves the combination of male and female **gametes**, for example in most animals and plants, is called **sexual reproduction**. Reproduction in which there is only one parent, for example in bacteria, is called **asexual reproduction**. → MEIOSIS, MITOSIS **2** [C] a copy of something, especially a work of art

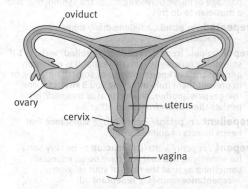

female reproductive system

reproductive /ˌriːprəˈdʌktɪv/ adj **BIOLOGY** relating to the process of having babies or producing young animals, plants, or other organisms

,reproductive 'cell noun [C] **BIOLOGY** a male or female cell that unites with a cell from the opposite sex to form a new organism in the process of sexual reproduction = GAMETE

reproving /rɪˈpruːvɪŋ/ adj formal expressing criticism or blame —**reprovingly** adv

reptile /ˈreptaɪl/ noun [C] BIOLOGY a vertebrate animal such as a snake or lizard that lays eggs, and whose body is covered in scales —picture → on next page —**reptilian** /repˈtɪliən/ adj

republic /rɪˈpʌblɪk/ noun [C] POLITICS a country that is not ruled by a king or queen

republican /rɪˈpʌblɪkən/ noun [C] POLITICS someone who thinks that their country should not have a king or queen —**republican** adj

the Reˈpublican ˌParty POLITICS one of the two main political parties in the US

repudiate /rɪˈpjuːdieɪt/ verb [T] formal to say formally that something is not true, or that you do not accept it —**repudiation** /rɪˌpjuːdiˈeɪʃ(ə)n/ noun [U]

repugnant /rɪˈpʌgnənt/ adj formal extremely unpleasant or offensive —**repugnance** noun [U]

repulse /rɪˈpʌls/ verb [T] formal 1 to stop a military attack 2 if someone or something repulses you, you think that they are very unpleasant

repulsion /rɪˈpʌlʃ(ə)n/ noun [U] 1 a strong feeling of dislike 2 PHYSICS a force such as electricity or magnetism that makes things move apart ≠ ATTRACTION —picture → MAGNET

repulsive /rɪˈpʌlsɪv/ adj extremely unpleasant = DISGUSTING

reˈpulsive ˌforce noun [C/U] PHYSICS a force such as electricity or magnetism that can make things move apart. Repulsive force causes the north pole of a magnet to move away from the north pole of another magnet.

reputable /ˈrepjʊtəb(ə)l/ adj generally considered to be honest and reliable

reputation /ˌrepjʊˈteɪʃ(ə)n/ noun [C/U] the opinion people have about how good or bad someone or something is: That part of town **has a bad reputation**. ♦ Clark had **a reputation for** arrogance. ♦ Our university has an international **reputation as** a centre of excellence.

reputed /rɪˈpjuːtɪd/ adj formal said or believed by a lot of people, but not definitely true —**reputedly** adv

request¹ /rɪˈkwest/ noun [C] 1 an act of asking for something in a polite or formal way: Evening meals are available **on request** (=if you ask). ♦ **Requests for** visas will be dealt with immediately. ♦ I've **made a request** for additional help. ♦ Treatment was stopped at the **request** of the patient. 2 a piece of music that you ask a musician or a **DJ** to play

request² /rɪˈkwest/ verb [T] to ask for something, or to ask someone to do something, in a polite or formal way

requiem /ˈrekwiəm/ or ˌ**requiem ˈmass** noun [C] RELIGION, MUSIC a Christian ceremony for someone who has died, or music which is written for this ceremony

require /rɪˈkwaɪə/ verb [T] 1 to need someone or something: Working with these children **requires** a great deal of **patience**. ♦ a medical condition **requiring treatment** 2 if a rule, law, contract etc requires something, you must do that thing: Car insurance is **required by law**.

requirement /rɪˈkwaɪəmənt/ noun [C] something that is necessary, or that a rule or law says that you

must do: a list of safety requirements ♦ Check the car's fuel requirements.

requisite /ˈrekwɪzɪt/ adj formal necessary for a particular purpose

requisition /ˌrekwɪˈzɪʃ(ə)n/ verb [T] to make an official request or order that something should be given or made available

resale /ˈriːseɪl/ noun [U] a situation in which someone sells something that they have bought previously

resat /ˌriːˈsæt/ the past tense and past participle of **resit¹**

rescind /rɪˈsɪnd/ verb [T] formal to state officially that something such as a law or an agreement has ended and no longer has legal authority

rescue¹ /ˈreskjuː/ verb [T] 1 to save someone from a dangerous or unpleasant situation: The crew of the ship were rescued just before it sank. 2 to prevent a business, project etc from failing: an attempt to rescue the peace process —**rescuer** noun [C]

rescue² /ˈreskjuː/ noun [C/U] an act of saving someone or something from danger or from an unpleasant situation: Soldiers carried out a dramatic rescue of the hostages last night. ♦ a rescue attempt

research¹ /rɪˈsɜːtʃ, ˈriːsɜːtʃ/ noun [U] the detailed study of something in order to discover new facts: medical research ♦ a research project ♦ He did some **research into** the causes of lung cancer. ♦ Scientists have **carried out** extensive **research** into the effects of these drugs.

PHRASE **research and development** the work that a company does when it is studying new ideas or developing new products, services, or methods. It is often simply called **R & D**.

research² /rɪˈsɜːtʃ, ˈriːsɜːtʃ/ verb [T] to make a detailed study of something in order to discover new facts —**researcher** noun [C]

resell /ˌriːˈsel/ (**resells, reselling, resold** /ˌriːˈsəʊld/) verb [T] to sell something that you previously bought

resemblance /rɪˈzembləns/ noun [C/U] if there is a resemblance between two people or things, they are similar

resemble /rɪˈzemb(ə)l/ verb [T] to be similar to someone or something: The animals make a sound that resembles a cat's miaow.

resent /rɪˈzent/ verb [T] to feel angry because you think that you have been treated unfairly

resentful /rɪˈzentf(ə)l/ adj feeling angry because you think that you have been treated unfairly

resentment /rɪˈzentmənt/ noun [U] an angry feeling that you have when you think that you have been treated unfairly: The decision caused a lot of resentment among the family.

reservation /ˌrezəˈveɪʃ(ə)n/ noun 1 [C] an arrangement to have something such as a room in a hotel or a seat in a theatre kept for you to use = BOOKING 2 [C/U] a feeling of doubt about whether something is good or right 3 [C] an area of land in the US where **Native Americans** live as a separate community

reserve¹ /rɪˈzɜːv/ noun 1 [C] a supply of something that a country, an organization, or a person can use: Norway's oil reserves ♦ We discovered **reserves of** strength that we didn't realize we had. 2 [C] SPORTS a player who has not been chosen to play in a particular match but who is available to play if he or she needed = SUBSTITUTE 3 [U] the behaviour of someone who tends not to talk about or show their feelings 4 [C] ENVIRONMENT an area of land where wild animals or plants are officially protected

reptiles

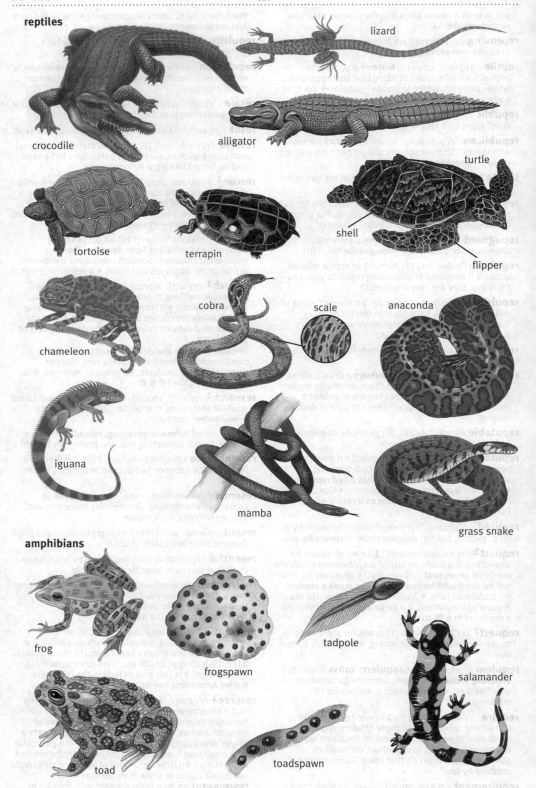

lizard

crocodile

alligator

turtle

shell

flipper

tortoise

terrapin

chameleon

cobra

scale

anaconda

iguana

mamba

grass snake

amphibians

frog

frogspawn

tadpole

salamander

toad

toadspawn

reptiles and amphibians

PHRASE **in reserve** available to be used: *Keep a few pounds in reserve to cover unexpected costs.*

reserve² /rɪˈzɜːv/ verb **1** [I/T] to make an arrangement so that something such as a room in a hotel or a seat in a theatre is kept for you to use: *We've reserved a table for 7.30.* **2** [T] to keep something for a particular person, purpose, or situation: *This area is reserved for non-smokers.*

PHRASE **reserve judgment** to wait until you have more information about someone or something before you form an opinion on them

reˈserve ˌcurrency noun [C] **ECONOMICS** a currency that is considered strong and reliable and is used a lot in international trade, for example the US **dollar**, the British **pound**, or the Japanese **yen**

reserved /rɪˈzɜːvd/ adj **1** available to be used only by a particular person or group **2** someone who is reserved tends not to talk about or show their feelings

reservist /rɪˈzɜːvɪst/ noun [C] a soldier who is not part of a country's permanent army, but who is trained to fight with the army if necessary

reservoir /ˈrezəˌvwɑː/ noun [C] **GEOGRAPHY** a lake, often an artificial one, where water is stored so that it can be supplied to houses, factories etc —*picture* → **DAM, WATER SUPPLY** **2** a container, often part of a machine, where liquid is kept for a particular purpose

reset /ˌriːˈset/ (**resets, resetting, reset**) verb [T] **1** to press a special button, or to make changes, so that a machine will work again or will work in a different way **2** **HEALTH** to put a broken bone back into its correct position

reside /rɪˈzaɪd/ verb [I] *formal* to live in a particular place

residence /ˈrezɪd(ə)ns/ noun **1** [C] *formal* a house or other place where someone lives: *the President's official residence* **2** [U] the fact that someone lives somewhere, or the period of time they spend living there: *He took up residence in Hollywood* (=started to live there) *in 1999.*

ˈresidence ˌpermit noun [C] **LAW** an official document allowing a foreigner to live in a country

residency /ˈrezɪd(ə)nsi/ noun [U] **LAW** the legal right to live in a country

resident /ˈrezɪd(ə)nt/ noun [C] someone who lives in a particular place: *Many local residents have objected to the new road.* ♦ *They are both residents of the same village.* —**resident** adj

residential /ˌrezɪˈdenʃ(ə)l/ adj **1** a residential area is one in which most of the buildings are houses **2** relating to the fact that someone lives in a place

residual /rɪˈzɪdjuəl/ adj remaining after the rest of something has gone

residue /ˈrezɪdjuː/ noun [C] **1** the part of something that remains after the rest has gone **2** **CHEMISTRY** a substance that remains after a chemical process —*picture* → **FILTER**

resign /rɪˈzaɪn/ verb [I/T] to state formally that you are leaving your job: *He made it clear that he was not resigning from active politics.* ♦ *He was forced to resign as mayor.*

PHRASE **resign yourself (to sth)** to accept that something unpleasant must happen and that you cannot change it: *I resigned myself to the fact that I'd never be a champion.*

resignation /ˌrezɪɡˈneɪʃ(ə)n/ noun **1** [C/U] the act of leaving a job permanently: *The scandal resulted in Allen's resignation from his post.* ♦ *She decided it was time to hand in her resignation.* **2** [U] the attitude of

someone who accepts that something unpleasant must happen and that they cannot change it

resigned /rɪˈzaɪnd/ adj accepting that something unpleasant must happen and that you cannot change it

resilient /rɪˈzɪliənt/ adj **1** able to quickly become healthy or strong again after an illness or a problem **2** **PHYSICS** a resilient substance or object can return to its original shape after being bent, stretched, or pressed —**resilience** noun [U]

resin /ˈrezɪn/ noun **1** [U] a transparent sticky substance that is used for making paints, glue, and plastic **2** [C/U] **CHEMISTRY** a chemical substance that is used instead of natural resin

resist /rɪˈzɪst/ verb **1** [I/T] to stop yourself from doing something that you would like to do: *It's difficult to resist a challenge like that.* ♦ *She couldn't resist asking him about his date.* **2** [T] to oppose someone or something, or to fight against them: *Antibodies help us resist infection.* ♦ *One protester was injured while resisting arrest.* **3** [T] to not be affected or harmed by something: *The shelters are designed to resist heat.*

resistance /rɪˈzɪst(ə)ns/ noun

1 slows electrical current	4 refusal of sth new
2 force	5 opposition
3 not being affected	6 opposition group

1 [U] **PHYSICS** the ability of a material or object to slow down an electric current. Good conductors, for example silver, have **low resistance**, and bad conductors, for example glass, have **high resistance**. **2** [U] **PHYSICS** a force that makes a moving object move more slowly: *wind resistance* **3** [singular/U] **BIOLOGY, HEALTH** the ability to not be affected or harmed by something, especially a disease or drug: *water resistance* ♦ *Vitamin C helps build resistance to infection.* **4** [singular/U] a refusal to accept something new: *political resistance* ♦ *This proposal is meeting some resistance* (=some people do not accept it) *at the UN.* **5** [singular/U] military opposition to someone who is attacking you: *There was some resistance in the north.* **6** [singular] a secret organization that fights against the group that controls their country

resistant /rɪˈzɪst(ə)nt/ adj **1** not harmed or affected by something: *a flame-resistant material* **2** opposed to something

reˌsistant ˈstrain noun [C] **BIOLOGY** a group of related organisms that are not affected by a particular disease, **antibiotic, pesticide** etc

resistor /rɪˈzɪstə/ noun [C] **PHYSICS** a piece of wire or other material that controls the level of current flowing in an electric circuit by providing resistance —*picture* → **ELECTRICITY**

resit¹ /ˌriːˈsɪt, ˈriːˌsɪt/ (**resits, resitting, resat** /ˌriːˈsæt, ˈriːˌsæt/) verb [T] **EDUCATION** to take an examination again

resit² /ˈriːˌsɪt/ noun [C] **EDUCATION** an examination that you take again because you failed it the first time

resold /ˌriːˈsəʊld/ the past tense and past participle of **resell**

resolute /ˈrezəluːt/ adj extremely determined —**resolutely** adv

resolution /ˌrezəˈluːʃ(ə)n/ noun **1** [C] a formal proposal that is considered by an organization and then voted on: *The UN passed a resolution* (=formally accepted it) *condemning the country's actions.* **2** [U] the act of solving a problem or of dealing with a disagreement: *a peaceful resolution of the conflict* **3** [C] a firm decision to do something: *Make a resolution to* *always do your homework on time.* **4** [U] the amount of detail that you can see on a television or computer screen

resolve¹ /rɪˈzɒlv/ verb **1** [T] to solve a problem, or to find a way of dealing with a disagreement **2** [I] *formal* to make a determined decision to do something

resolve² /rɪˈzɒlv/ noun [U] *formal* determination

resonance /ˈrezənəns/ noun [C/U] **1** PHYSICS a sound that something makes as a result of **sound waves** from another object **2** an emotional effect produced by something that reminds someone of something else —**resonant** adj

resonate /ˈrezəneɪt/ verb [I] PHYSICS to produce or be filled with a sound as a result of **sound waves** from another object

resort /rɪˈzɔːt/ noun [C] TOURISM a place where people go for a holiday: *a ski resort*

PHRASE **(as) a last resort** used for saying that you will do something only after trying everything else to solve a problem: *We would only expel a student as a last resort.*

reˈsort ˌhotel noun [C] TOURISM a hotel in a resort, for people who are on holiday rather than on business

resounding /rɪˈzaʊndɪŋ/ adj complete: used for emphasizing how successful or unsuccessful someone or something is

resource /rɪˈzɔːs/ noun [C] **1** something that you can use to achieve something: *We are increasing resources for the health service.* ♦ *The Internet has become a valuable resource in some schools.* ♦ *a lack of educational resources* **2** things that exist in nature and can be used by people: *Many of these countries are rich in mineral resources.* **3** resources [plural] the skills that someone has that they can use for dealing with problems: *He needed all his resources to escape alive.*

resourceful /rɪˈzɔːsf(ə)l/ adj good at finding effective ways to deal with problems —**resourcefulness** noun [U]

respect¹ /rɪˈspekt/ noun **1** [U] the attitude that someone is important and should be admired, and that you should treat them politely: *She has worked hard to **gain the respect of** her colleagues.* ♦ *Students **show** their **respect for** the teacher by not talking.* ♦ *Children should **treat** their parents **with respect**.* **2** [U] a feeling that something is important and deserves serious attention: *a **healthy respect for** the law* **3** [C] an aspect of something: *In many respects, we are no different from other people.*

PHRASE **in respect of** or **with respect to** *formal* concerning: *The two groups are very similar with respect to age.*

respect² /rɪˈspekt/ verb [T] **1** to treat someone in a way that shows that you think they are important and should be admired: *He is **highly respected** in his profession.* ♦ *People will **respect** you **for** telling the truth.* **2** to understand the importance of something: *We expect all governments to respect the rights of minorities.*

Word family: **respect**	
*Words in the same family as **respect***	
■ respectable *adj*	■ respectably *adv*
■ respectability *n*	■ respected *adj*
■ respectful *adj*	■ respectfully *adv*
■ disrespectful *adj*	■ disrespect *n*

respectable /rɪˈspektəb(ə)l/ adj **1** keeping to the accepted moral standards of your society, and not doing anything shocking or illegal **2** if an amount is respectable, it is enough: *a respectable salary*

—**respectability** /rɪˌspektəˈbɪləti/ noun [U], **respectably** adv

respected /rɪˈspektɪd/ adj admired and approved of by many people

respectful /rɪˈspektf(ə)l/ adj treating someone with respect —**respectfully** adv

respective /rɪˈspektɪv/ adj belonging to each of the people or things that you mentioned previously: *Jane and Patrick talked about their respective childhoods.*

respectively /rɪˈspektɪvli/ adv in the same order as the people or things that you have mentioned previously: *Walsh and O'Neill were jailed for 12 and 11 years respectively.*

respiration /ˌrespəˈreɪʃ(ə)n/ noun [U] BIOLOGY the process of making the energy present in organic compounds able to be used by the cells of living things. Oxygen is usually needed for this to take place, and this is called **aerobic respiration**. When oxygen is not used, it is called **anaerobic respiration**. The exchange of gases that is necessary for respiration to take place is called **gaseous exchange**, which takes place in the lungs of animals, leaves of trees, **gills** of fish etc. In humans and many other animals oxygen is taken into the lungs by breathing. —*picture* → CARBON CYCLE, WATER CYCLE

respiratory /rɪˈspɪrət(ə)ri, ˈresp(ə)rət(ə)ri/ adj BIOLOGY relating to the process of breathing: *the respiratory system*

ˈrespiratory ˌtube noun [C] BIOLOGY a long tube that sticks out from the **anus** of the larvae of some insects. The larvae use the tube to breathe when they are under water. —*picture* → MOSQUITO

respire /rɪˈspaɪə/ verb [I] BIOLOGY **1** to release energy from food so that it can be used by the body **2** to breathe

respite /ˈrespɪt, ˈrespaɪt/ noun [singular/U] a short period of time in which a difficult or unpleasant situation stops

respond /rɪˈspɒnd/ verb [I] **1** to react to something by doing or saying something: *She hugged him, but he didn't respond.* ♦ *Protesters threw stones at police, who **responded with** rubber bullets.* **2** to reply, especially in writing: *Thousands of readers **responded to** our questionnaire.* **3** HEALTH to react well to medical treatment: *The infection should **respond to** antibiotics.*

respondent /rɪˈspɒndənt/ noun [C] LAW the **defendant** in a court case, especially someone who is getting divorced

response /rɪˈspɒns/ noun [C] **1** something that someone does as a reaction to something else: *Her response was to leave the room and slam the door.* ♦ *There was an enthusiastic **response to** the suggestions.* ♦ *In response to complaints, the company reviewed its safety procedures.* **2** an answer to a question in a test: *I'm sorry; the correct response was 'B'.* **3** a reply to a question or letter: *I've left messages, but there's been no response.* **4** BIOLOGY the way that the body reacts to something, for example to bacteria: *We're studying the body's immune **response to** the virus.*

responsibility /rɪˌspɒnsəˈbɪləti/ noun **1** [C/U] something that you have to do as a duty or a job: *She has a lot of responsibility as a nurse.* ♦ *One of his responsibilities is the welfare of the pupils.* ♦ *She will **have responsibility for** marketing.* **2** [U] blame for something bad that has happened: *Allan has got to **take responsibility for** the failure of the deal.* ♦ *No one has **accepted responsibility for** the attack on the embassy.*

responsible /rɪˈspɒnsəb(ə)l/ adj **1** if you are responsible for something that has happened, you caused it, or you deserve to be blamed for it: *Parents feel responsible when things go wrong.* ♦ *He was responsible for the accident.* ♦ *The farmer was held responsible for the damage done by his animals.* **2** in charge of someone or something: *The manager is responsible for the running of the theatre.* **3** sensible, reliable, and able to be trusted ≠ IRRESPONSIBLE: *She may be only 14, but she's very responsible.*

responsibly /rɪˈspɒnsəbli/ adv in a sensible way that shows that you can be trusted

responsive /rɪˈspɒnsɪv/ adj **1** quick to react in the way that is right for a particular situation **2** willing to reply to a question or talk about something

rest¹ /rest/ noun **1** [singular] the part of something that remains, or the people or things that remain: *I'm not really hungry – do you want the rest?* ♦ *Rain will spread to the rest of the country by evening.* ♦ *The rest of the attackers were in jail.* **2** [C/U] a period of time that you spend relaxing or sleeping: *Can we stop for a minute? I need a rest.* ♦ *She has a rest after lunch.* ♦ *She took a well-earned rest from her studies.* **3** [C] an object that is used for supporting something → HEADREST **4** [C] MUSIC a pause of a particular length in a piece of music, or the symbol used to show this —*picture* → MUSIC

PHRASES **at rest** not moving
come to rest to finally stop moving: *The car skidded across the road before coming to rest against a wall.*
set/put sb's mind at rest to stop someone from worrying: *Tell me what happened, just to put my mind at rest.*

rest² /rest/ verb **1** [I] to spend a period of time relaxing or sleeping: *It would be nice to sit down and rest for a while.* **2** [T] to put something somewhere for support, especially a part of your body: *He rested the bag on the desk.* ♦ *John was asleep, with his head resting on my shoulder.* **3** [T] to not use a part of your body that is tired or injured, so that it can get better: *You'll need to rest your foot for at least two days.*

restart /ˌriːˈstɑːt/ verb [T] COMPUTING to start a computer again instead of shutting it down

restate /ˌriːˈsteɪt/ verb [T] to say or write something again, or using different words, in order to emphasize it or make it clearer

restaurant /ˈrest(ə)rɒnt/ noun [C] a building or room where meals and drinks are sold to customers sitting at tables → CAFÉ

restaurateur /ˌrest(ə)rəˈtɜː/ noun [C] *formal* someone who owns or manages a restaurant

restful /ˈrestf(ə)l/ adj relaxing and peaceful

restitution /ˌrestɪˈtjuːʃ(ə)n/ noun [U] *formal* payment or services that someone provides someone else with because they have done something bad or illegal to them

restless /ˈres(t)ləs/ adj **1** not willing or not able to keep still **2** someone who is restless is not satisfied with the way that they are living and wants to have new experiences —**restlessly** adv, **restlessness** noun [U]

reˈstorative ˌjustice noun [U] LAW the practice of making the person who committed a crime meet their **victim**, in order to repair some of the damage done by the crime

restore /rɪˈstɔː/ verb [T] **1** to make something exist again: *The lesson continued when order had been restored.* ♦ *The government is trying to restore confidence in the country's economy.* ♦ *Doctors say there's a possibility that his sight can be restored.* **2** to

clean and repair something that is old and dirty or damaged: *His uncle restores old furniture.* **3** to give something back to the person that it belongs to after it has been lost, taken, or stolen: *Most of the land has been restored to its original owners.* —**restoration** /ˌrestəˈreɪʃ(ə)n/ noun [C/U], **restorative** adj

restrain /rɪˈstreɪn/ verb [T] **1** to stop yourself or someone else from doing something **2** to control the movements of a person or animal

restrained /rɪˈstreɪnd/ adj controlled and not emotional

restraining order /rɪˈstreɪnɪŋ ˌɔːdə/ noun [C] LAW a legal document from a judge that stops someone from doing something

restraint /rɪˈstreɪnt/ noun **1** [U] an attempt to control your emotions, or to not do what you would like to do **2** [C/U] something that limits what you can do

restrict /rɪˈstrɪkt/ verb [T] **1** to keep something within strict limits: *Doctors have restricted the number of visits to two per day.* **2** to physically limit or control the movement of something: *The drug restricts blood flow.*

restricted /rɪˈstrɪktɪd/ adj **1** a restricted area is one that only particular people can go into **2** not able to develop, to happen, or to do things with complete freedom: *Freedom of the press is restricted here.*

reˌstricted ˈarticles noun [plural] TOURISM things that passengers must not carry onto planes, for example knives

reˌstricted ˈfare noun [C] TOURISM a type of plane, train etc ticket that you cannot change, for example to a different date

restriction /rɪˈstrɪkʃ(ə)n/ noun [C] something, for example a law, that limits what you can do

restrictive /rɪˈstrɪktɪv/ adj **1** strictly limiting or controlling something **2** LANGUAGE limiting the meaning of another part of the sentence → RESTRICTIVE RELATIVE CLAUSE

reˌstrictive ˈpractices noun [plural] BUSINESS unfair limits that workers put on the rights of their employers or other workers, in order to protect their own interests

reˌstrictive ˈrelative ˌclause noun [C] LANGUAGE a part of a sentence that is added in order to make clear which particular person or thing in a group you are talking about. For example, in the sentence 'The boys who arrived late sat at the back of the class', 'who arrived late' is a restrictive relative clause.

restroom /ˈrestˌruːm/ noun [C] *American* a room with a toilet in it, especially in a public building

restructure /ˌriːˈstrʌktʃə/ verb [T] to organize something such as a company in a different way so that it will operate better= REORGANIZE —**restructuring** noun [C/U]

result¹ /rɪˈzʌlt/ noun

1 sth caused by sth	5 success from sth
2 score	6 finance document
3 information obtained	7 votes in election
4 mark in exam	

1 [C/U] something that is caused directly by something else: *He said the argument was the result of a misunderstanding.* ♦ *York Road will be closed and delays are likely as a result.* ♦ *Colby died as the result of a heart attack.* ♦ *Whichever method you use, the end result is the same.*
2 [C] the final score in a sports game, the number of votes that someone gets in an election, or the number of points that someone gets in a competition: *The election result was a disaster for the party.*

3 [C] a piece of information that you get by examining, studying, or calculating something: *The results of the survey will be published shortly.*

4 [C] **EDUCATION** the mark that a student gets in an examination: *You should get your* **exam results** *next week.*

5 results [plural] success that you achieve: *He breaks rules, but he* **gets results**.

6 results [plural] **BUSINESS** a financial document that shows how well a company has done over a particular period of time

7 results [plural] **POLITICS** the number of votes that someone gets in an election: *We'll see who controls the parliament when* **the results are in** (=when the winner is announced).

> ### Build your vocabulary: words you can use instead of **result**
>
> - **consequence** [usually plural] something that happens as a result of something else, especially something bad or unwanted
> - **effect** a change that is caused by an action or event, and that may be good or bad
> - **outcome** the final result at the end of a discussion, a series of events etc
> - **repercussions** additional results that appear later, and have bad effects that were not expected or intended
> - **after-effects** bad or unwanted results that continue for a long time after the original cause

result² /rɪˈzʌlt/ verb [I] to be caused directly by something that happened previously: *The arrests* **resulted from** *an anonymous telephone call.*
PHRASAL VERB **re'sult in sth** to cause or produce something: *The crash resulted in the deaths of 14 passengers.*

resultant /rɪˈzʌltənt/ adj formal happening as a result of something that has just been mentioned

re'sultant ,force noun [C] **PHYSICS** the total force that is acting on an object. If the forces are acting in the same direction, you add them together. If they are acting in opposite directions, you subtract them.

resume /rɪˈzjuːm/ verb [I/T] formal to start something again after stopping temporarily, or to be started again after stopping temporarily: *Tom resumed his work.* ♦ *Talks will resume today.*

resumption /rɪˈzʌmpʃ(ə)n/ noun [singular/U] formal the act of starting something again after it had stopped

resurgence /rɪˈsɜːdʒ(ə)ns/ noun [singular/U] the start of something again that quickly increases in influence, effect etc

resurgent /rɪˈsɜːdʒ(ə)nt/ adj quickly becoming popular, important, or successful again

resurrect /ˌrezəˈrekt/ verb [T] **1** to make something exist again or start to be used again **2** to bring someone back to life after they are dead

the Resurrection /ˌrezəˈrekʃ(ə)n/ noun [singular] **RELIGION** the occasion on which Jesus Christ was brought back to life after his death, according to the Christian religion

resuscitate /rɪˈsʌsɪteɪt/ verb [T] **HEALTH** to make an unconscious person start to breathe again —**resuscitation** /rɪˌsʌsɪˈteɪʃ(ə)n/ noun [U]

retail¹ /ˈriːteɪl/ adj **BUSINESS** relating to the sale of goods directly to the public for their own use: *a retail outlet* (=a shop) → WHOLESALE¹ sense 1

retail² /ˈriːteɪl/ verb [I/T] **BUSINESS** to sell goods directly to the public for their own use, or to be sold directly to the public → WHOLESALE

retailer /ˈriːˌteɪlə/ noun [C] **BUSINESS** a person or company that sells goods directly to the public → WHOLESALER

'retail ,park noun [C] an area where there are several large shops together in one place, especially furniture shops and electrical shops

the ,retail 'price ,index noun **ECONOMICS** a list of the prices of some basic goods and services that is published each month by the government to show how much prices in general have risen or fallen

retain /rɪˈteɪn/ verb [T] formal **1** to keep someone or something: *We're trying to recruit and retain skilled staff.* **2** to remember ideas or information **3** to employ a professional person such as a lawyer or doctor by paying an amount of money called a **retainer** before the work is done

retake /ˌriːˈteɪk/ (**retakes, retaking, retook** /ˌriːˈtʊk/, **retaken** /ˌriːˈteɪkən/) verb [T] **1** to take control of something, or to get something again, after you have lost it: *The army launched an operation to retake land captured by rebels.* **2** to photograph or record something again because it was not satisfactory **3** **EDUCATION** to take an examination again because you did not pass it the first time

retaliate /rɪˈtælieɪt/ verb [I] to do something unpleasant to someone because they did something unpleasant to you —**retaliation** /rɪˌtæliˈeɪʃ(ə)n/ noun [U], **retaliatory** /rɪˈtæliət(ə)ri/ adj

retarded growth /rɪˌtɑːdɪd ˈɡrəʊθ/ noun [U] **HEALTH** a condition in which someone is not as tall as they should be

retch /retʃ/ verb [I] to behave and sound as if you are vomiting, without in fact bringing any food up from the stomach

retention /rɪˈtenʃ(ə)n/ noun [U] formal **1** the act of keeping something **2** the ability to remember ideas or facts

rethink /ˌriːˈθɪŋk/ (**rethinks, rethinking, rethought** /ˌriːˈθɔːt/) verb [I/T] to think about something such as an idea, plan, or system again in order to change it —**rethink** /ˈriːˌθɪŋk/ noun [singular]: *a rethink of educational policy*

reticent /ˈretɪs(ə)nt/ adj not willing to talk or provide information about something —**reticence** noun [U]

retina /ˈretɪnə/ noun [C] **ANATOMY** the part that covers the inside surface of the eye and sends signals to the brain along the **optic nerve**. The retina contains special cells called **rods** and **cones** that react to light of different strengths and colours. —*picture* → EYE, SHORT-SIGHTED and on next page

retire /rɪˈtaɪə/ verb **1** [I] to stop working permanently, especially when you are old: *He retired from the army last month.* ♦ *Mrs Kenny retired as headteacher in July.* **2** [I] formal to leave a place in order to go somewhere quieter: *In the evenings, Lloyd retired to his study to write.* **3** [I/T] to stop taking part in a game or sports competition because of injury or illness, or to make someone do this: *He retired hurt with a bloody nose.*

retired /rɪˈtaɪəd/ adj no longer working at a job, especially when you are old: *a retired teacher*

retirement /rɪˈtaɪəmənt/ noun [singular] the time after you permanently stop working, or the act of permanently stopping work: *her retirement from politics*

retiring /rɪˈtaɪərɪŋ/ adj shy and not likely to enjoy social activities

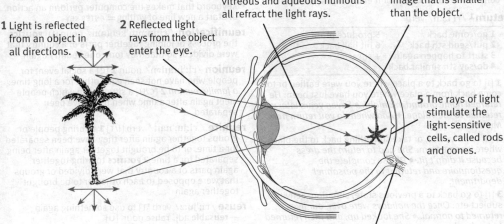

3 The light rays are refracted as they pass through the eye. The cornea, the lens, and the vitreous and aqueous humours all refract the light rays.

4 The light rays focus on the retina as a real and inverted (upside down) image that is smaller than the object.

1 Light is reflected from an object in all directions.

2 Reflected light rays from the object enter the eye.

5 The rays of light stimulate the light-sensitive cells, called rods and cones.

6 Nerve impulses are then transmitted through the optic nerve to the optic centre of the cerebral cortex where the image is interpreted as upright.

image formation on the retina

retook /ˌriːˈtʊk/ the past tense of **retake**

retort¹ /rɪˈtɔːt/ verb [T] to reply immediately in an angry or humorous way to something that someone has said

retort² /rɪˈtɔːt/ noun [C] **1 SCIENCE** a glass container, used in laboratories, that is wide at the bottom and narrow at the top, with a long **spout** at the top that points downwards **2** an angry or humorous reply that you make immediately after someone has said something

re'tort ˌstand noun [C] **SCIENCE** a piece of laboratory equipment for supporting **test tubes** etc while they are being heated with a Bunsen burner —*picture*
→ LABORATORY

retrace /rɪˈtreɪs/ verb **retrace your steps** to return along the same path that you have just travelled along

retract /rɪˈtrækt/ verb [I/T] to say that something that you previously said is not true —**retraction** /rɪˈtrækʃ(ə)n/ noun [C/U]

retractable /rɪˈtræktəb(ə)l/ adj able to be pulled backwards or inside something larger

retrain /ˌriːˈtreɪn/ verb [I/T] **EDUCATION** to learn, or to teach someone, new skills that are needed for a job —**retraining** noun [U]

retreat¹ /rɪˈtriːt/ verb [I] **1** to move back in order to avoid a dangerous or unpleasant situation: *The army was forced to retreat.* **2** to change your previous opinion or decision about something, especially because of opposition to it

retreat² /rɪˈtriːt/ noun **1** [C] a peaceful and private place where you can go in order to rest **2** [C/U] an act of moving back in order to avoid a dangerous or unpleasant situation **3** [C/U] a change in someone's opinion or decision, especially because there is opposition to it

retrenchment /rɪˈtrentʃmənt/ noun [C/U] **BUSINESS** action taken by a company to reduce its costs or the amount that it spends, in order to save money because of difficult economic conditions

retrial /ˈriːˌtraɪəl/ noun [C] **LAW** a second trial in a court of law that takes place because the first trial was considered not to be fair, or ended without a **verdict**

retribution /ˌretrɪˈbjuːʃ(ə)n/ noun [U] severe punishment for something bad, especially one that you think someone deserves

retrieve /rɪˈtriːv/ verb [T] **1** *formal* to go and get something back: *Bobby waded out into the lake to retrieve the ball.* **2 COMPUTING** to find information that is stored in a computer **3** to save something that was going to be damaged or destroyed —**retrieval** /rɪˈtriːv(ə)l/ noun [U]

retroflex /ˈretrəʊˌfleks/ adj **LANGUAGE** pronounced with the end of the tongue bent backwards

retrograde /ˈretrəʊˌɡreɪd/ adj *formal* returning to a condition or situation that is worse than the present one

retrospect /ˈretrəʊˌspekt/ noun **in retrospect** used for saying that, when you think about a situation in the past, you would have done something in a different way if you had known then what you know now: *In retrospect, I should have told her the truth.*

retrospective¹ /ˌretrəʊˈspektɪv/ adj relating to things that have already happened or that have already been done —**retrospectively** adv

retrospective² /ˌretrəʊˈspektɪv/ noun [C] **ARTS** an exhibition that includes examples of a particular artist's work from their whole career

retrovirus /ˈretrəʊˌvaɪrəs/ noun [C] **HEALTH** a virus that carries its genetic material in the form of RNA rather than DNA. The AIDS virus is a retrovirus.

retry /ˌriːˈtraɪ/ (**retries, retrying, retried**) verb **1** [I] to try to do something again after the first attempt was not successful **2** [T] **LAW** to judge a person or crime in a court of law again, because a previous trial was considered not to be fair or it ended without a **verdict**

return¹ /rɪˈtɜːn/ verb

1 go/come back	**5** produce profit
2 put/send sth back	**6** hit ball back
3 start to happen again	**+ PHRASE**
4 do/say sth similar back	

1 [I] to go back to a place where you were earlier, or to come back from a place where you have just been: *He returned home around midnight.* ♦ *Seven years later we returned to the village.* ♦ *And when do you return from Mombasa?*

2 [T] to put, send, or take something back to the place where it came from: *She had to return the dress because it didn't fit.* ♦ *Please complete the questionnaire and return it to the personnel department.*

3 [I] to go back to a previous state, situation, activity, subject etc: *Once the holidays were over, our lives returned to normal.* ♦ *She looked up, and then returned to her book.*

4 [T] to do or say something to someone that is similar to something that they have done or said to you: *I'm sorry I wasn't able to return your phone call earlier.* ♦ *Thanks for helping me. I'll try to return the favour some day.* → COMPLIMENT¹

5 [T] **BUSINESS** to produce a particular amount of profit: *The £10,000 she invested returned a handsome profit.*

6 [I/T] **SPORTS** to hit a ball back to an opponent in a game such as tennis

PHRASE return a verdict **LAW** to say whether someone is guilty or not guilty of a crime in a court of law: *After several hours the jury returned a verdict of not guilty.*

return² /rɪˈtɜːn/ noun

1 going/coming back	**5** ticket
2 starting again	**6** official (tax) form
3 sending sth back	**7** hitting ball back
4 profit	**+ PHRASES**

1 [singular/U] a situation in which you go back to a place or come back from a place: *Harry had met Olivia shortly after his return from India.* ♦ *John was packing for his return to Singapore.*

2 [singular/U] a situation in which a previous activity or condition starts again: **the country's return to** democratic rule ♦ *After a long winter, they eagerly awaited the return of spring.*

3 [C/U] the action of putting, sending, or taking something back to the place where it came from: *A reward is offered for the safe return of the medal.*

4 [C/U] a profit on money that you have invested: *We were able to get a return of 10% on our investment.*

5 [C] a ticket that allows you to travel to a place and back again

6 [C] an official form on which you say how much your income is, so that the amount of tax that you owe can be calculated

7 [C] **SPORTS** the action of hitting a ball back to an opponent in a game such as tennis

PHRASES in return as a payment, exchange, or way of thanking someone: *What can we do in return for your kindness?*

many happy returns used as a greeting on someone's birthday

return³ /rɪˈtɜːn/ adj relating to a journey to a place and back again, or to the journey that you take on the way back: *a return trip*

'return ˌkey noun [C] **COMPUTING** a key on a computer keyboard that makes the computer perform an action, or start a new line of writing = ENTER KEY

reunification /ˌriːjuːnɪfɪˈkeɪʃ(ə)n/ noun [U] **POLITICS** the process of joining together parts of a country that were divided, so that they form one country again

reunion /riːˈjuːniən/ noun **1** [C] a social event for people who have not seen each other for a long time: *a family reunion* **2** [C/U] a situation in which people meet again after a time when they have been separated

reunite /ˌriːjuːˈnaɪt/ verb [I/T] **1** to bring people or groups together again after they have been separated for a time, or to be brought together again after being separated for a time **2** **POLITICS** to bring together again parts of a country that were divided or groups that were opposed to each other, or to be brought together again

reuse /riːˈjuːz/ verb [T] to use something again —**reusable** adj, **reuse** noun [U]

Rev. abbrev **RELIGION** Reverend

revalidate /ˌriːˈvælɪdeɪt/ verb [T] **TOURISM** to change an airline ticket so that a passenger can fly on a different date or at a different time, but still on the same route

reveal¹ /rɪˈviːl/ verb [T] **1** to let something become known that was previously not known: *Cockpit recordings may reveal the cause of the crash.* ♦ *Neither side revealed what was discussed in the meeting.* ♦ *The survey revealed that many consumers are aware of the risks involved.* **2** to show something that was covered or hidden: *She pulled back the curtain to reveal a table.*

reveal² /rɪˈviːl/ noun [C] **CONSTRUCTION** the side surface of a door or window **opening**

revealing /rɪˈviːlɪŋ/ adj **1** providing new, surprising, or important information **2** showing a part of someone's body that is usually covered

revelation /ˌrevəˈleɪʃ(ə)n/ noun **1** [C] a surprising piece of information: *revelations about his private life* **2** [singular] a surprising and enjoyable experience that makes you realize something that you previously had not known: *His piano-playing was a revelation.*

revenge /rɪˈvendʒ/ noun [U] something that you do in order to hurt or punish someone because they have hurt you or someone else: *I wanted to get revenge on her for the trouble she had caused.*

revenue /ˈrevənjuː/ noun [U] **BUSINESS** income from business activities or taxes

'revenue ˌstream noun [C] **BUSINESS** the income that an organization gets from a particular activity

reverberate /rɪˈvɜːbəreɪt/ verb [I] if a sound reverberates, it is repeated many times as it hits two opposite surfaces —**reverberation** /rɪˌvɜːbəˈreɪʃ(ə)n/ noun [C/U]

reverberatory furnace /rɪˈvɜːbərətəri ˌfɜːnɪs/ noun [C] **TECHNOLOGY** a **furnace** in which the ore and the fuel are kept separate, and where the ore is melted by indirect heat from the walls and ceiling of the furnace

revere /rɪˈvɪə/ verb [T] to have a lot of respect and admiration for someone or something

reverence /ˈrev(ə)rəns/ noun [U] a strong feeling of respect and admiration

Reverend /'rev(ə)rənd/ RELIGION a title that is used for some Christian priests and ministers

reversal /rɪ'vɜːs(ə)l/ noun **1** [C/U] a change in something, so that it becomes the opposite of what it was: *The decision was **a** complete **reversal of** government policy.* **2** [C] a problem, difficulty, or failure that prevents someone from being successful = SETBACK

reverse¹ /rɪ'vɜːs/ verb **1** [T] to change something such as a process, situation, decision, or policy so that it becomes the opposite of what it was: *The judge reversed the court's previous decision.* **2** [I/T] to go backwards in a vehicle, or to make a vehicle do this: *She **reversed into** the parking space.* **3** [T] to exchange your status with that of another person: *He's always taught me, but now the **roles** are **reversed** and I can teach him.* **4** [T] to turn something so that the part that is usually on the outside is on the inside: *You can reverse the jacket so that the pattern is on the outside.*

reverse² /rɪ'vɜːs/ adj opposite to what is usual or to what existed previously: *Now arrange the numbers **in** reverse order.*

reverse³ /rɪ'vɜːs/ noun **1 the reverse** [singular] the opposite of something: *The situation is **the reverse of** what it seems.* **2 the reverse** [singular] the back side of a flat object **3** [U] the position in which you put a **gear** in a vehicle in order to make it go backwards: *Put the car **in** reverse.*

re,verse-charge 'call noun [C] a telephone call that the person you are calling agrees to pay for

re,verse os'mosis noun [U] CHEMISTRY a method of removing unwanted substances from sea water using membranes that allow only pure water to pass through

reversible /rɪ'vɜːsəb(ə)l/ adj **1** able to return or to be changed to a previous state ≠ IRREVERSIBLE: *The effects of the treatment are reversible.* **2** able to be used or worn with either side facing out: *a reversible jacket*

reversing light /rɪ'vɜːsɪŋ ˌlaɪt/ noun [C] a light at the back of a car that warns other drivers that the car is going backwards

review¹ /rɪ'vjuː/ noun **1** [C/U] the process of examining something again in order to check it or make a decision about it: *Several aspects of the system are currently **under review**.* ♦ *A review of all government policy affecting the environment was announced.* **2** [C] an article in which someone gives their opinion of a play, book, exhibition etc: *The film **got** really **good** reviews.*

review² /rɪ'vjuː/ verb [T] **1** to examine something again in order to check it or make a decision about it: *After reviewing the evidence, the committee decided he had a strong case.* ♦ *The progress of each child must be regularly reviewed.* **2** to write an article giving your opinion of a play, book, exhibition etc

revise /rɪ'vaɪz/ verb **1** [T] to change your judgment of someone or something **2** [T] to change, improve, or make additions to something: *a revised draft of the treaty* **3** [I/T] EDUCATION to study your notes and information again in order to prepare for an examination

revision /rɪ'vɪʒ(ə)n/ noun **1** [C/U] the process of changing, improving, or making additions to something: *He intends to undertake a **major revision** of the process.* ♦ *The article was published **with** a few revisions.* **2** [U] EDUCATION the work of studying for an examination: *I can't go out – I've got to **do** some revision for my exams.*

revisit /ˌriː'vɪzɪt/ verb [T] **1** to go again to a place **2** to consider or discuss something again

revitalize /riː'vaɪtəlaɪz/ verb [T] **1** to make something that is failing or weak become strong and successful again **2** to make someone feel healthy again

revival /rɪ'vaɪv(ə)l/ noun **1** [C/U] the process of becoming active, successful, or popular again: *a **revival of interest** in the subject* **2** [C] a new performance of something that has not been performed for a long time, such as a play

revive /rɪ'vaɪv/ verb **1** [I/T] to make someone become conscious or alive again, or to become conscious or alive again: *She had fainted, but soon revived.* **2** [I/T] to become active, successful, or popular again, or to make something do this: *His TV series **revived interest** in the war.* **3** [T] to perform something such as a play that has not been performed recently

revolt¹ /rɪ'vəʊlt/ verb **1** [I] POLITICS if people revolt, they try to remove the government of their country by using force **2** [I] to say that you will not accept someone's authority **3** [T] if someone or something revolts you, they are so unpleasant that you feel slightly ill = DISGUST

revolt² /rɪ'vəʊlt/ noun [C/U] **1** POLITICS an attempt to remove the government of a country by using force = REBELLION **2** a refusal to accept someone's authority

revolting /rɪ'vəʊltɪŋ/ adj extremely unpleasant = DISGUSTING

revolution /ˌrevə'luːʃ(ə)n/ noun **1** [C/U] POLITICS a situation in which people completely change their government or political system, usually by force: *the Russian Revolution* ♦ *a group committed to promoting revolution* **2** [C] a sudden or major change, especially in ideas or methods: *the **revolution in** information technology* **3** [C/U] the movement of something in a circle around something else: *the revolution of the Earth around the Sun*

revolutionary¹ /ˌrevə'luːʃ(ə)n(ə)ri/ adj **1** POLITICS relating to or supporting a political revolution: *a revolutionary movement* **2** new and completely changing the way that something is done or thought about: *a revolutionary idea*

revolutionary² /ˌrevə'luːʃ(ə)n(ə)ri/ (plural revolutionaries) noun [C] POLITICS someone who supports or takes part in a revolution

revolutionize /ˌrevə'luːʃəˌnaɪz/ verb [T] to completely change the way that something is done or thought about

revolve /rɪ'vɒlv/ verb [I/T] to turn or spin around a central point, or to make something do this —**revolving** /rɪ'vɒlvɪŋ/ adj

revolved section /rɪ'vɒlvd ˌsekʃ(ə)n/ noun [C/U] MATHS, PHYSICS a drawing of a section of a three-dimensional object that shows a part of the object revolved 90°

revolver /rɪ'vɒlvə/ noun [C] a small gun that holds several bullets

re,volving 'door noun [C] a set of doors that spin around a central post

revulsion /rɪ'vʌlʃ(ə)n/ noun [U] a feeling of dislike for someone or something that is enough to make you feel slightly ill = DISGUST

reward¹ /rɪ'wɔːd/ noun **1** [C/U] something good that happens or that you receive because of something that you have done: *Nursing is a tough job, but it **has its rewards**.* ♦ *You deserve a day off **as a reward for** working so hard.* **2** [C] money that is offered for help in finding someone or something: *There's **a** substantial **reward for** information leading to his capture.*

reward² /rɪˈwɔːd/ verb [T] to give someone something such as praise or money because of something good that they have done

rewarding /rɪˈwɔːdɪŋ/ adj giving you satisfaction, pleasure, or profit: *rewarding work*

rewind /ˌriːˈwaɪnd/ (**rewinds, rewinding, rewound** /ˌriːˈwaʊnd/) verb [I/T] if you rewind a video or a tape, or if it rewinds, it goes backwards to the beginning or to an earlier place

reword /ˌriːˈwɜːd/ verb [T] to express something using different words, in order to make it clearer or more correct

reworking /ˌriːˈwɜːkɪŋ/ noun **1** [C] a piece of music or writing that is different from its original form **2** [C/U] a new way of doing something that is intended to be an improvement

rewound /ˌriːˈwaʊnd/ the past tense and past participle of **rewind**

rewritable /ˌriːˈraɪtəb(ə)l/ adj **COMPUTING** a rewritable disk can be written on many times

rewrite /ˌriːˈraɪt/ (**rewrites, rewriting, rewrote** /ˌriːˈrəʊt/, **rewritten** /ˌriːˈrɪt(ə)n/) verb [T] to make changes to a piece of writing, a computer program, or a law

rezone /ˌriːˈzəʊn/ verb [T] **POLITICS** to officially make a particular area of land available for a purpose that was not originally allowed

RFID /ˈɑːfɪd/ noun [U] **BUSINESS** radio frequency identification: a technology that uses labels that produce radio signals to identify things such as goods, farm animals, and vehicles. RFID has replaced **bar codes** in some shops.

rhapsody /ˈræpsədi/ noun [C] **1** **MUSIC** a piece of classical music that is not regular in form and expresses strong emotion **2** a feeling of great enthusiasm, or the things you say or write to express this enthusiasm

rhenium /ˈriːniəm/ noun [U] **CHEMISTRY** a silvery-white heavy metallic element with a high melting point. Chemical symbol: **Re**

rheostat /ˈriːəstæt/ noun [C] **PHYSICS** a **resistor** that allows the flow of electricity in an electrical circuit to be controlled without breaking the circuit. The volume control in a radio is a rheostat.

Rhesus disease /ˈriːsəs dɪˌziːz/ noun [U] **HEALTH** a condition that can affect a **Rhesus positive** baby of a **Rhesus negative** mother. If the condition is not treated, the mother's antibodies pass through the **placenta** and attack the baby's Rhesus positive blood cells, causing serious health problems and sometimes even the death of the baby.

Rhesus factor /ˈriːsəs ˌfæktə/ noun [singular] **HEALTH** an antigen that is present in the red blood cells of about 85% of humans and some other **primates**

Rhesus negative /ˌriːsəs ˈnegətɪv/ adj **HEALTH** someone who is Rhesus negative does not have the Rhesus factor in their red blood cells

Rhesus positive /ˌriːsəs ˈpɒzətɪv/ adj **HEALTH** someone who is Rhesus positive has the Rhesus factor in their red blood cells

rhetoric /ˈretərɪk/ noun [U] a style of speaking or writing that is intended to influence people: *anti-American rhetoric* —**rhetorical** /rɪˈtɒrɪk(ə)l/ adj, **rhetorically** /rɪˈtɒrɪkli/ adv

rheˌtorical ˈquestion noun [C] **LANGUAGE** a question that you ask without expecting or wanting an answer

rheumatic fever /ruːˌmætɪk ˈfiːvə/ noun [U] **HEALTH** an illness that causes a fever and pain in the joints

rheumatism /ˈruːməˌtɪz(ə)m/ noun [U] **HEALTH** an illness affecting the joints or muscles so that they swell and become stiff and painful

rheumatoid arthritis /ˌruːmətɔɪd ɑːˈθraɪtɪs/ noun [U] **HEALTH** a serious illness that permanently damages your joints by making them swell and become stiff and painful

rheumatology /ˌruːməˈtɒlədʒi/ noun [U] **HEALTH** the area of medicine that deals with **rheumatism** —**rheumatologist** noun [C]

Rh factor /ˌɑː ˈeɪtʃ ˌfæktə/ noun [singular] **HEALTH** Rhesus factor

rhinoceros /raɪˈnɒs(ə)rəs/ (plural **rhinoceroses**) or **rhino** /ˈraɪnəʊ/ noun [C] a large African or Asian mammal with very thick grey skin and one or two horns on its nose —*picture* → MAMMAL

rhizoid /ˈraɪzɔɪd/ noun [C] **BIOLOGY** a long thin part in **mosses**, **liverworts**, and the reproductive cells of **ferns**. It absorbs nourishment in a similar way to a root.

rhizome /ˈraɪzəʊm/ noun [C] **BIOLOGY** a thick plant stem that grows along the ground and produces roots and new plant growth —**rhizomatous** /raɪˈzɒmətəs/ adj

rhodium /ˈrəʊdiəm/ noun [U] **CHEMISTRY** a silvery-white metallic element that is similar to **platinum**. It is used in jewellery and in alloys. Chemical symbol: **Rh**

rhomboid /ˈrɒmbɔɪd/ noun [C] **MATHS** a parallelogram

rhombus /ˈrɒmbəs/ (plural **rhombuses**) noun [C] **MATHS** a shape with four straight sides of equal length and angles that are not 90° —*picture* → SHAPE

rhotic /ˈrəʊtɪk/ adj **LANGUAGE** used for describing an accent in which the speaker pronounces the letter 'r' after a vowel, as most American and Scottish speakers do

rhubarb /ˈruːˌbɑːb/ noun [U] a plant with long red or pink stems that is cooked and eaten as a fruit

rhyme¹ /raɪm/ noun **LITERATURE** **1** [C] a short poem, often for children, that has lines ending in the same sound **2** [C] a word that ends with the same sound as another word **3** [U] the use of words that are rhymes, especially in poetry

rhyme² /raɪm/ verb [I] if two words or lines of poetry rhyme, they end with a similar sound: *'Boy' rhymes with 'toy'.*

rhythm /ˈrɪðəm/ noun **1** [C] a regular pattern of sounds or movements: *the slow rhythm of the rocking chair* **2** [C/U] **MUSIC** a regular pattern of sounds in music: *He tapped out the rhythm on the table.* **3** [C/U] **LITERATURE** a regular pattern of syllables in poetry —**rhythmic** /ˈrɪðmɪk/ adj, **rhythmical** /ˈrɪðmɪk(ə)l/ adj, **rhythmically** /ˈrɪðmɪkli/ adv

ˌrhythm and ˈblues noun [U] **MUSIC** a type of popular music that African American musicians developed from **blues** and jazz. Rhythm and blues is often called R and B.

ˈrhythm ˌsection noun [C] **MUSIC** the instruments or musicians in a band that provide the rhythm, for example the drums and **bass guitar**

rib /rɪb/ noun [C] **ANATOMY** one of the long curved bones in the chest —*picture* → LUNG, SKELETON, VERTEBRA

ribbon /ˈrɪbən/ noun **1** [C/U] a long narrow piece of coloured cloth or paper that is used for decorating or tying things **2** [C] a small piece of coloured cloth that is worn on a uniform as a military honour

ˈribbon ˌlake noun [C] **GEOLOGY** a long narrow lake formed in the valley that was created when a glacier moved over an area that contained bands of hard and soft rock

'rib ,cage noun [C] ANATOMY the bones that curve around and protect the organs in the chest —*picture* → SKELETON

riboflavin /ˌraɪbəʊˈfleɪvɪn/ noun [U] HEALTH a substance found in eggs, milk, liver, and green vegetables that the body needs for growth. Riboflavin is one of the **B vitamins**.

ribonucleic acid /ˌraɪbəʊnjuːˌkleɪɪk ˈæsɪd/ noun [U] BIOLOGY see RNA

ribosome /ˈraɪbəsəʊm/ noun [C] BIOLOGY a structure made up of proteins and RNA that exists in large numbers in the **cytoplasm** of living cells. Ribosomes control the way **amino acids** are made into proteins. —**ribosomal** /ˌraɪbəˈsəʊm(ə)l/ adj

rice /raɪs/ noun [U] **1** a food consisting of small white or brown grains that are eaten cooked **2** AGRICULTURE the plant that produces rice. It is often grown in fields called **paddy fields** or **paddies**. —*picture* → CEREAL

rich /rɪtʃ/ adj

1 with much money	5 expensive/high quality
2 rich people	6 of land/soil
3 having a lot of sth	7 strong/attractive
4 about food	8 interesting

1 having a lot of money, property, or valuable possessions= WEALTHY ≠ POOR: *a rich man* ♦ *one of the world's richest countries* ♦ *People wanted to get rich by investing in Internet companies.*
2 the rich people who have a lot of money, property, or valuable possessions
3 containing a large quantity of something: *a rich source of protein* ♦ *an area rich in natural resources*
4 containing a lot of things such as butter, eggs, or cream that make your stomach feel full very quickly: *a rich chocolate dessert*
5 beautiful, expensive, and of very high quality: *rich silks and cashmeres*
6 containing a lot of substances that are good for growing plants ≠ POOR: *rich agricultural land*
7 a rich colour, sound, or smell is strong in a nice way
8 interesting, with a lot of different qualities, experiences, or events: *a town with a rich cultural life* —**richness** noun [U]

-rich /rɪtʃ/ suffix full of something: *an oil-rich country*

,rich 'email noun [C/U] COMPUTING an email with a voice message attached to it, or this type of email in general

riches /ˈrɪtʃɪz/ noun [plural] *literary* large amounts of money, property, or valuable possessions

richly /ˈrɪtʃli/ adv **1** in a beautiful and expensive way: *a richly decorated palace* **2** with pleasant strong colours, flavours, or smells: *richly coloured silks* **3** completely: *He gave them the credit that they very richly deserved.* **4** with a lot of money or benefit: *He was richly rewarded for the help he gave.*

the Richter scale /ˈrɪktə ˌskeɪl/ noun [singular] GEOLOGY a scale from 1 to 10 which is used for measuring the strength of earthquakes according to how much energy is released. A higher number represents a stronger force.

,rich 'text noun [U] COMPUTING documents that include codes that show how the writing should look, for example to show **bold** and **italic**

,rich 'text ,format noun [U] COMPUTING see RTF

rickets /ˈrɪkɪts/ noun [U] HEALTH a disease that mainly affects children, in which the bones become

soft and bend. It is caused by a lack of **vitamin D** in food or by a lack of sunlight on the skin.

rickety /ˈrɪkəti/ adj a rickety structure or piece of furniture is likely to break if you put any weight on it

rickshaw /ˈrɪkˌʃɔː/ noun [C] a small vehicle with two wheels that is used for carrying passengers and is pulled by someone riding a bicycle or walking

rid /rɪd/ adj
PHRASE **get rid of 1** to throw away, give away, or sell something that you no longer want or need: *We're moving, so we have to get rid of a lot of our furniture.* **2** to do something so that you stop being affected by someone or something that is annoying or unpleasant: *I wish I could get rid of this cold.* ♦ *I'm sure he knew we were trying to get rid of him!*

ridden /ˈrɪd(ə)n/ the past participle of **ride**[1]

riddle /ˈrɪd(ə)l/ noun [C] **1** a question that seems impossible or silly but that has a clever or funny answer **2** someone or something that is mysterious or confusing

riddled /ˈrɪd(ə)ld/ or **'riddled ,with** adj containing a lot of things that are bad or not wanted: *a project riddled with problems*

ride[1] /raɪd/ (**rides, riding, rode** /rəʊd/, **ridden** /ˈrɪd(ə)n/) verb **1** [I/T] to sit on a bicycle, motorcycle, or an animal such as a horse and control it as it moves: *I learned to ride a bike when I was five.* ♦ *Have you ever ridden on a camel?* → DRIVE[1] sense 1 **2** [I] to be a passenger in a vehicle, especially a car or bus: *They rode to the wedding in a carriage.* **3** [I/T] SPORTS to take part in a race on a horse, bicycle, etc: *Are you riding in tomorrow's race?* **4** [I/T] to float, or to appear to float, on water or in the air: *Surfers rode the huge waves.*

ride[2] /raɪd/ noun [C] **1** a journey on a horse or other animal, on a bicycle, motorcycle, or other vehicle: *The bus ride from the airport was very pleasant.* ♦ *I went for a ride in Jason's new car.* ♦ *Joe let us have a ride on his horse.* **2** a machine at an **amusement park**

rider /ˈraɪdə/ noun [C] someone who rides on an animal such as a horse, or on a vehicle such as a bicycle or motorcycle

ridge /rɪdʒ/ noun [C] **1** GEOGRAPHY the long narrow top of a mountain or group of mountains **2** a long narrow raised line along the surface of something **3** GEOGRAPHY a long narrow area of high pressure in a weather system **4** CONSTRUCTION a piece of wood at the top of a roof that the **rafters** are attached to

ridicule[1] /ˈrɪdɪˌkjuːl/ verb [T] to try to make someone or something seem silly by making fun of them in an unkind way

ridicule[2] /ˈrɪdɪˌkjuːl/ noun [U] remarks or behaviour that are intended to make someone or something seem silly by making fun of them in an unkind way

ridiculous /rɪˈdɪkjʊləs/ adj silly or unreasonable and deserving to be laughed at= ABSURD: *a ridiculous idea* ♦ *She looks absolutely ridiculous in that hat.* —**ridiculously** adv: *The test was ridiculously easy.*

riding /ˈraɪdɪŋ/ noun [U] the activity or sport of riding horses

rife /raɪf/ adj if something that is bad is rife, there is a lot of it

riff /rɪf/ noun [C] MUSIC a short series of notes in jazz or popular music that is repeated often throughout a piece

rifle /ˈraɪf(ə)l/ noun [C] a large gun with a long **barrel**

rift /rɪft/ noun [C] **1 GEOLOGY** a crack or long narrow space that forms in a large mass of something such as rock **2** a disagreement between two people or groups

'rift ,valley noun [C] **GEOGRAPHY** a valley with steep sides, produced when the land between two parallel cracks in the ground sinks

rig¹ /rɪg/ (**rigs, rigging, rigged**) verb [T] to influence something such as an election in a dishonest way in order to produce a particular result

rig² /rɪg/ noun [C] a tall structure with equipment for getting oil or gas out of the ground

right¹ /raɪt/ adv

1 exactly	**4** towards the right
2 immediately	**5** correctly
3 all the way	**6** as would be normal

1 exactly: *Their office is **right in the middle** of town.* ♦ *'Am I late?' 'No, you're **right on time.'*** ♦ *Don't worry – I'm **right behind** you.*
2 immediately: *I liked her **right from the start.*** ♦ *Paul arrived **right after** me.* ♦ *She called and asked me to come over **right away.*** ♦ *Just a minute – **I'll be right there.***
3 all the way, or completely: *My foot went **right through** the floorboards.*
4 in the direction of your right side: ***Turn right** at the corner.*
5 correctly, or accurately: *You did it **right** the first time.*
6 in the way someone hoped: *Everything went just **right** and the party was a big success.*
→ RIGHTLY, SERVE¹

right² /raɪt/ adj

1 correct	**4** on one side of body
2 morally correct	**5** suitable
3 in correct state etc	**6** on the correct side

1 correct according to the facts ≠ WRONG: *'D' is the **right** answer.* ♦ *Is this the **right** way to the station?* ♦ *You were absolutely **right**. My sweater was on the chair.* ♦ *I think you were **right about** the colour – it doesn't match.*
2 morally correct ≠ WRONG: *You **did the right thing** by telling them you had lied.* ♦ *I think it's **only right** to warn you that I'm looking for another job.* ♦ *It wasn't **right of** her to take it without asking.*
3 in the position, state, or situation that you would normally expect someone or something to be in ≠ WRONG: *She hadn't been feeling **right** for weeks.* ♦ *I noticed that some of the pictures weren't in the **right** place.*
4 on or relating to the side of your body that is towards the east when you are facing north ≠ LEFT: *Hold the bat in your **right** hand.*
5 the right person or thing has exactly the qualities that you want or need ≠ WRONG: *I'm not sure this is **the right** time to go on holiday.* ♦ *Harry's definitely the **right** person **for** the job.*
6 relating to the side of something that should be seen or used ≠ WRONG: *Make sure the **right** side of the fabric is facing outwards.*
→ ALL RIGHT¹

right³ /raɪt/ noun

1 good behaviour	**4** a turn to the right
2 sth that is allowed	**5** in politics
3 side of your body	**+ PHRASES**

1 [U] behaviour that is considered good or moral ≠ WRONG: *Do children of that age know the difference between **right and wrong**?*
2 [C] something that you are morally or legally allowed to do or have: *We are fighting for workers' **rights**.* ♦ ***equal rights** for women* ♦ *the **right to** political asylum*

♦ *We **have every right to** complain.* ♦ *You **have no right to** come barging in here like that.* → CIVIL RIGHTS
3 [singular] the side of your body that is towards the east when you are facing north, or this direction ≠ LEFT: *Could you move a little **to the right**?* ♦ *It's the second door **on your right**.*
4 [C] a turn towards the right that is made by someone who is walking or driving: ***Take a right** at the art gallery.* ♦ *It's **the first right** (=the first street where you can turn right) after the hospital.*
5 the right [singular] **POLITICS** the political party or the group of people within a society who are conservative in their political views

PHRASES **in your own right** as a result of your own ability, achievements, qualifications etc and not because of anyone else: *Her father's a well-known author, but she's an excellent writer in her own right.*
right of way the legal right to go across someone's private land

right⁴ /raɪt/ interjection **1** used for making someone pay attention before you say something: *Right! Is everybody ready to start?* **2** used for asking whether what you have said is correct: *You told everyone about tomorrow's meeting, right?* **3** used for saying that you agree with a statement or accept a suggestion or an order: *'Get some more milk when you're out.' 'Right.'*

right⁵ /raɪt/ verb [T] to put someone or something back into their usual upright position

PHRASE **right a wrong** to correct something that is bad or wrong that someone has done

'right ,angle noun [C] **MATHS** an angle of 90° —picture → ANGLE

right-angled triangle /ˌraɪt æŋg(ə)ld 'traɪæŋg(ə)l/ noun [C] **MATHS** a flat shape with three straight sides and three angles, one of which is a right angle —picture → TRIANGLE

,right ,circular 'cone noun [C] **MATHS** a cone with its **vertex** (=point at the top) perpendicular to the centre of its circular base

'right-,click verb [I] **COMPUTING** to press the button on the right side of a computer mouse → LEFT-CLICK

'right ,cylinder noun [C] **MATHS** a cylinder with a circular top parallel to a circular base

righteous /'raɪtʃəs/ adj righteous feelings of anger are caused by a belief that you are right to feel angry

rightful /'raɪtf(ə)l/ adj formal officially or legally accepted as right or correct —**rightfully** adv

'right-,hand adj on the right, or towards the right of someone or something ≠ LEFT-HAND: *the right-hand side of the bed*

right-handed /ˌraɪt 'hændɪd/ adj naturally tending to use your right hand rather than your left to do things such as writing ≠ LEFT-HANDED —**,right-'handed** adv

rightly /'raɪtli/ adv **1** for a good reason: *Voters are rightly concerned about what is going to happen.* **2** correctly, or accurately: *As you rightly say, we must work carefully.*

'right ,prism noun [C] **MATHS** a prism with its sides perpendicular to its base

'right ,pyramid noun [C] **MATHS** a pyramid with its **vertex** (=point at the top) perpendicular to the centre of its base

rightsize /'raɪt,saɪz/ verb [I/T] **BUSINESS** if a company rightsizes, or if someone rightsizes it, it gets rid of some workers in order to save money or become more effective

,right-'wing adj POLITICS a person or organization that is right-wing is conservative in their political views ≠ LEFT-WING —**,right-'winger** noun [C]

rigid /'rɪdʒɪd/ adj **1** not easily changed: *a rigid class system* **2** done or applied in a strict and unreasonable way: *rigid discipline* **3** stiff, hard, and difficult to bend or move **4** not willing to change your ideas, attitudes, opinions etc —**rigidity** /rɪ'dʒɪdəti/ noun [U], **rigidly** adv

,rigid transfor'mation noun [C/U] MATHS a **transformation** that does not change the shape or size of a geometric shape or object

rigorous /'rɪgərəs/ adj **1** thorough and careful **2** strict, or severe —**rigorously** adv

rim /rɪm/ noun [C] the edge of an open container or circular object → PACIFIC RIM

rime /raɪm/ noun [C] LANGUAGE an identical string of letters in a word ending that do not always have the same sound, for example '-ear'

rind /raɪnd/ noun [C/U] **1** the outer skin of a fruit such as a lemon or an orange **2** the hard outer edge of **bacon** or some types of cheese

ring¹ /rɪŋ/ (**rings, ringing, rang** /ræŋ/, **rung** /rʌŋ/) verb

1 phone sb	6 surround sb/sth
2 of telephone	7 draw circle on sth
3 of bell	+ PHRASE
4 of ears	+ PHRASAL VERBS
5 of sound in a place	

1 [I/T] to call someone on the telephone = CALL, PHONE, TELEPHONE: *Ring me at home later.* ♦ *Sarah rang to say she couldn't come tonight.* ♦ *I'm ringing about the vacancy you advertised.*
2 [I] if a telephone rings, it makes a sound in order to show that someone is calling: *The phone rang again immediately.*
3 [I/T] if a bell rings, or if you ring it, it makes a sound: *He rang the doorbell.* ♦ *The bell rang, and the children stood up.*
4 [I] if your ears are ringing, you continue to hear a loud sound in your head, for example after a loud noise
5 [I] if a sound rings in a place, or if a place rings with sound, the sound is loud and you can hear it clearly: *A great cheer rang through the hall.*
6 (**ringed**) [T] to surround someone or something, especially in order to protect them or to prevent them from escaping: *Protesters carrying signs ringed the hotel.*
7 [T] to draw a circle around something = CIRCLE: *She ringed the date on the calendar in the kitchen.*

PHRASE **ring true** to sound true or sincere: *I didn't think Green's explanation rang true.*

PHRASAL VERBS **,ring 'back** to phone someone again: *I'll ring back later.*
,ring sb 'back to phone someone who phoned you earlier: *Can you ask him to ring me back when he gets home?*
,ring (sb) 'up same as **ring¹** sense 1: *She rang up yesterday to make an appointment.*

ring² /rɪŋ/ noun [C]

1 jewellery	5 in boxing etc
2 shape like circle	6 around planet
3 bell sound	+ PHRASES
4 group doing sth	

1 a piece of jewellery in the form of a circle that is worn on a finger: *She had a **ring** on every finger.* → WEDDING RING
2 something that is in the shape of a circle: *onion rings*

♦ *Kate had dark rings under her eyes.* ♦ *The kids sat in a ring around the fire.*
3 the sound that a bell or telephone makes: *the ring of the doorbell* ♦ *I answered the phone on the first ring.*
4 a group of people who are involved in an illegal activity: *an international drugs ring*
5 SPORTS a raised area that is surrounded by ropes where people take part in boxing or **wrestling**
6 ASTRONOMY a circle of extremely small pieces of dust or ice that moves around a planet —*picture* → SOLAR SYSTEM

PHRASES **give sb a ring** *informal* to phone someone
ring of fire GEOLOGY an area around the Pacific Ocean where there are frequent earthquakes and volcanic eruptions
→ RUN¹

ringed worm /,rɪŋ 'wɜːm/ noun [C] an invertebrate animal with no legs and a long body that is divided into a lot of **segments**. It usually lives in water or soil.

'ring ,finger noun [C] the third finger on the left hand, on which a **wedding ring** is traditionally worn —*picture* → BODY

ringleader /'rɪŋ,liːdə/ noun [C] a leader of a group of people who are doing something that is illegal or wrong

ringlet /'rɪŋlət/ noun [C] a piece of long hair that hangs down in curls

'ring ,main noun [C] CONSTRUCTION an electrical circuit that connects the **sockets** on the walls of a house

'ring ,road noun [C] a road that is built around a large town or city in order to keep traffic away from the town centre

ringtone /'rɪŋ,təʊn/ noun [C] the sound that a mobile phone makes when someone rings it, for example a series of short sounds or a musical tune

ringworm /'rɪŋ,wɜːm/ noun [U] HEALTH a disease that affects the skin, causing red areas in the shape of a ring

rink /rɪŋk/ noun [C] a large flat area where people go to **skate**

rinse¹ /rɪns/ verb [T] to wash something quickly in clean water to remove soap or dirt

rinse² /rɪns/ noun **1** [C] a quick wash in clean water **2** [C/U] something that someone puts on their hair to change its colour for a short time

riot¹ /'raɪət/ noun [C/U] a violent protest by a crowd of people

PHRASE **run riot 1** to behave in a noisy and uncontrolled way **2** if your imagination or emotions run riot, you cannot control them

riot² /'raɪət/ verb [I] if people riot, they protest violently about something —**rioter** noun [C], **rioting** noun [U]

rip¹ /rɪp/ (**rips, ripping, ripped**) verb **1** [I/T] to tear something quickly and with a lot of force, or to be torn in this way: *Stop pulling my shirt – it's going to rip.* ♦ *I ripped my jeans on a sharp nail.* ♦ *Jodie ripped the letter open.* **2** [T] to remove something quickly by pulling hard: *We've ripped out the old fireplace.* **3** [T] COMPUTING to copy music from a website or CD to a computer or **hand-held** device

PHRASAL VERB **,rip sth 'up** to tear something into small pieces

rip² /rɪp/ noun [C] a hole in something produced by tearing = TEAR: *My shirt has a big rip in it.*

ripe /raɪp/ adj ripe fruit or crops have grown to their full size and are ready to eat or use

PHRASE **be ripe for sth** to be ready for something, especially a change: *Some of the smaller firms are ripe for takeover.*
—**ripeness** noun [U]

ripen /'raɪpən/ verb [I/T] to become ripe, or to make something become ripe

riposte /rɪ'pɒst/ noun [C] *formal* a quick and clever reply to something that someone has said

ripper /'rɪpə/ noun [C] COMPUTING a program for copying **digital** music from a CD onto a computer, before changing it into a form that can be stored as a computer file

ripple¹ /'rɪp(ə)l/ noun [C] **1** a small wave or series of small waves on the surface of a liquid **2** an emotion or reaction that spreads gradually through a person or a group: *a ripple of applause*

ripple² /'rɪp(ə)l/ verb [I] if a feeling or sound ripples through someone or something, it spreads gradually through them

rise¹ /raɪz/ (**rises, rising, rose** /rəʊz/, **risen** /'rɪz(ə)n/) verb [I]

1 move upwards	**6** water increases
2 increase	**7** be tall/high
3 achieve success	**8** oppose government
4 stand up	**9** bread/cake grows
5 voice gets higher	

1 to move upwards or to a higher position: *The aircraft rose slowly into the air.* ♦ *Thick black smoke rose from the middle of the town.* ♦ *As the sun rose in the sky, the clouds disappeared.*
2 to increase in size, amount, quality, or strength: *Temperatures will rise steadily towards the end of the week.* ♦ *Tensions rose in the city as the day went on.* ♦ *Interest rates rise and fall according to the health of the economy.*
3 to achieve success, power, or a higher status: *I am sure she will rise to the top of her profession.* ♦ *He rose to power as a leader of the miners' union.*
4 *formal* to stand from a sitting, kneeling, or lying position: *He rose and went to the window.*
5 if your voice rises, it gets higher, often because of a strong feeling
6 if an area of water rises, its level goes up: *The river rose and burst its banks.*
7 if something such as a building or mountain rises somewhere, it is tall or high and can be seen clearly: *Grey mountains rose above the lakes.*
8 to start to protest and fight against a government or leader= REBEL, REVOLT: *Eventually the people rose against the regime.*
9 if something such as bread or a cake rises, it increases in size when it is cooked

rise² /raɪz/ noun **1** [C] an increase in size, amount, quality, or strength: *The proposed tax rise was not unexpected.* ♦ *Serious crime is once again on the rise.* ♦ *the rise and fall of share prices* ♦ *the threat of a sudden rise in oil prices* **2** [singular] an increase in the power or influence of someone or something: *Fidel Castro's rise to power* ♦ *the rise of nationalism in the 1930s* ♦ *The series covers the rise and fall of the Third Reich.* **3** [C] an increase in pay: *I'm going to ask for a rise next week.* **4** [singular] a movement upwards
PHRASE **give rise to sth** to make something happen or begin, especially something that is unpleasant or unexpected

riser /'raɪzə/ noun **1** CONSTRUCTION the vertical surface of a step **2** TECHNOLOGY a vertical pipe in a mould that holds a supply of **molten** (=melted) metal

to keep the mould full. The amount of metal in the mould becomes less as the metal cools.

rising damp /,raɪzɪŋ 'dæmp/ noun [U] CONSTRUCTION a problem in which the walls of a building become wet because moisture from the ground starts to rise up them

rising main /,raɪzɪŋ 'meɪn/ noun [C] CONSTRUCTION the pipes for the water supply in a building

risk¹ /rɪsk/ noun **1** [C/U] the possibility that something unpleasant or dangerous might happen: *There is a risk that the virus can be transferred from patient to doctor.* ♦ *The risks to consumers are being analysed.* ♦ *There is a serious risk of a major nuclear accident.* **2** [C] someone or something that is likely to be a danger or problem in the future: *a possible fire risk* (=something that could cause fire)
PHRASES **at your own risk** if you do something at your own risk, you are responsible for any harm or damage that you suffer as a result
at risk in a situation in which something that is unpleasant or dangerous could happen to you: *The laws will put many small businesses at risk.*
at the risk of doing sth used for saying that you realize that something bad or unpleasant may happen as a result of what you are going to say: *At the risk of seeming boring, I don't think we should try it.*
run the risk (of sth) to be in a situation in which something that is bad could happen: *I didn't want to run the risk of seeing Neil again.*
take a risk to do something although you know that something that is unpleasant or dangerous could happen: *A good pilot never takes a risk.* ♦ *I didn't want to take the risk of leaving John alone.*

risk² /rɪsk/ verb [T] to do something although you know that something that is bad could happen as a result: *We don't want to risk becoming involved in a civil war.*
PHRASE **risk your life** to put yourself in a situation in which you could be killed

'risk as,sessment noun [C/U] BUSINESS the process of calculating how much risk is involved in a particular action

risky /'rɪski/ adj involving the possibility of danger, harm, or failure —**riskily** adv

rite /raɪt/ noun [C] RELIGION a traditional ceremony, especially a religious one

ritual /'rɪtʃuəl/ noun [C/U] **1** RELIGION a formal ceremony, especially a religious ceremony **2** something that you do regularly and always in the same way: *Their meetings became a weekly ritual.*
—**ritual** adj

rival¹ /'raɪv(ə)l/ noun [C] **1** a person, team, or business that competes with another: *She scored twice as many points as her rival.* **2** someone or something that is as good as someone or something else: *The band has few rivals in the pop music world.* —**rival** adj: *rival companies*

rival² /'raɪv(ə)l/ (**rivals, rivalling, rivalled**) verb [T] to be as good as someone or something else: *This small restaurant rivals any that you will find in the city.*

rivalry /'raɪv(ə)lri/ (plural **rivalries**) noun [C/U] a situation in which people, teams, businesses etc compete with one another

river /'rɪvə/ noun [C] GEOGRAPHY a large area of water that flows towards the sea: *They were swimming in the river.* ♦ *the River Nile* ♦ *a river valley* —picture
→ on next page

riverbank /'rɪvə,bæŋk/ noun [C] GEOGRAPHY the land at the side of a river

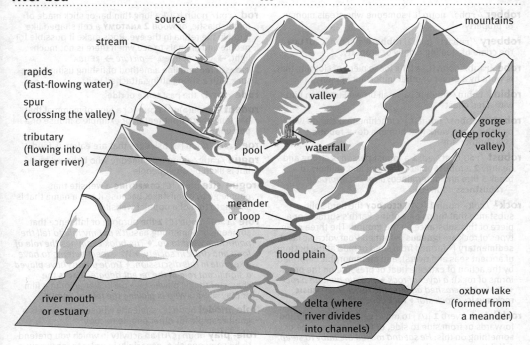

river

source
stream
rapids
(fast-flowing water)
spur
(crossing the valley)
tributary
(flowing into
a larger river)
mountains
valley
gorge
(deep rocky
valley)
pool
waterfall
meander
or loop
flood plain
river mouth
or estuary
delta (where
river divides
into channels)
oxbow lake
(formed from
a meander)

'river ˌbed noun [C] GEOGRAPHY the ground under the water of a river

'river ˌblindness noun [U] HEALTH a disease caused by a parasitic worm that is left under the skin by the bite of a fly. It can cause blindness.

riverside /ˈrɪvəˌsaɪd/ noun [singular] GEOGRAPHY the land at the side of a river

rivet /ˈrɪvɪt/ noun [C] a metal pin used for joining pieces of metal together

RNA /ˌɑː en ˈeɪ/ noun [U] BIOLOGY ribonucleic acid: an acid that is in all living cells. It uses information from DNA to make proteins. In some viruses it carries information to the genes.

road /rəʊd/ noun [C] **1** a way that leads from one place to another that cars and other vehicles can use: *They live in Lockwood Road.* ♦ *He was driving on the wrong side of the road.* ♦ *The journey is about three hours by road.* **2** a particular process or course of action = WAY: *I don't think we ought to go down that road.*

PHRASES **on the road** travelling in a car, bus, or truck, especially for a long distance or a long period of time
the road to sth a process or series of events that will achieve something or have a particular result: *It's an important step on the road to democracy.*

- A **road** is built for vehicles to travel along and can have buildings on each side. It can be wide or narrow, and it can be in a town or can join different towns: *My school is just down the road.* ♦ *the road from Hyderabad to Karachi*
- A **street** is a road in a town, with buildings such as houses and shops along its sides: *They live on a busy street.*
- A **path** is a way from one place to another for people to walk along: *a path leading into the forest*
- A **track** is a path or road with a rough surface, especially one that has been made by people walking along it

'road ˌmap noun [C] a map that shows all the main roads and motorways in a region or country

roadside /ˈrəʊdˌsaɪd/ noun [C] the area at the edge of a road

'road-ˌtest verb [T] to test whether a vehicle works well by driving it on the road

roam /rəʊm/ verb [I/T] to move or travel with no particular purpose: *Young men roamed the streets.*

roaming /ˈrəʊmɪŋ/ noun [U] the use of a mobile phone outside someone's home country

roar¹ /rɔː/ verb **1** [I/T] to shout, speak, or laugh very loudly: *The crowd roared as the team ran onto the pitch.* ♦ *Barney roared with laughter.* **2** [I] to make a continuous very loud noise: *Military planes roared overhead.* **3** [I] if a lion roars, it makes a deep loud sound **4** [I] if a vehicle roars somewhere, it travels there very quickly and noisily: *We sat and waited as the traffic roared past.*

roar² /rɔː/ noun [C] **1** a loud continuous sound: *the roar of the waves* ♦ *a roar of anger* **2** the loud deep sound that a lion makes

roaring /ˈrɔːrɪŋ/ adj **1** a roaring fire burns very brightly and produces a lot of heat **2** making a loud deep noise: *a roaring waterfall*

roast¹ /rəʊst/ verb [I/T] to cook meat or vegetables in an oven

roast² /rəʊst/ noun [C] a large piece of meat that has been cooked in an oven

roast³ /rəʊst/ adj cooked in an oven: *roast beef*

rob /rɒb/ (**robs, robbing, robbed**) verb [T] **1** LAW to take money or property from someone illegally: *They were planning to rob the museum.* **2** to take something such as an opportunity, ability, or quality from someone: *The shock had robbed her of the power of speech.*

robber /ˈrɒbə/ noun [C] someone who steals money or property

robbery /ˈrɒbəri/ (plural **robberies**) noun [C/U] LAW the crime of stealing money or property

robe /rəʊb/ noun [C] a long loose piece of clothing that is worn by a priest or other important person

robin /ˈrɒbɪn/ noun [C] a small brown European bird with a red chest

robot /ˈrəʊbɒt/ noun [C] a machine that can do work by itself, often work that humans do —**robotic** /rəʊˈbɒtɪk/ adj

robust /rəʊˈbʌst/ adj **1** a robust person is strong and healthy **2** a robust object is strong and unlikely to break **3** firm and determined: *a robust approach* —**robustness** noun [U]

rock¹ /rɒk/ noun **1** [C/U] GEOLOGY the hard solid substance that forms part of the Earth's surface, or a piece of this substance on the ground. The three main types of rock are **igneous** (=formed from volcanic lava), **sedimentary** (=formed from sand or mud at the bottom of ancient seas and rivers), and **metamorphic** (=formed by the action of extreme heat or pressure on the other forms of rock): *a layer of rock* ♦ *a castle built on a rock* ♦ *The waves crashed against the rocks.* **2** [U] MUSIC **rock music**: *a rock star* ♦ *rock concerts*

rock² /rɒk/ verb **1** [I/T] to move gently backwards and forwards or from side to side, or to make someone or something do this: *He sat and rocked the baby to sleep.* ♦ *Hold your knees close to your chest and rock from side to side.* **2** [T] if an explosion or earthquake rocks something, it makes it shake violently: *The blast rocked the houses in the street.*

‚rock ‘bottom noun [U] the lowest possible level: *Confidence in the company is* **at rock bottom**. —‘**rock-‚bottom** adj: *rock-bottom prices*

the ‘rock ‚cycle noun [singular] GEOLOGY the process over millions of years by which different types of rock get broken down into small pieces by processes such as erosion, and are then carried by water and wind to the sea. There they form sedimentary rock, which, if it is heated by the Earth's core, forms metamorphic rock. All the different types of rock then get eroded again, and the process continues. —*picture* → on next page

rocket¹ /ˈrɒkɪt/ noun [C] **1** ASTRONOMY a vehicle that is shaped like a tube that travels in space. Rockets consist of several sections, many of which contain only fuel. **2** a weapon that is shaped like a tube that flies through the air and explodes when it hits something **3** a **firework** that is shaped like a tube that flies up into the air when you light it and then explodes

rocket² /ˈrɒkɪt/ verb [I] to increase suddenly

rocking chair /ˈrɒkɪŋ ˌtʃeə/ noun [C] a chair on two curved pieces of wood that moves gently backwards and forwards when you are sitting in it

‘rock ‚music noun [U] MUSIC music that has a strong regular beat and that is played on electric guitars

‚rock ‘n’ ‘roll noun [U] MUSIC a type of music that was popular in the 1950s and combined simple **blues** structures, played on guitars, with strong regular beats

‘rock ‚ore noun [U] GEOLOGY rock containing a substance such as a mineral that can be dug out of the ground

‘rock ‚pool noun [C] a small pool of water that is left between rocks on a beach after a wave flows back into the sea

rocky /ˈrɒki/ adj covered with rocks, or made of rock

rod /rɒd/ noun [C] **1** a long thin bar or stick made of metal, plastic, or wood **2** ANATOMY a cell shaped like a rod in the retina in the eye. Rods make it possible for people and animals to see when there is not much light. → CONE sense 4 —*picture* → RETINA

PHRASE **rod and line** a method of fishing using a long stick with a strong string attached to it

rode /rəʊd/ the past tense of **ride¹**

rodent /ˈrəʊd(ə)nt/ noun [C] a type of mammal that has long sharp front teeth, for example a mouse or a **porcupine**

roe /rəʊ/ noun [U] fish eggs that are eaten as food

rogue /rəʊg/ noun [C] someone who behaves badly but is liked by other people

‘rogue ‚site noun [C] COMPUTING a website that people go to by mistake, because it has a name that is similar to that of a popular website

role /rəʊl/ noun [C] **1** the purpose or influence that someone or something has: *It's not my role to tell the politicians what to do.* ♦ *The book examines* **the role of** *food and drink in society.* ♦ *We expect parents to have* **a key role** *in this discussion.* ♦ *Trade unions have* **played** *a significant* **role** *in the recent debate.* **2** ARTS the character that is played by a particular actor in a film or play ＝ PART: *Who* **is playing the role of** *Hamlet?*

‘role ‚model noun [C] someone whose behaviour is a good example for other people to copy

‘role-‚play noun [C/U] an activity in which you pretend to be someone else, especially in order to learn new skills —‘**role-‚playing** noun [U]

roll¹ /rəʊl/ verb

1 move and turn	**6** flow
2 move on wheels	**7** make sth flat
3 move from side to side	**8** machine: work
4 change position	**+ PHRASES**
5 wrap sth	**+ PHRASAL VERBS**

1 [I/T] to move forwards while turning over and over, or to make something do this: *The pencil went rolling across the floor.* ♦ *Men were rolling tyres across the yard.*

2 [I/T] to move on wheels, or to move something that is on wheels: *The car rolled to a stop at the side of the road.* ♦ *We rolled the piano to the front of the stage.*

3 [I] to move from side to side: *The pigs were rolling in the mud.*

4 [I] to change the position of your body when you are lying down: *He* **rolled onto** *his back and looked up at me.*

5 [T] to fold something or wrap it around itself so that it forms a tube or a ball: *I always roll my clothes when I pack them.* ♦ *Take a piece of the mixture and roll it into a ball.*

6 [I] if a drop of liquid rolls, it moves across a surface without stopping: *Raindrops rolled down the window.*

7 [T] to make a substance flat by pushing something across it: *Roll the dough very thinly.*

8 [I] if a machine such as a camera is rolling, it is working: *Although the interview had ended, the cameras were still rolling.*

PHRASES **(all) rolled into one** if someone is several things rolled into one, they are all of those things at the same time

roll your eyes to move your eyes upwards in order to show that you are annoyed or impatient → BALL

PHRASAL VERBS **‚roll sth ‘out** BUSINESS to start to sell a new product or service

‚roll sth ‘up 1 if you roll your sleeves or the legs of your trousers up, you fold the cloth several times until they

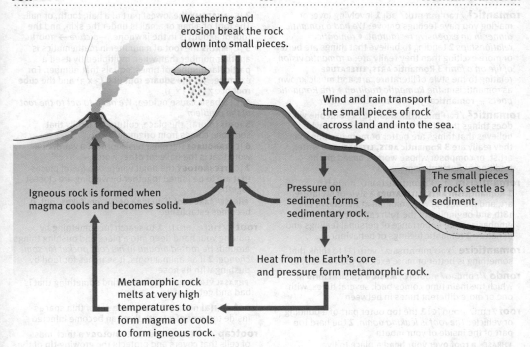

Weathering and erosion break the rock down into small pieces.

Wind and rain transport the small pieces of rock across land and into the sea.

The small pieces of rock settle as sediment.

Igneous rock is formed when magma cools and becomes solid.

Pressure on sediment forms sedimentary rock.

Heat from the Earth's core and pressure form metamorphic rock.

Metamorphic rock melts at very high temperatures to form magma or cools to form igneous rock.

the rock cycle

are shorter **2** same as **roll¹** sense 5: She rolled her scarf up and put it into her bag.

roll² /rəʊl/ noun [C]

1 sth rolled into tube	**4** list of names
2 small loaf of bread	**5** continuous sound
3 action of rolling	

1 a long piece of something such as paper or carpet that is rolled into the shape of a tube: We used ten **rolls of** wallpaper.
2 bread in the form of a small round or long shape
3 the action of turning over or rolling from side to side: The constant roll of the ship made her feel ill.
4 an official list of names, for example of students in a school
5 a continuous low sound made by drums or thunder

rollback /ˈrəʊlˌbæk/ noun [U] **COMPUTING** the process of loading software again after there has been a problem with the original software

'roll ,call noun [C/U] **EDUCATION** the process of reading out an official list of people's names in order to see who is present

roller /ˈrəʊlə/ noun [C] **1** something that is shaped like a tube that goes over a surface in order to make it flat, or in order to crush, spread, or print something **2** a small tube that you wind some of your hair around in order to make a curl= CURLER

'roller ,bearing noun [C] **ENGINEERING** a **bearing** (=machine part) in which metal tubes **rotate** (=move around an axis)

roller coaster /ˈrəʊlə ˌkəʊstə/ noun [C] **1** a structure like a tall railway with steep slopes that people ride on for fun at an **amusement park 2** a situation in which there are many big and sudden changes

'roller ,skates noun [plural] boots with four small wheels on the bottom —**'roller-,skate** verb [I], **'roller ,skating** noun [U]

rolling /ˈrəʊlɪŋ/ adj rolling land has a lot of gentle slopes

'rolling ,pin noun [C] a piece of kitchen equipment that you roll over **pastry** in order to make it flat and thin

rollout /ˈrəʊlˌaʊt/ noun [singular] **BUSINESS** the process of starting to sell a new product or service, especially when it gradually becomes available in a larger number of places

ROM /rɒm/ noun [U] **COMPUTING** read-only memory: the part of a computer's memory that is permanent and cannot be changed

Roman¹ /ˈrəʊmən/ adj of ancient Rome or its **empire**, or from ancient Rome or its **empire**

Roman² /ˈrəʊmən/ noun [C] someone from ancient Rome or its **empire**

the ,Roman 'alphabet noun **LANGUAGE** the alphabet developed by the ancient Romans that is used for writing English and many other European languages

,Roman 'Catholic noun [C] **RELIGION** a member of the part of the Christian Church that has the **Pope** as its leader —**,Roman 'Catholic** adj, **,Roman Ca'tholicism** noun [U]

romance /rəʊˈmæns/ noun **1** [C] a short exciting romantic relationship **2** [U] the behaviour that is typical of two people who love each other: She wasn't in a mood for romance. **3** [C] **ARTS, LITERATURE** a story, for example in a book or film, about a romantic relationship **4** [U] a feeling of excitement that you get from a particular place, activity, or experience: the romance of travel

Ro'mance ,language noun [C] **LANGUAGE** a language such as French, Spanish, or Italian that comes from Latin

,Roman 'numeral noun [C] **MATHS** one of the letters 'I', 'V', 'X', 'L', 'C', 'D', and 'M' that are sometimes used for representing numbers. For example VI represents the number 6.

romantic¹ /rəʊˈmæntɪk/ adj **1** involving love, or making you have feelings of love: *We had a romantic dinner in an expensive restaurant.* ♦ *romantic relationships* **2** tending to believe that things are better or more exciting than they really are: *a romantic vision of life on a farm* **3 Romantic ARTS, LITERATURE** relating to the style of literature, art, and music known as romanticism: *the Romantic tradition* ♦ *the Romantic poets* —**romantically** /rəʊˈmæntɪkli/ adv

romantic² /rəʊˈmæntɪk/ noun [C] **1** someone who does things that show their love **2** someone who believes that things are better or more exciting than they really are **3 Romantic ARTS, LITERATURE** a writer, artist, or **composer** whose work is based on the tradition of **Romanticism**

romanticism /rəʊˈmæntɪˌsɪz(ə)m/ noun [U] **1 Romanticism ARTS, LITERATURE** a style of literature, art, and music that was common at the end of the 18th and beginning of the 19th centuries and that emphasized the importance of personal feelings and of nature **2** romantic feelings or behaviour

romanticize /rəʊˈmæntɪsaɪz/ verb [T] to think that something is better or more exciting than it really is

rondo /ˈrɒndəʊ/ noun [C] **MUSIC** a musical form in which the main tune comes back several times, with one or more different tunes in between

roof /ruːf/ noun [C] **1** the top outer part of a building or vehicle: *The roof is leaking again.* **2** the hard top part of the inside of your mouth
    PHRASE a roof over your head a place to live

roofing /ˈruːfɪŋ/ noun [U] **1** material used for making roofs **2** the process of building or repairing roofs

rooftop /ˈruːfˌtɒp/ noun [C] the roof of a building

rook /rʊk/ noun [C] **1** a large black European bird that belongs to the **crow** family of birds **2** a piece in the shape of a tower used in chess

room /ruːm/ noun **1** [C] a part of a building with a floor, walls, and a ceiling: *Annie ran out of the room.* **2** [C] a bedroom in a home or a hotel: *I'm staying in Room 52.* ♦ *My mum told me to tidy my room.* **3** [U] the amount of space that you need for a particular purpose: *There isn't much room in here.* ♦ *This table takes up too much room.* ♦ *Is there room for another person in your car?* → PLACE¹ sense 1 **4** [U] the possibility for something to happen: *There is room for improvement in his work* (=it is not very good).

rooming slip /ˈruːmɪŋ ˌslɪp/ noun [C] **TOURISM** a piece of paper given to a hotel guest, with the room number and price on it

roommate /ˈruːmˌmeɪt/ noun [C] someone who you share a room with

'room ˌtemperature noun [U] the normal temperature inside a building

roomy /ˈruːmi/ (**roomier, roomiest**) adj large and providing you with a lot of space: *a roomy car*

roost /ruːst/ noun [C] a place where birds rest and sleep —**roost** verb [I]

rooster /ˈruːstə/ noun [C] a male chicken

root¹ /ruːt/ noun

1 part of plant	**5** origin of family
2 part of hair etc	**6** basic form of word
3 in mathematics	**7** in welding
4 main cause/idea	**+** PHRASE

1 [C] **BIOLOGY** the part of a plant that grows under the ground, through which the plant gets water and minerals, and where some plants store food: *Olive trees have deep roots.* —*picture* → TREE and on next page

2 [C] **ANATOMY** the lowest part of a hair, tooth, or nail. The root of a hair or a nail is under the skin, and the root of a tooth is in the jawbone. —*picture* → TOOTH

3 [C] **MATHS** the root of a number in mathematics is another number that, when multiplied by itself a particular number of times, equals that number. For example, 3 is the **square root** of 9 (3 x 3) and the **cube root** of 27 (3 x 3 x 3).

4 [C] a basic cause or idea: *We need to get to **the root of** the problem.*

5 roots [plural] the place, culture, or family that someone comes from originally

6 [C] **LANGUAGE** the most basic form of a word, or a word that is the base for other words

7 [C] **TECHNOLOGY** the point where two metal pieces that are to be joined together by welding are closest together
    PHRASE take root if an idea or system takes root, it becomes established

root² /ruːt/ verb [I] **1** to search for something by putting your hand deep into a place and pushing things around: *He rooted around in his coat pocket for some change.* **2** if an animal roots, it searches for food by pushing with its nose
    PHRASAL VERB ˌroot sth ˈout to find something that is bad and get rid of it

'root caˌnal noun [C] **ANATOMY** a set of thin spaces inside the root of a tooth that can become infected

rootcap /ˈruːtˌkæp/ noun [C] **BIOLOGY** a thick mass of cells that covers and protects the growing **tip** of the root of a plant

'root ˌcrop noun [C] **AGRICULTURE** a crop that is grown so that its roots can be used for food, for example **carrots**

rooted /ˈruːtɪd/ adj **rooted in sth** if one thing is rooted in another, it is based on it or it has developed from it

'root ˌhair noun [C] **BIOLOGY** a small thin growth from the root of a plant that takes water and minerals from the soil

'root ˌpass noun [U] **TECHNOLOGY** in welding, the first weld that joins the bottom edge of two pieces of metal together. It lies below the **first filler pass**.

'root ˌpressure noun [U] **BIOLOGY** the pressure inside the root of a plant, which increases when water enters the root by **osmosis**, through the many root hairs

'root weld ˌbead noun [C] **TECHNOLOGY** a **stringer bead** (=first layer of welded material)

rope¹ /rəʊp/ noun **1** [C/U] a type of very thick string that can be used for tying or pulling things **2 the ropes** [plural] the correct way of doing something: *You spend the first few days **learning the ropes**.* ♦ *One of our most experienced workers will **show** you **the ropes**.*

rope² /rəʊp/ verb [T] to tie people or things together with a piece of rope

rosary /ˈrəʊzəri/ (plural **rosaries**) noun [C] **RELIGION** a set of beads used by Catholics for counting prayers

rose¹ /rəʊz/ noun [C] a flower that has a sweet smell and sharp **thorns** on its stem, or the bush that it grows on

rose² /rəʊz/ the past tense of **rise¹**

rosé /ˈrəʊzeɪ/ noun [U] a type of wine that is pink

rosemary /ˈrəʊzməri/ noun [U] a European bush with narrow leaves that are used as a herb in cooking

rosette /rəʊˈzet/ noun [C] a circular decoration that is given to someone as a prize or worn by supporters of a political party

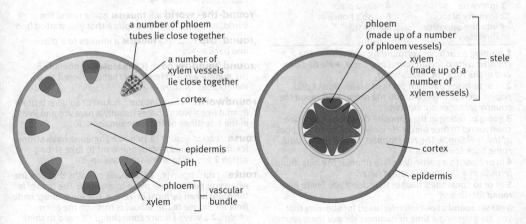

a transverse section through the stem of a dicotyledonous plant

the transverse section of a root of a dicotyledonous plant

a number of phloem tubes lie close together

a number of xylem vessels lie close together

cortex

epidermis

pith

phloem — vascular bundle

xylem

phloem (made up of a number of phloem vessels)

xylem (made up of a number of xylem vessels) — stele

cortex

epidermis

sections of roots and stems

roster /ˈrɒstə/ noun [C] a list of people's names that shows when each of them must work, and what they have to do

rostrum /ˈrɒstrəm/ noun [C] a small raised area that you stand on so that an audience can see you

rosy /ˈrəʊzi/ adj **1** pink **2** likely to be successful or happy: *a rosy future*

rot¹ /rɒt/ (**rots, rotting, rotted**) or **,rot aˈway** verb [I/T] to decay, or to make something decay

rot² /rɒt/ noun **1** [U] decayed material, or the process of decaying **2** **the rot** [singular] the process by which a situation gradually gets much worse: *This government has got to **stop the rot** in the economy.* ♦ *Once officers start accepting money, that's when **the rot sets in** (=starts).*

rota /ˈrəʊtə/ noun [C] a list of people's names that shows when each person has to do a particular job

rotary /ˈrəʊtəri/ adj with parts that turn around a central point

rotate /rəʊˈteɪt/ verb [I/T] **1** to move in a circle around a central point, or to move something in this way: *The Earth rotates 360 degrees every 24 hours.* **2** if people or things rotate, or if you rotate them, you change them regularly in a fixed order

rotating joint /rəʊˌteɪtɪŋ ˈdʒɔɪnt/ noun [C] ANATOMY a **pivot joint**

rotation /rəʊˈteɪʃ(ə)n/ noun **1** [C/U] movement in a circle around an axis, for example the movement of the Earth around its axis once every 24 hours **2** [U] the process of regularly changing people or things in a fixed order —**rotational** adj

rote /rəʊt/ noun **learn sth by rote** to learn something by repeating it many times rather than by understanding it

rotor /ˈrəʊtə/ noun [C] ENGINEERING, PHYSICS the part of an electric motor consisting of a magnet that turns inside a **stator** (=set of conductors) and produces electric current in them

rotten /ˈrɒt(ə)n/ adj **1** decayed: *rotten eggs* **2** *informal* unpleasant: *They were really rotten to him!* ♦ *We had a rotten time at the museum.* **3** *informal* of a low quality, standard, or ability: *She's a rotten singer.*

rotund /rəʊˈtʌnd/ adj *formal* round and fat

rough¹ /rʌf/ adj

1 not smooth	4 with crime etc
2 difficult	5 not finished/exact
3 not gentle	

1 with a surface that is not smooth: *The walls were built of dark rough stone.* ♦ *a rough dirt track* ♦ *strong winds and **rough seas***
2 *informal* difficult and full of problems: *I've had a really rough day at school.*
3 not gentle: *Don't be so rough with her, James. She's only a baby.*
4 a rough place is not pleasant because there is a lot of crime or violence there
5 not completely finished, or not exact: *Can you give me **a rough idea** of the cost?* ♦ *Here is **a rough draft** for you to read.*
—**roughness** noun [U]
→ ROUGHLY

rough² /rʌf/ noun [singular] SPORTS the part of a **golf course** where the grass is tall and not cut

PHRASE **in rough** if you do a piece of written work in rough, you do it in a form that you will finish or improve at a later time

rough³ /rʌf/ adv **sleep/live rough** to sleep or live outside because you do not have a home

roughage /ˈrʌfɪdʒ/ noun [U] HEALTH fibre in the food that you eat that cannot be digested and that helps the movement of food through the digestive system. It mainly consists of the **cellulose** that is found in grains, fruits, and vegetables.

,rough-and-ˈtumble noun [U] **1** the rough way in which a particular activity is usually done: *the rough-and-tumble of a political campaign* **2** the rough behaviour of children who are playing

,rough ˈjustice noun [U] treatment or punishment that is not fair

roughly /ˈrʌfli/ adv **1** used for showing that an amount or number is not exact = APPROXIMATELY: *The meeting lasted roughly 45 minutes.* **2** in a way that is not gentle: *He pushed roughly past her.* **3** in a way that is not tidy or exact: *The onions should be roughly chopped.*

,rough 'sleeper noun [C] someone who sleeps or lives outside because they have no home

round¹ /raʊnd/ adv, preposition

1 in a circle	**4** near a place
2 in many places	**5** at sb's house
3 into the opposite direction	**+ PHRASE**

1 forming a circle, or surrounding something: *The children were dancing round in a circle.* ♦ *He tied one end of the rope round his waist.*

2 in or to many different parts or areas: *Books and papers were scattered round the room.* ♦ *All round the country factories are closing.*

3 going or facing in the opposite direction: *Katharine spun round to face him.* ♦ *He walked round to the back of the building.* ♦ *The car stopped, turned round, and came back towards us.*

4 in or close to a particular place or area: *the hills round Jerusalem* ♦ *Do you live round here?*

5 at or to someone's house: *Why don't you invite him round for dinner?*

PHRASE **round about** *informal* used for showing that you are guessing a time or number: *We got there round about half past nine.*

→ ABOUT, AROUND, CIRCLE¹

round² /raʊnd/ adj **1** shaped like a circle or a ball: *a round table* **2** MATHS not exact, but given as a whole number or a number ending in zero: *They quoted a round figure of $100.* —**roundness** noun [U]

round³ /raʊnd/ noun [C]

1 (one of) a series	**5** set of drinks
2 in competition	**6** in boxing match
3 series of visits	**7** game of golf
4 bullet/shot	

1 one of a series of similar events: *The next round of peace talks will be held in Rome.*

2 a stage in a competition or election: *Brazil beat the United States in the second round of the World Cup.*

3 a series of visits to different places that is made as part of someone's job: *The body was found by a postman on his morning delivery round.*

4 a shot that is fired from a weapon: *Those guns are capable of firing 1,250 rounds per minute.*

5 a drink for each of the people in a group: *Tom bought a round of drinks.*

6 SPORTS one of the periods of fighting in a boxing or **wrestling** match: *He knocked out his opponent in the fourth round.*

7 SPORTS a complete game of golf: *He likes to play a round of golf on Saturdays.*

round⁴ /raʊnd/ verb [T] to go round something: *The van had just rounded the corner.*

PHRASAL VERBS **,round sth 'down** to reduce a number to the nearest whole number, or to the nearest number ending in zero

,round sth 'up to increase a number to the nearest whole number, or to the nearest number ending in zero

,round sb/sth 'up to bring people or animals together in one place for a particular purpose

roundabout /'raʊndə,baʊt/ noun [C] **1** a circular area where three or more roads meet **2** a circular structure in a **playground** that children sit on while someone pushes it round

'round ,angle noun [C] MATHS an angle of 360° —*picture* → ANGLE

rounded /'raʊndɪd/ adj something that is rounded has a curved shape or surface

rounders /'raʊndəz/ noun [U] SPORTS a game played in the UK that is similar to baseball

,round-pin 'plug noun [C] an electrical **plug** that has round pins —*picture* → PLUG

'round-the-,world adj TOURISM going round the world, and returning to the place that you started from

,round 'trip noun [C] TOURISM a journey to a place and back again

,round 'window noun [C] ANATOMY an opening in the **middle ear** and **inner ear** that is covered by a membrane —*picture* → EAR

roundworm /'raʊnd,wɜːm/ noun [C] an invertebrate animal like a worm that is usually a parasite and lives in the intestines of some mammals

rouse /raʊz/ verb [T] **1** to make someone have strong feelings, or to make someone want to take strong action **2** *formal* to wake someone up

route /ruːt/ noun [C] **1** the roads or paths that you use when you go from one place to another: *The tunnel is the route taken by most drivers.* ♦ *The most direct route from the house to the school is through the town centre.* **2** a way of doing something: *I'll need to think carefully before deciding what route to take next.* ♦ *the route to success* → EN ROUTE

router /'ruːtə/ noun [C] COMPUTING a piece of equipment or software that finds the best way of sending information between any two **networks**

routeway /'ruːt,weɪ/ noun [C] GEOGRAPHY a route for travelling to a place

routine¹ /ruː'tiːn/ noun **1** [C/U] your usual way of doing things: *It shouldn't take too long to get back to our old routine.* **2** [C] a set of things such as jokes or songs that a performer uses regularly: *a comedy routine* **3** [C] COMPUTING a set of instructions that a computer obeys

routine² /ruː'tiːn/ adj **1** usual and not done for any special reason: *a routine check* **2** ordinary and not interesting or special: *routine, repetitive work*

routinely /ruː'tiːnli/ adv as part of the normal way of doing something

row¹ /rəʊ/ noun [C] **1** a series of people or things that are arranged in a straight line: *a row of houses* **2** a line of seats in a theatre or cinema

PHRASE **in a row 1** in a straight line: *The children stood in a row against the wall.* **2** one after another, without anything different happening in between: *His job allows him to take several days off in a row.*

row² /rəʊ/ verb [I/T] to move a boat through water using poles with flat ends called **oars**

row³ /raʊ/ noun **1** [C] an argument or disagreement between people, organizations, or countries: *I had a row with my boyfriend last night.* ♦ *the continuing row over the terms of the ceasefire* **2** [singular] noisy behaviour

row⁴ /raʊ/ verb [I] if people row, they have a noisy argument with each other

rowdy /'raʊdi/ (**rowdier, rowdiest**) adj noisy and causing trouble

rowing /'rəʊɪŋ/ noun [U] the activity of moving a boat through water using **oars**, either for pleasure or as a sport

rowing boat /'rəʊɪŋ ,bəʊt/ noun [C] a small boat that you move by pulling on two poles with flat ends called **oars**

royal /'rɔɪəl/ adj relating to a king or queen, or to their family: *the royal palace* ♦ *a royal wedding*

,royal 'blue adj deep blue in colour —**,royal 'blue** noun [U]

,Royal 'Highness noun **Your/His/Her Royal Highness** used for speaking to or about a prince or princess

royalist /ˈrɔɪəlɪst/ noun [C] someone who believes that their country should have a king or queen

royalty /ˈrɔɪəlti/ noun [U] kings and queens and their families

RPG /ˌɑː piː ˈdʒiː/ noun [C] a role-playing game: a **computer game** in which people pretend to be different characters

RPI /ˌɑː piː ˈaɪ/ abbrev **ECONOMICS** the **retail price index**

rpm /ˌɑː piː ˈem/ abbrev **PHYSICS** revolutions per minute: a unit for measuring the speed at which something goes round in a circle

RSS feed /ˌɑː es ˈes ˌfiːd/ noun [C] **COMPUTING** a file that delivers information from a website, sometimes in a summary with **links** to the full document, to another website. RSS feeds are used mainly to supply the latest information to websites that are regularly **updated**.

RSVP /ˌɑː es viː ˈpiː/ abbrev used on written invitations for asking for a reply

RTF /ˌɑː tiː ˈef/ abbrev **COMPUTING** rich text format: a way of storing a computer document so that when you send it to someone, it will look exactly the same on their computer screen

rub¹ /rʌb/ (**rubs, rubbing, rubbed**) verb **1** [I/T] to move your hands or an object firmly over a surface: *Scott gently rubbed her back until the pain went away.* ♦ *Rub your hands together – it will help you to stay warm.* **2** [T] to spread a liquid or substance onto the surface of something: *She rubbed some tanning oil on his back.* ♦ *Rub the chicken with garlic before putting it in the oven.* **3** [I] to hurt or damage something by continuously pressing and moving against it: *Cindy's new shoes were rubbing and giving her blisters.*
    PHRASAL VERB **,rub sth 'out** to use a rubber to remove something that you have written or drawn in pencil: *If you make a mistake rub it out and rewrite the answer.*

rub² /rʌb/ noun [singular] the action of rubbing something: *Let the polish dry then give the shoes a good rub.*

rubber /ˈrʌbə/ noun **1** [U] **AGRICULTURE** a substance that is made from the **sap** (=fluid) taken from a rubber tree. Rubber is a strong but bends easily and is used for making things such as tyres and boots. **2** [C] a small piece of rubber that you use for removing pencil marks from paper= ERASER —*picture* → WORKSTATION

'rubber ,plant noun [C] a plant with large shiny green leaves that comes from South-East Asia

'rubber ,tree noun [C] a tropical tree whose **sap** is used to make natural rubber

rubbery /ˈrʌbəri/ adj similar to rubber

rubbish /ˈrʌbɪʃ/ noun [U] **1** things that you throw away because they are no longer useful: *The streets were littered with rubbish.* **2** things that someone says or writes that are not reasonable or sensible= NONSENSE: *As usual, he was talking complete rubbish.* **3** something that is of very low quality= JUNK: *Critics have described the paintings as worthless rubbish.*

rubble /ˈrʌb(ə)l/ noun [U] broken pieces of stone and brick from buildings that have been destroyed

rubella /ruːˈbelə/ noun [U] **HEALTH** an infectious viral disease that causes red spots on the skin. It is a minor illness in children and adults, but it can cause serious damage to the foetus if a pregnant woman catches it = GERMAN MEASLES

rubidium /ruːˈbɪdiəm/ noun [U] **CHEMISTRY** a soft silvery radioactive element that **ignites** (=starts to burn) in air. Chemical symbol: **Rb**

rubric /ˈruːbrɪk/ noun [C] *formal* **1** a set of instructions at the beginning of a document, for example at the top of an examination paper **2** the name of a particular group or section of something

ruby /ˈruːbi/ (plural **rubies**) noun [C] a valuable red jewel

ruck /rʌk/ noun [C] **SPORTS** in **rugby**, a group of players who are all trying to get the ball when it is on the ground

rucksack /ˈrʌkˌsæk/ noun [C] a bag that you carry on your back= BACKPACK

rudder /ˈrʌdə/ noun [C] a flat part at the back of a boat or plane that is moved in order to turn the boat or plane

rude /ruːd/ adj **1** not polite: *I don't want to seem rude, but I'd rather be alone.* ♦ *It's rude to keep people waiting.* **2** offensive because of referring to sex or using the toilet: *a rude word* —**rudely** adv: *I can't remember what I was saying before I was so rudely interrupted!* —**rudeness** noun [U]

rudimentary /ˌruːdɪˈment(ə)ri/ adj basic, and not detailed or developed

ruff /rʌf/ noun [C] **1** **BIOLOGY** the fur or feathers that grow around the neck of a bird or other animal **2** a large collar with upright folds that people wore in the 16th and 17th centuries

rug /rʌg/ noun [C] **1** a small carpet that covers part of a floor **2** a cloth made of wool that you use to keep yourself warm

rugby /ˈrʌgbi/ noun [U] **SPORTS** a game that is played by two teams of players with a ball that is shaped like an egg

rugged /ˈrʌgɪd/ adj **1** not smooth or flat: *a rugged landscape* **2** strong and able to deal with difficult conditions: *a rugged piece of equipment* **3** with a strong attractive appearance: *He had a tanned rugged face.*

ruin¹ /ˈruːɪn/ verb [T] **1** to spoil or destroy something: *She had ruined her mother's chances of getting a job.* **2** to make someone lose all their money or power: *The scandal totally ruined him.*

ruin² /ˈruːɪn/ noun **1** **ruins** [plural] the parts of a building that remain after it has been severely damaged: *People had built shelters among the ruins of the city.* **2** [U] the loss of all your money or power: *Many of these companies are facing ruin.*
    PHRASE **in ruins** destroyed, or severely damaged: *His marriage was over and his career was in ruins.*

rule¹ /ruːl/ noun **1** [C] a statement that explains what you can or cannot do in a particular situation: *grammatical rules* ♦ *Players who break the rules are sent off the field.* ♦ *You should always follow these simple rules when using electrical equipment.* ♦ *You can't do that, it's against the rules!* ♦ *the basic rules of the game* **2** [U] the person, group, or country that officially controls a place: *British rule over Hong Kong ended in 1997.*
    PHRASES **as a rule** usually: *As a rule, we go to bed at 8 o'clock.*
    bend/stretch the rules to allow something that is not normally allowed
    be the rule to be what usually happens, or what is thought to be normal: *Heavy rain is the rule at this time of year.*

rule of thumb a simple method or principle that is not exact, but that is effective
→ GOLDEN RULE, HOME RULE

rule² /ruːl/ verb **1** [I/T] to officially control a country or area= GOVERN: *Portugal ruled East Timor for nearly four centuries.* **2** [I/T] to make and announce an official decision: *The judge still has not ruled on the case.* ♦ *The court ruled that the strike was illegal.* **3** [T] to control someone's thoughts or actions: *We must not allow ourselves to be ruled by personal feelings.*

PHRASAL VERB ,rule sb/sth 'out to stop considering someone or something as a possibility: *The president has ruled out the use of troops.*

ruled /ruːld/ adj ruled paper has straight lines printed on it for writing on

ruler /'ruːlə/ noun [C] **1** MATHS a long flat object that you use for measuring or for drawing straight lines —picture → WORKSTATION **2** someone who controls a country: *Haiti's former military rulers*

ruling /'ruːlɪŋ/ noun [C] an official decision

rum /rʌm/ noun [U] a strong alcoholic drink made from sugar cane

rumble /'rʌmb(ə)l/ verb [I] to make a continuous deep sound —**rumble** noun [C]

rumbling /'rʌmblɪŋ/ noun **1** [singular] a continuous deep sound **2** rumblings [plural] signs that people are becoming unhappy about a situation

ruminant /'ruːmɪnənt/ noun [C] BIOLOGY a mammal such as a cow or sheep that brings food back from its stomach into its mouth to chew it a second time

rummage /'rʌmɪdʒ/ verb [I] to search for something among a lot of other things

rumour /'ruːmə/ noun [C/U] something that people are saying that may or may not be true: *He denied rumours that staff would lose their jobs.* ♦ *Someone had been spreading nasty rumours about her.* ♦ *Rumour has it that* (=there is a rumour that) *he's seriously ill.* ♦ *Now there are rumours of wedding plans.*

rump /rʌmp/ noun [C] the part of an animal's body that is above its back legs

rumpled /'rʌmp(ə)ld/ adj something that is rumpled is untidy because it is not smooth or flat

run¹ /rʌn/ (runs, running, ran /ræn/, run) verb

1 move quickly	**11** exist in a place
2 control/organize	**12** use program
3 machine: work	**13** in newspaper
4 take sb in car	**14** try to be elected
5 liquid: flow	**15** of liquid/colour
6 make water flow	**16** pay for car
7 continue to be shown	**17** do test/check
8 vehicle: travel	+ PHRASES
9 reach amount/rate	+ PHRASAL VERBS
10 move sth along	

1 [I] to move quickly using your legs and feet: *You'll have to run if you want to catch the bus.* ♦ *A cat ran across the road in front of me.* ♦ *I ran to the door and opened it.*
2 [T] to control and organize something such as a business, organization, or event= MANAGE: *He was the man who ran Clinton's election campaign.*
3 [I] if a machine or engine is running, it is operating: *Don't leave the car engine running.*
4 [T] to take someone somewhere in your car: *I'll run you there – it's no trouble.* ♦ *John kindly offered to run me into town.*
5 [I] if a liquid runs somewhere, it flows there: *Tears were running down his face.* ♦ *The River Congo runs into the Atlantic Ocean.*

6 [T] to make water flow into or from a container: *I'm going to run a bath.*
7 [I] if a play, film, or television programme runs, it continues to be performed or shown: *a soap opera that has been running for many years*
8 [I] if a bus or train runs, it travels somewhere at regular times: *The train only runs at weekends.*
9 [I] to continue at a particular amount or rate: *Inflation is running at 3%.*
10 [T] to move something through or along something else: *Fred ran his fingers gently through her hair.*
11 [I] if something such as a road or wall runs somewhere, it continues from one place to another: *There was a path running through the middle of the forest.*
12 [I/T] if you run a computer program, or if it runs, you start it or use it: *The software will run on any PC.*
13 [T] if newspapers run an article, advertisement, or photograph, they print it
14 [I] to try to be elected to an official job or position: *How many candidates are running?* ♦ *Jackson announced his intention to run for president.*
15 [I] if a piece of clothing or a colour runs, the colour spreads when you wash it
16 [T] to use and pay for a car: *He can't afford to run a car on his salary.*
17 [T] to perform something such as a test, or to check on someone or something: *The police run a check on all new government staff.*

PHRASES **run rings round sb** to do something much better than someone else
running late if you are running late, you do something or arrive somewhere later than you planned
run short/low if you run short of something, or if you run low on something, you do not have enough of it left: *We're running low on rice.* ♦ *I'm running short of ideas.*
sth runs in the family if something such as a quality or disease runs in the family, a lot of people in the family have it
→ COURSE, SHORT², STEAM¹

PHRASAL VERBS ,run 'after sb/sth to chase someone or something: *Velluci ran after the car waving his fists.*
,run a'way to secretly leave a place because you are not happy there: *When I was 13, I ran away from home.*
,run (sth) 'down if something such as a machine runs down, or if you run it down, it gradually stops working because it is losing power: *Switch your headlights off, or you'll run the battery down.*
,run sb/sth 'down to hit a person or animal with a car and injure or kill them: *She got run down outside school.*
,run 'off to suddenly leave a place or person: *Their dad ran off when they were little.*
,run 'off with sth to steal something, or to take it without permission
,run 'on to continue for longer than you expected or planned: *I hope this meeting doesn't run on too long.*
,run 'out **1** to use all of something and not have any left: *Many hospitals are running out of money.* **2** if something such as money or time runs out, there is no more of it left: *They returned home from South Africa when their money ran out.* **3** to stop being legal on a particular date= EXPIRE: *My contract runs out next July.* ♦ *When does your passport run out?*
,run sb/sth 'over to hit someone or something with a vehicle: *Keeley was run over by a car outside her house.*
,run 'through sth to explain or read something quickly: *Do you want me to run through the details with you?*
,run 'up sth if you run up a bill or a debt, you owe someone a lot of money: *My son ran up a huge phone bill.*

run² /rʌn/ noun **1** [C] **SPORTS** an act of running, or a race in which you run a long distance: *Lee is doing a six-mile run on Saturday.* **2** [singular] a period of time when something continues: *The play is enjoying a successful run.* ♦ *We've had a run of bad luck recently.* **3** [singular] a journey in a vehicle: *We took the new car out for a run in the country.* **4** [C] **SPORTS** one point in the game of **cricket** or baseball: *He has scored 90 runs in this match.*

PHRASE **on the run** trying to hide or escape from the police
→ LONG¹, SHORT¹

runaway /ˈrʌnəˌweɪ/ adj **1** a runaway vehicle or animal is moving fast without anyone controlling it **2** happening or increasing very quickly: *runaway inflation* **3** a runaway person has left their home or has escaped from somewhere

,run-'down adj **1** so tired that you do not feel well **2** in bad condition because no one has spent money on repairs: *a run-down hotel*

rung¹ /rʌŋ/ noun [C] **1** one of the bars across a ladder that you put your feet on when you climb up **2** a level of achievement: *You could be on the first rung of a great new career.*

rung² /rʌŋ/ the past participle of **ring¹**

runner /ˈrʌnə/ noun [C] **1** **SPORTS** a person or animal that runs in a race, or someone who runs for pleasure **2** a narrow part on which something such as a drawer or **sledge** slides **3** someone who carries drugs or weapons illegally from one place to another **4** **BIOLOGY** a stem that grows along the ground and has a new plant growing on it

'runner ,bean noun [C] a long green bean that is cooked and eaten

,runner-'up (plural **runners-up**) noun [C] someone who is second in a competition or race

running /ˈrʌnɪŋ/ noun [U] **1** **SPORTS** the activity of running for pleasure or as a sport **2** the activities that are involved in managing or organizing something: *The family is not involved in the day-to-day running of the company.*

,running 'total noun [C] a total amount that has new amounts added to it regularly

,running 'water noun [U] water that is supplied by pipes into a building

runny /ˈrʌni/ adj **1** a runny nose has liquid coming out of it **2** like a liquid

runoff /ˈrʌnɒf/ noun [U] **ENVIRONMENT** the flow of water from fields into rivers and streams. Runoff may contain fertilizers and other agricultural chemicals that can cause pollution. —*picture* → POLLUTION

,run-on 'sentence noun [C] **LANGUAGE** a sentence in which two main clauses are connected without any conjunctions, or without the correct punctuation

'run-,up noun **SPORTS** a run that someone makes before jumping, throwing a ball etc

PHRASE **the run-up to sth** the period of time just before an important event

runway /ˈrʌnweɪ/ noun [C] a long road that is used by planes when they land and **take off**

rupee /ˌruːˈpiː/ noun [C] **ECONOMICS** the unit of money used in India, Pakistan, and some other countries

rupture /ˈrʌptʃə/ verb [I/T] if something ruptures, or if you rupture it, it bursts or tears suddenly: *The impact ruptured both fuel tanks.* —**rupture** noun [C]

rural /ˈrʊərəl/ adj **GEOGRAPHY** relating to the countryside, or in the countryside ≠ URBAN: *a rural area*

rush¹ /rʌʃ/ verb **1** [I/T] to go somewhere in a hurry, or to take someone or send something somewhere in a hurry: *Suddenly the door burst open and Joe rushed in.* ♦ *Ambulance crews rushed to the scene of the accident.* ♦ *Frank was rushed to hospital with violent stomach pains.* **2** [I/T] to do something quickly, or to make someone do something quickly: *There's no need to rush. We've got plenty of time.* ♦ *Don't rush into a decision.* ♦ *Hayley rushed to answer the phone.* **3** [T] to attack someone suddenly = CHARGE

rush² /rʌʃ/ noun

1 sudden movement	4 sudden strong emotion
2 a hurry to do sth	5 time with heavy traffic
3 interest to do/have sth	6 tall plant like grass

1 [singular] a sudden strong movement forwards: *Everyone made a rush for the refreshments.* ♦ *Passengers jostled in a rush to get off the train.* **2** [singular/U] a situation in which you hurry to do something: *Sorry, I can't stop. I'm in a rush.* ♦ *There was a mad rush to get the house tidy before they arrived.* **3** [singular] an occasion when a lot of people suddenly want to do something or have something: *We've had a rush on cameras this week.* ♦ *There was a rush to buy tickets for the concert.* **4** [C] a sudden strong feeling of excitement or other emotion: *I felt an incredible rush as I jumped form the plane.* ♦ *a rush of affection/panic* **5** **the rush** [singular] the time of day when a place is very busy and there is a lot of traffic: *Lee left the city at six o'clock to avoid the rush.* **6** [C] a tall plant that looks like grass and grows in water. It is used for making baskets and covering floors.

rushed /rʌʃt/ adj done in a hurry

rushes /ˈrʌʃɪz/ noun [plural] tall plants like grass that grow in water

rust¹ /rʌst/ noun [U] **CHEMISTRY** the red-brown substance called **iron oxide**, that forms on the surface of iron or steel through a chemical reaction with water and air

rust² /rʌst/ verb [I/T] **CHEMISTRY** to become damaged by rust, or to make metal develop rust

rustic /ˈrʌstɪk/ adj made in the simple style of the countryside

rustle /ˈrʌs(ə)l/ verb [I/T] to produce a sound like the sound that leaves or sheets of paper make when they move, or to make something do this —**rustle** noun [singular]

rusty /ˈrʌsti/ (**rustier, rustiest**) adj **1** covered in **rust** **2** a skill that is rusty has not been used recently

rut /rʌt/ noun [C] **1** a situation that is boring and difficult to change: *If you're in a rut, change jobs.* **2** a deep narrow mark in the ground made by a wheel

ruthenium /ruˈθiːniəm/ noun [U] **CHEMISTRY** a silvery-white metallic element that is used to make **platinum** and **palladium** harder. Chemical symbol: **Ru**

ruthless /ˈruːθləs/ adj willing to hurt other people in order to get what you want —**ruthlessly** adv

rye /raɪ/ noun [U] **AGRICULTURE** a crop that produces grain used for making bread and **whisky** —*picture* → CEREAL

S s

s /es/ (plural **s's**) or **S** (plural **S's**) noun [C/U] the 19th letter of the English alphabet

S abbrev **1** small: used on clothes labels **2 GEOGRAPHY** South **3 GEOGRAPHY** Southern

-'s¹ short form **1** a way of saying or writing 'is' and 'has'. This is not often used in formal writing: *She's in the kitchen.* ♦ *John's gone out.* **2** the usual way of saying or writing 'us' when you use it with 'let' to make a suggestion: *Let's not tell him now.*

-'s² suffix **1** used with nouns for showing who or what something belongs to: *I've never met Andy's wife.* ♦ *The dog's leg was badly cut.* ♦ *the evening's activities* (=activities that happen in the evening) **2** used for talking about the home of a particular person: *We all went back to Alan's for lunch.*

the Sabbath /'sæbəθ/ noun [singular] **RELIGION** a day when the people of some religions rest and pray

sabbatical /sə'bætɪk(ə)l/ noun [C/U] **EDUCATION** a period away from work when people such as college or university teachers can study, rest, or travel

sabotage /'sæbətɑːʒ/ verb [T] **1** to deliberately damage or destroy something that belongs to an enemy **2** to deliberately prevent something from being successful —**sabotage** noun [U]

sabre /'seɪbə/ noun [C] a sword with a curved blade

sac /sæk/ noun [C] **BIOLOGY** a part of an animal or plant that is shaped like a small bag and is usually filled with liquid or air

saccharin /'sækərɪn/ noun [U] **CHEMISTRY** an artificial substance that is used instead of sugar for making food sweet

saccule /'sækjuːl/ noun [C] **ANATOMY** a space in the **inner ear** that is filled with fluid and is important for balance

sachet /'sæʃeɪ/ noun [C] a small flat plastic bag that contains a liquid or powder

sack¹ /sæk/ noun **1** [C] a large strong bag for storing and carrying things: *a sack of rice* **2** the sack [singular] *informal* a situation in which someone is forced to leave their job: *We didn't want to risk getting the sack by going on strike.* ♦ *He ought to be given the sack.*

sack² /sæk/ verb [T] **1** *informal* to force someone to leave their job = FIRE: *Hundreds of workers are to be sacked at the factory.* **2** if an army sacks a place, they steal property from it and destroy it

sacral vertebra /ˌseɪkrəl 'vɜːtəbrə/ noun [C] **ANATOMY** one of the spinal bones in the bottom part of the back, between the hip bones

sacrament /'sækrəmənt/ noun [C] **RELIGION** an important Christian ceremony such as marriage or baptism

  PHRASE Sacrament of the Sick RELIGION a religious ceremony performed by a Roman Catholic priest for someone who is dying

sacred /'seɪkrɪd/ adj **1 RELIGION** connected with religion: *sacred art* **2 RELIGION** holy: *Jerusalem is sacred to Christians, Muslims, and Jews.* **3** something that is sacred is so important that you should not change or criticize it: *He has broken one of the*

profession's most sacred rules. —**sacredness** noun [U]

sacrifice¹ /'sækrɪfaɪs/ noun [C/U] **1** a decision not to have or do something that is important to you, so that someone else will have a benefit or so that you will benefit later: *Making sacrifices is part of bringing up children.* **2 RELIGION** the act of killing a person or animal as part of a ceremony to honour a god or spirit —**sacrificial** /ˌsækrɪ'fɪʃ(ə)l/ adj: *a sacrificial animal*

sacrifice² /'sækrɪfaɪs/ verb [T] **1** to choose not to have something so that other people can have something else: *She sacrificed her career to bring up the children.* ♦ *Would you sacrifice some of your salary for more holiday time?* **2 RELIGION** to kill a person or animal as part of a ceremony to honour a god or spirit

sacrificial pro'tection noun [U] **CHEMISTRY** the use of a metal such as zinc to protect another metal such as iron from **rust**. The zinc rusts first, so that the iron will not rust provided there is some zinc left.

sacrilege /'sækrəlɪdʒ/ noun [U] **RELIGION** behaviour that shows that someone has no respect for something holy or important —**sacrilegious** /ˌsækrə'lɪdʒəs/ adj

the SACU /ˌes eɪ siː 'juː/ noun [singular] **ECONOMICS, POLITICS** the Southern African Customs Union: an organization of countries in Southern Africa that has **free trade** between its member states. They all charge the same rate of **duty** (=tax) on imports from countries that are not members of the Union.

sad /sæd/ (**sadder, saddest**) adj **1** feeling unhappy, making you feel unhappy, or showing that you feel unhappy: *sad eyes* ♦ *Reading her letter made us all feel a little sad.* **2** very bad in a way that makes you feel angry, upset, or shocked: *It's sad that some children don't get the chance to go to school.* ♦ *The sad truth is that many people never learn to read.*

the SADC /ˌes eɪ diː 'siː/ noun [singular] **ECONOMICS, POLITICS** the Southern African Development Community: an organization of countries in Southern Africa that organizes programmes to improve economic development in the region

sadden /'sæd(ə)n/ verb [T] *formal* to make someone feel sad

saddle¹ /'sæd(ə)l/ noun [C] **1** a leather seat that you put on a horse's back **2** the seat on a bicycle or motorcycle

saddle² /'sæd(ə)l/ verb [T] to put a saddle on a horse

sadhu /'sɑːduː/ noun [C] **RELIGION** *Indian English* a Hindu holy man who chooses to own nothing and to live by asking people for food

sadist /'seɪdɪst/ noun [C] someone who likes to hurt people —**sadism** noun [U]

sadistic /sə'dɪstɪk/ adj someone who is sadistic likes to hurt people

sadly /'sædli/ adv **1** used for showing that you think that something is bad or wrong: *Sadly, they chose to ignore our advice.* **2** in a way that shows that you are sad, or that makes you feel sad: *She smiled sadly.* ♦ *Mrs Shin was a wonderful teacher and she'll be sadly missed.*

sadness /'sædnəs/ noun [U] the feeling of being unhappy: *Her childhood was filled with pain and sadness.* ♦ *It is with great sadness that we announce the death of Pak Jaemin.*

sae /ˌes eɪ 'iː/ noun [C] stamped addressed envelope, or self-addressed envelope: an envelope with your name, address, and a stamp on it that you give to someone so that they can easily send you something

safari /sə'fɑːri/ noun [C] **TOURISM** a journey, especially to Africa, in order to see wild animals in their natural environment

safe¹ /seɪf/ adj

1 protected from harm	**4** not involving risk
2 not likely to cause harm	**5** in law: reliable
3 not damaged/hurt/lost	**+ PHRASE**

1 not likely to be harmed, lost, or stolen: *Will my car be safe if I park it in the street?* ♦ *It's difficult to make airports **safe from** terrorist attacks.* ♦ *Make sure to **keep** your credit card **safe**.*
2 not likely to cause damage or harm: *Travelling by plane is much safer than driving your own car.* ♦ *a safe environment for children*
3 not damaged, hurt, or lost: *Rescuers found the children safe inside the house.* ♦ *Everyone arrived **safe and sound**.*
4 not involving a lot of risk: *a safe investment*
5 LAW based on reliable evidence
PHRASE **in safe hands** protected from harm or danger by a particular person or organization

safe² /seɪf/ noun [C] a strong metal box that is used for storing valuable things

safeguard /'seɪf,gɑːd/ verb [T] to protect something or someone: *We hope that world leaders can agree on a plan to safeguard the environment.* —**safeguard** noun [C]

safe 'haven noun [C] a place where people are safe from danger or attack

safekeeping /,seɪf'kiːpɪŋ/ noun [U] protection from being damaged or lost: *Sheila gave me the rings **for safekeeping**.*

safely /'seɪfli/ adv **1** in a way that will not cause damage or harm: *Remember to drive safely.* ♦ *Keep plastic bags safely out of the reach of children.*
2 without being damaged, hurt, or lost: *All the children have been returned safely to their parents.* **3** in a way that does not involve a lot of risk

safe 'sex noun [U] **HEALTH** sexual activity in which people are careful to avoid getting diseases

safety /'seɪfti/ noun [U] **1** the fact that something is safe to do or use: *Their cars have a reputation for safety and reliability.* ♦ *The airline has a poor **safety record** (=a record of how safe something has been in the past).* ♦ *Do we know enough about **the safety of** these vaccines?* **2** a place or situation in which you are protected from danger: *Refugees walked for several days until they **reached safety**.* ♦ *We watched the storm from **the safety of** our home.* **3** a safe way of behaving: *We plan to have frequent training sessions on safety at work.*

'safety ,belt noun [C] a **seat belt**

'safety ,net noun [C] **1** a plan or system that is designed to protect people or prevent serious problems **2** a net that you put under something in order to catch people if they fall

'safety ,pin noun [C] a curved pin with a cover that fits over the sharp point

'safety ,valve noun [C] **1** a place that gas or liquid can escape through when there is too much pressure inside a container **2** a way of getting rid of strong emotions without harming anyone

saffron /'sæfrən/ noun [U] part of a flower that is used for adding flavour and yellow colour to food

sag /sæg/ (**sags, sagging, sagged**) verb [I] **1** to become soft and start to bend or hang downwards **2** to become weaker or less in amount or value

saga /'sɑːgə/ noun [C] **LITERATURE** a story about what happens to a group of characters over a long period of time

sage /seɪdʒ/ noun [U] a herb with grey-green leaves that are used for adding flavour to food

Sagittarius /,sædʒɪ'teəriəs/ noun [C/U] one of the twelve signs of the zodiac. A **Sagittarius** is someone who was born between 23 November and 21 December.

said¹ /sed/ adj **LAW** mentioned earlier

said² /sed/ the past tense and past participle of **say¹**

sail¹ /seɪl/ verb **1** [I] to travel somewhere by boat or ship: *Sail to Greece aboard the SS Monterey.* **2** [I/T] to control the movement of a boat or ship, especially one that uses the wind to move it: *It's a great opportunity to learn to sail.* **3** [I/T] if a boat sails, it moves across the surface of water: *The yacht sailed into harbour.* **4** [I] to move quickly and easily: *The ball **sailed over** his head and into the goal.*

sail² /seɪl/ noun **1** [C] a large piece of strong cloth fixed to the **mast** (=tall pole) on a boat. It uses the wind to move the boat across water. **2** [singular] a journey by boat or ship

sailboard /'seɪl,bɔːd/ noun [C] **SPORTS** a long board with a **mast** and sail, used for moving across water in **windsurfing**

sailing /'seɪlɪŋ/ noun [U] **SPORTS** the sport or activity of travelling across water in a sailing boat

'sailing ,boat noun [C] a small boat that uses a sail or sails to move along

sailor /'seɪlə/ noun [C] someone who works on a boat or ship, or who sails for pleasure

saint /seɪnt/ noun [C] **1 RELIGION** someone who the Christian Church officially honours after their death because they have lived a very holy life **2** someone who is very kind, patient, and helpful —**sainthood** /'seɪnt,hʊd/ noun [U]

sake¹ /seɪk/ noun
PHRASES **for sb's/sth's sake** or **for the sake of sb/sth** for the benefit or good of someone or something: *He agreed to resign for the sake of the party.* ♦ *We hope for her sake that the wedding goes as planned.*
for the sake of sth for the purpose of doing, getting, or achieving something: *I hope you're not doing this just for the sake of the money.*

sake² /'sɑːki/ noun [U] an alcoholic drink from Japan made from rice

salad /'sæləd/ noun [C/U] **1** a food containing a mixture of raw vegetables such as **lettuce**, tomatoes, and **cucumbers**: *a green salad* **2** food that has been cut into small pieces and mixed together, usually with a sauce, and served cold: *a fruit salad*

salamander /'sælə,mændə/ noun [C] a small amphibian with a long tail that breeds in water —*picture* → REPTILE

salami /sə'lɑːmi/ noun [C/U] a type of **sausage** containing strong spices. It is usually cut into thin pieces and served cold.

salaried /'sælərid/ adj someone who is salaried is paid a fixed amount of money for doing their job, for example each month or year

salary /'sæləri/ (plural **salaries**) noun [C] a fixed amount of money that someone earns each month or each year from their job: *What is her **annual salary**?*

warning signs (black on a yellow background)

danger

harmful or irritant

risk of electric shock

explosive

toxic

corrosive

highly flammable

radioactive

biohazard

oxidizing

laser radiation

non-ionizing radiation

mandatory signs (white on a blue background)

breathing mask
must be worn

ear protection
must be worn

eye protection
must be worn

hand protection
must be worn

safety symbols

sale /seɪl/ noun

1 process of selling	5 total sold
2 instance of selling	6 selling department
3 event for selling	+ PHRASES
4 with lower prices	

1 [C/U] the process of selling goods or services for money: *a ban on **the sale of** arms*

2 [C] a single instance of selling goods or services: *I'm willing to lower the price in order to **make a sale**.*

3 [C] an event at which people meet to buy and sell things: *a second-hand book sale*

4 [C] an event or period of time during which a shop reduces the prices of some of its goods: *Many of the shops have a sale on.*

5 sales [plural] BUSINESS the total number of things that a company sells within a particular period of time, or the money that it earns by selling things: *Sales are up for the month of May.* ♦ *We hope to **increase sales** this year to £50 million.* ♦ *Do you have **the sales figures** yet?*

6 sales [plural] BUSINESS the department of a company that sells its goods or services: *David works in sales.*

PHRASES **for sale** available for people to buy: *That chair is **not for sale**.*

on sale available for people to buy: *Tickets for the performance are on sale at the box office.*

up for sale available for people to buy: *The factory is up for sale.*

'**sales ,force** noun [C] BUSINESS a group of people whose job is to sell goods or services for their company

salesman /'seɪlzmən/ (plural **salesmen** /'seɪlzmən/) noun [C] BUSINESS a man whose job is to sell the products or services of a particular company

salesmanship /'seɪlzmənʃɪp/ noun [U] BUSINESS the skills and methods used to persuade people to buy goods or services

'**sales repre,sentative** or '**sales ,rep** noun [C] BUSINESS someone whose job is to travel to different places in order to sell the products or services of a particular company

saleswoman /'seɪlz,wʊmən/ (plural **saleswomen** /'seɪlz,wɪmɪn/) noun [C] BUSINESS a woman whose job is to sell the products or services of a particular company

salient /'seɪliənt/ adj formal very noticeable or relevant

saline¹ /'seɪlaɪn/ adj containing salt

saline² /'seɪlaɪn/ noun [U] HEALTH a liquid containing salt and water, used especially in medical treatments

salinization /,sælɪmaɪ'zeɪʃ(ə)n/ noun [U] CHEMISTRY, ENVIRONMENT an increase in the amount of salt in the ground over a period of time, especially to levels at which most plants cannot grow

saliva /sə'laɪvə/ noun [U] BIOLOGY the liquid that is produced in the mouth. It makes food easier to chew and swallow, and contains enzymes that help with the digestion of carbohydrates.

salivary amylase /sə,laɪvəri 'æmɪleɪz/ noun [U] BIOLOGY an enzyme that is found in human saliva

salivary gland /sə'laɪvəri ,glænd/ noun [C] ANATOMY a gland that produces saliva in the mouth —*picture* → DIGESTIVE SYSTEM

salivate /'sælɪveɪt/ verb [I] to produce more than the usual amount of saliva, because you see or smell food

salmon /'sæmən/ (plural **salmon**) noun [C/U] a large silver fish with pink flesh that is eaten as food

salmonella /,sælmə'nelə/ noun [C] HEALTH a type of bacterium that is found in food and can cause serious **food poisoning**

salsa /'sælsə/ noun [U] MUSIC a type of Latin-American **dance music** influenced by jazz and rock, or the dance performed to this

salt /sɔːlt/ noun **1** [U] a white substance that is often added to food to improve its flavour. Salt is found naturally in **sea water** and under the ground, and is also present in the fluids of all living things. Its scientific name is **sodium chloride**. **2** [C] CHEMISTRY a chemical compound formed from an acid. Solutions of salts can conduct electricity.

saltation /sælˈteɪʃ(ə)n, sɔːlˈteɪʃ(ə)n/ noun [U] GEOLOGY the carrying of particles of soil or sand in the wind or in running water. The particles rise and fall with bouncing movements.

'salt ,flats noun [plural] GEOGRAPHY a large area of flat land naturally covered with salt

'salt ,marsh noun [C] GEOGRAPHY a flat area of land that is frequently covered with salt water

'salt ,water noun [U] SCIENCE water containing salt, especially water from the sea

saltwater /ˈsɔːltˌwɔːtə/ adj BIOLOGY living in the sea or in water that contains salt ≠ FRESHWATER: *saltwater fish*

salty /ˈsɔːlti/ adj containing salt, or tasting like salt —**saltiness** noun [U]

salutary /ˈsæljʊt(ə)ri/ adj *formal* a salutary experience or warning is one that has a good effect, although it is unpleasant

salute /səˈluːt/ verb **1** [I/T] to put your hand to your head as a formal way of showing respect to a senior officer in the armed forces **2** [T] to express praise or respect for a person or an achievement, especially formally and in public —**salute** noun [C]

salvage /ˈsælvɪdʒ/ verb [T] **1** to save things from a ship or building that has been damaged or destroyed **2** to succeed in achieving something in a situation that has been a failure —**salvage** noun [U]

salvation /sælˈveɪʃ(ə)n/ noun [U] **1** RELIGION according to the Christian religion, the act of being saved by God from evil= REDEMPTION **2** someone or something that helps you in a bad or dangerous situation

the Sal,vation 'Army noun RELIGION an international organization that teaches Christianity and helps people who have problems

samarium /səˈmeəriəm/ noun [U] CHEMISTRY a silvery-grey metallic element in the **lanthanide** group of the periodic table. Chemical symbol: **Sm**

same /seɪm/ adj, adv, pronoun **1 the same** used for saying that a particular person or thing is the one that you are referring to, and not a different one: *We were all staying at the same hotel.* ♦ *My birthday is on the same day as hers.* **2 the same** exactly like another person, thing, or way of doing something: *She did not want to make the same mistake again.* ♦ *The twins looked the same to me – I couldn't tell them apart.* ♦ *Her eyes are the same colour as yours.* **3 the same** used for saying that someone or something has not changed: *The Government's policy has remained the same since 1997.* ♦ *This land looks the same as it did 200 years ago.* **4 the same** used for saying that one number, amount, price etc is equal to another: *The four sides of a square are all the same length.* ♦ *One centimetre is the same as ten millimetres.*

PHRASE **at the same time 1** happening together: *They all stood up at the same time.* **2** used for introducing another fact or opinion that needs to be considered as well as the one that has just been stated: *He wants to work hard for his family, but at the same time he wants to spend time with them.*
→ BOAT

Build your vocabulary: words you can use instead of same
- **alike** almost the same
- **constant** remaining at the same level
- **equal/equivalent** at the same level, or the same in quality or quantity
- **identical** exactly the same, with no differences
- **similar** almost the same, but with small differences

'same-,sex adj used for referring to sexual relationships involving either two men or two women

samosa /səˈməʊsə/ noun [C] an Indian food made with cooked meat or vegetables wrapped in thin **pastry** and cooked in oil

sample¹ /ˈsɑːmp(ə)l/ noun [C] **1** an example or small amount of something that shows you what all of it is like: *We had to bring some samples of our work to the interview.* **2** a small amount of a substance that is used for scientific or medical tests: *Tests were performed on hair and blood samples.* ♦ *Researchers are taking samples of the air close to the factory.* **3** a group of people that is used for getting information about a larger group, or about the whole population: *The study took a sample of 100 students from 3 schools.* **4** MUSIC a short piece of music that is copied from a record, and then used again as part of a new piece of music

sample² /ˈsɑːmp(ə)l/ verb [T] **1** to taste a small amount of food or drink in order to see what it is like: *They let us sample some of the wine.* **2** to try doing a new activity for a time: *Here you can relax and sample life in this island paradise.* **3** to use a group of people in order to get information about a larger group or about the whole population **4** MUSIC to copy a short piece of music from a record, then use it again as part of a new piece of music. This activity is called **sampling**.

sanatorium /ˌsænəˈtɔːriəm/ noun [C] HEALTH a hospital where people who have had a serious illness go so that doctors can take care of them until they get better

sanctify /ˈsæŋktɪfaɪ/ (**sanctifies, sanctifying, sanctified**) verb [T] RELIGION to make someone or something holy in a religious ceremony

sanction¹ /ˈsæŋkʃ(ə)n/ noun **1** [C] an official order to stop communication, trade etc with a country that has broken international law: *economic sanctions* ♦ *The Council wanted to impose sanctions* (=start to use them) *against the countries involved in the dispute.* **2** [U] official permission for taking action: *War was declared without the sanction of the United Nations.* **3** [C] a punishment for breaking a rule

sanction² /ˈsæŋkʃ(ə)n/ verb [T] *formal* to give approval or permission for something

sanctity /ˈsæŋktəti/ noun [U] RELIGION the quality of being holy or of having special religious importance

sanctuary /ˈsæŋktʃuəri/ (plural **sanctuaries**) noun **1** [C/U] a place that provides official protection for someone: *Refugees sought sanctuary in Thailand.* **2** [C] ENVIRONMENT an area where animals can live in a natural environment protected from people

sand¹ /sænd/ noun **1** [U] GEOLOGY a pale brown substance that forms a beach or covers a desert, formed from very small pieces of rock: *The children were playing in the sand.* ♦ *a grain of sand* **2 sands** [plural] GEOGRAPHY an area of sand

sand² /sænd/ or **,sand 'down** verb [T] to make something such as wood very smooth by rubbing it with **sandpaper**

sandal /'sænd(ə)l/ noun [C] a light shoe that is partly open on top and does not cover your heel or toes

sandalwood /'sænd(ə)l,wʊd/ noun [C] a tree with a pleasant-smelling wood, grown in India for its oil and used for making soap and perfume

sandbag /'sæn(d),bæg/ noun [C] a bag that is filled with sand, used for protecting a place from floods or explosions

sandbank /'sæn(d),bæŋk/ noun [C] GEOGRAPHY an area of sand that is formed in, or at the edge of, a river or sea

'**sand ,bar** noun [C] GEOGRAPHY a raised area of sand in a river or sea that is just below the surface of the water, or that sticks out above it —*picture* → LAGOON

'**sand-,cast** verb [T] TECHNOLOGY to **cast** an object from **molten** (=melted) metal using a mould made of sand

'**sand ,dune** noun [C] GEOGRAPHY a hill of sand that is formed by the wind in a desert or near a beach

'**sand ,fly** noun [C] a small fly that lives in warm regions of Asia, Africa, and southern Europe. It can spread disease when it bites.

sandpaper /'sæn(d),peɪpə/ noun [U] strong paper with a rough surface that you rub against wood or metal to make it smooth —**sandpaper** verb [T]

sandstone /'sæn(d),stəʊn/ noun [C] GEOLOGY a type of stone that is made mainly of grains of **quartz** and other minerals. It is a type of sedimentary rock, and can be red, yellow, grey, or brown.

sandstorm /'sæn(d),stɔ:m/ noun [C] GEOGRAPHY a strong wind in the desert in which clouds of sand are blown into the air

sandwich /'sæn(d)wɪdʒ, 'sæn(d)wɪtʃ/ noun [C] two pieces of bread with a layer of food such as meat, cheese, or egg between them: *a cheese sandwich* ♦ *I usually just* **have a sandwich** *for lunch.*

'**sandwich ,course** noun [C] EDUCATION an educational course in which students have practical experience of the subject between periods of study

sandy /'sændi/ adj **1** covered in sand **2** GEOGRAPHY, AGRICULTURE sandy soil contains a lot of sand, so that water passes through it very easily

sane /seɪn/ adj **1** able to think, speak, and behave in a reasonable and normal way ≠ INSANE **2** a sane action or decision is a sensible one

sang /sæŋ/ the past tense of **sing**

sanitary /'sænɪt(ə)ri/ adj HEALTH **1** relating to people's health, especially to the system of supplying water and dealing with human waste **2** keeping things healthy and clean

'**sanitary ,towel** or '**sanitary ,pad** noun [C] a thick band of soft material that women put inside their underwear during **menstruation**

sanitation /,sænɪ'teɪʃ(ə)n/ noun [U] HEALTH conditions and processes relating to people's health, especially the systems that supply water and deal with human waste

sanity /'sænəti/ noun [U] the ability to think and speak in a reasonable way and to behave normally: *I was beginning to doubt my own sanity* (=think I was possibly mentally ill).

sank /sæŋk/ the past tense of **sink**

Santa Claus /'sæntə ,klɔ:z/ or **Santa** /'sæntə/ an imaginary man with a long white beard and a red suit who brings presents for children at Christmas = FATHER CHRISTMAS

sap[1] /sæp/ noun [U] a sticky substance that is found in plants and trees

sap[2] /sæp/ (**saps**, **sapping**, **sapped**) verb [T] to make something become weak: *Years of illness had sapped his strength.*

sapling /'sæplɪŋ/ noun [C] a young tree

saponification /sə,pɒnɪfɪ'keɪʃ(ə)n/ noun [U] CHEMISTRY the process of making soap, by heating fat or oil with an alkali such as **sodium hydroxide**

sapphire /'sæfaɪə/ noun [C/U] a clear blue jewel

saprophyte /'sæprəʊ,faɪt/ noun [C] BIOLOGY an organism, especially a fungus or bacterium, that lives on and gets its food from dead organisms or decaying organic matter —**saprophytic** /,sæprəʊ'fɪtɪk/ adj, **saprophytism** noun [U]

sarcasm /'sɑ:kæz(ə)m/ noun [U] the activity of saying or writing the opposite of what you mean, in order to make someone feel stupid or to show them that you are angry: *'Fascinating,' said Sheila, her voice heavy with sarcasm.*

sarcastic /sɑ:'kæstɪk/ adj using sarcasm —**sarcastically** /sɑ:'kæstɪkli/ adv

sarcoma /sɑ:'kəʊmə/ noun [C] HEALTH a group of **diseased** cells in the body that can grow and spread very quickly and will cause serious illness or death if it is not removed. It is a type of cancer.

sardine /sɑ:'di:n/ noun [C] a small silver fish that is eaten as food

sardonic /sɑ:'dɒnɪk/ adj showing a lack of respect for what someone has said or done

sari /'sɑ:ri/ noun [C] a very long wide piece of cloth that women in South Asia wrap around their bodies to make a long dress

sarin /'sɑ:rɪn/ noun [U] CHEMISTRY a poisonous gas used as a weapon by some **terrorists**

SARS /sɑ:z/ noun [U] HEALTH severe acute respiratory syndrome: a serious illness that affects the chest. It was first reported in Asia in 2003.

sash /sæʃ/ noun [C] **1** a long piece of cloth that is worn around the waist or over one shoulder and across the chest, for example in an official ceremony **2** CONSTRUCTION a piece of glass in a wooden frame that forms part of a window

,**sash 'window** noun [C] CONSTRUCTION a window made with two panes of glass, each in a separate frame. One frame slides vertically past the other when the window is opened or closed.

sat /sæt/ the past tense and past participle of **sit**

Sat. abbrev Saturday

Satan /'seɪt(ə)n/ RELIGION the most powerful evil spirit in many religions such as Christianity and Islam = DEVIL

satanic /sə'tænɪk/ adj **1** RELIGION involving the worship of Satan **2** very evil and cruel

satay /'sæteɪ/ noun [U] an Indonesian or Malaysian meal that consists of meat or fish that is cooked on long thin sticks over a fire and usually served with **peanut** sauce

satchel /'sætʃ(ə)l/ noun [C] a bag with a long **strap** that goes over your shoulder, used for carrying school books

satellite /'sætəlaɪt/ noun **1** [C] ASTRONOMY an object that is sent into space to travel round the Earth in order to receive and send information: *a communications satellite* ♦ *We have pictures of the disaster live* **via satellite** (=by satellite). **2** [C] ASTRONOMY a natural object such as a moon that moves around a planet **3** [C] a country, city, or organization that depends on or is controlled by a larger, more powerful one **4** [U] **satellite television**

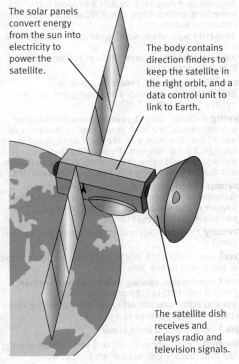

The solar panels convert energy from the sun into electricity to power the satellite.

The body contains direction finders to keep the satellite in the right orbit, and a data control unit to link to Earth.

The satellite dish receives and relays radio and television signals.

communications satellite

'satellite ,dish noun [C] a piece of equipment in the shape of a dish that receives signals from a satellite, especially one that allows you to watch satellite television —*picture* → SATELLITE

'satellite ,telephone noun [U] a mobile phone that can send voice messages over extremely long distances, using connections to communications satellites

,satellite 'television or **,satellite T'V** noun [U] television programmes that are sent to your television by satellite

satin /'sætɪn/ noun [U] a very smooth shiny cloth that is used for making expensive clothes

satire /'sætaɪə/ noun **ARTS, LITERATURE 1** [U] the use of humour to criticize someone or something and make them seem silly **2** [C] a play, book, film etc that uses this humour

satirical /sə'tɪrɪk(ə)l/ adj **ARTS, LITERATURE** using humour to criticize people or things and make them seem silly —**satirically** /sə'tɪrɪkli/ adv

satisfaction /,sætɪs'fækʃ(ə)n/ noun **1** [U] the feeling of pleasure that you get when you achieve or obtain something that you want ≠ DISSATISFACTION: *He expressed* **satisfaction with** *the results.* ♦ *At least we had the* **satisfaction of** *knowing we had done our best.* ♦ *I* **get** *a lot of* **satisfaction from** *my work.* **2** [C] something that gives you this feeling: *Being a parent is one of the great satisfactions in life.* **3** [U] *formal* the action of providing something that someone wants or needs

PHRASE **to sb's satisfaction** in the way that a particular

person likes or wants: *The problem was resolved to everyone's satisfaction.*

satisfactory /,sætɪs'fækt(ə)ri/ adj **1** good enough ≠ UNSATISFACTORY: *His work is far from satisfactory.* ♦ *I have still not received a satisfactory answer to my question.* ♦ *The patient was in a satisfactory condition.* **2** enjoyable and pleasing: *a satisfactory outcome* ♦ *This new arrangement proved* **highly satisfactory** *to us all.* —**satisfactorily** adv

satisfied /'sætɪsfaɪd/ adj **1** pleased with what has happened, or with what you have achieved: *a satisfied customer* ♦ *The President declared himself* **satisfied with** *the progress of the talks.* **2** if you are satisfied that something is true or correct, you do not need any more proof: *I am satisfied that they are doing all they can.*

satisfy /'sætɪsfaɪ/ (**satisfies, satisfying, satisfied**) verb

1 give sb what they want	4 convince sb sth is true
2 provide what is needed	5 in maths
3 meet requirements	

1 [T] to please someone by giving them something that they want or need: *an agreement that is unlikely to satisfy environmental campaigners*
2 [I/T] to provide what is needed or wanted: *There's nothing like a cold drink to satisfy your thirst.* ♦ *I just want to satisfy my curiosity – why did he do it?*
3 [T] to have all the qualities or features that are necessary according to a rule, condition, or standard: *Students must* **satisfy** *all* **requirements** *to be accepted on the course.*
4 [T] to provide someone with the evidence that they need in order to be certain that something is true = CONVINCE: *The prosecution has to satisfy the jury that the defendant is guilty.*
5 [T] MATHS if a number or group of numbers satisfies an equation, it is a correct solution to it

satisfying /'sætɪs,faɪɪŋ/ adj making you feel pleased or happy because you have got what you want or need: *a satisfying result* ♦ *a satisfying meal*

satnav /'sæt,næv/ noun [U] satellite navigation: a system for finding the best way to a place using information from satellites. It is often found in cars.

satsuma /sæt'su:mə/ noun [C] a fruit similar to a small orange, but with a loose skin and often without seeds

saturate /'sætʃəreɪt/ verb [T] **1** to make something completely wet **2** to fill something completely with a large number of things or a large amount of something **3** CHEMISTRY to put as much of a **solute** (=a solid that dissolves) into a chemical solution as you possibly can —**saturation** /,sætʃə'reɪʃ(ə)n/ noun [U]

saturated /'sætʃə,reɪtɪd/ adj **1** very wet **2** completely filled with things or people **3** CHEMISTRY a chemical solution that is saturated contains as much of a **solute** (=a solid that dissolves) as is possible

,saturated 'fat noun [C/U] CHEMISTRY, HEALTH fat from animal food such as meat or milk whose **fatty acids** do not contain any **double bonds**. Eating too much saturated fat can lead to high levels of **cholesterol** in the blood. → POLYUNSATURATED FAT, UNSATURATED FAT

satu'ration ,point noun [C] CHEMISTRY the point at which a chemical solution contains as much of a solid as is possible

Saturday /'sætədeɪ/ noun [C/U] the day after Friday and before Sunday: *I'm looking forward to the match* **next Saturday**. ♦ *See you* **on Saturday**. ♦ *I usually go for a walk* **on Saturdays** (=every Saturday).

Saturn /'sætɜːn, 'sæt(ə)n/ **ASTRONOMY** the planet that is sixth furthest from the Sun, between Jupiter and Uranus. Saturn is surrounded by large rings. —*picture* → SOLAR SYSTEM

sauce /sɔːs/ noun [C/U] a liquid food that you put on other foods to give them a particular flavour: *tomato sauce* ♦ *ice cream and chocolate sauce*

saucepan /'sɔːspən/ noun [C] a round deep metal container with a long handle. It is used for cooking food on a cooker.

saucer /'sɔːsə/ noun [C] a small round flat dish that you put a cup on

saunter /'sɔːntə/ verb [I] to walk in a slow relaxed way —**saunter** noun [C]

sausage /'sɒsɪdʒ/ noun [C/U] a food that consists of a tube of skin containing meat mixed with spices

savage¹ /'sævɪdʒ/ adj **1** extremely violent: *a savage attack* **2** extremely severe: *savage cuts in public services* —**savagely** adv

savage² /'sævɪdʒ/ verb [T] **1** to criticize someone or something severely **2** if an animal savages someone, it attacks them and injures or kills them

savagery /'sævɪdʒ(ə)ri/ noun [U] extremely violent behaviour

savannah or **savanna** /sə'vænə/ noun [C/U] **GEOGRAPHY** a large flat area of land covered with grass in a warm part of the world

save¹ /seɪv/ verb

1 help sb/sth avoid harm	6 keep sth for sb
2 help sb avoid sth	7 collect things
3 avoid using sth	8 in computing
4 put money in bank	9 in sport
5 keep sth for future	+ PHRASAL VERBS

1 [T] to make it possible for someone or something to avoid danger, harm, injury etc: *campaigns to save the planet* ♦ *A cure for cancer would save thousands of lives each year.* ♦ *Nothing can save this company from bankruptcy.*

2 [T] to make it possible for someone to avoid doing something: *Setting down clear rules from the start will save arguments later on.* ♦ *If you could tell her, that would save me phoning her.*

3 [T] to avoid using something such as money, time, or energy, or to use less of it: *You can save five dollars if you buy your tickets before Saturday.* ♦ *Travelling by plane is more expensive, but it saves time.* ♦ *These politicians argue their plan will save the government money in the future.*

4 [I/T] to regularly put money in a bank, or to invest it so that you can use it later: *I've managed to save a few dollars from my wages.* ♦ *He doesn't earn enough money to save for retirement.* ♦ *We've been saving to buy a new car.*

5 [T] to keep or store something so that you can use it in the future: *Save some energy for the end of the race.* ♦ *Let's have one piece of cake now and save the rest for later.*

6 [T] to keep something for someone by making sure that other people do not take it: *Would you please save a place in the queue for me?* ♦ *Save me some dinner and I'll have it when I get in.*

7 [T] to collect a set of things and keep them for a particular purpose: *Save eight tokens and you can get one of these amazing pens!*

8 [I/T] **COMPUTING** to make a computer keep information that you have put into it: *Where did you save the file you were working on?* ♦ *It's a good idea to save frequently.*

9 [I/T] **SPORTS** if a goalkeeper saves a ball in a sport

such as football, they prevent the ball from going into the net

PHRASAL VERBS ˌsave on sth **1** to spend less money on something than you would normally: *light bulbs that help you save on electricity bills* **2** to avoid using something, or to use less of it: *Keep your showers short to save on water.*

ˌsave (sth) 'up *same as* **save¹** sense 4: *I'm saving up for a new school bag.*

ˌsave 'up sth *same as* **save¹** sense 7: *You save up the tokens to get a prize.*

save² /seɪv/ noun [C] **SPORTS** an action by a **goalkeeper** that prevents a ball from going into the net in a sport such as football

saving /'seɪvɪŋ/ noun **1** **savings** [plural] money that you have saved in a bank or invested so that you can use it later: *The money for the flight came out of my savings.* **2** [C] an amount of something that you manage to avoid using or spending: *At only 25 dollars, this represents a saving of 5 dollars on the usual fee.*

saviour /'seɪvjə/ noun **1** [C] someone who saves someone or something from trouble or danger **2 the Saviour** or **Our Saviour** a name that Christians sometimes use for Jesus Christ

savoury /'seɪvəri/ adj tasting of salt or spices and not sweet

saw¹ /sɔː/ noun [C] a tool that is used for cutting wood or metal —*picture* → TOOL

saw² /sɔː/ (**saws**, **sawing**, **sawed**, **sawed** or **sawn** /sɔːn/) verb [I/T] to cut something with a saw

PHRASAL VERB ˌsaw sth 'off to remove something by cutting through it with a saw or knife

saw³ /sɔː/ the past tense of **see**

sawdust /'sɔːˌdʌst/ noun [U] very small pieces of wood like dust that are produced when you cut wood

sawmill /'sɔːˌmɪl/ noun [C] a building where wood is cut into boards using machines

sawn /sɔːn/ a past participle of **saw²**

sax /sæks/ noun [C] **MUSIC** *informal* a **saxophone**

saxophone /'sæksəˌfəʊn/ noun [C] **MUSIC** a musical instrument consisting of a long curved metal tube that you play by blowing into it as you press its keys with your fingers —*picture* → MUSICAL INSTRUMENT —**saxophonist** /sæk'spfənɪst/ noun [C]

say¹ /seɪ/ (**says** /sez/, **saying**, **said** /sed/) verb

1 express with words	4 show sth
2 have opinion	5 imagine sth
3 give information	+ PHRASES

1 [I/T] to express something using words: *She said that she liked dancing.* ♦ *Did he say who called?* ♦ *Tell me what he said to you.* ♦ *'Pleased to meet you,' he said with a smile.* ♦ *'When's he coming back?' 'He didn't say.'* ♦ *The committee said yes* (=gave permission), *so we can go ahead.* ♦ *I then said goodbye and left.*

2 [T] to think something, or to have a particular opinion: *He always said you'd be rich and famous one day.* ♦ *I think we should stop now. What do you say?* ♦ *'Will she meet the deadline?' 'I would say so* (=think it is likely).*'* ♦ *She is said to have great talent as an artist.*

3 [T] to give information or orders in writing, numbers, pictures etc: *My watch says quarter to twelve.* ♦ *Her letter says she's arriving at midday.* ♦ *The rules say that we need a two-thirds majority to win.* ♦ *Does it say on the box how much it costs?*

4 [T] to show indirectly what someone or something is like: *This problem says something about the way the company is run.*

5 [T] to imagine what will happen in a particular

situation: *Say you get 200 dollars for the car – you'll still need another hundred.*

PHRASES **go without saying (that)** to be completely obvious or true: *It goes without saying that I'm sorry.*
say sth to yourself to think something: *'This is the real thing,' he said to himself.*
to say the least used for saying that you could have expressed something in a much stronger way: *I found the flight rather uncomfortable, to say the least.*

- You **say** something to someone. **Say** is followed by the words that someone uses, or by reported speech: *She said no to me.* ♦ *'Hello,' he said.* ♦ *I said that I was cold.*
- You **tell** someone something when you give them information or an instruction. **Tell** is usually followed by the person who is spoken to: *'It's time to go,' he told us.* ♦ *I told Kate to shut up.*
- **Speak** and **talk** both mean to say something. They are not usually followed by an object: *Don't interrupt me when I'm speaking.* ♦ *Jade and Adele were talking in the corner.*

say² /seɪ/ noun [singular/U] the right to give your opinion and be involved in a discussion about something: *The junior staff **had no say in** this decision.*

saying /ˈseɪɪŋ/ noun [C] a well-known statement about what often happens in life

scab /skæb/ noun [C] **HEALTH** a hard layer of dried blood that forms on a cut on your skin

scabies /ˈskeɪbiːz/ noun [U] **HEALTH** a highly infectious skin disease caused by a very small parasite that lives in the skin of humans, causing severe **itching**

scaffold /ˈskæfəʊld/ noun [C] **1 CONSTRUCTION** a structure consisting of poles and boards on the outside of a building. People stand on it when they are working on the building. **2** a structure on which criminals were killed in the past by being **hanged** or **beheaded**

scaffolding /ˈskæfəʊldɪŋ/ noun [U] **CONSTRUCTION** poles and boards used for making a scaffold on the outside of a building

scalar /ˈskeɪlə/ adj **MATHS** used for describing a quantity that has size but no direction, for example area

scald /skɔːld/ verb [T] to burn your skin with very hot liquid or steam —**scald** noun [C]

scalding /ˈskɔːldɪŋ/ adj very hot

scale¹ /skeɪl/ noun

1 size/rate/level	5 for weighing
2 range	6 musical notes
3 set of marks	7 hard piece of skin
4 of map/model	+ PHRASE

1 [singular/U] the size, rate, or level of something: *Is the Government aware of **the scale of** the problem* (=are they aware of how big it is)*?*
2 [C] a range of numbers or amounts that form a system for separating things into different groups: *The rich are at the top of the **social scale**.* ♦ *We were told to rate the films **on a scale of** 1 to 10.*
3 [C] **MATHS, SCIENCE** a set of marks on a piece of equipment or a drawing, used for measuring something: *the vertical scale on the graph*
4 [C/U] **MATHS** the relationship between the actual distance or size of something and how it is shown on a map or in a drawing or model: *This map has a **scale of** 1:20,000.*
5 **scales** [plural] a piece of equipment that you use for weighing people or things: *a set of scales*
6 [C] **MUSIC** a series of musical notes in a fixed order from the lowest to the highest or the highest to the

lowest: *She was **practising scales** on her new piano.* —*picture* → MUSIC
7 [C] **BIOLOGY** one of the small hard flat pieces of skin on the body of a fish, snake, or similar animal —*picture* → REPTILE

PHRASE **to scale** with all the parts the right size in relation to each other

scale² /skeɪl/ verb [T] to climb to or over the top of a mountain, wall etc

ˈscale ˌfactor noun [C] **TECHNOLOGY** the number representing the amount by which the size of a shape or object is made larger or smaller when someone is drawing it to scale

scalene triangle /ˌskeɪliːn ˈtraɪæŋg(ə)l/ noun [C] **MATHS** a shape with three angles and three straight sides of different lengths

scallop /ˈskɒləp, ˈskæləp/ noun [C] a large sea mollusc with a shell shaped like a **fan**. Scallops are eaten as food in many countries.

scalp /skælp/ noun [C] the skin under the hair on the head

scalpel /ˈskælp(ə)l/ noun [C] **HEALTH** a small very sharp knife. Scalpels are used in medical operations or in laboratories, for example. —*picture* → LABORATORY

scaly /ˈskeɪli/ adj **1** a scaly animal has skin like that of a fish or a snake **2** scaly skin is so dry that small pieces of it fall off

scamper /ˈskæmpə/ verb [I] to move quickly with small light steps

scan¹ /skæn/ (**scans, scanning, scanned**) verb

1 look carefully at	4 photograph inside of
2 read quickly	sth
3 copy with equipment	5 about poetry

1 [T] to look at something very carefully in order to see a particular person or thing: *Ella scanned the crowd for any sign of Geoff.*
2 [I/T] to read something very quickly in order to get a general idea of its meaning or to find particular information
3 [I/T] **COMPUTING** to copy and store information in **digital** form using computer equipment
4 [T] **HEALTH** to use a piece of equipment to produce a picture of the inside of a part of the body
5 [I] **LITERATURE** if poetry scans, it has a regular rhythm

scan² /skæn/ noun [C] **HEALTH** a medical test that uses a piece of equipment to produce a picture of the inside of the body

scandal /ˈskænd(ə)l/ noun **1** [C/U] a situation in which people behave in a dishonest or immoral way that shocks people: *a sex scandal* **2** [U] talk or reports in the newspapers or on television about shocking behaviour: *the endless stream of scandal offered by the newspapers*

scandalize /ˈskændəlaɪz/ verb [T] to do something that shocks someone

scandalous /ˈskændələs/ adj shocking and immoral or dishonest

scandium /ˈskændiəm/ noun [U] **CHEMISTRY** a silvery-white metallic element that is found in **rare-earth** ores. Chemical symbol: **Sc**

scanner /ˈskænə/ noun [C] **1 COMPUTING** a piece of equipment that you use for copying a picture or document into a computer —*picture* → COMPUTER **2 HEALTH** a piece of equipment used for producing a picture of the inside of a part of someone's body for a medical examination

scansion /ˈskænʃ(ə)n/ noun [U] **LITERATURE** the regular pattern of syllables in a poem

scapegoat /ˈskeɪpɡəʊt/ noun [C] someone who is blamed for something that is not their fault

scapula /ˈskæpjʊlə/ (plural **scapulae** /ˈskæpjʊli/ or **scapulas**) noun [C] **ANATOMY** one of the two bones on the sides of the upper back —*picture* → SKELETON

scar¹ /skɑː/ noun [C] **1** a permanent mark on your skin where you have been injured: *He has a scar under his left eye.* **2** a permanent negative effect on someone's mind, caused by an unpleasant experience: *She bore the scars of an unhappy childhood.*

scar² /skɑː/ (**scars, scarring, scarred**) verb [T] **1** to leave a permanent mark on someone's skin as the result of an injury **2** if an unpleasant experience scars someone, it has a permanent negative effect on the way that they think and live

scarab /ˈskærəb/ noun [C] a large black beetle that ancient Egyptians believed was holy

scarce /skeəs/ adj if something is scarce, there is not very much of it ≠ ABUNDANT: *Fresh water and medicines were scarce in the disaster area.*

scarcely /ˈskeəsli/ adv **1** almost not, or almost none = BARELY, HARDLY: *There was scarcely any traffic.* **2** only just= BARELY: *We had scarcely driven a mile when the car broke down.* **3** used for showing that something is certainly not true or possible= HARDLY: *I can scarcely refuse to help after all he's done for me.*

scarcity /ˈskeəsəti/ noun [singular/U] a situation in which there is not enough of something for the people who want or need it= SHORTAGE ≠ ABUNDANCE

scare¹ /skeə/ verb **1** [T] to make someone feel frightened: *I'm sorry, I didn't mean to scare you.* **2** [I] to become frightened

scare² /skeə/ noun [C] **1** a situation that makes people suddenly feel frightened or worried about something: *a bomb scare* **2** a sudden feeling of fear: *It gave me quite a scare when the cat jumped on me.*

scarecrow /ˈskeəˌkrəʊ/ noun [C] **AGRICULTURE** an object in the shape of a person that farmers put in their fields to frighten birds away

scared /skeəd/ adj frightened, or worried: *I'm scared I'll fail all my exams.* ♦ *I'm scared stiff* (=extremely scared) *of having the operation.* ♦ *Louise is scared of flying.*

scarf /skɑːf/ (plural **scarves** /skɑːvz/) noun [C] a piece of cloth that you wear round your neck or head

scarlet /ˈskɑːlət/ adj bright red in colour —**scarlet** noun [U]

scarlet ˈfever noun [U] **HEALTH** a disease caused by bacteria that mainly affects children. It causes a fever, sore throat, and red spots on the skin.

scarp /skɑːp/ noun [C] **GEOGRAPHY** a steep slope or cliff

scarves /skɑːvz/ the plural of **scarf**

scary /ˈskeəri/ (**scarier, scariest**) adj frightening: *a scary story*

scathing /ˈskeɪðɪŋ/ adj criticizing someone or something in a very strong way

scatter /ˈskætə/ verb **1** [T] to throw or drop things so that they spread over an area **2** [I/T] if a group of people or animals scatter, or if something scatters them, they suddenly move away in different directions

ˈscatter ˌdiagram noun [C] **MATHS** a graph that shows numbers or amounts as points. A straight line is drawn

through as many points as possible in order to show the general pattern. —*picture* → CHART

scattered /ˈskætəd/ adj **1** spread over a large area: *My relatives are scattered all over the country.* **2** happening or existing in only a few places: *scattered showers*

scattering /ˈskætərɪŋ/ noun [C] a small number of people or things that are spread over a large area

ˈscatter ˌplot noun [C] **MATHS** a scatter diagram

scavenge /ˈskævɪndʒ/ verb [I/T] **1** if an animal scavenges, it eats anything that it can find **2** to search through things that other people have thrown away in order to see if there is anything that you want —**scavenger** noun [C]

scenario /səˈnɑːriəʊ/ (plural **scenarios**) noun [C] a situation that could possibly happen: *The most likely scenario is that Brooks will resign.* ♦ *According to the worst-case scenario, global temperatures could rise by 8 degrees in the next 30 years.*

scene /siːn/ noun [C] **1** **ARTS** a part of a play, book, film etc in which events happen in the same place or period of time: *a love scene* ♦ *the opening scene* of the play **2** a view that you can see in a picture or from the place where you are: *She stood in the doorway surveying the scene.* ♦ *paintings that depict scenes of village life* **3** a place where something happens: *the scene of the accident* ♦ *The paramedics will be at the scene within a few minutes.* **4** a particular interest or activity, and the people and places that are involved in it: *an important figure on the political scene* ♦ *the music scene*

PHRASES **behind the scenes** secretly: *These agreements have been drafted by officials behind the scenes.*
set the scene to create the conditions that make it possible for an event to happen: *These findings have set the scene for further debate on the system.*

scenery /ˈsiːnəri/ noun [U] **1** natural things such as trees, hills, and lakes that you can see in a particular place: *Switzerland has some spectacular scenery.* **2** **ARTS** the furniture and painted background on a theatre stage

scenic /ˈsiːnɪk/ adj providing beautiful views of nature

ˌscenic ˈrailway noun [C] **TOURISM** a very small railway that runs through artificial countryside, especially in an **amusement park**

scent¹ /sent/ noun **1** [C] a pleasant smell: *a fruit with a rich flavour and scent* **2** [C/U] a liquid that women put on their skin to make themselves smell nice = FRAGRANCE, PERFUME **3** [C/U] the smell that an animal or person has, that some animals can follow

scent² /sent/ verb [T] if an animal scents someone or something, it knows that they are there because of their smell

scented /ˈsentɪd/ adj having a pleasant smell

sceptic /ˈskeptɪk/ noun [C] someone who has doubts about things that other people think are true or right

sceptical /ˈskeptɪk(ə)l/ adj having doubts about something that other people think is true or right: *I'm very sceptical about the results of the survey.*

scepticism /ˈskeptɪˌsɪz(ə)m/ noun [U] doubts that someone has about something that other people think is true or right

sceptre /ˈseptə/ noun [C] a decorated rod that a king or queen carries at ceremonies

schedule¹ /ˈʃedjuːl/ noun [C] a plan of activities or events and when they will happen= TIMETABLE: *What's on your schedule today?* ♦ *Our MP has a very busy schedule.* ♦ *We're shooting the film on a very tight*

schedule (=with many things to do in a short time). ♦ *a project completed **ahead of schedule*** (=before the time that was planned)

schedule² /'ʃedjuːl/ verb [T] to plan for something to happen at a particular time= TIMETABLE: *Let's **schedule** another meeting **for** July.* ♦ *The exhibition **is scheduled to** run from January until March.*

scheduled /'ʃedjuːld/ adj planned to happen at a particular time, or at the same time each day, week etc: *a scheduled lecture* ♦ *a scheduled flight*

scheme¹ /skiːm/ noun [C] **1** a plan that is developed by a government or large organization in order to provide a particular service for people: *a training scheme* ♦ *The proposed scheme should solve the parking problem.* **2** a plan for achieving something, especially something illegal or dishonest: *a crazy money-making scheme*

scheme² /skiːm/ verb [I] to make secret plans to achieve something, especially in an illegal or dishonest way= PLOT: *She's convinced that they're **scheming against** her.* —**schemer** noun [C], **scheming** adj

scherzo /'skeətsəʊ/ noun [C] **MUSIC** a piece of music that is quick and lively

schism /'skɪz(ə)m, 'sɪz(ə)m/ noun [C/U] *formal* an occasion when one group divides into two groups because of a disagreement= SPLIT

schistosomiasis /ˌʃɪstəsəʊ'maɪəsɪs/ noun [U] **HEALTH** a serious tropical disease, also called **bilharzia**

schizogony /skɪt'sɒgəni, skɪ'zɒgəni/ noun [U] **BIOLOGY** a form of **asexual reproduction** that is found in some protozoans. It enables some parasites, including the malaria parasite, to multiply rapidly in the body of an infected **host**.

schizoid /'skɪtsɔɪd/ adj **HEALTH** typical of schizophrenia

schizophrenia /ˌskɪtsəʊ'friːniə/ noun [U] **HEALTH** a serious mental illness in which the way that someone thinks and feels is not connected with what is really happening

schizophrenic /ˌskɪtsəʊ'frenɪk/ adj **HEALTH** relating to schizophrenia, or affected by it —**schizophrenic** noun [C]

scholar /'skɒlə/ noun [C] **1** someone who studies a particular subject and knows a lot about it, especially a subject that is not scientific **2** **EDUCATION** someone who is given a scholarship to study at a particular school or university

scholarship /'skɒləʃɪp/ noun **1** [C] **EDUCATION** an amount of money that an organization gives to someone so that they can study at a particular school or university: *Sophie was awarded a scholarship to attend Boston University.* **2** [U] serious formal study and the knowledge that you get from it: *a work of great scholarship*

scholastic /skə'læstɪk/ adj **EDUCATION** *formal* connected with schools, teaching, or studying = ACADEMIC, EDUCATIONAL

school /skuːl/ noun

1 place of learning	5 where skill taught
2 period of education	6 group of artists
3 everyone in school	7 large group of fish etc
4 department	+ PHRASE

1 [C/U] **EDUCATION** a place where children go to be taught, or the time during the day when they are there: *the biggest school in the city* ♦ *The kids will be **at school***

until 3.00 today. ♦ *It's time to **go to school**.* ♦ *They go swimming **after school**.*
2 [U] **EDUCATION** the situation or period of years when you receive your education: *My younger sister is still **at school**.* ♦ *I left **school** when I was fifteen.*
3 [singular] **EDUCATION** all the students and staff at a school: *The whole school assembled in the hall.*
4 [C/U] **EDUCATION** a university department or a college that teaches a particular subject: *medical school* ♦ *the **School of** Management*
5 [C/U] a private institution that teaches a particular skill: *a driving school*
6 [C] **ARTS, LITERATURE** a group of writers, artists etc whose work or ideas are similar: *the Impressionist school of painting*
7 [C] **BIOLOGY** a large group of fish or sea mammals
PHRASE **school of thought** a way of thinking about a particular subject or idea that is shared by a group of people

schoolboy /'skuːlbɔɪ/ noun [C] **EDUCATION** a boy who goes to school

schoolchild /'skuːltʃaɪld/ (plural **schoolchildren** /'skuːltʃɪldrən/) noun [C] **EDUCATION** a child who goes to school

schooldays /'skuːldeɪz/ noun [plural] **EDUCATION** the time in your life when you go to school

schoolgirl /'skuːlgɜːl/ noun [C] **EDUCATION** a girl who goes to school

schooling /'skuːlɪŋ/ noun [U] **EDUCATION** the education that you get at school

school-leaver /'skuːl ˌliːvə/ noun [C] someone who has just left school and is looking for a job

ˌschool 'leaving examiˌnation noun [C] **EDUCATION** an examination taken by students at the end of their studies at a **secondary** school

schoolmaster /'skuːlˌmɑːstə/ noun [C] **EDUCATION** *old-fashioned* a man who teaches in a school

schoolmistress /'skuːlˌmɪstrəs/ noun [C] **EDUCATION** *old-fashioned* a woman who teaches in a school

ˈschool reˌfusal noun [U] **EDUCATION** fear of going to school

schoolteacher /'skuːlˌtiːtʃə/ noun [C] **EDUCATION** a teacher who works in a school

schoolwork /'skuːlwɜːk/ noun [U] **EDUCATION** work that students do for school or in school classes

ˈschool ˌyear noun [C] **EDUCATION** the period of the year when students go to school

schooner /'skuːnə/ noun [C] a sailing ship with at least two **masts** (=tall poles supporting the sails)

schwa /ʃwɑː/ noun [C] **LANGUAGE** a vowel sound used in **unstressed** syllables, for example the sound of 'a' in 'above'. Its symbol in this dictionary is /ə/.

sciatica /saɪ'ætɪkə/ noun [U] **HEALTH** severe pain in the lower back, or behind the top of the legs, caused by pressure on a nerve

science /'saɪəns/ noun **1** [U] **SCIENCE** the study and knowledge of the physical world and its behaviour, that is based on experiments and facts and is organized into a system: *recent advances in science* ♦ *a science teacher* **2** [C] **SCIENCE** a scientific subject, for example chemistry, physics, or biology **3** [C] an organized way of making, arranging, or dealing with something: *the science of brewing beer*

ˌscience 'fiction noun [U] **ARTS, LITERATURE** books and films about imaginary future events that often include space travel and creatures from other planets

scientific /ˌsaɪənˈtɪfɪk/ adj **1** SCIENCE relating to science, or based on the methods of science: *scientific research ♦ scientific instruments* **2** done in an organized way: *There's nothing scientific about the process they use to select people.* —**scientifically** /ˌsaɪənˈtɪfɪkli/ adv

scientist /ˈsaɪəntɪst/ noun [C] SCIENCE someone who is trained in science, especially someone whose job is to do scientific research

scion /ˈsaɪən/ noun [C] BIOLOGY a part that is cut from a plant and fixed to another plant in order to make it grow there

scissors /ˈsɪzəz/ noun [plural] a tool for cutting paper, with two blades that open and shut

sclera /ˈsklɪərə/ noun [C] ANATOMY the outer layer of the eyeball that forms the white of the eye —*picture* → EYE

sclerenchyma /sklɪəˈreŋkɪmə/ noun [U] BIOLOGY a type of tissue in plants that protects and supports them, made up of thick hard dry cells

scoff /skɒf/ verb [I] to laugh or say things to show that you do not respect someone or something

scold /skəʊld/ verb [T] *old-fashioned* to criticize someone angrily because they have done something that is wrong

scolex /ˈskəʊleks/ (plural **scolices** /ˈskəʊlɪsiːz/) noun [C] BIOLOGY the head of a tapeworm, which has hooks or **suckers** that enable it to attach itself to its **host**

scone /skɒn, skəʊn/ noun [C] a small soft cake that sometimes contains dried fruit

scoop¹ /skuːp/ verb [T] to dig something out, or to pick something up, using an object or your curved hand: *He scooped some water from the stream.*

scoop² /skuːp/ noun [C] a tool like a spoon that is used for measuring or serving something, or the amount that this tool holds

'scoop ,net noun [C] a net used in fishing that catches fish close to the surface of the water

scooter /ˈskuːtə/ noun [C] **1** a child's vehicle that consists of a board with two small wheels and an upright handle. You stand on the board with one foot and push with the other. **2** a vehicle with an engine and two small wheels that looks like a small motorcycle

scope /skəʊp/ noun [U] **1** the things that a particular activity, organization, subject etc deals with = RANGE: *The new law is limited in scope. ♦ These issues are beyond the scope of this book. ♦ Responsibility for office services is not within the scope of the department.* **2** the opportunity or freedom to do something: *There is still much scope for improvement.*

scorch /skɔːtʃ/ verb [T] **1** to burn something slightly so that it changes colour or is damaged on the surface **2** if extreme heat scorches someone, or part of their body, it is so hot it is painful

scorched /skɔːtʃt/ adj burnt on the surface

,scorched 'earth ,policy noun [C] the destruction by an army or a government of everything that might be useful to enemy forces moving into the area

scorching /ˈskɔːtʃɪŋ/ adj extremely hot

score¹ /skɔː/ verb **1** [I/T] to get a point in a game or sport: *No one scored in the first half. ♦ He scored the first goal after five minutes.* **2** [T] to achieve a particular amount, level etc in a test: *She's hoping to score full marks in the maths test.* **3** [I/T] to be successful in doing something: *She seems to have scored with her latest novel. ♦ They scored some big sales successes.* **4** [T] to

mark a line into the surface of something: *Score the meat lightly with a knife.*

score² /skɔː/ noun **1** [C] the number of points that someone gains in a game or test: *The average score for the test was 75. ♦ The final score was 4–3.* **2** [C] MUSIC a written copy of a piece of music **3** scores [plural] a large number of people or things: *Scores of volunteers offered to help.*

PHRASE **on that/this score** concerning the thing that has just been mentioned: *We wanted to attract new recruits, and on that score, the campaign has been successful.*
→ SETTLE

scoreboard /ˈskɔːbɔːd/ noun [C] SPORTS a large board that shows the score in a game or sports event

scorecard /ˈskɔːkɑːd/ noun [C] SPORTS a card on which someone records the score in a sports event while it is being played

scorer /ˈskɔːrə/ noun [C] SPORTS **1** a player who scores a point in a game **2** an official in a sports event who is responsible for keeping an accurate record of the points won

scorn¹ /skɔːn/ noun [U] a feeling that someone or something is not good enough to deserve your approval or respect

scorn² /skɔːn/ verb [T] to treat someone or something as if they do not deserve your approval or respect

scornful /ˈskɔːnf(ə)l/ adj feeling or expressing scorn —**scornfully** adv

Scorpio /ˈskɔːpiəʊ/ noun [C/U] one of the twelve signs of the zodiac. A **Scorpio** is someone who was born between 24 October and 22 November.

scorpion /ˈskɔːpiən/ noun [C] an invertebrate animal like a large insect that has a curved tail with a poisonous part on the end. Like spiders, scorpions are **arachnids.** —*picture* → INSECT

scour /ˈskaʊə/ verb [T] **1** to search a place or document thoroughly for something: *Police officers are scouring the area for the missing child.* **2** to clean something thoroughly by rubbing it hard with something rough

scourge /skɜːdʒ/ noun [C] *formal* something that causes a lot of trouble or harm

scouring powder /ˈskaʊərɪŋ ˌpaʊdə/ noun [C] a dry substance that is used for cleaning things

scout¹ /skaʊt/ noun [C] **1** a soldier who is sent by an army to get information about the position of the enemy **2** someone whose job is to find and employ people who have special abilities, for example in sports or entertainment: *a talent scout* **3** scout or Scout a **Boy Scout**

scout² /skaʊt/ verb [I/T] to search for someone or something

scowl /skaʊl/ verb [I] to put an angry expression on your face —**scowl** noun [C]

scrabble /ˈskræb(ə)l/ verb [I] to make a lot of small quick movements with your fingers, especially when you are trying to find something that you cannot see

scramble¹ /ˈskræmb(ə)l/ verb [I] **1** to climb somewhere quickly using your feet and hands = CLAMBER: *She managed to scramble over the wall.* **2** to move somewhere quickly and in a way that is not graceful: *He scrambled awkwardly to his feet.* **3** to try very hard to get something that other people are also trying to get: *Companies are scrambling to recruit skilled workers.*

scramble² /ˈskræmb(ə)l/ noun **1** [singular] a difficult climb in which you use your feet and hands **2** [singular] a situation in which people all compete for the same thing **3** [C] **SPORTS** a motorcycle race over rough ground

scrambled eggs /ˌskræmb(ə)ld 'egz/ noun [plural] eggs that are cooked with their white and yellow parts mixed together

scrap¹ /skræp/ noun **1** [C] a small piece of something: *a scrap of paper* ♦ *Every scrap of evidence has to be investigated.* **2** [U] old metal that can be used again after going through a special process: *The car was sold for scrap.* **3** [C] *informal* a fight, or an argument

scrap² /skræp/ (**scraps, scrapping, scrapped**) verb [T] **1** *informal* to decide not to continue with something such as a plan or event= ABANDON **2** to get rid of something **3** to take an old machine or vehicle apart and throw away all the parts that cannot be used

scrapbook /'skræpˌbʊk/ noun [C] a book in which you stick pictures, articles etc

scrape¹ /skreɪp/ verb **1** [T] to remove something by pulling a hard tool across the surface it is on: *Scrape the mud off your boots before you come inside.* **2** [I/T] if a sharp edge or point scrapes a surface, or if you scrape it across the surface, it moves across a surface: *He felt the knife blade scrape against the back of his neck.* **3** [T] to injure a part of your body or damage something by rubbing it against a rough surface = GRAZE: *I scraped my elbow when I fell over.* ♦ *He scraped his van while he was parking it.* **4** [I] to make a rough unpleasant noise by rubbing against a hard surface: *Simon's chair scraped as he pushed it back.*

scrape² /skreɪp/ noun [C] a slight injury or mark caused by rubbing against a rough surface

scraper /'skreɪpə/ noun [C] a tool with a handle and a sharp edge, used for removing a layer of something from a surface

scratch¹ /skrætʃ/ verb **1** [I/T] to pull your nails along your skin, especially because you have an **itch** that makes you want to do this: *Scratch my back for me.* **2** [T] to damage the skin or a surface by cutting it slightly or marking it with something sharp or rough: *Don't worry: the cat won't scratch you.* ♦ *Someone's scratched my car door.* **3** [I/T] to move something sharp or rough against a hard surface and make a noise: *I could hear the dog scratching at the back door.*

scratch² /skrætʃ/ noun [C] **1** a narrow mark on the skin or on a surface that is caused by cutting it slightly or marking it with something sharp or rough **2** the action of pulling your nails along your skin, especially because you have an **itch** that makes you want to do this

PHRASE **from scratch** from the beginning, doing everything yourself: *He built the company from scratch.*

scratch³ /skrætʃ/ adj **SPORTS 1** a scratch team is organized quickly, using any players who are available **2** a scratch player is one who does not have a **handicap**

'scratch ˌfile noun [C] **COMPUTING** a temporary computer file that is created to hold information while a program is being used

scrawl /skrɔːl/ verb [T] to write something carelessly or in a hurry, so that it is difficult to read —**scrawl** noun [C]

scrawny /'skrɔːni/ adj very thin, in a way that is not attractive or healthy

scream¹ /skriːm/ verb **1** [I] to make a loud high cry because you are hurt, frightened, or excited: *She opened her mouth to scream.* ♦ *They were screaming with delight.* ♦ *We could hear the passengers screaming in terror.* → SHOUT¹ sense 2 **2** [I] to make a

very loud high noise **3** [I/T] to shout something in a very loud voice = YELL: *Nobody heard them screaming for help.* ♦ *I felt like screaming at him.*

scream² /skriːm/ noun [C] **1** a loud high cry that you make because you are hurt, frightened, or excited = SHRIEK **2** a very loud high noise= SCREECH

scree /skriː/ noun [U] **GEOGRAPHY** small loose pieces of broken rock at the bottom of a cliff or along the slopes of a mountain

screech /skriːtʃ/ verb [I/T] to make a loud, high, and unpleasant cry or noise: *Seagulls were screeching over our heads.* ♦ *The car screeched to a halt.* —**screech** noun [C]

screed /skriːd/ noun [C] **CONSTRUCTION** a layer of concrete or other material that finishes the surface of a floor and makes it level for laying tiles, wood etc on it

screen¹ /skriːn/ noun

1 on television etc	4 for separating area
2 for showing film	5 for protecting/hiding
3 cinema	

1 [C] **COMPUTING** the flat surface on a computer, television, or piece of electronic equipment where words and pictures are shown: *Suddenly the screen went blank.* —**picture** → COMPUTER
2 [C] **ARTS** the flat surface in a cinema where the picture is shown: *a new 14-screen cinema*
3 [U] **ARTS** cinema in general: *a star of stage and screen*
4 [C] a flat structure that is used for separating one area of a room from another: *She got undressed behind a folding screen.*
5 [C] something that protects someone or allows them to hide: *The cattle provided a screen for the soldiers.*

screen² /skriːn/ verb [T] **1** **HEALTH** to test someone to find out if they have a particular disease **2** **ARTS** to broadcast a television programme, or to show a film: *The series is currently being screened on Fridays.* **3** to hide someone or something by being in front of them: *A line of trees screened the house from the road.* **4** to get information about someone in order to decide whether they are suitable for a job= VET

'screen ˌdump noun [C] **COMPUTING** the process of printing or saving what appears on your computer screen

screening /'skriːnɪŋ/ noun **1** [C/U] **HEALTH** tests done to check someone for a particular disease **2** [C/U] **ARTS** an occasion when a film is shown or a television programme is broadcast **3** [U] checks that an employer makes in order to be sure that someone they want to employ is suitable for a particular job

screen saver /'skriːn ˌseɪvə/ noun [C] **COMPUTING** a computer program that makes the screen black or shows a picture when the computer is on but not being used

screenshot /'skriːnˌʃɒt/ noun [C] **COMPUTING** a photograph or printed page showing what appears on a computer screen

screw¹ /skruː/ verb [T] **1** to fasten one thing to another using screws ≠ UNSCREW: *The rails need to be firmly screwed to the wall.* **2** to put something into its position by turning it ≠ UNSCREW: *Make sure you screw the lid on firmly to keep the contents fresh.* **3** to make something into a smaller shape by squeezing or twisting it: *She was nervously screwing her tissue into a ball.*

screw² /skruː/ noun [C] a thin pointed piece of metal that you push and turn with a **screwdriver** in order to fasten one thing to another. It has a raised line that curves around it called a **thread**.

screwdriver /'skruː,draɪvə/ noun [C] a tool used for turning screws —*picture* → TOOL

scribble /'skrɪb(ə)l/ verb **1** [T] to write something quickly and carelessly **2** [I/T] to make marks or drawings with no meaning —**scribble** noun [C/U]

scribe /skraɪb/ noun [C] **SOCIAL STUDIES** someone whose job was to copy documents and books before printing was invented

scriber /'skraɪbə/ noun [C] **TECHNOLOGY** a pointed steel tool that is used to mark out metal before shaping or forming it

script /skrɪpt/ noun **1** [C] **ARTS, LITERATURE** the written words of a play, film, television programme, speech etc **2** [C/U] **LANGUAGE** a system of written letters and symbols: *Roman script*

scripture /'skrɪptʃə/ noun [C/U] **RELIGION** the holy writings of a religion

scriptwriter /'skrɪpt,raɪtə/ noun [C] **ARTS, LITERATURE** someone whose job is to write the words for films or television programmes

scroll¹ /skrəʊl/ noun [C] a long roll of paper with ancient writing on it

scroll² /skrəʊl/ verb [I/T] **COMPUTING** to move words or images up or down a computer screen in order to read or look at something: *It shouldn't take long to scroll through the document and check the spelling.*

'scroll ,bar noun [C] **COMPUTING** a long narrow area at the edge of a computer screen that is used for moving information up, down, or across the screen

scrotal sac /'skrəʊtəl ,sæk/ noun [C] **ANATOMY** the **scrotum**

scrotum /'skrəʊtəm/ noun [C] **ANATOMY** in most male mammals, the bag of skin containing the **testicles**

scrub¹ /skrʌb/ (**scrubs, scrubbing, scrubbed**) verb [I/T] to wash or clean something thoroughly by rubbing it hard with a brush or cloth

scrub² /skrʌb/ noun **1** [U] small bushes and trees that grow in areas without much rain **2** [singular] a thorough wash or clean that you give something by rubbing it hard with a brush or cloth

scruffy /'skrʌfi/ (**scruffier, scruffiest**) adj untidy, or dirty

scrum /skrʌm/ noun [C] **SPORTS** an arrangement of players in a game of **rugby** when they all push together to try and get the ball

,scrum 'half noun [C] **SPORTS** a **rugby** player who plays in the middle of the field and who throws the ball into the scrum

scruples /'skruːp(ə)lz/ noun [plural] moral principles that prevent you from doing something that you think is bad

scrupulous /'skruːpjʊləs/ adj **1** very careful to be honest and to do what is morally right ≠ UNSCRUPULOUS **2** done very carefully, giving a lot of attention to details —**scrupulously** adv

scrutinize /'skruːtɪnaɪz/ verb [T] to examine someone or something very carefully

scrutiny /'skruːtɪni/ noun [U] careful examination of someone or something: *The industry comes **under scrutiny** in tonight's programme.*

scuba diving /'skuːbə ,daɪvɪŋ/ noun [U] the activity of swimming under water with a container of air on your back and a tube for breathing through

scuffle /'skʌf(ə)l/ noun [C] a fight that lasts for a short time and is not very violent

scullery /'skʌləri/ noun [C] a room next to the kitchen that some old houses have, used for washing dishes or clothes

sculptor /'skʌlptə/ noun [C] **ARTS** an artist who makes sculptures

sculpture /'skʌlptʃə/ noun **ARTS 1** [C/U] a solid object that someone makes as a work of art by shaping a substance such as stone, metal, or wood **2** [U] the art of making sculptures

scum /skʌm/ noun [U] **1** a layer of a dirty or unpleasant substance that forms on the surface of a liquid **2** *offensive* an insulting word for a person or people who are considered to be very unpleasant —**scummy** adj

scurry /'skʌri/ (**scurries, scurrying, scurried**) verb [I] to hurry to do something or get something

scurvy /'skɜːvi/ noun [U] **HEALTH** an illness caused by not eating enough foods that contain **vitamin C** (=a natural substance found in fruit and vegetables)

scythe /saɪð/ noun [C] **AGRICULTURE** a tool with a long curved metal blade for cutting long grass or grain

sea /siː/ noun **1** [singular/U] **GEOGRAPHY** the large area of salt water that covers most of the surface of the Earth: *He had a room overlooking the sea.* ♦ *Tim went swimming **in the sea**.* ♦ *They live in a house **by the sea** (=close to the sea).* ♦ *He died in an accident **at sea**.* ♦ *The goods will be transported **by sea**.* ♦ *She rowed the boat **out to sea**.* —*picture* → ISTHMUS **2** [C] the condition of the sea, especially the way it is affected by the weather: *The fishing boat went missing in **rough seas**.* **3** [C] a large area of salt water: *The dam will create an enormous **inland sea**.* → HIGH SEAS

sea anemone /'siː ə,neməni/ noun [C] a small brightly coloured invertebrate sea animal that looks like a flower and fixes itself onto a rock. Sea anemones are **echinoderms**.

the 'sea ,bed noun [singular] **GEOGRAPHY** the ground at the bottom of the sea

,sea 'breeze noun [C] **GEOGRAPHY** a gentle wind that blows from the sea onto the land

'sea ,cliff noun [C] **GEOGRAPHY** a steep or vertical side of a rock that has been formed by the action of the waves

the ,sea 'floor noun [singular] **GEOGRAPHY** the sea bed

seafood /'siː,fuːd/ noun [U] fish and **shellfish** that you can eat

seagrass /'siː,grɑːs/ noun [C/U] **BIOLOGY** a type of plant with very long roots that live under the sea, usually in water that is not very deep

seagull /'siː,gʌl/ noun [C] a large grey and white bird that lives near the sea —*picture* → BIRD

seahorse /'siː,hɔːs/ noun [C] a small sea fish with a head that looks like a horse's head and a long tail that can curl around objects —*picture* → SEA

seal¹ /siːl/ verb [T] **1** to close a container or space by covering it with something so that air or other substances cannot get in or out: *Small gaps can be **sealed with** wax.* **2** to close an envelope by sticking down the top edge

seal² /siːl/ noun [C] **1** a large sea mammal that eats fish and lives mainly in cold parts of the world —*picture* → SEA **2** something that seals a container and that you have to break before you can open the container: *Make sure that the seal on the bottle is intact.* **3** something

dolphin

shark

flipper

porpoise

squid

whale

ray

starfish

jellyfish

octopus

sponge

tentacle

coral

oyster

seaweed

sea urchin

mussel

seahorse

clam

tusks

seal

shell

walrus

crab

prawn

antennae

pincers/claws

shrimp

lobster

sea life

that stops air or other substances entering or leaving something: *I replaced the seal, but oil is still leaking out.* **4** a special mark that is put on a document to show that it is legal or official

sealant /ˈsiːlənt/ noun [C/U] a substance that is painted on a surface to protect it from air, water etc

ˈsea ˌlevel noun [U] GEOGRAPHY the average level of the sea. It is used for measuring the height of parts of the land.

ˈsea ˌlion noun [C] a large type of **seal**

seam /siːm/ noun [C] **1** a line of stitches that joins two pieces of cloth **2** a long thin layer of coal under the ground

seamless /ˈsiːmləs/ adj changing or continuing very smoothly and without stopping —**seamlessly** adv

seaplane /ˈsiːˌpleɪn/ noun [C] an aircraft that can take off from water and land on water

seaport /ˈsiːˌpɔːt/ noun [C] a town by the sea with a large port

search¹ /sɜːtʃ/ noun [C] **1** an attempt to find something: *Despite a thorough search, they found no drugs on him.* ♦ *The police have conducted an extensive search of the area.* ♦ *Many people had left their homes to go in search of food.* **2** an attempt to find an answer: *The committee is involved in a search for solutions to international problems.* **3** COMPUTING the process of using a computer to find information, especially on the Internet: *You can probably get the address by doing an Internet search.* **4** the process of examining official documents to find information: *A search of the parish records provided useful information.*

search² /sɜːtʃ/ verb **1** [I/T] to try to find something or someone by looking carefully in a place: *After three days searching, I gave up.* ♦ *Detectives have been brought in to help search for clues.* ♦ *Rescue teams are still searching through the wreckage for survivors.* **2** [T] to carefully examine something or someone for something that is hidden: *The police have arrested a man after searching his house.* **3** [T] COMPUTING to use a computer to look for information, especially on the Internet: *I got most of the answers by searching the Net.*

ˈsearch diˌrectory noun [C] COMPUTING a website that contains **links** to other websites, organized according to subject and in alphabetical order
→ SEARCH ENGINE

ˈsearch ˌengine noun [C] COMPUTING a computer program that is used for searching for information on the Internet

ˈsearch ˌparty noun [C] a group of people that is organized to search for someone who is lost or missing

ˈsearch ˌwarrant noun [C] LAW an official document that allows the police to enter a place and search it

searing /ˈsɪərɪŋ/ adj **1** extreme in degree or strength: *searing heat* **2** severe in your judgment of someone or something

seascape /ˈsiːˌskeɪp/ noun [C] ARTS a picture of the sea

seashell /ˈsiːˌʃel/ noun [C] the empty shell of a sea mollusc such as an **oyster** or a **mussel**

seashore /ˈsiːˌʃɔː/ noun [C] GEOGRAPHY a piece of land next to the sea

seasick /ˈsiːˌsɪk/ adj feeling ill from the movement of the boat that you are travelling on

seaside /ˈsiːˌsaɪd/ noun [singular] an area that is near the sea, especially one where people go for a holiday: *a seaside town* ♦ *This was their first holiday together at the seaside.*

season¹ /ˈsiːz(ə)n/ noun

1 period of year	4 period for films etc
2 of weather	5 period plants grow
3 time for activity	+ PHRASES

1 [C] one of the four periods into which the year is divided according to the weather: *She likes to paint the changing seasons in the garden.* ♦ *My mood is often affected by the season of the year.*
2 [singular] a period of the year when a particular type of weather is expected in some regions of the world: *the dry season*
3 [singular] a particular time or period of the year when something happens: *It's the peak of the holiday season, so the roads will be busy.* ♦ *Fruit trees need to be watered regularly during the growing season.*
4 [singular] ARTS a period of time when a series of films, plays, or television programmes are shown: *There is a short season of films by the French director Bertrand Tavernier.*
5 [singular] AGRICULTURE a time when plants grow, or when they produce flowers or fruit: *It's unusual to have a frost so late in the season.* ♦ *the planting season*

PHRASES **in season** BIOLOGY a female mammal that is in season is ready to have sex. Do not use this about humans.
season's greetings used as a greeting during the Christmas period, especially on cards

season² /ˈsiːz(ə)n/ verb [T] to add salt, pepper, or other spices to food

seasonal /ˈsiːz(ə)nəl/ adj available, or happening, at a particular time of year: *seasonal work* ♦ *seasonal changes in temperature* ♦ *seasonal vegetables*

seasoned /ˈsiːz(ə)nd/ adj experienced in a particular activity or job

seasoning /ˈsiːz(ə)nɪŋ/ noun [C/U] salt, pepper, or other spices that you add to food to improve the taste

ˈseason ˌticket noun [C] a ticket that you use several times within a particular period of time

ˈsea ˌstump noun [C] GEOLOGY a small rock left after a **stack** (=a tall vertical rock in the sea) collapses or is eroded

seat¹ /siːt/ noun [C] **1** something that you can sit on: *Some of the vans have leather seats.* ♦ *The seat next to me was empty.* ♦ *He was in the back seat of the car when the accident happened.* ♦ *She put her bag on the passenger seat* (=the seat next to the driver) *and started the car.* ♦ *I had a window seat on the plane.*
→ PASSENGER SEAT, WINDOW SEAT **2** a seat that you pay for as a passenger on a vehicle or as a member of the audience in a theatre: *I managed to get us the best seats in the theatre.* ♦ *We tried to get on the Friday flight, but there were no seats left.* **3** the part of a chair that you sit on **4** a position as a member of a parliament or committee: *The Green Party won four seats in the new parliament.* ♦ *a permanent seat on the UN Security Council*

PHRASE **take a seat** to sit down: *Hi, come on in, take a seat.*
→ BACK SEAT, EDGE¹

seat² /siːt/ verb [T] **1** *formal* to put someone or yourself in a seat somewhere: *He seated himself behind his desk.* **2** to have places for a particular number of people to sit: *The new stadium will seat up to 80,000 people.*

PHRASE **be seated** to be sitting down: *When she entered the room they were already seated.*

,seat-back 'television noun [C] TOURISM a small television screen set into the back of the seat on an aircraft

'seat ,belt noun [C] a strong belt in a car or plane that you fasten around yourself

seating /'siːtɪŋ/ noun [U] **1** the seats in a public place such as a cinema, or on a bus or train **2** the way in which seats are arranged

'seat ,pitch noun [C] TOURISM the distance between the front edge of a plane seat and the front edge of the seat in front

sea urchin /'siː ˌɜːtʃɪn/ noun [C] a small round invertebrate sea animal that has a hard shell with sharp points. Sea urchins are **echinoderms**. —*picture* → SEA

'sea ,water noun [U] water from the sea —*picture* → DESALINATION

seaweed /'siːˌwiːd/ noun [U] a simple green, red, or brown plant that grows in the sea —*picture* → SEA

sebaceous gland /sə'beɪʃəs ˌglænd/ noun [C] ANATOMY a gland in the skin that allows a type of oil called sebum to flow onto the skin and hair to keep them soft —*picture* → SKIN

sebum /'siːbəm/ noun [U] ANATOMY a substance like oil produced by the **sebaceous glands** that stops the hair and skin from drying out and also protects against some bacteria

secateurs /'sekətəz, ˌsekə'tɜːz/ noun [plural] a tool similar to a strong pair of scissors that is used for cutting plants —*picture* → AGRICULTURAL

secede /sɪ'siːd/ verb [I] POLITICS *formal* to officially leave an organization. This word is used especially about a state or region that chooses to become independent and govern itself.

secession /sɪ'seʃ(ə)n/ noun [U] POLITICS *formal* the act of seceding, especially from a country — **secessionist** adj

secluded /sɪ'kluːdɪd/ adj private, peaceful, and not near other people or places

second¹ /'sekənd/ number **1** in the place or position counted as number two: *the second of October* ♦ *This is the second programme in the series.* ♦ *Bulawayo is Zimbabwe's second largest city.* ♦ *He came second in the championship.* **2** in addition to the first one: *The fence needs a second coat of paint.* **3** next in quality or importance after someone or something that is the best or most important: *She was our second choice for the job.* ♦ *In terms of scoring goals, he's second only to Davies.*

PHRASES **have second thoughts (about sth)** to begin to doubt a decision that you have made
second to none the best

second² /'sekənd/ noun [C] **1** a period of time that is one of the 60 parts in a minute: *Each commercial lasts for 30 seconds.* **2** an extremely short period of time: *Just give me a second to put my coat on.* **3** a product that is not perfect, that you can buy at a reduced price **4** EDUCATION a **second-class** university degree

second³ /'sekənd/ verb [T] **1** /'sekənd/ to officially support a proposal made by another person in a meeting **2** /sɪ'kɒnd/ to send someone to work temporarily in another place

secondary /'sekənd(ə)ri/ adj **1** EDUCATION relating to the education of children between the ages of 11 and 16 or 18: *primary and secondary education* ♦ *secondary teachers* **2** less important than something else: *The colour of the car is secondary to its quality and price.* **3** happening after something else or as a

result of it: *a secondary infection* —**secondarily** adv

'secondary ,cell noun [C] PHYSICS an **electrolytic cell** that can be **recharged** after use

,secondary 'colour noun [C] **1** ARTS a colour produced by mixing two **primary colours** in equal amounts. For example, orange is produced by mixing red and yellow. **2** PHYSICS the secondary colours of light are yellow, **magenta**, and **cyan**

'secondary con,sumer noun [C] BIOLOGY, ENVIRONMENT a living thing that feeds on **primary consumers**, which feed on plants at the bottom of the **food chain**

'secondary ,school noun [C] EDUCATION a school for children between the ages of 11 and 16 or 18

,secondary 'stress noun [C/U] LANGUAGE the second-strongest emphasis on a part of a word or sentence

,second 'best noun [singular/U] **1** someone or something that is not what you wanted, or is not as good as others **2** someone or something that comes directly after the best in order of achievement or quality —**,second-'best** adj

,second 'class noun [U] **1** the ordinary method of sending post that is not urgent **2** TOURISM the ordinary seats and service on a train or ship

,second-'class adj **1** low in quality or importance **2** relating to post that is sent by second class **3** TOURISM travelling in second class **4** EDUCATION a second-class university degree is a good degree, but not as good as a **first**

,second-class 'lever noun [C] PHYSICS a type of lever where the **fulcrum** is at one end and the effort at the other, with the load in between. **Bottle openers** and **wheelbarrows** are second-class levers.

,second 'cousin noun [C] a child of your parent's cousin

,second-de'gree adj **1** HEALTH a second-degree burn is serious **2** LAW *American* second-degree crimes are less serious than **first-degree** crimes

,second 'filler ,pass noun [C] TECHNOLOGY a second layer of melted metal that has been welded on top of the first layer, usually along one side of the joint

,second-gener'ation adj **1** SOCIAL STUDIES used for describing someone who was born in the country that they live in but whose parents were not born there **2** developed and improved from an earlier form

,second-'hand adj **1** owned or used by someone else before you: *second-hand clothing* **2** heard from someone who was not directly involved: *second-hand reports* —**,second-'hand** adv

,second-hand 'smoke noun [U] smoke from other people's cigarettes —**,second-hand 'smoking** noun [U]

,second 'language noun [C] LANGUAGE a language that you can speak but that is not your main language

,second-'language acqui,sition noun [U] LANGUAGE the process by which people learn a language that is not their **native** language

,second law of 'motion noun [singular] PHYSICS one of the laws about movement that were first expressed by Isaac Newton. It states that a force accelerates the movement of an object.

secondly /'sekən(d)li/ adv used for introducing the second in a series of two or more things: *Firstly, I didn't know the neighbourhood and, secondly, it was night.*

the ˌsecond ˈperson noun LANGUAGE the pronoun or form of a verb that refers to the person you are talking to. In English the second person pronoun is 'you'.

ˌsecond-ˈrate adj not of good quality

ˌsecond vioˈlin noun [C] MUSIC a musician who plays the **violin** in an orchestra and belongs to the group of **violinists** that is less important than the **first violins** —picture ➔ ORCHESTRA

secrecy /ˈsiːkrəsi/ noun [U] a situation in which you keep something secret

secret¹ /ˈsiːkrət/ noun [C] **1** a piece of information that is known by only a small number of people, and is deliberately not told to other people: *I can't tell you what she said – it's a secret.* ♦ *Can you promise to keep a secret* (=not tell anyone)? **2** something that cannot be explained or is difficult to understand: *What secrets of the universe will the new telescope reveal?* **3** a particular way of achieving something: *The secret of our success is having highly skilled staff.*

PHRASE **in secret** without anyone else knowing: *The negotiations were conducted in secret.*

secret² /ˈsiːkrət/ adj **1** deliberately not told to other people, or kept hidden from other people: *The diary records her most secret thoughts and feelings.* ♦ *Campaigners have accused the government of keeping the results of the inquiry secret.* **2** not known about by many people: *We love coming here because it's like a secret garden.* —**secretly** adv: *The videotapes were secretly recorded by the investigators.*

secretarial /ˌsekrəˈteəriəl/ adj relating to the work or skills of a secretary

secretary /ˈsekrətri/ (plural **secretaries**) noun [C] **1** someone in an office who works for someone else and does jobs such as arranging meetings, making phone calls, and preparing letters **2** the member of a committee who writes letters and keeps records of meetings: *He was secretary of the local golf club.* **3** the politician in charge of a particular government department: *the Education Secretary*

PHRASE **Secretary of State** POLITICS the politician in charge of a particular government department

ˌsecretary-ˈgeneral noun [C] an official in charge of a large organization such as the United Nations

secrete /sɪˈkriːt/ verb [T] BIOLOGY to produce a liquid such as saliva

secretion /sɪˈkriːʃ(ə)n/ noun [C/U] BIOLOGY a liquid that is produced by a living thing, or the process of producing this liquid

secretive /ˈsiːkrətɪv/ adj deliberately not telling people things

ˌsecret ˈservice noun [C] POLITICS a government department that employs people to secretly find out information about the governments of other countries

sect /sekt/ noun [C] RELIGION a religious group whose beliefs are different from the beliefs of an established religion

sectarian /sekˈteəriən/ adj caused by disagreements among people from different religious groups

section /ˈsekʃ(ə)n/ noun [C] **1** a person, group, part, or area that forms part of something larger: *The food section is in the rear of the shop.* ♦ *A large section of the population lives in the cities.* **2** a part of a newspaper, book, or other piece of writing that may be considered separately: *The story was reported on the front page of the business section.* **3** an image that you would see if you cut through something and looked at the flat surface that is created by the cut: *Figure 2 shows a vertical section of the building.* **4** SCIENCE a thin piece cut from an animal or plant and examined

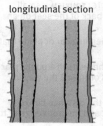
longitudinal section

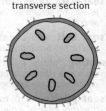
transverse section

sections of a plant stem

sectional /ˈsekʃ(ə)nəl/ adj **1** made in sections that you fit together **2** showing a **cross section** of something

ˈsectional ˌview noun [C/U] MATHS, PHYSICS a view of a flat surface inside a three-dimensional object that is shown by cutting straight through it

sector /ˈsektə/ noun [C] **1** ECONOMICS, BUSINESS a part of a country's economic or business activity: *the industrial sector* ♦ *A number of key sectors of the economy are in trouble.* **2** a part of an area: *the business sector of the town* **3** a group that is part of a larger group: *Some sectors of the community are opposed to the development plan.* **4** MATHS a part of a circle that is formed by drawing two straight lines from the centre to the outer edge —picture ➔ CIRCLE

secular /ˈsekjʊlə/ adj not religious, or not connected with religion —**secularism** noun [U]

secure¹ /sɪˈkjʊə/ verb [T] *formal* **1** to get or achieve something important: *The team secured their second victory of the season.* **2** to make an area or building safe: *We have done our best to secure the embassy against terrorist attacks.* **3** to hold something firmly in place by tying or fastening it: *Screws secure the steel bars to the window frame.*

secure² /sɪˈkjʊə/ adj **1** safe from attack, harm, or damage: *Make your home more secure with our burglar alarm system.* ♦ *No shop can be completely secure against theft.* **2** fastened firmly, in a safe way: *Make sure the pictures are secure.* **3** in a situation where you feel confident and do not need to worry ≠ INSECURE: *The important thing is that children feel secure about being loved.* **4** a secure situation or job is safe and reliable: *She wanted a job with a more secure future.* —**securely** adv: *Please make sure that your seat belt is securely fastened.*

seˌcure ˈserver noun [C] BUSINESS, COMPUTING a server that is suitable to use for doing business over the Internet because it can deal with information that has been **encrypted** (=made safe by putting it into a form that not everyone can read)

securities /sɪˈkjʊərətiz/ noun [plural] BUSINESS documents showing that someone owns shares in a company

security /sɪˈkjʊərəti/ noun [U] **1** safety from attack, harm, or damage: *The information received is highly confidential and relates to national security.* ♦ *The meeting took place amid extremely tight security.* ➔ NATIONAL SECURITY **2** a feeling of confidence and safety, or a situation in which you can feel confident and safe: *A predictable routine gives children a sense of security.* **3** the department within an organization that protects buildings and workers: *If you won't leave, I'll have to call security.* **4** BUSINESS property or goods that you agree to give to someone who has lent you money if you cannot pay the money back ➔ SECURITIES

se'curity ,guard noun [C] someone whose job is to guard something

se'curity ,service noun [C] **POLITICS** a government organization that deals with a country's security

sedate /sɪˈdeɪt/ adj quiet or slow, and not likely to shock people or attract attention —**sedately** adv

sedative /ˈsedətɪv/ noun [C] **HEALTH** a drug that makes someone calmer, or makes them sleep

sedentary /ˈsed(ə)nt(ə)ri/ adj involving a lot of sitting and not much exercise

sediment /ˈsedɪmənt/ noun [C/U] **1** a layer of a substance that forms at the bottom of a liquid —*picture* → DAM **2** GEOLOGY a layer of sand, stones, dirt etc that becomes a layer of rock

sedimentary /ˌsedɪˈmentəri/ adj GEOLOGY sedimentary rock, for example **limestone** and **sandstone**, is a type of rock that is formed from substances that have been left by water, wind, or ice and have become pressed together through time. The other types of rock are igneous rock and metamorphic rock. —*picture* → OIL WELL, ROCK CYCLE

sedimentation /ˌsedɪmenˈteɪʃ(ə)n/ noun [U] SCIENCE the process by which a **sediment** is formed as heavier material drops to the bottom of a liquid

sedimen'tation ,tank noun [C] ENVIRONMENT a large tank that water from a river or **reservoir** passes through in the process of being cleaned and supplied to homes, factories etc. The solids that are present in the water settle at the bottom of the tank and the remaining water passes on to the next stage of cleaning. —*picture* → WATER

seduce /sɪˈdjuːs/ verb [T] if one person seduces another person, they persuade the other person to have sex with them —**seduction** /sɪˈdʌkʃ(ə)n/ noun [C/U]

seductive /sɪˈdʌktɪv/ adj **1** sexually attractive **2** attractive and likely to persuade people to do something that may be harmful or wrong —**seductively** adv

see /siː/ (**sees, seeing, saw** /sɔː/, **seen** /siːn/) verb

1 notice with eyes	8 find sth out
2 watch film etc	9 experience sth
3 meet/visit sb	10 go with sb
4 understand sth	11 be in relationship
5 consider sb/sth	+ PHRASE
6 imagine sb/sth	+ PHRASAL VERBS
7 make sure	

1 [I/T] to notice someone or something using your eyes: *Didn't you see him talking to her earlier?* ♦ *She laughed when she saw the expression on his face.* ♦ *Did you see who it was?* ♦ *She can't see a thing without her glasses.* ♦ *I could see she was upset.*
2 [T] to watch something such as a film or television programme: *Have you seen American Beauty?*
3 [T] to meet or visit someone: *Are you seeing Jane tomorrow?* ♦ *When can Mr Martin see me?* ♦ *See you at the station at 6 o'clock.*
4 [I/T] to understand something: *I think I see the problem here.* ♦ *'You do it like this.' 'I see.'* ♦ *I see why you're angry.*
5 [T] to consider someone or something in a particular way: *A scientist sees things differently from an artist.* ♦ *This was seen as an attempt to fool the voters.*
6 [T] to imagine someone or something: *I just can't see them winning the game.* ♦ *Where do you see yourself in five years' time?*
7 [T] to make sure that someone does something or that something happens: *Could you see that everything's ready in time?*

8 [I/T] to find something out: *If you read his report, you'll see that he recommends a cautious approach.* ♦ *As we saw in Chapter 2, the reasons for the war were complex.* ♦ *He went back to see whether they needed any help.*
9 [T] to experience something: *The region has seen some of the fiercest fighting in the war.*
10 [T] to go with someone because you want to make sure that they arrive somewhere: *Can I see you home?*
11 [T] to be in a romantic relationship with someone: *Is she seeing anyone at the moment?*

PHRASE **see for yourself** to check what someone has told you by looking at it: *It's all gone – see for yourself.* → RED²

PHRASAL VERBS **'see a,bout sth** to deal with or organize something: *I must go and see about this job.* ♦ *Can you see about getting us a lift home?*
,see 'through sb/sth to recognize that someone is trying to trick you: *We can all see through your little game, Adam.*
'see to sb/sth to deal with someone or something: *You try to get some sleep, I'll see to the children's breakfast.*

- If you **see** someone or something, you become aware of them using your eyes: *I saw a flash of light.* ♦ *He saw someone run into the house.*
- If you **look at** someone or something, you deliberately move your eyes towards them so that you can **see** them: *Look at that car!* ♦ *I dropped a glass and everyone turned to look at me.*
- If you **watch** someone or something, you look at them for some time because they are moving or changing and you want to see what happens. You **watch** television or a piece of entertainment: *They were all watching the football match.* ♦ *He sat and watched her clean up.*

seed¹ /siːd/ noun **1** [C/U] BIOLOGY a usually small, hard part produced by a plant, that can grow into a new plant of the same type. A seed is an **ovule** that has been fertilized and contains the plant embryo and its food: *sesame seeds* ♦ *The traditional method of sowing seeds* (=putting them on or in the ground) *is by hand.* **2** [C] SPORTS a player who is given a number that shows how likely they are to win a competition

PHRASE **go/run to seed 1** to stop looking attractive and healthy, especially because you have not been looking after yourself **2** BIOLOGY if a plant goes or runs to seed, it starts producing seeds after it has produced flowers

seed² /siːd/ verb **1** [T] AGRICULTURE to put seeds in the ground so that they can grow **2** [I] BIOLOGY if a plant seeds, it produces seeds **3** [T] SPORTS to give a player or team a number showing how likely they are to win a competition

'seed ,leaf noun [C] BIOLOGY a **cotyledon**

seedless /ˈsiːdləs/ adj AGRICULTURE not containing any seeds

seedling /ˈsiːdlɪŋ/ noun [C] BIOLOGY a young plant that has very recently grown from a seed

seek /siːk/ (**seeks, seeking, sought** /sɔːt/) verb [T] *formal* **1** to ask for something, or to try to get something: *Seek medical advice if symptoms last more than a week.* ♦ *Hundreds of people sought refuge in the British Embassy.* **2** to try to find something or someone that you need in your life: *They are actively seeking employment.* —**seeker** noun [C]

seem /siːm/ linking verb [I] **1** to appear to be something, or appear to have a particular quality: *He seems happy enough to me.* ♦ *She seemed to take very good care of herself.* ♦ *Susan seems like a very sensible person.* **2** used when you want to say something in a more careful and less direct way: *I* **seem to have** *forgotten your name.* ♦ *We* **can't seem to** *get this computer to work.*

PHRASE **it seems** used for saying that something appears to exist or be true: *It seemed that he had never been away.* ♦ **It seems like** *their marriage is over.* ♦ **It seems as if** *everybody else knew except me.* ♦ **It seems to me** *this is his most important novel.*

seemingly /ˈsiːmɪŋli/ adv in a way that appears to have a particular quality, even though this is probably not true: *Heidi was seemingly calm when she left to take the test.*

seen /siːn/ the past participle of **see**

seep /siːp/ verb [I] to flow into or out of something through small holes: *Chemicals from the factory were seeping into the earth.*

seesaw /ˈsiːˌsɔː/ noun [C] a long board for children to play on. It is balanced on a support in the middle.

seethe /siːð/ verb [I] **1** to be extremely angry **2** to be full of a lot of people or animals that are moving around quickly

segment /ˈsegmənt/ noun [C]

1 part	**4** of solid shape
2 of insect/worm	**5** of circle
3 of fruit	

1 a part of something: *certain* **segments of the** *population*
2 **BIOLOGY** one of the parts of something such as an insect's body or an **earthworm** that has clearly separate parts
3 one of the parts of something such as an orange or a **grapefruit** that can easily be separated into parts
4 **MATHS** a part of a solid that is cut by a **plane** (=flat surface)
5 **MATHS** a part of a circle that is formed by a straight line going across it but not going through the centre —*picture* → CIRCLE

segregate /ˈsegrɪgeɪt/ verb [T] **SOCIAL STUDIES** to separate groups of people, especially according to race, sex, or religion —**segregation** /ˌsegrɪˈgeɪʃ(ə)n/ noun [U]

seismic /ˈsaɪzmɪk/ adj **GEOLOGY** relating to earthquakes: *seismic activity*

ˈseismic ˌwave noun [C] **GEOLOGY** a movement that travels through the Earth as a result of an earthquake

seismogram /ˈsaɪzməˌgræm/ noun [C] **GEOLOGY** a written record of an earthquake, produced by a **seismograph=** SEISMOMETER

seismograph /ˈsaɪzməˌgrɑːf/ noun [C] **GEOLOGY** an instrument used for measuring and recording the strength of earthquakes

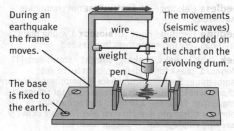

During an earthquake the frame moves.
The base is fixed to the earth.
wire
weight
pen
The movements (seismic waves) are recorded on the chart on the revolving drum.

seismograph

seismology /saɪzˈmɒlədʒi/ noun [U] **GEOLOGY** the scientific study of earthquakes —**seismological** /ˌsaɪzməˈlɒdʒɪk(ə)l/ adj, **seismologist** noun [C]

seismometer /ˌsaɪzˈmɒmɪtə/ noun [C] **GEOLOGY** a seismograph

seize /siːz/ verb [T] **1** to suddenly and firmly hold someone or something: *'Listen,' he said, seizing my wrist.* ♦ *Before he could run away, she* **seized** *him* **by** *the collar.* **2** to take something using official power or force= CONFISCATE: *Customs officials have seized 100 kilos of cocaine.* **3** to take control of a place or situation: *Their opponents had* **seized control** *of the army.* **4** if a feeling or emotion seizes someone, it suddenly affects them very strongly: *A wave of panic seized me.*

PHRASE **seize the opportunity/chance to do sth** to act quickly in order to use an opportunity that may not be available later: *If he looks away, his opponent will seize the opportunity to attack.*

PHRASAL VERB ˌseize ˈup to suddenly stop moving or working: *If you don't add oil, the engine will eventually seize up.*

seizure /ˈsiːʒə/ noun **1** [C/U] the action of taking something, or of taking control of something, using power or force **2** [C] **HEALTH** a sudden attack of an illness that makes the body shake

seldom /ˈseldəm/ adv not often= RARELY ≠ FREQUENTLY: *We seldom see each other any more.*

select¹ /sɪˈlekt/ verb [T] **1** to choose someone or something from a group: *You can select one of four colours.* ♦ *We're going to* **select** *two students* **to** *represent the school.* ♦ *The group had been carefully* **selected** *for the study because of their lifestyles.* **2** **COMPUTING** to mark something on a computer screen before changing it: *You can select a word by double-clicking on it.*

select² /sɪˈlekt/ adj **1** carefully chosen from a larger group: *Only a select few companies were allowed to compete for the contract.* **2** very good, or expensive: *a small, very select hotel*

selection /sɪˈlekʃ(ə)n/ noun **1** [C/U] the process of choosing one person or thing from a group: *There are strict rules that govern* **the selection of** *political candidates.* **2** [singular] a set of things for you to choose from: *a* **selection** *of local foods* ♦ *They have a* **wide selection** *of carpets to suit all tastes.* **3** [C] someone or something that you have chosen: *I'm very happy with my selection.* **4** [U] **EDUCATION** in the UK, a system in which schools choose the students they want

selective /sɪˈlektɪv/ adj **1** careful about what you choose or accept: *He is very selective in his reading.* **2** accepting or using only some things or people: *selective schools* —**selectively** adv

seˌlective ˈmenu noun [C] **TOURISM** a menu with a limited choice of foods for each part of the meal

selector mechanism /sɪˈlektə ˌmekənɪz(ə)m/ noun [C] **ENGINEERING** a piece of equipment that a driver uses to change from one **gear** to another. A **gear stick** is a type of selector mechanism.

selenium /səˈliːniəm/ noun [U] **CHEMISTRY** a chemical element that is not a metal and that the body needs in small amounts in order to be healthy. It can change light into electricity, and so is used in **photocopiers**, **photovoltaic cells**, and photography. Chemical symbol: **Se**

self /self/ (plural **selves** /selvz/) noun [C/U] who you are and what you think and feel, especially the conscious feeling of being separate and different from other people: *Young babies do not have a fully developed* **sense of self**.

self- /self/ prefix relating to yourself or itself: used with many nouns and adjectives: *self-respect ♦ a self-confident person*

self-'access noun [U] a way of learning in which students choose their own books and other materials and study by themselves

self-as'sessment noun [U] EDUCATION a process in which a student **assesses** (=judges the quality of) their own work

self-as'sured adj confident and relaxed because you are sure of your abilities —**self-as'surance** noun [U]

self-a'wareness noun [U] the quality of understanding what your own true thoughts, feelings, and abilities are —**self-a'ware** adj

self-'build noun CONSTRUCTION **1** [U] the process of building your own house **2** [C] a house that you build yourself —**self-'build** verb [I/T]

self-'care noun [U] HEALTH a situation in which individuals, families, or communities take responsibility for improving their own health and preventing illness

self-centred /,self 'sentəd/ adj *showing disapproval* too interested in yourself, so that you do not think about what other people feel or need

self-'centring noun [U] ENGINEERING the action of a **steering wheel** when it goes back to a central position after being turned

self-confessed /,self kən'fest/ adj admitting to being a particular bad type of person

self-'confidence noun [U] the feeling that you can do things well and that people respect you —**self-'confident** adj

self-'conscious adj **1** embarrassed or worried about how you look or what other people think of you **2** not successful in creating a particular effect because of being too obvious —**self-'consciously** adv, **self-'consciousness** noun [U]

self-contained /,self kən'teind/ adj **1** a self-contained flat is part of a larger house but has its own kitchen and bathroom **2** not needing the help or friendship of other people

self-con'trol noun [U] the ability to control your behaviour and not show strong emotions

self-correcting /,self kə'rektiŋ/ adj COMPUTING automatically correcting any typing mistakes made by the user as soon as they make them

self-de'fence noun [U] things that you do in order to protect yourself from being attacked: *Margaret claims she was acting in self-defence when she shot him.*

self-destruct /,self di'strʌkt/ verb [I] if something self-destructs, it destroys itself

self-de'structive adj doing things that are likely to harm you in some way —**self-de'struction** noun [U]

self-de,termi'nation noun [U] POLITICS the freedom of the people in a country to choose their own government and not be controlled by another country

self-de'velopment noun [U] EDUCATION a process is which someone takes personal responsibility for their own learning

self-'discipline noun [U] the ability to control your behaviour so that you do what you should do —**self-'disciplined** adj

self-dis'covery noun [U] new knowledge and understanding that someone gets about their feelings, and about the type of person that they are

self-'drive adj TOURISM a self-drive holiday is one where people drive to the place where they will stay, instead of taking a train or plane

self-effacing /,self i'feisiŋ/ adj someone who is self-effacing does not want to be noticed by other people and tends not to talk about their abilities or achievements

self-employed /,self im'plɔid/ adj working for yourself rather than being employed directly by a company or organization —**self-em'ployment** noun [U]

self-es'teem noun [U] the feeling that you are as good as other people and that you deserve to be treated well

self-evalu'ation noun [U] EDUCATION a process in which a student **evaluates** (=makes a judgment about) their own character, work, achievements, or goals

self-'evident adj obvious, and therefore not needing any explanation —**self-'evidently** adv

self-ex,ami'nation noun [C/U] HEALTH the process of checking parts of your own body for signs of disease

self-ex'planatory adj easy to understand without further explanation

self-ex'pression noun [U] ways in which someone can express their feelings and ideas, for example through painting, writing, or acting

self-'government noun [U] POLITICS a situation in which a country or region is governed by its own people, not by people from outside

self-'harm noun [U] HEALTH physical harm that someone with emotional problems deliberately does to their own body, for example by cutting their skin —**self-'harm** verb [I]

self-'help noun [U] things that someone does to solve their own problems instead of depending on other people. A **self-help group** consists of people who discuss their problems and find ways to deal with them. A **self-help book** is designed to help people to solve their own problems.

self-'image noun [singular] someone's opinions about their own looks, abilities etc

self-im'portant adj *showing disapproval* behaving in a way that shows you think you are very important

self-imposed /,self im'pəuzd/ adj self-imposed rules and conditions are those that you have chosen for yourself, rather than those that someone else has forced you to accept

self-in'dulgent adj *showing disapproval* doing things for your own pleasure, rather than for any other purpose: *an idle self-indulgent lifestyle* —**self-in'dulgence** noun [U]

self-inflicted /,self in'fliktid/ adj a self-inflicted injury, condition etc is one that you suffer from and that you have caused: *a self-inflicted gunshot wound*

self-'interest noun [U] the fact of caring only about what will bring advantages for you, rather than what will help other people —**self-'interested** adj

selfish /'selfiʃ/ adj thinking only about yourself and not caring about other people ≠ UNSELFISH: *a greedy selfish man* —**selfishly** adv, **selfishness** noun [U]

self-'knowledge noun [U] good understanding that someone has of their own thoughts, feelings, abilities etc

selfless /'selfləs/ adj caring about other people's needs and problems more than your own = UNSELFISH —**selflessly** adv, **selflessness** noun [U]

,self-'luminous adj PHYSICS something that is self-luminous produces its own light

,self-'made adj a self-made person has become successful despite starting with no particular advantages: *a self-made millionaire*

,self-moti'vation noun [U] the ability to achieve something because of enthusiasm and interest, without needing encouragement from other people

,self-'pity noun [U] the feeling that your situation is worse than other people's and that they should feel sorry for you —**,self-'pitying** adj

,self-polli'nation noun [U] BIOLOGY the process by which pollen passes from the **anthers** to the **stigma** of the same flower, or another flower on the same plant —**,self-'pollinate** verb [I]

,self-'portrait noun [C] ARTS a picture that you draw or paint of yourself

,self-preser'vation noun [U] the wish to stay alive and protect yourself from things that might hurt you

,self-regu'lation noun [U] a process in which a system or organization controls itself and makes its own rules —**self-regulatory** adj

,self-re'liant adj able to do things for yourself without depending on other people —**,self-re'liance** noun [U]

,self-re'spect noun [U] the feeling that you are as important or as good as other people, and that you should not allow them to treat you badly —**'self-re,specting** adj

,self-'righteous adj *showing disapproval* too proud of your own moral behaviour or beliefs, especially in a way that annoys other people —**,self-'righteously** adv

,self-'rule noun [U] POLITICS government of a country or region by its own people

,self-'satisfied adj *showing disapproval* feeling pleased about your own situation in a way that annoys other people: *a self-satisfied smile* —**,self-satis'faction** noun [U]

self-selected /,self sɪ'lektɪd/ adj chosen by someone offering to do something

,self-'starter noun [C] someone who is intelligent and confident enough to do a job without regular help and advice from other people

,self-'study noun [U] work that you do without the help of a teacher

,self-suf'ficient adj able to provide everything that you need for yourself, without help from other people —**,self-suf'ficiency** noun [U]

,self-'taught adj having learnt a particular skill by yourself, instead of being taught by someone

self-testing /,self 'testɪŋ/ noun [U] EDUCATION a process in which a student tests himself or herself

sell /sel/ (**sells, selling, sold** /səʊld/) verb **1** [T] to let someone have something in exchange for money: *We've decided to sell our house.* ♦ *I sold Chris my old car.* ♦ *Sheila sold her jewellery to an antiques dealer.* **2** [T] if a shop or company sells a particular product, people can buy that product from them: *Do you think they sell children's books here?* **3** [I] if a product sells, people buy it: *Her novel sold very well in the first six months.* **4** [T] *informal* to persuade someone to do, have, or use something: *I don't think we could sell the idea to our partners.* —**seller** noun [C]

PHRASAL VERB **,sell 'out 1** if a shop sells out of something, it sells all that it has so that there is no more available: *I went to get some bread, but the shop had sold out.* ♦ *They had sold out of rice.* **2** if products,

tickets etc sell out, there are none left for people to buy because they have all been sold

'sell-by ,date noun [C] BUSINESS a date printed on food products to show that they should not be sold after that date because they will no longer be good to eat

PHRASE **past its sell-by date** *informal* old-fashioned, or no longer useful or interesting

'seller's ,market noun [singular] BUSINESS a situation in which there are more people wanting to buy a product than the amount of the product that is available, so that prices are high and people selling the product have an advantage ≠ BUYER'S MARKET

'sell-,off noun [C] BUSINESS a situation in which a business or part of a business is sold

Sellotape /'seləˌteɪp/ TRADEMARK clear plastic material that is sticky on one side and is used for sticking things together

'sell-,out noun [singular] **1** ARTS, SPORTS a performance, sports event etc for which all the tickets are sold **2** *informal* a situation in which someone does something that is the opposite of what they had promised, or is against their principles

selves /selvz/ the plural of **self**

semantic /sə'mæntɪk/ adj LANGUAGE relating to the meaning of words —**semantically** /sə'mæntɪkli/ adv

semantics /sə'mæntɪks/ noun [U] LANGUAGE **1** the meaning of words and phrases **2** the study of words and their meanings

semen /'siːmən/ noun [U] BIOLOGY the liquid that contains sperm produced by the male sex organs

semester /sə'mestə/ noun [C] EDUCATION one of the two periods of about 18 weeks that the school year is divided into in some countries

semi- /semi/ prefix **1** exactly half: used with some nouns: *a semi-circle* **2** partly but not completely: used with some adjectives and nouns: *semi-naked*

semibreve /'semiˌbriːv/ noun [C] MUSIC a musical note that is as long as four ordinary notes called **crotchets** —*picture* → MUSIC

semicircle /'semiˌsɜːk(ə)l/ noun [C] **1** MATHS half of a circle —*picture* → SHAPE **2** a group of people or things arranged in a curved line —**semicircular** /ˌsemi'sɜːkjʊlə/ adj

,semicircular ca'nal noun [C] ANATOMY one of the three tubes in the **inner ear** that is shaped like half of a circle and is important for balance —*picture* → EAR

semicolon /ˌsemi'kəʊlɒn/ noun [C] LANGUAGE the symbol ; used in writing for separating words in a list or two parts of a sentence that can be understood separately

semiconductor /ˌsemikən'dʌktə/ noun [C] PHYSICS a solid substance such as **silicon** that allows some electricity to pass through it, used for making electronic equipment such as computers. A **conductor** allows more electricity to pass through it, and an **insulator** allows less.

,semi-de'tached adj a semi-detached house is joined to another house by one wall that they share

semifinal /ˌsemi'faɪn(ə)l/ noun [C] SPORTS one of the two games that are played immediately before the last game in a sports competition

semi-floating axle /ˌsemi ˌfləʊtɪŋ 'æks(ə)l/ noun [C] ENGINEERING an **axle** that is used to drive the wheels of a vehicle, hold them on, and carry some of the vehicle's weight

semilunar valve /ˌsemiluːnə ˈvælv/ noun [C] ANATOMY one of two **valves** in the heart that prevent blood from the **aorta** or **pulmonary artery** from flowing back into the **ventricles** —*picture* → CIRCULATION

semimetal /ˌsemiˈmet(ə)l/ noun [C] CHEMISTRY a **non-metallic** element such as **silicon** that has properties between those of a metal and a non-metal —**semimetallic** /ˌsemiməˈtælɪk/ adj

semi-molten /ˌsemi ˈməʊltən/ adj GEOLOGY semi-molten rock has almost become liquid because it is so hot

seminal /ˈsemɪn(ə)l/ adj *formal* a seminal piece of writing or music is new and different, and influences other literature or music that comes after it

ˈseminal ˌfluid noun [U] BIOLOGY **semen**, the liquid that contains sperm

ˈseminal ˌvesicle noun [C] ANATOMY a gland that produces semen

seminar /ˈsemɪnɑː/ noun [C] **1** a meeting at which a group of people discuss a subject **2** EDUCATION a class at a college or university in which a small group of students discuss a subject with a teacher

seminary /ˈsemɪnəri/ (plural **seminaries**) noun [C] RELIGION a college in which priests or ministers are trained

semiotics /ˌsemiˈɒtɪks/ noun [U] LANGUAGE the study of the way in which people communicate through signs and symbols —**semiotician** /ˌsemiəˈtɪʃ(ə)n/ noun [C]

semi-ˈpermanent adj something that is semi-permanent lasts for some time but not for ever

semipermeable /ˌsemiˈpɜːmiəb(ə)l/ adj BIOLOGY a semipermeable membrane or other material lets the **solvent** (=liquid part of a solution) pass through it, but not the **solute** (=substance that is dissolved)

semiquaver /ˈsemiˌkweɪvə/ noun [C] MUSIC a musical note that is half as long as a short note called a **quaver** —*picture* → MUSIC

ˌsemi-ˈskilled adj a semi-skilled job needs some basic skills. Someone who does this kind of job is called a **semi-skilled worker**.

semitone /ˈsemiˌtəʊn/ noun [C] MUSIC an amount by which one sound is higher or lower than another, equal to 1/12 of an **octave**

semi-trailing arm /ˌsemi ˌtreɪlɪŋ ˈɑːm/ noun [C] ENGINEERING a part of the **suspension** of the back wheels of some vehicles that **pivots** at an angle to the vehicle's body, in order to make the vehicle turn corners more efficiently

semitropical /ˌsemiˈtrɒpɪk(ə)l/ adj GEOGRAPHY **subtropical**

ˈsemi-ˌvowel noun [C] LANGUAGE a speech sound such as 'y' that is sometimes pronounced as a vowel but is considered to be a consonant

semolina /ˌseməˈliːnə/ noun [U] small grains of crushed wheat that are used for making pasta

senate /ˈsenət/ noun [C] POLITICS the more senior part of a law-making institution that has two parts

senator /ˈsenətə/ noun [C] POLITICS someone who is a member of a senate

send /send/ (**sends, sending, sent** /sent/) verb [T] **1** to arrange for something such as a letter or email to be delivered to someone in another place: *I sent the letters yesterday, so they should arrive today.* ♦ *Send me an email when you get there!* ♦ *I forgot to send a birthday card to Amy.* **2** to arrange for someone or something to go to a place, or to tell someone to go to a place: *Two*

warships have been **sent to** the area. ♦ *My mother sent me back to the shop to get the things I'd forgotten.* **3** to make someone move or fall suddenly: *The blow sent him crashing to the floor.* **4** to make a substance such as smoke or a chemical go out into the atmosphere: *Forest fires sent up smoke for miles around.*

PHRASAL VERBS **send sb aˈway** to tell someone to leave a place: *His solicitor was sent away by the security guards.*

ˌsend aˈway for sth to write to an organization asking them to send something to you

send sth ˈback to return something to the person who sent it, especially because it is not satisfactory: *If you're not happy with it, you can always send it back.*

ˈsend for sb/sth to ask or arrange for someone or something to come to you: *I think we should send for a doctor.*

ˌsend sth ˈin to send a letter or document to an organization: *Keep sending your letters and suggestions in to our office.*

ˌsend sb ˈoff to tell a sports player officially to leave the sports field because they have done something that is not allowed by the rules

ˌsend sth ˈoff to send a letter, email etc to someone: *I must get the parcel sent off tomorrow.*

sender /ˈsendə/ noun [C] the person who sent a letter, parcel, email etc

senile /ˈsiːnaɪl/ adj HEALTH someone who is senile is confused, forgets things, or behaves in a strange way, because they are old —**senility** /səˈnɪləti/ noun [U]

senior /ˈsiːniə/ adj **1** with a high position within an organization, or a higher position than someone else ≠ JUNIOR: *a senior officer* **2** belonging to an older age group

ˌsenior ˈcitizen or **senior** noun [C] SOCIAL STUDIES someone who is at or past the age when most people stop working

seniority /ˌsiːniˈɒrəti/ noun [U] greater age, or a more important position

senna /ˈsenə/ noun [U] a tropical plant with fruit that is used for making a **laxative**

sensation /senˈseɪʃ(ə)n/ noun **1** [C/U] the ability to feel something, or something that you feel: *When she awoke she had lost all sensation in her legs.* ♦ *The cream may cause a slight burning sensation.* **2** [C] a feeling in your mind, especially a strange or uncomfortable one: *He had the uncomfortable sensation that he was being watched.* **3** [singular] an event that causes a lot of excitement and interest: *The show caused a sensation when it was first performed.*

sensational /senˈseɪʃ(ə)nəl/ adj very exciting and impressive: *a sensational victory* —**sensationally** adv

sense¹ /sens/ noun

1 reasonable behaviour	4 natural ability
2 feeling/belief	5 meaning of word
3 way of understanding	+ PHRASES

1 [U] a reasonable way of thinking about something or doing something: *They must have had the sense to park the car in the shade.* ♦ *There's no sense in going ahead until the costs have been agreed.*

2 [singular] a feeling or belief that you have, especially about yourself: *All children need to feel a sense of pride in their achievements.* ♦ *Beth read Jake's letter with an increasing sense of panic.*

3 [singular] a way of understanding something, although there may be other ways: *My family's from this area, so in a sense it's like coming home.* ♦ *In one sense, Robertson is a typical politician.*

4 [C] a natural physical ability that most people have,

especially the ability to see, hear, smell, taste, and feel things: *Dogs have **a sense of smell** that is five times more sensitive than that of humans.*

5 [C] **LANGUAGE** the meaning of a word or phrase: *The word 'bank' has a number of senses.*

PHRASES **come to your senses** to start to behave in a reasonable way: *At last she's come to her senses and realizes that we just can't afford it.*

make sense 1 to be practical and sensible: *It makes sense to keep such information on disk.* **2** to be easy to understand: *These instructions don't make any sense to me.*

make sense of sth to understand something that is complicated or unusual

sense of humour the ability to laugh at things and recognize when they are funny

sense² /sens/ verb [T] to know about something through a natural ability or feeling, without being told: *I think she must have sensed there was something wrong.*

senseless /'sensləs/ adj **1** happening or done for no purpose: *the senseless killing of innocent people* **2** unconscious —**senselessly** adv

'sense ,organ noun [C] **ANATOMY, BIOLOGY** an organ that is used for seeing, hearing, smelling, tasting, or feeling something

sensible /'sensəb(ə)l/ adj reasonable and practical: *This seems to be a sensible way of dealing with the problem.* ♦ *It would be sensible to consult the others first.* —**sensibly** adv

sensitive /'sensətɪv/ adj

1 reacting quickly	**4** easily damaged
2 easily upset	**5** secret
3 caring about feelings	**6** likely to offend sb

1 reacting quickly or strongly to something: *Bats have extremely sensitive ears.* ♦ *Coral is very **sensitive to** changes in water temperature.*
2 likely to become upset very easily: *Paul was always a very sensitive little boy.*
3 caring about someone's feelings and not wanting to offend or upset them ≠ INSENSITIVE: *This is a case that needs sensitive and skilful handling.*
4 needing to be protected because of being easy to harm or destroy: *sensitive skin*
5 sensitive information should be kept secret
6 a sensitive issue needs to be dealt with carefully because it is likely to upset or offend people
—**sensitively** adv: *I thought she handled the situation very sensitively.*

sensitivity /,sensə'tɪvəti/ (plural **sensitivities**) noun **1** [U] the quality of understanding how someone feels and being careful not to offend them: *Delivering bad news requires sensitivity on the doctor's part.* **2** [C/U] a tendency to have a strong physical reaction to something: *The drug can cause **sensitivity to** sunlight.* **3** [U] a situation in which something needs to be dealt with carefully because people could be upset or offended

sensor /'sensə/ noun [C] a piece of equipment that reacts to physical changes such as the amount of heat or light that there is in a place

sensory /'sensəri/ adj **BIOLOGY** relating to the physical senses of sight, hearing, smell, taste, and touch

'sensory ,impulse noun [C] **BIOLOGY** a nerve signal that comes from a **receptor** (=sense organ)

'sensory ,neuron noun [C] **ANATOMY** a type of nerve cell that passes signals from the sense organs to the brain or **spinal cord** —*picture* → NEURON

sensual /'sensjuəl/ adj relating to or providing physical pleasure, especially sexual pleasure —**sensuality** /,sensju'æləti/ noun [U]

sensuous /'sensjuəs/ adj relating to physical pleasure

sent /sent/ the past tense and past participle of **send**

sentence¹ /'sentəns/ noun [C] **1** **LANGUAGE** a group of words, usually including a subject and a verb, that expresses a statement, question, or instruction **2** **LAW** a punishment that is officially given by a judge: *He is **serving a** three-year **sentence** for burglary.*

sentence² /'sentəns/ verb [T] **LAW** if a judge sentences someone, they officially say what that person's punishment will be: *He was **sentenced to** 15 years in prison.*

'sentence ,adverb noun [C] **LANGUAGE** an adverb that applies to the whole sentence that follows it rather than an individual word. For example, in the sentence 'Unfortunately, the train was delayed', 'unfortunately' is a sentence adverb.

sentential /sen'tenʃ(ə)l/ adj **LANGUAGE** relating to sentences

sentiment /'sentɪmənt/ noun [C/U] *formal* a feeling, or an attitude

sentimental /,sentɪ'ment(ə)l/ adj making people experience feelings of sadness, sympathy, love etc, especially in a deliberate or obvious way that many people do not like: *a sentimental song* —**sentimentality** /,sentɪmen'tæləti/ noun [U], **sentimentally** adv

sentry /'sentri/ (plural **sentries**) noun [C] a soldier who stands at the entrance to a place and guards it

sepal /'sep(ə)l/ noun [C] **BIOLOGY** one of the parts of a flower that surround the petals and other inner parts before the flower has opened. The group of sepals is called the **calyx**. —*picture* → FLOWER

separable /'sep(ə)rəb(ə)l/ adj capable of being separated ≠ INSEPARABLE

separate¹ /'sep(ə)rət/ adj **1** not together: *My brother and I always had separate rooms.* ♦ *Clients' funds should be kept **separate from** the firm's own money.* **2** different or new: *Answer each question on a separate sheet of paper.* **3** not connected with something that is similar: *Police have arrested seven drug smugglers in three separate incidents this week.* —**separately** adv: *They arrived at the party separately.*

separate² /'sepəreɪt/ verb **1** [I/T] to keep people or things apart from each other, or to stop being joined to something else: *The army was called in to help separate the warring factions.* ♦ *The newly formed cells will **separate from** the main organism.* ♦ *The child may **be separated from** his mother while she receives treatment.* **2** [T] to be between things or people so that they are kept apart: *A large river **separates** the north of the city **from** the south.* **3** [I/T] to divide something, or to become divided, into different parts: *The two issues need to be separated to discuss them fairly.* ♦ *The story then **separates into** several different strands.* **4** [I] if people who are married or are in a sexual relationship separate, they stop living with each other

separated /'sepə,reɪtɪd/ adj someone who is separated no longer lives with their husband, wife, or sexual partner → DIVORCED

separation /,sepə'reɪʃ(ə)n/ noun **1** [C/U] a period of time that people who are usually together spend apart: *a baby's **separation from** its mother* **2** [U] the act of separating two or more things, or the fact that they are separated: *Quebec wanted some form of **separation** from the rest of Canada.* **3** [C/U] an arrangement in which a husband and wife live apart even though they are not divorced

Sept. abbrev September

September /sep'tembə/ noun [U] the ninth month of the year, between August and October: *The last time I saw her was in September.* ♦ *The interview is on September 9th.*

septet /sep'tet/ noun [C] MUSIC a group of seven musicians or singers

septic /'septɪk/ adj HEALTH infected with bacteria

septicaemia /ˌseptɪ'siːmiə/ noun [U] HEALTH an illness in which the blood becomes infected by bacteria. The more usual word is **blood poisoning**.

septic 'tank noun [C] CONSTRUCTION a large container buried under the ground and used for collecting waste from toilets

septuagenarian /ˌseptjuədʒə'neəriən/ noun [C] someone who is between 70 and 79 years old

septum /'septəm/ noun [C] ANATOMY a layer of muscle that separates the two sides of the heart

sequel /'siːkwəl/ noun [C] LITERATURE, ARTS a book, film, play etc that continues the story of an earlier one = FOLLOW-UP

sequence /'siːkwəns/ noun [C/U] **1** a set of related things that happen or are arranged in a particular order: *A computer can store and repeat sequences of instructions.* ♦ *Are the numbers in sequence?* ♦ *Describe the exact sequence of events that evening.* **2** BIOLOGY the order in which the parts of a molecule or gene are arranged

sequencer /'siːkwənsə/ noun [C] COMPUTING a piece of software that allows a user to write music for electronic musical instruments, record notes from instruments, and mix together several pieces of music

sequential /sɪ'kwenʃ(ə)l/ adj forming a set with a particular order, or happening in a particular order —**sequentially** adv

se,quential 'access noun [U] COMPUTING a way of getting and reading a computer file by starting at the beginning → DIRECT ACCESS

sequester /sɪ'kwestə/ verb [T] LAW **1** to keep a group of people, especially a jury in a court trial, apart from other people **2** to **sequestrate**

sequestrate /'siːkwə,streɪt/ verb [T] LAW to take someone's property away from them until they pay the money that they owe —**sequestration** /ˌsiːkwə'streɪʃ(ə)n/ noun [C/U]

serenade /ˌserə'neɪd/ noun [C] MUSIC a song or piece of music that is usually performed by a man outside the house of the woman he loves

serene /sə'riːn/ adj calm, or peaceful —**serenely** adv, **serenity** /sə'renəti/ noun [U]

sergeant /'sɑːdʒ(ə)nt/ noun [C] **1** an officer of middle rank in the army or air force **2** a police officer of middle rank

sergeant 'major noun [C] an officer of fairly high rank in the army

serial /'sɪəriəl/ noun [C] ARTS, LITERATURE a story that is broadcast or published in a series of separate parts

serial ,killer noun [C] someone who murders several people one after the other, often in the same way

serial ,port noun [C] COMPUTING a part of a computer where you can connect another piece of equipment → PARALLEL PORT

series /'sɪəriːz/ (plural **series**) noun [C] **1** a set of similar things that come one after another: *We'll need to do a series of tests before we do anything else.* **2** ARTS a set of television or radio programmes that are all about a particular subject, person, or group of people: *Tonight's programme is the second in a three-part series.* **3** a set of things that are made with the same design, or made in the same way: *a popular new series of children's books*

'series ,circuit noun [C] PHYSICS an electric circuit in which the current passes through one part of the circuit after another → PARALLEL CIRCUIT —*picture* → CIRCUIT

serious /'sɪəriəs/ adj **1** bad or dangerous enough to make you worried: *It's not a serious problem.* ♦ *a serious head injury* ♦ *An accident like this poses a serious threat to the environment.* **2** meaning what you say or do, and not making a joke: *I'm sorry, I didn't realize you were being serious.* ♦ *Do you think Mike's serious about going to live in New Zealand?* **3** thinking carefully about things and not laughing much: *Peter seems serious but he actually has a good sense of humour.* **4** if you are in a serious romantic relationship with someone, you intend to stay together for a long time —**seriousness** noun [U]

seriously /'sɪəriəsli/ adv **1** in a way that is bad or dangerous enough to make you worried: *Was anyone in the car seriously hurt?* **2** in a way that shows that you think something is important and should be thought about carefully: *We have to think seriously about what we do next.* ♦ *I'm seriously considering moving to Hong Kong.*

PHRASE **take sb/sth seriously** to behave in a way that shows that you think that someone or something is important

sermon /'sɜːmən/ noun [C] RELIGION a religious speech that is made by a priest in church

seroconversion /ˌsɪərəʊkən'vɜːʃ(ə)n/ noun [U] HEALTH the process by which antibodies are produced in the blood after vaccination or an infection

serotonin /ˌsɪərə'təʊnɪn/ noun [U] BIOLOGY a substance in your body that affects your moods

serrated /sə'reɪtɪd/ adj a serrated object such as a knife has a row of regular sharp points along its edge

serum /'sɪərəm/ noun **1** [C/U] HEALTH a liquid obtained from the blood of an animal that is put into someone's blood in order to help their body to deal with an infection or a poison **2** [U] BIOLOGY the thin yellow liquid that is part of blood and separates from it when it clots

servant /'sɜːv(ə)nt/ noun [C] someone whose job is to cook, clean, or do other work in someone else's home

serve¹ /sɜːv/ verb

1 provide food/drink	6 help customers
2 do work	7 spend in prison
3 be used for purpose	8 give document
4 help achieve sth	9 hit ball to start play
5 provide sth useful	+ PHRASE

1 [I/T] to provide food or a drink for someone, especially at a meal: *A light meal will be served during the flight.* ♦ *Dinner is served between 7 and 10 pm.*

2 [I/T] to do a job, or to perform duties for a person or organization: *He served more than 20 years in the army.* ♦ *Mr Pak served as president of the Association for fifteen years.* ♦ *Henry served on numerous committees and commissions.*

3 [I/T] to be used for a particular purpose: *Their spare room also serves as an office.* ♦ *His death serves to remind us how dangerous drugs can be.*

4 [T] to help to achieve something: *They voted for a chairman who might better* **serve** *their* **interests**. ♦ *His ability to get on with people* **served** *him* **well** *in setting up his own business*.

5 [T] to provide a group of people or an area with something useful: *These gas pipes serve the whole area*. ♦ *a new hospital to* **serve the needs** *of the local community*

6 [I/T] to help customers to buy goods in a shop

7 [T] to spend time in prison: *He's* **serving** *a life* **sentence** *for murder*.

8 [T] **LAW** to officially give someone a legal document that orders them to do something: *She was* **served with** *a summons to appear in court*.

9 [I/T] **SPORTS** to hit a ball at the beginning of each point in a game such as tennis

PHRASE **it serves sb right (for doing sth)** used for saying that you think that someone deserves something unpleasant that happens to them

serve² /sɜːv/ noun [C] **SPORTS** a hit of a ball in order to start playing for a point in a game such as tennis = SERVICE

server /ˈsɜːvə/ noun [C] **1** **COMPUTING** a computer that stores information for all the computers in a **network** **2** **SPORTS** the player who hits the ball to start the play in a game such as tennis

'server ,farm noun [C] **COMPUTING** a building or a group of buildings that holds a large collection of **servers** for connecting to the Internet

service¹ /ˈsɜːvɪs/ noun

1 system to meet needs	**6** of machines
2 help for customers	**7** religious ceremony
3 type of business	**8** the armed forces
4 government work	**9** in tennis etc
5 sb's work	**10** giving of document

1 [C] a system that provides things that the public needs: *the education services* → HEALTH SERVICE
2 [U] help and advice that is given to customers in a shop, hotel, or business: *a shop with a reputation for excellent* **customer service**
3 [C] a business that provides help, information, or advice for the public: *financial services* ♦ *the service sector*
4 [C] an organization that does work for a government: *the prison service*
5 [C/U] work that someone does as a job or in order to help other people: *Jack had given 25 years of* **loyal service**. ♦ *She was praised for her* **services to the community**.
6 [C] an occasion when a vehicle or machine is examined to check that it works correctly, and to make repairs: *I need to take the car in for a service.*
7 [C] **RELIGION** a religious ceremony: *a church service*
8 the services [plural] the armed forces
9 [C] **SPORTS** a hit of a ball in order to start playing for a point in a game such as tennis = SERVE
10 [U] **LAW** the action of officially giving someone a legal document that orders them to do something → SERVICES

service² /ˈsɜːvɪs/ verb [T] to examine and repair a vehicle or machine as part of a regular check

'service ,area noun [C] a place beside a motorway where petrol, food, drinks, and toilets are available

'service ,centre noun [C] **BUSINESS** a shop where you can buy parts for the products that are sold there, and can have the products repaired

'service ,charge noun [C] **1** **BUSINESS** an amount of money that a company adds to the cost of something in order to be paid for their services **2** **TOURISM** an

amount of money added to your bill in a restaurant, that is for the person who brings your food **3** an amount of money that people who live in flats pay for services such as cleaning and keeping the garden tidy

'service ,contract noun [C] **BUSINESS 1** a contract with a company to keep equipment working correctly, at an agreed price during a fixed period of time **2** a contract between a company and a senior employee such as a senior manager

'service ,industry noun [C] **ECONOMICS** an industry that provides services instead of producing goods, for example banks, hospitals, and hotels

'service ,line noun [C] **SPORTS** the line on a tennis court that the ball has to land behind when a player is serving

serviceman /ˈsɜːvɪsmən/ (plural **servicemen** /ˈsɜːvɪsmən/) noun [C] a man who is a member of the armed forces

'service ,mark noun [C] **BUSINESS** an official sign or symbol used as a trademark by a person or company that provides a service

serviceperson /ˈsɜːvɪsˌpɜːs(ə)n/ noun [C] **BUSINESS** someone whose job is to keep equipment working correctly

'service pro,vider noun [C] **1** **BUSINESS, COMPUTING** a company that provides customers with a connection to the Internet = ISP **2** **BUSINESS** a company that provides a service, for example insurance or medical treatment

services /ˈsɜːvɪsɪz/ noun [C] a place beside a motorway where petrol, food, drinks, and toilets are available

'service ,station noun [C] a business that sells petrol, oil, and other things for vehicles

servicewoman /ˈsɜːvɪsˌwʊmən/ (plural **servicewomen** /ˈsɜːvɪsˌwɪmɪn/) noun [C] a woman who is a member of the armed forces

serving /ˈsɜːvɪŋ/ noun [C] an amount of food for one person = HELPING

sesame /ˈsesəmi/ noun [U] a plant that produces seeds and oil that are used in cooking, found in tropical regions of Asia

sessile /ˈsesaɪl/ adj **BIOLOGY 1** relating to a flower or leaf that has no stalk but is attached directly to the plant stem or branch **2** relating to an animal such as a **barnacle** that is permanently attached to something, rather than moving freely

session /ˈseʃ(ə)n/ noun [C] **1** a period of time that is used for a particular activity: *a question-and-answer session* ♦ *a recording session* **2** a formal meeting of an institution such as a parliament or a court of law: *an emergency session of the UN Security Council*

set¹ /set/ (**sets, setting, set**) verb

1 put sb/sth in place	**8** put story in place
2 of equipment	**9** when sun goes
3 decide time/place	**10** liquid: go solid
4 decide price/value	**11** join broken bone
5 establish rule etc	**+ PHRASE**
6 give sb sth to do	**+ PHRASAL VERBS**
7 put sb/sth in state	

1 [T] to put someone or something in a position, or to be in a particular place or position: *She set the baby on the floor to play.* ♦ *The bookcase was set into the wall.*

2 [T] to make a piece of equipment ready to operate, or ready to start at a particular time: *The bomb was set to go off at eight o'clock.* ♦ *I'm* **setting** *the* **alarm** *for 6.30.*

3 [T] to decide where or when an event will happen: *Have they **set a date** for the wedding?*
4 [T] to decide the price, value, or level of something: *The central bank is responsible for setting interest rates.*
5 [T] to establish a rule, standard, limit etc that people must follow: *Their teacher **sets** high **standards** and expects everyone to meet them.* ◆ *Opposition parties have **set conditions** for cooperating with the government.* ◆ *You should **set an example** for your younger brothers.*
6 [T] to give something to someone to do or achieve: *The teacher set us an essay to do over the weekend.* ◆ *You'll never get anywhere if you don't **set** yourself any **goals**.*
7 [T] to put someone or something in a particular state: *The suspect has been accused of **setting** the restaurant **on fire**.* ◆ *The hostages have been **set free** after 34 days in captivity.*
8 [T] if a play, book, film etc is set in a particular time or place, it happens in that time or place: *The film is set in southern Africa.*
9 [I] when the sun sets, it goes below the horizon at the end of the day ≠ RISE
10 [I] if a liquid sets, it forms a solid substance: *a type of concrete that sets in 15 minutes*
11 [I/T] HEALTH to put the two ends of a broken bone back together, or to be joined in this way
  PHRASE **set the stage for sth** to create the conditions in which something is likely to happen
  PHRASAL VERBS **'set a,bout sth** to begin doing something, especially in a determined or enthusiastic way: *She set about the problem with her usual energy.*
,set sth a'gainst sth to compare one thing with another: *This season's results have been disappointing set against last year's.*
,set sth a'side to keep or save something from a larger amount or supply in order to use it later: *Most of our money is **set aside for** food.*
,set sth 'back to delay the progress of something
,set sth 'down *formal* to state officially how something should be done
,set 'in if something unpleasant sets in, it starts to happen and is likely to continue: *If the wound is not kept clean, infection could set in.*
,set 'off to start a journey: *We set off early the next morning.*
,set 'out 1 to start a journey: *The group set out from Grand Cayman five days ago.* **2** to start doing something, or start trying to achieve something: *They set out to build their own house.*
,set sth 'up 1 to make a piece of equipment ready for use: *Will you be able to set up my PC?* **2** to organize or plan something: *I'll **set up a meeting** for Thursday.* **3** to start something such as a business, organization, or institution

set² /set/ noun [C]

1 group of things	**4** of play/film
2 piece of equipment	**5** of tennis match
3 group of people	**6** in mathematics

1 a group of things that belong together: *a **set of** keys* ◆ *Winners will receive **a complete set of** REM albums.*
2 a piece of equipment that receives television or radio signals: *a TV set*
3 a group of people who spend time together or share an interest: *New York's literary set* ◆ *He's made a completely new set of friends at university.*
4 ARTS a theatre stage, or a place where a film or television programme is made: *This photograph was taken **on the set of** her latest film.*
5 SPORTS a part of a tennis match consisting of at least six games

6 MATHS a group of numbers in mathematics

set³ /set/ adj **1** already decided or agreed: *There's no set time limit for the job.* ◆ *He charges **a set fee** for his services.* **2** not willing to change your opinion or way of doing things: *He's old and stubborn and **set in his ways**.* **3** ready to do something, or likely to do something: *Are you **all set for** the party tonight?* ◆ *The band is **getting set** to do a world tour.* ◆ *The system is **set to** rise under the new government.* **4** EDUCATION a set book or **text** contains information that students must study before an examination

setback /'set,bæk/ noun [C] a problem that delays or stops progress

,set 'piece noun [C] a performance or action that is planned very carefully

'set ,square noun [C] MATHS a flat plastic or metal tool with three straight sides and one right angle, used for drawing lines and measuring angles

settee /se'ti:/ noun [C] a long comfortable chair for two or three people = COUCH, SOFA

setting /'setɪŋ/ noun [C] **1** the place where someone or something is, and all the things that are part of that place: *The classroom setting must be calm and safe.* ◆ *a hotel in a charming mountain setting* **2** ARTS, LITERATURE the time or place in which the events of a play, book, film etc happen: *a love story in a desert setting* **3** a position on the controls of a piece of equipment: *Adjust the temperature setting on the oven.* **4** MUSIC a piece of music added to words, especially to the words of a poem

settle /'set(ə)l/ verb

1 end disagreement	**6** pay money owed
2 decide sth	**7** become calm
3 make sb relaxed	+ PHRASE
4 fall on place & rest	+ PHRASAL VERBS
5 go to live somewhere	

1 [T] to end an argument or legal disagreement: *The two sides are holding talks to **settle the dispute**.* ◆ *The case was **settled out of court** (=without asking a law court to decide).*
2 [T] to decide something definitely: *It was settled that they would leave before dark.*
3 [I/T] to make yourself or someone else comfortable and relaxed in a particular place or position: *I **settled back** into a comfortable chair and waited.*
4 [I] if something settles, it falls downwards and stays on the place where it has fallen: *Flakes of snow **settled on** the windscreen.*
5 [I] to go to live permanently in a particular place: *Her relatives had gone to America and **settled in** Boston.*
6 [T] to pay all the money that you owe to a particular person or company: *He has 30 days to **settle** his bill.*
7 [I/T] to become calm after being upset, nervous, or excited, or to make someone do this: *The kids will settle after they've had a nap.*
  PHRASE **settle a score (with sb)** to do something bad in order to harm someone, because they did something bad to you in the past
  PHRASAL VERBS **,settle (sb) 'down** *same as* **settle** sense 7
,settle 'in to become familiar with a new way of life, place, or job: *She seems to have settled in quickly at her new school.*

settled /'set(ə)ld/ adj **1** happy and relaxed because you are in a familiar or permanent situation **2** if you have a settled way of life, you stay permanently in one place or job or with one person **3** not changing, or not likely to change

settlement /'set(ə)lmənt/ noun **1** [C/U] a formal agreement that ends a disagreement: *They are negotiating a peace settlement.* ♦ *the settlement of disputes between employers and employees* **2** [C] GEOGRAPHY a place where people have come to live permanently: *These people made their first settlement at Mbembe.* **3** [C/U] the complete payment of an amount of money that someone owes to another person: *Your duties include dealing with the settlement of guests' accounts.* ♦ *Enclosed is a cheque in settlement of the bill.*

settler /'setlə/ noun [C] someone who goes to live in a place where not many people live

'set-up noun [C] **1** the way a particular group of people or things is organized **2** *informal* a situation in which someone cheats or tricks you

setup program /'setʌp ˌprəʊɡræm/ noun [C] COMPUTING a program that helps a user to start using their new computer or new software

seven /'sev(ə)n/ number the number 7

seventeen /ˌsev(ə)n'tiːn/ number the number 17

seventeenth /ˌsev(ə)n'tiːnθ/ number **1** in the place or position counted as number 17 **2** one of 17 equal parts of something

seventh /'sev(ə)nθ/ number **1** in the place or position counted as number 7 **2** one of 7 equal parts of something

seventies /'sev(ə)ntiz/ noun [plural]
PHRASES **the seventies 1** the years from 1970 to 1979: *She liked to wear seventies clothing.* **2** a temperature in the seventies is between 70 and 79 degrees Fahrenheit
in your seventies aged between 70 and 79

seventieth /'sev(ə)ntiəθ/ number **1** in the place or position counted as number 70 **2** one of 70 equal parts of something

seventy /'sev(ə)nti/ number the number 70

sever /'sevə/ verb [T] **1** to cut through a part of something so that it is separated completely from the main part **2** to end something such as a friendship or a connection completely and permanently

several /'sev(ə)rəl/ determiner, pronoun more than two or three, but not many: *He had been warned several times about not doing his homework.* ♦ *Several of the company's computers were stolen.*

severe /sɪ'vɪə/ adj **1** very serious and bad, worrying, or unpleasant: *The housing shortage is severe.* ♦ *a severe thunderstorm* ♦ *John had suffered severe bruising and serious cuts.* **2** severe weather is likely to cause harm or damage: *Severe thunderstorms are forecast for Tuesday night.* **3** very strict or extreme= HARSH: *The most severe penalty he could get is ten years in prison.* ♦ *The country has come under severe criticism for its human rights record.* **4** unfriendly and not smiling: *a severe expression* —**severely** adv, **severity** /sɪ'verəti/ noun [U]

sew /səʊ/ (**sews, sewing, sewed, sewed** or **sewn** /səʊn/) verb [I/T] to make or repair clothes, or to fasten something, using a needle and thread

sewage /'suːɪdʒ/ noun [U] ENVIRONMENT waste from people's bodies that is removed from houses and other buildings by a system of large underground pipes called **sewers**

sewer /'suːə/ noun [C] an underground pipe or passage that carries sewage

sewerage /'suːərɪdʒ/ noun [U] ENVIRONMENT **1** a system of pipes and passages that carry **sewage 2** waste and used water that is carried away from buildings through passages and pipes= SEWAGE

sewing /'səʊɪŋ/ noun [U] **1** work that people do using a needle and thread or a sewing machine **2** things such as clothes or curtains that people sew

'sewing ma,chine noun [C] a machine that is used for sewing clothes, curtains etc

sewn /səʊn/ a past participle of **sew**

sex /seks/ noun **1** [U] the activity in which people kiss and touch each other's sexual organs, that may also include **sexual intercourse**: *the impact of sex and violence in TV programmes* ♦ *Parents worry about their teenagers **having sex**.* **2** [C] males or females considered as separate groups: *equal treatment of the sexes* ♦ *The hostel has separate sleeping areas for each sex.* **3** [U] BIOLOGY the fact that a person, animal, or plant is either male or female: *They don't want to know the sex of their baby before it is born.*

'sex ,cell noun [C] BIOLOGY a **reproductive cell**

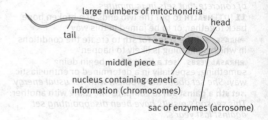

sperm (male gamete)

large numbers of mitochondria

head

tail

middle piece

nucleus containing genetic information (chromosomes)

sac of enzymes (acrosome)

ovum (female gamete)

nucleus containing genetic information (chromosomes)

cytoplasm

thin membrane and a jelly-like coat

male and female sex cells

'sex ,chromosome noun [C] BIOLOGY a chromosome that controls what the sex of an organism will be, for example the **X-chromosomes** and **Y-chromosomes** in humans and other mammals. Male mammals have one X-chromosome and one Y-chromosome, and female mammals have two X-chromosomes.

sexism /'seksɪz(ə)m/ noun [U] SOCIAL STUDIES unfair treatment of someone because they are a woman or a man —**sexist** adj

sextet /ˌseks'tet/ noun [C] MUSIC a group of six musicians or singers

sexual /'sekʃuəl/ adj **1** involving or relating to sex: *a sexual relationship* ♦ *sexual desire* **2** concerning relationships between men and women, or the way that people think that men and women should behave: *sexual stereotyping* —**sexually** adv

,sexual 'harassment noun [U] SOCIAL STUDIES unpleasant or annoying behaviour that involves making sexual comments to someone or touching them sexually when they do not want this

sexual 'intercourse noun [U] BIOLOGY sexual activity between a man and a woman in which the man puts his penis inside the woman's vagina

sexuality /ˌsekʃuˈæləti/ noun [U] sexual feelings, attitudes, and activities

sexual repro'duction noun [U] BIOLOGY the process of producing new organisms in which male and female **gametes** (=reproductive cells) are joined together and combine their genetic information to form a new cell, called a **zygote**

'sex ˌworker noun [C] a **prostitute**

SGML /ˌes dʒiː em ˈel/ noun [U] COMPUTING Standard Generalized Markup Language: a type of computer language using normal English words for publishing documents in electronic form → XML

shabby /ˈʃæbi/ (**shabbier, shabbiest**) adj **1** old and in bad condition: *shabby clothes* **2** not fair or honest: *the government's shabby treatment of trade unions* —**shabbily** adv

shack /ʃæk/ noun [C] a small plain building

ˌshackle and 'pin noun [C] ENGINEERING a U-shaped piece of metal that is closed with a metal bar across the top

shackles /ˈʃæk(ə)lz/ noun [plural] a pair of connected metal rings that can be locked onto the wrists or legs of a prisoner

shade¹ /ʃeɪd/ noun **1** [U] an area where the light and heat from the sun do not reach, that is slightly darker and cooler than other areas: *I spent the afternoon reading under **the shade of** an umbrella.* ♦ *We sat **in the shade** and ate our lunch.* **2** [C] a screen or cover that protects something from the sun or from a light **3** [C] a particular form of a colour: *a brilliant **shade of** red* **4** [C] a slightly different form or type of something: *All **shades of** political opinion were represented.*

shade² /ʃeɪd/ verb [T] to prevent light from shining directly onto or into something

shading /ˈʃeɪdɪŋ/ noun [U] ARTS lines or colours that represent areas of shadow in a drawing or painting

shadow¹ /ˈʃædəʊ/ noun **1** [C/U] an area of darkness that is created when something blocks light: *The dogs are always trying to chase their own shadows.* ♦ *Even on a bright day, the room was **in shadow**.* **2** [C] someone who follows another person wherever they go

PHRASES **beyond/without a shadow of a doubt** used for saying that you are completely certain of something **in sb's shadow** in a situation where your own qualities are not noticed or recognized because most people pay attention to someone else: *For years, she lived in her father's shadow.*

shadow² /ˈʃædəʊ/ verb [T] to secretly follow someone wherever they go

shadowy /ˈʃædəʊi/ adj **1** mysterious and secret, or not understood **2** hidden in darkness or shadows

shady /ˈʃeɪdi/ adj **1** probably dishonest or illegal **2** a shady area is slightly darker and cooler than other areas because the sun does not shine there

shaft /ʃɑːft/ noun [C] **1** a long narrow passage that goes down through a building or down through the ground: *a lift shaft —picture* → OIL RIG **2** ENGINEERING a metal bar in an engine that causes a part to move when another part moves **3** the handle of a tool

'shaft ˌmine noun [C] GEOLOGY a **mine** in which coal, gold etc is dug from a tunnel under the ground, which can only be reached by a vertical hole leading from above the ground —*picture* → OIL RIG —**shaft mining** noun [U]

shaggy /ˈʃægi/ adj shaggy fur or hair is long, thick, and untidy

shake¹ /ʃeɪk/ (**shakes, shaking, shook** /ʃʊk/, **shaken** /ˈʃeɪkən/) verb

1 make quick movements	**4** make less strong etc
2 get rid of problem etc	**5** when voice sounds weak
3 cause fear/emotion	**+ PHRASES**

1 [I/T] to make lots of quick small movements up and down, or from side to side, or to make someone or something do this: *Houses shook as a bomb exploded in the neighbourhood.* ♦ *An earthquake shook the region last year.* ♦ *'You're not listening!' she cried, shaking him.*
2 shake or **shake off** [T] to get rid of something bad such as a problem, illness, or fear: *She couldn't shake her fear of snakes.*
3 [T] to frighten someone, or to make them feel very shocked or upset: *He was shaken and upset by the accident.*
4 [T] to make something less strong, powerful, or confident: *You must believe in yourself and not allow anyone to **shake** your **confidence**.*
5 [I] if your voice shakes, it sounds weak, nervous, or emotional
PHRASES **shake hands (with sb)** or **shake sb's hand** to hold someone's hand and move it up and down, as a way of greeting them or to show that you agree to something: *'Nice to meet you,' Larry said, shaking my hand.*
shake your head to say no by turning your head from side to side

shake² /ʃeɪk/ noun [C] the action of shaking

'shake-up noun [C] an important change in the way that something such as a department or company is organized

shaky /ˈʃeɪki/ (**shakier, shakiest**) adj **1** feeling weak or unable to walk or move without shaking, for example because you are ill **2** likely to fail or be unsuccessful: *The Kenyan team overcame a shaky start to win the championship.* —**shakily** adv

shale /ʃeɪl/ noun [U] GEOLOGY a type of smooth dark rock that breaks easily into thin layers. It is a type of sedimentary rock, formed from layers of clay, **silt**, or mud that have become hard.

shall /strong ʃæl, weak ʃəl/ modal verb **1** used for offering help, suggesting something, or asking someone what to do: *Shall I open the window?* ♦ *Where shall we meet?* **2** formal used after 'I' or 'we' for saying what you intend to do in the future. **Shall** is much more formal than **will** or its short form **'ll**: *If he gets violent, I shall phone the police.* **3** LAW used in instructions and legal documents for saying that something must be done: *The Court shall have authority to demand the presence of witnesses.*

shallot /ʃəˈlɒt/ noun [C] a small vegetable similar to an onion —*picture* → VEGETABLE

shallow /ˈʃæləʊ/ adj **1** with only a short distance from the top or surface to the bottom ≠ DEEP: *He dug a shallow trench.* ♦ *Move to the **shallow end** of the pool.* **2** not interested in serious ideas, strong feelings, or other important things ═ SUPERFICIAL

ˌshallow-'focus adj GEOLOGY a shallow-focus earthquake starts at a point that is near the surface of the Earth

sham /ʃæm/ noun [singular] something that people pretend is good, serious, or honest, but that is not

shambles /'ʃæmb(ə)lz/ noun [singular] **1** something that is very badly organized **2** an extremely untidy place

shame¹ /ʃeɪm/ noun **1** [singular] a reason for feeling sad or disappointed: *It seems a shame to waste all this food.* ♦ *It was a shame that you couldn't come with us.* **2** [U] a guilty and embarrassed feeling that you have when you have behaved badly: *The people who let this happen should **hang their heads in shame**.* ♦ *He seems completely **without shame**.* **3** [U] loss of respect or a good reputation because of your own or someone else's bad behaviour or bad performance: *They accused her of bringing shame and disgrace on the family.* ♦ *There is no shame in failing.*

PHRASE **put sb/sth to shame** to make someone or something seem less good by comparison

shame² /ʃeɪm/ verb [T] to make someone feel guilty or embarrassed, especially so that they change their behaviour

shameful /'ʃeɪmf(ə)l/ adj so bad that you feel ashamed —**shamefully** adv

shameless /'ʃeɪmləs/ adj not feeling ashamed of behaving in a way that other people do not approve of: *a shameless liar* —**shamelessly** adv

shampoo /ʃæm'puː/ noun [C/U] a liquid that you use for washing your hair —**shampoo** verb [T]

shan't /ʃɑːnt/ short form the usual way of saying or writing 'shall not'. This is not often used in formal writing: *I shan't be away for long.*

shanty town /'ʃænti ˌtaʊn/ noun [C] an area where people live in houses made from sheets of wood, metal, or other thin material

shape¹ /ʃeɪp/ noun **1** [C/U] the outer form of something: *Trace the shape onto the card and cut it out.* ♦ *There were balloons of **all shapes and sizes** in the sky.* ♦ *a design **in the shape of** a cross* **2** [C] something that you cannot see well because it is far away or there is not enough light: *Ghostly shapes loomed out of the fog.* **3** [U] the condition of something: *The economy is **in bad shape**.* **4** [U] the features or qualities of something: *It's part of a plan to **change the shape of** local government.*

PHRASES **in/out of shape** in good or bad physical condition: *I can't believe how out of shape I am.* ♦ *I really want to **get in shape** for the match.*
take shape to develop into something that can be recognized: *The idea began to take shape about two years ago.*

shape² /ʃeɪp/ verb [T] **1** to influence the way that a person, idea, or situation develops: *We have all been shaped by our past experiences.* **2** to form something into a particular shape: ***Shape** the mixture **into** cubes.*

shaped /ʃeɪpt/ adj with a particular shape

shapeless /'ʃeɪpləs/ adj without a definite shape

share¹ /ʃeə/ verb

1 use/have with sb	**5** have same opinion
2 do sth with sb else	**6** tell sb sth
3 give part to sb	**+ PHRASAL VERB**
4 let sb use/have sth	

1 [I/T] to use or to have something at the same time as someone else: *Do you mind sharing a table?* ♦ *There's only one copy left, so we'll have to share.* ♦ *I share this flat **with** five other people.*
2 [I/T] to do something, or to be responsible for something, with someone else: *We **share responsibility** for meeting the targets.*
3 [T] to give a part of something to someone else: *The money will be **shared between** 30 different environmental organizations.*
4 [T] to allow someone to use or have something that you own: *He would never **share** his toys **with** me.*
5 [T] to have the same opinion or feeling as someone else: *Not everyone will share your enthusiasm for this scheme.*
6 [I/T] to tell someone something: *Newsgroups enable patients to share information.*

PHRASAL VERB ˌshare sth 'out same as **share¹** sense 3

share² /ʃeə/ noun **1** [C] a part of a total number or amount of something that is divided between two or more people or things: *The country's **share of** world trade had steadily declined.* ♦ *He has no right to **a share in** profits.* **2** [singular] a part of the total amount of work or responsibility of several people: *He does his **share of** the cooking.* ♦ *Jane has accepted her **share of** the blame.* **3** [singular] a reasonable or normal amount of something: *We certainly had our **share of** good fortune.* **4** [C] BUSINESS one of the equal parts of a company that someone can buy as a way of investing money: *The scheme allows employees to buy **shares in** the company.* ♦ ***Share prices** fell on the Tokyo Stock Exchange today.*

shareholder /'ʃeəˌhəʊldə/ noun [C] BUSINESS someone who owns shares in a company

'share ˌindex noun [C] BUSINESS, ECONOMICS an official list of the average price of the shares of companies on a **stock exchange**

shareware /'ʃeəˌweə/ noun [U] COMPUTING computer software that you can use for a period of time before paying for it

sharia /ʃəˈriːə/ noun [U] RELIGION the traditional system of Islamic law

shark /ʃɑːk/ noun [C] a very large fish with sharp teeth and a skeleton of cartilage that lives in the sea —*picture* → SEA

sharp¹ /ʃɑːp/ adj

1 able to cut	**6** showing annoyance
2 sudden & big	**7** clearly different
3 turning suddenly	**8** wind/frost: cold
4 clear & with detail	**9** higher in music
5 quick to notice	

1 a sharp object has an edge that can cut or an end that is pointed: *a sharp knife* ♦ *sharp teeth* ♦ *a sharp pencil* ♦ *These scissors aren't very sharp.*
2 sudden and very big or severe: *a **sharp drop** in unemployment* ♦ *I felt a **sharp pain** in my foot.* ♦ *a **sharp rise** in sales*
3 changing direction suddenly: *a sharp bend in the road*
4 clear and seen in a lot of detail: *a TV with a **razor-sharp** picture*
5 intelligent and quick to notice something or react to something: *Some of these kids are pretty sharp when it comes to maths.*
6 a sharp comment, voice, or expression shows that someone is unfriendly or annoyed: *The deal has come under sharp criticism from the opposition parties.*
7 clearly recognized as different: *Her kindness was **in sharp contrast** to the cruelty I'd experienced before.*
8 a sharp wind or frost is very cold
9 MUSIC used for showing that a musical note should be played or sung a **semitone** higher than usual ≠ FLAT —**sharply** adv: *The government has been sharply criticized.* ♦ *Interest rates have **fallen sharply**.* —**sharpness** noun [U]

sharp² /ʃɑːp/ adv **1** at a particular time exactly: *We're leaving at 5 o'clock sharp.* **2** in a way that changes direction suddenly: *Turn sharp left after the bridge.* **3** MUSIC at a higher than usual **pitch** ≠ FLAT

2D shapes

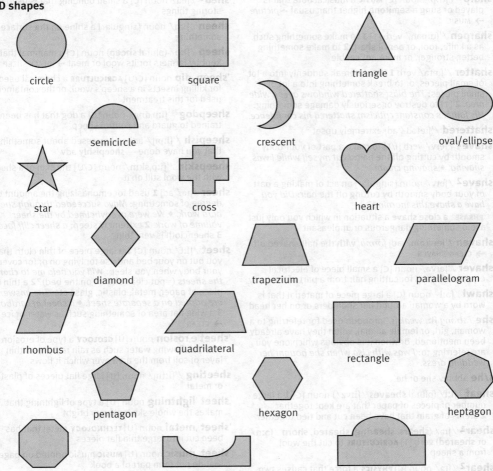

circle

square

triangle

semicircle

crescent

oval/ellipse

star

cross

heart

diamond

trapezium

parallelogram

rhombus

quadrilateral

rectangle

pentagon

hexagon

heptagon

octagon

concave surface

convex surface

3D shapes

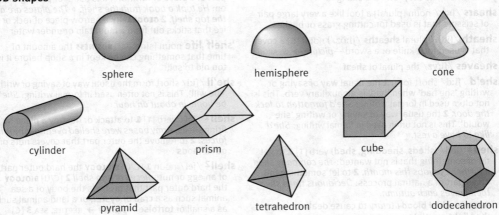

sphere

hemisphere

cone

cylinder

prism

cube

pyramid

tetrahedron

dodecahedron

shapes

sharp³ /ʃɑːp/ noun [C] **MUSIC** a musical note that is played or sung a **semitone** higher than usual —*picture* → MUSIC

sharpen /'ʃɑːpən/ verb [T] **1** to make something such as a knife, tool, or pencil sharp **2** to make something better, stronger, or more noticeable

shatter /'ʃætə/ verb **1** [I/T] to break suddenly into a lot of small pieces, or to break something into a lot of small pieces: *The blast shattered windows over a wide area.* **2** [T] to destroy or seriously damage something: *His father's constant criticism shattered his confidence.*

shattered /'ʃætəd/ adj extremely upset

shave¹ /ʃeɪv/ verb [I/T] to make a part of your body smooth by cutting off the hair: *I cut myself while I was shaving.* ♦ *shaving cream*

shave² /ʃeɪv/ noun [singular] an act of making a part of your body smooth by cutting off the hair: *Did you have a shave this morning?*

    PHRASE **a close shave** a situation in which you only just avoid something dangerous or unpleasant

shaven /'ʃeɪv(ə)n/ adj *formal* with the hair shaved off → CLEAN-SHAVEN

shaver /'ʃeɪvə/ noun [C] a small piece of electrical equipment used for cutting hair from a part of the body

shawl /ʃɔːl/ noun [C] a large piece of material that is worn by a woman around her shoulders or on her head

she /*strong* ʃiː, *weak* ʃɪ/ pronoun used for referring to a woman, girl, or female animal, when they have already been mentioned, or when it is obvious which one you are referring to: *I was with Lisa when she bought her wedding dress.*

s/he abbrev she or he

sheaf /ʃiːf/ (plural **sheaves** /ʃiːvz/) noun [C] **1** a large number of pieces of paper that are kept together **2** stems of grain that have been cut and tied together

shear¹ /ʃɪə/ (**shears, shearing, sheared, shorn** /ʃɔːn/ or **sheared**) verb [T] **AGRICULTURE** to cut the wool from a sheep

shear² /ʃɪə/ noun [C] **PHYSICS** a force that causes two parts of a body to slide past each other in opposite but parallel directions

shearing /'ʃɪərɪŋ/ noun [C/U] **MATHS** a **transformation** in which the parallel lines of a geometric shape or object remain parallel, but the distances between them and the angles they form are changed

shears /ʃɪəz/ noun [plural] a tool like a very large pair of scissors that is used for cutting grass or bushes

sheath /ʃiːθ/ (plural **sheaths** /ʃiːðz/) noun [C] a cover that is used for a knife or a sword —*picture* → WEAPON

sheaves /ʃiːvz/ the plural of **sheaf**

she'd /ʃiːd/ short form **1** the usual way of saying or writing 'she had' when 'had' is an auxiliary verb. This is not often used in formal writing: *She'd forgotten to lock the door.* **2** the usual way of saying or writing 'she would'. This is not often used in formal writing: *She'd like to have a rest.*

shed¹ /ʃed/ (**sheds, shedding, shed**) verb [T] **1** to get rid of something that is not wanted: *The company shed a further 250 jobs this month.* **2** to let something fall off as part of a natural process: *Deciduous trees shed their leaves each autumn.*

    PHRASES **shed blood** *literary* to cause death or injury
shed light on sth to suggest an explanation for something that is difficult to understand
shed tears to cry, or to feel very sad

shed² /ʃed/ noun [C] a small building that is used for storing things

sheen /ʃiːn/ noun [singular] a shine on the surface of something

sheep /ʃiːp/ (plural **sheep**) noun [C] a mammal that is kept by farmers for its wool or meat → BLACK SHEEP

'sheep ,dip noun [C/U] **AGRICULTURE** a chemical used for killing insects in a sheep's wool, or the container used for this treatment

sheepdog /'ʃiːp,dɒg/ noun [C] a dog that has been trained to guard and control sheep

sheepish /'ʃiːpɪʃ/ adj embarrassed about something that you have done —**sheepishly** adv

sheepskin /'ʃiːp,skɪn/ noun [C/U] the skin of a sheep with the wool still on it

sheer /ʃɪə/ adj **1** used for emphasizing the amount or degree of something: *Maya succeeded through sheer hard work.* ♦ *We were overwhelmed by the sheer volume of work.* **2** extremely steep: *a sheer cliff face* **3** sheer cloth is very thin

sheet /ʃiːt/ noun [C] **1** a large piece of thin cloth that you put on your bed and use for lying on or for covering your body when you sleep: *Will you help me to change the sheets* (=put clean sheets on the bed)? **2** a thin flat piece of paper, metal, plastic, glass etc: *The answers are printed on a separate sheet.* ♦ *a sheet of cardboard* **3** a wide flat area of something such as water or ice → CLEAN¹

'sheet e,rosion noun [U] **GEOLOGY** a type of erosion in which flowing water such as rain removes a thin layer of soil from the area over which it flows

sheeting /'ʃiːtɪŋ/ noun [U] large flat pieces of plastic or metal

,sheet 'lightning noun [U] a type of lightning that makes the whole sky look very bright

'sheet ,metal noun [U] **TECHNOLOGY** metal that has been cut into large thin flat pieces

'sheet ,music noun [U] **MUSIC** music printed on pages that do not form part of a book

sheik or **sheikh** /ʃeɪk, ʃiːk/ noun [C] **1** a male leader in an Arab country **2** **RELIGION** a Muslim religious leader

shelf /ʃelf/ (plural **shelves** /ʃelvz/) noun [C] **1** a flat piece of wood or glass that is attached to a wall or is part of a piece of furniture. It is used for putting things on: *He took a book from the shelf.* ♦ *The plates are on the top shelf.* **2** **GEOGRAPHY** a narrow piece of rock or ice that sticks out from a mountain or under water

'shelf ,life noun [singular] **BUSINESS** the amount of time that something can be kept in a shop before it is too old to sell

she'll /ʃiːl/ short form the usual way of saying or writing 'she will'. This is not often used in formal writing: *She'll be home in about an hour.*

shell¹ /ʃel/ verb [T] **1** to attack or destroy a place by firing shells: *Army bases were shelled overnight by rebel forces.* **2** to remove the outer part that covers nuts or other foods

shell² /ʃel/ noun **1** [C/U] **BIOLOGY** the hard outer part of an egg or nut: *pieces of egg shell* **2** [C/U] **BIOLOGY** the hard outer part that protects the body of a sea animal such as a **crab** or **oyster**, or a land animal such as a snail or **tortoise** —*picture* → REPTILE, SEA **3** [C] **PHYSICS, CHEMISTRY** one of several groups of electrons moving in orbit around the nucleus of an atom **4** [C] a metal container filled with a substance that explodes when it is fired from a large gun: *anti-aircraft shells*

'shell ,company noun [C] **BUSINESS** a company that does not own anything or trade as an independent company, but is used by its owners to carry out particular business or to control other companies

shellfish /'ʃel,fɪʃ/ (plural **shellfish**) noun [C/U] **BIOLOGY** an invertebrate sea animal with a shell, for example a **shrimp** or an **oyster**

shelter[1] /'ʃeltə/ noun **1** [C] a place where people are protected from bad weather or from danger: *We built a temporary shelter out of branches.* ♦ *a bus shelter* ♦ *a bomb shelter* **2** [U] protection from bad weather or danger: *People stood and watched from **the shelter of** shop doorways.* ♦ *We **took shelter from** the rain in a nearby café.* **3** [C] a temporary place to live for people who do not have their own homes, or for animals who have been treated in a cruel way= REFUGE: *a women's shelter* **4** [U] a place to live, considered as a basic human need: *Everyone has the right to food, clothing, and shelter.*

shelter[2] /'ʃeltə/ verb **1** [T] to protect someone or something from bad weather: *Hills **sheltered** the town from the winds.* **2** [T] to protect someone from unpleasant experiences or danger: *You cannot **shelter** your children **from** the realities of life.* **3** [I] to stay somewhere where you are protected from danger or bad weather: *We sheltered in an old barn for the night.*

sheltered /'ʃeltəd/ adj **1** not affected by bad weather **2** protected from unpleasant experiences

shelve /ʃelv/ verb **1** [T] to decide not to use something such as a plan or suggestion now, although you may use it later **2** [I] to slope gradually downwards

shelves /ʃelvz/ the plural of **shelf**

shepherd /'ʃepəd/ noun [C] **AGRICULTURE** someone whose job is to look after sheep

sheriff /'ʃerɪf/ noun [C] in some countries, the most senior police officer in a community or town

Sherpa /'ʃɜːpə/ noun [C] a member of a group of people from Tibet or Nepal. Many Sherpas work as guides to help people climbing in the Himalaya Mountains.

sherry /'ʃeri/ (plural **sherries**) noun [C/U] a strong wine from southern Spain

she's /ʃiːz/ short form **1** the usual way of saying or writing 'she is'. This is not often used in formal writing: *She's a psychiatrist.* **2** the usual way of saying or writing 'she has' when 'has' is an auxiliary verb. This is not often used in formal writing: *She's gone over to Kerry's house.*

Shia /'ʃiːə/ noun [U] **RELIGION** one of the main groups in the religion of Islam. A Muslim who belongs to this group is called a **Shia** or a **Shiite**. → SUNNI

shield[1] /ʃiːld/ noun [C] **1** a large transparent plastic object that police officers carry to protect them when they are controlling crowds: *Riot police with shields had surrounded the building.* **2** someone or something that protects you from harm or bad experiences **3** an object that soldiers carried in the past to protect themselves from being hit **4** an object shaped like a shield that is given to the winner of a competition

shield[2] /ʃiːld/ verb [T] to protect something or someone from something that is dangerous or unpleasant

shielding gas /'ʃiːldɪŋ ,gæs/ noun [C/U] **TECHNOLOGY** a gas that protects metal from the effects of gases and water vapour in the air during welding

'shield vol,cano noun [C] **GEOLOGY** a large volcano with gently sloping sides

shift[1] /ʃɪft/ verb **1** [I/T] to change, or to change something: *Public opinion had shifted sharply to the left following the war.* ♦ *The government has **shifted its attention** away from the fight against crime.* **2** [I/T] to move, or to move something: *We'll need to shift this table over to the wall.* ♦ *The children are **shifting** uncomfortably **in their seats**.* ♦ *She stared at him, then **shifted her gaze** to the suitcase on the bed.* **3** [T] to make someone or something else responsible for something: *The lawyers want to **shift the blame** from their client to our company.*

shift[2] /ʃɪft/ noun [C] **1** a period of work time in a place where some people work during the day and some work at night: *a 12-hour shift* ♦ *Rudolfo works the **day shift**.* **2** a change in someone's ideas or opinions: *the government's latest policy shift* ♦ ***shifts in** consumer demand* **3** **COMPUTING** a **shift key** on a computer keyboard

shifting cultivation /,ʃɪftɪŋ ,kʌltɪ'veɪʃ(ə)n/ noun [U] **AGRICULTURE** a method of farming used in tropical regions, in which an area of land is cleared and crops are grown on it until the soil is no longer good enough for growing them. The area is then not used until the soil has improved again.

'shift ,key noun [C] **COMPUTING** the key that you press on a computer keyboard when you want to write a capital letter

shifty /'ʃɪfti/ adj *informal* looking dishonest

Shiite /'ʃiːaɪt/ noun [C] **RELIGION** a Muslim who belongs to the **Shia** group within the religion of Islam → SUNNI

shimmer /'ʃɪmə/ verb [I] to reflect a gentle light that seems to shake slightly

shin /ʃɪn/ noun [C] **ANATOMY** the lower front part of the leg that is between the knee and the foot —*picture* → BODY

shinbone /'ʃɪn,bəʊn/ noun [C] **ANATOMY** the bone in the lower front part of the leg, between the knee and the ankle —*picture* → SKELETON

shine[1] /ʃaɪn/ (**shines**, **shining**, **shone** /ʃɒn/) verb **1** [I/T] to produce a bright light, or to aim a light in a particular direction: *Kobe shone the torch slowly around the room.* ♦ *Lights were shining from the windows of a few of the houses.* ♦ *The sun was **shining brightly**.* **2** [I] to have a bright attractive appearance: *The wooden tables had been polished until they shone.* **3** [I] if people's eyes or faces shine, they look extremely happy or excited **4** [I] to show that you have a lot of skill when you do something: *It's time we gave some of the younger players a chance to shine.*

shine[2] /ʃaɪn/ noun [singular] the bright appearance that something such as wood, metal, or leather has when it is in good condition

shingle /'ʃɪŋg(ə)l/ noun [U] small stones on a beach

shingles /'ʃɪŋg(ə)lz/ noun [U] **HEALTH** a disease of the nerves in which painful red spots cover a particular part of the body. It is caused by the same virus as **chickenpox**.

Shinto /'ʃɪntəʊ/ or **Shintoism** /'ʃɪntəʊ,ɪz(ə)m/ noun [U] **RELIGION** the traditional religion of Japan. It has many gods and spirits that are related to the natural world.

shiny /'ʃaɪni/ (**shinier**, **shiniest**) adj something that is shiny has a bright surface that reflects light: *a shiny red apple*

ship¹ /ʃɪp/ noun [C] a very large boat that is used for carrying people or goods long distances: *a cargo ship* ♦ *His ship sailed from Hong Kong on Monday.* ♦ *There were over 350 passengers aboard ship.*

ship² /ʃɪp/ (**ships, shipping, shipped**) verb [T] **1** BUSINESS to send goods to customers, usually by air or land **2** to send people somewhere by ship

shipbuilder /'ʃɪp,bɪldə/ noun [C] a company that builds ships —**shipbuilding** noun [U]

shipment /'ʃɪpmənt/ noun BUSINESS **1** [C] an amount of goods carried on a ship, plane, train, or truck **2** [U] the process of taking goods from one place to another

shipping /'ʃɪpɪŋ/ noun [U] **1** BUSINESS the business of carrying goods **2** ships and boats that are sailing

'shipping ,agent noun [C] BUSINESS a person or company that prepares the legal documents that are necessary for goods to be carried by ship

shipwreck¹ /'ʃɪp,rek/ noun [C/U] an accident in which a ship is destroyed during a journey

shipwreck² /'ʃɪp,rek/ verb **be shipwrecked** to be involved in a shipwreck

shipyard /'ʃɪp,jɑːd/ noun [C] a place where ships are built or repaired

shirk /ʃɜːk/ verb [I/T] to avoid doing something difficult, or to avoid accepting responsibility for something: *A good manager should never shirk difficult decisions.*

shirt /ʃɜːt/ noun [C] a piece of clothing that covers the top part of your body. It usually has long sleeves and buttons down the front: *a cotton shirt* ♦ *One of his shirt buttons was missing.*

shiver /'ʃɪvə/ verb [I] to shake slightly because you are cold or frightened —**shiver** noun [C]

shoal /ʃəʊl/ noun [C] a group of fish that swim together

shock¹ /ʃɒk/ noun **1** [singular/U] the feeling of being very surprised by something bad that happens unexpectedly: *Jessica's face was blank with shock.* ♦ *My mother got a shock when she saw my new haircut.* ♦ *It will give him a shock when he sees how much you've spent.* **2** [C] something that happens unexpectedly and makes you feel very surprised and upset: *The announcement came as a complete shock to me.* ♦ *It was a terrible shock to discover he was already married.* **3** [U] HEALTH a medical condition in which you suddenly become very weak and cold after a serious accident or injury **4** [C] a sudden flow of electricity that goes through your body

shock² /ʃɒk/ verb **1** [T] if something bad and unexpected shocks someone, they are very surprised and upset by it: *The news shocked everyone.* ♦ *We were all shocked by the lies he told.* **2** [I/T] to make someone feel embarrassed or offended by saying or doing something that is offensive or immoral: *He only says things like that to shock you.* —**shocked** /ʃɒkt/ adj: *We were deeply shocked to hear of his sudden death.* ♦ *They listened in shocked silence.*

shock absorber /'ʃɒk əb,zɔːbə/ noun [C] ENGINEERING a piece of equipment fitted to each wheel of a vehicle that prevents it bouncing too much when driving over rough roads

shocking /'ʃɒkɪŋ/ adj making you feel extremely worried, upset, or embarrassed —**shockingly** adv

'shock ,wave noun [C] **1** PHYSICS a wave with very sharp differences of pressure, temperature, and density that travels much faster than normal **sound waves 2** GEOLOGY a seismic wave —*picture* → EARTHQUAKE

shoddy /'ʃɒdi/ adj of a very low standard

shoe /ʃuː/ noun [C] **1** something that you wear on each foot, usually over socks: *leather shoes* ♦ *She bought several pairs of shoes.* ♦ *shoe polish* **2** a **horseshoe**
PHRASE **in sb's shoes** in the situation that someone else is in: *What would you do if you were in my shoes?*

shoelace /'ʃuː,leɪs/ noun [C] a thick string that you use for fastening a shoe on your foot

shone /ʃɒn/ the past tense and past participle of **shine¹**

shook /ʃʊk/ the past tense of **shake¹**

shoot¹ /ʃuːt/ (**shoots, shooting, shot** /ʃɒt/) verb **1** [I/T] to fire a gun, or to hit someone or something with a bullet from a gun: *We were ordered not to shoot until he gave the signal.* ♦ *Two of our officers were shot.* ♦ *They were shooting at bottles on a wall.* **2** [I/T] SPORTS to throw or kick a ball in an attempt to score points: *He shot the ball straight at the goalkeeper.* ♦ *We were all shouting for him to shoot.* **3** [I] to move somewhere very suddenly and quickly: *The car shot across the road at high speed.* **4** [I/T] ARTS to take photographs, or to make a film or video: *All the outdoor scenes were shot on location in Egypt.*

shoot² /ʃuːt/ noun [C] **1** BIOLOGY a plant that has recently started growing, or a new part growing on a plant **2** an occasion when someone takes a series of photographs or makes a film

shooting /'ʃuːtɪŋ/ noun **1** [C/U] an occasion when someone is attacked by a person with a gun: *the fatal shooting of two teenagers* **2** [U] any sport or activity in which guns are used: *hunting, shooting, and fishing*

,shooting 'star noun [C] ASTRONOMY a **meteor**

shop¹ /ʃɒp/ noun [C] **1** a place where you buy things or where you pay for a service: *I'm just going to the shop.* ♦ *The shops are closed on Sundays.* **2** a business where something is made or repaired: *a shoe repair shop*
PHRASE **set up shop** to start a business or activity

shop² /ʃɒp/ (**shops, shopping, shopped**) verb [I] to go to shops to look at and buy things: *We shop at the local market.*

'shop as,sistant noun [C] someone whose job is to serve people in a shop

,shop 'floor noun [C] **1** the area in a factory where products are made **2** the workers in a factory, not the managers

'shop ,front noun [C] the outside part of a shop that is on the street, where the main entrance is

shopkeeper /'ʃɒp,kiːpə/ noun [C] someone who owns or manages a shop

shoplifting /'ʃɒp,lɪftɪŋ/ noun [U] LAW the crime of stealing things from a shop —**shoplift** verb [I/T], **shoplifter** noun [C]

shopper /'ʃɒpə/ noun [C] someone who goes to a shop in order to look at or buy the things that are sold there

shopping /'ʃɒpɪŋ/ noun [U] **1** the activity of going to a shop to buy things: *I don't like shopping very much.* ♦ *I don't suppose you've had a chance to go shopping yet?* ♦ *Where do you go to do your shopping?* **2** all of the things that you have bought in a shop, especially food and products for cleaning the house: *Can you help me bring the shopping in?*

'shopping ,basket noun [C] COMPUTING a piece of software that runs on a **web server** and allows users to choose the things that they want to buy

'shopping ,centre noun [C] an area where different types of stores and businesses are built next to each other

shore /ʃɔː/ noun [C/U] GEOGRAPHY the land that is on the edge of a sea, river, or lake: *Three of the sailors managed to swim to the shore.* ♦ *a village on the shores of Lake Tanganyika* —*picture* → BACKWASH

- ■ The **shore** is the land that is on the edge of a lake, river, or sea: *They managed to swim to the shore.* ♦ *a village on the shores of the lake*
- ■ The **coast** is the land at the edge of a country, near the sea: *From the deck we could see the coast of Africa.* ♦ *a town on the south coast*
- ■ A **beach** is an area of sand or small stones next to the sea or by a river or lake, where people can sit and enjoy themselves: *Let's have a picnic on the beach.*

shoreline /ˈʃɔːˌlaɪn/ noun [C] GEOGRAPHY the edge of a sea or lake

shorn /ʃɔːn/ a past participle of **shear**[1]

short[1] /ʃɔːt/ adj

1 small in height etc	6 about memory
2 of time	7 rude & unfriendly
3 with few words	8 about vowel/syllable
4 with fewer letters	+ PHRASES
5 not having enough	

1 measuring a small height, length, or distance: *She's short and slim.* ♦ *The sleeves of this shirt are much too short.* ♦ *The theatre is a relatively short distance from here.*
2 a short period of time does not last very long, or seems to pass quickly: *I'm sorry this has been such a short stay.* ♦ *He was here for a short while last week.*
3 expressed in few words, or containing few pages: *Could you give us a short summary of what happened?* ♦ *It was a short book and she read it in one night.*
4 using fewer words or letters than the full form of something: *Memo is short for memorandum.* ♦ *My name is Elizabeth, or Liz for short.*
5 used for saying that you do not have enough of something: *Skilled workers are in short supply around here.* ♦ *Many of our clients are short of money.* ♦ *He's very bright but a little short on personality.* ♦ *Their family often went short of food.*
6 if you have a short memory, you are not able or willing to remember things
7 rude and unfriendly when speaking to someone
8 LANGUAGE a short vowel or syllable is one that you pronounce quickly

PHRASES **at short notice** without being given much warning before something happens: *I was asked to come at very short notice.*
in the short run/term during the period of time that is not very far into the future: *The policy served him well in the short term but later backfired.*

short[2] /ʃɔːt/ adv without reaching a particular place or position: *The plane came down just short of the runway.*

PHRASES **cut sth short** to end something before it is completely finished: *We cut our trip short because Rachel fell ill.*
fall short of sth to fail to reach your aim, or fail to reach a particular level: *Sales of the CD fell short of expectations.*
run short (of sth) used for saying that there is not much of something left: *Supplies were running short as winter came on.* ♦ *We're running short of time.*
short of (doing) sth except for: *Short of selling our houses, I don't know how we'll pay for this.* ♦ *Nothing short of a miracle can save us now.*
→ CUT[1], FALL[1]

short[3] /ʃɔːt/ noun [C] PHYSICS a **short circuit**
PHRASE **in short** used for introducing a summary of something that you have just said
→ SHORTS

shortage /ˈʃɔːtɪdʒ/ noun [C/U] a lack of something that you need or want: *The villagers are facing serious food and fuel shortages.* ♦ *a shortage of clean water*

short ˈcircuit noun [C] PHYSICS an electrical circuit that is completed, often accidentally, in a way that allows current to flow along a different path from the one intended. Short circuits cause a sudden increase in current that can damage equipment. —**short-ˈcircuit** verb [I/T]

short-ˈcircuit ˌvoltage noun [U] TECHNOLOGY the voltage between the terminals of a welding circuit when there is an **electric arc** (=continuous electric spark), and the electrode is in contact with the metal being worked on

shortcoming /ˈʃɔːtˌkʌmɪŋ/ noun [C] a fault that makes someone or something less effective

ˈshort ˌcut noun [C] **1** a path or route that is quicker and shorter than the usual way **2** a way of saving time or effort in doing something **3** COMPUTING a combination of keys on a keyboard that helps you to do something more quickly, or an **icon** on the screen that lets you start a program

shorten /ˈʃɔːt(ə)n/ verb [I/T] to become shorter, or to make something shorter

shortfall /ˈʃɔːtˌfɔːl/ noun [C] a lack of something that you need or want, or the amount that you lack

shorthand /ˈʃɔːtˌhænd/ noun [U] a quick way of writing that uses symbols to represent letters, words, or phrases

ˈshort-ˌhaul adj travelling a short distance, especially by air ≠ LONG-HAUL

shortlist /ˈʃɔːtˌlɪst/ noun [C] a list of people who have been chosen from a larger group by someone who is deciding who should get a job, prize etc —**shortlist** verb [T]

short-lived /ˌʃɔːt ˈlɪvd/ adj lasting for a short period of time

shortly /ˈʃɔːtli/ adv **1** soon, or happening within a short period of time of something: *We're going to break for lunch very shortly.* ♦ *Police arrived at the scene shortly after midnight.* **2** if you say something shortly, you sound annoyed or rude

shorts /ʃɔːts/ noun [plural] short trousers that end at or above the knees

short-ˈsighted adj **1** not able to see things clearly if they are far away from you ≠ LONG-SIGHTED —*picture* → on next page **2** failing to consider what will happen in the future —**short-ˈsightedness** noun [U]

ˌshort ˈstory noun [C] LITERATURE a short piece of writing about an imaginary situation

ˌshort-ˈterm adj lasting for a short period of time ≠ LONG-TERM: *a short-term solution*

ˈshort ˌwave noun [C] PHYSICS a type of radio wave that is used for broadcasting across large distances → LONG WAVE, MEDIUM WAVE

shot[1] /ʃɒt/ noun

1 when gun is fired	5 small drink
2 throw etc of ball	6 of drug
3 photograph/view	7 balls fired from
4 attempt to do sth	shotgun

1 [C] an act of firing a gun, or the sound of a gun being fired: *The man fired two shots from a handgun.* ♦ *The neighbours say they heard four shots.*

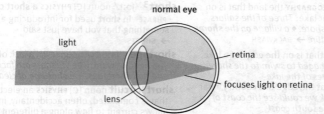

normal eye

light

retina

focuses light on retina

lens

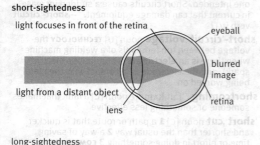

short-sightedness

light focuses in front of the retina

eyeball

blurred image

light from a distant object

lens

retina

long-sightedness

light focuses behind the retina

eyeball

blurred image

light from a near object

lens

retina

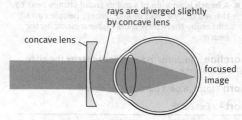

rays are diverged slightly by concave lens

concave lens

focused image

rays are converged slightly by convex lens

convex lens

focused image

short- and long-sightedness

2 [C] **SPORTS** an act of throwing, hitting, or kicking a ball: *That was another fine shot from Tiger Woods.* ♦ *They didn't manage to get a single **shot at** our goal.*
3 [C] **ARTS** a photograph, or the view of something that you have because of the position of a camera: *In the opening shot we see a man walking across a field.* ♦ *I got a great **shot** of the dogs playing together.*
4 [C] *informal* a chance or attempt to do or get something: *This is her first **shot at** an international title.* ♦ *We **had a shot at** bringing the ship round into the harbour.* ♦ ***Give it your best shot** (=try as hard as you can) – that's all you can do.*
5 [C] a small amount of a strong alcoholic drink
6 [C] **HEALTH** a medical treatment in which a small amount of a drug is put into the body with a needle
7 [U] small metal balls that are fired from a shotgun

shot² /ʃɒt/ the past tense and past participle of **shoot¹**

shotgun /'ʃɒt.ɡʌn/ noun [C] a long gun that is used especially for hunting birds and animals

the 'shot ,put noun [singular] **SPORTS** a sports event in which you throw a heavy metal ball as far as you can

should /ʃʊd/ modal verb **1** used for saying or asking about the right or sensible thing to do: *You shouldn't drive so fast.* ♦ *Should I look for another job?* ♦ *You should have taken my advice.* **2** used when you have strong reasons for believing or expecting something: *There should be a knife in the drawer.* ♦ *That was disappointing – we should have won that game easily.* **3** used for describing a situation that may possibly happen: *Should you need help, just give me a call.* ♦ *If anything should happen to me, please give this letter to my wife.*

shoulder¹ /'ʃəʊldə/ noun [C] **1** one of the two parts of the body between the neck and the top of the arms: *She injured her shoulder in the accident.* ♦ *The man*

tapped my friend **on the shoulder** and asked for a cigarette. ♦ *He just smiled and **shrugged his shoulders** (=moved them quickly up and down as a sign that he did not know something or did not care).* —*picture* → BODY, JOINT **2** [C/U] the upper part of the front leg of an animal, or meat from this part: *a shoulder of lamb*
PHRASE a shoulder to cry on someone who listens to you with sympathy when you talk about your problems

shoulder² /'ʃəʊldə/ verb [T] **1** to deal with or accept something difficult **2** to push someone with your shoulder

'shoulder ,blade noun [C] **ANATOMY** one of the two flat bones at the top of the back, near the shoulders = SCAPULA —*picture* → SKELETON

shoulder girdle /'ʃəʊldə ,ɡɜːd(ə)l/ noun [C] **ANATOMY** the **pectoral girdle** in humans —*picture* → SKELETON

shouldn't /'ʃʊd(ə)nt/ short form the usual way of saying or writing 'should not'. This is not often used in formal writing: *We shouldn't assume that everyone will agree.*

shout¹ /ʃaʊt/ verb [I/T] **1** to say something in a loud voice: *'Stop!' he shouted.* ♦ *Donna **shouted at** the men furiously.* ♦ *We **shouted to** the driver to tell him to switch off the engine.* **2** to make a sudden loud noise because you are afraid or you feel pain: *A man in the next bed was **shouting** wildly **in** pain.*
PHRASAL VERB ,shout (sth) 'out to say something suddenly in a very loud voice: *I wanted to shout out and stop her but she was already gone.* ♦ *An officer was shouting out orders.*

shout² /ʃaʊt/ noun [C] the sound of someone shouting, or the words that they shout: *They could hear angry shouts coming from the kitchen.*

shove /ʃʌv/ verb **1** [I/T] to push someone or something with force **2** [T] *informal* to move something, or put it somewhere, quickly and carelessly —**shove** noun [C]

shovel /'ʃʌv(ə)l/ noun [C] a tool that is used for lifting and moving something such as snow or soil. It consists of a long handle with a curved metal end. —**shovel** verb [I/T]

show¹ /ʃəʊ/ (**shows, showing, showed, shown** /ʃəʊn/) verb

1 prove sth is true	**7** of film/programme
2 let sb see sth	**8** put in exhibition
3 let sb know sth	**9** lead sb somewhere
4 give information	+ PHRASE
5 make noticeable	+ PHRASAL VERBS
6 explain sth to sb	

1 [T] to prove that something exists or is true: *The study shows an increase in the disease among the elderly.* ♦ *Accidents like this show what can happen when drivers are not alert.* ♦ *The test results show that he could not have committed the murder.*

2 [T] to let someone see something: *This is the first time the painting has been shown to the public.* ♦ *I couldn't wait to show him the letter.*

3 [T] to behave in a way that allows people to know your feelings, opinions, or personal qualities: *They have shown what they think of our suggestion.* ♦ *The government has shown that it is not willing to compromise.* ♦ *Try to show an interest in the customer's needs.*

4 [T] if a map, photograph, piece of equipment etc shows something, you can see or read that thing on it: *a map showing all the major tourist attractions* ♦ *The dial showed that the pressure had fallen to a dangerously low level.*

5 [I/T] to be easy to see or notice, or to make something easy to see or notice: *A deep sadness showed in his eyes.* ♦ *She had chosen a colour that really showed the dirt.*

6 [T] to explain something to someone by doing it once and letting them watch: *A young girl showed me how to operate the machine.* ♦ *Can you show me the right way to do this?*

7 [I/T] ARTS if someone shows a film or television programme, or if it is showing, people can see it: *It was the first time the film was shown on television.* ♦ *Now showing at a cinema near you!*

8 [T] ARTS to put something such as a work of art, an animal, or a plant in an exhibition or competition: *Her work was first shown at a gallery in Munich.*

9 [T] to lead someone somewhere: *Let me show you to your room.*

PHRASE **have something/nothing to show for sth** to have achieved something or nothing as a result of your efforts: *They had absolutely nothing to show for weeks of hard work.*

PHRASAL VERBS **,show sb a'round** to lead someone around a place for the first time, so that they can see all parts of it

,show sb 'in to lead someone into a room where they are going to meet other people

,show 'off *showing disapproval* to behave in a way that is intended to attract people's attention and make them admire you: *The children start showing off the minute anyone comes into the house.*

,show sb 'out to lead someone to the door when they are leaving a place

,show sb 'round *same as* **show sb around**

,show 'up if something shows up, people can see it: *The writing didn't show up very well on yellow paper.*

show² /ʃəʊ/ noun

1 performance	**4** making sth clear
2 programme	**5** pretending sth
3 exhibition	+ PHRASE

1 [C] ARTS a performance in a theatre

2 [C] ARTS a television or radio programme: *It's the funniest comedy show on television.*

3 [C] an exhibition: *a fashion show*

4 [singular] something that you do in order to make people realize what your opinions or intentions are: *The attack was clearly intended as a show of force.*

5 [singular/U] an occasion when you pretend to have particular feelings: *They put on a show of affection in front of the journalists.* ♦ *The friendly behaviour was clearly just for show.*

PHRASE **on show** available for people to see: *These are just some of the exciting works of art on show today.*

showcase¹ /'ʃəʊˌkeɪs/ noun [C] an event that emphasizes the good qualities of someone or something

showcase² /'ʃəʊˌkeɪs/ verb [T] to show someone or something in a way that attracts attention and emphasizes their good qualities

shower¹ /'ʃaʊə/ noun [C] **1** a piece of equipment that forces small drops of water into the air and is used for washing your body, or a small area with a shower in it: *The shower isn't working.* ♦ *Is your brother still in the shower?* **2** the activity of washing yourself by standing under a shower: *I'm going to have a shower.* **3** a short period when it rains: *Tonight there will be showers.* **4** a large number of things moving through the air or falling together: *a shower of sparks*

shower² /'ʃaʊə/ verb **1** [I] to wash yourself in a shower **2** [T] to give a very large number of things to someone: *He showered her with gifts.*

'shower ,cap noun [C] a plastic hat for wearing in a shower, so that the hair does not get wet

shower gel /'ʃaʊə ˌdʒel/ noun [C/U] a type of liquid soap used for washing yourself in a shower

showerhead /'ʃaʊəˌhed/ noun [C] the round part at the top of a shower that the water comes through

showing /'ʃəʊɪŋ/ noun [C] **1** an occasion when something such as a film or television programme is shown **2** the amount of success that someone or something has in an event or during a particular period: *She had a strong showing in the local elections.*

show jumping /'ʃəʊ ˌdʒʌmpɪŋ/ noun [U] SPORTS a sport in which someone riding a horse jumps over a set of fences

shown /ʃəʊn/ the past participle of **show¹**

showy /'ʃəʊi/ adj **1** brightly coloured and attractive: *a plant with large showy flowers* **2** *showing disapproval* big and expensive in a way that seems ugly = OSTENTATIOUS: *a showy ring*

shrank /ʃræŋk/ the past tense of **shrink**

shrapnel /'ʃræpn(ə)l/ noun [U] small pieces of metal that fly out of a bomb or bullet when it explodes

shred¹ /ʃred/ noun [C] **1** a long thin piece that has been cut or torn from something **2** a very small amount of something: *There's not a shred of evidence to support his claim.*

shred² /ʃred/ (**shreds, shredding, shredded**) verb [T] **1** to destroy a document by putting it into a shredder **2** to cut or tear something into long thin pieces

shredder /'ʃredə/ noun [C] a machine that destroys documents by cutting them into long thin pieces

shrew /ʃruː/ noun [C] a small mammal that looks like a mouse with a pointed nose

shrewd /ʃruːd/ adj able to make good decisions and to judge people and situations very well —**shrewdly** adv

shriek /ʃriːk/ verb [I] to shout in a loud high voice because you are frightened, excited, or surprised = SCREAM —**shriek** noun [C]

shrill /ʃrɪl/ adj a shrill noise or voice is very loud, high, and unpleasant

shrimp /ʃrɪmp/ noun [C] a small crustacean with a hard shell around it and a pair of claws —*picture* → SEA

shrine /ʃraɪn/ noun [C] RELIGION a religious place that has been built to remember a particular holy person or event

shrink /ʃrɪŋk/ (**shrinks, shrinking, shrank** /ʃræŋk/, **shrunk** /ʃrʌŋk/) verb **1** [I/T] to become smaller, or to make something become smaller: *Do you think this dress will shrink if I put it in the washing machine?* ♦ *Profits shrank from 32.5 per cent to 17 per cent.* **2** [I] to move back or away from someone or something because you are frightened or nervous: *He shrank away from her touch.*

shrinkage /ˈʃrɪŋkɪdʒ/ noun **1** [U] the process of becoming smaller in size **2** [singular/U] a reduction in something

shrivel /ˈʃrɪv(ə)l/ (**shrivels, shrivelling, shrivelled**) or ,**shrivel 'up** verb [I] if something such as a plant shrivels, it becomes smaller, thinner, and drier, and it does not look fresh and healthy —**shrivelled** /ˈʃrɪv(ə)ld/ adj

shroff /ʃrɒf/ noun [C] someone in South Asia who works in a bank, or exchanges money of one country for money of another country

shroud¹ /ʃraʊd/ noun [C] a piece of cloth that is wrapped around a dead body before it is buried

shroud² /ʃraʊd/ verb [T] to cover or hide something
PHRASE **be shrouded in secrecy/mystery** to be very secret or mysterious

shroud-waving /ˈʃraʊd ˌweɪvɪŋ/ noun [U] the use of sad or frightening events or figures to draw attention to issues or to get a political advantage

shrub /ʃrʌb/ noun [C] a woody plant that has a lot of thin branches growing from the lower part of the **trunk**

shrug /ʃrʌɡ/ (**shrugs, shrugging, shrugged**) verb [I/T] to move your shoulders up and let them drop, in order to show that you do not know something or do not care —**shrug** noun [C]

shrunk /ʃrʌŋk/ the past participle of **shrink**

shrunken /ˈʃrʌŋk(ə)n/ adj smaller than before, or smaller than is natural

shudder /ˈʃʌdə/ verb [I] **1** if you shudder, your body shakes several times, for example because you suddenly feel cold or frightened **2** if something shudders, it shakes violently several times —**shudder** noun [C]

shuffle /ˈʃʌf(ə)l/ verb **1** [I] to walk slowly and noisily without lifting your feet **2** [I/T] to keep moving your feet because you are nervous, embarrassed, or bored **3** [T] to change the order of papers or other things in a group **4** [I/T] to put cards into a different order before giving them out to the players at the beginning of a game —**shuffle** noun [C]

shun /ʃʌn/ (**shuns, shunning, shunned**) verb [T] to deliberately avoid a person, place, or activity

shunt¹ /ʃʌnt/ verb [T] to move someone or something to a different place or position, especially to avoid dealing with them: *The children are constantly shunted around to various relatives.*

shunt² /ʃʌnt/ noun [C] **1** HEALTH a small tube placed in the body to carry blood or fluid from one place to another **2** a situation in which several cars crash into each other in a line

shut¹ /ʃʌt/ (**shuts, shutting, shut**) verb [I/T] **1** to close something, or to become closed ≠ OPEN: *Sandra shut the book and put it down on the table.* ♦ **Shut** *the gate or the dog will get out.* ♦ *I heard the front door shut.* **2** to close a business at the end of the working day or for a short period of time ≠ OPEN: *We shut at 6 o'clock.*
PHRASAL VERBS ,**shut (sth) 'down 1** if a shop, school, factory, or business shuts down, or if someone shuts it down, it closes permanently **2** if a machine or computer shuts down, or if someone shuts it down, it stops operating
,**shut (sb) 'up** *impolite* to stop talking or making a noise, or to make someone stop talking or making a noise: *Why don't you shut up?* ♦ *Can't you shut your little brother up for just five minutes?*

shut² /ʃʌt/ adj **1** closed: *With the door shut, the room was hot and humid.* **2** not open for business: *The shops are all shut on public holidays.*

shutter /ˈʃʌtə/ noun [C] **1** a cover that can be closed over the outside of a window **2** the part inside a camera that quickly opens and closes to let in light —*picture* → CAMERA

shuttle /ˈʃʌt(ə)l/ noun [C] **1** a bus, train, or plane that makes frequent short journeys between two places **2** a **space shuttle**

shuttlecock /ˈʃʌt(ə)l,kɒk/ noun [C] SPORTS the object that you hit over the net in **badminton**

shy¹ /ʃaɪ/ (**shier, shiest**) adj **1** nervous and embarrassed in the company of other people, especially people who you do not know: *I'd love to meet her but I'm too shy to introduce myself.* ♦ *He gave me a shy smile and looked away.* **2** nervous about doing something or being involved in something: *He's not shy about saying what he wants.* —**shyly** adv, **shyness** noun [U]

shy² /ʃaɪ/ (**shies, shying, shied**) verb [I] if a horse shies, it moves suddenly away from something because it is afraid

sibilant /ˈsɪbɪlənt/ adj LANGUAGE *formal* making a sound like the letters 's' or 'sh' —**sibilant** noun [C]

sibling /ˈsɪblɪŋ/ noun [C] BIOLOGY your siblings are your brothers and sisters

sic /sɪk/ adv *formal* written in brackets after a word that is not spelled or used correctly in order to show that you have written it as someone else spelled or used it

sick /sɪk/ adj **1** if you are sick, food that you have eaten suddenly comes out of your stomach through your mouth: *I'm going to be sick!* → SEASICK **2** if you are sick, you have an illness: *He stayed at home caring for his sick wife.* **3** unpleasant in a way that would upset some people: *sick jokes* **4** the **sick** people who are ill
PHRASE **make sb sick** *spoken* to make someone very angry or upset: *The way he treats her makes me sick.*

sicken /ˈsɪkən/ verb [T] to make you feel shocked and angry

sickening /ˈsɪk(ə)nɪŋ/ adj very unpleasant and shocking

sickle /ˈsɪk(ə)l/ noun [C] AGRICULTURE a tool for cutting down grass and tall plants, consisting of a short handle and a curved blade —*picture* → AGRICULTURAL

,sickle-cell a'naemia noun [U] HEALTH a blood disease in which the red blood cells are damaged, making the blood flow more slowly. This prevents oxygen from getting to the bones and organs.

sickly /'sɪkli/ adj **1** HEALTH not healthy and often ill **2** a sickly smell or taste makes you feel sick

sickness /'sɪknəs/ noun **1** [U] HEALTH a condition in which you have an illness **2** [C] HEALTH a particular illness **3** [U] the feeling that food is going to come from your stomach out through your mouth, or the condition you have when this happens

side¹ /saɪd/ noun [C]

1 one part of area	**7** aspect of situation
2 surface of object	**8** of opposing groups
3 edge of sth flat	**9** sports team
4 surface of sth flat	**10** part of family
5 edge of body	**11** TV channel
6 slope of hill	**+ PHRASES**

1 either of the two parts or areas that something consists of: *Motorists in Japan drive on **the left side** of the road.*
2 a surface of an object or shape, especially one that is not its front, back, bottom, or top: *A cube has six sides.* ♦ *The ship was found lying **on** its **side**.* ♦ *The entrance is on **the side of** the building.*
3 any of the edges of a flat shape: *A square has four sides.*
4 either of the flat surfaces of something that is thin such as a piece of paper or a coin: *Use the lined side of the paper.*
5 the general area of your body from your shoulder down to your waist: *I had a sharp pain in **my right side**.* ♦ *His arms hung limply **by his sides**.*
6 the part of a hill that slopes and is between the top and the bottom
7 one aspect of a situation or subject: *I still haven't heard her **side** of the story.*
8 one of two or more groups of people who are opposing each other: *The agreement has been signed by both sides.* ♦ *Don't get annoyed with me – I'm on **your side** (=supporting you)! ♦ I'm not **taking sides** (=showing support for one person and not another) in this argument.* ♦ *Mary always **takes your side** (=supports you).*
9 SPORTS a sports team: *The winning side will get a place in the finals.*
10 a part of your family, either your father's set of relatives or your mother's: *Which **side of the family** is his uncle from? ♦ Rose is my cousin **on my mother's side**.*
11 a television **channel**: *Which side is the film on?*
PHRASES at/by sb's side 1 beside someone: *She sat by his side.* **2** supporting someone, or remaining loyal to them: *The family will be at her side throughout the trial.*
from all sides from all directions towards one object or person: *Suddenly the crowd came at him from all sides.*
from side to side moving from left to right, then from right to left, then back again
on the side in addition to what is usual: *The band's lead singer has been making solo appearances on the side.*
on the...side slightly, but not very: *It's a nice house, but the rooms are on the small side (=rather small).*
put sth to one side to not talk about something, deal with it, or use it now: *Let's put the question of blame to one side for a minute.*
side by side directly next to each other: *The two girls stood side by side.*
→ COIN

side² /saɪd/ adj **1** not in or on the central part of something: *a side door* **2** less important or less relevant: *a side issue*

sidebar /'saɪd,bɑː/ noun [C] COMPUTING a block of writing at the side of the main writing in an Internet document

'side ,benefit noun [C] something good that happens in addition to a main benefit or purpose

'side ef,fect noun [C] **1** HEALTH an effect of a medicine that is not intended and could be unpleasant **2** an additional result that you did not expect or want

'side ele,vation noun [C/U] MATHS, PHYSICS an **end view**

'side-,hung adj CONSTRUCTION a side-hung window swings open like a door

sideline /'saɪd,laɪn/ noun **1** [C] a job that someone does in addition to their main job, in order to earn extra money **2** [C] SPORTS either of the lines on the sides of a sports field that show where the edges of the field are **3 the sidelines** a situation in which someone watches something that is happening but is not involved in it

sidereal /saɪ'dɪəriəl/ adj ASTRONOMY relating to the stars, or measured by the movement of the stars in the sky

siderite /'saɪdəraɪt/ noun [U] CHEMISTRY, GEOLOGY a naturally occurring iron ore, containing about 30 per cent iron

'side ,street noun [C] a small street that is connected to a major street

sidetrack /'saɪd,træk/ verb [T] to delay the progress of something by causing people to waste time on something else that is less important

'side ,view noun [C/U] MATHS, PHYSICS an **end view**

sidewalk /'saɪd,wɔːk/ noun [C] American the **pavement** by the side of a road

sideways /'saɪdweɪz/ adj, adv **1** to, towards, or from one side: *He moved sideways along the bench.* **2** with one side facing forwards: *A car was sideways across the road, blocking it.*

SIDS /sɪdz/ noun [U] HEALTH sudden infant death syndrome: a medical condition that causes a baby to die suddenly in its bed= COT DEATH

siege /siːdʒ/ noun [C/U] **1** an attack in which an army surrounds a castle or city in order to prevent the people inside from receiving supplies → LAY¹ **2** a situation in which a group of soldiers or police surround a building in order to force the people inside to come out

siesta /si'estə/ noun [C] a short period of sleep in the middle of the day= NAP

sieve /sɪv/ noun [C] an object that you pour a liquid or mixture through in order to remove the large pieces —*picture* → AGRICULTURAL —**sieve** verb [T]

sift /sɪft/ verb [T] **1** to pour a dry substance through a sieve in order to remove the large pieces **2** to examine something carefully in order to find what you are looking for

sigh¹ /saɪ/ verb **1** [I] to breathe out slowly making a long soft sound, especially because you are disappointed, tired, annoyed, or relaxed: *Jan **sighed** **heavily** and shook her head.* **2** [T] to say something with a sigh: *'I wish you had told me earlier,' she sighed.*

sigh² /saɪ/ noun [C] a slow breath out that makes a long soft sound: *She let out a **deep sigh**.*

sight¹ /saɪt/ noun

1 ability to see	**5** places to visit
2 act of seeing sb/sth	**6** sth unpleasant/untidy
3 area you see	**7** part of a gun
4 sb/sth that you see	**+ PHRASES**

1 [U] the ability to see using your eyes= EYESIGHT, VISION: *people with **poor sight***

2 [U] the act of seeing someone or something: *I don't know him personally, but I **know him by sight** (=I know what he looks like).* ♦ *The captain ordered us to shoot any strangers **on sight** (=as soon as we saw them).* ♦ *I can't stand **the sight of** blood.*

3 [U] any place that you can see from where you are = VIEW: *They passed behind the hill and **out of sight**.* ♦ *The rocket **disappeared from sight**.* ♦ *The ship sank **within sight of** the harbour.*

4 [C] a person or thing that you see that has a particular feature: *Elephants are **a common sight** in this part of the country.*

5 **sights** [plural] interesting places that people go to see: *We enjoyed **seeing the sights** of Kuala Lumpur.*

6 [singular] a person or place that is very unusual, untidy, or unpleasant to look at: *You look a sight!* → PRETTY²

7 [C] the part of a gun or other piece of equipment that you look through in order to aim it

PHRASES catch sight of to suddenly see someone or something: *As she stood up she caught sight of her reflection in the mirror.*

in/within sight 1 in a place that you can see from where you are: *There was nobody in sight.* **2** going to happen soon: *Political independence seemed to be in sight.*

lose sight of 1 to no longer be able to see something or someone **2** to forget something that is important, or to forget how important it is: *We shouldn't lose sight of the reasons why we started this campaign.*

set your sights on sth to decide that you want to get or achieve something: *The team has set its sights on the national championship.*

sight² /saɪt/ verb [T] *formal* to see someone or something suddenly or in the distance

sighted /'saɪtɪd/ adj not blind

sighting /'saɪtɪŋ/ noun [C] an occasion when you see someone or something that you do not often see

sight-read /'saɪt ˌriːd/ (**sight-reads, sight-reading**, **sight-read** /'saɪt ˌred/) verb [I/T] MUSIC to sing or play written music the first time you look at it, without practising it first —**sight-reading** noun [U]

sightseeing /'saɪtˌsiːɪŋ/ noun [U] TOURISM the activity of travelling around a place in order to see the interesting things in it

sightseer /'saɪtˌsiːə/ noun [C] TOURISM someone who is travelling around a place and looking at interesting things

'sight-,sing (**sight-sings, sight-singing, sight-sang**, **sight-sung**) verb [I] MUSIC to sing music without having looked at it first

sigma /'sɪɡmə/ noun [singular] MATHS the Greek letter S, used as a symbol for representing the total of numbers or quantities added together

sign¹ /saɪn/ noun

1 piece of evidence	**4** written symbol
2 sth with information	**5** star sign
3 movement/sound	

1 [C/U] a piece of evidence that something exists or is happening= INDICATION: *He had somehow missed the signs that she was upset.* ♦ *I couldn't see any **sign of** progress.*

2 [C] a flat object with words or pictures on it, put in a public place in order to provide information or to advertise something: *a flashing neon sign* ♦ *Turn right and **follow the signs** to the zoo.*

3 [C] a movement or sound that you make in order to tell someone something= SIGNAL: *He made a sign to me to leave.*

4 [C] a written symbol that has a particular meaning, for example % meaning 'per cent' or $ meaning 'dollar': *a multiplication sign*

5 [C] a **star sign**: *I'm a Scorpio. What sign are you?*

sign² /saɪn/ verb **1** [I/T] to write your name on something in order to show that you have written it, or that you agree with what is written on it: *Please **sign** and date **the form**.* ♦ *A trade **agreement** was **signed** today by the US and China.* **2** [T] to officially employ someone to work for a particular organization: *The team needs to **sign** some new players.* **3** [I/T] to communicate using **sign language** → DOTTED LINE

PHRASAL VERBS ˌsign sth a'way to agree that a property or a right to something no longer belongs to you, by writing your name on a document

ˌsign 'up to agree to do something or to join a course or organization

signage /'saɪnɪdʒ/ noun [U] signs in a public place

signal¹ /'sɪɡn(ə)l/ noun [C] **1** a movement or sound that is made by someone and has a special meaning for another person: *We waited for them to **give** us **the signal to** move.* **2** a fact, event, or action that shows what someone intends to do, or that shows what is likely to happen= SIGN: *There were strong signals that she intended to resign.* **3** pictures, sounds, or other pieces of information that are sent by one piece of electronic equipment and received by another one: *an electronic signal* **4** a piece of equipment with coloured lights on it that tells the driver of a vehicle to stop, go, or slow down= TRAFFIC LIGHTS: *The signal was at green.*

signal² /'sɪɡn(ə)l/ (**signals, signalling, signalled**) verb **1** [I/T] to make a movement or sound that has a special meaning to another person: *The cyclist signalled and turned right.* ♦ *He flashed his torch to signal that he was ready.* ♦ *He **signalled to** his wife, who was on the other side of the room.* **2** [T] to show that something is happening or will happen: *This agreement signalled the end of the war.* **3** [T] to show what you intend to do about something: *The kidnappers have signalled their willingness to negotiate.*

signatory /'sɪɡnət(ə)ri/ (plural **signatories**) noun [C] a person or organization that has signed an official agreement

signature /'sɪɡnətʃə/ noun [C] a person's name that is written in a special way by that person: *Is this your signature on the letter?* → AUTOGRAPH

'signature ˌfile noun [C] COMPUTING a computer file that contains information about the person who sent an email

significance /sɪɡ'nɪfɪkəns/ noun [singular/U] **1** the importance that something has because it affects other things: *I do not think this case is really **of great significance**.* ♦ *the historical **significance of** these events* **2** the meaning of something, usually a special meaning or a meaning that is not obvious: *I didn't realize **the** true **significance of** this comment at the time.*

significant /sɪɡ'nɪfɪkənt/ adj **1** very large or noticeable ≠ INSIGNIFICANT: *A **significant proportion** of the population never actually votes in elections.* ♦ *I think we can save a **significant amount** of time.* **2** very important: *one of the most significant musicians of the last century* **3** having a special meaning that only some people understand: *The look he gave her seemed to be significant.* —**significantly** adv

sigˌnificant 'figures noun [plural] MATHS the individual numbers that make up a number, starting from the first number that is not zero. They are used for expressing it accurately.

signify /'sɪɡnɪfaɪ/ (**signifies, signifying, signified**) verb [T] **1** to be a sign or symbol of something **2** to mean something: *What does this symbol signify?*

signing /'saɪnɪŋ/ noun **1** [U] the action of agreeing to a document by writing your name on it **2** [C] a player who has recently signed a contract to join a sports team **3** [U] the use of sign language to communicate

'sign ,language noun [C/U] LANGUAGE a way of communicating with people who cannot hear by making signals with your hands

'sign-,off noun [C] a word or phrase used for ending a letter, for example 'Yours sincerely'

signpost /'saɪn,pəʊst/ noun [C] a sign that is next to a road, that shows where something is

Sikh /siːk/ noun [C] RELIGION a member of an Indian religious group that separated from **Hinduism** in the 16th century. Sikhs believe in one god, and their beliefs include some aspects of Islam. —**Sikh** adj, **Sikhism** /'siːk,ɪz(ə)m/ noun [U]

silage /'saɪlɪdʒ/ noun [U] AGRICULTURE grass and plants that are allowed to partly decay in a **silo** and are then used for feeding farm animals

silence¹ /'saɪləns/ noun **1** [U] complete quiet: *The silence was broken by the soft sound of rain.* **2** [C/U] a period of time when no one speaks: *Long silences make her uncomfortable.* ♦ *They walked home in silence.* **3** [singular/U] a refusal to talk about something or provide information: *Her silence on the subject has been interpreted as a sign of guilt.*

silence² /'saɪləns/ verb [T] **1** to stop someone or something from speaking or making a sound **2** to prevent someone from giving an opinion or criticizing you

silent /'saɪlənt/ adj **1** not talking or making any noise: *a crowd of silent onlookers* ♦ *Everyone fell silent* (=stopped talking) *as the president walked in.* **2** a silent place is very quiet: *The old house was completely silent.* **3** refusing to talk about something: *For now, I prefer to stay silent on the matter.* **4** LANGUAGE not pronounced: *The 'b' in 'thumb' is silent.* —**silently** adv

silhouette /,sɪlu'et/ noun [C] **1** the dark shape or shadow of someone or something with the light behind them **2** an image or drawing showing only the shape of something

silica /'sɪlɪkə/ noun [U] CHEMISTRY a hard white or clear compound of **silicon** and oxygen that exists in sand and **quartz**. It is used for making glass. Chemical formula: SiO_2

silicate /'sɪlɪkeɪt/ noun [C/U] CHEMISTRY a substance made from silica mixed with another substance

silicon /'sɪlɪkən/ noun [U] CHEMISTRY a **metalloid** element that is found in sand, clay, and other minerals. It is used especially for making computer chips. Chemical symbol: **Si**

,silicon 'chip noun [C] COMPUTING a small piece of silicon with a set of complicated electronic connections on it, used especially in computers

,silicon di'oxide noun [U] CHEMISTRY **silica**

silk /sɪlk/ noun **1** [U] a thin smooth cloth made from the fibres produced by insects called **silkworms 2** [C] LAW a QC, a lawyer of high status

'silk ,screen noun [U] ARTS a method of printing designs on a surface by forcing ink or paint through a thin cloth

silkworm /'sɪlk,wɜːm/ noun [C] AGRICULTURE the larva of an Asian moth that produces silk when it is young

silky /'sɪlki/ adj very soft, smooth, and shiny

sill /sɪl/ noun [C] a narrow shelf at the bottom of a window = LEDGE

silly /'sɪli/ (**sillier, silliest**) adj **1** not intelligent or sensible: *a silly mistake* ♦ *You've been very silly.* **2** not important: *Don't get upset over silly things that people say.* **3** unsuitable and annoying because it makes someone seem stupid or like a child: *a silly hat*

silo /'saɪləʊ/ (plural **silos**) noun [C] **1** AGRICULTURE a tall round tower on a farm, used for storing things such as grain or for making **silage 2** a large underground structure, used for storing or protecting something

silt /sɪlt/ noun [U] GEOLOGY small particles of rock that are smaller than sand particles and bigger than clay. It is often found at the bottom of rivers, lakes etc, where it settles.

silver¹ /'sɪlvə/ noun **1** [U] CHEMISTRY a light grey metal element that is the most effective conductor of electricity and heat of any substance. It is used for making jewellery, coins etc, and also in photography, **soldering**, and to make conductors. Chemical symbol: **Ag 2** [U] attractive objects made from silver that people collect: *They had some beautiful silver.* **3** [C/U] SPORTS a **silver medal**

silver² /'sɪlvə/ adj **1** made of silver **2** light grey in colour

silver halide /,sɪlvə 'heɪlaɪd, ,sɪlvə 'hælaɪd/ noun [C] CHEMISTRY a chemical compound of silver and a halogen element. Silver halides change when they are in the light, and give atoms of silver and the halogen.

,silver 'medal noun [C] SPORTS a round flat silver object that is given as a prize for being second in a competition —**,silver 'medallist** [C]

'silver-,soldering noun [U] TECHNOLOGY a type of **brazing** (=joining metals together at very high temperatures) in which the **filler metal** contains some silver —**'silver-,solder** verb [I]

,silver 'surfer noun [C] informal a **senior citizen** who uses the Internet

,silver 'wedding noun [C] the day when people celebrate 25 years of marriage

silvery /'sɪlvəri/ adj like silver in colour or appearance

SIM card /'sɪm ,kɑːd/ noun [C] a small piece of plastic inside a mobile phone that contains information about the person who uses the phone

similar /'sɪmɪlə/ adj **1** things that are similar are like each other but are not exactly the same ≠ DIFFERENT: *We have similar interests.* ♦ *A second study produced remarkably similar results.* ♦ *Their situation is very similar to ours.* ♦ *The two men are similar in appearance.* **2** MATHS similar objects have exactly the same shape but are different sizes

similarity /,sɪmə'lærəti/ (plural **similarities**) noun **1** [C/U] the degree to which one thing is similar to another thing, or the fact that they are similar: *The similarity between the two stories suggests Lowry wrote them both.* ♦ *His signature bears absolutely no similarity to mine.* **2** [C] something that makes one thing seem like another: *There are many similarities between Ron and his father.* ♦ *His music shows several similarities to that of other modern composers.*

similarly /'sɪmələli/ adv **1** used for showing that two ideas are related or connected: *High inflation usually leads to high interest rates. Similarly, interest rates decline when inflation is low.* **2** in a similar way: *similarly priced cars*

simile /'sɪməli/ noun [C] LANGUAGE a phrase that describes something by comparing it to something else using the word 'like' or 'as', for example 'his hands were as cold as ice'

SIMM /sɪm/ noun [C] **COMPUTING** single inline memory module: a part that is attached to the **motherboard** of a computer to add memory

simmer /'sɪmə/ verb [I/T] to cook slowly at a temperature that is near boiling, or to cook something in this way

simple /'sɪmp(ə)l/ adj

1 easy to understand/do	4 not divided into parts
2 not decorated	5 of sentences
3 not complicated by sth	

1 easy to understand or do: *Students were given a simple skills test.* ♦ *The machine is fairly simple to operate.*
2 plain, without any complicated features or decoration: *a simple meal* ♦ *simple tools*
3 used for emphasizing one important fact: *The simple truth is that I was scared.* ♦ *She came for the simple reason that she wanted to see you.*
4 BIOLOGY a simple leaf or organism is not divided into separate parts
5 LANGUAGE a simple sentence has only one subject and one verb

'simple ,eye noun [C] **BIOLOGY** an eye in insects and other invertebrates that has a single lens —*picture*
→ CATERPILLAR, INSECT

,simple 'interest noun [U] **BUSINESS** interest earned on money that someone has invested, calculated once a year on the **principal** (=the amount of money originally invested) → COMPOUND INTEREST

'simple ,leaf noun [C] **BIOLOGY** a single leaf on a stalk
→ COMPOUND LEAF

,simple 'sugar noun [C] **BIOLOGY, CHEMISTRY** a **monosaccharide**

simplicity /sɪm'plɪsəti/ noun [U] the quality of being simple

simplify /'sɪmplɪfaɪ/ (**simplifies, simplifying, simplified**) verb [T] **1** to make something less complicated or difficult **2 MATHS** to make something such as a fraction or an equation simpler by removing those numbers or symbols that are the same in each part of it —**simplification** /,sɪmplɪfɪ'keɪʃ(ə)n/ noun [C/U]

simplistic /sɪm'plɪstɪk/ adj *showing disapproval* treating something in a way that makes it seem much simpler than it really is

simply /'sɪmpli/ adv **1** used for emphasizing one important fact: *He lost simply because he wasn't good enough.* **2** in a way that is not complicated or confusing: *I've stated my intention as simply as possible.* **3** in a very ordinary or plain way: *We live very simply and don't spend a lot of money.*

simulate /'sɪmjʊleɪt/ verb [T] **1** to produce the features of something in a way that seems real but is not **2** to have features or qualities that are similar to a particular substance **3** to pretend to feel or think something —**simulated** adj: *simulated leather*

simulation /,sɪmjʊ'leɪʃ(ə)n/ noun **1** [C/U] something that produces the features of something in a way that seems real but is not **2** [U] **COMPUTING** the use of computers to create models of real situations and real events, for example weather conditions or processes in the body, that people can use for studying these situations and events

simulator /'sɪmjʊ,leɪtə/ noun [C] a piece of equipment that is used for training people to operate an aircraft or other vehicle, by **simulating** different situations

simultaneous /,sɪm(ə)l'teɪniəs/ adj happening or done at the same time —**simultaneously** adv

sin¹ /sɪn/ noun [C/U] **RELIGION** an action, thought, or way of behaving that is wrong according to religious laws: *the sin of pride*

sin² /sɪn/ (**sins, sinning, sinned**) verb [I] **RELIGION** to do something that is wrong according to religious laws

since /sɪns/ adv, conjunction, preposition **1** from a particular point in the past until now, or until another point in the past: *I've known Joanna since she was born.* ♦ *Turkey has been a republic since 1923.* ♦ *I had not seen her since she went to live in Pretoria.* ♦ *Since arriving in Nairobi, Thomas has had 15 job interviews.* ♦ *Paul started sailing in 1986 and he's been doing it ever since.* **2** because: *I shall not be able to attend the meeting since I shall be on holiday with my family.*

sincere /sɪn'sɪə/ adj showing that you really mean what you say ≠ INSINCERE: *His apology seemed sincere.*

sincerely /sɪn'sɪəli/ adv really, or honestly: *I sincerely hope you will succeed.*

PHRASE Yours sincerely used before your name as a way of ending a formal letter that starts with 'Dear Mr/Mrs/Ms' etc

sincerity /sɪn'serəti/ noun [U] an honest way of behaving that shows that you really mean what you say or do

sine /saɪn/ noun [C] **MATHS** in a right-angled triangle, the measurement of an **acute** angle that is equal to the length of the side opposite the angle divided by the length of the hypotenuse

'sine ,curve noun [C] **MATHS** a graph showing the sine **function**

sine qua non /,sɪni kwɑː 'nɒn/ noun [singular] *formal* a condition that must exist before something can happen

sinew /'sɪnjuː/ noun [C/U] **ANATOMY** the strong substance that connects muscles to bone, or a piece of this = TENDON

sinful /'sɪnf(ə)l/ adj **RELIGION** morally wrong according to religious laws

sing /sɪŋ/ (**sings, singing, sang** /sæŋ/, **sung** /sʌŋ/) verb [I/T] **MUSIC** to make music using your voice: *Grace was singing softly to herself.* ♦ *They sang several old familiar songs.* **2** [I] if a bird sings, it makes musical sounds

PHRASE sing sb's/sth's praises to talk about how good someone or something is

sing. abbrev singular

singe /sɪndʒ/ (**singes, singeing, singed**) verb [I/T] to burn something slightly, so that only the edge or surface is affected

singer /'sɪŋə/ noun [C] **MUSIC** someone who sings, especially someone who sings well or as their job

single¹ /'sɪŋɡ(ə)l/ adj **1** only one: *a single sheet of paper* **2** not married, or not in a romantic relationship: *Please state whether you are single, married, or divorced.* **3** designed for one person, or used by one person: *The room has two single beds.* **4** used for emphasizing one thing: *Drugs are the single biggest cause of crime here.* ♦ *Do we have to count every single penny we spend?*

PHRASE not a single not even one: *You didn't write a single letter the whole time you were away.*

single² /'sɪŋɡ(ə)l/ noun **1** [C] **MUSIC** a musical record with only one song or piece of music on each side **2 singles** [plural] people who are not married, or who are not in a romantic relationship **3 singles** [plural] **SPORTS** in tennis, a match that is played between two people **4** [C] **TOURISM** a ticket for travelling to a place, but not for returning from it

single³ /'sɪŋɡ(ə)l/ **PHRASAL VERB** **,single sb/sth 'out** to choose one person or thing from a group for special attention: *In her article, three schools were singled out for particular criticism.*

single-celled /'sɪŋɡ(ə)l ,seld/ adj **BIOLOGY** consisting of only one cell

,single 'currency noun [singular] **ECONOMICS** a system of money that is shared by several countries

,single 'file noun [C/U] a line of people or things in which one is directly behind the other —**,single 'file** adv

single-handed /,sɪŋɡ(ə)l 'hændɪd/ adj, adv done by one person without help from anyone else —**single-handedly** adv

single-minded /,sɪŋɡ(ə)l 'maɪndɪd/ adj **focused**

,single 'parent noun [C] **SOCIAL STUDIES** a parent who raises their children alone, without a partner

,single-parent 'family noun [C] **SOCIAL STUDIES** a family in which only one parent lives in the home and takes care of the children

,single-'plate ,clutch noun [C] **ENGINEERING** a type of **clutch** that has a single **clutch plate**

'single ,room noun [C] **TOURISM** a room that is large enough for one person to sleep in, especially one in a hotel or a rented property

,single 'supplement noun [C] **TOURISM** an extra amount of money that someone travelling alone has to pay for a hotel room or **package holiday**

singleton /'sɪŋɡ(ə)ltən/ noun [C] **1** a person who is not married, or is not in a romantic relationship **2** a single object of a type that sometimes comes in pairs or groups

singly /'sɪŋɡli/ adv separately: *You can buy stamps singly or in packs of ten.*

singular /'sɪŋɡjʊlə/ adj **1** **LANGUAGE** the singular form of a word is used for referring to one person or thing **2** *formal* strange, or unusual

the singular /'sɪŋɡjʊlə/ noun [singular] **LANGUAGE** the form of a word that is used for referring to one person or thing

sinister /'sɪnɪstə/ adj threatening to do something harmful or evil: *a sinister remark*

sink¹ /sɪŋk/ (**sinks, sinking, sank** /sæŋk/, **sunk** /sʌŋk/) verb

1 go under water	**6** become quiet
2 force liquid out of position	**7** push sth sharp into sth
3 move to lower level	**8** invest money
4 fall/sit/lie down	**9** shape metal
5 go down in amount	**+ PHRASE**
	+ PHRASAL VERB

1 [I/T] to disappear below the surface of water, or to make something do this ≠ **FLOAT**: *The ferry sank during a storm.* ♦ *The **ship** was **sunk** by an enemy submarine.*
2 [I] **PHYSICS** if a heavy object sinks, it moves downwards through a liquid or soft substance because it **displaces** (=forces out of its position) more of the liquid or soft substance than its own weight
3 [I] to move to a lower level: *The water level in the lake had sunk by several feet.* ♦ *We watched the sun **sinking below** the horizon.*
4 [I] to fall, sit, or lie down: *All I wanted to do was to **sink into** an armchair and rest.*
5 [I] to go down in value or amount: *Agricultural production had **sunk to** its lowest level in years.*
6 [I] to become quiet: *Their voices sank to a whisper.*

7 [T] to push something that is sharp into something that is solid: *The cat **sank** its claws **into** my leg.*
8 [T] to invest money in something: *We've **sunk** several thousand dollars **into** the project so far.*
9 [T] **TECHNOLOGY** to shape a piece of metal using a hammer, leaving a flat base and **rim** (=edge)

PHRASE **your spirits sink/your heart sinks** if your spirits sink or your heart sinks, you become sad or lose hope

PHRASAL VERB **,sink 'in** to become completely understood: *She had to repeat her words several times before they finally sank in.*

sink² /sɪŋk/ noun [C] a large open container for water that is fixed to a wall and connected to pipes that bring the water and carry it away

sinkhole /'sɪŋk,həʊl/ noun [C] **GEOLOGY** a circular hole in the ground, formed when a rock such as **limestone** dissolves

sinking /'sɪŋkɪŋ/ noun [U] **TECHNOLOGY** a technique in **metalwork** in which a piece of metal is curved inwards, using a hammer, to create an object such as a plate

'sinking ,fund noun [C] **BUSINESS** an amount of money that a business or organization puts into a **bank account** or invests, in order to pay for something in the future

sinner /'sɪnə/ noun [C] **RELIGION** someone who does not obey religious laws

sinus /'saɪnəs/ noun [C] **ANATOMY** one of several empty spaces that are in the bones of the face in the area behind the nose

sinusitis /,saɪnə'saɪtɪs/ noun [U] **HEALTH** an infection in which the inside of the sinuses becomes swollen

sinusoidal /,saɪnə'sɔɪd(ə)l/ adj **MATHS, PHYSICS** relating to or in the shape of a **sine curve**

sip¹ /sɪp/ (**sips, sipping, sipped**) verb [I/T] to drink in small amounts: *She sipped her tea.*

sip² /sɪp/ noun [C] a small amount of liquid that is taken into your mouth: *He **took a sip** of coffee.*

siphon /'saɪf(ə)n/ or **,siphon sth 'off** verb [T] **1** to move liquid from one container to another through a tube **2** to move money from one bank account to another illegally

sir /strong sɜː, weak sə/ **1** *spoken* used as a polite way of speaking to a man **2** Sir used before the name of a man who is a **knight**

PHRASE **Dear Sir** used for beginning a letter to a man whose name you do not know

sire¹ /saɪə/ noun [C] the male parent of an animal such as a horse or a cow

sire² /saɪə/ verb [T] to become the father of an animal such as a horse or a cow

siren /'saɪrən/ noun [C] a piece of equipment that makes a loud sound, used for warning people

sisal /'saɪs(ə)l/ noun [U] **AGRICULTURE** a white fibre used for making rope and **rugs**. It comes from a Mexican plant with spines on its leaves called an **agave**.

sister /'sɪstə/ noun [C] **1** a girl or woman who has the same parents as you: *I have two brothers and two sisters.* → HALF SISTER, STEPSISTER **2** **HEALTH** a female nurse in charge of a hospital **ward** (=a room for people who are ill) **3** **RELIGION** a **nun** (=a woman who is a member of a religious community): *Sister Mary* **4** used by women for referring to a woman who they feel loyalty and friendship towards: *support for our sisters who are the victims of war*

'sister-in-,law (plural **'sisters-in-,law**) noun [C] **1** the sister of someone's husband or wife **2** the wife of someone's brother

sit /sɪt/ (**sits, sitting, sat** /sæt/) verb

1 rest on seat	**6** be member of sth
2 put body into seat	**7** meet officially
3 make someone sit	**8** take examination
4 be in situation etc	**9** be model
5 be in a place	**+ PHRASAL VERBS**

1 [I] to be in a position in which the lower part of your body rests on a seat or the ground, while the upper part of your body is upright: *Sit still* (=without moving) *while I brush your hair.* ♦ *I usually sit next to Andrew in history.* ♦ *They were sitting in a café drinking coffee.* ♦ *I was sitting at my computer when the phone rang.* ♦ *Matt sat on a park bench, reading.* ♦ *Six of us were sitting around the table talking.*
2 [I] to lower your body into a sitting position: *He came over and sat on the sofa.*
3 [T] to put someone into a sitting position: *Joanna sat the child on her lap and read him a story.*
4 [I] to be in a particular situation or condition for a period of time: *I was sitting in traffic for over an hour.*
5 [I] to be in a particular place: *The house sits on top of a hill.*
6 [I] to be a member of a committee or other official group: *She sits on the boards of several large companies.*
7 [I] POLITICS, LAW if a parliament, a court of law, or a committee sits, it has an official meeting
8 [T] EDUCATION to take an examination: *I'm sitting my French exam tomorrow.*
9 [I] ARTS to be a model for a painter or a photographer
PHRASAL VERBS **,sit 'down** same as **sit** sense 2: *Do sit down by the fire.*
'sit ,on sth to delay dealing with something: *They've been sitting on my application for over a month now.*
,sit 'up 1 to sit with your back straight and upright: *Sit up straight* and pay attention. **2** to go from a lying position to a sitting position: *Would you like to sit up and read for a while?*

sitar /sɪ'tɑː/ noun [C] MUSIC an Indian musical instrument like a guitar with a long neck and a round body

sitcom /'sɪtkɒm/ noun [C] ARTS a humorous television or radio series about a group of characters

site¹ /saɪt/ noun [C] **1** an area of land where something is being built or could be built: *a construction site* **2** a place where something interesting or important happened: *We visited the site of the battle.* **3** a place used for a particular purpose: *a landing site for helicopters* **4** COMPUTING a website

site² /saɪt/ verb [T] to put something in a particular place

site datum /'saɪt ,deɪtəm/ noun [C] CONSTRUCTION a fixed point used for measuring the different levels of a building

,site lo'cation ,plan noun [C] CONSTRUCTION, TECHNOLOGY a drawing that shows details of the place where a building will be built, together with the area around it

'site ,plan noun [C] CONSTRUCTION, TECHNOLOGY a drawing that shows details of the place where a building will be built

sitter /'sɪtə/ noun [C] ARTS someone who sits or stands in a particular position while an artist paints or photographs them

sitting /'sɪtɪŋ/ noun [C] **1** a period of time during which a meal is served **2** POLITICS, LAW a period of time when a parliament or court meets **3** ARTS a period of time when someone is being painted or photographed by an artist

'sitting ,room noun [C] a **living room**

situate /'sɪtʃueɪt/ verb [T] formal **1** to describe or discuss something in relation to the things it is connected to **2** to put something, especially a building, in a particular place

situated /'sɪtʃueɪtɪd/ adj in a particular place= LOCATED

situation /,sɪtʃu'eɪʃ(ə)n/ noun [C] **1** the set of conditions that exist at a particular time in a particular place: *The country is facing a very difficult economic situation.* ♦ *I found myself in an embarrassing situation.* ♦ *What prospects are there for a person in his situation?* **2** formal a job —**situational** adj

SI unit /,es 'aɪ ,juːnɪt/ noun [C] SCIENCE Système International unit: a standard scientific unit of measurement in an international system. It is based on the metric system and uses **multiples** of 10. The main units are the metre, kilogram, second, **ampere, kelvin**, and **mole**.

six /sɪks/ number the number 6

sixteen /,sɪks'tiːn/ number the number 16

sixteenth /,sɪks'tiːnθ/ number **1** in the place or position counted as number 16 **2** one of 16 equal parts of something

sixth /sɪksθ/ number **1** in the place or position counted as number 6 **2** one of 6 equal parts of something

sixties /'sɪkstiz/ noun [plural]
PHRASES **the sixties 1** the years from 1960 to 1969 **2** a temperature in the sixties is between 60 and 69 degrees Fahrenheit
in your sixties the period of time from age 60 to age 69: *a woman in her sixties*

sixtieth /'sɪkstiəθ/ number **1** in the place or position counted as number 60 **2** one of 60 equal parts of something

sixty /'sɪksti/ number the number 60

size /saɪz/ noun **1** [C/U] a measurement of how large or small something is: *balloons of all shapes and sizes* ♦ *The president has promised to reduce the size of the army.* **2** [C] one of a series of standard measurements according to which goods are made or sold: *What size shoes do you take?* ♦ *This dress is a size 12.* **3** [U] the fact that something is very large: *The size of the organization makes communication difficult.*

sizeable /'saɪzəb(ə)l/ adj fairly large

sizzle /'sɪz(ə)l/ verb [I] to make the sound of food that is cooking in hot oil —**sizzle** noun [singular]

ska /skɑː/ noun [U] MUSIC a type of music that developed in Jamaica in the 1950s, combining US styles of jazz, **rock**, and **R & B** with traditional Jamaican music

skate¹ /skeɪt/ noun [C] **1** a type of shoe with a thin metal blade on the bottom, used for moving quickly on ice= ICE SKATE **2** a type of shoe with four thick wheels on the bottom, used for moving quickly on a smooth surface= ROLLER SKATES

skate² /skeɪt/ verb [I] to move over a surface using skates —**skater** noun [C], **skating** /'skeɪtɪŋ/ noun [U]

skateboard /'skeɪt,bɔːd/ noun [C] a board with four wheels on the bottom that you stand on and ride —**skateboarder** noun [C], **skateboarding** noun [U]

'skating ,rink noun [C] a place with an area of ice or a smooth floor, used for **skating**

skeletal /'skelɪt(ə)l/ adj **1** ANATOMY relating to the skeleton **2** extremely thin

skeleton /'skelɪt(ə)n/ noun [C] **1** ANATOMY, BIOLOGY the hard frame that supports the body of a human or other animal. In vertebrates it is usually made of bone that the muscles are attached to, and it protects the most important organs, for example the brain and the heart. → ENDOSKELETON, EXOSKELETON — *picture* → on next page **2** the basic parts of something such as a plan or organization, without any details

sketch¹ /sketʃ/ noun [C] **1** ARTS a drawing that is made quickly that does not have many details **2** ARTS a short funny scene performed within a longer show **3** a short account of something with only a few details

sketch² /sketʃ/ verb **1** [I/T] ARTS to draw a picture quickly and with few details **2** [T] to make a general plan of something, with only a few details

sketchbook /'sketʃ,bʊk/ or **sketchpad** /'sketʃ,pæd/ noun [C] ARTS a book with blank pages, used for drawing

skewed /skjuːd/ adj **1** results or opinions that are skewed are not accurate because they have been affected by something **2** not straight

skewer /'skjuːə/ noun [C] a long thin piece of metal or wood that you stick through food to hold it while it cooks

ski¹ /skiː/ (plural **skis**) noun [C] SPORTS a long thin object that is fitted to a boot to allow someone to slide easily over snow

ski² /skiː/ (**skis, skiing, skied**) verb [I] SPORTS to slide over snow on skis

skid /skɪd/ (**skids, skidding, skidded**) verb [I] to slide across the ground in an uncontrolled way —**skid** noun [C]

skier /'skiːə/ noun [C] SPORTS someone who moves over snow on **skis**

skiing /'skiːɪŋ/ noun [U] SPORTS the sport or activity of moving over snow on **skis**

'ski ,jump noun [C] SPORTS **1** a steep hill for skiing that turns up at the end so that when people ski off, they travel through the air before landing **2** a competition in which people go down and jump off a ski jump

skilful /'skɪlf(ə)l/ adj showing a lot of skill: *a skilful negotiator* ♦ *the artist's skilful use of colour* —**skilfully** adv

'ski ,lift noun [C] a machine that carries people to the top of a slope so they can **ski** down= CHAIRLIFT

skill /skɪl/ noun [C/U] the ability to do something well, usually as a result of experience and training: *I admired the skill and dedication of the nursing staff.* ♦ *computer skills*

skilled /skɪld/ adj **1** skilful ≠ UNSKILLED: *a skilled craftsman* **2** a skilled job needs someone who has ability and experience

skim /skɪm/ (**skims, skimming, skimmed**) verb **1** [T] to remove a substance that is floating on the surface of a liquid: *Skim the fat off the soup.* **2** [I/T] to move quickly over the surface of something: *Water skiers skimmed across the lake.* **3** [I/T] to read something quickly and not very carefully

skimmed milk /,skɪmd 'mɪlk/ noun [U] milk that has had the cream removed from it

skin¹ /skɪn/ noun [C/U] **1** the outer layer of a vertebrate's body. It consists of a thick inner layer of cells called the **dermis** and a thinner outer layer called the **epidermis**. Skin helps to protect against some diseases and the effects of sunlight, and is also important in helping to keep the body's temperature even: *She has beautiful soft skin.* ♦ *a skin disease* → HOMEOSTASIS —*picture* → on p.687 **2** the outer layer that is cut from an animal's body, used for making clothing and decorations= HIDE **3** the outer layer of a fruit or vegetable= PEEL: *banana skins* → THICK¹

skin² /skɪn/ (**skins, skinning, skinned**) verb [T] to remove the skin from an animal, fruit, or vegetable

'skin ,cancer noun [U] HEALTH cancer of the skin, often caused by **ultraviolet** light

skinny /'skɪni/ (**skinnier, skinniest**) adj **1** *informal* very thin **2** skinny clothes fit the body very tightly

skip¹ /skɪp/ (**skips, skipping, skipped**) verb **1** [I] to move forwards by jumping first on one foot and then the other: *Julie skipped along the pavement.* **2** [I] to jump over a rope that you or two other people swing above your head and then under your feet **3** [T] to not do or not have something: *Let's skip that chapter and move on to the next one.* ♦ *It's not a good idea to skip breakfast.* **4** [I] to move quickly from one place or thing to another: *They kept* **skipping from** *one topic* **to** *another.*

skip² /skɪp/ noun [C] **1** a very large metal container that is used in the building industry for rubbish **2** the action of skipping

skipper /'skɪpə/ noun [C] *informal* someone who is in charge of a small ship

skirt /skɜːt/ noun [C] a piece of clothing for a woman or girl. It hangs from the waist and is not joined between the legs: *She was wearing a long skirt.*

'ski ,slope or **'ski ,run** noun [C] a part of a hill or mountain that you **ski** on

skit /skɪt/ noun [C] LITERATURE, ARTS a short humorous performance or piece of writing

skull /skʌl/ noun [C] ANATOMY the bones of the head —*picture* → BRAIN, SKELETON

sky /skaɪ/ noun **1** [singular/U] the space above the Earth that you see when you look up into the air: *a clear blue sky* ♦ *Black smoke rose into the sky.* ♦ **The night sky** *was filled with stars.* **2** **skies** [plural] a way of referring to the sky, used especially when talking about the weather: *Tomorrow we expect* **clear skies** *and sunshine.*

'sky ,bed noun [C] TOURISM a seat on a passenger aircraft that turns into a bed

skylight /'skaɪ,laɪt/ noun [C] a window in a roof or ceiling

skyline /'skaɪ,laɪn/ noun [C] the shapes made by buildings or mountains when you see them against the sky

sky marshal /'skaɪ ,mɑːʃ(ə)l/ noun [C] TOURISM a guard who makes certain that passengers stay safe on plane flights

Skype /skaɪp/ TRADEMARK a network on the Internet that people use to make telephone calls

skyscraper /'skaɪ,skreɪpə/ noun [C] a very tall building containing offices or flats

slab /slæb/ noun [C] a large flat piece of something, especially something hard: *a concrete slab* ♦ *a slab of chocolate*

slack /slæk/ adj **1** loose and not pulled tight: *The rope suddenly* **went slack**. **2** not taking enough care to make

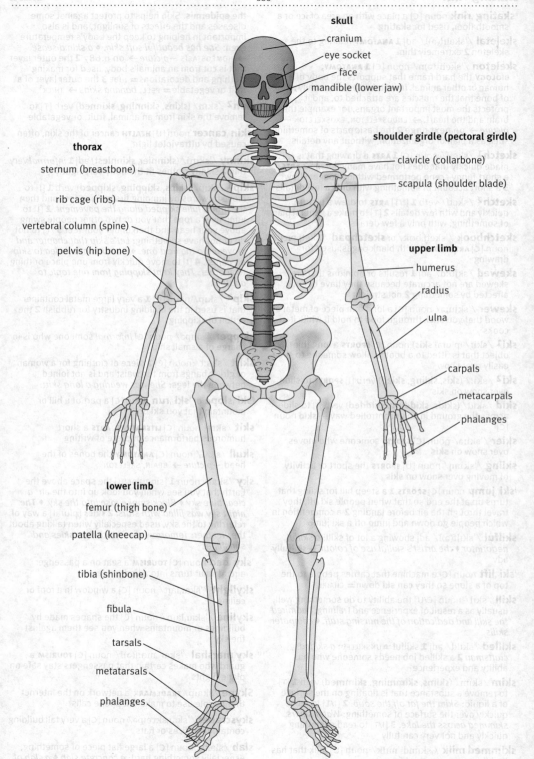

skull
- cranium
- eye socket
- face
- mandible (lower jaw)

thorax
- sternum (breastbone)
- rib cage (ribs)
- vertebral column (spine)
- pelvis (hip bone)

shoulder girdle (pectoral girdle)
- clavicle (collarbone)
- scapula (shoulder blade)

upper limb
- humerus
- radius
- ulna
- carpals
- metacarpals
- phalanges

lower limb
- femur (thigh bone)
- patella (kneecap)
- tibia (shinbone)
- fibula
- tarsals
- metatarsals
- phalanges

human skeleton

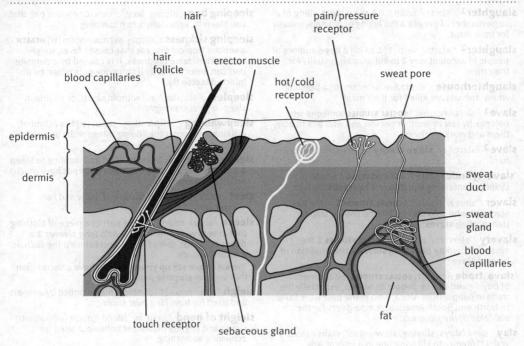

hair

pain/pressure receptor

hair follicle

erector muscle

sweat pore

blood capillaries

hot/cold receptor

epidermis

sweat duct

dermis

sweat gland

blood capillaries

touch receptor

sebaceous gland

fat

skin

sure that something is done well: *slack safety standards* **3** not as busy or successful as usual in business

slacken /'slækən/ verb [I/T] **1** to become slower or less active, or to make something become slower or less active **2** to become looser, or to make something looser

slag /slæg/ noun [U] a waste product that is left after coal or metal has been processed

slain /sleɪn/ the past participle of **slay**

slalom /'slɑːləm/ noun [C/U] **SPORTS** a race, especially on **skis**, in which people move around a series of poles

slam /slæm/ (**slams, slamming, slammed**) verb **1** [I/T] if a door or lid slams, or if you slam it, it shuts with great force so that it makes a loud noise: *He ran from the room, slamming the door behind him.* ♦ *The heavy gate slammed shut.* **2** [T] to put, move, or hit something somewhere with great force: *He slammed the groceries down on the table.* ♦ *She slammed the brakes on.* **3** [I] to hit against something with great force: *The bicycle slammed into a tree.*

slander¹ /'slɑːndə/ noun [C/U] **LAW** the crime of saying something about someone that is not true and that is likely to damage their reputation

slander² /'slɑːndə/ verb [T] **LAW** to say something about someone that is not true and is likely to damage their reputation

slanderous /'slɑːnd(ə)rəs/ adj **LAW** containing or using slander

slang /slæŋ/ noun [U] **LANGUAGE** words or expressions that are very informal and that are not considered suitable for formal situations

slant¹ /slɑːnt/ verb **1** [I] to be or move at an angle that is not 90°: *Sunlight slanted through the curtains.* **2** [T] to give information or ideas in a way that gives more attention or support to a particular person, group, or opinion: *He was accused of slanting his reports to protect his colleagues.*

slant² /slɑːnt/ noun [singular] **1** the angle at which something slopes **2** a particular way of showing or considering information: *Her recipes give us a new slant on Italian cooking.*

slanted /'slɑːntɪd/ adj **1** at an angle that is not 90°: *a room with a slanted ceiling* **2** done in a way that gives more attention or support to a particular person, group, or opinion: *The book is heavily slanted towards American business methods.*

slap¹ /slæp/ (**slaps, slapping, slapped**) verb **1** [T] to hit someone or something quickly with the palm of the hand **2** [T] to put something down quickly and noisily: *Annie slapped down her cards.* **3** [I] to hit a surface with a sound that is like someone slapping something: *The waves slapped against the stone pier.* **4** [T] to put something on a surface quickly and without much attention: *Just slap some paint on the wall and it will look fine.*

slap² /slæp/ noun [C] a sharp hit with the palm of the hand

slash¹ /slæʃ/ verb **1** [T] to reduce something by a large amount: *The budget had been slashed by £3 million.* **2** [I/T] to cut something in a violent way: *The tyres on the car had been slashed.* **3** [I] to try to cut or hit something by making several swinging movements: *She slashed wildly at the ball.*

slash² /slæʃ/ noun [C] **1** a long deep cut **2** a quick swinging movement, especially with something sharp **3** a line / that separates numbers, letters, or words in writing

PHRASE slash and burn AGRICULTURE slash and burn farming involves clearing an area by cutting down and burning trees and old plants to make it possible to plant crops

slate /sleɪt/ noun **1** [U] **GEOLOGY** a type of dark grey rock that breaks easily into flat thin pieces. It is a type of metamorphic rock that is formed from **shale**. **2** [C] a single flat piece of slate that is used with others for covering a roof → CLEAN¹

slaughter¹ /ˈslɔːtə/ noun [U] **1** the violent killing of a large number of people **2** the killing of animals, usually for their meat

slaughter² /ˈslɔːtə/ verb [T] **1** to kill a large number of people in a violent way **2** to kill animals, usually for their meat

slaughterhouse /ˈslɔːtəˌhaʊs/ noun [C] a building where animals are killed for their meat

slave¹ /sleɪv/ noun [C] **SOCIAL STUDIES** someone who belongs by law to another person and who has to obey them and work for them

slave² /sleɪv/ or **slave aˈway** verb [I] to work very hard

ˈslave ˌcylinder noun [C] **ENGINEERING** a small cylinder containing a **piston** in a **hydraulic** system

slaver /ˈsleɪvə/ noun [C] **SOCIAL STUDIES 1** in the past, someone who sold **slaves 2** in the past, a ship for transporting **slaves**

slavery /ˈsleɪvəri/ noun [U] **SOCIAL STUDIES 1** the system of owning people as **slaves 2** the condition of being a **slave**

ˈslave ˌtrade noun [U] **SOCIAL STUDIES** the business of buying and selling people as **slaves**, especially the trade in people from Africa, who in the past were taken to North and South America: *campaigners for the abolition of the slave trade*

slay /sleɪ/ (**slays, slaying, slew** /sluː/, **slain** /sleɪn/) verb [T] *literary* to kill someone in a violent way

sleazy /ˈsliːzi/ (**sleazier, sleaziest**) adj **1** dishonest, or immoral **2** a sleazy place is dirty and unpleasant

sledge /sledʒ/ noun [C] a small vehicle that someone sits on to slide over snow. It moves on smooth pieces of wood or plastic.

sledgehammer /ˈsledʒˌhæmə/ noun [C] a long heavy hammer that you swing with both hands

sleek /sliːk/ adj **1** sleek fur or hair is smooth and shiny **2** with a modern attractive smooth design: *a sleek red sports car*

sleep¹ /sliːp/ (**sleeps, sleeping, slept** /slept/) verb **1** [I] to go into a natural state in which your body rests and you are unconscious, especially for several hours at night: *The baby usually sleeps in the afternoon.* ♦ *'Did you sleep well?' 'Yes, thanks.'* **2** [T] to have enough room or beds for a particular number of people to sleep in: *The house sleeps six comfortably.*

PHRASAL VERB ˌsleep ˈin to continue sleeping after the time that you usually wake up: *The whole family sleeps in on Sundays.*

sleep² /sliːp/ noun **1** [U] a natural state in which your body rests and you are unconscious: *I can't get to sleep if there's any noise.* ♦ *You need to go home and get some sleep.* ♦ *The motion of the car sent me to sleep.* **2** [singular] a period of time when you are sleeping: *I think I'll have a sleep this afternoon.* ♦ *She lay down and soon fell into a deep sleep.*

PHRASES go to sleep to begin sleeping: *What time do the kids usually go to sleep?*

put sth to sleep to give an animal drugs so that it dies quickly without feeling any pain

sleeper /ˈsliːpə/ noun [C] **1** someone who is sleeping: *a light sleeper* **2 TOURISM** a train with beds for passengers to sleep in **3** one of the large pieces of wood that support a railway track

ˈsleeper ˌwall noun [C] **CONSTRUCTION** a low brick wall that supports the wooden **joists** of a floor and keeps them away from wet ground

sleeping bag /ˈsliːpɪŋ ˌbæg/ noun [C] a warm bag that you sleep in, especially when camping

sleeping sickness /ˈsliːpɪŋ ˌsɪknəs/ noun [U] **HEALTH** a serious tropical disease that causes fever, weight loss, and extreme tiredness. It is caused by a parasite that can enter the body if someone gets bitten by an infected **tsetse fly**.

sleepless /ˈsliːpləs/ adj without sleep, or unable to sleep: *a sleepless night*

sleepwalking /ˈsliːpˌwɔːkɪŋ/ noun [U] the action of walking and sometimes doing things while you are still sleeping

sleepy /ˈsliːpi/ adj **1** feeling tired and wanting to sleep **2** a sleepy place is very quiet and does not have much activity —**sleepily** adv

sleet /sliːt/ noun [U] a mixture of snow and rain —**sleet** verb [I]

sleeve /sliːv/ noun [C] **1** the part of a piece of clothing that covers your arm: *a dress with long sleeves* **2** a paper or plastic cover that protects something such as a record or book

PHRASE have sth up your sleeve to have a secret plan that you can surprise people with

sleigh /sleɪ/ noun [C] a vehicle that is pulled by animals and used for travelling over snow

sleight of hand /ˌslaɪt əv ˈhænd/ noun [singular/U] clever and slightly dishonest behaviour used for achieving something

slender /ˈslendə/ adj **1** tall or long and thin in an attractive way: *slender fingers* **2** very small in amount and only just enough: *They won by a slender majority.*

slept /slept/ the past tense and past participle of **sleep¹**

slew /sluː/ the past tense of **slay**

slice¹ /slaɪs/ noun [C] **1** a flat piece of food that has been cut from something larger: *Cut the bread into thick slices.* ♦ *a slice of bread* **2** *informal* a part or share of something: *We want a bigger slice of the tourist trade.* **3 SPORTS** a way of hitting a ball on its edge, so that it curves or spins

slice² /slaɪs/ verb **1** [T] to cut something such as a piece of food into flat pieces: *I'll slice some bread.* —*picture* → FOOD **2** [I] to cut something easily: *The saw quickly sliced through the board.* **3** [T] **SPORTS** to hit a ball on its edge, so that it curves or spins

slick¹ /slɪk/ adj **1** smooth and shiny or wet: *slick black hair* **2** clever and good at persuading people but probably not honest: *a slick car salesman* **3** done in an impressive way that seems to need little effort: *a slick advertisement*

slick² /slɪk/ verb [T] if someone slicks their hair back or down, they put oil or water on it in order to make it stay in place

slide¹ /slaɪd/ noun [C]

1 sth children play on	4 for microscope
2 reduction in sth	5 fall of rock/earth
3 piece of film/glass	

1 a structure for children to play on, with steps and a slope to slide down

2 a situation in which an amount gradually becomes less: *a slide in sales*

3 ARTS a small piece of film in a frame. You shine light through it in order to show the image on a screen. —*picture* → PROJECTOR

4 SCIENCE a small thin piece of clear glass used for holding an object that is being looked at under a microscope —*picture* → MICROSCOPE

5 GEOGRAPHY a sudden fall of rock, earth etc from the side of a mountain

slide² /slaɪd/ (**slides, sliding, slid** /slɪd/) verb **1** [I/T] to move smoothly and quickly across a surface, or to make something move in this way: *He slid down the hill on a sledge.* ♦ *The doors slid open.* ♦ *I slid the letter under her door.* **2** [I] to gradually get into a worse situation than before: *The company slid further into debt last year.*

'**slide ,rule** noun [C] MATHS a simple piece of equipment used for calculating, shaped like a ruler with a piece in the middle that slides along

'**slide ,show** noun [C] COMPUTING a feature of software that shows photographs one after the other, without the user having to give an instruction to look at the next image

sliding joint /ˌslaɪdɪŋ 'dʒɔɪnt/ noun [C] ANATOMY a joint in the body in which one bone can slide over the bone next to it. The **vertebrae** of the spine move in this way. —picture → JOINT

slight /slaɪt/ adj **1** small in size, amount, or degree: *a slight increase in temperature* **2** thin and small: *a slight young woman*

PHRASE **not in the slightest** not at all

slightly /'slaɪtli/ adv a little: *I feel slightly better today.* ♦ *He was limping slightly.* ♦ *'Do you know her?' 'Only slightly.'*

slim¹ /slɪm/ (**slimmer, slimmest**) adj **1** thin in an attractive way: *She had a slim youthful figure.* **2** very small: *There is still a slim chance that she may be alive.*

slim² /slɪm/ (**slims, slimming, slimmed**) verb [I] to try to lose weight by eating less

slime /slaɪm/ noun [U] a thick, wet, and unpleasant substance

slimy /'slaɪmi/ adj thick, wet, and unpleasant to touch

sling¹ /slɪŋ/ (**slings, slinging, slung** /slʌŋ/) verb [T] to put or throw something somewhere in a careless way: *He slung his jacket over one shoulder.*

sling² /slɪŋ/ noun [C] **1** a piece of cloth used for supporting your arm when it is injured **2** a set of belts or ropes used for supporting or lifting something heavy

slip¹ /slɪp/ (**slips, slipping, slipped**) verb

1 (almost) fall	4 slide sth somewhere
2 slide out of position	5 become less strong
3 go quickly & quietly	+ PHRASES

1 [I] if you slip, your feet slide accidentally and you fall or lose your balance: *Margaret slipped and broke her arm.* ♦ *Be careful you don't slip on the wet floor.*
2 [I] if something slips, it slides out of the position it should be in: *The knife slipped and cut my finger.* ♦ *The ball slipped out of my hands.*
3 [I] to go somewhere quickly and quietly, without anyone noticing you or stopping you: *Several people managed to slip past the guards.* ♦ *I slipped away before the end of the meeting.*
4 [T] to slide something into a place or position, often so that other people do not notice: *John slipped his arm around his wife's waist.* ♦ *He slipped the money into his pocket.*
5 [I] to gradually become less strong or good: *Profits slipped by 13% last year.*

PHRASES **let (it) slip** to tell someone something that is secret by mistake: *He let it slip that they intended to move to Canada.*
slip through your fingers if something such as an opportunity or a prize slips through your fingers, you fail to get it or to take advantage of it

slip² /slɪp/ noun [C]

1 small piece of paper	4 change to lower level
2 slight mistake	5 in cricket
3 piece of clothing	

1 a small piece of paper: *I left the message for you on a slip of paper.*
2 a small mistake: *Tom played well, despite a few slips at the beginning.*
3 a piece of women's underwear consisting of a loose skirt or dress with no sleeves
4 a small change from a higher level to a lower one
5 SPORTS in **cricket**, a place near the **batsman** where players stand when they are trying to catch the ball

slipped disc /ˌslɪpt 'dɪsk/ noun [C] HEALTH a round flat piece of cartilage between the **vertebrae** in the spine that has been forced out of its position so that it causes severe back pain

slipper /'slɪpə/ noun [C] a soft comfortable shoe that you wear in your house

slippery /'slɪpəri/ adj a slippery surface or object is difficult to move on or hold because it is smooth or wet

slit¹ /slɪt/ noun [C] a long narrow space or cut in something: *a skirt with a slit up the side*

slit² /slɪt/ (**slits, slitting, slit**) verb [T] to make a long thin cut in something: *She grabbed the envelope and slit it open.*

'**slit ,gong** noun [C] MUSIC a type of drum used in Africa that consists of a whole **log** whose inside has been removed through **slits** (=long narrow holes) along one side

slither /'slɪðə/ verb [I] to move along the ground like a snake

sliver /'slɪvə/ noun [C] a small thin piece of something: *slivers of glass*

slogan /'sləʊɡən/ noun [C] a short phrase that is used for advertising something, or for supporting someone in politics

slop /slɒp/ (**slops, slopping, slopped**) verb [I/T] if a liquid slops, or if you slop it, it moves inside its container, or some of it comes out of the container

slope¹ /sləʊp/ noun [C] **1** a surface or piece of ground that has one end higher than the other: *At the end of the garden there is a steep slope.* **2** the angle of a slope: *a 45-degree slope* **3** PHYSICS an **inclined plane**

slope² /sləʊp/ verb [I] to have one end higher than the other: *The floor slopes a bit.* —**sloping** adj

,**sloping 'surface** noun [C] PHYSICS a surface that is neither horizontal nor vertical

sloppy /'slɒpi/ (**sloppier, sloppiest**) adj **1** done in a very careless way: *a sloppy job* **2** sloppy clothes are loose and informal **3** expressing emotions in a way that seems silly or embarrassing

slot /slɒt/ noun [C] **1** a long narrow hole or space that you can fit something through or into: *He put a coin in the slot.* **2** a time between other events when it is arranged that something will happen: *We circled the airport waiting for a landing slot.*

slotted screw /ˌslɒtɪd 'skruː/ noun [C] TECHNOLOGY a screw that has a single **slot** (=line) cut in the top

slouch /slaʊtʃ/ verb [I] to sit, walk, or stand with your shoulders bent forwards

slough /slʌf/ or ,**slough 'off** verb [T] BIOLOGY to remove an outer layer of skin

slow[1] /sləʊ/ adj **1** not moving or happening fast: *This bus is really slow.* ♦ *She's a slow worker, but reliable.* ♦ *Progress has been **painfully slow*** (=very slow). ♦ *The government has been **slow to** respond.* **2** not busy, interesting, or exciting: *The first part of the film is very slow.* **3** a watch or clock that is slow shows a time that is earlier than the correct time: *Your watch is 15 minutes slow.* **4** someone who is slow is not intelligent, so that they need a lot of time in order to understand simple things

slow[2] /sləʊ/ verb [I/T] **1** if you slow something, or if it slows, you reduce the speed at which it happens or moves: *Drugs can slow the progress of the disease.* ♦ *Traffic on the motorway had slowed to walking pace.* **2** if you slow something, or if it slows, you reduce the level or amount of it: *Inflation slowed significantly in the 1990s.*

   PHRASAL VERB **,slow (sth) 'down** same as **slow**[2] sense 1: *The new government is slowing down the pace of reform.*

slowly /'sləʊli/ adv moving or happening at a slow speed: *The city is slowly getting back to normal after a three-day transport strike.* ♦ *Could you **speak** a little more **slowly**?*

'slow-,worm noun [C] a type of lizard that has no legs and looks like a small snake

sludge /slʌdʒ/ noun [U] **1** an unpleasant thick wet substance **2 ENVIRONMENT** a thick soft waste substance from an industrial process

slug /slʌg/ noun [C] a small mollusc that lives on land, similar to a snail without a shell

sluggish /'slʌgɪʃ/ adj not moving, performing, or reacting as well as usual: *a sluggish economy* ♦ *Sasha woke up feeling tired and sluggish.*

sluice /sluːs/ noun [C] a passage that water flows along, with a gate that can be closed to control the flow

slum /slʌm/ noun [C] a poor area of a town where the houses are in very bad condition

slump[1] /slʌmp/ verb [I] **1** to suddenly fall to a much lower level: *Profits slumped to under $250 million.* **2** to suddenly fall or sit down because you are very tired or unconscious: *Sam's body slumped to the floor.*

slump[2] /slʌmp/ noun [C] **1** a sudden large reduction in amount: *a slump in prices* **2 ECONOMICS** a period when someone or something is much less successful than before: *an economic slump*

slung /slʌŋ/ the past tense and past participle of **sling**[1]

slur[1] /slɜː/ noun [C] **MUSIC** a line written above musical notes to show that there should be no pause between them

slur[2] /slɜː/ (**slurs, slurring, slurred**) verb [I/T] to speak without pronouncing the words clearly or separately —**slurred** /slɜːd/ adj: *slurred speech*

sly /slaɪ/ adj *showing disapproval* clever at tricking people or at hurting them without them realizing it: *I noticed his sly smile.*

smack[1] /smæk/ verb [T] to hit someone with your flat hand or with a flat object

smack[2] /smæk/ noun [C] **1** a hit with your flat hand or with a flat object **2** a loud sound that is made when something hits a surface

small /smɔːl/ adj **1** not large in size, amount, or number: *These shoes are too small for me.* ♦ *I'd rather work for a smaller company.* ♦ *A small number of people have complained.* **2** not very important or difficult: *Can you do me a small favour?* ♦ *I noticed a few small mistakes.* **3** not worth a lot of money, or not involving a lot of money: *small investors* **4** small children are very young —**small** adv: *Write small so that everything will fit on one page.*

Both **small** and **little** can be used to describe something that is not big in size or number.
■ **Small** is a more general word: *a woman with a small dog* ♦ *Our house is fairly small.*
■ **Little** is usually used when you feel something about the thing that you like, dislike it, or feel surprised that it is so small: *Look at that little baby!* ♦ *She has such little feet.*

Build your vocabulary: words you can use instead of small

Small is a very general word. Here are some words with more specific meanings that sound more natural and appropriate in particular situations.
places/buildings/rooms little, compact, tiny, cramped
people short, little, petite, tiny
numbers/amounts low, insignificant, meagre, paltry
problems/effects/changes minor, considerable, slight, negligible, minimal

,small 'business noun [C] **BUSINESS** a business that has a small number of employees

,small 'claims ,court noun [C] **LAW** a law court in which people try to get back small amounts of money that they think other people or businesses owe them

smallholder /'smɔːl,həʊldə/ noun [C] **AGRICULTURE** a person who farms a small piece of land called a **smallholding**

smallholding /'smɔːl,həʊldɪŋ/ noun [C] **AGRICULTURE** a piece of farmed land that is smaller than the average farm

,small in'testine noun [C] **ANATOMY** the tube in the body that food goes into after it has passed through the stomach. It is where most of the digestion and absorption of food takes place. —*picture* → DIGESTIVE SYSTEM, ORGAN

smallpox /'smɔːl,pɒks/ noun [U] **HEALTH** an extremely infectious viral disease that killed many people in the past. Smallpox now only exists as a virus kept in some laboratories, because of a successful worldwide vaccination programme.

,small-'scale adj smaller or less important than other things of the same kind

smart[1] /smɑːt/ adj **1** clean and tidy in appearance and dressed in nice clothes: *smart new clothes* ♦ *Sandy's looking very smart today.* **2** intelligent: *Sophie is a smart hard-working student.* ♦ *Wilson made a few smart investments.* **3** used by rich fashionable people: *the city's smartest shopping district* **4** smart weapons and machines are very effective because they use computer technology —**smartly** adv: *a smartly dressed young man*

smart[2] /smɑːt/ verb [I] **1** to hurt with a sudden sharp pain **2** to be very upset by something that someone has said or done

'smart ,card noun [C] **COMPUTING** a small plastic card that stores information in electronic form

smash[1] /smæʃ/ verb **1** [I/T] if something smashes, or if you smash it, it breaks noisily into many pieces when it falls or when you break it: *Someone had smashed a window.* ♦ *The bottle fell and smashed on the floor.* **2** [I/T] to hit against an object or surface with a lot of force, or to hit something against something in this way: *His car smashed into a tree.* ♦ *He fell and smashed his head on the pavement.* **3** [T] to completely destroy or defeat an organization, system etc **4** [T] SPORTS in tennis, to hit a ball that is above your head downwards and very hard

smash² /smæʃ/ noun [C] **1** informal a car crash **2** SPORTS in tennis, the action of hitting a ball above your head downwards very hard

SME /ˌes em ˈiː/ noun [C] BUSINESS small and medium-sized enterprise: a business that has a small or medium number of employees

smear¹ /smɪə/ verb [T] **1** to spread a soft substance on a surface in an untidy way: *The kids had smeared glue all over the floor.* ♦ *His face was smeared with mud.* **2** to try to damage someone's reputation by telling lies about them **3** to make the surface of something dirty, for example glass, by rubbing it

smear² /smɪə/ noun [C] **1** a dirty mark made by rubbing something **2** an attempt to damage someone's reputation by telling lies about them **3** HEALTH a **smear test**

ˈsmear cam,paign noun [C] a series of attempts to damage someone's reputation by telling lies about them

ˈsmear ,test or **smear** noun [C] HEALTH a medical test in which a doctor takes cells from a woman's uterus and checks them for cancer

smell¹ /smel/ noun **1** [C] the quality of something that you notice when you breathe in through your nose: *This paint has a very strong smell.* ♦ *the delicious smell of fresh bread →* AROMA **2** [U] the ability to notice or recognize smells: *Dogs have an excellent sense of smell.* **3** [C] an instance of smelling something: *Have a smell of this perfume.*

smell² /smel/ (**smells**, **smelling**, **smelled** or **smelt** /smelt/) verb

1 have particular smell	4 put nose close to smell
2 have a bad smell	5 feel sth will happen
3 notice/recognize smell	

1 [linking verb] to have a particular smell: *That cake smells so good!* ♦ *The laboratory smelled strongly of chemicals.* ♦ *It smells like a bar in here.* **2** [I] to have an unpleasant smell: *It smells in here!* ♦ *His feet really smell.* **3** [T] to notice or recognize the smell of something: *Do you smell gas?* **4** [T] to experience the smell of something by putting your nose close to it: *Come and smell these roses.* **5** [T] to feel that something is going to happen, usually something bad: *I could smell trouble ahead.*

smelly /ˈsmeli/ adj with an unpleasant smell

smelt¹ /smelt/ a past tense and past participle of **smell²**

smelt² /smelt/ verb [T] TECHNOLOGY to heat and melt ore in a **furnace**, in order to remove the metal that it contains

smelter /ˈsmeltə/ noun [C] TECHNOLOGY a **furnace** used for obtaining metal from ore by heating and melting it, or the factory where this process takes place

smile¹ /smaɪl/ verb [I] to raise the corners of your mouth when you are happy or when you are being friendly: *James looked up and smiled at Karen.*

smile² /smaɪl/ noun [C] an act of smiling, or this expression on your face: *Tom had a huge smile on his face.* ♦ *a smile of satisfaction*

smirk /smɜːk/ verb [I] to smile in an unpleasant way because something bad has happened to someone else —**smirk** noun [C]

SMMEs /ˌes ˌdʌb(ə)l em ˈiːz/ noun [plural] BUSINESS small, medium, and microenterprises: businesses that are small, average, or extremely small in size

smock /smɒk/ noun [C] a long loose shirt

smog /smɒg/ noun [U] ENVIRONMENT polluted air that forms a cloud close to the ground

smoke¹ /sməʊk/ noun **1** [U] a grey, black, or white cloud that is produced by something that is burning: *A column of black smoke slowly rose above the building.* ♦ *The air was thick with cigarette smoke.* **2** [C] informal a cigarette, or an act of smoking a cigarette: *I'm just going out for a smoke.*

PHRASE **go up in smoke** informal to be destroyed

smoke² /sməʊk/ verb **1** [I/T] to suck smoke from a cigarette, pipe etc into the mouth and lungs: *Phil was reading the paper and smoking a cigarette.* **2** [I/T] to smoke cigarettes as a regular habit: *I didn't know he smoked!* **3** [I] to produce smoke: *By the time I got to the garage, the engine was smoking alarmingly.* **4** [T] to preserve and give flavour to food by hanging it in smoke

smoked /sməʊkt/ adj smoked food has a special flavour because it has been hung in smoke

ˈsmoke-free adj in which no people are smoking, or in which smoking is not allowed

smokeless zone /ˈsməʊkləs ˌzəʊn/ noun [C] an area of a town where people are not allowed to make any smoke

smoker /ˈsməʊkə/ noun [C] someone who smokes cigarettes, a pipe etc

smokescreen /ˈsməʊkˌskriːn/ noun [C] **1** something that you say or do as a way of hiding your real feelings, intentions, or activities **2** a cloud of smoke created to hide the movements of soldiers or military vehicles

smoking /ˈsməʊkɪŋ/ noun [U] HEALTH the activity of breathing smoke from cigarettes, pipes etc into the mouth and lungs. Smoking is very **addictive**, and causes many serious diseases, including cancer and heart disease.

smoky /ˈsməʊki/ adj **1** with a lot of smoke in the air **2** tasting or smelling of smoke

smooth¹ /smuːð/ adj **1** completely flat and even with no rough areas or lumps ≠ ROUGH: *smooth skin* **2** moving in a way that is steady and well controlled: *With a smooth swing, he hit the ball.* **3** causing no difficulty, problems, or delays: *a smooth process* ♦ *We are changing systems, but we expect a smooth transition.*

smooth² /smuːð/ verb [T] **1** to move your hand across the surface of something until it is flat and even: *Frances smoothed her skirt down over her knees.* **2** to carefully spread a substance over a surface: *Anne gently smoothed cream into the baby's skin.*

smoothly /ˈsmuːðli/ adv **1** without difficulty, problems, or delays **2** in a relaxed and confident way that usually persuades people to do things **3** with a movement that is steady and well controlled **4** in a way that produces a smooth, even surface

ˈsmooth ,muscle noun [C] ANATOMY a type of muscle inside the **gut** that is not made of long fibres and is not under voluntary control

smother /ˈsmʌðə/ verb [T] **1** to cover something completely **2** to kill someone by covering their face until they stop breathing **3** to stop a fire burning by covering it

smoulder /ˈsməʊldə/ verb [I] to burn slowly, producing smoke but no flames

SMS /,es em 'es/ noun [U] short message service: a method of sending a written message using a mobile phone

SMTP /,es em ti: 'pi:/ abbrev COMPUTING Simple Mail Transfer Protocol: the main method of sending emails on the Internet, consisting of rules for how programs sending email should work with programs receiving email

smudge¹ /smʌdʒ/ noun [C] a small untidy mark made by a substance such as dirt or ink

smudge² /smʌdʒ/ verb [I/T] if you smudge something such as ink, or if it smudges, you make it spread in an untidy way by touching it

smug /smʌg/ adj showing disapproval too satisfied with your abilities or achievements —**smugly** adv, **smugness** noun [U]

smuggle /'smʌg(ə)l/ verb [T] to take someone or something secretly or illegally into or out of a place —**smuggler** noun [C], **smuggling** noun [U]

snack /snæk/ noun [C] a small amount of food that you eat between meals: Coffee, tea, and snacks are available throughout the day. —**snack** verb [I]

snag /snæg/ noun [C] a problem or disadvantage

snail /sneɪl/ noun [C] a small mollusc that has a soft body, no legs, and a hard spiral shell on its back

'snail ,mail noun [U] informal letters that are sent by post. This expression is used mainly by people writing emails.

snake¹ /sneɪk/ noun [C] a long thin reptile with no legs and a smooth skin. Many snakes are **venomous** (=they produce a poison).

snake² /sneɪk/ verb [I] to move in a series of long curves: The path snakes through the trees and up the hill.

snap¹ /snæp/ (**snaps, snapping, snapped**) verb

1 break loudly	4 become upset
2 move sth noisily	5 speak angrily
3 (try to) bite	+ PHRASE

1 [I/T] to suddenly break something with a short loud noise, or to be broken in this way: When the rope snapped, Davis fell into the water. ♦ Ken **snapped off** the smaller branches.
2 [I/T] to quickly move something, for example a light switch or something else that makes a short sound, or to be moved quickly in this way: She quickly **snapped** her handbag **shut**. ♦ It's really simple to build – the bits just **snap together**.
3 [I/T] if an animal such as a dog snaps at you, it bites you or tries to bite you: A terrier was **snapping at** his heels.
4 [I] to suddenly lose control and become extremely angry or upset: She was bound to snap under all that pressure.
5 [I] to speak to someone in a sudden angry way: I'm sorry I **snapped at** you just now.
PHRASE **snap your fingers** to make a short sound by pressing your middle finger against your thumb and moving them suddenly apart

snap² /snæp/ noun **1** [singular] a short loud noise, made especially by something breaking or closing **2** [U] a card game in which players put down cards one after the other in piles and try to be the first to shout 'snap' when two cards are the same

snapper /'snæpə/ noun [C/U] a brightly coloured tropical fish with sharp teeth, eaten as food

snapshot /'snæp,ʃɒt/ noun [C] **1** a photograph that is taken without the use of professional equipment **2** a

short explanation or description that tells you what a particular place or situation is like

snare¹ /sneə/ noun [C] a piece of equipment that is used for catching an animal

snare² /sneə/ verb [T] **1** to catch an animal using a snare **2** to trick someone into an unpleasant situation that they cannot escape from

snarl /snɑːl/ verb **1** [I/T] to speak in an unpleasant angry way **2** [I] if an animal snarls, it makes an angry sound in its throat and shows its teeth —**snarl** noun [C]

snatch /snætʃ/ verb [T] **1** to quickly take something or someone away: Her brother snatched the letter and tore it open. **2** to take the opportunity to do something quickly: They managed to snatch a few hours' sleep. **3** to manage to get something that you almost did not get: They **snatched victory** with a goal in the last minute.

sneak /sniːk/ verb **1** [I] to move somewhere quietly and secretly so that no one can see you or hear you **2** [T] to take someone or something secretly or illegally

sneaky /'sniːki/ adj doing or saying things secretly, often in a dishonest or unfair way

sneer /snɪə/ verb [I/T] to smile or speak in an unpleasant way that shows that you do not respect someone or something —**sneer** noun [C]

sneeze /sniːz/ verb [I] to loudly blow air out of your nose in a sudden uncontrolled way —**sneeze** noun [C]

sniff /snɪf/ verb **1** [I] to breathe in noisily through your nose, for example because you have been crying: Amanda sniffed and wiped her nose. **2** [T] to breathe in through your nose in order to smell something: He took off the lid and sniffed the contents of the jar. —**sniff** noun [C]

sniffer dog /'snɪfə ,dɒg/ noun [C] a dog that is trained to find drugs, bombs etc by smelling

snigger /'snɪgə/ verb [I] to laugh quietly at something rude, or at something unpleasant that has happened to someone —**snigger** noun [C]

snip /snɪp/ (**snips, snipping, snipped**) verb [T] to cut something in a short quick movement using scissors —**snip** noun [C]

sniper /'snaɪpə/ noun [C] someone who shoots at people from a hidden place

snippet /'snɪpɪt/ noun [C] a small piece of something, especially information or news

snob /snɒb/ noun [C] showing disapproval someone who thinks that they are better than other people, usually because of their social class

snobbery /'snɒbəri/ noun [U] showing disapproval the attitude or behaviour of someone who thinks that they are better than other people

snobbish /'snɒbɪʃ/ adj showing disapproval behaving in a way that shows that you think you are better than other people

snooker /'snuːkə/ noun [U] a game that you play on a large table that is covered with green cloth. Players try to hit coloured balls into holes with a long stick called a **cue**.

snoop /snuːp/ verb [I] to secretly try to get information that someone would not want you to have

snooze /snuːz/ verb [I] informal to sleep for a short period of time, especially during the day —**snooze** noun [C]

snore /snɔː/ verb [I] to breathe noisily while you sleep —**snore** noun [C]

snorkel /'snɔːk(ə)l/ noun [C] a piece of equipment with a tube that fits in your mouth so that you can breathe when you are swimming under water

snorkelling /'snɔːk(ə)lɪŋ/ noun [U] the activity of swimming using a snorkel

snort /snɔːt/ verb [I] to make a sudden loud noise through your nose, for example because you are angry or laughing —**snort** noun [C]

snout /snaʊt/ noun [C] **BIOLOGY** the long nose of a pig or a similar animal

snow¹ /snəʊ/ noun **GEOGRAPHY** 1 [U] small soft white pieces of ice that fall from the sky and cover the ground: *Three inches of snow fell overnight.* ♦ *The path was hidden under a blanket of snow.* 2 **snows** [plural] the snow that falls over a period of time: *The first snows of winter are here.*

snow² /snəʊ/ verb [I] **GEOGRAPHY** when it snows, snow falls from the sky

> **PHRASE** **snowed under** if you are snowed under, you have too much work to deal with

snowboard /'snəʊˌbɔːd/ noun [C] **SPORTS** a long curved board that someone stands on with both feet and uses for sliding down a hill covered in snow —**snowboarding** noun [U]

snowfall /'snəʊˌfɔːl/ noun [C/U] **GEOGRAPHY** the amount of snow that falls during a particular period

snowflake /'snəʊˌfleɪk/ noun [C] a single piece of snow that falls from the sky

the 'snow-ˌline noun **GEOGRAPHY** on a mountain, the level above which the land is covered with snow, usually permanently

snowplough /'snəʊˌplaʊ/ noun [C] a large vehicle that pushes snow off the road

snowstorm /'snəʊˌstɔːm/ noun [C] **GEOGRAPHY** a storm with a lot of snow and strong winds

snowy /'snəʊi/ adj with a lot of snow

snub /snʌb/ (**snubs, snubbing, snubbed**) verb [T] to insult someone by ignoring them or being rude to them —**snub** noun [C]

snug /snʌg/ adj 1 warm and comfortable = COSY 2 fitting closely —**snugly** adv

so /səʊ/ adv, conjunction

1 very	4 as a result
2 used instead of repeating sth	5 states a purpose
3 also	6 starts new subject
	+ PHRASES

1 used for emphasizing a quality, feeling, or amount: *Why are we going so slowly?* ♦ *The road surface became so hot that it melted.*
2 used for referring back to what has just been said, instead of repeating it: *If you wanted to leave early, you should have said so.* ♦ *Does the President intend to go to Moscow? And if so, when?*
3 used for saying that something that was just said is also true about another person or thing: *Fatima is planning to come, and so is Sylvia.* ♦ *If I can learn how to drive a car, so can you.*
4 happening because of what you have just mentioned: *A tree had fallen across the road, so they had to turn round and go back.*
5 used for saying what the purpose of an action is: *He lowered his voice so no one would hear.*
6 *spoken* used for starting a new subject or introducing a question: *So, what are you hoping to study at university?*

> **PHRASES** **and so on/and so forth** used instead of mentioning more of a similar type of thing that has already been mentioned: *I use the computer to write letters, reports, and so on.*
>
> **not so...(as)** used for saying that one person or thing has less of a particular quality than another: *The idea is not so silly as it sounds.*
>
> **only so much/only so many** used for saying that a number or amount is limited: *There are only so many police officers available.*
>
> **or so** used for showing that a number or amount is not exact: *The job won't take long – about twenty minutes or so.*
>
> **so (what)?** *informal* used for saying in a slightly rude way that what someone has said does not matter or is not important
> → LONG²

soak /səʊk/ verb [I/T] 1 to put something into a liquid and leave it there for a period of time: *Leave the beans to soak overnight.* 2 to make something very wet, or to become very wet: *The rain poured in, soaking the cardboard boxes.* ♦ *Blood had soaked through the bandage.*

> **PHRASAL VERB** ˌsoak sth 'up if a dry or soft substance soaks up a liquid, the liquid goes into it

soakaway /'səʊkəˌweɪ/ noun [C] **CONSTRUCTION** a hole for collecting water that has soaked into the soil

soaked /səʊkt/ adj extremely wet

soaking /'səʊkɪŋ/ adj extremely wet

'soaking ˌpit noun [C] **TECHNOLOGY** a heated pit or hole in which **ingots** (=blocks of metal) are kept until they have the same temperature throughout

soap /səʊp/ noun [C/U] a substance that you use with water in order to wash your body or an object: *a bar of soap* ♦ *perfumed soaps*

soapless /'səʊpləs/ adj a soapless substance does not contain soap

'soap ˌopera noun [C] **ARTS** a television or radio series about the imaginary lives of a group of people

soapy /'səʊpi/ adj covered in soap, or containing soap

soar /sɔː/ verb [I] 1 to quickly increase to a high level: *Unemployment has soared.* 2 to rise or fly high in the sky 3 if someone's spirits or hopes soar, they suddenly feel very happy and hopeful —**soaring** adj

sob /sɒb/ (**sobs, sobbing, sobbed**) verb [I/T] to cry noisily while taking short breaths —**sob** noun [C]

sober /'səʊbə/ adj 1 not drunk 2 with a serious attitude 3 plain and not brightly coloured —**soberly** adv

so-called /'səʊ kɔːld/ adj 1 used for showing that you think a word used for describing something is not suitable: *His so-called friends betrayed him.* 2 used for saying that a particular word is usually used for referring to something: *They've found the flight recorder, the so-called black box.*

soccer /'sɒkə/ noun [U] **SPORTS** the game of **football**

sociable /'səʊʃəb(ə)l/ adj a sociable person is friendly and enjoys being with other people = OUTGOING ≠ UNSOCIABLE

social /'səʊʃ(ə)l/ adj

1 about society	4 about behaviour
2 about position	5 about animals
3 about activities	

1 **SOCIAL STUDIES** relating to society and to people's lives in general: *a period of enormous political and social change* ♦ *social problems such as unemployment*
2 **SOCIAL STUDIES** relating to the position that someone has in society in relation to other people: *someone's social background* ♦ *The evidence shows a relationship between crime and social class.*

3 relating to activities that involve being with other people, especially activities that you do for pleasure: *a social activity* ♦ *The worst thing about working from home is the lack of **social contact**.*
4 relating to rules about behaviour with other people: *We need someone with excellent **social skills**.*
5 BIOLOGY used for describing animals that live in groups rather than alone
—**socially** adv

,social 'housing noun [U] SOCIAL STUDIES houses that local councils and other organizations provide at a low cost

,social 'indicator noun [C] ECONOMICS something that shows how much progress has been made in improving the conditions in which people live and work

socialism /'səʊʃə,lɪz(ə)m/ noun [U] POLITICS a political system that aims to create a society in which everyone has equal opportunities and in which the most important industries are owned or controlled by the whole community —**socialist** adj, **socialist** noun [C]

socialize /'səʊʃəlaɪz/ verb [I] to spend time with other people socially —**socialization** /,səʊʃəlaɪ'zeɪʃ(ə)n/ noun [U]

,social 'networking noun [U] COMPUTING the activity of using special websites that allow people to communicate with friends, and make new friends with similar interests

,social psy'chology noun [U] SOCIAL STUDIES the study of how social conditions affect people

,social 'science noun [C/U] SOCIAL STUDIES the study of the way that people live in society, or one of the separate subjects that involve the study of human societies, for example **sociology** or history —**,social 'scientist** noun [C]

,social se'curity noun [U] SOCIAL STUDIES **1** the system by which the government regularly pays money to people who do not have a job, or are too ill or too old to work **2** money that you receive from social security

,social 'services noun [plural] SOCIAL STUDIES the services that are provided by a government or local council for people with social problems

social studies /'səʊʃ(ə)l ,stʌdiz/ noun [U] EDUCATION a school or college subject that includes the study of history, government, and cultures of the world

'social ,worker noun [C] SOCIAL STUDIES someone who is trained to give help and advice to people who have severe social problems —**'social ,work** noun [U]

societal /sə'saɪət(ə)l/ adj *formal* relating to society, or to the way that society is organized

society /sə'saɪəti/ (plural **societies**) noun **1** [U] SOCIAL STUDIES people in general living together in organized communities, with laws and traditions controlling the way that they behave towards each other: *Society has to be prepared to support its elderly people.* ♦ *The scheme aims to help prisoners who have been released into society.* **2** [C/U] SOCIAL STUDIES a particular community or type of community, or the people who live in it: *The protesters were drawn from a broad cross section of society.* ♦ *Never forget that we live in a multicultural society.* **3** [U] the group of people in a country who are rich and fashionable or from a high social class: *She moved in **high society** and had many aristocratic friends.* ♦ *a big society wedding* **4** [C] an organization or club for people who have a particular interest or who take part in a particular activity: *She joined the local history society.* → BUILDING SOCIETY

sociocultural /,səʊʃiəʊ'kʌltʃ(ə)rəl/ adj SOCIAL STUDIES involving a combination of social and cultural elements

socioeconomic /,səʊʃiəʊ,ekə'nɒmɪk/ adj SOCIAL STUDIES involving a combination of social and economic elements

sociolect /'səʊʃiəʊlekt/ noun [C] LANGUAGE a type of language spoken by people in a particular social class or group

sociology /,səʊʃi'ɒlədʒi/ noun [U] SOCIAL STUDIES the study of society, the way that it is organized, and the way that people behave in relation to each other —**sociological** /,səʊʃiə'lɒdʒɪk(ə)l/ adj, **sociologist** noun [C]

sociopolitical /,səʊʃiəʊpə'lɪtɪk(ə)l/ adj SOCIAL STUDIES involving a combination of social and political elements

sock /sɒk/ noun [C] a soft piece of clothing that you wear on your foot inside your shoe: *a pair of yellow **socks***

socket /'sɒkɪt/ noun [C] **1** PHYSICS a place on a wall or machine with holes that you use for connecting a piece of electrical equipment —*picture* → PLUG **2** a curved space that something fits into **3** ANATOMY an **eye socket** —*picture* → EYE **4** CONSTRUCTION the end of a pipe that a narrower pipe called a **spigot** fits into to form a joint

soda /'səʊdə/ or **'soda ,water** noun [C/U] water with gas in it that is added to an alcoholic drink

sodium /'səʊdiəm/ noun [U] CHEMISTRY a very reactive chemical element that is a silver-white metal and is found in salt. Chemical symbol: **Na**

sodium bicarbonate /,səʊdiəm baɪ'kɑːbənət/ noun [U] CHEMISTRY a chemical compound in the form of a white powder that is used in cooking. Chemical formula: $NaHCO_3$

,sodium 'chloride noun [U] CHEMISTRY the scientific name for salt. Chemical formula: $NaCl$

,sodium hy'droxide noun [U] CHEMISTRY a chemical compound that is very alkaline and is used in making paper, soap, chemicals, and medicines. Chemical formula: $NaOH$ = CAUSTIC SODA

,sodium 'nitrate noun [U] CHEMISTRY a chemical compound used in making fertilizers and for keeping meat fresh. Chemical formula: $NaNO_3$

sodium stearate /,səʊdiəm 'stɪəreɪt/ noun [U] CHEMISTRY the chemical name for a type of soap

sofa /'səʊfə/ noun [C] a large soft comfortable seat with arms and a back that two or three people can sit on

soffit /'sɒfɪt/ noun [C] CONSTRUCTION the underneath part of a roof that sticks out beyond the walls, or the material that covers this

soft /sɒft/ adj

1 not hard/firm	5 not strict enough
2 not rough/stiff	6 kind/sympathetic
3 not harsh	7 about water
4 pale/gentle	

1 a soft substance is easy to press or shape and is not hard or firm: *soft cheese* ♦ *The soil is fairly soft after the rain.*
2 a soft material or surface is nice to touch and not rough or stiff: *I want to get a nice soft carpet for the bedroom.* ♦ *Her skin **felt soft** to his touch.*
3 a soft sound is quiet and nice to listen to: *The engine noise was no more than a soft hum.*
4 a soft light or colour is pale, gentle, and nice to look

at: *Her bedroom was decorated in soft shades of pink and blue.*
5 not strict enough with other people and allowing them to do things they should not do: *You're too soft – I wouldn't let them behave like that.* ♦ *They accused the minister of being soft on crime.*
6 kind and sympathetic: *He must have a soft heart beneath that stern exterior.*
7 soft water does not contain many natural minerals and is easy to use with soap
—**softly** adv, **softness** noun [U]

softball /ˈsɒftˌbɔːl/ noun [U] **SPORTS** a game similar to baseball, played on a smaller field and with a larger softer ball

'soft ˌcopy noun [C/U] **COMPUTING** information that is in electronic form, not printed on paper ≠ HARD COPY

ˌsoft 'drink noun [C] a cold drink that does not contain any alcohol

ˌsoft 'drug noun [C] an illegal drug that is less harmful than other illegal drugs

soften /ˈsɒf(ə)n/ verb **1** [I/T] to become softer, or to make something become softer: *Simmer gently until the fruit has softened.* **2** [I/T] to become kinder and less severe, or to make someone or something do this: *When Jack spoke to the children his voice softened.* **3** [T] to make something look nicer by making its colour or shape less strong: *The warm light softened her features.*

ˌsoft 'error noun [C] **COMPUTING** a mistake caused by software that is very difficult to find, because it only appears in particular situations

ˌsoft 'palate noun [C] **ANATOMY** the soft part of the top of the inside of the mouth, at the back

ˌsoft-'spoken adj speaking or said in a quiet gentle voice

ˌsoft 'target noun [C] someone or something that is very easy to attack or criticize

software /ˈsɒf(t)ˌweə/ noun [U] **COMPUTING** the programs used by computers for doing particular jobs: *word-processing software* ♦ *You log onto our website, then download and install the software.* ♦ *a software company* → HARDWARE

ˌsoft 'water noun [U] **CHEMISTRY** water that does not contain many natural minerals and is easy to use with soap

soggy /ˈsɒɡi/ adj wet and soft

soh /səʊ/ noun [C] **MUSIC** the fifth note in the **sol-fa** musical **scale**

soil¹ /sɔɪl/ noun [C/U] **GEOLOGY, AGRICULTURE** the top layer on the surface of the Earth in which plants grow. Soil consists of extremely small pieces of rock, decayed organic matter, air, water, and minerals: *The dry rocky soil is suitable for planting vines.*

soil² /sɔɪl/ verb [T] *formal* to make something dirty —**soiled** /sɔɪld/ adj

'soil ˌcreep noun [U] **GEOLOGY** the very slow movement of soil down a hill, caused by gravity

'soil eˌrosion noun [U] **AGRICULTURE, ENVIRONMENT** the process by which soil is gradually removed by the rain, wind, or sea. It is sometimes made worse by farming practices such as cutting down trees, leaving the ground without any plant cover, or using heavy vehicles on slopes.

soil injector /ˈsɔɪl ɪnˌdʒektə/ noun [C] **AGRICULTURE** a piece of equipment like a large syringe that is used for putting liquids such as fertilizer and **insecticide** into the soil close to plants —*picture* → AGRICULTURAL

'soil ˌprofile noun [C] **AGRICULTURE** a deep section of soil in which different layers of material can be seen

solar /ˈsəʊlə/ adj **ASTRONOMY** relating to the Sun, or coming from the Sun

'solar ˌcell noun [C] **PHYSICS** a piece of equipment that uses the Sun's energy to produce electricity

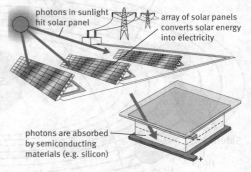

photons in sunlight hit solar panel
array of solar panels converts solar energy into electricity
photons are absorbed by semiconducting materials (e.g. silicon)
solar cell

ˌsolar e'clipse noun [C] **ASTRONOMY** an **eclipse** in which the Moon passes between the Sun and the Earth, preventing all or part of the Sun's light from reaching the Earth's surface → LUNAR ECLIPSE —*picture* → ECLIPSE

ˌsolar 'energy noun [U] **1** **SCIENCE, ENVIRONMENT** energy that uses the radiation of the Sun's light and heat —*picture* → SOLAR CELL **2** **ASTRONOMY, PHYSICS** the energy released by **nuclear fusion** reactions in stars such as the Sun

ˌsolar 'flare noun [C] **ASTRONOMY** a huge explosion of heat and energy from the surface of the Sun —*picture* → SUN

ˌsolar 'panel noun [C] a piece of equipment that uses energy from the Sun in order to create power —*picture* → SATELLITE, SOLAR CELL

solar plexus /ˌsəʊlə 'pleksəs/ noun [singular] **ANATOMY** the top part of the stomach just below the ribs

'solar ˌpower noun [U] **SCIENCE, ENVIRONMENT** solar energy

'solar ˌsystem noun [C] **ASTRONOMY** a star and the planets that go round it, especially the Sun and the group of planets that includes the Earth: *the outer reaches of our solar system* ♦ *the search for planets in other solar systems* —*picture* → on next page

sold /səʊld/ the past tense and past participle of **sell**

solder¹ /ˈsɒldə/ noun [U] **TECHNOLOGY** a soft metal that becomes liquid when it is heated, and is used for joining two metal surfaces together

solder² /ˈsɒldə/ verb [T] **TECHNOLOGY** to join two metal surfaces together by heating solder —**soldering** noun [U]

'soldering ˌiron noun [C] **TECHNOLOGY** a tool used for heating solder and joining metal surfaces together

soldier /ˈsəʊldʒə/ noun [C] someone who is a member of an army

ˌsold 'out adj if an event is sold out, all the tickets for it have been sold

sole¹ /səʊl/ adj the sole person or thing is the only one of a particular type= ONLY: *She is the sole survivor of the crash.* ♦ *His sole purpose in going there was to see Kelly.*

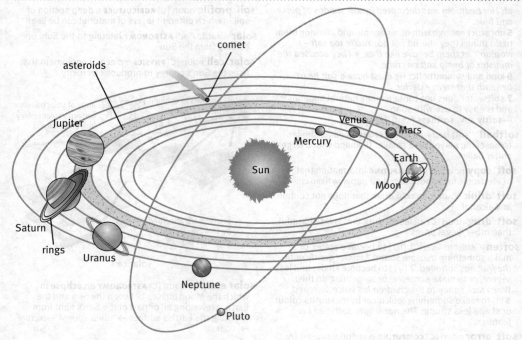

comet

asteroids

Jupiter

Venus

Mercury

Mars

Earth

Sun

Moon

Saturn

rings

Uranus

Neptune

Pluto

solar system

sole² /səʊl/ noun **1** [C] the flat bottom part of the foot —*picture* → BODY **2** [C] the bottom part of a shoe that goes under the foot **3** (plural **sole**) [C/U] a flat fish that lives in the sea, or this fish eaten as food

solely /ˈsəʊlli/ adv involving nothing except the person or thing mentioned

solemn /ˈsɒləm/ adj involving serious behaviour, attitudes, or intentions —**solemnity** /səˈlemnəti/ noun [U], **solemnly** adv

solenoid /ˈsɒlənɔɪd/ noun [C] ENGINEERING an object consisting of a coil of wire surrounding an iron core that moves along the length of the coil when an electric current is passed through it. Solenoids are used in vehicles to complete the circuit between the battery and the **starter motor**.

sol-fa /ˌsɒlˈfɑː/ noun [U] MUSIC the musical system in which the notes in a **scale** are represented by the seven short words 'doh', 're', 'mi', 'fah', 'soh', 'lah', and 'ti'

solicitor /səˈlɪsɪtə/ noun [C] in the UK, a lawyer who gives legal advice, writes legal contracts, and represents people in the lower courts of law

solicitous /səˈlɪsɪtəs/ adj *formal* if someone is solicitous, they behave in a way that shows they care about someone's health, feelings, safety etc

solid¹ /ˈsɒlɪd/ adj

1 not liquid/gas	5 with no pauses
2 with no holes	6 continuous
3 strong	7 of one substance/
4 with no bad parts	colour

1 SCIENCE relating to a substance that is not a liquid or a gas and does not change in shape or volume
2 a solid object or shape does not have any holes or empty space inside it: *a solid block of ice* → HOLLOW¹ sense 1
3 strong enough not to break or become damaged easily: *The containers have to be solid enough to withstand pressure.*

4 completely good, with no mistakes or bad parts: *She gave another solid performance.*
5 with no pauses or interruptions: *It rained for a solid week.* ♦ *I can't believe I slept for twelve hours solid.*
6 a solid line is continuous, with no breaks in it: *a solid line of traffic*
7 consisting of one substance or one colour only: *a solid oak bookcase* ♦ *a solid blue screen* —**solidity** /səˈlɪdəti/ noun [U], **solidly** adv

solid² /ˈsɒlɪd/ noun **1** [C] SCIENCE a substance that is not a liquid or a gas and does not change in shape or volume —*picture* → STATE **2** [C] MATHS a shape that is not flat but can be measured in height, depth, and width **3 solids** [plural] food that is not liquid

solidarity /ˌsɒlɪˈdærəti/ noun [U] the support that people in a group give each other because they have the same opinions or aims

solid 'fuel noun [C/U] ENVIRONMENT a fuel such as coal or wood, as opposed to oil or gas

solid ge'ometry noun [U] MATHS the part of geometry that deals with three-dimensional objects → PLANE GEOMETRY

solidify /səˈlɪdɪfaɪ/ (**solidifies, solidifying, solidified**) verb [I/T] to become solid, or to make something become solid —**solidification** /səˌlɪdɪfɪˈkeɪʃ(ə)n/ noun [U]

solid so'lution noun [C] TECHNOLOGY a solid material containing one substance uniformly distributed in another

'solid-ˌstate adj CHEMISTRY, PHYSICS **1** working by means of the flow of electric current through solid material, as in **semiconductors** and **transistors 2** relating to the electronic characteristics of solids, especially at the **atomic** or **molecular** level

solitary /ˈsɒlət(ə)ri/ adj **1** tending to spend a lot of time alone **2** done or experienced by someone who is alone **3** in a place or situation where there are no other people or things of the same type

,solitary con'finement noun [U] a punishment in which a prisoner is kept alone

solitude /'sɒlə,tjuːd/ noun [U] the state of being completely alone

solo¹ /'səʊləʊ/ (plural **solos**) noun [C] MUSIC a piece of music that is performed by one person

solo² /'səʊləʊ/ adj, adv **1** done by one person alone **2** MUSIC playing or singing alone

soloist /'səʊləʊɪst/ noun [C] MUSIC someone who performs a musical solo

solubility /,sɒljʊ'bɪləti/ (plural **solubilities**) noun CHEMISTRY **1** [U] the ability of a substance (**solute**) to dissolve in a liquid (**solvent**), forming a solution **2** [C] a measure of the ability of a **solute** to dissolve in a specific amount of a **solvent** at a specific temperature and pressure

soluble /'sɒljʊb(ə)l/ adj CHEMISTRY able to dissolve in a liquid ≠ INSOLUBLE

solute /'sɒljuːt/ noun [C/U] SCIENCE a substance that has dissolved in a liquid (**solvent**), forming a solution

solution /sə'luːʃ(ə)n/ noun [C] **1** a way to solve a problem or deal with a bad situation: *Putting children in prison is not the solution.* ♦ *The committee has failed to come up with any **solutions for** the crisis.* ♦ *UN leaders are working hard to find a peaceful **solution to** the conflict.* **2** the answer to a question in a game such as a **puzzle** or a **crossword 3** MATHS the answer to a problem in mathematics **4** CHEMISTRY a liquid mixture that is formed when a solute dissolves in a **solvent** and becomes part of the liquid

solve /sɒlv/ verb [T] **1** to find a solution to something that is causing difficulties: *an attempt to solve the dispute* ♦ *We can help you **solve** your financial problems.* **2** to find the reason or explanation for something: *He hopes to solve the mystery of the plane's disappearance.* ♦ *Police have still not solved this terrible crime.* **3** to find the answer to a question in a game such as a **puzzle** or a **crossword 4** MATHS to find the answer to a problem in mathematics: *Try to solve the equation on your own.* ♦ *solve an equation*

solvent¹ /'sɒlv(ə)nt/ noun [C] CHEMISTRY the liquid part of a solution in which a **solute** dissolves

solvent² /'sɒlv(ə)nt/ adj able to pay money that you owe

'solvent a,buse noun [U] HEALTH the dangerous practice of breathing in the gas from substances like glue in order to feel good

somatic /sə'mætɪk/ adj **1** relating to or affecting the body, especially the body considered as separate from the mind **2** ANATOMY relating to the outer walls of the body, not the inner organs **3** BIOLOGY relating to a somatic cell

so'matic ,cell noun [C] BIOLOGY any cell that is not a reproductive cell

sombre /'sɒmbə/ adj **1** serious, or sad **2** dark in colour

some /strong sʌm, weak səm/ determiner, pronoun **1** used for referring to an amount or number, without saying how much or how many: *Let me give you some advice.* ♦ *Tomatoes were only 80 pence a kilo, so I bought some.* ♦ *I met some really interesting people at the party.* ♦ *Would you like **some more** tea?* **2** used for referring to part of an amount, group, or number, but not all of it: *Some kids are more adventurous than others.* ♦ *Some of the water evaporates and turns into steam.* **3** used for emphasizing that you are talking about a fairly large amount or number: *We've been waiting here **for some time** already.* **4** used for referring

to a person or thing without saying exactly which one: *Some idiot drove into the back of my car.*

somebody /'sʌmbədi/ pronoun someone: *Somebody phoned while you were out.*

someday /'sʌm,deɪ/ adv at some time in the future, even though you do not know when: *Someday I'll meet the right woman and we'll get married.*

somehow /'sʌmhaʊ/ adv in some way or for some reason, although you do not know or understand exactly how: *Somehow he managed to pass all his exams.*

someone /'sʌmwʌn/ pronoun used for referring to a person when you do not know or do not say who the person is: *I can't find my calculator – someone must have taken it.* ♦ *I don't know the answer – you'll have to ask **someone else**.*

somersault /'sʌmə,sɔːlt/ noun [C] a movement in which you form your body into a ball and roll forwards or backwards on the ground —**somersault** verb [I]

something /'sʌmθɪŋ/ pronoun **1** used for referring to a thing, idea, fact etc when you do not know or do not say exactly what it is: *I need to buy something for Ted's birthday.* ♦ *Would you like **something to eat**?* ♦ *Jake looks pale – is there **something wrong** with him?* ♦ *I'd love to give up my job and do **something else**.* ♦ *Why doesn't the government **do something about** fuel prices?* **2** used for giving a description or amount that is not exact: *It sounded **something like** a bomb going off.*

PHRASES **be/have something to do with sth** to be related to something else: *I can't remember what his job is – it has something to do with computers.*
or something informal used for showing that you mean something in a general way, but you are not being specific: *We should call her or something, and make sure she is all right.*
→ UP¹

sometime /'sʌmtaɪm/ adv at a time that you do not know exactly or have not yet decided: *I'd love to visit New York sometime.* ♦ *Ewan returned from London sometime last week.*

sometimes /'sʌmtaɪmz/ adv on some occasions, but not always: *Sometimes it's so hot I don't even want to leave the house.*

somewhat /'sʌmwɒt/ adv to some degree, but not a lot: *The situation has improved somewhat during the past year.*

somewhere /'sʌmweə/ adv **1** used for referring to a place when you do not know or do not say exactly where: *I've lost my watch, but it must be somewhere in the house.* ♦ *Let's go somewhere quiet where we can talk.* ♦ *If we don't provide a good service, customers will go **somewhere else**.* **2** used when giving an amount that is not exact: *There were **somewhere around** 50 people at the meeting.*

PHRASE **be getting somewhere** to be making some progress: *I think at last we're getting somewhere.*

son /sʌn/ noun [C] someone's male child: *My younger son is a doctor.* ♦ *He was **the son of** an eminent scientist.*

sonar /'səʊnɑː/ noun [U] ENGINEERING a method for showing the position of objects under water by transmitting and receiving **sound waves** —*picture* → on next page

sonata /sə'nɑːtə/ noun [C] MUSIC a piece of classical music for one instrument, usually the piano, or for one instrument and a piano

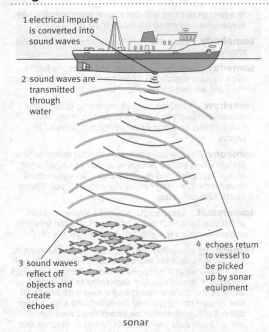

1 electrical impulse is converted into sound waves

2 sound waves are transmitted through water

3 sound waves reflect off objects and create echoes

4 echoes return to vessel to be picked up by sonar equipment

sonar

song /sɒŋ/ noun 1 [C] MUSIC a piece of music with words that you sing: *She knew the words to every song that came on the radio.* ♦ *He sang a beautiful love song.* 2 [U] MUSIC the art or activity of singing: *festivals of traditional music and song* 3 [C/U] the musical sound that a bird makes

songwriter /'sɒŋ,raɪtə/ noun [C] MUSIC someone who writes songs

sonic /'sɒnɪk/ adj PHYSICS relating to sound or **sound waves**

,sonic 'boom or **,sonic 'bang** noun [C] PHYSICS the loud sound that a plane makes as it starts to go faster than the speed of sound

'son-in-,law (plural **sons-in-law**) noun [C] the husband of someone's daughter

sonnet /'sɒnɪt/ noun [C] LITERATURE a type of poem with 14 lines

soon /suːn/ adv 1 within a short time: *If we don't leave soon, we're going to miss our bus.* ♦ *Danny arrived soon after you left.* 2 quickly: *How soon can this package be delivered to Brussels?* ♦ *Helen wants you to call her back as soon as possible.*
PHRASE **as soon as** immediately after something: *I'll call you as soon as I get home from work.*

sooner /'suːnə/ adv earlier than expected: *The announcement came sooner than we expected.*
PHRASES **no sooner... than** used for saying that something happens immediately after something else: *No sooner had I walked in the door than the phone rang.*
sooner or later definitely at some later time, although you do not know exactly when: *The whole thing was going to go wrong sooner or later.*
the sooner... the sooner... used for saying that you want something to happen soon so that something else can also happen: *The sooner you do your homework, the sooner you can go out.*
→ BETTER

soot /sʊt/ noun [U] a dirty black powder that is produced when you burn something such as coal —**sooty** adj

soothe /suːð/ verb [T] 1 to make someone more calm when they are feeling worried or upset 2 to make something less sore or painful —**soothing** adj, **soothingly** adv

sophisticated /sə'fɪstɪ,keɪtɪd/ adj 1 knowing and understanding a lot about a subject: *Consumers are getting more sophisticated.* 2 knowing a lot about things such as culture, fashion, and the modern world: *She was elegant and sophisticated.* 3 complicated and advanced in design: *highly sophisticated electronic equipment* —**sophistication** /sə,fɪstɪ'keɪʃ(ə)n/ noun [U]

soporific /,sɒpə'rɪfɪk/ adj formal something that is soporific makes people want to sleep

soprano /sə'prɑːnəʊ/ (plural **sopranos**) noun [C] MUSIC a girl, woman, or boy with the highest type of voice for singing

sorcery /'sɔːsəri/ noun [U] magic that is done with the help of evil spirits

sordid /'sɔːdɪd/ adj immoral, dishonest, or unpleasant

sore¹ /sɔː/ adj HEALTH painful and uncomfortable, usually as a result of an injury, infection, or too much exercise: *I always feel stiff and sore after gardening.* ♦ *a sore throat*
PHRASE **a sore point/spot/subject** something that makes you upset, angry, or embarrassed when someone mentions it

sore² /sɔː/ noun [C] HEALTH a small painful area of skin that is injured or infected

sorghum /'sɔːgəm/ noun [U] AGRICULTURE a plant that produces grain and grows mainly in tropical areas

sorrow /'sɒrəʊ/ noun 1 [U] great sadness 2 [C] an event or problem that makes someone very sad —**sorrowful** adj

sorry /'sɒri/ adj 1 used to say that you are ashamed, embarrassed, or unhappy about something that you have done: *I'm sorry I behaved in such a childish way.* ♦ *He wasn't sorry for hitting the other boy.* 2 feeling sadness or sympathy for someone because something bad has happened to them: *I'm sorry about your losing your job.* ♦ *I am sorry to hear that your father died.* 3 disappointed about a situation, and wishing you could change it: *I'm sorry you have decided to leave the company.*
PHRASES **feel sorry for sb** to feel sympathy for someone because they are in a difficult or unpleasant situation: *I feel sorry for the guys who have to work night shifts.*
feel sorry for yourself to feel sad about your life rather than trying to do things that could make you feel better: *Instead of sitting around feeling sorry for yourself, go out and socialize.*

sort¹ /sɔːt/ noun 1 [C] a group or type of people or things with the same qualities or features = KIND, TYPE: *What sort are you looking for?* ♦ *Is this a joke of some sort?* ♦ *Mistakes of this sort happen every day.* ♦ *He was asking us all sorts of questions about you.* 2 [singular/U] COMPUTING the process by which a computer arranges information in a particular order, for example by date or number, or in alphabetical order

sort² /sɔːt/ verb [T] 1 to arrange things in groups or in a particular order: *Sort the letters into three piles.* ♦ *Once the data is collected, the computer will sort it by date.* 2 informal to solve a problem or deal with someone or something: *Don't worry about the bill. I'll sort it.* ♦ *Did you get the tickets sorted?*
PHRASAL VERBS **,sort sth 'out 1** to get rid of things that

you do not need and arrange the things that you do need: *I need to* **sort out** *the* **mess** *on my desk.* **2** to deal with a difficult situation successfully: *This matter could be sorted out if they would just sit down and talk.*

'**sort through sth** to look at a lot of things in order to find something: *Police are now sorting through boxes of documents trying to find evidence.*

sought /sɔːt/ the past tense and past participle of **seek**

soul /səʊl/ noun

1 thoughts/feelings	4 sth's special qualities
2 spirit of person	5 soul music
3 person	

1 [C] the part of a person that is capable of thinking and feeling: *Deep in your* **heart and soul** *you must know that this is wrong.*
2 [C] **RELIGION** the spiritual part of a person that most religions believe continues to exist after the body dies
3 [C] a person: *There wasn't a soul to be seen.* ♦ *I promise I* **won't tell a soul**.
4 [U] the qualities that are typical of something and make it special: *The loss of local shops has destroyed the soul of the community.*
5 [U] **MUSIC soul music**

'**soul ,music** noun [U] **MUSIC** a type of African-American music that developed in the 1960s, combining **R & B** with **pop, rock 'n' roll**, and **gospel** styles. Soul music usually has a strong beat and places emphasis on singing.

sound[1] /saʊnd/ noun **1** [C] something that you can hear: *Laura didn't* **make a sound** *as she left the room.* ♦ *the sound of voices* **2** [U] the music, talking, and other noises that come from a radio, television, film etc: *Something was interfering with the sound during the broadcast.* **3** [U] the loudness of a radio, television etc = VOLUME: *Turn the sound up a bit – I can't hear.*

> **Build your vocabulary: types of sound**
>
> - **bang** a sound like an explosion
> - **clank** a sound like two heavy pieces of metal knocking together
> - **crash** a sound like a large object falling to the ground and breaking
> - **creak** a sound like the sound that is made by an old door when you push it open slowly
> - **rattle** a sound like a loose object hitting another object several times
> - **squeak** a sound like the noise that a mouse makes
> - **thud** a sound like something heavy falling to the ground

sound[2] /saʊnd/ verb **1** [linking verb] to seem good, bad, interesting, exciting etc as a result of what you have heard, have read, or know: *It sounds as if he's never home.* ♦ *You make it* **sound as though** *he is the most boring man in the world.* ♦ *Malta* **sounds like** *a great place for a relaxing holiday.* **2** [linking verb] to show a particular emotion or quality in your voice: *He sounded a bit annoyed.* ♦ *It sounds as if you're getting a cold.* **3** [I/T] to produce a sound, or to make something produce a sound: *The sirens sounded, warning of a tornado.* ♦ *Trains are required to sound their whistles as they approach a crossing.* **4** [T] to express a particular attitude or opinion: *The aim of the scheme is to* **sound a warning** *to teenagers about the dangers of smoking.*

sound[3] /saʊnd/ adj **1** involving the use of good judgment, and therefore likely to be effective or reliable ≠ UNSOUND: *He will be able to offer you sound advice and guidance.* **2** thorough: *a sound understanding of basic teaching skills* **3** safe, healthy, or in good condition: *Investigators found the plane to*

be structurally sound. ♦ *Doctors say his heart is perfectly sound.* **4** a sound sleep is one that it is difficult to wake someone from

sound[4] /saʊnd/ adv **sound asleep** sleeping very well

the 'sound ,barrier noun the very strong air pressure that presses against a plane when it starts to travel at the speed of sound

soundbite /'saʊndbaɪt/ noun [C] a short comment by a politician or other famous person that gets people's attention

'**sound ,card** noun [C] **COMPUTING** a part inside a computer that changes information into sounds that you can hear

'**sound ef,fects** noun [plural] **ARTS** the special recorded sounds in a film, television programme, or radio show

'**sound ,energy** noun [U] **PHYSICS** energy in the form of sound waves

sounding board /'saʊndɪŋ ,bɔːd/ noun [C] someone who listens to your ideas and opinions and tells you whether they think they are good or not

soundly /'saʊn(d)li/ adv if you sleep soundly, you sleep well and it is difficult to wake you

soundproof /'saʊnd,pruːf/ adj designed to stop sound from entering or leaving

soundtrack /'saʊnd(d),træk/ noun [C] **MUSIC** the music that is played during a film or television programme, or a CD of this music

'**sound ,wave** noun [C] **PHYSICS** a type of wave movement that can be heard. It starts when something vibrates and causes further vibrations. Sound waves can travel through gases, liquids, and solids but not through empty space. —*picture* → ACOUSTICS, SONAR

soup /suːp/ noun [C/U] a liquid food that is made by cooking meat, fish, or vegetables with water: *a bowl of soup* ♦ *chicken soup*

'**soup ,kitchen** noun [C] a place where poor people can go in order to get a free hot meal

sour[1] /'saʊə/ adj **1** with a taste like that of a lemon **2** sour milk has an unpleasant taste or smell because it is no longer fresh **3** unpleasant, unfriendly, or in a bad mood: *a sour look*

sour[2] /'saʊə/ verb [I/T] to stop being successful or satisfactory, or to make something do this

source /sɔːs/ noun [C] **1** a person, place, or thing that provides something that you need or want: *an energy source* ♦ *A garden was* **the source of** *inspiration for the painting.* **2** someone who provides information for a journalist: *The article quoted a senior source at the UN.* **3** the cause of a problem, or the place where it began: *Her son was* **a constant source of** *worry to her.* **4** the beginning of a river or stream

'**source ,code** noun [C] **COMPUTING** a set of instructions for a computer program that a computer **programmer** understands, and that are translated into instructions that a computer understands

'**source ,language** noun [C] **LANGUAGE** the language that someone is translating something from

sourly /'saʊəli/ adv in an unpleasant and unfriendly way, especially in the way that you speak

south[1] /saʊθ/ noun **GEOGRAPHY** **1** [U] the direction that is on your right when you are facing the rising sun: *driving from south to north* —*picture* → COMPASS **2 the south** [singular] the part of a place that is in the south: *Did you like living* **in the south**?

south[2] /saʊθ/ adv GEOGRAPHY towards the south: *A room that faces south gets more sunlight.* ♦ *They live 20 minutes **south of** Manchester.*

south[3] /saʊθ/ adj GEOGRAPHY **1** in the south, or facing towards the south **2** a south wind blows from the south

,**South A'merica** GEOGRAPHY the fourth largest continent in the world, between the Atlantic and Pacific Oceans. It is south-east of North America, and stretches from Panama in the north to Cape Horn in the south. —*picture* → CONTINENT

,**South 'Asia** GEOGRAPHY the part of Asia that contains the countries of India, Pakistan, and Bangladesh

,**south-'east**[1] noun GEOGRAPHY **1** [U] the direction that is between south and east —*picture* → COMPASS **2 the south-east** [singular] the part of a place that is in the south-east: *The weather gets much hotter **in the south-east.*** —,**south-'eastern** adj

,**south-'east**[2] adj GEOGRAPHY in the south-east, or facing towards the south-east —,**south-'east** adv

,**South-East 'Asia** GEOGRAPHY the part of Asia that includes the countries of Myanmar, Thailand, Laos, Vietnam, Cambodia, Malaysia, Indonesia, Singapore, and the Philippines

southerly /'sʌðəli/ adj GEOGRAPHY **1** a southerly wind blows from the south **2** towards or in the south

southern /'sʌðən/ adj GEOGRAPHY in or from the south of a place: *the southern shore of the lake* ♦ *southern India*

the ,Southern 'Cross noun ASTRONOMY a **constellation** (=group of stars) in the shape of a cross that can be seen in the sky in the southern half of the world

the ,southern 'hemisphere noun [singular] GEOGRAPHY the half of the Earth that is south of the equator —*picture* → EARTH

southernmost /'sʌðən,məʊst/ adj GEOGRAPHY furthest towards the south

,**Southern 'Ocean** GEOGRAPHY the ocean to the north of Antarctica —*picture* → CONTINENT

the ,South 'Pole GEOGRAPHY the point on the Earth that is the furthest south —*picture* → EARTH

southward /'saʊθwəd/ adj GEOGRAPHY towards or in the south

southwards /'saʊθwədz/ adv GEOGRAPHY towards the south

,**south-'west**[1] noun GEOGRAPHY **1** [U] the direction that is between south and west —*picture* → COMPASS **2 the south-west** [singular] the part of a place that is in the south-west: *They own a farmhouse **in the south-west** of France.* ♦ *The drought affected large areas of the south-west of the country.* —,**south-'western** adj

,**south-'west**[2] adj GEOGRAPHY in the south-west, or facing towards the south-west —,**south-'west** adv

souvenir /,suːvə'nɪə/ noun [C] something that you buy to remind you of a place that you visited on holiday or of a special event

sovereign[1] /'sɒvrɪn/ adj POLITICS a sovereign nation rules itself

sovereign[2] /'sɒvrɪn/ noun [C] *formal* a king or queen

sovereignty /'sɒvrɪnti/ noun [U] POLITICS **1** the right of a country to rule itself **2** the right to rule a country

soviet /'səʊviət, 'sɒviət/ noun [C] POLITICS one of the local elected councils that ruled the **Soviet Union** when it existed in the past

Soviet[1] /'səʊviət, 'sɒviət/ adj from or relating to the Soviet Union when it existed in the past

Soviet[2] /'səʊviət, 'sɒviət/ noun [C] someone who came from the Soviet Union when it existed in the past

,**Soviet 'Union** noun [singular] GEOGRAPHY the name for the group of 15 communist republics in Eastern Europe that formed a single country until 1991. Russia was the most important republic.

sow[1] /səʊ/ (**sows, sowing, sowed** /səʊd/, **sown** /səʊn/) verb [T] AGRICULTURE to plant seeds in the ground

sow[2] /saʊ/ noun [C] AGRICULTURE an adult female pig

soya bean /'sɔɪə ,biːn/ noun [C] the seed of a plant, used for making food and oil

soya milk /'sɔɪə ,mɪlk/ noun [U] a white liquid from soya beans, used as a drink and in cooking

soy sauce /,sɔɪ 'sɔːs/ noun [U] a dark brown sauce made from soya beans

spa /spɑː/ noun [C] a place with a natural supply of **mineral water** where people go to improve their health

space[1] /speɪs/ noun

1 available area	5 area everything is in
2 area for purpose	6 on computer
3 gap	7 period of time
4 beyond atmosphere	

1 [C/U] an empty or available area: *We replaced the bath with a shower to create more space.* ♦ *Their voices sounded loud in the small space.* ♦ *What we really need is more **green spaces** in cities.* ♦ *The nursery has **space** for 48 children.* → PLACE[1] sense 1

2 [C/U] an area used for a particular purpose: *a parking space* ♦ *Newspapers make money from selling advertising space.*

3 [C] an empty area between things = GAP: *Leave a space of about two feet.* ♦ *You can grow seeds in the spaces between the plants.*

4 [U] ASTRONOMY the whole of the universe outside the Earth's atmosphere: *The crew have been living **in space** for over three months.* ♦ *a space mission* → SEED[1]

5 [U] the area in which everything exists: *different points in space and time*

6 [U] COMPUTING the area that is available on a computer for storing information

7 [singular] a period of time: *It was an amazing achievement in such a short **space of time.*** ♦ *In the **space of** 36 hours, I had travelled halfway round the world.*

space[2] /speɪs/ verb [T] to arrange objects, events etc so that they are a particular distance or time apart: *Plant the seedlings at evenly spaced intervals.*

'**space ,bar** noun [C] COMPUTING the long narrow bar at the front of a computer keyboard that you press to make a space between words when you are typing

'**space ,capsule** noun [C] ASTRONOMY a small space vehicle or part of a large spacecraft in which astronauts travel

spacecraft /'speɪs,krɑːft/ (plural **spacecraft**) noun [C] ASTRONOMY a vehicle that can travel in space

'**space ,probe** noun [C] ASTRONOMY a vehicle containing cameras and other equipment that is sent into space to collect information and send it back to Earth

spaceship /ˈspeɪsˌʃɪp/ noun [C] ASTRONOMY a spacecraft

ˈspace ˌshuttle noun [C] ASTRONOMY a vehicle that travels into space and back to Earth and lands like a plane —*picture* ➔ on next page

ˈspace ˌstation noun [C] ASTRONOMY a laboratory in space where people can live and work for long periods

spacesuit /ˈspeɪsˌsuːt/ noun [C] ASTRONOMY a set of clothes that covers the whole body and allows someone to move and breathe in space

spacewalk /ˈspeɪsˌwɔːk/ noun [C] ASTRONOMY an occasion when an astronaut goes outside the spacecraft in space, for example in order to repair something

spacious /ˈspeɪʃəs/ adj with a lot of space inside

spade /speɪd/ noun **1** [C] a tool used for digging that consists of a handle and a flat part that you push into the earth **2** [C] a playing card with a pattern on it that is like a pointed black leaf **3 spades** [plural] the **suit** (=group) of playing cards that has a pattern on them that is like a pointed black leaf: *the ace of spades*

spaghetti /spəˈɡeti/ noun [U] a type of pasta that is in the form of long thin pieces like string

spam¹ /spæm/ noun [U] COMPUTING emails that are sent to large numbers of people on the Internet, especially when these are not wanted

spam² /spæm/ (**spams, spamming, spammed**) verb [T] COMPUTING to send emails to large numbers of people on the Internet, especially when these are not wanted —**spammer** noun [C], **spamming** noun [U]

span¹ /spæn/ (**spans, spanning, spanned**) verb [T] **1** to last for a particular period of time: *His career spanned half a century.* **2** to cross or cover an area of water or land: *a bridge spanning the River Jordan* **3** to include a number of different things

span² /spæn/ noun [C] **1** the amount of time that something lasts: *Kids these days have a very limited attention span.* ➔ LIFESPAN **2** the width of something **3** CONSTRUCTION the horizontal distance between two supporting parts of a structure

spaniel /ˈspænjəl/ noun [C] a type of small dog with long ears and long shiny hair

spanner /ˈspænə/ noun [C] a metal tool that is used for turning small pieces of metal called nuts —*picture* ➔ TOOL

spar¹ /spɑː/ noun [C] **1** a thick strong pole that supports something such as the sails on a boat or the wings of a plane **2** GEOLOGY a long thin piece of a mineral, or of rock

spar² /spɑː/ (**spars, sparring, sparred**) verb [I] SPORTS to practise fighting with someone

spare¹ /speə/ adj **1** a spare object is kept in addition to another similar thing or things, so that you can use it if you need it: *a spare key* ◆ *Bring a towel and some spare clothes.* **2** available: *Have you got any spare room in your car?*

spare² /speə/ verb [T]

1 give/lend sth	4 use sth
2 have time available	5 not harm sb/sth
3 of bad experience	+ PHRASE

1 if you can spare something, you can give or lend it to someone because you do not need it: *Can you spare a couple of pounds?* ◆ *We can't spare the staff for training sessions.*

2 if you can spare time, you have it available: *It's kind of you to spare me a moment.* ◆ *We arrived at the airport with just 20 minutes to spare.*

3 to prevent someone from experiencing something that is unpleasant or painful: *I want to spare her the embarrassment of asking for money.*

4 if you do not spare something, you use a lot of it in order to make something succeed: *We will spare no effort to find the murderer.* ◆ *No expense was spared in organizing the conference.*

5 *formal* to not harm or kill someone or something: *The commander was so impressed by their bravery that he spared them.*

PHRASE money/room/time etc to spare more than enough money, room, time etc: *We've got food to spare.*

spare³ /speə/ noun [C] something that you have in addition to another similar thing or things, that you can use if you need it

ˌspare ˈpart noun [C] a part for a vehicle or machine that you can use to replace one that breaks

ˌspare ˈtyre noun [C] an extra wheel with a tyre on it, that you keep in your car to use if a tyre gets damaged

sparingly /ˈspeərɪŋli/ adv in small quantities

spark¹ /spɑːk/ verb **1 spark** or **spark off** [T] to make something start: *The verdict sparked riots all over the city.* **2** [T] to start a fire or explosion **3** [I] to produce a very small fire or an electrical flash

spark² /spɑːk/ noun **1** [C] a very small fire or an electrical flash **2** [singular/U] a strong and exciting quality or feeling: *She felt a spark of enthusiasm.*

ˈspark igˌnition ˌengine noun [C] ENGINEERING a type of engine in which the mixture of fuel and air is **ignited** (=lit) with a spark

sparkle /ˈspɑːk(ə)l/ verb [I] **1** to shine with small points of reflected light **2** to be very lively and interesting —**sparkle** noun [C/U]

sparkling /ˈspɑːk(ə)lɪŋ/ adj **1** shining with small points of reflected light **2** very lively and interesting **3** sparkling drinks are full of bubbles

ˈspark ˌplug noun [C] ENGINEERING a small part in a vehicle's engine containing two electrodes that create a spark that makes the fuel burn

sparring partner /ˈspɑːrɪŋ ˌpɑːtnə/ noun [C] **1** SPORTS someone who helps a **boxer** to train for a fight by taking the part of an opponent **2** someone who you have regular arguments with but not in an unfriendly way, especially in politics

sparrow /ˈspærəʊ/ noun [C] a small brown bird that is common in the US and in northern Europe

sparse /spɑːs/ adj existing in small amounts, or spread over a large area in small amounts —**sparsely** adv

spartan /ˈspɑːt(ə)n/ adj very plain and simple, without the things that make life comfortable and pleasant

spasm /ˈspæz(ə)m/ noun [C/U] a sudden painful movement of a muscle

spat /spæt/ the past tense and past participle of **spit¹**

spate /speɪt/ noun
PHRASES a spate of sth a large number of things of the same type, usually bad things, that suddenly happen in a very short period of time
in spate if a river is in spate, it is much deeper than usual and the water in it is moving very fast, for example after snow melts in the spring

spatial /ˈspeɪʃ(ə)l/ adj relating to the size, shape, and position of things and their relation to each other in space

spatter /ˈspætə/ verb [I/T] to throw small drops of a liquid onto a surface with a lot of force, or to be thrown onto a surface in this way —**spatter** noun [C]

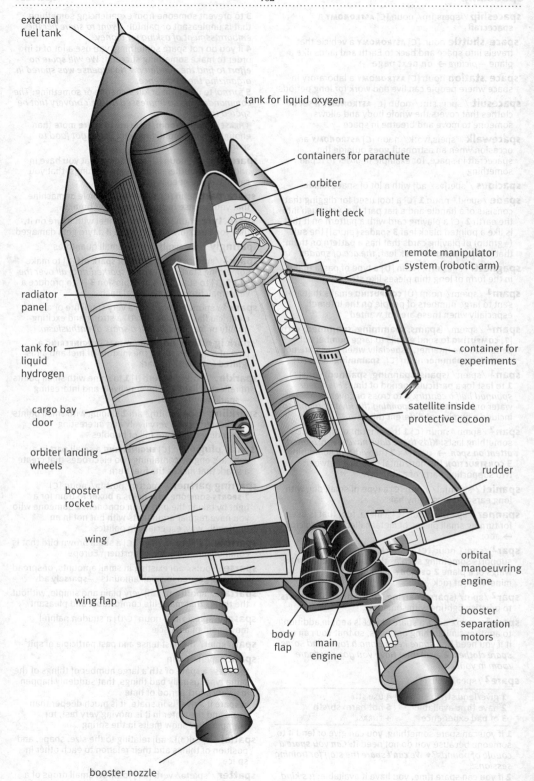

external
fuel tank

tank for liquid oxygen

containers for parachute

orbiter

flight deck

remote manipulator
system (robotic arm)

radiator
panel

container for
experiments

tank for
liquid
hydrogen

cargo bay
door

satellite inside
protective cocoon

orbiter landing
wheels

rudder

booster
rocket

wing

orbital
manoeuvring
engine

wing flap

booster
separation
motors

body
flap

main
engine

booster nozzle

space shuttle

spatula /ˈspætjʊlə/ noun [C] a tool with a handle at one end and a wide flat part at the other that is used for lifting hot foods or for spreading soft substances —picture → LABORATORY

spawn /spɔːn/ noun [U] the eggs of a **frog** or fish

speak /spiːk/ (**speaks, speaking, spoke** /spəʊk/, **spoken** /ˈspəʊkən/) verb

1 talk about sth or to sb	5 express
2 use voice to talk	ideas/thoughts
3 talk particular	+ PHRASES
language	+ PHRASAL VERBS
4 give formal speech	

1 [I] to talk to someone about something: *We spoke yesterday.* ♦ *I phoned your office and* **spoke to** *your assistant.* ♦ *Let me* **speak with** *Jennifer and see what she thinks.* ♦ *He* **spoke** *movingly* **about** *his son's struggle with cancer.* ♦ *People* **spoke of** *their fear as the flood waters rose.* ♦ *I know I* **speak for** *all of us when I say how sorry I am.* → SAY[1], TALK[1]
2 [I] to use your voice to talk: *There was a long pause before she spoke again.* ♦ *He spoke so softly it was difficult to hear what he said.*
3 [T] to be able to talk in a particular language: *Do you speak Chinese?* ♦ *He speaks three languages.*
4 [I] to give a formal speech: *The local MP will be* **speaking at** *our graduation ceremony.* ♦ *Petersen* **spoke to** *an audience of 2,000.*
5 [I/T] to express ideas, thoughts, or opinions about something: *Yvonne has* **spoken** *so* **highly** *of you.* ♦ *Only a small group of people dared to* **speak against** *the war.*
PHRASES **broadly/generally speaking** used for showing that what you are saying is usually true, but not in every instance
no...to speak of or **nothing to speak of** used for saying that something is very small or unimportant: *She has no money to speak of.*
speak for itself to be so clear or obvious that no argument is necessary: *His success as a lawyer speaks for itself.*
PHRASAL VERBS ,**speak 'out** to state your opinion firmly and publicly about something
,**speak 'up 1** to talk louder **2** to say what you think instead of saying nothing

> Word family: **speak**
>
> *Words in the same family as* **speak**
> - **speaker** *n*
> - **spoken** *adj*
> - **unspoken** *adj*
> - **outspoken** *adj*
> - **speech** *n*
> - **speechless** *adj*
> - **unspeakable** *adj*
> - **unspeakably** *adv*

speaker /ˈspiːkə/ noun [C] **1** someone who talks about a subject to a group: *She's a very interesting speaker.* **2** someone who is able to speak a particular language: *an English speaker* **3** someone who is talking: *expressions that show the speaker is annoyed* **4** a piece of electrical equipment that sends out sound —*picture* → COMPUTER

spear[1] /spɪə/ noun [C] a long weapon that is like a stick with one sharp pointed end and is thrown at someone —*picture* → WEAPON

spear[2] /spɪə/ verb [T] to push something that is sharp and pointed into something else

spearhead /ˈspɪəˌhed/ verb [T] to lead an organized effort or activity

special[1] /ˈspeʃ(ə)l/ adj **1** different from and usually better than what is normal or ordinary: *The children can only stay up late on* **special** *occasions.* ♦ *You're very* **special to** *me.* **2** more than usual: *Special care must be taken in handling very old books.* **3** relating to one

particular person, thing, or purpose: *Many sports have their own special equipment.*

special[2] /ˈspeʃ(ə)l/ noun [C] something that is produced for a particular time or day, for example a type of food in a restaurant or a programme on television

,**special ef'fects** noun [plural] ARTS the artificial images or sounds in a film that are created with technology

,**special 'interest ,holiday** noun [C] TOURISM a holiday arranged for people with particular interests, such as painting or cooking

specialist /ˈspeʃəlɪst/ noun [C] someone whose training, education, or experience makes them an expert in a particular subject: *a web design specialist*

speciality /ˌspeʃiˈæləti/ (plural **specialities**) noun [C] **1** a food or drink that a region or restaurant is well known for and that you cannot always get in other places **2** a particular part of a subject or profession that someone concentrates on or is an expert in

specialize /ˈspeʃəlaɪz/ verb [I] to concentrate on, or be an expert in, a particular part of a subject or profession —**specialization** /ˌspeʃəlaɪˈzeɪʃ(ə)n/ noun [C/U]

specialized /ˈspeʃəlaɪzd/ adj designed for a particular purpose, or concentrating on a particular subject

specially /ˈspeʃ(ə)li/ adv in a particular way, or for a particular purpose: *These coats are specially treated to be water repellent.*

,**special 'needs** noun [plural] EDUCATION the particular needs of people who have learning problems or physical problems

,**special 'pleading** noun [U] **1** LAW the introduction of new evidence in a trial **2** an unfair attempt to influence someone in authority to do something that will be of benefit only to you

'**special ,school** noun [C] EDUCATION a school for students who have physical, educational, or emotional problems

specialty /ˈspeʃ(ə)lti/ (plural **specialties**) noun [C] **1** HEALTH a particular area of medicine that someone is an expert in **2** a **speciality**

species /ˈspiːʃiːz/ (plural **species**) noun [C] BIOLOGY a group of living things whose members all have similar general features and are able to produce new organisms together: *the human species* ♦ *Over 120* **species of** *birds have been recorded in this National Park.* —*picture* → TAXONOMY

specific /spəˈsɪfɪk/ adj **1** involving or limited to only one particular thing or purpose: *You have to enter the information in a specific order.* ♦ *problems that are* **specific to** *this type of work* **2** exact and detailed: *For specific instructions, please refer to the guide.* ♦ *Can you be more specific?*

specifically /spəˈsɪfɪkli/ adv **1** for one particular thing or purpose: *They bought the land specifically in order to build a hotel on it.* **2** in an exact and detailed way: *She specifically stated that she went to the station because her brother told her to.*

specification /ˌspesɪfɪˈkeɪʃ(ə)n/ noun [C] an exact measurement or detailed plan about how something is to be made

spe,cific 'gravity noun [U] SCIENCE the mass of something divided by the mass of the same volume of water

spe,cific 'heat ca,pacity noun [C/U] CHEMISTRY the heat that is needed to raise the temperature of a particular mass of a substance by a particular amount

specifics /spə'sɪfɪks/ noun [plural] the details of something: *We'll leave the lawyers to deal with the specifics.*

specify /'spesɪfaɪ/ (**specifies, specifying, specified**) verb [T] to explain something in an exact and detailed way

specimen /'spesəmɪn/ noun [C] **1** HEALTH a small amount of something such as blood or urine that is taken from the body so that it can be examined **2** an example of something, especially of a plant or animal

speck /spek/ noun [C] a very small spot or mark

speckled /'spek(ə)ld/ adj covered with a lot of very small spots or marks

spectacle /'spektək(ə)l/ noun [C/U] an unusual, exciting, or impressive event or sight

spectacles /'spektək(ə)lz/ noun [plural] *formal* glasses that you wear to help you to see better

spectacular /spek'tækjʊlə/ adj extremely impressive —**spectacularly** adv

spectator /spek'teɪtə/ noun [C] someone who watches a public activity or event

spec'tator ,sport noun [C] SPORTS a sport that a lot of people enjoy watching

spectral /'spektrəl/ adj PHYSICS relating to a **spectrum**

spectre /'spektə/ noun [C] the possibility of something unpleasant that might happen in the future

spectrum /'spektrəm/ noun [singular] **1** the whole range of ideas, qualities, situations etc that are possible **2** PHYSICS the complete range of colours into which light can be separated **3** PHYSICS the whole range of the **electromagnetic spectrum**, including X-rays and light waves

speculate /'spekjʊleɪt/ verb **1** [I/T] to consider or discuss why something has happened or might happen **2** [I] BUSINESS to buy things such as shares and property, hoping to make a big profit later when you sell them —**speculator** noun [C]

speculation /ˌspekjʊ'leɪʃ(ə)n/ noun [C/U] guesses about why something has happened or what might happen

speculative /'spekjʊlətɪv/ adj **1** based on guesses or on only a little information **2** BUSINESS done in order to make a big profit, but with a high risk that money will be lost

sped /sped/ a past tense and past participle of **speed²**

speech /spiːtʃ/ noun **1** [C] a formal occasion when someone speaks to an audience, or the words that someone speaks to an audience: *She writes most of the president's speeches.* ♦ *She made a wonderful speech.* **2** [U] spoken language, or the ability to speak: *A stroke can cause difficulties with speech.* ♦ *tapes of recorded speech* ♦ *speech development*

'speech ,act noun [C] LANGUAGE something that you say

'speech im,pediment noun [C] a difficulty in speaking caused by nervousness or by a physical problem

speechless /'spiːtʃləs/ adj so surprised or angry that you cannot think of anything to say

'speech ,marks noun [plural] LANGUAGE **quotation marks**

'speech recog,nition noun [U] COMPUTING a system where you speak to a computer to make it do things, for example instead of using a keyboard = VOICE RECOGNITION

'speech ,synthesis noun [U] COMPUTING a process in which a computer produces sounds that are similar to human speech

,speech 'therapy noun [U] HEALTH exercises in talking that are designed to help someone who cannot say words correctly

speed¹ /spiːd/ noun **1** [C/U] the rate at which someone or something moves, works, or happens: *They were working with incredible speed.* ♦ *The main advantage of this method is its speed.* ♦ *The device measures the speed and direction of the wind.* → VELOCITY **2** [C] a **gear¹** sense 1: *a car with a 5-speed gearbox* **3** [U] *informal* an illegal drug that makes people feel as if they have a lot of energy

PHRASES **speed of light** PHYSICS the speed of light in a vacuum, which is equal to 3 x 108 metres per second
up to speed at the speed or level that is expected

speed² /spiːd/ (**speeds, speeding, sped** /sped/ or **speeded**) verb **1** [I] to move somewhere quickly: *an endless stream of traffic speeding towards the city* ♦ *I heard a car speed away.* **2** [I] to drive a car faster than the speed that is allowed **3** [T] to make something happen more quickly: *Regular exercise will help speed your recovery.*

PHRASAL VERB **,speed (sth) 'up** to move or happen faster, or to make something move or happen faster

speedboat /'spiːdˌbəʊt/ noun [C] a boat with a powerful motor that can go very fast

speed dating /'spiːd ˌdeɪtɪŋ/ noun [U] an event at which single people looking for a partner divide into pairs and have short conversations with each other, then decide who among those they have met they would like to meet again

'speed ,limit noun [singular] the fastest speed that is allowed for vehicles in a particular area

speedometer /spɪ'dɒmɪtə/ noun [C] the piece of equipment in a vehicle that shows how fast it is going

'speed ,skating noun [U] SPORTS a sport in which people wearing **skates** race each other on ice

speedy /'spiːdi/ (**speedier, speediest**) adj **1** happening very quickly **2** able to move very fast

spell¹ /spel/ (**spells, spelling, spelt** /spelt/ or **spelled**) verb **1** [I/T] to write or say the letters of a word in the correct order: *Can you spell 'beautiful'?* ♦ *You've spelt my name wrong.* ♦ *Her writing is neat, but she can't spell.* **2** [T] to be the letters that make up a word: *L-O-V-E spells 'love'.* **3** [T] to show that something bad is going to happen: *That look on her face spells trouble.*

PHRASAL VERB **,spell sth 'out 1** to say or write the letters of a word in the correct order **2** *informal* to explain something so that it is very clear

spell² /spel/ noun [C] **1** a period of time, usually a short one: *After a short spell in the army, I went to college.* ♦ *a spell of rain* **2** words or actions that are believed to make magic things happen: *The witch cast a spell on him.*

spellbound /'spelˌbaʊnd/ adj so impressed by something that you do not pay attention to anything else

spellchecker /'spelˌtʃekə/ noun [C] COMPUTING a computer program that checks and corrects the way that you spell words

spelling /'spelɪŋ/ noun **1** [U] the ability to spell **2** [C] the correct way of writing a word

spelt /spelt/ a past tense and past participle of **spell¹**

spend /spend/ (**spends, spending, spent** /spent/) verb **1** [I/T] to use money to pay for things: *How much money did you spend?* ♦ *You spend too much on clothes.*

2 [T] to stay somewhere, or to do something, for a period of time: *I'm going to spend Christmas with my family.* ♦ *He spent hours practising.* ♦ *We **spent the day** at the beach.* ♦ *We have **spent** too much time **on** this problem.* **3** [T] to use time, effort, or energy to do something: *Considerable energy is spent on making the costumes look perfect.*

spending /'spendɪŋ/ noun [U] money spent, especially by governments or large organizations

'spending ,power noun [U] **ECONOMICS** the amount of money that a person, business etc has available to spend

spent¹ /spent/ the past tense and past participle of **spend**

spent² /spent/ adj used, and therefore no longer useful: *spent nuclear fuel*

sperm /spɜːm/ (plural **sperm**) noun **BIOLOGY** **1** [C] the male **gamete** (=reproductive cell) produced by the male sex organs that fertilizes a female egg. The sperm are contained in **seminal fluid**, and together they form semen. They have half the number of chromosomes as other cells in the body. A single sperm is sometimes called a **spermatozoon**. —*picture* → FERTILIZATION, SEX CELL **2** [U] the liquid from a man's penis that contains sperm = SEMEN

'sperm ,duct noun [C] **ANATOMY** a long thin tube that carries sperm away from the **scrotum** to the **seminal vesicles**

spermicide /'spɜːmɪsaɪd/ noun [C] **HEALTH** a cream containing a chemical that kills sperm. It is used during sex to prevent a woman from becoming pregnant. —**spermicidal** /ˌspɜːmɪˈsaɪd(ə)l/ adj

spew /spjuː/ or, **spew (sth) 'out** verb [I/T] to flow out with a lot of force, or to make something do this

sphere /sfɪə/ noun [C] **1** **MATHS** an object that is shaped like a ball —*picture* → SHAPE **2** a particular area of interest, activity, or responsibility

spherical /'sferɪk(ə)l/ adj shaped like a ball

spheroid /'sfɪərɔɪd/ noun [C] **MATHS** an object shaped like a sphere, but not completely spherical

sphincter /'sfɪŋktə/ noun [C] **ANATOMY** a muscle that surrounds and controls an opening in the body, especially the **anus**

sphinx /sfɪŋks/ noun [C] **LITERATURE** an animal in ancient Greek and Egyptian **myths** that has a lion's body and a human head

sphygmomanometer /ˌsfɪɡməʊməˈnɒmɪtə/ noun [C] **HEALTH** an instrument that is used to measure blood pressure

spice /spaɪs/ noun **1** [C/U] a substance made from a plant and added to food to give it flavour **2** [U] extra interest or excitement

spicy /'spaɪsi/ (**spicier, spiciest**) adj with a strong hot flavour

spider /'spaɪdə/ noun [C] **1** an **arachnid** with eight legs that spins **webs** in order to catch insects —*picture* → INSECT **2** **COMPUTING** a program that searches for new websites on the Internet and builds them into a **database**. Users can use this to find documents containing a particular word, phrase, or subject.

spigot /'spɪɡət/ noun [C] **CONSTRUCTION** the end of a pipe that fits into a wider pipe called a **socket** in order to form a joint

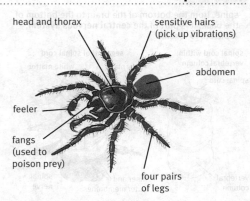

head and thorax

sensitive hairs (pick up vibrations)

abdomen

feeler

fangs (used to poison prey)

four pairs of legs

spider

spike /spaɪk/ noun [C] a sharp pointed piece of metal or wood —**spiky** adj

spill¹ /spɪl/ (**spills, spilling, spilled** or **spilt** /spɪlt/) verb **1** [I/T] if a liquid spills, or if you spill it, it accidentally flows out of its container: *Oil is still spilling from the ship.* ♦ *I spilt coffee all over my desk.* **2** [I] if people spill out of a place, a lot of them leave at the same time

PHRASAL VERB ,spill 'over to spread to other areas: *The violence has spilled over to other parts of the city.*

spill² /spɪl/ noun [C/U] an amount of liquid that has accidentally flowed out of its container: *an oil spill*

spin¹ /spɪn/ (**spins, spinning, spun** /spʌn/) verb

1 turn round quickly	**5** present sth certain way
2 of washing machine	**+** PHRASAL VERB
3 make thread	
4 insect, spider: create web, thread etc	

1 [I/T] to turn round and round quickly, or to make someone or something do this: *The dancers were spinning in circles.* ♦ *Spin the wheel with your hand.* **2** [I/T] when a washing machine spins clothes, it squeezes water out of them by turning them round and round quickly **3** [I/T] to twist fibres into thread in order to make cloth **4** [T] if an insect or spider spins something such as a **web**, it makes it from thread that it produces in its body **5** [T] *informal* to present information in a particular way, especially in a way that makes something seem good or less bad

PHRASAL VERB ,spin sth 'out to make something last for a long time

spin² /spɪn/ noun **1** [C/U] a quick turning movement round and round **2** [singular/U] *informal* a way of giving information that makes something seem less bad

spina bifida /ˌspaɪnə ˈbɪfɪdə/ noun [U] **HEALTH** a serious medical condition in which someone's **spinal cord** is damaged, making them **paralysed** (=unable to move parts of their body)

spinach /'spɪnɪdʒ/ noun [U] a vegetable with dark green leaves

spinal /'spaɪn(ə)l/ adj **ANATOMY** relating to the spine

'spinal ,column noun [C] **ANATOMY** the main bone structure of the spine

,spinal 'cord noun [C] **ANATOMY, BIOLOGY** the thick length of nerve tissue that goes down the hole in the

spine, from the bottom of the brain to the bottom of the back. It is part of the **central nervous system**.
—*picture* → ORGAN

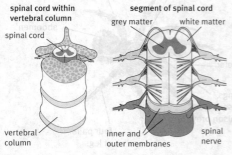

spinal cord within vertebral column

spinal cord

segment of spinal cord

grey matter   white matter

vertebral column

inner and outer membranes

spinal nerve

spinal cord

'spinal ,nerve noun [C] **ANATOMY** one of the 31 paired nerves in the **spinal cord** that carry information from the body to the spinal cord, and from the spinal cord and the brain to the rest of the body
—*picture* → SPINAL CORD

spine /spaɪn/ noun [C] **1 ANATOMY** the row of bones down or along the middle of the back of a vertebrate = BACKBONE, SPINAL COLUMN, VERTEBRAL COLUMN —*picture* → SKELETON **2** the edge of a book where all the pages are fixed together **3 BIOLOGY** a sharp point on a plant or animal

spineless /'spaɪnləs/ adj **1** not brave or determined **2 BIOLOGY** a spineless animal does not have a spine. Invertebrates such as insects are spineless.

spinnaker /'spɪnəkə/ noun [C] an extra sail sometimes fitted on the front of a boat when it is being used for racing

spinneret /'spɪnəret/ noun [C] **BIOLOGY** one of the organs in a spider's body that produce the liquid that the spider uses to make its **web**

spiracle /'spaɪrək(ə)l/ noun [C] **BIOLOGY 1** a small hole behind the eye of fishes such as **sharks** and rays **2** one of the small holes along the side of an insect's body that allow air in and out —*picture* → INSECT, MOSQUITO

spiral¹ /'spaɪrəl/ noun [C] **1** a shape that looks like a set of circles and is made by one line curving around a central point **2** a situation that gets worse and worse: *the endless **spiral** of violence and hatred* —**spiral** adj

spiral² /'spaɪrəl/ (**spirals, spiralling, spiralled**) verb [I] **1** to move in the shape of a spiral **2** to become worse and worse: *Crime has begun to spiral out of control.*

,spiral inclined 'plane noun [C] **PHYSICS** a sloping surface that has a spiral shape

spire /'spaɪə/ noun [C] the pointed top of a church tower

spirit /'spɪrɪt/ noun

1 attitude of group	5 real meaning
2 determination	6 non-physical part of sb
3 mood	7 imaginary creature
4 sb's attitude	8 alcoholic drink

1 [singular/U] the attitude of people in a group: *a spirit of cooperation* ♦ *We need more **team spirit**.*
2 [U] an enthusiastic or determined attitude: *She showed a lot of spirit.*
3 spirits [plural] your mood at a particular time: *She tried singing to **keep** her **spirits up**.* ♦ *Dad's **in high spirits** today, isn't he?*

4 [C/U] your attitude to life or to other people: *his independent spirit*
5 [U] the general or real meaning of something: *Their actions go against **the spirit of** the agreement.*
6 [C] **RELIGION** the part of a person that many people believe continues to exist after death: *His spirit will always be with us.*
7 [C] an imaginary creature with special powers: *evil spirits*
8 [C] a strong alcoholic drink such as **whisky** or **brandy**

spirited /'spɪrɪtɪd/ adj showing a lot of enthusiasm or determination

'spirit ,lamp noun [C] a small lamp that burns alcohol to produce light

'spirit ,level noun [C] a tool for measuring how level a surface is, usually used by someone who is building something such as a house or wall

spiritual¹ /'spɪrɪtʃuəl/ adj **RELIGION 1** relating to the part of a person that many people believe continues to exist after death: *a spiritual experience* **2** religious: *spiritual leaders* —**spirituality** /ˌspɪrɪtʃu'æləti/ noun [U], **spiritually** adv

spiritual² /'spɪrɪtʃuəl/ noun [C] **MUSIC** a type of religious song originally sung by African Americans

spiritualism /'spɪrɪtʃuə,lɪz(ə)m/ noun [U] **RELIGION** the belief that dead people are able to communicate with people who are still alive —**spiritualist** noun [C]

spirogyra /ˌspaɪrəʊ'dʒaɪrə/ noun [U] **BIOLOGY** a type of alga that contains chlorophyll and consists of strings of many cells

spit¹ /spɪt/ (**spits, spitting, spat** /spæt/) verb [I/T] **1** to force something that is liquid or solid out from your mouth **2** to rain slightly

spit² /spɪt/ noun **1** [U] *informal* the clear liquid that is in your mouth = SALIVA **2** [C] a long sharp piece of metal that is used for holding and turning meat as it cooks over a fire **3** [C] **GEOGRAPHY** a long narrow area of land that sticks out into the sea or a lake

spite¹ /spaɪt/ noun [U] a feeling of wanting to upset someone or to cause problems for them: *She refused out of spite.*

PHRASE in spite of sth used for referring to a fact that makes something else surprising = DESPITE: *In spite of feeling tired, we decided to go out.* ♦ *The house will certainly sell, **in spite of the fact that** it's overpriced.*

spite² /spaɪt/ verb [T] to deliberately upset someone or cause problems for them

spiteful /'spaɪtf(ə)l/ adj deliberately trying to upset someone or cause problems for them —**spitefully** adv

splash¹ /splæʃ/ verb **1** [I/T] if a liquid splashes, or if you splash it, it moves or hits something noisily **2** [I] to move around noisily in water

splash² /splæʃ/ noun [C] **1** the sound of liquid hitting something noisily, or the sound of something falling into a liquid **2** a mark made by a liquid splashing **3** a small amount of bright colour

'splash-type lubri,cation noun [U] **ENGINEERING** a method of **lubricating** (=putting oil on) an engine by **splashing** oil up from a container of oil at the bottom of a cylinder

spleen /spliːn/ noun [C] **ANATOMY** the organ in the body that removes dead red cells from the blood and produces white cells

splendid /'splendɪd/ adj *formal* very good, impressive, or enjoyable = WONDERFUL —**splendidly** adv

splendour /'splendə/ noun [U] the impressive beauty of something

splint /splɪnt/ noun [C] a piece of metal, plastic, or wood that is put next to a broken bone in order to hold it in place

splinter¹ /'splɪntə/ noun [C] a small sharp piece of wood or glass that has broken from a bigger piece

splinter² /'splɪntə/ verb [I/T] to break into small sharp pieces, or to make something do this

split¹ /splɪt/ (**splits, splitting, split**) verb **1** [I/T] to divide something into several parts, or to be divided into several parts: *Let's split into groups and work separately.* **2** [T] to share something by dividing it into separate parts: *I suggest we split the bill* (=divide it into equal amounts). **3** [I/T] if something splits, or if you split it, a long thin cut or break forms in it: *How did you split your trousers?* ♦ *One of the boxes fell and split open.* **4** [I] to separate from a group or organization: *1979 was the year they split from the Party.*
PHRASE split hairs to argue or worry about unimportant details

split² /splɪt/ noun [C] **1** a long thin cut or break in something **2** a disagreement that causes a group to divide into smaller groups **3** a way of dividing something

split in'finitive noun [C] **LANGUAGE** an infinitive in which there is an adverb between the word 'to' and the verb, as in the phrase 'to completely understand'. Some people avoid this because they think it is bad style.

'split ,pattern noun [C] **TECHNOLOGY** a **pattern** (=shape) made in two or more parts that is used for preparing complicated moulds in **sand-casting**

,split 'screen noun [C] **COMPUTING, ARTS** a way of showing two or more pictures or pieces of information on one screen

,split 'second noun [singular] an extremely small amount of time —**'split-,second** adj

splitting headache /,splɪtɪŋ 'hedeɪk/ noun [C] a very bad pain in the head

spoil /spɔɪl/ (**spoils, spoiling, spoiled** or **spoilt** /spɔɪlt/) verb

1 make worse	4 food: become too old
2 allow child everything	5 in election
3 treat sb with care	

1 [T] to make something worse, less attractive, or less enjoyable: *Radio towers spoilt the view.* ♦ *I really hope it doesn't rain – that would spoil everything.*
2 [T] to allow a child to get everything that they want, so that they behave badly if they do not get something: *His mother spoils him rotten* (=spoils him very much).
3 [T] to treat someone with a lot of care and kindness: *It's Mother's Day – let them spoil you a little!*
4 [I] if food spoils, it becomes not safe to eat because it is burnt or too old
5 [T] **POLITICS** to mark a voting paper so that it will not be officially accepted, usually to show unhappiness about the election

spoilage /'spɔɪlɪdʒ/ noun [U] the process of becoming decayed or damaged

spoilt¹ /spɔɪlt/ adj a spoilt child behaves badly if they do not get what they want because people have always given them everything that they want

spoilt² /spɔɪlt/ a past tense and past participle of **spoil**

spoke¹ /spəʊk/ noun [C] one of the thin metal bars that connect the centre of a wheel to the outside part

spoke² /spəʊk/ the past tense of **speak**

spoken¹ /'spəʊkən/ adj said, instead of being written: *examples of spoken and written English*

spoken² /'spəʊkən/ the past participle of **speak**

spokesman /'spəʊksmən/ (plural **spokesmen** /'spəʊksmən/) noun [C] a male spokesperson

spokesperson /'spəʊks,pɜːs(ə)n/ (plural **spokespeople** /'spəʊks,piːp(ə)l/ or **spokespersons**) noun [C] someone whose job is to officially represent an organization and to speak to journalists

spokeswoman /'spəʊks,wʊmən/ (plural **spokeswomen** /'spəʊks,wɪmɪn/) noun [C] a female spokesperson

spondee /'spɒndi/ noun [C] **LITERATURE** a set of two stressed syllables in poetry coming one after the other

sponge /spʌndʒ/ noun [C] **1** a piece of a soft substance that takes in water easily and is used for cleaning things or for washing yourself **2** **BIOLOGY** an invertebrate sea animal whose light soft skeleton can be used for washing or cleaning things —*picture* → SEA

spongy /'spʌndʒi/ adj light, soft, and full of small holes

'spongy ,bone noun [U] **ANATOMY** the light tissue that forms the inside of most bones. It contains bone marrow. —*picture* → BONE

,spongy 'mesophyll noun [U] **BIOLOGY** a part below the top surface of a leaf that has large air spaces between its cells, which makes **gaseous exchange** easier

sponsor¹ /'spɒnsə/ verb [T] **1** to pay for something such as an event or a radio or television programme as a way of advertising your company or products **2** to agree to give money to someone who is going to take part in an event in order to make money for charity **3** to organize and support an event or activity **4** **POLITICS** if an elected official sponsors a **bill**, they write the bill and organize support for it, in order to try get other officials in Parliament or Congress to vote for it —**sponsorship** noun [U]

sponsor² /'spɒnsə/ noun [C] **1** a person or business that pays for something such as an event or a radio or television programme as a way of advertising their company or products **2** someone who agrees to give money to someone who is taking part in an event in order to make money for charity **3** a country, organization, or group that organizes and supports an activity

spontaneous /spɒn'teɪniəs/ adj **1** happening in a natural way without being planned or thought about: *spontaneous applause* **2** **CHEMISTRY, BIOLOGY** used about chemical or biological processes or changes that happen suddenly in a natural way —**spontaneity** /,spɒntə'neɪəti/ noun [U], **spontaneously** adv

spon,taneous a'bortion noun [C] **BIOLOGY** an occasion when a foetus comes out of its mother's body before it has developed enough to live. It is more usually called a **miscarriage**.

spooky /'spuːki/ (**spookier, spookiest**) adj *informal* strange and frightening

spool¹ /spuːl/ noun [C] **1** a round object with a hole in the middle that you wind something such as string around **2** **COMPUTING** a part of a computer's memory where information is kept for a short period = BUFFER

spool² /spuːl/ verb [T] **1** to wind something around a spool **2** **COMPUTING** to move information for printing into a computer's memory, so that it can print later and not slow down the computer

spoon¹ /spuːn/ noun [C] an object that you use for eating soup and other liquid foods and for mixing and preparing food

spoon² /spuːn/ verb [T] to eat or serve food with a spoon

spoonful /ˈspuːnfʊl/ noun [C] the amount that a spoon contains

sporadic /spəˈrædɪk/ adj not regular or frequent —**sporadically** /spəˈrædɪkli/ adv

sporangium /spəˈrændʒiəm/ (plural **sporangia** /spəˈrændʒiə/) noun [C] **BIOLOGY** a spore case in which **asexual** spores are formed, in plants such as ferns and in fungi

spore /spɔː/ noun [C] **BIOLOGY** a structure consisting of one cell that is produced, for example, by a fungus, **moss**, or fern, and that can develop into a new organism of the same type

sporophyte /ˈspɔːrəfaɪt, ˈspɔːrəfaɪt/ noun [C] **BIOLOGY** the stage in the life of organisms such as fungi, algae, and **mosses**, which have both sexual and **asexual** forms, when spores are produced
→ GAMETOPHYTE

sport /spɔːt/ noun **1** [C] **SPORTS** a physical activity in which players or teams compete against each other: *Bob's favourite sport is tennis.* ♦ *the newspaper's sports section* **2** [U] **SPORTS** sports in general: *The school is keen to involve more young people in sport.* **3** [C] **BIOLOGY** a plant or animal that is different in a noticeable way from other plants or animals of the same type

'sports ,day noun [C] **EDUCATION** a day at school when children compete against one another in different sports and their parents watch

'sports ,drink noun [C] **SPORTS** a drink that usually contains sugar and a little salt and is suitable for people who are exercising

sportsman /ˈspɔːtsmən/ (plural **sportsmen** /ˈspɔːtsmən/) noun [C] **SPORTS** a man who plays sport

sportsmanship /ˈspɔːtsmənʃɪp/ noun [U] **SPORTS** fair and honest behaviour in sport

sportsperson /ˈspɔːtspɜːs(ə)n/ (plural **sportspeople** /ˈspɔːtspiːp(ə)l/) noun [C] **SPORTS** someone who plays sport

'sports ,supplement noun [C] **SPORTS** a food substance or drug that people can take to increase their energy

sportswoman /ˈspɔːtswʊmən/ (plural **sportswomen** /ˈspɔːtswɪmɪn/) noun [C] **SPORTS** a woman who plays sport

sporty /ˈspɔːti/ adj **1** a sporty car looks fast and expensive **2** a sporty person likes playing sport

spot¹ /spɒt/ noun [C]

1 place	4 red lump on face
2 small area of colour	5 small amount of sth
3 dirty mark	+ PHRASES

1 a particular place: *We found him sitting in a sunny spot in the garden.* ♦ *one of the region's best-known tourist spots*
2 a small round area of colour that is different from the colour of the area around it: *The flower is yellow with red spots.*
3 a small unpleasant or dirty mark on something
4 a small red lump on someone's face = PIMPLE
5 a small amount of something, usually liquid = DROP: *I felt a few spots of rain on my face.*
 PHRASES **on the spot** in the exact place where something is happening
put sb on the spot to ask someone a difficult or embarrassing question
→ BLIND SPOT, HOT SPOT, SORE¹

spot² /spɒt/ (**spots, spotting, spotted**) verb [T] to notice someone or something: *Maria spotted the book lying under the chair.*

spotface /ˈspɒt,feɪs/ verb [T] **TECHNOLOGY** to make a hole in an uneven surface with a special cutting tool, so that there is a level area for a **washer** or a **bolt**

spotless /ˈspɒtləs/ adj extremely clean —**spotlessly** adv

spotlight /ˈspɒt,laɪt/ noun **1** [C] **ARTS** a powerful light that shines on a small area, for example in a theatre **2 the spotlight** [singular] a situation in which someone gets a lot of public attention

spotted /ˈspɒtɪd/ adj covered with a pattern of spots

spotty /ˈspɒti/ adj covered with spots

'spot ,weld noun [C] **TECHNOLOGY** an act of joining two pieces of metal together by welding them at several separate points —**spot-weld** verb [I/T]

spouse /spaʊs/ noun [C] *formal* someone's husband or wife

spout¹ /spaʊt/ noun [C] a part of a container that is shaped like a tube and is used for pouring liquid

spout² /spaʊt/ verb [I/T] if a liquid spouts from somewhere, or if something spouts it, a lot of it comes out fast and continuously

sprain /spreɪn/ verb [T] **HEALTH** to injure a joint such as the wrist by suddenly turning it too much —**sprain** noun [C], **sprained** /spreɪnd/ adj: *a sprained ankle*

sprang /spræŋ/ the past tense of **spring²**

sprawl /sprɔːl/ verb [I] **1** to sit or lie with the arms and legs stretched out in a relaxed or careless way **2** to stretch over or across something in an ugly and untidy way —**sprawl** noun [singular/U]

spray¹ /spreɪ/ verb [I/T] **1** if you spray a liquid, or if it sprays, very small drops of it are forced out of a container through a small hole: *The chemical is sprayed onto the crops once a week.* **2** if something sprays very small drops or pieces of a substance, or if they spray, they are thrown into the air in different directions

spray² /spreɪ/ noun **1** [C/U] a liquid that is forced out of a container in very small drops when you push a button on it **2** [singular/U] many small drops of water that are forced into the air

'spray ,can noun [C] a small container that uses pressure to shoot out a stream of small drops of liquid

spread¹ /spred/ (**spreads, spreading, spread**) verb

1 affect larger area	5 of information
2 open sth folded	6 make happen in stages
3 put/be in wide area	7 move limbs apart
4 cover with layer	+ PHRASAL VERBS

1 [I/T] to gradually affect a larger area or a larger number of people or things, or to make something do this: *Rain will spread from the west this evening.* ♦ *Soldiers returning from the war spread the disease through the region.*
2 spread or **spread out** [T] to open something that is folded so that it covers a surface: *We **spread** the blanket **on** the grass and sat down on it.*
3 [I/T] to put things in many parts of an area, or to be present in many parts of a large area: *There are 54 community colleges **spread across** California.*
4 [T] to cover a surface with a thin layer of a soft food: *Maureen **spread** jam **on** her toast.* ♦ *First, **spread** the bread **with** mayonnaise.* —picture → FOOD
5 [I/T] if information spreads, or if you spread it, it becomes known by more people than before: *Someone has been **spreading** nasty **rumours** about Stella's private life.*

6 [T] to make something happen at several times during a long period, instead of all at once: *You can spread your payments over five years.*

7 [T] to move the arms, legs, or hands so that they are far apart= EXTEND

PHRASAL VERBS ,spread 'out 1 if people in a group spread out, they move away from one another so that they cover a large area *same as* **spread¹** sense 7: *He spread out his toes in the soft sand and wiggled them.*

,spread sth 'out *same as* **spread¹** sense 2: *We spread our papers out on the table.*

spread² /spred/ noun **1** [singular] the growth or development of something, so that it affects a larger area or a larger number of people: *There were concerns about the **spread of** fighting to other regions.* **2** [C/U] a soft food that you put on bread and similar foods: *a low-fat spread* **3** [C] a long article in a newspaper or magazine: *a double-page spread* **4** [singular] a number of different things= RANGE: *You minimize risk by investing in **a spread of** companies.*

spreadsheet /'spred,ʃiːt/ noun [C] COMPUTING a **chart** that is produced on a computer that shows numbers in a way that makes them easy to deal with or change

spree /spriː/ noun [C] a short period that you spend doing a lot of an enjoyable activity

sprig /sprɪg/ noun [C] a stem or very small branch that is cut from a plant

sprightly /'spraɪtli/ (**sprightlier, sprightliest**) adj healthy and full of energy despite being old

spring¹ /sprɪŋ/ noun **1** [C/U] the season between winter and summer: *These flowers bloom **in spring**.* **2** [C] GEOGRAPHY a place where water flows up from under the ground and forms a small stream or pool **3** [C] a long thin piece of metal that is twisted into the shape of a coil that quickly returns to its original shape after you stop stretching it **4** [C] a quick jump forward or up

spring² /sprɪŋ/ (**springs, springing, sprang** /spræŋ/, **sprung** /sprʌŋ/) verb [I] **1** to jump or move quickly and with a lot of energy in a particular direction: *The young man turned to hit him, but Corbett sprang back.* ◆ *Robert **sprang to his feet** (=stood quickly) to shout at the referee.* **2** to do something quickly and with energy or force: *'Let's get going,' my father cried, **springing into** action.* ◆ *'She was just trying to help!' said Eric, **springing to** her defence.* **3** to happen or appear somewhere suddenly or unexpectedly: *Tears **sprang to** his eyes as he thought of Helen.*

PHRASE **spring a leak** to crack or break so that water or another liquid can get in or out: *The boat sprang a leak and quickly sank.*
→ MIND¹

'spring ,balance noun [C] a piece of equipment used for weighing things, consisting of a spring that is measured to see how much it stretches when something is hung from it → BEAM BALANCE

springboard /'sprɪŋ,bɔːd/ noun [C] **1** something that helps you to become successful **2** SPORTS a strong board used for helping you to jump in sports such as diving

springbok /'sprɪŋ,bɒk/ noun [C] a brown and white African mammal that looks like a small **deer**

spring bow compass /sprɪŋ bəʊ ,kʌmpəs/ noun [C] TECHNOLOGY a pair of **compasses** with a screw for holding them in a fixed position

springer /'sprɪŋə/ noun [C] CONSTRUCTION the first stone or brick at either end of an **arch**

spring 'onion noun [C] a small white onion with a long thin green stem that is often eaten raw in salads —*picture* → VEGETABLE

'spring ,steel noun [U] ENGINEERING a type of steel that contains a medium amount of carbon. It is used for making objects that easily return to their original shape after being bent or twisted.

,spring 'tide noun [C] GEOGRAPHY a time when there is a big difference between the highest and lowest levels of the sea

springtime /'sprɪŋ,taɪm/ noun [U] the season of spring

springy /'sprɪŋi/ adj something that is springy quickly returns to its shape after you press it or walk on it

sprinkle /'sprɪŋk(ə)l/ verb [T] **1** to shake small amounts of a liquid or a substance such as sugar over the surface of something: ***Sprinkle** the chicken with soy sauce.* ◆ ***Sprinkle** the grated cheese **over** the pasta, and serve.* **2** used about other things that exist somewhere in separate small amounts

sprinkler /'sprɪŋklə/ noun [C] **1** a piece of equipment that is used for automatically sprinkling water on a garden —*picture* → AGRICULTURAL **2** a piece of equipment on the ceiling that spreads water over the room if a fire starts

sprinkling /'sprɪŋklɪŋ/ noun [C] a small amount of a liquid or a substance such as sugar that is shaken over the surface of something

sprint¹ /sprɪnt/ noun [C] **1** SPORTS a short race at a fast speed **2** a sudden burst of speed, energy, or activity

sprint² /sprɪnt/ verb [I] to run at a very fast speed for a short period

sprite /spraɪt/ noun [C] **1** COMPUTING on a computer, an independent part of a picture that you can move around easily on the screen **2** a small magical creature in traditional stories, especially one that lives in or near water

sprout¹ /spraʊt/ verb **1** [I/T] BIOLOGY if a plant sprouts, or if it sprouts something, new leaves or shoots begin to grow on it **2** sprout or sprout up [I] to suddenly appear or increase in number: *A lot of these modern buildings have sprouted suddenly along the shore of the lake.*

sprout² /spraʊt/ noun [C] **1** a Brussels sprout **2** BIOLOGY a new shoot on a plant

sprung /sprʌŋ/ the past participle of **spring²**

'sprung ,weight noun [C] ENGINEERING the part of a vehicle's weight that is supported by the **suspension**

spun /spʌn/ the past tense and past participle of **spin¹**

spur¹ /spɜː/ noun [C] **1** a metal object on the heel of a rider's boot that the rider presses into a horse's side in order to make it go faster **2** GEOGRAPHY a long piece of high land that sticks out into a valley. It is a result of **glaciation**. —*picture* → RIVER

spur² /spɜː/ (**spurs, spurring, spurred**) verb [T] **1** to encourage someone to do something **2** to cause something to happen

'spur ,gear noun [C] ENGINEERING, TECHNOLOGY a **gear** (=circular part of a machine) with **teeth** (=narrow pointed parts) that stick out parallel to its axis. Spur gears are the simplest form of gear.

spurious /'spjʊəriəs/ adj *formal* not based on true facts

spurt /spɜːt/ verb **1** [I/T] to come out in a sudden strong flow **2** [I] to suddenly increase in speed or energy —**spurt** noun [C]

sputum /'spjuːtəm/ noun [U] HEALTH a thick unpleasant substance that develops in the throat and lungs of someone who has an infection. It can be coughed up.

spy[1] /spaɪ/ (plural **spies**) noun [C] someone whose job is to find out secret information about a country or an organization

spy[2] /spaɪ/ (**spies, spying, spied**) verb [I] to work as a spy

PHRASAL VERB **'spy on sb** to watch someone secretly so that you know everything that they do

spyware /'spaɪˌweə/ noun [U] COMPUTING software put onto your computer without you realizing it that sends information about you and your Internet use over the Internet

sq. abbrev square

squad /skwɒd/ noun [C] **1** a small group of soldiers who do a particular job **2** a department in a police force that deals with a particular type of crime **3** SPORTS a sports team **4** SPORTS a larger group of players from which a team is chosen

squadron /'skwɒdrən/ noun [C] a section of the armed forces, especially of the air force

squalid /'skwɒlɪd/ adj a place that is squalid is dirty and unpleasant

squall /skwɔːl/ noun [C] a storm that happens suddenly

squalor /'skwɒlə/ noun [U] dirty and uncomfortable conditions that someone lives in or works in

squander /'skwɒndə/ verb [T] to not use something such as money, time, or an opportunity in a sensible way

square[1] /skweə/ noun [C] **1** a shape with four straight sides of equal length and four right angles: *The flower beds* **form a** perfect **square.** —*picture* → SHAPE **2** an open area of land in the shape of a square with buildings around it: *The hotel is in the main square.* ♦ *They have an office in Soho Square.* **3** MATHS the number that is the result of multiplying one number by itself: *The square of 3 is 9.*

PHRASE **back to square one** in the same situation that you were in before you started to do something, so that you have made no progress

square[2] /skweə/ adj **1** in the shape of a square: *a small square garden* **2** with edges or corners that are not as curved as usual: *He had broad* **square shoulders.** **3** MATHS used for talking about units for measuring the area of something: *an area of over 200 square miles* ♦ *The room only four yards square.*

PHRASE **all square** if a game is all square, both teams or players have the same number of points

square[3] /skweə/ verb [T] MATHS to multiply a number by itself

‚square 'bracket noun [C] MATHS, SCIENCE either of the symbols [or] that are often used in mathematics and scientific writing

‚square-‚pin 'plug noun [C] an electrical **plug** that has square pins —*picture* → PLUG

‚square 'root noun [C] MATHS a number that you multiply by itself in order to produce a particular number: *The square root of 9 is 3.*

‚square 'thread noun [C] TECHNOLOGY a **thread** (=raised line) curving around a screw that has straight sides at an angle of 90° to the screw, a flat top, and a flat space in between

squash[1] /skwɒʃ/ verb **1** [T] to damage something by pressing or crushing it so that it loses its normal shape

2 [I/T] to push someone or something so that they fit into a small space, or to fit into a small space with difficulty **3** [T] to prevent something from happening or being effective

squash[2] /skwɒʃ/ noun **1** [U] SPORTS an indoor game in which two players use **rackets** in order to hit a small ball against a wall **2** [singular] a situation in which there are too many people in a small space **3** (plural **squash** or **squashes**) [C/U] a large hard vegetable with very thick green or orange skin

squat[1] /skwɒt/ (**squats, squatting, squatted**) verb [I] **1** to bend your knees and lower yourself towards the ground so that you balance on your feet = CROUCH **2** to live in a place without permission and without paying the owner

squat[2] /skwɒt/ noun [C] a house where people live without permission and without paying the owner

squat[3] /skwɒt/ adj wide and not very tall or high

squatter /'skwɒtə/ noun [C] someone who lives in a place without permission and without paying the owner

squeak /skwiːk/ verb [I] to make a short high sound —**squeak** noun [C]

squeaky /'skwiːki/ (**squeakier, squeakiest**) adj making a short high sound

squeal /skwiːl/ verb [I] to make a long high sound —**squeal** noun [C]

squeamish /'skwiːmɪʃ/ adj easily upset by seeing something that is unpleasant

squeeze[1] /skwiːz/ verb **1** [I/T] to press something firmly: *Ruth smiled, squeezing his hand affectionately.* **2** [T] to press something such as a liquid out of something: *She squeezed some cream onto her hands.* **3** [I/T] to fit something into a small space with difficulty, or to fit into a small space with difficulty: *We can only squeeze one more thing into the bag.* ♦ *He had* **squeezed through** *a hole in the fence.* ♦ *Passengers were trying to* **squeeze onto** *the bus.* **4** [T] to make someone have financial trouble, for example by raising prices or cutting a supply of money: *Supermarkets are accused of squeezing both customers and suppliers.*

squeeze[2] /skwiːz/ noun **1** [C] an act of squeezing something **2** [C] a small amount of a liquid that is squeezed out of something **3** [singular] a situation in which there are too many people or things in a small space **4** [singular] ECONOMICS a situation in which there is strict control over money or goods

squelch /skweltʃ/ verb [I] to make the sound that your feet make when you walk on wet ground —**squelch** noun [C]

squid /skwɪd/ (plural **squid**) noun [C] a sea mollusc that is similar to an **octopus** but with ten arms instead of eight —*picture* → SEA

squiggle /'skwɪɡ(ə)l/ noun [C] a line with a lot of curves in it —**squiggly** adj

squint /skwɪnt/ verb [I] to close your eyes slightly in order to try to see something more clearly —**squint** noun [C]

squirm /skwɜːm/ verb [I] **1** to look or feel embarrassed and uncomfortable **2** to move by twisting and turning in a small space

squirrel /'skwɪrəl/ noun [C] a grey or red-brown mammal with a long thick tail. Squirrels live in trees. —*picture* → MAMMAL

squirt /skwɜːt/ verb **1** [I/T] if a liquid squirts somewhere, or if you squirt it, it comes out in a narrow stream with a lot of force **2** [T] to make someone or something wet by squirting a liquid —**squirt** noun [C]

Sr abbrev Senior: used after the name of someone who has a child with the same name

st abbrev **stones**

St abbrev **1** RELIGION Saint **2** Street

stab¹ /stæb/ (**stabs, stabbing, stabbed**) verb [T] to push a knife or other sharp object into someone or something
  PHRASE **stab sb in the back** to do something that is not loyal to someone who trusts you

stab² /stæb/ noun [C] **1** an act of stabbing someone **2** informal an attempt to do something that is difficult to do or that you have never done: They decided to **have a stab at** fixing the car themselves. **3** a sudden feeling of a negative emotion: a stab of jealousy

stabbing /'stæbɪŋ/ noun [C] an attack in which someone is **stabbed**

stability /stə'bɪləti/ noun [U] **1** a situation in which things continue without any major changes or problems ≠ INSTABILITY: The rise of nationalism could threaten the stability of Europe. **2** SCIENCE the ability of a substance to stay in the same state **3** PHYSICS the ability of an object to stay balanced so that it does not move

stabilize /'steɪbəlaɪz/ verb [I/T] to reach a state where there are no longer any major changes or problems, or to make something do this: Oil prices have stabilized for now. —**stabilization** /ˌsteɪbəlaɪˈzeɪʃ(ə)n/ noun [U]

stabilizer /'steɪbəlaɪzə/ noun [C] CHEMISTRY a substance added to some prepared foods to stop the taste or appearance from changing

stable¹ /'steɪb(ə)l/ adj **1** not changing frequently, and not likely to suddenly become worse ≠ UNSTABLE: a stable economic situation ♦ Tonight the baby is in a **stable condition** in hospital. **2** not likely to fall or move in the wrong way ≠ UNSTABLE: The suspension keeps the car stable when cornering. **3** HEALTH with a healthy mental and emotional state = BALANCED **4** PHYSICS able to stay balanced and not move ≠ UNSTABLE —**stably** adv

stable² /'steɪb(ə)l/ noun [C] a building where horses are kept

staccato /stə'kɑːtəʊ/ adj, adv MUSIC staccato notes are played or sung so that each note is clearly separate

stack¹ /stæk/ noun [C] **1** a pile of things that are placed one on top of another: a **stack of** unopened mail **2** informal a large amount of something: There's **stacks of** time left. **3** COMPUTING a system for storing information on a computer **4** GEOLOGY a tall steep piece of rock that rises out of the sea. It is formed as a result of being separated from a cliff by waves eroding the rock in between. —picture → EROSION

stack² /stæk/ verb [T] **1** to arrange things by putting one on top of another: Stack the chairs and put them in the corner when you're finished. **2** to fill something by arranging things in piles or rows in or on it: The shelves were stacked with books.

stadium /'steɪdiəm/ noun [C] SPORTS a large building, usually without a roof, where people watch sports events such as football matches or races

staff¹ /stɑːf/ noun **1** [singular/U] the people who work for a particular company, organization, or institution: Peter became a very valued **member of staff**. ♦ She **joined the staff** in 1996. ♦ The embassy employs around 50 people on its **full-time staff**. **2** [C] MUSIC the set of lines on which music is written = STAVE

Staff can be used with a singular or plural verb. You can say: The staff **has** worked very hard. OR: The staff **have** worked very hard.

staff² /stɑːf/ verb [T] to provide a company, organization, or institution with workers

'staff ,lines noun [plural] MUSIC the set of lines on which music is written

staffroom /'stɑːfruːm/ noun [C] EDUCATION a room for the teachers of a school or college, where they can go between classes

stag /stæg/ noun [C] a male **deer** —picture → MAMMAL

'stag ,beetle noun [C] a large dark beetle with large jaws that resemble the horns on the head of a male deer

stage¹ /steɪdʒ/ noun **1** [C] a particular point in time during a process or series of events: We were now on **the last stage of** our journey. ♦ They had the ball more often **in the early stages of** the game. ♦ There's no point arguing about it **at this stage**. **2** [C] ARTS the part of a theatre where the actors or musicians perform: They had now been **on stage** for over four hours. ♦ The band didn't **take the stage** (=come onto it) until after ten o'clock. —picture → ACOUSTICS **3** [C] a flat area or surface on which something takes place or on which you do something —picture → MICROSCOPE **4 the stage** [singular] ARTS the theatre, or the profession of acting: She's written a number of works for the stage.

stage² /steɪdʒ/ verb [T] **1** to organize an event: They staged a protest in front of the embassy. **2** ARTS to organize a performance of a play or opera —**staging** noun [C/U]

'stage di,rection noun [C] ARTS an instruction about what will happen in a play or other show

stagflation /stæg'fleɪʃ(ə)n/ noun [U] ECONOMICS a situation in which **inflation** (=a general increase in prices) and unemployment are high, and demand and economic activity are **stagnant** (=not growing)

stagger /'stægə/ verb **1** [I] to walk in an uncontrolled way, as if you are going to fall: He gave her a slight push, and she staggered backwards. **2** [T] to surprise and shock someone = ASTOUND: Rory was staggered by his answer. **3** [T] to arrange for events or activities to start at different times: We have to stagger mealtimes because there are so many of us now.

stagnant /'stægnənt/ adj **1** stagnant water does not flow and often smells bad **2** not growing or developing

stain¹ /steɪn/ verb **1** [I/T] to leave a mark on something accidentally: Sweat had stained his shirt. **2** [T] to colour wood with a special liquid **3** [T] SCIENCE to colour something before examining it under a microscope

stain² /steɪn/ noun **1** [C] a mark that is left accidentally on clothes or surfaces: oil stains **2** [C/U] a liquid that is used for colouring wood **3** [C/U] SCIENCE a dye used for colouring something such as biological tissue in order to make it easier to see and examine under a microscope

stained glass /ˌsteɪnd 'glɑːs/ noun [U] coloured glass that is traditionally used in church windows —**'stained-,glass** adj

stainless steel /ˌsteɪnləs 'stiːl/ noun [U] steel that has been treated to stop **rust** forming on its surface. It is used for making knives, tools etc. —**,stainless-'steel** adj

stair /steə/ noun **1 stairs** [plural] a set of steps that allow you to go from one level of a building to another: I **climbed the stairs** to Charles's office. ♦ John raced **down the stairs** to answer the door. ♦ Someone was waiting **at the top of the stairs**. **2** [C] one of the steps in a set of stairs: He was standing on the bottom stair.

staircase /ˈsteəˌkeɪs/ noun [C] a set of stairs in a building with a **banister** that you hold on to when you go up or down

stairway /ˈsteəˌweɪ/ noun [C] a set of stairs inside or outside a building

stake¹ /steɪk/ noun **1** [C] **BUSINESS** the part of a business that you own because you have invested money in it: *They took a 40% **stake in** the company last year*. **2** [C] an amount of money that you risk losing when you try to guess the result of a race or competition **3 stakes** [plural] the things that you can gain or lose by taking a risk: *The Americans have **raised the stakes** (=risked gaining or losing more) in a bitter fight over imports.* ♦ *With such **high stakes** (=a lot that could be won or lost), the atmosphere was tense.* **4** [C] a wooden or metal post with a pointed end that is used for supporting or marking something
PHRASE **at stake** likely to be lost or damaged if something fails: *People's lives are at stake.*

stake² /steɪk/ verb [T] to risk losing or damaging something that is valuable in order to get or do something = GAMBLE: *The government has **staked** its **reputation on** eliminating the deficit.*
PHRASE **stake a claim (to sth)** to say or show clearly that you believe that something is yours

stakeholder /ˈsteɪkˌhəʊldə/ noun [C] **1** **BUSINESS** a person or company that has invested in a business and owns part of it **2** someone who has an interest in the success of a plan, system, or organization

stalactite /ˈstæləktaɪt/ noun [C] **GEOLOGY, CHEMISTRY** a long pointed piece of rock that hangs down from the roof of a cave. It is formed over many years by drops of water containing dissolved chemicals. → STALAGMITE —*picture* → LIMESTONE

stalagmite /ˈstæləgmaɪt/ noun [C] **GEOLOGY, CHEMISTRY** a long pointed piece of rock that rises up from the floor of a cave. It is formed over many years by drops of water containing dissolved chemicals falling from the roof. → STALACTITE —*picture* → LIMESTONE

stale /steɪl/ adj **1** old and no longer fresh: *stale bread* **2** not smelling fresh or nice: *stale air* **3** not new, original, or interesting: *stale news* **4** someone who is stale has done something so often that they can no longer do it well or be interested in it

stalemate /ˈsteɪlˌmeɪt/ noun [C/U] **1** a situation in which progress is impossible because the people involved cannot agree: *Management and the unions have **reached stalemate** in their negotiations.* **2** the situation in chess when the game ends because neither player can win

stalk¹ /stɔːk/ noun [C] **BIOLOGY** a long thin part of a plant with a flower, fruit, or leaf at the end —*picture* → FLOWER, TREE

stalk² /stɔːk/ verb **1** [I] to walk in a way that shows that you feel angry or offended: *He shook his head in disgust and **stalked off**, muttering.* **2** [T] to hunt a person or animal by following them without being seen **3** [T] to follow and watch someone all the time in a threatening way, because of an extremely strong interest in them

stall¹ /stɔːl/ noun [C] **1** a large table or a small building that is open at the front. Stalls are used for selling things or for giving people information.
2 **AGRICULTURE** a narrow space for one animal such as a horse or pig **3 stalls** [plural] **ARTS** the seats in front of the stage on the lowest level of a theatre, cinema etc

stall² /stɔːl/ verb [I/T] **1** if a vehicle's engine stalls, or if the driver stalls it, it suddenly stops working **2** if a process stalls, or if someone stalls it, it stops making progress: *Talks have stalled and both sides are preparing for war.* **3** to delay, or to delay someone, in order to gain more time: *If he calls again, try to stall him until I get there.*

stallion /ˈstæljən/ noun [C] an adult male horse

stalwart /ˈstɔːlwət/ adj very loyal: *a stalwart supporter* —**stalwart** noun [C]

stamen /ˈsteɪmən/ noun [C] **BIOLOGY** the male part of a flower that produces pollen. It consists of an **anther** and a **filament**. —*picture* → FLOWER

stamina /ˈstæmɪnə/ noun [U] the ability to do something that needs a lot of effort over a long period of time without getting tired

stammer /ˈstæmə/ verb [I/T] to keep repeating a particular sound when trying to speak because you have a speech problem, or because you are nervous or excited = STUTTER —**stammer** noun [singular]

stamp¹ /stæmp/ noun **1** [C] a small official piece of paper that you buy and stick on an envelope in order to pay for the cost of posting a letter or parcel: *a first-class stamp* **2** [C] a small tool with a pattern or writing on one side that you press into ink and use for printing a mark on paper **3** [C] a mark that you make with a stamp: *Did you get a stamp in your passport?* **4** [singular] a particular quality that is clearly noticeable in someone or something: *The film **bears the** unmistakable **stamp of** its energetic director.* ♦ *He has a chance to **put his stamp on** government policy.*

stamp² /stæmp/ verb **1** [I/T] to put your foot down hard and noisily on something: *Mary tried to **stamp on** the spider.* ♦ *He **stamped his foot** angrily.* **2** [I] to walk putting your feet down hard and noisily on the ground, usually because you are angry: *Riley **stamped into** the editor's office.* **3** [T] to put a mark on something using ink and a stamp: *They didn't stamp my passport.*

stamped addressed envelope /ˌstæmpt əˌdrest ˈenvələʊp/ noun [C] an **sae**

stampede /stæmˈpiːd/ noun [C] a situation in which a group of people or animals all start to run in a very fast uncontrolled way because they are frightened or excited —**stampede** verb [I/T]

stance /stæns/ noun [C] **1** an attitude or view about an issue that you state publicly = POSITION **2** a particular way of standing

stand¹ /stænd/ (**stands, standing, stood** /stʊd/) verb

1 be upright on feet	9 still exist
2 get up	10 accept sth bad
3 be/put sth upright	11 have attitude
4 put foot on/in sth	12 not be affected
5 be a height	13 try to be elected
6 be in situation	14 perform job
7 of vehicle	+ PHRASES
8 reach level	+ PHRASAL VERBS

1 [I] to have your body in an upright position supported by your feet: *The train was full and we had to stand all the way to Edinburgh.* ♦ *Stand still and let me brush your hair.* ♦ *Mrs Carter was **standing by** the open window.* ♦ *The man **standing behind** him spoke.*
2 [I] to move from lying, sitting, or bending down into an upright position: *Everyone stood as the judge entered the court.*
3 [I/T] to put someone or something in an upright position, or to be in an upright position: *Stand the bookcase against the far wall.* ♦ *His statue stands in the city square.*

4 [I] to put your foot on or in something: *He apologized for **standing on** my foot.*

5 [I] to be a particular height: *The structure stands 40 metres high.*

6 [I] to be in a particular situation or state: *How do negotiations stand at the moment?* ♦ *As it stands, the law doesn't allow local government to take such action.*

7 [I] if a car, train, plane etc stands somewhere, it remains there without moving, waiting to be used: *Luckily, the train was still standing at the platform.*

8 [I] to reach a particular level or amount: *The total amount of money raised so far **stands at** over £3,000.*

9 [I] to remain in existence or use: *Her world record has stood for nearly 20 years.* ♦ *Tell him **my offer still stands.***

10 [T] to be willing to accept something that is unpleasant: *How can you stand all that noise?*

11 [I] to have a particular attitude or view about a person or subject: ***Where does** the Prime Minister **stand on** this issue?*

12 [T] to be good or strong enough not to be badly affected or damaged by something: *These are plants that do not stand the cold well.* ♦ *I wonder how many of these new businesses will **stand the test of time**.*

13 [I] **POLITICS** to take part in an election as a **candidate** (=someone who people vote for): *She is intending to **stand for** parliament.* ♦ *He'll be **standing as** the candidate for Falkirk West.*

14 [T] to perform a particular job or service: *Two men were **standing guard over** the prisoners.*

PHRASES **sb can't stand sb/sth** used for saying that a person dislikes someone or something very much: *James just can't stand his mother-in-law.* ♦ *I can't stand waiting for buses.* ♦ *She **couldn't stand to** see him leave.* ♦ *Sylvia **couldn't stand the sight of** blood.*

it stands to reason (that) used for saying that something is obvious because it is what most sensible people would expect: *If they don't like you, it stands to reason they won't give you the job.*

stand accused of sth LAW to be the person who has been formally accused in a court of law of committing a crime

stand a chance (of doing sth) to be likely to achieve something: *Do they stand any chance of winning against France?*

stand in sb's way to try to stop someone from doing something

stand in the way of sth to try to prevent something from happening

stand on your own two feet to behave in an independent way, especially by not asking for financial help from anyone

stand to do sth to be in a particular situation or state that makes something likely to happen to you: *Many small companies stand to lose financially if the new law is introduced.*

stand trial (for sth) LAW to be judged for a crime in a court of law

→ GROUND¹

PHRASAL VERBS **,stand 'back** to move away from something, or to stand at a distance from something

,stand 'by to be ready to do something if you are needed: *A boat will be standing by in case of emergency.*

,stand 'down to leave an important job or position: *She'll be **standing down as** president at the end of the year.*

'stand for sth 1 if an abbreviation or a symbol stands for something, that is what it means or represents: *The letters ERM stand for Exchange-Rate Mechanism.* **2** to be willing to accept something that someone does: *No one makes a fool of me. I **won't stand for it**!* **3** if someone stands for a particular principle, they believe that that

principle is important: *I hate them and everything they stand for.*

,stand 'out to be easy to see or notice because of being different: *His bright yellow tie **stood out against** his black suit.*

,stand 'up to put your body into an upright position from a sitting or lying position: *A man at the back stood up to ask a question.*

,stand 'up to sb to not allow yourself to be treated badly by someone who is more powerful than you

stand² /stænd/ noun

1 attitude/opinion	**4** for holding sth
2 attempt to oppose	**5** for watching sports
3 table	

1 [singular] an attitude or opinion about something that you state publicly: *I couldn't vote for them because of the **stand** they have **taken on** social issues.*

2 [singular] a determined attempt to oppose someone or something that you think is wrong: *support for their **stand against** racism* ♦ *The Prime Minister must **take a firm stand** against extremists in his party.*

3 [C] a large table or structure that is used for selling things or for providing information or services: *a hot-dog stand* ♦ *the Porsche stand at the Paris show*

4 [C] an object or a piece of furniture that is used for holding, supporting, or storing something: *a cake stand* ♦ *an umbrella stand*

5 [C] **SPORTS** a part of a sports **stadium** where people sit or stand in order to watch an event

'stand-a,lone adj **1** not connected to anything else, or not depending on anything else **2** **COMPUTING** used about an individual computer that is not part of a **network**

standard¹ /'stændəd/ noun **1** [C/U] a level of quality or achievement, especially one that most people think is normal or acceptable: *What can be done to **raise standards** in schools?* ♦ *The food was not **up to standard**.* ♦ *He **sets** himself high **standards**.* ♦ *higher **standards of** service in hospitals* **2** [C] a level of quality or achievement that is used for judging someone or something: *The first computers were terribly slow **by today's standards**.* ♦ *The building was still magnificent **by any standards**.* **3** **standards** [plural] traditional principles of good behaviour: *declining **moral standards*** **4** [C] a flag used in ceremonies

PHRASE **standard of living** the type of life that a person or society has according to the amount of money that they have

standard² /'stændəd/ adj **1** generally used or accepted as normal: *It's a standard reply that the company sends out to applicants.* ♦ *It is **standard practice** for the school to inform the parents whenever a child is punished.* **2** made or done according to a generally accepted set of rules, measurements etc: *The promotional pack was 20 per cent bigger than the **standard size**.* **3** a standard book or work is one that most people use because it is the most respected in a particular subject: *This condition is not mentioned in standard medical textbooks.* **4** generally accepted as correct

,standard devi'ation noun [C] **MATHS** a number that shows how much smaller or larger another number in a set of numbers is from the average of the set

Standard English /,stændəd 'ɪŋglɪʃ/ noun [U] **LANGUAGE** the form of spoken and written English that is considered acceptable by most English-speaking people

'standard ,form noun [U] **MATHS, SCIENCE** a way of writing very large or very small numbers, using one **digit** before the decimal point that is then multiplied by a power of 10. For example, 63400 in standard form is 6.34×10^4.

standby /'stæn(d)baɪ/ noun [C] someone or something that is always available to be used if they are needed

PHRASE on standby 1 available to be used if needed: *The troops are on standby and can return at a moment's notice.* **2 TOURISM** ready to get on a plane if there is a seat left when it is about to take off: *The flight is sold out, but we can put you on standby.* —**standby** adj: *standby passengers*

'stand-in noun [C] someone or something that takes the place of another person or thing for a short time, especially in order to do their job

standing¹ /'stændɪŋ/ noun [U] the status or reputation that someone or something has

standing² /'stændɪŋ/ adj always existing: *the members of the standing committee* ♦ *We've got a standing invitation to stay with Jen and Mike whenever we want.*

,standing 'army noun [C] a professional army that a country has all the time, not just in a war

,standing 'order noun [C/U] an instruction from someone to their bank to take a particular amount of money out of their account on a regular date, to pay a person or organization

'standing ,wave noun [C] **PHYSICS** a wave pattern produced when two waves of equal frequency and **intensity**, travelling in opposite directions, combine

standpoint /'stæn(d)ˌpɔɪnt/ noun [C] a way of thinking about something

standstill /'stæn(d)ˌstɪl/ noun [singular] a situation in which something stops moving or happening

stank /stæŋk/ the past tense of **stink**

stanza /'stænzə/ noun [C] **LITERATURE** a group of lines in a poem that form a unit with a pattern that is repeated through the whole poem

stapes /'steɪpiːz/ (plural **stapes**) noun [C] **ANATOMY** a small bone in the **middle ear** that is nearest to the **inner ear** = STIRRUP

staple¹ /'steɪp(ə)l/ noun [C] **1** a small piece of wire that you press through pieces of paper with a **stapler** in order to fasten them together **2** a very basic and important food or product that people eat or use regularly

staple² /'steɪp(ə)l/ adj a staple food or product is a very basic and important one for a particular place or group of people

staple³ /'steɪp(ə)l/ verb [T] to fasten pieces of paper together with a staple

,staple 'diet noun [singular] the main food or foods that a person or animal eats regularly

stapler /'steɪplə/ noun [C] a small object used for fastening pieces of paper with a **staple** —*picture* → WORKSTATION

star¹ /stɑː/ noun [C]

1 light in night sky	**4** shape with points
2 sb famous	**5** the best in a group
3 main actor	**6** sign of quality

1 ASTRONOMY a very large hot ball of gas that appears as a small bright light in the sky at night
2 a famous and popular actor, entertainer, or sports player: *a pop star*
3 ARTS the main actor or performer in a film, play, television programme etc: *Today, he's the star of a hundred-million-dollar movie.*

4 an object, shape, or sign with five or more points that looks like a star: *We always put a star at the top of our Christmas tree.* ♦ *the 50 stars on the US flag* ♦ *I've put stars next to the names I want you to check.* —*picture* → SHAPE
5 someone or something that is clearly better than all the other people or things in a group: *McAllister was most definitely the star of the Scottish team.* ♦ *Mick was a star pupil at his school.*
6 a sign that is shaped like a star that is given to a hotel or restaurant in order to show what level of quality it has: *a five-star hotel*

star² /stɑː/ (**stars, starring, starred**) verb [I/T] **ARTS** if someone stars in a film, play, television programme etc, or if it stars them, they are the main actor or performer in it: *The X-Files, starring David Duchovny and Gillian Anderson* ♦ *He starred in the school play.*

starboard /'stɑːbəd/ noun [U] the right side of a ship when you are looking towards the front → PORT

starch /stɑːtʃ/ noun **1** [C/U] **BIOLOGY, CHEMISTRY** a type of carbohydrate made from glucose molecules that is stored in rice, potatoes, and other vegetables. It is an important type of food that provides energy. It is also used to make some types of cloth, paper, and glue. **2** [U] a substance that is used for making clothes stiff

starchy /'stɑːtʃi/ (**starchier, starchiest**) adj starchy foods have a lot of starch in them

stare /steə/ verb [I] to look at someone or something very directly for a long time: *It's rude to stare.* ♦ *He lifted his head and stared at her.* —**stare** noun [C]

starfish /'stɑːˌfɪʃ/ (plural **starfish**) noun [C] a small flat sea animal with five or more arms that is shaped like a star. Starfish are **echinoderms**. —*picture* → SEA

starfruit /'stɑːˌfruːt/ noun [C] a tropical fruit with soft yellow skin that is the shape of a star when you cut it in half

stark¹ /stɑːk/ adj **1** very clear and plain to look at, in a slightly unpleasant or frightening way: *stark brick walls* **2** very obvious, or impossible to avoid: *The stark choice is between moving out or staying here and paying more.* **3** extreme and obvious: *His words were in stark contrast to what he had said earlier.* —**starkly** adv

stark² /stɑːk/ adv **stark naked** not wearing any clothes

starlight /'stɑːˌlaɪt/ noun [U] the light that comes from the stars

starlit /'stɑːlɪt/ adj bright with light from the stars

starry /'stɑːri/ adj a starry sky or night is one with a lot of stars

'star ,sign noun [C] one of the 12 signs of the zodiac that some people believe influence your character and your future

start¹ /stɑːt/ verb

1 begin to happen	**7** be the limit of sth
2 begin to do sth	**8** be the lowest price
3 begin a journey	**9** make sth happen
4 begin job etc	**10** make machine work
5 begin a period of time	**+ PHRASES**
6 of business/project	**+ PHRASAL VERBS**

1 [I] to begin to happen: *The World Championships start in two weeks.* ♦ *It's starting to rain.* ♦ *The leaves have started falling off the trees.*
2 [I/T] to begin doing something: *Please start when you are ready.* ♦ *I started to unpack my suitcase.* ♦ *Everyone in the class started laughing.* ♦ *The class starts with some gentle stretching exercises.*

3 [I/T] to begin a journey: *We started early enough but got caught in the London traffic.*

4 [I/T] to begin a new job, career, or period of education: *I start work on Monday.* ♦ *Things were very different when I started in politics.*

5 [T] to begin a period of time in a particular way: *I always start the day with a cup of coffee.*

6 [T] to bring a business or project into existence: *He decided to quit his job and start his own business.*

7 [I] used for talking about the nearest end or edge of something: *The new houses start immediately beyond the bridge.*

8 [I] used for talking about the lowest price or number: *Prices for theatre tickets start from £10.*

9 [T] to cause something, or to be the first person to do something: *Who wants to start the discussion?* ♦ *What she said started me thinking.*

10 [I/T] if you start a machine, or if it starts, it begins to work: *No matter how many times he tried, the car wouldn't start.* ♦ *Scott started the engine and drove off.*

PHRASES back where you started in the same place or situation where you were before, so that you have not made any progress

get started to begin doing something: *We couldn't wait to get started on the next job.*

get sb started to help or cause someone to begin doing something new: *It was his aunt who got him started in business.*

to start with 1 as a beginning, or as the first thing: *Let's do a few easy exercises to start with.* **2** used for introducing the first or the most important point that supports an opinion: *Well, to start with, you haven't got the right qualifications.*

→ START-UP

PHRASAL VERBS ,start (sth) 'off to begin, or to cause something to begin: *Let's start off with a few questions from the audience.*

,start 'out 1 to begin as something before developing into something different: *Some businesses start out as hobbies.* **2** to begin a journey= SET OUT: *We started out at five o'clock and got there at eight.*

,start (sth) 'up if you start up a business or project, or if it starts up, you bring it into existence: *She left last year to start up her own business.*

start² /stɑːt/ noun [singular]

1 of period of time	**5** in races and games
2 way sb begins sth	**6** new opportunity
3 of journey	**7** advantage
4 of film/story	**+ PHRASES**

1 the beginning of a period of time: *At the start of the final year, students do work experience.* ♦ *I hated her right from the start.* ♦ *The operation takes about 15 minutes from start to finish.*

2 the way that someone begins a period of time or activity: *There's no better start to the day than a healthy breakfast.* ♦ *Hakkinen made a good start and was in second place by the first corner.* ♦ *Her election campaign got off to a slow start.*

3 the beginning of a journey: *After an early start, we were soon out of the city.*

4 the beginning of a film, story, show etc: *Let's take a look at the start of the story in more detail.*

5 SPORTS the moment when a race begins, or the place where it begins: *The start has been brought forward by 30 minutes.* ♦ *The runners were all gathered at the start.*

6 a big change or new opportunity in your life: *She travelled to Hong Kong, hoping for a fresh start.*

7 an advantage that you have, especially in a race or competition= HEAD START: *The women runners are given a 50-metre start.*

PHRASES for a start used for introducing the first point in a series, especially in an argument: *They are too young for a start.*

make a start (on sth) to begin doing something: *I'll make a start on the cooking.*

starter /ˈstɑːtə/ noun [C] **1** a small amount of food that is eaten at the start of a meal **2 SPORTS** an official who signals the start of a race **3** used for talking about the time or manner in which someone starts something: *I've always been a slow starter in the mornings.*

'starter ,motor noun [C] **ENGINEERING** a motor that is part of a machine or engine and makes it start

starting block /ˈstɑːtɪŋ ˌblɒk/ noun [C] **SPORTS** one of a pair of small blocks against which a runner puts their feet at the start of a race

starting gate /ˈstɑːtɪŋ ˌgeɪt/ noun [C] **SPORTS** a gate that a person or horse must stay behind until a race begins

starting gun /ˈstɑːtɪŋ ˌgʌn/ noun [C] **SPORTS** a small gun used for signalling the start of a race

starting line /ˈstɑːtɪŋ ˌlaɪn/ noun [C] **SPORTS** the line or point where a race starts

starting point /ˈstɑːtɪŋ ˌpɔɪnt/ noun [C] **1** the place where a journey begins **2** something that you use as the first stage in a discussion or other activity

startle /ˈstɑːt(ə)l/ verb [T] to make a person or animal suddenly feel frightened or surprised —**startled** adj, **startling** adj

'start ,page noun [C] **COMPUTING** the words and pictures that first appear on a computer screen when you use the Internet

'start-up noun [C/U] **1 BUSINESS** the process of starting a business, or a small business that is just being started **2 COMPUTING** the process of switching on a computer, or the action of doing this —**'start-up** adj

starvation /stɑːˈveɪʃ(ə)n/ noun [U] **HEALTH** a situation in which people or animals suffer or die because they do not have enough food

starve /stɑːv/ verb [I/T] **HEALTH** to suffer or die because you do not have enough food, or to make someone do this

starved /stɑːvd/ adj prevented from having enough of what you need

starving /ˈstɑːvɪŋ/ adj **1** *informal* very hungry **2 HEALTH** ill or dying because you do not have enough food

state¹ /steɪt/ noun

1 condition of sth	**5** government
2 condition of person	**6** USA
3 nation	**+ PHRASES**
4 region	

1 [C] the condition of something at a particular time: *Experts believe the painting can be restored to its original state.* ♦ *We're collecting data on the state of the environment.* ♦ *The British transport system is in a sorry state* (=a very bad condition).

2 [singular] the physical or mental condition of a person, usually when this is bad: *By the time he got home, he was in a terrible state.* ♦ *I'd never seen you in such a state* (=very upset or nervous). ♦ *She was in a state of panic.*

3 [C] a nation, or a country

4 [C] a region of a country that has its own government: *the state of Michigan*

5 [singular/U] **POLITICS** the government of a country: *Should the state play a bigger role in industry?*

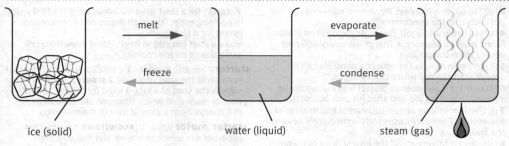

melt

freeze

evaporate

condense

ice (solid)

water (liquid)

steam (gas)

states of matter

6 the States *informal* the United States of America

PHRASES **state of affairs** a situation
state of mind the way you are feeling at a particular time
states of matter SCIENCE the forms in which a substance can occur. The three states of matter are liquid, solid, and gas.

state² /steɪt/ verb [T] to express something in speech or writing, especially in a definite or formal way: *'Jemma is going with me,' George stated firmly.* ♦ *He stated that the project would be completed by April.*

state³ /steɪt/ adj POLITICS **1** a state occasion or event involves a country's government or leader **2** a state institution is one that is run by the government **3** taking place in a state or relating to a state

the 'State De,partment POLITICS in the US, the government department that manages the country's relations with other countries. The **Secretary of State** is the head of this department.

stateless /'steɪtləs/ adj SOCIAL STUDIES not officially recognized as a citizen of any country

statement¹ /'steɪtmənt/ noun [C] **1** something that you say or write, especially officially or in public: *He refused to **make a statement** to the press.* **2** an official document that lists the amounts of money that have been put in or taken out of a bank account **3** a formal written account of events that a person gives to the police: *After several hours of questioning he agreed to **make a statement**.*

statement² /'steɪtmənt/ verb [T] EDUCATION to decide officially that a child has **learning disabilities** and that he or she should receive special educational help

'state ,school noun [C] EDUCATION in the UK, a school that is paid for by the government and provides free education

statesman /'steɪtsmən/ (plural **statesmen** /'steɪtsmən/) noun [C] POLITICS an experienced political leader that many people respect — **statesmanlike** adj, **statesmanship** noun [U]

static¹ /'stætɪk/ adj something that is static does not move or change

static² /'stætɪk/ noun [U] the unpleasant noise that you hear on a radio, television, or telephone that is caused by electricity in the air

,static elec'tricity noun [U] PHYSICS electricity that is produced when two objects rub together

,static 'friction noun [U] PHYSICS the force that keeps an object that is not moving from being pushed or pulled across a surface

statin /'stætɪn/ noun [C] HEALTH a drug that is used to reduce the amount of **cholesterol** in the blood

station¹ /'steɪʃ(ə)n/ noun [C] **1** a building or place where trains or buses stop so that passengers can get on or off: *It was dark when we arrived at the station.* **2** a building or place where a particular service or activity is based: *Astronomers at the Salyut Research Station discovered the star.* **3** ARTS a company that broadcasts television or radio programmes: *Listen to your local radio station for travel information.*

station² /'steɪʃ(ə)n/ verb [T] to send someone to a particular place in order to do a job, especially for the armed forces

stationary /'steɪʃən(ə)ri/ adj not moving

,stationary 'point noun [C] MATHS a point on a graph at which the **tangent** is either horizontal or vertical

stationery /'steɪʃən(ə)ri/ noun [U] **1** things that you use for writing such as paper and pens **2** paper used for writing letters, often with the name of a company on it and envelopes that match

statistic /stə'tɪstɪk/ noun [C] a number that represents a fact or describes a situation

statistician /,stætɪ'stɪʃ(ə)n/ noun [C] someone whose job is to study and work with statistics

statistics /stə'tɪstɪks/ noun **1** [plural] a group of numbers that represent facts or describe a situation **2** [U] MATHS the science of using numbers to represent facts and describe situations —**statistical** /stə'tɪstɪk(ə)l/ adj, **statistically** /stə'tɪstɪkli/ adv

stative /'steɪtɪv/ adj LANGUAGE used for describing verbs like 'know' or 'own' that deal with states, as opposed to verbs like 'listen', 'talk', or 'go' that deal with actions

stator /'steɪtə/ noun [C] ENGINEERING, PHYSICS the part of an electric motor that consists of a set of conductors in the shape of coils

statue /'stætʃuː/ noun [C] ARTS an image of a person or animal that is made of stone, wood, metal etc

stature /'stætʃə/ noun [U] *formal* **1** the degree to which someone or something is respected or admired **2** someone's height

status /'steɪtəs/ noun [U] **1** the legal position of someone or something: *Will I be officially self-employed, or will I have employee status?* **2** someone's position in a profession or society, especially in comparison with other people: *Our organization seeks to improve the **social status** of disabled people.* **3** a high social position that makes other people respect and admire you: *a **symbol of status** and wealth* **4** the level of importance or progress in a particular situation or discussion: *Officials are now discussing the current status of the health reform laws.*

'status ,bar noun [C] COMPUTING a bar across the bottom of a computer screen that gives information about a program and the job that it is doing

the status quo /ˌsteɪtəs ˈkwəʊ/ noun [singular] the present situation, or the way that things usually are

statute /ˈstætʃuːt/ noun [C] LAW formal a law or a rule
PHRASE **statute of limitations** LAW a law that sets a period of time during which legal action must begin in a court case

ˈstatute ˌlaw noun [U] LAW all the laws created by government

statutory /ˈstætʃʊt(ə)ri/ adj LAW formal controlled by a statute —**statutorily** adv

ˌstatutory ˈholiday noun [C] LAW a holiday that is fixed by law

staunch /stɔːntʃ/ adj loyal and showing strong support

stave /steɪv/ noun [C] MUSIC a set of lines used for writing music on = STAFF

stay¹ /steɪ/ verb [I] **1** to remain in a particular place: *Stay right here, please.* ♦ *I have to* **stay late** *at work every Thursday.* ♦ *He wanted her to* **stay at home** *and look after the children.* **2** to remain in a particular situation or state: *Interest rates should stay low for the next few months.* **3** to live or remain in a place for a while as a guest or visitor: *How long is he planning to* **stay with** *you?*
PHRASE **sth is here to stay** used for saying that something is generally accepted and is part of people's lives: *Do you think high unemployment is here to stay?*
PHRASAL VERBS **ˌstay beˈhind** or **ˌstay ˈback** to remain somewhere after everyone else has left: *Tony stayed behind and helped us clean the kitchen.*
ˌstay ˈin to remain in your home and not go out: *I think I'd rather stay in tonight.*
ˌstay ˈup to not go to bed: *Josh could stay up all night without getting tired.*

stay² /steɪ/ noun [C] a period of time that you spend somewhere
PHRASE **stay of execution/deportation etc** LAW an order given by a judge to stop or delay something such as an execution or deportation

STD /ˌes tiː ˈdiː/ noun [C] HEALTH sexually transmitted disease: a disease that someone gets from having sex with an infected person

steady¹ /ˈstedi/ (**steadier, steadiest**) adj **1** firmly held, without moving or shaking: **Hold** *the torch* **steady** *so I can see better.* ♦ *You have to have* **a steady hand** *to be a surgeon.* **2** slowly and gradually continuing to change, move, or happen: *A* **steady stream** *of people passed by.* ♦ *a* **steady increase** *in car sales* **3** staying at the same level, speed, value etc: *She listened to the steady rhythm of his breathing as he slept.* **4** likely to continue for a long period of time: *a steady boyfriend* ♦ *a steady relationship* ♦ *It would be nice to have* **a steady job.** —**steadily** adv

steady² /ˈstedi/ (**steadies, steadying, steadied**) verb [T] to hold something firmly without moving it
PHRASES **steady your nerves** to stop yourself from feeling nervous
steady yourself to try to get your balance again so that you will not fall

ˌsteady ˈstate ˌtheory noun [singular] PHYSICS the theory that the universe has always existed and that the movements of stars have always happened. It is opposed to the **Big Bang** theory.

steak /steɪk/ noun [C/U] a large flat piece of meat or fish

steal /stiːl/ (**steals, stealing, stole** /stəʊl/, **stolen** /ˈstəʊlən/) verb **1** [I/T] to take something that belongs to someone without permission: *She was caught stealing food from the supermarket.* **2** [I] to move

somewhere quietly and secretly: *While Sara wasn't looking, I* **stole across** *the hall to make a call.* **3** [I] if a feeling steals over someone, they gradually begin to feel it: *I felt a warm deep pleasure steal over me.*

> **Build your vocabulary: words you can use instead of steal**
> - **break into sth** to enter a building or vehicle illegally
> - **burgle** to steal from a house or flat that you have entered illegally
> - **mug** to attack a person in a public place and steal something from them
> - **nick** or **pinch** (*informal*) to take something that belongs to someone else without their permission
> - **rob** to steal things from a place using violence, or threatening to use violence
> - **shoplift** to steal goods from a shop

stealth tax /ˈstelθ ˌtæks/ noun [C] ECONOMICS a way of making people pay more tax that is hard to notice, for example by making a new tax, increasing a tax, or introducing a charge that operates as a tax

stealthy /ˈstelθi/ adj quiet and secret so that no one sees or hears you —**stealthily** adv

steam¹ /stiːm/ noun [U] PHYSICS **1** the small drops of water, like a hot cloud, that are produced when water vapour starts to condense: *The steam from the volcano rose into the air.* —picture → STATE **2** the power that is created when water is heated: *The equipment was originally powered by steam.* ♦ *a steam engine*
PHRASES **let off steam** to express feelings of anger or excitement without harming anyone: *The meeting will be a chance for the protesters to let off steam.*
run out of steam to lose energy, enthusiasm, or importance

steam² /stiːm/ verb **1** [I/T] to cook food with steam **2** [I] to move using steam power

ˈsteam ˌengine noun [C] an engine that gets its energy from steam, especially a railway engine

steamer /ˈstiːmə/ noun [C] **1** a container used for cooking food with steam **2** a steamship

ˈsteam ˌgenerator noun [C] PHYSICS part of a **nuclear reactor** where water passes through a system of tubes and is turned into steam, using the heat from the reactor —picture → NUCLEAR REACTOR

steamroller /ˈstiːmˌrəʊlə/ noun [C] a heavy vehicle that is used for making a road flat

steamship /ˈstiːmˌʃɪp/ noun [C] a ship that moves by steam power

steamy /ˈstiːmi/ adj very hot and full of steam

stearic acid /stiˌærɪk ˈæsɪd/ noun [U] CHEMISTRY a solid **fatty acid** that is obtained from vegetable or animal fat. Soap contains stearic acid.

steel /stiːl/ noun [U] CHEMISTRY a strong metal made from a mixture of iron and carbon

ˌsteel ˈpan noun [C] MUSIC a percussion instrument that is made out of an oil drum

steel toecap /ˌstiːl ˈtəʊkæp/ noun [C] a piece of steel at the front of a boot or shoe that protects the toes from being damaged by heavy objects falling on them

steelworks /ˈstiːlˌwɜːks/ (plural **steelworks**) noun [C] a factory where steel is made —**steelworker** noun [C]

steep¹ /stiːp/ adj **1** a steep slope goes up or down very quickly: *a steep hill* ♦ *Suddenly the plane went into a steep dive.* **2** a steep increase or fall in something is sudden and very big: *a* **steep rise** *in oil prices* **3** steep prices are very high —**steeply** adv, **steepness** noun [U]

steep² /stiːp/ verb [T] to leave something in a liquid for some time

steeple /'stiːp(ə)l/ noun [C] a tall pointed tower on a church

steeplechase /'stiːp(ə)l,tʃeɪs/ noun [C] **SPORTS** a race in which horses jump over fences and water → FLAT RACE

steer¹ /stɪə/ verb **1** [I/T] to control the direction in which a vehicle moves: *Jack steered while Ken gave directions.* ♦ *We **steered** the boat **into** the harbour.* **2** [T] to influence the way that something happens or the way that people behave: *I try to **steer** my children **towards** healthier foods.* ♦ *Ruth attempted to **steer** the conversation **away from** homework.* **3** [T] to control the direction in which someone moves, using your hand: *He took her arm to **steer** her **towards** the door.*
  PHRASE steer clear (of) *informal* to avoid someone or something that is dangerous or unpleasant: *Tourists are advised to steer clear of the area.*

steer² /stɪə/ noun [C] **AGRICULTURE** a young male bull that has had its **testicles** removed. Steers are kept for their meat.

steering /'stɪərɪŋ/ noun [U] the parts of a vehicle that allow you to control the direction that it travels in

'steering ,column noun [C] **ENGINEERING** the metal pole that connects a vehicle's wheels to the **steering wheel**

steering damper /'stɪərɪŋ ,dæmpə/ noun [C] **ENGINEERING** a piece of equipment on a motorcycle that prevents it from moving in an uncontrolled way when a rider **steers** it

'steering ,wheel noun [C] the wheel that you hold and turn in order to control the direction that a vehicle travels in

stegosaurus /,stegə'sɔːrəs/ noun [C] a dinosaur with large flat plates sticking up from its back

stele /stiːl, 'stiːli/ noun [C] **BIOLOGY** a structure that runs through the centre of a root. It contains the **vascular** tissue that carries water and food around the plant. —*picture* → ROOT

stem¹ /stem/ noun [C] **1 BIOLOGY** the long part of a plant that the leaves and flowers grow from **2** the long thin part of a wine glass that joins the bowl to the base **3 LANGUAGE** the part of a word that does not change when an ending is added, for example 'work' in the word 'working'

stem² /stem/ (**stems, stemming, stemmed**) verb [T] to stop something from spreading or increasing
  PHRASAL VERB 'stem from sth to be caused by something

,stem-and-'leaf adj **MATHS** relating to a method of showing numbers that uses **columns** called stems and rows called leaves

'stem ,cell noun [C] **BIOLOGY** a cell that can produce many cells exactly like itself or that can develop into different types of cell

'stem ,tuber noun [C] **BIOLOGY** the swollen part of some plants, for example the potato, that grows underground, stores food, and produces new plants

stench /stentʃ/ noun [C] a very unpleasant smell

stencil /'stens(ə)l/ noun [C] a piece of paper or plastic with a shape or letters cut out of it. You place it on a surface and paint over it in order to make a design on something.

step¹ /step/ noun [C]

1 movement/sound	4 stage
2 one act of series	5 dance movement
3 for walking up/down	+ PHRASE

1 a movement made by putting one foot in front of the other, or the sound that your feet make while you are walking: *I could hear the steps coming closer.* ♦ *The postbox is just a few steps from my front door.* ♦ *Tom **took a step** backwards.*

2 one of a series of actions that you take in order to achieve a particular aim: *The government must **take steps** to control inflation.* ♦ *This agreement is an important **step towards** our goal.* ♦ *This new law is the first **step in** making our city safer.* ♦ *The new microchip is a major **step forward** (=improvement) in computer technology.* → RIGHT²

3 a flat surface, usually one in a series, that you walk up or down in order to move to a different level: *I met him on the **front steps** of the bank.* ♦ *I climbed **a flight of** steps* (=a set of steps).

4 one of the stages in a process: *When you finish the exercise, repeat steps five to ten.*

5 a particular movement or set of movements that you make with your feet while dancing: *Juan was practising his new **dance steps.***
  PHRASE in step if people walk in step, each person moves their feet at exactly the same time as the others

step² /step/ (**steps, stepping, stepped**) verb [I] **1** to move somewhere by putting one foot down in front of the other: *I **stepped onto** the platform and started to speak.* **2** to move or walk a short distance in a particular direction: *Please **step outside** and wait for a moment.*

stepbrother /'step,brʌðə/ noun [C] the son of your **stepfather** or **stepmother**

,step-by-'step adj a step-by-step plan or set of instructions is easy to follow and explains each stage of a process in a clear and simple way

stepchild /'step,tʃaɪld/ (plural **stepchildren** /'step,tʃɪldrən/) noun [C] the son or daughter of your husband or wife from a previous relationship

stepdaughter /'step,dɔːtə/ noun [C] the daughter of your husband or wife, who is not your child

stepfather /'step,fɑːðə/ noun [C] the man who is married to your mother, but who is not your father

stepladder /'step,lædə/ noun [C] a short ladder consisting of two sloping parts, that can be folded and carried

stepmother /'step,mʌðə/ noun [C] the woman who is married to your father, but who is not your mother

stepping-stone /'stepɪŋ ,stəʊn/ noun [C] **1** a step in a process that helps you to move forward to another part of it **2** a flat piece of rock in a river that you stand on in order to cross to the other side

stepsister /'step,sɪstə/ noun [C] the daughter of your **stepfather** or **stepmother**

stepson /'step,sʌn/ noun [C] the son of your husband or wife, who is not your child

stereo /'steriəʊ/ (plural **stereos**) noun [C] a piece of electronic equipment with two speakers that you use for listening to the radio, CDs, or **cassettes**
  PHRASE in stereo recorded or broadcast using a system that sends the sound through two speakers
  —**stereo** adj

stereotype /'steriə,taɪp/ noun [C] **1** a firm idea about what a particular type of person or thing is like, especially an idea that is wrong **2** someone who is exactly what many people expect a person of their particular class, nationality, profession etc to be like
  —**stereotype** verb [T], **stereotypical** /,steriə'tɪpɪk(ə)l/ adj, **stereotypically** /,steriə'tɪpɪkli/ adv

sterile /'steraɪl/ adj **1** completely clean, with no bacteria ≠ DIRTY **2 BIOLOGY** not able to produce

children 3 a sterile argument or discussion does not contain any interesting new ideas —**sterility** /stə'rɪləti/ noun [U]

sterilize /'sterəlaɪz/ verb [T] **1** to kill all the bacteria on or in something and make it completely clean **2 HEALTH** to perform an operation on someone that makes them unable to produce children —**sterilization** /ˌsterəlaɪ'zeɪʃ(ə)n/ noun [C/U], **sterilizer** noun [C]

sterling /'stɜːlɪŋ/ noun [U] **1 ECONOMICS** the standard unit of money in the UK **2 sterling** or **sterling silver** silver that is of a standard quality

stern1 /stɜːn/ adj serious and severe —**sternly** adv

stern2 /stɜːn/ noun [C] the back part of a ship

sternum /'stɜːnəm/ noun [C] **ANATOMY** the flat bone in the middle of the chest= BREASTBONE —*picture* → SKELETON

steroid /'stɪərɔɪd, 'sterɔɪd/ noun [C] **HEALTH** a drug that is used by doctors for helping tissue to grow again. It is sometimes used illegally by athletes for building muscles and improving their performance.

stethoscope /'steθəˌskəʊp/ noun [C] **HEALTH** a piece of equipment that doctors use to listen to your heart or to your breathing

stew1 /stjuː/ noun [C/U] a dish made by cooking vegetables, and usually meat or fish, slowly in a liquid

stew2 /stjuː/ verb [T] to cook something slowly in a liquid

steward /'stjuːəd/ noun [C] someone who helps to organize people at an event such as a football match or a horse race

STI /ˌes tiː 'aɪ/ noun [C] **HEALTH** sexually transmitted infection: an infection that someone gets from having sex with an infected person, for example AIDS or **syphilis**

stick1 /stɪk/ (**sticks, sticking, stuck** /stʌk/) verb

1 push sth long into sth	**4** become fixed
2 remain in sth	**5** put quickly
3 fix sth to sth	**+ PHRASAL VERBS**

1 [T] to push something that is long and thin into or through something else: *He **stuck** the end of the post **in** the ground.* ♦ *a piece of cloth with a pin **stuck through** it*
2 [I] if something sticks in, into, or through something else, its end remains in it or through it: *The knife missed its target and **stuck in** the door.* ♦ *Something sharp was **sticking into** my back.*
3 [I/T] to fix one thing to another, or to become fixed to something, especially using a sticky substance such as glue: *Can you **stick** the pieces of this vase back **together**?* ♦ *She was **sticking** posters **on** her bedroom wall.* ♦ *The pasta has **stuck to** the bottom of the pan.*
4 [I] to become firmly fixed in one position, and therefore difficult or impossible to move: *The door is sticking, so give it a good push.* ♦ *The wheels had **stuck in** the mud.*
5 [T] *informal* to put something somewhere quickly and without taking much care= SHOVE

PHRASAL VERBS ,**stick 'out 1** to continue further than the end of a surface or the main part of an object: *His ears stick out.* ♦ *A magazine was **sticking out of** his coat pocket.* **2** to be easy to notice or remember because of being unusual or different: *One face in particular stuck out.*
,**stick to'gether** if objects stick together, they become fixed to one another
,**stick 'up** to continue upwards further than the end of a surface or the main part of an object: *You've got a bit of hair sticking up at the back.*

stick2 /stɪk/ noun [C] **1** a thin piece of wood, especially one that has been broken or cut from a tree: *I went out to find some sticks for a fire.* **2** a long strong piece of wood, usually with a handle at the top, that you use for helping you to walk **3 SPORTS** a long thin piece of wood that is used for hitting or carrying something in a sport: *a hockey stick* **4** a long thin piece of something

sticker /'stɪkə/ noun [C] a piece of paper or plastic with a picture, colour, or writing on one side and a sticky surface on the other that someone can stick to something

'**stick ,insect** noun [C] a long thin insect that looks like a small stick —*picture* → INSECT

sticky /'stɪki/ (**stickier, stickiest**) adj **1** made of or covered with a substance that sticks to other things: *The dough should be soft but not sticky.* ♦ *sticky fingers* **2** sticky weather is hot and damp= HUMID **3** *informal* a sticky situation is difficult or dangerous= TRICKY **4 BUSINESS, COMPUTING** a sticky website interests people so that they continue looking at it for a long time, or visit it many times

'**sticky ,tape** noun [U] a long thin clear piece of sticky plastic on a roll, used for sticking paper or other things to each other

stiff1 /stɪf/ adj

1 firm & not bending	**5** of mixture
2 severe/difficult	**6** with much alcohol
3 with pain in muscles	**7** formal/controlled
4 not moving easily	

1 firm and difficult to bend: *a stiff piece of card* ♦ *a small stiff brush*
2 more severe or difficult than usual: *Jarvis is up against some **stiff competition** in this race.* ♦ *Those caught breaking the new law face **stiff penalties.***
3 if a part of your body is stiff, you feel pain in your muscles and cannot move easily: *I've got a really stiff neck.*
4 not moving or operating as easily as you expect: *The drawer was rather stiff, so I pulled at it.*
5 a mixture that is stiff is very thick: *Whisk the egg whites until stiff.*
6 a stiff drink contains a lot of alcohol
7 formal in a way that is not friendly or relaxed: *He looked stiff and awkward in his new suit.*
—**stiffly** adv, **stiffness** noun [U]

stiff2 /stɪf/ adv **bored/scared/worried stiff** extremely bored, frightened, or worried

stiffen /'stɪf(ə)n/ verb **1** [I] to suddenly hold your body in a stiff way, often because you are afraid or angry **2** [I/T] to become stiff, or to make something stiff

stifle /'staɪf(ə)l/ verb **1** [T] to stop something from happening or developing **2** [I/T] to stop someone from breathing, or to have difficulty in breathing= SUFFOCATE

stifling /'staɪf(ə)lɪŋ/ adj so hot that you feel uncomfortable and are unable to breathe easily

stigma /'stɪgmə/ noun **1** [singular/U] a general attitude in which people treat something as wrong or embarrassing, especially in an unfair way **2** [C] **BIOLOGY** the female part of a flower that receives pollen —*picture* → FERTILIZATION, FLOWER

stile /staɪl/ noun [C] **CONSTRUCTION** the outer vertical piece of a door

still1 /stɪl/ adv **1** used for saying that a situation continues to exist up to and including a particular time: *Is Terry still in college?* → YET **2** used for emphasizing that a particular situation has not completely ended or changed: *I still have 50 pages to read before Friday.* **3** used for saying that something remains true despite what you have just said or done: *We knew we wouldn't win the game, but it was still exciting!* **4** used for emphasizing that although something is big, good, bad etc, something else is even bigger, better, worse etc: *The freezing cold weather made our task still more difficult.* ♦ *Greg's heavily in debt, and, **worse still**, he may lose his job.*

still² /stɪl/ adj **1** not moving: *The water appeared still from a distance.* ♦ *Just **sit still** for a minute and let me tie your shoe.* **2** quiet and calm, with nothing happening: *By 10.00 the streets are quite still.* **3** without gas bubbles ≠ SPARKLING: *still mineral water* —**stillness** noun [U]

still³ /stɪl/ noun [C] **1** ARTS a photograph that is taken from one of the scenes in a film or video **2** a piece of equipment that is used for making strong alcohol

stillbirth /ˈstɪl,bɜːθ/ noun [C/U] HEALTH a birth in which the baby is born dead

stillborn /ˈstɪl,bɔːn/ adj HEALTH a stillborn baby is born dead

,still 'life (plural **,still 'lifes**) noun [C/U] ARTS a type of art that represents objects instead of people, animals, or the countryside

stilts /stɪlts/ noun [plural] **1** a pair of long pieces of wood that you stand on so that you can walk high above the ground **2** a set of posts that a house is built on in order to raise it above the ground or above water

stimulant /ˈstɪmjʊlənt/ noun [C] a substance that makes you feel more lively or awake

stimulate /ˈstɪmjʊleɪt/ verb [T] **1** to encourage something to happen, develop, or improve: *The government should do more to stimulate investment in the north.* **2** to make someone feel interested in learning new things: *Such questions provide a useful way of stimulating students' interest.* **3** BIOLOGY to make plants, cells, or a part of someone's body grow or become more active —**stimulation** /,stɪmjʊˈleɪʃ(ə)n/ noun [U]

stimulating /ˈstɪmjʊˌleɪtɪŋ/ adj interesting and making you think

stimulus /ˈstɪmjʊləs/ (plural **stimuli** /ˈstɪmjʊlaɪ/) noun [C/U] **1** something that encourages something else to happen, develop, or improve **2** BIOLOGY something that produces a reaction in a living thing

sting¹ /stɪŋ/ (**stings, stinging, stung** /stʌŋ/) verb **1** [I/T] if an insect, animal, or plant stings you, it hurts you by putting poison on or into your skin **2** [I/T] HEALTH to be affected by a sudden pain or uncomfortable feeling, or to make something do this: *My eyes were stinging with the salt in the water.* **3** [T] to make someone feel angry and upset

sting² /stɪŋ/ noun [C] **1** the pain that you feel when an insect, animal, or plant stings you **2** HEALTH a sudden pain or uncomfortable feeling

stinging /ˈstɪŋɪŋ/ adj strong enough to upset you: *a stinging attack on government policy*

stingray /ˈstɪŋ,reɪ/ noun [C] a large flat fish with a skeleton made of cartilage and a narrow tail that can sting

stink /stɪŋk/ (**stinks, stinking, stank** /stæŋk/, **stunk** /stʌŋk/) verb [I] *informal* to smell very unpleasant

stipulate /ˈstɪpjʊleɪt/ verb [T] *formal* to say what is allowed or what is necessary —**stipulation** /,stɪpjʊˈleɪʃ(ə)n/ noun [C]

stir¹ /stɜː/ (**stirs, stirring, stirred**) verb **1** [I/T] to move food or a liquid around using a spoon or other object: *Stir the sauce gently over a low heat.* **2** [T] to make someone have a particular feeling or memory: *This*

crime has stirred a lot of anger in the community. ♦ *Seeing George again stirred old memories in me.* **3** [I/T] to move slightly, or to make someone or something move slightly: *The curtains stirred gently in the summer breeze.* ♦ *Mary was asleep and didn't stir.*

stir² /stɜː/ noun [singular] **1** a situation in which a lot of people feel interested or angry: *His speech caused quite a stir.* **2** the movement that you make with a spoon or other object when you move food or a liquid around

'stir-,fry verb [T] to cook food quickly by moving it around in hot oil —**'stir-,fry** noun [C]

stirring /ˈstɜːrɪŋ/ adj causing strong emotions

stirrup /ˈstɪrəp/ noun [C] **1** a metal object that supports your foot when you ride a horse **2** ANATOMY a small bone in the **inner ear** —*picture* → EAR

stitch¹ /stɪtʃ/ noun **1** [C] one of the short pieces of thread that you can see on cloth when it has been sewn **2** [C] HEALTH a short piece of thread that is used for joining someone's skin together after it has been cut **3** [C] a piece of wool that has been put round a needle when you are **knitting 4** [singular/U] HEALTH a sharp pain in the side of your body

stitch² /stɪtʃ/ verb [T] **1** to join pieces of cloth together by sewing them **2** HEALTH to join someone's skin together with thread after it has been cut

stock¹ /stɒk/ noun

1 amount kept	4 for soups/sauces
2 goods in shop	5 farm animals
3 shares in company	+ PHRASE

1 [C] an amount of something that is kept so that it can be used when it is needed: *Their **stocks of** ammunition were running low.*
2 [U] BUSINESS the goods that are available to buy in a shop: *We're having some new stock delivered this afternoon.* ♦ *Do you have any of these batteries **in stock** (=available to buy) at the moment?* ♦ *I'm afraid that size is **out of stock** (=not available to buy).*
3 [C] BUSINESS a group of **shares** in an individual company, or the value of the company based on the value of its shares: *stocks and shares*
4 [C/U] a liquid made by boiling meat, bones, or vegetables that is used for making soups and sauces: *chicken stock*
5 [U] AGRICULTURE animals such as cows and pigs that are kept on a farm= LIVESTOCK

  PHRASE take stock (of sth) to spend some time thinking about the situation that you are in before you decide what to do next

stock² /stɒk/ verb [T] **1** BUSINESS if a shop stocks goods, it has them available for sale **2** to fill a place with things that you will need

stockade /stɒˈkeɪd/ noun [C] a wall made of large wooden posts

stockbroker /ˈstɒk,brəʊkə/ noun [C] BUSINESS someone whose job is to buy and sell shares in companies for other people —**stockbroking** noun [U]

'stock ,car noun [C] an ordinary car that has been changed for racing, or an old car used for racing

'stock con,trol noun [U] BUSINESS the activity of checking a shop's **stock**

'stock ex,change noun **1** [C] BUSINESS a place where people buy and sell shares in companies **2 the stock exchange** [singular] BUSINESS, ECONOMICS the **stock market**

stocking /ˈstɒkɪŋ/ noun [C] a very thin piece of clothing that is worn on a woman's foot and leg

stockkeeping /'stɒk,kiːpɪŋ/ noun [U] **BUSINESS** stock control

the 'stock ,market noun [singular] **BUSINESS, ECONOMICS** the activities connected with buying and selling shares in companies

stockpile /'stɒk,paɪl/ verb [T] to collect large amounts of things that may be needed —**stockpile** noun [C]

stocktaking /'stɒk,teɪkɪŋ/ noun [U] **BUSINESS** the process of counting a business's goods

stocky /'stɒki/ adj a stocky person is not tall but looks strong

stodgy /'stɒdʒi/ adj **1** stodgy food is solid and not pleasant to eat **2** boring and not willing to do things

stoical /'stəʊɪk(ə)l/ or **stoic** /'stəʊɪk/ adj accepting things without complaining —**stoically** /'stəʊɪkli/ adv, **stoicism** /'stəʊɪˌsɪz(ə)m/ noun [U]

stoichiometry /,stɔɪki'ɒmɪtri/ noun [U] **CHEMISTRY 1** the branch of chemistry that studies the relative numbers of atoms of elements that combine during **chemical reactions 2** a measure of the amounts of the elements that combine in a **chemical reaction** —**stoichiometric** /,stɔɪkiə'metrɪk/ adj

stole /stəʊl/ the past tense of **steal**

stolen /'stəʊlən/ the past participle of **steal**

stolon /'stəʊlɒn/ noun [C] **BIOLOGY** a side stem that grows horizontally underground, and can start new roots and a new plant

stoma /'stəʊmə/ (plural **stomata** /'stəʊmətə/) noun [C] **BIOLOGY** one of the many very small holes in the outer layer of a leaf or stem that allow water vapour and other gases into and out of a plant

stomach /'stʌmək/ noun [C] **1** the soft part at the front of the body that is between the chest and the legs: *A horse had kicked her in the stomach.* —*picture* → BODY **2 ANATOMY** the organ at the bottom of the oesophagus where food goes after it is eaten: *She'll feel better when she has some food in her stomach.* —*picture* → DIGESTIVE SYSTEM, ORGAN

   PHRASE on an empty stomach if you do something on an empty stomach, you do not eat anything before you do it: *It's not good to drink alcohol on an empty stomach.*

'stomach ,ache noun [C/U] **HEALTH** pain in the stomach

stomata /'stəʊmətə/ **BIOLOGY** the plural of **stoma**

stomp /stɒmp/ verb [I] to walk angrily making a lot of noise with your feet

stone¹ /stəʊn/ noun

1 rock	4 unit of measurement
2 rock cut into shape	5 jewel
3 seed in fruit	

1 [C/U] **GEOLOGY** the hard substance that rocks are made of, or a small piece of rock: *a cottage built of stone ♦ Children threw stones at him.*
2 [C] a piece of rock that has been cut into a shape for a particular purpose: *a paving stone*
3 [C] a large hard seed that is inside a piece of fruit: *a peach stone*
4 (plural **stones** or **stone**) [C] a unit for measuring weight that contains 14 pounds and is equal to 6.35 kilograms: *I've lost nearly two stone.*
5 [C] a jewel

stone² /stəʊn/ verb [T] to throw stones at someone in order to kill them

the 'Stone ,Age noun [singular] the period of history when people made tools and weapons from stone

stoned /stəʊnd/ adj *informal* if someone is stoned, they are affected by an illegal drug that makes them feel very relaxed

stonewall /,stəʊn'wɔːl/ verb [I/T] *informal* to refuse to give information

stony /'stəʊni/ adj **1** covered with stones, or containing stones **2** not friendly and not showing any emotion

stood /stʊd/ the past tense and past participle of **stand¹**

stool /stuːl/ noun [C] **1** a seat that has legs but no support for your back or arms **2** a piece of faeces

stoop /stuːp/ verb [I] **1** to bend the top half of your body downwards **2** to do something bad in order to get something

stop¹ /stɒp/ (**stops, stopping, stopped**) verb

1 prevent sth	6 bus/train
2 no longer do sth	7 pause to do sth
3 no longer move	+ PHRASES
4 ask sb to stop	+ PHRASAL VERB
5 work no longer	

1 [T] to prevent someone from doing something, or to prevent something from happening: *Policies like this aren't going to stop crime. ♦ A broken leg won't stop me from going to the concert.*
2 [I/T] to no longer do something, or to no longer happen: *When the rain stops, I'm going out. ♦ He wants to stop smoking.*
3 [I/T] to no longer move: *The car stopped at the traffic lights. ♦ Lots of people stopped and stared at the accident.♦ Stop the car!*
4 [T] to prevent someone from continuing to walk or drive so that you can talk to them: *I stopped a woman and asked her for directions.*
5 [I/T] to no longer work, or to cause something to no longer work: *My watch has stopped. ♦ Can you stop the engine?*
6 [I] if a bus or train stops somewhere, it pauses while it is moving in order to let passengers get on or off: *Does the train stop at Cambridge?*
7 [I] to pause while you are moving or doing something so that you can do something else: *He stopped and listened before opening the door. ♦ Jeff stopped to get a drink of water.*

   PHRASES stop at nothing to do anything in order to get what you want, even if it is very bad
   stop short of (doing) sth to not do something, although you almost do it: *I stopped short of telling him what I really thought.*

   PHRASAL VERB ,stop 'off to visit somewhere before continuing to another place

stop² /stɒp/ noun [C] **1** a place where you stop on a journey, or the time that you are there: *The president's first stop on his tour will be Honolulu. ♦ After a brief stop for coffee, we were on our way.* **2** a place where a bus or train stops in order to let passengers get on or off: *I'm getting off at the next stop.*

   PHRASE come/jerk/skid etc to a stop to stop moving → PULL¹, PUT

stopclock /'stɒp,klɒk/ noun [C] a clock used for measuring a particular period of time, with a switch for starting and stopping it —*picture* → LABORATORY

stopcock /'stɒp,kɒk/ noun [C] **CONSTRUCTION** a short pipe that is opened and closed by turning a handle or key

stopgap /'stɒp,gæp/ noun [C] a person or thing that provides a temporary solution

'stop-,off noun [C] **TOURISM** a stopover

stopover /'stɒp,əʊvə/ noun [C] TOURISM a stop during a journey, especially during a flight

stoppage /'stɒpɪdʒ/ noun **1** [C] a time when people stop working as a protest **2** [C/U] SPORTS a period of time when a game stops because of injury or bad weather

stopper /'stɒpə/ noun [C] an object that is put into the top of a bottle in order to prevent the liquid from coming out —*picture* → LABORATORY

stopwatch /'stɒp,wɒtʃ/ noun [C] a small clock that is used for measuring the exact time that it takes to do something —*picture* → LABORATORY

storage /'stɔːrɪdʒ/ noun [U] **1** the act of storing something, or the space where something is stored: *The area underneath provides useful storage.* ♦ *Most of our furniture is in storage.* **2** COMPUTING the ability of a computer to store information, or the process of doing this

store¹ /stɔː/ noun [C] **1** a supply of something that is kept so that it can be used later= STOCK: *a store of food for the winter* **2** *American* a shop: *a grocery store* ♦ *The store manager will be happy to assist you.*
    PHRASES **in store (for sb)** if something is in store for you, it will happen to you in the future
    set (great) store by sth to think that something is very important

store² /stɔː/ verb [T] **1** to keep something in a particular place: *Store the cake in an airtight container.* **2** COMPUTING to save information in electronic form, for example in a computer's memory

stored energy /,stɔːd 'enədʒi/ noun [U] SCIENCE the energy that exists in something and that can be released, whether because of its position, for example at the top of a slope, its shape, for example a wound-up spring, or its structure, for example the chemical energy in a fuel

storefront /'stɔː,frʌnt/ noun [C] **1** *American* a shop front **2** COMPUTING a website that is similar to a shop because it provides product information and you can buy goods from it

storeman /'stɔːmən/ (plural **storemen**) noun [C] someone whose job is to look after goods that are being stored

storeroom /'stɔː,ruːm/ noun [C] a room where things are stored

storey /'stɔːri/ (plural **storeys**) noun [C] a level of a building

stork /stɔːk/ noun [C] a large bird with long legs and a long beak

storm¹ /stɔːm/ noun **1** [C] an occasion when a lot of rain or snow falls very quickly, often with very strong winds or thunder and lightning: *A fierce storm hit the west coast of Florida early this morning.* **2** [singular] a situation in which many people are upset or excited: *His arrest provoked a storm of protest.*
    PHRASE **take sth by storm** to be very successful in a particular place or among a particular group of people: *Jazz took London and Paris by storm in the 1920s.*

storm² /stɔːm/ verb **1** [T] to use force to enter a place and take control of it **2** [I] to go somewhere very quickly because you are angry or upset: *Rob stormed out of the house and slammed the door.*

'storm ,drain noun [C] ENVIRONMENT a large **drain** (=pipe for taking away water or waste) that carries water away from a road during heavy rain and prevents flooding

stormwater /'stɔːm,wɔːtə/ noun [U] AGRICULTURE, ENVIRONMENT water that falls as rain or snow, or that comes from melted snow

stormy /'stɔːmi/ (**stormier, stormiest**) adj **1** with a lot of rain or snow and very strong winds **2** involving a lot of anger or arguments

story /'stɔːri/ (plural **stories**) noun [C] **1** LITERATURE an account of something that is either imaginary, traditional, or true: *She was reading a story to the children.* ♦ *a story about a princess and a frog* ♦ *stories of his travels in Asia* ♦ *He's written several children's stories.* **2** an account of events in a newspaper report or news programme: *tonight's main news stories* **3** an excuse or reason that is not true: *Do you expect me to believe that ridiculous story?* **4** something that people are talking about that may not be true= RUMOUR: *I heard a story that he had moved to Australia.*

storyboard /'stɔːri,bɔːd/ noun [C] ARTS a series of pictures that the director of a film uses to plan the action that will be filmed

storyteller /'stɔːri,telə/ noun [C] ARTS someone who tells stories —**storytelling** noun [U]

stout /staʊt/ adj **1** slightly fat **2** strong and thick **3** very determined

stove /stəʊv/ noun [C] a piece of equipment that provides heat for cooking or for heating a room

stow /stəʊ/ verb [T] to put something somewhere while you are not using it

stowaway /'stəʊə,weɪ/ noun [C] someone who hides in a vehicle, ship, or plane in order to travel without permission

straight¹ /streɪt/ adj

1 not bending	**6** clean and tidy
2 not leaning	**7** having top marks
3 honest and true	**8** with only two choices
4 one after the other	**+** PHRASES
5 attracted to other sex	

1 without bends or curves: *Draw a straight line.* ♦ *She has long straight hair* (=no curls or waves).
2 in the correct position, not leaning to one side or the other: *The picture on that wall isn't straight.* ♦ *Make sure you keep your back straight.*
3 honest and true: *I want a straight answer.* ♦ *You have to be straight with her.*
4 happening one after the other: *It was the team's sixth straight win.* ♦ *There were five straight days of exams.*
5 *informal* sexually attracted to people of the opposite sex
6 clean and tidy: *I'll never get the house straight before my parents get home.*
7 a student who has straight A's has the highest mark in every subject or course: *She got straight A's this term.*
8 a straight choice or competition is one in which there are only two choices, or only two people who have any chance of winning: *The election is going to be a straight fight between Labour and the Conservatives.*
    PHRASES **a straight face** if someone has a straight face, they look serious even though they are being funny or they are in a funny situation
    get sth straight to correctly understand something: *Let me get this straight – you didn't know they had your car.*
    have your facts straight if you have or get your facts straight, you are sure they are correct
    set/put sb straight or **set/put the record straight** to tell someone the true facts about a situation after they have been told something that is not true

straight² /streɪt/ adv **1** without a bend or curve: *The car was coming **straight at** me.* ♦ *He stared **straight ahead**.* **2** directly and immediately: *I decided I'd leave **straight after** breakfast.* ♦ *We decided to go **straight home**.* ♦ *I'll **come straight to the point*** (=say immediately what I want to say). **3** in an upright position, not leaning: *Sit up straight.* **4** without stopping: *We drove for five hours straight.*
  PHRASE **straight out** said directly and immediately: *She asked straight out if I liked her.*

straight³ /streɪt/ noun [singular] SPORTS a straight part of a race track

,straight 'angle noun [C] MATHS an angle of 180°
  —*picture* → ANGLE

,straight a'way or **straightaway** /ˌstreɪtə'weɪ/ adv immediately: *They can't pay me straight away.*

straighten /'streɪt(ə)n/ verb [I/T] to make something straight, or to become straight: *He straightened his tie.*

straightforward /ˌstreɪt'fɔ:wəd/ adj **1** not complicated or difficult to understand: *a straightforward process* **2** clear and honest: *a straightforward answer*

,straight-line 'motion noun [U] PHYSICS movement along a straight line

strain¹ /streɪn/ noun

1 pressure	4 characteristic
2 physical pressure	5 change in shape
3 injury	

1 [C/U] worries or problems that are caused by a difficult situation: *This war will **put** a **strain on** the economy.* ♦ *She's been **under** a lot of **strain** since the divorce.*
2 [C/U] physical pressure or effort: *All that lifting is putting his back **under** severe **strain**.*
3 [C/U] HEALTH an injury that is caused by twisting or stretching a muscle too much: *a thigh strain*
4 [C] a particular type or aspect of something: *a new strain of the flu virus*
5 [C/U] PHYSICS a change in the shape of an object, as a result of force being applied to it

strain² /streɪn/ verb

1 try hard to do sth	4 separate solid and
2 make relationship bad	liquid
3 injure muscle	5 pull/push hard

1 [I/T] to try very hard to do something: *I strained to hear what they were saying.*
2 [T] to cause problems in a relationship: *Relations between the two countries have been strained by trade disputes.*
3 [T] HEALTH to injure yourself by twisting or stretching a muscle too much: *Reading in poor light can strain your eyes.*
4 [T] to separate a solid from a liquid by pouring it into a **strainer**
5 [I] to pull or push very hard: *The elephants strained at their ropes.*

strained /streɪnd/ adj **1** not relaxed or friendly: *a strained atmosphere* **2** done only by trying hard, in a way that is not natural: *a strained smile*

strainer /'streɪnə/ noun [C] an object like a bowl with holes, used for separating the liquid and solid parts of food

strait /streɪt/ noun [C] GEOGRAPHY a narrow area of water that joins two larger areas of water

strand /strænd/ noun [C] **1** a single thin piece of something: *a strand of hair* **2** one of many aspects of something: *the different strands of the story*

stranded /'strændɪd/ adj left in a place or situation that you cannot get away from

strange /streɪndʒ/ adj **1** unusual or unexpected in a way that surprises, worries, or frightens you: *Ian is a very strange person.* ♦ *It seemed strange that she would leave so early.* ♦ *For some strange reason, she didn't even say 'hello'.* **2** not familiar or known to you: *When you arrive in a new country, everything seems strange.* **3** making someone feel uncomfortable, embarrassed, or ill: *I always feel strange in a large group of people.* —**strangely** adv: *Everyone looked at him strangely.*

stranger /'streɪndʒə/ noun [C] **1** someone who you do not know: *I didn't want to share a room with a complete stranger.* **2** someone who does not know a place well

'stranger ,crime noun [U] violent crimes committed by someone who the person attacked does not know

strangle /'stræŋg(ə)l/ verb [T] **1** to kill a person or an animal by squeezing their throat **2** to stop the development of something

strap¹ /stræp/ noun [C] a narrow piece of cloth, plastic etc that you use for fastening or carrying something, or for holding something in position: *a bag with leather straps* ♦ *The dress had thin shoulder straps.*

strap² /stræp/ (**straps, strapping, strapped**) verb [T] to hold or keep something in position by fastening a strap around it: *He strapped down the lid of the basket.*

'strap ,hinge noun [C] CONSTRUCTION a hinge with a long part made of iron or steel that is screwed onto a door

strata /'strɑ:tə/ GEOLOGY, SOCIAL STUDIES the plural of **stratum**

strategic /strə'ti:dʒɪk/ adj **1** designed to achieve a particular goal in war, business, or politics: *strategic planning* ♦ *a strategic political move* **2** strategic weapons are designed to hit an enemy's country —**strategically** /strə'ti:dʒɪkli/ adv: *a strategically located military base*

stra,tegic 'planning noun [U] BUSINESS the process of planning the activities of a business so that it competes well with other businesses and makes a profit

strategy /'strætədʒi/ (plural **strategies**) noun **1** [C] a plan or method for achieving something: *a strategy to reduce government spending* ♦ *successful language-learning strategies* **2** [U] the skill of planning how to achieve something: *experts in military strategy*

stratification /ˌstrætɪfɪ'keɪʃ(ə)n/ noun [U] GEOLOGY the way in which rock forms different layers

stratified /'strætɪfaɪd/ adj GEOLOGY formed into layers of a particular type of rock

stratiform clouds /'strætɪfɔ:m ˌklaʊdz/ noun [plural] GEOGRAPHY clouds in layers that spread out over a large area

the stratosphere /'strætəˌsfɪə/ noun SCIENCE the part of the Earth's atmosphere that is 10 km to 50 km above the surface —*picture* → ATMOSPHERE

stratovolcano /ˌstreɪtəʊvɒl'keɪnəʊ, ˌstrætəʊvɒl'keɪnəʊ/ noun [C] GEOLOGY a tall volcano with steep sides that is formed of layers of lava and pieces of rock

stratum /'strɑ:təm/ (plural **strata** /'strɑ:tə/) noun [C] **1** SOCIAL STUDIES a group or class in society **2** GEOLOGY a layer of a particular type of rock

stratus /'strɑ:təs/ noun [U] GEOGRAPHY flat grey cloud that is low in the sky —*picture* → CLOUD

straw /strɔː/ noun **1** [U] AGRICULTURE the stiff yellow stems of dried crops such as wheat. Straw can be used for animals to sleep on. **2** [C] a long thin tube that you use for drinking

PHRASE **the last/final straw** the last of a series of bad events that makes you decide to try to change a situation

strawberry /ˈstrɔːb(ə)ri/ (plural **strawberries**) noun [C] a small soft red fruit with a lot of very small seeds on its skin —*picture* → FRUIT

stray¹ /streɪ/ verb [I] **1** to move away from the correct place or path **2** to start talking about a new subject without intending to

stray² /streɪ/ adj **1** lost, or without a home: *a stray dog* **2** separated from a group or from the main part of something: *a stray curl of hair*

stray³ /streɪ/ noun [C] a pet that is lost or has left its home

streak¹ /striːk/ noun [C] **1** a line or long mark that is a different colour from the colour surrounding it: *The bird has a dark streak on its breast.* ♦ *a streak of lightning* **2** a part of someone's character that is different from the rest of their character: *The child has a stubborn streak.*

streak² /striːk/ verb [I] to move very quickly: *Jet planes streaked overhead.*

PHRASE **be streaked (with sth)** to have lines or long marks of a different colour: *Jim's face was streaked with paint.*

stream¹ /striːm/ noun [C] **1** GEOGRAPHY a small narrow river **2** a continuous flow of liquid or gas: *A stream of blood was running down his face.* **3** a continuous flow of people or things: *a stream of visitors* **4** EDUCATION a group of school students of the same age and with the same level of abilities

stream² /striːm/ verb **1** [I] to flow continuously: *Tears streamed down his cheeks.* **2** [I] to move in large numbers in a continuous flow: *Students streamed into the building.* **3** [I] to shine, or to give off light: *Sunlight was streaming through the windows.* **4** [T] EDUCATION to put school students into different groups based on their abilities

streaming /ˈstriːmɪŋ/ noun [U] COMPUTING a technology for sending sound or pictures to your computer through the Internet

streamline /ˈstriːmˌlaɪn/ verb [T] **1** to improve something such as an organization or process by making it more modern or simple **2** to design something with a smooth shape so that it will move quickly through air or water

streamlined flow /ˈstriːmlaɪnd ˌfləʊ/ noun [U] PHYSICS a situation in which air flows smoothly over and under an object such as a moving car or aeroplane

street /striːt/ noun [C] a road in a town or city with buildings along it: *I just saw Bill walking down the street.* ♦ *Who lives across the street?* → ROAD

PHRASE **on the street(s) 1** with no house to live in: *After losing his job he ended up on the streets.* **2** in public places in a town: *More police officers are being put on the streets.*
→ HIGH STREET

'street ˌcrime noun [U] criminal activity that happens in a public place, usually in a town or city, for example stealing people's personal possessions or drug dealing

'street ˌfurniture noun [U] things that have been placed at the side of a street, for example lights, road signs, and containers for rubbish

streetlamp /ˈstriːtˌlæmp/ or **streetlight** /ˈstriːtˌlaɪt/ noun [C] a light on top of a long pole in a street

streetwise /ˈstriːtˌwaɪz/ adj able to deal with the difficult or dangerous situations that you often find in cities in a confident way

strength /streŋθ/ noun

1 physical power	6 influence
2 ability not to break	7 size of group needed
3 of sb's character	8 value of money
4 power of sth	+ PHRASE
5 sth sb does well	

1 [U] the physical energy that someone has to lift or move things: *upper body strength* ♦ *The job requires a lot of physical strength.* ♦ *I didn't have the strength to get out of bed.*
2 [C/U] the ability of something to pull, push, or support something without breaking: *Test the strength of the rope.*
3 [U] the ability to deal with difficult situations: *She has great strength of character.*
4 [U] power in a military, political, or economic situation: *the strength of the economy*
5 [C] something that someone does very well = ABILITY: *Ron's main strength is his ability to motivate players.* ♦ *The test shows the students' strengths and weaknesses.*
6 [U] the amount of influence that a person or group has: *the strength of public opinion*
7 [C/U] the size of a group of people needed to achieve something: *The military force numbered 14,000 at full strength.* ♦ *Local people turned out in strength to support us.*
8 [U] the value of one country's money compared to the money of other countries: *the strength of the dollar against the euro*

PHRASE **on the strength of** because of what you saw, heard, experienced etc: *I heard their new single, and on the strength of that I bought the album.*

strengthen /ˈstreŋθ(ə)n/ verb **1** [I/T] to make someone or something stronger, or to become stronger: *Aerobic exercise strengthens the heart.* ♦ *a sense of community that has strengthened over time* **2** [T] to give support to a position or argument: *The new evidence strengthens Wilkins' case.* **3** [I/T] if the value of a country's money strengthens, or if something strengthens it, it increases: *The dollar continues to strengthen against the yen.*

strenuous /ˈstrenjuəs/ adj **1** needing a lot of effort, energy, or strength: *strenuous exercise* **2** determined: *strenuous opposition*

streptococcus /ˌstreptəˈkɒkəs/ (plural **streptococci** /ˌstreptəˈkɒksaɪ/) noun [C] HEALTH a round-shaped bacterium that causes throat infections

streptomycin /ˌstreptəˈmaɪsɪn/ noun [U] HEALTH an antibiotic that is used for treating **tuberculosis** and other infections caused by bacteria

stress¹ /stres/ noun **1** [C/U] HEALTH a worried or nervous feeling that makes you unable to relax, or a situation that makes you feel like this: *Carol's been under a lot of stress lately.* ♦ *the stresses and strains of everyday living* **2** [U] special importance that is given to something so that you pay more attention to it = EMPHASIS: *The course puts great stress on communication.* **3** [C/U] physical pressure that can make something break or change its shape: *Judo puts a lot of stress on your knee joints.* **4** [C/U] LANGUAGE the emphasis that you put on a particular word or part of a word by saying it more loudly → INTONATION

stress² /stres/ verb [T] **1** to emphasize something such as an idea, fact, or detail: *I want to stress that I accept responsibility for these mistakes.* ♦ *The Prime Minister stressed the importance of controlling spending.* **2** LANGUAGE to say a particular word or part of a word more loudly

stressed /strest/ adj **1** stressed or stressed out HEALTH worried and unable to relax **2** LANGUAGE a stressed word or syllable is pronounced with greater force than others ≠ UNSTRESSED

stressful /ˈstresf(ə)l/ adj making you feel stressed: *My new job is much less stressful.*

'stress ,mark noun [C] LANGUAGE a mark that shows you which part of a word is pronounced more loudly

stressor /ˈstresə/ noun [C] HEALTH anything in the environment that causes stress

stress-timed /ˈstres ,taɪmd/ adj LANGUAGE in a stress-timed language, there is a regular pattern of stressed syllables → SYLLABLE-TIMED

stretch¹ /stretʃ/ verb

1 make longer/wider	4 continue
2 make smooth etc	5 use money/time
3 of body	+ PHRASAL VERB

1 [I/T] if you stretch something, or if it stretches, it becomes longer or wider when you pull it: *Can you stretch the material a little?* ♦ *My jumper stretched the first time I washed it.*
2 [T] to pull something so that it becomes smooth, straight, and tight: *The canvas is stretched across a metal frame.*
3 [I/T] to make your arms, legs, or body as long as they can be: *I leaned back in the chair and stretched.* ♦ *Todd stretched his hand towards the rope.*
4 [I] to continue for a particular distance or time: *The beach stretches for miles in each direction.* ♦ *The team has a history that stretches back to 1895.*
5 [T] to use all the money, time, or ability that is available: *I don't think this new job stretches him much.* ♦ *Medical services were stretched to the limit.*
PHRASAL VERB ,stretch 'out to lie down: *I'll just stretch out on the sofa.*

stretch² /stretʃ/ noun [C] **1** an area of land or water: *a narrow stretch of water* **2** a continuous period of time: *You can't learn it all in such a short stretch of time.* ♦ *He'll surf the Internet for six hours at a stretch* (=continuously). **3** a movement or exercise in which you make a part of your body as long as possible
PHRASE not by any stretch of the imagination used for emphasizing that you think that something is definitely not true or possible

stretcher /ˈstretʃə/ noun [C] **1** HEALTH a type of bed that is used for carrying someone who is injured or ill **2** CONSTRUCTION a brick laid in a wall so that the longest surface is showing

'stretcher ,bond noun [C] CONSTRUCTION an arrangement of bricks in a wall that forms a pattern with the long sides of the bricks showing

striated /straɪˈeɪtɪd/ adj a striated surface has long straight lines in it or on it

stri'ated ,muscle noun [C/U] ANATOMY the type of muscle in the arms or legs. It is made of long fibres.

stricken /ˈstrɪkən/ adj damaged, destroyed, or affected by serious problems

strict /strɪkt/ adj **1** someone who is strict expects people to obey rules completely, or obeys rules completely themselves: *The coach is very strict about our diet.* **2** strict rules or conditions must be obeyed completely: *They operate within strict time limits.*

♦ *Lynn gave us strict instructions to be good.* **3** exact, or accurate: *He was not depressed in the strict sense of the word.*

strictly /ˈstrɪk(t)li/ adv **1** in a strict way: *laws that are strictly enforced* **2** completely: *It's a strictly neutral organization.* ♦ *That's not strictly true.*

stride¹ /straɪd/ (strides, striding, strode /strəʊd/, stridden /ˈstrɪd(ə)n/) verb [I] to walk with energy and confidence: *She strode onto the platform.*

stride² /straɪd/ noun [C] a long confident step
PHRASES get into your stride to begin to do something confidently and well
take sth in your stride to not be upset by something

strife /straɪf/ noun [U] *formal* fighting or disagreement between people

strike¹ /straɪk/ (strikes, striking, struck /strʌk/) verb

1 hit against	7 make flame
2 hit with hand etc	8 clock: make sound
3 refuse to work	9 make agreement
4 affect sb/sth suddenly	10 find gold/oil etc
5 when you think sth	+ PHRASES
6 make attack	+ PHRASAL VERBS

1 [T] *formal* to hit against someone or something: *The car struck a tree.* ♦ *The ball struck her hard on the left shoulder.* ♦ *About 50 worshippers were inside the church when it was struck by lightning.*
2 [T] *formal* to hit someone or something with your hand, a tool, or a weapon: *We watched helplessly as she struck the child in the face.*
3 [I] to refuse to work for a period of time as a protest about your pay or conditions of work: *Car workers were threatening to strike over the job losses.*
4 [I/T] if something unpleasant or dangerous strikes, or if it strikes someone or something, it happens to them suddenly and unexpectedly: *Three earthquakes struck Peru on April 5th and 6th.* ♦ *That same year, tragedy struck again.*
5 [T] if a thought or idea strikes you, it enters your mind suddenly: *The first thing that struck me about Alex was her self-confidence.*
6 [I] to make a sudden violent or illegal attack: *Police are worried the man could strike again.*
7 [T] to rub a match against a hard surface in order to produce a flame
8 [I/T] if a clock strikes, or if it strikes a particular time, it makes a sound to show what the time is: *The town hall clock struck midnight.*
9 [T] to make an agreement: *The two sides had just struck a deal.*
10 [T] to find something such as gold or oil by digging or drilling
PHRASES strike sb as sth to make someone have a particular opinion or feeling: *He didn't strike me as the jealous sort.* ♦ *It struck me as a little bit odd that she was always alone.*
strike a balance (between sth and sth) to find a solution that is more reasonable and fair than either of two extreme possibilities
within striking distance (of sth) close to something, or close to achieving something
PHRASAL VERBS ,strike sth 'off to remove something from a list or record
,strike sth 'out or ,strike sth 'through to remove words from a document by drawing a line through them

strike² /straɪk/ noun **1** [C/U] a period of time during which people refuse to work, as a protest: *A train strike has crippled the city.* ♦ *Workers have been on strike since Friday.* → HUNGER STRIKE **2** [C] a military attack: *a strike on the airfield*

'strike-off ,bar noun [C] TECHNOLOGY a long piece of wood that is used to level sand packed into a **moulding flask** in **sand-casting**

striker /'straɪkə/ noun [C] **1** a worker who is taking part in a strike **2** SPORTS a football player whose job is to score goals

striking /'straɪkɪŋ/ adj attracting your interest or attention because of an unusual feature: *a striking young woman* ♦ *There are some striking differences in the two theories.* —**strikingly** adv

string¹ /strɪŋ/ noun

1 thin rope	**5** instruments/players
2 group of things	**6** on tennis racket etc
3 in computer program	**7** of staircase
4 on instrument	**+** PHRASE

1 [C/U] thin rope that you use for tying things together: *a piece of string* ♦ *The balloon was attached to a long string.*
2 [C] a group of things or events: *He owns a string of restaurants in Wales.* ♦ *We had a string of burglaries in the area last month.*
3 [C] COMPUTING a group of letters, numbers, or symbols used in a computer program and treated as a single unit
4 [C] MUSIC one of several long pieces of **nylon** or wire on a musical instrument. You touch them in order to produce sound.
5 the strings [plural] MUSIC the **stringed instruments** in an orchestra, or the people who play them —*picture* → ORCHESTRA
6 [C] SPORTS any of the long thin pieces of plastic or other material stretched across the frame of a tennis **racket**
7 [C] CONSTRUCTION a **beam** that supports the steps in a staircase
PHRASE **no strings (attached)** without any special conditions that limit an offer or agreement → PULL¹

string² /strɪŋ/ (**strings, stringing, strung** /strʌŋ/) verb [T] **1** to hang a string or rope somewhere, or to hang something that is like string or rope: *She strung a rope between two trees.* ♦ *Lights were strung all around the garden.* **2** to pass a string through several things in order to make a chain: *The children sat on the floor stringing beads.*

stringed instrument /,strɪŋd 'ɪnstrʊmənt/ noun [C] MUSIC a musical instrument with strings that you touch to produce sound, for example a **violin** —*picture* → MUSICAL INSTRUMENT

stringent /'strɪndʒ(ə)nt/ adj stringent rules or conditions are very strict —**stringently** adv

stringer bead /'strɪŋə ,biːd/ noun [C] TECHNOLOGY the first layer of weld at the **root** (=bottom) of a joint between two pieces of metal

,string quar'tet noun [C] MUSIC a group of four musicians who play instruments that have strings, normally two **violins**, a **viola**, and a **cello**

strip¹ /strɪp/ noun [C] a long narrow piece of something: *Cut the paper into strips.* ♦ *a strip of land*

strip² /strɪp/ (**strips, stripping, stripped**) verb **1** [I/T] to take off all of your clothes, or to take off all of another person's clothes: *They all stripped and ran into the water.* **2** [T] to remove something that covers something: *The wind had stripped the leaves from the trees.* **3** [T] to take something away using force or authority: *They stripped the prisoners of weapons and cash.*

stripe /straɪp/ noun [C] a line of one colour on a background of a different colour: *a white shirt with red stripes*

striped /straɪpt/ adj with a pattern of stripes: *a blue-and-white striped tablecloth*

strip planting /'strɪp ,plɑːntɪŋ/ noun [U] AGRICULTURE a way of reducing **soil erosion** by growing two or more different crops in alternate **strips** (=long narrow areas). The crops from the strips are collected at different times to avoid leaving large areas of bare land.

strive /straɪv/ (**strives, striving, strove** /strəʊv/, **striven** /'strɪv(ə)n/) verb [I] to make a lot of effort to achieve something: *We are **striving for** perfection in our products.*

strode /strəʊd/ the past tense of **stride¹**

stroke¹ /strəʊk/ noun

1 medical condition	**5** mark of pen etc
2 unexpected event	**6** hand movement
3 in sport	**7** movement of piston
4 in swimming	**+** PHRASE

1 [C/U] HEALTH illness caused by a blocked or broken blood vessel that can make someone suddenly unable to speak or move: *Leni **suffered a stroke** last year, and is unable to walk.*
2 [singular] an unexpected but important event or action: *I had a **stroke** of luck.* ♦ *It was a real **stroke of genius** (=an idea that shows great intelligence).*
3 [C] SPORTS a movement in which someone hits the ball in some sports, or the way in which they make this movement: *He slammed the ball with a powerful backhand stroke.*
4 [C] SPORTS a style of swimming, or one complete movement of the arms and legs in swimming
5 [C] a single short line or mark made with a pen or brush
6 [C] a gentle movement of your hand over skin, hair, or fur
7 [C] ENGINEERING a movement of a **piston** from one end of the limit of its movement to another
PHRASE **at a stroke** with a single action that changes a situation completely

stroke² /strəʊk/ verb [T] to gently move your hand over skin, hair, or fur: *She stroked his hair as he fell asleep.*

stroll /strəʊl/ verb [I] to walk without hurrying —**stroll** noun [C]

strong /strɒŋ/ adj

1 powerful/healthy	**6** firmly believed/felt
2 produced with power	**7** of high level
3 not easily damaged	**8** with power
4 with confidence	**9** very noticeable
5 good at doing sth	**+** PHRASES

1 physically powerful and healthy: *Are you strong enough to carry that?* ♦ *strong arms* ♦ *Two weeks after her surgery she was **feeling** much **stronger**.*
2 done with a lot of power or force: *a strong blow*
3 not easily broken, damaged, or destroyed: *a strong rope* ♦ *a strong friendship*
4 someone who is strong has confidence, determination, and emotional strength: *You've got to be strong and not let their jokes bother you.*
5 good at doing something: *She's a strong swimmer.*
6 firmly believed or felt: *a strong opinion*
7 of a high degree or level: *There's a **strong possibility** that they'll get married in the spring.*
8 with a lot of power or influence: *a strong leader* ♦ *Our lawyers say we have a very **strong case**.*

9 very noticeable: *a strong colour ♦ a strong British accent ♦ a strong taste ♦ a strong wind*

PHRASES going strong successful, or healthy: *The company was founded in 1860 and is still going strong.* **sb's/sth's strong point** a good quality that makes someone or something effective: *Paula's ability to work quickly is one of her strongest points. ♦ Patience is not my strong point* (=I am not a patient person).

,strong 'acid noun [C] **CHEMISTRY** an acid with a pH of between 1 and 3 that produces a large number of **hydrogen ions** in solution

,strong 'alkali noun [C] **CHEMISTRY** an alkali with a pH of between 12 and 14 that produces a large number of **hydroxyl ions** in solution

stronghold /'strɒŋ,həʊld/ noun [C] a place where the majority of people have the same political or religious beliefs

strongly /'strɒŋli/ adv used for emphasizing that someone is very serious about what they say, feel, or believe: *I feel strongly that the trial was unfair.*

strontium /'strɒntiəm/ noun [U] **CHEMISTRY** a chemical element that is a soft grey metal that burns easily. It is used in **fireworks**. Chemical symbol: **Sr**

strove /strəʊv/ the past tense of **strive**

struck /strʌk/ the past tense and past participle of **strike¹**

structural /'strʌktʃ(ə)rəl/ adj **1** related to the structure of something such as a building: *structural damage* **2** related to the way that something is organized: *structural changes in the industry* —**structurally** adv

,structural engi'neer noun [C] **ENGINEERING** someone whose job is to plan large building projects such as roads, bridges, or factories —**,structural engi'neering** noun [U]

structure¹ /'strʌktʃə/ noun **1** [C/U] the way in which the parts of something are organized or arranged into a whole: *sentence structure ♦ the structure of DNA ♦ the changing structure of agriculture in this country* **2** [C] an organization or system that is made up of many parts: *a social structure* **3** [C] **CONSTRUCTION** something large such as a building or a bridge that is built from different parts

structure² /'strʌktʃə/ verb [T] to plan or organize something

struggle¹ /'strʌg(ə)l/ verb [I] **1** to try hard to do something that is very difficult: *She was struggling to cope with her work.* **2** to try very hard to defeat someone or stop them having power over you: *We have to struggle to win our freedom. ♦ women struggling against oppression* **3** to use your strength to fight against someone or something: *The man grabbed him, but he struggled free.*

struggle² /'strʌg(ə)l/ noun **1** [C] an attempt to do something that takes a lot of effort over a period of time: *the struggle for democracy ♦ her struggle with the disease ♦ the community's struggle against racism* **2** [C/U] a fight or war: *the armed struggle against the government* **3** [singular] something that takes a lot of physical or mental effort: *Foreign languages were always a struggle for him. ♦ It was a struggle to get up the hill in the snow.*

strum /strʌm/ (**strums, strumming, strummed**) verb [T] **MUSIC** to play a musical instrument such as a guitar by moving your fingers across its strings

strung /strʌŋ/ the past tense and past participle of **string²**

strut¹ /strʌt/ (**struts, strutting, strutted**) verb [I] to walk in a confident and proud way

strut² /strʌt/ noun **1** [C] **CONSTRUCTION** a supporting part of a structure that is **under compression** (=being squeezed along its length by weight from above) **2** [singular] a proud and confident way of walking

strychnine /'strɪkniːn/ noun [U] **CHEMISTRY** a chemical from plants that is used for making poison or medicine

stub /stʌb/ (**stubs, stubbing, stubbed**) verb [T] to hit your toe against something accidentally so that it hurts

stubble /'stʌb(ə)l/ noun [U] **1** the short stiff hairs on a man's face that grow into a beard **2** **AGRICULTURE** the ends of plant stems that are left in the ground after a farmer cuts a grain crop

stubborn /'stʌbən/ adj **1** not willing to change your ideas or decisions: *Stop being so stubborn! ♦ stubborn pride* **2** very difficult to change, defeat, or remove: *stubborn opposition ♦ stubborn weeds* —**stubbornly** adv, **stubbornness** noun [U]

stuck¹ /stʌk/ adj **1** caught or held in a position so that no movement is possible: *Carl's car got stuck in the mud.* **2** unable to solve a problem that prevents you from continuing something: *I'm really stuck on this algebra problem.*

stuck² /stʌk/ the past tense and past participle of **stick¹**

stud /stʌd/ noun **1** [C] a small piece of jewellery on a short metal bar that is worn through a part of your body **2** [C] a small piece of metal that sticks up from a surface: *a jacket covered with metal studs* **3** [C] a piece of plastic or rubber on the bottom of a boot that prevents you from slipping **4** [C/U] a male horse or group of male horses used in breeding for producing young animals

student /'stjuːd(ə)nt/ noun [C] **EDUCATION** someone who goes to a university, college, or school: *Jennifer is one of my best students. ♦ a physics student ♦ a student organization*

,students' 'union noun [C] **EDUCATION** an organization at a university or college that helps its students by providing services and places to meet and play sport

studio /'stjuːdiəʊ/ noun [C] **1** **ARTS** a room in which someone such as a painter or photographer works **2** a small flat that has only one main room **3** **ARTS** a company that produces films **4** **ARTS** a set of rooms where music or a film, television show, or radio show is recorded

studious /'stjuːdiəs/ adj **1** tending to study and read a lot **2** giving a lot of attention and care to what you are doing or learning —**studiously** adv

'stud par,tition noun [C] **CONSTRUCTION** a light structure of pieces of wood to which **plasterboard** can be attached to make a dividing wall in a building

study¹ /'stʌdi/ (plural **studies**) noun

1 process of learning	**4** room for reading etc
2 research project	**5** first drawing/
3 college etc	model/plan
work/subject	

1 [U] the process of learning about a subject or problem: *a centre for the study of Asian languages*
2 [C] a research project that examines a problem or subject: *The study showed a link between the chemicals and cancer.*
3 studies [plural] **EDUCATION** the work that you do, or a subject that you can study, while you are at school, college, or university: *Sarah wants to continue her studies. ♦ social studies*
4 [C] a room in a house where you can read or work quietly

5 [C] ARTS a first drawing, model, or plan of a work by an artist

study² /'stʌdi/ (**studies, studying, studied**) verb
1 [I/T] EDUCATION to learn about a subject by going to school, university etc: *She's studying history at university.* ♦ *Michael was **studying to be** a lawyer.*
→ LEARN **2** [I] EDUCATION to do work such as reading and homework: *You need to study hard if you want to pass.* **3** [T] to read or look at something very carefully: *I studied various maps of the area.* **4** [T] to learn about a problem or subject using scientific methods: *They will study the effect of technology on jobs.*

'study ,tour noun [C] TOURISM a visit to an area in which people go to different places and have lectures and classes

stuff¹ /stʌf/ noun [U] *informal* **1** objects, or things: *What's all this stuff on my desk?* ♦ *By the time we got to the sale, all the good stuff was gone.* ♦ *I spend most of my time doing really boring stuff.* **2** a material, or a substance **3** general information

stuff² /stʌf/ verb [T] **1** to push something soft into a space or container: *Alice quickly **stuffed** her clothes **into** a suitcase and left.* **2** to fill a container or space with something, especially something soft

stuffed /stʌft/ adj **1** full of things: *The drawer was **stuffed with** money.* **2** stuffed meat or vegetables have been filled with another type of food

stuffing /'stʌfɪŋ/ noun [U] **1** food that has been cut into small pieces and put inside meat or vegetables **2** soft material that is used for filling something such as a toy or a seat

stuffy /'stʌfi/ (**stuffier, stuffiest**) adj **1** a stuffy room is unpleasant to be in because it is too warm and there is no fresh air in it **2** *informal* with strict or old-fashioned attitudes —**stuffiness** noun [U]

stumble /'stʌmb(ə)l/ verb [I] **1** to fall, or almost fall, while you are walking or running: *Derek stumbled over a fallen tree.* **2** to make a mistake when you are speaking —**stumble** noun [C]

stumbling block /'stʌmblɪŋ ,blɒk/ noun [C] a difficulty that causes mistakes or prevents progress

stump¹ /stʌmp/ noun [C]

1 part of tree	4 part left behind
2 part of limb	5 rock in sea
3 in cricket	

1 the part of a tree that is left above the ground after it has been cut off at the base
2 the remaining part of someone's arm, leg, or finger after the rest is cut off
3 SPORTS one of the three sticks that you try to hit in the game of **cricket**
4 a part that is left of something, which sticks out or sticks up after the rest of it has been broken off or worn away
5 GEOLOGY a piece of rock that sticks up out of the sea. It is formed after a taller piece of rock has fallen in as a result of the sea eroding it at the bottom. —*picture* → EROSION

stump² /stʌmp/ verb [T] SPORTS to end a cricket player's turn by hitting the **stumps** with the ball while the player is running towards them

PHRASE **be stumped by sth** to be unable to explain something mysterious, or to be unable to answer a question

stun /stʌn/ (**stuns, stunning, stunned**) verb [T] **1** to shock and surprise someone so much that they cannot react immediately: *His violent death stunned the nation.* **2** to hit someone so hard on the head that they

are unable to move or react for a short time —**stunned** /stʌnd/ adj

stung /stʌŋ/ the past tense and past participle of **sting¹**

stunk /stʌŋk/ the past participle of **stink**

stunning /'stʌnɪŋ/ adj **1** very impressive or beautiful: *The view from the top of the hill is stunning.* **2** surprising, powerful, and effective —**stunningly** adv

stunt¹ /stʌnt/ noun [C] **1** something that is done in order to impress someone or to get their attention: *a publicity stunt* **2** something dangerous that is done in order to entertain people, often as part of a film

stunt² /stʌnt/ verb **stunt sb's/sth's growth** to stop someone or something from growing or developing

stupid /'stju:pɪd/ adj **1** not intelligent, or showing bad judgment: *What a stupid question!* ♦ *I didn't ask because I was afraid of **looking stupid**.* **2** silly or annoying: *He kept singing the same stupid song.* —**stupidity** /stju:'pɪdəti/ noun [U], **stupidly** adv: *I stupidly loaned him some money.*

stupor /'stju:pə/ noun [singular/U] the condition of being unable to think or act normally because you are not completely conscious

sturdy /'stɜ:di/ (**sturdier, sturdiest**) adj strong and thick or solid: *sturdy legs*

stutter /'stʌtə/ verb [I/T] to repeat the sounds of words in an uncontrolled way when you speak, because you are nervous or you have a speech problem = STAMMER —**stutter** noun [singular]

sty /staɪ/ (plural **sties**) noun [C] AGRICULTURE a small building where pigs are kept on a farm

style /staɪl/ noun

1 way of doing sth	4 way of writing,
2 attractive way of	painting etc
behaving	5 part of flower
3 typical appearance	

1 [C] the individual way that someone behaves and does things: *I really dislike her teaching style.* ♦ *Having big parties is **not my style**.*
2 [U] an attractive or impressive way of behaving or doing something: *Greg **has** a lot **of style**.*
3 [C/U] the way that something is made or done that is typical of a particular group, time, or place: *I don't like **the style of** dresses that are in fashion now.* ♦ *traditional and modern **styles of** furniture*
4 [C] LITERATURE, ARTS the way that someone writes or produces art: *Joyce's writing style* ♦ *Picasso's **style of** painting*
5 [C] BIOLOGY a long thin part of the **carpel** of a flower, at the top of which is the **stigma** —*picture* → FERTILIZATION, FLOWER

stylish /'staɪlɪʃ/ adj attractive and fashionable: *stylish clothes* —**stylishly** adv

stylistic /staɪ'lɪstɪk/ adj LITERATURE, ARTS relating to ways of creating effects, especially in language and literature —**stylistically** /staɪ'lɪstɪkli/ adv

stylized /'staɪlaɪzd/ adj in a style that is artificial rather than realistic

sub- /sʌb/ prefix **1** one small part of a larger thing: *a subsection* **2** smaller or less important than someone or something: *a subheading* **3** below a particular level: *sub-zero temperatures*

subaqua /ˌsʌb'ækwə/ adj SPORTS relating to sports that people do under water

subarctic /ˌsʌb'ɑːktɪk/ adj GEOGRAPHY relating to the very cold parts of the world just south of the Arctic Circle

subatomic particle /ˌsʌbətɒmɪk ˈpɑːtɪk(ə)l/ noun [C] **PHYSICS** an extremely small part of matter that makes up part of an atom, or is smaller than an atom. Protons and neutrons are subatomic particles.
→ ELEMENTARY PARTICLE

subconscious[1] /ˌsʌbˈkɒnʃəs/ adj relating to thoughts or feelings that you have but do not think about, or that you do not realize that you have —**subconsciously** adv

subconscious[2] /ˌsʌbˈkɒnʃəs/ noun [singular] the part of your mind that contains thoughts and feelings that you do not think about, or that you do not realize that you have

subcontinent /ˌsʌbˈkɒntɪnənt/ noun [C] **GEOGRAPHY** a large area of land that forms part of a continent, especially the part of Asia that contains the countries of India, Pakistan, and Bangladesh

subcontract /ˌsʌbkənˈtrækt/ verb [I/T] **BUSINESS** to pay someone to do some of the work that you have agreed to do for someone else —**subcontractor** /ˌsʌbkənˈtræktə/ noun [C]

subculture /ˈsʌbˌkʌltʃə/ noun [C] **SOCIAL STUDIES** a group of people whose beliefs and ways of behaving make them different from the rest of society

subcutaneous /ˌsʌbkjuːˈteɪniəs/ adj **HEALTH** under the skin, or injected directly under the skin

subdirectory /ˈsʌbdɪˌrekt(ə)ri/ (plural **subdirectories**) noun [C] **COMPUTING** a small area in a computer where information is stored, or a list of the files and programs stored there, that is part of a larger area

subdivide /ˌsʌbdɪˈvaɪd/ verb [T] to divide the parts of something that has already been divided

subdivision /ˈsʌbdɪˌvɪʒ(ə)n/ noun **1** [C] one small part of something that has already been divided into several larger parts **2** [U] the process of subdividing something

subdue /səbˈdjuː/ verb [T] **1** to make someone stop behaving in an uncontrolled or violent way **2** formal to take control of a place or a group of people by using force

subdued /səbˈdjuːd/ adj **1** quiet and slightly sad or worried **2** not very loud or bright: subdued lighting

subframe /ˈsʌbˌfreɪm/ noun [C] **ENGINEERING** a metal frame on which a vehicle's body is built

subheading /ˈsʌbˌhedɪŋ/ noun [C] **LITERATURE** the title of one section of a longer piece of writing

subject[1] /ˈsʌbdʒɪkt/ noun [C]

1 sth you discuss	**4** sb in scientific test
2 sth taught at school	**5** sth in picture
3 in grammar	**6** sb ruled by king/queen

1 something that you discuss or write about: He's never mentioned **the subject of** money. ♦ Someone **raised the subject of** (=started talking about) sports facilities. ♦ Can we **change the subject** (=talk about something else), please?
2 **EDUCATION** something that you learn or teach in a school, for example English, mathematics, or biology
3 **LANGUAGE** in English grammar, the person or thing that does what the verb describes. In the sentence 'Mary threw the ball', 'Mary' is the subject.
4 a person or animal that is used in a medical or scientific test
5 **ARTS** someone or something that is shown in a picture
6 **POLITICS, LAW** someone who lives in a country that is controlled by a king or queen: a British subject

subject[2] /ˈsʌbdʒɪkt/ adj
PHRASE **subject to sth 1** likely to be affected by something: Train times are subject to change during bad weather. **2** in a situation where you have to obey a rule or law: All building firms are subject to tight controls. **3** depending on whether something happens: Goods will be sent out within 14 days, subject to availability.

subject[3] /səbˈdʒekt/ verb [T] to make someone experience something unpleasant: Her husband **subjected** her **to** years of physical abuse.

subjective /səbˈdʒektɪv/ adj **1** based on your own feelings and ideas, and not on facts **2** **LANGUAGE** relating to the subject of a sentence —**subjectively** adv, **subjectivity** /ˌsʌbdʒekˈtɪvəti/ noun [U]

'subject ˌline noun [C] **COMPUTING** the place in an email where you can type what the email is about

'subject ˌmatter noun [U] the things that a speech, a piece of writing, an article etc is about

sub judice /ˌsʌb ˈdʒuːdəsi/ adj, adv **LAW** a legal case or piece of evidence that is sub judice is being considered by a judge or in a court, and some details of it cannot be discussed in public

subjunctive[1] /səbˈdʒʌŋktɪv/ noun [singular] **LANGUAGE** the form of a verb that is used for expressing doubts and wishes. For example, in the sentence 'I wish I were taller', 'were' is in the subjunctive.

subjunctive[2] /səbˈdʒʌŋktɪv/ adj **LANGUAGE** the subjunctive form of a verb is used for expressing doubts and wishes

sublimation /ˌsʌblɪˈmeɪʃ(ə)n/ noun [U] **SCIENCE** a process in which a substance is changed from a solid into a gas or from a gas into a solid without first becoming a liquid

sublime /səˈblaɪm/ adj formal used for describing an extreme feeling or quality

submachine gun /ˌsʌbməˈʃiːn ˌɡʌn/ noun [C] a light machine gun that is held against the **hip** or the shoulder when shooting

submarine /ˈsʌbməriːn/ noun [C] a ship that can travel both on the surface of the water and under water

ˌsubmarine ˈearthquake noun [C] **GEOLOGY** an earthquake under the sea

submerge /səbˈmɜːdʒ/ verb [I/T] to go completely under water, or to put something completely under water —**submerged** /səbˈmɜːdʒd/ adj

submersed /səbˈmɜːst/ adj **BIOLOGY** submersed plants grow under water

submersion /səbˈmɜːʃ(ə)n/ noun [U] a situation in which something is under water, or the process of going under water

submission /səbˈmɪʃ(ə)n/ noun **1** [U] formal the action of accepting that someone has defeated you or has power over you **2** [C/U] the process of formally giving a document to someone for them to consider, or the document that you give them **3** [C] a statement that you make to a judge or official committee

submissive /səbˈmɪsɪv/ adj willing to do what other people tell you to do without arguing —**submissively** adv, **submissiveness** noun [U]

submit /səbˈmɪt/ (**submits**, **submitting**, **submitted**) verb **1** [T] to formally give something to someone for them to consider: The plans will be submitted next week. **2** [I/T] to accept that someone has defeated you or has power over you, so that you do what they want: The rebels have refused to **submit to** the national government. ♦ *Women were supposed to* **submit** *themselves totally* **to** *their husbands.*

submultiple /ˌsʌbˈmʌltɪp(ə)l/ noun [C] **MATHS** a number that you can divide into another number exactly: *3 is a submultiple of 9.*

subordinate¹ /səˈbɔːdɪnət/ adj **1** having less power or authority than someone else **2** less important than something else —**subordination** /sə,bɔːdɪˈneɪʃ(ə)n/ noun [U]

subordinate² /səˈbɔːdɪnət/ noun [C] someone who has less power or authority than someone else

sub,ordinate 'clause noun [C] **LANGUAGE** a group of words that gives extra information about a sentence but cannot form a sentence by itself. For example, in the sentence 'Marla stayed at home because she was tired', 'because she was tired' is a subordinate clause.

subordinating conjunction /sə,bɔːdɪneɪtɪŋ kənˈdʒʌŋkʃ(ə)n/ noun [C] **LANGUAGE** a word such as 'because', 'while', 'that', 'which', or 'who' that begins a subordinate clause and connects it to the main part of a sentence

'sub-,plot noun [C] **LITERATURE, ARTS** a story in a novel, play, or film that is separate from the main story and not as important as it

subpoena¹ /səˈpiːnə/ noun [C] **LAW** an official legal document that says you must come to a court of law to give information

subpoena² /səˈpiːnə/ verb [T] **LAW** to officially order someone to come to a court of law to give information

subroutine /ˈsʌbruːˌtiːn/ noun [C] **COMPUTING** a small part of a computer program that does one specific job

sub-Saharan /ˌsʌb səˈhɑːr(ə)n/ adj **GEOGRAPHY** in the part of Africa that is south of the Sahara Desert

subscribe /səbˈskraɪb/ verb [I] **1** to pay money regularly so that you receive a product such as a magazine, or a service such as an Internet connection **2 COMPUTING** to join an Internet **newsgroup** —**subscriber** noun [C]

subscript /ˈsʌbˌskrɪpt/ adj written or printed in very small print below, and after, a letter or number —**subscript** noun [C/U]

subscription /səbˈskrɪpʃ(ə)n/ noun [C] an agreement to pay an amount of money regularly so that you will receive something such as a magazine or a service, or the amount of money that you pay

subsection /ˈsʌbˌsekʃ(ə)n/ noun [C] a small section within another larger section of something

subsequent /ˈsʌbsɪkwənt/ adj *formal* happening or coming after something else: *In subsequent interviews, he denied the story.*

subsequently /ˈsʌbsɪkwəntli/ adv after something else happened: *The disease subsequently spread to the rest of the country.*

subservient /səbˈsɜːviənt/ adj too willing to obey other people —**subservience** noun [U]

subset /ˈsʌbˌset/ noun [C] a small group of people or things that is a part of a larger group

subside /səbˈsaɪd/ verb [I] **1** to become weaker, less violent, or less severe: *Gradually the pain subsided.* **2** if flood water, land, or a building subsides, it sinks to a lower level

subsidence /ˈsʌbsɪd(ə)ns, səbˈsaɪd(ə)ns/ noun [U] the process by which land or buildings sink to a lower level

subsidiary /səbˈsɪdiəri/ (plural **subsidiaries**) noun [C] **BUSINESS** a company that is owned by a larger company

subsidize /ˈsʌbsɪdaɪz/ verb [T] to pay some of the cost of a product or service so that it can be sold to people at a lower price

subsidy /ˈsʌbsədi/ (plural **subsidies**) noun [C] **ECONOMICS** an amount of money that the government or another organization pays to help to reduce the cost of a product or service

subsist /səbˈsɪst/ verb [I] to stay alive when you do not have much food or money

subsistence /səbˈsɪstəns/ noun [U] **1** the ability to stay alive when you do not have much food or money **2 ECONOMICS** the smallest amount of food or money that someone needs to stay alive

sub'sistence ,farming noun [U] **AGRICULTURE** a type of farming in which people produce enough food for themselves to live on, but not enough to sell —**sub'sistence ,farmer** noun [C]

subsoil /ˈsʌbˌsɔɪl/ noun [U] **AGRICULTURE** the layer of soil that is immediately above the level of the rock underneath

subsonic /ˌsʌbˈsɒnɪk/ adj **PHYSICS** slower than the speed of sound

subspecies /ˈsʌbˌspiːʃiːz/ noun [C] **BIOLOGY** a group of plants or animals within a species that have slight genetic differences from other plants or animals in that species

substance /ˈsʌbstəns/ noun **1** [C] a particular type of liquid, solid, or gas: *The wood is coated with a special substance that protects it from the sun.* **2** [U] the quality of being important, true, or useful: *The band is all show and* **no substance.** ♦ *There* **is no substance to** *his accusations* (=they are not true). **3** [C] a drug that people can become **addicted** to, especially an illegal drug **4** [U] the most important ideas or basic meaning of a discussion or piece of writing

'substance a,buse noun [U] **HEALTH** the use of alcohol, or illegal or dangerous drugs, in amounts that can damage health

substandard /ˌsʌbˈstændəd/ adj not as good as you would normally expect, or not good enough to be accepted

substantial /səbˈstænʃ(ə)l/ adj **1** large in amount or degree= CONSIDERABLE: *A* **substantial number** *of people have complained.* ♦ *a* **substantial sum** *of money* **2** large and strongly built: *a substantial brick building* **3** important or real: *His decision was based on nothing more substantial than his dislike of foreigners.*

substantially /səbˈstænʃ(ə)li/ adv by a large amount or degree: *We have substantially increased the number of courses.*

substantiate /səbˈstænʃieɪt/ verb [T] to provide evidence that proves something

substantive¹ /səbˈstæntɪv/ adj *formal* **1** important or serious, or referring to the most important or serious issues **2** large in amount, degree, or strength = SUBSTANTIAL —**substantively** adv

substantive² /ˈsʌbstəntɪv/ noun [C] **LANGUAGE** a noun

substation /ˈsʌbˌsteɪʃ(ə)n/ noun [C] **PHYSICS** a piece of equipment that changes the voltage of an electricity supply between the place where it is produced and the place where it is used

substitute¹ /ˈsʌbstɪˌtjuːt/ verb **1** [T] to use something new or different instead of what is normally used: *You can substitute chicken for beef in this recipe.* **2** [T] to remove one thing and put something else in its place: *She substituted a photo of herself for the one already attached to the form.* **3** [T] **SPORTS** to replace a member of a sports team with another player during a game **4** [I] **substitute for sb** to do someone else's job for a short period of time

substitute² /'sʌbstɪˌtjuːt/ noun [C] **1** something that is used instead of something else **2** someone who does someone else's job for a short time **3** **SPORTS** a player who replaces another member of his or her team during a sports game

substitution /ˌsʌbstɪˈtjuːʃ(ə)n/ noun [C/U] the action of replacing someone or something with someone or something else

substrate /'sʌbˌstreɪt/ noun [C] **1** **BIOLOGY** the material that a plant or an animal that does not move much feeds on or uses as support **2** **CHEMISTRY**, **BIOLOGY** a substance on which a **catalyst** or enzyme has a particular effect

substructure /'sʌbˌstrʌktʃə/ noun [C] **CONSTRUCTION** the part of a building that is under it and supports it

subsume /səb'sjuːm/ verb [T] *formal* to include something in a larger group and cause it to lose its own individual character

subtend /səb'tend/ verb [T] **BIOLOGY** to surround something from underneath

subterfuge /'sʌbtəˌfjuːdʒ/ noun [C/U] *formal* the use of lies and tricks = DECEIT

subterranean /ˌsʌbtəˈreɪniən/ adj under the ground

subtext /'sʌbˌtekst/ noun [C] **LANGUAGE** a true but not directly expressed meaning of something that someone says

subtitle /'sʌbˌtaɪt(ə)l/ noun **1** **subtitles** [plural] **ARTS** a **translation** of what people are saying in a foreign language film or television programme that appears at the bottom of the screen **2** [C] **LITERATURE** an additional title that appears after the main title of a piece of writing

subtle /'sʌt(ə)l/ adj **1** not obvious, and therefore difficult to notice: *subtle changes* ♦ *subtle threats* ♦ *subtle advertising* (=that persuades people in a subtle way) ♦ *a subtle hint* **2** showing an ability to notice and understand small things that other people do not: *subtle humour* **3** delicate and complicated in an attractive way: *a subtle pattern* **4** a subtle colour is pleasant because it is not too bright —**subtly** adv

subtlety /'sʌt(ə)lti/ (plural **subtleties**) noun **1** [U] the quality of being complicated, delicate, or difficult to notice **2** [C] a small detail or feature that is difficult to notice

subtract /səb'trækt/ verb [I/T] **MATHS** to take a number or amount from another number or amount —**subtraction** /səb'trækʃ(ə)n/ noun [U]

subtractive /səb'træktɪv/ adj **PHYSICS** relating to a theory of light that states that the colour we see from a coloured object depends on the colours of light that are reflected away from the object

subtropical /ˌsʌb'trɒpɪk(ə)l/ adj **GEOGRAPHY** from or relating to the warm parts of the world just north and south of the **tropics**

the subtropics /ˌsʌb'trɒpɪks/ noun [plural] **GEOGRAPHY** the warm areas of the Earth that are next to the **tropics** —*picture* → EARTH

suburb /'sʌbɜːb/ noun [C] an area or town near a large city but away from its centre, where there are many houses

suburban /sə'bɜːbən/ adj in, relating to, or typical of a suburb → URBAN

subversive /səb'vɜːsɪv/ adj intended to destroy the power or influence of a government or of an established principle

subway /'sʌbˌweɪ/ noun [C] **1** a tunnel that people can walk through to go under a road **2** *American* a railway that goes under the ground

sub-'zero adj sub-zero temperatures are lower than zero degrees

succeed /sək'siːd/ verb **1** [I] to achieve something that you planned to do or attempted to do ≠ FAIL: *Everyone wants the peace process to succeed.* ♦ *We finally succeeded in getting some extra funding.* **2** [I] to do well in school, in your career, or in another activity ≠ FAIL: *These days there is a lot of pressure on children to succeed.* **3** [T] to replace someone who was in a powerful job or position: *In 1603, Elizabeth was succeeded by James I.* **4** [T] *formal* to follow and replace something

Word family: **succeed**
Words in the same family as succeed
■ **success** *n*   ■ **unsuccessful** *adj*
■ **successful** *adj*   ■ **unsuccessfully** *adv*
■ **successfully** *adv*

succeeding /sək'siːdɪŋ/ adj coming after something else

success /sək'ses/ noun **1** [U] the achievement of something that you planned to do or attempted to do ≠ FAILURE: *The chairman thanked all those who had contributed to **the success of** the company.* ♦ *How do you explain their **success in** reducing crime?* **2** [C] a plan or attempt that achieves good results: *She set up her own business and **made a success of** it.* ♦ *The party **was a great success**.* **3** [U] the fact that you are successful in your career ≠ FAILURE: *Her success is due mainly to luck and determination.*

successful /sək'sesf(ə)l/ adj **1** achieving the result that you want ≠ UNSUCCESSFUL: *The team has had a **highly successful** season.* ♦ *We have been very **successful in** attracting top quality candidates.* **2** a successful person does well in their career ≠ UNSUCCESSFUL: *a successful businesswoman* **3** a successful business makes a lot of money ≠ UNSUCCESSFUL: *It was another very successful year for the bank.* —**successfully** adv

succession /sək'seʃ(ə)n/ noun **1** [singular] a series of people or things of the same type: *a succession of low-paid jobs* **2** [U] the process by which one person comes after another as a king, queen, or leader
PHRASE in succession in a series: *Hankins has won the tournament five times in succession.*

successive /sək'sesɪv/ adj coming or happening one after another in a series —**successively** adv

successor /sək'sesə/ noun [C] **1** someone who has an important position after someone else **2** an organization or machine that replaces something that did the same job before

succinct /sək'sɪŋkt/ adj expressed in a very short but clear way —**succinctly** adv

succulent¹ /'sʌkjʊlənt/ adj **1** succulent food is full of juice and tastes good **2** **BIOLOGY** succulent plants have thick stems or leaves that store a lot of water

succulent² /'sʌkjʊlənt/ noun [C] **BIOLOGY** a succulent plant

succumb /sə'kʌm/ verb [I] *formal* **1** to lose your ability to fight against someone or something **2** **HEALTH** to become very ill, or to die from a disease

such /sʌtʃ/ determiner, pronoun **1** of the type that has been mentioned or is being discussed: *What evidence do you have for such a conclusion?* ♦ *If this is not a genuine CD, it should not be sold as such.* **2** used for emphasizing a special or unusual quality in someone or something: *If it's such a secret, why did you tell me?* ♦ *She's such a lovely person.* **3** used for saying that a particular type of situation, behaviour, action etc causes the result that you are mentioning: *He speaks to me in such a way that I always feel he is insulting me.* ♦ *Their relationship was such that they spent every possible minute together.*

PHRASES not...as such not in the usual meaning of the word you have mentioned: *It's not a university as such, but you can study for degrees there.*

such as used for introducing more examples of the type of person or thing that you have just mentioned: *basic foods such as flour, rice, and cooking oil*

such...that used for emphasizing the degree of a quality by stating its result: *We had such a good time that we're planning to go again next year.*

there's no such thing/person as used for saying that a particular type of thing or person does not exist: *There's no such thing as luck.*

suck /sʌk/ verb **1** [I/T] to pull liquid, air, or smoke into your mouth: *He sucked in a lot of air, then jumped into the pool.* **2** [I/T] to put something in your mouth and move your tongue against it: *She sucked on a sweet and stared at us.* **3** [T] to pull something somewhere, especially with a lot of force: *The current nearly sucked us under the water.* **4** [T] to gradually take something from something else

sucker /sʌkə/ noun [C] **BIOLOGY 1** a round structure on the bodies of some animals that allows them to stick to surfaces **2** a plant that grows from the bottom of another plant's stem or roots

suckle /sʌk(ə)l/ verb [T] *old-fashioned* to feed a baby or young animal with milk from a breast or **udder**

sucrose /suːkrəʊs/ noun [U] **BIOLOGY, CHEMISTRY** a common type of sugar that comes from plants such as **sugar cane** and **sugar beet**. It is a **disaccharide**. Chemical formula: $C_{12}H_{22}O_{11}$

suction /sʌkʃ(ə)n/ noun [U] the process of sucking air or a liquid from somewhere by creating a space without air that it can flow into

sudden¹ /sʌd(ə)n/ adj happening very quickly and without any warning: *a sudden rise in violent crime* ♦ *She felt a sudden pain in her hip.* —**suddenness** noun [U]

sudden² /sʌd(ə)n/ noun **all of a sudden** if something happens all of a sudden, it happens quickly, and without any warning: *All of a sudden, the door slammed shut.*

sudden 'death noun [U] **SPORTS** an extra period of time added to the end of a game when both players or teams have the same score, in which the team that scores first wins

suddenly /sʌd(ə)nli/ adv quickly and without any warning: *A strange feeling suddenly came over him.*

sudoku /suˈdəʊkuː/ noun [U] a number game in which you fill a square of 81 smaller squares with the numbers 1 to 9 so that each row, **column**, and square of 9 squares contains each number only once

sue /suː, sjuː/ verb [I/T] **LAW** to make a legal claim against someone, usually in order to get money from them because they have done something bad to you

suede /sweɪd/ noun [U] leather with a soft brushed surface

suet /suːɪt/ noun [U] hard fat from around an animal's kidneys that is used for cooking

suffer /sʌfə/ verb **1** [I/T] to feel physical or mental pain: *When parents argue constantly, it's the children who suffer most.* ♦ *Don't worry, the animal won't suffer any pain.* **2** [I/T] to have a particular illness or physical problem: *patients suffering from heart disease* **3** [I/T] to experience something very unpleasant or painful: *In wars, it's usually innocent civilians that suffer.* ♦ *Our team suffered another humiliating defeat last night.* **4** [I] to become worse or less successful

sufferer /sʌfərə/ noun [C] someone who has a particular problem or disease

suffering /sʌfərɪŋ/ noun [C/U] mental or physical pain or problems

sufficient /səˈfɪʃ(ə)nt/ adj as much as is needed = ENOUGH ≠ INSUFFICIENT: *There is now sufficient evidence to prove his claims.* ♦ *The wages were not sufficient for people to live on.* —**sufficiently** adv

suffix /sʌfɪks/ noun [C] **LANGUAGE** a letter or group of letters added to the end of a word to make a different word. For example the suffix '-ness' is added to 'great' and 'happy' to make 'greatness' and 'happiness'.

suffocate /sʌfəkeɪt/ verb [I/T] to die because you cannot breathe, or to kill someone in this way —**suffocation** /ˌsʌfəˈkeɪʃ(ə)n/ noun [U]

suffocating /sʌfəkeɪtɪŋ/ adj so hot that you cannot breathe easily

suffrage /sʌfrɪdʒ/ noun [U] **POLITICS, SOCIAL STUDIES** the right to vote

Sufi /suːfi/ noun [C] **RELIGION** a member of an Islamic religious group whose aim is to communicate directly with God and understand spiritual mysteries —**Sufism** noun [U]

sugar /ʃʊɡə/ noun **1** [U] a sweet substance that is added to food or drinks to make them taste sweet: *Do you take sugar in your coffee?* **2** [C] the amount of sugar that is contained in a **teaspoon**: *How many sugars do you take?* **3** [C] **CHEMISTRY** one of a group of sweet substances contained in plants

'sugar ,beet noun [C/U] **AGRICULTURE** a plant with a round part that grows under the ground and is used for producing sugar

'sugar ,cane noun [C/U] **AGRICULTURE** a tall tropical plant with thick stems that are used for producing sugar

sugary /ʃʊɡəri/ adj tasting sweet from sugar

suggest /səˈdʒest/ verb [T] **1** to offer an idea or a plan for someone to consider: *He suggested that we have dinner first, and then watch the film.* ♦ *If you have computer problems, we suggest phoning the manufacturer direct.* **2** to tell someone about something that may be suitable for a particular purpose = RECOMMEND: *Can you suggest a good restaurant?* **3** to make people think that something exists or is true = IMPLY: *Evidence suggests a link between asthma and pollution.* ♦ *I'm not suggesting that giving up smoking will be easy.*

suggestion /səˈdʒestʃ(ə)n/ noun **1** [C] an idea or plan that you offer for someone to consider: *The suggestion that only rich people go to the opera is inaccurate.* ♦ *Could I make a suggestion?* ♦ *People had some helpful suggestions for improving the service.* **2** [U] the act of suggesting something: *It was at Larry's suggestion that I attended the meeting.* **3** [singular] the possibility that something is true, or evidence that shows that something might be true: *The government rejected any suggestion that it was to blame.*

suggestive /sə'dʒestɪv/ adj **1** making you think of sex **2** making you think or remember a particular thing

suicidal /ˌsuːɪ'saɪd(ə)l/ adj **1** someone who is suicidal is likely to try to kill themselves **2** very dangerous, and likely to lead to serious problems or to death

suicide¹ /'suːɪsaɪd/ noun **1** [C/U] the action by which someone deliberately kills themself: *Police believe he committed suicide.* **2** [U] something that you do that is likely to have very bad results for you

suicide² /'suːɪsaɪd/ adj a suicide attack will kill the person who makes it: *a suicide bombing*

'suicide ˌbomber noun [C] someone who attacks a person or a place with a bomb and who intends to die while killing or destroying them, usually for political aims

suit¹ /suːt/ verb [T] **1** to be convenient or suitable for someone: *It's important to find a form of exercise that suits your lifestyle.* ♦ *I work part-time, which suits me fine.* **2** if a style or something you wear suits you, it makes you look good: *The new hairstyle really suits her.*

suit² /suːt/ noun [C] **1** a set of clothes made from the same cloth, usually a jacket with trousers or a skirt: *He was wearing a dark suit and a tie.* **2** a type of clothing that you wear for a particular activity: *a diving suit* **3** LAW a claim or complaint that someone makes in a court of law= LAWSUIT **4** one of four sets of playing cards that together make a pack

suitability /ˌsuːtə'bɪləti/ noun [U] the degree to which someone or something is suitable for a particular job or purpose

suitable /'suːtəb(ə)l/ adj right for a particular purpose, person, or situation ≠ UNSUITABLE: *It's difficult for students to find suitable accommodation.* ♦ *This film is not suitable for young children.*

suitably /'suːtəbli/ adv **1** in a way that is right for a particular purpose or situation: *There is a shortage of suitably qualified and experienced teachers.* **2** used for saying that someone reacts in the way that you expected: *We all looked suitably impressed when she told us her exam results.*

suitcase /'suːtˌkeɪs/ noun [C] a large bag with flat sides and a handle that you use for carrying clothes and other things when you travel

suite /swiːt/ noun [C] **1** a set of rooms **2** COMPUTING a set of computer programs **3** MUSIC a series of pieces of music

suited /'suːtɪd/ adj **1** right for a particular purpose or situation **2** if two people are suited, they are likely to have a successful relationship= COMPATIBLE

sulfur /'sʌlfə/ the American spelling of **sulphur**

sulk /sʌlk/ verb [I] to show that you are angry about being treated badly by looking unhappy and not talking to anyone —**sulk** noun [C]

sulky /'sʌlki/ adj feeling angry and unhappy about being treated badly, and not wanting to talk to anyone —**sulkily** adv

sullen /'sʌlən/ adj angry, unhappy, and not wanting to talk to anyone —**sullenly** adv

sulphate /'sʌlfeɪt/ noun [C/U] CHEMISTRY a chemical compound produced from **sulphuric acid**. Chemical formula: SO_4

sulphide /'sʌlfaɪd/ noun [C/U] CHEMISTRY a mixture of sulphur and another chemical element

sulphur /'sʌlfə/ noun [U] CHEMISTRY a yellow chemical element that burns with a strong smell. It is used to make **sulphuric acid**, matches, **fungicides**, and **gunpowder**. Chemical symbol: **S**

ˌsulphur diˈoxide noun [U] CHEMISTRY a poisonous gas with a strong smell. It is used for preserving things. Chemical formula: SO_2 *—picture* → POLLUTION

sulphuric acid /sʌlˌfjʊərɪk 'æsɪd/ noun [U] CHEMISTRY a strong acid that has no colour and can harm flesh. It is used in batteries, fertilizers, and **detergents**, and in many other compounds. Chemical formula: H_2SO_4

sultan /'sʌltən/ noun [C] the leader in some Muslim countries

sultana /sʌl'tɑːnə/ noun [C] a dried white grape, used in cooking

sultanate /'sʌltənət/ noun [C] **1** a country that is ruled by a **sultan 2** the period during which a **sultan** rules

sultry /'sʌltri/ adj sultry weather is unpleasant because the air is hot and feels slightly wet

sum¹ /sʌm/ noun [C] **1** an amount of money: *We already spend large sums of money on advertising.* ♦ *The painting was sold for the sum of £1.3 million.* **2** MATHS a simple calculation **3** MATHS a total amount made by adding several numbers or amounts together: *What's the sum of those three numbers?*

sum² /sʌm/ (**sums, summing, summed**)   PHRASAL VERB
ˌsum (sth) 'up to give a summary of something

summarize /'sʌməraɪz/ verb [I/T] to provide a short account of the most important facts or features of something

summary¹ /'sʌməri/ (plural **summaries**) noun [C] a short account of something that gives only the most important information: *The text provides summaries of the plots of Shakespeare's plays.*

summary² /'sʌməri/ adj done immediately and without following the usual methods or processes: *summary executions*

summer /'sʌmə/ noun [C/U] the season between spring and autumn, when the weather is hottest: *the summer of 1973* ♦ *a warm summer evening* ♦ *This room is cold even in summer.*

'summer ˌcamp noun [C/U] a place where children can go to stay in the summer holiday and do various activities

'summer ˌschool noun [C/U] EDUCATION a course of study held at a college or university during the summer holiday

summer solstice /ˌsʌmə 'sɒlstɪs/ noun [C/U] ASTRONOMY the day of the year when the sun is above the horizon for the longest amount of time, around 21st June in the northern half of the Earth and 21st December in the southern half

summertime /'sʌməˌtaɪm/ noun [U] the period of the year when it is summer

summing-up /ˌsʌmɪŋ 'ʌp/ noun [C] LAW a statement made by a lawyer or judge that gives a summary of the evidence in a case

summit /'sʌmɪt/ noun [C] **1** a meeting or series of meetings between leaders of two or more countries: *a summit of EU leaders* **2** GEOGRAPHY the top of a mountain **3** the highest level of achievement in something: *His appointment as a cabinet minister was the summit of his career.*

summon /'sʌmən/ verb [T] **1** *formal* to officially order someone to come to a place: *He was urgently summoned to Washington for consultations.* **2** to manage to produce a quality or a reaction that helps you to deal with a difficult situation: *She could barely summon a smile.*

summons¹ /'sʌmənz/ noun [C] LAW an official document that orders someone to appear in a court of law

summons² /'sʌmənz/ verb [T] LAW to order someone to appear in court

sumo /'suːməʊ/ or ,sumo 'wrestling noun [U] SPORTS a Japanese sport in which two very large men wrestle —,sumo 'wrestler noun [C]

sump /sʌmp/ noun [C] ENGINEERING the bowl-shaped part at the bottom of a vehicle engine that holds the oil

sumptuous /'sʌmptʃuəs/ adj impressive, expensive, and of high quality —**sumptuously** adv

sun /sʌn/ noun **1 the Sun** or **the sun** ASTRONOMY the star that is nearest to the Earth and that provides the Earth with energy in the form of light and heat. All the planets in the solar system move in orbit around the Sun. —*picture* → ECLIPSE, SOLAR SYSTEM, WATER CYCLE **2** [singular/U] the light and heat that you feel from the sun: *Miriam was sitting **in the sun** reading a book.* **3** [C] ASTRONOMY a very bright star, especially one that a planet travels round

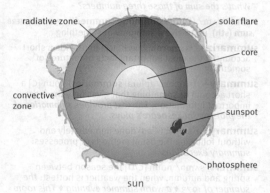

radiative zone

solar flare

core

convective zone

sunspot

photosphere

sun

Sun. abbrev Sunday

sunbathe /'sʌnˌbeɪð/ verb [I] to sit or lie in the sun so that your skin becomes darker —**sunbather** noun [C], **sunbathing** noun [U]

sunburn /'sʌnˌbɜːn/ noun [U] sore skin that is caused by staying in the sun for too long

sunburnt /'sʌnˌbɜːnt/ or **sunburned** /'sʌnˌbɜːnd/ adj skin that is sunburnt is sore from too much sun

Sunday /'sʌndeɪ/ noun [C/U] the day after Saturday and before Monday: *Our next meeting is on a Sunday.* ♦ *I'm going to visit my parents next Sunday.* ♦ *Are you doing anything nice **on Sunday**?* ♦ *We usually go to church **on Sundays** (=every Sunday).*

'Sunday ,school noun [C/U] RELIGION religious lessons for children that are given in a church on Sundays

sundial /'sʌnˌdaɪəl/ noun [C] an object that measures time by the position of a shadow made in sunny weather

'sun-,dried adj sun-dried fruit and vegetables have been put in the sun to dry in order to preserve them and give them a strong flavour

sunflower /'sʌnˌflaʊə/ noun [C] a very tall plant that has large yellow flowers with a round brown centre

sung /sʌŋ/ the past participle of **sing**

sunglasses /'sʌnˌglɑːsɪz/ noun [plural] dark glasses that you wear to protect your eyes when the sun is bright

sunk /sʌŋk/ the past participle of **sink**

sunken /'sʌŋkən/ adj **1** lying at the bottom of the sea **2** lower than the level of the surrounding land or floor **3** sunken eyes or cheeks curve inwards, often showing that someone is ill or old

sunlight /'sʌnˌlaɪt/ noun [U] the light from the sun: *strong sunlight* —*picture* → POLLUTION

sunlit /'sʌnlɪt/ adj brightly lit by the sun

Sunni /'sʊni/ (plural **Sunnis** or **Sunni**) noun RELIGION **1** [U] one of the two groups within the religion of Islam **2** [C] a Muslim who belongs to this group → SHIITE

sunny /'sʌni/ (**sunnier, sunniest**) adj **1** bright with light from the sun: *It was a beautiful sunny day.* **2** happy: *a sunny smile*

sunrise /'sʌnˌraɪz/ noun [C/U] the time in the early morning when the sun first appears in the sky, or the way that the sky looks at this time → SUNSET

'sunrise ,industry noun [C] BUSINESS a new industry, especially one using advanced technology, that is growing and developing quickly → SUNSET INDUSTRY

sunscreen /'sʌnˌskriːn/ noun [C/U] a cream that you can rub onto your skin to stop it from being burned by the sun

sunset /'sʌnˌset/ noun [C/U] the time in the evening when the sun goes down below the horizon and night begins, or the way that the sky looks at this time → SUNRISE

'sunset ,industry noun [C] BUSINESS an old industry that is becoming less successful or important, especially because demand for its products is falling → SUNRISE INDUSTRY

sunshine /'sʌnˌʃaɪn/ noun [U] light from the sun: *We set off in bright sunshine.*

sunspot /'sʌnˌspɒt/ noun [C] ASTRONOMY a dark area on the surface of the Sun —*picture* → SUN

suntan /'sʌnˌtæn/ noun [C] a darker colour that someone's skin gets when they have spent time in the sun —**suntanned** adj, **suntanning** noun [U]

super- /suːpə/ prefix more, better, or bigger than usual: *a superhero* ♦ *supersonic*

superb /sʊ'pɜːb/ adj of the highest quality = EXCELLENT —**superbly** adv

supercilious /ˌsuːpə'sɪliəs/ adj a supercilious person behaves as if they think they are better or more important than everyone else —**superciliously** adv, **superciliousness** noun [U]

superconductivity /ˌsuːpəˌkɒndʌk'tɪvəti/ noun [U] CHEMISTRY, PHYSICS the ability of some metals to allow electricity to pass through them at very low temperatures without any resistance

superconductor /ˌsuːpəkən'dʌktə/ noun [C] CHEMISTRY, PHYSICS a metal that allows electricity to pass through it at very low temperatures without any resistance

superficial /ˌsuːpə'fɪʃ(ə)l/ adj **1** affecting or involving only the surface or outside part of something = MINOR: *Her injuries were only superficial.* **2** not complete or thorough = CURSORY: *a superficial examination of the damage* **3** a superficial person does not think about serious or important things = SHALLOW **4** *formal* in or part of the top layer of something such as skin, soil, or rock —**superficially** adv

superfluous /suːˈpɜːfluəs/ adj not needed or wanted

superfood /ˈsuːpəˌfuːd/ noun [C] a food that is considered to be very good for people's health and that may even help some medical conditions

Superglue /ˈsuːpəˌgluː/ TRADEMARK a type of very strong glue that sticks things together very quickly

superhuman /ˌsuːpəˈhjuːmən/ adj superhuman qualities are much greater and more impressive than those of an ordinary person

superimpose /ˌsuːpərɪmˈpəʊz/ verb [T] **1** to put one image on top of another so that both can be seen **2** to add something such as a feature or idea from one system or situation to another

superintendent /ˌsuːpərɪnˈtendənt/ noun [C] **1** a senior police officer in the UK **2** someone whose job is to be in charge of an area or an activity

superior¹ /suːˈpɪəriə/ adj **1** of high quality, or better or bigger than something else: *The hotel's service is superior.* ♦ *The sound quality is **superior to** that on a regular CD.* **2** behaving as if you think that you are better than other people: *I can't stand that superior smile of his.* **3** having a higher status or position than someone or something else: *Rockwood was charged with disobeying a **superior officer**.*

superior² /suːˈpɪəriə/ noun [C] **1** someone who is senior to you in an organization or job **2** formal someone who is more skilful than you at an activity

superiority /suːˌpɪəriˈɒrəti/ noun [U] **1** the fact that one person or thing is better than another **2** a way of behaving that shows that you think you are better than other people

superlative¹ /suːˈpɜːlətɪv/ adj LANGUAGE a superlative adjective or adverb is one that expresses the greatest degree of a particular quality. For example the superlative form of 'happy' is 'happiest'. → COMPARATIVE¹

superlative² /suːˈpɜːlətɪv/ noun [singular] LANGUAGE the superlative form of an adjective or an adverb

supermarket /ˈsuːpəˌmɑːkɪt/ noun [C] a very large shop that sells food and other products for the home

supernatural /ˌsuːpəˈnætʃərəl/ adj used about things that seem to be caused by magic and do not have a natural or scientific explanation

the supernatural /ˌsuːpəˈnætʃərəl/ noun [singular] supernatural events, forces, or creatures

supernova /ˈsuːpəˌnəʊvə/ noun [C] ASTRONOMY an exploding star that produces an extremely bright light

superordinate /ˌsuːpərˈɔːdɪnət/ noun [C] LANGUAGE a word that includes the meaning of more specific words. For example, 'vehicle' is the superordinate of words such as 'car' and 'truck'.

superpower /ˈsuːpəˌpaʊə/ noun [C] a country that has great military, economic, and political power

superscript /ˈsuːpəˌskrɪpt/ adj written or printed in very small print above, and after, a letter, number, or symbol —**superscript** noun [C/U]

supersede /ˌsuːpəˈsiːd/ verb [T] if one thing supersedes another, it replaces the other thing, especially because it is more modern or more useful

supersonic /ˌsuːpəˈsɒnɪk/ adj faster than the speed of sound

superstition /ˌsuːpəˈstɪʃ(ə)n/ noun [C/U] a belief that things such as magic or luck have the power to affect your life —**superstitious** /ˌsuːpəˈstɪʃəs/ adj

superstructure /ˈsuːpəˌstrʌktʃə/ noun [C] CONSTRUCTION the part of a ship that is above the main deck, or the part of a building that is above its **foundations** (=the parts below ground)

supervise /ˈsuːpəvaɪz/ verb [I/T] to be in charge of people and check that they are behaving or working correctly: *His job was to supervise the loading of the ship.* —**supervision** /ˌsuːpəˈvɪʒ(ə)n/ noun [U]: *Here children can play safely **under supervision**.*

super'vision ˌorder noun [C] LAW a court order that says that a child must be looked after by a **social worker**

supervisor /ˈsuːpəˌvaɪzə/ noun [C] someone who is in charge of an activity, a place, or a group of people —**supervisory** /ˌsuːpəˈvaɪzəri/ adj

supper /ˈsʌpə/ noun [C/U] a meal that you eat in the evening → DINNER

supplant /səˈplɑːnt/ verb [T] formal to replace something or someone, often as a result of being more powerful

supple /ˈsʌp(ə)l/ adj able to move and bend easily —**suppleness** noun [U]

supplement¹ /ˈsʌplɪment/ verb [T] **1** to add something extra in order to improve something: *a balanced diet **supplemented with** vitamin tablets* **2** to add extra money to the amount that you normally earn: *He was able to supplement his income by writing stories.*

supplement² /ˈsʌplɪmənt/ noun [C] **1** something extra that you add to make something better **2** a separate part of a newspaper or magazine **3** an extra amount of money that you have to pay for special services, especially in a hotel

supplementary /ˌsʌplɪˈment(ə)ri/ adj additional

ˌsupplementary ˈangles noun [plural] MATHS two adjacent angles that make 180° when they are added together —*picture* → ANGLE

supplier /səˈplaɪə/ noun [C] a company, organization, or country that supplies or sells a product or service: *Colombia is our main **supplier of** coffee beans.*

supply¹ /səˈplaɪ/ (plural **supplies**) noun **1** [C] an amount or quantity of something that is available to use: *The crops need **a** constant **supply of** water.* ♦ *electricity supplies* **2** supplies [plural] things such as food, medicine, and equipment that you need to live or to perform a particular activity: *The trucks carried medicine and other supplies across the border.* **3** [U] the act or process of providing something that is needed: *This muscle controls the supply of blood to the heart.*

PHRASES **in short supply** available only in small quantities, so that there is not enough: *Water was in short supply.*

supply and demand ECONOMICS the relationship between how much of a particular product is available and how much of it people want, and especially the way this affects the level of prices

supply² /səˈplaɪ/ (**supplies, supplying, supplied**) verb [T] to provide someone or something with something that they need or want: *Two huge generators supply power to farms in the area.* ♦ *They used the money to supply the school with new textbooks.*

sup'ply ˌchain noun [C] BUSINESS the series of processes that is involved in producing goods and supplying them to customers

sup'ply-side eco,nomics noun [U] ECONOMICS economic policies that involve helping companies that supply goods and services, in order to improve the economy

support¹ /sə'pɔːt/ verb [T]

1 approve of/help	**5** help to prove sth
2 help a friend	**6** like a sports team
3 hold/bear weight	**7** in computing
4 provide sth necessary	

1 to approve of an idea or a person or organization, and help them to be successful: *Of course we all support the prime minister.*

2 to help someone and be kind to them when they are in a difficult situation: *My friends have supported me through the entire trial.*

3 to hold the weight of someone or something so that they do not move or fall: *The plants were supported with wire.* ♦ *She was sitting up in bed, supported by pillows.*

4 to provide someone with the money, food, shelter, or other things that they need in order to live: *How can we support our families on such low wages?* ♦ *She's been supporting herself since she was 18 years old.*

5 to show that an idea, statement, theory etc is true or correct: *Our **conclusions** are **supported** by extensive research.*

6 SPORTS to like a particular sports team and always want them to win: *I support West Ham – who do you support?* → SUPPORTER

7 COMPUTING to provide information and material that keep a computer system or program working: *Does the company still support that version of the program?*

support² /sə'pɔːt/ noun

1 help/approval	**4** sth that holds sth
2 money	**5** proof
3 kindness	**6** performer in show

1 [U] help and approval that you give to a particular idea, politician, organization etc: *I urge my colleagues to join me **in support of** this plan.*

2 [U] money that is provided to a person or organization in order to help them: *financial **support for** local bus services*

3 [U] help and kindness that you give to someone who is having a difficult time: *I am grateful to my family for their love and support.*

4 [C/U] CONSTRUCTION something that holds the weight of an object, building, or structure so that it does not move or fall

5 [U] proof that something is true or correct: *Do you have any **support for** your theory?*

6 [U] ARTS someone who performs in a show or concert but is not the main performer

supporter /sə'pɔːtə/ noun [C] **1** someone who supports a particular idea, person, or group: *Jarvis is a strong **supporter of** the European Union.* **2** SPORTS someone who likes to watch a particular sports team and wants that team to win= FAN: *Barcelona supporters*

supporting /sə'pɔːtɪŋ/ adj **1** ARTS used about a part in a play or film that is important but is not the main part: *a supporting role* **2** CONSTRUCTION holding the weight of something, especially in a building **3** helping to prove that a theory or claim is true: *supporting evidence*

supportive /sə'pɔːtɪv/ adj helpful and sympathetic to someone who is having a difficult time

suppose /sə'pəʊz/ verb [T] to think that something is probably true, right, or possible: *You don't suppose that he's going to hurt anyone, do you?* ♦ *I suppose I had*

better get back to work. ♦ *We have **no reason to suppose that** he's done anything illegal.*

PHRASES **be supposed to do/be sth 1** to be expected to behave in a particular way, especially according to a rule, an agreement, or someone in authority: *You're supposed to make a copy of the contract before you mail it.* **2** to be generally considered to have a particular quality or skill: *Latin America is supposed to be a pretty inexpensive place to travel in.* **3** to be expected or intended to happen in a particular way or have a particular result: *The new regulations are supposed to help single parents.*

suppose/supposing (that) used for introducing a possible situation or action and the results of it: *Suppose you won the lottery, what would you do with the money?*

supposed /sə'pəʊzd, sə'pəʊzɪd/ adj believed or said by some people to be true, although you may not agree with this: *the supposed economic benefits of lower taxes*

supposedly /sə'pəʊzɪdli/ adv as some people believe or say, although you may not agree with this: *The house is supposedly haunted.*

suppress /sə'pres/ verb [T] **1** to stop political opposition, protests, or other forms of disagreement, especially by using force or strict laws: *The revolt was brutally suppressed.* **2** to stop yourself from feeling or showing an emotion: *suppressed anger* **3** to stop a physical process from happening or developing: *chemicals that suppress weeds* —**suppression** /sə'preʃ(ə)n/ noun [U]

supremacy /sʊ'preməsi/ noun [U] a situation in which one person, group, or thing has more power or influence than any other

supreme /sʊ'priːm/ adj **1** most important or powerful: *the Supreme Commander of the Allied Forces* **2** very great: *The Church was of supreme importance in medieval Europe.*

su,preme 'court noun [C] LAW the most important court in some countries and in most states of the US

supremely /sʊ'priːmli/ adv extremely, or to the highest possible degree

surcharge /'sɜːtʃɑːdʒ/ noun [C] an extra amount of money that you must pay for something

sure¹ /ʃɔː, ʃʊə/ adj **1** certain that something is real, true, or correct: *I was sure I had left my keys on the counter.* ♦ *No one is really sure why he resigned.* ♦ *I think she's called Monica, but **I'm not sure**.* ♦ *If you're really **sure about** the facts, we'll publish them.* **2** certain to happen or succeed: *Everyone thought that the deal was **a sure thing** (=that it would definitely happen).* ♦ *If you stay up late, you're **sure to** feel rotten in the morning.* **3** used about something that is definite and cannot be questioned or doubted: *Bill was biting his nails, **a sure sign** that he was worried.*

PHRASES **for sure** definitely, or definitely true: *I will call you tomorrow for sure.* ♦ *Ashe was an incredible tennis player, **that's for sure**.*

make sure 1 to check something, so that you can be certain about it: *I just wanted to make sure you knew where to go.* ♦ *Always **make sure of** your facts before accusing anyone.* **2** to take the action that is necessary for something to happen: *Police were there to make sure there was no violence.*

sure of yourself confident

sure² /ʃɔː, ʃʊə/ adv *spoken* used for saying yes or agreeing to something: *'Can I borrow your green jumper?' 'Sure, no problem.'*

PHRASE **sure enough** used for saying that something happened exactly as you thought it would: *I had a feeling we'd get lost, and sure enough, we did.*

surely /'ʃɔːli, 'ʃʊəli/ adv used for showing that you think that something is very likely: *Surely you realized we were at home when you saw the lights on?*

surety /'ʃʊərəti/ noun **LAW** **stand surety (for sb)** to be responsible for paying money that is owed, or for making certain that someone goes to court when they should

surf¹ /sɜːf/ verb **1** [I] to ride on waves in the sea on a **surfboard 2** [I/T] **COMPUTING** to look at various places one after another on the Internet or on television: *She spends hours every day just surfing the Net.* —**surfer** noun [C], **surfing** noun [U]

surf² /sɜːf/ noun [U] waves that are falling onto a beach

surface¹ /'sɜːfɪs/ noun **1** [C] the top layer or outside part of something: *a rough surface* ♦ *Road surfaces are slippery from the rain.* ♦ *We saw fish swimming just under the surface of the water.* **2** [C] a flat area: *All surfaces in the kitchen should be carefully cleaned.* ♦ *Some players complained that the surface was too slippery.* **3** [singular] an appearance that is different from what someone or something is really like: *On the surface, they looked like a happily married couple.* **4** [C] **MATHS** one of the sides of an object

surface² /'sɜːfɪs/ verb **1** [I] if something surfaces, it appears, or people start to notice it: *New information about the murder is slowly surfacing.* **2** [I] to come up to the surface of water: *The divers were forced to surface after their equipment was damaged.* **3** [T] to put a smooth surface on a road

surface³ /'sɜːfɪs/ adj **1** on the surface of something: *the surface temperature of the lake* **2** travelling on the surface of land or water, rather than through the air: *surface mail*

'surface ,area noun [C] **MATHS, SCIENCE** the total area of a surface or surfaces, especially the outside surfaces of an object

'surface de,velopment noun [C] **MATHS, PHYSICS** a drawing that shows the shape of the outer surface of an object such as a box as a flat object

surface grinder /'sɜːfɪs ,ɡraɪndə/ noun [C] **ENGINEERING** a **machine tool** that **grinds** (=rubs) surfaces until they are smooth

'surface ,plate noun [C] **TECHNOLOGY** a flat metal plate that is used to check that other surfaces are completely level

'surface ,structure noun [U] **LANGUAGE** the structure that a sentence has when you consider only the classes of its words, as opposed to the **logical** relationships on which this structure is based → DEEP STRUCTURE

,surface 'tension noun [U] **PHYSICS** the force by which the molecules of a liquid stay close together at the surface to form the smallest possible area. Surface tension is what makes it possible for small insects to walk on the surface of water.

,surface-to-'air adj used to describe a missile that is fired from the ground or from a ship to hit aircraft or other missiles in the air

'surface ,water noun [U] **ENVIRONMENT** rain that falls on the surface of the ground, or in rivers, lakes, or the sea, that has not yet **drained away** or evaporated

surfboard /'sɜːfbɔːd/ noun [C] a long narrow board that someone stands or lies on to ride on waves

surfeit /'sɜːfɪt/ noun **a surfeit of sth** *formal* too much of something

surge¹ /sɜːdʒ/ noun [singular] **1** a sudden increase in something: *a surge in spending* **2** a sudden movement of a large group of people **3** a sudden strong feeling: *a surge of emotion*

surge² /sɜːdʒ/ verb [I] **1** if a crowd of people surges, they all move forward together very quickly **2** to increase a lot very quickly **3** if a feeling surges, you start to feel it very strongly: *Panic surged inside her.*

surgeon /'sɜːdʒ(ə)n/ noun [C] **HEALTH** a doctor who is trained to perform operations

'surge pro,tector noun [C] **COMPUTING** a piece of equipment used for protecting computers from damage caused by a sudden increase in electrical power

surgery /'sɜːdʒəri/ (plural **surgeries**) noun **HEALTH** **1** [U] medical treatment in which a doctor cuts open someone's body **2** [C] a place where people can visit a doctor or a dentist

surgical /'sɜːdʒɪk(ə)l/ adj **HEALTH** connected with surgery —**surgically** /'sɜːdʒɪkli/ adv

surly /'sɜːli/ adj unfriendly and rude

surmise /sə'maɪz/ verb [T] *formal* to guess that something is true, without having enough information to prove that it is true

surname /'sɜː,neɪm/ noun [C] the part of someone's name that is their family's name = FAMILY NAME, LAST NAME

surpass /sə'pɑːs/ verb [T] **1** to be better or bigger than something else = EXCEED: *Temperatures surpassed 42 degrees Celsius.* **2** to be even better than what was expected or hoped for: *Winning the gold medal surpassed my wildest dreams.*

surplice /'sɜːplɪs/ noun [C] **RELIGION** a loose white piece of clothing worn over other clothes by priests, church singers, and people who help during church ceremonies

surplus¹ /'sɜːpləs/ noun [C/U] **1** a larger amount of something than is necessary: *a surplus of oil* **2** **ECONOMICS** an amount of money by which the income and **assets** of a country, business, or organization is greater than its **expenditure** and **liabilities** (=debts)

surplus² /'sɜːpləs/ adj more than is needed: *They should use the surplus cash to help people who need it.*

surprise¹ /sə'praɪz/ noun **1** [C] an unusual event, or an unexpected piece of news: *I have a surprise for you.* ♦ *The news came as a big surprise to everyone.* **2** [U] the feeling that you have when something unusual or unexpected happens: *Many students expressed surprise at the news.* ♦ *Much to my surprise, the restaurant was actually very nice.*
PHRASE **take/catch sb by surprise** to surprise someone by happening unexpectedly: *The storm caught the fishermen completely by surprise.*

surprise² /sə'praɪz/ verb [T] **1** to give someone a feeling of surprise: *Her angry tone of voice surprised me.* ♦ *It wouldn't surprise me if it snowed tonight.* **2** to attack someone when they do not expect it **3** to discover someone doing something bad or embarrassing: *A teacher surprised the boys smoking.*

surprised /sə'praɪzd/ adj **1** feeling surprise because something unexpected has happened: *We were surprised at Ben's reaction to the news.* ♦ *I wouldn't be surprised if he got married again soon.* ♦ *I wasn't surprised to hear that their marriage had ended.* **2** showing surprise: *a surprised look*

surprising /səˈpraɪzɪŋ/ adj unusual or unexpected: *It's surprising what you can achieve with so little money.* ♦ *It's **hardly surprising** (=not at all surprising) that she's angry, considering what you said.* —**surprisingly** adv: *It's a small house, but the garden is surprisingly large.*

surreal /səˈrɪəl/ adj something surreal is so strange that you cannot believe that it is real

surrealism /səˈrɪə,lɪz(ə)m/ noun [U] **ARTS, LITERATURE** a 20th-century style of art and literature that tried to represent dreams and unconscious experience using unusual combinations of images —**surrealist** adj, **surrealist** noun [C]

surrender[1] /səˈrendə/ verb **1** [I] if soldiers surrender, they stop fighting and officially admit that they have been defeated **2** [T] to give something to someone in authority because you have to: *She was ordered to surrender her passport.*

surrender[2] /səˈrendə/ noun [U] **1** an occasion when soldiers stop fighting and officially admit that they have been defeated **2** the act of giving up something because someone in authority demands it

surreptitious /ˌsʌrəpˈtɪʃəs/ adj done quietly or secretly so that other people will not notice —**surreptitiously** adv

surrogate mother /ˌsʌrəgət ˈmʌðə/ noun [C] a woman who gives birth to a baby for another woman who cannot have children

surround /səˈraʊnd/ verb [T] **1** to be all around something or someone: *Armed police quickly surrounded the building.* ♦ *People are **surrounding** their homes **with** barbed wire fences.* **2** to be closely connected with a situation or an event: *Uncertainty surrounds the future of the industry.* **3** to be near someone all the time: *She grew up **surrounded by** older children.*

surrounding /səˈraʊndɪŋ/ adj around a place: *The hotel is ideally located for visiting the surrounding area.*

surˈrounding ˌnet noun [C] a net used in fishing that is laid out by a boat and that catches large numbers of fish close to the surface of the water

surroundings /səˈraʊndɪŋz/ noun [plural] a place and all the things in it: *She soon became accustomed to her new surroundings.*

surtax /ˈsɜː,tæks/ noun [C] **ECONOMICS** an additional tax on something on which people already pay tax, especially a high income

surveillance /səˈveɪləns/ noun [U] if the police keep someone under surveillance, they watch them closely

survey[1] /ˈsɜːveɪ/ (plural **surveys**) noun [C] **1** a set of questions that you ask in order to find out people's opinions: *We **carried out a survey** of local housing needs.* **2** an examination of the condition of something, especially a house **3 GEOGRAPHY** an examination of land by someone who is making a map **4** a general book or programme about a subject

survey[2] /səˈveɪ, ˈsɜːveɪ/ (**surveys, surveying, surveyed**) verb [T] **1** to ask people questions in order to find out their opinions: *19% of those surveyed say they haven't decided who they will vote for.* **2** to look at or examine something: *He sat quietly, **surveying the scene** around him.* **3 GEOGRAPHY** to examine an area of land in order to make a map of it, or in order to decide where buildings will go

surveyor /səˈveɪə/ noun [C] **1 GEOGRAPHY** someone whose job is to measure land in order to make maps **2** someone whose job is to examine a house or other building to see if it is in good condition, especially for someone who wants to buy it

survival /səˈvaɪv(ə)l/ noun [U] the fact that someone is still alive, or the fact that something still exists: *survival equipment* ♦ *These animals face a constant **fight for survival**.*

survive /səˈvaɪv/ verb [I/T] **1** to continue to exist or live despite a difficult or dangerous situation: *Only one of the museum's paintings survived the fire.* ♦ *How does the family **survive on** such a small monthly wage?* **2** to stay alive after an injury, illness, or attack: *Doctors don't think the victims will survive.* ♦ *Just eight passengers **survived** the plane **crash**.* **3** to manage to deal with something difficult or unpleasant: *Don't worry about Molly – she'll survive.*

surviving /səˈvaɪvɪŋ/ adj still alive or existing

survivor /səˈvaɪvə/ noun [C] someone who is still alive after an injury, illness, or attack

susceptible /səˈseptəb(ə)l/ adj likely to be influenced or affected by something: *Children are particularly **susceptible to** the disease.* —**susceptibility** /sə,septəˈbɪləti/ noun [U]

sushi /ˈsuːʃi/ noun [U] Japanese food that consists of cold rice with fish, egg, or vegetables

suspect[1] /səˈspekt/ verb [T] **1** to believe that something is true: *Police suspected that she had some connection with the robbery.* **2** to think that someone might have done something bad: *He wrote a letter naming the people whom he suspected.* ♦ *men **suspected of** involvement in the bombing* **3** to think that something might be bad: *Carl seemed very kind, but she suspected his motives.*

> **Word family: suspect**
>
> *Words in the same family as **suspect***
> - **suspected** adj
> - **suspicion** n
> - **suspicious** adj
> - **suspiciously** adv
> - **unsuspecting** adj

suspect[2] /ˈsʌspekt/ noun [C] **1** someone who might have committed a crime: *a murder suspect* **2** something that might have caused something bad

suspect[3] /ˈsʌspekt/ adj **1** something that is suspect might not be good, honest, or reliable: *suspect motives* **2** a suspect object might be dangerous or illegal: *a suspect package*

suspend /səˈspend/ verb [T] **1** to order someone to leave their job or school for a short period of time as a punishment **2** to officially stop something for a short time: *Operations at the plant have been suspended because of safety concerns.* **3** *formal* to hang something from something else

suspended sentence /sə,spendɪd ˈsentəns/ noun [C] **LAW** time that someone will have to spend in prison only if they commit another crime within a fixed period

suspense /səˈspens/ noun [U] the excited or worried feeling that you have when you are waiting for something to happen: *Please don't **keep** me **in suspense**. I need to know!*

suspension /səˈspenʃ(ə)n/ noun **1** [C/U] the act of officially stopping something for a period of time: *the **suspension of** the peace talks* **2** [C/U] a punishment in which someone is forced to leave their job or school for a short period of time **3** [U] **ENGINEERING** the equipment that makes a vehicle move smoothly when it goes over rough ground **4** [C] **CHEMISTRY** a liquid that contains very small pieces of solid material

susˈpension ˌbridge noun [C] a type of bridge that hangs from strong steel ropes that are fixed to towers

suspension damper /səˈspenʃ(ə)n ˌdæmpə/ noun [C] **ENGINEERING** a **shock absorber** in a vehicle's **suspension** system

suspensory ligament /sə,spensəri 'ligəmənt/ noun [C] **ANATOMY** a set of fibres within the body that supports an organ or another body part, especially the one that holds the lens of the eye in place —*picture* → EYE

suspicion /sə'spɪʃ(ə)n/ noun **1** [C/U] a feeling that something bad has happened: *She had a suspicion that Mr Engel was not being completely honest.* ♦ *They were both arrested on suspicion of murder.* **2** [U] a feeling that you do not trust someone: *an atmosphere of suspicion and hostility*

PHRASE under suspicion if someone is under suspicion, people think that they might have done something bad: *Several senior party members have come under suspicion.*

suspicious /sə'spɪʃəs/ adj **1** if you are suspicious, you do not trust someone or you think that something bad might have happened: *Colleagues became suspicious when he started acting strangely.* ♦ *a suspicious look* ♦ *People are often suspicious of strangers.* **2** if something is suspicious, you think that it might be bad or dangerous: *Customers noticed a suspicious package by the door.* —**suspiciously** adv

sustain /sə'steɪn/ verb [T] **1** to provide the conditions that allow something to happen or exist: *Can the country's economic growth be sustained?* ♦ *Only two of the planets could sustain life.* **2** *formal* to give someone strength, energy, or hope: *A cup of coffee isn't enough to sustain you until lunchtime.* **3** *formal* to experience something bad = SUFFER: *One of the officers sustained minor injuries in the fire.*

sustainable /sə'steɪnəb(ə)l/ adj **1** capable of continuing for a long time at the same level **2** **ENVIRONMENT** using methods that do not harm the environment —**sustainability** /sə,steɪnə'bɪləti/ noun [U], **sustainably** adv

su,stainable de'velopment noun [U] **ECONOMICS, ENVIRONMENT** the development of a country or region that does not use more **natural resources** than can be replaced and so does not harm the environment

sustained /sə'steɪnd/ adj continuing at the same level for a long time: *sustained economic growth*

sustenance /'sʌstənəns/ noun [U] *formal* food and drink

suture /'suːtʃə/ noun [C/U] **HEALTH** the stitch or stitches used for closing the edges of a cut

SW abbrev **PHYSICS** short wave

swab /swɒb/ noun [C] **HEALTH 1** a small piece of a soft substance that is used for cleaning injuries **2** a small amount of a substance from someone's body that a doctor is testing

swagger /'swægə/ verb [I] *showing disapproval* to walk in a proud confident way —**swagger** noun [singular]

swallow[1] /'swɒləʊ/ verb **1** [I/T] to make food or drink go down your throat and into your stomach: *She quickly swallowed the rest of her coffee.* ♦ *I had a sore throat and it hurt to swallow.* **2** [I] to make a movement in your throat as if you are swallowing food: *Tim swallowed nervously before replying.* **3** [T] *informal* to believe something that is unlikely to be true

PHRASE swallow your pride/disappointment etc to not allow your feelings of pride, disappointment etc to affect your behaviour: *He finally had to swallow his pride and ask for help.*

swallow[2] /'swɒləʊ/ noun [C] **1** a small bird whose tail has two long points —*picture* → BIRD **2** a movement in your throat that makes food or drink go down into your stomach

'swallow ,hole noun [C] **GEOLOGY** a sinkhole (=a circular hole in the ground)

swam /swæm/ the past tense of **swim**[1]

swamp[1] /swɒmp/ verb [T] **1** if someone is swamped, they have too much to deal with at one time: *Bookshops are always swamped with orders at Christmas.* **2** if a place is swamped, there are very large numbers of people in it: *The hotel foyer was suddenly swamped by reporters and photographers.* **3** to fill or cover something with water

swamp[2] /swɒmp/ noun [C/U] **GEOGRAPHY** an area of land that is covered by water —**swampy** adj

swampland /'swɒmp,lænd/ noun [C/U] **GEOGRAPHY** an area of land covered by a swamp

swan /swɒn/ noun [C] a large white bird with a long neck that lives near water —*picture* → BIRD

swap /swɒp/ (**swaps, swapping, swapped**) verb **1** [I/T] to give something to someone in exchange for something else: *If you like this one better, I'll swap with you.* ♦ *Members are encouraged to swap books with each other.* **2** [T] if people swap stories, ideas etc, they tell each other about their experiences or ideas

PHRASE swap places 1 if two people swap places, each person goes to the place where the other person was before **2** if two people swap places, each person goes into the situation in which the other person was before —**swap** noun [singular]

swarf /swɔːf/ noun [U] **TECHNOLOGY** small pieces of metal that are removed during operations such as **drilling** and **filing**

swarm[1] /swɔːm/ verb [I] **1** to go somewhere as a large crowd: *Fans swarmed onto the pitch to celebrate.* **2** if insects swarm, they fly together in a large group

swarm[2] /swɔːm/ noun [C] **1** a large group of insects flying together **2** a large number of people moving together as a group

swash /swɒʃ/ noun [C] **GEOGRAPHY** the water that goes onto the shore after a wave has reached its highest point and started to fall —*picture* → BACKWASH

swastika /'swɒstɪkə/ noun [C] a symbol in the shape of a cross with bent ends used as the symbol of the German Nazi party

swat /swɒt/ (**swats, swatting, swatted**) verb [T] to hit an insect and try to kill it

swathe /sweɪð/ noun [C] *formal* **1** a large area of land **2** a large number of people, or a large amount of something

PHRASE cut a (wide) swathe through sth to move through something and cause a lot of change or destruction

sway[1] /sweɪ/ verb **1** [I] to move or swing gently from side to side: *Their bodies swayed to the music.* **2** [T] to change someone's opinion: *Do not allow yourselves to be swayed by these arguments.*

sway[2] /sweɪ/ noun [singular] a gentle swinging movement from side to side

swear /sweə/ (**swears, swearing, swore** /swɔː/, **sworn** /swɔːn/) verb **1** [I] to use words that are deliberately offensive, for example because you are angry: *That's the first time I've ever heard him swear.* ♦ *She was shouting and swearing at everyone.* **2** [T] to make a sincere statement or promise: *She swears that this is the man who attacked her.* ♦ *Members have to swear an oath of secrecy.* ♦ *He swore to stay out of politics when he retired.*

swearing-in /,sweərɪŋ 'ɪn/ noun [C] an official ceremony in which someone beginning an important job formally promises to do their duty

swearword /'sweə,wɜːd/ noun [C] an offensive word that people use when they swear

sweat¹ /swet/ noun [U] **BIOLOGY** liquid containing waste substances that forms on the skin when someone is hot. The evaporation of sweat helps to cool the body: *She wiped the sweat off her forehead with a towel.*

sweat² /swet/ verb [I] **1 BIOLOGY** to produce sweat on the surface of the skin when you are hot, nervous, or ill: *She could feel the palms of her hands sweating.* **2** *informal* to feel very nervous or worried

'sweat ,duct noun [C] **ANATOMY** one of the many small tubes in the skin that take sweat up to the skin's surface —*picture* → SKIN

sweater /'swetə/ noun [C] a warm piece of clothing that covers the upper body and arms

'sweat ,gland noun [C] **ANATOMY** a gland in the skin that produces sweat —*picture* → SKIN

sweating /'swetɪŋ/ noun [U] **BIOLOGY** the process by which liquid containing waste produced by sweat glands forms on the skin as a result of hot conditions, physical exercise, illness, or **nervousness**

'sweat ,pore noun [C] **ANATOMY** a small hole in the skin through which sweat can leave the body —*picture* → SKIN

sweatshirt /'swet,ʃɜːt/ noun [C] a piece of clothing made of thick cotton that people wear on the upper part of the body for exercise or informal activities

sweatshop /'swet,ʃɒp/ noun [C] *informal* a factory where people work very hard in bad conditions and earn very little money

sweaty /'sweti/ adj covered in sweat, or smelling of sweat

swede /swiːd/ noun [C/U] a hard round yellow vegetable that grows under the ground

sweep¹ /swiːp/ (**sweeps, sweeping, swept** /swept/) verb **1** [T] to clean a floor using a long brush: *Her work consisted mainly of making coffee and **sweeping the floor**.* **2** [I/T] to move quickly or with a lot of force, or to take something somewhere quickly or with a lot of force: *The flood waters swept the car downstream.* ♦ *Fire swept through the building.* ♦ *Disease has swept through this remote city.* **3** [I] to go somewhere quickly and in a confident or angry way: *Several senior officials swept into the room.*
  PHRASE **sweep to power POLITICS** to win an election by a very large number of votes
  PHRASAL VERBS ,**sweep sth a'way** to destroy something, or to completely remove something: *Many people died when floods swept their homes away.*
  ,**sweep 'up** to clean a floor using a long brush

sweep² /swiːp/ noun [C] **1** a long wide curved area of land or water **2** a long smooth curved movement

sweeper /'swiːpə/ noun [C] **1 SPORTS** a player in a football team who plays behind the players in defence **2** a person or machine that sweeps a place clean, especially a street

sweeping /'swiːpɪŋ/ adj **1** a sweeping change or development has a major effect **2** a sweeping statement is too general to be true in every case **3** with a wide impressive curved shape

sweet¹ /swiːt/ adj **1** foods and drinks that are sweet taste like sugar ≠ SOUR: *This tea is too sweet.* **2** something that is sweet has a nice smell, sound, or appearance: *The room is filled with the sweet fragrance of flowers.* ♦ *a sweet little kitten* **3** kind and gentle: *He's such a sweet man.* ♦ *It was so sweet of you to help me.* —**sweetness** noun [U]

sweet² /swiːt/ noun **1** [C] a small piece of sweet food made with sugar **2** [C/U] a sweet food that you eat at the end of a meal = DESSERT

sweetcorn /'swiːt,kɔːn/ noun [U] the small yellow seeds of some types of **maize** plant that are cooked and eaten as a vegetable

sweeten /'swiːt(ə)n/ verb [T] **1** to make something taste sweeter **2** to make something such as an offer seem more attractive in order to persuade someone to accept it

sweetener /'swiːt(ə)nə/ noun [C/U] a substance that is added to food or drink to make it taste sweeter

sweetheart /'swiːt,hɑːt/ noun [C] **1** used especially by men for talking to a woman whose name they do not know. Many women find this use offensive. **2** *informal old-fashioned* a kind and helpful person

sweetly /'swiːtli/ adv **1** in a nice, kind, and gentle way **2** in a way that is nice to hear or smell

,**sweet 'pepper** noun [C] a **pepper**

,**sweet po'tato** noun [C] a vegetable with a sweet taste that is the swollen root of the plant. It has pink skin and pale pink or yellow flesh. —*picture* → VEGETABLE

swell¹ /swel/ (**swells, swelling, swelled** or **swollen** /'swəʊlən/) verb [I/T] **1** to become larger than normal, or to make something larger than normal: *My ankles tend to swell when I travel by air.* **2** to increase in amount or number, or to make something increase in amount or number
  PHRASAL VERB ,**swell 'up** to become larger than usual

swell² /swel/ noun [singular] the movement of the waves in the sea

swelling /'swelɪŋ/ noun [C] **HEALTH** an area of the body that has become bigger because of an injury or illness

sweltering /'swelt(ə)rɪŋ/ adj so hot that you feel uncomfortable

swept /swept/ the past tense and past participle of **sweep¹**

swerve /swɜːv/ verb [I] to change direction suddenly in order to avoid something —**swerve** noun [C]

swift /swɪft/ adj **1** happening quickly or immediately **2** moving quickly —**swiftly** adv

swim¹ /swɪm/ (**swims, swimming, swam** /swæm/, **swum** /swʌm/) verb **1** [I/T] to move through water by making movements with your arms and legs: *It's not safe to swim in the lake.* ♦ *Can you swim a length of the pool without stopping?* **2** [I] if your head is swimming, you cannot think or see clearly because you are tired or ill **3** [I] if things are swimming, they appear to be moving when you look at them, because you are tired or ill —**swimmer** noun [C], **swimming** noun [U]: *I go swimming every evening.*

swim² /swɪm/ noun [singular] an occasion when you swim: *Why don't we go for a swim this afternoon?*

'swim ,bladder noun [C] **BIOLOGY** a sac filled with air in the body of a fish that keeps it upright in water and prevents it from sinking

'swimming ,pool noun [C] a large structure filled with water for people to swim in

swindle /'swɪnd(ə)l/ verb [T] to cheat someone in order to get their money —**swindle** noun [C], **swindler** noun [C]

swine /swaɪn/ noun [C] **1** (plural **swines**) *informal* an extremely unpleasant man **2** (plural **swine**) an old word meaning 'pig'

swing¹ /swɪŋ/ (**swings, swinging, swung** /swʌŋ/) verb [I/T] **1** to move backwards and forwards from a point, or to make something move in this way: *Swing your **arms** loosely at your sides.* ♦ *The rope bridge was **swinging in** the breeze.* **2** to move with a wide curving movement, or to make something move in this way: *I swung the car into a narrow side street.* ♦ *She **swung round** and stared angrily at us.* **3** to change from one emotion or condition to another that is very different: *Public opinion has begun to **swing the other way** (=away from what it was before).* **4** to try to hit someone or something by making a smooth curving movement with the hand, a weapon, or a piece of sports equipment: *He **swung** the bat wildly **at** the ball, missing it completely.* ♦ *Mrs Shaw **swung at** the youth with her umbrella.*

swing² /swɪŋ/ noun [C] **1** an attempt to hit someone or something: *I clenched my fist and **took a swing at** him.* **2** SPORTS a curving movement that a player makes when they hit the ball with a **club** in golf **3** a change from one emotion or condition to one that is very different: *He suffers from severe **mood swings**.* **4** a seat that hangs from chains or ropes and moves backwards and forwards

PHRASE **in full swing** at a very busy or active stage: *The party was in full swing when they arrived.*

swipe /swaɪp/ verb [T] **1** to pass a plastic card through a piece of electronic equipment that reads the information on it **2** to swing your arm and hit someone or something

'swipe ,card noun [C] a plastic card that you pass through a piece of electronic equipment that reads the information stored on the card

swirl¹ /swɜːl/ verb [I] to move quickly in circles

swirl² /swɜːl/ noun [C] **1** a fast circular movement **2** a circular shape

swish /swɪʃ/ verb [I] to move quickly with a smooth gentle sound —**swish** noun [singular]

switch¹ /swɪtʃ/ verb **1** [I/T] to change from one thing to another, or to make something do this: *He used to vote Conservative, but he **switched to** Labour in 1997.* ♦ *Once you have learned the basics of word processing, **switching between** different programs is quite easy.* ♦ *They announced that the tournament would be **switched from** March **to** December.* **2** [T] to replace one object with another: *He was accused of switching price labels.*

PHRASAL VERBS **,switch (sth) 'off** if you switch off something such as a light or a machine, or if it switches off, it stops working: *The heating has switched off.* ♦ *I parked the car and switched off the engine.*
,switch (sth) 'on if you switch on something such as a light or a machine, or if it switches on, it starts working: *Don't switch on the light.* ♦ *The machine switches on automatically.*

switch² /swɪtʃ/ noun [C] **1** something such as a button or key that makes a piece of equipment work: *a light switch* ♦ *an on-off switch* —*picture* → ELECTRICITY **2** a change from one thing to another: *a major policy switch by Washington* ♦ *He said **the switch from** electric **to** solar power would be made soon.*

switchboard /'swɪtʃbɔːd/ noun [C] a large piece of equipment in an office, hotel, public building etc that a person called a **switchboard operator** uses to answer telephone calls, and connect the people calling with the people they want to speak to

swivel /'swɪv(ə)l/ (**swivels, swivelling, swivelled**) verb [I/T] to turn round a fixed point, or to make something turn in this way

swollen¹ /'swəʊlən/ adj **1** HEALTH bigger than usual because of an injury or illness **2** a swollen river or stream contains more water than normal

swollen² /'swəʊlən/ a past participle of **swell¹**

swoop /swuːp/ verb [I] **1** to move quickly and suddenly downwards through the air in order to attack something **2** to make an attack on a place suddenly and unexpectedly

sword /sɔːd/ noun [C] a weapon with a short handle and a long sharp blade —*picture* → WEAPON

swordfish /'sɔːd,fɪʃ/ (plural **swordfish**) noun [C] a large sea fish with a long upper jaw

swore /swɔː/ the past tense of **swear**

sworn¹ /swɔːn/ adj **1** done by someone who promises to tell the truth: *sworn testimony* **2** sworn enemies hate each other

sworn² /swɔːn/ the past participle of **swear**

swot¹ /swɒt/ (**swots, swotting, swotted**) verb [I] *informal* to study very hard, especially for an examination

swot² /swɒt/ noun [C] *informal, showing disapproval* a student who works extremely hard and has no time for other activities

SWOT analysis /'swɒt ə,næləsɪs/ noun [C/U] BUSINESS an examination of an organization's **strengths** and **weaknesses**, and the opportunities and threats it is likely to experience. It is used as a way of measuring how successful the organization can be, and as a way of planning for the future.

swum /swʌm/ the past participle of **swim¹**

swung /swʌŋ/ the past tense and past participle of **swing¹**

syllabic /sɪ'læbɪk/ adj LANGUAGE relating to or consisting of syllables

syllabification /sɪ,læbɪfɪ'keɪʃ(ə)n/ noun [U] LANGUAGE the division of words into syllables

syllable /'sɪləb(ə)l/ noun [C] LANGUAGE a part of a word that has only one vowel sound. For example, the word 'father' has two syllables.

syllable-timed /'sɪləb(ə)l ,taɪmd/ adj LANGUAGE in a syllable-timed language, each syllable has a regular rhythm and there are no **stresses** → STRESS-TIMED

syllabus /'sɪləbəs/ (plural **syllabuses** or **syllabi** /'sɪləbaɪ/) noun [C] EDUCATION a list of the main subjects in a course of study → CURRICULUM

symbiosis /,sɪmbaɪ'əʊsɪs/ noun [U] **1** a close relationship between two different things or people from which both get benefits **2** BIOLOGY a close connection between two different organisms from which both get benefits —**symbiotic** /,sɪmbaɪ'ɒtɪk/ adj: *a symbiotic relationship*

symbol /'sɪmb(ə)l/ noun [C] **1** someone or something that represents a particular idea or quality: *Many Catholics saw him as a **symbol of** hope.* **2** a mark, letter, or number that is used to represent something, for example in chemistry or music **3** a picture or shape that is used to represent something

symbolic /sɪm'bɒlɪk/ adj **1** representing something important: *This meeting has great symbolic importance for the people of Ireland.* **2** used as a symbol: *The wedding rings are **symbolic of** their love.* —**symbolically** /sɪm'bɒlɪkli/ adv

symbolism /'sɪmbə,lɪz(ə)m/ noun [U] **1** the use of symbols to represent something **2** the fact that an action or event is a sign of something important

symbolize /'sɪmbəlaɪz/ verb [T] **1** to be a symbol of something: *The cross symbolizes Christianity.* **2** to be considered as a perfect example of something: *For many people, cars symbolize personal freedom.*

symmetrical /sɪ'metrɪk(ə)l/ adj **MATHS** a symmetrical shape or object has two halves that are exactly the same —**symmetrically** /sɪ'metrɪkli/ adv

symmetry /'sɪmətri/ noun [U] **MATHS** the fact that something has two halves that are exactly the same

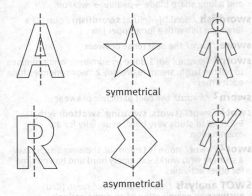

symmetrical

asymmetrical

sympathetic /ˌsɪmpə'θetɪk/ adj **1** willing to understand someone's problems and help them ≠ UNSYMPATHETIC: *You're not being very sympathetic.* ♦ *Jill was a sympathetic listener.* **2** if you are sympathetic to something such as a plan, you support it ≠ UNSYMPATHETIC **3** a sympathetic character is easy to like ≠ UNSYMPATHETIC —**sympathetically** /ˌsɪmpə'θetɪkli/ adv

sympathize /'sɪmpəθaɪz/ verb [I] **1** to behave in a kind way and show that you understand someone's problems: *We sympathize deeply with the families of the victims.* **2** to support something: *Many people admit they sympathize with the rebels' demands.*

sympathizer /'sɪmpəθaɪzə/ noun [C] someone who supports something

sympathy /'sɪmpəθi/ (plural **sympathies**) noun **1** [U] a feeling of kindness and understanding that you have for someone who is experiencing problems: *We all have great sympathy for the victims of the flood.* ♦ *It's his own fault, so he'll get no sympathy from me.* **2** [C/U] support for something such as a plan or a political party: *journalists with left-wing sympathies* ♦ *Do you have any sympathy with his point of view?* ♦ *Darwin himself had little sympathy for these ideas.*

symphony /'sɪmfəni/ (plural **symphonies**) noun [C] **MUSIC** a long piece of classical music played by an orchestra —**symphonic** /sɪm'fɒnɪk/ adj

'symphony ,orchestra noun [C] **MUSIC** a large orchestra that plays classical music

symposium /sɪm'pəʊziəm/ (plural **symposiums** or **symposia** /sɪm'pəʊziə/) noun [C] *formal* **1** a meeting where experts discuss a particular subject **2** a collection of articles on a particular subject that are published together in a book

symptom /'sɪmptəm/ noun [C] **1** **HEALTH** a sign that someone has an illness: *The symptoms include fever and vomiting.* ♦ *The symptoms of flu may last several days.* **2** a sign of a larger problem: *The fighting is a symptom of growing insecurity in the region.*

symptomatic /ˌsɪmptə'mætɪk/ adj **1** *formal* showing the existence of a problem or of a bad situation **2** **HEALTH** showing the symptoms of an illness

synagogue /'sɪnəgɒg/ noun [C] **RELIGION** a building that is used by Jewish people for religious services

synapse /'saɪnæps/ noun [C] **BIOLOGY** a space between nerve cells, across which nerve signals travel by means of **neurotransmitters**

synchromesh unit /'sɪŋkrəʊmeʃ ˌjuːnɪt/ noun [C] **ENGINEERING** a piece of equipment that makes a vehicle's **gears** move at the same speed, so that it is easier for the driver to change from one gear to another

synchronic /sɪŋ'krɒnɪk/ adj **LANGUAGE** relating to the study of something, especially a language, at one particular time without considering its history → DIACHRONIC

synchronize /'sɪŋkrənaɪz/ verb [T] to make two or more things happen at the same time or move at the same speed —**synchronization** /ˌsɪŋkrənaɪ'zeɪʃ(ə)n/ noun [U]

synchronized swimming /ˌsɪŋkrənaɪzd 'swɪmɪŋ/ noun [U] **SPORTS** a sport in which two or more swimmers perform complicated movements to music at the same time as each other

synchronous /'sɪŋkrənəs/ adj **PHYSICS** happening at the same time with the same frequency = SIMULTANEOUS

synclinal /sɪŋ'klaɪn(ə)l/ adj **GEOLOGY** in the form of a syncline

syncline /'sɪŋklaɪn/ noun [C] **GEOLOGY** a bend in a layer of underground rock that curves downwards in the shape of a **basin**. It has the youngest rocks at its core.

syncopated /'sɪŋkəˌpeɪtɪd/ adj **MUSIC** syncopated sounds or movements emphasize the weak beats instead of the strong beats

syncopation /ˌsɪŋkə'peɪʃ(ə)n/ noun [C/U] **MUSIC** a type of musical rhythm in which the weak beats are emphasized instead of the strong beats

syndicate /'sɪndɪkət/ noun [C] a group of people or organizations that work together to achieve something

syndrome /'sɪn,drəʊm/ noun [C] **1** **HEALTH** a set of different symptoms and conditions that are typical of a particular illness or medical condition **2** a set of feelings or actions that are typical in a particular situation

synonym /'sɪnənɪm/ noun [C] **LANGUAGE** a word that has the same meaning as another word → ANTONYM

synonymous /sɪ'nɒnɪməs/ adj **1** if one person or thing is synonymous with another, people think of one of them whenever they think of the other one **2** **LANGUAGE** if two words are synonymous, they have the same meaning

synonymy /sɪ'nɒnɪmi/ noun [U] **LANGUAGE** similar meaning in different words

synopsis /sɪ'nɒpsɪs/ (plural **synopses** /sɪ'nɒpsiːz/) noun [C] **LITERATURE, ARTS** a short summary of a book, play, or film

synoptic /sɪ'nɒptɪk/ adj **GEOGRAPHY** relating to or showing weather conditions experienced at the same time over a large area

synovial fluid /saɪ,nəʊviəl 'fluːɪd/ noun [U] **ANATOMY** liquid within the joints of the body that allows the bones to move smoothly —*picture* → JOINT

synovial joint /saɪ,nəʊviəl 'dʒɔɪnt/ noun [C] **ANATOMY** a type of joint in the body that contains fluid to help it to move smoothly

synovial membrane /saɪ,nəʊviəl 'membreɪn/ noun [C] **ANATOMY** the membrane that surrounds a synovial joint

syntactic /sɪn'tæktɪk/ adj **LANGUAGE** relating to syntax —**syntactically** /sɪn'tæktɪkli/ adv

syntax /'sɪntæks/ noun [U] **1 LANGUAGE** the rules about how words are arranged to make phrases and sentences **2 COMPUTING** rules about the ways in which computer languages can be used to make programs

synthesis /'sɪnθəsɪs/ (plural **syntheses** /'sɪnθəsiːz/) noun **1** [C] a combination of different ideas or styles that produces a new idea or style **2** [C/U] **SCIENCE** the process of producing a substance by a chemical reaction

synthesize /'sɪnθəsaɪz/ verb [T] **1 SCIENCE** to produce a new substance as a result of a chemical reaction **2** to combine different ideas or styles

synthetic /sɪn'θetɪk/ adj made from artificial substances

syphilis /'sɪfəlɪs/ noun [U] **HEALTH** a serious disease caused by a bacterium that is passed on through sexual contact

syringe /sɪ'rɪndʒ/ noun [C] **HEALTH** a plastic tube with a needle that is used for putting medicine, or sometimes illegal drugs, into the body through the skin. It can also be used for putting liquids into other substances. —*picture* → LABORATORY

syrup /'sɪrəp/ noun [C/U] a thick sweet liquid made from sugar and water

system /'sɪstəm/ noun

1 connected things	4 set of organs
2 way of organizing things	5 rules of society
3 body	+ PHRASE

1 [C] a set of connected things that work together: *a central heating system* ♦ *the public transport system* ♦ *a new computer system*
2 [C] a method of organizing things or doing things: *a political system* ♦ *the criminal justice system* ♦ *They are introducing a new system for delivering information to the public.* ♦ *a democratic system of government*
3 [U] **BIOLOGY** the body considered as a set of connected organs, tubes etc: *Lack of sleep can be hard on the system.*
4 [U] **BIOLOGY** a set of organs, tubes etc in your body that work together: *the circulatory system*
5 the system [singular] **SOCIAL STUDIES** the rules, laws, and structures that control how a society operates: *You can't **beat the system**.*
PHRASE get sb/sth out of your system *informal* to get rid of strong feelings about someone or something → IMMUNE SYSTEM

systematic /,sɪstə'mætɪk/ adj done according to a careful plan —**systematically** /,sɪstə'mætɪkli/ adv

syste,matic circu'lation noun [U] **BIOLOGY** the movement of blood from the left side of the heart to the rest of the body

systematize /'sɪstəmətaɪz/ verb [T] *formal* to organize something according to a system

'system ,disk noun [C] **COMPUTING** a disk that holds the **system software**

systemic /sɪ'stiːmɪk, sɪ'stemɪk/ adj **1** affecting all of something **2 BIOLOGY** affecting the whole body —**systemically** /sɪ'stiːmɪkli, sɪ'stemɪkli/ adv

,system 'operator noun [C] **COMPUTING** someone whose job is to manage a **bulletin board** or a computer system

'systems a,nalysis noun [U] **COMPUTING** the job of planning and improving the way businesses and organizations use computers

,systems 'analyst noun [C] **COMPUTING** someone whose job is to plan or improve the way that a business or organization uses computers

'system ,software noun [U] **COMPUTING** the **operating system** and programs used to operate a computer system → APPLICATION SOFTWARE

systolic pressure /sɪs'tɒlɪk ,preʃə/ noun [U] **HEALTH** a person's blood pressure when the heart is contracting. It is the first of the two numbers given when saying what someone's blood pressure is.

T t

t /tiː/ (plural **t's**) or **T** (plural **T's**) noun [C/U] the 20th letter of the English alphabet → T-SHIRT

tab¹ /tæb/ noun [C] **1 tab** or **tab key COMPUTING** a button on a computer keyboard that you press in order to move several spaces along the same line **2** a part that you pull to open something

tab² /tæb/ (**tabs, tabbing, tabbed**) verb [I] **COMPUTING** to press the tab on a computer keyboard

tabla /'tæblə/ noun [C] **MUSIC** an Indian musical instrument consisting of two drums joined together

table /'teɪb(ə)l/ noun [C] **1** a piece of furniture that consists of a flat surface that is supported by legs: *They sat around a long table in the conference room.* **2** a set of facts or numbers that are arranged in rows and **columns** on a page
PHRASES clear the table to take away from a table all the knives, forks, plates etc after people have finished eating
set the table to put knives, forks, plates etc on a table at each place where a person will eat

tableau /'tæbləʊ/ (plural **tableaux** /'tæbləʊz/) noun [C] **1** an unusual or impressive scene that someone remembers for a long time **2 ARTS** a form of silent theatre in which a group of actors stand or sit in certain positions to create a picture of a historical scene

tablecloth /'teɪb(ə)l,klɒθ/ noun [C] a large cloth for covering a table

table d'hôte /,tɑː'b(ə)l 'dəʊt/ noun [singular] **TOURISM** a menu in a restaurant that offers a fixed price for meals

'table ,salt noun [U] fine grains of salt that you can put on your food when you eat it

tablespoon /'teɪb(ə)l,spuːn/ noun [C] **1** a large spoon that you use for serving food or for measuring amounts of food or liquid **2 tablespoon** or **tablespoonful** /'teɪb(ə)l,spuːnfʊl/ the amount of food or liquid that a tablespoon holds

tablet /ˈtæblət/ noun [C] **1 HEALTH** a small hard round piece of medicine that you swallow = PILL **2** a flat piece of stone that has writing cut into it **3 COMPUTING** a flat square piece of equipment that sends information to a computer

'table ,tennis noun [U] **SPORTS** a game in which players use bats to hit a small light ball across a table with a low net across the middle

tableware /ˈteɪb(ə)l,weə/ noun [U] things such as knives, forks, dishes etc that people use when they are having a meal

tabloid /ˈtæblɔɪd/ noun [C] a newspaper that has small pages, a lot of photographs, and not much serious news —**tabloid** adj

taboo /təˈbuː/ adj if something is taboo, people do not do it or talk about it because it is considered offensive or shocking —**taboo** noun [C]

tabular /ˈtæbjʊlə/ adj formal in the form of a **table** (=a way of showing detailed information in rows)

tabulate /ˈtæbjʊleɪt/ verb [T] to show pieces of information in an organized way, for example in lists or rows —**tabulation** /,tæbjʊˈleɪʃ(ə)n/ noun [U]

tacit /ˈtæsɪt/ adj expressed or understood without being said directly —**tacitly** adv

tack¹ /tæk/ noun **1** [C] a small nail or short pin **2** [singular] a particular way of doing or achieving something: Let's try **a different tack**. **3** [U] the pieces of equipment that someone puts on a horse when they are going to ride it **4** [C] a direction that a boat sails in relation to the wind

tack² /tæk/ verb **1** [T] to fix something somewhere using small nails or short pins: There was a note **tacked to the door. 2** [T] to sew pieces of cloth together with long loose stitches, before you sew it more carefully **3** [I] if a boat tacks, it turns so that the wind is blowing on the other side of its sails

tackle¹ /ˈtæk(ə)l/ verb [T]

1 deal with problem	4 in sport: stop sb
2 in sport: take ball	5 talk about problem
3 push sb to ground	

1 to deal with a problem: Governments have failed to **tackle the question of** homelessness.
2 SPORTS to try to take the ball from an opponent in a game such as football
3 to take hold of someone and push them to the ground
4 [I/T] **SPORTS** to take hold of an opponent in a game such as **rugby** or American football and stop them from moving forward, usually by forcing them to the ground
5 to talk to someone about something that they have done that you do not approve of: The interviewer **tackled** him **about** his failed economic policies.

tackle² /ˈtæk(ə)l/ noun **1** [C] **SPORTS** an attempt to take the ball from an opponent in a game such as football **2** [U] **SPORTS** special equipment that people use for sports: fishing tackle **3** [C] an attempt to take hold of someone and push them to the ground

'tack ,weld noun [C] **TECHNOLOGY** a temporary joint in welding that is used to hold two pieces of metal together until the final weld is added

tact /tækt/ noun [U] a careful way of speaking or behaving that avoids upsetting other people

tactful /ˈtæk(t)f(ə)l/ adj careful to avoid upsetting other people —**tactfully** adv

tactic /ˈtæktɪk/ noun **1** [C] a method or plan for achieving something **2 tactics** [plural] the skill of effectively organizing and using soldiers, weapons, and equipment in battles

tactical /ˈtæktɪk(ə)l/ adj **1** done as part of a plan for achieving something **2** involving **tactics 3** tactical aircraft, missiles, and other weapons are designed to be used over short distances —**tactically** /ˈtæktɪkli/ adv

tactile /ˈtæktaɪl/ adj concerning the sense of touch

tactless /ˈtæk(t)ləs/ adj not careful about the way that you speak or behave towards other people, so that you often upset them

tadpole /ˈtæd,pəʊl/ noun [C] the larva of an amphibian that develops into an adult **frog, toad** etc —picture → REPTILE

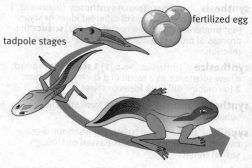

fertilized egg

tadpole stages

tadpole stages

tag¹ /tæg/ noun [C] **1** a small label: a name tag **2 LANGUAGE** a **question tag 3** a piece of electronic equipment that is attached to a criminal or a wild animal. It shows where they are.

tag² /tæg/ (**tags, tagging, tagged**) verb [T] **1** to fix a label to something **2** to put an electronic tag on a criminal or a wild animal **3** to touch another player in some children's games

'tag ,question noun [C] **LANGUAGE** a question that has a **question tag** at the end of it

t'ai chi /,taɪ ˈtʃiː/ noun [U] a Chinese activity that involves doing very slow physical exercises to make the mind relax and improve the body's balance

tail¹ /teɪl/ noun **1** [C] a part at the back of an animal's body that can move: The animal sprays liquid from a gland under its tail. ♦ the bright tail feathers of a peacock —picture → BIRD **2** [C] the part at the back of a plane **3** [singular] the back or end of something: at **the tail of** the queue → TAILS

tail² /teɪl/ verb [T] to secretly follow someone

tailback /ˈteɪl,bæk/ noun [C] a long line of traffic that is moving very slowly

tailor /ˈteɪlə/ noun [C] someone who makes clothes for men

,tailor-'made adj **1** extremely suitable **2** designed for a particular person

tails /teɪlz/ noun **1** [U] the side of a coin that does not have a picture of a person on it **2** [plural] a man's formal jacket that is long at the back and short at the front

tailwind /ˈteɪl,wɪnd/ noun [C] a wind that blows in the same direction in which a vehicle is moving → HEADWIND

take¹ /teɪk/ (**takes, taking, took** /tʊk/, **taken** /'teɪkən/) verb [T]

1 move sb/sth	**12** get control of sth
2 perform action	**13** use transport
3 need sth	**14** use food/drink etc
4 accept sth	**15** use milk/sugar
5 put sb in situation	**16** wear a size
6 win prize/election	**17** think of
7 reach and get sth	**18** do or have sth
8 study	**19** have opinion
9 remove/steal sth	+ PHRASE
10 get measure etc	+ PHRASAL VERBS
11 in calculation	

1 to move or carry someone or something from one place to another: *Remember to take a pen with you.* ♦ *The cat had to be taken to the vet.* ♦ *Our guide took us around the cathedral.* ♦ *On long journeys I always* **take** *my dog along.* ♦ *We* **took** *my mother for a drive in the country.* ♦ *Take Debbie this cup of coffee, will you?* ♦ *Let's* **take** *the presents to them tonight.* → BRING

2 to perform an action: *Take a deep breath.* ♦ *Let's take a walk down to the river.* ♦ *The government must take action to stop this trade.* ♦ *You need to take more exercise.*

3 to need something: *It takes talent and dedication to become a top dancer.* ♦ *The journey will take us about three days.* ♦ *Your odd behaviour is going to take a bit of explaining.* ♦ *It's going to take some doing* (=be difficult to do) *to persuade them!*

4 to accept something: *I've decided not to take the job.* ♦ *Sorry, we don't take credit cards.* ♦ *She won't take my advice.* ♦ *In this job you have to be able to take criticism.* ♦ *That's my final price, take it or leave it* (=the offer will not change). ♦ *You don't have to take my word for it* (=believe what I am saying) – *you can ask Tom.*

5 to cause someone or something to be in a new situation: *Her amazing energy has taken her to the top of her profession.* ♦ *The police took the thief into custody.* ♦ *They'll take us to court if we don't pay up soon.*

6 to win a prize in a competition or a vote in an election: *Who took the silver medal?* ♦ *The Labour Party took 45 per cent of the vote.*

7 to reach out and get something with your hand: *Take as many cakes as you like.* ♦ *Let me take your coats.*

8 EDUCATION to study a particular subject: *I took a course in computer programming.*

9 to remove something, or to steal something: *Who's taken my pencil?* ♦ *The thieves didn't take much.* ♦ *Take the knife away from her!*

10 to get a picture or a measurement using a machine: *May I take a photo of the two of you?* ♦ *A nurse took his temperature every hour.*

11 MATHS to remove one number or quantity from another number or quantity: *If you take five from ten, you're left with five.*

12 to get control of something from an opponent: *The town was finally taken after a six-week siege.*

13 to use a particular type of transport or a particular road: *Take the A14 as far as Cambridge.* ♦ *I usually take the bus to work.*

14 to put drugs or medicine into your body: *People worry that their children will start taking drugs.*

You **eat** food and **drink** drinks, but you **take** liquid or solid medicine: *She took a pill for her headache.* ♦ *You have to keep taking your antibiotics.*

15 to have milk or sugar in your tea or coffee: *Do you take milk in your coffee?*

16 to wear a particular size of clothes or shoes: *What size shoes do you take?*

17 to think about someone or something in a particular way: *He tries hard, but I just can't take him seriously.* ♦ *She took his remarks as a compliment.* ♦ *She looks so young that I took her for your sister.*

18 to do or have something: *Please take a seat* (=sit down). ♦ *They're shooting at us! Quick, take cover!* ♦ *I did all the work, but Gill took all the credit.* ♦ *The rebels are taking control of the city.* ♦ *We must encourage fathers to take full responsibility for their children.*

19 to have a feeling or opinion: *I'm afraid she took offence at my remarks.* ♦ *He's never taken much interest in his kids.* ♦ *Lisa took pity on us and invited us to dinner.* ♦ *I take the view that children should be told the truth.* → PITY¹

PHRASE **take place** to happen: *The Olympics take place every four years.*

PHRASAL VERBS **,take 'after sb** to look or behave like an older relative

,take sth a'part to separate an object into its pieces: *Ben was taking apart an old bicycle.*

,take sth 'back 1 to take something that you have bought back to the shop because it is broken or not suitable **2** to admit that something that you said as a criticism of someone or something was wrong: *I'm sorry – I take it back.*

'take sb for sth to believe something, usually wrongly, about someone or something: *She looks so young I took her for your sister.* ♦ *Do you take me for a complete idiot?*

,take sth 'in to understand and remember something that you hear or read: *I'm not sure how much of his explanation she took in.*

,take 'off if a plane takes off, it leaves the ground and starts to fly ≠ LAND

,take sth 'off to remove a piece of clothing from your body

,take sth/sb 'out to remove something from a place: *Henry took out his wallet.*

,take (sth) 'over 1 to begin to do something that someone else was doing: *Jane took over as director after Richard retired.* **2** BUSINESS to take control of something: *IBM is taking over the smaller company.*

'take to sb/sth to begin to like someone or something: *I took to John immediately.*

,take sth 'up to start doing something regularly as a habit, job, or interest: *Chris has taken up jogging.* ♦ *The new teacher will take up her post in May.*

take² /teɪk/ noun [C] ARTS a section of a film or television programme that is recorded without stopping

PHRASE **sb's take on sth** someone's opinion about something: *What's your take on the political crisis?*

takeaway /'teɪkə,weɪ/ noun [C] **1** a meal that you buy in a restaurant and take home to eat **2** a restaurant that sells meals that you take home to eat

taken /'teɪkən/ the past participle of **take¹**

'take-,off noun [C/U] an occasion when a plane leaves the ground and starts to fly ≠ LANDING

takeover /'teɪk,əʊvə/ noun [C] a situation in which one company or country takes control of another company or country → MERGER

takings /'teɪkɪŋz/ noun [plural] the money that a shop receives from customers

tala /'tælə/ noun [U] MUSIC a rhythm (=regular pattern of sounds) used in Indian classical music

tale /teɪl/ noun [C] **1** LITERATURE a story about imaginary events or people **2** a spoken account of someone's experiences

talent /'tælənt/ noun [C/U] a natural ability for doing a particular activity well: *She had an obvious **talent for** music.*

talented /'tæləntɪd/ adj very good at something

talisman /'tælɪzmən/ noun [C] an object that some people believe has the power to protect you from bad things

talk¹ /tɔːk/ verb **1** [I] to speak, or to have a conversation: *Can their baby talk yet?* ♦ *Am I talking too much?* ♦ *I saw her **talking to** Matt.* ♦ *Everyone was busily **talking with** their friends.* ♦ *We were **talking about** you last night.* → SAY² **2** [I/T] to discuss something: *You and I **need to talk**.* ♦ *John and Pete spent the evening **talking politics** (=discussing political issues).* **3** [I] to give information that should be secret: *Do you think the prisoners will talk?* **4** [I] to give a lecture on a subject: *In the hall a woman was **talking on** diet and health.*

> **PHRASAL VERBS** ,talk 'back to reply to someone rudely: *Melanie, don't **talk back** to your mother!*
> ,talk sb 'into sth to persuade someone to do something: *They talked their mother into taking a rest for a while.*
> ,talk sb 'out of sth to persuade someone not to do something: *We managed to talk him out of giving up his job.*
> ,talk sth 'over to discuss a problem or a plan: *You both need to talk over what happened that day.*

> **Build your vocabulary: words you can use instead of talk**
> - **chat** to talk informally in a friendly way
> - **discuss** to talk about a particular subject in detail
> - **gossip** to talk about other people's private lives
> - **speak** to talk to someone about something, or to be able to talk in a particular language

talk² /tɔːk/ noun **1** [C/U] a conversation, or conversations in general: *You need time to relax and **have a talk with** your children.* ♦ *There's **a lot of talk** in the school **about** the new exam system.* **2** [C] an informal lecture about a subject: *Williams **gave a talk on** his travels in Nepal.* **3 talks** [plural] discussions between important people that are designed to solve a problem: *peace talks* ♦ *the outcome of **talks between** the government and the rebels* ♦ *preliminary **talks on** the future of the steel industry* ♦ *He visited Egypt in March for **talks with** the president.* ♦ *The management will be **holding** informal **talks with** union officials.* **4** [U] statements, discussions, promises, or threats that are not worth listening to: *She says she's an expert on men, but it's **all talk**!*

talkative /'tɔːkətɪv/ adj someone who is talkative talks a lot

talkboard /'tɔːk,bɔːd/ noun [C] **COMPUTING** an Internet discussion group on a particular subject, sometimes involving people with special knowledge who answer questions

tall /tɔːl/ adj **1** a tall person or object has greater height than the average person or object: *a tall thin woman* ♦ *tall buildings* → HIGH¹ sense 1 **2** used for talking about measurements of height: *He must be over six feet tall.*

tally /'tæli/ (plural **tallies**) noun [C] a record of the number of things that someone has won or achieved

the Talmud /'tælmʊd/ **RELIGION** a collection of Jewish religious writings

talon /'tælən/ noun [C] **BIOLOGY** one of the sharp nails on the feet of some birds, especially **birds of prey** —*picture* → BIRD

tamarind /'tæmərɪnd/ noun [C/U] a small soft fruit with sticky brown skin, or the African tree that it grows on

tamboura /tæm'bʊərə/ noun [C] **MUSIC** an Asian musical instrument with strings, played like a guitar

tambourine /,tæmbə'riːn/ noun [C] **MUSIC** a musical instrument that you shake or hit with your hand. It consists of a round frame with small pieces of metal around the edge.

tame¹ /teɪm/ adj **1** a tame animal has been trained not to attack people ≠ WILD **2** not exciting, powerful, or dangerous enough —**tamely** adv

tame² /teɪm/ verb [T] to train an animal not to attack people

tamoxifen /tə'mɒksɪfen/ noun [U] **HEALTH** a drug used in the treatment of breast cancer

tamper /'tæmpə/   **PHRASAL VERB** 'tamper with sth to touch or change something that you should not touch or change, often because you want to spoil it

tampon /'tæmpɒn/ noun [C] an object that a woman puts inside her vagina to absorb the blood during her period

tan¹ /tæn/ noun **1** [C] a **suntan 2** [U] a light brown colour

tan² /tæn/ (**tans, tanning, tanned**) verb [I/T] if you tan, or if the sun tans your skin, the sun makes your skin darker than it was before

tan³ /tæn/ adj light brown in colour

tandem /'tændəm/ noun [C] a bicycle with seats for two people

tandoori /tæn'dʊəri/ (plural **tandooris**) noun [C] an Indian meal that is cooked in a clay container

tangent /'tændʒ(ə)nt/ noun [C] **MATHS** a straight line that touches the edge of a circle but does not pass through it —*picture* → CIRCLE

tangential /tæn'dʒenʃ(ə)l/ adj **MATHS** something such as a line that is tangential to something touches its edge but does not pass through it —**tangentially** adv

tangerine /,tændʒə'riːn/ noun [C] a fruit that is like a small orange

tangible /'tændʒəb(ə)l/ adj **1** able to be seen to exist or be true: *tangible evidence* **2** **BUSINESS** tangible **assets** are real things that a company has, for example buildings or equipment

tangle¹ /'tæŋg(ə)l/ noun [C] **1** the untidy shape that things make when they are twisted round each other or round something else **2** a situation that is difficult to deal with because things are not organized

tangle² /'tæŋg(ə)l/ verb [I/T] if something tangles, or if you tangle it, its parts become twisted round each other or round something else

tangled /'tæŋg(ə)ld/ adj **1** if something is tangled, its parts are twisted round each other in an untidy way **2** very complicated and difficult to deal with
> **PHRASE** tangled up in sth involved in a difficult situation

tangram /'tæŋgræm/ noun [C] **MATHS** a Chinese game consisting of a square made of seven pieces that are used to form different shapes

tank /tæŋk/ noun [C] **1** a large metal container for liquid or gas **2** a very strong military vehicle with a large gun on the top

tanker /'tæŋkə/ noun [C] a large ship or truck that carries petrol or oil

tanned /tænd/ adj someone who is tanned has darker skin than before because they have spent time in the sun

Tannoy /'tænɔɪ/ TRADEMARK a system of **loudspeakers** that is used for making announcements in public places and large buildings

tantalum /'tæntələm/ noun [U] CHEMISTRY a hard blue-grey metallic element that does not **rust**. It is used to repair damaged bones. Chemical symbol: **Ta**

tantrum /'tæntrəm/ noun [C] an occasion when someone, especially a young child, suddenly behaves in a very angry way that is unreasonable or silly

tap¹ /tæp/ noun [C] **1** an object that is used for controlling how much water comes out of a pipe: *Just turn the cold tap on for a few seconds.* **2** the action of touching someone or something gently, or the sound that the touch makes: *I felt a tap on my shoulder.* ♦ *We heard a tap at the window.* **3** a piece of electronic equipment that is used for secretly listening to someone's telephone conversations

tap² /tæp/ (**taps, tapping, tapped**) verb **1** [I/T] to touch someone or something gently: *We could hear someone tapping at the door.* ♦ *I tapped him on the shoulder and he jumped.* **2** [T] to get or use something: *Several other companies were already tapping this market.* **3** [T] to use electronic equipment in order to listen secretly to someone's telephone conversations

tape¹ /teɪp/ noun **1** [C] a **cassette** with something recorded on it or for recording something: *This is a great tape – have you heard it?* ♦ *We need a blank tape* (=one with nothing recorded on it). **2** [U] a very long thin piece of plastic that is used for recording sound, pictures, or information: *We've got the concert on tape.* **3** [U] a long thin band of plastic that is sticky on one side and is used for sticking things together **4** [C/U] a long thin band of cloth or plastic that is used for fastening things together or for marking the edges of an area: *Police roped off the area with yellow tape after the incident.*

tape² /teɪp/ verb **1** [I/T] to record sounds or pictures onto tape **2** [T] to stick something using sticky tape

'tape ,measure noun [C] a tool for measuring things that consists of a long narrow piece of cloth, soft plastic, or thin metal with numbers on it

taper /'teɪpə/ verb [I] to gradually become narrower towards one end

'tape re,corder noun [C] a piece of equipment for playing a tape or for recording sound on tape

'taper roller ,bearing noun [C] ENGINEERING a type of **roller bearing** that is thinner at one end than the other

tapestry /'tæpɪstri/ (plural **tapestries**) noun [C/U] a thick heavy cloth that has pictures or patterns woven into it

tapeworm /'teɪp,wɜːm/ noun [C] a long flat worm that can live inside the intestines of humans and other vertebrate animals and cause illness. The larva of the tapeworm usually gets into the human body from meat or fish that has not been completely cooked.

tapir /'teɪpə/ noun [C] a mammal that has a long nose and lives in tropical forests

taproot /'tæp,ruːt/ noun [C] BIOLOGY the main straight root of a **dicotyledon** plant that has smaller roots growing out from its sides. Some vegetables, for example **carrots**, are taproots.

tar¹ /taː/ noun [U] **1** a thick black liquid that is used for making the surfaces of roads **2** a sticky poisonous substance from tobacco

tar² /taː/ (**tars, tarring, tarred**) verb [T] to cover the surface of a road with tar

tarantula /təˈræntjʊlə/ noun [C] a large poisonous spider

target¹ /'taːgɪt/ noun [C] **1** someone or something that is being attacked: *military targets such as air bases* ♦ *Foreigners have become targets for attack by terrorists.* **2** a person, organization, or idea that is being criticized or blamed: *The policy has become the target of severe criticism.* **3** something that you try to achieve: *The organization is setting a target of 2,000 new members.* ♦ *The government hasn't met its target* (=achieved it) *for reducing unemployment.* ♦ *The economy was on target to grow by more than 4 per cent.* **4** an object that you have to hit in a game: *Few players managed to get their shots on target.*

target² /'taːgɪt/ verb [T] **1** to attack or criticize someone or something: *The terrorists were targeting government buildings.* ♦ *The company had been targeted because of its bad record on pollution.* **2** to try to persuade or influence a particular group of people: *television advertising targeted at children* **3** to direct money or help to a particular group of people

'target ,language noun [singular] LANGUAGE the language that you are translating something into

,target 'organ noun [C] BIOLOGY an organ in the body on which a particular hormone acts

tariff /'tærɪf/ noun [C] **1** ECONOMICS a tax that a government charges on goods that enter or leave their country **2** a list of the prices that a company charges for its goods or services

tarmac /'taːmæk/ noun **1** [U] a mixture of **tar** and stones that is used for making the surfaces of roads = ASPHALT **2 the tarmac** [singular] the part of an airport where the planes stop

tarn /taːn/ noun [C] GEOGRAPHY a mountain lake that forms in a **cirque** (=valley on a mountain slope)

tarnish /'taːnɪʃ/ verb **1** [T] if something tarnishes your reputation or image, it makes people have a bad opinion of you **2** [I/T] if metal tarnishes, or if something tarnishes it, it loses its colour and becomes less shiny

tarsal¹ /'taːs(ə)l/ adj ANATOMY relating to the tarsus

tarsal² /'taːs(ə)l/ noun [C] ANATOMY one of the bones of the tarsus —*picture* → SKELETON

tarsus /'taːsəs/ noun [C] ANATOMY the **ankle** (=the set of bones that connect the foot to the leg)

tart /taːt/ noun [C] **1** a pie with no top that is filled with fruit **2** *offensive* an offensive word for a woman who looks or behaves as if she wants to attract men and have sex

tartan /'taːt(ə)n/ noun [U] a pattern of colourful lines and squares on cloth that is typical of Scotland —**tartan** adj

tartaric acid /taːˌtærɪk 'æsɪd/ noun [U] CHEMISTRY an acid that is used in **baking powder** and as a food **additive**

tartrazine /'taːtrəziːn/ noun [U] CHEMISTRY a substance that is added to some prepared foods to make them a yellow colour

task /taːsk/ noun [C] something that you have to do, often something that is difficult or unpleasant: *a routine task* ♦ *Ken began the difficult task of organizing the information.*

taskbar /'taːsk,baː/ noun [C] COMPUTING a list that appears along the top or bottom of your computer screen and shows the programs that you are using or the activities that you can perform

'task ,management noun [U] **COMPUTING** the process in which the **system software** of a computer controls what **resources** are given to which programs

tassel /'tæs(ə)l/ noun [C] a decoration on cloth that consists of a group of strings tied together at one end

taste¹ /teɪst/ noun

1 flavour	4 experience of sth
2 ability to judge	5 sth eaten/drunk
3 things sb likes	

1 [C/U] the flavour that something creates in your mouth when you eat or drink it: *I love the taste of chocolate.*
2 [U] the ability to judge whether something is good or bad in things such as art, fashion, and social behaviour: *She has such good taste in clothes.* ♦ *The joke was in very bad taste.*
3 [C/U] the types of thing that you like: *The meals are designed to suit all tastes.* ♦ *The girls share his taste in music.* ♦ *Even at a young age he had a taste for books.*
4 [singular] a short experience of something that you are not used to: *After 16 years in prison, it was their first taste of freedom.*
5 [singular] a small amount of food or drink that you have in order to find out what flavour it has: *Have a taste of this cheese.*

taste² /teɪst/ verb **1** [linking verb] to have a particular flavour: *Although the meal was cold, it tasted delicious.* ♦ *This lemonade tastes more like water.* ♦ *These biscuits don't taste of ginger.* **2** [T] to eat or drink something and experience its flavour: *The dinner was one of the best meals I have ever tasted.* ♦ *Visitors will be able to taste different types of wines.* **3** [T] to experience something: *It is 13 years since they last tasted victory.*

'taste ,bud noun [C] **ANATOMY** one of the small parts on the surface of the tongue that are sensitive to different flavours

tasteful /'teɪs(t)f(ə)l/ adj showing good judgment about what is attractive or suitable —**tastefully** adv

tasteless /'teɪs(t)ləs/ adj **1** food or drink that is tasteless has no flavour **2** showing bad judgment about what is attractive or suitable

tasty /'teɪsti/ (**tastier, tastiest**) adj tasty food has a nice flavour

tattered /'tætəd/ adj torn and in very bad condition = RAGGED

tattoo /tæ'tuː/ (plural **tattoos**) noun [C] a permanent picture that is drawn on the skin —**tattoo** verb [T]

tatty /'tæti/ adj *informal* old and in bad condition = SHABBY

taught /tɔːt/ the past tense and past participle of **teach**

taunt /tɔːnt/ verb [T] to shout cruel things at someone in order to make them angry or upset —**taunt** noun [C]

Taurus /'tɔːrəs/ noun [C/U] one of the twelve signs of the zodiac. A **Taurus** is someone who was born between 22 April and 21 May.

taut /tɔːt/ adj stretched tight —**tautly** adv

tautological /,tɔːtə'lɒdʒɪk(ə)l/ or **tautologous** /tɔː'tɒləgəs/ adj **LANGUAGE** a tautological statement, sentence etc repeats its meaning in an unnecessary way by using different words to say the same thing —**tautologically** /,tɔːtə'lɒdʒɪkli/ adv

tautology /tɔː'tɒlədʒi/ noun [C/U] **LANGUAGE** a statement, sentence etc in which the meaning is repeated in an unnecessary way by using different words

tax¹ /tæks/ noun [C/U] **ECONOMICS** an amount of money that you have to pay to the government. It is used for providing public services and for paying for government institutions: *The government has promised to lower taxes after the election.* ♦ *I was earning £800 a month after tax* (=after paying tax). ♦ *an increase in the tax on petrol*

tax² /tæks/ verb [T] **1 ECONOMICS** to make someone pay a tax **2 ECONOMICS** to put a tax on something **3** *formal* to cause problems or make things difficult for someone

taxa /'tæksə/ the plural of **taxon**

taxation /tæk'seɪʃ(ə)n/ noun [U] **1 ECONOMICS** the system that a government uses for collecting money in the form of taxes **2** the money that a government collects as tax

tax-deductible /,tæks dɪ'dʌktəb(ə)l/ adj tax-deductible costs can be taken away from someone's total income before they pay tax on what remains

taxi¹ /'tæksi/ (plural **taxis**) noun [C] a car with a driver who you pay to take you somewhere = CAB: *It was late, so I took a taxi home.* ♦ *You won't have any problem getting a taxi.* ♦ *I tried to hail a taxi* (=stop one in the street) *but they all sped past.*

taxi² /'tæksi/ (**taxies, taxiing, taxied**) verb [I] if a plane taxies, it moves slowly along the ground

taxicab /'tæksi,kæb/ noun [C] *formal* a **taxi**

'taxicab ge,ometry noun [U] **MATHS** the study of paths and distances in a rectangular **grid** (=pattern of straight lines that cross each other to form squares)

'taxi ,rank noun [C] a place where taxis wait for customers

taxon /'tæksɒn/ (plural **taxa** /'tæksə/) noun [C] **BIOLOGY** a group in which organisms are placed according to the principles of taxonomy, for example a species, **genus**, or family

taxonomy /tæk'sɒnəmi/ noun [U] **SCIENCE** the process of organizing similar things, especially living things, into groups or types = CLASSIFICATION —*picture* → on next page —**taxonomic** /,tæksə'nɒmɪk/ adj

taxpayer /'tæks,peɪə/ noun [C] someone who pays tax

'tax re,lief noun [U] a reduction in the amount of tax that a person must pay

TB /,tiː 'biː/ noun [U] **HEALTH** tuberculosis: a serious infectious disease, caused by bacteria, that affects the lungs and can cause death

TBA /,tiː biː 'eɪ/ noun [C] **HEALTH** traditional birth attendant: in some countries, someone with experience, but not formal training, who helps a woman when she is giving birth to a baby

tbc abbrev to be confirmed: used for showing that something has not been decided yet

T cell /'tiː ,sel/ noun [C] **HEALTH** a type of white blood cell that helps the body fight disease

TCP/IP /,tiː siː siː ,piː aɪ 'piː/ abbrev **COMPUTING** transmission control protocol/Internet protocol: a set of rules used by all computers on the Internet that allow them to communicate with each other

TDC abbrev **ENGINEERING** top dead centre in an engine

tea /tiː/ noun **1** [C/U] a hot brown drink made by pouring boiling water onto the dried leaves of the tea bush, or a cup of this drink: *Do you want some more tea?* ♦ *Two teas, please.* ♦ *I'd love a cup of tea.* **2** [C/U] a hot drink made by pouring boiling water onto the dried leaves, fruit, or flowers of a particular plant, or a cup of this drink: *a cup of rosehip tea* **3** [U] the dried

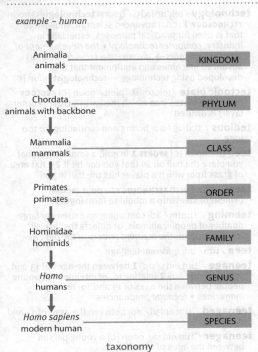

example – human

Animalia animals → KINGDOM

Chordata animals with backbone → PHYLUM

Mammalia mammals → CLASS

Primates primates → ORDER

Hominidae hominids → FAMILY

Homo humans → GENUS

Homo sapiens modern human → SPECIES

taxonomy

leaves of the tea bush, used for making tea: *a packet of tea* **4** [U] a small meal of sandwiches and cakes that is eaten in the afternoon with tea, or a cooked meal eaten in the early evening

teach /tiːtʃ/ (**teaches, teaching, taught** /tɔːt/) verb **1** [I/T] **EDUCATION** to help students to learn something in a school, college, or university by giving lessons: *She teaches children with learning difficulties.* ♦ *How long have you been teaching here?* ♦ *John* **teaches** *English* **to** *adult learners.* **2** [T] to help someone to learn a skill by showing them how to do it: *His mother had taught him some words in Spanish.* ♦ *My uncle is going to* **teach** *me* **to** *drive this summer.* **3** [T] to change the way that someone behaves or the way that someone thinks or feels about something: *The experience taught her the importance of having good friends.* ♦ *These children have to be* **taught to** *share with others.*

PHRASE **teach sb a lesson** *informal* to punish someone for doing something bad so that they do not do it again

teacher /ˈtiːtʃə/ noun [C] **EDUCATION** someone whose job is to teach: *a French teacher*

teacher training noun [U] **EDUCATION** training that prepares someone to become a teacher

teaching /ˈtiːtʃɪŋ/ noun **1** [U] **EDUCATION** the job of a teacher: *a career in teaching* **2** [C/U] the religious or political ideas of a particular person or group: *issues that are central to traditional Christian teaching* ♦ *the* **teachings of** *Buddha*

teaching hospital noun [C] **HEALTH, EDUCATION** a hospital where students who are learning to be doctors are trained

teak /tiːk/ noun **1** [C/U] a large Asian tree with valuable hard wood **2** [U] the wood of this tree, used especially for making furniture

team /tiːm/ noun [C] **1** **SPORTS** a group of people who play a sport or game against another group: *a football team* ♦ *Are you* **in the** *hockey* **team** *this year?* **2** a group

of people who work together: *a negotiating team* ♦ *a* **team of** *legal experts* **3** two or more animals that pull a vehicle or piece of farm equipment

Team can be used with a singular or plural verb. You can say: *The team* **has** *lost three games* OR: *The team* **have** *lost three games.*

teammate /ˈtiːmˌmeɪt/ noun [C] someone who is in the same team as you

teamwork /ˈtiːmˌwɜːk/ noun [U] work that you do together with other people

teapot /ˈtiːˌpɒt/ noun [C] a container with a handle and a **spout** (=small tube for pouring) that you use for making and pouring tea

tear¹ /teə/ (**tears, tearing, tore** /tɔː/, **torn** /tɔːn/) verb **1** [I/T] to pull something so that it separates into pieces or gets a hole in it, or to become damaged in this way= RIP: *He'd torn his raincoat.* ♦ *It's very thin material that tears easily.* ♦ *Mary* **tore** *the letter* **to pieces.** ♦ *He* **tore** *the envelope* **open.** **2** [T] to remove something by pulling it away from something else with force: *You'll need to* **tear** *the old wallpaper* **off** *the walls.* ♦ *The storm had* **torn** *the old tree* **up** *by the roots.* **3** [T] to damage something such as a muscle by stretching it until it pulls apart: *I tore a muscle playing football.* **4** [I] to move somewhere very quickly, usually in an excited or uncontrolled way: *Those kids are always* **tearing around** *here on their bicycles.*

PHRASE **be torn between** to be unable to decide which of two people or things you want most: *I was torn between my family and my career.*

PHRASAL VERBS **tear sth a'part** to damage or destroy something completely by breaking it into pieces: *The building was torn apart by the explosion.*

tear sth 'up to destroy something such as a piece of paper or cloth by pulling it into pieces: *I tore up all the old photos of us.*

tear² /teə/ noun [C] a hole in something where it has been torn: *There was* **a tear in** *her coat.*

tear³ /tɪə/ noun **1** [C] a drop of liquid that comes from your eye when you cry: *Her eyes filled with tears.* ♦ *She welcomed Ian with* **tears of joy.** **2 tears** [plural] the state of crying: *I was left standing there* **in tears** (=crying). ♦ *She slammed the phone down and* **burst into tears** (=suddenly started crying). ♦ *I was* **near to tears** (=almost crying) *when she said goodbye.*

tearful /ˈtɪəf(ə)l/ adj crying, or feeling as if you want to cry —**tearfully** adv

tear gas /ˈtɪə ˌgæs/ noun [U] a gas that makes the eyes sting. It is used by the police for controlling violent crowds.

tear gland /ˈtɪə ˌglænd/ noun [C] **ANATOMY** a gland in the eye where tears are produced —*picture* → EYE

tease /tiːz/ verb [I/T] to say something to someone in order to have fun by embarrassing or annoying them

teaspoon /ˈtiːˌspuːn/ noun [C] **1** a small spoon that you use for adding sugar to tea or coffee, or for measuring small amounts of liquid or powder **2 teaspoon** or **teaspoonful** /ˈtiːˌspuːnfʊl/ the amount of food or liquid that a teaspoon holds

teat /tiːt/ noun [C] **1** a piece of rubber or plastic fixed to a bottle, through which a baby sucks milk or juice **2 BIOLOGY** one of the small pointed parts of a female mammal's body through which a baby animal sucks milk

tea towel noun [C] a cloth that you use for drying things such as dishes and cups

technetium /tekˈniːʃiəm/ noun [U] CHEMISTRY a silvery-grey radioactive metallic element produced by **nuclear fission**. It is the lightest of the elements. Chemical symbol: **Te**

technical /ˈteknɪk(ə)l/ adj

1 involving science	**3** relating to machine
2 using difficult language	**4** relating to skills
	5 following rule strictly

1 involving science or industry: *technical experts ♦ The job requires someone with technical knowledge.*
2 LANGUAGE technical language is difficult to understand for someone who do not know about the subject: *The text is interesting and informative, without being too technical.* ♦ *a technical term in philosophy*
3 TECHNOLOGY relating to the way that a machine or piece of equipment works: *delays caused by technical problems*
4 relating to the skills that are needed to perform a particular activity: *The dancers reached extremely high levels of technical skill and ability.*
5 based on a strict way of understanding or explaining a law or rule: *This was not a mere technical violation of a statute.*

ˈtechnical ˌcollege noun [C] EDUCATION a college that trains people for jobs in technology and other practical subjects

ˈtechnical ˌdrawing noun TECHNOLOGY **1** [U] the skill, practice, or study of drawing objects in a very accurate and detailed way for use by someone making or building them **2** [C] a very accurate and detailed drawing of an object for use by someone making or building it

technicality /ˌteknɪˈkæləti/ (plural **technicalities**) noun **1 technicalities** [plural] details about a particular subject that are understood only by an expert **2** [C] LAW a minor detail of the law that can lead to an unfair result

technically /ˈteknɪkli/ adv **1** in a way that involves skill in doing something: *a technically accomplished player* **2** according to a strict way of understanding a rule or set of facts: *Technically the war was over, but there was still some fighting.* **3** in a way that involves the practical use of skills, processes, or equipment in science and industry: *The use of an alternative fuel is not technically feasible.*

ˌtechnical supˈport noun [U] COMPUTING a service provided by a computer company to help customers who are having problems using their products

technician /tekˈnɪʃ(ə)n/ noun [C] someone with technical training whose job involves working with and taking care of special equipment

technicon or **technikon** /ˈteknɪkɒn/ noun [C] EDUCATION a university of technology in South Africa

technique /tekˈniːk/ noun **1** [C] a method of doing something using a special skill that you have developed: *surgical techniques* ♦ *a useful technique for dealing with difficult customers* ♦ *modern techniques of business management* **2** [U] the skills that are needed to perform a particular activity: *Strength, speed, and technique are what you need to be a winner.*

techno /ˈteknəʊ/ noun [U] MUSIC a type of electronic **dance music** that developed in the 1980s, consisting of fast, hard, repeated beats and heavy drum sounds

technological /ˌteknəˈlɒdʒɪk(ə)l/ adj TECHNOLOGY relating to or involving technology —**technologically** /ˌteknəˈlɒdʒɪkli/ adv

technology /tekˈnɒlədʒi/ (plural **technologies**) noun TECHNOLOGY **1** [C/U] advanced scientific knowledge that is used for practical purposes, especially in industry: *computer technology ♦ the development of new technologies →* INFORMATION TECHNOLOGY **2** [U] advanced machines and equipment that are developed using technology —**technologist** noun [C]

tectonic plate /tekˌtɒnɪk ˈpleɪt/ noun [C] GEOLOGY one of the pieces into which the Earth's **crust** (=outer layer) is divided

tedious /ˈtiːdiəs/ adj boring and continuing for too long

tee /tiː/ noun [C] SPORTS **1** in golf, a small object that you place the ball on so that you can hit it **2** a flat area of grass from which a player hits the ball in golf

teem /tiːm/ verb TECHNOLOGY to pour **molten** (=melted) steel into a mould to form **ingots**

teeming /ˈtiːmɪŋ/ adj containing an extremely large number of people, animals, or objects that are all moving around: *the teeming streets of the old city*

teen /tiːn/ adj informal teenage

teenage /ˈtiːneɪdʒ/ adj **1** between the ages of 13 and 19: *a teenage boy* **2** relating to, or intended for, young people between the ages of 13 and 19: *teenage magazines ♦ teenage pregnancies*

teenaged /ˈtiːneɪdʒd/ adj between the ages of 13 and 19

teenager /ˈtiːneɪdʒə/ noun [C] a young person between the ages of 13 and 19

teens /tiːnz/ noun [plural] the years of your life between the ages of 13 and 19: *She became a tennis champion while she was still in her teens.*

ˈtee ˌshirt another spelling of **T-shirt**

teeth /tiːθ/ the plural of **tooth**

teetotal /ˌtiːˈtəʊt(ə)l/ adj never drinking alcohol —**teetotaller** noun [C]

TEFL /ˈtef(ə)l/ noun [U] EDUCATION the Teaching of English as a Foreign Language

Teflon /ˈteflɒn/ TRADEMARK a type of plastic often put on pans to prevent food from sticking to them

tel. abbrev telephone number

telco /ˈtelkəʊ/ noun [C] BUSINESS a **telecommunications** company

telecommunications /ˌtelɪkəˌmjuːnɪˈkeɪʃ(ə)nz/ noun [U] TECHNOLOGY, ENGINEERING the science and technology of sending information by telephone, radio, or television

telecomputing /ˈtelɪkəmˌpjuːtɪŋ/ noun [U] COMPUTING the process of sending information to another computer or receiving information from another computer, using the Internet, a **modem**, or a **local area network**

teledensity /ˈtelɪˌdensəti/ noun [U] BUSINESS a measurement of how many telephones are available, expressed as the number of telephone lines for every 100 people in a country

telegram /ˈtelɪˌgræm/ noun [C] a message that you send by telegraph

telegraph /ˈtelɪˌgrɑːf/ noun [U] an old-fashioned method of communicating, by sending signals through wires or by radio waves

ˈtelegraph ˌpole noun [C] a tall pole that supports telephone wires

telepathy /təˈlepəθi/ noun [U] the ability that some people believe exists by which someone can communicate directly with another person's mind, without using words —**telepathic** /ˌtelɪˈpæθɪk/ adj

telephone[1] /ˈtelɪˌfəʊn/ noun **1** [C] a piece of electronic equipment that you use for speaking to someone in a different place= PHONE: *Suddenly, the telephone rang.* ♦ *Pascoe answered the telephone and said 'Hello'.* ♦ *He's been on the telephone for the past two hours.* —*picture* → WORKSTATION **2** [U] the system of communicating using telephones: *a telephone line* ♦ *People are interviewed over the telephone.* ♦ *I placed my order by telephone two weeks ago.*

telephone[2] /ˈtelɪˌfəʊn/ verb [I/T] *formal* to speak to someone using the telephone= PHONE

'telephone ,banking noun [U] banking services provided to customers by telephone

'telephone ex,change noun [C] a place with equipment that connects one telephone line to another

'telephone ,number noun [C] a series of single numbers that you use for phoning a particular person

telephonist /təˈlefənɪst/ noun [C] someone who works for a business or organization answering the telephone and directing calls to the right people

telephony /təˈlefəni/ noun [U] BUSINESS, TECHNOLOGY the system, technology, or business of telephone communication

telesales /ˈtelɪˌseɪlz/ noun [U] BUSINESS the activity or job of using the telephone in order to sell goods or services

telescope /ˈtelɪˌskəʊp/ noun [C] ASTRONOMY, PHYSICS a piece of equipment shaped like a tube that makes distant objects look closer and larger. Telescopes contain a system of mirrors or lenses, or both.

televise /ˈtelɪvaɪz/ verb [T] to broadcast something on television

television /ˈtelɪˌvɪʒ(ə)n/ noun **1** [C] a piece of electrical equipment with a screen that is used for watching programmes= TV: *Kelly switched on the television and stared blankly at the screen.* **2** [U] the system of broadcasting pictures and sounds by electronic signals: *a television series* **3** [U] ARTS the programmes that are shown on television: *I spent the evening watching television.* ♦ *I'm sure I've seen him on television.* **4** [U] ARTS the business of creating and broadcasting television programmes: *She works in television.*

> **Build your vocabulary: types of television programme**
>
> - **chat show** a programme in which a well-known person interviews famous people
> - **current affairs programme** a programme about politics or other subjects that are being discussed in the news
> - **documentary** a programme that deals with facts or historical events
> - **drama** any serious programme that tells a story
> - **episode** a single programme of a series
> - **game show** a programme in which people compete to win prizes
> - **the news** a programme that provides the latest information about the day's events
> - **series** a group of related programmes that are broadcast over a period of time
> - **sitcom** a type of humorous programme in which the same characters regularly appear in funny situations

> - **soap** a type of programme in which the same characters regularly appear in situations that are like ordinary life

'television ,set noun [C] a **television**

tell /tel/ (**tells**, **telling**, **told** /təʊld/) verb

1 sb gives information	**6** have clear effect
2 sth gives information	**7** see difference
3 talk about story	**+ PHRASES**
4 advise to do sth	**+ PHRASAL VERBS**
5 know sth	

1 [T] to give information to someone: *If you see anything suspicious, tell the police.* ♦ *Didn't he tell you that I wanted to see you?* ♦ *Just tell me what she said.* ♦ *He finally told me the reason he was so upset.* ♦ *'Tell me about your day,' she said.* ♦ *I haven't been told anything about it.* → SAY[1]
2 [T] if something such as a fact, event, or piece of equipment tells you something, it gives you or shows you some information: *The flashing light tells you when the battery needs recharging.* ♦ *What does this room tell you about the person who lived here?*
3 [T] if you tell a story or a joke, you give someone a spoken account of it: *Grandpa tells wonderful stories about the old days.* ♦ *Shall I tell you a joke?*
4 [T] to order or strongly advise someone to do something: *I'm not asking you – I'm telling you!* ♦ *I told him what to do, but he wouldn't listen.* ♦ *I told you to be here on time this morning.*
5 [I/T] to recognize something as a result of experience or evidence: *It's never easy to tell whether he's being serious or not.* ♦ *He's lying. I can always tell.* ♦ *Peter could tell that she was bored.*
6 [I] to have an effect that can be clearly seen, especially a bad effect: *The strain of the last few days was beginning to tell.*
7 [I/T] to recognize the difference between one person or thing and another: *Which is which? I can't tell.* ♦ *These days it's hard to tell the difference between political parties.* ♦ *Can you tell butter from margarine?*
PHRASES **tell the time** to know what time it is when you look at a clock or watch
tell yourself (that) to make yourself consider something in order to understand it correctly or persuade yourself that it is true
→ TELLING
PHRASAL VERBS **,tell sb/sth a'part** to recognize the difference between two people or things that are very similar: *I couldn't tell the two pictures apart.*
,tell sb 'off *informal* to criticize someone angrily for doing something wrong: *The teacher told me off for talking again today.*

telling /ˈtelɪŋ/ adj **1** very important or effective **2** showing or suggesting the truth about a situation

tellurium /teˈljʊəriəm/ noun [U] CHEMISTRY a silvery-grey semi-metallic element, used in alloys and electronic equipment. Chemical symbol: **Te**

temper[1] /ˈtempə/ noun **1** [C/U] a tendency to get angry very quickly: *That temper of yours is going to get you into trouble.* **2** [singular/U] a particular emotional state or mood: *Mark was in a foul temper.*
PHRASE **lose your temper (with)** to become very angry

temper[2] /ˈtempə/ verb [T] TECHNOLOGY to heat metal again to a specific temperature then cool it, in order to make it stronger

tempera /ˈtempərə/ noun [U] ARTS a method of painting in which colour is mixed with egg or another thick liquid

temperament /'temprəmənt/ noun [C/U] someone's temperament is their basic character, for example their tendency to be happy or angry, or calm or worried

temperamental /,temprə'ment(ə)l/ adj someone who is temperamental gets angry easily or changes from one mood to another very quickly

temperate /'temp(ə)rət/ adj **1** GEOGRAPHY never having extremely hot or extremely cold weather —picture ➔ ECOSYSTEM **2** not extreme in behaviour or language

temperature /'tempritʃə/ noun [C/U] **1** SCIENCE a measurement of how hot or cold a place or object is. Temperature is measured in **degrees Celsius** or **degrees Fahrenheit**, using the symbols °C or °F. The SI unit of temperature is the **kelvin**: *The plants need a temperature of at least 15 °C to grow well.*
♦ *Temperatures dropped below freezing last night.*
♦ *The temperature rose steadily throughout the day.*
2 HEALTH the measurement of how hot your body is: *She had a very high temperature.* ♦ *The nurse took his temperature.*

'temperature ,gauge noun [C] ENGINEERING a piece of equipment for measuring the temperature of something

'temperature ,range noun [C] all the temperature measurements that are included within particular limits, from the lowest to the highest

'temperature-,sensitive adj reacting to changes in temperature:

tempest /'tempɪst/ noun [C] *literary* a severe storm

template /'tem,pleɪt/ noun [C] **1** something that is used as a pattern or example for something else **2** COMPUTING a computer file that can be used to make new files that are similar to it

temple /'temp(ə)l/ noun [C] **1** RELIGION a building that is used for worship in some religions **2** the flat area that is on either side of the forehead next to the eyes —picture ➔ BODY

tempo /'tempəʊ/ (plural **tempi** /'tempi:/ or **tempos**) noun **1** [singular] the speed at which something happens **2** [C/U] MUSIC the speed at which music is played or sung

temporal /'temp(ə)rəl/ adj *formal* relating to time —**temporally** adv

'temporal ,lobe noun [C] ANATOMY a part of the brain that is responsible for hearing

temporary /'temp(ə)rəri/ adj **1** existing, done, or used for only a limited period of time ≠ PERMANENT: *These measures are only temporary.* ♦ *a temporary job* **2** temporary workers do a job for a limited period of time: *a temporary lecturer* —**temporarily** /,tempə'reərəli/ adv: *Bucharest airport was closed down temporarily.*

tempt /tempt/ verb [T] to make you want to do or have something, especially something that is wrong or bad for you

temptation /temp'teɪʃ(ə)n/ noun **1** [U] a strong feeling of wanting to do or have something, especially something that is wrong or bad for you: *I resisted the temptation to have another piece of cake* (=stopped myself from having another piece). **2** [C] something that tempts you

tempting /'temptɪŋ/ adj something that is tempting makes you feel that you would like to do it or have it, even though it is wrong or bad for you

ten /ten/ number the number 10

tenacious /tə'neɪʃəs/ adj very determined and not willing to stop trying to do something —**tenaciously** adv

tenacity /tə'næsəti/ noun [U] **1** tenacious behaviour **2** TECHNOLOGY the ultimate **tensile strength** (=ability not to break when stretched) of a material

tenancy /'tenənsi/ (plural **tenancies**) noun [C/U] the right to use a flat, office, building, or piece of land that you rent from the person who owns it

tenant /'tenənt/ noun [C] someone who rents a flat, office, building, or piece of land from the person who owns it

,tenant 'farmer noun [C] AGRICULTURE a farmer who rents the land that they farm from someone else. The tenant farmer pays the owner with money or with food that they produce.

tend /tend/ verb **1** [I] to usually do a particular thing: *He tends to exaggerate.* ♦ *I tend not to go out so much in the winter.* **2** [I/T] to take care of someone or something: *Eddie kept himself busy tending the garden.* ♦ *Doctors were tending the wounded.* ♦ *I have to tend to the children before I go out.* **3** [I] to usually have a particular quality: *Her study found that sociologists tended towards liberalism and radicalism.*

tendency /'tendənsi/ (plural **tendencies**) noun [C] **1** an aspect of your character that you show by behaving in a particular way: *criminal tendencies* ♦ *You have a tendency to avoid arguments.* **2** a situation that is starting to develop in a particular way= TREND: *We continue to see a tendency towards globalization of brands.* ♦ *There is a growing tendency for students to use the Internet to do their research.*

tender /'tendə/ adj **1** gentle in a way that shows that you care about someone or something: *Her voice was low and tender.* **2** soft, and easy to cut and eat **3** if a part of your body is tender, it is painful when you touch it —**tenderly** adv, **tenderness** noun [U]

tendon /'tendən/ noun [C] ANATOMY a band of strong tissue that connects a muscle to a bone

tendril /'tendrəl/ noun [C] BIOLOGY a long thin part of some climbing plants that curls around things and helps to support the stem

tennis /'tenɪs/ noun [U] SPORTS a game in which two or four people hit a ball across a net using a **racket**

tenor /'tenə/ noun **1** [C/U] MUSIC the middle and higher range of musical notes written for men to sing, or a man who sings this range **2** [singular] **the tenor of sth** the feeling, mood, or main message that you get from something

tenpin bowling /,tenpɪn 'bəʊlɪŋ/ noun [U] a game played inside where players roll a heavy ball down a track in order to knock **tenpins** (=objects shaped like bottles) over

tense¹ /tens/ adj **1** making you feel nervous and not relaxed: *a tense situation* **2** feeling nervous and not relaxed: *He was too tense to sleep.* **3** stretched tight: *tense muscles*

tense² /tens/ noun [C/U] LANGUAGE a form of a verb that is used for showing when something happens. For example 'I go' is the present tense and 'I went' is the past tense of the verb 'to go'.

tense³ /tens/ or **,tense (sth) 'up** verb [I/T] if your muscles tense, or if you tense them, they become tight

tensile strength /,tensaɪl 'streŋθ/ noun [U] PHYSICS the amount of physical pressure that can be applied to a material before it breaks or changes its shape. Many metals have a high tensile strength.

tension /'tenʃ(ə)n/ noun

1 nervous feeling	**4** of muscle/rope:
2 lack of trust	tightness
3 problems	**5** force stretching object

1 [U] the feeling of being so nervous, worried, or excited that you cannot relax: *I tried to **ease the tension*** (=make it less strong) *with a joke.* ♦ *Symptoms include **nervous tension**, depression, and insomnia.*
2 [C/U] a situation in which there is a lack of trust between people, groups, or countries and they may attack each other: *racial tensions* ♦ *Measures are needed to **reduce tension** between the two states.*
3 [C/U] a situation in which opposing aims, ideas, or influences cause problems: *There is a certain **tension between** the freedom of individuals and the need for public safety.*
4 [U] the degree to which something such as a rope or muscle is pulled tight: *Can you feel the tension in your neck and shoulders?*
5 [U] **CONSTRUCTION, PHYSICS** a force that makes an object or part of a structure stretch

tent /tent/ noun [C] a structure made of cloth and supported with poles and ropes. You sleep in it when you are camping.

tentacle /'tentək(ə)l/ noun [C] **BIOLOGY** one of the long thin organs around the mouth or on the head of some invertebrate sea animals such as **squid**. Tentacles are used for holding, catching, feeling, and moving. —*picture* → SEA

tentative /'tentətɪv/ adj **1** not definite, or not certain **2** not confident —**tentatively** adv

tenth /tenθ/ number **1** in the place or position that is counted as number 10 **2** one of ten equal parts of something

tenure /'tenjə/ noun [U] **1** the period of time during which someone has an important job **2** LAW someone's right to live on land and own it

tepid /'tepɪd/ adj a tepid liquid is slightly warm

tera- /terə/ prefix one **trillion**: used with some units of measurement

terbium /'tɜːbiəm/ noun [U] **CHEMISTRY** a soft silvery-white metallic element in the **lanthanide** group of the periodic table. Chemical symbol: **Tb**

term /tɜːm/ noun

1 word/phrase	**5** in mathematics
2 aspects	**6** of agreement
3 division of year	**+** PHRASES
4 time sth lasts	

1 [C] a word or phrase that is used for referring to or describing someone or something: *a technical term*
2 terms [plural] the aspects of something that you are considering or including: *In practical terms, this change is unlikely to affect many people.* ♦ *The savings, both in terms of time and money, could be considerable.*
3 [C] **EDUCATION** one of the periods of time that the year is divided into for students: *What classes are you taking this term?* ♦ *How many weeks is it till the end of term?* ♦ *He trains five times a week during term time.*
4 [C] a period of time that something lasts: *In 1988 he was re-elected for a five-year term.* ♦ *He received a prison term of six months.*
5 [C] **MATHS** a number or symbol used in a calculation in mathematics
6 terms [plural] the conditions of a legal, business, or financial agreement that the people making it accept: *We have agreed the terms of the lease.* ♦ *Do you accept these terms and conditions?*
PHRASES be on good/bad/friendly etc terms to have a

good, bad, or friendly etc relationship with someone: *He's still on friendly terms with his first wife.*
come to terms with sth to learn to accept and deal with an unpleasant situation or event
on speaking terms feeling friendly towards someone, and not angry with them
→ LONG¹, SHORT¹

terminal¹ /'tɜːmɪn(ə)l/ noun [C] **1** the part of an airport where passengers arrive and leave **2** a large building where train, boat, or bus services start and finish **3** **COMPUTING** a computer screen and a keyboard connected to a computer **network 4 PHYSICS** a place where electricity enters or leaves a piece of electrical equipment

terminal² /'tɜːmɪn(ə)l/ adj **HEALTH** a terminal illness cannot be cured and will cause death —**terminally** adv

terminal mo'raine noun [C] **GEOLOGY** a line of rock, gravel, and soil across a valley at the end of a glacier

terminate /'tɜːmɪneɪt/ verb [I/T] *formal* to end, or to make something end

termination /ˌtɜːmɪ'neɪʃ(ə)n/ noun **1** [C/U] the end of an agreement, job, or situation **2** [C] **HEALTH** a medical operation in which a foetus is removed from a woman's body before it is completely developed, so that it is not born alive= ABORTION

terminology /ˌtɜːmɪ'nɒlədʒi/ noun [U] **LANGUAGE** the words and phrases that are used in a particular subject or profession

terminus /'tɜːmɪnəs/ (plural **terminuses**) noun [C] the place where a bus or train service ends

termite /'tɜːmaɪt/ noun [C] a small insect that eats wood and can damage buildings

ternary form /'tɜːnəri ˌfɔːm/ noun [U] **MUSIC** a musical form consisting of three sections, in which the first section is repeated after the second section

terrace /'terəs/ noun [C] **1** a flat area outside a building where you can sit and eat meals **2** **GEOLOGY** a slope with a flat top and steep sides beside a river. It is formed from mud left behind when the river floods. —*picture* → FLOOD PLAIN

terraced house /'terəst ˌhaʊs/ noun [C] a house in a row of houses that are joined together

terracette /ˌterə'set/ noun [C] **GEOLOGY** a narrow raised line on a hill, formed when soil particles that are full of moisture become dry and move slowly down the hill

terracing /'terəsɪŋ/ noun [U] **AGRICULTURE** land on the side of a hill that has been made into thin flat sections that look like steps so that it can be used for farming

terracotta /ˌterə'kɒtə/ noun [U] a brown-red clay

terrain /tə'reɪn/ noun [U] **GEOGRAPHY** an area of land with a particular physical feature

terrapin /'terəpɪn/ noun [C] a small reptile that lives in water and has a hard shell on its back. It is a type of **turtle**. —*picture* → REPTILE

terrestrial /tə'restriəl/ adj **1** existing on the Earth, or happening on the Earth **2** **BIOLOGY** living on land rather than in water: *terrestrial plants* → AQUATIC **3** terrestrial television consists of programmes that are not broadcast by **cable** or satellite

terrible /'terəb(ə)l/ adj **1** making you feel very upset or afraid: *A few minutes later there was a terrible scream.* ♦ *Her mother's sudden death came as a terrible shock.* **2** causing or involving serious harm or damage: *She suffered terrible injuries in the attack.* ♦ *A terrible storm hit the island last night.* **3** ill, unhappy, or feeling guilty: *I **feel terrible** about what I said.* ♦ *What's wrong? You **look terrible**.* **4** very bad: *The food was terrible.* ♦ *I've always been really **terrible at** maths.*

terribly /'terəbli/ adv **1** very, or extremely: *Something is terribly wrong.* **2** in a very bad way: *What's wrong? You're playing terribly today.*

terrier /'teriə/ noun [C] a type of small dog that is sometimes used for hunting small animals

terrific /tə'rıfık/ adj **1** very good or interesting **2** very big or great: *We suddenly heard a terrific bang.* —**terrifically** /tə'rıfıkli/ adv

terrified /'terəfaɪd/ adj extremely frightened

terrify /'terəfaɪ/ (**terrifies, terrifying, terrified**) verb [T] to make someone very frightened —**terrifying** adj

territorial /ˌterə'tɔːriəl/ adj relating to the land or the part of the sea that is controlled by a particular country

territorial 'sea noun [U] GEOGRAPHY the area of sea that covers a **continental shelf** —*picture* → OCEAN

territory /'terət(ə)ri/ (plural **territories**) noun **1** [C/U] an area of land that is controlled by a particular country, leader, or army: *Russian troops crossed into Austrian territory in February 1849.* **2** [C/U] BIOLOGY an area that an animal considers to be its own, and tries to prevent others from entering: *A lion will fearlessly **defend** its **territory**.* **3** [U] an area of knowledge, study, or experience: *Social work is **familiar territory** to her.*

terror /'terə/ noun **1** [singular/U] a strong feeling of fear: *I remember the **sheer terror** of those bombing raids.* ♦ *Thousands of people fled **in terror** as the volcano erupted.* **2** [U] violence that is used for achieving political aims: *the war against terror* ♦ *a deliberate **campaign** of terror* **3** [C] something or someone that makes you very frightened: *the terrors of the night*

terrorism /'terəˌrız(ə)m/ noun [U] the use of violence in order to achieve political aims: *They were charged with conspiring to commit **acts of terrorism**.*

terrorist /'terərıst/ noun [C] someone who uses violence in order to achieve political aims: *a suspected terrorist* ♦ *a terrorist bombing*

terrorize /'terəraɪz/ verb [T] to frighten someone by threatening them or by using violence

tertiary /'tɜːʃəri/ adj BUSINESS providing services

'tertiary con,sumer noun [C] BIOLOGY, ENVIRONMENT a **carnivore** (=meat-eating animal) that feeds on another carnivore, for example a sea bird that eats a fish that itself eats smaller fish

,tertiary edu'cation noun [U] EDUCATION education at a college or university

tessellation /ˌtesə'leɪʃ(ə)n/ noun [C/U] MATHS a pattern of geometric shapes that are fitted together with no spaces in between them

test¹ /test/ noun [C] **1** EDUCATION a set of questions that someone must answer, or a set of actions that someone must perform, in order to show their knowledge or ability in a subject: *Did you get a good mark **in your** physics **test**?* ♦ *You're going to have to **take** the test again.* ♦ *I **passed** my English **test** today.* ♦ *I know I'm going to **fail** this **test**.* **2** HEALTH an examination of a part of your body or of a substance that is taken from your body: *an eye test* ♦ *a test for HIV* ♦ *Your **test results** are fine.* **3** a process that is designed to find out whether something is satisfactory, whether something works correctly, or whether something exists somewhere: *nuclear tests in the Pacific* ♦ *Researchers **conducted tests on** more than 220 computers.* **4** a difficult situation that shows what

qualities someone or something has: *a test of strength* **PHRASE** **put sb/sth to the test** to find out how good or effective someone or something is

test² /test/ verb [T] **1** EDUCATION to find out how much someone knows or how well they can do something, by giving them a set of questions to answer or an activity to perform: *The aim of the examination is to **test** your writing skills.* ♦ *You won't be **tested on** anything that you haven't already studied.* **2** to try using something such as a machine or product in order to find out whether it works correctly or is satisfactory: *The theory will be tested by computer simulation.* ♦ *a skin-care product that isn't **tested on** animals* → TRIED² **3** HEALTH to examine someone's body in order to check that it is in good condition, or in order to find out whether they have a particular illness: *Debbie has to **have her eyes tested**.* ♦ *She was **tested for** hepatitis.* **4** to show how good or effective someone or something is by putting pressure on them: *They were never seriously tested by their opponents in the first half of the game.*

testa /'testə/ (plural **testae** /'testiː/) noun [C] BIOLOGY the hard layer that covers and protects the seed of a plant that produces flowers

testament /'testəmənt/ noun [C] LAW a **will²** sense 4 → NEW TESTAMENT, OLD TESTAMENT

testes /'testiːz/ ANATOMY the plural of **testis**

testicle /'testɪk(ə)l/ noun [C] ANATOMY in most male mammals, one of the two round male sex organs contained in a bag of skin behind the penis —**testicular** /te'stɪkjʊlə/ adj

testify /'testɪfaɪ/ (**testifies, testifying, testified**) verb [I/T] LAW to make a formal statement in a court of law about something that you saw, know, or experienced

testimonial /ˌtestɪ'məʊniəl/ noun [C] **1** an event that is organized as a formal way of thanking someone for their work **2** a formal statement about someone's qualities and character, usually provided by an employer. A more usual word is **reference**.

testimony /'testɪməni/ (plural **testimonies**) noun [C/U] LAW a formal statement that you make in a court of law about something that you saw, know, or experienced

testis /'testɪs/ (plural **testes** /'testiːz/) noun [C] ANATOMY in most male mammals, one of the two male sex organs contained in bag of skin behind the penis

'test ,match noun [C] SPORTS in cricket and rugby, a game between two teams from different countries

testosterone /te'stɒstərəʊn/ noun [U] BIOLOGY a sex hormone that causes men to develop the physical features that are typical of males, for example hair on the face and a deep voice. Testosterone belongs to the group of hormones called **steroids**.

'test ,tube noun [C] SCIENCE a long thin glass container that is rounded at one end and open at the other and is used in laboratories —*picture* → LABORATORY

'test-tube ,baby noun [C] BIOLOGY a human baby created in a laboratory using **in vitro fertilization**. The mother's egg is fertilized with the father's sperm outside the body, and the egg is then put back into the mother's uterus to develop naturally.

tetanus /'tet(ə)nəs/ noun [U] HEALTH a serious infection of the **nervous system** caused by an organism that is found in soil and animal waste. It gets into the body through a cut in the skin, and causes severe **convulsions** and often death.

tether /'teðə/ verb [T] to tie an animal to something so that it will stay in a particular area

tetrahedron /ˌtetrəˈhiːdrən/ noun [C] MATHS a solid shape consisting of four flat surfaces with straight sides —picture → SHAPE

tetraploid /'tetrəplɔɪd/ adj BIOLOGY having four matched sets of chromosomes in the cell nucleus —**tetraploidy** noun [U]

tetravalent /ˌtetrəˈveɪlənt/ adj CHEMISTRY relating to chemical elements that have a **valency** of four

text¹ /tekst/ noun **1** [U] the part of a book, magazine, or computer document that consists of writing and not pictures: *There are 200 pages of text and illustrations.* **2** [C/U] a written record of the words of a speech, lecture, programme, or play: *The text of the lecture is available from the departmental office.* **3** [C] EDUCATION a piece of writing such as a book or play that you study: *We'll be analysing the language of literary texts.* ♦ *The play is **a set text** for first-year students.* **4** [C] a text message —**textual** adj

text² /tekst/ verb [T] to send a written message to someone using a mobile phone: *Gemma didn't call or text me all day.* —**texting** noun [U]

textbook /'teks(t)bʊk/ noun [C] EDUCATION a book that contains information about a particular subject

'text ˌbox noun [C] COMPUTING a box on a computer screen in which you can type or change words and numbers

'text ˌchat noun [U] COMPUTING a way in which several Internet users can send messages to each other immediately

'text ˌeditor noun [C] COMPUTING a computer program that allows you to create and **edit** written documents

'text ˌfile noun [C] COMPUTING a file that contains only words and numbers and no codes to show how the document should look

textile /'tekstaɪl/ noun [C] any type of woven cloth = FABRIC

'text ˌmessage noun [C] a written message that you send or receive using a mobile phone —**'text ˌmessaging** /'teks(t) ˌmesɪdʒɪŋ/ noun [U]

texture /'tekstʃə/ noun [C/U] **1** the way that something feels when you touch it: *a rough texture* **2** used about the effect that is produced when different things combine, for example in music —**textural** adj, **textured** adj

thallium /'θæliəm/ noun [U] CHEMISTRY a soft toxic chemical element in the form of a silver-white metal. Chemical symbol: **Tl**

thallus /'θæləs/ (plural **thalli** /'θælaɪ/ or **thalluses**) noun [C] BIOLOGY the body of an organism such as an alga that has no separate leaves, stems, or roots —**thalloid** /'θælɔɪd/ adj

than /strong ðæn, weak ðən/ conjunction, preposition **1** used when making comparisons: *Nylon is considerably stronger than cotton.* ♦ *Is the world a safer place than it was a year ago?* **2** used when you are saying that a number or amount is above or below a particular level: *a city of **more than** 5 million people* ♦ *I'll be back in **less than** a week.* → RATHER

thank /θæŋk/ verb [T] to tell someone that you are grateful for something that they have done or given to you: *She didn't even thank me.* ♦ *I just wanted to **thank** you **for** the flowers – they're beautiful.* ♦ *I'd like to **thank** everybody **for** coming along today.*

PHRASE **thank God/goodness/heaven(s)** used for saying that you are pleased that something unpleasant has ended or has not happened: *Thank heaven nobody was injured in the crash.*

thankful /'θæŋkf(ə)l/ adj grateful for something, or pleased that something unpleasant is no longer happening or did not happen

thankfully /'θæŋkf(ə)li/ adv used for saying that you are pleased that something unpleasant is no longer happening or did not happen: *Thankfully the boys are safe.*

thankless /'θæŋkləs/ adj a thankless activity is unpleasant, and other people are not grateful to you for doing it

thanks¹ /θæŋks/ interjection *informal* **1** used for telling someone that you are grateful for something that they have said or done: *'You're looking well.' 'Thanks.'* ♦ *Thanks for dinner – it was great.* ♦ *Thanks for reminding me.* **2** used for politely accepting something that is offered to you: *'Do you want a chocolate?' 'Thanks, I'd love one.'*

PHRASE **no thanks** *spoken* used for politely saying you do not want something that someone has offered you: *'Would you like another drink?' 'No thanks.'*

thanks² /θæŋks/ noun [plural] things that you say or do in order to tell someone that you are grateful to them: *Please accept my heartfelt thanks for your concern and generosity.*

PHRASE **thanks to** because of someone or something: *Thanks to this treatment, her condition has improved.* ♦ *The railway system is in chaos, thanks to the government's incompetence.*

thanksgiving /'θæŋksˌgɪvɪŋ/ noun [C/U] *formal* an expression of thanks, often in the form of a prayer to God

Thanksgiving /'θæŋksˌgɪvɪŋ/ or **ˌThanksgiving ˈDay** noun [C/U] in the US and Canada, a holiday in the autumn when families have a special meal together

'thank ˌyou interjection **1** used for telling someone that you are grateful for something that they have said or done: *'That's a nice jacket.' 'Thank you.'* ♦ *Thank you for coming here today.* **2** used for politely accepting something that is offered to you: *'Would you like a cup of coffee?' 'Oh, thank you, that would be great.'*

PHRASE **no thank you** *spoken* used for politely and formally saying you do not want something that someone has offered you: *'Please sit down.' 'No thank you, I'd rather stand.'*

that /ðæt/ adv, conjunction, determiner, pronoun

1 one known about	**5** 'which' or 'who'
2 one looked at	**6** introducing a result
3 a past time or event	**7** very
4 introduces idea	

1 (plural **those** /ðəʊz/) used for referring to someone or something that has already been mentioned or is already known: *I know there's a problem, but I haven't got time to worry about that now.* ♦ *The engine's started making that noise again.* ♦ *Why don't you ask Carmen? That's who I'd ask.*

2 (plural **those** /ðəʊz/) *spoken* used for referring to someone or something that you can see or point at, although they are not near you: *Do you know who that woman in the blue dress is?* ♦ *I'm using these books, but you can borrow those.* ♦ *That's Jerry's car, over there.*

3 (plural **those** /ðəʊz/) used for referring to a period or event in the past: *Remember that time we all went to the lake?* ♦ *That was fun. We must do it again some time.* ♦ *There were no telephones **in those days**.*

4 /strong ðæt, weak ðət/ used after some verbs, adjectives, and nouns in order to state an idea, fact, or reason: *Dawkins believes that his sister was murdered.*

♦ *I'm sorry that I missed the first meeting.* ♦ *We can't ignore the fact that she lied to us.*

> The conjunction **that** is often left out, especially in spoken English, or with some very common verbs: *I told them I was busy.*

5 /strong ðæt, weak ðət/ used instead of 'which' or 'who' in order to give more information about a noun or pronoun: *We haven't met the people that live next door.* ♦ *It was the worst winter that anyone could remember.*

> The relative pronoun **that** is often left out when it is the object of a relative clause: *Did you find the book you were looking for?* In formal written English **that** is not generally left out.

6 /strong ðæt, weak ðət/ used after 'so' or 'such' for showing the result of something: *It was so cold that the sea froze in some places.*

> The conjunction **that** is often left out of expressions with 'so' and 'such', especially in spoken English: *I was so excited I couldn't sleep.*

7 spoken to a very great degree: *There's no need to get upset – it isn't that important.*
→ THIS

thatched /θætʃt/ adj with a roof made from dried plants such as **straw**

thaw¹ /θɔː/ verb **1** [I/T] if ice or snow thaws, or if something thaws it, it becomes warmer and changes into water **2** [I/T] if frozen food thaws, or if you thaw it, it becomes softer and ready to cook **3** [I] to become more friendly

thaw² /θɔː/ noun [singular] **1** a period of warmer weather that causes ice and snow to turn into water **2** an improvement in the relationship between people, countries etc

the /strong ðiː, weak ðə, ði/ determiner

1 used before sb/sth known about	**4** used to explain which is meant
2 used for general type of sth	**5** in dates and times
3 used before part of sth/body	**6** used for actions
	7 used before names
	+ PHRASE

1 used before a noun when that person or thing has already been mentioned or is already known, or when there is only one: *Have you locked the door?* ♦ *I had coffee and cake, but the cake was stale.* ♦ *the best hotel in Beijing*
2 used before a singular noun when making a general statement about things or people of a particular type: *Some people use the car as their only means of transport.* ♦ *The violin is a difficult instrument to play.* ♦ *The Japanese* (=Japanese people) *eat a lot of seafood.*

> DO NOT use **the** when you are referring to things or people in a general way: *Children need love and attention.*

3 used before a part of a particular thing, or a part of the body: *the sharp end of a pencil* ♦ *He had a gunshot wound in the neck.*
4 used when explaining which person or thing you are referring to: *Who was the actor who played Romeo?* ♦ *We live in the house with green shutters.*
5 used before dates or periods of time: *the 4th of July* ♦ *popular music of the 1960s*
6 used before a noun that refers to an action, especially when it is followed by 'of': *the destruction of a whole city* ♦ *the death of Princess Diana*
7 used before the names of seas, rivers, deserts, or

groups of mountains: *the Pacific Ocean* ♦ *the Sahara* ♦ *the Alps*

> **The** is not usually used before the names of streets, towns, countries, states, or continents: *My parents live in Kenya.*

PHRASE **the... the...** used with 'more', 'less', and other **comparatives** for showing that when one thing increases or is reduced, it causes something else to increase or be reduced at the same time: *The sooner we finish, the happier I'll be.*

theatre /ˈθɪətə/ noun **1** [C] ARTS a building or room that is used for performing plays: *We're going to the theatre tonight.* **2** [U] ARTS the activity or job of writing, performing, or organizing performances of plays **3** [U] ARTS plays considered as entertainment or art: *a compelling piece of theatre* **4** [C/U] HEALTH a room in a hospital that is used for medical operations = OPERATING THEATRE: *He's in theatre at the moment.*

theatrical /θiˈætrɪk(ə)l/ adj **1** ARTS relating to the theatre **2** theatrical behaviour is very emotional and aims to attract attention

theft /θeft/ noun [C/U] LAW the crime of stealing something

their /ðeə/ determiner **1** belonging to, or relating to, people or things that have already been mentioned or are already known: *chemical fertilizers and their effect on the environment* ♦ *They have children of their own.* **2** used instead of 'his or her', especially when you are referring back to a word such as 'everyone', 'someone', or 'anyone'. Some people disapprove of this use: *Everyone has their own way of doing things.*

theirs /ðeəz/ pronoun **1** used for referring to someone or something that belongs to or is connected with people who have already been mentioned: *Your house is big, but I think theirs is bigger.* ♦ *They introduced us to some friends of theirs.* **2** used instead of 'his or hers', especially when you are referring back to a word such as 'everyone', 'someone', or 'anyone'. Some people disapprove of this use: *I haven't had my lunch yet, but everyone else has had theirs.*

them /strong ðem, weak ðəm/ pronoun **1** the object form of 'they', used for referring to people or things that have already been mentioned or are already known: *They've taken their families with them.* ♦ *Sykes stole the paintings and then tried to sell them.* **2** used instead of 'him or her', especially when you are referring back to a word such as 'everyone', 'someone', or 'anyone'. Some people disapprove of this use: *Someone phoned, but I told them to call back later.*

thematic /θiˈmætɪk/ adj formal relating to ideas or subjects

theme /θiːm/ noun [C] **1** LITERATURE, ARTS the main subject of something such as a book, speech, discussion, or art exhibition: *Love and honour are the main themes of the book.* **2** theme or theme tune MUSIC a short piece of music that is played at the beginning and end of a radio or television programme or a film

ˈtheme ˌpark noun [C] a large park where people pay to play games and have fun and where all the entertainment is designed according to one theme

themselves /ðəmˈselvz/ pronoun **1** the reflexive form of 'they' that is used for showing that the people or things that do something are also affected by what they do: *They used sticks to defend themselves.* ♦ *They decided to build themselves a bigger house.* **2** used for emphasizing that a particular group of people are the ones that you are referring to: *The boys died in a fire that they themselves had started.*

PHRASES (all) by themselves 1 alone: *people who choose to live by themselves* 2 without any help: *They made the model all by themselves.*

(all) to themselves not sharing something with anyone else: *Helen and Philip were able to get a table to themselves.*

then /ðen/ adv 1 at a particular time in the past or in the future: *I can see you next weekend. Can you wait until then?* ♦ *I was at school in the 1970s, but things have changed a lot since then.* 2 used for introducing the next thing that happens: *He glanced quickly at Sally and then looked away again.* ♦ *We'll learn the rules first. Then we'll play the game.* 3 used for saying what you think the result must be if something is true: *'Sue and I grew up together.' 'You must know her fairly well then.'* ♦ *If no one else is willing, then I'll have to do the job myself.* → THERE

theocracy /θɪ'ɒkrəsi/ (plural **theocracies**) noun [C] **RELIGION** a government led by religious leaders —**theocratic** /ˌθiːə'krætɪk/ adj

theological /ˌθiːə'lɒdʒɪk(ə)l/ adj **RELIGION** relating to the study of God and religion —**theologically** /ˌθiːə'lɒdʒɪkli/ adv

theology /θɪ'ɒlədʒi/ (plural **theologies**) noun **RELIGION** 1 [U] the study of God and religion 2 [C/U] a set of religious beliefs

theorem /'θɪərəm/ noun [C] **MATHS** a statement that can be proved to be true

theoretical /ˌθɪə'retɪk(ə)l/ adj 1 based on theories instead of practical experience 2 possible but not definite

theoretically /ˌθɪə'retɪkli/ adv used for saying that something could be true or could exist: *Transmission of the virus is theoretically possible, but very unlikely.*

theory /'θɪəri/ (plural **theories**) noun 1 [C] an idea that explains how or why something happens: *Einstein's theory of relativity* ♦ *He had a theory that the germs caused disease.* 2 [U] the set of general principles that a particular subject is based on: *literary theory* 3 [C] an idea that you believe is true, although you have no proof: *I have my own theory about why he resigned.*
PHRASE in theory used for saying that something should be true, although it may not be true: *In theory the country is a democracy, but in practice the military holds most of the power.*

therapeutic /ˌθerə'pjuːtɪk/ adj 1 **HEALTH** helping to treat or cure illness 2 helping you to feel better or calmer

therapy /'θerəpi/ (plural **therapies**) noun **HEALTH** 1 [C/U] a form of treatment for an illness or medical condition 2 [U] treatment for someone with a mental illness or emotional problems that involves finding out about the reasons for the way they feel and behave —**therapist** noun [C]

there /ðeə/ adv, pronoun 1 /strong ðeə, weak ðə/ used for introducing a statement about someone or something that exists or happens: *There is plenty of time left.* ♦ *There are 24 teams competing in the tournament.* ♦ *Are there any other suggestions?* 2 in or to a place that has already been mentioned, or that you are looking at or pointing to: *They're going to Hawaii, and they plan to stay there for two months.* ♦ *It's only a hundred miles to Oxford. You could drive there and back in a day.* ♦ *Would you like to sit over there by the window?* ♦ *There's Angela now, coming up the path.* 3 at a particular point in a series of events, in a speech, or in a story: *I'll stop there, and answer questions.* 4 available, and ready to help or to be used: *The opportunity was there, so I took it.* ♦ *If you need me, I'll be there for you.*

PHRASE there and then or then and there immediately at that moment and in that place: *They wanted me to make a decision there and then.*

thereabouts /ˌðeərə'baʊts/ adv near a particular place, amount, or time that has just been mentioned

thereafter /ˌðeər'ɑːftə/ adv *formal* after a particular time that has just been mentioned

thereby /ðeə'baɪ/ adv *formal* because of, or by means of, what has just been mentioned

therefore /'ðeəfɔː/ adv as a result of the fact that you have just mentioned: *These boots are softer, and therefore more comfortable.* ♦ *This is a dangerous task. Therefore, you must be very careful.*

thermal¹ /'θɜːm(ə)l/ adj 1 **SCIENCE** relating to heat 2 thermal clothing is made of special material that keeps you warm —**thermally** adv

thermal² /'θɜːm(ə)l/ noun [C] **GEOGRAPHY** a rising current of warm air

thermal ex'pansion noun [U] **PHYSICS** the principle that substances **expand** (=become larger) when heated

thermal pol'lution noun [U] **ENVIRONMENT** damage to the environment caused by heat being released into streams, lakes, or other areas of water

thermocouple /'θɜːməʊˌkʌp(ə)l/ noun [C] **PHYSICS** a piece of equipment for measuring temperature in which two wires of different metals are joined. The **potential difference** between the wires is a measure of the temperature of something they touch.

thermo-cracking /'θɜːməʊ ˌkrækɪŋ/ noun [U] **CHEMISTRY** a process in which large **hydrocarbon** molecules are broken down into smaller, more useful ones by heating them at a high temperature without air

thermodynamic /ˌθɜːməʊdaɪ'næmɪk/ adj **PHYSICS** relating to the ways in which heat can be changed into other forms of energy

thermometer /θə'mɒmɪtə/ noun [C] **SCIENCE** a piece of equipment with a **scale** that measures temperature. The most common type of thermometer is a closed glass tube containing a liquid, usually **mercury**, that **expands** up the tube as the temperature rises. —*picture* → LABORATORY and on next page

thermonuclear /ˌθɜːməʊ'njuːkliə/ adj **PHYSICS** involving nuclear reactions in which atoms join together at very high temperatures and produce a lot of energy

thermoplastic /ˌθɜːməʊ'plæstɪk/ noun [C] **CHEMISTRY** one of the two main types of plastic. Thermoplastics melt when heated, and become hard when cooled. → THERMOSETTING PLASTIC

thermoregulation /ˌθɜːməʊregjuː'leɪʃ(ə)n/ noun [C] **BIOLOGY** the process of keeping body temperature the same, even when the temperature of the environment changes

Thermos /'θɜːməs/ or **'Thermos ˌflask** **TRADEMARK** a **vacuum flask** that keeps liquids hot or cold

thermosetting plastic /ˌθɜːməʊsetɪŋ 'plæstɪk/ noun [C] **CHEMISTRY** one of the two main types of plastic. Thermosetting plastics become permanently hard once they have been heated and shaped. → THERMOPLASTIC

the thermosphere /'θɜːməʊˌsfɪə/ noun [singular] **SCIENCE** the layer of the Earth's atmosphere above the mesosphere, beginning about 85 kilometres above the Earth's surface

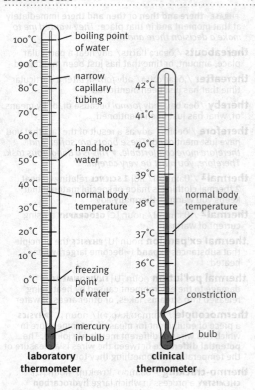

100°C — boiling point of water
90°C
80°C — narrow capillary tubing
70°C
60°C
50°C — hand hot water
40°C
30°C — normal body temperature
20°C
10°C
0°C — freezing point of water
— mercury in bulb

42°C
41°C
40°C
39°C
38°C — normal body temperature
37°C
36°C
35°C — constriction
— bulb

laboratory thermometer   **clinical thermometer**

thermostat /'θɜːməʊstæt/ noun [C] a piece of equipment that controls the temperature in a building, machine, or engine. It consists of a switch containing metals that **expand** to a different degree when heated. The thermostat switches the heat off as the temperature rises, and switches it on as the temperature falls. —**thermostatic** /ˌθɜːməʊ'stætɪk/ adj

thesaurus /θɪ'sɔːrəs/ (plural **thesauri** /θɪ'sɔːraɪ/ or **thesauruses**) noun [C] a book that contains lists of words that have similar meanings

these /ðiːz/ determiner, pronoun the plural of **this**

thesis /'θiːsɪs/ (plural **theses** /'θiːsiːz/) noun [C]
1 EDUCATION a long piece of writing that is the final part of an advanced university degree **2** formal a theory that is used for explaining something

they /ðeɪ/ pronoun **1** used for referring to people or things that have already been mentioned or are already known: I phoned her parents because I knew they were worried. ♦ It's hard to choose. They're all very nice. **2** used instead of 'he or she': We should give everyone a chance to say what they think.

- In spoken English and in informal written English, **they**, **them**, **their**, and **themselves** are used by many people for referring to a person without mentioning whether the person is male or female, especially when referring back to a pronoun such as 'everyone' or 'someone': What happens if someone changes their mind?
- In more formal English, 'he or she', 'him or her', or 'himself or herself' are used instead.

3 used for referring to people in general: They say there's going to be a war. **4** used for referring to a government, an organization, or a group of people in authority: They should change the law in order to protect children. → HE

they'd /ðeɪd/ short form **1** the usual way of saying or writing 'they would'. This is not often used in formal writing: They said they'd be happy to help. **2** the usual way of saying or writing 'they had' when 'had' is an auxiliary verb. This is not often used in formal writing: He knew they'd met somewhere before.

they'll /ðeɪl/ short form the usual way of saying or writing 'they will'. This is not often used in formal writing: Hurry up! They'll be here any minute.

they're /ðeə/ short form the usual way of saying or writing 'they are'. This is not often used in formal writing: They believe that what they're doing is right.

they've /ðeɪv/ short form the usual way of saying or writing 'they have' when 'have' is an auxiliary verb. This is not often used in formal writing: They've been talking about buying a new house for years.

thiacetazone /ˌθaɪə'setəzəʊn/ noun [U] HEALTH a medicine that is used for treating **tuberculosis**

thiamin /'θaɪəmɪn/ or **thiamine** /'θaɪəmiːn/ noun [U] HEALTH a vitamin found in the outer layer of rice and other grains that is important for keeping the nerves healthy. It belongs to the B group of vitamins.

thick¹ /θɪk/ adj

1 long between edges	6 of accent
2 of measurement	7 stupid
3 not flowing easily	8 full of sth
4 of plants/hair	+ PHRASE
5 filling air completely	

1 a thick object or material has a long distance between two opposite sides, edges, or surfaces ≠ THIN: a thick woollen sweater ♦ a thick layer of snow
2 used for stating the distance between the opposite surfaces or edges of a solid object: The walls are only a few inches thick.
3 a thick liquid is more stiff or solid than normal and does not flow easily ≠ THIN: a thick cream sauce
4 growing very close together ≠ THIN: her thick dark hair ♦ a thick coat of fur
5 thick smoke or cloud fills the air completely, so that it is difficult to see or difficult to breathe
6 a thick accent shows very clearly that the speaker comes from a particular place= BROAD
7 informal stupid
8 full of something: The air was thick with smoke.
PHRASE **have a thick skin** to not be easily upset or offended by what other people say about you —**thickly** adv

thick² /θɪk/ noun
PHRASES **in the thick of sth** in the most busy, active, or dangerous part of a situation, event, or activity
through thick and thin in all situations, especially the most difficult ones

thicken /'θɪkən/ verb [I/T] to become thick, or to make something become thick

thicket /'θɪkɪt/ noun [C] an area with a lot of bushes and small trees growing very close together

thickness /'θɪknəs/ noun **1** [C/U] the measurement of how thick something is **2** [C] a layer of something

thief /θiːf/ (plural **thieves** /θiːvz/) noun [C] someone who steals something

thigh /θaɪ/ noun [C] the top part of the leg, above the knee —picture → BODY

'thigh ˌbone noun [C] ANATOMY the **femur** —picture → SKELETON

thin¹ /θɪn/ (thinner, thinnest) adj

1 short between edges	**5** small in amount
2 with little fat	**6** not detailed
3 of hair/fur	**7** with little oxygen
4 flowing easily	**+** PHRASES

1 a thin object or material has only a short distance between two opposite sides, edges, or surfaces ≠ THICK: *a thin layer of dust* ♦ *Cut the tomatoes into thin slices.*
2 someone who is thin has very little fat on their body: *Charles was thin and very tall.*
3 thin hair or fur grows with spaces between the individual hairs ≠ THICK: *a thin moustache*
4 a thin liquid contains a lot of water, so that it flows easily ≠ THICK: *a plate of meat covered with thin gravy*
5 small in number or amount: *It was a day of thin trading on the stock market.*
6 without much detail or many facts: *The evidence for his theory is rather thin.*
7 thin air has less oxygen in it than usual
PHRASES **thin air** if something appears out of thin air or disappears into thin air, it appears or disappears in a sudden mysterious way
thin on the ground not available in large amounts or numbers
→ THINLY

> **Build your vocabulary: words you can use instead of thin**
> - **emaciated** extremely thin because you have been ill, or because you do not have enough food to eat
> - **lean/wiry** thin and strong
> - **skinny** (*informal*) thin in a way that is not attractive
> - **slender** thin in a graceful way
> - **slim** thin in an attractive way

thin² /θɪn/ (thins, thinning, thinned) verb

1 [I] to become less in number, amount, or **thickness**: *As it grew dark, the crowd started to thin.* ♦ *Did you notice that his hair is thinning on top?* **2** [T] to make a thick liquid become less thick by adding water or another liquid to it

thing /θɪŋ/ noun

1 object	**5** aspect/quality
2 possessions	**6** general situation
3 action/activity	**7** idea/information
4 situation/event	**+** PHRASES

1 [C] used for referring to an object that you cannot or do not want to refer to in a more specific way: *What's that thing over there on the table?* ♦ *It's one of those gadget things, isn't it?* ♦ *It's a thing for looking inside people's ears.*
2 things [plural] the objects that belong to a particular person or are used for a particular purpose: *I'll pack my things for the trip tomorrow.*
3 [C] an action, or an activity: *I have a lot of things to do today.* ♦ *I gave back the money. Did I do the right thing?*
4 [C] a situation or event: *A funny thing happened to me today.* ♦ *I think we should just forget the whole thing.* ♦ *She doesn't find that kind of thing funny.*
5 [C] an aspect of a situation, or a quality that someone has: *If you could change three things about your job, what would they be?* ♦ *The thing I really like about Theresa is her sense of humour.* ♦ *The funny thing is, I miss him now.* ♦ *It's a good thing that you don't need to work late.*
6 things [plural] used for talking about a situation in a general way: *Things have been getting better lately.* ♦ *The police soon got things under control.*

7 [C] an idea, comment, fact, or subject: *There are some interesting things in your report.* ♦ *I have a few things to say to you.*
PHRASES **be seeing/hearing things** to think that you see or hear something that is not really there
how are things? used as a general greeting when you meet someone

think /θɪŋk/ (thinks, thinking, thought /θɔːt/) verb

1 believe sth is true	**6** consider sb
2 have opinion	**7** have sth in mind
3 consider facts	**+** PHRASE
4 remember sb/sth	**+** PHRASAL VERBS
5 imagine sth	

1 [T] to believe something as a result of facts or ideas that you have: *I don't think there's a bank in the village.* ♦ *'Is Dan coming tonight?' 'I think so, but I'm not sure.'* ♦ *Faulty wiring is thought to have caused the fire.*
2 [I/T] to have a particular opinion about someone or something: *His colleagues think a lot of him* (=have a very good opinion of him). ♦ *I don't think much of Sam's new girlfriend* (=I don't like her very much). ♦ *Nobody seriously thought of him as a candidate for the job.*
3 [I] to carefully consider facts in order to understand something, make a decision, or solve a problem: *Let's stop and think before we do anything else.* ♦ *I need to think seriously about their offer.* ♦ *I've got to think of a way to earn more money.*
4 [I] to remember someone or something: *He could never think of the woman's name.* ♦ *I often think about the time we spent in Rome.*
5 [I/T] to imagine something: *I never thought that I'd end up working here.* ♦ *Just think of what she's suffered!*
6 [I] to consider someone and their needs or situation: *It was kind of you to think of our daughter.*
7 [I/T] to have something in your mind: *I wasn't worried – I just thought, 'Why is she doing that?'* ♦ *I expect we were all thinking the same thing.*
PHRASE **think twice/again** to carefully consider whether what you are planning to do is a good idea
PHRASAL VERBS ,think 'back to think about something that happened in the past: *I've been trying to think back to that last evening.*
,think sth 'over to consider a problem or decision carefully: *Let's think over his proposal before we see him again.*
,think sth 'up to invent or imagine something, especially an excuse: *She'd have to think up a good reason for being late.*

thinking /ˈθɪŋkɪŋ/ noun [U] **1** an opinion, or a set of ideas: *Can you explain the thinking behind your proposal?* **2** the way that you consider things or react to them: *What's needed here is some positive thinking.* **3** the process of considering something or reacting to something: *He had some serious thinking to do.*

thinly /ˈθɪnli/ adv **1** in a thin layer or piece: *thinly sliced tomatoes* **2** with only a few people or things that are far apart from each other: *a thinly populated area* **3** in a way that makes it easy to recognize what the true situation really is: *a thinly disguised threat*

third¹ /θɜːd/ number **1** in the place or position counted as number 3 **2** one of 3 equal parts of something

third² /θɜːd/ noun [C] EDUCATION in the UK or Australia, the lowest mark for a university degree

,third-class 'lever noun [C] PHYSICS a type of lever where the load is in the middle with the **fulcrum**, and the effort is at opposite ends. **Tweezers** and **fishing rods** are third-class levers.

the ,third 'degree noun a lot of questions that someone asks another person in a very determined way

'third-de,gree adj HEALTH a third-degree burn is the most serious type

,third law of 'motion noun [singular] PHYSICS one of the laws about movement that were first expressed by Isaac Newton. It states that every action has an equal and opposite reaction.

thirdly /'θɜːdli/ adv used for introducing the third idea in a list

,third 'party noun [C] formal a person or organization that is not one of the two main people or organizations involved in something

,third-'party adj **1** third-party insurance protects someone if they accidentally injure someone or accidentally damage their property **2** LANGUAGE relating to a person or organization that is not one of the two main people or organizations involved in a legal agreement or case

the ,third 'person noun [singular] LANGUAGE the set of pronouns and verb forms that are used for referring to someone or something that is not the speaker or the person who is being spoken to

,third-'rate adj of very low quality

the ,Third 'World noun [singular] ECONOMICS old-fashioned countries that are poor and do not have much industrial development. This word is now considered offensive, and most people use the expression **developing countries** or **emerging countries** instead.

thirst /θɜːst/ noun **1** [singular/U] the feeling or state of being thirsty **2** [singular] a strong feeling of wanting to have or do something: *a thirst for learning*

thirsty /'θɜːsti/ adj feeling that you want or need to drink something: *I'm really thirsty – could I have a glass of water?* —**thirstily** adv, **thirstiness** noun [U]

thirteen /,θɜː'tiːn/ number the number 13

thirteenth /,θɜː'tiːnθ/ number **1** in the place or position counted as number 13 **2** one of 13 equal parts of something

thirties /'θɜːtiz/ noun [plural]
PHRASES **the thirties 1** if the temperature is in the thirties, it is in the range of 30 to 39 degrees **2** the years from 1930 to 1939: *people who were born in the thirties*
in your thirties to be an age in the range of 30 to 39

thirtieth /'θɜːtiəθ/ number **1** in the place or position counted as number 30 **2** one of 30 equal parts of something

thirty /'θɜːti/ number the number 30

this /ðɪs/ adv, determiner, pronoun

1 the one here	4 so
2 the present one	5 saying who you are
3 the one known	

1 (plural **these** /ðiːz/) used for referring to a person, thing, or place that is near you: *I bought these shoes in Italy.* ♦ *This is my teacher, Mrs Adams.* ♦ *This is where I catch the bus.*
2 (plural **these** /ðiːz/) used for referring to the present time, or to a time that will happen soon: *Is this your first visit to Egypt?* ♦ *I'm going to be very busy this week.* ♦ *Benson was late again this morning* (=the morning of today).
3 (plural **these** /ðiːz/) used for referring to a particular fact, thing, person etc that has just been mentioned or that is already known: *Sometimes there's flooding, and*

this is why no one wants to live here. ♦ *This latest accident was more serious.*
4 spoken so, or to such a degree: *I haven't had this much fun since I was a kid.* ♦ *It was hot in Nairobi, but it wasn't as hot as this.*
5 used when you are saying who you are in a telephone conversation: *Hello, this is Kim Riley speaking.*

- **This** refers to something that you are holding or wearing, or that is nearest to you, and **that** refers to something that someone else is holding or wearing, or that is further away from you: *Do you like this shirt?* ♦ *Where did you get that hat?*
- **This** refers to things that are happening now or are just about to happen, but **that** refers to things that happened in the past, that have just ended, or that will happen in the future: *I'm enjoying this party.* ♦ *What happened at that meeting?*

thistle /'θɪs(ə)l/ noun [C] a wild plant with a thick round purple or white flower and leaves with sharp points

thoracic /θɔː'ræsɪk/ adj HEALTH relating to or affecting the thorax —**thoracically** /θə'ræsɪkli/ adv

tho,racic 'vertebra noun [C] ANATOMY one of the twelve spinal bones in the upper part of the back, to which the ribs are attached —picture → VERTEBRA

thorax /'θɔːræks/ noun [C] **1** ANATOMY the part of the body between the neck and the waist —picture → SKELETON **2** BIOLOGY the middle part of the body of an insect or **arachnid** that its legs and wings are joined to —picture → CATERPILLAR, INSECT, SPIDER

thorium /'θɔːriəm/ noun [U] CHEMISTRY a soft silvery-white radioactive metallic element in the **actinide** group of the periodic table. Chemical symbol: **Th**

thorn /θɔːn/ noun [C] a sharp point that sticks out from the stem of a plant

thorny /'θɔːni/ adj **1** difficult to deal with: *a thorny issue* **2** covered with thorns

thorough /'θʌrə/ adj **1** including everything that is possible or necessary: *a thorough investigation* ♦ *She has a thorough understanding of the business.*
2 someone who is thorough does everything that they should and leaves nothing out: *The doctor was very thorough and asked lots of questions.*
—**thoroughness** noun [U]

thoroughly /'θʌrəli/ adv **1** very much, or completely: *The children thoroughly enjoyed the show.* **2** very carefully, so that nothing is missed: *The case will be thoroughly studied before any decision is made.*

those /ðəʊz/ determiner, pronoun the plural of **that**

though /ðəʊ/ adv, conjunction **1** used for introducing a statement that makes your main statement seem surprising = ALTHOUGH: *Though they're only a small country, they're very rich.* ♦ *He went on fighting even though he was wounded.* **2** but = ALTHOUGH: *I enjoyed the book, though some parts were difficult to understand.* **3** used when adding a statement or question that seems surprising after the previous statement: *'It's very sunny.' 'Yes. It's quite cold, though.'* ♦ *'He's not very clever.' 'Isn't he a teacher, though?'* = AS

thought¹ /θɔːt/ noun **1** [C] a word, idea, or image that comes into your mind: *a comforting thought* ♦ *His mind was filled with thoughts of revenge.* ♦ *She couldn't bear the thought of seeing him again.* ♦ *The thought had crossed my mind that we were taking a big risk.* **2** [U] the mental effort that you make to understand something, make decisions, or solve problems: *Deep in thought, he did not hear the doorbell ring.* ♦ *I hope you'll give our conversation some thought* (=think

about it). **3** [C] an idea or opinion about something: *Does anyone want to express their **thoughts on** this matter?* **4** [C/U] an intention or wish to do something: *He insists he has no **thought of** running for office.*
PHRASE **with no thought for/of sth** without any feeling of being worried about what might happen as a result of an action

thought² /θɔːt/ the past tense and past participle of **think**

thoughtful /ˈθɔːtf(ə)l/ adj **1** kind and showing that you think that what other people want or need is important: *Thank you – the flowers were a very thoughtful gift.* **2** thinking seriously about something: *Beth stood there, silent and thoughtful.* **3** involving careful thought —**thoughtfully** adv

thoughtless /ˈθɔːtləs/ adj not thinking about what other people want or need —**thoughtlessly** adv, **thoughtlessness** noun [U]

thousand /ˈθaʊz(ə)nd/ number **1** the number 1,000 **2 thousands** or **a thousand** a large number or amount of people or things: *The floods have left thousands homeless.* ♦ *I still have a thousand things to do.*

thousandth /ˈθaʊz(ə)nθ/ number **1** in the place or position counted as number 1,000 **2** one of 1,000 equal parts of something

thrash /θræʃ/ verb **1** [T] to defeat an opponent very easily in a game or competition **2** [T] to hit someone hard several times as a punishment **3** [I] to move in a violent uncontrolled way

thread¹ /θred/ noun **1** [C/U] a long thin fibre used for sewing: *cotton thread* ♦ *You need a longer piece of thread.* **2** [C] an idea or quality that forms a connection between things: *There is a common thread running through all the problems.* **3** [C] **TECHNOLOGY** the raised line that curves around a screw in a continuous spiral **4** [C] **COMPUTING** a series of email messages about a particular subject

thread² /θred/ verb **1** [T] to put something long and thin through a hole or space in something: *Thread the rope through the rings.* **2** [T] to put a piece of thread through a hole in something: *Can you thread this needle for me?* **3** [I/T] to move carefully through a place, avoiding people or things that are in your way

threadbare /ˈθred,beə/ adj very thin because of being worn or used a lot: *a threadbare carpet*

threat /θret/ noun **1** [C] someone or something that could cause harm or danger: *She is not viewed as a threat by her former employer.* ♦ *a **threat to** freedom* ♦ *The dispute **poses a threat** (=is a threat) **to** peace.* **2** [C] an occasion when someone says that they will cause you harm or problems, especially if you do not do what they tell you to do: *He would not **make threats** he wasn't prepared to carry out.* ♦ *After **threats of** legal action they stopped the building work.* ♦ *He had received several **death threats**.* **3** [C/U] the possibility that something bad is going to happen: *They **face the threat** of terrorism every day.* ♦ *With the closure of the hospital, local jobs are **under threat**.*

threaten /ˈθret(ə)n/ verb **1** [T] to tell someone that you will cause them harm or problems, especially in order to make them do something: *He's been threatening me for months.* ♦ *The terrorists are **threatening to** kill the hostages.* ♦ *One man has been **threatened with** legal action.* **2** [T] to be likely to harm or destroy something: *Many workers feel that their jobs are threatened.* ♦ *Nearly 1,000 of the world's bird species are **threatened with** extinction.* ♦ *Nuclear testing **threatens to** destroy our environment.* **3** [I] if something bad or unpleasant threatens, it is likely to

happen or to affect you: *Rain was threatening.* —**threatening** adj, **threateningly** adv

three /θriː/ number the number 3

three-dimensional /ˌθriː daɪˈmenʃ(ə)nəl/ adj not flat, but able to be measured in height, depth, and width

three-dimensional ˌdrawing noun [C/U] **MATHS, PHYSICS** a drawing that shows a three-dimensional object

three-ˈquarters noun [plural] three of four equal parts of something: *It took an hour and three-quarters to get home.*

threshold /ˈθreʃ,həʊld/ noun [C] the point at which a limit is reached or a rule starts to apply
PHRASE **on the threshold of sth** starting a new stage in your life, or soon to discover something

threw /θruː/ the past tense of **throw¹**

thrift /θrɪft/ noun [U] the practice of spending money carefully so that it is not wasted

thrifty /ˈθrɪfti/ adj careful about how you spend money so that you do not waste any

thrill¹ /θrɪl/ noun [C] **1** a sudden feeling of being very pleased and excited **2** something that makes you feel very pleased and excited

thrill² /θrɪl/ verb [T] to make someone feel very pleased and excited

thrilled /θrɪld/ adj very pleased and excited: *We are thrilled that Kevin is going to join the team.*

thriller /ˈθrɪlə/ noun [C] **ARTS, LITERATURE** a book, play, or film that tells an exciting story

thrilling /ˈθrɪlɪŋ/ adj extremely exciting

thrive /θraɪv/ verb [I] to become very successful, happy, or healthy —**thriving** adj: *a thriving economy*

throat /θrəʊt/ noun [C] **1** **ANATOMY** the area at the back of the mouth and inside the neck: *She's in bed with a throat infection.* ♦ *Have we got any medicine for a **sore throat**?* **2** the front part of the neck: *The man grabbed him by the throat.* → CLEAR² —picture → BODY

throb /θrɒb/ (**throbs, throbbing, throbbed**) verb [I] **1** **HEALTH** if a painful part of your body throbs, the pain comes and goes in a fast regular pattern **2** to make a repeated low sound: *Loud dance music throbbed in the air.* —**throb** noun [C]

thrombocyte /ˈθrɒmbəʊsaɪt/ noun [C] **BIOLOGY** a platelet

thrombosis /θrɒmˈbəʊsɪs/ (plural **thromboses** /θrɒmˈbəʊsiːz/) noun [C/U] **HEALTH** a serious medical condition in which the blood gets thicker and forms a clot that stops it from flowing normally

throne /θrəʊn/ noun **1** [C] a special chair that a king or queen sits on **2 the throne** [singular] the position of being a king or queen

throng /θrɒŋ/ verb [I/T] if people throng somewhere, a lot of them go there —**throng** noun [C]

throttle¹ /ˈθrɒt(ə)l/ noun [C] a piece of equipment that controls how fast a vehicle is moving by controlling the amount of fuel going into the engine

throttle² /ˈθrɒt(ə)l/ verb [T] to hurt or kill someone by squeezing their throat so that they cannot breathe

throttle ˌvalve noun [C] **ENGINEERING** a valve that controls the supply of fuel to the engine in a vehicle

through /θruː/ adv, preposition

1 from one end or side to the other	**4** connected by phone
2 during a period of time	**5** in every part
3 by means of sth	**6** finished
	+ PHRASE

1 from one side of a hole, object, or area to the other: *The railway runs through a tunnel.* ♦ *The man at the gate would not let us through.* ♦ *The path climbs steeply through the trees.*
2 during the whole of a period of time until the end of it: *He lay awake **all through** the night.* ♦ *The project will continue **through to** the end of the year.*
3 by means of something, or because of something: *Most accidents occur **through** human error.* ♦ *skills that we can only learn **through** experience*
4 used for saying that you are connected to someone by phone: *Could you **put** me **through** to the manager, please?* ♦ *I tried phoning her, but I couldn't **get through**.*
5 affecting or looking at every part of something: *A rumour spread **through** the camp.* ♦ *Problems extend **through** the entire system.* ♦ *Read the instructions **through** carefully.*
6 finished doing or using something: *I'm not sure what time he'll be **through with** his meeting.*
 PHRASE **through and through** used for saying that someone has all the qualities of a particular type of person

throughout /θruːˈaʊt/ adv, preposition **1** in every part of a place: *The hotel has recently been redecorated throughout.* ♦ *Pollution is a serious problem in major cities throughout the world.* **2** during the whole of an event or a period of time: *The problem continued throughout the 1980s.*

throughput /ˈθruːˌpʊt/ noun [singular/U] the amount of work, people, or things that a system deals with in a particular period of time

through ˈticket noun [C] TOURISM a ticket that you can use to travel to a place, even though you may change trains or planes on the way

throw¹ /θrəʊ/ (throws, throwing, threw /θruː/, thrown /θrəʊn/) verb

1 send through air	6 look etc in direction
2 put sth somewhere	7 put sb/sth in state
3 move your body	8 say/ask sth suddenly
4 move sb/sth	+ PHRASES
5 confuse sb	+ PHRASAL VERBS

1 [I/T] to make something leave your hand and move through the air, by moving your arm quickly: *Kids were throwing stones at the windows.* ♦ *She threw the ball to the little boy.* ♦ *Can you throw me that rope?*
2 [T] to put something somewhere carelessly: *She hastily threw her books into the cupboard.*
3 [T] to suddenly move your body or a part of your body: *Throwing back his head, he started laughing.*
4 [T] to use force to move someone or something: *The door was thrown open.* ♦ *He threw his opponent to the ground.*
5 [T] if something throws you, it makes you confused because you were not expecting it and do not know how to deal with it
6 [T] to suddenly look, smile etc in a particular direction: *Marco threw an angry glance at her.*
7 [T] to cause someone or something to be in a particular state or situation, especially a bad one: *A single computer problem can **throw** the whole office **into** chaos.*
8 [T] if someone throws something such as questions, ideas, comments etc at someone, they suddenly ask them or mention them: *They stood in the street throwing insults at each other.*
 PHRASES **throw a party** to organize a party, especially in your own home
throw a punch to hit someone with your **fist** (=closed hand)
throw yourself into sth to start giving all of your

attention and energy to something: *After my girlfriend left me, I threw myself into my work.*
 PHRASAL VERBS **,throw sth a'way** to get rid of something that you no longer want: *Have you thrown the papers away?*
,throw sb 'out to force someone to leave a place or group: *Several people were **thrown out of** the party.*
,throw sth 'out same as **throw sth away**: *I've thrown out my old boots.*

throw² /θrəʊ/ noun [C] **1** an action of throwing something such as a ball **2** a large piece of cloth that you put over a chair, bed etc **3** SPORTS the action of throwing an opponent to the ground in a sport such as **wrestling**

'throw-in noun [C] SPORTS in football, an occasion when a player throws the ball back onto the field after it has gone out

thrown /θrəʊn/ the past participle of **throw¹**

thrush /θrʌʃ/ noun **1** [C] a brown bird with light spots on its breast **2** [U] HEALTH a fungal infection of the mouth or vagina

thrust¹ /θrʌst/ (thrusts, thrusting, thrust) verb [T] to put something somewhere with a quick hard push: *A reporter thrust a microphone under her nose.*

thrust² /θrʌst/ noun [U] **1** PHYSICS the force that an engine produces to push something forwards —*picture* → JET ENGINE **2** CONSTRUCTION, PHYSICS a force caused by one part of a structure pushing against another

'thrust ,bearing noun [C] ENGINEERING a **bearing** (=machine part) that can support a heavy load in the direction of the axis of the **shaft** (=metal rod) inside it

thruster /ˈθrʌstə/ noun [C] SCIENCE a rocket on a spacecraft or aircraft that controls in what direction and how high it flies

thud /θʌd/ noun [C] a low sound that is made by something heavy falling or hitting something —**thud** verb [I]

thug /θʌg/ noun [C] someone who behaves in an unpleasant and violent way, especially in a public place

thulium /ˈθjuːliəm/ noun [U] CHEMISTRY a soft silvery-grey metallic element in the **lanthanide** group of the periodic table. Chemical symbol: **Tm**

thumb /θʌm/ noun [C] the part like a wide finger at the side of the hand: *She held the jewel carefully between her finger and thumb.* —*picture* → BODY
 PHRASE **under sb's thumb** completely controlled by someone else

thumbnail /ˈθʌmˌneɪl/ noun [C] **1** the hard part over the top of the thumb **2** COMPUTING a small picture of something shown on a computer screen, especially on a web page

thump¹ /θʌmp/ verb **1** [T] to hit someone or something with your **fist** (=closed hand) = PUNCH **2** [I] if your heart is thumping, you can feel it beating very fast, for example because you are frightened or excited

thump² /θʌmp/ noun [C] **1** a low loud sound that is made when something heavy hits something else: *He brought his hand down on the table with a thump.* **2** an action of hitting someone or something with your **fist** (=closed hand) = PUNCH

thunder¹ /ˈθʌndə/ noun [U] GEOGRAPHY the loud noise that you sometimes hear in the sky during a storm

thunder² /ˈθʌndə/ verb [I] **1** GEOGRAPHY if it thunders, you hear thunder in the sky **2** to make a lot of noise while moving somewhere fast: *An express train thundered through the station.*

thunderstorm /'θʌndə,stɔːm/ noun [C] GEOGRAPHY a storm with thunder and lightning

Thurs. abbrev Thursday

Thursday /'θɜːzdeɪ/ noun [C/U] the day after Wednesday and before Friday: *The election is being held on a Thursday.* ♦ *I had lunch with Joe on Thursday.* ♦ *Adam has his piano lesson on Thursdays* (=every Thursday).

thus /ðʌs/ adv *formal* **1** as a result of the fact that you have just mentioned= HENCE, THEREFORE: *Fewer pupils will attend the schools, and they will thus need fewer teachers.* **2** by the method that has been mentioned: *The oil producers will raise prices, thus increasing their profits.*

thwart /θwɔːt/ verb [T] *formal* to prevent someone from doing something that they were planning to do

thylakoid /'θaɪləkɔɪd/ noun [C] BIOLOGY a **sac** (=small bag) enclosed in a membrane inside a **chloroplast**, where photosynthesis takes place. Thylakoids are often found on top of each other in structures called **grana**.

thyme /taɪm/ noun [U] a small plant with very small leaves, used for adding flavour to food

thymus /'θaɪməs/ noun [C] ANATOMY an **endocrine gland** that is situated near the top of the **spinal cord**

thyroid /'θaɪrɔɪd/ or **'thyroid ,gland** noun [C] ANATOMY a gland in the neck that produces hormones that control the **metabolism**

thyroxine /θaɪ'rɒksiːn/ noun [U] BIOLOGY the main hormone produced by the thyroid in humans and other vertebrates. It increases **metabolic rate** and controls growth and development.

ti /tiː/ noun [C] MUSIC the seventh note in the **sol-fa** musical **scale**

tibia /'tɪbiə/ noun [C] ANATOMY the wide bone at the front of the lower leg, between the knee and the ankle and next to the **fibula** —*picture* → SKELETON

tic /tɪk/ noun [C] a sudden movement of a muscle that you cannot control

tick¹ /tɪk/ verb **1** [I] if a clock or watch ticks, it makes a quiet sound every second **2** [T] to mark something with the symbol ✓ in order to show that it is correct or that you have dealt with it

PHRASAL VERB **,tick sth 'off** to put the symbol ✓ next to something on a list in order to show that you have dealt with it

tick² /tɪk/ noun [C] **1** the symbol ✓ that you write next to an answer in order to show that it is correct, or next to something on a list in order to show that you have dealt with it **2** the quiet sound that some clocks and watches make every second **3** a small **arachnid** that fastens itself onto the skin of a mammal and feeds on its blood —*picture* → INSECT

ticket /'tɪkɪt/ noun [C] **1** a piece of paper that shows that you have paid to do something such as go to a concert, visit a museum, or travel on a train, bus, plane etc: *a cinema ticket* ♦ *We'll send your tickets a week before your flight.* **2** a piece of paper that says you must pay an amount of money as a punishment for breaking a traffic law: *a speeding ticket*

'ticket col,lector noun [C] someone at a station who takes the tickets from passengers as they get off the train

ticketing /'tɪkɪtɪŋ/ noun [U] the process of producing and selling tickets for an event such as a concert or sports game

tickle /'tɪk(ə)l/ verb **1** [T] to move your fingers gently on someone's skin in order to make them laugh **2** [I/T] if a part of your body tickles, or if something that touches your skin tickles it, you have an uncomfortable feeling on your skin

tidal /'taɪd(ə)l/ adj GEOGRAPHY connected with the regular movement of the sea towards and away from the land

'tidal ,bulge noun [U] GEOGRAPHY the effect of the gravitational pull of the Moon and Sun on the ocean, which causes changes in sea level

'tidal ,energy noun [U] ENVIRONMENT energy produced by the movement of the tides of the sea. It can be used to produce electricity.

'tidal ,system noun [U] GEOGRAPHY the regular movement of the sea towards and away from the land

'tidal ,wave noun [C] **1** GEOGRAPHY a large wave or mass of water in the sea that is sometimes produced at **high tide 2** GEOLOGY a tsunami

tide /taɪd/ noun **1** [C] GEOGRAPHY the regular movement of the sea towards and away from the land **2** [singular] a tendency of people to think or feel in a particular way

tidemark /'taɪd,mɑːk/ noun [C] GEOGRAPHY a mark left on land by the sea that shows the highest point that the sea has reached

tidy¹ /'taɪdi/ (**tidier, tidiest**) adj **1** a tidy room, desk etc has everything in the correct place or arranged in the correct way= NEAT ≠ UNTIDY: *Try and keep your room tidy.* **2** a tidy person always puts their things in the correct place ≠ UNTIDY —**tidily** adv, **tidiness** noun [U]

tidy² /'taɪdi/ (**tidies, tidying, tidied**) verb [I/T] to make a place look better by putting things in the correct place

PHRASAL VERBS **,tidy sth a'way** to put something back in its correct place after you have used it

,tidy (sth) 'up *same as* **tidy²**

tie¹ /taɪ/ (**ties, tying, tied**) verb **1** [T] to fasten two ends of a piece of string, rope etc together with a knot, or to fasten things together with string, rope etc: *Sally bent down to tie her shoelaces.* ♦ *They **tied** one end of the rope **to** a tree.* ♦ ***Tie** the newspapers **together** before you throw them away.* **2** [T] to form a close connection between people or things: *This series **ties together** events from the past and present.* ♦ *Portugal's economy is closely **tied** to Spain's.* **3** [T] if something ties you to a particular place or situation, you cannot leave it: *Many young mothers feel **tied to** the home and children.* **4** [I/T] SPORTS if two players or teams tie, they both have the same number of points at the end of a game or competition= DRAW

PHRASAL VERB **,tie sth 'up** to tie the ends of something together

tie² /taɪ/ noun [C]

1 narrow cloth for neck	4 equal points/votes
2 connection	5 game in competition
3 for fastening	6 in building

1 a long narrow piece of coloured cloth that a man wears around his neck with a shirt: *a silk tie* ♦ *Do you have to wear a tie for work?*
2 a relationship or connection between people or things: *The treaty should **strengthen ties** between the two countries.*
3 a short piece of string or wire that is used for fastening something
4 SPORTS a result of a game or competition in which each person or team has the same number of points, votes etc= DRAW: *The game finished in a tie.*
5 SPORTS one game that is part of a competition

6 CONSTRUCTION a supporting part of a structure that prevents two other parts from moving apart

tiebreaker /'taɪˌbreɪkə/ or **tiebreak** /'taɪˌbreɪk/ noun [C] **SPORTS** in tennis and other sports, an extra game played to decide who will win when both players or teams have the same number of points

tied aid /ˌtaɪd 'eɪd/ noun [U] **ECONOMICS** money given to a country or area where people need it, but they have to agree to spend it only on goods and services provided by the country or organization that has given the money

tied up /ˌtaɪd 'ʌp/ adj **1** very busy **2** if your money is tied up in something, it is being used for that thing and you cannot use it for anything else

'tie-in noun [C] **BUSINESS** a product such as a toy or book that is connected with a successful film or television programme

tier /tɪə/ noun [C] **1** one of several levels in an organization or system: *the lower tiers of management* **2** one of several rows or layers of something that are all at different heights: *a wedding cake with three tiers*

tif /tɪf/ abbrev **COMPUTING** the last part of the name of a file that contains a **bitmap** image

tiger /'taɪgə/ noun [C] a large Asian wild mammal that has yellow fur with black lines. It is a member of the cat family. —*picture* → MAMMAL

'tiger e,conomy noun [C] **ECONOMICS** a very successful economy of a fairly small Asian country such as South Korea or Singapore

tight¹ /taɪt/ adj

1 close against body	**5** stretched flat
2 holding sth firmly	**6** of bend on a road
3 controlled carefully	**7** with close relationship
4 only just enough	**+ PHRASE**

1 fitting closely around the body or part of the body ≠ LOOSE: *a tight dress*
2 holding someone or fastening something very firmly ≠ LOOSE: *a tight knot* ♦ *Baxter kept a tight grip on the prisoner's arm.*
3 controlled very carefully and strictly ≠ LAX: *Security has been very tight throughout the Prince's visit.*
4 if something such as time or money is tight, you have only just enough of it: *holidays for people on **a tight budget***
5 if something such as cloth or rope is tight, it is stretched so that it is completely straight or flat
6 a tight bend on a road is difficult to drive round because it curves a lot
7 a tight group of people have a close relationship with each other
PHRASE **keep a tight grip/hold on sth** to control something in a very strict way
—**tightly** adv: *Keep the windows tightly closed.*
—**tightness** noun [U]

tight² /taɪt/ adv very firmly: *She **held on tight** to the railing.*

tighten /'taɪt(ə)n/ verb **1** [T] to turn something such as a screw or lid until it is tight and you cannot turn it any more ≠ LOOSEN **2** [I/T] to become tighter, or to make something become tighter ≠ LOOSEN: *He tightened his hold on the steering wheel.* **3** [I] if your hand tightens, or if your fingers tighten, you hold something more tightly **4** [T] to make a set of rules stricter or harder to avoid
PHRASE **tighten your belt** to spend less money

,tight-'knit or **,tightly-'knit** adj people in a tight-knit community or family have very strong and close relationships with each other

tightrope /'taɪtˌrəʊp/ noun [C] a piece of rope or wire high above the ground that a **circus** performer walks along
PHRASE **walk a tightrope** to be in a difficult situation that you have to deal with very carefully, because even a small mistake could have very bad results

tights /taɪts/ noun [plural] a piece of women's clothing that tightly covers the feet and legs up to the waist

tile¹ /taɪl/ noun [C] a flat piece of baked clay or stone that is used for covering a roof, floor, or wall

tile² /taɪl/ verb [T] **1** to cover a roof, floor, or wall with tiles **2** **COMPUTING** to arrange different windows on a computer screen so that you can see all of them next to each other

tiled /taɪld/ adj covered with **tiles**

till¹ /tɪl/ conjunction, preposition until: *You'll have to wait till tomorrow.* ♦ *Just sit here till I come back.*

till² /tɪl/ noun [C] a piece of equipment that is used in shops for adding up the amount of money that someone has to pay and for keeping the money in

tilt /tɪlt/ verb [I/T] to move, or to move something, so that one side is lower than the other: *The tray was tilted at an angle.* —**tilt** noun [singular]

timber /'tɪmbə/ noun [U] **1** wood that is used for building houses or making furniture **2** **AGRICULTURE** trees that are used for producing wood

timbre /'tæmbə/ noun [C/U] **MUSIC** the quality of sound that a particular voice or musical instrument has

time¹ /taɪm/ noun

1 hours, years etc	**7** when sth happens
2 measurement on clock	**8** time available
3 period	**9** part of history
4 occasion	**10** in a race
5 speed of music	**+ PHRASES**
6 moment/situation	

1 [U] **SCIENCE** the quantity that is measured in minutes, hours, days, years etc: *Einstein tried to define the relationship between space and time.*
2 [singular/U] the hours, minutes etc as shown on a clock: *Do you know **what time** it is?* ♦ ***What time** does the show start?* ♦ *Can your sister **tell the time** yet* (=is she able to say what time is shown on a clock)*?*
3 [C/U] a particular period of minutes, hours, days, years etc: *She thought about it for **a long time**.* ♦ *She left **a short time** ago.* ♦ *How much time did it **take to** get here?* ♦ *There have been improvements in **the length of time** patients have to wait for treatment.* ♦ *We've been waiting **for some time*** (=for a fairly long time).
4 [C] an occasion on which you do something or on which something happens: *It was **the first time** we'd met.* ♦ *Did you **have a good time** at camp?*
5 [U] **MUSIC** the speed at which a piece of music is played, measured as the number of beats in each **bar**: *a piece **in** 6–8 **time***
6 [singular/U] the moment or situation when something happens: ***By the time** we arrived, the other guests were already there.* ♦ *When would be **a good time** to discuss the proposal?* ♦ *It seemed like **the right time** to make the change.* ♦ *She was still living with her parents **at that time**.*
7 [U] the particular point when something should happen: *Is it **closing time** already?* ♦ *Come on, everyone. **It's time for** dinner.* ♦ *Did your plane arrive **on time**?* ♦ ***It's time** you children went to bed.*
8 [U] time that you have available for doing something in: *She will have less time to spend with family and friends now.* ♦ *Come and see me next week, if you **get the time**.* ♦ *I should be able to **find time** to phone him tomorrow.*

9 [C] a period in history or in someone's life: *The fort was built in Roman times.* ♦ *a time of political instability* ♦ *Mum thoroughly enjoyed her time as a teacher.*

10 [C] the amount of time that someone takes to finish a race: *She's cut two seconds off her previous best time.*

PHRASES **about time** used for saying that someone should do something soon: *Isn't it about time we went to bed?*

ahead of your/its etc time much more modern or advanced than most other people or things: *As an artist, he was years ahead of his time.*

all the time 1 often: *It's a very good restaurant. We go there all the time.* **2** continuously: *It rained all the time they were there.*

at a time used for saying how many things there are in each group or on each occasion: *Deal with each question separately, one at a time.*

at one time in the past, but not now: *At one time, that kind of thing would have made me really angry.*

at times sometimes, but not often: *She was fun to be with at times.*

for days/weeks etc at a time continuously for a period of several days, weeks etc

for the time being at the present time, but not permanently

from time to time sometimes, but not often

have no time for sb/sth to dislike someone or something
→ FOR, ONCE

in no time (at all) or **in next to no time** very soon or very quickly

in time 1 early enough to do something: *I want to be home in time for dinner.* ♦ *We got to the airport just in time.* ♦ *Luckily, they got there in time to warn him about what had happened.* **2** after a fairly long period of time: *He'll forget about it in time.* **3** MUSIC if you do something such as move your body in time to a piece of music, your movements are at the same speed and beat as the music

most of the time usually, or very often

of all time used for talking about people or things that are better than all others that have existed: *the greatest boxer of all time*

take your time to spend too much time doing something: *They're taking their time over that homework, aren't they?*

time after time or **time and again** happening so often that you become annoyed
→ FOR, ONCE

time² /taɪm/ verb [T] **1** to arrange something so that it happens at a particular time: *The exhibition has been timed to coincide with the publication of her new book.* **2** to use a clock to measure how long something takes or how often something happens: *a simple device for timing the human heartbeat* **3** SPORTS to hit a ball well or badly in sport because of the exact moment when you hit it

'**time ,bomb** noun [C] **1** a bomb that can be set to explode at a particular time **2** something that is likely to have a sudden and bad effect on a situation in the future

time-consuming /'taɪm kən,sjuːmɪŋ/ adj something that is time-consuming takes a long time to do

'**time ,frame** noun [C] the period of time in which something happens or should be done= TIMESCALE

timekeeper /'taɪm,kiːpə/ noun [C] SPORTS someone who records the time that is taken to do something, especially at a sports event

'**time ,lag** noun [C] the amount of time between two events

timeless /'taɪmləs/ adj not affected by time or by changes in fashion

'**time ,limit** noun [C] an amount of time in which you must do something

timeline /'taɪm,laɪn/ noun [C] a line showing particular dates, for example dates of historical events

timely /'taɪmli/ adj happening at the most suitable time ≠ UNTIMELY: *a timely reminder*

,**time 'off** noun [U] time when you are not at work or at school

,**time 'out** noun **1** [U] a period of time when you stop what you usually do and you rest or do something else instead **2** [C] SPORTS a short period of time in a game of basketball or **ice hockey** when players rest and plan their game

timeout /'taɪm,aʊt/ noun [U] COMPUTING a time when a computer connected to the Internet automatically **logs off** when no information is entered

timer /'taɪmə/ noun [C] a piece of equipment used for measuring time, or for turning a machine on or off at a particular time

times /taɪmz/ preposition MATHS informal multiplied by: *Two times four is eight.*

timeshare /'taɪm,ʃeə/ noun [C] TOURISM a flat or house that someone buys with other people, so that they can each use it for a particular amount of time every year

'**time ,signature** noun [C] MUSIC two numbers at the beginning of a line of music that tell you how many beats there are in a **bar** —picture → MUSIC

timetable /'taɪm,teɪb(ə)l/ noun [C] **1** a plan that shows the dates and times when something will take place = SCHEDULE **2** a list of the times when buses, trains etc arrive and leave **3** EDUCATION a list of the times of lessons or courses at a school, college, or university

'**time ,zone** noun [C] GEOGRAPHY one of the areas that the world is divided into for measuring time —picture → on next page

timid /'tɪmɪd/ adj shy and nervous —**timidity** /tɪ'mɪdəti/ noun [U], **timidly** adv

timing /'taɪmɪŋ/ noun **1** [C/U] the date or time when something happens or is planned to happen: *They objected to the timing of the election.* **2** [U] the ability to do or say things at the right moment **3** [U] ENGINEERING the measurement of the position that the **piston** in some vehicle engines should be in when the spark **ignites** the fuel and air mixture. Timing affects how efficiently a vehicle runs.

'**timing ,marks** noun [C] ENGINEERING points marked on an engine part that are used for setting the timing of a vehicle's **ignition** system

timpani /'tɪmpəni/ noun [plural] MUSIC a set of **kettledrums** (=large drums used in an orchestra) —**timpanist** noun [C]

tin¹ /tɪn/ noun **1** [U] CHEMISTRY a chemical element that is a soft light silver metal. Chemical symbol: **Sn**: *There used to be tin mines all around this area.* **2** [C] a closed metal container for food= CAN: *a tin of soup* **3** [C] a metal container with a lid, used for storing things: *a cake tin* **4** [C] an open metal container in which you cook food in an oven: *a baking tin*

tin² /tɪn/ verb [T] TECHNOLOGY to coat a **soldering iron** with **solder** when carrying out a soldering operation

tinfoil /'tɪn,fɔɪl/ noun [U] a substance that looks like shiny silver paper, used for wrapping and covering food

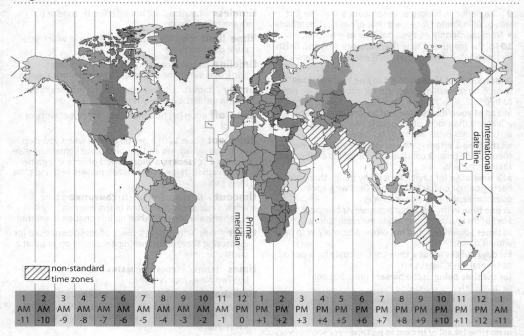

non-standard time zones

Prime meridian

International date line

1	2	3	4	5	6	7	8	9	10	11	12	1	2	3	4	5	6	7	8	9	10	11	12	1
AM	AM	AM	AM	AM	AM	AM	AM	AM	AM	AM	AM	PM	PM	PM	PM	PM	PM	PM	PM	PM	PM	PM	PM	AM
-11	-10	-9	-8	-7	-6	-5	-4	-3	-2	-1	0	+1	+2	+3	+4	+5	+6	+7	+8	+9	+10	+11	-12	-11

time zones

tingle /ˈtɪŋg(ə)l/ verb [I] if a part of your body tingles, it stings slightly, for example because it is very cold or hot —**tingle** noun [C]

tinker /ˈtɪŋkə/ or **,tinker aˈround** verb [I] to make small changes to a machine, plan, system etc, in order to improve or repair it

tinned /tɪnd/ adj tinned food has been preserved in a metal container= CANNED

tinnitus /ˈtɪnɪtəs/ noun [U] HEALTH a medical condition in which there is a continuous noise in the ears

'tin ,opener noun [C] an object that you use for opening **tins** of food

tint /tɪnt/ noun [C] a small amount of a particular colour

tinted /ˈtɪntɪd/ adj slightly coloured: *a car with tinted windows*

tiny /ˈtaɪni/ (**tinier, tiniest**) adj extremely small: *The floor was covered in tiny bits of paper.* ♦ *a tiny little baby*

tip¹ /tɪp/ noun [C] **1** a narrow or pointed end, especially of something long or thin: *the tip of your nose* ♦ *The village is on the southern tip of the island.* **2** an amount of money that you give to someone in addition to the price of a service: *Shall we leave a tip for the waiter?* **3** a useful suggestion or piece of information that someone gives you: *The booklet gives some good tips on getting the most out of your software.* **4** a place where you take rubbish and leave it = DUMP

PHRASES **on the tip of your tongue** if a word, name etc is on the tip of your tongue, you know it but cannot remember it at the time you are speaking

the tip of the iceberg a bad situation that shows that a much more serious problem exists: *The recent riots are just the tip of the iceberg.*

tip² /tɪp/ (**tips, tipping, tipped**) verb

1 (make sth) fall	4 give extra money
2 pour sth somewhere	5 say who will succeed
3 put/be at angle	+ PHRASAL VERB

1 [I/T] to fall to one side, or to make something fall onto its side

2 [T] to pour something from a container: *She tipped the sand out of her bucket.*

3 [I/T] to move into a position that is at an angle rather than upright, or to put something into a position like this: *He tipped his chair back and looked at me.*

4 [I/T] to give someone an amount of money in addition to what you owe for a service: *Don't forget to tip the driver.*

5 [T] to say who you think will get a particular job or be successful at something: *She is being tipped to take over from the managing director when he retires.*

PHRASAL VERB **,tip (sth) 'over** if something tips over, or if someone tips it over, it falls onto its side: *Be careful that the vase doesn't tip over.* ♦ *He tipped his drink over.*

tipper truck /ˈtɪpə ,trʌk/ noun [C] CONSTRUCTION a vehicle used for removing soil and stones from a building site. The back of the vehicle tips up and empties soil at the back of the vehicle.

Tipp-Ex /ˈtɪpeks/ TRADEMARK a white liquid used for covering mistakes in something that you are writing or typing

tipping point /ˈtɪpɪŋ ,pɔɪnt/ noun [C] **1** a time when important things start happening in a situation, especially things that you cannot change **2** HEALTH the time during an **epidemic** when the number of people who are infected with a disease increases very quickly

tiptoe¹ /ˈtɪp,təʊ/ noun **on tiptoe(s)** if you stand or walk on tiptoe, you stand or walk very quietly with only the front part of your foot touching the ground

tiptoe² /ˈtɪp,təʊ/ (**tiptoes, tiptoeing, tiptoed**) verb [I] to walk very quietly with only the front part of your foot touching the ground

tirade /taɪˈreɪd/ noun [C] a long angry speech criticizing someone or something

tire /'taɪə/ verb [I/T] to become tired, or to make someone feel tired

PHRASAL VERBS '**tire of sb/sth** to become bored with someone or something
,**tire sb 'out** to make someone feel very tired

tired /'taɪəd/ adj needing to rest or sleep: *Your mother looked tired.* ♦ *Kids can suddenly get very tired after playing for a time.*

PHRASE **tired of (doing) sth** not wanting something, or not wanting to do something, because you are bored or annoyed with it: *I'm tired of hearing about politics.*
—**tiredly** adv, **tiredness** noun [U]

tiresome /'taɪəs(ə)m/ adj making you feel bored or annoyed

tiring /'taɪərɪŋ/ adj making you feel tired

tissue /'tɪʃuː, 'tɪsjuː/ noun **1** [U] **ANATOMY** large numbers of similar cells working together. The four main types of tissue are nerve tissue, muscle tissue, **connective tissue**, and **epidermal** tissue: *brain tissue* **2** [C] a piece of soft thin paper that you use for wiping your nose: *a box of tissues* **3** tissue or **tissue paper** [U] a type of very thin paper used for wrapping or protecting things

'**tissue ,culture** noun **BIOLOGY 1** [U] the process of growing tissue cells taken from an organism in a **culture medium** (=substance that helps something to grow) for medical or scientific purposes **2** [C] an amount of tissue grown in a **culture medium**

Titan /'taɪt(ə)n/ noun **ASTRONOMY** the largest of the moons of the planet Saturn

titanium /taɪ'teɪniəm/ noun [U] **CHEMISTRY** a light strong greyish-white metallic element, used in alloys. Chemical symbol: **Ti**

tithe /taɪð/ noun [C] **RELIGION** in some churches, a tax that people pay regularly, usually one tenth of the money they earn

title /'taɪt(ə)l/ noun [C] **1** the name of a book, film, or other work of art: *What's the title of her new book?* **2** a word or abbreviation that is used before someone's name, for example 'Doctor', 'General', or 'Mrs' **3** a name for someone's job within a company or organization: *His new title is senior vice-president.* **4 SPORTS** the position of a winner in a sports competition: *She's won several important singles titles this year.*

'**title ,bar** noun [C] **COMPUTING** a coloured band across the top of a window on a computer screen that shows the name of the document or program that is open

'**title ,deed** noun [C] **LAW** an official document that shows who legally owns a building or piece of land

'**title-,holder** noun [C] **LAW** someone who owns a title deed

titration /taɪ'treɪʃ(ə)n/ noun [U] **CHEMISTRY** a way of calculating the strength of an unknown solution by adding a measured amount of another solution whose strength is known until a chemical reaction takes place

to /strong tuː, weak tə, tʊ/ preposition

1 part of an infinitive	**7** reaching sth
2 going somewhere	**8** before the hour
3 shows who action affects	**9** how numbers are related
4 in what direction	**10** for giving a score
5 shows relationship	**+ PHRASE**
6 shows connection	

1 used before a verb for forming an infinitive, or used without the following verb instead of an infinitive: *I hope to see you next week.* ♦ *The system is easy to understand.* ♦ *You don't need to come if you don't want to.*
2 used for saying the place or event where someone or something goes: *She rushed to the phone.* ♦ *There are daily flights to Boston.* ♦ *the road to the farm* ♦ *Robert hates going to parties.*
3 used for saying who or what gets something or is affected by something: *Prizes were presented to the winners.* ♦ *They were very kind to my mother when she was ill.* ♦ *advice to parents* ♦ *It seems to me that a lot of mistakes have been made.*
4 used for saying in which direction someone or something is, is pointing, or is looking: *She pointed to a notice on the wall.* ♦ *Henry was standing with his back to me.* ♦ *a large township just to the south of Johannesburg*
5 used for explaining a relationship between people or things: *a political party with ties to a terrorist group* ♦ *She is personal assistant to the Headteacher.* ♦ *the keys to my desk*
6 used for saying where something is fastened or where a connection is: *The carpet had been nailed to the floor.* ♦ *Your computer is connected to the main network.*
7 as far as a particular place, stage, time, or amount: *The disease had spread to his lungs.* ♦ *When will all this suffering come to an end?* ♦ *Only another three days to my birthday!* ♦ *How far is it from here to Nairobi?* ♦ *numbers from 10 to 20*
8 used when telling the time, for saying how many minutes it is before the hour: *I'll meet you at quarter to six* (=5.45).
9 used for showing the relationship between two numbers or amounts: *You get about ten of these apples to the kilo.*
10 used for saying what the score is in a game: *Our team won by five goals to three.*

PHRASE **to and fro** in one direction and then back again

toad /təʊd/ noun [C] a small amphibian that is similar to a **frog** but has brown skin and lives mainly on land —*picture* → REPTILE

toadspawn /'təʊd,spɔːn/ noun [U] **BIOLOGY** a soft floating mass of the fertilized eggs of a toad —*picture* → REPTILE

toadstool /'təʊd,stuːl/ noun [C] a fungus that is similar to a mushroom and is often poisonous

toast¹ /təʊst/ noun **1** [U] bread that has been heated until its outside is brown and hard **2** [C] an occasion when people all drink together and say someone's name in order to express their admiration or good wishes

toast² /təʊst/ verb [T] **1** to make bread into toast **2** to drink a toast to someone

tobacco /tə'bækəʊ/ noun [U] a substance that people smoke in cigarettes

today¹ /tə'deɪ/ adv **1** on this day: *I'm working today.* ♦ *Did you get any post today?* **2** at the period of time that is happening now: *Computers today are so sophisticated.*

today² /tə'deɪ/ noun [U] **1** this day: *Today is Wednesday.* **2** the present period of time: *Today's computers are so much more powerful than those of five years ago.*

toddler /'tɒdlə/ noun [C] a very young child who is learning how to walk

toe /təʊ/ noun [C] **1** one of the five individual parts at the end of your foot: *Vera slipped off her shoes and wiggled her toes.* —*picture* → BODY **2** the part of a shoe or sock that covers your toes: *shoes with pointed toes*

PHRASES **keep sb on their toes** to make someone

concentrate so that they are ready to deal with any problem

toe in ENGINEERING a way of setting a vehicle's wheels so that they point inwards

toe out ENGINEERING a way of setting a vehicle's wheels so that they point outwards

toenail /'təʊˌneɪl/ noun [C] the hard part over the top of a toe —picture → BODY

toffee /'tɒfi/ noun [C/U] a sticky brown sweet made by cooking together sugar, butter, and water

toga /'təʊɡə/ noun [C] a long loose piece of clothing worn by ancient Romans

together /tə'ɡeðə/ adv

1 combined or joined	4 at the same time
2 near each other	5 considered as whole
3 with each other	

1 if you put or join two or more things together, you combine or connect them: *Mix together the flour, eggs, and water.* ♦ *small patches of cloth sewn together* ♦ *Now add the numbers together.*

2 near each other, or in one place: *Get all your things together.* ♦ *The book brings together essays by several different authors.*

3 with each other: *Kevin, Jack, and Dave share a house together.* ♦ *Bob and I worked together many years ago.* ♦ *Are Tanya and Pete still together (=still in a romantic relationship)?*

4 at the same time: *Everyone arrived together at around four o'clock.*

5 considered as a whole: *Their two salaries together give them quite a nice income.*

toggle¹ /'tɒɡ(ə)l/ noun [C] **1** a small piece of wood or plastic that is used like a button for fastening clothes **2** COMPUTING a key or command on a computer that you use to move from one operation or program to another and back again

toggle² /'tɒɡ(ə)l/ verb [I/T] COMPUTING to move from one computer operation or program to another and back again by using a special key or command

toilet /'tɔɪlət/ noun [C] **1** a structure like a seat over a hole where you get rid of waste from your body **2** a room that contains a toilet

'toilet ˌpaper noun [U] soft thin paper that you use to clean yourself after using the toilet

toiletries /'tɔɪlətriz/ noun [plural] things such as soap and **shampoo** that you use for keeping yourself clean

'toilet ˌroll noun [C] a tube that has **toilet paper** wrapped around it

token¹ /'təʊkən/ noun [C] **1** a piece of paper that you can exchange for goods of a particular value in a shop **2** a small flat round piece of metal or plastic that you use instead of money in some machines **3** formal something that you do or give as a way of showing your feelings towards someone: *a token of your appreciation*

token² /'təʊkən/ adj done in order to pretend to people that you are trying to achieve something: *a token gesture*

told /təʊld/ the past tense and past participle of **tell**

tolerable /'tɒl(ə)rəb(ə)l/ adj formal acceptable, but not very good ≠ INTOLERABLE —**tolerably** adv

tolerance /'tɒlərəns/ noun **1** [U] the attitude of someone who is willing to accept other people's beliefs, way of life etc without criticizing them, even if they disagree with them ≠ INTOLERANCE: *We need to show greater tolerance towards each other.* **2** [U] the ability to experience something unpleasant or painful

without being harmed **3** [C/U] SCIENCE, TECHNOLOGY an acceptable variation in something that can be measured **4** [U] BIOLOGY the ability of plants or animals to exist in particular conditions

tolerant /'tɒlərənt/ adj **1** willing to accept other people's beliefs, way of life etc without criticizing them, even if you disagree with them ≠ INTOLERANT **2** BIOLOGY if plants or animals are tolerant of particular conditions, they are able to exist in those conditions

tolerate /'tɒləreɪt/ verb [T] **1** to allow someone to do something that you do not like or approve of: *He won't tolerate anyone questioning his decisions.* **2** to accept something that is unpleasant without becoming impatient or angry: *They have tolerated poor working conditions for too long.* **3** BIOLOGY if plants or animals tolerate particular conditions, they are able to exist in those conditions —**toleration** /ˌtɒlə'reɪʃ(ə)n/ noun [U]

toll¹ /təʊl/ noun **1** [C] an amount of money that you pay to use a bridge or road **2** [singular] the total number of people who have been killed or hurt: *The death toll from the earthquake is not yet known.* **3** [singular] the loud slow repeated sound of a large bell

PHRASE **take its toll** or **take a heavy toll** to harm or damage someone or something, especially gradually

toll² /təʊl/ verb [I/T] if you toll a bell, or if it tolls, it makes a slow repeated sound

tomato /tə'mɑːtəʊ/ (plural **tomatoes**) noun [C] a round red fruit that you eat raw in salads or cooked as a vegetable —picture → VEGETABLE

tomb /tuːm/ noun [C] a place or large stone structure where a dead person is buried

tombolo /'tɒmbələʊ/ noun [C] GEOGRAPHY a long narrow area of sand or small stones that links one island to another, or to the **mainland**

tombstone /'tuːmˌstəʊn/ noun [C] a large stone that is put over the place where a dead person is buried

tomorrow¹ /tə'mɒrəʊ/ adv **1** on the day after today: *Are you going back home tomorrow?* ♦ *They're arriving tomorrow morning.* **2** in the future: *Who can say what will happen tomorrow?*

tomorrow² /tə'mɒrəʊ/ noun [U] **1** the day after today: *Tomorrow is Tuesday.* **2** the future: *These students are the leaders of tomorrow.*

ton /tʌn/ noun [C] **1** a unit for measuring weight, containing 2,240 pounds and equal to 1,016 kilograms **2** informal a very large number or amount: *I've got tons of (=a lot of) things to do.* ♦ *That bag of yours weighs a ton (=is extremely heavy)!*

tonal /'təʊn(ə)l/ adj **1** relating to the **tone** of something, especially a colour or sound **2** MUSIC relating to music written in a particular **key** ≠ ATONAL

tonality /təʊ'næləti/ noun [C/U] **1** MUSIC the use of a particular **key** for writing a piece of music **2** ARTS the range of colours used in a painting

tone¹ /təʊn/ noun

1 sound of voice	4 phone sound
2 character of sth	5 colour
3 quality of sound	6 firm body

1 [C/U] the sound of someone's voice that shows what they are feeling: *His tone was angry.* ♦ *'Really?' Simone said in a surprised tone of voice.*

2 [singular/U] the general character of something: *The positive tone of the evening had changed completely.* ♦ *The opening remarks set the tone for the rest of the interview.*

3 [C/U] MUSIC the quality of a sound: *a flute with a clear bright tone*
4 [C] a sound made by a piece of equipment such as a telephone: *I picked up the phone and just got a beeping tone.*
5 [C] a colour, or a particular **shade** of a colour: *The room is decorated in cool blue tones.*
6 [U] a firm or healthy quality of the body, muscles, or skin: *The patient's general **muscle tone** is good.*

tone² /təʊn/ PHRASAL VERB ,tone sth 'down to make something less severe, shocking, or offensive

'tone ,language noun [C] LANGUAGE a language such as Chinese in which the meaning of some words changes when you say them in a different tone

tongs /tɒŋz/ noun [plural] a metal or plastic object that consists of two connected arms that you push together in order to pick something up —*picture* → LABORATORY

tongue¹ /tʌŋ/ noun **1** [C] the long soft piece of flesh that is fixed to the bottom of the mouth. In mammals it is used for swallowing and tasting, and in humans it is also used for speaking. **2** [C] an organ similar to a human tongue in animals such as **frogs**, snakes, and insects, that is used to help with swallowing and breathing, and sometimes to catch other animals **3** [C] a language: *English was clearly not his **mother tongue*** (=the one he first learned as a child). **4** [singular] a particular way of speaking or writing: *She has a rather sharp tongue.* → BITE¹, TIP¹

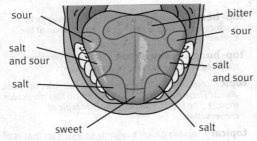

taste-sensitive areas of the tongue

tongue² /tʌŋ/ verb [I/T] MUSIC to produce a musical note on a **wind instrument** by using the tongue to prevent air from flowing through it for a short time

,tongue-in-'cheek adj intended to be humorous and not meant seriously: *a tongue-in-cheek answer* —,tongue-in-'cheek adv

tongue-tied /'tʌŋ ,taɪd/ adj unable to speak because you are nervous or embarrassed

tonic¹ /'tɒnɪk/ noun **1** tonic or **tonic water** [C/U] a type of **fizzy** water that has a bitter taste and is often mixed with a strong alcoholic drink **2** [singular] something that makes you feel happier or healthier **3** [C] HEALTH a medicine that someone takes to get more energy and feel healthier **4** [singular] MUSIC the first note in a musical scale

tonic² /'tɒnɪk/ adj MUSIC relating to the first note in a musical scale

tonight¹ /tə'naɪt/ adv in the evening or during the night of today: *Phone me tonight when you get home.*

tonight² /tə'naɪt/ noun [U] the evening or night of today: *tonight's performance*

tonne /tʌn/ noun [C] a unit for measuring weight, equal to 1,000 kilograms

tonsil /'tɒns(ə)l/ noun [C] ANATOMY one of the two small pieces of tissue on each side of the throat at the back of the mouth that make white blood cells as a protection against infection

tonsillitis /,tɒnsɪ'laɪtɪs/ noun [U] HEALTH an illness in which the tonsils become infected, swollen, and painful

too /tuː/ adv **1** more than is necessary or acceptable: *You're driving too fast.* ♦ *It's too cold to sit outside.* ♦ *You've put **too much** sugar in my coffee.* **2** used after mentioning an additional person, thing, or fact to show that they are included in what you are saying= ALSO: *Helen's got a lovely voice, and she's a good dancer too.* ♦ *'I'm starting to feel hungry.' 'Me too.'*

> Do not use **too** for making additions to negative sentences. Use **not... either**: *I didn't tell my friends and I didn't tell my wife either.*

took /tʊk/ the past tense of **take¹**

tool /tuːl/ noun [C] **1** a piece of equipment that you hold to do a particular type of work: *gardening tools* ♦ *a set of tools* —*picture* → on next page **2** something that you use in order to perform a job or achieve an aim: *The Internet has become an important research **tool for** students.*

toolbar /'tuːl,bɑː/ noun [C] COMPUTING a row of **icons** (=small pictures) on a computer screen that perform particular actions when you click on them

tooth /tuːθ/ (plural **teeth** /tiːθ/) noun [C] **1** ANATOMY one of the hard white objects inside the mouth that are used for biting: *a loose tooth* ♦ *It's important to **brush your teeth** at least twice a day.* —*picture* → BODY, DIGESTIVE SYSTEM on p.771 **2** one of a row of narrow pointed parts that form the edge of a tool or machine: *the teeth of a saw* → GRIT²

toothache /'tuːθeɪk/ noun [singular/U] HEALTH a pain in one or more of the teeth

toothbrush /'tuːθ,brʌʃ/ noun [C] a small brush that you use for cleaning your teeth

'tooth ,decay noun [U] HEALTH the gradual natural process in which the teeth start to decay, especially as a result of eating sweet foods

toothpaste /'tuːθ,peɪst/ noun [C/U] a soft thick substance that you put on a **toothbrush** to clean your teeth

toothpick /'tuːθ,pɪk/ noun [C] a thin pointed piece of wood that you use for removing bits of food from between your teeth

top¹ /tɒp/ noun

1 highest place/part	5 highest position
2 upper surface	6 furthest part
3 container lid/cover	+ PHRASES
4 piece of clothing	

1 [C] the highest place, point, part, or surface of something: *We could see mountain tops in the distance.* ♦ *I left my purse **at the top** of the stairs.* ♦ *He sprinkled sugar **on top of** the cake.*
2 [C] a flat upper surface of something: *a table top*
3 [C] a lid or cover for a container or pen: *the top of the shampoo bottle*
4 [C] a piece of clothing that covers the upper part of your body: *She was wearing a red skirt and a black top.*
5 the top [singular] the highest status or most important position: *Scott has reached **the top of** his profession.*
6 [singular] the part of something such as a street that is furthest away from you: *They've bought a new house at the top of our road.*

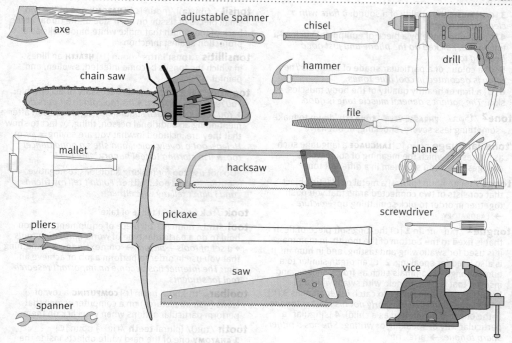

axe

adjustable spanner

chisel

drill

hammer

chain saw

file

mallet

plane

hacksaw

screwdriver

pickaxe

pliers

vice

saw

spanner

tools

PHRASES **from top to bottom** completely and thoroughly: *We cleaned the house from top to bottom.*
off the top of your head immediately and without thinking very much: *Off the top of my head, I'd say we have about 200 members.*
on top in a situation where you are in control or are winning: *United stayed on top throughout most of the match.*
on top of 1 in addition to something else: *On top of all his financial problems, his wife left him.* **2** in control of what is happening: *I try to stay on top of things.* **3** very close to someone or something: *The truck was almost on top of me.*
over the top more than what is considered normal or suitable

top² /tɒp/ adj **1** at or on the highest part of something: *Our room is on the top floor.* **2** highest in status, degree, or importance: *He's one of the top players in the league.* ♦ *Our **top priority** now is finding shelter for the flood victims.*

top³ /tɒp/ (**tops, topping, topped**) verb [T] **1** to be larger than a particular amount: *The costs for the project may top £50 million.* **2** to be in the most important or popular position in a list of things **3** to be better or more impressive than something else: *I don't think I can top your fishing story.* **4** to cover something with a layer of something else: *pizza topped with cheese*

PHRASAL VERB **,top sth 'up** to completely fill a container that is already partly full

,top dead 'centre noun [U] **ENGINEERING** in an engine, the position of a **piston** when it is furthest from the **crankshaft**

,top-'down adj starting at a general level and then moving to more specific things ≠ BOTTOM-UP

,top-'end adj top-end goods or services are more expensive and more advanced than other similar goods or services = HIGH-END

,top-'heavy adj something that is top-heavy lacks balance because it is heavier at the top than at the bottom

'top-,hung adj **CONSTRUCTION** a top-hung window has **hinges** at the top and opens outwards

topic /'tɒpɪk/ noun [C] a subject that you write or speak about: *There has been little research on this particular topic.* ♦ *She tried to think of another **topic of conversation**.*

topical /'tɒpɪk(ə)l/ adj **1** relating to a subject that is of particular interest at the present time **2** **HEALTH** relating to or used on a part of the body

topmost /'tɒp,məʊst/ adj highest

,top-of-the-'range adj of the best, most expensive, and most advanced kind available

topography /tə'pɒɡrəfi/ (plural **topographies**) noun [C/U] **GEOGRAPHY** the features of a particular area of land, such as hills, rivers, and roads —**topographical** /,tɒpə'ɡræfɪk(ə)l/ adj

topple /'tɒp(ə)l/ verb **1** [I/T] to fall, or to make someone or something fall **2** [T] to make someone in authority lose their power

,top 'secret adj containing or involving very important and secret information

topsoil /'tɒp,sɔɪl/ noun [U] **AGRICULTURE** the layer of soil that is near the surface of the ground and in which plants grow. **Soil erosion** can remove topsoil, making the land impossible to grow crops on.

topspin /'tɒp,spɪn/ noun [U] **SPORTS** the way that a ball spins forwards as it quickly flies through the air after someone has thrown or hit it in a particular way

the Torah /'tɔːrə/ **RELIGION 1** the first five books of the Jewish Bible **2** the principles and laws of the Jewish religion

cross section of a tooth

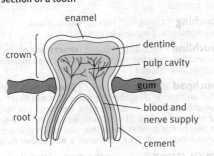

set of adult human teeth

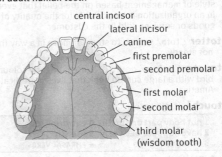

tooth

torch /tɔːtʃ/ noun [C] **1** a small electric light that you hold in your hand **2** a piece of wood with a flame at one end that is used as a light

tore /tɔː/ the past tense of **tear**[1]

torment[1] /ˈtɔːment/ noun [C/U] severe physical or mental pain, or something that causes this

torment[2] /tɔːˈment/ verb [T] to make someone suffer severe physical or mental pain —**tormentor** noun [C]

torn /tɔːn/ the past participle of **tear**[1]

tornado /tɔːˈneɪdəʊ/ (plural **tornadoes** or **tornados**) noun [C] **GEOGRAPHY** a very strong wind that spins in a circle and forms a **funnel** from the sky to the ground. Tornadoes usually cause severe damage on the ground.

torpedo /tɔːˈpiːdəʊ/ (plural **torpedoes**) noun [C] a weapon that is fired under water in order to hit a ship or a **submarine**

torque /tɔːk/ noun [U] **PHYSICS, ENGINEERING** the force that causes something to turn around a central point, for example the force produced by an **internal-combustion engine** to turn a vehicle's **driveshaft**

torque converter /ˈtɔːk kənˌvɜːtə/ noun [U] **ENGINEERING** a part of the **automatic transmission** in some vehicle engines that transfers and increases torque by **hydraulic** means

torrent /ˈtɒrənt/ noun **1** [C] a fast and powerful flow of water **2** [singular] a large amount of something: *a torrent of abuse*

torrential /təˈrenʃ(ə)l/ adj torrential rain falls hard and fast

torsion /ˈtɔːʃ(ə)n/ noun [U] **1** **PHYSICS** the effect caused by turning one end of an object while holding the other end still, or turning the other end in the opposite direction **2** **MATHS** the amount by which a curve twists

'torsion bar su,spension noun [C] **ENGINEERING** a steel rod fixed to the chassis at one end and the suspension at the other, which twists to absorb movement when the vehicle goes over rough ground

torso /ˈtɔːsəʊ/ (plural **torsos**) noun [C] the upper part of the body, not including the head or arms

tort /tɔːt/ noun [C] **LAW** an action that harms someone and for which you can be judged legally responsible, although it is not a crime

tortoise /ˈtɔːtəs/ noun [C] a land reptile that walks slowly and that can pull its head and legs into the shell on its back for protection —*picture* → REPTILE

tortuous /ˈtɔːtʃuəs/ adj **1** extremely complicated: *a tortuous process* **2** twisting and turning around many bends: *a tortuous route*

torture[1] /ˈtɔːtʃə/ noun [U] extreme physical pain that someone is forced to suffer as a punishment or as a way of making them give information

torture[2] /ˈtɔːtʃə/ verb [T] **1** to hurt someone deliberately in a very cruel way as a punishment, or in order to make them give information **2** to make someone feel extremely worried or upset about something —**torturer** noun [C]

toss[1] /tɒs/ verb [T] **1** to throw something somewhere gently or in a careless way: *Brendon tossed the ball into the air.* **2** to mix food with a liquid so that it becomes covered in the liquid: *Can you toss the salad for me?*

     PHRASES **toss a coin** to throw a coin into the air in order to make a decision based on which side the coin falls on

     toss and turn to be unable to sleep, or to sleep badly

     toss your head/hair (back) to move your head quickly upwards

toss[2] /tɒs/ noun [C] **1** the act of throwing something somewhere gently or in a careless way **2** the act of throwing a coin into the air in order to make a decision based on which side the coin falls on **3** the act of moving your head quickly upwards

total[1] /ˈtəʊt(ə)l/ adj **1** with all the numbers or things added together: *The total cost of the project came to about £700,000.* ♦ *The total number of votes was over one million.* **2** complete= ABSOLUTE: *Why would you let a total stranger into the house?* ♦ *They sat in almost total silence the whole evening.*

total[2] /ˈtəʊt(ə)l/ noun [C] the amount that you get when you add several numbers or things together: *The total for your books comes to £16.50.* ♦ *A total of 17 students signed up for the course.* ♦ *In total* (=counting everyone) *over 100 people attended.*

total[3] /ˈtəʊt(ə)l/ (**totals, totalling, totalled**) verb [T] to be a particular total as a result of everything being added together: *The company went bankrupt, with debts totalling £60 million.*

,total e'clipse noun [C] **ASTRONOMY** an **eclipse** in which all of the Sun or Moon is covered

totalitarian /təʊˌtælɪˈteəriən/ adj **POLITICS** controlling a country and its people in a very strict way, without allowing opposition from another political party —**totalitarianism** noun [U]

totality /təʊˈtæləti/ noun [U] *formal* **1** the state of being complete or whole **2** the total number or amount of something

totally /ˈtəʊt(ə)li/ adv completely: *I'd totally forgotten about the appointment.* ♦ *We have such totally different backgrounds.*

,total 'quality ,management noun [U] BUSINESS a style of management based on the belief that everyone in an organization is responsible for the quality of the goods or services sold to the customer

totter /'tɒtə/ verb [I] to stand or move in a way that is not steady

toucan /'tu:kən/ noun [C] a large, brightly coloured bird with a large curved beak that lives in tropical America

touch¹ /tʌtʃ/ verb

1 put body part on sb/sth	**4** eat/drink sth
2 have no space between	**5** use sth
3 affect emotions	**+ PHRASAL VERBS**

1 [T] to put your hand or part of your body on someone or something: *Beth reached out and touched his cheek.* ♦ *Please don't touch the paintings.* ♦ *He fell asleep as soon as his head touched the pillow.*
2 [I/T] if two things touch, or if something touches something else, there is no space between them: *They stood next to each other, barely touching.* ♦ *The chair was so high that his feet couldn't touch the ground.*
3 [T] to affect your emotions, so that you feel sad, sympathetic, pleased, or grateful: *His comments really touched me.* ♦ *Everyone was touched by the tragedy.*
4 [T] to eat or drink a particular thing: *I never touch meat or dairy products.*
5 [T] to use something: *Don't touch anything of mine while I'm away.*

PHRASAL VERBS **,touch 'down** if an aircraft or space vehicle touches down, it lands
,touch sth 'up to make a surface look better with small improvements

touch² /tʌtʃ/ noun

1 putting body part on sb/sth	**4** small feature
2 very small amount	**5** sb's particular quality
3 ability to feel things	**+ PHRASES**

1 [singular] the action of putting your hand or part of your body on someone or something: *Bill was wakened by her touch on his shoulder.*
2 [singular] a very small amount of something: *Add a touch of olive oil.*
3 [U] the sense that tells you what something feels like, through your skin, or when you put your fingers on it: *Children's imaginations can be stimulated through sight, touch, and smell.*
4 [C] a small feature that improves something: *The flowers in the room were a nice touch.* ♦ *The band is putting the finishing touches to their third album.*
5 [singular] a particular quality that someone can add to a situation: *The hotel provides good service and the personal touch.*

PHRASES **in touch (with sb)** in communication with someone by going to see them, speaking to them, or writing to them: *I'll be in touch next week about our trip to Hong Kong.* ♦ *I must get in touch with the bank and arrange an overdraft.* ♦ *They moved away five years ago, but we still keep in touch.*
out of touch (with sb) no longer seeing, speaking to, or writing to someone
out of touch (with sth) no longer having recent knowledge or information about something: *I haven't taught for a while so I'm a little out of touch.*
→ LOSE

,touch-and-'go adj not certain and with a risk of death or serious failure

touchdown /'tʌtʃ,daʊn/ noun [C] the moment when an aircraft lands on the ground

touched /tʌtʃt/ adj feeling sad, sympathetic, pleased, or grateful

touching /'tʌtʃɪŋ/ adj making you feel sad, sympathetic, pleased, or grateful

touchline /'tʌtʃ,laɪn/ noun [C] SPORTS one of the two lines that show the sides of a playing area in a sport, especially football

touchpad /'tʌtʃ,pæd/ noun [C] **1** COMPUTING a small flat surface on a **laptop** computer that you touch with your finger in order to move the cursor on the screen **2** a part of a piece of electronic equipment containing a number of smaller areas that you touch in order to make it operate, for example on a **microwave** oven

'touch ,screen noun [C] COMPUTING a computer screen that you touch in order to choose what you want to see next

touchstone /'tʌtʃ,stəʊn/ noun [C] a standard that is used for testing or judging other things

tough /tʌf/ adj

1 difficult	**5** with crime etc
2 strong	**6** of meat
3 determined	**7** hard to break
4 very strict/severe	

1 difficult: *He's having a really tough time at the moment.* ♦ *It was a tough decision to move to London.* ♦ *Many companies are facing tough competition.*
2 strong and able to deal with difficult situations or pain: *I think she'll be all right because she's very tough.*
3 confident and determined to get what you want: *a tough businesswoman*
4 very strict and severe: *tough criticism* ♦ *We must take tough action against terrorism.* ♦ *The new mayor promises to be tough on crime.*
5 a tough place is one in which there is a lot of crime and violence: *He grew up in a tough neighbourhood.*
6 tough meat is very difficult to cut and chew
7 TECHNOLOGY able to be bent, twisted, or hit without breaking
—**toughness** noun [U]

toughen /'tʌf(ə)n/ verb [I/T] to become mentally or physically stronger, or to make someone become mentally or physically stronger

tour¹ /tʊə/ noun **1** [C] a journey in which you visit several different places: *The president plans a European tour next month.* ♦ *We went on a 10-day tour of central Africa.* **2** [C/U] ARTS a journey in which a person or group visits several different places in order to perform: *The group is currently on tour in Europe.* **3** [C] TOURISM a short journey around a building or place in order to see what is there: *Every weekend there are free guided tours of the castle.*

tour² /tʊə/ verb [I/T] to visit several different places for pleasure or to perform

Tourette's syndrome /tə'rets ,sɪndrəʊm/ noun [U] HEALTH a condition in which a person makes frequent repeated sounds or movements that they cannot control

'tour ,guide noun [C] TOURISM someone whose job it is to show tourists around a place and give them information about its history, buildings etc

tourism /'tʊərɪz(ə)m/ noun [U] TOURISM the business of providing services for people who are travelling to places for a holiday

tourist /'tʊərɪst/ noun [C] TOURISM someone who is visiting a place on holiday: *The islands attract more than 17,000 tourists a year.* ♦ *a tourist hotel*

'tourist at,traction noun [C] TOURISM a place to visit that is very popular with tourists

'tourist ,board noun [C] TOURISM an official organization in a country or area that encourages tourists to visit it

'tourist ,class noun [U] TOURISM the cheapest set of seats on a plane or ship —**'tourist ,class** adj, adv

'tourist ,trap noun [C] TOURISM a place that is visited by many tourists and is therefore crowded and expensive

'tourist ,visa noun [C] TOURISM a **visa** that allows someone to visit a country for a short time on holiday

touristy /'tʊərɪsti/ adj TOURISM informal designed for tourists, or full of tourists

tournament /'tʊənəmənt/ noun [C] SPORTS a series of games in which the winner of each game plays in the next game until there is only one player or team left

tourniquet /'tɔːnɪkeɪ/ noun [C] HEALTH a piece of cloth that you tie very tight around someone's leg or arm in order to stop blood from flowing from a cut

'tour ,operator noun [C] TOURISM a company that organizes holiday **tours**

tousled /'taʊz(ə)ld/ adj tousled hair looks untidy in an attractive way

tow¹ /təʊ/ verb [T] to pull a vehicle or boat by fixing it to another vehicle or boat

tow² /təʊ/ noun [singular] the activity of pulling one vehicle or boat behind another

toward /tɔːd, tə'wɔːd/ preposition American **towards**

towards /tə'wɔːdz/ preposition **1** going in or facing a particular direction: I saw Joanna hurrying towards me. ♦ Victor was standing with his back towards me. ♦ a path leading towards the river **2** used when saying how you feel about someone or something, or how you treat them: He's not feeling very friendly towards you at the moment. ♦ my parents' attitude towards divorce **3** in a way that brings a process closer to a particular result: Not much has been done towards improving safety. ♦ progress towards peace in the region **4** near, or nearer, a time or place: I'll phone you some time towards the end of the week. ♦ Caroline's name appeared towards the bottom of the list.

towel /'taʊəl/ noun [C] a piece of material that you use for drying your hands or body, or for drying dishes

tower¹ /'taʊə/ noun [C] **1** a tall narrow structure, building, or part of a building: a water tower ♦ the Leaning Tower of Pisa ♦ a church tower —picture → CASTLE **2** COMPUTING a tall narrow box that contains the main working parts of a computer
PHRASE **a tower of strength** someone who you can depend on for help in a difficult situation

tower² /'taʊə/ PHRASAL VERB **'tower over sb/sth** to be much taller than the people or things that are near you

town /taʊn/ noun **1** [C] a place where people live and work that is larger than a village but smaller than a city: a small town ♦ a town on the River Ganges ♦ the northern Belgian **town of** Onkerzele → CITY **2** [U] the town or city that you live in or that you are talking about: He moved to another part of town. ♦ The crew was **in town** last week filming a new television series. ♦ His girlfriend flew in from **out of town**. **3** [U] the centre of a town where all the shops are: We're going **into town** this afternoon. **4** [singular] the people who live in a town: Most of the town was involved with the carnival.

township /'taʊnʃɪp/ noun [C] **1** a town in South Africa where black people were intended to live **2** an area within a **county** (=a division of a state) in the US or Canada that is responsible for running its own public services

townspeople /'taʊnz,piːp(ə)l/ noun [plural] the people who live in a town or city

toxaemia /tɒk'siːmiə/ noun [U] HEALTH a serious medical condition caused by bacteria in the blood and the **toxins** (=harmful substances) they produce

toxic /'tɒksɪk/ adj CHEMISTRY, HEALTH poisonous, and therefore harmful to humans and other animals, or to the environment

toxicity /tɒk'sɪsəti/ noun [U] CHEMISTRY, ENVIRONMENT the degree to which something is poisonous to a living organism, or to the environment

toxin /'tɒksɪn/ noun [C] CHEMISTRY, HEALTH a poisonous substance produced by living cells or living organisms

toxoid /'tɒksɔɪd/ noun [C] CHEMISTRY, HEALTH a toxin that is used in a weak form to produce antibodies to it. Toxoids are used in making some **vaccines**.

toy /tɔɪ/ noun [C] an object that is designed for a child to play with: boxes full of books, toys, and games ♦ a toy car

TQM /,tiː kjuː 'em/ abbrev BUSINESS **total quality management**

trace¹ /treɪs/ verb [T] **1** to find someone or something that you are looking for by asking questions and getting information: Detectives have failed to trace the missing woman. **2** to discover the origin or cause of something: The source of the infection was **traced to** a farm in Yorkshire. **3** to describe what happened in a long process or series of events: The book traces the history of the regiment. **4** ARTS, TECHNOLOGY to copy an image by putting transparent paper on top and following the lines with a pencil

trace² /treɪs/ noun **1** [C/U] a slight sign that someone has been present or that something has happened **2** [C] a very small amount of something

traceable /'treɪsəb(ə)l/ adj able to be found or followed

'trace ,element noun [C] **1** BIOLOGY a chemical element that an organism needs in only extremely small amounts in order to grow and develop normally, for example iron or zinc **2** CHEMISTRY a chemical element that is found in extremely small amounts in a mineral

trachea /trə'kiːə/ noun [C] ANATOMY the tube at the back of the throat that goes from the **larynx** to the **bronchi**. Air travels down it into the lungs = WINDPIPE —picture → LUNG, ORGAN

tracheotomy /,træki'ɒtəmi/ (plural **tracheotomies**) noun [C] HEALTH a medical operation in which a hole is cut in someone's trachea, in order to let air into their lungs

tracing paper /'treɪsɪŋ ,peɪpə/ noun [U] TECHNOLOGY transparent paper through which you **trace** (=copy) an image

track¹ /træk/ noun

1 rough path/road	**6** recorded music
2 train line	**7** distance between
3 marks on ground	sheels
4 racing course	**+** PHRASES
5 direction or way	

1 [C] a path or road with a rough surface: I walked along a track to the mountain village. ♦ There's **a dirt track** leading from the main road.

2 [C/U] a railway line: *a long stretch of track* ♦ *Roads and **railway tracks** were flooded in southern Germany.*

3 tracks [plural] marks that a person, animal, or vehicle leaves on the ground: *He followed the tracks of a car to the edge of the lake.*

4 [C] **SPORTS** a piece of ground that is used for running or racing

5 [C] the direction in which something moves: *the track of a hurricane/storm*

6 [C] **MUSIC** a song or piece of music that is recorded on a CD: *Which is your favourite track?*

7 [C] **ENGINEERING** the distance between two wheels, for example the front wheels of a vehicle

PHRASES keep track (of sth) to have information about how something is developing: *We need to keep track of how we are spending our money.*

lose track (of sth) to forget something, or to not know exactly what is happening: *I was so busy I **lost** all **track of time.***

on the right/wrong track doing or thinking the right or wrong things

on track doing things that are likely to be successful or correct: *a desperate attempt to keep the peace talks on track* ♦ *We're right on track to create two million new jobs.*

track and field SPORTS American **athletics**
→ BEATEN, COVER¹

track² /træk/ verb [T] **1** to follow someone or something by looking for evidence that shows where they have gone, or by using special equipment: *The radar system tracks planes up to 50 miles from the airport.* **2** to follow the development of something: *Live television coverage allows you to track the progress of the competitors.*

PHRASAL VERB ,track sb/sth 'down to find someone or something after a long search: *I finally managed to track him down in Manchester.*

trackball /'træk,bɔːl/ noun [C] **COMPUTING** a ball that is used instead of a computer mouse

'track ,record noun [C] **1** someone's reputation, based on the things that they have done **2 SPORTS** the fastest time for a race on a particular track

'track ,rod noun [C] **ENGINEERING** a metal bar that connects the two front wheels of a vehicle

tracksuit /'træk,suːt/ noun [C] loose trousers and a loose top that you wear before or after exercising

tract /trækt/ noun [C] **1** a large area of land **2 HEALTH** a group of organs and tubes that work together in the body

tractable /'træktəb(ə)l/ adj *very formal* easy to deal with

traction /'trækʃ(ə)n/ noun [U] **1 PHYSICS** the ability of something to move over a surface without slipping **2 HEALTH** the use of special equipment to hold someone's body in a particular position

'traction con,trol noun [U] **ENGINEERING** a system that prevents a vehicle from losing traction by reducing the engine power when this is about to happen

tractor /'træktə/ noun [C] **AGRICULTURE** a vehicle that is used on farms for pulling machines

trade¹ /treɪd/ noun **1** [U] **ECONOMICS** the activity of buying and selling goods or services: *The President's tour is designed to promote investment and trade.* ♦ *Spain wants to develop its **trade with** the Philippines.* ♦ *the illegal **trade in** drugs* **2** [C] **BUSINESS** a particular area of business or industry: *the book trade* **3** [C] a job

or type of work that someone is trained to do: *He learned his trade in the 1960s.*

trade² /treɪd/ verb **1** [I/T] **ECONOMICS** to buy and sell goods or services: *Investors can now trade stocks online.* ♦ *The group has issued threats against companies that **trade in** animal skins.* ♦ *Cuba continues to **trade with** other countries around the world.* **2** [I] **BUSINESS** to operate as a business: *The company will continue to trade under its original name.* **3** [T] to exchange something that you have for something else: *They **traded** freedom **for** security.*

'trade a,greement noun [C] **ECONOMICS** an agreement between two or more countries for controlling trade between them

'trade as,sociation noun [C] **BUSINESS** an organization formed to represent a number of businesses involved in the same type of work

'trade ,deficit noun [C] **ECONOMICS** a situation in which a country is buying more goods and services from other countries than it is selling to other countries

'trade ,discount noun [C] **BUSINESS** a reduction in the price of something offered by one business to another, especially by businesses that are involved in the same type of work

trademark /'treɪd,mɑːk/ noun [C] **BUSINESS, LAW** a name or design that belongs to a particular company and is used on its products

trader /'treɪdə/ noun [C] **BUSINESS** someone who buys and sells things: *market traders*

'trade ,surplus noun [C] **ECONOMICS** a situation in which a country is selling more goods and services to other countries than it is buying from other countries

,trade 'union noun [C] **SOCIAL STUDIES** an organization of workers that aims to improve pay and conditions of work

tradition /trə'dɪʃ(ə)n/ noun [C/U] a very old custom, belief, or story: *Native American culture and traditions* ♦ *His son **followed** the family **tradition** and entered politics.*

traditional /trə'dɪʃ(ə)nəl/ adj **1** relating to very old customs, beliefs, or stories: *traditional Mediterranean cooking* ♦ *All the dancers and musicians wore traditional costumes.* **2** typical of the things people have usually done: *Our house was built in a traditional style.* ♦ *Many women have abandoned their traditional role as wife and mother.* —**traditionally** adv

tra,ditional 'medicine noun [U] **HEALTH** medical treatment using methods that are different from the usual Western scientific methods, for example Chinese medicine or **herbal medicine**

traffic /'træfɪk/ noun [U] **1** the vehicles that are travelling in an area at a particular time: *At that time of night, there was no traffic on the roads.* ♦ *the huge volume of traffic in the city centre* ♦ *rush-hour traffic* ♦ *traffic noise* **2** aircraft, ships, and trains that travel from one place to another: *an increase in air traffic* **3** the information that passes through a communications system: *Internet traffic* **4** the process of buying and selling things such as drugs and weapons illegally: *measures to reduce the illegal **traffic in** heroin*

'traffic ,jam noun [C] a line of vehicles waiting behind something that is blocking the road

trafficking /'træfɪkɪŋ/ noun [U] the business of illegally buying and selling things such as drugs and weapons —**trafficker** noun [C]

'traffic ,lights noun [plural] a set of red, yellow, and green lights that control traffic

tragedy /'trædʒədi/ (plural **tragedies**) noun **1** [C/U] a very sad event that involves death or human suffering: *The trip ended in tragedy.* ♦ *We need new safety laws to prevent tragedies like this from happening again.* **2** [singular] a bad situation that makes people very upset or angry: *It's a tragedy that so many young people are out of work.* **3** [C] **LITERATURE, ARTS** a play in which people suffer or die, especially one in which the main character dies: *Shakespeare's tragedies*

tragic /'trædʒɪk/ adj **1** causing or involving great sadness, because someone suffers or dies **2** **LITERATURE** relating to tragedy in plays or literature —**tragically** /'trædʒɪkli/ adv

tragicomedy /,trædʒi'kɒmədi/ (plural **tragicomedies**) noun [C] **LITERATURE, ARTS** a play, story, or situation that is both sad and humorous —**tragicomic** /,trædʒi'kɒmɪk/ adj

trail¹ /treɪl/ noun [C] **1** a path through the countryside, especially one designed for walking for pleasure: *The trail led down to the lake.* **2** a series of marks that shows where someone or something has been: *a trail of blood* ♦ *He left a trail of muddy footprints.* **3** damage or harm caused by something bad: *Hurricane Andrew left a trail of destruction along the coast.* **4** many pieces of connected evidence that prove that someone did something wrong or illegal

trail² /treɪl/ verb

1 move slowly	**4** pull sth behind you
2 in competition	**5** leave marks
3 follow sb	**+ PHRASAL VERB**

1 [I] to move slowly behind someone in a tired or unhappy way: *My husband usually trails behind me when I'm shopping.*
2 [I/T] to be losing in a competition or election: *A recent poll shows the Democrats trailing the Republicans.*
3 [T] to follow someone secretly in order to learn something about them: *Detectives trailed Evans for weeks.*
4 [T] to pull something behind you, or to be pulled behind someone or something
5 [T] to leave something somewhere in an untidy way, often leaving it behind you as you go through a place: *The dogs came in, trailing mud everywhere.* ♦ *Avoid trailing cables across the room.*

PHRASAL VERB ,trail a'way or ,trail 'off if someone's voice trails away, they gradually become silent

trailer /'treɪlə/ noun [C] **1** a long container that can be fixed to a vehicle and used for moving heavy objects or large animals **2** an advertisement for a film or television programme that shows short parts of that film or programme

trailing wave /'treɪlɪŋ ,weɪv/ noun [C] **GEOGRAPHY** a wave that comes behind another wave

train¹ /treɪn/ noun [C] **1** a group of railway vehicles that are connected and pulled by an engine: *a passenger train* ♦ *We travelled across China by train.* ♦ *I met her on a train to Glasgow.* ♦ *More and more people got on the crowded train.* ♦ *We'll be waiting for you when you get off the train.* ♦ *If we don't leave now we'll miss the train.* ♦ *I'll meet you at the train station.* **2** a series of events or thoughts: *a disastrous train of events* ♦ *I'm sorry, I lost my train of thought* (=forgot what I was thinking). **3** a long part at the back of a formal dress that spreads out onto the ground

train² /treɪn/ verb **1** train or **train up** [T] to teach someone to do a particular job or activity: *We need to recruit and train more police officers.* ♦ *They were training him to use the new security system.* **2** [I] to learn how to do a particular job or activity: *He trained as a chef in Paris.* ♦ *I have an uncle who trained to be*

a pilot. **3** [I] **SPORTS** to practise a sport regularly before a match or competition: *The players train five days a week.* **4** [T] to teach an animal to obey you or to do something: *He had trained the dogs to attack.*

trainee /,treɪ'niː/ noun [C] someone who is learning how to do a particular job or activity

trainer /'treɪnə/ noun [C] **1** someone whose job is to teach people skills, or to help people to practise a sport **2** someone whose job is to train animals

trainers /'treɪnəz/ noun [plural] comfortable shoes that you wear in informal situations or for doing sport

training /'treɪnɪŋ/ noun [U] **1** the process of teaching or learning a particular job or activity: *Counselling is a difficult job requiring skill and training.* ♦ *Employees are given training in the use of safety equipment.* ♦ *The college provides vocational training for actors.* **2** physical exercise that someone does regularly in order to practise for a sport or to stay healthy: *McColgan is currently in training for the New York marathon.*

'training ,college noun [C/U] **EDUCATION** in the UK, a college where people train for a particular job or profession

trait /treɪt/ noun [C] a particular quality in someone's character

traitor /'treɪtə/ noun [C] someone who is not loyal to their country, friends, or family

trajectory /trə'dʒekt(ə)ri/ (plural **trajectories**) noun [C] the high curving line that is formed by the movement of an object through the air

tram /træm/ noun [C] a long narrow vehicle for carrying passengers that travels along metal tracks in the middle of a street

trammel /'træm(ə)l/ noun [C] **CONSTRUCTION** a board used for making a circle, for example when laying out the design of a circular building

tramp¹ /træmp/ noun [C] **1** someone without a home or a job who moves from one place to another **2** a long tiring walk

tramp² /træmp/ verb [I/T] to walk with slow heavy steps, or to walk a long way

trample /'træmp(ə)l/ verb [I/T] to put your feet down on someone or something in a heavy way that causes injury or damage

trampoline /'træmpə,liːn/ noun [C] a piece of equipment that you jump up and down on, consisting of a metal frame with a piece of strong material stretched tightly across it

trance /trɑːns/ noun [C] a state in which you are awake but not really conscious of where you are

tranquil /'træŋkwɪl/ adj calm, still, and quiet —**tranquillity** /træŋ'kwɪləti/ noun [U]

tranquillizer /'træŋkwɪlaɪzə/ noun [C] **HEALTH** a drug that makes people calmer when they are very worried or nervous

transaction /træn'zækʃ(ə)n/ noun [C] *formal* an occasion when someone buys or sells something: *a business transaction*

transatlantic /,trænzət'læntɪk/ adj **1** crossing the Atlantic Ocean **2** involving countries on both sides of the Atlantic Ocean

transcend /træn'send/ verb [T] *formal* to become free of things that limit what you can achieve

transcoding /trænz'kəʊdɪŋ/ noun [U] **LANGUAGE** the process of converting language from one form of coding to another

transcribe /træn'skraɪb/ verb [T] **1** to write, type, or record something exactly as it was said **2** music to change music so that a different instrument can play it **3** language to write something written in the alphabet of one language using the alphabet of another language

transcript /'træn,skrɪpt/ or **transcription** /træn'skrɪpʃ(ə)n/ noun [C] a written copy of the exact words that someone said

transducer /trænz'djuːsə/ noun [C] physics a piece of equipment that gets power from one **source** and then changes that power, so that it can be used by another system

transect /træn'sekt/ verb [T] maths to cut or divide something at an angle

trans fat /'trænz ,fæt/ or ,**trans ,fatty 'acid** noun [C/U] chemistry, health a type of solid fat such as **margarine** produced when vegetable oils are changed by a chemical process. These fats are considered bad for your health because they increase your **cholesterol** level.

transfer¹ /træns'fɜː/ (**transfers**, **transferring**, **transferred**) verb

1 move to somewhere else	**4** change phone line for else
2 give to sb/sth else	**5** make new owner of
3 move sb/sth somewhere	**6** copy to somewhere else

1 [I/T] to move, or to move someone, from one job or department to another in the same company or organization: *I'm* **transferring to** *our Tokyo office next year.* ♦ *Helen was* **transferred from** *marketing* **to** *sales.*
2 [T] to stop giving time or support to one person or thing and give it to another: *The time came to transfer their attention from study to practical life.*
3 [T] to move something or someone from one place to another: *Wait until the cakes cool before* **transferring** *them* **to** *a plate.* ♦ *The prisoner will be transferred to a maximum security unit.* ♦ *I need to transfer £500 to my daughter's account.*
4 [T] to let someone speak to another person by changing telephone lines for them: *Please hold the line while I transfer you.*
5 [T] to officially arrange for someone else to become the owner of something
6 [T] to copy information or images from one place or object to another: *I want you to transfer the files onto a disk.*
—**transferable** adj

transfer² /'trænsfɜː/ noun **1** [C/U] the process of moving, or being moved, from one job or place to another: *We're currently dealing with the paperwork for your transfer.* ♦ *the* **transfer** *of supplies* **2** [C] a piece of paper with a design or picture that can be printed on another surface, using heat and pressure

'**transfer ,coach** noun [C] tourism a coach that takes travellers from the airport to their hotel

'**transfer ,passenger** noun [C] tourism a traveller who is changing from one plane, train, or bus to another, or to another form of transport

transform /træns'fɔːm/ verb [T] to make someone or something completely different, especially in a positive way: *Email has transformed the way people communicate.* ♦ *They've* **transformed** *the old train station* **into** *a science museum.*

transformation /,trænsfə'meɪʃ(ə)n/ noun [C] **1** a complete change into something or someone very different, or the process during which this happens **2** maths a change made to a geometric shape or

object **3** maths a change in algebra in which one **expression** is changed to another by replacing the variables

transformer /træns'fɔːmə/ noun [C] physics a piece of electrical equipment that changes the voltage of a flow of electricity. A transformer can be used for connecting a piece of electrical equipment that uses one voltage to an electricity supply of a different voltage. —*picture* ➔ electricity, generator

transfusion /træns'fjuːʒ(ə)n/ noun [C/U] health a medical treatment in which blood from one person is put into another person's body, especially because the patient has lost a lot of blood from an injury or during a medical operation

transgenic /,trænz'dʒenɪk/ adj biology a transgenic plant or animal contains genes from a different plant or animal

transient /'trænziənt/ adj existing, happening, or staying somewhere for a short period of time only

transistor /træn'zɪstə/ noun [C] physics an object that controls the flow of electricity inside electronic equipment

transistorized /træn'zɪstəraɪzd/ adj physics made smaller by using **transistors**

transit /'trænzɪt/ noun [U] agriculture the movement of people or things from one place to another: *Our suitcases were damaged* **in transit**.

transition /træn'zɪʃ(ə)n/ noun [C/U] the process of changing from one situation, form, or state to another: *It's not always a smooth* **transition from** *school* **to** *university.* —**transitional** adj

tran'sition ,fit noun [U] technology a fit between two machine parts, for example a **shaft** and a hole, in which the specified limits of the sizes of each part produce either a **clearance fit** or an **interference fit**

tran'sition ,metal noun [C] chemistry a metallic element such as copper or gold whose **valency** (=ability to combine with other elements) can vary

transitive /'trænsətɪv/ adj language a transitive verb is always used with a **direct object**. For example 'hit' and 'make' are transitive verbs. They are marked [T] in this dictionary. ➔ intransitive

'**transit ,lounge** noun [C] tourism a room in an international airport where passengers can wait for their flight to another country

transitory /'trænsət(ə)ri/ adj temporary

'**transit ,passenger** noun [C] tourism a passenger at an airport who is there to change flights, and therefore does not have to go through **customs** or **immigration**

'**transit ,visa** noun [C] tourism an official document giving someone permission to travel through one country in order to get to another country

translate /træns'leɪt/ verb **1** [I/T] to change spoken or written words into a different language: *I don't speak Russian, so someone will have to translate.* ♦ *The book has been* **translated into** *more than 100 languages.* **2** [T] computing to change information in one computer program or language into a form that can be used by a different program or language **3** [I] to cause a particular situation or result: *Will the sales increase* **translate into** *more jobs?* **4** [I/T] to change something into a different form, or to express something in a different way: *These earnings, translated into pounds, represent half of our total profits.*

translation /trænsˈleɪʃ(ə)n/ noun **1** [C] a piece of work in which spoken or written words have been changed into a different language: *Some people like to make lists of words with translations in their own language.* ♦ *an English translation of Candide* **2** [U] the activity of changing spoken or written words into a different language: *Most legal translation is done by lawyers with foreign language training.* ♦ *Try to read Baudelaire in the original and not **in translation**.*

translator /trænsˈleɪtə/ noun [C] someone whose job is to translate spoken or written words into a different language

translocation /ˌtrænsləʊˈkeɪʃ(ə)n/ noun [U] **BIOLOGY** **1** the movement of dissolved substances within a plant, for example the movement of dissolved minerals upwards from the roots **2** a process by which part of a chromosome moves to a new position on the same, or on a different, chromosome. This causes a new arrangement of the genes. —**translocate** verb [T]

translucent /trænsˈluːs(ə)nt/ adj a translucent surface is clear enough for light to pass through it, but not completely clear. If you look through a translucent surface, you can see the general shape and colour of objects on the other side, but not the details. A surface that is completely clear is **transparent**. —*picture* → BEAM

transmission /trænzˈmɪʃ(ə)n/ noun **1** [C/U] **PHYSICS** the process of sending electronic signals such as radio or television signals, or a signal that is sent in this way: *New telephone lines allow faster data transmission by fax or modem.* **2** [U] **HEALTH** the process by which something spreads from one person to another: *the transmission of disease* **3** [C] **PHYSICS** the part of a vehicle that takes power from the engine to the wheels

transmit /trænzˈmɪt/ (**transmits, transmitting, transmitted**) verb [T] **1** **PHYSICS** to send an electronic signal such as a radio or television signal: *The Cup Final was transmitted via satellite to over 20 countries.* **2** *formal* to pass information, beliefs, or attitudes to other people: *We transmit our values to our children.* **3** **HEALTH** to spread a disease from one person to another: *HIV can be transmitted by sexual contact.* **4** **SCIENCE** if a substance transmits light, sound, or other form of energy, the form of energy can pass through it

transmitter /trænzˈmɪtə/ noun [C] **PHYSICS** a piece of electronic equipment that is used for sending radio, television, or telephone signals through the air

transom /ˈtræns(ə)m/ noun [C] **CONSTRUCTION** a bar of wood or stone that divides a window horizontally, or that divides a door from the window above it

transparency /trænsˈpærənsi/ (plural **transparencies**) noun [C] a photograph, drawing, or piece of writing on plastic that you shine light through in order to look at it on a screen

transparent /trænsˈpærənt/ adj **1** a transparent surface is clear enough to allow a lot of light to pass through it. If you look through a transparent surface, you can clearly see objects on the other side. A surface that allows some light to pass through it but is not completely clear is **translucent**: *a transparent substance* —*picture* → BEAM **2** not trying to keep anything secret: *a transparent system*

transpiration /ˌtrænspɪˈreɪʃ(ə)n/ noun [U] **BIOLOGY** the process in which water that has travelled from the roots of a plant up to its leaves passes out into the air. The holes that the water evaporates from are called **stomata**. —*picture* → WATER CYCLE

transpirational pull /ˌtrænspɪreɪʃ(ə)nəl ˈpʊl/ noun [U] **BIOLOGY** the effect by which water is pulled in through the roots, and up through the tissue of a plant, when water evaporates from the leaves

transpiration stream noun [U] **BIOLOGY** transpirational pull

transpire /trænˈspaɪə/ verb [I] **1** *formal* to become known: *It later transpired that the driver of her car was drunk.* **2** *formal* to happen **3** **BIOLOGY** if a plant transpires, water passes from the surface of its leaves into the air as vapour

transplant¹ /ˈtrænsˌplɑːnt/ noun [C/U] **HEALTH** a medical operation in which a new organ is put into someone's body

transplant² /ˌtrænsˈplɑːnt/ verb [T] **1** to take a plant out of the ground and put it in a different place **2** **HEALTH** to take an organ from one person's body and put it into another person's body

transponder /trænˈspɒndə/ noun [C] **PHYSICS** a piece of electronic equipment used for communicating with radio or **radar**. It sends a reply every time it receives a signal.

transport¹ /ˈtrænspɔːt/ noun [U] **1** the system that is used for travelling or for moving goods from one place to another: *road transport* ♦ *Auckland's **public transport** system is excellent.* → PUBLIC TRANSPORT **2** a method of travelling or moving things from one place to another: *Anyone needing transport should ring me.* ♦ *Have you got your own transport?* ♦ *Flying is still the safest **means of transport**.* **3** the action of moving goods from one place to another: *They have succeeded in stopping **the transport of** live animals.*

transport² /trænsˈpɔːt/ verb [T] to move people or things from one place to another, usually in a vehicle: *We will need a big truck to transport all the boxes.* ♦ *Volunteers will be **transported to** the island by boat.*

transportation /ˌtrænspɔːˈteɪʃ(ə)n/ noun [U] **1** the action of moving goods from one place to another **2** *American* **transport¹** sense 1

transport system noun [U] **BIOLOGY** the way in which something is moved from one place to another, for example the way that food and water are moved around within a plant

transpose /trænsˈpəʊz/ verb [T] **1** *formal* to change the order or position of something **2** **MUSIC** to change the **key** of a piece of music so that it can be performed using higher or lower notes —**transposition** /ˌtrænspəˈzɪʃ(ə)n/ noun [C/U]

transubstantiation /ˌtrænsəbˌstænʃiˈeɪʃ(ə)n/ noun [U] **RELIGION** the belief of some Christians that the bread and wine used in church ceremonies become the body and blood of Jesus Christ

transversal /trænzˈvɜːs(ə)l/ noun [C] **MATHS** a line that **intersects** (=crosses) two or more other lines

transverse /ˌtrænzˈvɜːs/ adj placed sideways or at an angle across something —*picture* → SECTION

transverse engine noun [C] **ENGINEERING** an engine in which the **crankshaft** runs left to right rather than front to back

transverse process noun [C] **ANATOMY** either of the two bony parts that stick out on the sides of a **vertebra** —*picture* → VERTEBRA

transverse section noun [C] **SCIENCE** an image that shows what you would see if you cut through something —*picture* → SECTION

transverse wave noun [C] **PHYSICS** a wave such as light that makes the medium through which it moves vibrate in a direction that is at right angles to the direction in which it is moving → LONGITUDINAL WAVE —*picture* → WAVE

trap[1] /træp/ (**traps, trapping, trapped**) verb [T] **1** to prevent someone from leaving a place: *Both men were trapped inside the burning car.* ♦ *The bomb exploded, trapping victims in the building.* **2** to make someone unable to change a bad situation or way of thinking: *The two communities are trapped in a cycle of violence.* ♦ *I felt trapped by my marriage.* **3** to catch an animal or a person such as a criminal using a trap: *Police officers trapped both suspects before they left the bank.* **4** to trick someone in order to make them do or say something that they did not mean to do or say: *I was trapped into admitting I had lied.*

trap[2] /træp/ noun [C] **1** a piece of equipment that is used for catching animals: *We set traps for the mice.* **2** a bad situation that is difficult to change or escape from: *He was caught in a trap of poverty.* **3** a trick that is designed to catch someone or make them do or say something that they did not mean to do or say: *We didn't know that we were walking straight into a trap.* **4** a mistake or problem that you should try to avoid: *I fell into the trap of putting work before family.*

trapdoor /'træp,dɔː/ noun [C] a small door that covers an opening in a floor, ceiling, or wall

trapezium /trə'piːziəm/ noun [C] MATHS a shape with four straight sides, two of which are parallel —*picture* → SHAPE

trapezoid /'træpɪzɔɪd/ noun [C] MATHS a shape with four straight sides that are not parallel to each other

trash /træʃ/ noun [U] *American* rubbish such as paper, plastic bags, used containers etc that you get rid of = RUBBISH: *There was trash all over the fairgrounds for weeks afterwards.*

trauma /'trɔːmə/ noun [U] **1** a feeling of being very upset, afraid, or shocked because of a bad experience, or the experience that causes this feeling **2** HEALTH a serious injury

traumatic /trɔː'mætɪk/ adj causing you to feel very upset, afraid, or shocked

traumatized /'trɔːmətaɪzd/ adj very upset, afraid, or shocked because of a bad experience —**traumatize** verb [T]

travel[1] /'træv(ə)l/ (**travels, travelling, travelled**) verb

1 go on (long) journey	**4** about light/sound
2 move: distance/speed	**5** in basketball
3 spread and affect people	

1 [I] to go on a journey, or to visit different places: *Matt spends much of his time travelling abroad.* ♦ *We travelled around Spain for two weeks.* ♦ *Joe recently travelled to Australia on business.* ♦ *I usually travel by bus.*
2 [I/T] to move a particular distance, or to move at a particular speed: *We travelled 300 miles on Saturday.* ♦ *The car was travelling at about 80 miles per hour.*
3 [I] to spread from one place to another in a way that affects or influences a lot of people: *The news travelled quickly.* ♦ *Rumours travel fast.*
4 [I] if light or sound travels from one place to another, it moves there
5 [I] SPORTS in basketball, to take more steps than the rules allow while holding the ball

travel[2] /'træv(ə)l/ noun [U] **1** the activity of travelling: *Foreign travel never really appealed to him until he retired.* ♦ *Our agency deals mostly with business travel.* ♦ *travel arrangements* **2** TECHNOLOGY the distance that a part of a machine can move

PHRASE **sb's travels** journeys that someone makes to different places: *We met a lot of interesting people on our travels.*

'**travel ,agent** noun [C] TOURISM someone whose job is to help people to plan holidays and to make travel arrangements

'**travel ,angle** noun [C] TECHNOLOGY the angle of an electrode as it moves along the direction of a weld

'**travel ,document** noun [C] TOURISM a passport or visa that allows someone to travel between countries

'**travel in,surance** noun [U] TOURISM a type of insurance that pays for someone's medical treatment when they are travelling abroad, or that gives them back their money if their holiday is cancelled

traveller /'træv(ə)lə/ noun [C] **1** someone who is travelling or who often travels: *Rail travellers are furious at the increase in fares.* **2** someone who does not have a permanent home and who travels from one place to another

'**traveller's ,cheque** noun [C] TOURISM a printed piece of paper that travellers can sign and use as money. It can be replaced if it is lost or stolen.

travelling companion /'træv(ə)lɪŋ kəm,pænjən/ noun [C] someone you are on a journey with

'**travel ,warning** noun [C] TOURISM an official notice by a government telling its citizens not to travel to a particular country or region because it is dangerous

traverse /trə'vɜːs/ verb [T] *formal* to move over or across an area

travesty /'trævəsti/ noun [singular] something that is shocking because it is unfair or very different from what you expect

travolator /'trævə,leɪtə/ noun [C] a type of floor that moves forwards and carries people along, used in places such as airports

trawl /trɔːl/ verb [I/T] to look for someone or something by searching through a large number of people or things —**trawl** noun [C]

trawler /'trɔːlə/ noun [C] a boat used for fishing that pulls a large net through the water

trawling /'trɔːlɪŋ/ noun [U] a method of fishing at sea in which one or two boats pull a large net behind them

tray /treɪ/ noun [C] **1** a flat piece of plastic, metal, or wood with raised edges, used for carrying food or drinks **2** a flat open container with raised edges, used for holding paper

treacherous /'tretʃərəs/ adj **1** very dangerous: *treacherous driving conditions* **2** someone who is treacherous cannot be trusted

treachery /'tretʃəri/ noun [U] the act of harming people who trusted you

treacle /'triːk(ə)l/ noun [U] a thick sweet black liquid that is used in cooking

tread[1] /tred/ (**treads, treading, trod** /trɒd/, **trodden** /'trɒd(ə)n/) verb [I/T] to walk, or to step on something
PHRASE **tread water** to stay upright in deep water by moving your legs and arms and keeping your head out of the water

tread[2] /tred/ noun [C] **1** the pattern of lines on a tyre **2** CONSTRUCTION the horizontal surface of a step

treason /'triːz(ə)n/ noun [U] LAW the crime of trying to harm your country's government

treasure[1] /'treʒə/ noun **1** [C] a valuable piece of art, or a valuable historical object: *the treasures of the Vatican Museum* **2** [U] a collection of valuable things, for example jewels, gold etc: *There are rumours of buried treasure in the old house.* **3** [C] something that is valuable or very important to someone

treasure² /ˈtreʒə/ verb [T] to think that something is very important because it gives you a lot of pleasure —**treasured** /ˈtreʒəd/ adj

treasurer /ˈtreʒərə/ noun [C] someone who is in charge of an organization's money

treasure trove /ˈtreʒə ˌtrəʊv/ noun [U] LAW valuable objects that someone finds buried in the ground and that no one seems to own

the Treasury /ˈtreʒəri/ noun [singular] POLITICS the government department that is responsible for a country's financial matters

treat¹ /triːt/ verb [T]

1 behave towards sb	4 protect sth
2 deal with sth	5 buy sb sth special
3 cure sb/sth	

1 to behave towards someone in a particular way: *Rachel felt she had been unfairly treated.* ♦ *They treat their guests very well.* ♦ *I wish you would stop treating me like a child!* ♦ *Dean always treated my grandfather with the greatest respect.*
2 to deal with something in a particular way: *You should treat this new evidence with caution.* ♦ *These payments will be treated as income.*
3 HEALTH to use medicine or medical methods to try to cure an illness: *Patients are treated using both medication and exercise.* ♦ *She was treated for minor injuries.*
4 to put a substance on something in order to protect it or to make it stronger: *The wood is treated with chemicals.*
5 to pay for something special for someone: *Bob treated us to dinner at a nice restaurant.*

treat² /triːt/ noun **1** [C] a very enjoyable event or occasion: *It's a real treat to see you again.* ♦ *The band is great – you're in for a treat* (=you will enjoy it). **2** [singular] an occasion when you pay for something special for someone else: *I'd like this lunch to be my treat.*

treatment /ˈtriːtmənt/ noun **1** [C/U] HEALTH the process of providing medical care, or a particular type of medical care: *the treatment of tropical diseases* ♦ *a new treatment for heroin addiction* ♦ *She was receiving treatment for breast cancer.* **2** [U] the particular way in which you deal with someone: *the treatment of prisoners* **3** [C] the way in which a subject is dealt with, especially in art or literature: *The book's treatment of village life is very realistic.*

ˈtreatment ˌplant noun [C] ENVIRONMENT, HEALTH a place where something such as **sewage** (=waste water and human waste products) is treated to make it safe

treaty /ˈtriːti/ (plural **treaties**) noun [C] an official written agreement between countries: *a treaty on arms reduction*

treble¹ /ˈtreb(ə)l/ noun **1** [C] SPORTS a situation in which a person or team wins three sports events or competitions within a particular period of time **2** [C/U] MUSIC the highest range of musical sounds or voices **3** [U] the part of a radio or **stereo** that controls the higher sounds —**treble** adj

treble² /ˈtreb(ə)l/ verb [I/T] to become three times bigger, or to make something three times bigger

treble³ /ˈtreb(ə)l/ determiner something that is treble the number or amount of another thing is three times bigger than it

ˌtreble ˈclef noun [C] MUSIC the symbol 𝄞, used at the beginning of a line of music to show that the note on

the second line of the **staff** represents G above **middle C** —*picture* → MUSIC

tree /triː/ noun [C] BIOLOGY a very tall plant that has branches and a thick woody **trunk**. Trees can be flowering plants, such as **mango** trees, or conifers, such as **fir** trees: *a pine tree* → FAMILY TREE —*picture* → on next page

ˈtree ˌdiagram noun [C] MATHS a diagram in which connections between the parts of a process or a whole are shown using lines that spread like the branches on a tree

treeline /ˈtriːˌlaɪn/ noun [singular] GEOGRAPHY the level on a mountain above which trees do not grow

trek /trek/ noun [C] a long tiring walk —**trek** verb [I]

trellis /ˈtrelɪs/ noun [C] an upright frame for plants to grow on

tremble /ˈtremb(ə)l/ verb [I] **1** if you are trembling, your body is shaking, for example because you are nervous or weak: *She was trembling with anger.* **2** if your voice trembles, you cannot talk in a steady calm way, especially because you are nervous, afraid, or excited

tremendous /trəˈmendəs/ adj **1** extremely great, important, or strong: *I have tremendous respect for my parents.* ♦ *We have a tremendous amount of work to do.* **2** extremely good: *We had a tremendous time on holiday.* —**tremendously** adv

tremor /ˈtremə/ noun [C] **1** GEOLOGY a small earthquake **2** a slight shaking movement in your body or voice that you cannot control

trench /trentʃ/ noun [C] a long narrow hole in the ground

trend /trend/ noun [C] a gradual change or development that produces a particular result: *His designs often set the trend* (=start something that becomes popular) *for the new season.* ♦ *We've seen a trend towards more violent films this year.* ♦ *the latest trends in popular music*

trepidation /ˌtrepɪˈdeɪʃ(ə)n/ noun [U] *formal* fear, or nervousness

trespass¹ /ˈtrespəs/ verb [I] LAW to go into a place without the owner's permission —**trespasser** noun [C]

trespass² /ˈtrespəs/ noun [C/U] LAW the crime of entering a place without the owner's permission

triage /ˈtriːɑːʒ/ noun [U] HEALTH the process of deciding which people in a hospital department should get medical treatment first, based on how serious their condition is

trial /ˈtraɪəl/ noun **1** [C/U] LAW the process of examining a case in a court of law and deciding whether someone is guilty of a crime: *a murder trial* ♦ *They're on trial for armed robbery.* **2** [C/U] the process of testing something over a period of time: *The system will operate for a six-month trial period.* **3** [C] SPORTS a sports competition in which people compete to be chosen for a later competition
PHRASES **trial and error** a way of finding a good method that involves trying several possibilities and learning from your mistakes
trial and improvement MATHS a method of finding a solution to a problem by guessing the solution and using an incorrect answer to improve the next guess

ˈtrial ˌhole noun [C] CONSTRUCTION a hole that is dug in the ground when examining an area of land to see if it is suitable for building on

ˌtrial ˈrun noun [C] an occasion when you try something for the first time in order to find out if it works

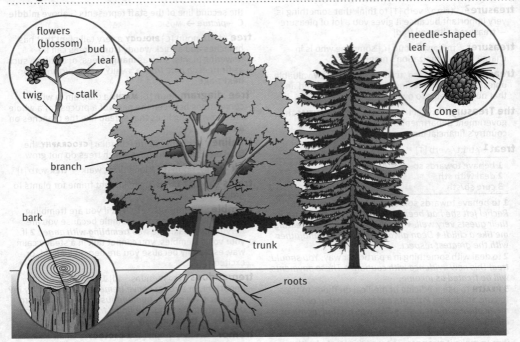

flowers
(blossom)
bud
leaf
twig
stalk
needle-shaped
leaf
cone
branch
bark
trunk
roots

tree

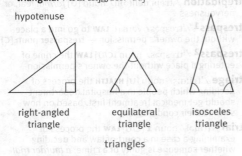

hypotenuse

right-angled
triangle

equilateral
triangle

isosceles
triangle

triangles

triangle /'traɪæŋg(ə)l/ noun [C] **1 MATHS** a flat shape with three straight sides and three angles —*picture* → SHAPE **2 MUSIC** a simple musical instrument that consists of a metal triangle that you hit with a bar —*picture* → MUSICAL INSTRUMENT, ORCHESTRA

PHRASE **triangle of forces PHYSICS** a triangle with sides that represent the sizes and directions of three forces in **equilibrium**
—**triangular** /traɪ'æŋgjʊlə/ adj

triangulation /traɪˌæŋgjʊ'leɪʃ(ə)n/ noun [C/U] **MATHS** the measurement of something using **trigonometry**

the Triassic /traɪ'æsɪk/ noun [singular] **GEOLOGY** the period of geological time from 248 million to 205 million years ago, when reptiles lived and the first dinosaurs developed

triathlon /traɪ'æθlən/ noun [C] **SPORTS** a type of race consisting of three parts in which each person swims, rides a bicycle, and runs

tribalism /'traɪbəˌlɪz(ə)m/ noun [U] **SOCIAL STUDIES** a way of thinking or behaving in which people are more loyal to their tribe than to their friends, their country, or any other social group

tribe /traɪb/ noun [C] **SOCIAL STUDIES** a large group of related families who live in the same area and share a common language, religion, and customs: *Native American tribes* —**tribal** adj

tribespeople /'traɪbzˌpiːp(ə)l/ noun [plural] **SOCIAL STUDIES** people who are members of a tribe

tribunal /traɪ'bjuːn(ə)l/ noun [C] **LAW** a special law court that is organized in order to judge a particular case: *a war crimes tribunal*

tributary /'trɪbjʊt(ə)ri/ (plural **tributaries**) noun [C] **GEOGRAPHY** a small river that flows into a larger river —*picture* → RIVER

tribute /'trɪbjuːt/ noun [C/U] something that you do, say, or make in order to show that you respect and admire someone: *They showed the programme as a tribute to Nelson Mandela.*

PHRASE **pay tribute to** to praise someone or something publicly

triceps /'traɪseps/ noun [C] **ANATOMY** the muscle at the back of the upper arm —*picture* → BODY

trick¹ /trɪk/ noun [C] **1** a deliberate attempt to make someone believe something that is not true, either as a joke or as an attempt to harm them: *At first I thought Joe was playing a trick on me.* **2** a way of entertaining people by doing something that looks like magic: *a street performer doing tricks for the crowd* **3** an effective and skilful way of doing something: *There's a trick to folding up this umbrella.* ♦ *If you want to see her, the trick is to go early.*

trick² /trɪk/ verb [T] to make someone believe something that is not true, either as a joke or as an attempt to harm them: *I suddenly realized that I'd been tricked.* ♦ *He tricked me into believing that he was somebody famous.*

trickery /'trɪkəri/ noun [U] the use of tricks to get what you want

trickle /ˈtrɪk(ə)l/ verb [I] **1** if a liquid trickles somewhere, a small amount of it flows there slowly: *A tear trickled down his cheek*. **2** if people or things trickle into or out of a place, a few of them arrive or leave —**trickle** noun [C]

'trickle-down ,theory noun [singular] ECONOMICS an economic theory according to which poor people benefit when richer people become even richer, because the rich will invest more, start new businesses etc

tricky /ˈtrɪki/ (**trickier, trickiest**) adj difficult to do or deal with: *a tricky situation*

tricuspid valve /traɪˈkʌspɪd ˌvælv/ noun [C] ANATOMY a **valve** on the right side of the heart. It prevents blood from flowing back from the right **ventricle** into the **atrium**. —*picture* → CIRCULATION

tried¹ /traɪd/ the past tense and past participle of **try¹**

tried² /traɪd/ adj **tried and tested** known to be good or effective

trigger¹ /ˈtrɪɡə/ verb [T] **1** to cause something to happen, especially something bad: *The news of his death triggered more violence*. **2** to make a machine or piece of equipment start to work: *Someone broke a window, and this triggered the alarm*.

trigger² /ˈtrɪɡə/ noun [C] **1** the part of a gun that you pull with your finger to make the gun fire **2** something that causes something to happen, especially something bad

trigonometry /ˌtrɪɡəˈnɒmətri/ noun [U] MATHS the part of mathematics that studies how the angles and sides of triangles are related —**trigonometric** /ˌtrɪɡənəˈmetrɪk/ adj

trill¹ /trɪl/ noun [C] MUSIC a musical sound made by singing or playing two similar notes one after the other very quickly

trill² /trɪl/ verb [I] MUSIC to sing or play a musical trill

trillion /ˈtrɪljən/ number the number 1,000,000,000,000

trilobite /ˈtraɪləʊbaɪt/ noun [C] GEOLOGY an **arthropod** that lived in the sea during the **Palaeozoic** period of geological time. Its **exoskeleton** (=hard cover of its body) was divided into three parts.

trilogy /ˈtrɪlədʒi/ (plural **trilogies**) noun [C] ARTS, LITERATURE a series of three books, films, or plays

trim¹ /trɪm/ (**trims, trimming, trimmed**) verb [T] **1** to cut a small amount off something so that it looks tidy: *I just wanted her to trim my hair*. **2** to reduce the amount or number of something: *The company has **trimmed** £6,000 **from** its advertising budget*. **3** to decorate something **4** to arrange the sails on a boat so that they are suitable for the wind

trim² /trɪm/ noun **1** [singular] the act of trimming something, especially hair **2** [singular/U] decoration on the edges of something: *cream leather seats with brown trim*

trimmings /ˈtrɪmɪŋz/ noun [plural] **1** extra parts that are added to a meal to make it traditional or more interesting **2** small objects or pieces of cloth that are used for decorating things such as clothes

the Trinity /ˈtrɪnəti/ noun [singular] RELIGION a name that Christians use for referring to the three parts that they believe God consists of. These are the **Father**, the **Son**, and the **Holy Ghost**.

trinomial /traɪˈnəʊmiəl/ noun [C] BIOLOGY a scientific name that consists of three elements. It names the **genus**, species, and **subspecies** or variety of an animal.

trio /ˈtriːəʊ/ (plural **trios**) noun [C] **1** a group of three people or things **2** MUSIC a group of three musicians who play together, or a piece of music for a trio

trip¹ /trɪp/ noun [C] an occasion when you go somewhere and come back again= JOURNEY: *a fishing trip* ♦ *a boat trip* ♦ *a trip to Brazil* ♦ *The whole family went on a trip to Florida*. → FIELD TRIP, ROUND TRIP

> ### Build your vocabulary: words you can use instead of **trip**
>
> - **crossing** a trip across water from one piece of land to another
> - **drive** a trip in a car
> - **excursion** an organized trip for a group of people
> - **expedition** a long and difficult trip to a place that is very far away, often made by people who are doing scientific research
> - **flight** a trip in a plane
> - **journey** a long trip from one place to another
> - **outing** a short trip made by a group of people who are visiting a place
> - **ride** a short trip in a car or bus, or on a bicycle or motorbike
> - **tour** a trip to a place where there are interesting things to see

trip² /trɪp/ (**trips, tripping, tripped**) verb **1** [I/T] to hit your foot on something and fall down, or to make someone hit their foot on something and fall down: *I'm sure she tripped me!* ♦ *I **tripped over** a rock*. **2** [T] to make a switch go on or off, especially by accident

tripartite /traɪˈpɑːtaɪt/ adj formal **1** involving three countries or organizations **2** consisting of three parts

triple¹ /ˈtrɪp(ə)l/ adj **1** involving three things of the same kind: *a triple killing* **2** three times bigger than the usual size or amount: *a triple vodka*

triple² /ˈtrɪp(ə)l/ determiner three times as much or as many: *The price they wanted was triple the amount we expected*.

triple³ /ˈtrɪp(ə)l/ verb [I/T] if something triples, or if you triple it, it increases so that it is three times bigger than before: *We had tripled our money by the end of the year*.

the 'triple ,jump noun [singular] SPORTS a sport in which you first jump forwards on one leg, jump again on the other leg, and jump a third time using both legs

triplet /ˈtrɪplət/ noun [C] one of three children who were born at the same time to the same mother

triploblastic /ˌtrɪpləʊˈblæstɪk/ adj BIOLOGY relating to an invertebrate animal in which the adult tissues come from the three layers of tissue in the embryo, called the **ectoderm**, **endoderm**, and **mesoderm** → DIPLOBLASTIC

tripod /ˈtraɪpɒd/ noun [C] an object with three legs, placed on the ground or on a surface and used for supporting a piece of equipment, a container for heating etc —*picture* → LABORATORY

trite /traɪt/ adj a trite remark is not interesting or original because people have used it too much

tritium /ˈtrɪtiəm/ noun [U] CHEMISTRY, PHYSICS a radioactive isotope of hydrogen. It has an **atomic mass** of 3 and a **half-life** of 12.3 years. Chemical symbol: **T**

Triton /ˈtraɪt(ə)n/ noun ASTRONOMY the largest of the moons of the planet Neptune

triumph¹ /ˈtraɪʌmf/ noun **1** [C/U] a great victory or success **2** [U] the proud or excited feeling that you get when you have been successful

triumph² /ˈtraɪʌmf/ verb [I] to win a great victory, or to have a great success

triumphant /traɪˈʌmfənt/ adj showing that you are very proud or excited about a victory or success: *a triumphant yell* —**triumphantly** adv

trivalent /traɪˈveɪlənt/ adj CHEMISTRY relating to chemical elements that have a **valency** (=ability to combine with other elements) of three

trivial /ˈtrɪviəl/ adj not very interesting, serious, or valuable: *Why are they so upset over such a trivial matter?*

trivialize /ˈtrɪviəlaɪz/ verb [T] to make something seem less important or serious than it really is

trochee /ˈtrəʊkiː/ noun [C] LITERATURE a set of two syllables in poetry in which you emphasize the first one when you read it, but not the second

trod /trɒd/ the past tense of **tread¹**

trodden /ˈtrɒd(ə)n/ the past participle of **tread¹**

Trojan horse /ˌtrəʊdʒən ˈhɔːs/ noun [C] COMPUTING a program that seems useful but is designed to be harmful, for example by destroying information

trolley /ˈtrɒli/ (plural **trolleys**) noun [C] **1** a large container with wheels that you push and use for carrying things in a supermarket or at an airport **2** a table with wheels used for serving food or drinks

trombone /trɒmˈbəʊn/ noun [C] MUSIC a musical instrument consisting of two metal tubes. You play it by blowing into it and sliding one tube forwards and backwards. —*picture* → MUSICAL INSTRUMENT, ORCHESTRA

troop /truːp/ verb [I] to walk somewhere in a group

troops /truːps/ noun [plural] soldiers

trope /trəʊp/ noun [C] LITERATURE a use of a word or expression in an unusual way by a writer, in order to achieve an effect = FIGURE OF SPEECH

trophic /ˈtrɒfɪk/ adj BIOLOGY relating to **nutrition** (=the effects of food on health and growth)

'trophic ˌlevel noun [C] ENVIRONMENT the position that a particular species has in the **food chain**. The species in each trophic level feeds on the level below it.

trophy /ˈtrəʊfi/ (plural **trophies**) noun [C] a large silver cup or similar object that is given as a prize to the winner of a sports competition

tropic /ˈtrɒpɪk/ noun [C] GEOGRAPHY one of the two imaginary lines around the Earth on either side of the equator. The **Tropic of Cancer** is 23° 27' north of it and the **Tropic of Capricorn** is 23° 27' south of it. —*picture* → EARTH

tropical /ˈtrɒpɪk(ə)l/ adj GEOGRAPHY in or from the hottest parts of the Earth —*picture* → ECOSYSTEM

ˌtropical 'cyclone noun [C] GEOGRAPHY a storm with heavy rain and strong winds that forms over warm waters in the tropics. **Typhoons** and **hurricanes** are tropical cyclones.

the tropics /ˈtrɒpɪks/ noun [plural] GEOGRAPHY the hottest parts of the Earth, that are near the equator. They are between the **Tropic of Cancer** and the **Tropic of Capricorn**. —*picture* → EARTH

tropism /ˈtrəʊpɪzəm/ noun [U] BIOLOGY the movement of part of a plant in a particular direction as it reacts to a **stimulus** such as light, water, chemicals etc

the troposphere /ˈtrɒpəˌsfɪə/ noun [singular] SCIENCE the part of the Earth's atmosphere that is closest to its surface —*picture* → ATMOSPHERE

trot /trɒt/ (**trots**, **trotting**, **trotted**) verb [I] if a horse trots, it walks quickly with short steps, but without running —**trot** noun [singular]

trouble¹ /ˈtrʌb(ə)l/ noun

1 problems/worries	**4** when blame is likely
2 additional effort	**5** violence
3 bad situation	**+** PHRASES

1 [C/U] problems, worries, or difficulties: *The plane had engine trouble and had to land in Miami.* ♦ *This old car has caused a lot of trouble for us.* ♦ *I'm having some trouble with my knee.* ♦ *He was having trouble hearing her* (=finding it difficult to hear her).
2 [U] additional or special effort that causes you problems: *I don't mind waiting – it's no trouble.* ♦ *Thank you for taking the trouble to reply.* ♦ *I'll do your shopping to save you the trouble of going out.*
3 [U] an unpleasant, difficult, or dangerous situation: *I knew we were in trouble when the lift stopped.* ♦ *The plane ran into serious trouble soon after take-off.*
4 [U] a situation for which you are likely to be blamed, criticized, or punished: *I hear she's in trouble with the police again.* ♦ *I got into trouble for being late.*
5 [C/U] fighting, violence, or bad behaviour: *There's been a lot of trouble in the neighbourhood recently.* ♦ *The trouble started after a youth was arrested.*

PHRASES **asking for trouble** doing something that is very likely to cause you problems or difficulties: *Delaying surgery is just asking for trouble.*
the trouble with sb/sth used for talking about something that causes problems, worries, or difficulties: *The trouble with my parents is they think I'm still a child.*

trouble² /ˈtrʌb(ə)l/ verb [T] to make someone worried: *I could tell that something was troubling her.*

troubled /ˈtrʌb(ə)ld/ adj **1** worried about the problems that you have **2** a troubled person, place, time, or situation is affected by many problems

troublemaker /ˈtrʌb(ə)lˌmeɪkə/ noun [C] someone who deliberately causes a lot of problems

troubleshooter /ˈtrʌb(ə)lˌʃuːtə/ noun [C] someone whose job is to solve problems that an organization is having

troubleshooting /ˈtrʌb(ə)lˌʃuːtɪŋ/ noun [U] the activity of finding out the cause of a problem and then solving it

troublesome /ˈtrʌb(ə)ls(ə)m/ adj causing annoying problems or difficulties

'trouble ˌspot noun [C] a place where there is often fighting between groups

trough /trɒf/ noun [C] **1** AGRICULTURE a long open container that is used for holding food or water for animals **2** a period when something that rises and falls regularly is at a low level: *the peaks and troughs in demand* —*picture* → WAVE

troupe /truːp/ noun [C] ARTS a group of performers

'trouser ˌpress noun [C] a piece of equipment consisting of two boards that you put a pair of trousers between in order to make them flat and smooth

trousers /ˈtraʊzəz/ noun [plural] a piece of clothing that covers the body from the waist to the feet, with separate parts for each leg: *a pair of trousers*

trout /traʊt/ (plural **trout**) noun [C/U] a fish that lives in rivers and lakes, or this fish eaten as food

trowel /ˈtraʊəl/ noun [C] **1** a small tool with a curved blade that is used in gardens for digging —*picture* → AGRICULTURAL **2** a small tool with a flat blade that is used for spreading substances such as cement

truancy /ˈtruːənsi/ noun [U] EDUCATION the act or habit of staying away from school without permission

truant /'truːənt/ noun [C] **EDUCATION** a child who stays away from school without permission

truce /truːs/ noun [C] a temporary agreement between two opponents to stop fighting

truck /trʌk/ noun [C] a large road vehicle that is used for carrying goods = LORRY

trudge /trʌdʒ/ verb [I] to walk somewhere with slow heavy steps

true /truː/ adj **1** based on facts or on things that really happened ≠ FALSE: *Is it true that you're looking for a new job?* ◆ *The film is based on a true story.* ◆ *It rains a lot in the north-west, and that is especially true of Cumbria.* **2** real or actual, especially when compared with how something seems to be: *Lara never shows her true feelings.* ◆ *The study shows that the true cost of the system is much higher than people think.* **3** having all the qualities that you expect in a particular type of person, thing, or feeling = GENUINE: *She was a true champion in every way.* ◆ *The country is not yet a true democracy.* ◆ **true love 4** if you are true to someone or something, you continue to be loyal to them: *Through the years, Doug stayed true to his wife.*

PHRASES **come true** if a wish, dream, fear etc comes true, it really happens: *Meeting Joe was like a dream come true* (=exactly what you have always wanted).
true to life similar to what really happens in people's lives: *The characters in this novel are so true to life.*

,true 'fruit noun [C] **BIOLOGY** a fruit such as a tomato that consists only of a fully developed ovary → FALSE FRUIT

,true 'leg noun [C] **BIOLOGY** one of the six legs on the **thorax** of an insect larva such as a caterpillar —*picture* → CATERPILLAR

,true 'length noun [C/U] **MATHS** the actual length of a line, which is established by looking at it at right angles to it

,true 'north noun [U] **GEOGRAPHY** the north of the Earth calculated according to the Earth's axis → MAGNETIC NORTH

truly /'truːli/ adv **1** completely: *a truly wonderful day* ◆ *She was someone who truly understood children.* **2** used for emphasizing that you really mean what you are saying: *I truly believe he's the right man for the job.*

trumpet /'trʌmpɪt/ noun [C] **MUSIC** a metal musical instrument that you play by blowing into it as you press buttons on the top —*picture* → MUSICAL INSTRUMENT, ORCHESTRA

truncate /trʌŋ'keɪt/ verb [T] *formal* to make something shorter, especially by removing the end or top of it —**truncated** adj, **truncation** /trʌŋ'keɪʃ(ə)n/ noun [C/U]

,truncated 'solid noun [C/U] **MATHS** a three-dimensional object that has had a part removed from its top or bottom by a **plane** (=flat surface) cutting it

,truncated 'surface noun [C] **TECHNOLOGY** the cut surface of a solid, for example a **prism** or **cone**, that has its top cut off by a **cutting plane**

truncheon /'trʌntʃ(ə)n/ noun [C] a short thick stick that a police officer carries as a weapon

trundle /'trʌnd(ə)l/ verb [I/T] to roll slowly on wheels, or to make something roll slowly on wheels

trunk /trʌŋk/ noun [C] **1** **BIOLOGY** the main part of a tree that the branches grow out of —*picture* → TREE **2** a large strong box with a lid, used for storing things **3** an elephant's long nose **4** **ANATOMY** the part of the body between the waist and the head, not including the arms or head

trunks /trʌŋks/ noun [plural] **shorts** that men wear for swimming

truss¹ /trʌs/ noun [C] **1** **CONSTRUCTION** a wooden or metal triangular support that strengthens a structure such as a roof or bridge **2** **HEALTH** a medical belt worn by someone with a **hernia**

truss² /trʌs/ verb [T] to tie someone's arms and legs very tightly so that they cannot move or escape

trust¹ /trʌst/ verb [T] to believe that someone or something is good, honest, or reliable: *Both communities have to trust each other.* ◆ *Never trust cheap locks like these.* ◆ *Can we trust you to give John the message?* ◆ *I trust Dana with all my secrets.*

Word family: trust

Words in the same family as trust:
- **trusting** adj
- **trustworthy** adj
- **distrust** n, v
- **trustee** n
- **trusty** adj
- **untrustworthy** adj
- **mistrust** n, v

trust² /trʌst/ noun **1** [U] a feeling that you trust someone or something: *The doctor-patient relationship has to be based on trust.* ◆ *We have to put our trust in the democratic system.* **2** [C/U] **LAW** an arrangement in which a person or an organization manages someone else's money or property, or the money or property that they manage: *The land will be held in trust by the Church.*

trustee /trʌ'stiː/ noun [C] **1** **LAW** someone who is responsible for looking after money or property that belongs to someone else **2** a member of a group of people who are chosen to manage an institution such as a hospital or school that is organized as a trust

trusteeship /trʌ'stiːʃɪp/ noun **1** [C/U] **LAW** the job or responsibilities of a trustee **2** [U] **POLITICS** the responsibility for governing a country while it is preparing to become independent

'trust ,fund noun [C] an amount of money that is invested and managed for someone, usually a child

trusting /'trʌstɪŋ/ adj willing to trust people, especially when it is not a sensible thing to do

trustworthy /'trʌs(t)ˌwɜːði/ adj someone who is trustworthy can be trusted ≠ UNTRUSTWORTHY

truth /truːθ/ noun **1** [U] the actual facts about something, rather than what people think or say is true: *We finally learned the truth about Gina's past.* ◆ *Tell me the truth: did you take the money?* ◆ *The truth is that they haven't solved the problem.* **2** [U] the quality of being true: *There is some truth to his story* (=it is at least partly true). ◆ *Are you questioning the truth of his accusations?* **3** [C] an idea that is accepted by most people as being true: *Is it a universal truth* (=something that is true in all situations) *that exercise is good for you?*

truthful /'truːθf(ə)l/ adj **1** a truthful person says what is true and does not lie: *He was sure she wasn't being completely truthful.* **2** a truthful statement only contains things that are true —**truthfully** adv

'truth ,table noun [C] **MATHS** a diagram consisting of rows and **columns** that shows whether something is true or false

try¹ /traɪ/ (**tries**, **trying**, **tried**) verb **1** [I/T] to attempt to do something: *Owen tried a shot at goal, but the ball went wide.* ◆ *Just try your best. I'm sure you'll be fine.* ◆ *We'll just have to try harder next time.* ◆ *Just try to stay calm.* ◆ *I will try and get the report to you today.* **2** [T] to do something in order to find out whether it is enjoyable, suitable, or effective: *Have you tried these biscuits? They're great!* ◆ *Let's try something different* with your hair this time. ♦ *She tried talking about it to Steve, but couldn't make him change his mind.* **3** [I/T] to go to a particular place in order to find something, or to go to a particular person in order to get information: *There's a hardware shop down the street – you could try there.* ♦ *Try Dina – she knows a lot about the law.* **4** [T] to judge a person or case in a court of law: *Franklin's case will be tried on 25th August.* ♦ *He was **tried for** murder and found guilty.*

PHRASE **try your hand at sth** to do an activity for the first time in order to find out whether you like it, or whether you are good at it

PHRASAL VERBS **,try sth 'on** to put on a piece of clothing in order to see how it looks and whether it fits
,try sth 'out to test something in order to see what it is like or whether it is suitable or effective

try² /traɪ/ (plural **tries**) noun [C] **1** an attempt to do something: *There are no guarantees that it will work, but it's **worth a try**.* ♦ *I'll **have a try** – I'm pretty good at fixing things.* **2 SPORTS** an occasion in **rugby** when a player touches the ground behind the goal line with the ball and scores points

trying /ˈtraɪɪŋ/ adj difficult to deal with in a way that makes you annoyed or tired: *We've all had a very trying day.*

trypsin /ˈtrɪpsɪn/ noun [U] **BIOLOGY** an enzyme produced by the pancreas that breaks down protein into **polypeptides** and **amino acids**

'try ,square noun [C] **TECHNOLOGY** a tool used for marking out right angles, or checking that something is square

tsar /zɑː/ noun [C] the king of Russia in the period before 1917

tsetse fly /ˈtetsi ˌflaɪ, ˈtsetsi ˌflaɪ/ noun [C] a flying insect in Africa that feeds on the blood of humans and other mammals. It can spread a serious disease called **sleeping sickness**.

T-shirt /ˈtiː ˌʃɜːt/ noun [C] a soft shirt that has short sleeves and no collar or buttons

T-square /ˈtiː ˌskweə/ noun [C] **TECHNOLOGY** a tool in the shape of the letter T that is used for drawing lines that are exactly parallel, or in the shape of a square

tsunami /tsuːˈnɑːmi/ noun [C] **GEOLOGY** a very large wave in the sea that is caused by an earthquake under the sea or by the **eruption** of a volcano. Tsunamis usually cause severe damage on land.

tub /tʌb/ noun [C] **1** a small container with a lid, used for holding or storing food: *ice cream tubs* **2** a large round container with a flat bottom: *tubs of flowers and shrubs*

tuba /ˈtjuːbə/ noun [C] **MUSIC** a large metal musical instrument that is a curved tube with a wide open end. You play it by blowing into it as you press buttons on the top. —*picture* → MUSICAL INSTRUMENT, ORCHESTRA

tubal ligation /ˌtjuːb(ə)l laɪˈɡeɪʃ(ə)n/ noun [U] **HEALTH** a medical operation in which a woman's **fallopian tubes** are cut and the ends of the tubes tied, so that she cannot have any more children

tube /tjuːb/ noun **1** [C] a long narrow object similar to a pipe that liquid or gas can move through: *Nurses had to feed Dan through a tube.* **2** [C] a long narrow plastic or metal container that you squeeze in order to push out the soft substance inside: *a tube of toothpaste* **3 the tube** [singular] *informal* the system of underground trains in London: *a tube train* ♦ *She goes to work **by tube**.*

tuber /ˈtjuːbə/ noun [C] **BIOLOGY** the swollen part of a plant such as a potato, that grows underground, stores food, and produces new plants

tuberculosis /tjuːˌbɜːkjʊˈləʊsɪs/ noun [U] **HEALTH** a serious infectious disease, caused by bacteria, that affects the lungs and can cause death

'tube ,well noun [C] **AGRICULTURE** a type of **well** (=hole in ground providing water) in which underground water is pumped to the surface of the ground using a tube made of **stainless steel**

tubing /ˈtjuːbɪŋ/ noun [U] a piece of tube, or a system of tubes

tubular /ˈtjuːbjʊlə/ adj shaped like a tube, or made from tubes

tubule /ˈtjuːbjuːl/ noun [C] **BIOLOGY** a part of a plant or animal that consists of a very small tube

tuck /tʌk/ verb [T] to put something in a place where it looks tidy or is hidden: *She tucked her glasses into her pocket.*

Tues. or **Tue.** abbrev Tuesday

Tuesday /ˈtjuːzdeɪ/ noun [C/U] the day after Monday and before Wednesday: *New Year's Day will be on a Tuesday this year.* ♦ *We are leaving **on Tuesday**.* ♦ *We close early **on Tuesdays** (=every Tuesday).*

tuft /tʌft/ noun [C] several pieces of grass, hair, feathers, or fibres that are all growing together

tug¹ /tʌɡ/ (**tugs**, **tugging**, **tugged**) verb [I/T] to pull someone or something by making a short strong movement: *The little boy tugged on his mother's skirt.*

tug² /tʌɡ/ noun [C] **1** a short strong pull **2 tug** or **tug boat** a small powerful boat that is used for pulling ships into and out of ports

tuition /tjuːˈɪʃ(ə)n/ noun [U] **EDUCATION 1** the work that a teacher does when they teach a particular subject, especially to one person or to a small group **2** money that you pay to take lessons, especially at a college, university, or private school

tulip /ˈtjuːlɪp/ noun [C] a plant with a colourful flower that is shaped like a cup

tumble /ˈtʌmb(ə)l/ verb [I] **1** if a price or value tumbles, it suddenly becomes much lower **2 tumble** or **tumble down** if an organization or system tumbles, it suddenly stops existing —**tumble** noun [C]

tummy /ˈtʌmi/ (plural **tummies**) noun [C] *informal* the stomach

tumour /ˈtjuːmə/ noun [C] **HEALTH** a mass of cells in the body that grow in a way that is not normal and can cause serious illness. Some tumours are made of cancer cells.

tuna /ˈtjuːnə/ (plural **tuna**) noun [C/U] a large fish that lives in the Pacific and Atlantic Oceans, or this fish eaten as food

tundra /ˈtʌndrə/ noun [C/U] **GEOGRAPHY** a large flat area of land without trees in very cold northern parts of the world. Its **subsoil** (=the layer under the top layer of soil) is permanently frozen.

tune¹ /tjuːn/ noun [C] **MUSIC** *informal* a song or simple piece of music: *a Russian folk tune* ♦ *the station that plays all your favourite tunes*

PHRASES **change your tune** to change your opinion or attitude

in tune MUSIC producing the right note when you sing or play music: *He can sing any song perfectly in tune.*

out of tune MUSIC producing the wrong note when you sing or play music: *One of the guitars sounded a little out of tune.*

to the tune of used for emphasizing how large an

amount of money is: *The company is in debt to the tune of £1.2 billion.*

tune² /tjuːn/ verb [T] **1** MUSIC to make small changes to a musical instrument so that it will produce the correct notes **2** to set a radio or television to a particular station or programme **3** ENGINEERING to make small changes to an engine or machine so that it works better

PHRASAL VERB ,**tune 'up** MUSIC if a group of musicians tune up, they make small changes to their instruments so that they can play well together

tungsten /'tʌŋstən/ noun [U] CHEMISTRY a very hard metal element that is used for making steel. Chemical symbol: **W**

tunic /'tjuːnɪk/ noun [C] **1** a long loose shirt **2** a short jacket that is part of a uniform

tuning fork /'tjuːnɪŋ ˌfɔːk/ noun [C] MUSIC a metal object that produces a particular note when you hit it and make it vibrate, used for testing that musical instruments are producing the correct note. It has a handle and two long thin parts.

tunnel¹ /'tʌn(ə)l/ noun [C] a passage through a hill or under the ground: *We watched the train enter a tunnel.*

tunnel² /'tʌn(ə)l/ (**tunnels, tunnelling, tunnelled**) verb [I] to dig a tunnel

,**tunnel 'vision** noun [U] **1** the tendency to think only about one goal or one part of something, without thinking about anything else **2** HEALTH a medical condition caused by damage to the retina in which someone can only see what is directly in front of them

turban /'tɜːbən/ noun [C] a long piece of cloth that is wrapped around the head like a hat. It is worn by some men in the Sikh, Hindu, and Muslim religions.

turbine /'tɜːbaɪn/ noun [C] PHYSICS a machine that produces power using the pressure of liquid or gas on a wheel. Turbines are used for **generating** electricity in **power stations** and for turning the **propellers** on ships. —*picture* → DAM, GENERATOR, JET ENGINE, NUCLEAR REACTOR

turbulence /'tɜːbjʊləns/ noun [U] **1** a confusing situation in which everything is changing in an uncontrolled way: *a period of turbulence after the death of the dictator* **2** sudden violent movements of air or water in different directions

turbulent /'tɜːbjʊlənt/ adj **1** a turbulent situation, place, or time is one in which there is a lot of uncontrolled change: *the country's turbulent history* **2** turbulent air or water moves suddenly and violently in different directions

turf /tɜːf/ noun [U] short grass and the earth that is under it

'**turf ,war** noun [C] arguments between people or groups who each want to control a particular area

turgor /'tɜːgə/ noun [U] BIOLOGY the outward pressure against the inside cell wall of a plant, caused by water trying to flow into the cell by **osmosis**. Turgor maintains the shape of the plant.

turkey /'tɜːki/ (plural **turkeys**) noun [C/U] a large bird that is similar to a chicken, or the meat from this bird — *picture* → BIRD

turmoil /'tɜːmɔɪl/ noun [U] a situation in which there is a lot of excitement or uncontrolled activity: *political turmoil* ♦ *Her life seemed to be in turmoil.*

turn¹ /tɜːn/ verb

1 move round	6 do/become sth else
2 move sth round	7 reach an age
3 change direction	8 shape sth using lathe
4 move in circle	+ PHRASES
5 move page	+ PHRASAL VERBS

1 [I/T] to change the position of your body or your head so that you are facing in a different direction: *She turned and stared at me.* ♦ *He turned his head and looked around the room.* ♦ *Maria turned to the reporters and said: 'I'm innocent.'* ♦ *Lopez just glared at the other man and then turned away.* ♦ *The girls in front turned round and smiled.*

2 [T] to change the position of something so that it is pointing in a different direction: *Turn your chairs round so you're facing me.*

3 [I/T] to change the direction in which you are moving or travelling, or to make something change direction: *We turned into our drive, glad to get home.* ♦ *Follow this road; then turn right after the school.* ♦ *They ordered the pilot to turn the plane around.*

4 [I/T] to make a circular movement, or to make something move in a circle: *I heard the key turn in the lock.*

5 [T] if you turn the page of a book or magazine, you move it in order to read a different page

6 [linking verb] to change and do something else, or to become something else: *The weather turned chilly in the afternoon.* ♦ *The crowd was beginning to turn violent.* ♦ *The lizard's skin turned green as we watched.*

7 [linking verb] to become a particular age: *He turned 40 in March.*

8 [T] ENGINEERING, TECHNOLOGY to give a particular shape to a piece of wood or metal using a **lathe**

PHRASES **turn your back on** to refuse to accept someone or something that you have previously accepted

turn a corner to reach a stage in which a situation improves, after a difficult period

PHRASAL VERBS ,**turn 'back** to return the same way that you came instead of continuing on your journey: *Bad weather forced them to turn back.*

,**turn sth 'down 1** to refuse to accept an offer or request: *How could you turn down such a fantastic job?* **2** to reduce the amount of sound, heat, or light that is produced by a piece of equipment, by pressing a button or by moving a switch ≠ TURN UP: *Can you turn the music down a bit?*

,**turn (sth) 'into sth** to change or develop into something different, or to make something change or develop into something different: *Our holiday turned into a nightmare.* ♦ *They turned her first book into a film.*

,**turn sth 'off** to stop using a piece of equipment or a supply of gas, electricity, or water by pressing, turning, or moving something: *Will you turn the television off, please?* ♦ *The emergency crew turned off the power and gas supplies.*

,**turn sth 'on** to start using a piece of equipment or a supply of gas, electricity, or water by pressing, turning, or moving something: *Is your computer turned on?* ♦ *Let's turn the radio on and see if it works.*

,**turn 'out** to develop in a particular way, or to have a particular result: *I'm sure it will all turn out well in the end.* ♦ *As it turned out, the storm missed Singapore.* ♦ *It all turned out to be a mistake.*

,**turn (sth) 'over** to turn a page in a book or a sheet of paper so that the other side is towards you: *You may turn over your exam papers now.*

,**turn 'up** to arrive somewhere: *She failed to turn up for work on Monday.*

,**turn sth 'up** to increase the amount of sound, heat, or light that is produced by a piece of equipment, by pressing a button or by moving a switch: *Can you turn the volume up a bit?*

turn² /tɜːn/ noun

1 time to do sth	4 change in situation
2 in a road	5 movement in circle
3 change of direction	+ PHRASES

1 [singular] the time when you can or must do something, because you are part of a group of people who are each doing the same activity, one after the other: *You've already moved your piece – it's my turn now.* ♦ *You'll just have to **wait your turn** (=be patient until it is your turn).* ♦ *I think **it's your turn to** wash the dishes.*
2 [C] a place where a road bends to the right or left: *There's **a very sharp turn** at the end of the road.*
3 [C] a change of direction made by a person or vehicle: *He made a left turn into a quiet street.*
4 [singular] a change in a situation: *The weather suddenly **took a turn for the worse** (=became worse).* ♦ *We wanted to express our shock at today's tragic **turn of events** (=unexpected change in the situation).*
5 [C] a circular movement, when something is turned around
PHRASES **in turn 1** one after the other in a particular order: *We will deal with each of these problems in turn.* **2** as a result of something that is part of a connected series of events: *Bad farming methods caused soil erosion, and this in turn made the land less productive.*
take turns or **take it in turn(s)** if people take turns doing something or to do something, each of them does their share of it, one after the other: *We took turns steering the boat.*

turning effect /'tɜːnɪŋ ɪˌfekt/ noun [U] PHYSICS the effect that is produced when a force acts along a line that does not pass through the centre of gravity of an object

turning point /'tɜːnɪŋ ˌpɔɪnt/ noun [C] a time when an important change takes place= CROSSROADS: *1956 marked a turning point in Franco's political and personal life.*

turnip /'tɜːnɪp/ noun [C] a large round orange vegetable that grows under the ground

turnout /'tɜːnaʊt/ noun [singular] the number of people who come to an event: *We're expecting a **good turnout** at tonight's meeting.*

turnover /'tɜːnˌəʊvə/ noun **1** [C/U] BUSINESS the value of the goods and services that a company sells in a particular period of time **2** [C/U] the rate at which people leave a business, school etc and new people arrive: *a high turnover of staff* **3** [U] BUSINESS the rate at which a shop sells products and replaces them with new ones

turnstile /'tɜːnˌstaɪl/ noun [C] a gate with metal bars that move in a circle so that only one person can go through at a time

turpentine /'tɜːpəntaɪn/ noun [U] ARTS an oil with a strong smell that you use for removing paint from things

turquoise /'tɜːkwɔɪz/ adj bright green-blue in colour —**turquoise** noun [U]

turret /'tʌrɪt/ noun [C] a small tower on the top of a building such as a castle —*picture* → CASTLE

turtle /'tɜːt(ə)l/ noun [C] a reptile with a shell and four short legs that lives mainly in water —*picture* → REPTILE

tusk /tʌsk/ noun [C] BIOLOGY one of the two very long pointed teeth of a mammal such as an elephant or a **walrus**

tut /tʌt/ interjection used for representing a sound that you make with your tongue when you do not approve of something

tutor /'tjuːtə/ noun [C] EDUCATION someone who teaches and advises a group of students in a university

tutorial /tjuːˈtɔːriəl/ noun [C] **1** EDUCATION a lesson in which a student or a small group of students discusses a subject with a tutor, especially at a

university or college **2** a book or a computer program that gives instructions on how to do something

tuyere /twiˈjeə/ noun [C] TECHNOLOGY a hole through which air is forced into a **furnace**

TV /ˌtiː ˈviː/ (plural TVs) noun [C/U] television: *a TV show* ♦ *What's **on TV** tonight?*

tweezers /'twiːzəz/ noun [plural] a tool that you use for picking up very small objects or for pulling out hairs. It consists of two narrow pieces of metal joined at one end.

twelfth /twelfθ/ number in the place or position counted as number 12

twelve /twelv/ number the number 12

twenties /'twentiz/ noun [plural]
PHRASES **the twenties 1** if the temperature is in the twenties, it is in the range of 20 to 29 degrees **2** the years from 1920 to 1929: *The twenties were a difficult time in Europe.*
in your twenties to be an age in the range of 20 to 29

twentieth /'twentiəθ/ number in the place or position counted as number 20

twenty /'twenti/ number the number 20

twenty-four 'seven adv informal all the time, without ever stopping, closing, or changing

twice¹ /twaɪs/ adv **1** two times: *He's phoned twice already this morning.* ♦ *I go to the gym twice a week.* **2** two times the amount or rate of something: *The United States has **twice as many** people as Japan.*

twice² /twaɪs/ determiner two times the amount or rate of something: *Wages are rising at twice the rate of inflation.*

twig /twɪg/ noun [C] a very small thin branch on a tree or bush —*picture* → TREE

twilight /'twaɪˌlaɪt/ noun [U] the time in the evening when the sky is beginning to get dark= DUSK

twin¹ /twɪn/ noun [C] one of two children who were born at the same time to the same mother

twin² /twɪn/ adj forming a pair of two similar things: *a plane with twin engines*

twin-bedded /ˌtwɪn ˈbedɪd/ adj TOURISM a twin-bedded room has two single beds

twin-engined /'twɪn ˌendʒɪnd/ adj a twin-engined plane has two engines

twinge /twɪndʒ/ noun [C] **1** a sudden unpleasant feeling: *a twinge of guilt* **2** HEALTH a sudden short pain

twinkle /'twɪŋk(ə)l/ verb [I] **1** if someone's eyes twinkle, they seem to shine because the person is happy **2** if lights or stars twinkle, the light from them seems to get brighter then weaker very quickly many times —**twinkle** noun [singular]

twinning /'twɪnɪŋ/ noun [U] TOURISM a system of formal connections between two towns in different countries that encourages their inhabitants to visit and exchange information

twirl /twɜːl/ verb [I/T] to move in circles, or to make something move in circles —**twirl** noun [C]

twist¹ /twɪst/ verb **1** [I/T] to bend or turn into a different shape, or to force something out of its original shape by bending it or turning it: *The force of the explosion had twisted the metal.* **2** [T] to turn something in a circle with your hands or fingers: *Kathryn sat anxiously twisting a handkerchief in her hands.* **3** [T] to injure a part of your body by suddenly bending it too much: *I've twisted my ankle so I won't be able to play.* **4** [T] to change the intended meaning of something slightly, so that it means what you want it to mean: *You're twisting my words.*

PHRASE twist sb's arm *informal* to persuade someone to do something that they do not want to do

twist² /twɪst/ noun [C] **1** a sudden unexpected change in a situation: *This is the final tragic twist in a long story.* **2** a bend in a road or river: *The island roads are full of twists and turns.* **3** a movement in which you turn something: *With a twist of his wrist, he untied the ropes.*

twisted /ˈtwɪstɪd/ adj bent into a shape that is not normal: *All that was left of the car was a tangle of twisted metal.*

twitch /twɪtʃ/ verb [I] if part of your body twitches, it makes a slight uncontrolled movement —**twitch** noun [C]

two /tuː/ number the number 2

PHRASES in two into two pieces: *The explosion had broken the plane in two.*
put two and two together to guess what is happening as a result of what you have seen or heard

two-dimensional /ˌtuː dɪˈmenʃ(ə)nəl/ adj **1** a two-dimensional shape is flat **2** a two-dimensional character in a book, play, or film does not have the complicated personality of a real person

ˈtwo-dimensional ˌdrawing noun [C/U] **MATHS, PHYSICS** a drawing that shows a three-dimensional object as a two-dimensional shape

twofold /ˈtuːˌfəʊld/ or **ˈtwo-ˌfold** adj **1** twice as much, or twice as many: *a twofold increase in the amount of traffic* **2** consisting of two parts: *The aim of the campaign is twofold.* —**twofold** adv

ˌtwo-pin ˈplug noun [C] an electrical **plug** that has two pins, one for a live wire and one for a **neutral** wire —*picture* → PLUG

ˌtwo-stroke ˈcycle noun [C] **ENGINEERING** an **internal-combustion engine** that completes the processes of **intake**, **compression**, **combustion**, and **exhaust** in only two **strokes** (=movements of the piston)

ˌtwo-ˈway adj **1** able both to send and to receive messages **2** moving in two opposite directions

txt abbrev **COMPUTING** the last part of the name of a file that contains a **text file**

tycoon /ˌtaɪˈkuːn/ noun [C] someone rich and powerful who is involved in business or industry

tying /ˈtaɪɪŋ/ the present participle of **tie¹**

tympanum /ˈtɪmpənəm/ noun [C] **ANATOMY** the eardrum

type¹ /taɪp/ noun **1** [C] a group of people or things with similar qualities that make them different from other groups= KIND, SORT: *What type of dog have you got?* ♦ *It's a good price for a bike of this type.* ♦ *We provide advice to all types of businesses.* **2** [C] someone with particular interests or qualities: *The bar is popular with arty types.* ♦ *Sam isn't the romantic type.* **3** [U] letters that are printed in a book, magazine, or newspaper, or typed using a keyboard: *The book is produced in large type.*

type² /taɪp/ verb **1** [I/T] to write something using a keyboard **2** [T] **SCIENCE, HEALTH** to find out what group a person or thing belongs to by doing tests

typeface /ˈtaɪpˌfeɪs/ noun [C] a set of letters and numbers of the same design, used in printing or computing

typewriter /ˈtaɪpˌraɪtə/ noun [C] a machine with a keyboard that you use for typing words directly onto a sheet of paper

typhoid /ˈtaɪfɔɪd/ noun [U] **HEALTH** a serious infectious disease that affects only humans. It is caused by bacteria that live in water or in the faeces of infected people.

typhoon /taɪˈfuːn/ noun [C] **GEOGRAPHY** a storm with very strong winds that forms over warm waters in the north-west Pacific Ocean. This type of storm over warm waters in the Atlantic Ocean is called a **hurricane**.

typical /ˈtɪpɪk(ə)l/ adj **1** like most people or things of the same type: *It's a typical working-class community.* ♦ *a typical response* ♦ *His opinions are fairly typical of people of his generation.* **2** behaving in a way that is usual for a particular person: *She responded with typical enthusiasm.* ♦ *It was typical of him to want to help.*

typically /ˈtɪpɪkli/ adv **1** usually: *The courses typically last for three days.* **2** with the typical qualities of a particular person or group of people **3** as you might expect from a particular person

typify /ˈtɪpɪfaɪ/ (**typifies, typifying, typified**) verb [T] to be a typical example or feature of something

typing /ˈtaɪpɪŋ/ noun [U] the skill of using a **typewriter** or computer keyboard to write documents

typist /ˈtaɪpɪst/ noun [C] someone who types using a **typewriter** or a computer keyboard, especially as their job

tyrannosaurus /tɪˌrænəˈsɔːrəs/ or **tyrannosaurus rex** /tɪˌrænəsɔːrəs ˈreks/ noun [C] a large dinosaur that walked on two legs and ate other animals

tyranny /ˈtɪrəni/ (plural **tyrannies**) noun [C/U] **1** a government that treats people in a cruel and unfair way, using force to control them **2** cruel and unfair treatment by someone in a position of power, especially a government —**tyrannical** /tɪˈrænɪk(ə)l/ adj

tyrant /ˈtaɪrənt/ noun [C] **1** someone who rules a country in a cruel and unfair way **2** someone in a position of power who behaves in a cruel and unfair way

tyre /ˈtaɪə/ noun [C] a thick rubber cover that fits round the wheel of a bicycle, car, or other vehicle: *a car tyre* ♦ *My bike's got a flat tyre.*

tzetze fly /ˈtetsi ˌflaɪ, ˈtsetsi ˌflaɪ/ another spelling of **tsetse fly**

u /juː/ (plural **u's**) or **U** (plural **U's**) noun [C/U] the 21st letter of the English alphabet → U-TURN

U /juː/ pronoun *informal* a written form of 'you', used in emails and **text messages**

UAI /ˌjuː eɪ ˈaɪ/ noun [singular] **EDUCATION** Universities Admissions Index: in some parts of Australia, a number based on the results of an exam that students take in their final year at school before going to university

ubiquitous /juːˈbɪkwɪtəs/ adj *formal* seeming to be everywhere

'U ,bolt noun [C] **ENGINEERING** a U-shaped piece of metal that has a **nut** and **threads** at each end. It is often used in the **suspension** systems of vehicles.

udder /ˈʌdə/ noun [C] **AGRICULTURE** the part under the body of a cow and some other female mammals that produces milk. The udder is a **mammary gland** like the human breast.

UFO /ˌjuː ef ˈəʊ/ (plural **UFOs**) noun [C] unidentified flying object: a mysterious object that flies through the sky, that some people think is a sign of life from other planets

ugh /ʊx, ʌg/ interjection used for writing the sound that people make when they think that something is extremely unpleasant

ugly /ˈʌgli/ (**uglier, ugliest**) adj **1** unpleasant to look at ≠ BEAUTIFUL **2** an ugly situation involves violent or angry behaviour: *an ugly confrontation*

UHF /ˌjuː eɪtʃ ˈef/ noun [U] **PHYSICS** Ultra High Frequency: a range of radio waves used for broadcasting television programmes

the UK /ˌjuː ˈkeɪ/ the United Kingdom

ulcer /ˈʌlsə/ noun [C] **HEALTH** a painful area on the skin or inside the body, where the surface layer has come away and the area gets infected: *a stomach ulcer* —**ulcerated** /ˈʌlsəˌreɪtɪd/ adj

ulna /ˈʌlnə/ (plural **ulnas** or **ulnae** /ˈʌlniː/) noun [C] **ANATOMY** the longer of the two bones that connect the wrist to the elbow, next to the **radius** —*picture* → SKELETON

ulterior motive /ʌlˌtɪəriə ˈməʊtɪv/ noun [C] a secret reason for doing something

ultimate¹ /ˈʌltɪmət/ adj **1** happening at the end of a process or activity = EVENTUAL: *Independence remains their ultimate political goal.* **2** if someone has something such as ultimate power or responsibility, they have more power or responsibility than anyone else: *Parents must have ultimate responsibility for their children's safety.* **3** as good or as bad as possible: *The Nobel Prize is the ultimate award for any scientist.* **4** relating to the origins or basic form of something = FUNDAMENTAL

ultimate² /ˈʌltɪmət/ noun **the ultimate in sth** the best or most perfect example of something: *Our stylish coaches offer the ultimate in luxury travel.*

ultimately /ˈʌltɪmətli/ adv **1** after a process or activity has ended: *Technological advances could ultimately lead to even more job losses.* **2** used for emphasizing the main point that you are talking about: *What worries them, ultimately, is the cost of the scheme.*

ultimatum /ˌʌltɪˈmeɪtəm/ noun [C] a statement that orders someone to do something and threatens to punish or attack them if they do not do it

ultra- /ˈʌltrə/ prefix **1** extremely: *an ultra-modern kitchen* **2** **SCIENCE** outside a particular range: used with some nouns and adjectives

ultrafiltration /ˌʌltrəfɪlˈtreɪʃ(ə)n/ noun [U] **BIOLOGY** the process that takes place in the **nephrons** of the kidney, where small molecules such as glucose, water, salt, and **urea** are removed from the blood and passed into the **Bowman's capsule**

ultrasonic /ˌʌltrəˈsɒnɪk/ adj **SCIENCE** relating to sounds that have a higher frequency than the range of sounds that humans can hear

ultrasound /ˈʌltrəˌsaʊnd/ noun [U] **1** **HEALTH** medical technology that uses sound waves of high frequency to produce an image of an organ or of a baby developing inside its mother's uterus **2** **SCIENCE** sound that has a higher frequency than the range of sounds that humans can hear

ultraviolet /ˌʌltrəˈvaɪələt/ adj **SCIENCE** ultraviolet light has waves with shorter wavelengths than light that humans can see. Natural ultraviolet light from the sun can cause skin cancer in people who are in sunlight too much = UV —**ultraviolet** noun [U]

ululate /ˈjuːljʊleɪt/ verb [I] **MUSIC** to sing using a long high sound, especially to celebrate or to show grief —**ululation** /ˌjuːljʊˈleɪʃ(ə)n/ noun [C/U]

umbilical cord /ʌmˈbɪlɪk(ə)l ˌkɔːd/ noun [C] **ANATOMY** a long tube that connects a baby to its mother in the uterus and through which it receives food and oxygen. It is cut immediately after birth. —*picture* → EMBRYO

umbra /ˈʌmbrə/ noun [C] **PHYSICS** a very dark shadow, sometimes inside an area of lighter shadow

umbrella /ʌmˈbrelə/ noun [C] **1** an object that you hold over your head in order to stay dry when it is raining **2** a single large group that separate groups belong to or are protected by

UML abbrev **COMPUTING** unified modelling language: a language used for designing complicated software before writing it

umma /ˈuːmə/ noun [C/U] **RELIGION** all Muslims in the world, considered as a group

umpire /ˈʌmpaɪə/ noun [C] **SPORTS** someone whose job is to make sure that players obey the rules in sports such as tennis, baseball, and **cricket** —**umpire** verb [I/T]

umpteen /ˌʌmpˈtiːn/ determiner *informal* a lot of —**umpteenth** adj

the UN /ˌjuː ˈen/ **SOCIAL STUDIES** the United Nations: an international organization that encourages countries to work together in order to solve world problems

un- /ʌn/ prefix used with many adjectives, adverbs, and verbs to give the opposite meaning: *unhappy* ♦ *unhurriedly* ♦ *unzip*

unabated /ˌʌnəˈbeɪtɪd/ adj *formal* without stopping

unable /ʌnˈeɪb(ə)l/ adj **unable to do sth** *formal* not able to do something: *Some of the children were unable to read.* ♦ *Many teenagers feel unable to talk to their parents about their problems.*

unabridged /ˌʌnəˈbrɪdʒd/ adj an unabridged book or article has not had any parts removed from it

unacceptable /ˌʌnəkˈseptəb(ə)l/ adj too bad to be allowed to continue —**unacceptably** adv

unaccompanied /ˌʌnəˈkʌmpənid/ adj **1** someone who is unaccompanied goes somewhere alone **2** **MUSIC** an unaccompanied singer or musician sings or plays alone

unaccounted for /ˌʌnəˈkaʊntɪd ˌfɔː/ adj if something is unaccounted for, you are unable to explain what happened to it, or where it is

unaccustomed /ˌʌnəˈkʌstəmd/ adj unusual
  PHRASE **unaccustomed to sth** not used to something

unaffected /ˌʌnəˈfektɪd/ adj **1** not changed or influenced by something **2** sincere and natural in your behaviour

unaided /ʌnˈeɪdɪd/ adv *formal* without help

unaltered /ʌnˈɔːltəd/ adj not changed

unambiguous /ˌʌnæmˈbɪɡjʊəs/ adj clear and with only one possible meaning —**unambiguously** adv

unanimous /juːˈnænɪməs/ adj **1** a unanimous decision, vote, agreement etc is one that everyone agrees with **2** a group of people who are unanimous about something all agree about it —**unanimity** /ˌjuːnəˈnɪməti/ noun [U], **unanimously** adv

unanswered /ʌnˈɑːnsəd/ adj **1** an unanswered question or problem has not been answered or solved **2** an unanswered letter, message, or phone call has not had a reply

unapologetic /ˌʌnəpɒləˈdʒetɪk/ adj showing that you do not think you have done something wrong, or that you do not think you need to **apologize** ≠ APOLOGETIC

unarmed /ʌnˈɑːmd/ adj not carrying a weapon ≠ ARMED

unarmed 'combat noun [U] the activity of fighting without weapons

unassisted /ˌʌnəˈsɪstɪd/ adj without help

unassuming /ˌʌnəˈsjuːmɪŋ/ adj showing approval behaving in a quiet pleasant way, without wanting to attract attention = MODEST

unattached /ˌʌnəˈtætʃt/ adj not married, or not having a boyfriend or girlfriend

unattainable /ˌʌnəˈteɪnəb(ə)l/ adj impossible to achieve or obtain

unattended /ˌʌnəˈtendɪd/ adj left without being looked after or dealt with

unattractive /ˌʌnəˈtræktɪv/ adj **1** ugly **2** unpleasant, or not enjoyable

unauthorized /ʌnˈɔːθəraɪzd/ adj done without official permission

unavailable /ˌʌnəˈveɪləb(ə)l/ adj **1** not able to go somewhere, meet someone, or do something **2** impossible to obtain

unavoidable /ˌʌnəˈvɔɪdəb(ə)l/ adj impossible to stop from happening = INEVITABLE —**unavoidably** adv

unaware /ˌʌnəˈweə/ adj not realizing that something exists or is happening

unawares /ˌʌnəˈweəz/ adv **catch/take sb unawares** to surprise someone, often making them feel confused or embarrassed

unbalanced /ʌnˈbælənst/ adj **1** mentally ill **2** giving only one view or opinion of a situation or subject

unbearable /ʌnˈbeərəb(ə)l/ adj too unpleasant or painful to deal with —**unbearably** adv

unbeatable /ʌnˈbiːtəb(ə)l/ adj **1** impossible to defeat **2** better than anything else of the same type

unbeaten /ʌnˈbiːt(ə)n/ adj if a team, player etc is unbeaten, they have not been defeated

unbelievable /ˌʌnbɪˈliːvəb(ə)l/ adj **1** informal used for emphasizing how good, bad, impressive etc something is **2** too unlikely to be true or to be believed —**unbelievably** adv

unbiased /ʌnˈbaɪəst/ adj fair in the way that you describe or deal with a situation

unblock /ʌnˈblɒk/ verb [T] to remove something that is blocking a pipe or tube

unborn /ʌnˈbɔːn/ adj an unborn child is still inside its mother's uterus

unbranded /ʌnˈbrændɪd/ adj **BUSINESS** unbranded goods are not marked with the name of the company that makes them

unbreakable /ʌnˈbreɪkəb(ə)l/ adj impossible to break

unbroken /ʌnˈbrəʊkən/ adj **1** continuing for a long time without stopping = CONTINUOUS **2** not broken or damaged **3** strong and determined despite problems

unbundle /ʌnˈbʌnd(ə)l/ verb [T] **BUSINESS** to sell related products and services separately, rather than as one unit

unburnt gas /ˌʌnbɜːnt ˈɡæs/ noun [C] **PHYSICS** gas that does not burn during **combustion**, for example the gas in the middle of a **candle** flame

uncanny /ʌnˈkæni/ adj strange and mysterious —**uncannily** adv

uncertain /ʌnˈsɜːt(ə)n/ adj **1** not clearly known or understood: *It is uncertain how they entered the property.* ♦ *The whole industry faces a very uncertain future.* **2** not feeling sure about something: *I left the meeting feeling uncertain about what to do next.* —**uncertainty** noun [C/U]

unchallenged /ʌnˈtʃælɪndʒd/ adj **1** accepted as right or correct **2** not stopped or prevented from going somewhere **3** **POLITICS** a leader or **candidate** who is unchallenged is not opposed by anyone

unchanged /ʌnˈtʃeɪndʒd/ adj remaining the same

unchanging /ʌnˈtʃeɪndʒɪŋ/ adj always remaining the same

unchecked /ʌnˈtʃekt/ adj formal not controlled or prevented from happening

uncivilized /ʌnˈsɪvəlaɪzd/ adj behaving in a rude or offensive way

uncle /ˈʌŋk(ə)l/ noun [C] the brother of one of your parents, or the husband of your aunt: *The business was owned by my uncle.* ♦ *a letter from Uncle Richard*

unclean /ʌnˈkliːn/ adj **1** formal dirty, or not pure **2** **RELIGION** unclean food or drink cannot be eaten or drunk by people belonging to a particular religion

unclear /ʌnˈklɪə/ adj not obvious, definite, or easy to understand

PHRASE **be unclear about/as to sth** to not understand something, or to not be certain about something

uncomfortable /ʌnˈkʌmftəb(ə)l/ adj **1** if you are uncomfortable, you have an unpleasant or slightly painful feeling in part of your body: *You'll be uncomfortable for a few days after the surgery.* ♦ *They were sitting in a very uncomfortable position.* **2** used for describing something that makes you have an unpleasant or slightly painful feeling in part of your body: *uncomfortable clothes* ♦ *an uncomfortable-looking chair* **3** feeling embarrassed or nervous, or making you feel embarrassed or nervous = UNEASY: *A long uncomfortable silence followed.* —**uncomfortably** adv

uncommercial /ˌʌnkəˈmɜːʃ(ə)l/ adj **BUSINESS** not attractive to customers and so not likely to make a profit

uncommon /ʌnˈkɒmən/ adj unusual, or rare

unconcerned /ˌʌnkənˈsɜːnd/ adj not worried about a situation or about what might happen

unconditional /ˌʌnkənˈdɪʃ(ə)nəl/ adj without limits or conditions —**unconditionally** adv

unconfirmed /ˌʌnkənˈfɜːmd/ adj with no definite proof to show that something is true: *unconfirmed reports of fighting*

unconscious[1] /ʌnˈkɒnʃəs/ adj **1** in a condition similar to sleep in which you do not see, feel, or think, usually because you are injured **2** an unconscious feeling or thought is one that you do not realize you have —**unconsciously** adv, **unconsciousness** noun [U]

unconscious[2] /ʌnˈkɒnʃəs/ noun [singular] the part of your mind that contains unconscious feelings and thoughts that influence your behaviour= SUBCONSCIOUS

uncontested /ˌʌnkənˈtestɪd/ adj if something is uncontested, no one opposes it or disagrees with it

uncontrollable /ˌʌnkənˈtrəʊləb(ə)l/ adj **1** impossible to control or stop **2** someone who is uncontrollable behaves badly and refuses to do what other people tell them —**uncontrollably** adv

uncontrolled /ˌʌnkənˈtrəʊld/ adj continuing without being controlled or stopped

unconventional /ˌʌnkənˈvenʃ(ə)nəl/ adj different from what most people consider to be usual or normal —**unconventionally** adv

unconvincing /ˌʌnkənˈvɪnsɪŋ/ adj **1** not capable of persuading someone that something is true or right **2** an unconvincing character, story, or performance is difficult to believe or enjoy, because it does not seem real or likely —**unconvincingly** adv

uncooked /ʌnˈkʊkt/ adj raw, or not yet cooked

uncooperative /ˌʌnkəʊˈɒp(ə)rətɪv/ adj not willing to work with or to help another person or group

uncoordinated /ˌʌnkəʊˈɔːdɪˌneɪtɪd/ adj **1** not graceful, or not able to fully control your movements = CLUMSY **2** badly planned or organized

uncorrupted /ˌʌnkəˈrʌptɪd/ adj COMPUTING an uncorrupted file or **database** has no mistakes or viruses

uncountable /ʌnˈkaʊntəb(ə)l/ or **uncount** /ˈʌnkaʊnt/ adj LANGUAGE an uncountable noun has no plural form and cannot be counted in individual units. Uncountable nouns are marked [U] in this dictionary.

uncouth /ʌnˈkuːθ/ adj behaving in a way that polite people think is rude or offensive

uncover /ʌnˈkʌvə/ verb [T] **1** to find out about something that has been hidden or kept secret **2** to take the lid or cover off something

uncultivated /ʌnˈkʌltɪˌveɪtɪd/ adj AGRICULTURE uncultivated land has not been used for growing crops

uncut /ˌʌnˈkʌt/ adj **1** allowed to grow longer without being cut: *uncut hair* **2** an uncut film or book is complete and has not had parts removed

undamaged /ʌnˈdæmɪdʒd/ adj not damaged

undaunted /ʌnˈdɔːntɪd/ adj not afraid to continue doing something, even though it might be difficult

undecagon /ʌnˈdekəgɒn/ noun [C] MATHS a geometric shape with eleven straight sides

undecided /ˌʌndɪˈsaɪdɪd/ adj **1** if someone is undecided, they have not yet made a decision about something **2** if a situation, problem, issue etc is undecided, no one has solved it or made a decision about it

undefeated /ˌʌndɪˈfiːtɪd/ adj not having been defeated in a particular period of time

undefined /ˌʌndɪˈfaɪnd/ adj **1** not clearly explained, or without clear rules or limits **2** without a clear shape or form

undelete /ˌʌndɪˈliːt/ verb [T] COMPUTING to make information that has been removed from a computer exist again

undemocratic /ˌʌndeməˈkrætɪk/ adj **1** POLITICS controlled by officials or politicians who have not been elected by the people **2** SOCIAL STUDIES not representing the wishes of the majority of people, and therefore unfair

under /ˈʌndə/ adv, preposition

1 below sth	**6** controlled by sb
2 less than	**7** using a name
3 affected by sth	**8** where to find sth
4 in certain conditions	**9** believing sth true
5 according to a rule	**10** getting treatment

1 in or to a position below something or covered by something: *I found the letter under a pile of books.* ♦ *The ball rolled under the table.* ♦ *Jump into the water and see how long you can stay under.*
2 less than a particular amount, or younger than a particular age ≠ OVER: *A visa is not required for a stay of under three months.* ♦ *The nursery is open for children aged four and under.* → UNDERAGE
3 in the process of being affected by a particular action, situation, or state: *Police claim the situation is now under control.* ♦ *A number of proposals are under consideration.*
4 used for saying that something happens when particular conditions exist: *His older brother was forced to leave Hong Kong the year before under similar circumstances.* ♦ *The UN inspectors would be allowed access to the eight sites, but only under certain conditions.* ♦ *Under the circumstances, Kane felt he had no option but to resign.*
5 according to a particular law, agreement, or system: *Under the terms of the agreement, our company will receive 40% of the profits.*
6 with a particular person or group in control of you as your leader, manager, or teacher: *He studied under Chomsky in the 1960s.*
7 using a particular name in some situations, often a name that is not your own: *Carson had been travelling under a false name.*
8 if something is under a particular title, letter etc, that is where it can be found: *I found information on whales in the encyclopedia under 'Mammals'.*
9 believing that something is happening or is true, especially when you are wrong about this: *I was under the impression that Faye had paid for the trip herself – but it seems I was wrong.*
10 receiving some type of medical treatment: *Many of the victims were under sedation after the attack.* → UNDERWAY

underage /ˌʌndərˈeɪdʒ/ adj not old enough to do something legally, for example drink alcohol or drive a car

undercarriage /ˈʌndəˌkærɪdʒ/ noun [C] the wheels of a plane and the whole structure that supports them

undercharge /ˌʌndəˈtʃɑːdʒ/ verb [I/T] BUSINESS to sell something to someone for too low a price, or accidentally not ask them for enough money in a shop etc

underclass /ˈʌndəˌklɑːs/ noun [C] SOCIAL STUDIES the lowest social class in a society, consisting of people who are the poorest and have the least power

undercoat /ˈʌndəˌkəʊt/ noun [C/U] a **coat** (=layer) of paint that is put on before the final coat

undercover /ˌʌndəˈkʌvə/ adj working or done secretly in order to catch criminals or get secret information —**undercover** adv

undercurrent /ˈʌndəˌkʌrənt/ noun [C] **1** GEOGRAPHY a current that moves below the surface in the sea or a river **2** a feeling that exists and affects the way people behave, but is not obvious or stated directly

undercut¹ /ˌʌndəˈkʌt/ (**undercuts, undercutting, undercut**) verb [T] **BUSINESS** to sell something at a cheaper price than another company or shop

undercut² /ˈʌndəˌkʌt/ adj **GEOLOGY** an undercut cliff or river bank has been eroded at the bottom but not at the top

underdeveloped /ˌʌndədɪˈveləpt/ adj **1 ECONOMICS** an underdeveloped country or region is poor. Many people think that this word is offensive, and prefer to use the word **developing**. **2** an underdeveloped person or body has not grown as much as it should have

underestimate /ˌʌndərˈestɪˌmeɪt/ verb [T] **1** to think that someone has less power or ability than they really have **2** to think or guess that something is smaller, less important etc than it really is ≠ OVERESTIMATE —**underestimate** /ˌʌndərˈestɪmət/ noun [C]

underfoot /ˌʌndəˈfʊt/ adv under your feet in the place where you are walking

underfunded /ˌʌndəˈfʌndɪd/ adj an institution or event that is underfunded does not have enough money to run properly

undergo /ˌʌndəˈɡəʊ/ (**undergoes, undergoing, underwent** /ˌʌndəˈwent/, **undergone** /ˌʌndəˈɡɒn/) verb [T] to experience something, especially a change or medical treatment: *Thompson underwent knee surgery in April.* ♦ *The bridge has undergone repairs.*

undergraduate /ˌʌndəˈɡrædʒuət/ noun [C] **EDUCATION** a student who is studying for a first degree at a college or university

underground /ˈʌndəˌɡraʊnd/ adj **1** below the surface of the ground **2** secret and usually illegal —**underground** /ˌʌndəˈɡraʊnd/ adv

undergrowth /ˈʌndəˌɡrəʊθ/ noun [U] small thick bushes that cover the ground

underline /ˌʌndəˈlaɪn/ verb [T] **1** to show or emphasize that something is important or true: *The recent violence underlines the need for continuing peace talks.* **2** to draw a line under something

underlying /ˌʌndəˈlaɪɪŋ/ adj **1** underlying causes, facts, ideas etc are the real or basic ones, although they are not obvious: *The underlying causes of the riots have been ignored.* **2** an underlying number or amount represents what the true amount or level of something is

undermine /ˌʌndəˈmaɪn/ verb [T] to make something or someone become gradually less effective, confident, or successful

underneath /ˌʌndəˈniːθ/ adv, preposition **1** in or to a place directly below something: *The ball rolled underneath the table.* ♦ *The photographer's name was printed underneath.* **2** on the lower surface of something: *The snake is green on top and yellow underneath.* **3** used for describing what someone or something is really like, despite how they may seem: *Gary acts tough, but underneath he's really very kind.*

undernourished /ˌʌndəˈnʌrɪʃt/ adj someone who is undernourished is not healthy because they do not get enough food —**undernourishment** /ˌʌndəˈnʌrɪʃmənt/ noun [U]

underpaid /ˌʌndəˈpeɪd/ adj someone who is underpaid does not earn enough money for the work that they do —**underpay** verb [I/T]

underpants /ˈʌndəˌpænts/ noun [plural] underwear for men worn on the lower half of the body

underpass /ˈʌndəˌpɑːs/ noun [C] part of a road or path that goes under another road or a railway

underperform /ˌʌndəpəˈfɔːm/ verb [I] to be less successful than people expect

underpin /ˌʌndəˈpɪn/ (**underpins, underpinning, underpinned**) verb [T] **1** to be an important basic part of something, allowing it to succeed or continue to exist **2** to support something such as a wall by putting a strong piece of metal or concrete under it

underprice /ˌʌndəˈpraɪs/ verb [T] **BUSINESS** to put a price on something for sale that is less than its actual value

underrated /ˌʌndəˈreɪtɪd/ adj if a person or thing is underrated, most people do not recognize how good that person or thing really is ≠ OVERRATED —**underrate** verb [T]

underside /ˈʌndəˌsaɪd/ noun [C] the bottom side or surface of something

understand /ˌʌndəˈstænd/ (**understands, understanding, understood** /ˌʌndəˈstʊd/) verb **1** [I/T] to know what someone or something means: *I didn't understand a word he was saying.* ♦ *I'm sorry, I don't understand French.* **2** [I/T] to know how or why something happens, or what effect or influence something has: *We are only beginning to understand how the brain functions.* ♦ *Do they fully understand the implications of their decision?* **3** [I/T] to know how someone feels, or why someone does something: *I understand your concern, but the operation is completely safe.* ♦ *Does she understand why he doesn't want to see her?* **4** [T] formal to believe that something is true because you have heard or read it somewhere: *We understand that a major announcement is to be made tomorrow.*

PHRASE make yourself understood to know enough of another language to be able to deal with ordinary situations

---

Word family: understand

Words in the same family as understand
- **understandable** adj
- **understandably** adv
- **understanding** n
- **misunderstand** v
- **misunderstood** adj
- **misunderstanding** n

---

understandable /ˌʌndəˈstændəb(ə)l/ adj **1** normal and reasonable in a particular situation **2** clear and easy to understand —**understandably** adv

understanding¹ /ˌʌndəˈstændɪŋ/ noun

1 knowledge	4 way you understand sth
2 sympathy	
3 informal agreement	5 ability to understand

1 [singular/U] knowledge about a particular subject, process, or situation: *The course will help you develop a deeper **understanding of** yourself.*
2 [U] sympathy that comes from knowing how other people feel and why they do things: *Suzy just needs a little understanding.*
3 [C] an agreement that is made in an informal way, or that is not expressed in words: *We **have an understanding** with them that we won't compete directly.* ♦ *We gave them the information **on the understanding that** it would not be made public.*
4 [C/U] the particular way in which you understand the meaning of something ≈ INTERPRETATION: *My understanding was that the meeting would end at 5 o'clock.*
5 [U] the ability to understand things: *A child with sufficient understanding may sometimes be asked to give a statement.*

understanding² /ˌʌndəˈstændɪŋ/ adj willing to forgive other people or to be sympathetic, because you understand how they feel

understatement /'ʌndə,steɪtmənt/ noun [C/U] something that you say that makes something seem less important or serious than it really is

understood /,ʌndə'stʊd/ the past tense and past participle of **understand**

undersurface /'ʌndə,sɜːfɪs/ noun [C] the bottom surface of something

undertake /,ʌndə'teɪk/ (**undertakes, undertaking, undertook** /,ʌndə'tʊk/, **undertaken** /,ʌndə'teɪkən/) verb [T] **1** to agree to be responsible for a job or project, and to do it: *The most recent survey of rare birds was undertaken in 1991.* ♦ *It is one of the largest dam projects ever undertaken.* **2** *formal* to promise to do something

undertaker /'ʌndə,teɪkə/ noun [C] someone whose job is to make arrangements for funerals= FUNERAL DIRECTOR

undertaking /'ʌndə,teɪkɪŋ/ noun [C] **1** something that you do that is difficult or complicated **2** *formal* a promise or agreement

undertone /'ʌndə,təʊn/ noun [C] an idea or feeling that exists, but is not obvious

undertook /,ʌndə'tʊk/ the past tense of **undertake**

undervalue /,ʌndə'væljuː/ verb [T] **1** to not recognize how important or valuable someone or something is **2** to think that something is worth less money than it really is —**undervalued** adj

underwater /,ʌndə'wɔːtə/ adj, adv existing, happening, or used under the surface of water

underway /,ʌndə'weɪ/ adj already started or happening: *Rescue efforts are underway.*

underwear /'ʌndə,weə/ noun [U] clothes that you wear next to your skin under your other clothes

underweight /,ʌndə'weɪt/ adj below the normal weight ≠ OVERWEIGHT

underwent /,ʌndə'went/ the past tense of **undergo**

underworld /'ʌndə,wɜːld/ noun **1** [singular] the criminals in a particular community, considered as a group **2** the Underworld LITERATURE in ancient Greek and Roman **mythology,** a place below the Earth's surface where people go when they die

underwrite /,ʌndə'raɪt/ (**underwrites, underwriting, underwrote** /,ʌndə'rəʊt/, **underwritten** /,ʌndə'rɪt(ə)n/) verb [T] BUSINESS **1** to invest money to help someone to start a new project **2** to sign an **insurance policy** and accept responsibility for making payment on it if a claim is made on it

underwriter /'ʌndə,raɪtə/ noun [C] BUSINESS a person or company that provides insurance

undesirable /,ʌndɪ'zaɪrəb(ə)l/ adj bad, or harmful

undetected /,ʌndɪ'tektɪd/ adj not noticed

undeveloped /,ʌndɪ'veləpt/ adj **1** not fully grown **2** undeveloped land has not been used for building or industry

undid /ʌn'dɪd/ the past tense of **undo**

undifferentiated /,ʌndɪfə'renʃieɪtɪd/ adj BIOLOGY an undifferentiated cell has not yet developed distinguishing features

undigested /,ʌndaɪ'dʒestɪd/ adj not broken down into smaller units that the body can use

undignified /ʌn'dɪgnɪfaɪd/ adj embarrassing or silly

undiluted /,ʌndaɪ'luːtɪd/ adj **1** an undiluted liquid is strong because no water has been mixed with it **2** without any attempt to make something less offensive or easier to accept

undisputed /,ʌndɪ'spjuːtɪd/ adj agreed or accepted by everyone

undisturbed /,ʌndɪ'stɜːbd/ adj **1** not touched or moved **2** not interrupted by anyone

undivided /,ʌndɪ'vaɪdɪd/ adj **1** complete and total: *You should give this matter your **undivided attention.*** **2** together as one unit, not separated into parts = UNITED

undo /ʌn'duː/ (**undoes, undoing, undid** /ʌn'dɪd/, **undone** /ʌn'dʌn/) verb **1** [T] to open something so that it is no longer closed, tied, or fastened: *He undid the screws that held the cassette together.* ♦ *I can't undo my belt.* **2** [T] to have the effect of changing something back into its original, usually worse, state: *One mistake could undo all our achievements.* **3** [I/T] COMPUTING to give a computer an instruction to ignore the last change that you made

undone /ʌn'dʌn/ adj **1** not closed or fastened **2** not finished

undoubtedly /ʌn'daʊtɪdli/ adv used for saying that something is certainly true or accepted by everyone —**undoubted** adj

undress /ʌn'dres/ verb [I/T] to remove your clothes, or to remove someone else's clothes

undue /ʌn'djuː/ adj *formal* not necessary or reasonable

undulating /'ʌndjʊ,leɪtɪŋ/ adj having slopes and curves, or moving gently up and down in the shape of waves —**undulate** verb [I]

unduly /ʌn'djuːli/ adv *formal* to a greater degree than is reasonable or necessary

undying /ʌn'daɪɪŋ/ adj continuing for ever

unearned income /,ʌnɜːnd 'ɪnkʌm/ noun [U] money that someone gets from something they have invested in, for example property or shares

unearth /ʌn'ɜːθ/ verb [T] **1** to discover someone or something that was not known before **2** to find something that is buried in the ground

uneasy /ʌn'iːzi/ adj **1** slightly nervous or worried about something= UNCOMFORTABLE **2** an uneasy situation is not settled, and it could quickly change and get worse —**unease** noun [U], **uneasily** adv

uneconomic /,ʌniːkə'nɒmɪk/ adj BUSINESS not capable of making a profit

uneducated /ʌn'edjʊ,keɪtɪd/ adj not having had much education

unelected /,ʌnɪ'lektɪd/ adj *showing disapproval* in a position of power without being elected

unemployed /,ʌnɪm'plɔɪd/ adj ECONOMICS **1** without a job: *He's been unemployed for over a year.* ♦ *an unemployed engineer* **2** the unemployed people who are unemployed

unemployment /,ʌnɪm'plɔɪmənt/ noun [U] ECONOMICS a situation in which people do not have jobs, or the fact that someone does not have a job: *Unemployment rose last month to its highest level in five years.* ♦ *a period of **high unemployment***

unending /ʌn'endɪŋ/ adj continuing without stopping, or seeming to last for ever

unequal /ʌn'iːkwəl/ adj **1** not giving the same treatment or opportunities to everyone, and therefore unfair **2** not the same in amount, number, or size **3** involving one person, team, army etc that is much stronger than another **4** not good enough or skilful enough to do something

unequivocal /ˌʌnɪ'kwɪvək(ə)l/ adj *formal* clear and definite —**unequivocally** adv

UNESCO or **Unesco** /juː'neskəʊ/ SOCIAL STUDIES the United Nations Educational, Scientific, and Cultural Organization

unethical /ʌn'eθɪk(ə)l/ adj morally wrong

uneven /ʌn'iːv(ə)n/ adj **1** not smooth or level **2** not the same in size or length **3** not fairly balanced or equally shared **4** not of the same quality in all its parts = PATCHY —**unevenly** adv, **unevenness** noun [U]

unexciting /ˌʌnɪk'saɪtɪŋ/ adj not interesting or exciting

unexpected /ˌʌnɪk'spektɪd/ adj surprising: *Her defeat was totally unexpected.* ♦ *an unexpected change of policy* —**unexpectedly** adv

unexplained /ˌʌnɪk'spleɪnd/ adj an unexplained event seems to have no explanation or reason

unexploded /ˌʌnɪk'spləʊdɪd/ adj an unexploded bomb has been dropped or left somewhere but has not exploded, usually because of a fault

unexplored /ˌʌnɪk'splɔːd/ adj **1** never visited by people **2** not thought about or considered before

unfailing /ʌn'feɪlɪŋ/ adj never changing or ending —**unfailingly** adv

unfair /ʌn'feə/ adj **1** not fair or reasonable= UNJUST: *It is grossly unfair* (=very unfair) *to suggest that the school was responsible for this accident.* **2** not treating people equally: *It is unfair that not everyone got the chance to vote.* ♦ *Their very low labour costs give them an unfair advantage in the market.* —**unfairly** adv

unfaithful /ʌn'feɪθf(ə)l/ adj if someone is unfaithful, they have a sexual relationship with someone who is not their husband, wife, or usual partner

unfamiliar /ˌʌnfə'mɪljə/ adj if you are unfamiliar with something, you have no knowledge or experience of it —**unfamiliarity** /ˌʌnfə,mɪli'ærəti/ noun [U]

unfashionable /ʌn'fæʃ(ə)nəb(ə)l/ adj not popular or fashionable

unfasten /ʌn'fɑːs(ə)n/ verb [T] to open something, especially a piece of clothing or a belt, so that it is no longer fastened or tied= UNDO

unfavourable /ʌn'feɪv(ə)rəb(ə)l/ adj **1** not positive, or not showing approval= CRITICAL **2** an unfavourable situation is one that is not suitable for doing something in: *unfavourable weather conditions* —**unfavourably** adv

unfinished /ʌn'fɪnɪʃt/ adj not finished, or not dealt with completely

unfit /ʌn'fɪt/ adj **1** below the accepted quality or standard for a particular use or purpose: *an unfit mother* **2** not feeling healthy or strong because you do not take enough exercise

unfold /ʌn'fəʊld/ verb **1** [T] to open something that was folded **2** [I] to happen, or to develop

unforeseeable /ˌʌnfɔː'siːəb(ə)l/ adj impossible to know about or expect

unforeseen /ˌʌnfɔː'siːn/ adj an unforeseen situation is one that you did not expect= UNEXPECTED

unforgettable /ˌʌnfə'getəb(ə)l/ adj something that is unforgettable will be remembered for a very long time = MEMORABLE —**unforgettably** adv

unforgivable /ˌʌnfə'gɪvəb(ə)l/ adj extremely bad and impossible to forgive

unforgiving /ˌʌnfə'gɪvɪŋ/ adj not willing to forgive people

unformatted /ʌn'fɔːmætɪd/ adj COMPUTING an unformatted computer disk has not been divided into the parts that are needed to allow information to be saved and stored

unfortunate /ʌn'fɔːtʃ(ə)nət/ adj **1** experiencing bad luck, or caused by bad luck= UNLUCKY: *The unfortunate woman had had all her bags stolen.* **2** *formal* if something is unfortunate, you do not approve of it, or you wish that it had not happened: *an unfortunate accident*

unfortunately /ʌn'fɔːtʃ(ə)nətli/ adv used for saying that you wish that something had not happened, or that it was not true: *Unfortunately, Jaswinder is leaving the school.* ♦ *Effective treatments do exist, but unfortunately they are very expensive.*

unfounded /ʌn'faʊndɪd/ adj not supported with facts or evidence

unfriendly /ʌn'fren(d)li/ adj not friendly

unfulfilled /ˌʌnfʊl'fɪld/ adj unhappy because you have not achieved what you want

ungainly /ʌn'geɪnli/ adj not moving in an attractive or graceful way

ungracious /ʌn'greɪʃəs/ adj not polite or friendly —**ungraciously** adv

ungrammatical /ˌʌngrə'mætɪk(ə)l/ adj LANGUAGE not correct according to the rules of grammar

ungrateful /ʌn'greɪtf(ə)l/ adj not grateful to someone who has helped you or been kind to you —**ungratefully** adv

unhappy /ʌn'hæpi/ (**unhappier, unhappiest**) adj **1** feeling sad or upset, or making someone feel sad or upset: *Why are you so unhappy?* ♦ *an unhappy childhood* **2** not satisfied: *People are very unhappy about the high ticket prices.* —**unhappily** adv, **unhappiness** noun [U]

unhealthy /ʌn'helθi/ adj **1** ill, or not physically fit **2** not good for you

unhelpful /ʌn'helpf(ə)l/ adj **1** not willing or able to help **2** not useful —**unhelpfully** adv

unhurt /ʌn'hɜːt/ adj not injured

unhygienic /ˌʌnhaɪ'dʒiːnɪk/ adj not clean, and likely to cause disease

unicellular /ˌjuːnɪ'seljʊlə/ adj BIOLOGY a unicellular organism consists of one cell only. Amoebas are unicellular organisms.

unicorn /'juːnɪˌkɔːn/ noun [C] an imaginary creature like a horse with a single long horn on its head

unidentified /ˌʌnaɪ'dentɪˌfaɪd/ adj not recognized or known

unification /ˌjuːnɪfɪ'keɪʃ(ə)n/ noun [U] the process of uniting groups or countries, or the fact that they have been united

uniform¹ /'juːnɪfɔːm/ noun [C] a set of clothes that you wear to show that you are part of a particular organization or school: *He was still wearing his school uniform.* ♦ *a police uniform*

PHRASE **in uniform** wearing a uniform: *soldiers in uniform*

uniform² /'juːnɪfɔːm/ adj the same everywhere: *a uniform standard of health care* —**uniformly** adv

unify /'juːnɪfaɪ/ (**unifies, unifying, unified**) verb [T] **1** to unite people or countries so that they will work together **2** to make things work well together —**unified** adj

unilateral /ˌjuːnɪˈlæt(ə)rəl/ adj done or decided by one country, group, or person without the agreement of others —**unilaterally** adv

unimaginable /ˌʌnɪˈmædʒɪnəb(ə)l/ adj very difficult to imagine —**unimaginably** adv

unimaginative /ˌʌnɪˈmædʒɪnətɪv/ adj unable to think of new and interesting things

unimportant /ˌʌnɪmˈpɔːt(ə)nt/ adj not important or relevant

uninhabited /ˌʌnɪnˈhæbɪtɪd/ adj an uninhabited place has no people living there

uninstall /ˌʌnɪnˈstɔːl/ verb [T] COMPUTING to remove a program or piece of software from a computer

unintelligible /ˌʌnɪnˈtelɪdʒəb(ə)l/ adj impossible to understand

unintended /ˌʌnɪnˈtendɪd/ adj not deliberate or planned

unintentional /ˌʌnɪnˈtenʃ(ə)nəl/ adj not deliberate or planned —**unintentionally** adv

uninterested /ʌnˈɪntrəstɪd/ adj not interested

uninterrupted /ˌʌnɪntəˈrʌptɪd/ adj **1** continuous **2** not hidden by anything, so that you can see a long way

union /ˈjuːnjən/ noun **1** [C] SOCIAL STUDIES an organization that represents the workers in a particular industry= TRADE UNION: *the National Union of Teachers* ♦ *They encourage all employees to join a union.* **2 Union** [C] POLITICS a group of states or countries that have joined together: *the European Union* **3** [C] an organization or club for people or groups that share an interest or aim, for example protecting the rights of particular groups: *the American Civil Liberties Union* **4** [singular/U] the process of joining things together, or the state of being joined together

Unionism /ˈjuːnjəˌnɪz(ə)m/ noun [U] POLITICS the belief that Northern Ireland should remain part of the UK —**Unionist** noun [C]

Union 'Jack the national flag of the UK

unique /juːˈniːk/ adj **1** very special, unusual, or good: *It is her use of colour that makes her work unique.* ♦ *Mark had a unique opportunity to travel with the President.* **2** not the same as anything or anyone else: *Each individual is unique.* **3** only existing or happening in one place or situation: *The problem is not unique to British students.* —**uniqueness** noun [U], **uniquely** adv

unisex /ˈjuːnɪˌseks/ adj BIOLOGY containing only the male or female reproductive structure

unit /ˈjuːnɪt/ noun [C]

1 individual part	**5** small machine
2 part of institution	**6** piece of furniture
3 team of people	**7** part of a book
4 for measuring	

1 an individual thing that is part of a larger group: *low-cost housing units* ♦ *The sen is the smallest unit of currency in Malaysia.* **2** a department of an institution that has a particular purpose: *an intensive care unit* **3** a group of people who work as a team within a larger group or organization: *an army unit* **4** a standard quantity that is used for measuring something: *The gram is a unit for measuring weight.* **5** a small machine that does a particular job: *an air-conditioning unit* **6** a piece of furniture that fits together with other pieces of the same type: *kitchen units* **7** EDUCATION one of the parts that an educational book or course of study is divided into

unitary bodywork /ˈjuːnɪt(ə)ri ˌbɒdiwɜːk/ noun [U] ENGINEERING a vehicle whose body and **chassis** are built as a single unit

unitary fraction /ˈjuːnɪt(ə)ri ˈfrækʃ(ə)n/ noun [C] MATHS a fraction with a **numerator** (=number above the line) that is 1, for example $\frac{1}{4}$

'unit ˌcost noun [C] BUSINESS the cost of producing a single example of a product that a company makes in large numbers

unite /juːˈnaɪt/ verb [I/T] to join together, or to join people or groups together: *Our community has united to demand a safer neighbourhood.*

united /juːˈnaɪtɪd/ adj **1** if people are united, they agree with each other: *Local people are united in their opposition to the site.* **2** joined together: *a united Germany*

the ˌUnited 'Kingdom POLITICS, GEOGRAPHY England, Scotland, Wales, and Northern Ireland, considered as a political unit

the Uˌnited 'Nations SOCIAL STUDIES the **UN**

unity /ˈjuːnəti/ noun [U] a situation in which people, groups, or countries join together or agree about something

univariate /ˌjuːniˈveəriət/ adj MATHS relating to or containing only one **variable**

universal /ˌjuːnɪˈvɜːs(ə)l/ adj involving or affecting everyone in the world, or all the members of a group or society: *universal human rights* ♦ *universal free education* —**universally** adv

ˌuniversal 'grammar noun [U] LANGUAGE rules about language that apply to all languages

ˌuniversal 'indicator noun [C] CHEMISTRY a chemical solution that changes to different colours over a range of pH values and is used for finding out the degree to which a substance is an acid or an alkali

ˌuniversal 'joint noun [C] ENGINEERING a joint between two shafts that allows the shafts to move in any direction as they **rotate**. It consists of two **hinges** set at 90° to each other.

ˌuniversal 'set noun [C] MATHS a set that contains all the relevant objects and all the related **subsets**

universe /ˈjuːnɪˌvɜːs/ noun [singular] **1 the universe** ASTRONOMY space and everything that exists in it, including the Earth, solar systems, and **galaxies**: *The origins of the universe are still a mystery.* ♦ *Do you think we are the only form of intelligent life in the universe?* **2** someone's life: *Music is the centre of her universe.*

university /ˌjuːnɪˈvɜːsəti/ (plural **universities**) noun [C/U] EDUCATION an educational institution where students study for degrees and where academic research is done: *They met while they were at university.* ♦ *He's taking a year off before going to university.* ♦ *He studied at Harare University.*

Unix /ˈjuːnɪks/ TRADEMARK COMPUTING a computer **operating system** that can be used by several people at the same time

unjust /ʌnˈdʒʌst/ adj not fair or reasonable= UNFAIR —**unjustly** adv

unjustified /ʌnˈdʒʌstɪfaɪd/ adj not fair, or not based on any good reason

unkempt /ʌnˈkempt/ adj dirty and untidy

unkind /ʌnˈkaɪnd/ adj unfriendly, insulting, or cruel: *an unkind remark* ♦ *You're being very unkind to your sister.* —**unkindly** adv, **unkindness** noun [U]

unknown[1] /ʌnˈnəʊn/ adj **1** if something is unknown, people do not know about it or do not know what it is:

For some unknown reason, the plane landed at the wrong airport. **2** not famous: *an unknown poet*

unknown² /ʌnˈnəʊn/ noun **1** [C] someone who is not famous **2 the unknown** [singular] things that you do not know about or have not experienced

unlawful /ʌnˈlɔːf(ə)l/ adj LAW considered to be illegal —**unlawfully** adv

unleaded /ʌnˈledɪd/ adj unleaded petrol does not contain lead

unleash /ʌnˈliːʃ/ verb [T] to do or cause something that has a very powerful or harmful effect

unless /ənˈles/ conjunction used for saying that if something does not happen, something else will happen or will be true as a result: *I can't help you unless you tell me what's wrong.* ♦ *Unless you come now, I'm going to leave without you.* ♦ *'Are you going to stay overnight?' 'Not unless* (=only if) *it's absolutely necessary.'*

unlike /ʌnˈlaɪk/ preposition **1** different from someone or something else: *The show was unlike anything we'd ever seen before.* **2** not typical of a particular person or thing: *It's so unlike Mary to go off without telling someone.*

unlikely /ʌnˈlaɪkli/ adj **1** not likely to happen: *It's highly unlikely we'll be invited.* ♦ *He's unlikely ever to find a job again.* ♦ *It seems unlikely that she will make the same mistake next time.* **2** not typical: *He's a very unlikely romantic hero.*

unlimited /ʌnˈlɪmɪtɪd/ adj with no limits

unlit /ʌnˈlɪt/ adj dark because there are no lights

unload /ʌnˈləʊd/ verb **1** [I/T] to take goods off a vehicle **2** [T] to take the bullets out of a gun, or the film out of a camera

unlock /ʌnˈlɒk/ verb [T] to open the lock on something, usually with a key

unlucky /ʌnˈlʌki/ adj **1** having bad luck **2** happening because of bad luck **3** believed to bring bad luck —**unluckily** adv

unmanned /ʌnˈmænd/ adj an unmanned building, vehicle, or machine does not have anyone working in it or on it

unmarked /ʌnˈmɑːkt/ adj **1** something that is unmarked has no words or symbols on it to show what or where it is **2** SPORTS in sport, an unmarked player has a lot of freedom to move because they are not being **marked** by a player from the other team **3** LANGUAGE an unmarked word or phrase is generally used in normal English rather than being, for example, formal or informal

unmarried /ʌnˈmærid/ adj not married = SINGLE

unmet /ʌnˈmet/ adj used for saying that what is needed or wanted has not been done or provided

unmetered /ʌnˈmiːtəd/ adj COMPUTING an unmetered Internet service allows people to use the Internet whenever they want for as long as they want, for a fixed monthly amount of money

unmistakable /ˌʌnmɪˈsteɪkəb(ə)l/ adj very easy to recognize

unnamed /ʌnˈneɪmd/ adj used for describing a person or thing whose name is not mentioned

unnatural /ʌnˈnætʃ(ə)rəl/ adj **1** different from what you would normally expect or experience, especially in a way that makes you feel nervous or afraid: *an unnatural silence* **2** used for describing behaviour that offends or shocks people because it is not considered normal **3** not like real life or like the way people really behave —**unnaturally** adv

unnecessary /ʌnˈnesəs(ə)ri/ adj **1** used for describing something that should not have happened because it could have been avoided: *The policy had caused thousands of families unnecessary suffering.* ♦ *The delay was totally unnecessary.* **2** not needed: *Remove all unnecessary files from your computer.* —**unnecessarily** /ˌʌnnesəˈserəli/ adv

unnoticed /ʌnˈnəʊtɪst/ adj, adv not seen or noticed by anyone

unobtrusive /ˌʌnəbˈtruːsɪv/ adj formal not attracting much attention —**unobtrusively** adv

unoccupied /ʌnˈɒkjʊpaɪd/ adj an unoccupied room, building, or seat is not being used by anyone

unofficial /ˌʌnəˈfɪʃ(ə)l/ adj **1** not organized or formally approved by anyone in authority **2** not having an official position or status —**unofficially** adv

unopposed /ˌʌnəˈpəʊzd/ adj, adv if someone does something unopposed, no one competes against them or tries to stop them

unorthodox /ʌnˈɔːθədɒks/ adj not following the usual rules or beliefs of a religion, society etc

unpack /ʌnˈpæk/ verb **1** [I/T] to take things out of a suitcase or other container that they were being carried in **2** [T] to explain something difficult by reducing it to small simple stages or by using simpler language **3** [T] COMPUTING to increase the size of a file to its original size after it has been reduced using a computer program = UNZIP

unpaid /ʌnˈpeɪd/ adj **1** unpaid work is work that someone is not paid for **2** not yet paid: *unpaid bills*

unpaired /ʌnˈpeəd/ adj not forming part of a pair

unparalleled /ʌnˈpærəleld/ adj formal much greater than anything else or anyone else

unplaced /ʌnˈpleɪst/ adj SPORTS not among the winners in a race or competition

unplanned /ʌnˈplænd/ adj not intended or expected

unpleasant /ʌnˈplez(ə)nt/ adj **1** if something is unpleasant, you do not like or enjoy it: *The smell was very unpleasant.* ♦ *an unpleasant experience* **2** not friendly or kind: *She was really unpleasant on the phone.* —**unpleasantly** adv

unplug /ʌnˈplʌg/ (**unplugs, unplugging, unplugged**) verb [T] to separate a piece of equipment from a power supply by taking its **plug** out of an electric **socket**

unpopular /ʌnˈpɒpjʊlə/ adj disliked by many people —**unpopularity** /ˌʌnpɒpjʊˈlærəti/ noun [U]

unprecedented /ʌnˈpresɪˌdentɪd/ adj something that is unprecedented has never happened or existed before —**unprecedentedly** adv

unpredictable /ˌʌnprɪˈdɪktəb(ə)l/ adj changing often, in a way that is impossible to prepare for = ERRATIC —**unpredictably** adv

unprepared /ˌʌnprɪˈpeəd/ adj not ready for a particular situation, event, or process

unprincipled /ʌnˈprɪnsəp(ə)ld/ adj someone who is unprincipled is willing to use dishonest or unfair methods in order to get what they want

unproductive /ˌʌnprəˈdʌktɪv/ adj not achieving any benefits or positive results

unprotected sex /ˌʌnprətektɪd ˈseks/ noun [U] sex that people have without using contraception to protect them against pregnancy or diseases

unproven /ʌnˈpruːv(ə)n/ adj LAW not proved in a court of law

unprovoked /ˌʌnprəˈvəʊkt/ adj an unprovoked attack is made on someone who has done nothing to deserve it

unqualified /ʌnˈkwɒlɪfaɪd/ adj **1** not having the education, experience, or right qualifications to do a particular job **2** complete and total, without any doubts

unquestionable /ʌnˈkwestʃ(ə)nəb(ə)l/ adj used for emphasizing how true something is, or for saying that most people believe it: *His commitment to his schoolwork is unquestionable.* —**unquestionably** adv

unravel /ʌnˈræv(ə)l/ (**unravels, unravelling, unravelled**) verb **1** [T] to understand something complicated by thinking about it for a long time **2** [I] if a process or project unravels, it begins to fail **3** [I/T] if a piece of clothing unravels, or if you unravel it, its fibres become separated from each other

unreal /ˌʌnˈrɪəl/ adj **1** extremely unusual and not normal **2** unlikely to ever happen or be true = UNREALISTIC —**unreality** /ˌʌnrɪˈæləti/ noun [U]

unrealistic /ˌʌnrɪəˈlɪstɪk/ adj based on hopes or wishes, and not on what is likely or possible —**unrealistically** /ˌʌnrɪəˈlɪstɪkli/ adv

unreasonable /ʌnˈriːz(ə)nəb(ə)l/ adj **1** not fair **2** not sensible —**unreasonably** adv

unrecognizable /ʌnˈrekəɡˌnaɪzəb(ə)l/ adj very different from the person or place that you remember

unrecoverable error /ˌʌnrɪkʌv(ə)rəb(ə)l ˈerə/ noun [C] COMPUTING a fault in computer equipment or software that causes a program to stop working

unrelated /ˌʌnrɪˈleɪtɪd/ adj **1** not connected with another event, situation, subject etc: *His decision to quit was **unrelated to** the team's performance.* **2** not part of the same family

unreliable /ˌʌnrɪˈlaɪəb(ə)l/ adj **1** someone or something that is unreliable cannot be depended on **2** unreliable information is not definitely true or accurate

unrest /ʌnˈrest/ noun [U] angry or violent behaviour by people who are protesting against something

unrewarded /ˌʌnrɪˈwɔːdɪd/ adj if something that you do goes unrewarded, you do not achieve or get what you wanted as a result

unrivalled /ʌnˈraɪv(ə)ld/ adj used for emphasizing that something is much better or more important than other similar things

unruly /ʌnˈruːli/ adj very difficult to control

unsafe /ʌnˈseɪf/ adj **1** dangerous **2** involving a lot of risk **3** LAW not based on reliable evidence

unsatisfactory /ˌʌnsætɪsˈfækt(ə)ri/ adj not good enough

unsaturated fat /ʌnˌsætʃəreɪtɪd ˈfæt/ noun [C/U] CHEMISTRY, HEALTH fat that is made mainly from vegetable oil that has **fatty acids** with one or more **double bonds**. It is considered to be better for your health than **saturated fat**. → POLYUNSATURATED FAT, SATURATED FAT

unsavoury /ʌnˈseɪvəri/ adj involving unpleasant, dishonest, or immoral things

unscathed /ʌnˈskeɪðd/ adj not harmed or damaged

unscrew /ʌnˈskruː/ verb [T] to open something by twisting its lid or top

unscrupulous /ʌnˈskruːpjʊləs/ adj willing to do things that are unfair, dishonest, or illegal

unseeded /ʌnˈsiːdɪd/ adj SPORTS not expected to win a tennis competition and not on the official list of best players

unseen /ʌnˈsiːn/ adj not seen or known about by anyone —**unseen** adv

unselfish /ʌnˈselfɪʃ/ adj thinking about what other people want or need rather than what you want or need yourself —**unselfishly** adv

unsettled /ʌnˈset(ə)ld/ adj **1** nervous, confused, or upset **2** an unsettled place, situation, or period of time is one in which people feel nervous because things are changing **3** unsettled weather changes a lot and there is a lot of wind and rain **4** something such as a problem or argument that is unsettled has not been dealt with successfully

unsettling /ʌnˈsetlɪŋ/ adj making you feel nervous, confused, or upset

unsightly /ʌnˈsaɪtli/ adj not pleasant to look at: *an unsightly scar*

unskilled /ʌnˈskɪld/ adj **1** not needing much education, training, or experience **2** not having enough education, training, or experience to do a job that needs skill

unsociable /ʌnˈsəʊʃəb(ə)l/ adj not interested in meeting people or in doing things with other people

unsold /ʌnˈsəʊld/ adj not sold

unsolved /ʌnˈsɒlvd/ adj an unsolved problem or **mystery** is one that has not been dealt with or explained

unsound /ʌnˈsaʊnd/ adj **1** not safe **2** not based on sensible ideas
PHRASE **of unsound mind** LAW mentally ill at the time of committing a crime

unspeakable /ʌnˈspiːkəb(ə)l/ adj used for emphasizing how bad something is —**unspeakably** adv

unspecified /ʌnˈspesɪfaɪd/ adj not mentioned or known

unspoiled /ʌnˈspɔɪld/ or **unspoilt** /ʌnˈspɔɪlt/ adj an unspoiled place has not been changed in ways that make it less beautiful or enjoyable

unspoken /ʌnˈspəʊkən/ adj not expressed in words but understood

unsprung weight /ˌʌnsprʌŋ ˈweɪt/ noun [U] ENGINEERING the weight of a vehicle's **suspension**, wheels, and any other parts connected to them

unstable /ʌnˈsteɪb(ə)l/ adj

1 person	4 chemical element
2 government	5 radioactive substance
3 situation	6 likely to move/change

1 an unstable person often becomes suddenly angry or upset
2 an unstable government changes often and must deal with a lot of fighting and protests
3 often affected by serious problems: *an unstable economy*
4 CHEMISTRY an unstable chemical element or compound reacts very easily with other substances. Some unstable substances, for example **nitroglycerine**, produce very violent reactions and are useful in making explosives ≠ STABLE
5 CHEMISTRY, PHYSICS relating to a radioactive substance whose nucleus breaks down to release radioactivity
6 PHYSICS an unstable object is likely to move or change because of the forces affecting it. For example, a pencil lying on a desk is **stable** (=not likely to move or change), but a pencil standing on its end on a desk is unstable and will fall over ≠ STABLE

unsteady /ʌn'stedi/ adj **1** not regular, calm, or normal **2** too weak or ill to walk well

unstressed /ʌn'strest/ adj **LANGUAGE** an unstressed word or syllable is pronounced more quietly or with less force than other words or syllables

unstructured /ʌn'strʌktʃəd/ adj not organized in a formal way

unsubscribe /ˌʌnsəb'skraɪb/ verb [I/T] **COMPUTING** to take your name off an Internet **mailing list** (=list of people who receive emails)

unsuccessful /ˌʌnsək'sesf(ə)l/ adj **1** something that is unsuccessful does not achieve what you want: *another unsuccessful attempt to reach agreement* **2** someone who is unsuccessful does not get what they want: *Letters are sent to all unsuccessful candidates.* —**unsuccessfully** adv

unsuitable /ʌn'su:təb(ə)l/ adj not suitable for a particular situation, purpose, or person: *These films are **unsuitable for** children.*

unsupervised /ʌn'su:pəvaɪzd/ adj someone who is unsupervised does not have a responsible person in charge of them or looking after them

unsure /ʌn'ʃʊə/ adj not certain about something
   PHRASE unsure of yourself not having much confidence

unsuspecting /ˌʌnsə'spektɪŋ/ adj not knowing that something bad is happening or will happen

unsustainable /ˌʌnsə'steɪnəb(ə)l/ adj **1** not capable of continuing at the same rate or level **2 ENVIRONMENT** unsustainable farming methods, industries etc damage the environment because they use up more energy, wood, coal etc than can be replaced naturally ≠ SUSTAINABLE

unsympathetic /ˌʌnsɪmpə'θetɪk/ adj **1** not kind enough to want to know about other people's problems **2** not willing to support something

untangle /ʌn'tæŋg(ə)l/ verb [T] **1** to understand a complicated situation, or to solve a difficult problem **2** to separate things that are twisted around each other

untenable /ʌn'tenəb(ə)l/ adj impossible to defend as fair, suitable, or true

unthinkable /ʌn'θɪŋkəb(ə)l/ adj impossible to imagine

untidy /ʌn'taɪdi/ (**untidier, untidiest**) adj **1** not arranged in a way that is tidy: *an untidy desk* **2** not keeping things tidy: *He's always criticizing me for being untidy.*

untie /ʌn'taɪ/ (**unties, untying, untied**) verb [T] to take the knot out of a piece of rope or string that fastens something

until /ən'tɪl/ conjunction, preposition **1** happening or done up to a particular point in time, and then stopping: *Baker is expected to be here until the end of the week.* ♦ *You'll just have to wait until they call your name.* **2** as far as a particular place: *Perry was leading the race until the final bend.*
   PHRASE not (...) until used for stating the point at which something finally happens, becomes possible, or becomes true: *They didn't see each other again until the autumn.*

untimely /ʌn'taɪmli/ adj **1** happening at a time that is not suitable, for example because it causes additional problems **2** happening earlier than you expected

untold /ʌn'təʊld/ adj too great to be measured

untouched /ʌn'tʌtʃt/ adj **1** not harmed or spoiled: *Few families were **untouched by** the war.* **2** food or drink that is untouched has not been eaten or drunk

untoward /ˌʌntə'wɔːd/ adj not suitable, usual, or normal

untrained /ʌn'treɪnd/ adj not trained to do a particular job

untreated /ʌn'tri:tɪd/ adj **1 HEALTH** receiving no medical treatment **2** in a natural state, and perhaps harmful

untrue /ʌn'truː/ adj not based on fact

untrustworthy /ʌn'trʌst,wɜːði/ adj not capable of being trusted or depended on

untruth /ʌn'truːθ/ noun [C] *formal* a lie

unusable /ʌn'juːzəb(ə)l/ adj not good enough to use

unused /ʌn'juːzd/ adj not used

unusual /ʌn'juːʒʊəl/ adj **1** not normal, common, or ordinary: *You're in a very unusual situation.* ♦ *Local residents should contact the police if they notice **anything unusual**.* ♦ *It's **unusual to** find so many different plants in one garden.* **2** different from other people or things in a way that is interesting, attractive, or impressive: *The designers have chosen unusual colour combinations.* ♦ *Ewing is a player of unusual talent.*

unusually /ʌn'juːʒʊəli/ adv **1** in a way that is not usual or typical: *Boris seemed unusually quiet.* **2** extremely: *Cambridge has several unusually good restaurants.*

unveil /ʌn'veɪl/ verb [T] **1** to announce something officially **2** to remove the cover from something as part of an official ceremony

unvoiced /ʌn'vɔɪst/ adj **LANGUAGE** an unvoiced sound such as 't', 's', or 'f' is produced without using the **vocal cords** ≠ VOICED

unwanted /ʌn'wɒntɪd/ adj **1** not wanted **2** not loved

unwarranted /ʌn'wɒrəntɪd/ adj not fair or necessary

unwelcome /ʌn'welkəm/ adj **1** unpleasant or annoying **2** an unwelcome guest or visitor is someone who you do not want to spend time with

unwell /ʌn'wel/ adj *formal* ill

unwieldy /ʌn'wiːldi/ adj *formal* **1** too big or complicated to work well **2** large or heavy and difficult to carry

unwilling /ʌn'wɪlɪŋ/ adj **1** if you are unwilling to do something, you do not want to do it or you refuse to do it: *Jane was **unwilling to** admit she was wrong.* **2** involved in doing something that you do not want to do: *an unwilling participant* —**unwillingly** adv, **unwillingness** noun [U]

unwind /ʌn'waɪnd/ (**unwinds, unwinding, unwound** /ʌn'waʊnd/) verb **1** [I] *informal* to begin to relax after you have been working hard or feeling nervous **2** [I/T] to become straighter or looser after being wrapped around something else, or to make something do this

unwise /ʌn'waɪz/ adj not sensible —**unwisely** adv

unwittingly /ʌn'wɪtɪŋli/ adv in a way that is not conscious or deliberate —**unwitting** adj

unworkable /ʌn'wɜːkəb(ə)l/ adj not practical, and therefore unlikely to be successful

unwound /ʌn'waʊnd/ the past tense and past participle of **unwind**

unwrap /ʌn'ræp/ (**unwraps, unwrapping, unwrapped**) verb [T] to remove the paper or plastic that is covering something

unwritten /ʌn'rɪt(ə)n/ adj known or understood by everyone but not official

unzip /ʌnˈzɪp/ (**unzips, unzipping, unzipped**) verb [T]
1 to open a piece of clothing or a bag by pulling a **zip**
2 COMPUTING to increase the size of a file to its original size after it has been reduced

up¹ /ʌp/ adj, adv, preposition

1 higher	**8** into smaller parts
2 upright	**9** completely
3 moving to sb/sth	**10** fastened
4 further along	**11** collected
5 to higher level	**12** working
6 not in bed	+ PHRASES
7 at an end	

1 in or towards a higher position: *I got off my bike and walked up the hill.* ♦ *Pick your clothes up off the floor.* ♦ *The hotel is 1,500 feet up in the mountains.* ♦ *We were jumping* **up and down** *on the bed.*
2 upright, or moving towards an upright position: *I found Hattie* **sitting up** *in bed.* ♦ *He* **stood up** *and walked out of the room.*
3 moving near to someone or something and then stopping: *A sales assistant* **came up** *and asked if she could help.* ♦ *Just go* **up to** *him and say hello.*
4 in or to a place that is further along: *He lives up the street from me.*
5 at or towards an increased amount or level: *Turn the volume up – I can't hear anything.* ♦ *The company's profits are up by £3 million this year.*
6 awake and out of bed: *I was up till midnight finishing my homework.* ♦ *Get up! It's almost 10.00.*
7 used for stating that a period of time has ended: *Come along now, please!* **Time's up!**
8 divided or broken into smaller pieces or equal parts: *The prize money will be divided up among the team members.*
9 completely done or used so that there is nothing left: *He ate up all his dinner.* ♦ *The stream dries up in summer.*
10 fastened or closed completely: *Did you lock the house up before you left?* ♦ *She keeps the letters tied up in a bundle.*
11 collected, added, or brought together in one place: *She was busy gathering up her papers.* ♦ *Check that you've added the amounts up correctly.*
12 a system that is up is working as it should: *By ten o'clock we had the computers up again.* ♦ *The new filing system should be* **up and running** *soon.*
PHRASES **up and down** backwards and forwards: *He kept walking up and down the hallway all night long.*
up to sb if something is up to you, you are responsible for deciding about it or doing it: *Do you want to stay or go? It's up to you.* ♦ *It's up to all of us to make our streets safe for children.*
up to sth 1 used for saying the most that an amount can be, or the highest level it can reach: *Some dinosaurs were up to twenty-seven metres long.* **2** used for giving a particular standard that something can reach: *I'm afraid the play wasn't up to our expectations.* **3** doing something wrong or secret: *When the children are quiet like this, I know they're up to something.* **4** well enough, strong enough, or good enough to do something: *She's supposed to leave hospital tomorrow, but I don't think she's up to it.*

up² /ʌp/ noun **ups and downs** *informal* a mixture of good and bad situations or experiences: *Like all teams, we've had our ups and downs.*

upbringing /ˈʌpˌbrɪŋɪŋ/ noun [singular] the way that parents look after their children and teach them to behave

update¹ /ʌpˈdeɪt/ verb **1** [I/T] to add the most recent information to something such as a book, document, or list: *The latest edition has been completely updated.*
2 [T] to tell someone the most recent news or information about something: *Dr Cooper can update us on the latest developments.* **3** [T] to make something more modern: *Our software is continually being updated and improved.* → UP-TO-DATE

update² /ˈʌpdeɪt/ noun [C] **1** a report or broadcast that contains the most recent information
2 COMPUTING a piece of software that contains recent improvements to a computer program

upfold /ˈʌpˌfəʊld/ noun [C] GEOLOGY an **anticline** (=a bend in a layer of rock that curves upwards)

up ˈfront or **upfront** /ʌpˈfrʌnt/ adv **1** if you pay for something up front, you pay for it before you receive it **2** if you tell someone something up front, you are very honest from the beginning about something that might affect them —**upfront** adj

upgrade¹ /ʌpˈɡreɪd/ verb **1** [I/T] COMPUTING to make a computer or machine more powerful or effective **2** [T] to officially give someone or something a higher status

upgrade² /ˈʌpˌɡreɪd/ noun [C] COMPUTING, COMPUTING a piece of equipment or software that is designed to make a computer more powerful or effective

upheaval /ʌpˈhiːv(ə)l/ noun [C/U] a sudden or violent change

upheld /ʌpˈheld/ the past tense and past participle of **uphold**

uphill /ˈʌphɪl/ adj **1** towards the top of a slope or hill ≠ DOWNHILL **2** difficult to do or achieve —**uphill** /ˌʌpˈhɪl/ adv

uphold /ʌpˈhəʊld/ (**upholds, upholding, upheld** /ʌpˈheld/) verb [T] **1** if a court of law upholds something, it says that it is correct: *The Appeals Court upheld the decision of the lower court.* **2** *formal* to show that you support something: *We have an obligation to uphold the law.*

upholstery /ʌpˈhəʊlst(ə)ri/ noun [U] soft material that is used for covering chairs and other seats

upkeep /ˈʌpˌkiːp/ noun [singular/U] the process or cost of keeping property in good condition

upland /ˈʌplənd/ adj GEOGRAPHY relating to an area of high land

uplands /ˈʌpləndz/ noun [plural] GEOGRAPHY areas of high land

upload /ˈʌpˌləʊd/ verb [T] COMPUTING to send information from a computer to a larger system using the Internet ≠ DOWNLOAD

upmarket /ʌpˈmɑːkɪt/ adj expensive, and of very good quality ≠ DOWNMARKET —**upmarket** adv

up-milling /ˈʌp ˌmɪlɪŋ/ noun [U] TECHNOLOGY **conventional milling**, in which the material being cut moves in the opposite direction to the equipment that is cutting it

upon /əˈpɒn/ preposition *formal* used after some verbs with the same meaning as 'on': *Your whole future depends upon your performance in these exams.*

upper /ˈʌpə/ adj **1** higher than something else, especially higher than one of two things that are a pair ≠ LOWER: *He had a scar on his upper lip.* **2** near the top, or at the top of something ≠ LOWER: *the upper slopes of the mountain* **3** higher in status or rank ≠ LOWER: *the upper ranks of the army*

ˌupper ˈcase noun [U] LANGUAGE the form in which capital letters are written, for example 'A', 'F', and 'T': *upper case letters* ♦ *a message typed* **in upper case**
→ LOWER CASE

the ,upper 'class noun SOCIAL STUDIES people who have the highest social status —,upper-'class adj
→ LOWER CLASS, MIDDLE CLASS, WORKING CLASS

,upper epi'dermis noun [C] BIOLOGY the top surface of a leaf

uppermost /'ʌpə,məʊst/ adj 1 more important than anything else 2 at or near the top

upright¹ /'ʌpraɪt/ adv 1 sitting or standing with a straight back: *Sangmin was wide awake, sitting upright in bed.* 2 in or into a straight or standing position: *Pictures were propped upright against all the walls.*

upright² /'ʌpraɪt/ adj 1 straight and tall: *Make sure your seat is in an upright position for landing.* 2 honest: *an upright citizen*

uprising /'ʌp,raɪzɪŋ/ noun [C] POLITICS a political situation in which a large group of people opposes and tries to defeat the government or the person who rules their country= REBELLION

uproar /'ʌp,rɔː/ noun [singular/U] 1 angry public criticism of something 2 a lot of noise made by people who are shouting

uproot /ʌp'ruːt/ verb [T] 1 to force someone to leave the place where they live 2 to pull a whole tree or plant from the ground

upset¹ /ʌp'set/ adj 1 sad, worried, or angry about something: *Why are you so upset?* ♦ *They felt too upset to talk about the incident.* ♦ *They're all still very upset about losing the match.* ♦ *It's nothing to get upset about.* ♦ *She feels upset that we didn't tell her the truth.* 2 if your stomach is upset, you have an illness affecting your stomach, usually caused by something that you have eaten or drunk: *Phone and tell them you've got an upset stomach.*

upset² /ʌp'set/ (**upsets, upsetting, upset**) verb [T] 1 to make someone feel sad, worried, or angry: *I'm sorry, I didn't mean to upset you.* ♦ *People were upset by his rude remarks.* 2 to spoil something: *I'm sorry if I've upset your plans for this evening.* ♦ *The introduction of a new species has upset the ecological balance of the lake.* 3 formal to knock something over accidentally = SPILL

upset³ /'ʌpset/ noun [C] 1 an occasion when someone defeats an opponent who is considered better than them 2 an illness that affects your stomach, usually caused by something that you have eaten or drunk 3 something that makes you feel sad, worried, or angry

upsetting /ʌp'setɪŋ/ adj making you feel sad, worried, or angry

upshot /'ʌp,ʃɒt/ noun **the upshot (of sth)** the result of a process or event

upside /'ʌpsaɪd/ noun [singular] the positive aspect of a bad situation ≠ DOWNSIDE

,upside 'down adv with the top part at the bottom or lower than the bottom part: *The car landed upside down in a ditch.*
PHRASES **turn sb's life/world upside down** to change someone's life completely
turn sth upside down to make a place very untidy while you are searching for something
—,upside-'down adj

upslope /'ʌp,sləʊp/ noun [C] GEOLOGY a slope that is considered to be at an upward angle

upstairs /ʌp'steəz/ adv 1 on an upper level of a building with stairs ≠ DOWNSTAIRS: *The children are upstairs in bed.* ♦ *Do you know who lives in the flat upstairs?* 2 to an upper level of a building ≠ DOWNSTAIRS: *I'm going*

upstairs for a rest. —**upstairs** /'ʌp,steəz/ adj: *an upstairs window*

upstream /ʌp'striːm/ adv GEOGRAPHY in the opposite direction to the way that a river or stream flows ≠ DOWNSTREAM

upsurge /'ʌp,sɜːdʒ/ noun [singular] a sudden increase in something

uptake /'ʌp,teɪk/ noun [singular/U] BIOLOGY the process in which living things use substances such as food or water to breathe, produce energy etc

,up-'tempo adj MUSIC up-tempo music has a fast beat

upthrust /'ʌp,θrʌst/ noun 1 [U] PHYSICS the force that a liquid or gas directs upwards on an object that is floating on it 2 [C/U] GEOLOGY a large piece of rock that has moved upwards in a crack in the Earth's surface

,up-to-'date adj 1 giving the most recent news and information: *Visit our website for the most up-to-date match reports.* ♦ *Make sure your passport is kept up-to-date.* 2 modern and using the latest ideas or knowledge: *up-to-date technology*

,up-to-the-'minute adj 1 containing all the most recent news and information 2 very modern

upturned /ʌp'tɜːnd/ adj 1 curving, pointing, or facing upwards 2 an upturned object has been moved so that its top part is at the bottom

uPVC /ˌjuː piː viː 'siː/ noun [U] CONSTRUCTION unplasticized polyvinyl chloride: a plastic material used for making pipes, doors, and window frames

upward /'ʌpwəd/ adj 1 moving or turned towards a higher position ≠ DOWNWARD: *strong upward currents of air* 2 moving towards a higher level or amount ≠ DOWNWARD

upwards /'ʌpwədz/ or **upward** /'ʌpwəd/ adv 1 towards a higher position ≠ DOWNWARDS: *She glanced upwards at the screen.* 2 towards a higher or more important level ≠ DOWNWARDS: *The initial estimate has been revised upwards.* 3 more than a particular number or amount: *It will take upwards of six months to complete the work.*

upwind /ʌp'wɪnd/ adv GEOGRAPHY moving in the direction from which the wind is blowing

uranium /jʊ'reɪniəm/ noun [U] CHEMISTRY a silver-white radioactive metallic element in the **actinide** group of the periodic table. It is used in the production of nuclear energy. Chemical symbol: **U**

Uranus /'jʊərənəs/ noun ASTRONOMY the planet that is seventh furthest away from the Sun, between Saturn and Neptune. It is made up mainly of the gases hydrogen and **helium**. —picture → SOLAR SYSTEM

urban /'ɜːbən/ adj GEOGRAPHY relating to towns and cities ≠ RURAL: *People moved to the urban areas for jobs.*

urbanization /ˌɜːbənaɪ'zeɪʃ(ə)n/ noun [U] GEOGRAPHY, SOCIAL STUDIES the process by which towns and cities grow bigger and more and more people go to live in them

urea /jʊ'riːə/ noun [U] BIOLOGY a substance found in urine that is used for making fertilizers and for some types of medicine

ureter /jʊ'riːtə/ noun [C] BIOLOGY one of the two tubes that carry urine from the kidneys to the bladder in most mammals, or to the place where waste collects in some vertebrates

urethra /jʊ'riːθrə/ noun [C] ANATOMY in most mammals, the tube that carries urine out of the body

urge^1 /ɜːdʒ/ verb [T] **1** to advise someone very strongly about what action or attitude they should take: *The chief of police has urged restraint in dealing with the protesters.* ♦ *The UN has **urged** them **to** honour the peace treaty.* **2** to make a person or animal move in a particular direction: *He urged the horse forwards.*

urge^2 /ɜːdʒ/ noun [C] a strong feeling of wanting or needing to do something: *Suddenly I had an overwhelming urge to laugh.*

urgency /'ɜːdʒ(ə)nsi/ noun [U] the need to deal with something immediately

urgent /'ɜːdʒ(ə)nt/ adj **1** urgent things are things that you need to deal with immediately: *The problem is becoming increasingly urgent.* ♦ *He had some urgent business to attend to.* ♦ *Some villages are **in urgent need of** food.* **2** expressing the feeling of wanting something very much or wanting it immediately: *an urgent whisper* —**urgently** adv

'urinary ,bladder noun [C] BIOLOGY the **bladder**

'urinary ,tract or **urinary system** noun [C] ANATOMY the system of tubes that carry urine from the kidneys to the bladder and out of the body

urinate /'jʊərmeɪt/ verb [I] BIOLOGY to get rid of urine from the body —**urination** /ˌjʊərɪ'neɪʃ(ə)n/ noun [U]

urine /'jʊərɪn/ noun [U] BIOLOGY a liquid that contains waste products such as **urea** and salts from the body that are filtered out through the kidneys. Urine collects in the bladder and passes from the body through the urethra. —**urinary** adj

URL /ˌjuː ɑː 'el/ noun [C] COMPUTING Uniform Resource Locator: an Internet address

urn /ɜːn/ noun [C] **1** a large metal container for making tea or coffee **2** a container for a dead person's **ashes** (=powder that is left after the body has been burnt)

urogenital /ˌjʊərəʊ'dʒenɪt(ə)l/ adj ANATOMY relating to or involving the organs that remove liquid waste from the body, and the sex organs

urology /ju'rɒlədʒi/ noun [U] HEALTH the study of diseases of the **urinary tract**, or medical treatment for them —**urologist** noun [C]

us /strong ʌs, weak əs/ pronoun the object form of 'we', used for referring to yourself and other people with you or in your group when you are the person speaking or writing: *It wasn't our idea, so don't blame us.* ♦ *We needed a guide to show us the way.* ♦ *Anansi came with us.*

the US /ˌjuː 'es/ GEOGRAPHY the United States

the USA /ˌjuː es 'eɪ/ GEOGRAPHY the United States of America

usability /ˌjuːzə'bɪlɪti/ noun [U] the usability of something is how easy it is to use

usable /'juːzəb(ə)l/ adj available or suitable to be used for a particular purpose

usage /'juːsɪdʒ/ noun **1** [C/U] LANGUAGE the way that words are used by people when they speak and write their language: *differences between British and American usage* **2** [U] the process of using something **3** [U] the amount of something that you use

USB /ˌjuː es 'biː/ noun [C] COMPUTING universal serial bus: a standard for connecting a piece of equipment such as a printer or mouse to a computer

US'B de,vice noun [C] COMPUTING a piece of equipment such as a printer, keyboard, or **modem** that can be connected to a computer through a USB port

US'B ,port noun [C] COMPUTING a place on a computer where you can attach a **cable** for connecting a printer, keyboard, **modem** etc —*picture* → COMPUTER

USD abbrev US dollars

use^1 /juːz/ verb [T]

1 do sth with tool etc	**4** treat sb in unfair way
2 get benefit from sth	**5** say particular words
3 take from supply	**+ PHRASAL VERB**

1 to do something with a machine, tool, skill, method etc in order to achieve a particular result: *Using a computer is so much quicker.* ♦ *What type of soap do you use?* ♦ *Don't use swearwords in front of your little brother.* ♦ *We **use** methane gas **for** heating.* ♦ *The land is being **used as** a car park.*
2 to get a benefit for yourself from something available to you: *Only about 30 people regularly use the bus service.*
3 to take an amount from a supply of something: *You've used all the hot water again.*
4 to treat someone in an unfair way, for example by pretending to care about them so that they do what you want: *You know he's just using you.*
5 to say or write particular words: *Don't use language like that in front of your little brother.*

PHRASAL VERB ,**use sth 'up** to use all of a supply of something: *All the world's coal and oil will be used up in 50 years.*

Word family: use

*Words in the same family as **use***
- usage *n*
- used *adj*
- useful *adj*
- usefully *adv*
- usefulness *n*
- reuse *v, n*
- user *n*
- disused *adj*
- misuse *n, v*
- useless *adj*
- uselessly *adv*
- reusable *adj*

use^2 /juːs/ noun

1 act of using sth	**4** ability to use
2 way of using sth	mind/body
3 right etc to use sth	**5** meaning etc of word
	+ PHRASES

1 [singular/U] the act of using something: *an unnecessary use of force* ♦ *the use of computers*
2 [C/U] a way of using something: *This material has a variety of manufacturing uses.* ♦ *This is not the best use of your talents.* ♦ *I kept hoping to find a use for it.*
3 [U] the right, an opportunity, or permission to use something: *We can **have the use of** the hall every Thursday.* ♦ *The pool was built **for the use of** local people.*
4 [U] the ability to use a part of your body: *He lost the use of his legs in a car crash.*
5 [C] a meaning of a word or a way of speaking or writing a word: *This use is common among young people.*

PHRASES **be of use (to sb)** to be helpful or useful: *Can I be of any use?* ♦ *This information may be of use to him.*
be (of) no use (to sb) to not be helpful or useful: *This book is no use whatever.* ♦ *Get some rest or you'll be of no use to anyone.*
come into/go out of use to start or stop being used by people: *Computers first came into use in the early 1950s.*
make use of to use someone or something for a particular purpose, especially one that brings a benefit to you: *Why doesn't she make use of her singing talent?* ♦ *I hope you've **made good use of** your time.*
put sth to good use to use something you have for a sensible purpose that brings a benefit to you: *Do you promise to put the money to good use?*

used /juːzd/ adj **1** owned by someone else before you = SECOND-HAND: *a used car* **2** no longer completely clean because of having been used: *a used towel*

used to[1] /ˈjuːst tuː/ modal verb used for saying what was true or what happened regularly in the past, especially when this is not true or does not happen now: *I used to enjoy gardening, but I don't have time for it now.* ♦ *Where did you use to live before you moved here?* ♦ *I didn't use to like him, but now we're good friends.*

> ■ **Used to** is usually followed by an infinitive: *We used to swim in the river.* But sometimes the following infinitive is left out: *I don't play golf now, but I used to.*
> ■ **Used to** only exists as a past tense.
> ■ Questions and negatives are usually formed with 'did' + **use to** (with no 'd'): *Did you use to work here?* ♦ *We didn't use to earn much.*
> ■ In formal English, negatives are often formed with **used not to**: *They used not to allow shops to be open on Sundays.*

used to[2] /ˈjuːst tuː/ adj familiar with something because you have often experienced it before, so that it no longer seems difficult or strange: *Dilip was used to working on difficult assignments.* ♦ *I'm tired – I'm not used to these late nights.* ♦ *I haven't **got used to** the new system yet.*

useful /ˈjuːsf(ə)l/ adj helpful for doing or achieving something: *a useful gadget* ♦ *Here's some useful information about the history of the Gonja people.* ♦ *I was **useful to** them because I could speak Hindi.* ♦ *That basket would be **useful for** carrying fruit.* ♦ *Keep a record of everything that might **prove useful**.* ♦ *Thanks. It's **useful to** know that.*

   PHRASE **come in useful** to be helpful in a particular situation: *Your medical training might come in very useful indeed.*

   —**usefully** adv, **usefulness** noun [U]

useless /ˈjuːsləs/ adj **1** useless objects have no purpose or cannot do what they were designed to do: *This technology is useless if you can't operate it.* ♦ *This bucket is full of holes – it's completely useless!* **2** useless activities are not effective in achieving the purpose they were intended to achieve: *All of my efforts to persuade him were useless.* ♦ *It's useless trying to talk to her because she never listens.* **3** if someone is useless, they are not capable of achieving anything: *I'm **useless at** cooking* (=very bad at it). ♦ *Don't ask Mehmet – he's useless!* —**uselessly** adv

Usenet /ˈjuːznet/ noun **COMPUTING** a system for sending news and information to people over the Internet

user /ˈjuːzə/ noun [C] **1** someone who uses something such as a service or a piece of equipment: *Software should be designed to meet the needs of users.* ♦ *Cyclists, like all **road users**, must obey traffic signs.* ♦ ***users of** mobile phones* **2** someone who regularly takes illegal drugs

user-ˈfriendly adj easy to use or understand

ˈuser ˌgroup noun [C] **COMPUTING** a group of people who are interested in computers and share information using the Internet

userID /ˈjuːzəraɪˌdiː/ noun [C] **COMPUTING** a name or password that allows a user to use a computer system

ˌuser ˈinterface noun [C] **COMPUTING** the part of a computer program that you see on the screen when you are using it

username /ˈjuːzəˌneɪm/ noun [C] **COMPUTING** the name that is used by someone for operating a computer program

usher[1] /ˈʌʃə/ verb [T] to lead someone politely somewhere

usher[2] /ˈʌʃə/ noun [C] someone whose job is to show people where to sit

USP /ˌjuː es ˈpiː/ noun [C] **BUSINESS** unique selling proposition, or unique selling point: the feature that makes a product or service special or different from others

the USSR /ˌjuː es es ˈɑː/ **GEOGRAPHY, POLITICS** Union of Soviet Socialist Republics: the name for the group of communist countries in Eastern Europe that formed a single country until 1991

usual /ˈjuːʒʊəl/ adj typical of what happens in most situations, or of what people do in most situations: *She gave us her usual polite smile.* ♦ *The journey to school took **longer than usual**.* ♦ *It's **usual practice** to ask permission before borrowing any equipment.*

   PHRASE **as usual** used for saying what usually happens: *We went to bed that evening around 8.30 as usual.*

usually /ˈjuːʒʊəli/ adv used for saying what happens in most situations, or what people do in most situations = NORMALLY: *What time do you usually eat in the evening?* ♦ *We don't usually see each other at weekends.* ♦ *She's usually home by this time.*

UTC /ˌjuː tiː ˈsiː/ noun [U] **PHYSICS** Coordinated Universal Time: the international standard for time

utensil /juːˈtens(ə)l/ noun [C] something that you use for cooking or eating with

utero *see* **in utero**

uterus /ˈjuːt(ə)rəs/ noun [C] **ANATOMY** the organ in the body of a female mammal where a fertilized egg grows and develops into a foetus —*picture* → EMBRYO, FERTILIZATION, REPRODUCTION

utility /juːˈtɪləti/ (plural **utilities**) noun **1** [C] a public service such as gas, water, or electricity that is provided to people **2** [U] *formal* the state of being useful **3** [C] **COMPUTING** a **utility program**

uˈtility ˌprogram noun [C] **COMPUTING** a computer program that does a basic job such as copying or saving information = UTILITY

utilize /ˈjuːtɪlaɪz/ verb [T] *formal* to use something —**utilization** /ˌjuːtɪlaɪˈzeɪʃ(ə)n/ noun [U]

utmost[1] /ˈʌtməʊst/ adj as much as possible: *We attach the utmost importance to public safety.*

utmost[2] /ˈʌtməʊst/ noun [singular] the greatest amount or degree possible

   PHRASE **do/try your utmost (to do sth)** to try as hard as possible

utopia /juːˈtəʊpiə/ noun [C/U] an imaginary place or situation in which everything is perfect —**utopian** adj

utricle /ˈjuːtrɪk(ə)l/ noun [C] **ANATOMY** a space in the **inner ear** that is filled with fluid and is important for balance

utter[1] /ˈʌtə/ adj complete: *It's been an utter waste of time.*

utter[2] /ˈʌtə/ verb [T] **1** to say something: *They followed her without uttering a single word of protest.* **2** to make a sound: *She uttered a sharp cry of pain.*

utterance /ˈʌt(ə)rəns/ noun [C] **1** *formal* a statement **2** **LANGUAGE** a word or phrase that someone speaks

utterly /ˈʌtəli/ adv completely: *You're being utterly unreasonable.*

U-turn /ˈjuː ˌtɜːn/ noun [C] **1** a movement in which someone turns a vehicle in order to travel in the opposite direction **2** a sudden and complete change of policy

UV /ˌjuː ˈviː/ abbrev **SCIENCE** ultraviolet: light with shorter wavelengths than humans can see: *UV radiation*

UVA /ˌjuː viː ˈeɪ/ noun [U] **SCIENCE** ultraviolet A-rays: light from the sun that has a fairly long wavelength and causes skin to go brown and look older

UVB /ˌjuː viː ˈbiː/ noun [U] **SCIENCE** ultraviolet B-rays: light from the sun that has a fairly short wavelength and causes skin to go brown and look older

uvula /ˈjuːvjʊlə/ noun [C] **ANATOMY** the small piece of flesh that hangs down at the back of the mouth

uvular /ˈjuːvjʊlə/ adj **LANGUAGE** uvular sounds are made when the back of the tongue touches the uvula —**uvular** noun [C]

Vv

v¹ /viː/ (plural **v's**) or **V** (plural **V's**) noun [C/U] the 22nd letter of the English alphabet

v² abbrev **1** **LANGUAGE** verb **2** versus **3** very

V abbrev volt

vacancy /ˈveɪkənsi/ (plural **vacancies**) noun [C] **1** a job that is available: *We have several vacancies to fill in the Sales Department.* **2** **TOURISM** a room in a hotel that is available: *We have no vacancies at all during July.*

vacant /ˈveɪkənt/ adj **1** a place that is vacant is available because no one else is using it **2** if a job is vacant, someone is needed to do it **3** looking as if you do not understand or are not paying attention —**vacantly** adv

vacant pos'session noun [U] **LAW** the fact that no one is living in a house when the new owner buys it

vacate /vəˈkeɪt/ verb [T] *formal* to leave a place or a job so that it is available for someone else

vacation /vəˈkeɪʃ(ə)n/ noun **1** [C] **EDUCATION** a period of time when a university is closed **2** [C/U] *American* a holiday: *We're taking a vacation in Europe this summer.* —**vacation** verb [I]

vaccinate /ˈvæksɪneɪt/ verb [T] **HEALTH** to treat a person or animal with a vaccine in order to protect them against a disease= IMMUNIZE —**vaccination** /ˌvæksɪˈneɪʃ(ə)n/ noun [C/U]

vaccine /ˈvæksiːn/ noun [C/U] **HEALTH** a dead or weak microorganism that is put into the body in order to provide protection against a disease by causing it to make antibodies

vacillate /ˈvæsɪleɪt/ verb [I] *formal* to keep changing your ideas about something —**vacillation** /ˌvæsɪˈleɪʃ(ə)n/ noun [C/U]

vacuolation /ˌvækjuəˈleɪʃ(ə)n/ noun [U] **BIOLOGY** the state of having small spaces or **vacuoles** in a cell —**vacuolate** /ˈvækjuələt, ˈvækjuəleɪt/ adj

vacuole /ˈvækjuəʊl/ noun [C] **BIOLOGY** a space inside a cell, filled with air, food, or waste products —*picture* → CELL

vacuum¹ /ˈvækjuəm/ noun **1** [C] **PHYSICS** an enclosed space with all the air and other gases removed from it **2** [singular] a situation in which something is missing: *the political vacuum left by his death*

PHRASE in a vacuum existing or happening separately from other people or things, and not influenced by them: *Learning cannot occur in a vacuum.*

vacuum² /ˈvækjuəm/ verb [I/T] to clean a room using a vacuum cleaner

'vacuum ˌcleaner noun [C] a piece of electrical equipment that cleans floors by sucking dirt into itself

'vacuum ˌflask noun [C] a container for keeping something such as food or drink at an even temperature. It has walls from which nearly all the air has been removed, forming a **vacuum** through which heat cannot easily travel.

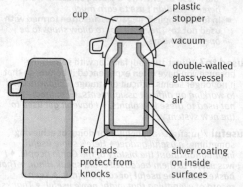

cup

plastic stopper

vacuum

double-walled glass vessel

air

felt pads protect from knocks

silver coating on inside surfaces

vacuum flask

vagaries /ˈveɪɡəriz/ noun [plural] *formal* unexpected changes that you cannot control

vagina /vəˈdʒaɪnə/ noun [C] **ANATOMY** in female mammals, a sex organ consisting of a tube from the opening of the uterus to the outside —*picture* → REPRODUCTION —**vaginal** adj

vagrancy /ˈveɪɡrənsi/ noun [U] **LAW** the crime of living on the street and asking people for money

vagrant /ˈveɪɡrənt/ noun [C] *formal* someone with no home or job who asks people for money

vague /veɪɡ/ adj **1** not clearly or fully explained: *Witnesses gave only a vague description of the driver.* ♦ *the vague promises of politicians* **2** a vague feeling or memory is not complete or definite: *Simon had only the vaguest idea of where she worked.* ♦ *I've got a vague memory of the hotel.* **3** someone who is vague does not clearly or fully explain something: *He was always vague when I asked about deadlines.* ♦ *She was rather vague about the details.* **4** a vague shape is not clear or not easy to see

vaguely /ˈveɪɡli/ adv **1** in a way that is not clear: *He vaguely remembered his mother talking about it.* **2** slightly: *The interview made him look vaguely ridiculous.* **3** in a way that shows that you are not paying attention

vain /veɪn/ adj **1** unsuccessful, or useless: *a vain attempt* **2** *showing disapproval* someone who is vain is very proud and thinks that they are attractive or special

PHRASE in vain without success —**vainly** adv

valency /ˈveɪlənsi/ (plural **valencies**) noun [C] **CHEMISTRY** a measurement of the ability of a chemical element to combine with other elements. The measurement is a number that shows how many atoms of the element combine with a single atom of the element hydrogen. Oxygen, for example, has a valency of 2, as is shown in the chemical formula for water, H_2O.

valentine /'væləntaɪn/ noun [C] **1** a card or present that someone gives to someone else on Valentine's Day, 14 February **2** the person who you give a valentine to

valet parking /ˌvælɪt 'pɑːkɪŋ, ˌvæleɪ 'pɑːkɪŋ/ noun [U] **TOURISM** an arrangement by which a staff member of a restaurant, hotel etc parks customers' cars for them

valet service /'vælɪt ˌsɜːvɪs, 'væleɪ ˌsɜːvɪs/ noun [U] **TOURISM** a service in a hotel for cleaning and pressing clothes

valiant /'væliənt/ adj *formal* very brave and determined —**valiantly** adv

valid /'vælɪd/ adj **1** legally or officially acceptable ≠ INVALID: *a valid claim ♦ You will need a valid passport. ♦ This offer is **valid for** travel before the end of April.* **2** reasonable and generally accepted ≠ INVALID: *a valid argument ♦ These are **valid reasons** why we should ban tobacco advertising.* **3** **COMPUTING** accepted by a computer system ≠ INVALID: *a valid password* —**validity** /və'lɪdəti/ noun [U]

validate /'vælɪdeɪt/ verb [T] *formal* **1** to officially prove that something is true or correct **2** to officially state that something is of a suitable standard —**validation** /ˌvælɪ'deɪʃ(ə)n/ noun [C/U]

valley /'væli/ (plural **valleys**) noun [C] **GEOGRAPHY** a low area of land between two mountains or hills, often with a river flowing through it: *Their house has wonderful views across the valley. ♦ the Thames valley*

valour /'vælə/ noun [U] *formal* the quality of being very brave, especially in war

valuable /'væljʊb(ə)l/ adj **1** worth a lot of money: *a valuable antique ♦ The necklace is not very valuable.* **2** very useful and important: *a valuable lesson ♦ an opportunity to gain valuable experience* **3** valuable time is important because there is not much of it available

valuables /'væljʊb(ə)lz/ noun [plural] small possessions that are worth a lot of money

valuation /ˌvæljʊ'eɪʃ(ə)n/ noun [C/U] a decision about how much money something is worth, or the process of making this decision

value¹ /'væljuː/ noun

1 amount sth is worth	**5** in mathematics
2 importance/usefulness	**6** length of musical
3 interesting quality	note
4 in terms of price	

1 [C/U] the amount that something is worth, measured especially in money: *The value of the painting is not known. ♦ a fall in value ♦ You can't put a value on a human life. ♦ The ring was **of little value**.* → MARKET VALUE
2 [U] the degree to which someone or something is useful or important: *educational value ♦ documents that will be **of great value to** future historians*
3 [U] the particular interesting quality that something has: *Some episodes are included purely for their shock value.*
4 [U] the amount that something is worth compared with the money that it costs: *This wine is excellent value at £4.99 a bottle. ♦ Customers are looking for **value for money**.*
5 [C] **MATHS** a number or amount that is not known and is represented by a letter
6 [C] **MUSIC** the length of time that a musical note lasts for

value² /'væljuː/ verb [T] **1** to believe that someone or something is important: *a valued friend ♦ a community in which people value the knowledge of their elders*

2 to state how much something is worth: *I had the necklace valued. ♦ a contract **valued at** approximately £3 billion* —**valuer** noun [C]

value 'added noun [U] **BUSINESS 1** the amount by which the value of a product increases as it goes through the different stages of production and **distribution** (=being supplied to shops) **2** the difference between the profit of a business before tax is paid and its **expenditure** on goods and services from other businesses

'value ˌchain noun [C] **BUSINESS** the series of activities that a company carries out as it designs, makes, sells, and delivers a product or service, with each activity adding value

values /'væljuːz/ noun [plural] the principles and beliefs that influence the behaviour and way of life of a particular group or community: *Christian values*

valve /vælv/ noun [C] **1** **PHYSICS** the part of a machine or piece of equipment that opens and closes in order to control the flow of air or liquid **2** **MUSIC** the part of some musical instruments that opens and closes to change the sound of the note **3** **ANATOMY** the part of an organ or tube in the body that opens and closes to keep liquid flowing in the right direction, for example in the heart

'valve ˌguide noun [C] **ENGINEERING** a tube of metal in a **cylinder head** that keeps a valve in a vehicle engine moving up and down smoothly

'valve ˌoverlap noun [C] **ENGINEERING** a situation in which the **valves** in a vehicle engine that let fuel and air into a cylinder and out of it are both open at the same time

vampire /'væmpaɪə/ noun [C] **ARTS, LITERATURE** a character in stories and films who appears at night to bite people's necks and suck their blood

van /væn/ noun [C] a vehicle that is used for carrying goods: *a delivery van ♦ We'll have to hire a van to move all this stuff.*

vanadium /və'neɪdiəm/ noun [U] **CHEMISTRY** a toxic silvery-grey metallic element, used in steel alloys. Chemical symbol: **V**

vandal /'vænd(ə)l/ noun [C] someone who deliberately damages or destroys things, especially public property

vandalism /'vændəˌlɪz(ə)m/ noun [U] the act of deliberately damaging or destroying things, especially public property

vandalize /'vændəlaɪz/ verb [T] to deliberately damage or destroy things, especially public property

vane /veɪn/ noun [C] **TECHNOLOGY** a long flat blade designed to be moved by wind or water, especially in order to provide power for a machine

the vanguard /'vænɡɑːd/ noun [singular] the people who introduce and develop new ways of thinking, new technologies etc

vanilla /və'nɪlə/ noun [U] a flavour from the bean of a tropical plant, used in some sweet foods

vanish /'vænɪʃ/ verb [I] **1** to disappear in a sudden or mysterious way: *One moment she was there, the next she had vanished. ♦ The plane circled the airport once, then vanished. ♦ He **vanished into** the darkness. ♦ My calculator's **vanished from** my desk.* **2** to stop existing completely: *another species that has vanished*

vanishing point /'vænɪʃɪŋ ˌpɔɪnt/ noun [C] the point in the distance where two parallel lines seem to become one line —*picture* → PERSPECTIVE

vanity /'vænəti/ noun [U] the quality of being too proud of your abilities, or too interested in your appearance

vantage point /'vɑːntɪdʒ ˌpɔɪnt/ noun [C] **1** a position from which you can see things well **2** the particular ideas or beliefs that influence the way that you think about things

vapour /'veɪpə/ noun [C/U] **SCIENCE** the gas that is produced when a liquid evaporates below its boiling point

variable¹ /'veəriəb(ə)l/ adj capable of being changed, or changing often: *a variable rate of interest* —**variably** adv

variable² /'veəriəb(ə)l/ noun [C] **1 MATHS** a letter representing a number that can change depending on the other numbers in an equation **2 SCIENCE** in a scientific experiment, a **factor** or feature that is allowed to change while others (the **constants**) are kept the same **3** something that can change and affect a situation

variable ˌcost noun [C] **BUSINESS** a cost that a company has to pay that changes according to **output** (=how much of a product it makes)

variance /'veəriəns/ noun [U] *formal* differences between two or more similar things

> **PHRASE** **at variance (with)** *formal* if one thing is at variance with another, they are completely different and seem to oppose each other

variant /'veəriənt/ noun [C] **1** something that is related to another thing but is not exactly the same **2 LANGUAGE** a different form, spelling, or pronunciation of a word

variant CJD noun [U] **HEALTH** variant Creutzfeldt-Jakob Disease: a form of **CJD** (=a serious brain disease) that has recently been recognized and that mainly affects younger people

variation /ˌveəri'eɪʃ(ə)n/ noun **1** [C/U] differences in amount, level etc: *There was **wide variation in** the test scores.* ♦ *variations in temperature* **2** [C] something that is slightly different from similar things: *The dessert is a **variation on** a classic recipe.* **3** [C] **MUSIC** a piece of music that is based on, or is similar to, another piece

varicose veins /ˌværɪkəʊs 'veɪnz/ noun [plural] **HEALTH** a medical condition in which the veins in the legs become swollen and painful

varied /'veərid/ adj including a wide range of things or people

variety /və'raɪəti/ (plural **varieties**) noun **1** [singular] a number of different people or things: *Adults study for **a variety of** reasons.* ♦ *We've interviewed **a wide variety of** people.* **2** [C] a particular type of thing: *different varieties of British cheese* **3** [C] **BIOLOGY** a group of plants that belongs to the same species **4** [U] the fact that something consists of different things: *Consumers are demanding more variety.*

various /'veəriəs/ adj several different: *There are various ways of solving the problem.* ♦ *vehicles of various shapes and sizes*

variously /'veəriəsli/ adv in different ways, by different people, or at different times

varnish /'vɑːnɪʃ/ noun [C/U] a clear sticky liquid that is put onto wood to protect it and make it shiny —**varnish** verb [T]

vary /'veəri/ (**varies, varying, varied**) verb **1** [I] to change according to the situation: *People's reactions to the drug can **vary widely**.* ♦ *Prices **vary according to** the size of the job.* **2** [I] if things vary, they are different from each other: *Rooms **vary in size** but all have a*

television and a telephone. **3** [T] to change something: *The software allows you to vary the size of the print.*

vascular /'væskjʊlə/ adj **1 ANATOMY** relating to the blood vessels in the body **2 BIOLOGY** vascular tissue in plants carries water, **mineral salts**, and food from one part of the plant to another

vascular 'bundle noun [C] **BIOLOGY** the structure inside the stem or root of a plant that consists of the **phloem** and **xylem** —*picture* → ROOT

vas deferens /ˌvæs 'defərənz/ noun [C] **ANATOMY** a thin tube that carries sperm from the testis to the urethra, where they are released

vase /vɑːz, *American* veɪz/ noun [C] a container for cut flowers

vasectomy /və'sektəmi/ (plural **vasectomies**) noun [C] **HEALTH** a medical operation in which the tube that a man's sperm passes through is cut. This makes him unable to have children.

vasoconstriction /ˌveɪzəʊkən'strɪkʃ(ə)n/ noun [U] **BIOLOGY** narrowing of the blood vessels, which reduces the blood flow or increases the blood pressure

vasodilation /ˌveɪzəʊdaɪ'leɪʃ(ə)n/ noun [U] **BIOLOGY** widening of the blood vessels, especially the arteries, which increases the blood flow or reduces the blood pressure

vassal /'væs(ə)l/ noun [C] **SOCIAL STUDIES** someone during the Middle Ages who was loyal to a king who gave them a home and protection

vast /vɑːst/ adj extremely large= HUGE: *I believe **the vast majority of** people* (=almost everyone) *will support us.* ♦ *Our dog eats **a vast amount** of food each day.*

vastly /'vɑːs(t)li/ adv to a great degree: *The hotel has been vastly improved.*

vat /væt/ noun [C] a large container for holding or storing liquids

VAT /ˌviː eɪ 'tiː, væt/ noun [U] **ECONOMICS** value added tax: a tax on goods and services

vault /vɔːlt/ verb [T] to jump over something, especially using your hands or a pole

v-CJD /ˌviː siː dʒeɪ 'diː/ noun [U] **HEALTH** variant CJD

VDR /ˌviː diː 'ɑː/ abbrev **COMPUTING** videodisk recorder: a machine for playing and recording **videodisks**

VDSL /ˌviː diː es 'el/ abbrev **COMPUTING** very-high-data-rate digital subscriber line: a very high-speed **DSL** (=a fast phone connection to the Internet)

VDT /ˌviː diː 'tiː/ noun [C] **COMPUTING** video display terminal: the part of a computer that contains the screen

VDU /ˌviː diː 'juː/ noun [C] **COMPUTING** visual display unit: a computer screen

've /əv/ short form the usual way of saying or writing 'have', added to the end of 'I', 'you', 'we', or 'they' to form the present perfect tense. This is not often used in formal writing: *We've been trying to reach you for days.*

veal /viːl/ noun [U] meat from a young cow

vector /'vektə/ noun [C] **1 PHYSICS, MATHS** a quantity such as velocity that can change and is measured by its size and its direction. It is usually represented by a line with an arrow on it. **2** an insect or other small organism that carries diseases between larger animals, including humans, but is not itself harmed by the disease. Mosquitoes and **ticks** are vectors.

vee engine /'vi: ,endʒɪn/ noun [C] ENGINEERING a vehicle engine that has two **cylinder blocks** arranged in a V shape

veer /vɪə/ verb [I] **1** to suddenly move in a different direction **2** to change in a sudden or noticeable way, for example in opinion or mood

vegan /'vi:gən/ noun [C] someone who chooses not to eat anything made from animals or fish, including eggs, milk, and cheese

vegetable /'vedʒtəb(ə)l/ noun **1** [C] BIOLOGY a part of a plant used as food that is not usually sweet. Potatoes, beans, and **cabbage** are all vegetables: *We grow all our own vegetables.* —*picture* → on next page **2** [C/U] a plant, not an animal or a mineral

vegetarian /ˌvedʒə'teəriən/ noun [C] someone who chooses not to eat meat or fish —**vegetarian** adj, **vegetarianism** noun [U]

vegetate /'vedʒəteɪt/ verb [I] **1** BIOLOGY to start producing leaves or flowers **2** to be lazy or not active

vegetation /ˌvedʒə'teɪʃ(ə)n/ noun [U] *formal* plants

vegetative /'vedʒətətɪv/ adj *formal* relating to plants, or to the growth of plants → PERSISTENT VEGETATIVE STATE

ˌvegetative propaˈgation noun [U] BIOLOGY the process of producing new plants whose genes are the same as the original ones by using **cuttings** (=pieces cut from plants), **grafts** (=pieces of one plant put into a cut in the stem of another plant), bulbs etc instead of seeds

ˌvegetative reproˈduction noun [U] BIOLOGY **vegetative propagation** → SEXUAL REPRODUCTION

vehement /'vi:əmənt/ adj involving extremely strong feelings or beliefs —**vehemence** noun [U], **vehemently** adv

vehicle /'vi:ɪk(ə)l/ noun [C] **1** a machine that you travel in or on, especially one with an engine that travels on roads, for example a car, bus, van, truck, or motorcycle **2** a way of expressing ideas or of making something happen: *He launched the newspaper as a vehicle for his campaign.* **3** a film, television show etc that is created for one actor: *The film was a vehicle for Tom Hanks.*

veil /veɪl/ noun [C] **1** a thin piece of cloth worn over a woman's head or face **2** a layer of something such as rain that prevents you from seeing very far **3** a lack of knowledge or information that prevents you from discovering the truth: *a veil of secrecy*

veiled /veɪld/ adj **1** a veiled threat, attack, or warning is not direct but is easily understood **2** covered with a veil

vein /veɪn/ noun **1** [C] ANATOMY one of the blood vessels in the body that carry blood towards the heart. The blood in nearly all veins, except for the **pulmonary vein**, has a low level of oxygen, as the oxygen has been used in respiration. → ARTERY —*picture* → BLOOD VESSEL, CIRCULATION **2** [C] BIOLOGY one of the tubes that carry substances through a plant —*picture* → LEAF **3** [C] GEOLOGY a thin layer of a metal or other substance inside the Earth **4** [singular] a supply or amount of a particular thing: *a rich vein of talent*

velar /'vi:lə/ adj LANGUAGE velar consonants such as 'k' and 'g' are pronounced with the back of the tongue near the upper back part of the mouth —**velar** noun [C]

Velcro /'velkrəʊ/ TRADEMARK two narrow bands of cloth with special surfaces that stick together, used for fastening clothes, shoes etc

velocity /və'lɒsəti/ (plural **velocities**) noun [C/U] PHYSICS the speed at which something moves in one direction. It is measured by dividing the distance travelled in metres by the time taken in seconds. → ACCELERATION

velodrome /'velə,drəʊm/ noun [C] SPORTS a **racetrack** for bicycles

velvet /'velvɪt/ noun [U] cloth that is very soft on one side and smooth on the other

vena cava /ˌvi:nə 'keɪvə/ (plural **venae cavae** /ˌvi:ni: 'keɪvi:/) noun [C] ANATOMY one of the two large veins that carry blood from the right side of the heart. The **anterior vena cava** brings blood from the upper body and the head, and the **posterior vena cava** brings blood from below the chest. —*picture* → CIRCULATION

venation /vi:'neɪʃ(ə)n/ noun [U] BIOLOGY **1** the pattern formed by the veins in an insect's wing or in a leaf **2** a system of veins in a human or animal

vendetta /ven'detə/ noun [C] a situation in which one person or group keeps trying to harm another, especially because of something that happened in the past

vending machine /'vendɪŋ mə,ʃi:n/ noun [C] a machine that people can buy things from, for example sweets, or drinks

vendor /'vendə/ noun [C] someone who sells something, but not in a shop

veneer /və'nɪə/ noun **1** [C/U] a thin layer of wood or plastic that covers something and improves its appearance **2** [singular] a pleasant appearance or polite way of behaving that is not sincere

vengeance /'vendʒ(ə)ns/ noun [U] the act of harming or killing someone because they have done something bad to you = REVENGE

PHRASE **with a vengeance** used for emphasizing that something happens in an extreme way or with a lot of force

venison /'venɪs(ə)n/ noun [U] meat from a **deer**

Venn diagram /'ven ,daɪəɡræm/ noun [C] MATHS a drawing of circles that go across the edges of each other, showing features shared by different **sets**

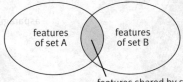

features shared by sets A and B

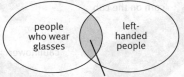

left-handed people who wear glasses

Venn diagrams

venom /'venəm/ noun [U] **1** BIOLOGY poison produced by some animals, especially snakes and insects **2** very strong anger or hate

venomous /'venəməs/ adj **1** BIOLOGY capable of producing poison **2** extremely unpleasant and full of very strong anger or hate

sweet potato

cassava/manioc

beetroot

ginger

potato

radish

carrot

spring onions

shallots

pumpkin

garlic

onion

courgette

tomato

peppers

mushrooms

lettuce

cucumber

lady's finger/ okra

fennel

celery

broccoli

Chinese cabbage/ pak choi

asparagus

Brussels sprouts

corn on the cob

aubergine

cauliflower

peas

cabbage

green beans

kidney beans

vegetables

vent¹ /vent/ verb [T] to express your feelings of anger very strongly

vent² /vent/ noun [C] **1** a hole that allows air, gas, or smoke to escape or fresh air to enter **2** BIOLOGY a small hole in the body of a fish, bird, reptile etc through which waste material or eggs come out **3** GEOLOGY a hole in the Earth's surface through which lava or gas comes out —*picture* → VOLCANO **4** CONSTRUCTION a pipe that releases pressure from a system such as a **drainage** system

ventilate /'ventɪleɪt/ verb [T] to allow fresh air to enter a room or building

ventilation /ˌventɪ'leɪʃ(ə)n/ noun [U] the movement of fresh air around a room or building

ventral fin /ˌventrəl 'fɪn/ noun [C] BIOLOGY the fin under the body of a fish

ventral root /ˌventrəl 'ruːt/ noun [C] BIOLOGY a structure in the **spinal cord** that carries **motor neurons** away from the spinal cord

ventricle /'ventrɪk(ə)l/ noun [C] ANATOMY one of the two lower parts of the heart that pumps blood to the rest of the body —*picture* → CIRCULATION

venture¹ /'ventʃə/ noun [C] a new business or activity

venture² /'ventʃə/ verb **1** [I] to go somewhere unpleasant, dangerous, or exciting **2** [I] to do something that is a risk **3** [T] to be brave enough to say something

'venture ˌcapital noun [U] BUSINESS money invested in a new business that has a high risk of being lost, but which may make a very large profit

venturi /ven'tjʊri/ noun [C] ENGINEERING a specially shaped tube for taking air into a **carburettor** that produces a drop in pressure. This sucks in drops of fuel, which mix with the air.

venue /'venjuː/ noun [C] the place where an activity or event happens

Venus /'viːnəs/ ASTRONOMY the planet that is second furthest from the Sun, between Mercury and Earth —*picture* → SOLAR SYSTEM

Venus flytrap /ˌviːnəs 'flaɪtræp/ noun [C] a plant with leaves that open and close to catch insects

veranda or **verandah** /və'rændə/ noun [C] a covered area along the outside of a house

verb /vɜːb/ noun [C] LANGUAGE a word that shows someone doing or being something, for example 'run' or 'remain'. **Transitive** verbs have an **object**, for example 'hit' and 'admire'. **Intransitive** verbs do not have an object, for example 'rise' and 'die'. Transitive verbs are marked [T] in this dictionary, and intransitive verbs are marked [I]. The basic form of a verb, for example 'to be', 'to see', or 'to sink' is called the **infinitive**.

verbal /'vɜːb(ə)l/ adj **1** using words, or relating to words: *verbal communication* **2** LANGUAGE acting as a verb, or relating to a verb **3** using spoken communication rather than writing: *a verbal agreement* **4** using words, not physical force: *verbal abuse* —**verbally** adv

ˌverbal 'noun noun [C] LANGUAGE a noun that is formed from a verb and ends in '-ing', for example 'swimming' in the sentence 'Swimming is my favourite sport'= GERUND

verbatim /vɜː'beɪtɪm/ adj, adv repeating the exact words that were used

verbose /vɜː'bəʊs/ adj *formal* using more words than necessary, and therefore long and boring —**verbosity** /vɜː'bɒsəti/ noun [U]

verdict /'vɜːdɪkt/ noun [C] **1** LAW an official judgment made in a court: *a verdict of accidental death* ♦ *The jury took 16 hours to reach a verdict.* **2** an opinion that you have or a decision that you make: *What's your verdict on the film?*

verge /vɜːdʒ/ noun **1** [C] a border along the side of a road, often covered with grass **2** CONSTRUCTION the edge of a roof that sticks out beyond a **gable** PHRASE **on the verge of sth** about to do something: *The two countries were on the verge of war.*

verify /'verɪfaɪ/ (**verifies**, **verifying**, **verified**) verb [T] *formal* to check or prove that something is true or correct —**verification** /ˌverɪfɪ'keɪʃ(ə)n/ noun [U]

vermin /'vɜːmɪn/ noun [plural] small animals or insects that cause damage or disease

vernier calliper /'vɜːniə ˌkælɪpə/ noun [C] TECHNOLOGY a tool that is used for taking very accurate measurements. It consists of a fixed and a moving scale, and a fixed and a moving **jaw** (=part that holds an object tightly).

vernier scale /'vɜːniə ˌskeɪl/ noun [C] TECHNOLOGY the moving scale on a vernier calliper

versa see **vice versa**

versatile /'vɜːsətaɪl/ adj **1** able to be used in many different ways: *a versatile summer jacket* **2** having a wide range of different skills and abilities: *a versatile actor* —**versatility** /ˌvɜːsə'tɪləti/ noun [U]

verse /vɜːs/ noun **1** [C] LITERATURE, MUSIC a group of words or sentences that form one section of a poem or song **2** [U] LITERATURE *formal* poetry **3** [C] RELIGION a small group of words or sentences in the Bible that has a number next to it

version /'vɜːʃ(ə)n/ noun [C] **1** a form of something that is different from other forms or from the original: *The software comes in several different versions.* ♦ *The latest version of the film is more like the book.* **2** a description of something that happened, according to one person: *I want to hear his version of the story now.*

versus /'vɜːsəs/ preposition **1** used for showing that two people, groups, or teams are competing against each other: *A huge crowd came to watch Manchester United versus Liverpool.* **2** used for saying that two things are being compared: *the grades of male versus female students at the university*

vertebra /'vɜːtəbrə/ (plural **vertebrae** /'vɜːtəbreɪ/) noun [C] ANATOMY one of the small bones that form a row down the centre of the back —*picture* → SKELETON and on next page

vertebral column /ˌvɜːtəbrəl 'kɒləm/ noun [C] ANATOMY the **spinal column** —*picture* → SKELETON, SPINAL CORD

vertebrarterial /ˌvɜːtebrɑː'tɪəriəl/ adj ANATOMY relating to a vertebra and an artery

vertebrate /'vɜːtɪbrət/ noun [C] BIOLOGY an animal with a backbone, for example a mammal, a bird, or a fish. Vertebrates form one of the main groups that the animal **kingdom** is divided into ≠ INVERTEBRATE —**vertebrate** adj

vertex /'vɜːteks/ (plural **vertexes** or **vertices** /'vɜːtɪsiːz/) noun [C] MATHS **1** the point where two lines join at an angle **2** the point that is opposite the base of a triangle

vertical¹ /'vɜːtɪk(ə)l/ adj standing, pointing, or moving straight up: *vertical lines* ♦ *The cliff face is almost vertical.* —**vertically** /'vɜːtɪkli/ adv

vertical² /'vɜːtɪk(ə)l/ noun [C] MATHS a vertical line or position, for example the vertical axis on a graph

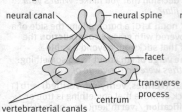

cervical vertebra
(has two small holes apart from
the large neural canal)

neural canal — neural spine

facet

transverse
process

vertebrarterial canals
(two small holes in vertebra, one on either side)

centrum

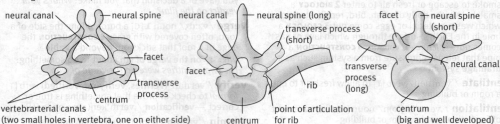

thoracic vertebra
(articulate with ribs as well
as other vertebrae)

neural canal — neural spine (long)

transverse process
(short)

facet

centrum

rib

point of articulation
for rib

lumbar vertebra
(has large centrum and long
transverse processes)

facet — neural spine
(short)

transverse
process
(long)

neural canal

centrum
(big and well developed)

sections of the vertebra

,vertical 'axis noun [singular] MATHS the **y-axis** in a
system of coordinates

,vertical inte'gration noun [U] BUSINESS the process
by which a single company takes control of another
business, so that it handles more or all of the stages of
producing and selling a product

'vertical ,plane noun [C] MATHS, PHYSICS a plane
(=flat surface) in **orthographic projection** that is
vertical

vertical shifting /,vɜːtɪk(ə)l 'ʃɪftɪŋ/ noun [U]
GEOLOGY an upward movement of the Earth's surface

vertical welding /,vɜːtɪk(ə)l 'weldɪŋ/ noun [U]
TECHNOLOGY a technique in **electric arc welding** in
which the direction of the weld is approximately vertical

vertices /'vɜːtɪsiːz/ a plural of **vertex**

very /'veri/ adj, adv **1** used for emphasizing that a
quality exists or is true to a great degree: *The building
looks very old.* ♦ *The traffic was moving very slowly.* ♦ *It
was a very good film.* ♦ *Thank you very much.* **2** used
for emphasizing a noun, especially a place or time that
is at the top, bottom, or end of something: *The bird
was sitting at the very top of the tree.* ♦ *We worked till
the very end of the day.*

    PHRASE **not very** used before adjectives and adverbs
for saying that something is only slightly true, or that
it is not true at all: *Victor's suggestions were not very
helpful.*

vesicle /'vesɪk(ə)l/ noun [C] **1** ANATOMY a small **sac**
(=small bag) in the body, especially one containing
fluid **2** BIOLOGY a very small swelling filled with clear
fluid= BLISTER **3** BIOLOGY a space filled with air inside
a **seaweed** or water plant

vessel /'ves(ə)l/ noun [C] **1** BIOLOGY a tube in people,
animals, or plants through which liquid flows **2** *formal*
a large boat or ship

vest /vest/ noun [C] a piece of underwear for the top
half of the body

vested interest /,vestɪd 'ɪntrəst/ noun [singular] a
special reason for wanting things to happen in a
particular way, because you will benefit from this

vestibular apparatus /ve'stɪbjʊlə ,æpəreɪtəs/ noun
[C] ANATOMY three **semicircular canals** filled with
fluid in the **inner ear** that are important for balance

vestibule /'vestɪ,bjuːl/ noun [C] **1** *formal* a room
between the outside door and the main part of a
building **2** ANATOMY the middle part of the **inner ear**,
between the **cochlea** and the **semicircular canals** —
picture → EAR

vestige /'vestɪdʒ/ noun [C] *formal* a very small sign
that remains when something has almost disappeared
= TRACE

vestigial /ves'tɪdʒiəl/ adj *formal* remaining after
almost all of something has disappeared

vestment /'vestmənt/ noun [C] RELIGION a **robe**
worn by a priest, or a piece of clothing worn with it

vet¹ /vet/ (**vets, vetting, vetted**) verb [T] **1** to check
someone's character or reputation in order to find out
whether they are suitable for a particular job= SCREEN
2 to examine something in order to decide if it is
allowed

vet² /vet/ noun [C] a doctor for animals

veteran /'vet(ə)rən/ noun [C] **1** someone who was in
the armed forces, especially during a war **2** someone
who has a lot of experience of doing a particular
activity: *jazz veteran Dave Brubeck*

veterinarian /,vet(ə)rɪ'neəriən/ noun [C] *American* a
vet (=animal doctor)

veterinary /'vet(ə)nri, 'vet(ə)rənəri/ adj relating to
the care of animals that are ill or injured

'veterinary ,surgeon noun [C] *formal* a **vet**

veto¹ /'viːtəʊ/ (**vetoes, vetoing, vetoed**) verb [T] to
officially refuse to approve or allow something

veto² /'viːtəʊ/ (plural **vetoes**) noun [C/U] an official
refusal to approve or allow something

vexed /vekst/ adj full of difficulties= PROBLEMATIC

VGA /,viː dʒiː 'eɪ/ abbrev COMPUTING video graphics
array: a standard system for showing pictures and
videos on computer screens

VHF /,viː eɪtʃ 'ef/ noun [U] PHYSICS very high
frequency: a range of radio waves that produces good
sound quality

VHS /,viː eɪtʃ 'es/ noun [U] video home system: a
system for recording television programmes at home

via /'vaɪə, 'viːə/ preposition **1** going through one place
on the way to another place: *They flew from New York
to New Delhi via Frankfurt.* **2** using a particular method
or person to send or deliver something: *News reports
are broadcast via satellite.*

viable /'vaɪəb(ə)l/ adj **1** able to be done, or worth doing
2 BIOLOGY able to live and grow in an independent
way —**viability** /,vaɪə'bɪləti/ noun [U]

viaduct /'vaɪə,dʌkt/ noun [C] a long bridge on high
posts, usually across a valley

vibrant /'vaɪbrənt/ adj **1** lively and exciting **2** bright
and colourful —**vibrancy** /'vaɪbrənsi/ noun [U],
vibrantly adv

vibraphone /'vaɪbrə,fəʊn/ noun [C] MUSIC an
electronic musical instrument with metal bars that you
hit with small hammers

vibrate /vaɪ'breɪt/ verb [I] to shake very quickly with small movements

vibration /vaɪ'breɪʃ(ə)n/ noun [C/U] **PHYSICS** a small, fast, backward and forward movement such as that which sets up a sound wave

vibrato /vɪ'brɑːtəʊ/ noun [C/U] **MUSIC** a shaking effect on a musical note

vibrator /vaɪ'breɪtə/ noun [C] **MUSIC** a pedal on some musical instruments that gives an effect of sound going on and off

vicar /'vɪkə/ noun [C] **RELIGION** a priest in the Church of England or the US **Episcopal Church**

vice /vaɪs/ noun **1** [C] a bad habit or personal quality ≠ VIRTUE **2** [U] crimes relating to sex **3** [C] a tool that holds an object firmly while you are working with it —*picture* → TOOL

vice-'president noun [C] **POLITICS** a politician who is next in rank to the president

viceroy /'vaɪs,rɔɪ/ noun [C] **POLITICS** someone chosen by a king or queen to rule another country

vice versa /,vaɪsi 'vɜːsə, ,vaɪs 'vɜːsə/ adv the opposite of what has been said: *Should I come to your house or vice versa?*

vicinity /və'sɪnəti/ noun [singular] *formal* the area near a particular place: *a university **in the vicinity of** London*

vicious /'vɪʃəs/ adj **1** extremely violent: *a vicious attack* **2** extremely unkind or unpleasant: *He had a vicious temper.* —**viciously** adv

vicious 'circle or **vicious 'cycle** noun [singular] a process in which the existence of a problem causes other problems, and this makes the original problem worse

victim /'vɪktɪm/ noun [C] **1** someone who has been harmed or killed as the result of a crime: *a murder victim* ♦ *victims of violence* **2** someone who has been affected by something such as an accident or illness: *an earthquake victim* ♦ *She **fell victim to** a rare disease.* **3** someone who has suffered as a result of the actions or attitudes of other people: *victims of discrimination*

victimize /'vɪktɪmaɪz/ verb [T] to treat someone in a deliberately unfair way —**victimization** /,vɪktɪmaɪ'zeɪʃ(ə)n/ noun [U]

victor /'vɪktə/ noun [C] *formal* the winner of a competition or battle

Victorian¹ /vɪk'tɔːriən/ adj **SOCIAL STUDIES** relating to the period from 1837 to 1901, when Queen Victoria was queen in the UK

Victorian² /vɪk'tɔːriən/ noun [C] **SOCIAL STUDIES** someone who lived during the Victorian period

victorious /vɪk'tɔːriəs/ adj having won a competition or battle

victory /'vɪkt(ə)ri/ (plural **victories**) noun **1** [C/U] the fact of winning a competition or battle, or an occasion when someone wins ≠ DEFEAT: *a decisive election victory for the Labour Party* ♦ *Spain's 3–2 victory over Russia in last night's game* **2** [C] a situation in which someone's principles or goals become officially accepted: *The judge's ruling has been hailed as a victory for freedom of speech.*

video¹ /'vɪdiəʊ/ (plural **videos**) noun **1** [C/U] a film or television programme recorded onto **videotape**: *The film will soon be available **on video**.* ♦ *We stayed in and watched a video.* ♦ *They **made a video** of the wedding.* **2** [U] the activity of making films using **videotape 3** [C] a **video recorder**

video² /'vɪdiəʊ/ (**videos, videoing, videoed**) verb [T] **1** to record a television programme onto **videotape 2** to film an event using a video camera

'video a,dapter noun [C] **COMPUTING** the part inside a computer that changes information into images

'video ,camera noun [C] a piece of equipment that you use for recording something onto **videotape**

'video ,card noun [C] **COMPUTING** a **video adapter**

'video ,clip noun [C] **COMPUTING** a short video recording that can be used on a website

videoconference /'vɪdiəʊ,kɒnf(ə)rəns/ noun [C] a meeting in which people in different places see and hear each other using electronic equipment, including video screens

videoconferencing /'vɪdiəʊ,kɒnf(ə)rənsɪŋ/ noun [U] the activity of having meetings at which people in different places can see and hear each other because they are connected by electronic equipment

videodisk /'vɪdiəʊ,dɪsk/ noun [C] **COMPUTING** a computer disk that can store **full-motion video**

videofilm /'vɪdiəʊ,fɪlm/ noun [C] a film or television programme recorded on **videotape**

'video ,game noun [C] **COMPUTING** a game in which players use electronic controls to move images on a television or computer screen

videographer /,vɪdi'ɒɡrəfə/ noun [C] someone who makes videos, especially as their job

'video re,corder noun [C] a piece of equipment that you use for watching videos or recording television programmes

videotape /'vɪdiəʊ,teɪp/ noun [C/U] a thin band of film in a plastic case, used mainly for recording television programmes

vie /vaɪ/ (**vies, vying, vied**) verb [I] *formal* to compete with other people for something that is difficult to get

the Vietnam War /vi,etnæm 'wɔː/ **SOCIAL STUDIES** a war between North and South Vietnam from 1954 to 1975, in which the US supported South Vietnam

view¹ /vjuː/ noun **1** [C] your personal opinion about something: *It's our view that women should get paid the same as men.* ♦ *What are your **views on** the election?* ♦ *He has strong **views about** global warming.* **2** [C/U] the things that you can see from a particular place: *We had a spectacular **view of** the mountains from our room.* ♦ *The showers were **in full view of** (=easily seen by) everyone in the pool.* ♦ *The castle **came into view** (=became able to be seen) as we turned the corner.* **3** [C] **ARTS** a picture or photograph of a place, especially an attractive place

PHRASES in view of sth because of something: *In view of the shortage of time, each person may only speak for five minutes.*
with a view to (doing) sth with the hope of doing something in the future

view² /vjuː/ verb [T] **1** to have a particular opinion or attitude towards something = REGARD: *The Internet is viewed by many **as** a revolutionary educational tool.* ♦ *These results must be **viewed with** caution.* **2** to look at or watch something: ***Viewed from** the road, the wall looked too high to climb.* **3** **COMPUTING** to look at information on a computer screen: *To view the next page, press 'tab'.*

viewdata /'vjuː,deɪtə/ noun [U] **COMPUTING** a type of computer technology that allows you to look at information from a computer on a television screen = VIDEOTEXT

viewer /'vjuːə/ noun [C] someone who is watching, or who watches, television programmes

viewfinder /'vjuː,faɪndə/ noun [C] a small window in a camera, used for seeing exactly what you are photographing or recording —*picture* → CAMERA

viewing /'vjuːɪŋ/ noun [C/U] **1** the activity of watching a television programme or film, or an occasion when someone does this **2** the activity of looking at something, or an occasion when someone does this

viewpoint /'vjuːpɔɪnt/ noun [C] **1** an opinion that you have about something **2** a place from which you can see or watch something

viewscreen /'vjuːskriːn/ noun [C] the screen on a **digital** camera on which you can see the image that you have just recorded

vigil /'vɪdʒɪl/ noun [C] a period of time when you stay quietly in a place, for example as a protest or when you are looking after someone who is ill

vigilant /'vɪdʒɪlənt/ adj *formal* watching a person or situation very carefully so that you will notice any problems immediately —**vigilance** noun [U]

vigilante /,vɪdʒɪ'lænti/ noun [C] someone who tries to catch and punish criminals by themselves, without waiting for the police

vignette /vɪn'jet/ noun [C] ARTS, LITERATURE a short but interesting piece of writing or section of a film

vigorous /'vɪg(ə)rəs/ adj **1** full of energy, enthusiasm, and determination: *a vigorous debate* **2** strong and healthy: *a vigorous young man* —**vigorously** adv

vigour /'vɪgə/ noun [U] energy, enthusiasm, and determination

vile /vaɪl/ adj extremely unpleasant = HORRIBLE

vilify /'vɪlɪfaɪ/ (**vilifies, vilifying, vilified**) verb [T] *formal* to criticize someone very strongly, especially in a way that is not fair —**vilification** /,vɪlɪfɪ'keɪʃ(ə)n/ noun [U]

villa /'vɪlə/ noun [C] a large house, especially one used for holidays

village /'vɪlɪdʒ/ noun [C] a very small town in the countryside: *a Scottish fishing village ♦ the village shop* → CITY

villager /'vɪlɪdʒə/ noun [C] someone who lives in a village

villain /'vɪlən/ noun [C] **1** a bad character in a story, play, film etc ≠ HERO **2** an evil person or criminal

villus /'vɪlʌs/ (plural **villi** /'vɪlaɪ/) noun [C] **1** ANATOMY one of a large number of small parts that stick out from the inner wall of the **small intestine**. They increase the amount of surface that is available for the absorption of food substances. **2** BIOLOGY a part like a hair that grows on a plant

vindicate /'vɪndɪkeɪt/ verb [T] to prove that someone is right, especially when most people believed that they were wrong —**vindication** /,vɪndɪ'keɪʃ(ə)n/ noun [C/U]

vindictive /vɪn'dɪktɪv/ adj someone who is vindictive will not forgive a person who has hurt them, and tries to hurt them back —**vindictiveness** noun [U]

vine /vaɪn/ noun [C] BIOLOGY a long climbing stem such as the plant on which grapes grow = GRAPEVINE

vinegar /'vɪnɪgə/ noun [U] a sour liquid that is used for adding flavour to food

vineyard /'vɪnjəd/ noun [C] AGRICULTURE a piece of land where grapes are grown and wine is produced

vintage car /,vɪntɪdʒ 'kɑː/ noun [C] an old car, especially one that was built between 1919 and 1930

vinyl /'vaɪn(ə)l/ noun [U] **1** CHEMISTRY a light strong plastic **2** MUSIC records, used for listening to music before CDs were invented

viola /vi'əʊlə/ noun [C] MUSIC a musical instrument that is like a large **violin** —*picture* → MUSICAL INSTRUMENT, ORCHESTRA

violate /'vaɪəleɪt/ verb [T] **1** to break a law, agreement etc **2** to enter an area or place without permission **3** to treat a holy place with no respect —**violator** noun [C]

violation /,vaɪə'leɪʃ(ə)n/ noun [C/U] an action that breaks a law, agreement etc

violence /'vaɪələns/ noun [U] **1** violent behaviour: *acts of violence ♦ Violence against women must stop.* **2** a strong force that something has, often one that causes a lot of damage: *the violence of the storm*

violent /'vaɪələnt/ adj **1** using physical force to cause harm or damage, or involving people who use physical force in this way: *a violent film ♦ a fall in violent crime ♦ He gets violent when he's been drinking.* **2** a violent wind, storm, or explosion happens with a lot of force and causes serious damage **3** painful and difficult to control: *a violent coughing fit* **4** involving very strong and angry emotions or opinions: *a violent argument* —**violently** adv

violet[1] /'vaɪələt/ noun **1** [C] a small plant with purple flowers and a sweet smell **2** [U] a blue-purple colour

violet[2] /'vaɪələt/ adj blue-purple in colour

violin /,vaɪə'lɪn/ noun [C] MUSIC a musical instrument that you hold under your chin and play by pulling a long object called a **bow** across its strings —*picture* → MUSICAL INSTRUMENT, ORCHESTRA —**violinist** noun [C]

VIP /,viː aɪ 'piː/ noun [C] very important person: someone who receives special treatment because they are powerful or famous

viper /'vaɪpə/ noun [C] a poisonous snake

viral[1] /'vaɪrəl/ adj **1** HEALTH caused by or relating to a virus **2** COMPUTING produced by or relating to a computer virus

viral[2] /'vaɪrəl/ noun [C] COMPUTING something such as a joke, a short film, or an advertisement that is funny or entertaining and is passed around among people using the Internet

viral 'load noun [C] HEALTH the amount of a virus that someone has in their blood

viral 'marketing noun [U] BUSINESS a type of marketing in which an organization's customers advertise a product simply by talking to other people about it, or by sending them emails about it

virgin /'vɜːdʒɪn/ noun [C] someone who has never had sex

virginity /və'dʒɪnəti/ noun [singular] the state of being a virgin

Virgo /'vɜːgəʊ/ (plural **Virgos**) noun [C/U] one of the 12 signs of the zodiac. A **Virgo** is someone who was born between 22 August and 22 September.

virile /'vɪraɪl/ adj a man who is virile is strong, active, and full of sexual energy

virility /və'rɪləti/ noun [U] the quality of being strong, active, and full of sexual energy that is considered typical of a man

virology /vaɪ'rɒlədʒi/ noun [U] HEALTH the treatment and study of illnesses caused by viruses

virtual /'vɜːtʃʊəl/ adj **1** very close to a particular condition, quality etc: *Over the years they had become*

virtual strangers. ✦ *It's a virtual impossibility.*
2 COMPUTING created or shown by computers, or existing on computers or on the Internet: *a virtual community*

,virtual 'image noun [C] **PHYSICS** an image that is formed by light rays from an object passing through a concave lens. The image has no real existence.

virtually /'vɜːtʃʊəli/ adv used for emphasizing that a statement is almost completely true= ALMOST: *It's virtually impossible to get him to eat vegetables.*

,virtual 'memory noun [U] **COMPUTING** space on a computer's hard drive that the software can use as a temporary place to store information

,virtual re'ality noun [U] **COMPUTING** images and sounds that are produced by a computer in a way that makes the user feel as if they are real

virtue /'vɜːtʃuː/ noun **1** [C] a good quality that someone has, especially a moral one ≠ VICE: *Patience is not one of my virtues.* **2** [U] *formal* a way of behaving in which you do what is morally good and right, and avoid doing things that are morally wrong **3** [C] an advantage or good feature that something has= MERIT: *The plan had the virtue of simplicity.*
PHRASE **by virtue of sth** because of something, or as a result of something: *I got this house by virtue of my job.*

virtuoso /,vɜːtʃu'əʊsəʊ/ (plural **virtuosos**) noun [C] **MUSIC** someone who is very good at playing a musical instrument

virtuous /'vɜːtʃʊəs/ adj behaving in a way that is morally good and right —**virtuously** adv

virulent /'vɪrʊlənt/ adj **HEALTH** a virulent illness is very dangerous and affects people very quickly —**virulence** noun [U], **virulently** adv

virus /'vaɪrəs/ noun [C] **1 BIOLOGY, HEALTH** a microorganism that is only able to exist and reproduce within a cell of another living thing. It is a parasite and is often the cause of serious diseases. For example, HIV is the virus that causes AIDS. → BACTERIA **2 HEALTH** an illness caused by a virus: *She caught some kind of virus at school.* **3 COMPUTING** a program that enters a computer and damages or destroys information that is stored on it: *Most viruses are spread over the Internet.*

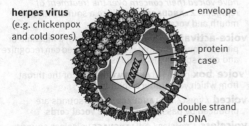

herpes virus
(e.g. chickenpox
and cold sores)

envelope

protein case

double strand
of DNA

'virus ,checker noun [C] **COMPUTING** software that finds and removes computer viruses from a computer

visa /'viːzə/ noun [C] an official document or mark in your passport that allows you to enter or leave a country

vis-à-vis /,viːz ə 'viː/ preposition *formal* compared with, or relating to someone or something

visceral muscle /'vɪsərəl ,mʌs(ə)l/ noun [C] **ANATOMY** the type of muscle in internal organs such as the intestines

viscosity /vɪs'kɒsəti/ noun [C/U] **ENGINEERING** the tendency of a fluid to **resist** flowing

viscous /'vɪskəs/ adj a viscous liquid is thick and sticky

visibility /,vɪzə'bɪləti/ noun [U] **1** the distance that you can see, depending on conditions such as the weather **2** a situation in which someone or something can be clearly seen or noticed

visible /'vɪzəb(ə)l/ adj **1** able to be seen: *The house is visible from the road.* **2** clear or obvious: *There has been a visible improvement in your work.*

the ,visible 'spectrum noun **PHYSICS** the seven colours that make up white light. It can be seen when white light passes through something such as drops of water or a diamond.

visibly /'vɪzəbli/ adv in a way that is easy to see or notice

vision /'vɪʒ(ə)n/ noun **1** [U] the ability to think about and plan for the future, using your intelligence and imagination: *Tackling these challenges will require real vision.* **2** [C] someone's idea of how something should be done, or of how it will be in the future: *The speech gives her vision of the country's economic future.* **3** [U] the ability to see= SIGHT: *He suffers from blurred vision and headaches.* **4** [C] **RELIGION** something that someone sees in a dream or as a religious experience

'vision ,statement noun [C] **BUSINESS** a general statement of what an organization aims or hopes to achieve in the future

visit¹ /'vɪzɪt/ verb **1** [I/T] to go and see someone and spend some time with them: *I visit my family every year at Christmas.* ✦ *We only use this room when friends come to visit.* **2** [T] to go to a place for a short period of time: *Have you visited Venezuela before?* **3** [T] **COMPUTING** to look at a particular page on the Internet: *For more information, visit our website.*

visit² /'vɪzɪt/ noun [C] **1** an occasion when you visit a person or place: *I've just come over on a visit.* ✦ *What did you see on your visit to India?* ✦ *I was surprised to receive a visit from an old friend.* ✦ *It's been a long time since I've paid my Gran a visit.* **2** an occasion when an important person such as a political leader visits a place: *The president arrived in Taiwan today for a three-day visit.* **3 COMPUTING** an occasion when someone looks at a particular page on the Internet

visitor /'vɪzɪtə/ noun [C] **1** someone who visits a person or place: *Did you have any visitors today?* ✦ *Visitors to the museum will notice many improvements.* **2 COMPUTING** someone who looks at a particular page on the Internet: *Visitors to our website can purchase books online.*

'visitor ,centre noun [C] **TOURISM** a building that gives information and services to people visiting a place such as a historical building

visking tubing /'vɪskɪŋ ,tjuːbɪŋ/ noun [U] **SCIENCE** an artificial substance that can be used as a membrane in laboratory experiments

visor /'vaɪzə/ noun [C] **1** a piece of clear plastic on the front of a **helmet** (=hard hat) that protects your face —*picture* → ASTRONAUT **2** a curved piece of plastic or other material on a band that you wear on your head to protect your eyes from the sun **3** a flat object at the top of the front window of a car that you pull down to protect your eyes from the sun

visual /'vɪʒʊəl/ adj **1** relating to things that you can see: *the visual arts* **2** relating to sight: *a visual impairment* —**visually** adv

,visual 'aid noun [C] **EDUCATION** a drawing, map, film etc that people can look at when they are learning about a particular subject

visual 'arts noun [plural] **ARTS** types of art in which you make something for people to look at, for example painting, drawing, and photography → PERFORMING ARTS

visualize /'vɪʒʊəlaɪz/ verb [T] to form a picture of someone or something in the mind —**visualization** /ˌvɪʒʊəlaɪˈzeɪʃ(ə)n/ noun [U]

vital /'vaɪt(ə)l/ adj **1** very important, or necessary = ESSENTIAL: *Skilful employees are **vital to** the success of any company.* ♦ *He played a **vital role in** setting up the organization.* **2** full of energy and life: *He was young, vital, and handsome.* **3** necessary to keep you alive: *vital organs*

vital ca'pacity noun [C/U] **BIOLOGY** the amount of air that moves through the lungs when someone breathes in and out as hard as they can

vitality /vaɪˈtæləti/ noun [U] **1** energy, or enthusiasm **2** the quality of being exciting or successful

vitally /'vaɪt(ə)li/ adv used for emphasizing that something is very important or necessary: *It is vitally important that we find him.*

vital 'signs noun [plural] **HEALTH** the signs that show a person is alive, for example their breathing or their **heartbeat**

vitamin /'vɪtəmɪn/ noun [C] **HEALTH** a natural substance in food that is necessary for good health

vitamin 'A noun [U] **HEALTH** a vitamin found in some vegetables, fish, milk, and eggs that is important for sight, the skin, and the growth of tissue. A lack of vitamin A causes blindness.

vitamin 'B noun [U] **HEALTH** any one of a group of vitamins found especially in cereal grains, liver, and yeast that is important for growth, for the blood, and for the nerves

vitamin 'C noun [U] **HEALTH** a vitamin found especially in **citrus fruits** and vegetables with green leaves that is important for the skin, teeth, bones, and blood. A lack of vitamin C causes **scurvy** = ASCORBIC ACID

vitamin 'D noun [U] **HEALTH** a vitamin found in fish and eggs that is important for bones and teeth. Vitamin D is also produced by the action of sunlight on the skin. A lack of vitamin D causes **rickets**.

viticulture /'vɪtɪˌkʌltʃə/ noun [U] **AGRICULTURE** the activity or science of growing grapes, especially for making wine

vitreous humour /ˌvɪtriəs 'hjuːmə/ noun [U] **ANATOMY** the liquid that fills the large space inside the eyeball between the lens and the retina —*picture* → EYE, RETINA

vitrified clay /'vɪtrɪfaɪd ˌkleɪ/ noun [U] **CONSTRUCTION** clay that has been baked at a very high temperature to make it **waterproof**

vitro *see* **in vitro**

vivid /'vɪvɪd/ adj **1** very clear and detailed: *a vivid description* **2** a vivid example of something shows very clearly that something exists or is true **3** a vivid colour is strong and bright —**vividly** adv, **vividness** noun [U]

vivisection /ˌvɪvɪˈsekʃ(ə)n/ noun [U] **SCIENCE** the practice of performing operations on living animals for scientific experiments

viz. /vɪz/ abbrev *formal* used, especially in writing, for giving more specific information about something that has just been mentioned

vocabulary /vəˈkæbjʊləri/ (plural **vocabularies**) noun [C/U] **LANGUAGE** all the words that someone knows, or all the words in a particular language, a

particular book etc: *exercises designed to increase your vocabulary*

vocal /'vəʊk(ə)l/ adj **1** **MUSIC** relating to the voice, or done with the voice **2** a vocal group of people express their opinions strongly with the result that people in authority notice them —**vocally** adv

'vocal ˌcords noun [plural] **ANATOMY** the very thin threads of tissue inside the throat that vibrate to make sounds —*picture* → LUNG

vocalic /vəʊˈkælɪk/ adj **LANGUAGE** relating to vowels, or consisting of a vowel

vocalist /'vəʊkəlɪst/ noun [C] **MUSIC** a singer, especially one who sings popular music

vocation /vəʊˈkeɪʃ(ə)n/ noun [C] a job that you do because you feel that it is your purpose in life and that you have special skills for doing it

vocational /vəʊˈkeɪʃ(ə)nəl/ adj relating to the skills that you need for a particular job: *a vocational course* —**vocationally** adv

vocative /'vɒkətɪv/ noun [C] **LANGUAGE** in some languages, the form of a noun that is used for showing that a particular person or thing is being spoken to

vociferous /vəʊˈsɪfərəs/ adj *formal* expressing opinions loudly and with force —**vociferously** adv

vodka /'vɒdkə/ noun [C/U] a strong clear alcoholic drink, or a glass of this drink

voice¹ /vɔɪs/ noun **1** [C/U] the sounds that someone makes when they speak, or the way that someone speaks: *We could hear voices in the next apartment.* ♦ *The woman at the desk greeted him **in a** bored **voice**.* ♦ *The children were very well-behaved, and I never had to **raise my voice** (=speak louder or shout).* ♦ *She started screaming **at the top of her voice** (=very loudly).* **2** [singular] the right or opportunity to express your opinions or feelings and influence what happens **3** [singular] a person, organization etc that represents a particular type of opinion or group of people: *Carter is **the voice of** the black minority in this area.* ♦ *the voice of reason* **4** [singular] **LANGUAGE** the form of a verb that shows whether the subject of the verb does the action (**the active voice**) or whether the action is done to it (**the passive voice**) → RAISE

voice² /vɔɪs/ verb [T] **1** *formal* to express your opinions or feelings about something: *Human rights groups have **voiced their concern** over the treatment of refugees.* **2** **LANGUAGE** to produce a sound with the mouth and **vocal cords**

voice-activated /'vɔɪsˌæktɪveɪtɪd/ adj a machine or piece of equipment that is voice-activated can recognize and obey spoken instructions

'voice ˌbox noun [C] **ANATOMY** the part of the throat from which you produce sounds

voiced /vɔɪst/ adj **LANGUAGE** voiced sounds are produced by passing air over the **vocal cords**

voiceless /'vɔɪsləs/ adj **LANGUAGE** voiceless sounds are produced without passing air over the **vocal cords**

voicemail /'vɔɪsmeɪl/ noun [U] an electronic system that records and stores phone messages

'voice recogˌnition noun [U] **COMPUTING** the ability of a computer to know the voice of a person speaking into it, so that only voices that the computer knows can use the system

void¹ /vɔɪd/ noun [singular] *formal* **1** a situation in which someone or something that is important to you is no longer there **2** an extremely large empty space

void² /vɔɪd/ adj **LAW** no longer legal or effective → NULL

void[3] /vɔɪd/ verb [T] **LAW** to make something no longer legal or effective

VoIP /vɔɪp/ noun [U] **COMPUTING** voice over Internet protocol: a technology that allows voice messages to be sent over the Internet

volatile /ˈvɒlətaɪl/ adj **1** a volatile situation can suddenly change or become more dangerous **2 CHEMISTRY** a volatile liquid or solid can easily change into a vapour —**volatility** /ˌvɒləˈtɪləti/ noun [U]

volcanic /vɒlˈkænɪk/ adj **GEOLOGY** coming from, or relating to, a volcano: *a layer of volcanic ash* ♦ *volcanic activity*

volcanism /ˈvɒlkənɪzəm/ noun [U] **GEOLOGY** the processes involved in the creation of volcanoes, and in the movement of **magma** (=hot liquid rock) from inside the Earth to its surface

volcano /vɒlˈkeɪnəʊ/ (plural **volcanoes** or **volcanos**) noun [C] **GEOLOGY** an opening in the surface of the Earth through which hot gas, rocks, ash, and lava are pushed. Some volcanos are in the form of mountains, and some are under the sea. Some are not dangerous at the present time because they are not **active** and have become **dormant**. Others will never be dangerous again because they are completely **extinct**.

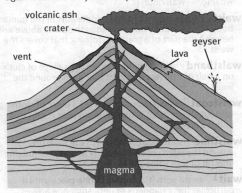

volcanic ash
crater
geyser
vent
lava
magma

volcano

vole /vəʊl/ noun [C] a small mammal similar to a mouse but with a short tail

volition /vəˈlɪʃ(ə)n/ noun [U] *formal* the power or ability to decide something without help from others, and to take action to get something. A more usual word is **will**.

volley[1] /ˈvɒli/ noun [C] **1 SPORTS** the action of hitting or kicking a ball back to an opponent before it touches the ground **2** a lot of questions, insults etc that are all spoken or made at the same time

volley[2] /ˈvɒli/ (**volleys, volleying, volleyed**) verb [I/T] **SPORTS** to hit or kick a ball back to an opponent before it touches the ground

volleyball /ˈvɒliˌbɔːl/ noun [U] **SPORTS** a sport in which two teams use their hands and arms to hit a ball to each other over a high net

volt /vəʊlt/ noun [C] **PHYSICS** a unit for measuring the **potential difference** of an electric current. The unit of electric current is the **amp**, and the unit of electrical power is the **watt**.

voltage /ˈvəʊltɪdʒ/ noun [C/U] **PHYSICS** the amount of **potential difference** in an electric current, measured in volts. Symbol V

volte-face /ˌvɒlt ˈfɑːs/ noun [C] *formal* a sudden and complete change of opinion or plan

voltmeter /ˈvəʊltˌmiːtə/ noun [C] **PHYSICS** a piece of equipment used for measuring voltage —*picture* → ELECTRICITY

volume /ˈvɒljuːm/ noun **1** [U] **MATHS, SCIENCE** the amount of space that is contained in something or that is filled by something, measured in cubic units: *How do you calculate the volume of a cube?* **2** [U] the loudness of a sound, especially from something such as a television, CD player etc **3** [C/U] an amount of something: *an increase in the volume of traffic* ♦ *Some students cannot cope with the huge volume of work.* **4** [C] *formal* a book

voluntary /ˈvɒlənt(ə)ri/ adj **1 BIOLOGY** a voluntary muscle is a muscle that you can control, for example any of the muscles that you use for moving your arms and legs, and a voluntary movement is a movement that you choose to make ≠ INVOLUNTARY **2** something that is voluntary is done because you choose to do it, and not because you have to ≠ COMPULSORY, MANDATORY **3** voluntary work is done for no pay: *My job at the hospital is purely voluntary.* **4** a voluntary organization does important work for the community but does not make a profit, and usually has to raise all its own money: *the voluntary sector* —**voluntarily** /ˌvɒlənˈteərɪli/ adv

volunteer[1] /ˌvɒlənˈtɪə/ noun [C] **1** someone who works without expecting to be paid for what they do **2** someone who offers to do something and does not have to be made to do it **3** someone who joins the armed forces without being forced to

volunteer[2] /ˌvɒlənˈtɪə/ verb **1** [I/T] to offer or choose to do something for someone else **2** [I/T] to work without expecting to be paid for what you do **3** [I/T] to say something or give information without being asked **4** [I] to join the armed forces without being forced to

vomit[1] /ˈvɒmɪt/ verb [I/T] if you vomit, or if you vomit something, food comes up from your stomach and out through your mouth because you are ill

vomit[2] /ˈvɒmɪt/ noun [U] food or other substances that come up from your stomach when you vomit

voodoo /ˈvuːduː/ noun [U] **RELIGION** a religion whose followers believe in magic and **witchcraft**

voracious /vəˈreɪʃəs/ adj *formal* **1** a voracious person or animal eats a lot **2** enjoying something very much and wanting to do it a lot: *a voracious reader* —**voraciously** adv

vote[1] /vəʊt/ verb [I/T] **POLITICS** to decide something, or to choose a representative or winner, by officially stating your choice, for example in an election: *The Council will vote on the proposal next Friday.* ♦ *68 per cent of the union voted against striking.* ♦ *I'm going to vote for Jackson.* ♦ *The committee voted unanimously to allocate the funds.*

vote[2] /vəʊt/ noun **1** [C] an official choice that you make between two or more issues, people etc, for example in an election: *There were only 62 votes for the proposal, compared with 740 against.* **2** the vote [singular] **POLITICS** the right to vote in an election

voter /ˈvəʊtə/ noun [C] someone who votes in an election

voucher /ˈvaʊtʃə/ noun [C] a piece of paper that you buy something with instead of using money

vow[1] /vaʊ/ noun **1** [C] a serious promise **2 vows** [plural] a set of formal promises that people make to each other, for example during a wedding ceremony

vow² /vaʊ/ verb [I/T] *formal* to promise that you will do something

vowel /'vaʊəl/ noun [C] LANGUAGE in English, one of the letters a, e, i, o, or u, or the sounds that they represent

voyage /'vɔɪdʒ/ noun [C] a long journey, especially on a ship

VP /ˌviː 'piː/ noun [C] MATHS, PHYSICS a **vertical plane**

vs abbrev versus

vulcanism /'vʌlkənɪzəm/ noun [U] GEOLOGY **volcanism**

vulcanite /'vʌlkənaɪt/ noun [U] CHEMISTRY a type of hard rubber produced by heating rubber with **sulphur**

vulgar /'vʌlgə/ adj **1** a vulgar joke, comment, action etc has a sexual meaning that is rude or offensive **2** someone who is vulgar is rude, unpleasant, and offensive **3** showing a lack of ability to judge what is attractive, suitable etc —**vulgarly** adv

ˌvulgar ˈfraction noun [C] MATHS *old-fashioned* a **proper fraction**

vulnerable /'vʌln(ə)rəb(ə)l/ adj weak and therefore easy to hurt, harm, or attack: *the most vulnerable groups in society* —**vulnerability** /ˌvʌln(ə)rə'bɪləti/ noun [U]

vulture /'vʌltʃə/ noun [C] a large bird that eats the bodies of dead animals —*picture* → BIRD

vulva /'vʌlvə/ noun [C] ANATOMY the outer parts of a woman's sexual organs

W w

w /'dʌb(ə)ljuː/ (plural **w's**) or **W** (plural **W's**) noun [C/U] the 23rd letter of the English alphabet

W abbrev **1** PHYSICS watt **2** GEOGRAPHY West **3** GEOGRAPHY Western

W3 /ˌdʌb(ə)ljuː dʌb(ə)ljuː 'dʌb(ə)ljuː/ abbrev COMPUTING the **World Wide Web**

wad /wɒd/ noun [C] **1** a thick pile of papers, documents, or banknotes **2** a round mass of something soft

waddle /'wɒd(ə)l/ verb [I] to walk with short steps that make your body move from side to side —**waddle** noun [C]

wade /weɪd/ verb [I] to walk in water that is not very deep

wading bird /'weɪdɪŋ ˌbɜːd/ noun [C] a bird with long legs that stands in the water while it hunts for fish

waffle /'wɒf(ə)l/ noun **1** [C] a flat cake that has deep square marks on both sides **2** [U] *informal* talk or writing that uses a lot of words but does not say anything important

waft /wɑːft/ verb [I] if a smell or a noise wafts, it floats through the air

wag /wæg/ (**wags, wagging, wagged**) verb [I/T] **1** if a dog wags its tail, it moves its tail from one side to the other several times **2** to move a finger quickly from side to side several times, especially in order to show that you do not approve of something

wage¹ /weɪdʒ/ noun [C] a regular amount of money that you earn for working: *a weekly wage* ♦ *I've usually spent all my wages by Tuesday.* ♦ *What is the **minimum wage** here?*

wage² /weɪdʒ/ verb [T] to start and continue a war or fight: *The government has pledged to **wage war on** drugs.*

ˈwage ˌcurve noun [C] ECONOMICS a line on a graph that shows the relationship between the average pay for workers in a region or industry and the rate of unemployment in that region or industry

ˈwage diffeˌrential noun [C] ECONOMICS a difference in pay between workers with different skills who work in the same industry, or workers with similar skills who work in different industries or regions

waggle /'wæg(ə)l/ verb [I/T] to move up and down or from side to side with short quick movements, or to make something move in this way

wagon /'wægən/ noun [C] **1** a covered vehicle with four wheels that is usually pulled by horses **2** a large open container that is pulled by a train

wail /weɪl/ verb **1** [I/T] to shout or cry with a long high sound because you are in pain or are very sad **2** [I] to make a long high sound: *We could hear the sirens wailing.* —**wail** noun [C]

waist /weɪst/ noun [C] **1** the middle part of the human body that is usually narrower than the parts above and below **2** the part of a piece of clothing that covers the waist

waistband /'weɪs(t)ˌbænd/ noun [C] a piece of cloth on a pair of trousers or a skirt that goes around the waist

waistcoat /'weɪs(t)ˌkəʊt/ noun [C] a piece of clothing without sleeves that is usually worn over a shirt and under a jacket

waistline /'weɪs(t)ˌlaɪn/ noun [C] the measurement around the waist, used especially as a way of judging how fat or thin someone is

wait¹ /weɪt/ verb [I] **1** to stay in one place until a particular thing happens or until someone arrives: *Sheryl said she'd be waiting in the lobby.* ♦ *He was attacked while he was **waiting for** a bus.* ♦ *They **waited** anxiously for news of survivors.* ♦ *Let's sit down and **wait until** Bob gets here.* **2** to delay doing something until something happens or until someone arrives: *I'm busy right now so you'll just have to wait.* ♦ *Should we start eating or should we **wait for** the others?* **3** to be hoping or expecting that something will happen: *I've been **waiting for** a refund cheque for several months.* ♦ *There's no point **waiting for** her to change her mind.* **4** to be ready for someone to take or use: *There's a package **waiting for** you in the office.*

PHRASES **sb can't wait/can hardly wait** used for saying that someone is very excited about something that is going to happen: *I can't wait for the holidays.*

keep sb waiting to make someone stay in one place or do nothing until you are ready to see them or talk to them: *We were kept waiting outside his office for over an hour.*

PHRASAL VERBS **ˈwait ˌon sb** TOURISM to serve people in a restaurant

ˌwait ˈup to not go to bed until someone comes home

Wait for and **expect** have different meanings.

■ If you **wait for** something to happen, you do not leave a place or do something else until it happens: *We waited for Alex to finish his lunch.* ♦ *I'm waiting for a bus.*

■ If you **expect** something to happen, you believe that it will happen: *We expected Lee to be upset.* ♦ *I'm expecting a phone call later.*

wait² /weɪt/ noun [singular] a period of time during which you wait for something: *Expect a long wait if you intend to buy tickets.* → LIE¹

waiter /'weɪtə/ noun [C] a man who brings food and drink to your table in a restaurant

waiting room /'weɪtɪŋ ˌruːm/ noun [C] a room where you wait for something such as a train, or for someone such as a doctor to be ready to see you

waitress /'weɪtrəs/ noun [C] a woman who brings food and drink to your table in a restaurant

waive /weɪv/ verb [T] to choose to officially ignore a rule, right, or claim

wake¹ /weɪk/ (**wakes, waking, woke** /wəʊk/, **woken** /'wəʊkən/) verb [I/T] to stop sleeping, or to make someone stop sleeping: *I woke at 5 o'clock this morning.* ♦ *Be quiet or you'll wake the baby.*

    PHRASAL VERB ,**wake (sb)** '**up** same as **wake¹**: *Wake up! It's nearly ten o'clock!* ♦ *Don't wake me up when you come in.*

wake² /weɪk/ noun [C] **1** a meeting of friends and relations before or after a funeral in order to remember the person who died **2** the track that appears in the water behind a moving boat

waken /'weɪkən/ verb [I/T] *formal* to wake up, or to wake someone up

'**wake-up** ,**call** noun [C] **1** a bad experience that makes you take action in order to improve a situation: *The low test scores should serve as a loud wake-up call to teachers.* **2 TOURISM** a telephone call that you receive in order to wake you up

waking /'weɪkɪŋ/ adj relating to the time when you are awake: *I spent every waking hour working on the report.*

waling /'weɪlɪŋ/ noun [C] **CONSTRUCTION** a horizontal wooden board that strengthens a row of vertical **poling boards**

walk¹ /wɔːk/ verb **1** [I] to move forwards by putting one foot in front of the other: *Has your little boy learned to walk yet?* ♦ *It takes me 25 minutes to* **walk to** *work.* ♦ *Greg* **walked** *slowly* **towards** *her, smiling.* ♦ *Howard* **walked in** *with two men I'd never seen before.* ♦ *As we* **walked along** *she talked about her plans.* **2** [T] to go a particular distance by walking: *She walked three miles each day.* **3** [T] to walk somewhere with someone in order to be sure that they reach the place safely: *When Valerie worked late, Carl always* **walked** *her* **home.**

    PHRASE walk all over sb to treat someone very badly → TIGHTROPE

    PHRASAL VERBS ,**walk** '**off** to leave somewhere, usually without telling people that you are going to leave
    ,**walk** '**out** to suddenly leave a job or relationship: *Her husband had* **walked out on** *her a year before.*

Build your vocabulary: words you can use instead of **walk**

■ **march** to walk in a military way or with a lot of energy
■ **shuffle** to walk slowly without lifting your feet off the ground
■ **stagger** to walk with uneven steps, almost falling over
■ **step** to move one foot forward
■ **stride** to walk fast, taking big steps
■ **stroll** to walk for pleasure in a relaxed way

■ **tiptoe** to walk very quietly, standing on your toes
■ **trudge** to walk slowly because you are very tired

walk² /wɔːk/ noun [C] **1** a short journey that you make by walking, or the distance of this journey: *It's a five-minute walk from our house to the post office.* ♦ *It's a beautiful walk down to the beach.* ♦ *Does anyone want to* **go for a walk**? ♦ *Let's* **take a walk** *after we eat.* **2** the way that someone walks

    PHRASE from all walks of life used for saying that a group consists of all types of people with different backgrounds, jobs etc

walker /'wɔːkə/ noun [C] **1** someone who walks for pleasure or for exercise: *Davis is a keen walker and cyclist.* **2** used for describing the speed that someone walks at

walking /'wɔːkɪŋ/ noun [U] the activity of going for walks for pleasure or for exercise: *a pair of strong walking boots* ♦ *We* **went walking** *in the Malvern hills.*

'**walking** ,**tour** noun [C] **TOURISM** a trip on which people walk from one place to another, spend the night, and then continue walking the next day

Walkman /'wɔːkmən/ **TRADEMARK** a type of small **cassette** or CD player with **headphones** that you can carry with you

walkthrough /'wɔːk,θruː/ noun [C] **COMPUTING** a set of instructions on how to use a piece of software, or how to complete a computer game

wall /wɔːl/ noun [C] **1** an upright side of a room or building: *The walls of the factory were covered in graffiti.* ♦ *Several paintings hung on the wall.* **2** an upright structure made of stone or brick that surrounds or divides an area of land: *The children got into the yard by climbing over the wall.* **3** a large amount of something that forms a tall mass: *A wall of dark water approached their small boat.*

wallaby /'wɒləbi/ (plural **wallabies**) noun [C] a mammal like a small **kangaroo** that lives mainly in Australia

wallchart /'wɔːl,tʃɑːt/ noun [C] a large piece of paper that contains information on a particular subject and is fastened to a wall

'**wall** ,**cloud** noun [C] **GEOGRAPHY** an area of low cloud below a **thunderstorm**. **Tornadoes** often start at the edge of wall clouds. —*picture* → HURRICANE

walled /wɔːld/ adj surrounded by a wall

,**walled** '**garden** noun [C] **COMPUTING** a website that you need a **username** and password to use, or that limits what you can look at

wallet /'wɒlɪt/ noun [C] a small flat case that you keep money, credit cards etc in

wall-mounted /'wɔːl ,maʊntɪd/ adj fixed to a wall

wallow /'wɒləʊ/ verb [I] **1** *showing disapproval* to spend a lot of time feeling sad or upset: *George still seems determined to* **wallow in** *self-pity.* **2** to lie down and roll around in water, dirt, or mud

wallpaper¹ /'wɔːl,peɪpə/ noun [C/U] **1** thick paper that you can stick on the walls inside a house in order to decorate them **2 COMPUTING** the background colour or pattern that you can put on your computer screen

wallpaper² /'wɔːl,peɪpə/ verb [I/T] to put wallpaper onto walls= PAPER

'**Wall** ,**Street 1 BUSINESS, ECONOMICS** the US **stock market 2** the area in New York City where the US **stock exchange** and other major financial institutions are based

'wall ,tie noun [C] CONSTRUCTION a metal part that connects internal and external walls together

walnut /'wɔːlnʌt/ noun [C/U] the tree that this nut grows on, or the wood of a walnut tree

walrus /'wɔːlrəs/ (plural **walruses**) noun [C] a large sea mammal that has two very long **tusks** —*picture* → SEA

waltz /wɔːls/ noun [singular] MUSIC a dance in which a pair of dancers turns continuously while moving around the dance floor, or the music for this dance

wan /wɒn/ adj **1** someone who is wan looks very pale and weak because they are ill **2** a wan light is not bright

WAN /wæn/ noun [C] COMPUTING wide area network: a system that allows computers over a wide area to communicate with one another

wander /'wɒndə/ verb **1** [I/T] to go from place to place without a particular direction or purpose: *Jim wandered into the kitchen and made some tea.* ♦ *We spent the afternoon in the old city, just wandering the streets.* **2** [I] if your mind or thoughts wander, you stop concentrating and start thinking about other things **3** [I] if your gaze wanders or your eyes wander, you stop looking at one thing and start looking at another **4** [I] *same as* **wander off** —**wanderer** noun [C]
PHRASAL VERB **,wander 'off** to move away from a place where you are usually, or where people expect you to be: *Don't let the kids wander off on their own.*

wane /weɪn/ verb [I] **1** to become weaker or less important **2** when the moon is waning, you see less and less of it each night ≠ WAX

waning moon /'weɪnɪŋ ,muːn/ noun [U] ASTRONOMY the moon when it is between a full moon and a new moon, and less of it appears each night

want¹ /wɒnt/ verb [T] **1** to feel that you would like to have, keep, or do something: *Do you still want these old letters?* ♦ *She wants a ticket to the concert for her birthday.* ♦ *Liz wants to see the gardens.* **2** to feel that you would like someone to do something, or would like something to happen: *I want you to come with me.* ♦ *I'm not sure what he wants from me.* **3** to ask for someone because you would like to see or speak to them: *Mum wants you – she's in the kitchen.* ♦ *You're wanted on the phone.* **4** to need something: *We desperately want rain.* ♦ *She wants help if she's going to sort out her financial problems.* ♦ *You won't want much money on a camping holiday.*

want² /wɒnt/ noun **1** [C/U] *formal* a situation in which people do not have basic things such as food or money **2 wants** [plural] things that you want or need
PHRASE **for want of a better word/phrase/term** used for saying that you cannot think of a more exact way of describing or explaining what you mean

wanted /'wɒntɪd/ adj **1** being looked for by the police in connection with a crime **2** loved by other people: *All children need to feel wanted.*

wanting /'wɒntɪŋ/ adj something that is wanting is not as good as it should be: *UN peacekeeping forces were found wanting.*

WAP /wæp/ noun [U] COMPUTING wireless application protocol: a type of technology that allows you to send emails and look at information on the Internet using a mobile phone or **pager**

war /wɔː/ noun **1** [C/U] SOCIAL STUDIES fighting between two or more countries or groups that involves the use of armed forces and usually continues for a long time: *the Vietnam War* ♦ *They have been at war for five years.* ♦ *He volunteered for the Navy when war broke out.* ♦ *The Allies declared war* (=officially said they were at war) *in 1939.* **2** [C] ECONOMICS a situation in which countries, organizations, or businesses compete with

each other in order to gain economic advantages: *This could easily start a trade war.* **3** [C/U] a determined effort to control or stop something, for example a disease or crime: *This is a major victory in the war against drugs.* ♦ *the war on poverty* → WARRING

'war ,crime noun [C] LAW the crime of killing or harming people during a war for reasons that are not allowed by international law —'**war ,criminal** noun [C]

ward /wɔːd/ noun [C] **1** HEALTH a large room in a hospital with beds for people to stay in **2** LAW someone, especially a child, who is officially being looked after by a court of law or by someone who is not their parents. The person who looks after them is their **guardian**.

warden /'wɔːd(ə)n/ noun [C] someone whose job is to be responsible for a particular place or thing, and to check that rules are obeyed

wardrobe /'wɔːdrəʊb/ noun [C] **1** a piece of furniture like a large cupboard where you can hang your clothes **2** all the clothes that someone has

ware /weə/ noun **1** [U] **pottery** (=dishes or other objects made of clay) **2 wares** [plural] goods that someone is selling, especially at a market or on the street

warehouse /'weə,haʊs/ noun [C] a big building where large amounts of goods are stored

warfare /'wɔːfeə/ noun [U] the activity of fighting a war, or the methods that are used for fighting wars: *the rules of warfare* ♦ *germ warfare*

warfarin /'wɔːf(ə)rɪn/ noun [U] HEALTH a drug used for treating some illnesses by making the blood thinner

warhead /'wɔː,hed/ noun [C] the front part of a missile that explodes

warlike /'wɔː,laɪk/ adj likely to start wars, or always ready to go to war

warlord /'wɔː,lɔːd/ noun [C] a military leader who controls part of a country but does not belong to the country's official armed forces

warm¹ /wɔːm/ adj **1** fairly hot in a comfortable, pleasant way ≠ COOL: *It was warm enough for us to sit outside.* ♦ *I walked fast to keep warm.* **2** warm clothes and buildings prevent you from feeling cold: *The kitchen was the warmest room in the house.* ♦ *a thick warm coat* **3** kind and friendly in a way that makes other people feel comfortable: *a warm smile* ♦ *Please give a warm welcome to tonight's special guests.* **4** warm colours have red, orange, or yellow in them —**warmly** adv

warm² /wɔːm/ verb [T] to make someone or something warm: *The morning sun warms the room nicely.*
PHRASAL VERB **,warm (sb/sth) 'up 1** to become warm, or to make someone or something become warm: *I'll warm up some soup for lunch.* ♦ *Drink this and you'll soon warm up.* **2** to prepare for a sport or activity by doing gentle exercises or practising just before it starts: *The players are already on the field warming up.*

warm-blooded /,wɔːm 'blʌdɪd/ adj BIOLOGY warm-blooded animals have a body that stays warm in both hot and cold environments → COLD-BLOODED

'war me,morial noun [C] a structure that is built to remind people of the soldiers and other people who were killed in a war

,warm 'front noun [C] GEOGRAPHY the front edge of a mass of warm air that brings warm weather when it moves into an area —*picture* → CLOUD

warm-hearted /,wɔːm 'hɑːtɪd/ adj friendly, kind, and generous ≠ COLD-HEARTED

,**warm** '**sector** noun [C] GEOGRAPHY an area of warm air within the low-pressure region between the **cold front** and **warm front** of a storm → COLD SECTOR

warmth /wɔːmθ/ noun [U] **1** heat that is comfortable and pleasant: *We sat near the warmth of the fire.* **2** a kind, friendly quality in someone or something

warn /wɔːn/ verb [I/T] **1** to tell someone about a possible problem or danger, so that they can avoid it or deal with it: *The report warns that consumers could end up paying higher prices.* ♦ *Recent studies **warn against** drinking too much caffeine.* ♦ *Scientists **warned of** the threat to beaches and rivers from pollution.* ♦ *Police are **warning** all women in the area **to** take extra care when going out alone.* ♦ *Travel agents are not **warning** tourists **about** the dangers of crime in holiday resorts.* **2** to tell someone that they will be punished or that something bad will happen if they do something: *Behave yourself! That's the last time I'm warning you.*

warning /'wɔːnɪŋ/ noun **1** [C/U] an action or statement telling someone of a possible problem or danger: *a **warning against** driving on the icy roads* ♦ *a **warning of** severe thunderstorms* ♦ *By law, cigarette packets must carry **a health warning**.* **2** [C] a statement telling someone that they will be punished or that something bad will happen if they do something: *This is your last warning – if you're late again, you'll lose your job.*

warp /wɔːp/ verb [I/T] to become bent or curved because of damage by heat or water, or to make something do this

warrant /'wɒrənt/ noun [C] LAW a document written by a judge that gives the police permission to do something, for example to arrest someone or to search a house

warranty /'wɒrənti/ (plural **warranties**) noun [C] a company's written promise to repair or replace a product that you buy from them if it breaks or does not work≡ GUARANTEE

warren /'wɒrən/ noun [C] a place that is very difficult to find your way around because there are so many ways that you could go

warring /'wɔːrɪŋ/ adj arguing or fighting with each other

warship /'wɔːˌʃɪp/ noun [C] a large ship with a lot of weapons, used for fighting in wars

wart /wɔːt/ noun [C] HEALTH a small hard lump that grows on the skin

wartime /'wɔːˌtaɪm/ noun [U] the period when a war is taking place ≠ PEACETIME —**wartime** adj

'**war-ˌtorn** adj a war-torn country or place has been badly damaged by a war

wary /'weəri/ (**warier, wariest**) adj careful or nervous about someone or something, because you think that they might cause a problem —**warily** adv

was /strong wɒz, weak wəz/ 3rd person singular of the past tense of **be**

wash[1] /wɒʃ/ verb **1** [T] to clean something with water or with soap and water: *I've got to wash the car.* ♦ *You should always wash fruit before eating it.* ♦ *a freshly washed shirt* **2** [I/T] to clean yourself or a part of your body with water and with soap and water: *He washed and dressed quickly.* ♦ ***Wash your hands** before you touch the food.* **3** [T] if water washes a person or object somewhere, it carries them there: *Some very strange things get **washed ashore** here.* **4** [I/T] to flow, or to flow to a place: *Waves were washing against the side of the boat.*

PHRASAL VERBS ,**wash sth a**'**way** if water washes

something away, it carries it away: *Heavy rains have washed away the bridge.*

,**wash (sth)** '**off** if you wash dirt off, or if dirt washes off, you remove it by washing: *Wash all the soil off before you cook the potatoes.* ♦ *Don't worry – that'll wash off easily.*

,**wash (sth)** '**up** to wash the plates, cups, spoons etc after a meal: *I can help to cook and wash up.* ♦ *The breakfast things haven't been washed up yet.*

wash[2] /wɒʃ/ noun **1** [C] the process of washing someone or something: *These trousers need a wash.* ♦ *After a few washes the colour faded.* **2** [singular] the flowing movement of water in the sea

washable /'wɒʃəb(ə)l/ adj able to be washed without being damaged

washbasin /'wɒʃˌbeɪs(ə)n/ noun [C] the container in a bathroom that you use for washing your face and hands

'**wash ˌcoat** noun [U] TECHNOLOGY a **cover pass** (=top layer) in welding

washed-out /ˌwɒʃt 'aʊt/ adj informal very pale and ill or tired

washer /'wɒʃə/ noun [C] **1** a small flat ring that is used for filling the space between two metal parts, for example between a surface and the top of a screw **2** informal a **washing machine**

washing /'wɒʃɪŋ/ noun [U] clothes that need to be washed or that have just been washed

'**washing ˌline** noun [C] a rope tied between poles that is used for hanging wet clothes on to dry

'**washing maˌchine** noun [C] a machine for washing clothes

'**washing ˌpowder** noun [U] soap in the form of a powder that you use for washing clothes

'**washing ˌsoda** noun [U] CHEMISTRY a substance that is used to make soap, and is added to water in order to reduce the amount of unwanted minerals in it

,**washing-'up** noun [U] **1** the dishes, cups, knives, forks etc that need to be washed after a meal **2** the activity of washing the dishes and other things used for a meal

wasn't /'wɒz(ə)nt/ short form the usual way of saying or writing 'was not'. This is not often used in formal writing: *The food looked good, but I wasn't hungry.*

wasp /wɒsp/ noun [C] a black and yellow flying insect that can sting you —*picture* → INSECT

wastage /'weɪstɪdʒ/ noun [U] the amount of something that is wasted, or a situation in which something is wasted

waste[1] /weɪst/ noun **1** [singular/U] the failure to use something that is valuable or useful in an effective way: *All this uneaten food – what a waste!* ♦ *It's **a waste of time** trying to get her to change her mind.* ♦ *The cherries will just **go to waste** (=be spoiled or thrown away) if we don't pick them soon.* **2** [C/U] the useless materials, substances, or parts that are left after you have used something: *nuclear waste*

waste[2] /weɪst/ verb [T] to use more of something than is necessary, or to use it in a way that does not produce the best results: *There were accusations that the government was **wasting** public **money**.* ♦ *A great deal of time was wasted arguing over the details of the contract.* ♦ *Why do you **waste** your money **on** lottery tickets?*

PHRASES **be wasted on sb** if something is wasted on someone, they do not understand it or realize how good it is: *Don't give the smoked salmon to the children – it'd just be wasted on them.*

waste no time (in) doing sth to do something immediately

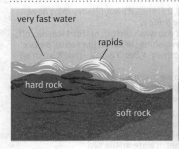
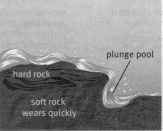
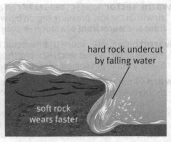

very fast water

rapids

hard rock

soft rock

hard rock

soft rock
wears quickly

plunge pool

hard rock undercut
by falling water

soft rock
wears faster

formation of waterfalls

waste³ /weɪst/ adj **1** waste substances are what is left of something after the valuable parts of it have been used **2** waste land or waste ground is land that is not being used or has not been built on

'**waste ,basket** noun [C] COMPUTING the place on your computer that stores files that you have deleted
= RECYCLE BIN

'**waste ,bin** noun [C] a container that you put rubbish in

wasted /ˈweɪstɪd/ adj **1** not used effectively: *a wasted day* **2** extremely thin and weak

wasteful /ˈweɪst(t)f(ə)l/ adj using something carelessly, so that some of it is wasted

wasteland /ˈweɪs(t),lænd/ noun [C/U] an area of land that is empty or that cannot be used

wastepaper basket /weɪs(t)ˈpeɪpə ,bɑːskɪt/ noun [C] a small open container for rubbish such as used paper —*picture* → WORKSTATION

'**waste ,pipe** noun [C] a pipe used for carrying used water and waste from a building

'**waste ,product** noun [C] BIOLOGY, ENVIRONMENT an unwanted material or substance that is left after something has been processed

wasting /ˈweɪstɪŋ/ adj HEALTH a wasting disease makes you thin, weak, and tired

watch¹ /wɒtʃ/ verb **1** [I/T] to look at someone or something for a period of time: *Did you watch the news last night?* ♦ *We watched helplessly as the car rolled into the river.* ♦ *Jill watched the children build sandcastles.* ♦ *We arrived early to watch the players warming up.* → LOOK¹ **2** [T] to be careful of something: *Watch the knife! It's sharp!* ♦ *Watch you don't get your bag stolen.* ♦ *They need to watch what they spend quite carefully.* **3** [T] to look after someone or something for a short time and make sure that nothing bad happens to them: *Could you just watch the baby for a minute?*

PHRASAL VERBS ,**watch 'out** used for telling someone to be careful: *Watch out – you're going to hit that car!*
,**watch 'out for sb/sth** to be careful so that you can avoid someone or something
,**watch 'over sb/sth** to guard, protect, or be in charge of someone or something

watch² /wɒtʃ/ noun [C] **1** a small clock that you wear on your wrist **2** an organization that continuously watches something to make sure that bad things do not happen: *members of the local neighbourhood watch*

PHRASE **keep (a) watch 1** to pay attention to a situation carefully so that you can deal with any changes or problems: *Scientists are* **keeping** *a close* **watch on** *pollution levels.* **2** to watch someone carefully in order to make sure that they are safe or that they do not do something bad: *Keep a watch on him in case he gets worse.*

watchdog /ˈwɒtʃ,dɒg/ noun [C] **1** a person or organization whose job is to make sure that companies that provide a particular type of service or product do not break the law or do anything harmful: *the water industry watchdog* **2** a dog that is used for guarding a building

watchful /ˈwɒtʃf(ə)l/ adj looking at something carefully, or noticing everything that is happening
= VIGILANT

watching brief /ˈwɒtʃɪŋ ,briːf/ noun [C] LAW written instructions to a lawyer to watch a particular legal case

watchman /ˈwɒtʃmən/ (plural **watchmen** /ˈwɒtʃmen/) noun [C] a **night watchman**

watchtower /ˈwɒtʃ,taʊə/ noun [C] a tower from where guards can see the whole area that they are guarding

water¹ /ˈwɔːtə/ noun **1** [U] GEOGRAPHY, CHEMISTRY the clear liquid that falls as rain, covers two-thirds of the Earth's surface, and is used for drinking, washing, and cooking. Water is a compound of hydrogen and oxygen. It exists in frozen form as ice and in gas form as water vapour. It boils at 100°C and freezes at 0°C. Water is necessary to all living things on Earth and is necessary for most biological processes. Chemical formula: H_2O: *Wash your hands thoroughly with soap and water.* —*picture* → DAM, STATE, WATER SUPPLY, WAVE **2** [U] an area of water such as a lake or sea: *From the hotel there's a beautiful view of the water.* **3** [C/U] the surface of a lake or the sea: *I was swimming under the water near the beach.* **4 waters** [plural] GEOGRAPHY an area of water that belongs to a particular place, state, country etc: *British waters*

water² /ˈwɔːtə/ verb **1** [T] to pour water on plants in order to keep them healthy **2** [I] if your eyes water, tears form in them because something is hurting them **3** [I] if your mouth waters when you see or smell nice food, saliva begins to form in your mouth

waterborne /ˈwɔːtə,bɔːn/ adj a waterborne disease is spread through water

'**water ,buffalo** noun [C] a large Asian mammal similar to a cow, that has black or white fur and horns. It is used for farming and pulling vehicles.

'**water ,chestnut** noun [C] **1** a small hard round white fruit, often used in Asian cooking **2** a vegetable that is the swollen stem of the plant, used in Asian cooking

watercolour /ˈwɔːtə,kʌlə/ noun ARTS **1** [C/U] a type of paint that is mixed with water for painting pictures **2** [C] a painting that is done with watercolour paints

water cooler /ˈwɔːtə ,kuːlə/ noun [C] a machine that makes cool water available for people to drink, especially in an office or other place where people work

watercourse /ˈwɔːtə,kɔːs/ noun [C] GEOGRAPHY a river, canal, or stream

the ,water 'cycle noun [singular] GEOGRAPHY the continuous process by which water in seas, rivers, soil, living things etc evaporates into the atmosphere, where it forms clouds that produce rain, snow, or hail

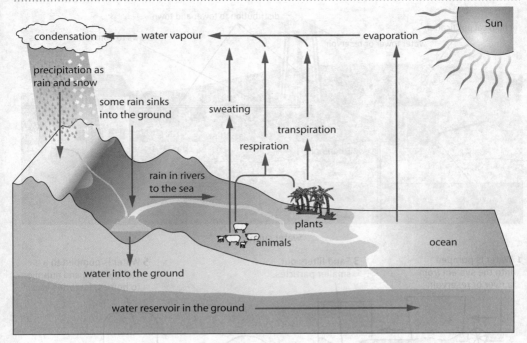

the water cycle

so that it goes back into the seas, rivers, soil etc again

waterfall /'wɔːtəˌfɔːl/ noun [C] **GEOGRAPHY** a place where water flows over the edge of a steep place onto another level below —*picture* → RIVER and on previous page

waterfront /'wɔːtəˌfrʌnt/ noun [C] an area that is next to a river, lake, or the sea

waterhole /'wɔːtəˌhəʊl/ noun [C] a small area of water in a hot country where wild animals go to drink

watering can /'wɔːt(ə)rɪŋ ˌkæn/ noun [C] a container used for pouring water on plants. It has a handle and a long **spout**. —*picture* → AGRICULTURAL

watering hole /'wɔːt(ə)rɪŋ ˌhəʊl/ noun [C] a **waterhole**

water level noun [C/U] **GEOGRAPHY** the height of the surface of a river, lake, or other area of water

water lily noun [C] a flowering plant that grows in water and has very big flat leaves that float on the surface

waterlogged /'wɔːtəˌlɒgd/ adj waterlogged ground is too wet to walk on or play sports on

water mark noun [C] **GEOGRAPHY** a mark showing the level that a river has reached

water meadow noun [C] a field next to a river that fills with water when the river floods

watermelon /'wɔːtəˌmelən/ noun [C/U] a large round fruit that has a hard green skin and is red with small black seeds inside —*picture* → FRUIT

water-of-Ayr stone /ˌwɔːtə əv ˈeə ˌstəʊn/ noun [U] **TECHNOLOGY** a special type of stone that is used for removing marks from the surface of metal

water park noun [C] **TOURISM** a park with water slides, swimming pools, and rides with flowing water

water polo noun [U] **SPORTS** a game played in water by two teams of seven players who get points by throwing a ball into the opponent's goal

waterproof /'wɔːtəˌpruːf/ adj waterproof clothes or materials do not let water pass through them

water pump noun [C] **ENGINEERING** a pump in the **cooling system** of a vehicle's engine that makes the water move around the system

watershed /'wɔːtəˌʃed/ noun **1** [singular] a time or event when a major change takes place = TURNING POINT **2** [C] **GEOGRAPHY** a high piece of land that divides the flow of water in rivers in a particular area

water-skiing noun [U] **SPORTS** an activity in which you stand on **skis** and ride on the surface of water while being pulled behind a boat —**'water-ski** verb [I], **'water-skier** noun [C]

water softener /'wɔːtə ˌsɒf(ə)nə/ noun [C] a substance or piece of equipment used for removing unwanted minerals from water

water supply noun [C/U] water that is available for people to use in a particular area —*picture* → on next page

water table noun [C] **GEOGRAPHY** the level below the Earth's surface where water is found —*picture* → on next page

watertight /'wɔːtəˌtaɪt/ adj **1** a watertight container or room is made so that water cannot enter it **2** a watertight excuse, argument, or case is so good that no one can find anything wrong with it

water tower noun [C] a tower used for storing and supplying water in a particular area —*picture* → on next page

water vapour noun [U] **SCIENCE** water in the form of a gas produced by evaporation below its boiling point —*picture* → DESALINATION

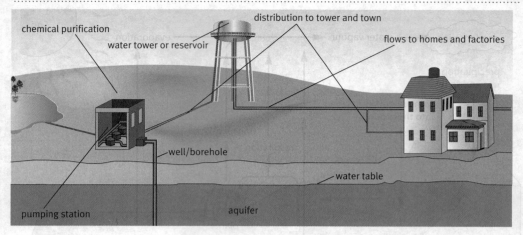

chemical purification

water tower or reservoir

distribution to tower and town

flows to homes and factories

well/borehole

water table

pumping station

aquifer

water supply

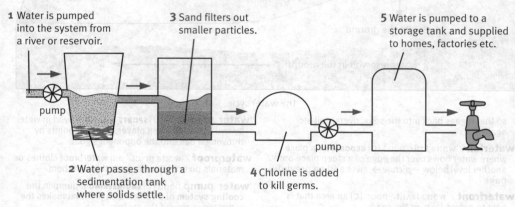

1 Water is pumped into the system from a river or reservoir.

3 Sand filters out smaller particles.

5 Water is pumped to a storage tank and supplied to homes, factories etc.

pump

pump

2 Water passes through a sedimentation tank where solids settle.

4 Chlorine is added to kill germs.

water purification

waterway /ˈwɔːtəˌweɪ/ noun [C] GEOGRAPHY a river or canal that boats use for travelling from one place to another

ˈwater ˌwell noun [C] a hole in the ground that is dug in order to bring water to the surface

watery /ˈwɔːt(ə)ri/ adj **1** containing or filled with water: *watery eyes* **2** watery food or drink contains a lot of water and has a weak taste **3** weak or pale: *watery sunlight*

watt /wɒt/ noun [C] PHYSICS a unit for measuring electrical power, measured in **joules** per second. The unit of electric current is the **amp** and the unit of **potential difference** is the **volt**. Symbol W

wattage /ˈwɒtɪdʒ/ noun [U] PHYSICS the measure of power, measured in watts

wav abbrev COMPUTING the last part of the name of a sound file

wave¹ /weɪv/ noun [C]

1 of water	4 increase
2 movement	5 sudden emotion
3 of sound/light etc	6 lots of people

1 a line of water that rises up on the surface of a sea, lake, or river: *The boat was smashed by a huge wave.* ♦ *Children swam and played in the waves.*
2 a movement that you make with your hand or with an object as a way of saying hello or goodbye to someone or as a signal to them

3 PHYSICS the form that energy such as light or radio waves takes as it travels from one place to another. The line representing the wave curves upwards to a **crest**, then downwards to a **trough**, then upwards again, and so on. The distance between two **crests** or two **troughs** is the **wavelength**. → ELECTROMAGNETIC SPECTRUM —*picture* → on p.822
4 a sudden increase in a particular type of behaviour or activity: *a frightening **wave** of drug-related killings* ♦ *a new **wave** of company bankruptcies*
5 a sudden strong emotion that affects a person or group: *The invasion caused a **wave** of anti-American feeling.*
6 a large number of people moving or arriving somewhere at the same time: ***Waves** of protesters began arriving at the stadium.*
→ NEW WAVE

wave² /weɪv/ verb **1** [I/T] to move your hand in order to say hello or goodbye: *He smiled and waved when he saw me.* ♦ *We **waved goodbye** to them as the car drove off.* **2** [T] to move your hand in order to tell someone to move, to leave, or to stop annoying you: *He **waved** me **away** when I offered to help.* **3** [T] to move something around in the air: *People clapped and cheered and children waved flags.* **4** [I] to move smoothly and gently from side to side: *The tall trees were waving in the wind.*

waveband /ˈweɪvˌbænd/ noun [C] PHYSICS a range of radio waves that have lengths that come between particular limits

'wave-built ,terrace noun [C] GEOLOGY a narrow flat area made from loose stones, sand etc that have been carried along by waves

'wave-cut ,terrace noun [C] GEOLOGY a narrow flat area of rock at the bottom of a sea cliff, caused by the action of the waves

'wave ,file noun [C] COMPUTING a file that contains sound

waveform /'weɪv,fɔːm/ noun [C] PHYSICS a picture of the shape of a wave, especially one showing a characteristic such as frequency or **amplitude** in relation to time

wavelength /'weɪv,leŋθ/ noun [C] **1** the length of the radio wave that a radio station uses for broadcasting. This is in one of the groups **long wave**, **medium wave**, or **short wave**. **2** PHYSICS the distance between two waves of light or radio waves —*picture* → WAVE

'wave ,power noun [U] ENVIRONMENT power that is produced by the movement of waves in the sea

waver /'weɪvə/ verb [I] **1** to not be certain about what to do= HESITATE **2** to shake and not be steady: *Her voice wavered as she said goodbye.*

wavy /'weɪvi/ adj a wavy line or wavy hair has a lot of waves or curls in it

wax¹ /wæks/ noun [U] **1** a solid substance that becomes liquid when it is heated. Wax is used, for example, to make **candles**. —*picture* → REFINE **2** a dark yellow substance in the ears —**waxy** adj

wax² /wæks/ verb **1** [T] to make wood shiny by rubbing wax onto it **2** [I] if the moon is waxing, you see more and more of it each night ≠ WANE

waxing moon /'wæksɪŋ ,muːn/ noun [U] ASTRONOMY the moon when it is between a new moon and a full moon, and more of it appears each night

way¹ /weɪ/ noun [C]

1 method	5 distance in space
2 manner/style	6 distance in time
3 road/path	7 aspect
4 direction/position	+ PHRASES

1 a method for doing something: *There are so many delicious ways you can prepare chicken.* ♦ *Is there any* **way of** *contacting you while you're in Africa?* ♦ *The students are learning new* **ways to** *communicate in writing.* → EASY, HARD¹
2 the manner or style in which something happens or is done: *I love to watch the way she plays with the children.* ♦ *That's* **no way to** *talk to your mother.*
3 the particular road, path, or track that you use in order to go from one place to another: *I don't think this is* **the right way**. ♦ *The tourists* **lost their way** (=became lost) *and had to ask for directions.* ♦ *Is this* **the way to** *the Eiffel Tower?* ♦ *Does Tim* **know the way** *to your house from here?* ♦ *Could you please* **show me the way** *to the bus station?* ♦ *Don't bother picking me up. It's really* **out of your way** (=far from the road you use). → LEAD¹
4 the direction or position where something is, or the direction in which something is moving: *The bathroom is* **this way**. ♦ *The car was going* **the wrong way**.
5 the distance from one place to another: *The nearest shop is quite* **a long way** *from here.* ♦ *The children were arguing* **all the way** *home.*
6 a distance in time from one event to another: *The Christmas holidays were still* **a long way off**.
7 a particular aspect of something: *The evening was a great success,* **in more ways than one**. ♦ **In a way**, *I agree with you.*
    PHRASES **be/get in the/sb's way** to be in the area where someone is, so that it is difficult for them to do

something: *Can I move your bags? They're in my way.*
be/get/keep out of the/sb's way to be away from, or to stay away from, the area where someone is, so that you do not make it difficult for them to do something: *Make sure the kids keep out of the way while I'm working.*
be on the/its way to be about to arrive or happen: *Economists fear a recession is on the way.*
get/have your (own) way to be allowed to do what you want, although other people want something different
get in the way of sth to prevent something from happening: *The new rules are just getting in the way of progress.*
get sth out of the way to finish doing something that is difficult or unpleasant: *I want to get this out of the way before the weekend.*
give way 1 if something gives way, it breaks because there is too much weight or pressure on it **2** to agree to something that someone else wants instead of what you want: *We will not* **give way to** *terrorism.*
go out of your way to do sth to make an extra effort to do something, even though it is not convenient or easy to do
know your way around (sth) to be very familiar with a particular place or activity
make way to move in order to allow someone to go forward or get past: *The crowd made way as police officers entered the building.*
make way for sth to provide space for something new by removing what was there before: *They plan to demolish the houses to make way for a petrol station.*
one way or another used for saying that something will definitely happen, even though you do not know how it will happen: *One way or another, I'm going to go to Europe.*
way of life the way people normally live in a place, or the things that they normally do or experience: *Fishing has been a way of life here for centuries.* ♦ *People see this as a threat to their way of life.*
→ BY, FIND¹, LONG¹

Build your vocabulary: words you can use instead of way

- **means** a way that makes it possible to do something
- **method** a way of doing something that involves following a detailed plan
- **procedure** a way of doing something that involves doing specific activities in a particular order
- **strategy** a way of achieving an aim that involves detailed planning
- **system** a way of doing something that involves following an organized set of rules
- **technique** a way of doing something that involves using particular skills

way² /weɪ/ adv informal by a large amount or distance: *Michael was way ahead of the other runners.*

,way 'out noun [C] **1** an **exit** from a place **2** a way of dealing with a problem

wayward /'weɪwəd/ adj difficult to control and tending to do unexpected things

the WB /,dʌb(ə)l ju: 'bi:/ noun [singular] ECONOMICS the **World Bank**

WC /,dʌb(ə)lju: 'si:/ noun [C] a toilet

we /wiː/ pronoun **1** used for referring to yourself and one or more other people when you are the person speaking or writing: *We moved here soon after we were married.* ♦ *We were all glad to get back home.* **2** used for referring to people in general: *We live in a competitive world.*

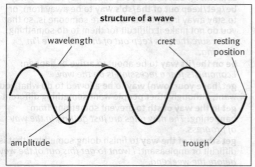

structure of a wave

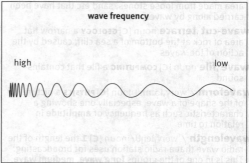

wave frequency

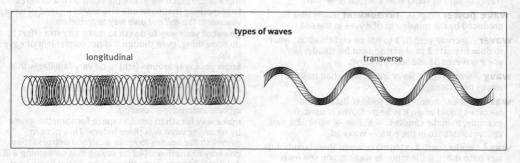

types of waves

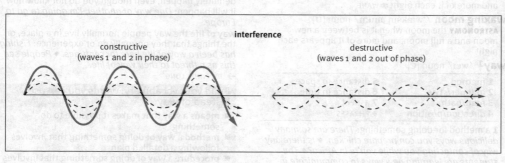

interference

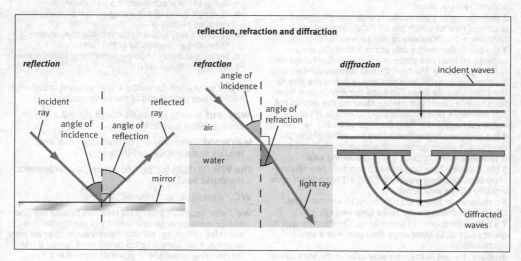

reflection, refraction and diffraction

waves

weak /wiːk/ adj

1 not strong	**6** easily criticized
2 not strongly built/ formed	**7** with a lot of water
3 not effective	**8** hard to see/hear
4 easily persuaded	**9** not stressed
5 bad in quality	**10** of verbs

1 HEALTH lacking physical strength or good health ≠ STRONG: *The illness had left him too weak to speak.* ♦ *He has always had a weak heart.*

2 not strongly built and easily damaged or destroyed: *The floorboards are weak in some places.*

3 not powerful or effective, and unlikely to be successful ≠ STRONG: *We are in a weak negotiating position.* ♦ *a weak economy*

4 lacking determination and easily persuaded to do something that you should not do: *weak, indecisive leadership*

5 bad in quality or ability ≠ STRONG: *Her written work is good, but her oral skills are rather weak.*

6 a weak argument or idea is one that you can easily criticize or prove to be wrong ≠ STRONG: *The government's case is very weak.*

7 a weak liquid contains a lot of water and does not have much taste ≠ STRONG: *a cup of weak coffee*

8 a weak light or sound, or weak heat is one that you cannot easily see, hear, or feel ≠ STRONG

9 LANGUAGE a weak word, or a weak part of a word, is not emphasized when you say the word

10 LANGUAGE a weak verb forms the past tenses in a regular way. Weak verbs in English do this by adding '-ed', '-d', or '-t' to the infinitive.
—**weakly** adv

,**weak 'acid** noun [C] CHEMISTRY an acid with a pH of 5 or 6 that produces only a few **hydrogen ions**

,**weak 'alkali** noun [C] CHEMISTRY an alkali with a pH of 8 or 9 that produces only a few **hydroxyl ions**

weaken /'wiːkən/ verb [I/T] **1** to become less strong or healthy, or to make someone or something do this **2** to become less powerful, effective, or determined, or to make someone or something do this

weakling /'wiːklɪŋ/ noun [C] *showing disapproval* a person or animal that is physically weak

weakness /'wiːknəs/ noun **1** [U] the state or condition of being weak: *the increasing **weakness of** the government* **2** [C] a fault or problem that makes someone or something less effective or attractive: *They listed **the strengths and weaknesses of** their product.* **3** [C] a love or enjoyment of something: *You know my **weakness for** chocolate.*

wealth /welθ/ noun [U] **1** a large amount of money and other valuable things: *a man of immense wealth* **2** the state of being rich ≠ POVERTY: *He had an obsession with power and wealth.* **3** a large amount of something that is useful or interesting: *a **wealth of** exciting opportunities*

wealthy /'welθi/ (**wealthier**, **wealthiest**) adj rich: *a wealthy businessman*

weapon /'wepən/ noun [C] an object that can be used for hurting people or damaging property, for example a gun, knife, or bomb —*picture* → on next page

     PHRASE **weapons of mass destruction** weapons that can cause great damage to very large areas, including **nuclear weapons**, **chemical weapons**, and **biological weapons**. They are often simply referred to as **WMD**.

weaponry /'wepənri/ noun [U] weapons

wear¹ /weə/ (**wears**, **wearing**, **wore** /wɔː/, **worn** /wɔːn/) verb **1** [T] to have something on your body as clothing, decoration, or protection: *He was wearing jeans and a T-shirt.* ♦ *She wasn't wearing any make-up.* ♦ *He wears glasses now.* **2** [T] to have a particular hairstyle: *It was fashionable for men to wear their hair long then.* **3** [T] to have a particular expression on your face: *They all wore puzzled frowns.* **4** [I/T] to become damaged because of being used a lot, or to cause damage to something by using it a lot: *The carpet has **worn thin** in places.* ♦ *He had **worn a hole in** his sleeve.*

     PHRASE **wear thin** if something such as a feeling or explanation wears thin, it becomes gradually weaker or harder to accept

     PHRASAL VERBS ,**wear (sth) a'way** to disappear, or to make something disappear, because it has been used or rubbed a lot: *The inscription on the ring had almost worn away.*

,**wear sth 'down** to make something gradually disappear or become thinner by using or rubbing it: *The old stone steps had been worn down by years of use.*

,**wear 'off** if a feeling wears off, it gradually disappears

,**wear sb 'out** to make someone feel very tired: *Those kids wore me out today.*

wear² /weə/ noun [U] **1** the continuous use that something has over a period of time **2** a type of clothes for a particular activity or a particular group of people: *I didn't bring any evening wear.*

     PHRASE **wear and tear** the changes or damage that normally happen to something that has been used a lot

wearing /'weərɪŋ/ adj making you physically or mentally tired

weary /'wɪəri/ (**wearier**, **weariest**) adj **1** very tired **2** bored or annoyed with something that you feel has continued for too long —**wearily** adv, **weariness** noun [U]

weasel /'wiːz(ə)l/ noun [C] a small thin wild mammal with brown fur, short legs, and a long tail

weather¹ /'weðə/ noun [U] GEOGRAPHY the conditions that exist in the atmosphere, for example, whether it is hot, cold, sunny, or wet: *The hot weather will continue through the weekend.* ♦ *We couldn't paint the fence because of the weather.*

     PHRASE **under the weather** *informal* not feeling well

weather² /'weðə/ verb **1** [I/T] GEOGRAPHY, GEOLOGY if rocks and minerals weather, or if they are weathered, they are broken into very small pieces by the action of rain, snow, frost, water etc **2** [T] to manage a difficult experience without being seriously harmed

'**weather ,forecast** noun [C] GEOGRAPHY a report on what the weather will be like for a period of time in the future —'**weather ,forecaster** noun [C]

weathering /'weðərɪŋ/ noun [U] GEOGRAPHY, GEOLOGY the process by which rocks and minerals are broken into very small pieces by the action of rain, snow, frost, water etc → EROSION —*picture* → ROCK CYCLE

'**weather ,station** noun [C] GEOGRAPHY a place where instruments record information about the weather. Large weather stations also contain equipment that scientists use for studying the weather.

'**weather ,vane** noun [C] GEOGRAPHY an object fixed to the top of a building that points in the direction the wind is coming from = WIND VANE

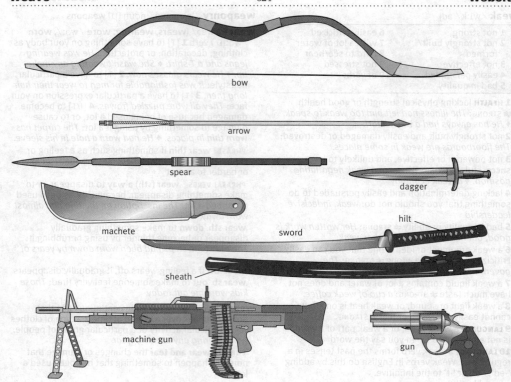

bow

arrow

spear

dagger

machete

sword

hilt

sheath

machine gun

gun

types of weapon

weave /wiːv/ (**weaves, weaving, wove** /wəʊv/, **woven** /ˈwəʊv(ə)n/) verb **1** [I/T] to make cloth by crossing long threads over and under each other on a special machine **2** [T] to create an object by weaving or by twisting pieces of things together: *She was weaving a basket.* **3** (**weaved**) [I/T] to move somewhere by going around and between people or things —**weaver** noun [C]

weaverbird /ˈwiːvəˌbɜːd/ noun [C] a common African and Asian bird that weaves a nest that a lot of weaverbirds live in together

web /web/ noun [C] **1** a net of thin threads that a spider makes in order to catch insects= COBWEB **2** a complicated set of related things: *a web of lies*

the Web /web/ noun [singular] COMPUTING all the websites that organizations have created on their computers for people using the Internet to look at = WORLD WIDE WEB

webbed /webd/ adj if a bird or mammal has webbed feet, it has skin between its toes to help it to swim

ˈweb ˌbrowser noun [C] COMPUTING a software program that you use for finding and looking at pages on the Internet

webcam /ˈwebˌkæm/ noun [C] COMPUTING a camera that is connected to a computer and produces images on a website —*picture* → COMPUTER

webcast /ˈwebˌkɑːst/ noun [C] COMPUTING a broadcast that is shown on the Internet —**webcast** verb [I/T]

web crawler /ˈweb ˌkrɔːlə/ noun [C] COMPUTING a program used for searching through websites on the Internet for documents containing a particular word, phrase, or subject

ˈweb-eˌnable verb [T] COMPUTING to make a piece of electronic equipment or software able to connect to the Internet

ˈweb ˌfarm noun [C] BUSINESS, COMPUTING a **web server farm**

web hosting /ˈweb ˌhəʊstɪŋ/ noun [U] BUSINESS, COMPUTING the business of supplying computer space for websites, which sometimes also includes other related services such as advice in creating the websites themselves

weblink /ˈwebˌlɪŋk/ noun [C] COMPUTING a word or image in a computer document that you can click on, in order to move to a related website

weblog /ˈwebˌlɒg/ noun [C] COMPUTING a **website** that frequently has new information added to it and is designed to provide information instead of things

webmaster /ˈwebˌmɑːstə/ noun [C] COMPUTING someone whose job is to manage a website

ˈweb ˌpage noun [C] COMPUTING a page or document that you can read on a website

webphone /ˈwebˌfəʊn/ noun [C] COMPUTING a phone that uses the Internet to make connections and carry voice messages

ˈweb ˌserver noun [C] COMPUTING a program that finds and provides the web pages that an Internet user wants to see

ˈweb server ˌfarm noun [C] BUSINESS, COMPUTING a business that has a group of computers connected to each other for **web hosting**

website /ˈwebˌsaɪt/ noun [C] COMPUTING a place on the Internet where information is available about a particular subject, company, organization etc

we'd /wiːd/ short form the usual way of saying or writing 'we had' or 'we would'. This is not often used in formal writing: *We'd like to hear from you.* ♦ *Although we'd only just met, I knew that I liked her.*

wed /wed/ (**weds, wedding, wed** or **wedded**) verb [I/T] to marry, or to marry someone

Wed. abbrev Wednesday

wedding /'wedɪŋ/ noun [C] a ceremony in which two people get married: *We wanted a quiet wedding.* ♦ *a wedding present*

'wedding ,ring noun [C] a ring that someone wears in order to show that they are married

wedge¹ /wedʒ/ noun [C] **1** a piece of wood, plastic, or other material that is thin at one end and wider at the other. You press it into a space to hold something in place or to force things apart. **2** a piece of something that is shaped like a wedge: *a wedge of lemon* **3** SPORTS a golf club with a thick flat head that slopes away from the ball

wedge² /wedʒ/ verb [T] **1** to fix something in position with a wedge **2** to push something tightly into a small space: *I wedged a piece of paper into the crack.*

Wednesday /'wenzdeɪ/ noun [C/U] the day after Tuesday and before Thursday: *I was born on a Wednesday.* ♦ *They are arriving on Wednesday.* ♦ *I go swimming on Wednesdays* (=every Wednesday).

Weds abbrev Wednesday

weed¹ /wiːd/ noun **1** [C] a wild plant that grows in a place where it is not wanted, and that blocks light or takes nutrients from other plants **2** [C/U] a plant or a mass of plants growing in water → SEAWEED **3** [U] *informal* the drug **cannabis**

weed² /wiːd/ verb [I/T] to remove weeds from the ground

weedkiller /'wiːdˌkɪlə/ noun [C/U] AGRICULTURE a chemical used for killing plants that are growing where they are not wanted

week /wiːk/ noun [C] **1** a period of seven days, usually counted from a Sunday: *They spent two weeks in Florida.* ♦ *He works from home two days a week.* ♦ *He will meet his uncle in Geneva next week.* ♦ *We're seeing Jim a week on Tuesday* (=seven days from next Tuesday). ♦ *I'll be home Thursday week* (=the Thursday after next Thursday). **2** the five days from Monday to Friday, when most people work: *They work a 35-hour week.* ♦ *She stays in the city during the week.*

weekday /'wiːkdeɪ/ noun [C] a day that is not Saturday or Sunday

weekend /ˌwiːk'end/ noun [C] Saturday and Sunday: *Let's go away for the weekend.* ♦ *The bus service is free at weekends.*

weekly¹ /'wiːkli/ adj happening or published once every week

weekly² /'wiːkli/ adv every week

weep /wiːp/ (**weeps, weeping, wept** /wept/) verb [I/T] to cry

weevil /'wiːv(ə)l/ noun [C] AGRICULTURE an insect that eats plants and can destroy crops

weigh /weɪ/ verb **1** [linking verb] to have a particular weight: *How much do you weigh?* ♦ *The baby weighed 7 pounds at birth.* ♦ *Your suitcase weighs a ton* (=is very heavy). **2** [T] to measure how heavy someone or something is: *She weighed herself once a week.* **3** [T] to consider all the aspects of a situation carefully before making a decision: *The judge weighed all the facts before reaching a verdict.* ♦ *Those costs must be weighed against the environmental benefits.*

PHRASAL VERBS **,weigh sb 'down 1** to be very heavy and prevent someone from moving easily **2** to cause problems for someone or something
,weigh sth 'out to measure an exact amount of something by weighing it
,weigh sth 'up to consider the good and bad aspects of something in order to reach a decision about it

'weigh-,in noun [C] SPORTS an occasion when someone who is taking part in a sport such as boxing is officially weighed

weight¹ /weɪt/ noun

1 measurement	4 sth hard to move
2 being heavy	5 influence
3 for exercise/sport	6 sth causing trouble

1 [U] PHYSICS a measurement of how heavy something is. For scientists, weight is a measure of the force that attracts an object towards the Earth, and the scientific unit of weight is the **newton**. A 100g mass is attracted to the Earth with a force of about 10 newtons (=10 N): *It was about 12 pounds in weight.*
2 [U] the fact or effect of being heavy: *The weight of the backpack made the child fall over.*
3 [C] SPORTS a piece of heavy metal that is designed for lifting for exercise or as a sport
4 [C] a heavy object that is difficult to lift or move
5 [U] the influence or importance that someone or something has: *Simpson's opinions carry a lot of weight with* (=have a lot of influence on) *the President.* ♦ *The Chief Executive is throwing his full weight behind the proposal.*
6 [singular] something that causes you trouble or difficulty: *Obviously the verdict is a huge weight off my mind* (=something I no longer have to worry about).

weight² /weɪt/ or **'weight sth ,down** verb [T] to make something heavier by putting a weight on it in order to stop it from moving

weighted /'weɪtɪd/ adj designed to produce a particular effect or result by giving more importance to one thing than to another: *The tax laws are heavily weighted in favour of the wealthy.*

weightless /'weɪtləs/ adj having no weight, because of being outside the Earth's atmosphere —**weightlessness** noun [U]

weightlifting /'weɪtˌlɪftɪŋ/ noun [U] SPORTS the sport of lifting heavy weights —**weightlifter** noun [C]

Weil's disease /'waɪlz dɪˌziːz/ noun [U] HEALTH a disease affecting animals and sometimes humans, caused by bacteria from the urine of an infected animal

weir /wɪə/ noun [C] a place in a river or stream where a wall has been built across it in order to control the flow of water

weird /wɪəd/ adj strange and unusual —**weirdly** adv

welcome¹ /'welkəm/ verb [T] **1** to greet someone in a polite and friendly way when they arrive: *My aunt and uncle were waiting at the door to welcome us.* **2** to say that you approve of something that has happened, or that you are pleased about it: *They welcomed the new proposals.* **3** to say that you are pleased to accept or consider something such as an opportunity or a question: *We welcome suggestions from our readers.* ♦ *The faculty welcomes prospective students wishing to visit departments.* **4** to celebrate an event: *Fireworks welcomed the New Year in Moscow's Red Square.*

welcome² /'welkəm/ adj **1** if you are welcome somewhere, people are pleased that you are there ≠ UNWELCOME: *Your friends are always welcome here.* ♦ *The neighbours made us feel very welcome.* **2** if something is welcome, people are happy about it because it is pleasant or because they need it

≠ UNWELCOME: *A cold drink would be very welcome.* **3** if someone tells you that you are welcome to do something, they mean that you are allowed to do it if you want to: *Members of the public are* **welcome to** *attend the meeting.* ♦ *You're* **more than welcome** *to stay overnight.* **4** if someone tells you that you are welcome to something, they mean that you can have it or use it, because they do not want it themselves

PHRASE you're welcome used as a reply to someone who has thanked you

welcome³ /'welkəm/ noun **1** [C/U] an act of welcoming someone to a place: *He gave us a* **warm welcome** *and invited us to lunch.* **2** [C] a reaction to a suggestion or decision

welcome⁴ /'welkəm/ interjection used for welcoming someone to a place: **Welcome to** *Edinburgh.*

weld¹ /weld/ verb [T] **TECHNOLOGY** to join two pieces of metal together by using heat and sometimes pressure, or by melting the edges of the metals so that they flow together. Sometimes metal is added to strengthen the joint.

weld² /weld/ noun [C] **TECHNOLOGY** a joint made between two pieces of metal by welding

'weld ,angle noun [C] **TECHNOLOGY** the angle of an electrode as it travels along the direction of a weld

'weld ,bead noun [C] **TECHNOLOGY** a line of weld made during the **electric arc welding** process

welder /'weldə/ noun [C] **TECHNOLOGY** someone whose job is to weld metal

welding goggles /'weldɪŋ ,gɒg(ə)lz/ noun [plural] **TECHNOLOGY** special glasses that are worn to protect the eyes during welding

welfare /'welfeə/ noun [U] **1** the health, happiness, and safety of a person or group= WELL-BEING: *Police are concerned for* **the welfare of** *the child.* **2 SOCIAL STUDIES** care that is provided by the government or another organization for people in need: *the welfare system*

,welfare 'state noun **SOCIAL STUDIES 1 the welfare state** [singular] the system by which a country looks after its citizens by providing them with education, medical care, or money if they are unable to work **2** [C] a country that looks after its citizens by providing social and financial support

we'll /wiːl/ short form the usual way of saying or writing 'we shall' or 'we will'. This is not often used in formal writing: *We'll come to meet you at the airport.*

well¹ /wel/ (**better** /'betə/, **best** /best/) adv **1** skilfully, or effectively: *She speaks Japanese really well.* **2** in a satisfactory way: *The boys were not behaving very well.* **3** completely, or thoroughly: *Shake the can well before opening.* ♦ *I don't know these people very well.* **4** very, or very much: *Rostov was* **well aware of** *the scandal he was creating.* ♦ *A trip to the new museum is* **well worth** *the effort.* ♦ *Pete left the party* **well before** *you got there.*

PHRASES as well (as) in addition to someone or something else: *I'd like a cup of coffee, and a glass of water as well.* ♦ *I need to go to the bookshop as well as the bank.* → ALSO
be doing well to be getting better after an illness
could/may/might well used for saying that something is likely: *The two murder cases may well be connected.*
may/might (just) as well do sth *informal* used for saying that it might be a good idea to do something, although it is not essential: *We might as well wait a little longer for them.*
well done used for giving someone praise when they do something well

well² /wel/ interjection **1** used for introducing a statement or question, often one that you make or ask as a reply: *Well, I agree with you about that.* ♦ *'So you told him what you thought of his idea, then?' 'Well, not exactly.'* ♦ *Well, what did they say?* **2** used after a pause, for continuing with what you were saying: *Well, as I was saying... 'So 3* used for expressing surprise or anger: *Well, they have a nerve!* **4** used for ending a discussion or talk: *Well, thanks for calling. I'll get back to you again tomorrow.*

well³ /wel/ (**better** /'betə/, **best** /best/) adj healthy: *'How are you?' 'Very well, thank you.'* ♦ *I'm not feeling very well today.* ♦ *You don't look too well.* ♦ *Take care and* **get well soon**!

PHRASES just as well helpful or convenient in the situation that exists: *It's just as well we have neighbours who don't mind noise.*
leave well alone to avoid trying to improve or change something that is fairly satisfactory: *Sometimes it's better to just leave well alone.*

well⁴ /wel/ noun [C] a deep hole that is dug in the ground where there is a supply of water, oil, or gas —*picture* → WATER SUPPLY

well-advised /,wel əd'vaɪzd/ adj sensible and following good advice

,well-'balanced adj **1** made up of various things that form a satisfactory or healthy combination: *a well-balanced diet* **2** sensible and mentally strong

well-behaved /,wel bɪ'heɪvd/ adj behaving in a way that is polite and quiet and does not upset people

,well-'being noun [U] a satisfactory state in which you are happy, healthy, and safe, and have enough money = WELFARE

well-brought-up /,wel brɔːt 'ʌp/ adj knowing how to behave politely because you have been taught well by your parents

,well-'built adj a well-built person has an attractive, strong body

,well-con'nected adj knowing a lot of people who are important or who have influence

,well-'defined adj clearly shown or explained

,well-'done adj well-done meat has been cooked thoroughly until all of it is brown → RARE sense 3

,well-'dressed adj wearing good, fashionable clothes

well-earned /,wel 'ɜːnd/ adj earned or deserved because of hard work or a difficult experience

,well-'educated adj a well-educated person has a lot of knowledge about many subjects, usually because they have studied a lot at college or university

,well-es'tablished adj having existed for a long time, and having been successful or accepted for a long time

,well-'fed adj getting a lot of good food to eat

well-formed /,wel 'fɔːmd/ adj **LANGUAGE** a well-formed sentence follows the rules of a language correctly. This would usually be called a **grammatically correct** sentence.

,well-in'formed adj **1** knowing a lot about a subject or a situation **2** based on accurate information

wellington /'welɪŋtən/ or **,wellington 'boot** noun [C] a long rubber or plastic boot that does not let water in

well-intentioned /,wel ɪn'tenʃ(ə)nd/ adj trying to help, but often making a situation worse= WELL-MEANING

,well-'kept adj a well-kept place looks good because someone looks after it carefully

PHRASE **a well-kept secret** a fact that some people know but do not share with everyone

,well-'known adj known by many people, or by the people involved in a particular situation

well-mannered /,wel 'mænəd/ adj polite ≠ ILL-MANNERED, IMPOLITE

,well-'meaning adj trying to help, but often making a situation worse= WELL-INTENTIONED

wellness /'welnəs/ noun [U] health

,well-'off adj informal **1** rich **2** in a good situation, or very lucky

well-read /,wel 'red/ adj having read many books so that you know about a lot of things

,well-'rounded adj **1** including a good balance of various subjects **2** with a strong attractive shape

well-timed /,wel 'taɪmd/ adj effective because of happening at the right time= TIMELY

,well-to-'do adj rich and belonging to a family from a high social class

well-wisher /'wel ,wɪʃə/ noun [C] someone who expresses their good wishes or sympathy to a person who they do not know

went /went/ the past tense of **go¹**

wept /wept/ the past tense and past participle of **weep**

we're /wɪə/ short form the usual way of saying or writing 'we are'. This is not often used in formal writing: We're having a party on Saturday.

were /strong wɜː, weak wə/ a past tense of **be**

weren't /wɜːnt/ short form the usual way of saying or writing 'were not'. This is not often used in formal writing: You weren't listening.

west¹ /west/ noun GEOGRAPHY **1** [U] the direction that is behind you when you are facing the rising sun: We've driven from east to west. —picture → COMPASS **2 the west** [singular] the part of a place that is in the west: The country's major cities are all in the west. ♦ I work in **the west of** the city. **3 the West** [singular] the western part of the world, especially Europe and North America

west² /west/ adv GEOGRAPHY towards the west: You drive west to get to the lake. ♦ We'll camp ten miles **west of** town.

west³ /west/ adj GEOGRAPHY **1** in the west, or facing towards the west: a city on the west coast **2** a west wind blows from the west

the 'West ,Coast GEOGRAPHY the western part of the US, along the Pacific Ocean

the 'West ,Country GEOGRAPHY the south-western part of England

westerly /'westəli/ adj GEOGRAPHY **1** towards or in the west **2** a westerly wind blows from the west

western¹ /'westən/ adj GEOGRAPHY **1** in the west of a place: the western United States **2** relating to or typical of the western part of the world, especially Europe and North America: western attitudes ♦ Wages there are much lower than western levels.

western² /'westən/ noun [C] ARTS a film about cowboys in the western United States in the 19th century

Westminster /'wes(t),mɪnstə/ POLITICS the UK parliament, based in Westminster, London

westward /'westwəd/ adj GEOGRAPHY towards or in the west

westwards /'westwədz/ adv GEOGRAPHY towards the west

wet¹ /wet/ adj **1** covered with water or another liquid: You'd better come in or you'll get wet. ♦ My socks and shoes were **soaking wet** (=very wet). ♦ Her forehead was **wet with** sweat. ♦ Where have you been? You're **wet through** (=completely wet)! **2** not yet dry or solid: wet paint **3** if the weather is wet, it is raining **4** showing disapproval lacking confidence or determination

wet² /wet/ (**wets, wetting, wet** or **wetted**) verb [T] **1** to make something wet with water or another liquid **2** to make something such as a bed or clothes wet with urine

wetlands /'wetlændz/ noun [plural] GEOGRAPHY low land that is often covered with water from the lake, river, or sea next to it —**wetland** adj

,wet oxi'dation noun [U] CHEMISTRY the process of metal becoming destroyed by chemical action, where water and air are both present

the 'wet ,season noun [C] GEOGRAPHY in tropical regions, the part of the year when large amounts of rain fall= RAINY SEASON, THE

'wet-sump lubri,cation noun [U] ENGINEERING a system of supplying oil to an engine in which the **oil pump** pumps oil from the **sump** through a tube, and then to the rest of the engine

we've /wiːv/ short form the usual way of saying or writing 'we have'. This is not often used in formal writing: We've been waiting for a long time.

whack /wæk/ verb [T] informal to hit someone or something with a lot of force —**whack** noun [C]

whale /weɪl/ noun [C] a very large sea mammal that looks like a fish but breathes air through a hole on the top of its head —picture → SEA

whale watching /'weɪl ,wɒtʃɪŋ/ noun [U] TOURISM the activity of watching **whales**

whaling /'weɪlɪŋ/ noun [U] the activity of hunting **whales**

wharf /wɔːf/ (plural **wharves** /wɔːvz/) noun [C] a structure built at the edge of the land where boats can stop= DOCK

what /wɒt/ determiner, interjection, pronoun **1** used for asking which thing or which type of thing something is: What's your name? ♦ What time is it? ♦ I asked her what kind of music she liked. **2** used for referring to a particular thing that is being described or explained: You haven't given me what I asked for. ♦ I told him what the problem was. ♦ What annoyed me was their rudeness. **3** used for asking someone to repeat what they have just said because you did not hear it, or for replying to someone who calls your name: 'Turn the radio down, will you?' 'What?' ♦ 'Hey, Julie!' 'What?' **4** spoken used for introducing a remark which emphasizes how big, good, bad etc someone or something is: What awful weather we've been having! ♦ What a kind man!

PHRASES **what about...?** spoken **1** used for making a suggestion: 'When shall we meet?' 'What about Tuesday?' **2** used for reminding someone that a particular person or thing needs to be considered: What about Eileen? Shouldn't we invite her too?

what for spoken used for asking the reason for something: 'I'm waiting.' 'What for?' ♦ What did you hit him for?

what if...? 1 used for asking what would happen in a particular situation, especially an unpleasant situation: What if something goes wrong? **2** used when you are making a helpful suggestion: What if I lend you the money?

whatever /wɒt'evə/ adv, determiner, pronoun

1 anything or everything	**3** sth you do not know
2 when sth does not matter	**4** at all
	5 an annoyed reply

1 used for referring to anything or everything that happens or is available, needed, wanted etc: *Now you are free to do whatever you want.* ♦ *We shall be grateful for whatever help you can give us.*
2 used for saying that what happens or what is true makes no difference to the situation: *You know that you have our full support whatever you decide.*
3 used for referring to something when you do not know what it is: *He said there were 'technical difficulties', whatever that means.*
4 used with a noun for emphasis in a negative statement: *I have **no** intention **whatever** of leaving.*
5 *spoken* used for showing that you are annoyed about something, or that you do not care about it, but that you will accept it: *'They say we all have to come in for the meeting on Saturday.' 'Whatever.'*

whatsoever /ˌwɒtsəʊ'evə/ adv used for emphasizing a negative statement **=** WHATEVER: *It had no effect whatsoever.*

wheat /wiːt/ noun [U] **1** AGRICULTURE a plant that produces grain used for making bread and many other foods. Wheat is a type of grass and is an important crop in many regions of the world. —picture → CEREAL
2 wheat grains, or food made from them

wheel¹ /wiːl/ noun **1** [C] a circular object that turns round in order to make a car, bicycle, or other vehicle move **2 the wheel** [singular] the **steering wheel** of a vehicle: *Would you like me to **take the wheel** (=to drive) for a while?* ♦ *He fell asleep **at the wheel**.*
PHRASE wheel and axle PHYSICS a wheel with a metal bar passing through the centre of it

wheel² /wiːl/ verb **1** [T] to move something that has wheels by pushing it **2** [T] to move someone in or on an object that has wheels **3** [I/T] to move in a circle in the air, or to make something do this

'wheel a,lignment noun [C] ENGINEERING the process of changing the angles of a vehicle's wheels, so that they are in the correct position

wheelbarrow /'wiːlˌbærəʊ/ noun [C] a large open container with a wheel at the front and handles at the back. You use it outside for moving things such as dirt, wood, or supplies. —picture → AGRICULTURAL

wheelbase /'wiːlˌbeɪs/ noun [C] ENGINEERING the distance between the front and back **axles** of a vehicle

wheelchair /'wiːlˌtʃeə/ noun [C] a chair with large wheels that someone who cannot walk uses for moving around

wheeze /wiːz/ verb [I] to breathe in a noisy way that is uncomfortable, because you are ill —**wheezy** adj

when /wen/ adv, conjunction **1** used for asking at what time or in what situation something happens: *When will we know our test results?* ♦ *I asked him when he was going to start work.* **2** at the same time as something, or just after it has finished: *When it stops raining, we'll go outside.* ♦ *I wear a hat when I work in the fields.* ♦ *I was in the kitchen when I heard the noise.* **3** used for referring to a particular occasion or situation: *He didn't say when he was leaving.* ♦ *Do you remember **the time when** we got lost in the city?* **4** used for making a general statement about something that is always true or correct: *We use 'an' when the next word begins with a vowel.*

whenever /wen'evə/ adv, conjunction **1** every time that something happens: *Whenever I hear that song, I think of you.* **2** *spoken* used for saying that it does not matter when something happens, because all times are equally convenient: *'When shall we meet?' 'Thursday night? Friday?' 'Whenever. I don't mind.'* **3** at any time: *You can come and stay with us whenever you want.* ♦ *Give me a call on Saturday, **or whenever** (=at any other time that is possible or convenient).* **4** used for showing that you do not know when something happened or will happen: *We'll have to wait until the next committee meeting, whenever that is.*

where /weə/ adv, conjunction **1** used for asking what place someone or something is in, or what place they go to: *Where would you like to sit?* ♦ *I wonder where Jack's gone.* ♦ *Do you know where the road leads to?* **2** used for referring to a particular place: *She didn't say where she works.* ♦ *Put the picture where I can see it.* ♦ *We were led to the dining room, where lunch was being served.* **3** used for referring to a situation or a point in a process, discussion, story etc: *Where shall I start?* ♦ *Eventually I reached the point where I was beginning to enjoy my work.*

whereabouts /'weərəˌbaʊts/ adv used for asking in general where someone or something is: *Whereabouts was he born?*

whereas /weər'æz/ conjunction used for showing that there is an important difference between two things or situations: *She likes dancing and singing, whereas her brother is very shy and quiet.*

whereby /weə'baɪ/ adv *formal* done according to the method, arrangement, rule etc that has been referred to

whereupon /ˌweərə'pɒn/ conjunction *formal* used for showing that something happens just after, or because of, something that has been mentioned

wherever /weər'evə/ adv, conjunction **1** everywhere, or anywhere: *Wherever he went, he took his dog with him.* ♦ *The plant grows wherever there's water nearby.* **2** used for emphasizing 'where' in a question to show that you are surprised, interested, upset, or annoyed: *I've been looking all over the place for that letter. Wherever did you find it?* **3** used for showing that you do not know where something is: *He said he was phoning from Landsford Park, **wherever that is**.*

the wherewithal /'weəwɪðˌɔːl/ noun [singular] the money or other things that you need in order to be able to do a particular thing

whether /'weðə/ conjunction **1** used when someone does not know which of two possibilities is true: *They asked us whether we were married.* ♦ *She doesn't even know **whether** her daughter is dead **or** alive.* **2** used when someone can choose between two possibilities: *We haven't decided **whether to** accept their offer.* ♦ *There was a debate over **whether or not to** send troops.* **3** used for saying that it does not matter which of two possibilities is true, because the situation will be the same: ***Whether you like it or not**, you'll have to change your lifestyle.*

- Both **whether** and **if** can be used to introduce indirect questions: *She asked if/whether I liked jazz.*
- Use **whether**, not **if**, before an infinitive or after a preposition: *She can't decide whether to tell him.* ♦ *I was worried about whether he would come.*
- Use **whether**, not **if**, before 'or not': *I don't know whether or not we can afford it.*

which /wɪtʃ/ determiner, pronoun **1** used for asking for a specific choice from a limited number of possibilities: *Which would you like, tea or coffee?* ♦ *Which way did they go?* ♦ ***Which of** the teachers do you like best?* **2** used for referring to a particular person or thing: *Did he say which hotel he was staying at?* ♦ *It* was either blue or green – I forget which. **3** used for adding information or a comment: *It's a story which every child will enjoy.* ♦ *They come from Harare, which is in Zimbabwe.*

whichever /wɪtʃ'evə/ determiner, pronoun **1** used for saying that it does not matter which person or thing is involved: *I'm sure you'll enjoy whichever book you choose.* **2** used for referring to any person or thing from a group: *Whichever of us gets home first will cook the dinner.*

while¹ /waɪl/ conjunction **1** during the time that something is happening: *Someone called while you were out.* **2** used when comparing things, situations, or people and showing how they are different: *While most children learn to read easily, some need extra help.* **3** *formal* despite a particular fact: *While I support you, I do not believe that you will succeed.*

while² /waɪl/ noun [singular] a fairly long period of time: *We haven't seen Barry for a while.* ♦ *I've been waiting here quite a while* (=a fairly long time). → ONCE

whilst /waɪlst/ conjunction *formal* while

whim /wɪm/ noun [C] a sudden feeling that you must have or must do something that other people think is unnecessary or silly

whimper /'wɪmpə/ verb [I] to make small sounds of pain, fear, or sadness —**whimper** noun [C]

whimsical /'wɪmzɪk(ə)l/ adj **1** slightly strange and funny **2** slightly strange or old-fashioned

whine /waɪn/ verb [I] **1** to complain in a way that annoys other people **2** if a dog whines, it makes a high noise, usually because it wants something —**whine** noun [C]

whip¹ /wɪp/ noun [C] **1** a long thin piece of leather with a handle on one end that is used for making horses move faster **2** POLITICS someone in a political party whose job is to make certain that other members are present and vote in the correct way when they are needed

whip² /wɪp/ (**whips, whipping, whipped**) verb [T] **1** to hit a person or animal with a whip **2** to move something somewhere very quickly: *Sykes whipped out a gun and demanded the money.* **3** to mix a food such as cream very quickly in order to make it thicker = BEAT

whipworm /'wɪp,wɜːm/ noun [C] BIOLOGY a worm that lives as a parasite in human intestines. It can cause diarrhoea.

whirl¹ /wɜːl/ verb **1** [I/T] to move quickly in circles, or to make something move in this way **2** [I] if your mind, thoughts, or feelings whirl, you feel very confused or upset **3** [I/T] to turn quickly, usually to look at someone or something

whirl² /wɜːl/ noun [C] **1** a lot of confused activity and movement **2** a quick movement round in circles

whirlpool /'wɜːl,puːl/ noun [C] an area in a river or stream where the water moves round in circles very quickly and pulls things under the surface

whirlwind /'wɜːl,wɪnd/ noun [C] **1** a situation that changes very quickly, in a way that is confusing or out of control: *a whirlwind of emotions* **2** a very powerful dangerous wind that spins extremely fast

whirr /wɜː/ (**whirrs, whirring, whirred**) verb [I] to make a fast repeated quiet sound —**whirr** noun [singular]

whisk /wɪsk/ verb [T] **1** to mix something such as eggs or cream using a whisk or a fork = BEAT —*picture* → FOOD **2** to move someone or something very quickly: *The police whisked her away in a van.*

whisker /'wɪskə/ noun [C] one of several long stiff hairs that grow near the mouth of an animal such as a cat

whisky /'wɪski/ (plural **whiskies**) noun [C/U] a strong alcoholic drink from Scotland that is made from **barley**, or a glass of this drink

whisper¹ /'wɪspə/ verb [I/T] to speak very quietly to someone, so that other people cannot hear you: *Stop whispering, you two!* ♦ *Dad whispered a warning to us to keep quiet.*

whisper² /'wɪspə/ noun [C] a very quiet way of saying something to someone so that other people cannot hear you

whistle¹ /'wɪs(ə)l/ noun [C] **1** a small metal or plastic object that you put in your mouth and blow in order to make a high sound **2** a sound that you make by blowing through a whistle or by forcing air through your lips

whistle² /'wɪs(ə)l/ verb **1** [I/T] to make a high sound by blowing through a whistle or by forcing air through your lips **2** [I] to produce a high sound as a result of air passing quickly through or over something **3** [I] to move very quickly through the air

white¹ /waɪt/ adj

1 of colour of milk	4 ill/upset
2 with pale skin	5 of tea/coffee
3 of white people	6 of wine

1 something that is white is the same colour as milk or snow: *a white tablecloth* ♦ *The hills were white with snow.* → BLACK¹ sense 1
2 a white person belongs to a race of people with pale skin: *The attacker was described as white, with short hair.* → BLACK¹ sense 2
3 relating to white people, or consisting of white people: *a white neighbourhood*
4 with a very pale face because you are frightened, angry, or ill: *She suddenly turned very white and fainted.* ♦ *Luke's face was white with anger.*
5 white tea or coffee has milk in it → BLACK¹ sense 3
6 white wine is a pale yellow colour
—**whiteness** noun [U]

white² /waɪt/ noun **1** [C/U] the colour of milk or snow: *We painted the walls a creamy white.* ♦ *The sign was written in white on a black background.* ♦ *The bride wore white* (=white clothes). **2** [C] someone who belongs to a race of people with pale skin **3** [C/U] the clear part inside an egg that surrounds the yolk

white blood cell noun [C] BIOLOGY a type of blood cell. Many types of white blood cells protect the body against infection and produce antibodies. Unlike red blood cells, white blood cells have a nucleus. They are formed in the bone marrow and **lymph nodes**. → RED BLOOD CELL —*picture* → CELL

whiteboard /'waɪt,bɔːd/ noun [C] EDUCATION a white plastic board in a classroom that a teacher writes on with large thick pens

white cast iron noun [U] TECHNOLOGY cast iron in which all the carbon is present in the form **cementite**

white-collar adj SOCIAL STUDIES white-collar workers work in offices → BLUE-COLLAR

white dwarf noun [C] ASTRONOMY a star that does not shine very brightly and is at the end of its life

white goods noun [plural] BUSINESS large pieces of electrical equipment, for example **washing machines** and **fridges**

the White House POLITICS **1** the official home of the President of the US, in Washington, DC **2** the people who work at the White House, including the President

ˌwhite ˈknight noun [C] **BUSINESS** a person or company that helps another company by investing money in it, in order to prevent it being **taken over** (=taken control of) by a larger company

ˈwhite ˌmatter noun [U] **ANATOMY** the white tissue in the brain and **spinal cord** of vertebrate animals. It consists mainly of nerve fibres. → GREY MATTER —*picture* → BRAIN, SPINAL CORD

ˌwhite ˈmeat noun [U] meat such as chicken or **pork** that is pale after you have cooked it

ˌwhite ˈspirit noun [U] a liquid made from petrol, used for removing paint marks and making paint thinner

whitewater rafting /ˌwaɪtwɔːtə ˈrɑːftɪŋ/ noun [U] **SPORTS** the activity of floating in a **raft** along rivers where the current is very fast and rough

whitish /ˈwaɪtɪʃ/ adj almost white in colour

Whitworth thread or **Whitworth screw thread** /ˈwɪtwɜːθ ˌθred/ noun [C] **TECHNOLOGY** a **thread** (=raised line) curving around a screw that has sides at an angle of 55° to the screw, a space shaped like the letter U in between, and a rounded top

who /huː/ pronoun **1** used for asking which person is involved in something, or what someone's name is: *Who works in that office?* ♦ *Who did you speak to?* ♦ *'Who is that?' 'It's Karen – don't you recognize her?'* ♦ *Who else did you tell the secret to?* **2** used when someone knows or says which person is involved in something or what their name is: *Curry refused to say who had organized the meeting.* **3** used for adding more information about a person: *I recently talked to Michael Hall, who lectures in music at the university.* ♦ *We only employ people who already have computer skills.*

who'd /huːd/ short form the usual way of saying or writing 'who had' or 'who would'. This is not often used in formal writing: *He was the one who'd complained the loudest.* ♦ *Do you know anyone who'd be able to help us?*

whodunnit /ˌhuːˈdʌnɪt/ noun [C] **ARTS, LITERATURE** *informal* a book or film usually about a murder, in which you do not know who committed the murder until the end

whoever /huːˈevə/ pronoun **1** someone, or anyone: *Whoever finishes first will get a prize.* ♦ *You may choose whoever you would like to represent you.* **2** used for saying that it does not matter who is involved: *Whoever you ask, the answer is always the same.* **3** *spoken* used when you do not know who someone is or what their name is: *The film is about Celia Daniels, whoever that is.*

whole¹ /həʊl/ adj **1** all of something= ENTIRE: *My whole family came to watch me playing in the concert.* ♦ *The whole process will take months.* ♦ *Come on, let's just forget the whole thing.* ♦ *She told me the whole story.* **2** not divided or broken: *Some of the statues were broken, but others were still whole.* **3** used for emphasizing what you are saying: *We've had a whole host of problems.* ♦ *The whole point of this meeting was to discuss finances.* ♦ *They're the best ice creams in the whole world.* —**wholeness** noun [U]

whole² /həʊl/ noun [C] a complete thing made of several parts: *Two halves make a whole.*

PHRASES **as a whole** considering all the parts of something as one unit: *His views are not popular with the townspeople as a whole.*
on the whole used for talking about the general situation: *It was a pretty good conference on the whole.* ♦ *On the whole, she felt that the report was fair.*
the whole of all of something: *I was off work for the*

whole of January. ♦ *The problem will affect the whole of Europe.*

whole³ /həʊl/ adv **1** as a single piece: *The bird swallowed the fish whole.* **2** *informal* completely: *E-commerce is a whole new way of doing business.*

wholehearted /ˌhəʊlˈhɑːtɪd/ adj enthusiastic and complete —**wholeheartedly** adv

wholemeal /ˈhəʊlmiːl/ adj made from flour that contains all the wheat grain, including the outer part

ˌwhole ˈnumber noun [C] **MATHS** a number such as 1, 32, 144 etc, rather than a number such as 0.1, 0.32, 1/2, 3/4 etc

wholesale¹ /ˈhəʊlˌseɪl/ adj **1** **BUSINESS** relating to the business of buying and selling large quantities of goods, especially to people who are going to sell them in a shop **2** affecting every part of something, or affecting every person: *the wholesale destruction of entire communities* —**wholesale** adv

wholesale² /ˈhəʊlˌseɪl/ noun [U] **BUSINESS** the business of buying and selling large quantities of goods, especially in order to sell them in a shop

wholesaler /ˈhəʊlˌseɪlə/ noun [C] **BUSINESS** a person or company that sells large quantities of goods to shops or small businesses

wholesome /ˈhəʊls(ə)m/ adj **1** wholesome food is good for you **2** thought to have a good influence on people

ˌwhole ˈtone noun [C] **MUSIC** a musical interval consisting of two **semitones**, for example between the notes D and E, or A and B

who'll /huːl/ short form the usual way of saying or writing 'who will'. This is not often used in formal writing: *You're the one who'll have to decide.*

wholly /ˈhəʊlli/ adv *formal* completely: *His behaviour is wholly unacceptable.*

whom /huːm/ pronoun *formal* **1** used for adding more information about a person: *This is the gentleman whom I mentioned a moment ago.* **2** used for asking which person is involved in something: *To whom did you speak?*

whooping cough /ˈhuːpɪŋ ˌkɒf/ noun [U] **HEALTH** a very infectious disease that mainly affects children under five. It makes them cough in an uncontrolled way and make a loud noise when they try to breathe air into the lungs.

who's /huːz/ short form the usual way of saying or writing 'who is' or 'who has'. This is not often used in formal writing: *Do you know anyone who's been to New Zealand?* ♦ *Who's that talking to Michael?*

whose /huːz/ determiner, pronoun **1** used for showing that someone or something belongs to the person or thing that you have just mentioned: *Help is needed for families whose homes were destroyed in the floods.* ♦ *a school whose reputation is excellent* **2** used for asking who someone or something belongs to or who they are connected with: *What about these glasses? Whose are they?* ♦ *Whose little girl is she?* **3** used when someone knows or says who someone or something belongs to: *He wouldn't say whose names were on the list.*

who've /huːv/ short form the usual way of saying or writing 'who have'. This is not often used in formal writing: *Talk to people who've been doing the job for a while.*

wh-question /ˌdʌb(ə)lju: ˈeɪtʃ ˌkwestʃ(ə)n/ noun [C] **LANGUAGE** a question that begins with any of the words 'who', 'where', 'when', 'what', 'why', or 'how'

why /waɪ/ adv **1** used for asking the reason for something: *Why are you so angry?* ♦ *He asked me why I was leaving early.* **2** used when someone knows or says the reason for something: *I don't know why she's always so rude.* ♦ *There's no reason why Frank should be jealous.*

PHRASE **why not...?** *spoken* **1** used for making a suggestion: *Why not stay for lunch?* **2** used for agreeing to a suggestion or request: *'Perhaps we could all meet up at your house?' 'Yes, of course, why not?'*

wicked /ˈwɪkɪd/ adj **1** morally wrong and deliberately intending to hurt people **2** slightly cruel, but in a way that is intended to be funny: *a wicked sense of humour* —**wickedly** adv, **wickedness** noun [U]

wicker /ˈwɪkə/ noun [U] long thin pieces of wood that are woven together to make furniture or baskets

wicket /ˈwɪkɪt/ noun [C] SPORTS in the game of cricket, the set of three sticks that the **bowler** tries to hit with the ball

wide¹ /waɪd/ adj **1** measuring a large distance from one side to the other: *Beijing's wide avenues and boulevards* ♦ *An earthquake shook a wide area of southern Italy on Saturday.* **2** measuring a particular distance from one side to the other: *The stream is about 4 feet wide.* ♦ *The roads are barely wide enough for cars.* **3** including or involving many different things or people: *Her proposal has gained wide support.* ♦ *his wide experience of the business world* ♦ *Workers must carry out a wide range of tasks.* **4** large: *There can be wide differences in temperature between the north and the south.* ♦ *a wide smile* → MARK¹, WIDTH

wide² /waɪd/ adv **1** as much as possible: *The door opened wide and people came streaming out.* ♦ *He was now wide awake and sitting up in bed.* **2** over a large area: *The news spread far and wide.*

,wide ,area ˈnewtork noun [C] COMPUTING *see* WAN

wide-floored /ˈwaɪd ˌflɔːd/ adj GEOGRAPHY a wide-floored valley has a wide bottom part

widely /ˈwaɪdli/ adv **1** by a lot of people, or in a lot of places: *He has travelled widely in South America.* ♦ *The drug is widely used in the treatment of cancer.* **2** by a large amount, or to a large degree: *widely different views* ♦ *Prices vary widely for products that appear to be very similar.*

widen /ˈwaɪd(ə)n/ verb [I/T] **1** to become wider, or to make something wider ≠ NARROW **2** to increase, or to make something increase ≠ NARROW

wide-ranging /ˌwaɪd ˈreɪndʒɪŋ/ adj dealing with a large variety of subjects

widespread /ˈwaɪdspred/ adj happening or existing in many places, or affecting many people: *the widespread use of antibiotics* ♦ *The project has received widespread support.* ♦ *These facilities are becoming more widespread in urban areas.*

widow /ˈwɪdəʊ/ noun [C] a woman whose husband has died

widowed /ˈwɪdəʊd/ adj if someone is widowed, their husband or wife has died

widower /ˈwɪdəʊə/ noun [C] a man whose wife has died

width /wɪdθ/ noun **1** [C/U] the distance from one side of something to the other: *The path is about two metres in width.* **2** [U] the quality of being wide: *the width of his shoulders* **3** [C] SPORTS the distance from one side of a swimming pool to the other

wield /wiːld/ verb [T] **1** to have power or influence and be able to use it: *The organization wielded enormous political power.* **2** to hold a weapon or tool and use it

wife /waɪf/ (plural **wives** /waɪvz/) noun [C] the woman that a man is married to: *I'd better phone my wife and tell her I'll be late.* ♦ *a reception for the wives of the ambassadors*

wi-fi /ˈwaɪ faɪ/ noun [C] COMPUTING a set of standards for **wireless local area networks**. Any wi-fi product can be used with any other wi-fi product.

wig /wɪg/ noun [C] a cover of artificial hair that you wear on your head

wiggle /ˈwɪg(ə)l/ verb [I/T] to make short quick movements from side to side, or to move something in this way —**wiggle** noun [C]

wiki /ˈwiki/ noun [C] COMPUTING a website that allows its readers to freely add and edit content, and to create **links** between different pieces of content

wild¹ /waɪld/ adj

1 not raised by humans	**4** with no people
2 with strong emotions	**5** of weather/sea
3 not accurate	**6** exciting

1 a wild animal or plant lives or grows on its own in natural conditions and is not raised by humans: *The wild rose is a familiar sight in woods and hedges.* ♦ *This trait is common to both domestic and wild dogs.*
2 expressing or feeling strong emotions: *Hernandez entered the boxing ring to wild cheers.* ♦ *When Pascal scored, the fans went wild.*
3 not accurate, or not thought about carefully: *wild accusations* ♦ *They make all sorts of wild promises.*
4 a wild area is one where people do not live or cannot live: *wild mountainous regions*
5 if the weather or the sea is wild, there is a storm with strong winds: *a wet and wild night*
6 exciting and enjoyable: *They have some pretty wild parties.*
—**wildness** noun [U]

wild² /waɪld/ adv in a natural or uncontrolled way: *I found these daisies growing wild in the meadow.*

wild³ /waɪld/ noun **in the wild** in a natural environment

ˈwild ˌcard noun [C] **1** COMPUTING a sign or symbol used for representing any letter or number **2** SPORTS permission for someone to take part in a sports competition that they would not normally be allowed to play in

ˈwild ˌcat noun [C] **1** a wild mammal that is similar to a pet cat but larger **2** a cat that lives in natural conditions rather than with people

wildebeest /ˈvɪldəˌbiːst/ noun [C] an African wild mammal that is a type of **antelope** with curved horns = GNU

wilderness /ˈwɪldənəs/ noun **1** [C] an area of land where people do not live or grow crops and where there are no buildings **2** [singular] a period when someone is not as successful or powerful as they were previously

wildfire /ˈwaɪldˌfaɪə/ noun **spread like wildfire** if information spreads like wildfire, a lot of people hear about it in a short period of time

ˈwild ˌflower noun [C] a flower that grows in fields or in the countryside rather than in gardens

wildlife /ˈwaɪldˌlaɪf/ noun [U] animals and plants that live in natural conditions

wildly /ˈwaɪldli/ adv **1** in an uncontrolled way: *Italian fans cheered wildly.* **2** extremely: used for emphasizing what you are saying: *The figures are wildly inaccurate.*

wilful /ˈwɪlf(ə)l/ adj **1** done deliberately in order to cause damage or harm **2** someone who is wilful is determined to do what they want and does not care if they upset other people —**wilfully** adv

will¹ /wɪl/ modal verb **1** used for saying what is planned or expected for the future: *The President will attend a lunch hosted by the Queen.* ♦ *Let's finish the job now – it won't take long.* **2** used for saying that you are willing to do something or that you intend to do it: *If you won't tell him the truth, I will.* **3** used for asking or inviting someone to do something or for offering them something: *Will you please listen to what I'm saying!* ♦ *Won't you stay for lunch?* **4** used for saying whether something is possible: *Will these gloves fit you?* ♦ *The money will buy enough food for a week.*

will² /wɪl/ noun **1** [C/U] someone's determination to do what they want: *a child with a very strong will* ♦ *Without the will to win, the team won't go far.* **2** [singular] what someone wants to happen: *the will of the people* ♦ *He was kept in the room against his will* (=someone forced him to stay in the room although he did not want to stay). → GOODWILL **3** [singular] an ability to make decisions and take action: *This machine seems to have a will of its own.* → FREE WILL **4** [C] LAW a legal document that explains what you want to happen to your money and possessions after you die: *Ed's father didn't leave him anything in his will.*

willing /'wɪlɪŋ/ adj **1** if you are willing to do something, you do it when someone asks you ≠ UNWILLING: *They are very willing to give her the job.* ♦ *I wasn't willing to accept his gifts.* **2** enthusiastic about doing something ≠ UNWILLING: *a willing helper* —**willingly** adv: *She would willingly give up her spare time to help you.* —**willingness** noun [U]

willow /'wɪləʊ/ noun [C] a tree with long thin branches and narrow leaves that grows near water

willpower /'wɪl,paʊə/ noun [U] the ability to control your thoughts and behaviour in order to achieve something

wilt /wɪlt/ verb [I] if a plant wilts, it gradually bends towards the ground because it needs water or is dying

win¹ /wɪn/ (**wins, winning, won** /wʌn/) verb **1** [I/T] to defeat everyone else by being the best, or by finishing first in a competition ≠ LOSE: *Every time we play tennis, she wins.* ♦ *Who won the race?* ♦ *The Liberals won the election.* ♦ *I never win at cards.* **2** [I/T] to achieve victory in a war, battle, or argument ≠ LOSE: *In an argument like that, nobody wins.* ♦ *No one knows who will win the war.* **3** [T] to get something as a prize for defeating other people or because you are lucky: *He won £4,000 in the lottery.* ♦ *Our skiing team won a gold medal at the Olympics.* ♦ *Raoul won first prize in a spelling contest.* **4** [T] to succeed in getting something that you want because of hard work or ability: *We've won a £3 million contract to build the new bridge.* ♦ *The bill is winning a lot of support from farmers.* —**winning** adj: *the winning team*

PHRASAL VERB ,**win sb** '**over** to persuade someone to agree with you: *We've finally won him over to our point of view.*

win² /wɪn/ noun [C] an occasion when someone wins something: *This is their fourth win of the season.*

wince /wɪns/ verb [I] to make a sudden expression or movement that shows that you are embarrassed or feel pain —**wince** noun [C]

winch /wɪntʃ/ noun [C] TECHNOLOGY a piece of equipment that uses a rope or chain for lifting or pulling things or people —**winch** verb [T]

wind¹ /wɪnd/ noun **1** [C/U] GEOGRAPHY a natural current of air that moves fast enough for you to feel it: *A cold wind blew.* ♦ *During the night the wind picked*

up (=got stronger). ♦ *The helicopter can't reach them until the wind drops* (=becomes less strong). ♦ *A large gust of wind swept his hat into the sea.* **2** [singular] the air in your lungs: *The heavy blow knocked the wind out of him.* **3** [U] gas produced in the stomach that makes you feel uncomfortable

wind² /waɪnd/ (**winds, winding, wound** /waʊnd/) verb

1 wrap sth around	4 about watch/clock
2 move in a curve	5 about car window
3 move tape	

1 [T] to wrap or twist something around something else: *I put on my coat and wound a scarf round my neck.* **2** [I/T] to follow a course or path that curves or twists a lot: *The bus wound its way up the mountain.* ♦ *The River Nile winds through Sudan and Egypt.* **3** [T] to make the tape in a video or a **cassette** move forwards or backwards in a machine: *I've wound it back to the beginning.* → REWIND **4** [T] if you wind a watch or clock, you make it operate by turning a part of it round and round **5** [T] to make the window of a vehicle move up or down: *Wind down the window and let some air in.*

wind³ /wɪnd/ verb [T] to hit someone hard in the stomach, so that they have difficulty breathing

wind chill /'wɪnd ,tʃɪl/ noun [U] GEOGRAPHY the fact that the wind makes the air temperature feel colder

wind current /'wɪnd ,kʌrənt/ noun [C] GEOGRAPHY a movement of the wind in a particular direction:

windfall tax /'wɪn(d)fɔːl ,tæks/ noun [C] BUSINESS, ECONOMICS an extra amount of tax that the government charges a company that has made a lot of money unexpectedly

wind farm /'wɪnd ,fɑːm/ noun [C] ENVIRONMENT a place where **wind turbines** are used for producing electricity from the power of the wind

winding /'waɪndɪŋ/ adj with a lot of bends: *a winding lane*

wind instrument /'wɪnd ,ɪnstrʊmənt/ noun [C] MUSIC a musical instrument that you play by blowing through it, for example a **flute** or **clarinet**

windlass /'wɪndləs/ noun [C] TECHNOLOGY a piece of equipment used for lifting heavy things. It uses a motor to wind a rope or chain around a large round cylinder.

wind load /'wɪnd ,ləʊd/ noun [C] CONSTRUCTION the amount of pressure on walls and roofs from the wind

windmill /'wɪn(d),mɪl/ noun [C] a tall building with long pieces of wood or metal that turn in the wind, used for producing power or crushing grain

window /'wɪndəʊ/ noun [C] **1** a hole with a frame in a wall or vehicle that lets in light and air and lets you see outside, or the glass that covers this hole: *She was watching him from an upstairs window.* ♦ *a car with electric windows* ♦ *She just stood there staring out of the window.* ♦ *Do you mind if I open a window?* ♦ *Rioters set fire to cars and smashed shop windows.* **2** COMPUTING one of the different work areas on a computer screen: *Click on the X to close the window.* **3** a short period of time when you can do something: *I've got a window on Friday when I could see you.*

'**window ,pane** noun [C] a piece of glass used in a window

'**window ,seat** noun [C] a seat that is next to a window on a plane, train, or bus

windowsill /'wɪndəʊ,sɪl/ noun [C] a shelf under a window

windpipe /'wɪn(d),paɪp/ noun [C] **ANATOMY** the tube that carries air into the lungs from the nose or mouth = TRACHEA

wind-pollinated /'wɪnd ,pɒlənetɪd/ adj **BIOLOGY** wind-pollinated plants are fertilized by pollen that is blown by the wind from other plants of the same type —**wind pollination** noun [U]

wind power /'wɪnd ,paʊə/ noun [U] electricity that is created using the power of wind

windscreen /'wɪn(d),skriːn/ noun [C] the large window at the front of a vehicle

windscreen wiper /'wɪn(d)skriːn ,waɪpə/ noun [C] a long thin piece of equipment that moves across a vehicle's windscreen in order to wipe and clean it

wind speed /'wɪnd ,spiːd/ noun [U] **GEOGRAPHY** the speed at which the air is moving when the wind is blowing

windsurfing /'wɪn(d),sɜːfɪŋ/ noun [U] **SPORTS** a sport in which someone moves across water standing on a flat board with a sail —**windsurfer** noun [C]

wind turbine /'wɪnd ,tɜːbaɪn/ noun [C] **ENVIRONMENT** a large machine like a **windmill** used for producing electricity from the wind

wind vane /'wɪnd ,veɪn/ noun [C] **GEOGRAPHY** a **weather vane**

windy /'wɪndi/ adj with a lot of wind: *a windy day*

wine /waɪn/ noun [C/U] an alcoholic drink made from grapes, or a glass of this drink: *a bottle of wine* ♦ *Spanish wines* ♦ *I'll have a red wine, please* (=a glass of red wine).

wing /wɪŋ/ noun [C]

1 part of bird/insect	5 in sports
2 part of plane	6 wheel cover on car
3 part of building	7 in a theatre
4 part of group	

1 one of the parts on a bird or insect that move up and down and allow it to fly: *a moth's delicate wings* ♦ *a blackbird flapping its wings* —picture → BIRD, INSECT
2 one of the long flat parts on both sides of a plane that allow it to fly
3 a part of a building that sticks out from the main part, especially one with a particular purpose: *the west wing* ♦ *He works in the psychiatric wing of the hospital.*
4 a part of an organization or political party that has particular responsibilities or opinions: *the Green Party's youth wing*
5 SPORTS the left or right side of a sports field, or a player who plays on the side of a sports field
6 the part of a car that covers the wheel
7 the wings [plural] **ARTS** the right or left side of a stage that you cannot see if you are in the audience

winged /wɪŋd/ adj with wings

wing ,mirror noun [C] a small mirror on each side of a vehicle

wing ,nut noun [C] a **nut** with a flat piece on either side to make it easier to hold

wink /wɪŋk/ verb [I] to quickly close and open one eye as a sign to someone: *Marcus winked at me.* —**wink** noun [C]

winner /'wɪnə/ noun [C] **1** someone who wins a competition, race, or prize: *The winner of the tournament gets £50,000.* ♦ *She was a gold medal winner at the last Olympics.* ♦ *The winner will be announced in October.* **2** informal something that is

very popular or successful: *Her latest book looks like another winner.*

'winning ,post noun [singular] **SPORTS** the post that shows where the end of a horse race is

winnings /'wɪnɪŋz/ noun [plural] money that you win

'winning ,streak noun [C] a period of time when you win a series of things

winnow /'wɪnəʊ/ verb [T] **AGRICULTURE** to remove the **husk** (=outer cover) from grain, either by throwing the grain in the air or by blowing air through it

winter¹ /'wɪntə/ noun [C/U] the season after autumn and before spring, when it is usually cold: *a cold winter* ♦ *a winter's night* ♦ *We usually go skiing in winter.* ♦ *This town is deserted in the winter.* ♦ *She wore a heavy winter coat.*

winter² /'wɪntə/ verb [I] to spend the winter in a particular place

winter solstice /,wɪntə 'sɒlstɪs/ noun [C/U] the day of the year when the sun is above the horizon for the shortest amount of time

,winter 'sports noun [plural] **SPORTS** sports that are done on snow or ice

wintry /'wɪntri/ adj cold and typical of winter

wipe¹ /waɪp/ verb [T] **1** to clean or dry something by moving something such as a cloth over it: *Let me just wipe the table before you sit down.* ♦ *She wiped away her tears.* ♦ *He wiped his mouth with his serviette.* **2** to clean or dry something by moving it over a surface: *Wipe your feet before you come inside.* ♦ *I wish you wouldn't wipe your hands on your clothes!* **3** to remove something, or to make something disappear: *Nearly $20 billion was wiped off share prices yesterday.* ♦ *This new virus could wipe all the data from your hard drive.*
PHRASAL VERB **,wipe sth 'out** to destroy or get rid of something completely = ERADICATE: *We want to wipe out world hunger by the year 2010.*

wipe² /waɪp/ noun [C] **1** the action of wiping something to make it clean **2** a small wet cloth for cleaning something that you use only once

wire¹ /'waɪə/ noun [C/U] **1** a long piece of metal like a very thin piece of string: *The sticks were tied in bundles with wire.* ♦ *a wire cage* **2** a long thin piece of metal that carries electricity or telephone signals: *telephone wires*

wire² /'waɪə/ verb [T] **1** to connect a piece of electrical equipment to something, or to connect the wires inside a piece of equipment **2** to send money using an electronic system

wireless /'waɪələs/ adj not using wires: *wireless phones* ♦ *wireless data transfer* —**wirelessly** adv

'Wireless Appli,cation ,Protocol noun **COMPUTING** see **WAP**

wiring /'waɪərɪŋ/ noun [U] the electric wires in a building, vehicle, or machine

wiry /'waɪəri/ adj **1** a wiry person is thin but looks strong **2** wiry hair is stiff and rough

wisdom /'wɪzdəm/ noun [U] the ability to make good decisions based on knowledge and experience: *The Egyptian leader was praised for his courage and wisdom.*
PHRASE **question/doubt the wisdom of (doing) sth** to feel that something is probably not a sensible thing to do

'wisdom ,tooth noun [C] **ANATOMY** one of the four large teeth that grow at each of the back corners of the mouth of an adult —picture → TOOTH

wise /waɪz/ adj **1** a wise action or decision is sensible and shows that you have good judgment: *You made a* **wise decision** *when you chose to study Spanish.* ♦ *I don't think* **it's wise to** *teach your children at home.* **2** a wise person is able to make good choices and decisions because they have a lot of experience —**wisely** adv: *They spent the money wisely.*

wish¹ /wɪʃ/ verb **1** [T] to want something to happen although it is unlikely: *I wish I was rich!* ♦ *Andy wished that he could think of a way of helping.* ♦ *I wish Beth would stop interfering.* **2** [T] used for saying that you feel sorry or disappointed about something that you did or did not do: *I wish I'd never come!* ♦ *Now he wished that he had listened more carefully.* **3** [I/T] *formal* to want something, or to want to do something: *You may attend the meeting* **if you wish.** ♦ *Please do not hesitate to contact me if you wish to discuss the matter.* **4** [T] **wish sb sth** used for saying that you hope someone enjoys something or that something good happens to them: *May I* **wish you** *all* **a very Merry Christmas.** ♦ *I* **wish you** *every* **success.** ♦ *The crowd* **wished them well** *as they left for their honeymoon.*

PHRASAL VERB '**wish for sth** *formal* to want something: *What more could anyone wish for?*

wish² /wɪʃ/ noun [C] **1** a feeling that you want something or want to do something: *He'd* **expressed a wish to** *go there.* ♦ *I have to* **respect the wishes of** *my client.* **2** a thing that you want to have or to do: *Our one wish is to find a cure for this disease.* **3** something that you hope will happen by magic or by the power of your mind: **Make a wish** *and then blow out the candles.*
→ BEST

wishful thinking /ˌwɪʃf(ə)l ˈθɪŋkɪŋ/ noun [U] a belief that something is true, based only on the fact that you want it to be true, not on the real situation

wisp /wɪsp/ noun [C] something that has a long, thin, delicate shape: *a wisp of smoke* —**wispy** adj

wit /wɪt/ noun **1** [singular/U] the ability to use words in a clever way that makes people laugh: *a novel of great inventiveness and wit* **2 wits** [plural] the ability to think quickly and make sensible decisions: *You can't afford to make mistakes. You've got to* **keep your wits about you.**

PHRASE at your wits' end so worried and tired because of your problems that you cannot think of any more ways of solving them

witch /wɪtʃ/ noun [C] a woman with magic powers

witchcraft /ˈwɪtʃˌkrɑːft/ noun [U] the practice of magic, especially for evil purposes

with /wɪð, wɪθ/ preposition

1 together	**6** against sb
2 having sth	**7** in a particular way
3 by means of sth	**8** covered by sth
4 concerning sb/sth	**9** sharing
5 caused by sth	**10** relating to sth

1 if one person or thing is with another or does something with them, they are together or they do it together: *Hannah lives with her parents.* ♦ *chicken served with rice*
2 used for saying what someone or something has or is holding: *a girl with red hair* ♦ *a room with a high ceiling* ♦ *My father came in with the letter.*
3 used for saying what is used for doing something: *Stir the mixture with a spoon.* ♦ *Stan wiped his eyes with his hand.*
4 used for saying what person or thing you have a particular feeling towards: *Why are you angry with me?* ♦ *We were disappointed with the court's decision.*
5 used for saying what feeling causes someone or something to be in a particular state: *She was*

trembling with rage. ♦ *The air was* **thick with smoke.**
6 used for showing who you compete, fight, or argue against: *Don't argue with me.* ♦ *The war with France lasted for nearly 20 years.*
7 used for describing the qualities that someone shows in their behaviour: *He spoke with great confidence.*
8 used for saying what is in or on something: *Fill the jug with boiling water.* ♦ *The hills were covered with snow.*
9 used for saying that people share or exchange things: *She shares her food with all the family.* ♦ *Most countries had stopped trading with South Africa.*
10 used for saying what something is related to: *There's nothing wrong with my eyesight.* ♦ *We're making good progress with our investigations.*

withdraw /wɪðˈdrɔː/ (**withdraws, withdrawing, withdrew** /wɪðˈdruː/, **withdrawn** /wɪðˈdrɔːn/) verb **1** [T] to take something back, or to stop providing something: *The bus service in many rural areas has been withdrawn.* ♦ *Some parents have* **withdrawn** *their support* **from** *the school.* **2** [I/T] to leave a place or a situation, or make someone leave a place or situation: *The injury has forced him to* **withdraw from** *the competition.* ♦ *The party* **withdrew** *their candidate* **from** *the election.* ♦ *The US is* **withdrawing** *its troops* **from** *the northern region.* **3** [T] to take money from a bank account: *You can* **withdraw cash** *at any of our branches.* **4** [T] to say that something that you said earlier is not in fact true: *He withdrew his remarks and apologized.*

withdrawal /wɪðˈdrɔːəl/ noun **1** [C/U] the act of stopping something or removing something: *Their* **withdrawal of** *support forced the minister to resign.* ♦ *Illness led to her* **withdrawal from** *the contest.* **2** [C/U] the process of taking an amount of money out of your bank account, or the amount of money that you take out: *You can* **make a withdrawal** *from most cash machines.* **3** [U] **HEALTH** a period during which someone feels ill because they have stopped taking a drug that they have been taking regularly and have become **addicted** to **4** [singular] a statement that says that someone wants people to ignore a remark that they made

with'drawal ,symptoms noun [plural] **HEALTH** the unpleasant physical and mental effects suffered by someone who stops taking a substance that they have been taking regularly, especially a drug they are **addicted** to

withdrawn¹ /wɪðˈdrɔːn/ adj very quiet and preferring not to talk to other people

withdrawn² /wɪðˈdrɔːn/ the past participle of **withdraw**

withdrew /wɪðˈdruː/ the past tense of **withdraw**

wither /ˈwɪðə/ verb [I] **1** if a plant withers, it becomes dry and starts to die **2** to become weaker and then disappear

withhold /wɪðˈhəʊld/ (**withholds, withholding, withheld** /wɪðˈheld/) verb [T] *formal* to deliberately not give something to someone

within /wɪðˈɪn/ adv, preposition **1** during a period of time, or before a period of time ends: *Within the past few weeks, 215 people have been arrested.* ♦ *We expect an announcement within the next 24 hours.* **2** inside a place, organization, or person: *There were four churches within the walls of the ancient city.* ♦ *There was a lack of leadership within the company.* ♦ *She has a kind of spiritual strength that comes* **from within.** **3** not more than a particular distance or amount: *A bomb exploded within 50 metres of the building.* **4** included in the range of things that are possible, reasonable, or allowed: *The organization must operate* **within** *the limits of* **the law.**

without /wɪð'aʊt/ adv, preposition **1** used for saying what someone or something does not have: *I can't find the answer without a calculator.* ♦ *a dress without sleeves* ♦ *I can't afford new shoes, so I'll have to* **do without** (=manage despite not having them). **2** used for saying that someone is not with you: *If the others don't want to come, we'll go without them.* **3** used for saying what does not happen when something else happens: *Liz closed the door without making a sound.* ♦ *an attack that came without any warning*

withstand /wɪð'stænd/ (**withstands, withstanding, withstood** /wɪð'stʊd/) verb [T] to be strong enough not to be harmed or destroyed by something

witness¹ /'wɪtnəs/ noun [C] **1** someone who sees a crime, accident, or other event happen: *Witnesses reported hearing two gunshots.* ♦ *Any* **witnesses to** *the incident are asked to contact the police.* **2 LAW** someone who tells a court what they know about a crime: *More than 20 witnesses will be called.* ♦ *a* **witness for** *the defence* **3** someone who watches you sign an official document and then signs it to state that they have watched you

witness² /'wɪtnəs/ verb [T] **1** to see something happen, for example a crime or an accident: *Several journalists witnessed the incident.* **2** to be present when something important happens: *We are witnessing the third change of government in three years.* **3** used for saying that something happened at a particular time or in a particular place: *The 1980s witnessed enormous growth in the financial sector.* **4** to watch someone sign an official document, and then sign it yourself to state that you have watched them: *Could you witness my signature on this visa application?*

'witness ,box noun [C] **LAW** the place in a court of law where **witnesses** stand or sit when they are answering questions

witty /'wɪti/ (**wittier, wittiest**) adj clever and funny

wives /waɪvz/ the plural of **wife**

wizard /'wɪzəd/ noun [C] **1** a man in stories who has magic powers **2** someone who is very good at something: *a financial wizard*

wizened /'wɪz(ə)nd/ adj old and with a lot of **wrinkles** (=lines on the skin)

WMD /,dʌb(ə)lju: em 'di:/ noun [plural] weapons of mass destruction: nuclear, chemical, and biological weapons

wobble /'wɒb(ə)l/ verb [I/T] to move slightly from side to side, or to make something do this —**wobbly** adj

woe /wəʊ/ noun [plural] *formal* **woes** problems and worries

wok /wɒk/ noun [C] a metal pan that is shaped like a large bowl, and is used for cooking Chinese food

woke /wəʊk/ the past tense of **wake¹**

woken /'wəʊkən/ the past participle of **wake¹**

wolf /wʊlf/ (plural **wolves** /wʊlvz/) noun [C] a wild mammal that looks like a large dog and hunts in a **pack** (=a large social group) —*picture* → MAMMAL

woman /'wʊmən/ (plural **women** /'wɪmɪn/) noun [C] an adult female person: *We need more women in parliament.* ♦ *a study of women writers*

womanhood /'wʊmən,hʊd/ noun [U] the state of being a woman

womb /wu:m/ noun [C] **ANATOMY** a uterus

women /'wɪmɪn/ the plural of **woman**

won /wʌn/ the past tense and past participle of **win¹**

wonder¹ /'wʌndə/ verb **1** [I/T] to think about something because you want to know more facts, or because you are worried: *'How did they find out?' she wondered.* ♦ *I wonder what we can do to help Sylvia.* ♦ *I was* **wondering about** *the best place for a holiday.* ♦ *I* **wonder if** *they'll get married.* ♦ *I* **wonder whether** *it was wise to let her travel alone.* **2** [I] to be very impressed or surprised by something: *It's hard not to* **wonder at** *the miracle of a newborn baby.*

PHRASE **I wonder if/whether** a polite way of asking something: *I wonder if you would do me a favour?* ♦ *I was wondering whether you would like to come to the theatre with me?*

wonder² /'wʌndə/ noun **1** [U] a strong feeling of surprise or admiration: *She gazed at the ocean* **in wonder.** ♦ *Where is the* **sense of wonder** *we felt when we were younger?* **2** [C] something that is very impressive or surprising: *the* **wonders of** *modern technology* ♦ *Coral reefs are among* **the** *natural* **wonders of the world.**

PHRASES **do/work wonders** to have a very good effect on someone or something: *Fresh air and exercise* **do wonders for** *your health.* ♦ *They have* **worked wonders with** *kids that other schools had rejected.*
it's a wonder (that) used for saying that something is so bad that it is surprising that a good result can come from it: *Your writing is so small, it's a wonder anyone can read it.*

wonder³ /'wʌndə/ adj extremely good or effective: *The treatment was first regarded as a wonder cure.*

wonderful /'wʌndəf(ə)l/ adj extremely good: *There was a wonderful view from the window.* ♦ *Thank you so much – I had a wonderful time!* —**wonderfully** adv

won't /wəʊnt/ short form the usual way of saying or writing 'will not'. This is not often used in formal writing: *I'm sorry I won't be able to come to your party.*

woo /wu:/ (**woos, wooing, wooed**) verb [T] to try to persuade people to support you or buy something from you

wood /wʊd/ noun **1** [U] the substance that trees are made of, used for making furniture and other objects: *a piece of wood* ♦ *a wood floor* ♦ *tables* **made of wood** **2** [C] a small forest: *We walk the dog in the woods behind our house.*

woodblock /'wʊd,blɒk/ noun [C] **MUSIC** a piece of wood used as a **percussion** instrument

woodcarving /'wʊd,kɑːvɪŋ/ noun [C] **ARTS** an object used as a decoration, made by cutting and shaping a piece of wood

woodcut /'wʊd,kʌt/ noun [C] **ARTS 1** a square piece of wood with a pattern on it, used for printing pictures **2** a picture printed using a woodcut

wooded /'wʊdɪd/ adj covered with trees

wooden /'wʊd(ə)n/ adj made of wood: *a wooden box*

woodland /'wʊdlənd/ noun [C/U] an area of land that is filled with trees

woodlouse /'wʊd,laʊs/ (plural **woodlice** /'wʊd,laɪs/) noun [C] a small land crustacean that lives in decaying wood and slightly wet places. It can curl into a ball to protect itself if it is threatened.

woodpecker /'wʊd,pekə/ noun [C] a bird that makes holes in trees using its long beak

'wood ,pulp noun [U] a substance made from very small pieces of crushed wood, used for making paper

woodwind /'wʊd,wɪnd/ noun [U] MUSIC musical instruments made of wood that you play by blowing into them → BRASS —picture → MUSICAL INSTRUMENT, ORCHESTRA

woodwork /'wʊd,wɜːk/ noun [U] 1 the doors, window frames, and other wooden parts of a room 2 the activity or skill of making objects from wood

woodworm /'wʊd,wɜːm/ noun 1 [C] a small insect that makes holes in wood 2 [U] damage to wood that is caused by woodworms

woody /'wʊdi/ adj BIOLOGY a woody plant has a strong hard stem made of wood

woof /wʊf/ noun [C] the sound that a dog makes when it **barks**

wool /wʊl/ noun [U] 1 AGRICULTURE thick hair that grows on sheep and some other mammals, for example **llamas** and **alpacas** 2 fibre or cloth made from wool: a ball of wool ♦ a wool jacket → COTTON WOOL

woollen /'wʊlən/ adj made from wool

woolly /'wʊli/ adj informal made from wool, or similar to wool

word¹ /wɜːd/ noun

1 unit of language	4 news/information
2 things sb says	5 of advice/praise etc
3 short conversation	+ PHRASES

1 [C] LANGUAGE a single unit of language that expresses a particular meaning by itself: The first word that many babies say is 'Mama'. ♦ Can you read the words on this page? ♦ The Latin word for a table is 'mensa'.
2 **words** [plural] someone's words are the things that they say: The nation was facing – **in the words of** the Prime Minister – a choice between two evils.
3 [singular] a short conversation or discussion, usually without other people listening: David **wants a word with** you. ♦ Can I **have a word with** you?
4 [singular/U] news, or information: We've had no **word from** Brian yet. ♦ He **sent word** that they had arrived safely.
5 [C] if someone gives you a word of something such as advice, praise, or warning, they advise, praise, or warn you: a few **words of** encouragement
PHRASES from the word go from the beginning of something
give/say the word to give someone an order to do something
give (sb) your word to promise to do something: You gave me your word that you would look after them.
in other words used for introducing a simpler way of saying something
keep your word to do what you promised to do
put in a (good) word for sb to praise someone so that someone else will like them, choose them, or employ them
put words into sb's mouth to claim that someone said or meant a particular thing that they did not really say or mean
word for word if you repeat something word for word, you repeat it exactly as someone said it or wrote it
word of mouth informal conversations between people: Most of our customers hear about us **by word of mouth.**

word² /wɜːd/ verb [T] to use words to express something in a particular way: You could have worded your message a bit more clearly.

'word ,class noun [C] LANGUAGE a **part of speech**

'word e,quation noun [C] CHEMISTRY a **chemical equation** written in words instead of chemical symbols

wording /'wɜːdɪŋ/ noun [U] the words that are used in a particular piece of writing

'word ,processing noun [U] COMPUTING the work or skill of producing written documents on a computer or word processor

'word ,processor noun [C] COMPUTING a computer program that you use for creating documents

wordwrap /'wɜːd,ræp/ noun [U] COMPUTING a feature in a **word processing** program that fits all the words in a document automatically within the **margins**

wore /wɔː/ the past tense of **wear¹**

work¹ /wɜːk/ verb

1 have job	5 operate equipment
2 use effort on sth	6 move gradually
3 operate well	7 shape a substance
4 have effect	+ PHRASAL VERBS

1 [I] to have a job: Dominic works part-time. ♦ She **works for** a big law firm in the city. ♦ She **worked as** a journalist. ♦ I hope to **work in** marketing when I'm older.
2 [I] to spend time and use effort trying to achieve something: I've been working in the field all day. ♦ Our thanks go to everybody who has **worked on** this project. ♦ He **worked** hard **to** improve safety conditions in the mines.
3 [I] to operate in a satisfactory way: The new telephone system seems to be working perfectly. ♦ This pen doesn't work. ♦ My brain's not working very well today.
4 [I] to succeed, or to have a particular effect: If this plan doesn't work, we'll have to think of something else. ♦ The drug works by blocking the spread of the virus. ♦ Criticizing your former employer usually **works against** you in an interview. ♦ The new tax system is **working in** the company's **favour.**
5 [T] to operate a piece of equipment: I don't know how to work this thing.
6 [I/T] to move gradually, or to move something gradually: He managed to work one hand free of the rope.
7 [T] TECHNOLOGY to shape a material such as wood or metal in a particular way, especially using tools → WONDER²
PHRASAL VERBS 'work at sth to try hard to develop or improve something: Successful relationships don't just happen – you have to work at them.
'work on sth to spend time producing or improving something: He'll have to work on getting fit before the game.
,work sth 'out 1 to find a way of dealing with a problem: We can't work out how to get the Internet connection going. **2** to find an answer to something by calculating it: Use the chart to work out how much tax you have to pay.
'work through sth to deal with something such as a problem or a strong feeling by thinking and talking about it: He needs to work through some of the guilt he's feeling.

work² /wɜːk/ noun

1 job	4 sth made/done in job
2 activity needing effort	5 in physics
3 place sb does their job	+ PHRASES

1 [U] a job that you are paid to do: It's not easy to **find work** (=get a job). ♦ I **started work** (=got my first job) when I was 16. ♦ She's been **out of work** (=unemployed) for over a year.
2 [U] activity that involves physical or mental effort: I know you've got a lot of work to do. ♦ Thank you for all your **hard work.**
3 [U] a place where someone goes to do their job: I walk to work and take the bus home.

4 [C/U] something that someone makes or does: *As a writer, she did some of her best work in her late twenties.* ♦ *It's not the best **piece of work** you've ever done.* ♦ ***works of** literature*

5 [U] **PHYSICS** the process of changing energy from one form into another, usually in order to make something move or operate. Work is equal to the amount of force used on the object, measured in **newtons**, multiplied by the distance, measured in metres, over which it is used. Work is measured in units called **joules**. Symbol *W*

PHRASES at work 1 at the place where you work: *If he's not at home, he must still be at work.* **2** in the process of doing or making something: *She's currently **at work on** a new book.*

get/go/set to work (on sth) to start doing something: *Let's get to work on finding a solution to the problem.*

have your work cut out to have something difficult that you have to do

work of art 1 **ARTS** something such as a painting or **sculpture** that an artist produces **2** something that is very impressive

- You can refer to what someone does in order to get paid as their **work** or their **job**: *Do you find your work OR your job interesting?* ♦ *What kind of work OR job does he do?*
- **Work** is uncountable with this meaning, so it never has **a** in front of it and is never plural: *He's looking for work.* ♦ *It's fascinating work.* ♦ *Has he found a job?* ♦ *She has had many different jobs.*

workable /ˈwɜːkəb(ə)l/ adj practical and likely to be effective

'work ,angle noun [C] **TECHNOLOGY** in welding, the angle between the electrode and the joint being welded

workbook /ˈwɜːkˌbʊk/ noun [C] **EDUCATION** a book for students that contains exercises

worked up /ˌwɜːkt ˈʌp/ adj upset, angry, or excited

worker /ˈwɜːkə/ noun [C] **1** someone who works in a company or industry and is below the level of a manager= EMPLOYEE: *About 1,000 workers at the factory lost their jobs.* ♦ *farm workers* **2** someone who works for a particular organization, especially a political party: *a mood of optimism among party workers* **3** used for describing how well or how quickly someone works: *He's a nice man, but quite a slow worker.*

,worker partici'pation noun [U] **BUSINESS** the idea of involving ordinary employees in making decisions at all levels in a business

workflow /ˈwɜːkˌfləʊ/ noun [U] **COMPUTING** software designed to improve the flow of electronic documents around an office **network**, from user to user

workforce /ˈwɜːkˌfɔːs/ noun [singular] **BUSINESS** the total number of people who work in a particular company, industry, or country

working /ˈwɜːkɪŋ/ adj **1** a working person has a job: *working parents* **2** relating to or involving work: *After the meeting there will be **a working lunch**.* ♦ *The strikers are demanding better **working conditions**.* **3** something that is working can be operated or used: *The dining room has an attractive **working fireplace**.* **4** satisfactory, but not perfect or completely developed: *Applicants should have **a working knowledge** of Greek.*

PHRASE in working order working correctly, without any problems

,working 'capital noun [U] **BUSINESS** the money that a business has available for immediate use in running its operations

the ,working 'class noun **SOCIAL STUDIES** the social class that consists of people who do not have much money, education, or power and who work mainly in **manual** jobs (=jobs that involve physical work) — **,working-'class** adj → LOWER CLASS, MIDDLE CLASS, UPPER CLASS

,working 'day noun [C] **1** a day of the week when people have to work **2** the period of time that you work in one day

'working ,drawing noun [C/U] **MATHS, PHYSICS** a detailed drawing of an object in **orthographic projection**, for use by someone making or building it

,working 'holiday noun [C] a holiday during which someone works, for example doing unpaid work to benefit the community in which they are staying

workings /ˈwɜːkɪŋz/ noun [plural] the parts of something such as a system, organization, or piece of equipment that control it or make it work

,work-life 'balance noun [singular] **BUSINESS** the relationship between the amount of time and effort that someone gives to work, and the amount that they give to other aspects of life, such as their family

workload /ˈwɜːkˌləʊd/ noun [C] the amount of work that a person or organization has to do

workman /ˈwɜːkmən/ (plural **workmen** /ˈwɜːkmən/) noun [C] a man whose job is building or repairing things

workmanship /ˈwɜːkmənʃɪp/ noun [U] the standard of someone's work, or the skill that they use in making something

workpiece /ˈwɜːkˌpiːs/ noun [C] **TECHNOLOGY** a piece of wood, metal etc that is being worked on

workplace /ˈwɜːkˌpleɪs/ noun [C] the place where you work, or all the places where people work

worksheet /ˈwɜːkˌʃiːt/ noun [C] **EDUCATION** a piece of paper with exercises on it that help you to learn something

workshop /ˈwɜːkˌʃɒp/ noun [C] **1** a room or building where things are made using tools and machines **2** **EDUCATION** an occasion when a group of people meet in order to learn about a particular subject

workstation /ˈwɜːkˌsteɪʃ(ə)n/ noun [C] **COMPUTING** **1** a desk with a computer for one person to work at **2** a powerful computer used in an office —*picture* → on next page

world¹ /wɜːld/ noun **1 the world** [singular] **GEOGRAPHY** the planet that we live on: *changes in the world's climate* **2** [singular] people and society in all countries: *We want to create a safer world for our children.* ♦ *They control about a quarter of the world's oil supply.* ♦ *The terrorists pose a threat to **the whole world**.* ♦ *The same problems are faced by workers **throughout the world**.* **3** [C] a particular group of countries: *the economies of **the western world** (=the countries of western Europe and North America)* ♦ *It is the oldest institution in **the English-speaking world**.* **4** [C] the particular type of place or situation in which someone lives or works: *the entertainment world*

PHRASES do sb a/the world of good to make someone feel very happy or healthy

in the world 1 used for emphasizing a particular quality that something has: *They produce some of the finest wines in the world.* **2** used for adding emphasis to a question in order to show that you are surprised or

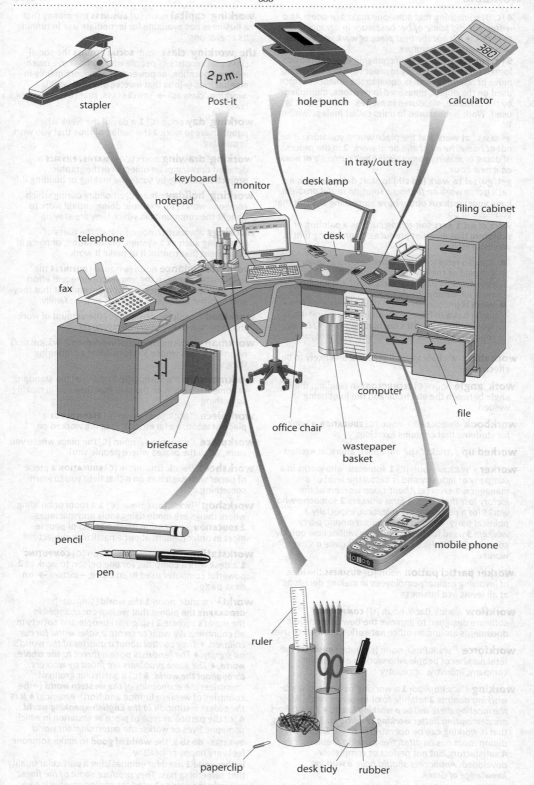

stapler

Post-it

2 p.m.

hole punch

calculator

in tray/out tray

keyboard

desk lamp

monitor

notepad

desk

filing cabinet

telephone

fax

computer

file

office chair

briefcase

wastepaper basket

pencil

mobile phone

pen

ruler

paperclip

desk tidy

rubber

workstation

annoyed: *How in the world did they make a mistake like that?*

the outside world ordinary society, rather than places such as prisons or religious communities where people live separately from the rest of society
→ BEST²

world² /wɜːld/ adj involving all the countries of the world: *the world championships* ♦ *a world war*

the ,World 'Bank ECONOMICS an international organization that lends money to countries that are members of the United Nations

world-'class adj at a level where you are one of the best in the world

world e'conomy noun [singular] ECONOMICS the economy of the world, considered as an international exchange of goods and services

world-'famous adj known by people in all parts of the world

,World 'Heritage ,Site noun [C] a place of great historical and cultural importance that is officially protected and preserved

worldly /ˈwɜːldli/ adj a worldly person has a lot of experience and knowledge of life
PHRASE **sb's worldly goods/possessions** all the things that someone owns

,world 'music noun [U] MUSIC in western Europe and North America, music from other cultures

the ,World 'Trade Organiz,ation ECONOMICS an international organization that controls trade between countries

,world 'view noun [C] the way that someone sees and understands world events, especially in relation to their religious or political beliefs and ideas

worldwide /ˌwɜːldˈwaɪd/ adj, adv happening or existing all over the world: *a worldwide network of more than 100 organizations* ♦ *Our company employs 1,500 staff worldwide.*

the ,World Wide 'Web noun [singular] COMPUTING the **Web**

worm /wɜːm/ noun [C] **1** BIOLOGY a small invertebrate animal with a long soft body and no bones or legs **2** COMPUTING a program that deliberately damages computer systems by making copies of itself

worn¹ /wɔːn/ adj **1** something that is worn looks old and damaged because it has been used a lot **2** looking tired and old

worn² /wɔːn/ the past participle of **wear¹**

,worn 'out adj **1** extremely tired= EXHAUSTED **2** too old or damaged to be used any longer

worried /ˈwʌrid/ adj nervous and upset because you are thinking about your problems or about bad things that could happen= ANXIOUS: *Everyone was very worried when John didn't show up.* ♦ *a worried look* ♦ *I'm worried that he might have got lost.* ♦ *We are very* **worried about** *our future.* ♦ *Your parents are* **worried sick** *about you* (=extremely worried).

worry¹ /ˈwʌri/ (**worries, worrying, worried**) verb **1** [I/T] to feel nervous and upset because you keep thinking about your problems or about bad things that could happen: *She worried that she might have taken on too much work.* ♦ **Try not to worry** *so much.* ♦ *People* **worry** more **about** *their health than they used to.* ♦ *If companies are following the rules, they've got* **nothing to worry about**. **2** [T] to make someone feel nervous and upset: *What worries me most is the possibility of complete failure.* ♦ *Tell them not to worry themselves about the financial position.*

worry² /ˈwʌri/ (plural **worries**) noun **1** [C] a problem or possibility that makes you feel worried: *financial worries* ♦ *My biggest worry now is how we are going to pay for it.* **2** [U] the feeling of being worried: *She was making herself* **ill with worry**.

worrying /ˈwʌriɪŋ/ adj making you feel worried
—**worryingly** adv

worse¹ /wɜːs/ adj **1** less pleasant or less good than something else, or than before ≠ BETTER: *Our performance got worse as the game went on.* ♦ *The company's financial problems are getting* **worse and worse**. ♦ *The injury looked a lot* **worse than** *it really was.* **2** more ill than before ≠ BETTER: *She's* **feeling** *much* **worse** *today.*
PHRASE **make matters/things worse** to make a bad situation even worse

worse² /wɜːs/ adv **1** less well ≠ BETTER: *They played even worse in the second half.* **2** more severely: *His leg seemed to be hurting* **worse than** *ever.*

worse³ /wɜːs/ noun [U] something that is less pleasant or less good: *Things were looking bad, but worse was to follow.*
PHRASE **for the worse** in a way that makes a situation worse
→ NONE

worsen /ˈwɜːs(ə)n/ verb [I/T] to become worse, or to make something worse ≠ IMPROVE —**worsening** adj

,worse 'off adj **1** in a worse situation than someone else or than before ≠ BETTER OFF **2** having less money than someone else, or than before ≠ BETTER OFF

worship¹ /ˈwɜːʃɪp/ noun [U] RELIGION the activity of showing respect and love for God or a god

worship² /ˈwɜːʃɪp/ (**worships, worshipping, worshipped**) verb **1** [I/T] RELIGION to show respect and love for God or a god **2** [T] to love and admire someone or something very much —**worshipper** noun [C]

worst¹ /wɜːst/ adj worse than all others, or worse than at all other times: *It was the worst accident in the company's history.* ♦ *The noise from the airport is worst at night.*

worst² /wɜːst/ noun [singular] **the worst** someone or something that is worse than all others: *Even if the worst happens, you shouldn't give up hope.*
PHRASE **at worst** used for talking about the worst possibility in a situation: *At worst, we'll lose £100.*

worst³ /wɜːst/ adv less well than all others or than at all other times: *the areas that were worst hit by Monday's heavy rains*

worth¹ /wɜːθ/ adj **1** if you say how much something is worth, you state its value in money: *a car worth £1,000* ♦ *How much do you think the house is worth?* **2** used for saying that there is a good reason for doing something, because it is important, enjoyable, useful etc: *The book is definitely worth reading.* ♦ *It was hard work, but* **it was worth it** *in the end.* **3** used for saying how rich someone is: *She is now worth 20 million dollars.*

worth² /wɜːθ/ noun [U] **1** the degree to which someone or something is good, useful, or important: *We never recognized her* **true worth** *as a player.* **2** the financial value of something: *millions of pounds'* **worth of** *equipment* ♦ *The animals are being sold at prices far below their true worth.* **3** an amount measured by the time it lasts: *a week's* **worth of** *work*

worthless /ˈwɜːθləs/ adj **1** with no value, or not useful **2** a worthless person has no good qualities

worthwhile /ˌwɜːθˈwaɪl/ adj if something is worthwhile, it is worth the time, money, or effort that you spend on it: *We felt the meeting had been very worthwhile.* ♦ *It might be worthwhile to remember a few important facts.*

worthy /ˈwɜːði/ adj **1** *formal* deserving something: *He had shown himself to be **worthy of** their respect.* **2** a worthy person or thing has qualities that make people respect them: *a worthy winner* ♦ *The money will go to a **worthy cause** (=an activity or organization that helps people).*

would /wʊd/ modal verb

1 for talking about what was going to happen in the past	**3** for talking about past habits
2 for talking about results of an unlikely situation	**4** in requests/offers
	5 to be willing
	6 expresses wish

1 used for showing what someone expected, intended etc when they were thinking or talking in the past about what was going to happen in the future: *James said he would never forgive her.*
2 used for talking about the possible results of a situation that is unlikely to happen or did not happen: *I'd buy a car if I could afford it.* ♦ *If I'd known you were coming, I'**d have** got your room ready.*
3 used for saying what someone used to do in the past: *On winter evenings we'd all sit around the fire.*
4 used for politely asking someone for something or for offering them something: ***Would you like** a cup of coffee or something?* ♦ ***Would you mind** waiting outside?*
5 used when you think that someone is willing to do something: *Bruce would lend you the money, I'm sure.*
6 used for saying what someone wants to do or wishes that they could do: *I wish it would stop raining.* ♦ *I think David **would like** to see you alone.*

wouldn't /ˈwʊd(ə)nt/ short form the usual way of saying or writing 'would not'. This is not often used in formal writing: *I told you he wouldn't come.*

wound¹ /wuːnd/ noun [C] an injury in which your skin or flesh is seriously damaged: *a head wound* ♦ *a stab wound* ♦ *He **had** serious **wounds to** his stomach.*

wound² /wuːnd/ verb [T] **1** to injure someone so that their skin or flesh is seriously damaged: *Two soldiers died and three others were wounded in the attack.* **2** to hurt someone's feelings by doing or saying something unpleasant: *Her remark had deeply wounded him.*

wound³ /waʊnd/ the past tense and past participle of **wind²**

wounded /ˈwuːndɪd/ adj **1** seriously injured: *wounded soldiers* ♦ *his wounded arm* **2** feeling emotional pain: *wounded pride*

wound up /ˌwaʊnd ˈʌp/ adj *informal* nervous, worried, or angry

wove /wəʊv/ the past tense of **weave**

woven /ˈwəʊvən/ the past participle of **weave**

WP /ˌdʌb(ə)ljuː ˈpiː/ noun **COMPUTING 1** [C] word processor **2** [U] word processing

wrap /ræp/ (**wraps, wrapping, wrapped**) verb [T] to cover someone or something by putting paper, cloth etc round them ≠ UNWRAP: *Keep the cheeses fresh by wrapping each one individually.* ♦ *We **wrapped** the baby **in** a blanket to keep it warm.*

PHRASE **be wrapped up in sth** to spend so much time doing something that you do not notice anything else

wrapper /ˈræpə/ noun [C] a piece of paper or plastic that is wrapped around something that you buy: *sweet wrappers*

wrapping /ˈræpɪŋ/ noun [U] the paper or plastic that is wrapped around something

ˈwrapping ˌpaper noun [U] paper that you use for wrapping presents

wrath /rɒθ/ noun [U] *formal* very great anger

wreak /riːk/ verb **wreak havoc (on)** to cause very great harm or damage

wreath /riːθ/ (plural **wreaths** /riːðz/) noun [C] a circle of flowers that you put on a dead person's **grave**

wreck¹ /rek/ verb [T] to destroy something, or to damage it badly

wreck² /rek/ noun [C] something that has been badly damaged or is in very bad condition

wreckage /ˈrekɪdʒ/ noun [singular/U] the parts of a vehicle or building that remain after it has been severely damaged

wrench¹ /rentʃ/ verb [T] **1** to injure a part of your body by twisting it suddenly **2** to pull and twist something strongly: *The door had been wrenched off its hinges.*

wrench² /rentʃ/ noun **1** [singular] a strong movement of pulling and twisting something **2** [singular] a feeling of sadness that you get when you leave a place or a person that you love **3** [C] an **adjustable spanner**

wrest /rest/ verb [T] *formal* to pull something away from someone using force

wrestle /ˈres(ə)l/ verb [I/T] **SPORTS** to fight by holding someone and trying to push or throw them to the ground, especially as a sport —**wrestling** /ˈres(ə)lɪŋ/ noun [U]

wrestling /ˈres(ə)lɪŋ/ noun [U] **SPORTS** the sport of holding someone and trying to push or throw them to the ground —**wrestler** noun [C]

wretch /retʃ/ noun [C] someone who is in a difficult situation and who people feel sorry for

wretched /ˈretʃɪd/ adj **1** very unhappy or ill **2** very unpleasant, or in very bad condition

wriggle /ˈrɪg(ə)l/ verb [I/T] to move by twisting or turning quickly, or to make something move in this way

wring /rɪŋ/ (**wrings, wringing, wrung** /rʌŋ/) or **ˌwring sth ˈout** verb [T] to twist and squeeze something in order to remove liquid from it

wrinkle /ˈrɪŋk(ə)l/ noun [C] **1** a line that appears on the skin when someone gets older **2** a fold in clothes that makes them look untidy —**wrinkle** verb [I/T], **wrinkled** adj, **wrinkly** adj

wrist /rɪst/ noun [C] the part of the body that joins the hand to the arm —*picture* → JOINT

ˈwrist supˌport noun [C] **COMPUTING** a long object in front of a keyboard on which a user rests their wrists, so that they do not develop problems with their arm or hand muscles

writ /rɪt/ noun [C] **LAW** an official document that orders someone to do something

write /raɪt/ (**writes, writing, wrote** /rəʊt/, **written** /ˈrɪt(ə)n/) verb **1** [I/T] to use something such as a pen or pencil to make words, numbers, or symbols: *Emily is just learning to write.* ♦ *Write your full name in Box A.* **2** [I/T] to create something such as a book, a piece of music, or a computer program, by putting together words or symbols: *I have to write a review of my favourite film.* ♦ *Matt writes software for games machines.* ♦ *He travelled around Mexico and **wrote about** his experiences.* ♦ *She **writes for** several fashion* magazines. **3** [I/T] to create a letter or other message and send it: *I wrote to Kate last week.* ♦ *She'd written a letter to the newspaper to complain.* **4** [T] to create a formal document by writing: *I'll write you a cheque for the full amount.*

PHRASAL VERBS ,write 'back to send a reply to someone who has sent you a letter

,write sth 'down to write something on a piece of paper

,write 'in to send a letter to an organization

,write 'off to send a letter to an organization in order to ask for something: *You can write off for a free book of recipes.*

,write-'down noun [C/U] **BUSINESS** a reduction in the value of the **assets** that a company owns

,write-pro'tected adj **COMPUTING** containing information that cannot be changed or removed

writer /'raɪtə/ noun [C] **LITERATURE** someone who writes books, stories, or articles as their job

writhe /raɪð/ verb [I] to twist your body because you are feeling a lot of pain

writing /'raɪtɪŋ/ noun **1** [U] **LITERATURE** the skill of producing written material by putting words together: *In the first two years, the children focus on **reading and writing**.* **2** [U] **LITERATURE** the activity of creating things such as books, poems, or newspaper articles, or books, poems, and articles that have been created: *He teaches **creative writing**.* ♦ *a course on women's writing* **3** [U] words that are written or printed on something: *The label was torn and I couldn't read the writing.* **4 writings** [plural] **LITERATURE** all the books, poems, or articles that someone has written

PHRASE in writing in the form of a document that you can keep as proof of something: *Customers are expected to **put their complaints in writing**.*

written¹ /'rɪt(ə)n/ adj in the form of a letter or other document

written² /'rɪt(ə)n/ the past participle of **write**

wrong¹ /rɒŋ/ adj **1** if there is something wrong, there is a problem: *You don't look well. Is anything wrong?* ♦ *I checked the engine, but I couldn't find anything wrong.* ♦ *There was **something wrong with** one of the tyres.* ♦ *She had some blood tests, but they still don't know **what's wrong with** her.* **2** not accurate, correct, or sensible= INCORRECT: *We must have gone the wrong way.* ♦ *the wrong answer* ♦ *If you think carefully, you won't make the wrong decision.* **3** not morally right = UNJUST: *Do you think it's wrong to use animals for testing new medicines?* ♦ *There's **nothing wrong with** living with your boyfriend in my opinion.* **4** not suitable: *It's **the wrong place** to build a factory.* ♦ *The colours just look **wrong for** a room this size.*

PHRASE the wrong way round with one part in the position where the other part should be

wrong² /rɒŋ/ adv in a way that is not correct: *Someone had tied the rope on wrong.*

PHRASES get sth wrong to make a mistake about something: *The police got the name wrong and arrested an innocent man.*

go wrong **1** to stop working: *Then something went wrong with the engine.* **2** used when a problem happens and causes something to fail: *It's difficult to say when the relationship started to go wrong.*

wrong³ /rɒŋ/ noun **1** [U] behaviour that is morally wrong or breaks a rule: *Small children do not know **the difference between right and wrong**.* **2** [C] a particular action or situation that is morally wrong or that breaks a rule

PHRASE in the wrong someone who is in the wrong has made a mistake and deserves the blame for it

wrong⁴ /rɒŋ/ verb [T] *formal* to treat or judge someone unfairly

wrongdoing /'rɒŋˌduːɪŋ/ noun [C/U] *formal* behaviour that is illegal or immoral

wrongful /'rɒŋf(ə)l/ adj unfair or illegal: *a wrongful arrest*

wrongly /'rɒŋli/ adv not correctly, or by mistake

wrote /rəʊt/ the past tense of **write**

wrought iron /ˌrɔːt 'aɪən/ noun [U] **TECHNOLOGY** a type of strong iron that is easy to shape and is used for making gates, fences etc, especially for decoration. It is the purest form of iron.

WRT abbrev with regard to: used in emails and **text messages** before the subject that you are going to mention

wrung /rʌŋ/ the past tense and past participle of **wring**

wry /raɪ/ adj showing that you think that something is funny but not very pleasant: *a wry smile* —**wryly** adv

wt abbrev weight

the WTO /ˌdʌb(ə)lju: ti: 'əʊ/ **ECONOMICS** the World Trade Organization

WWI abbrev **SOCIAL STUDIES** World War I: a war fought in Europe from 1914 to 1919

WWII abbrev **SOCIAL STUDIES** World War II: a war fought in Europe, Africa, and Asia from 1939 to 1945

www /ˌdʌb(ə)lju: dʌb(ə)lju: 'dʌb(ə)lju:/ abbrev **COMPUTING** the World Wide Web: used in some website addresses

WYSIWYG /'wɪziwɪg/ adj **COMPUTING** what you see is what you get: used for describing computer systems in which the information that you see on the screen is exactly what will appear when you print it on paper

x /eks/ (plural **x's**) or X (plural **X's**) noun [C/U] **1** the 24th letter of the English alphabet **2** a symbol that you use for showing that an answer is wrong **3** X [U] used instead of saying the name of a person or place when you do not know it, or when you want to keep it secret: *Mr X* **4** *informal* a symbol that you use for writing a kiss at the end of a letter

x-axis /'eks ˌæksɪs/ noun [singular] **MATHS** the line of figures that go from left to right in a system of coordinates= HORIZONTAL AXIS

X-chromosome /'eks ˌkrəʊməsəʊm/ noun [C] **BIOLOGY** the chromosome that makes a human or other mammal female instead of male. Females have two X-chromosomes and males have one X-chromosome and one **Y-chromosome.** → Y-CHROMOSOME

xenon /'zenɒn, 'ziːnɒn/ noun [U] **CHEMISTRY** an element that is a gas with no colour or smell. It is used for making some types of electric lights. Chemical symbol: **Xe**

xenophobia /ˌzenəˈfəʊbiə/ noun [U] a feeling of deep dislike towards people from other countries and cultures —**xenophobic** adj

xerophyte /'zɪərəfaɪt/ noun [C] **BIOLOGY** a plant that is suitable for growing in a dry environment, for example a **cactus** → HYDROPHYTE, MESOPHYTE

XL /,eks 'el/ abbrev extra large: used on labels showing clothes sizes

XML /,eks em 'el/ noun [U] **COMPUTING** a computer language that is used for creating websites

X-ray /'eks ,reɪ/ noun [C] **1 SCIENCE** radiation with a very short wavelength. X-rays are used for producing images of the inside of things such as the human body, but can cause cancer if used too much. **2 HEALTH** a picture of the inside of someone's body that is taken using X-rays

xylem /'zaɪləm/ noun [U] **BIOLOGY** a type of tissue in the veins of plants through which water and minerals are carried up from the roots through the stem to the leaves. Xylem also provides support for the softer or weaker parts of the plant. In trees, the middle part of the **trunk** is made of xylem. —*picture* → ROOT

xylophone /'zaɪlə,fəʊn/ noun [C] **MUSIC** a musical instrument with a row of narrow wooden pieces that you hit with a wooden hammer —*picture* → MUSICAL INSTRUMENT

y /waɪ/ (plural **y's**) or **Y** (plural **Y's**) noun [C/U] the 25th letter of the English alphabet

yacht /jɒt/ noun [C] a boat that is used for racing or sailing

yachting /'jɒtɪŋ/ noun [U] the activity of racing or sailing a yacht

yachtsman /'jɒtsmən/ (plural **yachtsmen**) noun [C] someone who sails or owns a **yacht**

yachtswoman /'jɒts,wʊmən/ (plural **yachtswomen**) noun [C] a woman who sails or owns a **yacht**

yak /jæk/ noun [C] a large mammal like an **ox** with long hair and horns that comes from Tibet and Central Asia

yam /jæm/ noun [C/U] a long vegetable that is the swollen root of a tropical vine. It has brown skin and white flesh.

yank /jæŋk/ verb [I/T] to pull something suddenly using force= JERK

yap /jæp/ (**yaps, yapping, yapped**) verb [I] if a dog yaps, it makes short high sounds

yard /jɑːd/ noun [C] **1** a unit for measuring length that is equal to 0.91 metres **2** an enclosed area around a large building where people can do activities outside: *a prison yard* **3** a large open area that is used for a particular purpose: *a builder's yard*

yardstick /'jɑːd,stɪk/ noun [C] something that you compare similar things to, as a way of judging their quality or value

yawn /jɔːn/ verb [I] to open your mouth wide and take a big breath, because you are tired or bored —**yawn** noun [C]

yaws /jɔːz/ noun [U] **HEALTH** an infectious tropical disease that produces red spots on the skin and causes pain in the bones and joints

y-axis /'waɪ ,æksɪs/ noun [singular] **MATHS** the line of figures that go from top to bottom in a system of coordinates= VERTICAL AXIS

Y-chromosome /'waɪ ,krəʊməsəʊm/ noun [C] **BIOLOGY** the chromosome that makes a human or other mammal male instead of female. Males have one Y-chromosome and one **X-chromosome**. → X-CHROMOSOME

yd abbrev yard

year /jɪə/ noun

1 12 months	**5** a long time
2 January to December	**6** level at school
3 in astronomy	**+** PHRASE
4 period for institution	

1 [C] a period of 365 or 366 days divided into 12 months: *He lived in Paris for a few years.* ♦ *I started my job two* **years ago.** ♦ *He returned to China* **year after year** (=continuously for many years).
2 [C] a year beginning on 1 January and ending on 31 December: *We're hoping to sell the house by the end of the year.* ♦ *one of this year's best films*
3 [C] **ASTRONOMY** the amount of time that a planet takes to travel round the Sun
4 [C] the period during which an institution operates, or the system it uses for dividing time: *the school year* ♦ *the tax year*
5 **years** [plural] a very long time: *He hasn't been back to his country* **for years.** ♦ *It wasn't until* **years later** *that I realized how foolish I'd been.*
6 [C] **EDUCATION** the level that a student is at in school: *She's in the same year as me.* ♦ *We did this subject in year 10.* ♦ *one of the first years* (=a student who is in his or her first year)
PHRASE **five/ten etc years old** the number of years that someone has lived or that something has existed: *Their son is six years old.*

,year 'end noun [C] **BUSINESS** the end of a **financial year**, used by a company or organization when producing its accounts

yearly /'jɪəli/ adj, adv happening every year, or once every year= ANNUAL

yeast /jiːst/ noun [U] a white substance that is used in making bread and beer

'yeast in,fection noun [C] **HEALTH** the medical condition **thrush**

yell /jel/ verb [I/T] to shout loudly —**yell** noun [C]

yellow /'jeləʊ/ adj something that is yellow is the same colour as the sun or the middle of an egg: *yellow flowers* —**yellow** noun [C/U]

,yellow 'card noun [C] **SPORTS** in football, a small yellow card used for warning a player that they have done something wrong → RED CARD

,yellow 'fever noun [U] **HEALTH** a serious tropical illness caused by a virus and spread by a mosquito. It causes fever, bleeding, and the skin to turn yellow.

yellowing /'jeləʊɪŋ/ noun [U] the process of becoming yellow

yellowish /'jeləʊɪʃ/ or **yellowy** /'jeləʊi/ adj similar to yellow

'yellow ,spot noun [C] **ANATOMY** a small yellow area in the eyeball near the middle of the retina, opposite the centre of the lens. The eye sees things very well in this area because there are many sensitive cells called **cones** there. —*picture* → EYE

yen /jen/ (plural **yen**) noun **1** [C] **ECONOMICS** the unit of money used in Japan. Its symbol is ¥. **2** [singular] a strong feeling that you want to do something

yes¹ /jes/ adv **1** used for saying that something is true or correct, for giving permission, or for agreeing to do something: *'Is that your car?' 'Yes, it is.'* ♦ *'Can I borrow your pen for a minute?' 'Yes, of course.'* ♦ *'Can you get it for me by this afternoon?' 'Yes, I can.'* ♦ *'Would you like me to open a window?'* **'Yes, please.'** **2** used for answering someone who calls you in order to show that you have heard them: *'Erica!' 'Yes?'* **3** used for correcting someone when they make a wrong negative statement: *'She won't go.' 'Yes, she will. She just told me she would.'*

yes² /jes/ (plural **yesses** or **yeses**) noun [C] an answer or a vote that expresses agreement or gives permission

yeshiva or **yeshivah** /jə'ʃiːvə/ noun [C] RELIGION **1** a school for Orthodox Jewish students where they can train to become rabbis **2** a school for Jewish boys that teaches both religious and other subjects

yesterday¹ /'jestədeɪ/ adv on the day before today: *Yesterday, we went to the zoo.* ♦ *I saw her* **yesterday afternoon.**

yesterday² /'jestədeɪ/ noun [C/U] **1** the day before today **2** *formal* a time in the past

yet /jet/ adv, conjunction **1** used for talking or asking about something that has not happened or cannot happen now, but will happen or may happen in the future: *She hasn't decided yet if she wants to come.* ♦ *The team* **may yet** *make it to the finals.* ♦ *'Are you feeling hungry?'* **'Not yet.'** **2** used for saying that someone or something is the best, worst, biggest etc of their kind up to now: *This will be the Prime Minister's most important speech yet.* **3** used for introducing a statement that is surprising after what has just been mentioned: *The new computer is much more powerful; yet it costs the same.* **4** used for emphasizing that someone or something is even bigger, better, worse, more etc: *Seth knew that he had failed* **yet again.** ♦ *We had* **yet another** *problem to deal with.*

> Already, **yet**, and **still** are sometimes confused. Both **already** and **yet** are used for talking about something that happened before a particular time or before now.
> ■ Use **already** in positive sentences or in questions when you think it is likely that something has happened, or when you know it has happened and are surprised: *Thanks, but I've already eaten.* ♦ *Have I already given you my email address?* ♦ *Is John married already? He hardly looks old enough.*
> ■ Use **yet** in negative sentences and in questions, especially when you think that something should happen soon: *Kim hasn't seen the film yet, so don't tell her how it ends.* ♦ *Have you told her yet that you're leaving?*
> ■ Use **still** for talking about things that continue happening without changing: *Are you still working at the factory?* ♦ *I still love him.*
> ■ You can also use **still** for expressing surprise that a situation has not changed: *Why are you still here?*

yield¹ /jiːld/ verb **1** [T] to produce something: *We're hoping the farm will* **yield** *a big harvest in the autumn.* ♦ *The search for truth is beginning to* **yield results.** **2** [I] to finally agree to do what someone wants you to do: *The sport should not* **yield to** *every demand from the television companies.* **3** [T] to give something to someone else: *After the war, Mexico yielded a large amount of its territory to the United States.* **4** [I] *formal* if something yields when you push or pull it, it moves or bends

yield² /jiːld/ noun [C] the amount of something that is produced

the YMCA /ˌwaɪ em si: 'eɪ/ the Young Men's Christian Association: an organization that provides places for people to exercise, take courses, and sometimes rent a room for the night while travelling

yoga /'jəʊɡə/ noun [U] an activity that involves exercises that are intended to make you stronger and more relaxed

yoghurt or **yogurt** /'jɒɡət/ noun [C/U] a food made from milk that has become thick and slightly sour

yogi /'jəʊɡi/ noun [C] **1** someone who knows a lot about **yoga 2** RELIGION a student of Indian religion

yoke /jəʊk/ noun [C] a wooden object used for connecting animals that are pulling a vehicle, especially a plough
> PHRASE **the yoke of sth** *formal* a situation or experience that limits someone's freedom

yolk /jəʊk/ noun [C/U] BIOLOGY the yellow part of an egg, for example the egg of a bird. The yolk contains protein and fat that provide food for the embryo. The clear substance that surrounds the yolk is called the **albumen**.

you /strong juː, weak jə, jʊ/ pronoun **1** used for referring to the person or people that you are talking or writing to: *Do you like oranges?* ♦ *I'll give it to you if you want it.* **2** used for referring to people in general: *You don't have to be a great athlete to enjoy sport.*

you'd /juːd/ short form **1** the usual way of saying or writing 'you had' when 'had' is an auxiliary verb. This is not often used in formal writing: *You look very tired – you'd better take a break.* **2** the usual way of saying or writing 'you would'. This is not often used in formal writing: *The doctor can see you at 3 pm if you'd like to come then.*

you'll /juːl/ short form the usual way of saying or writing 'you will'. This is not often used in formal writing: *You'll get cold if you don't wear a coat.*

young¹ /jʌŋ/ adj **1** someone who is young has lived for only a short time: *a young woman* ♦ *They told him he was too young to understand.* ♦ *She has two young children.* **2** something that is young has existed for only a short time: *It's still quite a young organization.* **3** suitable for young people: *That dress is a little young for you.*

young² /jʌŋ/ noun [plural] **1** a group of young animals that belong to the same family **2 the young** children and young adults in general

younger /'jʌŋɡə/ adj not as old as you are, or not as old as someone else who you are discussing: *My younger sister, Karen, is moving to Japan.*

your /strong jɔː, weak jə/ determiner **1** used for showing that something belongs to the person or people who you are talking to: *You never really talk to your parents, do you?* ♦ *What's your address?* **2** used for showing that something is connected with people in general: *You never forget your first kiss.*

you're /jɔː/ short form the usual way of saying or writing 'you are'. This is not often used in formal writing: *You're looking well, Peter.*

yours /jɔːz/ pronoun used for referring to something that belongs to the person or people who you are talking to: *My pen isn't working – can I borrow yours?* ♦ *A friend* **of yours** *called while you were out.*
> PHRASE **Yours** or **Yours faithfully/sincerely** used at the end of a letter before your name. Use 'Yours faithfully' when you have started the letter with 'Dear Sir/Madam'. Use 'Yours sincerely' when you have

started the letter with 'Dear Mr/Mrs/Ms etc'. Use 'Yours' when you have started the letter with 'Dear John/Maria etc'.

yourself /jəˈself/ (plural **yourselves** /jəˈselvz/) pronoun **1** the reflexive form of 'you', used for showing that the person or people who you are talking to are affected by something that they do: *Did you hurt yourself?* ♦ *Go and get yourselves something to eat.* **2** used with 'you' for emphasizing that you mean the person or people who you are talking to, and no one else: *Think about how* **you yourself** *would like to be treated in a similar situation.* **3** used for referring back to the person or people you are talking or writing to when they have already been mentioned in the sentence: *I'll give you a little time to get yourself comfortable.* **4** used instead of 'you' in order to be formal or polite. Many people think that this use is incorrect: *Someone like yourself would be a good person to give him advice.*
PHRASES **(all) by yourself 1** without help from anyone else: *Did you paint the room all by yourself?* **2** alone: *I'm sure you like to be by yourself sometimes.*
(all) to yourself not shared with anyone else: *You have the house to yourself until five o'clock.*
be/feel/look etc yourself to be, or appear to be, in your normal mental or physical state: *Take a rest – you're not quite yourself today.*

youth /juːθ/ noun **1** [U] the time in your life when you are young: *the energy of youth* ♦ *In his youth, he travelled around the world.* **2** [C] a male teenager: *a gang of youths* **3** [U] young people in general: *the youth of the nation* ♦ *youth culture*

ˈyouth ˌclub noun [C] a place where young people can go to meet and take part in activities

youthful /ˈjuːθf(ə)l/ adj **1** typical of young people **2** looking or behaving like a young person, although you are no longer young

ˈyouth ˌhostel noun [C] a cheap place where travellers can stay for a short period of time

you've /juːv/ short form the usual way of saying or writing 'you have' when 'have' is an auxiliary verb. This is not often used in formal writing: *You've got a letter.*

yr abbrev year

ytterbium /ɪˈtɜːbiəm/ noun [U] CHEMISTRY a soft silvery-white metallic element in the **lanthanide** group of the periodic table. Chemical symbol: **Yb**

yttrium /ˈɪtriəm/ noun [U] CHEMISTRY a silvery-grey metallic element that is found in **rare-earth** ores. Chemical symbol: **Y**

yuan /juˈɑːn/ (plural **yuan**) noun [C] ECONOMICS the unit of money used in China

the YWCA /ˌwaɪ dʌb(ə)ljuː siː ˈeɪ/ the Young Women's Christian Association: an organization that helps women by providing them with a place to live, giving them information etc

Zz

z /zed, *American* ziː/ (plural **z's**) or **Z** (plural **Z's**) noun [C/U] the 26th and last letter of the English alphabet

zeal /ziːl/ noun [U] great energy, effort, and enthusiasm

zebra /ˈzebrə/ noun [C] an African mammal that is similar to a horse but has black and white stripes on its body —*picture* → MAMMAL

zeitgeist /ˈzaɪtˌɡaɪst/ noun [singular] *formal* the ideas, beliefs, and interests that are typical of most people during a particular time in history, and are expressed in the culture of that time

zenith /ˈzenɪθ/ noun [C] the point in the sky where the Sun or Moon is highest above the Earth

zero /ˈzɪərəʊ/ (plural **zeros** or **zeroes**) noun **1** [C/U] MATHS the number 0= NOUGHT: *Add a zero to the figure 3 and you get 30.* **2** [U] SCIENCE the temperature on the Celsius scale at which water freezes: *The temperature was 40 degrees* **below zero**. **3** used for showing that there is no amount at all of something: *We're likely to see zero growth in the market this year.* ♦ *astronauts in zero gravity*

ˌzero ˈgrowth noun [U] ECONOMICS a situation in which there is no increase in the growth or development of something

zest /zest/ noun [U] **1** a feeling of great enthusiasm or interest **2** the skin of an orange or lemon when it is used in cooking

zeugma /ˈzjuːɡmə/ noun [U] LANGUAGE the use of a word once in a sentence, but with two different meanings, often for humorous effect. The sentence 'She broke the record and her leg' is an example of zeugma.

zigzag¹ /ˈzɪɡzæɡ/ noun [C] a line or movement that makes very sharp angles, because it suddenly changes from one direction to another

zigzag² /ˈzɪɡzæɡ/ (**zigzags, zigzagging, zigzagged**) verb [I] to move forwards in a line that makes very sharp angles, by suddenly changing from one direction to another

zinc /zɪŋk/ noun [U] CHEMISTRY a chemical element that is a blue-white metal. It is used to make alloys and as a surface layer to protect other metals, especially iron and steel. Chemical symbol: **Zn**

zip¹ /zɪp/ noun [C] a long narrow metal or plastic object with two rows of **teeth**. It is used for opening or closing something such as a piece of clothing.

zip² /zɪp/ (**zips, zipping, zipped**) verb [T] **1** to close or fasten something with a zip ≠ UNZIP **2** COMPUTING to make a computer document fill less space by **compressing** it ≠ UNZIP

ˈZip ˌdrive noun [C] COMPUTING a part of a computer or a separate small machine that you connect to your computer, used for copying large documents onto a special disk

ˈZip ˌfile noun [C] COMPUTING a computer document that has been **compressed** so that it fills less space and can be stored more easily or sent by email more quickly

zirconium /zɜːˈkəʊniəm/ noun [U] CHEMISTRY a soft greyish-white metallic element, used in alloys and **nuclear reactors**. Chemical symbol: **Zr**

zither /ˈzɪðə/ noun [C] MUSIC a small musical instrument consisting of a box with strings across the top. It is played using the fingers.

the zodiac /ˈzəʊdiˌæk/ noun [singular] 12 groups of stars that some people believe affect your character according to the positions that they are in when you are born

zonation /zəʊˈneɪʃ(ə)n/ noun [U] ENVIRONMENT the arrangement of different plants and animals at different points along the shore. It depends on how long they are under the sea as the sea level rises and falls.

zone /zəʊn/ noun [C] **1** an area where a particular thing happens: *an earthquake zone* ♦ *a traffic-free zone* **2** GEOGRAPHY one of the large areas that the world is divided into according to its temperature

zoo /zuː/ (plural **zoos**) noun [C] a place where many types of wild animals are kept so that people can see them

'zoo-ˌkeeper noun [C] someone whose job is to look after the animals in a zoo

zoologist /zuˈɒlədʒɪst/ noun [C] BIOLOGY a scientist who studies animals

zoology /zuˈɒlədʒi/ noun [U] BIOLOGY the scientific study of animals

zoom /zuːm/ verb [I] **1** to move with a lot of speed and energy **2** if a camera zooms in or out, it makes something seem much closer or further away: *The camera **zoomed in on** a cat stuck in the tree.*

zooplankton /ˌzəʊəˈplæŋktən/ noun [U] BIOLOGY tiny animals that float in the surface water of the sea and feed on **phytoplankton** (=microscopic organisms in the sea)

Zoroastrianism /ˌzɒrəʊˈæstriəˌnɪz(ə)m/ noun [U] RELIGION a religion in parts of Iran and India. It is based on the continuing battle between good and bad and light and darkness.

zucchini /zʊˈkiːni/ noun [C] *American* a **courgette**

zygote /ˈzaɪɡəʊt/ noun [C] BIOLOGY a fertilized egg in living things that have sexual reproduction —*picture* → FERTILIZATION

REFERENCE SECTION

CONTENTS

STUDY SKILLS

These pages have been specially prepared to help you with your schoolwork, and also your written correspondence in English – with friends, or with future employers for example.

The articles on schoolwork cover basic skills you will need in all your subject areas. They contain information on taking notes (**Taking Notes**) and writing up your work (**Writing up Experiments and Project Work**). There is an account of the different types of composition and the tools you can use to improve your composition skills (**Essay Writing**). The assessment of the work you do in school is of great importance. We have therefore included a section to help you to revise, and given some advice on how you can do well on the different kinds of question you will have in your exams (**Preparing for Exams**).

The pages on writing formal and informal letters explain what language is suitable in different situations (**Writing Letters**). There is also a guide to interview skills and writing your CV (**Writing CVs** and **Preparing for Interviews**). Because of the importance of email as a form of communication nowadays, we have included a section on composing formal and informal emails (**Writing Emails**). A summary of basic language skills is also included (**Capital Letters and Punctuation**).

Being able to present information in different ways is an essential skill, and so we have included a section on preparing and interpreting tables, pie charts, bar charts, histograms, and line graphs (**Dealing with Data**). The importance of new technology in all subject areas has also been recognized with the inclusion of a section on computer hardware and software, and computer language and the Internet (**Information and Communication Technology**, or **ICT**).

Finally, there is a description of the different literary genres and figures of speech (**Literary Terms).**

We hope that you will find these pages interesting and useful, and that they will increase your appreciation of a wide range of communication skills.

DEALING WITH DATA

by Dr June Hassall

Data is information, often in the form of numbers, which you may have collected during an experiment or research acitivty. This section helps you to prepare and interpret tables, pie charts, bar charts, histograms, and line graphs.

Tables

What they are: Boxes with a grid of crossing lines: vertical columns and horizontal rows.

Use tables to: Record similarities and differences between organisms, and to enter the readings you take during an experiment.

Making tables

- Use a title to describe the information.

- Columns are labelled with the things being described or the quantities being measured (and their units, such as %, g, °C).

- Across the rows, enter your observations or readings.

Comparison of the composition of two foods:

Foods	Percentage of food constituents			
	Protein%	Fat%	Carbo-hydrate%	Inedible%
Peanut	26	46	10	18
Corn	10	5	70	15

Interpreting tables

- First find the information that is needed.

- You will usually need to do some simple arithmetic on numerical data:
  - add, subtract, multiply, and divide whole numbers, decimals and fractions
  - work out ratios, percentages, and fractions
  - find the mean and median.

For example, from the table above:

1 How many grams of protein would there be in 50 g of peanuts?

For peanuts, the % of protein is 26; this means 26 g of protein are present in 100 g of peanuts.

So in 50 g there are 26/100 x 50 = 13 g (Half of 26, as 50 is half of 100.)

Now work out the answer for the corn.

2 What fraction of peanuts is made up of carbohydrate?

For peanuts, the % of carbohydrates is 10%. This means 10 parts out of a hundred, or 10/100 = 1/10 (one tenth). This can also be written as 0.1.

Now work out the answer for the corn.

Pie charts

What they are: Pie charts are circles with lines dividing them into parts (sectors), like cutting a pizza. Each sector is labelled and represents the amount of a certain thing as part of the whole.

Use pie charts to: Show parts of the whole as a diagram, for example of food constituents in a certain food, different uses of chemicals, or various kinds of music, books etc.

Making pie charts

We start with a table.

Percentage of food constituents				
	Protein	Fat	Carbo-hydrate	Inedible
Peanut	26	46	10	18

The angle at the centre of a circle is 360°. We divide this angle in the same proportion as the constituents:

$$\frac{\text{Percentage of constituent}}{100} \times 360° = \text{angle of segment}$$

Protein = 26/100 x 360° = 93.6°

Fat = 46/100 x 360° = 165.6°

Carbohydrate = 10/100 x 360° = 36°

Inedible part = 18/100 x 360° = 64.8°

The sectors are then drawn onto the circle using a protractor to measure the angles. They are shaded or coloured, and labelled.

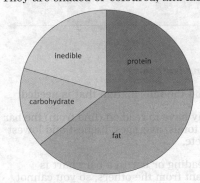

Interpreting pie charts

Do the reverse of making the pie chart.

- Use a protractor to find an angle, e.g. 36° for the sector of carbohydrate in peanuts.

- Find what percentage this is of the whole by dividing by 360 and multiplying by 100:

$$36/360 \times 100 = 10\%.$$

- If the total weight of the item of food is 250g, for example, then this sector represents:

10% of 250, which is 10/100 x 250 = 25g of carbohydrate in the item of food.

Bar charts

What they are: Bar charts have vertical or horizontal bars. The lengths of bars represent the value of the variable being measured.

Use bar charts: When one variable is numerical (for example amount of rainfall), and the other variable is a description (for example days of the week).

Making bar charts

Rainfall (cm) for five days					
	Days				
	Mon	Tues	Wed	Thurs	Fri
Rainfall (cm)	0	2	4	3	6

- On the horizontal axis, enter the names of the descriptive variable.

- On the vertical axis, enter the scale for the numerical variable.

- Draw bars of equal width to represent the values. Bars do not usually touch each other.

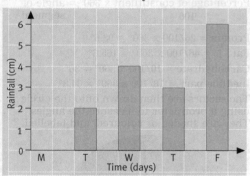

Interpreting bar charts

- First find the information that is needed.

- You may have to read off (find from) the bar chart the totals, averages, highest and lowest readings etc.

- Each reading or bar in a bar chart is independent from the others, so you cannot use a bar chart to predict other readings.

For example, for the bar chart above:

1 On which day did it rain a) most, b) least?
a) Most was on Friday, b) Least was on Monday.

2 What is the average rainfall during the week?

(Add together all the values, and divide by the number of readings.)

$$\frac{0 + 2 + 4 + 3 + 6}{5} = 15/5 = 3 \text{ cm rain/day}$$

Histograms

What they are: Histograms also have bars, the heights of which represent values.

Use histograms: When information on both the axes is numerical, for example the number of seedlings that are different specified heights.

Making histograms

- We often combine the readings of one variable into groups (or classes) and the scale for these is put along the horizontal axis.

- On the vertical axis, enter the scale for the readings that were taken.

- Draw bars of equal width to represent the values. Bars touch each other because they are showing values of the same variable.

Number of seedlings of different height			
	Height (cm)		
	0-4 cm	5-9 cm	10-14 cm
Number	6	20	4

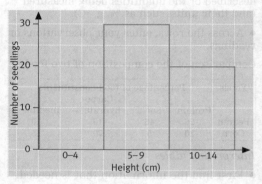

Interpreting histograms

- First find the information that is needed.

- You may have to read off various values, and work out totals, averages etc.

- You may have to explain how and why the experiment was set up as it was.

For example, for the histogram above:

1 What is the most common height range for the seedlings?
This is 5-9 cm.

2 How many seedlings were used?
(Add the total number of readings.)
Total = 6 + 20 + 4 = 30.

3 Why were so many seedlings used?
When we do experiments with living things we need to use large numbers, because some may die.

4 Why is the first height range listed as 0–4?
For this experiment what is the significance of a reading of 0? A reading of 0 would mean the plant died – it didn't grow.

Line graphs

What they are: Line graphs are points recorded on graph paper (marked with squares) that are then joined by lines.

Use line graphs: To show how one numerical variable changes in relation to another. For example a line graph can record how children increase in height as they become older.

Making graphs

a) *Draw the axes*

• Draw the lines for the axes at right angles and as long as you can, in order to fill the space that you have.

• On the horizontal (x) axis put the values you decide, called the independent variable. This could be time (minutes, days, years etc) or temperature.

• On the vertical (y) axis put the readings you take of the experiment (what you are investigating). This is called the dependent variable, and could be height, mass, or number.

b) *Label and choose scales*

• Add the units in which readings will be made, for example time (days), height (cm) etc.

• *Decide on the scales*: These usually begin from zero (but they don't have to). Look at your lowest and highest readings and mark these on the axes. Then divide the space between them into equal parts and add numbers.

c) *Plot the points*
Use the numerical data you have collected or have been given in a table. Read the scales carefully and then run an imaginary line up from a value on the horizontal axis, and another across from the corresponding value on the vertical axis. Where these two lines meet, make a cross or a dot inside a circle.

d) *Join the points*
Check each point is in the correct place, then join the points with straight lines.

e) *Add a title*
Include both the dependent and the independent variables.

Prepare a line graph of this information that shows the relation between time and the increase in height of seedlings.

	Height (cm)						
	3	3.5	4.2	4.8	5.5	6.1	6.7
Time (days)	1	2	3	4	5	6	7

Axes: The values chosen by the experimenter are the days on which readings are made – so this is the horizontal axis. The values that depend on these are the readings of height that are recorded – so these go on the vertical axis.

Scales: You can chose one large square for each day and for each cm.

Plot points: Record with a cross or a dot the intersection of each pair of values.

Join points: Use a ruler.

Add a title: 'Graph to show the relation between height of seedlings and time'.

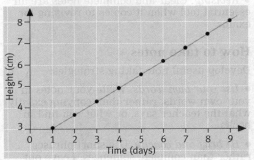

Interpreting graphs

• Use the graph line to find values on the axes:

– On which day is the height 3.5 cm?

– A height of 5.5 cm is found on which day?

• You can make predictions. If a reading had been missed, then the line could be used to estimate it. The line can also be extended to predict new values, as shown by a dotted line on the graph above. This shows a predicted value of 7.4 cm for an 8-day-old seedling.

• Describe the graph.

– If the line is steep, it means a high rate of growth.

– If the line is less steep, then the growth rate is also less.

Have fun dealing with data!

TAKING NOTES

by Elizabeth Potter

Why take notes?

Note-taking is one of the most essential study skills for a number of reasons.

- *Recording.* Well-organized notes provide a useful record of what you have learned in class

- *Understanding.* Writing things down in note form can help you understand the subjects that you are studying

- *Writing.* By developing good note-taking skills you will develop your writing skills in general

- *Remembering.* Well-organized notes will help you remember what you have learned

- *Revising.* Clear and complete notes are an essential tool when it comes to revising for exams

How to take notes

Develop useful note-taking strategies:

- *Use your own words.* Write your notes in your own words, rather than copying exactly what the teacher says, or what you find in books

- *Be brief and concise.* Use short phrases rather than complete sentences. Leave out words that are not essential, such as articles and auxiliary verbs

- *Use shortcuts.* Use abbreviations and symbols wherever possible

- *Use signposts.* Make the different points stand out, for example by numbering them, or by using symbols such as dashes or asterisks

- *Be accurate.* Make a note of the exact source of the information that you are recording, for example the title and author of a book, and the page or chapter number

- *Go over your notes.* If you have taken notes in class, go over them soon afterwards to make sure you understand what you have written, and fill in any gaps

Find the strategies that suit you:

- *Find your style.* Different people find different strategies useful when they are taking notes. Some people find it helpful to organize their notes in columns or lists, while others find more visual techniques are useful. Experiment with different techniques to find the ones that suit your learning style.

Things to avoid:

- *Avoid writing too much.* Do not write in full sentences or copy out chunks from books word for word (unless you are going to use them as quotations)

- *Neatness is not the point.* There is no point in writing out notes several times to make them tidier: as long as you can read them and understand what you meant by them, that is all that is necessary

Symbols and abbreviations

Using symbols and abbreviations will help you save time when you are making notes, and will make your notes more concise.

- *Symbols.* Some of the most common and useful symbols are:

%	per cent or percentage
$, R, P	for currencies
&	and
<	less than
>	more than
≠	not equal to
≈	roughly equal to

- *Abbreviations.* Some of the most common and useful abbreviations are:

etc.	etcetera
e.g.	for example
i.e.	that is
NB	note well

There are standard abbreviations for things like days of the week (**Fri.**), months (**Dec.**), countries (**US, UAE**), weight and measures (**kg, cc**) and so on.

Many other abbreviations are made by shortening words, for example:

approx.	approximate or approximately
esp.	especially
max	maximum
opp.	(opposite)

while others are contractions:

wt	weight
govt	government
Mt	mount or mountain

- You can make up your own abbreviations and symbols, but make sure that you will remember their meanings easily when you come to look at the notes again.

Organize your notes

An untidy bundle of pieces of paper covered with notes on a range of different subjects is not much more useful than no notes at all. You should organize your notes according to subject and topic, and if possible keep each subject in a separate folder or binder.

WRITING UP EXPERIMENTS AND PROJECT WORK

by Dr June Hassall and Elizabeth Potter

Writing up experiments

- *Report what was done*. Experiments are recorded using a formal and impersonal style. They are usually written in the past tense and the passive voice, as though they were done by someone else. This means that you write

  'Water was added to the sand'

  rather than

  'We added water to the sand'.

- *Use scientific words carefully*. For example, do not confuse *mass* (the amount of substance in an object, measured in g or kg), with *weight* (the force acting on an object, measured in newtons).

Headings for experiments

You use headings under which you answer certain questions.

- *Date*. When did you do the experiment?
- *Aim*. What were you trying to do? What were you trying to find out? What idea or hypothesis were you testing?
- *Equipment and materials*. What did you use? What equipment, materials, and chemicals did you need?
- *Method*. What did you do? How did you use the science equipment? Do you need to give a diagram of what you used? What were the steps in your method?
- *Results*. What happened? What did you record using your senses? What changes or measurements did you record?
- *Conclusion*. What have you learned from the experiment? What have you found out? How can you explain your results? Have you found an answer to your aim?

Fair tests

You will not be able to draw proper conclusions if you do not set up a fair test.

In a fair test only one feature or *variable* is changed at a time. Then when you find your results, you can say that they were due to that particular variable.

For example, if you want to find out the effect of moisture on the growth of mould, you could set up wet and dry bread and see which grows most mould. But you must use the same kind of bread and leave the pieces at the same temperature and with the same amount of light, so that you can be sure it was the moisture that accounted for any differences that you see.

Project work

The steps you follow in setting up and recording a project are similar to those above. However, a project runs over a longer time and you may be working with a larger group of people.

- *Plan*. Clearly identify your aim. Do not make it too large, or you may be discouraged before you have finished. If finding out about your aim involves an experiment, then make sure you set up a fair test by controlling variables.

- *Gather information*. Decide where you will look for information. It can come from books, people, or observation and experiment. You may also be able to use electronic resources such as CD-ROMs or the Internet. Gathering information may involve doing experiments, making and testing models, collecting and classifying living things, or researching historical and other information.

- *Organize the work*. Divide up the work between members of the group. Try to identify with the group the parts of the project and when you will try to complete each step. This is called 'setting deadlines.' It is important that team members keep to the deadlines.

- *Interpret your results*. You need to look at the data you have collected and think about how to organize it. You may also have found opinions that are different; now you have to decide how to present them in a fair way. Set down your results and the conclusions that you can draw.

- *Report your findings*. Try to use a variety of presentations, including charts, graphs, and tables as well as discussions, talks, and typed reports. Again, divide the work to be done between the group members and set up deadlines for completion.

ESSAY WRITING

by Dr June Hassall

Composition skills cover the planning and writing of material for a variety of purposes. There are also certain useful tools you can use.

Guide to becoming a good writer

- *Observe* carefully everything around you.

- *Record* interesting ideas in a notebook.

- *Choose* a subject you really like.

- *Decide* what you want to achieve from your writing – think about which kind of composition you are writing.

- *Plan* the main outline and write it down.

- *Use* your ideas and your plan for a first draft.

- *Revise* what you have written.

- *Prepare the final version* either in neat handwriting, or using a computer.

- *Show* your writing to others.

Different kinds of composition

- *Narratives*: These tell a story or give an account of something that happened. They can repeat facts or can be imaginary (made up). They are often written in the past tense and may include speech to add variety. You will find the tools of Planning, Sentence structure, Parts of Speech, and Paragraphs especially useful.

- *Journal writing*: This is a personal record of the things that happen to you, and of the feelings you have. You can decide if you are going to keep the journal just for yourself, or share it with others. You can use an informal style and develop your own abbreviations and codes.

- *Descriptive writing*: This 'paints a picture' using words. Descriptions tell what something or someone is like, or how to do something. When you write a description, imagine you are writing it for someone who has never seen, felt, smelt, heard, or tasted what you are describing.

  You can also include sections of descriptive writing within narratives and journal writing.

- *Explanatory writing*: First make sure you understand what you want to explain. Imagine you are telling a younger person what they should do. Use facts and not opinions. Use diagrams if these help. Also see the section on **Writing up Experiments and Project**

Work. The tools of Planning, Sentence structure, and Linking words will be useful.

- *Persuasive writing*: This covers describing different points of view – opinions – about something. You write in order to convince your reader to agree with you. This style of writing is often used in the Essay section of examinations. Useful tools are Planning, Vocabulary and Spelling, Sentence structure, and Punctuation.

- *Playscripts*: These list the dialogue (words spoken by the characters), together with descriptions of the actions and the way in which the words should be said. Useful tools are Planning, Vocabulary and Spelling, Sentence structure, and Punctuation.

- *Summaries*: Read and understand the material. Then pick out the main ideas, and list them. Now put the main ideas together in your own words to write your summary. Writing summaries is also a good way to revise: see **Preparing for Exams**.

- *Book reports*: This is a summary about a book you have read that gives enough information to other people for them to decide if they would like to read it. You summarize the story and say if you enjoyed it. List the title, publisher, and author and describe the setting, characters, and plot. Useful tools are Planning, Vocabulary and Spelling, Sentence structure, and Punctuation.

- *Poetry*: This often has short lines that are not complete sentences. It uses rhyme and rhythm to express feelings. Poems describe a person, place, or idea about which the writer feels strongly. You can use a pattern for writing a poem, or make up your own style. Useful tools are Parts of speech (especially adjectives and adverbs) and Figurative language.

Useful tools

- *Planning*: First decide on the kind of writing you are going to do. Then write down any ideas related to the topic that you have chosen or been given. Use this for recalling facts in an exam, for listing steps in an explanation, for creating new characters and plot in a narrative or playscript, or for planning a book report or poem.

  For persuasive writing it is useful to make a table of alternative opinions, and for poetry to note down sets of rhyming words. Then add numbers to your ideas to put them into a sensible order. As you do this you will think of other ideas to add.

• *Vocabulary and Spelling*: Your vocabulary (words you use) is related to the composition. For example, you can use informal vocabulary in your Journal, in a poem, or in text messages, but not in an essay for an exam. Also use proper scientific terms in Science. Expand your vocabulary by recording new words and meanings in a notebook.

In an exam there will be some marks awarded for spelling, so it is always useful to check new words using a dictionary. Try to find and remember similar patterns in spelling words.

• *Sentence structure*: Poems have their own patterns, and the style used in Journals can be very personal. For other writing, try to vary the style, length, and complexity:

– Phrases are incomplete sentences: they do not have a verb or a subject.
in the long term
according to experts
first of all

– Sentences have a verb and a subject and make complete sense. Some examples are statements, questions, and exclamations.
Most crimes are not reported to the police.
When did you hear the news?
There must be some mistake!

– Simple sentences have just one main clause, containing one subject and one verb.
Vitamins are important for health.

– Compound sentences are made by joining two simple sentences and so have two main clauses.
They dry the crops and then store them for the winter.

– Complex sentences contain one main clause and two or more minor or subordinate clauses.
Because there was a risk of flooding, people had to leave the city.

• *Parts of speech*: Use these correctly:

– Noun: a naming word. Common nouns (lower case letters) are general names such as *baby* and *idea*. Proper nouns (capital letters) name special people, places, or things, such as *Lin Thomas*.

– Verb: an action word. This describes what something does, for example 'Tom *kicked* the ball', or the state of being, for example 'I *slept*'. The verb 'kicked' has an object (ball) and so it is called a transitive verb. The verb 'slept' does not have an object and so it is called an intransitive verb.

– Adjective: a describing word. It usually, but not always, comes before the noun or pronoun it describes, for example 'she had a *pretty* face'.

– Adverb: a word that describes a verb – how, when, or where something happens, for example 'he drove *quickly*'. It also describes adjectives or other adverbs, for example 'she had an *extremely* pretty face' or 'he drove *very* quickly'.

In descriptive writing several adjectives or adverbs can be used together. They can also be used to compare two or more things, for example 'taller, tallest' and 'quickly, more quickly'.

– Pronoun: stands in for a noun, for example *he, she, it, him, her, them*.

– Preposition: describes how one person or thing relates to another: The cat is *under* the table.

– Conjunction: a joining word, and one that introduces another part of a sentence, for example *and, but, or, because, although*.

• *Figurative language*: Some examples:

– Similes: these compare two things using 'as', 'like', and 'as...as', for example 'swift *as* the wind'.

– Metaphors: these say one thing is another, for example 'She is a rock' (very dependable).

– Onomatopeia: using words that sound like the actual sound, for example 'a creaking chair'.

See the section on **Literary Terms** for more help on how to use figurative language.

• *Paragraphs*: A paragraph is a set of sentences that go together. You need a new paragraph when you introduce a new person or place, or a change of time or idea. One pattern to use is:

– The first sentence gives the main idea.

– This is followed by the body of the paragraph that develops the idea and gives examples.

– The last sentence sums up the information or gives the main idea in a slightly different way.

• *Linking words*: These are words and phrases such as *first, next, after that,* and *finally* that help the reader to follow the order of a book report or of explanatory or persuasive writing.

Other linking words and phrases, such as *however, besides, moreover,* or *in addition* can be used to introduce new or contrasting ideas in persuasive writing.

You can also use linking words and phrases such as *overall, in general,* or *in conclusion*, to summarize your ideas for the reader, especially in explanatory writing.

PREPARING FOR EXAMS

by Dr June Hassall

How can you improve the results you will get on your examinations? Here are some useful hints.

Work hard during the term

• *Make good notes.* Underline headings and important words so you can see them easily. See also the section on **Taking Notes** for more help with this.

• *Learn as you go.* When you finish a piece of work, check that you understand it.

• *Take class tests seriously.* Try to do well on all your tests.

• *Complete assignments on time.* Projects and practicals done during term-time may form part of your overall exam mark, so do them well.

Revise effectively

• *Know your course.* Make a list of the topics that you have to learn.

• *Make a revision timetable.* Write down when you will revise each topic. Leave the week before your exam free for last-minute revision.

• *Make revision blocks short.* Short blocks of 30 minutes, with a 5-minute break, are better than long ones.

• *Make your revision active.* For example:

– use a highlighter pen to mark important words in your notes;

– write out summaries of your notes;

– write the important words from your notes and then try to fill in the details;

– draw and label diagrams, then check them;

– try to repeat your notes from memory. Cover over a small part, then try and write or say it;

– ask someone to test you by asking questions on the topic that you have done.

• *Learn from your mistakes.* Check the answers to questions, and if you made mistakes try to think where you went wrong, and learn from it.

• *Keep a record.* Record what you have revised, and tick off the topics as you do them.

Answering multiple-choice questions

• *Know the format.* Multiple-choice questions usually have an incomplete statement (stem) followed by four possible answers from which you have to choose the best one.

• *Using an answer sheet.* For each question there will be four blank areas labelled A, B, C, and D. You have to blacken the letter that is the same as the answer that you think is correct. Use a pencil for this, in case you want to change it.

• *Don't just guess.* If you are not sure of the right answer, *don't* just guess. First cross off the options that you know are wrong. Then choose between those that are left.

• *Do answer every question.* Each question is worth one mark, and should only take a minute.

• *Making corrections.* If you want to change an answer, rub out the first one very carefully before marking the new one. You will be marked wrong if dark smudges show in two letters.

Answering structured questions

• *Know the format.* A structured question is divided into several numbered parts.

• *Writing your answers.* The question has lines on which you write your answers. The number of marks for each part of the question is usually listed. As a guide, make one point or write one sentence for each mark available.

• *Getting help.* If you are not sure of an answer, first read carefully all parts of the question. Check that you are clear where to write each part of the answer, and don't repeat yourself.

• *Use the space.* If you don't have enough to write in the space, check that you have understood the question. Also don't try and write more than can easily fit each space.

• *Answer all parts.* You must answer each part of the question in the correct place. If not, you won't get the marks.

• *Leave extra time for difficult questions*, such as those involving graphs. Check through your answers at the end.

Answering essay questions

• *Know the format.* An essay question is usually divided into only a few parts. Each part has more marks than for a structured question.

• *Choosing questions.* You usually have a choice of questions. Spend time on this so that you make wise choices. Select questions on which you can answer most of the parts.

• *Divide your time.* Be very careful to allow time for answering all the questions that you are required to do. If you miss out an entire question you will lose a lot of marks.

• *Answer the question.* Don't just write down everything you know about a topic. Make sure that you answer the exact question that is asked.

• *Be careful.* Check especially for *either ... or,* and *not* or *and.* Don't waste time if all you are asked for is a list. But don't leave out the explanation if you are asked to explain.

• *Check if diagrams are needed.* If they are needed, you'll lose marks if you don't do them.

• *Plan your answer.* Note down the main points before you write your answer. See also the section on **Essay Writing**.

• *If you are short of time at the end.* A well-drawn and labelled diagram is a quick way to record information and will gain you marks.

Answering practical questions

• *Know the format.* A practical question tests your ability to make and label drawings, and to design and carry out experiments.

• *Make and label drawings.* Specimens will be given to you to draw, for example: bones, flowers, insects, and their parts. Remember:

– drawings should look like the real thing

– make the drawing large enough, and the parts in proportion

– make a pale outline first of the main parts

– erase the outline as you complete the drawing

– check the original often to make sure you are making a good copy of it

– arrows, shading, and colouring are not used

– use a ruler for drawing label lines

– label lines should not cross each other

– give your drawing a title.

• *Design an experiment.* List and collect all the materials, apparatus, and chemicals that you will need. You may also have to set up a fair test:

– set up a control that contains all the *variables* you think are important;

– the parts of the experiment should test the effect of just one *variable*;

– compare the same numbers, masses, volumes etc to make it fair

– use large numbers of, for example, seeds or seedlings to reduce problems due to chance.

• *Carry out an experiment.* Remember:

– decide how you will measure or describe your results, for example a change in colour;

– do your experiment and record the results in a table;

– beware of any reading that is very different from the others – you may have made a mistake;

– if you have time, repeat your experiments and take the average of three readings.

See also the section on **Writing up Experiments and Project Work**.

Close to the examination

• *The last week.* This is the time to skim through your revision notes and answer exam questions. You can also check previous years' papers to find the topics that are most often tested. Ask a friend to test you on topics that you are not confident about.

• *The night before.* Put together your pencils, pens, eraser, ruler, calculator etc. Do *not* cram new information. Have a good night's sleep so that you can think clearly the next day.

In the examination

• *Read all the instructions very carefully.* Make sure you notice:

– questions that are compulsory. You have to do these to get the marks.

– questions on which you have a choice. Make sure that you answer the correct number of these, and from the correct sections.

• *Divide up your time.* Spend *roughly* one minute for each mark. For example:

– spend no more than one minute for each multiple-choice item;

– for longer questions, divide your time. *Don't* spend so long over one or two questions that you run out of time and cannot answer the others.

• *Leave time for checking.* Read through your answers and make corrections.

Good luck in your exams!

WRITING LETTERS

by Elizabeth Potter

Formal letters

Formal letters, including business letters and job applications, require a more formal style than letters written to family members or friends. Although many business communications now take place by email, formal letters still have their place. They have a standard layout and often include set phrases and formulae, some of which are listed below. When writing a formal letter you should observe these conventions and avoid informal features such as contractions, colloquial expressions and slang. For example, say *I am writing...*, *I have been working...* rather than *I'm writing...*, *I've been working...*

---

146 Maple Road
Newtown
NT4 6PU
Tel: 0678 123 4567
Mobile: 07777 472737
Email: emmajenks@yahoo.co.uk (1)

Ms Marie Read
Senior Events Officer
Capital City Events
35 Charlotte Lane
Edinburgh EH9 4PT (2)

11th July 2008 (3)

Ref no: EO4/8 (4)

Dear Ms Read (5)

I wish to apply for the post of Events Officer advertised on the Guardian website this week. (6)

I completed a Master's Degree in International Event Management at Brighton University last year, obtaining a distinction in my final assessment. Since then I have been working for Brighton Museums as Marketing Events Assistant, helping to plan, market and carry out a number of prestigious events including champagne suppers for supporters of the museums, two open days for the general public and several receptions marking the opening of special exhibitions. I have greatly enjoyed this work, but the post is only funded for one year and it seems no further funding will be available, so I am looking for a similar but broader role elsewhere. (7)

My previous experience includes a period of two years working on a wide range of events in Melbourne, where I completed my undergraduate studies, and my home city of Sydney. It was this that made me decide that I wanted a career in events management.

I am available for interview at any time, as my current employers know I am looking for another position. However, I shall need a few days' notice in order to arrange travel to Edinburgh.

I enclose a copy of my CV and look forward to hearing from you. (8)

Yours sincerely (9)

Emma Jenkinson (10)

---

1 Your address normally goes on the right-hand side of the page. Businesses often have their address, including email address and phone and fax numbers, at the top of the page in the centre.

2 The recipient's address goes on the left-hand side of the page. If you know the name and title of the person you are writing to, add these above the address.

3 The date can go either on the right-hand side under your address or on the left-hand side under the address of the recipient.

4 If you have a reference number, for example the reference for the job, add this under the address. **Ref** is short for 'reference'.

5 You can start your letter in one of the following ways:

1. If you know the name of the person you are writing to, put *Dear Mr [surname]* or *Dear Ms [surname]*. Only use *Miss* or *Mrs* if the person you are writing to has used that title in a previous letter.

2. If you don't know the name of the person, put *Dear Sir/Madam* or *Dear Sir or Madam*.

3. Some people use *Dear [first name] [second name]* (eg *Dear Marie Read*) but this is less suitable for a formal business letter.

6 Give the reason for your letter here. Other useful phrases include:

Thank you for your letter of... regarding ...

I am writing to enquire about/ ...in response to/ ... to inform you that/ ... to complain about/...

Further to my letter of July 6th ... I wish to inform you ...

7 Give further details about the purpose of your letter here.

8 Other expressions you can use to close your letter include:

Thank you in advance for your help.

I would be most grateful if you could let me know...

Please let me know as soon as possible if...

I look forward to receiving your reply.

9 You can write the following expressions before your name:

1. *Yours faithfully* or *Yours truly* if you don't know the name of the person you are writing to.

2. *Yours sincerely* or *Sincerely* if you are writing to a named person.

3. Other expressions such as *Best wishes, Regards, Best* are too informal for business letters.

10 Write your full name below your signature.

Informal letters

There are far fewer rules for informal letters than for formal ones. Some features of informal letters are:

- They usually start with *Dear* followed by the person's first name
- In slightly more formal letters you can use the person's first and second name
- Although it is usual to put your address and the date at the top right-hand side, you don't usually include the name and address of the person you are writing to
- You can use contractions, abbreviations, colloquial expressions and even slang as you would in speech
- You can end the letter in a number of ways including:

  1. All the best   *4. Love* (from)

  2. Best wishes   *5. Love to* (Auntie Gill/everyone/the boys...)

  3. Regards to (you all/Jamie...)   *6. Lots of love* (only in very informal letters)

---

141 Maple Road
Newtown
25th July 2008

Dear Amy

Sorry I haven't written for so long, I've been really busy. I'm actually writing this on the train from Edinburgh, where I've just been for a job interview. I think it went well so fingers crossed — they said they'd let me know by the end of next week. It's a small company, really friendly, with only 5 or 6 staff, quite a change from the museum. But I'd have a lot more responsibility right away, which is good. And the women who interviewed me were really nice and seemed impressed with my experience.

Edinburgh is BEAUTIFUL but rather chilly, even in the middle of July. Bit of a shock to the system after Brighton, never mind home. I shall need lots of woolly sweaters if I do get the job. Anyway I think I'm ready for a change so here's hoping it all works out.

Nothing much to report apart from the job. I've applied for another couple but they are in London and I really don't see how anyone can afford to live there, certainly not on the salaries they are paying.

Talking of London the train will be getting in in a few minutes so I'll stop.

Lots of love to you all, write back soon,

Emma

WRITING EMAILS

by Elizabeth Potter

Writing emails

Since emails are a relatively new form of communication, there are no set formulae for how they should be written, as there are for traditional business letters. Most emails tend to be informal, but there are occasions when you might need to write a formal email, for example when you are applying for a job, responding to an invitation to an interview, or requesting information. It is usual to use a formal style when emailing someone you do not know for the first time, but even in these cases the style of any subsequent emails is likely to be less formal.

Writing a formal email

From: Emma Jenkinson
To: Marie Read
CC:
Date: Fri, 11/07/08 17:40
Subject: Application for position of Events Officer **(1)**

Dear Ms Read **(2)**
(3) I attach my application for the position of Events Officer with Capital City Events, together with a copy of my CV. **(4)**

I am available for interview at any time and can be contacted either by email or phone (my home and mobile numbers are on my CV).

I look forward to hearing from you.

Yours sincerely **(5)**

Emma Jenkinson **(6)**

1 Make sure that the subject line is relevant to your email and easily identified (for example, not just 'job application').

2 When you are writing a formal email to someone you have never met, use their surname and title in the first email you send them. Use **Mr** for men, and **Ms** for women, since it is unlikely you will know their marital status. If they have another title such as **Dr** or **Professor**, use that.

If you do not know the name of the person you are writing to, for example when you are writing to an organization's general email address, it is acceptable to start with *Hello*.

3 People often send documents or pictures with the email: these are known as attachments.

4 Although people often do not write in complete or grammatically correct sentences when they are writing emails, if you are writing a formal email such as an application for a job or a place on a course, it gives a better impression if you use full sentences and correct grammar and punctuation.

5 If you are writing to someone you do not know well, end your email with **Yours sincerely** or **Yours**. **Best wishes** is also acceptable.

6 When writing to someone you don't know for the first time, it is best to use your full name.

From: Marie Read
To: Emma Jenkinson
CC: Jack Cheetham, Rosie March **(1)**
Date: Wednesday, July 16, 2008 9:54 AM
Subject: Re: Application for position of Events Officer

Dear Emma **(2)**

Thank you for your application for the position of Events Officer. Your CV
is very impressive and we would like to invite you for an interview here at
our offices at 11.30 on Thursday 24th July. The interview will be conducted
by myself and our MD Rosie March and should last about an hour. Please
phone my assistant Jack Cheetham on our general office number below to
confirm that you can attend. **(3)**

Please prepare a short presentation (5–8 minutes) on an event you have
successfully organized. You can use any format; let us know if you will
need computers, screens etc.

I attach a map showing the location of our offices in central Edinburgh
which are easily accessible by public transport. It's best not to bring a car
as parking is difficult and expensive.

I look forward to seeing you on the 24th.

Best wishes **(4)**

Marie **(5)**

Marie Read
Events manager
Capital City Events
35 Charlotte Lane
Edinburgh EH9 4PT
t: +44 131 400 7780
dd: +44 131 400 7789
e: m.read@capitalcity.co.uk

1 'CC' is used to send copies of the email to other people who are involved or might be
interested.

2 It is acceptable to use someone's first name in the first email you send them after they have
written to you. 'Dear Ms Jenkinson', although possible, would sound very formal.

3 When sending formal emails, it is better to use full sentences and correct grammar.

4 Best wishes and **Regards** are both suitable sign-offs for formal emails. **All the best** is
another possibility, but is a little more informal.

5 Once contact has been established, you usually use just your first name.

Writing an informal email

> From: Emma Jenkinson
> To: Lizzie Adams
> CC:
> Date: Thu, 17/07/08 10:45
> Subject: visit hi there **(1)**
>
> long time no see…hope you're OK **(2)**
>
> I've got a job interview! in Edinboro, Thurs next week. v excited and a bit
> nervous…**(3)**
>
> can I stay with you Weds nite, we can catch up and u can listen to my
> presentation (!) there's a train gets in around 6, I can find my way to yours
> let me know asap, cu soon **(4)**
>
> luv **(5)**
>
> Emma **(6)**

1 You do not need to begin informal emails with a formal greeting. **Dear Lizzie**, **Hello Lizzie**, **Hi Lizzie** or even just **Hello** or **Hi** are all acceptable ways of starting an email.

2 It is very easy to sound abrupt in an email, so a short greeting helps to sound friendly.

3 Emails are usually written at speed, so people very often do not write in complete or grammatically correct sentences.

4 Abbreviations are also often used to save time. For example, **asap** means 'as soon as possible', **cu** means 'see you', **u** means 'you'.

5 You usually end emails with something short like **Best** (short for 'Best Wishes') or **Regards**. Only use **love** for close friends and family.

6 People usually sign informal emails with their first name.

CVs AND INTERVIEWS

by Elizabeth Potter

Writing a CV

Employers receive many CVs and it is important that yours should stand out for all the right reasons.

- Keep it brief: never more than two pages, and one page is often enough

- Target the information you give to the job that you are applying for. For example, if you have a lot of work experience, give priority to those jobs that are directly relevant to the post that you are applying for

- Be careful not to leave gaps. Any unexplained periods in your life could make employers wonder what you were doing that you don't want to talk about

- Make sure the layout is clear, with plenty of white space and with the relevant information under the correct headings

- Check your grammar and spelling several times over to ensure that there are no careless mistakes

---

CURRICULUM VITAE

Personal details

Name	Emma Jenkinson
Address	146 Maple Road, Newtown, NT4 6PU
	Tel: 0678 123 4567
	Mobile: 07777 472737
	Email: emmajenks@yahoo.co.uk
Nationality	Australian (with permanent residence in UK)

Personal profile (1)

I am reliable, well-organized and used to working on my own initiative. I am adaptable and flexible, having lived, studied and worked on three continents. I have excellent interpersonal skills and enjoy working in a team, but am also comfortable working on my own. I thrive on pressure and am not intimidated by deadlines or tight schedules.

Key Skills (2)

Excellent computer skills	Self-starter
Confident communicator	Fluent in French
Able to cope under pressure	Clean driving licence

Work experience (3)

2007–present	Marketing and Events Assistant, Brighton Museums (one year post). Responsibilities include supporting all aspects of the museums' programme of events, including planning, marketing, visitor attendance and satisfaction, ensuring local and national media coverage of events, and maintaining the press office's database
2004–2006	Various positions in events management in Melbourne and Sydney, Australia
2003–2004	Teaching English in a school in Arusha, Tanzania

Education (4)

2006–2007	MA in International Event Management, University of Brighton
2003	Diploma in teaching English, Melbourne
2000–2003	Bachelor of Arts/Bachelor of Business (Marketing), Monash University, Melbourne, Australia
1994–2000	Sydney Girls High School, Sydney, Australia. High School Certificate with UAI of 96

References (5)

Available on request

1 Give a brief description of your most important personal qualities relevant to the post that you are applying for.

2 Key skills relevant to the job are often listed before employment history. Useful phrases include:

- **Experienced ...**
- **Experienced in ...**
- **with a good knowledge of ...**
- **Fluent/near-native command of French**
- **adequate spoken/written Italian**
- **Fully computer-literate**
- **Self-starter** (someone who can take responsibility, and work without supervision)

3 This can also be called **Experience** or **Employment history**. Start the list with your most recent job and finish with the earliest one. If you have had many jobs, include only your relevant work experience. You should also include relevant training courses, voluntary work etc.

4 This can also be called **Qualifications** or **Educational qualifications**. Start with your most recent qualifications and finish with your secondary education. It is not necessary to include details of your primary education.

5 **References** (the people that the employer can contact to get information about you) can be listed either at the end of the CV or included in a separate letter.

Interview skills

Preparing for interview

- Make sure you find out everything you can about the employer and the job that you have applied for. Look at the website, if there is one, or research the organization using the library

- Think about how you will answer questions that are likely to come up

- Think of a few relevant questions about the job and the organization that you want to ask yourself

- Dress appropriately for the organization that you are applying to. Some employers will expect very smart standards of dress, while others will expect you to be slightly more casual

- Arrive in good time – there's nothing worse than arriving late or in a rush

- Practise your handshake. A recent survey showed that employers were put off candidates whose handshakes were weak, wet, or excessively strong

- Smile and make eye contact (but not too much). The interviewer knows you're nervous, but try not to show it by mumbling or looking down

Typical questions asked at an interview

Of course, all interviews are different, but here are some questions you may be asked:

- Tell me/us a bit about yourself
- Tell me what qualities you will bring to this organization
- What has been your greatest achievement to date?
- Give me an example of how you have dealt with pressure/a heavy workload
- Tell me about a time when you changed someone's mind
- How would you describe your strengths and weaknesses?

CAPITAL LETTERS AND PUNCTUATION

by Michael Vince and Dr June Hassall

Capital letters

Capital (or upper case) letters are used:

- to begin a sentence or phrase
  You've done a fantastic job. Fresh fish!

- for the names of people
  Lin, Mary, Yiqun Wang

- for calling people by their title
  Mrs Brown, Uncle Kwame, Mum

- for the personal pronoun 'I'
  Can I help you?

- for the titles of books, films etc
  Alice in Wonderland, Treasure Island

Note: Small words like *and, a, the,* and prepositions do not usually have capitals, unless they are the first word of the title:
  The film was based on The Lord of the Rings *by J.R.R. Tolkien*

- for names and abbreviations of organizations
  Friends of the Earth, United Nations Educational Scientific and Cultural Organization UNESCO

- for the names of places (towns, countries etc)
  Singapore, Kuala Lumpur, P.R.C. (People's Republic of China)

- for nationalities and languages
  Malaysian, English, Chinese

- for adjectives made from proper nouns
  China, Chinese; Jamaica, Jamaican

- for days, months, celebrations etc
  Wednesday, March, Divali

Note: Some words can be written with capitals or in lower case, depending on the meaning:

- jobs
  Lee was a good president (general use)
  Paul met President Chin. (job title)

- compass points
  I live in the north of Malaysia. (description)
  Lyn works in the Far East. (place name)

Full stop (.)

Full stops are used:

- at the end of a statement (information and instructions) and after a polite request
  His sister's name is Adjoa.
  Please come here.

- in some abbreviations to show that letters at the end of a word are missing
  Sat. (Saturday), pl. (plural), approx. (approximately)

Note: In modern British English, full stops are not usually added when the abbreviation contains the last letter of the full word:
  Mr, Dr Mister, Doctor (used in titles)
  Rd, Ave Road, Avenue (used in addresses)

- In British English, full stops are also omitted from many abbreviations
  UK, IDB, IMF

- Full stops are not used after abbreviations of scientific units
  cm, g, kg, sec etc

Comma (,)

Commas are used:

- in writing to represent a brief pause in a long sentence
  Everyone agrees that Efua is a very intelligent girl, but she is rather lazy.

- in lists of two or more items
  I bought some bananas, some oranges, and a pineapple.

Note: This is the style used in this dictionary, but the *final* comma (before 'and') can be left out.

- in lists of adjectives that appear before a noun
  a hot, dry, sunny day

Note: In the above example, commas can be left out. Commas are not used to separate adjectives in this dictionary.

- after linking words at the beginning of a sentence
  First of all, I will tell you how it works.

- before and after linking words in the middle of a sentence
  Chen, on the other hand, did not agree.

- when giving additional information that can be left out
  John, who is usually late, turned up at 10.30.

- before question tags
  You're from China, aren't you?

- in large numbers to separate sets of digits
  6,550   17,500   387,100   2,000,000

Note: In some languages a full stop (.) is used instead. In English, a full stop would mean a decimal point (so 3.5 million = 'three and a half million' or 'three point five million').

- to separate the speaker from the words spoken
  Bo said, 'I'll be late.'

Note: Commas are *not* used:

- if there is other punctuation
  'Don't be too late!' said her mother.

- in reported speech
  Bo said she would be late.

Semicolon (;)

Semicolons are used:

- to join together two sentences with related meanings
  We need better technology; better technology costs money.

- to separate long items in a list
  Students are asked not to leave bicycles by the entrance; not to leave bags in the sitting room; and not to leave coats in the dining room.

Colon (:)

Colons are used:

- to introduce items in a list
  You will need to provide one of the following pieces of identification: a passport, a student's card, or a driving licence.

- to introduce an explanation of the previous part of the sentence
  Finally, we had to stop: we were tired and it was very dark.

Quotation marks (' ')

Quotation marks (also called speech marks or inverted commas) can be single (' ') or double (" ").

Quotation marks are used:

- around direct speech
  'Why are we leaving so early?' Susie asked.

- around words you want to emphasize or treat in a special way.
  What is a 'blog'?

Question mark (?)

Question marks are used:

- after a question
  What's the time?

Exclamation mark (!)

Exclamation marks are used:

- to show strong emotion such as surprise, joy, or anger
  You'll never guess! I passed my test!

- with commands that should be obeyed
  Come here immediately!

- with short exclamations that are called interjections
  Ouch! Help! Oh dear!

Note: Exclamation marks are used in informal writing, but should be limited in formal writing.

Apostrophe (')

Apostrophes are used:

- with 's' to show who or what someone or something belongs to or is connected with
  Chen is having dinner with Lin's sister.
  Did you go to yesterday's meeting?

Note: -'s is used when referring to a single person or thing.
  The boy's father (= the father of one boy) asked for an explanation.

Note: -s' is used when referring to more than one person or thing.
  The boys' father (= the father of more than one boy) asked for an explanation.

- in contractions (short forms) to show that some letters are missing
  The talk wasn't (= was not) any good.
  I'm (= I am) only here for a week.
  That can't (= cannot) be true.

Note: Remember that **its** (= belonging to or connected with 'it') does *not* have an apostrophe
  The dog was chasing its tail.

Note: Remember that **it's** (= 'it is' or 'it has') *does* have an apostrophe to show the missing letters.
  It's (= it is) too late now to do anything.
  It's (= it has) been raining all day.

Dash (–)

Dashes are used:

- alone or in pairs, to separate a comment from the rest of the sentence
  He claimed he was innocent – but was he?
  Her exam results during the year – with one exception – have been outstanding.

- in informal English, instead of a colon, to introduce a summary of what has just been said
  Friends, neighbours, distant relatives – all were invited to the celebration.

INFORMATION AND COMMUNICATION TECHNOLOGY (ICT)

by Dr June Hassall and Elizabeth Potter

Computer hardware

Computer hardware is the equipment. There are five main parts to the computer.

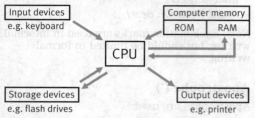

- *Input devices*: These change information into digital signals that can be used by the CPU. Examples of input devices are: keyboard, mouse, keypad, touch screen, microphone, scanner, digital camera, and webcam.

- *CPU*: Central processing unit. This controls what the computer does. It interprets the program instructions and performs the computer's activities.

- *Computer memory*: ROM and RAM

– ROM: read-only memory. This is the permanent memory that can be used but not changed. It contains programs needed for start-up, for example for loading the operating system.

– RAM: random access memory. This is the memory where you can save and change information. RAM is used by programs that are part of the operating system, or that are put in by the user of the computer.

- *Output devices*: These change digital signals from the CPU into a useful form for humans. Some examples of output devices are: the VDU (Visual Display Unit – the screen or monitor), printers, and loudspeakers.

- *Storage devices*: These write information onto storage media and read it back. Some examples of storage media are:

– hard disk: This is built into the computer itself. It can contain many gigabytes of information.

– USB flash drive: These can be put in and out of the computer and transported. They can hold several gigabytes of data.

– CDs and DVDs: These are read by laser beams in the CD drive. There are three kinds:

1. CD-ROMs (Compact disc read-only memory) are used for example to distribute software programs. They cannot be changed ('written to') by the user.

2. CD-R (CD-Recordable) and CD-RW (CD-Rewritable) can have data added by the user. CD-RWs allow the old files to be deleted as new files are added, so the CDs can be used as many times as required.

3. DVDs (Digital versatile discs) have a capacity of around 20 gigabytes and can store movies that can be viewed on a computer or TV screen.

Computer software

These are the programs for instructing the computer. There are two main types.

- *Operating systems*, such as Windows Vista, Linux, and Mac OS X. These control the hardware.

- *Applications*, such as word-processing and spreadsheet programs, and web browsers. Applications work through the operating system to gain access to the hardware, so that their programs can run.

Computer language: bits and bytes

- *Bit*: This is short for **bi**nary digi**t**. The binary system is a way of counting that uses only two digits, 0 and 1, to make a digital code. Electronic circuits transfer information written in digital code, by being either switched ON (which counts as 1) or OFF (which counts as 0). Strings of 0's and 1's are used to make codes for all the letters, numbers, and punctuation that we use.

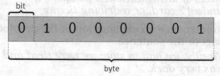

- *Byte*: This is a string of 8 bits. Each position in the code has a value based on powers of 2, so that each position to the left is twice the value of that on the right.

	2^7	2^6	2^5	2^4	2^3	2^2	2^1	2^0
	128	64	32	16	8	4	2	1
A	0	1	0	0	0	0	0	1
a	0	1	1	0	0	0	0	1

Using this system, the numerical value of 'A' is 64+1=65, and of 'a' is 64+32+1= 97. All the letters and symbols etc have a value between 1 and 255.

- *Bigger bytes:* One byte is only enough to make codes for one letter, number, or symbol. For coding larger amounts of data we also have:

– one kilobyte (kb) or 1K (1,024 bytes);
– one megabyte (Mb) (1,024 kilobytes);
– one gigabyte (Gb) (1,024 megabytes).

The Internet

The Internet or Net is an electronic system that connects people and allows them to exchange information.

- *ISPs*: Internet Service Providers. These allow computers to access the Net. They may also provide services such as search engines for finding information on the Net.

- *Modem*: This connects the computer, through the telephone lines, to the Net.

- *Broadband*: This is a system of connecting to the Net that works very quickly and uses a special broadband modem.

- *Wireless*: Wireless technology allows computers to connect to the Net using electronic signals rather than through fixed telephone lines. This means that instead of being kept in one place, computers can be used wherever a wireless network is available, for example on trains and in hotels.

Features of the Net

- *Website*: This is a place on the Net where particular information is available on web pages.

- *World Wide Web (www)*: This is the huge collection of web pages that can be searched using a search engine.

- *Search engines*: Search requests can be entered, and matching information (called 'hits') is found.

- *Email*: This is electronic information sent from one user 'address' to another. Attachments (additional files) can also be added and sent.

- *E-commerce*: Many companies now advertise and sell their products via the Net or 'online'.

- *Chat rooms*: These are groups of users who can have live conversations with each other via the Net.

- *Social networking*: Social networking websites are sites such as MySpace, Facebook and Bebo that allow users to post and access personal information and communicate with their friends.

- *Blogs*: A blog is a type of personal website that is changed regularly, to give the latest news. The page usually contains someone's personal opinions, comments, and experiences.

Problems with the Net

- *Spam*: This is advertising and emails sent via the Net to people who don't want them.

- *Fraud*: Criminals target people using e-commerce and online banking, trying to steal their bank or credit card details, or even take over their identities in order to commit

further fraud. E-commerce sites use coding (encryption techniques) to overcome these problems.

- *Viruses, worms, Trojans*: These are computer programs, usually spread via the Net, that can damage or destroy information you have on your computer.

Other uses of ICT

- *Scanning of bar codes*: This allows the shopper to have an itemized list of purchases, and makes the ordering of new stock easier for the store.

- *Computer programs*: These are used to operate microwave ovens, video recorders, automated assembly lines, robots etc.

- *Mobile phones*: As well as text messaging and phone calls, the latest mobile phones allow users to access the Internet and email services, play music, and take photographs and video film. Some also have GPS (a system for finding out where you are that uses satellites).

Text messaging

- Text messages sent between mobile phone users have two advantages:
  - they are cheaper than normal phone calls
  - you can send text messages from wherever you are

- However, as the screen of a mobile phone is small, text has to be shortened

- Text messages send the most important part of a message, so, for example, pronouns, articles (*a, an, the*), and prepositions are left out

- Abbreviations are used as much as possible, and letters are used to stand for whole words.

Here are some examples of commonly used abbreviations using first letters:

AFAIK As Far As I Know (you are not completely sure about something)

BFN Bye for now

BTW By The Way

CUL See You Later

FYI For Your Information

GTG Got To Go

IMO In My Opinion

Here are some that use letters and numbers for words:

B4 before

CUL8R see you later

GR8 great

NE1 anyone

LITERARY TERMS

by Julia Sander

Genres

A **genre** is a particular style of writing, such as poetry or drama. The main written genres are **poetry** and **prose** (the ordinary form of writing as opposed to poetry). Prose writing can be either **non-fiction** or (about things which are true or have really happened) or **fiction** (about imaginary events or people). **Narrative** writing tells a story or gives an account of something that has happened.

These are some of the main literary genres.

- **Allegory**: a story, play or poem where the events and characters are used to express a moral or political idea: *Animal Farm (George Orwell)*

- **Fable**: a traditional story about animals used to teach a lesson: *the Anansi stories.*

- **Myth**: an ancient story about gods, heroes and magic: *Kikuyu myths about the origins of mankind.*

- **Legend**: an old story about famous people and events in the past: *the Ashanti legend of the golden stool*

- **Autobiography**: an account someone writes about their own life: *Long Walk to Freedom (Nelson Mandela)*

- **Biography**: an account written about someone's life: *The Life of Bob Marley (Timothy White).*

- **Novel**: a long written story about imaginary characters and events: *Things Fall Apart (Chinua Achebe)*. Novels sometimes have a **sequel** (another book continuing the story begun in the first book) *No Longer at Ease* is a sequel to *Things Fall Apart.*

- **Short story**: a short written story about imaginary characters. Short stories are often published in collections or **anthologies**: *No Sweetness Here and Other Stories (Ama Ata Aidoo).*

- **Science-fiction**: stories about imaginary future events, often describing space travel and life on other planets: *The War of the Worlds (H.G. Wells)*

- **Eulogy**: a speech or piece of writing which praises a person's achievements, often delivered at that person's funeral.

Elements of a story

The basic elements of a story are as follows:

- **Setting**: the time and place where the story is set: *The story is set in a fishing village during the last century*. The **setting** of the story helps to create the **atmosphere** (the mood or feeling the story creates in the reader).

- **Characters**: the people in the story. The way the characters are developed throughout the story is known as **characterization.**

- **Plot**: the events that make up the story.

Drama

The main dramatic **genres** are:

- **Comedy**: a type of play which is humorous or does not have a serious theme: *The Trials of Brother Jero (Wole Soyinka).*

- **Tragedy**: a play in which people suffer or die: *Macbeth (William Shakespeare)*

The following **elements** are found in drama:

- **Acts**: the sections of play, usually divided into two or more **scenes**.

- **Dramatis personae**: the Latin term for the characters in a play, also known as the **cast**.

- **Script**: the written words of the play.

- **Dialogue**: the words spoken by the characters in a play.

- **Soliloquy**: a speech where a character who is alone on stage speaks about their thoughts and feelings.

- **Stage directions**: Instructions to the actors that tell them how to speak their lines, or what to do:

JERO: (rising.) God bless you, brother! (turns around) Chume!

The direction **aside** tells actors to speak so that only the audience can hear them.

Poetry

There are many different forms of poetry. These are some of the best known.

- **Ballad:** a long poem that tells a story.

- **Epic:** An **epic** poem is similar to a ballad, but tells the story of ancient people and their gods.

- **Dirge:** a slow, sad poem, often recited at a funeral.

- **Elegy:** a poem which expresses sorrow, often about someone's death.

- **Lyric:** a poem which expresses personal feelings

- **Haiku:** a short poem of 17 syllables and 3 lines which originated in Japan.

- **Ode:** a poem written for a particular person or event.

- **Sonnet:** a 14 line poem which follows a set pattern.

Prosody

Prosody refers to the pattern of sounds and rhythm in poetry. Poetry is written in **lines** and is often divided into **stanzas**, also known as **verses**. A lot of poems have a regular **beat**, known as **metre**, that gives a poem its **rhythm**. The verse below has three **beats** in each line, indicated by underlining the stressed syllable.

When the dark clouds gather
In the stormy sky
The boats return to harbour
Before the wind's too high.

In the above example alternate lines of the poem **rhyme** with one another. Many poems are written in **rhyming couplets**: pairs of lines which rhyme with one another. **Free verse** is poetry that does not have a regular beat or rhyme:

Waves
Creep up the shore
And curl around a stranded plank

Literary Devices

Writers use a variety of devices to make their writing more expressive, for example:

- **Simile:** a phrase which compares one thing to another using the words *like* or *as*:
The rain fell like bullets on the roof.

  The rain on the roof was as loud as thunder.

- **Metaphor:** a phrase which describes one thing as if it were something else:
The setting sun was a ball of flame.

- **Personification:** writing about something as if it were a person:
The wind whispered in my ear.

- **Oxymoron:** a phrase which unites two words with opposite meanings:
a bitter sweet experience, a deafening silence.

- **Hyperbole:** using exaggerated language for effect:
It's boiling hot today.

- **Euphemism:** an expression used to avoid mentioning something embarrassing or unpleasant:
He passed away (instead of: *He died.*)

- **Irony:** form of humour using words which express the opposite of what is meant:
'Exams start next week. I can hardly wait.'

- **Satire:** the use of humour to criticise people or things by making them look foolish:
The story is a satire on political life in Africa today.

- **Flashback:** part of a story which goes back in time and tells the reader what happened earlier.

- **Paradox:** a person or situation which has features not normally associated with one another:
It is a paradox that Marie, who loves nature, wants to live in the town.

Sound effects:

- **Alliteration:** placing words using the same consonant sound close together to create an effect: *a slow, slimy snail*

- **Assonance:** placing words with similar vowel sounds close together:
The flames of the fire rose higher and higher.

- **Onomatopoeia:** words in which the meaning and the sound match:
fizz, splash

THE PERIODIC TABLE

KEY: metals | metalloids | non-metals

Each chemical element is represented by its symbol. Atomic numbers are shown above each symbol and relative atomic masses shown below. Relative atomic masses shown in brackets are for longest-lived isotopes.

Transition metals

Period	I	II												III	IV	V	VI	VII	VIII
1	1 H 1																		2 He 4
2	3 Li 7	4 Be 9												5 B 11	6 C 12	7 N 14	8 O 16	9 F 19	10 Ne 20
3	11 Na 23	12 Mg 24												13 Al 27	14 Si 28	15 P 31	16 S 32	17 Cl 35.5	18 Ar 40
4	19 K 39	20 Ca 40	21 Sc 45	22 Ti 48	23 V 51	24 Cr 52	25 Mn 55	26 Fe 56	27 Co 59	28 Ni 59	29 Cu 64	30 Zn 65		31 Ga 70	32 Ge 72.5	33 As 75	34 Se 79	35 Br 80	36 Kr 84
5	37 Rb 85.5	38 Sr 88	39 Y 89	40 Zr 91	41 Nb 93	42 Mo 96	43 Tc (99)	44 Ru 101	45 Rh 103	46 Pd 106	47 Ag 108	48 Cd 112		49 In 115	50 Sn 119	51 Sb 122	52 Te 127.5	53 I 127	54 Xe 131
6	55 Cs 133	56 Ba 137	57–71 see below	72 Hf 178	73 Ta 181	74 W 184	75 Re 186	76 Os 190	77 Ir 192	78 Pt 195	79 Au 197	80 Hg 200.5		81 Tl 204	82 Pb 207	83 Bi 209	84 Po 209	85 At (210)	86 Rn (222)
7	87 Fr (223)	88 Ra (226)	89–103 see below																

Lanthanides

57 La 139	58 Ce 140	59 Pr 141	60 Nd 144	61 Pm (145)	62 Sm 150	63 Eu 152	64 Gd 157	65 Tb 159	66 Dy 162.5	67 Ho 165	68 Er 167	69 Tm 169	70 Yb 173	71 Lu 175

Actinides

89 Ac (226)	90 Th (232)	91 Pa (231)	92 U 238	93 Np (237)	94 Pu (244)	95 Am (243)	96 Cm (247)	97 Bk (247)	98 Cf (251)	99 Es (254)	100 Fm (257)	101 Md (258)	102 No (255)	103 Lr (256)

CHEMICAL ELEMENTS

Elements are listed with their symbol, atomic number, and relative atomic mass (RAM) to the nearest 0.5. RAMs for the longest-lived or most important isotopes are shown in brackets. Elements with at. no. (atomic number) 104–116 and 118 have been made or detected by scientists but only in small amounts and for a very short time.

Element	symbol	at. no.	RAM	Element	symbol	at. no.	RAM
actinium	Ac	89	(226)	mendelevium	Md	101	(258)
aluminium	Al	13	27	mercury	Hg	80	200.5
americium	Am	95	(243)	molybdenum	Mo	42	96
antimony	Sb	51	122	neodymium	Nd	60	144
argon	Ar	18	40	neon	Ne	10	20
arsenic	As	33	75	neptunium	Np	93	(237)
astatine	At	85	(210)	nickel	Ni	28	59
barium	Ba	56	137	niobium	Nb	41	93
berkelium	Bk	97	(247)	nitrogen	N	7	14
beryllium	Be	4	9	nobelium	No	102	(255)
bismuth	Bi	83	209	osmium	Os	76	190
boron	B	5	11	oxygen	O	8	16
bromine	Br	35	80	palladium	Pd	46	106
cadmium	Cd	48	112	phosphorus	P	15	31
caesium	Cs	55	133	platinum	Pt	78	195
calcium	Ca	20	40	plutonium	Pu	94	(244)
californium	Cf	98	(251)	polonium	Po	84	209
carbon	C	6	12	potassium	K	19	39
cerium	Ce	58	140	praseodymium	Pr	59	141
chlorine	Cl	17	35.5	promethium	Pm	61	(145)
chromium	Cr	24	52	protactinium	Pa	91	(231)
cobalt	Co	27	59	radium	Ra	88	(226)
copper	Cu	29	64	radon	Rn	86	(222)
curium	Cm	96	(247)	rhenium	Re	75	186
dysprosium	Dy	66	162.5	rhodium	Rh	45	103
einsteinium	Es	99	(254)	rubidium	Rb	37	85.5
erbium	Er	68	167	ruthenium	Ru	44	101
europium	Eu	63	152	samarium	Sm	62	150
fermium	Fm	100	(257)	scandium	Sc	21	45
fluorine	F	9	19	selenium	Se	34	79
francium	Fr	87	(223)	silicon	Si	14	28
gadolinium	Gd	64	157	silver	Ag	47	108
gallium	Ga	31	70	sodium	Na	11	23
germanium	Ge	32	72.5	strontium	Sr	38	88
gold	Au	79	197	sulphur	S	16	32
hafnium	Hf	72	178.5	tantalum	Ta	73	181
helium	He	2	4	technetium	Tc	43	(99)
holmium	Ho	67	165	tellurium	Te	52	127.5
hydrogen	H	1	1	terbium	Tb	65	159
indium	In	49	115	thallium	Tl	81	204
iodine	I	53	127	thorium	Th	90	(232)
iridium	Ir	77	192	thulium	Tm	69	169
iron	Fe	26	56	tin	Sn	50	119
krypton	Kr	36	84	titanium	Ti	22	48
lanthanum	La	57	139	tungsten (wolfram)	W	74	184
lawrencium	Lr	103	(256)	uranium	U	92	238
lead	Pb	82	207	vanadium	V	23	51
lithium	Li	3	7	xenon	Xe	54	131
lutetium	Lu	71	175	ytterbium	Yb	70	173
magnesium	Mg	12	24	yttrium	Y	39	89
manganese	Mn	25	55	zinc	Zn	30	65
				zirconium	Zr	40	91

USING NUMBERS

Cardinal and Ordinal Numbers

A cardinal number represents an amount or quantity. An ordinal number shows what position something has in a series.

	Cardinal		Ordinal
1	one	1st	first
2	two	2nd	second
3	three	3rd	third
4	four	4th	fourth
5	five	5th	fifth
6	six	6th	sixth
7	seven	7th	seventh
8	eight	8th	eighth
9	nine	9th	ninth
10	ten	10th	tenth
11	eleven	11th	eleventh
12	twelve	12th	twelfth
13	thirteen	13th	thirteenth
14	fourteen	14th	fourteenth
15	fifteen	15th	fifteenth
16	sixteen	16th	sixteenth
17	seventeen	17th	seventeenth
18	eighteen	18th	eighteenth
19	nineteen	19th	nineteenth
20	twenty	20th	twentieth
21	twenty-one	21st	twenty-first
22	twenty-two	22nd	twenty-second
30	thirty	30th	thirtieth
40	forty	40th	fortieth
50	fifty	50th	fiftieth
60	sixty	60th	sixtieth
70	seventy	70th	seventieth
80	eighty	80th	eightieth
90	ninety	90th	ninetieth
100	hundred	100th	hundredth
101	hundred and one	101st	hundred and first
200	two hundred	200th	two hundredth
1,000	thousand	1,000th	thousandth
10,000	ten thousand	10,000th	ten thousandth
100,000	hundred thousand	100,000th	hundred thousandth
1,000,000	million	1,000,000th	millionth

Examples:

94	ninety-four	2,347	two thousand three hundred and forty-seven
569	five hundred and sixty-nine	34,608	thirty-four thousand six hundred and eight

In numbers over one thousand you use a comma or small space to separate thousands from hundreds: 2,347 or 2 347.

Telephone numbers

You say each number in a telephone number separately, usually with a pause after each set of numbers. The number zero is pronounced as 'zero' or 'oh':

8297 0449   *you say*   eight two nine seven – oh (*or* zero) four four nine

If you are calling a number in a different country you have to use the international dialling code before the phone number. You also have to drop the first number of the area code: *44 is the international dialling code for the UK.* ♦ *It's a central London number – 44 207 494 6879.*

Money

$1	one dollar	£1	one pound
10¢	ten cents	10 p	ten pence (say 'ten pee')
25¢	twenty-five cents	25 p	twenty-five pence (say 'pee')
$1.50	one dollar fifty *or* a dollar fifty *or* one fifty	£2.50	two pounds fifty pence (say 'pee') *or* two pounds fifty

Time

	Informal use	*More formal use*
08.00	eight o'clock	(oh) eight hundred hours
08.05	five past eight	(oh) eight oh five
08.10	ten past eight	(oh) eight ten
08.15	(a) quarter past eight	(oh) eight fifteen
08.20	twenty past eight	(oh) eight twenty
08.25	eight twenty-five	(oh) eight twenty five
08.30	half past eight	(oh) eight thirty
08.35	twenty-five to nine	(oh) eight thirty-five
08.40	twenty to nine	(oh) eight forty
08.45	(a) quarter to nine	(oh) eight forty-five
08.50	ten to nine	(oh) eight fifty
08.55	five to nine	(oh) eight fifty-five
14.00	two o'clock	fourteen hundred (hours)
20.58	two minutes to nine	twenty fifty-eight

In informal use you can add 'in the morning' for times between midnight and midday. For times between midday and midnight you add 'in the afternoon', 'in the evening', or 'at night'. In writing, people use 'a.m.' (for times up to midday) and 'p.m.' for times up to midnight.

Dates

This is how you say dates that are years:

1907	nineteen oh seven	2000	two thousand
1952	nineteen fifty-two	2009	two thousand and nine

This is how you say dates that give the day, month, and year:

14th October 2009	the fourteenth of October two thousand and nine
October 14, 2009	October the fourteenth two thousand and nine

You can also write dates as numbers only: 14/10/09 *or* 14.10.09

In American English the month comes before the day: 10/14/09

Fractions and Decimals

Fractions		Decimals	
½	a half, one half	0.5	(nought *or* zero) point five
⅓	a third, one third	0.33	(nought *or* zero) point three three
¼	quarter, a quarter, one quarter	0.25	(nought *or* zero) point two five
¾	three quarters	0.75	(nought *or* zero) point seven five
⅘	four fifths	0.8	(nought *or* zero) point eight
3 ½	three and a half	3.5	three point five
4 ⅗	four and three fifths	4.62	four point six two

SI UNITS AND CONVERSIONS

The SI system is an internationally accepted system of units used in science. It is based on the metric system that works in multiples of 10. There are seven base units that can be multiplied or divided by each other to give derived units. The SI units that you will use in school, and the units based on them, are shown below.

Base units

Unit	Quantity	Symbol
metre	length	m
kilogram	mass	kg
second	time	s
ampere	electric current	A
kelvin	absolute temperature	K
mole	amount of substance	mol
candela	luminous intensity (=strength of light)	cd

Some derived units without special names and symbols

Unit	Quantity	Symbol
cubic metre	volume	m^3
kilogram per metre cubed	density	kg/m^3
metre per second	linear speed	m/s
newton metre	torque	Nm
square metre	area	m^2

Some derived units with special names and symbols

Unit	Quantity	Relation to other SI units	Symbol
becquerel	radioactivity		Bq
coulomb	electric charge	ampere per second (A/s)	C
degree Celsius	temperature		°C
farad	electric capacitance	coulomb per volt (C/V)	F
henry	inductance		H
hertz	frequency		Hz
joule	energy or work	newton metre (Nm)	J
newton	force, weight		N
ohm	resistance	volt per ampere (V/A)	Ω
pascal	pressure	newton per square metre (N/m^2)	Pa
radian	angle		rad
volt	potential difference	watt per ampere (W/A)	V
watt	power	joule per second (J/s)	W

Other units used with the SI system

Some units that do not strictly belong to the SI system are used with it, because they are practical, or because they have been in use for some time. Apart from the litre and tonne, they are not used with prefixes.

Unit	Quantity	Symbol
astronomical unit	length	AU
hectare	area	ha
knot	linear speed (at sea)	kn
litre	volume	l, L
millibar	pressure	mbar
nautical mile	length (at sea)	M
tonne	mass	t

Prefixes used with SI units

The values of the base units and derived units can be changed by adding standard SI prefixes that indicate multiples or submultiples of 10. For example, 100 cm equals 1 m, and 10 mm equals 1 cm.

Multiples	Prefix	Symbol	Example
10 (10^1)	deca-	da	dam
100 (10^2)	hecto-	h	hm
1,000 (10^3)	kilo-	k	km
1,000,000 (10^6)	mega-	M	Mm
1,000,000,000 (10^9)	giga-	G	Gm
1,000,000,000,000 (10^{12})	tera-	T	Tm

Submultiples	Prefix	Symbol	Example
0.1 (10^{-1})	deci-	d	dm
0.01 (10^{-2})	centi-	c	cm
0.001 (10^{-3})	milli-	m	mm
0.000001 (10^{-6})	micro-	μ	μm
0.000000001 (10^{-9})	nano-	n	nm
0.000000000001 (10^{-12})	pico-	p	pm
0.000000000000001 (10^{-15})	femto-	f	fm

Converting imperial and metric units

Imperial to metric	Metric to imperial
1 inch = 2.54 cm	1 cm = 0.39 inch
1 foot = 0.305 m	1 m = 3.28 feet
1 yard = 0.914 m	1 m = 1.09 yard
1 mile = 1.61 km	1 km = 0.62 mile
1 sq inch = 6.45 cm^2	1 cm^2 = 0.16 sq inch
1 sq foot = 0.093 cm^2	1 m^2 = 10.76 sq feet
1 sq mile = 2.59 km^2	1 km^2 = 0.39 sq mile
1 cu inch = 16.39 cm^3	1 cm^3 = 0.061 cu inch
1 cu foot = 0.028 m^3	1 m^3 = 35.3 cu feet
1 pint = 0.57 l (litres)	1 l = 1.76 pint
1 gallon = 4.55 l	1 l = 0.22 gallon
1 ounce = 28.35 g	1 g = 0.04 ounce
1 pound = 0.45 kg	1 kg = 2.2 pound
1 stone = 6.35 kg	1 kg = 0.16 stone
1 calorie = 4.19 J	1 J = 0.24 calorie
°F to °C: -32, x 5, ÷ 9	°C to °F = x 9, ÷ 5, +32

GEOGRAPHICAL NAMES AND NATIONALITIES

The following lists show you the names and pronunciations of places (including continents) and the adjectives that are related to them. Most adjectives can be used as nouns to describe a person from a particular place (e.g. a **Belgian** is a person from **Belgium**). Where the adjective cannot be used as a noun, it is followed by an asterisk (*) and the correct term is given in the Nationalities table at the end.

NOTE: Inclusion in the following list does not imply status as a sovereign state.

Name	Adjective
Afghanistan /æf'gænɪstɑːn/	Afghan /'æfgæn/
Africa /'æfrɪkə/	African /'æfrɪk(ə)n/
Albania /æl'beɪnɪə/	Albanian /æl'beɪnɪən/
Algeria /æl'dʒɪərɪə/	Algerian /æl'dʒɪərɪən/
Andorra /æn'dɔːrə/	Andorran /æn'dɔːrən/
Angola /æŋ'gəʊlə/	Angolan /æŋ'gəʊlən/
Antigua and Barbuda /æn,tiːgə ən bɑː'bjuːdə/	Antiguan /æn'tiːgən/
Argentina /,ɑːdʒən'tiːnə/	Argentine* /'ɑːdʒəntaɪn/
Armenia /ɑː'miːnɪə/	Armenian /ɑː'miːnɪən/
Asia /'eɪʒə, 'eɪʃə/	Asian /'eɪʒ(ə)n, 'eɪʃ(ə)n/
Australia /ɒ'streɪlɪə/	Australian /ɒ'streɪlɪən/
Austria /'ɒstrɪə/	Austrian /'ɒstrɪən/
Azerbaijan /,æzəbaɪ'dʒɑːn/	Azerbaijani* /,æzəbaɪ'dʒɑːni/
Bahamas, the /bə'hɑːməz/	Bahamian /bə'heɪmɪən/
Bahrain /bɑː'reɪn/	Bahraini /bɑː'reɪni/
Bangladesh /,bæŋglə'deʃ/	Bangladeshi /,bæŋglə'deʃi/
Barbados /bɑː'beɪdɒs/	Barbadian /bɑː'beɪdɪən/
Belarus /,belə'ruːs/	Belarusian /,belə'ruːsi(ə)n/
Belgium /'beldʒəm/	Belgian /'beldʒ(ə)n/
Belize /bə'liːz/	Belizian /bə'liːzɪən/
Benin /be'niːn/	Beninese /,benɪ'niːz/
Bermuda /bə'mjuːdə/	Bermudan /bə'mjuːdən/
Bhutan /buːˈtɑːn/	Bhutanese /,buːtə'niːz/
Bolivia /bə'lɪvɪə/	Bolivian /bə'lɪvɪən/
Bosnia-Herzegovina /'bɒznɪə ,hɜːtsə'gɒvɪnə/	Bosnian /'bɒznɪən/
Botswana /bɒt'swɑːnə/	Botswanan /bɒt'swɑːnən/
Brazil /brə'zɪl/	Brazilian /brə'zɪlɪən/
Brunei /'bruːnaɪ/	Bruneian /bruː'naɪən/
Bulgaria /bʌl'geərɪə/	Bulgarian /bʌl'geərɪən/
Burkina Faso /bɜː,kiːnə 'fæsəʊ/	Burkinan /bɜː'kiːnən/
Burundi /bʊ'rʊndi/	Burundian /bʊ'rʊndɪən/
Cambodia /kæm'bəʊdɪə/	Cambodian /kæm'bəʊdɪən/
Cameroon /,kæmə'ruːn/	Cameroonian /,kæmə'ruːnɪən/
Canada /'kænədə/	Canadian /kə'neɪdɪən/
Cape Verde /,keɪp 'vɜːd/	Cape Verdean /,keɪp 'vɜːdɪən/
Caribbean, the /,kærə'biːən/	Caribbean /,kærə'biːən/
Cayman Islands, the /'keɪmən ,aɪləndz/	Cayman Island* /'keɪmən ,aɪlənd/
Central African Republic, the /,sentr(ə)l ,æfrɪkən rɪ'pʌblɪk/	Central African /,sentr(ə)l 'æfrɪkən/
Chad /tʃæd/	Chadian /'tʃædɪən/
Chile /'tʃɪli/	Chilean /'tʃɪlɪən/
China /'tʃaɪnə/	Chinese /,tʃaɪ'niːz/
Colombia /kə'lʌmbɪə/	Colombian /kə'lʌmbɪən/
Comoros /'kɒmərəʊz/	Comoran /kə'mɔːrən/
Democratic Republic of the Congo, the /,deməkrætɪk rɪ,pʌblɪk əv ðə 'kɒŋgəʊ/	Congolese /,kɒŋgə'liːz/
Republic of Congo, the /rɪ,pʌblɪk əv 'kɒŋgəʊ/	Congolese /,kɒŋgə'liːz/
Costa Rica /,kɒstə 'riːkə/	Costa Rican /,kɒstə 'riːkən/
Côte d'Ivoire /,kəʊt di:'vwɑː/	Ivorian /aɪ'vɔːrɪən/
Croatia /krəʊ'eɪʃə/	Croatian* /krəʊ'eɪʃ(ə)n/
Cuba /'kjuːbə/	Cuban /'kjuːbən/
Cyprus /'saɪprəs/	Cypriot /'sɪprɪət/
Czech Republic, the /,tʃek rɪ'pʌblɪk/	Czech /tʃek/
Denmark /'denmɑːk/	Danish* /'deɪnɪʃ/
Djibouti /dʒɪ'buːti/	Djiboutian /dʒɪ'buːtɪən/

Dominica /ˌdɒmɪˈniːkə/
Dominican Republic, the /dəˌmɪnɪkən rɪˈpʌblɪk/
East Timor /ˌiːst ˈtiːmɔː/
Ecuador /ˈekwədɔː/
Egypt /ˈiːdʒɪpt/
El Salvador /el ˈsælvədɔː/
England /ˈɪŋglənd/
Equatorial Guinea /ˌekwətɔːriəl ˈgɪni/
Eritrea /ˌerɪˈtreɪə/
Estonia /eˈstəʊniə/
Ethiopia /ˌiːθiˈəʊpiə/
Europe /ˈjʊərəp/
Fiji /ˈfiːdʒiː/
Finland /ˈfɪnlənd/
France /frɑːns/
Gabon /gəˈbɒn/
Gambia, the /ˈgæmbiə/
Georgia /ˈdʒɔːdʒə/
Germany /ˈdʒɜːməni/
Ghana /ˈgɑːnə/
Gibraltar /dʒɪˈbrɔːltə/
Great Britain /ˌgreɪt ˈbrɪt(ə)n/
Greece /griːs/
Greenland /ˈgriːnlənd/
Grenada /grəˈneɪdə/
Guatemala /ˌgwɑːtəˈmɑːlə/
Guinea /ˈgɪni/
Guinea-Bissau /ˌgɪni bɪˈsaʊ/
Guyana /gaɪˈænə/
Haiti /ˈheɪti/
Honduras /hɒnˈdjʊərəs/
Hungary /ˈhʌŋgəri/
Iceland /ˈaɪslənd/
India /ˈɪndiə/
Indonesia /ˌɪndəˈniːʒə/
Iran /ɪˈrɑːn/
Iraq /ɪˈrɑːk/
Northern Ireland /ˌnɔːð(ə)n ˈaɪələnd/
Republic of Ireland, the /rɪˌpʌblɪk əv ˈaɪələnd/
Israel /ˈɪzreɪl/
Italy /ˈɪtəli/
Ivory Coast, the /ˌaɪvəri ˈkəʊst/
Jamaica /dʒəˈmeɪkə/
Japan /dʒəˈpæn/
Jordan /ˈdʒɔːd(ə)n/
Kazakhstan /ˌkæzækˈstɑːn/
Kenya /ˈkenjə/
Kiribati /ˌkɪrəˈbæs, ˌkɪrɪˈbɑːti/
North Korea /ˌnɔːθ kəˈriːə/
South Korea /ˌsaʊθ kəˈriːə/
Kuwait /kʊˈweɪt/
Kyrgyzstan /ˌkɜːgɪˈstɑːn/
Laos /laʊs/
Latvia /ˈlætviə/
Lebanon /ˈlebənən/
Lesotho /ləˈsuːtuː/
Liberia /laɪˈbɪəriə/
Libya /ˈlɪbiə/
Liechtenstein /ˈlɪktənstaɪn/
Lithuania /ˌlɪθjuˈeɪniə/
Luxembourg /ˈlʌksəmbɜːg/
Madagascar /ˌmædəˈgæskə/
Malawi /məˈlɑːwi/
Malaysia /məˈleɪziə/
Maldives, the /ˈmɔːldiːvz/
Mali /ˈmɑːli/
Malta /ˈmɔːltə/
Marshall Islands, the /ˈmɑːʃ(ə)l ˌaɪləndz/
Mauritania /ˌmɒrɪˈteɪniə/
Mauritius /məˈrɪʃəs/

Dominican /ˌdɒmɪˈniːkən/
Dominican /dəˈmɪnɪkən/

East Timorese /ˌiːst ˌtiːmɔːˈriːz/
Ecuadorian /ˌekwəˈdɔːriən/
Egyptian /ɪˈdʒɪpʃ(ə)n/
Salvadorian /ˌsælvəˈdɔːriən/
English* /ˈɪŋglɪʃ/
Equatorial Guinean /ˌekwətɔːriəl ˈgɪniən/
Eritrean /ˌerɪˈtreɪən/
Estonian /eˈstəʊniən/
Ethiopian /ˌiːθiˈəʊpiən/
European /ˌjʊərəˈpiːən/
Fijian /fiːˈdʒiːən/
Finnish* /ˈfɪnɪʃ/
French* /frentʃ/
Gabonese /ˌgæbəˈniːz/
Gambian /ˈgæmbiən/
Georgian /ˈdʒɔːdʒən/
German /ˈdʒɜːmən/
Ghanaian /gɑːˈneɪən/
Gibraltarian /ˌdʒɪbrɔːlˈteəriən/
British* /ˈbrɪtɪʃ/
Greek /griːk/
Greenlandic* /ˌgriːnˈlændɪk/
Grenadian /grəˈneɪdiən/
Guatemalan /ˌgwɑːtəˈmɑːlən/
Guinean /ˈgɪniən/
Guinea-Bissauan /ˌgɪni bɪˈsaʊən/
Guyanese /ˌgaɪəˈniːz/
Haitian /ˈheɪʃ(ə)n/
Honduran /hɒnˈdjʊərən/
Hungarian /hʌŋˈgeəriən/
Icelandic* /aɪsˈlændɪk/
Indian /ˈɪndiən/
Indonesian /ˌɪndəˈniːʒ(ə)n/
Iranian /ɪˈreɪniən/
Iraqi /ɪˈrɑːki/

Irish* /ˈaɪrɪʃ/

Israeli /ɪzˈreɪli/
Italian /ɪˈtæliən/
Ivorian /aɪˈvɔːriən/
Jamaican /dʒəˈmeɪkən/
Japanese /ˌdʒæpəˈniːz/
Jordanian /dʒɔːˈdeɪniən/
Kazakh /kəˈzæk/
Kenyan /ˈkenjən/
Kiribati /ˌkɪrəˈbæs, ˌkɪrɪˈbɑːti/
North Korean /ˌnɔːθ kəˈriːən/
South Korean /ˌsaʊθ kəˈriːən/
Kuwaiti /kʊˈweɪti/
Kyrgyz /ˈkɜːgɪz/
Laotian /ˈlaʊʃ(ə)n/
Latvian /ˈlætviən/
Lebanese /ˌlebəˈniːz/
Sotho* /ˈsuːtuː/
Liberian /laɪˈbɪəriən/
Libyan /ˈlɪbiən/
Liechtenstein* /ˈlɪktənstaɪn/
Lithuanian /ˌlɪθjuˈeɪniən/
Luxembourg* /ˈlʌksəmbɜːg/
Malagasy /ˌmæləˈgæsi/
Malawian /məˈlɑːwiən/
Malaysian /məˈleɪziən/
Maldivian /məlˈdɪviən/
Malian /ˈmɑːliən/
Maltese* /ˌmɔːlˈtiːz/
Marshallese* /ˌmɑːʃəˈliːz/
Mauritanian /ˌmɒrɪˈteɪniən/
Mauritian /məˈrɪʃ(ə)n/

Melanesia /ˌmeləˈniːziə/	Melanesian /ˌmeləˈniːziən/
Mexico /ˈmeksɪkəʊ/	Mexican /ˈmeksɪkən/
Micronesia /ˌmaɪkrəˈniːziə/	Micronesian /ˌmaɪkrəˈniːziən/
Moldova /mɒlˈdəʊvə/	Moldovan /mɒlˈdəʊvən/
Monaco /ˈmɒnəkəʊ/	Monegasque /ˌmɒnɪˈgæsk/
Mongolia /mɒŋˈɡəʊliə/	Mongolian /mɒŋˈɡəʊliən/
Montserrat /ˌmɒn(t)səˈræt/	Montserratian /ˌmɒn(t)səˈreɪʃ(ə)n/
Morocco /məˈrɒkəʊ/	Moroccan /məˈrɒkən/
Mozambique /ˌməʊzæmˈbiːk/	Mozambican /ˌməʊzæmˈbiːkən/
Myanmar /ˈmiːənmɑː/	Burmese /bɜːˈmiːz/
Namibia /nəˈmɪbiə/	Namibian /nəˈmɪbiən/
Nauru /nɑːˈuːruː/	Nauruan /nɑːˈuːruən/
Nepal /nəˈpɔːl/	Nepalese /ˌnepəˈliːz/
Netherlands, the /ˈneðələndz/	Dutch* /dʌtʃ/
New Zealand /ˌnjuːˈziːlənd/	New Zealand* /ˌnjuːˈziːlənd/
Nicaragua /ˌnɪkəˈræɡjuə/	Nicaraguan /ˌnɪkəˈræɡjuən/
Niger /niːˈʒeə, ˈnaɪdʒə/	Nigerien /niːˈʒeəriən, naɪˈdʒɪəriən/
Nigeria /naɪˈdʒɪəriə/	Nigerian /naɪˈdʒɪəriən/
North America /ˌnɔːθ əˈmerɪkə/	North American /ˌnɔːθ əˈmerɪk(ə)n/
Norway /ˈnɔːweɪ/	Norwegian /nɔːˈwiːdʒ(ə)n/
Oman /əʊˈmɑːn/	Omani /əʊˈmɑːni/
Pakistan /ˌpɑːkɪˈstɑːn/	Pakistani /ˌpɑːkɪˈstɑːni/
Panama /ˈpænəmɑː/	Panamanian /ˌpænəˈmeɪniən/
Papua New Guinea /ˌpæpuə njuːˈɡɪni/	Papua New Guinean /ˌpæpuə njuːˈɡɪniən/
Paraguay /ˈpærəɡwaɪ/	Paraguayan /ˌpærəˈɡwaɪən/
Peru /pəˈruː/	Peruvian /pəˈruːviən/
Philippines, the /ˈfɪlɪpiːnz/	Philippine* /ˈfɪlɪpiːn/
Poland /ˈpəʊlənd/	Polish* /ˈpəʊlɪʃ/
Polynesia /ˌpɒlɪˈniːziə/	Polynesian /ˌpɒlɪˈniːziən/
Portugal /ˈpɔːtʃəɡ(ə)l/	Portuguese /ˌpɔːtʃəˈɡiːz/
Puerto Rico /ˌpwɜːtəʊ ˈriːkəʊ/	Puerto Rican /ˌpwɜːtəʊ ˈriːkən/
Qatar /kæˈtɑː/	Qatari /kæˈtɑːri/
Romania /rʊˈmeɪniə/	Romanian /rʊˈmeɪniən/
Russia /ˈrʌʃə/	Russian /ˈrʌʃ(ə)n/
Russian Federation, the /ˌrʌʃ(ə)n fedəˈreɪʃ(ə)n/	
Rwanda /ruˈændə/	Rwandese /ruˈændiːz/
Saint Kitts and Nevis /sənt ˌkɪts ən ˈniːvɪs/	Kittitian /kɪˈtɪʃ(ə)n/
	Nevisian /nəˈviːʃ(ə)n/
Saint Lucia /sənt ˈluːʃə/	Saint Lucian /sənt ˈluːʃ(ə)n/
Saint Vincent and the Grenadines /sənt ˌvɪns(ə)nt ən ðə ˌɡrenəˈdiːnz/	Vincentian /vɪnˈsenʃ(ə)n/
Samoa /səˈməʊə/	Samoan /səˈməʊən/
San Marino /ˌsæn məˈriːnəʊ/	Sanmarinese /ˌsænmærɪˈniːz/
São Tomé and Príncipe /sau təˌmeɪ ən ˈprɪnsɪpeɪ/	Sao Tomean /ˌsau təˈmeɪən/
Saudi Arabia /ˌsaʊdi əˈreɪbiə/	Saudi Arabian /ˌsaʊdi əˈreɪbiən/
	Saudi /ˈsaʊdi/
Scandinavia /ˌskændɪˈneɪviə/	Scandinavian /ˌskændɪˈneɪviən/
Scotland /ˈskɒtlənd/	Scottish* /ˈskɒtɪʃ/
Senegal /ˌsenɪˈɡɔːl/	Senegalese /ˌsenɪɡəˈliːz/
Serbia and Montenegro /ˌsɜːbiə ən(d) ˌmɒntɪˈniːɡrəʊ/	Serbian and Montenegran /ˌsɜːbiən ən(d) ˌmɒntɪˈniːɡrən/
Seychelles, the /seɪˈʃelz/	Seychellois /ˌseɪʃelˈwɑː/
Sierra Leone /siˌerə liˈəʊn/	Sierra Leonean /siˌerə liˈəʊniən/
Singapore /ˌsɪŋəˈpɔː/	Singaporean /ˌsɪŋəˈpɔːriən/
Slovakia /sləˈvækiə/	Slovak /ˈsləʊvæk/
	Slovakian /sləˈvækiən/
Slovenia /sləˈviːniə/	Slovene /ˈsləʊviːn/
	Slovenian /sləˈviːniən/
Solomon Islands, the /ˈsɒləmən ˌaɪləndz/	Solomon Island* /ˈsɒləmən ˌaɪlənd/
Somalia /səˈmɑːliə/	Somali /səˈmɑːli/
South Africa /ˌsaʊθ ˈæfrɪkə/	South African /ˌsaʊθ ˈæfrɪkən/
South America /ˌsaʊθ əˈmerɪkə/	South American /ˌsaʊθ əˈmerɪk(ə)n/
Spain /speɪn/	Spanish* /ˈspænɪʃ/
Sri Lanka /srɪ ˈlæŋkə/	Sri Lankan /srɪ ˈlæŋkən/
Sudan /suːˈdɑːn/	Sudanese /ˌsuːdəˈniːz/
Suriname /ˌsʊərɪˈnæm/	Surinamese* /ˌsʊərɪnæˈmiːz/
Swaziland /ˈswɑːzilænd/	Swazi /ˈswɑːzi/
Sweden /ˈswiːd(ə)n/	Swedish* /ˈswiːdɪʃ/
Switzerland /ˈswɪtsələnd/	Swiss /swɪs/
Syria /ˈsɪriə/	Syrian /ˈsɪriən/

Tajikistan /tɑːˌdʒiːkɪˈstɑːn/	Tajik /tɑːˈdʒiːk/
Tanzania /ˌtænzəˈniːə/	Tanzanian /ˌtænzəˈniːən/
Thailand /ˈtaɪlænd/	Thai /taɪ/
Togo /ˈtəʊgəʊ/	Togolese /ˌtəʊgəˈliːz/
Tonga /ˈtɒŋə/	Tongan /ˈtɒŋən/
Trinidad and Tobago /ˌtrɪnɪdæd ən təˈbeɪgəʊ/	Trinidadian /ˌtrɪnɪˈdædiən/
	Tobagan /təˈbeɪgən/
Tunisia /tjuːˈnɪziə/	Tunisian /tjuːˈnɪziən/
Turkey /ˈtɜːki/	Turkish* /ˈtɜːkɪʃ/
Turkmenistan /tɜːkˌmenɪˈstɑːn/	Turkmen /ˈtɜːkmen/
Tuvalu /tuːˈvɑːluː, ˌtuːvəˈluː/	Tuvaluan /ˌtuːvəˈluːən/
Uganda /juːˈgændə/	Ugandan /juːˈgændən/
Ukraine /juːˈkreɪn/	Ukrainian /juːˈkreɪniən/
United Arab Emirates, the /juːˌnaɪtɪd ˌærəb ˈemɪrəts/	Emirati /ˌemɪˈrɑːti/
United Kingdom, the /juːˌnaɪtɪd ˈkɪŋdəm/	British* /ˈbrɪtɪʃ/
United States of America, the /juːˌnaɪtɪd ˌsteɪts əv əˈmerɪkə/	American /əˈmerɪkən/
Uruguay /ˈjʊərəgwaɪ/	Uruguayan /ˌjʊərəˈgwaɪən/
Uzbekistan /ʊzˌbekɪˈstɑːn/	Uzbek /ˈʊzbek/
Vanuatu /ˌvænuˈɑːtuː/	Vanuatuan /ˌvænuɑːˈtuːən/
Vatican City /ˌvætɪkən ˈsɪti/	Vatican /ˈvætɪkən/
Venezuela /ˌvenɪˈzweɪlə/	Venezuelan /ˌvenɪˈzweɪlən/
Vietnam /ˌviːetˈnæm/	Vietnamese /ˌviːetnəˈmiːz/
Wales /weɪlz/	Welsh* /welʃ/
Western Sahara /ˌwestən səˈhɑːrə/	Sahrawian /sɑːˈrɑːwiən/
Yemen /ˈjemən/	Yemeni /ˈjeməni/
Zambia /ˈzæmbiə/	Zambian /ˈzæmbiən/
Zimbabwe /zɪmˈbɑːbweɪ/	Zimbabwean /zɪmˈbɑːbwiən/

Nationalities

Country	Person
Argentina /ˌɑːdʒənˈtiːnə/	Argentinian /ˌɑːdʒənˈtɪniən/
Azerbaijan /ˌæzəbaɪˈdʒɑːn/	Azeri /æˈzeəri/
	Azerbaijani /ˌæzəbaɪˈdʒɑːni/
Cayman Islands, the /ˈkeɪmən ˌaɪləndz/	Cayman Islander /ˌkeɪmən ˈaɪləndə/
Croatia /krəʊˈeɪʃə/	Croat /ˈkrəʊæt/
Denmark /ˈdenmɑːk/	Dane /deɪn/
England /ˈɪŋglənd/	Englishman /ˈɪŋglɪʃmən/
Finland /ˈfɪnlənd/	Finn /fɪn/
France /frɑːns/	Frenchman /ˈfrentʃmən/
Great Britain /ˌgreɪt ˈbrɪt(ə)n/	Briton (mainly journalism) /ˈbrɪt(ə)n/
Greenland /ˈgriːnlənd/	Greenlander /ˈgriːnləndə/
Iceland /ˈaɪslənd/	Icelander /ˈaɪsləndə/
Republic of Ireland, the /rɪˌpʌblɪk əv ˈaɪələnd/	Irishman /ˈaɪrɪʃmən/
Lesotho /ləˈsuːtuː/	Mosotho /məˈsuːtuː/
	plural Basotho /bəˈsuːtuː/
Liechtenstein /ˈlɪktənstaɪn/	Liechtensteiner /ˈlɪktənstaɪnə/
Luxembourg /ˈlʌksəmbɜːg/	Luxembourger /ˈlʌksəmbɜːgə/
Marshall Islands, the /ˈmɑːʃ(ə)l ˌaɪləndz/	Marshall Islander /ˌmɑːʃ(ə)l ˈaɪləndə/
Netherlands, the /ˈneðələndz/	Dutchman /ˈdʌtʃmən/
New Zealand /ˌnjuː ˈziːlənd/	New Zealander /ˌnjuː ˈziːləndə/
Philippines, the /ˈfɪlɪpiːnz/	Filipino /ˌfɪlɪˈpiːnəʊ/
Poland /ˈpəʊlənd/	Pole /pəʊl/
Scotland /ˈskɒtlənd/	Scot /skɒt/
Serbia and Montenegro /ˌsɜːbiə ən(d) ˌmɒntɪˈniːgrəʊ/	Serb, Montenegran /sɜːb/, /ˌmɒntɪˈniːgrən/
Solomon Islands, the /ˈsɒləmən ˌaɪləndz/	Solomon Islander /ˌsɒləmən ˈaɪləndə/
Spain /speɪn/	Spaniard /ˈspænjəd/
Suriname /ˌsʊərɪˈnæm/	Surinamer /ˌsʊərɪˈnɑːmə/
Sweden /ˈswiːd(ə)n/	Swede /swiːd/
Turkey /ˈtɜːki/	Turk /tɜːk/
United Kingdom, the /juːˌnaɪtɪd ˈkɪŋdəm/	Briton (mainly journalism) /ˈbrɪt(ə)n/
Wales /weɪlz/	Welshman /ˈwelʃmən/

IRREGULAR VERBS

Infinitive	past tense	past participle	Infinitive	past tense	past participle
arise	arose	arisen	fly	flew	flown
awake	awoke	awoken	forbid	forbade	forbidden
babysit	babysat	babysat	forecast	forecast	forecast
be	was/were	been	foresee	foresaw	foreseen
bear	bore	borne	foretell	foretold	foretold
beat	beat	beaten	forget	forgot	forgotten
become	became	become	forgive	forgave	forgiven
begin	began	begun	forgo	forwent	forgone
bend	bent	bent	forsake	forsook	forsaken
beseech	besought,	besought,	freeze	froze	frozen
	beseeched	beseeched	get	got	got, US gotten
bet	bet	bet	give	gave	given
bid	bid	bid	go	went	gone
bind	bound	bound	grind	ground	ground
bite	bit	bitten	grow	grew	grown
bleed	bled	bled	hang	hung	hung
blow	blew	blown	have	had	had
break	broke	broken	hear	heard	heard
breastfeed	breastfed	breastfed	hide	hid	hidden
breed	bred	bred	hit	hit	hit
bring	brought	brought	hold	held	held
broadcast	broadcast	broadcast	hurt	hurt	hurt
build	built	built	interweave	interwove	interwoven
burn	burnt,	burnt,	keep	kept	kept
	burned	burned	kneel	knelt,	knelt,
burst	burst	burst		kneeled	kneeled
buy	bought	bought	know	knew	known
cast	cast	cast	lay	laid	laid
catch	caught	caught	lead	led	led
choose	chose	chosen	lean	leant,	leant,
cling	clung	clung		leaned	leaned
come	came	come	leap	leapt,	leapt,
cost	cost	cost		leaped	leaped
creep	crept	crept	learn	learnt,	learnt,
cut	cut	cut		learned	learned
deal	dealt	dealt	leave	left	left
dig	dug	dug	lend	lent	lent
do	did	done	let	let	let
draw	drew	drawn	lie	lay	lain
dream	dreamt,	dreamt,	light	lit	lit
	dreamed	dreamed	lose	lost	lost
drink	drank	drunk	make	made	made
drive	drove	driven	mean	meant	meant
dwell	dwelt,	dwelt,	meet	met	met
	dwelled	dwelled	mimic	mimicked	mimicked
eat	ate	eaten	mislay	mislaid	mislaid
fall	fell	fallen	mislead	misled	misled
feed	fed	fed	misspell	misspelt	misspelt
feel	felt	felt	mistake	mistook	mistaken
fight	fought	fought	misunderstand	misunderstood	misunderstood
find	found	found	mow	mowed	mowed,
fit	fitted,	fitted,			mown
	fit	fit	outdo	outdid	outdone
flee	fled	fled	overcome	overcame	overcome
fling	flung	flung	overfly	overflew	overflown

Infinitive	past tense	past participle	Infinitive	past tense	past participle
overhang	overhung	overhung	spell	spelt, spelled	spelt, spelled
overhear	overheard	overheard	spend	spent	spent
overrun	overran	overran	spill	spilled, spilt	spilled, spilt
oversee	oversaw	overseen			
overspend	overspent	overspent	spin	spun	spun
overtake	overtook	overtaken	spit	spat	spat
overthrow	overthrew	overthrown	split	split	split
pay	paid	paid	spoil	spoilt, spoiled	spoilt, spoiled
prove	proved	proved, proven	spread	spread	spread
put	put	put	spring	sprang	sprung
quit	quit, quitted	quit, quitted	stand	stood	stood
			steal	stole	stolen
read	read	read	stick	stuck	stuck
rebuild	rebuilt	rebuilt	sting	stung	stung
redo	redid	redone	stink	stank	stunk
repay	repaid	repaid	stride	strode	strode
resell	resold	resold	strike	struck	struck
reset	reset	reset	string	strung	strung
resit	resat	resat	strive	strove	striven
retake	retook	retaken	swear	swore	sworn
rethink	rethought	rethought	sweep	swept	swept
rewind	rewound	rewound	swell	swelled	swollen, swelled
rewrite	rewrote	rewritten			
ride	rode	ridden	swim	swam	swum
ring	rang	rung	swing	swung	swung
rise	rose	risen	take	took	taken
run	ran	run	teach	taught	taught
saw	sawed	sawn	tear	tore	torn
say	said	said	tell	told	told
see	saw	seen	think	thought	thought
seek	sought	sought	throw	threw	thrown
sell	sold	sold	thrust	thrust	thrust
send	sent	sent	tread	trod	trodden
set	set	set	undercut	undercut	undercut
sew	sewed	sewn, sewed	undergo	underwent	underwent
shake	shook	shaken	understand	understood	understood
shear	sheared	shorn, sheared	undertake	undertook	undertaken
			underwrite	underwrote	underwritten
shed	shed	shed	undo	undid	undone
shine	shone	shone	unwind	unwound	unwound
shoot	shot	shot	uphold	upheld	upheld
show	showed	shown	upset	upset	upset
shrink	shrank	shrunk	wake	woke	woken
shut	shut	shut	wear	wore	worn
sing	sang	sung	weave	wove	woven
sink	sank	sunk	wed	wed, wedded	wed, wedded
sit	sat	sat			
slay	slaid	slain	weep	wept	wept
sleep	slept	slept	wet	wet, wetted	wet, wetted
slide	slid	slid			
sling	slung	slung	win	won	won
slit	slit	slit	wind	wound	wound
smell	smelt, smelled	smelt, smelled	withdraw	withdrew	withdrawn
			withhold	withheld	withheld
sow	sowed	sown	withstand	withstood	withstood
speak	spoke	spoken	wring	wrung	wrung
speed	sped	sped	write	wrote	written

PRONUNCIATION GUIDE

This dictionary uses the following symbols from the International Phonetic Alphabet:

Consonants

p	press	h	hot
b	bag	x	loch
t	time	tʃ	chair
d	day	dʒ	jam
k	can	m	more
g	gap	n	snow
f	fast	ŋ	sing
v	vote	w	water
θ	thin	r	ring
ð	that	l	list
s	sit	j	you
z	zebra		
ʃ	shine		
ʒ	measure		

Vowels and diphthongs

ɪ	bit	ɔː	caught
e	bed	uː	boot
æ	bad	ɜː	bird
ɒ	hot	eɪ	bay
ʌ	cut	aɪ	buy
ʊ	book	ɔɪ	boy
ə	about	əʊ	go
i	pretty	aʊ	now
u	casual	ʊə	tour
iː	bee	eə	hair
ɑː	far	ɪə	hear

Stress

The main stressed syllable in an entry is shown by the symbol / ' /, and the second-most important stressed syllable is shown by the symbol /ˌ/, for example **correspond** /ˌkɒrɪˈspɒnd/. Compound entries that are made up of two or more separate words have stress marks on them if the pronunciation for each individual word is already given in the dictionary, for example ˌice ˈcream.

Alternative pronunciations

The dictionary shows alternative pronunciations for entries only if the second pronunciation is so different from the main one that it might not be understood easily, for example at **cervical** /ˈsɜːvɪk(ə)l, səˈvaɪk(ə)l/. American pronunciations are shown only when they are so different from the British pronunciation that they might not be understood easily, for example at **lieutenant** /lefˈtenənt, *American* luːˈtenənt/.

Weak forms and strong forms

Some grammar words (common words like prepositions and pronouns) have more than one pronunciation. The weak form is used when the syllable is unstressed, and the strong form is used when the syllable is stressed. These two forms are shown like this in the dictionary: **but** /*strong* bʌt, *weak* bət/.

Normal rapid speech

Pronunciations of words often change in normal rapid speech. The schwa /ə/ often disappears between certain consonants and the sounds /d/ and /t/ can often not be heard when they are found between two other consonants. If these sounds are given in brackets, it means that they are often not pronounced by fluent speakers of English, for example **station** /ˈsteɪʃ(ə)n/, **friendly** /ˈfren(d)li/, and **postman** /ˈpəʊs(t)mən/.

Nasalized vowels

Some French words that have entered the English language contain a nasalized vowel sound that is common in French but rare in English. These vowels are shown with the symbol /~/ above them, for example **Grand Prix** /ˌgrõn ˈpriː/.

SOFTWARE LICENCE FOR THE MACMILLAN STUDY DICTIONARY CD-ROM, FIRST PUBLISHED 2010